THE
SOCIAL SCIENCE
ENCYCLOPEDIA

Second Edition

THE
SOCIAL SCIENCE
ENCYCLOPEDIA

Second Edition

Edited by

Adam Kuper and Jessica Kuper

London and New York

First published in 1996

by Routledge
11 New Fetter Lane
London EC4P 4EE

29 West 35th Street, New York, NY 10001

Typeset in Monotype Baskerville 9½ on 10½ by
Florencetype Ltd, Stoodleigh, Devon

Printed and bound in Great Britain by
Clays Ltd, St. Ives plc

Printed on acid-free paper

British Library Cataloguing in Publication Data
A catalogue record for this book is available from the British Library

Library of Congress Cataloging-in-Publication Data
A catalog record for this book is available on request

ISBN 0–415–10829–2

Contents

Editorial preface

The Social Science Encyclopedia aims to provide a broad, authoritative, accessible and up-to-date coverage of the social sciences in a convenient format. It is intended for a sophisticated but not necessarily specialist readership, including social scientists, students, journalists, managers, planners and administrators, and indeed all those with a serious interest in contemporary academic thinking about the individual in society.

Major entries survey the central disciplines in the social sciences, and there are substantial reviews of important specialisms. Theories and topics of special interest are covered in shorter entries, and there are also surveys and specialist entries on methods and in the philosophy of the social sciences. There are profiles of key historical figures, and on the schools of thought that have shaped the social sciences. Finally, the Encyclopedia deals with applications of the social sciences, in management and industrial relations, in economic and financial analysis and in planning, in communications and opinion polls, in therapy, in aptitude testing and the measurement of intelligence, in social work, in criminology and in penology.

The first edition of this Encyclopedia appeared in 1985, to a generous welcome, but a decade later it clearly required renewal. Many fields had moved on from the preoccupations of the 1980s. There were urgent new debates, influential books and popular courses on subjects that had barely appeared on the horizon when the first edition was published. Post-modernism had just begun to make an impact on the social sciences in the mid-1980s, feminism was still widely regarded as an embattled, radical fringe movement, sociobiology was associated with a simplistic genetic determinism, and Marxism was still a protean source of argument in a number of disciplines. Privatization and regulation and new versions of liberalism were not yet the burning topics of debate that they became in the following years. Communication, culture and media studies had already started to establish themselves, but they began to flourish only in the mid-1980s. The 1990s have seen the coming of age of new fields of enquiry, such as environmental, evolutionary and experimental economics, civil society and citizenship in political science, and connectionism in psychology; the revitalization of some cross-disciplinary projects, including cultural studies, cultural geography and cultural history, sociolegal studies, and economic and psychological anthropology; and the fresh influence of new or revived ideas, including rational choice theory, game theory, neo-Darwinism and reflexivity.

Clearly, then, a new edition was required. Indeed, the Encyclopedia had to be radically recast. The new edition is a similar size to the original, and the format has been retained, but nearly 50 per cent of the approximately 600 entries are new or have been completely rewritten; a further 40 per cent have been substantially revised; and only about 10 per cent have been retained in their original form.

Introducing the first edition we noted that the various social science disciplines clearly form a single arena of discourse, comparable debates cropping up in a variety of fields, new ideas crossing easily

92932

from one discipline to another. As editors, we have often found it difficult to decide whether the author of a particular entry should be a psychologist or an anthropologist, an economist or a sociologist, a demographer or a geographer, a political scientist or a historian. Is rational choice theory the primary concern of political scientists, economists or sociologists? Are the notions of the body and the self especially salient to the current interests of psychologists or sociologists, or would it be more interesting to tap the debates of anthropologists or historians? On reflexity, rationality and rationalism, or relativism, should the floor be given to philosophers, sociologists, or anthropologists? Is the welfare state better explained by a political scientist, a historian or a social worker? In the event, these problems proved to be less difficult to resolve than might be imagined. We found that the choices we made did not necessarily make a great deal of difference, since a great many central ideas and arguments cross-cut the disciplines.

To a considerable extent this Encyclopedia necessarily illustrates the extent of interconnectedness, of overlap, if not of cohesion among the intellectual traditions which comprise the social sciences. This is not to deny the diversity of theoretical perspectives. However, a single field of discourse does not necessarily require a shared paradigm. Through interchange, by a process of challenge and response, shared standards and concerns develop. The attentive reader will find that certain themes recur, cropping up in the most unexpected places, and that an initial enquiry may lead from an obvious starting-point right across disciplinary boundaries to perhaps hitherto unheard of destinations.

Another aspect of this unity in diversity appears from the fact that although the bulk of our 500-odd contributors are drawn – in almost equal numbers – from the USA and Britain, there are a substantial number of contributions from other western European countries and also from Australia, Canada, India, Israel, Japan and South Africa. The fluidity of disciplinary boundaries is matched by the international character of the modern social sciences.

But we should not exaggerate the convergences, or the areas in which a certain degree of consensus reigns. There is certainly more than enough diversity to raise questions about emphasis, or even bias. We have selected our contributors for their individual expertise, but inevitably they represent a very broad cross-section of opinion and a variety of intellectual orientations: indeed, that is surely one of the strengths of this volume. The balance comes from reading further, following up cross-references, so that one perspective is balanced by another.

It is, of course, precisely this sort of diversity that has led some to query the scientific status of the social sciences (though social scientists have raised interesting questions about what constitutes a proper science). Desirable or not, the divergences are real enough. The new edition of the Encyclopedia accordingly reflects the controversies as well as the common assumptions. Our ambition remains to review the whole gamut of ideas on the individual and society that have emerged from a century of academic research, criticism and discussion.

Adam Kuper
Jessica Kuper
London, July 1994

Advisory editors

Contributors

Arthur Brittan, University of York, UK.

Andrew Britton, National Institute of Economic and Social Research, London, UK.

Martin Bronfenbrenner, Duke University, NC, USA.

A. J. Brown, University of Leeds, UK.

Archie Brown, University of Oxford, UK.

C. V. Brown, University of Stirling, UK.

Richard K. Brown, University of Durham, UK.

Rupert Brown, University of Kent, UK.

Stanley C. Brubaker, Colgate University, NY, USA.

Ronald D. Brunner, University of Colorado, Boulder, CO, USA.

Peter Bull, University of York, UK.

Martin Bulmer, University of Surrey, UK.

Valerie Bunce, Cornell University, NY, USA.

Robert G. Burgess, University of Warwick, UK.

Peter Burke, University of Cambridge, UK.

Michael L. Burton, University of California, Irvine, CA, USA.

K. J. Button, Loughborough University of Technology, UK.

W. F. Bynum, Wellcome Institute for the History of Medicine, London, UK.

John C. Caldwell, Australian National University, Canberra, Australia.

Craig Calhoun, University of North Carolina, Chapel Hill, NC, USA.

Fenella Cannell, London School of Economics and Political Science, UK.

Margaret Canovan, University of Keele, UK.

James G. Carrier, University of Durham, UK.

Michael Carrithers, University of Durham, UK.

Janet Carsten, University of Edinburgh, UK

Rosalind D. Cartwright, Rush-Presbyterian-St Luke's Medical Center, Chicago, IL, USA.

Mark Casson, University of Reading, UK.

Martin Cave, Brunel University, UK.

William J. Chambliss, George Washington University, Washington, DC, USA.

Victoria Chick, University College London, UK.

Nils Christie, University of Oslo, Norway.

Robert B. Cialdini, Arizona State University, AZ, USA.

Claudio Ciborra, University of Bologna, Italy.

Eve V. Clark, Stanford University, CA, USA.

J. A. Clark, University of Sussex, UK.

Dennis Chong, Northwestern University, IL, USA.

Gillian Cohen, Open University, Milton Keynes, UK.

Percy S. Cohen, London School of Economics and Political Science, UK.

Stanley Cohen, Hebrew University, Jerusalem, Israel.

David Collard, University of Bath, UK.

Andrew M. Colman, University of Leicester, UK.

Noshir S. Contractor, University of Illinois, Urbana-Champaign, IL, USA.

Martin A. Conway, University of Bristol, UK.

Karen S. Cook, University of Washington, WA, USA.

Peter J. Cooper, University of Reading, UK.

John Cornwall, Dalhousie University, NS, Canada.

Denis Cosgrove, Royal Holloway, University of London, UK.

Daniel Courgeau, Institut National d'Etudes Démographiques, Paris, France.

Charles D. Cowan, Bureau of the Census, US Dept of Commerce, Washington, DC.

Frank A. Cowell, London School of Economics and Political Science, UK.

N. F. R. Crafts, London School of Economics and Political Science, UK.

Thomas J. Csordas, Case Western Reserve University, OH, USA.

John Curtice, University of Strathclyde, UK.

Keith Cuthbertson, City University Business School, London, UK.

Ralf Dahrendorf, University of Oxford, UK.

Roy D'Andrade, University of California, San Diego, CA, USA.

Regna Darnell, University of Western Ontario, Canada.

Paul Davidson, University of Tennessee, TN, USA.

S. W. Davies, University of East Anglia, UK.

J. Davis, University of Oxford, UK.

Phyllis Deane, University of Cambridge, UK.

Rutledge M. Dennis, George Mason University, VA, USA.

Donald Denoon, Australian National University, Canberra, Australia.

Philippe Descola, Ecole des Hautes Etudes en Sciences Sociales, Paris, France.

René F. W. Diekstra, University of Leiden, The Netherlands.

R. Emerson Dobash, University of Wales, Cardiff, UK.

Russell P. Dobash, University of Wales, Cardiff, UK.

Peter C. Dodwell, Queen's University, Kingston, Ontario, Canada.

Patrick Doreian, University of Pittsburgh, PA, USA.

Keith Dowding, London School of Economics and Political Science, UK.

Juris G. Draguns, Pennsylvania State University, PA, USA.

Vic Duke, University of Salford, UK.

William Dutton, Brunel University, UK, and University of Southern California, CA, USA.

Thráinn Eggertsson, University of Iceland, Reykjavik, Iceland, and Indiana University, IN, USA.

Ed Elbers, University of Utrecht, The Netherlands.

Walter Elkan, Brunel University, UK.

R. F. Ellen, University of Kent, UK.

Stanley L. Engerman, University of Rochester, NY, USA.

Milton J. Esman, Cornell University, NY, USA.

Saul Estrin, London Business School, UK.

H. David Evans, Institute of Development Studies, University of Sussex, UK.

Jonathan St B. T. Evans, University of Plymouth, UK.

Mary Evans, University of Kent, UK.

Douglas C. Ewbank, University of Pennsylvania, PA, USA.

Michael W. Eysenck, Royal Holloway, University of London, UK.

Robert M. Farr, London School of Economics and Political Science, UK.

Walter Feinberg, University of Illinois, Urbana-Champaign, IL, USA.

Marcus W. Feldman, Stanford University, CA, USA.

W. L. F. Felstiner, University of California, Santa Barbara, CA, USA.

Agneta A. Fischer, University of Amsterdam, The Netherlands.

Shirley Fisher, University of Strathclyde, UK.

Joshua A. Fishman, Yeshiva University, NY, USA.

Peter Fitzpatrick, University of Kent, UK.

Duncan Forbes, formerly, University of Cambridge, UK.

Robin Fox, Rutgers University, NJ, USA.

Wayne L. Francis, University of Florida, FL, USA.

Ronald Frankenberg, Brunel University, UK.

Colin Fraser, University of Cambridge, UK.

Lawrence Freedman, King's College, University of London, UK.

Christopher French, Goldsmiths' College, University of London, UK.

Bruno S. Frey, University of Zurich, Switzerland.

Jonathan Friedman, University of Lund, Sweden.

Victoria A. Fromkin, University of California, Los Angeles, CA, USA.

Giulio M. Gallarotti, Wesleyan University, CT, USA

Philippa A. Garety, Institute of Psychiatry, University of London, UK.

David Garland, University of Edinburgh, UK.

Alan Garnham, University of Sussex, UK.

Viktor Gecas, Washington State University, WA, USA.

Dimitra Gefou-Madianou, Panteion University, Athens, Greece.

Ernest Gellner, University of Cambridge, UK.

Arthur R. Gilgen, University of Northern Iowa, IA, USA.

K. J. Gilhooly, University of Aberdeen, UK.

Ian Goldin, World Bank, Washington, DC, USA.

Jack A. Goldstone, University of California, Davis, CA, USA.

Erich Goode, State University of New York, Stony Brook, NY, USA.

Barbara Goodwin, Brunel University, UK.

Jan Gorecki, University of Illinois, Urbana-Champaign, IL, USA.

John Goyder, University of Waterloo, Ontario, Canada.

Harvey J. Graff, University of Texas, Dallas, TX, USA.

Karl Grammar, Max-Planck Institut für Verhalten-physiologie, Forschungsstelle für Humanethologie, Germany.

Ryken Grattet, Louisiana State University, LA, USA.

Sarah Green, University of Cambridge, UK.

Joseph Greenberg, Stanford University, CA, USA.

Keith Grint, University of Oxford, UK.

Henry Grunebaum, Harvard University, MA, USA.

Stephen Gudeman, University of Minnesota, MN, USA.

Josef Gugler, University of Connecticut, CT, USA.

Thomas G. Gutheil, Harvard University, MA, USA.

Claude Hagège, Ecole Pratique des Hautes Etudes, Paris, France.

Lesley A. Hall, Wellcome Institute for the History of Medicine, London, UK.

Thomas D. Hall, De Pauw University, IN, USA.

A. H. Halsey, University of Oxford, UK.

Koichi Hamada, Yale University, CT, USA.

Ulf Hannerz, University of Stockholm, Sweden.

Lorraine M. Fox Harding, University of Leeds, UK.

B. E. Harrell-Bond, University of Oxford, UK.

David M. Harrington, University of California, Santa Cruz, CA, USA.

Haim Hazan, Tel-Aviv University, Israel.

Suzette Heald, Lancaster University, UK.

David M. Heer, University of Southern California, CA, USA.

A. Heertje, University of Amsterdam, The Netherlands.

Martin Herbert, University of Exeter, UK.

Peter Herriot, Sundridge Park: Corporate Research, Bromley, Kent, UK.

Luc de Heusch, Free University of Brussels, Belgium.

Rosalyn Higgins, UN Committee on Human Rights and London School of Economics and Political Science, UK.

Paul Hirst, Birkbeck College, University of London, UK.

Peter S. Hlebowitsh, University of Iowa, IA, USA.

Ian Hodder, University of Cambridge, UK.

Walter W. Holland, Guy's and St Thomas's Medical and Dental Schools, University of London, UK.

Peter Holmes, University of Sussex, UK.

Ladislav Holy, University of St Andrews, UK.

Christopher Hood, London School of Economics and Political Science, UK.

Keith Hope, Southern Illinois University, IL, USA.

Kevin Howells, University of Leicester, UK.

Andrzej Huczynski, University of Glasgow, UK.

Gordon Hughes, University of Cambridge, UK.

Maggie Humm, University of East London, UK.

S. C. Humphreys, University of Michigan, Ann Arbor, MI, USA.

Jane Humphries, University of Cambridge, UK.

James G. Hunt, Texas Tech University, TX, USA.

Richard Hyman, University of Warwick, UK.

David Ingleby, University of Utrecht, The Netherlands.

Tim Ingold, University of Manchester, UK.

A. M. Iossifides, Panteion University, Athens, Greece.

Norman Ireland, University of Warwick, UK.

Jonathan I. Israel, University College London, UK.

Catherine Itzin, University of Bradford, UK.

Dudley Jackson, University of Wollongong, NSW, Australia.

Peter Jackson, University of Sheffield, UK.

P. M. Jackson, University of Leicester, UK.

Ian Jarvie, York University, Toronto, Canada.

Richard Jenkins, University of Wales, Swansea, UK.

Sut Jhally, University of Massachusetts, Amherst, MA, USA.

Per-Olov Johansson, Stockholm School of Economics, Sweden.

Geraint Johnes, Lancaster University, UK.

R. J. Johnston, University of Essex, UK.

Alan Jones, Analytical Services Division, Dept of Social Security, UK.

Edward E. Jones, formerly, Princeton University, NJ, USA.

Grant Jordan, University of Aberdeen, UK.

P. E. de Josselin de Jong, University of Leiden, The Netherlands.

Jasna Jovanovic, University of Illinois, Urbana-Champaign, IL, USA.

Roger Jowell, Social & Community Planning Research, London, UK.

P. N. Junankar, Australian National University, Canberra, Australia.

Stephen Kalberg, Boston University, MA, USA.

S. M. Ravi Kanbur, University of Essex, UK.

Victor Karady, Centre National de la Recherche Scientific, Paris, France.

Dennis Kavanagh, University of Nottingham, UK.

John Kay, London School of Economics and Political Science, UK.

Allen C. Kelley, Duke University, NC, USA.

Douglas Kellner, University of Texas, Austin, TX, USA.

Philip C. Kendall, Temple University, PA, USA.

Nathan Keyfitz, Harvard University, MA, USA and International Institute for Applied Systems Analysis, Austria.

Charles P. Kindleberger, Massachusetts Institute of Technology, MA, USA.

Paul Kline, University of Exeter, UK.

Paul L. Knox, Virginia Polytechnic Institute and State University, VA, USA.

Stephen M. Kosslyn, Harvard University, MA, USA.

Deirdre A. Kramer, Rutgers University, NJ, USA.

David R. Krathwohl, Syracuse University, NY, USA.

Robert P. Kraynak, Colgate University, NY, USA.

Philip Kreager, University of Oxford, UK.

J. A. Kregel, University of Groningen, The Netherlands.

Louis Kriesberg, Syracuse University, NY, USA.

Anton O. Kris, Boston Psychoanalytic Institute, MA, USA.

Krishan Kumar, University of Kent, UK.

Adam Kuper, Brunel University, UK.

Frank J. Landy, Pennsylvania State University, PA, USA.

Roger Lass, University of Cape Town, South Africa.

Peter Lassman, University of Birmingham, UK.

Aaron Lazare, Massachusetts General Hospital, MA, USA.

John Lazarus, University of Newcastle upon Tyne, UK.

Richard Lecomber, University of Bristol, UK.

David Lehmann, University of Cambridge, UK.

Herschel W. Leibowitz, Pennsylvania State University, PA, USA.

Jacqueline V. Lerner, Michigan State University, MI, USA.

Richard M. Lerner, Michigan State University, MI, USA.

Bernard S. Levy, Harvard University, MA, USA.

Arendt Lijphart, University of California, San Diego, CA, USA.

David T. Llewellyn, Loughborough University of Technology, UK.

Brian J. Loasby, University of Stirling, UK.

Grahame Lock, Catholic University of Nijmegen, The Netherlands.

Karl-Gustav Löfgren, University of Umeå, Sweden.

Norman Long, University of Bath, UK.

C. A. Knox Lovell, University of Georgia, GA, USA.

Michael Lynch, Brunel University, UK.

David Lyons, Cornell University, NY, USA.

Dean MacCannell, University of California, Davis, CA, USA.

Peter McDonald, Australian Institute of Family Studies, Melbourne, Australia.

Alan MacFarlane, University of Cambridge, UK.

Peter McGuffin, University of Wales College of Medicine, UK.

Henry M. McHenry, University of California, Davis, CA, USA.

N. J. Mackintosh, University of Cambridge, UK.

David McLellan, University of Kent, UK.

Klim McPherson, London School of Hygiene and Tropical Medicine, University of London, UK.

Denis McQuail, University of Amsterdam, The Netherlands.

Melvin Manis, University of Michigan and Ann Arbor Veterans Administration Medical Center, MI, USA.

Antony S. R. Manstead, University of Amsterdam, The Netherlands.

Peter Marris, University of California, Los Angeles, CA, USA.

David Marsden, London School of Economics and Political Science, UK.

Dwaine Marvick, University of California, Los Angeles, CA, USA.

Roger D. Masters, Dartmouth College, NH, USA.

Thomas Mayer, University of California, Davis, CA, USA.

Andrew Mayes, University of Manchester, UK.

Alan Maynard, University of York, UK.

Ivan N. Mensh, University of California, Los Angeles, CA, USA.

Kenneth Menzies, University of Guelph, Ontario, Canada.

J. S. Metcalfe, University of Manchester, UK.

Alice G. B. ter Meulen, University of Indiana, IN, USA.

Alfred G. Meyer, University of Michigan, Ann Arbor, MI, USA.

David Miller, University of Oxford, UK.

Robert Millward, University of Manchester, UK.

Chris Milner, University of Nottingham, UK.

Patrick Minford, University of Liverpool and Cardiff Business School, UK.

Kenneth Minogue, London School of Economics and Political Science, UK.

Donald Moggridge, University of Toronto, Canada.

Peter R. Monge, University of Southern California, CA, USA.

Mark Monmonier, Syracuse University, NY, USA.

Sally Falk Moore, Harvard University, MA, USA.

Howard Morphy, Pitt Rivers Museum, Oxford, UK.

John Muellbauer, University of Oxford, UK.

Andy Mullineux, University of Birmingham, UK.

Gareth D. Myles, University of Exeter, UK.

J. Peter Neary, University College Dublin, Ireland.

Edward J. Nell, New School for Social Research, NY, USA.

Michael Nelson, Vanderbilt University, TN, USA.

John C. Nemiah, Dartmouth Medical School, NH, USA.

Kenneth Newton, University of Essex, UK.

D. P. O'Brien, University of Durham, UK.

Peter R. Odell, Erasmus University, Rotterdam, The Netherlands.

Brendan O'Leary, London School of Economics and Political Science, UK.

D. L. Olmsted, University of California, Davis, CA, USA.

W. M. O'Neil, University of Sydney, Australia.

Timothy O'Riordan, University of East Anglia, UK.

Carlos P. Otero, University of California, Los Angeles, CA, USA.

J. P. Parry, London School of Economics and Political Science, UK.

Gianfranco Pasquino, University of Bologna, Italy.

Dorothy Pawluch, McMaster University, Ontario, Canada.

Stanley G. Payne, University of Wisconsin, WI, USA.

Terry Peach, University of Manchester, UK.

David W. Pearce, University College London, UK.

J. D. Y. Peel, School of Oriental and African Studies, University of London, UK.

Mark Philp, University of Oxford, UK.

Ann Phoenix, Birkbeck College, University of London, UK.

Harold Alan Pincus, American Psychiatric Association, Washington, DC, USA.

M. Pinto-Duschinsky, Brunel University, UK.

Ken Plummer, University of Essex, UK.

Christopher Pollitt, Brunel University, UK.

George H. Pollock, Institute for Psychoanalysis, Chicago, IL, USA.

Michael Poole, Cardiff Business School, University of Wales, UK.

Harrison G. Pope, Mailman Research Center, Belmont, MA, USA.

Jonathan Potter, Loughborough University of Technology, UK.

Jean Pouillon, Collège de France, Paris, France.

Michael Prestwich, University of Durham, UK.

John Purcell, University of Oxford, UK.

John Radford, University of East London, UK.

Gloria Goodwin Raheja, University of Minnesota, MN, USA.

Alastair J. Read, University of Cambridge, UK.

Michael I. Reed, Lancaster University, UK.

W. Duncan Reekie, University of the Witwatersrand, Johannesburg, South Africa.

R. Reiner, London School of Economics and Political Science, UK.

Stanley A. Renshon, City University, New York, USA.

Jack Revell, University of Wales, Bangor, UK.

P. A. Reynolds, Lancaster University, UK.

John T. E. Richardson, Brunel University, UK.

James C. Riley, Indiana University, IN, USA.

Roland Robertson, University of Pittsburgh, PA, USA.

Kevin Robins, University of Newcastle upon Tyne, UK.

Mark Robinson, Institute of Development Studies, University of Sussex, UK.

Paul Rock, London School of Economics and Political Science, UK.

Paul Rogers, University of Bradford, UK.

Paul Roman, University of Georgia, Athens, GA, USA.

Michael Roper, University of Essex, UK.

Hilary Rose, University of Bradford, UK.

Frederick Rosen, University College London, UK.

Robert Ross, University of Leiden, The Netherlands.

Alvin E. Roth, University of Pittsburgh, PA, USA.

Loren H. Roth, University of Pittsburgh, PA, USA.

William McKinley Runyan, University of California, Berkeley, CA, USA.

Peter H. Russell, University of Toronto, Canada.

Robert Sack, University of Wisconsin, Madison, WI, USA.

Ashwani Saith, Institute of Social Studies, The Hague, The Netherlands.

Todd Sandler, Iowa State University, IA, USA.

Gigi Santow, University of Stockholm, Sweden.

Donald Sassoon, Queen Mary's and Westfield College, University of London, UK.

Lawrence A. Scaff, Pennsylvania State University, PA, USA.

Roberto Scazzieri, University of Bologna, Italy.

Bernard Schaffer, formerly, Institute of Development Studies, University of Sussex, UK.

John Scott, University of Essex, UK.

Maurice Scott, University of Oxford, UK.

Peter Self, Australian National University, Canberra, Australia.

John Sharp, University of Cape Town, South Africa.

William H. Shaw, San José State University, CA, USA.

James F. Short, Jr, Washington State University, WA, USA.

S. Siebert, University of Birmingham, UK.

Paul Sillitoe, University of Durham, UK.

Herbert A. Simon, Carnegie Mellon University, PA, USA.

H. W. Singer, Institute of Development Studies, University of Sussex, UK.

Jerome L. Singer, Yale University, CT, USA.

A. S. Skinner, University of Glasgow, UK.

David F. Sly, Florida State University, FL, USA.

Carol Smart, University of Leeds, UK.

James E. Smith, Cambridge Group for the History of Population and Social Structure, UK and Westat Inc., Rockville, MD, USA.

Neil Smith, Rutgers University, NJ, USA.

Susan Smith, University of Edinburgh, UK.

Paul Spencer, School of Oriental and African Studies, University of London, UK.

David Spiegel, Stanford University, CA, USA.

Charles D. Spielberger, University of South Florida, FL, USA.

Elizabeth A. Stanko, Brunel University, UK.

Liz Stanley, University of Manchester, UK.

Emilia Steuerman, Brunel University, UK.

Richard Stevens, Open University, Milton Keynes, UK.

Charles Stewart, University College London, UK.

Alan A. Stone, Harvard University, MA, USA.

Andrea B. Stone, Westfield Area Mental Health Clinic and University of Massachusetts Medical Center, MA, USA.

John Stone, George Mason University, VA, USA.

M. Stone, University College London, UK.

John Storey, University of Sunderland, UK.

John S. Strauss, Yale University, CT, USA.

Erich Streissler, University of Vienna, Austria.

Bob Sutcliffe, University of the Basque Country, Bilbao, Spain.

P. Swann, London Business School, UK.

James L. Sweeney, Stanford University, CA, USA.

Conrad Taeuber, Georgetown University, Washington, DC, USA.

Vincent J. Tarascio, University of North Carolina, Chapel Hill, NC, USA.

Sidney Tarrow, Cornell University, NY, USA.

Mark Taylor, University of Liverpool.

Maye Taylor, Manchester Metropolitan University, UK.

Peter J. Taylor, University of Newcastle upon Tyne, UK.

Keith Tester, University of Portsmouth, UK.

Pat Thane, University of Sussex, UK.

H. S. Thayer, City University, New York, USA.

A. P. Thirlwall, University of Kent, UK.

Jonathan Thomas, University of Warwick, UK.

John B. Thompson, University of Cambridge, UK.

Rodney Tiffen, University of Sydney, Australia.

Noel Timms, University of Leicester, UK.

Gary L. Tischler, Yale University, CT, USA.

Phillip V. Tobias, University of the Witwatersrand, Johannesburg, South Africa.

B. R. Tomlinson, University of Birmingham, UK.

Jim Tomlinson, Brunel University, UK.

Elizabeth Tonkin, Queen's University Belfast, UK.

Christina Toren, Brunel University, UK.

Jean Tournon, University of Grenoble, France.

Peter Townsend, University of Bristol, UK.

John Toye, Institute of Development Studies, University of Sussex, UK.

Bruce G. Trigger, McGill University, Montreal, Canada.

Stephen Trotter, University of Hull, UK.

Bryan S. Turner, Deakin University, Geelong, Victoria, Australia.

Michael Twaddle, Institute of Commonwealth Studies, University of London, UK.

David Unwin, Birkbeck College, University of London, UK.

John Urry, Lancaster University, UK.

George E. Vaillant, Harvard Medical School, MA, USA.

E. R. Valentine, Royal Holloway, University of London, UK.

Pierre van den Berghe, University of Washington, WA, USA.

Jaap van Ginneken, University of Leiden, The Netherlands.

John Van Maanen, Massachusetts Institute of Technology, MA, USA.

Nancy E. Vettorello, American Psychiatric Association, Washington, DC, USA.

Joan Vincent, Columbia University, NY, USA.

David Vines, University of Oxford, UK.

Fred W. Vondracek, Pennsylvania State University, PA, USA.

E. Voutira, University of Oxford, UK.

Ian Waddington, University of Leicester, UK.

Alan Walker, University of Sheffield, UK.

Carol Walker, Sheffield Hallam University, UK.

Nigel Walker, University of Cambridge, UK.

Richard Wall, Cambridge Group for the History of Population and Social Structure, UK.

Roy Wallis, formerly, Queen's University Belfast, UK.

Michael Ward, Institute of Development Studies, University of Sussex, UK.

Michael Waterson, University of Warwick, UK.

E. D. Watt, University of Western Australia, Perth, Australia.

P. A. Watt, University of Birmingham, UK.

Martin Weale, University of Cambridge, UK.

Kenneth Wexler, University of California, Irvine, CA, USA.

Richard Whipp, Cardiff Business School, University of Wales, UK.

John K. Whitaker, University of Virginia, VA, USA.

Douglas R. White, University of California, Irvine, CA, USA.

Geoffrey M. White, East-West Center, Honolulu, HI, USA.

Geoffrey Whittington, University of Cambridge, UK.

Ronald W. Wilhelm, University of North Texas, TX, USA.

Fiona Williams, Open University, Milton Keynes, UK.

Roy Willis, University of Edinburgh, UK.

Deirdre Wilson, University College London, UK.

David Winter, Barnet Health Care, London, UK.

Sue Wise, Lancaster University, UK.

Charlotte Wolf, Memphis State University, TN, USA.

Janet Wolff, University of Rochester, NY, USA.

Normund Wong, Walter Reed Army Medical Center, Washington, DC, USA.

Robert Woods, University of Liverpool, UK.

Steve Woolgar, Brunel University, UK.

Peter Worsley, University of Manchester, UK.

Michael Wright, Brunel University, UK.

Guillaume Wunsch, University of Louvain, Belgium.

Toshio Yamagishi, Hokkaido University, Japan.

Kaoru Yamamoto, University of Colorado, Denver, CO, USA.

Aubrey J. Yates, University of Western Australia, Perth, Australia.

John W. Yolton, Rutgers University, NJ, USA.

Michael W. Young, Australian National University, Canberra, Australia.

Abraham Zaleznik, Harvard University, MA, USA.

George Zeidenstein, Harvard University, MA, USA.

Entries listed by discipline and subject

Anthropology

age organization
anthropology
archaeology
Asiatic mode of production
Boas, Franz
body
cannibalism
cargo cults
caste
community
cultural anthropology
culture
Darwin, Charles
divine kingship
division of labour by sex
dual economy
Durkheim, Emile
ecology
economic anthropology
environment
ethnicity
ethnography
evolutionism and progress
exchange
family

feud
folklore and myth
functional analysis
gender and sex
genealogies
groups
habitus
hermeneutics
hierarchy
house
household
human evolution
human nature
human needs
hunters and gatherers
incest
individualism
kinship
language and culture
Lévi-Strauss, Claude
magic
Malinowski, Bronislaw Kasper
marriage
material culture
medical anthropology
nature
oral history

oral tradition
Orientalism
pastoralism
patriarchy
peasants
person
political anthropology
post-modernity
primitive society
psychological anthropology
race
racism
reason, rationality and
   rationalism
religion and ritual
rites of passage
role
Rousseau, Jean-Jacques
self-concept
semantics
semiotics
social anthropology
social Darwinism
social networks
social structure and structuration
sociobiology
state, origins of

Education

Piaget, Jean
social skills and social skills
   training
thinking
vocational and career
   development

Family and kinship

adolescence
childcare
childhood
division of labour by sex
divorce
domestic violence
family
family history
family therapy
feminist practice
feminist research
feminist theory
fertility
gender and sex
genealogies
household
kinship
marriage
nuptiality
patriarchy
women
women's studies

Feminism, gender and women's studies

body
division of labour by sex
divorce
domestic violence
family
feminist practice
feminist research
feminist theory
gender and sex
homosexualities
marriage
patriarchy
pornography
sexual behaviour
women
women's studies

Geography

business concentration
cartography
centre and periphery
cultural geography
ecology
energy
environment
geographical information systems
geography
historical geography
landscape
nature
place
political geography
population and resources
population geography
region
social geography
space
spatial analysis
territoriality
transport, economic and
   planning
urban geography
urban planning
world-system theory

Government, politics and public policy

aid
authoritarian and totalitarian
   systems
authority
Bentham, Jeremy
bureaucracy
capital punishment
centre and periphery
charisma
citizenship
civil society
collective action
colonialism
committees
community
conflict, social
conformity
constitutions and constitutionalism
corporatism
corruption
decision making

democracy
democratization
economic growth
elections
elites
employment and unemployment
energy
ethnic politics
federation and federalism
game theory
globalizaton
governance
government
hierarchy
human rights
industrial democracy
institutions
intellectuals
interest groups and lobbying
international relations
international trade
judicial process
law
law and economics
leadership
legitimacy
Marx's theory of history and
   society
media and politics
metropolitan and urban
   government
military regimes
modernization
nationalism
nationalization
organizations
parties, political
patronage
peace studies
penology
police
pluralism, political
policy sciences
political anthropology
political culture
political economy
political geography
political psychology
political recruitment and careers
political science
political theory
populism
power
prisoners' dilemma
privacy

Psychiatry, psychoanalysis and clinical psychology

Psychology

consciousness
constitutional psychology
counselling psychology
creativity
Darwin, Charles
delusions
developmental psychology
dreams
eating disorders
educational psychology
emotion
fantasy
Freud, Sigmund
gender and sex
genetics and behaviour
group dynamics
human nature
human needs
industrial and organisational
  psychology
instinct
learning
learning curve
life cycle
life history
life-span development
memory
mental disorders
mental health
mental imagery
mind
nervous system
neuroses
non-verbal communication
norms
occupational psychology
parapsychology
personal construct theory
personality
personality assessment
phenomenology
physiological psychology
Piaget, Jean
political psychology
prejudice
prisoners' dilemma
problem solving
projective methods
psychiatry
psychoanalysis
psychological anthropology
psychology
psychopathic personality
psychopharmacology
psychoses

pschosomatic illness
reference groups
role
self-concept
sensation and perception
sexual behaviour
sleep
social identity
social psychology
social skills and social skills
  training
sociobiology
stereotypes
stigma
stress
thinking
unconscious
vision
vocational and career
  development

Social administration, social work, 'social problems'

adolescence
alcoholism and alcohol abuse
basic needs
childcare
childhood
clinical psychology
community
community development
conflict, social
crime and delinquency
criminology
deviance
disability
divorce
domestic violence
family therapy
feminist practice
gangs
gerontology, social
homosexualities
human nature
human needs
human rights
labelling theory
media effects
police
pornography
poverty
prejudice

privacy
public administration
public choice
public goods
public health
public management
public sector economics
public sphere
punishment
racism
refugees
rehabilitation
social problems
social welfare
social welfare policy
social work
stigma
subculture
suicide
violence
welfare economics
welfare state

Sociology

adolescence
advertising
alienation
altruism
art, sociology of
authority
basic needs
body
bureaucracy
capitalism
case study
centre and periphery
charisma
childhood
city
civil society
class, social
collective action
community
community development
Comte, Auguste
conflict, social
conformity
crime and delinquency
criminology
culture
deviance
divorce
Durkheim, Emile

A

accelerator principle

In contrast to the (Keynesian) multiplier, which relates output to changes in investment, the accelerator models investment as determined by changes in output. As the principle that investment responds to the changes in output which imply pressure on capacity, the accelerator has a long history, but its formal development dates from the realization that its combination with the multiplier could produce neat models of cyclical behaviour. J. M. Clark originally noted the possibilities inherent in such models, but their first formal development was by Lundberg (1937) and Harrod (1936), and subsequently by Samuelson (1939a; 1939b) with Hicks (1949; 1950) and Goodwin (1948) and others providing refinements.

Suppose the optimal capital stock stands in fixed proportion to output, that is, formally:

$$K^* = \alpha Y$$

where

    K^* is the desired stock of fixed capital
    Y is annual output
    α is the average and marginal ratio of optimal capital to output, i.e. $(K^*/Y = \Delta K^*/Y)$

Now let the subscripts t and t–1 refer to the variables in years t and t–1

$$K^*_{t-1} = \alpha Y_{t-1}$$

$$K^*_t = \alpha Y_t$$

so $K^*_t - K^*_{t-1} = \alpha(Y_t - Y_{t-1})$

Assume that the optimal capital stock was achieved in year t–1,

$$K_{t-1} = K^*_{t-1}$$

therefore

$$K^*_t - K_{t-1} = \alpha(Y_t - Y_{t-1})$$

To understand investment, that is, the flow of expenditure on capital goods, it is necessary to know how quickly investors intend to close any gap between the actual and optimal capital stocks. Let λ be an adjustment coefficient which represents the extent to which the gap between the realized and the desired capital stocks is to be closed.

Then

$$I_t = \lambda\alpha(Y_t - Y_{t-1})$$
or $I_t = V(Y_t - Y_{t-1})$

The λ and α coefficients together link investment to first differences in output levels and are described as the accelerator coefficient, here V. Even at this elementary level the accelerator has several interesting implications. First, net investment determined by the accelerator will be positive (negative and zero respectively) if and only if $(Y_t - Y_{t-1})$ is positive (negative and zero respectively). Second, such net investment will fall if the *rate* at which output is increasing declines.

However, even at this simple level the weaknesses of the approach are also apparent. First, the results above relate *only* to investment determined by the accelerator, that is motivated as described above by a desire to expand capacity in line with output. It may well be that while entrepreneurs are influenced by relative pressure on their capital stocks, other factors also act as an inducement/disincentive to investment such as expectations, availability of new technology, and so on. Thus, the accelerator describes only a part of investment which might not stand in any fixed relation to total investment. Furthermore, the capacity argument really only models the *optimal capital stock*. To make the jump to the flow of investment requires the introduction of the λ coefficient which can be justified only by *ad-hoc* references to supply conditions in the investment goods industries and/or the state of expectations. In the absence of such additional assumptions it would only be possible to say that I $\lessgtr$ O according to whether $K^*_t \lessgtr K_{t-1}$.

As suggested above, the accelerator has been fruitfully combined with the multiplier in models designed to explicate economic dynamics. Here the problem has been that while such models are useful in understanding the origins of cyclical fluctuation, realistic estimates of V predict an unreasonable degree of dynamic instability. This problem has generally been solved by combining the accelerator with other determinants of investment in more general models, and more specifically by theorizing the existence of 'floors' and 'ceilings' to income fluctuation, hence constraining potentially explosive accelerator multiplier interactions. In addition, generalized accelerator models themselves have provided the basis for empirical investigation of investment behaviour.

Jane Humphries
University of Cambridge

References

Goodwin, R. M. (1948) 'Secular and cyclical aspects of the multiplier and the accelerator', in *Income Employment and Public Policy: Essays in Honor of Alvin H. Hansen*, New York.
Harrod, R. F. (1936) *The Trade Cycle: An Essay*, Oxford.
Hicks, J. R. (1949) 'Mr Harrod's dynamic theory', *Economica* XVI.
—— (1950) *A Contribution to the Theory of the Trade Cycle*, Oxford.
Lundberg, E. (1937) *Studies in the Theory of Economic Expansion*, London.
Samuelson, P. A. (1939a) 'A synthesis of the principle of acceleration and the multiplier', *Journal of Political Economy* 47.
—— (1939b) 'Interactions between the multiplier analysis and the principle of acceleration', *Review of Economic Statistics* 21.

accounting

Accounting deals with the provision of information about the economic activities of various accounting entities, the largest of which is the whole economy, for which national accounts are prepared. However, the traditional province of the accountant is the smaller unit, typically a business firm. Here, a distinction is often made between financial accounting and management accounting.

Financial accounting deals with the provision of information to providers of finance (shareholders and creditors) and other interested parties who do not participate in the management of the firm (such as trade unions and consumer groups). This usually takes the form of a balance sheet (a statement of assets and claims thereon at a point in time), and a profit and loss account (a statement of revenue, expenses and

profit over a period of time), supplemented by various other statements and notes. The form of financial accounting by companies is, in most countries, laid down by statute, and the contents are usually checked and certified independently by auditors. In some countries, there are also accounting standards laid down by the accounting profession or by the independent bodies which it supports, such as the United States Financial Accounting Standards Board, which determine the form and content of financial accounts. The auditing and regulation of financial accounts is a natural response to the potential moral hazard problem arising from the information asymmetry which exists between managers and providers of finance. In the absence of such quality assurance, users of accounts would have little confidence in the honesty and accuracy of statements that could be distorted by management to represent its performance in the most favourable light.

Management accounting is concerned with the provision of information to management, to assist with planning, decision making and control within the business. Because planning and decision making are inevitably directed to the future, management accounting often involves making future projections, usually called budgets. Important applications of this are capital budgeting, which deals with the appraisal of investments, and cash budgeting, which deals with the projection of future cash inflows and outflows and the consequent financial requirements of the entity. Management accounting is also concerned with controlling and appraising the outcome of past plans, for example, by analysing costs, and with assessing the economic performance of particular divisions or activities of the entity. Because the demand for management accounting information varies according to the activities, size and management structure of the entity, and because the supply of such information is not subject to statutory regulation or audit, there is a much greater variety both of techniques and of practice in management accounting than in financial accounting. Management has, of course, direct control over the information system of the business, so that formal regulation of the management accounting system is less important. However, within large organizations, there are information asymmetries and potential moral hazard problems between different groups (e.g. between branch managers and head office), and such organizations typically have internal auditing systems to reduce such problems.

Both management accounts and financial accounts derive from an accounting system which records the basic data relating to the transactions of the entity. The degree to which management accounting and financial accounting information can both derive from a common set of records depends on the circumstances of the individual accounting entity and, in particular, on the form of its management accounting. However, all accounting systems have a common root in double-entry bookkeeping, a self-balancing system, based on the principle that all assets of the entity ('debits') can be attributed to an owner (a claim on the entity by a creditor or the owners' 'equity' interest in the residual assets of the entity, both of which are 'credits'). This system owes its origin to Italian merchants of the fifteenth century, but it is still fundamental to accounting systems, although records are now often kept on computers, so that debits and credits take the form of different axes of a matrix, rather than different sides of the page in a handwritten ledger. The design of accounting systems to avoid fraud and error is an important aspect of the work of the accountant.

The traditional orientation of accounting was to record transactions at their historical cost, that is, in terms of the monetary units in which transactions took place. Thus, an asset would be recorded at the amount originally paid for it. Inflation and changing prices in recent years have called into question the relevance of historical cost, and inflation accounting has become an important subject. It has been proposed at various times and in different countries that accounts should show current values, that is, the specific current prices of individual assets, or that they should be adjusted by a general price level index to reflect the impact of inflation on the value of the monetary unit, or that a combination of both types of adjustment should be employed. Intervention by standard-setting bodies on this subject has been specifically directed at financial accounting, but it has been hoped that the change of method would also affect management accounting.

Financial accounting has also been affected, in recent years, by an increased public demand for information about business activities often supported by governments. Associated with this has been demand for information outside the scope of traditional profit-oriented accounts, resulting in research and experimentation in such areas as human asset accounting, environmental (or 'green') accounting and corporate social reporting. There has also been more interest in accounting for public-sector activities and not-for-profit organizations. Recent developments in management accounting, facilitated by the increased use of computers, include the greater employment of the mathematical and statistical methods of operational research and greater power to simulate the outcomes of alternative decisions. This development has, however, been matched by a growing interest in behavioural aspects of accounting, for example, studies of the human response to budgets and other targets set by management accountants. The whole area of accounting is currently one of rapid change, both in research and in practice.

Geoffrey Whittington
University of Cambridge

Further reading

Arnold, J. and Hope, A. (1990) *Accounting for Management Decisions*, 2nd edn, Englewood Cliffs, NJ.
Arnold, J., Hope, A., Southworth, A. and Kirkham, L. (1994) *Financial Accounting*, 2nd edn, Englewood Cliffs, NJ.
Ashton, D., Hopper, T. and Scapens, R. (eds) (1990) *Issues in Management Accounting*, Englewood Cliffs, NJ.
Kellas, J. and Nobes, C. (1990) *Accounting Explained*. Harmondsworth.
Parket, R. H. (1988) *Understanding Company Financial Statements*, 3rd edn, Harmondsworth.
Whittington, G. (1992) *The Elements of Accounting: An Introduction*, Cambridge, UK.

See also: capital consumption; stock-flow analysis.

activation and arousal

The terms activation and arousal have often been used interchangeably to describe a continuum ranging from deep sleep or coma to extreme terror or excitement. This continuum has sometimes been thought of as referring to observed behaviour, but many psychologists have argued that arousal should be construed in physiological terms. Of particular importance in this connection is the ascending reticular activating system, which is located in the brain-stem and has an alerting effect on the brain.

Some question the usefulness of the theoretical constructs of activation and arousal. On the positive side, it makes some sense to claim that elevated arousal is involved in both motivational and emotional states. It appears that individual differences in personality are related to arousal levels, with introverts being characteristically more aroused than extroverts (H. J. Eysenck 1967). In addition, proponents of arousal theory have had some success in predicting performance effectiveness on the basis of arousal level. In general, performance is best when the prevailing level of arousal is neither very low nor very high. Particularly important is the fact that there are sufficient similarities among the behavioural effects of factors such as intense noise, incentives and stimulant drugs to encourage the belief that they all affect some common arousal system.

On the negative side, the concepts of activation and of arousal are rather amorphous. Different physiological measures of arousal are often only weakly correlated with one another, and physiological, behavioural and self-report measures of arousal tend to produce conflicting evidence. Faced with these complexities, many theorists have suggested that there is more than one kind of arousal. For example, H. J. Eysenck (1967) proposed that the term arousal should be limited to cortical arousal, with the term activation being used to refer to emotional or autonomic arousal.

It may be desirable to go even further and identify three varieties of arousal. For example, a case can be made for distinguishing among behavioural, autonomic and cortical forms of arousal (Lacey 1967). Alternatively, Pribram and McGuinness (1975) argued for the existence of stimulus-produced arousal, activation or physiological readiness to respond, and effort in the sense of activity co-ordinating arousal and activation processes.

In sum, the basic notion that the behavioural effects of various emotional and motivational manipulations are determined at least in part by internal states of physiological arousal is plausible and in line with the evidence. However, the number and nature of the arousal dimensions that ought to be postulated remains controversial. In addition, there is growing suspicion that the effects of arousal on behaviour are usually rather modest and indirect. What appears to happen is that people respond to non-optimal levels of arousal (too low or too high) with various strategies and compensatory activities designed to minimize the adverse effects of the prevailing level of arousal (M. W. Eysenck 1982). Thus, the way in which performance is maintained at a reasonable level despite substantial variations in arousal needs further explanation.

Michael W. Eysenck
University of London

References

Eysenck, H. J. (1967) *The Biological Basis of Personality*, Springfield, IL.

Eysenck, M. W. (1982) *Attention and Arousal: Cognition and Performance*, Berlin.

Lacey, J. I. (1967) 'Somatic response patterning and stress: some revisions of activation theory', in M. H. Appley and R. Trumbull (eds) *Psychological Stress*, New York.

Pribram, K. H. and McGuinness, D. (1975) 'Arousal, activation, and effort in the control of attention', *Psychological Review* 82.

See also: aggression and anger; emotion; stress.

administration, public *see* public administration

adolescence

Definitions of adolescence typically indicate that it is the period during which those who have previously been encompassed within the category 'children' grow up. The very vagueness of when children can be said to have grown up is reflected in the lack of precision about when adolescence is supposed to occur. Most definitions indicate that it occurs between puberty and the attainment of physiological and/or psychological maturity. Both the onset (and end) of puberty and the attainment of maturity are extremely difficult to specify because it is possible to define them in a variety of ways and they occur at different times for different people. As a result, some writers concentrate more on adolescence as a hypothetically constructed period rather than as a precise age range. Those who do specify the adolescent years vary slightly in the ages they define, but generally indicate an extremely long period, from about 9 years to 25 years. The focus on puberty as crucial to the definition of adolescence has produced a concentration on biological, individualistic development rather than social development, although these areas are, in fact, inextricably linked.

The US psychologist Granville Stanley Hall is usually credited with the 'discovery' of adolescence in the late 1880s when he brought together a range of ideas which were current at the time. These ideas were similar to those described by Aristotle and Plato more than 2000 years ago and some of the themes identified by Hall have continued to generate interest. Hall borrowed the term *Sturm und Drang* (storm and stress) from German literature and applied it to the period of adolescence. This phrase is still often used, but rather imprecisely, to encompass both antisocial conduct and emotional turmoil, often also invoking psychological notions of an 'identity crisis' (borrowed from psychoanalytic theory) or a 'generation gap' between young people and their parents (Coleman and Hendry 1990).

Investigations of these phenomena (identity crisis and generation gap) indicate that a minority of adolescents do experience difficulties, but have not provided support for the belief that such difficulties are universal, or even widespread. However, twentieth-century concerns with (and moral panics about) political and social issues such as youth unemployment, juvenile delinquency, drug abuse and adolescent sexuality (both heterosexuality and homosexuality) have resulted in a profusion of publications on adolescence. More often than not, such publications take it for granted that adolescence is problematic (Griffin 1993).

Writing on adolescence highlights epistemological contradictions between the study of adolescence and work in other areas. Following the work of the psychoanalyst Erik Erikson, it is often asserted that adolescence is a critical phase or period in the life course when identity has to be established in order for young people to become ready to assume adult sexuality and other adult responsibilities. However, this formulation runs counter to theoretical movements in developmental psychology which have shifted away from both age-stage thinking and from notions of critical periods. Furthermore, much of the outpouring of work on identity in adolescence has assumed that identities are coherent, unitary and hierarchically organized. Other work on identities or subjectivities from a range of disciplines has theorized it differently: as fragmented, potentially contradictory and multiple. This idea of fluidity and change in identities has become increasingly influential.

The problems of adolescence are generally assumed to be creations of late modernity. Yet historical analyses indicate that, far from being novel, many generations have considered that young people (and it is mostly young men who have been studied) are problematic (Cohen 1986). Those who refer to adolescence as a twentieth-century creation are generally referring to the fact that young people reach puberty earlier, stay in full-time education and hence remain dependent for longer than previous generations. There have also been suggestions that it is the absence, in western societies, of status markers signalling entry into adulthood that produces the interim state of adolescence.

The area of adolescence demonstrates commonalities and differences between psychology and other disciplines. Sociologists, for example, tend to refer to youth rather than to adolescence. However, the difference in terminology does not necessarily indicate different approaches to the age group. Some European traditions of sociological analysis of youth began with the psychological idea of adolescence as that phase of life in which individuals seek and formulate a self-concept and identity. The reason for this was the premise that the formation of subjectivity is significant for social integration and aspects of social change (Chisholm *et al.* 1990).

Another joint adolescence/youth research tradition has been concerned with transitions to (un)employment. In psychology this has been particularly concerned with the psychological impact of youth unemployment, since, at least for young men, employment has long been considered one of the indicators of the attainment of independent adult status. In sociology, it has been largely macroanalytic and concerned with the ways in which school students experience school as well as how the educational system and pedagogic practices have an impact on social reproduction and social change.

A tradition which has been particularly influential was started at the Centre for Contemporary Cultural Studies in Britain. Their approach dominated youth research in the 1970s and early 1980s, gained influence in a range of countries and had an impact on subsequent research. Their orientation was a cultural studies one that challenged the tendency for adolescence to be discussed as if all young people pass through it at the same time and in the same way. Work in this tradition deconstructed notions that the category 'youth' is unitary and universal and argued that young people are differentiated by race and social class, but that, in themselves, young people also constitute a class fraction. A major part of youth studies within sociology came to be the study of youth subcultures, usually male working-class subcultures, with a focus on leisure pursuits and style. Some have argued that the result of this was a trivializing of the whole 'youth question' to one of 'storm and dress' instead of the psychological 'storm and stress' (Cohen 1986). The lack of attention to young women in such work has also been much criticized (McRobbie 1991).

While there are similarities between the sociological study of youth and the psychological study of adolescence, there are also some notable differences. One important focus of sociology is the study of social divisions as a means to the understanding of structured systems of inequality along divisions of gender, race, social class and geography. The issue of the underclass and the polarization between relatively affluent and poor people has been consistently discussed since the late 1970s in sociology. Although the treatment of race and ethnicity in sociology has presented a rather two-dimensional picture of black and other minority young people, they continue to be absent within most of psychology, except when their racialized identities are being discussed. Social class and structural position have also been neglected within much of psychology although they are inextricably linked to definitions of adolescence and the ways in which young people spend their time. Gender among young people has not received a great deal of attention either in sociology or in psychology. However, it has also tended to receive rather different treatment in the two disciplines because sociologists have focused on young women's cultures while psychologists have tended to compare young women and young men.

The study of adolescence is thus a burgeoning field which, since it draws on a range of competing traditions from a number of disciplines, is far from unified.

Ann Phoenix
University of London

References

Chisholm, L., Buchner, P., Kruger, H.-H. and Brown, P. (eds) (1990) *Childhood, Youth and Social Change*, London.

Cohen, P. (1986) *Rethinking the Youth Question*, London.

Coleman, J. and Hendry, L. (1990) *The Nature of Adolescence*, 2nd edn, London.

Griffin, C. (1993) *Representations of Youth: The Study of Youth and Adolescence in Britain and America*, London.

McRobbie, A. (1991) *Feminism and Youth Culture: From Jackie to Just Seventeen*, London.

Further reading

Adams, G., Gullotta, T. and Montemayor, R. (eds) (1992) *Adolescent Identity Formation*, London.

Brooks-Gunn, J., Lerner, R. and Petersen, A. (eds) (1991) *The Encyclopedia on Adolescence*, New York.

Carnegie Council on Adolescent Development (1992) *A Matter of Time: Risk and Opportunity in the Non-School Hours*, New York.

Heath, S. B. and McLaughlin, M. (eds) (1993) *Identity and Inner-City Youth: Beyond Ethnicity and Gender*, New York.

Moore, S. and Rosenthal, D. (1993) *Sexuality in Adolescence*, London.

See also: childhood; life cycle; life-span development.

advertising

Advertising, at its simplest, can be defined as the market communication of sellers of goods and services. Much of the early attention to advertising came from economists and was based around the key concept of *information* operating within a national market structure. A great deal of empirical research has been conducted on the effectiveness of advertising in raising product demand (both for individual campaigns as well as aggregate market consumption). The overall results have been inconclusive with regard to the economic effectiveness of advertising (Albion and Farris 1981).

Among the first theorists to develop alternatives to the concept of information were Marxist economists, who stressed instead its persuasive and manipulative functions. Advertising was viewed as a key component in the creation of demand, upon which capitalism increasingly came to rely as its productive capacity outstripped the provision of basic needs. In this view advertising is an indispensable institution to the very survival of the system, solving the growing difficulties of 'realization' in late capitalism (the transformation of value embedded in commodities into a money form) (Mandel 1978).

The location of advertising within this broader set of factors has prompted a great deal of historical work on the origins of the institution of advertising. Stuart Ewen (1976) pioneered this field, arguing that advertising fulfilled a key double function for capitalism at the turn of the century: both creating demand for the unleased industrial capacity of industry, as well as attempting to deflect attention away from class conflict at the workplace by redefining identity as being based around consumption rather than production. It was seen as a new and vital institution as capitalism transformed from its industrial to its consumer stage. Many other critical social theorists continue to see this as the most important function of advertising for capitalism. The cultural theorist Raymond Williams (1980) called advertising 'a magic system' that deflected attention away from the class nature of society by stressing consumption. In much of this literature advertising is seen as being the chief vehicle for the creation of *false needs*.

In this shift away from seeing the effects of advertising solely in economic terms, research space was opened up for a view of advertising that stressed its much broader and general effects. Leiss *et al.* (1990) argued for locating advertising within an institutional perspective (mediating the relations between business and media) in which the question of advertising's role in influencing sales was seen as much less important (and interesting) than its role as a vehicle of *social communication* (how it tried to sell goods by appealing to consumers along a whole range of dimensions not directly connected to goods – individual, group and family identity; the sense of happiness and contentment; the uses of leisure; gender and sexual identity, etc.). Advertising here was described as an important part of the 'discourse through and about objects' that any society has to engage in. In this extension beyond a strictly economic orientation to a *cultural* perspective, the power of advertising was redefined also. Its influence was seen as being based on its ubiquitous presence in the everyday lives of people, stemming from its *privileged* position within the discursive structures of modern society. It is an institution that not only reflects broader cultural values but also plays a key role in re-directing and emphasizing some of these values over others. In this regard it was seen as performing a function similar to myth in older societies (Leymore 1975). Viewed from this perspective, advertising became seen as an important historical repository for shifting cultural values during the course of the twentieth century. Social historians (e.g. Marchand 1985) as well as anthropologists (e.g. McCracken 1988) used the data provided by this repository for their own broader historical and cross-cultural analysis.

Much of the recent (academic and social) concern with advertising is based on this view of it as a vital component of *popular culture*. The most sustained social science analysis of advertising has concerned the role it plays in *gender socialization*. Based largely on the methodology of content analysis, it has been conclusively shown that men and women are portrayed in very different types of social roles in advertising: women are represented in much narrower and subordinated ways (largely as sex objects or in domestic activities) than men (Courtney and Whipple 1983). There has been much speculation on the link between commercial images of gender and the subordination of women within society. The most advanced theoretical work on gender came from Erving Goffman (1979) who argued that the visual subordination of women was based on advertising presenting 'real-life' subordination in a 'hyper-ritualiziatic' form – again reflecting dominant cultural values as well as powerfully reinforcing them.

Another important area of concern around advertising is the effect that it has on *children's socialization* along a broad range of dimensions, especially health (in terms of nutrition) as well as the development of intellectual and imaginative capacities. In the most comprehensive analysis of its kind, Kline (1994) has argued that the marketing of children's toys has had a severe negative impact upon the kind of play that children engage in (limiting imagination and creativity), as well as inter-gender interaction and child–parent interaction.

Advertising is also connected with *health* concerns to do with the marketing of products such as alcohol, tobacco and pharmaceutical drugs. In particular, a great deal of attention has been paid to the relationship between tobacco advertising and tobacco addiction, with critics arguing that the nicotine industry uses advertising to maintain present markets by reassuring smokers about possible health concern, as well as drawing new users (largely children) into the market.

Increasingly, the techniques learned from product advertising have extended their reach into other areas of social life, such that more and more of the discourses of modern society are mediated through a commercial lens. Modern *political campaigns* are run the same as any other marketing campaign for a consumer good. Commentators have wondered about the impact this may have on the nature of democracy and the types of candidates that the process brings forth. Public health campaigns (e.g. for AIDS education) are also using the techniques and the services developed first in the advertising industry (leading to the field labelled as social marketing).

There has also been much concern about the effect that global advertising will have on the cultural values of traditional societies hitherto outside the communication influence of the market, as well as the influence on media editorial content (entertainment and news) of income revenues that stem from advertisers (Collins 1993).

Sut Jhally
University of Massachusetts

References

Albion, P. and Farris, M. (1981) *The Advertising Controversy*, Boston, MA.

Collins, R. (1993) *Dictating Content*, Washington, DC.

Courtney, A. and Whipple, T. (1983) *Sex Stereotyping in Advertising*, Lexington, MA.

Ewen, S. (1976) *Captains of Consciousness*, New York.

Goffman, E. (1979) *Gender Advertisements*, New York.

Kline, S. (1993) *Out of the Garden*, London.

Leiss, W., Kline, S. and Jhally, S. (1990) *Social Communication in Advertising*, New York.

Leymore, V. (1975) *Hidden Myth: Structure and Symbolism in Advertising*, London.

McCracken, G. (1988) *Culture and Consumption*, Bloomington, IN.

Mandel, E. (1978) *Late Capitalism*, London.

Marchand, R. (1985) *Advertising the American Dream*, Berkeley, CA.

Williams, R. (1980) 'Advertising: the magic system', in R. Williams (ed.) *Problems in Materialism and Culture*, London.

age organization

All societies share (up to a point) two components of age organization. These are age itself and the principles that govern seniority within each family, such as birth order and generational differences. In most pre-industrial societies, family position determines status, and age is a moderating factor only when there is an obvious discrepancy. In certain areas, however, and especially among males in East Africa, age is a major principle of social organization reckoned normally from the time at which groups of adolescents are initiated together into adulthood and share a bond that unites them for the remainder of their lives. Where ranking by age is controlled outside the family, this may inhibit competition between males that might otherwise be generated within the family. In other instances, anomalies between age and generational seniority may be critical and provide essential clues for exploring age organization in the wider social context; in extreme instances this should more accurately be described as a *generational system* rather than an *age system*. In other words, age organization has to be viewed as a principle which may in some way structure the anomalies thrown up by the kinship system.

No age organization can be satisfactorily studied as an entity separated from its wider social context; for this reason many existing accounts of such systems which imply that they are self-contained and self-explanatory do not in fact explain very much, while those that seek to pursue the ramifications of the age system are inevitably daunting in their scope.

In the analysis of age organizations, the term *age-set* (sometimes age group, or *classe d'âge* in French) may be used to refer to all those who are initiated in youth during a definite span of time, and as a group share certain constraints and expectations for the remainder of their lives; and *age grade* (*échelon d'âge* in French) refers to a status through which all individuals pass at some period of their lives unless they die first. Each is an institutionalized arrangement governed by an explicit set of rules. The Nuer of the Southern Sudan have age-sets into which boys are initiated, but beyond this point they have no age grades. In our own society, we have age grades relating to infancy, schooling, adulthood and retirement, but (schools apart) we have no age-sets; members pass through these successive grades of their lives as individuals, and alone. In the more formalized instances of age organization, both institutions exist, and members of an age-set pass together through the various age grades, rather like pupils in a school. Using a ladder as an analogy for the system of age stratification, each rung (*échelon*) would represent an age grade, and successive age-sets would pass up it in procession, with youths climbing on to the lowest rung on initiation.

This procession involves a regulated cycle of promotions with a new age-set formed on the lowest rung once every cycle. The example of our own school system, stratified by year and with mass promotions once a year, is extremely rudimentary and consciously contrived to fulfil a task. In age organizations that span the entire lives of adults, the procession is more complex and the precise span of the periodic cycle is less predictable. A constantly changing configuration of roles occurs as members of each age-set mature and step up the ladder. Spacing tends to be uneven, with a certain jostling between successive age-sets at one point and sometimes a vacant rung elsewhere – an intermediate age grade with no incumbent. Changes in this configuration are predictable, however, and one complete cycle later there will be jostling and unoccupied rungs at precisely the same levels on the ladder, although each age-set meanwhile will have climbed to the position previously held by its predecessor. The anthropologist who normally only sees the system during one phase of the cycle, which may span fifteen years or more in some societies, has to use indirect evidence to piece together the profile of a complete cycle, but the existence of such regularities – the predictability of each successive phase – clearly indicates that this is indeed a system with its own inner logic and feedback mechanisms.

It is probably significant that formalized age systems are especially widespread in Africa, where there is a pronounced respect for older men in the more traditional areas and generally a higher polygyny rate than in any other part of the world. The older men are the polygynists, and the younger men correspondingly often face a prolonged bachelorhood. The existence of an age organization tends to structure the balance of power among men between the young who have reached physical maturity, and the old whose experience and widespread influence remain their principal assets despite failing strength and falling numbers. This may be regarded as a balance between nature and culture, and is reflected in much of the symbolism associated with age organization which often emphasizes the depravity of youth and the respect due to old age, and imposes circumcision as a major step in the civilizing process administered by older men. It is they who control the rate at which younger men advance, when they can marry, and what privileges they can enjoy. Unlike the more widely reported opposition between males and females, a dynamic transformation constantly in play is between young and old, and the young have a long-term interest in the status quo which women can never enjoy in male-dominated societies. It is never a question of *if* they will take over from the older men, but when and in what manner. They have to assert themselves to show their mettle, and yet restrain themselves from any flagrant violation of the system that might undermine the gerontocratic system and damage their own reputation when they become older men. In nature, it is often males at their physical prime who control the females of the herd. In gerontocratic culture there is a displacement towards the men who are past their physical prime. They are the polygamists, while the younger men must wait as bachelors. The age organization, with its frequent emphasis on ritual and moral values, provides a system which the older men must control if they are to maintain their advantage.

Paul Spencer
University of London

Further reading

Baxter, P. T. W. and Almagor, U. (eds) (1978) *Age, Generation and Time: Some Features of East African Age Organisations*, London.

Spencer, P. (1976) 'Opposing streams and the gerontocratic ladder: two models of age organisation in East Africa', *Man* (ns) 12.

—— (1983) 'Homo ascendens et homo hierarchicus', in M. Abélès and C. Collard (eds) *Aînesse et générations en Afrique*, ICAES.

Stewart, F. H. (1977) *Fundamentals of Age-Group Systems*, New York.

See also: life cycle; life-span development; rites of passage.

age-sex structure

The age-sex structure of a population is its distribution by age and sex. The classification of the population according to age and sex can be given either in absolute numbers or in relative numbers, the latter being the ratio of the population in a given age-sex category to the total population of all ages by sex or for both sexes. The age distribution is given either in single years of age or in age groups, for example, five-year age groups. Broad age groups such as 0 to 14, 15 to 59, 60 and over are also sometimes used. The grouping of ages depends on the degree of precision desired, and on the quality of the data at hand. If data are defective, as in some developing countries where people do not know their precise age, the classification by age groups is often to be preferred to the distribution by individual year of age, even if this implies a loss of information.

A graphic presentation of the age-sex structure of the population is the so-called *population pyramid*. This is a form of histogram, absolute or relative population figures being given on the axis of the abscissa, and age or age groups being represented on the ordinate. Male data are given on the left-hand side of the axis of ordinates and female data on the right-hand side. The areas of the rectangles of the histogram are taken to be proportional to the population numbers at each age or age group.

Figure 1 presents, as an example, the population pyramid of Algeria in 1966. Population figures at each age are given here per 10,000 persons of all ages and of both sexes. One sees that the population of Algeria is young: the population under 15 years of age, for example, is quite large compared to the rest. One also sees that the classification by age in the Algerian census of 1966 is defective. People tend to round off the age they declare, yielding higher population numbers at ages ending by digits 0 and 5. In the Algerian case, this age-heaping effect is more pronounced for females than for males.

Another useful graph shows the differential distribution of sexes by age, presenting sex ratios by age or age group. Sex ratios are obtained by dividing the number of males in each age group by the corresponding number of females. The results are often called *masculinity ratios*. Masculinity ratios tend to decrease with age. At young ages there are usually more boys than girls: approximately 105 male births occur per 100 female births. As age increases, masculinity ratios decline and become lower than 1, due to the prevalence of higher age-specific risks of dying for males than for females. On the whole, there

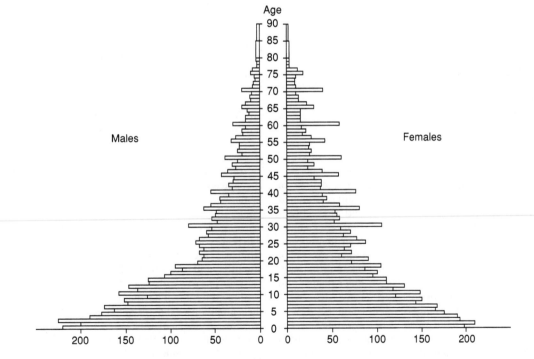

Figure 1   Population pyramid of Algeria (1966) (per thousand inhabitants)

are usually more females than males in the total population, due to excess male mortality. Masculinity ratios by age are also dependent on the impact of migration. If migration is sex-specific, masculinity ratios will reflect this phenomenon at the ages concerned.

One often speaks of young or old age structures. In the former case, the proportion of young in the population is high; the opposite is true in the second case. Young population age structures are essentially linked to high fertility. Ageing population structures are observed as fertility declines. The impact of mortality decline on age structure is much smaller than that of fertility decline, as the decrease in risks of dying affects all ages simultaneously. If decreases in risks of dying occur mainly at young ages, lower mortality will actually rejuvenate the population; the converse is true if gains in life expectancy are obtained principally at old ages.

If fertility and mortality remain constant over time and the population is closed to migration, a *stable* age structure will eventually result in the long run: the age distribution becomes invariant and depends solely on the age-specific fertility and mortality schedules. This property has been demonstrated by A. J. Lotka and is known as *strong ergodicity*.

Guillaume Wunsch
University of Louvain

Further reading

Coale, A. J. (1957) 'How the age distribution of a human population is determined', *Cold Spring Harbor Symposia on Quantitative Biology* 22.

—— (1964) 'How a population ages or grows younger', in R. Freedman (ed.) *Population: The Vital Revolution.*

ageing

The proportion of older adults in the populations of western countries continues to increase and is estimated to reach around 13 per cent by the end of the twentieth century. An understanding of the kinds of changes in cognitive processes and mental abilities that accompany normal ageing is important for many aspects of social policy, such as the appropriate age of retirement, the provision of housing suitable for older people and the need for support services.

The process of ageing is often confounded with other associated factors, such as deteriorating physical health, poor nutrition, bereavement, social isolation and depression, which also affect mental abilities so that it is difficult for researchers to isolate and identify the effects of ageing. In addition, poor performance may be the product of sensory deficits, anxiety or lack of motivation rather than of mental deterioration.

Many mental abilities do show age-related deficits but others are unimpaired. In the words of Rabbitt (1993) it is quite wrong to suppose that 'it all goes together when it goes'. Different abilities show quite different rates and patterns of deterioration. Moreover, differences between individuals tend to increase in older populations. Most individuals begin to show some slight decline by the mid-sixties; with others problems begin earlier and are more severe; and about 10 per cent, the so-called 'super-old', preserve their faculties unimpaired into late old age. Traditional psychometric testing has yielded age norms for performance on batteries of standard intelligence tests. The results have led to a distinction between crystallized (or age invariant) intelligence and fluid (age sensitive) intelligence. Tests which measure intellectual attainments such as vocabulary, verbal ability and factual knowledge reflect crystallized intelligence and show relatively little effect of age. Tests measuring mental processes such as the speed and accuracy with which information can be manipulated as in backward digit span, digit-symbol substitution and reasoning, reflect fluid intelligence and generally reveal an age-related decline. Nevertheless, the pattern of decline within the category of fluid abilities is not uniform. The relationship between chronological age and performance on memory tasks is not necessarily the same as the relationship between age and speed of information processing. These complex patterns pose problems for theorists such as Salthouse (1992) who attribute age-related decline to the single global factor of 'general slowing'.

Experimental techniques reveal not only which tasks are impaired by ageing but also which of the component stages or processes are affected. For example, experimental studies of memory indicate that the retrieval stage is relatively more affected than encoding or storage and that short-term or 'working' memory is relatively more impaired than long-term memory. Semantic memory, which stores general knowledge, is stable, whereas episodic memory, which records events and experiences, is more likely to be defective. Age differences are most evident in demanding and unfamiliar tasks which require conscious effortful attention and the observed age difference tends to increase linearly with task complexity.

Since the mid-1980s many researchers have turned their attention to the systematic study of the effects of cognitive ageing on performance in everyday life. Using questionnaires, observations and naturalistic experiments which mimic real-life situations, the practical problems which commonly confront older adults have been identified (Cohen 1993) and, in some cases, remedial therapies have been devised. For example, older people tend to have particular difficulty in calling proper names; in remembering to carry out intended actions; and in remembering whether an action such as taking medicine has been performed or only thought about. Memory for the location of objects and for novel routes is unreliable. Memory for the details of texts and conversations is less efficient, and memory for the source of information (who said what) also tends to be poorly retained. Skills which require rapid processing of information from several sources such as driving also deteriorate markedly. Nevertheless, older people often develop effective compensatory strategies for coping with such problems, making more use of mnemonic devices, making adjustments in lifestyle and devoting more effort and attention to selected activities.

Although the effects of cognitive ageing have been catalogued in considerable detail, much work remains to be done in developing a comprehensive theoretical framework and in mapping the cognitive changes on to the neurophysiological changs in the ageing brain.

Gillian Cohen
Open University

References

Cohen, G. (1993) 'Memory and ageing', in G. M. Davies and R. H. Logie (eds) *Memory in Everyday Life: Advances in Psychology*, vol. 100, Amsterdam.

Rabbit, P. M. A. (1993) 'Does it all go together when it goes? The Nineteenth Bartlett Lecture', *Quarterly Journal of Experimental Psychology 46A*.

Salthouse, T. A. (1992) *Theoretical Perspectives on Aging*, Hillsdale, NJ.

Further reading

Craik, F. I. M. and Salthouse, T. A. (1992) *Handbook of Aging and Cognition*, Hillsdale, NJ.

See also: gerontology, social.

agency, agent *see* principal and agent

aggression and anger

Biological/instinctual, psychoanalytic, ethological, social learning and cognitive theorists have all attempted to further our understanding of aggression, often spurred by a stated concern about humans' capacity to inflict suffering on others and by fears for the future of the species. While most would accept that some progress has been made, the actual achievements of social scientists to date are thought by some to be limited. The reasons for these limitations are of interest in themselves. Marsh and Campbell (1982) attribute lack of progress to a number of factors, including the difficulties in studying aggression, both in laboratory and naturalistic settings, and the compartmentalization of the academic world, such that researchers fail to cross the boundaries dividing psychology from sociology, physiology and anthropology, or even the subdivisions within psychology itself.

There are, however, two even more basic problems which have inhibited progress. The first is the difficulty in arriving at any generally acceptable definition of aggression, and the second is the related problem of the over-inclusiveness of the theories themselves. An important starting-point in providing an adequate definition is to distinguish aggression from anger and hostility. Anger refers to a state of emotional arousal, typically with autonomic and facial accompaniments. A person may be angry without being behaviourally destructive and vice versa. Hostility refers to the cognitive/evaluative appraisal of other people and events. It would be possible to appraise a particular group in society in very negative terms without their eliciting anger or overt aggression, though in most cases cognition and affect will be intimately linked (see below).

Aggression itself refers to overt behaviour, though precisely what sort of behaviour should be labelled aggressive is controversial. Bandura (1973) proposes cutting through the 'semantic jungle' in this area by restricting the term to acts resulting in personal injury or destruction of property, while accepting that injury may be psychological as well as physical. There then remain problems in defining what is injurious and in dealing with 'accidental' aggression (where injury is inflicted but not intended) and 'failed' aggression (as when a person tries to shoot another person but misses). In general, the definition of an act as aggressive involves a social judgement on the part of the observer. For this reason, injurious acts may not be labelled as aggressive when socially prescribed (for example, capital punishment) or when they support values the observer endorses (for example, a parent beating a child to instil godfearing virtue). In this sense, labelling a behaviour as aggressive inevitably has a social and political dimension to it.

The second difficulty lies in the breadth of activities addressed by most theories. Stabbing another person in a fight, battering a baby, being abusive in a social encounter and waging warfare may all be behaviours that meet the definition of aggression, but they are also disparate activities with little obvious functional unity. This should, but often does not, preclude attempts to provide general theories which would account for them all. Many different theories are likely to be required to account for these different forms of aggressive behaviour.

In recent years the utility of one particular distinction has become apparent – that between 'angry' and 'instrumental' or what some have called 'annoyance-motivated' and 'incentive motivated' aggression (Zillman 1979). The former is preceded by affective arousal. The person is in an emotional, physiologically activated state, often induced by environmental frustration of some sort. In instrumental aggression, on the other hand, the aggressive act is used as a way of securing some environmental reward and emotional activation may not be present, as in the case of someone using violence to rob a bank. The two classes are not entirely independent in that environmental reinforcement is also involved in angry aggression, though the reward obtained is likely to be that of inflicting pain or injury itself.

The many sources of instrumental aggression have been well documented in psychological research. That some aggressive behaviour is indeed learned socially because it is effective in securing environmental rewards or because aggressive models for imitation exist is now widely accepted (for a review see Bandura 1973). The powerful effects of pressures towards obedience to authority in producing cruelty have also been shown in laboratory investigations. Recent years, however, have witnessed a renewal of interest in angry forms of aggression and it is on this work that I shall focus for the remainder of this article.

Angry aggression is an important feature of much of the violence which causes social concern. Studies of homicide, for example, suggest that the violent act is often a response to intense anger arousal. The violent person is often described as in a 'fury' or a 'rage', directed in many cases at a person with whom they have an intimate relationship (a wife or husband). Anger may also be involved in less obvious forms of violence. There is evidence, for example, that many rapes show features of angry aggression. A substantial number of rapists are in an angry/frustrated state preceding the assault and appear to be motivated to hurt and degrade the victim rather than to obtain sexual relief (Groth 1979).

Research on anger

Until the early 1980s, much less attention was directed by social scientists at the affect of anger than at its direct behavioural manifestations. Anger has been widely discussed by philosophers and poets but rarely by the experimental psychologist. The renewed interest in this phenomenological aspect of aggression stems in part from a general reconsideration of the emotions within psychology and also from developments in the field of cognition and its relationship to affect.

Anger seems to have four components – the environment, cognition, emotional/physiological arousal, and behaviour itself, and these components interact recip-

rocally in a complex fashion (Novaco 1978). The first two of these elements, in particular, have been the focus for experimental investigation. Anger and angry aggression are generally preceded by a triggering environmental event. There are a number of theories of what kind of event is likely to be important (the frustration-aggression theory, for example). Berkowitz (1982) argued persuasively that environmental events elicit aggression to the extent that they are *aversive*. Thus the absence of reward where it is expected or the blocking of goal-directed activity provoke aggression because they are unpleasant. Experiencing failure, being insulted, unjustly treated or attacked share the property of aversiveness and are capable, therefore, of producing anger and aggression. Berkowitz suggests that both humans and animals are born with a readiness to flee or to fight when confronted by an aversive stimulus. Which reaction will occur will depend on learning experiences (flight, for example, may have been found to be more effective) and on the nature of the particular situation (a situation where the person has expectations of control may make fight more likely). Consistent with Berkowitz's thesis that aversiveness is critical are a number of laboratory and naturalistic studies showing, for example, that pain is a potent elicitor of angry aggression. Unpleasant smells, 'disgusting' visual stimuli and high temperatures have also been found to lower the threshold for aggression, though in the latter case the relationship is curvilinear.

Diary studies of what makes people angry in everyday life not only confirm the importance of aversive/frustrating events but also suggest a feature of anger not always apparent in laboratory studies – that it is predominantly elicited by *interpersonal* events. Other people, rather than things or impersonal occurrences, make us angry. James Averill (1982) found that people reported becoming mildly to moderately angry in the range of several times a day to several times a week and that only 6 per cent of incidents were elicited by a non-animate object. The frustrating person in over half the episodes was someone known and liked – friends and loved ones are common sources of aversive experiences.

The second component of anger is the cognitive processing of social and internal events. The concerns of cognitive theorists are typically with how people appraise, interpret and construct the social environment. Attribution theory has been a major force in cognitive theorizing, and attributional processes are now widely acknowledged to be relevant to angry aggression. Such processes are best viewed as mediating the emotional and behavioural responses to the aversive/frustrating events described above. The power of attributions can be appreciated by considering the differing emotional and behavioural consequences of various attributions for an event such as being knocked off one's bicycle on the way home from work. This painful and aversive occurrence might be attributed by the cyclist to personal inadequacies ('not looking where I was going') or to chance ('given the number of cars and bicycles it is inevitable some people are knocked down'). Neither of these attributions is, intuitively, likely to produce an aggressive response. Suppose, however, that the attribution was made that the car driver had deliberately intended to knock me off my bicycle. The threshold for aggression, at least towards the driver, might be expected to be considerably lowered by such an appraisal. Attributions of 'malevolent intent' of this sort have been shown to be important for anger and aggression (see Ferguson and Rule 1983).

The third and fourth components of anger are emotional/physiological arousal itself and the aggressive act which may or may not follow anger arousal. Anger is undoubtedly accompanied by autonomic activation (increases in blood pressure, heart rate, respiration and muscle tension and so on), but it is still unclear whether the pattern of activation can be discriminated from arousal caused by other emotions. Most experiences of anger in everyday life are not followed by physical aggression. Averill (1982) found that less than 10 per cent of angry episodes induced physical aggression. What he called 'contrary reactions', activities opposite to the instigation of anger, such as being very friendly to the instigator, were twice as frequent as physical aggression. Anger may produce a range of other reactions – the previous learning experiences of the individual are clearly important in determining whether frustration and anger are responded to with withdrawal, help-seeking, constructive problem-solving or what Bandura (1973) called 'self-anaesthetization through drugs and alcohol'.

The reciprocal bi-directional influence between the components of anger is something that has been stressed by Novaco (1978). Cognitions may induce anger and aggression, but behaving aggressively may activate hostile cognitions and also change the environment in such a way as to make the person even more frustrated. Hostile appraisals of other people are often self-fulfilling. Untangling the complex interrelationships between these environmental, cognitive, physiological and behavioural component processes will be the major task for future aggression researchers.

Kevin Howells
University of Leicester

References

Averill, J. R. (1982) *Anger and Aggression: An Essay on Emotion*, New York.

Bandura, A. (1973) *Aggression: A Social Learning Analysis*, Englewood Cliffs, NJ.

Berkowitz, L. (1982) 'Aversive conditions as stimuli to aggression', in L. Berkowitz (ed.) *Advances in Experimental Social Psychology* 15, New York.

Ferguson, T. J. and Rule, B. G. (1983) 'An attributional perspective on anger and aggression', in *Aggression: Theoretical and Empirical Reviews* Vol. 1, New York.

Groth, A. N. (1979) *Men who Rape*. New York.

Marsh, P. and Campbell, A. (eds) (1982) *Aggression and Violence*, Oxford.

Novaco, R. W. (1978) 'Anger and coping with stress', in J. P. Foreyt and D. P. Rathjen (eds) *Cognitive Behavior Therapy*, New York.

Zillman, D. (1979) *Hostility and Aggression*, Hillsdale, NJ.

See also: activation and arousal; emotion; social psychology.

agricultural economics

The first formal conceptualization of agriculture within economic theory can be attributed to the Physiocrats or, more specifically, to Quesnay's *Tableau Economique*, which modelled economic flows between different sectors on the eve of industrialization in France. Agriculture was held to be the only productive sector, since it allowed for extended reproduction in terms of grain, while the embryo manufacturing sector was seen merely to transform agricultural produce into other forms of artisanal or manufactured articles, and it was assumed that this latter process did not generate any additional economic value. A contrasting stance was adopted by English classical political economists. The key Ricardian argument was that the rising demand for food would extend the margin of cultivation to inferior lands and raise the price of grain as well as the rents accruing on all non-marginal land. Ricardo's pessimism about technological progress then led inexorably to the deduction that rent would erode the share of profit in the national product. Such a conceptualization of the economic process provided the theoretical underpinnings of the anti-landlord class bias of the classical economists. An exception was Malthus, who argued that agriculture was thus the generator not only of foodstuffs for the manufacturing sector, but also, crucially, of demand for its products.

From the common roots of classical political economy emerge two divergent systems of economic theorizing of agriculture: the Marxian and the neoclassical. The former focused special attention on the analysis of the role of agriculture in the transition from the feudal to the capitalist mode of production, a process characterized by primitive capital accumulation and surplus transfer from the pre-capitalist, mostly agrarian, sectors to the capitalist, mainly industrialist, ones. Both the classical and the Marxian approaches analyse the agricultural sector within a macroeconomic framework dealing with the structural position and functional role of agriculture in terms of intersectoral and national economic linkages; both emphasize the importance of the generation and extraction of agricultural surplus – in the form of industrial crops, food and labour – for industrialization; both treat, though to different degrees, the dynamic intrarural dimensions of production relations and organization as necessary parts of the analysis. Thus, agriculture and industry are treated as distinct sectors, characterized by different internal technological and production conditions, social and political organization, and by different functional roles in the process of economic development.

The second offshoot of classical economy, neoclassical economics, now forms the disciplinary mainstream, and agricultural economics (as generally defined in the curricula of most universities) is identified closely with the method and schema of neoclassical theory. In sharp contrast to other traditions, neoclassical agricultural economics focuses primarily on microeconomic issues dealing with the static efficiency of resource use in agricultural production. The optimal choice of products, and combinations of inputs to produce these, form virtually its exclusive concerns. The central problem of agricultural economics is then reduced to one of profit maximization by an individual farmer operating with specified resources and technologies in an economic environment marked by perfect competition in all input and output markets. There is no analysis of the structure of agrarian production relations and organization or its transformation *vis-à-vis* the stimulus of economic growth. In general, production relations, for example, share-cropping, are analysed specifically from the vantage point of their impact through implicit (dis)incentive effects on the efficient allocation of available resources by decision makers. Within this framework, there has been a plethora of empirical studies which have asked the question: are peasants efficient in their resource-use? The methodology has involved assuming perfect competition, and then deriving an econometric estimate – using cross-sectional data on a group of peasants – of a production function, frequently of the Cobb-Douglas type. A simple test for the equality of the estimated marginal productivity of each factor of production with respect to its relative price (with respect to the output) then reveals, within this paradigm, whether this decision maker could be adjudged to be efficient or not.

This framework was amplified initially in debates over sharecropping systems in the American South, but it has been advanced further in the contemporary context of rural development in the Third World. If one believes, as some celebrated neo-classical empirical studies argue, that peasants are poor but efficient, then additional agricultural growth is possible either if the relative price and hence the profitability of the

agricultural sector is boosted, or if there is technological progress. The recipe is thus an improvement in agriculture's terms of trade alongside the use of improved methods such as those characterizing the so-called green revolution. While policies for rural education, health, agricultural extension services and credit are justified as necessary for expediting rapid technological absorption, the prime emphasis is on the role of relative prices in guiding resource allocation. Another crucial corollary is that poor countries should not hesitate to concentrate resources on commercial crops and rely on heavy food imports so long as they enjoy a comparative trade advantage in the former at the going world prices. The validity of this policy package depends crucially on the realism of the fundamental premises underlying the neo-classical edifice. With regard to distribution, the twin assumptions of infinite factor substitution and perfectly competitive markets have been held to imply that growth would tend to increase the incomes of the landless labourers, leading to the contention that the benefits of agricultural growth would trickle down to the bottom echelons, even in highly inegalitarian property ownership structures. As such, neo-classical agricultural economics has provided the intellectual underpinnings for a conservative political programme.

Far from being perfectly competitive, however, agricultural product and factor markets are heavily segmented, interlocked and frequently governed by an unequal and personalized power equation between landed patrons and (near) landless clients; as such, peasants are frequently not independent decision makers. The production system has inherent externalities, for example, in soil conservation and irrigation, and uncertainties arising from information gaps and the elemental unpredictability of the delivery system and a changing technological matrix. A second criticism of the neo-classical approach applies to the behavioural postulates and the notion of efficiency. The economic calculus of rich farmers might be determined considerably by the longer-term objective of maximizing 'power' rather than short-term profits, while that of the poor is influenced by the immediate objective of guaranteeing survival in the face of price and output risks and uncertainty. The method ignores the realistic situation where the pursuit of efficient maximization algorithms of peasant profit-maximizers would lead dynamically to a process of collective deterioration, as in the widely observable illustrations of the vicious circle of ecological destruction. Neither is the question of the efficiency of the production relations themselves considered: alternative forms of production organization, *ceteris paribus*, could provide a powerful source of growth unrecognized by the paradigm of neo-classical agricultural economics. Finally, there are problems with the neo-classical modelling of agricultural production. For example, when the peasant farm is treated virtually as an industrial firm, the critical importance of the timing and interdependence of sequential cultivation operations is ignored. More significantly, the methodological validity of attempts to test for the economic efficiency of peasants through the use of a cross-sectional production function is highly dubious. The joint burden of these objections is to undermine the theoretical basis of the policy recommendations offered by the neoclassical approach.

Experience of Third World development in the post-colonial period has stimulated the discipline in several directions. Empirical studies have stimulated lively, theoretically eclectic debates, and resulted in the introduction of multidisciplinary approaches to the arena of conventional agricultural economics. Notable here are the resuscitation of Chayanov's theory of the demographic differentiation within the pre-1917 Russian peasant economy, Geertz's speculative interpretation of colonial rural Java, using the concept of agricultural involution, and Lipton's attribution of the persistence of rural poverty to the phenomenon of urban bias. However, underlying this multifaceted diversity of agricultural economics are the latent roots of further disagreement and debate.

Ashwani Saith
Institute of Social Studies, The Hague

Further reading

Bhaduri, A. (1883) *The Economic Structure of Backward Agriculture*, New York.
Bliss, C. J. and Stern, N. H. (1982) *Palanpur: The Economy of an Indian Village*, Oxford.
Rudra, A. (1982) *Indian Agricultural Economics*, Delhi.
Schultz, T. W. (1964) *Transforming Traditional Agriculture*, New Haven, CT.

See also: peasants; rural sociology.

aid

The terms aid or development aid (often also foreign aid or development assistance) are not entirely unambiguous and are often used with slightly different meanings by different writers and organizations. However, there is agreement that in essence resource transfers from a more developed to a less developed country (or from a richer country to a poorer country) qualify for inclusion in 'aid' provided they meet three criteria:

1 The objective should be developmental or charitable rather than military.
2 The donor's objectives should be non-commercial.
3 The terms of the transfer should have a concessional element ('grant element').

Each of these criteria gives rise to some conceptual difficulty. The first one neglects the factor of 'fungibility', that is, that up to a point the use of resources by the recipient country is somewhat flexible. For example, aid may be given and ostensibly used for developmental purposes, but in fact the recipient country may use its own resources set free by this transaction in order to buy armaments; or the aid may lead to leakages and abuses and result in the building up of bank accounts in Switzerland, rather than to the ostensible developmental objectives.

The second criterion, that the objective should be non-commercial, also presents difficulties. Much of the bilateral aid, that is, aid given by a single government to another government, is 'tied', which means that the proceeds must be spent on classified goods produced in the donor country. Here we clearly have a commercial objective mixed in with the developmental objective; it is again impossible to decide statistically at what point the transaction becomes a commercial transaction rather than aid. The line of division between export credits and tied aid of this kind is clearly a thin one. Moreover, many acts of commercial policy, such as reduction of tariffs or preferential tariff treatment given to developing countries under the internationally agreed GSP (Generalized System of Preferences) can be more effective aid than many transactions listed as aid – yet they are excluded from the aid concept.

The third criterion – that the aid should be concessional and include a grant element – is also not easy to define. What, for example, is a full commercial rate of interest at which the transaction ceases to be aid? The grant element may also lie in the duration of any loan, in the granting of a 'grace period' (a time lag between the granting of the loan and the date at which the first repayment is due). The DAC (Development Assistance Committee of the OECD, the Organization for Economic Cooperation and Development in Paris) makes a valiant attempt to combine all these different aspects of concessionality in to one single calculation of the grant element. However, such calculations are subject to the objection that the grant element from the donor's point of view may differ from that from the recipient's point of view. In DAC aid in 1990/91, some 72 per cent was direct grants and the loans had a 59 per cent grant element, resulting in an 'overall grant element' for total aid of 85 per cent. The Development Assistance Committee is the main source of aid statistics, and its tabulations and definitions are generally recognized as authoritative. DAC publishes an Annual Report under the title *Development Cooperation*;

the 1992 volume contained detailed tables and break-downs of aid flows.

The OECD countries (the western industrial countries including Japan, Australia and New Zealand) and the international organization supported by them, such as the World Bank, the Regional Development Banks, the UN Development Programme, and so on, account for the bulk of global aid. DAC also provides some data on other aid flows such as from OPEC (Organization of Petroleum Exporting Countries) countries and from former USSR countries. Private investment, lending by commercial banks and private export credits are by definition treated as commercial and thus excluded from aid, although they compose a significant proportion of inflows into developing countries. Bank lending and export credits were exceptionally high by historical standards during the late 1970s and early 1980s. These levels proved unsustainable due to changes in the external environment and imprudent fiscal policy. The ensuing 'debt crisis' resulted in a sudden collapse of resource flows into developing countries. The total resource flow into developing countries in 1991 was $131 billion, of which $57 billion was ODA (Overseas Development Administration) from DAC countries (excluding forgiveness of non ODA debt), an average ODA/GNP ratio of 0.33 per cent (OECD 1992).

There is a growing concern over the unbalanced geographical mix of these flows. An increasing percentage of official development assistance is being directed to Sub-Saharan Africa, which has very low foreign direct investment, hence becoming increasingly aid dependent, which is not desirable in the long term. There is a broad consensus among donors and recipients that the aim of aid should be to assist in basic objectives of sustainable, participatory economic and social development. The role of aid is increasingly considered to be one of poverty alleviation rather than growth creation.

One of the main distinctions is between bilateral aid and multilateral aid (contributions of multilateral institutions such as the World Bank, the Regional Development Banks, and so forth). This distinction is also not entirely clear. For example, the western European countries give some of their aid through the EU (European Union). EU aid is not bilateral nor is it fully multilateral as the World Bank is; it is therefore to some extent a matter of arbitrary definition whether EU aid should be counted as bilateral or multilateral. Multilateral aid is more valuable to the recipient than tied bilateral aid, because it gives a wider choice of options to obtain the imports financed by aid from the cheapest possible source. Untied bilateral aid would be equally valuable to the recipient; however, on political grounds, the recipient (and some donors, too)

may prefer the multilateral route. Multilateral aid constitutes about 25 per cent of total aid.

It has been frequently pointed out that aid donors could increase the value of their aid to the recipients without any real cost to themselves, either by channelling it multilaterally or by mutually untying their aid by reciprocal agreement. However, this might lose bilateral aid some of the political support which it acquires by tying and which gives national producers and workers a vested interest in aid. This is particularly important in the case of food aid. Nongovernmental organizations (NGOs), often in partnership with southern NGOs, are being increasingly recognized as holding an important role in aid distribution, particularly as a channel for official aid.

The 1980s saw a growing disenchantment with aid and consideration of the possibility that aid may even be damaging to the poor. Critics from the left have claimed that aid leads to the extension of international capitalism and supports the political motives of neo-colonial powers (the high percentage of US aid flowing to Israel and Egypt is an example of aid fulfilling political interests). From the right, critics have claimed that aid supports the bureaucratic extension of the state, acting against the interest of free market forces and long-term development (e.g. Bauer 1984) and that developing countries have a limited capacity to absorb aid.

Aid appraisals at a micro level have generally concluded that aid had a positive impact. A World Bank study in 1986 estimated a rate of return of 14.6 per cent for its projects (White 1992). Cassen found that 'projects on average do produce satisfactory results in a very large proportion of cases' (Cassen 1986: 307). However, some macroeconomic studies have failed to find a significant relationship between aid and growth. The macroeconomic role of aid can be modelled by a two gap model, shortages in capital creating savings and foreign exchange gaps, or bottlenecks, which can be bridged with foreign aid. However, whether or not aid does fulfil a positive macroeconomic role has not been empirically proven. Fears are often expressed that aid may be used to displace savings, particularly public sector savings. Additionally aid may have 'Dutch disease' effect, inflows of foreign aid increasing the price of non-tradable goods relative to tradables, hence creating the equivalent of a real exchange rate appreciation. This leads to a reduction in export competitiveness which may leave the country increasingly dependent upon aid.

Emergency relief is a part of ODA which is used in handling the consequences of an abnormal event which results in human suffering, including refugee assistance. Emergency aid is often considered as a separate category from a budget and planning perspective, although more effort is being made to link relief and long-term development assistance. In 1991 food aid comprised 6.1 per cent of total ODA aid by members of DAC (1993 Food Aid Review: 138), with a multilateral share of 23 per cent, similar to the multilateral share in financial aid. One-third of total food aid went to Sub-Saharan Africa, but Egypt and Bangladesh were the two largest recipients.

H. W. Singer
University of Sussex

References

1993 Food Aid Review, World Food Programme, Rome.

Bauer, P. (1984) *Reality and Rhetoric: Studies in the Economics of Development*, London.

Cassen, R. and associates (1986) *Does Aid Work?* Report to an intergovernmental task force, Development Committee, Oxford.

OECD (1992) *Development Cooperation 1992 Report*, Paris.

White, H. (1992) 'The macroeconomic impact of development aid: a critical survey', *Journal of Development Studies* 28(2).

Further reading

Krueger, A., Michalopoulos, C. and Ruttan, V. (1989) *Aid and Development*, Baltimore, MD.

Mosely, P., Harrigan, J. and Toye, J. (1991) *Aid and Power: The World Bank Policy-based Lending*, 2 vols, London.

See also: economic development; technical assistance; underdevelopment; World Bank.

alcoholism and alcohol abuse

Alcohol use typically becomes a social problem with the emergence of industrialized, urban forms of social organization. Social disruption is more likely to accompany drinking in densely populated environments, and where person–machine interaction is central to work. In such contexts, alcohol use is causally linked to many disruptive behaviours: violence, low productivity and jeopardizing others through driving, boating or bicycling while intoxicated. While conclusive evidence that drinking causes these behaviours is rare, public opinion in North America tends not to question the destructive impacts of alcohol.

Social science involvement in alcohol studies began after the 1933 repeal of Prohibition in the USA. Social scientists promoted the conception of alcoholism as a disease rather than as a moral weakness (Bacon 1958; Jellinek 1960). This 'disease model' links chronic destructive drinking to biochemical mechanisms that are still unspecified.

The dependence of drinking outcomes on cultural norms is a key contribution of social science. Anthropologists have documented the widely variant outcomes associated with similar levels of alcohol consumption across cultures, notwithstanding the fact that its biochemical interactions with the human organism should be similar everywhere. Studies of ethnic differences in rates of drinking and alcoholism brought out the importance of variant forms of socialization, social definition and social support (Marshall 1980).

There are, however, few widely adopted aetiological theories of alcohol abuse and alcoholism that are based in social science. While such theories exist (Akers 1977; Roman 1991; Trice 1966), their influence has been impeded by the premises underlying alcoholism intervention, especially Alcoholics Anonymous, and the treatment modalities that reflect its ideology. Furthermore, in most parts of the western world research funding flows toward medically linked science. Thus the alcoholism research establishment routinely presses for increased research allocations for work that adopts biological approaches.

Social scientists have been critical of the logic and internal consistency of the disease model of alcoholism (Fingarette 1988; Peele 1991). Their alternative proposals are unclear, however, especially as to how 'alcohol problems' should be treated differently from 'alcoholism'. What is called a new public health approach tends to muddle conceptions of deviant drinking, alcohol abuse, and alcohol dependence (Pittman 1991; Roman 1991).

A related body of research explores the consequences of different national and regional policies of alcohol distribution. These studies indicate that distribution policies influence the incidence of alcohol problems and alcoholism (Moore and Gerstein 1981). Given the heretofore myopic focus of alcohol research on North America and western Europe, a broader research base is vital as emerging nations struggle with radical changes in drinking norms accompanying both industrialization and the commercialization of alcohol distribution. Research by historians on all aspects of drinking and social policy is mushrooming and provides a critical background for cross-national considerations in the development of alcohol-related policies (Barrows and Room 1991).

While inconclusive, international comparisons have also put in question the view, common in Alcoholics Anonymous and in the treatment community, that abstinence is the only possible solution to alcohol abuse. A reduction of alcohol intake or a routinization of intake may also provide viable solutions (Heather and Robertson 1981). However, the diffusion of commercialized alcoholism treatment throughout the world tends to further the belief that the only cure is abstinence. This is fundamental to the medicalized model of alcoholism.

Social scientists are also involved in applied studies associated with alcohol problems. In the USA, Canada and Australia, social scientists have promoted the workplace as a setting within which persons with alcohol problems may be identified, confronted and rehabilitated without the costs of job loss and displacement (Sonnenstuhl and Trice 1990). In parallel fashion, social scientists have challenged the efficacy of educational strategies directed toward preventing alcohol problems among young people (Mauss *et al.* 1988).

In general, however, social science research on alcoholism is vastly overshadowed by the emphasis on biological aetiology and increasingly upon the potential of biomedical intervention. Fruitful social science research potential lies in understanding the dynamics of the various paradigms that ebb and flow across time and across nations, paradigms around which cultural conceptions of alcohol abuse and alcoholism are organized.

Paul Roman
University of Georgia

References

Akers, R. (1977) *Deviant Behavior and Social Learning*, Belmont, CA.

Bacon, S. (1958) 'Alcoholics do not drink,' *Annals of the American Academy of Political and Social Science* 315.

Barrows, S. and Room, R. (1991) *Drinking: Behaviors and Beliefs in Modern History*, Berkeley, CA.

Fingarette, H. (1988) *Heavy Drinking: The Myth of Alcoholism as a Disease*, Berkeley, CA.

Heather, N. and Robertson, I. (1981) *Controlled Drinking*, London.

Jellinek, E. M. (1960) *The Disease Concept of Alcoholism*, New Haven, CT.

Marshall, M. (ed.) (1980) *Beliefs, Behaviors, and Alcoholic Beverages*, Ann Abor, MI.

Mauss, A., Hopkins, R., Weisheit, R., and Kearney, K. (1988) 'The problematic prospects for prevention in the classroom: should alcohol education programmes be expected to reduce drinking by youth?', *Journal of Studies on Alcohol* 49.

Moore, M. and Gerstein, G. (eds) (1981) *Alcohol and Public Policy*, Washington, DC.

Peele, S. (1991) *The Diseasing of America: Addiction Treatment Out of Control*, New York.

Pittman, D. (1991) 'The new temperance movement', in D. Pittman and H. White (eds) *Society, Culture and Drinking Behavior Re-examined*, New Brunswick, NJ.

Roman, P. (1991) *Alcohol: The Development of Sociological Perspectives on Use and Abuse*, New Brunswick, NJ.

Sonnenstuhl, W. and Trice, H. (1990) *Strategies for Employee Assistance Programs*, 2nd edn, Ithaca, NY

Trice, H. M. (1966) *Alcoholism in America*, New York.

See also: drug use.

alienation

Alienation (in German *Entfremdung*), sometimes called estrangement, is a psychological, sociological or philosophical-anthropological category, largely derived from the writings of Hegel, Feuerbach and Marx.

In Hegel (1971 [1807]), we find the claim that the sphere of Spirit, at a certain stage in history, *splits up* into two regions: that of the 'actual world ... of self-estrangement', and that of pure consciousness, which is, says Hegel, simply the 'other form' of that same estrangement. In this situation, self-consciousness is in absolute disintegration; personality is split in two. Here we have the *'entire estrangement'* of reality and thought from one another. This alienation will be overcome only when the division between Nature and Spirit is overcome – when Spirit becomes 'divested of self', that is, itself externalized.

This massive, objective, idealist philosophy of history was challenged by Feuerbach (1936[1841]) whose critique of Hegel centred precisely around a rejection of the latter's conception of the process of alienation. It is not that Feuerbach takes the 'separation' between subject and object to be a philosophical mythology. But this separation, he thinks, is assigned the status of a 'false alienation' in Hegel's work. For while man is real, God is an imaginary projection: 'the consciousness of God is the self-consciousness of man, the perception of God the self-perception of man'. Nor is nature a self-alienated form of the Absolute Spirit. But this reference to a 'false' alienation in Hegel suggests the existence of something like a 'true' – that is, really existing or operative – form of alienation. And Feuerbach does indeed believe in such a form; for it is only in some relation of contact with the objects which man produces – thus separating them off from himself – that he can become properly conscious of himself.

Marx (1975[1844]) seems to disagree. He argues that it is just by creating a world of objects through his practical activity that man proves himself as a conscious species-being. Under capitalism, however, the objects produced by human labour come to confront him as something *alien*. So the product of labour is transformed into an alien object 'exercising power over him', while the worker's activity becomes an alien activity. Marx adds that man's species-being then turns into a being alien to him, estranging him from his human aspect, and that man is thus estranged from man.

Marx's early writings, including the so-called *1844 Manuscripts*, were (re)discovered in the 1930s. Thus it was that some of their themes, including that of 'alienation', found their way into political, sociological and philosophical writings of the following period, including works of a non-Marxist character. A psychological line in alienation theory can also be identified, partially derived from Hegel (see below). The concept also, of course, has an ethical aspect: alienation is generally considered (whatever theory it derives from) a bad thing. It has even been said (Sargent 1972) to be 'a major or even the dominant condition of contemporary life'. An abundant literature exists on uses of the term (see Josephson and Josephson 1962).

Lukes (1967) has clearly identified the fundamental difference between two concepts which are apparently often confused: that of alienation, and that – introduced by Durkheim – of anomie. For Durkheim the problem of anomic man is that he needs (but misses) rules to live by, limits to his desires and to his thoughts. Marx's problem is rather the opposite: that of man in the grip of a system from which he cannot escape.

Althusser (1969[1965]) developed a powerful critique of the notion of alienation as used by the young Marx, claiming that it was a metaphysical category abandoned by Marx in his later works.

It may finally be noted that the same term has appeared in the psychoanalytical writings of Lacan (1977[1966]), in the context of his theory of the 'mirror stage' in child development. This stage establishes an initial relation between the organism and its environment, but at the cost of a 'fragmentation' of the body. This may sound like a materialist version of Hegel's notion of the divided personality; and Lacan is indeed influenced by Hegel's analyses. It is, according to Lacan, in the relation between human subject and language that 'the most profound alienation of the subject in our scientific civilization' is to be found.

Grahame Lock
Catholic University of Nijmegen

References

Althusser, L. (1969[1965]) *For Marx*, London. (Original edn, *Pour Marx*, Paris.)
Feuerbach, L. (1936[1841]) *Das Wesen des Christentums*, Berlin.
Hegel, G. W. F. (1971[1807]) *The Phenomonology of Mind*, London. (Original edn, *System der Wissenschaft: Erster Teil, die Phänomenologie des Geistes*, Leipzig.)
Josephson, E. and Josephson, M. (1962) *Man Alone*, New York.
Lacan, J. (1977[1966]) *Ecrits*, London. (Original edn, *Ecrits*, Paris.)
Lukes, S. (1967) 'Alienation and anomie', in P. Laslett and W. C. Runciman (eds) *Philosophy, Politics and Society*, Oxford.
Marx, K. (1975[1844]) *Economic and Philosophic Manuscripts of 1844*, in K. Marx and F. Engels, *Collected Works*, vol. 3, London. (Original edn, *Ökonomisch-philosophische Manuskripte*.)
Sargent, L. T. (1972) *New Left Thought: An Introduction*, Homewood, IL.

Further reading

Blauner, R. (1964) *Alienation and Freedom: The Factory Worker and his Industry*, London.
Schaff, A. (1975) 'Alienation as a social and philosophical problem', *Social Praxis* 3.
Sykes, G. (ed.) (1964) *Alienation: The Cultural Climate of Modern Man*, 2 vols, New York.

See also: Marx, Karl Heinrich; Marx's theory of history and society.

altruism

Parents sacrifice themselves for their children. Gift giving and sharing are universal. People help others in distress, give blood and may even donate a bodily organ to a stranger while still alive. In the Second World War some hid Jews from the Nazis at the risk of their own lives, and in 1981 IRA hunger strikers died voluntarily for their cause.

Theories of the origin of such altruistic acts, intended to benefit others at a cost to oneself, have come from both evolutionary and cultural sources. While Darwinian evolution is commonly equated with a competitive struggle for existence, theories developed since the 1960s have shown that altruism towards kin (Grafen 1991; Hamilton 1964), and reciprocal altruism (co-operation) between unrelated individuals (Axelrod 1984) are both favoured by natural selection under certain conditions. Kin-directed altruism is favoured because relatives have a high chance of carrying the genes predisposing the altruist to selfless behaviour. This means that if the altruist's loss of fitness is outweighed by the relative's gain (devalued by the chance that the genes in question are carried by the relative), genes predisposing individuals to altruism will be favoured overall and spread through the population. The ubiquitous favouring of close kin is probably the result of such evolutionary forces.

The problem for the evolution of altruism between unrelated individuals is cheating, since those who receive without giving do best of all. When cheating can be punished, however, a game theory analysis shows that tit-for-tat reciprocation, that rewards altruism with altruism and punishes selfishness with selfishness, results in greater rewards than egoism (Axelrod 1984). When all individuals behave reciprocally in this way selfishness never arises.

This analysis fails to explain altruism between strangers, however, since it predicts reciprocation only when the same individuals interact frequently. Of more generality is a model in which self-sacrifice is culturally transmitted and benefits the social group. Here children adopt the commonest adult trait as their role model, such conformism itself being favoured by natural selection (Boyd and Richerson, in Hinde and Groebel 1991). This model fits well with the demonstrated tendency to favour individuals in one's own social group, and with ethnocentrism and xenophobia.

These models leave open the psychological issue of what motivates an individual to behave altruistically. This question has been central to the study of human nature since classical times, philosophers disagreeing over whether egoistic or altruistic impulses are at the root of human action, and consequently over the possibilities for ethical and political obligation. Under the hedonistic view all behaviour is motivated by the desire to avoid pain and secure pleasure, so that altruism is ultimately selfish. However, if all that is being claimed is that the achievement of goals is pleasurable, then hedonism indeed explains altruism but misses the interesting points that the goal in this case is to help another individual, and that some cost is suffered even though goal achievement might be enjoyed. There remains the difficult question of whether altruistic acts are performed to ameliorate the suffering of others or the saddened mood that normally accompanies empathy for a victim. Social psychologists who have disentangled these associated motivations have found conflicting results (Fultz and Cialdini, in Hinde and Groebel 1991), although empathic individuals do tend to show more helping behaviour. In addition, people may help even when they believe they would remain anonymous if they declined to do so, demonstrating that the good opinion of others is not a necessary motive for altruism.

In western societies altruistic tendencies are enhanced by the development in childhood of empathy, moral reasoning and the ability to take the perspective of others. These traits develop most readily in children whose parents are caring and supportive, set clear standards, enforce them without punishment, encourage responsibility and are themselves altruistic. These mechanisms may not be universal however; in the Utkuhikhalingmiut, an Eskimo group, for example, kindness is taught as a response to fear, reflecting its adult use as a means of defusing potential antagonism by feared individuals.

Norms of altruistic behaviour vary between cultures – western individualism contrasts with the collectivism of China and Japan, for example – and have their developmental roots in the way children are taught. Within small-scale egalitarian societies altruism may be valued more highly where there is little competition for resources or where a harsh environment favours co-operation.

John Lazarus
University of Newcastle upon Tyne

References

Axelrod, R. (1984) *The Evolution of Cooperation*, New York.

Boyd, R. and Richerson, P. J. (1991) 'Culture and Cooperation', in Hinde, R. A. and Groebel, J. (1991).

Fultz, J. and Cialdini, R. B. (1991) 'Situational and Personality Determinants of the Quantity and Quality of Helping', in Hinde, R. A. and Groebel, J. (1991).

Grafen, A. (1991) 'Modelling in behavioural ecology', in J. R. Krebs and N. B. Davies (eds) *Behavioural Ecology: An Evolutionary Approach*, 3rd edn, Oxford.

Hamilton, W. D. (1964) 'The genetical evolution of social behaviour, I and II', *Journal of Theoretical Biology* 7.

Piliavin, J. and Hong-Wen Charng (1990) 'Altruism: A review of recent theory and research' *Am. Rev. of Soc.* 16: 27–65.

Further reading

Hinde, R. A. and Groebel, J. (eds) (1991) *Cooperation and Prosocial Behaviour*, Cambridge, UK.

See also: social psychology; sociobiology; trust and co-operation.

analysis, cohort *see* cohort analysis

analysis, cost-benefit *see* cost-benefit analysis

analysis, discourse *see* discourse analysis

analysis, event-history *see* event-history analysis

analysis, functional *see* functional analysis

analysis, input-output *see* input-output analysis

analysis, labour market *see* labour market analysis

analysis, life tables and survival *see* life tables and survival analysis

analysis, marginal *see* **marginal analysis**

analysis, national income *see* **national income analysis**

analysis, risk *see* **risk analysis**

analysis, spatial *see* **spatial analysis**

analysis, stock-flow *see* **stock-flow analysis**

anarchism

Anarchism is a political philosophy which holds that societies can and should exist without rulers. Anarchists believe that this will not, as is commonly supposed, lead to chaos – anarchy in the popular sense – but on the contrary to an increase in social order. Anarchists see the state as the decisive source of corruption and disorder in the body politic. They point to many examples where people freely co-operate, without coercion, to achieve common purposes. Among traditional societies they find much to interest them in the 'ordered anarchies' of certain African tribes such as the Nuer, as well as in the workings of autonomous peasant communities such as the Russian *mir* and the self-governing cities of medieval Europe. In modern times they have hailed the anarchist experiments of the German Anabaptists of sixteenth-century Münster; the Diggers and Fifth Monarchists of the English Civil War; the popular clubs and societies of the French revolution; the Paris Commune of 1871; the Russian soviets of 1905 and 1917; and the anarchist ventures in Catalonia and Andalusia during the Spanish Civil War.

Christ and Buddha have been claimed among earlier anarchists; and there were many social movements in both medieval Europe and medieval China which drew a fundamentally anarchist inspiration from Christianity and Buddhism. Religious anarchism continued into modern times with Tolstoy and Gandhi. But the modern phase of anarchism proper opens with the eighteenth-century Enlightenment, and can be traced equally from Rousseau's romanticism and William Godwin's rationalism. An early exponent was Godwin's

son-in-law, the poet Shelley. Later advocates included the French socialist Proudhon, the German philosopher of egoism Max Stirner, the American individualist Thoreau, and the Russian aristocratic rebels Michael Bakunin and Peter Kropotkin. Anarchism was a strong current during the Russian revolution and its immediate aftermath; the suppression of the Kronstadt rising in 1921 and the emasculation of the soviets signalled its defeat. But the ideas lived on, to surface not only in Spain in the 1930s, but also in Hungary in 1956, and in Paris in 1968, where the student radicals achieved a dazzling blend of anarchism and surrealism.

Anarchism has been incorporated into the political philosophy of a number of ecological groups, especially in Germany and the United States. It is strongly marked in such ecological utopias as Ursula Le Guin's *The Dispossessed* (1974) and Ernest Callenbach's *Ecotopia* (1975). These in turn have been influenced by earlier anarchist 'ecotopias' such as William Morris's *News from Nowhere* (1890) and Aldous Huxley's *Island* (1962).

Krishan Kumar
University of Kent

Further reading

Bookchin, M. (1982) *The Ecology of Freedom*, Palo Alto, CA.
Joll, J. (1964) *The Anarchists*, London.
Marshall, P. (1993) *Demanding the Impossible: A History of Anarchism*, London.
Miller, D. (1984) *Anarchism*, London.
Ritter, A. (1980) *Anarchism: A Theoretical Analysis*, Cambridge, UK.

anger *see* **aggression and anger**

Annales School

The journal *Annales d'histoire économique et sociale*, long planned, was founded in 1929 by two historians at the University of Strasbourg, Lucien Febvre and Marc Bloch, because they were unhappy with the manner in which history was studied in France and elsewhere, and wished to offer an alternative. They considered orthodox history to be too much concerned with events, too narrowly political, and too isolated from neighbouring disciplines. In their attempt to construct a 'total' history, as it came to be called (total in the sense of dealing with every human activity, not in that of trying to include every detail), Febvre and Bloch were concerned to enlist the collaboration of workers in the social sciences. They were both admirers of the work of Paul Vidal de la Blache in human geography, and interested in the ideas of Lucien Lévy-Bruhl on primitive mentality, while Bloch was also inspired by Durkheim's concern with the social and by his comparative method. The first editorial board of *Annales* included the geographer Albert Demangeon, the sociologist Maurice Halbwachs and the political scientist André Siegfried.

The movement associated with the journal can be divided into three phases. In the first phase (to about 1945), it was small, radical and subversive. After the Second World War, however, the rebels took over the historical establishment. Febvre became president of the new interdisciplinary École Pratique des Hautes Études. He continued to edit *Annales: Economies, Sociétés, Civilisations*, as it became in 1946, thus extending its range to the 'history of mentalities' practised by Febvre in his own work on the Reformation. He was aided by Fernand Braudel, whose doctoral thesis on *The Mediterranean and the Mediterranean World in the Age of Philip II* (1949) quickly made him famous. Braudel dominated the second generation of the movement, which was most truly a 'school' with distinctive concepts and methods. Braudel himself stressed the importance of the long term (*la longue durée*) of historical geography, and of material culture (*civilisation matérielle*) Pierre Chaunu emphasized quantitative methods (l'histoire sérielle), notably in his vast study of trade between Spain and the New World, *Seville et l'Atlantique*. Pierre Goubert, a former student of Bloch's, integrated the new historical demography, developed by Louis Henry, into a historical community study of the Beauvais region. Robert Mandrou remained close to Febvre and the history of mentalities.

A third phase in the history of the movement opened in 1968 (a date which seems to mark the revenge of political events on the historians who neglected them). Braudel reacted to the political crisis by deciding to take a back seat and confiding the journal to younger men, notably Emmanuel Le Roy Ladurie. Le Roy Ladurie made his reputation with *The Peasants of Languedoc* (1966), a total history from the ground up in the Braudel manner, which used quantitative methods wherever possible, but he has since moved 'from the cellar to the attic', towards the history of mentalities and historical anthropology, as in his bestselling study of a fourteenth-century village, *Montaillou* (1975). The 1980s saw a fragmentation of the former school, which has in any case been so influential in France that it has lost its distinctiveness. It is now a 'school' only for its foreign admirers and its domestic critics, who continue to reproach it for underestimating the importance of political events. Some members of the *Annales* group, notably Le Roy Ladurie and Georges Duby, a medievalist, who has moved, like Ladurie, from rural history to the history of mentalities, are presently concerned to integrate both politics and events into their approach, and to provide narrative as well as analysis.

Others, notably Jacques Le Goff, Roger Chartier and Jean Claude Schmitt, have developed a new approach to the history of culture, in a wide sense of this term, including the history of rituals, gestures and ways of reading.

Since Braudel had a quasi-filial relationship with Febvre and a quasi-paternal relationship with Ladurie, the development of the *Annales* movement into a school and its fragmentation into a loosely organized group might be interpreted in terms of the succession of three generations. It also illustrates the cyclical process by which the rebels become the establishment and are in turn rebelled against. However, the journal and the people associated with it still offer the most sustained long-term example of fruitful interaction between historians and social sciences.

Peter Burke
University of Cambridge

Further reading

Burke, P. (1990) *The French Historical Revolution: The Annales School, 1929–1989*, London.
Fink, C. (1989) *Marc Bloch: A Life in History*, Cambridge, UK.
Review special issue (1978) 'The impact of the Annales School on the social sciences' *Review* 1.

See also: Braudel, Fernand; cultural history; social history.

anthropology

The central issue in anthropology is human variation. In the nineteenth century the guiding idea was that there were significant biological differences between human populations, and that these biological differences – notably in the development of the brain – explained variations in rationality, technical sophistication and social complexity. On one theory, each human 'race' had specific inherent capacities and therefore produced more or less sophisticated cultural forms and social institutions. The Darwinian discourse suggested, however, that there had been an evolutionary movement from more primitive to more advanced human types. On this view, there were still some primitive human populations, closer in every way to the primate ancestors of humanity. There were also relatively more advanced populations, who had progressed further from this common point of origin. This suggested that 'primitive' peoples – like, it was thought, the Fuegians, Australian aboriginals, and the South African Bushmen – were physically less evolved than other humans, lived in a 'primitive' society based on kinship and had a 'primitive' totemic religion. They were very like our own ancestors, who had lived many millennia ago. Dead civilizations revealed by archaeology and also many living populations represented intermediate stages of development between 'primitive' and 'civilized' peoples.

A major paradigm shift occurred in the first decades of the twentieth century, associated particularly with the father of American cultural anthropology, Franz Boas (1858–1942). Boas and his students were among the pioneering critics of racial theory, and they helped to establish that biological differences between extant human populations cross-cut the racial classifications; that these racial classifications were crude and unreliable, being based on a few phenotypical features; and that there were were no apparent differences in intellectual capacity between populations. It was not race that caused the differences between cultures. Cultural differences were themselves the main source of human variation. Anthropologists in the Boasian mould accordingly distinguished between biological and cultural processes.

Culture was conceived as that part of the human heritage that was passed on by learning rather than by biological inheritance. There were, however, two very different views of culture. E. B. Tylor and other evolutionist writers had typically treated culture or civilization as a single, cumulative attribute of humankind: some communities simply enjoyed more or less 'culture' as they advanced. The Boasian scholars were critical of these evolutionist speculations, and were more concerned with the differences between cultures. For them, culture was a distinct historical agency, the cause of variation between populations and the main determinant of consciousness, knowledge and understanding. In contradiction to the evolutionists, they insisted that cultural history did not follow any set course. A culture was formed by contacts, exchanges, population movements. Each culture was a historically and geographically specific accretion of traits. There was no necessary course of cultural development, and in consequence cultures could not be rated as more or less advanced.

If cultural and biological processes were largely independent of each other, the history of culture could be studied independently of the biological study of human evolution and variation. Although Boas himself contributed to 'physical anthropology' or 'biological anthropology', this became a distinct specialism in the USA. In Europe, physical anthropology (often confusingly termed 'anthropology') developed independently of what had initially been called ethnology, the study of peoples.

Some influential figures in American anthropology saw human evolution as the organizing theme of anthropology and tried to preserve the 'four fields' approach, which linked cultural anthropology, physical anthropology, archaeology and linguistics, but increasingly the specialisms within anthropology diverged from each other. By the middle of the twentieth century the intellectual links between the four fields had become increasingly exiguous. Certainly there is some mutual influence. Archaeology has increasingly drawn on cultural and social theory, and under the influence of sociobiology some physical anthropologists have attempted to revive biological explanations for cultural behaviour. In general, however, cultural anthropology in North America and social anthropology and ethnology in Europe can be treated in isolation from the other anthropological disciplines. Cultural anthropology has been more influenced by developments in the study of language than by biology, and social anthropology has been particularly influenced by social theory and historiography.

Ethnographic research

Europeans had accumulated a considerable body of information on the peoples of Asia, the Americas and Africa since the sixteenth century, but the reports were often unsystematic and unreliable. Since the eighteenth century, scholars had increasingly concerned themselves with the study of the literary and religious traditions of the east. Reliable, detailed, descriptions of the peoples beyond the great centres of civilization were, however, hard to come by, and the universal historians of the Enlightenment had to rely on scattered and generally unsatisfactory sources. Even the pioneer anthropologists had to make do with decontextualized and often naïve reports of customs and practices, but in the last decades of the nineteenth century pioneering ethnographic expeditions were undertaken by professional scientists, typically surveys of extensive regions. Metropolitan anthropologists began to organize the systematic collection of ethnographic information. Their model was the field reports of botanists and zoologists, and the ethnographies they favoured typically took the form of lists of cultural traits and techniques, and often included physical measurements and data on natural history.

In the early twentieth century there was a shift to longer, more intensive field studies of particular cultures. Franz Boas made a long-term study of the native peoples of southern, coastal British Columbia, collecting a huge archive of vernacular texts from key informants. Russian scientists made intensive studies of the Siberian peoples, and European scholars began to publish studies of small societies in the tropical colonies. Between 1915 and 1918 Bronislaw Malinowski (1884–1942) engaged in a field study of the Trobriand Islands in Melanesia, which introduced a new approach to ethnographic research. He spent two years in the field, working in the Trobriand language, and systematically recorded not only the idealized systems of rules, values and ceremonies but also the daily practices of social life. Influenced by the sociology of Durkheim, he conceived of the Trobrianders as constituting a social system with institutions that sustained each other and served to meet a series of basic needs. But he did not provide a merely idealized account of the social order, insisting rather that even in small-scale and homogeneous communities social practices diverged from the rules and individuals engaged in strategic behaviour to maximize personal advantage.

This form of fieldwork, which came to be termed 'participant observation', eventually became the standard mode of ethnographic research. In particular, the British school of social anthropology exploited the potential of this method and produced a series of classic ethnographies that may prove to be the most enduring achievement of twentieth century social and cultural anthropology (see e.g. Firth 1936; Evans-Pritchard 1937; Malinowski 1922; 1935; Turner 1957). Some regions of Africa, Indonesia, Melanesia and the Amazon were gradually covered by a set of interlinked ethnographic studies that provided a basis for intensive regional comparison.

The ethnographies produced between about 1920 and 1970 were typically holistic in conception. The guiding notion was that the institutions of the society under study formed an integrated and self-regulating system. As a heuristic device this was undoubtedly fruitful, since it directed attention to the links between different domains of social and cultural life and resulted in rounded accounts of communities. However, this perspective tended to exclude history and social change, and it was not adapted to the investigation of the effects of the colonial institutions that impinged on local social life. From the 1960s, ethnographers increasingly began to develop historical perspectives, drawing on oral traditions as well as archival sources, particularly as more studies were undertaken in peasant societies in Europe and the Near and Far East.

Comparison and explanation

Ethnography was perhaps the most successful enterprise of social and cultural anthropology, but what was the purpose of piling up meticulous ethnographies that dealt mainly with small and remote communities? There were four possible responses to this challenge. The first, historically, was the evolutionist notion that living so-called primitive peoples would provide insights into the ways of life of our own ancestors. Second, drawing on the social sciences (particularly after 1920), many anthropologists argued that ethno-

graphic research and comparison would permit the development of genuinely universal social sciences, which embraced all the peoples of the world, and did not limit themselves to the study of modern western societies. Third, particularly under the influence of ethnology, and later sociobiology, some anthropologists believed that comparative ethnography would reveal the elements of a universal human nature. Finally, humanists, often sceptical about generalizations concerning human behaviour, and critical of the positivist tradition, argued that the understanding of strange ways of life was valuable in itself. It would extend our appreciation of what it means to be human, inculcate a salutary sense of the relativity of values, and extend our sympathies.

The evolutionist faith was that the social and cultural history of humankind could be arranged in a series of fixed stages, through which populations progressed at different speeds. This central idea was badly shaken by the critiques of the Boasians and other scholars in the early twentieth century, but it persisted in some school of archaeology and was sustained by Marxist writers. There have been attempts to revive a generalized evolutionist history in a more sophisticated form (e.g. Gellner 1988). There have also been detailed studies of type cases designed to illuminate evolutionary processes. Richard Lee (1979) undertook a detailed account of !Kung Bushman economic life, for example, with the explicit aim of seeking clues to the way of life of Upper Palaeolithic foraging populations. His study revealed that the !Kung could sustain a viable way of life using simply technologies in a marginal environment, and the details of !Kung social and economic organization were widely referred to as a paradigmatic example of hunter-gatherer life now and in the distant past (Lee 1979; Lee and DeVore 1968). An influential critique has argued that on the contrary the !Kung are to be understood in terms of their particular modern history. They are the heirs of centuries of contact with Bantu-speaking pastoralists and with European colonists, and their way of life represents a defensive adaptation to exploitation (Wilmsen 1989.) Others argued that the culture of the !Kung could best be understood as a local example of a specific cultural tradition, shared by pastoralist Khoisan peoples as well as other Kalahari Bushmen groups. These critiques are reminiscent of the Boasian critiques of the evolutionist theories of their day.

A related tradition was concerned rather with human universals, and with the relationships between human capacities and forms of behaviour and those of other primates. Since the mid-1970s the sociobiological movement has given a fresh impetus to this project, combining the ethological emphasis on human nature with a theory of selection: institutions (such as the incest taboo) could be explained in terms of their evolutionary payoff. The social and cultural anthropologists were in general more impressed with the variability of customs and the speed with which cultures could change, and objected to the down-playing of cultural variation which this programme required.

An alternative approach to human universals was offered by the structuralism of Claude Lévi-Strauss, who argued that common intellectual processes – determined by the structure of the human mind – underlay all cultural products (see e.g. Lévi-Strauss 1963; 1977). Lévi-Strauss was inspired by structural linguistics, but more recent approaches draw rather on modern theories of cognition.

Social science approaches were dominant in social and cultural anthropology for much of the twentieth century, and fitted in with the behaviourist, positivist approaches favoured more generally in the social sciences. In Europe, the term social anthropology became current, reflecting the influence of the Durkheimian tradition of sociology. Ethnographic studies were typically written up in a 'functionalist' framework, that brought out the interconnections between institutions in a particular society. Some were also influenced by Marxist currents of thought in the 1960s and 1970s. Since the mid-1980s, individualist sociologies have become more popular, but the structuralist tradition also persists, and European scholars are more open than formerly to ideas emanating from American cultural anthropology (see Kuper 1992). Many American anthropologists were particularly interested in psychology, and a whole specialism developed that attempted to apply psychological theories in non-western settings. Initially the main interest was in socialization, but recently there has been more emphasis upon the study of cognition (D'Andrade 1994).

Attempts were also made to develop typologies of societies, religions, kinship and political systems, etc. (e.g. Fortes and Evans-Pritchard 1940). In the USA, G. P. Murdock produced a cross-cultural database to permit the testing of hypotheses about the relationships between particular variables, such as family form and economy, or between the initiation of young men and the practice of warfare, and so on (Murdock 1949). There is also a long tradition of regional cultural comparison, that takes account of historical relationships and seeks for local structural continuities.

Boas and his students tended to emphasize the variety of local cultural traditions and the accidental course of their development. Some of his most creative associates came to see cultural anthropology as one of the humanities, and this became the dominant cast of American cultural anthropology in the last decades of the twentieth century. Its leading exponent is Clifford Geertz, who argued generally that 'interpretation' rather than 'explanation' should be the guiding aim of cultural anthropology (Geertz 1973). Anthropologists of this persuasion are sceptical about social science approaches, harbour a suspicion of typologies, and reject what they describe as 'reductionist' biological theories. A major early influence was the humanistic linguistics of Edward Sapir, but later other movements in linguistics, hermeneutics and literary theory made converts. Respect for foreign ways of thinking also induced a critical and reflexive stance. Claims for the superiority of a western rationalist or scientific view of the world are treated with grave suspicion (see Clifford and Marcus 1986).

Recent developments

The broad field of anthropology is sustained by its ambition to describe the full range of human cultural and biological variation. The ethnographic record provides a rich documentation of the cultural variety of humanity. Archaeology traces the full sweep of the long-term history of the species. Biological anthropology studies human evolution and biological variation. The use to which these empirical investigations are put are many and diverse. Evolutionist approaches attempt to find common themes in the history of the species; social and psychological anthropologists engage in a dialogue with contemporary social science, confronting the models current in the social sciences with the experiences and models of people in a great variety of cultural contexts; and a humanist tradition aspires to provide phenomenological insights into the cultural experience of other peoples. Once criticized as the handmaiden of colonialism, anthropology is increasingly a truly international enterprise, with major centres in Brazil, Mexico, India and South Africa, where specialists concern themselves mainly with the study of the peoples of their own countries. In Europe and North America, too, there is a lively movement that applies the methods and insights of social and cultural anthropology to the description and analysis of the western societies that were initially excluded from ethnographic investigation.

Applied anthropology developed in the 1920s, and was initially conceived of as an aid to colonial administration. With the end of the European colonial empires, many anthropologists were drawn into the new field of development studies. Others began to apply anthropological insights to problems of ethnic relations, migration, education and medicine in their own societies. As local communities of anthropologists were established in formerly colonial societies, they too began more and more to concern themselves with the application of anthropology to the urgent problems of health, demography, migration and economic development. Medical anthropology is today probably the largest speciality within social and cultural anthropology, and a majority of American PhDs in anthropology are now employed outside the academy.

Adam Kuper
Brunel University

References

Clifford, J. and Marcus, G. (eds) (1986) *Writing Culture: The Poetics and Politics of Ethnography*, Berkeley, CA.

D'Andrade, R. (1995) *The Development of Cognitive Anthropology*, Cambridge, UK.

Evans-Pritchard, E. E. (1937) *Witchcraft, Oracles and Magic among the Azande of the Anglo-American Sudan*, Oxford.

Firth, R. (1936) *We the Tikopia*, London.

Fortes, M. and Evans-Pritchard, E. E. (eds) (1940) *African Political Systems*, London.

Geertz, C. (1973) *The Interpretation of Cultures*, New York.

Gellner, E. (1988) *Plough, Sword and Book: The Structure of Human History*, London.

Kuper, A. (1992) *Conceptualizing Society*, London.

Lee, R. (1979) *The !Kung San: Men, Women, and Work in a Foraging Society*, Cambridge, UK.

Lee, R. and DeVore, I. (eds) (1968) *Man the Hunter*, Chicago.

Lévi-Strauss, C. (1963) *Structural Anthropology*, New York.

Lévi-Strauss, C. (1977) *Structural Anthropology Vol. 11*, London.

Malinowski, B. (1922) *Argonauts of the Western Pacific*, London.

Malinowski, B. (1935) *Coral Gardens and their Magic*, London.

Murdock, G. P. (1949) *Social Structure*, New York.

Turner, V. (1957) *Schism and Continuity in an African Society: A Study of Ndembu Village Life*, Manchester.

Wilmsen, E. (1989) *Land Filled with Flies: A Political Economy of the Kalahari*, Chicago.

Further reading

Borofsky, R. (ed.) (1994) *Assessing Cultural Anthropology*, New York.

Carrithers, M. (1993) *Why Humans have Culture: Explaining Anthropology and Social Diversity*, Oxford.

Kuper, A. (1994) *The Chosen Primate: Human Nature and Cultural Diversity*, Cambridge, MA.

anthropology, cultural *see* cultural anthropology

anthropology, economic *see* economic anthropology

anthropology, medical *see* medical anthropology

anthropology, psychological *see* psychological anthropology

anthropology, social *see* social anthropology

anxiety

The term anxiety is currently used in psychology and psychiatry to refer to at least three related, yet logically different, constructs. Although most commonly used to describe an unpleasant emotional state or condition, anxiety also denotes a complex psychophysiological process that occurs as a reaction to stress. In addition, the concept of anxiety refers to relatively stable individual differences in anxiety proneness as a personality trait.

Anxiety states can be distinguished from other unpleasant emotions such as anger, sorrow or grief, by their unique combination of experiential, physiological and behavioural manifestations. An anxiety state is characterized by subjective feelings of tension, apprehension, nervousness and worry, and by activation (arousal) and discharge of the autonomic nervous system. Such states may vary in intensity and fluctuate over time as a function of the amount of stress that impinges on an individual. Calmness and serenity indicate the absence of anxiety; tension, apprehension and nervousness accompany moderate levels of anxiety; intense feelings of fear, fright and panic are indicative of very high levels of anxiety.

The physiological changes that occur in anxiety states include increased heart rate (palpitations, tachycardia), sweating, muscular tension, irregularities in breathing (hyperventilation), dilation of the pupils, and dryness of the mouth. There may also be vertigo (dizziness), nausea, and muscular skeletal disturbances such as tremors, tics, feelings of weakness and restlessness. Individuals who experience an anxiety state can generally describe their subjective feelings, and report the intensity and duration of this unpleasant emotional reaction.

Anxiety states are evoked whenever a person perceives or interprets a particular stimulus or situation as potentially dangerous, harmful or threatening. The intensity and duration of an anxiety state will be proportional to the amount of *threat* the situation poses for the individual and the persistence of the individual's interpretation of the situation as personally dangerous. The appraisal of a particular situation as threatening will also be influenced by the person's skills, abilities and past experience.

Anxiety states are similar to fear reactions, which are generally defined as unpleasant emotional reactions to anticipated injury or harm from some external danger. Indeed, Freud regarded fear as synonymous with 'objective anxiety', in which the intensity of the anxiety reaction was proportional to the magnitude of the external danger that evoked it: the greater the external danger, the stronger the perceived threat, the more intense the resulting anxiety reaction. Thus, fear denotes a process that involves an emotional reaction to a perceived danger, whereas the anxiety state refers more narrowly to the quality and the intensity of the emotional reaction itself.

The concept of anxiety-as-process implies a theory of anxiety as a temporally ordered sequence of events which may be initiated by a stressful external stimulus or by an internal cue that is interpreted as dangerous or threatening. It includes the following fundamental constructs or variables: stressors, perceptions and appraisals of danger or threat, anxiety state and psychological defence mechanisms. Stressors refer to situations or stimuli that are objectively characterized by some degree of physical or psychological danger. Threat denotes an individual's subjective appraisal of a situation as potentially dangerous or harmful. Since appraisals of danger are immediately followed by an anxiety state reaction, anxiety as an emotional state is at the core of the anxiety process.

Stressful situations that are frequently encountered may lead to the development of effective coping responses that quickly eliminate or minimize the danger. However, if people interpret a situation as dangerous or threatening and are unable to cope with the stressor, they may resort to intraphsychic manoeuvres (psychological defences) to eliminate the resulting anxiety state, or to reduce its level of intensity.

In general, psychological defence mechanisms modify, distort or render unconscious the feelings, thoughts and memories that would otherwise provoke anxiety. To the extent that a defence mechanism is successful, the circumstances that evoke the anxiety will be less threatening, and there will be a corresponding reduction in the intensity of the anxiety reaction. But defence mechanisms are almost always inefficient and often maladaptive because the underlying problems that caused the anxiety remain unchanged.

While everyone experiences anxiety states from time to time, there are substantial differences among people in the frequency and the intensity with which these states occur. Trait anxiety is the term used to describe these individual differences in the tendency to see the world as dangerous or threatening, and in the frequency that anxiety states are experienced over long periods of time. People high in trait anxiety are more vulnerable to stress, and they react to a wider range of situations as dangerous or threatening than low trait anxiety individuals. Consequently, high trait anxious people experience anxiety state reactions more frequently and often with greater intensity than do people who are low in trait anxiety.

To clarify the distinction between anxiety as a personality trait and as a transitory emotional state, consider the statement: 'Ms Smith is anxious'. This statement may be interpreted as meaning either that Smith is anxious *now*, at this very moment, or that Smith is *frequently* anxious. If Smith is 'anxious now', she is experiencing an unpleasant emotional state, which may or may not be characteristic of how she generally feels. If Smith experiences anxiety states more often than others, she may be classified as 'an anxious person', in which case her average level of state anxiety would generally be higher than that of most other people. Even though Smith may be an *anxious person*, whether or not she is *anxious now* will depend on how she interprets her present circumstances.

Two important classes of stressors have been identified that appear to have different implications for the evocation of anxiety states in people who differ in trait anxiety. People high in trait anxiety are more vulnerable to being evaluated by others because they lack confidence in themselves and are low in self-esteem. Situations that involve psychological threats (that is, threats to self-esteem, particularly ego-threats when personal adequacy is evaluated), appear to be more threatening for people high in trait anxiety than for low trait anxious individuals. While situations involving physical danger, such as imminent surgery, generally evoke high levels of state anxiety, persons high or low in trait anxiety show comparable increases in anxiety state in such situations.

Individuals very high in trait anxiety, for example, psychoneurotics or patients suffering from depression, experience high levels of state anxiety much of the time. But even they have coping skills and defences against anxiety that occasionally leave them relatively free of it. This is most likely to occur in situations where they are fully occupied with a non-threatening task on which they are doing well, and are thus distracted from the internal stimuli that otherwise constantly cue state anxiety responses.

Charles D. Spielberger
University of South Florida

Further reading

Freud, S. (1936) *The Problem of Anxiety*, New York.

Lazarus, R. S. (1966) *Psychological Stress and the Coping Process*, New York.

Levitt, E. E. (1980) *The Psychology of Anxiety*, Hillsdale, NJ.

See also: stress.

aptitude tests

Aptitude tests are standardized tasks designed to indicate an individual's future job proficiency or success in training. Some tests have been specifically developed for this purpose (for example, name and number comparison tests for selecting clerical workers), while others have been borrowed from educational, clinical and research use (for example, Cattell's 16 Personality Factor Questionnaire). Tests may be administered to an individual or to a group. The main types now in use are of intellectual, spatial, mechanical, perceptual and motor abilities, and of interests and personality traits.

Tests must be shown to be job-relevant, the most persuasive evidence usually being the demonstration of a relationship between pre-entry tests scores and later training or job performance (predictive validity). For example, Flanagan (1948) showed in one study that none of the very low scorers (grade 1) on a pilot aptitude test battery graduated from pilot training, as against some 30 per cent of average scorers (grade 5) and over 60 per cent of the very high scorers (grade 9). Ghiselli (1973) concluded that aptitude tests are generally better at predicting training success rather than job proficiency, but that for every type of job there is at least one type of test which gives a moderate level of prediction. Combining tests into a battery would tend to improve prediction.

Until the 1970s it was generally accepted that a test had to show predictive validity in each specific instance of use, but many psychologists now believe that validity can be generalized given an adequate specification of the test and of the job. Thus, an organization need no longer rely solely on its own research, since evidence from a number of organizations can be collected to serve as a national or international database.

The financial benefit to an organization from test use depends on other factors besides validity, notably on how selective it can be when choosing job applicants and the nature of the job (variation in performance in monetary terms). The reductions in costs or increase in profits can be impressive; Schmidt *et al.* (1979) estimated that the selection of computer programmers using a programmer aptitude test could produce productivity gains of some 10 billion dollars per year for the US economy.

There has been increasing criticism of aptitude tests in personnel selection because of alleged unfairness to minority groups. Some of the specific instances raised in the law courts indicated that the necessary validation research had not been carried out; test use was therefore potentially unfair to all applicants and disadvantageous to the organization. A number of statistical techniques are available to help evaluate test fairness, and increasingly the developers and suppliers of tests provide information about the performance of different groups (defined by gender and ethnicity, for example) and other data relevant to equal opportunities.

Most aptitude tests are paper-and-pencil. Only a small proportion involve other types of material or apparatus. Recent developments include the production of computerized versions of existing tests, and computer scoring. It is likely that tests designed to benefit from computer technology, for example tests involving the display of dynamic material on the visual display unit, and the interpretation of test results using computer software, for example expert systems, will become common (see, e.g. Bartram 1989).

Alan Jones
Dept of Social Security (UK)

References

Bartram, D. (1989) 'Computer-based assessment', in P. Herriot (ed.) *Assessment and Selection in Organizations*, Chichester.

Flanagan, J. C. (1948) *The Aviation Psychology Program in the Army Air Forces*, Report no. 1, Washington DC.

Ghiselli, E. E. (1973) 'The validity of aptitude tests in personnel selection', *Personnel Psychology* 26.

Schmidt, F. L., Hunter, J. E., McKenzie, R. C. and Muldrow, T. W. (1979) 'Impact of valid selection procedures on workforce productivity', *Journal of Applied Psychology* 64.

See also: industrial and organizational psychology; occupational psychology; vocational and career development.

archaeology

Archaeology often appears to mean different things, from the particular to the general, in different contexts. At one extreme it can refer to the recovery of ancient remains by excavation, 'digging up pots and bones'. But even field archaeology now includes a wide range of activities from survey, the cleaning and recording of industrial machines (industrial archaeology), underwater archaeology to air photography. Excavation itself involves both archaeological concepts such as context, association and assemblage, and external techniques, such as methods of probing below the surface soil with magnetometers, pollen analysis to reconstruct past environments, and data processing with computers. More generally, archaeology is often used to refer to what archaeologists do, including what is more properly termed prehistory or history. All reconstruction of the past which is based on material remains other than written records might be termed archaeology. Yet within historical archaeology use is often made of written records as part of the interpretative process.

The boundary between archaeology and history (including prehistory) is blurred, because the interpretation of layers on a site is closely dependent on accumulated knowledge about what went on at any particular place and time in the past. Since there are few Pompeiis, and archaeological remains are typically fragmentary and ambiguous, the burden on theory is great. Theories and paradigms often change with little contradiction from the data. There is much scope for historical imagination.

Views differ as to the degree of rigour and certainty that can be obtained in reconstructing the past from archaeological remains, at least partly in relation to whether one thinks archaeology is really an historical or an anthropological science. Unfortunately, the two approaches have normally been opposed. Those who claim that the purpose of archaeology is historical emphasize the particularity of past cultures, the unpredictability of human action, and the role of individuals. They state that each past culture has its own value system which it is difficult for archaeologists to reconstruct with any confidence. Prehistory and archaeology are interpretative by nature. For those who claim that 'archaeology is anthropology or it is nothing', and who believe in the cross-cultural method, allied with positivism and with laws of evolution and systematic relationships, rigorous explanation of events in past societies is feasible. The concern with scientific explanation has been particularly strong in the USA, but the two views of archaeology, as history or science, have a long tradition in the discipline.

The history of archaeology

Speculation about the human past began in classical antiquity, but investigation of monuments and artefacts dates back to the Renaissance and increased markedly in the eighteenth and nineteenth centuries as part of national interests, pride and identity. This early archaeology had its origin in the study of oriental and classical antiquities such as Pompeii, the recording of European monuments such as Stonehenge and Carnac, and the interest in human origins as an outcome of developments in geology and biology.

The initial concern was to establish a chronological sequence, and in the early nineteenth century in Denmark C. J. Thomsen grouped antiquities into stone, bronze and iron and gave them chronological significance, while J. J. A. Worsaae provided stratigraphical evidence for the sequence. The scheme was argued on ethnographic grounds to relate to a development from savagery to civilization. This idea of Sven Nilsson was, in the second half of the nineteenth century, developed by Sir Edward Tylor and Lewis H. Morgan, and it influenced Marx and Engels.

An evolutionary emphasis in archaeology was, in the debates about the origins of humankind, also closely linked to Charles Darwin.

In this early period of archaeology, an evolutionary approach was closely allied to a cross-cultural emphasis, scientific optimism, and notions of progress from barbarism to industrial societies. Yet in the early twentieth century, and particularly after the First World War, the main concern in archaeology became the building up of local historical sequences, the identification of cultural differences and the description of the diffusion and origin of styles and types, V. Gordon Childe crystallized earlier German and English uses of the term culture and defined it as a recurring association of traits in a limited geographical area. These spatial and temporal units became the building blocks for the definition of local historical sequences and the diffusion of traits. Childe described the prehistory of Europe as at least partly the result of diffusion from the Near East, 'ex Oriente lux'.

But Childe was already responsible for reintroducing an evolutionary emphasis in European archaeology by taking up Morgan's scheme, while in the USA Julian Steward and Leslie White embraced similar ideas. Rather than describing sites, processes were to be examined. In particular, attention focused on the economic relationships between a site and its environment. The work of Grahame Clark in Europe and Willey and Braidwood in the USA pioneered this new, functional, integrative approach which owed much to developments in anthropology. The discovery of physical dating methods such as radiocarbon (C^{14}) measurement freed the archaeologist from a reliance on typology, types, cultures and associations in establishing chronologies.

A full mixture of evolutionary theory, anthropology, and science in archaeology was attempted in the 'New Archaeology', a development of the 1960s and 1970s, spearheaded by Lewis Binford in the USA and David Clarke in Britain. Although there were many differences between these and other New Archaeologists, the overall concern was to introduce scientific, rigorous methods of explanation into archaeology. Rather than describing what happened in the past (the perceived view of earlier, historical approaches in archaeology), they tried to explain why events occurred. Ethnography and anthropology provided the theories for the explanation of past events, and a subdiscipline, 'ethnoarchaeology', developed in order to study more closely the relationship between material culture residues and processes in the living world. From such studies they hoped to build laws of cultural process from which particular archaeological occurrences could be deduced. They frequently referred to positivism and Hempel's hypothetico-deductive method.

The current scene

Much archaeology, particularly in the USA, remains within the grip of ecological functionalism, evolutionary theory and positivism, in the aftermath of the New Archaeology. The enduring concerns have been with process, the application of systems theory, positivism and scientific methods, including the widespread use of computers for the storing and sorting of field data, statistical manipulations, taxonomy and simulation. Cemeteries are examined in order to identify age, sex and status groupings as part of 'social archaeology', and settlement data are searched for organizational clues. Evolutionary theory is referred to in the definition of bands, tribes, chiefdoms and states and in discussions of the transformation of these categories through time. There are both Neo-Darwinian and Neo-Marxist schools.

Yet for many archaeologists, particularly in Europe, archaeology remains an historical discipline. Many field archaeologists, funded by central or local government or by development contractors, find that the academic rhetoric of their university colleagues has little relevance to their problems and interests. The split between theory and application is widening. Similarly, museum curators are aware that popular interest centres on local and regional historical continuity, and on the material achievements of foreign cultures, rather than on cross-cultural laws of social process. In addition, many academic archaeologists cling to the historical tradition in which they had been taught and reject the claims of the New Archaeology.

An emerging feeling in archaeology is that the old battle between historical and scientific-anthropological views of the past is inadequate. The concern is to allow the particularity of historical sequences, and the individuality of culture, while at the same time focusing on social process and cultural change.

Ian Hodder
University of Cambridge

Further reading

Barker, P. (1983) *Techniques of Archaeological Excavation*, London.
Binford, L. (1972) *An Archaeological Perspective*, New York.
Renfrew, C. and Bahn, D. (1991) *Archaeology: Theories, Methods and Practice*, London.
Trigger, B. (1989) *A History of Archaeological Thought*, Cambridge, UK.

See also: anthropology; material culture.

Aristotle (384–322 BC)

Aristotle was born in Stagira, a small Greek town on the coast of the Chalcidice peninsula in the northern Aegean, close to the Macedonian kingdom. His father was court physician to Amyntas III of Macedon. He studied with Plato in Athens from 367 to 348 BC, then moved to the court of Hermias of Atarneus, in the Troad, another pupil of Plato, one of whose relatives became Aristotle's wife. After a period in Lesbos, Aristotle joined Philip of Macedon's court as tutor to Alexander in 342. After Philip's death in 335 he returned to Athens and stayed there until Alexander's death in 323 when the anti-Macedonian reaction forced him to withdraw to Chalcis, the Euboean city from which his mother had come.

Aristotle was thus exposed both socially and intellectually to contradictory influences. Socially, he belonged to the Greek polis in the last generation of its struggle to retain autonomy – a limited local autonomy in the case of Stagira, the claim of a fading imperial power in the case of Athens – but at the same time he had firsthand experience of living in the new form of society which was to succeed the polis. Intellectually, his father was part of the empiricist tradition of Greek medicine with its emphasis on careful reporting and observation as the only basis for accurate prediction of the likely future course of a disease, while his teacher Plato believed that the visible world was merely an imperfect reflection of a reality which could be apprehended only intellectually, and thought it the right and duty of the philosopher to reason out the correct course for humankind and society and then – if only he could – impose his prescriptions on his fellow-citizens.

This second source of tension in Aristotle's life, between opposing epistemologies, was much more productive than the first. It led him firmly to assert the intellectual satisfactions, as well as the practical utility, of studying apparently low forms of animal life and engaging in the messy activity of dissection (Lloyd 1968), and to extend the methods of research developed in medicine to the whole field of biology; it also led him to reflect systematically on logic and processes of reasoning, both human and animal. The characteristics which humans shared with animals, instead of being seen in a negative way as inescapable defects (mortality) of a 'lower nature' which had to be subdued, became a basis for understanding, a transformation with particularly far-reaching implications for psychology. At the same time the principles of argument which had been being worked out piecemeal in law courts, assembly debates, medical practitioners' disputes and treatises (see Lloyd 1979), mathematical proofs and philosophical dialectic were drawn together in a systematic way which helped to establish methodology or 'second-order thinking, thinking about thinking' (Elkana 1981) as a problem in its own right. Aristotelian logic eliminated many of the sophistic puzzles that had perplexed earlier philosophers, extended the idea of 'proof' from mathematics to other areas of scientific and philosophical thought, and even, by implication, anticipated modern concern with the relation between logic and language. Aristotle's comprehensive interests and systematic organization of research provided the first foundations for the idea of a university as a place where students are taught how to extend knowledge in all its branches. Discussion and criticism of earlier views was part of the method.

In principle, Aristotle's procedure of taking earlier opinions, particularly those of Plato, and criticizing them on the basis of observation, coupled with his experience of the Macedonian court, might have produced important transformations in political theory. In practice it hardly did so; Aristotle's political and social thought remained enclosed within the frame of the city-state. His view that *chrematikē*, the art of money-making, was morally wrong prevented him from developing an understanding of the growing importance of trade and commodity production in the economy, and in general his empirical attitude tended to lead to a confusion between the statistically normal and the normative. Since domination of males over females, parents over children and masters over slaves was so widespread, it must be right. Belief in the superiority of Greeks over barbarians led Aristotle to assert that some ethnic groups are naturally fit only for slavery, a view which had a long career in the service of racism, though Aristotle himself thought of culturally rather than physically transmitted qualities. The view that the family, observable in animals as well as humans, is the basic form of society had already been put forward by Plato in the *Laws* (earlier Greek thinkers had pictured primitive human society as a herd rather than a family: Cole 1967). Aristotle took it up and extended it, producing the model of development from family to *gens* and from *gens* to phratry, tribe and city which was to have such an important influence on anthropological kinship theory in the nineteenth and early twentieth centuries. Possibly the growing importance of private life in fourth-century Greece, particularly for those not directly involved in politics, helped to make this view of kinship ties as the basic bonds of society attractive (see Humphreys 1983a, 1983b).

The fact that Aristotle lived an essentially 'private' life (whatever his relations with the ruling Macedonian elite may have been) is also responsible for his marked interest in the study of friendship, which plays a large part in his *Ethics*. Friends were the philosopher's reference-group, the people who assured him that the philosophical life was indeed the best life; Aristotle's discussion of friendship supplied the basis for the stoic idea of the 'cosmopolitan' community of wise men.

At the same time Aristotle's relations with the Macedonians had given him plenty of experience of patronage and friendship between unequals: his acute remarks here were to prove useful to later Hellenistic philosophers grappling with the problems of royal power and patronage.

There is no doubt that Aristotle was a shrewd observer of human behaviour. He firmly rejected the Socratic view that virtue is knowledge, on the grounds that people often know what they should do but fail to do it; what we call virtues are consistent patterns of behaviour, though conscious thought must also enter into them. How the habit of virtuous behaviour is to be inculcated Aristotle does not really tell us. He accepted social conflict as inevitable; rich and poor have opposed interests and the best way to achieve stability in society is to have a large middle class of intermediate wealth who will hold the balance between them. This emphasis of the middle class as the key element in society is part of his more general belief that virtue and right action is a mean between two extremes, an adaptation of the Delphic maxim *méden agan*, 'nothing to excess'.

Medical theory helped Aristotle fit a much more liberal attitude than Plato's towards the arts into this framework. Though care must be exercised in choosing music and stories for children, adults can benefit from having their emotions stirred by music and tragedy because this purges them of excess emotion. In an important book, Jones (1962) has argued that Aristotle's remarks on tragedy have been misunderstood in the European tradition and, when correctly interpreted, can throw light on the difference between Greek conceptions of the person and of action and those of the modern western world.

In a sense Aristotle seems to be a consolidator rather than an innovator, a systematizer and synthesizer of ideas originally raised by others. Nevertheless, the new fields of research he opened up, his contributions to methodology and scientific terminology, and the intelligence of his criticisms of earlier views and proposed solutions to philosophical problems make him a founding figure in many branches of research. The works which survive were written for teaching purposes rather than for the general public: their inelegant, rather jerky style gives an attractive impression of an unpretentious thinker who faced difficulties and objections to his own views honestly.

S. C. Humphreys
University of Michigan

References

Cole, T. (1967) *Democritus and the Sources of Greek Anthropology*, Cleveland, OH.

Elkana, Y. (1981) 'A programmatic attempt at an anthropology of knowledge', in E. Mendelssohn and Y. Elkana (eds) *Sciences and Cultures* 5.

Humphreys, S. C. (1983a) 'The family in classical Athens', in S. C. Humphreys, *The Family, Women and Death*, London.

—— (1983b) 'Fustel de Coulanges and the Greek "genos" ', *Sociologia del diritto* 9.

Jones, H. J. (1962) *Aristotle and Greek Tragedy*, London.

Lloyd, G. E. R. (1968) *Aristotle: The Growth and Structure of his Thought*, Cambridge, UK.

—— (1979) *Magic, Science and Religion*, Cambridge, UK.

Further reading

Guthrie, W. K. C. (1981) *History of Greek Philosophy, VI. Aristotle: An Encounter*, Cambridge, UK.

Wood, E. and Wood, N. (1978) *Class Ideology and Ancient Political Theory: Socrates, Plato and Aristotle in Social Context*, Oxford.

arousal *see* activation and arousal

art, sociology of

The term sociology of art usually serves as a convenient, if confusing, shorthand for sociology of the arts or, sometimes, sociology of art and literature. In fact, the sociology of the visual arts is probably far less developed than the sociology of literature, drama or even film. The generic nature of the subject matter of this subdiscipline does unavoidably create difficulties for analysis, since it is not always possible to draw exact parallels between, say, music and the novel, in their social or political contexts.

The sociology of art is an extremely diverse body of work. There is no single, or even dominant, model of analysis or theory of the relationship between the arts and society. In Britain and in some other European countries, Marxist and neo-Marxist approaches have been particularly influential since the mid-1970s, though there are plenty of studies and contributions by non-Marxist scholars too; in the USA, Marxism is rarely the foundation for a sociology of the arts. It is useful to begin to survey work in this area by starting from these two very different traditions.

The American sociology of art is often referred to as the production-of-culture approach. It is very much in the mainstream of sociological analysis, and focuses on the study of the institutions and organizations of cultural production (see Becker 1982; Coser 1978; Kamerman and Martorella 1983; Peterson 1976). The interest is on the social relations in which art is produced. Sociologists have looked at the role of gatekeepers (publishers, critics, gallery-owners) in mediating between artist and public; at the social relations and decision making processes in a college of art, or an opera company; or at the relation between particular cultural products (for example, photographs) and the social organizations in which they are produced (Adler 1979; Bystryn 1978; Rosenblum 1978). The emphasis is often, though by no means exclusively, on the performing arts, where the complexity of social relations merits analysis; in Britain, the performing arts take second place to literature as a central focus for sociologists.

The Marxist tradition

A criticism sometimes levelled at the so-called production-of-culture approach is that it often ignores the cultural product itself, taking it simply as a given object, and paying no attention to its content, symbolic nature, or conventions of representation. Work in the Marxist tradition, on the other hand, has increasingly come to recognize the importance of looking critically and analytically at the novel, or painting, or film, as well as at its conditions of production. Marxist aesthetics has moved away from the simple and misleading metaphor of base-and-superstructure, with its constant risk of an economic reductionist account of culture, and of conceiving of literature and art as merely 'reflections' of class or economic factors. Here the earlier work of continental European authors (Gramsci, Adorno, Althusser, Goldmann) has been crucial in refining the model, stressing the mediating levels of social group, individual (authorial) consciousness and experience, and, more recently, of textual specificity. In this last case, there has been a fruitful incorporation of structuralist, semiotic, and psychoanalytic insights into a more sociological perspective, which has facilitated an attention to such things as narrative, visual imagery, cinematic techniques and conventions, and televisual codes. Thus, as well as demonstrating that, for example, a television news programme is produced in the particular context of capitalist social relations, governmental or commercial financing, and professional and political ideologies, it is also possible to look at the 'text' itself (the programme, in this case), and to analyse the ways in which meanings (aesthetic, political, ideological) are constituted in a variety of ways – through visual and aural codes, narrative commentary, camera angles and so on.

The strengths of the sociology of art to date, particularly in the USA and in Britain, have been, first, the development of a methodology for the study of the institutions and practices of cultural production and, second, the analysis of culture as part of a wider social and historical framework. The sociology of cultural production and the sociology of the text, as complementary analyses, provide a valuable corrective to the more traditional, uncritical approaches to the arts dominant in art history, literary criticism, and aesthetics. It is worth noting, however, that a major contribution to the development of the sociology of art, at least in Britain, has come from people working in those disciplines. Concerned to expose the ideological nature of their subject matter as well as of their disciplines, they have argued that the 'great tradition' and the 'literary canon' are much better perceived as social and historical products, constituted in particular institutions and through specific values, than as presenting any 'natural' or 'transcendent' values (Eagleton 1976; Widdowson 1982).

Another area of great importance to the sociology of art is the study of reception – of audiences and their responses. This aspect of culture has so far been neglected, although developments in literary criticism in the USA, in Germany and in Scandinavia (hermeneutics, reception-aesthetics, psychoanalytic approaches) provide the possibility of an approach to the constitution of meaning in the reader/viewer. It is now realized by several sociologists that the critical study of texts needs to be supplemented by a sociology of readers and audiences, their nature, constitution, and modes of reception (Eco 1980).

The sociological approach to the arts has been able to demonstrate the contingent, and class-related, development and separation of 'high art' from 'popular culture', and thus to render more problematic the elitist conceptions of art which obtain among those involved in support and funding for the arts, as well as in society in general (including, incidentally, among many of its sociologists). The notion of 'cultural capital' (Bourdieu 1984), suggesting the use made by dominant social groups of specific forms of culture as a way of securing their identity by the exclusion of other groups, is a useful way of demonstrating the historical and continuing production of boundaries and aesthetic judgements in culture.

Recognition of the interdisciplinary character of the sociology of art must also include mention of work by feminist critics and historians, who have noted and challenged the exclusion of women from both the production of art and the history of art (Moers 1977; Parker and Pollock 1981; Pollock 1982). The answer to the question 'why have there been no great women artists?' (Nochlin 1973) is certainly a sociological or social-historical one, and feminist analysis enables us to comprehend the one-sided nature of the production of culture, in terms of gender, and also the dominance of patriarchal ideology in artistic representation. The way in which women (and men) are represented in art and literature is both a product of their actual position in society and the ideologies which maintain this, and also a contributing factor *to* those ideologies. And as post-colonial criticism has shown, an exactly parallel argument can be made about ethnic minorities and non-western culture (Hiller 1991; Lipparet 1990; Said 1978). For culture is not simply a reflection of social structures: it is also the producer of meanings and the determinant and support of ideologies. In this sense, the metaphor of base and superstructure is clearly reversible, since art and culture can also sustain, and in some cases subvert, the *existing* order.

Janet Wolff
University of Rochester

References

Adler, J. (1979) *Artists in Office: An Ethnography of an Academic Art Scene*, New Brunswick, NJ.

Becker, H. (1982), *Art Worlds*, Berkeley, CA.

Bourdieu, P. (1984) *Distinction: A Social Critique of the Judgement of Taste*, Cambridge, MA.

Bystryn, M. (1978) 'Art galleries as gatekeepers: the case of the Abstract Expressionists', in L. A. Coser (ed.) *The Production of Culture, Social Research* 45.

Coser, L. A. (ed.) (1978) *The Production of Culture, Social Research* 45.

Eagleton, T. (1976) *Criticism and Ideology*, London.

Eco, U. (1980) 'Towards a semiotic enquiry into the television message', in J. Corner and J. Hawthorn (eds) *Communication Studies*, London.

Hiller, S. (ed.) (1991) *The Myth of Primitivism*, London.

Kamerman, J. B. and Martorella, R. (eds) (1983) *Performers and Performances*, New York.

Lippard, L. (1990) *Mixed Blessings: New Artina Multicultural America*, New York.

Moers, E. (1977) *Literary Women*, New York.

Nochlin, L. (1973) 'Why have there been no great women artists?', in T. B. Hess and E. C. Baker (eds) *Art and Sexual Politics*, New York.

Parker, R. and Pollock, G. (1981) *Old Mistresses: Women, Art and Ideology*, London.

Peterson, R. A. (ed.) (1976) *The Production of Culture*, Beverly Hills, CA.

Pollock, G. (1982) 'Vision, voice and power: feminist art history and Marxism', *Block* 6.

Rosenblum, B. (1978) *Photographers at Work: A Sociology of Photographic Styles*, New York.

Said, E. W. (1978) *Orientalism*, New York.

Widdowson, P. (ed.) (1982) *Re-reading English*, London.

artificial intelligence

Research in artificial intelligence (AI) represents an attempt to understand intelligent behaviour (and its prerequisites: perception, language use, and the mental representation of information) by making computers reproduce it. It has historical precedents in the work of Pascal, Leibniz and Babbage, who all devised schemes for intelligent machines that were impractical, given the mechanical components from which it was envisaged that those machines would be constructed. The existence of AI as an independent discipline, however, can be traced to the invention of the digital computer, and, more specifically, to a conference at Dartford College, New Hampshire, in 1956. At that conference, Allen Newell, Cliff Shaw and Herbert Simon (see, e.g. Newell *et al.* 1957) described the use of heuristic, rule of thumb, procedures for solving problems, and showed how those procedures could be encoded as computer programs. Their work contrasted sharply with immediately preceding attempts to explain intelligent behaviour by modelling the properties of brain cells.

Newell *et al.*'s work led to the development of more sophisticated programming languages (in particular John McCarthy's LISP), and their general approach, dubbed *semantic information processing* by Marvin Minsky, was applied to fields as diverse as visual object recognition, language understanding and chess playing. The advent of larger, faster computers forced AI researchers to confront the problem of whether their programs would scale up so that they could operate in the real world, rather than on small-scale laboratory tasks. Could a program that conversed about wooden blocks on a table top be generalized so that it could talk about poverty in the developing world, for example?

Often the answer was: no. Tricks that worked in a limited range of cases would fail on other cases from the same domain. For example, ideas used in early object recognition programs were later shown to be restricted to objects with flat surfaces. Many aspects of intelligence came, therefore, to be seen as the exercise of domain-specific knowledge, which had to be encoded in detail into computer programs, and separately for each subdomain. This conception of intelligence led to the construction of *expert systems*. DENDRAL (see Lindsay *et al.* 1980), which computed the structure of complex organic molecules, and MYCIN (see Shortliffe 1976), which diagnosed serious bacterial infections, were the first such systems, and they remain among the best known. Expert systems have become commercially important, usually in the guise of sophisticated *aides memoires* for human experts, rather than as replacements for them. One of their principal strengths is their ability to process probabilistic information, which contributes to many kinds of diagnosis.

A different attack on the semantic information processing research of the 1960s came from David Marr (see, in particular, Marr 1982), who argued that AI researchers had failed to provide a *computational theory* of the tasks their machines were trying to carry out. By a computational theory he meant an account of what outputs those machines were trying to produce from their inputs, and why. Marr wanted to combine evidence from neurophysiology and perceptual psychology with computational techniques from AI, and other parts of computer science, to produce a detailed and explanatory account of human vision. Although he did not wholly succeed before his untimely death in his mid-thirties, his work on the lower levels of the human visual system remains the paradigmatic example of successful research in cognitive science.

Marr's computational models contained units that were intended to mimic the properties of cells in the visual system. He therefore reintroduced techniques that had been sidelined by Newell *et al.*'s information processing approach. *Connectionism* is a more direct descendant of the earlier neural modelling approach. However, the units from which connectionist models are built are not based on specific classes of nerve cells, as those in Marr's models are.

Marr questioned whether traditional AI could generate *explanations* of intelligent behaviour, and connectionists asked whether it could model *biological*, and in particular human, intelligence. Not surprisingly, therefore, many AI researchers in the 1980s embraced the engineering side of the discipline, and focused their attention on its applications. This orientation was also sensible at a time when funding was more readily available for projects with short- to intermediate-term returns. Ideas from AI, albeit not always in a pure form, found their way into commercial expert systems, learning aids, robots, machine vision and image processing systems, and speech and language technology. Indeed, techniques that have their origin in AI are now widespread in many types of software development, particularly of programs that run on personal computers. Object-oriented programming was first introduced in the AI language SMALLTALK. It is now a staple of programming in C++, one of the standard languages for windows applications.

Learning posed another problem for traditional AI. The semantic information processing approach assumed that the analysis of an ability, such as chess playing, should be at an abstract level, independent of the underlying hardware – person or machine – and independent of how the hardware came to have the ability, by learning or by being programmed. The ability to learn is itself an ability that might be modelled in an AI program, and some AI programs *were* programs that learned. However, a vague unease that learning was not receiving the attention it deserved grew, in some quarters, to the feeling that machines could never be really intelligent unless they could learn for themselves. Furthermore, the kinds of learning modelled in AI programs were limited. For example, concept learning programs were capable only of making slightly more complex concepts out of simpler ones that were programmed into them. For some kinds of *machine induction* this kind of learning is satisfactory, and it can produce impressive results on large machines. However, it leaves doubts about the limitations of such methods of learning unanswered.

Connectionism, with its techniques of pattern abstraction and generalization, has been seen by many as at least a partial solution to the problems about learning that beset traditional AI. A different approach is based on the analogy between evolution and learning, and on the idea that many types of intelligent behaviour are the product of evolution, rather than of learning in individual animals. *Genetic algorithms* were originally invented by John Holland (see 1992) who showed, perhaps surprisingly, that computer programs can be evolved by a method that parallels evolution by natural selection. The programs are broken into pieces that can be recombined according to fixed rules (as bits of genetic material are recombined in sexual reproduction). The new programs then attempt to perform the to-be-learned task, and the ones that work best are selected to enter the next round, and to leave offspring of their own. As in evolution, this process must be iterated many times if order is to emerge, in the form of a program that can carry out the required task. The use of genetic algorithms is closely allied to the emerging discipline of artificial life, which is broader in scope and more controversial than AI.

Many of the controversies that surround artificial life are philosophical ones, and they often parallel those generated by AI research. Two main questions have been prompted by work in AI. First, can machines really exhibit intelligence, or can they only simulate it in the way that meteorological computers simulate weather systems? Second, if there were intelligent machines, what moral issues would their existence raise? Potentially, intelligent machines are different from weather-predicting computers, since those computers do not produce rain, whereas robots could act intelligently in the real world. The moral question, like all moral questions raised by scientific advances, must be addressed by society and not specifically by AI researchers.

Alan Garnham
University of Sussex

References

Holland, J. H. (1992) *Adaptation in Natural and Artificial Systems: An Introductory Analysis with Applications to Biology, Control, and Artificial Intelligence*, 2nd edn, Cambridge, MA.

Lindsay, R., Buchanan, B. G., Feigenbaum, E. A. and Lederberg, J. (1980) *Applications of Artificial Intelligence for Chemical Inference: The DENDRAL Project*, New York.

Marr, D. (1982) *Vision: A Computational Investigation into the Human Representation and Processing of Visual Information*, San Francisco, CA.

Newell, A., Shaw, J. C. and Simon, H. A. (1957) 'Empirical explorations with the Logic Theory Machine: A case study in heuristics', *Proceedings of the Western Joint Computer Conference* 15.

Shortliffe, E. H. (1976) 'A model of inexact reasoning in medicine', *Mathematical Biosciences* 23.

Further reading

Boden, M. A. (1987) *Artificial Intelligence and Natural Man*, 2nd edn, London.

Garnham, A. (1988) *Artificial Intelligence: An Introduction*, London.

Rich, E. and Knight, K. (1991) *Artificial Intelligence*, 2nd edn, New York.

Winston, P. H. (1992) *Artificial Intelligence*, 3rd edn, Reading, MA.

See also: computer simulation; connectionism; mind.

Asiatic Mode of Production

The Asiatic Mode of Production refers to a much debated concept in Marxist social science. In the writings of Marx and Engels (1955; 1970 [1845–6]), discussions of 'Asiatic forms' appear on numerous occasions although almost never in combination with the term 'mode of production', a concept which was not systematized until after Marx's death. Moreover, they employ the term in reference to two quite different phenomena. In the newspaper articles and correspondence on India, the concept would appear to extend and elaborate a more economic version of older eighteenth- and nineteenth-century ideas of 'Oriental Despotism', referring here to the great Asiatic empires with their complex political organization. In the justly famous section of the *Grundrisse der Kritik der politischen Ökonomie* (1857–8), called *Pre-Capitalist Economic Formations* (1964), the concept is used to characterize the most primitive form of state society where a collection of self-sufficient agricultural communities are ruled by a higher instance, the theocratic representative of the higher unity of collectivity – sacralized nature, deity or ancestor – of primitive society. Similarly, economic exploitation is a simple extension of a potential already present in primitive society: 'Surplus labour belongs to the higher community, which ultimately appears as a person' (Marx 1964).

The Oriental Despotic version of the Asiatic Mode concept is that which dominated the intellectual development of the late nineteenth and early twentieth centuries. The Asiatic empires were conceived of as historically stagnant societies dominated by a state class that controlled the totality of the land and organized supra-local irrigation works, but whose economic base consisted of self-sufficient village communities whose contact with one another was minimal and who supported the state-class by means of the taxation of their surplus product. With the emergence of a formalized historical materialism in the work of Engels and the Second International (Kautsky, Plekhanov), the concept became increasingly linked to a techno-ecological kind of explanation. This tendency reached its climax in the subsequent work of Wittfogel and emerged finally in the hydraulic hypothesis, which posits a causal relation between the ecologically determined necessity of large-scale irrigation and the emergence of the despotic-bureaucratic state machine (Wittfogel 1957). The Asiatic Mode was not a particularly welcome concept among the higher echelons of post-revolutionary Soviet society for obvious reasons, and both Wittfogel and the Asiatic Mode of Production were purged from the Third International, whose project for a Chinese revolution was incompatible with the suggestion that Asia was fundamentally different from the west, that it possessed a stagnant mode of production, or that a bureaucracy could in any way constitute a ruling class.

While the work of Wittfogel significantly influenced American neo-evolutionism (Steward 1955), theoretical discussion of the Asiatic Mode of Production was not again revived until the late 1950s and 1960s, after the Twentieth Congress of the Communist Party officially announced the reopening of Marxist debate. Discussions began first in eastern Europe and then spread to Paris, where they have played a central role in the development of structural Marxist theory in general, and anthropology in particular (Althusser and Balibar 1969 [1965]; Godelier 1969). The new discussion has been based primarily on Marx's *Pre-Capitalist Economic Formations* and has focused on the problem of early state formation in general, the relation between 'primitive' communal forms and class formation, the symbolism of state power and theocracy, and the specifics of 'Asiatic' social forms in evolutionary as well as concrete historical frames of reference (Friedman 1979; Hindness and Hirst 1975; Krader 1975).

Jonathan Friedman
University of Lund

References

Althusser, L. and Balibar, E. (1969 [1965]) *Reading Capital*, London. (Original edn, *Lire le capital*, Paris.)
Friedman, J. (1979) *System, Structure and Contradiction in the Evolution of 'Asiatic' Social Forms*, Copenhagen.
Godelier, M. (1969) 'La Notion de "mode de production asiatique" et les schémas marxistes d'évolution des sociétés', in R. Garaudy (ed.) *Sur le mode de production asiatique*, Paris.
Hindess, B. and Hirst, P. (1975) *Pre-Capitalist Modes of Production*, London.
Krader, L. (1975) *The Asiatic Mode of Production*, Assen, Netherlands.
Marx, K. (1964) *Pre-Capitalist Economic Formations*, ed. E. Hobsbawm, London.
Marx, K. and Engels, F. (1955) *Selected Correspondence*, Moscow.
——(1970 [1845–6]) *The German Ideology*, London. (Original edn, *Die Deutsche Ideologie*.)
Steward, J. (1955) 'Introduction' and 'Some implications of the symposium', in *Irrigation Civilizations*, Washington, DC.
Wittfogel, K. (1957) *Oriental Despotism*, New Haven, CT.

See also: *Marx's theory of history and society.*

associationism

The concept of the association of ideas is as old as Aristotle, but its use as the basic framework for a complete account of mental life is essentially British, beginning with John Locke and ending with Alexander Bain. There were some near contemporary continental associationists and some Scottish philosophers who made considerable but subsidiary use of the concept. They were not as thoroughgoing, or perhaps as single-minded, as the group recognized as British Empiricists.

Locke, Berkeley and Hume used associationism to provide support for the empiricist epistemology they were developing in opposition to Descartes's basically rationalist view. They maintained that knowledge and belief derived from, and could only be justified by, reference to sensory experience, as distinct from the innate ideas and necessary truths argued for by Descartes. They also held that such sense-based experience could be divided into elementary units such as sensations (experiences brought about by the impact of external objects on the senses), images (re-evoked or remembered sensations) and feelings (affective values attached to sensations and images). This resort to atomistic elements was probably made in the belief that such experiences were incorrigible and hence beyond dispute; what I experience on one occasion is not corrected by what I experience on comparable occasions, even though the series may build up a web of experience. This web or set of patterned knowledge is built up as the separate ideas become associated or linked in synchronous groups or chronological chains.

British associationism reached its peak as a psychological system when a series of thinkers, David Hartley, James Mill, John Stuart Mill and Bain, concentrated on erecting a free-standing theory of mental life and not just a psychological foundation for an epistemology.

It is important to note the growing positivist sensationism of the three early philosophers. Locke had assumed a mind or self on which external objects made an impact through the senses; Berkeley accepted the mind or self but denied that we could have any direct knowledge of external objects (all we could directly know were our 'ideas'); Hume went further and claimed that the so-called mind or self was no more than the passage of our 'ideas'.

Hartley, a physician rather than a philosopher, tried to give sensations, images, feelings and their associations a neurophysiological basis. He suggested that the impact of external objects on the senses set up vibrations in the sensory nervous apparatus and that these were experienced as sensations. Images were the result of later minor vibrations, which he called 'vibratiuncles', induced by associated sensations or images. James Mill, an historian and political theorist, abandoned Hartley's premature and rather fantastic neurophysiology but developed the psychological thinking on more systematic and positivistic lines. His treatment was strictly atomistic and mechanical. John Stuart Mill and Alexander Bain softened these tendencies, arguing for 'mental compounds' in the chemical sense as well as for 'mental mixtures' in which the totality was no more than the sum of the associated elements.

There was much disagreement over the 'laws' or conditions of the association of 'ideas'. It was universally accepted that frequency and contiguity (two or more 'ideas' often occurring together or in close succession) constituted a basic condition, for example 'table' and 'chair' are said to be associated because these two 'ideas' are frequently experienced in conjunction. (Some modern learning theories would call this assumption into question.) In addition to this basic law, some associationists added one or more qualitative laws, such as the 'law of similarity' governing the association of 'dark' and 'black', the 'law of contrast' 'dark' and 'light', and the 'law of cause and effect', 'boiling' with sustained 'heat'. Bain added a 'law of effect' which claimed that an experience followed by another became associated if the latter satisfied a need related to the former; this was given a prominent place in later S-R learning theory.

Though claiming to be based on observation or sensory experience, British associationism was based largely on common sense and anecdotal evidence. Later, von Helmholtz, Wundt, Ebbinghaus, Kulpe, G. E. Muller and others developed experimental methods to provide a sounder empirical basis for somewhat revised associationist theorizing.

W. M. O'Neil
University of Sydney

Further reading

Peters, R. S. (ed.) (1953) *Brett's History of Psychology*, London.

attachment

Attachment refers to the tie between two or more individuals; it is a psychological relationship which is discriminating and specific and which bonds one to the other in space and over enduring periods of time. Researchers and clinicians have been particularly concerned with two types of attachment: parental attachment (which sadly, in the literature, usually means *maternal*) and infantile attachment. It is widely agreed that the infants of many vertebrate species become psychologically attached to their parents; human babies first acquire an attachment to their mothers and (usually a little later) significant others during the second half of their first year of life.

Proximity seeking (for example, following) is commonly interpreted as an index of infant-to-parent attachment; other indicators include behaviour in 'strange situations' and activities such as differential smiling, crying and vocalization, as well as protest at separation (see Ainsworth 1973). Multiple criteria are used to specify attachment phenomena because of individual differences in the way attachment is organized and manifested – differences that seem to be related to variations among mothers in their infant-care practices. Indeed, because the child's attachment system is, in a sense, the reciprocal of the parents', it may be preferable to speak of, say, the mother and young child as forming a single, superordinate attachment system. The delicate and complementary intermeshing of their respective, individual attachment repertoires is such that it is not possible to describe one fully without also describing the other.

There is little agreement on the nature of this powerful motivational process: a plethora of explanatory ideas have been put forward, in the name of learning theory (Gerwitz 1972; Hoffman and Ratner 1973), psychoanalysis (Freud 1946) and ethology (Ainsworth 1973; Bowlby 1969). Bowlby – to take one example – sees attachment behaviour as the operation of an internal control system. Children are biologically predisposed to form attachments. It could be said that they are genetically programmed to respond to social situations and to display forms of behaviour (smiling, crying, clinging, and so on) from the beginning of life up to and beyond the point in time when they make a focused attachment to parental figures. What is new, then, when the infant becomes attached, is not the display of new forms of behaviour or new intensities of social responses, but a pattern of organization of these responses in relation to one significant person. Virtually all the elements in the child's behaviour repertoire become capable of being functionally linked to a controlling system or plan, which is hierarchical in its organization and target-seeking in its effect. The 'target' is defined as the maintenance of proximity to the care-giver, and the hierarchical nature of the organization is revealed in the fact that a particular response can serve a number of different functions in maintaining this proximity.

It is argued (Belsky and Nezworski 1988) that the 1980s witnessed a 'virtual revolution' in our understanding of the child's early development, and in particular a recognition that individual differences measured within the first years of life are predictive of later development. This applies, *inter alia*, to the child's socio-emotional development within the context of his or her attachments (see Herbert 1991). The measurement of the *security* of infant-to-mother attachment (at the end of the first year of life) has come into its own as a predictor of *competence* as far forward as the early school years (see Bretherton 1985).

The preoccupation of researchers and clinicians with the influence of the mother on the infant's development, and the foundational significance of the first attachment has had salutary effects: highlighting the psychological needs of the young child and humanizing substitute child-care arrangements. The cost was a professional ideology, particularly rampant in the 1950s, whereby mothers were inculpated in the causation of psychopathology varying from infantile autism to juvenile delinquency. Rutter (1972), among others, was instrumental in producing a more balanced view of the role of attachment and maternal care in the development of normal and abnormal behaviour.

Mother-to-infant attachment is usually referred to as maternal bonding. Put briefly, it proposed that in some mammalian species, *including our own*, mothers become bonded to their infants through close contact (e.g. skin-to-skin) during a short critical period, soon after birth. This is an awesome claim considering that no other adult human behaviour, and a complex pattern of behaviour and attitude at that, is explained in such 'ethological' terms. To spell it out, the suggestion is that sensory stimulation from the infant soon after its delivery is essential if the mother is to fall in love with her baby. During the critical hours following birth, tactile, visual and olfactory stimulation of the mother by her baby is thought to be particularly significant.

The close-contact, critical-period bonding theory is said to be justified on two grounds (see Klaus and Kennel 1976). One is rooted in studies of animal behaviour. The ethological support for the bonding doctrine, derived from early experiments with ewes and goats (olfactory imprinting) has not stood the test of time. Nor has evidence from human longitudinal studies comparing mothers who, after giving birth to a baby, have either been separated from it or have been allowed extended skin-to-skin contact with it, supported a 'sensitive' period, 'ethological' explanation. The impact of the doctrine upon the thinking of practitioners in obstetric, paediatric and social work fields has been considerable, particularly in relating bonding failures (allegedly due to early separation experiences) to serious problems such as child abuse. These clinical applications have also been challenged (see Herbert and Sluckin 1985; Sluckin *et al.* 1983). It seems more likely that exposure learning, different forms of conditioning, imitation and cultural factors, all influence the development of mother-to-infant (and, indeed, father-to-infant) attachments and involve a process of learning gradually to love an infant more strongly – a process characterized by ups and downs, and one which is often associated with a variety of mixed feelings about the child.

It is as well to remember that maternal bonding is only one more idea in the long history of child care ideologies. Ideas and prescriptions for the early management of children are like fashions; they have come and gone, like the influence of their proponents.

Martin Herbert
University of Exeter

References

Ainsworth, M. D. S. (1973) 'The development of infant–mother attachment', in B. M. Caldwell and H. N. Ricciuti (eds) *Review of Child Development Research* vol. 3, Chicago.

Belsky, J. and Nezworski, T. (eds) (1988) *Clinical Implications of Attachment*, Hillsdale, NJ.

Bowlby, J. (1969) *Attachment and Loss*, vol. 1, *Attachment*, New York.

Bretherton, I. (1985) 'Attachment theory: retrospect and prospect', in I. Bretherton and E. Waters (eds) *Growing Points in Attachment Theory and Research*, Monographs of the Society for Research in Child Development, 50(209).

Freud, A. (1946) 'The psychoanalytic study of infantile feeding disturbances', *Psychoanalytic Study of the Child* 2.

Gerwitz, J. L. (1972) 'Attachment, dependence, and a distinction in terms of stimulus control', in J. L. Gerwitz (ed.) *Attachment and Dependency*, Washington, DC.

Herbert, M. (1991) *Clinical Child Psychology: Social Learning, Development and Behaviour*, Chichester.

Herbert, M. and Sluckin, A. (1985) 'A realistic look at mother–infant bonding', in M. L. Chiswick (ed.) *Recent Advances in Perinatal Medicine*, Edinburgh.

Hoffman, H. S. and Ratner, A. M. (1973) 'A reinforcement model of imprinting: implications for socialization in monkeys and men', *Psychological Review* 80.

Klaus, M. H. and Kennell, J. N. (1976) *Maternal Infant Bonding*, St Louis, MO.

Rutter, M. (1972) *Maternal Deprivation Reassessed*, Harmondsworth.

Sluckin, W., Herbert, M. and Sluckin, A. (1983) *Maternal Bonding*, Oxford.

See also: developmental psychology.

attitudes

In a classic article published in the mid-1930s, Gordon Allport (1935) contended that the attitude concept was 'the most distinctive and indispensable concept in contemporary social psychology'. While this confident assertion may perhaps be more debatable now, the study of attitudes continues to occupy the attention of many researchers.

Attitudes are predominantly a matter of affective evaluation. They represent the evaluations (positive or negative) that we associate with diverse entities, for example, individuals, groups, objects, actions and institutions. Attitudes are typically assessed through a direct inquiry procedure in which respondents are essentially asked to indicate their evaluative reaction (like–dislike, and so on) to something or someone. A number of indirect (disguised) measurement procedures have also been developed (Kidder and Campbell 1970), but these are sometimes difficult to apply and have not been widely utilized.

Some theorists contend that attitudes should not be defined solely in affective (or evaluative) terms, suggesting instead that attitudes are normally found in combination with 'related' cognitive and behavioural components. Thus, people who *like* unions will usually hold characteristic beliefs; they may believe, for example, that union activities have often been treated unfairly in the press. In addition, people with pro-union attitudes will often *act* accordingly, by joining a union, or by purchasing union goods in preference to those produced by non-unionized labour. Despite the plausibility of these assertions, however, they have not gone unchallenged; in particular, the relationship between attitudes and behaviour has often proven to be weak or nonexistent.

Rather than defining attitudes such that associated beliefs and behaviours are included as essential components (by definition), contemporary researchers have preferred to focus on the evaluative aspect of attitudes, to judge from the assessment procedures they have developed, and have gone on to study *empirically* the relationship between attitudes and beliefs and the relationship between attitudes and behaviour.

Attitudes and beliefs

A commonsensical approach suggests that our attitudes, pro or con, derive from our beliefs. For example, if we learn that a newly opened store offers excellent service, superior goods and low prices, we are likely to evaluate it positively. Advertising campaigns are often based on an implicit model of this type; they may attempt to change our beliefs about a product or institution by telling us of the good qualities it possesses, in the hope that this will ultimately influence our attitudes and buying behaviour.

While it is clear that attitudes can be influenced by changes in belief (as outlined above), there is also evidence for the reverse proposition. That is, attitudes may not only be influenced by beliefs, but they may also contribute to the things that we believe (Rosenberg *et al.* 1960). In one study, for example, respondents were led (through direct post-hypnotic suggestion) to accept a new position with respect to foreign aid. Subsequent inquiry indicated that these hypnotically induced attitudes were accompanied by a spontaneous acceptance of new beliefs that had not been mentioned during the induction procedure, beliefs that were supportive of the respondents' new views. Other studies suggest that attitudes may also play a type of filtering role, influencing the extent to which we accept new information that bears on the validity of our attitudes (Lord *et al.* 1979).

Attitudes and behaviour

Attitudes are generally thought to influence behaviour. People who favour a given candidate or political position are expected to vote for that person, or to provide other concrete support (for example, in the form of donations), in contrast to those who hold relatively negative views. Despite the seeming obviousness of this proposition, however, many studies have found only weak, unreliable relations between attitudes and everyday behaviour. Part of the difficulty here derives from the fact that behaviour is often dependent on situational factors that may override the influence of the individual's preferences. Despite the fact that someone holds extremely positive views towards organized religion, she may none the less be unresponsive to requests for financial donations to her church if she has recently lost her job. Similarly, a hotel clerk may override his personal prejudices and politely serve patrons of diverse ethnic origins, if this is what his job requires. On the other hand, there is now persuasive evidence that attitudes may be more substantially associated with everyday actions if we take a broader view of behaviour, tracking the individual's reactions in a wide range of settings rather than just one. For example, although religious attitudes (positive–negative) may be weakly associated with financial contributions to the church, a more clearcut linkage between religious attitudes and religious behaviour may be observed if a composite behavioural index is employed, one that takes account of such matters as weekly religious observance, observance during holiday celebrations, saying Grace before meals, and so on (Fishbein and Ajzen 1974). Attitudes may also be effectively related to overt actions if they are action-oriented and are measured with appropriate specificity. Thus, church donations may be related to people's attitudes toward the concrete act of 'donating to the church', as contrasted with their general attitude towards 'organized religion'.

One of the most firmly established phenomena in contemporary attitude research is the fact that behaviours may have a causal impact on attitudes, rather than simply reflecting the actor's previously held views. This proposition has been supported in a wide range of experiments. In a classic study by Festinger and Carlsmith (1959), some respondents were led to describe a certain laboratory activity as 'interesting', despite the fact that they actually regarded it as rather dull. People who had enacted this form of counter-attitudinal behaviour for a modest (one-dollar) incentive subsequently rated the dull laboratory task in relatively favourable terms, compared to those who had not been required to produce counter-attitudinal statements. Other researchers have employed a procedure in which a person who was supposed to be 'teaching' something to another seemingly punished the learners with electric shocks whenever they made an error. Subsequent enquiry revealed that people who had served as 'teachers' in this type of situation became increasingly negative to their 'pupils' as a consequence.

The continuing vitality of the attitude construct may derive, in part, from the seemingly universal importance of evaluation (Osgood 1964). We are apparently disposed to respond evaluatively to the people, objects, events and institutions that we encounter. These evaluative (attitudinal) reactions, their origins, correlates and consequences, continue to constitute a fertile domain for academic and applied research.

Melvin Manis
University of Michigan

References

Allport, G. W. (1935) 'Attitudes', in C. Murchison (ed.) *A Handbook of Social Psychology*, Worcester, MA.
Festinger, L. and Carlsmith, J. M. (1959) 'Cognitive consequences of forced compliance', *Journal of Abnormal and Social Psychology* 58.
Fishbein, M. and Ajzen, I. (1974) 'Attitudes toward objects as predictive of single and multiple behavioral criteria', *Psychological Review* 81.
Kidder, L. H. and Campbell, D. T. (1970) 'The indirect testing of social attitude', in G. I. Summers (ed.) *Attitude Measurement*, Chicago.
Lord, C. G., Ross, L. and Lepper, M. R. (1979) 'Biased assimilation and attitude polarization: the effects of prior theories in subsequently considered evidence', *Journal of Personality and Social Psychology* 37.
Osgood, C. E. (1964) 'Semantic differential technique in the comparative study of cultures', *American Psychologist* 66.
Rosenberg, M. J., Hovland, C. I., McGuire, W. J., Abelson, R. P. and Brehm, J. W. (1960) *Attitude Organization and Change*, New Haven, CT.

Further reading

McGuire, W. J. (1969), 'The nature of attitudes and attitude change', in *The Handbook of Social Psychology*, 2nd edn, vol. 3, Reading, MA.
Petty, R. E. and Cacioppo, J. T. (1981) *Attitudes and Persuasion: Classical and Contemporary Approaches*, Dubuque, IA.

See also: prejudice; social psychology.

Austrian School

The Austrian School of Economics is one of the branches of economic thought which grew out of the Marginalist or neo-classical revolution (1870–90). Although basically similar to the teachings stemming from Jevons, Leon Walras and Marshall, the Austrian School's unique ideas were already contained in Menger's relatively slim volume, *Grundsätze der Volkswirtschaftslehre* (1871), thus giving the school its alternative name, the Menger School. Menger was the sole professor of economic theory in the law faculty of Vienna University between 1873 and 1903. Wieser succeeded him in 1904 and held the position until 1922. But from 1904 until 1913, Böhm-Bawerk, too, was an economics professor in the university, which is why the school is also known as the Vienna School.

Menger (1950 [1871]) tried to create a unified theory of prices, encompassing commodity as well as distributional prices. He based this on subjective valuation of the buyers at the moment of purchase, that is, on their direct utility for consumption goods or their indirect utility for productive services. These ideas are similar to other marginalist traditions. But what was unique to Menger's approach was his stress on problems of information in economics (taken up later by Hayek), consequent upon the time structure of production which entails the likelihood of forecasting errors, especially by producers of 'higher order commodities' – those far removed from final demand ('first order commodities'). From this developed the Austrians' concern with both capital and business cycle theory, the two being seen as closely linked (Böhm-Bawerk, Mises, Hayek, Schumpeter). Another unique contribution by Menger was his vision of price formation, with monopolistic pricing or even individual bargains at the fore, and perfect competition only a limiting case. Thus prices are not fully determinate, but subject to bargaining. This approach developed via Morgenstern into the Theory of Games. Menger regarded commodities as typically unhomogeneous; the constant creation of new varieties of final commodities, aside from offering insights into productive possibilities, were to him the most important aspects of development, another idea taken up by Schumpeter. Finally, Menger was the first of many Austrians to be concerned with monetary theory. He saw in money the most marketable commodity, and a medium of reserve held for precautionary reasons, with, consequently, a volatile velocity of circulation.

The best known contributions of Menger's successors are Böhm-Bawerk's (1959) attempts to measure capital in terms of waiting time, and his determinants of 'the' rate of interest. Wieser (1927 [1914]) should be remembered for his notion that prices are, above all, informative, and therefore necessary for all private and social calculations (an idea which is now usually associated with Mises's strictures on the impossibility of efficient socialist economies without market prices). Wieser also propounded the leadership role of the creative entrepreneur, an idea which Schumpeter (1952 [1912]) expanded into his theory of innovation and economic development. Mises (1949) and Hayek created a monetary ('Austrian') theory of the business cycle: investment booms are caused by bouts of bank credit at a market rate of interest below the rate of return on capital, a credit creation which cannot be prolonged indefinitely without additional saving, so that much new capital formation must be prematurely terminated.

A new Austrian School has developed, particularly in the USA. Taking up the strands of Austrian thought, it stresses the non-static nature of economic processes and the informational uniqueness of entrepreneurial decision taking. It must be noted, however, that both in respect of the full scope of thought and in its personal links, its connection with the now defunct former Austrian School is rather tenuous.

Erich Streissler
University of Vienna

References

Böhm-Bawerk, E. (1959) *Capital and Interest*, 3 vols, South Holland, 1.
Menger, C. (1950 [1871]) *Principles of Economics: First General Part*, ed. J. Dingwall and B. F. Hoselitz, Glencoe, IL. (Original edn, *Grundsätze der Volkswirtschaftslehre*, Vienna.)
Mises, L. (1949) *Human Action: A Treatise on Economics*, 3rd edn, New Haven, CT.
Schumpeter, J. (1952 [1912]) *The Theory of Economic Development: An Inquiry into Profits, Capital, Credit, Interest and the Business Cycle*, 5th edn, Cambridge, MA. (Original edn, *Theorie der wirtschaftlichen Entwicklung*, Leipzig.)

Wieser, F. (1927 [1914]) *Social Economics*, New York. (Original edn, 'Theorie der gesellschaftlichen Wirtschaft' in *Grundriss der Sozialökonomik*, Tübingen.)

Further reading

Böhm-Bawerk, E. (1890) 'The Austrian economists', *Annals of the American Academy of Political and Social Science* 1.
Hicks, J. R. and Weber, W. (eds) (1973) *Carl Menger and the Austrian School of Economics*, Oxford.
Streissler, E. (1969) 'Structural economic thought – on the significance of the Austrian School today', *Zeitschrift für Nationalökonomie* 29.

See also: Hayek, Friedrich A.

authoritarian and totalitarian systems

Authoritarian systems are political regimes which are characterized by a concentration of political power in the hands of a small group of elites who are not in any institutional sense accountable to the public. Thus, they lack those traits which distinguish liberal democratic orders – in particular, extensive civil liberties, rule of law, inter-party competition and representative government.

There are many forms of authoritarian government. Rule can be by the military or by civilian politicians, and political power can be exercised directly by individuals or through a political party. Perhaps the most important distinction among authoritarian regimes, however, is on the dimensions of despotism and penetration (Mann 1986). Despotism refers to the extent to which political power is capricious and exercised without constraint, and penetration refers to the extent to which the authoritarian state orchestrates everyday life. At one end of this continuum would be one-party dictatorships which none the less have limits on the exercise of political power and violence and which have limits as well on the reach of the state, for example, Mexico. At the other end of the continuum would be totalitarian states, such as we find in its purist form in Stalinist Russia from 1927 to 1953. Totalitarianism features an interlocking and highly centralized party-state directorate which uses terror, detailed organization and ideological indoctrination to control virtually all aspects of social life. In practice, this means control not only over the selection of the political elite and the policy agenda, but also over the society and the economy – through control over the media, elaborate socialization of the public, prevention of any organization autonomous from the party-state structure, and, finally, ownership and planning of the economy (Arendt 1951; Friedrich and Brzezinski 1956). Thus, in totalitarianism the familiar boundaries separating politics, economics and society disappear. This allows for a degree of penetration and despotism which is distinctive to this modern form of dictatorship.

The rise of states as forms of political organization were accompanied by the rise of authoritarianism. In this sense, authoritarianism is as old as the state itself, because it was through authoritarian political practices that states began to form (Anderson 1974; Tilly 1975). However, beginning in the eighteenth century in Europe, states began to differentiate themselves in terms of the degree of their accountability to the public. This process – which eventually led in England and France, for example, to the rise of democracy – has produced a spirited set of debates about the rise of democracy versus the consolidation of authoritarian rule in fascist and communist forms (Moore 1967; Rueschemeyer et al. 1992).

Debates have also flourished on two other issues. One is why some democracies evolve into authoritarian systems (Collier 1979; Linz and Stepan 1978; Luebbert 1991). The other is why some authoritarian systems collapse and give way to more liberalized political orders (Bunce 1985; Di Palma 1990).

Valerie Bunce
Cornell University

References

Anderson, P. (1974) *Lineages of the Absolutist State*, London.
Arendt, H. (1951) *The Origins of Totalitarianism*, New York.
Bunce, V. (1985) 'The empire strikes back: the evolution of the Eastern Bloc from a Soviet asset to a Soviet liability', *International Organization* 39.
Collier, D. (1979) *The New Authoritarianism in Latin America*, Princeton, NJ.
Di Palma, G. (1990) *To Craft Democracies: An Essay on Democratic Transitions*, Berkeley, CA.
Friedrich, K. and Brzezinski, Z. (1956) *Totalitarian Dictatorship and Autocracy*. Cambridge, MA.
Linz, J. and Stepan, A. (1978) *The Breakdown of Democratic Regimes*, Baltimore, MD.
Luebbert, G. (1991) *Liberalism, Fascism or Social Democracy: Social Classes and the Political Origin of Regimes in Interwar Europe*, Oxford.
Mann, M. (1986) *Sources of Social Power*, Cambridge, UK.
Moore, B. (1967) *Social Origins of Dictatorship and Democracy*, Boston, MA.
Rueschemeyer, D., Stephens, E. H. and Stevens, J. D. (1992) *Capitalist Development and Democracy*, Chicago.
Tilly, C. (1975) *The Formation of National States in Western Europe*, Princeton, NJ.

See also: communism; democratization; fascism; military regimes.

authority

Six distinctions must be drawn in any account of the concept of authority (Friedman 1973; Lukes 1978; Raz 1989).

First, the failure to explain the unity and order of social life and the compliance of subjects solely in terms of coercion and/or rational agreement opens a space for the concept of authority. Authority refers to a distinctive form of compliance in social life. Three accounts exist of the basis of this special compliance. One sees authoritative institutions as reflecting the common beliefs, values, traditions and practices of members of society (Arendt 1963; Parsons 1960); a second sees political authority as offering a co-ordination solution to a Hobbesian state of nature, or a lack of shared values (Hobbes 1651); a third view argues that although social order is imposed by force, it derives its permanence and stability through techniques of legitimation, ideology, hegemony, mobilization of bias, false consensus and so on, which secure the willing compliance of citizens through the manipulation of their beliefs (Lukes 1978; Weber 1978 [1922]).

Second, what is special about the compliance that B renders A which marks off authority from coercion and rational agreement? Coercion secures B's compliance by the use of force or threats; persuasion convinces B by appeal to arguments that an action is in B's interests, is, for example, morally right, or prudent; but B complies with authority when B recognizes A's right to command B in a certain sphere. B voluntarily surrenders the right to make compliance contingent on an evaluation of the content of A's command, and obeys because A's order comes from an appropriate person and falls within the appropriate range. Where authority exists there will be 'rules of recognition' (Hart 1961) or 'marks' by which to identify those eligible to exercise it.

Third, we must also distinguish between *de facto* and *de jure* authority (Peters 1967; Winch 1967). *De facto* authority is evidenced whenever B complies with A in the appropriate manner; *de jure* authority exists where A has a right to B's compliance in a given area which derives from a set of institutional rules. That A has one form of authority in no way entails that A will also have the other.

Fourth, many writers have referred to authority as 'legitimate power'. This may mean either that coercion is exercised by someone with *de jure* authority, although the coerced agent is not responding to A's authority; or that A's orders in fact produce this distinctive form of non-coerced deferential obedience (A thus has *de facto* authority) – this being in sharp contrast to cases where compliance is based on fear.

Fifth, authority is thus a two-tier concept: it refers

to a mode of influence and compliance, and to a set of criteria which identify who is to exercise this influence. For this influence to take effect it must be exercised 'within a certain kind of normative arrangement accepted by both parties' (Friedman 1973). This normative arrangement may be a common tradition, practice or set of beliefs (MacIntyre 1967; Winch 1967), or it may be simply a common acknowledgement that some set of rules is required to avoid chaos. B's compliance with A's authority may take two forms: it may be unquestioning (as with Weber's 'charismatic authority') or B may be able to criticize A's command, yet still complies because B recognizes A's right to command, even if B privately disagrees with its content.

Sixth, a further important distinction is that between being *an* authority and being *in* authority. The former concerns matters of belief; the latter concerns A's place in a normative order with recognized positions of *de jure* authority. When A is *an* authority, A is held to have, or successfully claims, special knowledge, insight, expertise, and so on, which justifies B's deference to A's judgement. When A is *in* authority, A claims, and is recognized as occupying, a special institutional role with a co-ordinate sphere of command (as with Weber's legal-rational authority (1978 [1922])). When B complies with A's judgement where A is *an* authority, B's compliance involves belief in the validity of A's judgement; whereas, when A is simply *in* authority, B may disagree yet comply because B recognizes A's *de jure* authority. Traditional and charismatic leaders are authoritative over belief and value; leaders in legal-rational systems are granted authority in certain spheres of action for convenience. Where A is *an* authority, A's influence over B relies on B's continued belief in A's guaranteed judgement. Where A is *in* authority,

A relies on B continuing to recognize that A fulfils a valuable co-ordination function. Both systems may face legitimation crises when B no longer believes A, or no longer believes that A successfully co-ordinates. However, both systems may seek to maintain B's belief through a variety of techniques: ideology, hegemony, mobilization of bias, and so on (Habermas 1976 [1973]).

Mark Philp
University of Oxford

References

Arendt, H. (1963) 'What is authority?', in *Between Past and Future*, New York.

Friedman, R. B. (1973) 'On the concept of authority in political philosophy', in R. E. Flathman (ed.) *Concepts in Social and Political Philosophy*, New York.

Habermas, J. (1976 [1973]) *Legitimation Crisis*, London. (Original edn, *Legitimations problem in Spatkapitalismus*, Frankfurt.)

Hart, H. L. A. (1961) *The Concept of Law*, Oxford.

Hobbes, T. (1651) *Leviathan*, London.

Lukes, S. (1978) 'Power and authority', in T. Bottomore and R. Nisbett (eds) *A History of Sociological Analysis*, London.

MacIntyre, A. (1967) *Secularisation and Moral Change*, London.

Parsons, T. (1960) 'Authority, legitimation, and political action', in *Structure and Process in Modern Societies*, Glencoe, IL.

Peters, R. S. (1967) 'Authority', in A. Quinton (ed.) *Political Philosophy*, Oxford.

Raz, J. (ed.) (1989) *Authority*, Oxford.

Weber, M. (1978 [1922]) *Economy and Society*, 2 vols, ed. G. Roth and C. Wittich, Berkeley, CA.

Winch, P. (1967) 'Authority', in A. Quinton (ed.) *Political Philosophy*, Oxford.

See also: charisma; legitimacy; power; Weber, Max.

B

balance of payments

A balance of payments is an accounting record of a country's international transactions with the rest of the world. Foreign currency receipts from the sale of goods and services are called exports and appear as a credit item in what is termed the current account of the balance of payments. Foreign currency payments for purchases of goods and services are called imports and appear as a debit item in the current account. In addition, there are transactions in capital which appear in a separate capital account. Outflows of capital, to finance overseas investment, for example, are treated as debits, and inflows of capital are treated as credits. A deficit on current account may be offset or financed by a surplus on capital account and vice versa. Since the foreign exchange rate is the price of one currency in terms of another, total credits (the supply of foreign exchange) and debits (the demand for foreign exchange) must be equal if the exchange rate is allowed to fluctuate freely to balance the supply of and demand for foreign currency. If the exchange rate is not free to vary, however, deficits or surpluses of foreign currency will arise. Deficits may be financed by government borrowing from international banks and monetary institutions, such as the International Monetary Fund, or by selling gold and foreign currency reserves. Surpluses may be dissipated by accumulating reserves or lending overseas.

The fact that a flexible exchange rate guarantees a balance in the foreign exchange market does not mean that a country is immune from balance of payments difficulties. A country may experience a decline in real income and employment because of the inability of exports to pay for imports on current account. Such a deficit financed by capital inflows will not preserve jobs, nor will a depreciating currency necessarily guarantee that the current account deficit will be rectified. Neither can a country be indifferent to the international value of its currency. Widely fluctuating exchange rates may adversely affect international trade. A rapidly depreciating currency, which raises the domestic price of imports, can be highly inflationary, which necessitates further depreciation, and so on.

In considering measures to adjust the balance of payments, therefore, it is highly desirable that countries should focus on the current account if they are concerned with the functioning of the real economy, and (if in deficit) wish to avoid turbulent exchange rates round a declining trend. Three major approaches to balance of payments adjustment have been developed by economists, corresponding to how deficits are viewed. First, the elasticities approach sees deficits as a result of distorted relative prices or uncompetitiveness in trade. Adjustment should work through exchange rate depreciation provided the sum of the price elasticities of demand for imports and exports exceeds unity. Second, the absorption approach views deficits as a result of excessive expenditure relative to domestic output, so that favourable adjustment must imply that expenditure falls relative to output. Third, the monetary approach ascribes deficits to an excess supply of money relative to demand, so that adjustment can be successful only if it raises the demand for money relative to the supply. In many contexts, particularly in developing countries, none of the approaches may be relevant where the problem is one of the characteristics of goods produced and exported, so that the price of balance of payments equilibrium is always slow growth. In this case, there is an argument for structural adjustment through planning and protection. If economic objectives are to be obtained simultaneously, a necessary condition is that the form of adjustment should be related to the initial cause of the disequilibrium.

A. P. Thirlwall
University of Kent

Further reading

Thirlwall, A. P. (1982) *Balance of Payments Theory and the United Kingdom Experience*, 2nd edn, London.

See also: international trade; Marshall-Lerner criterion.

banking

The word for a bank is recognizably the same in many European languages, and is derived from a word meaning 'bench' or 'counter'. The bench in question appears to have been that of the money-changer at the medieval fairs rather than that of the usurer, and the link of banking with trade between nations and communities has been maintained. The early banks were often started as a subsidiary business by merchants, shippers, cattle drovers and, more recently, by travel agents. Other banks grew out of the business of the goldsmiths, and some of the earliest were founded for charitable reasons. In the last two centuries, however, banking has become a recognizable trade in its own right, and companies and partnerships have been founded to carry on the specific business of banking.

Each legal system has its own definition of a bank. One common element present in nearly all definitions is the taking of deposits and the making of loans for the profit of the owners of the bank, although in some cases the proviso is made that both the deposits and the loans should be short term. An economist would be more likely to seize on the fact that bankers are able to use a relatively small capital of their own to pass large sums from ultimate lenders to ultimate borrowers, taking a margin on each transaction in the form of higher interest rates for loans than for deposits. Both these approaches credit banks with only one function, the macroeconomic function of intermediation. In reality all banks perform many more functions, while some recognized banks are not particularly active as intermediaries. Many provide payment services, and most act as insurers by giving guarantees on behalf of their customers. Services of this sort could plausibly be regarded as facilitating intermediation, but there are many other services that are purely incidental – investment management, computer services and travel agency are among them. Increasingly important in many countries is the part of the bank's income that comes from fees and commission rather than from the interest margin. Non-interest income had already risen to around 44 per cent of total income for the group of eight large British banks by 1992.

Because the liabilities of banks form a large part of the accepted definitions of the money supply, banks attract government regulation on a scale that is greater than that applying to almost every other sector. This regulation can be divided into two main areas. The first is regulation for the purposes of furthering monetary policy. The other area of regulation covers prudent behaviour of banks in an effort to ensure the safe and efficient functioning of the banking system.

Monetary policy seeks to influence the behaviour of the real economy by changing various financial variables like interest rates, the stock of money, the volume of credit and the direction of credit. Since bank deposits account for a large part of the stock of money, and since bank loans are a very important part of the total volume of credit, it is only natural that banks should be the most important channel for monetary policy measures. The measures that have been imposed on banks include control of their interest rates, primary and secondary requirements on holdings of reserves with the central bank and of government securities, limitation of the amount of credit extended, and control over the direction of credit. Many of these measures built on constraints that the banks had previously observed on their own initiative for prudential reasons.

Banking is a business that depends completely on the confidence of the public, and for the most part banks have always been very careful not to endanger that confidence. After the banking crisis of the early 1930s, the self-regulation that banks had practised for prudential reasons was supplemented in most countries by an elaborate set of prudential regulations and often by detailed supervision; the same intensification of prudential regulation and supervision occurred after the 1974–5 banking crisis. The various measures adopted are often said to be motivated by a desire to protect the interests of the depositor, but an even more important motive is the need for any government to protect the stability and soundness of the entire financial system. The measures laid down in regulations are designed to prevent bank failures by ensuring that the capital and reserves are adequate to cover all likely risks of loss, and that there are sufficient sources of liquidity to meet cash demands day by day. Many sets of regulations seek to achieve these aims by detailed and rigid balance-sheet ratios, and since 1989 banks of all kinds in most developed countries have been required to observe a minimum ratio devised by bankers from the largest countries meeting at the Bank for International Settlements in Basle. Under this scheme banks must hold capital equal to at least 8 per cent of the total of risk-weighted assets, the weights ranging from zero for government securities up to 100 for normal bank loans.

The agent for carrying out monetary policy is always the central bank, which is in a specially favourable position for influencing financial flows because it is usually the banker to the government, the main domestic banks and the central banks of other countries; it thus stands at the crossroads between the banking system and the private, public and external sectors and can influence the behaviour of all of them to various degrees by its regulations and its market operations.

It has always been thought desirable that the central bank should not be a government department but should have some autonomy. This is sometimes shown, as in the USA and in Italy, by the fact that the central bank is wholly or partly owned by private banks and not by the government; the Bank of England was not nationalized until 1946. In the early 1990s there was considerable pressure for the autonomy to be taken further by granting the central bank complete independence in the formulation and carrying out of monetary policy, subject only to a broad brief from the parliament, to which it would be accountable. Several countries, including France, Italy and Spain, have already granted this independence, following the examples of Germany and the USA.

Prudential regulation and supervision are often carried out by the central bank, as in Britain, Spain and Italy, but many countries, including Germany and the Scandinavian countries, have separate supervisory bodies; the USA has several. The Bank of England has always resisted pressure to give up its supervisory duties. The inevitable bank failures demonstrate that supervision is a poisoned chalice, but the Bank of England claims that the intimate knowledge of individual banks that it yields is essential for carrying out its other duties.

Since the 1960s the banking systems of most developed countries have changed considerably in several directions. The first major trend has been the internationalization of banking. Until the mid-twentieth century, banks conducted most of their international business through correspondent banks in the various countries, but most large and many medium-sized banks now reckon to have branches in all important international financial centres. This move was led by the large banks from the USA, and they and branches of banks from other countries have introduced new techniques and been the catalysts for change in many countries whose banking markets were previously sheltered. Banking has also become internationalized through the establishment of a pool of international bank deposits (the eurodollar market) and through syndicated lending by numbers of large banks to multinational corporations and to governments. During the recession that started in 1978, the inability of many governments and other borrowers to meet the conditions of loan repayments has been a considerable source of instability, which continued into the recession that started at the end of the 1980s. The heavy

provisions that banks had been forced to make against sovereign debt in the first of the two recessions were joined by provisions against domestic loans in the second. The banking systems of developed countries were considerably weakened by these two bouts of provisions against bad loans, and their large customers turned to the capital market for a much higher proportion of their funding needs. Banks have proved very flexible in this situation by themselves acquiring subsidiaries in the securities industry and in insurance and by the switch to non-interest income referred to earlier, but the balance of power in the financial system has moved considerably away from banking to the securities markets and to the institutional investors that are the biggest holders of most types of security.

On the domestic scene, the methods of operation of the international banking market have been adopted in what is termed wholesale banking, in which banks deal with large organizations. The technique is essentially the mobilization of large deposits through an interbank money market to provide funds for loans of up to ten years, often at rates of interest that change every three or six months.

In retail banking, with households and small businesses, the number of personal customers has increased, especially through the payment of wages into bank accounts rather than by cash. Competition has intensified, and savings banks, building societies and co-operative banks are becoming more like the main banks in their powers and kinds of business. The new electronic technology of payments, using the plastic card, will further increase competition, because it will enable institutions without branch networks to compete successfully with those that have branches.

Jack Revell
University of Wales

Further reading

Goodhart, C. A. E. (1994) *The Central Bank and the Financial System*, London.

Lewis, M. K. J. and Davis, K. T. (1987) *Domestic and International Banking*, Oxford.

Molyneux, P. (1990) *Banking: An Introductory Text*, London.

Peccioli, R. (1983) *The Internationalisation of Banking*, Paris.

Revell, J. R. S. (1983) *Banking and Electronic Fund Transfers: A Study of the Implications*, Paris.

See also: credit; financial system.

bargaining (economic theories)

Economists are interested in bargaining not only because many transactions are negotiated (as opposed to being entirely determined by market forces) but also because, conceptually, bargaining is precisely the opposite of the idealized 'perfect competition' among infinitely many traders, in terms of which economists often think about markets. Bargaining situations concern as few as two individuals, who may try to reach agreement on any of a range of transactions which leave them both at least as well off as they could be if they reached no agreement. As early as Edgeworth (1881), it was noted that modelling traders only by their initial endowments and indifference curves, while often adequate to determine a unique competitive equilibrium in a market, would nevertheless leave indeterminate the outcome of bargaining, although it could determine a 'contract curve' in which the outcomes of successful bargaining might be found.

With the advent of game theory, attempts were made to develop theories of bargaining which would predict particular outcomes in the contract curve. John Nash (1950; 1953) initiated two related, influential approaches. In his 1950 paper he proposed a model which predicted an outcome of bargaining based only on information about each bargainer's preferences, as modelled by an expected utility function over the set of feasible agreements and the outcome which would result in case of disagreement. In his 1953 paper, Nash considered a simple model of the strategic choices facing bargainers, and argued that one of the strategic equilibria of this game, which corresponded to the outcome identified in his 1950 paper, was particularly robust.

Nash's approach of analysing bargaining with complementary models – abstract models which focus on outcomes, in the spirit of co-operative game theory, and more detailed strategic models, in the spirit of non-cooperative game theory – has influenced much of game theory. Modern contributions to this tradition include influential work on bargaining by Ariel Rubinstein and Ken Binmore. One direction this work has taken has been to connect bargaining theory with the theory of competitive equilibrium in markets, by examining market models in which agents meet and negotiate transactions, with the option of returning to the market in case of disagreement (see, e.g. Binmore and Dasgupta 1987: Osborne and Rubinstein 1990).

One shortcoming of the classical game theoretic models of bargaining was that they provided little help in understanding disagreements, except to suggest that disagreements resulted primarily from bargainers' mistakes. Incomplete information models help to remedy this, by showing how a positive probability of disagreement may be inescapable at equilibrium, when agents do not know how other agents value all transactions. The underlying intuition is that if you reach an agreement whenever there are gains from trade, then you are not making as much profit on each agreement as you could (see, e.g. the papers in Roth 1985).

Because many game theoretic models of bargaining depend on information difficult to observe in the field (e.g. bargainers' detailed information and preferences over alternatives), these models were long resistant to all but the most indirect empirical tests. However, with the growth of experimental economics, many laboratory experiments were designed to test the predictions of these theories. Although some of their qualitative predictions have received some support, the existing models have performed poorly as point predictors. Most recently, this has led to new (or sometimes renewed) interest in different kinds of theories, having to do with co-ordination and/or learning and adaptive behaviour. (For an account of experimental work see Roth 1995.)

Alvin E. Roth
University of Pittsburgh

References

Binmore, K. and Dasgupta P. (eds) (1987) *The Economics of Bargaining*, Oxford.
Edgeworth, F. Y. (1881) *Mathematical Psychics*, London.
Nash, J. (1950) 'The bargaining problem', *Econometrica* 18.
—— (1953) 'Two-person cooperative games', *Econometrica* 21.
Osborne, M. J. and Rubinstein, A. (1990) *Bargaining and Markets*, San Diego, CA.
Roth, A. E. (ed.) (1985), *Game-Theoretic Models of Bargaining*, Cambridge, UK.
—— (1995) 'Bargaining experiments', in J. Kagel and A. E. Roth (eds) *Handbook of Experimental Economics*, Princeton, NJ.

basic needs

The concept of basic needs has played a big part in analysing conditions in poor countries in recent years. In reports produced by international agencies, the term has a long history (see, e.g. Drewnowski and Scott 1966). The term was given particularly wide currency after the International Labour Office's World Employment Conference at Geneva in 1976, where it was formally adopted. Basic needs were said to include two elements:

Firstly, they include certain minimum requirements of a family for private consumption: adequate food, shelter and clothing, as well as certain household furniture and equipment. Second, they include essential services provided by and for the community at large, such as safe drinking water, sanitation, public transport and health, education and cultural facilities.... The concept of basic needs should be placed within a context of a nation's overall economic and social development. In no circumstances should it be taken to mean merely the minimum necessary for subsistence; it should be placed within a context of national independence, the dignity of individuals and peoples and their freedom to chart their destiny without hindrance.

(ILO 1976: 24–5)

The idea has played a prominent part in a succession of national plans (see, e.g. Ghai *et al.* 1979) and in international reports (see, e.g. Brandt 1980; UNESCO 1978).

The term is quite clearly an enlargement of the subsistence concept, the older idea that families could be assessed as to whether their incomes were 'sufficient to obtain the minimum necessaries for the maintenance of merely physical efficiency' (Rowntree 1901). However, the basic needs formulation differs to the extent that it adds a new emphasis on minimum facilities required by local communities. The arbitrariness of the criteria used to select the items on the list is very evident. Moreover, the needs of populations cannot be defined adequately just by reference to the physical needs of individuals *and* the reference to a few of the more obvious physical provisions and services required by local communities. The exposition of need depends on some assumptions about the functioning and development of societies. The emerging *social* expectations laid upon the citizens of poor countries during periods of development are not adequately acknowledged. The disproportionate poverty and deprivation experienced by tribal groups, ethnic minorities, women, elderly people, children and people with disabilities in such countries is not adequately allowed for in this formulation.

It is important to recognize the function of basic needs in the debates going on about the relationship between the First and Third Worlds. The more that social aspects of need are acknowledged, the more it becomes necessary to accept the relativity of need to the world's and national resources. The more the concept is restricted to physical goods and facilities, the easier it is to argue that economic growth alone, rather than a complex combination of growth, redistribution and reorganization of trading and other institutional relationships, is implied.

Peter Townsend
University of Bristol

References

Brandt, W. (chairman) (1980) *North–South: A Programme for Survival*, London.
Drewnowski, J. and Scott, W. (1966) *The Level of Living Index*, UN Research Institute for Social Development, Research Report 4, Geneva.
Ghai, D., Godfrey, M. and Lisk, F. (1979) *Planning for Basic Needs in Kenya*, Geneva.
ILO (1976) *Employment Growth and Basic Needs: A One-World Problem*, Geneva.
Rowntree, B. S. (1901) *Poverty: A Study of Town Life*, London.
UNESCO (1978) *Study in Depth on the Concept of Basic Human Needs in Relation to Various Ways of Life and its Possible Implications for the Action of the Organizations*, Paris.

See also: human needs.

behaviour, consumer *see* consumer behaviour

behaviour, sexual *see* sexual behaviour

behaviour therapy

The movement that has come to be known as behaviour therapy (or behaviour modification) arose shortly after the end of the Second World War, having its origins independently in the USA, Britain and South Africa. In Britain, behaviour therapy developed mainly out of dissatisfaction with the traditional role of the clinical psychologist who worked within a medical model which likened mental disease to bodily disease, except that the former was a disease of the mind rather than the body. There was also dissatisfaction with the psychodynamic approach that viewed patients' symptoms as indicators of some underlying conflict requiring their resolution in-depth analysis, and with the diagnostic (testing) approach resulting in patients being labelled, but without any obvious consequent implications for therapy.

To replace these traditional approaches, it was proposed that psychologists make use of the entire body of knowledge and theory that constituted psychology as a scientific discipline and in which only the psychologist was an expert. In practice, the aim was to be achieved by stressing experimental investigation of the single case (that is, the presenting patient), in which the precise nature of the patient's problem was to be elucidated by systematic investigations. Behaviour therapy was simply the extension of this method to attempts to modify the maladaptive behaviour by similar controlled experimental procedures. In the USA, behaviour therapy developed mainly out of the efforts to apply the principles of operant conditioning to the description and control of human behaviour, especially, in its early stages, the bizarre behaviours of psychotics. In South Africa, the impetus for behaviour therapy came largely from the work of Wolpe (1958). His reciprocal inhibition theory, developed from studies of animal neuroses, underlay the technique of systematic desensitization which was applied to the treatment of phobias with great success, and served more than anything else to bring behaviour therapy to notice as a significant new way of approaching the therapy of maladaptive behaviours.

Between 1950 and 1970 behaviour therapy developed rapidly, its achievements being critically reviewed in three simultaneous publications (Bandura 1969; Franks 1969; Yates 1970). Although Eysenck's definition of behaviour therapy as 'the attempt to alter human behaviour and emotion in a beneficial manner according to the laws of modern learning theory' (Eysenck 1964) has been very widely accepted, Yates (1970) has stressed that behaviour therapy is a much broader endeavour than Eysenck's definition suggests, since, in principle, the whole body of the knowledge and theory that constitutes psychology is available to the behaviour therapist when dealing with a presenting patient. But for some behaviour therapists, the development of techniques that 'work' is more important than the use of theory and the experimental method, even though the best known technique of all (Wolpe's systematic desensitization) was based on specific theoretical considerations. Justification for a technique-oriented approach, however, stems in part from the demonstration that flooding, a technique directly contradicting Wolpe's theory, appears to be as effective as systematic desensitization in the therapy of phobias. There are few other standard techniques available, one notable successful example being the bell-and-pad method of treating enuresis (bedwetting).

The rapid growth of behaviour therapy has led to its application to a far wider range of problems than could earlier have been envisaged (Yates 1981). In its early stages behaviour therapy was mainly concerned with the investigation of individuals, either alone or in hospital settings. Now it is widely used by professional social workers, in marital therapy, in the design of social communities, in crime prevention and the treatment of criminals, to name but a few areas. The approach has been utilized in the control of littering, energy consumption and refuse disposal; in community aid to the disadvantaged (such as persuading low-income parents to have their children accept dental care). A good indication of the vastly expanded range of behaviour therapy can be gained by perusing successive volumes of the *Journal of Applied Behavior Analysis* (1968+), *Progress in Behavior Modification* (1975+) and the *Annual Review of Behavior Therapy* (1969+).

An important development since the early 1970s has been the attempt to reconcile behaviour therapy with psychodynamic psychotherapy and even to integrate them. Yates (1970) had argued that the two approaches differed so fundamentally in their theories about the genesis and maintenance of abnormalities of behaviour that any reconciliation and inte-gration was impossible. However, such moves had started as early as 1966 and by 1980 had achieved considerable progress (Yates 1983). The strength of the movement is indicated by the appearance of a symposium in *Behavior Therapy* (1982 13: articles by Kendall, Goldfried, Wachtel and Garfield). While admitting the strength of the evidence in favour of a reconciliation and integration, a fundamental difficulty remains, namely the relationship between theory and therapy which makes it difficult, if not impossible, for agreement to be reached on the appropriate therapy for disorders such as enuresis and stuttering; this consequently undermines the apparent integration achieved in relation to more complex disorders such as anxiety (Yates 1983).

Behaviour therapy has become as prominent an approach to the explanation and treatment of disorders of behaviour in the second half of the twentieth century as psychoanalysis was in the first half. There seems no doubt that it has fundamentally and irrevocably altered the framework within which disorders of behaviour are viewed. Its greatest virtue is perhaps its relative open-endedness and therefore its capacity for change and self-correction in the light of empirical evidence. It seems unlikely that it will suffer the fate of many of its predecessors, which became prematurely frozen within a rigid conceptual and methodological framework.

Aubrey J. Yates
University of Western Australia

References

Bandura, A. (1969) *Principles of Behavior Modification*, New York.

Eysenck, H. J. (1964) 'The nature of behaviour therapy', in H. J. Eysenck (ed.) *Experiments in Behaviour Therapy*, London.

Franks, C. (1969) *Behavior Therapy: Appraisal and Status*, New York.

Wolpe, J. (1958) *Psychotherapy by Reciprocal Inhibition*, Stanford, CA.

Yates, A. J. (1970) *Behaviour Therapy*, New York.

—— (1981) 'Behaviour therapy: past, present, future – imperfect?', *Clinical Psychology Review* 1.

—— (1983) 'Behaviour therapy and psychodynamic psychotherapy: basic conflict or reconciliation and integration?', *British Journal of Clinical Psychology* 22.

Further reading

Kazdin, A. E. (1978) *History of Behavior Modification: Experimental Foundations of Contemporary Research*, Baltimore, MD.

Wachtel, P. L. (1977) *Psychoanalysis and Behavior Therapy: Toward an Integration*, New York.

See also: clinical psychology; cognitive-behavioural therapy; conditioning, classical and operant; mental disorders.

behavioural economics

As the topic of economics is human behaviour in economic affairs, the phrase behavioural economics might be thought redundant. Nevertheless, 'behavioural' must somehow be distinguished from 'neo-classical' economics because the latter generally eschews a detailed empirical study of human choice in favour of deducing the behaviour logically from axioms of perfect rationality. The neo-classical axioms postulate a consistent utility function that the economic actor uses to choose the action which maximizes utility (or, under uncertainty, maximizes expected utility).

Contrast between behavioural and neo-classical theory

Empirically, actual choice behaviour commonly departs widely from the behaviour predicted by the axioms of perfect rationality (see Kahneman *et al.* 1982). Moreover, decision making within business firms is heavily concerned with the discovery of choice alternatives (e.g. Cyert and March 1993 [1963]), and frequently seeks satisfactory rather than optimal choices; whereas in neo-classical theory, alternatives are generally assumed to be given in advance (but see Stigler 1961), and the goal is the optimum.

In response to these and other major discrepancies between neo-classical assumptions and actual behaviour, neo-classical theorists seldom defend the literal correctness of the axioms, but prefer to argue, first, that departures from the behaviour called for by the axioms are not sufficiently large to have significant consequences for markets or the whole economy, and second, that actors may behave 'as if' they were maximizing utility without actually carrying out the implied calculations. The best known defence of neo-classical theory along these lines is Milton Friedman's (1953).

With respect to the first argument, behavioural economists would reply that changes in behavioural assumptions do, in fact, have major macroeconomic implications: for instance, the differences between Keynesian and neo-classical predictions all stem from departures of the Keynesian model from the assumptions of perfect rationality, Keynes's appeal to 'animal spirits' and to money illusion being two of the most obvious examples. The classical theory also cannot usually arrive at definite predictions about the economic effects of economic policies without making numerous auxiliary assumptions. For example, economic analyses commonly assume that people equate utility with wealth, and that altruism is absent from their economic calculations. But both of these are empirical assumptions, and the evidence indicates that they are false. Current practice in neo-classical economics is highly tolerant of *ad hoc* empirical assumptions of these kinds without requiring empirical support for them.

With respect to the second argument, behavioural economists regard discovering the actual mechanisms underlying economic decisions as a major goal of economic science. Just as molecular biology seeks to explain life processes in terms of chemistry and physics, positive economics seeks to explain the behaviour of firms and individuals in terms of psychological laws. 'As if' assumptions that ignore the computational and knowledge limits of human actors cannot provide a basis for understanding economic choice behaviour.

Hence, on the critical side, behavioural economics is concerned with altering those core and auxiliary assumptions of neo-classical theory that are empirically unsound, and with challenging conclusions drawn from theory that depend on these assumptions. On the positive side, behavioural economics is concerned with building an empirically founded theory of human decision making.

Behavioural theories

Behavioural theory in economics resembles theory in biology more than theory in physics. There are not just a few central phenomena to be explained, but a large number, which interact to produce the behaviour of economic systems. These phenomena are not produced by a few underlying processes, but by numerous interdependent mechanisms. In particular, the theory is much more inductive than deductive, emerging out of empirical investigation. There is a substantial body of theory about human economic behaviour, supported by extensive data.

One part of the behavioural theory explains phenomena that do not depend at all on assumptions of rationality (Simon 1979). For example, the observed average relation of executive salary to size of firm (salaries are proportional to logarithm of firm size) is explicable in terms of the relative constancy of span of control (number of immediate subordinates per executive) and a social norm for the ratio of salaries at adjacent organizational levels. Neo-classical theory had explained this relation only by making strong, *ad hoc* untested assumptions about the distribution of executives by ability. Similarly, the observed logarithmic rank-size distribution of business firms is explicable on the assumption that average growth rates of firms are independent of present size. The neo-classical literature 'explains' this distribution by contrary-to-fact assumptions about the change of cost of production with company size.

Another part of behavioural theory seeks to establish the human motivations that underlie economic decision making, and the circumstances under which particular motives display themselves. Of particular importance is evidence that people sometimes behave altruistically, especially by identifying with particular social groups, ranging from the family and business organizations to ethnic and national groups. As a consequence, the 'I' becomes a 'we', which evaluates alternatives by their consequences for the relevant group instead of the self.

A third part of behavioural theory explains the operation of business firms and the choice between firms and markets. Here organizational identification gives firms a comparative advantage over markets. A second important mechanism accounting for the efficiency of firms is the employment contract, which shifts from employees to employers the management of uncertainty in matters where decisions have much larger consequences for the firm than for the employee. Particular attention is being paid to the information flows, in addition to information about prices, that are required for the conduct of economic affairs. These flows also have strong impact on the choice between organizational and market arrangements. At a more abstract level, and drawing upon both the behavioural and neo-classical viewpoints, the 'new institutional economics' (Williamson 1975) explains the choice between intra-firm and inter-firm arrangements in terms of transaction costs and opportunism (unenforceability of contract conditions).

A fourth part of behavioural theory explains rationality in decision making in the face of people's limited information and limited capabilities for computing consequences ('bounded rationality'). It studies the focus of attention (the small part of the decision context that is actually considered); how problems that reach the agenda are represented and structured; the processes for generating potential problem solutions (design processes); and how design and problem-solving processes are organized in business firms.

New concepts have emerged from this fourth component of the theory and have been investigated empirically, including the respective roles of satisficing (looking for good-enough solutions) and maximizing in making decisions; the formation of aspiration levels that determine what is 'good enough'; the development of individual and organizational expertise by acquiring large knowledge bases and 'indexes' that give access to the knowledge; the routinization of organizational decision making by using the knowledge bases to recognize decision situations and handle them on a rule-governed basis, and many more.

Research methods

Because of the empirical emphasis of the behavioural theory, much attention has been paid to methods of enquiry. Neo-classical economics, when undertaking empirical verification of its theories, has mostly relied on econometric methods applied to aggregated data. Most often, the data were originally assembled with other purposes than economic analysis in mind.

While not ignoring such data, behavioural economists have sought more direct ways to observe actual decision making in organizations, as well as the behaviour of consumers. Survey research aimed at collecting data about expectations provided much of the early information about departures of actual behaviour from perfect rationality. Techniques have gradually developed for direct observation of decision making in individual business firms; but better methods are needed for aggregating individual case studies into evidence for general theories. Computer simulation of individual and organizational problem solving and decision making has become an important way of stating theories in rigorous and testable form. Finally, there has been a vigorous development of experimental economics, especially the laboratory study of markets. All of these improved and new techniques facilitate progress in our understanding of human decision making, and, as a consequence, our understanding of human bounded rationality in the operation of business firms, markets and the economy.

Herbert A. Simon
Carnegie Mellon University

References

Cyert, R. M. and March, J. G. (1993 [1963]) *A Behavioral Theory of the Firm*, Englewood Cliffs, NJ.
Friedman, M. (1953) *Essays in Positive Economics*, Chicago.
Kahneman, D., Slovic, P. and Tversky, A. (eds) (1982) *Judgment under Uncertainty*, Cambridge, UK.
Simon, H. A. (1979) 'On parsimonious explanations of production relations', *Scandinavian Journal of Economics* 81.
—— (1983) *Reason in Human Affairs*, Stanford, CA.
Stigler, G. J. (1961) 'The economics of information', *Journal of Political Economy* 69.
Williamson, O. E. (1975) *Markets and Hierarchies*, New York.

behaviourism

Behaviourism is mainly a twentieth-century orientation within the discipline of psychology in the USA. The behavioural approach emphasizes the objective study of the relationships between environmental manipulations and human and animal behaviour change, usually in laboratory or relatively controlled institutional settings. Emerging as a discrete movement just prior to the First World War, behaviourism represented a vigorous rejection of psychology defined as the introspective study of the human mind and consciousness. Early behaviourists eschewed the structuralism of Wundt and Titchener, the functional mentalism of James, Dewey, Angell and Carr, and the relativism and phenomenology of Gestalt psychology.

John B. Watson is credited with declaring behaviourism a new movement in 1913, but the foundations of the development extend back to the ancient Greeks and include empiricism, elementism, associationism, objectivism and naturalism. The direct antecedents of behaviourism during the late nineteenth and early twentieth centuries were the studies of animal behaviour and the functional orientation inspired by Darwin's theory of evolution; the conditioning research of Russian physiologists Ivan Pavlov and Vladimir Bekhterev emphasizing stimulus substitution in the context of reflexive behaviour; and the puzzle box studies of US psychologist Edward Thorndike concerned with the effects of the consequences of behaviour on response frequency. The two predominant and often competing theoretical-procedural models of conditioning research have been classical conditioning derived from the work of Pavlov and Bekhterev, and Skinner's operant conditioning.

While it is generally claimed that behaviourism as a distinct school ceased to exist by the 1950s, behaviourism as a general orientation has gone through the following overlapping periods: classical behaviourism (1900–25), represented by the work of Thorndike and Watson; neo-behaviourism (1920s–40s), an exciting time when the theories of Clark Hull, Edward Tolman, Edwin Guthrie and Burrhus F. Skinner competed for pre-eminence; Hullian behaviourism (1940–50s), when Hull's complex hypothetico-deductive behaviour theory appeared most promising; Skinnerian behaviourism (1960s–mid-1970s), during which time operant conditioning techniques, emphasizing the control of behaviour implicit in the consequences of behaviour, afforded the most powerful methodologies; and, finally, cognitive behaviourism (1975–present) when the limits of a purely Skinnerian approach to behaviour change became increasingly apparent, and cognitive perspectives, such as social learning theories, seemed necessary to account for behaviour change.

A behavioural orientation has been central to twentieth-century psychology in the USA primarily because of a strong faith in laboratory research and experimental methodologies; an interest in studying the process of learning; a preference for quantitative information; the elimination from the discipline of ambiguous concepts and investigations of complex and therefore difficult to describe private (subjective) experiences; and, since the late 1950s, a very conservative approach to theory building.

While each of the major behavioural programmes from Thorndike's to Skinner's failed to provide a comprehensive account of behaviour change, the behavioural orientation has led to the development of behaviour-control methodologies with useful application in most areas of psychology. In addition, the movement has inspired precision and accountability in psychological enquiry.

Behavioural methodologies have, of course, been employed by psychologists in countries other than the USA, particularly those with strong scientific traditions such as Britain and Japan. Behavioural assumptions have also influenced other social sciences, especially sociology and political science. But because laboratory animal research is central to the behavioural orientation, behaviourism as a major movement developed only in psychology.

Albert R. Gilgen
University of Northern Iowa

Further reading

Marx, M. H. and Hillix, W. A. (1979) *Systems and Theories in Psychology*, New York.

See also: conditioning, classical and operant.

Bentham, Jeremy (1748–1832)

Jeremy Bentham was undoubtedly one of the most important and influential figures in the development of modern social science. His numerous writings are major contributions to the development of philosophy, law, government, economics, social administration and public policy, and many have become classic texts in these fields. To these subjects he brought an analytical precision and careful attention to detail which, especially in matters of legal organization and jurisprudence, had not been attempted since Aristotle, and he transformed in method and substance the way these subjects were conceived. He combined a critical rationalism and empiricism with a vision of reform and, latterly, radical reform, which gave unity and direction to what became Philosophic Radicalism. Although he was not the first philosopher to use the greatest happiness principle as the standard of right and wrong, he is rightly remembered as the founder of modern utilitarianism. Many of Bentham's writings were never published in his lifetime or were completed by various editors. The new edition of the *Collected Works* (1968–in progress) will replace in approximately sixty-five volumes the inadequate *Works of Jeremy Bentham* (1838–43), edited by John Bowring, and will reveal for the first time the full extent and scope of Bentham's work.

Bentham is best known for some of his earliest writings. *An Introduction to the Principles of Morals and Legislation* (printed in 1780 and published in 1789) and *Of Laws in General* (not published until 1945) are important texts in legal philosophy and, together with his critique of William Blackstone's *Commentaries on the Laws of England* in the *Comment on the Commentaries* (published first in 1928) and *A Fragment on Government* (1776), represent major landmarks in the development of jurisprudence. The *Introduction to the Principles of Morals and Legislation* was also intended to serve as an introduction to a penal code, which was an important part of a lifelong ambition, never fully realized, of constructing a complete code of laws (latterly called the *Pannomion*). At this time Bentham also turned to economic questions which were to occupy him in various forms throughout his life. His first publication was the *Defence of Usury* (1787), a critique of Adam Smith's treatment of this subject in *The Wealth of Nations*.

From the outset of his career, Bentham was devoted to reform and especially to the reform of legal institutions. His attitude towards fundamental political reform developed more slowly. Although at the time of the French Revolution he was not part of the radical movement in England, he wrote numerous manuscripts in support of democratic institutions in France. He eventually reacted strongly against the excesses of the revolution, but earlier contacts, largely developed through Lord Lansdowne, and the publication of his *Draught of a New Plan for the Organisation of the Judicial Establishment of France*, led to his being made an honorary citizen of France. One important development of this period was his friendship with Etienne Dumont, the Swiss reformer and scholar, whose French versions of Bentham's works, especially the *Traités de législation, civile et pénale* (1802), were read throughout Europe and Latin America and earned for Bentham a considerable international reputation. Following the French Revolution much of Bentham's practical energies were devoted, in conjunction with his brother Samuel, to establishing model prisons, called Panopticons, in various countries. His main effort in England failed, and this failure, though ultimately compensated by the government, was one factor leading him to take up the cause of radical political reform. The influence of James Mill was perhaps the most important factor (there were many) in his 'conversion' to radicalism in 1809–10, and the publication of *A Plan of Parliamentary Reform* in 1817 launched the Philosophic Radicals in their quest for parliamentary reform. In the 1820s, though now in his seventies, Bentham resumed the task of codification and the construction of the *Pannomion* in response to requests from governments and disciples in Spain, Portugal, Greece and Latin America. In his massive, unfinished *Constitutional Code* (1822–), he set forth a theory of representative democracy which was a grand synthesis of many of his ideas and a classic of liberal political thought.

Frederick Rosen
University of London

Further reading

Dinwiddy, J. (1989) *Bentham*, Oxford.
Halévy, E. (1901–4) *La Formation du radicalisme philosophique*, 3 vols, Paris.
Hart, H. L. A. (1982) *Essays on Bentham: Jurisprudence and Political Theory*, Oxford.
Kelly, P. (1990) *Utilitarianism and Distributive Justice: Jeremy Bentham and the Civil Law*, Oxford.
Rosen, F. (1983) *Jeremy Bentham and Representative Democracy*, Oxford.
—— (1992) *Bentham, Byron and Greece: Constitutionalism, Nationalism and Early Liberal Political Thought*, Oxford.
Semple, J. (1993) *Bentham's Prison: A Study of the Panopticon Penitentiary*, Oxford.

See also: liberalism; utilitarianism.

black economy *see* informal economy; informal sector

Boas, Franz (1858–1942)

Franz Boas, born in Germany in 1858, naturalized US citizen in 1892, unquestionably dominated both the intellectual paradigm and institutional development of twentieth-century American anthropology until the Second World War, presiding over the emergence of anthropology as a professional discipline based on the concept of culture, and establishing a subdisciplinary scope including cultural, physical and linguistic anthropology as well as prehistoric archaeology.

In spite of his focus on professionalism in science, Boas himself was trained in (psycho)physics in his native Germany, thereby coming into contact with the folk psychology of Wundt and the anthropology of Bastian (European folk cultures) and Virchow (anthropometry). Boas's dissertation at the University of Kiel in 1881 on the colour of sea water led to concern with the inherent subjectivity of observer perception. His work in geography with Fischer initially supported environmental determinism, but his expedition to the Eskimo of Baffin Land in 1882–3 led to a more flexible argument stressing the interaction of culture and environment.

Boas settled permanently in North America only in 1887, recognizing greater opportunities there for an ambitious young Jewish scholar. In the ensuing years, he was crucially involved in the development of American anthropology in all of its early major centres. The institutional framework for the emerging Boasian anthropology was usually collaboration between a university, ensuring the academic training of professional anthropologists, and a museum to sponsor field research and publication. Boas himself settled in New York, teaching at Columbia from 1896 until 1936. He had previously served as Honorary Philologist of the Bureau of American Ethnology, which dominated Washington and government anthropology. Through F. W. Putnam of Harvard, he organized anthropology at the Chicago World's Fair of 1892 and acquired ties to archaeological work centring at Harvard. Boas's own students established programmes elsewhere, particularly Kroeber at Berkeley, Speck at Pennsylvania, and Sapir in Ottawa. By about 1920, Boasian anthropology was firmly established as the dominant paradigm of the North American discipline.

Boas's theoretical position, often characterized as historical particularism, claimed that unilinear evolution was an inadequate model for the known diversity of human cultures. Human nature was defined as variable and learned tradition. Although he was extremely interested in particular historical developments, Boas argued that progress did not necessarily follow a fixed sequence, nor was it always unidirectional from simple to complex. He further parted from evolutionary theorists like E. B. Tylor in his contention that cultural learning is basically unconscious rather than rational. Boas produced particular ethnographic examples to argue the limits of theoretical generalization in anthropology, indeed in social science generally. 'Laws' comparable to those of the natural sciences were possible in principle though usually premature in practice. The ultimate generalizations of anthropology would be psychological (1911b), but Boas's own studies rarely transcended the prior level of ethnographic description. Later students, especially Margaret Mead and Benedict, elaborated these ideas in what came to be called culture and personality.

Particular histories could not be reconstructed in detail for societies without written records. In contrast, Boas stressed the historical dimensions of synchronically observable, particular cultural phenomena. For example, distribution was the primary reconstructive method to trace the diffusion (borrowing) of folklore motifs and combinations on the Northwest Coast. Elements in a single culture had diverse sources rather than a single common origin. Boas applied this same argument to linguistic work, assuming that language was a part of culture. His scepticism about distant genetic relationships of American Indian languages was consistent with his lack of training in Indo-European philology, and brought him into frequent disagreement with his former student Edward Sapir, whose linguistic work was far more sophisticated.

On the other hand, Boas made important contributions to linguistics, being the first to establish the theoretical independence of race, language and culture as classificatory variables for human diversity (1911a). He broke with the Indo-European tradition in insisting on the 'inner form' (Steinthal) of each language in its grammatical patterning, developing new analytic categories appropriate to American Indian languages.

Boas insisted on the importance of firsthand fieldwork in living cultures, and he returned again and again to the Kwakiutl and other Northwest Coast tribes. He trained native informants to record their own cultures, and collected native language texts for folklore as well as linguistics. He was particularly concerned to record the symbolic culture of these tribes, focusing on art, mythology, religion and language, and was influential in the development of the disciplines of folklore and linguistics as well as anthropology.

Boas's own research spanned the scope of anthropology in its North American definition. In archaeology, he pioneered in Mexico and the Southwest in developing research programmes to reconstruct the history of particular cultures. In physical anthropology, he demonstrated that the head-form of descendants of immigrants can change in a single generation, thereby illustrating the essential variability and plasticity of the human form. He further developed important statistical methods for human growth studies, using longitudinal studies and family-line variation to show the role of environment in modifying heredity. Moreover, Boas was dedicated to the idea that anthropology had practical consequences for society generally, arguing, particularly in response to events in Nazi Germany at the end of his life, for the essential equality of races (defined in terms of statistical variability) and the validity of each cultural pattern.

Boas is, then, more than any other individual, responsible for the characteristic form which the discipline of anthropology has taken in North America. During his long career, he and several successive generations of students stood for a particular scope, method and theory, applied largely to the study of the American Indians. The increasing diversity of North American anthropology since The Second World War still has Boasian roots.

Regna Darnell
University of Western Ontario

References

Boas, F. (1911a) 'Introduction', in *Handbook of American Indian Languages*, Washington, DC.
—— (1911b) *The Mind of Primitive Man*, New York.

Further reading

Boas, F. (1888 [1964]) *The Central Eskimo*, Lincoln, NB.
—— (1940) *Race, Language and Culture*, New York.
Goldschmidt, W. (ed.) (1959) *The Anthropology of Franz Boas: Memoir of the American Anthropological Association* 89.
Harris, M. (1968) *The Rise of Anthropological Theory*, New York.
Stocking, G. (1968) *Race, Culture and Evolution*, New York.

See also: cultural anthropology.

body

Since the early 1970s the human body has become a vivid presence in the human sciences and inter-disciplinary cultural studies. Feminist theory, literary criticism, history, comparative religion, philosophy, sociology, psychology and anthropology are all implicated in the move towards the body. It has been suggested that this widespread interest in the body may be due to the current historical moment in which 'we are undergoing fundamental changes in how our bodies are organized and experienced' such that we are seeing 'the end of one kind of body and the beginning of another kind of body' (Martin 1992: 121).

Recent scholarship (Bynum 1989; Frank, 1991) appears to support this claim. The body has been typically assumed, by scholarly and popular thought alike, to be a fixed, material entity subject to the empirical rules of biological science, and characterized by unchangeable inner necessities. The new body beginning to be identified can no longer be considered a brute fact of nature. A chorus of critical statements has declared that 'the body has a history' in that it behaves in new ways at particular historical moments, that neither our personal nor social bodies are natural because they exist only within the self-creating process of human labour, and that as the existential ground of culture the body is characterized by an essential indeterminacy and flux. With biology no longer a monolithic objectivity, the body is transformed from object to agent.

Others argue that the human body can no longer be considered a 'bounded entity' due to the destabilizing impact of social processes of commodification, fragmentation, and the semiotic barrage of images of body parts (Kroker and Kroker, 1987). In the milieu of late capitalism and consumer culture, the body/self is primarily a performing-self of appearance, display, and impression management. Fixed life-cycle categories are blurred, and the goals of bodily self-care have changed from spiritual salvation, to enhanced health, and finally to a marketable self. The asceticism of inner body discipline is no longer incompatible with outer body hedonism and social mobility, but has become a means towards them.

The contemporary cultural transformation of the body is also observable in the problematizing of the boundaries of corporeality itself. These include the boundaries between the physical and non-physical, between animal and human, between animal/human and machine or automaton, and between human and gods or deities. Yet another inescapable transformation of the contemporary body is being wrought by the incredible proliferation of violence: ethnic violence, sexual violence, self-destructive violence, domestic violence, and gang violence. From the dissolution of self in torture and the denaturing of the body in situations of chronic political violence, from unarticulated bodily resistance to hegemonic oppression among the impoverished and again to the madness of 'ethnic cleansing' and rape as political weapons, the body is the threatened vehicle of human being and dignity.

Across these transformations, several general approaches to the body can be identified in current literature. A premise of much writing is an 'analytic body' that invites discrete focus on perception, practice, parts, processes or products. Other literature concentrates on the 'topical body', that is, an understanding of the body in relation to specific domains of cultural activity: the body and health, the body and political domination, the body and trauma, the body and religion, the body and gender, the body and self, the body and emotion, the body and technology are examples. Finally, there is the 'multiple body', with the number of bodies dependent on how many of its aspects one cares to recognize. Douglas (1973) called attention to the 'two bodies', referring to the social and physical aspects of the body. Scheper-Hughes and Lock (1987) give us 'three bodies', including the individual body, social body, and body politic. O'Neill (1985) ups the ante to 'five bodies': the world's body, the social body, the body politic, the consumer body, and the medical or medicalized body.

To greater or lesser degrees these approaches study the *body* and its transformations while taking *embodiment* for granted. Emphasis on embodiment problematizes conceptual dualities between mind and body, pre-objective and objectified, subject and object, culture and biology, mental and material, culture and practice, gender and sex. There is among champions of the body in contemporary theorizing a tendency to vilify what is usually called Cartesian dualism as a kind of moral abjection. Yet Descartes in part introduced the doctrine as a methodological distinction and a way to free scientific thought from subjection to theology and strict institutional supervision by the Church. The philosopher is doubtless not entirely to blame for the ontologization of the distinction, and the way it has become embedded in our thinking (cf. Leder 1990).

The possibility that the body might be understood as a seat of subjectivity is one source of challenge to theories of culture in which mind/subject/culture are placed in contrast to body/object/biology. Much theorizing is in fact heir to the Cartesian legacy in that it privileges the mind/subject/culture set in the form of representation, whether cast in terms of rules and principles by social anthropology and sociology, signs and symbols by semiotics, text and discourse by literary studies, or knowledge and models by cognitive science. In such accounts the body is a creature of representation, as in the work of Foucault (1979; 1986), whose primary concern is to establish the discursive conditions of possibility for the body as object of domination. In contrast, the body can be comprehended as a function of being-in-the-world, as in the work of Merleau-Ponty (1962), for whom embodiment is the existential condition of possibility for culture and self. If indeed the body is in a critical historical moment, the corresponding theoretical moment is the tension between representation and being-in-the-world.

Thomas J. Csordas
Case Western Reserve University

References

Bynum, C. W. (1989) 'The Female Body and Religious Practice in the Later Middle Ages', in M. Feher (ed.) *Fragments for a History of the Human Body, Part One*, New York.
Douglas, M. (1973) *Natural Symbols*, New York.
Foucault, M. (1979) *Discipline and Punish: The Birth of the Prison*, New York.
—— (1986) *The Care of the Self: The History of Sexuality*, vol. 3, New York.
Frank, A. (1991) 'For a Sociology of the Body: An Analytical Review', in M. Featherstone, M. Hepworth and B. S. Turner (eds) *The Body: Social Process and Cultural Theory*, London.
Kroker, A. and Kroker, M. (1987) *Body Invaders: Panic Sex in America*, New York.
Martin, E. (1992) 'The end of the body?', *American Ethnologist* 19.
O'Neill, J. (1985) *Five Bodies: The Shape of Modern Society*, Ithaca, NY.
Scheper-Hughes, N. and Lock, M. (1987) 'The mindful body: a prolegomenon to future work in medical anthropology', *Medical Anthropology Quarterly* 1.

Further reading

Csordas, T. (ed.) (1994) *Embodiment and Experience: The Existential Ground of Culture and Self*, Cambridge, UK.

Featherstone, M. Hepworth, M. and Turner, B. S. (eds) (1991) *The Body: Social Process and Cultural Theory*, London.
Feher, M. (ed.) (1989) *Fragments for a History of the Human Body*, 3 vols, New York.
Haraway, D. (1991) *Simians, Cyborgs, and Women: The Reinvention of Nature*, New York.
Jacobus, M., Keller, E. F. and Shuttleworth, S. (eds) (1990) *Body/Politics: Women and the Discourses of Science*, New York.
Leder, D. (1990) *The Absent Body*, Chicago.
Lock, M. (1993) 'The anthropology of the body', *Annual Review of Anthropology* 22.
Merleau-Ponty, M. (1962) *Phenomenology of Perception*, trans. J. Edie, Evanston, IL.
Scarry, E. (1985) *The Body in Pain: The Making and Un-Making of the World*, New York.

See also: medical anthropology.

Braudel, Fernand (1902–85)

Fernand Braudel was one of the most influential historians of the twentieth century. The third of the founding fathers of the so-called Annales School of French historians, he followed the lead of such pre-Second World War historians as Lucien Fèbvre and Marc Bloch in seeking to revitalize the study of history in the light of the methods and concerns of the social sciences. However, Braudel went considerably further along this path than his predecessors, developing an entirely new concept of, and approach to, historical studies. In a more systematic way than his precursors, Braudel sought to emancipate history from its traditional division into political, economic and cultural history and to achieve a 'total' history of society. The objective was to integrate all aspects of humankind's past, placing the chief emphasis on the changing environment and lifestyle of the common person and of society as a whole. Inevitably, the new approach involved a marked de-emphasizing and distancing from the political and constitutional history, which had always been the central preoccupation of historians and which Braudel and his followers term 'histoire événementielle'.

Braudel's most famous and important work, on the Mediterranean world in the age of Philip II, was first published in 1949 and was greeted with widespread and eventually almost universal acclaim. A revised and considerably expanded second edition was published in 1966. In this vast undertaking, Braudel transcended all political and cultural borders, as he did in all historical practice and procedure. He sought to reveal the immense scope and implications of the decline of Mediterranean society in the sixteenth century, achieving a majestic and often elegant synthesis of economic, demographic, cultural and political data and interpretation. It was by no means Braudel's intention to disregard political phenomena; rather he wished to tackle these in a new way, within the context of long- and medium-term socioeconomic trends. Thus one of his principal objectives was to throw new light on the shift in the policy concerns of Philip II of Spain away from the Mediterranean and towards the Atlantic, a change in the direction of Spanish policy making which dates from the 1580s.

Basic to Braudel's approach was his novel categorization of history into simultaneous processes proceeding on different levels at quite different speeds. He envisaged these various trends as taking place on three main levels and, on occasion, compared the processes of historical change to an edifice consisting of three storeys. On the lowest level, he placed the slow, long-term changes in humankind's agrarian, maritime and demographic environment. On the middle level, Braudel placed the medium-term economic and cultural shifts which take place over one or two centuries rather than millennia. Finally, on his uppermost storey, he located all short-term fluctuations and 'events' in the traditional sense.

This novel approach to history is further developed in Braudel's second major work, an ambitious trilogy entitled *Civilisation matérielle et capitalisme* (1967–79) (English trans., 1973–82 *Civilization and Capitalism*), which deals with the evolution of the world economy and of society generally from the end of the Middle Ages to the industrial revolution. Despite Braudel's insistence on material factors as the determinants of social change, and his readiness to borrow concepts from Marx, including the term capitalism which figures prominently in his later work, Braudel's system, like the work of the Annales School more generally, is in essence quite outside the Marxist tradition in that it allocates no central role to class conflict. In the view of some scholars, certain weaknesses evident in the earlier work are much more pronounced in the later study. A less secure grasp of detail, frequent errors both of fact and interpretation of data and, generally, much less convincing evaluations detract considerably from the value of the later work. Certain historians now also see serious defects in Braudel's overall approach, running through his entire *œuvre* which, besides the two major works, includes a number of noteworthy short books and essays. In particular it is felt that Braudel's method of handling the interaction between socioeconomic and political history is unconvincing and unsatisfactory. Thus, his radical de-emphasizing of political and military power, and the impact of 'events' on socioeconomic development, gives rise in his writing to numerous, often major, distortions.

The influence of Braudel's ideas and the extent to which they have been adopted as the modern approach to historical studies varies from country to country, but is pervasive in several European and many Latin American countries as well as in North America. It has been repeatedly asserted that he was 'indisputably the greatest of living historians', but it must also be said that a tendency towards uncritical adulation of his work has become fashionable in many quarters on both sides of the Atlantic. Some history departments in universities, and a number of collaborative historical research projects and publications, have professed Braudel and his approach as the guiding principle directing their studies.

Jonathan I. Israel
University of London

References

Braudel, F. (1966) *La Méditerranée et le monde méditerranéen à l'époque de Philippe II*, 2nd enlarged edn, 2 vols, Paris. (English edn, *The Mediterranean and the Mediterranean World in the Age of Philip II*, 2 vols, New York.)
—— (1967–79) *Civilisation matérielle et capitalisme*, Paris. (English edn, *Material Civilization and Capitalism, 15th–18th Century*, vol. 1: *The Structure of Everyday Life*, London, 1982; vol. 2: *The Wheels of Commerce*, London, 1983; vol. 3: *The Perspective of the World*, London, 1984.)

Further reading

Israel, J. I. (1983) 'Fernand Braudel – a reassessment', *The Times Literary Supplement* 4, 164.
Journal of Modern History (1972) vol. 44: special issue on Braudel with articles by H. R. Trevor-Roper and J. H. Hexter, and Braudel's own 'Personal testimony'.

See also: Annales School.

bureaucracy

Agreement as to when and how the word bureaucracy was invented is widespread and precise. 'The late M. de Gornay ...' notes Baron de Grimm, the French philosopher, in a letter dated 1 July 1764, 'sometimes used to ... invent a fourth or fifth form of government under the heading of *bureaucratie*.' Within a very short time, the physiocrat economist's word entered the international language of politics: the Italian *burocrazia*, the German *Bureaukratie* (later *Bürokratie*), and the English 'bureaucracy' (Albrow 1970).

Agreement about what the word means, however, could hardly be *less* widespread or precise. In political debate, writes Martin Albrow, ' "bureaucracy" has become a term of strong emotive overtones and elusive connotations'. Social scientists have been no more precise. 'Sometimes "bureaucracy" seems to mean administrative efficiency, at other times the opposite. It may appear as simple as a synonym for civil service, or it may be as complex as an idea summing up the specific features of modern organizational structure. It may refer to a body of officials, or to the routines of office administration' (Albrow 1970).

This confusion may be more apparent than real. From the plethora of definitions, two stand out: bureaucracy as rule by officials, and bureaucracy as a particular form of organization. Even these meanings, though distinct, are not unrelated.

Rule by officials was Vincent de Gornay's intention when, in the style of 'democracy' and 'aristocracy', he attached the Greek suffix for rule to the French word 'bureau', which already included 'a place where officials work' among its definitions. It also was the meaning of Harold Laski when he defined bureaucracy in the 1930 *Encyclopaedia of the Social Sciences* as 'A system of government the control of which is so completely in the hands of officials that their power jeopardizes the liberties of ordinary citizens', and of Harold Lasswell and Abraham Kaplan (1950), who defined it in *Power and Society* as 'the form of rule in which the élite is composed of officials'.

Twentieth-century heirs to de Gornay's definition of bureaucracy have characteristically shared his observations on 'bureaumania' – the spread of bureaucracy – as well. They regard rule by officials to be the most prevalent form of government in modern society. Some have traced this rise to officials' organized concentration of expert knowledge. Others, such as Robert Michels (1962 [1911]), have explained it in terms of the imperatives of large-scale organization itself: 'Who says organization, say oligarchy.'

Most modern authors of the de Gornay school have also inherited his displeasure with what he called the 'illness' of bureaucracy. Yet their shared distress belies the polarity of their diagnoses. Sometimes bureaucracy is looked upon as 'intolerably meddlesome', 'a demanding giant', 'an oppressive foreign power', and sometimes as 'timid and indecisive', 'flabby, overpaid, and lazy'. The same critics often seem to regard bureaucracy as both aggressive and passive. Laski, for example, having identified bureaucracy as a form of rule that 'jeopardizes the liberties of ordinary citizens', adds in the next sentence that: 'The characteristics of such a regime are a passion for routine in administration, the sacrifice of flexibility to rule, delay in the making of decisions and a refusal to embark upon experiment.'

In all cases, however, officials tend to be judged by subscribers to this first definition as the real power in any political system in which the ranks of officialdom are large. It was this view that Max Weber (Gerth and Mills 1946) challenged in the early part of the twentieth century, with arguments that set the stage for the development of bureaucracy's second definition, as a particular form of organization.

To Weber, those who equated large numbers of officials with rule by officials sometimes confused appearance and reality. They saw official orders given and obeyed, and assumed from this that officials were wielding independent power. In truth, Weber argued, orders were more likely obeyed because their recipients believed that it was right to obey. Not power *per se*, but 'authority' – power cloaked with legitimacy – was at play. In modern society, such authority characteristically was 'legal' rather than 'charismatic' or 'traditional' in nature: officials' orders were considered legitimate when officials were seen to be acting in accordance with their duties as defined by a written code of laws, including statutes, administrative regulations, and court precedents.

As Weber conceived it, bureaucracy was the form of organization best suited to the exercise of legal authority. If legal authority calls for 'a government of laws and not of men', bureaucracy may be thought of as 'an organization of positions and not of people'. Bureaucratic organizations consist of offices whose powers and duties are clearly defined, whose activities are recorded in writing and retained in files, and whose arrangement in relation to one another is hierarchic. Offices are filled on the basis of 'merit', as measured by diplomas, examinations, or other professional qualifications. Officeholders occupy, but in no sense own, their positions or the powers, duties, and other resources that go with them. Their personal relationships with the organization are defined by contracts that specify salary and career structure.

'Rule by officials' and 'a particular form of organization' are very different understandings of bureaucracy. But they also are related: as this history has shown, one definition was formed in reaction to the other. There may even be grounds for reconciling, if not fusing, the two.

Weber, for example, seemed most provoked by the connotations that were usually attached to the 'rule by officials' definition – the easy assumption that wherever officials proliferated, they governed. He was right in seeing that this assumption was often made, but one would be wrong in thinking it necessarily must be made. One can think of bureaucracy as a form of government without assuming that it is the most prevalent form of government.

Conversely, it is not uncommon for those who define bureaucracy in organizational terms to be concerned about rule by officials, either as dangerously efficient (a 'demanding giant') or as hopelessly inefficient ('flabby, overpaid, and lazy'). For Weber's part, he warned in one of his most widely remembered passages of the potential power of bureaucracy at its most efficient:

Under normal conditions, the power position of a fully developed bureaucracy is always overtowering. The 'political master' finds himself in the position of the 'dilettante' who stands opposite the 'expert', facing the trained official who stands within the management of administration. This holds whether the 'master' whom the bureaucracy serves is a 'people' . . . or a parliament . . . a popularly elected president, a hereditary and 'absolute' or a 'constitutional' monarch.

(Gerth and Mills 1946)

Other social scientists who basically accept Weber's definition of bureaucracy direct their concerns about bureaucratic power to the inefficiency of such organizations. Robert Merton (1952), for example, notes the danger, inherent in any rules-bound organization, that the rules will become ends in themselves, blinding officials to the organization's service functions and making them resistant to change. In the same spirit, Michel Crozier (1964) describes bureaucracy as 'an organization that cannot correct its behaviour by learning from its errors'.

Michael Nelson
Rhodes College

References

Albrow, M. (1970) *Bureaucracy*, New York.
Crozier, M. (1964) *The Bureaucratic Phenomenon*, London.
Gerth, H. and Mills, C. W. (1946) *From Max Weber: Essays in Sociology*, New York.
Laski, H. (1930) 'Bureaucracy', in *Encyclopaedia of the Social Sciences*, vol. 3, New York and London.
Lasswell, H. D. and Kaplan, A. (1950) *Power and Society: A Framework for Political Inquiry*, New Haven, CT.
Merton, R. (1952) 'Bureaucratic structure and personality', in R. Merton (ed.) *Reader in Bureaucracy*, Glencoe, IL.
Michels, R. (1962 [1911]) *Political Parties*, New York.

See also: government; management theory; public administration; public management; Weber, Max.

Burke, Edmund (1729–97)

Edmund Burke, the British statesman and political theorist, was born in Dublin in 1729. He came to London in 1750 and soon acquired a reputation as a philosopher and man of letters. In 1765 he was elected to the House of Commons, acting as party secretary and chief man of ideas to the Whig connection led by the Marquis of Rockingham. He wrote voluminously, and the eloquence he brought to expressing a high-minded but by no means unrealistic view of political possibilities has never been surpassed. He could bring out the universal element in the most parochial of issues.

Burke's enduring importance in articulating a political tendency is particularly evident in the *Reflections on the Revolution in France* (1790) and subsequent late works in which he defended his criticism of the Revolution against fellow Whigs who had welcomed it as an act of liberation from an odious Bourbon absolutism. Attacked as one who had betrayed the cause of liberty, Burke agreed (in the *Appeal from the Old to the New Whigs*) that consistency was the highest virtue in politics, but proceeded to theorize its complex nature. In supporting the American colonists, he argued, he was in no way committed to support every movement which raised the banner of liberty, for in his view the Americans 'had taken up arms from one motive only; that is, our attempting to tax them without their consent' (Burke 1855, *Appeal*, vol. 3). Real political consistency must take account of circumstances, and cannot be deduced from principles. And it was in terms of the contrast between historical concreteness and abstract principle that Burke interpreted the challenge posed by the revolutionaries in France.

The revolutionaries were, Burke argued, amateur politicians attempting to solve the complex problems of French society with a set of theories or what he called 'metaphysic rights'. They believed that an ideal rational constitution, in which a republic guaranteed the rights of humankind, was suitable for all societies. This belief constituted a revelation which stigmatized most existing beliefs as prejudice and superstition, and all existing forms of government as corrupt and unjust. On Burke's historical understanding of the specificity of different societies, the beliefs and practices of any society revealed their character; indeed, properly understood, they revealed a kind of rationality much more profound than the propositional fantasies of revolutionaries. To condemn what whole societies had long believed as merely mistaken was in the highest degree superficial. Society is a delicate fabric of sentiments and understandings which would be irreparably damaged if subjected to the butchery of abstract ideas. Burke judged that, as the revolutionaries discovered that the people were not behaving according to the rationalist prescriptions, they would have increasing recourse to violence and terror. At the end of every prospect would be found a gallows. He predicted that the outcome would be a military dictatorship.

Burke's genius lay in breaking up the conventional antitheses through which politics was then understood. He had never been, he wrote, 'a friend or an enemy to republics or to monarchies in the abstract' (Burke 1855, *Appeal*, vol. 3), and this refusal to take sides on an abstractly specified principle became a dominant strain in conservatism. The real clue to wisdom politics lay not at the level of high principle but of low and humble circumstance. This was the level of actual human experience, and, at this level, there was not a great deal that governments could achieve, and most of what they could was to prevent evils rather than promote goods. No stranger to paradox, Burke insisted that one of the most important of the rights of humankind is the right to be restrained by suitable laws. Again, Burke was prepared to agree that society was indeed a contract, but he instantly qualified this conventional judgement by insisting that it was a contract of a quite sublime kind, linking the living, the dead and those yet to be born. It is in these hesitations and qualifications of conventional wisdom to which he was impelled by the excitements of his time that Burke's contribution to political understanding lies.

More philosophically, Burke adapted to political use the empiricist doctrine that the passions, especially as entrenched in and shaped by social institutions, are closer to reality than the speculations of philosophers, and especially of *philosophes*. His defence of prejudice threw down a gauntlet to the superficial rationalism of his opponents, and has sometimes been seen as expressing an irrationalism endemic to conservative thought. It is, however, an argument about the relations between reason and passion similar to that of Hegel, though in a quite different idiom.

Burke's political judgement is a conservative modification of the English political tradition and covers many areas. On the nature of representation, for example, he argued that the House of Commons was not a congress of ambassadors from the constituencies. His defence of the place of parties in British politics contributed to the acceptance and development of party government, however limited in intention it may have been (Brewer 1971). In the indictment of Warren Hastings, he stressed the trusteeship of power and property which was never far from his thoughts. But in all his political writings, Burke wrote to the occasion, and it is perilous to generalize about him too far. His personal ambitions required manoeuvring in the complex world of late eighteenth-century politics which have led some writers (e.g. Namier 1929; Young 1943) to regard him as little more than a silver-tongued opportunist. This is to do less than justice to the suggestiveness of his prose and the momentousness of the occasions to which he so brilliantly responded.

Kenneth Minogue
London School of Economics and
Political Science

References

Brewer, J. (1971) 'Party and the double cabinet: two facets of Burke's thoughts', *Historical Journal* 14.
Burke, E. (1855) *Works*, London.
Namier, L. (1929) *The Structure of Politics at the Accession of George III*, London.
Young, G. M. (1943) *Burke* (British Academy Lecture on a Mastermind), London.

Further reading

Canavan, F. P. (1960) *The Political Reason of Edmund Burke*, Durham, NC.
Cruise O'Brien, Conor (1992) *The Great Melody*, London.

business concentration

Business seller concentration refers to the extent to which sales in a market, or economy, are concentrated in the hands of a few large firms. At the level of an individual market or industry, *market concentration* is thus an (imperfect) indicator of the *degree of oligopoly*, and measures thereof are widely used by industrial economists in empirical tests of oligopoly theory. The most popular operational measure is the *concentration ratio*, which records the share of industry size (usually sales, but sometimes employment or value added) accounted for by the k largest firms (where, usually, $k = 3$ or 4 or 5). Its popularity derives more from its regular publication in Production Census reports than from a belief in its desirable properties (either economic or statistical). The multitude of other concentration measures include the Hirschman-Herfindahl index, which is the sum of squared market shares of all firms in the industry, the Hannah-Kay index, a generalization of the former, and various statistical inequality measures borrowed from the study of personal income distribution. While there is general agreement that a respectable measure of concentration should be inversely related to the number of sellers and positively related to the magnitude of size inequalities, these criteria are satisfied by a large number of the alternative indexes, and there is no consensus on what is the ideal measure.

Evidence on market concentration is readily available for most western economies, and although differences in methods of data collection and definitions make most international comparisons hazardous, three broad facts are indisputable. First, the pattern of concentration is similar within most countries, with high concentration prevalent in consumer good and capital-intensive industries. Second, typical levels of market concentration are higher in smaller economies. Third, in-depth studies of the UK and the USA suggest that, on average, the five firm ratio may be as much as fourteen points higher in the UK. Studies of trends over time show a steady and pronounced increase in the UK from 1935 to 1968, with a levelling off in the 1970s. In the USA, market concentration has remained fairly constant since the Second World War.

Theories on the causes of concentration include the technology and entry barrier explanation (emanating from the Structure-Conduct-Performance paradigm), and a range of stochastic models based on Gibrat's Law of Proportionate Effect. The latter are largely (statistically) successful in accounting for the characteristic positive skew observed in most firm size distributions and for the steady increase in concentration ('spontaneous drift'). They do not, however, provide a true economic understanding of the forces at work. Empirically, mergers have also been identified as a major source of concentration increases.

Aggregate concentration is often measured as the share in GDP, or aggregate manufacturing of the top 100 corporations. In the UK this rose dramatically from 16 per cent in 1909 to 40 per cent in 1968 and then remained constant up to 1980.

S. W. Davies
University of East Anglia

Further reading

Curry, B. and George, K. D. (1983) 'Industrial concentration: a survey', *Journal of Industrial Economics* 31.

See also: corporate enterprise; multinational enterprises.

business cycles

Business cycles are recurring cycles of economic events involving a period of more rapid than normal or average growth (the *expansionary phase*) and culminating in a peak, followed by a phase of slower than average growth (a *recession*), or a period of negative growth (a *depression*) culminating in a trough. In the post-war literature, business cycles are normally assumed to be forty to sixty months in duration, and they are distinguished from various longer cycles that have been discussed in the economics literature, such as the six- to eight-year Major trade cycle, the fifteen- to twenty-five-year Kuznets or building cycle, and the fifty- to sixty-year Kondratieff wave.

Business cycles have commonly been viewed as evolving around a long-term growth trend, especially in the post-war period, and this has typically led to a divorce of 'business cycle theory', which attempts to explain the fluctuations around the trend, from 'growth theory', which attempts to explain the trend growth itself. In the 1970s, interest in long waves revived, and

an alternative view is that business cycles are short-term fluctuations in economic activity around longer cycles or waves. In this case, business cycles are analysed as growth cycles, with alternating rapid growth expansionary phases and slower growth contractionary phases (or recessions) during the upswing of the long wave; while during the downswing of the long wave they will involve periods of positive growth in the expansionary phase followed by periods of zero or negative growth in the contractionary phase (or depression).

There has been some debate about whether business cycles are systematic economic fluctuations, or whether they are instead purely random fluctuations in economic activity. It is certainly true that business cycles are not regular, in the sense of a sine wave with constant period and amplitude. But the weight of evidence, largely due to the accumulated studies produced through the National Bureau of Economic Research, indicates that business cycles are sufficiently uniform to warrant serious study.

Business cycle modelling in the post-war period has usually adopted the approach, suggested by the work of Frisch (1966 [1933]) and Slutsky (1937 [1927]), of regarding the economic system as fundamentally stable but being bombarded by a series of shocks or unexpected events. Economists commonly attempted to devise a 'propagation model' of the economy capable of converting shocks, generated by an impulse model, into a cycle. Using this strategy, many different models have been devised; these vary according to the degree of stability assumed in the 'propagation model', the form of the series of shocks emanating from the 'impulse model', and the sources of the shocks and sectors of the economy described by the propagation model. The various models have commonly involved linear stochastic second order equation systems. The linearity assumption serves both to simplify analysis and to allow an easy separation of business cycle and growth theory, because growth can be represented by a linear or log linear trend. There have been exceptions to this general modelling strategy that have used nonlinear equa-tion systems capable of generating – in the absence of shocks – self-sustaining 'limit cycles'. These can be stable and self-repeating even in the face of shocks, which merely impart some additional irregularity. Since the late 1970s catastrophe theory and bifurcation theory have been used to develop models of the cycle in which nonlinear discontinuities play a key role. Chaos theory, which can explain the seeming irregularity of business cycles using simple nonlinearities, has also been employed. Such contributions have been relatively rare but may become more common as economists increasingly familiarize themselves with nonlinear techniques of mathematical and statistical analysis. The possibility of modelling the business cycle as a limit cycle, as an alternative to the Frisch-Slutsky approach, raises the general question of whether the business cycle is something that would die out in the absence of shocks, or whether it is endogenous to the economic system.

The nonlinear models have also commonly treated business cycles and growth theory as separable. There is, however, an alternative view, which is that business cycles and growth should be explained together, and that a theory of dynamic economic development is required. This view is most frequently associated with the work of Schumpeter (1989).

In 1975 papers by Nordhaus (1975) and Lucas (1975) discussing the political and the equilibrium theories of the business cycle had a major impact. The political theory of the business cycle argues that business cycles are in fact electoral economic cycles which result from governments manipulating the economy in order to win elections. This contrasts with the broad Keynesian consensus view of the mid-1960s that governments, through anti-cyclical demand management policies, had on the whole been successful in reducing the amplitude of the cycle, although it was accepted that at times they may have aggravated it because of the problems involved in allowing for the lag in the effect of policy interventions. The equilibrium theory of the business cycle assumes that economic agents are endowed with 'rational expectations' but must make decisions based on inadequate information about whether price changes are purely inflationary, so that no real response is required, or whether they indicate a profitable opportunity. In models based on this theory, systematic anti-cyclical monetary policy can have no effect, and the only contribution the government can make is to reduce the shocks to the economy by pursuing a systematic monetary policy. The equilibrium theory of the business cycle contrasts with most other theories, which view business cycles as being fundamentally a disequilibrium phenomenon. Although the political and equilibrium theories have many contrasting features, they both raise questions concerning the appropriate treatment of the government in business cycle models. The Keynesian consensus view was that the government could be treated exogenously. In contrast, the political and equilibrium theories of the business cycle indicate that the government should be treated endogenously in business cycle models. A promising new approach to business cycle modelling is the game theoretic analysis of government policy making.

Both the political and equilibrium theories of the business cycle have their origins in much earlier literature. The evidence in their support is rather less than conclusive. Nevertheless, these modern theories revived interest in the nature and causes of business cycles, and spawned a large literature on 'real business cycles', which are equilibrium cycles driven by real, rather than monetary, shocks. They also provoked a reconsideration of the appropriate policy responses to business cycles, based on the analysis of policy credibility and reputation, which led to support for central bank independence.

Andy Mullineux
University of Birmingham

References

Frisch, R. A. K. (1966 [1933]) 'Propagation and impulse problems in dynamic economics', in R. A. Gordon and L. R. Klein (eds) *Readings in Business Cycles*.

Lucas, R. E. Jr (1975) 'An equilibrium model of the business cycle', *Journal of Political Economy* 83.

Nordhaus, W. D. (1975) 'The political business cycle', *Review of Economic Studies* 42.

Schumpeter, J. A. (1989) *Business Cycles: A Theoretical, Historical and Statistical Analysis of the Capitalist Process*, Philadelphia, PA.

Slutsky, E. (1937 [1927]) 'The summation of random causes as the source of cyclic processes' (in Russian), *Problems of Economic Conditions* 3(1), Moscow. (Revised English version, *Econometrica* April.)

Further reading

Dore, M. H. Z. (1993) *The Macroeconomics of Business Cycles*, Oxford.

Goodwin, R. M. (1990) *Chaotic Economic Dynamics*, Oxford.

Mullineux, A. W. (1984) *The Business Cycle after Keynes: A Contemporary Analysis*, Brighton.

—— (1990) *Business Cycles and Financial Crises*, Ann Arbor, MI.

Mullineux, A. W. *et al.* (1993) *Business Cycles: Theory and Evidence*, Oxford.

Zarnowitz, V. (1992) *Business Cycles: Theory, History, Indicators and Forecasting*, Chicago.

business studies

The term business studies is a loose generic title for several related aspects of enterprises and their environments, foremost among these being administration and management, accounting, finance and banking, international relations, marketing, and personnel and industrial relations. There is considerable disagreement, however, on the extent to which scholastic, managerial or professional values should predominate in the framing of the curriculum and in research and teaching objectives.

It is usual to trace modern ideas on business studies to formative developments in the USA, where the Wharton School of Finance and Commerce was the first of 20 schools of business administration and commerce to be founded between 1881 and 1910. But it was particularly in the next two decades, when a further 180 schools were established, that the distinctive US style of business education, with a high degree of abstraction and a quantitative approach to the solution of problems, became firmly rooted (Rose 1970). Management education developed much later in Europe, originally under the tutelage of practitioners from the USA. Indeed, in Britain, it was not until 1947 that the first major centre, the Administrative Staff College at Henley, was inaugurated. There are now several leading European institutes for business and management studies. In both Europe and Japan, there have been active attempts to develop programmes which are distinctive from the original North American model, a change which has been facilitated by the considerable interest in business studies in Third World nations and by the rigorous analytical techniques which have latterly evolved in the USA.

The precise causes of the expansion of business education are open to some doubt, although processes of rationalization in modern societies and the rapid growth in numbers of managerial personnel have been signal influences. Further favourable trends have been increased international competition and investment, major technical changes, a larger scale and greater complexity of modern enterprises and a facilitative role of governments.

However, opinion differs on whether business studies should become an empirical social science or whether, to the contrary, it should be founded on a series of prescriptive values (what should be accomplished) and ideas (what can be achieved) in actual employing organizations. A particular problem of internal coherence in business education also stems from the varied subject backgrounds of research workers and teachers, a situation which has militated against an adequate interdisciplinary synthesis.

In principle, the theoretical linkages between the main areas of business studies are examined in business policy, although this has in practice become a highly specialized area dealing primarily with the intertemporal concept of strategy. In substantive terms, organizational behaviour is the most obvious branch of study that connects the disparate approaches within the business field. Nevertheless, its excessive reliance on contingency theory (which implies that whether a particular organizational form is effective depends on the nature of the environmental context) has proved to be an encumbrance, since challenges to this approach have ensured that there is no longer a generally accepted model for conceptualizing business behaviour.

A further critical issue in business studies is the extent to which, regardless of cultural, socioeconomic or political conditions, common administrative practices are appropriate on a worldwide scale. The earliest perspectives tended to assume a considerable uniformity, the various strands being combined in the 'industrial society' thesis in which a basic 'logic of industrialism' was seen to impel all modern economies towards similar organizational structures and modes of administration (Kerr *et al.* 1960). This complemented the earlier work on classical organization theory, which postulated universal traits of business management, and on studies of bureaucracy, which arrived at similar conclusions. In this approach, too, a key assumption was that there had been a divorce of ownership from control in the business enterprise that, in turn, had ensured the convergence of decision-making processes between societies with ostensibly irreconcilable political ideologies and economic systems.

More recently, however, the 'culturalist' thesis has emerged as a check-weight to these universalist approaches. This assumes great diversity in business behaviour and ideology occasioned either by variations in the 'task' environment (community, government, consumer, employee, supplier, distributor, shareholder) or, more especially, in the 'social' environment (cultural, legal, political, social). Above all, it emphasizes that each new generation internalizes an enduring strain of culture through its process of socialization, with people in different countries learning their own language, concepts and systems of values. Moreover, such deep-rooted cultural forces are continually reasserted in the way people relate to one another and ensure that organizational structures which are not consonant with culturally derived expectations will remain purely formal.

Divergence in business organization and practice can also stem from temporal as well as spatial differences between societies. Indeed, 'late development' would appear to enhance a mode of industrialization quite distinct from the earliest western models, with the state being more predominant at the expense of a *laissez-faire* ideology, educational institutions preceding manufacturing, more substantial technical and organizational 'leaps', human relations and personnel management techniques being more advanced, and large-scale enterprises being deliberately constructed as a spearhead for economic advancement (Dore 1973). In this respect, too, the choices of strategic elites are as important as the constraints of environment and organizational structure in determining which types of business conduct become ascendant in any given society.

Since the Second World War, business studies have been influenced by notions of 'human resource management' (Blyton and Turnbull 1992). The issue here is whether business managers have wider moral obligations, beyond seeking to enhance profitability and efficiency. 'External social responsibility' is particularly relevant to marketing policies. Various ethical questions are raised by the strategies and techniques for promoting different types of goods and services (Baird *et al.* 1990).

'Internal social responsibility' has to do with employee welfare and satisfaction, and human relations in the enterprise. More broadly, there has been a major expansion of research and teaching in the fields of personnel management and industrial relations (Schuler and Huber 1993).

The structure of business studies courses often shows evidence of a tension between professional and managerial approaches. Another unresolved issue is the extent to which business studies should concentrate on the development of empirical social science, perhaps at the expense of consultancy work.

Michael Poole
University of Wales

References

Baird, L. S., Post, J. E. and Mahon, J. F. (1990) *Management: Functions and Responsibilities*, New York.

Blyton, P. and Turnbull, P. (1992) *Reassessing Human Resource Management*, London.

Dore, R. P. (1973) *British Factory – Japanese Factory*, London.

Kerr, C., Dunlop, J. T., Harbison, F. H. and Myers, C. A. (1960) *Industrialism and Industrial Man*, Cambridge, MA.

Rose, H. (1970) *Management Education in the 1970s*, London.

Schuler, R. S. and Huber, V. H. (1993) *Personnel and Human Resource Management*, Minneapolis, MN.

C

cannibalism

Cannibalism, as the customary consumption of human flesh in some other time or place, is a worldwide and time-honoured assumption. This pervasive, and in many ways appealing, characterization of others has also found its place in contemporary anthropology, which has tended to accept uncritically all reports of cannibalism in other cultures as ethnographic fact. This propensity has led to the development of a variety of categories for the conceptualization of the pattern and motivation for the purported behaviour. These have included the recognition of endocannibalism (eating one's own kind) as opposed to exocannibalism (eating outsiders), and ritual in contrast to gustatory or nutritional cannibalism. Uncondoned survival cannibalism, under conditions of extreme privation, has also been noted. Yet, despite the uncounted allusions and the elaborate typologies, there is reason to treat any particular report of the practice with caution, and the entire intellectual complex with some scepticism.

This estimation is warranted for a number of reasons. Depending on time or place, written accounts of alleged cannibalism entered the historical record long after the cessation of the purported custom – often after the obliteration of the culture itself and the decimation of its population. Moreover, reporters were representatives of the very society that was then engaged in the subjugation and exploitation of the people in question. Those responsible for our contemporary impressions rarely took an unbiased view of the traditional culture, and at best relied upon informants who claimed that 'others', such as the nobility or priesthood, engaged in such reprehensible practices. Consequently, rather than reliably documenting a custom, between the early sixteenth and late nineteenth centuries the allegation of cannibalism in western literature often merely legitimized the conquest of foreign cultures by expansionist European states.

These suspect conditions could have been rectified by modern anthropologists actually resident among presumed cannibals in the remoter regions of the world. However, contemporary reports continue to be secondhand; indeed, no anthropologist has ever provided an account of cannibalism based on observation. While reasonable explanations are offered for these circumstances, for example, that the practice has been discontinued or is now hidden, the overall pattern continues to be one of circumstantial rather than direct evidence.

Thus, is it reasonable to assume that cannibalism ever occurred? The answer is yes, but neither as often nor in the context usually assumed. There is as indicated survival cannibalism, but also an antisocial or criminal variety and sometimes subcultural cannibalism practised by a deviant segment of the population (see Parry 1982). In rare instances, 'inversion' cannibalism has also occurred. The first three types are sporadically noted in every part of the world, where they are frowned upon by the majority. The final instance, of which there are a few accounts, involves rituals in which members of a society are constrained to act for the moment in ways prohibited under ordinary moral circumstances (Poole 1983). Such occasions of inversion underscore the basic rules of society by intentional violations but should not be construed as custom in the general sense. There is a simplistic and unwarranted tendency to label non-western societies with such restricted practices of any aforementioned type as cannibalistic. This suggests that the portrayal of others as man-eaters, rather than the deed itself, is the pervasive human trait.

W. Arens
State University of New York at Stony Brook

References

Parry, J. (1982) 'Sacrificial death and the necrophagous ascetic', in M. Bloch and J. Parry (eds) *Death and the Regeneration of Life*, Cambridge, UK.

Poole, F. P. (1983) 'Cannibals, tricksters and witches', in D. Tuzin and P. Brown (eds) *The Ethnography of Cannibalism*, Washington, DC.

Further reading

Arens, W. (1979) *The Man-Eating Myth*, New York.

capital, credit and money markets

Production requires capital to be laid down in advance; capitalist economies have developed markets to allow the division of function between the person undertaking the production, the 'entrepreneur', and the ultimate owner of capital. The modern capital market, as this nexus of markets is called, extends across frontiers and embraces a wide variety of contracts, from debt and credit through preferential shares to ordinary equity (i.e. shared ownership). Investors of capital are able through diversification, between different types of projects and contracts, to obtain the most favourable combination of risk and return. The entrepreneur is able to tap into sources of funds that similarly offer the best combination of risk and cost.

In addition to the primary markets in debt and equity, 'derivative' markets have developed that allow investors and entrepreneurs to adjust their portfolios of assets and liabilities to a quite precise mix. This mix is defined by the events that would trigger costs and returns: through options and futures one may protect one's position against a particular event such as the outcome of an election while being exposed to, say, the economy's growth rate. (An option is a contract for someone to pay or receive a sum contingent on an event, while a future is a purchase or sale of a primary instrument made for a future date.)

The modern theory of finance suggests that in capital markets free from controls the multitude of people buying and selling will drive the expected return on (or, seen from the other side, the cost of) investment to a risk-free rate plus a risk-premium that should reflect (besides the average investor's dislike of risk or 'risk-aversion') 'systematic' risk, by which is meant the contribution to the overall risk on a portfolio made by holding this asset. This contribution will depend on the correlation between returns on this asset and on other assets, which is taken advantage of by diversification. Since this correlation should be reasonably stable, this risk-premium ought to be stable too and invariant to the amounts of the asset being traded, provided these are small relative to the market as a whole. Furthermore if people make proper use of available information (rational expectations) then the expected return should change only when new information arrives in the market.

This theory is that of 'efficient markets', efficient in the sense that information is being reflected appropriately in market prices (and hence in expected returns): this also implies that the capital markets allocate capital in the most economical way between uses, so that government intervention could not (using the same information) improve matters. At an international level it implies extremely high capital mobility between countries: a country's entrepreneurs or government will be able to raise as much capital as they can profitably employ at a cost that will reflect the general international cost of capital adjusted for their particular risk-premium.

This smoothly functioning world of capital may seem too good to be true; certainly in empirical testing the results have been mixed. Statistical tests over past data generally reject the hypothesis of strict efficiency (such rejection could be partly explained by variability of risk-premiums though this should normally be modest). Nevertheless, it has also proved hard to make above-normal returns by investment strategies other than those which used information unavailable to the market: this suggests a fair degree of efficiency. There is clearly a tension between the exploitation of information driving above-normal returns to zero and there being sufficient above-normal returns available to motivate the research into an analysis of information that makes such exploitation possible: it may well be, therefore, that the markets are 'nearly efficient' – with just enough inefficiency to enable analysts to make a living. This state of affairs would justify using the theory as a working approximation.

So far we have made no mention of money. Indeed it would be quite possible to envisage this world of capital markets functioning without money. If everyone had a balance in a gigantic clearing system, whose unit was some amount of a consumer good or combination of several (a 'basket'), then money would be unnecessary. However, it is a fact that many goods are paid for by money by most people and most goods are paid for by money by some people. The reason is to do with the cost of doing business (transactions cost): clearing systems are good value typically for large transactions by people with some security to offer, money is typically good value for small transactions and for people with no security. The costs of both sorts of exchange technology also depend on how intensively and widely they are used, the size of their network – rather like a telephone system.

Notice that money and capital markets are quite separate things. Money is a means of exchange (of anything), one way of permitting exchange in any set of markets; while capital markets trade capital and could use various means of exchange to carry out this trade, including a clearing system or money. (Cash could also be used as part of the portfolio, as a store of value, but being non-interest-bearing it would make better sense to hold a savings deposit in a bank.)

However, once money exists as the means of exchange it acquires potential importance for the functioning of the whole economy. The usual institutional set-up will be one in which money (cash) is used for a limited set of goods and clearing systems (such as credit cards and cheques) for the rest, with cash as their unit of account. By this is meant that to close a balance in these systems one must produce cash. Therefore ultimately cash might have to be used; of course in practice cash may well not be used. For example in bank accounts cash is virtually never used to close them; rather they continue in credit or overdraft. With credit card balances, again cash is rarely used: instead bank account balances are transferred to settle them.

How does money affect the economy and capital markets in such a set-up? Money, being the unit of account, now implies a price level: the amount of money needed to pay for a basket of goods. Also the rate of interest is expressed in money; other capital contracts may not be (equity gives part-ownership of a company, for example) but their prices in the market are, and are related as above to the risk-free rate of interest. It follows that the government (or the central bank if it has the authority) can either fix the quantity of money (cash which it prints), or the price level (through a conversion rule for example as under the early gold standard, where it offers to buy goods, or print money, if their price level falls below a certain level and vice versa), or the rate of interest.

Given that people want cash in order to carry out transactions, printing money will give them more than they initially require. The oldest of theories, the quantity theory, views this requirement as related to the volume of transactions, the price level, and the period over which money turns over (basically the gap between wage payments). The latter should be sensitive to the rate of interest because non-interest-yielding cash creates an incentive to economise by more frequent payment. Hence these different policies of government are in certain conditions equivalent: printing money creates an excess supply of money which must induce higher demand by lowering the rate of interest; lowering the rate of interest increases the demand and this can only be met by printing more money. These two equivalent policies then raise spending on capital and consumption so that, assuming that the economy is fully employed and cannot produce extra quantities, the price level will be driven up. Direct action by government to raise the price level would equivalently have raised the price level, and this would have raised demand for money which would have required extra to be printed.

This way of thinking – in which full employment was assumed to be normal – dominated economics before the First World War. Money was seen as the way to control the price level. It was considered fairly immaterial whether the control was carried out by direct printing control, or indirectly, by fixing interest rates or pegging the price level. After the First World War the Great Depression focused minds (particularly that of J. M. Keynes) on how monetary contraction could depress output and employment rather than only prices: the answer seems to be that most contract prices for goods and labour are written in money terms and are renegotiated at intervals, so that prices change only slowly. Hence sharp unexpected changes in monetary conditions (whether the gold parity, interest rates, or money printed) could have their first effect on output. When this happens these three monetary policy interventions will have different effects: it will depend on the shocks that may hit the economy, whether policies that stabilize money supply, the price level, or interest rates are preferable. The recurring debate over whether exchange rates should be fixed or flexible can be seen in this light. (The evidence tends to suggest that a modern economy facing a wide variety of demand and supply shocks will be better served by flexible rates that permit competitiveness to adjust quickly and also allow interest rates to vary flexibly to maintain employment stability; experience within the European Exchange Rate Mechanism has reinforced the point.) Modern thought (following the work of monetarists such as Milton Friedman and Karl Brunner) accepts such ideas for the short run while maintaining the classical position for the long run, when monetary policy should have its sole impact on prices (or if it is persistently expansionary, on inflation in which case it will also affect interest rates as capital providers protect their returns against it). However, there is no general agreement on the precise short-run mechanisms.

Some monetary theorists have stressed that credit availability rather than cost (interest rates) is the channel by which monetary policy works. However, while this appears superficially attractive from experiences of 'credit crunches', such episodes (for example in 1980 in the USA) tend to occur when controls on credit or other capital markets are introduced. When capital markets are free of controls it is hard to see why availability of finance should be limited given the wide variety of instruments through which capital can be made available.

Patrick Minford
University of Liverpool and Cardiff Business School

Further reading

Allen, D. E. (1985) *Introduction to the Theory of Finance*, Oxford.

Brunner, K. (1970) 'The "Monetarist" Revolution in Monetary Theory', *Weltwirtschaftliches Archiv* 105.

Friedman, M. (1968) 'The role of monetary policy', *American Economic Review* 58.

Keynes, J. M. (1936) *The General Theory of Employment, Interest and Money*, London.

Minford, P. (1992) *Rational Expectations Macroeconomics: An Introductory Handbook*, Oxford.

Parkin, M. and Bade, R. (1988) *Modern Macroeconomics*, London.

See also: capital theory; derivative markets and futures markets; financial system; markets; Marx's theory of history and society.

capital consumption

Understanding capital consumption (that is, the using up of fixed capital) must be based on an understanding of the distinction between fixed capital and circulating capital. In this context, the term capital refers to tangible assets (i.e. as excluding financial assets). Items of circulating capital have only a once-for-all (or 'once-over') use in the process of production; items of fixed capital have a continuing and repeated use in the process of production. A dressmaker has a stock of cloth and a sewing machine: the cloth has a once-for-all use in the process of dressmaking; the sewing machine can be used repeatedly. The cloth is *circulating capital*; the sewing machine is *fixed capital*. The universal feature of items of fixed capital (apart from land) is that, for more than one reason, they have finite working lifetimes and will eventually have to be replaced (as the cloth has immediately to be replaced) if the production process is to continue.

Suppose the working lifetime of a sewing machine is ten years: at the beginning of Year 1 the dressmaker starts business with a (new) sewing machine valued at $1,000 and at the end of Year 10 the sewing machine is worth nothing (assuming it has no residual scrap-metal value). In order to continue in business, the dressmaker has then to spend $1,000 on replacing the sewing machine (abstracting from inflation – a very significant proviso). Now, if over the years the dressmaker has not gathered in from all the customers an aggregate amount of $1,000, then the effect is that those customers have had the free gift of the services of the sewing machine. Therefore, customers should be charged for the use of fixed capital. Suppose the dressmaker makes 200 dresses a year; over ten years 2,000 dresses will have been made and customers should be charged 50 cents per dress, reckoned as: $1,000 (original capital cost of sewing machine) *divided by* 2,000 (dresses) *equals* $0.50 per dress. The 50 cents is the charge for (fixed) capital consumption per dress, and is analogous to the charge made for the cloth used. The price charged must include the cost of capital consumption per dress.

However, most enterprises do not proceed in this direct way to incorporate capital consumption into the price(s) of the item(s) they produce. Instead, the same result may be achieved by making an overall deduction of annual capital consumption from annual gross income (income gross of – including – capital consumption). The dressmaker may deduct from gross income an *annual* charge for capital consumption, reckoned as: $1,000 (original capital cost of sewing machine) *divided by* 10 (years – the lifetime of the sewing machine) *equals* $100 per annum.

If 'income' is to be taxed, then net income rather than gross income is the appropriate tax-base. Hence tax authorities have regulations concerning the deduction of (annual) capital consumption, otherwise known as depreciation provisions.

There are various methods of calculating the flow of depreciation provisions. The formula just given is known as the 'straight-line' method, because it gives a linear decline in the depreciated value of the fixed capital stock and a linear increase in the cumulated depreciation provisions (that is, there is a constant annual charge for depreciation), as follows: beginning Year 1, $1,000 capital, $0 cumulated depreciation provisions; end Year 1, $900 depreciated value of capital, $100 cumulated depreciation provisions; end Year 2, $800 depreciated value of capital, $200 cumulated depreciation provisions; and so on until end Year 10, $0 depreciated value of capital, $1,000 cumulated depreciation provisions. Together the sum of depreciated capital and cumulated depreciation provisions always equal $1,000 and so 'maintains' capital (i.e. wealth) intact.

This arithmetic example illustrates the definitions that: 'Depreciation is the measure of the wearing out, consumption or other loss of value of a fixed asset' (Accounting Standards 1982); or that capital consumption is the fall in the value of fixed capital between two accounting dates; or that charging depreciation provisions is a method of allocating the (original) cost of a long-lived asset to the time periods in which the asset is 'used up'. It also illustrates how the purpose of charging capital consumption against gross income to arrive at net (true) profit is to prevent an enterprise from 'living off its capital': 'A provision for depreciation reduces profit by an amount which might otherwise have been seen as available for distribution as a dividend' (Pizzey 1980). It is not essential that the depreciation provisions be re-invested in the same item: it is quite in order for the dressmaker to invest, in an ongoing way, the depreciation provisions in, say, a knitting machine. What is essential is that sufficient capital equipment for production purposes continues to be available.

Dudley Jackson
University of Wollongong

References

Accounting Standards (1982) *Statements of Standard Accounting Practice 12*, 'Accounting for depreciation', London.
Pizzey, A. (1980) *Accounting and Finance: A Firm Foundation*, London.

See also: capital theory; stock-flow analysis.

capital punishment

Capital punishment, accompanied by torture, is widely applied and taken for granted in most pre-industrial societies, past and present (see, e.g. Diamond 1971). In modern industrial societies there has been a tendency towards decreasing severity of criminal punishments, and, especially, towards decreasing use of the death penalty (Gorecki 1983). This pattern has been particularly marked in European history, although the total abolition of capital punishment became a publicly articulated demand only after the Enlightenment. Most liberal democracies do not now have the death penalty, but many authoritarian societies readily apply capital punishment.

Among the democracies, the USA is the most conspicuous exception. Following a protracted struggle, the American abolitionists resorted, in the 1960s, to judicial review: they petitioned Federal courts rather than lawmakers to ban the penalty on the ground of the constitutional prohibition of 'cruel and unusual punishments'. Abolitionist scholars supplied the Supreme Court with relevant sociolegal empirical data which some Justices cited in their opinions. However, the abolitionists lost the struggle in the wake of a crucial Supreme Court decision of 1976; following that decision, the majority of the states in the USA continue to punish the most abominable cases of murder by death. This development was precipitated by the increasing public anger against high rates of violent crime in the USA.

The arguments of both abolitionists and retentionists are many and hotly debated. The most forcefully stressed retentionist plea is utilitarian (or, strictly speaking, teleological): capital punishment is claimed to deter wrongdoing even better than lifelong confinement. There are further utilitarian contentions as well: that capital punishment constitutes the only secure incapacitation, and that it increases respect for criminal law. Non-utilitarian retentionists believe in the ultimate retributive value of capital punishment as the only 'just desert' for the most abhorrent crimes. In rejoinder, the abolitionists question the superior deterrent value of the death penalty. Furthermore, they stress the sanctity of human life and immorality of the state killing anyone. They argue that the penalty brutalizes society, and endangers the innocent, because judicial errors do occur. Moreover, they claim that the penalty is arbitrarily imposed, and often tainted by prejudice, especially if the perpetrator is black and the victim white (Baldus *et al.* 1990). They also feel that the suffering of convicts who are led to execution and of those who wait on death row is appalling. Believers in the re-education of wrongdoers rather than in retribution as the basic goal of criminal justice complain that execution not only is vindictive but also precludes rehabilitation.

The logical status and empirical validity of these arguments vary. The non-utilitarian arguments constitute moral axioms, like any ultimate ethical norms. The utilitarian arguments are questionable on purely empirical grounds. This is particularly true of the deterrence idea, which has stimulated a wealth of statistical inquiries. Despite their increasing refinement – especially by Ehrlich (1975) and his opponents – the enquiries have been inconclusive; we do not know and may never learn whether capital punishment deters most effectively. But while the impact of the death penalty on the functioning of criminal justice remains unproved and uncertain, the question as to whether we send criminals to their death presents a moral dilemma of utmost importance. That is why interest in the issue remains intense, particularly in the USA.

Since the defeat of the abolitionists in 1976, the US crime rates have risen dramatically. This generated such continuing growth of punitive attitudes that politicians hardly dare to appear 'soft on crime', and often use (and abuse) advocacy of the gallows for political purposes. Since the 1980s, the consistently retentionist Supreme Court stopped utilizing sociolegal empirical studies, which were designed to test the factual assertions underlying the normative views of individual Justices (Acker 1993; Ellsworth 1988; Zimring 1993). In this climate the abolitionists, active and influential in the late 1970s, have lost most of their clout.

Will the USA join the abolitionist club of the most advanced societies? This will probably happen if and when violent crime is brought under control by a conjunction of new social and legal policies. This would have to include the implementation of a viable family and educational policy, guaranteeing adequate upbringing and training for all of America's children and adolescents, and, on the legal front, an overhaul of the criminal justice system. With crime under control, and the pervasive anger and fear of crime disappearing, the tendency towards declining harshness of criminal punishments cannot but start working again, and the day of the abolitionists will probably come. But, for constitutional reasons, it should come through legislative process rather than the action of the Supreme Court. Since legislatures constitute an audience obviously more open to scholarly expertise than the judicial branch, empirical data relevant to the struggle for and against abolition will once more be granted attention.

Jan Gorecki
University of Illinois

References

Acker, J. R. (1993) 'A different agenda: the Supreme Court, empirical research evidence, and capital punishment', *Law and Society Review* 27.

Baldus, D., Woodward, G. and Pulaski, C. Jr (1990) *Equal Justice and Death Penalty: A Legal and Empirical Analysis*, Boston, MA.

Diamond, A. S. (1971) *Primitive Law Past and Present*, London.

Ehrlich, I. (1975) 'The deterrent effect of capital punishment: a question of life and death', *American Economic Review* 65.

Ellsworth, P. C. (1988) 'Unpleasant facts: the Supreme Court's response to empirical research on capital punishment', in K. C. Haas and J. A. Inciardi (eds) *Challenging Capital Punishment: Legal and Social Science Approaches*, Newbury Park, CA.

Gorecki, J. (1983) *Capital Punishment: Criminal Law and Social Evolution*, New York.

Zimring, F. E. (1993) 'On the liberating virtues of irrelevance', *Law and Society Review* 27.

See also: penology; punishment.

capital theory

Capital's role in the technological specification of production and as a source of income called interest or profit encompasses theories of production and accumulation and theories of value and distribution. The subject has perplexed economists because capital produces a return which keeps capital intact and yields an interest or profit which is thus permanent, while consumption goods produce a unique return (utility) equal to cost and are destroyed in use.

The pre-industrial classical economists thought of capital as stocks of food and provisions advanced to labour; it was the accumulation of stocks making possible the division of labour which was of importance. This position is reflected in J. S. Mill's (1886 [1848]) statement that to 'speak of the "productive powers of capital" . . . is not literally correct. The only productive powers are those of labour and natural agents.' Capital was at best an intermediate good determined by technology and thus subject to exogenous or 'natural' laws, rather than human or economic 'laws'.

By Marx's time, factory-labour working with fixed machinery had become widespread, and he was impressed by the increase in the ratio of 'dead' labour, which had gone into producing the machines, to the living labour which operated them. Marx's idea of a 'mode of production' made capital a social, rather than a purely technological, relation; it was not the machinery, but the operation of the laws of value and distribution under capitalism that produced revolutionary implications. This integration of production and distribution challenged Mills's separation and clearly raised the question of the justification for profit or interest as a permanent return to capital.

Jevons was among the first to note the importance of the time that labour was accumulated in stock. Böhm-Bawerk's Austrian theory of capital built on time as a justification for interest in answer to Marx. The Austrians considered human and natural powers as the original productive factors, but 'time', which allowed more 'roundabout' production processes using intermediate inputs, was also productive. Longer average periods of production would produce greater output, but in decreasing proportion. It was the capitalists' ability to wait for the greater product of longer processes, and the workers' haste to consume, which explained the former's profit.

Clark extended Ricardo's classical theory of differential rent of land to physical capital goods, considering diminishing returns to be a 'natural law' of production. In Clark's explanation it is the capital goods themselves which are considered productive, their return equal to their marginal product. Determination of capital's 'marginal' contribution requires that it be 'fixed' while the amount of labour employed varies, but 'transmutable' into the appropriate technical form when different quantities are used with a 'fixed' quantity of labour.

L. Walras shifted emphasis from physical capital goods to their services as the 'productive' inputs and the return to owning the goods themselves which can then be analysed as the exchange and valuation of the permanent net revenues they produce.

Wicksell (1934) was critical of Walras, rejected 'time' as a productive factor, and was sceptical of the application of marginal theory to aggregate capital, for the 'margin' of the capital stock could not be clearly defined. The problem was in the fact that 'land and labour are measured each in terms of their own technical unit' while 'capital . . . is reckoned as a sum of exchange value . . . each particular capital good is measured by a unit extraneous to itself', which meant that the value of capital, equal in equilibrium to its costs of production, could not be used to define the quantity used to calculate its marginal return because 'these costs of production include capital and interest. . . . We should therefore be arguing in a circle' (Wicksell 1934). Wicksell's argument recalls the original classical view of capital as an intermediate good, a produced means of production, rather than an 'original' productive factor.

Fisher made a sharp distinction between the flow of income and the capital stock that produced it; since discounting future income converts one into the other, the key to the problem is in the role of individual preferences of present over future consumption, or the 'rate of time preference' in determining the rate of interest. The greater the preference for present goods, the higher the rate of time discount and the lower the present value of future goods represented by the stock of capital.

Keynes's *General Theory* assumption of a fixed stock of capital and the absence of a clear theory of distribution left open the analysis of capital and the determination of the rate of interest or profit to complement the theory. Neoclassical theorists (based in Cambridge, USA) added a simplified version of Clark's theory via an aggregate production function relating homogeneous output to the 'productive' factors: labour and aggregate capital, in which the 'quantity' of capital would be negatively associated with its price, the rate of interest. This preserved the negative relation between price and quantity of traditional demand theory. Cambridge (UK) economists rejected capital as a productive factor, arguing that the value of the heterogeneously produced means of production comprising 'aggregate capital' could not be measured independently of its price, which was a determinant of the value used to identify its quantity. These theoretical disputes came to be known as the 'Cambridge Controversies' in capital theory.

A crucial role was played in these debates by Sraffa's (1960) theory of prices, which furnished formal proof of Wicksell's criticisms by demonstrating that changes in the rate of interest (or profit) in an interdependent system could affect the prices of the goods making up the means of production in such a way that the sum of their values representing the aggregate 'quantity' of capital might rise or fall, or even take on the same value at two different rates of interest. These demonstrations came to be known as 'capital reversal' and 'reswitching' and clearly demonstrated that the negative relation between the quantity of aggregate capital and the rate of interest had no general application. Such criticism does not apply to the analysis of individual capital goods, although a general equilibrium in which the rate of return is uniform requires the comparison of competing rates of return and thus ratios of profits to the value of the capital goods that produce them. Modern theorists agree only on the inappropriateness of aggregate capital concepts.

J. A. Kregel
University of Groningen

References

Mill, J. S. (1886 [1848]) *Principles of Political Economy*, London.
Sraffa, P. (1960) *Production of Commodities by Means of Commodities*, Cambridge, UK.
Wicksell, K. (1934) *Lectures on Political Economy*, London.

Further reading

Harcourt, G. C. (1972) *Some Cambridge Controversies in the Theory of Capital*, Cambridge, UK.
Kregel, J. A. (1976) *Theory of Capital*, London.

See also: capital, credit and money markets; capital consumption; capitalism; factors of production; human capital; investment.

capitalism

The term capitalism relates to a particular system of socioeconomic organization (generally contrasted with feudalism and socialism), the nature of which is more often defined implicitly than explicitly. In common with other value-loaded concepts of political controversy, its definition – whether implicit or explicit – shows a chameleon-like tendency to vary with the ideological bias of the user. Even when treated as a historical category and precisely defined for the purpose of objective analysis, the definition adopted is often associated with a distinctive view of the temporal sequence and character of historical development. Thus historians such as Sombart (1915), Weber (1930 [1922]) and Tawney (1926), who were concerned to relate changes in economic organization to shifts in religious and ethical attitudes, found the essence of capitalism in the acquisitive spirit of profit-making enterprise and focused on developments occurring in the sixteenth, seventeenth and early eighteenth centuries. Probably a majority of historians have seen capitalism as reaching its fullest development in the course of the Industrial Revolution and have treated the earlier period as part of a long transition between feudalism and capitalism. Marxist historians have identified a series of stages in the evolution of capitalism – for example, merchant capitalism, agrarian capitalism, industrial capitalism and state capitalism – and much of the debate on origins and progress has hinged on differing views of the significance, timing and characteristics of each stage. Thus Wallerstein (1979), who adopts a world-economy perspective, locates its origins in the agrarian capitalism that characterized Europe of the sixteenth, seventeenth and eighteenth centuries; while Tribe (1981), who also takes agrarian capitalism as the original mode of capitalist production, sees the essence of capitalism in a national economy where production is separated from consumption and is co-ordinated according to the profitability of enterprises operating in competition with each other.

Whatever the historical or polemical objective of writers, however, their definition is likely to be strongly influenced by Karl Marx (1867–94), who was the first to attempt a systematic analysis of the 'economic law of motion' of capitalist society and from whom most of the subsequent controversy on the nature and role of capitalism has stemmed. For Marx, capitalism was a 'mode of production' in which there are basically two classes of producers: the capitalists, who own the means of production (capital or land), make the strategic day-to-day economic decisions on technology, output and marketing, and appropriate the profits of production and distribution; and the labourers, who own no property but are free to dispose of their labour for wages on terms which depend on the numbers seeking work and the demand for their services. This was essentially the definition adopted, for example, by non-Marxist economic historians such as Lipson and Cunningham and by Marxists such as Dobb (1946).

Given this perspective, it is primarily the emergence of a dominant class of entrepreneurs supplying the capital necessary to activate a substantial body of workers which marks the birth of capitalism. In England, and even more emphatically in Holland, it can be dated from the late sixteenth and early seventeenth centuries. Holland's supremacy in international trade, associated with its urgent need to import grain and timber (and hence to export manufactures) enabled Amsterdam to corner the Baltic trade and to displace Venice as the commercial and financial centre of Europe. The capital thus amassed was available to fund the famous chartered companies (Dutch East India Company 1602; West India Company 1621) as well as companies to reclaim land and exploit the area's most important source of industrial energy – peat. It also provided the circulating capital for merchants engaged in the putting-out system whereby they supplied raw materials to domestic handicrafts workers and marketed the product. Specialization within agriculture drew the rural areas still further into the money economy, and the urban areas supplied a wide range of industrial exports to pay for essential raw material imports.

Dutch capitalists flourished the more because they were subject to a Republican administration which was sympathetic to their free market, individualist values.

In England, where similar economic developments were in progress in the sixteenth and early seventeenth centuries, the rising class of capitalists was inhibited by a paternalistic monarchical government bent on regulating their activities for its own fiscal purposes and power objectives and in terms of a different set of social values. The Tudor system of state control included checking enclosures, controlling food supplies, regulating wages and manipulating the currency. The early Stuarts went further in selling industrial monopolies and concessions to favoured entrepreneurs and exclusive corporations and infuriated the majority whose interests were thus damaged. The English capitalists carried their fight against monopolies to the Cromwellian Revolution. When the monarchy was restored in the 1660s, the climate of opinion had been moulded by religious, political and scientific revolution into an environment which favoured the advancement of capitalism and laid the foundations for its next significant phase – the Industrial Revolution.

Orthodox economic theorists eschew the concept of capitalism: it is too broad for their purposes in that it takes into account the social relations of production. Modern economic historians adhering to an orthodox framework of economic theory also tend to avoid the term. They do, however, recognize a significant aspect of capitalism by emphasizing the rational, profit-maximizing, double bookkeeping characteristics of capitalist enterprise; and in the post-Second World War debates on economic development from a backward starting-point, there has been a tendency to regard the emergence of this 'capitalist spirit' as an essential prerequisite to the process of sustained economic growth in non-socialist countries (see, e.g. Landes 1969; Morishima 1982; North and Thomas 1973).

The modern debate on capitalism in contemporary advanced economies has revolved around its being an alternative to socialism. Marxist economists follow Marx in seeing capitalism as a mode of production whose internal contradictions determine that it will eventually be replaced by socialism. In the aftermath of the Second World War, when the governments of most developed countries took full employment and faster economic growth as explicit objectives of national economic policy, there was a marked propensity for the governments of capitalist economies to intervene actively and extensively in the process of production. At that stage the interesting issues for most Western economists seemed to be the changing balance of private and public economic power (see Shonfield 1965), and the extent to which it was either desirable or inevitable for the increasingly 'mixed' capitalist economies to converge towards socialism. In the late 1960s and 1970s, when the unprecedented post-war boom in world economic activity came to an end, Marxist economists were able to point confidently to the 'crisis of capitalism' for which they found evidence in rising unemployment and inflation in capitalist countries; but non-Marxist economists had lost their earlier consensus. The economic debate on capitalism is now taking place in a political context which is relatively hostile to state intervention; and those economists who believe that the 'spirit of capitalism', or free private enterprise, is the key to sustained technological progress and that it is weakened by socialist economic policies, seem to carry more conviction than they did in the 1950s and 1960s.

Phyllis Deane
University of Cambridge

References

Dobb, M. (1946) *Studies in the Development of Capitalism*, London.
Landes, D. (1969) *Prometheus Unbound*, Cambridge, UK.
Mark, K. (1867–94) *Das Kapital*, 3 vols, Moscow.
Morishima, M. (1982) *Why has Japan Succeeded?*, Cambridge, UK.
North, D. C. and Thomas, R. P. (1973) *The Rise of the Western World*, Cambridge, UK.
Shonfield, A. (1965) *Modern Capitalism*, London.
Sombart, W. (1915) *The Quintessence of Capitalism*, New York.
Tawney, R. H. (1926) *Religion and the Rise of Capitalism*, London.
Tribe, K. (1981) *Genealogies of Capitalism*, London.
Wallerstein, I. (1979) *The Capitalist World-Economy*, Cambridge, UK.
Weber, M. (1930 [1922]) *The Protestant Ethic and the Spirit of Capitalism*, New York. (Original edn, Tübingen.)

See also: capital theory; feudalism; Marx's theory of history and society; socialism; world-system theory.

career development *see* vocational and career development

cargo cults

Cargo cults is the name given to millenarian movements of Melanesia, which centre on a belief that specified ritual manipulations and observances will soon bring to the people concerned material rewards, notably manufactured goods, and a better, even paradisiacal, life. The name originates from the frequent use by participants of the Pidgin word *kago* (derived from the English 'cargo') to describe the returns they intend their activities to bring, although having a wider, and in the cult context uniquely Melanesian, connotation.

These small-scale and intense cults usually have messianic leaders who rise up to direct their activities, using relevant traditional belief, reinterpreting myths and manipulating associated symbols to promulgate their syncretized and appealing message. The activities inspired and directed by these 'prophets' frequently disrupt everyday life, as they divert people from subsistence tasks (at times even forbid them), and encourage the pursuit of preparations for the coming millennium. One example is clearing airstrips, and surrounding them with bamboo landing lights, to receive the prophesied aircraft coming with cargo, sometimes to be piloted by the ancestors.

One cult reported in the late 1970s, from the Vanuatuan island of Tanna, centres on the Duke of Edinburgh and his autographed photograph. The people believe that the duke was spirited from their midst at birth, and they have prepared for his return, which they believe is imminent, to cure sickness, rejuvenate the elderly and bring material wealth to all. They have a site ready on a nearby beach where the duke's boat will berth on arrival.

Early reports interpreted such cults as the actions of irrational and deluded people, even in states of temporary collective madness. Sensitive research in post-war years has refuted this dismissive conclusion, showing that cargo cults are a rational indigenous response to traumatic culture contact with western society. Although precipitated by familiarity with, and a desire to possess, the goods of the industrialized world, they have a traditional focus and logic. They turn to traditional beliefs and idioms to cope with a bewildering invasion, and although inappropriate, even comical to us in their misunderstanding of our society and their bizarre interpretation of unintelligible aspects of it (like the role of the Royal Family or aircraft technology), they are neither illogical nor stupid.

The newcomers have material wealth and technical capabilities beyond local people's understanding and imagination and – for tribal societies – irresistible political and military power emanating from incomprehensible nation-states. Europeans apparently do no physical work to produce these goods, unlike the politically subjugated local population, many of whom they put to hard labour for paltry returns. Neither do Europeans share their fabulous wealth with others, a direct assault on a cardinal Melanesian value, where giving and receiving is an integral aspect of social life.

Clearly Europeans know something, and the problem for the Melanesians is how to gain access to this knowledge. Unable to comprehend western society and the long-term nature of education, which they interpret as a scheme to dupe them, or the worldwide capitalist economic system and the life of a factory worker, they turn to millenarian cults. A recurring feature in these cults is a belief that Europeans in some past age tricked Melanesians and are withholding from them their rightful share of material goods. In cargo cults the Melanesians are trying to reverse this situation, to discover the ritual formula that will facilitate access to their misappropriated manufactured possessions. They conclude that material goods come from the spirit world and that the wealthy whites are stealing their share; so it is a case of manipulating rituals in order to gain access to them.

An oft-repeated aim is to secure the cargo of the ancestors, who some cultists believe will return at the millennium. They will come to right current injustices. Some cults take on a disturbing racist tone here, probably reflecting the attitudes of the white newcomers, which signal people's discontent with European domination and feelings of impotence. With the coming of the millennium, blacks will become whites, and the whites turn black, and white domination will end.

The relatively frequent pan-Melanesian occurrence of cargo cults in a wide range of disparate cultures, and their recurrence time and again, with modified dogma and ritual, in the same region, testify to their importance to the people concerned. In their expression of tensions, they lend themselves to a range of sociological and psychological interpretations. Although frenetic, short-lived and – to outsiders – disruptive, these cults allow Melanesians who find themselves in a confusing and inexplicable world invaded by technically superior outsiders to cope with the changed situation, even manipulate it, for in some cases their behaviour brings results: desperate governments supply processed food and other provisions to alleviate the resulting, sometimes chronic, food shortages following the disruption of subsistence activities.

Paul Sillitoe
University of Durham

Further reading

Cohen, N. (1961) *The Pursuit of the Millennium*, 2nd edn, New York.
Lawrence, P. (1965) *Road Belong Cargo*, Manchester.
Steinbauer, F. (1979) *Melanesian Cargo Cults*, St Lucia, Queensland.
Worsley, P. (1957) *The Trumpet Shall Sound*, London.

See also: sects and cults.

cartels and trade associations

Cartels are a common form of collusion in oligopolistic markets. In a market with many sellers (perfect competition) each seller can take the market price as parametric, but in an oligopolistic market firms will be aware that their pricing decisions will affect the decisions of others. It is commonly agreed that isolated profit maximization in an oligopolistic market will lead all producers to have lower profits than would be possible if they colluded. Cartels and trade assoc-iations are descriptions for collusion, the former in markets with a small number of firms, the latter in markets where there are many (100). Cartels vary from gentlemen's agreements to legally binding contracts. In most countries they are illegal, but have often also been formed at government behest, as in Germany and the USA in the 1930s. The objective of a cartel is to raise price and cut quantity to increase industry profits. Although they are commonly observed (and more commonly exist), they are often unstable, as each firm has an incentive to cheat by offering small discounts to gain increased sales. Because every firm can cheat, many will, and cheating will occur unless the cartel is properly policed. Cartels can take many forms, from overt (or covert) agreements to tacit agreements on price leadership in the market. Agreement appears to be easier to reach when numbers involved are modest, products are homogeneous and government regulation lax. Developments in the theory of games, using infinite dynamic game theory with time discounting and plausible retaliation for cheating, have aided our understanding of the topic (see Friedman 1982), but have served only to emphasize the indeterminateness of possible solutions in cartelized markets.

Ray Barrell
National Institute of Economic and
Social Research

Reference

Friedman, J. (1982) *Oligopoly Theory*, Cambridge, UK.

Further reading

Scherer, F. M. (1980) *Industrial Structure and Economic Performance*, 2nd edn, Chicago.

See also: monopoly; multinational enterprises; regulation.

cartography

Cartography is the art and technology of making and using maps to represent locations and spatial relationships. It is an art because these representations typically, but not always, are graphic, and thus instruments of visual communication and visual aesthetics. It is also a technology because map makers use, develop and adapt a wide variety of electronic, mechanical and photographic techniques for storing, retrieving, selecting, generalizing and displaying geographic information. These techniques can affect the appearance of graphic maps as well as the efficacy of map-making and map use. Dramatic changes in the cartographic image reflect profound changes in map-making technology over the past five centuries, particularly since 1970. Maps have become dynamic and interactive, and electronic technology has encouraged an ever more diverse range of specialized cartographic applications.

Most geographers and other scholars regard cartography largely as map authorship, that is, the design and crafting of geographic illustrations to accompany a verbal narrative. Often there is a division of labour in expository cartography between the author-cartographer, who compiles the maps and writes the text, and a cartographic illustrator or drafter, who produces the artwork. But as word-processing and electronic-publishing technology are displacing the typesetter by making fuller use of the author's key strokes, electronic cartography is displacing the drafter who retraces the map author's delineations. Because the cartographic technician serves as a design filter, to advise authors ignorant or uncertain about map projections, symbols and generalization, electronic cartography calls for a greater awareness of graphic and cartographic principles and practices by both authors and their editors. Electronic cartography also fosters a closer integration of maps and words in multimedia and hypertext presentations as well as in traditional publishing formats of articles, books and atlases. Computers, too, are weakening distinctions between cartographic presentation and cartographic analysis, in which maps are a tool for discovering and understanding geographic patterns and for testing and refining hypotheses.

Map making is also an institutional enterprise, in which government cartographic units compile and publish a wide variety of topographic maps, navigational charts, geographic inventories, and other cartographic products essential for economic development, national defence, environmental protection, and growth management. In addition, commercial firms not only serve governments as contractors but also produce a still wider range of derivative, value-added maps and cartographic databases tailored to the needs of travellers, industries, businesses, local governments, and educators. Because expository cartography depends heavily on institutional cartography for source materials, map authors must be aware of the availability, utility and reliability of government and commercial maps.

Cartography is also a subdiscipline of geography in which scholars either seek more effective means of cartographic communication or treat the map, its derivation and its impact as an object of study. Most academic cartographers are concerned with training geographers and others in the design and use of maps as well as with developing improved methods of cartographic display. Studies of map design rely on a variety of approaches, including semiotic theory, psychophysics, colour theory, statistics, policy analysis, and subject-testing. Because maps can be largely or subtly rhetorical, other cartographic scholars focus on mapping as a social or intellectual process and on the map's role as an instrument of power and persuasion. Despite the hyperbole of cartographic chauvinists who assert that the field is fundamentally a science, maps are subjective texts that reflect the biases of their authors and sources as well as the limitations of technology.

Mark Monmonier
Syracuse University

Further reading

Brunet, R. (1987) *La Carte: mode d'emploi*, Montpellier.
Keates, J. S. (1989 [1973]) *Cartographic Design and Production*, London.
Monmonier, M. (1991) *How to Lie with Maps*, Chicago.
—— (1993) *Mapping It Out: Expository Cartography for the Humanities and Social Sciences*, Chicago.
Parry, R. B. and Perkins, C. R. (eds) (1987) *World Mapping Today*, London.
Perkins, C. R. and Parry, R. B. (eds) (1990) *Information Sources in Cartography*, London.
Robinson, A. H. and Petchenik, B. B. (1976) *The Nature of Maps*, Chicago.
Wright, J. K. (1942) 'Map makers are human: comments on the subjective in mapping', *Geographical Review* 32.

See also: geographical information systems; landscape.

case study

The case study is widely and variously used across the whole range of social science disciplines. It refers to both an organizing principle for and a method of social research. Simply put, case study describes any form of single unit analysis. An individual may be the focus for a case study, as in psychotherapy or medicine, but so may an organization, a group, an event or a social process. The point is that the focus is upon a naturally occurring social phenomenon rather than an experimentally constructed activity or selected sample. Thus, Smith (1990: 11); writing about educational research, says:

> The relative emphasis on what I call an 'intact', 'natural' or 'ongoing' group versus some kind of sampled set of pupils, teachers, classes, curricula or schools also seems very important. I believe that this is what some of the case study advocates mean by 'case'.

Cases are not normally selected by criteria of typicality but on the basis of theoretical significance or particular critical qualities.

Case study is based upon depth; more specifically it is holistic and exhaustive. The aim is for what Geertz (1973) calls 'thick description', which is so essential to an understanding of context and situation. An eclectic variety of types of data are collected and set against one another in the processes of analysis and in the representation of 'the case' in writing. Where appropriate and feasible, researchers themselves are central to the conduct of case study research. Data are collected by direct presence in the site, or face-to-face exchange with the subject. The researcher aims to share experiences with the researched, to witness events firsthand, to question action within the setting. The design and conduct of case study research is responsive and creative, accommodating to the form, rhythm and possibilities of the setting. 'Any case study is a construction itself, a product of the interaction between respondents, site and researcher' (Lincoln and Guba 1990: 54). This is typically reflected in the language of case study reporting; 'case studies will rhetorically exemplify the interpersonal involvement which characterized that form of inquiry' (Lincoln and Guba 1990: 59). This contrasts with the 'stripped down, cool' style of 'scientific' reporting. Case studies are written to convey authenticity, to recapture the natural language of the setting and to evoke a vicarious response from the reader.

Case study research is frequently attacked for its lack of generalizability (Bolgar 1965; Shaunhessy and Zechmeister 1985) although in some respects the importation of generalization arguments from the field of quantitative research is based upon misunderstandings of the purposes of case study research. The case study is not premised on the generation of abstract, causal or law-like statements. Rather, it is intended to reveal the intricate complexities of specific sites or processes and their origins, interrelations and dynamics. However, the evolution of the approach and the defence against the generalization argument, the escape from what is called 'radical particularism', has led, in some fields, to the use of multi-site case study research designs. These concentrate upon a limited range of issues across a number of settings, collecting the same data and using the same analytical procedures. Firestone and Herriot (1984) examined twenty-five such studies, which ranged in scope from three sites to sixty. Both the number and the heterogeneity of sites have been used as a basis for claims about more robust generalizability. However, the basic issue of the value of breadth rather than depth applies as much when considering single as against multi-site case studies as it does when the single case study is set over and against survey research. The key question is, what is lost and gained in the trade-off between exhaustive depth and more superficial breadth?

Stephen J. Ball
King's College London

References

Bolgar, H. (1965) 'The case study method', in B. B. Wolman (ed.) *Handbook of Clinical Psychology*, New York.
Firestone, W. A. and Herriot, R. E. (1984) 'Multisite qualitative policy research: some design and implementation issues', in D. M. Fetterman (ed.) *Ethnography in Educational Evaluation*, Beverly Hills, CA.
Geertz, C. (1973) *The Interpretation of Cultures*, New York.
Lincoln, Y. S. and Guba, E. G. (1990) 'Judging the quality of case study reports', *International Journal of Qualitative Studies in Education* 3(1).
Shaunhessy, J. J. and Zechmeister, E. B. (1985) *Research Methods in Psychology*, New York.
Smith, L. M. (1990) 'Critical introduction: whither classroom ethnography?', in M. Hammersley (ed.) *Classroom Ethnography*, Milton Keynes.

See also: ethnography; life history; methods of social research.

caste

Caste systems have been defined in the most general terms as systems of hierarchically ordered endogamous units in which membership is hereditary and permanent (e.g. Berreman 1960). On such a definition a whole range of rigidly stratified societies would be characterized by caste – Japan, for example, or certain Polynesian and East African societies, or the racially divided world of the American Deep South. Hindu India is generally taken as the paradigmatic example. Many scholars would argue, however, that the difference between this case and the others are far more significant than the similarities, and that the term caste should properly be applied only to this context.

The morphology of the Hindu caste system can be described in terms of three key characteristics (Bouglé 1971 [1908]), all of which are religiously underpinned by the religious values of purity (Dumont 1970). First, there is a *hierarchy* of castes which is theoretically based on their relative degree of purity. As the purest of all the Brahmans rank highest, and are in principle both distinct from and superior to the caste which actually wields politico-economic power. Second, as the pure can maintain their purity only if there are impure castes to remove the pollution that they inevitably incur by their involvement in the natural world, there is a *division of labour* between castes resulting in their *interdependence*. Third, pollution is contagious, and a caste must therefore restrict its contacts with inferiors in order to maintain its status. This *separation* takes many forms: a rule of endogamy precluding marital alliances with inferiors; restrictions on commensality; the outcasting of those who transgress the rules lest they pollute the rest of the group, and the phenomenon of Untouchability debarring physical contact between 'clean' and 'polluted' groups. (We even have historical reports of theoretically Unseeable castes; while in parts of traditional Kerala the relative status of non-Brahman castes was in theory precisely reflected in the number of paces distant they had to keep from the highest Brahmans.)

While the (upward) mobility of *individuals* is theoretically impossible and empirically rare, the group as a whole may lay claim to a higher status by emulating the customs and practices of its superiors, and may succeed in validating its claims by using a new-found political or economic leverage to persuade erstwhile superiors to interact with it on a new basis (the crucial test being their acceptance of its food and water). As the actors present it, however, this is not a matter of social climbing but of reasserting a traditional status quo which was temporarily disrupted. A theory of timeless stasis is thus preserved despite a good deal of actual mobility.

The system is often visualized as being like a layer-cake with each layer as an occupationally specialized group characterized by endogamy and unrestricted commensality. A better image is of a set of Chinese boxes. At the most schematic level, contemporary Hindus, following the scriptures, represent the caste order in terms of a fourfold division: Brahman, Kshatriya, Vaishya and Shudra. At the local level (the details vary considerably), the Brahmans may be subdivided into priestly and non-priestly subgroups, the priestly Brahmans into Household-priests, Temple-priests and Funeral-priests; the Household-priests into two or more endogamous circles; and each circle into its component clans and lineages, who may be the only people who will freely accept one another's food. The answer to the question 'What is your caste?' will depend on context and might legitimately be phrased in terms of any of these levels. At each level the group is referred to as a *jati*, a term which is conventionally translated as 'caste' but is more accurately rendered as 'breed' or 'species'. Groups which share a common status in relation to outsiders are internally hierarchized: all Brahmans are equal in relation to non-Brahmans, but non-priestly Brahmans are superior in relation to priestly ones, and Household-priests in relation to Funeral-priests. It will be seen that the occupationally specialized group is not necessarily coterminous with the endogamous group, which may not coincide with the unit of unrestricted commensality. It is therefore impossible to define caste by listing a series of characteristics (e.g. occupation, endogamy, etc.) common to all. The universe of caste is a relational universe, rather than one made up of a given number of fixed and bounded units.

J. P. Parry
London School of Economics and Political Science

References

Berreman, G. D. (1960) 'Caste in India and the United States', *American Journal of Sociology* 66.
Bouglé, V. (1971 [1908]) *Essays on the Caste System*, Cambridge, UK. (Original French edn, *Essais sur le régime des castes*, Paris.)
Dumont, L. (1970) *Homo Hierarchicus: The Caste System and its Implications*, London.

See also: hierarchy; stratification.

census of population

A census of population, as defined in United Nations reports, is the total process of collecting, compiling, evaluating, analysing and publishing, or otherwise disseminating, demographic, economic and social data pertaining to all persons in a country, or to a well delimited part of a country at a specified time.

The census of population is the oldest and most widely distributed statistical undertaking by governments throughout the world. Censuses have also been developed to provide information on housing, manufactures, agriculture, mineral industries and business establishments. Many of the principles applying to the census of population apply equally to these other censuses.

It is not known which ruler first ordered a count of the people in order to assess the numbers potentially available for military service or to determine how many households might be liable to pay taxes. Population counts were reported from ancient Japan, and counts were compiled by Egyptians, Greeks, Hebrews, Persians and Peruvians. Many of these early censuses were limited as to the area covered and in some instances dealt with only a part of the population, such as men of military age. The results were generally treated as state secrets. In Europe, censuses on a city-wide basis were reported in the fifteenth and sixteenth centuries. India reported a census in 1687. Various censuses have been claimed as the first in modern times.

Data collected in a population census have often been used as the basis for the allocation of a territory to one or the other claimant governments. Census data are widely used by governments for planning and carrying out a variety of governmental functions. In some countries representation in legislative bodies and distribution of funds by the central government are significantly affected by the census results. The powers and duties of many municipalities depend on the size of their population. The private economy makes extensive use of the data for site locations, marketing strategies, and many other activities. Health, education and welfare programmes depend very heavily on such data.

The oldest continuous census taking is that of the USA where a census has been taken every ten years since 1790. The United Kingdom began taking a census in 1801 and followed the ten-year pattern except in 1941 when wartime requirements led to its cancellation. The ten-year pattern is widely observed. In many countries the census is authorized anew whenever the government finds a need for the data. In a few countries censuses are taken at regular five-year intervals. During the 1970s special efforts by the United Nations and some donor countries were directed to assisting African countries which had not previously taken a census. In 1982 the People's Republic of China completed the largest census ever taken. By 1983 virtually every country in the world had taken at least one census of population.

Early censuses often utilized household lists or similar sources as the basis of their tabulations. A modern census is one in which information is collected separately about each individual. Such practices became common during the last half of the nineteenth century.

The information assembled in a census depends in large part on the needs of the government for such information and on the availability of alternative sources. The United Nations has identified a set of topics which appear most essential. They include place where found at time of census, place of usual residence, place of birth, sex, age, relationship to head of household, marital status, children born alive, children living, literacy, school attendance, status (employer, employee, etc.). International comparability will be facilitated to the extent that national census offices utilize the standard definitions which have been developed by the United Nations.

A question which needs careful attention prior to a census is who is to be counted as part of the national and local population. Special consideration needs to be given to such persons as members of the Armed Forces, including those stationed outside the home country, migratory workers, university students, technical assistance personnel outside their home countries, long-term visitors, and guest workers.

Having determined who is to be included in the census, it becomes necessary also to determine in which part of the national territory they are to be counted. The classic distinction is that between a *de facto* and a *de jure* census. In a *de facto* census people are generally counted as a part of the population of the place where they encountered the census enumerator. This differs from the practice in a *de jure* census where an effort is made to ascertain where the person 'belongs'. This may be a usual residence, a legal residence, or an ancestral home. Persons who spend part of the time in one place and the remainder in one or more other places, and persons in long-stay institutions (prisons, hospitals, etc.) need to be recorded in a uniform manner within the country. Special procedures may need to be developed for persons who have no fixed place of residence, such as persons who live on the streets, nomads, refugees, or illegal aliens.

Customarily two basic methods of taking the census are recognized – direct enumeration and self-enumeration. Under the former method the enumerator collects information directly from the household. Self-enumeration means that the household members are given a questionnaire with the request that they enter the appropriate information and deliver the completed form to the designated census office or to an enumerator who comes to collect the completed forms.

The law establishing the census normally makes provision for the authority of the census office and its employees to conduct the census and establishes the obligation of the residents to provide the answers to the best of their ability. There are normally legal penalties for refusal or for providing false information.

An important part of the legal provision for the census is the guarantee that the individually identifiable information will be held in strict confidence and will be used only for statistical purposes, and violation of pledge of confidentiality is a punishable offence.

The almost universal availability of computers for the processing, tabulation and printing of the data collected in the census has greatly facilitated the work of census offices. A more complete and thorough review of the raw data as well as of intermediate and final tabulations is possible, and where the research community also has access to computers the provision of summary tapes and of public use microdata sample tapes has enabled them to use the data more effectively.

The improved access of the public to the census products has greatly increased the concern over errors in the census from whatever source, whether in coverage of the population, errors by the respondents, errors in recording the information supplied by respondents, or errors made in the processing of the data, and census officials are alerted to this problem.

Computers and the development of sampling procedures have brought about significant changes in the conduct of population censuses. The effective use of computers has brought about changes in field procedures and has speeded up the tabulation and release of the results. They have led to the preparation of data for specialized purposes. They have contributed to procedures for making microdata available for research purposes, while protecting the confidentiality of the individual records.

The quality of census results has come under increasing study. The completeness of the coverage is critical for many governmental actions. Special efforts have been undertaken to ascertain the completeness of the census results. Methods of ascertaining the degree of under- or overcounting of the population of a given area have yielded valuable information. Special attention has been given to sources of data within the census operation which can yield the information required. The treatment of members of minority groups – ethnic, age, occupation, country of birth, etc. – can have profound effects on the data and public actions for or against members of the groups.

Related sources of information, such as a population register, can be used very effectively in all phases of the census. Training and supervision of the staff are critical to the success of a census. Special arrangements may be needed if the census work in essence is a part-time activity by persons who have other duties. A different set of procedures is needed if the bulk of the census is carried on by persons who are recruited for the census.

Conrad Taeuber
Georgetown University

Further reading

Alonso, W. and Starr, P. (eds) (1983) *The Politics of Numbers*, New York.
Mitrof, I., Mason, R. and Barabba, V. P. (eds) (1983) *The 1980 Census: Policymaking Amid Turbulence*, Lexington, MA.
National Academy of Sciences, Committee on National Statistics (1993) *A Census that Mirrors America*, Washington, DC.
Shryock, H. S. and Taeuber, C. (1976) *The Conventional Population Census*, Chapel Hill, NC.
United Nations (1980) *Principles and Recommendations for Population and Housing Censuses*, New York.

See also: vital statistics.

centre and periphery

The two concepts centre and periphery form part of an attempt to explain the processes through which capitalism is able to affect the economic and political structure of underdeveloped or developing societies. Drawing on the Marxist tradition, this view assumes that in the central capitalist countries there is a high organic composition of capital, and wage levels approximate the cost of reproducing labour. By contrast, in the peripheral countries, there is a low organic composition of capital, and wages are likely to be low, hardly meeting the cost of reproducing labour. This happens because in peripheral areas reproduction of labour is often dependent on some degree of non-capitalist production, and the wages paid to workers are subsidized by subsistence production. In some cases, such as with plantation workers, smallholder plots may contribute as much as the actual money wage paid, or in mining, the migrant male wage labourer may receive a wage which supports him but not his family, who depend on subsistence production elsewhere. In the centre, wages are determined largely by market processes, whereas at the periphery non-market forces, such as political repression or traditional relations of super- and subordination (as between patrons and clients), are important in determining the wage rate.

The use of the concepts centre and periphery implies the world-system as the unit of analysis, and 'underdevelopment' as an instituted process rather than a mere descriptive term. Underdevelopment is the result of contradictions within capitalist production relations at the centre. It is the outcome of attempts to solve these problems and is a necessary part of the reproduction of capitalism on a world scale.

Attempts to analyse the processes of surplus extraction, together with the claim that the world economy had become capitalist, gave rise to two major interrelated debates. One concerned the precise definition of capitalism and whether it is to be satisfactorily characterized by a specific system of production or of exchange relations. The other tried to identify the links between centre and periphery, and thus the nature of the system, in terms of the relations or articulations between different modes of production. In trying to clarify these theoretical issues together with their political implications, the use of the terms centre and periphery was elaborated and empirically researched. This gave rise to various forms of world-system theory, represented in the writing of Wallerstein (1974), Frank (1978) and Amin (1976); it also revived interest in theories of national and global economic cycles, for example in the work of Mandel (1980). In addition, in attempting to explain the position of countries such as Brazil, Argentina and Mexico, the concept of the semi-periphery was developed. This concept involves the idea that their particular political cultures and the mixed nature of their industrialization places these countries in a buffer position, particularly in their international political stance, between central capitalist countries and those of the true periphery.

Tony Barnett
University of East Anglia

References

Amin, S. (1976) *Unequal Development*, New York.
Frank, A. G. (1978) *Dependent Accumulation and Underdevelopment*, London.
Mandel, E. (1980) *Long Waves of Capitalist Development*, Cambridge, UK.
Wallerstein, I. (1974) *The Modern World System*, New York.

Further reading

Hoogvelt, A. M. (1982) *The Third World in Global Development*, London.

See also: Third World; underdevelopment; world-system theory.

charisma

Charisma is one of the more contentious sociological concepts, in part because it has been absorbed into popular, or at least mass media, usage in a considerably adulterated form. The term derives from a theological conception which referred to the divine gift of grace. Max Weber developed its sociological use by extending it to refer to the recognition in individual leaders by their followers of supernatural or superhuman powers or qualities of an exemplary kind or of transcendental origin.

Weber's formulation gave rise to ambiguities. On the one hand, it could be argued that the nature of charisma inhered in the powers or qualities displayed by the individual, and thus was to be explained primarily in terms of the personal psychological attributes of the leader. On the other hand, it could be argued that the character of charisma lay in the recognition extended by the following, and thus was to be explained primarily in terms of the social psychological features of the interpersonal relationship between leader and followers. Common usage bears elements of both approaches, identifying the charismatic figure as one who displays personal attractiveness or forcefulness of a kind which leads to great popularity or popular devotion. However, this is quite antithetical to Weber's central thrust.

Weber sharply contrasts charisma with forms of authority deriving from tradition and from rationalistic or legal considerations. The charismatic leader is one who breaks with tradition or prevailing legal norms, and demands obedience on specifically irrational grounds of devotion as God's Prophet, the embodiment of transcendental forces, or as possessor of supernatural powers. Conventionally elected leaders, or heirs of an established tradition, cannot therefore be construed as charismatic because of their attractiveness or popularity or even both.

The following of a charismatic leader offers its obedience and devotion in virtue of the mission upon which it believes the leader to be engaged and the transcendental forces which the leader manifests. But it may require periodically to be reassured of the possession of those powers, demanding signs of the miraculous as the price of commitment.

The charismatic leader operates through a body of disciples or other personally devoted inner circle rather than an established administrative staff. Often – especially in the case of religious charisma – it may consist of members of the leader's immediate household, living in an intimate and emotionally laden communal relationship with the leader. They receive their appointment not on the basis of technical expertise, but rather because of the intensity of their devotion or willingness to subordinate themselves to the leader's will. They are commissioned to carry out that will on an *ad hoc* basis. There is no administrative routine, or any such routine is short-lived, constantly disrupted by the intervention and revelation of the leader. The economic basis of the movement is irregular and founded on booty or free-will offerings. Decision making is erratic and inspirational.

Charisma is inevitably a precarious form of authority. Max Weber maintained that it could exist in its pure form for only a relatively brief period. In the course of time it tends to become transformed into a less spontaneous or less unpredictable form of leadership, towards traditionalism or rational-legal authority. Such a development appears to be an ineluctable consequence of perpetuating the movement's mission or of spreading it beyond an immediate, local band of disciples. Endurance over time or wider spread is likely to introduce the need for mechanisms of co-ordination, supervision and delegation. In consequence there will arise increasing impersonality and routine and the desire for greater stability and predictability on the part of officials.

The problem of succession often accelerates the process of routinization. The charisma of the founder is vested in another by virtue of hereditary succession or a ritual of consecration. Thus, such forms as 'hereditary charisma' or 'charisma of office' become an intervening step in the transformation of authority in a traditionalistic or rational-legal direction.

Roy Wallis
Formerly, Queen's University Belfast

Further reading

Weber, M. (1947 [1922]) *The Theory of Social and Economic Organization*, London. (Part 1 of *Wirtschaft und Gesellschaft*, Tübingen.)
Willner, A. (1984) *The Spellbinders: Charismatic Political Leadership*, New Haven, CT.
Wilson, B. (1975) *The Noble Savages: The Primitive Origins of Charisma and its Contemporary Survival*, Berkeley, CA.

See also: authority; leadership; political psychology; Weber, Max.

Chicago School

The so-called Chicago School of economics, chiefly American, is a neo-classical counter-revolution against institutionalism in economic methodology, against Keynesian macroeconomics, and against 'twentieth-century liberalism', i.e. interventionism and *dirigisme*, in economic policy generally. Its centre has been the University of Chicago, where it first achieved prominence in the 1930s. Its intellectual leaders until about 1950 were Frank H. Knight in matters of theory and methodology and Henry C. Simons in matters of economic policy. During the next generation, the leaders have been Milton Friedman, George Stigler and Gary Becker. Many economists not trained at Chicago have aligned themselves with many 'Chicago' positions, and many members of the Chicago economics faculty, to say nothing of its graduates, have dissociated themselves from 'Chicago' doctrine.

Some characteristic Chicago School views have been as follows:

1 Methodological positivism. The validity of a theory depends neither upon its generality nor upon the plausibility of its initial assumptions, but exclusively upon the confirmation or disconfirmation (primarily statistical) of such of its implications as diverge from the implications of alternative theories.
2 Acceptance of market solutions for economic problems, not in any Utopian or optimal sense but in aid of political and intellectual freedom. Chicago School economists see the market economy as a *necessary* condition for free societies generally. It is not, however, a *sufficient* condition.
3 Distrust of administrative discretion and *ad hoc* intervention in economic policy. Preference for 'rules versus authorities' in matters of monetary and fiscal policy.
4 Monetarism rather than fiscalism in macroeconomic regulation.
5 The use of fiscal measures to alleviate poverty, but distrust of redistributionism above the poverty line.
6 Disciplinary imperialism, by which is meant the applicability of economic analysis by economists to problems normally restricted to other disciplines, such as history, politics, law and sociology.

The school's positions with regard to a number of topics, especially trade regulation and monetary policy, have changed over the years. Simons, for example, believed in the active maintenance of competition by a strong anti-monopoly or 'trust-busting' policy, while Friedman and Stigler thought monopoly and oligopoly to be only short-term problems of minor long-term significance. Simons also believed that monetary policy should be guided by a price-level rule – expansionary when the price level was falling and contractionary when it was rising. Friedman, impressed by the long and variable time-lags involved in price-level reactions to monetary change, has favoured a constant rate of monetary growth.

Following the retirement and death of Stigler, and the retirement of Friedman and his move to the Pacific coast, Chicago's own economists have become at once less directly concerned with public policy and more frequently honoured by Nobel Prizes and other awards for pure economic, financial and historical scholarship. In macroeconomics, Robert Lucas has become a leader in the 'new classical' or 'rational expectations' approach to research in monetary and financial economics. In fact, in the mid-1990s, Lucas and Gary Becker may be considered the guiding spirits if not yet the elder statesmen of the Chicago School, replacing Friedman and Stigler.

The two best summaries of Chicago doctrine are Simons's (1938) *Economic Policy for a Free Society* and Friedman's (1962) *Capitalism and Freedom*.

Martin Bronfenbrenner
Duke University

References

Friedman, M. (1962) *Capitalism and Freedom*, Chicago.
Simons, H. C. (1938) *Economic Policy for a Free Society*, Chicago.

Further reading

Patinkin, D. (1981) *Essays On and In the Chicago Tradition*, Durham, NC.

See also: Friedman, Milton; monetarism.

childcare

Childcare is taken to refer to state policy regarding the care of children, and more generally to ideas and practices concerning the care of children. State agencies may be involved with the provision of substitute or alternative care where family caring mechanisms have broken down, and with the provision or regulation of care for children during the day or for short periods when parents are not available to care. An extension of this role may be to provide support and supervision for families where there is some doubt about the standards of childcare.

A major concern since the 1970s is the abuse of children, both physical and sexual, due partly to the discovery that both forms of abuse were more common than previously thought, and to 'scandal' cases where care agencies were unable to prevent child deaths at the hands of a parent or parent figure (for example the case of Maria Colwell in Britain in 1973). This led to anxiety about the risk to children from their own birth or genetic parents, about returning children from substitute care to a parental home where care might be inadequate, and about situations where children's lives were disrupted by constant moves back and forth from substitute to birth parent care. The focus on abuse and the debate about the appropriate role for the state continued into the 1980s and 1990s.

A number of perspectives have been outlined by Fox Harding (1991) on how the state might proceed in relation to children and their families where there is concern about the quality of care. These views connect with wider ideas about child psychology, the importance of genetic relatives, and the broader role of the state. The first perspective is concerned with independent and secure, permanent families, be these birth families or substitute families, and a minimum role for the state. The second perspective is concerned primarily with poor parental care and the necessity of firm state action to protect children. The third perspective is concerned above all with the original family unit, its importance for the child, and the need to support deprived families by means of various services. Finally, there is a 'children's rights' perspective.

Of interest for the future is the fourth perspective emphasizing the *rights* of children as actors independent of adults or state agencies. At its extreme, this allocates to children rights identical to those of adults such as the franchise and the right to work (see, e.g. Farson 1978; Holt 1975). While most would find the granting of all adult rights and freedoms to children impracticable, and not necessarily in the interests of children themselves, a more moderate form of the 'rights' emphasis has found expression in the greater ability of children under the law to express a view, give evidence, and apply to live in a particular home (e.g. under the Children Act 1989 in Britain); in campaigns against corporal punishment of children (e.g. Newell 1989); and in the UN Convention on the Rights of the Child 1989, the first international legal instrument on children's rights, which explicitly states that children have a right to a say in processes affecting their lives (Freeman 1993).

The 1980s and 1990s saw matters of childcare policy debated against a background of policies of reducing public expenditure and contracting of the role of the state. In the childcare context this has meant an increased emphasis on parental rather than state responsibility. There has also been a concern about the increased number of mother-headed families, and the loss of the father's role from the family, both in terms of financial support, and his disciplinary and general caring role. Attempts have been made to extract more by way of maintenance payments from 'absent' fathers, for example under the Child Support Act 1991 in Britain, which was itself modelled on schemes operating in Wisconsin and in Australia. The concern about the 'disappearance' of the father's role has also been linked with wider problems of social breakdown and disorder (e.g. Dennis and Erdos 1992).

Childcare remains a controversial area, and differences of view arise between those who hold different ideas about the role of the state, the role of the family, the roots of abuse and poor childcare, and the nature of childhood itself.

Lorraine M. Fox Harding
University of Leeds

References

Dennis, N. and Erdos, G. (1992) *Families Without Fatherhood*, London.

Farson, R. (1978) *Birthrights*, Harmondsworth.

Fox Harding, L. (1991) *Perspectives in Child Care Policy*, Harlow.

Freeman, M. (1993) 'Laws, conventions and rights', in G. Pugh (ed.) *30 Years of Change for Children*, London.

Holt, J. (1975) *Escape from Childhood*, Harmondsworth.

Newell, P. (1989) *Children are People Too*, London.

Further reading

Finkelhor, D. *et al.* (eds) (1986) *A Source Book on Child Sexual Abuse*, Beverly Hills, CA.

Freeman, M. D. A. (1983) *The Rights and Wrongs of Children*, London.

Frost, N. and Stein, M. (1989) *The Politics of Child Welfare*, Hemel Hempstead.

Packman, J. (1993) 'From prevention to partnership: child welfare services across three decades', in G. Pugh (ed.) *30 Years of Change for Children*, London.

Parton, N. (1985) *The Politics of Child Abuse*, Basingstoke.

Violence Against Children Study Group (1990) *Taking Child Abuse Seriously*, London.

Pecora, P. J., Whittaker, J. K. and Maluccio, A. (1992) *The Child Welfare Challenge: Policy, Practice, Research*, New York.

See also: childhood; domestic violence.

childhood

For most periods of history and for most children in the world, childhood is *not* ideally cosy, protected, playful and free from adult responsibilities; in practice, a child's survival in hostile conditions is often the first challenge that the child faces (see Scheper-Hughes 1987). The UN Convention on the Rights of the Child 1976 accordingly sought to establish not 'the best' but progressive realization of the 'best possible' standards respecting the economic, social and cultural rights of children.

The idea of childhood is historically and culturally variable. Philippe Aries (1962 [1960]) argues that in Europe childhood began to be marked as a distinctive stage of life only in the thirteenth century. The conception of childhood altered radically in the seventeenth century with the rise of modern notions of the family and of the school, and again in the nineteenth century. The modern world is 'obsessed by the physical, moral and sexual problems of childhood' (Aries 1962 [1960]: 411).

If Aries is right, it cannot be sheer coincidence that the most influential theorists in the history of psychology – Sigmund Freud and Jean Piaget – were concerned to understand childhood and how children come to be adults. Freud focused on sexual identification and the development of conscience. The child becomes a moral being via the control by guilt of sexual and aggressive impulses. Piaget (e.g. 1926; 1935) devoted his life to describing how the child cognitively constructs the concepts that allow for an effective adult engagement in the world, such as those of number, time, physical causality, measurement, etc.

Behaviourist psychologists tried to show how, like other animals, children are 'conditioned' to behave in certain ways through encounters with their environment, including other people, that yielded rewards and punishments. The increasing sophistication of biology-based studies of animal behaviour and cognitivist studies of humans revealed difficulties with learning theory, but the notion that children are 'conditioned' by their environment proved particularly congenial to sociologists and anthropologists who were less concerned with the child as 'individual' than they were with the child as a member of a collectivity. For example, the anthropologist Margaret Mead, whose best known works focus on childhood and adolescence, ascribed to cultural conditioning the fact that *what* children learn is culturally appropriate and *how* they learn is culturally mediated too. Data on child-rearing practices were also of special significance for those 'culture and personality' theorists who were interested in the cross-cultural applicability of psychoanalytic theory (see, e.g. Whiting and Child 1953).

However, with the export of Piaget's ideas to the USA and the increasing dominance of cognitivist explanations in psychology during the 1960s and 1970s, the idea of the child as conditioned by the environment or, more radically, as imitating adult behaviour, gave way to 'socialization' theories, according to which the child was actively engaged in knowledge processes.

Piaget was criticized by his Russian contemporary Vygotsky for failing to incorporate historical (i.e. socio-cultural) parameters and social interaction in his account of childhood cognition (see, e.g. Vygotsky 1962 [1934]), and by others because he did not recognize how extensive are a child's earliest cognitive abilities (see, e.g. Smith *et al.* 1988), nor how early infants form a sense of an emergent self which actively shapes their interactions with others (e.g. Stern 1985).

While psychological models of childhood long stressed the active and *transformative* nature of cognitive developmental processes, they also tended to suggest that the end-products of cognition are known. Particularly in anthropology and sociology the child was regarded as a more or less passive receiver of collectively constituted, and adult, ideas. However, since the 1980s there have emerged a number of inter-disciplinary approaches to the project of understanding childhood. These studies emphasize the idea of the child as *agent*, as a producer as well as a product of the dynamic collective processes we characterize as 'history' (see, e.g. Kessel and Siegel 1983; James and Prout 1992). Children inevitably differentiate themselves from their parents and, in so doing, they establish historically specific forms of social relations that will manifest at once both cultural continuity and cultural change. This approach directs attention to how children cognitively construct over time concepts that refer to domains that we have been used to think of as distinctively adult – kinship or political economy or religion (see, e.g. Toren 1990). Under the stimulus of new theoretical approaches, the study of childhood in anthropology and sociology may come to have the same importance for theory in these disciplines as it has always had in psychology.

Christina Toren
Brunel University

References

Aries, P. (1962 [1960]) *Centuries of Childhood*, London. (Original edn, Paris.)

James, A. and Prout, A. (eds) (1992) *Constructing and Reconstructing Childhood*, London.

Kessel, F. S. and Siegel, A. W. (eds) (1983) *The Child and Other Cultural Inventions*, New York.

Piaget, J. (1926) *The Child's Conception of the World*, London.

—— (1935) *The Moral Judgement of the Child*, New York.

Scheper-Hughes, N. (1987) *Child Survival: Anthropological Perspectives on the Treatment and Maltreatment of Children*, Dordrecht.

Smith, L. G., Sera, M. and Gattuso, B. (1988) 'The development of thinking', in R. J. Sternberg and E. E. Smith (eds) *The Psychology of Human Thought*, Cambridge, UK.

Stern, D. N. (1985) *The Interpersonal World of the Infant*, New York.

Toren, C. (1990) *Making Sense of Hierarchy: Cognition as Social Process in Fiji*, London.

Vygotsky, L. S. (1962 [1934]) *Thought and Language*, Cambridge, MA. (Original edn, Moscow.)

Whiting, J. W. M. and Child, I. L. (1953) *Child Training and Personality: A Cross-Cultural Study*, New Haven, CT.

Further reading

Briggs, J. L. (1970) *Never in Anger: Portrait of an Eskimo Family*, Cambridge, MA.

La Fontaine, J. S. (1979) *Sex and Age as Principles of Social Differentiation*, London.

Middleton, J. (ed.) (1970) *From Child to Adult: Studies in the Anthropology of Education*, New York.

Richards, M. and Light, P. (eds) (1986) *Children of Social Worlds*, Cambridge, MA.

Schieffelin, B. B. (1990) *The Give and Take of Everyday Life: Language Socialization of Kaluli Children*, Cambridge, UK.

Wertsch, J. V. (1985) *Culture, Communication and Cognition*, Cambridge, UK.

See also: adolescence; childcare; life cycle; life-span development.

Chomsky, Noam (1928–   )

Noam Chomsky, language theoretician, philosopher, intellectual historian and social critic, is one of the most profound and influential thinkers of the modern period, and one of the few scientists whose works are widely read.

After receiving a PhD in linguistics from the University of Pennsylvania in 1955, he joined the faculty at the Massachusetts Institute of Technology, where he was promoted to full professor in 1961, appointed to an endowed chair in 1966, and made institute professor (one of a handful, most of them Nobel laureates) in 1976. Many of the most distinguished contemporary linguists were once his students, some of whom continue to find his work inspiring. (He has supervised about one hundred doctoral dissertations to date.)

His most original contribution has been to open the way to the cognitive natural sciences, for which he has provided a model that is still without equal. (He received the Kyoto Prize for 'basic sciences' in 1988.) His specific model for human language, often referred to as (transformational) generative grammar, can be regarded as a kind of confluence of traditional, and long-forgotten, concerns of the study of language and mind (as in the work of Wilhelm von Humboldt or Otto Jespersen) and new understanding provided by the formal sciences in the late 1930s, specifically, recursive function theory, also known as the theory of computation. His rather unusual knowledge of philosophy, logic and mathematics also allowed him to make use of more sophisticated techniques in linguistics than were being used when he appeared on the scene (and to go on to develop, in the late 1950s, algebraic linguistics, a branch of abstract algebra which is now part of computer science).

However, his original theory of language led in due course (by 1980) to the principles-and-parameters model (greatly improved in his 'minimalist programme' of the early 1990s) and this new model – the first one ever to suggest a substantive solution to the fundamental problem of language acquisition – constitutes a radical break from the rich tradition of thousands of years of linguistic enquiry, which in a way cannot be said of early generative grammar. It is true that the entire (modern) generative grammar period appears to be in many ways a new era. In retrospect it is clear that it has brought with it quite significant changes and progress in the study of language. New areas of enquiry have been opened to serious investigation, leading to many insights and deeper understanding. Furthermore, the current rate of change and progress is rapid even by the standards of the 1960s, so that the generative grammar of the first decade of the twenty-first century may be as novel to us as present-day generative grammar would be to linguists of the not too distant past. If the thinking along the lines of the minimalist programme is anywhere near accurate, it might not be unreasonable to expect that 'a rich and exciting future lies ahead for the study of language and related disciplines', as Chomsky believes in the mid-1990s.

One of the most important consequences of his technical work is that it provides what appears to be decisive evidence in support of epistemological rationalism, as he was quick to point out. It is no secret that Chomsky was greatly influenced by developments in philosophy from the very beginning, and that he turned to the serious study of the Cartesian tradition, which he was to revive and update, shortly after he made his revolutionary discoveries. It was these discoveries that made it possible for him to go well beyond the programmatic, nonspecific insights of the Cartesians, and give substance, at long last, to central Cartesian claims, in the process reconstructing the enduring ideas of the first phase of the age of modern philosophy (a not always recognized antecedent of the cognitive revolution of the 1950s), on which Chomsky has shed much light as a very insightful intellectual historian.

For Chomsky, as for Descartes, there is no essential

variation among humans (no 'degrees of humanness') apart from superficial physical aspects: a creature is either human or it is not. Racism, sexism and other inegalitarian tendencies are then a logical impossibility under this conception, if consistently applied. This conviction, which his technical linguistic work shores up to some extent, is at the root of his broader, more searching studies of human nature and society, and on the grounding of concepts of a social order in features of human nature concerning which empirical enquiry might provide some insight. This is not to say that he, or anyone else, has been able to provide a specific model for the study of social structures, that is, a sort of 'universal grammar' (a new cognitive science) of possible forms of social interaction comparable in depth to the model he has provided for linguistic structures, something possible in principle for other cognitive domains, in his view (which provides an entirely new perspective on the humanities and the social sciences). Still, his social and political theory, which takes an 'instinct for freedom' and the associated urge for self-realization as our basic human need (as distinct from our merely animal needs) – drawing heavily on his superb sympathetic acquaintance with the modern history of social struggle and the ideals underlying it – does not lack inner coherence, is consistent with what is currently known, and compares favourably with any available alternative.

However, the bulk of Chomsky's 'non-professional' writings, which by now are voluminous, and of his numerous and well-attended talks, is devoted not to social and political theory but to a painstaking analysis of contemporary society, to which he brings the intellectual standards taken for granted in scrupulous and profound disciplines (in addition to a hard-to-match brilliance and just plain decency). Because of the broad range, the massive documentation and the incisiveness of this work he is widely recognized as the foremost critic of the foreign and domestic policies of the world's number one (and now only) superpower.

Carlos P. Otero
University of California, Los Angeles

Further reading

Achbar, M. (ed.) (1994) *Manufacturing Consent: Noam Chomsky and the Media*, Montreal.
Chomsky, N. (1986) *Knowledge of Language: Its Nature, Origin, and Use*, New York.
—— (1987) *The Chomsky Reader*, New York.
—— (1988) *Language and Problems of Knowledge*, Cambridge, MA.
—— (1993) *Year 501: The Conquest Continues*, Boston, MA.
Freidin, R. (1992) *Foundations of Generative Syntax*, Cambridge, UK.
Haley, M. C. and Lunsford, R. F. (1994) *Noam Chomsky*, New York.
Leiber, J. (1975) *Noam Chomsky: A Philosophic Overview*, New York.
Lightfoot, D. (1982) *The Language Lottery: Toward a Biology of Grammars*, Cambridge, UK.
Lyons, J. (1991) *Chomsky*, 3rd edn, London.
Newmeyer, F. (1983) *Grammatical Theory: Its Limits and Possibilities*, Chicago.
Otero, C. P. (ed.) (1994) *Noam Chomsky: Critical Assessments*, 8 vols, London.
Salkie, R. (1990) *The Chomsky Update: Linguistics and Politics*, London.
Smith, N. (1989) *The Twitter Machine: Reflections on Language*, Oxford.

See also: linguistics.

citizenship

Only a state, that is, an internationally recognized entity, can grant a person citizenship. One cannot be a citizen of an ethnic group or of a nationality which is not organized as a state. Nor is citizenship confined to democratic states. The distinction between citizens (who belong to a republic) and subjects (who belong to a monarchy) became obsolete when democracy matured in states that retained a monarchical façade. Non-democratic states would not now tolerate the international stigmatization of their population by a refusal to term them 'citizens'.

Citizenship is a legal status defined by each state. Rights and obligations are nowadays ascribed equally to all citizens, since it has become inexpedient to acknowledge the existence of second-class citizens, whether on the basis of place of birth or residence, gender, beliefs, behaviour, race or caste. 'Civil' rights protect their safety and their ability to act. Raymond Aron (1974) affirms that 'modern citizenship is defined by the Rights of Man', but ancient polities (e.g. the Roman Empire) emphasized liberties and procedural guarantees on behalf of their recognized members. In addition to these civil rights, other rights, again supposedly modern, are termed social rights or entitlements. These entitle the citizen to some level of well-being and of social (i.e. socially guaranteed and organized) security. It should not be forgotten, however, that ancient states had their own forms of entitlements, the *panem et circenses* of Rome being inconsiderable when compared to the state socialism of some ancient empires in America or Asia. Moreover, civil rights, true prerequisites of democracy, have for centuries been viewed as 'natural' possessions of individuals, which had only to be protected from the state (hence their often negative description: 'Congress shall make no law . . . abridging the freedom of speech or of the press'). Social rights, in contrast, are popular aspirations which are not always enforceable, even where they are endorsed by the state, because of socioeconomic or ideological constraints. Westbrook (1993: 341) therefore suggests that 'a civil right is thus defined in spite of ordinary politics; a social right is defined by the grace of ordinary politics'.

The duty of the citizens is to obey the laws of the state: 'subjection to the sovereign is the defining characteristic of citizenship' (Camilleri and Falk 1992: 18). Serving the state, from paying taxes up to risking one's life in its defence, is part of civic duty. However, most political philosophers have stressed that the state exists to serve the citizens: hence it is necessary for the citizens to assert political control over the state in order to ensure that their civic responsibilities do not become too heavy in proportion to their rights.

It is therefore easy to understand why citizenship, originally merely a classification of membership, has become enmeshed with the three most formidable ideological currents of modern times: nationalism and democracy, which advocate an active, dedicated citizenship, and tend to reject on the one hand the non-patriots and on the other hand the non-democrats; and third, but not least, the ideology of the welfare state, which emphasizes a passive, consumer-like citizenship and which merges easily with the Hobbesian view of a profitable authority. These three conflicting ideologies are themselves internally divided on such issues as the relevance of ethnicity for the nation, and of majority rule for democracy. In consequence of these ideological conflicts being grafted upon it, the juridical notion of citizenship is sure to remain a matter of urgent public debate for many years to come.

Jean Tournon
University of Grenoble

References

Aron, R. (1974) 'Is multi-national citizenship possible?', *Social Research* 16(4).

Camilleri, J. and Falk, J. (1992) *The End of Sovereignty?*, Aldershot.

Westbrook, D. A. (1993) 'One among millions: an American perspective on citizenship in large polities', *Annales de Droit de Louvain* 2.

Further reading

Faculté de Droit de Nantes (1993) *De la citoyenneté, notions et définitions*, Paris.

Habermas, J. (1992) 'Citizenship and national identity', *Praxis International* 12(1).

Roche, M. (1992) *Rethinking Citizenship: Welfare, Ideology and Change in Modern Society*, Cambridge, UK.

See also: civil society; democracy; human rights; political recruitment and careers; representation, political; state.

city

Terms like the city, urban and urbanism relate to a wide range of phenomena, which have varied greatly through history and between world regions. Different disciplines develop their own perspectives towards urban phenomena: there is an urban anthropology, an urban economics, an urban geography, an urban sociology, etc. Conceptions of the urban community are not congruent between different languages: the English town/city distinction does not have direct counterparts even in closely related languages.

We may regard a reasonably large and permanent concentration of people within a limited territory as the common characteristic of all cities and other urban places. Scholarship has focused on the role of such communities within the wider society, and on the particular characteristics of their internal life.

The beginnings of urbanism are now usually identified with a broad-type of ritual-political centre which developed apparently independently in six areas: Mesopotamia, the Nile and Indus Valleys. North China, Mesoamerica, the Andes, and Yorubaland in West Africa (Wheatley 1971). In these centres divine monarchs and priesthoods, with a corps of officials and guards, controlled the peasants of the surrounding region and extracted a surplus from them. What may have begun as modest tribal shrines were elaborated as complexes of monumental architecture: temples, pyramids, palaces, terraces and courts. We find here the early history not only of the city, but also of civilization and the state. The Yoruba towns, last of the kind to emerge independently, but the only ones still existing as ongoing concerns in a form at all resembling the original, have not exhibited the complexity of architecture and other technology of the earlier and more famous cases but show similarities of social form.

The early centres were urban especially through their capacity to organize the countryside around them, evidently mostly through symbolic control. Yet they might have small residential populations, and most of the people under their rule came to them only for major ritual events. In this sense, one may see the centres as marginally urban. Over time, however, warfare and other factors tended to lead to more secular forms of political control, as well as to greater population concentrations at the centres themselves. The same development can be discerned in European antiquity. In *La Cité antique* (1864) (*The Ancient City*), Fustel de Coulanges has described its urban beginnings as once more a complex of ritual politics, but at the height of their power, the cities of the Graeco-Roman world had elites of landowners and warriors, in control of enormous slave workforces.

These were cities of power, and cities of consumers. Commerce and industry played a minor part within them. But the ancient empires and their cities would decline, and in the Middle Ages, a new urbanism came into being in western Europe. It was mostly commercially based, and with business as the dominant element, the cities developed a considerable autonomy and independence from the feudal social structures surrounding them. The Belgian historian Henri Pirenne is one of the scholars who have been concerned with these medieval European cities. Another is Max Weber, who developed an ideal type in *The City* (1958 [1921]): an urban community must have a market as its central institution, but also a fortification, an at least partially autonomous administrative and legal system, and a form of association reflecting the particular features of urban life (the guild was a conspicuous example).

This frequently quoted formulation constituted a very restrictive definition of urbanism. The distinctiveness of the town in relation to the surrounding countryside is clear, but the institutional apparatus belonged in a particular phase of European history. Weber also contrasted this occidental city with its oriental counterparts. The latter were more internally fragmented and at the same time more closely integrated into imperial administrations. As cities of power rather than of commerce, often with some emphasis on the symbolic expression of pre-eminence, the great urban centres of the east as seen by early European travellers may appear more related to the first urban forms.

Industrialism, of course, has given shape to yet other kinds of cities. One important account of the misery of the huge new concentrations of labouring people in rapidly growing cities is Friedrich Engels's in *The Condition of the Working Class in England* (1969 [1845]), based on his experience in Manchester. Another classic set of studies of urban life under industrialism were carried out by the Chicago school of sociologists – Robert E. Park, Louis Wirth and others – in the 1920s and 1930s. The Chicago sociologists drew attention to the spatial organization of the industrial city and its apparently orderly changes, and thus launched an 'urban ecology'. At the same time, they located a series of smaller-scale ethnographies of particular 'natural areas' within the wider spatial order. Thus they simultaneously pioneered the study of many topics now central to urban anthropology – ethnic quarters, youth gangs, occupations, deviant groups and public places.

In a well-known formulation, Louis Wirth (1938) described urban social contacts as 'impersonal, superficial, transitory, and segmental', and the Chicago sociologists were generally pessimistic about the possibilities of achieving a satisfying human life under urban conditions, as a great many other thinkers have also been. (Yet one celebrates the contribution of urbanism to intellectual life.) On the whole, they concerned themselves more with the internal characteristics of the city, rather than with its place in society. This probably contributed to their tendency to generalize about urbanism on the basis of their Chicago experience, instead of emphasizing that this city was a product of a particular American context, including expansive industrial capitalism as well as ethnic diversity in a somewhat unsettled state.

Partly in response to such generalizations, a considerable body of ethnographically inclined research has emphasized the great variety of forms of life which can be found under urban conditions, and not least the fact that informal social organization may indeed be quite different from the type summarized by Wirth's phrase. William F. Whyte's *Street Corner Society* (1943), describing a close-knit Italian-American neighbourhood in Boston, was a noteworthy early study in this vein, and it is by now generally understood that while city life may have its share of impersonality and anonymity, it also contains a web of friendship, kinship, and occupational linkages: in part, it may be a mosaic of 'urban villages'. With the growth of new subcultures and lifestyles, and a new appreciation for cultural diversity in the city, urban ethnography has been further revitalized in North America and Europe.

Similar perspectives have also been important in the study of contemporary urbanism in the Third World. Especially as the process of urbanization accelerated greatly in Africa, Asia and Latin America in the mid-twentieth century, there was first a tendency by commentators to emphasize 'disorganization', 'detribalization', and the weakening of traditional social ties generally. Later studies have tended to point to the security still provided by kinship and ethnicity, the economic and political uses to which they may be put, and the ability of urbanites to evolve new adaptations, even without significant economic means. Research on squatter settlements, especially in Latin American cities, has thus often made the point that such 'informal housing' is often superior in its efficiency to large-scale public housing projects, and a wave of studies of the 'informal sector' of the urban economy has shown that a very large number of people in Third World urban centres make some kind of living through self-employment or less formal employment arrangements, without occupational training in formal educational structures, and with very limited material resources. This sector includes artisans, petty traders, rickshaw drivers, ice cream vendors, shoe shiners, truck pushers and a multitude of other more or less legitimate ways of supporting oneself, as well as a variety of illicit occupations.

One must not exaggerate the capacity of informal modes of organization to solve the problems of urban living, however, in Third World countries or elsewhere, and the debate on such issues is not yet concluded. What is clear is that generalizations about cities and city life must almost always be qualified. There are in fact a great many types of urban centres, each city has many kinds of inhabitants, and every urbanite engages in social contacts and activities of multiple sorts.

This diversity obviously depends to a great extent on the varying relationships between cities and society. Several different research perspectives thus concern themselves with setting urban centres in a wider context. In economic geography and regional science, different models have been developed to deal with the spatial distribution of urban functions within larger areas. Central place theory, first developed by Walter Christaller (1933) in the 1930s, has been a prominent example, dealing with the location of commercial, administrative and transport centres. Geographers have also concerned themselves with the problem of classifying cities according to their major societal functions, and analysing their internal structure as determined by these functions. Among early well-known classifications, for example, is one showing eight types of urban communities in the United States: retail, wholesale, manufacturing, mining, transport, resort and retirement, university, and diversified. Since the 1960s, one strong interdisciplinary trend has been to view urban processes especially in western Europe and North America within the framework of the political economy of industrial capitalism. This trend, partially under Marxist inspiration, has related urbanism more closely to issues of class, power and social movements (Castells 1977).

In the years since Max Weber drew his contrast between occidental and oriental cities, there have also been numerous further attempts at delineating various regional urban types, such as the Middle Eastern City or the Latin-American City. Cultural historians and other area specialists have played an important part in evolving such constructs, and they have not always been guided by a desire to arrive at a comprehensive comparative understanding of world urbanism. Because of colonialism and other kinds of western expansion, of course, the urban forms of different regions have not all been equally autonomous in their development. Often they must be seen within the context of international centre–periphery relationships. In Africa, Asia and Latin America the large port cities which grew with western domination – Dakar, Bombay, Calcutta, Shanghai, Buenos Aires and others – are an example of this. A recurrent pattern in the colonial and post-colonial Third World has also been the growth of 'primate cities', which through a strong concentration of the commercial, administrative, industrial, cultural and other functions of a country or a territory become much larger and more important than any other urban centre there. Yet colonialism has also created other kinds of urban communities – mining towns, small administrative centres, 'hill stations' for resort purposes, and so forth – and its products may have coexisted with more indigenous urban traditions. Due to such variations, it would seem wiser to look at regional forms of urbanism not always as single types but as typologies in themselves, generated through an interplay of international influences and local forces of social and spatial differentiation.

As for present and future changes in urbanism, these depend in complex ways on demographic, economic, technological and other factors. The twentieth century has witnessed urban growth on an unprecedented scale. 'Megalopolis' and 'conurbation' are new concepts applicable to phenomena of both the western and the non-western world. With increasing globalization, the growing economic and cultural importance of 'world cities' has drawn more attention since the 1980s (Sassen 1991). Yet new modes of transport and communication tend to make human beings less dependent on crowding themselves in limited spaces. 'Counter-urbanization' is thus another modern phenomenon.

Ulf Hannerz
University of Stockholm

References

Castells, M. (1977) *The Urban Question*, London.
Christaller, W. (1933) *Central Places in Southern Germany*, Englewood Cliffs, NJ.
Engels, F. (1969 [1845]) *The Condition of the Working Class in England*, London.
Fustel de Coulanges, N. D. (nd [1864]) *The Ancient City*, Garden City, NY. (Original French edn, *La Cité antique*, Paris.)
Sassen, S. (1991) *The Global City*, Princeton, NJ.
Weber, M. (1958 [1921]) *The City*, New York.
Wheatley, P. (1971) *The Pivot of the Four Quarters*, Edinburgh.
Whyte, W. F. (1943) *Street Corner Society*, Chicago.
Wirth, L. (1938) 'Urbanism as a way of life', *American Journal of Sociology* 44.

See also: metropolitan and urban government; urban geography; urban planning; urbanization.

civil society

This is an old concept in social and political thought that has recently been revived, especially in eastern Europe but also in the west. Traditionally, up to the eighteenth century, it was a more or less literal translation of the Roman *societas civilis* and, behind that, the Greek *koinónia politiké*. It was synonymous, that is, with the state or 'political society'. When Locke spoke of 'civil government', or Kant of *bürgerliche gesellschaft*, or Rousseau of *état civil*, they all meant simply the state, seen as encompassing – like the Greek *polis* – the whole realm of the political. Civil society was the arena of the politically active citizen. It also carried the sense of a 'civilized' society, one that ordered its relations according to a system of laws rather than the autocratic whim of a despot.

The connection of citizenship with civil society was never entirely lost. It forms part of the association that lends its appeal to more recent revivals of the concept. But there was a decisive innovation in the second half of the eighteenth century that broke the historic equation of civil society and the state. British social thought was especially influential in this. In the writings of John Locke and Tom Paine, Adam Smith and Adam Ferguson, there was elaborated the idea of a sphere of society distinct from the state and with forms and principles of its own. The growth of the new science of political economy – again largely a British achievement – was particularly important in establishing this distinction. Most of these writers continued to use the term civil society in its classical sense, as in Adam Ferguson's *Essay on the History of Civil Society* (1966 [1767]); but what they were in fact doing was making the analytical distinction that was soon to transform the meaning of the concept.

It is to Hegel that we owe the modern meaning of the concept of civil society. In the *Philosophy of Right* (1958 [1821]), civil society is the sphere of ethical life interposed between the family and the state. Following the British economists, Hegel sees the content of civil society as largely determined by the free play of economic forces and individual self-seeking. But civil society also includes social and civic institutions that inhibit and regulate economic life, leading by the ineluctable process of education to the rational life of the state. So the particularity of civil society passes over into the universality of the state.

Marx, though acknowledging his debt to Hegel, narrowed the concept of civil society to make it equivalent simply to the autonomous realm of private property and market relations. 'The anatomy of civil society', Marx said, 'is to be sought in political economy'. This restriction threatened its usefulness. What need was there for the concept of civil society when the economy or simply 'society' – seen as the effective content of the state and political life generally – supplied its principal terms? In his later writings Marx himself dropped the term, preferring instead the simple dichotomy 'society—state'. Other writers too, and not only those influenced by Marx, found less and

less reason to retain the concept of civil society. The 'political society' of Alexis de Tocqueville's *Democracy in America* (1835–40) recalled the earlier sense of civil society as education for citizenship; but Tocqueville's example did little to revive the fortunes of what was increasingly regarded as an outmoded term. In the second half of the nineteenth century 'civil society' fell into disuse.

It was left to Antonio Gramsci, in the writing gathered together as the *Prison Notebooks* (1971 [1929–35]), to rescue the concept in the early part of the twentieth century. Gramsci, while retaining a basic Marxist orientation, went back to Hegel to revitalize the concept. Indeed he went further than Hegel in detaching civil society from the economy and allocating it instead to the state. Civil society is that part of the state concerned not with coercion or formal rule but with the manufacture of consent. It is the sphere of 'cultural politics'. The institutions of civil society are the Church, schools, trade unions, and other organizations through which the ruling class exercises hegemony over society. By the same token it is also the arena where that hegemony is challengeable. In the radical decades of the 1960s and 1970s, it was Gramsci's concept of civil society that found favour with those who attempted to oppose the ruling structures of society not by direct political confrontation but by waging a kind of cultural guerrilla warfare. Culture and education were the spheres where hegemony would be contested, and ended.

New life was also breathed into the concept by the swift-moving changes in central and eastern Europe in the late 1970s and 1980s. Dissidents in the region turned to the concept of civil society as a weapon against the all-encompassing claims of the totalitarian state. The example of Solidarity in Poland suggested a model of opposition and regeneration that avoided suicidal confrontation with the state by building up the institutions of civil society as a 'parallel society'. In the wake of the successful revolutions of 1989 throughout the region, the concept of civil society gained immensely in popularity. To many intellectuals it carried the promise of a privileged route to the post-communist, pluralist society, though they were vague about the details. Western intellectuals too were enthused anew with the concept. For them it suggested a new perspective on old questions of democracy and participation, in societies where these practices seemed to have become moribund.

Civil society, it is clear, has renewed its appeal. As in the eighteenth century, we seem to feel once more the need to define and distinguish a sphere of society that is separate from the state. Citizenship appears to depend for its exercise on active participation in non-state institutions, as the necessary basis for participation in formal political institutions. This was Tocqueville's point about American democracy; it is a lesson that the rest of the world now seems very anxious to take to heart. The question remains whether 'civil society' will simply be a rallying cry and a slogan, or whether it will be given sufficient substance to help in the creation of the concrete institutions needed to realize its goals.

Krishan Kumar
University of Kent

References

Ferguson, A. (1966 [1767]) *Essay on the History of Civil Society*, ed. D. Forbes, Edinburgh.
Gramsci, A. (1971 [1929–35]) *Selections from Prison Notebooks*, trans. Q. Hoare and G. Nowell Smith, London. (Original edn, *Quaderni del Carcere*, 6 vols, Turin.)
Hegel, G. W. F. (1958 [1821]) *Philosophy of Right*, trans. T. W. Knox, Oxford.
Tocqueville, A. de (1835–40) *Democracy in America*, ed. J. P. Mayer, trans. G. Lawrence, 2 vols, New York.

Further reading

Arato, A. and Cohen, J. (1992) *Civil Society and Democratic Theory*, Cambridge, MA.
Keane, J. (ed.) (1988) *Civil Society and the State*, London.
Lewis, P. (ed.) (1992) *Democracy and Civil Society in Eastern Europe*, London.
Seligman, A. (1992) *The Idea of Civil Society*, New York.

See also: citizenship; state.

class, social

In the course of the first three decades of the nineteenth century the term class gradually replaced estates, ranks and orders as the major word used to denote divisions within society. The change of vocabulary reflected the diminishing significance of rank and ascribed or inherited qualities in general, and the growing importance of possessions and income among the determinants of the social position. Taken over by social theory from its original context of political debate, class came to refer to large categories of population, distinct from other categories in respect of wealth and related social position, deriving their distinctive status mainly from their location in the production and distribution of social wealth, sharing accordingly in distinctive interests either opposing or complementing other group interests, and consequently displaying a tendency to a group – distinctive political, cultural and social attitudes and behaviour. At the very early stage of the debate, class was given a pronounced economic meaning, arguably under the influence of David Ricardo, who identified the social category of labourers with the economic category of labour, understood as one of the factors of capitalist production. Political economists of the 'Ricardian socialist' school (William Thompson (1824), Thomas Hodgskin (1825) and others) developed Ricardo's suggestions into a comprehensive economic theory of class division, which was then adopted and elaborated upon by Karl Marx.

The many usages of class in social-scientific theory and research are invariably influenced by Marx's magisterial vision of class division as, simultaneously, the principal source of social dynamics and the main principle of its interpretation. Even if historiosophic aspects of Marx's class theory (all history is a history of class struggle; social change occurs through class revolutions; the conflict between capitalists and workers, arising from the capitalist form of production, is bound to lead to a proletarian revolution and to a new, socialist form of production) are questioned or rejected, the enduring interest in class and, indeed, the unfaltering centrality of the category of class in social-scientific discourse are due to Marx-inspired belief in a high predictive and explanatory value of (primarily economic) class in respect of both individual and collective behaviour.

The resilience to this latter aspect of Marx's theoretical legacy is in no small part due to its overall harmony with the dominant liberal world-view, which interprets individual action as, by and large, rational pursuit of interest, and assigns to 'gain' the role of the central motive of human conduct. The continuous popularity of Marx's class theory has been helped by the incorporation of these tacit premises of common sense and the resulting strategy of interpreting social antagonisms as conflicts of economic interests (that is, incompatibility of goals rationally pursued by various groups differently located within the economic process).

Defining classes as large groups united by their common location within the economic process and aspiring, against efforts of other classes, to an increased share of the surplus product, was a habit firmly established inside the classic political economy before Marx. The fateful contribution of Marx consisted in the reading into the class conflict of another dimension – the struggle for the management of social surplus. Since, within the capitalist order, the right to the surplus was the prerogative of the managers of the productive process, rational effort to amplify a class share in the surplus product must be aimed at the management of production; since, again in the capitalist system, the right to manage productive process as a prerogative of the owners of capital (or means of production), a class barred from access to the surplus can defy its deprivation only through dissociating the right to manage from the right of ownership – through the expropriation of the owners of the capital. In the succession of historical forms of class struggle, the conflict between capitalists and their workers was thus presented by Marx as the modern equivalent of *both* the conflict between pre-capitalist landlords and their serfs *and* the conflict between landowning aristocracy and industry-owning capitalists. Indeed, the specifically Marxist approach to class analysis of industrial society consists in conflating the two dimensions of class conflict and the tendency to interpret the first (the redistribution of surplus) as an immature manifestation, or an early stage, of the second (the management of the production of surplus).

In consequence, the Marx-inspired study of class and class conflict focuses its attention on the combat between owners of capital and industrial workers. More specifically, in this conflict, considered central for the current historical era, this study is interested in the progression of industrial workers from their objective situation as a factor in the process of capitalist production ('class in itself') to the acquisition of a consciousness of their situation and, finally, to the appropriation of a political strategy aimed at radically overcoming their subordination to capital by abolishing the capitalist mode of production itself ('class for itself').

For the Marx-inspired class theory, therefore, the major difficulty arises from the evident failure of industrial workers to make any notable advance along the line of anticipated progression. A century and a half after the essential historiosophical assumptions of Marx's class theory had been made public in the *Communist Manifesto* (1980 [1848]), the workers of the industrialized world seem to come nowhere near the threshold of the socialist transformation of society.

The gap between predictions generated by class theory and the actual tendency of historical development was brought into sharp relief in the wake of the October Revolution in Russia in 1917: a revolution claiming to fulfil the Marxist promise of socialist transformation occurred in a society little advanced in its capitalist development, while all the timid attempts at socialist revolution in truly capitalist countries with a large industrial working population failed. What, from the theoretical perspective, appeared a bewildering incongruity of historical praxis, triggered off recurring attempts among Marxist thinkers to provide auxiliary theories accounting for the failure of the anticipated historical tendency to materialize.

The first, and tone-setter, in the long chain of such auxiliary theories was Lukács's (1967 [1923]) 'false consciousness' theory. Lukács distinguished 'consciousness of class' from 'class consciousness'; the first was

the empirically ascertainable state of ideas and motives of the class members arising from the experience accessible within their daily business of life, while the second could be arrived at only through a bird's-eye survey of the total situation of the society, and a rational study of the totality of the information related to the social system (Lukács was here influenced by Weber's method of 'ideal types'). In Lukács's view, there was no automatic passage from the first to the second: the information necessary to construct ideal-typical 'class consciousness' was not available within the individual experience constrained by the tasks of daily survival. The empirical consciousness of class displayed a tendency, therefore, to remain a 'false consciousness', misguided and misled as it were by the narrow horizons of individual experience – unless assisted by scientific analysis filtered into the minds of the workers through the channels of their political organizations. In Lukács's subtle revision of the original model, the passage from 'class in itself' to 'class for itself', far from being an automatic process guaranteed by the logic of capitalist economy, has now become a matter of ideological struggle. Without such battle of ideas the passage would not be probable, let alone inevitable.

Numerous suggestions have been made in the sociological literature since the mid-1960s to render the discrepancy between the objective deprivation of the workers, and the apparent lack of radical opposition to the system responsible for it, amenable to empirical study, leading eventually to the location of factors either furthering the persistence of deprivation or prompting opposition to it. An early attempt was made by Dahrendorf (1959) to analyse the problem in terms of the passage from 'quasi-groups', united only by 'latent interests', to 'interest groups', whose consciousness of the common fate renders their interests 'manifest'. Sharing of latent interests is a necessary, but insufficient, condition of the passage; the latter demands that a number of additional factors must be present. Developing this insight, Morris and Murphy (1966) suggested that class consciousness should be seen as 'a processual emergent', and that from 'no perception of status difference' to a 'behaviour undertaken on behalf of the stratum interests and ideology' lead a number of stages, each subject to a somewhat different set of factors. In a highly influential collective study of *The Black-Coated Worker*, Lockwood (1958) departed from the 'stages' or 'progression' framework heretofore dominant in post-Marxian study of class consciousness and proposed that depending on the technologically determined type of employment, presence or absence of communal living and other cultural aspects of the mode of life, different types of consciousness ('traditional', 'deferential' or 'privatized') may develop among workers, each acquiring a degree of permanence grounded in its congruence with specific conditions of life. The early study of class consciousness by Parkin (1974) prompted similar conclusions: Parkin singled out, as an attitudinal type most likely to arise from life experience of the workers, a 'subordinate' ideology, taking either a 'deferential' or 'aspirational' form, but in both cases inducing the workers to make peace with the system responsible for their subordinate position.

These auxiliary theories all assume that the life situation of the workers within the capitalist mode of production necessarily produces an anti-capitalist tendency in their consciousness. It is this assumption, and this assumption only, which renders the evident absence of anti-capitalist action problematic and gives both meaning and urgency to the study of factors responsible for the empirical departure from a theoretically grounded expectation.

Not so in the case of another large family of class theories, tracing its origin to Max Weber. Weber revised Marx's theory of class in three important respects. First, having accepted Marx's notion of class as a category articulated first and foremost within the network of economic relations, he denied to these relations the determining role in respect of the articulation of society on its sociocultural and political planes. Status groups (the nearest equivalent of the Marxist idea of class consciousness) as well as political groupings (the nearest equivalent of the Marxist idea of class action) are categories in their own right, parallel to but not necessarily overlapping with economically determined classes, and subject to their own constitutive rules and developmental logic. In short, Weber denied that economic divisions were necessarily mirrored in the cultural and political articulation of the society. Then, having related class, as an economic phenomenon, to the market (specifically, to the chances of access to marketable goods), Weber questioned the possibility of determining *a priori* which of the many conflicts of interests that the market may generate at various times should be assigned a paramount role. And in contrast to Marx, Weber argued that interests vary with respect to different goods and market chances. Consequently they divide the population exposed to the market in more than one way, each individual belonging in principle to a number of classes whose boundaries need not overlap. (The concept of 'housing classes', advanced by Rex (1967), is a good example of a category of economic classes articulated in relation to just one, though highly important, marketable commodity.) The relative importance attached by a given individual to each of the classes to which they belong is not, therefore, determined in advance. It may change, depending on the structure of the market situation, and no one class can be credited in advance with a capacity to command an overwhelming allegiance, displacing all other classes as the major determinant of action.

Weber's insight into the multiplicity of classes and the role of the market in their articulation has been applied, particularly by British sociologists, in a novel analysis of the self-perception of classes and their responses to class inequality. Theoretical models emerging from these analyses refuse to be constrained by the idea of a structurally assigned class consciousness organizing the field of class attitudes and opinions, and instead attempt to gear themselves, with some success, to the empirically accessible evidence of actual ideologies, policies and actions of labour. Among these developments two are perhaps most seminal. One is W. G. Runciman's (1966) concept of 'relative deprivation' (akin to Moore's concept of 'outraged justice'), according to which groups, in their effort to assess their own social position, tend to 'compare with comparable' only: that is, they do not perceive as inequality, at least not as an 'unjust' inequality, the differences between their situation and that of groups distant on the scale of possessions – but they keenly guard their parity with groups they consider their equals, and are goaded into collective action when overtaken by those occupying a lower rung of the ladder. A somewhat similar analysis of class conflicts has been advanced by Parkin (1979) in his later study, drawing on the little used concept of 'closure', introduced but left largely undeveloped by Weber. According to Parkin, the mechanism of class behaviour can best be understood in terms of a tendency to preserve, and if possible enhance, whatever privileged access to coveted market commodities a given class may possess. Subject to this tendency, rational action would consist in the policy of either 'closure by exclusion' (to prevent dilution of the privilege by an influx of those below), or 'closure by usurpation' (to acquire a share in the privileges of those above). In the light of both analyses, organized labour's notorious lack of concern with the extremes of the social distribution of surplus, the paramount importance attached in the practice of trade unions to the preservation of 'differentials', or the puzzling indifference of the same unions to the conditions of the unemployed poor (as distinct from the defence of members' jobs), are all manifestations of a sociological regularity, rather than aberrations calling for special explanations in terms of unusual factors.

The American reception of Weberian ideas pointed in a somewhat different direction. It was guided by the Weberian image of the essential multidimensionality of social differentiation, and was concerned above all with the investigation of correlation (or lack of correlation) between wealth, prestige and influence. In practice most American sociology (particularly until the 1960s) tended to assign a central role to the dimension of prestige (as exemplified by the widespread studies of social deference in relation to occupations). In the context of these practices, however, the term 'class' was employed but rarely (when used outside the Weberian current, for example by Warner or Centers, the term was given a primarily psychological meaning). The specifically American approaches to the question of socially induced inequality are not an exact equivalent (or an alternative to) class theory, and are better analysed in their own framework, as theories of stratification (based on the master-image of gradation, rather than division).

As for class theory proper, both post-Marxian and post-Weberian approaches remain faithful to the ground premises articulated early in the nineteenth century: class is first and foremost an economic phenomenon, and class conflict is above all about the defence or the improvement of economic position, that is, of the share in the distribution of social surplus. One can say that the discursive formation of class has been shaped in its present form in the period of reinterpretation, in economic terms, of social conflicts spanning the course of west European history between the French Revolution and the 'Spring of Nation' of 1848. It was only quite recently that the rethinking of the class model of society has developed sufficiently to put in question the very premises on which the discourse of class is grounded. One of the important lines of questioning comes from the work of Foucault (1980) which revealed a close association of the modern social system, not so much with the invention of machine technology or the spread of the capitalist form of labour, as with the establishment of a new type of 'disciplinary' power, aimed directly at the control of the human body and using surveillance as its main method. From this perspective the intense social conflicts of the early nineteenth century, later interpreted as manifestations of the inchoate labour movement, are seen as the last stage of the defensive struggle against new forms of controlling power; while the economically oriented organizations of factory workers, portrayed within class theory as specimens of a mature labour movement, are seen as a product of displacing the original conflict, centred around control, on to the field of distribution.

Whatever the view of the applicability of class theory to the understanding of the past two centuries, other doubts are raised about its usefulness in the study of the current stage in social development. Habermas (1978 [1973]), Offé (1964), Gorz (1982) and Touraine (1971) among others drew attention, each in a slightly different way, to the rapidly shrinking size of the industrial labour force, to the diminishing role of bargaining between owners of capital and industrial workers in organizing the distribution of surplus, and to the growing mediation and, indeed, initiative of the state in reproducing the essential conditions of the social production of surplus. In view of these developments, it is increasingly difficult to maintain that class membership remains a major key to the mechanism of reproduction of societally inflicted deprivations (and, more generally, social differentiation as such) or, for that matter, a major explanatory variable in the study of individual and group behaviour. Thus far, however, no alternative concept of similar comprehensiveness and cogency has been proposed to replace class in the description and interpretation of socially produced inequality.

Some sociologists have attempted to replace class as the overriding determinant of identity with other criteria, notably gender, ethnicity, race, or culture. On the whole, however, contemporary sociologists are not inclined to accept that one dimension of stratification subsumes all others. Identity is generally treated as multidimensional, and the ability of individuals to construct and deconstruct their social identities is acknowledged. Indeed, the degree to which this freedom is enjoyed may be seen as the most salient element in defining social status. The wider social categories, previously treated as given, are now also analysed as the products of human agency. Moreover, no principle of division or stratification is believed to apply to all members of a society. The notion of the underclass, for example, tacitly suggests that a part of the population is excluded from the 'class system'.

Zygmunt Bauman
University of Leeds

References

Dahrendorf, R. (1959) *Class and Conflict in Industrial Society*, London.

Foucault, M. (1980) *Power and Knowledge*, ed. C. Gordon, Brighton.

Gorz, A. (1982) *Farewell to the Working Class*, London.

Habermas, J. (1978 [1973]) *Legitimation Crisis*, London. (Original German edn, *Legitimationsprobleme in Spatkapitalismus*.)

Hodgskin, T. (1825) *Labour Defended Against the Claims of Capital*, London.

Lockwood, D. (1958) *The Black-Coated Worker*, London.

Lukács, G. (1967 [1923]) *History and Class Consciousness*, London. (Original edn, *Geschichte und Klassenbegrips*, Berlin.)

Marx, K. (1980 [1848]) *Communist Manifesto*, London. (Original edn, *Manifest der Kommunistisch Partei*, London.)

Offé, K. (1964) 'Political authority and class structures', in D. Senghaas (ed.) *Politikwissenschaft*, Frankfurt.

Parkin, F. (1974) *Class Inequality and Political Order*, London.

—— (1979) *Marxism and Class Theory*, London.

Rex, J. (1967) *Race, Community and Conflict*, Oxford.

Runciman, W. G. (1966) *Relative Deprivation and Social Justice*, London.

Thompson, W. (1824) *An Inquiry into the Principles of the Distribution of Wealth most Conducive to Human Happiness*, London.

Touraine, A. (1971) *The Post-Industrial Society*, New York.

Further reading

Argyle, M. (1994) *The Psychology of Social Class*, London.

Bottomore, T. (1965) *Classes in Modern Society*, London.

Giddens, A. (1973) *Class Structure of the Advanced Societies*, London.

Lasch, S. and Friedman, J. (eds) (1992) *Modernity and Identity*, Oxford.

See also: stratification.

classical and operant conditioning *see* conditioning, classical and operant

classical economics

The term classical economics, although sometimes given the rather broader meaning of any economics which is not Keynesian, is generally taken to refer to the body of economic ideas stemming from the work of David Hume, whose most important work was published in 1752, and Adam Smith, whose great *Wealth of Nations* was published in 1776. These ideas came to dominate economics particularly, but far from exclusively, in Britain throughout the last quarter of the eighteenth and the first three quarters of the nineteenth century.

Hume's contributions principally concerned money and the balance of payments. But Smith's work is a virtual compendium of economics, focusing on the key question of economic growth, and covering division of labour, distribution, capital accumulation, trade and colonial policy, and public finance. Among their successors was T. R. Malthus; though chiefly famous for his writings on population, he covered the whole field of economic inquiry (Malthus 1820). A major impetus to the development of classical economics was provided by David Ricardo (1951–73). He read Smith's work critically and from it constructed a 'model' which, unlike Smith's work, produced fairly clear and definite predictions. Ricardo succeeded initially in attracting disciples, notably J. Mill (1821–6; see also Winch 1966) and – though he later drifted away from Ricardo's influence – J. R. McCulloch

(1825) as well as Thomas De Quincey. But his influence waned after his death and the work of J. Mill's son, J. S. Mill (1848; 1963–85), is much closer to Smith in range, reliance upon empirical material, and the avoidance of precise predictions.

Classical economics covered the whole field of economic enquiry, but with an emphasis on questions dealing with large aggregates – economic growth, international trade, monetary economics and public finance – rather than with the analysis of the behaviour of the maximizing individual which came to be of dominant interest after 1870. (In the field of value theory, in particular, the classical economists generally made do with various sorts of production theories emphasizing, in varying degrees, the importance of labour cost in total cost.) At the same time a fundamental premise lying behind the analysis of aggregates, and stemming from Smith, was that individuals were motivated by the pursuit of self-interest, and that their pursuit had to be limited by a framework of law, religion and custom, to ensure coincidence of private and social interest. This in turn meant that in the field of economic policy classical economics, while predisposed against government interference (partly because of the way in which such interference could be used for purely sectional interest, and partly because of a belief that decentralized individual knowledge was superior to state knowledge), was pragmatic – the necessary legislative framework could be learned only by experience and enquiry.

At the heart of the classical vision is the idea of economic growth occurring through the interaction of capital accumulation and division of labour. Capital accumulation made it possible to postpone the sale of output, permitting the development of specialization and division of labour. Division of labour in turn increased total output, permitting further capital accumulation. Economic growth would be increased by allowing capital to flow to where it was most productive; thus, other things being equal, it was desirable to remove restraints on the free allocation of resources. Division of labour itself was limited by the extent of the market. The extent of the home market depended on population and income per head. As capital was accumulated, the available labour supply found itself in greater demand and wages rose above the necessary minimum – 'subsistence' which could be either psychological or physiological. Population responded to the rise in wages by increasing; this in turn increased the labour supply which pushed wages back towards subsistence, though, if subsistence was a psychological variable – as it was with many classical writers – population growth might well stop before wages had fallen to the old level of subsistence. As wages rose, profits fell; this might check capital accumulation, but as long as profits were above a necessary minimum, capital accumulation would continue. Output, population, and capital thus all grew together. However, a brake on growth was provided by the shortage of a third input, land. With the progress of economic growth, food became more and more expensive to produce, while landlords enjoyed the benefit of an unearned rent arising from ownership of this scarce but vital resource – this aspect was particularly stressed by Malthus and Ricardo. The rising cost of food also meant that the floor below which subsistence could not fall – the minimum wage necessary to procure basic physical necessities of life – rose; and Ricardo in particular emphasized that such a rise would depress profits .and might eventually stop capital accumulation and growth altogether. (Smith had believed that growth would stop only when investment opportunities were exhausted.) He then argued that repeal of the Corn Laws (restricting food imports) was urgent, since subsistence could be obtained more cheaply abroad. (Later classical economists such as McCulloch and J. S. Mill were, however, optimistic about technical progress in agriculture which could postpone any slowdown in economic growth by lowering the cost of agricultural output.)

The argument for repeal of the Corn Laws provided one part of a general classical case for freedom of trade; the desire to widen the market to maximize possible division of labour provided another. However, a more general and sophisticated argument for freedom of trade was provided by R. Torrens (1820; 1821) and Ricardo, in the form of the theory of comparative costs (later refined and developed by J. S. Mill) which showed that a country could gain from importing even those commodities in which it had a competitive advantage if it had an even greater competitive advantage in the production of other commodities – it should concentrate its scarce resources on the latter.

Balance of payments equilibrium was ensured by a mechanism which was due to David Hume, and which was also basic to classical monetary theory, the price-specie-flow mechanism. A balance of payments deficit would, through gold outflow, reduce the money supply, and thus the price level, making exports competitive and imports less attractive, and this equilibrating mechanism would continue until the gold outflow stopped and payments came into balance. The price level was thus dependent on the money supply; and the predominant classical view from Ricardo to Lord Overstone (1837) was that the note issue, as part of the money supply, should be contracted if gold was flowing out, since the outflow was a symptom of a price level which was too high. Monetary control was also necessary to dampen the effects of an endogenous trade

cycle, an element introduced into classical economics, chiefly by Overstone, from the late 1830s. (A minority of classical economists, however, viewed the money supply as demand-determined.)

Classical economics represented a major intellectual achievement. The foundations which it laid in the fields of monetary and trade theory, in particular, are still with economics. Eventually it lost some of its momentum; it was always policy-oriented, and as the policy questions were settled – usually along the lines indicated by the classical analyses – and as economists came to take continuing economic growth for granted, they turned their attention to different questions requiring different techniques of analysis.

D. P. O'Brien
University of Durham

References

Hume, D. (1752) *Political Discourses*, Edinburgh.
McCulloch, J. R. (1825) *The Principles of Political Economy: With Some Inquiries Respecting their Application and a Sketch of the Rise and Progress of the Science*, 2nd edn, Edinburgh.
Malthus, T. R. (1820) *Principles of Political Economy*, London.
Mill, J. (1821–6) *Elements of Political Economy*, np.
Mill, J. S. (1848) *Principles of Political Economy with Some of their Applications to Social Philosophy*, np.
—— (1963–85) *Collected Works of J. S. Mill*, ed. J. M. Robson, Toronto.
Overstone, Lord (1837) *Reflections Suggested by a Perusal of Mr J. Horsley Palmer's Pamphlet on the Causes and Consequences of the Pressure on the Money Market*, London.
Ricardo, D. (1951–73) *The Works and Correspondence of David Ricardo*, ed. P. Sraffa with M. H. Dobb, 10 vols, Cambridge, UK.
Smith, A. (1981 [1776]) *An Inquiry into the Nature and Causes of the Wealth of Nations*, ed. R. Campbell and A. Skinner, Indianapolis, IN.
Torrens, R. (1820) *An Essay on the External Corn Trade*, London.
—— (1821) *An Essay on the Production of Wealth*, London.
Winch, D. (ed.) (1966) *James Mill: Selected Economic Writings*, Edinburgh.

Further reading

Blaug, M. (1958) *Ricardian Economics*, New Haven, CT.
O'Brien, D. P. (1975) *The Classical Economists*, Oxford.

See also: Keynesian economics.

clinical psychology

Clinical psychology is one of the speciality areas of applied psychology, together with such other specialities as industrial, physiological, measurement and developmental psychology. The science and profession of clinical psychology, as one of the mental health disciplines, utilizes the principles of psychology to understand, diagnose and treat psychological problems; to teach and train students in these principles and their applications; and to conduct research in human behaviour as well as function as consumer of research advances as a means of upgrading the delivery of health care.

The two world wars and the major development of public schools in the USA between the wars vastly accelerated the growth of clinical psychology, first as purely a psychological or 'mental' test application in assessing intellectual and other psychological responses and capabilities, and then, after the Second World War, expanding into other roles, in the psychotherapies as well as in research and training and in formal graduate programmes in clinical psychology. In the USA alone, it has been estimated that during the Second World War 16 million military candidates and recruits were given psychological tests for classification and assignment to duties. In the First World War psychologists did psychometric assessment only; in the Second World War they also carried out treatment responsibilities for mentally ill personnel, together with psychiatrists, social workers, nurses and technicians.

Two major developments after the Second World War furthered the growth of clinical psychology in the USA: the establishment of the National Institute of Mental Health and its support for training and research; and the decision of the Veterans Administration to fund training for clinical psychology as one of the disciplines in mental health to assess and treat veterans with psychological illness. There followed the accreditation, by the American Psychological Association (APA), of doctoral training programmes (over 190 in 1993) and internship programmes (over 435 in 1993) in professional psychology (clinical, counselling, school and professional-scientific psychology); and certification and licensing by states.

Two other standards organizations developed, the first in 1947 and thus growing during the great 'spurt' since the early 1950s, and the second initially an outgrowth of the former. The American Board of Professional Psychology (ABPP) was established in 1947 by the Council of Representatives of the American Psychological Association 'to define the standards, conduct examinations, grant diplomas, and encourage the pursuit of excellence in professional psychology' (1980). The five fields of specialization are clinical; counselling; industrial and organizational; school; and neuropsychology.

In 1957, there were 15,545 life members, fellows and associates in the APA, of whom 1,907 fellows and associates were in the Division of Clinical Psychology. By 1993 there were over 113,000 fellows, members and associates, nearly 13,000 of whom were in the Division of Clinical Psychology or in closely related divisions. There are nearly 16,000 registrants in the National Register.

Clinical psychology has moved towards a reintegration with other fields of psychology; new specialities have also been created within clinical psychology. Health psychology has drawn to it scientists and professionals from other domains of psychology, principally clinical, social, physiological and learning or cognitive areas. This field was initially a research area and increasingly has become an applied field. An interesting cycle in the history of clinical psychology concerns psychological or 'mental' tests, which have played a prominent role in development of clinical psychology since the end of the nineteenth century. After the Second World War, primarily in the USA, graduate programmes decreased their commitment to teaching assessment methods, and their graduates increasingly turned to psychotherapy as a principal activity. Then, research training support, litigation over the effects upon individuals of toxic and other industrial and environmental pollutants, and mounting interest in psychological changes in disease and accident victims and in elderly people all contributed to bringing assessment again into prominence, especially neuropsychological assessment; there are now local, state, regional, national and international societies of neuropsychologists.

Ivan N. Mensh
University of California, Los Angeles

Further reading

American Board of Professional Psychology (1989) *Directory of Diplomates*, Washington, DC.

Cattell, R. B. (1983) 'Let's end the duel', *American Psychologist* 38.

Council for the National Register of Health Science Providers in Psychology (1993) *National Register of Health Service Providers in Psychology*, Washington, DC.

Mensh, I. N. (1966) *Clinical Psychology: Science and Profession*, New York.

See also: behaviour therapy; cognitive-behavioural therapy; counselling psychology; mental disorders; mental health.

cliometrics

The term cliometrics (a neologism linking the concept of measurement to the muse of history) was apparently coined at Purdue University, Indiana, USA, in the late 1950s. Originally applied to the study of economic history as undertaken by scholars trained as economists (and also called, by its practitioners and others, the new economic history, econometric history and quantitative economic history), more recently cliometrics has been applied to a broader range of historical studies (including the new political history, the new social history, and, most inclusively, social science history).

The historians' early interest in cliometrics partly reflects the impact of two important works in US economic history. The detailed estimates by Conrad and Meyer (1958) of the profitability of slavery before the Civil War and the quantitative evaluation of the role of the railways in economic growth by Fogel (1964) triggered wide-ranging debate, with much attention to questions of method as well as substance. While these two works, combining economic theory and quantitative analysis, attracted the most attention, other books and articles published at about the same time also highlighted the quantitative aspect, although in a more traditional (and less controversial) manner. A National Bureau of Economic Research (NBER 1960) conference volume, edited by Parker, presented a number of important studies (by, among others, Easterlin, Gallman, Lebergott, and North) pushing back many important times-series on economic variables to the early nineteenth century, an effort complemented by the publication, several years later, of another NBER (1966) conference dealing mainly with nineteenth-century economic change. North (1961) combined his new estimates of pre-1860 foreign trade with a familiar regional approach to describe the basic contours of US economic growth from 1790 to the Civil War. These works had important implications for discussions of economic growth in the USA, particularly in the period before the Civil War. The concentration of major publications within a short time period, together with the start of an annual conference of cliometricians at Purdue University, organized by Davis, Hughes, and others, which, with several changes of venue, still continues, generated the momentum which led to major shifts in the nature of the writing of US economic history, as well as revisions of many interpretations of past developments. The late 1950s and 1960s saw similar changes in other subfields of history, particularly political and social history, although it was in economic history that the concentration on theory, quantitative data, and statistical methods was most complete.

In perhaps the most controversial work of cliometrics, Fogel (who was, with North, to win the Nobel Prize in Economics for 1993) co-authored, with Engerman, a work on the economics of US slavery, *Time on the Cross* (1974) whose conclusions as to the profitability, viability and efficiency of slavery triggered considerable debate among cliometricians and other historians. Fogel's subsequent work on slavery, *Without Consent or Contract* (1989) did not lead to a similar debate, although the basic conclusions were similar to those of the earlier work. The 1970s and 1980s saw a broadening of the interests of cliometricians from those of the earlier decades. For example, there was considerable attention given to the study of demographic and anthropometric issues, while North (see, e.g. Davis and North 1971; North 1990), and various other scholars, focused attention on the study of the development of economic institutions and organizations. An indicator of these expanding horizons is seen in the third of the NBER (1986) volumes dealing with economic history, edited by Engerman and Gallman.

The most general characteristics of cliometric work (in economic history) have been the systematic use of economic theory and its concepts to examine economic growth in the past, and the widespread preparation and formal statistical analysis of quantitative material. While none of this may seem to provide a new approach in historical studies (as is often pointed out in criticizing claims of novelty), the more explicit attention to theory and the more frequent reliance on quantitative materials and statistical procedures have had an important impact upon the manner in which historical questions have been approached and interpreted. However, cliometricians still differ in how they make use of quantitative and statistical methods. To some, the major work is the preparation of quantitative data, either of detailed information for a particular time period (based on, e.g. the samples of population, agriculture, and manufacturing records drawn from the decadal federal census) or of long-period time-series (e.g. national income and wealth, wages, labour force) to be used in measuring and understanding past economic changes. These estimates require imaginative reconstructions from the available samples of past data, but do not often involve sophisticated statistical tools. Others emphasize the use of more formal statistical methods, most frequently regression analysis, to test hypotheses. Some cliometricians restrict themselves to the use of economic theory to analyse institutional and economic changes, which are difficult to describe quantitatively.

Continued interest in economic (and political and sociological) theory has led to a more frequent attempt to find historical generalizations based upon social science concepts and methods than some, more traditionally trained, historians seem comfortable with. Nevertheless, the ability to collect and examine data, from archival and published sources, furthered by the development of the computer, has permitted a considerable expansion in the amount of material relevant to questions of interest to historians, as well as better methods of organizing, analysing, and testing data. The heat of earlier debates on method has apparently declined as the use of quantitative methods and theoretical constructs has become a part of the standard tool-kit of historians, while cliometricians have broadened the range of questions they have discussed and the varieties of evidence utilized.

While the first cliometric studies were done principally by North American scholars and, for reasons of data availability, most frequently concerned the USA in the nineteenth century, since the mid-1970s the temporal and geographic scope has widened, as have the types of questions to which cliometric analysis is applied. Much work has been done on the colonial period, as well as the twentieth century, in the USA. Not only have the interests of American cliometricians expanded to include studies of other parts of the world, but also cliometric work has developed in a number of other countries, most particularly in Britain and other parts of western Europe. Although, as with most attempts at categorization, a sharp dividing line is often difficult to draw, cliometric history continues to emphasize the systematic application of social science theory and the use of quantitative data and statistical analysis to understand the historical past.

Stanley L. Engerman
University of Rochester

References

Conrad, A. H. and Meyer, J. R. (1958) 'The economics of slavery in the ante-bellum South', *Journal of Political Economy*.

Davis, L. E. and North, D. C. (1971) *Institutional Change and American Economic Growth*, Cambridge, UK.

Fogel, R. W. (1964) *Railroads and American Economic Growth: Essays in Econometric History*, Baltimore, MD.

—— (1989) *Without Consent or Contract: The Rise and Fall of American Slavery*, New York.

Fogel, R. W. and Engerman, S. L. (1974) *Time on the Cross: The Economics of American Negro Slavery*, Boston, MA.

National Bureau of Economic Research (1960) Conference on Research in Income and Wealth, *Trends in the American Economy in the Nineteenth Century*, Princeton, NJ.

—— (1966) Conference on Research in Income and Wealth, *Output, Employment, and Productivity in the United States after 1800*, New York.

—— (1986) Conference on Research in Income and Wealth, *Long-Term Factors in American Economic Growth*, Chicago.

North, D. C. (1961) *The Economic Growth of the United States, 1790–1860*, Englewood Cliffs, NJ.

—— (1990) *Institutions, Institutional Change and Economic Performance*, Cambridge, UK.

Further reading

Engerman, S. L. (1977) 'Recent developments in American economic history', *Social Science History*.

Kousser, J. M. (1980) 'Quantitative social-scientific history', in M. Kammen (ed.) *The Past Before Us*, Ithaca, NY.

McCloskey, D. N. (1978) 'The achievements of the cliometric school', *Journal of Economic History*.

McCloskey, D. N. and Hersh, G. A. (1990) *A Bibliography of Historical Economics to 1980*, Cambridge, UK.

Williamson, S. H. (1991) 'The history of cliometrics', in J. Mokyr (ed.) *The Vital One: Essays in Honor of Jonathan R. T. Hughes*, Greenwich, CT.

See also: economic history.

cognition *see* cognitive psychology; cognitive science; intelligence and intelligence testing; memory; sensation and perception; thinking

cognitive-behavioural therapy

Cognitive-behavioural interventions preserve the demonstrated efficiencies of behavioural therapy within a less doctrinaire context by incorporating the congitive activities of the client in the efforts to produce therapeutic change (Kendall and Hollon 1979). It is a major force in psychotherapy today, both in theory and in application.

Basic to the cognitive-behavioural approach is a set of principles captured briefly as follows. Client and therapist work together to evaluate problems and generate solutions (e.g. collaborative empiricism). Most human learning is cognitively mediated. Cognition, affect and behaviour are causally interrelated. Attitudes, expectancies, attributions and other cognitive activities are central in producing, predicting and understanding behaviour and the effects of therapy. Cognitive processes can be integrated into behavioural paradigms, and it is possible and desirable to combine cognitive treatment strategies with enactive and contingency management techniques (Kendall *et al.*, Mahoney 1977).

Within the boundaries of these fundamental principles, the actual implementation of the cognitive-behavioural therapies varies. The major strategies within cognitive-behavioural therapy include cognitive-behavioural therapy of depression; rational-emotive therapy; systematic rational restructuring; stress inoculation; cognitive-behavioural training with children.

Cognitive-behavioural therapy of depression (Beck *et al.* 1979) is structured, active and typically time-limited. Learning experiences are designed to teach clients to monitor their negative thinking, to examine the evidence for and against their distorted (negative) thinking, to substitute more reality-oriented interpretations for negative thinking, and to begin to alter the dysfunctional beliefs and lifestyle associated with negative thinking. Behavioural strategies such as self-monitoring of mood, activity scheduling, graduated task assignments, and role-playing exercises are integrated with more cognitive procedures such as focusing on changing negative thinking, reattribution, and decentring.

Rational-emotive therapy (RET) offers both a theoretical and therapeutic system consistent with cognitive-behavioural therapy (Ellis 1980). In RET, events do not cause emotional and behavioural consequences; private beliefs do. When the individual's beliefs (salient assumptions) are inaccurate/irrational and are framed in absolutistic or imperative terms, maladjustment is likely to result. RET teaches clients to identify and change the illogical notions that underlie their distressing symptoms.

Systematic rational restructuring (SRR) is a derivative of RET which offers a clear description of the procedures of treatment. SRR offers specific techniques for modifying anxiety and irrational beliefs and is implemented in four stages: presenting the rationale for the treatment to the clients; reviewing the irrationality of certain types of beliefs and assumptions; analysing the client's problems in terms of irrational thinking and undesirable self-talk; and teaching the client to modify self-talk and irrationality (e.g. Goldfried 1979).

Stress inoculation (Meichenbaum 1985) is a three-stage intervention which focuses on teaching cognitive and behavioural skills for coping with stressful situations. In the first, educational, phase, clients are taught a conceptual framework for understanding stress in cognitive terms. The second phase, skills training, teaches clients cognitive (imagery, changing irrational self-talk) and behavioural (relaxation, breathing) skills. In the final stage, clients practise the new skills in stressful situations.

Cognitive-behavioural training with children is designed to teach thinking skills (Kendall 1993; Kendall and Braswell 1993). For example, children who lack foresight and planning (e.g. impulsive, uncontrolled, hyperactive/attention disorder) are exposed to training procedures that involve the rehearsal of overt, then covert, self-guiding verbalizations. Using tasks and role-plays, the therapist and child practise thinking out loud.

Cognitive-behavioural therapies are consistent with therapeutic integration, where varying resources are tapped as sources of effective treatment. In one sense they are prototypical of integration: performance-based behavioural treatments with a focus on the cognitive representation, or meanings, of events and the merits of thinking; in other words, the purposeful interface of thought and action in psychotherapy.

Philip C. Kendall
Temple University

References

Beck, A. T., Rush, A. J., Shaw, B. F. and Emery, G. (1979) *Cognitive Therapy of Depression*, New York.

Ellis, A. (1980) 'Rational-emotive therapy and cognitive behavior therapy: similarities and differences', *Cognitive Therapy and Research* 4.

Goldfried, M. R. (1979) 'Anxiety reduction through cognitive-behavioral intervention', in P. C. Kendall and S. D. Hollon (eds) *Cognitive-Behavioral Interventions: Therapy, Research, and Procedures*, New York.

Kendall, P. C. (1993) 'Cognitive-behavioral therapies with youth', *Journal of Consulting and Clinical Psychology* 61.

Kendall, P. C. and Braswell, L. (1993) *Cognitive-Behavioral Therapy for Impulsive Children*, 2nd edn, New York.

Kendall, P. C. and Hollon, S. D. (1979) *Cognitive-Behavioral Interventions: Therapy, Research, and Procedures*, New York.

Kendall, P. C., Vitousek, K. B. and Kane, M. (1991) 'Thought and action in psychotherapy: cognitive-behavioral interventions', in M. Hersen, A. E. Kazdin and A. Bellack (eds) *The Clinical Psychology Handbook*, 2nd edn, New York.

Mahoney, J. M. (1977) 'Reflections on the cognitive learning trend in psychotherapy', *American Psychologist* 32.

Meichenbaum, D. (1985) *Stress Inoculation Training*, New York.

See also: behaviour therapy; clinical psychology; mental disorders.

cognitive psychology

According to Drever's (1964) *Dictionary of Psychology*, 'cognition' is 'a general term covering all the various modes of knowing – perceiving, imagining, conceiving, judging, reasoning'. It picks out those forms of abstract thinking and problem solving that are based upon the manipulation of either linguistic symbols (propositions) or iconic symbols (images). Cognitive psychology refers to the attempt to understand these various human faculties by means of systematic empirical observation and theory construction. Its origins lie in research conducted during the 1950s by Donald Broadbent, Jerome Bruner and George Miller (see Gardner 1985), although it was probably first generally acknowledged as a distinctive intellectual development with the publication of Ulric Neisser's (1967) book, *Cognitive Psychology*. It was also encouraged by cognate movements in other areas of psychology, such as the work by Jean Piaget and David Ausubel in developmental psychology and by Alan Newell and Herbert Simon in artificial intelligence. Cognitive psychology has in turn promoted developments in related areas of psychological research, of which cognitive neuropsychology is a notable example, and it is a central pillar of cognitive science.

The methods and theories of cognitive psychology have been influenced by two rather different traditions.

First, cognitive psychology is the natural heir to what used to be called 'human experimental psychology', and it has incorporated (perhaps too uncritically) the behaviourist methodology which dominated psychological research earlier in the twentieth century. It therefore involves most typically the objective description of human behaviour within formal laboratory experiments. These experiments usually seek to differentiate well-articulated theoretical alternatives within an established (though relatively narrow) research paradigm. This approach encourages a degree of artificiality in cognitive research, as it has always been recognized that the degree of naturalism in a laboratory study is likely to be inversely related to the extent to which the subjects' performance can be adequately described and to which the task itself can be conceptually analysed.

Cognitive psychology also stems from the field of human factors research which developed during the Second World War in order to tackle problems concerning human–machine interaction. This work led to an interest in the control mechanisms governing intelligent behaviour, to the idea of human thought and action as consisting of discrete stages of information processing, and inevitably to the use of the structure and function of the digital computer as a metaphor in theorizing about human cognition. (This is, of course, distinct from the use of the digital computer itself as a research tool.) An early though highly influential account of such notions was contained in Miller *et al.*'s (1960) *Plans and the Structure of Human Behavior*. Research carried out within this tradition is rather more pragmatic in its orientation: it aims to produce general frameworks which are of direct benefit in the design and construction of complex systems but which may not be amenable to rigorous experimental evaluation (Reason 1987).

Human cognition is undoubtedly a complex object of study, and researchers within cognitive psychology are faced with a number of options with regard to the most fruitful way to conduct their investigations. Eysenck (1984) identified three such decisions: the pursuit of basic or applied research; the focus upon general or specific problems; and the inclusion or exclusion of the motivational and emotional states of the subjects from their domain of analysis. Eysenck observed that the contemporary emphasis was upon 'basic research into specific problems that is conducted with a total disregard for emotional and motivational factors', although he for one has certainly been concerned to address issues concerning the role of emotional and motivational factors in human cognition.

Cognitive psychology does provide sophisticated theoretical accounts based upon experimental manip-ulations and procedures which have been extensively employed in laboratory-based research. However, there are various respects in which it has proved difficult to relate such research to practical issues, and Eysenck (1984) pointed to three interrelated problems. First, what is studied in laboratory research may be of little relevance to ordinary human functioning; second, laboratory research has very often ignored important characteristics of the cognition of everyday life; and third, at least some laboratory findings may not extrapolate to real-life events because of the artificiality of the experimental situation. Eysenck pointed out that the goal of laboratory-based research was not simply to mimic aspects of everyday cognitive functioning, but he concluded that genuine theoretical progress in cognitive psychology would be achieved only by means of a cross-fertilization between laboratory studies and more applied research.

Accounts of this sort given by cognitive psychologists themselves tend to assume that it is simply an empirical matter whether the cognitive processes that are being tapped in a particular psychological experiment are actually employed in the everyday task which the experiment is intended to model. Such an assumption is often made when the methods of cognitive psychology are criticized for their dubious 'ecological validity' (to use the prevalent jargon), for the latter tends to be regarded as a purely technical characteristic of particular experimental procedures. Whether or not a psychological experiment involves cognitive processes that are used in everyday life is then a matter to be settled by further empirical research. For instance, Yuille (1986) argued that laboratory-based research revealed little or nothing about the real-life functions of basic cognitive processes, but his criticisms of a purely experimental approach to the study of human cognition were based predominantly upon evidence obtained from formal laboratory experiments.

However, more radical critics have argued that the social situation of the psychological experiment is qualitatively different from the concrete tasks that confront individual human beings in their everyday lives. It is this point which is behind criticisms of the artificiality and worthlessness of laboratory experiments (Harré 1974). Some critics have pointed to the power relationships inherent in the experimental situation, and have put forward political and moral arguments concerning the effects of laboratory research upon both subjects and researchers (Heron 1981). Rowan (1981) suggested that experimental laboratory work exemplified the various forms of alienation which according to Marx would operate in any economic system where the workers (in this case, the subjects) did not own the means of production. There is thus perhaps a perverse sense in which laboratory experiments successfully (though unwittingly) capture certain aspects of the social situation of workplace, though certainly not of those situations in which individual human beings engage in autonomous and self-motivated cognition. Nevertheless, on this account, to compare the results of laboratory-based research either with the findings of applied studies or with 'natural history' observations would simply fail to set like against like (though Rowan included conventional forms of 'applied' research in his criticisms).

These criticisms are not trivial ones, and some call into question the whole enterprise of cognitive psychology. They clearly need to be addressed, perhaps by means of more sophisticated conceptual analyses, perhaps by means of theoretical developments, or perhaps by means of methodological innovations. However, many of these criticisms are already being addressed, and this in itself has led to significant advances within the field of cognitive psychology. In addition to the concern with practical applications which has always been inherent in the human factors tradition, the 1970s and 1980s saw a lively interest in accommodating mainstream research to the realities of everyday life, most obviously with regard to research on human memory (Gruneberg et al. 1978; 1988). Nowadays, most cognitive psychologists would agree that attention to the potential or actual applications of research is likely to provide a major impetus in the development and elaboration of theories and research within cognitive psychology itself.

John T. E. Richardson
Brunel University

References

Drever, J. (1964) *A Dictionary of Psychology*, rev. H. Wallerstein, Harmondsworth.

Eysenck, M. W. (1984) *A Handbook of Cognitive Psychology*, London.

Gardner, H. (1985) *The Mind's New Science: A History of the Cognitive Revolution*, New York.

Gruneberg, M. M., Morris, P. E. and Sykes, R. N. (1978) *Practical Aspects of Memory*, London.

—— (1988) *Practical Aspects of Memory: Current Research and Issues*, Chichester.

Harré, R. (1974) 'Some remarks on "rule" as a scientific concept', in T. Mischel (ed.) *Understanding Other Persons*, Oxford.

Heron, J. (1981) 'Philosophical basis for a new paradigm', in P. Reason and J. Rowan (eds) *Human Inquiry: A Sourcebook of New Paradigm Research*, Chichester.

Miller, G. A., Galanter, E. and Pribram, K. H. (1960) *Plans and the Structure of Human Behavior*, New York.

Neisser, U. (1967) *Cognitive Psychology*, New York.

Reason, J. (1987) 'Framework models of human performance and error: a consumer guide', in L. Goodstein, H. B. Anderson and S. E. Olsen (eds) *Tasks, Errors and Mental Models*, London.

Rowan, J. (1981) 'A dialectical paradigm for research', in P. Reason and J. Rowan (eds) *Human Inquiry: A Sourcebook of New Paradigm Research*, Chichester.

Yuille, J. C. (1986) 'The futility of a purely experimental psychology of cognition: imagery as a case study', in D. F. Marks (ed.) *Theories of Image Formation*, New York.

Further reading

Eysenck, M. W. and Keane, M. T. (1995) *Cognitive Psychology: A Student's Handbook*, 2nd edn, Hove.

Smyth, M. M., Morris, P. E., Levy, P. and Ellis, A. W. (1987) *Cognition in Action*, London.

See also: cognitive science; consciousness; memory; thinking.

cognitive science

The term cognitive science refers to the interdisciplinary study of information processing in human cognition. Although there are obvious precursors in the work of mathematicians such as Alan Turing and John von Neumann, of neurophysiologists such as Warren McCulloch and Walter Pitts, and of communications theorists such as Norbert Wiener and Claude Shannon, it is generally agreed that cognitive science came into being in 1956. This year marked the beginnings of genuine collaboration among research workers in artificial intelligence (Allen Newell and Herbert Simon), cognitive psychology (Jerome Bruner and George Miller), and linguistics (Noam Chomsky); Gardner (1985) has identified cognate movements in epistemology, anthropology, and the neurosciences. Kosslyn (1983) has summarized the manner in which cognitive science has taken advantage of developments in these different disciplines:

> From computer science it draws information about how computers and computer programs work; from philosophy it has adopted not only many of its basic questions and a general orientation toward the mind, but many of the fundamental ideas about information representation (e.g. 'propositions'); from linguistics it draws a basic way of thinking about mental events and theories of language; and from cognitive psychology it draws methodologies and specific findings about human information-processing abilities.

Cognitive science has been inspired very much by insights within the discipline of psychology, and in particular has developed in step with the field of cognitive psychology. However, it is intrinsically at odds with much of mainstream cognitive psychology, which grew out of what used to be called 'human experimental psychology', and which has incorporated the behaviourist methodology which dominated research earlier this century. Cognitive science owes rather more to the 'human factors' tradition within cognitive psychology, which developed during the Second World War in order to tackle problems concerning human–machine interaction. An illustration of the disparity between cognitive psychologists and cognitive scientists arises in their attitudes to introspective reports of conscious experience. Cognitive psychologists tend to be suspicious of introspective reports and sceptical of their value as empirical data, whereas in cognitive science the use and analysis of such verbal 'protocols' is widely accepted (see, e.g. Ericsson and Simon 1984). As an excellent case study within the field of cognitive science, Kosslyn (1983) has given an autobiographical account of his work on mental imagery, which combines systematic experimentation with introspectionist methodology.

Gardner (1985) has identified two core assumptions in contemporary research in cognitive science. The first assumption is that to explain intelligent behaviour it is necessary to incorporate the idea of 'internal' or 'mental' representations as a distinctive and irreducible level of theoretical analysis. Indeed, theories in cognitive science are often based upon the structuralist notion that internal representations intervene between experience and behaviour. Human cognition is regarded as the symbolic manipulation of stored information, and in order to understand intelligent human behaviour, it is necessary to investigate the properties of these internal representations and of the processes that operate upon them. Nevertheless, it should be noted that sociologists have argued that descriptions of mental experience are socially constructed and are at the very least problematic as explanations of behaviour (see Woolgar 1987).

The second core assumption is that the computer is a useful model of human thought and a valuable research tool. Precisely because digital computers are artefactual systems that have been specifically designed for the symbolic manipulation of stored information, the language of computer science seems to provide a convenient and congenial means of articulating notions concerning human cognition. As Kosslyn (1983) has noted, cognitive scientists have therefore borrowed much of the vocabulary that was originally developed to talk about computer functioning and use it to talk about mental representation and processing in human beings. Indeed, the language of computer science tends to function as a theoretical *lingua franca* among the variety of disciplines that make up cognitive science; as Levy (1987) has put it, the computational representation of models is the 'common test-bed' of cognitive science. Of course, the contemporary digital computer may not provide the best model for characterizing

human information processing, and alternative system architectures may prove to be more useful (Kosslyn 1983): a very fashionable approach based upon the notion of parallel distributed processing is claimed to be much more appropriate for modelling human cognition because it is more akin to the known physiology of the central nervous system (McClelland *et al.* 1986). Nevertheless, the supposed functional similarity between computers and human brains provides a distinctive means of evaluating the theories of cognitive science: the computer simulation of behaviour. The point has been elegantly summarized by Kosslyn (1983):

> If the brain and computer both can be described as manipulating symbols in the same way, then a good theory of mental events should be able to be translated into a computer program, and if the theory is correct, then the program should lead the computer to produce the same overt responses that a person would in various circumstances.

A fundamental criticism of research in cognitive science is that it has tended to view cognition in abstract terms, devoid of any personal, social or ecological significance. As Gardner (1985) remarks, cognitive science tends to exclude (or at least to de-emphasize) 'the influence of affective factors or emotions, the contribution of historical and cultural factors, and the role of the background context in which particular actions or thoughts occur'. Gardner implies that this feature of cognitive science is the result of a deliberate strategic decision in order to render the problems under investigation more tractable. However, it has to be recognized that the pattern of much research within cognitive science (as in other areas of scholarly investigation) is set by existing traditions, and therefore such strategic choices have typically gone by default. The relevance of cognitive science to everyday human experience and its practical application in real-life situations will undoubtedly be enhanced by the incorporation of emotional, cultural and contextual factors into theoretical accounts of human cognition.

John T. E. Richardson
Brunel University

References

Ericsson, K. A. and Simon, H. A. (1984) *Protocol Analysis: Verbal Reports as Data*, Cambridge, MA.

Gardner, H. (1985) *The Mind's New Science: A History of the Cognitive Revolution*, New York.

Kosslyn, S. M. (1983) *Ghosts in the Mind's Machine: Creating and Using Images in the Brain*, New York.

Levy, P. (1987) 'Modelling cognition: some current issues', in P. Morris (ed.) *Modelling Cognition*, Chichester.

McClelland, J. L., Rumelhart, D. E. and Hinton, G. E. (1986)

'The appeal of parallel distributed processing', in D. E. Rumelhart, J. L. McClelland and the PDP Research Group, *Parallel Distributed Processing: Explorations in the Microstructure of Cognition*, vol. 1, Cambridge, MA.

Woolgar, S. (1987) 'Reconstructing man and machine: a note on sociological critiques of cognitivism', in W. E. Bijker, T. P. Hughes and T. Pinch (eds) *The Social Construction of Technological Systems*, Cambridge, MA.

See also: cognitive psychology.

cohort analysis

Cohort analysis (also known as longitudinal analysis) refers to studies that measure characteristics of cohorts through their lives, a cohort being a group of persons who have experienced the same life event during a specified period of time (normally one year). If the life event is birth, one speaks of a birth cohort, or generation. Similarly one may speak of marriage cohorts, divorce cohorts, educational cohorts, etc., life events in these cases being respectively marriage, divorce, or the attainment of a certain level of education, during a particular period of time. For instance one may follow a cohort of marriages over time in order to ascertain how many couples eventually divorce, and to determine the risk of divorcing at each duration of marriage.

Cohort data are usually obtained by comparing the characteristics of a cohort at two or more points in time, using census or sample survey data. When the *same* individuals are compared, the term 'panel study' is often used. Demographic and epidemiological data on cohorts can frequently be derived from records or registers, such as vital statistics or cancer registers. Other important sources of cohort data are retrospective studies, in which respondents are asked to provide information about past characteristics and events.

Cohort data may be affected by selection effects. People die, or move, between censuses or surveys, and retrospective questions can be answered only by those who survive. Bias may be introduced if those who are lost tend to have other characteristics that differentiate them from those interviewed. Retrospective studies are also influenced by recall lapses.

Cohort measures may relate to the characteristics of the cohort, or to events experienced by it. For example, an inter-cohort study might compare the proportions of single people in different cohorts, or focusing on birth, compare the average number of children borne by women at the end of their reproductive period. An intra-cohort study would be concerned rather with changes in characteristics over a lifetime, or in the distribution of events by age, such as changes in the proportion surviving by age, or the distribution of deaths or risks of dying by age.

Cohort studies are often undertaken in order to distinguish cohort effects (i.e. effects particular to each cohort) from age (or duration) effects and period effects. Ordinary statistical methods are unsatisfactory here, due to the *identification problem*. Age, period and cohort (APC) are not independent variables: knowing two yields the third. The three variables cannot therefore be used simultaneously in statistical procedures that require linear independence between variables. One way out of this difficulty is to place constraints on the model, for example to suppose that one of the effects (e.g. the period effect) is nil, or that the effect of being in one age group is a particular constant. APC models, moreover, do not usually incorporate terms measuring interaction effects between age and cohort, or between period and cohort. Alternatively, the period variable (such as the year), may be used as an indicator of an underlying variable, for example, yearly income per head. If data are available, one may then substitute the underlying variable for the year. This is a simple resolution of the identification problem, as the underlying variable is not a linear construct of age and cohort. The choice of the procedure or constraint must rest on supplementary information, or on an appeal to theoretical considerations: it cannot be made on purely statistical grounds.

Guillaume Wunsch
University of Louvain

Further reading

Glenn, N. D. (1977) *Cohort Analysis, Quantitative Applications in the Social Sciences*, Beverly Hills, CA.

Wunsch, G. (ed.) (1993) 'Cohort analysis of vital processes,' in D. J. Bogue, E. E. Arriaga and D. L. Anderton (eds) *Readings in Population Research Methodology*, vol. 5, Chicago.

See also: event-history analysis; life tables and survival analysis.

collective action

Unlike rational individuals who act to fulfil their own self-interest, a group of rational actors may not engage in collective action to pursue a common interest. Groups often value collective or public goods that are available, once they are produced, to contributors and non-contributors alike. As people can potentially receive the benefits of these collective goods without paying for them, they will not readily contribute to their provision.

The logic of collective action (Olson 1965), which has proved applicable to a remarkably broad range of social and economic situations, proceeds from the assumption that co-operation must be explained in terms of the individual's cost-benefit calculus rather than the group's, because the group is not itself rational, but can only consist of rational individuals. In the classic examples of collective action problems, such as preserving the environment, sharing a common natural resource, participating in national defence, voting in mass elections, and engaging in social protests, group members gain when all individuals do their share, but the marginal benefit of a single contribution is outweighed by its cost. What is best for the group therefore is not necessarily best for the individual. The study of collective action using laboratory experiments, game theory, and historical cases has tried to identify the conditions under which rational actors are likely to co-operate when they have a strong incentive to be free riders.

The collective action problem is most often represented by a game theoretic model known as the prisoners' dilemma (Hardin 1982). The prisoners' dilemma is a non-co-operative game in which the players' choices are independent and agreements and promises cannot be enforced. A group of n individuals must decide to contribute (i.e. co-operate) or not to contribute to a collective good (i.e. defect). Depending on whether the public good is divisible, the utility of a contribution is either the additional amount of the good that is produced or it is the increase in the probability that an indivisible public good will be generated as a result of the contribution. Unanimous co-operation is preferred by everyone to unanimous defection, but the payoff structure of the game also specifies that no matter how many individuals contribute, each person does better by defecting and thereby enjoying the public good for free; in this sense, defection is a dominant strategy. However, should each rational individual choose his or her dominant strategy, the outcome – total defection – is Pareto-suboptimal, for everyone can improve his or her position if all co-operate in the supply of the public good.

A group may succeed in providing itself with some amount of the public good if it is 'privileged'; that is, if it contains a single member who receives a sufficiently large benefit from the good that it is economical for the person to pay for it even if no one else contributes. In Mancur Olson's (1965) terminology, this results in the exploitation of the great by the small. Groups that are not privileged have to devise other means to encourage contributions, either by changing the incentive structure facing individuals, or by inducing co-operative behavior through repeated social interaction.

Many groups alter cost-benefit calculations by offering selective incentives in the form of rewards to co-operators and punishments to free riders. Members of professional organizations, for example, receive trade publications and journals, reduced fare travel packages, subsidized health insurance programmes, and other products or services. Shame, praise, honour and ostracism can likewise be viewed, in this regard, as non-material social selective incentives. The provision of selective incentives, however, usually entails a separate collective action problem that demands its own explanation, as successful organization for collective ends characteristically precedes the provision of selective incentives to members.

Another potential selective incentive is the benefit inherent in the activity itself, in which case the motivation behind co-operation is not the outcome sought by collective action, but the process or experience of participation (Hirschman 1982). It is undeniable that, for some people, political and organizational activity builds self-esteem and feelings of political efficacy, symbolizes political citizenship, reinforces moral convictions, and constitutes an enthralling experience. The non-instrumental nature of these motives, however, makes them problematic in theories of instrumental rational action.

Aside from changing the incentive structure of the prisoners' dilemma (thus removing the dilemma), co-operation in groups can be fostered, in the absence of selective incentives, by repeated social interactions that introduce long-term calculations (Taylor 1987). In iterated social interaction, a person can try to influence the behaviour of others by making his or her choices contingent upon their earlier choices. In a two-person prisoners' dilemma, for example, a person might co-operate on the first exchange and thereafter co-operate only if the other player co-operated on the previous exchange. If both players use this strategy – known as tit for tat – mutual co-operation will be the equilibrium outcome as long as future benefits are not discounted too heavily. Co-operation is therefore possible among self-interested players if they care sufficiently about future payoffs to modify their present behaviour.

Ongoing social interaction is less likely to solve the collective action problem when the group is large because defection is harder to identify and to deter when many people are involved. One possible equilibrium in the n-person prisoners' dilemma occurs when everyone co-operates initially and continues to do so as long as everyone else does, but not otherwise. Co-operation is therefore sustained by the expectation that, as soon as one person defects, everyone else defects in retaliation. A less stringent equilibrium occurs when there is a subset of co-operators, some proportion of which co-operates contingent upon the co-operation of every other member of the subset. These equilibria, how-ever, may be difficult to realize in practice if threats of disbanding given a single or a small number of defectors are not credible. Such is the case, for example, when the remaining co-operators can still profitably produce the collective good, so that they would have to hurt themselves in order to punish free riders. Incredible threats open the door to mass defection: if some individuals free ride on the assumption that others will continue to provide the collective good, then everybody might be so tempted and the collective good may never be produced.

For this reason, contingent co-operation in large-scale ventures is facilitated when collective action comprises a federated network of community groups and organizations. Monitoring is feasible in these smaller groups and co-operation or defection can be rewarded or punished in the course of everyday inter-action with friends and associates. Consequently, individuals who refuse to contribute to a community-wide effort may suffer damage to their reputations and lose companionship and future opportunities for bene-ficial exchanges with those in their immediate reference groups (Chong 1991).

There is no reason to suppose that successful collec-tive action will be driven by a single motivation, either coercive or voluntary. Self-interested calculations based on selective material incentives and ongoing social exchange often have to be supplemented by moral and psychological considerations in order for people to contribute to collective goods. Nor is it neces-sary to assume that all contributors to collective action will employ the same cost-benefit calculus. Collective action frequently relies on the initiative of committed leaders who supply information, resources and monitoring, and lay the foundation for subsequent conditional co-operation among more narrowly self-interested actors.

Dennis Chong
Northwestern University

References

Chong, D. (1991) *Collective Action and the Civil Rights Movement*, Chicago.
Hardin, R. (1982) *Collective Action*, Baltimore, MD.
Hirschman, A. (1982) *Shifting Involvements*, Princeton, NJ.
Olson, M. (1965) *The Logic of Collective Action*, Cambridge, UK.
Taylor, M. (1987) *The Possibility of Cooperation*, Cambridge, UK.

Further reading

Axelrod, R. (1984) *The Evolution of Cooperation*, New York.
Elster, J. (1989) *The Cement of Society*, Cambridge, UK.
Rapoport, A. and Chammah, A. M. (1965) *Prisoner's Dilemma*, Ann Arbor, MI.

See also: prisoners' dilemma.

colonialism

When most of the world's colonial dependencies attained independence as sovereign nation-states in the middle of the twentieth century, it seemed that an epoch had ended logically as well as historically. Colonies had been particular forms of imperialism, created during the tide of western European expansion into other continents and oceans from the sixteenth century onwards. At high noon – the end of the nine-teenth century – almost every society outside Europe had become or had been the colony of a western European state. Colonialism began as a series of crude ventures. Whether by force or by treaty, sovereignty was seized, and exercised by governors responsible to foreign states. If indigenous rulers were retained, they mainly veiled the reality of power. As colonial states became more secure and elaborate, they intruded more pervasively into the daily life of subject popula-tions; popular resentment seemed to foreshadow the gradual transfer of governmental machinery to indige-nous nationalist leaders.

The actual outcomes were much less orderly. Dislodged or dislocated by the Second World War, and assailed by the United Nations rhetoric of national self-determination, many colonial states in South and South-east Asia passed without ceremony into the hands of nationalists; several in Africa negotiated independence before they had trained indigenous bureaucracies; others had to mount and endure sus-tained warfare to reach the same goal; and yet others – usually islands with small populations – chose to remain dependencies, with rights of individual entry into the former metropolitan country. A few fragments were retained by metropolitan powers, either as conve-niently remote nuclear testing facilities or as significant entrepôts. Despite this messy variety, most scholars believed that a logical narrative had come to an end: western colonialism, born in the sixteenth century and maturing until the twentieth, had reached its apothe-osis in the sovereign states which succeeded them and took their places in the community of nations.

Yet colonialism continues to fascinate social scien-tists, both applied and theoretical. The successor-states were often bounded by arbitrary frontiers which exacerbated ethnic identities, and were vulnerable to the rivalries of the Cold War. Brave attempts to generate solidarity on the basis of the whole Third World, or even more modest efforts such as Afri-can unity, failed to reorient the ex-colonies' long-established links with the former metropolitan powers. Their inherited bureaucracies were better equipped to control than to mobilize the populace, and their formal economies were well designed to export unprocessed commodities. Their scanty education and training institutions could not immediately cope with the rising expectations of burgeoning populations. Independence was expected to liberate national energies in escaping from underdevelopment and backwardness, in pursuit of development and modernization. The United Nations Development Decade focused international attention on these goals, and academic centres of development studies graduated platoons of experts to assist in achieving them by finding technical solutions.

Few ex-colonies responded as planned, to strategies of agricultural intensification and economic diversification. Most of tropical Africa and some other parts of the world have performed so poorly that they have, in effect, retired from the global economy, their peoples committed to environmentally dubious practices in order to survive, their cities swelling and their recurrent budgets dependent upon aid flows. These catastrophes contrast sharply with the performance of the economic tigers of South-east and East Asia, whose success owes rather little to the advice of development experts. In either case, the imperatives of economic development legitimized authoritarian styles of government, which often adopted and elaborated the colonial structures of control in ways which hardly meet the old criteria of modernization.

These disconcerting tendencies add grist to the post-modernist mill and its critique of academic positivism. Stage theories of human progress have suffered especially badly at the hands of post-modern writers. Colonialism was not, after all, an aberration. Some see it as inherent in the western Enlightenment, quoting (for example) John Locke's opinion that 'God gave the world to men in Common, but since He gave it them for their benefit and the greatest conveniencies of life they were capable to draw from it, it cannot be supposed He meant it should always remain common and uncultivated. He gave it to the use of the industrious and rational'. Edward Said's (1978) seminal *Orientalism*, and the Subaltern Studies pioneered and elaborated by expatriate South Asian scholars (Guha 1994), insist that colonialism was neither a finite era nor a particular set of governmental mechanisms. The desired achievement of post-colonialism therefore requires a great deal more than the application of technical solutions to discrete problems. Colonial apologetics and the triumphalist narratives of anti-colonial nationalism are portrayed as two sides of the same coin, alternative stage theories of social evolution which distort rather than illuminate past and present human experience. Only their deconstruction may exorcise colonialism's diffuse influences in the minds and practices of subalterns and superiors alike.

Just as colonialism has been applied beyond its earlier chronological limits, so it has burst its conventional boundaries in space. Ethnic identities which survived the homogenizing pressures of the modern nation-state have been unleashed by the end of the Cold War. When communities seek shelter from open competition, in solidarities which transcend market relations, ethnic identities are reasserted and historic charters invoked. Whether the immediate demands are political recognition and decentralized institutions, or land rights or other tangible benefits, the spectre of ethnic nationalism walks abroad, wearing the bloody robe of colonialism. Curiously, this extension of the term's application severs the ties with capitalism and imperialism, and brings it closer to an earlier usage, whereby the movement of any group of settlers into territory claimed or occupied by others could be described quite interchangeably as colonialism or colonization.

Donald Denoon
Australian National University

Further reading

Guha, R. (ed.) (1994) *Subaltern Studies: Writings on South Asian History and Society*, 2 vols, Delhi.
Said, E. (1978) *Orientalism*, New York.

See also: imperialism; plural society.

committees

The most notable committees are those that help govern nations – cabinet committees, legislative assemblies, party committees, and higher courts. But there are also boards of directors of corporations, labour union councils, state or provincial assemblies, and city councils, all of which are involved in governance. The term committee normally refers to a face-to-face group of people who arrive at a decision through some means of polling member opinions. The types of committees mentioned have a firm institutional grounding and will have well-defined means of voting the issues that come before them. Their decisions have a semi-binding nature to them, perhaps subject to appeals or approvals elsewhere.

In contrast, there are many committees that are no more than advisory in nature, acting as a source of information for an administrator, a supervisor, or even a larger organization. For a larger organization, advisory committees offer a division of work, specialization, and economies of scale. For a single administrator or supervisor, advisory committees offer balanced judgement and a diversification of information sources beyond the ordinary chain-of-command. The growth of the seemingly infinite variety of committee organization and function has in many ways marked a decline in the traditional efficient chain-of-command method of conducting business. In a purely practical sense, technology has made it easier for committees to function effectively. Duplicating services and electronic transmission have made it more convenient to share information and communication and to arrange for meetings. Transportation advances have also facilitated the convening of committees.

The study of committees has progressed in two directions: in the study of single committees and in the study of committee systems. The study of single committees has concentrated on the justification of their use and voting strategies of members (see, e.g. Black 1958), or on the substantive decision making norms of very important groups. There has been increased attention given to committee systems, primarily in relation to legislatures. An eight-nation study of committee systems in national legislatures was completed in 1979 by Lees and Shaw which tried to determine the significance of the various committee systems in relation to other decision-making foci. The study confirmed, for example, as others suspected, that committee systems have the most central role in US legislatures, while political parties have a weaker role.

The organizers of committee systems are faced with several decisions: how to divide up the subject matter; how many committees; how many members on each committee; how many committee assignments per member; how much authority to delegate; and whether or not to have subcommittees within committees. In representative bodies, small committees sacrifice representativeness, yet they may be necessary under a heavy agenda (Francis 1989). The US Congress and state legislatures legislate through committees, and in Congress, the committees legislate through subcommittees. In other words, in the latter case, the subcommittees debate the subject before the committees deal with it. In Britain, India and Canada, the issues are debated on the floor before they are assigned to committee. In essence, committee systems are becoming complex forms of organization, and serve as an ample challenge in future theories of decision making.

Wayne L. Francis
University of Florida

References

Black, D. (1958) *The Theory of Committees and Elections*, Cambridge, UK.

Francis, W. L. (1989) *The Legislative Committee Game*, Columbus, OH.

Lees, J. D. and Shaw, M. (eds) (1979) *Committees in Legislatures*, Durham, NC.

Further reading

Eulau, H. and McCluggage, V. (1984) 'Standing committees in legislatures', *Legislative Studies Quarterly*.

Sibley, J. H. (ed.) (1994) *Encyclopedia of the American Legislative System*, New York.

commodity stabilization schemes

Schemes for the stabilization of primary commodity prices have always been an important item on the agenda of international policy discussions. This is because the prices of these commodities are volatile, and because exports of them are large sources of revenue for many countries, particularly those of the Third World. One of the most famous schemes was proposed by Keynes in 1942, as a companion to his International Clearing Union (which later became the IMF). Keynes's argument for commodity price stabilization led to political opposition from those opposed to market intervention and had to be shelved. More recently the same fate has befallen the Integral Program for Commodities put forward by UNCTAD (the United Nations Conference on Trade and Development). Those schemes which exist have developed in a piecemeal fashion. 'Only [schemes for] wheat, sugar, tea and coffee have lasted a number of years, and few appear to have achieved much before their demise' (MacBean and Snowden 1981).

Price stabilization is usually put forward as a means of stabilizing the incomes of producers and consumers. It could also be used as a means of raising the average incomes of producers, but would then need to be buttressed by quota schemes to restrict production.

Price stabilization will normally succeed in stabilizing revenues to producers in the face of shifts in demand for commodities of the kind which occur because of the world business cycle. The managers of the scheme need to operate some kind of buffer stock. When demand is high, the extra can be satisfied by sales from the buffer stock: producers' revenue is unaltered by the demand increase. The reverse is true when demand falls. Stabilization of prices will, it is true, allow fluctuations in producers' incomes to remain in the face of fluctuations in the quantity produced, as a result, say, of changes in harvests. However, without stabilization of prices, producers' incomes might be even more unstable, if good harvest produced very large falls in prices (and vice versa). Price stabilization will also isolate consumers of primary commodities from shocks to the purchasing power of their incomes in a wide variety of circumstances.

Economists differ in their assessment of the benefits to be obtained from such stabilization of prices.

Newbery and Stiglitz (1981) have argued, in a powerful modern study, that the benefits to producers are small. Newbery and Stiglitz would clearly be correct if producers could adjust their spending in line with fluctuations in their income. However, they ignore the great hardships which could arise when primary commodity producers (both individuals and nations) have to make unexpected cuts in expenditures. Such hardships will indeed arise when average incomes are not much above subsistence or when the revenue from sales of primary commodities is used to pay for development projects which are hard to stop and start at will. Newbery and Stiglitz also argue that the potential benefits to consumers would be small. But they largely ignore the inflationary difficulties for consumers which primary-commodity-price instability creates, and it was those which concerned Keynes. It must be admitted that contemporary proponents of primary commodity price stabilization schemes have been slow to produce good evidence about the size of those effects which Newbery and Stiglitz ignore.

There are fundamental difficulties in the way of setting up any stabilization scheme. It is necessary to choose not only the price level at which stabilization is to take place, but also the optimum size for the buffer stock. An obvious candidate for the price level is one which would balance supply with demand, averaging over the normal fluctuations in both supply and demand. But the amount of information required accurately to determine this price would be formidable for most commodities. As for the buffer stock, it should presumably be able to deal with the normal fluctuations in supply and demand. But in order to avoid running absurdly large stocks the objective of *complete* price stabilization would need to be abandoned, at least in extreme circumstances. Even so, the cost of operating the required buffer stock might be very large for many commodities. It is thus easy to see why those stabilization schemes which have been established have always been on the verge of breaking down.

David Vines
University of Glasgow

References

MacBean, A. I. and Snowden, P. N. (1981) *International Institutions in Trade and Finance*, London.

Newbery, D. M. G. and Stiglitz, J. E. (1981) *The Theory of Commodity Price Stabilization: A Study on the Economics of Risk*, Oxford.

communication networks

A network can be defined as a particular type of relation that links a set of people or objects, called the nodes of the network (Wasserman and Faust 1994). A communication network is a structure that is built on the basis of communication relationships between individuals, groups, organizations or societies. A networks perspective is a distinct research tradition within the social and behavioural sciences because it is based on the assumption that the attitudes and behaviours of the nodes (be they individuals or collectives) are significantly enabled or constrained by the networks in which they are embedded.

Communication networks have been studied in various social systems and at differing levels of analysis. At the *intrapersonal level*, research has shown that individuals who have similar positions in the organization's network are more likely to have similar cognitions about the firm's products and processes (Krackhardt 1987; Pattison 1995; Walker 1985). In the area of *interpersonal relations*, researchers have shown that the degree of overlap between individuals' networks positively influences the development and stability of romantic relationships (Bott 1971; Parks and Adelman 1983). Research has also shown that an individual's interpersonal and community networks serve an important social support role in overcoming difficult life events (Albrecht and Adelman 1984; Wellman and Wortley 1990). In the context of small group behaviour, studies have shown that characteristics of the network's structure have a significant impact on the performance and satisfaction of group members involved in problem solving (Collins and Raven 1969; Shaw 1964). Considerable research has been conducted on communication and information flow in production, innovation, and informal social networks *within organizations*. For instance, Monge *et al.* (1983) showed that proximity, propensity to communicate, and commitment to the organization were important antecedents to the involvement of individuals in organizational networks. Researchers have noted that individuals' decisions to adopt new communication technologies are significantly predicted by the decisions of others in their communication network. Inversely, the adoption of new communication technologies significantly alters individuals' communication networks (Burkhardt and Brass 1990; Contractor and Eisenberg 1990). Likewise, there is a rapidly growing literature on the communication linkages among *inter-organizational* systems (Eisenberg *et al.* 1983; Mizruchi and Schwartz 1987). For instance, Galaskiewicz and Burt (1991) report that corporate decisions about making a philanthropic donation to specific non-profit organizations are positively influenced by the decisions of other donating officers in their inter-organizational communication network. At the broader *societal and cultural levels*, Rogers and Kincaid (1981) describe the uses of network analysis for the diffusion of ideas. Typical of this approach is their analysis of the communication patterns for the diffusion of family planning among sixty-nine women in a Korean village. These examples all employ 'people' as the nodes of the communication network, but this need not be the case. For example, Rice *et al.* (1988) used communication network analysis to demonstrate the influence of citation patterns among core journals in the field of communication.

Monge (1987) notes that two major objectives of network analysis are network articulation and metrics. In network articulation, individuals are assigned to various network role classifications such as clique member, liaison, and isolate. Liaisons do not belong to particular groups but have information linkages with people in two or more groups; they frequently figure importantly in linking groups together. As the name implies, isolates have few, if any, connections within the network. Research has shown that liaisons, isolates, and group members have different characteristics and function quite differently in communication networks (Monge and Eisenberg 1987). Network metrics refers to quantitative indices of various aspects of the network. The most frequently studied indices include density and centrality (Knoke and Kuklinski 1982). The density of a network is the ratio of the number of observed links connecting nodes to the number of possible links between the nodes. A node is central in a network if it is connected to nodes that are not directly connected to each other.

Techniques for observing communication networks are many and varied (Monge and Contractor 1988). Often people are asked to recall their interactions with all other network members and to report the frequency, duration and importance of these contacts. In some studies, participants have been asked to keep diaries of their interactions during a given time period. In other research, participant-observers have logged the frequency of interactions among people in an organization. In one interesting series of studies, Milgram (1967) asked people to send a message to an unknown target by sending it through someone they knew personally. That process was repeated at each step until a person was eventually found who knew the target and delivered the message. An average of seven steps was required to reach the target. Bernard and Killworth (1980) collected data about the communication networks among ham radio operators by recording their public dialogue on the radio waves. Another example is the work of Rice (1995), who describes the use of computer-mediated communication systems to record the frequency and duration of communication linkages among individuals.

Analysis of communication network data, whether network articulation or metrics, is too unwieldy to be undertaken without a computer. While many network researchers write their own programs, there are a handful of network analysis and graphics packages available for use on microcomputers (for a review, see Wasserman and Faust 1994). The programs differ considerably in terms of the assumptions that they make about network data, objectives of the analysis, and computational algorithms.

Networks perspectives have emerged as an influential intellectual force in the social and behavioural sciences. While individual attributes (such as an individual's gender, age and education) are important sources of explanation for human behaviour, a number of social theorists (e.g. Burt 1982; 1992) have argued that they are incomplete and, in some cases, misleading. These theorists suggest that there are group and social phenomena that cannot be explained by the attributes of its constituents. In such cases, a networks perspective with its focus on the relationships between the constituents offers unique insights into collective phenomena.

Peter R. Monge
University of Southern California

Noshir S. Contractor
University of Illinois
at Urbana-Champaign

References

Albrecht, T. L. and Adelman, M. B. (1984) 'Social support and life stress: new directions for communication research', *Human Communication Research 11.*

Bernard, H. H. and Killworth, P. D. (1980) 'Informant accuracy in social network data IV: a comparison of the clique-level structure in behavioral and cognitive network data', *Social Networks* 2.

Burt, R. S. (1982) *Toward a Structural Theory of Action*, New York.

—— (1992) *Structural Holes: The Social Structure of Competition*, Cambridge, MA.

Collins, B. E. and Raven, B. H. (1969) 'Group structure: attraction, coalitions, communication, and power', in G. Lindsey and E. Aronson (eds) *The Handbook of Social Psychology* 2nd edn, Reading, MA.

Contractor, N. S. and Eisenberg, E. M. (1990) 'Communication networks and new media in organizations', in J. Fulk and C. Steinfield (eds) *Organizations and Communication Technology*, Newbury Park, CA.

Eisenberg, E. M., Farace, R. V., Monge, P. R., Bettinghaus, E. P., Kurchner-Hawkins, R., Miller, K. I. and White, L. (1983) 'Communication linkages in interorganizational systems: review and synthesis', in B. Dervin and M. Voight (eds) *Progess in Communication Science*, vol. 6, Norwood, NJ.

Galaskiewicz, J. and Burt, R. (1991) 'Interorganization contagion in corporate philanthropy', *Administrative Science Quarterly 36.*

Knoke, D. and Kuklinski, J. H. (1982) *Network analysis*, Newbury Park, CA.

Krackhardt, D. (1987) 'Cognitive social structures', *Social Networks 9*.

Milgram, S. (1967) 'The small world problem', *Psychology Today 1*.

Mizruchi, M. S. and Schwartz, M. (1987) *Intercorporate Relations: The Structural Analysis of Business*, Cambridge, UK.

Monge, P. R. (1987) 'The network level of analysis', in C. R. Berger and S. H. Chaffee (eds) *Handbook of Communication Science* Newbury Park, CA.

Monge, P. R. and Contractor, N. S. (1988) 'Measurement techniques for the study of communication networks', in C. Tardy (ed.) *A Handbook for the Study of Human Communication: Methods and Instruments for Observing, Measuring, and Assessing Communication Processes*, Norwood, NJ.

Monge, P. R. and Eisenberg, E. M. (1987) 'Emergent communication networks', in F. Jablin, L. Putnam and L. Porter (eds) *Handbook of Organizational Communication*, Newbury Park, CA.

Monge, P. R., Edwards, J. A. and Kirste, K. K. (1983) 'Determinants of communication network involvement: connectedness and integration', *Group and Organizational Studies 8*.

Parks, M. R. and Adelman, M. B. (1983) 'Communication networks and the development of romantic relationships', *Human Communication Research 10*.

Pattison, P. (1995) 'Social cognition in context: some applications of social network analysis', in S. Wasserman and J. Galaskiewicz (eds) *Advances in the Social and Behavioral Sciences from Social Network Analysis*, Newbury Park, CA.

Rice, R. E. (1995) 'Network analysis and computer-mediated communication systems', in S. Wasserman and J. Galaskiewicz (eds) *Advances in the Social and Behavioral Sciences from Social Network Analysis*, Newbury Park, CA.

Rice, R. E., Borgman, C. L. and Reeves, B. (1988) 'Citation networks of communication journals, 1977–1985: cliques and positions, citations made and citations received', *Human Communication Research 15*

Rogers, E. M. and Kincaid, D. L. (1981) *Communication Networks: Toward a New Paradigm for Research*, New York.

Shaw, M. E. (1964) 'Communication networks', in L. Berkowitz (ed.) *Advances in Experimental Social Psychology*, vol. 1, New York.

Walker, G. (1985) 'Network position and cognition in a computer software firm', *Administrative Science Quarterly 30*.

Wasserman, S. and Faust, K. (1994) *Social Network Analysis: Methods and Applications*, Cambridge, UK.

Wellman, B. and Wortley, S. (1990) 'Different strokes from different folks: community ties and social support', *American Journal of Sociology 96*.

See also: communications; globalization; information society; mass media; social networks; sociology of science.

communication, non-verbal *see* non-verbal communication

communications

The social scientific study of human communication began during the late 1930s in the USA (Delia 1987). Schramm (1983) attributes the birth of this movement to four scholars: the political scientist, Harold Lasswell, the sociologist, Paul Lazarsfeld, and the social psychologists, Kurt Lewin and Carl Hovland. Though the parentage of any scholarly movement is bound to be ambiguous, many communication researchers would doubtless concur with Schramm's attribution, for these four pioneers not only authored much of the early influential communication research, but were also responsible for training a second generation of scholars who carried on their work.

The work of two of these founders, Lasswell and Lazarsfeld, centred almost exclusively on the impact of mass media on public information and attitudes, with some of Hovland's work at Yale University focusing on the same problem (see Hovland *et al.* 1949). Katz and Lazarsfeld (1955) note that the early traditions of communication research focused either on the media of public communication as instruments of clandestine manipulation or hope for them as agencies of social integration. Scholars in both traditions forwarded the 'hypodermic needle' model of media effects, positing that the media could 'inject' new information and attitudes into individual citizens in much the same way as a doctor could inject serum into a patient. As a result of the classic election studies conducted in the 1940s by Lazarsfeld and his colleagues (1948), a different, less communicatively hegemonous view of the mass media emerged, one positing that the media transmitted information to opinion leaders who, in turn, employed it to influence others in face-to-face settings – a process labelled 'the two-step flow hypothesis'. Although later research revealed that both the hypodermic needle model and the two-step flow hypothesis were oversimplified explanations of the impact of mass media on individual attitudes and behaviours, these two notions exerted a strong influence on the thinking of mass communication researchers for several decades.

During roughly the same period, Lewin was conducting his famous studies at the University of Iowa concerning the effects of group decision making (Lewin 1958) and group leadership (Lewin 1939; Lippitt and White 1943) on the productivity and morale of group members, studies motivated at least partially by his repugnance for the fascist regimes emerging in Germany and Italy. With the advent of the Second World War, concern for ways of mounting effective public information campaigns against these Axis powers spawned the remarkably fruitful programme of research on communication and persuasion carried out by Hovland and his associates at Yale, a programme that produced an influential set of volumes which began appearing around the mid-1900s (Rosenberg *et al.* 1960; Sherif and Hovland 1961). Their work influenced communication researchers interested in the areas of small group communication and persuasion.

As the preceding chronicle suggests, most ground-breaking early work was problem-oriented and was conducted by scholars of varying disciplinary commitments. Communication did not emerge as an academic discipline until the late 1940s, one of the earliest signs of its emergence being the establishment, in 1947, of the Institute of Communications Research at the University of Illinois under the directorship of Wilbur Schramm. Influenced by the success at Illinois, research units were formed at other major midwestern universities including, most notably, at Michigan State University, University of Minnesota, and the University of Wisconsin. The growth of communication as a discipline accelerated rapidly in the 1960s and 1970s. Two Annenberg Schools of Communication were founded, the first at the University of Pennsylvania and the second at the University of Southern California. The newly christened departments were staffed by faculty whose degrees were from departments of journalism, speech, sociology, psychology, economics, and political science. But they all shared a common commitment to studying human communication processes.

As with most fledgling academic enterprises, consensus regarding conceptual delineation for the field has emerged slowly and equivocally. One approach to defining the field has focused on the various situational contexts in which communication may occur. This category system has produced researchers interested in mass communication, cross-cultural communication, health communication, technologically mediated communication, organizational communication, educational communication, small-group communication, family communication, marital communication, communication among children, interpersonal communication, non-verbal communication, and intrapersonal communication. A second approach has focused on various functions of communication, including socialization, conflict resolution, negotiation and bargaining, with persuasion and social influence receiving the lion's share of attention. Indeed, until the late 1960s, most of the theoretical, methodological, and empirical literature was devoted to the persuasion process. McGuire's (1969) ambitious summary of attitude and attitude-change work through the late 1960s has forty-two pages of references dealing with the topic.

Though persuasion research is certainly not a dead issue (Miller and Burgoon 1978), students of communi-cation have diversified their interests considerably. Spurred by several important educational and schol-arly occurrences, including the growth of interpersonal classes in the universities and the publication of Watzlawick *et al.*'s (1967) *Pragmatics of Human Communi-cation*, a number of researchers have turned to the study of symbolic transactions in more intimate, face-to-face settings. A lively interest has developed in examining the design of messages (O'Keefe and Lambert 1995) and message exchanges from a transactional, relational perspective (Folger and Poole 1982). Rather than using individual communicators as the unit of analysis, this approach uses the relationship: 'the focus of analysis is on the systemic properties that the participants have collectively, not individually' (Rogers and Farance 1975). Furthermore, greater emphasis has been placed on investigating communication relationships develop-mentally; that is, in looking at the evolution of relationships over time (Cappella 1984).

Three major paradigmatic alternatives have emerged to the earlier approaches. The *systems* per-spective (Monge 1977; Watzlawick *et al.* 1967) stresses the structure and organization of all components of a system, rather than focusing on one or more under-lying elements as would a reductionist approach. Contemporary treatments (Contractor 1994; Watt and Van Lear 1995) focus on studying how communication systems move from order into chaos (i.e. chaotic systems) or from chaos into order (i.e. self-organizing systems). The second major paradigm, the *interpretive* perspective (Putnam 1983) underscores the centrality of meaning in social interactions. It aims to unravel the subjective and consensual meanings that constitute social reality, by conducting naturalistic studies to document how symbols are invested with interpret-ations during interaction. A third paradigm, the *critical* perspective, is also concerned with the study of subjec-tive social realities. However, unlike scholars from the interpretive paradigm, critical scholars assume a political stance in treating society as circumscribed by power relations (including materialistic forces such as capital) and conflict. Their efforts, which have been focused primarily in the arena of popular culture (Grossberg 1992), gender issues (Treichler and Kramarae 1988), and sexuality (Vance 1987), often incorporate interventionist strategies for changing both discursive and material conditions.

As the study of communication moves into the twenty-first century, these paradigmatic debates, buttressed, one hopes, by more durable research foundations, will doubtless continue. In addition, the burgeoning communication technology is likely to generate more intensive efforts to identify the inter-faces between mediated and face-to-face communi-cation systems (McGrath and Hollingshead 1994). The precise nature of these influences constitutes an important priority for future communication research.

Noshir S. Contractor
University of Illinois at Urbana-Champaign
(revision of text by the late Gerald Miller)

References

Cappella, J. N. (1984) 'The relevance of microstructure of interaction to relationship change', *Journal of Social and Personal Relationships* 1.

Contractor, N. S. (1994) 'Self-organizing systems perspective in the study of organizational communication', in B. Kovacic (ed.) *New Approaches to Organizational Communication*, Albany, NY.

Delia, J. G. (1987) 'Communication research: a history', in C. R. Berger and S. H. Chaffee (eds) *Handbook of Communication Science*, Newbury Park, CA.

Folger, J. P. and Poole, M. S. (1982) 'Relational coding schemes: the question of validity', in M. Burgoon (ed.) *Communication Yearbook 5*, New Brunswick, NJ.

Grossberg, L. (1992) *We Gotta Get Out of This Place: Popular Conservatism and Postmodern Culture*, New York.

Hovland, C. I., Lumsdaine, A. A. and Sheffield, F. D. (1949) *Experiments on Mass Communication*, Princeton, NJ.

Katz, E. and Lazarsfeld, P. F. (1955) *Personal Influence*, New York.

Lazarsfeld, P., Berelson, B. and Gaudet, H. (1948) *The People's Choice*, New York.

Lewin, K. (1958) 'Group decision and social change', in E. E. Maccoby, T. M. Newcomb and E. E. Hartley (eds) *Readings in Social Psychology*, New York.

Lippitt, R. and White, R. K. (1943) 'The social climate of children's groups', in R. G. Barker, J. Kounin and H. Wright (eds) *Child Behavior and Development*, New York.

McGrath, J. E. and Hollingshead, A. B. (1994) *Groups Interacting with Technology*, Newbury Park, CA.

McGuire, W. J. (1969) 'The nature of attitudes and attitude change', in G. Lindsey and E. Aronson (eds) *Handbook of Social Psychology*, vol. 3, Reading, MA.

Miller, G. R. (1982) 'A neglected connection: mass media exposure and interpersonal communicative competency', in G. Gumpert and R. Cathcart (eds) *Intermedia: Interpersonal Communication in a Media World*, 2nd edn, New York.

Miller, G. R. and Burgoon, M. (1979) 'Persuasion research: review and commentary', in B. D. Ruben (ed.) *Communication Yearbook 2*, New Brunswick, NJ.

Monge, P. R. (1977) The systems perspective as a theoretical basis for the study of human communication, *Communication Quarterly 25*.

O'Keefe, B. and Lambert, B. L. (1995) 'Managing the flow of ideas: A local management approach to message design', in B. Burleson (ed.) *Communication Yearbook 18*, Newbury Park, CA.

Putnam, L. L. (1983) 'The interpretive perspective: an alternative to functionalism', in L. L. Putnam and M. E. Pacanowsky (eds) *Communication and Organizations: An Interpretive Approach*, Newbury Park, CA.

Rogers, L. E. and Farace, R. V. (1975) 'Analysis of relational communication in dyads: new measurement procedures', *Human Communication Research* 1.

Rosenberg, M. J. *et al.* (1960) *Attitude Organization and Change*. New Haven, CT.

Schramm, W. (1963) 'The unique perspective of communication: a retrospective view', *Journal of Communication* 33.

Sherif, M. and Hovland, C. I. (1961) *Social Judgment: Assimilation and Contrast Effects in Communication and Attitude Change*, New Haven, CT.

Treichler, P. and Kramarae, C. (1988) 'Medicine, language and women: whose body?', *Women and Language News 7* (spring 4).

Vance, C. S. (ed.) (1987) *Pleasure and Danger: Exploring Female Sexuality*, London.

Watt, J. and Van Lear, A. (1995) *Cycles and Dynamic Patterns in Communication Processes*, Newbury Park, CA.

Watzlawiek, P., Beavin, J. and Jackson, D. D. (1967) *Pragmatics of Human Communication*, New York.

See also: communication networks; cultural studies; information society; mass media.

communism

Communism connotes any societal arrangement based on communal ownership, production, consumption, self-government, perhaps even communal sexual mating. The term refers both to such societies and practices and to any theory advocating them. Examples of the former can be found in religious orders throughout history and in radical communities, from the sixteenth-century Anabaptists to the contemporary 'counterculture'; and the most famous example of advocacy of communism may well be the regime proposed for the guardian caste in Plato's *Republic*.

In the middle of the nineteenth century, the most radical schools of the growing socialist movement, including that of Marx and Engels, called themselves communists in order to dissociate themselves from other, allegedly less consistent, socialist groups. Hence when reference is made to that period, communism often is synonymous with the system of ideas developed by Engels and Marx, even though they often used the terms communism and socialism interchangeably. Communism in this sense connotes the sum-total of Marxist doctrines; hence it is the Marxist critique of capitalism and liberal theory and the project for the proletarian revolution, though at times it connotes specifically the ultimate goal of that revolution – the society visualized as emerging out of it, which is dimly foreseen as a society without property, without classes or a division of labour, without institutions of coercion and domination. The precise features of this society are not delineated in the writings of Marx and Engels, and among Marxists there are controversies about the degree of residual alienation and oppression (if any) that one ought to expect in the communist society of the future. Some of the hints Marx and Engels themselves gave come from their notion of a primitive communism allegedly prevailing among the savage early ancestors of the human race.

Among the earliest followers of Engels and Marx, the term fell into disuse; most Marxists around the turn of the century called themselves Social-Democrats. The term was revived after the Russian Revolution of 1917 by V. I. Lenin, who renamed his faction of the Russian Marxist movement the Communist Party and compelled all those parties who wished to join the newly-created Third (or Communist) International to adopt the same designation, so as to dissociate themselves from the Social-Democratic parties. As a consequence, communism since then connotes that interpretation of Marxism which considers the ideas and actions of Lenin and his Bolshevik faction to be the only correct interpretation of Marxism, and the sum-total of parties that subscribe to this interpretation.

Leninism is characterized by the insistence that meaningful social change can come only through revolution, while reforms threaten to corrupt the oppressed. Further, it implies the application of Marxism to countries where capitalism is under-developed, hence the development of flexible political strategies, including the mobilization of peasants and ethnic minorities for revolution. Foremost, it insists on the need for a 'vanguard party' of revolutionaries-by-profession to whom correct knowledge of the laws of history and politics ('consciousness') is attributed. Within the party and its numerous auxiliary organizations designed to mobilize the working class and its presumed allies, the vanguard is expected to ensure the prevalence of enlightened consciousness over blind passion by a combination of mass initiative and bureaucratic control that Lenin called 'democratic centralism'. Finally, Leninism implies the accumulated experience of the Russian Communist Party in governing their country. Communism thus connotes the theory and practice of rule by communist parties.

Although the leaders of ruling communist parties have generally refrained from claiming that the systems they were ruling were communist, it has become customary in the western world to refer to them as communist systems. Communism thus refers to any society or group of societies governed by communist parties.

The mature form of communist rule was developed in the USSR under the rule of J. V. Stalin. Hence communism since the 1930s has become synonymous with Stalinism or Neo-Stalinism. This is a system in which the communist party proclaims itself the enlightened leadership and claims authority to speak for the entire nation. It enforces this claim through control over all organizations and associations, all forms of communication, education, and entertainment, individual appointments and careers. The chief aim of these systems is rapid economic growth through crash programmes of industrialization, carried out through a centralized command economy. Communism in its Stalinist form thus is a species of entrepreneurship.

Contemporary communist societies thus bear no resemblance to the vision of communism sketched by Marx and Engels or even to that provided by Lenin in his unfinished work, *The State and Revolution*. Yet the memory of that vision lingers and has repeatedly led to attempts within communist parties to define alternatives to Leninist and Stalinist theories and practices. Contemporary communism therefore is not one single orthodoxy, but an ever growing cluster of orthodoxies and heresies, all of them backing up their arguments by reference to Engels and Marx, yet fiercely contending with each other.

Twentieth-century communism began as a dream to create an ideal society and an empowered human being. It turned into a clumsy crash programme of anti-capitalist capital accumulation, of westernization despite the west. That project has now collapsed in the European part of the communist world; the command economies have yielded to various modes of privatization and the market, doctrinal orthodoxy and the leadership claims of communist parties have been replaced by a multiplicity of parties and ideologies. Ethnic hatreds long tabooed and suppressed have erupted into the open, tearing empires and states apart in bloody conflict. The agony of this revolutionary process has led many citizens of the formerly communist countries to look back to the rule of the communist parties with nostalgia, while for others everything connected with communism has been thoroughly and irreversibly discredited. General opinion in the 'west' considers communism to be dead; but that may be premature.

Alfred G. Meyer
University of Michigan

Further reading

Claudin, F. (1975) *The Communist Movement: From Comintern to Cominform*, London.

Daniels, R. V. (ed.) (1965) *Marxism and Communism: Essential Readings*, New York.

——(1993) *The End of the Communist Revolution*, London and New York.

Kolakowski, L. (1978) *Main Currents of Marxism*, 3 vols, Oxford.

Meyer, A. G. (1984) *Communism*, 4th edn, New York.

Rosenberg, A. (1967) *A History of Bolshevism*, New York.

See also: political culture; social democracy; socialism.

community

The term community relates to a wide range of phenomena and has been used as an omnibus word loaded with diverse associations. Hillery (1955) unearthed no fewer than ninety-four definitions of community and its definition has continued to be a thriving intellectual pastime of sociologists.

A preliminary confusion arises between community as a type of *collectivity* or social unit, and community as a type of *social relationship* or sentiment. The root of the problem could be traced to Tönnies's *Gemeinschaft*, which uses the term to describe both a collectivity and a social relationship. Subsequently, most scholars have used community to connote a form of collectivity (with or without *Gemeinschaft* ties), but some, such as Nisbet (1953), have kept the community-as-sentiment approach alive in their emphasis on the quest for community and their concern with the loss of community in modern life. These approaches are clearly mixed with some nostalgia for a glorious past in which people were thought to be more secure, less alienated and less atomized. But, as Schmalenbach (1960) pointed out, Tönnies's *Gemeinschaft* implied a spontaneous, taken-for-granted relationship. Fellowship ties which are consciously sought and are more emotionally laden better fit what he called communion (*bund*) ties, such as those found in religious sects or ideological groups. Communion ties are often created by precisely those people who are dissatisfied with the routinization (hence loss of meaning and involvement) of the extant community ties.

Community, in the sense of type of collectivity, usually refers to a group sharing a defined physical space or geographical area such as a neighbourhood, city, village or hamlet; a community can also be a group sharing common traits, a sense of belonging and/or maintaining social ties and interactions which shape it into a distinctive social entity, such as an ethnic, religious, academic or professional community. The differences are between what may be called territorial and non-territorial approaches. For some scholars (Hawley 1950; Park 1929) the most important bases of commonality is common territory. While they do not dismiss the essential element of common ties, these ties are not sufficient in themselves to constitute a community. The non-territorial approach stresses the common ties at the expense of territory. Community still denotes a *social entity* with common ties and not the ties themselves, but territory is not a necessary ingredient of commonality. Common ties and a sense of belonging may derive from beliefs in a common past or a common fate, common values, interests, kinship relations and so on, none of which presuppose living together, as illustrated by ethnic or religious communities whose members might be geographically dispersed. We still do not know, however, what is distinctive about community ties compared to ties of other collectivities. Since locality is not the distinctive feature in this approach, one looks for distinctiveness in the type of ties. This may in turn re-create the confusion between community as a form of collectivity or community as a form of human bond. The non-territorial approach has gained force as a result of modern advances in communication which have reduced the importance or territorial proximity as a bases for human association, increasingly creating what Webber (1964) called 'community without propinquity'. A related non-territorial approach is found among social network theorists, some of whom also object to treating communities as social entities in their own right, regarding this a legacy of Durkheimian corporationist tendencies as opposed to Simmel's interactionist approach (Boissevain 1968).

Hillery (1968) and Gottschalk (1975) have made the most systematic attempt to differentiate between formal organization and community (or rather communal organization). The formal organization's primary orientation towards a specific, defining goal is contrasted with the communal organization's primarily diffuse goal orientation. Azarya (1984) has added that formal organizations are basically instruments established to attain external goals whereas communities' goals are mostly inner-oriented: they strive to maintain a set of desired relationships among fellow members and a state of affairs within the collectivity. In their goal-related activities, members of formal organizations relate to one another as specific role-bearers, while relations among members of communal organizations are more diffuse, encompassing a larger aspect of one another's life. Corporations, schools, churches, armies, political movements and professional associations are all formal organizations, while families, ethnic groups and neighbourhoods are communal organizations. Communal and formal organizations can, of course, include sub-units of the opposite kind, as for example informal community-like friendship groups among workers of an industrial plant, or, by contrast, voluntary associations created within a neighbourhood or an ethnic community.

Delineating the boundaries of communities is one of the greatest difficulties hampering their proper identification. The lack of clear boundaries is indeed one of the major properties of communities as compared to formal organizations (Hillery 1968). In non-territorial communities, clear boundaries and sharp differentiation between members and non-members are signs of association formation within the community, which brings it closer to the formal organization pole. In territorial communities, if no size limitations are set on 'the people living together' which the community is said to represent, the concept may be stretched to include an entire nation or even the world at large (Warren 1973). Some scholars (Hawley 1950) prefer to limit community to a size which enables the inhabitants to have a diffuse familiarity with the everyday life of the area. While one knows about special events that occur outside the community, familiarity with one's own community includes ordinary events which would not draw attention elsewhere. This would exclude global, national and metropolitan areas from being called communities.

However a measure of maximal size may be specified, what would be the minimal size of a territorial community? The smaller the community, the greater its members' familiarity with routine life, but would that make a single house (or an apartment building) a community? According to Warren, some basic functions have to be performed in each community, including the provision of basic economic needs, socialization, social control, social participation and mutual support (Warren 1973). The community might depend on external organizations in performing these functions, and community members do not have to prefer locally offered services to external ones, but some activity has to take place in the community in each of these spheres. This would exclude an apartment building or a modern nuclear family from being a community in its own right, though not necessarily the pre-modern extended family household. A related feature of community stressed in the literature is its being a microcosm of society. The community, unlike other collectivities, is a social system in itself, including such subsystems as government, economy, education, religion, and family found in a larger society. A certain size has to be attained for these institutional spheres to manifest themselves. It is also possible that the community loses some of its multifaceted characteristics in more developed societies, becoming less differentiated as societies become more so (Elias 1974).

The conceptual disarray of social science regarding community has not prevented an abundance of community studies, some of which are among the best known pieces of social science literature. The various urban studies of the Chicago school in the 1920s and 1930s, Warren and Lunt's (1941) *Yankee City*, Redfield's (1949) *Tepotzlan: A Mexican Village*, Whyte's (1961) *Street Corner Society*, Gans's (1962) *Urban Villagers* and (1967) *Levittowners* are just a few examples of a much longer list. Scholarly interest in community has included units of greatly different size, autonomy, demographic composition, technological, economic or cultural traits. Community characteristics have been used to explain other phenomena – inequality, deviance, transform-

ative capacity. Special attention has focused on the extent to which urban–rural differences can explain variations in community structure and interactions (Wirth 1938). Doubts have been raised about the narrative style and idiosyncratic methodology of most community studies which make them irreproducible and hard to compare. Ruth Glass called them 'the poor sociologist's substitute for the novel' (Bell and Newby 1971), but perhaps this concrete quality and the 'story' that they carried has been their greatest advantage.

Victor Azarya
Hebrew University

References

Azarya, V. (1984) *The Armenian Quarter of Jerusalem*, Berkeley, CA.
Bell, C. and Newby, H. (1971) *Community Studies*, London.
Boissevain, J. (1968) 'The place of non-groups in the social sciences', *Man* 3.
Elias, N. (1974) 'Towards a theory of communities', in C. Bell and H. Newby (eds) *The Sociology of Community*, London.
Gans, H. J. (1962) *The Urban Villagers*, New York.
—— (1967) *The Levittowners*, New York.
Gottschalk, S. (1975) *Communities and Alternatives*, Cambridge, MA.
Hawley, A. (1950) *Human Ecology: A Theory of Community Structure*, New York.
Hillery, G. A. Jr (1955) 'Definitions of community: areas of agreement', *Rural Sociology* 20.
—— (1968) *Communal Organizations*, Chicago.
Nisbet, R. A. (1953) *The Quest for Community*, New York.
Park, R. E. and Burgess, E. W. (1929) *Introduction to the Science of Sociology*, 2nd edn, Chicago.
Redfield, R. (1949) *Tepoztlan: A Mexican Village*, Chicago.
Schmalenbach, H. (1961) 'The sociological category of communion', in T. Parsons *et al.* (eds) *Theories of Society*, 2 vols, New York.
Warren, R. (1973) *The Community in America*, Chicago.
Warren, W. L. and Lunt, P. S. (1941) *Yankee City: The Social Life of a Modern Community*, New Haven, CT.
Webber, M. M. (1964) 'The urban place and the nonplace urban realm', in M. M. Webber *et al.* (eds) *Explorations into Urban Structure*, Philadelphia, PA.
Whyte, W. F. (1961) *Street Corner Society*, Chicago.
Wirth, L. (1938) 'Urbanism as a way of life', *American Journal of Sociology* 44.

See also: community development

community development

In the context of public policy, the phrase community development has most often been used to describe projects initiated by, or with the active participation of, the inhabitants of a locality, which are intended to benefit them collectively. The projects may concern education, social welfare, health, infrastructure such as roads, wells or irrigation, farming, manufacture or commerce. While much of the benefit may accrue to individual families, the projects are intended to enhance the community as a whole, in self-confidence and political skills, for instance, even if not more tangibly.

This conception of community development was widely adopted by British, French and Belgian colonial administrations in Africa and Asia, especially after the Second World War, as a social and political as much as economic strategy for rural areas. In British Africa; for example, departments of community development were created with community development officers trained according to increasingly self-conscious principles of professional community development practice (du Sautoy 1968; Batten 1962). The stimulation of local leadership, the growth of capacity to initiate projects and organize self-help, and the learning of skills were characteristically considered more important than the achievements of any particular project. The ideal community development officer was therefore a facilitator, adviser and sensitive guide, who sought to encourage a collective capacity for initiative and organization that would then continue independently.

In practice, the community development officer's role was more ambivalent than this ideal allowed. As a government employee, he was bound to favour local initiatives which corresponded with national policy and discourage others. His intervention was often crucial in drawing local factions into co-operation and in securing resources. Hence community development remained essentially an aspect of government policy, although a variety of mutual aid and village development associations evolved independently of government – as for instance in Eastern Nigeria.

After independence, community development was seen as a means of mobilizing rural people for such endeavours as mass literacy or education, as for instance in the movement for self-reliance in Tanzania, or the Harambee movement in Kenya. But the inherent ambiguity remains of a strategy intended both to encourage self-help and initiative while implementing national government's goals.

In the 1960s, the term community development came to be applied to projects in predominantly urban neighbourhoods of America and later Britain, where poverty and social pathologies were believed to concentrate. Like their colonial predecessors, these projects were intended both to provide practical benefits, such as improved social services, more relevant vocational training, legal aid, low-cost housing and more jobs, and, in doing so, to increase the community's sense of its collective competence. In the United States, this approach became national policy under Title II of the Economic Opportunity Act of 1964, following earlier experiments by the Ford Foundation and the President's Committee on Juvenile Delinquency (Marris and Rein 1980) and was continued in many subsequent policies, such as the Model Cities Program and Community Development Block Grants from the federal to local governments. Besides community action agencies, largely concerned with social welfare and educational programmes, community development corporations were funded to promote housing and commercial enterprises, especially in neighbourhoods of high unemployment. The Watts Labor Community Action Coalition, for instance, has, at various times, developed produce markets, a bus service, a large shopping centre, and housing in a black district of Los Angeles (Hampden-Turner 1974). Apart from housing, development corporations have experienced great difficulties in sustaining viable commercial enterprises in their communities. In most instances, the attempt to fulfil social purposes, such as employment opportunities for local residents, in market settings which more experienced commercial enterprises have already judged unprofitable, proves too difficult even with the help of subsidies. Over time, therefore, the corporations tend either to withdraw from commercial endeavours or to defer many of their original social reasons for starting them.

The British Community Development Project, modelled on American community action agencies, was initiated in 1969 by the Home Office with a similar hope of stimulating self-help and innovative solutions in neighbourhoods of concentrated social problems, choosing for the experiment twelve mostly urban neighbourhoods in Britain (Marris 1982). Over time, as concern shifted from social pathology – which was neither as apparent nor as concentrated as had been assumed – to unemployment, the project had to confront the difficulty of applying very localized resources to remedy the effects of large-scale changes of economic structure.

Both the British and American projects were regarded as experimental by the governments which initiated them. Community development, in this context, was intended to discover inexpensive solutions to problems of poverty and unemployment, through self-help and innovative, more relevant and efficient use of resources already allocated. It has therefore never received funding on a scale commensurate with the problems it addressed. Its most lasting achievement, especially in the United States, probably lies in the growing sophistication and organizational capacity of neighbourhood groups in dealing with economic and physical changes which affect them.

Peter Marris
University of California, Los Angeles

References

Batten, T. R. (1962) *Training for Community Development*, London.
du Sautoy, P. (1958) *Community Development in Ghana*, London.
Hampden-Turner, C. (1974) *From Poverty to Dignity: A Strategy for Poor Americans*, Garden City, NY.
Marris, P. and Rein, M. (1980) *Dilemmas of Social Reform*, 3rd edn, Chicago.
Marris, P. (1982) *Community Planning and Conceptions of Change*, London.

See also: community; social problems

competition

The simplest meaning of the term is rivalry between alternative buyers and sellers, each seeking to pursue their own ends. It is central to economics because it provides the mechanism through which the actions of agents can be co-ordinated. It is the basis for Adam Smith's claim that every individual 'is led by an invisible hand to promote an end which was no part of his intention' (Smith 1979 [1776]: 456). It requires both a plurality of potential buyers and sellers and a competitive attitude. Thus its opposite may be either monopoly (the usage in most modern economics) or custom and co-operation (as was the case for J. S. Mill).

When Adam Smith and the classical economists used the term competition, they referred to the process whereby prices were forced down to costs of production, and wages and profits to their 'ordinary' levels. The requirement for this was what Smith termed 'perfect liberty' in which there are no barriers to mobility and 'every man, as long as he does not violate the laws of justice, is left perfectly free to pursue his own interests in his own way, and to bring both his industry and his capital into competition with those of any other man' (Smith 1979 [1776]: 687). This is what has since been termed the long period aspect of competition, the process whereby capital and labour are moved from one activity to another taking considerable time. In contrast, the short period aspect of competition concerns the way markets operate. For the classical economists, the short period aspect of competition was summarized by the law of one price: the proposition that there cannot be two prices in the same market. It embodies a static notion of competition, for the process whereby price differences are eliminated is ignored.

Between the 1870s and the 1930s a number of economists (notably W. S. Jevons, L. Walras, F. Y. Edgeworth, V. Pareto, A. Marshall and K. Wicksell, J. Robinson and E. H. Chamberlin) developed the concept of perfect competition. Like the law of one price, and in contrast to what the classical economists understood by competition, perfect competition is a static concept. It is not a process but a type of market in which each agent is so small as to be unable to influence the price at which goods are bought and sold. Agents are price-takers. It is contrasted with imperfect competition, a state in which individual agents are sufficiently large to be able to have some control over the price of what they are buying or selling. Imperfect competition covers a variety of market structures ranging from monopoly (one seller) and monopsony (one buyer) to oligopoly (a small number of sellers) and bilateral monopoly (one buyer and one seller).

Perfect competition is a situation where most of the phenomena commonly associated with competition (brands and product differentiation, advertising, price wars – phenomena that were extensively discussed in the late nineteenth-century US literature) are absent, yet it has provided the dominant theory of competition in economic theory since the 1940s. Economists have explored, with great rigour, the conditions under which perfect competition will occur. Perfect competition has been shown to be efficient in the sense that in a perfectly competitive equilibrium it is impossible to make any individual better off without simultaneously making someone else worse off (Pareto efficiency). Perfect competition was, at least until the 1980s, the almost universally used assumption about market structure in diverse areas of economics such as international trade, inflation and unemployment.

The main reason why economists rely so heavily on models of perfect competition is that imperfect competition, in particular oligopoly, is much more difficult to analyse, one of the main problems being that in order to work out what is the best action to take, agents (usually firms) have to take into account how their competitors are likely to respond. Nowadays the most widely accepted solution to this problem is to use game theory. Using game theory economists have managed to construct theoretical models of aspects of competition such as entry deterrence, strategic investment, product variety and R&D expenditure.

While the focus of most economic theory has been on perfect competition, dynamic aspects of competition such as concerned Smith and the classical economists have not been neglected. The Austrian School, based on the work of C. Menger, sees competition as a dynamic process of discovery, dominated by the figure of the entrepreneur. It is entrepreneurs who see the possibilities for making profits by producing new goods, or by producing existing goods in new ways. The competitive process involves the continual creation and subsequent elimination of opportunities for profit. The contrast between orthodox and

Austrian conceptions of competition is shown by the debate, in the 1920s and 1930s, over whether rational (i.e. efficient) economic calculation was possible under socialism. Market socialists such as O. Lange focused on the static concept of perfect competition, arguing that it was possible to design a set of rules for a socialist economy (in which there was no private ownership of capital) that would produce the same allocation of resources as would occur in a competitive, capitalist economy. Against them, Austrians such as L. von Mises and F. A. von Hayek argued that competition in the sense of rivalry was necessary if new products and new technologies were to be discovered: that those aspects of competition that K. Marx saw as wasteful (e.g. the building of two factories, one of which was subsequently eliminated by competition) were a vital feature of capitalism that could not be emulated under socialism.

Perhaps the best-known economist working in the Austrian tradition was J. A. Schumpeter. His vision was of competition as a process of 'creative destruction'. Entrepreneurs discover new technologies, earning large profits as a result. Over time their discoveries are imitated by others, with the result that competition forces profits down. This theory fits into a longer tradition of evolutionary theories of competition, whose history goes back to the social Darwinism of the late nineteenth century in which competition was seen as eliminating the unfit. Among the most prominent modern exponents of evolutionary theories of competition are R. R. Nelson and S. G. Winter, who combined the Austrian idea that entrepreneurs explore alternative ways of responding to novel situations with the Darwinian idea that those who make good choices survive, with competition eliminating those who make bad ones.

The Austrian emphasis on innovation also results in a different attitude towards the role of numbers in competition. The standard view is that the smaller the number of firms, the less is the degree of competition. Attempts have therefore been made to measure competition by measuring variables such as concentration ratios – the share of output produced by, say, the largest five firms. Austrians, however, emphasize potential competition, which may be unrelated to the number of firms in the industry. A similar line has been pursued by W. J. Baumol who has developed the notion of a 'contestable' market. A perfectly contestable market is one in which entry and exit are absolutely costless, the result being that potential competition will keep prices low even if there are few firms in the industry.

Roger E. Backhouse
University of Birmingham

Reference

Smith, A. (1979 [1776]) *An Inquiry into the Nature and Causes of the Wealth of Nations*, ed. R. H. Campbell and A. S. Skinner, Oxford.

Further reading

Backhouse, R. E. (1990) 'Competition', in J. Creedy (ed.) *Foundations of Economic Thought*, Oxford.

Lavoie, D. (1985) *Rivalry and Central Planning: The Socialist Calculation Debate Reconsidered*, Cambridge, UK.

McNulty, P. J. (1987) 'Competition: Austrian conceptions', in J. Eatwell, M. Milgate and P. Newman (eds) *The New Palgrave Dictionary of Economics*, London.

Morgan, M. (1993) 'Competing notions of "competition" in late-nineteenth-century American economics', *History of Political Economy* 25(4).

Schumpeter, J. A. (1976) *Capitalism, Socialism and Democracy*, 5th edn, London.

Stigler, G. J. (1957) 'Perfect competition, historically contemplated', *Journal of Political Economy* 65(1). Reprinted in G. J. Stigler (1965) *Essays on the History of Economics*, Chicago.

—— (1987) 'Competition', in J. Eatwell, M. Milgate and P. Newman (eds) *The New Palgrave Dictionary of Economics*, London.

See also: equilibrium; firm, theory of; markets; monopoly.

computer simulation

Computer simulation is a methodology for building, testing and using computer programs which imitate (Latin *simulare*, to imitate) some aspect of social system behaviour. Since its inception in the 1960s, computer simulation has continued to be a specialized and useful tool for addressing a variety of social science topics, including settlement patterns in archaeology, small population dynamics in anthropology, voting behaviours in political science, family and kinship processes in demography, and outcomes assessment in social policy analysis.

A computer simulation model is embodied in a computer program which uses numbers or symbols to represent observed variables in a social system, along with programming statements that attempt to mimic the behaviour of the system. In order to start the simulation, initial values are set for the variables and for the parameters which determine the behaviour of the system. Then, the simulation program executes and produces outputs showing how the values of variables change over time. By re-specifying initial values and parameters the modeller can experiment with alternative hypotheses in ways that might be impossible, impractical or unethical in a real social system.

Experiments with computer simulation models yield insight into the operation of complex social systems.

While some simulation models might also be useful for making limited predictions of the future, most social scientists are pessimistic about the reliability of such predictions. Thus, the goal of simulation experiments is usually to obtain a better understanding of complex social processes and our theories and hypotheses rather than to make predictions of the future.

Computer simulation models can be conveniently classified as *macro-simulation* models or *micro-simulation* models. A macro-simulation model operates much like an accounting system. It presents the state of a social system in a numerical accounting statement, such as counts of numbers of people by age, gender and social characteristics in a population. The macro-simulation program then adds and subtracts from these numbers in ways that imitate social processes operating over time, such as by adding to counts of infants and subtracting from counts of people at all ages to simulate birth and death processes, respectively. Many macro-simulation models can be expressed as mathematical equations, so that the computer simulation model is simply a tool for deriving results from the mathematical model.

Micro-simulation models are usually more complex and detailed than macro-simulation models. Micro-simulation models operate by keeping track of each individual entity (e.g. person, institution, family) and its attributes (e.g. age, gender, size, social characteristics) in a small artificial population maintained in computer memory. Using a simulation clock to imitate the passage of time, the micro-simulation program schedules events (e.g. birth, death, marriage, change in status) which happen to these simulated individuals at specified times. At various times during the simulation a statistical output or perhaps a 'census' listing of the simulated individuals and their characteristics is produced for later analysis. Micro-simulation models are usually difficult or impossible to express with traditional mathematical methods, so that micro-simulation methods open new vistas in social science research.

Micro-simulation models are usually stochastic models, meaning that some degree of controlled randomness is included in the models. Random variables are created from pseudo-random numbers generated on the computer and these random variables can be created to conform to any of a wide variety of probability distributions. In this way micro-simulation models typically represent patterns of variation, randomness, and uncertainty in social systems as an integral part of the simulation model. The results produced by the simulations therefore display patterns of variability between individuals, and over time, similar to real-world data. Because of their random component, micro-simulation models are part of the larger class of statistical and computational techniques known as Monte Carlo methods.

A complete micro-simulation experiment consists of numerous replications (computer runs) which differ from each other due to the random component. The principles of experimental design and analysis, including analysis of variance, apply to designing and analysing micro-simulation experiments just as they do to empirical research. But unlike empirical research, micro-simulation research allows the modeller to control the patterns of randomness so that it is also a subject for investigation and experiment. Moreover, because the random component of a simulation is controlled by the modeller, special variance reduction techniques can be employed to increase the statistical efficiency of the results (Rubinstein 1981).

A critical, but often slighted, task in computer simulation work is testing the model. Among the tests which should be conducted and reported on any computer simulation model are verification, validation and tuning. Verification examines a simulation program for logical errors and programming mistakes; validation compares simulation outputs to real data as an empirical check on the model; tuning refines the model to increase its validity and reduce its sensitivity to extraneous factors. It can be particularly difficult to test a micro-simulation model thoroughly because some errors surface only when rare events or combinations of events happen to occur. Thus, the more complex and the more probabilistic the micro-simulation model is, the harder it is to test. This is a good reason for keeping simulation models as simple as possible while at the same time engaging in thorough testing under a wide variety of initial inputs and parameter values.

As with any scientific model, the simulation modeller faces difficult choices between creating a more complex and comprehensive model that is more difficult to understand and test, versus devising a simpler and more limited model that is more thoroughly tractable and testable (for discussions see the essays by Nathan Keyfitz and Kenneth Wachter in Bongaarts, Burch, and Wachter, 1986). As one example of this tension, in the United States, the National Research Council has given strong endorsement to the use of micro-simulation modelling in policy analysis while at the same time strongly emphasizing the need for much better validation and documentation of existing and future simulation models (Citro and Hanushek 1991).

The practice of computer simulation is closely tied to the technology of computing. The early micro-simulation experiments of Orcutt *et al.* (1961) consumed vast amounts of computer time on a large computer that was many times slower and had many times less memory than today's inexpensive desktop or portable microcomputers. But even with modern computers, micro-simulation models typically require relatively large amounts of computing time and memory, partly because of the need for many replications in a simulation experiment. However, the task of efficient simulation programming is greatly enhanced by special programming languages (e.g. Schriber 1991) which provide efficient memory management, mechanisms for event timing, and fast generation of pseudo-random numbers. Many texts (e.g. Mitrani 1982; Payne 1982) introduce the concepts, issues and programming languages relevant to computer simulation.

James E. Smith
Cambridge Group for the History of Population and
Social Structure and Westat Inc., Rockville, MD

References

Bongaarts, J., Burch, T. and Wachter K. (eds) (1986) *Family Demography: Methods and their Applications*, Oxford.

Citro, C. and Hanushek E. A. (eds) (1991) *Improving Information for Social Policy Decisions: The Uses of Microsimulation Modeling*, Washington, DC.

Mitrani, I. (1982) *Simulation Techniques for Discrete Event Systems*, Cambridge, UK.

Orcutt, G. H., Greenburger, M., Korbel, J. and Rivlin, A. M. (1961) *Microanalysis of Socioeconomic Systems: A Simulation Study*, New York.

Payne, J. A. (1982) *Introduction to Simulation: Programming Techniques and Methods of Analysis*, New York.

Rubinstein, R. (1981) *Simulation and The Monte Carlo Method*, New York.

Schriber, T. (1991) *An Introduction to Simulation Using GPSS/H*, New York.

Comte, Auguste (1798–1857)

Auguste Comte, philosopher of science and social visionary, is perhaps best known for giving a name to a subject he outlined rather than practised: sociology. As the Comtist motto 'Order and Progress' suggests, the keynote of his thought is his search, in chaotic times, for principles of cultural and political order that were consistent with the forward march of society. Born at Montpellier in southern France of a conservative, middle-class family, Comte received a good scientific education at the Ecole Polytechnique in Paris, a centre of advanced liberal thought. From 1817 to 1824 he was closely associated with the radical prophet of a new industrial order, Henri de Saint-Simon, to whom he owed a considerable (and largely disavowed) intellectual debt. At the same time, despite the loss of his Catholic faith, he was drawn to some of the ideas of the conservative thinker, Joseph de Maistre, and eventually based much of the 'religion of humanity' on medieval, Catholic models.

Comte's writings fall into two main phases, which express different aspects of a single, unified vision of knowledge and society, rather than a change in fundamental emphasis. Of the first, the major work is the six-volume *Cours de philosophie positive* (1830–42). (*The Positive Philosophy of Auguste Comte*, 1896), which sets forth a developmental epistemology of science. In his later writings, especially the *Discours sur l'esprit positif*, (1844) (*Discourse on the Positive Spirit*), the *Système de politique positive* (1848–54) (*System of Positive Polity*, 1875–77), and the *Catechism of Positive Religion* (1858), Comte gives the blueprint of a new social order, including the 'religion of humanity' which was to provide its ethical underpinning. For Comte, 'positivism' was not merely the doctrine that the methods of the natural sciences provide the only route to a knowledge of human nature and society (as it has latterly come to mean), but also a source of value for social reorganization. 'Sociology' is, in fact, the specific knowledge requisite to this task.

In the *Cours* Comte sets forth the famous 'Law of the three stages'. In its origins, human thought is 'theological', making use of an idiom of spiritual forces; later, in a phase which culminates in the Enlightenment, it moves to a 'metaphysical' stage, which is conjectural and largely negative; finally, when it is able to grasp real causal relations between phenomena, it achieves the scientific or 'positive' stage. To these stages there also correspond characteristic social and political institutions. Individual sciences develop in the same manner, emerging at the positive stage in the order of their complexity: mathematics, astronomy, physics, chemistry, biology and, finally, sociology. Comte's view of sociology is highly programmatic: he argues for an analytic distinction between social 'statics' and 'dynamics', and for society to be analysed as a system of interdependent parts, based upon a consensus.

Despite his religious eccentricities, Comte exercised an immediate influence on his comtemporaries. J. S. Mill introduced his work to the English-speaking world, where the positive philosophy appealed as a check to the extremes of liberal individualism, and even Spencer adopted the name 'sociology'. Though he is little read today, the functionalist and natural scientific paradigms which Comte advocated have remained in sociology's mainstream.

J. D. Y. Peel
University of London
School of Oriental and African Studies

Further reading

Lenzer, J. (ed.) (1975) *Auguste Comte and Positivism: The Essential Writings*, New York.

Pickering, M. (1993) *Auguste Comte: An Intellectual Biography*, vol. 1 Cambridge, UK.

Thompson, K. (1975) *Auguste Comte: The Foundation of Sociology*, London.

conditioning, classical and operant

The Russian physiologist, Ivan Pavlov, was not the first scientist to investigate how animals learn, but he was certainly one of the first to undertake a systematic series of experiments intended to provide precise quantitative information on the subject, and it is to his work that we owe the term conditioning to describe one form of that learning. In the course of his work on the digestive system of dogs, Pavlov had found that salivary secretion was elicited not only by placing food in the dog's mouth but also by the sight or smell of food, and that eventually a dog might start to salivate at the sight or sound of the attendant who usually provided the food. These 'psychic secretions', although initially interfering with the planned study of the digestive system, provided the basis for the study of conditional reflexes for which Pavlov is now far more famous.

Pavlov's experimental arrangement was simple. A hungry dog is restrained on a stand; every few minutes, the dog receives some meat powder, the delivery of which is signalled by an arbitrary stimulus, such as the ticking of a metronome or the flashing of a light. The food itself elicits copious salivation, which is measured by diverting the end of the salivary duct through a fistula in the dog's cheek. After a number of trials on which the delivery of food is always preceded by the ticking of the metronome, the dog does not wait for the food, but starts to salivate as soon as the metronome is sounded. Food is referred to as an unconditional stimulus because it unconditionally elicits salivation; the metronome is a conditional stimulus which comes to elicit salivation conditional on its relationship to the food. By similar reasoning, salivation to food is an unconditional response, but when the dog starts salivating to the metronome, this is a conditional response, strengthened or reinforced by the delivery of food whenever the metronome sounds, and weakened or extinguished whenever the metronome occurs without being followed by food. In translation from the original Russian, 'conditional' and 'unconditional' became 'conditioned' and 'unconditioned' and the verb 'to condition' was rapidly introduced to describe the procedure which brought about this change in the dog's behaviour.

At about the same time as Pavlov was starting his work on what is now called classical conditioning, a young American research student, Edward Thorndike, was undertaking an equally systematic series of experiments which are now regarded as providing the first analysis of operant conditioning. Thorndike was more catholic in his choice of animal to study than was Pavlov, using cats, chickens and monkeys impartially. The impetus for his work was also different. While Pavlov was a physiologist who saw himself as studying the brain and how it controlled not only inborn but also acquired reflexes, Thorndike was concerned to study how animals learned in an objective and scientific manner in order to dispel the myths that he thought had arisen about the amazing feats of intelligence of which animals were capable, myths that owed much to a post-Darwinian desire to prove the mental continuity of humans and other animals.

In a typical experiment, Thorndike would place a cat in a puzzle box from which the animal could escape, and so get access to a dish of food, only by performing some arbitrary response such as pressing a catch or pulling on a piece of string. Thorndike recorded the time it took the animal to perform the required response on successive trials, and observing a gradual decline in this time, interpreted the learning in terms of his celebrated 'law of effect': the reward of escaping from confinement and obtaining food strengthened the one response that was successful in achieving this, while all other responses, being followed by no such desirable effects, were weakened.

The term operant conditioning was introduced by the American psychologist, B. F. Skinner, who refined Thorndike's procedure by the simple device of delivering food to the animal (via, for example, an automatic pellet dispenser) while it remained inside the box. In this apparatus, a rat could be trained to perform hundreds of responses, usually pressing a small bar protruding from one wall, in order to obtain occasional pellets of food. The response of pressing the bar was termed an operant because it operated on the animal's environment, and the procedure was therefore operant conditioning, which was reinforced by the occasional pellet of food, and extinguished if pressing the bar was no longer followed by food.

Although Skinner, unlike Thorndike, took over much of Pavlov's terminology, he interpreted the learning he observed in a way much more closely related to Thorndike's analysis. For Skinner, as for Thorndike, the central feature of learning and adaptation is that an animal's behaviour should be modified by its consequences. The rat presses the bar because this response produces a particular outcome – the delivery of food; when it no longer does so, the rat stops pressing the bar, just as it will also stop if pressing the bar produces some other, less desirable outcome such as the delivery of a brief shock. The schedules according to which the experimenter arranges these outcomes have orderly and appropriate effects on the animal's behaviour.

The law of effect, which summarizes these observations, is entirely in accord with common sense: parents hope and believe that rewarding children for good behaviour or punishing them for bad will also have appropriate effects, and when they are mistaken or disappointed we are more inclined to look for other sources of reward or to question the efficacy of their punishment than to question the underlying logic of the argument. Operant conditioning, therefore, although no doubt only one, rather simple form of learning or way of modifying behaviour, is surely an important and pervasive one. It is not so immediately obvious that the process of classical conditioning identified by Pavlov is of such importance. Why does the dog start salivating at the sound of the metronome? The experimenter delivers the food regardless of the dog's behaviour (this, of course, is the precise distinction between classical and operant conditioning, for in Skinner's experiments the rat gets food only *if* it presses the bar). It has been argued that salivation does actually achieve something – for example, it makes dry food more palatable and this is why the dog learns to salivate in anticipation of food. The explanation attempts to interpret classical conditioning in operant terms, for it seeks to identify a desirable consequence of salivation responsible for reinforcing the response. But the explanation is probably false. Another popular example of classical conditioning is that of blinking by a rabbit to a flash of light which signals the delivery of a puff of air to the rabbit's eye. Since this is a classical experiment, the puff of air is delivered on every trial regardless of the rabbit's behaviour. Just as in the case of the dog's salivary response, however, it seems reasonable to argue that the rabbit's eye blink serves to protect the eye from the puff of air and is therefore reinforced by this desirable consequence. The argument implies that if the experimenter arranged that on any trial on which the rabbit blinked in anticipation of the puff of air, the experimenter cancelled its delivery altogether, the rabbit would learn to blink even more readily. Here, after all, blinking has an even more beneficial consequence than usual: it completely cancels an aversive consequence. But in fact such a procedure significantly interferes with the conditioning of the rabbit's eye blink.

A more plausible interpretation, then, is that classical conditioning simply reflects an animal's anticipation of a particular consequence, not necessarily an attempt to obtain or avoid that consequence – this latter being the provenance of operant conditioning. Classical conditioning probably has its most important application in the area of emotions and attitudes: the anticipation of an unpleasant event may generate a variety of emotional changes, such as fear or alarm which are not necessarily under voluntary control. Voluntary

behaviour, that is, that directly affected by its consequences, is the sphere of operant conditioning.

N. J. Mackintosh
University of Cambridge

Further reading

Domjan, M. and Burkhard, B. (1986) 2nd edn, *The Principles of Learning and Behavior*, Monterey, CA.
Flaherty, C. E. (1985) *Animal Learning and Cognition*, New York.
Mackintosh, N. J. (1983) *Conditioning and Associative Learning*, Oxford.
—— (1994) *Handbook of Perception and Cognition*, vol. 9, *Animal Learning and Cognition*, New York.

See also: behaviourism; behaviour therapy; learning.

conflict, social

Social conflict can be considered in two ways: as a perspective in which conflict permeates and shapes all aspects of human interaction and social structure, or as one of innumerable specific fights or struggles such as wars, revolutions, strikes and uprisings.

Conflict perspective

Stated at a necessarily high level of generality, analysts using the conflict approach (as opposed to, say, a functionalist, exchange, or systems approach) seek to explain not only how social order is maintained despite great inequalities, but also how social structures change. They view societies, organizations, and other social systems as arenas for personal and group contests. (Complementary and common interests are not excluded, but the incompatible character of interests are emphasized.) Coercion is viewed as a major way in which people seek to advance their interests. It is assumed that humans generally do not want to be dominated or coerced, and therefore resist attempts at coercion, and struggles ensue.

Conflict theory has a long tradition going back to the earliest historical accounts and counsel to rulers, as can be seen in the writings of Thucydides, Machiavelli and Hobbes. Marx and Engels stressed the material conditions underlying conflict, especially the class struggles based upon property relations. Other conflict theorists such as Gumplowitz, Ratzenhofer and Novicow worked in the context of evolutionary thought and posited a group struggle for existence; they variously stressed military power in conflict, and interests – for example, ethnic differences – as bases for conquest. Simmel was another classical sociologist concerned with the forms and consequences of conflict.

Interest in the conflict perspective revived, at least in English-speaking countries, in the 1960s. In preceding decades the dominant social-science theories portrayed societies as based on consensus and consent, but the political turmoil of the 1960s, both domestic and international, directed attention to social conflicts and to the conflict approach.

Conflict theorists have emphasized different combinations of elements from the rich conflict tradition. Many contemporary social scientists draw from Marxism, but they differ a great deal in their interpretations of Marx and how they have developed elements of it. For example, Gramsci (1971) stresses the cultural hegemony of the ruling class as a mode of domination. Many conflict theorists stress their differences with Marxism, or otherwise emphasize authority, ethnicity, gender or other factors and processes which Marxists do not. For example, Dahrendorf (1959) argued that authority relations, not property relations, underlie social conflict. Collins (1975) considered coercion, including violence, as important means of control, but he also drew from the symbolic-interaction tradition to stress the importance of meanings in the organization of people for struggle, both at the interpersonal and the social-structural levels.

The study of economic development exemplifies how the conflict perspective has become important for many topics of enquiry. The conflict approach in this context stresses the use of economic, political, and military power to impose unequal exchanges which lead to a world-system marked by dependency; many analysts have sought to account for underdevelopment in the Third World using this perspective.

Types of social conflicts

Social scientists seek to understand specific conflicts in the context of interdependent relations and institutionalized means of changing relations. Many such kinds of conflicts have long been studied, as testified by the literature on wars, revolutions, labour strikes, communal riots and interpersonal fights. Social scientists have sought to develop explanations for social conflicts in general, examining their sources, patterns of escalation, de-escalation, settlement and consequences. There are important similarities among all kinds of conflicts as adversaries mutually define each other, perceive incompatible goals, strive to attain them, and resolve the conflict through various combinations of imposition and implicit and explicit negotiations. To specify such ideas, types of conflicts need to be distinguished. Variations in types of social conflicts affect the way they emerge, escalate, and de-escalate. Among the many variations are three particularly significant and interrelated factors: the character of the parties, the nature of the goals, and the means used in the struggle.

First, conflicting parties differ in their degree of organization and boundedness. At one extreme are governments, trade unions and other entities with membership rules and generally recognized roles for forming and executing policy towards adversaries. At the other extreme are more nebulous entities such as social classes and believers in a common ideology where boundaries of adherence may be disputed or in flux, and which generally lack recognized roles for contending with adversaries. Moreover, every social conflict is likely to include many adversaries: some overlapping and cross-cutting, or encompassing others. For example, a government head may claim to speak for a government, a state, a people, an ideology, a political party faction, and a social class. Each such claim helps constitute a corresponding adversary. Herein lies one of the bases for the interlocking character of conflict.

Second, social conflicts are about incompatible goals, and the nature of these goals are another basis for distinguishing different kinds of conflicts. Adversaries may contest control over land, money, or other resources which they all value: such disputes are *consensual* conflicts. Alternatively, they may come into conflict about differently held values. These are *dissensual* conflicts. Of course, in specific conflicts both consensual and dissensual components are usually present. In addition, goals differ in their significance for the adversaries, e.g. whether they pertain to peripheral interests or to basic human needs.

Third, conflicts are waged in a variety of ways. Conflict analysts are usually interested in struggles involving violence or other forms of coercion, whether employed or threatened, and which are relatively non-institutionalized. But an adversary often uses persuasion and even the promise of rewards to influence the other side to agree to what is being sought. In many conflicts, the adversaries adhere to well-developed and highly institutionalized rules; indeed, these are often not regarded as social conflicts at all. This may be the case, for instance, in electoral campaigns, where different parties seek to control the government. Certain kinds of conflicts may become increasingly institutionalized and regulated over time, and that transformation is a matter of paramount significance. We can recognize such a change in labour-management conflicts in many countries during the nineteenth century (Dahrendorf 1959).

Aside from the theoretical issues, the value orientations of the investigators are also crucial in the study of conflicts. Some tend to approach social conflict from a partisan perspective, trying to learn how to advance the goals of their side. This is the case for military strategists and many advocates of national liberation. Others want to minimize violence and look for alternative ways of defending or attaining their goals. Still others are primarily interested in attaining a new social order, justified in terms of universal claims for justice or equity; they may see conflicts as the natural process towards this end. Finally, the intellectually curious adopt a disinterested, relativistic view of social conflicts.

Such judgements of social conflicts are affected by a variety of social conditions, intellectual changes, and the course of major paradigm-shifting conflicts. For example, in the USA during the 1950s, conflicts were often viewed as unrealistic and disruptive and as instigated by socially marginal individuals; during the late 1960s and 1970s, they were often viewed as realistic efforts to redress injustices; in the 1980s, all contenders in a struggle tended to be accorded some legitimacy.

Origins of social conflicts

Social scientists mostly find the bases of social conflicts in social, political and economic relations and not in the biological nature of humans. But social conditions and processes internal to one party in a conflict may be stressed in accounting for a fight or for the means used in waging the struggle (Ross 1993). For example, feminists note the prevalence of gender role socialization which produces aggressiveness among men, and psychologists note that resentments arising from dissatisfaction from one source may be displaced upon easily targeted scapegoats. This produces an unrealistic conflict, in the sense that it is not based on objective conditions, or that the means employed are disproportionate to the issues at stake. It is difficult to assess the objective basis or appropriate means for solving a conflict, although various studies are contributing something in this direction.

Most conflict theorists stress that conflicts arise from adversaries striving for the same limited matters, and one underlying basis for such conflicts is inequality. Other conflicts may arise from differences in goals – when groups have different values but one group seeks to impose its own upon the other. In addition to differences which underlie the emergence of conflicts, the potential adversaries may have qualities which reduce the likelihood of a conflict erupting, such as high levels of interdependence and shared norms.

The system within which possible adversaries act can also effect the eruption of conflicts. The existence of legitimate means for managing conflicts usually reduces the likelihood of a conflict emerging. Functionalist theorists stressing the functional integration and consensual character of social systems, believe that many conflicts result from unequal rates of social change (Johnson 1966). Such conflicts tend to exhibit

behaviour which analysts regard as expressive rather than instrumental.

Awareness by adversaries that they are in conflict is necessary for a conflict to exist. Some analysts argue that awareness arises from absolute deprivation, while others regard relative deprivation as more important (Gurr 1970). In any event, the group members' beliefs that they are able to improve their conditions are crucial, and these beliefs vary with developments in each contending party and in their relations with each other. The strength and cohesion of the dominant group is critical to the emergence and success of challengers to domination (Goldstone 1991). Groups seeking to change others must also be able to mobilize to pursue their goals (Tilly 1978). Pre-existing interpersonal linkages help mobilization, as do charismatic leaders and shared ideologies of possible recruits.

The fact that dominant groups are relatively able to attain their goals helps explain why they often initiate further demands leading to overt conflict. If a subordinate group believes that it can effectively challenge the status quo, the dominant group may react by attempting to suppress the challengers by persuading others to regard the status quo as legitimate.

Conflict escalation, de-escalation and settlement

Most studies of social conflicts have focused on the emergence of coercive behaviour and its escalation, but interest in conflict de-escalation and conflict resolution has grown. The coercive means used in waging a conflict vary greatly in intensity and extent, and non-coercive inducements are also used in conflicts. While coercion encompasses a variety of violent and non-violent means, non-coercion includes efforts at persuasion and positive sanctions, such as promised benefits (Kriesberg 1982). Escalation and de-escalation are affected by the internal developments in each of the adversary groups, the interaction between them, and the conduct of actors not initially involved in the conflict.

First, internal factors include various social-psychological processes and organizational developments which lead to an increasing commitment to the cause of the struggle. Sub-units engaged in the conflict may derive power, status and economic gains by building up their fighting resources, while those who suffer in the struggle, especially if they are much more severely affected than their adversaries, may become less committed.

Second, how adversaries interact significantly affects a conflict's development. Adversary actions can be provocatively hostile and hence escalating, or successfully intimidating and thereby de-escalating; or the actions can be conciliatory and thus de-escalating, or appeasing and thereby encouraging escalation. Many conditions affect which specific patterns of conduct have which effects (Kriesberg 1982).

Third, parties not initially involved in a conflict affect its course of development by joining in to advance their own interests or by setting limits to the conflict. Intermediaries can also mitigate the undesired aspects of conflicts by mediation, thus facilitating communication and providing face-saving options. Every fight ends, but the end may be the prelude to the next fight. An understanding of the nature of a conflict's conclusion is a critical aspect in the study of social conflicts.

Adversaries in conflicts generally evaluate the outcomes in terms of victories or defeats, wins or losses. In addition, mutual losses are likely, as a conflict destructively escalates. It is also possible, however, that mutual gains are achieved, because of the interlocking character of conflicts and the reframing of a conflict to achieve a mutually beneficial settlement. The longer term and indirect consequences of social conflicts are also important. Functionalists point to the functions of social conflicts not only for the contending parties, but for the larger system in which the conflicts occur (Coser 1956). Analysts adopting a conflict perspective observe that not only are conflicts endemic, but also they are ways of bringing about needed changes.

Louis Kriesberg
Syracuse University

References

Collins, R. (1975) *Conflict Sociology*, New York.
Coser, L. (1956) *The Functions of Social Conflict*, New York.
Dahrendorf, R. (1959) *Class and Class Conflict in Industrial Society*, London.
Goldstone, J. A. (1991) *Revolution and Rebellion in the Early Modern World*, Berkeley, CA.
Gramsci, A. (1971) *Selections from the Prison Notebooks*, London.
Gurr, T. R. (1970) *Why Men Rebel*, Princeton, NJ.
Johnson, C. (1966) *Revolutionary Change*, Boston, MA.
Kriesberg, L. (1982) *Social Conflicts*, 2nd edn, Greenwich, CT.
Ross, M. H. (1993) *The Culture of Conflict*, New Haven, CT.
Tilly, C. (1978) *From Mobilization to Revolution*, Reading, MA.

Further reading

Boulding, K. E. (1962) *Conflict and Defense*, New York.
Galtung, J. (1980) *The True World: A Transnational Perspective*, New York.
Kriesberg, L. (1992) *International Conflict Resolution*, New Haven, CT.

Schelling, T. C. (1980) *The Strategy of Conflict*, Cambridge, MA.

See also: feud; peace studies; war studies.

conformity

Early attempts to explain the many uniformities observable in human social behaviour in terms of either a limited number of instincts (McDougall) or some general principle of learning such as imitation or suggestion (Tarde, Le Bon) proved to be unsatisfactory because they were essentially circular explanations. Research on conformity *per se* did not commence until the question of accounting for regularities in behaviour was tackled experimentally in the laboratory.

In the 1930s Sherif (1935) investigated, under laboratory conditions, the formation and functioning of social norms. He chose a task, based on the autokinetic effect, for which there were no pre-established norms or standards which might aid his subjects in making their judgements. When a fixed point of light is viewed in an otherwise totally darkened room it will appear to move. Sherif's subjects had to estimate, in inches, the extent of this apparent movement. Individuals, making a series of such judgements alone, established their own particular norm. When several such individuals subsequently performed the task in each other's presence, a convergence in their estimates was noted, i.e. the emergence of a group norm. Other individuals, who made their initial estimates under group conditions, subsequently maintained the group norm when responding alone. It was Durkheim (1966) who had first identified the state of anomie or normlessness. Sherif, by selecting the autokinetic effect, was able to investigate scientifically this social phenomenon, and he demonstrated how a social norm acts as a frame of reference to guiding individual action.

Enlightened liberals, who value the autonomy of the individual, disliked a possible implication of Sherif's findings: that humans are gullible. In the early 1950s Asch hoped to demonstrate individual autonomy by removing the ambiguity in the stimuli to be judged. Naïve subjects in his experiment found themselves, on certain critical trials, in a minority of one when making simple judgements about the equivalence of length of lines (Asch 1956). They were unaware of the fact that the other participants were, in reality, stooges of the experimenter who, on the pre-selected trials, were unanimous in making a wrong choice. On each trial the naïve subject responded either last or last but one. On approximately two-thirds of the occasions when this conflict occurred, the naïve subject remained independent. So Asch had proved his point. Or had he? It was the minority response in the Asch situation, however, that riveted people's attention, i.e. yielding to the opinion of the false majority. Individuals differed quite widely in the extent to which they conformed. That naïve subjects should conform on as many as one-third of such occasions deeply shocked many Americans and also, one suspects, Asch himself.

The experiment had an immediate impact outside of Asch's own laboratory. Much was written, of a popular nature, about the prevalence of conformity in social life. By varying both the size and the unanimity of the false majority, Asch showed that the effect depended crucially upon the majority being unanimous and that it was maximal in strength with a majority of four. Crutchfield (1955) mechanized the Asch procedure by standardizing on a group of five and substituting electronic for live stooges. All five were naïve subjects, believing themselves to be subject number five. This greatly increased the efficiency of data collection without significantly reducing the level of conformity. Deutsch and Gerard (1955) increased the individual's independence in the Asch situation by either increasing the salience of self to self (by requiring subjects to note down their own responses *before* hearing the responses of the others) or by decreasing the salience of self to others (with anonymous responding).

Milgram's (1974) experimental studies of obedience were as controversial in the mid-1960s as Asch's studies had been in the early 1950s. Milgram identified the conditions conducive to the carrying out of instructions coming from a legitimate source of authority (i.e. the experimenter). In response to Asch's studies, Moscovici (1976) has developed a theory of minority influence. He is concerned with identifying how it is that minorities, over time, come to influence the majority. While his theory is based on laboratory evidence, Moscovici is more broadly interested in how creative individuals (like Freud, Einstein or Darwin) manage to convert the majority to their own way of thinking. He is thus more interested in studying creativity and change than in studying the maintenance of the status quo.

Robert M. Farr
London School of Economics and
Political Science

References

Asch, S. E. (1956) 'Studies of independence and submission to group pressure: 1. A minority of one against a unanimous majority', *Psychological Monographs* 70.

Crutchfield, R. S. (1955) 'Conformity and character', *American Psychologist* 10.

Deutsch, M. and Gerard, H. B. (1955) 'A study of normative and informational social influences upon individual judgment', *Journal of Abnormal and Social Psychology* 51.

Durkheim, E. (1966) *Suicide*, Glencoe, IL.

Milgram, S. (1974) *Obedience to Authority: An Experimental View*, London.

Moscovici, S. (1976) *Social Influence and Social Change*, London.

Sherif, M. (1935) 'A study of some social factors in perception', *Archives of Psychology* 27.

See also: deviance; group dynamics; norms; social psychology.

connectionism

The term connectionism has been used in a variety of senses in the history of psychology. Carl Wernicke's (1874) model of language functioning, which emphasized connections between different areas of the brain, was dubbed connectionist, as was Donald Hebb's (1949) account of memory as the strengthening of neural connections. The modern use of the term is related to Hebb's, and applies to computational models of human performance that are built from neuron-like units. These models can be traced back to the work of McCulloch and Pitts (1943) on the simulation of neural functioning. Their ideas were simplified and made computationally viable by Rosenblatt (1962), in his work on *perceptrons* in the 1950s and 1960s. However, interest in perceptrons waned when Minsky and Papert (1969) showed that the best understood perceptrons had severe limitations. In particular they could not solve so-called *exclusive-OR* problems, in which a stimulus was to be classified in a particular way if it had one property or another property, but not both. More complex perceptrons were difficult to analyse mathematically, but interest in them revived in the late 1970s, with the availability of cheap computer power. Such computer power enabled a practical, rather than a mathematical, demonstration of what problems could be solved by complex *neural networks*.

Since the mid-1980s neural network computing has seen a wide variety of applications, most of which lie outside of psychology. The term connectionism, though not strictly defined, is usually applied to the use of neural networks in psychological models of a kind made popular by Rumelhart, McClelland, Hinton and others (McClelland *et al.* 1986; Rumelhart *et al.* 1986). A connectionist model contains three groups of neuron-like units called *input units, hidden units and output units*. The basic property of a unit is to have a *level of activation*, corresponding roughly to a rate of neural firing. Activation is passed along the connections that link the units into a network, so that the activation of a particular unit is affected (either positively or negatively) by the activation of the units it is linked to. Passing of activation takes place in a series of cycles, one at each tick of a (computational) clock.

The stimulus that a connectionist net is currently responding to is encoded as a pattern of activation in the input units. Cycles of activation passing lead to a pattern of activation in the output units, which encodes the net's response. The hidden units come between the input units and the output units, and allow considerable complexity both in the responses that the net can make and in the relations between the ways it responds to different stimuli.

It is possible to specify the function of units in a connectionist network and the strengths of the connections between them. For example, a unit in a word identification system might correspond to a letter *A* at the beginning of the word, and this unit will be highly activated by a word that actually begins with *A*. In addition, this unit will have strong positive connections to units that represent words beginning with *A*. However, one of the most important properties of connectionist networks is that they can *learn* to perform tasks. But, if they are to learn, all that can be specified is the methods of encoding used by the input and the output units. The interpretation of activation of the hidden units, and of the strengths of the connections between the units cannot be predetermined. In fact, learning in such systems is defined as a change in strength of the connections.

The best known method of learning in connectionist nets is *back propagation*. Initially the strengths of the connections are set at random, and an input is presented to the system. It produces a random output, but is told by its teacher (usually another part of the program) what the correct output should be. The difference between the actual output and the correct output is then used to adjust the strengths of the connections, working back from the output units to the input units (hence *back* propagation). This procedure is repeated many times for different inputs, selected from a so-called *training set*. The changes to the strengths of the connections are always (very) small, because the net must not get its response to the last input right by messing up its responses to other inputs. Eventually, a set of connection strengths should emerge that allows accurate response to all the stimuli in the training set and to other stimuli from the same class, on which it might be tested. Unsupervised methods of learning are also available for connectionist nets. *Competitive learning* is the best known in psychology, but a technique called *adaptive resonance* may be more useful.

Connectionist networks have found a variety of applications, both in psychological modelling and in the real world. In psychological modelling, the area that has seen the most successful application of pure connectionist techniques has been the identification of spoken and written words. In other domains, particularly those thought of as 'higher level', *hybrid* models are more popular. These models combine connectionist techniques with more traditional symbolic ones. Interestingly, in commercial applications (see, e.g. Lisboa 1992), such as industrial process control (including robotics and machine vision) and pattern classification, hybrid system are also often used.

Although strong claims have been made for them, connectionist nets suffer certain limitations. First, despite their success in models of, in particular, spoken word identification, connectionist nets in their basic form are not able to represent sequential information in a natural way. However, the recurrent (or sequential) nets developed by Jordan (1986) do have this capability, since they feed information from the output units back to the input units (with a time delay), so that temporal sequences may be learned. A more important limitation is that current connectionist networks appear to be incapable of explaining some of the inevitable relations between bits of information stored in the human mind. As Fodor and Pylyshyn (1988: 48) point out

> You don't . . . get minds that are prepared to infer *John went to the store* from *John and Mary and Susan and Sally went to the store* and from *John and Mary went to the store* but not from *John and Mary and Susan went to the store.*

Unfortunately it is all too easy for connectionist nets to have this property.

Alan Garnham
University of Sussex

References

Fodor, J. A. and Pylyshyn, Z. W. (1988) 'Connectionism and cognitive architecture: a critical analysis', *Cognition* 28.

Hebb, D. O. (1949) *The Organization of Behavior: A Neuropsychological Theory*, New York.

Jordan, M. I. (1986) 'Attractor dynamics and parallelism in a connectionist sequential machine', in *Proceedings of the Eighth Annual Conference of the Cognitive Science Society*, Hillsdale, NJ.

Lisboa, P. J. G. (ed.) (1992) *Neural Networks: Current Applications*, London.

McClelland, J. L., Rumelhart, D. E. and the PDP Research Group (1986) *Parallel Distributed Processing: Explorations in the Microstructure of Cognition*, vol. 2, *Psychological and Biological Models*, Cambridge, MA.

McCulloch, W. S. and Pitts, W. H. (1943) 'A logical calculus of ideas immanent in nervous activity', *Bulletin of Mathematical Biophysics* 5.

Minsky, M. and Papert, S. (1969) *Perceptrons*, Cambridge, MA.

Rosenblatt, F. (1962) *Principles of Neurodynamics*, New York.

Rumelhart, D. E., McClelland, J. L. and the PDP Research Group (1986) *Parallel Distributed Processing: Explorations in the Microstructure of Cognition*, vol. 1, *Foundations*, Cambridge, MA.

Wernicke, C. (1874) *Der aphasische Symptomenkomplex*, Breslau.

Further reading

Levine, D. S. (1991) *Introduction to Neural and Cognitive Modeling*, Hillsdale, NJ.

See also: artificial intelligence; nervous system.

consciousness

Consciousness in the core sense refers to a state or continuum in which we are able to feel, think and perceive. Certain popular and social science usages, such as class consciousness, consciousness raising and self consciousness, refer to the content, style or objects of consciousness rather than the primary fact of being aware.

Consciousness is paradoxical because we have direct and immediate personal knowledge of it, but, at the same time, it seems to evade the explanatory frameworks of the social and natural sciences. Let us assume that it can be shown that a particular group of neurons in the brain fires whenever the observer sees something red, and that another group of neurons fires whenever the observer sees something green. This might explain how the observer can make different responses to different colours, but does not seem to explain the subjective appearance of those colours. Acquisition of the appropriate linguistic usages of the term red (as a child) might explain why we can all agree that ripe strawberries and English post boxes are red, but can it explain their redness? This point is illustrated in the puzzle of the inverted spectrum; suppose what you see as having the subjective quality of redness, I see as having the subjective quality of greenness. We nevertheless can agree in our use of colour names because the same (publicly describable) objects always cause similar (private) sensations for a given individual.

Philosophers have given the name *qualia* to specific sensory qualities, such as the smell of freshly baked bread, the sound of a breaking glass, or the colour and texture of the bark of an oak tree. To know these things vividly and precisely, it is not good enough to be told about them, one must experience them for oneself. Consciousness seems to depend on a privileged observer and unique viewpoint, and it might be argued that the subjective aspects of consciousness are thus outside the explanatory systems of science which are based on shared knowledge (Nagel 1986), and, by extension, beyond all socially constructed meanings.

William James (1890) provided a critique and synthesis of the nineteenth-century debate about whether the mind originated from the material brain or a non-material soul. He concluded that thought was founded on brain physiology but followed its own laws. His analysis of consciousness began with introspection.

Consciousness, or the stream of thought, is continuous and ever-changing. Thought is personal, related to an 'I' or self; it always has objects; it is selective and evaluative. Consciousness has a span: there are a limited number of objects which we can attend to simultaneously, and there is a span of immediate memory, for events which are just past and have not yet left consciousness.

Problems with introspection as a scientific tool contributed to the ascendancy of behaviourism from the 1920s to the 1950s. Behaviourists held that behaviour could be observed unambiguously, but mental states could not. Establishing the laws relating stimuli and responses would provide a complete explanation of behaviour, denying a causal status to mental events; consciousness was redundant.

With the growth of cognitive psychology in the 1960s, the causal status of mental events was re-affirmed; cognition (by analogy with computer programs) was identified as the processing of information received by the senses. It became legitimate to investigate such topics as mental imagery, objective measures such as reaction times providing corroboration of subjective reports. Much of cognitive processing, including early stages of perceptual analysis, was shown to be unavailable to consciousness, which was linked with focal attention.

Compelling evidence that consciousness depends upon specific brain functions comes from studies of patients with brain injuries. If the visual cortex on one side of the brain is destroyed following a stroke, vision is lost in the opposite half of the visual field. Such patients report a complete absence of any visual sensations from the blind hemifield. Some of these patients nevertheless can point, quite accurately, to a visual target in the 'blind' hemifield, while denying that they see anything. There is thus a dissociation between the conscious experience of seeing and the visual processing required for pointing; vision without conscious awareness is termed 'blindsight' (Weiskrantz 1986). If right parietal cortex is damaged, patients tend to exhibit a syndrome known as unilateral neglect. They appear not to be conscious of bodily or extra-personal space on the side opposite the lesion. The sensory input appears to be intact, because if a stimulus is applied in isolation to the neglected side, it can usually be detected. However, under everyday conditions patients may misjudge the centre of doors, eat only the right half of food on a plate or dress only the right half of the body. Bisiach and Luzzatti (1978) have shown that unilateral neglect applies to imagined as well as real scenes. It would appear that conscious awareness of an external world, of the body, and of an imagined scene, requires brain processes over and above the simple registration of sensory inputs. A key component of consciousness is deliberate or voluntary action: Luria (1973) described patients who, after massive frontal lobe lesions, were completely passive, expressed no wishes or desires and made no requests. Luria showed that this was a disturbance only of the higher forms of conscious activity, not a global paralysis or stupor. Involuntary or routine behaviours were intact or intensified, emerging sometimes at inappropriate moments, due to the loss of conscious regulation. Incidental stimuli such as the squeak of a door could not be ignored; a patient might respond involuntarily to an overheard conversation with another patient, while being unable to respond directly to questions.

Shallice (1982) has proposed that the frontal lobes are part of a supervisory attentional system which controls and modulates the routine, involuntary and habitual processes of behaviour and perception, and it is tempting to identify conscious thought with the normal operation of systems of this kind. Velmans (1992) has argued, however, that it is mistaken to abandon a first-person for a third-person perspective in this way, and that it is focal attention, not consciousness, which has a role in human information processing.

What are the developmental origins of consciousness? Vygotsky (1986) saw individual subjective awareness as secondary and derivative of social awareness; an internalization of processes and concepts derived from the wider culture via speech (Kozulin 1990). In keeping with this view, the ability to monitor one's own experiences and the intentions of others are facets of the same developmental achievement (metarepresentation). According to Perner (1991), children below the age of 4 years do not know that they have intentions: moreover, in solving a puzzle they did not know whether they chose the right answer because they knew it was correct, or by guessing.

Social and cognitive theories of consciousness are broadly compatible with a functionalist stance on the mind–body problem. Thus, Dennett (1991) has argued that enough is now known, from psychology, social sciences, neuroscience and computer science, to provide an explanation (in principle) of consciousness. Only the philosophers' puzzles remain, and Dennett marshals arguments to strip them of their power: qualia, for instance, are ultimately nothing more than the sum total of our reactive dispositions, and there is no Cartesian theatre where conscious events are played out for us.

Crick (1994) argues that a neurophysiology of consciousness is within the scope of science. It should be possible, for example, to identify the neural correlates of visual awareness. Neurons in higher visual areas, such as V4 and V5, have responses which correlate more closely with perceptual responses than do neurons in lower visual areas such as V1: V4 cells responding to colour patches are influenced in their firing by surrounding colour patches in a way that parallels human perception of colour; cells in V1 tend simply to respond to the wavelength of light. Crick reviews evidence that 'back projections' from higher to lower visual areas are important in visual awareness; they may unify the isolated visual features which bottom-up, hierarchical analysis has identified.

The demystification of consciousness by such means is unlikely to satisfy everyone, and for many, the paradox endures. Penrose (1994), for example, implies that the primacy of conscious experience places it outside the functionalist paradigm. He explains with great clarity fundamental problems in the theory of computation and quantum physics, and argues (more obscurely) that there is a deep connection between these problems and that of consciousness.

Michael Wright
Brunel University

References

Bisiach, E. and Luzzatti, C. (1978) 'Unilateral neglect, representational schema and consciousness', *Cortex* 14.

Crick, F. (1994) *The Astonishing Hypothesis: The Scientific Search for the Soul*, New York.

Dennett, D. C. (1991) *Consciousness Explained*, New York.

James, W. (1890) *The Principles of Psychology*, New York.

Kozulin, A. (1990) *Vygotsky's Psychology: A Biography of Ideas*, New York.

Luria, A. R. (1973) *The Working Brain: An Introduction to Neuropsychology*, Harmondsworth.

Nagel, T. (1986) *The View from Nowhere*, Oxford.

Penrose, R. (1994) *Shadows of the Mind*, Oxford.

Perner, J. (1991) *Understanding the Representational Mind*, Cambridge, MA.

Shallice, T. (1982) 'Specific disorders of planning', *Philosophical Transactions of the Royal Society of London* 298.

Velmans, M. (1992) 'Is human information processing conscious?', *Behavioral and Brain Sciences* 14.

Vygotsky, L. S. (1986) *Thought and Language*, ed. A. Kozulim, Boston, MA.

Weiskrantz, L. (1986) *Blindsight*, Oxford.

See also: cognitive psychology; mental imagery; mind; unconscious.

conservation

Conservation is essentially a stockholding activity. Holding back today allows greater use tomorrow or perhaps 100 years hence. Economists' attention, and ours, is generally focused on natural phenomena – fish, oil, environmental quality and suchlike – although machines, literature and culture may also be conserved and many of the same principles apply.

The earth is finite, its resources and its ability to carry population and absorb pollution are limited.

Some economists believe that continued growth in output and population will bring the world to these limits perhaps rather quickly. According to this view both non-renewable stocks (such as oils and metals) and renewable resources (for example, fish and land) will come under increasing and perhaps irreparable strain. Environmental damage (through erosion, build-up of carbon dioxide) will likewise become excessive, and habits of high consumption, once built up, will be difficult to break. Radical and Marxist economists often blame such problems on capitalism, even if the countries of eastern Europe appear to have fared equally badly.

A more characteristic view among economists is that *markets* provide adequate incentives to conservation. Resource use will be determined mainly by expected price movements and the discount rate. Scarcity involves high prices, expected scarcity expected high prices, increasing the advantage both of conserving the resource and of taking other resource-saving measures such as recycling and appropriate technical change. Only where market failure occurs is there perhaps cause to worry, and even then such failure may tend to excessive conservation. Moreover, market failure can generally be recognized and alleviated. Occasionally the view emerges that such difficulties present a challenge, which mighty humankind must and will overcome. Wise use of resources to build up capital and develop new techniques and skills may be a crucial part of this fight.

The 1973 oil crisis exhibited vividly the possibilities and dangers of a resource crisis. The sudden fourfold rise in oil prices caused worldwide disruption; the ensuing slumpflation (though doubtless partly due to earlier causes) has been an obvious disaster, economically, medically and socially. Even an oil-rich country like Britain has been depressed. Econometric studies have indicated great responsiveness to price, but building up slowly over decades as capital, technologies and habits change. It is the slowness of these changes that has created the current crisis, while in the longer run technological changes may bring unwelcome side-effects.

Renewable resources (like fish) are constantly replenished by nature, hence permitting (up to a point) continued use without depletion. There is a maximum sustainable yield, although it may be desirable to hold yield below this level because of harvesting cost, or above it because of discounting. With non-renewable resources (like oil), use now precludes use later, although reserves can be extended by improved extraction techniques and by exploration. Metals are normally considered non-renewable, although recycling can extend their use.

The natural environment is another kind of resource. To some extent it is the concern of the rich, for example, as a source of landscape and recreational experiences. However, in this it differs little from other parts of market and indeed non-market systems. But not all environmental problems are of this type. Water pollution and air pollution damage those who live in the areas concerned – often the poor, as the rich can afford to move away (into conservation areas perhaps). Erosion, flooding and pesticides will affect everyone. There are also international problems, such as global overheating and the excessive build-up of carbon dioxide leading to difficult-to-reverse melting of the polar ice caps and very extensive flooding. Problems associated with nuclear radiation are widely feared.

There are two reasons for including population in this discussion: first, population size and growth are major determinants of problems of resources and environment; second, childbearing involves the characteristic externality problem of unpaid burdens on others, especially if fiscal help is given to large families. Currently the world's population is doubling every forty years. In some countries, such as China and Taiwan, dramatic downward shifts in birth rate are occurring. But elsewhere, as in India and most Muslim and Roman Catholic countries, signs of change are very weak. Even in most developed countries population growth continues, with particularly strong resource effects. The causes are complex and poorly understood, although cost has been found relevant.

Many factors underlie inadequate conservation (see Pearce 1976), for example, difficulties of prediction and the appropriate treatment of uncertainty. Particularly important are common access problems, applying not only to fishing, but also to forestry, hunting, extraction of oil and deep sea nodule mining, and to population growth. Tax regimes can be strongly anti-conservationist – childbearing and US mining are important examples. Another possible problem is that the discount rate used is too high, giving undue favour to the present; the difficulties here are, first, that this is an economy-wide problem, by no means confined to resources, and indeed some writers have used it to justify greater investment and faster growth; second, governments may hesitate to override the preferences of the current generation; and, third, more radical authors suggest that growth itself uses resources and damages the environment, although this is disputed.

Remedies are difficult to summarize. Characteristically those used (and supported by most non-economists) are regulations, whereas much of the economic debate is over the superiority of taxes. Regulations include net size, limited seasons and outright bans in fishing, limits or bans for pollution, including pesticides, and planning regulations for building and land use. The objection is that lack of discrimination leads to inefficiency; sometimes extreme inefficiency, as when limited fishing seasons invite the multiplication of boats, which stand idle over the rest of the year. Direct controls also tend to be narrowly specific, leaving no incentive to achieve more than the specified cut-back or to undertake R&D to improve control. Fiscal measures are occasionally used but with little finesse, and subsidies or tax concessions (as for airlines, heavy industries or children) are generally preferred to taxes. More promising examples, such as fuel-saving subsidies and also the emerging systems of penalizing pollution in several European countries, incidentally (and unlike controls) generating substantial revenue. There are many other possible remedies, such as nationalization, diversification (often favoured by ecologists) indirect measures (recycling, durability and curbs on advertising and so on), auctioned rights (for example to cull a resource or to pollute), public expenditure (on sewage or agricultural infrastructure and so on), provision of information, including forecasts, and attempts to influence attitudes. As Baumol and Oates (1979) emphasize, each of these methods, or indeed various combinations, will be appropriate in particular circumstances.

Richard Lecomber
University of Bristol

References

Baumol, W. J. and Oates, W. E. (1979) *Economics, Environmental Policy and the Quality of Life*, Englewood Cliffs, NJ.
Pearce, D. W. (1976) *Environmental Economics*, London.

Further reading

O'Riordan, T. (1976) *Environmentalism*, London.
Pearce, D. W., Turner, R. K. and Bateman, I. (1993) *An Introduction to Environmental Economics*, London.
Schultz, T. P. (1981) *Economics of Population*, Reading, M.A.

See also: energy; environment; environmental economics; population and resources.

conservatism

Conservatism is the doctrine that the reality of any society is to be found in its historical development, and therefore that the most reliable, though not the sole, guide for governments is caution in interfering with what has long been established. Clearly distinctive conservative doctrine emerged in the 1790s, in reaction to the rationalist projects of the French revolutionaries, and its classic statement is to to found in Edmund Burke's *Reflections on the Revolution in France* (1790). Burke's historical emphasis was itself the outcome of deep currents in European thought, currents rejecting abstract reasoning as a method for understanding the human world. The sheer flamboy-ance of Burke's rhetoric was necessary to bring conservatism into the world, however, since the doctrine in its purest form consists of a few maxims of prudence (concerning the complexity of things and the wisdom of caution) which, in the intellectualist atmosphere of the last two centuries, make a poor showing against the seductive philosophical pretensions of modern ideologies. These competing doctrines claim to explain not only the activity of politics, but humankind and its place in the universe. Burke himself thought that this wider picture was supplied for us by religion, and thus he was prone to extend the reverence appropriate to divine things so that it embraced the established institutions of society. This fideist emphasis, however, ought not to conceal the fact that conservatism rests upon a deep scepticism about the ability of any human being, acting within the constraints of a present consciousness, to understand the daunting complexities of human life as it has developed over recorded time.

Conservatism construes society as something that grows, and conservatives prefer pruning leaves and branches to tearing up the roots. The latter view is taken by radicals who believe that nothing less than a revolutionary transformation both of society and of human beings themselves will serve to save us from what they believe to be a deeply unjust society. Generically, then, all are conservative who oppose the revolutionary transformation of society. Specifically, however, conservatism is one of three doctrinal partners, each of which may plausibly claim centrality in the European political tradition. One of these is liberalism, constituted by its allegiance to liberty and the values of reform, and the other is constitutional socialism, whose fundamental preoccupation with the problem of the poor leads it to construe all political problems as issues of realizing a truer community. Modern politics is a ceaseless dialogue between these three tendencies and movements.

Conservatism in this specific sense emerged from a split in the Whig Party in late eighteenth-century Britain, and it was only in the 1830s, when the present nomenclature of each of the three doctrines crystallized, that Tories began calling themselves 'conservatives'. This name failed to catch on in other countries, most notably perhaps the USA, where 'conservative' until recently connoted timidity and lack of enterprise. From the 1960s onwards, however, the tendency of American liberals (predominantly but not exclusively in the Democratic Party) to adopt socialist policies has provoked a reaction which calls itself '*neo*-conservative' in testimony to its adherence to many classical liberal positions.

As it is conservative doctrine that political parties must respond to changing circumstances, it would be not merely futile but also paradoxical to discover a doctrinal essence in the changing attitudes of any particular Conservative party. Nevertheless, conservatism is not only a doctrine but also a human disposition; many conservative temperaments have influenced the British Conservative Party, whose response to the successive problems of the modern world may give some clue to conservatism. Under Disraeli it organized itself successfully to exploit successive nineteenth-century extensions of the franchise, and its electoral viability has since largely depended upon the allegiance of the figure known to political scientists as the 'Tory workingman'. In the latter part of the nineteenth century, it rode a tide of imperial emotion and economic protection and stood for the unity of the United Kingdom against attempts to grant self-government to Ireland. Between the two world wars, Baldwin saw it as the task of the party to educate an electorate, now enjoying universal suffrage, in the responsibilities of power. After Attlee's creation of the Welfare State from 1945 to 1951, Churchill and Macmillan found conservative reasons for sustaining a welfarist consensus, but since 1976, Mrs Thatcher and a dominant wing of the party identified the expense of the welfare state in its present form as one of the emerging problems of politics.

A principle of conservation offers little substantive guide to political action, and is vulnerable to the objection brought by F. A. Hayek: 'By its nature, it cannot offer an alternative to the direction we are moving' (*The Constitution of Liberty*, 1960). It is a mistake, however, to identify conservatism with hostility to change; the point is rather the *source* of change. It is characteristic of all radicals to seek one big change, after which a perfected community will be essentially changeless. On this basis, they often seek to monopolize the rhetoric of change. Liberals consider it the duty of an active government to make the reforms that will dissipate social evils. While refusing to erect limitation of government into an absolute principle, conservatives tend to think that, within a strong framework of laws, society will often work out for itself a better response to evils than can be found in the necessary complexities of legislation, and worse, of course, in the simple *dictat* of the legislator. Conservatism is, in this respect, a political application of the legal maxim that hard cases make bad law. It is thus a central mistake to think of conservatism as mere hostility to change. It poses, rather, the issue of where change should originate.

Like all political doctrines, conservatism is loosely but importantly associated with a particular temperament, a view of the world. It is characteristic of the conservative temperament to value established identities, to praise habit and to respect prejudice, not because it is irrational, but because such things anchor the darting impulses of human beings in solidities of custom which we often do not begin to value until we are already losing them. Radicalism often generates youth movements, while conservatism is a disposition found among the mature, who have discovered what it is in life they most value. The ideological cast of contemporary thought has provoked some writers to present conservatism as if it contained the entire sum of political wisdom; but this is to mistake the part for the whole. Nevertheless, a society without a strong element of conservatism could hardly be anything but impossibly giddy.

Kenneth Minogue
London School of Economics and Political Science

Reference

Hayek, F. A. (1960) *The Constitution of Liberty*, London.

Further reading

Baker, K. (ed.) (1993) *The Faber Book of Conservatism*, London.
Kirk, R. (1953) *The Conservative Mind*, Chicago.
Oakeshott, M. (1962) *Rationalism in Politics*, London.
O'Sullivan, N. (1976) *Conservatism*, London.
Quinton, A. (1978) *The Politics of Imperfection*, Oxford.
Scruton, R. (1980) *Meaning of Conservatism*, London.

constitutional psychology

Constitutional psychology is an obvious and widely accepted feature of psychological thinking. At the same time it is a controversial view held by relatively few psychologists. It may be defined as the study of the relation between, on the one hand, the morphological structure and the physiological function of the body and, on the other hand, psychological and social functioning. Few psychologists would disagree with the idea that bodily structure and functioning are related to psychosocial functioning, and in fact considerable data support this relation (see e.g. Lerner and Jovanovic 1990).

The early work of Kretschmer (1921) and the later, more comprehensive research of Sheldon (e.g. 1940) were criticized on conceptual, methodological and data analytic grounds (Humphreys 1957). The scientific community had little confidence in the strengths of association between physique type and temperament reported in this work (e.g. correlations on the order of +0.8 between theoretically related physique and temperament types; Sheldon 1940). However, more methodologically careful work has established that significant associations do exist between somatotypes (endomorphs, mesomorphs, and ectomorphs) and/or other features of the body (such as physical attractiveness), and personality or temperament characteristics theoretically related to these somatotypes (e.g. viscerotonic traits, somatotonic traits and cerebrotonic traits, respectively) or to the other bodily features, for example physically attractive children and adolescents are more popular with peers than are their physically unattractive counterparts (Lerner 1987). But the strengths of the association are considerably less than that reported by Sheldon; for example, correlations more typically cluster around +0.3 (e.g. Lerner *et al.* 1991). Moreover, research relating pubertal change (such as early, on-time, and late maturation) to psychosocial functioning during adolescence has also established that significant relations exist between physiological (such as hormonal) changes or morphological characteristics and youth behaviour and development (Adams *et al.* 1992).

The controversy involved in constitutional psychology surrounds the explanation of the empirical relations between bodily characteristics and psychosocial functions. These explanations involve the well-known nature–nurture controversy. Only a minority of psychologists working in this area subscribe to nature-based interpretations of body–behaviour relations. Such interpretations stress that hereditary and/or other biological variables provide a common source of morphology, physiology and psychosocial functioning. For example, the biological variables thought to provide the source of a mesomorphic somatotype are thought also to provide the source of aggressive or delinquent behaviours (Hall and Lindzey 1978). Nurture-based explanations of body–behaviour relations stress that environmental events (for example, socialization experiences) influence both bodily and behavioural characteristics (e.g. McCandless 1970). An example of this type of interpretation is that the socialization experiences that lead to a chubby body build also will lead to dependency and/or self-indulgence (Hall and Lindzey 1978).

Finally, most contemporary interpretations propose that biological and experiential variables interact or fuse to provide a basis of physical, physiological and psychosocial characteristics (see, e.g. Adams *et al.* 1992; Lerner 1987; 1992). A representative idea here, one associated with a 'developmental contextual' theory of human development (Lerner, 1992), is that children with different physical characteristics evoke differential reactions in significant others, and that these reactions feed back to children and provide a differential basis for their further psychosocial functioning; this functioning includes personality and social behaviour and also self-management behaviours (e.g. in regard to diet and exercise) which may influence their physical characteristics.

However, there are still no crucial or critical tests of key hypotheses derived from any of the extant interpretative positions. Indeed, data in this area, although increasingly more often theoretically derived from various instances of interactionist theory, are still typically open to alternative explanations (cf. Adams, *et al.* 1992 versus Lerner 1992). Nevertheless, activity in this area of research continues to be high, especially in research on the adolescent period of life (Adams *et al.* 1992; Lerner 1987; 1992). It is likely that the theoretical debates framing this activity will continue to promote research for some time.

Richard M. Lerner
Michigan State University

Jacqueline V. Lerner
Michigan State University

Jasna Jovanovic
University of Illinois, Urbana-Champaign

References

Adams, G. R., Day, T., Dyk, P. H., Frede, E. and Rodgers, D. R. S. (1992) 'On the dialectics of pubescence and psychosocial development', *Journal of Early Adolescence* 12.

Hall, C. S. and Lindzey, G. (1978) *Theories of Personality*, New York.

Humphreys, L. G. (1957) 'Characteristics of type concepts with special reference to Sheldon's typology', *Psychological Bulletin* 54.

Kretschmer, E. (1921) *Körperbau und Charakter*, Berlin.

Lerner, R. M. (1987) 'A life-span perspective for early adolescence', in R. M. Lerner and T. T. Foch (eds), *Biological– Psychosocial Interactions in Early Adolescence: A Life-Span Perspective*, Hillsdale, NJ.

—— (1992) 'Dialectics, developmental contextualism, and the further enhancement of theory about puberty and psychosocial development', *Journal of Early Adolescence* 12.

Lerner, R. M. and Jovanovic, J. (1990) 'The role of body image in psychosocial development across the life-span: a developmental contextual perspective', in T. T. Cash and T. Pruzinsky (eds), *Body Image: Development, Deviance, and Change*, New York.

Lerner, R. M., Lerner, J. V., Hess, L. E., Schwab, J., Jovanovic, J., Talwar, R. and Kucher, J. S. (1991) 'Physical attractiveness and psychosocial functioning among early adolescents', *Journal of Early Adolescence* 11.

McCandless, B. R. (1970) *Adolescents*, Hinsdale, IL.

Sheldon, W. H. (1940) *The Varieties of Human Physique*, New York.

constitutionalism *see* constitutions and constitutionalism

constitutions and constitutionalism

The constitution of a state is the collection of rules and principles according to which a state is governed. In antiquity the most important function of a constitution was to determine who should rule. The criterion which served as the basis for assigning political power reflected the ethos of the society. Thus each constitutional form exercised a moulding influence on virtue; the good citizen was a different being in an oligarchy, a democracy and an aristocracy (Aristotle). Although modern constitutions are far more complex, still the rules they establish for acquiring and exercising governmental power will usually embody the underlying norms and ideology of the polity.

The constitution of the modern nation state contains three main elements. First, it establishes the principal institutions of government and the relationships among these institutions. These institutions may be structured on traditional western lines of a division of executive, legislative and judicial responsibilities. The constitutions of one-party states gives greater emphasis to the structures of the governing party, while those based on theocratic principles assign a dominant position to religious offices and institutions. Second, constitutions provide for a distribution of governmental power over the nation's territory. In a unitary state, local units of government are established as agencies of the central government. The constitution of a federal state assigns power directly to central and local levels of government. Third, constitutions provide a compendium of fundamental rights and duties of citizens including their rights to participate in the institutions of government. Some constitutions emphasize economic and social rights as much, if not more, than political and legal/procedural rights.

In most countries there is a single document called 'The Constitution' which contains most of the significant elements of the constitutional system. But this is not the only form in which the rules of a constitution may be expressed. They may also take the form of ordinary laws such as statutes or decrees, judicial decisions or well-established customs and conventions. The United Kingdom is distinctive in that it does not have a document known as the Constitution; all of its constitutional rules are expressed more informally as statutes, judicial opinions, customs and conventions. Since the American Revolution the worldwide trend has been very much towards the codification of constitutional norms. New states established in the aftermath of revolution, the withdrawal of empire and world war have relied on a formal constitutional text to set out their basic governmental arrangements. However, even in these new nations, statutes, judicial decisions and conventions usually supplement the formal constitution.

A country may have a constitution but may not enjoy constitutionalism. Constitutionalism is a political condition in which the constitution functions as an effective and significant limit on government. Where constitutionalism characterizes a regime, the constitution is antecedent to government, and those who

govern are constrained by its terms. The constitutional rules of such a regime are not easily changed – even when they are obstacles to policies supported by leading politicians. Thus, constitutional government is said to be 'limited government' (Sartori 1956). The limits imposed by a constitution are sometimes said to embody a 'higher law' – the enduring will of a people – which constitutes the basis of a legitimate check on the will of governments representing transient majorities (Corwin 1955; McIlwain 1947).

Constitutionalism may be maintained by the practice of judicial review, whereby judges with a reasonable degree of independence of the other branches of government have the authority to veto laws and activities of government on the grounds that they conflict with the constitution. Constitutionalism in the European Union has been largely promoted by the European Court of Justice, whose decisions have given the treaties on which the Union is based the status of constitutional law with supremacy over the laws of the member states (Mancini 1991). Constitutionalism may also be manifest in a formal amendment process that requires much more than the support of a dominant political party or a simple majority of the population to change the formal constitution. The British situation demonstrates, however, that neither of these practices is a necessary condition for constitutionalism. In that country the most important constitutional precepts are maintained and enforced more informally through well-established popular attitudes and the restraint of politicians (Dicey 1959).

The reality of constitutionalism depends on whether there are political forces genuinely independent of the government of the day powerful enough to insist on the government's observance of constitutional limits. Critics of those liberal democracies that claim to practise constitutionalism contend that in reality the constitutions imposing constitutional limits (e.g. the judiciary or the opposition party) are not independent of government, because they are controlled by social or economic interests aligned with the government. However, defenders of these regimes may point to occasions on which the maintenance of constitutional rules has forced political leaders to abandon major policies or even to abandon office (e.g. US President Nixon in the Watergate affair).

In countries that have formal written constitutions, whether or not they practise constitutionalism, the constitution may serve an important symbolic function. Constitutions are often employed as instruments of political education designed to inculcate public respect for political and social norms. A constitution may also be a means of gaining legitimacy, both internally and externally, for a regime. This is a primary function of constitutions in communist states (Brunner 1977). The development of codes of fundamental human rights since the Second World War has prompted many states to include such rights in their domestic constitutions in order to ingratiate themselves in the international community.

Peter H. Russell
University of Toronto

References

The Politics of Aristotle, (1948) trans. E. Barker, Oxford.

Brunner, G. (1977) 'The functions of communist constitutions', *Review of Socialist Law* 2.

Corwin, E. S. (1955) *The 'Higher Law' Background of American Constitutional Law*, Ithaca, NY.

Dicey, A. V. (1959) *Introduction to the Study of the Law of the Constitution*, 10th edn, London.

McIlwain, C. H. (1947) *Constitutionalism: Ancient and Modern*, revised edn, Ithaca, NY.

Mancini, G. F. (1991) 'The making of a constitution for Europe', in R. O. Keohane and S. Hoffmann (eds) *The New European Community*, Boulder, CO.

Sartori, G. (1956) 'Constitutionalism: a preliminary discussion', *American Political Science Review* 56.

Further reading

Andrews, W. G. (1961) *Constitutions and Constitutionalism*, Princeton, NJ.

Friedrich, C. J. (1950) *Constitutional Government and Democracy*, New York.

See also: federation and federalism.

consumer behaviour

In his authoritative review of the development of utility theory, Stigler (1950) wrote, 'If consumers do not buy less of a commodity when their incomes rise, they will surely buy less when the price of the commodity rises. This was the chief product – so far as the hypotheses on economic behaviour go of the long labours of a very large number of able economists [who] had known all along that demand curves have negative slopes, quite independently of their utility theorizing.' So what use is utility theory, the reigning paradigm among economists interested in consumer behaviour?

Data on consumer behaviour have expanded enormously since the 1950s, computing costs have plummetted, statistical numeracy has spread and the range of applied studies has multiplied. Simultaneously more content has been put into choice theory and more accessible links forged via the cost and other 'dual' functions between the structure of preferences and behaviour. A comprehensive modern treatment of choice theory and its application to most types of consumer behaviour can be found in Deaton and Muellbauer (1980).

The existence of an ordinal utility function defined on bundles of goods implies that certain axioms of choice are fulfilled, the key ones being transitivity or consistency of choice, continuity (small differences matter only a little) and non-satiation. Preferences can also be represented through the cost function. This defines the minimum cost of reaching a given utility level for a consumer facing given prices. Among its properties: it is concave in prices and its price derivatives give purchases as functions of prices and the utility level, i.e. compensated demands. The great advantage is that a simple step – differentiation – leads from a representation of preferences to a description of the behaviour of a consumer faced with a linear budget constraint. Concavity then immediately implies the law of demand described above. In fact, considerably more is implied: the matrix of compensated price derivatives is symmetric negative semidefinite. A great deal of econometric effort has gone into applying and testing these very considerable restrictions on behaviour.

Systems of demand equations are usually estimated for annual or quarterly observations on aggregate consumer spending on such categories as food, clothing, housing, fuel, etc. More is now understood about the links between individual and aggregate behaviour. For example, under quite restrictive conditions, average behaviour is like that of a single consumer so that then one can say a 'representative consumer' exists. Specific assumptions on the structure of preferences yield further implications. Thus an additive utility function strongly restricts the cross-price responses of demands. These and many other properties are analysed in Gorman (1976), who makes elegant use of cost and profit functions. Almost invariably, some kind of separability assumptions are made in applied work: thus, preferences for current period goods need to be separable from the allocation of leisure and of consumption in other periods if demands are functions only of current prices and total expenditure on these goods. However, such static demand functions are, by most empirical evidence, misspecified. A widely applied hypothesis which can explain why is that preferences are conditioned by past behaviour, not only of the consumer but also of others, so that demand functions are dynamic (more on this below).

By assuming that the consumer can lend or borrow at the same interest rate, the utility maximizing consumer's inter-temporal choices are subject to a linear budget constraint. In this life-cycle theory of consumption, developed by Modigliani and his co-workers, the budget is life-cycle wealth consisting of initial asset holdings, income and discounted expected income, and relative prices depend on real interest rates. Extensions to the demand for money and durables have yielded interesting insights into, for example, the role of interest rates.

The treatment of income expectations has been the most controversial issue for empirical workers using this theory. The simple treatment by Friedman in his book on the permanent income hypothesis of consumption, as well as his suppression of a separate role for assets, is now seen as less than satisfactory. Hall (1978) has shown that, under certain conditions, the life cycle model together with rational expectations implies that consumption follows a random walk. There is significant empirical evidence against both the random walk hypothesis and simple forms of the life cycle model (see Deaton 1992).

One of the major criticisms of life cycle theory is that the budget constraints are not in fact linear for credit constrained consumers, though the implications are hard to model on aggregate data. Much attention has been paid to non-linear budget constraints in the analysis of behaviour from household surveys. Labour supply decisions are the major example; others are the choice of housing tenure and transport models where choice has discrete elements. An integrated statistical framework with rational and random elements for such decisions now exists. In this context too, restrictions on preferences have major empirical content, for example, additive preferences allow great simplifications in the analysis of repeated surveys of the same households. A more traditional use of household budget surveys collected to derive weights for cost of living indices and to analyse inequality has been the derivation of Engel functions which link expenditures on different goods with the total budget and household demography. A major use has been derivation of equivalence scales used to standardize budgets in studies of poverty and inequality for variations in household size and structure.

Another way to put more content into the theory is to regard the household as a producer, using market goods and time, of utility yielding commodities. This household production approach has proved useful, for example, in the measurement of quality change, in welfare measurement of the provision of public leisure facilities, and in the economics of fertility and other aspects of family life. There has been increasing interest in how decisions by individual family members are co-ordinated.

Most decisions are, of course, made under uncertainty and the expected utility approach has been widely used by economists. Under the axioms assumed here, subjective probabilities are themselves defined and this gives rise to a theory of learning founded on Bayes' Theorem. The intuitive notion of risk averting behaviour here has a formal basis and applications to the behaviour of financial markets have proved particularly popular. Evidence against some of the axioms has accumulated from laboratory experiments on volunteers. So far no agreement exists on a better set of axioms.

There have been many criticisms of the utility maximizing approach, ranging from 'it is tautologous' to the introspective doubt that anyone could be so good at absorbing and storing information and then computing consistent decisions. H. A. Simon's notion of bounded rationality has much intuitive appeal. Certainly one can interpret the role of costs of adjustment or habits based on own or others' behaviour in this light. The implication of a stimulus response smaller in the short run than in the long is suggestive. Psychologists have suggested models such as that of 'cognitive dissonance' which appeal in particular contexts but do not yield a general behavioural theory. Market researchers have developed distinct approaches of their own based on the interpretation of attitude surveys used as marketing tools and with the major focus on brand choice, repeat buying and the introduction of new varieties. They have drawn relatively little out of the utility maximizing hypothesis, though not all these approaches are necessarily inconsistent with it.

John Muellbauer
University of Oxford

References

Deaton, A. (1992) *Understanding Consumption*, Oxford.

Deaton, A. and Muellbauer, J. (1980) *Economics and Consumer Behavior*, New York.

Gorman, W. M. (1976) 'Tricks with utility functions', in M. Artis and R. Nobay (eds) *Essays in Economic Analysis*, Cambridge, UK.

Hall, R. E. (1978) 'Stochastic implications of the life cycle-permanent income hypothesis: theory and evidence', *Journal of Political Economy* 86.

Stigler, G. (1950) 'The development of utility theory', *Journal of Political Economy* 58.

See also: consumer surplus; consumption function; microeconomics.

consumer surplus

There can be few areas of economics where more ink has been spilled in obfuscating an essentially simple idea. The basic idea of the change in consumer surplus is to measure the loss or gain to a consumer from a change in consumption or from a change in one or more prices. The early formulation by Dupuit in 1844 was justified by Marshall in 1880. It consists of taking the area under the demand curve which traces out the effect of changes in the good's price, holding constant the budget in order to measure the change in utility in money terms. Already in 1892 Pareto criticized Marshall's assumption of a constant marginal utility of the budget. Indeed, there are only two circumstances where Marshall's formulation is correct: either the proportions in which goods are consumed are independent of the budget, which is grossly untrue empirically, or, for the particular good whose price is changing, the demand is unaffected by changes in the budget.

Hicks in 1939 recognized that the correct measure is to take the change in area under the compensated demand curve. However, as Samuelson remarked in 1947, consumer surplus was essentially a superfluous concept since there was already an established theory of economic index numbers. The modern theory of index numbers is based on the cost or expenditure function which gives the minimum cost of reaching a given indifference curve at a specified set of prices. The money value of a change in utility is then given by the change in cost at some reference prices. When the change in utility is caused by some price changes, Hicks's 'compensating variation' can be viewed as the measure which uses the new prices as reference and his 'equivalent variation' as that which uses the old prices as reference.

There is a widespread impression that the computation of such correct concepts is intrinsically harder or requires more information than computing Marshallian consumer surplus. However, simple and accurate approximations to the correct measures are available, and straightforward algorithms exist to calculate them with any required degree of accuracy. Finally, it should be noted that *aggregating* utility changes over different consumers raises a new issue: is a dollar to the poor worth the same in social terms as a dollar to the rich? Consumer surplus as such does not address this question, though it is an inescapable one in cost benefit analysis.

John Muellbauer
University of Oxford

Reference

Deaton, A. and Muellbauer, J. (1980) *Economics and Consumer Behavior*, New York.

See also: consumer behaviour.

consumption function

The consumption function expresses the functional dependence of consumption on variables thought to influence the level of consumption expenditure by individuals, such as income, wealth and the rate of interest. The consumption function was an important innovation introduced into economic theory by J. M. Keynes in his *General Theory of Employment, Interest and Money* (1936), to undermine the classical orthodoxy that the rate of interest acts to equilibriate savings and investment at the full employment level of income. Keynes made consumption, and therefore saving, a function of income, and by doing so divorced the savings function from the investment function. He then showed that if plans to invest fall short of plans to save out of the full employment level of income, there will be a tendency for the level of income (not the rate of interest) to fall to bring saving and investment into equilibrium again, the extent of the fall being given by the value of the income multiplier which is the reciprocal of the marginal propensity to save. By means of the consumption function, Keynes had apparently demonstrated the possibility that an economy may find itself in an equilibrium state at less than full employment. This demonstration was part of the Keynesian revolution of thought which undermined the idea that there are macroeconomic forces at work which automatically guarantee that economies tend to long-run full employment. This is the theoretical importance of the consumption function.

The practical interest in the consumption function relates to the relation between consumption and income through time. Keynes seemed to suggest that the long-run consumption function was non-proportional, so that as societies became richer they would spend proportionately less on consumption, implying that a higher proportion of income would have to be invested if economies were not to stagnate. Fears were expressed that mature economic societies might run out of profitable investment opportunities. The international cross-section evidence reveals an interesting pattern. The savings ratio does rise with the level of development but at a decreasing rate, levelling off in maturity at about 25 per cent of national income. There is a voluminous literature concerning why this should be the case. It is as if saving is a luxury good which then loses its appeal. James Duesenberry (1949) developed the relative income hypothesis, which predicts that the savings–income ratio will remain unchanged through time if the personal distribution of income remains unchanged. Ando and Modigliani (1963) developed the life-cycle hypothesis of saving, which predicts a constant savings ratio if the rate of growth of population and per capita income are steady. Milton Friedman (1957) developed the permanent income hypothesis, arguing that individuals wish to maintain a constant relation between their consumption and a measure of permanent income determined by wealth and other factors. To discriminate between the hypotheses is virtually impossible. As societies develop, both growth and income inequality first increase and then decelerate and stabilize, which would explain the historical savings behaviour observed. Other factors that might be important relate to the increased monetization of an economy, which then yields diminishing returns. However, the fears of a lack of investment opportunities to match growing saving, owing to the saturation of markets, seems to be unfounded.

A. P. Thirlwall
University of Kent

References

Ando, A. and Modigliani, F. (1963) 'The life cycle hypothesis of saving: aggregate implications and tests', *American Economic Review* 1(53).

Duesenberry, J. (1949) *Income, Saving and the Theory of Consumer Behavior*, Cambridge, MA.

Friedman, M. (1957) *A Theory of the Consumption Function*, Washington, DC.

Keynes, J. M. (1936) *General Theory of Employment, Interest and Money*, London.

See also: consumer behaviour.

control, social *see* social control

co-operation and trust *see* trust and co-operation

co-operatives

Co-operatives are economic organizations run by their members on the basis of one person, one vote, with their trading surplus being distributed among the membership in an agreed manner. Membership can therefore be seen as an extension of corporate shareholding except that, in co-operatives, decision making is based on democratic principles. Hence the defining characteristic of the co-operative is the principle of one member, one vote. Unlike conventional firms, a capital stake is not necessarily the crucial element conferring decision-making rights. Indeed, the return on capital holdings is generally fixed at a low level, leaving the bulk of the surplus to be allocated according to member transactions. Decision-making authority derives from the characteristic of the democratic collective, such as consumers, farmers or workers. For example, in consumer co-operatives, membership derives from the act of purchase and profits are distributed according to the amount spent. In agricultural co-ops, the members are private farmers who join forces for production, retailing and services. Other important co-operative forms include credit unions and housing co-operatives,

in which the membership are borrowers and lenders and tenants respectively, and producer co-operatives, in which the workers jointly share the profits as income.

In 1844 the first co-operative was opened in Toad Lane, Rochdale, by twenty-eight Lancashire workers, who developed the seven 'Co-operative Principles' which still form the basis of the international co-operative movement. These are open membership; one member, one vote; limited return on capital; allocation of surplus in proportion to member transactions; cash trading; stress on education; and religious and political neutrality. They were reviewed by the International Co-operative Alliance (ICA), the worldwide organization of all co-ops, in 1966, and the last two principles were dropped in favour of a new one supporting inter-co-operative collaboration.

The international co-operative movement has grown to enormous proportions, with more than 700,000 co-operatives affiliated to the ICA in 1980 containing 350 million members in 65 countries. The largest number of societies were agricultural and credit co-operatives, with 250,000 each worldwide covering 180 million members between them. However, the largest number of members are in consumer co-operatives, containing 130 million in 60,000 societies. There are also 45,000 industrial co-operatives with a labour force in excess of 5.5 million workers. Co-operatives started in Europe and North America and the movement still has a solid basis there, especially consumer and agricultural co-operatives. Since the Second World War there has been rapid expansion of the co-operative movement in less developed countries, where agricultural co-operatives, for example, allow smallholders to combine their resources for harvesting, production or marketing. The co-operative form has become significant in the former communist countries of central and eastern Europe, representing a compromise between the socialist and capitalist form of work organization.

Inspired by the system of workers' self-management of industry that operated in former Yugoslavia between 1952 and 1989, and following the seminal work of Ward (1958) and Vanek (1970), these producer co-operatives, or labour-managed firms as they have become known, have been studied extensively (see Ireland and Law 1982 for a survey). Analysts interested in how enterprise decisions change when the interests of workers replace profitability as the corporate objective, have focused on five main areas. First, it has been argued that producer co-operatives are not very market-oriented firms, and may have sluggish or even perverse production responses because the membership's motivation is to increase wages and secure employment rather than to increase profit by satisfying consumer demand. Second, it is feared that such firms will under-invest, because workers will prefer higher wages now to future income increases to be obtained through investment. Third, many observers have suggested that there will be deficiencies in managerial competence and an unwillingness to bear risks. These factors together indicate that producer co-operatives might find it difficult to survive in a free market environment, a view encapsulated in the fourth proposition that producer co-operatives are founded to secure jobs in declining sectors, but when conditions improve they degenerate back to the capitalist form. Such a pessimistic argument is often countered by the final observation that employee involvement in decision making and profits can act as a decisive boost to labour productivity. This has stimulated interest in schemes for worker participation in management as a way of obtaining the positive incentive effects without the presumed deficiencies of full workers' control.

There are producer co-operative sectors in most western economies, the largest and most successful being the Mondragon group in the Basque area of Spain. Since its formation in the mid-1950s, an integrated productive, retail, financial and educational structure has emerged providing 16,000 industrial jobs. Empirical work establishes the group to be relatively more productive and profitable than comparable capitalist firms, as well as being better able to meet social goals (see H. Thomas in Jones and Svejnar, 1982). Other studies isolate a positive productivity effect in the 20,000 Italian producer co-operatives, the 700 French ones and the 800 societies in the USA (Estrin *et al.* 1987). However, apart from Mondragon, producer co-operative have tended to be relatively small, under-capitalized, concentrated in traditional sectors like textiles and construction, and short lived. The co-operative form has probably failed to displace joint stock companies despite their democratic structure and the productivity benefits because of difficulties with risk bearing; entrepreneurial workers cannot spread their risks by working in a number of activities in the way that capital owners can spread theirs by holding a diversified portfolio of assets. Hence capital has historically hired workers rather than labour hiring capital. However, many new producer co-operatives have been founded as a way of maintaining employment – about 1600 in the UK between 1975 and 1990 – and if risk-bearing problems can be solved this may prove to be an important type of enterprise in the future.

Saul Estrin
London Business School

References

Estrin, S., Jones, D. C. and Svejnar, J. (1987) 'The productivity effect of worker participation: producer co-operatives in Western economies', *Journal of Comparative Economics* 11.
Ireland, N. J. and Law, P. J. (1982) *The Economics of Labour-Managed Enterprises*, London.
Jones, D. C. and Svejnar, J. (1982) *Participatory and Self-Managed Firms*, Lexington, MA.
Vanek, J. (1970) *The General Theory of Labour-Managed Market Economics*, Ithaca, NY.
Ward, B. (1958) 'The firm in Illyria; market syndicalism', *American Economic Review* 55.

corporate enterprise

The most common form of capitalist business enterprise, the limited liability company, has a legal status or a *persona* separate from owners or shareholders. Three features arise: debts incurred are the firm's, not the shareholders', whose maximum liability is restricted to their original financial outlay; the identity of the firm is unchanged should any shareholders transfer their ownership title to a third party; contractual relations are entered into by the firm's directors.

It is widely agreed that the move to large-scale industrial enterprise was facilitated, and indeed made possible, by limited liability. The threat of potential confiscation of an individual's total wealth should part of it be invested in an unsuccessful company was removed. Moreover risk could be further reduced by investing in several and not just one firm. Large sums of untapped personal financial capital became available after the advent of limited liability. Transferability of shares permitted continuity of business operation not present in other forms of enterprise. The existence of the firm as a separate contracting *persona* permitted a productive division of labour between risk-bearing capitalist and business administrators.

Schumpeter (1950) criticized this division of labour as 'absentee ownership' which pushes 'into the background all . . . the institutions of property and free contracting . . . that expressed the needs of economic activity'. Others, such as Hessen (1979), take the contrary view: limited liability and the joint stock firm are creatures of private agreement, not the state. Freely negotiated contractual specialization is a device for greater efficiency in meeting private wants, not a shirking of responsibility.

Historically limited liability was a state-created benefit awarded by fifteenth-century English law to monastic communities and trade guilds for commonly held property. Likewise in the seventeenth century, joint stock charters were awarded as circumscribed monopoly privileges to groups such as the East India and Hudson's Bay Companies. The two properties were amalgamated by a 1662 Act of Parliament (Clapham 1957). Many entrepreneurs, banned by law from adopting the corporate form, simply copied it

using the common law provisions of transferable partnership interests alone or together with those of trusteeship. Indeed it was through those mechanisms that
the British canal and railway systems were financed and
managed in the 1780s–90s and the 1830s–40s respectively. The Bubble Act 1720, which was passed to
suppress such innovations, failed (Du Bois 1938) and in
1844 the Companies' Registration Act effectively
repealed it, setting up a registry for corporations which
made their establishment cheap and easy; the state's
role became simply that of a recording agency. The
1844 Act was amended in 1856 to provide limited
liability to all registered companies. Thus it could be
argued that either the selective legal privilege of limited
liability was extended to all or alternatively that legislation was merely catching up with the reality in the
financial market-place, namely that the characteristics
of the corporation appeared without the need for
government intervention. Nevertheless, corporations
appeared in large numbers after the institution of
limited liability. Prior to that, and still numerically
important in the 1990s, most businesses were
conducted by sole traders and unlimited partnerships
of two or more people. Incorporation encouraged firm
growth and, except in the smallest corporations, shareholders participated less in day-to-day management. In
the UK this growth continued well into the twentieth
century resulting in an increasing concentration of
industry.

Firms initially grew to obtain the advantages of scale
economies and of monopoly power. The latter was
perceived to be especially true in the USA where men
like Rockefeller and Carnegie built industrial empires
in the oil and steel industries. Congress, fearful of the
consequences of industrial size, passed the Sherman
Anti-trust Act in 1890, and firms such as Standard
Oil and American Tobacco were ordered to divest
themselves of assets and split into separate firms. In the
next three-quarters of a century many US firms
took alternative growth routes, partly to minimize
their visibility to trust-busters and partly to obtain the
benefit of diversification. Risk-avoidance was obtained
by spreading the company's efforts over a range of
domestic markets for different products, or by expanding abroad with the original product range. These
activities were mirrored elswhere by British, German,
Dutch and Swiss firms such as ICI, Hoechst, Philips
and Nestlé respectively.

Some observers are concerned at the levels of industrial concentration. They argue that as a consequence
prices are uncompetitively high, that very large firms
become inefficient and reluctant to change and innovate. Others argue that concentration varies industry
by industry and is determined by technology or is
a reward for innovation and efficiency. Large firms

become large only by winning the consumer's approval.
The leading firms are also changing and the leading
100 firms of 1900 were very different in both identity
and in ranking from the leading 100 in 1990. Firms
must either change as demand and supply conditions
change or forfeit any position they have won through
previous successful responsiveness to market conditions.
This view holds that provided entry to and exit from
an industry are easy, concentration levels need not be
a cause for concern. The issue of whether industrial
structure determines firm conduct and performance, or
whether firm performance and conduct determines
industrial structure, is still unsettled. If there are
barriers to entry imposed by regulations, the truth may
embody both theses.

A further area of debate is the degree to which incorporation and what Berle and Means (1968) called the
consequential 'divorce of ownership from control' has
resulted in managers pursuing goals different from the
maximization of profit. Alternative theories have been
put forward suggesting that managers pursue sales or
asset growth, size *per se*, or maximize utility functions
containing both financial and psychic variables. In most
cases these alternative goals are subject to a minimum
profit constraint which, if not met, would result in a
takeover by another firm, loss of managerial job security and so a return to a profit target closer to that of
maximization. Proponents of these views argue that
these alternative goals result in different patterns of
firm behaviour if the external environment changes
(for example, a flat rate tax on profits does not affect a
profit maximizer's behaviour, but a sales maximizer
subject to a minimum profits constraint would reduce
output and raise price). Defenders of the traditional
theory (such as Manne 1965) argue that efficient
stock markets, via the takeover mechanism, ensure that
managers depart but little from profit maximization. To
the extent that they do, this is a cost borne willingly by
owners to achieve the net benefits of specialization of
function between risk capital providers and the more
risk-averse providers of managerial expertise.

The issue then becomes one of how best to minimize
this agency cost (Jensen and Meckling 1976). In countries such as Sweden, Switzerland and South Africa,
pyramidal holding companies controlled by a few dominant shareholders are common. Proprietorial family
groups such as the Wallenbergs or the Oppenheimers
control an array of companies while owning only a
small percentage of the total capital. But this small fraction notwithstanding, it represents a large proportion of
the proprietors' wealth, motivating them to control
management rather than to sell out if the companies
controlled are not run in the proprietors' interests.

In Anglo-Saxon countries, such as the UK and the
USA such forms of corporate control are either discour-

aged or illegal. Roe (1991) documents the history of legal and political restraints on the control of US corporations by financial institutions such as J. P. Morgan at the turn of the century and others such as insurers, banks and unit trusts today. Black and Coffee (1993) argue that similar less formal restraints were placed on British bank ownership of shares by the Bank of England, and that while UK institutions have been major shareholders for some decades they have been reactive rather than proactive owners. Thus the divorce of ownership from control in Anglo-Saxon countries, where not offset by the takeover mechanism, is, on this view, exaggerated – by governmentally created constraints and prohibitions on minority proprietorial ownership structures which give disproportionate power to such owners, or by constraints on bank and institutional ownership, or by the 'free-rider' problem. (Thus an institution with 5 per cent of shares acting on its own to improve corporate performance would gain 5 per cent of the benefits, the remaining shareholders would reap the remaining benefits while incurring none of the costs.)

W. Duncan Reekie
University of the Witwatersrand

References

Berle, A. A. and Means, G. C. (1968) *The Modern Corporation and Private Property*, rev. edn, New York.

Black, B. and Coffee, J. (1993) *Hail Britannia? Institutional Investor Behaviour under Limited Regulation*, Columbia, NY.

Clapham, J. (1957) *A Concise Economic History of Britain from the Earliest Times to 1750*, Cambridge, UK.

Du Bois, A. (1938) *The English Business Company after the Bubble Act*, New York.

Hessen, R. (1979) *In Defense of the Corporation*, Stanford, CA.

Jensen, M. C. and Meckling, W. H. (1976) 'Theory of the firm: managerial behaviour, agency costs and university structures', *Journal of Financial Economics* 3.

Manne, H. (1965) 'Mergers and the market for corporate control', *Journal of Political Economy* 73.

Roe, M. J. (1991) 'A political theory of American corporate finance', *Columbia Law Review* 91.10.

Schumpeter, J. A. (1950) *Capitalism, Socialism and Democracy*, New York.

See also: business concentration; firm, theory of; limited liability; monopoly.

corporatism

Corporatism, whether corporate, clerical or fascist in origin, is an ideology of organization which assumes that a variety of parties will co-operate on the basis of shared values. Corporatism (also called neo-corporatism or liberal corporatism) presupposes, on the contrary, the existence of fundamental conflicts which, however, need not produce organizational disruption but can be mediated with the help of the state. The concept first appeared in Scandinavian writings after the Second World War (Heckscher, St Rokkan), but was only made generally known by Schmitter (1979; 1981). However, functional equivalents of the concept, labelled 'organized capitalism' can be traced back to Hilferding (1915) in the social democratic debate in Germany and Austria. The concept was thus developed in countries where state sponsorship of trade unions had a certain tradition, but where unions had achieved positions of considerable power.

Corporatism has been greatly extended. Left-wing theorists invoke it to explain how – despite expectations – through successful manipulation, crises did not come to a head, and class struggles were not exacerbated. More conservative scholars embraced neo-corporatism as a solution to what was termed the 'problem of ungovernability' (Schmitter 1981). Ungovernability in modern democracies was widely thought to be a consequence of the over-burdening of the system of communication. There was also said to be a weakening of legitimacy, from the point of view of the citizen. Schmitter pointed rather to the inadequate co-ordination of interests and of demands by state agencies. Corporatism offered itself as an alternative to the syndicalist view that a multitude of uncoordinated and sharply antagonistic groups confronted one another. In countries where the ideas of a social contract is undeveloped – as in Italy – or where a kind of 'bargained corporatism' is beginning to crystallize – as in Britain (Crouch 1977) – the notion of corporatism has been rejected by the unions.

Where strategies of negotiation and conflict are in a more differentiated fashion, it is often apparent that the possibilities of neo-corporatism have been over-estimated. Great strides have been made in spatial planning, health policies and to some extent in education (Cawson 1978); but where many economic interests are involved, it seems that pluralist market models are more effective in articulating interests. Where ideologically founded alternatives are in question, as in environmental policy, negotiated settlements and compromise proposals tend to meet with strong opposition.

Corporatism was a 'growth sector' in the 1980s. Hardly any book on decision making could do without the key notion of corporatism. By the end of the 1980s increasingly non-corporatist strategies for growth and economic stability were discovered, by students of comparative policy research, especially in Japan, Switzerland and the USA. Corporatism in retrospect was linked to a basic social-democratic consensus. It withered away with Keynesianism and the optimism that state agencies are able to steer the society via 'moral suasion'. The erosion of socialism in eastern Europe was explained in some countries, such as Poland and Hungary, as a corporatist strategy. But most communist countries collapsed. New paradigms of transition to democracy overshadowed partial explanations, such as corporatism.

Scepticism against the steering capacities of the political system spread in the paradigm shift of system's theories towards autopoietic and self-referential systems and contributed to the end of the corporatist debate. Other scholars – who were pioneers of corporatist theories in the early 1980s – turned to new variations of partial theories to explain new forms of co-operation between state and interest groups, such as the theory of private interest governments (Schmitter, Streeck). Others worked on a more general theory of 'generalized political exchange' (Pizzorno, Marin, Mayntz) which tried to overcome the theoretical shortcomings of corporatist theories which had remained too close to empirical fact-finding in order to explain the development of modern and post-modern societies.

Klaus von Beyme
University of Heidelberg

References

Cawson, A. (1978) 'Pluralism, corporatism, and the role of the state', *Government and Oppositions* 13.
Crouch, C. (1977) *Class Conflict and Industrial Relations Crisis: Compromise and Corporatism in the Policies of the British State*, London.
Schmitter, P. C. (1979) 'Still the century of corporatism?' in P. C. Schmitter and G. Lehmbruch (eds) *Trends Towards Corporatist Intermediation*, Beverly Hills, CA.

Further reading

Beyme, K. von (1983) 'Neo-corporatism: a new nut in an old shell', *International Political Science Review*.
Lehmbruch, G. and Schmitter, P. C. (eds) (1982) *Pattern of Corporatist Policy-Making*, Beverly Hills, CA.
Marin, B. (ed.) (1990) *Generalized Political Exchange*, Frankfurt and Boulder, CO.
Williamson, P. J. (1989) *Corporatism in Perspective*, London.

See also: decision making; trade unions.

corruption

In its most general sense, corruption means the perversion or abandonment of a standard. Hence it is common to speak of the corruption of language or of moral corruption. More narrowly, corruption refers to the abandonment of expected standards of behaviour by those in authority for the sake of unsanctioned personal advantage. In the business sphere, company directors are deemed corrupt if they sell their private property to the company at an inflated price, at the expense of the shareholders whose interests they are supposed to safeguard. Lawyers, architects and other professionals are similarly guilty of corruption if they take advantage of their clients to make undue personal gains.

Political corruption can be defined as the misuse of public office or authority for unsanctioned private gain. Three points about the definition should be noted. First, not all forms of misconduct or abuse of office constitute corruption. An official or a government minister who is merely incompetent or who betrays government secrets to a foreign power for ideological reasons is not generally considered corrupt. Second, legislators and public officials in most countries are entitled to salaries and other allowances. Corruption occurs only when they receive additional *unsanctioned* benefits, such as bribes. In practice, it is frequently hard to draw the line between authorized and unauthorized payments; in any case, this will change over time and will be drawn differently in different countries. A benefit regarded as a bribe in one country may be seen as normal and legitimate in another. Legal definitions of corrupt practices are only an imperfect guide because benefits forbidden by law are often sanctioned by social custom, and vice versa. The boundaries of accepted behaviour can be especially difficult to determine in countries affected by rapid political and social change. Third, *electoral corruption* needs to be defined differently from other forms. Whereas most political corruption involves the abuse of public office, electoral corruption is the abuse of the process by which public office is won.

Common forms of corruption are bribery, extortion (the unauthorized extraction of money by officials from members of the public) and misuse of official information. Bribery need not consist of a direct payment to a public official. 'Indirect bribery' may take the form of a promise of a post-retirement job, the provision of reduced-price goods, or the channelling of business to legislators or to members of their family.

Corruption was a serious problem in biblical and classical times, and was found in most periods of history. Cases of judicial corruption were particularly frequent. By the 1960s, an influential school of 'revisionist' political scientists nevertheless presented an optimistic view about the decline of corruption in advanced western democracies (Heidenheimer 1970). Some of the revisionists maintained that corruption did not present as grave a problem as previous writers had suggested. In many newly independent nations, where corruption was supposedly rampant, the practices condemned by western observers as corrupt (for example, making payments to low-level officials for routine services) were accepted as normal by local standards. Moreover, some forms of corruption, far from damaging the process of social and economic development, could be positively beneficial. Bribery enabled entrepreneurs (including foreign companies) to cut through red tape, thereby promoting the economic advance of poor nations. Corruption was seen as a transitory phenomenon, which was likely to decline as economic and social progress was achieved. The general trend was to be seen, it was argued, in the history of Britain and the USA. In Britain, electoral corruption, the sale of titles and government jobs, and corruption relating to public contracts had been rife until the nineteenth century. The introduction of merit systems of appointment to the civil service, the successful battle against electoral corruption and a change in public attitudes towards the conduct of government had led to a dramatic decline in corruption – a decline which coincided with the nation's economic development. Similarly, in the USA, corruption had been rampant in the late nineteenth and early twentieth centuries, which had been a period of intense economic and social change. As suggested by Robert Merton, the corrupt urban party machines, such as the Democratic Party organization in New York City (Tammany Hall) had provided avenues for advancement for underpriviliged immigrant groups. After the Second World War, full employment, the advance of education, the decline of political patronage and the growth of public welfare benefits combined to eliminate the deprivation that had previously led to corruption. A new civic culture replaced the former loyalties to family and to ethnic group. According to a common view, the party machine and the corruption that had accompanied it withered away.

This interpretation has come under challenge. Corruption is neither so benign in underdeveloped countries, nor is it so rare in advanced ones as previously thought. It is unrealistic to suppose that advances in education or in techniques of public administration, the development of a 'public-regarding ethos' or economic development can lead to the virtual disappearance of corruption. The growth of governmental activity and regulation in the modern state increases the opportunities and the temptations for corruption. Improvements in education need not lead to the elimination of corruption but to its perpetuation in new, sophisticated forms.

Revelations since the 1970s have led scholars to give increased attention to the contemporary problems of corruption in advanced democracies and in communist countries. In the USA, the Watergate affair of 1972–4 led to a wave of investigations that resulted in hundreds of convictions for corruption, including that of Vice-President Spiro Agnew. Others convicted included the governors of Illinois, Maryland, Oklahoma and West Virginia. Rampant corruption was uncovered in a number of states including Florida, New Jersey, Pennsylvania and Texas. In Britain, the conventional view about the virtual elimination of corruption was shattered by several major scandals in the 1970s. The far-reaching Poulson scandal, involving local government corruption in the north of England as well as Members of Parliament, erupted in 1972. Local government corruption was proved in South Wales, Birmingham and in Scotland, while in London several police officers were imprisoned.

Since the 1980s, corruption has re-emerged as one of the most contentious and damaging issues in a number of countries. In the western democracies, some of the most serious scandals have involved large-scale, illegal funds to politicians for use in election campaigns. From 1981, all the major parties in the former West Germany were shaken by the Flick affair. Even more far-reaching have been the consequences of revelations that have led to the overthrow of the ruling Liberals in Japan and of the Christian Democrats in Italy.

The destabilizing effects of allegations of top-level corruption were also seen in the former Soviet Union, where the attack on graft was a central feature of Gorbachev's policy of perestroika and, in particular, of his criticism of the Brezhnev regime. The downfall of communist systems since the late 1980s has, however, merely led to the replacement of an old style of corruption by a new one. Mafia-type activities and corruption relating to privatization have emerged as barriers to the consolidation of stable democracies in these countries.

The 1990s have also seen the emergence of corruption as an issue of concern to western governments and to international organizations in their policies relating to aid to the Third World. Organizations ranging from the World Bank to the Organization for Economic Co-operation and Development have taken the view – in contrast to the revionism mentioned earlier – that corruption has severely damaged the prospects for economic growth, especially in Africa and Latin America.

The definitions, causes and effects of corruption and techniques of reform continue to be matters of controversy among sociologists and political scientists. What is increasingly accepted in the 1990s is that political corruption is a widespread, pervasive and serious phenomenon.

Michael Pinto-Duschinsky
Brunel University

Reference

Heidenheimer, A. J. (ed.) (1970) *Political Corruption: Readings in Comparative Analysis*, New York.

Further reading

Heidenheimer, A. J., Johnston, M. and LeVine, V. J. (eds) (1989) *Political Corruption: A Handbook*, New Brunswick, NJ.
Journal of Democracy (1991) Special issue 2(4).
Rainer, N., Philp, M. and Pinto-Duschinsky, M. (eds) (1989) *Political Corruption and Scandals: Case Studies from East and West*, Vienna.
Theobald, R. (1990) *Corruption, Development and Under-development*, Durham, NC.

See also: patronage.

cost-benefit analysis

In terms of its practical application, cost-benefit analysis (CBA) is usually regarded as having its origins in the US Flood Control Act 1936. Without reference to the body of welfare economics that had already arisen by then, and before the introduction of compensation criteria into the literature, the Act argued that flood control projects had their social justification in a weighing up of the costs and benefits, with the latter being summed regardless of to whom they accrued. It is this reference to the *social* dimension of investment appraisal that distinguishes CBA from the more orthodox techniques which deal with the cash flow to a firm or single agency.

Oddly, CBA grew in advance of the theoretical foundations obtained from welfare economics that subsequently provided its underpinning. The notion that the benefits to individuals should be measured according to some indicator of consumer's surplus was well established by nineteenth-century writers, especially Dupuit and Marshall, but Hicks's work (1943) established the exact requirements for such measures. Similarly, the notion of a *shadow price* is crucial to CBA as, even if a project's output is marketed, CBA does not necessarily use market prices as indicators of value. Rather, reference is made to the marginal cost of providing the extra output in question. Despite the ambiguous relationship between marginal cost pricing in an economy where some sectors have unregulated pricing policies which force price above marginal cost, CBA and shadow pricing have flourished as an appraisal technique. CBA secured widespread adoption in US public agencies in the 1950s and 1960s, and was both used and advocated in Europe in the 1960s. It suffered a mild demise in the early 1970s in light of critiques based on the alleged fallacy of applying monetary values to intangible items such as peace and quiet, clean air and the general quality of life. Significantly, post-1973 recession revived its use as governments sought value for money in public expenditure. Unease with the monetization of many unmarketed costs and benefits remained, however, resulting in a proliferation of alternative techniques such as environmental impact assessment, cost-effectiveness analysis (in which only resource costs are expressed in money and benefits remain in non-monetary units), and some multi-objective approaches. CBA retains its strength because of its ability potentially to identify optimal expenditures (where net benefits are maximized) and to secure a well-defined project ranking. However, few practitioners would argue that it has a role outside the ranking of expenditures within a given budget. That is, it has a highly limited role in comparing the efficiency of expenditures across major budget areas such as defence, education, health and so on.

As generally formulated, CBA operates with the efficiency objectives of welfare economics. The maximization of net social benefits is formally equivalent to securing the largest net welfare gain as defined by the Kaldor-Hicks compensation principle. Academic debate in this respect has centred on the appropriate choice of the measure of consumer's surplus, with the dominant advocacy being of the use of the 'compensating variation' measure introduced by Hicks (1943). Use of social prices based on consumer valuations implicitly assumes that the distribution of market power within the relevant economy is itself optimal. As this is a value judgement, it is open to anyone to substitute it with an alternative distributional judgement. Some would argue that this apparent arbitrariness defines the inadequacies of CBA, while others suggest that no society has ever operated with disregard for distributional criteria and that distributional judgements are no less arbitrary than efficiency judgements.

Much of the practical effort in CBA has gone into actual mechanisms for discovering individuals' preferences in contexts where there is no explicit market. The most successful have been the hedonic price techniques and the use of bidding techniques ('contingent valuation'). Hedonic prices refer to the coefficients defining the relationship between property prices and changes in some unmarketed variable affecting property prices. An example would be clean air, which should raise the price of a property, other things being equal. Bidding techniques involve the use of questionnaires which ask directly for consumers' valuations of the benefits.

As costs and benefits accrue over time, CBA tends to adopt a discounting approach whereby future cash and non-cash flows are discounted back to a present value by use of a discount rate. The determination of the discount rate has occupied a substantial literature. In theory, one would expect consumers to prefer the present to the future because of impatience ('myopia') and expectations of higher incomes in the future (thus lowering their marginal valuation of a unit of benefit in the future). In turn, the resulting rate of time preference should be equal to interest rates ruling in the market which also reflect the productivity of capital. In practice, time preference rates and cost of capital estimates can vary significantly because of imperfections in capital markets. Moreover, the rate of discount relevant to *social* decisions can differ from the average of individual valuations, because choices made as members of society will differ when compared to choices made on an individualist basis. Further controversy surrounds the issue of intergenerational fairness since positive discount rates have the potential for shifting cost burdens forward to future generations. Thus the risks of, say, storing nuclear waste appear small when discounted back to the present and expressed as a present value. Conversely, zero discount rates may discriminate against projects which offer the highest potential for leaving accumulated capital for the use of future generations. To pursue the nuclear power example, non-investment because of the waste disposal problem could reduce the inherited stock of energy availability to future generations, by forcing a rapid depletion of finite stock resources such as coal or oil. The intergenerational issue is thus complex and raises the fundamental issue of just how far into the future CBA should look. Because of its foundations in consumer sovereignty, there is a temptation to argue that the time-horizon is set by the existing generation and, at most, the succeeding one or two generations.

CBA has enjoyed a revival of interest in recent years. Not only has there been a return of concern over the social value of public expenditure, but also the alternative techniques developed in the 1970s have been shown to be even more limited in their ability to discriminate between good and bad investments. In particular, CBA has resurfaced through *environmental economics*, particularly with reference to the economic valuation of environmental costs and benefits. As an aid to rational thinking its credentials are higher than any of the alternatives so far advanced. That it cannot substitute for political decisions is not in question, but social science has a duty to inform public choice, and it is in this respect that CBA has its role to play.

David W. Pearce
University of London

Reference

Hicks, J. (1943) 'The four consumer's surplus', *Review of Economic Studies* LL.

Further reading

Mishan, E. J. (1975) *Cost Benefit Analysis*, 2nd edn, London.
Pearce, D. W. (1986), *Cost Benefit Analysis*, 2nd edn, London.

See also: environmental economics; microeconomics; welfare economics.

cost functions *see* production and cost functions

counselling psychology

Counselling psychology is an applied psychological discipline concerned with generating, applying and disseminating knowledge on the remediation and prevention of disturbed human functioning in a variety of settings (Brown and Lent 1992). It has been a recognized discipline in the USA since 1947, and it is also well established in Australia and Canada, but it is really only since 1982, when the Counselling Psychology Section of the British Psychological Society was formed, that it became so established in Britain.

Counselling is essentially a psychological process. Its theories are concerned with helping individuals to understand and change their feelings, thoughts and behaviour. Counselling psychology, however, goes beyond this and provides a broader base. It is

a speciality in the field of psychology whose practitioners help people improve their well-being, alleviate their distress, resolve their crises, and increase their ability to solve problems and make decisions. Counselling psychologists utilise scientific approaches in their development of solutions to the variety of human problems resulting from interactions of intrapersonal, interpersonal, and environmental forces. Counselling psychologists conduct research, apply interventions, and evaluate services in order to stimulate personal and group development, and prevent and remedy developmental, educational, emotional health, organisational, social and/or vocational problems and adheres to strict standards and ethics.

(American Psychological Association 1985)

This definition can be broken down to reveal the most commonly identified tasks in the work of the counselling psychologist, namely collecting data about clients (assessment), personal adjustment counselling, specific problem identification and diagnosis, vocational counselling and long-term psychotherapy. Nelson-Jones (1982) stresses the importance of assessment, if the counselling psychologist is to be able to offer appropriate interventions beyond the fundamental counselling relationship. Given that counselling psychologists work one-to-one and with groups, in a variety of contexts such as industry, commerce, education, medical settings (in particular primary health care), community work and the private sector, it is evident that they intervene in a range of related areas and need to call upon a wide range of psychological knowledge. The recognition and awareness of the existence of post-traumatic stress, for example, demonstrated the need to develop specific and focused psychological counselling intervention.

Importantly, the helping relationship itself is seen as a crucial therapeutic variable, in that *counselling* psychology involves more than just the application of specific psychological treatment techniques in a standardized fashion (Woolfe 1990). Effective helping, whatever the theoretical model being used, is seen by counselling psychologists as a transactional encounter between people in order to explore their objective *and* subjective experience, which is best served when the relationship is characterized by the manifestation of personal qualities such as empathy, non-possesive warmth and authenticity on the part of the helper (Rogers 1951). That the self of the helper is an active ingredient in this process means that personal development work and the experience of being a client are mandatory ingredients in the training of counselling psychologists if they are to be able to monitor the process between themselves and the clients, and here lies the distinctiveness of counselling psychology with its emphasis on the issue of process as well as content and technique.

As well as an emphasis on the nature of the relationship between client and helper, counselling psychology generally emphasizes the distinction between well-being and sickness, and concerns itself with enhancing the psychological functioning and well-being of individuals. This is underlined by adopting a more holistic view of clients in that their mental health is considered in the location of an individual in the life cycle, in their lifestyle and relationships and in their social and political context, including the influence of gender (Taylor 1994). One of the strengths of counselling psychology lies in this humanistic way of looking at personal change and development grounded in a modern sociological imagination. Furthermore, when employed in organizational structures, counselling psychologists are in a position to provide feedback about how those structures affect the quality of life of individuals within the organization and so play a part in facilitating constructive organizational change and good management practice.

Thus counselling psychology is a field notable for its diversity, influenced by diverse political and social forces as well as developments within mainstream psychology. Counselling psychology has overlaps with other areas of psychology, particularly with clinical psychology, However, a useful distinguishing factor is the issue of intentionality and the way counselling psychologists think about what they do. To quote Woolfe (1990):

'Counselling psychology brings a humanistic perspective to looking at human problems in that it perceives them not so much as deficits but as adaptations. In this sense it can be said to involve a paradigmatic shift from traditional psychological ways of looking at problems.'

Maye Taylor
Manchester Metropolitan University

References

American Psychological Association (1985) *Minutes of Midwinter Executive Committee Meeting*, Chicago.
Brown, S. D. and Lent, R. W. (1992) *Handbook of Counselling Psychology*, Chichester.
Nelson-Jones, R. (1982) *The Theory and Practice of Counselling Psychology*, London.
Rogers, C. R. (1951) *Client Centred Therapy*, London.
Taylor, M. (1994) 'The feminist paradigm', in M. Walker (ed.) *In Search of a Therapist*, Milton Keynes.
Woolfe, R. (1990) 'Counselling psychology in Britain', *The Psychologist* 3.12.

See also: clinical psychology.

creativity

Creativity is the ability to bring something new into existence. It shows itself in the acts of people. Through the creative process taking place in a person or group of persons, creative products are born. Such products may be quite diverse: mechanical inventions, new chemical processes, new solutions or new statements of problems in mathematics and science; the composition of a piece of music, or a poem, story or novel; the making of new forms in painting, sculpture or photography; the forming of a new religion or philosophical system; an innovation in law, a general change in manners, a fresh way of thinking about and solving social problems; new medical agents and techniques; even new ways of persuasion and of controlling the minds of others.

Implicit in this diversity is a common core of characteristics that mark creative products, processes and persons. Creative products are distinguished by their originality, their aptness, their validity, their usefulness, and very often by a subtle additional property which we may call aesthetic fit. For such products we use words such as fresh, novel, ingenious, clever, unusual, divergent. The ingredients of the creative process are related functionally to the creative forms produced: seeing things in a new way, making connections, taking risks, being alerted to chance and to the opportunities present by contradictions and complexities, recognizing familiar patterns in the unfamiliar so that new patterns may be formed by transforming old ones, being alert to the contingencies which may arise from such transformations. In creative people, regardless of their age, sex, ethnic background, nationality or way of life, we find certain traits recurring: an ability to think metaphorically or analogically as well as logically, independence of judgement (sometimes manifesting itself as unconventionality, rebellion, revolutionary thinking and acting), a rejection of an insufficient simplicity (or a tendency to premature closure) in favour of a search for a more complex and satisfying new order or synthesis. A certain *naïveté* or innocence of vision must be combined with stringent requirements set by judgement and experience. The act of verification is a final stage in the creative process, preceded by immersion in the problem, incubation of the process subliminally, and illumination or new vision.

The birth of 'creativity'

The creative aspects of Mind and of Will engaged the attention of all the major philosopher-psychologists of the late nineteenth and early twentieth centuries. Alfred Binet, the famed constructor of intelligence tests, was known first through the pages of *L'Année Psychologique* in the 1880s and 1890s as the author of widely ranging empirical studies of creativity (including research by questionnaire and interview of leading French writers) and the originator of dozens of tests of imagination (devised first as games to play with his own children). The fateful decision to exclude such occasions for imaginative play from his compendium of tasks prototypical of needed scholastic aptitudes has led to much mischief in educational application and to continuing confusion about the relationship of intelligence to creativity. The former as generally measured is important to certain aspects of the latter, but people of equal intelligence have been found to vary widely in creativity; and, alas, some notably creative persons have also been found notably lacking in whatever it takes to get on successfully in school.

Of the two most famous psychoanalysts, Carl Jung made a greater contribution than Freud in this field, developing especially the notions of intuition and of the collective unconscious as the sources of creation. Henri Bergson (1911 [1907]), in *Creative Evolution*, distinguished intuition from intellect as the main vehicle of the creative process in mind-in-general and in what, in retrospect, is more than mere vitalism he attributed to will, as *élan vital*, the chief motivating force of the creative process in nature. Nearly a century after Bergson's initial formulations, Gregory Bateson (1979) was writing in that same tradition, and his gradual development of 'an ecology of mind' found expression in his *Mind and Nature: A Necessary Unity*.

The modern empirical study of creativity

New methods of observation and measurement have produced a marked proliferation of articles and books about creative persons, processes and products since the Second World War. A commonly recognized milestone in the systematic research effort is an address in 1950 by J. P. Guilford who, as president of the American Psychological Association, pointed out that up to that time only 186 out of 121,000 entries in *Psychological Abstracts* dealt with creative imagination. In the following decades there was a surge of publications in the field. Studies at the University of California of highly creative contemporary writers, architects, artists, mathematicians and scientists by intensive methods of personal assessment contributed important impetus to the study of personality and creativity (work funded mostly by foundations such as Carnegie, Ford, Rockefeller, and Richardson), while the US Office of Education gave significant support to research on creativity in education. A bibliography published in the late 1960s by the Creative Education Foundation contains 4,176 references, nearly 3,000 of them dated later than 1960.

Yet this abundance of effort also produced a mixed picture of results based on psychological measurement, due mainly to inconsistencies in the choice of measures, their relative unreliability, and the equally inconsistent, somewhat unreliable, and factorially and definitionally complex criteria. Psychologists generally have restricted the term creativity to the production of humanly *valuable* novelty in an effort to exclude from consideration the relatively mundane expressions of creativity in everyday life, but this introduction of value to the definition of creativity, and the consequent invocation of historically bound and subjective judgements to assess such value, necessarily raise theoretical and methodological questions which have bedevilled and divided students of creativity for decades. *Whose* values, for example, must be met for an act to be creative – the values of the creative agent alone, or the values of a social group? And if so, which group?

Further, should the term creative be restricted to novel activities valued by connoisseurs of achievement in the classically 'creative domains' of literature, music and other arts, or can it be applied also to novel behaviour valued by those able to recognize achievement in mathematics, science and technology? While most creativity scholars and investigators extend 'creative' to these latter domains with few qualms, they do not generally assume that the creative processes involved in producing good literature, good music, good art and good science are the same, or that the personality and intellectual characteristics associated with creative achievement in these various domains are highly similar. Whether the term creative can be extended to novel activities of value in domains such as business, sports, teaching, therapy, parenting and homemaking is an even more controversial question among creativity scholars.

Nor can the issue of values and standards be resolved simply by accepting as legitimate a particular domain of activity, for even within a specific domain, such as art, the question remains: whose values or standards are to be met – the values and standards of the artist who produced the piece, of other artists, of art critics, of art historians, or the audience in general? And if other artists, *which* artists; if art critics, *which* art critics; and if art historians, *which* art historians – from which schools and what eras? If behaviour in less public domains (for example, therapy and parenting) is considered, who is to assess the novelty and effectiveness of the behaviour and how is scholarship and investigation to proceed?

Intimately related to the question of values and standards are questions concerning the nature or form of the act's impact. Several theorists, for example, have drawn distinctions between acts of 'primary' creativity – acts whose values derive from their power to transform in a basic way our perception of reality or our understanding of the universe of human experience and possibility – and acts of 'secondary' creativity – acts which merely apply or extend some previously developed meaning, principle or technique to a new domain or instance.

While it would be comforting to be able to report that the definitional differences and distinctions reviewed here are relatively trivial compared to the core of common meaning contained within them, it is not at all clear that this is so. Whether creative individuals are identified on the basis of their achievements, or their skills and abilities, or their activities, or their personality characteristics, shapes answers to frequently asked substantive questions about creativity. (For example, can creativity be taught or fostered? Can creativity be predicted? How are creativity and intelligence related?) Definitional differences and variations in emphasis have led, and will continue to lead, to many misunderstandings, misreadings and confusions in the study of creativity. Readers of the psychological literature on creativity are therefore well advised to ascertain the conceptual perspectives and operational definitions of the scholars and investigators whose works they are examining. Thus, not only measurement unreliability in both predictors and criteria but also basic definitional questions as well as the genuine role of chance itself in both the genesis and the recognition of creativity have served to confound results. Overall, none the less, a strong impressionistic consensus of the sort reported at the outset of this article prevails; the research enterprise continues undeterred.

A critical review of the professional literature on creativity in the decade 1970–80 (Barron and Harrington 1981) turned up approximately 2,500 studies, produced at a steady rate of about 250 per year during that decade. The literature has grown since. Emerging new themes in the 1980s and early 1990s include creativity in women, computer-assisted creativity and creativity in the moral domain. There is renewed interest in the apparent relationships between bipolar affective disorders and creativity, the development and developmental significance of creativity over the lifespan, and a heightened consciousness that creativity is deeply embedded in social, historical, economic and cultural circumstances. This awareness has led to the development of 'ecological' or 'systems' perspectives that attempt to integrate what is known about creative people, creative processes, and creative social contexts and to connect the intrapsychic, interpersonal, social and cultural properties of creativity in theoretically useful ways. Such broadened theoretical efforts have led naturally to calls for more vigorous multidisciplinary approaches to the study and understanding of creativity.

Frank Barron

David M. Harrington
University of California, Santa Cruz

References

Barron, F. and Harrington, D. M. (1981) 'Creativity, intelligence, and personality', *Annual Review of Psychology* 32.

Bergson, H. (1911 [1907]) *Creative Evolution*, London.

Further reading

Albert, R. S. (1992) *Genius and Eminence: The Social Psychology of Creativity and Exceptional Achievement*, 2nd edn, New York.

Barron, F. (1969) *Creative Person and Creative Process*, New York.

Feldman, D. H., Csikszentmihalyi, M. and Gardner, H. (1994) *Changing the World: A Framework for the Study of Creativity*, Westport, CT.

Gardner, H. (1993) *Creating Minds*, New York.

Ghiselin, B. (1952) *The Creative Process*, Berkeley, CA.

Harrington, D. M. (1990) 'The ecology of human creativity: a psychological perspective', in M. A. Runco and R. S. Albert (eds) *Theories of Creativity*, Newbury Park, CA.

Jamison, K. R. (1993) *Touched with Fire: Manic Depressive Illness and the Artistic Temperament*, New York.

Koestler, A. (1964) *The Act of Creation*, New York.

Simonton, D. K. (1988) *Scientific Genius*, Cambridge, UK.

Sternberg, R. J. (1988) *The Nature of Creativity*, Cambridge, UK.

credit

The term credit, derived from the Latin *credere* (to believe), has several meanings, many of which are outside the field of finances. Even in finance it can be used to indicate a positive accounting entry, an increase in wealth or income, but the main use, with which we are concerned here, involves an element of deferred payment. It thus covers not only formal loans but also the multitude of informal arrangements whereby payment for a transaction is made some time after the physical transfer of the goods or services, and by extension it is also used where payment is made in advance. In accounting terms it refers not only to trade credit between businesses but also to the various items known as accruals. Examples of such accruals are the payment of salaries after a person has worked for a week or a month and, on the other side, the advance payment of a year's premium for insurance.

In macroeconomies the term is used with a special meaning to refer to those items of credit that are measurable for the economy as a whole; in practice this restricts it to credit extended by the banking system. As bank loans are made, the proceeds are used to pay for goods and services, and the recipients of these payments pass the cheques to the credit of their own bank deposits: bank loans can be said to create bank deposits. By controlling the volume of bank credit, the monetary authorities can thus indirectly control the volume of bank deposits, which are the most important element in the money supply. The control of bank credit, both in total volume and in the selection of favoured and unfavoured borrowing sectors, is thus often a weapon of monetary policy.

Credit plays an important part in the theory of financial intermediation. The first stage of development of a financial system can be taken as the move from barter to the use of commodity money. Although this move frees the exchange of commodities from the restrictions of barter, by itself it does nothing for the growth of business enterprises because the only funds available for capital investment come from the current income or the previously accumulated money balances of the entrepreneur. The development of credit, in the form of direct lending and borrowing, enables the accumulated money balances of others to be transferred to the entrepreneur, who can thus put to profitable use the savings of many other people. Because this development was associated with the levying of interest, it faced religious and social obstacles; these still persist in Muslim countries, where an alternative form of banking (Islamic banking) has been developed on the basis of profit-sharing by the depositor.

For several centuries, credit, both as formal loans and as trade credit, was restricted to businesses and the wealthier households, but since the mid-1930s all but the poorest households have obtained access to formal and informal credit. This extension of credit has been achieved by a number of innovations in the forms in which credit is granted. Few of these forms were completely new; the innovations came in the use to which they were put and in the ways in which they were combined.

All lenders need to satisfy themselves on two points before granting credit: these are the ability of the borrower to repay and his willingness to do so. Traditionally, the ability to repay was assured by requiring the borrower to give the lender a mortgage or charge on assets to a value greater than that of the loan, and willingness to repay was assessed on the past record of the borrower and personal knowledge of his character. Unless the loan is for the purchase of a house, the problem raised in giving credit to the ordinary household is that there are no suitable assets to pledge as security. The solution has taken several forms. The first was to obtain a mortgage on the asset (car or television set, for example) that was being purchased with the loan; where the legal system did not permit this (as under English law), the asset was hired to the 'borrower', with a final nominal payment to transfer ownership – hire purchase. Even where this legal subterfuge was not necessary, there was a growth in leasing and straight hiring to households to overcome many of the credit problems.

The key change in this form of consumer lending was a realization that current income rather than accumulated assets was the real security for a loan. In lending on consumer durables, this came about because there is a poor secondhand market, but even with houses lenders prefer to avoid the trouble of auctioning the property to secure repayment. During the 1960s this change of attitude towards the nature of the security for a loan was also adopted in corporate lending; it came to be known as lending on the cash flow. For large corporate loans, banks often use their computers for simulating the cash flows of prospective borrowers under a number of hypothetical conditions.

It is obvious from the previous analysis that the key point in granting credit is the assessment of the creditworthiness of the borrower. In the past much of this depended on the personal judgement of local bank managers and on adequate collateral. With the growth in the number of customers, branch managers cannot now claim a close knowledge of all their customers, and more formal methods of assessment have become necessary. This is particularly necessary when loans can be obtained by post through the filling in of a simple questionnaire or even through answering questions posed by an electronic terminal. Most of the methods used are based on credit scoring, which uses a statistical technique known as multivariate discriminant analysis (MDA) or one of its variants. Applicants are scored according to such characteristics as ownership of their home, steady employment, and possession of a telephone, and the loan is granted if the score exceeds a predetermined level based on past experience of bad debts.

The experience of the 1980s and early 1990s brought to the fore several new aspects of assessing creditworthiness. During the 1970s banks throughout the world had vied to take part in syndicated lending to developing countries on the assumption that loans to governments were relatively risk-free. The international debt crisis starting in 1982 showed this belief to be wide of the mark, and banks began to develop schemes for taking into account the risks involved in worldwide movements of commodity prices – country or sovereign risk. The huge provisions that banks had to make against these international loans were more than matched during the recession of the early 1990s by defaults on domestic loans of all sorts, from corporate loans to consumer debt and mortgage loans. It would be nice to think that banks had learned the lesson that the most creditworthy of borrowers is vulnerable when economic circumstances change enough and to allow for this possibility in their risk assessments, but experience shows that banks nearly always begin to lend carelessly in periods of strong competition.

Jack Revell
University College of North Wales, Bangor

Further reading

Beckman, T. N. (1969) *Credits and Collections: Management and Theory*, 8th edn, New York.
Gurley, J. G. and Shaw, E. S. (1960) *Money in a Theory of Finance*, Washington, DC.
Krayenbuehl, T. E. (1985) *Country Risk: Assessment and Monitoring*, Lexington, MA.

See also: banking; capital, credit and money markets; financial system; interest; risk analysis.

crime and delinquency

In everyday language crime and delinquency are terms that carry substantial emotional content. One hears people speak of all sorts of unseemly behaviour as being 'criminal' or the finger pointed at unruly children as 'delinquents'. In this usage, the terms carry considerable cultural baggage which for the scientific study of crime and delinquency not only is excess, but also makes systematic study impossible. No reasonable generalizations could be made about the actors or acts to which some people would normally apply the terms. For this reason, scholars have attempted to

conceptualize crime and delinquency in a more restricted fashion in order to give more precise meaning to the terms. Although there is not consensus on the matter, the prevailing view among criminologists is that crime should be restricted to those acts which are defined as violations of the criminal law. Even this more restricted definition, however, is troublesome when general theories of crime are sought because it encompasses so much: government officials who plan and carry out criminal acts (conspiracies to commit political assassinations such as the numerous US intelligence agencies plots to assassinate Fidel Castro), corporate executives who violate health and safety laws or engage in illegal economic transactions, juveniles who are truant from school or who hang about in gangs, acts of physical abuse of spouses and children, murder, rape, theft and robbery.

Despite the conceptual problems that inhere in the acceptance of the legal definition of crime and delinquency there are advantages as well. For one, the legal definition provides an objective criterion for what is included in the study of crime and delinquency. To determine whether or not an act is a crime one need only look to see if a law has been passed which provides for punishment by state officials. Another analytical advantage of limiting crime and delinquency to the legal definition is that it allows for cross-cultural comparisons which reveal that some acts are defined as criminal in all state societies and, equally important, that what is crime in one nation-state or at one historical period is not crime in another country or at a different time. For example, murder, rape and theft are criminal in every state society, but acts of business executives or journalists that are a crime in one country are not in another. If the Secrecy Act of Great Britain were in force in the USA and US journalists exposed governmental crime as they presently do, US journalists would be well represented in the prison population. Heroin addicts can obtain drugs through state-monitored programmes in some countries and in others they face long prison sentences merely for possessing the drug. Marijuana may be purchased in cafés in The Netherlands but possession of small amounts can land a person in prison for many years in others. Even within a country different jurisdictions define criminality differently: in the USA marijuana possession is a felony for which a conviction can earn a defendant forty years in prison in one state but in an adjoining state it is a misdemeanour punishable by a very small fine or it is not criminal at all. Even acts which we accept today as 'clearly criminal' such as murder and rape once were viewed as wrongs which should be settled in accordance with the wishes of the aggrieved party or the party's relatives rather than acts which the state should punish. In many countries local courts still operate on this principle. In the USA American Indian communities emphasize the importance of providing transgressors a right of passage back into legitimate roles, and in many Mexican and African villages there is a similar emphasis as well. The anthropologist Laura Nader (1990), in her cross-cultural studies of law and crime, found that stateless societies and small communities are much more likely to invoke the principle of 'give a little, get a little', rather than 'winner take all' when members of the community deviate from accepted norms.

The definition of crime and variations in what constitutes crime in time and space is, of course, only the beginning of the systematic study of crime and delinquency by social scientists. The heart of the discipline is determined by what questions are asked in the effort to understand. The study of crime and delinquency is as diverse as are the social sciences, but three sets of questions have dominated the field.

First, the question most often asked in the field is 'Why do some people commit crime and others do not?' From the first studies of crime and delinquency in Italy, England and France the search for an adequate answer to this question has led researchers to seek biological, sociological, psychological, economic and even geographical variables associated with and presumably causally related to criminal and delinquent behaviour. That this quest has been somewhat less than successful is not surprising when it is realized that practically everyone commits some types of crimes in the course of a lifetime. The search for an answer to why some people commit crime, then, is nothing less than a search for a theory of human action. It is probably safe to say that the cross-fertilization of general social psychological theories of human action and social psychological theories of criminal and delinquent behaviour is to date the most valuable contribution made by this orientation.

Second, social science research on crime and delinquency also has asked the sociological (as contrasted with social psychological) question, 'Why do rates and types of crimes and delinquency vary from one society or group to another?' The answers to this question are as diverse and contradictory as are those of the social psychologists. As with sociology generally, the answers offered invariably invoke some combination of cultural and subcultural values with economic and social position in a given society. The different theories that try to answer the question can be divided between the relative importance attributed to these different sociological forces.

Third, since the mid-1980s there has been rapid growth in efforts to answer two other fundamental questions about crime and delinquency: 'What are the social forces that lead to the definition of some acts as criminal and not others?' and 'How does the criminal justice system of police, prosecutors, courts and prisons work and what effect does it have on the perception, reporting and incidence of crime and delinquency?' These questions dovetail the study of crime and delinquency with the sociology of law and they have provided for a great deal of valuable cross-fertilization between the fields. As might be expected, the theories put forth to answer this question are dominated by the theoretical traditions of Durkheim, Marx and Weber, and equally predictably there has not emerged a consensus among scholars as to which paradigm best answers the question.

There is no reason to suppose that the future of studies of crime and delinquency will veer very far away from these basic questions. In view of the salience of crime as a political and economic issue, however, it is likely that rather more resources will be devoted to questions about the appropriateness of defining acts as criminal and the functioning of the criminal justice system. The issue of whether using drugs should be criminalized is preoccupying most western countries, and the growth and power of what the Norwegian criminologist Nils Christie (1993) calls 'the crime industry' is deservedly receiving a great deal more attention than heretofore. Regardless of these changes, it is safe to say that the search for answers to and the gathering of empirical data on all three questions will occupy the social-scientific study of crime and delinquency for the future as it has for the past two hundred or more years.

William J. Chambliss
George Washington University

References

Christie, N. (1993) *Crime Control as Industry*, London.
Nader, L. (1990) *Harmony, Ideology, Justice and Control*, Stanford, CA.

Further reading

Beirne, P. and Messerschmidt, J. (1991) *Criminology*, New York.
Braithwaite, J. (1979) *Inequality, Crime and Public Policy*, London.
Chambliss, W. J. and Zatz, M. (1994) *Making Law: The State, Law and Structural Contradictions*, Bloomington, IN.
Cohen, S. (1988) *Against Criminology*, New Brunswick, NJ.
Feeley, M. (1992) *The Process is the Punishment*, New York.

See also: criminology; penology; police; punishment; social problems.

criminology

Standard textbook accounts find two scriptural beginnings to the history of criminology: the 'classical school' and the 'positivist school', each one marking out a somewhat different fate for the discipline. More sophisticated criminologists have rewritten this history (Beirne 1993; Garland 1985; 1994) but the conflict between these two trajectories still remains a useful way of understanding the shape of a discipline conventionally defined as 'the scientific study of crime and its control'.

The classical trajectory dates from the mid-eighteenth century and tells of the revolutionary contribution of Enlightenment thinkers like Beccaria and Bentham in breaking with a previously 'archaic', 'barbaric', 'repressive' or 'arbitrary' system of criminal law. For these reformers, legal philosophers and political theorists, the crime question was predominantly the punishment question. Their programme was to prevent punishment from being, in Beccaria's words, 'an act of violence of one or many against a private citizen'; instead it should be 'essentially public, prompt, necessary, the least possible in given circumstances, proportionate to the crime, dictated by laws'.

Classicism presented a model of rationality: on the one side, the 'free' sovereign individual acting according to the dictates of reason and self interest; on the other hand, the limited liberal state, contracted to grant rights and liberties, to prescribe duties and to impose the fair and just punishment that must result from the knowing infraction of the legal code and the knowing infliction of social harm.

This 'immaculate conception' of the birth of the classical school as a humanistic reform has been challenged by revisionist histories of law and the state. Dates, concepts and subjects have been reordered. Classicism is now more likely to be conceived in terms of the broader rationalization of crime control associated with the emergence of the free market and the new capitalist order. But whatever their origins, the internal preoccupations of classicism – whether they appear in utilitarianism, Kantianism, liberalism, anarchism or indeed any political philosophy at all – have never really disappeared from the criminological agenda. This is where the subject overlaps with politics, jurisprudence and the sociology of law.

A century after classicism, though, criminology was to claim for itself its 'real' scientific beginning and a quite different set of influences. This was the positivist 'revolution', dated in comic-book intellectual history with the publication in 1876 of Lombroso's *Delinquent Man*. This was a positivism which shared the more general social-scientific connotations of the term (the notion, that is, of the unity of the scientific method) but which acquired a more specific meaning in criminology. As David Matza (1964; 1969) suggests in his influential sociologies of criminological knowledge, criminological positivism managed the astonishing feat of separating the study of crime from the contemplation of the state. Classicism was dismissed as

metaphysical speculation. The new programme was to focus not on crime (the act) but on the criminal (the actor); it was to assume not rationality, choice and free will, but determinism (biological, psychic or social). At the centre of the new criminological enterprise was the notion of causality. No longer sovereign beings, subject to the same pulls and pushes at their fellow citizens, criminals were now special creatures or members of a special class.

The whole of the last century of criminology can be understood as a series of creative yet eventually repetitive variations on these late nineteenth-century themes. The particular image conjured up by Lombroso's criminal type – the atavistic genetic throwback – faded away, but the subsequent structure and logic of criminological explanation remained largely within the positivist paradigm. Whether the level of explanation was biological, psychological, sociological or a combination of these ('multifactorial' as some versions were dignified), the Holy Grail was a general causal theory: why do people commit crime? This quest gave the subject its self-definition: 'the scientific study of the causes of crime'.

At each stage of this search, criminology strengthened its claim to exist as an autonomous, multi-disciplinary study. Somewhat like a parasite, criminology attached itself to its host disciplines (law, psychology and, dominantly, sociology) and drew from them methods, theories and academic credibility. At the same time – somewhat like a colonial power landing on new territory – each of these disciplines descended on the eternally fascinating subjects of crime and punishment and claimed them as their own. In this fashion, the theories, methods and substance of criminology draw on Freudianism, behaviourism, virtually every stream of sociology (the Chicago School, functionalism, anomie theory, interactionism, etc.), Marxism, feminism, rational choice theory and even post-modernism. Each of these traces can be found in any current criminological textbook; it would be difficult to think of a major system of thought in the social sciences which would not be so represented.

All the time, however, that this positivist trajectory was being established, criminologists retained their interest in questions of punishment and control. If, in one sense, all criminology became positivist, then also all criminology has always been concerned with classical matters. But instead of thinking about the limits and nature of the criminal sanction, this side of criminology (sometimes called penology) took this sanction as politically given. True, there was (and still is) an important debate about whether the discipline's subject matter should be confined to conventional legal definitions of crime or broadened to include all forms of socially injurious conduct. And the criminalization versus decriminalization debate is still very much alive, in areas such as corporate wrong-doing, pornography and drug abuse.

Questions of punishment and social control, however, became part of a more scientific discourse: the construction of empirical knowledge about the workings of the criminal justice system. Research findings were built up about the police, courts, prisons and various other agencies devoted to the prevention, control, deterrence or treatment of adult crime and juvenile delinquency. The structure and ideologies of these agencies are analysed, their working practices and relations to each other observed, their effectiveness evaluated. This is now a major part of the criminological enterprise.

Behind this work, the classical tradition remains alive in another sense. Modern criminologists became the heirs of the Enlightenment belief in rationality and progress. Their scientific task was informed by a sense of faith: that the business of crime control could be made not only more efficient, but also more humane. As reformers, advisers and consultants, most criminologists claim for themselves not merely an autonomous body of knowledge, but also the status of an applied science or even profession.

It is this simultaneous claim to knowledge and power that links the two sides of the criminological discourse: causation and control. In positivism, this is an organic link: to know the cause is to know the appropriate policy. But the history and status of this link is more complicated. The early nineteenth-century penitentiary system was dependent on theories of rehabilitation, behaviour modification and anomie well before their supposed 'discovery' by scientific criminology. There is a lively debate about Foucault's characterization of criminological knowledge as wholly utilitarian, an elaborate alibi to justify the exercise of power.

In the general climate of radical self-scrutiny which descended on the social sciences in the 1960s, criminology too began to fragment. There were three major attacks against what was visualized as the positivist hegemony. Each in its own peculiar and quite distinct way represented a revival of classicist concerns.

First, labelling theory – a loose body of ideas derived from symbolic interactionism – restated some simple sociological truths about the relativity of social rules and normative boundaries. Crime was only one form of that wider category of social action, deviance; criminology should be absorbed into the sociology of deviance. Beyond such conceptual and disciplinary boundary disputes, the whole quest for causality was regarded with scepticism. In addition to the standard behavioural question (why do some people do these bad things?) there were a series of definitional questions. Why are certain actions defined as rule-breaking? How

are these rules applied? What are the consequences of this application? These definitional questions took causal primacy: it was not that deviance led to control, but control to deviance. Social control agencies – the most benevolent as well as the most punitive – only made matters worse. Sympathy and tolerance for society's outsiders were preferable to the conformity and scientific pretensions of mainstream criminology.

Second, this liberal criticism became harder in the 1960s onslaught on mainstream criminology. This came from what was labelled variously as conflict, new, critical, radical or Marxist criminology. Combining some strands of labelling theory and conflict sociology with classical Marxist writing about law, class and the state, this critique moved even further from the agenda of positivism. Traditional causal inquiries, particularly individualistic, were either dismissed or subsumed under the criminogenic features of capitalism. Legalistic definitions were either expanded to include the 'crimes of the powerful' (those social harms which business and the state license themselves to commit) or subjected to historicist and materialist enquiry. Labelling theory's wider category of deviance was refocused on law: the power of the state to criminalize some actions rather than others. The analytical task was to construct a political economy of crime and its control. The normative task was to eliminate those systems of exploitation that cause crime.

The third critique of the positivist enterprise came from a quite different theoretical and political direction, one that would prove more enduring. Impressed by the apparent failure of the causal quest and of progressive policies such as treatment, rehabilitation and social reform ('nothing works' was the slogan), loose coalitions appeared in the 1970s under such rallying calls as 'realism', 'back to justice' and 'neo-classicism'. Some of this was neo-liberalism – sad disenchantment with the ideals and policies of progressive criminology. Some was neo-conservativism – satisfaction about the supposed progressive failures. But politics aside, all these criminologists began turning back to classical questions. The notion of justice allowed liberals to talk of rights, equity and fairness and to advance the Kantian-derived 'just-deserts' model of sentencing. In the face of massively escalating crime rates throughout the west, conservatives (and just about everyone else) talked about law and order, social defence, deterrence and the protection of society. The traditional positivist interest in causation seemed less important than devising rational crime control policies.

By the beginning of the 1990s, the fragmented discourse of criminology was settling into yet another pattern. The original labelling and radical moments all but disappeared, most of their cohort denouncing its own earlier romantic excesses in favour of what is called 'left-realist criminology'. This is more receptive to reformist social policy and more interested in victimization and causation. 'Victimology' has become a major subfield in itself. The mainstream non-positivist position has become highly influential in various forms of managerial or administrative criminology. These emphasize 'situational crime prevention' (designing physical and social space to reduce criminal opportunity) and rest on an image of the new 'reasoning criminal' (Cornish and Clarke 1986) derived from rational choice theory. At the same time, traditional positivist inquiry remains very much alive in the form of massive birth cohort or longitudinal studies about the development of criminal careers. A more theoretically innovative direction comes from Braithwaite's neo-Durkeimian theory of reintegrative shaming (Braithwaite 1989).

Most criminologists now work in what has been separated off in the USA as the applied field of criminal justice studies. Basic theoretical debates – whether about the nature of the subject or the nature of criminality – are still alive but less prestigious. The subject remains ethnocentric: seldom engaging with the less developed world or with crimes of the state or with political violence.

The diversity in modern criminology arises from two tensions. First, crime is behaviour, but it is behaviour which the state is organized to punish. Second, crime raises matters of pragmatic public interest, but it has also created its own theoretical discourse.

Stanley Cohen
Hebrew University, Jerusalem

References

Beirne, P. (1993) *Inventing Criminology: The Rise of 'Homo Criminalis'*, Albany, NY.
Braithwaite, J. (1989) *Crime, Shame and Reintegration*, Cambridge, UK.
Cornish, D. B. and Clarke, R. V. (eds) (1986) *The Reasoning Criminal: Rational Choice Perspectives on Offending*, New York.
Garland, D. (1985) *Punishment and Welfare*, Aldershot.
—— (1994) 'Of crimes and criminals: the development of criminology in Britain', in M. Maguire *et al.* (eds) *The Oxford Handbook of Criminology*, Oxford.
Matza, D. (1964) *Delinquency and Drift*, New York.
—— (1969) *Becoming Deviant*, Englewood Cliffs, NJ.

Further reading

Christie, N. (1981) *Limits to Pain*, Oxford.
Cohen, S. (1988) *Against Criminology*, New Brunswick, NJ.
Gottfredson, M. and Hirschi, T. (1990) *A General Theory of Crime*, Stanford, CA.
Maguire, M., Morgan, R. and Reiner, R. (1994) *The Oxford Handbook of Criminology*, Oxford.
Sutherland, E. and Cressey, D. (1989) *Principles of Criminology*, Philadelphia, PA.
Young, J. and Mathews, R. (eds) (1992) *Rethinking Criminology: The Realist Debate*, London.

See also: crime and delinquency; critical legal studies; deviance; penology; police; punishment; sociolegal studies.

critical legal studies

Critical legal studies is an intellectual and political movement accommodating a diversity of resistances to the orthodox study of law in doctrinal terms. Consistent with origins in the radical political culture of the 1960s, critical legal studies (CLS) has sought to effect libertarian reforms in legal education, but its success with this has been less conspicuous than the large impact it has had on legal theory. CLS has specific institutional presences in various loose organizations and annual conferences in Europe and the USA. It can also claim a significant literature for itself.

CLS has thrived on opposition. Rarely can an intellectual endeavour so diverse and eclectic have caused such hostility within academic orthodoxy. CLS has been a persistent provocation to mainstream legal scholarship from its earliest guise as variants of phenomenology and critical social theory to its later inclusion of post-modernism, feminism and anti-racism. This conflict is in one way unsurprising. What has united the several strands of CLS has been a radical interrogation of the academic adequacy and the operative autonomy of doctrinal approaches to law. In another way the opposition to CLS does seem surprising because there are social perspectives on law, such as those provided by the sociology of law, which have long questioned the self-sufficiency of the legal domain. This questioning has, however, largely taken the integrity of law as given and then related law to various social influences or determinations. The dangerous dimension of CLS has consisted in its scrutiny of law from within, a scrutiny that has revealed basic division and contradiction within law itself, not only as an academic field but also as the very rule of law held necessary for the viability of liberal society. In particular, by looking closely at legal doctrine in operation, CLS has shaken law's claims to consistency, certainty and predictability.

The cunning of law, however, knows no bounds. The disorientation of law effected by CLS does raise the issue of why such a precarious entity as law endures. CLS has in ways added to law's mystery, and even its potency, by showing, at least obliquely, that law survives in the face of its own incoherence. Perhaps this is why CLS has come to explore the arcanum of law's distinct 'force' or its (paternal) authority by resort to deconstruction and psychoanalysis. Another influential response in CLS to law's radical uncertainty has been the discovery that there is an ineluctable place within law for ethics and justice – elements which were supposedly excluded in doctrinal claims to completeness. This marks something of a return to law, to finding sources of critique within law itself.

In all, the old enemy of doctrine persists and CLS continues to provide expansive protocols of combat which themselves would find coexistence difficult without this common adversary.

Peter Fitzpatrick
University of Kent

Further reading

Douzinas, C., Goodrich, P. and Hachamovitch, Y. (eds) (1994) *Politics, Postmodernity and Critical Legal Studies: The Legality of the Contingent*, London.
Fitzpatrick, P. and Hunt, A. (eds) (1987) *Critical Legal Studies*, Oxford.
Kelman, M. (1987) *A Guide to Critical Legal Studies*, Cambridge, MA.

See also: criminology; judicial process; law; sociolegal studies.

crowding out

The concept of the crowding out of private sector activity by expansions of government sector has become increasingly important in political/academic debates. All participants in the debate accept that if the economy is at full employment, an increase in government spending will reduce private sector spending. The debate is concentrated on the effect of increases in government spending away from full employment. If government spending rises by $100 million and national income increases by less than $100 million, then crowding out is said to have occurred. In other words, crowding out is associated with a *multiplier* of less than unity. Even if national income rises by more than $100 million, it would normally be the case that the higher interest rates associated with higher borrowing will reduce productive private sector investment and so 'crowd out' some elements of national income.

The resurgence of interest in crowding out has been associated with the monetarist critique of macroeconomic policy and has received its main theoretical (Carlson and Spencer 1975) and empirical (Anderson and Jordan 1968) support from work undertaken at the Federal Reserve Bank of St Louis in the USA. Although much of this work has been discredited (see Goldfeld and Blinder 1972), the political impact has been increasing. Apart from the interest rate effect on a number of other possible sources for crowding out have been suggested. Increased government expenditure may have a depressing effect on people's expectations about the future possible productivity of the economy, and so causing them to reduce investment. Alternatively, investment could be so interest sensitive that even a small rise in the interest rate will reduce investment fully in line with the increase in government spending (this is sometimes known as the Knight case, after the Chicago economist Frank Knight).

The major case emphasized by monetarist economists comes from an analysis of the financing of a government deficit. To have an impact on the economy a deficit has to be sustained for a number of years, but each year that deficit has to be financed by borrowing or printing money. Continual financing by borrowing will raise interest rates as the government competes for funds, and the gradual increase in interest rates will reduce investment. As well as this effect, it may be stressed that government debt is safer than private debt, so dollar for dollar substitution will increase the liquidity of the economy and reduce the impulsion to save (and therefore reduce investment funds).

However lacking in persuasiveness these arguments may be, there is strong empirical support for the proposition that multipliers are very low in the UK at least (Cook and Jackson 1979). In versions of the Treasury Model and the Keynesian National Institute model, long-run multipliers vary from 1.1 to 0.4 giving considerable credence to the arguments in favour of crowding out. This does not demonstrate that fiscal policy is impossible, but that it is just difficult to sustain.

Ray Barrell
National Institute of Economic and
Social Research

References

Anderson, L. C. and Jordan, J. L. (1968) 'Monetary and fiscal actions: a test of their relative importance in economic stabilisation', *Federal Reserve Bank of St Louis Review*.
Carlson, K. M. and Spencer, R. W. (1975) 'Crowding out and its critics', *Federal Reserve Bank of St Louis Review*.
Cook, S. T. and Jackson, P. M. (eds) (1979) *Government Issues in Fiscal Policy*, London.
Goldfeld, S. and Blinder, A. (1972) 'Some implications of endogenous stabilisation policy', *Brookings Papers on Economic Activity*.

See also: mixed economy; monetarism.

cults *see* cargo cults; sects and cults

cultural anthropology

Cultural anthropology is the study of the social practices, expressive forms, and language use through which meanings are constituted, invoked and often contested in human societies. The term cultural anthropology is generally associated with the American tradition of anthropological research and writing. In the early part of the twentieth century, Franz Boas (1940) was critical of the assumptions of evolutionary anthropology and of its racial implications; in developing his critique, he focused on the particularities of different ways of life rather than upon broad comparison and generalization, and on demonstrating that race and culture were not coterminous. Boasian anthropology, as George Stocking (1974: 19) has suggested, elaborated a concept of culture as a 'relativistic, pluralistic, holistic, integrated, and historically conditioned framework for the study of the determination of human behavior', a concept that involved an emphasis on language as an embodiment of culturally significant classificatory systems.

The Boasian emphasis on culture as a particularized, patterned and shared set of categories and assumptions that often did not rise into conscious awareness directed anthropologists working in this tradition to focus upon the meanings rather than the functions of social and cultural practices, and upon the specificities of these meanings rather than upon the construction of cross-cultural sociological laws and principles.

This way of thinking about culture is a significant and enduring paradigm that continues to inform American anthropology, and it was influential in the development of French structural anthropology as well. Edward Sapir, a student of Boas, adumbrated later critiques of some Boasian assumptions with his stress on individual creativity in culture and in language, and with his writings on the diversity of perspectives within societies (1949). Since at least the late 1970s cultural anthropologists, while retaining the emphasis on culture as a set of signs and meanings, have been further challenging some Boasian assumptions about culture as a shared, integrated and taken-for-granted unified whole; as a result, they are experimenting with a variety of novel interpretive and writing strategies.

Broadly speaking, these challenges have resulted from a rethinking of the idea of culture on four inter-related fronts: considerations of the politics of representing other cultures and societies; considerations of the power relations in which cultural meanings are always situated; reconsiderations of the relation of language to culture; and considerations of person, self and emotion in relation to cultural meanings. Together these frame a broad spectrum of research and writing in cultural anthropology.

The politics of representation

Edward Said's enormously influential argument in *Orientalism* (1978) was that western descriptions of other (usually formerly colonized) cultures typically represent them as static, mired in an unchanging and unchallengeable tradition, and as exercising such control over behaviour and attitudes that people are unable consciously to critique or transform their own societies or to exercise agency with respect to them. Said views this as a dehumanizing mode of writing that not only serves the political interests of the colonizing and formerly colonizing west, but also allows the west to define itself as advancing rather than static, and as scientific and rational rather than traditional. Cultural anthropologists have considered the implications of these and other critiques of western writing about other societies, and the way that older conceptions of culture reinforced such representations. As a result they have transformed their modes of writing and analysis to highlight the historically changing nature of all societies, the active construction and deployment of tradition in the cultures they study, and to reflect on the inevitably political nature of all anthropological writing and to make this explicit in their writing.

Culture and power

Boasian and structural definitions of culture typically involve assumptions about the degree to which culture is shared within a given community, and the degree to which cultural propositions are part of everyday taken-for-granted and unquestioned common sense. Cultural anthropology, often drawing upon the work of Pierre Bourdieu (1977), has come to emphasize instead the tactical uses of cultural discourses in everyday social practice, and influenced as well by the writings of Michel Foucault (1977; 1978), the ways that cultural propositions are upheld by and serve the interests of certain segments of a society. Feminist anthropology and research on the politics of class and race have been of critical importance in this move to interpret culture as an arena characterized as much by struggle and contestation as by consensus. Thus, for example, many feminist anthropologists have turned their attention to the poetics and politics of ritual, story, song and other expressive traditions that offer implicit or explicit critiques of authoritative cultural discourses concerning gender, kinship, and economic and political institutions.

Ethnographic writing has come to focus upon the relationship of culture to power and, reflecting upon the work of James C. Scott (1985; 1990) and others on the nature of resistance, to emphasize the fact that cultural discourses may be challenged, contested or negotiated by those whom they disadvantage. Cultural anthropologists have also analysed the deployment of cultural traditions as responses to power relations on a global scale, to specific colonial and postcolonial political and economic situations, belying earlier assumptions about the fixity and timelessness of 'tradition'.

Language in cultural anthropology

The shift in anthropology from a definition of culture stressing stasis, internal consistency and homogeneity to one stressing heterogeneous meanings deployed for different persuasive purposes is paralleled and in some ways foreshadowed by the shift away from the Boasian and structuralist concern with language as a formal system of abstract cultural categories to a concern with the linguistic strategies through which speakers rhetorically construct and reconstruct status, identity and social relationships in varied situations of everyday life. Speech, these anthropologists argue, is always produced in specific historical and micropolitical contexts, and it both reflects and is constitutive of the power relationships implicit in the speech situation. Cultural anthropologists frequently use the term *discourse* to characterize language envisioned as a set of resources that speakers draw upon to construct and negotiate their social worlds in specific contexts. The word is intended to evoke the idea of language and culture as implicated in a universe of power relationships, and to focus analytic attention on the pragmatic uses of linguistic forms rather than on language as a fixed and formal set of features or cultural categories that somehow transcend the actual social circumstances of the speech community.

Person, self and emotion

In veering away from styles of ethnographic writing that view cultures as monolithic and homogeneous and moving towards modes of writing that see human subjectivity as both social and individual, and culture as both shared and contested, cultural anthropologists have been increasingly concerned with the role that emotions and talk about emotions play in social life, and with the possibility of an anthropology of experience that would convey the distinctive qualities of life in another culture while at the same time portraying an individual's complex and often contradictory experiences within that culture. Earlier work, beginning with that of Ruth Benedict (1934), for example, saw both personality and culture as consistent unified wholes. More recent analyses of the language of personal narrative, of cultural discourses of emotion, of life history, of the micropolitics of everyday life, and psychoanalytic modes of analysis have all contributed to the effort to write convincingly of the fluidity and contextuality of the self and of culture.

Gloria Goodwin Raheja
University of Minnesota

References

Benedict, R. (1934) *Patterns of Culture*, Boston.
Boas, F. (1940) *Race, Language and Culture*, New York.
Bourdieu, P. (1977) *Outline of a Theory of Practice*, Cambridge, UK.
Foucault, M. (1977) *Discipline and Punish: The Birth of the Prison*, New York.
—— (1978) *The History of Sexuality*, vol. 1, *An Introduction*, New York.
Said, E. (1978) *Orientalism*, New York.
Sapir, E. (1949) *Selected Writings of Edward Sapir*, Berkeley, Los Angeles and London.
Scott, J. (1985) *Weapons of the Weak: Everyday Forms of Peasant Resistance*, New Haven, CT.
—— (1990) *Domination and the Arts of Resistance: Hidden Transcripts*, New Haven, CT.
Stocking, G. (1974) *The Shaping of American Anthropology: 1883–1911*, New York.

Further reading

Abu-Lughod, L. (1993) *Writing Women's Worlds: Bedouin Stories*, Berkeley, CA.
Clifford, J. and Marcus, G. (eds) (1986) *Writing Culture: The Poetics and Politics of Ethnography*, Berkeley, CA.
Fox, R. (ed.) (1991) *Recapturing Anthropology: Working in the Present*, Santa Fe, NM.
Marcus, G. and M. Fischer (1986) *Anthropology as Cultural Critique: An Experimental Moment in the Human Sciences*, Chicago.
Sherzer, J. (1987) 'A discourse-centered approach to language and culture', *American Anthropologist* 89.
Tsing, A. L. (1993) *In the Realm of the Diamond Queen: Marginality in an Out-of-the-Way Place*, Princeton, NJ.

See also: Boas, Franz; cultural history; cultural studies; culture; medical anthropology; orientalism; political culture; psychological anthropology; social anthropology.

cultural geography

Cultural geography is concerned with understanding the diversity of human cultures across the surface of the earth and with exploring the spatial constitution of cultural difference. Its origins can be traced to the nineteenth-century German conception of *Kultur* (referring to the specific and variable cultures of different nations and periods). The geographical expression of culture in the landscape was central to the German tradition of *Landschaftskunde*, an approach that was assimilated and transformed in North America through the work of Carl Sauer (1889–1975) and his students at what became known as the 'Berkeley school'. Sauer was implacably opposed to environmental determinism and approached the study of landscape change as an indication of the scope of human agency in transforming the face of the earth (Thomas 1956). To investigate such transformations, Sauer used a range of evidence including settlement patterns, the domestication of plants and animals, the distribution of material artefacts and the diffusion of innovations. Drawing on the work of contemporary anthropologists such as Alfred Kroeber and Robert Lowie, Sauer (1925: 46) distinguished between natural and cultural landscapes, arguing that, 'The cultural landscape is fashioned out of a natural landscape by a culture group. Culture is the agent, the natural area is the medium, the cultural landscape the result.'

Sauer's work is still widely respected for his command of languages and dedication to fieldwork, his emphasis on human agency and ecological concern, and his scorn for narrow disciplinary boundaries. But his work has been criticized for its static, disembodied, 'superorganic' theory of culture (Duncan 1980) and for its antiquarian preoccupation with rural landscapes of the distant past (Cosgrove and Jackson 1987). Cultural geographers in Britain and North America have challenged Sauer's unitary view of culture, suggesting that landscapes are contested cultural constructions, socially invested with conflicting meanings that derive from different material interests. Treating landscapes as a reflection of diverse ways of seeing, new methods of interpretation have arisen, including studies of the iconography of landscape and the relationship between social formation and landscape symbolism (Cosgrove 1984; Cosgrove and Daniels 1988).

Reflecting the 'cultural turn' throughout the social sciences and the humanities, cultural geographers have begun to explore post-structuralist concerns with discourse and text, developing a sensitivity to the politics of representation (Barnes and Duncan 1992; Duncan and Ley 1993). Some have also been influenced by developments in feminist theory and cultural studies, concerning the cultural politics of gender and sexuality, language, race and nation, as these are played out across the contested boundaries of public and private space (Jackson 1989). Such departures from the Berkeley school tradition have not been universally welcomed (see Price and Lewis 1993 and subsequent commentaries).

As people's experiences of environment and nature are increasingly mediated through television and popular culture, places have come to be recognized as the product of invented traditions (Anderson and Gale 1992). Unitary definitions have given way to a plurality of conflicting cultures and to a conception of modern identities as inherently hybrid. These developments have led to a more sharply politicized conception of cultural geography in which notions of ideology and power now play a central role. Cultural geographers have returned to the question of nature, bringing new perspectives such as ecofeminism, psychoanalysis and post-modernism to issues that were originally raised by Berkeley school scholars such as Clarence Glacken (1967). Cultural geography is also coming to terms with its historical links with imperialism, exploring a range of post-colonial debates over issues such as native land rights. The diversity of cultural geography truly reflects the contested nature of its core concept, culture, which, as Raymond Williams (1976: 87) observed, is 'one of the two or three most complicated words in the English language'.

Peter Jackson
University of Sheffield

References

Anderson, K. J. and Gale, F. (eds) (1992) *Inventing Places*, Melbourne.
Barnes, T. and Duncan, J. S. (eds) (1992) *Writing Worlds*, London and New York.
Cosgrove, D. (1984) *Social Formation and Symbolic Landscape*, London.
Cosgrove, D. and Daniels, S. (eds) (1988) *The Iconography of Landscape*, Cambridge, UK.
Cosgrove, D. and Jackson, P. (1987) 'New directions in cultural geography', *Area* 19.
Duncan, J. S. (1980) 'The superorganic in American cultural geography', *Annals, Association of American Geographers* 70.
Duncan, J. S. and Ley, D. (eds) (1993) *Place/Culture/Representation*, London and New York.
Glacken, C. (1967) *Traces on the Rhodian Shore*, Berkeley, CA.
Jackson, P. (1989) *Maps of Meaning*, London.
Price, M. and Lewis, M. (1993) The reinvention of cultural geography, *Annals, Association of American Geographers* 83.
Sauer, C. O. (1925) 'The morphology of landscape', *University of California Publications in Geography* 2, reprinted in J. Leighly (ed.) (1963) *Land and Life*, Berkeley, CA.
Thomas, W. L. (ed.) (1956) *Man's Role in Changing the Face of the Earth*, Chicago.
Williams, R. (1976) *Keywords*, London.

See also: culture; economic geography; landscape; social geography.

cultural history

The term cultural history came into use in the late eighteenth century, originally in Germany, inspired by the attempts of Herder, Hegel and others to view the different parts of culture as a whole (histories of literature, art and music go back much further). The most famous nineteenth-century example of the genre was the Swiss scholar Jacob Burckhardt's *Civilization of the Renaissance in Italy* (1860), which was concerned not so much with painting or literature as with attitudes, notably with individualism, with the admiration for antiquity, with morality and with festivals and even the organization of the state as 'works of art'. In the early twentieth century, the Dutch historian Johan Huizinga produced a masterly study of Franco-Flemish culture, *The Waning of the Middle Ages* (1919), more or less on the Burckhardtian model (*see* Huizinga 1959 [1929]), while in Hamburg Aby Warburg wrote a handful of important articles and built up a marvellous library (transferred to London in 1933) devoted to the history of the classical tradition and to the science of culture (*Kulturwissenschaft*). However, these attempts to write a general history of culture found few emulators. At much the same time, between the two world wars, French attempts to go beyond political and economic history took the form of the history of collective mentalities associated with the Annales School, while in the USA attention was focused on the history of ideas.

The history of culture did not go uncriticized. Marxists in particular pointed out that the classical studies of cultural history depend on a postulate which it is extremely difficult to justify, the postulate of cultural unity or consensus. Thus Burckhardt wrote of 'the culture of the Renaissance', while Huizinga once described history as the form in which 'a culture accounts to itself for its past'. In similar fashion, the non-Marxist Ernst Gombrich rejected the work of Burckhardt and Huizinga on the grounds that it was built on 'Hegelian foundations' which had 'crumbled' (Gombrich 1969).

The rise or revival of interest in a holistic history of culture goes back to the 1970s or thereabouts, a time of reaction against socioeconomic determinism and archive positivism. Just as late eighteenth-century historians were inspired by Herder and Hegel, so late twentieth-century historians – especially in France and the USA – draw on cultural anthropology (especially on Clifford Geertz, whose essay on the cock-fight is cited again and again), and on cultural theory more generally. The ideas of Lévi-Strauss evoked some response from historians in the 1970s, but the influence of Elias, Bakhtin, Foucault and Bourdieu has been considerably more substantial and long-lasting, while a few brave souls are attempting to make use of Derrida.

In recent work, the term culture has extended its meaning to embrace a much wider range of activities. Historians study popular culture as well as elite culture. They are concerned not only with art but also with material culture, not only with the written but also with the oral, not only with drama but also with ritual. The idea of political culture stretches the concept still further. Everyday life is included, or more precisely the rules or principles underlying everyday practices.

Traditional assumptions about the relation between culture and society have been reversed. Cultural historians, like cultural theorists, now claim that culture is capable of resisting social pressures or even that it shapes social reality. Hence the increasing interest in the history of representations (whether verbal or visual), the history of the imaginary, and especially the story of the construction, invention or constitution of what used to be considered social facts such as social class, nation or gender.

Another approach, partly inspired by anthropology, focuses on cultural encounters, clashes or invasion. Historians have attempted to reconstruct the way in which the Caribs perceived Columbus, the Aztecs saw Cortés, or the Hawaiians viewed Captain Cook and his sailors. The point to emphasize here is the relatively new interest in the way in which the two sides understood or failed to understand one another. There is also increasing interest in the process of borrowing, acculturation, reception, and resistance, in cases of encounters not only between cultures but also between groups within them.

Peter Burke
University of Cambridge

References

Gombrich, E. H. (1969) *In Search of Cultural History*, Oxford.
Huizinga, J. (1959 [1929]) 'The task of cultural history', in J. Huizinga, *Men and Ideas*, New York.

Further reading

Chartier, R. (1988) *Cultural History*, Cambridge, UK.
Hunt, L. (ed.) (1989) *The New Cultural History*, Berkeley, CA.

See also: cultural anthropology; culture; history of medicine; political culture; social anthropology; social history.

cultural studies

John Fiske (1992) maintains that 'culture' (in cultural studies) 'is neither aesthetic nor humanist in emphasis, but political'. Thus, the object of study in cultural studies is not culture defined in the narrow sense, as the objects of aesthetic excellence ('high art') nor culture defined in an equally narrow sense, as a process of aesthetic, intellectual and spiritual develop-ment, but culture understood, in Raymond Williams's (1961) famous appropriation from anthropology, as 'a particular way of life, whether of a people, a period or a group'. This is a definition of culture which can embrace the first two definitions, but also, and crucially, it can range beyond the social exclusivity and narrowness of these, to include the study of popular culture. Therefore, although cultural studies cannot (or should not) be reduced to the study of popular culture, it is certainly the case that the study of popular culture is central to the project of cultural studies. Finally, cultural studies regards culture as political in a quite specific sense, one which reveals the dominant political position within cultural studies. Stuart Hall (1981), for example, describes popular culture as

> an arena of consent and resistance. It is partly where hegemony arises, and where it is secured. It is not a sphere where socialism, a socialist culture – already fully formed – might be simply 'expressed'. But it is one of the places where socialism might be constituted. That is why 'popular culture' matters.

Others within cultural studies might not express their attitude to popular culture quite in these terms, but they would certainly share Hall's concern to think of culture politically.

All the basic assumptions of cultural studies are Marxist. This is not to say that all practitioners of cultural studies are Marxists, but that cultural studies is itself grounded in Marxism. Marxism informs cultural studies in two fundamental ways. First, to understand the meanings of culture we must analyse it in relation to the social structure and its historical contingency. Although constituted by a particular social structure with a particular history, culture is not studied as a reflection of this structure and history. On the contrary, cultural studies argues that culture's importance derives from the fact that it helps constitute the structure and shape the history. Second, cultural studies assumes that capitalist industrial societies are societies divided unequally along ethnic, gender, generational and class lines. It is argued that culture is one of the principal sites where this division is established and contested: culture is a terrain on which takes place a continual struggle over meaning, in which subordinate groups attempt to resist the imposition of meanings which bear the interests of dominant groups. It is this which makes culture ideological.

Ideology is without doubt the central concept in cultural studies. There are many competing definitions of ideology, but it is the formulation established by Hall (1982), which is generally accepted as the dominant definition within cultural studies. Working within a framework of Gramsci's (1971) concept of hegemony, Hall developed a theory of 'articulation' to explain the processes of ideological struggle (Hall's use of 'articulation' plays on the term's double meaning: to express and to join together). He argues that cultural texts and practices are not inscribed with meaning, guaranteed once and for all by the intentions of production; meaning is always the result of an act of 'articulation' (an active process of production in use). The process is called articulation because meaning has to be expressed, but it is always expressed in a specific context, a specific historical moment, within a specific discourse(s). Thus expression is always connected (articulated) to and conditioned by context. Hall also draws on the work of the Russian theorist Valentin Volosinov (1973 [1929]) who argues that meaning is always determined by context of articulation. Cultural texts and practices are 'multi-accentual', that is, they can be articulated with different accents by different people in different contexts for different politics. Meaning is therefore a social production: the world has to be made to mean. A text or practice or event is not the issuing source of meaning, but a site where the articulation of meaning – variable meaning(s) – can take place. Because different meanings can be ascribed to the same text or practice or event, meaning is always a potential site of conflict. Thus the field of culture is for cultural studies a major site of ideological struggle; a terrain of incorporation and resistance; one of the sites where hegemony is to be won or lost.

There are those, within and outside cultural studies, who believe that cultural studies' model of ideological struggle leads (in some versions almost inevitably) to an uncritical celebration of popular culture: 'resistance' is endlessly elaborated in terms of empowerment and pleasure, while incorporation is quietly forgotten. An advocate of this thesis is Jim McGuigan (1992), who claims to identify 'an *uncritical* populist drift' within cultural studies; an uncritical celebration of the 'popular' reading. Against this, cultural studies would insist that people *make* popular culture from the repertoire of commodities supplied by the cultural industries. Cultural studies would also insist that making popular culture ('production in use') can be empowering to subordinate and resistant to dominant understandings of the world. But this is not to say that popular culture is always empowering and resistant. To deny the passivity of consumption is not to deny that sometimes consumption is passive; to deny that the consumers of popular culture are not cultural dupes is not to deny that at times we can all be duped. But it is to deny that popular culture is little more than a degraded culture, successfully imposed from above, to make profit and secure ideological control. The best of cultural studies insists that to decide these matters requires vigilance and attention to the details of the production, distribution and consumption of culture. These are not matters that can be decided once and for all (outside the contingencies of history and politics) with an elitist glance and a condescending sneer. Nor can they be read off from the moment of production (locating meaning, pleasure, ideological effect, etc., in, variously, the intention, the means of production or the production itself). These are only aspects of the contexts for production in use, and it is, ultimately, in production in use that questions of meaning, pleasure, ideological effect, and so on can be (contingently) decided.

John Storey
University of Sunderland

References

Fiske, J. (1992) 'British cultural studies and television', in R. C. Allen (ed.) *Channels of Discourse, Reassembled*, London.
Gramsci, A. (1971) *Selections from Prison Notebooks*, London.
Hall, S. (1981) 'Notes on deconstructing "the popular" ', in R. Samuel (ed.) *People's History and Socialist Theory*, London.
—— (1982) 'The rediscovery of ideology: the return of the repressed', in M. Gurevitch, T. Bennett, J. Curran and J. Woollacott (eds) *Culture, Society and the Media*, London.
McGuigan, J. (1992) *Cultural Populism*, London.
Volosinov, V. N. (1973 [1929]) *Marxism and the Philosophy of Language*, New York.
Williams, R. (1961) *The Long Revolution*, London.

Further reading

Brantlinger, P. (1990) *Crusoe's Footprints: Cultural Studies in Britain and America*, London.
During, S. (ed.) (1993) *The Cultural Studies Reader*, London.
Fiske, J. (1989) *Understanding Popular Culture*, London.
Franklin, S., Lury, C. and Stacy, J. (eds) (1991) *Off-Centre: Feminism and Cultural Studies*, London.
Grossberg, L., Nelson, C. and Treichler, P. (eds) (1992) *Cultural Studies*, London.
Hall, S., Hobson, D., Lowe, A. and Willis, P. (eds) (1980) *Culture, Media, Language*, London.
Inglis, F. (1993) *Cultural Studies*, Oxford.
McRobbie, A. (1994) *Postmodernism and Popular Culture*, London.
Mukerji, C. and Schudson, M. (eds) (1991) *Rethinking Popular Culture: Contemporary Perspectives in Cultural Studies*, Berkeley, CA.
Storey, J. (1993) *An Introductory Guide to Cultural Theory and Popular Culture*, London.
—— (ed.) (1994) *Cultural Theory and Popular Culture: A Reader*, London.
Turner, G. (1990) *British Cultural Studies: An Introduction*, London.

See also: communications; cultural anthropology; culture; mass media; political culture.

culture

Culture is one of the basic theoretical terms in the social sciences. In its most general sense within the social sciences, culture refers to the socially inherited body of learning characteristic of human societies. This contrasts with the ordinary meaning of the term, which refers to a special part of the social heritage having to do with manners and the arts. Both the ordinary and the social science uses are derived from the Latin *cultura*, from the verb *colere*, 'to tend or cultivate'. An excellent history of the term culture can be found in Kroeber and Kluckhohn's (1963) classic work, *Culture: A Critical Review of Concepts and Definitions*.

In the social sciences the term culture takes much of its meaning from its position within a model of the world which depicts the relations between society, culture and the individual.

The social science model

Human society is made up of individuals who engage in activities by which they adapt to their environment and exchange resources with each other so that the society is maintained and individual needs are satisfied.

These activities are learned by imitation and tuition from other humans, and hence are part of the social heritage, or culture, of a society. These learned activities persist from generation to generation with only a small degree of change unless external factors interfere with the degree to which these activities succeed in satisfying social and individual needs.

Learned activities are only one part of the society's culture. Also included in the social heritage are *artefacts* (tools, shelters, utensils, weapons, etc.), plus an ideational complex of constructs and propositions expressed in systems of *symbols*, of which natural *language* is the most important. By means of symbols it is possible to create a rich variety of special entities, called culturally constructed objects, such as money, nationhood, marriage, games, laws, etc., whose existence depends on adherence to the rule system that defines them (D'Andrade 1984). The ideational systems and symbolic systems of the social heritage are necessary because human adaptive activities are so complex and numerous that they could not be learned and performed without a large store of knowledge and a symbolic system to communicate this knowledge and co-ordinate activities.

Much, but not all, of the social heritage or culture has a normative character; that is, the individuals of a community typically feel that their social heritage – their ways of doing things, their understandings of the world, their symbolic expressions – are proper, true and beautiful, and they sanction positively those who conform to the social heritage and punish those who do not.

Individuals perform the activities and hold the beliefs of their social heritage or culture not just because of sanctions from others, and not just because they find these activities and beliefs proper and true, but because they also find at least some cultural activities and beliefs to be motivationally and emotionally satisfying.

In this formulation of the model the terms social heritage and culture have been equated. The model ascribes to culture or social heritage the properties of being socially and individually adaptive, learned, persistent, normative, and motivated. Empirical consideration of the content of the social heritage leads directly to an omnibus definition of culture, like that given by Tylor: 'Culture ... is that complex whole which includes knowledge, belief, art, law, morals, custom, and any other capabilities and habits acquired by man as a member of society (1958); that is, to an enumeration of the kinds of things that can be observed to make up the social heritage.

However, many social scientists restrict the definition of culture to only certain aspects of the social heritage. Most frequently, culture is restricted to the non-physical, or mental part of the social heritage. The physical activities that people perform and the physical artefacts they use are then treated as consequences of the fact that people learn, as part of their social heritage, how to perform these activities and how to make these artefacts. Treating actions and artefacts as the result of learning the social heritage gives causal efficacy to culture; in such a definition culture not only is a descriptive term for a collection of ideas, actions and objects, but also refers to mental entities which are the necessary cause of certain actions and objects.

The current consensus among social scientists also excludes emotional and motivational learnings from culture, focusing on culture as knowledge, or understandings, or propositions. However, it is recognized that some cultural propositions may arouse strong emotions and motivations; when this happens these propositions are said to be internalized (Spiro 1987).

Some social scientists would further restrict the term culture to just those parts of the social heritage which involve representations of things, excluding norms or procedural knowledge about how things should be done (Schneider 1968). Other social scientists would further restrict the definition of culture to symbolic meanings, that is, to those symbolic representations which are used to communicate interpretations of events. Geertz (1973), for example, uses this further restriction of the social heritage not only to exclude affective, motivational and normative parts of the social heritage, but also to argue against the notion that culture resides *in* the individual. According to Geertz, culture resides in the intersubjective field of public meaning, perhaps in the same transcendent sense in which one might speak of algebra as something that exists outside of anyone's understanding of it (Geertz 1973).

Many of the disagreements about the definition of culture contain implicit arguments about the causal nature of the social heritage. For example, there is a controversy about whether or not culture is a 'coherent, integrated whole', that is, whether or not any particular culture can be treated as 'one thing' which has 'one nature'. If it were found that cultures generally display a high degree of integration, this would be evidence that some causal force makes different parts of the culture consistent with one another. However, social scientists are now more likely to stress the diversity and contradictions to be found among the parts of a culture. Although almost any element of the culture can be found to have multiplex relations to other cultural elements (as Malinowski (1922), in his great book, *Argonauts of the Western Pacific*, demonstrated), there is little evidence that these relations ever form a single overall pattern which can be explicitly characterized, Ruth Benedict's (1934) *Patterns of Culture* notwithstanding.

Issues involving the integration of culture are related to issues concerning whether or not culture is a bounded entity. If culture is conceived of as a collection of elements which do not form a coherent whole, then the only thing that makes something a part of a particular culture is the fact that it happens to be part of the social heritage of that particular society. But if one believes that cultures are coherent wholes, then the collection of cultural elements which make up a particular culture can be bounded by whatever characterizes the whole.

The boundary issue leads in turn to the problem of sharedness, that is, if culture is not a bounded entity with its own coherence and integration, then *some* number of individuals in a society must hold a representation or norm in order for it to qualify as a part of the social heritage. However, no principled way has been found to set a numerical cut-off point. In fact, there is some evidence that cultural elements tend to fall into two types: first, a relatively small number of elements that are very highly shared and form a core of high consensus understandings (e.g. red lights mean stop); second, a much larger body of cultural elements which need to be known only by individuals in certain social statuses (e.g. a *tort* is a civil wrong independent of a contract) (Swartz 1991).

These and other problems have led to disenchantment with the term culture, along with a number of replacement terms such as 'ideology' and 'discourse'. It is not that the importance of the social heritage is being questioned within the social sciences; rather, it is that splitting the social heritage into various ontological categories does not seem to carve nature at the joints. For example, for a culture to work as a heritage – something which can be learned and passed along – it must include all kinds of physical objects and events, such as the physical sounds of words and the physical presence of artefacts – otherwise one could not learn the language or learn how to make and use artefacts. Since the cultural process necessarily involves mental and physical, cognitive and affective, representational and normative phenomena, it can be argued that the definition of culture should not be restricted to just one part of the social heritage.

Behind these definitional skirmishes lie important issues. The different definitions of culture can be understood as attempts to work out the causal priorities among the parts of the social heritage. For example, behind the attempt to restrict the definition of culture to the representational aspects of the social heritage lies the hypothesis that norms, emotional reactions, motivations, etc. are dependent on a prior determination of what's what. The norm of generalized exchange and feelings of amity between kin, for example, can exist only if there is a category system that distinguishes kin from non-kin. Further, a cultural definition of kin as 'people of the same flesh and blood' asserts a shared identity that makes exchange and amity a natural consequence of the nature of things. If it is universally true that cultural representations have causal priority over norms, sentiments, and motives, then defining culture as representation focuses attention on what is most important. However, the gain of sharp focus is offset by the dependence of such a definition on assumptions which are likely to turn out to be overly simple.

Roy D'Andrade
University of California,
San Diego

References

Benedict, R. (1934) *Patterns of Culture*, Boston, MA.
D'Andrade, R. (1984) 'Cultural meaning systems', in R. A. Shweder and R. A. LeVine (eds) *Culture Theory: Essays on Mind, Self, and Emotion*, Cambridge, UK.
Geertz, C. (1973) *The Interpretation of Cultures*, New York.
Kroeber, A. L. and Kluckhohn, C. (1963) *Culture: A Critical Review of Concepts and Definitions*, New York.
Malinowski, B. (1922) *Argonauts of the Western Pacific*, London.
Schneider, D. (1968) *American Kinship: A Cultural Account*, Englewood Cliffs, NJ.
Spiro, M. E. (1987) *Culture and Human Nature*, Chicago.
Swartz, M. (1991) *The Way the World is: Cultural Processes and Social Relations among the Mombassa Swahili*, Berkeley, CA.
Tylor, E. B. (1958 [1871]) *Primitive Culture: Researches in the Development of Mythology, Philosophy, Religion, Art and Custom*. Gloucester, MA.

See also: cultural anthropology; cultural geography; cultural history; cultural studies; language and culture; political culture.

culture, material *see* material culture

culture, political *see* political culture

customs unions

A customs union is a form of regional economic integration where countries join together to eliminate all barriers to their mutual trade while imposing common restrictions to trade from non-member states. Customs unions therefore imply preferential or discriminatory trade policy which conflicts with one of the basic tenets of the GATT (General Agreement on Tariffs and Trade). However, the GATT permits customs unions (Article XXIV) if they entail the removal of trade restrictions on most of the trade between members and if the average restrictiveness of external trade barriers does not increase.

In the late 1940s when the GATT was created it was generally felt that since customs unions represented a movement towards the goal of global free trade they would be economically beneficial. In the 1950s this favourable economic view was undermined by the development of the theory of second best in which the analysis of customs unions played a prominent role. Since customs unions involve the movement from one distorted allocation of resources (trade restrictions on all sources of imports) to another (trade restrictions on certain sources of imports) there can be no presumption that economic welfare will increase.

The principal contribution to the analysis of customs unions was provided by Viner (1950) who introduced the concepts of 'trade creation' and 'trade diversion'. Trade creation arises when demand which was formerly satisfied by domestic production is met by imports from a more efficient partner, leading to a saving in the real cost of satisfying a given level of demand. Trade diversion arises if the removal of internal trade restrictions results in demand which was previously satisfied by imports from the rest of the world being met by imports from the comparatively less efficient partner. There is a real cost in terms of the tariff revenue forgone. Whether a customs union is beneficial for a particular member depends upon whether on balance trade creation exceeds trade diversion. A beneficial consumption effect was later identified; the more efficiently produced output from the partner is provided at a lower price thus enabling a greater level of consumption.

Since joining a customs union may reduce welfare, why do countries not remove trade barriers to all sources of imports? The benefits of trade creation are maximized and there is no trade diversion. One answer is that countries join customs unions for non-economic reasons; for example, a desire to increase the size of the industrial sector can be satisfied at a lower cost inside a union. Alternatively there may be economic benefits which were ignored by Viner. There may be gains from the exploitation of economies of scale, improvements in the terms of trade, greater efficiency stimulated by greater competition, increased innovation and faster growth. Further, unilateral tariff reduction directly affects only a country's imports. For that country's exports to increase it must encourage others to reduce their tariffs.

Paul Brenton
University of Birmingham

Reference

Viner, J. (1950) *The Customs Union Issue*, New York.

Further reading

Robson, P. (1987) *The Economics of International Integration*, London

See also: GATT; international trade.

D

Darwin, Charles (1809–82)

Charles Darwin is widely regarded as the founder of modern evolutionism. Although not the first to propose a theory of the transmutation of species, his *Origin of Species* (1859) sparked the debate which converted the scientific community to evolutionism. This book not only provided the basic argument for evolution, but also proposed a new mechanism of change: natural selection. Although this mechanism remained controversial until synthesized with Mendelian genetics in the twentieth century, it has now become the basis for most biologists' approach to the question. Darwin also confronted the human implications of evolutionism in his *Descent of Man* (1871) exploring the link between humans and their ape-like ancestors and the implications of such a link for the nature of society.

Charles Robert Darwin was born in Shrewsbury, England. His father was a wealthy doctor. His grandfather, Erasmus Darwin, also a successful physician, had proposed an evolutionary theory in the 1790s. During an abortive attempt to study medicine at Edinburgh, Darwin met the Lamarckian evolutionist R. E. Grant, who aroused his interest in fundamental biological problems. Darwin then went to Cambridge, where he studied for a BA in the expectation of becoming an Anglican clergyman, but also came into contact with the botanist John Henslow and the geologist Adam Sedgwick. After taking his degree he spent five years as ship's naturalist aboard the survey vessel HMS *Beagle* (1831–6). On the voyage he studied both the geology and zoology of South America. He soon accepted the uniformitarian geology of Charles Lyell, in which all change was supposed to be slow and gradual. He proposed important geological theories, especially on the formation of coral reefs. The fauna of the Galapagos islands (off the Pacific coast of South America) forced him to reassess his belief in the fixity of species. It was clear that closely related forms on separate islands had diverged from a common ancestor when the populations were isolated from each other.

On his return to England, Darwin spent the years 1836–42 as an active member of the scientific community in London. Family support enabled him to marry and then to set up as a country gentleman at Down in Kent. Darwin had already turned his attention to the problem of the evolutionary mechanism. He realized that evolution adapted each population to its local environment, but did not think that the Lamarckian explanation of the inheritance of acquired characteristics was adequate. He studied the techniques of artificial selection used by animal breeders and then encountered the principle of population expansion proposed in T. R. Malthus's *Essay on the Principle of Population*. This led to his theory of natural selection: population pressure created a struggle for existence in which the best adapted individuals would survive and breed, while the least adapted would die out. The extent to which the selection theory embodies the competitive ethos of capitalism remains controversial. Darwin wrote outlines of his theory in 1842 and 1844, but had no intention of publishing at this time. Although now affected by a chronic illness, he continued his researches. He studied barnacles, in part to throw light on evolutionary problems, and also worked on biogeography. A few naturalists were informed of the evolutionary project lying behind these studies, especially the botanist J. D. Hooker. In the mid-1850s he realized the significance of divergence and specialization in evolution and began to write an account of his theory for publication. This was interrupted by the arrival in 1858 of A. R. Wallace's paper on natural selection, which prompted Darwin to write the 'abstract' which became the *Origin of Species*.

The *Origin* aroused much controversy, but Darwin had primed a group of sympathetic naturalists, including J. D. Hooker and T. H. Huxley, who ensured that his theory would not be dismissed. By 1870 the general idea of evolution was widely accepted, although natural selection remained controversial. Both scientists and non-scientists found natural selection too harsh a mechanism to square with their religious and philosophical beliefs. Darwin himself accepted a role for Lamarckism, and this mechanism became widely popular in the late nineteenth century. Much evolutionary research was based on an attempt to reconstruct the tree of life from anatomical and paleontological evidence, but Darwin's own later work concentrated on botany, explaining the origin of various structures in plants in terms of natural selection. He also studied the effects of earthworms upon the soil.

Darwin had become aware of the human implications of evolutionism in the 1830s, but avoided this topic in the *Origin* to minimize controversy. His *Descent of Man* of 1871 was the first detailed attempt to explain the origin of the human race in evolutionary terms and to explore the implications of this approach for human affairs. Darwin used T. H. Huxley's work as evidence that the human species was closely related to the great apes. Much of his book took it for granted that mental and social evolution were progressive. Darwin was convinced that the white race was the most advanced, while darker races were closer to the ancestral ape. Yet he also pioneered ideas about human origins that would not be taken seriously until the mid-twentieth century. He identified Africa rather than Asia as the most probable centre of human evolution and proposed that the key breakthrough separating the ape and human families was the latter's adoption of bipedalism. This freed the hands for making weapons and tools, introducing a selection for intelligence and a consequent increase in the size of the brain. He explained the moral faculties as rationalizations of the instinctive behaviour patterns that had been programmed into our ancestors because of their social life. His *Expression of the Emotions in Man and the Animals* (1872) explained many aspects of human behaviour as relics of our animal ancestry.

Peter J. Bowler
Queen's University Belfast

References

Darwin, C. R. (1859) *On the Origin of Species by Means of Natural Selection: or the Preservation of Favoured Races in the Struggle for Life* London.
—— (1871) *The Descent of Man and Selection in Relation to Sex*, London.
—— (1872) *The Expression of the Emotions in Man and the Animals*, London.

Further reading

Bowler, P. J. (1990) *Charles Darwin: The Man and his Influence*, Oxford.

De Beer, G. (1963) *Charles Darwin*, London.
Desmond, A. and Moore, J. (1991) *Darwin*, London.

See also: human evolution.

decision making

In a sense, the study of decision making is so fundamental to social science that all of its disciplines have some claim to contribute to our knowledge of how decisions are, or should be, made. Throughout the twentieth century, some of these themes have come to be studied under the heading of a single discipline known as decision theory. Many of the key contributions come from experts in mathematics, philosophy, economics and psychology and partly because of this strong interdisciplinary theme, the subject has not found an obvious institutional foothold in the university system. North America is an exception to this, though there is a tendency for university departments to focus on decision science, which is perhaps better understood as a branch of operations research. With these caveats in mind, an interpretation of decision theory broad enough to take in contributions from game theory's insights into strategic choice (decisions made in competition with reasoning agents) as well as those from the areas of organizational behaviour and sociology gives one access to a corpus of ideas that provide a bedrock for understanding the logic of reasoned (and sometimes seemingly unreasoned) action in most human spheres.

Mathematical and qualitative analyses of decision making emphasize different aspects of decision making, but there are three themes that recur. First, there are questions about the appropriate modelling of risk and uncertainty. Second, it is recognized that options need to be evaluated according to a number of different, potentially incommensurable criteria. Third, there are questions about the meaning (and truth) of the assumption that human agents are rational. A fourth issue arises in practice and concerns the apparent gap between planning (rational decision making) and the implementation of those plans within organizations (Langley 1991). We deal with each in turn.

Decision theorists are particularly interested in how decision makers cope with uncertainty. Probability theory provides the basic tools, but there are a number of ways in which the concept can be interpreted and each has pros and cons. The practice of using the relative frequency of an event (a ratio of successes to trials) has a long history though the first theoretical account, associated with the name of Laplace, suggested that probability was a measure of ignorance concerning equally likely events (so regarded because there was insufficient reason to make any other ascription (Weatherford

1982)). To the question, what should we do when relative frequencies do not exist, are undefined, or are unknown the answer is taken to be that we can think of probability as measuring belief and infer subjective probabilities from people's choices over certain gambles. The ability to infer coherent beliefs, that is, ones which satisfy basic laws of probability, depends on the truth of certain assumptions about people's preferences and their beliefs. The experimental literature that has resulted shows that the axioms of classical decision are violated both often and systematically (Baron 1988; Kahneman and Tversky 1979).

One of the classic experiments (Ellsberg 1961) to show how and when the subjective interpretation of probability might fail, also makes a direct link with the notion of uncertainty, as opposed to risk. If the term risk is reserved for situations in which probabilities can be attached to different states of the world, then it is clear that there are many situations (ranging from the adoption of some innovation through to the evaluation of environmental policy) in which even the qualitative nature of the decision problem is poorly understood, and for which probabilities are inappropriate. There is no consensus about how to model uncertainty, as opposed to risk, though ideas in Chapter 6 of Keynes's (1921) treatise have drawn considerable attention. The fact of experimental failings does not in itself touch normative claims (this is how people should behave if only they were rational) but it turns out that many of the philosophical arguments are invalid (Anand 1993).

Turning to the second issue, that of weighing up different aspects associated with options, the customary method of evaluation in economics and finance is to use some form of cost-benefit analysis which requires the aggregation of considerations in terms of costs and benefits. Every general decision-making tool must handle situations in which different considerations must be weighed against each other even though decision makers might object to the explicitness of certain tradeoffs. An alternative, which avoids the description of attributes in monetary terms, can be found in multi-attribute utility theory (MAUT), which allows decision makers to rate options on a number of criteria. This turns out to be a useful practical tool. Often it is impossible to be precise about the relative weights given to different criteria or the criteria scores of different actions so that extensive sensitivity analysis is required: the procedure can be time-consuming but it has the merit of contributing substantially to our understanding of the dilemmas and conflicts in a decision problem. An unexpected finding by those using such tools with decision makers (Phillips 1984) is that the process of using them helps foster consensus and commitment, the absence of which can undermine even the most sophisticated planning systems.

The assumption that humans are rational is often the occasion for more heated debate than enlightened discussion. Some of this might be avoided if there were more clarity about what the assumption entails. The following list of definitions is undoubtedly partial but contains those that recur most frequently. An older philosophical view (which still curries favour in lay circles) is that rationality identifies things which we ought to pursue – though the rise of countries and supranational states where cultural diversity is the norm sees this view on the wane. An alternative, more widely accepted, 'instrumental' view is that rationality is about choosing means appropriate to ends, whatever the ends are. A third possibility, due to Herbert Simon (1955), is implied by the observation that human beings are not *maximizers* of anything given: that they are cognitively limited and seek only to satisfy their desires within the bounds of expectation. Another view, namely that rational agents have transitive preferences (if you prefer *a* to *b*, and *b* to *c*, then you also prefer *a* to *c*), predominates in the higher reaches of economic theory. Yet more accounts of what it is rational to do can be found in game theory. Suffice to say, the term had no unique meaning and accusations of irrationality are made at the risk of not understanding the logic that underpins a particular behaviour.

A new discipline, known as risk studies, may be about to emerge (Turner 1994). If it does, decision theory will no doubt make an important contribution to its development though the gulf between mathematical and institutional analyses remains. There are many aspects of good decision making in practice about which decision theory has had little to say, such as the creative acts required to conceive of options (de Bono 1970). It is, for example, apparent that good risk communication is essential if increasingly publicized crises, from oil spills to faulty breast implants, are to be handled successfully, though there is no substantial body of theory to help with this as yet. A more methodological lesson that we might draw from this subject is the possibility that theories might be useful even if they are false.

P. Anand
University of Oxford

References

Anand, P. (1993) *Foundations of Rational Choice under Risk*, Oxford.

Baron, J. (1988) *Thinking and Deciding*, Cambridge.

de Bono, E. (1970) *Lateral Thinking*, Harmondsworth.

Ellsberg, D. (1961) 'Risk ambiguity and the savage axioms', *Quarterly Journal of Economics* 75.

Kahneman, D. and Tversky, A. (1979) 'Prospect theory', *Econometrica* 47.

Keynes, J. M. (1921) *A Treatise on Probability*, London.

Langley, A. (1991) '*Formal Analysis and Strategic Decision Making*' Omega, 19.

Phillips, L. (1984) 'A theory of requisite decision models', *Acta Psychologica* 56.

Simon, H. A. (1955) 'A Behavioral Model of Rational Choice', *Quarterly Journal of Economics*, 99.

Turner, B. A. (1994) 'The future for risk research', *Journal of Contingencies and Crisis Management* 2.

Weatherford, R. (1982) *Philosophical Foundations of Probability Theory*, London.

defence economics

Since the beginning of the Second World War, economists have applied their tools to the study of war and the preservation of peace. Defence economics is the study of defence and peace with the use of economic analysis and methods, embracing both microeconomics and macroeconomics and including static optimization, growth theory, distribution theory, dynamic optimization, comparative statics (i.e. the comparison of equilibria) and econometrics (i.e. statistical representations of economic models). In defence economics, agents (e.g. defence ministries, bureaucrats, defence contractors, Members of Parliament, allied nations, guerrillas, terrorists and insurgents) are characterized as rational agents who seek their well-being subject to constraints on their resources and actions. As such, agents are viewed as responding in predictable fashions to alteration in their tastes or environment. Thus, for example, a terrorist, who confronts higher prices (costs) for engaging in, say, skyjackings owing to the installation of metal detectors in airports, is expected to substitute skyjackings with a related mode of attack (e.g. kidnappings) that are relatively cheaper to perform.

When analysing the behaviour of government agents (e.g. bureaucrats or elected officials), defence economists often employ public choice methods that account for the self-interests of the agents. These agents may, consequently, trade off the welfare of their constituency in the pursuit of their own well-being, incurring costs that are not justified by defence needs.

Topics relevant to defence economics include the study of arms races, alliances and burden-sharing, economic warfare, the arms trade, weapons procurement policies, defence and development, defence industries, arms control agreements and their net benefits, the economics of treaty verification, evaluation of disarmament proposals, and defence industry conversion. Relevant studies of economic efficiency in the defence sector deal with budgeting, evaluation of alternative organizational forms, internal markets in the armed forces, recruitment, military personnel, incentive contracting, and performance indicators.

During the Cold War, much of the attention of defence economists focused on the following issues: defence burdens and their impact on economic growth; defence burden sharing among allied nations; the measurement and instability of arms races; the efficient allocation of resources within the defence sector; and the regional and national impact of defence spending on income distribution. In the post-Cold-War era, researchers have focused their attention on industrial conversion, the resource allocative aspects of disarmament, the economics of peacekeeping forces, and the measurement of a peace dividend.

When applying economic methods to defence economic issues, researchers must take into account the unique institutional structures of the defence establishment. Thus, for example, cost-plus contracts make more sense when one realizes that the buyer (e.g. the Ministry of Defence) may reserve the option to change the performance specification of a weapon system at a later stage. Institutional considerations are relevant to procurement practices, arms trade policies, defence industries' performance, alliance burden sharing, defence and growth, and a host of related defence economic topics.

Policy issues have centred around whether large allies shoulder the burdens of the small, and, if so, what can be done about it. Another policy concern involves the impact of defence spending on growth: that is, does defence promote or inhibit growth? For most developed countries, defence is expected to impede growth by channelling resources (including research scientists) away from investment. The outcome is less clear cut in developing economies where military service can train personnel and build social infrastructure. The relative profitability of the defence sector has also been a policy concern, since firms tend to face little competition and may earn high profits. Another policy issue has focused on the costs and benefits of an all-volunteer military force.

Todd Sandler
Iowa State University

Further reading

Intriligator, M. D. (1990) 'On the nature and scope of defence economics', *Defence Economics* I.

Reppy, J. (1991) 'On the nature and scope of defence economics: a comment', *Defence Economics* II.

Sandler, T. and Hartley, K. (1995) *The Economics of Defense*, Cambridge, U.K.

defences

The conceptualization of ego mechanisms of defence presents one of the most valuable contributions that

Sigmund Freud and psychoanalysis have made to psychology. Modern psychiatrists, including non-Freudians, define defence mechanisms in a more generic sense, as innate coping styles which allow individuals to minimize sudden, often unexpected, changes in internal and external environment and to resolve cognitive dissonance (psychological conflicts). Defences are deployed involuntarily, as is the case in physiological homeostasis, and in contrast to so-called coping strategies. Evidence continues to accumulate that differences in how individuals deploy defences – their unconscious coping styles – are a major consideration in understanding differential responses to environmental stress. For example, some people respond to stress in a calm, rational way, whereas others become phobic or paranoid, or retreat into fantasy. These different responses are intelligible in terms of different defences.

Sigmund Freud (1964 [1894]) suggested that psychopathology was caused by upsetting affects, or emotions, rather than disturbing ideas. Freud observed that the ego's defence mechanisms can cause affects to become 'dislocated or transposed' from particular ideas or people, by processes that Freud later called dissociation, repression and isolation. In addition, affects could be 'reattached' to other ideas and objects through processes called displacement, projection and sublimation.

Freud identified four significant properties of the defences: they help manage instincts and affects; they are unconscious; they are dynamic and reversible; and although the hallmarks of major psychiatric syndromes, in most people they reflect an adaptive, not a pathological, process.

The use of defence mechanisms usually alters the individual's perception of both internal and external reality. Awareness of instinctual 'wishes' is often diminished; alternative, sometimes antithetical, wishes may be passionately adhered to. While ego mechanisms of defence imply integrated and dynamic – if unconscious – psychological processes, they are more analogous to an oppossum playing dead in the face of danger than to a reflexive eye-blink or to conscious tactics of interpersonal manipulation.

Some inferred purposes of ego mechanisms of defence are: first, to keep affects within bearable limits during sudden changes in one's emotional life (for example, following the death of a loved one); second, to restore psychological homeostasis by postponing or deflecting sudden increases in biological drives (such as heightened sexual awareness and aggression during adolescence); third, to create a moratorium in which to master critical life changes (for example, puberty, life-threatening illness, or promotion); and fourth, to handle unresolved conflicts with important people, living or dead.

In 1936, Freud advised the interested student: 'There are an extraordinarily large number of methods (or mechanisms, as we say) used by our ego in the discharge of its defensive functions ... My daughter, the child analyst, is writing a book upon them.' He was referring to his eightieth-birthday present from Anna Freud; her monograph, *The Ego and the Mechanisms of Defense* (1937), is still the best single reference on the subject.

George E. Vaillant
Harvard Medical School

Reference

Freud, S. (1964 [1894]) *The Neuro-psychoses of Defence, Standard Edition of the Complete Psychological Works of Sigmund Freud*, ed. J. Strachey, Vol. 3, London.

Further reading

Vaillant, G. E. (1992) *Ego Mechanisms of Defense*, Washington, DC.

See also: ego; free association; repression; unconscious.

deflation *see* inflation and deflation

delinquency *see* crime and delinquency

delusions

Although the notion that a bizarre or irrational belief may reflect a state of insanity has a long history (Sims 1988), most contemporary accounts of delusions have been influenced by the work of the Heidelberg school of psychiatry, particularly Karl Jaspers (1963 [1912]). Jaspers advocated a phenomenological approach in which the clinician attempts to understand mental *ill*ness by empathizing with the patient and sharing the patient's experiences. On his view, the hallmark of psychotic illness is that it is not amenable to empathy and is therefore ultimately *ununderstandable*. Jaspers observed that abnormal beliefs in general are held with extraordinary conviction, are impervious to counterargument, and have bizarre or impossible content. However, he further distinguished between *delusion-like ideas*, which arise understandably from the individual's personality, mood or experiences, and *primary delusions*, which arise suddenly from a more fundamental change of personality and which are not mediated by inference. The American Psychiatric Association (1987) defined a delusion as simply

A false personal belief based on incorrect inference about external reality that is firmly sustained despite of what almost everyone else believes and despite what constitutes incontrovertible and obvious proof or evidence to the contrary. The belief is not one ordinarily accepted by other members of the person's culture or subculture.

The concept of *paranoia* has been used to describe psychotic disorders in which delusions (particularly of persecution) are the main feature. Kraepelin (1907), also a Heidelberg psychiatrist who had a major influence on the development of modern systems of psychiatric classification, initially took the view that dementia paranoides was a discrete type of psychotic disorder but later held that it was a subtype of dementia praecox (renamed schizophrenia by Bleuler). The American Psychiatric Association (1994) now uses the term *delusional disorder* to describe schizophrenia-like illnesses in which delusions are the main feature.

Delusions observed in clinical practice tend to concern themes of persecution, reference (when a patient believes that apparently meaningless or innocuous events, comments or objects refer to the self) or grandiosity (Sims 1988). Morbid jealousy (characterized by a delusion that a loved one is being unfaithful) and misidentification syndromes (for example, the Capgras syndrome in which a patient believes that a loved one has been replaced by an impostor) are less often observed (Enoch and Trethowan 1979).

The social context of delusional thinking has hardly been investigated, although Mirowsky and Ross (1983) have suggested that paranoid ideation is particularly evident in social and economic circumstances characterized by powerlessness. Following his analysis of the memoirs of Daniel Schreber, a German judge who suffered from a severe mental illness, Freud (1958 [1911]) suggested that paranoia is a product of homosexual longings which are unacceptable to consciousness. This theory has been disputed by other commentators who have attributed Schreber's illness to the authoritarian childrearing practices advocated by his father (Schatzman 1973).

Two further accounts of delusional thinking have been proposed in the psychological literature. Maher (1974) has suggested that delusions are the product of rational attempts to explain anomalous experiences including abnormal bodily sensations; on this view the reasoning of deluded people is normal. Although perceptual abnormalities do seem to be implicated in some types of delusions (particularly the misidentification syndromes; cf. Ellis and Young 1990), empirical studies have failed to establish a general relationship between anomalous experiences and abnormal beliefs (Chapman and Chapman 1988).

Other psychologists have argued that reasoning processes may be abnormal in deluded patients and recent empirical studies would tend to support this view. Garety *et al.* (1991) have shown that many deluded patients perform abnormally on probabilistic reasoning tasks, sampling less evidence before making a decision than non-deluded controls. Taking a different approach, Bentall *et al.* (1994) have shown that deluded patients have an abnormal tendency to explain negative experiences by reference to causes which are external to self. This attributional style, which seems to reflect the abnormal functioning of a normal defensive mechanism, is hypothesized to protect the deluded individual from low self-esteem. This account is consistent with the view that paranoia is a camouflaged form of depression (Zigler and Glick 1988).

There is evidence that cognitive-behavioural strategies may be effective in the treatment of some kinds of delusional beliefs (Chadwick and Lowe 1990).

Richard Bentall
University of Liverpool

References

American Psychiatric Association (1994) *Diagnostic and Statistical Manual of Mental Disorders, 4th Edition*, Washington, DC.

Bentall, R. P., Kinderman, P. and Kaney, S. (1994) 'The self, attributional processes and abnormal beliefs: towards a model of persecutory delusions', *Behaviour Research and Therapy* 32.

Chadwick, P. and Lowe, C. F. (1990) 'The measurement and modification of delusional beliefs', *Journal of Consulting and Clinical Psychology* 58.

Chapman, L. J. and Chapman, J. P. (1988) 'The genesis of delusions', in T. F. Oltmanns and B. A. Maher (eds) *Delusional Beliefs*, New York.

Ellis, H. D. and Young, A. W. (1990) 'Accounting for delusional misidentification', *British Journal of Psychiatry* 157.

Enoch, D. and Trethowan, W. H. (1979) *Uncommon Psychiatric Syndromes*, Bristol.

Freud, S. (1958[1911]) 'Psychoanalytic notes upon an autobiographical account of a case of paranoia (dementia paranoides)', *Standard Edition of the Complete Psychological Works of Sigmund Freud*, ed. J. Strachey, vol. 12, London.

Garety, P. A., Hemsley, D. R. and Wessely, S. (1991) 'Reasoning in deluded schizophrenic and paranoid patients', *Journal of Nervous and Mental Disease* 179.

Jaspers, K. (1963[1912]) *General Psychopathology*, Manchester.

Kraepelin, E. (1907) Textbook of Psychiatry, 7th edition (Diefendorf, A. R., trans.) London.

Maher, B. A. (1974) 'Delusional thinking and perceptual disorder', *Journal of Individual Psychology* 30.

Mirowsky, J. and Ross, C. E. (1983) 'Paranoia and the structure of powerlessness', *American Sociological Review* 48.

Schatzman, M. (1973) *Soul Murder: Persecution in the Family*, London.

Sims, A. (1988) *Symptoms in the Mind*, London.

Zigler, E. and Glick, M. (1988) 'Is paranoid schizophrenia really camoflaged depression?' *American Psychologist* 43.

Further reading

Oltmanns, T. F. and Maher, B. A. (eds) (1988) *Delusional Beliefs*, New York.

See also: fantasy.

demand for money

The demand for money has often played a central role in the debate concerning the appropriate stance for monetary policy. Changes in the money supply have a direct impact on interest rates, which provides the first link in the chain of the monetary transmission mechanism. Monetarists believe that the money supply has an effect on real output in the short run (three to five years) but in the long run real output returns to its 'natural rate' and any monetary expansion is dissipated in price rises (inflation). In an open economy the money supply also influences the exchange rate and may even cause the latter to overshoot, with consequent short-run effects on price competitiveness, exports, imports and hence real output.

In analysing money demand we assume that in the long run, desired nominal money holdings rise one-for-one with the price level so that the purchasing power of money (i.e. real money balances) remains constant (*ceteris paribus*). In economies that suffer from hyperinflation (e.g. some Latin American countries, emerging economies of eastern Europe and Russia) the main determinant of *real* money demand is the expected rate of inflation. The higher that the latter is, the more people wish to move out of money and into goods. Here the rate of inflation represents the rate of loss of purchasing power of money or, more technically, the opportunity cost of money.

In industrialized countries (with moderate inflation rates) a key determinant of (real) money holdings is the level of (real) transactions undertaken. If the desired demand for money M^d is proportional to money income PY then $M^d = kPY$. In equilibrium money supply M^s must equal money demand so that $M^s = kPY$. Hence as long as 'k' remains constant, any increase in the money supply M^s will cause an increase in prices P or real output Y. If, in the long run, real output growth is determined by the underlying growth in productivity, then the price level rises one-for-one with an increase in the money supply.

Given the underlying growth in output and a desired path for prices and an estimate of k, one can calculate the required growth of the money supply. Often debates about monetary policy are conducted in terms of the 'velocity of circulation' which is defined as PY/M.

Given our above assumption about proportionality in the demand for money, we see that this implies that velocity is a constant (i.e. $V = 1/k$).

As well as the transactions motive for holding money, we have the 'asset motive', which is based on the fact that money is a 'store of value'. Faced with the choice between two assets, money which earns interest r_m and bonds which earn interest r_b, the individual will (in general) choose to hold both assets (i.e. diversified portfolio). However, the individual will hold more wealth in money (and less in bonds) if either the interest rate on bonds falls or the interest rate on money rises, or if bonds are perceived to have become more risky. This model of the demand for money has its origins in the so-called mean-variance approach to asset demands. If we consider the transactions motive and the asset motive together, this more complex demand for money function poses much greater problems in setting monetary targets.

To predict the demand for money consistent with a desired or feasible path for output and prices one needs to be able to predict the behaviour of the interest rate spread, namely the own rate of interest on money less the rate on bonds. Movements in this spread depend in part on the objectives (e.g. profit maximizing behaviour) of commercial banks. If the authorities by open market sales of bonds, raise interest rates on bonds in an attempt to reduce the demand (and hence supply) for money, the commercial banks may respond by raising the interest rate they pay on large deposits (e.g. certificates of deposit), thus 'attracting back' the funds to the banks and keeping monetary growth high. Also, the financial sector will look for ways of creating new types of deposits (i.e. financial innovation). For example, in the USA, 'money market mutual funds' are deposits which are invested in a portfolio of short-term assets (e.g. Treasury bills, commercial bills), yet customers of the bank can easily draw cheques on such funds. In addition, if there are no capital controls, residents can either place funds in offshore banks in the home currency (e.g. US dollars of US residents held in the Caribbean) or in foreign currencies. Currency substitution may then take place between the domestic and foreign currencies. This may provide an additional source of difficulty when trying precisely to define what constitutes 'money' and in determining the demand for the domestic currency.

All in all, while the demand for narrow (i.e. transactions) and broad money (which includes savings accounts) tended to move broadly together in the 1950s and 1960s, this has ceased to be the case in the 1980s and 1990s in many industrialized countries. In technical language, the demand for money (or 'velocity') has become more unpredictable in the 1970s (UK and US broad money), the early 1980s (e.g. 'the great velocity decline' in the USA) and even in Germany, in the 1992–4 period. Hence for any given change in the money supply, it is much more difficult to predict the course of prices (inflation) over the ensuing five years (i.e. there are 'long and variable lags' in the system). This has led to a move away from sole reliance on the money supply as the means of combating inflation. Instead there has been either a move towards setting nominal interest rates (to achieve a desired level of real interest rates) in closed economies (like the USA) or in open economies, fixing the domestic exchange rate to a low inflation anchor currency (e.g. to the Deutsche Mark in European countries).

Keith Cuthbertson
City University Business School

Further reading

Cuthbertson, K. (1985) *The Supply and Demand for Money*, Oxford.
Cuthbertson, K. and Gripaios, P. (1993) *The Macroeconomy: A Guide for Business*, 2nd edn, London.
Laidler, D. E. W. (1992) *The Demand for Money Theories and Evidence*, 3rd edn, New York.

See also: monetarism; monetary policy.

democracy

In the classical Greek *polis*, democracy was the name of a constitution in which the poorer people (*demos*) exercised power in their own interest as against the interest of the rich and aristocratic. Aristotle thought it a debased form of constitution, and it played relatively little part in subsequent political thought, largely because Polybius and other writers diffused the idea that only mixed and balanced constitutions (incorporating monarchic, aristocratic and democratic elements) could be stable. Democracies were commonly regarded as aggressive and unstable and likely to lead (as in Plato's *Republic*) to tyranny. Their propensity to oppress minorities (especially the propertied) was what Burke meant when he described a perfect democracy as the most shameless thing in the world.

Democracy as popular power in an approving sense may occasionally be found in early modern times (in the radical thinkers of the English Civil War, the constitution of Rhode Island of 1641, and in the deliberations of the framers of the American Constitution), but the real vogue for democracy dates from the French Revolution. The main reason is that 'democracy' came to be the new name for the long-entrenched tradition of classical republicanism which, transmitted through Machiavelli, had long constituted a criticism of the dominant monarchical institutions of Europe. This tradition had often emphasized the importance of aristocratic guidance in a republic, and many of its adherents throughout Europe considered that the British constitutional monarchy with an elected parliament was the very model of a proper republic. This idea fused in the nineteenth century with demand to extend the franchise, and the resulting package came generally to be called 'democracy'.

It is important to emphasize that democracy *was* a package, because the name had always previously described a source of power rather than a manner of governing. By the nineteenth century, however, the idea of democracy included representative parliaments, the separation of powers, the rule of law, civil rights and other such liberal desirabilities. All of these conditions were taken to be the culmination of human moral evolution, and the politics of the period often revolved around extensions of the franchise, first to adult males, then to women, and subsequently to such classes as young people of 18 (rather than 21) and, recently in Britain, to voluntary patients in mental hospitals.

Democracy proved to be a fertile and effervescent principle of political perfection. Inevitably, each advance towards democracy disappointed many adherents, but the true ideal could always be relocated in new refinements of the idea. The basis of many such extensions had been laid by the fact that democracy was a Greek term used, for accidental reasons, to describe a complicated set of institutions whose real roots were medieval. The most important was representation, supported by some American founding fathers precisely because it might moderate rather than reflect the passions of an untutored multitude. The Greekness of the name, however, continually suggests that the practice of representation is not intrinsic to modern democracy, but rather a contingent imperfection resulting from the sheer size of modern nations by comparison with ancient city states. In fact, modern constitutional government is quite unrelated to the democracy of the Greeks.

Although modern democracy is a complicated package, the logic of the expression suggests a single principle. The problem is: what precisely is the principle? A further question arises: how far should it extend? So far as the first question is concerned, democracy might be identified with popular sovereignty, majority rule, protection of minorities, affability, constitutional liberties, participation in decisions at every level, egalitarianism, and much else. Parties emphasize one or other of these principles according to current convenience, but most parties in the modern world (the fascist parties between 1918 and 1945 are the most important exception) have seldom failed to claim a democratic legitimacy. The principle of democracy was thus a suitably restless principle for a restless people ever searching for constitutional perfection.

Democracy is irresistible as a slogan because it seems to promise a form of government in which rulers and ruled are in such harmony that little actual governing will be required. Democracy was thus equated with a dream of freedom. For this reason, the nationalist theories which helped destroy the great European empires were a department of the grand principle of democracy, since everybody assumed that the people would want to be ruled by politicians of their own kind. The demographic complexities of many areas, however, were such that many people would inevitably be ruled by foreigners; and such people often preferred to be ruled on an imperial principle – in which all subjects are, as it were, foreigners – rather than on a national principle, which constitutes some as the nation, and the rest as minorities. In claiming to be democratic, rulers might hope to persuade their subjects that they ruled in the popular interest.

Democracy is possible only when a population can recognize both sectional and public interests, and organize itself for political action. Hence no state is seriously democratic unless an opposition is permitted to criticize governments, organize support, and contest elections. But in many countries, such oppositions are likely to be based upon tribes, nations or regions, which do not recognize a common or universal good in the state. Where political parties are of this kind, democratic institutions generate quarrels rather than law and order. In these circumstances, democracy is impossible, and the outcome has been the emergence of some other unifying principle: sometimes an army claiming to stand above 'politics', and sometimes an ideological party in which a doctrine supplies a simulacrum of the missing universal element. One-party states often lay claim to some eccentric (and superior) kind of democracy – basic, popular, guided and so on. In fact, the very name 'party' requires pluralism. Hence, in one-party states, the party is a different kind of political entity altogether, and the claim to democracy is merely window-dressing. This does not necessarily mean, however, that such governments are entirely without virtue. It would be foolish to think that one manner of government suited all peoples.

Democracy as an ideal in the nineteenth century took for granted citizens who were rationally reflective about the voting choices open to them. Modern political scientists have concentrated their attention upon the actual irrationalities of the democratic process. Some have even argued that a high degree of political apathy is preferable to mass enthusiasm which endangers constitutional forms.

Kenneth Minogue
London School of Economics and
Political Science

Further reading

Macpherson, C. B. (1973) *Democratic Theory: Essays in Retrieval*, Oxford.
Plamenatz, J. (1973) *Democracy and Illusion*, London.
Sartori, G. (1962) *Democracy*, Detroit, MI.
Schumpeter, J. (1943) *Capitalism, Socialism and Democracy*, London.

See also: citizenship; democratization; elections; freedom; pluralism, political; populism; representation, political.

democracy, industrial *see* industrial democracy

democracy, social *see* social democracy

democratization

The process through which authoritarian regimes are transformed into democratic regimes is called democratization. It must be kept analytically distinct both from the process of liberalization and from the process of transition. Liberalization is simply the decompression of the authoritarian regime taking place within its framework. It is controlled by the authoritarian rulers themselves. It consists in the relaxation of the most heinous features of authoritarianism: the end of torture, the liberation of political prisoners, the lifting of censorship and the toleration of some opposition. Liberalization may be the first stage in the transition to democracy. However, the transition to democracy truly begins when the authoritarian rulers are no longer capable of controlling domestic political developments and are obliged to relinquish political power. At that point, an explosion of groups, associations, movements and parties signals that the transition has started.

There is no guarantee that, once begun, a transition from authoritarianism will necessarily lead to a democratic regime. Though it will simply be impossible to restore the previous authoritarian regime, in many cases the political transition will be long, protracted and ineffective. In other cases, the major features of a democratic regime will come into being. Usually, political parties re-emerge representing the old political memories of the country or new parties are created to represent the dissenting groups and the adamant oppositions during the authoritarian regime. Depending on the tenure of the previous authoritarian regimes, there will appear different leadership groups. If the authoritarian regime has lasted for some decades, then few old political leaders retain enough social popularity and political support to be able to play a significant role in the transition and new young leaders will quickly replace them. If the authoritarian regime has lasted less than a decade, it will be possible for the political leaders ousted by the authoritarian regime to restructure their political organizations and to reacquire governmental power. During the process of democratization new institutions will be created. The once atomized and compressed society enters into a process of self-reorganization and provides the social basis for new political actors.

The reorganization of society has proved easier in non-communist authoritarian regimes. In former communist authoritarian regimes, all social organizations have been destroyed by the communist party. Only groups supporting the communist party and dominated by it were allowed to function. Few dissenting associations and movements were tolerated and allowed to be active in politics. On the contrary, in southern European and Latin American countries, the various authoritarian regimes never succeeded in destroying all forms of pluralism, or organized groups. Moreover, their rate of economic growth, though limited, created the premises of a pluralist society almost ready-made for the process of democratization. Eastern European communist authoritarian regimes collapsed in a sort of sociopolitical void. Only in Poland a powerful organized movement existed, *Solidarnosc*, that could inherit political power. Otherwise, citizens' forums and umbrella associations had to emerge while former communists slowly reorganized themselves. For these reasons, free elections have determined a new distribution of political power in eastern Europe without yet stabilizing a democratic regime.

According to Harvard political scientist Samuel P. Huntington (1991) so far there have been three waves of democratization and two reversals: the first wave took place from 1828 to 1926 and the first reverse wave from 1922 to 1942. The second wave appeared from 1943 to 1962 and the second reverse wave from 1958 to 1975. Finally, the third wave materialized starting from 1974 and is still going on. The overall process of democratization has moved from the Anglo-Saxon and northern European countries to the southern European rim and to the Latin American continent. It has now reached all eastern European and several Asian countries. Democratization is no longer a culturally bounded phenomenon and, contrary to previous periods, it has found a largely supportive international climate. Though not all newly created democratic regimes are politically stable and socioeconomically effective, they appear to have won the bitter and prolonged struggle against authoritarian actors and mentalities. Only Muslim fundamentalist movements now represent a powerful and dogmatic alternative to the attempts to democratize contemporary regimes.

Gianfranco Pasquino
University of Bologna

Reference

Huntington, S. P. (1991) *The Third Wave: Democratization in the Late Twentieth Century*, London.

Further Reading

O'Donnell, G., Schmitter, P. and Whitehead, L. (eds) (1986) *Transitions from Authoritarian Rule: Prospects for Democracy*, Baltimore, MD.
Vanhanen, T. (1990) *The Process of Democratization: A Comparative Study of 147 States, 1980–1990*, New York.

See also: authoritarian and totalitarian systems; democracy; military regimes.

demographic transition

Demographic transition, also known as the demographic cycle, describes the movement of death and birth rates in a society from a situation where both are high to one where both are low. In the more developed economies, it was appreciated in the nineteenth century that mortality was declining. Fertility began to fall in France in the late eighteenth century, and in north-west and central Europe, as well as in English-speaking countries of overseas European settlement, in the last three decades of the nineteenth century. Fertility levels were believed to have approximated mortality levels over much of human history, but the fact that fertility declined later than mortality during demographic transition inevitably produced rapid population growth. In France this situation appeared to have passed by 1910, as birth and death rates once again drew close to each other, and by the 1930s this also seemed to be happening in the rest of the countries referred to above.

Thompson (1929) categorized the countries of the world into three groups according to their stage in this movement of vital rates (later also to be termed the vital revolution). This process was to be carried further by C. P. Blacker (1947), who discerned five stages of which the last was not the reattainment of nearly stationary demographic conditions but of declining population, a possibility suggested by the experience of a range of countries in the economic depression of the 1930s. However, it was a paper published in 1945 by Notestein, the director of Princeton University's Office of Population Research, which introduced the term demographic transition. Notestein implied the inevitability of the transition for all societies and, together with another paper published seven years later, began to explore the mechanisms which might explain the change. Notestein argued that the mortality decline was the result of scientific and economic change, and was generally welcomed. However, fertility had been kept sufficiently high in high-mortality countries to avoid population decline only by a whole array of religious and cultural mechanisms which slowly decayed once lower mortality meant that they were no longer needed. He also believed that the growth of city populations, and economic development more generally, created individualism and rationalism which undermined the cultural props supporting uncontrolled fertility.

Demographic transition theory is less a theory than a body of observations and explanations. Coale (1973) has summarized research on the European demographic transition as indicating the importance of the diffusion of birth control behaviour within cultural units, usually linguistic ones, with diffusion halting at cultural frontiers. Caldwell (1976) has argued that high fertility is economically rewarding in pre-transitional societies to the decision makers, usually the parents, and that, if subsequent changes in the social relations between the generations mean that the cost of children outweighs the lifelong returns from them, then fertility begins to fall. The Chicago Household Economists (see Schultz 1974) place stress on the underlying social and economic changes in the value of women's time as well as on the changing marginal value of children.

After the Second World War doubt was cast as to whether the transition necessarily ended with near-stationary population growth because of the occurrence in many industrialized countries of a baby boom, but by the 1970s this was regarded as an aberrant phenomenon related largely to a perhaps temporary movement toward early and universal marriages. By this time the demographic transition's claim to be globally applicable had received support from fertility declines (usually assisted in developing countries by government family planning programmes) in most of the world with the major exceptions of Africa and the Middle East.

Although demographic transition refers to the decline of both mortality and fertility, social scientists have often employed it to refer almost exclusively to the latter phenomenon. Because the world's first persistent fertility decline began in north–west and central Europe in the second half of the nineteenth century, demographers were tempted to employ the term *second demographic transition* for subsequent large-scale movements of this type, such as the somewhat later fall of the birth rates in southern and eastern Europe or the fertility decline in much of Latin America and Asia from the 1960s. However, second demographic transition has now found acceptance as the description of the fertility decline which followed the baby boom in developed countries and which began first in those countries which earliest participated in the first demographic transition, north–west and central Europe and the English-speaking countries of overseas European settlement. Between the mid-1960s and early 1980s fertility fell by 30–50 per cent in nearly all these countries so that by the latter date fertility was below the long-term replacement level in nearly all of them and the rest of Europe as well.

Philippe Ariès (1980) wrote of 'two successive motivations for the decline of the Western birth rate', stating that, while the first had aimed at improving the chances of the children in achieving social and occupational advancement in the world, the second was parent-oriented rather than child-oriented and had in fact resulted in the dethroning of the *child-king* (his term). Ariès and others agreed that in a faster changing world parents were now planning for their own futures as well as those of their children, that the process had been accelerated by later and fewer marriages and the trend towards most women working outside the home, and that it had been facilitated by the development of more effective methods of birth control, such as the pill and IUD, and readier resort to sterilization. Henri Léridon (1981) wrote of the *second contraceptive revolution*, Ron Lesthaege and Dirk van de Kaa (1986) of two *demographic transitions* and van de Kaa (1987) of the *second demographic transition*.

John C. Caldwell
Australian National University

References

Ariès, P. (1980) 'Two successive motivations for the declining birth rate in the West', *Population and Development Review* 6(4).

Blacker, C. P. (1947) 'Stages in population growth', *Eugenics Review* 39.

Caldwell, J. C. (1976) 'Toward a restatement of demographic transition theory', *Population and Development Review* 2 (3–4).

Coale, A. J. (1973) 'The demographic transition', in *International Population Conference*, Liège, 1973, *Proceedings*, vol. 1, Liège.

Léridon, H. (1981) 'Fertility and contraception in 12 developed countries', *International Family Planning Perspectives* 7(2).

Notestein, F. W. (1945) 'Population: the long view', in T. W. Schultz (ed.) *Food for the World*, Chicago.

Schultz, T. W. (ed.) (1974) *Economics of the Family: Marriage, Children, and Human Capital: A Conference Report of the National Bureau of Economic Research*, Chicago.

Thompson, W. S. (1929) 'Population', *American Journal of Sociology* 34.

van de Kaa, D. J. (1987) 'Europe's second demographic transition', *Population Bulletin* 42(1).

See also: fertility; health transition; mortality; population policy.

demography

Demography is the analysis of population variables. It includes both methods and substantive results, in the fields of mortality, fertility, migration and resulting population numbers. Demographers collect data on population and its components of change, and construct models of population dynamics. They contribute to the wider field of population studies that relate population changes to non-demographic – social, economic, political or other – factors. In so far as it reaches into population studies, demography is interdisciplinary: it includes elements of sociology, economics, biology, history, psychology and other fields. Its methods include parts of statistics and numerical analysis. Public health officials and actuaries have had their part in its development. Most demographers have professional knowledge of one or more of these disciplines.

Population variables are of two kinds – stock and flow. The important source of information on stock variables is national censuses, whose modern form goes back to the seventeenth century in Canada, Virginia, Sweden, and a few other places, and which are now carried out periodically in nearly all countries of the world. Among the cross-sectional information collected in censuses are age and sex distribution, labour force status and occupation, and birthplace.

The flow variables, the components of population change, include birth and death registrations, initiated before the nineteenth century in Sweden and in Britain, and now routine in all industrial countries. Efforts to attain completeness are slowly making their way elsewhere. Migration statistics, collected at national frontiers, are less available and less reliable than birth and death registrations. Much additional information, including statistics of birth expectations, is collected by sample surveys.

These four sources (censuses, vital registration, migration records, and sample surveys) differ in the ease with which they may be instituted in a new country. Censuses and surveys are the easiest to initiate. With care the completeness of a census can reach 97 per cent or more. It is true that a large number of enumerators have to be mobilized (over 100,000 in the USA in 1980, over 5 million for China's 1982 census), but that is easier to arrange than the education of the entire population to the need for birth registration. The USA first attained 90 per cent complete birth records in the first quarter of the twentieth century; contemporary poor countries are unlikely to reach this level of completeness until their residents come to have need for birth certificates. Migration statistics will not be complete as long as many of those crossing international borders can conceal their movement from the immigration authorities. Apart from illegal crossings there is the difficulty that migrants are a small fraction of those passing national boundaries, the majority being tourists, persons travelling on business, commuters, and other non-immigrants. American sentiment that people ought to be able to leave their country of residence without hindrance is so strong that outgoing residents are not even stopped at the border to be asked whether they intend to return.

The special characteristics of demography are the quantitative and empirical methods that it uses. Once data in the form of censuses and registrations are available, demographic techniques are needed for valid comparisons among these. Mexico has a death rate of 6 per thousand, against France's 10; this does not signify that Mexico is healthier, but only that it has a younger age distribution as a result of high fertility; standardized comparison consists in finding what Mexico's death rate would be if it had France's age distribution but retained its own age-specific rates.

Partly for purposes of comparing mortality, but originally more for the conduct of pension and insurance business, life tables were developed in The Netherlands and in Britain during the course of the eighteenth century. The first technical problem that actuaries and demographers solved was how to go from statistics of deaths and of populations exposed to probabilities of dying. With data in finite age intervals the probabilities are not uniquely ascertainable, and a variety of methods for making life tables are currently in use.

The concerns of public health have led to the improvement of mortality statistics along many lines, including drawing up the International List of Causes of Death, now in its ninth revision. Unfortunately uniformity in applying the classification among physicians in all countries is still a distant goal. One object of the International List is the making of cause-related tables. The expectation of life in the USA is 75 years. If all deaths from cancer were eliminated this would be increased by about 3 years; elimination of all heart disease would increase the expectation by over 15 years.

Increasing populations have lower proportions of deaths than stationary populations. In effect the age distribution pivots on the middle ages as population growth slows. A sharp drop in the birth rate does not show its full effect immediately; births remain high as the large cohorts of children already born themselves come into childbearing; population growth thus has a kind of momentum. Replacement is the condition where each child is replaced in the next generation by just one child, so that ultimately the population is stationary. After birth rates fall to bare replacement a population can still increase by 60 per cent or more.

Births are not as sensitive to the pivoting of age distribution as are deaths, since the fertile ages, intermediate between childhood and old age, are a relatively constant fraction of a population. Fast-growing countries have more children below reproductive age but fewer old people. But births are greatly affected by a bulge of individuals in the reproductive ages; births in the USA have risen from about 3.1 million in the early 1970s to about 3.6 million currently, almost entirely due to change in age distribution as the large cohorts of the 1950s reach reproduction.

The pioneer in demographic methods and models was Alfred J. Lotka, who in a series of papers extending from 1907 to 1948 showed how to answer a number of questions that are still being asked. A central one was, 'How fast is a given population really growing, as determined by its age-specific birth and death rates in abstraction from its age distribution?' Any population that grows at a fixed rate for a long period develops a stable or fixed age distribution which Lotka showed how to calculate, and its increase when it reaches this stage is its intrinsic rate.

After a long period of neglect, Lotka's work came to be applied and further developed during the 1960s. It turned out that his approach could help the estimation of birth and death rates for countries of known age distribution but lacking adequate registration data.

The techniques of birth and death analysis have been carried over to migration, especially in the form of Markov chains that describe movement or transition between countries, and other areas, just as they describe transition between life and death. Such Markov chains are capable also of representing transitions between the married and single condition, among working, being unemployed, and leaving the labour force, and many other sets of states. A literature has now been built up in which changes of state, including migration, are represented by matrices, particularly easy to handle on a computer. The first extensive calculation of this kind was due to P. H. Leslie in the 1940s.

Communities living under 'primitive' conditions grow slowly; their high birth rates are offset by high deaths. The movement of a community from this condition to one of low birth and death rates as it modernizes is known as the demographic transition. Since the fall in the birth rate lags behind the fall in the death rate, very large increases can be recorded during the transition. Britain's population multiplied fourfold between the censuses of 1801 and 1901. Contemporary less developed countries are increasing even more rapidly.

This effect of rising income is contrary to what has often been thought: that people want children and will have as many as they can afford – a view commonly attributed to Malthus, although Malthus's writings, after the first edition of his *Essay*, are much more subtle than this. Apparently at a certain point the causal mechanism flips over: for very poor people a rise of income results in a faster rate of increase; once people are better off a further rise slows their increase.

The modernization that brings down the birth rate affects subgroups of national populations at different times. In consequence the demographic transition shows itself as differential fertility: the rich, the urban and the educated have for a time lower birth rates than the poor, the rural and the illiterate in cross-sections taken during the transition. Such differentials close up as incomes generally rise and income distributions narrow.

Some of the most puzzling questions concern the causal mechanisms that lie behind contemporary demographic changes. In what degree the fall of fertility is due to education, in what degree to income, cannot yet be answered in a way that applies to all countries. Less developed countries have far greater rates of increase now than did the countries of Europe when these were at a comparable stage of development. To what extent is the difference due to higher birth rates among presently poor countries than among the poor countries of the eighteenth century, and to what extent to lower death rates? Population models can provide answers to such questions; they show that birth differences are much more influential than death differences.

More difficult are questions on the direction of causation between two variables clearly related to each other. In most advanced countries more women are working outside the home now than in the 1950s, at a time when their partners are for the most part earning higher real wages; at the same time women's fertility has diminished, when their income and that of their partners would enable them to have more children if they wanted. Is the fall in fertility the result of women seeking jobs, and so finding it inconvenient to have children, the wish to work being primary, or do they no longer wish to have children and so take jobs to fill their time? A wealth of data exists, but the techniques for answering such questions are elusive. Again, are the present low birth rates a cohort or a period phenomenon? Do they result from present generations intending to finish up with fewer births, or are they a conjunctural phenomenon due, say, to the world recession since the mid-1970s?

A task that demographers are often called on to perform is population forecasting. Professional demographers describe their statements on future population as projections, the working out of the consequences of a set of assumptions. Users believe that the assumptions are chosen by the demographers because they are realistic, and they accept the results as forecasts. Forecasting has gone through many styles, starting with extrapolation of population numbers by exponential, logistic or other curves. More acceptable is extrapolating the components of population – birth, death, and migration – and assembling the population from the extrapolated values of these. Sampling to ascertain childbearing intentions of women has been extensively tried. Demographers have no illusions about the predictability of the long-term future, but estimates made by those who have studied the past are more worthy of attention than the simple-minded extrapolations that are the alternative. Some numbers on future population are indispensable for virtually any kind of economic planning, whether by a corporation or a government.

One aspect of the future that has become of interest to several disciplines since the mid-1980s is the relation of a deteriorating planetary environment to population growth. How far are the loss of forests, emissions of carbon dioxide and other greenhouse gases with consequent danger of global warming, thinning of the ozone layer, declining catches in the fishing areas off western Europe, due to population increase, to what extent to expanding economies, to what extent to inadequate environmental regulation? The facts are the same for everyone, but scholars of different disciplines read them differently, and come to very different conclusions.

Biology works above all with direct observation: the facts are plain to the naked eye; no sophisticated theory is needed to see that forests are invaded and destroyed by the need of increasing populations for wood and food, that crowded countries of Asia with growing economies will suffer more pollution of water, land and air if their populations continue to increase at present rates, that Africa may have been thinly settled in the past but its present population increase with stagnant economies will bring increasing misery and destruction. For many biologists population control is humankind's first priority; the US National Academy of Sciences and the Royal Society of London introduce their joint statement with the words, 'If current predictions of population growth prove accurate and patterns of human activity on the planet remain unchanged, science and technology may not be able to prevent either irreversible degradation of the environment or continued poverty for much of the world'. No vote was taken of the membership representing all the sciences, but this statement would surely have commanded the assent of a large majority

Economics finds the matter more complicated. Population growth has advantages that could well compensate for its apparent disadvantages. With more people there will be more inventive geniuses; with larger markets there will be more opportunity for division of labour and so more economic progress; once people are rich enough they will be able to use any necessary small fraction of their wealth to counter environmental damage. So it is increasing wealth rather than population control that ought to have priority.

When biology and economics find such opposite relations of population to environment, only the blandest of statements can be made without contradicting one or another scientific authority. Before such contradiction one ought to examine the contending disciplines more closely, and try to find what of their features and methods lead them to such opposite conclusions. Study of the intimate detail of the several disciplines is the only hope for breaking the deadlock, and the only way of making full use of the positive knowledge of those disciplines.

The richness of demography is in part due to the commitment of scholars from many disciplines. Actuaries developed much of the early theory, and statisticians and biostatisticians add to their work the techniques of numerical analysis and determination of error. Sociologists see population change as both the cause and the result of major changes in social structures and attitudes; they study the increase of labour force participation by women, of divorce, of single-person households, the apparently lessening importance of marriage, and the decline in fertility rates. Economists see fertility rising and falling as people try to maximize utility. Biologists employ an ecological framework relating human populations to the plant and animal populations among which they live and on which they depend. Psychologists have brought their survey and other tools to the study of preferences of parents for number and sex of children. Historians, in a particularly happy synthesis with demography, are putting to use the enormous amount of valuable data in parish and other records to gain new insights on what happened to birth and death rates during the past few centuries.

Nathan Keyfitz
Harvard University and the International Institute
for Applied Systems Analysis

Reference

(1992) *Population Growth, Resource Consumption and a Sustainable World*. A joint statement by the officers of the Royal Society of London and the US National Academy of Sciences. Sir Michael Atiyah, President of the Royal Society of London, and Frank Press, President of the US National Academy of Sciences.

Further reading

Coale, A. J. (1972) *The Growth and Structure of Human Populations: A Mathematical Investigation*, Princeton, NJ.

Keyfitz, N. (1977) *Applied Mathematical Demography*, New York.

— (1993) 'Are there limits to population?' *Proceedings of the US National Academy of Sciences* 90.

Petersen, W. (1969) *Population*, 2nd edn, Toronto.

Pressat, R. (1969) *L'Analyse demographique*, 2nd edn, Paris.

Shryock, H. S. and Siegel, J. S. (1971) *The Methods and Materials of Demography*, 2 vols, Washington, DC.

See also: Malthus, Thomas Robert.

demography, historical *see* historical demography

depressive disorders

Depressive disorders are a heterogeneous group of conditions that share the common symptom of dysphoric mood. Current psychiatric classification divides major depressive disorders into bipolar and non-bipolar categories, depending on whether there is evidence of associated manic episodes. Less severe depressive states are categorized as dysthymic, cyclothymic and atypical depressive disorders.

The diagnosis of a depressive disorder is made only when the intensity and duration of depressive symptoms exceed those usually provoked by the stresses of normal life. Major depressive episodes are characterized by a pervasive dysphoric mood, which may be associated with feelings of worthlessness, suicidal ideation, difficulty with concentration, inability to feel pleasure, and neurovegetative changes in appetite, sleep patterns, psychomotor activity and energy levels. In severe cases, psychotic symptoms may also be present.

The prevalence of depressive disorders is relatively high. Lifetime incidence is thought to be 15–30 per cent, with women affected twice as often as men.

Although the cause of depressive disorders is not known, it is probably multifactorial. A minority of cases have clear-cut origins in medical conditions. For the remaining cases, most experts would endorse a diathesis-stress model of causation. Some factor is believed to predispose the depressed person to experience the disorder, but this latent diathesis leads to overt symptomatology only when a precipitating stress occurs. Theories of causation focus on the following potentially interactive factors: genetic predisposition, personality development, losses in early life, environmental factors and learned dysfunctional patterns of cognition and interpersonal behaviour.

Precipitating factors for acute episodes are often easily identifiable events. In other cases, external stresses seem to be absent. Psychodynamic theorists maintain that even in these patients a seemingly minor event has been idiosyncratically interpreted as a major loss, or that something has led patients to recognize the dysfunctional nature of their existence. More biologically oriented investigators believe that some physiological dysfunction precipitates most episodes.

Whether the cause or the result of a depressive disorder, a number of physiological abnormalities have been associated with subgroups of depressed patients. Shortened rapid eye movement (REM) latency, an abnormally short time between the onset of sleep and the first REM sleep cycle, is well established. There is sufficient evidence of deficiencies in both the noradrenergic and serotonergic neurotransmitter systems to suggest that there may be two neurophysiological subgroups of depressed patients.

The natural history of depression is variable, reinforcing the argument that we are considering a number of disorders under this general rubric. Onset of major depressive disorders can occur at any time in the life cycle, although bipolar disorders usually appear in the second or third decades of life. Dysthymic disorders, especially those that occur in families of patients with bipolar disorder, often begin in young adulthood. Epidemiological studies suggest that the majority of depressive episodes are untreated, either resolving on their own, or developing into chronic disorders.

Treatments of depression include psychotherapies and medication. Psychoanalytically oriented psychotherapy is often employed, although without more than anecdotal evidence of success. Enthusiasm for short-term psychotherapies in depression has been stirred by studies demonstrating success with time-limited interpersonal and cognitive therapies. The combination of interpersonal psychotherapy and medication has been shown to be more effective than either treatment alone.

Antidepressant medications which include the heterocyclic antidepressants, monoamine oxidase inhibitors, serotonin reuptake inhibitors and several novel agents are effective in as many as 80 per cent of episodes of major depression, and in many instances of dysthymic conditions. Electroconvulsive therapy remains an important treatment for life-threatening conditions, depressions refractory to drug therapy, or for people who cannot take medication safely, such as many elderly people. Long-term maintenance medication with antidepressants or mood stabilizers, such as lithium, demonstrably decreases the frequency and intensity of repeated episodes. Frequent recurrences may adversely affect the course of the illness.

The scope, nature and cause of depressive disorders may be further elucidated by the greater understanding of the relationship between depression and other psychiatric disorders that often have accompanying dysphoria, especially anxiety disorders, obsessive compulsive disorder and substance abuse disorders.

Paul S. Appelbaum

Andrea B. Stone
University of Massachusetts Medical Center

Further reading

Cooper, J., Bloom, F. and Roth, R. (eds) (1991) *The Biochemical Basis of Neuropharmacology*, New York.
Weissman, M., Leaf, P., Tischler, G., Blazer, D., Karno, M., Bruce, M. and Florio, L. (1988) 'Affective disorders in five United States communities', *Psychological Medicine* 141.
Wolman, B. and Stricker, G. (1990) *Depressive Disorders: Facts, Theories, and Treatment Methods*, New York.
Woods, J. and Brooks, B. (eds) (1984) *Frontiers of Clinical Neuroscience*, Baltimore, MD.

See also: DSM-IV; mental disorders; psychoses.

derivative markets and futures markets

A financial instrument which is derived from, or is written on, some other asset is known as a derivative and is traded on a derivatives market. The asset on which the derivative is written can be a commodity or a financial asset. While trading in derivatives based on commodities has a much longer history, the value of trading in these instruments is greatly outweighed by the value of trading in derivatives on financial assets.

The main forms of derivative instruments are forward, futures, options and swaps contracts. Forward and futures contracts involve two parties contracting to trade a particular asset at some point in the future for a price agreed now. Options contracts give the buyer the right, but not the obligation, to buy from, if it is a call option, or sell to, if it is a put option, the writer of the contract a particular commodity or asset at some point in the future for a price agreed now. Swaps contracts involve two parties contracting to exchange cash flows at specified future dates in a manner agreed now. Forward, swaps and some types of options are traded on over-the-counter markets where the details of the contract are tailored to the specific needs of the two parties. In contrast, some other options contracts and futures are traded through organized exchanges where trading takes place at a specified location and contracts are standardized. The standardized nature of futures and exchange traded options enhances the liquidity of these markets. Almost all futures and traded options contracts are settled not by delivery of the asset but by the parties to the contract taking an offsetting position.

Trading of derivatives based on commodities through organized exchanges dates back to the nineteenth century, with the establishment of the Chicago Board of Trade in 1848 and the introduction of futures trading there in the 1860s. However, it was not until the 1970s that trading in financial derivatives through organized exchanges began. Derivative markets represent one of the major advances in financial markets since this time. The early 1970s saw the breakdown of the Bretton Woods fixed exchange rate regime. The move to floating exchange rates, together with other major changes in the global economy in the early 1970s, led to increased volatility in both exchange rates and interest rates. Such volatility is a source of uncertainty for firms and led to a demand for financial instruments which would assist risk management. Financial futures and exchange traded options were developed to help meet this demand. Within twenty years of their establishment financial futures accounted for in excess of 60 per cent of all futures trading.

The main purpose of derivative trading is to allow risk to be managed or hedged. For example, consider a firm which is selling overseas and is due to receive payment in a foreign currency in three months' time. Changes in exchange rates over the next three months could lead to the amount of domestic currency received being much less than anticipated, possibly rendering the sale a loss-making enterprise. By using currency futures the firm can remove the uncertainty associated with exchange rate movement and lock in an exchange rate for the currency to be received. When futures are used to hedge, the risk associated with the position is transferred from the hedger to the counter-party to the trade. This counter-party may be another hedger with opposite requirements or a speculator. Speculators are willing to take on the risk in the expectation that they can profit from the activity.

In addition to their hedging role, derivatives also fulfil a price discovery role. Futures prices, for example, provide a forecast of expected future asset prices. Futures prices thus provide important information which can assist the planning of both individuals and companies. While derivative markets provide important benefits in the form of hedging and price discovery, they have also been criticized. This criticism is largely due to the fact that they are attractive to speculators who are believed to have a destabilizing impact on the market for the underlying asset. However, there is little evidence to suggest that this negative view of derivatives is justified.

Antonios Antoniou
Brunel University

Further reading

Dixon, R. and Holmes, P. (1992) *Financial Markets: The Guide for Business*, London.

Edwards, F. R. and Ma, C. W. (1992) *Futures and Options*, New York.

Kolb, R. W. (1988) *Understanding Futures Markets*, 2nd edn, Glenview, IL.

Tucker, A. L. (1991) *Financial Futures, Options, and Swaps*, New York.

See also: capital, credit and money markets; financial system; markets.

design, experimental *see* experimental design

development *see* economic development

developmental psychology

Developmental psychology studies change in psychological structures and processes during the life cycle. Although traditionally focused on childhood and adolescence, it has extended its scope to adulthood and old age as well.

Two factors stimulated the rise of developmental psychology towards the end of the nineteenth century. First, Darwin's claim of continuity between humans and nature revived the discussion among philosophers such as Locke, Kant and Rousseau regarding the origins of mind. It was hoped that the study of childhood would unlock the secrets of the relationship between animal and human nature. Darwin himself kept notebooks on the development of his first child, setting a trend which was to be followed by many of the great names in the discipline.

Given Darwin's role in the genesis of developmental psychology, it is hardly surprising that biological views, in which development is regarded as the unfolding of genetically programmed characteristics and abilities, have been strongly represented in it. (Indeed, the etymological root of the word development means 'unfolding'). Typical of such views are Stanley Hall's theory that development recapitulates evolution, Sigmund Freud's account of the stages through which sexuality develops, Arnold Gesell's belief in a fixed timetable for growth, John Bowlby's notion of attachment as an instinctive mechanism and Chomsky's model of inborn language-processing abilities. Current research on developmental neurobiology continues this tradition.

Nevertheless, those who place their faith in the influence of the environment have also had an important say in the discipline. Behaviourism, which attributes all change to conditioning, may have failed to account satisfactorily for many developmental phenomena, but its attempts to imitate the methodology of the natural sciences have left an indelible imprint on the discipline. Most developmental psychologists now eschew extreme nature or nurture viewpoints and subscribe to one form or other of interactionism, according to which development is the outcome of the *interplay* of external and internal influences.

The second factor which stimulated the growth of developmental psychology was the hope of solving social problems. Compulsory education brought about a growing realization of the inadequacy of traditional teaching methods and a call for new ones based on scientific understanding of the child's mind. The failures of nineteenth-century psychiatry prompted a search for the deeper causes of mental disturbances and crime, widely assumed to lie in childhood. The application of developmental psychology to these social problems led to the creation of cognitive, emotional and social subdisciplines, with the unfortunate side-effect that the interrelatedness of these facets of the person has often been overlooked.

In the field of *cognitive development*, the contribution of the Swiss psychologist Jean Piaget (1896–1980) has been unparalleled, though by no means unchallenged. Piaget developed his own form of interactionism (constructivism) in which the child is biologically endowed with a general drive towards adaptation to the environment or equilibrium. New cognitive structures are generated in the course of the child's ongoing confrontation with the external world. Piaget claimed that the development of thought followed a progression of discrete and universal stages, and much of his work was devoted to mapping out the characteristics of these stages. His theory is often regarded as a biological one – yet for Piaget the developmental sequence is not constrained by genes, but by logic and the structure of reality itself.

Full recognition of Piaget's work in the USA had to await a revival of interest in educational problems during the mid-1950s and the collapse of faith in behaviourism known as the cognitive revolution which followed in 1960. Subsequently, however, developmental psychologists such as Jerome Bruner challenged Piaget's notion of a solitary epistemic subject and revived ideas developed in Soviet Russia half a century before by Lev Vygotsky (1896–1934). As a Marxist, Vygotsky had emphasized the embeddedness of all thought and action in a social context; for him, thinking was a *collective* achievement, and cognitive development largely a matter of internalizing culture.

His provocative ideas exert an increasing fascination on developmental psychologists. Others, however, maintain Piaget's emphasis on the child as solitary thinker, and seek to understand the development of thought by reference to computer analogies or neurophysiology.

The study of *social and emotional development* was mainly motivated by concerns over mental health, delinquency and crime. The first serious developmental theory in this area was that of Sigmund Freud; invited to the USA by Stanley Hall in 1909, his psychoanalytic notions were received enthusiastically for a time. For Freud, however, the origin of psychopathology lay in the demands of civilization (above all the incest taboo), and no amount of utopian social engineering could – or should – hope to remove these. From 1920 onwards, American psychology increasingly abandoned Freud in favour of the more optimistic and hard-nosed behaviourism.

However, the emotional needs of children were of scant interest to behaviourists, and it was not until the 1950s that John Bowlby (1907–90) established a theoretical basis for research on this topic by combining elements of psychoanalysis, animal behaviour studies and system theory into attachment theory. Bowlby's conception of the biological needs of children was informed by a profoundly conservative vision of family life, and his initial claims about the necessity of prolonged, exclusive maternal care were vigorously challenged in the rapidly changing society of the 1960s and 1970s. Nevertheless, his work helped to focus attention on relationships in early childhood, which have now become a major topic in developmental psychology. New awareness of the rich and complex social life of young children has undermined the traditional assumption that the child enters society (becomes socialized) only *after* the core of the personality has been formed.

Critics of developmental psychology point to its tendency to naturalize middle-class, western ideals as universal norms of development, to its indifference to cultural and historical variations, and to the lack of a unified theoretical approach. However, its very diversity guarantees continued debate and controversy, and its own development shows no signs of coming to a halt.

David Ingleby
University of Utrecht

Further reading

Burman, E. (1994) *Deconstructing Developmental Psychology*, London.

Butterworth, G. and Harris, M. (1994) *Principles of Developmental Psychology*, Hove.

Cole, M. and Cole, S. R. (1993) *The Development of Children*, 2nd edn, New York.

See also: attachment; first language acquisition; Piaget, Jean.

deviance

Although the term deviance has been employed for over 300 years, its sociological meanings are rather recent and distinct. In the main, sociologists and criminologists have taken deviance to refer to behaviour that is banned, censured, stigmatized or penalized. It is often portrayed as a breaking of rules. It is considered more extensive than crime, crime being no more than a breach of one particular kind of rule, but it includes crime and its outer margins are unclear and imprecise. What exactly deviance comprises, what it excludes, what makes it interesting, and how it should be characterized, are not settled. There have been studies of very diverse groups in the name of the sociology of deviance. There have been descriptions of the deaf, the blind, the ill, the mad, dwarves, stutterers, strippers, prostitutes, homosexuals, thieves, murderers, nudists and drug addicts. Sociologists are not in accord about whether all these roles are unified and what it is that may be said to unify them. They can appeal to no common convention within their own discipline. Neither can they turn to lay definitions for guidance. On the contrary, commonplace interpretations are often elastic, contingent and local. What is called deviant can shift from time to time and place to place, its significance being unstable.

Common sense and everyday talk do not seem to point to an area that is widely and unambiguously recognized as deviant. It is not even evident that people *do* talk about deviance with any great frequency. Instead, they allude to specific forms of conduct without appearing to claim that there is a single, overarching category that embraces them all. They may talk of punks, addicts, glue-sniffers, extremists, thieves, traitors, liars and eccentrics, but they rarely mention *deviants*. It may be only the sociologist who finds it interesting and instructive to clump these groups together under a solitary title.

The apparent elusiveness and vagueness of the idea of deviance has elicited different responses from sociologists. Some have refrained from attempting to find one definition that covers every instance of the phenomenon. They have used *ad hoc* or implied definitions that serve the analytic needs of the moment and suppress the importance of definition itself. Others, like Liazos, have questioned the intellectual integrity of the subject, alleging that it may amount to little more than an incoherent jumble of 'nuts, sluts and perverts'. Phillipson has actually described the analysis of deviance as 'that antediluvian activity which sought to show oddities, curiosities, peccadilloes and villains as central to sociological reason'.

A number of sociologists have chosen to represent 'that antediluvian activity' as important precisely because its subject is so odd: the inchoate character of deviance becomes a remarkable property of the phenomenon rather than a weakness in its description. Matza, for example, held that 'plural evaluation, shifting standards, and moral ambiguity may, and do, coexist with a phenomenal realm that is commonly sensed as deviant'. His book, *Becoming Deviant* (1969), proceeded to chart the special contours of that realm by following the passage of an archetypal deviant into its interior. In such a guise, deviance is taken to offer a rare glimpse of the fluid and contradictory face of society, showing things in unexpected relief and proportion. Garfinkel (1967), Goffman (1963) and others have taken to repairing to the deviant margins because they offer new perspectives through incongruity or strain, perspectives that jolt the understanding and make the sociologist 'stumble into awareness'. Deviants are required to negotiate problems of meaning and structure that are a little foreign to everyday life. The study of their activity may force the sociologist to view the world as anthropologically strange. Indeed, some sociologists have implicitly turned the social world inside out, making deviance the centre and the centre peripheral. They have explored the odd and the exotic, giving birth to a sociology of the absurd that dwells on the parts played by indeterminacy, paradox and surprise in social life.

Absurdity is perhaps given its fullest recognition in a number of essays by structuralists and phenomenologists. It is there asserted that deviance is distinguished by its special power to muddle and unsettle social reality. Deviation is described by its ability to upset systems of thought and methods of classification. Deviant matters are things out of place, things that make no sense. As Scott (1972) argued, 'The property of deviance is conferred on things that are perceived as being anomalous.' The meaninglessness of deviance is thus forced to become substantially more than a simple lack of intellectual coherence in sociology. People are thought to find it disturbing, and phenomenologists have replied by turning their gaze towards the problems which disturbance can raise. The phenomenologists' difference with Marxist and radical sociologists probably turns on their emphasis on flux and disorder. Radical sociologists tend to stress the solidity of the social world and the importance of what Gouldner (1970) called 'overpowering social structures'. Phenomenologists and others tend to stress the openness and plasticity of things, arguing that social structure is actually rather delicate and negotiable.

What *is* certain is that the analysis of deviance echoes many of the unities and disunities of sociology at large. Sociological definition is not neutral and independent. It will refract wider debates, problems and pursuits. It is in this sense that sociologists do not necessarily mean the same thing when they talk of deviance. Their ideas sometimes contradict one another, although contradiction is often no more than a trick of language, an effect of the different vocabularies that have become attached to theories.

A list of examples should reveal a little of that diversity.

Probably the most elementary definition of deviance describes it as behaviour that is *statistically infrequent*. A contrast is traced between the normal, which is common, and the abnormal or deviant, which is uncommon. That definition is deployed characteristically in clinical or psychological analysis that relies on counting: normal distribution curves are drawn, and the deviant is that which falls at the poles. Those who wet their beds with unusual frequency, who are very tall or very short, who read obsessively or not at all are deviant for practical numerical purposes. It is a definition that serves well enough in certain settings, but it can sometimes fail to make sense of deviance as it is presented in everyday life. Thus, the statistically infrequent may be socially unremarked and inconsequential. The statistically frequent may be exposed to control, disapproval and stigma. What is *assumed* to be infrequent, acquiring some of its identity from that assumption, may actually be quite common. (Homosexuality, adultery and chastity are all rather more abundant than many people suppose, but they are *taken* to be unusual.) It may indeed be *beliefs* about statistical incidence that are occasionally more significant than the incidence itself. Statistical analysis can then be rephrased to produce a commentary about the interplay between ideas about deviance and convention.

A second major strand of sociological thought is *Marxism*, but many Marxists have relegated deviance to the margins of analysis. Its pettiness has been emphasized both in the explicit arguments of some sociologists and in the practical neglect of deviance by others. Deviation is commonly thought to be a process that is relatively trivial in a world that is dominated by the massive structures of political economy. It has been maintained that little can be gained from studying deviance that cannot be achieved more directly, efficiently and elegantly from the analysis of class and state. Some, like Hirst (1975), Bankowski *et al.* (1977) and Mungham, have actually reproached Marxist and radical sociologists of deviance for discussing inappropriate and minor problems. Marxists, they claim, should concentrate on the class struggle.

When Marxists *do* explore deviance, they tend to stress its bearing on the class struggle and the state. Thus Hill (1961), Thompson (1975) and Hobsbawm (1965) have developed a social history of crime that emphasizes the scale of popular opposition to the emergence of capitalism in England. Hall *et al.* (1976), Cohen (1972) and Willis (1977) have talked of youthful deviance as 'resistance through ritual', a fleeting and probably doomed act of refusal to accede to the authority of institutions that oppress the working class. Sumner (1976) has taken the unity of deviance to stem from the censures that reside in the core of capitalist ideology; Taylor (1980) has lodged the origins of deviance in the contradictions of the ailing political economy of late capitalism in crisis; Platt (1978) and Quinney (1975) cast deviants as those who have been defeated in the class war; Box and Pearce present them as the scapegoats who divert the gaze from the major pathologies of capitalism; and so it goes on. Marxists deposit deviation in a world made up of resistance, protest and conflict. Few have occupied themselves with processes outside that world. After all, that is the world of Marxism. Lea and Young (1984) *have* ventured outside but their place within Marxism may have become a little unsure in consequence.

A third major representative strand is *functionalism*, and Talcott Parsons (1951) is the pivot of functionalism. Parsons typified one version of deviance as the disorganized phenomena that can attend institutions and individuals that have become out of joint. He argued that, as the social world changes, so its parts may move with unequal velocities and in different directions, straining against one another and creating problems of cohesion. Deviance then became activity that sprang from defective integration. It could evolve to become a new conformity; persist as a source of stress within the social system; or disappear altogether as coherence returned to society.

Parsons (1951) also focused on a very special form of deviance in his essay on the 'sick role'. He depicted illness as the status of those who should not be rewarded for occupying what could become a dangerously seductive and useless position. The sick are pampered and, without discouragement, people might learn to malinger. Illness had to be controlled by the threat of stigma.

Almost all other functionalists have diverged from Parsons's insistence on the dysfunctions of deviance. Instead, they have elected to illustrate the surprising fashion in which deviation has unintentionally buttressed the social order. Durkheim (1933) pointed to the solidarity conferred by collective sentiments outraged by the breaking of rules. Erikson (1966) wrote of how dramatized encounters between deviants and agents of social control beat the bounds of the moral community. Deviance was to be described as a dialectical foil to themes that infuse the moral centre of society. Without a vividly reproduced deviance, it was held, the centre would lose its structure and integrity. Good requires the bad, God Satan, and morality immorality. Within the borders of society, too, deviance was to be depicted as a kind of dangerous but necessary zone between major regions and classes of phenomena. The revulsion said to surround the homosexual and the hermaphrodite enforces morally charged divisions between the genders. Deviance then supports convention, and it does so in numerous ways. Bell (1960) and Merton (1957) talked of the part played by organized crime in repairing economic and political defects in the USA, suggesting that the criminal offers power, influence and services where none is provided by the respectable order. Davis (1961) remarked how prostitution supports monogamy and bastardy primogeniture. Most functionalist essays on deviance are brief and unsystematic. Yet their recurrent theme is that deviance upholds what it seems to disrupt. Their paradox is the interesting symbiosis of rule making, rule enforcement and rule breaking.

There are other postures: feminists writing about the rooting of deviation in patriarchy; control theorists taking deviance to be the wildness that erupts when social disciplines become weak; and ecologists charting the interlacing of deviance and conformity in the lives of people who live in the same territory. Each gives rule breaking a place in a distinct theoretical environment. Each imparts a distinctiveness that is sometimes quite marked and sometimes a little superficial. Without much effort, it is quite possible to transcribe some of those definitions so that they begin to resemble one another more closely. Thus functionalism resonates the assertions made by Marxists about the interdependence of crime and capitalism, by feminists about the links between patriarchy and rule breaking, and by phenomenologists about the work done in the social regulation of anomaly.

The sociology of deviance has probably been allied most prominently to the symbolic interactionism, labelling theory and phenomenology that came to the fore in the 1960s. So intimate is that connection that the sociology of deviance is often taken to be a wholly interactionist undertaking, bearing with it a crowd of unstated assumptions about methods, history and focus. *Deviance* is then held to refer not only to rule breaking but also to a special method of interpreting rule breaking. Those who chose to explore deviance in the late 1950s, 1960s and 1970s sought to advertise their distance from criminologists described as positivist and correctionalist. They took their task to be the symbolic reconstruction of deviance, learning how rule breaking had become possible, what meanings it attained, and how it progressed from stage to stage. The cast of performers was enlarged to include all those who significantly affected critical passages in the evolution of deviant histories. The influence of people and events was held to change with each new phase, being interpreted and reinterpreted by participants. Developments were thought to be intelligible only within the emergent logic of an unfolding career. The importance of interpretation, the processual character of social life and the centrality of deviant identity led interactionists to redefine deviation as a moving transaction between those who made rules, those who broke rules and those who implemented rules. Deviance was held to be *negotiated* over time, its properties reflecting the practical power and assumptions of those who propelled it from phase to phase. At the very core of the negotiating process are deviants themselves, and their conduct responds to the attitudes which are taken towards them at various junctures. Becoming deviant entails a recasting of the self and a redrafting of motives. It entails a supplying of accounts, meanings, purposes and character. In that process, deviant and conventional identities are manufactured, and the interactionist sociologists of deviance furnished portrait after portrait of hustlers, police officers, prostitutes, delinquents and drug users. Their work continues although it has become a little overshadowed by more recent models of conduct.

In retrospect, it is clear that the chief importance of the word deviance was connotative rather than denotative. It signified the break made in the 1960s by sociologists who sought symbolically to distance themselves and their work from what was taken to be the excessive positivism and correctionalism of orthodox criminology. In the American Society for the Study of Social Problems and the British National Deviancy Conference, in the writings of Howard Becker (1963), David Matza and Stanley Cohen, there was an attempt to champion a new beginning for criminology, a beginning that conceived rule breaking processes to be meaningful and emergent, that did not judge or refrain from making conventional moral and political judgements, and that attached importance to the consequences of the signifying work performed by audiences and by representatives of the state in particular. What was actually studied tended, in the main, to be much the same as before, although there was a new attention to rule making and rule enforcement.

The effects of the new sociology of deviance were profound. They fed into orthodox criminology and made it rather less analytically threadbare and empiricist. But, conversely, the sociology of deviance itself began to take on some of the political and moral preoccupations it had once derided. In the 1980s, especially, civil disorder, social disorganization, crimes against women and children, and victim surveys persuaded many sociologists that correctionalism and social intervention were not really inappropriate responses to the sufferings of victims, and of female, young and black victims above all. The distinctions between crime and deviance, and between criminologists and sociologists of deviance, blurred and faded, no longer seeming to be of such great interest, and the very word deviance itself acquired a somewhat dated ring.

Paul Rock
London School of Economics and
Political Science

References

Bankowski, Z., Mungham, G. and Young, P. (1977) 'Radical criminology or radical criminologist?', *Contemporary Crises* 1.
Becker, H. (1963) *Outsiders*, New York.
Bell, D. (1960) *The End of Ideology*, New York.
Cohen, P. (1972) 'Working class youth cultures in East London', in *Working Papers in Cultural Studies*, Birmingham.
Davis, K. (1961) 'Prostitution', in R. Merton and R. Nisbet (eds) *Contemporary Social Problems*, New York.
Downes, D. and Rock, P. (1982) *Understanding Deviance*, Oxford.
Durkheim, E. (1933) *The Division of Labour in Society*, New York (*De la division du travail social*, 1893, Paris).
Erikson, K. (1966) *Wayward Puritans*, New York.
Garfinkel, H. (1967) *Studies in Ethnomethodology*, Englewood Cliffs, NJ.
Goffman, E. (1963) *Stigma*, Englewood Cliffs, NJ.
Gouldner, A. (1970) *The Coming Crisis in Western Sociology*, New York.
Hall, S. *et al.* (eds) (1976) *Resistance Through Ritual*, London.
Hill, C. (1961) *The Century of Revolution*, Edinburgh.
Hirst, P. (1975) 'Marx and Engels on law, crime and morality', in I. Taylor *et al.* (eds) *Critical Criminology*, London.
Hobsbawm, E. (1965) *Primitive Rebels*, New York.
Lea, J. and Young, J. (1984) *What Is To Be Done About Law and Order?*, London.
Merton, R. (1957) *Social Theory and Social Structure*, New York.
Parsons, T. (1951) *The Social System*, New York.
Platt, A. (1978) ' "Street Crime" – A view from the Left', *Crime and Social Justice* 9.
Quinney, R. (1975) 'Crime control in capitalist society', in I. Taylor *et al.* (eds) *Critical Criminology*, London.
Scott, R. (1972) 'A proposed framework for analyzing deviance as a property of social order', in R. Scott and J. Douglas (eds) *Theoretical Perspectives on Deviance*, New York.
Scott, R. and Douglas, J. (eds) (1972) *Theoretical Perspectives on Deviance*, New York.
Smart, C. (1977) *Women, Crime and Criminology*, London.
Sumner, C. (1976) 'Ideology and deviance', PhD dissertation, Sheffield.
Taylor, I. (1980) 'The law and order issue in the British General Election and the Canadian Federal Election of 1979', *Canadian Journal of Sociology*.
Taylor, I., Walton, P. and Young, J. (1973) *The New Criminology*, London.
Thompson, E. (1975) *Whigs and Hunters*, London.
Willis, P. (1977) *Learning to Labour*, Farnborough.

See also: conformity; criminology; labelling theory; norms; social problems.

Dewey, John (1859–1952)

John Dewey was born in 1859. He was a child of pre-industrial New England, born and raised in Burlington, Vermont, where his father was a storekeeper, and where Dewey himself would grow to maturity and eventually attend the University of Vermont at age 16 (Wirth 1989). Graduating in 1879, Dewey became a high school teacher. Within three years, however, he entered into a doctoral programme at Johns Hopkins University. Dewey took only two years to complete his doctoral studies, which culminated with a dissertation on Kant's psychology. His first academic appointment was at the University of Michigan as an instructor of psychology and philosophy. In 1884 he moved to the University of Chicago, where he put a great deal of energy into the development of a laboratory school that allowed him to test his school-related ideas against the actual experience of teaching children (see *School and the Society*, 1902). But in 1905, in a squabble over the leadership of the laboratory school, Dewey left Chicago for Columbia University. He remained at Columbia until his retirement and died in New York City at the age of 92.

During his long life, Dewey engaged in a philosophy that not only addressed traditional philosophic pursuits in logic, ethics, political science, religion, psychology and aesthetics, but also spoke to issues in the public arena. Dewey, for instance, had substantive things to say about issues related to the suffragette movement, labour unions, birth control, world peace, social class tensions and societal transformations in Mexico, China and Russia (Dworkin 1954). A complete corpus of Dewey's work has been captured in a thirty-seven volume edition edited by Jo Ann Boydston (1979).

Although Dewey started his career in the field of psychology while still under the philosophical influence of German idealism, he soon came to know and appreciate the work of the American pragmatists, William James, Charles Peirce and George Herbert Mead, who inspired a social psychology that examined human behaviours. Dewey eventually made his own contributions to American pragmatism by stressing the role that the scientific method could play in improving the human condition, and by openly committing his philosophy to the values and aims of democracy. To Dewey, democracy was less of a political concept than a moral one. When married to a method of enquiry (essentially found in science), democracy represented a moral method of understanding. Dewey, in this sense, became the chief axiologist for American pragmatism, a role that likely led George Herbert Mead to observe that 'in the profoundest sense John Dewey is the philosopher of America' (quoted in Morris 1970: 8).

Dewey's social philosophy focused on the worth of the individual in the context of the collective, and aimed to empower the judgements of the common people. Scientific enquiry was favoured because it represented a method of deliberation that provided provisional answers to situational or emergent problems. These emergent problems comprised the main focal points for enquiry. To Dewey, problems were always seen as opportunities for growth and improvement. He believed that by subjecting the problems of the present to a method of enquiry, humanity could reconstruct and improve itself.

Dewey's programme for American pragmatism yoked together science, democracy and education (Dewey 1916). He bridged conserving and transforming agendas by fashioning a method of understanding within a democratic ethic. He argued that education should always be responsive to the organic interplay between the nature of the learner, the values of the society and the world of knowledge embodied in organized subject matter (Tanner and Tanner 1990). Despite a variety of criticisms, some of which was overtly ideological, Dewey continues to attract a diverse scholarly audience.

Peter S. Hlebowitsh
University of Iowa

References

Boydston, J. A. (1979) *The Complete Works of John Dewey*, Carbondale, IL.
Dewey, J. (1902) *The School and the Society*, Chicago.
—— (1916) *Democracy and Education*, New York.
Dworkin, M. (1954) *Dewey on Education*, New York.
Morris, C. (1970) *The Pragmatic Movement in American Philosophy*, New York.
Tanner, D. and Tanner, L. N. (1990) *The History of the School Curriculum*, New York.
Wirth, A. (1989) *John Dewey as Educator*, Landam, MD.

Further reading

Dykhuizen, G. (1973) *The Life and Mind of John Dewey*, Carbondale, IL.
Mayhew, K. and Edwards, A. (1936) *The Dewey School*, New York.
Rockefeller, S. (1991) *John Dewey*, New York.
Westbrook, R. (1991) *John Dewey and American Democracy*, Ithaca, NY.

See also: education.

disability

Despite the fact that between 4 and 5 per cent of the populations of the industrialized nations can be categorized as significantly disabled, disability has been relatively slow to capture the imagination of social scientists. Most research is basically descriptive, tied to agendas of policy formulation and evaluation, advocacy or demographic monitoring.

Disability has become a more visible social phenomenon for four reasons. First, people are living longer, resulting in an increase in age-related physical impairments. Second, advances in medical technology pose ever more difficult questions concerning the survival of babies born with serious impairments. Third, community care policies have rendered people with disabilities socially more visible. Finally, the development of a politicized disability movement means that people with disabilities are resisting their social stigmatization and questioning the social provisions which others make for them.

The most basic question, and perhaps the most controversial, is that of definition. The World Health Organization distinguishes between *impairment*, the absence or defect of a limb, organ or bodily mechanism, *disablement* or *disability*, the reduction or loss of function or ability consequent upon impairment, and *handicap*, the disadvantage or constraint which follows from disability. Social conditions may intervene to make an impairment more or less disabling, while handicap is likely in large part to be due to social factors rather than an inevitable consequence of disability. Handicap can also result from a non-disabling impairment such as disfigurement.

Without denying the 'reality' of impairment, this model has been challenged for placing insufficient emphasis upon the social and cultural construction of disablement. In one view, which dispenses with the category of handicap, disability is wholly the product of social exclusion and marginalization (Oliver 1990). Elsewhere, it is argued that the focus of attention should, for example, be upon disabling built environments and the inadequate nature of the social response to impairments, not upon disabling conditions or people with disabilities (Swain *et al.* 1993).

A number of important themes are clear in the analytical social science literature. Drawing upon the labelling perspective in the sociology of deviance, there is a long-standing interest in how people with disabilities manage and respond to their social stigmatization (Goffman 1963). A more recent concern is with the interaction between the social construction of disability and handicap and stratification, poverty and social closure (Jenkins 1991). This is linked to the question of the social reproduction of disadvantage and disability. Reflecting the new-found voice of the disability movement, perhaps the most significant recent social science development emphasizes the *meaning* of disability for people with disabilities and their experiences and testimony (Ferguson *et al.* 1992). One of the most eloquent

contributions to this literature is anthropologist Robert Murphy's personal account of his own paralysis and gradual assumption of a social identity as disabled (Murphy 1990).

Many questions and issues remain for social science. Two further examples will suffice. First, what in Britain is known as learning difficulties or mental handicap, and in the USA as mental retardation, presents a specific set of difficulties and research questions. For example, community care philosophies as they apply to people with intellectual impairments problematize the cultural construction and imposition of 'normality' (Baldwin and Hattersley 1991; Chappell 1992). In terms of interpretation, how we may best document and understand the social experiences of people with learning difficulties is a question of some methodological and epistemological moment.

Second, the comparative study of disability has been neglected. Our understanding of cross-cultural variation in the interpretation and definition of disability is unsystematic and shallow. Nor is this a matter of purely intellectual interest. For the developing nations, disability is a subject of pressing practical concern (Coleridge 1993). Impairments are caused, *inter alia*, by dietary deficiency, inadequate health care and poor social provision; in turn, disability makes its own contribution to poverty and underdevelopment. In this respect, as in so many others, disability offers challenges to the social sciences which are theoretical, methodological and ethical.

Richard Jenkins
University College of Swansea

References

Baldwin, S. and Hattersley, J. (eds) (1991) *Mental Handicap: Social Science Perspectives*, London.
Chappell, A. L. (1992) 'Towards a sociological critique of the normalisation principle', *Disability, Handicap and Society* 7.
Coleridge, P. (1993) *Disability, Liberation and Development*, Oxford.
Ferguson, P. M., Ferguson, D. L. and Taylor, S. J. (eds) (1992) *Interpreting Disability: A Qualitative Reader*, New York.
Goffman, E. (1963) *Stigma: Notes on the Management of Spoiled Identity*, Englewood Cliffs, NJ.
Jenkins, R. (1991) 'Disability and social stratification', *British Journal of Sociology* 42.
Murphy, R. F. (1992) *The Body Silent*, New York.
Oliver, M. (1990) *The Politics of Disablement*, Basingstoke.
Swain, J., Finkelstein, V., French, S. and Oliver, M. (eds) (1993) *Disabling Barriers – Enabling Environments*, London.

See also: medical anthropology; medical sociology.

discourse analysis

Discourse analysis refers to a lively but theoretically contested crossroads between several social science disciplines. Here social and cognitive psychologists have come into creative but sometimes rather uncomfortable contact with sociologists, philosophers, rhetoricians, linguists and literary theorists as they rework their theoretical ideas in the terrain of discourse (itself a contested notion). To further the confusion, discourse analysis is sometimes treated as a generic term to refer to virtually all work on language use in its social or cognitive context and at other times as a label for specific bodies of work, or as a contrast to text linguistics or conversation analysis. It is perfectly possible to have two books on discourse analysis which have no overlap in content at all.

At the boundary of cognitive psychology and linguistics there is work done in the tradition of discourse processes. Discourse analysis is here defined as the study of linguistic units that are larger than the sentence, and the hope is that some of the successes of linguistic analysis with smaller units could be repeated in this domain. Work in this tradition considers the way that individual utterances or sentences cohere into spoken or written discourse, and the relation between such patterning and the psychological phenomena involved in representing and comprehending such organizations. For example, it might ask whether there is a regular grammar underlying a written narrative, and it might consider whether the reader is using a cognitive representation such as a script or schema to recover the sense from the narrative.

Another distinctive area of discourse analysis has been developed principally using the example of classroom interaction. Sinclair and Coulthard (1975) attempted to provide a systematic model which would account for some of the typical interaction patterns that take place in teaching in terms of initiation-response-feedback (IRF) structures. For example,

> **Teacher**: What's the capital of Austria? (*Initiation*)
> **Pupil**:   Berne, Miss.   (*Response*)
> **Teacher**: Close Jenny, have another go. (*Feedback*)

The ambition was to provide a model that would ultimately account for discourse structure in a range of settings such as doctor–patient interactions, news interviews and committee meetings. Despite some success in characterizing features of rather formal kinds of classroom interaction, this model has encountered a series of difficulties which are mainly a consequence of applying a basically linguistic approach to the complex social practices taking place in classrooms and similar locations.

If linguistic forms of analysis take the upper hand in these first two areas, a separate tradition of discourse analysis has been more driven by developments in sociology and literary theory. The ambition here is rather different. Instead of being primarily concerned with extending linguistics, or connecting it to cognition, it is attempting to provide an alternative way of doing social science which is much more responsive to the idea that talk and writing – whether in an interview, a questionnaire, or an everyday conversation – is oriented to action.

In its simplest form, this tradition started with the observation that, when researching a complex social domain such as science, there are wide variations in the accounts given by different scientists and even by the same scientist in different settings. Rather than treat this as a methodological problem to be resolved by 'triangulation' from the different accounts, or by the use of ethnographically acquired knowledge of the setting, these discourse analysts endorsed the virtue of taking such variation as a research topic in its own right. In an influential study of a group of biochemists, Gilbert and Mulkay (1984) show how they construct versions of their social world using two very different 'interpretative repertoires', or interrelated vocabularies of terms, metaphors and tropes. The 'empiricist repertoire' predominates in research papers and is used by scientists to warrant their own beliefs in the manner of textbook science; the 'contingent repertoire' is a much more fragmentary set of notions which are used in informal settings to explain away beliefs seen as false in terms of social, political and psychological influences. Work of this kind has not only focused attention on the workings of scientists' texts but also raised questions about the literary forms with which social scientists construct and authorize their own versions of reality.

This approach has been reworked by social psychologists who have built a more explicit theoretical grounding which draws upon ideas from both ethnomethodology and post-structuralist thinking (particularly the work of Barthes and of Foucault, who has sometimes been described as a continental discourse analyst). Ironically, this form of discourse analysis has been used to question the status of some of the very cognitive notions which are central to the 'discourse processes' tradition. It has also been used in a critical manner to throw light on ageism, sexism and racism. For example, Wetherell and Potter (1992) mapped the interpretative repertoires that white middle-class New Zealanders used to construct versions of their world in talk and writing which justified inequalities and undermined arguments for social change. A striking conclusion from this study was the way that egalitarian and liberal notions were selectively drawn upon to support racist claims.

Some social scientists have been discomforted by the relativist thrust to this line of discourse analysis. For its proponents it is a way of studying the resources (interpretative repertoires, devices, category systems) that people use for constituting versions of their world, and the practices through which these resources are brought to life.

Jonathan Potter
Loughborough University of Technology

References

Gilbert, G. N. and Mulkay, M. (1984) *Opening Pandora's Box: A Sociological Analysis of Scientists' Discourse*, Cambridge, UK.

Sinclair, J. and Coulthard, M. (1975) *Towards an Analysis of Discourse: The English Used by Teachers and Pupils*, Oxford.

Wetherell, M. and Potter, J. (1992) *Mapping the Language of Racism: Discourse and the Legitimation of Exploitation*, London.

Further reading

Atkinson, P. (1989) *The Ethnographic Imagination: Textual Constructions of Reality*, London.

Brown, G. and Yule, G. (1983) *Discourse Analysis*, Cambridge, UK.

Fairclough, N. (1992) *Discourse and Social Change*, Cambridge, UK.

Potter, J. and Wetherell, M. (1987) *Discourse and Social Psychology: Beyond Attitudes and Behaviour*, London.

van Dijk, T. A. (ed.) (1985) *Handbook of Discourse Analysis*, 4 vols, London.

See also: ethnomethodology; language and culture; pragmatics; sociolinguistics.

disorders, depressive *see* depressive disorders

disorders, mental *see* mental disorders

distribution of incomes and wealth

The distribution of income is usually understood by economists in two main senses: the distribution of income among *factors* (sometimes known as the *functional* distribution of income), and the distribution of income among *persons* (alternatively known as the *size* distribution of income).

The distribution of income among factors is an integral part of the economic analysis of relative prices, output and employment. In this sense there are several theories of income distribution corresponding to different theoretical and ideological stances on these central issues. However, these various analyses usually focus on the same basic economic concepts: employment of the factors of production – land, labour and capital – and the rates of remuneration of their services – rent, wages and profit. This tripartite classification is by no means the only functional decomposition which is useful in economic theory; in some analyses, for example, a finer subdivision is attempted, distinguishing specifically between interest and profits as rewards to 'waiting' and 'entrepreneurship' respectively, or distinguishing between rewards to different types of labour. In many practical applications the characteristics of national data make it expedient to subdivide the functional categories simply as income from work and income from property. When these categories are applied to the income of an individual, household or subgroup of the population, a third type must be added, transfer income, although items in this category, such as welfare payments and alimony, net out when the economy as a whole is considered. Some macroeconomists gave much attention to the supposed constancy or stability of the share of wages in national income. This interest now appears to have been somewhat misplaced, since it is clear that over long periods this share does change significantly. In many industrialized countries during the twentieth century it has been increasing, and now stands at about three-quarters (UK) to four-fifths (USA).

The distribution of income among persons – the size distribution – and the distribution of wealth may both be thought of as particular applications of a statistical frequency distribution, although they are often represented by other statistical devices such as the Lorenz curve (which in the case of income distribution graphs cumulative proportions of income received against cumulative proportions of income receivers). The frequency distribution of each quantity is generally positively skewed with a long upper tail indicating the presence of relatively small numbers of very well-off people. The dispersion of these frequency distributions, which can be measured in a number of ways, is taken as an indicator of the inequality of the size distributions of income and of wealth.

The size distribution of income is noted almost everywhere for two remarkable qualities: the great inequality of personal incomes that is revealed, and the stability of the distribution over time. This is true even though the exact shape of the size distribution is significantly affected by the particular definition of income one employs (for example whether one includes transfer incomes and incomes received in 'kind' rather than cash, and deducts personal taxes), and the definition of the income-receiving 'unit' (for example whether one looks at the distribution of income among households, or incomes among persons). In the case of the USA, the top one-fifth of income receivers in 1947 received about 45.5 per cent of total personal income before tax and the bottom fifth then received about 3.5 per cent of total income; in 1977 the shares in total personal income of these two groups were about 45 and 4 per cent respectively (although there was some variation in intervening years) (Blinder 1980). While the composition of personal incomes in the lower tail of the distribution has changed substantially as the scope of government transfers has altered, it is still true to say that in most western-style economies the component of personal income that comes from various forms of property is primarily associated with the upper tail of the distribution. In order to understand the size distribution of *incomes* in the upper tail, therefore, it is important to examine the size distribution of wealth.

One of the most difficult problems in analysing the wealth distribution within any community with reasonably extensive holdings of private property is to decide exactly what one means by wealth. This is not a point of semantics, nor is it one of purely arcane, theoretical interest. While *marketable* wealth – including financial assets such as stocks and cash balances, and physical assets such as land, houses and jewellery – is fairly readily recognizable for what it is, other forms of wealth may also need to be taken into account in estimating the people's effective command over economic resources. These include various pension rights, which represent substantial *future* claims against economic goods (and are thus in that sense substitutes for cash or negotiable securities that have been held as a precaution against old age), but which may have little or no immediate surrender value. As is the case with the size distribution of incomes, estimates of the distribution of wealth are sensitive to assumptions one makes about the definition of wealth itself and the 'units' of population among whom the wealth is distributed. Moreover, parts of the wealth distribution are also very sensitive to different methods of valuing the components of wealth and to short-term changes in the prices of assets. However, it is virtually incontestable that the size distribution of wealth is much more unequal than the size distribution of income. For example, in the UK in 1976 the top 1 per cent of wealth holders possessed at least 14 per cent of personal wealth (this is on the most generous assumptions which include state and occupational pension rights as personal wealth; were these to be excluded the figure would have been 25 per cent), but the top 1 per cent of income recipients received about 5.5 per cent of personal income before tax (3.5 per cent after tax). Furthermore, it is clear that a substantial proportion of this implied inequality in the distribution of wealth is attributable to the effects of inheritance, rather than to the process of wealth accumulation that takes place during the course of people's lives (Harbury and Hitchens 1979).

Finally, if one switches one's attention from the analysis of the size distribution of income (or wealth) within national economies to the size distribution in the world as a whole, not only do the problems of measurement and comparison become much greater, so also does the dispersion. However one resolves the difficult practical questions of defining and quantifying personal or household incomes on this inter-country basis, it is clear that income inequality within national economies is usually much smaller than the income inequality that persists between countries.

Frank A. Cowell
London School of Economics and
Political Science

References

Blinder, A. S. (1980) 'The level and distribution of economic well-being', in M. Feldstein (ed.) *The American Economy in Transition*, Chicago.
Harbury, C. and Hitchins, D. M. W. N. (1979) *Inheritance and Wealth Inequality in Britain*, London.

Further reading

Atkinson, A. B. and Harrison, A. J. (1978) *Distribution of Personal Wealth in Britain*, Cambridge, UK.
Pen, J. (1971) *Income Distribution*, London.

See also: income distribution, theory of; taxation.

divine kingship

It was Frazer (1890) who first perceived that political power in archaic societies was intimately related to ritual functions, to the control which political leaders exercised over nature and, especially, rainfall. The sacred leader had to be put to death when his strength waned, since it was feared that his physical decline would result in a parallel weakening of the cosmic forces mysteriously associated with his person.

Evans-Pritchard denied the ritual character of regicide, seeing in it no more than the disguised expression of political conflict between rival factions. Studies in Africa have shown, however, that the putting to death of the sovereign forms an integral feature of the symbolic complex of sacred kingship (which Frazer called divine kingship).

This mystical institution, which was supposed to assure fecundity and prosperity, is characterized by a set of traits which are constant, though more or less developed in particular instances. The sacred king or chief commits fundamental transgressions: during his investiture he breaks the law of exogamy and commits real or symbolic incest (as among the Kuba, Lunda, Rwanda and Swazi) or even a sort of cannibalism, which consists in eating the flesh of his clan totem (for example,

Rukuba). A formidable and august figure, the sacred chief is hedged about by interdictions which regulate his conduct. This extraordinary being is potentially dangerous, and he may himself be contaminated. If he is regarded as an ambiguous creature, outside culture, this is because he has responsibility for the natural order. The Kuba identify their sovereign at once with a good natural spirit and with a powerful sorcerer.

Very often the king's body, isolated from the group, cannot fulfil its magical function when it begins to age. In some cases he must disappear after an arbitrarily fixed period, at least unless a substitute can be sacrificed to regenerate him. This is, for example, the Swazi conception (see Kuper 1947). Every year, during the summer solstice, the naked king, proclaimed 'bull of the nation', is seated on the principal ox of the herd and then thrown to the ground beside another beast, which has been stolen from a commoner, and which is tortured and sacrificed. The Mundang of Chad put their king himself, the master of the rain, to death at the end of a reign which may not exceed ten years (Adler 1982).

Sacred chiefship is based on a radical separation of political power (ritual in essence) and the society over which it is exercised. It is no accident that many African myths represent the founder of the sacred kingship not as a powerful warrior but as a foreign hunter who possesses powerful magic and bears the stigma of his outsider's status (de Heusch, 1972). This symbolic structure, which recurs in the most diverse historical contexts, is not a mystifying ideological representation of the state. One finds the same elements in tiny Rukuba polities no larger than a single village. The sacred chief here is the prisoner of the group which depends on his magical power to guarantee general prosperity. One cannot assume that this is the primitive form of kingship, but many African examples do show that various state institutions may develop from this representation of power. The state, in so far as it implies the existence of a system of coercion, requires the emergence of magico-religious institutions which do not fall within the domain of the kinship system, and which are in fact capable of breaking the monopoly of kinship institutions in the field of social organization.

Luc de Heusch
Free University of Brussels

References

Adler, A. (1982) *La Mort est le masque du roi*, Paris.
Frazer, J. G. (1890) *The Golden Bough*, London.
Heusch, L. de (1972) *Le Roi ivre ou l'origine de l'état*, Paris (English edn. *The Drunken King*, Bloomington, IN, 1982).
Kuper, H. (1947) *An African Aristocracy*, London.

See also: political anthropology.

division of labour by sex

The sexual division of labour is a basic structural element in human social organization. Interest in this topic began in the nineteenth century, but understanding was clouded by major misconceptions. These concerned the original human division of labour by sex, changes in this division of labour in the course of human evolution, and consequences for the relations between the sexes. A widespread view was that primitive subsistence was based mainly on tasks performed by males; hunting, fishing and herding. Marx and Engels (1947 [1932]), for example, inferred from this premise that masculine economic superiority was the order of nature, with slavery latent in the human family. Engels (1972 [1884]) compounded this misconception by assuming relative constancy of the sexual division of labour over time. He attributed a decline in female status to the larger societal division of labour and the rise of private property, with monogamy a corollary of property relations. A different misconception, found in Durkheim (1933 [1893]), is that the original sexual division of labour was minimal. He viewed differentiation between the sexes as increasing with time, moving towards organic solidarity and strong marriage ties.

Bias towards under-reporting women's contribution to subsistence is common across studies of many types of societies. Reporting biases will be reviewed where relevant in discussion of evidence on the following four topics: the original human division of labour; ethnological variability in sexual division of labour; changes in sexual division of labour with societal complexity; and consequences of the sexual division of labour.

First, evidence for the original human division of labour comes from two sources: primate ethology and the ethnology of foragers. Male specialization in hunting is consistent with the tendency of male terrestrial primates to specialize in defence. The latter specialization gives a selective advantage to larger males. Sexual dimorphism is a consequence of this original division of labour. Humans are alone among the primates in having a marked sexual division of labour in food production and in having food sharing on a regular basis. Early studies of foragers, while noting that men tend to hunt and women to gather, greatly underestimated the importance of female gathering, and in so doing fostered a view of the human family which overemphasizes the dependence of wives on their husbands. Studies of foragers (Lee and DeVore 1968) show that women's gathering often contributes more than half of the subsistence calories.

Second, variability in sexual division of labour is also much greater than commonly assumed for both pre-industrial and industrial societies. The rise of cross-cultural and cross-national research makes it possible to estimate the relative frequencies of allocations of male and female effort to various tasks. As a result of Murdock's work (Murdock 1937; Murdock and Provost 1973) we now have cross-cultural codes on sexual division of labour for fifty tasks. These codes confirm earlier generalizations about near-universals. Tasks done by males in more than 95 per cent of the sample societies include hunting large land animals, metal-working, wood- and bone-working, boatbuilding, and trapping. Tasks done by females in more than 95 per cent of the sample include only cooking and care of infants. Patterns of sexual division of labour appear to have only a partial basis in biology, and most tasks exhibit high variability. This is especially true of the important food production tasks pertaining to agriculture and the care of domesticated animals.

These variations, however, fall within constraints of a relative rather than universal nature. Many researchers have sought rules of consistency in the variable allocation of tasks. While earlier researchers emphasized the male strength advantage, research in the 1970s placed more emphasis on constraints due to the reproductive specialization of women. Brown (1970) emphasized the compatibility of women's tasks with simultaneous child-care responsibilities. Women's tasks are likely to be relatively close to home not dangerous, and interruptible. Burton *et al.* (1977) proposed that these relative constraints produce entailments within production sequences. Women tend to take on additional tasks within production sequences in an order which begins with tasks closer to the home and ends with tasks farther afield. Men take on additional tasks in the opposite order, from the more distant to those closer to home. Burton and colleagues found entailment chains for the following production sequences: animal tending, animal products, textiles, fishing and agriculture. An example from agriculture: if women clear the land, they also prepare the soil; if the latter, they also plant, tend crops, and harvest. If they tend crops, they also fetch water, and if they plant, they also prepare vegetables for cooking.

Third, in pre-industrial societies female participation in many tasks declines with societal complexity. For example, women build houses in nomadic societies but not in sedentary societies; and female participation in pottery-making declines with increasing population density. For crafts, the explanation for these changes seems to be the evolution of occupational specialization, which displaces craft activity from the domestic arena to the workshop. Agricultural intensification is accompanied by dramatic decreases in female contributions to farming. For Boserup (1970) agricultural intensification results from population pressure and introduction of the plough, and pulls men into agriculture to meet the increased demand for labour. Ember (1983) suggested a second mechanism in the shift to male farming: women are pulled out of farming into the household economy by increased time spent on food processing, household chores, and child care. Burton and White (1984) carried this work further with a model of four factors – population density, a short growing season, presence of the plough, and high dependence on domesticated animals – which lead to the displacement of women's labour from agriculture to the domestic and less economically visible activities.

The four-factor intensification model accounts for many empirical observations concerning female subsistence participation: that it is higher in tropical climates and in horticultural societies and that it is higher with root crops than with cereal crops, for these attributes are correlated with a long rainy season, low dependence on domesticated animals, absence of the plough, and low population density.

Finally, several researchers following Boserup (1970) hypothesized that agricultural intensification has a negative impact on female control of economic resources. This research suggests that high female subsistence contributions are a necessary prerequisite to female control of economic resources, and to women's freedom of choice in life events. In searching for other consequences of the sexual division of labour, Heath (1958) and several other researchers found that low female subsistence contributions lead to monogamy. Such studies shed light on puzzles such as the rise of monogamy and decline in women's status, originally noted by nineteenth-century theorists.

Michael L. Burton

Douglas R. White
University of California, Irvine

References

Boserup, E. (1970) *Woman's Role in Economic Development*, New York.

Brown, J. K. (1970) 'A note on the division of labor by sex', *American Anthropologist* 72.

Burton, M. L. and White, D. R. (1984) 'Sexual division of labor in agriculture', *American Anthropologist* 86.

Burton, M. L., Brudner, L. A. and White, D. R. (1977) 'A model of the sexual division of labor', *American Ethnologist* 4.

Durkheim, E. (1933 [1893]) *The Division of Labor in Society*, New York. (Original edn, *De la division du travail social: étude sur l'organization des sociétés supérieures*, Paris.)

Ember, C. R. (1983) 'The relative decline in women's contribution to agriculture with intensification', *American Anthropologist* 85.

Engels, F. (1972 [1884]) *The Origin of the Family, Private Property and the State*, New York. (Original edn, *Der Ursprung der Familie, des Privateigentums und des Staats*.)

Heath, D. (1958) 'Sexual division of labor and cross-cultural research', *Social Forces* 37.

Lee, R. B. and De Vore, I. (1968) *Man the Hunter*, Chicago.

Marx, K. and Engels, F. (1947 [1932]) *The German Ideology*, London. (Original edn, *Die deutsche Ideologie*, Moscow.)

Murdock, G. P. (1937) 'Comparative data on the division of labour by sex', *Social Forces* 15.

Murdock, G. P. and Provost, C. (1973) 'Factors in the division of labor by sex: a cross-cultural analysis', *Ethnology* 12.

See also: gender and sex; women's studies.

divorce

Divorce is the legal procedure by which marriage can be formally ended. Not all societies permit divorce (e.g. the Republic of Ireland) but in the majority of western countries, not only is divorce now possible but also legal constraints and obstacles to divorce have been gradually reduced since the end of the Second World War. It is usually possible to divorce on the grounds of incompatibility, and it is no longer necessary to prove that a spouse has committed a matrimonial offence such as adultery or desertion. The fact that divorce is now easier to obtain has, however, led to a belief that divorce itself is easy. Moreover, the idea that couples divorce simply because they are incompatible masks the seriousness of problems that may exist within the institution of marriage. Such problems may include violence, economic deprivation and cruelty to children. It is a mistake to imagine that couples divorce readily for whimsical reasons.

In the European Union, Denmark had the highest rate of divorce in 1990 (12.8 divorces per 1,000 existing marriages) with the United Kingdom close behind (12.6 per 1,000). The USA has the highest divorce rate of all developed societies and some statistics suggest that one in two marriages will end in divorce. It is necessary to be cautious about such statistics and it is particularly difficult to compare trends across countries. It would, for example, be wrong to presume that marriages do not break down in some countries where legal divorce is not available or where it is restricted. Couples in Catholic countries, for example, may rely on the process of annulment or may simply separate without going through any legal or formal process.

The rise in divorce in the west, particularly immediately following the Second World War, led to concerns over declining moral standards and fears about the stability of society. Rising divorce rates have often been (popularly) associated with rising rates of illegitimacy and of delinquency; such trends can be seen as generating moral panics and tendencies to blame individuals rather than understanding the deeper structural changes which may be giving rise to such developments. These sorts of moral concerns continue in the 1990s but they have been largely overtaken by two questions of social policy: first, the relationship between divorce and poverty, especially for women and children; and second, concern over the welfare of children who have experienced their parents' divorce.

It has become clear that divorce causes poverty because, at the very least, the same resources have to spread across two households (Eekelaar and Maclean 1986; Weitzman 1985). This problem is exacerbated if the main wage-earner re-partners and has additional children. Evidence suggests that the resulting hardship is most acutely felt by divorced mothers who typically retain the care of children. This is because they may not be able to return to the labour market or because they can do so only a part-time basis, often returning to lower status, more poorly paid jobs than those they held before their marriage. Such women tend to become reliant on low levels of state support, or on inadequate wages. In addition, in countries where health care is based on private insurance, divorced women often find they lose access to decent health care provision because it is typically attached to a husband's employment and/or record of contributions. On divorce a wife can no longer claim on such schemes because she is no longer next of kin or family member, and it is unlikely that she will have sufficient contributions of her own to generate sufficient cover. Divorced wives also lose entitlement to their husbands' occupational pension schemes and so, later in life, they are forced to become reliant on low state provisions or their own partial contributions. Thus divorce 'stores up' long-term poverty for many women if they have left the labour market to care for children and if they do not remarry (Glendinning 1992; Maclean 1991).

On the issue of children's welfare, the main concerns relate to the effects of poverty and the effects of emotional disturbance on children. It is not easy to disentangle these two issues because typically children experience the loss of a parent (usually a father) at the same time as facing a significant decline in living standards. But research on the impact of divorce on children is quite contradictory with some claiming that divorce *per se* has little impact and others suggesting that it is very harmful. There has been an interesting shift in research focus since the 1960s and 1970s. In these decades the focus was on the potential harms of maternal deprivation. This research was often used to blame working mothers for producing delinquent children. In the 1990s, however, the focus became the absent father. It is now his loss which has become associated with disturbed or antisocial behaviour. As a consequence many countries in the European Union, the USA, Australia and New Zealand are now developing divorce laws which try to encourage fathers to remain in contact with children after divorce. Equally many are striving harder to make fathers pay more realistic amounts towards childrearing costs (for example the Child Support Act 1991 in England and Wales). Such policies *could* shift the economic burden of divorce on to men and away from women, but the complexities of many benefit systems and the difficulties involved in this redistribution may produce conflicting outcomes in which women and children do not necessarily benefit. It is clear, however, that many national governments wish increasingly to avoid paying for the economic costs of divorce through systems of state benefits. It remains to be seen what the consequence will be of these new strategies to deal with divorce.

Carol Smart
University of Leeds

References

Eekelaar, J. and Maclean, M. (1986) *Maintenance after Divorce*, Oxford.
Glendinning, C. (1991) *The Costs of Informal Care*, London.
Maclean, M. (1991) *Surviving Divorce*, London.
Weitzman, L. (1985) *The Divorce Revolution*, New York.

Further reading

Clark, D. (ed.) (1991) *Marriage, Domestic Life and Social Change*, London.
Gibson, C. (1993) *Dissolving Wedlock*, London.
Mitchell, A. (1985) *Children in the Middle*, London.
Pahl, J. (1989) *Money and Marriage*, London.

See also: family; marriage; nuptiality.

domestic violence

There have been three historical periods during which the problem of domestic violence has become a public issue and been responded to by reformers and agencies of the state – 1870s, 1910s and 1970s to present. At each of these junctures, the problem was publicly recognized, statistics were gathered, explanations were proffered and policy reforms were introduced. On each occasion, the move to public recognition and reform was led by a vigorous women's movement.

The issue has been variously described as wife-beating and, more recently, as violence against women, woman abuse or domestic violence. Research findings show that across time and across cultures violence in marital and marital-like relationships is overwhelmingly asymmetrical, with men using violence against their female partners. While much of this violence remains unreported, current findings from crime statistics, victim surveys and depth-interviews reveal that between 10 and 25 per cent of all 'married' women have experienced violence from their male partner at some time during their life. The nature of the violence ranges from slapping and shoving to domestic homicide. The most common form is punching and kicking resulting in injuries such as bruising, broken bones and teeth, and cuts. Evidence further suggests that this physical violence is usually accompanied by other acts of aggression, coercion and intimidation, and is sometimes associated with sexual violence.

Across societies, homicide in domestic settings is, for the most part, the killing of wives, uxoricide. This usually occurs in the context of a history of sustained violence by the man against his female partner. Occasionally women kill husbands and the rate of these acts varies across societies, but this usually occurs in the context of a history of male violence directed at the woman. While death is an unusual outcome of domestic assaults, it none the less represents an important proportion of all the homicides of women, and in some countries uxoricide accounts for a considerable proportion of all the homicides. The evidence about domestic violence tells a common story, of a problem that is serious and widespread in most societies and of violence perpetrated by males against females.

Various explanations have been proposed by social scientists to account for this violence: social and individual pathologies; interactional, situational and family dynamics; and institutional, cultural and ideological forces. In many of these perspectives, male power, domination and control are emphasized to varying degrees. Historical, anthropological and contemporary research consistently reveal that conflicts associated with the use of violence typically include male concerns about power and authority, about jealousy and sexual possessiveness and about the domestic labour of women (e.g. food preparation and child-care). Individual backgrounds and learning experiences have also been shown to be important.

Domestic violence is a problem that has simultaneously involved researchers, social activists and policy makers. Activists have introduced the problem into the public agenda, secured its definition as a social problem and engaged the state in the process of policy making. Researchers have added systematic knowledge and policy makers have engaged in efforts to respond with measures intended to reduce or eliminate the problem and/or to provide support to its victims. The women's movement has been at the forefront in recognizing the problem internationally, providing the major response in the form of refuge or shelter for abused women and their children, and engaging the state in seeking reforms.

In addition to studying the nature of violence, social scientists have investigated the responses of the state, including their shortcomings and the effectiveness of existing responses and innovative policies and programmes. In this respect, initial attention was focused primarily on housing and refuge provision for abused women and criminal justice responses to violent men and the women they victimized. Evidence shows that housing and shelter provide important sanctuaries for women and children; traditional justice responses are not usually effective in reducing violence or supporting victims; and there is now a climate of change in law and law enforcement in some countries. An emerging area of research focuses on the effectiveness of innovative legal responses to violent men. Studies of the social services show a similar history of ineffective responses followed by innovations whose effectiveness is yet to be studied. Health and health care services have become the focus of growing academic and policy attention.

Within the social sciences, the disciplines of sociology, criminology and psychology have to date provided the greatest amount of research and scholarship. Anthropology, evolutionary psychology, medicine and nursing have begun to study the problem to add new explanations and enhance, modify or challenge existing ones.

Russell P. Dobash

R. Emerson Dobash
University of Wales,
Cardiff

Further reading

Browne, A. (1987) *When Battered Women Kill*, New York.

Daly, M. and Wilson, M. (1988) *Homicide*, New York.

Dobash, R. E. and Dobash, R. P. (1979) *Violence Against Wives*, New York.

—— (1992) *Women, Violence and Social Change*, London and New York.

Dobash, R. P., Dobash, R. E., Daly, M. and Wilson, M. (1992) 'The myth of sexual symmetrical in marital violence', *Social Problems* 39.

Edwards, S. S. M. (1989) *Policing Domestic Violence*, London.

Fagan, J. and Browne, A. (1994) 'Violence between spouses and intimates: Physical aggression between women and men in relationships', in A. J. Reiss, Jr and J. A. Roth (eds) *The Understanding and Control of Violent Behavior, vol. 3,* Washington, DC.

Gordon, L. (1988) *Heroes of their Own Lives*, New York.

Kelly, L. (1988) *Surviving Sexual Violence*, Cambridge.

Pahl, J. (ed.) (1985), *Private Violence and Public Policy: The Needs of Battered Women and the Response of the Public Service*, London.

Schechter, S. (1982) *Women and Male Violence: The Visions and Struggles of the Battered Women's Movement*, Boston, MA.

Smith, L. (1989) *Domestic Violence: An Overview of the Literature*, Home Office Research Study 107, London.

Straus, M. A. and Gelles, R. J. (eds) (1990) *Physical Violence in American Families*, New Brunswick, NJ.

See also: childcare; family; social problems; violence; women's studies.

dreams

Despite their power to bewilder, frighten or amuse us, dreams remain an area of human behaviour little understood and typically ignored in models of cognition. As the methods of introspection were replaced with more self-consciously objective methods in the social sciences of the 1930s and 1940s, dream studies dropped out of the scientific literature. Dreams were not directly observable by an experimenter and subjects' dream reports were not reliable, being prey to the familiar problems of distortion due to delayed recall, if they were recalled at all. More often dreams are, of course, forgotten entirely perhaps due to their prohibited character (Freud, 1955 [1900]). Altogether, these problems seemed to put them beyond the realm of science.

The discovery that dreams take place primarily during a distinctive electrophysiological state of sleep, rapid eye movement (REM) sleep, which can be identified by objective criteria, led to a rebirth of interest in this phenomenon. When REM sleep episodes were timed for their duration and subjects woken to make reports before major editing or forgetting could take place, it was determined that subjects accurately matched the length of time they judged the dream narrative to be ongoing to the length of REM sleep that preceded the awakening. This close correlation of REM sleep and dream experience was the basis of the first series of reports describing the nature of dreaming: that it is a regular nightly, rather than occasional, phenomenon, and a high-frequency activity within each sleep period occurring at predictable intervals of approximately every 60 to 90 minutes in all humans throughout the life-span. REM sleep episodes and the dreams that accompany them lengthen progressively across the night, with the first episode being shortest, of approximately 10–12 minutes duration, and the second and third episodes increasing to 15–20 minutes. Dreams at the end of the night may last as long as 45 minutes, although these may be experienced as several distinct stories due to momentary arousals interrupting sleep as the night ends. Dream reports can be retrieved from normal subjects on 50 per cent of the occasions when an awakening is made prior to the end of the first REM period. This rate of retrieval is increased to about 99 per cent when awakenings are made from the last REM period of the night. This increase in ability to recall appears to be related to an intensification across the night in the vividness of dream imagery, colours and emotions. The dream story itself in the last REM period is furthest from reality, containing more bizarre elements, and it is these properties, coupled with the increased likelihood of spontaneous arousals allowing waking review to take place, that heighten the chance of recall of the last dream. The distinctive properties of this dream also contribute to the reputation of dreams being 'crazy'. Reports from earlier dreams of the night, being more realistic, are often mistaken for waking thoughts.

Systematic content analysis studies have established that there are within-subject differences between dreams collected from home versus laboratory sleep periods, with home dreams being on the whole more affect-laden. This calls into question the representativeness of laboratory-collected dreams, particularly when subjects have not been adapted to the laboratory and the collections are carried out only for a limited period. More often, between-group comparisons are being made. Here clear differences have been reported between the home-recalled dreams of males and females, old and young, rich and poor, and between those of different ethnic groups living in the same geographical area. These differences reflect the waking sex-role characteristics, personality traits, and sociocultural values and concerns of these groups. These findings raise the question of whether dreams make some unique contribution to the total psychic economy, or merely reflect, in their distinctive imagistic, condensed language and more primitive logic, the same mental content available during wakefulness by direct observation or interviewing techniques.

The question of uniqueness of dream data and function may well be answered differently for home and laboratory retrieved dreams. Home dreams are so highly selected, whether from dream diaries or those recalled in response to questionnaires, that they yield culturally common material much like the study of common myths. In the laboratory, where the database includes all of the dreams of a night in sequence and where experimental controls can be instituted to ensure uniform collection, the yield is more individual and varied. Despite this, the question of dream function has continued to be an area of controversy in modern sleep research since the mid-1950s. It has been approached empirically through studies of the effects of dream deprivation with little progress. Neither awakenings at REM onset to abort dreams nor nights of drug-induced REM sleep deprivation have been followed by reliable deficits in waking behaviour or the appearance of dream-like waking hallucinations.

It is possible that these studies have not been carried out long enough or that the dependent measures have not been appropriately designed. Other studies have proceeded by manipulating the pre-sleep state to heighten a specific drive, such as thirst or sex, or to introduce a problem requiring completion such as a memory task and testing for the effects on dream content or subsequent waking behaviour. Again, effects have been small and rarely replicable. The laboratory

setting and experimenter effects have been implicated in masking the very phenomenon the studies were designed to reveal, being more powerful stimuli than the experimental manipulation itself (Cartwright and Kaszniak 1978).

Seldom have theoretical models of dream function been tested. These have varied widely in the psychological processes implicated. Learning and memory have been prominent, as in the Hughlings Jackson (1932) view that sleep serves to sweep away unnecessary memories and connections from the day. This has been revised by Crick and Mitchison (1983) and stated as a theory that dream sleep is a period of reversed learning. However, the opposite view that dreaming has an information-handling, memory-consolidating function (Hennevin and Leconte 1971) is also common. Other writers stress an affective function. Greenberg and Pearlman (1974) and Dewan (1970) hold that during dreaming, reprogramming of emotional experiences occurs, integrating new experiences and updating existing programmes. The modern psychoanalytically oriented view is an adaptation of Freud's conception of dreams as safe ways for unconscious drive discharge to take place (Fisher 1965; French and Fromm 1964). Beyond the issue of what psychological process is involved is the further problem posed by those who deny that studies of dream content can make any headway without taking into account their latent as well as their manifest content. This requires obtaining waking associations to each dream to plumb their function fully. Such a design would produce confounding effects on subsequent dreams.

Despite the theoretical morass and methodological problems rife in this field, systematic headway in understanding dreams has been made. One such advance came from a ground-breaking longitudinal collection of home and laboratory dreams of boys and girls by Foulkes (1982). These were analysed to explore the age- and sex-related changes in dream structure and content in terms of the cognitive and other aspects of the developmental stages of these children. Another advance came in the area of methodology with the development of standardized content analysis systems (Foulkes 1978) and rating scales (Winget and Kramer 1979). Another improvement in design combines the advantages of the methods of the laboratory with the reality of a field study by predicting dream-content differences in the laboratory retrieved dreams among groups of persons differing in response to a major affect-inducing life event. For example, Cartwright (1991) has shown that those who dream directly of the emotionally disturbing person (the former spouse in a divorcing sample) more often made a good waking adjustment to the change.

The study of dreams is ready to move beyond the descriptive. Many factors have been amassed about this

distinctive mental activity, without any clear understanding of its basic nature. Many points of view on
dream function still compete (see Moffitt *et al.* 1993).
How is a dream put together into a dramatic format
without the contribution of any voluntary intent of the
dreamer? How are the new perceptions formed that
often express in such highly economical terms a coming
together of old memories and current waking experiences? Do dreams have effects despite the fact that they
are forgotten? What do these processes tell us about
how the mind works? Dreams are a difficult challenge.
They deserve our best response.

Rosalind D. Cartwright
Rush-Presbyterian-St Luke's Medical Center,
Chicago

References

Cartwright, R. (1991) 'Dreams that work', *Dreaming* 1.
Cartwright, R. and Kaszniak, A. (1978) 'The social
    psychology of dream reporting', in A. Arkin *et al.* (eds) *The
    Mind in Sleep*, Hillsdale, NJ.
Crick, F. and Mitchison, G. (1983) 'The function of dream
    sleep', *Nature* 304.
Dewan, E. (1970) 'The programming "P" hypotheses for
    REM sleep', in E. Hartmann (ed.) *Sleep and Dreaming*,
    Boston, MA.
Fisher, C. (1965) 'Psychoanalytic implications of recent
    research on sleep and dreaming. II. Implications of psycho-
    analytic theory', *Journal of American Psychoanalytical Associ-
    ation* 13.
Foulkes, D. (1978) *A Grammar of Dreams*, New York.
—— (1982) *Children's Dreams*, New York.
French, T. and Fromm, E. (1964) *Dream Interpretation: A New
    Approach*, New York.
Freud, S. (1955 [1900]) *The Interpretation of Dreams, Standard
    Edition of the Complete Psychological Works of Sigmund Freud*, ed.
    J. Strachey, vols 4 and 5, London.
Greenberg, R. and Pearlman, C. (1974) 'Cutting the REM
    nerve: an approach to the adaptive role of REM sleep',
    Perspectives in Biology and Medicine.
Hennevin, E. and Leconte, P. (1971) 'La fonction du sommeil
    paradoxal: faits et hypotheses', *L'Ann. Psychologique* 2.
Jackson, J. H. (1932) *Selected Writings of John Hughlings Jackson*,
    ed. J. Taylor. London.
Moffitt, A., Kramer, M. and Hoffman, R. (1993) *The Functions
    of Dreaming*, New York.
Winget, C. and Kramer, M. (1979) *Dimensions of Dreams*,
    Gainesville, FL.

Further reading

Cartwright, R. and Lamberg, L. (1992) *Crisis Dreaming*, New
    York.
Cohen, D. (1979) *Sleep and Dreaming*, New York.
Fishbein, W. (1981) *Sleep, Dreams and Memory*, New York.

See also: fantasy; sleep.

drug use

The concept 'drug' is both socially constructed and
concretely real. That is, first, what a drug is depends
on the perspective of the definer; certain definitions
are relevant only within specific social contexts.
Second, once drugs are defined in a certain fashion,
their concrete reality is no longer a matter of definition
but of empirical fact, subject, of course, to the usual
scientific debate and confirmation. Put another way,
drugs are physical entities with concrete properties
and objective, measurable effects, but the properties and effects may or may not be relevant, according
to the observer's definitional and conceptual framework.

Of all definitions of drugs, the one most widely
accepted in the social sciences is substances that are
psychoactive, or influence the mind in significant ways.
Among other things, drugs influence how the human
mind works, they have an impact on mood, emotion,
feeling, perception, and thinking processes. This definition excludes substances used within a medical
context, such as penicillin and antibiotics, which are
not psychoactive. This definition includes those
substances that strongly influence the mind but which
are legally obtainable and, as a result, may not be
widely regarded as drugs by the general public, such as
alcohol and tobacco cigarettes.

The ingestion of mind-altering substances is very
nearly a human universal; in practically every society
on earth, a sizeable proportion of its members take at
least one drug for psychoactive purposes. This has been
true for a significant stretch of human history.
Fermentation is one of the earliest of human discoveries, predating even the fashioning of metals; humans
have been ingesting alcoholic beverages for at least
10,000 years. Strands of the marijuana plant embedded
in Chinese pottery have been found by archaeologists
in sites estimated to date back some ten millennia (Abel
1980). Dozens of plants containing chemicals that
influence the workings of the mind have been smoked,
chewed, or sniffed by members of societies all over the
world: coca leaves, the opium poppy, marijuana, psilocybin (or the 'magic' mushroom), *Amanita muscaria*,
the peyote cactus, quat leaves, nutmeg, coffee beans,
the yagé vine, and tea leaves. During the past century
or so, hundreds of thousands of psychoactive chemicals
have been discovered, isolated or synthesized by scientists, physicians or technicians. Thousands have been
marketed for medicinal purposes. According to the
journal, *Pharmacy Times*, roughly 1.5 billion prescriptions for drugs are written each year in the USA alone,
roughly one in six or one in seven of which are
psychoactive. In the USA, roughly two-thirds of the
population age 12 and older has drunk alcohol one or

more times in their lives, and half the population has done so during the past month; one-quarter of all Americans are current smokers of tobacco cigarettes; one-third has at least tried marijuana, 10 per cent have used it in the past year, and 5 per cent have done so in the past month (Goode 1993). Drug-taking is a widespread and extremely commonly indulged-in activity.

Most of the time that psychoactive chemicals are ingested, they are used 'in a culturally approved manner' (Edgerton 1976), with little or no negative impact on the user or on society. However, in a significant number of cases, drugs are taken in a culturally unacceptable or disapproved fashion: a condemned drug is taken instead of an approved one, it is taken too frequently or under the wrong circumstances, for the wrong reasons, or with undesirable consequences. With the establishment of the modern nation-state and, along with it, the elaboration of an explicit legal code, certain actions came to be judged illegal or criminal. The use, possession or sale of certain drugs, taking drugs in certain contexts, or the ingestion of drugs for disapproved motives, have been regarded as crimes in nearly all countries, punishable with a fine or imprisonment of the offender.

The catch-all term drug 'abuse' has been used variously by different observers. Some experts argue that drug abuse should be defined by its *illegal* and *extra-medical* character (Abadinsky 1989), a definition which would exclude the excessive and abusive consumption of alcohol. Others specify that drug 'abuse' must be defined by the deleterious effects that users and others suffer as a consequence of the use of psychoactive chemicals (White 1991). The controversy underlines the socially constructed character of drugs and their use.

It must be emphasized that drug use is not a unitary phenomenon. There exist, to begin with, different types of drugs, classified according to their action. Drugs are commonly categorized on the basis of their impact on the central nervous system (CNS), that is, the brain and the spinal column. Some drugs speed up signals passing through the CNS; pharmacologists refer to them as *stimulants*. Stimulants include cocaine, the amphetamines and caffeine. Nicotine, the principal psychoactive ingredient in tobacco cigarettes, also has a simulating effect, but some of its other effects are sufficiently distinct as to merit a separate classification. Other drugs retard, slow down, or depress signals passing through the CNS, and are referred to as *depressants*. The two major types of depressants include *narcotics* or *narcotic analgesics* (such as opium, morphine, heroin and methadone), which dull the sensation of pain, and sedatives or 'general depressants' (such as alcohol, barbiturates, methaqualone and Valium),

which are anti-anxiety agents. Most psychoactive drugs are not classifiable by the stimulant–depression continuum. A wide and miscellaneous range of psychoactive substances are used to treat mental disorder or mental illness; the two major types are the *antipsychotics* (or phenothiazines), which are administered to schizophrenics, and *antidepressants* (or mood elevators), which are administered to the clinically depressed. Hallucinogens or 'psychedelics' are capable of producing dramatic perceptual changes (although they very rarely produce genuine hallucinations); examples include LSD, mescaline and psilocybin. The cannabis products, marijuana and hashish, are usually thought to occupy a separate and distinct category of psychoactive substances.

Even the same psychoactive substance may be taken by different individuals for different motives, to achieve different goals. Indeed, even the same individual may take the same drug at different times for different purposes. Attaining religious or mystical insight or ecstasy, healing the mind or body, suppressing fatigue, hunger or anxiety, enhancing pleasure or hedonism, facilitating interpersonal intimacy, following the dictates of a particular group or social circle, and establishing an identity as a certain kind of person include some of the more commonly expressed motives for psychoactive drug use. A drug's psychoactive properties may be central to the user's motive for taking it, or they may be incidental; the intoxication or 'high' may be experienced for intrinsic reasons, that is, as an end in itself, or the drug may be taken for instrumental purposes, that is, to attain a specific and separate goal, such as alleviating pain. Of the many varieties of drug use, perhaps the three most common and important are legal recreational use, illegal recreational use, and legal instrumental use, mainly medical. Each of these modes attract strikingly different users and have strikingly different consequences. It is a fallacy to assume that the pharmacological properties of a drug dictate the consequences of its use; factors such as motives for use, the social context in which use is embedded, the social norms surrounding use, methods of use or 'route of administration,' all play a role in influencing the impact of the use of psychoactive substances.

First, *legal recreational use* refers to the use of a psychoactive drug, whose possession and sale are not against the law, for pleasurable purposes. In western nations, this refers mainly to alcohol consumption. Although, in the USA, there has been an effort to redefine alcohol as a drug in the educational curricula, even today, much of the public does not see alcohol as a drug. When this term is used to apply to substances consumed outside a medical context, it typically connotes those whose possession has been criminalized and whose use is condemned. However, in the pharmacological sense, that is, in terms of its effects, alcohol is psychoactive, it is used for this purpose, it can produce a physical dependence or addiction, in heavy, long-term, chronic users, and it causes or is associated with a wide range of medical maladies. Many estimates place the proportion of alcoholics at roughly one drinker in ten, and argue that alcoholism is the west's most serious drug problem. In short, alcohol 'is a drug by any other name'.

Second, of all types of drug use, *illegal recreational use* has attracted the most attention and interest. In the generation following the early 1960s, western Europe and North America experienced an unprecedented rise in the recreational use of illegal psychoactive drugs. The most widely used of these are the cannabis products, marijuana and hashish. In a number of western countries, there are as many episodes of cannabis use as episodes of all other illegal drugs combined. Of all illegal drugs, cannabis is the one that users are most likely to 'stick with' or continue using regularly, and least likely to abandon or use only episodically. In other words, among illegal drugs, marijuana has the highest continuance rate. At the same time, as a general rule, legal drugs such as alcohol and cigarettes have far higher continuance rates than illegal drugs, marijuana included (Sandwijk *et al.* 1991). Hallucinogens, such as LSD, tend to be taken on an experimental or episodic basis, and are extremely rarely taken heavily or abusively. As with alcohol, the vast majority of cannabis users take the drug on a moderate, controlled fashion. Still, some illegal drugs do attract heavy, chronic, abusive users. In the USA the number of heroin addicts has been estimated at half a million; in the UK, the number of registered addicts has increased tenfold since the mid-1980s. It has been estimated that there are several million daily cocaine users in the USA. However, for all illegal substances, the vast majority of at-least one-time user or triers either abandon the drug after a few experimental trials or use it moderately, in a controlled fashion, on a once-in-a-while basis (Zinberg 1984).

Third, the *legal instrumental or medical use* of psychoactive drugs in the western world has undergone dramatic changes over the course of the twentieth century. At the turn of the nineteenth century, preparations containing psychoactive substances such as morphine and cocaine were freely available and were widely used to cure or treat medical and psychiatric ailments. Legal controls on the sale of these nostrums, or even what they contained, were practically nonexistent (Berridge and Edwards 1987; Musto 1987). In contrast, the twentieth century has witnessed an avalanche of legal controls on psychoactive substances for medical purposes. In western countries, the primary mode of dispensing drugs is via medical prescription. In the USA, the number of prescriptions written for psychoactive drugs rose steadily until the early 1970s, when misuse and abuse of these substances was widely publicized. Since that time, there has been a steep decline in the number of prescriptions written for psychoactive drugs. (In contrast, the number of prescriptions written for non-psychoactive drugs has remained stable, or even risen somewhat, because the west has an ageing population.) Between 1970 and the 1990s, prescriptions for the amphetamines generally and the barbiturates have declined 90 per cent; Valium, once the USA's best-selling prescription drug, has dropped to 47th place; and some drugs, such as methaqualone, a sedative, and Benzedrine, an amphetamine, are no longer obtainable via prescription (Goode 1993). The sales of a small number of recently introduced psychoactive drugs – such as Prozac, an antidepressant, and Xanax, a sedative – have boomed largely because they have been perceived as safer and/or more effective alternatives to previously popular prescription drugs. As a general rule, the overall decline in the prescription use of psychoactive pharmaceuticals has produced a decline in recreational 'street' usage; this has been the case, most dramatically, for amphetamine, barbiturate and methaqualone use.

In the 1950s, it was discovered that the phenothiazine drugs suppress the symptoms of mental disorder, especially schizophrenia. Since that time, the administration of antipsychotic drugs, such as Thorazine, Stelazine and Mellaril, to mental patients has been increasing dramatically. There were just under 560,000 resident patients in publicly funded mental hospitals in the USA in 1955; in the mid-1990s there are a shade over 100,000. Some three-quarters of all individuals diagnosed as mentally disordered are taking phenothiazine drugs on an outpatient basis. While the number of admissions to mental hospitals more than doubled between the 1950s and the 1990s, the length of stay of mental patients then was six to eight months; currently it is two weeks (Ray and Ksir 1993). Mentally disordered individuals who once would have been confined to mental institutions are now outpatients.

Since the mid-1980s in the USA, there has been a growing call for the full legalization or decriminalization of all currently illegal psychoactive substances, including cocaine and heroin. The pro-legalization argument is based on three assumptions: first, that use and abuse will not increase when legal controls are removed; second, that the currently illegal drugs are not as harmful as those that are legal, nor as harmful as legislators and the public believe; and third, that criminalization is both ineffective and counter-productive (Nadelmann 1989).

The vast majority of the American public is strongly opposed to full legalization, however, and legislators, even were they convinced of the proposal's feasibility, would be voted out of office were they to support it. Moreover, the assumption of no increase in use or abuse is not entirely convincing, for seven main reasons. First, there is a strong correlation between cost and use, and it is criminalization that keeps the cost of illegal drugs high. Second, if we take them both at their word and their actions, current abusers and heavy users would use substantially *more* were their substances of choice readily available. Third, in social contexts where psychoactive substances are or were readily available, such as among physicians and other medical workers, and among military personnel during the Vietnam War, use has been high. Fourth, during the period of national alcohol Prohibition in the USA, the consumption of alcohol did decline (Lender and Martin 1987). Fifth, where risk-taking activities remain beyond the reach of the law, a certain proportion of individuals will engage in them – motorcyclists refusing to wear helmets, motorists not wearing seat belts – while, when those same activities are legally controlled, a much lower proportion do so. Sixth, as we saw, continuance rates for the legal drugs are significantly higher than they are for the illegal drugs. Finally, in the USA, outlawing the sale of alcohol to persons under the age of 21 has been accompanied by a significant decline in the number of alcohol-related automobile fatalities in this age group.

It is possible that, while criminalization has produced higher rates of drug-related crime, disease and violence, it has also resulted in lower levels of use than would otherwise have been the case. In other words, as measured by the criterion of *containment*, legal controls may have been successful. Perhaps a 'third path' located somewhere between the current punitive policy and full legalization would be most effective. The Dutch policy of flexible enforcement, *de facto* decriminalization for the 'soft' cannabis products, and harm reduction might be explored by other western countries, including the USA.

Erich Goode
State University of New York at Stony Brook

References

Abadinsky, H. (1989) *Drug Abuse: An Introduction*, Chicago.
Abel, E. L. (1980) *Marihuana: The First Twelve Thousand Years*, New York.
Berridge, V. and Edwards, G. (1987) *Opium and the People: Opiate Use in Nineteenth-Century England*, New Haven, CT.
Edgerton, R. B. (1976) *Deviance: A Cross-Cultural Perspective*, Menlo Park, CA.
Goode, E. (1993) *Drugs in American Society*, 4th edn, New York.
Lender, M. E. and Martin, J. K. (1987) *Drinking in America: A History*, rev. and exp. edn, New York.
Musto, D. F. (1987) *The American Disease: Origins of Narcotic Control*, exp. edn, New York.
Nadelmann, E. A. (1989) 'Drug prohibition in the United States', *Science* 245.
Ray, O. and Ksir, C. (1993) *Drugs, Society, and Human Behavior*, 6th edn, St Louis, MI.
Sandwijk, J. P., Cohen, P. D. A. and Musterd, S. (1991) *Licit and Illicit Drug Use in Amsterdam*, Amsterdam.
White, J. M. (1991) *Drug Dependence*, Englewood Cliffs, NJ.
Zinberg, N. E. (1984) *Drugs, Set, and Setting: The Basis for Controlled Intoxicant Use*, New Haven, CT.

Further reading

Beck, J. and Rosenbaum, M. (1994) *Pursuit of Ecstasy: The MDMA Experience*, Albany, NY.
Inciardi, J. A. (ed.) (1991) *The Drug Legalization Debate*, London and Newbury Park, CA.
Stephens, R. C. (1991) *The Street Addict Role*, Albany, NY.
Venturelli, P. J. (ed.) (1994) *Drug Use in America: Social, Cultural, and Political Perspectives*, Boston, MA and London.
Williams, T. (1992) *Crackhouse: Notes from the End of the Line*, London and New York.

See also: alcoholism and alcohol abuse.

DSM-IV

DSM-IV is the fourth edition of the American Psychiatric Association's Diagnostic and Statistical Manual of Mental Disorders (published in 1994). The DSM-IV is a categorical classification which groups mental disorders based on primarily phenomenological features which are organized into specifically defined sets of criteria. Although developed primarily for its utility in clinical practice, the DSM-IV is also used in training, research, and medical record keeping.

Attempts to classify mental illness date back thousands of years (e.g. Egyptian and Sumerian references to senile dementia, melancholia, and hysteria date back to 3000 BC), and a variety of approaches has been applied. While some systems were based on a large number of narrowly defined conditions, others were established on more inclusive, broad conceptualizations. Classification systems have also differed in the extent to which classification of disorders should be based on aetiology, the course of the illness, or the descriptive presentation of symptom patterns. In the later half of the nineteenth century, Emil Kraepelin developed a classification which combined aspects of various systems: he studied groups of patients whose disorders had the same course, in order to determine their shared clinical symptomotology. Kraepelin's (1917) general methodology has been largely retained in the development of the current DSM system.

Other classification systems were developed in the USA prior to the publication of the DSM-I in 1952; however, the DSM system was the first to emphasize clinical utility. DSM-I was a variant of the World Health Organization's (1948) *International Classification of Diseases, Injuries, and Causes of Death*, 6th edn (later editions are entitled *International Classification of Disease* (ICD)), which was the first edition of the ICD to include a section on mental disorders. The relationship with the ICD system has continued; revisions were closely timed and recent efforts have ensured a greater compatibility between the two systems. The DSM-III (published in 1979) represented a major shift in the approach to psychiatric diagnosis and for the first time included explicit criteria (rather than glossary definitions), multiaxial assessment, and a descriptive approach that was neutral with regard to aetiology. The major innovation of the DSM-IV lies in its documentation and explicit reliance on empirical data in the revision process, the inclusion of over one thousand health and mental professionals in the development of the manual, expanded text sections describing symptom presentations that may vary according to age, gender and cultural differences, and the inclusion of more specifiers, subtypes and course modifiers. A three-step process was utilized in the development of the DSM-IV: comprehensive literature reviews, data reanalyses and focused field trials.

The DSM-IV disorders are grouped into sixteen major diagnostic classes, beginning with mental disorders Usually First Diagnosed in Infancy, Childhood, or Adolescence. Although almost all disorders in the DSM are neutral in regard to aetiology, the next three sections of the manual – Delirium, Dementia, Amnestic, and Other Cognitive Disorders; Mental Disorders Due to a General Medical Condition; and Substance-Related Disorders – are by definition based on aetiology and are listed before the remaining disorders because of their importance in differential diagnosis. These disorders were formerly referred to as Organic Disorders. The term organic has been eliminated from the DSM because of the erroneous implication that all other disorders in the system have no organic basis. The remaining disorders (except for Adjustment Disorders, which vary in their presentation, but are reactions to stressful events) are grouped based on common presenting symptoms. They are Schizo-phrenia and Other Psychotic Disorders; Mood Dis-orders; Anxiety Disorders; Somatoform Disorders; Factitious Disorders; Dissociative Disorders; Sexual and Gender Identity Disorders; Eating Disorders; Sleep Disorders; Impulse-Control Disorders Not Elsewhere Classified; Adjustment Disorders; and Personality Disorders. An additional section describes conditions which may be a focus of clinical attention (e.g. bereavement, relational problems) but which are not considered mental disorders.

In addition to the criteria set for each disorder, explanatory text describes diagnostic features (e.g. examples of criteria); subtypes and specifiers; recording procedures; commonly associated features and disorders; specific culture, age and gender features; prevalence rates; typical lifetime pattern and evolution of the disorder; familial pattern; and differential diagnosis pointers.

DSM-IV utilizes multi-axial assessment to ensure a comprehensive assessment of the individual's health, environment and functional level. Axis I includes all mental disorders except Mental Retardation and the Personality Disorders, which are listed on Axis II. General Medical Conditions (i.e. any condition listed in the ICD outside of the mental disorders section) are listed on Axis III. Psychosocial and environmental stressors (e.g. occupational or economic problems) are listed on Axis IV, while Axis V is used to record a Global Assessment of Functioning score (i.e. the clinician's assessment of the individual's level of occupational, social and psychosocial functioning; this information is helpful in planning a treatment regimen and in predicting likely treatment outcome).

Numeric codes for each disorder or condition listed in the manual are provided, and are derived from those used in the ICD, 9th edn, Clinical Modification, the official coding system in the USA (US Government Department of Health and Human Services 1979). An appendix lists all disorders with the *International Statistical Classification of Diseases and Related Health Problems*, 10th edn (ICD-10) codes as well (World Health Organization 1992). The ICD-10 is used in most other countries. Thus, the complete compatibility of DSM-IV with both systems facilitates medical record keeping and statistical comparison both in the United States and internationally.

Several caveats in the use of the DSM-IV are noted. First, although the inclusion of specific criteria sets aids in the diagnosis of mental disorders, the criteria are provided as guidelines and require specialized clinical training in their application. Also, additional information beyond that needed to make a diagnosis is necessary in the formulation of an appropriate treatment plan. Special consideration should be given when the clinician is unfamiliar with the cultural reference of the individual that he or she is evaluating; a clinician may mistake thoughts or actions that are an accepted and typical part of that person's culture as symptoms of a mental disorder.

The manual is intended to be comprehensive and reflect current knowledge but may not include all conditions for which individuals seek treatment, or for which research may be appropriate. Inclusion in the manual of a mental disorder does not imply that the condition meets legal or other non-medical criteria for what constitutes disability, mental disease, or a mental disorder. Clinical diagnosis in itself does not have a one-to-one relationship with issues of control, competence, criminal responsibility, disability or impairment.

Harold Alan Pincus

Nancy E. Vettorello
American Psychiatric Association

References

American Psychiatric Association (1952) *Diagnostic and Statistical Manual of Mental Disorders*, 1st edn, Washington, DC.
—— (1968) *Diagnostic and Statistical Manual of Mental Disorders*, 2nd edn, Washington, DC.
—— (1980) *Diagnostic and Statistical Manual of Mental Disorders*, 3rd edn, Washington, DC.
—— (1994) *Diagnostic and Statistical Manual of Mental Disorders*, 4th edn, Washington, DC.
Kraepelin, E. (1917) *Lectures on Clinical Psychiatry*, 3rd edn, New York.
US Government Department of Health and Human Services (1979) *International Classification of Diseases*, 9th edn, Clinical Modification, Washington, DC.
World Health Organization (1948) *International Classification of Diseases, Injuries, and Causes of Death*, 6th edn, Geneva.
—— (1992) *International Statistical Classification of Diseases and Related Health Problems*, 10th edn, Washington, DC.

See also: depressive disorders; mental disorders; neuroses; psychiatry; psychoses; schizophrenia.

dual economy

The term dual economy has at once a technical academic meaning and a broader, more general meaning. In the former sense it relates to the simultaneous co-existence within the same economy of two different sectors, divided by different culture, different laws of development, different technology, different demand patterns, and so on. In certain models or theories of development, such as two-sector division, and the inter-action between the two sectors, that is, a dual economy is taken as a foundation for theoretical analysis.

The best known of such models is the Arthur Lewis model, based on his famous article 'Economic development with unlimited supply of labour' (1954). Lewis distinguishes between a rural low-income subsistence type sector in which there is surplus population (zero or very low marginal productivity of labour), and a developing urban capitalist sector in which wages are held down by the pressure of rural surplus population with resulting rapid development, ultimately exhausting the labour surplus. A considerable literature has followed in the wake of the Lewis model. The main

modification of this model has been through Harris and Todaro (1970), who pointed out that the transfer of the labour surplus from rural to urban sectors could lead to urban unemployment and the development of an urban 'informal sector' rather than a reduction in wages in the capitalist sector to subsistence level.

The concept of the dual economy was originally developed by Boeke (1953), to describe the coexistence of modern and traditional sectors in a colonial economy. The term dual (or more frequently dualistic) economy is now applied more broadly to the coexistence of rich and poor sectors (either rich and poor countries in the global economy or rich and poor people in the national economy), where there is often a tendency for the 'rich to become richer, while the poor remain poor or become poorer'. For a discussion and literature survey of the concept in this broader sense see Singer (1970).

H. W. Singer
University of Sussex

References

Boeke, J. H. (1953) *Economics and Economic Policy of Dual Societies*, New York.
Harris, J. R. and Todaro, M. P. (1970) 'Migration, unemployment and development: a two-sector analysis', *American Economic Review*.
Lewis, W. A. (1954) 'Economic development with unlimited supply of labour', *The Manchester School*.
Singer, H. W. (1970) 'Dualism revisited: a new approach to the problems of dual society in developing countries', *Journal of Development Studies* 7.

See also: economic development.

Durkheim, Emile (1858–1917)

Emile Durkheim was the founding father of academic sociology in France and the most influential early theoretician of archaic or primitive societies. A Jew from north-east France, Durkheim followed the educational and ideological path of the positivist generation of great Republican academics. He was educated at the *Ecole Normale Supérieure*, taking a teacher's degree in philosophy and a doctorate (1893). After a short period as a *lycée* teacher, he spent a year in German universities studying social theory. On his return, he was appointed the first ever lecturer in 'social science and pedagogy' in a French university, at Bordeaux (1887). In 1902 he transferred to the Sorbonne, where he held a chair for the rest of his life.

Durkheim's seminal teaching and publications, included *De la division du travail social* (1893) (*The Division of Labor in Society* 1933), *Les Règles de la méthode sociologique* (1894) (*The Rules of Sociological Method* 1938), *Le Suicide*

(1897) (*Suicide* 1952), and work on socialism, family organization, the scope and development of German social theories. He attracted a cluster of gifted young scholars – mostly philosophers but also historians, economists and jurists (including Mauss, Hubert, Simiand, Fauconnet, Richard and Bouglé) – with whom he founded the *Année Sociologique* (1898). This was an essentially critical journal intended to cover the whole range of emerging social disciplines (social geography, demography, collective psychology, social and economic history, history of religion, ethnology and sociology proper). It was to become instrumental in developing and promoting a synthetic theory of social facts which overrode earlier disciplinary divisions.

Durkheim's later work included studies and lecture courses on the sociology of education, morality and moral science, pragmatism, family sociology, history of the social sciences, vital statistics and several other topics, but after the birth of the *Année* he was primarily concerned with the study of archaic societies, and especially with primitive religion and social organization. The problem of social cohesion in so-called polysegmentary societies which, according to Durkheim, were based on mechanical solidarity (as against the organic solidarity of modern societies, based on a division of labour) had been a major theme in his doctoral thesis (1893), but there it lacked any significant ethnological underpinning. Durkheim developed an intense interest in primitive society much later, after reading contemporary British 'religious anthropologists', above all, Robertson Smith and Frazer. This resulted in a reorientation of his work towards the study of 'collective representations' and, more specifically, of religion, from 1896 onwards.

There were two sets of reasons, theoretical and methodological, for this shift. First, religion was considered to serve an essential social function, creating a strong community of beliefs and providing a basis for social cohesion. The sacred and the profane became the two essential categories in Durkheim's sociology, which ordered the system of social facts. Second, primitive religion, either because it was believed to be more simple and consequently easier to study, or because it appeared to be functionally interconnected with most other 'social facts' (like economy, law, technology and so on, which had gained a measure of functional autonomy in the course of later development) seemed to provide the key to a theory of social order. The religious system of archaic societies thus became a privileged topic of research for Durkheim and some of the most gifted scholars of his cluster, notably Mauss, Hubert and Hertz. One out of four review articles published in the *Année* was dedicated to social anthropology, and primitive societies now supplied, for the first time in French intellectual history, a central topic in public philosophical debate, which soon engaged other leading academics (like Bergson and Lévy-Bruhl) as well.

In his anthropological work, Durkheim never surmounted the basic ambiguity of his approach to 'primitives', who were regarded either as prototypes, or as exemplifying the simplest imaginable occurrences of observable social types, or both at the same time. Moreover, he was initially sceptical about the heuristic utility of ethnographic data, and believed that preference should be given to historical documents over ethnographic information. His attitude changed, however, especially with the publication of more professional ethnographies, like Spencer and Gillen (on the Australian aborigines), Boas (on the Kwakiutl Indians) and the Cambridge scholars of the expedition to Torres Straits. He discussed all these new studies in painstakingly detailed critical reviews. They also supplied the data for his own contributions in the contemporary international debate concerning archaic societies. These fall broadly under two thematic headings: social organization and belief systems (and various combinations of the two).

The essay on 'La Prohibition de l'inceste et ses origines' (1898) (*Incest: The Nature and Origin of the Taboo*, 1963) obeyed to the letter his own prescription, 'Explain the social fact by other social facts'. Social institutions could not be explained by invoking instinctive behaviour. They must be accounted for purely in terms of social causes. Incest and exogamy derived from the nature of the elementary, that is, uterine, clan. Respect for the clan's totem manifested itself by a religious aversion to the blood of fellow clanspeople and, by extension, to sexual contact with the clan's women. The prohibition of incest was accompanied by prescriptions concerning interclan marriage. Some modern writers on kinship (for example, Lévi-Strauss 1949) recognize their debt to Durkheim, though they have submitted his theory to substantial criticism. Similarly, in his essays on totemism (1902) and Australian kinship (1905a), Durkheim seemed clearly to anticipate much later structuralist approaches. He identified, beyond the social categories of kinship, truly logical categories which, he suggested, could be understood as 'mathematical problems' (Durkheim 1905a). He went further in the exploration of such logical categories in a famous study, written together with Mauss, 'De quelques formes primitives de classification: contribution à l'étude des représentations collectives' (1903) (*Primitive Classification* 1963). This essay related ideas about space among some Australian and North-American tribesmen to their social organizations. Durkheim and Mauss argued that men 'classified things because they were divided into clans'. The model of all classification (especially of spatial orientation) is the society, because it is the unique whole (or totality) to which everything is related, so that 'the classification of things reproduces the classification of men'. Primitive classifications generated the first concepts or categories, enabling men to unify their knowledge. They constituted the first 'philosophy of nature'. Durkheim and Mauss suggested that in these classifications could be discerned 'the origins of logical procedure which is the basis of scientific classifications'. Durkheim would systematize these intimations in his last great work which focused on the social functions of religion proper.

Les Formes élémentaires de la vie religieuse (1912) (*The Elementary Forms of Religious Life*, 1915) was the culmination of Durkheim's anthropological studies. His focus upon Australians (and to some extent on American Indians) was grounded on the methodologically essential (and still ambiguous) assumption that their clan system was the most 'elementary' observable. The elementary religion is that of totemic clans. It contains the germ of all essential elements of religious thought and life.

Durkheim starts from the proposition that religious experience cannot be purely illusory and must refer to some reality. The reality underlying religious practice is society itself. Religion is 'above all a system of ideas by which individuals represent the society they belong to'. Moreover, 'metaphorical and symbolic as it may be, this representation is not unfaithful'. Certain types of 'collective effervescence' produce religious beliefs, or help to reconfirm beliefs and values of religious relevance. The type of religion is also determined by social structure. For example, the cult of the 'great god' corresponds to the synthesis of all totems and to the unification of the tribe.

Religion also helps to interpret or represent social realities by means of their projection in a special symbolic language. Thus, mythologies 'connect things in order to fix their internal relations, to classify and to systematize them'. They represent reality, as does science. The function of religion is ultimately social integration, which is effected by 'constantly producing and reproducing the soul of the collectivity and of individuals'. Symbolism is the very condition of social life, since it helps social communication to become communion, that is, 'the fusion of all particular sentiments into one common sentiment'.

Durkheim's religious anthropology has been severely criticized by field researchers, yet without ceasing to inspire scholars concerned with archaic religions. At the time, his sociology of religion had an immediate public appeal in consequence of the conflict then raging between the Church and the Republican State.

The study of primitive religion allowed Durkheim to adopt a purely scientific posture, while offering an historical criticism and a sociological evaluation of contemporary religious institutions. (He once described the Catholic Church as a 'sociological monster' (1905b).)

Ethnographic evidence drawn from primitive societies also led to heuristic generalizations concerning the nature of social cohesion, its agents and conditions. Ethnology, moreover, lent itself more easily than other established disciplines (like history or geography) to Durkheimian theorizing, because it was an intellectually weak and institutionally marginal branch of study (see Karady 1981). Durkheim's theoretical anthropology, together with the work of his followers and debating partners (such as Lévy-Bruhl, Mauss, Hubert and Hertz) contributed decisively to the birth of French academic field anthropology between the two world wars. A later generation of French anthropologists, including Griaule, Métraux, Dumont and Lévi-Strauss, continued to exploit Durkheim's heritage, while critically re-evaluating it. As a consequence of its Durkheimian roots, French social anthropology never broke with the other social sciences, and retained a penchant for high-level generalization.

Victor Karady
Centre National de la Recherche Scientifique

References

Durkheim, E. (1902) 'Sur le totémism', *L'Année Sociologique* 5.
—— (1905a) 'Sur l'organisation matrimoniale des sociétés australiennes', *L'Année Sociologique* 8.
—— (1905b) 'Conséquences religieuses de la séparation de l'Eglise et de l'Etat', republished in E. Durkheim (1975) *Textes*, Paris.
Karady, V. (1981) 'French ethnology and the Durkheimian breakthrough', *Journal of the Anthropological Society of Oxford* 12.
Lévi-Strauss, C. (1949) *Les Structures élémentaires de la parenté*, Paris. (English edn, *The Elementary Structures of Kinship*, London, 1969.)

Further reading

Besnard, P. (ed.) (1983) *The Sociological Domain: The Durkheimians and the Founding of French Sociology*, Cambridge, UK.
Lukes, S. (1972) *Emile Durkheim: His Life and Work. A Historical and Critical Study*, London.
Pickering, W. S. F. (ed.) (1975) *Durkheim on Religion: A Selection of Readings with Bibliographies and Introductory Remarks*, London.

See also: Annales School; social structure and structuration.

E

eating disorders

The term eating disorder is used in psychiatry to denote two closely related syndromes, anorexia nervosa and bulimia nervosa (and their variants). The central feature of these disorders is a set of characteristic beliefs and values concerning the pre-eminence of body shape and weight in self-evaluation. These beliefs and values, which are extreme in form, drive much of the disturbed behaviour in people suffering from these disorders, such as the pursuit of thinness in anorexia nervosa and the extreme methods of compensating for overeating in bulimia nervosa.

Epidemiology

Anorexia nervosa is a disorder mainly affecting young women in economically developed countries. The typical age of onset is 14 to 16 years, although childhood onset is well recognized and may be increasing (Lask and Bryant-Waugh 1992). The community studies of prevalence suggest that around 1 per cent of the at-risk population (i.e. young women) have the disorder. Case register studies have revealed a marked rise in the number of cases of anorexia nervosa coming to specialist attention. Thus, in Rochester (Minnesota) over the 50-year period from 1935 to 1984 the rate among young women rose from 7.0 to 26.3 per 100,000 person years (Lucas *et al.* 1991). There is a definite possibility that these findings reflect a true increase in the incidence of the disorder.

Bulimia nervosa was first described as a distinct syndrome in 1979 (Russell 1979). The disorder is almost exclusively found in women with a wide age range affected. The consensus is that 1–2 per cent of young women fulfil strict diagnostic criteria for bulimia nervosa with a greater number suffering from variants of the disorder (Fairburn and Beglin 1991).

Clinical features

People with anorexia nervosa markedly restrict their food intake, typically by adhering to a low carbohydrate diet. There is an associated preoccupation with food and eating. About half alternate between periods of marked restriction and bulimic episodes. Vomiting and laxative abuse are common. People with anorexia nervosa often deny that they have any problems and frequently insist, despite their emaciated state, that they are fat.

The profound weight loss in anorexia nervosa has a number of adverse effects on physical health (Mitchell 1986), such as amenorrhoea, low body temperature, low blood pressure and rapid heart beat. Starvation carries a marked risk of numerous complications including osteoporosis, liver function abnormalities and impaired cardiac function, as well as adverse psychological effects, including concentration impairment, irritability and depression.

The striking clinical feature in bulimia nervosa is the grossly disturbed eating habits, particularly the bulimic episodes. These are episodes of gross overeating which are experienced as occurring outside of voluntary control. They can occur many times a day. Bulimic episodes are fairly uniform in character: the eating is invariably carried out in secret with the food usually eaten quickly with little attention paid to taste; and the food eaten is typically those items the person is at other times attempting to avoid. Body weight tends to remain within the normal range, reflecting a balance between the episodes of overeating and various compensatory behaviours designed to counteract the effects of bulimic episodes. The most common method is self-induced vomiting which frequently terminates bulimic episodes. Purgatives are also used, sometimes in considerable quantities, as is exercise and further efforts at dietary restriction. People with bulimia nervosa have concerns about their body weight and shape similar to those found in people with anorexia nervosa. They tend to overestimate their own body size and persistently feel fat. Symptoms of depression and anxiety are marked in these people, and suicidal ideas and acts not uncommon.

Aetiology and maintenance

The aetiology of eating disorders is poorly understood, but it is widely accepted that a combination of biological, psychological and social factors are implicated. The relevant aetiological factors can be divided into those which predispose, those which precipitate and those which maintain the disorder.

Predisposing factors

Being a young woman in an economically developed country is a clear risk factor for eating disorders, presumably because of the social pressures to be slim. Eating disorders run in families. This is consistent with both a genetic and an environmental explanatory account. There is little firm evidence that a particular family environment is pathogenic, but this may be because the critical prospective comparative work has not been conducted. Twin studies suggest a genetic contribution to aetiology. A family history of obesity and of affective disorder have also been found to be important. While childhood sexual abuse is raised in people with eating disorders compared to psychiatrically well controls, the rate is no higher than in those with other psychiatric disorders. Finally, a history of anorexia nervosa is a definite predisposing factor for the development of bulimia nervosa.

Precipitating factors

The onset of eating disorders is often (though not always) preceded by a significant life event, but there appears to be no specificity in the form of such events. Loss of control over eating of the form seen in bulimia nervosa is almost invariably preceded by a period of dietary restriction. Such dieting itself may be preceded by teasing or adverse comments about the person's appearance.

Maintaining factors

Two consequences of weight loss are important in the maintenance of anorexia nervosa. First, the sense of achievement and the associated boost in self-confidence is often a spur to further dieting. Second, when the weight loss is extreme certain starvation effects serve to perpetuate dietary restriction: depressive symptoms lower self-esteem which encourages further dieting; and slow gastric emptying, by heightening the sense of fullness following eating, is a disincentive to eat. In bulimia nervosa the disturbed behaviours and cognitions drive each other in a vicious circle: concerns about weight and shape provoke dieting; dieting leads to lapses and overeating; overeating provokes further concerns about weight and shape and leads to vomiting and further dietary restriction; and this in turn leads to further overeating. This cycle can maintain itself without interruption for many years.

Treatment

There has been little systematic research into the treatment of anorexia nervosa. The mainstay of treatment has been hospitalization and nursing care, involving the refeeding of patients together with nutritional education in the context of emotional support (Russell 1970). The short-term results of such an approach are good with most patients being restored to a healthy body weight within three or four months. Day-patient treatment programmes have been described and encouraging results reported (Piran and Kaplan 1990). An impressive improvement to the general management of anorexia nervosa has been reported in controlled research by adding family therapy to post-hospital care (Russell et al. 1987).

There has been a considerable amount of controlled research into both the pharmacological and the psychological treatment of bulimia nervosa (Fairburn et al. 1992). It has become clear that, although a modest antibulimic effect is achieved with antidepressant medication, the clinical benefits are generally not maintained with patients relapsing whether or not they persist with the treatment. Far better results have been obtained using psychological treatments. There is some support for the use of a focal psychotherapy, but most of the research concerns the use of cognitive behaviour therapy (Fairburn and Cooper 1989). Excellent results have been found using this treatment with improvements well maintained (Fairburn et al. 1992). This cognitive behaviour therapy for bulimia nervosa has been produced in a self-help format (Cooper 1995) and good results have been reported.

Outcome

Studies of the outcome of patients with anorexia nervosa have revealed high rates of persisting disturbance (Ratnasuria et al. 1991). The mortality rate appears to be around 15 per cent with the most common cause of death being suicide (Hsu 1990). The outcome of less severe cases of the disorder is unknown but likely to be considerably more favourable.

Few studies of the outcome of bulimia nervosa have been reported. Although there have been no natural history studies it appears that without treatment the disorder runs a chronic course. Follow-up of patients who have received cognitive behaviour therapy has revealed a favourable prognosis for the great majority.

Peter J. Cooper
University of Reading

References

Cooper, P. J. (1995) *Bulimia Nervosa: A Guide to Recovery*, London.

Fairburn, C. G. and Beglin, S. (1991) 'Studies of the epidemiology of bulimia nervosa', *American Journal of Psychiatry* 147.

Fairburn, C. G. and Cooper, P. J. (1989) 'Cognitive behaviour therapy for eating disorders', in K. Hawton, P. Salkovskis, J. Kirk and D. M. Clark (eds) *Cognitive-Behavioural Approaches to Adult Psychiatric Disorders: A Practical Guide*, Oxford.

Fairburn, C. G., Agras, W. S. and Wilson, G. T. (1992) 'The research on the treatment of bulimia nervosa', in G. H. Anderson and S. H. Kennedy (eds) *The Biology of Feast and Famine: Relevance to Eating Disorders*, New York.

Hsu, L. K. (1990) *Eating Disorders*, New York.

Lask, B. and Bryant-Waugh, R. (1992) 'Childhood onset anorexia nervosa and related eating disorders', *Journal of Child Psychology and Psychiatry* 3.

Lucas, A. R., Beard, C. M., O'Fallon, W. M. and Kurkland, L. T. (1991) '50-year trends in the incidence of anorexia nervosa in Rochester, Minneapolis: a population based study', *American Journal of Psychiatry* 148.

Mitchell, J. E. (1986) 'Anorexia nervosa: medical and physiological aspects', in K. D. Brownell and J. P. Foreyt (eds) *Handbook of Eating Disorders: Physiology, Psychology and Treatment of Obesity, Anorexia and Bulimia*, New York.

Piran, N. and Kaplan, A. S. (1990) *A Day Hospital Group Treatment Program for Anorexia Nervosa and Bulimia Nervosa*, New York.

Ratnasuria, R. H., Eisler, I., Szmukler, G. and Russell, G. F. M. (1991) 'Anorexia nervosa: outcome and prognostic factors after 20 years', *British Journal of Psychiatry* 158.

Russell, G. F. M. (1970) 'Anorexia nervosa: its identity as an illness and its treatment', in J. H. Price (ed.) *Modern Trends in Psychological Medicine*, London.

—— (1979) 'Bulimia nervosa: an ominous variant of anorexia nervosa', *Psychological Medicine* 9.

Russell, G. F. M., Szmukler, G., Dare, C. and Eisler, I. (1987) 'An evaluation of family therapy in anorexia nervosa and bulimia nervosa', *Archives of General Psychiatry* 44.

Further reading

Brownell, K. D. and Foreyt, J. P. (eds) (1986) *Handbook of Eating Disorders: Physiology, Psychology and Treatment of Obesity, Anorexia and Bulimia*, New York.

Fairburn, C. G. and Wilson, G. T. (eds) (1993) *Binge Eating: Nature, Assessment and Treatment*, New York.

Hsu, L. K. (1990) *Eating Disorders*, New York.

ecology

The concept of ecology finds its immediate historical origins in Darwin's 'web of life', although such a non-Aristotelian view of the relationship between entities had been increasingly common since the eighteenth century. The term itself (*ökologie*) we owe to Ernst Haeckel (1834–1919). By the opening years of the twentieth century, crude generalizations and theory had been translated into empirical studies, beginning with the natural history of plants.

Ecology might briefly be described as the study of relations between living species, associations of different species, and their physical and biotic surroundings through the exchange of calories, material and information. As such it has been centrally concerned with the concept of adaptation and with all properties having a direct and measurable effect on the demography, development, behaviour and spatio-temporal position of an organism. Within this framework, the main preoccupations of contemporary biological ecology have been with population dynamics, energy transfer, systems modelling, nutrient cycles, environmental degradation and conservation; and, since the 1970s, especially with the application of neo-Darwinian thinking to socio-ecology.

In the social sciences, the concept of ecology in the strict sense was introduced first into human geography, via biogeography, and many geographers soon came to redefine their subject in explicitly ecological terms. By the 1930s, the Chicago school of urban sociology under the tutelage of R. E. Park and E. W. Burgess was describing its conceptual baggage as human ecology. Such an epithet was claimed to be justified on the grounds that analogies were drawn directly from the biological lexicon to explain spatial relationships, such as 'succession' for the movement of different class groups through urban areas. For a short time Chicago ecology was extremely influential, but it finally floundered on its own naïve analogies, crude empiricism and functionalist inductivism.

A number of the most fruitful applications of ecological approaches in the human and social sciences have been associated with anthropology. This has been so despite the dual intellectual dominance of Emile Durkheim (1858–1917) and Franz Boas (1858–1942) during the first three decades of the twentieth century, which had thoroughly crushed a nineteenth-century concern with environmental determinism. But although environmental issues were considered for the most part peripheral, and the environment accorded a constraining rather than a determinant role, there have been a number of important studies dealing with environmental interactions in this tradition. Boas's (1888) own work on the central Eskimo might be mentioned, as well as that of Mauss and Beuchat (1979) on the same subject. The general theoretical position is set out clearly in Daryll Forde's (1934) *Habitat, Economy and Society*.

The first really explicit use of the concept of ecology in anthropology is found in the work of Julian Steward during the 1930s (Steward and Murphy 1977). In Steward's theory the concept of cultural adaptation becomes paramount, and the key adaptive strategies of a particular culture are located in an infrastructural core of social institutions and technical arrangements directly concerned with food-getting activities. The recognition of distinctive adaptive strategies provided the basis for the delineation of cultural types, which Steward maintained evolved multilineally, rather than in the unilinear fashion subscribed to by many nineteenth-century thinkers. Steward's work has been very influential (and has found admirers in other disciplines), but his theory of cultural ecology entailed an interpretation of the concept of adaptation, together with a fundamental division between organic and super-organic levels of explanation, and between a core of key adaptive traits and a neutral periphery, which more recent writers (Ellen 1982) have been inclined to reject.

Advances within biological ecology linked to the notion of ecosystem, the empirical measurement of energy flow and the employment of the language of cybernetics and systems theory, led during the 1960s to a new formulation of ecological problems in the social sciences: in archaeology, geography, and also in anthropology. The prominence given by Steward to the superorganic level of organization was passed over in favour of a view of human behaviour in many respects functionally equivalent to that of other animals. The description of ecological interactions became more sophisticated, involving computations of carrying-capacity, estimates of energy intake, output and efficiency for different groups and activities. There also developed an interest in the way in which cultural institutions might serve to regulate certain systems of which human populations are part. All of these trends are demonstrated in the seminal work of Rappaport (1968), undertaken on a Maring clan from Highland New Guinea.

Sustained interest in the theoretical problems of systems approaches, plus an increasing number of detailed empirical analyses of particular cases, has, however, bred scepticism concerning simplistic notions of adaptation and system, and the more extreme proposition that certain kinds of small-scale society have built-in mechanisms for maintaining environmental balance through homeostasis (Ellen, 1982; Moran, 1990). Recent work has emphasised much more how people actually cope with environmental hazards (Vayda and McCay, 1975), employing the methods of economic individualism and, in the case of optimal foraging theory, evolutionary ecology (Winterhalder and Smith, 1981). This trend has been countered in the work of Ingold (1986) who has explicitly attempted to disaggregate post-Stewardian general ecology, and who speaks instead of humans being simultaneously involved in a field of ecological relations and a field of consciousness which cannot be reduced to adaptionist or other Darwinian explanations. There has been a general rekindling of interest in the evolution of social and ecological systems (Ingold, 1980), focusing on positive (rather than negative) feedback, and moving towards more explicitly historical approaches. Work in this latter area has drawn in particular on historical demography and on the French Annales school (Viazzo, 1989).

The other major impact of ecological concepts in the social sciences has been in relation to political environmentalism, and to environment and development. Under the guidance of figures such as Garrett Hardin and Kenneth Boulding, economic thinking has been placed in a broader biospheric context, and the 'growth model' rejected both in relation to advanced industrial and developing societies. Practical concern for environmental degradation, the profligate use of finite resources, the calculated advantages of 'alternative' technologies and worries for biodiversity conservation have spawned theories of sustainable development (Oldfield and Alcorn 1991; Redclift 1989). Some writing in this vein is distinctively utopian, some is concerned with practical matters of implementing specific controls; some seeks to modify the existing world-system though retaining capitalist relations of production, others a rapprochement between Marxism and environmentalism (see Redclift 1984). Increasing attention is also being paid to the cultural construction of nature (Croll and Parkin 1992), indigenous technical knowledge (e.g. Richards 1986), the management of collectively owned resources (McCay and Acheson 1987), and environmental history (Crosby 1986).

R. F. Ellen
University of Kent

References

Bennett, J. W. (1976) *The Ecological Transition: Cultural Anthropology and Human Adaptation*, New York.

Boas, F. (1888) *The Central Eskimo*, Washington, DC.

Croll, E. and Parkin, D. (eds) (1992) *Bush Base: Forest Farm: Culture, Environment and Development*, London.

Crosby, A. W. (1986) *Ecological Imperialism: The Biological Expansion of Europe, 900–1900*, Cambridge, UK.

Ellen, R. F. (1982) *Environment, Subsistence and System: The Ecology of Small-Scale Formations*, Cambridge, UK.

Forde, C. D. (1934) *Habitat, Economy and Society*, London.

Ingold, T. (1980) *Hunters, Pastoralists and Ranchers: Reindeer Economies and their Transformation*, Cambridge, UK.

— (1986) *The Appropriation of Nature: Essays on Human Ecology and Social Relations*, Manchester.

McCay, B. M. and Acheson, J. M. (eds) (1987) *The Question of the Commons: The Culture and Ecology of Communal Resources*, Tucson, AZ.

Mauss, M. and Beuchat, H. (1979) *Seasonal Variations of the Eskimo*, London.

Moran, E. F. (ed.) (1990) *The Ecosystem Approach in Anthropology: From Concept to Practice*, Ann Arbor, MI.

Oldfield, M. L. and Alcorn, J. (eds) (1991) *Biodiversity: Culture, Conservation and Ecodevelopment*, Boulder, CO.

Rappaport, R. A. (1968) *Pigs for the Ancestors: Ritual in the Ecology of a New Guinea People*, New Haven, CT. New edition 1984.

Redclift, M. (1984) *Development and the Environmental Crisis: Red or Green Alternatives*, London.

— (1989) *Sustainable Development: Exploring the Contradictions*, London.

Richards, P. (1986) *Coping with Hunger: Hazard and Experiment in an African Rice-Farming System*, London.

Steward, J. and Murphy, R. F. (1977) *Evolution and Ecology*, Urbana, IL.

Vayda, A. P. and McCay, B. J. (1975) 'New directions in ecology and ecological anthropology', *Annual Review of Anthropology* 4.

Viazzo, P. P. (1989) *Upland Communities: Environment, Populations, and Social Structure in the Alps since the Sixteenth Century*, Cambridge, UK.

Winterhalder, B. and Smith, E. A. (eds) (1981) *Hunter-Gatherer Foraging Strategies: Ethnographic and Archaeological Strategies*, Chicago.

See also: environment; population and resources.

econometrics

As the main concern of economics has shifted away from description and institutional analysis, economists have sought to quantify the relationships underpinning their models more precisely. In part this concern has been prompted by the desire to forecast the future behaviour of economic variables – for example, the response of aggregate consumption expenditure to changes in disposable income, or the effect of income tax changes on labour supply and the willingness of individuals to participate in the labour market. For such quantitative forecasts to have any value, it is essential that the empirical relationships on which the predictions rest should be relatively stable, both in terms of their structural characteristics and their coefficient values. It is less important that the empirical relationships should conform to the specification of a fully articulated economic model of the phenomenon under consideration, since, in practice, 'naïve' models may yield good forecasts and it may be quite impossible to observe the variables or to estimate the parameters in an elaborate model. There is, however, another reason for quantifying economic relationships which necessarily implies that careful model specification is essential if the resulting empirical estimates are to be of any value. This arises when the economist wishes to use the estimates to test hypotheses about the relative importance of different factors or economic variables which simultaneously determine some particular aspect of economic behaviour.

These distinct uses of quantitative economic relationships – i.e. forecasting and the investigation of economic hypotheses – have meant that econometrics, which is the branch of economics and statistics devoted to the empirical estimation of economic models, has developed in a number of quite separate directions. This tendency has been encouraged by the nature of the data available to econometricians. Much of classical statistical theory was developed for the purpose of making inferences from data collected in controlled experiments, typically involving some kind of randomized design in which all combinations of variables have an equal – or, at least, a known – probability of occurring. Economists must be satisfied either with time-series data produced by governments or other bodies, or with responses to sample surveys of a cross-section of the population during some period of time. Because their data is not experimentally generated, econometricians have been obliged to develop special techniques to deal with the characteristics of different types of data. For example, the user of aggregate time-series data must always check for the possibility that the errors about a particular equation are systematically correlated over time – this is called serial correlation. For the user of cross-section data, there is the consistent problem that the sample of observations may be non-random because, for example, self-selection means that certain types of individuals either refused to answer the questions or were excluded from the sample.

These and many other similar considerations mean that it is never simple to interpret data concerning economic relationships. Since the classical statistical assumptions rarely hold, econometricians are unable to separate questions concerning the validity of their statistical assumptions from issues relating to the specification of the model which they are estimating. As a result, the progress of empirical economic work has been characterized by interlocking disputes about econometric methodology and the relevance of the equations modelling aspects of economic behaviour. This means that it is often difficult to set up decisive econometric tests of particular hypotheses, especially as the underlying theoretical models may be specified in terms of variables which can, at best, only be approximately measured in practice. Nonetheless, econometric work has frequently prompted economists to reformulate or extend their models, either because the estimated equations had a poor forecasting record or because their explanatory power was rather low.

Historically, the development of econometric techniques has run parallel with changes in the availability of economic data and in the amount of computing power. Econometrics began to establish itself as a distinct discipline in the late 1920s and early 1930s – the Econometric Society was founded in 1931 with help from Alfred Cowles who was interested in forecasting stock market price movements – but it grew most rapidly in the years after the Second World War. This was because the political commitment to full employment using Keynesian policies prompted governments to monitor macroeconomic developments much more closely. The availability of time-series data on aggregate economic variables, and interest in forecasting aggregate demand encouraged econometric work on the relationships which comprise a simple Keynesian model of the economy. Two elements of such a model attracted particular attention: the consumption function in which consumption (or saving) is linked to disposable income, and the investment function which expresses aggregate investment in terms of the growth of aggregate demand (or production), interest rates, and other variables. While there are a number of competing formulations of the consumption function, econometric work on this has always appeared to be much more successful than that dealing with the investment function. It was found to be very difficult to forecast aggregate investment reliably, and estimated relationships differ significantly between time periods so that even though work has continued since the early 1950s there is no general agreement on the best specification for this relationship.

Interest in making forecasts of individual components of effective demand gradually evolved into the estimation of large macroeconometric models designed to forecast the overall macroeconomic behaviour of particular economies, as well as to investigate the implications of changes in aggregate variables for specific sectors of the economy or categories of expenditure. Work of this kind was initiated by Klein in the early 1950s (e.g. Klein and Goldberger 1955), but by the late 1960s advances in data and computing power had allowed econometricians to compile and simulate large-scale macroeconometric models. Despite considerable scepticism about the reliability of the forecasts produced by these models, their use has become an indispensable part of the process of making macroeconomic policy in all developed countries, so that argument tends now to revolve around the merits of competing models rather than about the value of making such forecasts. As macroeconomic models have become larger and more specialized, it has also become increasingly difficult to understand the factors which determine the way in which they behave as a whole. Hence, during the 1970s, econometricians started to focus more on the properties of complete models rather than on the performance of individual equations within the model.

Another application of econometrics that has been developing since the 1950s combines the interest in forecasting with the scope provided by econometric models for testing propositions derived from theoretical models. This is the estimation of single, or systems of, demand equations using either aggregate data on prices and consumption patterns or information collected in surveys of household expenditure. Initially, the main purpose of this work was to estimate income and price elasticities of demand for specific goods. This remains an important consideration, but theoretical work on consumer behaviour has shown that, if consumer expenditure decisions are derived from some kind of maximizing model, it is necessary to impose quite stringent conditions on the specification and parameter values of systems of demand equations. These restrictions include homogeneity in income and prices, symmetry of cross-price effects, and negative substitution effects. The results of testing these restrictions illustrate the difficulties of using econometric work to test theoretical models. Most studies have found that some or all of these restrictions are rejected by the data, but the response of economists has not been to discard the maximizing model of consumer behaviour but rather to investigate more elaborate specifications of the demand equations until the restrictions are not rejected. It is never possible to test the general restrictions implied by theoretical analysis except by adopting specific functional forms for the equations under investigation, so that statistical evidence against some hypothesis may be interpreted as implying either that the functional specification is inadequate, or that the basic theoretical model is wrong. In cases such as demand analysis, where the underlying theory is highly developed, econometricians have inevitably tended to regard their results as tests of specification rather than of general theoretical propositions. Only by the accumulation of negative evidence for a wide range of specifications is it possible to regard such work as undermining prior theoretical assumptions.

The availability of large-scale cross-section surveys – and of panel data sets in which individuals/households are interviewed at regular intervals over a period of years – has prompted the recent development of econometric techniques to deal with qualitative or limited dependent variables. These are variables which take on discrete values – e.g. 0 or 1 corresponding to 'no' or 'yes' responses to certain choices – or for which the range of permissible values is limited – e.g. it is not possible to work for a negative number of hours. The estimation of such microeconometric models is typically much more expensive than for classical regression models, and in most cases the amount of data to be handled is many times greater than for macroeconometric work. Hence, this work would have been impossible without the great improvements in computer hardware and software since the late 1960s. The principal applications of these techniques have been in the area of labour economics to the analysis of choices concerning labour supply and participation, education, job movement, retirement and migration. The results of this work have generated much interest among economists working on other topics, so that the range of applications may be expected to continue to increase rapidly as also will the techniques of analysis and estimation.

Econometrics has developed to the extent that it dominates applied work in most branches of economics. Indeed, even economic historians use econometric analysis – often under the title 'cliometrics' – in discussing issues such as the impact of railways on US or British economic growth, and of technical change in both agriculture and industry. The major improvements in the volume and quality of economic statistics and in the availability of large-scale sample surveys which stimulated many econometric developments during the period 1950–80 are not likely to be repeated. Thus, future developments in the subject will necessarily focus on methods of extracting more information from the data which are available. In practice, this will mean that applied economists and econometricians will have to devote more attention to the theoretical and statistical specification of their models in order to clarify the assumptions underpinning tests of particular hypotheses. Fortunately, the speed of technical change in computing is such that the cost of investigating more complex models, which has been prohibitive in the past, will not be a significant consideration in the future.

Gordon Hughes
University of Cambridge

Reference

Klein, L. R. and Goldberger, A. S. (1955) *An Econometric Model of the US 1929–1952*, Amsterdam.

Further reading

Griliches, Z. (1983) *Handbook of Econometrics*, vols 1 and 3, Amsterdam.

Harvey, A. C. (1981) *The Econometric Analysis of Time Series*, Oxford.
Maddala, G. S. (1983) *Limited–Dependent and Qualitative Variables in Econometrics*, Cambridge, UK.
Pindyck, R. S. and Rubinfeld, D. (1981) *Econometric Models and Economic Forecasts*, 2nd edn, New York.

See also: cliometrics; macroeconomic policy; microeconomics.

economic anthropology

Economic anthropologists study the ways that humans maintain and express themselves through the use of material goods and services. The field includes research on technology, production, trade and consumption as well as studies of the social and ideological arrangements humans develop for their material lives. In scope, economic anthropology embraces all contemporary and past societies, but early studies were carried out in 'non-western' communities. Economic anthropologists have now turned their attention to change and to the ways that different economic forms are mixed together, especially in contexts of differences in power and assertions of ideological superiority.

Economic anthropology has both ethnographic and theoretical aspects; one challenge for its practitioners is to join the two. The field also serves as a testing ground for major theories in economics. Contemporary macroeconomics has had little sway, but microapproaches from neo-classical economics have had a marked influence, as made evident in many anthropological studies of decision making in markets, agriculture and domestic groups. Use of neo-classical theory, however, brings into play assumptions about the universal presence of human rationality, calculation and optimization; these assumptions do not always rest well with broader approaches in anthropology. For example, microeconomic theorists find that shared habits and culture are especially difficult to explain, except as illustrations of non-rational constraints on market-like behaviour.

Marxism has provided a different theoretical impetus in economic anthropology. In the 1960s and 1970s, Marxists raised important questions about the origin and use of surplus in society. Focusing on the control and use of labour, they identified several modes of production that were encountered outside the European context. In the 1980s and 1990s, Marxist influence may be seen in studies of world-systems and their connection to local contexts; in interpretations of ideologies either as reflections or forms of resistance to dominant economies; and, in research, on the ways that productive modes are now combined in larger constellations.

Karl Polanyi and his associates, who developed an institutional approach, insisted that an economy based upon markets is not universal and that material life in many other societies is embedded within social relationships, such as reciprocity and redistribution. The Polanyi school, however, received less attention than Marxism and neo-classical thought, and the perspective has not been extensively developed.

The advocates of a fourth approach, cultural economics, urge that material life itself is a human construction. Some economic anthropologists of this type have looked at consumption and exchange as expressive modes that humans use and manipulate to advantage. Others have examined the models that a people construct of their productive system and their relation to the environment. Such local models often are built by projecting images of the human body or group upon the earth, crops or natural forces. Under the umbrella of this perspective as well, anthropologists have turned their attention to western economic theories and analysed them in light of their cultural assumptions and social contexts of production. By showing how western economics uses metaphors, folk notions of the self or ideas from other fields, these anthropologists would blur the line between modern and non-modern knowledge, challenge neo-classical claims to universality, and point to a different way of studying economic systems.

Advocates of these four approaches find few points of agreement, yet the several perspectives and ethnographic reports are cross-cut by a dualism that provides coherence to the field. In all material systems, humans face the practical choice between producing for the self and producing for the other. In the first case, material activities assume a reproductive pattern, and this supports group independence. In the second case, production is set within exchange: humans trade with others to secure needed and desired things. The first form may be termed community economy, the second is market economy. Real economies are complex, shifting combinations of the two, and humans often are pulled in both directions at once.

Community economies are formed around many types of association, such as households, compound groups, lineage segments, agglomerations of kinfolk, religious sodalities and settled villages. These locally based communities often are stacked one inside another, with each undertaking distinct material functions. Holding a commons is central to community economy. Consisting of land, material resources, knowledge, and even the ancestors, the commons is what a community shares and the source of its maintenance. Loss of the commons means dissolution of the community, while fracturing mutuality and trust within the community leads to loss of its commons. Rules of inheritance, access, use and disposal determine the differential allocation of the commons among community members. For example, game caught by a hunter may be distributed so that specific animal parts go to certain positions in the hunter's community, such as a chief, mother's brother and grandmother. Members of a community economy may expect or hope to achieve adequacy or sufficiency in their material lives.

The market economy is based upon competition among buyers and sellers who exchange between themselves. Unbounded in space, these exchanges ideally occur between anonymous transactors. The goal of participation in the market is to secure a money profit which is private property. Profit may be saved, competitively displayed, or invested: accumulated profit or capital is the analogue of the community commons. For its participants, the market promises efficiency in the allocation of resources, but it never pledges adequacy in meeting the needs of all.

Many of the economies that anthropologists once studied conformed rather closely to the community model. But ethnographers always found pure exchanges within them by which persons traded with anonymous others in order to secure wanted items. By contrast, in market economies today many pure exchanges are leavened with communal features that temper the competitive element, as in the cases of oligopolies, corporations, unions and households. In like manner, most theories used in economic anthropology pertain to one or the other side of the economic dualism, but usually they must be blended to make sense of practical situations. Economic anthropology suggests that the inherent tension between the two forms of material life is ever-present; this dualism, with its shifting modes of expression, will likely remain a central focus of the field.

Stephen Gudeman
University of Minnesota

Further reading

Dilley, R. (1992) *Contesting Markets*, Edinburgh.
Godelier, M. (1977) *Perspectives in Marxist Anthropology*, Cambridge, UK.
Gudeman, S. and Rivera, A. (1990) *Conversations in Colombia*, Cambridge, UK.
Polanyi, K. (1968) *Primitive, Archaic and Modern Economies*, Garden City, NY.

See also: exchange; social anthropology.

economic development

A central question in the study of economic development has turned out to be 'in what precisely does the economic development of a society consist?' For about twenty years after 1945, the accepted view was that the prolonged and steady increase of national income was an adequate indicator of economic development. This was held to be so because it was believed that such an increase could be sustained over long periods only if specific economic (and social) processes were at work.

These processes, which were supposed to be basic to development, can be briefly summarized as follows:

1 The share of investment in national expenditure rises, leading to a rise in capital stock per person employed.
2 The structure of national production changes, becoming more diversified as industry, utilities and services take a larger relative share, compared with agriculture and other forms of primary production.
3 The foreign trade sector expands relative to the whole economy, particularly as manufactured exports take a larger share in an increased export total.
4 The government budget rises relative to national income, as the government undertakes expanded commitments to construct economic and social infrastructure.

Accompanying these structural changes in the economy, major changes of social structure also occur:

5 The population expands rapidly as death rates fall in advance of birth rates. Thereafter, a demographic transition occurs in which improved living conditions in turn bring the birth rate down, to check the rate of overall population increase.
6 The population living in urban areas changes from a small minority to a large majority.
7 Literacy, skills and other forms of educational attainment are spread rapidly through the population.

This conceptualization of economic development as the interrelation of capital accumulation, industrialization, government growth, urbanization and education can still be found in many contemporary writers. It seems to make most sense when one has very long runs of historical statistics to look back over. Then the uniformities which this view implies are most likely to be visible. One doubt has always been whether generalizing retrospectively from statistics is not an ahistorical, rather than a truly historical, approach. It presupposes some theory of history which links the past to the future. The theory may not be transparent, or it may be unsubtly mechanistic and deterministic.

Another major doubt about the adequacy of the view of development described in processes 1–7 centres around the question of income distribution. If the basic development processes described above either do not

make the distribution of income more equal, or actually worsen the degree of inequality for more than a short period, some theorists would argue that economic development has not taken place. They prefer to distinguish economic growth from economic development which, by their definition, cannot leave the majority of the population as impoverished as they originally were. For them, indicators of growth and structural change must be complemented by indicators of improvement in the quality of everyday life for most people.

The latter can be of various kinds. They can focus on the availability of basic needs goods – food, shelter, clean water, clothing and household utensils. Or they can focus on life expectation tables and statistics of morbidity. The availability and cost of education opportunities are also relevant. Although the distribution of income may be a good starting-point, the distribution of entitlements (to use a concept expounded by A. K. Sen 1981) to consume of all kinds is the terminus. Similar kinds of consideration arise when one examines the role of political liberty in economic development. Is rapid growth and structural change induced by an oppressive, authoritarian regime true development? Those who object to the 'costs' of the development strategies of the former Soviet Union or the People's Republic of China do not think so. From a libertarian standpoint, they refuse to accept the standard account of economic development as sufficiently comprehensive.

The difficulty here is clearly with weighting all of the different indices involved to arrive at a single measure of the degree of development in this extended sense. Perhaps it cannot be done; and perhaps, if policy rather than international league tables is our main concern, this failure is not very important. The most familiar recent attempt in this vein is the United Nations Development Programme's *Human Development Report* series (UNDP 1990–   ).

Linked with these questions about the meaning of development is the problem of conceptualizing the process of development. Perhaps the most famous of all models of this process is the classically-based model of Sir Arthur Lewis (1954). This attempts to capture the simultaneous determination of income growth and income distribution. Its key assumptions are the availability within traditional, technologically backward agriculture of surplus population (surplus in the sense that their marginal product in agriculture is zero); and the existence of a conventional subsistence wage in the industrial sector which does not rise as the surplus agricultural population is transferred to industrial employment. The transfer of labour from agriculture to industry at a constant wage rate (which may or may not involve physical migration, but usually does) permits industrial capitalists to receive an increasing share of a rising national income as profit and to reinvest their profits in activities which progressively expand the share of industry in the national output. Thus Lewis explained what he regarded as the central puzzle of economic development, namely to understand the process which converted economies which habitually saved and invested 4–5 per cent of the national income into economies which save and invest 12–15 per cent.

The Lewis model can be elaborated to explain other stylized facts of development. If labour transfer involves physical migration, urbanization will follow. If capitalists are defined as those with an accumulation mentality (as Lewis does), they can operate in the public as well as the private sector, and expansion of the government share in national output can be understood in these terms. If industrial employment in some sense requires labour to be healthy and educated, these major social changes – including a demographic transition – may be set in train.

Much of the subsequent literature on economic development can be read as an extended commentary on the Lewis model. Neo-classical economists have criticized the assumptions of the model, questioning whether labour in the agricultural sector does have a zero marginal product, and whether labour transfer can be effected without raising the real wage rate (Lal 1983). Alternatives to the Lewis model as an account of rural–urban migration have been proposed (e.g. by Harris and Todaro 1970).

The Lewis model's sharp focus on physical capital formation has been strongly questioned. Some critics have gone so far as to deny that physical capital formation is necessary at all to economic development (e.g. Bauer 1981). A less extreme view is that human capital formation or investment in the acquisition of good health and skills is a prerequisite, rather than an inevitable consequence, of the successful operation of physical capital. A balance is therefore required between physical and human investments to ensure that an economy raises its level of technological capability in advance of a physical investment drive.

The sectoral destination of investment in the Lewis model also provoked a strong reaction. Although less narrowly focused than Dobb's model (1955) where investment priority was given to the capital goods sector of industry, the Lewis model's focus on investment in the modern industrial sector was seen as inimical to the development of agriculture, and the failure of agricultural development was increasingly identified as a cause of slow growth and income maldistribution in developing countries (as argued by Lipton 1977). The debate about sectoral investment balance has since been subsumed into the analysis of project appraisal,

as pioneered by Little and Mirrlees (1974) and others. This provides, in principle, a calculus of social profitability of projects in all sectors of the economy. It is worth noting, however, that the rationale for the social pricing of labour in the Little and Mirrlees method is based on the Lewis conception of agriculture-industry labour transfer.

The Lewis model recognized the possibilities of state capitalism as well as private capitalism. The infrequency in practice with which such potential has been realized has led to demands that governments confine themselves to their so-called 'traditional functions' and the creation of an incentive and regulatory framework for the promotion of private enterprise. This has been one of the major thrusts of the counter-revolution in development thinking and policy of the 1980s (Toye 1993).

Foreign trade plays a minor role in the Lewis model and other early models of economic development. This reflected the pessimism of many pioneers (such as Prebisch (1959) and Singer (1950) about the tendency of the terms of trade of primary commodity producers to decline. It also responded to a belief that, historically, isolation from the world economy had spurred development in Meiji Japan (Baran 1973) and Latin America in the 1930s (Frank 1969). More recently, the expansion of manufactured exports has been seen as a major element in the astonishingly successful development performances of East Asian countries like South Korea and Taiwan. Debate still rages, however, about whether this kind of trade expansion experience validates liberal trade and finance policies, or an intelligent and selective style of government intervention in these markets (as argued by Wade 1990).

The concessional transfer of finance and technical assistance from developed to developing countries fitted well with the Lewis emphasis on physical capital formation as the key to growth and income distribution. More recently, the effectiveness of aid has been questioned. Although simple supporters and enemies remain vocal, it is common now to see more clearly the complexities of the aid process, and to stress the many lessons that have been learned from hard experience to improve the likelihood of aid achieving its desired objectives (e.g. Cassen and Associates 1986; Lipton and Toye 1990).

Somewhat greater agreement exists on the facts of recent economic development than on the methods of bringing it about. That many poor countries have experienced much economic growth and structural change since 1945 is widely accepted. Few still claim that growth in developed countries systematically causes increased poverty in other, poorer countries. A weaker version of this thesis is that there is an ever-widening gap between richest and poorest, which can arise when the welfare of the poorest is constant or rising. Even this weaker version is controversial, on the grounds that countries are ranged evenly along a spectrum of wealth/poverty, and thus to split this spectrum into two groups of rich and poor in order to compare group statistics of economic performance can be somewhat arbitrary. In fact, the measured growth rates of developed and developing countries since the early 1960s show relatively small differences and ones that may well lie within the margins of error that attach to such estimates. The countries classified as developing also show increasing differentiation among themselves.

But, although the overall record of economic growth at least need not give cause for deep gloom, certain geographical regions do appear to have markedly unfavourable development prospects. Such regions include sub-Saharan Africa and parts of South Asia, and of Central and South America. The reasons for their poor prospects vary from place to place. Some are held back by severe pressure of population on cultivable land; some by inability to generate indigenous sources of appropriate technical progress; some by the persistence of intense social and political conflict; some by unenlightened policy making; and some by the continuing failure to evolve a worldwide financial system which does not tend to amplify the inherent unevenness (over place and time) of economic development.

It is also true that the rapid increase in the world's population makes it possible for the *absolute* number of people whose consumption falls below a given poverty line to increase, even when the *percentage* of the world's people who are poor on this definition is falling. This is what seems to be happening at the moment. Despite all the evidence of widespread economic development, theoretical and practical work on poverty alleviation has, therefore, a growing urgency and relevance.

John Toye
Institute of Development Studies

References

Baran, P. (1973) *The Political Economy of Growth*, Harmondsworth.

Bauer, P. T. (1981) *Equality, the Third World and Economic Delusion*, London.

Cassen, R. H. and associates (1986) *Does Aid Work?*, Oxford.

Dobb, M. (1955) *On Economic Theory and Socialism*, London.

Frank, A. G. (1969) *Latin America: Underdevelopment or Revolution?*, New York.

Harris, J. and Todaro, M. P. (1970) 'Migration, unemployment and development: a two-sector analysis', *American Economic Review* March.

Lal, D. (1983) *The Poverty of 'Development Economics'*, London.

Lewis, W. A. (1954) 'Economic development with unlimited supplies of labour', *The Manchester School* 22(2).

Lipton, M. (1977) *Why Poor People Stay Poor*, London.

Lipton, M. and Toye, J. (1990) *Does Aid Work in India?*, London.

Little, I. M. D. and Mirlees, J. A. (1974) *Project Appraisal and Planning for Developing Countries*, London.

Prebisch, R. (1959) 'Commercial policy in the underdeveloped countries', *American Economic Review* 49.

Sen, A. K. (1981) *Poverty and Famines: An Essay on Entitlement and Deprivation*, Oxford.

Singer, H. W. (1950) 'The distribution of the gains between investing and borrowing countries', *American Economic Review* 40.

Toye, J. (1993) *Dilemmas of Development: Reflections on the Counter-Revolution in Development Economics*, 2nd edn, Oxford.

United Nations Development Programme (UNDP) (1990–) *Human Development Report*, New York.

Wade, R. (1990) *Governing the Market*, Princeton, NJ.

Further reading

Kitching, G. (1982) *Development and Underdevelopment in Historical Perspective*, London.

Little, I. M. D. (1983) *Economic Development: Theory, Policy and International Relations*, New York.

See also: aid; dual economy; economic growth; industrial revolutions; modernization; technical assistance; underdevelopment.

economic dynamics

The concept of economic dynamics denotes both the movement of an economic system (or parts of it) over time, and the body of theory that provides an analytical understanding of the former type of phenomenon. The analytical representation of dynamics, that is, the identification of features giving identity to any given economic system over time, is the critical link between economic history and the theory of economic dynamics. Thus it provides a connection between the two views of economic dynamics (Baranzini and Scazzieri 1990). The consideration of change as a regular feature of modern economic systems is at least as old as the early recognition of persistent forces or repeated once-for-all impulses as a normal factor shaping the structural evolution of an economic system over time (the contributions by Adam Smith, Thomas Robert Malthus (*Essay on the Principle of Population*) and David Ricardo are instances of the former approach; Malthus's *Principles of Political Economy* are an instance of the latter approach). The recurrence of phases of contraction and expansion also received early recognition. The literature on economic crises provides an early example of the importance of the time-horizon in the analysis of economic dynamics (distinction among short, medium and long waves).

The concept of general economic crisis (Aftalion 1913; Robertson 1914; 1915; Tugan-Baranovsky

1894) is rooted in the idea that both contraction and expansion affect in due course the whole economic system, even if they would normally originate in particular subsystems (such as construction sector, machine tools sector or railways). Subsequent analysis often considered dynamic patterns relative to the whole economic system, thus overlooking a fine distinction of structural elements and dynamic factors. In this way, the attention paid to structural evolution (the change in the composition of aggregate magnitudes, or aggregate forces, as the economic system moves across time) receded into the background, and economic dynamics came to be considered as the analysis of long-run factors of change (such as capital accumulation, technical progress and population dynamics) and of their interaction. This type of investigation was often carried out on the assumption that long-run dynamic factors are constant and that the saving-investment equality is maintained throughout (steady growth under equilibrium assumption) (see Domar 1946; Harrod 1939; Kaldor 1957; Pasinetti 1962; Robinson 1956; Solow 1956; see also Baranzini 1991; Kregel 1973).

Recent work in the field of economic dynamics has pursued a number of distinct, yet interconnected, research lines. First, the interest in long-run dynamic factors has led to the consideration of learning and increasing returns as the most important endogenous phenomenon influencing economic evolution (Aghion and Howitt 1992; Romer 1986; 1990). Second, the mathematical theory of dynamic systems has been applied to the consideration of economic issues ranging from the stability of economic equilibrium (Gandolfo 1981) to cyclical patterns (Goodwin and Punzo 1987; Lucas 1987) and the emergence of new structures associated with qualitatively new features taken up by the dynamic relationships between economic variables (Anderson *et al.* 1988; Arthur *et al.* 1991a; 1991b). Third, the decomposition of economic aggregates and forces has stimulated renewed interest in the analysis of structural economic dynamics, which may be associated with the stage-structure of economic transitions (Hicks 1973; Lowe 1976; Quadrio-Curzio 1986), the long-run transformation of broad economic aggregates (Pasinetti 1981; 1993), the emergence of new and relatively persistent patterns of economic organization and their diffusion across economic sectors and over time (Landesmann and Scazzieri 1994).

Roberto Scazzieri
University of Bologna

References

Aftalion, A. (1913) *Les Crises periodiques de surproduction*, Paris.

Aghion, P. and Howitt, P. (1992) 'A model of growth through creative destruction', *Econometrica* 60.

Anderson, P. W., Arrow, K. J. and Pines, D. (eds) (1988) *The Economy as an Evolving Complex System: The Proceedings of the Evolutionary Paths of the Global Economy Workshop*, Redwood City, CA.

Arthur, B., Landesmann, M. A. and Scazzieri, R. (eds) (1991a) 'Contributions to economic dynamics', *Structural Change and Economic Dynamics* 2(1).

— (1991b) 'Dynamics and structures', *Structural Change and Economic Dynamics* 2(1).

Baranzini, M. (1991) *A Theory of Wealth Distribution and Accumulation*, Oxford.

Baranzini, M. and Scazzieri, R. (eds) (1990) *The Economic Theory of Structure and Change*, Cambridge, UK.

Domar, E. D. (1946) 'Capital expansion, rate of growth and employment', *Econometrica* 14.

Gandolfo, G. (1981) *Economic Dynamics: Methods and Models*, Amsterdam.

Goodwin, R. M. and Punzo, L. F. (1987) *The Dynamics of a Capitalist Economy. A Multi-Sectoral Approach*, Cambridge, UK.

Harrod, R. (1939) 'An essay in dynamic theory', *Economic Journal* 49.

— (1948) *Towards a Dynamic Economics: Some Recent Developments of Economic Theory and their Application to Policy*, London.

Hicks, J. (1973) *Capital and Time: A Neo-Austrian Theory*, Oxford.

Kaldor, N. (1957) 'A model of economic growth', *Economic Journal* 67.

Kregel, J. A. (1973) *The Reconstruction of Political Economy*, London.

Landesmann, M. A. and Scazzieri, R. (eds) (1994) *Production and Economic Dynamics*, Cambridge, UK.

Lowe, A. (1976) *The Path of Economic Growth*, Cambridge, UK.

Lucas, R. E. (1987) *Models of Business Cycles*, Oxford.

Pasinetti, L. L. (1962) 'The rate of profit and income distribution in relation to the rate of economic growth', *Review of Economic Studies* 29.

— (1981) *Structural Change and Economic Growth: A Theoretical Essay on the Dynamics of the Wealth of Nations*, Cambridge, UK.

— (1993) *Structural Economic Dynamics: A Theory of the Economic Consequences of Human Learning*, Cambridge, UK.

Quadrio-Curzio, A. (1986) 'Technological scarcity: an essay on production and structural change', in M. Baranzini and R. Scazzieri (eds) *Foundations of Economics: Structures of Inquiry and Economic Theory*, Oxford.

Robertson, D. H. (1914) 'Some material for a study of trade fluctuations', *Journal of the Royal Statistical Society* 77.

— (1915) *A Study of Industrial Fluctuation*, London.

Robinson, J. V. (1956) *The Accumulation of Capital*, London.

Romer, P. M. (1986) 'Increasing returns and long run growth', *Journal of Political Economy* 94.

— (1990) 'Endogenous technical change', *Journal of Political Economy* 98.

Solow, R. M. (1956) 'A contribution to the theory of economic growth', *Quarterly Journal of Economics* 70.

Tugan-Baranovsky, M. I. (1894) *Promyshlennye krizisy v sovremennoi Anglii* (*Industrial Crises in England*), St Petersburg.

Further reading

Baranzini, M. and Scazzieri, R. (1990) 'Economic structure: analytical perspectives', in M. Baranzini and R. Scazzieri (eds) *The Economic Theory of Structure and Change*, Cambridge, UK.

Eltis, W. A. (1984) *The Classical Theory of Economic Growth*, London.

Georgescu-Roegen, N. (1988) 'Closing remarks: about economic growth – a variation on a theme by David Hilbert', *Economic Development and Cultural Change* 36(3).

Hicks, J. (1985) *Methods of Economic Dynamics*, Oxford.

Schumpeter, J. A. (1912) *Theorie der wirtschaftlichen Entwicklung*, Leipzig. (English edn, *The Theory of Economic Development*, Cambridge, MA, 1934.)

Scott, F. M. (1989) *A New View of Economic Growth*, Oxford.

Solow, R. M. (1970) *Growth Theory: An Exposition*, Oxford.

See also: economic growth.

economic efficiency

In a restricted sense, economic efficiency is often taken to mean that resources or inputs should be used so as to produce an output in the cheapest possible way. It is the cost of a combination of inputs which is of interest, not the use of a single input. The economically efficient input combination is the one which yields a specified output level at the least possible cost. The use of a single input (e.g. energy) can, of course, be further reduced, but so much extra is then needed of other inputs that the total cost increases. Alternatively, one can speak of efficiency when a firm produces as much as possible (maximizes output) at a specified total cost. This illustrates the fact that the concept of efficiency is used in different production contexts. Similarly, one can speak of efficiency in consumption. Individuals who aim at achieving the highest possible level of utility, subject to their income, will allocate their income between goods in such a way that the marginal rate of substitution between any two goods (the satisfaction derived from an extra unit of the first commodity divided by the satisfaction derived from an extra unit of the second commodity) is equal to the ratio between their prices. This is the criterion for efficiency in consumption.

The concept of economic efficiency, as attributed to the Italian economist Vilfredo Pareto (1848–1923), is usually interpreted in a broader sense. Pareto specified a condition of optimal or efficient allocation of resources which is referred to as the *Pareto condition*. According to this criterion, a policy change is socially desirable if everyone is made better off by the change (the weak Pareto criterion), or at least some are made better off, while no one is made worse off (the strong Pareto criterion). When the possibilities for making such policy changes have been exhausted, society is left with an allocation of commodities that cannot be altered without someone being made worse off. Such an allocation is called *Pareto-optimal* or *efficient*.

Under certain conditions, a market economy will be Pareto efficient. The important relationship between competitive equilibria and Pareto optimality is that, when a competitive equilibrium exists, it attains Pareto optimality. This result, which is known as the *First Theorem of Welfare Economics*, provides a strong argument for the advocates of a pure market economy. The result says that the perfect market economy simultaneously yields efficiency in production and consumption.

Per-Olov Johansson
Stockholm School of Economics

Karl-Gustaf Löfgren
University of Umeå

Further reading

Johansson, P.-O. (1991) *An Introduction to Modern Welfare Economics*, Cambridge, UK.

Pareto, V. (1971) *Manual of Political Economy*, London.

Varian, H. R. (1992) *Microeconomic Analysis*, New York.

See also: Pareto efficiency; welfare economics.

economic geography

Economic geography is a sub-discipline within human geography concerned with describing and explaining the production, distribution, exchange and consumption of goods and services within an explicitly spatial economy. Economic geography was first institutionalized in the late nineteenth century, and arose in large part because of its potential contribution to European colonialism. Early economic geographers attempted to provide, first, a global inventory of tradeable resources and their conditions of production (Chisholm 1889), and, second, an intellectual justification for the marked differences in levels of economic development between colonized and colonizing countries based upon environmental determinism (Huntington 1915).

From the 1920s onwards, however, economic geographers increasingly looked inwards, and practised a regional approach that involved delineating the unique character of the economy of a given place. Employing a standardized typology, one based upon such categories as production, transportation, markets, and so on, facts were carefully compiled and organized for a particular region and then compared to those of another. By so doing, the uniqueness of place was proven.

Following the post-war enthusiasm for things scientific, economic geography's young Turks mounted a quantitative and theoretical revolution in the mid-1950s, transforming the discipline into spatial science. Initially this movement was defined by the use of a set of sophisticated parametric inferential statistical techniques, but increasingly it involved the importation of rigorous abstract theories and models drawn from at least four different sources. First, from neo-classical economics came general models of competition and rational behaviour. Second, from physics came gravity, potential and entropy models that, in turn, were used to explain patterns of spatial interaction. Third, from the recouping of a hitherto forgotten nineteenth-century German location school came a series of locational models: von Thunen's theory of agricultural location, Weber's theory of industrial location, and later, Loesch's and Christaller's central place theory. Finally, from geometry came a slew of axioms, lemmas and theorems that could be used to underpin a set of explanatory spatial morphological laws (Bunge 1962). More generally, economic geographers who prosecuted spatial science believed that an autonomous set of spatial forces regulated the geography of the economy, and that they were identifiable only by applying the scientific method.

From the mid-1970s onwards spatial science was increasingly criticized. Spatial science's main mistake was in assuming that the spatial was independent of the social. Rather, as the Marxist geographer David Harvey (1982) argued, the spatial must be conceived as thoroughly socialized by the dominant mode of production, capitalism. Under Harvey's approach, if economic geographers were to understand capitalism's changing economic landscape they needed to grasp the basic tensions within the non-spatial core of the capitalist system itself. For Harvey this was possible only by returning to Marx; in particular, by making use of Marx's idea of the 'annihilation of space by time' Harvey (1982) provided a brilliant reconstruction of capitalism's geography of accumulation.

The political economy approach that Harvey introduced into economic geography in the mid-1970s still remains the dominant paradigm. Subsequently, it has been elaborated and constructively criticized in at least five different ways, thereby defining the current agenda of the discipline.

First, in the mid-1980s Doreen Massey (1984) embellished Harvey's argument by suggesting that just as the spatial is socialized, so the social is spatialized. 'Geography matters', as she crisply put it. To show that it mattered, Massey (1984) argued that the character of a place is a result of the specific combination of past layers of investment made there. That character, however, reacts back and recursively influences the nature of yet future rounds of investment. As such, place is not passive, but an active component in the determination of the spatial division of labour. More generally, Massey's conception of the relationship between place and economy became the basis of the British 'localities project' that subsequently generated an enormous amount of research and debate within economic geography (Cooke 1989).

Second, there has been an attempt to flesh out the institutional structure that comprised Harvey's social relations. Of particular importance has been the French Regulationist school, and their twin concepts of a regime of accumulation and a mode of regulation, along with the historical instantiation of the two as Fordism and post-Fordism. These last two terms have become central to the work of economic geographers interested in contemporary industrial restructuring. The works of Allen Scott and Michael Storper (Storper and Scott 1992) are especially important, combining as they do theories of the French regulationists with detailed research on flexible production systems and industrial districts. Their post-Weberian theory, as they term it, has been especially useful in understanding the rise of both new high-tech industrial spaces, such as Silicon valley, and the renaissance of older craft centres, such as the Veneto region in Italy.

Third, following hints by Harvey, there emerged a burgeoning literature on financial services, and, more broadly, on the quaternary service sector of which they are part. Such work is often centred around corporate decision making within a broader context of globalization. The argument is that higher echelon business services (producer services), including financial ones, are concentrated in a few very large world cities, for example, London. Those centres, in turn, are linked by complex flows of information made possible by recent innovations in telecommunications. Furthermore, while such world cities are the loci of power and control within the global economy, they are also world consumption centres, spawning an urban underclass that provides many of the services necessary for that consumption to be maintained.

Fourth, stemming from Harvey's concern with the geography of accumulation, there continues work on economic development both at the regional and the international scales. At the international level, much of the emphasis has been on analysing the strategies and effects of transnational corporations, and the emergence of both a new international division of labour, and new growth complexes, particularly those in South-east and East Asia (Dicken 1992).

Finally, as a reaction to Harvey's implicit conception of the social as equivalent only to class, there have been a number of attempts to widen the discussion so as to include gender and race. Feminist economic geographers have sought both to criticize what they see as the phallocentric basis of the discipline, as well as to offer a series of case studies that demonstrate that gender matters (MacDowell 1991). Works that explicate racialization within economic geography are less numerous, but a cluster of studies exist on ethnic entrepreneurs and enclaves.

In sum, economic geography has been the great borrower, taking ideas conceived in one discipline, and refashioning them so that they are useful in understanding the economics of a *geographical* world. Such a task seems especially pertinent as that world is becoming, if not everyone's oyster, at least the oyster of capital.

Trevor Barnes
University of British Columbia

References

Bunge, W. (1962) *Theoretical Geography*, Lund.

Chisholm, G. (1889) *Handbook of Commercial Geography*, London.

Cooke, P. (1989) *Localities: The Changing Face of Urban Britain*, London.

Dicken, P. (1992) *Global Shift: The Internationalization of Economic Activities*, 2nd edn, London.

Harvey, D. (1982) *Limits to Capital*, Chicago.

Huntington, E. (1915) *Civilization and Climate*, New Haven, CT.

MacDowell, L. (1991) 'Life without father Ford: the new gender order of post-Fordism', *Transactions: Institute of British Geographers* 16.

Massey, D. (1984) *Spatial Divisions of Labour: Social Structures and the Geography of Production*, London.

Storper, M. and Scott, A. J. (eds) (1992) *Pathways to Industrialization and Regional Development*, London.

Further reading

Dicken, P. and Lloyd, P. (1990) *Location in Space: Theoretical Perspectives in Economic Geography*, 3rd edn, New York.

See also: cultural geography; energy; Fordism; social geography; transport, economics and planning.

economic growth

Economic growth is usually taken to mean the growth of the value of real income or output. The word 'real' signifies that only changes in quantities, and not changes in prices, are allowed to affect the measure. It is not equivalent to growth in welfare or happiness, although it may have important consequences for both, and there has been much debate about its benefits and costs (Beckerman 1974; Olson and Landsberg 1975). Measurable real income means, in turn, the maximum rate of measurable real consumption of goods and services that could be sustained indefinitely from the chosen point of time forward. It therefore presupposes that the costs of maintaining that rate of consumption are fully met, for example, that flocks are renewed, that roads are maintained, as also are the numbers of

people and levels of their health and education. In principle, properly measured income would be net of the costs of environmental degradation, and would allow for depletion of minerals, thus acknowledging concerns which, however, have often been exaggerated (Meadows *et al.* 1972; World Bank 1992). If income were all consumed, we would have a static economy in which all outputs would be maintained, but in which economic arrangements would be essentially unchanged.

To make the economy grow requires economic arrangements to change, and the cost of making these changes is *investment*. This can take many different forms, for example, increasing flocks, building more or better roads, making more or better machinery, educating more people, or to a higher standard, undertaking research and development, and so on. Countries will grow faster the more of their incomes they devote to investment and the more efficient that investment is. The former Soviet Union invested a large fraction of its income, but it was so inefficiently done that little benefit accrued to its people. Experience suggests that efficiency is best secured through a free market system, although there are some important large-scale investments that need to be centrally planned. In a market system, profits are important for investment for several reasons. They generally provide most of the savings and finance. High profits strengthen business confidence to undertake investment. Apart from taxation, the higher the share of profits, the lower must be the share of wages, and the stronger the incentive to employ more labour. But profits must not be the result of monopolistic agreements to raise prices and restrict output. Such agreements reduce growth, as does government protection from foreign competion.

The above emphasis on investment as the source of economic growth may seem little more than common sense. For a long time, however, economists have placed their emphasis on technical progress. This is because of the seemingly well-established empirical finding that, taken together, investment and employment growth can account for little more than one-half of the growth of many developed economies. The residual, unexplained, part of growth is then attributed to technical progress, which, according to theory, is the discovery of new ways to increase output from given inputs of labour and capital (Denison 1967; Solow 1957; and many others). Unfortunately, the residual in these studies results from the mistaken way in which the contribution of investment to growth has been estimated. In reality, this contribution has been far greater, and there is no residual to be explained (see Scott 1989; chs 1 and 3).

The earlier growth theories of Solow and others not only attributed too little growth to investment but also claimed that in the long run increasing the share of investment in output would leave the rate of growth unchanged. What mattered was technical progress, but its causes were left unexplained. Subsequently, attempts were made to explain it, usually by attributing it to some narrow category of investment such as research and development expenditure (Grossman and Helpman 1991; Romer 1990). These theories have erred in implicitly treating most investment as if it were just reduplication of existing assets. Since investment is the cost of *changing* economic arrangements, it is never mere reduplication. It is this which explains why investment opportunities are continually present, and are not steadily eliminated as they are taken up. Undertaking investment creates new opportunities as fast as it eliminates others. In the nineteenth century, for example, it was the railways and the telegraph which opened up the interior of the USA and which led to the development of much larger manufacturing and distributing enterprises able to take advantage of economies of scale and scope (Chandler 1990). Research and development are important, especially for some industries (e.g. aerospace, electronics and pharmaceuticals), but they are by no means the only important generators of investment opportunities. The fastest growing countries in the world are not those with the greatest expenditures on research and development. They are those Asian countries in which wages are low and profitability and investment are both high, as businesspeople take advantage of their ability to imitate and catch up the more developed countries in a relatively free market system. They have also benefited through a large transfer of workers from agriculture to manufacturing and other enterprises. Perhaps the chief constraint on growth in the west is the fact that a prolonged boom, which is needed to generate high rates of profit and investment, results too soon in unacceptably high rates of inflation, and leads western governments to slam on the brakes. By contrast, the Asian countries seem able to sustain their booms for much longer.

Maurice Scott
University of Oxford

References

Beckerman, W. (1974) *In Defence of Economic Growth*, London.
Chandler, A. D. with Hikimo, T. (1990) *Scale and Scope: The Dynamics of Industrial Capitalism*, Cambridge, MA.
Denison, E. F. assisted by Poullier, J.-P. (1967) *Why Growth Rates Differ*, Washington, DC.
Grossman, G. M. and Helpman, E. (1991) *Innovation and Growth in the Global Economy*, Cambridge, MA.
Meadows, D. H., Meadows, D. L., Randers, J. and Behrens III, W. W. (1972) *The Limits to Growth: A Report for the Club of Rome's Project on the Predicament of Mankind*, London.
Olson, M. and Landsberg, H. H. (eds) (1975) *The No-Growth Society*, London.
Romer, P. (1990) 'Endogenous technical change', *Journal of Political Economy* 98.
Scott, M. F. G. (1989) *A New View of Economic Growth*, Oxford.
Solow, R. M. (1957) 'Technical change and the aggregate production function', *Review of Economics and Stastics 39*.
World Bank (1992) *World Development Report 1992: Development and the Environment*, Oxford.

See also: economic development; economic dynamics; supply-side economics.

economic history

Economic history, as a combination of two disciplines, has had a rather varied evolution. Whereas in Britain and most other European countries economic history has been regarded as a separate discipline, such an academic distinction has not existed in the USA where, indicating the dual nature of the subject, economic historians can be found in either the history department or the economics department. Since the 1960s there has been a marked change in the study of economic history, first in the USA, then elsewhere, with the expansion of quantification and social-science model building, changes that have affected other sub-disciplines of history. Economic history in the USA has now become dominated by scholars trained as economists.

The definition of a field of study can be a rather uncertain thing, although there are generally two somewhat overlapping approaches to delimiting a discipline. One definition relates to the set of questions being studied. Economic history can be defined as the study of the economic aspects of the past, or as the study of the solution to the problems of the allocation and the distribution of goods and services that arise from the problem of scarcity. The second definition is based on the methods, techniques and concepts applied by scholars in studying problems. Applications of the basic tools of economics to historical problems would thus be considered to fall within the discipline. Given these two, at times inconsistent, definitions, it is sometimes difficult to be precise on the boundaries of economic history. This has become particularly so since the 1960s, where the basic concepts of economic analysis have been applied to wider sets of issues, and to problems which were until recently generally held to be outside the province of economics and of economic history.

Although the works of some earlier economists, including Smith, Steuart, and Malthus, contained historical data, the modern evolution of economic history in Britain from the latter part of the nineteenth century dates from the Irish historical economists,

Cliffe, Leslie and Ingram, and the first of the Ox-bridge economic historians, Rogers, Toynbee, and Cunningham. Toynbee's student, Ashley, who was also influenced by the German, Schmoller, came to hold the first chair in economic history in the English-speaking world, at Harvard in 1892, before returning to Britain. The first chair in economic history in Britain went to Unwin at Manchester, followed by a London School of Economics (LSE) chair to Cunningham's student, Knowles, in 1921, with chairs over the decade between 1928 and 1938 to Clapham (Cambridge), Clark (Oxford), Power (LSE), Tawney (LSE) and Postan (Cambridge). The acceptance of economic history as a field of study was marked by the founding of the Economic History Society in 1926; publication of the *Economic History Review* began in 1927.

The development of economic history in the USA lagged behind that in Britain, with more attention in the earlier part of the twentieth century given to the histories prepared for the Carnegie Institution, dealing with agriculture, manufacturing, transportation and commerce, among other issues. These scholarly writings and document collections are still central in the work of many contemporary economic historians. There was no 'historical school' in the British sense, but the American 'institutional school' filled its role as critic of economy theory and was to play a key role in influencing the study of economic history and its offshoot, business history. The latter emerged with the appointment of Gras to a chair at the Harvard Business School in 1927. Also important in influencing the development of economic history in the USA was the founding of the National Bureau of Economic Research in 1920. Among the founders was the Harvard economic and business historian, Gay, but most influential was its long-time director of research, Mitchell, and his student, Kuznets, with their emphasis on data collection and the studies of business cycles and economic growth. The Economic History Association was founded in 1940; its journal, the *Journal of Economic History* began publication in 1941. The work of most American (and British) economic historians prior to the Second World War, however, still reflected primarily the historian's orientation.

Economic history, being at the intersection of two disciplines, has often been involved in debates about methods and techniques. Before the 1960s, however, these debates were most frequently between economic historians and economists, and were concerned with the relative usefulness of abstract theory as contrasted with detailed institutional knowledge in understanding the past world and in prescribing policies for the contemporary situation. The German and English historical schools of the late nineteenth century arose primarily in reaction to what was felt to be the extreme abstractions of Austrian and Ricardian economic theory, with their extensive claims in regard to the universal applicability of economic theory as a guide to understanding past (and present) developments. Further, at this time the prescriptions of economic historians often pointed to the desirability of a wider range of state interference in the economy than was advocated by theoretical economists, a position buttressed by their claims of knowledge obtained from detailed examination of 'real' historical developments. Following Toynbee in Britain, there was often a social reform purpose central to historical studies. The classic *Methodenstreit* between Menger and Schmoller, which also raised questions about the usefulness and importance of induction and deduction as basic scientific approaches, is indicative of these debates with economists. Related points on the applicability of theoretical constructs arose in other debates between economic historians and economists, such as those at Cambridge between Marshall and Cunningham, and the 1920s series of articles, by Clapham and Pigou, on 'Empty Economic Boxes' (e.g. Clapham 1922; Pigou 1922)

There were some critiques stressing the advantages of the use of economic theory in the study of history. Heckscher's 1928 address to the International Historical Congress was not unique, nor was it the first, although it remains among the clearest examples of 'A plea for theory in economic history' (Heckscher 1929). Clapham's *Encyclopedia of the Social Sciences* essay (Clapham *et al.* 1931) sounded the call of the quantitatively oriented, with its reminder of the importance of 'the statistical sense, the habit of asking in relation to any institution, policy, group or movement the questions: how large? how long? how often? how representative?' Yet it seems safe to say that prior to the Second World War most economic historians fought their interdisciplinary battles mainly against economic theorists, and, in their own work, more often followed the style and methods of historians rather than those of economists. As historians, the economic historians did broaden the range of questions and approaches to reflect some of the concerns of economists, but the work remained closer to the historical mainstream than it was to be in subsequent years.

In the USA, beginning in the late 1950s and 1960s, there occurred a significant shift in the training and interests of economic historians. The work of the post-1950s generation of economic historians, including Davis, Fogel, Gallman, North and Parker, as well as others trained as economists, generally falls under the rubric of the new economic history, but is also known as econometric history and cliometrics. It contains three different, and not always compatible, aspects, features seen somewhat in earlier works of economic historians, but not to such a pronounced degree. The first feature, one which reflected the interests of many social scientists in the post-Second World War period, was a heightened concern with problems relating to the long-term economic growth of nations (in the sense of an increase in the measured output of goods and services per capita). These studies rested more heavily on economic analysis and quantitative measures than did earlier work. The questions to be studied by economic historians were often guided by a search for messages to those nations currently underdeveloped, and the economic histories of the developed nations were regarded as case studies to be looked at for the secrets of their success. This focus on growth was to be found among economic historians in Britain and elsewhere in Europe, with important works by Rostow (1960) and by Deane and Cole (1962) on British growth in the eighteenth and nineteenth centuries helping to shape subsequent studies.

A second important influence was a growing reliance upon quantitative constructs, such as measures of aggregate national income, as a means both of describing the past and of posing questions for study. Economic history has always been quantitatively oriented because much of the basic data, such as prices and wages, are numerical. There had been a major multinational collection of price data under the auspices of the International Scientific Committee on Price History in the 1930s. In explaining the increased attention to statistical measurement, the crucial role of the National Bureau of Economic Research can be seen. It was the direct contribution of Kuznets (1941), in making national income an operational construct, that led to much of the work in preparing estimates of national income and of output and input by industrial sector for the late nineteenth and twentieth centuries which was undertaken beginning in the 1930s. It was only in, and after, the 1950s that detailed estimates, based on census data, of United States national income from 1839 onwards, and of British national income in the nineteenth century, were generated, and even later before similar estimates were presented for other countries and, in some cases, for earlier times. Quantitative work, both by cliometricians and what might be called more traditional economic historians, greatly expanded after the 1960s with the development of the computer. The increased analysis of quantitative data by economic historians mirrors the expansion of econometrics as a tool used by economists, as well as the greater occurrence of quantification within other fields of historical study.

The third feature of recent work in economic history is the systematic use of economic analysis, particularly the application of conventional neo-classical supply and demand analysis. It should be noted that the claims to scientific history of the economic historians who used these methods differs from the claims of earlier scholars. To the earlier writers, scientific history meant the uncovering of the laws of motion of the social system, providing a key to understanding the past as well as predicting the future. Recently it has meant applying the tools of economics to answer specific questions that fit into the broader historical picture. As the critique of neo-classical economics has emerged among economists, however, so has criticism of its use in the study of historical problems. Similarly, the concern among economists with issues related to income distribution and power relations in society, whether influenced by neo-classical or Marxist models, has been reflected in the work of economic historians who have utilized census manuscripts, tax lists, and probate records to provide a fuller historical record of the course of inequality over the past centuries. The general attempt to expand the tools of economic analysis to what have been regarded as exogenous elements in the study of economic history has many applications: in the study of institutional changes, the examination of causes of technological change, the analysis of the causes and consequences of demographic movements (including both fertility and mortality changes), and the determination of the varieties of labour control to be found in different economies and over time.

In the post-Second World War period leadership in the new approach to economic history has been in the USA, with other nations generally following after a period of years. Yet the more traditional approaches to economic history, updated somewhat in method and approach, have continued to flourish in Britain and elsewhere, and economic history has retained its status as a separate discipline in Britain and other countries. In the USA, economic historians have again made the critique that mathematical economic theory has become too abstract and divorced from real-world issues, and that economics would benefit from reintroducing a more historical and empirical bent to the discipline, a practice that has, however, developed successfully in various fields of applied economics. Thus economic history has continued to contribute to both economics and to history.

Stanley L. Engerman
University of Rochester

References

Clapham, J. H. (1922) 'Of empty economic boxes', *Economic Journal* 32.
Clapham, J. H., Pirenne, H. and Gras, N. S. B. (1931) 'Economic history', in E. R. A. Seligman (ed.) *Encyclopedia of the Social Sciences*, vol. 5, New York.

Deane, P. and Cole, W. A. (1962) *British Economic Growth, 1688–1959*, Cambridge, UK.

Heckscher, E. F. (1929) 'A plea for theory in economic history', *Economic Journal*, Historical Supplement 4.

Kuznets, S. (1941) *National Income and its Composition, 1919–1938*, New York.

Pigou, A. C. (1992) 'Empty Economic Boxes: A Reply', *Economic Journal* 32.

Rostow, W. W. (1960) *The Stages of Economic Growth*, Cambridge, UK.

Further reading

Cole, A. H. (1968) 'Economic history in the United States: formative years of a discipline', *Journal of Economic History* 28.

Coleman, D. C. (1987) *History and the Economic Past: An Account of the Rise and Decline of Economic History in Britain*, Oxford.

Fishlow, A. and Fogel, R. W. (1971) 'Quantitative economic history: an interim evaluation', *Journal of Economic History* 31.

Harte, N. B. (ed.) (1970) *The Study of Economic History: Collected Inaugural Lectures, 1893–1970*, London.

Koot, G. M. (1987) *English Historical Economics, 1870–1926: The Rise of Economic History and Neomercantilism*, Cambridge, UK.

Maloney, J. (1985) *Marshall, Orthodoxy and the Professionalization of Economics*, Cambridge, UK.

North, D. C. (1968) 'Economic history', in D. L. Sills (ed.) *International Encyclopedia of the Social Sciences*, vol. 6, New York.

Wright, C. D. (1905) 'An economic history of the United States', *American Economic Review, Papers and Proceedings, Part II (b)*.

See also: cliometrics; Marx's theory of history and society; Marxist history.

economic man

In his classic work, *History of Economic Analysis*, Joseph Schumpeter (1954: 887) refers to the concept of economic man as one 'particularly effective in promoting the critics' mirth or wrath'. This response reflects the fact that the concept is extremely vague and general, and in some versions undoubtedly does suggest an extremely crude perception of how to understand human behaviour.

The concept in a broad sense can be traced back far into the history of social thought, but first becomes important with the growth of economic analysis founded upon the assumption of rational individualism in the nineteenth century. In the strong version eventually developed by economists, economic man is characterized by a complete set of ordered preferences, perfect information about the world, and infinite computing power to calculate with. With this formidable equipment, he is able to maximize his individual welfare subject to constraints. Economic man embodies then the strongest possible notion of instrumental rationality, where the ends of action are immaterial but those ends are rationally pursued.

From within economics the problems of this approach have been much debated. The uncertainty attached to outcomes has been emphasized, and the need to attach some probability to them stressed. The problem of the costs of acquiring information has also led to a wide-ranging literature, especially regarding how far we can make a rational assessment of the costs and benefits of acquiring information, when by definition we cannot know the content of that information. One popular general way of dealing with such problems is to stress the *limits* of human reason, and to work with a concept of 'bounded rationality' (Simon 1957), which stresses how humans attempt to make rational choices from among a small range of options, so overcoming the insuperable computational obstacles to assessing all possibilities. For Simon, humans 'satisfice' rather than maximize.

A quite different approach is to treat the assumptions of economic man as a purely deductive device, which can be used to develop certain predictions about the world, and which can then be checked against the evidence. In this approach, the character of the unrealistic assumptions about economic man are irrelevant, its usefulness as a concept is solely measured by the accuracy of the predictions derived from it (Friedman 1953).

Non-economists have not generally found this 'as if' defence of economic man persuasive. They have tended to regard its assumptions as relevant to judgements of its usefulness, but those assumptions as implausible. Those assumptions, for example, disregard any Freudian notions about different layers of human motivation. Human beings are always fully conscious of their motives, and lack conflicts in determining their behaviour. They also seem to bypass any discussion of how the *means* of calculation employed by economic agents are constructed. For example, what does it mean to maximize profit, when profit is an ambiguous word, with widely varying meanings in different contexts?

Whatever the philosophical and methodological problems, economic man remains a concept implicit in much modern economics. Partly this reflects a widespread belief that, by and large, humans roughly conform to the concept. In addition, the maximizing subject to constraint approach, which economic man underpins, is open to extensive mathematical manipulation, which any more complex picture of human motivation would tend to undermine.

Jim Tomlinson
Brunel University

References

Friedman, M. (1953) *Essays in Positive Economics*, Chicago.
Schumpeter, J. (1954) *History of Economic Analysis*, London.
Simon, H. (1957) *Models of Man*, New York.

Further reading

Hollis, M. and Nell, E. (1975) *Rational Economic Man*, Cambridge, UK.

See also: transaction costs.

economic planning see planning, economic

economics

In the draft of the introduction to his monumental study of the history of economic analysis, Joseph Schumpeter (1954) writes as follows:

> This book will describe the development and the fortunes of scientific analysis in the field of economics, from Graeco-Roman times to the present, in the appropriate setting of social and political history and with some attention to the developments in other social sciences and also in philosophy.

Few contemporary economists view their subject as stretching back continuously to Graeco-Roman civilizations, and some would regard a close association with history or philosophy as unnecessary, if not positively undesirable. Yet Schumpeter's account takes up nearly 200 pages before reaching Adam Smith's (1776) *The Wealth of Nations*, which is where economics began according to a vulgar view.

There is no great contradiction here. A reading of Schumpeter shows that he, as much as any other commentator, recognizes that the study of economic questions underwent radical changes of method, and an accelerated pace of development, in the late eighteenth century. Yet contemporary historians of economic thought agree with Schumpeter in not attributing the beginning of modern economics to the European Enlightenment, still less to the Scottish Enlightenment and Adam Smith. On examination the mercantilist and liberal writers turn out to share as much in common as they have differences. As in other cases, a sharper contrast exists between modern and early thinkers together, and their pre-modern predecessors (on mercantilism, see Magnusson 1994).

What began, whenever it began, and accelerated in the late eighteenth century, was not the description, not even the analysis, of economic institutions and questions, all of which are ancient. It was a redefinition of the centre of focus for such studies. A part justification of the simple belief that it all began with *The Wealth of Nations* is that the way in which Smith defined the subject is, in broad outline at least, recognizably the same as the subject defines itself today.

First, the renaissance idea that humankind is part of nature is sovereign. This frees economic analysis to apply rationalist and reductionist methods in order to attack economic superstitions, such as the belief that true wealth consists in the possession of gold.

Second, economics is liberated from morality, but not in the direction of an amoral political economy of nation-state power, which the mercantilists and others had explored. Rather many simple 'moral' views are discredited, often by the device of showing that their intentions fail to translate into moral outcomes. A phrase frequently used by Adam Smith captures this change of philosophy perfectly. Mercantilist restrictions are *unreasonable*. This means, of course, that like all institutions they are subject to critical rational review, and that they fail that test.

Third, if economics is not about selecting policies to promote the power of the sovereign, then what is it about? A view characteristic of the liberal individualism of the seventeenth and eighteenth centuries, again inherited by the modern discipline, has it that it is about the individual (or the individual family) and about the proper field, conceived as a wide one, for the pursuit of self-interest. The understanding that self-interest may be a socially constructive force is what separates the economist from the one who derives his views on economic issues solely from common sense. Equally, the understanding that self-interest may need to be channelled or even constrained to achieve good social outcomes is essential to a sophisticated economic insight.

Finally, this last tension, between the field for liberal policy, even *laissez-faire*, and the field for intervention, makes economics essentially concerned with policy. True there exist economic questions which are inherently abstract; questions addressed to the formalized issues which considerations of preference, decision and equilibrium throw up. Yet policy is never far away. As an illustration of the point, consider that no one would ever have wasted time on determining what is the level of normal prices if normal price was not considered as, at least potentially, an input to economic policy.

Description and analysis sound like science, but what of policy? Can there be a science of policy? Is indeed economics itself a science? The question is often asked thoughtlessly, without the enquirer having a clear notion of what counts as a science. Yet it conceals serious issues. Obviously economics is not physics, however physics may be conceived. Biology, or even climatology seem to be closer cousins. Economics has models, data and, certainly, simplifying assumptions. But it also concerns itself with values, with what is good or bad in economic states. Science is usually conceived of as value free; not in the sense that subject matter is chosen at random, but with the meaning that it concerns itself with what is, not with what ought to be.

Economics has tried to wriggle around this dilemma for most of its modern history. If there can be no ought to be, how can there be policy? And without policy, will not economics reduce to a kind of descriptive anthropology of economic life? If, however, values enter into economic discourse – a higher gross national product is good, fluctuations are bad, etc. – how is economics to escape from a mire of relativism in which its values are shown to be just one of many possibilities?

The question was posed most sharply by Professor Lionel Robbins (1952), who asked by what right economists maintained that the abolition of the Corn Laws in nineteenth-century Britain was a good thing. While it was good for manufacturers, and possibly for their workers, it was surely bad for landlords. Who were economists to say that landlords losses counted for less than the gains of manufacturers?

Showing that history was on the side of the manufacturers would hardly settle the matter. History after all was on the side of Cortés and against the South American aborigines at one time, but few people today regard that as settling the value issues. A different tack was tried by Kaldor (1939), and a similar argument explored by Hicks (1969). An economic change could be regarded as an improvement, argued Kaldor, if it carried the potential of making everyone in the economy better off. This fascinating argument, and its problems, almost define what the modern field of welfare economics is about.

The assumption that individual tastes are sovereign was not contentious for economists, although others might question it. Preferred by all had to mean better. Making individual self-interest basic to welfare evaluation goes back to Pareto and beyond. Hicks (1969) is a striking challenge to this view. Later investigation showed that even if the sovereignty of individual preference is conceded, there remain serious conceptual problems for welfare evaluation. The most fundamental statement of these difficulties is the hugely influential work of Arrow (1963), which shows that a social welfare function derived from individual preferences, according to weakly constrained principles, implies the dictatorship of one individual over the ranking of at least three possibilities. Arrow's axioms for the social welfare function have proved controversial (see Sen 1979) but there is no trick solution to a problem which just reformulates itself when the question is redefined.

Some economists have elected to throw away value neutrality and to investigate the implications for policy of specific value weights. Others have relied upon the important and useful fact that several important results in economic theory are value neutral in the sense that they hold true for all value weights. An example would be the very general result of public finance theory which says that lump sum taxation imposes less cost on those taxed (has a lower excess burden), for a given revenue collected, and regardless of how the burden of taxation is distributed, than any other form of taxation (see Atkinson and Stiglitz 1980: ch. 11).

This is not to say that one can easily manoeuvre around the problem that economic pronouncements are heavily value-laden. Lump-sum taxation completely severs the link between efficiency and distribution, and creates a utopian world in which economic institutions function perfectly to take the economy to its utility possibility frontier, while leaving the policy maker to select a point on that frontier. In general, efficiency and distribution are more closely bound together when policy is designed with feasible taxes and other instruments to hand. Modern economics has made much of *incentive compatibility*, which means the design of institutions, including taxation, but much more as well, so that the individual agents involved will find it in their self-interest to do what the policy maker intends. On incentive compatibility and the associated concept of mechanism design, see Fudenberg and Tirole (1991: ch. 7).

Policy design as conceived by modern economic theory is hugely more complicated and sophisticated than its eighteenth-century ancestor, with its sometimes simple 'get rid of irksome interference' approach. The role of the state and how it should best operate are well modelled in the context of the design of systems of taxation and regulation. Outside those particular areas, policy design needs a good deal of improvement, a point to which I shall return.

A good measure of how economics has grown and changed over its recent centuries of history is provided by the story of GNP (gross national product) or its equivalents. Before the twentieth century it would be no exaggeration to say that there was no well-developed flow concept of economic well-being. The wealth of nations, or regions or peoples, were the object of comment and investigation. Naturally, wealth and income, as the writings of Cantillon (1697–1734), Petty (1623–87) and Quesnay (1694–1774) confirm, are closely related concepts (see Cantillon 1755; Petty 1927; Quesnay 1759). Yet they part company in the short run, as when a depression lowers incomes substantially while little affecting wealth. To record fluctuations in national income at all precisely demands a systematic collection of statistics, via a census of production, which had to wait until the mid-twentieth century to become reality.

Before that happened, the theory of national income as a concept and as a measure of economic welfare had been developed. Pigou (1955) is a good short exposition. The theoretical framework was implemented in modern GNP accounting which has graduated in half a century from an academic exercise to perhaps the most important objective and indicator of government policy.

It is no surprise that the success of GNP accounting in measuring the level of activity for the economy has been followed by deep criticism of GNP as an objective of policy. More than one type of issue is involved and limitations of space prohibit a full discussion here. Yet two basic points are frequently encountered. They can be briefly labelled consumerism and the environment. In short, the consumerism argument says that GNP is biased towards a market notion of human welfare which overweighs capitalist lifestyle and consumption and underweighs non-market activities and lifestyle. Thus transport to commute to work, and health costs associated with commuting, enter into GNP, while the value of home-grown vegetables does not. Similar arguments become even more heated where the environment and finite resources are concerned. Modern industrial production based on the burning of fossil fuels boosts GNP. Yet the cost which is the reduction of the levels of those fuels remaining in the ground is not deducted from GNP. There are no easy answers to any of these issues; yet their existence reminds us of the change in focus of economic thought among professionals and non-professionals alike.

Probably the ideological side to economics explains why the subject has been prone to controversy and to discord between competing schools. In the Anglo-Saxon world, however, the predominant method has become the neo-classical approach. Most economists would agree with that view even when some would regret the fact. But what exactly is neo-classical economics, and what are the alternatives which have failed while the neo-classical variety has flourished?

In summary, neo-classical economics is built on the assumption that efficient markets arrive at an equilibrium in which the separate actions of rational maximizing agents are made consistent via market equilibrium (or market clearing) conditions. In the absence of externalities, it is then a *theorem* that the resulting allocation of resources is efficient in the sense of Pareto. This is the so-called first fundamental theorem of welfare economics. The second fundamental theorem states that any Pareto efficient allocation can be made a market equilibrium when suitable lump-sum transfers place each agent on the right budget constraint. These two results fully clarify the relationship between efficiency and market equilibrium for competitive economies.

Such a clear intellectual framework makes it easy to classify the main lines of attack for anti-neo-classical economics. These concern

1 Motivation: are real-life economic agents maximizers who concentrate mainly on economic on self-interest?

2 Information: are these agents well-informed about prices – current and future – and about technology, and even about their own tastes?

3 Calculation: even given the information, and the objective, how can agents calculate the right action? And how can the market, or the market-maker, calculate the equilibrium?

4 Do markets function as the neo-classical model has it, or are they subject to price rigidities, imperfect competition or monopoly, market failure or missing markets?

Some of these arguments are old, some more or less modern. The economist's assumption about the motivation of 'economic man' have always seemed absurd, and immoral as well, to many outsiders. Thorstein Veblen (1857–1929) articulated passionately the problems with the computational abilities implied by the assumption that economic agents maximize (Veblen 1904). Keynes, on one interpretation, is partly about the macroeconomic effects of sticky prices. The idea that imperfect information is crucial to market failure may have been mentioned in the nineteenth century, but until recent years there is no analysis of the idea worthy of the name. Imperfect competition, especially duopoly, was analysed by Antoine-Augustin Cournot (1801–77) amazingly ahead of his time in the mid-nineteenth century, and analysis continued ever since. The idea that markets may be *missing*, as opposed to just not functioning well, is certainly modern, and is tied up with the again modern concept that sources of information and transaction costs should be modelled explicitly.

Now we come to a powerful paradox. As models developed from the shortcomings of neo-classical theory listed above become increasingly refined and sophisticated, they frequently and typically emerge from the work of economists of the neo-classical stable. Indeed the neo-classical critique of neo-classical economics has become an industry in its own right. In this situation a truly anti-neo-classical economics has not been easy to construct. Akerlof (1984) is one of the most interesting attempts to do so, and the frequently neo-classical nature of approaches based on highly non-neo-classical assumptions is suggestive.

It must of course be easy to construct an entirely non-neo-classical economics if one is willing to ditch enough baggage. In particular, theories in which agents behave according to more or less arbitrary rules produce radically different conclusions. But is the theory that results economics? This debate tends to separate theory and empirical investigation. *Ad-hoc* behavioural assumptions are hard to motivate or to formalize. Yet empirical studies have sometimes forced economists to recognize them as fact. A notable case in point is choice under uncertainty. There some evidence is solidly against the most powerful and appealing theoretical model. Yet the evidence seems to indicate what may be going on, and formalization of that has been attempted (see Machina 1987).

If there is little truly anti-neo-classical economics but mainly neo-classical economics in need of more refinement and sophistication, where does that leave the Keynesian revolution? Keynes (1973) saw himself as correcting a (neo)classical economics, the root specifications of which he was to a great extent willing to accept. Specifically, he argued that his unemployment could be encountered in a competitive economy in some kind of equilibrium. How far he was correct is a controversial question.

A modern North American school of New Keynesian thinkers maintains that Keynesian economics can be made to work only by introducing the specific modelling of market imperfections, information asymmetries and missing markets (see Blanchard and Fischer 1989). Certainly the treatment of expectations differs notably between Keynes and his modern successors in macroeconomic theory. Keynes argued for the subjectivity and irrationality of expectations concerning the future. Some modern theorists, by contrast, have gone to the opposite extreme by studying *rational expectations* – expectations as efficient and perfect as it is possible to be in the circumstances (Begg 1982). Although taken to its logical limit, this approach soon becomes mathematically elaborate and even indeterminate, there lies at the bottom of the debate some fundamental questions concerning Keynes's economics which have asserted themselves from the start of the Keynesian revolution.

With the flexible output prices assumed by Keynes, the theory asserts that an increase in effective demand will generate an increased output from the supply side by raising output prices relative to wage costs, that is, by cutting the real wage. How will this do when workers become aware of the fall in their living standards even when employed? There are various answers, none 100 per cent satisfactory. Keynes's discussion suggests that price inflation co-ordinates real wage cuts for all workers which they cannot achieve acting on their own, but will willingly accept when generalized because imposed by price inflation. New classical macroeconomists argued that output could not be increased by a boost to effective demand, as workers willing to accept a cut in their real wage could have taken it anyway. Hence only inflation surprises would increase output from the supply side. With rational expectations the scope for policy using inflation surprises would be severely limited. These arguments contained a germ of truth, as with the conclusion that rapid and expected inflation is soon discounted and has few real effects. Experience has shown that Keynesian effects continue to exist but that their scope is shorter run than the earlier Keynesian theorists assumed. Unemployment, however, has proved to be a growing problem for industrial countries, leading some to conclude that structural factors and dual labour markets may now be more important than the demand side.

The intricacies of rational expectations analysis provides an example of the growing use, and eventual dominance, of mathematics in economic theorizing. Economics in the 1990s is an applied mathematical subject to an extent unimaginable a century ago. This is not because the mathematically literate have conspired to squeeze out their less advantaged colleagues. Rather, mathematics is a natural language for economic reasoning. Obviously mathematics, including the differential calculus, lends itself to maximization. Yet for all the arguments ever since Veblen, maximization is seldom vital; it often serves to provide a definiteness which could in principle be provided by alternative means. More important, however, is the power of mathematics in dealing with systems in which many influences make themselves felt simultaneously – a typical situation for social science models. Solving simultaneous equations really requires mathematics, and anyone who thinks that they can do it intuitively is practising self-deception.

Another great merit of mathematical reasoning is that it facilitates connections between theoretical and empirical work. For all the hostility of Keynes himself to mathematical economics and econometrics, the Keynesian revolution served to bring theoretical and applied economics closer together than had ever previously been the case. The development of national income accounting is a leading instance of this point. Yet economics and econometrics, though always second cousins, have never married. Rather, they have developed sufficiently separately to retain distinctive methods and styles. Hence the Econometric Society at its regular conferences in different parts of the world divides its programmes into economics and econometrics. Some resent this but no one could claim it to be an absurd division.

Growing specialization within economics does not affect only econometrics and is a result of the huge growth of the discipline and the proliferation of journals. Economists now tend to be development economists, labour economists, game theorists or specialists in other fields. The generalist hardly exists. Also, as a general category, *economist* is now more like *architect* than *man of letters*. It defines a profession. And clearly the number of people who can be said to earn a living by the practice of economics has increased massively since the Second World War. The total cannot easily be known but 150,000 worldwide would certainly not be an absurd guess.

That raises an obvious question: how successful is economics in the late twentieth century? In a crude ecological sense, economics is undoubtedly successful. It is reproducing itself with an awesome efficiency. However, on the test of its power as a problem-solving method, the success of economics must be regarded as more questionable. Indeed since the mid-1970s the subject has spent much of the time writing itself out of policy relevance. This is particularly marked with macroeconomics, where policy ineffectiveness theorems are central to a dominant mode of thought. It is true that the subject has always recognized that policy may be unable to improve on the market. With Adam Smith, however, that view owed more to scepticism about the usefulness of policy interference than to a faith in the perfection of unregulated markets as such. Recently, however, a faith in the perfection of markets, sometimes, but not always, qualified by the recognition of imperfect information and similar problems has attracted many and enthusiastic adherents.

The sometimes unfortunate effects of ill-considered deregulation exercises in the west may be blamed on that intellectual fashion. Of hugely greater importance in this context, however, has been the general failure of economics to provide useful modelling and advice for the former Soviet economies of eastern Europe following the fall of communism. That reform, which has required the creation of markets more than their liberalization, found economists more or less empty-handed. The result has too often been a flood of inconsistent advice derived from partial models based on western economies. It is too soon to write the history of the reform of former Soviet economies and economic thought but it must be hoped that some deep lessons will have been learned from an experience which underlines the fact that economics, for all its modern reach and power, remains a subject embedded in particular historical experiences and presumptions.

Christopher Bliss
Nuffield College

References

Akerlof, G. A. (1984) *An Economic Theorist's Book of Tales*, Cambridge, UK.

Arrow, K. J. (1963) *Social Choice and Individual Values*, 2nd edn, Chichester.

Atkinson, A. B. and Stiglitz, J. E. (1980) *Lectures on Public Economics*, Maidenhead.

Begg, D. K. H. (1982) *The Rational Expectations Revolution in Macroeconomics*, Baltimore, MD.

Blanchard, O. J. and Fischer, S. (1989) *Lectures on Macroeconomics*, Cambridge, MA.

Cantillon, R. (1755) *Essai sur la nature du commerce en général*, Paris. (English edn, ed. H. Higgs, London, 1931.)

Cournot, A. (1927), *Researches into the Mathematical Principles of the Theory of Wealth*, (English translation by Nathaniel T. Bacon), New York.

Fudenberg, D. and Tirole, J. (1991) *Game Theory*, Cambridge, MA.

Hicks, J. R. (1969) 'Preface and a manifesto', in K. J. Arrow and T. Scitovsky (eds) *Readings in Welfare Economics*, London. Corrected text from J. R. Hicks (1959) *Essays in World Economics*, Oxford.

Kaldor, N. (1939) 'Welfare propositions of economics and interpersonal comparisons of utility', *Economic Journal* 49.

Keynes, J. M. (1973) *The General Theory*, Royal Economic Society edn, London.

Machina, M. J. (1987), 'Choice under uncertainty: problems solved and unsolved', *Journal of Economic Perspectives* 1.

Magnusson, L. (1994) *Merchantilism: The Shaping of an Economic Language*, London.

Petty, W. (1927) *Papers*, ed. H. Lansdowne, London.

Pigou, A. C. (1955) *Income Revisited*, London.

Quesnay, F. (1759) *Tableau economique*, 3rd edn, Paris. (English edn, London, 1972.)

Robbins, L. (1952) *The Theory of Economic Policy in English Classical Political Economy*, London.

Schumpeter, J. A. (1954) *History of Economic Analysis*, New York.

Sen, A. K. (1979) *Collective Choice and Social Welfare*, Amsterdam.

Smith, A. (1981 [1776]) *An Inquiry into the Nature and Causes of the Wealth of Nations*, ed. R. Campbell and A. Skinner, Indianapolis, IN.

Veblen, T. (1904) *The Theory of Business Enterprise*, New York.

economics, agricultural *see* agricultural economics

economics, behavioural *see* behavioural economics

economics, classical *see* classical economics

economics, defence *see* defence economics

economics, environmental *see* environmental economics

economics, evolutionary *see* evolutionary economics

economics, experimental *see* experimental economics

economics, health *see* **health economics**

economics, institutional *see* institutional economics

economics, Keynesian *see* **Keynesian economics**

economics, Marxian *see* **Marxian economics**

economics, mathematical *see* mathematical economics

economics, natural resource *see* natural resource economics

economics, neo-classical *see* **neo-classical economics**

economics, public sector *see* public sector economics

economics, supply-side *see* **supply-side economics**

economics, welfare *see* **welfare economics**

economics and law *see* **law and economics**

economies of scale

The term economies of scale refers to the situation in which, at a given and unchanging set of input prices, the unit cost of production is lower in a plant of larger scale of (annual) output than in a plant of smaller scale. This happens because the physical requirement for labour and capital inputs per unit of output each tends to be lower the larger is the scale of annual output which the plant is designed to produce. This situation is contrasted with 'pecuniary economies of scale' in which the plant of larger scale may obtain inputs at lower prices. An example of economies of scale may be given for ethylene production in 1964 (Jackson 1982; adapted from Pratten 1971).

	100	200	300
Scale of ethylene plant, output in thousands of tons per year	100	200	300
Acquisition cost of equipment ($£$million)	8.4	13.5	16.6
Acquisition cost of equipment per unit of output, or unit capital requirement ($£$ per ton per year	84	67.5	55.3
Unit cost ($£$ per ton)			
Unit materials cost	41.2	41.2	41.2
Unit labour cost	3.5	2.7	2.1
Unit capital cost (depreciation only)	8.4	6.8	5.5
Unit total cost	53.1	50.7	48.8

The main reason for lower unit labour cost is that an increase in the scale of this (process) plant requires a less than equi-proportionate increase in the number of workers and so unit labour requirement decreases with the scale of output.

The reason for lower unit capital cost is that the proportionate increase in the acquisition cost of the equipment (for a plant of larger scale) tends, systematically, to be less than the proportionate increase in the capacity of the equipment to produce annual output. (It must be made clear that, in economies of scale, each piece of equipment of smaller capacity is replaced by a piece of equipment (of the same type) but with a larger capacity (the meaning of 'scaled up'.) Conversely, the larger annual output is *not* achieved by simply duplicating or replicating pieces of equipment each of the same capacity.)

The relationship between the acquisition cost of a piece of equipment and the capacity of the piece of equipment is expressed in what may be called the 'power rule' (or 'six-tenths factor'; due to Chilton 1950;

Williams 1947a; 1947b). The power rule is a most important basis for economies of scale.

The power rule is as follows. Let K denote the acquisition cost of a piece of equipment and V the capacity (however measured) of a piece of equipment; the subscripts i and j denote, respectively, pieces of equipment of the same type but different capacity, i being the larger capacity and j the smaller capacity; let s denote a parameter of the power rule. Then one version of the power rule is

$$(K_i/\mathrm{K}_j) = (V_i/\mathrm{V}_j)^s$$

Generally, $0 < s < 1$, and empirical values of s centre around two-thirds with values frequently approximating six-tenths. The value of s fundamentally derives from the two-thirds relationship between the surface area of a regularly shaped container (which is a basic determinant of the cost of the container) and the cubic capacity of the regularly shaped container (which determines the capacity of the container to produce a flow of output per period of time). Take the example of two cubes: the ratio between the surface areas is equal to, and varies as, the ratio of cubic capacities raised to the power two-thirds. Much fixed capital equipment is of the basic form of containers and so is subject to the power rule, but cost may not be exactly proportional to surface area and output may not be exactly proportional to cubic capacity, and such non-proportionality means that the parameter s may be either greater or less than the value two-thirds (hence the frequently observed value six-tenths).

If j the comparison piece of equipment is held constant, then for any i we can write a rearranged version of the power rule as

$$K_i = A \ V_i^s$$

(where $A = K_j V_j^{-s}$). Because plants are basically assemblages of pieces of equipment, the power rule can also apply to plants (with K then denoting the acquisition cost of a *plant* and V the capacity of the plant measured in terms of *annual output*). For instance, in the case of the ethylene plant the following power rule may be estimated (for the data as given):

$$K_i = 0.473 \times V_i^{0.627}$$

If $s < 1$, then the acquisition cost of the piece of capital equipment or of the plant increases less than proportionately to the increase in capacity, so giving rise to economies of scale in relation to fixed capital: that is, the larger the scale of the plant, the lower is the acquisition cost of capital installed per unit of output per year. This relationship between scale of plant and unit capital requirement is a systematic one: dividing the rearranged version of the power rule through by annual output V gives:

$$(K/V)_i = A \ V_i^{(s-1)}$$

so that, with $s < 1$, the exponent $(s - 1)$ is negative, and (K/V), the unit capital requirement, systematically declines as V, the scale of annual output, increases. Taking the example of the ethylene plant, doubling the scale of output would lead, according to the estimated relationship, to a change in unit capital requirement by proportion $2^{(0.627-1)} = 2^{-0.373} = 0.772$, or a reduction of 22.8 per cent.

Handbooks of engineering publish tables giving, for each of a wide variety of types of equipment, values of K_j and V_j (the comparison values) and of s, the parameter of the power rule. These tables are used by engineers for preliminary cost estimation when proposals for 'scaling up' a plant are under consideration (Perry *et al.* 1984).

For the economist, the interest of such data lies in the value of s for each type of equipment; nearly always less than 1 and centring around approximately $\frac{2}{3}$. For example, in a sample of 288 types of equipment the average value of s was 0.6559 (with a standard deviation of 0.2656) (calculated from Woods 1975: Appendix C). Consequently we may conclude that economies of scale is a widespread and inherent feature of the behaviour of the acquisition cost of equipment or of a plant as capacity is 'scaled up'.

Diseconomies of scale may be defined, at the plant level, as an increase in the unit cost of production associated with an increase in the scale of output per period. Diseconomies of scale is adduced as one possible explanation for limitations on the size of a plant and is hence associated with the concept of a 'minimum efficient scale' of production and with the related concept of a 'U-shaped long-run average cost curve'. Diseconomies of scale explain the putative upward (right) part of the curve, with the bottom of the curve being at the minimum efficient scale (economies of scale explain the downward (left) part of the curve). Some reasons for diseconomies of scale are: the need technically for capital-labour substitution and/or automation as the scale of plant, and hence materials handling, increases; increasing managerial difficulties of co-ordinating work processes as plants become larger; increased unit transport and/or distribution costs arising from the need to sell the increased quantity of output over a larger geographic area.

Dudley Jackson
University of Wollongong

References

Chilton, C. H. (1950) ' "Six tenths factor" applies to complete plant costs', *Chemical Engineering* April.

Jackson, D. (1982) *Introduction to Economics: Theory and Data*, London.

Perry, R. H., Green, D. W. and Maloney, J. O. (eds) (1984) *Perry's Chemical Engineers' Handbook*, New York.

Pratten, C. F. (1971) *Economies of Scale in Manufacturing Industry*, Cambridge, UK.

Williams, R. (1947a) 'Standardising cost data on process equipment', *Chemical Engineering* June.

— (1947b) ' "Six-tenths factor" aids in approximating costs', *Chemical Engineering* December.

Woods, D. R. (1975) *Financial Decision Making in the Process Industry*, Englewood Cliffs, NJ.

economy, dual *see* dual economy

economy, informal *see* informal economy

economy, mixed *see* mixed economy

economy, political *see* political economy

education

Although dominated by psychology, the field of educational research was once largely restricted to the general discipline of philosophy. Other disciplines, such as anthropology, economics, political science and sociology, have become increasingly prominent.

The status of education as an applied field makes it difficult to identify any specific method or conceptual domain which would single it out from other fields. For most scholars and researchers, however, the study of education has meant investigating activities related to learning, usually within the context of the schools. The problems studied and the method employed vary a great deal, depending largely on the training and background of the researchers. However, in contrast to the earlier, philosophical studies which focused on the *aims* of education, the prominence of the behavioural and social sciences has signalled a shift in concern to questions of *means*.

As an applied field of study, the problems investigated in the area of education tend to follow closely the concerns articulated by leaders in business, government and the media. For example, in the late 1950s and early 1960s when US political leaders were primarily concerned with the space race with the Soviet Union and the so-called missile gap, a series of reports by the well-known educator, James B. Conant

(1959) focused on the lagging academic quality of education in the USA. Educational research in that country then turned towards developing curriculum units, teaching strategies, school procedure and design that would produce more scientists and engineers. In this period, for example, the 'New Math' flourished, and influential educators, such as the psychologist Jerome Bruner, proposed the teaching of science, mathematics and other academic programmes in the lower grades (Bruner 1960).

In the mid-1960s, social pressure built up over the civil rights issue, and the concern of much of the educational research community again shifted towards issues related to equality of opportunity. The work of Jean Piaget provided the intellectual basis for British and US curriculum researchers, who argued for relaxing the structure of the curriculum by allowing more room for the individual expression of interests. Some opposed these moves because they were too permissive, but the intention was to create a fruitful interaction between the developmental patterns found among children and the structure and pacing of curriculum knowledge. However, the apparently reduced emphasis on a hierarchy of knowledge (with science, maths and other college preparatory subjects at the top and vocational subjects at the bottom), and the renewed recognition of the importance of the interest of the individual child as a major factor in the learning process, appeared to be consistent with the wider concern for equality of opportunity.

Equality has continued to be a major issue in educational research and debate in a number of different areas. For example, James Coleman's (1968) analysis of data from thousands of American schools explored the extent to which different variables affect school achievement across racial lines. His finding that the class and racial characteristics of the student body had an important influence on individual achievement was rapidly used as intellectual support for the bussing of children across racially distinct neighbourhoods in an effort to achieve greater racial balance. At the same time other studies explored the effectiveness of preschool programmes in raising the achievement levels of blacks and other children from lower socioeconomic classes.

At the time that educational research was exploring the pedagogical factors involved in maintaining inequality, the traditional meaning of equality of opportunity was first challenged. Coleman (1973), in an important article on equality of educational opportunity, suggested that the extent to which this ideal has been realized should be measured not in terms of equality of input – the resources spent on different children – but rather in terms of equality of results – whether or not the pattern of achievement is similar among different racial groups and minorities. Had this conception of equal opportunity been widely accepted, it would have significantly changed the rules of the game. This proposal would thus have mandated the allocation of unequal resources in some cases in order to achieve equal results.

Coleman's proposed conception was never fully accepted (Coleman himself offered it only tentatively). However, educational policy makers and politicians in the USA did begin to assign federal resources to special groups, such as handicapped people, blacks, women and non-native speakers of English; legal efforts were increased to redress racial imbalance in schools; and affirmative action programmes tried to increase the opportunities for minority students and women in universities and professional schools.

Even prior to Coleman's attempt to redefine the concept of equal opportunity, there had been other challenges to compensatory policies. The most publicized was an article by Arthur Jensen (1969) which claimed that most compensatory programmes had failed, and therefore children of different intellectual ability should be taught differently. Children with high IQ scores, Jensen argued, should be taught conceptually by problem-solving methods. Children with low IQ scores should be taught through associative or rote methods. Jensen's article was controversial because of three propositions: IQ tests measure intelligence; in a population intelligence is 80 per cent explained by genetic factors; and blacks as a population score on the average consistently lower than whites on both standard IQ tests and culture-fair tests. Jensen concluded that environmental enrichment programmes were severely limited in their ability to raise IQ scores, and that educators would better spend their time and resources identifying conceptual and associative learners and teaching them through the methods appropriate to their learning style. Jensen himself believed that when IQ tests were appropriately refined to identify the two types of learners, blacks and other minority students would be more fairly treated. He also believed that teaching style would become more consistent with learning style and that conceptual learners from these groups would be less likely to fall victim to the prejudicial judgement of a few teachers. However, he also strongly implied that because of genetic factors blacks would continue to achieve at a lower rate than whites.

An uproar followed the publication of Jensen's article. The twin studies on which he had built much of his case for the prominence of genetic over environmental factors were discredited. Questions were raised about the whole concept of measurement as applied to intelligence and about the appropriateness of such tests for culturally distinct, minority children. In addition, Jensen's argument traded on the ambiguity of the claim that 'IQ tests measure intelligence'. The claim could mean that a conceptual limit exists beyond which an individual cannot reach and an IQ test measures it, or it could mean that IQ tests measure the speed at which different individuals learn. This ambiguity is especially significant when it is understood that Jensen's view of associative and conceptual learning is inaccurate in at least one important respect. He believes that children can learn essentially the same basic material either through associative or conceptual methods, depending upon the learning style of the child. But, in fact, the children would be learning the same skills in only the most superficial sense. They might be learning how to translate symbols on a page into oral sounds, or learning to repeat number facts, thus giving the *appearance* of learning the same thing. However, each group also would be learning something about learning. One group would be learning that learning is a rote affair, while the other would be learning that it is essentially a conceptual and problem-solving activity. Jensen's article provides no evidence to support the view that such learning styles were irreversible, even though his own proposal seemed to rest upon this assumption.

The debate over Jensen's article was significant for a number of reasons. One of these went to the very heart of the question of equality of opportunity. For if equality of opportunity means that everyone is to be given the same chance, presumably ability differences should be the sole determinant of outcomes. However, if the major measure of ability, that is, IQ tests, is put into question, so too is the justification for different outcomes.

Some scholars, while dismissing the significance of IQ tests, continued to justify differential outcomes and to argue against 'extraordinary' measures to achieve educational equality. These arguments were often based on the view that governmental intervention creates unrealistic expectations and increases frustration and, possibly, violence. Environmental factors were considered important, but the most significant aspect of environment, the habits, discipline and foresight developed through class culture were thought extremely difficult to change. Because these studies took 'class-culture' and the habits and attitudes associated with it as an independent variable, they failed to examine the relationship between a student's habits, attitudes and achievement, and the work structures that were available to children from certain social classes.

This enlarged focus came only with a renewed interest in Marxist scholarship and, especially, with the work of two economists, Bowles and Gintis (1976). Their study concluded that schooling provided very little mobility, even when research controlled for IQ scores, and that schools largely served to reproduce and legitimize the personality characteristics required by the hierarchical relations found in advanced capitalistic countries.

The findings of Bowles and Gintis were challenged on a number of methodological grounds. However, one of the more significant effects of their work for educational scholarship was to reintroduce a Marxist perspective into the study of education in the USA. This perspective continued a tradition that was already established in Britain, western Europe, Australia, and in a number of Third-World countries. In effect Marxists have shifted some of the focus of educational research from the individual to the larger social, historical, cultural and political context of schooling (Apple 1982; Giroux 1981).

There is no uniform Marxist perspective. For example, the Brazilian educator, Paulo Freire (1973), draws not only on Marxist literature for many of his insights, but also on French existentialism, phenomenology, and Christian theology. Some analysts have adopted a structural approach and have examined the limits placed on the educational system by a hierarchical mode of production. Others, utilizing an ethnographic methodology, have explored the way in which a critical working-class consciousness is both developed and blunted in schools. There have been insightful studies on the reproduction of classroom knowledge for different social classes, on the production of educational materials and texts, and on the dilemmas created by radical educational thought for teacher education (Apple 1982; Giroux 1981).

While Marxist-oriented research represents a significant redefinition of the problem of education, it has remained a largely critical movement which only occasionally penetrates mainstream thinking about education. When inequality was a major issue for the educational community and the wider public, Marxism was able to gain a reasonable hearing. However, as unemployment rates in the USA, Britain and western Europe hit post-depression records, educational policy makers steered the agenda away from the issue of equality and towards the educational needs of the high technology revolution. Educational research is following suit as more concern is expressed about developing computer literacy, and about increasing the pool from which future scientists and engineers can be drawn. There have been calls to tighten up the curriculum, raise standards for admission into and matriculation out of higher education, and to reduce the 'frills' in the public schools. These concerns seem to signal a return to the era dominated by Conant.

Various forms of feminist scholarship have had an important influence on educational scholarship, focusing it on questions of gender-specific learning styles, knowledge and moral reasoning. Moreover, under the influence of post-modernism, there has been a developing concern with issues of identity, and in the relationship between identity and knowledge. There is also renewed interest in the non-cognitive aspects of schooling and education.

The applied nature of educational research, and its failure to develop an independent research programme, suggests that its future direction will depend on political and economic developments. The last attempt to provide an independent focus for the study of education was developed by the American philosopher, John Dewey (see Boydston 1979). Since Dewey, educational philosophy has taken a different turn, one that emphasizes the anaylsis of concepts and linguistic clarity. Yet the deeper questions about education involve the understanding of intergenerational continuity and change, and the normative concerns that guide the process of social and cultural reproduction. While little systematic effort has been undertaken to explore the process and patterns of social identity, it is possible to specify some of the factors that such a research programme would involve. They would include an analysis of the kind of knowledge that is prized by a given society, the institutional arrangements to protect and carry on such knowledge, the methods used to identify and train those who will bear that knowledge in the future, and the way in which knowledge is distributed among different groups in the society. Such a programme would maintain the interdisciplinary character of educational studies but would provide a focus that has been lacking. It would also provide a critical point from which to appraise present educational practice.

Walter Feinberg
University of Illinois,
Urbana-Champaign

References

Apple, M. (1982) *Education and Power*, London.

Bowles, S. and Gintis, H. (1976) *Schooling in Capitalist America: Educational Reform and the Contradictions of Economic Life*, New York.

Boydston, J. (ed.) (1979) *The Complete Works of John Dewey* Carbondale, IL.

Bruner, J. (1960) *The Process of Education*, Cambridge, MA.

Coleman, J. S. (1968) 'The concept of equality of educational opportunity', *Harvard Educational Review* 38.

—— (1973) 'Equality of opportunity and equality of results', *Harvard Educational Review* 43.

Conant, J. B. (1959) *The American High School Today*, New York.

Freire, P. (1973) *Pedagogy of the Oppressed*, New York.

Giroux, H. A. (1981) *Ideology, Culture and the Process of Schooling*, Philadelphia, PA.

Jensen, A. R. (1969) 'How much can we boost I.Q. and scholastic achievement?', *Harvard Educational Review* 39.

Further reading

Bourdieu, P. and Passeron, J.-C. (1977) *Reproduction in Education, Society and Culture*, London.
Feinberg, W. (1983) *Understanding Education: Toward a Reconstruction of Educational Inquiry*, Cambridge, UK.
Sharp, R. and Green, A. (1975) *Education and Social Control: A Study in Progressive Education*, London.

See also: Dewey

education, multicultural *see* multi-cultural education

educational psychology

The enduring difficulties that face both the academic and the professional sectors of educational psychology are due to three factors. First, educational psychology mirrors all the propensities and peculiarities of psychology. Second, and perhaps as a consequence, no distinctive approach or unified understanding of the field has evolved. Third, despite the professed concern with educational problems in general, the primary focus has in fact been schooling, as if all educational concerns are localized in schools.

Psychology in general has placed an enormous emphasis on quantification. Within educational psychology this trend has given rise to a huge testing industry, making tests, selling tests, giving tests, scoring tests, interpreting scores, categorizing and labelling people on the basis of scores, coaching test taking, doing research on and with tests, and so on. These activities have become so widespread, particularly in schools, as to make them a hallmark of the whole field, and educational psychologists have become effectively technicians of tests, measurements and evaluation, especially in the cognitive domain dealing with intelligence, aptitude and achievement (USA) or attainment (UK). The technical bias is so pervasive as to blind many practitioners to the damage that may be done to the test subjects (Hanson 1993).

This preoccupation with the tools of research has, of course, affected the substance. Persons *qua* persons tend to be diminished even as they are counted, aggregated, classified, labelled and treated. Not surprisingly, many significant questions have been ignored – for instance, how to handle young children's napping and sleeping patterns and their disruptions; what they dream, and how that affects their life awake; how one's temperament contributes to the formation of a worldview; how to help a person develop courage and a sense of honour; or what nurtures maturity, integrity and wisdom.

Substantively, educational psychology remains a hodgepodge. Indeed, a cursory survey of graduate programmes reveals large portions of courses devoted to research design and analysis, measurements and evaluation, and computer applications. Side by side with these are courses on learning, development (mostly focused on child–adolescent phases), personality formation and pathology. The last category is heavily dependent upon the psychiatric tradition of diagnosis and classification. Among the relevant areas of enquiry which are normally absent from such courses are group dynamics, the process of teaching, or the nature of curriculum. It is still rarer for such a course to pay attention to other disciplines. On the level of theory, what is typically found is a doctrinaire adherence to a single fashionable approach. In the 1950s the Skinnerian school was dominant, to be replaced, in turn, by the approaches of Piaget, Chomsky, Vygotsky, and others.

There is little sense of the history of the field, and perhaps in consequence it is hardly surprising that the same mistakes tend to be repeated both in theory and in practice. One error has been to view the school experience in a linear, causal fashion, within its narrowest and most immediate context, without interpreting it in interactional, systemic terms against the broader backdrop of human meaning. As important as schooling has become, particularly to the young, an educational psychology that centres its attention exclusively upon this process is unlikely to achieve that rounded understanding of the person in the world which is required if we are to provide appropriate support, assistance and guidance (Bronfenbrenner 1979; Ianni 1989).

Kaoru Yamamoto
University of Colorado, Denver

References

Bronfenbrenner, U. (1979) *The Ecology of Human Development*, Cambridge, MA.
Hanson, F. A. (1993) *Testing Testing*, Berkeley, CA.
Ianni, F. A. J. (1989) *The Search for Structure*, New York.

See also: education; learning.

efficiency *see* economic efficiency

ego

The ego is part of Freud's tripartite conception of the psyche. The ego emerges during the course of early development as that part of the mind concerned with perceptual awareness and sense of self. The ego also serves an integrating function and mediates between the individual and the external world. Like the id (instinctual energy), it is directed at obtaining pleasure but, because it is capable of reflecting the conditions of the outside world, it is tempered as well by concern for the demands of reality. Thus, although ego and id both serve the same end (pleasure), by sometimes seeking to postpone immediate gratification, the ego may conflict with the id. The third aspect of the psyche, the superego, which is roughly equivalent to conscience, develops through identification with a parent and integrating or assimilating that parent's values.

It is important to note that Freud did not mean to imply that the id, ego and superego are identifiable processes in the human brain. Rather, they are conceptualizations or abstractions used to refer to the interacting forces which govern behaviour. While 'ego' is the usual translation of the term used by Freud, *das Ich*, this ordinary German personal pronoun means literally 'the I'. By using this term, Freud firmly anchors this aspect of the psyche in our conscious awareness of ourselves. As Bettelheim (1983) has noted, the translators' use of Latin terms rather than everyday words serve to give the concepts spurious, scientific or medical connotations. The effect can be to reify them so that they become a formalized system rather than living tools which can help us to gain insights into the experience of being a person.

In his later formulations, Freud believed that one consequence of intrapsychic conflict (i.e. between the three aspects of the psyche) is the experience of anxiety. Such conflict may be alleviated by means of various defensive devices. One way would be to *repress* the conflicting desire from consciousness. This defence might be supplemented by *projecting* the repressed desire on to others so that they are seen as, say, being sexually motivated (even though they may not in fact be so). Or it may be *displaced*, as when repressed aggression is directed at another target. Another more productive way of alleviating conflict is to *sublimate* the repressed desire: as when sexual feelings are converted into concern for others, or into creative effort. Repression, projection, displacement and sublimation are all examples of ego defence mechanisms. In his later writings Freud, and also his daughter Anna among others, described a number of these. Note that defence mechanisms are considered to operate in largely an unconscious way. So, while the ego is the focus of consciousness, it should not be regarded as synonymous with it. Ego psychology offers a set of concepts which helps us to understand the processes whereby individuals cope with conflict, both within themselves and between themselves and aspects of the outside world.

In his later writings, the focus of Freud's interests shifted to (among other topics) such processes of inner conflict and integration and they have been taken up and developed by later psychoanalysts (e.g. Hartmann 1964).

Richard Stevens
Open University

References

Bettelheim, B. (1983) *Freud and Man's Soul*, New York.
Hartmann, H. (1964) *Essays in Ego Psychology: Selected Problems in Psychoanalytic Theory*, New York.

Further reading

Freud, A. (1936) *The Ego and Mechanisms of Defence*, London.
Freud, S. (1923) *The Ego and the Id, Standard Edition of the Complete Psychological Works of Sigmund Freud*, ed. J. Strachey, Vol. 19, London.
—— (1933) *New Introductory Lectures in Psychoanalysis, Standard Edition of the Complete Psychological Works of Sigmund Freud*, ed. J. Strachey, Vol. 22, London.
Stevens, R. (1983) *Freud and Psychoanalysis*, Milton Keynes.

See also: defences; Freud, Sigmund; id; latency period; psychoanalysis.

elections

In politics elections are a device whereby popular preferences are aggregated to choose an officeholder. Choice by elections is now almost inseparable from representative democracy. Some see the opportunity for choice at periodic elections as the key element of western democracy (Lipset 1960; Schumpeter 1942). In 1975, thirty-three states did not hold elections to choose political leaders. For other states the crucial question is: what sort of elections? A further thirty-three states allowed only one candidate for each office. These are 'consent' elections (Mackenzie 1958). States which allow competitive elections and the possibility of replacing the government are largely western.

Election systems provide guidelines on such matters as who votes and how, frequency of election, how votes are counted, who stands for office and so on. In the twentieth century, most states have granted the vote to all (with a few exceptions) adult resident citizens. Over time, the suffrage has been extended from estates to individuals, and in the twentieth century to large categories formerly excluded on grounds of race, sex and property qualifications. The change has also been to equality or 'one man one vote one value' (Rokkan 1970).

In most states, responsibility for registering eligible voters lies with the government. A significant exception is the USA, where states leave registration to individuals. This partly explains why the turn-out in presidential elections since 1960 has averaged 60 per cent, compared to over 80 per cent in many western states. But US voters have more opportunities to cast votes, in federal, state, local and primary elections, and in long ballots. At the other extreme, political and cultural pressures may produce remarkable turn-outs and verdicts, for example 99.9 per cent turn-out in the former German Democratic Republic in 1964.

Elections have several functions (Rose and Mossawir 1967). These include designating, directly or indirectly, the government; providing feedback between voters and government; demonstrating public support for or repudiation of a regime: providing a means for the recruitment of political leaders; and making the government answerable to the electorate. Functions may differ in states which have elections without choice, where a party's hegemonic or monopolistic position makes the outcome a foregone conclusion (Hermet *et al.* 1978).

In some countries (Belgium, Italy, Denmark and The Netherlands, for example) it is not the election but the inter-party bargaining following the election which determines the composition of government. Where the party system provides a choice between alternative potential majorities, voters do have such a choice. The impact of elections on policies depends in part on a programmatic disciplined majority party being in government. Until recently, the British two-party system was admired for providing a model of 'responsible party government'. More direct popular verdicts on issues may be made through referendums.

The nature of the electoral choice in each state is shaped by three sets of factors. First, the *object* of election, which may be to choose a constituency representative, party list or president. Second, the *party system*, or pattern of voting alignments (Lipset and Rokkan 1967), which in turn is shaped by cleavages in society, the electoral system, and the manoeuvres of elites. Third, the *electoral system*, particularly those provisions which aggregate votes and translate them into seats, that is, rules for counting and weighing votes.

A distinction may be drawn between the absolute majoritarian system, as in France, in which the winner has to achieve at least half the votes; the plurality (first past the post) system in many English-speaking countries; the various forms of proportionalism, including the pure proportional representation (PR) in The Netherlands (where 0.67 per cent of the vote gives a group a seat in the legislature); and those that combine elements of different systems (for example, Germany has PR for half the seats, subject to a party gaining at least 5 per cent of the vote).

Proportionalism was introduced at the turn of the century in divided societies to provide guarantees to minorities which felt threatened by universal suffrage or majority rule. Proportionalism furthers the goals of representativeness but, in the absence of a clear party majority, makes the choice of government less certain.

The British plurality system has usually achieved certainty in choice of the government while sacrificing representativeness. In October 1974 Labour had 51 per cent of the seats in the House of Commons with 39 per cent of the votes. The two systems maximize different values; most western states have opted for proportionalism, subject to qualifications.

We lack a good typology of elections. One may distinguish between degrees of choice, which in turn depends on the number of effective parties and the prospects of turnover in government. The USA has two parties, The Netherlands and Denmark a dozen. Italy, Sweden and Norway have had very long spells of dominant one-party rule, and there has been only one change in France since 1958. In the USA Key (1955) distinguished between elections which were *maintaining* (reflecting normal party loyalties), *deviating* (in which short-term factors produced a short-term surge or decline in support for the parties) and *realigning* (in which there is a long-term change in the balance of party strengths).

There are limits on the decisiveness of elections as authoritative arbiters of policy. Incumbents of the bureaucracy and judiciary, and leaders of powerful interests, who are not elected by the voters, constitute checks. At present 'votes count, resources decide' (Rokkan 1966). The debate about the relative influence of socioeconomic factors or party political factors (and therefore elections) has not been conclusive. The influence of the government depends on the power centralization in society. In pluralist and market societies the government is only one decision maker among others, and competitive elections and majority rule are only two elements in representative democracy. Competitive elections do not ensure the political responsiveness of an elite; they have to operate in favourable conditions. There are alternative methods of facilitating popular choice and eliciting and demonstrating popular consent (for example, acclamation, seniority, rotation, and elite bargaining), but election is still the birthmark of a government claiming to be democratic.

Dennis Kavanagh
University of Nottingham

References

Hermet, G. *et al.* (1978) *Elections Without Choice*, Paris.
Key, V. O. Jr (1955) 'A theory of critical elections', *Journal of Politics*.
Lipset, S. (1960) *Political Man*, London.

Lipset, S. and Rokkan, S. (eds) (1967) *Party Systems and Voter Alignments*, New York.

Mackenzie, W. J. M. (1958) *Free Elections*, London.

Rokkan, S. (1966) 'Norway: numerical democracy and corporate pluralism', in R. Dahl (ed.) *Political Oppositions in Western Democracies*, New Haven, CT.

—— (1970) *Citizens, Elections, Parties*, New York.

Rose, R. and Mossawir, H. (1967) 'Voting and elections: a functional analysis', *Political Studies*.

Schumpeter, J. A. (1942) *Capitalism, Socialism and Democracy*, New York.

See also: democracy; parties, political; voting.

elites

The term elite is part of a tradition which makes modern social scientists uneasy. At the same time, its use facilitates historical and contemporary analysis by providing an idiom of comparison that sets aside institutional details and culture-specific practices, and calls attention instead to intuitively understood equivalencies. Typically, an adjective precedes the word elite, clarifying its aim (oligarchic elite, modernizing elite) or its style (innovating elite, brokerage elite) or its institutional domain (legislative elite, bureaucratic elite) or its resources base (media elite, financial elite) or the decisional stage it dominates (planning elite, implementing elite) or its eligibility grounds (birth elite, credentialled elite).

Two quite different traditions of inquiry persist. In the older tradition, elites are treated as exemplars: fulfilling some historic mission, meeting a crucial need, possessing superior talents, or otherwise demonstrating qualities which set them apart. Whether they stabilize the old order or transform it into a new one, they are seen as pattern setters.

In the newer approach, elites are routinely understood to be incumbents: those who are collectively the influential figures in the governance of any sector of society, any institutional structure, any geographic locality or translocal community. Idiomatically, elites are thus roughly the same as leaders, decision makers or influentials, and not too different from spokespersons, dignitaries or central figures. This second usage is more matter-of-fact, less normative in tone.

Still, elites are seen by many as selfish people in power, bent upon protecting their vested interests, contemptuous of the restraints on constitutional order, callous about the needs of larger publics, ready to manipulate opinion, to rig elections, to use force if necessary to retain power. A conspiratorial variant worries those who fear revolutionary subversive elites: fanatical, selfless, disciplined, competent and devoted to their cause, equally contemptuous of political democracy, constitutional order or mass contentment, willing to exploit hatred and misery, to misrepresent beliefs and facts, and to face personal degradation and social obloquy. Whether to preserve old patterns of life or to exemplify new ones, elites are those who set the styles.

When most social scientists talk about elites, they have in mind 'those who run things' – that is, certain key actors playing structured, functionally understandable roles, not only in a nation's governance processes but also in other institutional settings – religious, military, academic industrial, communications, and so on (Czudnowski 1982; 1983; Eulan and Czudnowski 1979).

Early formulations lacked this pluralist assumption. Mosca (1939 [1896]) and Pareto (see Meisel 1958) both presumed that a ruling class effectively monopolized the command posts of a society. Michels (1959 [1911]) insisted that his 'iron law of oligarchy' was inevitable; in any organization, an inner circle of participants would take over, and run it for their own selfish purposes. By contrast, Lasswell's (1936) formulation in the 1930s was radically pluralistic. Elites are those who get the most of what there is to get in any institutionalized sector of society and not only in the governing institutions and ancillary processes of organized political life. At every functional stage of any decision process – indeed, in any relevant arena – some participants will be found who have sequestered disproportionate shares of those values, whether money, esteem, power or some other condition of life which people seek and struggle for. They are the elite at that stage and in that context. For Lasswell (1977), the question whether a situation is fully egalitarian – that is, extends elite status to every participant – is an empirical question, not a conceptual one. Nor is there necessarily any institutional stability. Macro-analysis of history shows periods of ascendancy for those with different kinds of skills, such as in the use of violence, propaganda, organization, or bargaining strategy.

The social formations – classes, communities and movements – from which elites derive are not fixed. Elites are usefully studied by asking which communities they represent or dominate, which classes they are exponents or products of, which interests they reflect or foreshadow, which personality types they are prone to recruit or to shunt aside, which circumstances of time and place (periods of crisis, tranquillity or transition) seem to provide missions and challenges for them.

Elites may change their character. Elite transformation has often been traced. Pareto saw vitality and decay as an endless cycle. Students of Third-World modernization often note the heightened tensions within a governing elite that accompany the shift in power from a revolutionary-agitational generation to a programmatic-executive generation. Specialized elites

– engineers, soldiers or priests – have often served as second-tier elites, recruited in the service of a ruling class that continues to set a governing style but whose members lack the skills to cope with new and pressing problems. Some scholars hold that a true elite emerges when those who perform the historic mission – whether to bring change, adapt to change, or resist to the end – become convinced that only they can carry out the mission properly. Self-consciously, they come to think of themselves as superior by nature – for example, able to think like scientists or soldiers, willing to take risks like capitalists or revolutionaries (Thoenes 1966).

For some centuries, the historical forces that have been shaping the institutions of modern, urban, industrial, interdependent, institutionally differentiated societies have had a net effect that enlarges, democratizes and equalizes the life chances for elitehood. Everywhere the political stratification system typically resembles a pyramid, reflecting the striking cross-national uniformity that only tiny fractions of a country's citizens have more than an infinitesimal chance of directly influencing national policy or even translocal policies. At the same time, fewer disadvantages linked to social status, educational attainment, geographic residence, cultural claims, age and sex attributes, or institutional credentials now appear to operate as conclusively or comprehensively as in the past.

Viewed as incumbents, those who hold key positions in the governing institutions of a community are, collectively, the elite. They are the custodians of the machinery for making policy. Once a sector of society becomes institutionally differentiated, its ability to adjust to conditions on its own terms is likely to be seriously constrained. Even within its semi-autonomous domains, a custodial elite finds it hard to sustain a liaison network or co-ordinate sector-wide efforts (Field and Higley 1980). Medical elites are typically locality-rooted. Military services feud with one another. Scientists are engrossed with specialized lines of inquiry. Commercial elites are fragmented. Industrial giants are rivals.

In the modern world, when elites are seen as housed within conventionally recognized establishments such as military, diplomatic, legislative or party organizational structures, mid-elites and cadres are linked hierarchically to top elites and specialized to implement the specific public and system goals of their domains. When elites are viewed as the top talent in a vocational field – lawyers, academics, entrepreneurs, and so on – the elite structure is much more disjointed. Mid-elites are the source of eligible talent, engaged in tasks having no necessary articulation with what top elites do, but nonetheless tasks that train and test, groom and screen individuals who may in due course reach top elitehood in their field (Putnam 1976).

Top elites in a custodial structure do not necessarily work well together. The structural complexity of legislatures is such that they typically have rather segmented power structures. In characterizing a military elite, the rivalries of services and branches, the geographic deployment and the generational gaps between echelons all must be acknowledged (Janowitz 1966). The illusion of homogeneity about the administrative elite is dispelled when one looks closely (Dogan 1975). Career services give some coherence to relatively autonomous fields, like police, fire, diplomacy and health. But in specific policy domains, clientele elites often dominate the picture (Armstrong 1973).

Especially when talking about elites in rather amorphous fields of endeavour, the implications of structural disjunctions on the perspectives of those in top positions seem far reaching. Most communications elites are set at working odds with one another in the various media where their contacts and skills apply. At community levels, civic leaders rarely sustain close contacts with their counterparts in other localities.

Elites are studied both in context, in what can be called elite characterization work, and out of context, in what is referred to as elite survey work. There are two main genres of the former: those in which elites are characterized by their mission or function, and those in which elites are seen in a custodial capacity, and characterized by the performance of the institutional processes they control. In a corresponding way, elite surveys – in which elites are taken out of context – also have two main genres: those in which the investigator is mainly interested in what elites think, in the acumen, loyalty and ideological bent of mind typical of certain elite perspectives, and those which explore the recruitment of elite figures by looking at the changing opportunity structure, at social credentials, screening criteria, processes of sponsorship, grooming and socialization, and at those who are the gatekeepers, brokers and mentors who affect the *corsus honorum* of a career. In modern systematic survey work, it is customary at the outset to say how, when and where the elite status of those studied has been established, whether by reputation, position held, or process participated in. Interviews are then held, often rather long interviews, to learn their beliefs, perceptions, preferences and appraisals. Necessarily, in survey work, elites are not studied 'in action'.

Dwaine Marvick
University of California, Los Angeles

References

Armstrong, J. A. (1973) *The European Administrative Elite*, Princeton, NJ.

Czudnowski, M. N. (ed.) (1982) *Does Who Governs Matter?*, DeKalb, IL.

— (1983) *Political Elites and Social Change*, DeKalb, IL.

Dogan, M. (ed.) (1975) *The Mandarins of Western Europe*, New York.

Eulau, H. and Czudnowski, M. (eds) (1979) *Elite Recruitment in Democratic Polities*, New York.

Field, G. L. and Higley, J. (1980) *The Professional Soldier*, Glencoe, IL.

Janowitz, M. (1966) *The Professional Soldier*, Glencoe, IL.

Lasswell, H. D. (1936) *Politics: Who Gets What, When, How*, New York.

— (1977) 'The study of political elites', in D. Marvick (ed.) *Harold D. Lasswell on Political Sociology*, Chicago.

Meisel, J. H. (1958) *The Myth of the Ruling Class*, Ann Arbor, MI.

Michels, R. (1959 [1911]) *Political Parties*, New York.

Mosca, G. (1939 [1896]) *The Ruling Class*, ed. A. Livingston, New York. (Original edn, *Elementi di Scienza parlamentare*.)

Putnam, R. D. (1976) *The Comparative Study of Political Elites*, Englewood Cliffs, NJ.

Thoenes, P. (1966) *The Elite in the Welfare State*, Glencoe, IL.

See also: leadership; political recruitment and careers; social mobility; stratification.

embodiment *see* body; medical anthropology

emotion

William James wrote that he would 'as lief read verbal descriptions of the shapes of the rocks on a New Hampshire farm' as toil again through the classic works on emotion, which lacked a 'central point of view, a deductive or generative principle'. Over one hundred years after James's (1884) famous essay in *Mind*, we are still debating the issues posed by James, in particular the role of physiological changes in emotions, and the central components that determine an emotion. Since James, many theories of emotion and definitions of emotion have been advanced, but there is still a lack of consensus on central issues that preoccupy the emotion area. This diversity of views is due partly to an upsurge during the past two decades of interest in emotion from scholars in different disciplines, all advocating a particular perspective on emotions. In this respect the area of emotion research has changed from a situation in which physiologists and psychologists dominated the field, to a multidisciplinary endeavour in which sociologists and anthropologists are also heavily engaged.

The issues that preoccupy modern emotion theory are in some respects similar to those that arose from James's theory of emotion. Three major disputes may be distinguished. The first concerns the role of physiological changes in emotion. James advocated what has come to be called a peripheral theory of emotion, in which he argued that the perception of an arousing stimulus causes changes in peripheral organs such as the viscera (heart, lungs, stomach, and so on) and the voluntary muscles, and that emotion is quite simply the perception of these bodily changes. To use James's own example, it is not that we tremble and run because we are afraid; rather, we are afraid because we tremble and run. This view clearly implies that there should be as many discrete patterns of physiological activity accompanying emotion as there are discernible emotional states. Cannon (1927) published what was widely regarded as a devastating critique of James's theory, although subsequent research has shown that some of Cannon's objections were ill founded. Although Cannon's critique reduced the influence of James's peripheral theory of emotion, this theory has by no means been completely discarded. In particular, the idea that the perception of bodily changes may elicit an emotion still inspires various contemporary researchers. Indeed, there is recent experimental evidence (Laird and Bresler 1992; Strack, Martin and Stepper 1988) that the induction of a mere posture or facial expression may elicit or enhance emotional feelings. However, evidence for the existence of discrete physiological patterns that differentiate the various emotions is still rather weak and this limits the extent to which James's ideas are accepted by modern researchers.

The essence of Cannon's critique was that the visceral changes that occur during emotion are too non-specific to serve as the basis for differentiated emotional experience. This point led later researchers to abandon the search for an explanation of emotion couched exclusively in terms of bodily changes, and to consider more carefully the role played by cognitive factors – the individual's interpretation of external and internal events.

There are several theories that pay attention to cognitive factors, and the question of the precise role played by cognition in emotion is a second major issue in current emotion theory and research. A classic theory is Schachter's (1964) two-factor theory. Schachter reasoned that the mere awareness of bodily changes does not necessarily result in emotional experience: emotion is the joint product of two factors, namely a general state of physiological arousal, and the cognition that this arousal is caused by an emotional stimulus. The arousal creates the condition necessary for any emotion to be experienced, while the cognition determines which emotion is actually experienced. Thus the same physiological arousal could, in principle, be experienced as any of a variety of emotions, depending on cognitive factors. Although this theory has an appealing elegance and simplicity, there is little evidence to support it (Manstead and Wagner 1981). More complex cognitive theories are proposed by Lazarus and his associates (Lazarus and Folkman 1984) and others (e.g. Frijda 1986). They agree that emotions should be seen as temporally extended processes in which cognitions are one of the central components. More specifically, people appraise their circumstances with respect to their well-being, and these appraisals elicit different emotions. This means that different emotions can be distinguished by different appraisal patterns. Indeed, there is abundant evidence that emotions are characterized by different patterns of appraisal. For example, anger is associated with the appraisal of a negative event caused by another person who is held responsible for this, whereas anxiety is characterized by a negative event with an uncertain outcome, and which is mainly situationally caused; guilt is linked to the appraisal of a negative event for which one blames oneself. Although there is consensus about the major dimensions of these appraisal patterns, debates in the early 1990s centred on the question of whether the role of appraisal really is a causal one (Parkinson and Manstead 1992). Much of the empirical evidence does not preclude a different conclusion, namely that appraisal is the result of the emotion, rather than its cause.

The third major issue governing current emotion research is concerned with its social and cultural aspects. One important question that elicits much theorizing and research is whether emotions are universal or culturally specific phenomena. The advocates of basic emotions (e.g. Ekman 1992) claim that there are a few basic emotions (among others fear, anger, sadness, happiness and disgust) that are expressed in similar ways across cultures and can therefore be recognized universally. Evidence for this claim comes mainly from studies on facial expressions: photographs showing faces posing particular emotional expressions appeared to be correctly recognized by people from a great variety of cultures (Ekman 1982). However, both theoretical and methodological objections have been raised against this view (Russell 1994). The opposite of the basic emotion view is defended by theorists who argue that emotions are simply social constructions. Harré (1986), for example, reasons that in order to gain more insight into emotions, we have merely to study the emotion vocabularies in different cultures. Although there is evidence that the richness, size and content of emotion language differs from one culture to another, there is little support for the view that emotion language is the major determinant of what we feel. However, emotions are influenced by social and cultural factors. Research, much of it conducted by sociologists and cultural anthropologists, has shown

how culture socializes our emotions by means of emotion rules, beliefs about emotions, emotion rituals, and so on. Thus, the answer to the question of the cultural-specificity versus universality of emotions seems to lie somewhere in the middle: there are both cross-cultural similarities and differences in emotions. What one finds depends on the level of analysis and the specific aspects of emotions that are taken into account (Mesquita and Frijda 1992).

Agneta H. Fischer
University of Amsterdam

Antony S. R. Manstead
University of Amsterdam

References

Cannon, W. B. (1927) 'The James-Lange theory of emotions: a critical examination and an alternative theory', *American Journal of Psychology* 39.

Ekman, P. (ed.) (1982) *Emotion in the Human Face*, 2nd edn, Cambridge, UK.

—— (1992) 'An argument for basic emotions', *Cognition and Emotion* 6.

Frijda, N. H. (1986) *The Emotions*, Cambridge, UK.

Harré, R. (ed.) (1986) *The Social Construction of Emotions*, Oxford.

James, W. (1884) 'What is an emotion?', *Mind* 5.

Laird, J. D. and Bresler, C. (1992) 'The Process of Emotional Experience: A Self-Perception Theory', in M. S. Clark (ed.) *Emotion (Review of Personality and Social Psychology 13)*.

Lazarus, R. S. and Folkman, S. (1984) *Stress, Appraisal and Coping*, New York.

Manstead, A. S. R. and Wagner, H. L. (1981) 'Arousal, cognition and emotion: an appraisal of two-factor theory', *Current Psychological Reviews* 1.

Mesquita, B. and Frijda, N. H. (1992) 'Cultural variations in emotions: a review', *Psychological Bulletin* 112.

Parkinson, B. and Manstead, A. S. R. (1992) 'Appraisal as a cause of emotion', in M. S. Clark (ed.) *Emotion (Review of Personality and Social Psychology 13)*.

Russell, J. A. (1994) 'Is there universal recognition of emotion from facial expression? A review of cross-cultural studies', *Psychological Bulletin* 115.

Schachter, S. (1964) 'The interaction of cognitive and physiological determinants of emotional state', in L. Berkowitz (ed.) *Advances in Experimental Social Psychology*, vol. 1, New York.

Strack, F., Martin, L. L. and Stepper, S. (1988) 'Inhibiting and Facilitating Conditions of the Human Smile: A Nonobtrusive Test of the Facial Feedback Hypothesis', Journal of Personality and Social Psychology 54.

Further reading

Frijda, N. H. (1986) *The Emotions*, Cambridge, UK.
Oatley, K. (1992) *Best Laid Schemes*, Cambridge, UK.

See also: activation and arousal; aggression and anger.

employment and unemployment

The concepts of employment and unemployment are more easily defined for a developed capitalist economy which has a market for wage labour. Employment is defined as working for at least one hour a week for some payment, either for a wage or for profit, or commission, or without pay in a family business. However, this definition usually excludes people (mainly women) who provide unpaid household services. Unemployment is defined in terms of not being employed, and available and looking for work. In less developed countries (LDCs), where wage labour is not a predominant form of employment, the concept of unemployment becomes fuzzy: the line between employment in the informal sector (selling cigarettes on the street corners) and unemployment is not clearly defined (see Turnham 1993). In most economies people may not look for work when there are no obvious vacancies available and dropout of the labour force (i.e. the participation rate varies). Since the concept of unemployment may not be well defined, labour economists sometimes use the concept of employment–population ratios (or the not-employed to population ratio).

In OECD countries (see OECD 1993), the post-war decades have seen a growth of the service sector and a relative decline of the industrial and agricultural sectors. At the same time there has been a growth in part-time female employment and a decline in full-time male employment. Further, there has been an increase in white-collar employment and a decline in blue-collar employment and wage inequality has increased. After a short period of full employment in the 1950s and 1960s, most of the OECD economies have faced increasing unemployment and long-term unemployment (the latter defined, at present, as continuous durations of unemployment of twelve months or more). This has led to economists (see Matthews 1968) asking whether the period of the 1950s and 1960s was unusual and whether the norm for developed capitalist economies is of periods of high unemployment. The only OECD countries which appear to have avoided the problems of high unemployment have been Japan, and to a lesser extent the USA. However, the USA appears to have lowered its unemployment rate at the expense of increasing the working poor and creating an underclass, and perhaps, as in LDCs, by a growth of informal sector activities like hustling on the streets.

In conventional economics, employment is determined by demand for labour and supply of labour. Demand for labour is determined in the same way as the demand for non-human inputs (e.g. raw materials, or capital): by firms maximizing profits. Labour supply is determined by individuals maximizing utility choosing between leisure and work (where work is considered to be a necessary evil). In this paradigm wages clear the labour market and unemployment is purely voluntary. In Keynesian and post-Keynesian theories, wages do not adjust instantaneously to clear the labour market and involuntary unemployment eventuates. Employment is determined by labour demand: the excess of labour supply at the market wages is called unemployment.

Full employment is defined as a state where labour demand equals labour supply at existing wage rates. More recently, the concept of the NAIRU has been proposed: this is the non-accelerating inflation rate of unemployment (Johnson and Layard 1986). This level of unemployment, sometimes called the natural rate of unemployment, is often thought of as the full employment level. Many economists argue that the labour market operates in such a way as to make the present level of unemployment depend on the previous history of the time path of unemployment: the idea of *hysteresis* in the labour market which leads to unemployment rates increasing with time in a 'ratchet' fashion. The reasons for hysteresis are thought to be the lower probability of the long-term unemployed finding work because of decreased search by them due to a loss of self-esteem, because of skill atrophy, and employers rejecting them because they see unemployment as a sign of poor qualities. In addition, in the macroeconomic sphere the long-term unemployed have no impact on wage bargaining and the NAIRU increases. In contrast to this view, new classical economists argue that employment and unemployment follow a random path: exogenous shocks simply perturb the natural rate. For the few countries for which we have data spanning a long period (say over fifty years) there is no obvious trend in the unemployment rate (Layard *et al.* 1991).

Unemployment is usually separated into the following components: seasonal, frictional (due to temporary mismatch between workers and vacancies), cyclical (due to aggregate demand changes), and structural (due to long-term changes in the economic structure, including technological change). Sometimes we distinguish hidden unemployment (people who leave the labour force in times of recession) from open unemployment. We also consider underemployment where workers would prefer to work longer hours, e.g. workers who are placed on short-time working, or those who can find only part-time work who would prefer full-time work.

The major explanations of unemployment (and fluctuations in unemployment) are as follows: aggregate demand, technological and structural change, wage rigidity, information problems, and aggregate supply. More recently, it has been postulated that unemployment in OECD countries has been caused by the growth of low wage Newly Industrialized Countries (NICs, like Korea, Singapore, Thailand, etc.) who are taking away markets from the richer high wage economies (Economist 1994; Krugman and Lawrence 1994).

Keynesians explain unemployment by a lack of aggregate demand for goods and services with a labour market where wages do not adjust instantaneously. Marx and Schumpeter argued that technological and structural change were inherent in a capitalist economy, and, due to the volatility of investment, unemployment would also be cyclical. Marx also argued that the industrial reserve army (unemployment) would act as a brake on wage growth as well as controlling the 'pretensions of the workers' (Junankar 1982). Neoclassical economists explain unemployment in terms of misinformation in the labour market which leads to some unemployed people not accepting wage offers in the (sometimes mistaken) belief that a better wage offer is round the corner. This is made possible by the availability of unemployment benefits. In some versions this is simply an optimizing strategy where the unemployed are carrying out an intertemporal substitution of leisure. In other versions, unemployment is due to random supply shocks. However, it is not explained why these 'random' shocks hit all countries simultaneously.

Most theories of unemployment focus on reasons for wages not adjusting downwards in textbook fashion in the face of excess supply (unemployment). Neo-classical theories tend to emphasize the rigidities introduced by unions, unemployment benefits, and minimum wage legislation. An alternative explanation, the insider-outsider hypothesis, has wage bargaining conducted between employers and unions such that they only concern themselves with the employed labour force (the insiders) while the unemployed (the outsiders) are ignored (Lindbeck 1993).

In the 1980s and 1990s theories of employment and unemployment have focused on emphasizing the distinctive properties of the labour market and the role of wages in providing incentives to offer more or higher quality (more productive) labour services (Solow 1990). Explanations are offered for the wage rate to be determined in such a manner that higher than market clearing wages are set by employers either to get a more skilled labour force (adverse selection models), or to provide the workers with an incentive to be more productive. These efficiency wage models (Akerlof and Yellen 1986) suggest that wages are set higher than necessary and workers who do not perform adequately would be fired (shirking model): the threat of unemployment or a poorly paid job provides workers with an incentive to be productive. In another version, higher wages decrease turnover and hence provide employers with a more stable and hence more productive workforce. In another version, suggested Akerlof, social custom plays a part and a partial gift-exchange takes place: workers get paid a wage higher than necessary and workers provide more (better) labour services than they are required to.

Unemployment imposes severe costs on the economy in terms of lost GDP (both now and in the future), costs to the government in terms of lost revenues, loss of earnings for the unemployed individuals and families, and a loss in terms of physical and mental illness, social disruption, and crime in society (Junankar 1986).

Many OECD governments have given up their commitment to full employment, either because they believe that the free market would eventually solve the problem, or that the danger of inflationary forces is too great to introduce explicit policies for full employment. Recent pronouncements have been in terms of introducing more flexible labour markets (i.e. increased downward flexibility of wages, fewer constraints on employers in hiring and firing practices, weakening of the powers of the unions, etc.). The major policy interventions have been in introducing labour market training programmes, improving the efficiency of labour market exchanges, and deregulating of the labour markets.

P. N. Junankar
Australian National University

References

Akerlof, G. A. and Yellen, J. L. (1986) (eds) *Efficiency Wage Models of the Labor Market*, Cambridge, UK.

Economist (1994) 'The global economy: a survey', *The Economist* 233 (7883).

Johnson, G. E. and Layard, P. R. G. (1986) 'The natural rate of unemployment: explanations and policy', in O. Ashenfelter and R. Layard (eds) *Handbook of Labor Economics*, Amsterdam.

Junankar, P. N. (1982) *Marx's Economics*, Oxford.

—— (1986) *Costs of Unemployment: Main Report*, Luxembourg.

Krugman, P. R. and Lawrence, R. Z. (1994) 'Trade, jobs and wages', *Scientific American* 270(4).

Layard, R., Nickell, S. and Jackman, R. (1991) *Unemployment: Macroeconomic Performance and the Labour Market*, Oxford.

Lindbeck, A. (1993) *Unemployment and Macroeconomics*, London.

Matthews, R. C. O. (1968) 'Why has Britain had full employment since the war?', *Economic Journal* 78.

OECD (1993) *Employment Outlook*, Paris.

Solow, R. (1990) *The Labour Market as a Social Institution*, Oxford.

Turnham, D. (1993) *Employment and Development: A Review of the Evidence*, Paris.

See also: labour market analysis; macroeconomic policy; stagflation.

energy

Any society's ability to survive depends on its continued access to energy in appropriate quantities and at acceptable costs. The relationship over time between the level of development in an economy and the use of energy is illustrated in Figure 1.

Given this relationship, then the transformation of the world since the 1840s from a world which consisted mainly of peasant economies largely subsistent in their organization to one consisting of post-industrial, industrial and industrializing economies, has produced a global use of energy which is now over twenty-five times greater than it is estimated to have been in 1860. Figure 2 shows what a remarkably consistent rate of growth in energy use there has been over the whole of this period (at about 2.2 per cent per year), except for the years between 1950 and 1973 when the rate of growth was almost 5 per cent per year.

The demand for energy

Though attitudes to the world energy situation and outlook have been heavily dependent on the idea that this exceptional period of rapid energy growth represents the norm, it was, on the contrary, a unique combination of time-coincident factors which produced an energy growth rate so much higher than the long-term trend; to which (as shown in Figure 2) the world has returned since 1973.

Between 1950 and 1973 virtually all the world's nations happened to be on the steepest part of the curve in Figure 1; in a situation, that is, in which their economies were in the most highly energy intensive period of development. First, the rich countries of the western economic system were going through the later stages of the industrialization process with an emphasis on products with high energy inputs – such as motor vehicles, household durable goods and petrochemical products. As a result, the use of energy on the production side of the economy greatly increased. On the consumption side, the increase in energy use was even more dramatic as a result of the mass use of motor cars, the suburbanization of cities, the switch from public to private transport, the expanded availability of leisure time and the 'annihilation of space' in the public's use of such time, the mechanization of households by the use of electricity-intensive equipment and

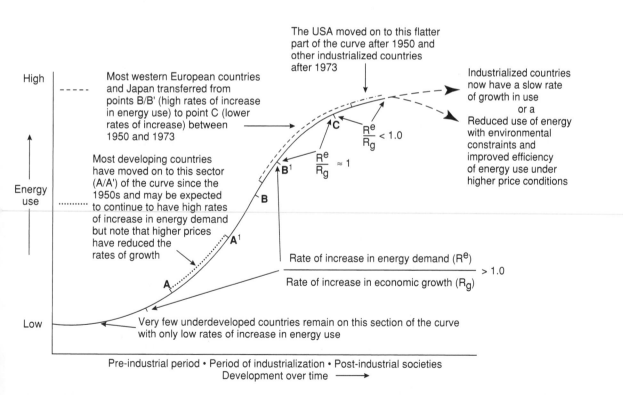

Figure 1   Relationship between energy use and economic development over time: the rate of increase (decrease) in energy use is a function of the stage of economic development. © EGI 113/86

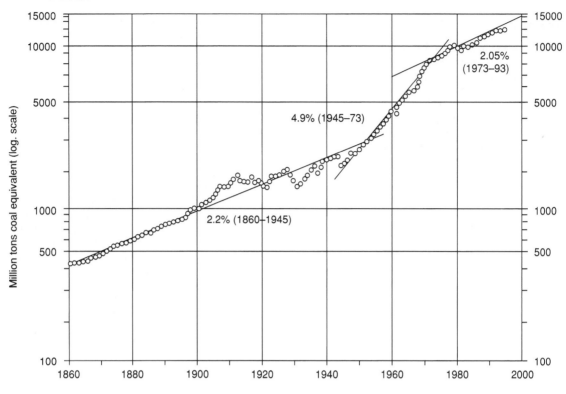

Figure 2 Trends in the evolution of world energy use, 1860–1993 © EGI 144/83 (rev 91)

the achievement of much higher standards of comfort (by heating and/or cooling) in homes and other buildings.

Second, many of the same factors positively influenced the rate of growth in energy use in the centrally planned economies of the former Soviet Union and eastern Europe. This was particularly the case in respect of those countries' industrialization, with its special emphasis on the rapid expansion of heavy, energy-intensive industry. To a smaller, but, nevertheless, a still significant extent, consumers in the centrally planned economies also increased their levels of energy use as a result of higher living standards and changes in lifestyle. The centrally planned economies were, moreover, extremely inefficient in their use of energy: partly because of technical inefficiencies and partly because the price of energy was kept very low.

Third, in the Third World most countries had moved off the lowest part of the curve shown in Figure 1, as policies of industrialization, accompanied by urbanization, were deliberately pursued in the search for higher living standards. The sort of industry which was established was either energy-intensive heavy industry, such as iron and steel and cement, or relatively energy-intensive industry, such as textiles and

household goods. The urbanization process, moreover, meant that peasants and other rural inhabitants abandoned their low-energy ways of living (in which most of the energy required was collected rather than purchased) for lifestyles in the city environment which were, no matter how poor the living standards achieved, much more demanding in their use of energy.

It was essentially the temporal coincidence of these basic societal change factors in most parts of the world which caused the high rate of growth in energy use in the 1950s and 1960s. The high energy growth rate was, moreover, increased by the continuing decline in the real price of energy during that period. This can be seen in Figure 3 in which the evolution of the real price of Saudi Arabian light crude oil (measured in terms of the 1974 value of the US dollar) over the period from 1950 is illustrated. From this one can see that the value of a barrel of oil fell by almost 60 per cent from 1950 to 1970. This decline brought about a falling market price for other forms of energy during this period throughout the world, and most especially in the western industrial countries with their open – or relatively open – economies. In these areas local energy production (such as coal in western Europe and oil and natural gas in the USA) either had to be reduced in price to enable it to compete, or it went out of business. (This phenomenon was also important for the supply side of the global energy situation. We shall return to this later.) Thus, both the actual decline in the price of energy and the perception created among energy users that energy was cheap, getting cheaper and so hardly worth worrying about in terms of the care and efficiency with which it was used, created conditions in which the careless and wasteful consumption of energy became a hallmark of both technological and behavioural aspects of societal developments – with a consequential emphasis on systems of production, transport and consumption which were, unnecessarily, too energy-intensive.

The impact of higher prices

Post-1970 changes in the price of oil (also shown in Figure 3), and hence in the price of energy overall, brought these attitudes to an end, so that the use of energy has since been curbed. The results of this change have (as shown in Figure 2) been dramatic. The rate of increase between 1973 and 1993 has fallen right back to the historic rate of only 2 per cent per year.

The most important element in this reduction in the rate of growth has been the fall in the energy-intensity of economic activities in the industrialized countries. For western European countries, for example, the energy-intensity of economic growth from 1973 to 1982 declined to little more than half that of the preceding ten years, and since 1982 the ratio has fallen by another 20 per cent. There have been both technological and behavioural components in this change; the latter include consumers' decisions to save energy through the expenditure of effort and money on insulating their homes and on living with lower temperatures, and on their more efficient use of their motor cars by driving more carefully and by combining trips to save mileage. It is, however, the technological improvements that have been the more important in saving energy: through more efficient processes in factories, more efficient lighting in offices, the development of motor vehicles, planes and ships which give more kilometres per litre (ton) of fuel, and the expansion of inherently more energy efficient systems of electricity production. For example, the production of electricity from natural gas in combined cycle gas turbines is up to 50 per cent more efficient than in

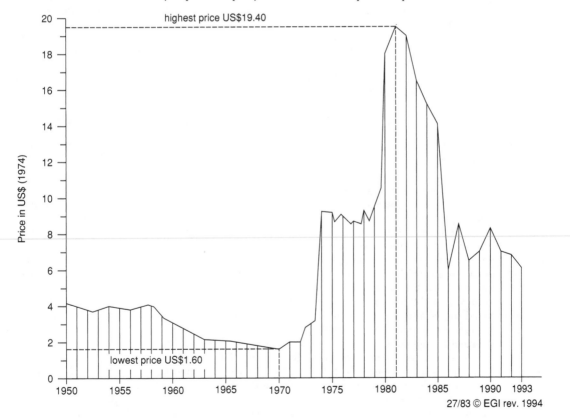

27/83 © EGI rev. 1994

Figure 3   Price of Saudi light crude oil, 1950–93 (shown in 1974 US$ values: the actual price in 1993 was US$16 per barrel)

conventional power stations. Nevertheless, both the behavioural and the technological aspects of more effective energy use still have far to go before the existing energy inefficient systems of the period of low and decreasing-cost energy are finally replaced, even in the richer countries where the required investment funds and other inputs (of knowledge, managerial and technical expertise and so on) are available. The diffusion of more effective energy-using systems to the modern sectors of most Third-World countries is an even slower process because of the scarcity of the inputs involved. Change is, however, taking place under the stimulus of the high foreign exchange cost of energy (particularly oil) imports to the economies concerned. Thus, enhanced levels of energy-use efficiency are being achieved in the Third World. This is an important consideration for the longer-term evolution of global energy demand, as the percentage of world energy use in these countries is steadily increasing under the joint impact of expanding populations and of economies which are going through the most energy intensive period of development (see Figure 1). The countries which had centrally planned economies lie somewhere in between the industrialized and the Third-World countries in respect of energy use and prospects patterns. To date they have not done as well as the market economies in saving energy, but the importance of energy conservation has now become generally recognized by the post-communist governments of the countries concerned so that the implementation of measures in these countries now has a much higher priority.

The supply of fossil fuels

Meanwhile, on the supply side the search for a higher degree of energy self-sufficiency by nations in all parts of the world became a key element in energy policy making after 1973. This was because of widely shared fears for recurring supply problems, emerging from the dependence on oil from the Middle East and a few other OPEC countries. This caused a reversal of what had hitherto been an increasingly concentrated geography of energy production of post-Second World War period, during which the prolific and extremely low cost oil resources of the Middle East and other areas undermined the economic production of most energy sources in most other parts of the world. Thus, not only did hitherto important energy-producing regions such as western Europe (where the economy had been built on the use of indigenous coal) become dependent on oil imports from the low-cost countries, but so did much of the developing world, where the required rapidly increasing supply of energy was easier to secure on the basis of oil imported through the aegis

of the international oil companies than through the efforts to expand the indigenous production of energy. It was only in the case of the few countries, including the USA, which protected their indigenous energy-supply industries to a high enough degree that the contribution of low-cost imported oil was restricted to a relatively small part of total energy supply.

By the early 1970s even the USA, with its wealth of energy resources, finally had to reduce the degree to which it protected its indigenous production in order to reduce the energy cost disadvantage it had come to suffer compared with competing industrial nations, where energy costs were related to the cheap oil available from the Middle East.

This situation changed drastically once OPEC increased the price of oil – as shown in Figure 3. The approximately fivefold real price increase of OPEC oil between 1970 and 1975 and the subsequent further doubling of the price by 1981 removed the economic restraints on investment in locally available energy resources, so there was thus a general reappraisal of the prospects for indigenous energy production in most countries. Some developments were possible in the short term, notably in the USA where underutilized capacity in already established energy-supply industries was quickly brought into production. In western Europe a massive stimulus was given to the efforts to exploit North Sea oil and gas and the hitherto deteriorating prospects for the continent's coal industry were temporarily reversed. Similar developments occurred elsewhere in the non-communist world and produced the changes, shown in Table 1, in the relative importance of OPEC exports to non-OPEC energy demand by 1986.

Table 1 shows how dramatically OPEC's contribution to the non-communist world's energy supply fell. Other oil supplies came to exceed imports of OPEC oil by a very wide margin. OPEC's 1986 oil exports were, moreover, less important than both natural gas and coal supplies. World energy supplies thus became geographically more dispersed, a process which continued as long as the price of OPEC oil remained so far above the cost of alternatives, and as long as oil supplies from most OPEC countries continued to be perceived as unreliable. In essence, the low-cost, but high-price, oil reserves of the OPEC countries became 'the energy source of last resort'. This involved real economic costs for the world economy as a result of the higher-than-necessary costs of energy inputs to both production and consumption activities – so reducing economic growth in most parts of the world in the 1980s.

These changes in energy supply and demand conditions soon led, however, to the reversal of the upward trend in prices. This can be seen in Figure 3, which

Table 1

Sources of energy used in the non-communist world
(excluding the OPEC countries) in 1973 and 1986

	1973		1986	
	mtoe*	% of total	mtoe*	% of total
Imports of OPEC oil	1480	36.5	674	16.2
Other energy supplies	2565	63.5	3474	83.8
of which				
oil	810	20.0	1318	31.8
natural gas	795	19.5	865	20.9
coal	825	20.5	1049	25.3
other	135	3.5	242	5.5
Total	4045	100	4148	100

Sources: Derived from UN Energy Statistics (Series J) and BP's
Annual Statistical Review of World Energy.

Note: * mtoe = million tons oil equivalent.

shows a more or less continuing fall in the oil price
since 1982. By 1993 the price was, indeed, back to its
level of the mid-1970s, yet supplies remained plentiful,
while global demand for energy continued to grow
only slowly (see Figure 2). Increasing geological knowledge, technical innovations and rising efficiency in
production have eliminated the earlier fears of scarcity
of fossil fuels and have made the international supply
system much more competitive. While there are some
residual concerns for the security of supply – largely
related to geopolitical factors – a new issue has now
emerged to justify continuing concern for energy,
that is, the regional and global environmental impacts of the use of increasing volumes of fossil fuels.
In particular, the likely global warming consequence of
carbon dioxide emissions is now central to policies
which seek to constrain energy use, with increases in
taxes generally agreed to be the most effective way of
achieving this objective. This, of course, implies limitations on the supply required, to the consternation of
the countries whose economies depend on fossil fuel
exports.

Alternative energy sources

Prospects for the exploitation of renewable energy
sources attracted much attention in the 1970s and
1980s through the fears of scarcity of fossil fuels: alternative energy prospects are now, by contrast, related
principally to environmental considerations. Thus,
there are enthusiastic lobbies for the rapid expansion
of benign energy systems based on solar, wind, water,

wave and biomass energy potential. There has been an
increasingly significant response to this enthusiasm by
energy policy makers in most parts of the world,
mainly in the form of more research and development
funds. However, apart from the continued expansion
of hydroelectricity production (a long-established
source of energy), relatively little success has been
achieved to date in 'commercializing' the potential
contribution of the benign energy sources. This is
partly because of the long gestation period required for
technical innovation, partly because their successful
utilization depends on locating appropriate physical
geographical conditions, and partly because their use
also depends on changes in the structure of societies
and the reorganization of national energy supply
networks. These are formidable problems so that the
relative contribution of such sources of energy to the
world's now slowly rising total energy needs still seems
unlikely to grow very quickly until well into the twenty-
first century.

By contrast, nuclear power which initially secured
the support of many governments as a means of
reducing dependence on imported oil is now also
presented as an environmentally cleaner form of
energy. Its expansion has thus been generously, even

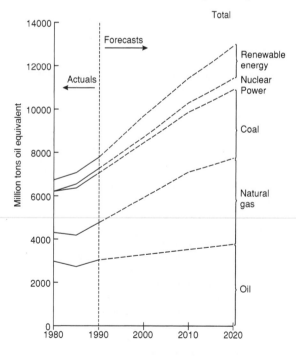

(forecasts = midpoint values of a range dependent on price)

Figure 4 Growth in world energy use, 1980–2020, showing
the contributions of individual main sources of energy
© EGI 61/91

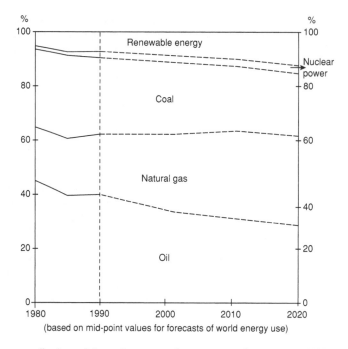

Figure 5 Percentage contributions of the main sources of energy to total energy use, 1980–2020 © EGI 62/91

extravagantly, funded (partly, at least, because it was linked to the development of the major powers' nuclear arsenals). There has been a tenfold expansion in nuclear electricity production since the mid-1970s, albeit from a very small initial level of output. In spite of all the efforts and money devoted to it, nuclear power remains globally no more important than water power, and it still contributes less than 2 per cent to the world's total energy use. Some governments and other authorities remain convinced of nuclear power's potential, but cost escalation, public concern for the safety of the reactors and of the irradiated waste products from the power stations, and, most important of all, its inability to compete effectively with electricity from fossil fuels in most countries where nuclear power is a practicable proposition from the standpoints of available finance and technology have severely undermined the prospects for nuclear power. It, too, seems destined to make little additional contribution to world energy supplies between 1995 and 2015. Figure 4 summarizes the outlook for world energy over the period up to 2020. Growth in use will continue to be modest and in this context the contribution of fossil fuels will remain dominant.

The relative importance of coal, oil and natural gas will, however, change as shown in Figure 5. Plentiful supplies, consumer preference and its more acceptable use from the environmental point of view will eventu-ally make natural gas the world's single most impor-tant energy source.

The poor world's energy problem

Outside the framework of the discussion of energy presented here is one element that remains important for large parts of the world, that is, the supply of locally available energy in societies which remain largely or partly subsistent in their economic organization. The *per capita* use of energy in such societies is small (see Figure 1), as it depends on the immediately available supply of combustible materials (such as wood and dung) which can provide for cooking and heating needs. Collectively, however, this pattern of energy use in the world is still large given the numbers of people involved in such societies. Overall, it is estimated still to account for almost 20 per cent of total world energy use, ranging from near zero in the industrialized coun-tries, to about 15 per cent in Latin America and to over 90 per cent in some of the poorest countries of Africa. In almost all of the latter areas the local scarcity of wood is becoming an increasingly difficult problem. The solution requires 'energy-farming' and new, albeit simple, technological developments which bring improved efficiencies in the use of the combustible materials. This is a world energy problem of which little is known and about which even less is being done, compared, that is, with the attention which is given to the problems of oil and the other energy sources required for intensive use in the developed world and in the modernized sectors of the developing countries' economies.

Peter R. Odell
Erasmus University,
Rotterdam

Further reading

Beck, P. (1994) *Prospects and Strategies for Nuclear Power*, London.
Clark, J. G. (1990) *The Political Economy of World Energy*, London.
Davis, J. D. (1984) *Blue Gold: The Political Economy of Natural Gas*, London.
Gordon, R. L. (1987) *World Coal; Economics, Politics and Prospects*, Cambridge, UK.
Grubb, M. (1990/1) *Energy Policies and the Greenhouse Effect*, Aldershot.
Mounfield, P. R. (1991) *World Nuclear Power*, London.
Odell, P. R. (1986) *Oil and World Power*, Harmondsworth.
Odell, P. R. and Rosing, K. E. (1983) *The Future of Oil: World Resources and Use*, London.
Office of Technology Assessment (US Congress) (1992) *Fueling Development: Energy Technologies for Developing Countries*, Washington, DC.
Schipper, L. and Meyers, S. (1992) *Energy Efficiency and Human Activity*, Cambridge, UK.
Simon, J. L. and Khan, H. (eds) (1984) *The Resourceful Earth*, Oxford.
Smil, V. and Knowland, W. E. (1980) *Energy in the Developing World: The Real Crisis*, New York.
World Energy Council (1993) *Energy for Tomorrow's World*, London.

See also: conservation; economic geography; environmental economics; natural resource economics; population and resources.

enterprise *see* corporate enterprise; multinational enterprises

entrepreneurship

The term entrepreneur seems to have been introduced into economic theory by Cantillon (1931 [1755]) and was first accorded prominence by Say (1803). It was variously translated into English as merchant, adventurer or employer, though the precise meaning is the undertaker of a project. John Stuart Mill (1848) popularized the term in Britain.

In the neo-classical theory of the firm, entrepreneurial ability is analogous to a fixed factor endowment because it sets a limit to the efficient size of the firm. The static and passive role of the entrepreneur in the neo-classical theory reflects the theory's emphasis on

perfect information – which trivializes management and decision making – and on perfect markets – which do all the co-ordination that is necessary and leave nothing for the entrepreneur.

According to Schumpeter (1934), entrepreneurs are the prime movers in economic development, and their function is to innovate or carry out new combinations. Five types of innovation are distinguished: the introduction of a new good (or an improvement in the quality of an existing good); the introduction of a new method of production; the opening of a new market – in particular an export market in new territory; the 'conquest of a new source of supply of raw materials or half-manufactured goods'; and the creating of a new type of industrial organization – in particular the formation of a trust or some other type of monopoly.

Schumpeter is also very clear about what entrepreneurs are not: they are not inventors, but people who decide to allocate resources to the exploitation of an invention; they are not risk-bearers: risk-bearing is the function of the capitalist who lends funds to the entrepreneur. Essentially, therefore, Schumpeter's entrepreneur has a managerial or decision-making role.

This view receives qualified support from Hayek (1937) and Kirzner (1973), who emphasize the role of entrepreneurs in acquiring and using information. Entrepreneurs' alertness to profit-opportunities, and their readiness to exploit these through arbitrage-type operations, makes them the key element in the market process. Hayek and Kirzner regard entrepreneurs as responding to change – as reflected in the information they receive – while Schumpeter emphasizes the role of entrepreneurs as a source of change. These two views are not incompatible: a change effected by one entrepreneur may cause spill-over effects, which alter the environment of other entrepreneurs. Hayek and Kirzner do not insist on the novelty of entrepreneurial activity, however, and it is certainly true that a correct decision is not always a decision to innovate; premature innovation may be commercially disastrous. Schumpeter begs the question of whether someone who is the first to evaluate an innovation, but decides (correctly) not to innovate, qualifies as an entrepreneur.

Knight (1921) insists that decision making involves uncertainty. Each business situation is unique, and the relative frequencies of past events cannot be used to evaluate the probabilities of future outcomes. According to Knight, measurable risks can be diversified (or laid off) through insurance markets, but uncertainties cannot. Those who take decisions in highly uncertain environments must bear the full consequences of those decisions themselves. These people are entrepreneurs: they are the owners of businesses and not the salaried managers that make the day-to-day decisions.

Leibenstein (1968) regards the entrepreneur as someone who achieves success by avoiding the inefficiencies to which other people – or the organizations to which they belong – are prone. Leibenstein's approach has the virtue of emphasizing that, in the real world, success is exceptional and failure is the norm.

Casson (1982) defines the entrepreneur as someone who specializes in taking decisions where, because of unequal access to information, different people would opt for different strategies. Casson shows that the evaluation of innovations, as discussed by Schumpeter, and the assessment of arbitrage opportunities, as discussed by Hayek and Kirzner, can be regarded as special cases. Casson also shows that if Knight's emphasis on the uniqueness of business situations is used to establish that differences of opinion are very likely in all business decisions, then the Knightian entrepreneur can be embraced within his definition as well. Because the definition identifies the *function* of the entrepreneur, it is possible to use conventional economic concepts to discuss the valuation of entrepreneurial services and many other aspects of the market for entrepreneurs.

Perhaps the aspect of entrepreneurship that has attracted most attention is the motivation of the entrepreneur. Hayek and Kirzner take the Austrian view that the entrepreneur typifies purposeful human action directed towards individualistic ends. Schumpeter, however, refers to the dream and will to found a private dynasty, the will to conquer and the joy of creating, while Weber (1930) emphasizes the Protestant Ethic and the concept of calling, and Redlich (1956) the role of militaristic values in the culture of the entrepreneur. Writers of business biographies have ascribed a whole range of different motives to people whom they describe as entrepreneurs. For many students of business behaviour, it seems that the entrepreneur is simply someone who finds adventure and personal fulfilment in the world of business. The persistence of this heroic concept suggests that many people do not want a scientific account of the role of the entrepreneur.

Successful entrepreneurship provides an avenue of social advancement that is particularly attractive to people who are denied opportunities elsewhere. This may explain why it is claimed that immigrants, religious minorities and people denied higher education are over-represented among entrepreneurs. Hypotheses of this kind are difficult to test without carefully controlled sampling procedures. The limited evidence available suggests that, in absolute terms, the most common type of entrepreneur is the son of an entrepreneur.

Mark Casson
University of Reading

References

Cantillon, R. (1931 [1755]) *Essai sur la nature du commerce en générale*, ed. H. Higgs, London.

Casson, M. C. (1982) *The Entrepreneur: An Economic Theory*, Oxford.

Hayek, F. A. von (1937) 'Economics and knowledge', *Economica* 4.

Kirzner, I. M. (1973) *Competition and Entrepreneurship*, Chicago.

Knight, F. H. (1921) *Risk, Uncertainty and Profit*, ed. G. J. Stigler, Chicago.

Leibenstein, H. (1968) 'Entrepreneurship and development', *American Economic Review* 58.

Mill, J. S. (1848) *Principles of Political Economy*, London.

Redlich, F. (1956) 'The military enterpriser: a neglected area of research', *Explorations in Entrepreneurial History* 8.

Say, J.-B. (1803) *Traité d'économie politique*, Paris.

Schumpeter, J. A. (1934) *The Theory of Economic Development*, trans. R. Opie, Cambridge, MA.

Weber, M. (1930) *The Protestant Ethic and the Spirit of Capitalism*, trans. T. Parsons, London.

See also: leadership; profit; risk analysis; Weber.

environment

Einstein is reported to have defined environment as 'everything that isn't me'. This aphorism symbolizes one feature of the environmental dilemma. Unlike any other living creature, humans can view the natural world as if they were separate from it. Toynbee (1976) remarked that humans have rational minds and emotional souls. They can order ideas and rank feelings. They can care passionately about salvation and fear for what they bequeath to their offspring. They can overslaughter bison yet create a lasting international Antarctic sanctuary for whales.

Environment is a metaphor for the enduring contradictions in the human condition: the power of domination yet the obligation of responsibility; the drive for betterment tempered by the sensitivity of humility; the manipulation of nature to improve the chances of survival, yet the universal appeal of sustainable development; the individualism of consumerism and the social solidarity of global citizenship. These points are made in books by Atkinson (1991), Dickens (1992), Dobson (1990), Eckersley (1992) and Sachs (1993). Throughout time, human excesses have been tamed by a combination of pragmatic caution and fearful guilt. The best statement here is Glacken (1967) but more accessible references can be found in Simmons (1989; 1993).

The balancing zone has never been static, nor confined to a single point. More often than not the tension has never been clearly recognized in day-to-day human behaviour. The traditional clash between developers and preservationists that has characterized environmental disputes since the days when the great American naturalist-philosopher John Muir fought to save the Hetch Hetchy valley in the California Yosemite, is no longer the battleground. The real struggle is to reunite humanity with the natural world. That world is resilient beyond anything that humans can do to alter it. But in adjusting to its human-induced transformation, the natural world can and will eliminate much of its meddlers. The tragedy is that those who will suffer are the victims, not the perpetrators of this transformation. Environment is now the process of combining social justice with global survival, of integrating civil rights with natural rights, and of linking all the sciences with the political processes that seek to make democracy work properly.

Humans are beginning to realize how unique life on earth actually is. The cosmos of which we are all a part is the outcome of almost unimaginable chance. The enormously complicated physical, chemical and biological processes that maintain life on earth appear to have a marvellous capacity for self-organization with no apparent ulterior design. This point is best expressed by Lovelock (1992) in the *Gaia thesis*. The biosphere is simply the zone in which life exists on earth. Gaia is defined as a self-regulating system that emerges from the tightly coupled evolution of biota and the material elements and fluxes that circulate substances and energy around the globe. In an important sense, Gaia is a very special scientific concept. It utilizes traditional scientific enquiry to reveal how the totality of physics, chemical and biological process interact to retain the conditions vital for the survival of all life on earth. Gaia has no morality, nor a purpose. It has no special place for humans. The history of evolution is littered with the remains of lost species and the wholesale removal of habitats. If Gaia tells us anything, it is that humans must adapt to survive, and that the process of adjustment is part of the totality of self-regulation. Otherwise the earth will do it for us.

At the heart of environmentalism are three views of the world, namely technocentric, ecocentric and deep green. First, the *technocentric* mode (O'Riordan 1981) visualizes humanity in manipulate or heroic mould, capable of transforming the earth for the betterment of both people and nature. This is the essence of the progressive conservationists of the turn of the century in the USA (Hays 1959). Technocentrism is optimistic, interventionist, dominant and, for some at least, male-led and hierarchical (Mies and Shiva 1993). It is the product of, and the provider for, conventional science with its bias in favour of objective observation, replicative experimentation, obedience to laws and hypothesis, and productive use of models. It also thrives on the purported efficiency of market forces, of minimum intervention by the state, and of opportunism in improving individual advancement. Technocentrism is regarded as not only the cause of environmental destitution, but also its salvation (Simon and Kahn 1984). It is seen as the progenitor of environmentally benign technology, environmentally friendly product substitution, and the wealth-creating engine that will allow the poor to be emancipated from their prisons of enforced environmental and social debasement.

The second view is *ecocentric* (Dobson 1990; O'Riordan 1981; Pepper 1986). This is also optimistic, but recognizes the need to incorporate the limits of arrogance in the conduct of human affairs. The aim is to incorporate the costs of altering the natural world, and of removing the civil rights and native knowledge of indigenous peoples by ensuring that these costs and obligations are duly placed on the accounts ledger. This in turn has spawned a host of manipulative middle ground, accommodationist mechanisms aimed at making economic development more socially tolerable and environmentally sustainable. Examples of five of these devices are as follows.

First, *sustainable development*, the buzz phrase of the Brundtland Commission (1987) and the UN Conference on Environment and Development (UNCED) held in Rio de Janeiro in 1992 and the basis of *Agenda 21*, the programme for integrating development and environment: for contrary views see International Union for the Conservation of Nature (1989) and Sachs (1993).

Second, the *precautionary principle*, the up-and-coming concept that accepts that scientific knowledge may never be complete, or ready in time to take justifiable action in anticipation of disaster. Precaution places the spotlight on *civic science*, or the integration of all the conventional sciences within a meaningful democratic process, or *ecological space*, or the provision of room for manoeuvre in the allocation of controls between the developed and developing nations, allowing for the latter to take time to adjust while the former accommodate more quickly and more comprehensively, and on *altering the burden of proof* to ensure that would-be victims can legitimately protest in advance of development so that those who seek to change the status quo must guarantee that no one is actually made worse off (see O'Riordan and Cameron 1994).

Third, *ecological economics*, the incorporation of valuation studies to calculate the worth of environmental services provided by natural systems such as stratospheric ozone or the tropical moist forests, so as to ensure that the full costs of development or of protection of *critical natural capital*, namely the life-sustaining habitats and processes are built into all future economic accounts in the form of parallel *natural resource accounts* or even environmental welfare indices (see Pearce *et al.* 1993).

Fourth, *environmental impact assessment*, or the complete analysis of the full social and natural environmental consequences of both specific projects and the policies upon which they are promoted (O'Riordan and Sewell 1981). This has spawned a whole enterprise of environmental consultancy and is slowly turning the planning, engineering and accountancy professions more environmentally sensitive.

Fifth, *ecoauditing* of industry using techniques such as *life cycle analysis* and *environmental burden analysis*. This is part of the environmental management systems approach to quality assurance in business practice. It is also likely to become internationally standardized as the basis of good corporate commitment to sustainable development. The various techniques involve systematic recording of the total energy, materials and economic flows associated with products and choice processes organized into comprehensive and public accounts.

All of this is still emerging in the frantic desire to make economic progress environmentally tolerable and socially acceptable. Advocates believe that this is the dynamic zone of ecological adaptation necessary to ensure both wealth creation and human survival. It also recognizes the vital necessity of incorporating all environmental costs, including possible danger to future generations, into the day-to-day behaviour of those alive today. Critics (especially Sachs 1993) regard this as face saving and posturing, allowing business as usual with minor variations to absorb environmentalists and so reinforce its domination under the green trappings of environmental conscience.

Finally, the *deep green* interpretation of environment is profoundly radical both in terms of ethics and social structure. It is sometimes termed *deep ecology* or *steady-state economics* and promotes the cause of small-scale self-reliant and politically empowered communities benefiting from ultra-modern information technology, but essentially running their own affairs on the basis of local resources and local needs. It confronts globalism in the economy and in political dependency, promotes the causes of pacifism, ecofeminism, consumer rights and animal welfare generally, and seeks to emancipate the soul from the oppression of economic and military dependency. Deep ecology is rooted in traditions of anarchism and community empowerment, but it regards the imperative for sustainable development as an opportunity to link social welfare policies, disarmament strategies and peaceful coexistence to create a strategy for collective survival.

Timothy O'Riordan
University of East Anglia

References

Atkinson, A. (1991) *The Principles of Political Ecology*, London.
Brundtland, H. G. (chair) (1987) *Our Common Future*, Oxford.
Dickens, P. (1992) *Society and Nature: Towards a Green Social Theory*, London.
Dobson, A. (1990) *Green Political Thought*, London.
Eckersley, R. (1992) *Environmentalism and Political Theory: Towards an Ecocentric Approach*, London.
Glacken, C. (1967) *Traces on the Rhodian Shore*, Berkeley, CA.
Hays, S. P. (1959) *Conservation and the Gospel of Efficiency*, Cambridge, MA.
International Union for the Conservation of Nature (1989) *Caring for the Earth*, Oxford.
Lovelock, J. (1992) *Gaia: The Practical Science of Planetary Medicine*, Stroud.
Mies, M. and Shiva, V. (1993) *Ecofeminism*, London.
O'Riordan, T. (1981) *Environmentalism*, London.
— (ed.) (1994) *Environmental Science for Environmental Management*, Harlow.
O'Riordan, T. and Cameron, J. (eds) (1994) *Interpreting the Precautionary Principle*, London.
O'Riordan, T. and Sewell, W. R. D. (eds) (1981) *From Project Appraisal to Policy Review*, Chichester.
Pearce, D. W., Turner, R. K. and Bateman, I. (1993) *An Introduction to Environmental Economics*, London.
Pepper, D. (1986) *The Roots of Environmentalism*, London.
Sachs, W. (ed.) (1993) *The Politics of Global Ecology*, London.
Simmons, I. (1989) *Changing the Face of the Earth*, Oxford.
— (1993) *Interpreting Nature: Cultural Construction of the Environment*, London.
Simon, J. L. and Kahn, H. (1984) *The Resourceful Earth*, New York.
Toynbee, A. (1976) *Mankind and Mother Earth*, Oxford.

See also: conservation; ecology; environmental economics; landscape; nature.

environmental economics

Environmental economics has its origins in the writings of Gray (the early 1900s), Pigou (1920s) and Hotelling (1930s), but did not develop as a coherent discipline until the 1970s, the era of the first environmental revolution. There are three central features of environmental economics.

First, human well-being is seriously affected by environmental degradation and the depreciation of natural resources. These linkages can be as obvious as the scarcity of fuelwood because of deforestation, landslides brought about by loss of vegetation cover, and mortality and morbidity due to contaminated water supplies. Or they can be more subtle and complex, as with the effects of certain trace gases on the stratospheric ozone layer and the resulting increase in ultraviolet radiation which affects human health (skin cancers and cataracts) through to marine productivity. That part of environmental economics that deals with demonstrating the *size* of such effects involves *economic valuation*, the process of placing money values on human preferences for, or against, environmental change.

Second, the *causes* of environmental degradation are invariably to be found in the workings, or failures, of the economic system. Such failures generally encompass *market failure*, the inability of free market systems to account adequately for the third party effects of economic activity (externalities); and *intervention failure*, the environmental degradation brought about by government interventions in the working of the economy. Examples of the former include conventional externality situations – such as upstream pollution of a river affecting downstream users – but need to be extended to *global missing markets*. An example of a global missing market is the carbon stored in tropical forests. If the forest is cleared by burning (to convert the land for agricultural use), then the carbon is released as carbon dioxide, contributing to the greenhouse effect and hence global warming. Yet there is no market in carbon storage, so the 'owner' of the forest has no incentive to conserve it to prevent the warming damage. Intervention failures are commonplace, as with the detrimental effects on the environment of the Common Agricultural Policy (e.g. lost hedgerows) and the underpricing of irrigation water, energy and fertilizers in many countries. The underpricing encourages wasteful use and hence creates environmental problems.

Third, the *solutions* to environmental problems are often most efficiently found in correcting the economic causes of degradation. Thus, underpricing of products and resources causes environmental degradation. The solution is therefore to charge the right price by imposing environmental taxes equal to the marginal external costs involved. Ideally, such taxes should equal the marginal externality at the optimum point. In practice, measurement problems result in approximations to such ideal taxes. An alternative to a tax is a *tradeable permit or quota*. These involve issuing quotas for pollution or resource use (e.g. fish catches) equal to the desired level, and then allowing holders of the quotas to buy and sell them. Such markets have emerged in practice for sulphur dioxide permits in the USA, and for fisheries in a number of the world's main fishing grounds. In general, the choice of an *economic instrument* such as a tax or tradeable permit, can be shown to be cheaper, and hence more cost effective, than the alternative command and control regulation.

In the area of natural resource economics, issues such as the optimal rate at which to deplete an exhaustible resource, and the optimal harvest rate for renewable resources have been analysed in great detail. Renewable resource problems probably dominate current work in resource economics due to concerns about overuse of fisheries, deforestation, excess use of groundwater and so on. Indeed, global problems such as ozone layer depletion and global warming can be thought of as renewable resource issues – an excessive use of the world's 'sinks' for everyday pollutants.

In recent years, *sustainable development* has absorbed a lot of attention from environmental economists. Sustainable development involves making sure that economic development paths do not make future generations worse off because of current policies. This non-declining utility definition has been shown by several authors to involve leaving the next generation a capital stock no less than that possessed by the current generation. This constant capital rule has two variants. If all capital is substitutable, then it does not matter if environmental capital (oil, forests, ozone layer) is lost so long as other forms of capital (roads, machinery, education) are built up. This is the weak sustainability rule. If, however, it is not possible to substitute between forms of capital – if, for example, some forms of environmental capital are 'special' – then not only must the overall stock of capital be kept constant but so, too, must the stock of critical environmental capital. In this way sustainable development becomes an added rationale for natural resource conservation.

Finally, the early 1990s witnessed the emergence of *ecological economics*, an as yet ill-defined body of thought that stresses ecological limits to economic activity, the essential nature of environmental assets, and the presence of discontinuities and thresholds in economic-ecological systems.

From being a somewhat fringe activity in the 1970s environmental economics has emerged as one of the most exciting and socially relevant disciplines of the 1990s. It is still a young science, and much more is to come.

David W. Pearce
University College London

Further reading

Pearce, D. W. and Turner, R. K. (1990) *Economics of Environment and Natural Resources*, Hemel Hempstead.
Pearce, D. W., Markandya, A. and Barbier, E. (1989) *Blueprint for a Green Economy*, London.

See also: conservation; energy; environment; natural resource economics.

epidemiology

Epidemiology is a multidisciplinary enterprise which assesses the causes, natural history and treatment of disease. It originates from the study of epidemics of communicable diseases, but is now much more concerned with chronic disease and health care delivery. The change of emphasis is determined by the relative burden of diseases and consequent expenditure of effort. Essentially the objectives of epidemiology are to minimize the unwanted consequence of diseases by informing appropriate policy to enable them to be prevented, or appropriately and efficiently treated.

Thus epidemiology is primarily the science of the causes of disease. It is concerned to study the variation in incidence of (or mortality from) disease with respect to persons, time and place so that patterns can be observed from which the component parts of a biologically plausible aetiological process can be constructed. This involves statistical methods, social observation and understanding, as well as biological knowledge. Epidemiology forms a basic science for public health, preventive medicine, health services research and health promotion.

In the development of epidemiology key figures have been John Snow (1813–58) who in the nineteenth century removed the handle from the Broad (now Broadwick) Street water pump in Soho, London, and at a stroke discovered the method of transmission of cholera, because people were no longer able to draw up the water, which was contaminated by raw sewage (Snow 1949). Florence Nightingale (1820–1910) was a seminal figure in epidemiology by emphasizing in her practice the importance of systematic observation of patients in order to learn the distinctive features that a disease course took.

Thomas McKeown (1979) identified and discussed the broad determinants of disease and sought to attribute the role of organized medicine in alleviating this burden, which he found to be importantly less than was supposed. Archie Cochrane (1972) took the argument further by identifying the extent of knowledge about outcomes consequent upon treatment, which he argued needed much more rigorous evaluation in medical practice by randomized trials. Richard Doll and Bradford Hill elucidated the relationship of cigarettes with disease by identifying a cohort of willing doctors who answered periodic questions about their smoking habits and enabled rigorous comparison of their death rates accordingly (Doll and Hill 1964).

Such is the legacy of epidemiology which currently has several branches and factions. Its methods consist of studying and encouraging the improvement of vital statistics on disease incidence and mortality. Sometimes cross-sectional studies are undertaken to look at particular patterns of disease prevalence and population characteristics. More often case control studies are used to investigate the relationships of past exposure to putative risk factors and a disease. Final assessment of causal relationships often has to await prospective cohort studies in which individuals who have been exposed are compared with those who have not. In exceptional circumstances randomized controlled trials are used to compare outcomes between those allocated at random to a particular exposure.

Since epidemiology is almost entirely itself empirical, the development of the subject depends on the amount of variation in disease incidence which is explained by established risk factors. The important theoretical components of epidemiology are largely statistical, social and biological. The statistical provides efficient means of deriving estimates of qualitatively different measures of risk and the biological constrains and informs the epidemiological investigation and their results. The social informs the transfer from discerning risk factors and measuring health to effective health promotion.

In terms of measuring risk, the most useful is the *relative risk*. This measure simply compares the incidence of a disease among groups of subjects exposed to a risk factor with that among those not exposed. Thus the relative risk of lung cancer among heavy cigarette smokers is around twenty, which says that over both genders and all ages, in any country, the annual incidence of lung cancer among heavy smokers is twenty times as high as among similar people who have never smoked. This then gives an indication of the potency of the aetiological effect. Clearly a relative risk of twenty is a good deal more potent than a relative risk of two. This latter might describe the potency of obesity with respect to coronary heart disease or, indeed, environmental tobacco smoke and lung cancer. This number is an aggregated statistic and in circumstances when the relative risk for a risk factor and a disease varies importantly the phenomenon is called *effect modification*. There is no intrinsic reason to suppose constant relative risks across heterogenous populations, but often effect modification is much less important than the aggregate effect itself.

An alternative measure of risk is estimated as the *attributable risk per cent*. This measures the amount of disease which is attributable to the risk factor being considered. Thus it estimates the proportion by which the current overall incidence of lung cancer would decrease if nobody had ever smoked. Thus around 86 per cent of the current incidence of lung cancer is attributable to cigarette smoking. In this respect epidemiology has achieved this degree of understanding, and the policy implication for an individual is importantly informed.

In contrast, another disease, more common among women in most communities than lung cancer, is breast cancer. For this disease the highest determined relative risk is around three, for women with an early age of starting periods, a late age of first pregnancy and a late menopause for instance. The magnitude of the attributable risks depend not only on the relative risks but also on the prevalence of these risk factors. In this case the attributable risk per cents are no higher than 15 per cent for each risk factor, and worse still the risk factors themselves are not readily amenable to incidental change.

Thus as time progresses the role of epidemiology becomes increasingly difficult as the larger effects are found and validated. The smaller effects of relative risks of around 1.5 are exceptionally difficult to establish epidemiologically because of measurement errors and the problem of confounding, where an association is observed which cannot be distinguished between an association with an unknown risk factor or a direct causal relationship.

However, these small effects are of paramount importance for common diseases because they represent the rule and not the exception and offer the greatest hope for the prevention of disease not amenable to treatment. Since most chronic diseases are not particularly amenable to treatment, progress must happen by constructive synergy between epidemiology with statistics, the social sciences and biology. Thus new genes which predispose to cancer, for incidence, will give rise to more precise estimates of other risks in new epidemiological studies.

Klim McPherson
London School of Hygiene and Tropical Medicine

References

Cochrane, A. L. (1972) *Effectiveness and Efficiency*, Oxford.
Doll, R. and Hill, A. B. (1964) 'Mortality in relation to smoking: ten years' observation of British doctors', *British Medical Journal* 269.
McKeown, T. (1979) *The Role of Medicine: Dream, Mirage or Nemesis?*, Oxford.
Snow, J. (1949) *Snow on Cholera*, Cambridge; MA.

Further reading

Ashton, J. (1994) *The Epidemiological Imagination*, Buckingham.
Buck, C., Llopis, A., Najera, E. and Rerris, M. (eds) (1989) *The Challenge of Epidemiology: Issues and Selected Readings*, Buckingham.

See also: medical sociology; morbidity; public health.

equality

'We hold', wrote Thomas Jefferson (1747–1826), 'these truths to be sacred and undeniable; that all men are created equal and independent'. No natural scientist *qua* scientist could do other than dismiss such a statement as either meaningless or empirically false.

Equality for a mathematician is a concept of some complexity in relation, for example, to identity or correlation, but one of no moral significance. Social scientists by contrast are latecomers to a debate about equality which is unresolved because it adds to the mathematician's complexity the further complications of moral argument. Equality refers to the principles on which human society ought to, as well as might, be based. Jefferson's was a moral declaration, not an empirical description. Social science attempts to explore the empirical validity of such declarations. The question is whether, and in what sense, social, political and economic equalities are possible. The answer is tentative, requiring the determination of the origins of inequality, the significance of inequality, and the viability of action intended to establish equality. All three aspects are disputed.

Traditional discussion of the origins of inequality turned on a crude distinction between nature and society. Modern recognition of cultural evolution complicates that distinction and tends to substitute a more elaborate matrix out of the consequences of interaction between genetic and environmental influences. But in neither simple nor sophisticated discussion is there denial of natural inequalities, the Jeffersonian declaration notwithstanding. Humans are not clones, and Mendelian genetics guarantees variation. Dispute, however, continues in important areas of scientific ignorance. For example, there is not adequate scientific evidence to settle the dispute between those who believe in the genetic basis of differences between ethnic or racial or class groups in educational attainment or performance in intelligence tests, and those who hold such differences to be socially created. Resolution of such disputes is, in principle, possible through the further advance of empirically tested theories of the interaction between heredity and environment.

Meanwhile dispute about the significance of natural differences continues its long history. Plato confidently argued from natural to political inequalilty. Hobbes in *Leviathan* (1934 [1651]) expressed the opposite view:

> Nature hath made man so equall, in the faculties of body, and mind; as that though bee found one man sometimes manifestly stronger in body, or of quicker mind than another; yet when all is reckoned together, the difference between man, and man, is not so considerable, as that one man can thereupon claim to himself and benefit, to which another may not pretend, as well as he.

Hobbes's formulation still defines the debate. Egalitarian claims, especially with respect to race and gender, are more strident now than they were in the seventeenth century, and we would now say that

Hobbes was making empirical propositions from both genetics and sociology, the one referring to natural differences and the other (about claiming and pretending) referring to the social psychology of human perceptions of social rights. But the central assertion is fundamentally about the values which ought to be reflected in the actual relations of men and women in society.

In this sense the debate, turning as it does on ethical priorities between such values as equality, liberty and fraternity, may never be finally resolvable. There have been, to be sure, notable contributions to greater conceptual clarity as to the meaning of terms. John Rawls (1971) adopts the device of the 'original position' – an 'if so' story of the rational choices that might be expected from an individual contemplating different societies with known different equalities or inequalities of positions but an unknown placement for the contemplator – to illuminate the problems of value choice. Brian Barry (1973) takes the discussion further to demonstrate how a small adjustment to Rawls's social and psychological assumptions opens the possibility of a crucial shift of preference towards egalitarian rather than liberal forms of society. But no amount of conceptual clarification, sophisticated or erudite, solves the problem of evaluation.

The social sciences can, however, note the provenance of different priorities. One mundane but momentous perspective recurs down the ages – the recognition of mortality. Thus Horace (BC 65–8) wrote: 'Pale death kicks his way equally into the cottages of the poor and the castles of kings.' And James Shirley (1596–1666) reminds us that

Death lays his icy hand on kings
  Sceptre and crown
  Must tumble down
And in the dust be equal made
With the poor crooked scythe and spade.

This attitude is integral to Christian social teaching, which dominated the evaluation of equality at least until the eighteenth century. It was not that natural inequalities between individuals were denied so much as deemed irrelevant in discussing the rights and wrongs of dictatorship or democracy, freedom or slavery. Christians were not only 'equal before the Cross' but, as the early Church Fathers insisted, would, if they eschewed sin, live like brothers without inequalities of property and power. Sin, since the fall of Adam, had created earthly inequality. Political inequality might be necessary to protect order and restrain evil, but it did not arise, as Plato had imagined, from natural inequality. Political inequality in Christian tradition must be endured but by no means implied a necessary respect or admiration for the rich and the powerful.

On the contrary, position in the next world was typically held to be threatened by privilege in this. 'He hath put down the mighty from their seat and hath exalted the humble and meek,' says the Magnificat.

The break with Christian attitudes of submission to inequality dates from the eighteenth century, with the decline of religious belief and the beginnings of a secular optimism with respect to the possibility of social transformation. Egalitarianism as a movement is commonly associated with Rousseau. But Rousseau, though believing that the evils of unfreedom and inequality were socially created, was a remorseless pessimist. He held that freedom was impossible except in a community of equals, but held out no hope of social transformation towards equality. In this sense he was a child of Christianity, and if the early socialists (Fourier, Proudhon, Saint-Simon, Robert Owen, William Thompson) were his intellectual children they were also crucially different in entertaining the hope of progress. Modern egalitarianism derives from this form of sociological optimism, and it was encouraged by, if by no means identical with, either the Hegelian idealist or Marxist materialist theories of the inevitability of social transformation. Hegel's elaborate analysis of the relation between masters and slaves, and Marx's development of it into a prediction of the future history of the working class hold out the possibility of a community of equals.

However, egalitarianism does not presuppose either the Hegelian or the Marxist theory of history. Its more fruitful contemporary discussion in the social sciences proceeds on assumptions of openness or voluntarism as opposed to necessitous history. These debates are the substance of the third aspect of the equality problem – the viability of deliberate social action aimed at reducing inequality. One theoretical approach deserves mention here because it avoids both liberal evolutionist determinism and the alternative Marxist historicism. This is T. H. Marshall's (1950) interpretation of the development of citizenship in advanced industrial societies. Marshall shows in the case of Britain how the basic equality of membership in a society, which is rooted in the civil rights established in the eighteenth century, was extended to include political rights in the nineteenth century and certain social rights in the twentieth century, when citizenship and class have been at war as opposing principles of social distribution. Marshall's analysis also brings out the important truth that the forces which influence the distribution of life-chances are neither mechanical nor irreversible. Class displaced feudal status with formal equality of market relations, as well as ushering in new inequalities of social condition. Citizenship promotes unequal rewards as well as equal rights, for example, state scholarships to selective university admission and universal political franchise. More generally, it may be noted that no social goal, equality, efficiency, liberty, order or fraternity may be regarded as absolute. Public policies are perforce compromises aiming at optimal balance between desired ends.

Three illustrations of the limits to egalitarianism are prominent in the form of arguments against the viability of egalitarian theory.

The first illustration concerns the immutability of occupational hierarchy, postulating a *de facto* necessity for some jobs to be more distasteful, unrewarding and injurious to health than others. Given that life-chances are largely determined by the individual's occupation, a hierarchy of social advantage seems to be inescapable, and equality, as opposed to equality of opportunity, therefore unobtainable. But, egalitarians reply, a less inegalitarian society is not sociologically impossible. It is not difficult to imagine a wide range of counteracting social policies. Apart from progressive taxation and levies on wealth, there could be national service specifically designed to direct the advantaged to a period of distasteful labour. The obvious rejoinders are lodged in the name of liberty and economic efficiency, again emphasizing the relativist character of claims for any social principle. Value choice is always the nub of the issue.

A second illustration may be had from Christopher Jencks's *Inequality* (1972) which essentially argues the importance of educational reform as an instrument of egalitarianism and stresses the role of chance or luck in the unequal distribution of income and occupational status. Schooling explains only 12 per cent of the variance in US incomes. But Jencks's argument is flawed in that his evidence is about the distribution of individuals over a given structure of occupations and wages. The explanation of inequality of income accruing to jobs is not what would explain who happens to hold those jobs. Whether the inequality of the job structure is immutable remains an open question.

Finally, there is the alleged obstacle of genetic differences between races and classes of which Jensen (1972) has been an outstanding proponent. As to classes, and against Jensen's marshalling of the evidence from studies of twins reared apart, there is the opposed conclusion of Schiff (1982) from his studies of cross-class adopted children in France. As to race, it has to be said that we do not yet have the techniques or the data to measure definitively the genetic and environmental influences on race–IQ differences. Nor does the answer really matter, for there are more important issues of equality and justice in present-day society which do not have to wait upon further advances in the social sciences.

A. H. Halsey
University of Oxford

References

Barry, B. (1973) *The Liberal Theory of Justice*, Oxford.
Hobbes, T. (1934 [1651]) *Leviathan*, Everyman edn, London.
Jencks, C. (1972) *Inequality*, New York.
Jensen, A. (1972) *Genetics and Education*, London.
Marshall, T. H. (1950) *Citizenship and Social Class*, Cambridge, UK.
Rawls, J. (1971) *A Theory of Justice*, Cambridge, MA.
Schiff, M. (1982) *L'Intelligence Gaspillée*, Paris.

Further reading

Letwin, W. (ed.) (1983) *Against Equality: Readings on Economic and Social Policy*, London.
Runciman, W. G. (1966) *Relative Deprivation and Social Justice*, London.
Tawney, R. H. (1952) *Equality*, 4th rev. edn, London.

See also: hierarchy; stratification.

equilibrium

In a static context, two distinct but related definitions of equilibrium can be given. The first defines equilibrium as a position of balance in the economy; the equality of demand and supply is an equilibrium under this definition because the forces of supply are balanced by the forces of demand. Alternatively, equilibrium can be defined as being achieved when no agent in the economy has any incentive to modify their chosen action or chosen strategy. This latter definition is derived from that used in the theory of games and is illustrated by the equilibrium of an oligopolistic market in which all firms are satisfied with their choice of output level. It is easily seen that these definitions are related. When supply is equal to demand, it is also true that no firm will wish to produce any more or less since each will have sold its profit-maximizing quantity. Similarly, each consumer will have been able to carry out their chosen consumption plan and this will be utility-maximizing. In the context of a competitive economy, the two definitions are identical: as shown by Arrow and Debreu (1954), the equilibrium of the competitive economy can be represented as the equilibrium point of a suitably defined game. For dynamic economies, the tradition since Hicks (1946) has been to divide time into discrete periods. When markets are balanced within a period, a temporary equilibrium is achieved. An equilibrium for the economy is a sequence of temporary equilibria.

Despite the existence of research into the economics of disequilibrium, the concept of equilibrium remains at the heart of economic analysis. Much effort is directed towards proving the existence of equilibrium in economic models and demonstrating the welfare properties of equilibrium. Equally important are the analysis of the uniqueness and stability of equilibrium and the determination of how changes in exogenous parameters affect the equilibrium. Positions of equilibrium are also contrasted to those of disequilibrium.

This emphasis upon equilibrium can be given several explanations. Historically, the economy was viewed as self-correcting so that, if it were ever away from equilibrium, forces existed that move it back towards equilibrium. In the long run, equilibrium would then always be attained. Although such adjustment can be justified in simple single-market contexts, both the practical experience of sustained high levels of unemployment and the theoretical study of stability (Arrow and Hahn 1971) have shown that it is not justified more generally. The present justifications for focusing upon equilibrium are more pragmatic. The analysis of a model must begin somewhere, and the equilibrium has much merit as a starting point. Sometimes the focus can be justified by showing that the equilibrium is the outcome of playing the underlying game correctly. In addition, even if the final focus is on disequilibrium, there is much to be gained from comparing the properties of points of disequilibrium to those of equilibrium. Finally, no positions other than those of equilibrium have any obvious claim to prominence.

Gareth D. Myles
University of Exeter

References

Arrow, K. J. and Debreu, G. (1954) 'Existence of equilibrium for a competitive economy', *Econometrica* 22.
Arrow, K. J. and Hahn, F. H. (1971) *General Competitive Analysis*, Amsterdam.
Hicks, J. (1946) *Value and Capital*, Oxford.

Further reading

Benassy, J.-P. (1982) *The Economics of Market Disequilibrium*, New York.
Hahn, F. H. (1973) *On the Notion of Equilibrium in Economics*, Cambridge, UK.

See also: competition; general equilibrium theory; mathematical economics.

ethics in social research

Social research ethics involve the consideration of the moral implications of social science enquiry. Ethics is a matter of principled sensitivity to the rights of others, in such a way that human beings who are being studied by social scientists are treated as ends rather than as means. Such ethical issues frequently also lead to consideration of the politics of research, the place of the investigator in the power structure, and the wider social impact of research. Those conducting social research need increasingly to be aware of the ethical and political implications of their actions.

The protection of human subjects is enshrined in the doctrine of informed consent, first developed in biomedical research. This stipulates that the voluntary consent of the human subject is essential, and this should be freely given without duress, and knowing and understanding what the research involves. Most social research, whether by experimental, social survey or observational methods, respects this principle, but there have been occasional sharp controversies where experimental or observational subjects have been left in ignorance of research, or have had research misrepresented to them. In observing the principle, most social scientists do not follow the formal procedures used in medical research such as signed consent forms.

A related controversy has concerned the use of deception in social research. The majority of social scientists are open about their purposes and aims, but in rare cases deception has been used on the grounds that, because of practical methodological or moral considerations, research could not otherwise be carried out. (Such studies include research on obedience to authority, and sexual deviance.) Objections to deception include its degrading and false character, its harmful social consequences, harm to the investigator, the creation of suspicion among subjects, and the breach of informed consent.

Research may in certain circumstances impinge upon the privacy of research subjects (that is, the freedom of the individual to decide how much of the self to reveal to others, when and to whom). Some information about the individual may be sensitive. Some settings (for example, jury rooms, Cabinet meetings) may be entirely closed to outsiders. The wider dissemination of research results may affect subjects adversely. Such problems may be handled by obtaining informed consent or by various forms of making data anonymous. In the latter case, for example, the location in which research was carried out may be concealed and the identities of particular individuals hidden under pseudonyms. A distinction may be made between the circumstances under which data are collected, and their subsequent storage, dissemination, analysis and re-analysis. Issues of confidentiality are raised by the latter, though also impinging upon collection. What will happen to data once collected? To whom will they be available? What repercussions might there be for the individual in providing certain data to a social researcher?

The importance of these questions has been intensified by the advent of the electronic computer, with immensely powerful means of large-scale data storage and retrieval. This has a major impact upon census data and large-scale social survey data. Various techniques have been developed to ensure that individual identities cannot be linked to published information. These include the deletion of individual identifiers such as name, address or local area of residence; the suppression of tables containing small numbers of cases; and processes of random error injection. In addition to physical security, technical means exist for making anonymous the data held in computer files, including the separation of identifiers from the main body of data and their linkage by suitable codes. Randomized response is a method of ensuring the confidentiality of data while it is being collected.

The ethical issues raised by research go wider than the treatment of research subjects and handling of data once collected. The social impact of research has been of concern and controversy both within particular societies (as in the Moynihan Report on black families in the USA) and internationally (as in Project Camelot in Chile in the 1960s). There is increasing concern about the sponsorship of research (Who pays? For whom, and in whose interest, is research conducted?), the negotiation of research access (especially the role played by gatekeepers, who may give or withhold permission), and about the possible adverse effects of the publication of research results on certain weaker groups or lower status sections of society. The investigator can rarely control any of these factors, but awareness of them can help to produce more effective work. Particular care is also required to review the ethical implications of action research and applied research leading to social intervention (for example, of some of the large-scale social experiments for social policy). Consideration of these broader issues leads on to an examination of the political role of social science research and its place in the society in which it is carried out.

There is no agreed theory of research ethics with which to evaluate the merits of undertaking particular pieces of research. It is difficult to determine whether, and if so to what extent, research subjects may be harmed by particular research practices. One widespread approach is in terms of a utilitarian risk/benefit calculus, but this leaves several issues unresolved. Both risks and benefits are difficult to predict and to measure, harm to the individual can only with difficulty be weighted against societal benefits, and the investigator is usually the judge in his own case. Another approach is in terms of situational ethics, where the investigator weighs up the morally appropriate course of action in the actual research context. A different approach is in terms of absolute moral principles to be followed in all situations. No approach receives universal approval, and ethical decision making in research remains ultimately a matter of individual judgement as well as professional controversy.

One practical consequence both of the societal impact of research and the indeterminacy of ethical decision making about research has been a move toward greater regulation. Many professional associations of social scientists have their own ethical codes, to which members are expected to adhere. Various forms of peer review by a researcher's own department or institution are a more rigorous and direct form of oversight. The Institutional Review Boards established by universities in the USA are one example of efforts to prevent unethical behaviour by social researchers.

Martin Bulmer
University of Surrey

Further reading

Barnes, J. A. (1980) *Who Should Know What? Social Science, Privacy and Ethics*, Cambridge, UK.
Beauchamp, T. L. *et al.* (eds) (1982) *Ethical Issues in Social Science Research*, Baltimore, MD.

ethnic politics

More than 80 per cent of contemporary states that comprise the United Nations are ethnically plural, in that they contain two or more mobilized ethnic communities. These communities compete, sometimes by civic methods, sometimes by violence for hegemony (control of the state apparatus), for autonomy (ranging from regional self-government to secession), or for incorporation into the society and polity on more favourable terms. Inter-ethnic relations may vary from stratificational (one group dominating the others politically and economically), to segmentational (each party controlling significant resources and institutions). In the contemporary era, ethnic politics implicate the state, because the state has become the principal allocator of the values that affect the relative power, status, material welfare, and life-chances of ethnic collectivities and their individual constituents. The values at stake may be political – control of territory, citizenship, voting rights, eligibility for public office and the symbols of the state; economic – access to higher education, employment, land, capital, credit and business opportunities; or cultural – the position of religion, the relative status of language in education and in government transactions.

Ethnic politics may be generated by the grievances of territorially concentrated peoples, demanding greater autonomy for their homeland and more equitable representation in the central government; or by immigrant diasporas asking for more equitable terms of inclusion in the polity, combined often with claims for recognition and official support for their distinctive cultural institutions. These initiatives often trigger counter-mobilization in the interest of ethnic groups that feel threatened by these claims and by state authorities committed to the ethnic status quo.

The latter have the principal responsibility for managing or regulating ethnic conflicts. Their strategies may be directed in three ways: first, at maintaining pluralism by coercive domination of subordinated ethnic communities or by consensual processes such as federalism and power sharing; second, at eliminating pluralism by genocide, expulsion or induced assimilation; or third, at reducing the political salience of ethnic solidarity by cultivating crosscutting affiliations, delegitimizing ethnic organizations and ethnic political messages, and emphasizing individual participation in the economy and polity. Ethnic conflicts are seldom settled or resolved; though specific issues may be successfully compromised, the parties remain to focus their grievances and demands on other issues. Thus ethnic politics is a continuing feature of ethnically divided states.

Government policies may contribute to stimulating and rewarding ethnic mobilization, as well as to mitigating ethnic conflict. Complicating inter-ethnic relations is the inevitability of factions within ethnic communities, each competing for available resources, for support within their constituency, and for the right to represent it to outsiders. Factional conflicts within ethnic communities may result in expedient, often tacit, understandings and coalitions with counterparts across hostile ethnic boundaries or with representatives of the state.

Many ethnic disputes spill over the borders of individual states, especially where ethnic kinfolk inhabit neighbouring states. Domestic ethnic conflicts thus intrude into international relations, prompting intervention by other states, by sympathizers with one of the parties to the dispute, and by international organizations attempting to mediate, restore and maintain order or mitigate the suffering of civilians and refugees. With the termination of the Cold War, violent ethnic conflicts including full-scale civil wars have emerged as a major source of international instability that preoccupies national politicians and attentive publics; they have overwhelmed the diplomatic, financial and operational capacities of the United Nations.

Liberals, Marxists and modernizers, despite their differences, have joined in perceiving ethnic solidarity as the residue of earlier stages of human development and in predicting and advocating its early disappearance in favour of more rational forms of association. They continue to treat it as a dangerous and essentially illegitimate phenomenon. Others explain the resurgence of politicized ethnicity and thus ethnic politics variously as, first, the search for community in increasingly bureaucratized and impersonal industrialized societies; second, more reliable sources of security and material opportunity than class-based organizations or weak, unrepresentative Third-World governments; third, efficient vehicles for mobilization and representation of individual and collective interests in modern societies; or fourth, the consequence of the disintegration of colonial empires and multi-ethnic states that leave ethnic collectivities as their residual legatees. These explanations relate to an ongoing dispute between 'primordialists', who argue that collective ethnic identies are deeply-rooted historical continuities nurtured by early socialization and reinforced by collective sanctions, and 'instrumentalists', who hold that ethnic identities and solidarities are fluid, pragmatic and opportunistic, often constructed by ethnic entrepreneurs to justify demands for political and especially material advantages.

Self-determination is the ideology that legitimizes ethnic activism on behalf of peoples who demand independence or increased territorial autonomy. Multiculturalism justifies demands for institutional separation and self-management where territorial autonomy is not feasible. Demands for non-discriminatory inclusion which may run parallel to cultural pluralism are inspired by universalistic liberal principles. State nationalism may either confirm the superordinate position of a dominant ethnic community or claim a higher order allegiance to the state that amalgamates and supersedes constituent loyalties in an ethnically plural society.

Milton J. Esman
Cornell University

Further reading

Esman, M. J. (1994) *Ethnic Politics: Conflict and Coexistence in the Modern State*, Ithaca, NY.

Horowitz, D. L. (1985) *Ethnic Groups in Conflict*, Berkeley, CA.

Moynihan, D. P. (1993) *Pandaemonium: Ethnicity in International Politics*, New York.

Rothschild, J. (1970) *Ethnopolitics: A Conceptual Framework*, New York.

Schermerhorn, R. A. (1970) *Comparative Ethnic Relations: A Framework for Theory and Research*, New York.

See also: *ethnicity; multicultural education; nationalism; plural society; tribe.*

ethnicity

Ethnicity is a fundamental category of social organization which is based on membership defined by a sense of common historical origins and which may also include shared culture, religion or language. It is to be distinguished from kinship in so far as kinship depends on biological inheritance. The term is derived from the Greek noun *ethnos*, which may be translated as 'a people or nation'. One of the most influential definitions of ethnicity can be found in Max Weber's *Economy and Society* (1968 [1922]) where he describes ethnic groups as 'human groups (other than kinship groups) which cherish a belief in their common origins of such a kind that it provides a basis for the creation of a community'.

The difficulty in reaching a precise definition of the term is reflected in the many different words employed in the literature to describe related or similar concepts, such as race and nation. While usage varies, 'race', like kinship, has biological connotations, although these are frequently without foundation, and nation implies a political agenda – the goal of separate statehood – beyond that generally associated with ethnic groups. According to Weber (1968 [1922]), 'a nation is the political extension of the ethnic community as its members and leadership search for a unique political structure by establishing an independent state'.

In predominantly immigrant societies, like the USA, Argentina, Australia and Canada, the study of ethnic groups forms a central theme of their social, economic and political life. Systematic research on American ethnic groups can be traced to the sociologists of the Chicago School during the 1920s, led by W. I. Thomas and Robert Ezra Park (Lal 1990), who were concerned with the processes of ethnic group assimilation into the dominant white, Anglo-Saxon, Protestant (WASP) mainstream. Park's 'race relations cycle', outlining a sequence of stages consisting of 'contact, competition, accommodation and assimilation', implied that successive ethnic groups would be absorbed into a relatively homogeneous US society. The underlying assumption of ethnic group theory was that a gradual process would result in the disappearance of separate ethnic groups into an American melting pot.

This unilinear interpretation gave way to more pluralistic conceptions of ethnicity in the USA, in which various dimensions of assimilation were identified by sociologists like Milton Gordon (1964). Gordon distinguished between cultural assimilation (acculturation) and structural assimilation, the former signifying the adoption of the language, values and ideals of the dominant society, while the latter reflected the incorporation of ethnic groups into the institutions of mainstream society. While cultural assimilation did not necessarily result in an ethnic group's inclusion within the principal institutions of society, structural assimilation invariably meant that assimilation on all other dimensions – from personal identification to intermarriage – had already taken place.

This conceptualization contrasts with that of M. G. Smith (1987), who argued that the key issue involved in a general theory of ethnic relations was the differential incorporation of ethnic groups into larger social units. Smith distinguished between three types of social incorporation: the *universalistic* type, where individuals are incorporated directly and on identical conditions in a common society; the *differential* mode, which is the same process except that individuals are incorporated on an unequal basis, either in a superior or inferior position; and *segmental* incorporation, where ethnic groups are incorporated in a common society 'as units of equivalent status on identical terms'. In this third case, individuals are incorporated indirectly, either on an egalitarian or unequal basis, giving a variety of possible ethnic outcomes.

Scholarly concern with ethnicity and ethnic groups has become increasingly salient since the 1960s. Faced with the proliferation of separatist movements throughout the world, and the rise of the so-called 'unmeltable ethnics' in North America, the inadequate assumptions underlying theories of modernization have been exposed in all types of societies, whether they are in the capitalist, socialist or developing world. The notion that modernity would result in a smooth transition from *gemeinschaft* (community) to *gesellschaft* (association), with the gradual dissolution of ethnic affiliations, simply did not fit the facts. Some social scientists argued that there was a primordial basis to ethnic attachments (Geertz 1963), while others explained the apparent persistence of ethnicity in largely instrumental terms, as a political resource to be mobilized in appropriate situations (Glazer and Moynihan 1975). Not only has ethnic loyalty taken on new meaning in many industrial societies (Esman 1977), but also ethnic divisions have continued to frustrate the efforts of nation-building in most post-colonial societies. Even the countries of the Communist bloc could contain the ethnic demands of their multinational, subject populations only by a judicious blend of co-optation and political oppression (Connor 1984; 1994).

The focus of research on ethnicity has shifted away from studies of specific groups to the broad processes of ethnogenesis, the construction and perpetuation of ethnic boundaries, and the meaning of ethnic identity. The question of the ethnic origin of nations (A. Smith 1986) has produced the same tension between those who stress the continuity of ethnic history and others who emphasize its situational nature. While most social scientists recognize the flexibility of ethnic identification, that under certain circumstances ethnicity becomes salient whereas in others it remains a dormant capacity waiting to be mobilized, some take the position that its impact has been greatly exaggerated. It is often merely 'symbolic ethnicity' (Gans 1979), or its influence is largely an illusion based on the 'invention of tradition' (Hobsbawm and Ranger 1983) to serve the interests of ethnic political entrepreneurs or, in the neo-Marxist literature, the ruling class.

One of the most influential writers on ethnic boundaries has been the anthropologist Fredrik Barth (1969), whose stress on the processes of group inclusion and exclusion can be seen as a parallel development to the sociological insights of Max Weber. Weber pointed to the tendency of social groups to attempt to monopolize wealth, prestige and political power by systematically excluding outsiders from achieving membership. Immigration restrictions are one way this can be attempted in modern societies. Another is the manner in which citizenship is defined by the state, so that in the case of Germany, for example, the dominant principle reflects a sense of shared ancestry, *jus sanguinis*, while in France the critical factor has been residence, *jus soli* (Brubaker 1992). While some writers have stressed the voluntary nature of ethnic group membership and the variety of ethnic options available to individuals in many post-industrial societies (Waters 1990), others point to the coercive element to be found in all forms of ethnic stratification that can be viewed as more crucial in most situations than any hypothetical elements of preference and choice (Jenkins 1994).

A central concern of social scientists has been the attempt to understand the nature of ethnic conflict and violence. Few issues have been of greater practical importance as the post-Cold War era has been marked by a resurgence of ethnic warfare and genocide in societies as diverse, and remote from each other, as Bosnia and Rwanda. In other societies, like South Africa, a relatively peaceful transfer of power in the elections of April 1994, from a white minority to the black majority, rests on a volatile sub-structure of ethnic divisions and fragile compromises (Adam and Moodley 1993).

A wide variety of theoretical perspectives can be found supporting contemporary studies of ethnicity and ethnic conflict (Rex and Mason 1986). Some, like rational choice theory, are methodologically individualistic and apply a cost-benefit formula to account for ethnic preferences and to explain the dynamics of ethnic group formation. These have been criticized on the grounds that they fail to appreciate the collective dynamics of much ethnic behaviour and underestimate the irrational side of ethnic violence. Other common perspectives focus on ethnic stratification: neo-Marxist theories stress the economic components underlying much ethnic discrimination; while those following in the tradition of scholars like Weber and Furnivall provide a more pluralistic interpretation of differences in ethnic power. In general, these originate from conquest and migration, and are used to account for the hierarchical ordering of ethnic and racial groups. Further theories point to psychological factors, like prejudice and ethnocentrism, as important explanations for the persistence of ethnicity. Two highly controversial arguments centre on genetic imperatives, which operate through the mechanism of kin-selection, and form part of the application of sociobiological thinking to ethnic relations; and neo-conservative theories that concentrate attention on cultural characteristics, which (it is asserted) are disproportionately distributed among certain ethnic groups (Sowell 1994; van den Berghe 1990). Such theories have been vigorously challenged because of their deterministic implications. The heat of the debate reinforces the conclusion that no one theory provides a generally accepted and comprehensive paradigm to explain the complexity of ethnic group formation or the persistence of ethnic conflict in the world today.

John Stone
George Mason University

References

Adam, H. and Moodley, K. (1993) *The Opening of the Apartheid Mind*, Los Angeles, CA.

Barth, F. (1969) *Ethnic Groups and Boundaries*, Boston, MA.

Brubaker, R. (1992) *Citizenship and Nationhood in France and Germany*, Cambridge, MA.

Connor, W. (1984) *The National Question in Marxist-Leninist Theory and Strategy*, Princeton, NJ.

—— (1994) *Ethnonationalism: The Quest for Understanding*, Princeton, NJ.

Esman, M. (1977) *Ethnic Conflict in the Western World*, Ithaca, NY.

Gans, H. (1979) 'Symbolic ethnicity', *Ethnic and Racial Studies* 2.

Geertz, C. (1963) 'The integrative revolution: primordial sentiments and civil politics in the new states', in C. Geertz (ed.) *Old Societies and New States*, New York.

Glazer, N. and Moynihan, D. P. (eds) (1975) *Ethnicity: Theory and Experience*, Cambridge, MA.

Gordon, M. (1964) *Assimilation in American Life*, New York.

Hobsbawm, E. and Ranger, T. (eds) (1983) *The Invention of Tradition*, Cambridge, UK.

Jenkins, R. (1994) 'Rethinking ethnicity: identity, categorization and power', *Ethnic and Racial Studies* 17.

Lal, B. (1990) *The Romance of Culture in an Urban Civilization*, London.

Rex, J. and Mason, D. (eds) (1986) *Theories of Race and Ethnic Relations*, Cambridge, UK.

Smith, A. (1986) *The Ethnic Origin of Nations*, Oxford.

Smith, M. G. (1987) 'Some problems with minority concepts and a solution', *Ethnic and Racial Studies* 10.

Sowell, T. (1994) *Race and Culture: A World View*, New York.

van den Berghe, P. (ed.) (1990) *State Violence and Ethnicity*, Boulder, CO.

Waters, M. (1990) *Ethnic Options: Choosing Ethnicities in America*, Berkeley, CA.

Weber, M. (1968 [1922]) *Economy and Society*, New York.

See also: ethnic politics; race; tribe.

ethnography

Ethnography is a term that carries several historically situated meanings. In its most general sense, the term refers to a study of the culture that a given group of people more or less share. The term is double-edged and has implications for both the method of study and the result of such study. When used as a method, ethnography typically refers to fieldwork (alternatively, participant-observation) conducted by a single investigator who 'lives with and lives like' those who are studied, usually for a year or more. When used as a result, ethnography ordinarily refers to the written representation of a culture. Contemporary students of culture emphasize the latter usage and thus look to define ethnography in terms of its topical, stylistic and rhetorical features.

There are three moments (discernible activity phases) associated with ethnography. The first moment concerns the collection of information or data on a specified culture. The second refers to the construction of an ethnographic report; in particular, the compositional practices used by an ethnographer to fashion a cultural portrait. The third moment of ethnography deals with the reading and reception that an ethnography receives across relevant audience segments both narrow and broad. Each phase raises distinctive issues.

The greatest attention in the social sciences has been directed to the first moment of ethnography – fieldwork. This form of social research is both a product of and a reaction to the cultural studies of the mid- to late nineteenth century (Stocking 1987; 1992). Early ethnography is marked by considerable distance between the researcher and researched. The anthropologists of the day based their cultural representations not on firsthand study but on their readings of documents, reports and letters originating from colonial administrators, members of scientific expeditions, missionaries, adventurers and, perhaps most importantly, faraway correspondents guided by questions posed by their stay-at-home pen-pals. Not until the early twentieth century did ethnographers begin to enter, experience and stay for more than brief periods of time in the strange (to them) social worlds about which they wrote. Bronislaw Malinowski (1922: 1–25) is most often credited with initiating by example a modern form of fieldwork that requires of the ethnographer the sustained, intimate and personal acquaintance with 'what the natives say and do'.

There is, however, a good deal of variation in terms of just what activities are involved in fieldwork and, more critically, just how such activities result in a written depiction of culture. Current practices include intensive interviewing, count-and-classify survey work, participation in everyday routines or occasional ceremonies engaged in by those studied, the collecting of samples of native behaviour across a range of social situations, and so on. There is now a rather large literature designed to help novice or veteran fieldworkers carry out ethnographic research (e.g. Bernard 1994; Hammersley and Atkinson 1983; Spradley 1979).

Yet much of the advise offered in fieldwork manuals defies codification and lacks the consensual approval of those who produce ethnographies. Fieldnotes, for example, are more or less *de rigueur* in terms of documenting what is learned in the field but there is little agreement as to what a standard fieldnote – much less a collection of fieldnotes – might be (Sanjek 1990). Moreover, how one moves from a period of lengthy *in situ* study to a written account presumably based on such study is by no means clear. Despite seventy or so years of practice, fieldwork remains a sprawling and quite diverse activity (Kuper 1983).

The second moment of ethnography – writing it up – has by and large been organized by a genre labelled 'ethnographic realism' (Clifford and Marcus 1986; Van Maanen 1988). It is a genre that has itself shifted over time from a relatively unreflective, closed and general (holistic) description of native sayings and doings to a more tentative, open and partial interpretation of native sayings and doings (Geertz 1973). Yet realism remains a governing style for a good deal of ethnography, descriptive or interpretative. It is marked by a number of compositional conventions that include, for example, the suppression of the individual cultural member's perspective in favour of a typified or common denominator 'native's point of view' the placement of a culture within a timeless ethnographic present and a claim for descriptive or interpretive validity based on the author's 'being there' (fieldwork) experience.

Some ethnographers, though by no means all, express a degree of dissatisfaction with ethnographic realism (Marcus and Fischer 1986). Partly a response to critics located outside ethnographic circles who wonder just how personal experience serves as the basis for a scientific study of culture, some ethnographers make visible – or, more accurately, textualize – their discovery practices and procedures (Agar 1980). *Confessional ethnography* results when the fieldwork process itself becomes the focus in an ethnographic text. Its composition rests on moving the fieldworker to centre stage and displaying how the writer comes to know a given culture. While often carefully segregated from an author's realist writings, confessional ethnography often manages to convey a good deal of the same sort of cultural knowledge put forth in conventional realist works but in a more personalized fashion (e.g. Rabinow 1977).

Other genres utilized for ethnographic reporting are available as well. *Dramatic ethnographies*, for example, rest on the narration of a particular event or sequence of events of apparent significance to the cultural members studied. Such ethnographies present an unfolding story and rely more on literary techniques drawn from fiction than on plain-speaking, documentary techniques – 'the style of non-style' – drawn from scientific reports (e.g. Shore 1982). *Critical ethnographies* provide another format wherein the represented culture is located within a larger historical, political, economic, social and symbolic context than is said to be recognized by cultural members, thus pushing the writer to move beyond traditional ethnographic frameworks and interests when constructing the text (e.g. Nash 1979). Even self or auto-ethnographies have emerged in which the culture of the ethnographer's own group is textualized. Such writings offer the passionate, emotional voice of a positioned and explicitly judgemental fieldworker and thus obliterates the customary distinction between the researcher and the researched (e.g. Young 1991).

A good deal of the narrative variety of ethnographic writing is a consequence of the post-1970s spread of the specialized and relatively insular disciplinary aims of anthropology and, to a lesser degree, sociology. Growing interest in the contemporary idea of culture – as something held by all identifiable groups, organizations and societies – has put ethnography in play virtually everywhere. No longer is ethnography organized simply by geographic region, society or community. Adjectival ethnographies have become common and sizeable literatures can be found in such areas as medical ethnography, organizational ethnography, conversation ethnography, school ethnography, occupational ethnography, family ethnography and many more. The results of the intellectual and territorial moves of both away and at-home ethnography include a proliferation of styles across domains and an increase in the number of experimental or provisional forms in which ethnography is cast.

The expansion of ethnographic interests, methods and styles is a product of the third moment of ethnography – the reading of ethnographic texts by particular audiences and the kinds of responses these texts appear to generate. Of particular interest are the categories of readers that an ethnographer recognizes and courts through the topical choices, analytic techniques and composition practices displayed in a text. Three audience categories stand out. First, collegial readers are those who follow particular ethnographic domains most avidly. They are usually the most careful and critical readers of one another's work and the most familiar with the past and present of ethnography. Second, general social science readers operate outside of ethnographic circles. These are readers attracted to a particular ethnography because the presumed facts (and perhaps the arguments) conveyed in the work helps further their own research agendas. Third, there are some who read ethnography for pleasure more than for professional enlightenment. Certain ethnographic works attract a large, unspecialized audience for whom the storytelling and allegorical nature of an ethnography is salient. Such readers look for familiar formats – the traveller's tale, the adventure story, the investigative report and, perhaps most frequently, the popular ethnographic classics of the past – when appraising the writing. Ironically, the ethnographer charged with being a novelist manqué by colleagues and other social scientists is quite likely to be the ethnographer with the largest number of readers.

For each reader segment, particular ethnographic styles are more or less attractive. Collegial readers may take in their stride what those outside the field find inelegant, pinched and abstruse. The growing segmentation across collegial readers suggests that many may be puzzled as to what nominal ethnographic colleagues are up to with their increasingly focused research techniques and refined, seemingly indecipherable, prose styles. This creates something of a dilemma for ethnographers for it suggests the distance between the general reader and the ethnographic specialist as well as the distance between differing segments of ethnographic specialists themselves is growing. While ethnography itself is in little or no danger of vanishing, those who read broadly across ethnographic fields may be fewer in number than in generations past. This is a shame, for strictly speaking an unread ethnography is no ethnography at all.

John Van Maanen
Massachusetts Institute of Technology

References

Agar, M. (1980) *The Professional Stranger*, New York.

Bernard, H. R. (1994) *Research Methods in Cultural Anthropology*, 2nd edn, Newbury Park, CA.

Clifford, J. and Marcus, G. E. (eds) (1986) *Writing Culture*, Berkeley, CA.

Geertz, C. (1973) *The Interpretation of Cultures*, New York.

Hammersley, M. and Atkinson, P. (1983) *Ethnography*, London.

Kuper, A. (1983) *Anthropology and Anthropologists*, 2nd edn, London.

Malinowski, B. (1922) *Argonauts of the Western Pacific*, London.

Marcus, G. E. and Fischer, M. (1986) *Anthropology as Cultural Critique*, Chicago.

Nash, J. (1979) *We Eat the Mines and the Mines Eat Us*, New York.

Rabinow, P. (1977) *Reflections on Fieldwork in Morocco*, Berkeley, CA.

Sanjek, R. (ed.) (1990) *Fieldnotes*, Ithaca, NY.

Shore, B. (1982) *Sala'ilua: A Samoan Mystery*, New York.

Spradley, J. P. (1979) *The Ethnographic Interview*, New York.

Stocking, G. W. (1987) *Victorian Anthropology*, New York.

—— (1992) *The Ethnographer's Magic*, Madison, WI.

Van Maanen, J. (1988) *Tales of the Field*, Chicago.

Young, M. (1991) *An Inside Job*, Oxford.

See also: case study; methods of social research.

ethnomethodology

The term ethnomethodology was coined by Harold Garfinkel, whose *Studies in Ethnomethodology* (1967) set the directions for a unique field of sociological investigation. As the word ethnomethodology implies, it is the study of 'people's methods'. It is partly akin to the anthropological ethnosciences (the study of folk systems of measurement, botanical classification, colour categories, astronomy and music), but its domain – everyday methods for producing social order – is more inclusive. In most cases, ethnomethodologists study commonplace activities in their own native societies. When they study exotic or specialized domains of practice they attempt to master the relevant linguistic and embodied competencies, preparatory to explicating their endogenous organization.

Ethnomethodology is defined not only by its subject matter, but also by a distinctive, and often controversial, conception of social order. From Talcott Parsons (1937), Garfinkel inherited a general sociological orientation to social action and social structure, but he radically transformed the theoretical *problem* of order into a descriptive orientation to the quotidian *production* of social order. Garfinkel's solution was not framed as a coherent theoretical answer to the foundational question of how order is created out of disorder; instead, it pointed to how the relentless, *ad hoc* production of ordinary social activities obviates any need for a formal theoretical solution. The idea was to identify and describe the diverse language games through which social order is *performed* on the street. This proposal borrowed liberally from existential phenomenology and Wittgenstein's later writings, but above all it was developed through Garfinkel's and his students' detailed investigations of everyday activities.

In addition to studying ordinary practical and communicative actions – for example, conversation, wayfinding, driving in traffic – ethnomethodologists investigate the embodied, communicative performance of social and natural scientific methods (Garfinkel *et al.* 1981). In line with the effort to describe the *accomplishment* of social order, ethnomethodologists try to detail the production of natural order without suggesting that scientific facts necessarily become any less factual for being so described. Unlike social constructivists, they do not frame the 'construction of facts' in causal or quasi-causal terms, and generally they do not attempt sceptically to undermine the objectivity of science and mathematics (Lynch 1993). Instead, they endeavour to show what can be *meant*, under different circumstances of enquiry and for all practical purposes, by fact, artefact, discovery, objectivity and the like. The policy with regard to such topics is one of 'indifference' rather than scepticism (Garfinkel and Sacks 1970).

Ethnomethodology is not itself a social science method. Leading figures in the field have repeatedly emphasized that there is no obligatory set of methods, and no prohibition against using any research procedure whatsoever, if it is *adequate* to the particular phenomena under study. Nevertheless, ethnomethodologists tend to use particular research techniques. Especially in the associated programme of conversation analysis, practitioners typically analyse audio and videotapes of conversations, meetings, interrogations, and continuous sequences of embodied action. These data are understood less as empirical evidence about an external world than as intelligible constituents of a life-world inhabited by participants and analysts alike. As the late Harvey Sacks, the founder of conversation analysis, noted, the 'single virtue' of tape-recorded materials is that they provide detailed records of activities, which permit extended and repeated study in a community of investigators (Sacks 1984: 26). Accordingly, rather than representing *facts* in an invisible, pre-theoretical domain of natural order, the data act as strong *reminders* of commonplace scenes of action, which touch off, supplement and sometimes challenge the analyst's reflections about the genealogy of social order. The point of such investigations is to *recover* – through a kind of technical *anamnesis* – the 'oriented to' sense of spontaneously produced communicative actions.

Ethnomethodology's scientific status remains doubtful and contentious. Although ethnomethodologists attempt rigorously to describe actual, singular occasions of conduct, they do not develop causal theories or explanatory models. To an extent, the results of ethnomethodological study can be likened to *manuals* of instruction that describe how the language games under study are performed. When done well, such praxiological descriptions delve into non-obvious properties of situated conduct that elude general cognitive schemes and rule-governed models. For that reason, ethnomethodology's long-term promise is not limited to its contribution to the knowledge base of the social science disciplines. It also can contribute to a variety of other academic and non-academic efforts to document the diverse tacit knowledges – the mundane, but virtually impossible to codify, competencies – that are part of innumerable organizations of practice.

Michael Lynch
Brunel University

References

Garfinkel, H. (1967) *Studies in Ethnomethodology*, Englewood Cliffs, NJ.

Garfinkel, H. and Sacks, H. (1970) 'On formal structures of practical actions', in J. C. McKinney and E. A. Tiryakian (eds) *Theoretical Sociology: Perspectives and Development*, New York.

Garfinkel, H., Lynch, M. and Livingston, E. (1981) 'The work of a discovering science construed with materials from the optically discovered pulsar', *Philosophy of the Social Sciences* 11.

Lynch, M. (1993) *Scientific Practice and Ordinary Action: Ethnomethodology and Social Studies of Science*, New York.

Parsons, T. (1937) *The Structure of Social Action*, New York.

Sacks, H. (1984) 'Notes on methodology', in J. M. Atkinson and J. C. Heritage (eds) *Structures of Social Action: Studies on Conversation Analysis*, Cambridge, UK.

Further reading

Button, G. (ed.) (1991) *Ethnomethodology and the Human Sciences*, Cambridge, UK.

Fehr, B. J., Stetson, J. and Mizukawa Y. (1990) 'A bibliography for ethnomethodology', in J. Coulter (ed.) *Ethnomethodological Sociology*, London.

Heritage, J. (1984) *Garfinkel and Ethnomethodology*, Oxford.

Maynard, D. and Clayman S. (1991) 'The diversity of ethnomethodology', *Annual Review of Sociology* 17.

Sacks, H. (1992) *Lectures on Conversation*, Oxford.

Sacks, H., Schegloff, E. A. and Jefferson, G. (1974) 'A simplest systematics for the organization of turn-taking in conversation', *Language* 50(4).

Sharrock, W. (1989) 'Ethnomethodology', *British Journal of Sociology* 40.

See also: discourse analysis; phenomenology; reflexivity.

ethology

Konrad Lorenz defined ethology as 'the discipline which applies to the behaviour of animals and humans all those questions asked and those methodologies used as a matter of course in all other branches of biology since Charles Darwin's time'. Ethology is concerned with causality and the functions of behaviour, and it tries to establish the influence on behaviour of genetic, physiological and ecological variables. Ethologists also ask how and why forms of behaviour develop in interaction with the environment in the ontogeny of the individual, as well as how behaviour could have developed phylogenetically. Behaviour is thus interpreted as a contribution to adaptation to a particular environment. The methods of ethology involve primarily observation of a species in their natural environment. Having collected the data, ethologists then develop an ethogram, an inventory of behaviour of a species. This step is followed by systematic experiments and interspecific comparisons.

The origins of ethology can be traced back to Darwin. His book, *On the Origin of Species* (1859), established the basis for the concept of instinct, while even more important was his theory that natural selection underlies the behaviour of an animal as well as its morphology and physiology. Whitman (1898) also claimed that an evolutionary perspective on behaviour was necessary; independently of Whitman, Heinroth (1910) discovered the existence of 'patterns of movements' which, like morphological structures, are comparable between species. Through such comparisons, particular behaviours could be called homologous and could be traced back to a common ancestor.

Another antecedent of ethology is purposive psychology developed by McDougall in *An Outline of Psychology* (1923) and later by Tolman in *Purposive Behavior in Animals and Man* (1932). Both postulated a factor called 'instinct' and noted that the behaviour of animals follows a purpose governed by this instinct. Craig (1918) differentiated the end of a chain of behaviours (the consummatory act) from its beginning (appetitive behaviour). Appetitive behaviour is a specific seeking behaviour for a stimulus situation in which the consummatory act can begin.

Modern ethology dates back to 1931 with Lorenz's 'Contributions to the study of the ethology of social *corvidae*'. This article and others that followed represented a synthesis of previously isolated efforts in ethology and led to a new model of animal behaviour. Lorenz stressed that the interpretation of animal behaviour is possible only after detailed observation of the animal in its natural environment, and that it is necessary to compare behaviours of different species.

Lorenz used a hydraulic model to describe the interaction between internal and external factors, and he redefined Craig's 'consummatory' act as the 'fixed action pattern' (FAP); the preliminary 'appetitive' behaviour was the phase leading to the performance of the FAP. Appetitive behaviour causes the animal to look for a configuration of stimuli which release the FAP. These stimuli are recognized innately according to a hypothetical mechanism, the 'innate releasing mechanism'. These signals are not only objects in the environment but also signals emitted by other members of the species, in which case signals serve a social function and are called 'releasers'. Releasers are not always equally efficient: this is because the efficiency is modulated by an 'action specific energy' which is diminished by the execution of an FAP. If only a little of the action specific energy is present, then the FAP can be executed only incompletely and thus becomes an 'intention' movement. When the FAP has not been executed for a long stretch of time, the threshold for the execution decreases and the FAP can be released even by a weak or inadequate stimulus; Lorenz termed this a 'vacuum activity'.

Lorenz's model was often criticized because it was so simple. Niko Tinbergen (1942) elaborated on Lorenz's original model. He expanded the techniques of observation through simple but ingenious experiments, and he evolved more sophisticated notions of releasers and instincts. Tinbergen defined instinct as

> a hierarchical organized nervous mechanism which reacts to priming, releasing and directing stimuli of either endogenous or exogenous character. The reaction consists of a co-ordinated series of movements that contribute to the preservation of the individual and species.

Tinbergen worked mainly on the reproductive behaviour of the stickleback and through his findings expanded our understanding of the hierarchical organization of instincts. His experiments were mostly concerned with motivational conflicts, redirected activities, ambivalent behaviour and displacement.

Following Lorenz's and Tinbergen's seminal work, ethology spread rapidly all over Europe and (at a slower rate) to the USA. Progress was halted during the Second World War and commenced again in the 1950s with the first international publication of Tinbergen's *The Study of Instinct* (the first ecology textbook) in 1951, and Lorenz's *King Solomon's Ring*, a popularized account of ethology, in 1952.

With the growth of ethology came a major conflict between two opposing views of behaviour. First, American experimental psychology adopted a behaviourist orientation that stressed the influence of environment and learning factors; they carried out laboratory experiments using rats, cats, dogs and apes as models for humans. Second, ethology, with its systematic observation of species in their natural setting, tried to discover evolutionary and adaptive mechanisms underlying animal behaviour – the genetic basis for behaviour. Unlike experimental psychologists, ethologists studied many and diverse species, thus strengthening their case for innateness and instinct. The neglect of learning by ethologists provoked a strong reaction against the discipline from members of the opposing camp, notably by Lehrman (1953), who based his criticisms on the work of Kuo (1932).

The innate versus acquired dichotomy resulting from the debate now seems somewhat sterile and false: innate and learned are no longer regarded as exclusive categories. Contemporary ethologists would agree that behaviour develops ontogenetically through the interaction between genetic information and environment. This does not imply that an apparently innate characteristic is really learned, or that every phylogenetically pre-programmed behaviour must be adaptively modifiable through learning. But everything learned must have as its foundation a phylogenetically provided programme if appropriate and adaptive behaviour patterns are to be produced. It seems logical to postulate that certain behaviour elements – those which conduct learning processes – should never be modifiable through learning. Learned behaviour does contain genetic information, to the extent that the basis of learning is a physiological apparatus which evolved under the pressure of selection. Lorenz termed this mechanism the 'innate school-marm'. Thus the question is not whether behaviour patterns are innate or acquired but rather how behaviour can be modified, or what can be learned, and when.

From the beginning, ethology was also interested in aspects of social behaviour such as territorial behaviour, group structure, and communication. A milestone in the ethological study of communication was the development of the concept of 'ritualization' (Huxley 1966), referring to the modification of a behaviour pattern by natural selection in order to serve a communicative function. Such expressive movements mostly occur in courtship and in displays of aggression or submission. Their social function is largely to channel aggression – thus ritualized fighting or submissive behaviour hinders escalation of a fight. Bonding is another function of ritualized behaviour.

Ethologists also investigated ranking as an aspect of social behaviour. Schielderup-Ebbe (1935) found that among a flock of hens a few enjoyed privileges during feeding and had first access to the feeding site and pecked at other, lower-ranking, hens. This led on to the study of dominance, defined as having priority access to scarce resources, and measured by the number of conflicts won. This concept is now generally limited to description of relationships, while other forms of behaviour are referred to in the construction of social hierarchies where high-ranking individuals are the focus of attention of other group members.

Other areas of interest to ethologists are the relationship between social organization and ecology (DeVore 1965); play behaviour; imprinting, or how individuals become attached to other members of the group, first observed by Lorenz in birds and studied by Hess (1973) and others. Ethologists have also considered the link between behaviour and the nervous system. Holst and St Paul (1963) elicited different behavioural reactions in hens through electrical stimulation of the brain, and Delgado (1967) was able to control aggressive behaviour using similar techniques. Neurophysiological research led to the discovery of neurons in the brain that are responsible for the control of different aspects of behaviour (Ewert 1976).

One development in ethology is sociobiology. Sociobiologists propose a global theory of behaviour which derives from the 'selfish interest' of the gene to reproduce itself; this selfishness leads to the concept of kin-selection, for related individuals share a determinable number of genes. Sociobiology's primary tools are intriguing mathematical models that consider phylogenetic adaptation and ecological pressures. When, in certain situations, different possible behaviours exist, pressures result in the development of 'evolutionary stabile strategies' (ESS) of behaviour. Sociobiologists try to include the social sciences in a modern synthesis of evolutionary theory, arguing that all forms of social organization – in animals ranging from termites to primates, including humans – can be described using the same parameters and the same quantitative theory. They are criticized for their overemphasis on genetic determinism and for their analytical models which are strongly reminiscent of the Social Darwinism of the early twentieth century. Nevertheless they can provide new insights into the structure and organization of individuals and their behaviour, and their importance is acknowledged in the study of insects, fish and birds. But the general applicability of sociobiological laws to primates and humans has yet to be proved.

The originality of the ethological approach in the study of human behaviour was in its methods of systematic observation and qualitative description, its considerations of phylogenetic roots, and the functions of behaviour deduced from a comparative approach. Human ethology in turn influenced areas of anthropology, psychology and sociology. However, the construction of an appropriate theoretical framework still remains a problem for the human ethologist.

Development of speech is a distinguishing primary characteristic of human behaviour. This made it possible to transmit information between generations by non-genetic means. Cultural evolution then assumed a major role in the adaptation of the species. It is possible that cultural evolution follows rules comparable to those which govern phylogenetic evolution, and also leads to the modification in behaviour. Moreover, humans are capable of altering their environment, thus changing selective pressures. These possibilities make it more difficult to determine the genetic adaptive value of a behaviour, and blur the distinction between phylogenetic and cultural traits.

Finally, human ethologists have tended to neglect the adaptive modification of behaviour, that is, learning processes.

Several popular books on human ethology – Ardrey's *The Territorial Imperative* (1966), Lorenz's *On Aggression* (1963), Morris's *The Naked Ape* (1967) and Wilson's *On Human Nature* (1978) – brought the subject to the attention of a wider public. These authors tried to present a biological explanation for human behaviour, but they often worked with naïve analogies and simplistic comparisons. At the same time, however, an authentic human ethology was being developed. Research focused on human-ethological interpretations of child development (child ethology), as in the work of Blurton-Jones (1972) and McGrew (1972); others described children's relationships and resulting group structures. Intercultural comparisons were made in the work of Eibl-Eibesfeldt on non-verbal behaviour (1972), who also observed the expressive behaviour of children born deaf and blind (1973). These studies have shown the complexities and the multidimensional nature of ontogeny, as well as confirmed the existence of invariant transcultural traits in human behaviour, such as expressive behaviour and its ritualization.

Human ethology has moved away from its descriptive beginnings and no longer restricts itself to investigating phylogenetic adaptations in behaviour: cultural patterns are also studied in relation to adaptation, and already a number of universal social interaction strategies have been observed through cross-cultural comparison. Their apparent variation can be attributed to the fact that phylogenetic and cultural patterns can be substituted as functional equivalents for one another, or they can be verbalized. Nevertheless, the underlying structural rules remain the same. This opens the way for the study of a grammar of human social behaviour encompassing verbal and non-verbal strategies. Such an approach could provide a theoretical framework and together with the empirical research in progress could give human ethology the refinement of animal ethology.

The results of human ethological studies could have an important impact on social questions, and the dangers arising from the neglect of human nature should be clear. While the modifiability of human behaviour, especially through educational programmes, is limited, this knowledge should not be used to justify a freeze on social changes, as extreme conservatives have already suggested. Indeed, this view was possible only because of the oversimplification of the field by popular writers. Rather, the universals identified by human ethology, especially in communication and in mechanisms of group cohesion and seclusion, could be the basis for shared concern and a common understanding and could provide a means to overcome ethnocentric political strategies.

Karl Grammar
Max-Planck Institut für Verhaltensphysiologie
Forsdiungsskelle für Humanethologie
Germany

References

Blurton-Jones, N. G. (1972) *Ethological Studies of Child Behaviour*, Cambridge, UK.

Bowlby, J. (1969) *Attachment and Loss, vol. I, Attachment*, London.

Craig, W. (1918) 'Appetites and aversions as constituents of instincts', *Biological Bulletin* 34.

Dawkins, R. (1976) *The Selfish Gene*, London.

Delgado, J. M. R. (1967) 'Aggression and defense under cerebral radio control', in C. D. Clemente and D. B. Lindsley (eds) *Aggression and Defense*, Berkeley, CA.

DeVore, I. (1965) *Primate Behavior: Field Studies of Monkeys and Apes*, New York.

Eibl-Eibesfeldt, I. (1972) 'Similarities and differences between cultures in expressive movements', in R. A. Hinde (ed.) *Non-Verbal Communication*, London.

— (1973) 'The expressive behaviour of deaf and blindborn', in M. von Cranach and I. Vine (eds) *Non-Verbal Behaviour and Expressive Movements*, London.

Ewert, J. P. (1976) *Neuro-Ethologie*, Berlin.

Heinroth, O. (1910) 'Beitrage zur Biologie, insbesondere Psychologie und Ethologie der Anatiden', *Verh. J. Int. Orthin. Kong.*, Berlin.

Hess, E. H. (1973) *Imprinting: Early Experience and the Development of Attachment*, New York.

Holst, E. V. and St Paul, U. V. (1963) 'On the functional organization of drives', *Animal Behaviour* 11.

Huxley, J. S. (1966) 'A discussion on ritualization of behaviour in animals and man', *Philosophical Transactions of the Royal Society* 251.

Kuo, Z. Y. (1932) 'Ontogeny of embryonic behavior in Aves I and II', *Journal of Experimental Zoology* 61.

Lehrman, D. S. (1953) 'A critique of Konrad Lorenz's theory of instinctive behaviour', *Quarterly Review of Biology* 28.

McGrew, W. C. (1972) *An Ethological Study of Children's Behavior*, New York.

Schielderup-Ebbe, T. (1935) 'Social behavior of birds', in A. Murchinson (ed.) *A Handbook of Social Psychology*, New York.

Tinbergen, N. (1942) 'An objective study of the innate behavior of animals', *Biblioth. Biotheor.* 1.

Whitman, C. C. (1898) 'Animal behavior', *Biol. Lect. Mar. Lab.*, Woods Hole, MA.

Further reading

Bateson, P. P. G. and Hinde, R. A. (eds) (1976) *Growing Points in Ethology*, London.

Eibl-Eibesfeldt, I. (1975) *Ethology: The Biology of Behavior*, 2nd edn, New York.

Lehner, P. N. (1979) *Handbook of Ethological Methods*, New York.

See also: genetics and behaviour; instinct; sociobiology.

European economic and monetary union

The countries of the European Union are formally committed to full economic and monetary union provided the conditions set out in the Maastricht Treaty 1992 are achieved. A monetary union between nation-states is distinct from an economic union. An economic union consists of a single market for goods, services, capital and labour with no imposed barriers or distortions to impede their free flow within the area. A monetary union also requires irrevocably fixed exchange rates between the component parts, possibly a common currency, and a centralized union-wide monetary policy.

To date (with the exception of Belgium and Luxembourg) the only viable and sustained monetary unions have been based on nation states. Attempts have been made to link countries in monetary unions (such as in Africa) but none has been conspicuously successful. The basic characteristics required for an effective full monetary union are strict:

1 There is no exchange control between the component parts, which means that capital is free to flow without impediment within the union.

2 There is no possibility of any internal exchange rate change as there is a common currency or an internal regime of complete and irrevocably fixed exchange rates.

3 There is a single union-wide central bank which is responsible for the conduct of monetary policy.

4 Monetary policy is conducted at the level of the union and not the component regions.

5 A common payments system exists throughout the union.

6 There is a union-wide capital market and banking system both subject to a common regulatory regime.

7 Although subsectors (e.g. states or countries) may have their own budgets, there is also a union-wide budget of the central government. Through this central budget there are in-built regional transfers such as when a depressed region automatically pays less tax and receives more government payments. There may also be explicit regional policy mechanisms built into fiscal policy.

Thus the essential features of a monetary union are centralized policy decision making with reference to the economic and financial circumstances of the union as a whole. Regions become subservient to the union despite the fact that their economic circumstances may be different. The major policy implication is that members of a European Monetary Union (EMU) would surrender sovereignty to pursue independent national policies in two main areas: with respect to setting the level of national currencies exchange rates, and over the conduct of monetary policy (the setting of interest rates and the growth of the money supply). If a common currency is created (though this is not a necessary condition for a monetary union) the possibility of internal exchange rate adjustments is by definition removed. It is for these reasons that the establishment of a EMU would also require the creation of a European Central Bank to determine the union's monetary policy.

The argument for European Monetary Union is that, as the degree of economic and financial integration between member states increases (and this will develop further with the complete abolition of exchange control and the completion of the internal market during the 1990s), so the relationship between member countries approaches that which exists between different regions or counties within countries. Proponents argue that to make the internal market effective (as it is in the USA where there are semi-independent states with different laws and budgets) it needs to be set within a monetary union with a single currency; it is a means of making the internal market effective which is a major reason why the issue of EMU has resurfaced in the 1990s following the commitment to complete the internal market programme.

Several benefits could derive from this, not the least being that there are no internal balance of payments financing problems or speculative capital flows which may, from time to time, induce financial crises. The major advantage is that, as uncertainty associated with exchange rate risks is eliminated, and there are no transactions costs involved in having trade conducted in several currencies, the volume of interregional trade is higher. At the same time capital and savings are allocated within the union to where the rate of return is highest. A further advantage is that it removes the potential conflicts and uncertainties that can arise through the conduct of divergent and non-cooperative national economic and monetary policies.

However, it also means that policy of any region is determined nationally and in the interests of the union as a whole rather than that of the region, and that monetary policy is not differentiated to reflect the particular economic circumstances of different regions. It also means that high unemployment in a region associated with uncompetitiveness cannot be offset by an exchange rate adjustment. It removes the policy autonomy and sovereignty of the component parts to choose their own economic policy and objectives (most especially with respect to any trade-off that might exist between unemployment and inflation) and to respond to asymmetric shocks. It is also argued that the condi-

tions required to make Europe an optimal currency area (high mobility of labour, etc.) do not exist. In addition, and compared to the operation of the European Monetary System (EMS), the issue arises as to whether the credibility of a newly created European Central Bank would be as great as that of the Bundesbank within the EMS.

In the final analysis, the objection to creating a monetary union is the implied loss of policy sovereignty. But the question arises as to how much effective sovereignty governments in practice have in countries which are highly integrated with other countries. The issue is therefore about how powerful national independent policy mechanisms are in an increasingly integrated Europe. The fact that a country has its own currency, conducts its own monetary policy, and sets its own budget, does not guarantee that it has a truly independent policy; it may have unimpaired *nominal* sovereignty but little *effective* sovereignty.

A major milestone en route to a European Monetary Union was set in the Maastricht Treaty of 1992. An irrevocable process was agreed which implies a binding commitment to creating a monetary union providing stated conditions are met. As the treaty stands, a monetary union *could* be created in 1997 if the majority of member states agree, and *will* be created in 1999 but only for those members which satisfy strict convergence criteria with respect to inflation, interest rates, size of budget deficits, etc. A distinct possibility is that only a limited number (possibly as few as two or three) of members will form a monetary union which gives rise to the possibility of a 'two-speed Europe'.

David T. Llewellyn
Loughborough University

Further reading

Cecchini Report (1988) *The European Challenge 1992*, Brussels.

Cohen, D. and Wyplosz, C. (1989) 'The European Monetary Union: an agnostic evaluation', CEPR Discussion Paper no. 453, September.

Commission of the European Communities (1990) 'One market, one money', *European Economy* 44.

De Cecco, M. and Giovannini, A. (eds) (1988) *A European Central Bank?*, Cambridge, UK.

Eichengreen, B. (1990a) 'Currency union', *Economic Policy* 10.

—— (1990b) 'Costs and benefits of the European monetary unification', CEPR Discussion Paper no. 453, September.

Giovannini, A. (1990) 'European monetary reform: progress and prospects', *Brookings Papers on Economic Activity*.

Llewellyn, D. T. (1988) 'European Monetary Union', *Banking World* November and December.

event-history analysis

Event-history analysis bases itself principally on the hypothesis that human behaviour is generated by a stochastic process. Its more general aim therefore is to estimate the probability distribution of the life courses followed by a given population over time. An individual event-history appears as a result of a complex process, which develops during the life course, yet is situated within given historical, economic, political and social conditions. This process is affected by social structures but in turn may alter them in a dualistic way.

During the 1970s and 1980s, the amount of reliable life-history data produced by surveys (fertility, family, occupation and migration surveys) increased considerably. At the same time, probability theories and statistical methodologies developed, resulting in techniques for handling such data. One such technique, event-history analysis, is now used in a growing number of disciplines, notably demography (Courgeau and Lelièvre 1992), econometrics (Lancaster 1990) and sociology (Tuma and Hannan 1984).

Traditional models focus on a single event or on a sequence of similar events, such as successive births for a woman. Their occurrence is studied from a dynamic temporal perspective, modelling via the events' probability functions and accounting for incomplete information by different censoring mechanisms, of which right-censoring at the end of an observation is the most widely known and studied example. However, as individuals experience events in different spheres of life (occupational, educational, migration, family and other histories), the study of such parallel and interacting histories requires much more complex multistate models, enabling us to examine interaction between two or more processes and to extend the analysis to more intricate situations. These models lead to new concepts of dependency in social sciences, for example, local dependence. We can thus formalize the notion that one given process may influence the local development of another without reciprocity. Simultaneously it is necessary to deal with heterogeneity in populations and to investigate the impact of certain individual characteristics, possibly time-dependent, on the occurrence of events. Semiparametric regression models, first introduced by Cox (1972), are extensively used to analyse the observed heterogeneity of populations and its effect on the timing of given events. This heterogeneity comes from family origins, educational characteristics or, more generally, from the past life history of the individual. Unlike standard regression models, these models have no error term and omission of important covariates raises problems of unobserved heterogeneity. Such problems have led to much

discussion in the field since the same observed outcomes may be generated by different models.

Event-history analysis had led to numerous innovations in various fields of the social sciences and is bringing new challenges to research into more complex social units such as households or families.

Daniel Courgeau
Institut National d'Etudes Démographiques
Paris

References

Courgeau, D. and Lelièvre, E. (1992) *Event History Analysis in Demography*, Oxford.

Cox, D. (1972) 'Regression models and life tables', *Journal of the Royal Statistical Society* B34.

Cox, D. and Oakes, D. (1984) *Analysis of Survival Data*, London.

Kalbfleisch, J. and Prentice, R. (1980) *The Statistical Analysis of Failure Time Data*, New York.

Lancaster, T. (1990) *The Econometric Analysis of Transition Data*, Cambridge, UK.

Trussel, J., Hankinson, R. and Tilton, J. (1992) *Demographic Applications of Event History Analysis*, Oxford.

Tuma, N. and Hannan, M. (1984) *Social Dynamics: Models and Methods*, Orlando, FL.

See also: cohort analysis.

evolution *see* evolutionary economics; evolutionism and progress; human evolution

evolutionary economics

The central concern of evolutionary economic analysis is to explain why and how the economic world changes, its subject matter is dynamics, and its purpose is to make sense of the immense variety of behaviour which comprises the rich tapestry of historical change. Evolution does not mean change *simpliciter* but change in the relative frequencies of specified entities within a population and subject to the operation of specific mechanisms. This is a theme to which the historical record speaks with great eloquence and persistence (Landes 1968; Mokyr 1991). The ever-changing structure of the economic fabric, as witnessed in the growth and decline of firms, cities, regions and nations, reflects evolution operating at different levels and with different speeds, as does the emergence over time of completely new areas of economic activity. The displacement of gas by electricity, the spread of robotic tools in the workplace, the displacement of corner shops by supermarkets, the growth of part-time relative to full-time employment and the shifting balance of employment between agriculture, manufacturing and services in their different ways draw upon the same mechanism, whose mainspring is variety in behaviour. That is the fundamental fact which makes any social science the investigation of interaction between individuals and organizations.

As with modern evolutionary theory, the process is applicable at many different levels of economic activity depending on what are taken to be the appropriate units of selection. But whatever the level the issues are the same, the specification of variety in behaviour, the identification of the selection mechanisms which resolve that variety into economic change, and the analysis of feedback and other mechanisms which shape and regenerate variety over time. Inherently this involves a population perspective in which any idea of representative behaviour is utterly redundant except as a statistic artefact. Before illustrating these remarks it is useful to remember Lewontin's (1982) famous requirements for an evolutionary theory, namely entities possessing different characteristics or behavioural traits; a mechanism which assigns differential fitness to entities as they interact with other rival entities in a selection environment; and heritability, the transmission through time of the behavioural traits. We should dispose of this last point first because, *contra* naïve views on evolution, no reference to any genetic mechanism is involved or implied. What is important is stability and persistence of behaviour over time, that tomorrow's behavioural traits are correlated with those of today. Thus, inertia is an important conserving element in the picture and it will be obvious that evolution cannot occur in a world where individuals or organizations behave randomly. As to the origins of variety in economic behaviour, there is a natural emphasis on matters of technology, organization and management, that is, upon the knowledge of how to act in order to acquire beneficial behavioural traits. The entrepreneur is fully at home in an evolutionary world, and perhaps no other, for the very definition of entrepreneurship entails variety in behaviour of individuals or organized groups. Does evolution entail rationality? Apparently not. In a world in which knowledge is costly to acquire, and computational competence is bounded there is little ground for invoking omniscient optimization as a behaviour yardstick. There is nothing amiss with the idea that individuals seek the best outcome of any set of options, but such calculations as are involved are necessary local solutions not global solutions. Here lies a powerful source of differential behaviour; individuals know different things, they live in the same world but perceive (imagine?) different worlds. Hence it is not surprising that evolutionary analysis finds the idea of bounded rationality to be of central importance; that it specifies

behaviour in terms of stable rules which themselves evolve over time; and, that it insists upon the benefits to be gained from the study of the internal working of organizations (Nelson and Winter 1982). Since the foundation of many of these issues is the acquisition of knowledge it is evident that there are close affinities with the emerging field of evolutionary epistemology (Hull 1988; Plotkin 1994). Nor is intentionality of economic behaviour a problem; quite the contrary, it helps us to understand how economic variation is guided and channelled while underpinning the central point of individuals and organizations behaving differently (Hodgson 1993). The simple point to grasp is that the sources of economic variety are far richer than the sources of biological variety.

A typical if basic picture of economic microevolution is as follows. It concerns a population of rival firms each producing one or more products, each product with its own methods of production as dictated by the firm's technology, organization and management rules. The firm is a vehicle for many co-ordinating activities which ultimately result in the production of saleable output, co-ordinating activities which evolutionists call replicators for they result in the firm generating copy after copy of its own behaviour. The firm interacts in markets with other firms to sell its products and purchase production inputs and the result of these market interactions determines the economic quality of its products, the prices at which it can sell them and the economic costs of their production. Users are continually comparing one product with another, and switching their allegiance to what they perceive to be better quality and price combinations, while firms deploy their profits in part to accumulate productive and marketing capabilities. In short, the underlying differences in behavioural rules lead to different prices, costs and levels of profitability which provide the basis for dynamic change: the general rule being that more profitable firms expand at the expense of less profitable rivals. Or to put it more accurately, there is market selection *for* products and their methods of production and consequent selection *of* the rival firms (Sober 1984). It is these differential rates of increase which correspond to the notion of economic fitness. If such a process is imagined to run in unchanged circumstances, the frequency distribution of output will concentrate on the firms with lower costs and superior products and it will gradually eliminate other firms according to the prevailing rules of bankruptcy.

Evolution and market concentration go hand in hand, which means that competition destroys the very variety on which it depends. Thus, if economic evolution is not to cease, mechanisms must be in play to regenerate that variety. Innovation is thus a central component of the macroevolutionary story, and economists have learned to think of this in terms of guided variation within existing technological activities, together with the less frequent emergence of conceptually new productive opportunities. What is important for present purposes is the dependence of innovative creativity on feedback from the selection process. Internally generated profits are a principal source of funds for such risky activity, while experience gained in pursing particular activities is a major stimulus to push the pattern of improvement in particular directions. Seeing innovation as random mutation, as in genetics, is not necessarily misplaced but this is certainly not the whole story. In this regard, innovation can gain a self-reinforcing momentum of its own as the process of competition reveals fresh possibilities, and, in the presence of such positive feedback, small historical events can have lasting consequences. In making sense of variety, evolution also makes sense of history.

Implicit in the above is a dual perspective on economic evolution. Much of it is concerned with the traditional role of markets as co-ordinating mechanisms. It is in market interactions that the profitability of different behaviours is determined and thus the resources to invest and innovate in the corresponding activities to which those behaviours relate. This involves competition within and between industries; it is an externalist view of evolution taking the unit of selection in relation to its environment. Equally important is an internalist perspective concerning the process of conjecture formation and selection which takes place within organizations and defines how the relevant bundle of behavioural rules evolves over time. Internal and external processes interact at different speeds and at different levels in complex intriguing ways. What happens within the community of science, for example, as it selects from novel hypotheses, provides material which firms can adopt and adapt as they seek sustainable competitive advantages. Equally, how governments perceive their regulatory role has clear implications for the dual perspective in economic evolution.

Many scholars have found an evolutionary perspective in economics to be appealing. Cut free from any dependence on biology and with the tools of modern mathematics and computation at its disposal, there is a rich agenda to be explored, an agenda which ultimately reduces to a question of the processes which generate and which limit the generation and spread of economic variety. In this it tackles one of the oldest of philosophical questions: how does order and structure emerge from diverse behaviours? If not universal Darwinism at least a broader picture of evolution and its place in shaping history.

J. S. Metcalfe
University of Manchester

References

Hodgson, G. (1993) *Economics and Evolution*, London.
Hull, G. (1988) *Science as a Process*, Chicago.
Landes, D. (1968) *The Unbound Prometheus*, Cambridge, UK.
Lewontin, R. (1982) *Human Diversity*, New York.
Mokyr, J. (1991) *The Lever of Riches*, Oxford.
Nelson, R. and Winter, S. (1982) *An Evolutionary Theory of Economic Change*, Cambridge, MA.
Plotkin, H. (1994) *The Nature of Knowledge*, London.
Sober, E. (1984) *The Nature of Selection*, Cambridge, MA.

Further reading

Witt, U. (1994) *Evolutionary Economics*, London.

evolutionism and progress

Evolutionism is the label now commonly used for a current of thought which was strongly represented in the anthropology and sociology of the nineteenth century. Although it fed on biological analogies, it must be clearly distinguished from Darwinian thinking. Its inspiration came rather from the older tradition of Lamarckian evolutionary theory, which provided the main rival to Darwinian theory until well into the twentieth century. Key elements in this tradition were the beliefs that organisms were intrinsically bound to improve themselves, that changes were progressive and often radical and sudden, and that acquired characters could be transmitted genetically. Typically, the stages of ontogeny, or the individual life history, were taken to exemplify the stages of phylogeny, the development of a species.

Herbert Spencer, one of the most consistent exponents of the organic analogy in the social sciences, was perhaps the leading evolutionist in sociology, but these general ideas were taken for granted by authors as diverse as Marx, Freud and Durkheim, and they survived in some modern theories in anthropology (e.g. Childe 1951), in the psychological theory of Piaget, in 'Whig' history, and so on. The evolutionist assumptions were, however, directly in contradiction to the Darwinian theory of evolution by variation and natural selection, which did not assume the existence of any progressive line of change. On the contrary, Darwin stated emphatically that 'I believe in no fixed law of development'.

Evolutionist theory in the social sciences should perhaps be regarded as part of a broader tradition of theories of progress, which represents the most deeply entrenched way of conceptualizing social history in the west. It has a particular appeal to progressive radicals and utopians, while the mirror-image theory, that the trend of history is towards social and cultural decadence, is, on the other hand, associated rather with right-wing political theories and with religious revivalism. Whether the unit of perfectibility was assumed to be humanity or a particular civilization or race, the theory was so abstract and value-laden as almost to defy empirical reference. Nisbett (1980), nevertheless, argues that the faith in progress has been eroded by a widespread scepticism about the unique superiority of contemporary western civilization.

Adam Kuper
Brunel University

References

Childe, G. (1951) *Social Evolution*, London.
Nisbett, R. (1985) *History of the Idea of Progress*, New York.

Further reading

Collini, S., Winch, D. and Burrow, J. (1984) *That Noble Science of Politics*, Cambridge, UK.
Kuper, A. (1988) *The Invention of Primitive Society*, London.
Stocking, G. (1987) *Victorian Anthropology*, New York.

See also: primitive society; Social Darwinism.

exchange

Exchange is interesting for five reasons: it is the means by which useful things pass from one person to another; it is one of the ways in which people create and maintain social organization; it is always regulated by religion, law, convention and etiquette; it is always meaningful because it carries a symbolic load, and is often a metaphor for other kinds of activities; finally, in many societies people speculate about its origins, about the motives for and the morality of it, about its consequences and what its essence might be. It is rare to find a scholar who gives equal attention to each of these aspects of the topic.

Exchange is universal: we know of no peoples who admire individuals who do not exchange, or who expect a category of people to refrain from it. Although people in industrial and market-organized countries sometimes imagine the attractions of self-sufficiency, and try to achieve it, it would be a new creation if they succeeded. It is true that in every social group some individuals are more engaged in exchange than others, but it is probably a mistake to imagine that some peoples exchange more than other peoples.

People distinguish among kinds of exchange: in English-speaking countries they talk of altruism, barter, charity, commerce, gifts, taxation and theft, among others. These distinctions are based on expectations of return: whether there should be one, whether it should be immediate or after a period of time, whether it should be equivalent or greater or less. This too is

universal, although the kinds available to different peoples are variable. People also categorize kinds of goods as being more suited to one kind of exchange than another: some peoples have goods which are exchanged only as gifts (greetings cards in many countries, *vaygua* in the Trobriands, and so on). They also prohibit the exchange of certain kinds of goods: in Christian thought, for instance, the purchase of spiritual office is distinguished as a named sin (Simony). People also often categorize kinds of exchange as particularly suited to kinds of relationships: friends and family should give gifts in Britain, judges and litigants should not. Where a kind of exchange is reserved to a kind of relationship, people may try to establish the relation by making the exchange. Marcel Mauss (1954 [1925]) noted that a refusal to accept a gift, or to return one, caused great offence, and could be equivalent to a declaration of war.

Social scientists, and in particular anthropologists, have tried to identify systems of exchange. They have done this in various ways. The pioneer was Mauss, who explored gift-giving as a type of exchange based on three obligations: to *give*, to *receive* and to *return*; these are still taken to be the key principles. Mauss's archetypal gift was one so heavily laden with symbolic meaning and consequence that it involved the 'total social personality' of the exchangers (who might be either individuals or groups of people), and success or failure in making exchanges affected their social standing. The potlatch (in which groups try to overwhelm competitors with gifts) was thus interested, but not directly profit-motivated. This is the first attempt to identify a non-market system of exchange by the principles on which the exchanges are made. Malinowski's (1922) exploration of *kula* exchanges between a number of Melanesian islands showed that ceremonial goods circulated by reciprocal gift-giving in the *kula* ring affording the opportunity for trade and establishing peace between neighbouring islands as well as maintaining hierarchy on particular islands: some people were more successful in the *kula* than others. Studies suggest that the ring was less systematic than Malinowski thought (Leach and Leach 1983). In later elaborations, deriving also in part from the work of Karl Polanyi (1944), the principle of reciprocity has been taken to identify a kind of economy: some economies are based principally on reciprocity, others on markets, others on the redistributive activities of chiefs and governments. Sahlins (1972) is noted for his unique attempt to show that different principles were consequential, and were not just *amusettes folkloriques*: economies performed differently as a result. This was especially important because economists and others attempted to show that forms of rational profit-seeking underlay all exchange, and that the differences shown in the ethnographic record were either imperfections (this a term of art of economists) or a manifestation of false consciousness.

The attempt by Lévi-Strauss (1969) and his followers to link formal structures of kinship and marriage to systems of exchange of women has proved most fruitful in kinship studies.

The principle of rational exchange was the basis of exchange theory, derived from the work of von Mises, and elaborated in sociology by Homans (1961) and Blau (1964) and in anthropology by Barth (1966) and Bailey (1969). The attractiveness of such theories derived in part from the shock of describing all social activity as profit-motivated. It also probably derived from the apparent ease with which market principles diffused so quickly in the 1950s and 1960s. This process was widely recorded, perhaps most successfully in the analysis by Bohannan and Bohannan (1968) of the decline of Tiv categories of exchange, when confronted with national markets: the apparent success of 'the modern economy' seemed to justify the adoption of a modern economics to explain everything. Anthropologists and some economists are now less sure. It is possible that some valuable lines for future research have already been established: these include Appadurai's (1986) investigations of the ways that things change meaning as they change hands, and Strathern's (1988) work on symbolism; Gregory's (1982) exploration of the distinction between *gift* and *commodity*, and work by economists and others on the mixed motives with which people engage in exchange, even in so-called market economies.

J. Davis
University of Oxford

References

Appadurai, A. (ed) (1986) *The Social Life of Things*, Cambridge, UK.
Bailey, F. G. (1969) *Stratagems and Spoils: A Social Anthroplogy of Politics*, Oxford.
Barth, F. (1966) *Models of Social Organisation*, London.
Blau, P. M. (1964) *Exchange and Power in Social Life*, New York.
Bohannan, P. and Bohannan, L. (1968) *Tiv Economy*, Evanston, IL.
Davis, J. (1992) *Exchange*, Milton Keynes.
Gregory, C. A. (1982) *Gifts and Commodities*, London.
Homans, G. C. (1961) *Social Behaviour: Its Elementary Forms*, London.
Leach, J. W. and Leach, E. R. (eds) (1983) *The Kula: New Perspectives on Massim Exchange*, Cambridge, UK.
Lévi-Strauss, C. (1969) *The Elementary Structures of Kinship* (*Les Structures élémentaires de la parenté*), revised edn trans. J. H. Bell and J. R. von Sturmer, and ed. R. Needham, London.
Malinowski, B. (1922) *Argonauts of the Western Pacific*, London.
Mauss, M. (1954[1925]) *The Gift*, trans. I. Cunnison, London.
Polanyi, K. (1944) *The Great Transformation*, New York.
Sahlins, M. D. (1972) *Stone Age Economics*, Chicago.
Strathern, M. (1988) *The Gender of the Gift*, Berkeley, CA.

See also: economic anthropology; Polanyi, Karl.

exchange rate

The exchange rate is a price: the price of one currency in terms of another. A distinction is made between the *nominal, effective* and *real* exchange rate. The *nominal* rate is a bilateral price expressed and quoted either as the number of units of the domestic currency per unit of another, or vice versa.

The *effective* exchange rate is an index of a currency's value in terms of a weighted basket of other currencies. Movements in this index show how a currency has moved, not against a single currency, but against the group of currencies in the basket. Movement in the effective rate is a weighted average of divergent changes in nominal rates.

The exchange rate (nominal or effective) determines the competitive position of domestic output in international markets. At constant domestic prices it gives the foreign currency price of a country's exports and hence influences foreign demand for domestically produced goods. Similarly, at constant foreign currency prices, the exchange rate determines the domestic currency price of imports and hence influences the demand for imports. Movements in the exchange rate can, therefore, have a powerful influence on the competitive position of goods and services produced in different countries and thereby influence the pattern of international trade flows.

The *real* exchange rate calculation adjusts movements in either a nominal or effective exchange rate for relative changes in the domestic price of goods in the country of production. Thus, if a currency depreciates by 10 per cent while its rate of inflation is 4 per cent more than its competitors, the real exchange rate has declined by 6 per cent.

The theory and empirical evidence about the determination of the exchange rate are far from settled. Flow theories tend to concentrate on the current account of the balance of payments and therefore on the factors (such as relative price and income movements between countries) influencing trade flows. The exchange rate is viewed as an equilibrating mechanism for the current account. Portfolio theories, or the asset-market approach (of which the monetary theory of the exchange rate is one of many variants), concentrate on the required conditions for equilibrium in wealth-holders' portfolios. In these models, movements in the exchange rate reflect an excess supply or demand for financial assets as between countries. A depreciation is viewed as a sympton of an excess supply of domestic financial assets. Stability in exchange rates requires, in these models, consistent monetary policies as between countries.

Governments have an interest in the level and stability of exchange rates. As movements influence the domestic price of imports, they have an effect on the domestic price level and, dependent upon how wage bargainers respond, the rate of inflation also. Through the same mechanism the exchange rate affects the level of real income and wages at each level of output. To the extent that the international competitive position of domestic goods is affected, movements in the exchange rate have implications for the level of output and employment. Thus governments might resist an appreciation because of its adverse employment effects, but also a depreciation because of the prices effect.

David T. Llewellyn
Loughborough University of Technology

Further reading

Isard, P. (1978) *Exchange Rate Determination*, Princeton, NJ.
Llewellyn, D. T. (1981) *International Financial Integration*, London.

experimental design

The function of experimental design

Experiments involve introducing a planned intervention (usually referred to as a treatment) into a situation, with the intent of inferring the association of treatment with a resulting change or outcome. Good experimental design facilitates this inferential process in three ways.

First, it translates all aspects of one's hypothesis – the statement of expected relation of treatment to outcome – into operational terms: subjects, behaviours, situation, equipment, procedures, and so on. These permit the hypotheses to be tested empirically.

Second, it rules out those alternative explanations which provide the most serious challenge to the treatment as the explanation for change. For example, because of faulty design, an experimental group was tested, exposed to a treatment, and post-tested. Improvement on the second testing could be attributed to familiarity with the test, thus providing an alternative explanation.

Third, it facilitates relating the change to other variables, thus permitting better understanding of the relationship. For example, with proper design, one could tell whether a treatment was more successful with men than women and with older than younger subjects, or its relation to any other variable included in the design.

The logic of experimental design

The first step in experimental design is to translate expectations expressed in one's hypotheses into operational terms. For example, given the hypothesis 'outlining in advance improves writing' one must specify what constitutes sufficient prior organization to be considered outlining and in what aspects of writing one expects gains. The accuracy of this translation is critical. If what passes for outlining in the study does not accurately reflect what is typically intended by the term, or the writing measure is inaccurate or insensitive, misleading conclusions could result.

Following operationalization, one must create a situation in which the treatment can occur as intended and changes can be sensed. Sometimes one compares the pre- with the post-intervention condition of the experimental subjects. In other instances, experimental subjects may be compared with an untreated comparable group, a control group. In still other instances, post-treatment condition is compared with estimates of the untreated state, for instance, test norms or regression estimates made from previous data on comparable groups.

By appropriate choice of design, one rules out whatever alternative explanations may be important rivals to that intended. For example, if a control group is used, the groups may not have been equivalent to begin with, or dropouts may make them nonequivalent at the end. Alternative explanations common to many studies have been identified (see below) but some may be unique to a study. For example, if subjects are allowed to complete a test at home, their score may reflect more their ability to seek help than their own achievement.

Assuming that the data support one's expectations, these steps in the logic follow: since the results were as predicted; and since there is no reasonable explanation for the phenomenon other than the treatment (others having been ruled out by one's design); then the hypotheses escaped disconfirmation. While one cannot test the hypothesis in every situation, one infers from this that similar predictions would prove accurate in like instances. With each such confirmation, confidence in the hypothesis increases, but a single disconfirmation, without a reasonable explanation, is sufficient to disprove it.

Experimental control

It is difficult to provide sufficient experimental control to protect against every possible alternative explanation. Further, one typically buys protection at a price. For example, a laboratory gives more complete control, but laboratory circumstances are rarely like those to which one hopes to generalize. Yet, natural circumstances may provide too little control. Zimbardo *et al.* (1981) supply an interesting example of this dilemma and its solution. They hypothesized that the paranoid behaviour frequent in elderly people was due to the gradual unnoticed loss of hearing common in old age. An expensive longitudinal design following subjects over time would have been inconclusive because of the subjects' varying social experiences. In addition, it would involve the unethical behaviour of withholding hearing loss information to see if the paranoid behaviour developed.

The researchers devised a creative experimental design. Post-hypnotic suggestion produced a temporary unnoticed hearing loss in college student volunteers with resulting display of paranoid behaviour. To eliminate rival alternative explanations, two control groups of similar subjects were established: one received the post-hypnotic suggestion of a hearing loss of which they would be *aware* and another received a neutral post-hypnotic suggestion in order to show that the hypnotic process itself did not induce paranoid behaviour. The paranoia was shown to follow only unnoticed induced hearing loss, and all subjects were exposed to controlled similar social experiences following hypnosis. Altogether, this is a clever use of experimental design for an otherwise difficult problem.

But using a laboratory-like setting may not be without costs to the validity of one's inferences. Impressed by the scientific laboratory, subjects may have tried to please the researcher; in addition, the researchers, knowing which was the experimental group, may have unintentionally cued subjects to appropriate behaviour (Rosenthal 1976). The verisimilitude of the hypnotically induced hearing loss to that which occurs in older people may be questioned, as may the use of college students.

Nearly every design choice involves trade-offs in the use of resources which might have been used to control something else. Part of the art of design is finding a suitable middle ground, one realistic enough to allow generalization of the results as broadly as one wishes but permitting sufficient control to make valid inferences.

The criteria of good design

A good design reduces one's uncertainty that the variables are indeed linked in a relationship and the linkage has generality. Showing that they are linked requires internal validity (LP) where (LP) stands for 'linking power' – the power of the study to link the treatment with the outcome (Krathwohl 1993). A study has strong internal validity (LP) when the explanation advanced for the relationship is credible, when the translation of variables into operational terms is faithful to that originally intended, where a relationship is demonstrated in the data, where rival explanations for the relationship are eliminated, and when the results are consistent with previous studies (Krathwohl 1993).

Similarly, demonstrating generality requires external validity (GP) where GP stands for 'generalizing power' – the power of the results to be generalized beyond the instance in which they were demonstrated (Krathwohl 1993). External validity (GP) assures the applicability of the results to other persons, places and times, and that the generalizability was not restricted by the conditions of the study. A study has strong external validity (GP) when the generality implied by the hypothesis, or inferred from it, is consistent with the choices made in operationalization of the study; that results were appropriately found throughout the instances of the study as expected; that there were no conditions of the study that limited generalization; and that the same results would have been expected were the study operationalized and designed in alternative ways.

Good designs accomplish the above with the best use of all available resources, time and energy. They fit the design to the problem rather than changing the problem definition to fit design requirements. They appropriately balance internal and external validity: strengthening internal validity is generally done at the expense of external validity. They accurately anticipate those alternative explanations to be eliminated that are most plausible to one's audience. Finally, ethical standards, resource limitations and institutional and social constraints are observed: altogether, a complex but manageable set of criteria (Krathwohl 1993).

Common alternative explanations

Certain common conditions provide as plausible explanations of an outcome as the treatment. Called 'threats to validity', they were described by Campbell and Stanley (1963) and Cook and Campbell (1979):

1 *Testing*: pre-treatment testing may affect post-treatment testing, especially if the same test is used. A control group provides protection since its post-test would be equally affected.

2 *Selection*: those selected for the experimental group differ from their controls, for example, when the experimental group consists of all volunteers and the control group comprises the remainder. One remedy is to use volunteers randomly assigned to experimental and control groups.
3 *Testing by treatment interaction*: subjects sensitized to aspects of a treatment by pre-testing react differently to post-testing. A post-test only design provides protection.

Common designs

Single group designs

These are often called time-series designs; relations are inferred from the pattern of treatment and response over time:

1 For static situations: pre-measure, treat, post-measure.
2 For situations with a regular pattern: observe it, treat, and determine if the pattern was disturbed.
3 With either an irregular pattern or for an especially conclusive demonstration, relate the pattern of change to that of treatment, intentionally varying the latter's timing, length, strength, and such other factors as affect outcome.

Also referred to as AB, ABA, or ABABA designs (A is the untreated condition, B the treated), ABABA and more complex designs are useful only where the change under the B condition is impermanent. (For information on such designs see Kratochwill and Levin 1992.)

Multiple group designs

These designs may involve both multiple experimental and control groups (Zimbardo used two control groups). Groups are alike as far as possible except for the conditions to which change is to be attributed. But only one condition can be different between groups being compared. Assuring group equivalency is usually achieved by randomly assigning subjects. *On the average* this will equate them for everything, from length of eyelashes to motivation.

The simplest, yet very effective, design involves post-testing only. Let R indicate random assignment of subjects to groups, O a test or observation, and X treatment. Then it is diagrammed as:

R   X   O
R   O

To assure that the groups were equivalent at the outset, a pre-test may be added:

R   O   X   O
R   O   O

But this introduces both testing and testing by treatment interaction as possible alternative explanations. For better control, the Solomon four group design combines the previous two:

R   X   O
R   O
R   O   X   O
R   O   O

Designs in which groups are not created by random assignment of subjects (same designs as above without the R) are designated quasi-experimental designs. Their strengths and weaknesses are explored in Campbell and Stanley (1963) and in Cook and Campbell (1979).

Blocking equates treatment groups. It does so by dividing the sample into blocks or strata on one or more characteristics (for example, intelligence and rank in birth order) where non-equivalence might affect the outcome. Individuals are randomly assigned to treatments within blocks. The matched pairs design is an extreme form of blocking.

Factorial designs

Factorial designs permit analysis of the simultaneous effects of two or more treatments or related variables by providing a group for each possible combination. For instance, to study the effect on speed of prose memorization of bold, italics and underlining of important parts, and of printing them in black or in red would require six groups – a 2×3 factorial design:

	Bold	Italics	Underlining
Black type			
Red type			

From this design one could learn which emphasis, treatment or colour was best alone, and if these factors interact, what combination of emphasis and colour is best. The latter is called interaction effect. If a pre-test were given this would be a repeated measures 2×3 factorial design.

Other designs

The variety of designs is limited mainly by one's ingenuity. A number of designs have been borrowed from agriculture such as the Latin and Graeco-Latin square and the split plot designs. These and others are described in Bow *et al.* (1978), Cochran (1992), Fisher (1966), Kirk (1982) and Winer (1971).

David R. Krathwohl
Syracuse University

References

Bow, G. E. P., Hunter, W. G. and Hunter, J. S. (1978) *Statistics for Experimenters: An Introduction to Design, Data Analysis and Model Building*, New York.

Campbell, D. T. and Stanley, J. C. (1963) 'Experimental and quasi-experimental designs for research on teaching', in N. L. Gage (ed.) *Handbook of Research on Teaching*, Chicago.

Cochran, W. G. (1992) *Experimental Designs*, 2nd edn, New York.

Cook, T. D. and Campbell, D. T. (1979), *Quasi-Experimentation*, Chicago.

Fisher, R. A. (1966) *Design of Experiments*, 8th edn, New York.

Kirk, R. (1982) *Experimental Design*, 2nd edn, Belmont, CA.

Krathwohl, D. R. (1993) *Methods of Educational and Social Science Research: An Intergrated Approach*, New York.

Kratochwill, T. R. and Levin, J. R. (1992) *Single-Case Research Design and Analysis: New Directions for Psychology and Education*, Hillsdale, NJ.

Rosenthal, R. (1976) *Experimenter Effects in Behavioral Research*, New York.

Solomon, R. L. (1949) 'An Extension of Control Group Design', *Psychological Bulletin* 46.

Winer, B. S. (1971) *Statistical Principles in Experimental Design*, 2nd edn, New York.

Zimbardo, P. G., Anderson, S. M. and Kabat, L. G. (1981) 'Induced hearing deficit generates experimental paranoia', *Science* 212.

See also: methods of social research.

experimental economics

There was a time when the conventional wisdom was that, because economics is a science concerned with complex, naturally occurring systems, laboratory experiments had little to offer economists. But experimental economics has now become a well-established tool of economic research. The initial impetus for this transformation came from studies of individual choice behaviour. As economists focused on microeconomic theories which depend on individuals' preferences, the fact that these are difficult to observe in natural environments made it increasingly attractive to look to the laboratory to see if the assumptions made about individuals were in fact descriptive of their behaviour.

In 1944 the publication of von Neumann and Morgenstern's *Theory of Games and Economic Behavior* accelerated the interest in experimentation. The expected utility theory they presented gave a new focus to experiments concerned with individual choice, while the predictions of game theory – and how these depend on the rules of the game – sparked a wave of experimental tests of interactive behaviour. This has blossomed into large literatures on topics as diverse as bargaining behaviour, the provision of public goods, co-ordination and equilibration, and the effects of different rules of market organization.

Formal tests of economic theories of individual choice go back at least as far as L. L. Thurstone (1931), who used experimental techniques common in psychology to investigate whether the indifference curve representation of preferences could coherently organize individuals' choices (he concluded that it could). Expected utility theory made more pointed predictions which allowed more powerful tests, and while some early experiments (e.g. Mosteller and Nogee 1951) supported the conclusion that utility theory could serve as an adequate approximation of behaviour, others, such as Allais (1953) identified systematic violations of utility theory. There have since been hundreds of experiments designed to explore further systematic violations of utility theory, and of the alternative choice theories that have been proposed to account for various parts of the experimental data. Considerably less experimental work has been devoted to assessing the extent to which utility theory is or is not an adequate approximation on different domains, and given the importance of utility theory in economic theory generally, this probably deserves more attention. Camerer (1995) gives a comprehensive survey.

An early game theoretic experiment, conducted by Melvin Dresher and Merrill Flood in 1950 (1958), first introduced the much studied game which subsequently came to be called the Prisoner's Dilemma. They observed that, even in a game with a unique equilibrium, the observed behaviour may deviate from the game theoretic prediction. But these experiments also confirm the game theoretic prediction that the incentives for individuals to act in their own interest may in some circumstances make it difficult to achieve the gains available from co-operative action. One body of experimental research which pursues this investigation concerns the provision of public goods; this literature is surveyed by Ledyard (1995).

A different kind of problem emerges in games having multiple equilibria, in which the players must co-ordinate their expectations and actions. Early experiments on co-ordination were reported by Thomas Schelling (1960). Bargaining presents an important class of problems in which co-ordination of expectations is of the essence, and it is a subject in which there has been considerable interplay between theory and experiment. Surveys of modern experiments concerning co-ordination and bargaining may be found in Ochs (1995) and Roth (1995a).

Experiments are particularly useful for isolating the effects of the rules of the game by which markets are organized. (For example, cattle and flowers are auctioned by different rules, but are also very different commodities, so one cannot isolate the effect of the different rules by relying only on field studies of cattle and flower auctions.) Chamberlin (1948) introduced a design, now widely used by experimenters, to create markets for artificial commodities in which the reservation prices of buyers and sellers can be controlled by the experimenter. Chamberlin's design permits experiments in which different rules of market organization (e.g. different forms of auction) can be compared while holding all else constant. Kagel (1995) surveys the large modern literature on auctions, Sunder (1995) considers markets for commodities (such as financial securities) in which information plays a dominant role, and Holt (1995) surveys experiments in industrial organization generally.

Much modern work has gone into understanding when equilibrium predictions will be descriptive, and when they will not. Experimental evidence has helped spark an interest in theories of learning and adaptation, in contrast to theories of static equilibrium. A general overview of experimental economics, including details of its early history, may be found in Roth (1995b).

Alvin E. Roth
University of Pittsburgh

References

Allais, M. (1953) 'Le Comportement de l'homme rationnel devant le risque: critique des postulats et axiomes de l'école américaine', *Econometrica* 21.

Camerer, C. (1995) 'Individual decision making', in J. Kagel and A. E. Roth (eds) *Handbook of Experimental Economics*, Princeton, NJ.

Chamberlin, E. H. (1948) 'An experimental imperfect market', *Journal of Political Economy* 56(2).

Flood, M. M. (1958) 'Some Experimental Games, Research Memorandum RM-789, RAND Corporation' *Management Science* (5).

Holt, C. A. (1995) 'Industrial organization: a survey of laboratory research', in J. Kagel and A. E. Roth (eds) *Handbook of Experimental Economics*, Princeton, NJ.

Kagel, J. H. (1995) 'Auctions: a survey of experimental research', in J. Kagel and A. E. Roth (eds) *Handbook of Experimental Economics*, Princeton, NJ.

Ledyard, J. (1995) 'Public goods: a survey of experimental research', in J. Kagel and A. E. Roth (eds) *Handbook of Experimental Economics*, Princeton, NJ.

Mosteller, F. and Nogee, P. (1951) 'An experimental measurement of utility', *Journal of Political Economy* 59.

Ochs, J. (1995) 'Coordination problems', in J. Kagel and A. E. Roth (eds) *Handbook of Experimental Economics*, Princeton, NJ.

Roth, A. E. (1995a) 'Bargaining experiments', in J. Kagel and A. E. Roth (eds) *Handbook of Experimental Economics*, Princeton, NJ.

—— (1995b) 'Introduction to experimental economics', in J. Kagel and A. E. Roth (eds) *Handbook of Experimental Economics*, Princeton, NJ.

Schelling, T. C. (1960) *The Strategy of Conflict*, Cambridge, MA.

Sunder, S. (1995) 'Experimental asset markets: a survey', in J. Kagel and A. E. Roth (eds) *Handbook of Experimental Economics*, Princeton, NJ.

Thurstone, L. L. (1931) 'The indifference function', *Journal of Social Psychology* 2.

See also: prisoners' dilemma

externalities

Economic externalities are (positive or negative) goods or services generated by an economic activity whose costs or benefits do not fall upon the decision-taking agent. Pollution is a leading and important example. They may, alternatively, be thought of as residuals, the difference between 'social' and 'private' costs and benefits. The divergence was first popularized and elaborated by Pigou in *The Economics of Welfare* (1920) and is believed to be a major reason for market failure: for example, the market will overproduce goods with high external costs. For that reason a main principle of cost-benefit analysis is that *all* costs and benefits, no matter to whom they accrue, should be included. Popular discussion rightly emphasizes external costs associated with production, but one should not entirely ignore positive production effects (apples and honey) or effects on the consumption side, either positive (attractive dress) or negative (radio noise).

Various policies are, in principle, available for dealing with externalities. For example, the extent of an activity may be *regulated*, as in the case of the discharge of industrial effluent into estuaries. Using partial equilibrium analysis the regulation should set the amount of discharge at an optimum, that is, where marginal social cost and benefit are equal to one another. This is, of course, very difficult to calculate, so rough rules of thumb are used instead. Economists often argue for the direct use of *pricing*: the agent is charged a tax (or paid a subsidy) equal to the value of the externality at the margin. The congestion tax is an example of this. Such taxes and subsidies are referred to as Pigouvian: they are intended to internalize the externality. Internalization may also come about spontaneously by the *merger* of two units inflicting large externalities upon one another (as in industrial integration).

The tax-subsidy solution is often objected to on the ground that it is open to injured parties to bring an action in tort against the offending agent. If agents know this to be the case, they will take expected compensation for damages into account and externalities will automatically be internalized. On this view not only would Pigouvian taxes not be needed but also they would, if imposed, lead to an over-restriction of activity (Coase 1960). Property rights are seen to be crucial, as they define rights to compensation: defenders of the market system therefore argue that externalities do not constitute market failure provided that property rights are adequately delineated. The direction of compensation naturally depends on the initial distribution of legal rights.

The alternative solutions are closely related to one another. Take the case of a major oil spillage which fouls beaches and destroys fishing and wildlife. If spillages are to be 'banned' the fine must be at least equal to the Pigouvian tax. If there is to be a legal contest, it will have to be fought between states and oil companies rather than through improvised groups of holiday-makers, workers in the fishing industry and wildlife enthusiasts. And fines/compensation must not give an outcome which is totally unreasonable in relation to the optimum (possibly, though not certainly, zero) amount of spillage.

David Collard
University of Bath

Reference

Coase, R. H. (1960) 'The problem of social cost', *Journal of Law and Economics* 3.

Further reading

Pearce, D. W. (ed.) (1978) *The Valuation of Social Cost*, London.

F

factors of production

Factors of production, or (in more modern terminology) 'inputs', are the things which are used in the process of producing goods or services. An early typology of inputs was provided by Jean-Baptiste Say, whose classification separately defined land, labour and capital as factors of production.

A distinction is often made between flow inputs (which are embodied in the final product and cannot therefore be used more than once in the act of production) and stock inputs (which can be used repeatedly). The distinction is somewhat artificial, however, because stock inputs characteristically depreciate in value over time, and this depreciation can itself usefully be regarded as a flow.

All factors of production can, in principle, be hired by the producer. In a non-slavery society, labour can be hired – at a per period cost defined by the wage – but not bought. Capital may, at the discretion of the producer, be bought rather than hired; it remains the case, however, that producers implicitly pay a rent ('user cost') on the capital under their ownership, because by using that capital they forgo the opportunity to hire it out to a third party. Land, likewise, may be bought or rented; in the former case producers implicitly pay a rent in order to use land as a factor of production, because they forgo the opportunity to earn a landlord's income.

Labour will in general be hired by a profit-maximizing producer up to that point where the wage is just offset by the value of the marginal product of labour. In a similar fashion, long-run equilibrium requires that capital should be employed up to the point where the user cost equals the value of the marginal product of capital. A similar condition applies to land. A change in production technology which disturbs the productivity of any factor of production will generally alter the equilibrium employment of each input. Likewise a change in the price of any input (for example, the wage or the user cost of capital) will, so long as inputs are to some degree substitutable, cause a change in the mix of factors of production employed.

Simple models of the production process typically employ two factors of production, often labour and capital. The first of these is defined to be variable in the short run, while the second is assumed fixed. In effect, the minimum timescale within which the latter input can be varied defines the length of the short run. Given information about the producer's objective function, this allows a distinction to be drawn between the behaviour of the producer which is optimal in the short run and that which is optimal in the long run.

The precise manner in which factors of production are converted into outputs is modelled by means of a production function. The simplest type of production function in common use postulates that the production of a single type of output is determined by a geometric weighted average of the various inputs employed. This is known as a Cobb-Douglas production function, the parameters of which may statistically be estimated by means of a regression which is linear in natural logarithms. The Cobb-Douglas function can be shown to produce downward sloping and convex isoquants – a characteristic which is conventionally deemed attractive because it establishes the existence of unique solutions to the constrained optimization problems characteristic of neo-classical economics.

The more general constant elasticity of substitution (CES) and transcendental logarithmic (or 'translog') production functions have become increasingly popular among applied economists. The Cobb-Douglas is a special case of both of these. The translog function adds to the list of explanatory variables used in a Cobb-Douglas type regression a full set of logged quadratic terms and interaction terms between the logged inputs.

An appealing property of all the production functions described above is their implication that the marginal product of variable inputs (eventually) falls as the employment of those inputs increases. This ensures the finiteness of the equilibrium level of output of the individual firm, regardless of demand conditions. The translog specification of the production function is particularly appealing because, depending upon the estimated parameters, it is consistent with the popular presumption that the long run average cost curve is U-shaped.

The production technology described by these functions is closely related to the way in which the producer's costs are determined. Given the prices of the various factors of production, producers use their knowledge of the production technology to decide, for each level of output, what mix of inputs optimizes their objective function (usually profits). Once this input mix is chosen, the total cost of production at each output level is straightforwardly calculated as the product of the vectors of input prices and input quantities.

It is only recently that economists have begun rigorously to tackle the analytical problems posed by firms which produce many distinct types of output. Multi-product firms of this type might exist because of synergies which arise from the co-ordinated production of different goods and services. These synergies may in turn arise from characteristics possessed by inputs which can simultaneously be put to more than one use. In the case of firms which produce more than one type of output, output cannot be represented as a scalar, and so the technology of production is best understood by investigating the dual problem: that is by estimating a (quadratic or CES) multi-product cost function.

The simplistic view of labour as a variable input has been relaxed in recent work which views skilled labour as an investment in 'human capital'. Such an investment takes time, and so in the short run skilled labour may be fixed. However, where more than two inputs are employed, the distinction between the short and long run becomes blurred. Indeed, an issue which has remained underdeveloped in the economics research programme concerns the application of methods commonly used in the literature on product differentiation to the case of heterogeneous factors of production.

Geraint Johnes
Lancaster University

Further reading

Heathfield, D. F. and Wibe, S. (1987) *An Introduction to Cost and Production Functions*, Basingstoke.

See also: capital theory; human capital; input-output analysis; labour market analysis; production and cost functions.

family

In the mid-third of the twentieth century, anthropologists and sociologists spent much time and energy debating the universality of the family, specifying its functions and undertaking comparative analysis of different family systems. At the end of the century, such concerns with the naturalness and consequent inevitability of the family seem somewhat barren, though moral arguments about which forms of family life are legitimate and which pathological remain politically contentious. While all societies are necessarily concerned with matters of biological and social reproduction, the social and economic organization of this reproduction is inherently bound with the wider social and economic formation in which it occurs.

Indeed the concept of the family can be recognized as a construction which developed its potency with modernity, if not industrialization. This was implicit in sociological debates about the impact of industrialization on the dominant family system, often simplistically expressed as a shift from an extended form to a nuclear one. That is, under the conditions of late nineteenth and early twentieth-century industrialization, the family seemed to be developing in an increasingly uniform and predictable fashion, marked by a gendered division of responsibility and a higher commitment to spouses and dependent children than to other kin (Harris 1983). Under these conditions the family came to take on particular meanings, though not ones which necessarily resonated very strongly in other types of society where social reproduction was organized in a different fashion. Inherent here too is the notion of family as itself complex and variable, with the term being used in both academic discourse and everyday talk in a variety of different ways depending on context.

Two broad strands of meaning are evident in much routine discussion of the family. First, there is the sense of family as a subset of an individual's kinship universe. That is, by family we refer to those who are linked by blood and marriage to us, though the linkages which are included in any particular instance is an open matter. Second, the term family is often used as a virtual synonym of household. Here kinship linkage remains important, but in addition there is implicit reference to a shared housekeeping and a common domestic economy. A main distinction behind the variable uses of the term family concerns the boundaries that are constructed delineating those who are family from those who are not. The closer the genealogical link, the more likely an individual is to be referred to as family, though genealogy itself is not the only factor. What also comes into play is the relative strength of the consequent social relationships and the nature of the obligations which have developed.

Family life has become rather more complex in the latter part of the twentieth century than it had been in the earlier part. Whereas for much of the century it was appropriate, albeit with a degree of caution, to conceive of a broad uniformity and standard order in family relationships, this is now a rather less convincing characterization. Within most western societies at least, the latter part of the twentieth century has seen significant shifts in the demography of family life, with consequences for the permeability of family boundaries and the nature of some family obligations. Thus whereas social scientists once talked of the 'family cycle', meaning a common route through a structured series of family phases involving different responsibilities and opportunities, this has given way to the idea of 'family course', implying the existence of phases which make differential demands on the individuals involved, but which do not necessary entail a tidy progression. For example, the increase in rates of divorce, cohabitation, births to unmarried mothers, and reconstituted families throughout the western world have resulted in more diverse family pathways emerging than in the recent past.

Equally, the same changes have led to networks of family relationships becoming more complex, with greater variation and less clarity about who can appropriately be regarded as family and how such relationships should properly be framed. In particular, the increased incidence of divorce and remarriage has meant that many more people have ex-spouses, absent parents, step-parents, step-siblings, half-siblings, and the like. The specific family circumstances of these relationships are themselves highly variable, for instance, in terms of whether step-parents or half-siblings are co-residential, and whether ex-spouses continue to parent children in an active way. Moreover the relationships have not been socially institutionalized, in the sense that there is little societal guidance as to how they are most appropriately patterned. Furthermore, marital separation and divorce often have ramifications for other family ties, affecting for example the form and content of grandparent, aunt/uncle and cousin relationships.

If in this sense the boundaries constructed around the family are more permeable than they once were, there is still a strong element within western cultures of the family being an essentially private institution. Indeed theories about the growing privatization of the family with industrialization are common, though not without their difficulties (Pahl and Wallace 1988). This covers more than ideas of a shift from extended to nuclear family forms; it also implies that families, predominantly in the sense of households, have managed to construct physical and symbolic boundaries around themselves which ensure that what goes on in the domestic arena is outside the gaze or control of others. Although privacy has long been sought by families in all classes, general improvements in the material conditions of home life have encouraged the self-containment of aspects of family life, with reduced involvement between those who happen to be neighbours (Allan 1985). At the same time though, the state through its various welfare measures has become more concerned with defining and monitoring appropriate standards of family behaviour. This applies particularly with regard to children where a range of welfare professionals – health visitors, social workers, teachers, doctors – play a part in regulating families, especially those seen as pathological or potentially so (Donzelot 1979).

Some of the most interesting research on families has focused on the issue of reproduction, in social and economic senses more than the biological. The division of household labour, the changes and continuities there have been in this, and its impact on gender inequalities, have been much analysed. Increased recognition has been given to the unpaid economic, as well as emotional and supportive, work which family life entails (Morris 1990; Pahl 1984). Thus the production of a particular standard of living for a household and the transformation of wages into well-being warrant analysis just as much as other forms of work. The social and economic relationships that this work involves have often been depicted as somehow natural because of their family basis, but in reality they contain issues about the social distribution of power and inequality as much as any other system of exchange does (Delphy and Leonard 1992).

In addition, families play a significant role in material and cultural reproduction across the generations. In particular, despite changes there have been in patterns of social mobility, the inheritance of private property and the transmission of 'cultural capital' (Bourdieu 1973) within families remains important in the maintenance of advantage and disadvantage. Equally numerous studies have demonstrated the continued link between health and educational success and the material conditions of home and family life (Graham 1993). Put simply, family environment, itself shaped by structural parameters whose roots lie elsewhere, has significant impact on the perpetuation of social and economic inequality.

For this and other reasons, the well-being of the family remains a highly charged political and moral issue throughout the western world. Matters like domestic violence and child abuse, the impact of unemployment and poverty on families, the problems facing lone-parent households, especially those headed by young, economically disadvantaged women, and the increase in cohabitation and step-families, have all led to a heightened consciousness of the ways in which the family is changing. Within this context, it becomes even more important to recognize the socially constructed character of the family. Family life has never been static; the forms it takes have always been influenced by the socioeconomic structures within which it develops. The significant changes occurring in family patterns in the late twentieth century need interpreting in this light rather than in a socially disconnected fashion.

Graham Allan
University of Southampton

References

Allan, G. A. (1985) *Family Life*, Oxford.
Bourdieu, P. (1973) 'Cultural reproduction and social reproduction', in R. Brown (ed.) *Knowledge, Education and Cultural Change*, London.
Delphy, C. and Leonard, D. (1992) *Familiar Exploitation*, Cambridge, UK.
Donzelot, J. (1979) *The Policing of Families*, London.
Graham, H. (1993) *Hardship and Health in Women's Lives*, Hemel Hempstead.
Harris, C. C. (1983) *The Family in Industrial Society*, London.
Morris, L. (1990) *The Workings of the Household*, Cambridge, UK.
Pahl, R. E. (1984) *Divisions of Labour*, Oxford.
Pahl, R. E. and Wallace, C. (1988) 'Neither angels in marble nor rebels in red', in D. Rose (ed.) *Social Stratification and Economic Change*, London.

See also: divorce; domestic violence; family history; household; kinship; marriage.

family history

Family history as a research field emerged in the 1950s as part of the growth of interest in economic and social history. Historians seeking information on the family sought to exploit a multitude of sources. Reference to legal texts, court cases, choice of forename, paintings of family groups, medieval treatises and excavations of private dwellings have enabled inferences to be drawn about the nature of family life in ancient Greece and Rome and the Middle Ages (Gardner 1986; Gotein 1978; Humphreys 1983; Klapisch-Zuber 1985; Rawson 1986; see also Ariès 1962, but see Burton 1989 for a critique of Ariès's interpretation of the representations of children in medieval and Renaissance art).

The largest number of people involved in family history, however, are those who devote their leisure time to researching the history of their own families.

Many family historians are no longer content just to collect names and dates, but try to study their ancestors in their context by learning about their occupations, friends and neighbours. A diverse literature has been produced by and for these family historians, providing both introductory and detailed guides, transcriptions and indexes of the most useful sources (Federation of Family History Societies 1993; Hey 1993). The Federation of Family History Societies also publishes a bi-annual newsletter, *Family History News and Digest*, detailing both activities and publications. In 1994 there were over eighty family history societies active in England and Wales.

Writing in 1980, Anderson identified four principal approaches adopted by historians when writing on the family: psychohistorical, demographic, sentiments and household economic (Anderson 1980). Each approach has had both champions and detractors. Psycho-historians promise the closest perspective on the motivations, conscious and unconscious, of past generations, but many of their conclusions have not been accepted by other historians (Anderson 1980; de Mause, 1974). Changes in attitudes to relations between parent and child, and to marriage, sex and privacy have been investigated by historians of the sentiments school, primarily using a range of literary sources. This has resulted in excessive attention to the lives of the elite, who produced the bulk of the literary records, an assumption that their behaviour would sometime later be adopted by the rest of society, and a tendency to focus on the origins of aspects of the family which are of contemporary concern, rather than considering the role of the family in a specific time and place (Stone 1977; for a criticism see Laslett 1987).

Demographic historians, by contrast, have been much more obviously constrained by the nature of the surviving evidence. In measuring what can be measured, most attention has been devoted to the form and structure of the household, age at first marriage, patterns of child-bearing and illegitimacy (Hanley and Wolf 1985; Laslett and Wall 1972; Mitterauer 1983; van Poppel 1992; Shorter 1976). Weaknesses with this approach are the inability to identify the attitudes which might account for the observed behaviour. Anderson argued, for example, that a similarity in age between husband and wife was insufficient proof of the presence of companionate, more egalitarian, relationships within marriage, and that the form of the family and household might be more appropriately viewed as the by-product of economic and social forces, rather than having any particular social meaning for the family members concerned (Anderson 1980).

The attempt to relate family forms to wider economic processes is represented by the work of historians who have adopted the household economics approach to study the significance for the family of inheritance customs and practices, and the work patterns of peasant and proletarianized populations. Some of the results have been surprising, for instance, the absence of a correlation between early marriage and partible inheritance and between late marriage and impartibile inheritance. Historians have also discovered a considerable degree of continuity in family patterns between pre-industrial and industrial societies (findings summarized in Anderson 1980). However, as a rule, the household economics approach is better adapted to the examination of distinct micro-economic environments rather than broader economic processes, due to the difficulty of measuring the indirect, as opposed to the direct, effects of economic change. Other problems arise because of biases in the nature of the surviving data, for example, transfers of property taking place after death are usually much better recorded than are lifetime transfers. Nor have historians favouring the household economics approach been any more successful than household demographers in measuring the extent to which cultural factors helped to shape family forms. The acknowledgement of the limited explanatory power of demographic and economic factors as determinants of family patterns has forced cultural factors on to the research agenda (Alter 1991). However, no way has yet been found to measure the impact of these cultural factors other than by assuming that these account for all of the variation in family patterns that cannot be explained in any other way (Ruggles 1987).

Few attempts have been made to integrate the various approaches to the history of the family. Hareven's (1987) assessment of a decade's work in family history largely ignores the sentiments and psycho-history approaches. Burgière *et al.*'s (1986) two-volume history of the family, drawing on a wide range of source material, is an effective summary of much research but provides little in the way of critical comment. Other studies have considered the power of key institutions, such as the church and the state, to determine family behaviour. It has been argued, for example, that the medieval church framed its marriage laws in such a way that land would accrue to the church from families left without heirs (Goody 1983; for a criticism see Bonfield 1991). The border between the spheres of influence of the eastern and western church, in conjunction with the pattern of colonization in early medieval times, has also been seen as influencing the perduring boundary between eastern and western Europe in terms of marriage ages and household patterns, with earlier age at marriage and more complex households located in eastern areas (Mitterauer 1994). In England, the Poor Law alleviated, if it did not entirely remove, disparities in income

between men and women and young and old, and families with many children and between families with few (Henderson and Wall 1994). To minimize expenditure, the Poor Law authorities would even on occasion actively promote the formation of households in which a younger recipient of poor relief would be paid to provide care to an older one (Sokoll 1993).

A great variety of family relationships could exist within the framework allowed by any one legal system. Historians now realize that in addition to the major differences in family patterns between eastern and western Europe, there was also extensive variation regionally and locally, and between richer and poorer and high and low status families, reflecting in particular the extent to which families functioned as welfare and work units, and the work patterns and status of women.

Richard Wall
ESRC Cambridge Group for the History of
Population and Social Structure

References

Alter, G. (1991) 'New perspectives on European marriage in the nineteenth century', *Journal of Family History* 16.

Anderson, M. (1980) *Approaches to the History of the Western Family 1500–1914*, Basingstoke.

Ariès, P. (1962) *Centuries of Childhood*, London.

Bonfield, L. (1991) 'Church law and family law in medieval Western Christendom', *Continuity and Change* 6.

Burgière, A., Klapisch-Zuber, C., Segalen, M. and Zonabend, F. (1986) *Histoire de la famille*, Paris.

Burton, A. (1989) 'Looking forward from Ariès? Pictorial and material evidence for the history of childhood and family life', *Continuity and Change* 4.

Federation of Family History Societies (1993) *Welsh Family History: A Guide to Research*, Birmingham.

Gardner, J. F. (1986) *Women in Roman Law and Society*, London.

Goody, J. (1983) *The Development of the Family and Marriage in Europe*, Cambridge, UK.

Gotein, S. D. (1978) *A Mediterranean Society: The Jewish Communities of the Arab World as Portrayed in the Documents of the Cairo Geniza*, vol. III, *The Family*, Berkeley.

Hanley, S. B. and Wolf, A. P. (1985) *Family and Population in East Asian History*, Stanford, CA.

Hareven, T. (1987), 'Family history at the crossroads', *Journal of Family History* 12.

Henderson, J. and Wall, R. (1994) *Poor Women and Children in the European Past*, London.

Hey, D. (1993) *The Oxford Guide to Family History*, Oxford.

Humphreys, S. C. (1983) *The Family, Women and Death: Comparative Studies*, London.

Laslett, P. (1987) 'The character of familial history, its limitations and the conditions for its proper pursuit', *Journal of Family History* 12.

Klapisch-Zuber, C. (1985) *Women, family and ritual in Renaissance Italy*, Chicago.

Laslett, P. and Wall, R. (eds) (1972) *Household and Family in Past Time*, Cambridge, UK.

Mause, L. de (1974) *The History of Childhood*, New York.

Mitterauer, M. (1983) *Ledige Mutter: Zur Geschichte unehelicher Geburten in Europa*, Munich.

—— (1994) 'Medieval roots of European family developments', unpublished paper in the library of ESRC Cambridge Group.

Poppel, F. van (1992) 'Trouwen in Nederland: Een historisch-demografische studie van de 19e en vroeg-20e eeuw', *AAG Bijdragen* 33.

Rawson, B. (ed.) (1986) *The Family in Ancient Rome*, London.

Ruggles, S. (1987) *Prolonged Connections: The Rise of the Extended Family in Nineteenth Century England and America*, Madison, WI.

Shorter, E. (1976) *The Making of the Modern Family*, London.

Sokoll, T. (1993) *Household and Family among the Poor*, Bochum.

Stone, L. (1977) *The Family, Sex and Marriage in England 1500–1800*, London.

See also: family; historical demography; household.

family therapy

Family therapy is both a theory of family functioning and a treatment technique for troubled couples or families. The theory maintains that the family is a functioning and cohesive system with rules or patterns, which it maintains when faced with stress. Thus the family system is different from and greater than the sum of its parts and must be observed as a whole in action. Malfunctioning or pathological family systems often lead to individual symptomatology.

To understand and change the family, the therapist requires certain information, including details about its culture, ethnicity and socioeconomic status, the facts about each member, and the family's history and life-cycle phase. Each family has its own traditions, marital contracts, myths, secrets and loyalties to the past. Individuals in the family have their own dynamics, expectations, hopes and life experiences. Direct observations are necessary in order to assess the roles, coalitions, hierarchies and alliances between members, the communicational patterns and their clarity, the patterns of rewards and punishments, and the distribution of power. Finally, the experimental and ethical aspects must be ascertained. This last step involves assessing the empathic experience of the family from the perspective of each member, learning whether they have been treated fairly and justly and what debts and credits they have *vis-à-vis* other family members.

The family therapist uses these observations to form a therapeutic alliance and meets with the appropriate family members to design suitable interventions in order to change family functioning. In maximally distressed families, interventions should initially be aimed at preventing physical harm to members, strengthening the parental-marital coalition, appropriately controlling the children, and promoting suitable distance between over-involved pairs. Other goals include encouraging clear and open communication, exploring mistaken attributions made of members, particularly as these are related to the past, and re-balancing the family towards fairness and justice.

Three techniques are commonly employed. First, the exploration of projective identification, where disowned aspects of the self are attributed to others, who are both related to as though the attribution was correct, and are often pressured to act in accordance with it. Second, the assignment of tasks to the family with the purpose of altering behavioural reinforcements, interrupting malfunctioning aspects of the family system, particularly when the family resists change, and providing a new and novel experience. Third, helping the family to find ways of redressing past injustices and finding new and fairer ways of functioning.

Family therapy is considered more effective than individual treatment when the problems involve a dysfunctional marriage, and at least as effective in the treatment of disturbed children and adolescents, particularly if the problems are neurotic or psychosomatic. Psycho-educational work with families has been found valuable in preventing relapse in schizophrenia. The family is educated about the disease, its course and treatment, and is helped to attend to and comment on the patient's behaviour rather than to criticize thoughts and feelings. Finally, meetings with the families of individual psychotherapy patients have been found to be a useful adjunct to the treatment of adults in marital difficulties.

Henry Grunebaum
Harvard University

Further reading

Grunebaum, H. and Glick, I. (1983) 'The basics of family treatment', in L. Grinspoon (ed.) *Psychiatry Update: The American Psychiatric Association Annual Review*, vol. 2.

McFarlane, W. R., Beels, C. C. and Rosenheck, S. (1983) 'New developments in the family treatment of the psychotic disorders', in L. Grinspoon (ed.) *Psychiatry Update: The American Psychiatric Association Annual Review*, vol. 2.

fantasy

Fantasy, our capacity to 'give to airy nothing a local habitation and a name', has long intrigued poets, playwrights and painters but only during the twentieth century has the phenomenon become a formal area of scientific inquiry in psychology. In current usage the term is almost synonymous with daydream. Within the area of experimental or clinical study, however, the term fantasy has a broader significance, as it deals not only with imaginary activity spontaneously produced as part of the ongoing stream of thought (daydreams) but also with products of thought elicited upon demand from a clinician in response to inkblots or ambiguous pictures. It also refers to literary or artistic representations of the mental processes.

Fantasy refers to the human being's remarkable ability to create an 'as if' world either spontaneously or upon demand. It is possible that people at one time were more prone to regard their own fleeting imagery or brief daydreams as actual visions, as omens, or as appearances of deities, much as they responded to nocturnal dreams (Jaynes 1977). Prophetic visions, such as Ezekiel's 'wheel' or John's Apocalypse, probably represent literary expressions of elaborate daydreams or fantasies used for expository or hortatory purposes.

In 1890 William James in *The Principles of Psychology* devoted portions of several chapters, including the famous one on the 'stream of thought', to issues closely related to fantasy processes. James called attention to what he termed the reproductive and memorial facets of imagery, or the degree to which the image is of an object recently perceived or one called forth from the distant past. The fantasy presumably may represent a response to a stimulus perceived momentarily which triggers off a complex associative process in the ongoing stream of thought. In James Joyce's novel *Ulysses* the young Stephen, gazing seaward from his tower apartment, first sees the waves whose foamy curves remind him of a childhood song, then of his mother's death, his refusal (as a lapsed Catholic) to pray, and finally these associations generate a vivid fantasy of her confronting him in her graveclothes to denounce him (Singer 1994).

Psychoanalytic contributions

Freud's elucidation of the structure and interpretative possibilities of the phenomenon of nocturnal dreaming, based largely on remarkable self-observation and intensive clinical work, also led quite naturally to explorations of other dreamlike phenomena, such as daydreams. Freud (1962 [1908]; 1962 [1911]) speculated on the psychological significance of the daydream in papers like 'Creative writers and daydreaming'. The free-association process of psychoanalysis itself also led to patients' frequent reports of memories of childhood fantasies or recent daydreams.

The most important fantasies from a technical psychotherapeutic sense were those involving the relationships between analyst and patient. Throughout the twentieth century psychoanalysts have made regular use of reports of spontaneous fantasies and published many papers in which myths or popular stories and literature were interpreted as outgrowths of fantasy.

Projective methods

With the indications of the widespread nature of human fantasy processes emerging from psychoanalysis and other psychiatric efforts, there was gradually an attempt to find procedures that could elicit fantasies from individuals providing significant diagnostic evidence ultimately for treatment plans and specific therapeutic interventions as well as for research purposes. The most prominent projective methods were the Rorschach Inkblots and the Thematic Apperception Test. They have been subject to literally hundreds of research studies which to some degree have also contributed to general personality research and to diagnostic understanding.

The *Rorschach Inkblots* represent an attempt to use spontaneous associations made to the ambiguous nature of the blots as a means of identifying structural properties of the personality, such as tendencies towards imaginativeness, emotional impulsivity, indications of anxiety or cognitive organization and self-control. Hermann Rorschach observed that associative responses to the ambiguous ink blots which involved reports of humans in action ('two men playing patty cake') were linked systematically not only to a considerable tendency to engage in fantasy but also to a capacity for self-restraint and inner control. Extensive research studies have generally supported this observation (Singer and Brown 1977). These so-called M responses to the Rorschach Inkblots do seem to reflect an adaptive capacity for restraint, self-knowledge and creative thought.

The Thematic Apperception Test, in which the respondent makes up stories to simple pictures (such as a boy staring at a violin) that are somewhat ambiguous, has also proven to be a significant indicator of fantasy. This measure has been perhaps even more precisely analysed in the work of David McClelland because of its linkage to motivation following its original development by Henry A. Murray of Harvard University. The scoring of these fantasy-like stories for indications of motives such as *achievement, power, affiliation* and *intimacy* needs has proven to predict the social behaviour of individuals in other settings to a considerable degree (McClelland 1961; 1992).

Current research methods and theoretical considerations

Psychologists under the influence of behaviourism were at first reluctant to study ephemeral thought processes or fantasies. Since the 1950s there has been an accelerating interest in such inner processes, furthered by the emergence of many improved methods for studying the nature of fantasy processes as they emerge in the course of normal ongoing thought (Klinger 1990; Singer 1966; 1993). The methods currently in active use by researchers include questionnaire surveys; self-recordings of daydreams under controlled conditions; laboratory studies of daydreams and fantasies that emerge during a variety of simple or complex task performances; psychophysiological measurement of brain functions or eye movements during the process of creating fantasies; and the assessment of fantasies as they occur naturally through having individuals carrying paging devices or bleepers which signal randomly when an individual must immediately report ongoing thought or fantasy.

What have we learned by the application of these methods? The questionnaire approaches allow us to sample the self-reports of hundreds of individuals about the frequency, content and patterns of their fantasy; it is possible to conclude that daydreaming and the generation of fantasies is a normal process, one that occurs almost daily in every individual. Three general styles of fantasizing have been identified: one involves more positive and future oriented explorations, a second more guilt-ridden or unpleasant and frightening considerations of past events or future possibilities, and the third pattern involves the ability to sustain elaborate fantasies or to organize one's private imagery into consistent story-like structures. Questionnaire studies have also brought various cultural differences in the content of fantasies with such differences often reflecting phenomena such as the relative upward mobility of a sociocultural group in this society. Sexual fantasies are nearly universal in western society if, however, not nearly as frequent as one might think from popular literature or film. There is no evidence that fantasy is in itself a sign of serious emotional disturbance; on the contrary severely disturbed individuals such as schizophrenics or extremely impulsive or aggressive individuals are often characterized by less varied or rich fantasy lives and more by single-minded and limited fantasy tendencies (Klinger 1990; Singer 1976).

Laboratory studies have shown the persistent and ubiquitous nature of human fantasy, even under conditions in which the individual is performing a relatively demanding task. For example, individuals may be sitting in small booths listening to signals presented to them via earphones and must be constantly pressing buttons to show that they comprehend the targeted signals as they appear as fast as one per second. If they are interrupted every fifteen seconds and must report on extraneous thoughts it turns out that even while processing signals quite accurately over an hour's time, they still generate a fantasy as often as 50 per cent of the time. It is possible to show that certain types of individuals, who on questionnaires report more fantasy tendencies, are often more inclined to report fantasies during such precisely measured laboratory interruptions.

Other types of laboratory studies have demonstrated that when individuals are engaged in a fantasy activity their eyes tend to become unfocused and relatively motionless, particularly if there are movements or other visual signals presented in front of them. This would suggest that the visual images, which are the predominant characteristics of human fantasy for most people, involve the same brain system as that of normal vision when processing externally generated stimuli. There are also research suggestions that particular types of brain waves, such as alpha rhythms or theta rhythms, may be the ones most prominently in evidence during waking fantasy activity.

Studies making use of paging devices are able to capture the way that fantasies occur during ordinary day-to-day activities. Extensive work in this area has been carried out especially by Russell Hurlburt, Mihailyi Csikszentmihalyi and Eric Klinger (1990). These studies also show how closely daydreams or fantasies are linked to fundamental motivational processes called 'current concerns', both short and longer term unfulfilled intentions.

Early theorizing about the nature of fantasy processes were strongly influenced by Sigmund Freud's important insight which linked the human being's capacity to delay gratification, a vitally significant step in our adaptive development, to our imaginative capacity. While certainly, as Freud suggested, the daydreams of the poet can be transformed into artistic productions, there is much less evidence for his position that only 'unsatisfied wishes are the driving power behind fantasies' or as he put it another time 'happy people never daydream' (1962 [1908]).

The research evidence since the late 1960s suggests rather that daydreaming is a fundamental human capacity which not only can reflect our unfulfilled wishes, of course, but also is inherent in our normal and healthy adaptive approach to exploring the physical and social environment through playing out mentally a series of possible scenarios. A more useful conclusion from current evidence would be that unhappy people are more likely to have unhappy daydreams and that people who are functioning effectively will be characterized by a great variety of daydreams, the majority of which are more likely to involve playful and fanciful explorations of possible futures as well as some consideration of the negative alternatives in life. For the most part, most fantasy tends to be more realistic and geared to relatively mundane, practical issues in the individual's life.

Another influential conception introduced by Sigmund Freud was that the daydream or fantasy could partially discharge a drive, such as sex or aggression, and thus reduce the likelihood of an impulsive act. This *catharsis* theory has been extremely influential among literary individuals or persons in film and television. It is widely used as an explanation for encouraging children or adults to watch a variety of violent sports activities or films or encouraging children's exposure to violent fairy tales, with the notion that such exposure will reduce the likelihood of overt aggressive action. The evidence from dozens of laboratory studies of adults and children and from field studies of children exposed to violence in film and television overwhelmingly suggests that vicarious fantasy *increases* tendencies towards aggressive behaviour rather than reducing them. Our human fantasy capacity involves not a drainage of drive but a preparation for action. Those persons, however, who have developed a varied and complex imaginative life are often also more likely to recognize the unreality of many of their wishes; they can envisage a host of self-defeating consequences of impulsive action.

The current approach to fantasy and daydreaming processes casts such phenomena within a broader context of modern cognitive, affective and social scientific research. Human beings are viewed as continuously seeking to make sense of the novelty and complexity of their environment. They seek to organize and label experiences and form them into meaningful structures called schemata or scripts. At the same time they seek to anticipate possible futures. Fantasy represents the effort (influenced by religious symbols, folk legends, popular literature and, increasingly, films and television) of individuals to rehearse their memories and to create possible futures. Studies of early imaginative play in children point to the origins of the fantasy process where the dilemmas or cognitive complexities of the big world (social and physical) are miniaturized or re-enacted in a controlled play form. Adults continue this process privately through their mental imagery and interior monologues. Nocturnal dreams as well as daydreams reflect this continuing effort and suggest the inherent creativity of almost all individuals. Artists are especially adept at noticing such fantasies and incorporating them into their productions. Psychotherapists from a variety of schools have increasingly also encouraged the fantasy and imagery capacities of their clients as resources in the treatment process.

Jerome L. Singer
Yale University

References

Freud, S. (1962 [1908]) 'Creative writers and daydreaming', in *Standard Edition of the Complete Psychological Works of Sigmund Freud*, ed. J. Strachey, vol. 9, London.
—— (1962 [1911]) 'Formulations regarding the two principles in mental functioning', in *Standard Edition of the Complete Psychological Works of Sigmund Freud*, ed. J. Strachey, vol. 12, London.
James, W. (1890) *The Principles of Psychology*, New York.
Jaynes, J. (1977) *The Origin of Consciousness in the Breakdown of the Bicameral Mind*, New York.
Klinger, E. (1990) *Daydreaming*, Los Angeles, CA.
McClelland, D. C. (1961) *The Achieving Society*, Princeton, NJ.
—— (1992) 'Is personality consistent?', in R. A. Zucker, A. I. Rabin, J. Aronoff and S. J. Frank (eds) *Personality Structure in the Life Course: Essays on Personology in the Murray Tradition*, New York.
Singer, D. G. and Singer, J. L. (1990) *The House of Make-Believe: Children's Play and the Developing Imagination*, Cambridge, MA.
Singer, J. L. (1966) *Daydreaming: An Introduction to the Experimental Study of Inner Experience*, New York.
—— (1976) *Daydreaming and Fantasy*, Oxford.
—— (1993) 'Experimental studies of ongoing conscious experience', Ciba Foundation Symposium 174, Experimental and Theoretical Studies of Consciousness, London.
—— (1994) 'William James, James Joyce and the stream of consciousness', in R. Fuller (ed.) *Behaviour and Mind*, London.
Singer, J. L. and Brown, S. (1977) 'The experience-type: some behavioral correlates and theoretical implications', in M. C. Rickers-Orsiankina (ed.) *Rorschach Psychology*, Huntington, NY.

Further reading

Klinger, E. (1971) *The Structure and Function of Fantasy*, New York.
Singer, J. L. (1974) *Imagery and Daydream Methods in Psychotherapy and Behavior Modification*, New York.

See also: delusions; dreams; Freud, Sigmund; projective methods.

fascism

Of all the major terms in twentieth-century political usage, fascism has tended to remain one of the most vague. At the popular level, it has become during the past two generations little more than a derogatory epithet employed to denigrate a bewildering variety of otherwise mutually contradictory political phenomena. It has been applied at one time or another to virtually every single form of twentieth-century radicalism or authoritarianism, as well as many more moderate phenomena. More specifically, in terms of political regimes, there has developed since the 1930s a broad tendency to refer to any form of right-wing authoritarian system that is not specifically socialist as fascist. In this usage the Italian regime of Benito Mussolini is used as terminological prototype for all non-Marxist or non-socialist authoritarian systems, however they may differ from Italian Fascism or among themselves.

Rigorous scholarly and historical definition of fascism, however, refers to the concrete historical phenomena of the European fascist movements that emerged between the two world wars, first in the Italian Fascist and German National Socialist movements founded in 1919–20 and then among their numerous counterparts in many European countries. An adequate political and historical definition of fascism must define common unique characteristics of all the fascist movements in Europe during the 1920s and 1930s while at the same time differentiating them from other political phenomena. Such a criterial definition must specify the typical fascist negations, fascist doctrine and goals, and the uniqueness of fascist style and organization.

The uniqueness of fascism lay in its opposition to nearly all the existing political sectors, left, right and centre. It was anti-liberal, anti-communist (as well as anti-socialist in the social democratic sense), and anti-conservative, though willing to undertake temporary alliances with other groups, primarily rightist.

In their ideology and political goals, fascist movements represented the most intense and radical form of nationalism known to modern Europe. They aimed at the creation of a new kind of nationalist authoritarian state that was not merely based on traditional principles or models. Though fascist groups differed considerably among themselves on economic goals, they all hoped to organize some new kind of regulated, multiclass, integrated national economic structure, diversely called national corporatist, national socialist or national syndicalist. All fascist movements aimed either at national imperial expansion or at least at a radical change in the nation's relationship with other powers to enhance its strength and prestige. Their doctrines rested on a philosophical basis of idealism and voluntarism, and normally involved the attempt to create a new form of modern, self-determined secular culture.

Fascist uniqueness was particularly expressed through the movements' style and organization Great emphasis was placed on the aesthetic structure of meetings, symbols and political choreography, relying especially on romantic and mystical aspects. Fascist movements all attempted to achieve mass mobilization, together with the militarization of political relationships and style and with the goal of a mass party militia. Unlike some other types of radicals, fascists placed strong positive evaluation on the use of violence, and strongly stressed the masculine principle and male dominance. Though they espoused an organic concept of society, they vigorously championed a new elitism and exalted youth above other phases of life. In leadership, fascist movements exhibited a specific tendency toward an authoritarian, charismatic, personal style of command (the *Führerprinzip*, in German National Socialist parlance).

Radical rightist groups shared some of the fascists' political goals, just as revolutionary leftist movements exhibited some of their stylistic and organizational characteristics. The uniqueness of the fascists, however, lay in their rejection of the cultural and economic conservatism, and the particular social elitism of the right, just as they rejected the internationalism, nominal egalitarianism and materialist socialism of the left. The historical uniqueness of fascism can be better grasped once it is realized that significant political movements sharing all – not merely some – of these common characteristics existed only in Europe during the years 1919–45.

Fascists claimed to represent all classes of national society, particularly the broad masses. Marxists and some others, conversely, claimed that they were no more than the tool of the most violent, monopolistic and reactionary sectors of the bourgeoisie. Both of these extreme interpretations are not supported by empirical evidence. In their earliest phase, fascist movements drew their followers from among former military personnel and small sectors of the radical intelligentsia, in some cases university students. Though some fascist movements enjoyed a degree of backing from the upper bourgeoisie, the broadest sector of fascist support, comparatively speaking, was provided by the lower middle class. Since this was one of the largest strata in European society during the 1920s and 1930s, the same might also have been said for various other political groups. In both Italy and Germany, a notable minority of party members were drawn from among urban workers. In Hungary and Romania primary social backing came from university students and poor peasants, and there was also considerable agrarian support in some parts of Italy.

A bewildering variety of theories and interpretations have been advanced since 1923 to explain fascism. Among them are, first, theories of socioeconomic causation of various kinds, primarily of Marxist inspiration; second, concepts of psychocultural motivation related to social psychology and personality and social structures; third, the application of modernization theory, which posits fascism as a phase in modern development; fourth, the theory of totalitarianism, which interprets fascism as one aspect of the broader phenomenon of twentieth-century totalitarianism; and finally, historicist interpretations, which attempt multi-causal explanation in terms of the major dimensions of central European historical development in the early twentieth century.

The only fascist movements to establish independent regimes of their own were those of Benito Mussolini (1922–43) and Adolf Hitler (1933–45), and only in the latter case did the movement's leader achieve complete power over the state. The other countries in which fascist movements were strongest were Austria (Austrian National Socialists), Hungary (Arrow Cross), Romania (Iron Guard) and Spain (Spanish Phalanx). In general, fascism had most appeal in countries defeated or destabilized by the effects of the First World War. Though fascist movements appeared in every single European country during these years (and also, very faintly, in the countries of the western hemisphere and Japan, paralleled by more vigorous expression in South Africa), very few of them enjoyed any degree of success. In nearly all countries anti-fascists were generally much more numerous than fascists. The extreme radicalism and calls to war and violence of the fascists limited their appeal, as did the non-rationalist, voluntarist nature of their doctrines. The great expansion of military power by Hitler's Germany was mainly responsible for the broader influence and historical importance achieved by fascism for a few years. Similarly, the complete defeat of Germany and Italy in the war condemned fascism to such total political destruction and historical discredit that all attempts at revival have enjoyed only miniscule support since 1945.

Stanley G. Payne
University of Wisconsin, Madison

Further reading

Griffin, R. (1991) *The Nature of Fascism*, London.
Laqueur, W. (ed.) (1976), *Fascism: A Reader's Guide*, Berkeley, CA.
Larsen, S. U. et al. (eds) (1980) *Who were the Fascists: Social Roots of European Fascism*, Bergen-Oslo.
Payne, S. G. (1980) *Fascism: Comparison and Definition*, Madison, WI.

See also: nationalism; populism; radicalism; socialism.

federation and federalism

A federation is a state organized on the basis of a division of power between general and regional governments, each independent within a sphere (Wheare 1946). The territory of a federal state is divided into units (for example, states, cantons, principalities, republics) which often coincide with distinctive geographic, cultural or historic divisions of the country. Many of the institutions of government are duplicated at the national and local levels with both levels of government exercising effective control over the same territory and population. Thus the citizens of a federal state belong simultaneously to two political communities: for those functions that are constitutionally assigned to the local level of government, the relevant community is the citizen's particular state, canton, province or republic; for functions assigned to the national government, the entire nation is the relevant community.

In the true federal state, both levels of government derive their powers directly from the constitution and neither is able to eliminate the other's jurisdiction. In this way a federal state is distinguished from a unitary state with territorial sub-units (such as counties, department, districts) that receive all of their powers by delegation from a central government. At the other extreme, a federal system of government should be distinguished from a confederation, or league of states, in which the central level of government receives all its powers from the member states and has no autonomous powers of its own.

The USA was the first modern nation-state to adopt a federal constitution. In the nineteenth century some of the new states of South and Central America (e.g. Venezuela, Colombia, Argentina, Brazil and Mexico) were organized on federal lines. But federal constitutions have been of less enduring significance there than in Switzerland (1848), Canada (1867) and Australia (1901) which, along with the USA, are the countries that have been practising federal constitutionalism without interruption for the longest time. Constitutions adopted by many of Britain's former colonies (e.g. India, Pakistan, Malaysia and Nigeria) incorporated the federal principle (Watts 1966). In Europe, the federal principle is prominent in the constitution of the Federal Republic of Germany. South Africa under its new constitution is to be organized as a federation.

The balance of power and of citizens' allegiance between the two levels of government is a dynamic element in the politics of a federal state. In some federations, the forces of centralization, especially when fostered by a single unified political party, may be so strong as to negate the autonomy of the local level of government. In others the forces of decentralization may be such that they lead to the break-up of the federal state (as in the cases of the British West Indian Federation and Yugoslavia). For a federal system to endure, there must be significant independent political forces supporting each level of government.

Federalism is a political movement advocating and working towards federation. A federalism movement can work in a centralizing or decentralizing direction. In the context of the European Union (EU), for example, federalists are considered to be centralizers as they attempt to increase the powers of EU institutions, while federalism in Belgium has had a decentralizing effect, converting a unitary state into a federal state.

Peter H. Russell
University of Toronto

References

Watts, R. L. (1966) *New Federations: Experiments in the Commonwealth*, Oxford.
Wheare, K. C. (1946) *Federal Government*, Oxford.

Further reading

Bowie, R. R. and Friedrich, C. J. (1954) *Studies in Federalism*, Boston, MA.
Burgess, M. and Gagnon, A. G. (1993) *Comparative Federalism and Federation: Competing Traditions and Future Directions*, London.
MacMahon, A. W. (ed.) (1962) *Federalism: Mature and Emergent*, New York.
Riker, W. H. (1964) *Federalism: Origin, Operation, Significance*, Boston, MA.

See also: constitutions and constitutionalism; nationalism; pluralism, political; state.

feminist practice

The women's movement has challenged the conventional binary distinction between theory and practice, arguing there should be a symbiotic relationship between them. This relationship is best seen in terms of praxis: the unity of theory and practice in the enactment of small revolutions in the here-and-now. Manifestations of feminist practice can be seen in the overtly political arena, as well as in activities not conventionally seen as political. Scrutinizing feminist practice shows continuities between 'first wave' (Victorian and Edwardian) and 'second wave' (1960s onward) feminism; it should be recognized, however, that these are First World responses and that feminisms globally have taken rather different forms.

Direct action involves a variety of unlawful acts designed to bring to public awareness particular injustices. Thus, for example, the later stages of Edwardian feminism is associated with arson attacks against public buildings, while protests against pornography saw feminists firing sex shops in the 1970s.

Civil disobedience includes behaviours on the threshold of lawfulness but outside of correct behaviour. Here, for example, Victorian feminists shocked convention by publicly opposing the Contagious Diseases Acts, while 1990s lesbian feminists did so by abseiling into the House of Lords when it was debating Clause 28 of the Local Government Bill 1988, which made unlawful so-called 'pretended family relationships'.

Pressure group politics is now considered one of the main forms of political action within parliamentary democracies; Victorian feminists were among the pioneers of what was then considered to be outrageous behaviour. Then, feminists lobbied MPs and staged sit-ins in front of the House of Commons, while in the 1960s and 1970s feminists lobbied for the Sex Discrimination Act and for lawful abortion within the National Health Service.

Self-help involves feminist provision of services which are either unavailable, or available only in unsatisfactory forms, from central and local government and their agencies. Thus Victorian feminists provided safe houses for abused children and refuges for women who were subject to violence from men, while 1970s feminists set up a national system of Rape Crisis Centres which offer help to women and children who have been subject to sexual abuse and sexual violence. Self-help provision is one means by which feminist practice has successfully challenged the boundaries of politics, moving attention away from the public of parliaments, armies and economies, and towards the private of everyday life and relationships. It has thereby also challenged dichotomized ways of thinking about the public and the private, for example, male violence and abuse within the family and also marital rape are now socially unacceptable, whereas earlier they were treated as part of private life in which state agencies should not interfere.

There are additional challenges to the boundaries of the political which feminism has pioneered; here again there are continuities between first-wave and second-wave feminisms. Thus the music of Victorian composer Ethel Smyth and the novels and essays of modernist Virginia Woolf, along with the poetry of contemporary black American feminist poet Audre Lorde and American artist Judy Chicago (best known for her exhibition 'The Dinner Party'), are powerful expressions of feminist practice as well as radical interventions in cultural representation. These and other examples demonstrate the strong feminist concern with acting against the grain, bringing together feminist theory and feminist practice in – and against – all aspects of social life. There has been an equally strong concern with living against the grain; examples here include living independently of men, sexually and also economically, and raising children in a non-sexist way.

In western societies, perhaps the most wide-reaching aspect of feminist practice is Women's Studies, which proposes a revolutionary remaking of knowledge. Its main areas of activity include critiquing the biases and omissions of 'malestream' theories and practices; filling the gaps occasioned by masculinist methodologies; reconceptualizing subject areas, theories and concepts from a woman-centred viewpoint; and challenging how knowledge is theorized and defined, thus politicizing questions of epistemology.

Sue Wise
Lancaster University

Further reading

Caine, B. (1992) *Victorian Feminists*, Oxford.
Coote, A. and Campbell, B. (1987) *Sweet Freedom*, Oxford.
Kramarae, C. and Spender, D. (eds) (1993) *The Knowledge Explosion: A Decade of Feminist Scholarship*, New York.
Morgan, R. (ed.), (1984) *Sisterhood is Global*, Harmondsworth.
Rowbotham, S. (1989) *The Past is Before Us: Feminism in Action since the 1960s*, Harmondsworth.
Rowbotham, S. (1992) *Women in Movement: Feminism and Social Action*, London.

See also: feminist research; feminist theory; women; women's studies.

feminist research

The ideas covered by the term feminist research have changed emphasis considerably since the start of the feminist renaissance in the 1960s and 1970s. At least four sets of meanings and research practices are involved and are now coexistent. Feminists in the social sciences are likely to draw on ideas taken from each of these: they are by no means to be seen as mutually exclusive, nor indeed as necessarily antithetical positions.

Displacing the male knower

From the start of the feminist renaissance of the 1960s and 1970s, the sociology of knowledge issues involved in the feminist critique of the social sciences were clearly signalled. Academic feminism, at that time located predominantly in sociology, questioned the objective, rational, dispassionate and removed 'knower' and displaced *him* from his actually gendered – and raced and classed – position at the centre of knowledge-production. An associated critique of the dichotomies of positivism – subjective/objective, rational/emotional, science/life, masculine/feminine, male/female – is central to the arguments involved here, together with the insistence that feminist knowledge should be rooted in, and work out from, women's experiences.

'Hard' and 'soft' methods: recovering subjectivities

The feminist critique also focused on questions of method and methodology and it pinpointed particular methods – quantitative and 'hard' science ones – as central to the organizational apparatus of masculinism in the social sciences. This work proposed an alternative qualitative approach which would map subjectivities, the private as counterposed by the public face of objective masculinity. The arguments here focus on the question of method ('hard' v. 'soft') and its relationship to the devaluing of subjectivity as somehow innately – essentially – irrational and emotional, that is, associated with notions of 'science' and scientific method. However, this concern with recovering subjectivities can with hindsight be seen to leave intact the dichotomies of male/objectivity and female/subjectivity that other feminist work has been concerned to challenge.

Interviewing: feminism and friendship?

Arguments about 'recovering subjectivities' have particularly influenced feminist ideas about interviewing, seeing this as a method that would not only enable the investigation of subjectivities but also position research as a form of 'friendship' between feminist researchers and women research subjects. However, even as such ideas were first mooted, other voices raised the deeper issues of power involved. Nonetheless, throughout the 1980s interviewing and variants upon it, importantly including different styles of action research, dominated the feminist social science research agenda.

Epistemology and the politics of location

From the late 1980s on there has been a renewed interest in questions of epistemology, fuelled at least in part by the greater influence of feminist philosophy, including the epistemological aspects of a feminist politics of location. 'Who you are' makes a difference: to *what* is seen, to *what* cannot be seen, to *how* seeing occurs, and to what interpretational conclusions are drawn. Thus 'knowledge' and its constitution – including who are seen to be knowers, how knowledge is distinguished from mere opinion, how competing knowledge-claims are adjudicated, how gatekeeping across the boundaries between knowers and others occurs and by whom – has returned to centre stage within academic feminism.

Method, methodology and epistemology

As this overview suggests, there has been effectively no interest in the idea of developing a feminist method, in the sense of a distinct, unique feminist technique of research. Relatedly, there is no longer the view that particular methods are innately either good or bad. The distinction between method (or techniques), methodology (or broad theoretical and programmatic statements) and epistemology (or a theory of knowledge and knowledge-production) is useful here, for it shifts feminist debate about research away from method narrowly conceived and on to the far-reaching and fundamental questions of epistemology. That is, method is seen as the product of wider methodological and epistemological assumptions and stances, so that, for example, there can be positivist and masculinist interviewing, and feminist and radical surveys.

Developments in feminist epistemology

Subsequent developments in feminist epistemology have focused on overlapping debates concerned with method, methodology and epistemology, the relationship between mind and body, a feminist ethic, the category 'women' and feminist deconstructionism, ideas about essentialism and difference, and representation and history. There are three related developments here worth particular comment.

Knowledge, method and praxis

Initially feminist writing on method/ology and epistemology addressed issues of particular concern to the social sciences. Subsequently, with the development of deconstructionist and post-modernist influences, the emphasis shifted first to the humanities, and then the debates became particularly marked by the concerns and language of feminist philosophy. One far-reaching consequence has been that the eminently practical and ethical issues that confront feminist researchers carrying out research in the social world, not just within and about texts, have, if not vanished, then been shifted to the epistemological sidelines. Indeed, questions of epistemology are becoming seen as part of feminist social theory and increasingly treated as the preserve of a small group of specialist elite theorists. What started as the practical questions of feminist praxis have become questions of feminist theory conceived in largely abstract terms. Thus for many feminist social scientists there is now an urgent need to return these debates back to the practical issues that face those who endeavour to carry out social research in feminist ways.

Epistemology and science

Writing about feminist research has from its inception been concerned with providing a critique of the natural sciences, seen as the paradigm case of science and its attendant binaries of subjectivity/objectivity, rationality/emotionality, and so on, while more recently the connections between these Cartesian binaries and the precepts of foundationalism elsewhere in academic life have been theorized. However, there have been feminist researchers and theorists working in the natural sciences as well as the social sciences and humanities, and writing attendant on their practices has developed along different lines. This latter strand of thinking has been more concerned with how feminist science can become possible, politically, ethically, methodologically and epistemologically. This latter strand of work, for example, has been concerned with the development of a feminist epistemological position that might heal the breach between 'heart, brain and hand' in the natural sciences.

Contra binaries

Academic feminism has provided a long-standing and stringent critique of binary ways of thinking, from its 1960s and 1970s critique of sexism in the social sciences, through to the arguments of feminist deconstructionism with its critique of binary gender and thus of the defining terms of feminism itself. It is, then, paradoxical that some work concerned with feminist research and epistemology has left effectively intact the binary divisions used to separate epistemological positions and indeed to caricature the 'submerged' binary of each pair: realism v. idealism, and foundationalism v. relativism. Thus attempts to shift debate away from realist (there is a world of facts independent of any social construction) and foundationalist (knowledge can be founded in such external and independent facticity) claims within feminism have sometimes been caricatured as proposing radical idealist (only social construction exists, there is no reality) and relativist (no knowledge-claims are ever possible) positions. However, it has been argued that alternatives to binary thinking exist, in the form of a feminist approach which seeks knowledge and makes knowledge-claims, but which also sees knowledge as necessarily local and provisional. A similar position has been argued in relation to 'feminist fractured foundationalism', the view that what is seen as foundational coexists in social life with what is recognized as contingent, provisional and socially constructed, and that the exploration and analysis of such competing local knowledges should be the basis of academic feminist research and theorizing.

Where does 'knowledge' come from

At the basis of many of the debates sketched out here are two related questions: Can epistemology be onto-logically based? Can epistemology ever be anything else? The first question expresses the view that femi-nist knowledge should be general and trans-situational and therefore not tied to the specificities of particular persons and places. The second question expresses the view (held by perhaps the majority of academic feminists) that there is no way of producing feminist or any other knowledge apart from through the minds of particular knowers, and that this politics of location requires a scrupulous attendance to unpacking the processes involved, including a detailed exposition of the processes of grounded feminist research.

As these two questions make clear, the feminist concern with research is actually a concern with the organizational and intellectual practices involved in knowledge-production, with assumptions about the definition and nature of knowledge, with how the rela-tionship between being and knowing is theorized, and with the very conditions and constitution of science within the academy and its status *vis-à-vis* everyday life. These are of course the most fundamental questions and issues for all social science; it is noteworthy that they are central to academic feminism across the acad-emic disciplines and occupy a particularly crucial place within feminist social science.

Liz Stanley
University of Manchester

Further reading

Fonow, M. and Cook, J. (eds) (1991) *Beyond Methodology: Feminist Scholarship as Lived Experience*, Buckingham.

Fuss, D. (1989) *Essentially Speaking: Feminism, Nature and Difference*, London.

Harding, S. (1986) *The Science Question in Feminism*, Bucking-ham.

—— (ed.) (1987) *Feminism and Methodology*, Buckingham.

—— (1991) *Whose Science? Whose Knowledge? Thinking From Women's Lives*, Buckingham.

Reinharz, S. (1992) *Feminist Methods in Social Research*, Lon-don.

Roberts, H. (1991) *Doing Feminist Research*, 2nd edn, Lon-don.

Stanley, L. (ed.) (1990) *Feminist Praxis: Research, Theory and Epistemology in Feminist Sociology*, London.

Stanley, L. and Wise, S. (1990) 'Method, methodology and epistemology in feminist research processes', in L. Stanley (ed.) (1990) *Feminist Praxis: Research, Theory and Epistemology in Feminist Sociology*, London.

—— (1993) *Breaking Out Again: Feminist Ontology and Epistemology*, London.

See also: feminist practice; feminist theory; women; women's studies.

feminist theory

All variants of feminist theory tend to share three major assumptions: gender is a social construction that oppresses women more than men; patriarchy (the male domination of social institutions) shapes these construc-tions; women's experiential knowledge best helps us to envision a future non-sexist society. These shared premises shape a double agenda: the task of critique (attacking gender stereotypes) and the task of construc-tion, sometimes called feminist praxis (constructing new models). Feminist theory focuses particularly on women's experiences of sexuality, work and the family, and so inevitably challenges traditional frameworks of knowledge and puts in question many assumptions of the social sciences, such as universalism.

Although foremothers like Mary Wollstonecraft (1759–97) are often claimed as feminist, the term femi-nism began to be used only in the 1890s (Offen 1988). In the twentieth century Virginia Woolf (1882–1941) and Simone de Beauvoir (1908–86) anticipate second wave feminism's attack on women's oppression. In the 1960s student and civil rights movements gave an impetus, shaping the topics and language of current feminist theory. As an identifiable area of the social sciences then, feminist theory dates from the 1970s with the publication of Kate Millett's *Sexual Politics*.

Feminist theory is, first, intensely interdisciplinary, ranging across customary subject divisions in the social sciences, including history, philosophy, anthropology, and the arts among others. Second, certain themes recur: reproduction, representation and the sexual divi-sion of labour. Third, and most striking, are new concepts such as sexism and essentialism created to address absences in existing knowledge as well as the social discriminations these concepts describe. Fourth, women's subjective experiences are drawn upon to enrich scholarship and scientific theories. The starting-point is often consciousness raising where the personal can become political. MacKinnon (1989) argues that feminist theory is the first theory to emerge from those whose interest it affirms. Androcentric knowledge, feminist psychoanalysts claim, derives from masculine experiences of *separation* learned in childhood.

Since feminism developed at a time when the par-ticipation of women in the workforce was rising fast but while discrimination persisted, critics first focused on the sexism of language and of cultural and economic institutions. While intellectual ideas rarely present themselves in neat chronological order, the 1970s tackled the *causes* of women's oppression (capitalism/masculinity) describing society as a struc-ture of oppressors (male) and oppressed (female). This moment is usually divided into *forms* of feminism (liberal, Marxist/socialist, cultural/radical). Liberal feminism argues that women's liberation will come with equal legal, political and economic rights, and Friedan attacked the 'feminine mystique' preventing women from claiming equality (Friedan 1963). More comprehensive Marxist/socialist assessments of economic gender exploitations were made by Juliet Mitchell (1966) and others. The key questions were: Did women form a distinct sex-class? How far is capitalism structured by patriarchy? By widening the Marxist concept of production to include household labour and child-care, feminists could highlight further sexual divisions ('domestic labour' debate) as well as women's unequal status at work ('reserve army of labour'). For example, Firestone (1970) argued that the 'material' of woman's reproductive body was as much a source of oppression as material inequality.

While dual systems theory argues that both capitalism and patriarchy construct gender, requiring a synthesis of Marxism with radical feminism, MacKinnon (1989) suggests that only radical feminism *is* feminism because it is post-Marxist. In opposition to a Marxist focus on *production*, cultural and radical feminists (e.g. Rich 1976) focused on reproduction and mothering and creativity. Although the labels cultural or radical are often misapplied, in general radical theorists take the view that sexuality, specifically male violence, is the cause of women's oppression condoned by the institutionalization of heterosexuality (see Dworkin 1981). This is the theme of Rich's (1980) milestone essay 'Compulsory Heterosexuality' which builds on de Beauvoir's premise that women are originally homosexual, to propose that lesbianism can be part of every women's cultural, if not physical, experience. This argument that 'lesbian' is shaped as much by ideological preferences as by explicit practice built on 'women identified women' and 'feminism is the theory, lesbianism is the practice' in second wave feminism.

A major rethinking of symbolic and social structures of gender difference was undertaken by French feminists (*écriture féminine*). They claimed that the cultural and gendered binaries man/woman, culture/nature always made 'woman' inferior (Cixous 1976). Binaries ignore women's fluid identity and the semiotic world of mother/infant bonding. American feminists drew on object relations psychoanalysis to locate the source of male power and fear of women in men's early experience of learning to be 'not the mother' (Chodorow 1978). These accounts of gender identity and objectification greatly enriched feminist film and media study. The notion that there is a distinctive and gendered perception (the male 'gaze') is supported by the feminist standpoint theorists who challenge false notions of rationality and universalism in the social sciences (Harding 1986).

The 1980s saw a crucial shift in feminist theory when black feminist writers directed attention to ethnic differences. Criticizing the three form, or phase, typology (liberal/Marxist/cultural) as a white women's mental map which ignored the experiences of black women, they describe discrimination as an *interlocking* system based on race, class and gender (hooks 1984). They also introduced fresh theoretical arguments, suggesting, for example, that the family was not necessarily patriarchal but could be a site of resistance. Black theory derives from Afrocentric history, as well as from a 'both/or' reality (the act of being simultaneously inside and outside society) and has a particular view of mothering experience (Lorde 1984; Walker 1984).

These critiques of white essentialism were paralleled by feminist post-structuralist and post-modern critiques of structured systems of subjectivity. Drawing on ideas from deconstruction and discourse analysis, feminists argued that gender structures are historically variable and not predetermined. This led to what Barrett calls 'the turn to culture' and a renewed interest in cultural symbols (Barrett and Phillips 1992). Italian feminists, for example, created the term *autocoscienza* or the collective construction of new identities. Through cultural study many of these themes were brought together in feminist peace theory which argues that violence stems from traditional gender socialization. In opposition, pacifists created women-centred symbolic models of environmental action.

Feminist challenges to mainstream social science are diverse and influential, a central claim being that *all* science is motivated by gendered ideologies whether these are conscious or unconscious. The academic future of feminist theory is now more secure with the growth of women's studies.

Maggie Humm
University of East London

References

Barrett, M. and Phillips, A. (1992) (eds) *Destabilising Theory*, Cambridge, UK.

Chodorow, N. (1978) *The Reproduction of Mothering*, Berkeley, CA.

Cixous, H. (1976) 'The laugh of the Medusa', *Signs* 1(4).

Dworkin, A. (1981) *Pornography*, London.

Firestone, S. (1970) *The Dialetic of Sex*, New York.

Friedan, B. (1963) *The Feminine Mystique*, New York.

Harding, S. (1986) *The Science Question in Feminism*, Ithaca, NY.

hooks, b. (1984) *Feminist Theory: From Margin to Center*, Boston, MA.

Lorde, A. (1984) *Sister Outsider*, Trumansberg.

MacKinnon, C. (1989) *Toward a Feminist Theory of the State*, Cambridge, UK.

Millett, K. (1970) *Sexual Politics*, New York.

Mitchell, J. (1966) 'Women the longest revolution', *New Left Review*, 40.

Offen, K. (1988) 'Defining feminism', *Signs* 14(11).

Rich, A. (1976) *Of Woman Born*, New York.

—— (1980) 'Compulsory heterosexuality and lesbian existence', *Signs* 5(4).

Walker, A. (1984) *In Search of Our Mothers' Gardens*, London.

Further reading

Collins, P. H. (1990) *Black Feminist Thought*, London.

Humm, M. (1995) *The Dictionary of Feminist Theory*, 2nd edn, Hemel Hempstead.

See also: feminist practice; feminist research; gender and sex; patriarchy; sexual behaviour; women; women's studies.

fertility

Fertility (also referred to as natality) always refers in demographic usage to the achievement of live births. This is in keeping with its Latin etymological derivation from *ferre* (to bear) but in contrast to the verb, fertilize, which relates to conception. In English-language social science, the capacity to bear children is described as fecundity and the fact of giving birth as fertility. This is the reverse of the usage in French and other Romance languages. It also conflicts with much popular, medical and biological usage where infertility means not childlessness but infecundity or sterility (confusingly, the last can be employed in both senses even by demographers).

Fertility has long been identified with fruitfulness and productiveness, not only in terms of human reproduction but also with regard to the availability of game for hunters and the yield of crops. Indeed, the perceived relationship has played a major role in religion since palaeolithic times. The dependence of fertility upon preceding sexual relations has meant that both fertility and coitus play a central role in much of human culture and morality. In some cultures, particularly in the Middle East, the fact of pregnancy or childbirth to a married woman is usually the cause of pleasure, but should she not be married the reaction of her relatives might be so antagonistic as to result in her death and in great problems in securing the marriage of her siblings.

In spite of the biblical advice to be fruitful and multiply, and its mirroring in the adages of many pre-industrial societies, the maximization of fertility is usually constrained by other competing social objectives. Fertility is usually not favoured outside marriage partly because it may interfere with achieving the desired marriage. It may be discouraged soon after the birth of another child, because of the risk to health and life of both mother and children, or by grandmothers, because of the conflict between grandmaternal and maternal duties. Traditionally these constraints have been embedded in religion and mores rather than being expressed solely in terms of conflicting roles and danger to health.

Fertility may be expressed as a measure of the behaviour of a society, a couple or an individual. In theory, reproductive measures are just as valid for individual males as females, but estimates for the former are rarely attempted because the fact of a man's fathering a child is less obvious to the community and may be unknown to the progenitor himself. The most meaningful measures of a woman's reproduction is the number of births she experiences between menarch (or puberty) and menopause. For the whole society, the average for all women is known as completed fertility. However, this measure can be determined only in retrospect, a quarter of a century after the peak in fertility for most women completing their reproductive spans, and societies frequently demand more immediate measures which are necessarily those for aggregate populations of different ages for a specified period (usually one year and hence described as an annual rate). The most common aggregate measure is the crude birth rate or the number of live births per year per thousand population. For national populations, this varied in 1993 from 53 in Malawi to 10 in Germany, Greece, Italy and Spain. The crude birth rate can prove to be an unsatisfactory measure in a society where immigration or other social changes have distorted the distribution of the population by sex or age, and more statistically refined measures relate births only to women of specified age or marital condition. The general fertility rate is the ratio of the births during a year to the total number of women 15–49 years of age. The relating of births to women of a specific age, or age range, for a specified period (usually one year), is termed the age-specifc birth rate (or fertility rate) and its sum over the whole reproductive age range is the total fertility rate, which in a society characterized by constant fertility over several decades, is an annual measure of the same magnitude as completed fertility. The total fertility rate ranged in 1993 from 7.7 in Malawi to 1.2 in Hong Kong, 1.3 in Italy and Spain and 1.4 in Germany and Macao. In former East Germany it was lower still, while in Asia levels of 1.5 were found in Japan, 1.6 in South Korea, 1.7 in Singapore and 1.9 in China. Attention may be confined to married women so as to determine marital age-specific birth rates and the total marital fertility rate. If only female births are related to mothers of each age, then the cumulative measure is known as the gross reproduction rate. Because for societies the effective measure of reproduction is not live births but surviving children, a measure known as the net reproduction rate has been devised. This may be defined as the ratio of female births in the next generation to those in this generation in conditions of constant fertility and mortality, and hence measures the eventual multiplication of societies' numbers from one generation to the next, once the age structure changes so as to conform with these stable conditions. If the society maintains a rate of unity for a considerable period (half a century or more in societies which were previously growing rapidly) it will become stationary, while a lower rate will imply eventually declining population size, and a higher rate, a growing population. In 1980, levels below unity were recorded by thirty-six European countries (the exceptions being Iceland, Ireland and Moldavia), seven East Asian countries (including China), seven Caribbean countries, and also the USA, Canada, Australia and Georgia. However, only Hungary also exhibited a decline in numbers (Bulgaria, Czechoslovakia, Denmark, Greece, Ireland, Italy, Latvia and Romania being stationary), because such rates have been achieved so recently that there are still disproportionatley more women in the potentially most fertile ages than would be the case in a population which had exhibited a net reproduction rate at or below unity for may years. Births within marriage may be described as nuptial or legitimate and those outside as exnuptial or illegitimate.

The female reproductive span varies between women and between societies (or the same society at different dates), but approximately spans ages from around 15 years to the late forties. If fertility were in no way constrained, not even by the institution of marriage or by the practice of breast-feeding which tends to depress fertility, completed family size would be around 15 (Bongaarts (1982) employs 15.3 in his model). The total marital fertility rate of the Hutterites, a religious community opposed to deliberate fertility control, was in the western USA in the late 1920s at least 12.4 – a level employed by Coale (1967) in his model – but this figure was almost certainly rising because of the reduction of the period of breast-feeding. Where breast-feeding is of traditional duration (two years or more) the following completed family sizes are found if deliberate control of marital fertility is not practised. First, where female marriage is early and widow remarriage is common, as among the Ashanti of West Africa (who practise only short periods of postpartum abstinence), around 8. Second, where female marriage is early and widow remarriage is discouraged, as in India prior to the family planning programme, around 6.5. Third, where female marriage is late and there are no strong feelings about widow remarriage, as in western Europe before the Industrial Revolution, around 6. The term natural fertility has been employed to describe the level of fertility, and its

structure by female age, found in societies which do not deliberately restrict marital fertility (but in which sexual abstinence may be practised after childbirth and terminal sexual abstinence after becoming a grandmother).

However, contemporary interest in fertility largely arises from the decline in fertility in all industrialized and many other societies and the possibility of further reduction in developing countries. The latter has been assisted by family planning programmes which have now been instituted by a majority of Third-World governments (beginning with India in 1952). The determinants of fertility have been classified (by Davis and Blake 1956) as first, intercourse variables (age at first entrance to sexual union; the proportion of women never entering a union; the period spent after or between union; voluntary and involuntary abstinence, and frequency of intercourse); second, conception variables (subfecundity or infecundity; contraception, and sterilization), and third, gestation variables (spontaneous or induced abortion). The list does not separately identify the duration of breast-feeding, which was undoubtedly in most traditional societies the major determinant of marital fertility, or sexual activity outside stable unions. Bongaarts (1982) has demonstrated that only four factors – the proportion of the female reproductive period spent in a sexual union (in many societies the period of marriage), the duration of postpartum infecundability (that is, the period without menstruation or ovulation plus any period beyond this of postpartum sexual abstinence), the practice of contraception and its effectiveness, and the extent of induced abortion – provide 96 per cent of the explanation of the variance in fertility levels in nearly all societies.

Beginning in France in the late eighteenth century, and becoming more general in industrialized countries from the late nineteenth century, fertility has fallen in economically developed countries so that most appear likely to attain zero population growth. This has been achieved largely through the deliberate control of marital fertility, in most countries by contraception (before the 1960s by chemical or mechanical means as well as rhythm, abstinence, and withdrawal or coitus interruptus and subsequently increasingly by the use of the Pill, intra-uterine devices and sterilization), supplemented by different levels of abortion. By 1993 fertility was clearly low or declining in every major world region except sub-Saharan Africa (where birth rates had begun to fall in South Africa, Botswana, Zimbabwe and Kenya – too few countries to affect the regional rate). Fertility also remained high and constant in parts of the Middle East and South-west Asia. Increasingly the relationship between the sexual act and conception has been weakened, and this has allowed a weakening in the relation between sexual activity and marriage.

John C. Caldwell
Australia National University

References

Bongaarts, J. (1982) 'The fertility-inhibiting effects of the intermediate fertility variables', *Studies in Family Planning* 13.

Coale, A. J. (1967) 'Factors associated with the development of low fertility: an historic summary', in *Proceedings of the World Population Conference, Belgrade, 1965*, vol. II, New York.

Davis, K. and Blake, J. (1956) 'Social structure and fertility: an analytical framework', *Economic Development and Cultural Change* 4.

Further reading

United Nations (1965) *Population Bulletin of the United Nations, No. 7–1963, with Special Reference to Conditions and Trends of Fertility in the World*, New York.

Wrong, D. H. (1977) *Population and Society*, 4th edn, New York.

See also: demographic transition; morbidity; nuptiality; population geography; population policy; population projections; vital statistics.

feud

In pre-industrial societies, there tend to be three levels of homicide. At the most intimate level, killing within the family or local descent group is felt to bring the threat of permanent mystical misfortune, because it violates the most fundamental bonds of kinship. At the most remote level, like warfare, it lies outside the boundaries of society and social order, in an amoral cosmos beyond. Between these two levels, any homicide tends to mobilize groups that work towards some resolution. *Feud* may be said to exist where the principle of blood-debt between groups is the expected response to homicide. It tends to be associated with societies in which local agnatic descent forms the basis of corporate grouping. Ideally, a feud is strictly limited by the convention that hostilities should be discriminating and that ultimately there should be a negotiated settlement with compensation. Those that are not directly involved in the feuding have an interest in ensuring that the conventions are upheld, or society itself is threatened. In practice, a satisfactory settlement may be evasive and the state of feud may persist indefinitely as the tally of injury mounts on both sides and resistance to any negotiated compromise increases.

It is revealing to compare feud with marriage alliance. Both are middle-range institutions, incompatible with close blood-ties, where the possibility of fratricide or incest evokes horror. Feud goes beyond the immediate relationship between killer and killed, just as marriage alliance goes beyond the union of husband and wife. The asymmetry of both may lead to further incidents of the same kind: retaliatory killings and exchange marriages. In other respects, they are neatly inverted. A marriage is initiated in the same manner as a feud may be terminated through a negotiated agreement which is confirmed by the payment of compensation (bride-wealth and blood-wealth). A feud is initiated in the same manner as a marriage may be terminated: through precipitate action between the principals (homicide and divorce). Permanence of the relationship is an ideal in marriage and a threat in feud, and vice versa. It is this structural transformation between them that accounts for their frequent association. It is the complementarity between one institution that fosters the reproduction of kin groups and of the wider society, and another that poses a threat to this reproduction. This has been summarized by Black-Michaud (1975): 'They are two aspects of precisely the same process. The ambiguities inherent in marital alliance often cause feuds, just as feuds are also frequently the "cause" of the marriages contracted to "conclude" hostilities.' In practice, any marriage to perpetuate the dead man's line is as likely to perpetuate the feud as to resolve it. In such circumstances, it is the blood-debt that has the binding force of a contract, and any settlement emerges as little more than a truce.

Paul Spencer
School of Oriental and African Studies
University of London

Reference

Black-Michaud, J. (1975) *Cohesive Force: Feud in the Mediterranean and the Middle East*, New York.

See also: conflict, social; war studies.

feudalism

There is no agreement on a definition of feudalism. The word can be used in very general terms to describe the totality of the economic and political relationships of medieval European society and of similar societies elsewhere. If such a view is taken, stress is normally laid upon the exploitation of the peasantry by the exaction of labour services in a closed, or natural, economy. The institution of the manor is of great importance; the main social relationships are seen in terms of lordship exercised over both people and land. Frequently such a definition becomes so wide as to be little more than synonymous with medieval, and so loses any real value, but even when used more carefully, there are still considerable problems.

During the medieval period, the economy underwent such transformations as to make the application of a single model of feudalism very dangerous. Money was far more important than was once thought, and production for the market more widespread. There were wide variations, both chronological and geographical, in the degree of the subjection of the peasantry. In England many labour services were commuted in the twelfth century, when feudalism could be thought to have been at its apogee, only to be reimposed in the thirteenth century. At best, society was only partly feudal, and it is significant that in his definition of feudalism one of its greatest historians, Marc Bloch (1961 [1939–40]), allowed for 'the survival of other forms of authority, family and state', alongside the structures of feudal lordship. Attempts at redefinition of the broad concept of feudalism, seeing small-scale peasant production under the political constraints of aristocratic lordship as the key element, have not proved satisfactory.

The alternative tradition to that which seeks a general model of feudalism is one which centres upon a specific type of landholding in return for military service. The word feudalism is derived from the Latin *feudum* (fief), the land held by a knight in return for service usually performed on horseback for forty days. It is possible to provide a much more satisfactory description and explanation for feudalism in such terms. The system had its origins in the collapse of public authority in the ninth century as the Carolingian Empire declined. Men commended themselves to lords, who granted them lands as fiefs. The knight and the castle were central to this feudalism, in which lordship resulted from the man, or vassal, performing a specific ceremony known as homage to his lord. The system evolved gradually, save in countries such as England and southern Italy, where it was imported by the Normans in the eleventh century. Fiefs came to be held in primogeniture, and the rights of the lord to certain dues, or feudal incidents, were given increasing definition. A lord could, for example, demand aid from his vassals to help pay for the knighting of his eldest son, and payment was expected when the son of a vassal succeeded his father in his estates. A complex legal system developed: the jurisdictional rights of lords over their tenants were an important element in a feudal society.

Such a definition is largely satisfactory, provided that it is understood that no society was ever wholly feudalized. In the case of England, the king was never solely dependent upon his feudal cavalry, but relied extensively upon mercenaries and infantry levies. The last effective feudal summons was issued in 1327, but in the first half of the thirteenth century the levels of service had been radically reduced, so that the quotas of knights came to bear little relationship to the feudal landholding structure. Castles were initially an integral part of the feudal organization of the country, but when Edward I came to build his great castles in Wales in the late thirteenth century, he used paid workmen and employed paid troops as garrisons. Such castles can hardly be described as feudal. The system of hiring soldiers by means of contracts and the issue of livery in the later Middle Ages has been described as 'bastard feudalism', but the true feudal elements of landed fiefs, heritability and homage were all absent. Yet the legal aspects of feudalism in England long outlasted the military utility of the system; there was even a revival of feudal techniques of money-raising in the early seventeenth century.

If it is only with care that the term feudalism in a strict sense can be applied to a western European country in the Middle Ages, then it is only with great difficulty that it can be used with reference to different regions and periods. Medieval Byzantium and Islam, with the *pronoia* and *iqta* respectively, had types of land grants which were not entirely dissimilar to fiefs. The *iqta* could only exceptionally be passed on by a holder to his children, but by the twelfth century the Byzantine system was moving towards the heritability which characterized western feudalism. The legal structure of European feudalism was largely lacking in these parallel systems. Japan is frequently cited as developing something very akin to the military feudalism of western Europe, but an economy based on rice production, and a wholly different cultural and legal tradition, made for contrasts as well as similarities. For those who are influenced by Marxist theories, however, feudalism represents a stage through which most societies must pass in the course of their development. Such a view involves using an extremely general definition of feudalism, with its attendant difficulties.

Many of the arguments of scholars over feudalism have been the result of a failure to agree upon definitions. No one word, no single model, can ever sum up the complex and varying structures of medieval societies. As a term describing a very specific set of relationships within the noble and knightly classes of medieval Europe, feudalism is convenient, but the word should only be used with great circumspection.

Michael Prestwich
University of Durham

Reference

Bloch, M. (1961 [1939–40]) *Feudal Society*, trans. L. A. Manyon, London. (Original French edn, *La Société féodale*, Paris.)

Further reading

Brown, R. A. (1973) *Origins of English Feudalism*, London.

Ganshof, F. (1961) *Feudalism*, New York.

Postan, M. M. (1983) 'Feudalism and its decline: a semantic exercise', in T. H. Aston *et al.* (eds) *Social Relations and Ideas: Essays in Honour of R. H. Hilton*, Cambridge, UK.

See also: capitalism; Marx's theory of history and society.

financial crisis

A financial crisis is defined as a sharp, brief, ultra-cyclical deterioration of almost all financial indicators – short-term interest rates, asset (stock, real estate, land) prices, commercial insolvencies and failure of financial institutions (Goldsmith 1982).

The process of a financial crisis is often described (e.g. Kindleberger 1989; Minsky 1986) as a succession of several phases: a displacement (exogenous shock), a speculative mania (with euphoria, overtrading and excessive gearing), financial distress, and, finally, catastrophe.

First is an exogenous shock to the economic system, some unexpected change that alters profit opportunities and induces changes in investment. It may be outbreak of war, the end of a war, or political revolution. It may be more narrowly economic, such as discovery of a new resource, a major innovation, good crops or bad crops. It can be narrowly financial – the unexpected success of a security issue, conversion of debt to lower interest rates, leading holders to try to maintain their returns in new investments. Whatever the event that perturbs the system, it alters investment opportunities and leads usually to speculation for capital gains.

If the change is sufficiently pervasive, euphoria and overtrading are likely to follow. The objects traded depend on the nature of the shock, and may consist of many things: commodities, stocks, bonds (foreign or domestic), railways, factories, mines, office buildings, houses, land, virtually anything substantial in value. Rising prices lead to further price increases, called 'bubbles'. Success of early investors induces others to participate. As more funds are borrowed, credit becomes distended, interest rates rise, and some marginal buyers may be forced to liquidate. Some, who anticipate that prices of assets almost reached their peak, cash in their gains. Prices stop rising, may level off or may start to slip. There follows a period called 'financial distress', as the confident expectation that prices will continue to climb gives way to doubt. If expectations of a price rise are replaced by expectations of a fall, a financial crisis is likely. A rush from real or financial assets into money drives down the prices of those assets and in acute cases leads to bankruptcy of individuals or concerns still holding them with borrowed funds, and even to bank failures.

Examples of financial crises abound in modern economic history. Among well-known earlier cases are the tulip mania in The Netherlands (1637) and the South Sea Bubble in Britain (1719). During the nineteenth century, the British economy experienced business cycles that recurred approximately every ten years. The great depression that started with the stock market crash in 1929 affected most of the world. (Similarly, 'Black Monday' in October 1987 created a fear for financial instability.)

Examples of significant excessive lending have been loans by international syndicates of banks, notably to Mexico, Brazil and Argentina. This was initiated by easy money in the USA beginning in 1970, and accelerated by rises in oil prices in 1973 and 1979 that increased not only the surplus of oil producing countries as supplier of funds, but also the need for loans by non-oil producing countries as well as the capacity to borrow from oil producing developing economies. Suddenly, interest rates in the US market jumped upward. Accordingly, governments of borrowing countries became insolvent, or at least they claimed to be so.

In the USA, when inflation pushed market interest rates above Regulation Q, the maximum ceilings on the deposit interest rates in the 1970s, the Savings and Loans Associations (S&Ls) suddenly lost saving customers. Deregulation of interest rates was implemented to help S&Ls, but it backfired. S&Ls that were protected by the Federal Deposit Insurance Corporation (FDIC) engaged in risky investments, and more than a thousand of S&Ls went into financial trouble. Eventually they were to be rescued by tax money that was estimated to be in excess of US $80 billion in 1992.

Oriental countries share the incidence of financial crises. For example, a boom in the Japanese economy during the First World War was interrupted by a severe stock market crash in 1920 and a devastating earthquake in 1923. To reduce the unfavourable impact to the credit system, the Bank of Japan extended loans as a lender of last resort and most likely weakened the discipline of the banking sector. The loans extended after the earthquake was not recovered, and triggered bank-runs when the finance minister mis-announced a bank failure in the Diet. These bank-runs and credit collapse are now known as the 'financial crisis' of 1927. After this incident, banking regulation was substantially tightened in Japan.

Incidentally, the relative intensity of disturbances to the financial sector at present, namely in the early 1990s in Japan, is at least comparable to that of the financial crisis of 1927. The current distress stems most likely from the overly expansionary monetary policy of the Bank of Japan during 1987 to 1989 undertaken with the excuse of defending the dollar by policy co-ordination, and the sudden monetary contraction that immediately followed (Hamada, 1995).

Whether financial distress ends in a financial crisis depends on a variety of factors, including the fragility of the earlier extensions of credit, the speed of the reversal of expectations, the disturbance to confidence produced by some financial accident (such as a spectacular failure or revelation of swindles), the regulation of banking industry, and the degree of the financial community's confidence in the central bank's role as a lender of last resort.

Expectations are important. Conventional views (e.g. Kindleberger 1989; Minsky 1986) recognize explicitly the role of irrational expectations and group psychology in critical stages of a financial crisis. People are often motivated by fear, rumour, and panic psychology in critical situations, and accordingly behave differently from what rational expectations economists usually postulate.

Economics of asymmetric information provides models that generate bank runs and financial panic even under the assumption of rational expectations by agents. For example, Diamond and Dybvig (1983) characterize a bank-run situation where the very expectations by the public that bank reserves may drain do indeed realize bank-runs even if there is no fundamental weakness in the business of the bank. In other words, the wrong co-ordination of expectations among people leads the society into a trap of choosing the worst equilibrium among multiple self-fulfilling equilibria.

Whether a financial crisis becomes serious or ephemeral depends to a considerable extent on how it is handled by monetary authorities. One doctrine is that the central bank supports a market in a case of crisis as a 'lender of last resort', a concept fully rationalized in Walter Bagehot's *Lombard Street* (1873).

There is, however, an incentive problem in using a lender of last resort: the more a financial market knows it will be helped in emergency, the more likely it is to take the chances that will land it in one. This is the 'moral hazard' principle in insurance, that the more insurance one has, the less motivated one is to be careful. It is on this ground that monetary authorities usually leave some doubt as to whether they will rescue markets and banks in difficulty.

A financial crisis may be shared in several countries. Propagation of the boom takes place through the rise of internationally traded commodities or securities, through capital flows which increase the recipient's monetary base and induce credit expansion, or through the mere communication of euphoria.

In the world depression of 1929, the crisis started in Germany and smaller European countries when the USA, in its fascination in 1928 with the rising New York stock market, cut off long-term lending to those areas. The stock market crash in 1929 itself was precipitated by short-term capital withdrawals from London in response to the Hatry crisis of September 1929 (Kindleberger 1986).

An international financial crisis requires an international lender of last resort. In the nineteenth century the City of London played such a role, occasionally helped by other central banks when London itself faced a crisis. In the 1929 depression, Britain, financially weakened by the First World War, ceased to act as the international lender of last resort, and the USA (and France) were unwilling to take on the role on an adequate scale.

The USA undertook to stabilize the world economy from the Second World War to about 1971. When the debt crisis reached the stage of distress in 1981 and 1982, the world turned not to the USA but to the International Monetary Fund (IMF). The IMF successfully organized rescue operations from Mexico, Argentina and Brazil on a temporary basis by using its own resources, those of the Bank for International Settlements, and advances from the US Federal Reserve System, and by persuading commercial banks not to halt lending, but in fact to lend more.

Koichi Hamada
Yale University

Charles P. Kindleberger
Massachusetts Institute of Technology

References

Bagehot, W. (1873) *Lombard Street*, repr. 1978 in N. St John Stevas (ed.) *The Collected Works of Walter Bagehot*, London.

Diamond, D. W. and Dybvig, P. H. (1983) 'Bank runs, deposit insurance, and liquidity', *Journal of Political Economy* 91.

Goldsmith, R. W. (1982) 'Comment on Hyman P. Minsky, *The Financial Instability Hypothesis*', in C. P. Kindleberger and J. P. Laffargue (eds) *Financial Crises, Theory, History and Policy*, Cambridge, UK.

Hamada, K. (1995) 'Bubbles, bursts and bailouts: a comparison of three episodes of financial crises in Japan', in Mitsuaki Okabe (ed.) *The Structure of the Japanese Economy*, New York.

Kindleberger, C. P. (1989) *Manias, Panics and Crashes: A History of Financial Crises*, New York.

—— (1986) *The World in Depression, 1929–39*, revised edn, Berkeley, CA.

Minsky, H. P. (1986) *Stabilizing an Unstable Economy*, New Haven, CT.

See also: financial system.

financial system

Financial systems provide society with a mechanism for facilitating trade, a machinery for transferring resources from savers to investors, and a means of holding wealth in a convenient form. Their origin lies in the need for a satisfactory payments system; further development has had more to do with the requirements of savers and investors, of wealth-owners and those who control the use of physical capital assets.

It is these physical assets – lands, buildings, equipment and other assets comprising the physical capital stock – which form the foundation on which the superstructure of the financial system is created. Financial instruments are claims whose value depends ultimately on physical resources (including human capital) or the income derived from them. The institutions within the financial system attempt to divide up or combine these ultimate claims in ways which match their clients' needs. The result in a sophisticated system is a great variety of instruments, handled by a broad and diverse range of institutions and financial markets.

The provision of notes and coins as generally acceptable means of payments has usually been regarded as a duty (or profitable right) of the state – the sovereign, government or central bank. These suffice only for small payments and are nowadays supplemented in even the most rudimentary financial system by banks, which take deposits and make payments by effecting transfers between accounts. Allied to this function is the provision of finance for trade – short term loans to bridge the gap between the dispatch of goods and the receipt of payment for them. Though important, activities associated with trade and payments now tend to comprise only a small part of the activities of financial systems.

Much more significant are activities associated with saving, investment and the ownership of wealth. The financial system enables society to separate the ownership of wealth from the control of physical capital and to ensure that savers and wealth-holders have access to financial assets whose characteristics are attractive to them and differ from those of the physical assets which underpin their value. For example, savers frequently seek safety and liquidity in the asset: they hold, whereas physical assets are durable, liable to lose their value, and difficult to turn into cash quickly; the scale of investment is often of an order which dwarfs the amount available from individual savers.

Financial systems thus facilitate effective capital accumulation. By *intermediating* between savers and investors, financial institutions enable surplus resources to be transferred to those who are able to use them. By *mobilizing* saving from many savers, they provide finance for large-scale investment projects. By *trans-forming* securities, the system allows the risk inherent in productive activity to be concentrated on wealth-holders who are prepared to take it, while others obtain the safe and liquid assets that they want. In a properly functioning system these activities can be expected both to increase the saving which is available for investment, and to raise the productivity of the investment that takes place.

Most financial systems consist largely of *intermediaries* – institutions which issue their own liabilities, and hold as assets the liabilities of ultimate borrowers or of other intermediaries. They fall into three broad groups: banks and other deposit-taking institutions, such as building societies, savings and loan associations, or credit unions; long-term investing institutions, such as life assurance companies, pension funds and investment companies or trusts; and special credit institutions, usually set up by governments to provide long-term finance for particular purposes. These institutions often compete with each other in the market for savings, loans, or both. In addition, most sophisticated financial systems, and some that are not yet highly developed, contain organized markets. These are security markets, such as the Stock Exchange, where long-term securities are issued and traded, and money markets, where short-term deposits and loans are made.

Economic and political conditions are the principal factors governing the evolution of financial systems. Goldsmith (1969) has suggested that three broad categories of systems can be identified, distinguished according to the scale and composition of the economy's financial superstructure. First, in the systems found in Europe and North America up to the mid-nineteenth century, the total value of financial instruments was low, financial institutions accounted for a low share of the outstanding assets, and commercial banks were pre-eminent. Risk-capital was predominantly in the hands of the owners of (comparatively small-scale) enterprises, and did not play a large part in the financial system. The second structure is similar to the first one, and was found in non-industrialized countries in the first half of the twentieth century. But in this case governments and government-supported institutions played a larger part, thanks to the mixed nature of the economies. A similar situation can be found in many developing countries, with government-supported institutions supplying capital for particular purposes. The third category, common among industrial countries in the twentieth century, shows a considerably greater degree of financial development, a higher proportion of risk-assets, and increased diversity among financial institutions. Some (e.g. The Netherlands, UK and USA) have strong long-term institutions supplying risk-capital; others (e.g. France and Italy) rely more heavily on special credit institutions. Socialist countries might be thought to form a fourth category: their financial systems are generally less highly developed than in market economies, with banks dominant among financial institutions.

While the tendency for financial and economic development to proceed in tandem is well documented, the direction of causation is still the subject of controversy. Some argue that financial development is a response to economic growth, others (e.g. Drake 1980), that improved financial facilities act as an independent stimulus. There is probably some truth in both views: financial innovation, in the form of new instruments or institutions, often results from changes in the economy; but, once created, new facilities are made available to others and help to stimulate further growth. Thus, even if financial development seldom sparks off economic growth, there is a positive feedback from the financial to the economic system.

A. D. Bain
University of Strathclyde

References

Drake, P. J. (1980) *Money, Finance and Development*, Oxford.
Goldsmith, R. W. (1969) *Financial Structure and Development*, New Haven, CT.

See also: banking; capital, credit and money markets; credit; derivative markets and futures markets; financial crisis.

firm, theory of

The role of specialization in economic progress was emphasized by Adam Smith. Now specialized activities need to be co-ordinated, either by conscious integration within an organization or through market relationships; the effects of both organizational forms and market structures on economic performance are topics which date back at least to Smith. But few economists have tried to treat the firm simultaneously as an organization and as a component of an industry or market. Marshall (1919; 1920) was one of the few, and business enterprise was at the core of his theory of economic development. The problems of the firm were problems of acquiring, generating and using knowledge: knowledge of production methods, existing and potential markets, and of the ways to construct an organization and to motivate its members to create opportunities for profit. The firm's customers, suppliers and competitors, including potential competitors, at once constrained its actions and provided opportunities to those who had the wit to perceive and the ability to exploit them; those opportunities were enhanced by the development of trade connections. For the analysis

of this complex evolutionary process the methods of static equilibrium offered some useful guidance, but could be misleading if rigorously pressed; there was no substitute for the detailed investigation of particular organizational and market arrangements, in relation to the technical conditions and demand characteristics of each case.

Marshall's successors ignored his advice, and the study of the firm disintegrated. The major activities of firms were defined away by the assumption of fully specified demand and cost functions, and the firm itself became a fictitious person whose actions were completely determined by its situation. The 'theory of the firm' was the label given to a set of exercises in constrained optimization, by which equilibrium price and output were derived for a series of market structures – perfect and imperfect competition, oligopoly and monopoly – and the effects of change read off from shifts in demand or cost curves. Cournot's analysis was reinvented. Robinson's *Economics of Imperfect Competition* (1933) epitomized the triumph of the formal model, and with it the dominance of problems generated within the theoretical structure, for the origins of imperfect competition theory lay in the logical impossibility of reconciling increasing returns (statically defined) with perfectly competitive equilibrium. Both were concepts which Marshall had avoided.

Chamberlin's (1933) conception of monopolistic competition was substantially different. Whereas Marshall had insisted that elements of competition and monopoly were usually blended in practice, Chamberlin set out to blend them in theory, and tried to incorporate both product variation and selling costs within a formal analysis which used the method (though often not the language) of static equilibrium. Despite his limited success, he provided the primary inspiration for the strong American tradition in industrial economics, though some of its practitioners borrowed their welfare criteria from Robinson. Chamberlin's approach was also distinguished by his attention to oligopoly, which steadily increased over the years. His insistence that oligopolistic behaviour (like all behaviour) depends on expectations, and that there could be no general theory of oligopoly because there could be no general theory of expectations, has haunted theorists ever since.

There are many specific models of oligopoly, though it is noteworthy that most restrict themselves either to relationships within the group (as, for example, the dominant firm and kinked demand models) or to the barriers, natural or artificial, against new entrants, and do not attempt to deal with both issues together – an example of economists' aversion to multi-level analysis. Andrews (1949) exceptionally tried to develop a non-formal theory of competitive oligopoly, in which the threat of cross-entry and the desire of managers to show themselves worthy of promotion might combine to ensure good value for the customer's money – especially if the customer was another firm – but neither his methods nor his conclusions were acceptable. However, the situational determinism which is apparently so effective in producing general solutions for other market structures will not deliver equivalent results for oligopoly, and the application of game theory, still heavily dependent on Cournot for its equilibrium concepts, has multiplied the possibilities, without so far encouraging economists to study business practice in order to improve their predictive ability and their understanding.

This failure provided a theoretical opportunity for Baumol (1959): instead of examining a standard firm in different market structures, he proposed to deduce the effects of different managerial objectives in oligopoly. He assumed that a firm's decision makers sought to maximize, not profit, but sales revenue; his lead was followed by Williamson (1963), who proposed a managerial utility function, and Marris (1964), who favoured growth. In all three models, the decision makers were constrained not only by market opportunities but also by their shareholders: in the first two by the need to provide an acceptable profit, and in the third by the risk of takeover. Each model generated some plausible contrasts to the results of profit maximization; yet, despite assuming oligopoly, none attempted to deal seriously with interdependence, and, though invoking organizational factors to justify their choice of managerially oriented objectives, none offered any analysis of organizational influences on behaviour. The firm remained a fictitious person.

In 1937 Coase had argued that firms came into existence when formal organization could undercut the costs of market transactions, but his implicit invitation to examine how and when this might be possible has elicited a tardy and sparse response, which has been dominated by Williamson (1975; 1985; 1986). Most economists (e.g. Alchian and Demsetz 1972; Fama 1980; Jensen and Meckling 1976) have preferred to extend market analysis into the firm, especially through the use of agency and game theory, which give scant attention to the fundamental uncertainties of technology and markets. In a comprehensive and detailed exposition Milgrom and Roberts (1992) focus on the efficient outcomes of free bargaining, effectively implemented and enforced through incentive compatibility. Though Williamson also argues that governance structures are chosen for their efficiency, he believes that bounded rationality often precludes the *ex-ante* assurance of incentive compatibility, and insists that firms make extensive use of hierarchical fiat.

Yet even Williamson has given rather little attention to the actual problems and processes of decision making, which are the focus of what is usually called (in economics) behavioural theory. This kind of theory is characterized by its emphasis on the inadequacy of knowledge, and on the limited ability of people to make use even of what knowledge they think they have. Simon's (1976) proposal to substitute procedural for substantive rationality makes obvious sense at a time of much concern over control systems, information systems, techniques of planning, and the machinery of government. To Simon's (1978) problem of how to decide what to do should be added the prior question of how to decide what to think about – a question which might also be addressed to economists analysing the firm. Cyert and March's (1963) study of short-term decision making has not been widely followed up, but Nelson and Winter (1982) have shown how the approach may be adapted and applied to technical change.

The firm as an agent of discovery and progress is once more receiving attention. It was a key element in Schumpeter's (1943) theory of economic development through 'creative destruction', but Schumpeter is not usually thought of as a theorist of the firm. There has been some interest in the concept of the entrepreneur as the agent of change; although neo-Austrians have so far studied the entrepreneur only as an individual in the market, Casson (1982) depicts the entrepreneur as the creator of an organization, facing some of the problems discussed by Marshall. Meanwhile, studies of innovation and technical change have increasingly recognized the need to investigate how organizational form as well as market structure influences the generation, transmission and exploitation of knowledge, and also the effects of these processes on markets and organizations. For this purpose there is no better definition of a firm than Penrose's (1959) 'pool of resources the utilisation of which is organised in an administrative framework' and no better application of that definition than the historical studies of Chandler (1962; 1977; 1990). The capabilities of a firm reside in its institutions as well as its skills. But these institutions embody the unintended consequences of rational choice: co-ordination, in firms as well as markets, reflects spontaneous order as well as conscious design. Indeed, we may be returning to Marshall's conception of a population of specialized firms generating variety within an evolutionary process. If so, we should remember Marshall's recognition of inter-firm linkages – a theme explored by Richardson (1972) – and the importance of markets as a pool of resources offering variety (Langlois 1992). Firms and markets would then feature as complementary and competitive institutions which both shape and are shaped by the course of evolution.

Brian J. Loasby
University of Stirling

References

Alchian, A. A. and Demsetz, H. (1972) 'Production, information costs, and economic organization', *American Economic Review* 62.

Andrews, P. W. S. (1949) *Manufacturing Business*, London.

Baumol, W. J. (1959) *Business Behavior, Value and Growth*, New York.

Casson, M. (1982) *The Entrepreneur: An Economic Theory*, Oxford.

Chamberlin, E. H. (1933) *The Theory of Monopolistic Competition*, Cambridge, MA.

Chandler, A. D. (1962) *Strategy and Structure*, Cambridge, MA.

—— (1977) *The Visible Hand*, Cambridge, MA.

—— (1990) *Scale and Scope*, Cambridge, MA.

Coase, R. H. (1937) 'The nature of the firm', *Economica* ns 4.

Cournot, A. (1838) *Recherches sur les Principes Mathématiques de la Théorie des Richesses*, Beacon, N.T. trans. (1927) New York.

Cyert, R. M. and March, J. G. (1963) *A Behavioral Theory of the Firm*, Englewood Cliffs, NJ.

Fama, E. (1980) 'Agency problems and the theory of the firm', *Journal of Political Economy* 88.

Jensen, M. C. and Meckling, W. (1976) 'Theory of the firm: managerial behavior, agency costs, and ownership structure', *Journal of Financial Economics* 3.

Langlois, R. N. (1992) 'Transaction cost economics in real time', *Industrial and Corporate Change* 1.

Marris, R. L. (1964) *The Economics of 'Managerial' Capitalism*, London.

Marshall, A. (1919) *Industry and Trade*, London.

—— (1920) *Principles of Economics*, 8th edn, London.

Milgrom, P. and Roberts, J. (1992) *Economics, Organization and Management*, Englewood Cliffs, NJ.

Nelson, R. R. and Winter, S. G. (1982) *An Evolutionary Theory of Economic Change*, Cambridge, MA.

Penrose, E. T. (1959) *The Theory of the Growth of the Firm*, Oxford.

Richardson, G. B. (1972) 'The organisation of industry', *Economic Journal* 82.

Robinson, J. V. (1933) *The Economics of Imperfect Competition*, London.

Schumpeter, J. A. (1943) *Capitalism, Socialism and Democracy*, London.

Simon, H. A. (1976) 'From substantive to procedural rationality', in S. J. Latsis (ed.) *Method and Appraisal in Economics*, Cambridge, UK.

—— (1978) 'On how to decide what to do', *Bell Journal of Economics* 9.

Smith, A. (1976) *An Inquiry into the Nature and Causes of the Wealth of Nations*, ed. R. H. Campbell, *et al.* Oxford.

Williamson, O. E. (1963) *Economics of Discretionary Behavior: Managerial Objectives in a Theory of the Firm*, Englewood Cliffs, NJ.

—— (1975) *Markets and Hierarchies: Analysis and Anti-Trust Implications*, New York.

—— (1985) *The Economic Institutions of Capitalism: Firms, Markets, Relational Contracting*, New York.

—— (1986) *Economic Organisation: Firms, Markets and Policy Control*, Brighton.

See also: competition; corporate enterprise; limited liability; markets; Marshall, Alfred; microeconomics; organizations.

first language acquisition

When infants acquire a first language, they learn one of the most complex skills of their lives and they attain adult levels of skill in many domains by the age of 5 or 6. How do they learn a system that requires mastery of the sound system, a huge vocabulary, grammatical rules, meanings, and rules for usage, as well as articulatory skill, auditory discrimination, memory storage, recognition, and retrieval? What may be innate and what learned in this complex task has long intrigued psychologists, linguists and philosophers (Bloom 1993). In their efforts to answer this question, researchers have kept records of how children advance from babbling, to words, to complex utterances. Since the 1960s, they have paid increased attention to the acquisition of different languages (Slobin 1985; 1991) and to the stages children go through.

Children hear language all around them. Adults display for them the syntactic structures and also demonstrate how words partition conceptual spaces (Slobin 1985; 1991). Adults offer essential information about the conventions of the language being acquired, and often direct children's attention by repeating, rewording, and re-casting child utterances into conventional forms.

When children start to produce words (anywhere from 12 to 18 months), they usually use just one at a time. But soon they begin to combine two or more, moving from utterances like *Raisin* to *More raisin* to *Me want raisin* (Brown 1973). Their early nouns pick out objects, often in such roles as agent, patient, or location. They mark what is 'given' and what 'new' in the conversation, and also grammatical relations like Subject-of and Direct-Object-of.

To do this, children need to learn how to modulate the meanings of nouns and verbs. In English, they can add a plural *-s* ending to nouns, for example, and mark limited duration (*-ing*) or past (*-ed*), on verbs. In more highly inflected languages, they may learn case and gender endings for nouns and adjectives, and verb endings to mark tense, aspect, person and number. Such inflections show which pieces of an utterance belong together and, for instance, which noun agrees with the verb. To learn inflections, children must identify stems and endings in words, and the meanings of each, together with any variants in form. For example, the plural of *cat* in English is pronounced [kats] (with an 's') while the plural of *dog* is [dogz] (with a 'z'). Learning variants takes time.

In addition, some common words are irregular. Compare regular *cat/cats* or *dog/dogs* with *mouse/mice*, *child/children* or *sheep/sheep*; or regular *jump/jumped* or *look/looked* with *go/went*, *sit/sat* or *bring/brought*. Children are pattern makers; they regularize irregulars to produce plurals like *foots* and *mans*, and past tense verbs like *comed*, *buyed* and *hitted*, before learning the irregular forms (Bloom 1993; Brown 1973; Clark 1993).

Most children produce word combinations and inflections by age 2–2½. In the next few months, they elaborate their utterances: they add demonstratives, articles and quantifiers (*that, the, some*); adjectives (*stuck, wet*); auxiliary and modal verbs (*do, be, can, will*). They add adverbs and prepositional phrases (*there, in the cupboard; loudly, in a hurry*); adverbial clauses (*They were tired WHEN THEY GOT HOME*); relative clauses (*the boy WHO WAS WATCHING THEM*); and complements (*They wanted TO RUN AWAY, She said THAT SHE WAS COMING*) (Bloom 1993). But acquiring syntax takes time. Many early elaborations omit the appropriate conjunctions (*before, while*) and complementizers (*that, to*), or contain the wrong one for the meaning intended.

Acquisition of vocabulary is a major ingredient in language. Children learn words very rapidly, moving from a vocabulary of 100–400 words at age 2 to around 14,000 by age 6. By the time they are adults, they may have up to 50,000 at their disposal. During acquisition, children identify word-forms and map meanings on to them (Bloom 1993; Clark 1993). They analyse complex words into their component parts (*pram-pusher > pram+push+er, blackness > black + ness*), and use these, when needed, to coin words with new meanings (*to scale* for adult 'weigh', *sander* for one who grinds pepper, or *far-see-er* for 'telescope'). Such coinages emerge from about age 2 onwards to fill gaps in the child's current vocabulary (Clark 1993).

Words work only if they are recognized, and children try hard to produce recognizable forms. While their earliest words may bear little resemblance to adult forms ([ga] for *squirrel*), by age 3, much of what children say is readily understood. But to get words right, children need to listen and store what they hear, hone their articulatory skills and identify the relevant sounds in each word attempted. When they produce words, they must match adult versions (stored in memory), moving closer with practice, for example, from simple consonant–vowel combinations (e.g. [do] for *dog*), to adding final consonants (e.g. [dog]), and mastering consonant clusters (e.g. from [kai] to [krai], for *cry*) (Ferguson *et al.* 1992).

Learning the structure of a language is only one side of acquisition. Children must also learn how to *use* language appropriately. They need to know how to make requests and what counts as polite (Andersen 1990). By age 4, many children distinguish among *Give me some cake, Can I have some cake?, Could I have some cake please?*, and *That cake looks very good, doesn't it?* As their knowledge of form and meaning expands, they also try out other language skills such as story-telling (Berman and Slobin 1994).

Finally, children seem to learn two languages just as easily as one (McLaughlin 1984). But the point at which they start on the second makes a difference. The earlier they start, the more acquisition of the second looks like acquisition of the first. How well a second language is learned also depends on the social value it carries in the community.

Eve V. Clark
Stanford University

References

Andersen, E. S. (1990) *Speaking with Style: The Sociolinguistic Skills of Children*, London.

Berman, R. A. and Slobin, D. I. (1994) *Relating Events in Narrative: A Crosslinguistic Developmental Study*, Hillsdale, NJ.

Bloom, P. (ed.) (1993) *Language Acquisition: Core Readings*, Hemel Hempstead.

Brown, R. W. (1973) *A First Language: The Early Stages*, Cambridge, MA.

Clark, E. V. (1993) *The Lexicon in Acquisition*, Cambridge, UK.

Ferguson, C. A., Menn, L. and Stoel-Gammon, C. (eds) (1992) *Phonological Development: Theories, Research, Implications*, Timonium, MD.

McLaughlin, B. (1984) *Second-language Acquisition in Childhood*, 2 vols, Hillsdale, NJ.

Slobin, D. I. (ed.) (1985; 1991) *The Crosslinguistic Study of Language Acquisition*, 3 vols, Hillsdale, NJ.

See also: developmental psychology; language; learning.

folklore and myth

The discipline of folklore was given its name by William Thoms only in 1846, but its origins go back to the beginning of the nineteenth century. It was a product of an intellectual movement opposed to the philosophy of the Enlightenment and associated with pre-Romanticism and, especially in Germany, with *Sturm und Drang*.

The publication in 1760 of James MacPherson's *Fragments of Ancient Poetry Collected in the Highlands of Scotland and Translated from the Gaelic or Erse Language* caused shock-waves throughout Europe. The Celtic bard Ossian was regarded as a Nordic Homer. The modern sensibility welcomed a poetry which, while ignorant of formal rules, was original, authentic and bursting with energy. The success of Ossian's poems was both profound and enduring, although it was gradually established that they were the work of MacPherson himself.

J. G. Herder, the spokesman for *Sturm und Drang* in Germany, provided the conceptual basis for the academic study of folklore. Popular poetry was an emanation of the popular spirit. Various cultures, which were 'equal in necessity, equal in originality, equal in value, equal in happiness' functioned in an organic manner.

The next generation developed these ideas. For the brothers Grimm, there was no question but that popular cultural products, stories, legends, *lieder*, beliefs and customary law shared the same source as mythology itself. They were various forms, perhaps modified in the course of history, of natural poetry (*Naturpoesie*). This poetry was born and evolved in an organic unconscious fashion in the human spirit. Its creation and functioning were controlled by the same mechanisms as those which ordained living organisms or natural phenomena, or, more to the point, human language. This ancient poetry was the product not of invention but of divine revelation. In time it generated a variety of epics, legends and stories. While it may sometimes be convenient to distinguish these genres of popular literature, they may equally legitimately be merged with each other since their content is the same – they all participate in the nature of myths. In the preface to the 1819 edition of *Kinder- und Hausmärchen*, the Grimms suggested that the ancient German myths could be recognized in the surviving folktales. In the postscript to the 1857 edition, Wilhelm Grimm expressed the same idea with greater precision. The stories were survivals, (the debris), of ancient beliefs which are figuratively expressed in them, and which are to be identified, however fictionalized, in the motifs of a performance. The mythical content fragments, because the story is a living organism. Continually evolving, it sheds beliefs which are no longer comprehensible, and integrates new elements. However, the further back one goes in time, the more the mythical element (*das Mythische*) predominates, until it constitutes the essence or sole foundation. This mythical context, which is retained in a fragmentary form in the stories, satisfies our taste for the extraordinary, the marvellous. It accounts for a certain category of stories (nos 300–749 in Aarne-Thompson's typology) in which mythical features are presented in a figurative fashion, in and through the narrative.

This conception of the nature of the popular story and of folklore more generally was accepted by scholars in the nineteenth and early twentieth centuries. Stories developed out of ancient myths and tended to erode as, with the passage of time, they were distanced from their ancient source in natural poetry. The scholars of the nineteenth century regarded folklore as a product of the degeneration of myths, which eroded and degenerated over the centuries. One had to trace them back in order to discover their pure and noble structure.

The concern of scholars was consequently with the mode of degeneration (or 'devolution', to use the expression of Dundes 1975) from myth to folklore. The English school, represented by Tylor (1871) and Lang (1884; 1887), developed the idea of 'survivals' in an evolutionist perspective. Survivals were the remains of dead civilizations which persisted in a living culture in the form of beliefs, practices, rituals or tales. The idea was accepted in France, where Sébillot (1908) wrote of 'contemporary paganism' and Saintyves (1923) congratulated the anthropologists for providing scholars with 'the historico-scientific notion of survivals', permitting them to recognize in popular stories commentaries on rituals which had fallen into disuse. As late as 1928, V. Propp took the view that rites, myths, the forms of primitive thought, and certain social institutions were anterior to particular stories and provided the means for their interpretation.

Modern scholars have abandoned this 'archaic illusion', which is ideological in nature, but without investigating its rationale or its origin. In consequence, they have instituted a radical distinction between myth and folklore, limiting themselves to the collection of items of folklore or to the study of their social function, and applying both to myths and to popular stories formalist methods which pass over questions of content. Yet it is surely the case that folkloric products may have a mythic content, even though this may be masked by superficial and formal features. This presence of the 'mythic' is not the consequence of what Lévi-Strauss (1952) called 'historical viscosity'. Folklore retains its functions, especially the permanent necessity of transmitting myth, by whatever means.

Nicole Belmont
Ecole des Hautes Etudes en Sciences Sociales

References

Dundes, A. (1975) *Analytic Essays in Folklore*, The Hague.
Grimm, J. and Grimm, W. (1819; 1857) *Kinder-und Hausmärchen*, Berlin.
Lang, A. (1884) *Custom and Myth*, London.
—— (1887) *Myth, Ritual and Religion*, London.
Lévi-Strauss, C. (1952) 'Le Père Noël supplicié', *Les Temps Modernes* 77.
Propp, V. (1908 [1928]) *Morphology of the Folktale*, Austin, TX.
Saintyves, P. (1923) *Les Contes de Perrault et les récits parallèles*, Paris.

Sebillot, P. (1908) *Le Paganisme contemporain chez les peuples celto-latins*, Paris.

Tylor, E. B. (1871) *Primitive Culture*, London.

Further reading

Dorson, R. M. (1968) *The British Folklorists: A History*, London.

Dundes, A. (1965) *The Study of Folklore*, Englewood Cliffs, NJ.

See also: oral history; oral tradition.

Fordism

Fordism is generally understood as a post-war affair, often synonymous with the long post-war boom from the 1950s to the early 1970s, and centred largely on the US and European economies. Antonio Gramsci is attributed with the first use of the term to convey something distinctive about the cultural values emanating from the American way of life in the 1930s (1971); indeed, it is the broad vision of Fordism as more than just an economic phenomenon which has tended to hold sway. For many, Fordism symbolizes the arrival of a new type of mass worker, a different kind of mass lifestyle, and the onset of an interventionist, welfare state. Put another way, Fordism acts as a metaphor for *modern* capitalism. The looseness of the term has been reduced, however, by Sayer's (1989) specification of four different senses of Fordism.

The first sense of Fordism takes its cue from the mass production systems pioneered by Henry Ford and his engineers at the Detroit car factory in 1913/14. Fordism essentially refers to a *labour process* based upon assembly-line techniques, specialized machinery, a fragmentation of tasks, and control by management over the line. The influence of Frederick Taylor's form of scientific management is to be found in the standardization of work tasks and the more detailed division of labour, as well as in the use of semi-skilled labour. Where Fordism differs from *Taylorism*, however, is in the use of technology to impose a work discipline upon the labour force, rather than rely upon the reorganization of work.

The second sense of Fordism goes beyond the labour process to include the *economic role* of the mass production industries within an economy as a whole. In relation to their size, Fordist industries are seen to have a disproportionate effect on economic growth through their ability to generate and transmit growth to other sectors, many of which will include small-scale producers. Growth in the car industry, for example, creates a demand for a whole range of inputs, from electrical components to glass fittings and plastic accessories. Such industries may grow by meeting the demands of the mass producers. Equally, the mass producers may generate disproportionate amounts of growth through the economies that arise from their scale of production. Although Fordist plants have high fixed costs, once in place they can realize increasing returns to scale as output rises. They are thus able to exert a dominant role in an economy.

A third meaning attached to Fordism refers to its *hegemonic role* in an economy. This again refers to the disproportionate role of the mass production industries, although in this instance it refers to the influence of the Fordist model outside of the mass production sector. So, for example, the extent to which collective bargaining agreements, rate-for-the-job contracts, or the imposition of managerial hierarchies occurs among small batch producers or even in the public services sector would be regarded as an indication of how widespread the Fordist model had become.

A fourth sense of Fordism comes closest to the notion of Fordism as an industrial era. It refers to Fordism as a *mode of regulation* aimed at sustaining a particular kind of economic growth; namely one that attempts to maintain the balance between mass production and mass consumption. Institutions such as the state are seen as central to the maintenance of such a balance and, in the case of the long post-war boom, the Keynesian interventionist, welfare state is held up as an example of how a mode of regulation may hold together a particular industrial era. Michel Aglietta's account of Fordism set out in *A Theory of Capitalist Regulation: The US Experience* (1979) is perhaps the best known regulationist study of the long post-war boom and, indeed, equally well known for drawing attention to the much heralded crisis of Fordism.

The crisis of Fordism which dates from the early 1970s is said to mark the end of an industrial era and the movement towards a new era based upon more flexible forms of economic organization and production, together with more diverse patterns of consumption and lifestyles. The terms used to describe this shift are neo- or post-Fordism, depending upon which characteristics of the route out of Fordism are stressed. *Neo-Fordism* emphasizes the continuity of the labour process under Fordism, whereas *post-Fordism* stresses a break with all that is Fordism. The hallmark of both, however, is that flexibility is said to represent a solution to the rigidities of an economy organized along Fordist lines.

Such solutions are far from unanimously held, however, as indeed is the notion of Fordism itself. One weakness of the concept of Fordism, noted by post-industrialists in particular, is the inability to see beyond large-scale mass production and to take into consideration the development of the service industries in the post-war period. At root here is the assumption, disputed by post-industrialists, that manufacturing, not services, represents the 'engine of growth' within a modern economy.

John Allen
Open University

References

Aglietta, M. (1979) *A Theory of Capitalist Regulation: The US Experience*, London. (Original French edn 1976, Paris.)
Sayer, A. (1989) 'Postfordism in Question', *International Journal of Urban and Regional Studies* 13(4).

Further reading

Boyer, R. (1990) *The Regulation School: A Critical Introduction*, New York.
Hounshell, A. (1984) *From the American System to Mass Production 1800–1932*, Baltimore, MD.

See also: industrial relations; industrial sociology; Taylorism.

forecasting *see* planning, economic; population projections; prediction and forecasting

Foucault, Michel (1926–84)

Michel Foucault, the French philosopher, was successively a university teacher, professor at Clermont-Ferrand, Paris-Vincennes, and from 1970, professor of the history of systems of thought at the Collège de France.

At first sight – and on account of the title of his chair – one might take Foucault to be engaged in a kind of history of ideas. In fact, he refuses any such definition of his work. His *L'Archéologie du savoir* (1969) (*The Archaeology of Knowledge*, 1972) is directed against the discipline called 'the history of ideas', which he takes to be something like a totalizing overview that rewrites the past in order to produce a unified object of study. In the same book he criticizes certain aspects of his own earlier work: for example, the presupposition of the existence of a 'general subject of history' contained in *Histoire de la folie à l'âge classique* (1961) (*Madness and Civilization*, 1967). In *Les Mots et les choses* (1966) (*The Order of Things*, 1970) Foucault claims that humankind is a modern invention and destined to disappear. Such an opinion might lead us to call him a structuralist, for he takes the idea of *man*, in any sense recognizable to the contemporary reader, to be a product of nineteenth-century structures (in fact, of structures of knowledge or *savoir*). But in *L'Archéologie*

du savoir he had also turned against the structuralist leanings of his earlier writings.

The problem appears to have lain in the use made in those writings of the concept of an *episteme*: roughly, a structure of knowledge or (in his own terms) a 'discursive formation', which determines the manner in which the world is experienced in a given epoch. Can a study of the history of the appearance and disappearance of epistemic formations itself make use of the concept of *episteme* as an *explanatory* tool? If not, what does explain epistemic ruptures and eruptions? Foucault insists that the explanation must lie in 'the regime of materiality', which he then interprets as consisting in the *institutions* in which the material relations structuring discursive events are embodied.

Knowledge therefore has to be explained in terms of institutions, and of the events which take place in the latter – events of a technical, economic, social and political nature. But institutions cannot function without the exercise of *power*. Foucault therefore turns to an examination of the question of power, which, being institutional, is not and cannot be personal in origin or character. Unlike Marxists, however, he wants to study not some mechanical process whereby power in general is explained in terms of economic ownership, but rather what he calls the 'strategies' of power. In order to avoid any semblance of anthropocentrism, he explains that he means by the term 'strategy' not the conscious plan or design of some human individual or group but 'the effect of a strategic position'.

The merely descriptive – and structuralist – notion of the *episteme* is now subordinated to a genuinely historical conception of the eruption of new epistemic configurations, including new sciences, a conception which (as mentioned) is avowedly materialist.

Power, he says, is located in strategies which are operative at every level: they cannot be reduced to the power of, for example, the state or of a ruling class. Power is productive (and in particular productive of knowledge). He talks about a 'microphysics of power', power disseminated throughout the whole of society. There are of course clashes between the multifarious and multi-levelled strategies of power. What is not clear is how the outcome of such clashes and similar processes is to be explained, given that no general mechanism of the generation of power is provided. Foucault has thus been criticized for offering, at the theoretical level, no more (nor less) than a *metaphysics* of power.

This critique does not detract from the interest of the detailed studies carried out by him (often in collaboration with pupils): for instance, his study of prisons and imprisonment (*Surveiller et punir*, 1975) (*Discipline and Punish*, 1977) and of the history of sexuality (*La Volonté de savoir*, 1976) (*The History of Sexuality*, vol. I, 1979).

Foucault's metaphysics of power – if such it is – is in any case, as we have seen, a microphysics. This point is worth underlining in the light of the exploitation made of his work by the so-called 'nouveaux philosophes' (André Glucksmann and others), who have drawn on some of its themes or vocabulary in order to produce a violently anti-Marxist metaphysics of the state – otherwise called a theory of totalitarianism – which reintroduces the idea, rejected by Foucault, of a single centre of power (see Glucksmann 1977).

Grahame Lock
Catholic University of Nijmegen

Reference

Glucksmann, A. (1977) *Les Maitres penseurs*, Paris.

Further reading

Dreyfus, H. and Rabinow, P. (1982) *Michel Foucault: Beyond Structuralism and Hermeneutics*, Brighton.
Foucault, M. (1977) *Language, Counter-Memory, Practice*, ed. D. Bouchard, Oxford.
— (1979) *Power, Truth, Strategy*, ed. M. Morris and P. Patton, Sydney.
— (1980) *Power/Knowledge*, ed. C. Gordon, Brighton.
Sheridan, A. (1981) *Michel Foucault: The Will to Truth*, London.
White, H. (1979) 'Michel Foucault', in J. Sturrock (ed.) *Structuralism and Since*, Oxford.

Frankfurt School

The Frankfurt School refers to the work of members of the *Institut für Sozialforschung*, which was established in Frankfurt, Germany, in 1923 as the first Marxist-oriented research centre affiliated with a major German university. Under its director, Carl Grunberg, the institute's work in the 1920s tended to be empirical, historical and oriented towards problems of the European working-class movement, although theoretical works by Karl Korsch, Georg Lukács and others were also published in its journal, *Archiv für die Geschichte des Sozialismus und der Arbeiterbewegung*.

Max Horkheimer became director of the institute in 1930, and gathered around him many talented theorists, including Erich Fromm, Herbert Marcuse and T. W. Adorno. Under Horkheimer, the institute sought to develop an interdisciplinary social theory which could serve as an instrument of social transformation. The work of this era was a synthesis of philosophy and social theory, combining sociology, psychology, cultural studies and political economy. The results appeared in

its own journal, *Zeitschrift für Sozialforschung* (1932–41), which contains a rich collection of articles and book reviews still worth reading.

The first major institute project in the Horkheimer period was a systematic study of authority, an investigation into individuals who submitted to irrational authority in authoritarian regimes. This culminated in a two-volume work, *Studien über Autorität und Familie* (1936). Fascism was a major interest during the 1930s. Most members were both Jews and Marxist radicals and were forced to flee Germany after Hitler's ascendancy to power. The majority emigrated to the USA and the institute became affiliated with Columbia University from 1931 until 1949, when it returned to Frankfurt.

From 1936 to the present, the institute referred to its work as the 'critical theory of society'. For many years, 'critical theory' stood as a code for the institute's Marxism and was distinguished by its attempt to found a radical interdisciplinary social theory rooted in Hegelian-Marxian dialectics, historical materialism, and the Marxian critique of political economy and theory of revolution. Members argued that Marx's concepts of the commodity, money, value, exchange and fetishism characterize not only the capitalist economy but also social relations under capitalism, where human relations and all forms of life are governed by commodity and exchange relations and values.

Horkheimer (1937) claimed in a key article 'Philosophie und Kritische Theorie' (Traditional and critical theory) that since 'the economy is the first cause of poverty, theoretical and practical criticism has to direct itself primarily at it'. Institute members were convinced that the capitalist economy was driving bourgeois society to catastrophe through its underlying cycle of production, anarchy, depressions, unemployment and wars. They believed that increasing tendencies toward bureaucratization and social rationalization were destroying the features of individuality and freedom which the capitalist system extolled as its prize creation.

Horkheimer (1937) wrote that critical theory's 'content consists of changing the concepts that thoroughly dominate the economy into their opposites: fair exchange into a deepening of social injustice; a free economy into monopolistic domination; productive labour into the strengthening of relations which inhibit production; the maintenance of society's life into the impoverishment of the people's'. The goal of critical theory is to transform these social conditions, and provide a theory of 'the historical movement of an epoch that is to come to an end'.

Critical theory produced aspects of a theory of the transformation of competitive capitalism into monopoly capitalism and fascism, and hoped to be part of a historical process through which capitalism would be replaced by socialism. Horkheimer claimed that 'The categories which have arisen under its influence criticize the present. The Marxist categories of class, exploitation, surplus value, profit, impoverishment, and collapse are moments of a conceptual whole whose meaning is to be sought, not in the reproduction of the present society, but in its transformation to a correct society.' Critical theory is thus motivated by an interest in emancipation and is a philosophy of social practice engaged in 'the struggle for the future'. Critical theory must remain loyal to the 'idea of a future society as the community of free human beings, in so far as such a society is possible, given the present technical means'.

In a series of studies carried out in the 1930s, the Institute for Social Research sketched out theories of monopoly capitalism, the new industrial state, the role of technology and giant corporations in monopoly capitalism, the cultural industries and the decline of the individual. It articulated theories which were to occupy the centre of social theory for the next several decades. Rarely, if ever, has such a talented group of inter-disciplinary workers come together under the auspices of one institute. They managed to keep alive radical social theory during a difficult historical era and provided aspects of a neo-Marxian theory of the changed social reality and new historical situation in the transition from competitive capitalism to monopoly capitalism.

During the Second World War, the institute tended to split up due to pressures of the war. Adorno and Horkheimer moved to California, while Lowenthal, Marcuse, Neumann and others worked for the US government as their contribution in the fight against fascism. Adorno and Horkheimer worked on their collective book *Dialectic of Enlightenment* (1947), which contains implicit critiques of Marxism, as well as fascism and consumer capitalism. Departing from the Marxian theory of history, they presented a philosophy of history that traced the fate of the Enlighten-ment from the beginning of scientific thought with the Greeks to fascist concentration camps and the cultural industries of US capitalism. They showed how western rationality served as instruments of domination and how 'Enlightenment' turned into its opposite, mystification and oppression. The book criticized enlightenment scientism and rationalism, and im-plicitly implicated Marxism within the 'dialectic of Enlightenment'.

After the Second World War, Adorno, Horkheimer and Pollock returned to Frankfurt to re-establish the institute in Germany, while Lowenthal, Marcuse and others remained in the USA. In Germany, Adorno, Horkheimer and their associates published a series of books and became a dominant intellectual current in Germany. At this time, the term Frankfurt School became widespread as a characterization of their version of interdisciplinary social research and of the particular social theory developed by Adorno, Horkheimer and their associates. They engaged in frequent methodological and substantive debates with other social theories, most notably 'the positivism dispute', where they criticized more empirical and quantitative approaches to social theory and defended their own more speculative and critical brand of social theory. The German group around Adorno and Horkheimer was also increasingly hostile toward orthodox Marxism and were in turn criticized by a variety of types of 'Marxism-Leninism' and 'scientific Marxists' for their alleged surrender of revolutionary and scientific Marxian perspectives.

The Frankfurt School eventually became best known for their theories of 'the totally administered society' or 'one-dimensional society', which theorized the increasing power of capitalism over all aspects of social life and the development of new forms of social control. During the 1950s, however, there were divergences between the work of the institute relocated in Frankfurt and the developing theories of Fromm, Lowenthal, Marcuse and others who did not return to Germany, which were often at odds with both the current and earlier work of Adorno and Horkheimer. Thus it is misleading to consider the work of various critical theo-rists during the post-war period as members of a mono-lithic Frankfurt School. Whereas there were both a shared sense of purpose and collective work on inter-disciplinary social theory from 1930 to the early 1940s, thereafter critical theorists frequently diverge, and during the 1950s and 1960s the term the 'Frankfurt School' can really be applied only to the work of the institute in Germany.

It is thus impossible to characterize the Frankfurt School as a whole, since their work spanned several decades and involved a variety of thinkers who later engaged in sharp debates with one another. Rather one should perceive various phases of institute work. (1) the empirical-historical studies of the Grunberg era. (2) attempts in the early to mid-1930s to establish a materialist interdisciplinary social theory under Horkheimer's directorship. (3) attempts to develop a critical theory of society during the exile period from about 1937 to the early 1940s. (4) the dispersion of institute members in the 1940s and new directions sketched out by Adorno and Horkheimer. (5) the return of the institute to Germany and its work in Frankfurt during the 1950s and 1960s. (6) the development of critical theory in various ways by Fromm, Lowenthal, Marcuse and others who remained in the USA. (7) the continuation of institute projects and development of critical theory in Germany by Jürgen Habermas, Oskar Negt, Alfred Schmidt, and others in the 1970s and 1980s. (8) contributions to critical theory by younger theorists and scholars currently active in Europe and the USA.

In surveying the field of critical theory, one observes a heterogeneity of theories, theorists and projects loosely connected by commitment to interdisciplinary social theory, and an interest in social critique and transformation, all influenced by the work of theorists like Adorno, Horkheimer, Marcuse, Habermas or others. Critical theorists tend to be critical of empirical and quantitative social theory and more sympathetic to theoretical construction, social critique and social transformation. It continues to be an active, though frequently marginal, tendency of social theory; thus the legacy of the Frankfurt School endures.

Douglas Kellner
University of Texas

References

Adorno, T. W. and Horkheimer, M. (1947) *Dialectic of Enlightenment*, New York.
Horkheimer, M. (1937) 'Philosophie und kritische Theorie', *Zeitschrift für Sozialforschung* 6.

Further reading

Bottomore, T. (1984) *The Frankfurt School*, London.
Horkheimer, M. (1972) *Critical Theory*, New York.
Jay, M. (1973) *The Dialectical Imagination*, Boston, MA.
—— (1984) *Adorno and the Frankfurt School*, London.
Marcuse, H. (1984) *One-Dimensional Man*, Boston, MA.

See also: Habermas, Jürgen.

free association

The requirement for free association is often referred to as the fundamental rule of psychoanalysis. The patient in psychoanalytic treatment attempts to express in words all thoughts, feelings, wishes, sensations, images and memories without reservation, as they spontaneously occur. Originally, Sigmund Freud introduced free association to assist in the abreaction of traumatic experiences. Later it served him especially well in deciphering the language and grammar of dreams and in describing the vicissitudes of human passion, emotion and motivation. Gradually, as psychoanalysis progressed, free association became the vehicle for elucidation of unconscious conflicts and of the history of their formation in the life of the individual.

Free association replaced hypnosis in Freud's early investigative and psychotherapeutic work in the 1890s. The approach was consonant with his general conviction about the determinism of mental life and the importance of unconscious influences. It served and continues to serve as the principal method of psychoanalysis and of psychoanalytic psychotherapy. The word 'free' in this term indicates relative freedom from *conscious* determination. Unconscious determinants, both those that seek expression and those that oppose it (resistance), can be inferred from the many varieties of sequence, content and form of the free associations. The analyst's interventions, based on a grasp of conscious and unconscious determinants, aim to expand the patient's *freedom* of association mainly through clarification and interpretation, with a concomitant development of the patient's insight. Analysts are guided by their own associations and by the requirement of maintaining a non-judgemental attitude characterized by relative personal anonymity, neutrality and abstinence.

The systematic use of the method of free association leads to the psychoanalytic process (or processes), in which *transference* and *counter-transference* occupy a central position. Free association can be seen to promote continuity in mental functioning – the continuity, for example, of thought, feeling, memory, styles of loving, and sense of self. Discontinuities in these functions and corresponding restrictions in the freedom of association are characteristic of the psychopathology which may be expected to respond favourably to psychoanalytic treatment. In a narrower sense, free association aims to make conscious what is unconscious, to revive lost experience, to expand what is condensed, to express the components of inner conflict, and to put thought and feeling, as much as possible, into words. Although not all of mental life can be put into words, emphasis on the intimate connection between language, reason, consciousness, and the capacity for decision and resolution has been an explicit feature of the psychoanalytic method from the beginning. The considerable variety of perspectives and theoretical formulations with which psychoanalysts perform their work can regularly be shown to relate to these features of the free association method. The implicit tension between the relational and self-observational components of the method of free association are reflected in the corresponding theoretical and technical approaches.

Anton O. Kris
Boston Psychoanalytic Institute

Further reading

Kris, A. O. (1982) *Free Association: Method and Process*, New Haven, CT.
—— (1990) 'The analyst's stance and the method of free association', *Psychoanalytical Study of the Child* 45.

—— (1992) 'Interpretation and the method of free association', *Psychoanalytic Inquiry* 12(2).

Spacal, S. (1990) 'Free association as a method of self-observation in relation to other methodological principles of psychoanalysis', *Psychoanalytic Quarterly* 59.

Wilson, A. and Weinstein, L. (1992) 'Language and the psychoanalytic process: psychoanalysis and Vygotskian psychology, Part II', *Journal of the American Psychoanalytic Association.*, 40.

See also: defences; Freud, Sigmund; projective methods; psychoanalysis; unconscious.

freedom

Freedom is the constitutive value of European political life, in that slaves, lacking freedom, must submit to a master, while free persons, being equal in respect of being free, constitute for themselves a government which secures order by law, and not by the unchecked will of a master. It is on this basis that Europeans have always distinguished their civil societies from the despotisms of the Orient, in which (according to the account commonly given in western political thought) all submit to a master.

Among the ancient Greeks, *eleutheria* was the adult condition in which a free male left behind the tutelage of childhood and took his place among fellow citizens in the public life of the *agora*, ruling and being ruled in turn. For the Romans, *libertas* was the quality of the free plebeian and corresponded to the *dignitas* of the patrician. The concrete reality of freedom for the Romans lay in their intense constitutionality, and their aversion, for many centuries after the expulsion of the Tarquins, to submitting themselves to a king. When the civic humanists of the medieval Italian cities revived the republican ideal, Julius Caesar stood as the man who extinguished freedom and gave Rome at last a master.

Medieval Europe, however, had its own indigenous sources of freedom, derived from both Christianity and from the practices of the barbarians who replaced the Romans. Regarding the situation in which one person rules another as sufficiently unusual to require justification (*omne potestas est a deo* was a common statement of the sentiment), they explored the forms of consent and the constitution of authority with great inventiveness: parliaments, juries, inquests the principle of representation and much else in what we call 'democracy' descend from the civil experience of that period.

In early modern Europe, these monarchical institutions and the classical republican tradition of freedom supplied a joint inheritance, and by no means a harmonious one. In the monarchical tradition, freedom was essentially a condition sustained by public life but enjoyed within the private realm. It came to be defined as a set of rights, which could be distinguished as the civil rights of the subject and the political rights of the citizen. Freedom, argued Thomas Hobbes, is 'the silence of the law', and, in this tradition, freedom has always resided in the ability of individuals, as judges of their own best interests, to order their lives within a structure of rules which are clear, predictable and known to all. The republican tradition, by contrast, took freedom as the moral ideal which identified being fully human with participation in public life. Active citizens, thus understood, were self-determining in that they participated in making the laws under which they lived. This view ultimately rested upon ideal memories of the virtuous and public-spirited cities of the ancient world. From Montesquieu onwards, many writers have judged that modern freedom, which is individualistic, is quite different from the civic freedom of those earlier times, but the ideal of a truly participatory community has never lost its power to influence European thought.

It was Rousseau who most notably elaborated this latter view of freedom, with a clarity of mind which led him to the paradoxical implication that citizens who have been compelled to abide by a law for which they are in principle responsible are being 'forced to be free'. In the extreme development of this view, individuals can properly be described as free only when they act virtuously, which seems, in terms of the modern view of freedom, to be self-contradictory. These two views of freedom are often discussed, following Isaiah Berlin (1969), as the negative and positive view of freedom. The negative view tends to be strongly associated with Anglo-Saxon societies, while continental life is more receptive to the positive view.

The issue is important because the ideal of freedom has become the ratchet of European social and political development. Philosophers and politicians alike make use of slogans and images developed from the contrast between slave and free. 'Man is born free and everywhere he is in chains', begins Rousseau's *Social Contract* (1762), while Marx and Engels end the *Communist Manifesto* (1848) by telling workers that they have nothing to lose but their chains. Hegel argued in his *Philosophy of History* (1837) that a universal freedom has been the great achievement of the modern Germanic world. In the despotisms of the east, he argued, one was free; among the Greeks and Romans, some were, but in modern Europe, all were free. Indeed, within a few decades of Hegel's death in 1831, slaves had been freed throughout European possessions, and also in the USA. Paradoxically, it was in exactly this period that a new type of politician arose – communist, anarchist, nationalist and so on – to proclaim that modern Europe was, contrary to all appearances, the most cunningly contrived system of domination the world had ever seen. This doctrine launched the idea of liberation. But whereas freedom and liberty refer to the removal of arbitrary interferences with the way that individuals govern their lives, liberation was the project of removing *all* conditions thought to frustrate human satisfaction. It stands for a vision of human life in which desire flows freely and uninterruptedly into satisfying action. This is a vastly more ambitious project than that of liberty, and has appealed to a correspondingly less sophisticated audience.

Kenneth Minogue
London School of Economics and Political Science

Reference

Berlin, I. (1969) *Four Essays on Liberty*, London.

Further reading

Barker, E. (ed.) (1995) *LSE on Freedom*, London.
Cranston, M. (1953) *Freedom: A New Social Analysis*, London.
Mill, J. S. (1859) *On Liberty*, London.
Miller, D. (ed.) (1991) *Liberty*, Oxford.

See also: democracy; human rights.

Freud, Sigmund (1856–1939)

Ernest Jones, the foremost biographer of Freud, commented that Freud gave the world an incomplete theory of mind, but a new vista on man (Jones 1953–7). The insights that Freud arrived at and shared with the world changed and developed as he expanded his knowledge and understanding of himself, pursued his clinical work with patients, and broadened his interest in the world of science and letters. The perilous times in which he lived had a profound impact on his personal and professional life.

Freud was born on 6 May 1856 in Schlossergasse, Moravia, a small town in what is now Czechoslovakia (Freud 1959 [1925]). His parents were Jewish, and though he was an agnostic he always maintained his identity as a Jew. The family moved to Vienna when Freud was 4, and he lived there until 1938, when he and his family fled the Nazis to London (Hampstead). He died a year later, on 23 September 1939.

Although the family was not well off, no pressure was put on Sigmund, the oldest child, to seek a career that would be economically advantageous. Stimulated by Darwin's theories, he saw new hopes for understanding human nature. An essay by Goethe, 'On Nature', read at a popular lecture, sparked his interest in becoming a natural scientist and strengthened his desire to go to medical school. Freud's interests in social sciences, human interactions, developmental processes and ancient history were already evident during his childhood and youth; they were later to give richness to the discipline he founded: psychoanalysis.

At the university, he experienced serious disappointments. Yet the fact that his Jewishness made him an outsider seemed to strengthen his independence of mind. In Ernst Brücke's physiological laboratory, where he *was* allowed to work, he found role models he could respect, not only Brücke himself but also his assistants, Sigmund Exner and Ernst Fleischl von Marxow. Brücke asked Freud to work on the histology of the nervous system, which he did before undertaking his own independent research. In 1882, when he had been at the laboratory for six years, Brücke strongly advised him, in view of his 'bad financial position', to abandon his research and theoretical career for a clinical one.

Freud entered the General Hospital in Vienna, where he pursued his neurohistological interests at the Institute of Cerebral Anatomy, published several short papers, and was encouraged by Professor Theodore Meynert to devote himself to the study of the anatomy of the brain.

In 1882 Freud's friend Josef Breuer told him about his work with a patient suffering from hysterical symptoms. After putting the patient into deep hypnosis, Breuer had asked her to tell him what was on her mind. In her awakened state she could not repeat what she had revealed under hypnosis. The major contribution of the case of Anna O. (whose real name was Bertha Pappenheim) was the discovery of a technique that was a precursor to psychoanalytic treatment – free association.

In 1885 Freud won a travelling grant and went to Paris, where he became a student at the Saltpêtrière of the eminent neurologist, Jean-Martin Charcot. Freud's interest in Breuer's work had made him eager to find out more about Charcot's studies on hysteria. Charcot demonstrated quite convincingly the genuineness of hysterical phenomena and their conformity to laws, the frequent occurrence of hysteria in men (contrary to current theories), the production of hysterical paralyses and contractures by hypnosis, and the finding that artificially induced states showed features similar to those of spontaneous attacks that were initiated traumatically. Freud determined to study neuroses in greater depth. Before returning to Vienna, he spent a few weeks in Berlin in order to gain more knowledge of childhood disorders. During the next few years he published several monographs on unilateral and bilateral cerebral palsies in children.

In 1886 he settled in Vienna as a physician, married Martha Bernays, to whom he had been engaged for several years, and became known as a specialist in nervous diseases. He reported to the Vienna Society of Medicine on his work with Charcot, an account which the medical society did not receive with favour. Some of his critics doubted that there could be hysteria in males. In response to their scepticism he found a male with a classical hysterical hemianesthesia, demonstrated it before the medical society, and was applauded – but ultimately ignored. Once again he was an outsider. He was excluded from the laboratory of cerebral anatomy, had no place to deliver his lectures, withdrew from academic life, and ceased to attend meetings of the professional societies.

Freud's therapeutic armamentarium was limited. He could use electrotherapy or hypnotism. Since it became known that the positive effects of electrotherapy were in fact the effects of suggestion, Freud turned his sole attention to hypnosis. With this shift he thus became more firmly committed to psychological rather than organic treatment. He had observed in Paris how hypnotism could produce symptoms similar to hysteria and could then remove them again. In 1889 he went to Nancy where he observed the technique developed by Liébeault and Bernheim which used suggestion, with or without hypnosis, for therapeutic purposes. As he wrote in his autobiographical study (1925), '[I] received the profoundest impression of the possibility that there could be powerful mental processes which nevertheless remained hidden from the consciousness of men.' This was one of the first statements presaging Freud's monumental discovery of the unconscious.

In the early 1890s, Freud attempted to persuade Breuer to renew his interest in the problems of hysteria and to share with the world the discoveries he had made in the case of Anna O. *Studien über Hysterie* (1895) (*Studies on Hysteria*) was the result – a collaborative effort in which Breuer and Freud presented their ideas on the origin and treatment of hysterical symptoms. Freud described the unconscious in detail and introduced two key concepts: that a symptom arises through the restraining of a conflictful affect, and that it results from the transformation of a quantum of energy which, instead of being used in other ways, was converted into the symptom. Breuer described the way in which the technique he used with Anna O. allowed for the cathartic discharge of feelings (abreaction) with symptom relief. Although subsequent clinical research has questioned the universality of the effectiveness of this technique, it was *Studies on Hysteria* that introduced psychoanalysis to the world.

Breuer ultimately left the field of psychological treatment, but Freud, undeterred by the unfavourable reception given to the *Studies* by the experts of the day, pursued his studies of patients. He discovered that what was strangulated in neurosis was not just any kind of emotional experience but those that were primarily sexual in nature. Freud then began to study the so-called neurasthenics as well as the hysterics.

As a consequence of these investigations, he believed at that time that the neuroses, without exception, resulted from disturbances in sexual function.

Freud's study of Breuer's patient, Anna O., led to the discovery of the concept of 'transference', a key to clinical and applied psychoanalysis. In patients' relationships with their analyst, Freud thought, patients re-experience the early emotional relations that they had with their parents. It is the analysis of this transference that becomes the most fruitful instrument of analytic treatment. As a result of his discovery of transference, Freud abandoned hypnotism and began to use other procedures that evolved into the technique used in psychoanalysis today. The patient lies on a couch with the analyst sitting behind. The patient associates freely, and the analyst listens for patterns of transference, linkages, feelings, dreams, and other products of the associative process.

Once he had abandoned the use of hypnosis, Freud came to understand that there were forces which he called 'resistances' which kept certain patterns, linkages, and connections from awareness. An impulse barred from access to consciousness was in fact retained and pushed into the unconscious (that is, 'repressed'), from which it was capable of re-emerging when the counterforces were weakened or the repressed impulses strengthened. Freud considered repression a mechanism of defence, comparable to the flight mechanism used to avoid external conflict. In order to keep the debarred impulse repressed in the unconscious, the mental apparatus had to deploy energy. The amount of energy available for other non-conflicted activities was thereby depleted, and as a result symptoms appeared. The theory of repression became the cornerstone of the newer understanding of the neuroses, which in turn affected the task of therapy.

Freud's early 'topographic model' of the mind separated the unconscious into the preconscious and the unconscious proper. The topographic model was later to evolve into the 'structural model' of the mind, which consisted of the id, the ego, and the ego ideal, or superego.

As Freud investigated his patients' lives, he was struck by the significance of events that had seemingly occurred during the first years of childhood. The impressions of that early period of life, though buried in the unconscious, still played a significant role in the individual's personality and vulnerability to later emotional disturbance. Freud's assertion that sexuality is present from the beginning of life and has a subsequent course of development was a pivotal concept of psychoanalysis and one that evoked a good deal of controversy.

At the time of this discovery, Freud believed that experiences of sexual seduction in childhood were universally the basis of neurosis. The evidence for this was derived from his clinical work. Subsequently, however, he came to realize that the seductions had not actually taken place but were fantasies. That such wishful fantasies were of even greater importance than actual external reality, however, was one of Freud's most significant discoveries.

Freud's ideas of infantile and childhood sexuality became the basis of his developmental theory of sexual progression. Initially, he believed that sexuality is connected with what he called 'component instincts', that is, instincts which are connected with erotogenic zones of the body but which have an independent wish for pleasure. These are usually connected with the vital biological activities necessary for survival. For example, oral activities involve sucking and feeding as well as oral pleasures; anal activities involve excretion as well as anal pleasures; and genital pleasures are related to reproduction and conception. Freud called the energy of sexual instincts 'libido'. In the course of psychosexual development, fixations of libido may occur at various points which may be returned to when later threats force a withdrawal to an earlier level. Freud called this process 'regression'. Freud also noted in *An Autobiographical Study* (1925) that 'The point of fixation is what determines the *choice of neurosis*, that is, the form in which the subsequent illness makes its appearance.'

The first object of libidinal gratification and fulfilment is the mother. Her breasts serve as the source of oral pleasure, and she takes on the significance of the external source from which later confidence, self-esteem, and self-regulation are derived. This relationship with the mother plays a pivotal role in a developmental stage that Freud named the Oedipus complex, after the famous Greek tragic hero. Using the male child as an illustration, and reducing this developmental stage to a simple formulation that did not take into account variations, complexities and consequences, Freud noted that boys focus their sexual wishes upon their mothers and become hostile to and rivalrous with their fathers. This incestuous object choice and its feared and fantasied consequences of genital damage and retaliation give rise to a stage of 'latency' during which the conscience (super-ego) becomes evident through feelings of morality, shame and disgust. At puberty, the earlier conflicts, including the Oedipus complex, may become reanimated. Although Freud's discoveries of the sexuality of children were made from the psychoanalyses of adults, direct observation of children as well as the analyses of children and adolescents have confirmed, extended, detailed and modified his ideas.

Freud also made a major contribution to the study of dreams – their meaning and their use in the thera-peutic situation. In one of his major works, *Die Traumdeutung* (1900) (*The Interpretation of Dreams*, 1913), Freud described his researches on dreams, dream work and formation, symbolism, and his wish-fulfilment theory of the function of dreams.

In *Zur Psychopathologie des Alltagslebens* (1904) (*The Psychopathology of Everyday Life*), Freud turned his attention to slips and lapses of memory. Such symptomatic acts, so common in everyday life, he believed, have meaning, can be explained and interpreted, and indicate the presence of conflicting impulses and intentions. The study of dreams and of symptomatic acts has applicability to both pathological situations and normal healthy mental functioning.

For ten years after he and Breuer parted (1895–6 through 1906–7) Freud worked in isolation, rejected by the German-Austrian establishment. In 1900–2, however, Bleuler and Jung, working at the Burghölzli, a large hospital near Zurich, became interested in psychoanalysis and began to extend the application of Freudian theories beyond the confines of upper-middle-class Vienna.

In 1909, Freud, Jung and Sandor Ferenczi, a member of Freud's circle in Vienna, gave lectures at Clark University in Worcester, Massachusetts. James J. Putnam, a neurologist at Harvard, and William James were among those present. The trip was a success, and marked the beginning of international recognition. In 1910 the International Psycho-Analytic Association was founded, an organization that still exists. Several journals, institutes and societies were organized in Vienna, Berlin, Moscow, New York, Zurich and London.

Although many of the earlier pioneers remained loyal to Freud and to psychoanalysis, some of his followers ultimately left him to found their own movements (for example, Adler, Jung, Reich, Rank and Stekel).

Freud's research continued at an intense pace, but gradually his students and colleagues took over increasingly from him. In 1923 he became ill with a malignancy of the jaw which was to give him pain and anguish for the rest of his life. His contributions to our understanding of art and artists, literature and writers, jokes, the psychology of religion, anthropology, myths and fairy tales, rituals, the emotional aspects of group psychology, philosophy, education, childcare and rearing, and the question of educating non-physicians to be psychoanalysts were some of the by-products of his lifelong struggle to penetrate the science of the mind.

Freud was a brilliant and a learned man, a researcher, clinician, theoretician and writer. Psychoanalysis allowed us to understand what previously was seen as irrational human behaviour from a new perspective. His contributions to psychiatry, psychology, sociology and biology are monumental. The science of psychoanalysis has moved on since Freud's time, correcting some of his errors and expanding into areas that he did not develop. One can only do so much in a lifetime, and Freud gave us so much that it will be many lifetimes before we have fully understood him.

George H. Pollock
Institute for Psychoanalysis, Chicago

References

Freud, S. (1953–74) *Standard Edition of the Complete Psychological Works of Sigmund Freud*, ed. J. Strachey, 24 vols, London.
—— (with J. Breuer) [1893–5] *Studies on Hysteria*, vol. 2.
—— [1900–1] *The Interpretation of Dreams*, vols 4 and 5.
—— [1904] *The Psychopathology of Everyday Life*, vol. 6.
—— [1925–6] *An Autobiographical Study, Inhibitions, Symptoms, Anxiety, Lay Analysis, and Other Works*, vol. 20.
Jones, E. (1953–7) *The Life and Work of Sigmund Freud*, London.

Further reading

Schur, M. (1972) *Freud: Living and Dying*, London.
Sulloway, F. J. (1979) *Freud: Biologist of the Mind*, New York.
Wollheim, R. (1971) *Sigmund Freud*, London.

See also: ego; fantasy; free association; latency period; libido; Oedipus complex; psychoanalysis.

Friedman, Milton (1912–   )

Since 1950, Milton Friedman has been a leader of international monetarism, methodological positivism and traditional liberalism, as well as of the so-called Chicago School which embodies these ideas. He was Nobel Laureate in 1976; his presidencies include the American Economic Association and the Mont Pelerin Society. His best-known book among the general public remains probably *Capitalism and Freedom* (1962), followed by selections from his *Essays in Positive Economics* (1953) and his *Monetary History of the United States* (1963, with Anna J. Schwartz).

Born in New Jersey of immigrant parents, Friedman was trained almost simultaneously in mathematics, economics and statistics (AB Rutgers University, MA University of Chicago, PhD Columbia University). He was initially known primarily as a mathematical statistician specializing in decision theory. His broader interests in economic theory, history and methodology became apparent in university teaching at the Universities of Wisconsin (1949–50), Minnesota (1945–7) and Chicago (1947–77), and dominate his later work. Since his retirement from Chicago, Friedman has been affiliated with the Hoover Institute on the Stanford University campus in California.

Friedman the methodologist believes that the widely ridiculed differences of opinion and advice among economists relate primarily to questions of *what is* (positive economics) rather than of *what should be* (normative economics), and that once the positive questions are satisfactorily answered the normative ones will be manageable. Friedman maintains that questions in positive economics can in principle be answered at least tentatively by comparing (evaluating) the quantitative predictions, which themselves result from alternative 'models' of how the world – or the economy – works. It makes no difference to him whether the basic assumptions underlying these models are or are not themselves intuitively realistic; also, any general case theory, into which wide ranges of alternative results fit equally well as special cases, is untestable and thus of little value.

Friedman's monetarism and his 'modernized' quantity theory of money illustrate his methodological position. He interprets the quantity theory as a theory of nominal income, and as maintaining only that the quantity of money in a country (however defined) is a more accurate determinant of both the levels and changes of that country's nominal income than is the country's autonomous expenditures, in the sense of Keynesian theory. As for the division of nominal-income effects between real income and the price level and, also, as for the precise structure relating money and income, the quantity theory (in Friedman's version) has little to say. We should also note that Friedman has favoured exchange-rate flexibility, whereas most international monetarists prefer a fixed-rate system.

In their *Monetary History of the United States* and related works, Friedman and Schwartz apply their monetary insights to the period since the American Civil War, tracing changes in both price levels and business activity to monetary uncertainties – fluctuations of monetary growth above and below any smooth relationship with the long-term growth rate of the real economy. It contains two disconcerting results. First, the inauguration of the Federal Reserve System in 1914 seems to have made things worse rather than better than they were previously – Friedman favours 'rules', including the pre-1914 gold standard, over 'authorities', like the Federal Reserve Board, as regulators of the money supply. Second, the main explanation for the depth and the persistence of the Great Depression of the 1930s is a series of errors in Federal Reserve policy, whose fears of 'going off gold' permitted the US money supply to fall by approximately one-third over the three-year period following the stock-market collapse of October 1929, without preventing the USA's departure from the gold standard.

Friedman's overall liberal faith in the market as an economic regulator is a matter of 'second best' and does not regard market determinations as utopian. This liberalism arises primarily from Friedman's understanding and interpretation of the record of intervention, extending even to attempts like the US Anti-Trust Laws at enforcement of closer approaches to 'pure and perfect competition' upon an imperfectly competitive market-place. Friedman's negative judgement embraces both the errors of well-intentioned voting majorities and of well-intentioned intellectual meritocrats, along with the errors of tyrants, dictators, and despots. A secondary Friedman argument for the market is the shelter that its anonymity offers to social, religious, racial and ideological minorities doomed to failure so long as success requires employment of licensure by the majority or by the Establishment. At the same time, Friedman's liberal individualism does not go so far as the 'libertarianism' of some other American writers for whom the state is illegitimate and taxation, in particular, is robbery. Friedman's major concession to the contemporary (twentieth-century) concept or distortion of liberalism has been his advocacy of a minimum income below which individuals and families should not be required to fall, but which should replace the myriad of social services programmes embodied in the contemporary welfare state.

Martin Bronfenbrenner
Duke University

Further reading

Breit, W. and Ransom, R. (1982) *The Academic Scribblers*, rev. edn, Chicago.
Thygessen, N. (1975) 'The scientific contributions of Milton Friedman', *Scandinavian Journal of Economics*.
Tobin, J. (1972) 'Friedman's theoretical framework', *Journal of Political Economy* 80.

See also: Chicago School; monetarism.

functional analysis

The terms functional analysis and functionalism are often equated, yet to equate them is to beg a number of questions, is misleading and perhaps even mistaken.

Functionalism is a doctrine which asserts that the principal task of sociology and social anthropology is to examine the contribution which social items make to the social and cultural life of human collectivities; it may additionally assert that to examine social phenomena in this way is to explain why those items occur at all, and/or why they have persisted.

Functional analysis is a method of sociological or anthropological enquiry which consists in examining social and cultural items by locating them in a wider context. This usually means showing how these items affect and are affected by others with which they coexist over time.

From these descriptions it is clear why the doctrine is named functionalism: it claims that cultural phenomena either have uses, and otherwise would not endure, or that they come into being, and then persist, because they are useful. But it is not initially clear why a method of examining cultural phenomena within the context of other such items should be called functional, in the sense of 'useful'. The most obvious reason is that functional analysis has been seen as so necessary to functionalism that the two have been treated almost as one. To explain the function(s) of a social item does itself require locating it within the context of a wider system or subsystem. For example, in order to show that the function of kinship terminology is to express the shared recognition of a set of kinship categories, which are necessary to sustain rules of co-operation, alliance, marital eligibility, succession, inheritance, and so on, one has to examine kinship terms of reference and address in the contexts of rules governing different degrees and directions of kinship interaction. So much is obvious. What is not at all obvious is that the practice of functional analysis also presupposes that the doctrine of functionalism is true: in short, from the decision to locate the use of kinship terminology within the context of its various uses, it does not follow that terminology owes its existence to those uses; it might be equally plausible to argue that the usages are consequent upon linguistic rules.

Here we encounter a second article of faith endorsed, unquestioningly in some cases by earlier functionalist anthropologists: that in the absence of written histories, or other reliable clues to the past, one must assume that some features of the here-and-now must be taken as given and as accounting for others; and that both sets of features are readily identifiable. For example, it would be assumed that the level of technology, the system of ordering economic and political relations through kinship, and the form of that kinship system could be taken as given, and that certain other practices, such as linguistic and ritual norms (symbolic representations) could be explained as functioning to maintain those given features of social and cultural life.

Furthermore, it seems also to have been assumed that the effectiveness of the method of functional analysis attested to the strength of the theory, and that the theory justified the method.

Whether or not the theory could have justified the method, what did justify it were two sets of circumstances in which ethnographers of preliterate societies worked. First, they dealt with societies with no written records and, it was often believed, with no other clear evidence which could illuminate the past and, consequently, the processes whereby the societies' existing features could have developed. Thus it seemed that all that ethnographers could do well was to examine certain existing practices and beliefs in their context, so as to make sense of them in comparison with the practices and beliefs of the societies in which ethnographic reports would be read. Second, they dealt with societies which, unlike their own, were relatively simple and slow-changing and, therefore, in which there appeared to be a high degree of interdependence of the different features of social and cultural life (Cohen 1968).

To qualify the first point, the absence of evidence for recounting reliable histories of certain societies had not inhibited the anthropological precursors of functionalists from constructing histories that were informed either by the theory of evolutionary parallelism or by that of diffusionism. Functionalism and functional analysis emerged in reaction to these so-called histories. Given the reaction against these seemingly untestable theories of pseudo-history and, moreover, their distracting effect on the examination of the here-and-now, it is likely that the commitment to functionalist doctrine was regarded not only as a necessary justification of the method, but also as a rationalized refutation of the two doctrines of conjectural history.

To qualify the second point, it should not be thought that functionalists explicitly acknowledged the greater interdependence of different features of social life to be found in the technologically simpler and smaller-scale societies. Rather, it can be said that the significant degree of functional autonomy possessed by different features of social life in most complex societies is expressed in a language which treats different areas of social and cultural activity as separable, even when they are not altogether separate. This language, fashioned not for self-conscious social scientific discourse, but, rather, for everyday use, was imposed on societies within which such categories were for the most part foreign. Thus, certain activities were separated out by the use of the ethnographers' taken-for-granted language and then shown to be more or less strongly interrelated. But few, if any, such ethnographers recognized that the degree of interconnectedness which constitutes a social and cultural system might itself vary from one such system to another. Moreover, some interpretations of the method encouraged an undue emphasis on the degree and nature of the interconnectedness of social and cultural phenomena in even the simplest societies, and, also, promoted an even greater error in the excessive search for it in more complex societies.

The almost casual equation of method and doctrine by some social anthropologists was highly misleading: the doctrine that functional analysis could also yield explanations of the existence of social and cultural phenomena was in many instances not even demonstrated, and was, in any case, at worst erroneous and at best confusing.

But what use of functional analysis of the here-and-now has ever explained why the Bemba are matrilineal, why the Tallensi have no centralized political authority, why the Nuer have a form of monotheism, or why some Australian aboriginal societies have moeities and others, in almost the same physical environment, do not? While a functional analysis of Nuer feuds might be thought to account for their forms by showing how these forms serve to maintain particular patterns of kin-based alignments, it could hardly account for the segmentary structure of that society. Of course, if one knows that the Nuer have a particular type of segmentary structure, characterized by particular processes of alignment and division, that knowledge might help explain why, if certain other conditions remain constant, that structure tends to perpetuate and to resist transformation into a more centralized type of society. Such an explanation of social reproduction – which could be called an equilibrium analysis, since it shows that the processes which inhere in this type of structure are self-correcting with regard to the non-centralization of power – does not itself rest on any part of the functionalist doctrine.

As philosophical critics, followed in turn by social scientists, have long shown, those explanations of social phenomena which are truly and simply functionalist are seriously flawed: they are teleological in that they account for items by examining their positive consequences in maintaining a wider system of which they are a part; and they reify such systems by treating them as though they were either mechanical or organic wholes (Nagel 1956).

The only reply to such critics is to argue that functional analysis may demonstrate a continuous, circular flow of causes and effects – that is, of so-called feedback processes – which show how a system persists, and therefore explains why particular items are to be found at a particular time and place. But even if this can be done convincingly – and it requires empirical confirmation, not simply an intuitive judgement that coexisting phenomena must interrelate in this self-maintaining way – it hardly attests to the value of a functionalist doctrine. Rather, it illustrates the point that social and cultural persistence may in some cases be explained in terms of 'systemic feedback' or, if one prefers, in terms of benign chains of cause and effect which are at some points recursive.

But, of course, the outcome of such causal chains may not be benign, at least to some sections of a society. For example, the educational systems of (most) industrial societies favour the children of the advantaged, whose environments not only facilitate educational performance but may also strengthen and channel motivations to succeed in it. But, since structured inequalities of performance contradict the principle of equality of opportunity, it could be argued that while the system 'functions' for the advantaged it does not do so for the disadvantaged and, especially, not where the latter are aware of the discrepancy between principle and reality. However, ardent functionalists might show that the system works effectively at creating only a low level of motivation among those who are least likely to succeed and, thus, in this way *does* function to maintain both itself and a degree of wider social stability. It could be said that the symbols of alienation with which the disadvantaged young adorn themselves signify an ill-contained and, perhaps, ill-defined discontent which they occasionally express in more overt fashion. But then one could also argue that those expressive symbols also serve the wider system, and so on (Merton 1949).

But what of those situations in which the working of the system benefits no one? In some circumstances of low, or even zero, economic growth, the institutionalized forms of conflict over income levels and differentials could become so intensified as to contribute to a negative growth rate and to an uneven but overall fall in real incomes. One could argue even here that the seeming dysfunctions of the systems are, after all, functional for it: since the contending parties cannot unite to change a system which no one wants in its existing form, their inactions contribute to its persistence.

What such an example demonstrates is that the term functional, meaning 'useful', pertains only to those circumstances in which the gratification of the conscious or unconscious motives of social actors is (intentionally or unintentionally) facilitated by certain enduring practices, which sustain those motives, and which in turn contribute to the continuation of the practices themselves. No other use of the term can be permitted. Certainly, to refer to social practices as functioning to maintain a system, regardless of whether any groups or collectivities have an interest in maintaining it, is either to state the obvious – that a system persists – or it is to beg the very question that needs to be answered. If the answer is negative, then either the use of the term function creates a self-contradiction or it is meretriciously redundant.

What has been called functional analysis should, in fact, be seen as a particular form of the systems approach in the social sciences. To state that there is a system is to imply that discernibly separable processes interact so as to endure in this state over a period of time. To enquire as to why particular features of that system persist is to locate those features in the wider system. To establish that some social practice, which is part of a system, gratifies the motives of some social members, is to ascribe a function to that practice.

Percy S. Cohen
London School of Economics and Political Science

References

Cohen, P. S. (1968) *Modern Social Theory*, London.
Merton, R. K. (1949) 'Manifest and latent functions', in *Social Theory and Social Structure*, Glencoe, IL.
Nagel, E. (1956) 'A formalization of functionalism', in *Logic Without Metaphysics*, Glencoe, IL.

Further reading

Davis, K. (1959) 'The myth of functional analysis as a special method in sociology and anthropology', *American Sociological Review* 24.

futurology

Futurology is not so much a social science as a social movement that sprang up in Europe and North America in the late 1950s and has since spread throughout the world. Its pretensions are scientific: to predict future developments in society by an intensive study of past and present trends. In this it follows the lead given by the first systematic futurological exercise, H. G. Wells's *Anticipations* (1901). From Wells, too, it takes its strongly technological bias, as reflected in the *chef d'oeuvre* of the movement, Herman Kahn and Anthony Wiener's *The Year 2000* (1967) and *The United Kingdom in 1980* (1974). But beyond this general orientation there is no agreement on scientific method, as revealed by the variety of techniques practised by its numerous acolytes. These range from imaginative, one-off shots, like Michael Young's satirical *The Rise of the Meritocracy* (1958) and Dennis Gabor's *Inventing the Future* (1963), through the civilized speculations of Bertrand de Jouvenel's *The Art of Conjecture* (1967), to the solemn computer-based team reports such as the EC's *Europe 2000* projections, and the Club of Rome's *The Limits to Growth* (1972). A notable contribution from eastern Europe in the latter vein is the report of Radovin Richta's Czech team, *Civilization at the Crossroads* (1967). Somewhere in the middle come the projections and speculations of experts working from their home disciplinary bases, as in the collections edited by Daniel Bell, *Towards the Year 2000* (1968), and Robert Jungk and Johan Galtung, *Mankind 2000* (1969). The centrality of technology in futurological thinking is underlined by the movement's frequent reference to Erich Jantsch's *Technological Forecasting in Perspective*

(1967), which is for many the Old Testament, if not the Bible, of futurology. Other popular techniques include a kind of team game known as Delphi forecasting, where experts revise their initial forecasts in the light of forecasts by other members of the team. The results are understandably not usually very exciting.

Most products of futurology, again following Wells, breathe a spirit of confidence, not to say complacency. They look forward to a 'post-industrial society' or even a 'super-industrial society', where the fruits of applied science have produced an era of leisure and abundance. The basic expectation seems to be that the future will be the present writ large. Some form of extrapolation is the method common to most futurologists, and given that the movement received its main impetus in the prosperous years of the 1960s, it is hardly surprising that the future appears largely as a bigger and better version of the 1960s, above all in the technological sphere. Differences of ideology and values are played down, in the belief that the technological imperative largely commands social systems. Here futurology shows its kinship with certain kinds of science fiction and utopianism; but an added and somewhat spurious dimension of serious science is given by the team and think-tank basis of much of its activities. This has made it attractive to governments, the more especially as it appears to offer the materials for long-range planning, and also because much of the thinking has been about 'the unthinkable', namely the prospect and possibility of nuclear war. Large private corporations have shown interest for the same reasons, and some, such as Shell, Unilever and Xerox, have themselves gone in for large-scale exercises in futurology.

In the wake of the oil crisis of 1973, and the world recession of the later 1970s, something of the gloss has gone off futurological speculation. There has been greater readiness to include the thinking of alternative and radical futurologists, especially those of an ecological persuasion. Groups such as Friends of the Earth, and magazines like *The Ecologist*, can see many of their ideas taken up in mainstream futurological journals such as *Futures* and *The Futurist*. In addition to the physical limits to growth indicated by the Club of Rome report, there has been a new awareness of the 'social limits to growth', as persuasively discussed in Fred Hirsch's book of that name (1977). The world no longer seems quite so amenable to western patterns of development, nor indeed so open to western or Soviet penetration. Fears about nuclear war have revived. The rosy glow that hovered over the millennial year 2000 now carries a more apocalyptic connotation. Futurology has not given up all the hopes implicit in its supposedly neutral scientific enterprise; but it has come to balance these with a greater realization of the limited historical and cultural context that inspired it in the heady days of the 1960s.

Krishan Kumar
University of Kent

Further reading

Clarke, I. F. (1979) *The Pattern of Expectation 1644–2001*, New York.
Toffler, A. (1970) *Future Shock*, New York.
Wagar, W. (1992) *A Short History of the Future*, London.

See also: post-industrial society.

G

game theory

The theory of games is a branch of mathematics devoted to the study of interdependent decision making. It applies to any social situation in which there are two or more decision makers, called *players*, each with a choice of two or more courses of action, called *strategies*; the outcome depends on the strategy choices of all the players; and each player has well-defined preferences among the possible outcomes, so that numerical payoffs reflecting these preferences can be assigned. Games such as chess and poker, together with many social, economic, political and military conflicts which are not commonly thought of as games, possess these properties and are therefore amenable in principle to game theory analysis. The primary goal of the theory is to determine, through formal reasoning alone, what strategies the players ought to choose in order to pursue their interests rationally, and what outcomes will result if they do so.

Although some progress was made by Zermelo in 1912, and by Borel during the early 1920s, the theory was not firmly established until John von Neumann proved the fundamental minimax theorem in 1928. This theorem applies to two-person, strictly competitive (zero-sum) games, in which one player's payoffs are simply the negatives of the other player's. If the number of strategies is finite, and the players are permitted to use randomizing devices to 'choose' weighted averages of their strategies, then each player can adopt a strategy that yields the best payoff given the most damaging counter-strategies available to the adversary. The minimax theorem asserts that these payoffs are equal, and that every game of this type therefore has a well-defined solution.

Applications of game theory in the social sciences have focused chiefly on non-zero-sum games. A famous example is the two-person *Prisoners' Dilemma*, identified in 1951 by Merrill Flood and later explicitly formulated and named by Albert W. Tucker. This game has the paradoxical property that whereas each player has a *dominant* strategy that yields the best payoff against both of the opponent's available counter-strategies, each player obtains a better payoff if both choose *dominated* strategies. A multi-person generalization of this, the *N-Person Prisoners' Dilemma*, was discovered in the early 1970s; in this game, every player is better off if all choose dominated strategies than if all choose dominant strategies. The N-Person Prisoners' Dilemma is a model of many familiar social problems, including resource conservation, wage inflation, environmental pollution, and arms races.

Experimental games have been used by psychologists to study co-operation and competition in two-person and multi-person groups, and economists have applied game theory to the study of bargaining and collective choice. In political science and sociology, game theory has been used to analyse voting behaviour and coalition formation, and numerous other applications of the theory in social anthropology and other fields have been attempted. During the 1970s, applications of the theory to the study of the evolution of social behaviour began to flourish in sociobiology.

Andrew M. Colman
University of Leicester

Further reading

Colman, A. M. (1982) *Game Theory and Experimental Games: The Study of Strategic Interaction*, Oxford.
Von Neumann, J. and Morgenstern, O. (1953) *Theory of Games and Economic Behavior*, 3rd edn, Princeton, NJ.

See also: game theory, economic applications; prisoners' dilemma; rational choice theory.

game theory, economic applications

Game theory is concerned with situations in which several decision makers interact, in the sense that the degree of satisfaction achieved by any one of them depends not only on his or her choices but also on the choices made by all the other players. Situations of this type are referred to as 'games'. Game theory tries to define what would be *rational* in the context of such a game, and it tries to predict the *actual* behaviour of the players.

Games are pervasive in economic life. Examples of economic games are the interaction among employees within a firm, the rivalry among firms operating in the same market, the negotiations between a firm and its suppliers, and the economic policy-making of governments in interdependent economies. The inventors of game theory recognized early that it was applicable to economics, but it was only in the 1980s that game theory became widely used in the field. It is now one of the most frequently used research tools in economics.

Game theory is divided into co-operative and non-cooperative branches, the distinction being that co-operative game theory assumes that decision makers can enter into binding agreements about their strategies, whereas non-cooperative game theory assumes that no such agreements can be made. Initially, it was mainly co-operative game theory that attracted the attention of economists, but non-cooperative game theory has become more important.

To see how game theory can be applied in economics, consider as an example the situation where different firms, competing in the same market, must make decisions about the choice of products, the prices to charge buyers, the extent of advertising, etc. Can firms be induced through competition to make choices that serve the interests of buyers even if this is at the expense of profits? Game theoretic analysis predicts that small groups of firms operating in transparent environments can maintain high profits and evade the forces of competition even if no binding, collusive agreements are permitted. Typically, the firms involved will develop accepted norms of behaviour, with the implicit threat that deviants will be punished through aggressive competitive behaviour. Such punishments are easier to implement in more transparent markets, which suggests that the transparency of markets may not be socially desirable.

Often the terms of economic transactions are not determined through market competition but are an outcome of bilateral bargaining: for example, wages which are negotiated between trade unions and employers' organizations. In this context, game theory has illuminated the precise way in which factors like patience or the willingness to take risks contribute to the success of a negotiator. Negotiators may be advantaged if they can create the impression that they have an alternative option, excluding the other party, should negotiations fail. This threat may not work, however, if it can be shown to lack credibility, for example because such an option would be less desirable than any outcome of the negotiations that could reasonably be anticipated. Game theory has clarified the distinction between credible and empty threats in bargaining.

Other examples of economic applications of game theory range from the analysis of the internal structure of firms to theories of economic policy-making in an international context. One of the major fields of application concerns games in which some participants lack important pieces of information. Beginning in the 1970s, economics has become increasingly concerned with the question of information, and a field known as 'economics of information' has developed, which, for example, studies markets in which goods come in different qualities, and in which buyers cannot observe quality before buying. This may drive high-quality products out of the market, or it may force the suppliers of such goods to make special efforts to distinguish themselves from other suppliers. Game theory has had limited success resolving the problems raised by the economics of information, since the predictions that emerged from its application were not adequately specific. Whether this difficulty can be resolved, perhaps by refining the notions of game theory, is the subject of ongoing research.

Tilman Börgers
University College London

Further reading

Bierman, H. S. and Fernandez, L. (1993) *Game Theory with Economic Applications*, Reading, MA.
Dixit, A. and Nelbuff, B. (1991) *Thinking Strategically*, New York.
Gibbons, R. (1992) *A Primer in Game Theory*, New York.
Rasumusen, E. (1989) *Games and Information*, Oxford.

See also: game theory; prisoners' dilemma; rational expectations.

gangs

The term 'gangs' has been used to refer to groups ranging from 'play groups' (as in 'that old gang of mine') to groups of organized criminals. As a public concern, the term refers to troublesome groups, usually of young people. Controversy over definition of the term focuses on whether to include criminal behaviour and self-identification in the definition of gangs.

Reduced to the simplest terms, youth gangs are *non-adult-sponsored adolescent groups*, that is, groups whose members meet together somewhat regularly, and over time, on the basis of *self-defined* criteria of membership (Short 1990). Identification with a 'hanging' or 'ranging' area typifies *street gangs*, while adult-sponsored groups typically identify with an institution, such as a school, church or agency.

Distinctions between adult-sponsored groups and gangs, and between gangs as a generic category and street gangs constitute the beginnings of a typology of gangs. The need for such a typology is great, in part because media portrayals, law-enforcement strategies and common public perceptions often blur distinctions between gangs that are critical both to understanding and to control of gangs.

Among the most troublesome behaviours associated with gangs, for example, are violence, drug use and drug trafficking. While there is strong evidence that many street gang members use and sell drugs, there is little evidence that street gangs play a major role in drug selling. Successful drug selling requires strong leadership, organizational skills, and cohesiveness, as well as focused efforts on drug sales and avoidance of other criminal involvement, none of which characterizes most street gangs (Klein 1994). While violence is common among both street gangs and drug gangs, among the former it is mainly about status (within as well as between gangs); among drug gangs violence is a means of controlling markets and enforcing discipline among gang members and payment by customers.

A substantial body of research suggests that street gangs become delinquent/violent as a result of, first, conflict with rival groups, often involving competition or conflict over territory or status-enhancing behaviours (e.g. graffiti, dancing or athletic contests); second, definitions or actions of others that push a gang identity on the group; and, third, group processes that create/reinforce group cohesion based on delinquent/violent behaviours. The last often involves individual and group status considerations.

Systematic research on youth gangs began only in the second half of the twentieth century. A complete typology of gangs is not yet possible, and any such attempt confronts a number of daunting tasks, including further distinguishing among a multitude of groups (e.g. 'wilding groups', skinheads, bikers, taggers, stoners, and many others), and specifying the nature of relationships between such groups and adults, which research suggests is of critical importance. A typology of gangs must not be static, because new forms and behaviours among such groups occur frequently. It must provide a basis for understanding changes in gang orientation and behaviour, e.g. how tagger groups become street gangs and how drug gangs evolve from street gangs. We know that such transitions occur – and that previously essentially non-delinquent gangs sometimes become more heavily involved in delinquent behaviours – but we know little about how and why they occur.

The existence and continuity of gangs is heavily influenced by forces external to the gang, including macroeconomic forces. In the USA and in some other countries, for example, the declining industrial base of some cities has resulted in persistent and pervasive poverty in inner-city communities. The impact on young people and on family and community life has been devastating. Among the hypothesized results are that street gangs have proliferated in the USA and are found in some cities in other countries where similar social and economic conditions exist. Many gang members continue gang affiliation well into adulthood, in some cases transforming the youth-oriented quality of street gangs into more economically instrumental gangs. Without systematic, rigorous research concerning the impact of social and economic changes such as these, there is little prospect of greater understanding and control of gangs.

James F. Short, Jr
Washington State University

References

Klein, M. W. (1995) *The American Street Gang*, New York.
Short, J. F. Jr (1990) 'Gangs, neighborhoods, and youth crime', *Criminal Justice Research Bulletin* 5(4).

Further reading

Spergel, I. I. (1995) *Youth Gangs: Problems and Response*, New York.

See also: subculture.

GATT

The General Agreement on Tariffs and Trade (GATT) is a treaty between states (contracting parties) under which they undertake to adhere to specific rules and principles relating to trade policies and to participate in periodic rounds of multilateral trade negotiations (MTNs) to lower trade barriers. MTN rounds have in fact lowered average tariffs substantially, restricted domestic pressures for protection and contributed significantly to post-war reconstruction, growth and globalization of the world economy. From its creation in 1947, GATT has evolved from a replacement for the stillborn International Trade Organization into a pillar of the international trading system. Under the Uruguay Round agreement (1994) it will be subsumed into the World Trade Organization (WTO) in 1995.

The WTO is to oversee the GATT, as well as two further agreements arising from the Uruguay Round: the General Agreement on Trade in Services (GATS) and the Agreement on Trade-related Intellectual Property Rights (TRIPs). The GATT will continue as a separate body concerned with trade in goods, indeed with its range of influence expanded and basic disciplines reinforced.

The influence of GATT has increased steadily over time, as the number of contracting parties (over 120 by 1994 and set to grow further as more developing and eastern European countries join) and as the policy instruments subject to GATT rules have increased. Agricultural and industrial producer lobbies, consumer associations and political parties are concerned with the outcome of MTNs. As a result, GATT and MTNs are the focus of major political debate, national and international, and of the mass media.

There are a number of possible reasons for GATT's longevity as an institution. There has, for instance, been a significant momentum for trade liberalization during much of the post-Second World War era, particularly up until the first oil shock of 1973–4. Memories of the beggar-thy-neighbour policies that were pursued in the 1930s have remained sufficiently vivid. This historical perspective has been reinforced by the experience of the growth of incomes in the major trading nations that accompanied liberal trade policies. Clearly trade liberalization was not the sole factor at work here, but the association between trade liberalization and growth has certainly not been harmful to GATT's status.

The Articles of the GATT unambiguously call for open markets and the use of transparent and non-discriminatory policies so as to foster free and fair competition in international trade. In practice GATT has tended to be a rather more pragmatic and flexible institution. The MTNs have largely ignored at times certain sensitive issues, such as protectionism in agriculture and textiles, or have introduced different treatment for special cases such as the developing countries. Similarly GATT rules have often been broken by contracting countries without GATT trying to enforce its obligations, in order to avoid serious conflict between important members. In large part this has been a reflection of the nature of its relatively small, Geneva-based secretariat, which has had limited power and resources to police the international trading system and has had therefore to serve the wishes of its members, in particular its most powerful members. But GATT has demonstrated a capacity to respond to new challenges and to widen its competence. Initially largely restricted to customs duties, GATT first shifted its attention to other non-tariff measures in the Kennedy Round (1964–7) and now is more concerned with regulating the use of a potentially enormous array of non-border controls (including subsidies, competition policies and anti-dumping procedures) that may be used by national governments to restrict international competition. Following the Uruguay Round and the creation of the WTO, that competence and power to regulate the trading system is likely to increase.

Chris Milner
University of Nottingham

Further reading

Bhagwati, J. (1991) *The World Trading System at Risk*, New York.
Finger, J. M. and Olechowski, A. (eds) (1987) *The Uruguay Round: A Handbook for the Multilateral Trade Negotiations*, Washington, DC.
Hudec, R. E. (1975) *The GATT Legal System and World Trade Diplomacy*, New York.

See also: customs unions; international trade.

gender and sex

The study of gender has its roots in the anthropology of women and for this reason is often mistakenly taken to be solely about women. Gender studies, however, are concerned with the cultural construction of embodied human beings, women and men. They examine the differences and similarities as experienced and interpreted in various contexts, taking this to mean all relationships whether they involve subjects of the same or different genders. Gender has often implied and/or been contrasted to sex, the biologically defined categories of male and female.

Despite the fact that the biologically determining nature of sexual differences had been questioned by Margaret Mead as early as 1935, gender studies began essentially in the 1960s with the growing awareness of the need to 'write women into' male-biased ethnographies. This women-centred approach, the anthropology of women as it came to be known, did not, as Moore (1988) notes, arise from the absence of women in the traditional ethnographies, but was rather due to a growing concern that women and their world-views were not being adequately represented.

In order to redress this imbalance, women's views had to be heard in the ethnographies. It was felt that women researchers, as women, were more capable of approaching and understanding women in other cultures. Underlying this belief was the view, often identified as essentialist, that there exists a universal women's nature: that despite cultural variations, biological sexual differences are stable and pre-social and are reflected in the socially constructed gender categories, men and women.

Many anthropologists felt that this position was untenable. In order to avoid the ghettoization that would occur with an anthropology of women, and equally important in order to surpass past, male-biased theories and biological determinism, they had to develop new theoretical and analytical approaches. They had to shift their interests from the study of women to gender studies, that is, to the study of women and men. In constructionist terms they asked how sexual differences were constituted through social and historic discourse and interaction. The question which remained central to their thesis was why and how women in nearly all societies seemed to experience some form of subordination to men.

One of the first to adopt such an approach was Edwin Ardener (1972). He proposed a theory of 'muted groups' in which dominance was explained as a group's ability, the group often identified with men, to express a worldview while in turn muting alternative, often women's, models. Other authors noted the western bias for language as a means of expression often controlled by men, as opposed to other non-verbal forms of expression such as bodily gestures, weaving and cooking. Furthermore, anthropologists, both men and women, use male models which have been drawn from their own culture to interpret models present in other cultures.

By pointing out that women anthropologists were not necessarily privileged in their studies of women of other cultures, researchers were able to pursue the study of gender as a cultural and sociological construction. Two theoretical approaches can be discerned in the study of the position of women and of gender. The first, influenced by Engels's distinction between production and reproduction and his analysis of the sexual division of labour, took economic relations as central to its thesis (1972). This approach preceded the anthropology of women but later fed into the study of gender. The second based its analysis on the separation between nature and culture, rooted in the works of Freud and Lévi-Strauss.

Marxist-oriented researchers (e.g. Leacock 1972; Reiter 1975; Sacks 1974) associated the subordination of women with the domestic/public dichotomy and the sexual division of labour. This analysis aligned the subordination of women with their exclusion from the public sphere of production and their subsequent relegation to reproductive labour within the household. They sought to explain women's position in society on the basis of women's access to the means of production. This view proved to be too narrow and ethnocentric, its theoretical premises rooted in industrialized, class-based societies. For example, some anthropologists noted that in hunter-gatherer societies where there is no sharp distinction between the public and private domains, the sexual division of labour is not based on

relations of inequality and asymmetry but on relations of complementarity. Other ethnographic evidence showed how women often took part in both productive and reproductive labour. Although the definition of reproduction was expanded in some instances to include social reproduction, the subordination of women was still often linked to their role in biological reproduction.

By contrast, adopting a structuralist approach and in line with Simone de Beauvoir's position, Sherry Ortner (1974) argued that women's universal subordination was a result of their association with nature due to their ability to bear children, whereas men were everywhere associated with the implied superior domain of culture and its production. Michelle Rosaldo (1974), in the same vein, pointed out that women were identified with the domestic domain because of their roles as mothers. She stressed the distinction between the ascribed status of women and the achieved status of men. For Rosaldo, women could overcome their subordinate role only if they moved out of the domestic and into the public, male domain.

These propositions were widely criticized for making too simple a universalisation. For example, in MacCormack and Strathern (1980), the contributors showed that the structuralist dichotomy between nature and culture was a western construct, historically constituted. In many societies, it was noted, this dichotomy was differently constructed and in some it was questioned whether it existed at all. Rosaldo (1980), too, later modified her position noting that the distinction between the domestic and the public could not necessarily be universally applied.

In view of this critique, gender categories and the relations between gender have to be understood in a different manner. Ortner and Whitehead (1981) proposed that gender could be understood as 'prestige structure' and had to be correlated with other systems of social evaluation. Errington (1990), for example, notes that in island South-east Asia, the differences between men and women are not highly marked. This may be due to their social invisibility to western-trained researchers. It might also have to do with how Euro-Americans define power and status. Women in these societies have instrumental power and control over practical matters and money. Yet their economic power may be the opposite of the spiritual power which brings the greatest prestige.

In short, the universals that had been proposed, that is the dichotomy between nature and culture, and its companion, domestic and public, had been questioned and undermined by the ethnographic evidence. Similarly questioned was the universality of such categories as subordination and inequality since these categories were shown to be context bound. Also brought to light were the multiple experiences of women and men, even within the same society. Women of different race, class and ethnic backgrounds did not necessarily share the experiences of white, middle-class women. It also challenged those theories which viewed the categories of women and men as universally given. Gender categories, it was argued, had to be observed and interpreted within a particular time and place.

Of equal importance was that the sex categories, male and female, were increasingly being viewed as presumed rather than proven by researchers. It was increasingly becoming evident that though the distinction between biological determined sex and culturally determined gender had assisted researchers in examining the relations between men and women and in viewing gender categories as socially and culturally constituted, this dichotomy in the end echoed that of nature and culture. Sex, as biologically given and therefore pre-social and causally prior to gender, was being challenged (Caplan 1987).

Social historians, prominent among them Michel Foucault (1978), laid bare the historical construct of sex as a western category. Laqueur (1990) for example notes how recent the two-sex model of Euro-America is. For centuries people held a one-sex model in which women were seen as inverted men. The two-sexed model developed not only in consequence of the dominance of the Cartesian model but also due to the growing power of biomedical discourses (see also Scheper-Hughes and Lock 1987).

In line with Schneider's critique on kinship (1968, 1972, 1984), Yanagisako and Collier (1987) argued that the two different and exclusive biologically defined categories, male and female, are derived from the Euro-American folk model of heterosexual reproduction – the same model underlying concepts of kinship. Therefore, in order to free ourselves from the blinkering category of sex, Collier and Yanagisako proposed that the study of gender should be disengaged from sex; that cultural construction alone should be studied.

Some reacted to this proposition. Errington (1990), for example, makes the distinction between 'sex', 'Sex', and 'gender'. By 'Sex' she refers to a particular social construct of human bodies. The term 'sex' by contrast refers to the physical nature of human bodies, while 'gender' refers to what different cultures make of sex. Given these distinctions she suggests that Yanagisako and Collier have conflated the meaning of sex and Sex. To disassociate gender from sex, that is from physical bodies, would lead to a confusion about what gender means and would simply reaffirm the distinction between nature and culture and the presumed hierarchical relations between them. Rather, the relation

between sex and gender, biology and culture is interactive, the one not predetermining the other.

Yet if sex as a biological category is itself a product of western history, can it exist independently outside of a social matrix? Moore (1994) notes this, taking issue with both Yanagisako and Collier and with Errington. She argues that if the category sex does not exist independently of a social context we can only really speak of Sex in any given society. As is shown by historical studies as well as by ethnographic research (e.g. Strathern 1980; 1988; Wikan 1978), not all societies have two mutually exclusive sexual categories but they do have a model of Sex. Given this, the analytic distinction, as Moore and others note, between sex and gender is no longer clear.

This does not mean that we must necessarily do away with the analytical categories of sex and gender; rather we must explore them further, and examine how they define and encompass one another in different contexts and discourses. Anthropologists seem to be moving towards new ways of understanding peoples' views of themselves and their relations, towards what some would define as an anthropology of identity.

Dimitra Gefou-Madianou

A. M. Iossifides
Panteion University, Athens

References

Ardener, E. (1972) 'Belief and the problem of women', in S. Ardener (ed.) *Perceiving Women*, London.

Caplan, P. (1987) *The Cultural Construction of Sexuality*, London.

Engels, F. (1972) *The Origins of Family, Private Property and the State*, E. Leacock (ed.) New York.

Errington, S. (1990) 'Recasting sex, gender, and power: a theoretical and regional overview', in J. M. Atkinson and S. Errington (eds) *Power and Difference: Gender in Southeast Asia*, Stanford, CA.

Foucault, M. (1978) *The History of Sexuality*, Vol. I, *An Introduction*, Harmondsworth.

Laqueur, T. (1990) *Making Sex: Body and Gender from the Greeks to Freud*, Cambridge, MA.

Leacock, E. (1972) 'Introduction to F. Engels', in *The Origins of the Family, Private Property and the State*, New York.

MacCormack, C. and Strathern, M. (eds) (1980) *Nature, Culture and Gender*, Cambridge, UK.

Mead, M. (1935) *Sex and Temperament in Three Primitive Societies*. New York.

Moore, H. L. (1988) *Feminism and Anthropology*, London.

—— (1994) 'Understanding sex and gender', in T. Ingold (ed.) *Companion Encyclopedia of Anthropology*, London.

Ortner, S. B. (1974). 'Is female to male as nature is to culture', in M. Z. Rosaldo and L. Lamphere (eds) *Women, Culture and Society*, Stanford, CA.

Ortner, S. B. and Whitehead, H. (eds) (1981). *Sexual Meanings: The Cultural Construction of Gender and Sexuality*, Cambridge, CA.

Reiter, R. R. (ed.) (1975) *Toward an Anthropology of Women*, London.

Rosaldo, M. Z. (1974) 'Women, culture, and society: a theoretical overview', in M. Z. Rosaldo and L. Lamphere (eds) *Women, Culture and Society*, Stanford, CA.

—— (1980) 'The use and abuse of anthropology', *Signs* 5(3).

Sacks, K. (1974) 'Engels Revisited: "Women, the Organization of Production, and Private Property" ', in M. Z. Rosaldo and L. Lamphere (eds) *Women, Culture, and Society*. Stanford, CA.

Scheper-Hughes, N. and Lock, M. (1987) 'The mindful body: a prolegomenon to future work in medical anthropology', *Medical Anthropology Quarterly*, 1 (1).

Schneider, D. ([1968] 1980) *American Kinship: A Cultural Account*, 2nd edn, Chicago.

—— (1972) 'What is kinship all about?', in P. Reining (ed.), *Kinship Studies in the Morgan Centennial Year*, Washington DC.

—— (1984) *A Critique of the Study of Kinship*, Ann Arbor, MI.

Strathern, M. (1980) 'No nature, no culture: the Hagen case', in C. MacCormack and M. Strathern (eds) *Nature, Culture and Gender*, Cambridge, UK.

—— (1988) *The Gender of the Gift*, Berkeley, CA.

Wikan, U. (1978) 'The Omani Xanith: the third gender role?', *Man* 13(3).

Yanagisako, J. and Collier, S. (1987) 'Essays towards a unified analysis', in J. Collier and S. Yanagisako (eds) *Gender and Kinship: Essays toward a Unified Analysis*, Stanford, CA.

Further reading

Atkinson, J. M. and Errington, S. (eds) (1990) *Power and Difference: Gender in Island in Southeast Asia*, Stanford, CA.

Broch-Due, V., Rudie, I. and Bleie, T. (eds) (1993) *Carved Flesh, Cast Selves: Gendered Symbols and Social Practices*, Oxford.

Collier, J. and Yanagisako, S. J. (eds) (1987) *Gender and Kinship: Essays toward a Unified Analysis*, Stanford, CA.

del Valle, T. (ed.) (1993) *Gendered Anthropology*, London.

Oakley, A. (1972) *Sex, Gender and Society*, London.

Rosaldo, M. Z. and Lamphere, L. (eds) (1974) *Woman, Culture and Society*, Stanford, CA.

Strathern, M. (ed.) (1987) *Dealing with Inequality: Analysing Gender Relations in Melanesia and Beyond*, Cambridge, CA.

See also: division of labour by sex; feminist theory; homosexualities; patriarchy; pornography; women; women's studies.

genealogies

Genealogies comprise verbal or diagrammatic representations of people's kin, and sometimes affinal, relationships. Their study, especially in relation to other aspects of kinship, has long been important in anthropology.

Interest in genealogies is most strongly associated with W. H. R. Rivers (e.g. 1914). In his fieldwork in the Torres Straits, in India, and in the Pacific, they provided him with both a ready means to understand the relationships between individuals and a means to work out the complexities of relationship terminology usage. The latter was important because of his belief in the conservative nature of relationship terminologies. He believed that embedded in their structures would be clues to the social organization of earlier times, and late in his life he also looked to such terminological structures for clues as to the connections between ethnic groups.

It is important to distinguish genealogical relationship from biological relationship. In anthropology, genealogies are always taken to indicate social relationships, which may or may not be truly biological. They may include, for example, presumed relatives, adoptive relatives, or even fictive relatives. Their extent is determined by what is culturally relevant, but they always include relatives on both sides of a given family; it should be possible to match one person's genealogy up with another to produce a 'map' of kin relationships which connect family to family. It is thus also important for a fieldworker to distinguish a person's genealogy from his or her pedigree. The latter is a subjective account provided by an informant and often emphasizes important kin relationships (such as descent from a unilineal ancestor) over other genealogical ties (Barnard and Good 1984). Thus, genealogies, as anthropologists usually understand the term, lie somewhere between the biological facts of reproduction (whose objective truth is anthropologically irrelevant) and indigenous statements of how individuals are related. The collection of genealogies both employs and helps to verify the truth of the latter.

There are a number of common problems in the collecting of genealogies. Informants 'collapse' them (forgetting unimportant ancestors), treat sibling relationships as genealogically equivalent (especially if they are terminologically equivalent), or claim ties which are not recognized by other members of the community. Where marriages are between close kin, the same person may legitimately be traced as a relative through more than one genealogical tie, and one of these ties (not always the closer) may be given precedence. Widespread adoptions, fictive egocentric kin relationships (like godparenthood), or culturally-specific equivalents to 'kinship' (like namesake-equivalence or age-mate equivalence) may complicate things further. However, in spite of all this, anthropologists generally agree that there is something universal about the 'genealogical grid', which consists of all (or all culturally-significant) relationships through parenthood and marriage, whatever the specific meaning of parenthood and marriage in any given culture. Without the recognition of such a device, the comparative study of relationship terminologies would be impossible.

There is little doubt that genealogies are useful for understanding social structure, and also simply for getting to know the individuals among whom an ethnographer works. Almost invariably, genealogies are more important in the cultures which non-indigenous anthropologists study than in the cultures from which those anthropologists come.

Alan Barnard
University of Edinburgh

References

Barnard, A. and Good, A. (1984) *Research Practices in the Study of Kinship*, London.

Rivers, W. H. R. (1914) *Kinship and Social Organisation*, London.

Further reading

Barnes, J. A. (1967) 'Genealogies', in A. L. Epstein (ed.) *The Craft of Social Anthropology*, London.

See also: kinship.

general equilibrium theory

The motivation for general equilibrium theory is the belief that an economy can be understood only as a set of interrelated markets and that any change, for example in economic policy or in preferences, may affect the equilibrium on all markets. Moreover, the direct effects of a change which affects one market may well be outweighed by the indirect effects on other markets. To be successful as a tool for policy analysis and prediction, an economic model representing such an economy should reflect this interdependence. General equilibrium theory is the study of such economic models.

Walras (1874) is traditionally credited with the development of the first formal general equilibrium model, but there can be little doubt that many earlier economists had appreciated the importance of links between markets. The model of Walras was competitive, so that both firms and consumers treated prices as parametric when determining their behaviour, but relied on a linear production technology. Walras's contribution was to formalize the concept of general equilibrium and to show that the formal model had as many equations as unknowns so that, potentially, it could have a well-defined solution. The model of Walras was developed in the German-language literature of the 1930s around the group of economists led by Menger in Vienna, culminating in Wald's (1936) proof that the model possessed an equilibrium when it satisfied the strong axiom of revealed preference. Essentially, this assumption restricts the consumption sector to act as if it were a single consumer.

Under more general assumptions, but still retaining competitive behaviour, the existence of equilibrium was established by Arrow and Debreu (1954) and McKenzie (1954). That an equilibrium exists under weak conditions can be judged as fairly remarkable and establishes the internal consistency of the model. What is more surprising is that the equilibrium also possesses properties of efficiency. As shown by Arrow (1951), the competitive equilibrium is Pareto optimal and any Pareto optimum can be decentralized as a competitive equilibrium. It has also been shown that the existence and efficiency properties apply in economies with an infinite number of goods (Bewley 1972) or with an infinite number of consumers (Aumann 1964). However, the efficiency properties do not apply when both the number of goods and consumers is infinite (Samuelson 1958). The latter case, which represents an economy that has an infinite future with some new consumers being born in each period and some old consumers reaching the end of their lives, is important in demonstrating that the competitive outcome is not always efficient. The Arrow-Debreu model of general equilibrium has been the basis of countless analyses in economics and has also formed the foundation for modern finance theory (Merton 1990).

When imperfect competition is introduced, the existence of equilibrium can be established only under strong assumptions. Existence results have been given by Negishi (1960–1), Arrow and Hahn (1971) and Cornwall (1977), but these have been undermined by the demonstration of Roberts and Sonnenschein (1977) that economies could be constructed that failed to satisfy the required assumptions. Despite this, imperfectly competitive general equilibrium economies can still be valuable in the analysis of policy (Myles 1989). In the late 1980s a development in the theory of general equilibrium has been the introduction of increasing returns to scale and the proof of the existence of equilibrium when firms operate bounded-loss pricing rules (Cornet 1988).

Gareth D. Myles
University of Exeter

References

Arrow, K. J. (1951) 'An extension of the basic theorems of classical welfare economics', in J. Neyman (ed.) *Proceedings of the Second Berkeley Symposium on Mathematical Statistics and Probability*, Berkeley, CA.

Arrow, K. J. and Debreu, G. (1954) 'Existence of equilibrium for a competitive economy', *Econometrica* 22.

Arrow, K. J. and Hahn, F. H. (1971) *General Competitive Analysis*, Amsterdam.

Aumann, R. J. (1964) 'Markets with a continuum of traders', *Econometrica* 32.

Bewley, T. F. (1972) 'Existence of equilibria in economies with infinitely many commodities', *Journal of Economic Theory* 4.

Cornet, B. (1988) 'General equilibrium and increasing returns: presentation', *Journal of Mathematical Economics* 17.

Cornwall, R. R. (1977) 'The concept of general equilibrium

in a market economy with imperfectly competitive producers', *Metroeconomica* 29.

McKenzie, L. W. (1954) 'On equilibrium in Graham's model of world trade and other competitive systems', *Econometrica* 22.

Merton, R. C. (1990) *Continuous-Time Fnance*, Oxford.

Myles, G. D. (1989) 'Ramsey tax rules for economies with imperfect competition', *Journal of Public Economics* 37.

Negishi, T. (1960–1), 'Monopolistic competition and general equilibrium', *Review of Economic Studies* 28.

Roberts, J. and Sonnenschein, H. (1977) 'On the foundations of the theory of monopolistic competition', *Econometrica* 45.

Samuelson, P. A. (1958) 'An exact consumption-loan model of interest with or without the social contrivance of money' *Journal of Political Economy* 66.

Wald, A. (1936) 'Uber einige Gleichungssyteme der mathematischen Okonomie', *Zeitschrift für Nationalökonomie* 7.

Walras, L. (1874) *Elements d'economie politique pure*, Lausanne.

Further reading

Ellickson, B. (1993) *Competitive Equilibrium*, Cambridge, UK.

Hildenbrand, W. and Kirman, A. (1988) *Equilibrium Analysis*, Amsterdam.

Koopmans, T. C. (1957) *Three Essays on the State of Economic Science*, New York.

See also: equilibrium; markets; mathematical economics; value and distribution.

genetic aspects of mental illness

The idea that 'insanity' may be hereditary is an ancient one, but it was not until the twentieth century that this began to be explored in a systematic and scientific fashion. Two major developments at the beginning of the century allowed this to occur. The first was the rediscovery in 1900 of Mendel's laws of inheritance (which had lain ignored since their publication in 1866) signalling the birth of a new science which in 1909 Bateson called *genetics*. The second was the elaboration of a workable and widely accepted system of classification of mental disorders largely based upon the work of the German psychopathologist Emile Kraepelin. However, from the outset, attempting to reconcile observations on the patterns of inheritance of common mental disorders within families with Mendelian laws proved to be problematic. Although some comparatively uncommon disorders with neuropsychiatric manifestations such as Huntington's disease clearly showed dominant inheritance (50 per cent of the offspring of affected parents showing the disorder), and some forms of mental retardation showed a recessive pattern (25 per cent of the offspring affected when both parents are unaffected 'carriers'), the more severe forms of common mental disorders such as schizophrenia or manic depressive illness showed a more complicated picture. Both of these disorders appeared

to be more common in the relatives of sufferers than in the population at large, but there appeared to be no regular pattern within families and many patients had no known family history at all.

The question therefore arose as to whether schizophrenia and manic depression ran in families simply because of some shared environmental effects rather than through genetic mechanisms. The answer came by researchers capitalizing on an 'experiment of nature' afforded by twins. Identical, or monozygotic (MZ), twins have all of their genes in common as well as sharing a common environment. Non-identical, or dizygotic (DZ), twins share, on average, 50 per cent of their genes and it is assumed, particularly when they are the same sex, that they share environments to roughly the same extent as MZ twins. Therefore if MZ twins are more often concordant (i.e. both affected) than DZ twins for a disorder such as schizophrenia or manic depression, this should indicate that genetic factors are playing a part. The use of twins as a tool for studying the genetics of human behaviour was first suggested by Francis Galton in the late nineteenth century, but the methodologies were not fully worked out until the 1920s and 1930s by Luxenberger and other psychiatrists of the Munich school. These researchers were able to demonstrate higher MZ than DZ concordance for schizophrenia, manic depression and a variety of other conditions. Tragically, the mounting evidence that genes played a part in mental disorders was taken up by the Nazi party and used to support its eugenics policies, eventually leading to sufferers from mental disorder being sterilized or exterminated under the naïve assumption that this would lead to the eradication of such disorders in future generations. Although this was both morally repugnant and scientifically idiotic, Nazi eugenics received some support from the medical profession. The eventual outcome after the Second World War was the eradication, not of mental illness, but of modern psychiatric genetics in the country of its birth. A popular mistrust of genetics generally and psychiatric genetics in particular still persists in Germany.

Fortunately researchers elsewhere, such as the British psychiatrist Eliot Slater and the Dane, Eric Strömgren, both of whom had been Visiting Fellows in Munich, kept psychiatric genetics alive. Twin studies focusing mainly on schizophrenia but also on manic depression, alcoholism and neurotic disorders were carried out deriving their samples from registers. These provided a method of systematic ascertainment (or sampling) overcoming the potential bias of earlier twin studies which tended to oversample the most conspicuous pairs, that is, those who are both monozygotic and concordant. For the first time researchers also attempted to overcome diagnostic biases by using explicit criteria and keeping investigators 'blind fold' to zygosity and the diagnosis in the other member of the twin pair.

The other method developed to separate the effects of genes and family environment was to study those removed from their biological parents early in life by fostering or adoption. The first adoption study of schizophrenia was carried out by Heston in the late 1960s who found strikingly that five out of forty-seven individuals adopted away from their schizophrenic mothers themselves developed schizophrenia. This contrasted with none of fifty control adoptees. Publication of other adoption study results quickly followed, and particularly influential was the work of Kety and others who matched up psychiatric and adoption registers in Denmark and in a series of studies confirmed that the vital factor in predisposing to schizophrenia was having a biological rather than an adoptive relative with the disorder. This took place at a time when 'anti-psychiatrists' such as R. D. Laing were attacking orthodox medical approaches towards schizophrenia, and others, such as T. Szasz, were claiming that the whole concept of mental illness was mythical. Kety was thus provoked to remark that if 'schizophrenia is a myth, then it is a myth with a strong genetic basis'.

Studies using twin and/or adoption methods have gone on to demonstrate a probable genetic contribution to a wide range of disorders, including both typical bipolar manic depression (episodes of mania and depression) and unipolar depression (episodes of depression alone) as well as certain types of anxiety disorders and, more controversially, alcoholism and even antisocial personality and criminality. Research in psychiatric genetics is attempting to move beyond merely demonstrating that a genetic contribution exists to using statistical model fitting techniques to estimate how much of the variance in liability to a disorder can be attributed to genes, to shared family environment and to individual specific environments. Model fitting techniques have also been used to try and differentiate between modes of transmission such as single gene, polygenic (many genes of small effect) or oligogenic (a handful of genes). Such statistical approaches provide a preliminary for the next stage, which is to attempt to localize and eventually identify the genes responsible for mental disorders using the methods of genetic linkage or association. Such methods have been dramatically successful in rarer single-gene neuropsychiatric disorders such as Huntington's disease and familial early onset Alzheimer dementia. The task is much more difficult with more common and complex disorders such as schizophrenia because of uncertainties over the mode of transmission. Nevertheless advances in molecular genetics have provided a nearly complete linkage map of the human genome (i.e. the twenty-three pairs of chromosomes carrying genetic material) which means that it is now feasible to search for markers linked to even complex traits. It seems likely therefore that genes for the more severe types of common inherited mental disorders will be localized within the foreseeable future.

Peter McGuffin
University of Wales

References

Bateson, W. (1909) *Mendel's Principles of Heredity*, Cambridge.

Galton, F. (1876) 'The history of twins as a criterion of the relative powers of nature and nurture', *Royal Anthropological Institute of Great Britain and Ireland Journal* 6.

Heston, L. L. (1966) 'Psychiatric disorders in foster-home-reared children of schizophrenic mothers', *British Journal of Psychiatry* 112.

Kety, S. S. (1971) 'Mental illness in the biological and adoptive families of adopted schizophrenics', *American Journal of Psychiatry* 112.

Krapelin, E. (1904) *Clinical Psychiatry: A Textbook for Students and Physicians* (trans. A. R. Diezendof), New York.

Laing, R. D. (1965) *The Divided Self*, Harmondsworth.

Strömgren, E. (1994) 'Recent history of European psychiatry – ideas, developments and personalities: The annual Eliot Slater Lecture', *American Journal of Medical Genetics (Neuropsychiatric Genetics)* 54.

Szasz, T. S. (1961) *The Myth of Mental Illness. Foundations of a Theory of Personal Conduct*, New York.

Further reading

Gottesman, I. I. (1991) *Schizophrenia Genesis: The Origins of Madness*, San Francisco, CA.

McGuffin, P., Owen, M. J., O'Donovan, M. C., Thapar, A. and Gottesman, I. I. (1994), *Seminars in Psychiatric Genetics*, London.

Tsuang, M. T. and Faroane S. V. (1990) *The Genetics of Mood Disorders*, Baltimore, M.D.

See also: genetics and behaviour; mental disorders; psychoses.

genetics, population *see* population genetics

genetics and behaviour

In the late nineteenth century, Sir Francis Galton collected information on accomplishments, physical traits and occupational status of members of families and began the correlational approach to behaviour genetics. In agreement with the prevailing sentiment of the British establishment, the finding that these characters aggregated in families was used as a biological justification for the social class structure of the time and even for the predominance of the British Empire. Kamin (1974) points out that similar reasoning by American psychologists responsible for the administration of intelligence tests to immigrants to the USA led to Congressional passage of the Immigration Act 1924 which restricted immigration to the USA from southern and eastern Europe. Thus over the past hundred years the issues involved in the relationship between genetics and behaviour have had serious political ramifications.

R. A. Fisher (1918) reconciled particulate Mendelian transmission genetics with the continously varying phenotypes that interested the biometricians. This paper led to the variance-analysis approach to familial data on continuously varying traits, in particular, behavioural characters. The idea is that overall phenotypic variance, P, can be partitioned into contributions due to variation in gene action, G, those due to environmental variation, E, and interactions between genes and environment. Later, animal breeders termed the ratio of G to P the 'heritability' of the trait. The sense in which animal breeders used heritability was as an index of amenability to selective breeding. Of course, this is inappropriate in the context of human behaviour, and in this context it unfortunately developed the connotation of an index of biological determination and refractivity to environmental intervention.

The use of heritability in situations where experimental controls are lacking has been criticized by geneticists, who prefer to think in terms of the 'norm of reaction'. The norm of reaction for a given genotype is the graph of the phenotype against the environment. It emphasizes the dependence of gene action on the particular environment; a genotype that performs better than another in one environment may do worse in a second. An example is the human genetic disease phenylketonuria, PKU, in which sufferers accumulate toxic concentrations of phenylalanine resulting in extreme mental retardation. Under a diet that restricts intake of phenylalanine from birth, normal mental function occurs. The norm of reaction approach informs us that even if the heritability of IQ were 100 per cent, this would say nothing about its potential for environmental manipulation.

Fisher's approach to the genetics of continuous variation produces expected values for correlations between relatives of all degrees which can then be compared to observed correlations and heritability estimated. In principle the most powerful data of this kind use adoptions and, in particular, identical twins reared apart. Such twins are extremely difficult to find and unfortunately the largest sample, that published by Burt in his analysis of the heritability of IQ, has been shown to be fraudulent. The remaining samples of this kind normally suffer from non-randomness in the adoption procedure. Nevertheless, until about 1970 the estimates obtained using data that included Burt's produced the widely accepted statistic that genes accounted for about 80 per cent of variation in IQ.

Wright's (1934) method of path analysis became the predominant one for estimating heritability. In 1974 this method produced an estimate of genetic heritability of 67 per cent. Path-analytic treatments make allowances for assortative mating and for the transmission of environments within families, that is, cultural transmission. Estimates by Rice *et al.* (1980) and Rao *et al.* (1982) suggest that genetic and cultural transmission each account for about one-third of the variance in IQ. As with Fisher's variance analysis, the path-analysis approach is based on linear models of determination and has been criticized for that reason. Among the other criticisms are that most adoptions are not random, that the increase in mean IQ of adoptive children over that of their biological parents is ignored, and that the estimates of genetic and cultural heritability depend on how the environment is defined and its transmission modelled.

It has frequently been claimed that a high heritability of a trait within a group makes it more likely that average differences between groups, for example, races, are genetic. This is false since heritability is strictly a within-group measure strongly dependent on the range of environments in which it is measured.

In studies of the distribution of human behaviours within families, where the database is not as large as that used for IQ and where the trait in question is a clinically defined disorder, the twin method and the method of adoptions have been widely used. In the twin method the fraction of identical (monozygous or MZ) twin pairs in which both members are affected is compared to that in fraternal (dizygous or DZ) twin pairs. A significant margin in favour of the former is taken as evidence of genetic aetiology. Numerous studies of these concordance rates for criminality, neuroses, homosexuality, drinking habits, affective disorders such as manic depression, and schizophrenia have generally shown greater agreement among MZ than DZ twins. In these studies the twins are usually not reared apart and the role of special environmental influences, especially on MZ twins, cannot be discounted. Other problems such as the mode of ascertainment of the proband, heterogeneity in syndrome definition and variation among the concordance rates in different studies also raise doubts about the efficacy of the twin method.

In the adoption method, the incidence of a trait in the adoptive relatives of an affected adoptee is compared with that in the biological relatives. If the latter is higher than the former the inference is usually drawn that there is some genetic aetiology to the disease. Adoption studies of behavioural disorders from among those mentioned above have generally produced higher agreements between biological than between adoptive relatives. Again the interpretation of a genetic basis for the behavioural abnormality must be viewed with circumspection, since truly random adoption is extremely rare and frequently adoption occurs relatively late in childhood. In none of the behavioural disorders mentioned above has any biochemically distinguishable genetic variant been identified, although research directed at the role of variation in properties of catecholamine and indole metabolism still continues.

The evolution of social behaviour has provided something of a puzzle to natural historians since Darwin. This field of study was subsumed under ethology and behavioural ecology, and until the mid-1970s was relatively immune to the developments in evolutionary population genetics by Fisher, Wright (1934) and Haldane (1932; 1955). The year 1975 saw the publication of E. O. Wilson's book *Sociobiology* in which he not only stressed that social behaviours were similar across the animal kingdom from termites to humans, but also claimed that these behaviours were genetically determined. Ethology and much of behavioural ecology were then subsumed under a new name, 'sociobiology'.

J. B. S. Haldane had speculated in 1932 as to how alarm calls in birds might have evolved genetically but concluded that a simple genetic basis for the evolution of self-sacrifice might only apply to the social insects. In 1955 he foreshadowed sociobiology by asking for how many cousins should one's self-sacrifice be equivalent to that for a brother. These speculations were formalized by Hamilton (1964), who modelled the evolution of a gene, one allele of which conferred altruistic behaviour on its carrier. Altruism here means that the fitness of the altruistic individuals is reduced by their performance of a behaviour which increases the fitness of others in the population. Hamilton arrived at conditions on the degree of relatedness between the donor and recipient of the behaviour that would enable altruistic genotypes to increase in the population. The condition is usually stated in the form $\beta r > \gamma$ where β and γ measure the gain in fitness to recipients and loss in fitness to donors, and r is a coefficient of relatedness. Hamilton noted that in the haplodiploid insects like the hymenoptera his measure of relatedness between sisters is higher than for any other relationship. Since the above inequality is then easier to satisfy than in species where both sexes are diploid, this could explain on a simple genetic basis the evolution in the social hymenoptera of the social caste system with sterile workers. This theory of the evolution of the kin-directed behaviours is now called 'kin selection'.

Hamilton's theoretical analysis was made using a mathematical approximation that allows the allele frequency of the altruistic variant, the altruistic gene frequency, to play the central role. With this approximation the mathematics gives the impression that it is possible to add fitness contributions from all relatives affected by the altruism to produce the inclusive fitness of the allele. It has been shown that inclusive fitness is an unnecessary concept and that the theory of kin selection can be developed in terms of classical population genetic models with frequency-dependent Darwinian fitness differences. Hamilton's formulation contains many assumptions, but when these are removed his theory remains qualitatively true: the closer is the degree of the relatedness between the donor and recipient of an individually disadvantageous behaviour (controlled by a single gene), the easier it is for that behaviour to evolve.

In *Sociobiology* E. O. Wilson extrapolated from Hamilton's theory to posit that the evolution of social behaviour throughout the animal kingdom including *Homo sapiens* has followed these rules of kin selection. Of course this position ignores the general criticism that none of the social behaviours discussed have been shown to have a genetic basis and are certainly not under simple genetic control. Although many behavioural ecologists took Wilson's position in the years immediately following the publication of his book, the difficulty of empirical measurement of relatedness, and fitness gains and losses, as well as technical criticism by population geneticists, have had a moderating effect. Kinship still plays a central role in behavioural ecology, but the explanatory limitations of the simple kin selection theory are now more widely appreciated.

In *Homo sapiens* the position of sociobiology is to minimize the role of learning and cultural transmission of social behaviours. In particular, the human sociobiologists have taken the position that such phenomena as aggression, incest taboos, sex-differentiated behaviours, sexual preferences, conformity and spite have largely genetic antecedents. There is clear political danger in acceptance of this assertion that such human behaviours have a genetic basis. We have the precedent of the politics of IQ based on erroneous inferences drawn from data of dubious quality. Sociobiology adopts a position of pan selectionism in which the terms adaptive and genetic are interchangeable. Cultural transmission, under which the properties of evolution are obviously different from those under genetic transmission, is ignored. Clearly sociobiology tried to claim too much: 'Sooner or later, political science, law, economics, psychology, psychiatry and anthropology will all be branches of sociobiology' (Trivers in *Time*, 1 August 1977). Fortunately, we are all biologists enough to tell the tail from the dog.

Marcus W. Feldman
Stanford University

References

Fisher, R. A. (1918) 'The correlation between relatives on the supposition of Mendelian inheritance', *Transactions of the Royal Society* 52.

Haldane, J. B. S. (1932) *The Causes of Evolution*, New York.

—— (1955) 'Population genetics', *New Biology* 18.

Hamilton, W. D. (1964) 'The genetical evolution of social behaviour, I and II', *Journal of Theoretical Biology* 7.

Kamin, L. (1974) *The Science and Politics of IQ*, Hillsdale, NJ.

Rao, D. C., Morton, N. E., Lalouel, J. M. and Lew, R. (1982) 'Path analysis under generalized assortative mating, II, American IQ', *Genetical Research Cambridge* 39.

Rice, J., Cloninger, C. R. and Reich, T. (1980) 'The analysis of behavioral traits in the presence of cultural transmission and assortative mating: application to IQ and SES', *Behavior Genetics* 10.

Wilson, E. O. (1975) *Sociobiology*, Cambridge, MA.

Wright, S. (1934), 'The method of path coefficients', *Annual of Mathematical Statistics* 5.

Further reading

Cavalli-Sforza, L. L. and Feldman, M. W. (1978) 'Darwinian selection and altruism', *Theoretical Population Biology* 14.

—— (1981) *Cultural Transmission and Evolution*, Princeton, NJ.

Feldman, M. W. and Lewontin, R. C. (1975), 'The heritability hangup', *Science* 190.

See also: genetic aspects of mental illness; population genetics; sociobiology.

geographical information systems

Geographical information systems (GIS) are integrated computer systems for the capture, storage, updating, manipulation, analysis and display of all forms of geographically referenced information. Although this definition stresses software, any successful application of GIS must also include appropriate data, hardware, and personnel. The basic concepts underlying GIS were developed by geographers during the 1960s, but use of complete systems grew dramatically during the 1980s as the costs of computer power fell and workstation computing became commonplace. GIS find application in all academic disciplines in which the element of location in space is important, such as geography, archaeology, land use planning, natural resource management and demography. In industry and commerce they are used in retailing, the public utilities, and local government. Because of the ubiquity of spatial location, it can be argued that GIS will become one of the largest of all computer applications.

GIS differ from standard database management systems and from computer mapping systems in one important respect. This is their ability to answer intrinsically spatial questions such as 'How many people live within 500m of this road?' If GIS were simply 'maps' in computers, they could not answer this type of question. Instead, they consist of a database describing, or modelling, selected aspects of the geography of the real world. Although systems vary, typically this is achieved by holding a number of 'layers', each of which describes some thematically related aspect of the geography, together with computer software tools to link these layers in various ways. Within each layer various approaches are used to describe the geography of interest. It is necessary to know where each feature of interest is, what it is, and how it relates to other, similar, features. Some systems use a *vector* approach in which each feature is described by lines (vectors), each made up of a series of point locations, which are coded into tables in the database. What the feature consists of and how it relates to other features are similarly coded. Vector systems grew out of older mapping programs and are usually used in socioeconomic applications. Other systems make use of a *raster* model to describe each layer. In this the earth's surface is subdivided into small, regular, elements (typically grid squares), and the presence or absence of the feature, or its numerical value, is recorded and stored for every single element. Raster systems grew out of image processing programmes and find most use in resource management and other environmental applications. Most commercial systems implement both of these approaches to varying degrees and provide software to enable conversion between them. Finally, some systems are totally *object oriented*, dispensing with the concept of a single layer and recording instead all the properties of each feature of interest as a single entity. In each case, the volume of data required is likely to be large, and the initial capture and organization of these data forms a major part of the total cost of implementing a GIS.

David Unwin
Birkbeck College University of London

See also: cartography.

geography

Geography is an academic discipline whose main concerns are describing and understanding areal differentiation in the distribution of various phenomena across the earth's surface. It focuses on the nature and interrelationships of three concepts – environment, space and place. This has produced a threefold division of the discipline into physical geography, human geography and regional geography respectively, with the first two containing separate systematic subfields.

As an academic discipline, with a major presence in universities and similar institutions, geography is about a century old. It was introduced, in Germany and elsewhere, to provide a source of ordered information about places; such material was of particular value to the civil services and (especially in times of conflict) armed forces of imperial nations (Taylor 1985). Geography was also promoted as an important subject in school education in a number of countries, to advance both 'world knowledge' as an end in itself and the ideological bases of national views.

With the development of universities as research as well as teaching institutions, geographers sought coherent frameworks for their discipline which would establish them as the equal of scholars in the burgeoning sciences and social sciences. This stimulated a number of proposed definitions of the discipline's content and methods, of which the most notable in the English language were probably Hartshorne's *The Nature of Geography* (1939) and Wooldridge and East's (1951) *The Spirit and Purpose of Geography*. Such prospectuses were largely rejected in the 1960s and thereafter, although the ideas of some of the discipline's founders – notably Paul Vidal de la Blache (Buttimer 1971) – continue to attract interest and support.

For a variety of reasons, some related to the subject's strengths in the relevant country's school system (as in the UK), geography became a very popular university discipline in many countries: to cater for the student demand, large numbers of academic staff were appointed. From the 1960s on these adopted the ethos of the modern university, with its emphasis on research as the base on which degree-level teaching is founded and with research achievement as the major criterion for career advancement. This provided the context for a rapid growth of research output and much experimentation with alternative epistemologies, methodologies and subject matters. Thus geography is an extremely broadly based discipline, and most academic departments of geography are catholic in their subject matter coverage (Johnston, 1991a).

Subject matter and divisions

Areal differentiation of the contents of the earth's surface covers both the physical environment and the many human modifications to that environment created in the struggle to exist and to enhance material and cultural living standards. The various approaches to the study of such areal differentiation have loosely coalesced around three major themes.

Environment

The 'natural' environment of an area comprises the land surface itself (relatively few geographers study the oceans), the hydrology of the water bodies on that surface, the fauna and flora which occupy it, the soils which form a thin layer on its surface, and the atmosphere immediately above. All are linked in complex environmental systems – the flora of an area, for example, influence the climate above it and the formation and erosion of soils beneath. Many physical geographers focus their attention on one aspect of the environmental complex only, however, in their detailed search for understanding its genesis and continual change (K. J. Gregory 1985).

These separate focuses are represented by the various subdivisions of physical geography, with most individuals claiming to specialize in one subdivision only rather than to be generalist physical geographers. Most of the subdivisions are linked to allied disciplines, to which some physical geographers claim more affinity than they do to the rest of their 'home' subject (Johnston 1991b).

Of the subdivisions, the largest is *geomorphology*, the study of landforms at a variety of spatial scales, and the processes which create them. Many geomorphologists pay particular attention to the role of water as a landscape-forming agent, thereby creating close ties with hydrology: others, especially those interested in the longer-term processes of landform genesis, have closer affinities with geologists, whereas those concerned with soils have links with pedologists. Much smaller groupings are those of *climatologists* (with links to meteorology) and *biogeographers*, who focus much more on plants than on animals and so associate with ecologists and botanists rather than zoologists.

Although most physical geographers work within just one of these subdisciplinary groupings, there is increasing recognition of the importance of studying the interactions among the various components of the environmental complex – not least because of the impacts of each on the others, as illustrated by the current concern with rapid environmental change.

There has also been increased recognition of the impact of human occupancy of the earth's surface, soils and atmosphere on the operation of geomorphological, hydrological, biological and atmospheric processes, with consequences for the ability of the environment to sustain human life in the long term if not the short term (Turner *et al.* 1990). This is leading to more team research which combines the various specialist skills.

Whereas the study of the physical environment is almost exclusively the preserve of physical geographers, there has always been some interest in the physical landscape among human geographers, mainly those concerned with the analysis of landscapes as part of the milieu of human life. To some, interpretation of physical landscapes is central to human endeavour, and so popular conceptions of how 'the earth works' (of the hydrological cycle, for example) are important sources of geographical understanding. To others, the concept of nature itself is a social construction and so interpretations of the physical world are part of the ideological superstructure of society.

Space

While physical geographers have focused their studies on the so-called 'natural' environment, the main concern of human geographers has been the occupation and use of that resource base. Land use was a major topic of interest for several decades, at a variety of scales (e.g. the difference between urban and rural areas at one scale and the agricultural use of different fields at another). Much of this work was descriptive, chronicling what was done where, with little attempt at explanation other than through the relationship with the physical environment.

In the late 1950s, the influence of pioneering geographical work in Scandinavia and of spatially oriented studies by economists and sociologists led to the promotion of an alternative perspective for human geography which focused on the spatial organization of human activity on the earth's surface. The goal was a scientific reconstruction of the discipline, whose rationale was to be the identification of the laws of both individual spatial behaviour and spatial patterns in the distributions of their artefacts. Distance is an impediment to human behaviour, because it takes time and costs money to cross space in the movement of goods, people and ideas. In order to minimize such costs, interaction patterns are organized on distance-minimizing principles, producing spatial organizations (of, for example, the pattern of settlements in an area) which ensure least-effort solutions. Human geography was thus presented as a 'discipline in distance', with distance the key concept that distinguished it from the other social sciences: spatial concepts were presented as the discipline's theoretical base (Johnston 1991a).

Numerous attempts were made in the 1960s and 1970s to codify this approach to human geography and its subject matter, and to identify its fundamental concepts. The most successful and widely cited was produced by Haggett (Haggett 1965; Haggett *et al.* 1978), who divided the discipline's subject matter into: point patterns (such as farm buildings in an agricultural area); hierarchical point patterns (such as shopping centres of various sizes and importance within an urban region); line patterns (notably transport networks); movement patterns (such as the flows along networks, whether of people, goods or information); surfaces of variations in a continuous phenomenon (such as maps of the density of population and of the value of land within an urban area); and diffusions over

space (such as the spread of a disease along a network, across a surface and/or down a hierarchy). To this can be added territories, the divisions of continuous space into discrete entities – whether nation-states, ghettos, or personal spaces within an open-plan office. Others sought the fundamental basic concepts of a spatial discipline: for Nystuen (1963) these primitives were direction, distance, connectiveness and, perhaps, boundary.

The goal was to identify spatial laws, which involved adopting a scientific methodology based on the quantitative evaluation of hypotheses. Thus both physical and human geographers switched from describing patterns cartographically to analysing them statistically and (to a lesser extent) modelling them mathematically. The discipline developed a very strong quantitative core in the 1970s, with a great deal of hope that it could attain scientific respectability through its methods and the generality of its finding (Harvey 1969).

This new geography ·of the 1960s and 1970s was introduced at a time of rapid growth in the study of geography in universities, especially in most of the English-speaking world. The 'quantitative and theoretical revolutionaries' could therefore promote their view of the discipline in a context of expansion: the large number of available staff positions and research studentships enabled them to 'take over' the discipline very substantially, and to advance their particular view of what geography studies, and how.

Rapid expansion of a discipline, most of whose practitioners were strong adherents to the research ethos of the modern university, meant that these new ideas were applied to a wide range of subject matters. Prior to the 1960s, human geography had some important subdisciplines (such as historical geography), but to a considerable extent it was divided by areal rather than sectoral interests (i.e. it was divided according to practitioners' interests in the geography of certain parts of the world). This changed rapidly, and the incipient sectoral divisions soon achieved predominance over disciplinary practice.

Those subdisciplines are cross-cutting, in a variety of ways. Four of the most enduring reflect links with the main other social sciences: economic geography with economics; social geography with sociology; political geography with political science; and cultural geography with anthropology. Practitioners of the first two were more numerous in the 1960s and 1970s. The others grew more slowly, and later; the link with anthropology has been much stronger in the USA than elsewhere. There were also subdivisions of the subdivisions, notably the several distinct areas of specialization within economic geography: industrial geography, agricultural geography, transport geography, retail geography, and the geography of service industries, for example.

A second set of subdivisions involved the separation of urban geography from rural geography (with the latter largely distinct from agricultural geography). Urban geography was the focus of much of the early quantitative and theoretical work, and became heavily populated in the 1960s and 1970s. It had its own subdivisions: urban social geographers who studied residential segregation in cities, for example, were largely separate from those who studied economic aspects of urban places, (such as the group influenced by the ideas encapsulated in 'central place theory' regarding the spatial organization of shopping centres and of the spatial behaviour of individuals who visited them).

By the mid-1970s, therefore, human geographers interested in the study of spatial organization were divided into a number of somewhat independent sub-groups, each with strong links outside the discipline. Their commonality within geography was defined by the procedures that they used rather than the subjects that they studied, and by their emphasis on distance as a key concept. (There were other, smaller, sub-disciplines, such as medical geography.) This work continues, and the strength of the subdivisions is marked by the proliferation of academic journals concentrating on the specialist parts of geography (Johnston 1994).

During the 1970s, however, unease about the discipline's fragmentation grew and a number of geographers, many of a Marxian persuasion, argued that society should be studied as a whole (Harvey 1973). Areal differentiation is an outcome of the processes of uneven development which involve social, political and cultural as well as economic factors, so important theoretical work by Harvey (1982) and others promoted the study of spatial organization as both an outcome of and a constraint to processes of capitalist development and underdevelopment. This stimulated a very different orientation to the study of space, and much debate (see, e.g. Sayer 1992) over whether spatial patterns are contingent outcomes of social, economic, political and other processes or whether, as those who promoted the 'geography as a discipline in distance' approach contended, distance is a determinant influence on human behaviour. Work in the Marxian and realist moulds was concerned with elucidating the general processes of uneven development rather than with statistically analysing patterns of development and of spatial behaviour within them. This led to conflict over epistemology and methodology.

The growth of interest in what has variously been termed a political economy approach, a structural approach, and a realist approach to uneven develop-

ment, in its many forms and at a variety of spatial scales, took place during a period of very rapid change in the societies being studied (Peet and Thrift, 1989). During the 1980s, in particular, there was very substantial economic restructuring which involved considerable rewriting of the map of uneven development; there were major cultural shifts, too, with the promotion of 'enterprise societies' and attacks on welfare states; and nationalism grew as a response to several forms of political hegemony in many parts of the world. This rapidly changing scene attracted much geographical attention.

Place

As already noted, geography emerged as an academic discipline to promote knowledge about places; it involved the collection, collation and presentation of information about different parts of the world. As it matured, so its practitioners perceived the need for more sophisticated methods of working than mere collecting, mapping and cataloguing: they wanted an intellectual framework which allowed them to advance knowledge as well as order information.

Various attempts were made to produce such a framework. Considerable support went in the early decades of the twentieth century to *environmental determinism*, in which the basic argument was that human occupancy of and action upon any part of the earth is determined by its physical character. This was widely discredited by the 1930s, and replaced by *regional geography*, whose rationale was description of the individual character of each region (a defined area of the earth's surface, delimited according to certain criteria). Individual geographers thus became regional geographers of defined areas – usually of continental or sub-continental scale – and their major publishing activities involved describing those areas, often in substantial regional texts.

Regional geography was methodologically weak – over the defining criteria, the means of determining regional boundaries, and descriptive protocols, for example. Much of it was strongly influenced by the environmental determinism paradigm; most regional geographies started with descriptions of the area's physical environment, as the context for, if not determinant of, the patterns of human occupancy there. To some, regional geography was an advanced art-form, whose goal was accurate description of a place's character.

This approach was becoming increasingly discredited by the 1960s, among geographers attracted to the spatial science paradigm of 'geography as a discipline in distance'. It was condemned as little more than mere fact gathering and presentation in woolly analytical frameworks – unscientific and not respectable for an academic discipline. It languished with the rapid growth in the number of geographers adhering to other approaches, and has never recovered, although there are still some who identify themselves as regional geographers and see their discipline's task as describing and analysing the world's complex mosaic of places to wide audiences. (Those audiences were for long schoolchildren, taught by the graduates of university departments. Few geography graduates become teachers now, and few school syllabuses emphasize regional geography.)

The study of place was thus very substantially devalued within geography, but it revived – albeit in a different form – from the 1970s on. This renewed interest was initially promoted by those – many of them historical or cultural geographers – who were disenchanted with the spatial science paradigm and its search for laws of patterns and behaviour. Such laws, they argued, denied individual free will and thereby denigrated human individuality, culture and decision making (D. Gregory 1978; Ley and Samuels 1978). Similar criticisms were addressed at some of the early Marxian work on uneven development, which implied that capitalist processes were structural determinants within which individuals had few degrees of freedom to act. Neither approach – spatial science or structural Marxism – corresponded with some geographers' perceptions of the empirical world, within which there was much cultural, social and political variation that could not be ascribed to economic determinants, however important material concerns were as impulses to human behaviour.

This alternative view, which became associated with the cultural turn in other social sciences in the 1980s, was linked to several contemporary intellectual developments. The rise of feminism, for example, not only demonstrated the oppression of women in most societies and the male dominance in the construction of academic disciplines such as geography (Rose 1992), but also showed that different groups within society have different perspectives on it: there is no one predominant view, though one may dominate academic and other discourse (D. Gregory 1994). Similarly, reactions to imperialism – cultural as well as economic and political – showed how the map of the world and the construction of understandings of its various parts was structured by the ideological goals of hegemonic groups. The growth of ecological and environmental movements, promoting different interpretations of the relationships between peoples and environments, similarly advanced an alternative conception of how society could be organized.

Difference rather than similarity became a focus of geographical scholarship, therefore. Place was central

to this because of its role as a constraining factor in cultural development and of the importance of place to constructions of the world. People learn who and what they are in places, and they develop notions of identity (their 'sense of place') within places. Places are milieux, created by people in the context of their perceptions of nature there, and in which people are created as new residents and socialized into the dominant construction of that place and what it is to be part of it. An important component of the construction of a place identity involves its opposition to that which it is not: part of the definition of what characterises one place is its difference from others – mainly but not only its neighbours, and so people in places develop images of other places and their residents.

Much of this work on place is not antithetic to that on the processes of uneven development, therefore, although it is largely opposed to spatial science. It enriches the political economy approach by stressing the importance of people and their positions within society as strong influences on what they do – whether in very local contexts or as world politicians. The understanding of the spatial organization of the world and its many component parts requires full appreciation of the nature of the people who are continually reconstructing that world, in the context of their place-contingent views of both their place in the world and those of all others.

Approaches and methods

Geography has been characterized since the Second World War by three main approaches to its subject matter and, within human geography at least, considerable debate about their merits and disadvantages (Johnston 1991a). In addition, there has been debate and dispute within each approach over the relative advantages and disadvantages of different methods.

As both physical and human geography moved from a descriptive to an analytical stance during the 1950s and 1960s, so the attractions of the positivist approach to science, with its emphasis on testable hypotheses leading to the formulation of laws and the derivation of theories, became seductive. This approach was strongly associated with quantification, and the belief that statistical regularities were the proof of the existence of theoretically suggested empirical cause-and-effect relationships. Thus measurement and the statistical manipulation of data replaced verbal and cartographic description as the dominant geographical procedures.

As with any discipline seeking to adopt and adapt procedures developed elsewhere, this switch to the positivist epistemology involved much trial and error analytical work and many relatively trivial empirical analyses. By the late 1960s, however, some geographers realized that statistical procedures developed in other disciplines could not readily be adopted for geographical work because of the particular features of spatial data sets: spatial autocorrelation was recognised as an impediment to drawing causal inferences from many analyses of spatial data, and led to sophisticated development of spatial statistical methods. (Many geographers ignored these important arguments, however, and either disregarded the problem or assumed that it didn't matter.) Geographers have thus been involved in the burgeoning work on the development of applicable statistical procedures for the analysis of spatial patterns and spatial behaviours. Whether they have identified many strong regularities indicative of the operation of causal laws is doubted by some, however: many intriguing findings have been reported, but such is the complexity of the physical and human contexts being studied that it is very difficult to disentangle the general from the locally particular. Many of the hopes of the early disciples of the 'quantitative and theoretical revolution' have been dashed on the difficulties of successfully testing meaningful hypotheses. They have provided much sophisticated description of the world, however, even if they have provided few clues to how it works (Harvey 1989).

The measurement-based approach to the discipline involved much experimentation and innovation in means of collecting data in the field, both in the operation of processes in the physical environment and from individuals pursuing their spatial behaviours. These have been assisted by major revolutions in the technology of data capture, storage, display and analysis, in many of which geographers have played important pioneering roles. The first of these involved the field of *remote sensing*, which is usually, but far from exclusively, associated with imaging the earth from space (Curran 1987). Vast quantities of data are produced by satellites and other airborne carriers of imaging equipment, and geographers have been at the forefront of developing means of interpreting the information provided – through large-memory computing devices – in order to portray detailed environmental variations over time and space. Remote sensing has provided not only much new material with which to analyse the earth but also many technical puzzles over how to transform and interpret that material in the pursuit of research goals.

Most geographical data refer to two- (if not three-) dimensional contexts. These have traditionally been represented in map form, but developments since the late 1970s in *geographical information systems* (GIS) have very significantly advanced the ability to store, visualize and analyse such spatial data in computer systems. The presentation of data and their analysis, through the ability to layer data sets on to each other (for example, rainfall observations at individual sites on to topographic maps), substantially enhances both the ability to suggest hypotheses for empirical testing and the conduct of those tests (Maguire *et al.* 1991).

Reaction to the deterministic cast of much of the argument for a spatial science of human behaviour led to interest among human geographers in what became widely known as humanistic geography, which emphasized individuality and difference rather than conformity and similarity. A range of epistemologies was investigated – including phenomenology, idealism, existentialism, and pragmatism (Jackson and Smith 1984) – but the main impact of this work was its opposition to the alternative paradigm being promoted, especially in the early 1970s.

The emphasis in this humanistic work was on interpretation – both interpretation of the world by those acting in it and interpretation of their actions and the outcomes (landscapes, for example) by geographers. The enterprise was strongly hermeneutic in flavour, therefore. Geographers were exploring the interpretations behind people's actions, often, especially in the case of historical work, through the study of texts, both written and visual (i.e. maps, works of art, and landscapes), and then transmitting those interpretations to their own readers. This resulted, apart from the programmatic essays advancing the humanistic cause and attacking the positivist approach, in a range of essays on a diversity of topics.

Key to much of this hermeneutic work was language, since most understandings are transmitted through words, which are very imperfect because of their openness to differences in interpretation (Barnes and Duncan 1992). The importance of language and difference in the later post-modernism project has been important to the advance of this approach to geography, with its very strong antagonism to notions of grand theory and totalizing explanation. Place is central to this, in part because much learning of language and its nuances is place-bound.

The methods of humanistic geography are those of interpretation, therefore, which raises a variety of issues relating to sources of information and their treatment. As already indicated, some of those sources are texts which have to be interpreted in the context of their production (the language and ideology of the time and place, for example); others involve collecting material directly from the individuals concerned, which means that much research is ethnographic in character, with all the associated ethical and other concerns.

The implicit determinism of the positivist approach to human geography, and the voluntarism of its humanistic counter, were together the focus of a third major approach to the discipline, also initiated in the early 1970s. As indicated above, much of this work was Marxist-inspired and represented the economic imperatives of capitalist processes as underpinning the ever-changing map of uneven development. Some of the early work was overly determinist also, however, and portrayed a set of socio-spatial processes which individuals and collectivities were largely impotent to combat. Within a few years, however, the structural thinking of the approach was being married with the arguments for difference and individuality within a humanistic one (Kobayashi and Mackenzie 1989). This generated a rich and sophisticated framework for appreciating how space, place and nature are constructed and reconstructed by knowing individuals, acting within the limits of their own appreciation and constrained by the structural imperatives of the capitalist mode of production. The perspectives of postmodernism have added to this, emphasizing difference and individuality (Soja 1989).

As with the humanistic approach, the structuralist/realist relies very heavily on textual interpretation. It is not as antagonistic to the use of quantitative data, however, though little of it involves sophisticated analysis of such material. More importantly, its goal is to identify not only specific causes but also general processes which underpin them, and which cannot be apprehended empirically. In some ways, this is similar to approaches to the understanding of large-scale environmental systems whose empirical complexities, which reflect locally contingent factors, obscure the underlying fundamental physical laws and their interactions.

Applying geography

Geography was invented as an academic discipline because of its potential applied value in promoting world-understanding. Since then, the importance of an applied stance has varied, in part at least because of the demands made on the discipline, and indeed on academia in general. Taylor (1985), for example, has argued that states, which provide much of universities' income, are more likely to press for applied work – with academics meeting the needs of society – in periods of economic recession than in times of relative prosperity, when pure research can flourish: in some societies, of course, such as those of the USSR and eastern Europe between 1945 and 1989, the practice of geography, and all other academic disciplines, was almost entirely determined by the demands of the state apparatus.

The applied value of geography was appreciated in the Second World War with the ability of geographers to provide information about other countries; their cartographic and photogrammetric skills were widely employed in intelligence work. From the 1950s on,

the role of geographical work, first in data collection and later in their analysis and use in prescription, as in the preparation of town and regional plans, was increasingly recognized and some of the technical developments since (as in GIS) have been oriented to such practical applications: indeed, some argue that one of the geographer's most important roles is to add value to data, which can then be 'sold' to spatial decision makers (Rhind 1989).

The growing concern over environmental issues – local, regional, national and global – has attracted much attention. Geographers' stress on both the processes that operate in the physical environment and the impact of human activity on those processes and their outcomes has generated much work, in the conduct of environmental impact assessments, for example.

Much of this applied work sees geographers applying the methods and goals of the positivist approach in seeking solutions to a variety of perceived problems: they are involved in the engineering of social futures on the basis of their scientific understanding. This technocratic view has been challenged by other geographers, who see such work as promoting the status quo within society, thereby maintaining its many inequalities and injustices and sustaining both the capitalist mode of production and the state apparatus whose goal is to promote and legitimize what is perceived as an unjust system. For such critics, there are other applied roles for geographers, in promoting awareness of the nature of the changing world in which we live (both self-awareness and awareness of others) and in advancing the cause of emancipation, whereby people are enabled to obtain control over society and steer it towards their own ends. Each is a political goal and is contested by adherents to other views: all involve geography as the servant of particular political causes, although some would deny this and argue that theirs is a neutral, scientific role within constraints set by a society – of which, of course, the geographers are members.

Summary

Geography is a large and vibrant academic discipline, with roots in the sciences, the social sciences and the humanities. It comprises a number of overlapping communities of researchers and teachers, all seeking to advance our understanding of environment, space and place in a great variety of ways.

The differences among these communities in their approaches to the discipline ensure continued debate about the relative merits of alternative perspectives. Alongside those, however, there is a great deal of substantial research and scholarly activity which is advancing our appreciation of how the physical environment is constructed and operated, of how human life is organized spatially, and of how places are created as the milieux within which most people are socialized.

R. J. Johnston
University of Bristol

References

Barnes, T. J. and Duncan, J. S. (eds) (1992) *Writing Worlds: Discourse, Text and Metaphor in the Representation of Landscape*, London.

Buttimer, A. (1971) *Society and Milieu in the French Geographical Tradition*, Chicago.

Curran, P. J. (1987) 'Remote sensing methodologies and geography', *International Journal of Remote Sensing* 8.

Gregory, D. (1978) *Ideology, Science and Human Geography*, London.

—— (1994) *Geographical Imaginations*, Oxford.

Gregory, K. J. (1985) *The Nature of Physical Geography*, London.

Haggett, P. (1965) *Locational Analysis in Human Geography*, London.

Haggett, P., Cliff, A. D. and Frey, A. E. (1978) *Locational Analysis in Human Geography*, 2nd edn, London.

Hartshorne, R. (1939) *The Nature of Geography: A Critical Survey of Current Thought in the Light of the Past*, Lancaster, PA.

Harvey, D. (1969) *Explanation in Geography*, London.

—— (1973) *Social Justice and the City*, London.

—— (1982) *The Limits to Capital*, Oxford.

—— (1989) 'From models to Marx: notes on the project to "remodel" contemporary geography', in B. Macmillan (ed.) *Remodelling Geography*, Oxford.

Jackson, P. and Smith, S. J. (1984) *Exploring Social Geography*, London.

Johnston, R. J. (1991a) *Geography and Geographers: Anglo-American Human Geography since 1945*, 4th edn, London.

—— (1991b) *A Question of Place: Exploring the Practice of Human Geography*, Oxford.

—— (1994) 'Geography journals for political scientists', *Political Studies* 42.

Kobayashi, A. and Mackenzie, S. (1989) *Remaking Human Geography*, Boston, MA.

Ley, D. F. and Samuels, M. S. (eds) (1978) *Humanistic Geography: Prospects and Problems*, Chicago.

Maguire, D. J., Goodchild, M. F. and Rhind, D. W. (eds) (1991) *Geographical Information Systems: Principles and Applications*, London.

Nystuen, J. D. (1963) 'Identification of some fundamental spatial concepts', *Proceedings of the Michigan Academy of Science, Arts and Letters*, 48.

Peet, R. and Thrift, N. J. (eds) (1989) *New Models in Geography: The Political-Economy Perspective*, 2 vols, Boston, MA.

Rhind, D. W. (1989) 'Computing, academic geography, and the world outside', in B. Macmillan (ed.) *Remodelling Geography*, Oxford.

Rose, G. (1992) *Feminism and Geography: The Limits of Geographical Knowledge*, Cambridge, UK.

Sayer, A. (1992) *Method in Social Science: A Realist Approach*, 2nd edn, London.

Soja, E. W. (1989) *Postmodern Geographies: The Reassertion of Space in Social Theory*, London.

Taylor, P. J. (1985) 'The value of a geographical perspective', in R. J. Johnston (ed.) *The Future of Geography*, London.

Turner, B. L. *et al.* (eds) (1990) *The Earth as Transformed by Human Action: Global and Regional Changes in the Biosphere over the last 300 Years*, Cambridge, UK.

Wooldridge, S. W. and East, W. G. (1958), *The Spirit and Purpose of Geography*, 2nd edn, London.

Further reading

Abler, R. F., Marcus, M. G. and Olson, J. M. (eds) (1992) *Geography's Inner Worlds: Pervasive Themes in Contemporary American Geography*, New Brunswick, NJ.

Gaile, G. and Willmott, C. J. (1989) *Geography in America*, Columbus, OH.

Johnston, R. J., Gregory, D. and Smith, D. M. (1994) *The Dictionary of Human Geography*, 3rd edn, Oxford.

Livingstone, D. N. (1992) *The Geographical Tradition: Episodes in the History of a Contested Enterprise*, Oxford.

Unwin, T. (1992) *The Place of Geography*, London.

geography, cultural *see* cultural geography

geography, economic *see* economic geography

geography, historical *see* historical geography

geography, political *see* political geography

geography, population *see* population geography

geography, social *see* social geography

geography, urban *see* urban geography

gerontology, social

Gerontology is the scientific study of biological, psychological and sociocultural aspects of the ageing process. Social gerontology is concerned only with its sociological-anthropological component. Although public interest in old age commonly stems from the association of ageing with social problems, such considerations will be excluded from this discussion.

Social gerontology emerged in the late 1950s and has become established as a recognized subject of study and research in academic institutes throughout the world, especially in the USA. The conceptual approaches and methodologies applied in this field reflect a wide gamut of theoretical frameworks and techniques. Nonetheless, three core issues in the study of behavioural phenomena in later life can be identified: the relative importance in ageing of universal human processes and specific cultural factors; the dialectic between stability and change in later life; questions concerning the place of the elderly in a social structure, and in the symbolic worlds of both aged and non-aged persons.

First, the quest for universal, generic characteristics of ageing has taken several theoretical forms. Some anthropologists have imputed common needs and aspirations to all old people, such as the desire for a prolonged life and dignified death, and they have tried to identify general role features, such as a shift from active participation in economic production to sedentary advisory roles. Similarly, 'disengagement theory' states that there is a gradual process of mutual disengagement between aged persons and their society in all cultures. Critics have cited cross-cultural and cross-sectional data to show that there have been a variety of context-bound, behavioural responses to old age. It has also been argued that patterns of active behaviour among elderly people, as well as manifestations of retreatism and inertia, are conditioned by environmental constraints and cultural configurations. However, some psychologists with a similar universalist bias have maintained that the process of ageing is governed by an increased concentration on the inner self, and especially on a retrospective life review.

Second, ageing is a dynamic process of concurrent transformations in various spheres of life. In a complex, changing society, where life transitions are generally equated with social mobility and progress within a given career opportunity structure, the changes associated with old age engender a paradoxical perception of later life. In a social structure which allocates statuses and prestige according to mastery of information, control of wealth and command of physical resources and mental faculties, aged persons are conceived of as a stagnant, marginal social category. This stereotype persists, in spite of the growing numbers of elderly people whose life expectancy is increasing and whose functioning capacities are improving relative to previous generations. Such incongruity between social definition and personal experience generates ambivalence and ambiguity. In the experience of the temporal universe of old people, long-term planning becomes problematic, if not impossible. The past is recalled selectively, and is mined in order to construct a meaningful present. The struggle of old people for continuity in identity is often expressed through their review and reinterpretation of life histories, as well as through their reorganization of social relationships and systems of meaning. Temporal asynchrony and disorganization of this kind usually does not exist in so-called simple societies, where the position of old people accurately reflects the balance between their control of valuable resources and their diminishing ability to protect their interests. In some economically 'hand-to-mouth' preliterate societies, an aged person whose presence becomes a burden may be abandoned or ritually killed. In agricultural societies, however, knowledge and spiritual powers are attributed to aged people. Elders have social and ritual roles entailing a honourable place in society.

Third, social roles are often associated with age categories. Passage through a series of age grades represents an important organizing principle of social life in most simple societies. In modern societies, age is less significant than occupational specialization. Yet the phases of 'childhood' and 'old age' are, by definition, social categories circumscribed by age norms, which are decisive in shaping individuals' social identities. The very fact that age alone is enough to define 'the old' reflects the disappearance of the normally decisive occupational and other roles and values, which in turn generates negative images and stereotypes of elderly people. This phenomenon has led a number of scholars to consider the potential development of subcultural or counter-cultural social units made up exclusively of the aged. Research on such groups, mainly in age-homogeneous communities, day centres and residential settings, shows that in many cases a new alternative system of social relationships and symbolic meanings is developed to supersede those of the prior, stigmatizing and alienating social milieu.

Social gerontology is currently in a transitional phase. Many aspects of ageing can be analysed and explained by other disciplines, but the growing reservoir of data and theory on old age encourages social research into such specific issues as the politics of ageing, ageing and the law, and the existential problems connected with old age. Much research is also directed to aged persons as a social problem and the object of public social concern. The central issues have been defined, but there is as yet no adequate theoretical treatment of them.

Haim Hazan
Tel-Aviv University

Further reading

Binstock, R. H. and Shanes, E. (eds) (1976) *Handbook of Aging and the Social Sciences*, New York.

Hareven, T. K. and Adams, K. J. (eds) (1982) *Ageing and Life Course Transitions*, London.

Hazan, H. (1994) *Old Age*, Cambridge, UK.

Holmes, L. (1983) *Other Culture, Elder Years*, St Paul, MN.

Myerhoff, B. G. and Simic, A. (eds) (1978) *Life's Career and Aging: Cultural Variations on Growing Old*, Beverly Hills, CA.

See also: ageing; life cycle; life-span development; mortality.

globalization

The development of the world economy has a long history, dating from at least the sixteenth century, and is associated with the economic and imperial expansionism of the great powers. By globalization we refer to a more advanced stage of this process of development. The global economy is one in which all aspects of the economy – raw materials, labour information and transportation, finance, distribution, marketing – are integrated or interdependent on a global scale (Carnoy *et al.* 1993). Moreover, they are so on an almost instantaneous basis. By global economy, 'we mean an economy that works as a unit in real time on a planetary basis' (Castells 1994: 21). The forces of globalization thereby tend to erode the integrity and autonomy of national economies.

Newly emerging and consolidating global corporations are the driving force behind these developments. Where multinational corporations in the past operated across a number of national economies, economic globalization now requires corporate interests to treat the world as a single entity, competing in all major markets simultaneously, rather than sequentially. This may involve the marketing of global products or world brands such as Coca Cola, McDonald's or Kodak (Levitt 1983). In most cases, however, global competitiveness will require more complex and differentiated strategies. Managing in a borderless world in fact necessitates the segmentation of corporate organization and marketing according to transnational regions, notably those of Europe, North America and the Far East (Ohmae 1990). Some global corporations describe their approach, more precisely, as one of global localization, recognizing the continuing significance of geographical difference and heterogeneity. The globalization of economies is more accurately seen in terms of an emergence of global-local nexus.

Globalization has been made possible through the establishment of worldwide information and communication networks. New telecommunication and computer networks are overcoming the barriers of time and space, allowing corporate and financial interests to operate on a twenty-four-hour basis across the planet. The inauguration of information superhighways promises to further extend this compression of our spatial and temporal worlds (Harvey 1989). Global media are also part of this complex pattern of transborder information flows. Using new satellite and cable systems, channels like CNN and MTV have begun to create truly global television markets and audiences (though here too, there is growing realization of the need to be sensitive to local differences). Instantaneous and ubiquitous communication gives substance to Marshall McLuhan's idea, first put forward in the 1960s, that the world is becoming a global village.

As national economic spaces become less functional in the global context, cities and city-regions are assuming a new role as the basing points in the spatial organization of international business. Cities are consequently compelled to attract and accommodate the key functions of the global economy (services, finance, communications, etc.). This results in inter-urban competition across national borders, leading to the formation of a new international urban hierarchy. Cities must aim to become key hubs in the new global networks. Metropolitan centres such as New York, Tokyo and London may be described as truly 'world cities' (Friedmann 1986) or 'global cities' (Sassen 1991), the command centres in the global economy. Competition among second-level global cities involves the struggle to achieve ascendancy within particular zones of the world. This competition also requires cities to distinguish their assets and endowments through strategies of place marketing and differentiation: in a context of increasing mobility, the particularities of place become a salient factor in the global positioning of cities (Behrman and Rondinelli 1992). As well as attracting global investors and tourists, cities are also the destinations of migrant and refugee populations from across the world. Global cities are also microcosms in which to observe the growing dualism between the world's rich and poor and the encounter of global cultures.

We should consider what globalization means for the world's cultures. Is there a global culture? What might we mean by this (Featherstone 1990)? In the case of commercial culture (film and television, popular music, etc.), there are certainly aspirations towards creating a unitary, worldwide market. Global media corporations, such as Time Warner, Sony and News Corporation, are thinking in terms of global products and global audiences. This is possible only with certain kinds of programming, however, and for the most part global media interests operate in terms of transnational media spaces (e.g. the 'Eurovision' region; the 'Asian' region served by Murdoch's Star TV). At the same time, there are contrary tendencies, towards the proliferation of national and also regional (e.g. Basque, Gaelic) media. This may be seen in terms of the (re)assertion of cultural difference and distinction in the face of globalising tendencies. Again it is the relation between the global and local that is significant (Sreberny-Mohammadi 1991). The globalization of the media should be understood, then, in terms of the construction of a complex new map of transnational, national and subnational cultural spaces.

Cultural globalization – associated with flows of media and communication, but also with flows of migrants, refugees and tourists – has brought to the fore questions of cultural identity. For some, the proliferation of shared or common cultural references across the world evokes cosmopolitan ideals. There is the sense that cultural encounters across frontiers can create new and productive kinds of cultural fusion and hybridity (Rushdie 1991). Where some see cosmopolitan complexities, others perceive (and oppose) cultural homogenization and the erosion of cultural specificity. Globalization is also linked, then, to the revalidation of particularistic cultures and identities. Across the world, there are those who respond to global upheaval by returning to their 'roots', by reclaiming what they see as their ethnic and national homelands, by recovering the certainties of religious tradition and fundamentals. Globalization pulls cultures in different, contradictory, and often conflictual, ways. It is about the deterritorialization of culture, but it also involves cultural reterritorialization. It is about the increasing mobility of culture, but also about new cultural fixities.

We may see globalization in terms of the new possibilities opened up by global communications, global travel and global products. Or, alternatively, we may consider it from the perspective of those for whom it represents unwelcome destabilization and disorientation. To some extent, this difference may be a matter of who will gain from global change and who will lose or be marginalized. Globalization occurs as a contradictory and uneven process, involving new kinds of polarization (economic, social and cultural) at a range of geographical scales. The encounter and possible confrontation of social and cultural values is an inevitable consequence. We have a global economy and global culture: we do not, however, have global political institutions that could mediate this encounter and confrontation.

Kevin Robins
University of Newcastle upon Tyne

References

Behrman, J. N. and Rondinelli, D. (1992) 'The cultural imperatives of globalisation: urban economic growth in the 21st century', *Economic Development Quarterly* 6(2).

Carnoy, M., Castells, M., Cohen, S. and Cardoso, F. H. (1993) *The New World Economy in the Information Age*, University Park, PA.

Castells, M. (1994) 'European cities, the informational society, and the global economy', *New Left Review* 204.

Featherstone, M. (1990) *Global Culture*, London.

Friedmann, J. (1986) 'The world city hypothesis', *Development and Change* 17(1).

Harvey, D. (1989) *The Condition of Postmodernity*, Oxford.

Levitt, T. (1983) 'The globalisation of markets', *Harvard Business Review* May–June.

McLuhan, M. (1964) *Understanding Media: The Extensions of Man*, London.

Ohmae, K. (1990) *The Borderless World: Power and Strategy in the Interlinked Economy*, New York.

Rushdie, S. (1991) *Imaginary Homelands*, London.

Sassen, S. (1991) *The Global City: New York, London, Tokyo*, Princeton, NJ.

Sreberny-Mohammadi, A. (1991) 'The global and the local in international communications', in J. Curran and M. Gurevitch (eds) *Mass Media and Society*, London.

Further reading

Johnston, R., Taylor, P. and Watts, M. (eds) (1995) *Geographies of Global Change: Remapping the World in the Late Twentieth Century*, Oxford.

King, A. (ed.) (1991) *Culture, Globalisation and the World-System*, London.

Mlinar, Z. (ed.) (1992) *Globalization and Territorial Identities*, Aldershot.

Sklair, L. (1991) *Sociology of the Global System*, London.

See also: communication networks; multinational enterprises; world-system theory.

gold standard

A gold standard represents a style of monetary organization in which gold fulfils the functions of a central money (i.e. numeraire). Gold becomes the main store and measure of value as well as a central medium of exchange. In this respect, a gold standard is a metallist rule for organizing money since a metal, in this case gold (but historically various other metals have been used), becomes the foundation for managing a money supply. Although it has fallen out of use as a means of managing national money after the Second World War, historically this type of monetary system has prevailed at both the national level (practised most widely as a form of organizing national money from the 1850s up to the First World War) and international level (especially 1880–1914 and 1947–71). National and international monetary organization is now founded on a fiat standard where the value and acceptability of monies does not derive from the intrinsic value of some commodity like metal, but derives instead from the decrees of governments.

Although there has not been a uniform means of practising a gold standard, such an organization of money at the national level has traditionally been oriented around several central practices or rules. First, money is defined in terms of some fixed quantity of gold. For example, in 1879 a US dollar was defined as 23.22 grains of fine gold. Since one fine ounce of gold equalled 480 grains, then one fine ounce of gold was equal to 20.67 dollars. All denominations of money are defined in either multiples or fractions of the central unit of account (in this case the dollar), hence all money has a clear correspondence to some quantity of gold. Traditionally, these domestic par values have been kept stable over time. Second, individuals enjoy perfect interconvertibility between gold money and non-gold-monies (principally notes) at rates which are legally determined. In this respect, notes ultimately represent claims on gold itself. Hence both notes and gold become widely acceptable as means of clearing debts and making purchases to unlimited amounts (i.e. acquire legal tender). This has become known as the practice of domestic convertibility.

Third, coins made of metals other than gold can circulate only as token money (small-denomination coin). These coins normally possess an intrinsic value which is significantly below their nominal value. Fourth, monetary authorities stand ready to coin all gold brought to them (usually for a slight charge referred to as seigniorage) and stand ready to convert notes into gold at legally specified rates. Fifth, individuals can hold gold in whatever form they choose (bullion or coin) and can freely import and export gold in whatever amounts they desire. Sixth, international reserves are held principally in gold. Hence gold becomes the principal reserve and vehicle currency between nations which are practising gold standards. Finally, monetary authorities institute a rule which links the creation of money (i.e. growth in the money supply) to the stock of gold. In this latter respect, a gold standard (or any metallist-standard for that matter) represents a classic 'rule' governing the management of a money supply.

At the international level, the currencies of nations practising gold standards become interchangeable at fixed exchange rates which derive from the respective domestic pars. Gold fulfils the function of an international numeraire in that it becomes the foundation for international transactions. Historically, such an international regime has both arisen spontaneously (as in the period 1880–1914) and been intentionally orchestrated by economically powerful nations (as the USA did in creating the Bretton Woods regime 1944–71).

Advocates of such rules have traditionally supported gold standards as means of escaping the unstable and inflationary effects of discretionary fiat monetary regimes where growth in the money supply is free from binding rules and subject to the whims of monetary and political elites. This support for a gold standard is all the more enhanced by a preference for fixed over flexible exchange rates. Critics of such rules have argued that a gold standard is too rigid to allow for the management of the business cycle (i.e. it does not allow authorities the luxury of inflating out of depression), and that developments in the money supply are overly dependent on the vagaries of mining. The case against a gold standard is enhanced by a preference for flexible over fixed exchange rates.

Giulio M. Gallarotti
Wesleyan University

Further reading

Bordo, M. and Schwartz, A. (1984) *A Retrospective on the Classical Gold Standard*, Chicago.
de Cecco, M. (1974) *Money and Empire: The International Gold Standard, 1890–1914*, Totowa, NJ.
Eichengreen, B. (1985) *The Gold Standard in Theory and History*, New York.
Gallarotti, G. (1995) *The Anatomy of an International Monetary Regime: The Classical Gold Standard 1880–1914*, New York.

See also: money; reserve currency.

governance

Governance is a term that applies to the exercise of power in a variety of institutional contexts, the object of which is to direct, control and regulate activities in the interests of people as citizens, voters and workers. For political scientists, governance refers to the process of political management which embraces the normative basis of political authority, the style in which public affairs are conducted, and the management of public resources. It is a broader concept than government, which is specifically concerned with the role of political authorities in maintaining social order within a defined territory and the exercise of executive power. Three terms are central to most definitions of governance: accountability, which denotes the effectiveness with which the governed can exercise influence over their governors; legitimacy, which is concerned with the right of the state to exercise power over its citizens, and the extent to which those powers are perceived to be rightly exercised; and transparency, which is founded on the existence of mechanisms for ensuring public access to decision making.

Governance is not restricted to the formal political realm; it also operates at the level of the firm or the community. Corporate governance is concerned with the processes by which corporate entities are governed, namely the exercise of power over the direction of the enterprise and mechanisms for ensuring executive acountability and the regulation of corporate actions. In more localized contexts, governance can refer to endogenously evolved sets of rules or authority structures within particular communities which play a role in resource management and in the maintenance of social order.

From the early 1990s the concept of governance attracted considerable interest from international aid donors concerned with political and administrative obstacles to successful economic development in the Third World. The analysis of the World Bank and other donors centres on a perceived crisis of governance stemming from self-interest, corruption and a loss of political legitimacy, which are associated with weak and undemocratic states. This concern with governance has also raised questions about the appropriate role of international institutions such as the World Bank and the United Nations in global economic and political management, and the nature of their mandate.

In the developed world, there are two main sources of pressure shaping ideas about governance. One stems from problems of governability manifest in a breakdown of law and order and despondency with formal political institutions which raises concerns about the manner in which the institutions of government should interact with citizens. A second set of influences derive from a neo-liberal political agenda which advocates a diminished role for the state and transforming it from a provider of services to a purchaser and regulator.

Proposals for bringing about improved governance centre on mechanisms to promote the decentralization of power and responsibility, and to increase consultation and participation in decision making. In developing countries, proposals for better governance often imply a return to liberal democratic politics and controls on executive power, along with civil service reform and bureaucratic reorientation with a view to increasing the accountability, legitimacy and effectiveness of public management. This is challenged by an alternative view which suggests that strong government is essential for political stability which in turn provides the best guarantee of successful development.

Mark Robinson
University of Sussex

Further reading

Hyden, G. and Bratton, M. (eds) (1992) *Governance and Politics in Africa*, Boulder, CO.

Kooiman, J. (ed.) (1993) *Modern Governance: New Government–Society Relations*, London

World Bank (1992) *Governance and Development*, Washington, DC.

government

The study of government lies at the heart of political science, but there is little unanimity within the discipline as to how it should be studied or as to the types or forms that exist. Indeed, the term itself has a multiplicity of distinct, if related, meanings. Only an overview of the confusion and controversy can be given here.

Following Finer (1974) we can discern four different meanings of the term government. First, government refers to the process of governing, that is, the authoritative exercise of power. Second, the term can be used to refer to the existence of that process, to a condition of ordered rule. Third, the government often means the people who fill the positions of authority in a society or institution, that is, the offices of government. Finally, the term may refer to the manner, method or system of government in a society, that is, to the structure and arrangement of the offices of government and the relationship between the government and the governed.

The existence of some institution of sovereign government is a distinguishing feature of the state. The study of such sovereign governments has been a major preoccupation of political scientists. But not all governments are sovereign; any institution, such as a trade union, a church group or a political party, which has a formal system of offices endowed with the authority to make binding decisions for that organization, can be said to have a government. Equally, government (in the sense of ordered rule) may exist in the absence of the state. A number of anthropological studies have revealed the existence of primitive societies in which conflict is resolved by various social processes without resort to the coercive powers of a formalized state. Indeed, in any society there are many social situations (such as a bus or theatre queue) where potential conflict over an allocative decision is avoided by a non-coercive social process.

Sovereign government in advanced societies is normally regarded as consisting of three distinct sets of offices, each set having a particular role: First, the role of the *legislature* is to make the law. Second, the *executive* (also sometimes confusingly referred to as the government) is responsible for the implementation of the law and in most advanced polities has come to play a predominant role in the formulation of proposals for new laws. Third, the *judiciary*, meanwhile, is responsible for the interpretation of the law and its application in individual cases.

Classification schemes

The precise arrangement of the offices of government varies from state to state. Ever since Aristotle, the study of government attempted to classify the varieties of governments according to different types. The purpose of such classification exercises has varied, and has included both a desire to make normative statements about the best type of government and positive statements concerning the behavioural implications of different governmental structures. But all the classification exercises have in common an attempt to produce conceptual categories that make it possible to make meaningful generalizations about government in the face of a bewildering variation in the ways governments are organized.

Classifications of government are legion, yet some common threads can be discerned. Classifications have tended to concentrate on two criteria: the arrangement of offices, which is more narrow in conception; and the relationship between the government and the governed.

The first criterion has produced two classification schemes which are in wide currency among political scientists, particularly among students of democratic government. The first classification scheme is based on the relationship between the executive and the legislature. In a parliamentary system, the executive is dependent for its continuance in office upon maintaining the support of the legislature. Members of the executive are commonly also members of the legislature. While a prime minister may be the most powerful member of the executive, important decisions within the executive are usually made collectively by a group of ministers. In a presidential system, the executive is independent of the legislature. Members of the executive are not normally also members of the legislature, while the ultimate source of decision-making authority within the executive lies with one person – the president. The second classification scheme concentrates on the distribution of power between different levels of government. In a unitary state, all authority to make laws is vested in one supreme legislature whose jurisdiction covers the whole country. While it may permit local legislatures to exist, they do so only on the sufferance of the main legislature. In a federal state, there exist local legislatures which have at least a measure of guaranteed autonomous decision-making authority. Both forms of government can be distinguished from a confederation, where a group of states combine for certain purposes but with each state retaining its sovereignty.

Classifications based on the second criterion – the relationship between the government and the governed – have commonly concentrated on the extent to which governments attempts to achieve their aims by coercion of their citizens rather than persuasion, and on the extent to which limits are placed on the legitimate authority of government. The precise formulation of classification schemes based on this criterion varies widely, but not uncommonly a distinction is drawn between, at one extreme, liberal democratic government and, at the other, totalitarian governments. Under liberal democratic government, government is seen as primarily responsive to the wishes of society, and clear limitations are placed upon its ability to coerce society or to mould it in any particular way. Totalitarian governments have few limits placed upon them and are seen as instruments whereby society may be changed.

New approaches

The study of government has changed considerably since the Second World War. Historically, the study of government grew out of the study of constitutional law. It was characterized by a concentration on the formal institutions of government and upon constitutional provisions, while individual countries tended to be studied in isolation rather than in comparative framework. However, under the influence of the behavioural revolution, scholars have paid increasing attention to how governments actually operate, to institutions outside the formal apparatus of the state but which play a vital role in its operation (such as political parties and pressure groups), and to explicitly comparative study. Particularly influential in the development of comparative study have been approaches derived from systems theory, especially structural-functionalism. These approaches have attempted to develop a conceptual language, based upon the functions that are performed within any society, that could be applied to the study of government in any country, including developing as well as advanced societies.

John Curtice
University of Strathclyde

Reference

Finer, S. E. (1974) *Comparative Government*, Harmondsworth.

Further reading

Almond, G. A. and Coleman, J. S. (eds) (1960) *The Politics of the Developing Countries*, Princeton, NJ.
Easton, D. (1965) *A Systems Analysis of Political Life*, New York.

See also: bureaucracy; power; state.

government, metropolitan and urban *see* metropolitan and urban government

group dynamics

Group dynamics was originally the term used, from the 1930s to the early 1950s, to characterize the study of changes in group life by Kurt Lewin and his followers. Gradually, however, the term lost its restricted reference and came to be more or less synonymous with the study of small groups. This broader, second sense will be used here.

A small group consists of from three to about thirty persons, every one of whom can recognize and react to every other as a distinct individual. The members are likely to manifest: perception of group membership; sustained interaction; shared group goals; affective relations; and norms internal to the group, which may be partially organized around a set of roles. Those are the most commonly invoked defining criteria of small social groups.

According to Hare (1976), by the end of the first decade of the twentieth century about twenty social scientific articles on small groups had appeared and many of the subsequent concerns of small group research had been identified. In 1898 Triplett reported laboratory and field experiments on the effect of the group on individual performance. Within the next half-dozen years, Cooley wrote about the importance of the primary group; Simmel discussed some of the consequences of group size; Taylor, the apostle of scientific management techniques, started to examine pressures on individuals to conform to group norms regarding productivity; Terman studied group leaders and leadership. From about 1920 onwards, the rate of publication started to increase. The 1930s saw the appearance of three classic lines of research: the work of Lewin *et al.* on different styles of leadership; the best-known parts of the programme of research at the Western Electric Company's Hawthorne plant, together with Mayo's selective and misleading popularization of their findings; reports by Moreno and others of sociometric techniques designed to represent choices, preferences or patterns of affect in a group.

By the late 1930s, the developing study of group processes was seen, in the USA at any rate, as part of the defence of conventional democratic practices in the face of authoritarian threats, and high hopes and expectations continued through the 1940s to the heyday of small group research, the 1950s and early 1960s. During that period Bales produced his category system for the relatively detailed description of group interaction processes, the sensitivity or experiential group appeared on the scene, and those not preoccupied with experiential groups increasingly studied laboratory experimental ones. In the 1970s the quantity of work did not abate but some of the sense of excitement and enthusiasm did. Mainly via labora-

tory experiments, a variety of delimited issues, often refinements of earlier topics, provided successive focuses for attention. These included co-operation and competition; aspects of group cohesion; leadership styles; social influence processes, including a new interest in minority influence; group decision making and group polarization; personal space and density; and interpersonal attraction. Increasing methodological sophistication was claimed and the absence of major theoretical advances bemoaned.

Initially the study of group dynamics, in the original, narrow sense, was held to offer answers to a number of democracy's problems (Zander 1979), but eventually the most tangible legacies of the group dynamics movement were the spawning of, first, group-centred training groups and, then, individual-centred existential groups. This shift from a concern with the world's problems to the soothing of personal anxieties perhaps was symptomatic of the failure of the study of small groups to fulfil its potential (Steiner 1974). All too often, narrow questions were studied with increasingly restricted methods, leading, at best, to mini-theories which failed to sustain interest in the issues. Some of the reasons for this reflect North American experimental social psychology more generally. But the nature of the groups studied must have been a contributing factor. In practice, the study of small groups came to be concerned not with families, friends, committees and the multitude of social groups that mediate between individual and society but with small collectivities of student strangers meeting for no more than an hour; it is likely that a majority of groups studied manifested few, if any, of the defining properties of actual social groups. In an analogy with nonsense syllables, Fraser and Foster (1984) dubbed those small collectivities 'nonsense groups'. In the late 1970s and early 1980s, the field seemed to be in the doldrums.

However, the study of small groups has been showing some signs of revival. Academic social psychologists not only have begun to generate new theoretical ideas for the investigation of standard topics in the laboratory (e.g. Turner 1991) but also are revealing more concern for the contexts in which naturally occurring groups function (Levine and Moreland 1990) and for some selected real-world issues, including crowding, the operation of social support, and relations between groups (Baron *et al.* 1992). These real-world issues, however, are still frequently studied in social psychologists' laboratories rather than in the worlds of lay people. But a major change in the study of small groups appears to be that the dominance of social psychology is no longer as marked as it had been since the 1940s. The study of real social groups is increasingly being tackled by researchers from other domains, such as family researchers and, especially, researchers in the area of organizations and work, where many of the newer developments regarding leadership, group effectiveness and the like are now located. It remains to be seen whether these changes in emphases will be sufficient finally to create a study of group dynamics which can adequately illuminate the major part played by small social groups in the relations between individuals and the societies they live in.

Colin Fraser
University of Cambridge

References

Baron, R. S., Kerr, N. L. and Miller, N. (1992) *Group Process, Group Decision, Group Action*, Buckingham.

Fraser, C. and Foster, D. (1984) 'Social groups, nonsense groups and group polarization', in H. Tajfel (ed.) *The Social Dimension: European Developments in Social Psychology*, vol. II, Cambridge, UK.

Hare, A. P. (1976) *Handbook of Small Group Research*, 2nd edn, New York.

Levine, J. M. and Moreland, R. L. (1990) 'Progress in small group research', *Annual Review of Psychology* 41.

Steiner, I. D. (1974) 'Whatever happened to the group in social psychology?', *Journal of Experimental Social Psychology* 10.

Turner, J. C. (1991) *Social Influence*, Buckingham.

Zander, A. (1979) 'The psychology of group processes', *Annual Review of Psychology* 30.

See also: conformity; groups; leadership; social psychology.

groups

The concept group features prominently in sociology and anthropology because of their interest in social relationships that are habitual, institutionalized and relatively enduring. Group has been used in many different ways, but it commonly refers to a plurality of individuals bounded by some principle of recruitment and by a set of membership rights and obligations. Everyone fulfilling the recruitment criteria is a member of the group and occupies a specific status in the group, and every group member automatically has the rights and discharges the obligations of membership. Groups are, in turn, the main elements of the social structure.

Critics of such a conceptualization of groups stress the fact that the notion of a society as consisting of permanent discrete groups is not a generalization from the observable social processes, but is either the analyst's model or a model that the members themselves have of their own society. When the object of the analysis is not to explain actual social processes, but rather the actors' cultural notions, or the cognitive structure of a given society, then the group can be defined simply in terms of the ideology of group membership.

Reference group (Merton and Kitt 1950) refers to a collection of persons with which individuals identify, or which they use as a point of reference for their aspirations; it is a typical example of a group as a notional entity. But the manifestation of groups in actual interactional situations cannot be assumed to follow automatically from their existence as notional phenomena. Instead, the interactions of specific individuals are seen to derive from their decisions about which of their numerous statuses or group memberships, or which of their interpersonal relationships, they wish to activate. In turn, these decisions cannot be generalized in terms of permanent groups but only in terms of cultural preferences. The distinction between the cognitive model of the society as consisting of permanent discrete groups, and the actual social processes in which the society's members are involved, led to the conceptual distinction between the social structure and social organization (Firth 1951) and to the development of network analysis. It also led to a more rigorous conceptualization of a group and to the analytical distinction between social groups and social categories.

A *social category* is a collection of individuals grouped conceptually because of some shared socially relevant features or characteristics (age, sex, occupation, religious beliefs, common ancestry, mutual genealogical relationship, and so on). A *social group* consists of individuals who interact in an interconnected set of roles (such as economic, political, ritual, occupational). While membership of a specific category usually defines eligibility for membership in a group, taking up group membership is not an automatic process; whether eligible persons will activate their group membership depends on many contingent factors other than belonging to the category. Depending on the nature of the interaction of its members, it is customary to distinguish *primary* groups whose members interact face to face (for example, a household or family) from *secondary* groups, all of whose members do not necessarily interact directly and personally with one another (for example occupational or political groups). Some groups have the character of corporations in that they control a body of property or estate which may be either material (such as land or capital equipment) or immaterial (such as skills, privileges, ritual names, titles). Ownership of this property is held by the group as a single entity, and all its members acquire certain rights in the joint property. In consequence, corporate groups typically exhibit greater continuity than non-corporate groups: they retain their identity as groups over time although their personnel changes.

At the other extreme is an action group or task group. It consists of individuals who assemble in some organized fashion to perform jointly a specific task. Action groups have only a limited existence in time, and they dissolve once the task for which they organized themselves has been completed. What distinguishes most groups from a task group and other units like crowds, or gatherings whose existence is also temporary, is their more or less permanent existence deriving from the fact that their members interact recurrently and that they have a more or less enduring internal organization and discreteness, though these characteristics may be variously defined and stressed by different analysts.

Ladislav Holy
University of St Andrews

References

Firth, R. (1951) *Elements of Social Organisation*, London.
Merton, R. K. and Kitt, A. (1950) 'Contributions to the theory of reference group behavior', in R. K. Merton and P. Lazarsfeld (eds) *Continuities in Social Research*, Glencoe, IL.

Further reading

Bales, R. F. (1951) *Interaction Process Analysis*, Reading, MA.
Hare, A. P., Borgatta, E. and Bales, R. F. (eds) (1955) *Small Groups*, New York.
Homans, G. C. (1950) *The Human Group*, New York.

See also: group dynamics; reference groups.

H

Habermas, Jürgen (1929–   )

Jürgen Habermas has been the most prolific and influential representative of the second generation of the Frankfurt School. He has not only continued the theoretical tradition of his teachers Adorno and Horkheimer and his friend Marcuse, but also significantly departed from classical critical theory and made many important contributions to contemporary philosophy and social theory. In particular, he has opened critical theory to a dialogue with other philosophies and social theories such as the hermeneutics of Gadamer, systems theory and structural functionalism, empirical social sciences, analytic and linguistic philosophy, and theories of cognitive and moral development. He has been synthesizing these influences into a theory of communicative action, which presents the foundation and framework of a social theory that builds on the tradition of Marx, Weber and classical critical theory, but also criticizes his predecessors and breaks new theoretical ground.

Habermas was born on 18 June 1929 in Düsseldorf, and grew up in Gummersbach, Germany. His father was head of the Bureau of Industry and Trade, and his grandfather was a minister and director of the local seminary. He experienced the rise and defeat of fascism, and was politicized by the Nuremberg trials and documentary films of the concentration camps shown after the war. Habermas began his university studies in Göttingen in 1949 and finished a dissertation of *Das Absolute und die Geschichte* in 1954. In the 1950s, Habermas studied – and was strongly influenced by – Lukács's *History and Class Consciousness* and Adorno and Horkheimer's *Dialectic of Enlightenment* which he first read in 1955. He studied the young Marx and the young Hegelians with Karl Löwith, one of Germany's great scholars and teachers.

Habermas resolved to work with Adorno and Horkheimer because he believed that they were establishing a dialectical and critical theory of society from within a creative and innovative Marxist tradition. He thus went to Frankfurt and continued his studies in the Institute for Social Research. In this context, he wrote his first major book *Strukturwandel der Öffentlichkeit* (1962). Combining historical and empirical research with the theoretical framework of critical theory, Habermas traced the historical rise and decline of what he called the 'bourgeois public sphere' and its replacement by the mass media, technocratic administration and societal depoliticization. This influential work continues to animate discussion concerning problems of representative democracy in contemporary capitalist-societies and the need for more participatory, democratic and egalitarian spheres of sociopolitical discussion and debate.

In the 1960s, Habermas taught at the universities of Heidelberg (1961–4) and Frankfurt (1964–71). At this time he also became more interested in politics and with others in 1961 published *Student und Politik*, which called for university reforms, and *Protestbewegung und Hochschulreform* (1969), which continued his concern with university reform and also criticized what he saw as the excesses of the German student movement in the 1960s. Habermas was also engaged in intense theoretical work during this period. His *Theorie und Praxis* appeared in 1963 (*Theory and Practice*, 1973), which contained theoretical papers on major classical and contemporary social and political theorists, as well as anticipations of his own theoretical position; *Zur Logik der Sozialwissenschaften* in 1967 contained a detailed and critical summary of contemporary debates in the logic of the social sciences; *Erkenntnis und Interesse* in 1968 (*Knowledge and Human Interests*, 1971) traced the development of epistemology and critical social theory from Kant to the present; and several collections of essays: *Technik und Wissenschaft als Ideologie* (1968); *Arbeit-Erkenntnis-Fort-schritt* (1970); and *Philosophische-politische Profile* (1971).

During the 1970s Habermas intensified his studies of the social sciences and began restructuring critical theory as communication theory. Key stages of this enterprise are contained in a collection of studies written with Niklas Luhmann, *Theorie der Gesellschaft oder Sozialtechnologie* (1971); *Legitimationsprobleme im Spät-kapitalismus* (1973); *Zur Rekonstruktion des Historischen Materialismus* (1976); and essays collected in several other books. In these works, Habermas sharpened his critique of classical Marxism and his critical theory predecessors. He attempted to develop his own recon-struction of historical materialism, a critical theory of society, and a philosophical theory rooted in analyses of communicative action. During much of this period, since 1971, Habermas was director of the Max Planck Institute in Starnberg where he involved himself in various research projects and was in close touch with developments in the social sciences. After a series of disputes with students and colleagues, he resigned in 1982 and returned to Frankfurt where he is now Professor of Philosophy and Sociology.

In 1981, Habermas published his two-volume magnum opus, *Theorie des kommunikativen Handelns*. This impressive work of historical scholarship and theoret-ical construction appraises the legacies of Marx, Durkheim, Weber, Lukács and western Marxism, including critical theory, and criticizes their tendencies towards theoretical reductionism and their failure to develop an adequate theory of communicative action and rationality. Habermas also contributes his own analysis of the importance of communicative action and rationality for contemporary social theory. The book points both to his continuity with the first gener-ation of the Frankfurt School and his significant depar-tures. *Theorie des kommunikativen Handelns* also manifests Habermas's continued interest in the relationship between theory and practice with his discussion of new social movements. The concluding section is a testa-ment to his interest in systematic social theory with a practical intent in his summation of the current status of critical theory. The work as a whole thus sums up Habermas's theoretical work in the 1970s and points to some issues and topics that constitute future projects.

Since 1981 Habermas has indeed continued to pursue development of a systematic articulation of his theory of communicative action in the fields of moral discourse and legal and political discourse. *Moral Consciousness and Communicative Action* (1990) contains contributions towards developing a discourse ethics, while *Faktizitat und Gultung* (1992) articulates a discourse theory of law, democracy and rights. *Postmetaphysical Thinking* (1992) contains articles that articulate Habermas's attempts to reformulate modern theory in terms of a theory of communicative action that over-comes the metaphysical presuppositions of the philo-sophical tradition.

In addition, Habermas has published collections of essays commenting on contemporary political, cultural and historical events such as *The New Conservativism* (1989) and he edited a collection of *Observations on 'the spiritual situation of our time'* (1984). Perhaps his most controversial book, however, was *The Philosophical Discourse of Modernity* (1987) where Habermas launched an attack on French postmodern theory (especially Derrida and Foucault) and its predecessors (Nietzsche, Heidegger and Bataille). In this text and other essays of the period, Habermas defended the heritage of modernity, Enlightenment, and reason against the postmodern attacks.

A vast number of books and articles have appeared which defend or criticize Habermas, and he often responds to collections of books containing essays on his work, such as *Habermas and Modernity* (Berstein 1985). A collection of interviews *Autonomy and Solidarity* (Dews 1992) also provides answers to his critics and insights into his life and intellectual development. *The Past as Future* (1994) provides interviews in which Habermas expresses his views on contemporary political and intellectual developments. Habermas thus continues to be highly productive and controversial as he enters his sixth decade and he has emerged as one of the great intellectual figures of our time.

Douglas Kellner
University of Texas

References

Berstein, R. (ed.) (1985) *Habermas and Modernity*, Cambridge, UK.
Dews, P. (ed.) (1992) *Autonomy and Solidarity: Interviews with Jürgen Habermas*, London.

Further reading

Holub, R. (1991) *Jürgen Habermas: Critic in the Public Sphere*, London.
McCarthy, T. (1978) *The Critical Theory of Jürgen Habermas*, London.

See also: Frankfurt School; post-modernism.

habitus

With a distinguished philosophical pedigree stretching from Hegel to Husserl, the notion of the *habitus*, although used by Weber, Durkheim and Mauss, has established itself in the social science lexicon through the work of Pierre Bourdieu. It is central to Bourdieu's attempt to develop a sociology of human practice which, as he sees it, avoids the errors of both individ-ualistic voluntarism and structuralist determinism.

In Bourdieu's usage it refers to an area of human being which is neither conscious nor unconscious, neither wholly social nor wholly individual. Residing in embodied individuals, it is the product of primary and secondary socialization, having its deepest roots in the earliest years of childhood. It is constituted in and by typically unreflexive processes of habituation and habit-formation.

The habitus is made up of classificatory schemes and practical dispositions, the two being intimately implicated in each other. Both are in a state of ongoing adjustment to the objective conditions of the social world of which the acting subject is a constituent. These schemes and dispositions, particularly the basic practical taxonomies in which classification and disposition most intimately coincide, are transposable from one social domain to another, as the logic of practice characteristic of a group or culture.

Embodiment is fundamental to the habitus. The body represents the point of view on which the most influential practical taxonomies – up:down, back:front, female:male, etc. – are centred. For Bourdieu the body, via the habitus, is a mnemonic device within and on which the foundations of culture are inscribed. The habitus is also constitutive of *hexis*, the socially and culturally distinctive physical style of being in the world (stance, movement, gesture).

Socially competent performances are, however, generated by the habitus without the actors necessarily appreciating what they are doing. Bourdieu is explicit that the habitus is not a set of rules governing behaviour, nor does it work through processes of conscious ratiocination. Rather, it is a framework within and out of which actors, to some extent thoughtlessly, improvise practices as a consequence of the interaction between their culturally specific dispositions and classificatory schema and the constraints, demands and opportunities of any specific social field or domain. A particular habitus will have origins in and most affinity with particular fields. It is in these encounters that internal subjectivity is ongoingly adjusted to the objective external world. This adjustment is one of the key processes by means of which the social world is reproduced.

In Bourdieu's own work this concept has been applied to a range of topics, from formal education, to cultural consumption to peasant marriage strategies. In its translation into anglophone sociology it seems to have been largely subsumed within an anthropologized model of culture. Although it can be criticized as overly dismissive of conscious decision making and residually deterministic, it offers an intriguing model of the social and cultural constitution of individual practice.

Richard Jenkins
University of Wales, Swansea

Further reading

Bourdieu, P. (1990) *The Logic of Practice*, Cambridge, UK.
Bourdieu, P. and Wacquant, L. (1992) *An Invitation to Reflexive Sociology*, Cambridge, UK.
Jenkins, R. (1992) *Pierre Bourdieu*, London.

See also: house; place.

Hayek, Friedrich A. (1899–1993)

Recipient of the Nobel Prize in Economic Science (together with Gunnar Myrdal) in 1974, Friedrich August von Hayek was born in Vienna on 8 May 1899. He earned two doctorates at the University of Vienna – Dr jur. (1921) and Dr rer. pol. (1923) – and became Privatdozent in Political Economy in 1929. He was director of the Austrian Institute for Economic Research from 1927 to 1931. In 1931 he accepted an appointment at the University of London as Tooke Professor of Economic Science and Statistics. He was awarded a DSc degree by that institution in 1944. He remained at London until 1950, when he accepted a position at the University of Chicago. He returned to Europe in 1962 as Professor of Economic Policy at the University of Freiburg, and upon retirement from that institution in 1967 he accepted a position as honorary professor at the University of Salzburg, from which he received an honorary doctor's degree in 1974.

Hayek was instrumental in the founding of the Mont Pelerin Society in April 1947, a society whose aims were to contribute to the preservation and improvement of the free society. He served as president of the society for twelve years.

Hayek's broad scope of inquiry is reflected in his contributions to economic science. These include the theory of economic fluctuations; the pure theory of capital; the theory of economic planning under socialism and competitive capitalism; and the methodology of economics.

In addition to many articles, his theory of economic fluctuations was presented in two books: *Monetary Theory and the Trade Cycle* (1926 and 1933) and *Prices and Production* (1931). Beginning with Wicksell's theory of the 'cumulative process', Hayek expanded and modified Wicksell's theory and then proceeded to develop his own theory of economic fluctuations which included such elements as how changes in the quantity of money affect relative prices, rather than general price levels, as well as allocation of resources, especially between producer and consumer goods; the related disturbances in investment period and voluntary saving, as well as 'forced saving', bank credit and its effects on 'forced saving' and capital deepening; a model of the price mechanism and its operation in the context of fluctuations.

In 1941, Hayek published *The Pure Theory of Capital*, a treatise on capital theory. Among the topics treated and which represented a contribution to the theory of capital were the concept of 'intertemporal equilibrium'; physical productivity of investment; the phenomenon of natural growth; 'period of investment', the idea of the 'force of interest'; and finally, 'durable goods'.

In spite of his contributions to economic theory, Hayek was never accorded the recognition of his contemporary, J. M. Keynes, whose *General Theory* (1936) was accepted as the standard paradigm of economic fluctuations in economics. Also, the Austrian theory of capital had fallen out of fashion by the time his *Pure Theory of Capital* appeared, and his work in this area was largely ignored. The later period of his career was devoted to political and social philosophy and methodology, the most popular publications on these being *The Road to Serfdom* (1944) and *The Counter-Revolution in Science* (1952).

Vincent J. Tarascio
University of North Carolina

References

Hayek, F. A. (1928) *Geldtheorie und Konjunkturtheorie*, Vienna. (English edn, *Monetary Theory and the Trade Cycle*, London, 1933.)
—— (1931) *Price and Production*, London.
—— (1941) *The Pure Theory of Capital*, London.
—— (1952) *The Road to Serfdom*, London.
—— (1952) *The Counter-Revolution in Science*, Glencoe, IL.

Further reading

Machlup, F. (1974) 'Friedrich von Hayek's contribution to economics', *Scandinavian Journal of Economics* 76.
—— (ed.) (1976) *Essays on Hayek*, New York.

See also: Austrian School; liberalism.

health, mental *see* mental health

health economics

Health economics is concerned with the analysis of health care inputs such as expenditure and employment, and an appraisal of their impact on that desired outcome, the health of society.

Clearly, many inputs may affect an individual's health. In a world of scarce resources it is necessary to ensure that these resources are used efficiently – that the cost of producing care and health is minimized and the benefits are maximized. At the individual level, this can be modelled in a human capital framework (Grossman 1972). Grossman's model permits an exploration of the links between inputs (such as education, income, wealth, health care and nutrition) and their impact on health status; this work indicates that the relative importance of income and nutrition on health is greater than that of health care.

The evaluation of health care is seriously deficient. Cochrane (1971) has argued that most health care therapies in use have not been evaluated scientifically. By scientifically, he means the application of randomized controlled trials which administer the therapy under investigation to a randomly selected (experimental) group of patients, and a placebo or alternative therapy (a control) to another randomly selected group of patients. The difference, if any, between the therapeutic results for the experimental and control groups gives an indication of the relative impact of the therapies. Such results require replication to ensure validity, and such methods are noticeable by their relative absence (see Bunker *et al.* 1977).

Such clinical evaluation informs decision makers about the benefits of health care, but an economic component is needed to assess costs. The economist's role is to elicit the social opportunity costs of the alternative therapies, that is, the costs to all decision makers, both public (the government) and private (for example, individuals and their families). A guide to the application of such techniques and an appraisal of over a hundred case studies is provided by Drummond (1980; 1981).

The dominant (monopolist) role of the medical profession in the health care market-place has resulted in an investigation of physicians' capacity to create demand for their own and other people's services (Department of Health and Human Services 1981). This, together with the fact that third parties (governments and insurance companies, rather than patients or producers) usually pay for health care, has led to cost containment problems (McLachlan and Maynard 1982). To control such inflation, user charges (prices) can be introduced, a policy that has both costs and benefits (Maynard 1979; Newhouse *et al.* 1981); or more effective incentives must be devised to encourage producers (doctors) to economize, for example, through health maintenance organizations (Luft 1981).

The inefficient use of health care resources is clearly unethical; it deprives patients of care from which they could benefit. The aim of health economists is to generate information about the costs and benefits of alternative ways of achieving health and health goals. It is hoped that such information will improve the efficiency and equity of health care systems across the world.

Alan Maynard
University of York, UK

References

Bunker, J. P., Barnes, B. A. and Mosteller, F. (eds) (1977) *The Costs, Benefits and Risks of Surgery*, New York.

Cochrane, A. L. (1971) *Effectiveness and Efficiency*, London.

Department of Health and Human Services (1981) *Physician Induced Demand for Surgical Operations*, Washington, DC.

Drummond, M. F. (1980) *Principles of Economic Appraisal in Health Care*, Oxford.

—— (1981) *Case Studies in Economic Appraisal in Health Care*, Oxford.

Grossman, M. (1972) *The Demand for Health*, New York.

Luft, H. (1981) *Health Maintenance Organisation*, New York.

McLachlan, G. and Maynard, A. (eds) (1982) *The Public Private Mix for Health*, London.

Maynard, A. (1979) 'Pricing, insurance and the National Health Service', *Journal of Social Policy* 8.

Newhouse, N. P. *et al.* (1981) 'Interim results from a controlled trial of cost-sharing in health-insurance', *New England Journal of Medicine* 305.

See also: public health.

health transition

Health transition means the changes over time in a society's health, as measured by both morbidity and mortality levels, and the determinants of those changes, especially the cultural, social or behavioural ones. Related terms include *mortality transition* and *epidemiologic (or epidemiological) transition*. Mortality transition was part of the vocabulary of *demographic transition* theory, which described the movement of societies from high birth and death rates to low ones, a phenomenon that was posited to consist of separate – although probably related – fertility and mortality transitions. The latter is now a worldwide phenomenon, and has been shown to have begun in England as early as the seventeenth century. *Epidemiologic transition* is due to Omran (1971) and refers not only to the decline in mortality but also to the change in the balance of disease and the causes of death as mortality declines. There is still controversy as to whether the level of sickness declines as death rates do, and some researchers (e.g. Riley 1990) deny that it does.

The term *health transition* was coined at a meeting organized by the Rockefeller Foundation at the Bellagio Conference Center in 1987. The intention was to include not only mortality but also morbidity, as well as indicating that the focus of interest would be improvements in health and well-being beyond what might be indicated merely by a reduction in illness. It was also intended that the field should embrace the determinants of morbidity and mortality decline, especially giving recognition to the growing body of evidence that this was determined not merely by the provision of modern medical services and rising levels of material well-being (as indicated by income, nutrition, housing, etc.) but by cultural, social and behavioural factors. The term met a need, as is testified by its increasing use and by its acceptance as an understood phrase by a range of journals and publishers. It is also included in the title of the journal, *Health Transition Review* (Caldwell and Santow, from 1991). In addition there are various collections of papers by writers on the subject (Caldwell and Santow 1989; Caldwell *et al.* 1990; Chen *et al.* 1993; Halstead *et al.* 1985).

The need to lay greater stress on social determinants of health has become ever clearer since the 1970s. In developed countries increasing emphasis has been placed on healthy lifestyles or behaviour, and some of the gains against adult mortality have been attributed to compliance with this advice. The international programmes of population surveys, the World Fertility Surveys of the 1970s and the Demographic and Health Surveys of the 1980s, had shown that child survival was associated with parental, especially maternal, education. Caldwell (1979) demonstrated that the influence of parental education was not merely a reflection of income levels but a powerful influence in its own right, and this was confirmed throughout the Third World by Hobcraft *et al.* (1984) and Cleland and van Ginnekan (1988). Mensch *et al.* (1985) calculated from a study of fifteen developing countries that the direct effect of female education was a decline of 3.4 per cent in their children's mortality for each additional year of schooling.

There was other compelling evidence of the importance of social factors in determining mortality decline. Life expectancy in Third-World countries bore little relation to per capita income levels. Sri Lanka and the Indian State, Kerala, achieved during the 1980s life expectancies of 70 years, not far behind the industrialized countries, with per capita incomes only one-fortieth of that of the rich countries and health expenditure similar to that found in other poor countries. Conversely, a range of Middle Eastern and North African countries, where women's education was low and where their autonomy was restricted, exhibited surprisingly high mortality. Caldwell (1986) attributed the successful health transitions of Sri Lanka and Kerala to a radical tradition and a high level of female autonomy in their cultures which had allowed both an early spread of female schooling and, at the individual level, a confident taking of health and treatment decisions by women with regard to their children and themselves. He pointed out that such social factors and the provision of modern health services interacted to produce low mortality, and that Sri Lanka had not achieved such success with regard to health before these services were available. The most successful health services were the most democratic ones which gave first priority to providing all sectors of the community with cheap and easy access to modern medical treatment. Mensch *et al.* (1985) showed that Third-World child survival was most strongly influenced by mother's education, father's education and ethnicity, pointing out that, in eleven plural societies investigated, there were in every case large differences in child mortality between ethnic groups even after education, income and access to medical services had been controlled. They believed their findings to 'emphasize the importance of "technique" such as childcare practices and personal hygiene relative to the importance of the sheer volume of material and monetary inputs that is reflected in such variables as income, housing facilities and residence in urban areas'. However, it might be noted that the evidence is still ambiguous as to whether the social factors involved in achieving low child mortality operate mainly through such mechanisms as care, especially in ensuring that children suffer from fewer bouts of sickness or from accidents, or whether the impact is mainly achieved through greater efficiency in interacting with the medical system once treatment is needed.

Preston and colleagues in a series of publications (e.g. Preston and Haines 1991) analysed US data at the beginning of the twentieth century and showed that the strong influence of maternal education on reducing child mortality found in the contemporary Third World was not evident in the USA of that time. Caldwell (1991) suggested that the reason was that effective treatment requires not only modern medicine but also a belief in it and a scientific outlook that leads to unhesitating and wholehearted collaboration with health services; these attitudes were part of western society at the beginning of the twentieth century but they have largely been imported into the Third World by western education systems. Hence the effectiveness of the health system is a function of an individual's or parent's duration of education.

Efforts have been made to develop analytical methods suited to exploring the health transition (e.g. Cleland and Hill 1991). In spite of a commitment to take health or ill-health as seriously as survival or death, most health transition analyses still support their conclusions with mortality statistics. This is the case not so much because of the finality of death and because it is the ultimate proof that health interventions did not succeed, but because it can be clearly defined in contrast to measures of sickness which are often ambiguous, especially when they are the product of retrospective reports on themselves or their children by respondents in household surveys. The cultural, social and behavioural measures are even more difficult, for, while some measures of education can be agreed upon,

this is far from being true with regard to female autonomy or the degree of radicalism or egalitarianism in a society.

John C. Caldwell
Australian National University

References

Caldwell, J. C. (1979) 'Education as a factor in mortality decline: an examination of Nigerian data', *Population Studies* 33.
—— (1986) 'Routes to low mortality in poor countries', *Population and Development Review* 12.
—— (1991) 'Major new evidence on health transition and its interpretation', *Health Transition Review* 1.
Caldwell, J. C. and Santow, G. (1989) *Selected Readings in the Cultural, Social and Behavioural Determinants of Health*, Canberra.
—— (from 1991) *Health Transition Review*, 2 issues annually.
Caldwell, J. C., Findley, S., Caldwell, P., Santow, G., Cosford, W., Braid, J. and Broers-Freeman, D. (eds) (1990) *What We Know about Health Transition: The Cultural, Social and Behavioural Determinants of Health*, Canberra.
Chen, L., Kleinman, A. and Ware, N. (eds) (1993) *Health and Social Change: An International Perspective*, Cambridge, MA.
Cleland, J. G. and van Ginnekan, J. K. (1988) 'Maternal education and child survival in developing countries: the search for pathways of influence', *Social Science and Medicine* 27.
Cleland, J. G. and Hill, A. G. (1991) *The Health Transition: Methods and Measures*, Canberra.
Halstead, S. B., Walsh, J. A. and Warren, K. S. (1985) *Good Health at Low Cost*, New York.
Hobcraft, J. N., McDonald, R. W. and Rutstein, S. O. (1984) 'Socio-economic factors in infant and child mortality: a cross-national comparison', *Population Studies* 38.
Mensch, B., Lentzner, H. and Preston, S. (1985) *Socio-economic Differentials in Child Mortality in Developing Countries*, United Nations, New York.
Omran, A. R. (1971) 'The epidemiologic transition: a theory of the epidemiology of population change', *Millbank Memorial Fund Quarterly* 49.
Preston, S. H. and Haines, M. R. (1991) *Fatal Years: Child Mortality in Late Nineteenth Century America*, Princeton, NJ.
Riley, J. C. (1990), 'Long-term morbidity and mortality trends: inverse health transitions', in J. C. Caldwell *et al.* (eds) *What We Know about Health Transition: The Cultural, Social and Behavioural Determinants of Health*, Canberra.

See also: demographic transition; morbidity; mortality; public health.

Hegel, Georg Wilhelm F. (1770–1831)

Probably no other philosophy dominates the modern European consciousness to the same extent as Hegel's. Yet few great thinkers have been so consistently misunderstood and their teaching so distorted by friend and foe alike, even today, in spite of the work of specialist Hegel scholars, who since the 1970s have swarmed as never before. The old stereotypes still persist: the allegedly 'tender-minded' reality-behind-appearance Idealist; the arch-rationalist; the professional historian's *bête noire* with his *a priori* philosophy of history; the apologist of Prussian authoritarianism and the conservatism of the Restoration, the apostle of *Machtpolitik* and totalitarianism, if rarely in their cruder shapes yet often nowadays in more subtle and sophisticated kinds of criticism. Scholars are reluctant, even timid, to start at the other end of the spectrum: to accept Hegel without reserve as the thoroughly down-to-earth realist that he always was, interested especially in what we would call sociological phenomena (and Hegel's *Volksgeist*, for instance, is to be seen in this light and not that of Romantic nationalism); or to see him as the lifelong enthusiast for the ideals of the French Revolution, in many ways closer to Benthamite radicalism than Burkeian conservatism, who tried to use philosophy to expound the logic of the claim of modern human beings to self-realization and freedom and therefore the rationale of the modern democratic state as such, a thinker who is not outside the liberal democratic tradition, but sociologically realistic within it.

It is a strange paradox that Marx did accept much of this, precisely because in his critique of Hegel's political philosophy he was attacking the idea of the state as such, in its most plausible form, and wanted to show that it was self-contradictory, because it was an illusion of the alienated false consciousness of bourgeois society or, rather, non-society, which could not possibly become a reality in the modern world. Marx admired the detail and clarity of Hegel's account of modern society and its sociological realism – only it was 'upside down', like a photographic negative. For modern Marxists it is an unshakeable dogma that Marx demystified Hegel, removed the centre of gravity from *Geist* to humankind, and so on. In fact they have created a new myth: not the state, but what in Hegel is one of its 'moments', namely 'civil society', is all-in-all, and the state is powerless to intervene and correct the self-destructive evils of this sphere of rampant economic liberalism that he analysed so acutely, especially the production of an alienated '*pöbel*' or proletariat. Hegel is said to be describing something on its way out. Although this sort of interpretation involves too much looking down the wrong end of the telescope, it does come closer to the real Hegel than traditional liberal distortions, for example, that Hegel equated state and society, in so far as Hegel's view of modern industrial and commercial civilization was not only profoundly critical but also closely related to a dialectic designed to develop fully the inherent self-contradic-

tions in all partial truths, and which applies not only to thinking but also to the reality that is thought.

An interpretation which spotlights the theme of alienation generally and the need for community need not be Marxist, and in Britain and the USA especially this has been fashionable. The influence of the *Zeitgeist* seems fairly obvious in this concentration on community rather than state in Hegel, a concentration which is inclined to lean heavily on certain aspects of his immature thought, especially his enthusiasm for the 'beautiful wholeness' of the lifestyle of the ancient Greeks. The mature Hegel is then interpreted in this light.

All these interpretations suffer from failure to understand the meaning and significance of the religious dimension of Hegel's philosophy, his claim that philosophy is the fully rational truth of Christianity, and how this is reflected in the Hegelian concept or notion, the concrete universal that is the tool of Reason, as opposed to the scientific Understanding which knows its objects by separating and dividing. This means accepting the reality and necessity of continuing division and conflict for true harmony and unity in the human spirit and society, and rejecting all belief in a 'beyond' as a pathological symptom of alienation. A true unity is a unity of differences, unlike the primitive undifferentiated wholeness of the Greek *polis*, and a rational state, as understood by philosophy, will be the reverse of totalitarian: it must in fact be pluralistic, since the universal needs the particular as much as the particular needs the universal. It is the 'prodigious strength' of the modern state that it is able to contain its negation: the world of self-seeking particularity that destroyed the primitive unity of the Greek *polis*. This is the fully developed freedom (fully developed in every relevant objective sense, ethical, legal, political and social) of the modern state that makes sense of history, and whose development the philosopher can trace in history. Beyond history and the state is the timeless absolute freedom of art, religion and philosophy; the state and its freedom is not an end in itself. Hegel was in fact describing something on its way in: the *Geist* of modern humans, their claim to freedom and the institutions necessary to make that claim real. In many ways he anticipated Max Weber in his account of the modern rational state as an essentially public impersonal institution that belongs to no one but which all individuals recognize as their own in so far as it is seen to uphold their own particular interests, and which generates a perpetual tension between freedom and control, liberty and order.

In the *Grundlinien der Philosophie des Rechts* (1821) (*Philosophy of Right*), Hegel spells this out in meticulous detail far surpassing anything to be found in most philosophers who call themselves empirical, and in this he was unnecessarily and dangerously extending his lines into matters that were contingent and time-bound. But it is a superficial view that writes off this sort of thing as out-of-date: it is more rewarding to seek the rationale that underlies such obvious anachronisms. This is in accordance with the Hegelian dialectic, which is not a strict and logically brittle deduction of 'thesis, antithesis and synthesis', but a way of thinking concretely and multidimensionally about human experience and of exhibiting such thought, which is one reason why Hegel is difficult. The only test is trueness to life. But anyone who approaches the *Philosophy of Right* in the correct spirit, a book which it should be remembered is not a 'book', but a compendium for a course of lectures, will be repeatedly struck by his soundness and common sense and be able to appreciate the force of his criticism of all abstract thinking about freedom and the state in purely legal or purely ethical or, for that matter, purely sociological modes. But a proper understanding of Hegel requires a sound knowledge of the historical background (which most critics do not have), so that one can make the necessary adjustments in order to arrive at its relevance. The beginner, however, should start with the lectures on the philosophy of history, which Hegel himself designed for beginners, though this too has its dangers. There is simply no short-cut to this philosophy, which is a circle, whose end is its beginning. Hegelian dialectic was able to bring home the bacon of sociological realism, as Marx in his own way realized, and political liberalism would have been a lot sounder and healthier if its exponents had realized it too, and not been so busy hunting "totalitarian and 'conservative' hares, in country for which they did not possess an adequate map.

Duncan Forbes
University of Cambridge

Further reading

Hegel, G. H. (1991) *Elements of the Philosophy of Right*, ed. A. W. Wood, Cambridge, UK.

hermeneutics

Hermeneutics is a term used to describe the views of a variety of authors who have been concerned with problems of understanding and interpretation. Some of the themes of hermeneutics were introduced to English-speaking social scientists by the writings of Max Weber. As a participant in the methodological debates which occurred in Germany during the late nineteenth and early twentieth centuries, Weber was familiar with the views of philosophers and historians such as Wilhelm Dilthey, Heinrich Rickert and Wilhelm Windleband, who all argued that the study of the social and historical world requires the use of methods which are different from those employed in the investigation of natural phenomena. These arguments were reflected in Weber's own emphasis on the concept of understanding (*verstehen*).

While Weber played an important role in introducing many social scientists to the ideas of hermeneutics, the latter tradition stretches back to a period well before Weber's time. Hermeneutics derives from the Greek verb *hermēneuein*, which means to make something clear, to announce or to unveil a message. The discipline of hermeneutics first arose, one could say, with the interpretation of Homer and other poets during the age of the Greek Enlightenment. From then on, hermeneutics was closely linked to philology and textual criticism. It became a very important discipline during the Reformation, when Protestants challenged the right of tradition to determine the interpretation of the holy scriptures. Both classical scholars and theologians attempted to elaborate the rules and conditions which governed the valid interpretation of texts.

The scope of hermeneutics was greatly extended by Wilhelm Dilthey (in the nineteenth century). An historian as well as a philosopher, Dilthey was aware that texts were merely one form of what he called 'objectifications of life'. So the problem of interpretation had to be related to the more general question of how knowledge of the social-historical world is possible. Such knowledge is based, in Dilthey's view, on the interrelation of experience, expression and understanding. Cultural phenomena, such as texts, works of art, actions and gestures, are purposive expressions of human life. They are objectified in a sphere of conventions and values which are collectively shared, in the way that a person's attitude may be objectified in the medium of language. To understand cultural phenomena is to grasp them as objectified expressions of life; ultimately it is to re-experience the creative act, to relive the experience of another. While reorienting hermeneutics towards a reflection on the foundations of the *Geisteswissenschaften* or 'human sciences', Dilthey's writings preserved a tension between the quest for objectivity and the legacy of Romanticism.

The key figure in twentieth-century hermeneutics is Martin Heidegger. Whereas in Dilthey's work the hermeneutical problem is linked to the question of *knowledge*, in Heidegger's it is tied to the question of *being*: problems of understanding and interpretation are encountered while unfolding the fundamental features of our 'being-in-the-world'. For Heidegger, 'understanding' is first and foremost a matter of projecting what we are capable of. This anticipatory character of understanding is a reformulation, in ontological terms, of what is commonly called the 'hermeneutical circle'.

Just as we understand part of a text by anticipating the structure of the whole, so too all understanding involves a 'pre-understanding' which attests to the primordial unity of subject and object. We are beings-in-the-world, familiar with and caring for what is ready-to-hand, before we are subjects claiming to have knowledge *about* objects in the world.

Heidegger's work has implications for the way that the human sciences are conceived, as Hans-Georg Gadamer has attempted to show. In *Truth and Method*, Gadamer (1975 [1960]) establishes a connection between the anticipatory character of understanding and the interrelated notions of prejudice, authority and tradition. The assumption that prejudices are necessarily negative is itself an unjustified prejudice stemming, in Gadamer's view, from the Enlightenment. It is an assumption which has prevented us from seeing that understanding always requires pre-judgement or 'prejudice', that there are 'legitimate prejudices' based on the recognition of authority, and that one form of authority which has a particular value is tradition. We are always immersed in traditions which provide us with the prejudices that make understanding possible. Hence there can be no standpoint outside of history from which the totality of historical effects could be grasped; instead, understanding must be seen as an open and continuously renewed 'fusion' of historical 'horizons'.

Gadamer's provocative thesis was challenged in the mid-1960s by Jürgen Habermas and other representatives of 'critical theory'. While acknowledging the importance of Gadamer's hermeneutics for the philosophy of the human sciences, Habermas attacked the link between understanding and tradition. For such a link underplays the extent to which tradition may *also* be a source of power which distorts the process of communication and which calls for critical reflection. Appealing to the model of psychoanalysis, Habermas sketched the framework for a 'depth-hermeneutical' discipline which would be oriented to the idea of emancipation.

The debate between hermeneutics and critical theory has been reappraised by Paul Ricoeur (1981). As a hermeneutic philosopher concerned with critique, Ricoeur has tried to mediate between the positions of Gadamer and Habermas by re-emphasizing the concept of the text. In contrast to the experience of belonging to a tradition, the text presupposes a distance or 'distanciation' from the social, historical and psychological conditions of its production. The interpretation of a text, involving both the structural explanation of its 'sense' and the creative projection of its 'reference', thus allows for the possibility of establishing a critical relation *vis-à-vis* 'the world' as well as the self. Ricoeur shows how the model of the text and the method of text interpretation can be fruitfully

extended to the study of such varied phenomena as metaphor, action and the unconscious.

As debates have indicated, the issues which for centuries have been discussed under the rubric of hermeneutics are still very much alive. The appreciation of texts and works of art, the study of action and institutions, the philosophy of science and social science: in all of these spheres, problems of understanding and interpretation are recognized as central. While few contemporary hermeneutic philosophers would wish to draw the distinction between the natural sciences and the *Geisteswissenschaften* in the way that their nineteenth-century predecessors did, many would nevertheless want to defend the peculiar character of social and historical enquiry. For the *objects* of such enquiry are the product of *subjects* capable of action and understanding, so that our knowledge of the social and historical world cannot be sharply separated from the subjects who make up that world.

John B. Thompson
University of Cambridge

References

Gadamer, H.-G. (1975 [1960]) *Truth and Method*, London. (Original edn, *Wahrheit und Methode*, Tübingen.)

Ricoeur, P. (1981) *Hermeneutics and the Human Sciences: Essays on Language, Action and Interpretation*, ed. and trans. J. B. Thompson, Cambridge, UK.

Further reading

Palmer, R. E. (1969) *Hermeneutics: Interpretation Theory in Schleiermacher, Dilthey, Heidegger, and Gadamer*, Evanston, IL.

See also: Habermas, Jürgen

hierarchy

Hierarchy is an organization in grades or orders or ranks of descending power, authority or prestige. In this general meaning, the concept has been absorbed into the social sciences and into common use. But its etymological reference is ecclesiastic. It refers to priestly government, usually to the Roman Catholic Church, but more widely to the graded organization of either angels or clergy. In classical enumeration there were nine functions or orders of the heavenly host subdivided into triads (also called hierarchies) in descending order: Seraphim, Cherubim, Thrones; Dominations, Virtues, Powers; Principalities, Archangels, Angels. The clerical hierarchy reflects the heavenly orders. Its highest triad is formed by baptism, communion and chrism (anointing). Second come the three orders of the ministry, bishops, priests and deacons. Third is the lowest triad of monks, 'initiated' and catechumens (those being prepared for baptism).

The celestial hierarchy is presumably of marginal interest to social scientists, but the earthly hierarchy is part of the complicated history of human organizations. In its modern secular usage, the word hierarchy has lost, or at least obscured, its connotation of sacredness and function as denoted in the triads described above. Yet these were essential aspects of the organization of the early Christian churches. St Paul appointed bishops at local churches with the pre-eminently spiritual function and spiritual authority of reproducing the Last Supper. As this duty became ritualized into the symbolic ceremony of the Eucharist the bishop was thought of as the representative of the Apostles. It may be that the original churches were collegiate, and therefore almost the opposite of the modern conception of hierarchical, in their organization, holding the authority of Christ collectively. But if so, collegial authority was soon superseded by power vested in a bishop with the presbyters as his council, and deacons appointed by him as administrative assistants. The theory thus emerged of the transmission of authority through the laying on of the bishop's hands.

Further development of the priestly hierarchy followed when Constantine made Christianity the state religion of Rome, willing that the Church be co-extensive with his empire. Civil and ecclesiastical administration became standardized, the areas of civil administration being formed to coincide with the ecclesiastical diocese, larger civil regions with patriarchal regions, and the whole Church centred on the supreme patriarchate at Rome. Papal authority thus became supreme in the Church and survived the fall of the Roman Empire.

The hierarchy was challenged at various times in the Middle Ages, notably as a result of the widespread inconsistency between the personal lives of local priests and the official claims of the priesthood to authority over their parishioners. The Lutheran revolt and the ensuing Protestant Reformation challenged the evolved theory of priestly hierarchy as it had developed in imperial and medieval Rome. Luther revived the medieval concept of the secular monarch as the vicar of God on earth in opposition to papal autocracy. The monarch provided the external or secular authority of the Church; internal authority was provided by religious dedication and spiritual grace among the Church members. Calvinism, while also rejecting the Roman hierarchy, gave greater power to its ministers and did not accord supremacy to the state. Calvin's ministers were held to be recipients of divine authority, but it was a collegiate authority vested not in Pope or bishop, but in the representatives chosen from a single united order. In the Church of England the reformed hierarchy is best described as the continuation of Catholicism without the Pope.

Thus the forms of authority and the division of powers and functions between state and church, ministry and laity, vary considerbly within Christendom. But all remain hierarchical in the original sense of organizing a divine spiritual authority.

The use of the term hierarchy in modern social science typically lacks this religious reference. Dumont (1970) defines it as 'a ladder of command in which the lower rungs are encompassed in the higher ones in regular succession'. He has in mind here a version of the *Shorter Oxford Dictionary* definition – 'a body of persons or things ranked in grades, orders or classes one above another'. He refers to Talcott Parsons's (1954) conception of social stratification as a system of ranking based on *evaluation*, which fundamental process of human interaction tends to differentiate individuals and groups into a rank order. From this starting-point Dumont develops a comprehensive analysis of the caste system as a hierarchical order.

Caste systems, viewed as a special case of status systems, are essentially hierarchical in the Parsonian sense. Hierarchy can be detached from its religious context and used to describe systems of rank where the elements or strata are judged in relation to the whole. Hierarchy then takes its place as a special form of what is treated in modern sociology and anthropology under the heading of social stratification.

A. H. Halsey
University of Oxford

References

Dumont, L. (1970) *Homo Hierarchicus*, London.
Parsons, T. (1954), 'A revised analytical approach to the theory of social stratification', in T. Parsons, *Essays in Sociological Theory*, Glencoe, Ill.

Further reading

Tocqueville, A. de (1875), *Democracy in America*, London.
Tocqueville, A. de (1952–3), *L'Ancien Régime et la Révolution*, 2 vols, Paris.
Bendix, R. (1978), *Kings or People*, London.
Bendix, R. and Lipset, S. M. (eds) (1967), *Class, Status and Power*, 2nd edn, London.

historical demography

The relative growth and decline of populations has been a fundamental concern of modern political and economic theorists since Machiavelli and Boisguilbert, and a sophisticated algebra of human numbers began as early as the seventeenth century. Malthus (1986) and his nineteenth-century contemporaries observed that human numbers are checked not only by mortality but also by institutions and customs which keep fertility well below biological maximum for the species, like delayed marriage. The development of a general method of analysing how these and other factors structured populations in the past, however, dates only to the 1950s, when a new approach was initiated by the French demographer, Louis Henry. He formulated rules which showed how to codify the mass of baptisms, burials and marriages recorded in parish records before 1800, defining each individual as a member of a reconstituted family over a specific duration (Fleury and Henry 1965). While Henry's method created new opportunities for technical demographic innovation, its main impact as the field has developed has been to show how the demographic constitution of a society can act as a primary factor shaping social and economic change. Historical demography has in consequence come to play an important interdisciplinary role, entering into concepts and methods employed by anthropologists, geographers and sociologists, as well as social and economic historians.

This breadth of interest reflects the shift in historical focus implied in Henry's approach. Detailed family histories had hitherto been available for some elite populations, but, following Henry, it became possible to trace, individual and family life courses for a substantial sample of an entire community. At base, the method entails systematic tracing of individual and family names in parish records ('nominal linkage'). The changing family structures to which this process gives rise then serve as a framework for integrating information on the same names or lives as they appear in a wider body of sources: civil, ecclesiastical and manorial court records; wills and inventories; census lists; Poor Law records; diaries and memoirs; and so forth. Once articulated in this way, many features of local society may be examined, notably the operation of social control, social and geographical mobility, interrelations between economic and health conditions, and the operation of land tenure and inheritance systems. Although developed initially with reference to European populations, this methodology has proven applicable to sources elsewhere, notably in China, Japan and the Americas.

One of the most fruitful lines of enquiry has addressed what Henry called 'natural fertility', that is, analysis of the set of factors (nuptiality, breastfeeding, foetal mortality, coital frequency, etc.) which regulate reproduction in the absence of modern contraceptive methods and strategies of fertility control. Reconstitution studies have established that a tremendous diversity characterized pre-industrial demographic systems. Very few groups practised birth control, yet completed family sizes have been found to vary from 2.9 to 11.4 births per woman. At the same time, infant mortality rates ranged from 140 to 280 per 1,000, rising in unfavourable circumstances to more than 400 per 1,000. These results overturn generally accepted notions that large families were everywhere the norm in past times, and that traditional rural societies were locked in a race that pitted high fertility against high mortality in an inexorable struggle to ensure social survival.

Debunking common myths about our demographic pasts has, in turn, encouraged rethinking the conventional view of population as a dependent variable in socioeconomic theory. Hajnal (1965), for instance, has identified a characteristic European marriage pattern, extant as early as the sixteenth century, in which women did not marry on average until age 23, and up to 15–20 per cent remained unmarried. In places like England, relatively small family sizes consequent on this pattern preceded rather than followed modern economic development. Viewed in aggregate terms, this marriage pattern carried important economic advantages: delayed marriage and correspondingly lower fertility were mechanisms which helped families to cope when times were hard and new economic opportunities scarce; conversely, the 'nuptiality valve' was flexible, opening up as circumstances improved to allow earlier marriage and renewed population growth, with their implications for expanding labour resources and markets. However, viewed at the local level, with the assistance of record linkage, it becomes clear that the timing of marriage carried strategic advantages with regard to much more than aggregate economic conditions. Even within the same community, different occupational, class, ethnic and religious groups could have different reproductive patterns and family compositions, reflecting the interplay of natural fertility and mortality with local institutions and values. These findings are echoed in research on a more recent phase in population history, known as the demographic transition. Coale and Watkins (1986), in reanalysing European census data on a province-by-province basis, have shown that declining family size in the late nineteenth and twentieth centuries cannot be accounted for adequately in terms of macro-level socioeconomic correlations. Attention has turned instead to examining how aggregate shifts in marriage and reproduction were expressions of a welter of institutional and cultural arrangements operating at several subnational levels.

Opening up new perspectives and extensive bodies of data has inevitably posed technical problems for historical demography. Perhaps the greatest difficulties arise in the attempt to move from local to aggregative levels of analysis. The calculation of conventional demographic measures requires record both of the incidence of births, deaths and marriages, and of the total populations at risk of experiencing these events. Family reconstitution, in supplying the former, provides many checks on the internal consistency of data. But it generally cannot supply the latter owing to well-known limitations of parish registers in most countries. These sources tend to give a very partial picture of migrants. They exclude members of important religious and ethnic groups. In many places records have been lost or were badly kept, especially for crucial urban populations. The distribution of reliable records, therefore, when viewed from a regional or national perspective, is far from uniform, and requires careful selection and adjustment. Pioneering work on these problems by Wrigley and Schofield (1981) has shown how representative samples may be established, and also how conventional demographic techniques used to forecast future population structures can be modified to generate population sizes and structures at successively earlier historical periods. The limitations and possible generalizability of their approach are currently the focus of much discussion.

Philip Kreager
University of Oxford

References

Coale, A. J. and Watkins, S. C. (eds) (1986) *The Decline of Fertility in Europe*, Princeton, NJ.

Fleury, M. and Henry, L. (1965) *Nouveau manuel de depouillement et d'exploitation de l'etat civil ancient*, Paris.

Hajnal, J. (1965) 'European marriage patterns in perspective', in D. V. Glass and D. E. C. Eversley (eds) *Population in History*, London.

Malthus, T. R. (1986) *Works*, vols. 1–4, Wrigley, E. A. and Souden, D. London.

Wrigley, E. A. and Schofield, R. (1981) *The Population History of England, 1541–1871*, London.

Further reading

Livi-Bacci, M. (1992) *A Concise History of World Population*, Oxford.

See also: family history; household.

historical geography

Historical geography has had a variety of meanings. Once used as a synonym for the history of geographical thought, it has long since ceased to be so employed. In the nineteenth and early-twentieth centuries it was commonly used to embrace the history of exploration and discovery, of mapping the earth, and of changes in political and administrative boundaries. But the birth and infancy of modern historical geography as the geographical study of the past can be traced to the 1920s and 1930s; by the mid-1960s it had matured into a distinctive discipline concerned not only with reconstructing past geographies but also with studying geographical changes.

A significant definition of the discipline was provided by H. C. Darby (1962) in a major statement which integrated old and new views by identifying four main approaches to historical geography: first, geographies of the past – 'horizontal' cross-sections of the geography of an area at some past time; second, changing landscapes – 'vertical' themes of landscape transformation, such as the clearing of woodlands and the draining of marshes; third, the past in the present – historical explanations of the present-day geography of a place; fourth, geographical history – investigation of the influence of geographical conditions (environmental and locational) upon the course of history. Historical geography within this mould came to be characterized as an approach in which the data were historical but in which the problems and methods were geographical: it emphasized mapping historical sources in order to demonstrate regional differences in past times and changing landscapes during past periods. The method was demonstrated *par excellence* in Darby's work on the Domesday geographies and on the draining of the Fens (Darby 1940; 1952–77).

From the early 1970s the Darbian tradition of an historical geography grounded in source-based empiricism and methodological pragmatism came increasingly and importantly to be interrogated in the light of developments in contemporary human geography and in the social sciences in general. An initial willingness by some historical geographers to participate in attempts to 'explain' the world though general theories of spatial organization was soon replaced by a wider rejection, or at best limited acceptance, of positivist spatial science when applied to historical studies, and then by a deliberate endeavour to explore other approaches to historico-geographical enquiry, involving encounters with historical materialism and humanistic idealism. Significantly, historical geographers have been in the forefront of the attack on positivist spatial science while at the same time deploying social theory in geography and arguing the case for the geographical imagination in social science. With a renewed recognition both of the need for an historical perspective within contemporary human geography and for a geographical perspective within history (and the social sciences), historical geography is making a vital contribution both to its parent and to cognate disciplines.

Historical geography as the study of past (largely human) geographies reflects the diversity of geography itself. It embraces not only geography's traditional, central concerns with regions, places and areas but also the modern, peripheral concerns of the ecological, locational and landscape schools of geography.

First, some notable books and atlases have been published treating the historical geographies of particular countries, areas and continents. Second, other studies focus upon the changing relationships of people with their physical environments, with the impact of cultures upon natural ecologies. Such studies themselves take a variety of forms: some are concerned with tracing historically the interactions between peoples and their physical environments which provide the material resources for sustaining both life and distinctive lifestyles in particular places; others are concerned with reconstructing historical geosophies, with questions about people's perceptions (and misperceptions) of their physical environments; while other studies monitor the impact of peoples upon their physical environments, engaging with questions about environmental management (and mismanagement) in the past.

Third, within historical geography there is a long-established school of location and diffusion studies, concerned with the spread of phenomena over space and through time. For long associated with the work of Carl Sauer and the Berkeley school of cultural geography in North America, diffusion studies have themselves changed under the impact of Torsten Hägerstrand, a Swedish geographer, so that they now range from informal, qualitative studies of the spread of the domestication of plants and animals to formal, quantitative studies of the spread of agricultural innovations and of diseases.

Finally, the landscape school within historical geography is similarly represented by contrasting approaches: some studies remain focused upon reconstructing the transformation of landscapes by human (principally economic) activity, while others explore the symbolic design and representation of landscapes, and the decoding of their meanings and iconographies.

Alan R. H. Baker
University of Cambridge

References

Darby, H. C. (1940) *The Draining of the Fens*, Cambridge, UK.
—— (ed.) (1952–77) *The Domesday Geographies of England*, 7 vols, Cambridge, UK.
—— (1962), 'Historical geography', in H. P. R. Finberg (ed.) *Approaches to History*, London.

Further reading

Baker, A. R. H. (ed.) (1972) *Progress in Historical Geography*, Newton Abbot.
Baker, A. R. H. and Billinge, M. (eds) (1982) *Period and Place: Research Methods in Historical Geography*, Cambridge, UK.
Baker, A. R. H. and Gregory, D. (1984) *Explorations in Historical Geography*, Cambridge, UK.
Brooks Green, D. (ed.) (1991) *Historical Geography: A Methodological Portrayal*, Savage, MD.
Butlin, R. A. (1993) *Historical Geography: Through the Gates of Time and Space*, London.
Driver, F. (1988) 'The historicity of human geography', *Progress in Human Geography* 12.
Earle, C. (1989) 'Historical geography', in G. L. Gaile and C. J. Willmot (eds) *Geography in America*, Columbus, OH.
—— (1992) *Geographical Inquiry and American Historical Problems*, Stanford, CA.
Genovese, E. D. and Hochberg, L. (eds) (1989) *Geographic Perspectives in History*, Oxford.
Gregory, D. (1985) 'Space and time in social life', *Wallace W. Atwood Lecture Series, Clark University*, 1.
—— (1991) 'Interventions in the historical geography of modernity: social theory, spatiality and the politics of representation', *Geografiska Annaler B* 73.
—— (1994) *Geographical Imaginations*, Oxford.
Gregory, D. and Urry, J. (eds) (1985) *Social Relations and Spatial Structures*, Basingstoke.
Hochberg, L. J. and Earle, C. (eds) (1995) *Geography of Social Change*, Stanford, CA.
Norton, W. (1984) *Historical Analysis in Geography*, London.
Pacione, M. (ed.) (1987) *Historical Geography: Progress and Prospect*, London.
Pred, A. (1990) *Making Histories and Constructing Geographies: The Local Transformation of Practice, Power Relations and Consciousness*, Boulder, CO.

See also: social history.

historical linguistics

Historical linguistics, as opposed to the history of linguistics, is the study, reconstruction, theoretical explication and modelling of language change over time. It is the linguistic counterpart of (diachronic) cultural anthropology, cultural or social history, or evolutionary biology.

In the nineteenth century, linguistics *was* predominantly historical: it was the study of evolution and change, not of structure. Following Saussure's (1916) radical dichotomy of linguistics into synchronic and diachronic studies as mutually exclusive pursuits, there was a reversal of interest, a period lasting well into the 1960s, when (in the English-speaking world at least) 'prestige' linguistics was synchronic ('structural'), and historical linguistics was either a minority pursuit of general linguists, or, from the linguist's point of view, an autonomous backwater institutionalized in the universities and journals as comparative philology, or history of English/German, and so on. (There are notable European exceptions, for example the work of the Prague School, and American exceptions in the work of Sapir, Bloomfield, Hockett, and others – but the generalization holds overall.)

As interest shifted from primary concern with data-processing to deeper theoretical concerns, often with explanatory pretensions (Lass 1980), historical linguistics gradually became integrated as a subfield of general linguistics. Each succeeding or competing school (paradigm) developed a synthesis, in which techniques of synchronic description and analysis and explanatory claims were applied to historical data, and often (partly at least) validated by their diachronic success. (This assumed, perhaps reasonably, that theories of what something *is* ought to bear on theories of its mutations over time: this could be compared to the largely successful wedding of synchronic genetics and evolutionary theory in biology.)

Historical linguistics follows four main lines of enquiry.

'Factual'/'Reconstructive'

This area covers three traditional activities: first, reconstructing unattested *états de langue* on the basis of comparison of descendant forms in different languages (for example, Proto-Indo-European *yúg-o-m* 'yoke' on the basis of Latin *jug-u-m*, Greek *zúg-o-n*, Sanskrit *yúg-a-m*, and so on; second, construction of chronicle histories of languages or language families (including reworkings of older histories on the basis of new evidence or interpretation); third, etymology or constructing phonological and semantic histories of particular words or groups, often showing up relations among forms that seem at first unrelated (such as the connection between *feather*, Greek *pétros* 'rock', and Latin *petere* 'strive' established by Maher 1973). These activities were the foundation of the discipline and are still practised, applied in some cases to unwritten or exotic language families (see Dixon 1980 on Australian) or to microhistories of unexplored aspects of familiar languages (see Lass 1976 on neglected pieces of the history of English).

Theoretical interpretative

The reinterpretation of known histories of languages in terms of current (often competing) research paradigms, and the use of historical data to make general theoretical points or validate particular models. Examples are the structuralist synthesis in Hoenigswald (1960) and the generativist synthesis in King (1969). Lightfoot (1979) attempted to reinterpret aspects of the history of English syntax in the light of a 'restrictive' transformational theory. Harris (1979) produced a history of French syntax drawing on work in word-order typology and theories of syntactic universals.

Sociolinguistic

Contemporary quantitative methods of studying linguistic variation in speech communities, especially the covariation of linguistic and social variables, have led to apparent observations of change in progress (something formerly thought impossible). These studies (e.g. Labov *et al.* 1972; Trudgill 1974), while not strictly historical, have none the less had a profound impact on historians, as they have for the first time made clear the primary mechanism of historical change – variation, cumulatively weighted in particular directions.

Sociohistorical linguistics

Sociolinguistic theory has been projected into history to form a new subdiscipline, sociohistorical linguistics, which is a major synthesis of these two directions, and is perhaps the most important contemporary development in the field (Romaine 1980).

Roger Lass
University of Cape Town

References

Dixon, R. M. W. (1980) *The Languages of Australia*, Cambridge, UK.

Harris, M. (1979) *The Evolution of French Syntax: A Comparative Approach*, London.

Hoenigswald, H. (1960) *Language Change and Linguistic Reconstruction*, Chicago.

King, R. D. (1969) *Historical Linguistics and Generative Grammar*, Englewood Cliffs, NJ.

Labov, W., Yeager, M. and Steiner, R. (1972) *A Quantitative Study of Sound Change in Progress*, 2 vols, Philadelphia, PA.

Lass, R. (1976) *English Phonology and Phonological Theory: Synchronic and Diachronic Studies*, Cambridge, UK.

—— (1980) *On Explaining Language Change*, Cambridge, UK.

Lightfoot, D. (1979) *Principles of Diachronic Syntax*, Cambridge, UK.

Maher, J. P. (1973) 'Neglected reflexes of Proto-Indo-European *pet* – 'fly': Greek *pétros* 'stone' *pétra* 'cliff'; with notes on the role of syntax (IC structure) in polysemy and semantic change, and the situational motivation of syntax', *Lingua e Stile* 8.

Romaine, S. (1980) *Sociohistorical Linguistics*, Cambridge, UK.

Saussure, F. de (1916) *Cours de Linguistique Générale*, Paris.

Trudgill, P. (1974) *The Social Differentiation of English in Norwich*, Cambridge, UK.

Further reading

Antilla, R. (1972) *An Introduction to Historical and Comparative Linguistics*, New York.

Bynon, T. (1977) *Historical Linguistics*, Cambridge, UK.

Pedersen, H. (1962) *The Discovery of Language*, tr. J. W. Spargo, Bloomington, IN.

history

History has some claim to be considered one of the world's oldest professions, and the subject was taught in some European universities, from Oxford to Göttingen, in the seventeenth and eighteenth centuries (Gilbert 1977). However, the rise of history as an academic discipline in the west coincided with the rise of the social sciences in the nineteenth century. The relation of historians to these subjects was often one of rivalry and conflict. Inspired by the work of Leopold von Ranke (1795–1886), historians were moving away from the history of society which some of them had practised in the eighteenth century and concentrating their attention on the production of narratives of political events firmly based on official documents. They tended to define their discipline by contrast to the social sciences, especially to sociology, although they were often interested in geography as a handmaid to their subject, while a handful of economic historians, such as Gustav Schmoller (1838–1917) had an interest in economic theory. Karl Lamprecht (1856–1915) in Germany and James Harvey Robinson (1863–1936) and others in the USA advocated a new kind of history which would pay considerable attention to culture and society and also draw on the concepts and theories of social scientists, but these historians were isolated among their professional colleagues. At the end of the nineteenth century, the conventional wisdom of the historian's craft, expressed in philosophical form by Wilhelm Dilthey (1833–1911), Wilhelm Windelband (1848–1915), Heinrich Rickert (1863–1936) and Benedetto Croce (1866–1952), was that history was concerned with unique events (leaving the establishment of general laws to the social sciences), and that historians tried to understand the past from within (while social scientists attempted to explain it from outside). For their part, sociologists such as Auguste Comte (1798–1857) and Herbert Spencer (1820–1903) regarded historians as at best collectors of raw material for theorists to utilize.

This intellectual landscape had not changed very much by the middle of the twentieth century. In Britain, for example, the views associated with Dilthey and Croce were reiterated with force by R. G. Collingwood (1888–1943), the one philosopher of history to be taken seriously in the English-speaking world (perhaps because he doubled as a historian of Roman Britain). There had been a few rebellions against the hegemony of political narrative, but in 1950 they could not yet be described as successful. Marxist historians had not yet produced many important works – the exceptions include Jan Romein's *The Lowlands by the Sea* (1934) and Emilio Sereni's *Capitalism in the Countryside* (1947). Only in two areas was change truly visible. Economic historians had become a significant group within the profession, with their own journals, such as the *Economic History Review*, their own heroes, such as the Belgian Henri Pirenne (1862–1935) and the Swede Eli Heckscher (1879–1952), and their own debates, which often had more in common with debates among economists than with those of their fellow-historians.

In France, a broader approach to history, inspired by Lucien Febvre (1878–1956) and Marc Bloch (1886–1944) and associated with the journal *Annales*, had begun to attract attention, and a remarkable work on the Mediterranean world in the age of Philip II was published in 1949 by Fernand Braudel (1902–85), particularly original in its exploration of what the author called 'geohistory', a historical geography influenced by the work of Vidal de la Blache but rather more deterministic.

Retrospectively, the 1950s now appear to be something of a historiographical turning-point. Serious Marxist history finally came on stream, generally produced outside the communist bloc (by Eric Hobsbawm and Edward Thompson in Britain, Pierre Vilar in France, etc.), but occasionally within it – an outstanding example being the work of the Polish economic historian Witold Kula (1916–88). In France, the *Annales* group, under Braudel's leadership, came to dominate the profession, both intellectually and institutionally. In the USA, France, and elsewhere, the 'new economic history', like economics, became increasingly ambitious in its aims, and quantitative in its methods. It was sometimes taken as a model for other kinds of history. Historical demography, for instance, which emerged as a sub-discipline in the 1950s (inspired by increasing concern with contemporary population growth), is a form of quantitative social history (Wrigley 1969). Other social historians and historical sociologists also took a quantitative turn at this time, though some resisted; E. P. Thompson's classic study *The Making of the English Working Class* (1963) contains a characteristically savage critique of what the author called sociology, more exactly the quantitative historical sociology of Talcott Parsons's follower Neil Smelser, who had recently written about the Industrial Revolution. Quantification also played an important role in the 'new political history', practised in the USA in particular, whether the emphasis fell on election results, voting patterns in Congress, or attempts to count strikes and other forms of protest (Bogue 1983). Similar methods were applied to religious history, particularly in France, with statistics for annual confession and communion taking the place of voting figures. For example, in his original and controversial book on 'baroque piety and dechristianisation', Michel Vovelle (1973) studied some 30,000 wills from eighteenth-century Provence, using them as indexes of views of death and of changes in religious attitudes. His work offered a possible link between cliometrics and another concern of the 1950s, 'psychohistory'. In France, following the tradition of Durkheim and Lucien Lévy-Bruhl (1857–1939), interest in historical psychology focused not on individuals but on collective mentalities, as in a series of studies by Philippe

Ariès (1914–84) on changing attitudes to childhood and to death over the centuries. A few bold spirits, among them the French medievalist Jacques Le Goff, attempted to study mentalities in the manner of Claude Lévi-Strauss, emphasizing binary oppositions in general and the opposition between nature and culture in particular. In the USA, where the ideas of Sigmund Freud were more deeply embedded in the culture than elsewhere, some historians and psychoanalysts attempted to study the motives and drives of religious and political leaders such as Martin Luther, Woodrow Wilson, Lenin and Gandhi, while a president of the American Historical Association invited his colleagues to consider psychohistory as their 'next assignment' (Langer 1958).

With few exceptions, historians failed to respond to Langer's invitation. What some of them did do in the 1970s, like their colleagues in related disciplines, to some extent as a reaction to the events of 1968, was to reject determinism (economic or geographical), as they rejected quantitative methods and the claim of the social sciences to be scientific. In the case of history, this rejection of the work of the previous generation was accompanied by new approaches to the past, four in particular, which can be summed up by four slogans in four languages: 'history from below', *microstoria*, *Alltagsgeschichte*, and *histoire de l'imaginaire*.

First, 'history from below', is an ambiguous term, and both meanings are important: not only the history of ordinary people in the past but also history written from the point of view of ordinary people. It is perhaps the most important change in the discipline in the twentieth century, a true Copernican Revolution in historical writing which compensates for the inadequacies of a tradition of elitist historiography that ignored the experiences, the culture and the aspirations of dominated groups (Guha 1982). This shift has encouraged and has in turn been encouraged by the rise of oral history, giving ordinary people an opportunity to describe their experience of the historical process in their own words. However, the practice of history from below has turned out to be much less simple than was originally thought, largely because of differences between different kinds of dominated groups – the working class, the peasantry, the colonized, and of course women. It was around the 1970s that the movement for women's history became generally visible, thanks to the rise of women's studies and feminism, and the result was to undermine any assumption of the unity of the 'subordinate classes'. In the second place, the study of the working class, or of women, or of popular culture, in isolation from the study of the middle class, or men, or elite culture, is now generally considered to be misleading, and attention is turning to the relations between these different groups.

Second, *microstoria* or microhistory may be defined as a concern with the past at the level of a small community, whether village, street, family or even individual, an examination of 'faces in the crowd' which allows concrete experience to re-enter social history. This approach was put on the historical map by Carlo Ginzburg's *Cheese and Worms* (1976), a study of the cosmos of a sixteenth-century Italian miller, as revealed in his replies to interrogations by the Inquisition, and by Emmanuel le Roy Ladurie's *Montaillou* (1975), which was also based on inquisitorial records and used them to produce a portrait of a fourteenth-century village which the author himself compared to community studies such as Ronald Blythe's *Akenfield*. These two books were not only bestsellers but also exemplary in the sense of inspiring a school or at least a trend. Condemned by more traditional historians as a kind of antiquarianism and as a dereliction of the historian's duty to explain how the modern world emerged, microhistory has been defended by one of its leading practitioners, Giovanni Levi (1991), on the grounds that the reduction of scale reveals how political and social rules often do not work in practice and how individuals can make spaces for themselves in the interstices between institutions.

Third, *Alltagsgeschichte* or 'the history of the everyday' is an approach which developed, or was at least defined in Germany, drawing on a philosophical and sociological tradition which includes Alfred Schutz (1899–1959) and Erving Goffman (1922–82), Henri Lefebvre and Michel de Certeau (1925–86). Like microhistory, with which it overlaps, the history of the everyday has been important as a way of reinserting human experience into social history, which was perceived by some of its practitioners as becoming increasingly abstract and faceless. The approach has been criticized for its concern with what the critics call trivialities, as well as for ignoring politics, but it has been defended, in much the same way that microhistory has been defended, on the grounds that it shows how trifles may be clues to important, subterranean changes (Lüdtke 1982).

Fourth, *histoire de l'imaginaire* or the history of mentalities might be defined as the everyday version of intellectual history or the history of ideas, in other words the history of habits of thought or unspoken assumptions rather than of ideas which have been consciously formulated by philosophers and other theorists. This approach, which originated in France in the 1920s and 1930s, has gone through something of a revival. As not infrequently happens in these cases, however, what is revived is not quite the same as what had existed earlier. Historians working in this area show an increasing concern with 'representations' (literary, visual or mental), and also with what French historians, following Jacques Lacan and Michel Foucault, call the *imaginaire* (perhaps best translated as the 'imagined' rather than the 'imaginary'). With this shift has come what is often called a new emphasis on the construction, constitution or 'social production' not only of different forms of culture – the 'invention of traditions', for example – but also of states and societies, which are now often viewed not as hard or objective structures, but rather as 'imagined communities' (Anderson 1991; Hobsbawm and Ranger 1983). In other words, historians like their colleagues in other disciplines are experiencing the effects of the 'linguistic turn'.

It is worth noting that all four of the approaches described are linked in some way to social anthropology, since anthropologists are concerned with 'the native's point of view' and work in small communities, observing everyday life and studying modes of thought or belief systems. Indeed, a number of historians practising these approaches would describe themselves as historical anthropologists, and introduce their work with references to E. E. Evans-Pritchard, to Victor Turner or, most often, to Clifford Geertz (Walters 1980).

Despite the importance of these four linked trends, they are not sufficient to describe recent changes in historical writing (let alone to characterize the work of more traditional historians). As was only to be expected, there are movements in different and even in opposite directions. While some scholars try to observe social change through the microscope, others, in the spirit of the 'total history' preached and practised by Fernand Braudel, try to look at the world as a whole. The best-known representative of this approach, apart from Braudel himself, is Immanuel Wallerstein, a sociologist of Africa turned historian of capitalism, in a series of volumes on 'the modern world-system'. Marxist in inspiration, these influential volumes draw on the economics of development and world systems theory in order to show connections between the rise of Venice and Amsterdam and the underdevelopment of eastern Europe and South America (Wallerstein 1974–). As might have been predicted, other attempts to see the history of planet earth as a whole have adopted an ecological viewpoint, examining, for instance, the consequences of the encounter between Europe and America as a 'Columbian exchange' of plants, animals, and, not least, diseases, and so 'placing Nature in History' (Crosby 1972). Braudel's geo-history has come to look rather static in the light of current concerns with the interaction between the landscape and its human and animal populations (Cronon 1990; Worst 1988).

At the same time as these new developments, and in reaction to some of them, readers of history have witnessed two revivals, the revival of politics and the revival of narrative. There have been many pleas by historians to put politics back into history, if not to restore its former dominance. In some respects the climate of the 1980s and 1990s has been favourable to a revival of politics, since the general rejection of determinism has made room for discussions of strategy and tactics which we may call political. However, under the influence of the trends discussed above, political history has been reconstructed to include what Michel Foucault described as micropolitics – in other words, strategies and tactics at the level of the village or the family as well as that of the state. Even diplomatic history, necessarily focused on states, has widened its concerns to include an interest in mentalities and in rituals.

More frequently discussed and more controversial is the trend towards the revival of narrative and of the history of events once so forcefully dismissed by the leaders of the *Annales* School (Stone 1979). As in the case of politics, the term revival is somewhat misleading. The history of events used to be written as if the past included nothing else, whereas historians, like some sociologists and anthropologists, are now explicitly concerned with the relation between events and structures (whether these structures are social or cultural, if that distinction still makes sense). As for narrative, it has returned in a new form, or more exactly a variety of new forms, since at least a few historians – like their sociological and anthropological colleagues – are conscious of their use of rhetoric, interested in literary experiment, and even (like some contemporary novelists) in transgressing the traditional boundaries between fact and fiction (White 1978). One of these new forms is the narrative of small-scale events, a technique commonly deployed by microhistorians, and a considerable contrast to the traditional Grand Narrative which emphasized key events and dates such as 1066, 1492, 1789, 1914, and so on. Another is the story told from more than one viewpoint, in order to accommodate differences in the perception of events from above and from below, by opposite sides in a civil war, and so on. Given current interest in encounters between cultures, it is likely that this dialogic form of narrative will be practised more and more frequently in the future. As this entry takes the form of a monologue, this is perhaps the moment to draw attention to the fact that it has itself been written from a particular point of view, that of a middle-class Englishman, and that – like most articles in this volume – it is especially though not exclusively concerned with developments in the west.

Peter Burke
University of Cambridge

References

Anderson, B. (1991) *Imagined Communities*, revised edn, London.

Bogue, A. G. (1983) *Clio and the Bitch Goddess: Quantification in American Political History*, Beverly Hills, CA.

Cronon, W. (1990) 'Placing nature in history', *Journal of American History* 76.

Crosby, A. W. (1972) *The Columbian Exchange: Biological and Cultural Consequences of 1492*, Westport, CT.

Gilbert, F. (1977) 'Reflections on the history of the professor of history', in F. Gilbert, *History: Choice and Commitment*, Cambridge, MA.

Guha, R. (1982) 'Some aspects of the historiography of colonial India', in *Subaltern Studies* I, Delhi.

Hobsbawm, E. J. and Ranger, T. O. (eds) (1983) *The Invention of Tradition*, Cambridge, UK.

Langer, W. L. (1958) 'The next assignment', *American Historical Review* 63.

Levi, G. (1991) 'On microhistory', in P. Burke (ed.) *New Perspectives on Historical Writing*, Cambridge, UK.

Lüdtke, A. (1982) 'The historiography of everyday life', in R. Samuel and G. Stedman Jones (eds) *Culture, Ideology and Politics*, London.

Stone, L. (1979) 'The revival of narrative', *Past and Present* 85.

Vovelle, M. (1973) *Piété baroque et déchristianisation en Provence au 18e sièecle*, Paris.

Wallerstein, I. (1974–) *The Modern World System*, New York.

Walters, R. G. (1980) 'Signs of the times: Clifford Geertz and historians', *Social Research* 47.

White, H. V. (1978) *Tropics of Discourse*, Baltimore, MD.

Worsten, D. (ed.) (1988) *The Ends of the Earth: Perspectives on Modern Environmental History*, Cambridge, UK.

Wrigley E. A. (1969) *Population and History*, London.

Further reading

Burke, P. (ed.) (1991) *New Perspectives on Historical Writing*, Cambridge, UK.

Iggers, G. G. (1984) *New Directions in European Historiography*, 2nd edn, Middletown, CT.

history, cultural *see* cultural history

history, economic *see* economic history

history, family *see* family history

history, Marxist *see* Marxist history

history, oral *see* oral history

history, social *see* social history

history of medicine

Doctors have long been conscious of traditions of the past. One of the Hippocratic treatises (third century BC) was entitled *Ancient Medicine*, and the veneration long accorded to the Hippocratics, Galen and other ancient medical writers guaranteed a steady stream of editions of classical authors well into the seventeenth century. From the eighteenth century, historical surveys of medicine began to be produced by doctors such as John Freind, Daniel Leclerc and Kurt Sprengel. Physicians seeking membership in the Royal College of Physicians of London were still expected to be literate in the literature of antiquity until the mid-nineteenth century, but the growth of science within medicine, the development of national traditions within Europe and places where European influences dominated, and the increased use of the vernacular in teaching and writing gradually raised awareness of the present at the expense of the past, rendering the ancients genuinely *historical* figures.

In late nineteenth-century Germany, the history of medicine was energetically pursued by a number of doctors and philologists, and Institutes for the History of Medicine were established in several universities, most importantly in Leipzig, where Karl Sudhoff held the chair from 1905 to 1925. Henry Sigerist, Owsei Temkin and Erwin Ackerknecht all worked in Leipzig before emigrating to the USA, from the late 1920s. Whereas the history of medicine had previously been viewed as part of cultural or intellectual history, Sigerist brought to his scholarship a vision of the wider social forces which have always shaped notions of health and disease, and the doctor–patient encounter. As director of the Institute of the History of Medicine at Johns Hopkins University from 1932, Sigerist helped create a small professional discipline in his adopted country, and encouraged doctors to take seriously the study of their profession's past.

By the 1950s, medical history was being taught within a few medical schools in the USA, Germany, Spain and several other countries, and most professional medical historians came to the subject from a medical background. At the same time, parallel developments in the history of science helped foster a wider scholarly community. Most historians were comfortable operating within the ordinary conventions of 'Whiggism' (Herbert Butterfield's phrase), in which the study of medical history revealed the gradual triumph of truth over error, and science over superstition.

Since the 1960s, the practice of medical history has changed. From being a subject pursued largely by doctors for doctors, it has become the concern of scholars from many disciplines, including (*inter alia*) economic and social history, historical demography, sociology and anthropology. This has meant that the centre of gravity of academic history of medicine has shifted from the medical schools to social sciences departments.

Allied to this has been the greater range of sources brought to the discipline. Traditionally, medical historians concentrated on the great names and famous achievements of the past. Medical historians are now as likely to be interested in health as in the history of disease and discovery, to be concerned with the ordinary and mundane as with the elite, to write about the patient as the doctor. To this end, new kinds of printed and manuscript sources as well as artefacts have been put to the service of medical history. These include such materials as self-help manuals and advice books, diaries and personal papers of ordinary doctors as well as sufferers, the administrative and financial records of medical institutions, case books and iconographical material, legal records and theological tracts. Once health is included in the discipline's brief, the terrain becomes very wide.

The medical history being written today is more probing than of old. It has challenged comfortable notions of inevitable progress and disinterested professional behaviour. Several topics have been actively pursued. Following Michel Foucault's pioneering work in the 1960s, the history of psychiatry has attracted much attention. Historians have argued that definitions of mental disorder are historically contingent and psychiatry itself has been an agent of social control. Fringe and alternative practitioners have been rescued from historical oblivion. Tropical medicine has been revealed to be a tool of empire. Women, both as healers and as sufferers, have been minutely scrutinized. The politics of health and welfare have been analysed.

To accommodate these kinds of enquiries, a number of new journals and societies have been established. These have supplemented rather than replaced more traditional outlets and associations, and tensions between doctors and historians occasionally surface. The social history of medicine has been accused of having left the medicine out. Nevertheless, the subject has expanded and become more confident, even in an era of widespread academic retrenchment.

W. F. Bynum
Wellcome Institute for the History of Medicine

Further reading

Brieger, G. H. (1980) 'The history of medicine', in P. J. Durbin (ed.) *A Guide to the Culture of Science, Technology and Medicine*, New York.

—— (1993) 'The historiography of medicine', in W. F. Bynum and R. Porter (eds) *Companion Encyclopedia of the History of Medicine*, London.

Porter, R. and Wear, A. (eds) (1987) *Problems and Methods in the History of Medicine*, London.

Webster, C. (1983) 'The historiography of medicine', in P. Corsi and P. Weindling (eds) *Information Sources in the History of Science and Medicine*, London.

See also: cultural history; medical anthropology; medical sociology; social history.

Hobbes, Thomas (1588–1679)

Thomas Hobbes is one of the most important figures in the development of modern science and modern politics. As a contemporary of Bacon, Galileo and Descartes, he contributed to the radical critique of medieval Scholasticism and classical philosophy that marked the beginning of the modern age. But he alone sought to develop a comprehensive philosophy – one that treated natural science, political science and theory of scientific method in a unified system. He published this system in three volumes, under the titles *Body* (1655), *Man* (1657) and *Citizen* (1642). In the course of his long career, Hobbes also published treatises on mathematics, on free will and determinism, on the English common law system, and on the English Civil War. Although his work covered the whole of philosophy, Hobbes made his greatest contribution to modern thought in the field of political philosophy. On three separate occasions, he presented his theory of humankind and the state; the most famous of his political treatises, the *Leviathan* (1651), is generally recognized as the greatest work of political philosophy in the English language.

In all branches of knowledge, Hobbes's thought is characterized by a pervasive sense that the ancient and medieval philosophers had failed to discover true knowledge, and that a new alternative was urgently needed. It is this sense that defines Hobbes as a modern thinker and gives his work its originality, verve and self-conscious radicalism. In natural science (metaphysics and physics), he rejected the Scholastic and Aristotelian ideas of abstract essences and immaterial causes as nothing more than vain and empty speech. The nature of reality is matter in motion, which implied that all phenomena of nature and human nature could be explained in terms of mechanical causation. In the theory of science, Hobbes dismissed the disputative method of Scholasticism and classical dialectics as forms of rhetoric that merely appealed to the authority of common opinion and produced endless verbal controversies. The correct method of reasoning combined the resolutive-compositive method of Galileo and the deductive method of Euclidean geometry. By combining these, Hobbes believed that every branch of knowledge, including the study of politics, could be turned into an exact deductive science.

In political science proper, Hobbes was no less radical in his rejection of the tradition. He opposed the republicanism of classical antiquity, the ecclesiastical politics of medieval Europe, and the doctrine of mixed-monarchy prevalent in seventeenth-century England. All these doctrines, Hobbes claimed, were seditious in intent or effect, because they were derived from 'higher' laws that allowed people to appeal to a standard above the will of the sovereign. Hobbes blamed such appeals, exploited by ambitious priests and political demagogues, for the political instability of his times, culminating in the English Civil War. The solution he proposed was political absolutism – the unification of sovereignty in an all-powerful state that derived its authority not from higher laws but from *de facto* power and the consent of the people.

With these three teachings – mechanistic materialism, exact deductive science, and political absolutism – Hobbes sought to establish science and politics on a new foundation that would produce certain knowledge and lasting civil peace.

From the first, Hobbes's philosophical system generated controversy. In the seventeenth century, Hobbes was treated as a dangerous subversive by all who believed in, or had an interest in, the traditional order. Christian clergymen condemned his materialist view of the world as atheistic and his mechanistic view of humankind as soulless; legal scholars attacked his doctrine of absolutism for placing the sovereign above the civil laws; even kings, whose power Hobbes sought to augment, were wary of accepting the teaching that political authority rested on force and consent rather than on divine right (Mintz 1962). In the eighteenth and nineteenth centuries his defence of absolute and arbitrary power ran counter to the general demand for constitutional government. Hobbes has been treated more favourably in the twentieth century then ever before. Although some scholars have seen certain parallels between Hobbes's Leviathan state and twentieth-century tyrannies (Collingwood 1942), most clearly recognize that Hobbes's enlightened despot, whose primary goal is to secure civil peace, is vastly different from the brutal and fanatical heads of totalitarian states (Strauss 1959).

Such studies can be divided into four groups, each reflecting the perspective of a contemporary school of philosophy as it probes the origins of modernity. First, guided by the concerns of contemporary analytical philosophy, one group argues for the primacy of method and formal logic in Hobbes's system and views his politics as a set of formal rules which serve as utilitarian guidelines for the state (McNeilly 1968; Watkins 1965). A second group has examined Hobbes's theory of political obligation from a Kantian point of view. According to this interpretation, Hobbes's argument for obedience goes beyond calculations of utility by appealing to a sense of moral duty in keeping the social contract, and by requiring citizens to have just intentions (Taylor 1938; Warrender 1957). Developed by Marxist scholars, a third interpretation uses Hobbes to understand the ideological origins of bourgeois society and to provide a critical perspective on bourgeois liberalism by exposing its Hobbesian roots (Coleman 1977; Macpherson 1962). The fourth interpretation reflects the concerns of the natural law school. According to the foremost scholar of this school, Hobbes is the decisive figure in transforming the natural law tradition from classical natural right to modern natural 'rights'; Hobbes accomplished this revolution by asserting that the right of self-preservation, grounded in the fear of violent death, is the only justifiable moral claim (Strauss 1936).

Robert P. Kraynak
Colgate University

References

Coleman, F. M. (1977) *Hobbes and America: Exploring the Constitutional Foundations*, Toronto.
Collingwood, R. G. (1942) *The New Leviathan*, Oxford.
McNeilly, F. S. (1968) *The Anatomy of Leviathan*, London.
Macpherson, C. B. (1962) *The Political Theory of Possessive Individualism*, Oxford.
Mintz, S. I. (1962) *The Hunting of Leviathan*, Cambridge, UK.
Strauss, L. (1936) *The Political Philosophy of Hobbes*, Chicago.
—— (1959) 'On the basis of Hobbes's political philosophy', in *What is Political Philosophy?*, New York.
Taylor, A. E. (1938) 'The ethical doctrine of Hobbes', *Philosophy* 13.
Warrender, H. (1957) *The Political Philosophy of Hobbes: His Theory of Obligation*, Oxford.
Watkins, J. W. N. (1965) *Hobbes's System of Ideas: A Study in the Political Significance of Philosophical Theories*, London.

See also: social contract.

homosexualities

Homosexuality is a category invented as an object of scientific investigation by a Hungarian doctor, Benkert, in 1869, amidst a flurry of attempts to classify sexuality (Foucault 1979). It is hence a distinctively modern term. By contrast, same-sex erotic experiences have existed across time and space with varying degrees of visibility, frequency and social organization. In different parts of the world, homosexualities assume widely divergent forms from male cult prostitution to female romantic friendships; they may be patterned by age as in ancient Greece or some societies like the Sambia; by gender as in the North American Berdache; or by class, as in master–slave relations in antiquity (Faderman 1981; Greenberg 1988). There is no unitary experience.

It is not quite clear when the distinctive modern or western form emerged. Some connect it to the rise of capitalism, others to the emergence of a modern medicine, still others to the emergence of major urban centres. However it emerged, throughout the past two centuries, homosexuality has been seen negatively – as sin, sickness or crime. Until the 1970s, the dominant mode of thinking about homosexuality in the west was clinical: caused by degeneracy, biological anomaly or family pathology, and treatments ranging from castration to psychoanalysis were advocated. While such approaches do still continue, since 1973 the American Psychiatric Association has officially removed homosexuality from its nomenclature. Homosexuality is no longer a sickness (Lewes 1988). Male homosexuality has also been illegal in most European countries and US states; not until the 1960s – a decade after the decriminalizing proposals of the British Wolfenden Report and the American model penal code of 1955 proposed by the American Law Institute – did the legal situation significantly change.

Throughout this time of hostility, there were always challenges. Magnus Hirschfield established the Institute for Sexual Science in Berlin in 1897 and campaigned for acceptance of homosexuality till the 1930s when the Nazis started their policy of extermination (Plant 1986). Others – Carpenter and Wilde in England, Gide and Genet in France – were pursuing literary defences (Dollimore 1991). It was not until the period after the Second World War that a substantial body of published research suggested the ubiquity and normality of homosexual experience. The Kinsey Reports in 1948 and 1953 suggested that 37 per cent of men had some post-adolescent homosexual orgasm and 4 per cent had a preponderance of such experience (13 per cent and 3 per cent, respectively, for women). Kinsey also suggested there was a continuum of homosexual–heterosexual attraction (on a scale of 1 to 6) and that homosexuality was to be found in all walks of life.

There was a progressive build-up of homophile organizations through the twentieth century, but it is the New York Stonewall Riots of 27–8 June 1969 that is generally considered to symbolize the birth of the modern international Gay and Lesbian Movement (Adam 1987). The scientifically imposed term 'homosexual' was shifted to the self-created ones of 'lesbian' and 'gay'; pathological medical rhetoric was converted to the political language of 'gay is good'; a wide array of organizations for gays and lesbians became widespread in most large cities; and millions of gay men and women started to 'come out' and identify positively with the category 'gay'. Over the next twenty-five years, the gay and lesbian community was to become a visible and powerful social community, political lobby and 'pink economy' on a global scale.

A striking, and unexpected, development was the arrival of AIDS and HIV infection around 1981. Although AIDS concerns many people, in the western world it has had a disproportionate impact upon gay men – both as sickness and as symbol. As sickness, many gay men in major cities (like San Francisco) have found their lives disrupted by a life-threatening disease, and have developed self-help institutions of support to cope with this AIDS crisis. Lesbians, too, have been involved in developing major programmes of community care. But as symbol, AIDS has been used as part of a conservative backlash to renew the stigmatizing attacks on homosexuality which were so prevalent in the earlier part of the twentieth century. At times, it has looked as if homosexuality was about to become 'remedicalized' as disease. But, ironically, in resisting these attacks the lesbian and gay communities appear to have become stronger, more visible and more political (Kayal 1993).

Since the late 1960s there has been a major development in research, writing and publication around homosexuality – the rise of 'lesbian and gay studies' (Abelove et al. 1993; Plummer 1992). In the 1970s, psychologists debunked the 'sick homosexual' and refocused on homophobia – the fear of homosexuality. Sociologists initiated a debate on the homosexual role, the ways in which 'homosexualities' were always 'socially constructed'; and the processes through which people came to identify themselves as gay. Historians and anthropologists researched homosexualities in different settings across the world (Duberman et al. 1989). Feminist scholars shaped many important debates on a wide range of matters like sexuality, female relationships, literary texts, and race (Douglas 1990). On all these areas, debates, conflicts and international conferences have proliferated (Altman et al. 1989; Weeks 1985).

By the late 1980s a younger generation was bringing a new and challenging strategy: 'queer' theory, 'queer' politics and 'queer' lifestyles. These deconstruct heterosexuality as an organizing assumption of everyday life and replace it with a much wider sense of transgressive differences around sexualities and genders (Sedgwick 1990). It remains to be seen whether this will become a widespread new construction of same-sex desires.

Ken Plummer
University of Essex

References

Abelove, H., Barale, M. and Halperin, D. (eds) (1993) *The Lesbian and Gay Studies Reader*, New York.

Adam, B. (1987) *The Rise of a Lesbian and Gay Movement*, Boston, MA.

Altman, D. *et al.* (1989) *Which Homosexuality?*, London.

Dollimore, J. (1991) *Sexual Dissidence: Augustine to Wilde, Freud to Foucault*, Oxford.

Douglas, C. A. (1990) *Love and Politics: Radical Feminist and Lesbian Theories*, San Francisco, CA.

Duberman, M., Vicinus, M. and Chauncey, G. (eds) (1989) *Hidden from History: Reclaiming the Gay and Lesbian Past*, New York.

Faderman, L. (1981) *Surpassing the Love of Men: Romantic Friendships between Women from the Renaissance to the Present*, London.

Foucault, M. (1979) *The History of Sexuality*, vol. 1, *An Introduction*, London.

Greenberg, D. (1988) *The Construction of Homosexuality*, Chicago.

Kayal, P. M. (1993) *Bearing Witness: Gay Men's Health Crisis and the Politics of AIDS*, Boulder, CO.

Kinsey, A., Pomeroy, W. B. and Martin, C. E. (1948) *Sexual Behavior in the Human Male*, Philadelphia.

Kinsey, A. *et al.* (1953) *Sexual Behavior in the Human Female*, New York.

Lewes, K. (1988) *The Psychoanalytic Theory of Male Homosexuality*, New York.

Plant, R. (1986) *The Pink Triangle: The Nazi War Against Homosexuals*, New York.

Plummer, K. (ed.) (1992) *Modern Homosexualities: Fragments of Lesbian and Gay Experience*, London.

Sedgwick, E. K. (1990) *Epistemology of the Closet*, Berkeley, CA.

Weeks, J. (1985) *Sexualities and its Discontents*, London.

See also: gender and sex; sexual behaviour.

house

The relationship between house form, environment and culture is a theme that has been explored by architects, archaeologists and anthropologists (Guidoni 1979; Rapoport 1969; Wilson 1988). An anthropological focus on the house derives from the way houses have importance in particular cultures, as material constructions, as social groups, and as the subject of symbolic elaboration (Waterson 1991). For example, in many societies, important principles of social classification, such as age and gender, are embodied in the internal arrangement of space within houses. Houses thus become the vehicles of acquiring and perpetuating social distinctions (e.g Bourdieu 1990).

Houses also endure over time and provide fixed points of reference for people. Anthropologists confronted with societies which do not conform to the models of classic kinship theory have turned to the house as a way of comprehending sociality. These societies do not necessarily have lineages, or else these do not function as described in classic ethnographies. Seeing these societies as made up of enduring houses is one attempt – to fit their analysis more closely to indigenous categories.

Lévi-Strauss's (1983a; 1983b; 1987) concept of 'sociétés à maison', house-based societies, is one such attempt which brings together the material, social and symbolic aspects of the house. Lévi-Strauss's argument relates principally to the Kwakiutl *numayma*, the medieval noble house in Europe, the houses of eleventh-century Japan and of certain Indonesian societies. The house 'reunites' or 'transcends' (1983a) a series of opposing principles, such as filiation/residence, patri-/matrilineal descent, close/distant marriage.Characteristically, filiation and marital alliance are equally important as well as mutually substitutable (1983b: 1224).

Lévi-Strauss (1987) emphasizes how 'alliance' acts as both a principle of unity and of antagonism in house-based societies where neither descent, property nor residence, taken alone, are criteria for the constitution of groups. The married couple is at once the centre of the family but also a source of tension between families – particularly over residence. The house then becomes 'the objectification' of the unstable relation of alliance to which it gives an illusory solidity. In this respect Lévi-Strauss has applied the notion of 'fetishism' to the house, using as examples certain Indonesian cultures with highly elaborated architecture. In other respects, however, Lévi-Strauss pays rather little attention to the material properties of the houses he examines.

Lévi-Strauss's writings have inspired other studies of the house in these terms. Anthropologists have tried to apply his model to the analysis of various societies in South-East Asia (Macdonald 1987). This in turn has led to a critique of his paradigm which appears to subvert the old categories of kinship analysis only to substitute another, equally rigid, one (Carsten and Hugh-Jones 1995). If a focus on the house is to provide an escape from the constraints of kinship theory, it can only do so through a more flexible approach which pays close attention to what people do with houses and how they conceive them in particular cultures. It will bring together the study of architecture with that of kinship, religion and economy, and be based on an understanding of houses and the people who live in them as involved in a single, dynamic process of living.

Janet Carsten
University of Edinburgh

References

Bourdieu, P. (1990 [1970]), 'The Kabyle house or the world reversed', (reprinted as appendix to) *The Logic of Practice*, Cambridge.

Carsten, J. and S. Hugh-Jones (eds) (1995), *About the House: Levi-Strauss and Beyond*, Cambridge.

Guidoni, E. (1979), *Primitive Architecture*, London.

Lévi-Strauss, C. (1983a) *The Way of the Masks*, London.

—— (1983b) 'Histoire et Ethnologie', *Annales* 38.

—— (1987) *Anthropology and Myth: Lectures 1951–1982*, Oxford.

Macdonald, C. (ed.), (1987) *De la hutte au palais: sociétés 'à maison' en Asie du Sud-Est insulaire*, Paris.

Rapoport, A. (1969) *House Form and Culture*, Englewood Cliffs, NJ.

Wilson, P. J. (1988) *The Domestication of the Human Species*, New Haven.

Waterson, R. (1991) *The Living House: An Anthropology of Architecture in South-East Asia*, Singapore.

See also: family; habitus; household; kinship.

household

The defining characteristic of household membership is the occupation of living space which is reserved for the exclusive use of that household. In certain populations, however, many other ties may unite members of the household including the pooling of incomes, the taking of at least one main meal together, responsibility for the socialization of the young and the welfare of all members, while the household may even serve as the locus of production. Households are likely to have been largest and most complex when they fulfilled all of these functions. When more of such activities took place elsewhere, as was increasingly likely from the late nineteenth century, the ties between household members were loosened and it became more feasible to live in smaller residential groups or even alone. In increasing numbers of households since the 1960s, it is no longer the case that members of the household take even one main meal together. In Britain the definition of the household as a unit of co-residence and housekeeping was replaced in 1983 with a more flexible definition referring to co-residence in combination with either the sharing of one meal a day or the sharing of living accommodation (*Social Trends* 1984 and 1985).

In 1991, 27 per cent of all British households contained just one person, 11 per cent of the population lived alone and households on average contained 2.5 persons (*Social Trends* 1994). Such small households are not at all unusual in developed populations. For example, an average household size of at least three persons was recorded for only three west European countries at the beginning of the 1990s: Portugal, Spain and the Irish Republic (Begeot *et al.* 1993). In the past larger households were more common. In pre-industrial England the average was 4.75 persons per household and less than 6 per cent of households consisted of persons living on their own (Laslett and Wall 1972). Households were somewhat larger still in rural parts of Denmark in 1787 and in Norway in 1801 (averages of 5.0 and 5.5 persons per household respectively) and considerably larger (over 7.0 persons per household) in many Austrian populations of the seventeenth and eighteenth centuries, and in northern Sweden in the seventeenth century (Lundh 1995; Wall

et al. 1983). An average of over 9.0 persons per household was reached by a Russian serf population in the early nineteenth century (Czap 1983).

Differences in the kinship structure of the household sometimes underlay these differences in household size. In much of north-western Europe nuclear family households comprising parents and unmarried children predominated, even before industrialization, while complex households involving the co-residence of two or more related couples were more readily formed in parts of southern and in eastern Europe. Within western Europe the composition of households also varied considerably in terms of the numbers of children and servants present and the frequency with which unmarried persons headed households (Wall 1991).

In the case of England two factors in particular account for the fact that in the late twentieth century households are much smaller than those of pre-industrial times: the decline in marital fertility and the virtual elimination from the household of the resident domestic and farm servants. The incidence of farm service for men declined markedly in most areas of England in the latter part of the eighteenth and early part of the nineteenth centuries, while domestic service (largely performed by women) persisted into the early decades of the twentieth century. The number of children per household (including households where there were no children) fell from 2.1 in 1911, little above the level typical of pre-industrial times, to 1.8 in 1921, 1.3 in 1947 and 0.9 in 1981. Since the end of the Second World War there has also been a marked decline in the frequency with which households are extended to include relatives outside the core couple and parent–child group (Wall 1991; 1995).

Demographic change explains many of the modifications that have occurred in the composition of the household. For example, the fall in fertility of the late nineteenth and early twentieth centuries initiated an immediate decline in the size of the average household and later made it less likely that parents approaching old age would still have unmarried children resident in their households (Wall 1994). Another demographic change to have a profound impact on household and family patterns of elderly people in the post-war period has been the greater improvement in female than in male life expectancy. This has prolonged the period that women spend as widows and therefore at risk of living on their own, while ensuring that many more elderly men than in the past have a spouse to provide primary care in their old age. In England in the eighteenth century, the structure of the household responded to demographic change (Wall *et al.* 1983). An earlier age at first marriage and higher proportions marrying than in the late seventeenth century, together with a fall in adult mortality, increased the proportions of households headed by married couples and led to an expansion in the size of the child population and in the average size of the household. Population growth, by making labour relatively more abundant and therefore cheaper, may also have encouraged farmers in arable areas to switch in the eighteenth century from the use of resident male labour (servants) to labourers who had households of their own and could be employed on a more casual basis.

However, improvements in living standards over the course of the twentieth century, and particularly since the 1950s, have enabled many more people to live alone, who in earlier times would have either lived with relatives or lodged with a non-relative. Variations in the standard of living also exert important but indirect influences on household patterns through alternatively lowering or raising the age at first marriage or cohabitation, thereby increasing or decreasing the pace of household formation. Nevertheless, in England neither urbanization nor industrialization appear to have promoted a major modification in the structure of the household. Even in the middle of the nineteenth century, there were no major differences between the structure of urban and rural households, apart from the greater number of lodgers attached to urban households. The modest increase between pre-industrial times and the middle of the nineteenth century in the number of relatives in the household other than members of the immediate family of the household head was at one time thought to be associated with industrialization (Anderson 1971). However, this increase is now known to have occurred in both rural and urban areas in response to demographic, as well as economic, change (Wall *et al.* 1983).

The impact of cultural influences on the household is less easy to measure. No written rules or customs recommended the formation of specific types of households, identified an appropriate age for children to leave the parental home, or ordered that elderly people should be cared for in the households of their children. Yet the relative uniformity of household and family patterns in the English past, despite contrasting economic and demographic circumstances, implies that residence patterns were influenced by norms, even if these were never written down, and no penalties applied if the norms were not followed.

Richard Wall
ESRC Cambridge Group for the History of
Population and Social Structure

References

Anderson, M. (1971) *Family Structure in Nineteenth Century Lancashire*, Cambridge, UK.

Begeot, F., Smith, L. and Pearce, D. (1993) 'First results from West European censuses', *Population Trends* 74.

Central Statistical Office (1982; 1983; 1994) *Social Trends* 12, 13, 24.

Czap, P. (1983) 'A large family: the peasant's greatest wealth', in R. Wall, J. Robin and P. Laslett (eds) *Family Forms in Historic Europe*, Cambridge, UK.

Laslett, P. and Wall, R. (eds) (1972) *Household and Family in Past Time*, Cambridge, UK.

Lundh, C. (1995) 'Households and families in pre-industrial Sweden', *Continuity and Change* 10.

Wall, R. (1991) 'European family and household systems', in Société de Démographie Historique (ed.) *Historiens et populations: Liber amicorum Étienne Hélin*, Louvain-la-Neuve.

—— (1994) 'Elderly persons and members of their households in England and Wales from pre-industrial times to the present', in D. Kertzer and P. Laslett (eds) *Aging in the Past: Demography, Society and Old Age*, Los Angeles, CA.

—— (1995) 'Historical development of the household in Europe', in E. Van Imhoff (ed.) *Household Demography and Household Modelling*, New York.

Wall, R., Robin, J. and Laslett, P. (eds) (1983) *Family Forms in Historic Europe*, Cambridge, UK.

See also: family; family history; historical demography; house.

human capital

Human capital is the stock of acquired talents, skills and knowledge which may enhance a worker's earning power in the labour market. A distinction is commonly made between *general* human capital – which is considered as affecting potential earnings in a broad range of jobs and occupations – and *specific* human capital, which augments people's earning power within the particular firm in which they are employed but is of negligible value elsewhere. An example of the former would be formal education in general skills such as mathematics; an example of the latter would be the acquired knowledge about the workings of, and personal contacts within, a particular firm. In many cases human capital is of an intermediate form, whether it be acquired 'off the job', in the form of schooling or vocational training, or 'on the job' in terms of work experience.

In several respects the economic analysis of human capital raises problems similar to that of capital as conventionally understood in terms of firms' plant and equipment. It is likely to be heterogeneous in form; it is accumulated over a substantial period of time using labour and capital already in existence; further investment usually requires immediate sacrifices (in terms of forgone earnings and tuition fees); its quality will be affected by technical progress; the prospective returns to an individual are likely to be fairly uncertain, and the capital stock will be subject to physical deterioration and obsolescence. Nevertheless there are considerable differences. Whereas one can realize the returns on physical or financial capital either by receiving the flow of profits accruing to the owner of the asset or by sale of the asset itself, the returns on human capital can usually be received only by the person in whom the investments have been made (although there are exceptions, such as indentured workers), and usually require further effort in the form of labour in order to be realized in cash terms. The stock of human capital cannot be transferred as can the titles to other forms of wealth, although the investments that parents make in their children's schooling and in informal education at home are sometimes taken as analogous to bequests of financial capital.

While the idea of investment in oneself commands wide acceptance in terms of its general principles, many economists are unwilling to accept stronger versions of the theory of earnings determination and the theory of income distribution that have been based on the pioneering work of Becker (1964) and Mincer (1958). This analysis generally assumes that everywhere labour markets are sufficiently competitive, the services of different types of human capital sufficiently substitutable and educational opportunities sufficiently open, such that earnings differentials can be unambiguously related to differential acquisition of human capital. On the basis of such assumptions estimates have been made of the returns (in terms of increased potential earnings) to human investment (measured in terms of forgone earnings and other costs) by using the observed earnings of workers in cross-sectional samples and in panel studies over time. The rates of return to such investment has usually been found to be in the range of 10–15 per cent. However, it should be emphasized that such estimates often neglect the impact of other economic and social factors which may affect the dispersion of earnings.

Frank A. Cowell
London School of Economics and Political Science

References

Becker, G. S. (1964) *Human Capital*, New York.
Mincer, J. (1958) 'Investment in human capital and personal income distribution', *Journal of Political Economy* 66.

Further reading

Mincer, J. (1974) *Schooling, Experience and Earnings*, New York.
Schultz, T. W. (1972) *Investment in Education*, Chicago.

See also: capital theory; factors of production.

human evolution

Evolution

The term evolution implies transformation through a sequence of stages. Although the term is a general one which is used in many fields of study (Lewontin 1968), in biology it is a fundamental unifying theory. Biological evolution specifically refers to *genetic* transformation of populations between organisms and their environment (Dobzhansky *et al.* 1977). The fact that life evolved is accepted by almost all modern biologists, although the exact mechanisms by which organic evolution occurs are the subject of intense research.

Principles of evolution

The benchmark for the beginning of research on biological evolution is the 1859 publication of Charles Darwin's *The Origin of Species*, although evolutionary ideas were common before that date. Darwin and Alfred Russel Wallace independently developed the idea of natural selection as the chief mechanism of causing life to evolve. The key feature of natural selection is that it is indirect: inherited variability exists in all species and the best adapted variants tend to leave more offspring so that through time there is gradual change. In this view, evolution is not directed by the processes that create the inherited variability, but rather by how that variability is shaped or pruned through time by natural selection.

Natural selection is a major feature of the synthetic theory of evolution, a term used to describe the modern view of the mechanisms of organic evolution. This synthesis was forged in the first half of the twentieth century by combining the theory of natural selection, Mendelian genetics, and other features to explain how life evolves. There has never been complete agreement on all aspects of the synthetic theory, however, with current controversy centering on topics such as the importance of random processes, the mechanisms of speciation, and the extrapolation from observable genetic changes over a short time span to patterns of phylogeny (Ridley 1993).

At the core of the synthetic theory of evolution are the processes that result in genetic transformation from generation to generation. These processes occur in two phases: first, the production and arrangement of genetic variation by gene mutation, chromosomal changes, genetic recombination, and gene migration, and second, the reduction of genetic variation by natural selection and genetic drift. Genetic variability is ultimately produced by gene mutation, which is a chemical change in the DNA molecule. Most mutations are deleterious or relatively neutral to the survival of the organism. Mutations with small effects probably accumulate and eventually have a greater role in evolution than macromutations. Mutation rate has little relationship with evolutionary rate. Genetic recombination is also a source of genetic variation, but at a different level. Whereas gene mutation is a change in the DNA molecule, genetic recombination is the formation of different combinations of genetic factors that occur during the sexual cycle from the formation of the sex cells to fertilization. Theoretically this process can create nearly an infinite number of different organisms simply by reshuffling the immense amount of genetic differences between the DNA of any two parents. Gene migration or flow is a source of new variability at the population level. A local population, for example, can undergo profound genetic change by the introduction of genes from other populations.

The second phase of genetic transformation is the reduction of genetic variation which is done primarily by natural selection. As far more sex cells are fertilized than can possibly survive and reproduce there is immense loss of potential life at each generation. In humans it is estimated that only about 12 per cent of all fertilized eggs survive, grow to adulthood and reproduce. The loss is probably mostly selective: genetic variants that do not survive to reproduce are lost because of deleterious mutations or combinations of genetic factors that tend to decrease vitality. Even resistance to disease often has a genetic component that can be selected. Simple chance may also be a factor in loss of genetic variability from generation to generation, a process called genetic drift. The importance of this random factor in evolution has been controversial ever since Sewall Wright proposed it in the 1930s.

The formation of new species involves mechanisms which reproductively isolate populations that were once part of the same species. In animals this usually requires physical isolation and no gene flow between populations that then undergo divergent genetic change. Naturalistic studies show that this can occur relatively rapidly in small isolated populations.

A common misunderstanding of evolution is that it occurs because of mutations that arise and directly change the genetic composition of a species through the generations. This view, called the mutation theory of evolution, was common in the early part of the twentieth century, but is now discredited for complex organisms. Genetic variability in species is immense as has been shown by biochemical research showing that a large percentage of genetic loci have one or more mutant variants. According to the synthetic theory, the direction of genetic change is determined by the selection and random loss of this vast store of existing genetic variability.

Another common misunderstanding of the synthetic theory of evolution is that it explains why the organic world evolved in the way that it did. The *pattern* of evolution revealed in the fossil record and by interference from living organisms cannot be predicted by the processes of production and reduction of genetic variation any more than human history can be explained by the processes by which individuals learn from birth to death.

Human evolution

There are twenty-one living orders of mammals. The one in which humans are classified (Primates) may have originated in the late Cretaceous (*c.*70–65 million years, Myr) but only by Eocene times (54–35 Myr) do primates of the modern aspect become abundant (Martin 1990). These Eocene forms resemble modern lemurs and tarsiers. By late Eocene to early Oligocene times (38–24 Myr) there are primates which share some derived characteristics seen in the group containing modern monkeys, apes and people (Anthropoidea). Not until the Miocene (24–5 Myr) are there fossils which have traits shared uniquely with the superfamily containing apes and people (Hominoidea). Although some middle to late Miocene (*c.*16–8 Myr) hominoids have a chewing apparatus that looks like early members of the human family (Hominidae), the resemblance is probably due to the fact that the common ancestor of the great apes and people also shared these traits. The earliest fossils that can be linked unequivocally and uniquely to modern humans are grouped in the genus *Australopithecus* and date back at least to 4 Myrs and probably to 5 or 5.5 Myr (Aiello and Dean, 1990; Klein 1989; McHenry 1994). The earlier date is from a fragment of jaw which appears to share unique characteristics with later and better known members of *Australopithecus*. All members of this genus are confined to Africa.

The earliest fossil species that is undoubtedly a member of the human family is *Australopithecus ramidus* known in East Africa from geological strata dating to 4.4 Myr (White *et al.*, 1994). Overall it is quite ape-like, but it does share a few unique features with later hominids such as broader and less projecting canines, a shorter cranial base, and some details of the elbow. It has thinner molar enamel than later hominids implying perhaps a diet more similar to African apes. Its habitat was closed woodland. Unfortunately there are as yet no hindlimb fossils to ascertain its form of location.

The next oldest hominid species, *A. afarensis* (4–2.9 Myr) is also quite ape-like in dental and cranial anatomy, but does share more derived features with later hominids than does *A. ramidus*. The most conspicuous of these traits include a much broader deciduous molar, smaller canine, less ape-like premolar, larger cheek teeth and thicker molar enamel. The brain size relative to body size is much closer to modern apes than to modern people, being less than one-half the relative size of *H. sapiens*. The body below the head (postcranium) is reorganized away from the common plan seen in all other Primates and shares the uniquely human bipedal pattern. Some primitive traits are retained in the postcranium, such as long and curved toes, which may imply a retention of greater tree climbing ability than that seen in *H. sapiens*.

Australopithecus afarensis was highly dimorphic with males weighing about 45 kg and females 29 kg (McHenry 1994). This level of sexual dimorphism implies that, by analogy with other mammalian species, *A. afarensis* was not monogamous. The forelimbs of the male were relatively very large, perhaps exceeding the dimorphism of living gorillas and orangs. This may imply strong sexual selection and male–male competition analogous to the role played by the large male canine in other mammalian species.

Between 3 and 2 Myr ago the fossil record reveals a diversification of hominid species. In East Africa, *A. aethiopicus* appears by 2.5 Myr as a species combining the primitive traits of *A. afarensis* with specialized features related to heavy chewing. These specialized features include huge cheek teeth and heavily buttressed crania for chewing musculature. In South Africa, *A. africanus* appears at about 3.0 Myr and persists to perhaps 2.4 Myr, but dating is uncertain. This species is similar to *A. afarensis* except that it is more derived toward *Homo* in key respects relating to its anterior dentition, reduced muzzle, fingers and encephalization. Cheek-tooth size is much larger than that of *A. afarensis*.

Beginning sometime between 2.4 and 2.1 Myrs the genus *Homo* appears. Its appearance is marked by reduction in cheek-tooth size from that seen in earlier hominid species, expansion of the brain, and the appearance of stone-tool culture. It is known from fossil deposits in South and East Africa. Variability is high and there is a strong case to be made for more than one species of *Homo* before 1.8 Myrs including *H. habilis* and *H. rudolfensis*. By 1.8 Myrs a new species of *Homo* appears in East Africa that in many ways resembles *H. erectus* of Asia.

Other species of hominid apparently coexisted with *Homo*. In South Africa, *A. robustus* overlapped in time and geography with early *Homo*. This species shared with *Homo* many derived characteristics relative to earlier species of hominid including encephalization, loss of a muzzle, bending of the base of the skull, and human-like hand morphology. At the same time it possessed highly derived morphology related to heavy chewing, including massive cheek teeth, huge jaws, and

strong buttressing for the chewing muscles. In East Africa, *A. boisei* appeared by 2.1 Myrs with a similar combination of *Homo*-like traits with an adaptation for even more extreme heavy chewing. Both of these species, *A. robustus* and *boisei*, are often referred to as 'Paranthropus' or 'robust' australopithecines. Their robustness was in chewing-related features only, however. Both species were quite petite in body size with males about 40–50 kg and females 32–4 kg (McHenry 1994).

The first appearance of human populations outside of Africa may precede 1 Myr, but certainly by about 0.9 Myr *H. erectus* has occupied parts of tropical Asia. The exact chronology is still uncertain, but sometime after this and before 0.5 Myr some populations had adapted to life in the temperate climatic zone of Asia and Europe. The appearance of *H. sapiens* depends on the definition, but by 0.3 Myr the fully modern brain size had evolved although the skull still retained many *H. erectus*-like traits. These archaic *H. sapiens* persisted in most areas of Eurasia until about 40,000 years ago. The earliest traces of anatomically modern *H. sapiens* are in Africa, perhaps as early as 130,000 years ago, although in Eurasia this form becomes abundant only after 40,000. By at least 32,000 years ago and perhaps by 50,000 Australia is inhabited by anatomically modern *H. sapiens*. America was settled by immigrants from Asia who migrated across a landbridge connecting Siberia and Alaska perhaps at 20,000 to 15,000 years ago but the successful colonization of most of the Americas began at 12,000 years ago. People first reached some of the Pacific islands several thousand years ago from the east, reaching the Marquesas Islands by about AD 300 and New Zealand by about AD 900.

Technological development in human evolution appears to be erratic in pace, but it certainly shows a pattern of acceleration. Relatively crude stone tools persist for over 1.5 Myr. Finely worked blade tools are much more recent. Humans have had agriculture, cities, and writing for less than one-quarter of 1 per cent of their evolutionary development as a separate mammalian lineage.

Behaviour

Human locomotor behaviour probably evolved from an ape-like ancestor with a short back, a flat chest, and a highly mobile shoulder and forelimb adapted to climbing and suspending the body below tree branches (Fleagle 1988). Like modern apes (but unlike monkeys) this hypothetical ancestor was relatively awkward and energetically inefficient at walking on the ground either quadrupedally or bipedally. But as has happened to many other primate groups, terrestrial travel was taken up with greater and greater frequency. Why our ancestors took up bipedality instead of quadrupedality is unknown, but certainly the unique ape-like body plan made either gait equally efficient in terms of energetic cost at normal speeds. Free hands for carrying makes bipedality more advantageous. Fossil evidence at about 3.5 Myr shows that bipedality had been established in the human evolutionary lineage, but before that time the paleontological record is not yet complete enough.

The evolutionary history of human feeding behaviour is documented by fossil dental remains spanning millions of years. The earliest hominids were quite different from modern African apes, having thick molar enamel, exceptionally large cheek teeth, and powerful chewing muscles. Microscopic studies of dental scratches show that these early humans were probably not eating seeds and grass, nor were they crushing bones. By about 2 Myr ago meat eating was certainly practised as evidenced by bone remains with stone tool cut marks. Relative cheek-tooth size reduces fairly gradually from 2 Myr to the present which may be because extra-oral food preparation to some extent took over the function of the grinding teeth.

Many other aspects of human behavioural evolution are related to the fact that absolute brain size tripled and relative brain size more than doubled over the last 2.5 Myr of human evolution. Human fossils dating between about 3.5 and 2.5 Myr ago have endocranial volumes the size of modern chimpanzees, although relative to body size they are slightly larger.

The biological evolution of most aspects of human behaviour are much more difficult to document. The basic method of enquiry involves comparisons with other living animals. From this perspective it is clear that spoken symbolic language is the most unique human attribute in the organic world. Field studies of monkeys reveal that they possess a form of vocal symbolic communication, but there is a vast, quantitative gap in speech capabilities between human and non-human primates.

The primary difficulty of studying the biological evolution of human behaviour is determining the genetic component of behaviour. Often the only genetic component is genetically conditioned developmental plasticity. There is a genetic basis for the development of the neurophysiology required for speech, for example, but a great deal of plasticity in the kind of language that is learned. There is a genetic basis for most aspects of human sexuality, but an enormous flexibility in how it is expressed. One method for approximating the extent of genetic contribution to specific behaviours is by comparing differences between identical twins (and hence genetically identical individuals) with the difference among unrelated individuals. Twin studies are complicated by the fact that most twins are raised in the same environment and that the sample of identical twins raised apart is still very small.

One theoretical breakthrough in the study of behavioural evolution came in 1964 with the publication of W. D. Hamilton's 'The genetical theory of social behavior'. He suggested that even genetically controlled behaviours that were detrimental to an organism's survival could be favoured by natural selection because of what has become known as kin selection. Kin selection refers to the 'selection of genes because of their effect in favoring the reproductive success of relatives other than offspring' (Barash 1982: 392). Kin selection theory has been successfully employed to explain several aspects of the social behaviour of non-human animals, especially social insects, but application of this and other sociobiological theories to the evolution of human social behaviour has not yet resulted in universally accepted principles. The enormity of human behavioural plasticity makes the search for evolutionary principles difficult, but a great deal of research on this topic is currently being pursued. Even more difficult, if not impossible, is the search for any behavioural evolutionary divergence between human groups that have a genetic basis.

Henry M. McHenry
University of California

References

Aiello, L. and Dean, C. (1990) *An Introduction to Human Evolutionary Anatomy*, San Diego, CA.

Barash, D. P. (1982) *Sociobiology and Behavior*, New York.

Darwin, C. (1859) *On the Origin of Species by Means of Natural Selection*, London.

Dobzhansky, T., Ayala, F. J., Stebbins, G. L. and Valentine, J. W. (1977) *Evolution*, San Francisco, CA.

Fleagle, J. G. (1988) *Primate Adaptation and Evolution*, San Diego, CA.

Hamilton, W. D. (1964) 'The genetical theory of social behavior', *Journal of Theoretical Biology* 12.

Klein, R. G. (1989) *The Human Career*, Chicago.

Lewontin, R. C. (1968) 'Concept of evolution', *International Encyclopedia of the Social Sciences*, New York.

McHenry, H. M. (1994) 'Tempo and mode in human evolution', *Proceedings of the National Academy of Sciences*, USA.

Martin, R. D. (1990) *Primate Origins and Evolution*, London.

White, T. D., Suwa, G. and Asfau, B. (1994) '*Australopithicus ramidus*, a new species of early hominid from Aramis, Ethiopia', *Nature* 371, pp. 306–311.

Further reading

Jones, S., Martin, R. and Pilbeam, D. (eds) (1992) *The Cambridge Encyclopedia of Human Evolution*, Cambridge, UK.

Ridley, M. (1993) *Evolution*, Boston, MA.

Tattersall, I., Delson, E. and Van Couvering, J. (1988) *Encyclopedia of Human Evolution and Prehistory*, New York.

See also: Darwin, Charles.

human nature

The concept of human nature, central to the study of human social life, can be traced to the ancient Greeks who elaborated the idea of 'nature' underlying western science. After Thales, Anaxagoras and other cosmologists began the quest for universal principles that explain the world; Sophists like Antiphon and Gorgias concluded that such rules of nature were different from – and contradicted by – human-made rules of law or cultural conventions (Wheelwright 1966). Socrates and his students challenged such a division between human nature and law or social virtue, claiming that what is 'right' or 'just' is 'according to nature' (Plato, *Republic*) and that humankind is 'the political animal' (Aristotle, *Politics*). Ever since, some political and social theorists (e.g. Hobbes, Locke and Rousseau) have viewed human nature as essentially selfish and derived society from the behaviour of individuals, whereas others (e.g. Hegel, Marx and Durkheim) have argued that humans are naturally sociable and traced individual traits to society and its history (Strauss 1953). The former assumption has generally been adopted in such disciplines as behaviourist psychology and classical economics, the latter in sociology, cultural anthropology and history.

Contemporary scientific research has demonstrated the impossibility of reducing this ancient controversy to the simplistic nature vs nurture dichotomy. Some aspects of human behaviour seem primarily shaped by individual experience, the present social situation or the cultural environment, while others can be influenced by genetic predisposition, prenatal events or critical periods in childhood development. Many individual variations in physiology and behaviour are controlled by hormones, neurotransmitters or innate structures in the brain, but such biological response systems depend in turn on individual development or experience.

Due to this interaction of genetic, developmental and social factors, human nature is complex and highly adaptable. Individuals of our species are thus by nature both co-operative and competitive, both selfish and altruistic (Eibl-Eibesfeldt 1989; Masters 1989). As a result, 'mankind viewed over many generations shares a single human nature within which relatively minor hereditary influences recycle through ever-changing patterns between sexes and across families and entire populations' (E. O. Wilson 1978: 50).

An evolutionary perspective clarifies the age-old debates concerning human nature by distinguishing relatively invariant and universal aspects of human behaviour from sources of variability that are, at least in part, under biological control. Not only does human nature entail the development of linguistic and cultural abilities that vary from one social environment to another, but also many differences among humans need to be understood as natural.

Common traits shared with other species

Among those attributes shared by every human being, some can be traced to our earliest vertebrate ancestors and are generally found among sexually reproducing animals: the overall bodily structure of vertebrates and basic drives, including food, sex, security and – for social species – predictable status. Like mammals, humans are warm-blooded, develop social bonds, and express emotions in ways that serve as social signals. Like primates, we are a highly intelligent species adopting varied social patterns and individual behavioural strategies in response to food supplies, physical environments, and individual or group experiences. This evolutionary history is reflected in the 'triune' structure of the human central nervous system, in which the brain stem controls the basic drives common to all vertebrates, the limbic system modulates the mammalian emotions, and the enlarged primate neocortex permits extraordinary learning and behavioural plasticity (MacLean 1992).

Each of these levels of evolution has behavioural consequences for all members of our species. Like most vertebrates, humans exhibit what ethologists call fixed action patterns, including social displays and the consummatory behaviours satisfying needs of nutrition and reproduction. Like most mammals, human females give birth after gestation, breastfeed and care for neonates (unless the mother–infant bond has been disturbed) and hence usually invest more than males in the reproductive process. Like most primates, humans recognize other members of the group individually and use a repertoire of non-verbal displays, including facial expressions, to modulate social interactions.

Also common to all humans are traits unique to our species. Most obvious are speech (the complex of linguistic abilities, utilizing grammar and syntax to produce a truly 'open' means of communication and information processing), complex productive technologies (including domestication of other species, elaborate manufacture of tools or weapons, irrigated agriculture, and industrial machinery) and of course cultural systems that use symbolic and linguistic skills to elaborate religious, political and artistic achievements unknown to other animals. Although chimpanzees exhibit many aspects of cultural variability (de Waal 1982; McGrew 1992; Maryanski and Turner 1992), human nature cannot be reduced to its evolutionary roots.

Variable traits shared by all humans

The amazing diversity of our species' social and cultural behaviours is itself a characteristic of human nature. Some elements of this variability are themselves influenced by biological factors. Personality differences can be traced to heritable temperaments which vary along multiple dimensions such as shyness and sociability, risk-taking and harm-avoidance, or novelty-seeking and predictability (Cloninger 1986; 1987; Eaves *et al.* 1989; MacDonald 1989). Individual variations in mate choice and sexual behaviour may be partly due to genetics, partly due to prenatal hormonal exposure, and partly due to individual experience or social setting (LeVay 1993; Posner 1992). Although the evidence on IQ is highly contested, differences in such specific abilities as fine or gross motor co-ordination, musical or artistic skills, and excellence in mathematics, while requiring training for full expression, seem to some degree heritable (Gardner 1983; Plomin 1990). Some have also found evidence of genetic susceptibility to cancer, mental disease, learning disabilities, alcoholism and crime, though each of these categories can apparently be produced by different combinations of inherited, developmental and environmental factors.

The exploration of a heritable component in gender differences has been particularly controversial, in part because both critics and proponents often ignore the way that patterns of variation overlap. For example, although the personality dimensions described above are normally distributed, males are on average more predisposed to risk-taking than females. As a result, a given personality type may be widely observed among both males and females even though there is a significant gender difference in the overall distribution of the trait. Often, such statistical patterns can be traced to hormonal differences during neonatal development (Hampson and Kimura 1993).

Some behavioural traits reflect physiological responses to specific situations of evolutionary significance. In humans as in many primates, for instance, dominant males have elevated levels of the neurotransmitter serotonin which depend on the sight of submissive behaviour by subordinates; after social status has changed, there are corresponding modifications in neurotransmitter levels (McGuire *et al.* 1995). It seems likely that such natural mechanisms of plastic behavioural response will be greatly elucidated by research in the late 1990s.

Cultural variation and the environment

At the level of entire societies, there seem to be natural relationships between cultural practices and the natural or social environment comparable to those studied in other species by behavioural ethologists (Alexander 1987; Eibl-Eibesfeldt 1989; McGrew 1992; Maryanski and Turner 1992; Masters 1989). Among hunter-scavengers or hunter-gatherers like the Kalahari San, egalitarian status patterns with informal group leadership can be viewed as an adaptive response to the environment, whereas hypergamous patterns of social stratification and gender inequality are characteristic responses to an environment of chaotic resource flows and interspecific or intraspecific predation (Chagnon and Irons 1979).

Although many social scientists assume that such variations have little to do with human nature, many facultative traits depend on a specific environment for their expression. As a result, human nature is in many respects a variable rather than a constant. Because the environment plays such an important role in shaping the expression of natural potentialities, for example, it is no longer possible to assert that a specific social institution like monogamous marriage is always and everywhere more 'natural' than alternatives, such as polygamy, homosexuality or (in some situations) celibacy (Posner 1992).

References to 'human nature' in the singular, therefore, need to be understood as describing a central tendency that is often subject to shaping or variation, depending on time and place. While there are indeed broad universals, such as the sense of justice expressed when moralistic aggression is directed at violations of group norms (Gruter and Masters 1991; J. Q. Wilson 1993), these general patterns can rarely be used to decide social conflicts in complex societies undergoing rapid change. While future scientific research will add further details to this picture, contemporary evidence confirms the view that human nature is a hodgepodge that is complex and changeable (E. O. Wilson 1978: 23) rather than a fixed essence that could be deduced from an eternal and immutable natural law.

Roger D. Masters
Dartmouth College

References

Alexander, R. D. (1987) *The Biology of Moral Systems*, New York.

Chagnon, N. and Irons, W. (eds) (1979) *Evolutionary Biology and Human Social Behavior*, N. Scituate, MA.

Cloninger, C. R. (1986) 'A unified biosocial theory of personality and its role in the development of anxiety states', *Psychiatric Developments* 167.

—— (1987) 'A systematic method of clinical description and classification of personality variants', *Archives General of Psychiatry* 573.

de Waal, F. (1982) *Chimpanzee Politics: Power and Sex among Apes*, London.

Eaves, L. J., Eysenck, H. J. and Martin, N. G. (1989) *Genes, Culture, and Personality: An Empirical Approach*, New York.

Eibl-Eibesfeldt, I. (1989) *Human Ethology*, New York.

Gardner, H. (1983) *Frames of Mind*, New York.

Gruter, M. and Masters, R. D. (1991) *The Sense of Justice: Biological Foundations of Law*, Newbury Park, CA.

Hampson, E. and Kimura, D. (1993) 'Sex differences and hormonal influences on cognitive function in humans', in J. B. Becker, S. M. Breedlove and D. Crews (eds) *Behavioral Endocrinology*, Cambridge, MA.

LeVay, S. (1993) *Sex and the Brain*, Cambridge, MA.

MacDonald, K. B. (1989) *Social and Personality Development: An Evolutionary Synthesis*, New York.

McGrew, W. C. (1992) *Chimpanzee Material Culture: Implications for Human Evolution*, Cambridge, UK.

McGuire, M. T., Fairbanks, L. A. and Raleigh, M. J. (1995) 'Life history strategies, adaptive variation, and behavior – physiology interactions: the sociophysiology of vervet monkeys', in P. Barchas (ed.) *Sociophysiology*, New York.

MacLean, P. (1992) 'A triangular brief on the evolution of the brain and law', in M. Gruter and P. Bohannan (eds) *Law, Biology, and Culture*, 2nd edn, New York.

Maryanski, A. R. and Turner, J. H. (1992) *The Social Cage: Human Nature and the Evolution of Society*, Stanford, CA.

Masters, R. D. (1989) *The Nature of Politics*, New Haven, CT.

Plomin, R. (1990) 'The role of inheritance in behavior', *Science* 183.

Posner, R. (1992) *Sex and Reason*, Cambridge, MA.

Strauss, L. (1953) *Natural Right and History*, Chicago.

Wheelwright, P. (1966) *The Presocratics*, New York.

Wilson, E. O. (1978) *On Human Nature*, Cambridge, MA.

Wilson, J. Q. (1993) *The Moral Sense*, New York.

See also: ethology; genetics and behaviour; human needs; human rights; nature; sociobiology.

human needs

Most of the authors who sought to use human need as a political norm during the 1960s and early 1970s wrote with frankly polemical intent, rejecting the notion that politics is about who gets what, when and how, and that the proper task of government is to meet people's wants, reconciling them in so far as they can be reconciled. In that account of politics, responsiveness is the chief virtue, and paternalism the corresponding vice; individuals normally know best what their wants are; expert knowledge is confined to the most effective means of satisfying demands, because nobody can speak with authority on the merits of the various demands; all wants *must* be considered equal, and pushpin must be as good as poetry.

It was in answer to such a 'politics of wants' that Fromm (1955), Marcuse (1964; 1969), Macpherson (1966; 1973), Bay (1965; 1968) and others proposed a 'politics of needs'. Need, not want, was to be the norm: politics was to be the pursuit of justice, and justice was seen as the meeting of human needs. All these writers agreed that it can be shown objectively what human needs are; indeed, human need could not serve as a

political norm unless it were believed to have the status of ascertainable fact. All of these writers held that, though in principle individuals may be capable of recognizing their own needs, in present circumstances most people are so indoctrinated as to be incapable of seeing what their true needs are, or of distinguishing them from false needs or mere wants (Fitzgerald 1977). Consequently, for the time being, knowledge of human needs will be unevenly distributed; some people will know much more about them than others do, and most people's ideas about their needs will be confused, incomplete, even mistaken. Important needs are related to important objectives, and not all objectives are important. Some, like burglary, are not even licit. The proponents of a politics of needs did not advocate the indiscriminate satisfaction of all needs, but only of those needs which they believed to be related to human fulfilment, to the actualization of human potential as they understood it. Their approach, then, like that of Marx (to whose ideas about human needs most of them referred with approval), was teleological. They identified and evaluated human needs, as Marx did, by reference to a model of humankind, a conception of human excellence which they held, in some sense, to be the sole valid one (Fitzgerald 1977).

One attack made on the politics of needs position is an attack on its teleological structure: models of humankind are many, not one, and the attackers asserted that a reasoned choice among models of human excellence is impossible, for any attempt would necessarily fall into the 'naturalistic fallacy'. Hence, there can be no such things as knowledge of human needs or experts on human needs. Another line of attack was to argue that among human *wants* no reasoned choice is possible, and that *needs* are simply what we require to meet our wants; accordingly, there can be knowledge of needs, and experts on needs, but these experts (architects or lawyers, for instance) advise us about what we need can only after we have told *them* what we want. Accordingly, the critics held that the politics of needs position is conceptually confused. They also held that its practical tendency is politically despotic, as it may be used to justify extensive coercion over those who are said to know less about their own needs than some group of needs-experts know (Fitzgerald 1977).

The politics of needs protagonists have clearly expressed their admiration for the governments of such countries as Cuba and Vietnam, so there is nothing conjectural about the association of needs-theory with political despotism (Fitzgerald 1977). But their critics have not succeeded in showing that needs-theory is necessarily despotic in tendency. Nor have they been able to show that needs-theory is conceptually confused. Statements about needs are not, as they say, dependent upon statements about wants. Nor have they shown that between models of excellence there can be no reasoned choice, so that any choice must be arbitrary. It is true that statements about the needs of an organism are related to notions of what constitutes a good specimen of that kind of organism and of how a specimen can be recognized as flourishing; but it is not true that these notions are arbitrary, and can express nothing more than the personal tastes of observers. That a plant is flourishing is a fact about it, no less than its height or its colour. It is, moreover, quite independent of wants. Plants cannot have wants, and human beings, who can have wants, are not expressing those wants in recognizing a plant to be a good specimen. The drug squad, the growers, and any competent person may agree in recognizing a cannabis plant as a flourishing specimen, though they do not all agree in wanting it to flourish.

The needs of a plant are the conditions which will enable it to fulfil its potential and become a flourishing specimen. These needs, too, are a matter of fact, not in the least subjective, though to establish what they are may be a more difficult procedure than to recognize a good specimen (Anscombe 1958).

Some human needs would seem to be very closely comparable with the needs of animals and plants. In matters of nutrition and exercise we may speak of needs which must normally be met if human beings are to fulfil their (physical) potential and become good (physical) specimens. These are objective statements about matters of fact; they are not statements about wants, nor do they depend upon statements about wants. I may need a vitamin I have never heard of, and so cannot possibly want. Other people, such as dieticians and gym instructors, may know more about my needs for nutrition and exercise than I do. To accept these statements is not, of course, to advocate a despotism of dieticians and gym instructors over everyone else's nutrition and exercise. Nor is it necessary, for fear of endorsing such a despotism, to fall into the absurdity of denying that some people may know more than we do about some of our needs.

Human non-physical needs, if there are any, will depend upon the possibility of similarly clear and sufficiently objective knowledge of what constitutes a flourishing specimen of the human *psyche*. The politics of needs writers have certainly propounded their notions of human excellence, though usually only in outline, and often in a crudely tendentious form, excluding, for instance, such 'socially harmful' activities as watching American films and making profits (Fromm 1955). They have, then, done little to engender confidence in their own capacity to make reasoned choices among models of human excellence and related human needs. But it has not been shown that what they failed to do

cannot be done. In Bowlby's (1969) account of the process of attachment in infancy, there is scarcely more subjectivity or arbitrariness in saying of people in whom such needs have not been met that they are (psychologically) handicapped specimens of humanity, than in saying that people whose nutritional needs have not been met are (physically) handicapped specimens of humanity. In both areas, it is a case of grave deprivation that is most readily recognizable. Whatever physical, psychological or moral needs there may be reason to recognize in human beings, those needs will still have no political significance unless it can also be shown that there is something in the public forum that can be done, and ought to be done, to meet them.

E. D. Watt
University of Western Australia

References

Anscombe, G. E. M. (1958) 'Modern moral philosophy', *Philosophy* 33.
Bay, C. (1965) 'Politics and pseudopolitics' *American Political Science Review* 59.
—— (1968) 'Needs, wants and political legitimacy', *Canadian Journal of Political Science* 1.
Bowlby, J. (1969) *Attachment and Loss*, vols I and II, London.
Fitzgerald, R. (ed.) (1977) *Human Needs and Politics*, Sydney.
Fromm, E. (1955) *The Sane Society*, New York.
Macpherson, C. B. (1966) *The Real World of Democracy*, Oxford.
—— (1973) *Democratic Theory: Essays in Retrieval*, Oxford.
Marcuse, H. (1964) *One-Dimensional Man*, London.
Marcuse, H. *et al.* (1969) *A Critique of Pure Tolerance*, London.

Further reading

Flew, A. G. N. (1977) 'Wants or needs, choices or commands', in R. Fitzgerald (ed.) *Human Needs and Politics*, Sydney.
Minogue, K. R. (1963) *The Liberal Mind*, London.

See also: basic needs; human nature; human rights; poverty; social welfare policy.

human resource management

Human resource management (HRM) is now the term most commonly used in academic circles to encompass the range of policies and practices used by 'modern' organizations in the management of employees. The shortened term human resource (HR) is increasingly found to describe the personnel department, director or manager. UK practice is beginning to follow the USA in this respect. The terms, however, are both confused and confusing. HRM as a term was first used by Miles (1965) in the *Harvard Business Review* to differentiate the human relations school which focused on managerial leadership from the creation of 'an environment in which the total resources of [the organization] can be utilized' (1965: 150). This meant finding a means of utilizing the untapped resources of all organizational members, be it skills, tacit knowledge, commitment or competences. This presumption that certain forms of management can release or empower employees to work more effectively for the organization took hold in the 1980s and 1990s as industrial relations problems receded and many firms found that better management of their existing resources was required to meet more competitive markets.

In 1984 two books were published in the USA which established HRM but simultaneously revealed a fundamental division in the meaning of the term. Beer *et al.* (1984) emphasized, like Miles, the 'soft' elements of HRM, arguing that an integrated set of approaches focused on the individual employee linked to the strategic needs of the company could create what became known as high-value work systems. Fombrun *et al.* (1984), however, developed the 'matching model' where the organization's approach to its employees derived from and fitted the wider business strategy. This was taken further by Schuler and Jackson (1987) to suggest that firms in different market segments will develop very different types of HRM systems. A firm in a price-sensitive market with relatively low-skilled workers is unlikely to invest heavily in training and development to empower the employees. This has been described by Storey (1992) in the definitive UK book as 'hard' HRM. As Legge (1989) has noted, the first is *human* resource management, the second human *resource* management.

This distinction between the optimistic soft model and the potentially exploitative hard version is sometimes linked with the notions of loose–tight to assess the extent to which HR policies are closely linked to corporate and business strategies. It is generally agreed that HRM requires a tight link to the strategy of the firm, whereas a loose connection is seen to typify personnel management, the term which predated HRM. Personnel management was restricted to the supply-side concerned to ensure that the right labour was available. In contrast HRM operates more on the demand side and involves all managers, not just the specialists. Here all factors which impinge on the performance of the worker – the design of jobs and relations with others, the types of contracts and pay systems, and the use of forms of individual and group communication, consultation and representation systems – are all designed in the light of strategic need to maximize economic outcomes whether by the soft or hard approach to labour force management.

The final distinguishing characteristic of HRM is that it is concerned with the internal policies and practices of the organization at the micro level and tends to ignore or take for granted wider macro issues of societal culture, the political economy and the role of the state. At the micro level, however, by the link with business strategy and focus on performance it does offer the prospect of a new theoretical sophistication (Boxall 1992).

John Purcell
University of Oxford

References

Beer, M., Spector, B., Lawrence, P. R., Quinn Miles, D. and Walton, R. E. (1984) *Managing Human Assets*, New York.

Boxall, P. F. (1992) 'Strategic human resource management: beginning of a new theoroectical sophisitication?', *Human Resource Management Journal* 2(3).

Fombrun, C. J., Tichy, N. M. and Devanna, M. A. (1984) *Strategic Human Resource Management*, New York.

Legge, K. (1989) 'Human resource management: a critical analysis', in J. Storey (ed.) *New Perspectives in Human Resource Management*, London.

Miles, R. (1965) 'Human relations or human resources?', *Harvard Business Review* 43(4).

Schuler, R. S. and Jackson, S. E. (1987) 'Organizational strategy and organizational level as determinants of human resource management practices', *Human Resource Planning* 10.

Storey, J. (1992) *Developments in Human Resource Management: An Analytical Review*, Oxford.

See also: industrial relations; management theory; organizations; strategic management.

human rights

Human rights are rights which all persons hold by virtue of the human condition. They are thus not dependent upon grant or permission of the state and they cannot be withdrawn by fiat of the state. While laws under different national legal systems may vary, the human rights to which each person is entitled are rights in international law. For example, the human right to a fair trial is the same for a person who lives under a legal system of common law, civil law or Roman law. States have the obligation to ensure that their discrete legal systems reflect and protect the international human rights which those within their jurisdiction hold.

Are human rights universal?

There has been a long-running debate on whether human rights are universal or whether they are necessarily the product of particular cultures and societies. The suggestion that human rights represent western values, and are imposed upon others, is more a product of liberal democratic sensitivity than a reflection of the views of non-western states or their populations. The very wide acceptance of the International Covenants on Human Rights of 1966 (themselves based on the unanimously adopted Universal Declaration of Human Rights) appeared to have answered this issue in favour of the perceived universality of the rights. Over 140 states are parties to the International Covenant on Civil and Political Rights. These include the former socialist countries of eastern Europe as well as many developing countries. Egypt, Tunisia, Iraq and Iran are among the Islamic countries that have freely chosen to ratify this instrument. Large numbers of socialist, non-Christian and developing states have accepted that their citizens are as entitled as those residing in western countries to fundamental freedoms and human rights. Human rights constitute the common language of humanity. If individuals choose to identify with a particular culture, which may restrict the rights to which they would otherwise be entitled by international law, that is their prerogative choice. But that identification with a culture or religion may not be imposed by a state against the wish of an individual. This is not to insist upon 'western' human rights, but rather to insist that human rights are for people and not for states.

From the entry into force of the Covenants until the early 1990s there was an incremental growth in the concept of the universality of human rights. In 1989, shortly after the fall of the Berlin Wall, it was decided to convene a World Conference on Human Rights. The conference took place in Vienna in 1993 and the preparations therefore, and the conference meetings themselves, were used by some states who had never undertaken the obligations of the Covenants to try to persuade others that human rights represented a western cultural imperialism. This was coupled with proposals for new regional human rights treaties that would be more reflective of cultural particularity. These efforts did not in fact prevail. Article 5 of the Vienna Declaration, in the formulation of which all UN members participated and which was adopted by consensus, proclaims that

> while the significance of national and regional particularities and various historical, cultural and regional backgrounds must be borne in mind, it is the duty of states, regardless of their political, economic and cultural systems, to promote and protect all human rights and fundamental freedoms.

Article 57 makes clear that the role of regional arrangements is not to detract from universal standards, but to reinforce them.

The content of human rights

Human rights do not consist only of civil and political rights. There also exist economic, social and cultural rights, notably those reflected in the International Covenant on Economic, Social and Cultural Rights. Western countries have been sceptical about whether the requirements contained in that instrument (for example, the right to housing, the right to education) should properly be described as rights, or whether they are mere aspirations. It has also been suggested that if a stated obligation is not justiciable in the courts, it is not a legal right. Developing countries have been anxious about their ability to deliver these rights in the short term. However, the International Covenant on Economic, Social and Cultural Rights is now ratified by countries from all parts of the world. The work of its monitoring Committee has done much to address these concerns. It has made clear, for example, that while the full attainment of an economic right may not be immediate, there is an immediate obligation to take designated and agreed steps to that end. Economic, social and cultural rights entail immediate obligations of 'best efforts', coupled with obligations of result. All of these factors are to be taken into account in determining whether, at any given moment, a specific country is or is not in violation of its obligations regarding such rights. Certain aspects of this category of rights may be justiciable, for example, if housing is being provided in a discriminatory manner. But the absence of justiciability in any event reflects not an absence of entitlement but a need for diverse mechanisms for guaranteeing such entitlements.

Individual and group rights

The beneficiaries of human rights, as reflected in the major international instruments, are individuals. This is true even of minority rights, which are articulated as the right of individuals to pursue their culture, or speak their language, or engage in worship, with others from their group. The sole exception arises in relation to the right to self-determination, which stands in a separate part of each of the Covenants, and is a right of 'all peoples'. From the western perspective, the emphasis on the individual as the beneficiary of rights is a necessary antithesis to the power of the state, and also to the power of groups that serve the purposes of the state. There is, however, now an interest in exploring again whether some rights do not properly adhere to groups. The cataclysmic events in the former Yugoslavia and in eastern Europe in the early 1990s have led to the perception that minority rights may need to be more broadly fashioned than is possible so long as they remain rights of individuals. The question of group rights has also become relevant in the context of new 'third and fourth generation' rights now being proposed, such as the right to a clean environment, the right to sustainable development, the rights of indigenous peoples, and others. With regard to these 'new generation' rights, there is still considerable debate as to their status as human rights, not only because of the novelty of groups or peoples as the beneficiary, but also because of the uncertainty of the content of the right or the obligations imposed thereby and on whom.

The sources and institutions of human rights law

General international law is the source of some human rights, but they are most clearly set out in a remarkable system of international treaties, all developed since the mid-1960s. The two International Covenants on Human Rights (1966) cover between them all the major civil and political, and economic, social and cultural rights. They are open to all states. Certain of those have been made the subject of single topic treaties, which specify the right concerned in more detail and provide for further procedural guarantees. These, too, are open to all states. These UN treaties have monitoring bodies, which receive reports, examine the states parties, and, in certain cases, sit as quasi-judicial tribunals in respect of individual claims. The Committee under the Covenant on Civil and Political Rights in particular has developed a significant jurisprudence. At the regional level, too, there are treaties that cover the generality of human rights and treaties that address single topics. These are open to the states of the region, or the regional institutions. The American Convention on Human Rights, which has its own Commission and Court, is an important instrument for the Americas. The Commission does much important work, much of it *in loco*. In the last fifteen years the Court has begun to develop its jurisprudence. All members of the Council of Europe adhere to the European Convention on Human Rights. Those newly seeking admission to the Council of Europe must also be prepared to ratify the European Convention and to accept the right of their citizens to bring cases against them. The European Commission of Human Rights and the European Court of Human Rights have since 1950 developed the most detailed and important jurisprudence on the rights. They also deal with some inter-state cases. The jurisprudence of the European Court of Human Rights is relied on in the courts of those states that have made the European Convention part of their own domestic law, whether by incorporation or otherwise. Even in those few countries that have not – for example, the United Kingdom – the decisions of the European Court are binding and an adverse finding may require alterations to legislation or to administrative practices. In 1994 a Protocol was signed which envisages important alterations to the institutions of the European Convention, most notably replacing the Commission and Court with a new permanent Court.

Limitations on rights

The balance between the rights of individuals and the legitimate concerns of the state, which has to take into account the general good, is met through the device of permitted limitations. Very few human rights are absolute. The prohibition against torture is such a right. Most rights may be qualified, in a particular case, if certain conditions are met. A law prescribing the limitation must pre-exist its use and be accessible and known. A restriction upon the right must be shown to be necessary. There are usually further conditions to be met, for example, that a restriction be for reasons of public order, public health or state security.

In times of national emergency states are permitted to derogate from human rights – that is to say, to suspend their obligations to guarantee these rights for the duration of the emergency. Again, certain rights may not be derogated from, whatever the circumstances. For example, no emergency justifies torture, nor can it remove a person's freedom of thought, conscience or of religion.

Rosalyn Higgins
UN Committee on Human Rights

Further reading

Commonwealth Secretariat/Interights (1988–93) *Developing Human Rights Jurisprudence, Judicial Colloquia*, 5 vols, London.
Meron, T. (1984) *Human Rights in International Law*, 2 vols, Oxford.
United Nations (1988) *United Nations Action in the Field of Human Rights*, New York.
Van Dijk, P. and Van Hoof, G. (1990) *Theory and Practice of the European Convention on Human Rights*, Dordrecht, The Netherlands.

See also: citizenship; freedom; human nature; human needs; social welfare policy.

Hume, David (1711–76)

Though it is now a cliché that Hume's philosophy is a Newtonian science of humankind, and that all through the twentieth century students of it have noticed such things as the role played by sympathy as a mechanism of communication and factor in the development of self-consciousness and attacked the view of its allegedly atomistic, unhistorical individualism, it seems fair to say that Hume has not occupied a particularly important place in the history of social science, except perhaps negatively. His friends Ferguson and Adam Smith have attracted more attention as founding fathers of a truly sociological method and outlook, and there are some good reasons for this: Hume's social theory, compared with theirs, was in many ways 'backward'. Its negative side has attracted those who value it as a useful political hygiene. There has been too much use of hasty generalizations and abridgements of a philosophy which is controversial and difficult to interpret. His social and political thought is no less complex and many-sided, as anyone knows who has tried to make sense of it as a whole. Those determined to place him in the tradition of conservative politics ignore his republicanism; those who collect evidence of his civic humanism, or the politics of nostalgia of the country gentleman, neglect what is forward looking and sociologically positive in him.

Hume's contribution to politics, which he defined as the science of 'men united in society and dependent on each other', can be divided roughly into three main sections or phases: a theory of justice and government as such, as part of a naturalistic ethics; essays covering a wide range of topics in economics and politics; and a *History of England*. All three can be seen as parts of a programme not only of political moderation but also of modernization, an attempt to give the Revolution and Hanoverian regime a proper, that is, philosophical or scientific and empirical foundation, and to understand the nature of modern European political civilization.

The natural law that Hume accepted as the ground of political science was, in its contemporary modes, open to the attacks of sceptics, moral relativists and Hobbists, but what Hume provided in his account of Justice – the three natural laws concerning property without which settled society is impossible and which government is instituted to uphold – was wholly secular and too avant-garde for his contemporaries. It was regarded, as was Hume's philosophy generally, as sceptical in a wholly destructive sense, a socially dangerous virus, not a healthy vaccine producing moderation, and the view that it destroyed the rational foundations of natural law became canonical in the textbook histories of jurisprudence and political thought. Even when Hume was praised for the sociological realism of his account of the origin of justice and government, allegedly doing away with the state of nature and the social contract, this was usually misunderstood, and Hume's real contribution to social science was overlooked: an empirical, secular and one-dimensional idea of society as the exclusive locus of justice and all moral obligation and social ties and rules. Hume had no use for the idea of a God-governed society of people *qua* rational agents as such; his philosophy could not accommodate it.

Hume's philosophical approach to politics had little more success in the other parts of his programme. Contemporaries in England did not appreciate his ability, both as a cosmopolitan Scotsman and a Newtonian scientist, to take a detached view of the British government and political scene or its history, and to compare them, not altogether favourably, with the 'civilized' absolute monarchies of Europe. The *History* became notoriously the Tory apologia for the Stuarts: its broader theme, the development of regular government in Europe, was invisible through the keyhole of English party politics.

A broader-based, more thorough and intensive study of Hume's politics is a comparatively recent development.

Duncan Forbes
formerly, University of Cambridge

Further reading

Forbes, D. (1975) *Hume's Philosophical Politics*, Cambridge, UK.
Miller, D. (1981) *Philosophy and Ideology in Hume's Political Thought*, Oxford.
Stewart, J. B. (1963) *The Moral and Political Thought of David Hume*, New York.

See also: Scottish Enlightenment, social theory.

hunters and gatherers

Hunters and gatherers, gatherer-hunters and foragers are all more or less synonymous terms, and are usually applied to those populations who live entirely by these two means of subsistence. Sometimes the terms are used more loosely to refer to populations who obtain *most* of their subsistence by hunting and gathering, who until recently subsisted entirely by hunting and gathering, or who subsist by hunting, gathering and fishing.

In 10,000 BC, the world's population consisted solely of hunters, gatherers and fishermen. By AD 1500, with the spread of pastoralism and agriculture, this total was down to 1 per cent. By AD 1900 it was a mere 0.001 per cent (Lee and DeVore 1968). In the 1990s hunter-gatherers include small, scattered groups on several continents, and they usually live encapsulated by and in contact with non-hunter-gatherers. Well-known examples include the Australian Aborigines, the African Bushmen and Pygmies, and the Inuit or Eskimo of northern North America. In all these cases full-time hunting and gathering is dying out, though many modern members of these groups, as well as South American horticulturists and African pastoralists, engage in part-time hunting and gathering and retain a foraging ethos which governs their economic activities. Throughout the world the basic sexual division of labour is the same: the men do the hunting and the women do the gathering.

In spite of their small numbers, 'pure' hunter-gatherers have been of great significance in social theory. Evolutionary anthropologists and human ethologists have emphasized that the overwhelming part of cultural humankind's 2 million-year existence has been spent in hunting and gathering societies. Some argue that humans' 'natural' biological make-up is best exemplified in these societies, rather than in agricultural or industrialized ones. The counter-argument is that present-day foragers are both biologically modern and fully 'cultural', and therefore the means of subsistence bear no necessary relation to any primeval human mentality.

Prehistoric archaeologists also use studies of present-day foragers, in this case as aids to interpreting the archaeological record. Yet the difficulty is that contemporary foragers, who are largely confined to deserts and jungles and in continual contact with non-foraging peoples, may be quite different from the ancient hunter-gatherers who inhabited the archaeological sites of Europe and temperate North America.

Another area of theoretical interest has been in economic anthropology. According to Sahlins (1974), hunters and gatherers represent 'the original affluent society'. If affluence is measured in free time rather than in accumulated wealth, hunters and gatherers are often far more affluent than their agricultural neighbours. Except in times of scarcity, hunter-gatherer populations need spend only a few hours per day in subsistence-related activities, and they survive times of general severity, such as drought, better than neighbouring agricultural peoples.

Yet in spite of all this theoretical interest in hunter-gatherers, some specialists have come to question the utility of hunter-gatherers as a meaningful category. Ellen (1982) argues that there is little difference between the subsistence pursuits of 'pure' hunter-gatherers and horticulturalists who hunt and gather for part of their food supply. Likewise, Ingold (1980) considers the case for a fuzzy boundary between hunting and herding. A number of writers have attacked the commonplace notion that foragers are somehow 'purer' than other branches of humanity. In earlier texts, foragers had been described as more 'natural' and therefore, but contradictorily, more 'human' than other peoples. Part-time foragers were thus seen as tainted by exposure to non-forager culture and less worthy of study.

Woodburn (1980) has suggested a way out of these impasses, but one which also questions the category hunters and gatherers. He draws the line not between hunter-gatherers and non-hunter-gatherers, but between 'immediate-return' hunter-gatherers and others.

Immediate-return economies are characterized by a hand-to-mouth existence, that is, a lack of time-investment in activities designed to pay off later, such as making fishing nets, keeping horses for use in hunting, or the cultivation of crops. In contrast, hunter-gatherers who invest in horses, nets, etc., and all non-hunter-gatherers, have 'delayed-return' economies. Immediate-return economies are characteristically egalitarian, with social life based on the wide sharing of goods.

Since the mid-1980s there has been a major debate sparked off by the 'revisionist' critique. Revisionists, such as Wilmsen (1989), have attacked the notion that modern hunter-gatherers have long been isolated from their neighbours. They emphasize the impact of the regional and even the world economy, not only recently but also in the centuries before European exploration and colonization. Ironically, say some commentators, the encapsulation of hunter-gatherers in the last century has led to a 'purer' foraging lifestyle, rather than the destruction of that lifestyle.

Alan Barnard
University of Edinburgh

References

Ellen, R. F. (1982) *Environment, Subsistence and System*, Cambridge, UK.
Ingold, T. (1980) *Hunters, Pastoralists and Ranchers*, Cambridge, UK.
Lee, R. B. and DeVore, I. (1968) 'Problems in the study of hunters and gatherers', in R. B. Lee and I. DeVore (eds) *Man the Hunter*, Chicago.
Sahlins, M. (1974) *Stone Age Economics*, London.
Wilmsen, E. N. (1989) *Land Filled with Flies: A Political Economy of the Kalahari*, Chicago.
Woodburn, J. (1980) 'Egalitarian societies', *Man* 17.

Further reading

Burch, E. L. Jr and Ellanna, L. J. (1994) *Key Issues in Hunter-Gatherer Research*, Oxford.
Ingold, T., Riches, D. and Woodburn, J. (eds) (1988) *Hunters and Gatherers*, 2 vols, Oxford.

See also: pastoralism.

hypnosis

Hypnosis is an altered state of mind, usually accompanied by some or all the following:

1 Increases in the intensity of focal concentration as compared with peripheral awareness
2 Changes in perception, memory and temporal orientation
3 Alternations in the sense of control over voluntary motor functions

4 Dissociation of certain parts of experience from the remainder
5 Intensification of interpersonal relatedness, with an increase in receptivity and suspension of critical judgement.

Individuals capable of experiencing some or all of these changes associated with a shift into the hypnotic trance state may learn to employ them as tools in facilitating therapeutic change. This applies especially to people with disorders which involve the psychosomatic interface.

Hypnosis is not sleep but rather a shift in attention which can occur in a matter of seconds, either with guidance or spontaneously. Highly hypnotizable individuals are more prone to intensely absorbing and self-altering experiences, for example when reading novels or watching good films. All hypnosis is really self-hypnosis. Under guided conditions, hypnotizable individuals allow a therapist or other person to structure their own shift in attention. However, not everyone can be hypnotized. Research using a variety of standardized scales indicates that hypnotizability is highest toward the end of the first decade of life, and declines slowly through adulthood and more rapidly late in life. Approximately two-thirds of the adult population is at least somewhat hypnotizable, and about 5 per cent are extremely hypnotizable. Among psychiatric patients, this capacity for hypnotic experience has been shown to be higher in certain disorders, such as dissociative and post-traumatic stress disorders and lower in others, such as schizophrenia. In general, the capacity to experience hypnosis is consistent with good mental health and normal brain function. Neurophysiological studies of hypnotized subjects indicate brain electrical activity consistent with resting alertness.

Hypnosis has been used successfully as an adjunctive tool in the treatment of a variety of psychiatric and medical conditions, including the control of pain; anxiety and phobias; habits, especially smoking; and in the treatment of acute and post-traumatic stress disorders. When used in treatment, the hypnotic state provides a receptive and attentive condition in which the patient concentrates on a primary treatment strategy designed to promote greater mastery over the symptom. Some individuals with dissociative fugue states and multiple personality disorder are treated with hypnosis because their high hypnotizability becomes a vehicle for the expression of symptoms. Dissociative amnesias can be uncovered, and shifts between different personality states can be facilitated with the goal of teaching the patient greater control over these transitions in states of mind.

All psychotherapies are composed of interpersonal and intrapsyphic components which facilitate change. Hypnotic trance mobilizes focused concentration, demonstrates the ability to change both psychological and somatic experience, and intensifies receptivity to input from others. This makes the hypnotic state a natural tool for use in psychotherapy and a fascinating psychobiological phenomenon.

David Spiegel
Stanford University

Further reading

Fromm, E. and Nash, M. R. (eds) (1992) *Contemporary Hypnosis Research*, New York.
Spiegel, H. and Spiegel, D. (1987) *Trance and Treatment: Clinical Uses of Hypnosis*, Washington, DC.

See also: unconscious.

id

In *The Ego and the Id* Freud (1923) drew together ideas initiated in earlier works and presented a more formalized conceptualization of the *psyche* or mind as an energy system taking the form of a confluence of interacting forces which may and often do, conflict. These forces, Freud suggested, were broadly of three types. The most basic and primitive of these, and the source of all instinctual energy, he called the id. (The others are the ego – the perceptual, integrative aspect of self – and the superego, which is roughly equivalent to conscience). Discharge of the energy of the id, either through consummatory actions or appropriate fantasy, is experienced as pleasure. Where the urge cannot be directly gratified in action or fantasy, tension results. According to Freudian theory, young babies are dominated by id impulses. If their needs are not met, tension builds up and they cry until breast or bottle is produced. Once they are satisfied, tension is relieved and they rest back content.

The id is the instinctual, hereditary part of the psyche. In developing this concept, Freud extended the idea of the unconscious to include not only that which is repressed but also the biological basis of personality. The id is the repository of sexual drive or libido and of the destructive power of the death instinct (thanatos). It follows only the pleasure principle without regard for reality or logic ('primary process'). Gratification may come through fantasy and urges may be displaced on to other objects. (In contrast the ego, while it also seeks pleasure, follows the reality principle and its secondary process thinking takes account of the external world.) Although the ego is the executive of the psyche and the id 'has no will of its own', Freud clearly accorded primacy to the id, seeing it as the source of all energy and as expressing the 'true purpose of the individual organism's life'. In describing the relation between ego and id, he drew the analogy between a horse and rider. 'Just as there often remains nothing for the rider, if he does not want to be separated from the horse, but to lead it where it wants to go, so the ego, too, is accustomed to translating the will of the id into actions as if that will were its own'. Because psychoanalysis was for Freud primarily the study of the unconscious, so 'psychoanalysis is to be described as a psychology of the id and of its effects on the ego'.

It is worth noting that Freud himself never used the word id. His original term was *das Es*, literally 'the it'. This effectively puts across the notion of a different kind of impulsion capable of acting outside and sometimes in spite of our conscious intention. Bettelheim (1985) has criticized Freud's English translators for introducing terms which 'reek of erudition' but whose effect is to distance us from Freud's ideas.

Richard Stevens
Open University

References

Bettelheim, B. (1985) *Freud and Man's Soul*, Harmondsworth.
Freud, S. (1923) *The Ego and the Id, Standard Edition of the Complete Psychological Works of Sigmund Freud*, ed. J. Strachey, vol. 19, London.

Further reading

Freud, S. (1933) *New Introductory Lectures in Psychoanalysis, Standard Edition of the Complete Psychological Works of Sigmund Freud*, ed. J. Strachey, vol. 22, London.
Stevens, R. (1983) *Freud and Psychoanalysis*, Milton Keynes.

See also: ego; psychoanalysis.

identity *see* social identity

imagery *see* mental imagery

imperialism

Imperialism has acquired so many meanings that the word ought to be dropped by social scientists, complained Professor Hancock in 1950. 'Muddle-headed historians in Great Britain and America use this word with heaven-knows how many shades of meaning, while Soviet writers are using it to summarize a theory and wage a war.' Alas, these errors continue. Autocratic rule over a diversity of otherwise roughly equal peoples goes back in time at least as far as the Indo-European Empire of Alexander the Great, but nowadays imperialism also means to Marxists the triumph of (mostly western European) monopoly finance capital over a still larger array of non-European peoples at the end of the nineteenth century, a very different kind of empire indeed. For some underdevelopment theorists, the term is simply synonymous with capitalism in general, not just its monopolistic stage. Demythologizing imperialism is therefore a rather slippery task.

Marxist theories of imperialism were first fleshed out during the 1900s and 1910s principally to explain why the expected final collapse of capitalism was taking so long to happen. Later the outbreak of the First World War, and the promptness with which European working peoples attacked one another rather than their bosses, added fresh urgency to thought. Nationalism, in retrospect, seems to have had something to do with this, as well as the autonomy of political choice at the time of outbreak of war from anything approaching economic rationality. But Marxist writers mostly looked elsewhere for explanations and for ammunition with which to pursue more sectarian concerns. Just before the war, Rosa Luxemburg provided in *Die Akkumulation des Kapitals* (1913) an analysis of imperialism which is still read respectfully today because of its pioneer probing of articulations between expanding capitalism and pre-capitalist social formations outside Europe. But during and after the First World War it was her advocacy of the mass revolutionary strike in order to speed up the final collapse of capitalism, otherwise given a new lease of life by imperialist expansion, that excited more immediate attention.

Marx himself had seen the expansion of capitalism outside its original heartlands as both a less important phenomenon and a more benign one than Luxemburg: it was a marginal matter, in at least two senses. Luxemburg, however, considered that capitalism could survive only if it continually expanded its territory. One problem with this view, as Mommsen (1981) pointed out, is that 'Rosa Luxemburg's basic adherence to Marx's complicated and controversial theory of surplus value, which by definition accrued to capitalism alone, prevented her from considering whether, if the consumer capacity of the masses were increased, internal markets might not afford suitable opportunities for the profitable investment of "unconsumed" i.e. reinvestable, surplus value.' Another defect was that Luxemburg undoubtedly misunderstood the significance of the enormous rise in overseas investment at the start of the twentieth century. Along with Hobson before and Lenin subsequently, she assumed that it was closely associated with colonial annexations. In fact, as Robinson and Gallagher (1961) pointed out, it diverged widely from it. Hilferding had taken a slightly different view. In *Das Finanzkapital* (1910), he was more concerned to explain why capitalist crises had become less frequent (there had not been one since 1896), and he argued that free trade had been replaced by finance capital, whose dominance and ability to intervene with state help anywhere in the world had temporarily delayed the final catastrophe. But it was the British journalist and free-trader Hobson, with his wide array of attacks upon overseas investment and colonial annexations in *Imperialism* (1902), whom Lenin used most extensively in his own famous study of *Imperialism, The Highest Stage of Capitalism* (1917). This was written in order not only to explain the First World War but also to attack the reformism of Karl Kautsky, who had suggested that the coming final collapse of capitalism might be still further delayed by the emergence of an 'ultra-imperialism' stopping for the time being further intra-imperialist wars. In retrospect, Lenin's work on imperialism reads more like a tract than a treatise, but its subsequent importance was of course vastly increased by the success of Lenin's faction in seizing power in Russia in 1917; for many years afterwards it retained unquestionable status as unholy writ.

Shortly after the Russian Revolution, Lenin also latched on to one of the greatest uses of imperialism as political ideology, namely as a weapon against non-communist empires. This tendency was continued by Stalin, who told the Twelfth Congress of the Russian Communist Party in 1923: 'Either we succeed in stirring up, in revolutionizing, the remote rear of imperialism – the colonial and semi-colonial countries of the East – and thereby hasten the fall of imperialism; or we fail to do so and thereby strengthen imperialism and weaken the force of our movement.' Such statements reversed Marx's original view that imperialism was good for capitalism but only of marginal importance in its development, and substituted a new conventional wisdom that, first, imperialism was bad news for all backward areas of the world, and, second, imperialism was of utterly central importance to the development of capitalism itself.

The first view was then widely popularized by the underdevelopment school associated with André Gundar Frank, and attacked later from both right and left. The second view led to an oddly focused debate among historians over the colonial partition of Africa at the close of the nineteenth century, the 'theory of economic imperialism' being something of a straw man in this debate, as imperialism (on most Marxist views) did not arise until after the Scramble for Africa had taken place; even after this date Lenin was clearly wrong about the direction of most overseas investment, let alone its political significance. Only in the case of South Africa (and possibly Cuba) is there even a plausible case for economic imperialism being identical with colonial annexation: the South African War indeed was popularly called 'les Boers contre la Bourse' in continental Europe at the time.

Other difficulties with Marxist views of imperialism derive from Lenin's use of Hobson's *Imperialism* (1902). Hobson was a very bitter critic of British overseas investment, but for very un-Marxist reasons. He was a free-trade liberal who saw colonial annexations and wars as a hugely expensive way of propping up the power and profits of a very small class of *rentier* capitalists, who pursued profit abroad to the detriment of investment at home. Only by manipulating the masses by appealing to their patriotism did this small class of capitalists get away with this (in his view) huge confidence trick and, ideally, social reform should increase the purchasing powers of the masses and thereby render imperialism powerless. Lenin ignored Hobson's theories and simply used his facts. In retrospect, the facts about the coincidence of overseas investment with colonial annexation appear very wrong-headed, his theories much less so. Hobson's views on underconsumption were later taken up and given some seminal twists by John Maynard Keynes, while his intuitions about connections between overseas annexations and metropolitan social structures were later taken up by Joseph Schumpeter and Hannah Arendt (for her analysis of the origins of Fascism).

Schumpeter wrote his essay *Zur Soziologie der Imperialismen* (1919) as an explicit attack upon Marxist theories of imperialism. Capitalism itself he considered to be essentially anti-imperialist in nature, and such monopolistic and expansionist tendencies characterizing pre-1914 capitalism he put down to the malevolent influence of an anachronistic militarism surviving from the European feudal past. Schumpeter defined imperialism as 'the objectless disposition on the part of a state to unlimited forcible expansion' (Schumpeter 1951 [1919]). The basic trouble with this particular formulation is that while the European colonial annexations of the late nineteenth and early twentieth centuries were certainly sometimes this, they were not always so. Similarly, while much European overseas investment in the late nineteenth century did not go to areas of European colonial annexation, sometimes it

did. Furthermore, while the theory of economic imperialism may well be a straw man as far as the debate about the causes of the Scramble for Africa is concerned, it would be absurd to suggest that the partitioners did not believe that there was *something* economically useful about Black Africa. Imperialism needs to be demythologized, not simply wished away.

Probably imperialism is best defined in some median manner. As the etymology of the word itself denotes, imperialism is closely concerned with empires and colonialism, but this is not necessarily always the case. In the Americas the Monroe Doctrine (1823) vetoed new formal empires by European countries – but not subsequent 'dollar diplomacy' by the USA, sometimes supported by the overt use of force, sometimes with mere threats and unequal financial practices. Capitalism, too, is not necessarily linked with territorial imperialism, but sometimes has been, especially in the many African and Asian colonial dependencies established during the second half of the nineteenth century. In these circumstances, imperialism is probably best separated analytically from both capitalism and colonialism and treated principally as the pursuit of intrusive and unequal economic policy in other countries supported by significant degrees of coercion.

Thus defined, imperialism as formal empire (or 'colonialism') may well be largely a thing of the past, except for strategic colonies (*colonies de position*). But imperialism as informal empire (or 'neo-colonialism', to employ Nkrumah's terminology) probably has an assured future ahead of it – in what remains of both the non-communist and the communist-dominated worlds in the post-Cold War era.

Michael Twaddle
University of London

References

Hancock, W. K. (1950) *Wealth of Colonies*, Cambridge, UK.
Mommsen, W. J. (1981) *Theories of Imperialism*, New York.
Porter, A. (1994) *European Imperialism: 1860–1914*, Basingstoke.
Robinson, R. and Gallagher, J. (1961) *Africa and the Victorians: The Official Mind of Imperialism*, London.
Schumpeter, J. A. (1951 [1919]) *Imperialism and Social Classes*, Oxford. (Includes translation of *Zur Soziologie der Imperialismen*)

See also: colonialism; world-system theory.

incest

Incest, defined as sexual relations between close kin (usually members of the same nuclear family), has received relatively scant theoretical attention compared to its prohibition – the incest taboo. The latter arrangement has been the subject of numerous and often contradictory explanations by almost all the major figures in western social science, including Freud (1950), Marx and Engels (1942), Durkheim (1963) and Lévi-Strauss (1969), as well as a host of other contributors to the present. This ambition has prevailed because the prohibition has been assumed to provide the basis for a distinctly human form of social organization, and thus allowing for the emergence of culture itself. Consequently any general theory of society must initially provide an explanation for the existence of the incest taboo. Incest itself has been assumed to be a natural human inclination to be guarded against. Yet this conclusion is in itself a profound theoretical statement about human nature – and one which has gone unconsidered. It is apparent, though, that the prohibition and the deed can be understood only in relation to each other.

In some form or another, the incest prohibition or avoidance has characterized all human societies for the overwhelming majority of its members. (Exceptions to this rule are accounted for below.) Recognizing this fact sociological explanations have noted that the rule effectively excludes sexual competition among members of the nuclear family, and in addition precludes the role confusion that would result from reproduction by father and daughter, mother and son, or brother and sister. At a more general level, the prohibition of these kinds of sexual activities requires that at maturity children will seek external partners, creating a series of social alliances among families. As such society itself – a series of linked co-operative groups – comes into existence as the consequence of these exchanges. Such functional explanations for the incest prohibition highlight obvious advantages of the custom. However, it is equally important to note that these arguments do not account for the origin of the prohibition, as opposed to its contemporary consequences.

From a biological perspective it has been argued that nuclear family inbreeding has deleterious effects on offspring. This assumption is borne out by contemporary genetics, but there is no evidence that human beings instituted the incest prohibition to achieve this purpose. Freud's famous scenario, of the primeval human horde in which the patriarch dies at the hands of his own sons for his monopoly of all available females, is a compelling image, and instructive in understanding human psychological development. However, there is no evidence from either human history or primate studies to substantiate such an argument. (Indeed primatology indicates the very opposite arrangement.)

In sum, these arguments merely assume without evidence that humans instituted the incest prohibition to prevent the deed, and that we are naturally inclined to engage in it. The implication subsumed here is that our social arrangements are morally superior to natural inclinations.

In the late nineteenth century, the Swedish moral philosopher Edward Westermarck (1894) took an entirely different tack in suggesting that humans were naturally (i.e. instinctually) inclined to avoid incest. The reasonable reaction at the time – to which Westermarck was unable to respond satisfactorily – was: Why then do all societies have the prohibition? However, we are now aware of some societies in which incest is not explicitly prohibited, but nevertheless does not occur. Moreover, ethnographic studies from China (Wolf and Huang 1980), the Middle East (McCabe 1983) and Israel (Shepher 1983) demonstrate that children raised together make for unappealing or unsatisfactory marriage partners. Finally, both field and controlled laboratory studies of primates and other mammals also indicate mate preference for individuals other than those raised together in either the wild or captivity. In the former instance, this outcome is achieved by either male or female troop transfer, so that the evolutionary disadvantages of inbreeding are unintentionally avoided. Since this social arrangement is a feature of all contemporary primate societies, it is assumed to have characterized our last common ancestor of some 400,000 years ago (Maryanski and Turner 1992). In the latter instance of laboratory experimentation – where this natural outbreeding option was prevented – a severe depression in normal mating and reproductive rates was the result (McGuire and Getz 1981).

If incestuous inbreeding is indeed naturally avoided then why does it exist for humans in the form of the uncondoned variety, as in our society? Moreover, there is every indication that the incidence of such behaviour is greater than previously assumed (Herman 1981). There are also numerous other cultures, such as Pharaonic Egypt, where incestuous marriages were characteristic of royalty. (These may have been purely symbolic arrangements; sex and reproduction were not necessarily at issue, especially for the males who had numerous other wives and sexual partners.) In addition, there is the now well-documented example of the Greek ethnic minority in Roman Egypt (first to fourth century AD) which regularly engaged in sibling marriage to prevent reproduction with the indigenous population (Hopkins 1980).

Although separate in space and time and different in their own ways, these incestuous episodes suggest that our species has the unique cultural capacity to overcome evolutionary inclinations against inbreeding and its negative consequences. Thus, in accounting for the existence of incest in any and all of its forms, we must look to human culture as opposed to human nature. In effect human beings have invented incest.

In recognition of this inclination most societies have generated rules against incest while proclaiming that the culprit lurks in our animal nature rather than our human imagination. Interestingly (but perhaps not surprisingly) the most popular theories attempting to account explicitly for the prohibition and implicitly the deed have followed a similar mystifying path by merely assuming that culture is superior to nature. There is enough evidence from history and ethnography to indicate that this is not always the case.

W. Arens
State University of New York

References

Durkheim, E. (1963) *Incest*, New York.
Engels, F. (1942) *The Origin of the Family, Private Property and the State*, New York.
Freud, S. (1950) *Totem and Taboo*, New York.
Herman, J. (1981) *Father–Daughter Incest*, Cambridge, MA.
Hopkins, K. (1980) 'Brother–sister marriage in Roman Egypt', *Comparative Studies in Society and History* 22.
Lévi-Strauss, C. (1969 [1949]) *The Elementary Structures of Kinship*, London.
McCabe, J. (1983) 'FBD Marriage', *American Anthropologist* 85.
McGuire, M. and Getz, L. (1981) 'Incest taboo between sibling microtus ochrogaster', *Journal of Mammalogy* 62.
Maryanski, A. and Turner, H. (1992) *The Social Cage*, Stanford, CA.
Shepherd, J. (1983) *Incest*, New York.
Westermarck, E. (1894) *The History of Human Marriage*, London.
Wolf, A. and Huang, H. (1980) *Marriage and Adoption in China, 1845–1945*, Stanford, CA.

Further reading

Arens, W. (1986) *The Original Sin*, New York.
Fox, R. (1980) *The Red Lamp of Incest*, New York.
Kuper, A. (1994) *The Chosen Primate*, Cambridge, MA.

See also: Oedipus complex; sexual behaviour.

income distribution, theory of

While economists have not always given such primacy to an explicit discussion of distributional questions, income distribution theory has almost always been central to the analysis of economic systems. The theory deals not only with the functional distribution of income but also with the size distribution of income.

Orthodox economic theory treats questions of income distribution as an integral part of the neoclassical analysis of prices, output mix and resource allocation. Briefly, each competitive firm takes the price it can get for its output and the prices it must pay for inputs as given in the market: it selects its level of output and adjusts its demand for inputs so as to maximize profits at those prices. Each household likewise takes as given the prices it must pay for goods and services, and the prices paid to it for goods and services (for example the labour services supplied by members of the household): it adjusts the quantities of the goods and services demanded or supplied in the market so as to maximize satisfaction within the limitations imposed by its budget. All these prices adjust so as to clear the markets: aggregate supply is at least as great as aggregate demand for every good and service. The reward to any factor of production – whether it be a particular type of labour, a natural resource or the services of capital equipment – is determined by its market clearing price. If the technology changes, or the stock of natural resources alters, or if there is a shift in the preference patterns of households, this will shift the pattern of supply and/or demand in one or more markets, and in general prices of goods and factors alter accordingly to clear the markets anew. The functional distribution of income is thus apparently automatically determined by the market mechanism, Moreover, the details of the distribution of income between persons or between households can be readily worked out within this framework: the time pattern of consumption and saving by households, and the educational investments which people make in themselves or in their offspring – each of which plays a significant role in the size distribution of incomes that is realized – can each be analysed as particular cases of the household's optimization problem.

However, one other piece of information is required for a complete theory of income distribution within this framework: the system of property rights that prevails within the community. The importance of this as regards the size distribution of income is obvious: the question of who owns which natural resources, of who owns the capital equipment and of who is entitled to a share in the profits of the firms is central to the determination of household incomes. Household budgets are determined jointly by these property rights and the market prices and may be dramatically affected by a change in the pattern of ownership, or by a shift in the *system* of ownership (for example from a system of private property to one of state ownership). But this system of ownership will *also* affect the market prices and thus the functional distribution of income. For if households' rights of ownership are changed, the consequent change in household budgets will change the pattern of demand for goods and services, and hence the market prices of consumption goods and of labour and other resources. Thus orthodox theory might be criticized for evading one of the principal issues of income determination, by passing the question of property rights on to the historian or the political philosopher.

However, the neo-classical orthodoxy has been challenged not only because of such shortcomings, but also on account of its restrictive assumptions concerning the economic processes involved. Because these assumptions lie at the heart of the theory rather than being merely convenient simplifications, many economists have questioned the relevance of various aspects of the standard account of income distribution. We may cite three particular examples which have led to the construction of useful alternative theories.

First, note that the orthodox theory neglects barriers to competition and the exercising of monopoly power as being of secondary or transitory importance in the competitive market story. It has been argued that restraints on competition – in the form of segmentation of the labour market and outright discrimination – are of major importance in analysing the lower tail of the size distribution of earnings; and monopoly power may be particularly important in the upper tail, for example, in the determination of earnings in professions with restricted entry. Monopolistic pricing by firms has also been seen as of prime importance in the *functional* distribution of income (see e.g. Kalecki 1939). Indeed such power has an important part to play in the Marxian concept of exploitation and of theories of distribution that are based on struggle between the classes representing different factors of production. The assumption of pure competition is also likely to be inadequate in analysing economics that have a substantial public sector.

A second feature of the orthodox approach which many theorists find unsatisfactory is the assumption of perfect information by individuals and firms. Indeed it is argued that uncertainty is itself a potent force generating inequality in both earned and unearned income alike, in that the rich not only are better able to bear risk but also may have superior information which can be exploited in the stock market and the labour market. Moreover, some of the barriers to competition may have been erected by firms in response to such uncertainty. Hence considerable interest has developed in the distributional implications of theories of output, employment and the structure of wages that explicitly incorporate imperfect information.

The third point arises from the second: the predominant interest of the neo-classical orthodox theory of income distribution in smooth adjustments to market clearing equilibria is considered by some writers to be inappropriate to a theory of the functional distribution of income. As a response to this, economists who are strongly influenced by J. M. Keynes's approach to macroeconomics have developed a number of alternative theories of the functional distribution of income using components of the Keynesian system, for example the work of Kaldor (1956) and Pasinetti

(1961). Key features of such alternative theories are rule-of-thumb savings decisions by capitalists and workers and a rigid technique by which labour and capital are combined to produce output.

Frank A. Cowell
London School of Economics and Political Science

References

Kaldor, N. (1956) 'Alternative theories of distribution', *Review of Economic Studies* 23.
Kalecki, M. (1939) *Essays in the Theory of Economic Fluctuations*, London.
Pasinetti, L. L. (1961) 'Rate of profit and income distribution in relation to the rate of economic growth', *Review of Economic Studies* 29.

Further reading

Atkinson, A. B. (1983) *The Economics of Inequality*, 2nd edn, London.
Phelps Brown, E. H. (1977) *The Inequality of Pay*, London.

See also: distribution of incomes and wealth.

individualism

Individualism is a modern word. Its first recorded use is in 1840 when it was used in the English translation of de Tocqueville's *Democracy in America*. In a later work Tocqueville (1856) noted that

> Our ancestors had not got the word 'Individualism' – a word which we have coined for our own use, because in fact in their time there was no individual who did not belong to a group, no one who could look on himself as absolutely alone.

In modern societies, such as the USA,

> Men being no longer attached to one another by any tie of caste, of class, of corporation, of family, are only too much inclined to be preoccupied only with their private interests . . . to retire into a narrow individualism.

The contrast between societies based on the group and the individual was part of the nineteenth-century attempt to understand the massive changes brought about in the wake of the French and Industrial Revolutions. All the founding fathers of the modern social sciences – Marx, Durkheim, Weber, Tönnies, Simmel and others – reflected on the new relations between the individual and the group. For example, Maine (1861) noted that the 'unit of an ancient society was the Family, of a modern society the individual'. It was generally agreed that the separation of the spheres of life, economics from society, religion from politics and so on had not only given the individual more liberty, in Mill's sense, but also destroyed both meaning and warmth.

Thus individualism came to be seen as the essential feature of 'modernity'. Bell (1976) wrote that the 'fundamental assumption of modernity . . . is that the social unit of society is not the group, the guild, the tribe or the city, but the person'. The belief in the primacy of the individual was not only powerful, but also peculiar. Dumont (1977) argued that 'among the great civilizations the world has known, the holistic type of society has been overwhelmingly predominant. Indeed it looks as if it had been the rule, the only exception being our modern civilization and its individualistic type of society'. The heart of the matter is summarized by Gellner (1988): 'a society emerged in which single individuals could apparently carry the entire culture within themselves, unaided.'

These views need to be qualified in various ways. First, it is clear that all human societies have the concept of the separate 'person'. As Mauss wrote, 'it is plain . . . that there has never existed a human being who has not been aware, not only of his body, but also at the same time of his individuality, both spiritual and physical' (quoted in Carrithers et al. 1985). Furthermore, anthropologists have noted that many of the features of individualism are to be found in societies ranging from the simplest hunting-gathering societies to the most complex civilizations, such as Japan over the last thousand years. An over-stark contrast between the 'west' and the 'rest' is not justified.

It is also clear that the water-shed theory of individualism is too simple. Although it is usually conceded that there was a long individualistic tradition in western civilization, somehow linked to Christianity, it is often assumed that the eighteenth century, with the rise of market capitalism, saw a new order of things. Yet, whether we look at the property system of Anglo-Saxon England where Maitland (1921) found a system compatible with 'the most absolute individualism' of ownership, or the medieval philosophy of Ockham and his successors, or, many centuries earlier, the extreme individualism of much Greek philosophy, it is clear that there is no clear progressive story. Again, too simple a dichotomy between the 'past' and the 'present' is not warranted.

This makes the future much less easy to predict. Some believe that the trend is towards heightened individualism and egotism. The greater division of labour and the penetration of market values, the spread of political concepts of equality and innate human rights will lead to increased individualism as de Tocqueville predicted. Others argue that we are now moving towards a global village where, in Donne's words, 'no man is an island'. We will be electronically, if not organically, returned to a holistic society. Some writers, for instance Foucault, Derrida and Lacan, have questioned the very notion of an independently constituted individual. Developments in medical technology, in particular organ transplants and reproductive technology, have indeed made the boundaries between individuals much less precise than they once were. The future of individualism is as contested as its meaning and value.

Alan Macfarlane
University of Cambridge

References

Bell, D. (1976) *The Cultural Contradictions of Capitalism*, New York.
Carrithers, M., Collins, S. and Lukes, S. (eds) (1985) *The Category of the Person*, Cambridge, UK.
Dumont, L. (1977) *From Mandeville to Marx*, Chicago.
Gellner, E. (1988) *Plough, Sword and Book*, London.
Maine, H. (1861) *Ancient Law*, London.
Maitland, F. W. (1921) *Domesday Book and Beyond*, Cambridge, UK.
Tocqueville, A. de (1856) *Ancien Regime*, trans. M. Patterson (1956), Oxford.

Further reading

Lukes, S. (1973) *Individualism*, Oxford.
Morris, B. (1991) *Western Conceptions of the Individual*, Oxford.

industrial and organizational psychology

Industrial and organizational (IO) psychology is the application of psychological principles to commerce and industry. It is defined in terms of where and how it is practised rather than according to distinct principles or propositions. There are three clear areas within IO psychology: personnel psychology, industrial/social or industrial/clinical psychology, and human factors or human engineering psychology.

Personnel psychology

Every organization has to make decisions about personnel selection, training, promotion, job transfer, lay-off, termination, compensation, and so on. In each case, the characteristics of both workers and jobs must be assessed. In job selection, for example, the personnel psychologist must be able to determine what are the demands of the job in question and which human abilities are required to meet these demands, and then find the most suitable candidate. Similarly, training (or retraining) requires knowledge of the job demands and the current skills levels of an employee. The personnel psychologist's task is to minimize the discrepancy between demands and skills levels. Other decisions, such as promotion or changes in amount of compensation, represent the same basic challenge for the personnel psychologist: to match the environmental characteristics with the individual's.

The personnel psychologist uses various tools, the two most common being job analysis and psychological aptitude testing. Job analysis helps to determine the most important and/or frequently occurring tasks in a particular job as well as the associated knowledges, skills, abilities and personal characteristics which support performance of those tasks. It may involve surveys, observations, interviews or combinations of these techniques, and data from current incumbents and supervisors are an important source of information. Psychological aptitude testing tries to identify the capacities and limitations of the candidates in meeting the demands of the job in question. In the past, popular methods were short tests of intellectual ability, particularly verbal and arithmetic skills. Two of the most popular tests of this kind are the Wonderlic Personnel Test and the Otis Intelligence Test. Since 1960 special ability tests, such as the Differential Aptitude Test Battery and the Flanagan Aptitude Classification Tests have been more prominent. Psychological testing implies a standardized sample of behaviour. The sample may be gathered by means of a standardized paper-and-pencil test with specific questions and limited alternative answers. Alternatively the sample might include broad questions and open-ended answers, with structure imposed by the respondent rather than by the test or test administrator. The sample could also include motor performance, interview behaviour, and even physiological measures, for example, resting heart rate or tests of vulnerability to stress factors in the work environment.

Industrial/social or industrial/clinical psychology

This area of IO psychology concerns the reciprocal adjustment between the person and the environment, the emotional capacities of the individual and the environmental climate being the key factors under investigation. The individual worker is assessed on the following criteria: adjustment, motivation, satisfaction, level of performance, tendency to remain within the organization and absenteeism rates. The organizational characteristics which are looked at include, for example, efforts to facilitate a positive emotional climate, reward systems used, leadership styles, and the actual structure and operation of the organization. Most adjustment strategies involve real or imagined others: this is the province of industrial social

psychology. The industrial/clinical aspect considers the employee's psychological well-being, and the fact that poor adjustment often creates stress and occasionally transient abnormal behaviour.

Human factors or human engineering psychology

This area makes assumptions which are just the opposite to those of the personnel psychologist. The problem is still the same: accomplishing a match between the individual and the job. But the human factors psychologist assumes that the person is constant and the job is variable. The psychologist must arrange or design the environment in such a way that it is more compatible with the capacities and limitations of human operators. In order to effect a better match, the job must be changed, which usually involves modifications in operations or equipment according to the capacities of the operators. These capacities could be sensory (for example, visual acuity), or cognitive (for example, information processing time). The information input and output system is emphasized: display devices (digital read-out devices, gauges or dials, and so on) and control devices (such as knobs, levers and switches) are examined and modified if found to have a negative effect on performance.

The three areas of IO are seldom, if ever, independent of one another: they are all components of an interrelated system. Selection strategies will define the capacities and shortcomings of the operators. This will yield a range for equipment design and modification. Similarly, available equipment will determine desirable capacities and characteristics of applicants. Finally, the interaction of worker characteristics, equipment and task design, and administrative practices will influence adjustment.

Frank J. Landy
Pennsylvania State University

Further reading

Dunnette, M. D. and Hough, L. (1992) *The Handbook of Industrial and Organizational Psychology*, Palo Alto, CA.
Landy, F. J. (1989) *The Psychology of Work Behavior*, 4th edn, Homewood, IL.

See also: aptitude tests; industrial sociology.

industrial democracy

Industrial democracy may be best understood as a generic term for the exercise of power by workers or their representatives over decisions within their places of employment, coupled with a modification in the locus and distribution of authority within the workplace. The principal debates concern the precise characteristics of participatory organizations, the theories of the genesis of this movement and the conditions which ensure effective outcomes within the enterprise. Industrial democracy has interested both politicians and scholars and has become the mainstay of several legislative programmes for the reform of industrial relations.

Classifactory schemes take several forms: some use geographic location, others initiating agents (Poole 1978), or underlying ideologies, or internal structure properties. The main types are workers' self-management (involving substantial workers' participation in the main decision-making bodies together with either workers' ownership or the rights to use the assets of the enterprise); participation of workers' representatives in management organs (for example, co-determination or worker-director schemes); trade union action (including disjunctive types based on conceptions of conflicting interests and *integrative* or harmonious practices); and shop floor experiments (such as job enrichment and quality of working life programmes).

The advocates of the so-called evolutionary and cyclical approaches are theoretically at odds. The evolutionary school argues that structural movements in modern societies (especially advances in technology and the growth of complex and interdependent roles in modern industry), changes in values (including the increasing concern for social justice) and a redistribution of power in favour of working people and their associations have led to durable institutional procedures for industrial democracy. Further evidence in support of this view is the considerable interest shown by developing countries in schemes of this type. But cyclical theorists observe that waves of institutional advance have been followed by periods of decline or decay and even of the abandonment of previously well-established participatory forms. Latterly, comparative approaches which focus on international similarities and differences of type have tried to transcend these divisions.

Views about actual outcomes also diverge, but existing research suggests that a relatively democratic enterprise possesses an elaborate and integrated system of formal representation covering a number of levels (such as boardroom and shopfloor). It has carefully drawn-up rules for participation that prescribe employees' involvement in decision making over a wide range of issues, and that grant representatives strong powers. It applies a democratic style of leadership and has a high level of unionization, and also recruits young and female supervisors. Moreover, while opportunities for individual involvement are superior in fairly small businesses, a relatively more egalitarian distribution of power is normally found in large organizations. And finally, a democratic leadership style would appear to be closely correlated with positive attitudes towards work and feelings of involvement in the job on the part of the labour force, regardless of country.

Michael Poole
Cardiff Business School, University of Wales

Reference

Poole, M. (1978) *Workers' Participation in Industry*, London.

Further reading

Industrial Democracy in Europe (IDE) (1993) *Industrial Democracy in Europe Revisited*, Oxford.

See also: industrial organization; industrial relations.

industrial organization

'Industrial organization is a curious name, distinctive mainly in its inability to communicate to outsiders what the subject is all about' (Scherer and Ross 1990: 1). So, preconceptions cast aside, how might the subject be described? One way is to say that it is the investigation of a number of key economic questions, none of which is answered satisfactorily by standard price theory or microeconomic analysis. In rough order of importance, these questions may be formulated as follows. How is it that some firms, or sections of industries, are able to maintain consistently high profitability? Why do some industries remain concentrated, with the same firms often holding key positions for a considerable time? Is it socially desirable that some industries are highly concentrated and/or profitable in this way? Why do firms on occasion choose marketing or purchasing arrangements so different from competitive supply or purchase? What are the implications of imperfect knowledge regarding research and development, and advertising, for rivalrous behaviour between firms? The term industrial economics, widely used as an alternative in the UK and elsewhere in Europe, additionally covers questions relating more specifically to the firm and internal organization.

Clearly, one of the underlying elements prompting this area of study is a series of stylized facts regarding the organization of industry. The subject's antecedents include Cournot's (1927 [1838]) notable mathematical treatise on industries with small numbers of firms, Marshall's (1890; 1899) views on the development of firms and industry equilibrium, and a number of writers between the world wars on imperfect competition, including Chamberlin (1933), Hotelling (1929) and Berle and Means (1932). However it is only since the Second World War that the subject developed into its modern form in North America and western Europe. The 'structure-conduct-performance' paradigm was developed as a sorting device by writers such as Bain (1956). It provides a means by which cross-industry empirical observations on relative profitability could be thought of as flowing from rather slowly changing elements of industry structure, characterized by concentration and barriers to entry.

Since the 1970s, there has been a gradual shift of direction away from broad empirical analysis informed theoretically only by general price theory towards the development of a considerable body of economic theory, and later empirical modelling, specific to the area of industrial organization (IO) itself. This development has been labelled by some 'the new IO'. A key feature is the use of game theory, and with it a recognition of the crucial importance of the underlying structural and particularly behavioural assumptions in determining the outcome. An algebraic story-telling tradition has developed. Following the insights of Schelling (1960) and others, strategic considerations have been extensively analysed in formal models. Indeed, some would say too extensively; if an appropriate theoretical explanation can be created for every unusual stylized fact, then the theory is over-determined.

In turn, these developments have led to a greater modesty in empirical work, with the realization that cross-industry analysis is valid only under restrictive conditions. Highly specified situations, as found for example in many auction markets, may enable rather precise predictions to be tested (see e.g. Hendricks and Porter 1988), while only comparatively weak predictions may be applicable more broadly (Sutton 1991). Nevertheless, certain broad regularities, accepted by most workers in the field, can be discerned. One would be that firms in relatively concentrated industries are on average equally or more profitable than those in broadly equivalent less concentrated industries.

It should be said that there are minority views of the subject, the most strident being the Chicago School. Broadly speaking, this rejects much of the detailed analysis of the mainstream approach. The Chicago view would agree that collusion between powerful market participants can lead to relatively high profits and socially undesirable outcomes. But it would place more emphasis on a wide range of practices (for example vertical contracting arrangements involving exclusive dealing) having an efficiency rather than a strategic rationale (Bork 1978).

Writers in the IO tradition have had an impact well outside the subdiscipline. Competition policy in the USA and the European Union is an example. It takes the (Chicago-consistent) stance that collusion is some-thing to be dealt with relatively harshly. From mainstream analysis it takes the use of various structural features of an industry as indicators of when firms' actions are more likely to have socially undesirable outcomes. IO writers have also had an influence on the design of economic regulation and the deregulation movement (Baumol et al. 1982). Finally, IO analysis has had a substantial influence on the theory of international trade, for example in explaining intra-industry trade and strategic use of tariff and non-tariff barriers, and on some elements of macroeconomics.

Michael Waterson
University of Warwick

References

Bain, J. S. (1956) *Barriers to New Competition*, Cambridge, MA.

Baumol, W. J., Panzar, J. C. and Willig, R. D. (1982) *Contestable Markets and the Theory of Industry Structure*. New York.

Berle, A. A. and Means, G. (1932) *The Modern Corporation and Private Property*, New York.

Bork, R. H. (1978) *The Antitrust Paradox*, New York.

Chamberlin, E. H. (1933) *The Theory of Monopolistic Competition*, Cambridge, MA.

Cournot, A. A. (1927 [1838]) *Researches into the Mathematical Principles of the Theory of Wealth*, trans. N. Bacon, New York. (Original edn, Paris.)

Hendricks, K. and Porter, R. H. (1988) 'An empirical study of an auction with asymmetric information', *American Economic Review* 78.

Hotelling, H. H. (1929) 'Stability in competition', *Economic Journal* 39.

Marshall, A. (1890) *Principles of Economics*, London.

—— (1899) *Economics of Industry*, 3rd edn, London.

Schelling, T. C. (1960) *The Strategy of Conflict*, Cambridge, MA.

Scherer, F. M. and Ross, D. (1990) *Industrial Market Structure and Economic Performance*, Boston, MA.

Sutton, J. (1991) *Sunk Costs and Market Structure*, Cambridge, MA.

Further reading

Hay, D. A. and Morris, D. J. (1991) *Industrial Economics and Organization: Theory and Evidence*, Oxford.

Reid, G. (1987) *Theories of Industrial Organization*, Oxford.

Schmalensee, R. and Willig, R. (1989) *Handbook of Industrial Organization*, 2 vols, Amsterdam.

Stigler, G. J. (1968) *The Organization of Industry*, Homewood, IL.

Tirole, J. (1988) *The Theory of Industrial Organization*, Cambridge, MA.

See also: industrial democracy; industrial relations; industrial sociology; organizational change; organizations.

industrial relations

The concept and the study of industrial relations originated in the USA in the early twentieth century, and soon extended to Britain. Until the 1980s, however, they have been unfamiliar outside English-speaking countries. The meaning of industrial relations is imprecise, and both the scope of the subject and its disciplinary status have long been debated. At the close of the twentieth century, as many employers – particularly in North America – have come to reject the principle of collective bargaining over conditions of employment, some scholars question whether industrial relations can survive.

The term entered public discourse in 1912, when the US Senate in the aftermath of violent industrial conflicts appointed a Commission on Industrial Relations with a wide-ranging investigative brief. Its agenda was comprehensive: a heterogeneous catalogue of aspects of what was conventionally described as 'the labour question'. However, the notion of industrial relations soon acquired a rather narrower meaning: the processes and institutions through which employment is managed, such as trade unions and employers' associations, collective negotiations and agreements, labour legislation, and organized conflict.

This definition provided the basis for the development of academic research and teaching, on both sides of the Atlantic, in the decades between the two world wars. In both Britain and the USA, the impetus was primarily pragmatic and reformist. Early academic writers on union-management relations (the Webbs and Cole in Britain, Hoxie and Commons in the USA) were for the most part sympathetic to labour and regarded trade unions as a positive force for social improvement; their perspectives converged with those of progressive employers and civil servants. Their common belief was that social peace could be encouraged by a better understanding of the sources of industrial conflict and the mechanics of collective regulation.

The Second World War enhanced interest in industrial relations: trade unions played a key role as guarantors of national consensus, while the demands of military production increased the importance of conflict avoidance. In the USA this was reflected in the creation of a War Labor Board, employing many young scholars who went on to manage a post-war expansion of industrial relations institutes and degree programmes. In Britain a similar though more modest extension of the subject received a further boost in the 1960s, when industrial relations problems became widely perceived as an important source of relative economic decline.

Early writers on industrial relations came from a variety of academic backgrounds: sociology, economics, law, psychology and history. But as the study became increasingly institutionalized, many in the field proclaimed industrial relations as a discipline in its own right. The most notable exponent of this view was the American economist John Dunlop, whose *Industrial Relations Systems* appeared in 1958. 'An industrial-relations system,' he argued, 'is to be viewed as an analytical subsystem of an industrial society on the same logical plane as an economic system' (Dunlop 1958: 5). Its defining characteristic was 'the full range of rule-making governing the work place'. The analysis of the rules of employment, the actors (employers, workers and their organizations, and governments) involved in their formulation and administration, and the contextual influences (technological, economic and political) required, in Dunlop's view, a distinctive theoretical apparatus which identified industrial relations as a separate discipline.

To some extent, insistence on the subject's disciplinary credentials stemmed from a specifically American style of academic politics. Most British exponents have been content to regard the subject merely as an interdisciplinary field of study. Dunlop's work was, however, influential in Britain in at least three respects: by stimulating debates about the precise definition of industrial relations; by encouraging the proliferation of formal models of industrial relations as an interactive system; and by inspiring theoretical analysis, notably in the writings of Allan Flanders (1970), which located 'job regulation' as the central object of analysis.

It is noteworthy that industrial relations developed as an academic subject almost exclusively in the English-speaking world. Such translations as *relations industrielles, industrielle Beziehungen* or *relazioni industriali* have always appeared self-conscious and artificial: in continental Europe the study of job regulation has normally been rooted within (and thus often fragmented between) such (sub)disciplines as labour law, industrial sociology and labour economics. One possible explanation is the relative autonomy of management–union relations within the Anglo-American world. In both Britain and the USA, the state was far less actively involved in the formative process of industrialization than in most of Europe, and the individualistic common-law tradition militated against systematic legal regulation of employment. The consequence was a considerable degree of discretion for employers (and to a lesser extent, workers and unions) in determining the terms and conditions of employment. In more regulated societies, by contrast, the processes of industrial relations were more obviously integrated within broader sociopolitical dynamics; to study them in isolation seemed futile.

Even in its home countries, the study of industrial relations has been in some disarray since the 1970s.

The reasons are partly intellectual and partly material. American systems approaches to the subject were strongly influenced by structural-functionalist sociology (Dunlop based his model explicitly on Parsons's *Social System*); it assumed an inherent bias towards order and stability. Mainstream writers argued that mature industrial relations systems inevitably functioned to contain and routinize conflict, often inferring a logic of capitalist development diametrically opposed to that of Marx. British writers in the field developed an analogous thesis, usually termed industrial relations pluralism. This challenged conceptions of industry based on the functional integration of interests, but also rejected any idea of class polarization. Following the ideas of such political theorists as Schumpeter, Dahl and Dahrendorf, the dominant British school of the 1960s and 1970s argued that economic interests were multiplex and cross-cutting, creating scope for negotiated accommodation through appropriate institutional arrangements. Collective bargaining was an effective recipe, not for eliminating industrial conflict but for rendering it manageable.

The challenges to conservative orthodoxies in the social sciences from the late 1960s made their mark in industrial relations also. Three aspects of this radicalization may be noted: first, a reassertion of the importance of class in the analysis of employment issues; second (post-Braverman), an insistence that any study of the world of work must attend to the dynamics of the labour process, not merely the wage-centred agenda of collective bargaining; third, the argument that processes of employment regulation must be analysed as part of a far broader political economy of capitalism. Such questioning of the prevailing intellectual foundations of the study of industrial relations undermined its academic coherence.

Material developments reinforced these challenges. The incidence of industrial disputes, which in most developed economies had fallen sharply in the 1950s and early 1960s, began to rise substantially; arguments for the institutionalization of conflict lost their plausibility. The changing structure of the economy and of employment also eroded the relevance of a field of study founded largely on the situation of male manual workers in manufacturing industry: traditional notions of industrial relations did not readily connect with the expanding milieux of work (female, white-collar, service-sector). In the 1970s, the traditional assumption of a substantial disjuncture between the worlds of politics and industrial relations also lost its purchase: western governments increasingly attempted to regulate wage bargaining, often pursued new initiatives in individual and collective labour law (a process which German scholars termed juridification), and in some cases – at least in the 1980s – imposed new restrictions on trade union organization and collective bargaining.

Employers also challenged the established institutions and procedures. This was most obvious in the USA, where many leading employers successfully attacked union organization in order to create a union-free workforce, replacing collective bargaining by internal company mechanisms of communication and employee involvement. Increasingly, firms gave their industrial relations departments a new title: human resource management (HRM). By the 1990s, American academics had in large measure followed suit: the number of chairs, institutes and courses in industrial relations has declined, to be overtaken by a rapid growth in HRM. In Britain this process has been far less dramatic, but still significant. Union membership declined substantially after the Conservative election victory of 1979, the coverage of collective bargaining falling below half the workforce by the end of the 1980s, and many former industrial relations scholars switched allegiance to more managerially popular concerns.

In its heyday, the study of industrial relations derived its appeal and seeming coherence from an historically conditioned convergence of orientations among trade unionists, leading employers and public policy makers. By the end of the twentieth century, in Britain and the USA, this basis has broken down: academics are forced to choose between an explicitly managerial focus on employment policy and a more critical social-science approach to the analysis of work. Paradoxically perhaps, the prospects for revival in the field seem greatest in countries with no academic industrial relations tradition: interest in cross-disciplinary analysis of employment regulation has been expanding in many countries of continental Europe – both west and east – and also in many 'less developed' economies. Also noteworthy has been the growth, since the 1980s, of systematic cross-national comparison in the subject.

Richard Hyman
University of Warwick

References

Dunlop, J. T. (1958) *Industrial Relations Systems*, New York.
Flanders, A. (1970) *Management and Unions*, London.

Further reading

Hyman, R. (1989) *The Political Economy of Industrial Relations*, London.
—— (1994) 'Theory and industrial relations', *British Journal of Industrial Relations* 32.
—— (1995) 'Industrial relations in Europe: theory and practice', *European Journal of Industrial Relations*.
Kaufman, B. E. (1993) *The Origins and Evolution of the Field of Industrial Relations*, Ithaca, NY.

Morris, R. (1987) 'The early uses of the industrial relations concept', *Journal of Industrial Relations* 39.

See also: Fordism; human resource management; industrial democracy; industrial organization; industrial sociology; Taylorism; trade unions.

industrial revolutions

The term industrial revolution is of fundamental importance in the study of economic history and economic development. The phrase is, however, full of pitfalls for the unwary, partly because it has been used with several different meanings, and has, of course, generated a good deal of controversy.

An early use of 'industrial revolution' referred to what are best seen as periods of industrial growth with quite limited implications for overall economic development. Well-known examples include Carus-Wilson (1941) on the thirteenth and Nef (1932) on the sixteenth centuries. This usage is now seen as unhelpful and is generally disparaged.

Still very much extant is thinking of 'industrial revolution' in the sense of technological revolution, as does Freeman (1987). This approach is often used by researchers concentrating on science and technology to describe developments which they feel had widespread economic and social ramifications. This school of thought envisages successive technological or (if you will) industrial revolutions. These would typically include the famous inventions of the period 1750–1850 based on steam power, the so-called second industrial revolution of the late nineteenth and early twentieth centuries involving new chemicals, electricity and automobiles, and the information technology revolution of the years after 1970.

Among economists and economic historians 'industrial revolution' most frequently relates to a fundamental part of the experience of economic development, namely the spread of industrialization in the economy as a whole. Since Kuznets (1966), this has been associated with the onset of modern economic growth. Econometric research has confirmed the existence of systematic patterns of change in the structure of economies as real incomes rise (Chenery and Syrquin 1975), although it is widely recognized that countries have not followed identical routes to modernity (O'Brien 1986). Industrialization is typically accompanied by acceleration in economic growth, increases in investment in both physical and human capital, and improvements in technology and urbanization.

Perhaps the most common use of all refers to the classic and pioneering example of industrialization which occurred in Britain during the late eighteenth and early nineteenth centuries, famously described by Rostow (1960) as featuring a spectacular take-off into self-sustained growth. It now seems more probable that this episode was characterized by particularly rapid changes in economic structure but quite slow growth (Crafts 1985). In this sense the British industrial revolution not only subsumed technological innovation in industry but also embraced much wider organizational changes in agriculture, finance, commerce, trade, etc. Indeed the term 'industrial revolution' is a metaphor which should not be taken literally in this context.

A large literature has sought the ultimate causes of the first industrial revolution and has produced a great variety of hypotheses, many of which are unpersuasive, although hard completely to refute (Hartwell 1967). What is generally accepted is that British industrialization resulted from prowess in technology and investment but ultimately depended on the institutions of a market economy which had their origins in the distant past (Mokyr 1993). While the structural changes and their implications for living standards can fairly be described as revolutionary, this does not detract from the point that the industrial revolution was the culmination of evolutionary changes which had been proceeding for centuries.

N. F. R. Crafts
London School of Economics and Political Science

References

Carus-Wilson, E. M. (1941) 'An industrial revolution of the thirteenth century', *Economic History Review* 11.

Chenery, H. B. and Syrquin, M. (1975) *Patterns of Development, 1950–1970*, London.

Crafts, N. F. R. (1985) *British Economic Growth during the Industrial Revolution*, Oxford.

Freeman, C. (1987) *Technology Policy and Economic Performance*, London.

Hartwell, R. M. (ed.) (1967) *The Causes of the Industrial Revolution in England*, London.

Kuznets, S. (1966) *Modern Economic Growth: Rate, Structure and Spread*, New Haven, CT.

Mokyr, J. (ed.) (1993) *The British Industrial Revolution: An Economic Perspective*, Oxford.

Nef, J. (1932) *The Rise of the British Coal Industry*, 2 vols, London.

O'Brien, P. K. (1986) 'Do we have a typology for the study of European industrialization in the nineteenth century?', *Journal of European Economic History* 15.

Rostow, W. W. (1960) *The Stages of Economic Growth*, Cambridge, UK.

Further reading

Ashton, T. S. (1948) *The Industrial Revolution, 1760–1830*, London.

Maddison, A. (1982) *Phases of Capitalist Development*, Oxford.

See also: economic development.

industrial sociology

Although industrial sociology's origins lie in the ideas of Marx, Weber and Durkheim, and perhaps beyond, as a discrete subject it really began only between the world wars, came to fruition in the late 1960s and early 1970s, and subsequently fragmented into myriad forms. Industrial sociology still remains important, though it often masquerades under different labels, such as the sociology of work and organizational behaviour, or has become merged along with some elements of industrial relations into Human Resource Management.

The history of industrial sociology can be read against the changing backdrop of the founding authorities. It might seem obvious that Marx, with his theory of proletarian revolution generated by alienation and exploitation, would prevail during the interwar period, when mass unemployment and economic crisis prevailed, but in fact Marx's influence was minimal: the limited success of the communist revolutions shifted the focus of many Marxists from industry to culture. Paradoxically, the contemporary Marxist approach to industrial sociology, the Labour Process perspective (Thompson 1983), traces its roots to the same period when Taylor's 'scientific management' theory suggested that managers should separate the conception of work (a managerial task) from its execution (an employee's task). Taylor also suggested that economic incentives, channelled through individuals not groups, were the 'one best way' to motivate workers, and that, wherever possible, jobs should be deskilled to enhance productivity and reduce labour costs. It was Braverman's (1974) seminal work, *Labor and Monopoly Capital*, which argued that managerial control, premised upon Taylorism, was the benchmark of capitalist management, and from this point Marxists became increasingly interested in the employment relationship. The hegemony of the Labour Process approach disintegrated during the 1980s, with the new right's political dominance, but it still remains an important strand of industrial sociology.

Earlier on, the ideas of Durkheim, particularly his *Division of Labour* (1933) with its notion of norms and solidarity, were more influential than Marx's. It was also the issue of social solidarity that led Elton Mayo (1946) to interpret the results of the interwar Hawthorne experiments as evidence of an irrational desire on the part of workers to form small groups. These experiments comprised a series of experimental, survey and anthropological approaches to worker behaviour. The results, considerably criticized then and now (Gillespie 1991), were nevertheless instrumental in the development of the Human Relations approach. Taylor's assertion, that the best way to manage people

at work was by keeping them isolated from one another, had apparently been dealt a death blow, but since individual contracts and payment systems came back into favour during the 1980s and 1990s we must assume that Taylorism's death was much exaggerated. So too was Durkheim's, for although his influence waned during the 1970s it was never extinguished, finding a home in the writings of Fox and Flanders (1969), and also proving an important foundation for the development of organizational symbolism in the writings of Turner (1990).

The interpretation of industrial phenomena, including symbols, was also at the heart of Weber's approach to industrial sociology. Disputing Marx's materialist explanation of the rise of capitalism, Weber (1948) argued that ideas also played a crucial role, particularly those associated with the Protestant work ethic. However, Weber's most telling analysis was reserved for his account of bureaucracy, and the crucial significance of rationality in the domination of 'legal rational' forms of authority, that is, those where legitimacy was rooted in formal rules and procedures. Subsequently challenged, originally by Gouldner (1954), and later in the attempts to de-bureaucratize work by reducing managerial hierarchies during the 1980s and 1990s, Weber's dire warnings about the decreasing significance of the individual within the 'iron cage of bureaucracy' still remain pertinent. Weber's triple heritage, in which ideas, interpretation, and domination by experts prevail, later formed the crux of a series of non-Marxist approaches, ranging from the more phenomenologically oriented work of Silverman (1970) through to the rather more middle line taken by Goldthorpe *et al.* (1969).

Since the early 1980s, four new themes have emerged. First, the patriarchal overtones of much traditional industrial sociology have stimulated the rise of a feminist line of research. In this approach the assumption that 'work' can be reduced to blue collar men employed in factories is sharply contrasted to, and linked with, both the unpaid domestic work of women and the rise of part-time women employed in clerical or service jobs. Furthermore, the very idea of technology as neutral and deterministic is shown to be an important element in the perpetuation of patriarchy (Cockburn 1983; Wajcman 1991). Second, the collapse of communism, the globalization of industry, the shift from Fordism to post-Fordism, the developments of surveillance technology and the rise of unrestrained individualism in the 1980s, ushered in a renewed concern with the roles of expertise, norms and self-domination, often explicitly linked to the ideas of Foucault and other post-modernists (Reed and Hughes 1992). Third, developments in information technology, and their applications to manufacturing and financial trading in particular, have encouraged a renewed concern to apply the social constructivist ideas from the sociology of science and technology to the sociology of work and industry (Grint and Woolgar 1994). Fourth, the assumption that occupation and production are the keys to social identity have been challenged by counter-arguments suggesting that consumption patterns are the source of individual identity (Hall 1992). Industrial sociology has certainly been transformed from its origins, but it retains an axial position in explaining contemporary life.

Keith Grint
University of Oxford

References

Braverman, H. (1974) *Labor and Monopoly Capital*, London.
Cockburn, C. (1983) *Brothers*, London.
Durkheim, E. (1993) *The Division of Labour*, New York.
Fox, A. and Flanders, A. (1969) '*The reform of collective bargaining: from Donovan to Durkheim*', British Journal of Industrial Relations 2.
Gillespie, R. (1991) *Manufacturing Knowledge*, Cambridge, MA.
Goldthorpe, J. H. *et al.* (1969) *The Affluent Worker*, London.
Gouldner, A. W. (1954) *Patterns of Industrial Bureaucracy*, New York.
Grint, K. and Woolgar, S. (1994) *Deus ex Machina*, Cambridge, UK.
Hall, S. (1992) 'The question of cultural identity' in S. Hall D. Held and A. McGrew (eds.) *Modernity and its Futures*, Cambridge, UK.
Mayo, E. (1946) *The Human Problems of an Industrial Civilization*, London.
Reed, M. and Hughes, M. (1992) *Rethinking Organization*, London.
Silverman, D. (1970) *The Theory of Organizations*, London.
Thompson, P. (1983) *The Nature of Work*, London.
Turner, B. (1990) *Organizational Symbolism*, Berlin.
Wajcman, J. (1991) *Feminism Confronts Technology*, Cambridge, UK.
Weber, M. (1948) *From Max Weber*, H. H. Gerth and C. W. Mills (eds), London.

Further reading

Brown, R. K. (1992) *Understanding Industrial Organizations*, London.
Eldridge, J., Cressy, P. and MacInnes, J. (1991) *Industrial Sociology and Economic Crisis*, Hemel Hempstead.
Grint, K. (1991) *The Sociology of Work*, Cambridge, UK.
Reed, M. (1992) *The Sociology of Organizations*, Hemel Hempstead.

See also: Fordism; industrial and organizational psychology; industrial organization; industrial relations; Taylorism; trade unions.

inflation and deflation

Inflation is generally taken to be the rise of all or most prices, or (put the other way round) the fall of the general purchasing power of the monetary unit. Since the mid-1930s, inflation has been continuous in the UK and nearly continuous in the USA. Over that period, consumer prices rose thirty-fivefold in the UK and more than twelvefold in the USA. Only the official prices in some centrally planned economies escaped the worldwide trend, until these regimes collapsed.

The corresponding sense of deflation – the general fall of prices – is less familiar because it has not been experienced for some time, though deflation prevailed in most countries from the early 1920s to the mid-1930s, and in many for long periods in both the earlier and the later nineteenth century. Deflation is perhaps more often used to refer to a fall in total money income or in the total stock of money, or, more loosely, to falls in their rate of growth. Inflation is sometimes used in corresponding, looser senses.

The idea that the value, or purchasing power, of money depends simply on the amount of it in relation to the amount of goods goes back in a fairly clear form at least to the mid-eighteenth century. So long as money consisted wholly or mainly of gold and/or silver coins, the application of this doctrine was easy. A reasonably convincing account of the main changes in price-trend even in the nineteenth century can be given in terms of the gold discoveries of the mid-century and those (together with the ore-processing innovations) of the 1890s, set against the continuous rise of physical output of goods. From early on, however, paper claims on trusted debtors began to constitute further means of payment, and such claims, in the form of liabilities of banks and quasi-banking institutions, have now replaced 'commodity money' (coined gold or silver, circulating at virtually its bullion value) almost completely. This makes the definition of money harder – and inevitably somewhat arbitrary. Moreover, the supply of money, though subject also to other influences, has always been to a considerable extent responsive to the demand for it, so that it cannot be taken as independently given.

The simplest kind of modern inflationary process is that where a government, perhaps for war purposes, needs to acquire an increased flow of goods and services, and pays at least partly for it with newly printed money (in practice, borrowed from the banking system). If the economy was fully employed to start with, and if we exclude the possibility of the need being met by imports, the effect is to raise prices in proportion to the increase in total (government and non-government) expenditure. As the money spent by the government goes into private hands, private expenditure rises, and the government can get an increased share of the national real output only by printing money faster and faster to keep ahead in the race. In the absence of complications from price rigidities and taxation, an indefinite, exponential inflation is generated. In practice, such complications exist and slow the process down; governments often try to increase price-rigidity by price control, which has usually to be supplemented by rationing. Inflation can, however, become completely explosive in the extreme cases of 'hyperinflation', like that in Germany in 1923, and the even bigger one in Hungary in 1946, when prices eventually doubled (or more) each day. These hyper-inflations were assisted by special circumstances; their very speed made revenue collection ineffective, so that nearly all government expenditure had to be financed by new money, expectations of their continuation made for very rapid adjustment of wages and salaries to the rate of inflation, and the disruption of the economy (by a general strike in one case, foreign occupation in the other) reduced the real flow of goods for which the government and other spenders were competing. True 'hyperinflation' has occurred only where something like this last condition has been present.

More usually, inflation has to be considered in the light of the fact that prices are formed in different ways. The prices of many raw materials and foodstuffs, in the world market, are flexible and strongly and quickly influenced by supply and demand conditions. The great upward surge of these prices in 1972–4 was induced partly by the boom in industrial production and demand (which, however, was no greater in relation to trend than the one in the late 1960s), partly by particular conditions affecting mainly cereals – the breakdown a few years earlier of the World Wheat Agreement, the widespread running down of stocks thereafter, and the failure of the harvest in the USSR. Petroleum, the price of which quadrupled, is a special case; its price is 'administered' rather than formed in the market, but the administration of it had passed from the international oil companies to the Organization of Petroleum Exporting Countries (OPEC). In addition, the outlook both for future discoveries of oil and for alternative sources of energy (on which a rational pricing of oil largely depends) had worsened. The immediate occasion for the biggest oil price increase was the Arab–Israeli War of 1973. (Events in Iran caused another increase in 1979.)

In contrast, the prices of manufactures, though also largely administered rather than determined on 'auction' principles in free markets, seem to be governed fairly closely by costs of production, which depend on wages, raw material and fuel costs, and labour productivity.

The determination of wages is more complex. They are hardly anywhere formed on the 'market-clearing' principle that unemployed workers will underbid current rates until they get jobs; labour solidarity and the need for a minimum of security and trust in the relations of employers with existing employees are too great for that. In fact, collective bargaining determines most wages in some countries (three-quarters of them in the UK), and even where the proportion is lower, as in the USA, the main collective agreements exercise widespread influence as 'price-leaders'. The result is that wage claims – and settlements – show considerable sensivity to rises in the cost of living, but that they also show a tendency to creep upward in response to the natural ambitions of trade unionists and their leaders, and sometimes as a result of jockeying for relative position between different trades.

The most noteworthy attempt to generalize about wage-inflation was that of A. W. Phillips (1958), who derived empirically, from British data, a negative relation between the level of unemployment and the rate of wage increases, which was for a time thought by some to be practically usable evidence of a possible policy trade-off. Unfortunately, within ten years of its formulation current data began to show that the Phillips Curve in the UK (and also in the USA, though the same is not true, for instance, of Germany) was shifting rapidly upwards – the unemployment rate needed to keep wage-inflation down to a given level was rising. At the same time, Milton Friedman (1968) argued that such a relation was inherently implausible; experience of wage-inflation would lead people to expect more of the same, and so raise bids and settlements. The curve would become vertical, only one rate of unemployment (the natural rate) being consistent with a rate of wage-inflation that was not either accelerating upwards or accelerating downwards. Examination of evidence from a number of countries suggests that the extent to which experience leads to expectations which have this effect varies greatly, and the time taken to convince people that inflation will continue, rather than subside, is also variable, but has often been a matter of years or even decades rather than months. Attempts to explain the formation of wages econometrically have been only partially successful.

From early in the post-war years, various governmental attempts were made to curb the tendency towards inflationary wage increases in conditions of low unemployment. Exhortation, informal agreements with trade unions or employers' organizations, legislative limits, temporary wage freezes, conferences in which potential negotiators were confronted with the average increases the economy was estimated to be able to bear without inflation, have all been tried somewhere, singly or in combination, sometimes in succession, in the USA and the countries of western Europe. The results have been mixed. The more drastic policies have sometimes been successful, but only temporarily, and there has been some rebound afterwards. Nevertheless, some countries, notably Austria and Germany, have achieved relatively high degrees of wage-restraint and low average levels of inflation over a long period with the help of their institutional arrangements. Japan has also been successful (with one or two lapses), mainly because in the large firms, guarantees of employment reconcile employees to arrangements which make their earnings sensitive to conditions in the product markets.

It is important to distinguish between inflation which arises from demand for a country's final output ('demand-pull') and that which comes, immediately at least, from rises in its import prices or in its labour costs of production ('cost-push'). The former tends to increase output, the latter to depress it.

It is natural to ask how cost-push can raise prices in a country without a concomitant rise in the supply of money; indeed, some writers do not recognize cost-push as a useful concept in explaining inflation, and the monetarist school, associated with Milton Friedman (but with many and various subdivisions) holds, generally, that the price level varies with the supply of money, and could be controlled, without detriment to the level of real output and employment, by increasing the money supply uniformly in line with the estimated physical capacity of the economy.

The relevant facts are complex. Controlling the supply of money is not easy; money is created by commercial bank lending, which will normally respond in some degree to demand, and central banks cannot fail to act as lenders of last resort to the commercial banks without risking collapse of the monetary system. The need for increased money payments, whether created by a rise in import prices or by an increase in physical output, can be and normally is met, to a substantial extent, by more rapid turnover of money (increase in the velocity of circulation) rather than by increase in the stock of money – though this is a short-term accommodation, normally reversed eventually. 'Tightnesss' in the supply of money curtails spending plans, and normally reduces physical output and employment before (and usually more than) it reduces prices, at least in the short run of two to four years. In the longer run, tightness of money tends to induce a proliferation of 'quasi-monies', the liabilities of institutions outside the banking system as for the time being defined.

Since the mid-1970s, control of the growth of the money stock as a means of controlling inflation has been much in vogue. Experience has shown the diffi-culty of hitting the target rates of increase, for the reasons just stated, and has demonstrated, not for the first time, that monetary stringency, sometimes combined with parallel fiscal policies, reduces inflation only at the cost of severe unemployment and the reduction of growth in real living standards.

In contrast with the damage to output which seems to be inseparable from deflationary policies (though its severity varies greatly with the institutional arrangements in the country concerned), it is hard to demonstrate any comparable material damage from, at all events, moderate demand-pull inflation (or moderate cost-push inflation which is accommodated by sufficient creation of purchasing power). It can cause arbitrary changes in income distribution, but they are not normally of a kind to depress output (rather the contrary) and they are mostly avoidable by suitable indexing arrangements. The worst aspect of any prolonged inflation is its tendency to accelerate, through the conditioning of expectations, and this is a serious problem, even though, as already noted, the extreme phenomenon of hyperinflation has occurred only where the economy has been disrupted by some external cause. Inflation is, however, unpopular even with those to whom it does no material harm; it is certainly inconvenient not to be able to rely upon the real value of the money unit, and it may create an illusion of impoverishment even when money incomes are periodically and fairly closely adjusted to it.

In the present writer's view, some, at least, of the main market economies can avoid inflation without the depressing concomitants of deflationary policies only if they are able to develop permanent incomes policies, or modify their wage- and salary-fixing institutions, so as to enjoy reasonably full employment without upward drift of labour costs such as became established in them at least by the end of the 1960s. But it must be remembered that the severest general peacetime inflation on record, that of the 1970s, was also largely propelled by supply and demand mal-adjustments in the world economy, plus special circumstances in the oil industry. This experience points to the need for better co-operation between the main industrial countries to stabilize the growth rate of their total activity, and for some co-ordinated forward planning of aggregate supplies of the main raw materials, fuels and foodstuffs. This would require a programme of international co-operation perhaps even more ambitious than that which, from the end of the Second World War, made possible a generation of unparalleled economic progress.

A. J. Brown
University of Leeds

References

Friedman, M. (1968) 'The role of monetary policy', *American Economic Review* 58.

Phillips, A. W. (1958) 'The relationship between unemployment and the rate of money wage-rates in the United Kingdom, 1861–1957', *Economica* 25.

Further reading

Bosworth, B. P. and Lawrence, R. Z. (1982) *Commodity Prices and the New Inflation*, Washington, DC.

Brown, A. J. (1955) *The Great Inflation 1939–51*, Oxford.

—— (1985) *World Inflation since 1950*, Cambridge, UK.

Bruno, M. and Sacks, J. D. (1985) *Economics of Worldwide Stagflation*, Oxford.

Fleming, J. S. (1976) *Inflation*, Oxford.

Organization for Economic Co-operation and Development (1977) *Towards Full Employment and Price Stability* (McCracken Report), London.

Trevithick, J. A. (1977) *Inflation: A Guide to the Crisis in Economics*, Harmondsworth.

See also: macroeconomic policy; macroeconomic theory; monetarism; stagflation; supply-side economics.

informal economy

The terms informal economy, underground economy, black economy or unobserved economy refer to all kinds of economic transactions not reflected in the official statistics. Such undeclared sources of income may result from criminal activities, but they may be legal, or they may involve the evasion of the law, as in tax schemes that exploit loopholes in the law. In short, these terms refer to legal or illegal transactions that may result in differences between the actual workings of an economy and the picture provided of it by official data.

Official employment figures do not fully reflect the unemployment situation. People who are registered as unemployed may in fact be gainfully occupied, in which case there is greater employment than officially registered. Similar problems arise when private consumption is studied. Those who acquire 'black' money by not declaring their income to the tax authorities will then spend part of it. If shops do not invoice purchases, then actual consumption will be higher than registered consumption. Consequently, in many countries the depression seems actually to have been less severe for consumers than one would have expected on the basis of reported developments. Real income distribution is also different from what the records suggests, because registered salaries often fail to take into account various fringe benefits such as free telephone calls, free meals and travel perks, while, at the lower end of the income scale, people often receive unrecorded payments. Similar arguments apply to statistics regarding production, national income and the economic growth rate, official estimates underestimating the true figures.

The informal economy has always existed, but it is difficult to quantify its significance, partly because much of it is illegal or doubtfully legal, and partly because the estimates will vary according to what aspects are being considered. However, empirical studies suggest that non-declared income and/or hidden production account for between 20 and 30 per cent of real national income in the major economies. There are strong indications, supported by econometric research in Europe and the USA, that the informal economy is now relatively more significant than it was in the first half of the century, having grown from a marginal phenomenon to be a major feature of modern states since the Second World War. Since 1985 the informal economy, and its illegal hard core, the black economy, have flourished, and it appears that the role of organized crime, in particular the drug economy, has been especially important.

What are the purely economic costs and benefits, for an individual, of participation in the informal economy? The level of taxation is a significant factor here, but in the USA, where taxes are lower and the consequences of being caught more severe, the size of the informal or black economy seems to be roughly the same as in Europe. It may be significant that people are more critical of government spending than was the case in the past. There may also be a tendency for individuals to defer less to the views and decisions of authorities.

If policy makers react by tightening laws and punishing offenders, they may simply stimulate tax avoidance and the export of capital. Policies should be based on an understanding of decision making processes in the informal economy, and this is a field to which economists have devoted increased attention since the early 1980s.

In most developing countries the informal sector of the economy is significant, particularly in the urban sector, and it is now often regarded as a dynamic and valuable element in the total economy. More generally, however, it is a difficult matter to weigh up the advantages and disadvantages of the informal sector, and to assess its contribution to employment and growth. Judgments are bound to be value-laden, and ultimately the decisions taken must be political ones. However, the black economy does erode standards and values on which the main economy depends. This is a major drawback, and suggests that efforts should be made gradually to reduce its size.

A. Heertje
University of Amsterdam

Further reading

Feige, E. L. (1989) *The Underground Economies*, Cambridge, UK.
Heertje, A., Allen, M. and Cohen, A. (1982) *The Black Economy*, London.
Mars, G. (1983) *Cheats at Work*, London.
Turnham, D., Salome, B. and Schwartz, A. (1990) *The Informal Sector Revisited*, Paris.

See also: informal sector.

informal sector

The term informal sector was coined in the early 1970s (Hart 1973). It relates to Third World countries and is used to describe small-scale, non-agricultural activities which provide a livelihood for people who make simple goods, such as chairs and paraffin lamps, or who provide a range of basic services, like carrying water from a standpipe. Unlike those who work in factories, government offices or the larger commercial undertakings, their activities tend not to be recorded in official statistics, nor was their economic significance or importance properly recognized until the 1970s.

People in the informal sector who make things as distinct from providing services, generally use only hand tools, and often recycle scrap wood or metal. Typical examples are simple furniture made from discarded crates, paraffin lamps made from empty oil cans, or charcoal stoves made from scrap metal. They are made in microenterprises, employing perhaps three to eight people, often working in the open air, protected from sun and rain by no more than a tarpaulin supported on four poles. The informal sector also provides services: hawkers sell empty gin bottles for storing paraffin; route taxis offer cheap transport; individuals may brew, cut hair, take photographs, repair cars and mend bicycles.

What all these activities have in common is that they are economically efficient. They use materials that would otherwise go to waste, like empty crates, scrap metal and empty bottles. They use skills that are in surplus supply, like carpentry and metalwork, which have been widely taught in schools in the mistaken belief that they would help school leavers to find jobs in factories (Foster 1966). They economize on scarce capital, using only hand tools instead of power-driven machinery, whose operation does not require a building of any kind. There are generally no barriers to entry and as a result there is near perfect competition, which helps to keep prices down. The informal sector exists because it produces goods and services that ordinary people want to buy, at prices they can afford. The consumers are not 'the poor', as is sometimes suggested, but small farmers growing crops for sale, or clerks, or shop assistants, or junior civil servants

who for the first time ever can afford the sorts of things that the informal sector purveys, and who would not be able to buy a factory-made upholstered bed, for example. Being without electricity, they would have no use for an electric cooker.

The informal sector has tended to respond rather than to lead. It has responded to the growth of incomes in agriculture and in urban activities, but has in turn added to the growth of consumer expenditure. It has also provided innumerable income-earning opportunities in countries where industrial development has failed to generate much employment. It has sometimes been inferred from the difference between recorded urban population growth and the much more modest increases in recorded employment that there must be massive urban unemployment. In the absence of state unemployment benefit, that has always seemed implausible. Many of those formerly thought to be unemployed were in fact working in the informal sector, often very hard and for long hours, but also sometimes earning more, albeit more precariously, than their customers.

The informal sector has been denigrated by some, under the influence of Marx, who have argued that it is really 'petty commodity trade' and as such the most vulnerable and exploited part of what they call the capitalist system. Attempts to improve the performance of microenterprises are bound to fail, and only fundamental changes in the political and economic structure can alter things (*World Development* 1979).

Governments, especially in eastern and southern Africa, have often seen the informal sector as the antithesis of modernization and as perpetuating outmoded methods of production. It has also often been seen as flying in the face of creating modern towns, and as being a haven for criminals, sellers of illegal beer, or stolen goods. Consequently there is a long history of attempts either to regulate informal sector activities by restrictive licensing, or to make them illegal. This attitude has begun to change, partly as a result of the influence of a number of International Labour Office reports, and especially one on Kenya (ILO 1972) which was the first to give a systematic account of the operation of the informal sector, and which urged the government to recognize its usefulness. But official thinking in many African countries, and elsewhere, has also been influenced by the manifest failure of many of the large-scale industries set up to provide substitutes for imports. There has thus been a growing recognition that indigenous microenterprises, operating without subsidies or protection from competing imports, not only provide useful business experience but also help to raise living standards for a majority in a way that most import substituting industries had not. This recognition has given rise to much discussion of what governments and foreign aid donors might do to help such microenterprises in the informal sector: should they provide better premises, easier credit, business training, and so forth (Elkan 1989)?

Walter Elkan
Brunel University

References

Elkan, W. (1989) 'Analysis of policy for small scale industry', *Journal of International Development* 1(2).

Foster, P. J. (1966) 'The vocational school fallacy in development planning' reprinted in M. Blaug (ed.) (1970) *Economics of Education*, vol. 1., Harmondsworth.

Hart, J. K. (1973) 'Informal income opportunities and urban unemployment in Ghana', *Journal of Modern African Studies* 11.

International Labour Office (1972) *Employment Incomes and Equality: A Strategy for Increasing Productive Employment in Kenya*, Geneva.

World Development (1979) 6(9/10), special issue devoted to urban informal sector. See especially articles by Bromley, Gerry and Moser.

Further reading

Elkan, W. (1988) 'Entrepreneurs and entrepreneurship in Africa', *World Bank Research Observer* 3 (2).

Weeks, J. (1975) 'Policies for expanding employment in the informal urban sector of developing countries', *International Labour Review* 111.

See also: informal economy.

information society

The information society is a broad concept which has been used since the 1970s to refer to the wide range of social and economic changes linked to the growing impact of information technology. It highlights the role that information technology plays in the way that individuals live, work, travel and entertain themselves. The use of the term information society has now become so widespread that the concept cannot be understood as a reference to any specific thesis. Journalists, futurists and social scientists often use this term to denote a more information-centric society in the same vein as others use such concepts as the information economy, the wired nation, the communications revolution, the microelectronics revolution and the knowledge society.

Others see the information society in terms of a prescription rather than a forecast. In Japan and Europe, as well as North America, the information society is often promoted as a vision for the twenty-first century as a means to help policy makers anticipate and nurture the information sector in local, national and regional economies. In the 1990s US and other national initiatives to build modern information infrastructures – the so-called 'information super-highway' – were based on such visions (Dutton *et al.* 1987).

For social scientists interested in the role of information and communication technology in social and economic development, the information society is a central idea. It builds on seminal work by the American sociologist Daniel Bell (1974), who focused on forecasting the 'post-industrial society'. Bell posited information as the defining technology of the post-Second World War era, while raw materials were the core technology of the agricultural society, and energy was the core technology of the industrial society.

Broadly speaking, information technology refers to knowledge about how to create, manage and use information to accomplish human purposes, and so includes not only advances in computing and telecommunications, but also advances in the techniques and skills for using these systems for such purposes as modelling and computer simulation.

Bell identified major trends in what he called the post-industrial society, focusing on the USA as the exemplary case. The principal trends tied to the development of an information society include the growth of employment in information-related work; the rise of business and industry tied to the production, transmission and analysis of information; and the increasing centrality of technologists – managers and professionals skilled in the use of information for planning and analysis – to decision making.

The most significant trend is the shift in the majority of the labour force from agriculture (the primary sector) and manufacturing (the secondary sector) to services (the tertiary sector). Growth in information work, primarily white-collar occupations, has contributed to growth in service sectors. Information work includes a broad array of jobs, ranging from programmers and software engineers to teachers and researchers. New information industries, such as the providers of on-line data and communication services, account for some of this growth, but information work has also become more central to every sector of the economy, including agriculture and manufacturing. In this respect, the occupational shifts associated with the information society do not necessarily imply a decline in the relevance of primary or secondary sectors to national or global economies, as some critics have argued, but rather a diminishing need for labour within these sectors as computing, telecommunications and management science techniques are used to redesign the way in which work is accomplished.

A second trend identified in post-industrial information societies is the increasing importance of knowledge – including theoretical knowledge and methodological techniques, and its codification – to the management of social and economic institutions. Knowledge and technique, such as systems theory, operations research, modelling and simulation, are viewed as critical to forecasting, planning and managing complex organizations and systems, which Bell posited as central problems of the post-industrial era. According to Bell, the complexity and scale of emerging social and economic systems requires systematic forecasting and foresight rather than a previously trusted reliance on common sense or reasoning based on surveys and experiments.

A third set of trends involves power shifts, particularly the growing prominence of a professional and managerial class – the knowledge workers. These are the individuals who understand and know how to work with knowledge, information systems, simulation and related analytical techniques. They will become increasingly vital to decision-making processes in situations of growing complexity (Dutton *et al.* 1987: 12–33). Thus, the relative power of experts should rise with the emergence of an information society.

Despite the significance and longevity of the concept, there remains no consensus on the definition of an information society, or indeed whether we are in fact living in an increasingly information-oriented society. Controversy over the trends and historical underpinnings of an information society generated a lively debate within the social sciences. Critics of Bell's theory focus on his identification of information technology as central to long-term macrolevel changes in society – particularly in the structure of occupations and social strata – and the resultant deterministic view of social change. Whether or not this is an oversimplification of the information society thesis, it has led to a valuable shift in the focus of social science enquiry. This no longer looks only at the social implications of technological change, but also considers the social, political and economic factors that have shaped the design and use of information and communication technologies.

William Dutton
Brunel University and University of
Southern California

References

Bell, D. (1974) *The Coming of Post-Industrial Society*, London. (Original edn 1973, New York.)
Dutton, W., Blumler, J. and Kraemer, K. (eds) (1987) *Wired Cities*, New York.

Further reading

Bell, D. (1980) 'The social framework of the information society', in T. Forester (ed.) *The Microelectronics Revolution*, Oxford.

Porat, M. (1976) 'The information economy', unpublished PhD Dissertation, Stanford University, CA.
Robins, K. (ed.) (1992) *Understanding Information*, London.

See also: communication networks; communications.

input-output analysis

An input-output table records transactions between industries, and input-output (I-O) analysis uses these data to examine the interdependence between sectors and the impact which changes in one sector have on others. This can be seen as a quantitative development of neoclassical general equilibrium analysis used by economists such as L. Walras. Its origins can be traced back to Quesnay's 'Tableau Économique' in 1758. The key figure has been Wassily Leontief, who completed the first I-O table in the USA in 1936 and has done much pioneering development work.

An I-O table (such as that shown in Figure 1) records in its columns the purchases by each industry, A, B, and C (that is, the inputs into the production process), and in the rows the sales by each industry. Also included are sales to final purchasers and payments for factors of production (labour and capital), thus showing the necessary integration into the rest of the national accounts.

Payments to \ Payments by	Industry A	B	C	Final demand	Total output
Industry A		20	45	35	100
Industry B	30		30	140	200
Industry C		80		70	150
Factors of production	70	100	75		
Total input	100	200	150		

Figure 1

The production of a commodity requires inputs from other industries, known as *direct inputs*, and from the I-O table a matrix of *technical coefficients* can be derived which shows direct inputs per unit of output, for example, in matrix A below 0.1 = 20/200. In turn the production of each of these commodities used as inputs requires inputs from the other industries, and this second round of production then imposes demands on other industries, and so on. All these subsequent inputs are known as *indirect inputs*. Tracing all these ramifications is a laborious process in a large I-O system, but it can be shown mathematically that the solution lies in the matrix $(I - A)^{-1}$ where I is the unit matrix and A is the matrix of direct input coefficients. Such a matrix, known as the *Leontief Inverse*, shows in its columns the total direct plus indirect inputs required per unit of output of the column industry (see Figure 2). This matrix is the key to I-O analysis as it encapsulates the interdependence of industries in the economy. For instance, a demand from, say, consumers for 1000 units of A requires the production of 1077 units of A, 351 of B and 141 of C (using col. A of matrix $(I - A)^{-1}$). The extra 77 units of A are needed by B and C to produce the inputs which A takes from them and which they take from each other.

Matrix A				Matrix $(I-A)^{-1}$		
	Ind A	Ind B	Ind C		Ind A	Ind B	Ind C

	Ind A	Ind B	Ind C		Ind A	Ind B	Ind C
A	–	0.1	0.3	A	1.077	0.257	0.375
B	0.3	–	0.2	B	0.351	1.171	0.340
C	–	0.4	–	C	0.141	0.468	1.136

Figure 2

Using such a model it is possible to calculate the effect of a change in demand in an economy on the output in all industries. The analysis can be extended to cover the inputs of factors of production which are closely related to the output levels, and in this way the precise effect which a change in demand for one product has on employment in that industry and in all others can be calculated with perhaps additional information on types of skill. The I-O table can be extended to include purchases of imports, thus enabling the import requirements of any given level of demand to be calculated; of particular interest to the balance of payments is the import content of exports.

Just as the production of a commodity has ramifications back through the chain of production, so a change in the price of an input has effects forward on to many other products, both directly and indirectly. The price of any product is determined by the prices of its inputs, and these can all in turn be traced back to the 'price' of labour, capital and imports, using the formal Leontief Inverse. It is thus possible to calculate the effects on final prices of, for example, an increase in wages in one industry or of a change in import prices due perhaps to changes in the exchange rate or changes in foreign prices.

All the above aspects of input-output analysis can be combined into a planning model which will give a comprehensive and internally consistent picture of the economy 5–10 years ahead. This enables policy makers to see the implications which, say, a certain growth in the economy has for particular industries, employment, prices, the balance of payments and so on, and

to locate key sectors. Most countries compile I-O tables, usually identifying fifty or more industries, although models have lost some of their popularity in western Europe. They are, however, extensively used in the CIS and eastern Europe and in developing economies. Here they are well suited to measuring the impact of marked changes in demand and supply patterns which are expected. Further refinements of I-O analysis include disaggregation by region and making a dynamic model so that investment needs are incorporated.

A. G. Armstrong
University of Bristol

Further reading

Leontief, W. (1966) *Input-Output Economics*, New York.
United Nations (1973) *Input-Output Tables and Analysis, Studies in Methods*, New York.

See also: factors of production; production and cost functions.

instinct

In common parlance instinct has a variety of meanings. For example, it can refer to an impulse to act in some way that is purposeful yet 'without foresight of the ends and without previous education in the performance' (James 1890); to a propensity, aptitude, or intuition with which an individual appears to be born, or a species naturally endowed; to motives, compulsions, or driving energies instigating behaviour serving some vital functions. This multiple meaning seldom causes a problem in everyday conversation. However, a tendency to assume that evidence for one of the meanings entails the others as well has been a cause of confusion in scientific contexts (Beer 1983).

Darwin

Most modern scientific uses of 'instinct' derive from Darwin. He dodged the question of definition, in view of the fact that 'several distinct mental actions are commonly embraced by the term' (Darwin 1964 [1859]). He used the word to refer to impulses such as that which drives a bird to migrate, dispositions such as tenacity in a dog, feelings such as sympathy in a person, and in other senses. However, he frequently argued as though 'instinct' stood for something that combined its several meanings into a single concept, licensing inference from one meaning to another. For example, when there was reason to think that some behaviour pattern was genetically inherited, he would assume its development to be independent of experience; conversely, he took opportunity for learning as a reason to doubt that he was dealing with an instinct, as though what is instinctive must be both hereditary and unlearned. But the relationship between hereditary transmission and ontogenetic development admits of all sorts of combination between the inborn and the acquired. To take one of Darwin's examples, there is no contradiction between a bird's having an inborn migratory urge, and its having to learn the flypath to follow. You can breed dogs for sheep-herding, but they will not be much use without a lot of training.

In *The Descent of Man* (1971) Darwin focused on instinct as the underlying source of feeling, wanting and willing. Construed thus as impulse to action, instinct manifests itself as behaviour directed towards a goal. However, if the only evidence for an instinct in this sense is the goal-directed behaviour that it is supposed to account for, the account will be uninformative. Unless there are independently identifiable correlates, such as physiological variables, the inventory of an animal's instincts will amount to an inventory of the goals towards which the animal's behaviour can be seen to be directed. However, observers can differ about what and how many kinds of goals govern an animal's behaviour; it is an open question whether all the behaviour directed at a particular goal is internally driven and controlled by a single and unitary motivational system. For Darwin these difficulties did not greatly affect his argument for psychological continuity between beast and human. They have been a bother to more recent theories of instinct, such as those of Freud, McDougall, and classical ethology.

Freud

Freud held several theories about instinct. In an early version he viewed the psyche as subject to biologically based instinctive drives for self-preservation and reproduction; later he envisaged a single supply of psychic energy giving rise to and dispersed among the psychic structures of the id, ego and superego, with their rival imperatives of appetite, accommodation and morality; finally this trio incorporated contending instincts of life (*eros*) and death (*thanatos*). For Freud the manifest goals of overt behaviour were false guides to the underlying instincts, since experience works through the ego to suppress or disguise their natural expression, in accordance with social constraints. Only by the techniques of psychoanalysis, such as those using word association and dream description, can the true inner dynamics of human action and preoccupation be revealed.

However, Freud made little effort to get independent empirical validation of his theories. Also he wrote at times as though instinct were a kind of blind energy, at least analogous to the energy of physics, and at other times as though instinct were an intentional agent employing strategies in the pursuit of ends. Consequently, to some critics, psychoanalysis lacks sufficient empirical anchorage and conceptual consistency to count as science. Other critics have contended that Freud's reliance on outmoded ideas from nineteenth-century biology (for example, Haeckel's biogenetic 'law' of recapitulation, and Lamarck's notion of the inheritance of acquired characteristics), anthropology, and other life sciences undermined the foundations of his theorizing (Kicher 1992; Sulloway 1992). Psychoanalysis itself has come to question the usefulness of its instinct theories. Without denying the existence of biologically grounded forces affecting behaviour and mental life, analysts such as Horney (1937) and the British 'object-relations' theorists (e.g. Guntrip 1961) have emphasized the roles of society, culture and interpersonal relationships in the development, differentiation and dynamics of the psyche.

McDougall

In his *Introduction to Social Psychology* (1908) William McDougall defined an instinct as

> an inherited or innate psychological disposition which determines its possessor to perceive, and to pay attention to, objects of a certain class, to experience an emotional excitement of a particular quality upon perceiving such an object, and to act in regard to it in a particular manner, or, at least, to experience an impulse to such action.

He thought of the connection among the three aspects of instinct as neural, yet insisted that the system is psychophysical, by which he meant that perception, emotion and impulse, as mentally manifested, are essential to and active in the instigation, control and direction of instinctive action.

Although McDougall, being an instinctivist, is often represented as ignoring effects of experience, he did allow that instincts are capable of modification through learning. But he held that such modification could occur only in the cognitive and conative divisions; the emotional centre was supposed to be immune. Accordingly he argued that identification of the distinct primary emotions is the way to discover what and how many instincts there are, and that this is a necessary preliminary to understanding the derived complexes and secondary drives patterning behaviour and mental life. He gave a list of the primary emotions and hence principal instincts of humans, together with speculation about their probable adaptive significance and hence evolutionary basis.

The plausibility of this analysis led to a fashion for instinct in psychology and adjacent fields (e.g. Trotter

1919; Veblen 1914). However, as the lists of instincts multiplied so did their variety. Different people parsed their emotions differently, and there was no agreed way of deciding among them. Also McDougall's conception of the psychophysical nature of instincts led him to vacillate between accounts in terms of causes and effects and accounts in terms of intentions and actions; his theory and speculation gave little purchase for empirical correlation or experimental test.

Behaviourist critics were provoked into mounting an 'anti-instinct revolt'. This was led by Dunlap (1919), who argued that McDougall's theory was scientifically vitiated by appeal to unobservable subjective purposiveness. Other attacks struck at the prominence given to innateness, contending that wherever evidence was available it supported the view that all behaviour, apart from the simplest reflexes, is shaped by experience. By and large the behaviourists got the better of the fight in their insistence on the priority of hard facts and the requirement of experimental testability. McDougall's theory has little following today (however, see Boden 1972).

Ethology

Ethology's classical phase covers the period beginning with Lorenz's publications in the 1930s (e.g. Lorenz 1937) and culminating with Tinbergen's *The Study of Instinct* (1951). Lorenz began with animal behavioural characteristics that are like certain anatomical features in being correlated with taxonomic relatedness in their distribution and variation. This evidence of genetic basis implied for Lorenz the other instinctive attributes: such behaviour must also be independent of experience in its development, independent of peripheral stimulation in its motorpatterning, and internally driven by endogenously generated 'action specific energy'. This action specific energy also causes 'appetitive behaviour' leading to encounter with 'sign stimuli' necessary to 'release' the instinctive act, and to which the mechanism controlling the act is innately tuned (Lorenz 1950). Tinbergen (1951) built the components of this conception into a more comprehensive theory in which each of the major functional classes of behaviour – feeding, reproduction, and so forth – is organized hierarchically, the underlying machinery consisting of control centres receiving motivational energy from above and distributing it to others below, depending on the sequence of alternative releasing stimuli encountered through the associated appetitive behaviour. For Tinbergen, the whole of such a functional system constituted an instinct, and to it he connected his conceptions of sensory and motor mechanisms, behavioural evolution, development, function and social interaction to make the classical ethological synthesis.

However, the next phase of ethology's history was given largely to criticism of the Lorenz-Tinbergen instinct theories. Both within and without ethology, critics pointed to lack of agreement between the quasi-hydraulic properties of the models, and what was known of how nervous systems actually work; the inadequacy of unitary motivational theories in general and ethological instinct theories in particular to deal with the full complexity of behavioural fact (e.g. Hinde 1960); the fallacy of arguing from evidence of hereditary transmission to conclusions about individual development and motivational fixity (Lehrman 1953; 1970). Tough-minded reaction to what was perceived as tender-minded speculation led to conceptual reform to meet empirical demands, and methodological refinement to bring experimental test to theoretical implications, and quantitative rigour to behavioural analysis. Even Tinbergen (1963) came to emphasize the importance of distinguishing among the different kinds of questions applying to behaviour. The general trend in later ethology has been division of 'the study of instinct' among the several distinct kinds of problem it encompasses. The conception of instinct as a form of motivational energy has been undercut by evidence that the control of behaviour involves numerous factors related in a complex causal nexus, as represented in the motivational 'state space' conceptions of McFarland (1989). Likewise the classical view of instinct as a passively produced product of natural selection developmentally dictated by a rigid genetic programme comes up against more recent arguments for an active role of behaviour in evolution, and novelty-generating plasticity in behavioural development (Bateson 1988; Gottlieb 1992; Plotkin 1988). Indeed ethologists now rarely talk of instinct, except to reflect on past uses and abuses, and on the present ambiguity of the word (e.g. Dawkins 1986).

The ambition to arrive at an overall theory of animal and human behaviour persists, as some of the claims of sociobiologists demonstrate (e.g. Wilson 1975). A reconstituted concept of instinct perhaps remains a possibility for incorporation in a future synthesis. But unless history is to repeat itself yet again, anyone deploying such a concept would do well to heed the lesson of its forerunners: they thrived on blurred distinctions, but to their ultimate undoing.

C. G. Beer
Rutgers University

References

Bateson, P. P. G. (1988) 'The active role of behaviour in evolution', in M.-W. Ho and S. Fox (eds) *Evolutionary Processes and Metaphors*, Chichester.

Beer, C. G. (1983) 'Darwin, instinct, and ethology', *Journal of the History of the Behavioral Sciences* 19.

Boden, M. (1972) *Purposive Explanation in Psychology*, Cambridge, MA.

Darwin, C. (1964 [1859]) *On the Origin of Species*, Cambridge, MA.

—— (1948 [1871]) *The Descent of Man*, New York.

Dawkins, M. S. (1986) *Unravelling Animal Behaviour*, Harlow.

Dunlap, K. (1919) 'Are there instincts?', *Journal of Abnormal Psychology* 14.

Gottlieb, G. (1992) *Individual Development and Evolution: The Genesis of Novel Behavior*, New York.

Guntrip, H. (1961) *Personality, Structure and Human Interaction*, London.

Hinde, R. A. (1960) 'Energy models of motivation', *Symposia of the Society of Experimental Biology* 14.

Horney, K. (1937) *The Neurotic Personality of our Time*, New York.

James, W. (1890) *The Principles of Psychology*, New York.

Kitcher, P. (1992) *Freud's Dream*, Cambridge, MA.

Lehrman, D. S. (1953) 'A critique of Konrad Lorenz's theory of instinctive behavior', *Quarterly Review of Biology* 28.

—— (1970) 'Semantic and conceptual issues in the nature–nurture problem', in L. R. Aronson, E. Tobach, D. S. Lehrman and J. S. Rosenblatt (eds) *Development and Evolution of Behavior*, San Francisco, CA.

Lorenz, K. Z. (1937) 'Über die Bildung des Instinktsbegriffes', *Naturwissenschaften* 25.

—— (1950) 'The comparative method in studying innate behaviour patterns', *Symposia of the Society for Experimental Biology* 4.

McDougall, W. (1908) *An Introduction to Social Psychology*, London.

McFarland, D. (1989) *Problems of Animal Behaviour*, Harlow.

Plotkin, H. C. (ed.) (1988) *The Role of Behavior in Evolution*, Cambridge, MA.

Sulloway, F. J. (1992) *Freud: Biologist of the Mind*, Cambridge, MA.

Tinbergen, N. (1951) *The Study of Instinct*, Oxford.

—— (1963) 'On the aims and methods of ethology', *Zeitschrift für Tierpsychologie* 20.

Trotter, W. (1919) *Instincts of the Herd in Peace and War*, New York.

Veblen, T. (1914) *The Instinct of Workmanship and the State of the Industrial Arts*, New York.

Wilson, E. O. (1975) *Sociobiology*, Cambridge, MA.

See also: ethology; motivation; sociobiology.

institutional economics

Institutional economics is concerned with the social systems that constrain the use and exchange of scarce resources and attempts to explain both the emergence of alternative institutional arrangements and their consequences for economic performance. By controlling the access of actors to resources, institutions affect economic performance in various ways:

1 Lack of control encourages wasteful attempts to capture wealth (consider open-access fisheries).

2 Credible controls lower the expectations of actors that their assets will be appropriated and reduce the expected transaction costs of protecting the assets, which in turn encourages specialization in production and long-term investments.

3 The social division of controls shapes the distribution of wealth.

4 Organization-specific controls influence the choice of economic organization (for instance, by outlawing certain ownership structures of firms).

5 Use-specific controls directly assign resources to particular activities, which may or may not be their most valued uses.

6 The structure of controls influences the long-term development of economic systems by affecting the relative value of investments and the nature of projects undertaken.

The social control of resources reflects the structure of institutions in communities. Institutions are human-made constraints that control and direct human interaction and consist of both formal rules such as laws and regulations and informal rules including norms and custom. Institutions are exogenous to individual actors, and the extent of social enforcement of the relevant rules determines the significance of particular institutions. The institutional structure varies both with people's social positions and with time, and in the long run actors may invest in attempts to alter their institutional environment.

The command that actors have over resources depends not only on the power granted them by social controls but also on power established through private controls (monitoring and enforcing contracts, fencing, or employing guards). These private efforts give rise to transaction costs, which are inversely related to the support provided by social controls. To further their ends, owners of resources contract to form organizations, but they are constrained by the institutional environment.

Until the 1980s standard economic analysis focused on exchange in secure markets. By limiting the enquiry to specific ideal type transactions – and by ignoring the complex factors of control, transaction costs, and incomplete information – economic theory profitably could employ relatively simple mathematical methods and powerful tools, particularly the rational choice model, optimization subject to constraints, explanations of social outcomes in terms of individual behaviour (methodological individualism), and the concept of equilibrium.

Many institutional economists have long argued for abandoning standard economic method and analysis, but these critics have not developed a coherent alternative research programme for analysing economic performance and institutional change. However, attempts to use traditional economic analysis outside the setting of secure markets frequently have given misleading results, sometimes with serious consequences. Many scholars, not only in economics but also in other social sciences, have attempted to resolve the quandary by modifying and extending the traditional economic model to make it appropriate for general institutional analysis (Eggertsson 1990). Pioneering contributions were made by Alchian (1977 [1961]) on property rights, Coase (1937; 1960) on transaction costs, Coleman (1990) on social capital, North (1981) on historical institutional change, and Williamson (1985) on the logic of economic organization.

Attempts to develop a general economic theory of institutions, which gathered momentum in the 1980s, are still incomplete, but valuable lessons have been learned. An extended version of the standard economic approach, neo-institutional economics, which explicitly allows for incomplete information, transaction costs and property rights, has become a powerful tool for analysing transactions, economic performance and the logic of economic organization in various institutional environments. Increasingly, these modifications of the standard approach are recognized by mainstream economists, for instance in the field of industrial organization (Milgrom and Roberts 1992). Similarly, the economics of law has become a legitimate branch of economics (Posner 1994). Neo-institutional economics also has had considerable success in analysing elements of institutional environments and institutional change. Transaction cost analysis and the rational choice model have provided important insights into the structure of democratic political organizations, such as legislatures, and the generation of formal rules (Alt and Shepsle 1990). Many studies have employed game theory to explore the nature, emergence and decay of informal institutions, such as norms and custom, giving special attention to explaining co-operation when enforcement by a third party is absent (Hechter et al. 1990).

Yet it is particularly for studying informal institutions that many scholars doubt the usefulness of neo-institutional economics. Informal institutions are closely related to the concept of preferences (tastes) in neo-classical economic theory, which builds on the core assumption of stable and exogenous preferences. The model of humankind employed in economics may be ill suited for explaining mentalities and the formation of social values. The concept of bounded rationality is an early attempt to modify the rational choice model, but in most applications bounded rationality is essentially equivalent to unlimited rationality with incomplete information and generates similar hypotheses. A more radical departure, and a logical extension of the information revolution in social science, is attempts to explain the formation of shared mental models of the moral and physical world. Elements of new theories have emerged, in some instances drawing on evolutionary biology and cognitive science, but obvious breakthroughs and consensus on common approaches are yet to appear.

Institutional change can be either purposive or non-purposive. Usually changes in formal rules are purposive whereas informal institutions often emerge as unintended by-products of social interactions. One can envision a two-tier theory of institutional change for coping with both purposive and non-purposive change. The first level, the level of the individual, would apply theories of learning and of mentalities to explain how individuals perceive their environment, possibly employing findings in biology and the cognitive sciences. The second level, the social level, would treat mentalities as exogenous and apply some versions of the rational choice model and methodological individualism to analyse how actors respond to changes in their environments and how their responses are aggregated to produce social outcomes.

Thráinn Eggertsson
University of Iceland and Indiana University

References

Alchian, A. A. (1977 [1961]) 'Some economics of property rights', in A. A. Alchian, *Economic Forces at Work*, Indianapolis, IN.

Alt, J. E. and Shepsle, K. A. (eds) (1990) *Perspectives on Positive Political Theory*, Cambridge, UK.

Coase, R. H. (1937) 'The nature of the firm', *Economica* 4.

—— (1960) 'The problem of social cost', *Journal of Law and Economics* 3.

Coleman, J. S. (1990) *Foundations of Social Theory*, Cambridge, MA.

Eggertsson, T. (1990) *Economic Behaviour and Institutions*, Cambridge, UK.

Hechter, M., Opp, K.–D. and Wippler, R. (1990) *Social Institutions: Their Emergence, Maintenance and Effect*, Berlin.

Milgrom, P. and Roberts, J. (1992) *Economics, Organization and Management*, Englewood Cliffs, NJ.

North, D. C. (1981) *Structure and Change in Economic History*, New York.

Posner, R. A (1994) *Economic Analysis of Law*, 4th edn, Boston, MA.

Williamson, O. E. (1985) *The Economic Institutions of Capitalism*, New York.

Further reading

Libecap, G. D. (1989) *Contracting for Property Rights*, Cambridge, UK.

North, D. C. (1989) *Institutions, Institutional Change and Economic Performance*, Cambridge, UK.

Ostrom, E., Gardner, R. and Walker, J. (1994) *Rules, Games, and Common Pool Resources*, Ann Arbor, MI.

See also: transaction costs.

institutions

Many, perhaps most, sociological concepts are derived from an existing commonsensical image, adapted to meet the requirements of the discipline. In commonsense usage the term institutions has various meanings. Most commonly it is used to refer to organizations which *contain* people, as in the case of hospitals, prisons, mental hospitals, homes for people mentally handicapped and the like. This sense of the term has been taken up by Erving Goffman in his work on *total institutions.*

Goffman (1961) describes the total institution as an environment in which a large number of like-situated individuals reside, cut off from the wider society and subjected to a common regime, often for the purpose of effecting a transformation in their identities. Apart from the examples above, Goffman includes such cases as boarding schools, monasteries, army training camps and deep-water naval vessels. He shows that such environments possess a number of common features, including the stripping away of former supports to the individual's identity through the use of institutional dress, limitations on personal possessions and appearance, strict timetabling of activities, and common subjection to the staff of the institution.

However, although Goffman's concept provides considerable insight into a wide range of organizations, it also blurs a fundamental distinction between those in which the lower members come to the setting already committed to its values and ethos (such as a monastery, a religious commune, or an officer training academy), and those in which they are involuntarily committed to the institution and largely reject its aims and methods (such as prisons, concentration camps, or some mental hospitals). The latter may generate a countervailing culture among inmates which often inhibits the achievement of the organization's goals in the long-term transformation of individual identity. Prisons are relatively unsuccessful in permanently changing the identities of their inmates, as is demonstrated by the high level of recidivism.

A second commonsensical use of the concept institution refers to widespread or large-scale entities which deal with major interests and problems of social concern: the family, the law, the state, the church. It is this sense of the term which has been most vigorously taken up by the discipline of sociology. The functionalist tradition from Herbert Spencer to Talcott Parsons drew a basic distinction between the structures and the processes of a society – analogous to the physical and organic structures of an organism and the activities which these perform. Thus social institutions were seen as the structural components of a society through which essential social activities were organized and social needs were met. They could take the form of organizations, groups or practices of an enduring kind, to which there was a high level of social commitment that integrated, ordered and stabilized major areas of social life, providing approved procedures and forms for the articulation of relationship and interests.

This use of the term remained of theoretical and analytical significance only as long as the functionalist approach to understanding society carried conviction. (There is no space here to detail the decline in persuasiveness of functionalism as an explanatory theory.) However, once the case for construing society as a complex organism had lost its force, so the importance of a sharp distinction between structure and process, institution and function, diminished.

Indeed, it became clearer that institutions were always in the course of formation, negotiation and decline, and that this process was itself of major significance as a focus of analysis. In this account, institutions are simply patterns of behaviour which persist and crystallize in the course of time and to which people become attached as a result of their role in the formation of identity, or through investments of energy or social interests. Thus social activities or patterns of behaviour are *more or less* institutionalized, that is, involve greater or lesser degrees of formalization, infusion of value and emotional attachment, and, therefore, of resistance to change and orientation to their survival.

Entirely new patterns of behaviour or relationship may emerge – as under the authority of a charismatic leader, or through innovations by political, social or cultural rebels. While people may embrace change, they also strive to render their environment relatively predictable and permanent. Thus, they may grow attached to a particular innovation and seek to perpetuate it, repeating the same pattern in an increasingly routine manner. This development of social habits or highly recognized patterns of behaviour changing little over the course of time, and valued intrinsically, is what is now commonly understood by *institutionalization*, a use of the term which draws upon the commonsensical usage that identifies as institutions *The Times*, the two-martini lunch, or even admired figures whose highly predictable eccentricities render them endearing. Thus, curiously, while 'institution' was once contrasted with 'process', now the emergence of institutions (institutionalization) *as a process* is more the focus of attention. How do new forms of behaviour or styles of life gain a foothold or following in our society, how do they spread and gain respectability and become integrated with other features of the culture and social structure? This forms a major focus of the sociology of collective behaviour and the sociology of social movements, often the vehicles for such changes.

The functionalist account of institutions saw them as essentially a good thing, assisting society to perform its necessary activities, but both Goffman's concept of the total institution and subsequent focus upon institutionalization as a process point up a greater moral ambivalence in the term. While routine and predictability, stability and persistence are features without which social life would be largely impossible, and thus are sought after and valued by human beings, the structures thus engendered come to possess a life of their own; they impose themselves upon social actors and may constrain their choices. A once helpful routine may become an inflexible requirement; a formerly instrumental pattern of action may become an empty formalism; once meaningful expressions of sentiment or value may become a rigid dogma. As they become institutionalized, ideas, actions and relationships may lose their excitement, their vitality, their idealism, and come to be valued simply because thay are familiar. This may be no bad thing in some cases (many a marriage survives usefully and happily despite the disappearance of the heady euphoria of first love). But it may sometimes act as a mechanism of control over innovation, repressing the human spirit beneath powerful institutional structures which have long outlived their usefulness.

Roy Wallis
formerly Queen's University Belfast

Reference

Goffman, E. (1961) *Asylums: Essays on the Social Situation of Mental Patients and Other Inmates*, New York.

Further reading

Berger, P. L. and Luckmann, T. (1966) *The Social Construction of Reality*, New York.

See also: functional analysis.

intellectuals

A strict definition of intellectuals would be that they are persons whose role is to deal with the advancement and propagation of knowledge, and with the articulation of the values of their particular society. In that sense all societies have their intellectuals, since even the most so-called primitive will maintain priests or other interpreters of the divine will and natural order. For most of history, intellectuals have of necessity been supported by the political and religious institutions of their societies, so that rebels against accepted institutions and mores have tended to be critical of what they regarded as the over-intellectual approach of the recognized teachers of their time.

The role of intellectuals was altered in major respects by the advent of printing, and consequently of a public for a wide variety of reading matter including freer discussion of basic problems in science, morals, politics and even religion. The French *philosophes* of the eighteenth century, later to be saddled by some historians with responsibility for the advent of the great Revolution, gave a precedent for the modern idea that intellectuals stand somehow outside the power structure and are, by definition, critical of existing social arrangements.

In the nineteenth century, the concept and its resonance differed in different societies. In France and the other advanced countries of western Europe, intellectuals were distinguished from scientists and scholars who depended upon institutions and academies funded by the state, and from those practitioners of literature whose appeal was strictly aesthetic. To be an intellectual was to claim a degree of independence of outlook; and the word in general parlance implied respect and approval. In central Europe, where the state was more suspicious of radical ideas, intellectuals, while courted by the political parties, were looked upon with suspicion by the authorities especially if they were recruited largely from minority groups. Nationalist (and later fascist) movements appealed to populist anti-intellectual prejudice against the Jewish intellectuals of Vienna at the turn of the century, and in the German Weimar Republic.

Britain differed from its neighbours in that, although there were eminent social critics in the Victorian age, the interaction between the world of the intellect and the political and administrative worlds was very close. Intellectuals could preach reform and hope to have an influence. For this reason the word intellectuals was held to represent a foreign rather than a British reality and was given a slightly scornful edge, as implying a lack of contact with everyday life. Few British people would have wished or would now wish to be called intellectuals. In the USA the similar role of intellectuals was diminished after their triumph in the success of the anti-slavery movement. Towards the end of the nineteenth century, a new movement of radical social criticism did develop among what can be seen as the American equivalent of European intellectuals, and this was renewed after the First World War and Woodrow Wilson's temporary mobilization of some of them in pursuit of his domestic and international ideals. So great was their alienation in this second phase that they became susceptible to Communist penetration and influence to a greater extent than was common in Europe in the 1930s, although Marxism was to enjoy an efflorescence in liberated Europe after the Second World War, notably in the Latin countries.

In tsarist Russia the differentiation between intellectuals and the members of learned professions was narrower, and they were grouped together as members of the intelligentsia. Faced with an absolutist regime, to be a member of the intelligentsia was almost by definition to be a critic of the social order and an opponent of the regime, although on occasion from a right-wing rather than a left-wing angle. In the former Soviet Union, and subsequently in eastern Europe as well, the monopoly of the communist party in defining and expounding the ruling doctrine, and the monopoly of state and party in access to the media, forced intellectuals seeking to follow their own bent to go underground so that, as under tsarism, to be intellectual is to be classed as an opponent of regimes whose instruments of repression are greater and used with less scruple than those of earlier times.

In the overseas European empires of the nineteenth and twentieth centuries, a class of intellectuals influenced by their western-style education came into being alongside the more traditionally educated and motivated intellectuals of the indigenous tradition. The ideas to which they were exposed, combined with the limited roles available to them, produced a similar effect to that noted in relation to tsarist Russia, predisposing them towards political opposition. Another similarity was the extension of the concept to include more than the small minority who were full-time intellectuals in the western sense. What was created was again an intelligentsia. This important aspect of the prelude to independence of the countries of the so-called Third World has had strong repercussions. Ingrained habits of criticism and opposition proved difficult to discard when these intelligentsias took power. Intellectuals, when called upon to rule, rarely perform well and usually have to give way to more disciplined elements such as the military.

A reaction against the adoption of western values and attitudes by intellectuals in Third-World countries has produced a revival of a traditional, largely religious-oriented leadership, notably in parts of the Islamic world, and a specific repudiation of intellectuals thought to be tarnished by western liberal or Marxist contacts.

Intellectuals whose mission is to examine everything are naturally prone to examine their own roles. This self-consciousness has been heightened by the anti-intellectualism of some populist movements, an anti-intellectualism which has surfaced more than once on the American political scene. There are a number of recurring problems for intellectuals generally. Should they seek solitude to produce and develop their own ideas, or does the notion itself imply a constant commerce between intellectuals such as took place in the salons of eighteenth-century Paris and Regency London, or later in the cafés of Paris and Vienna, or as it now takes place in the many international congresses and seminars supported by American foundations? Should intellectuals engage directly in current controversies or content themselves with publishing their own ideas, leaving the arena to others? Should they accept public office or even seek the suffrages of the people for themselves? Should philosophers be kings?

Max Beloff
University of Buckingham

Further reading

Beloff, M. (1970) *The Intellectual in Politics and Other Essays*, London.
Benda, J. (1927) *La Trahison des Clercs*, Paris.
Hofstadter, R. (1963) *Anti-Intellectualism in American Life*, New York.
Joll, J. (1969) *Three Intellectuals in Politics*, London.
Lasch, C. (1966) *The New Radicalism in America: The Intellectual as a Social Type*, New York.
Shils, E. (1972) *The Intellectuals and the Powers and Other Essays*, Chicago.

intelligence, artificial *see* artificial intelligence

intelligence and intelligence testing

The testing of intelligence has a long history (for psychology) going back to the turn of the century when Binet in Paris attempted to select children who might profit from public education. Since that time the notion of intelligence has been the subject of considerable scrutiny, especially by Spearman in Britain in the 1930s, and of much and often bitter controversy.

The meaning of intelligence

Intelligence is defined as a general reasoning ability which can be used to solve a wide variety of problems. It is called general because it has been shown empirically that such an ability enters into a variety of tasks. In job selection, for example, the average correlation with occupational success and intelligence test scores is 0.3. This is a good indication of how general intelligence is, as an ability.

This general intelligence must be distinguished from other abilities such as verbal ability, numerical ability and perceptual speed. These are more specific abilities which, when combined with intelligence, can produce very different results. A journalist and engineer may have similar general intelligence but would differ on verbal and spatial ability. The illiterate scientist and innumerate arts student are well-known stereotypes illustrating the point.

Intelligence tests

Most of our knowledge of intelligence has come about through the development and use of intelligence tests. In fact, intelligence is sometimes defined as that which intelligence tests measure. This is not as circular as it might appear: what intelligence tests measure is known from studies of those who score highly and those who do not, and from studies of what can be predicted from intelligence test scores. Indeed the very notion of intelligence as a general ability comes about from investigations of intelligence tests and other scores. Well-known tests of intelligence are the Wechsler scales (for adults and children), the Stanford-Binet test and the British Intelligence Scale. These are tests to be used with individuals. Well-known group tests are Raven's Matrices and Cattell's Culture Fair test.

The IQ (intelligence quotient) is a figure which makes any two scores immediately comparable. Scores at each age group are scaled such that the mean is 100 and the standard deviation is 15 in a normal distribution. Thus a score of 130 always means that the individual is two standard deviations beyond the norm, that is, in the top $2\frac{1}{2}$ per cent of the age group.

Modern intelligence tests have been developed through the use of factor analysis, a statistical method that can separate out dimensions underlying the observed differences of scores on different tests. When this is applied to a large collection of measures, an intelligence factor (or, strictly, factors, as we shall see) emerges which can be shown to run through almost all tests. Factor loadings show to what extent a test is related to a factor. Thus a test of vocabulary loads about 0.6, that is, it is correlated 0.6 with intelligence. Such loadings, of course, give a clear indication of the nature of intelligence.

The results of the most modern and technically adequate factor analysis can be summarized as follows (for a full description see Cattell 1971). Intelligence breaks down into two components.

Fluid ability (g_f) is the basic reasoning ability which in Cattell's view is largely innate (but see below) and depends upon the neurological constitution of the brain. It is largely independent of learning and can be tested best by items which do not need knowledge for their solution. A typical fluid ability item is:

$\bigcirc$ is to $\boxed{\bigcirc}$ as $\triangledown$ is to ... with a multiple choice of five drawings. An easy item (correct answer: $\boxed{\triangledown}$.

Crystallized ability (g_c) is a fluid ability as it is evinced in a culture. In Cattell's view crystallized ability results from the investment of fluid ability in the skills valued by a culture. In Britain this involves the traditional academic disciplines, for example, physics, mathematics, classics or languages. In later life, professional skills, as in law or medicine, may become the vehicles for crystallized ability. A typical Crystallized Ability Item is: Samson Agonistes is to Comus as Bacchae are to.... A difficult item (correct answer: Cyclops).

Many social class differences in intelligence test scores and educational attainment are easily explicable in terms of these factors especially if we remember that many old-fashioned intelligence tests measure a mixture of these two factors. Thus in middle-class homes, where family values and cultural values are consonant, a child's fluid intelligence becomes invested in activities which the culture as a whole values (verbal ability, for example). Performance in education is thus close to the full ability, as measured by g_f of the child. In children from homes where educational skills are not similarly encouraged there may be a considerable disparity between ability and achievement. On intelligence tests where crystallized ability is measured, social class differences are greater than on tests where fluid ability is assessed.

Thus a summary view of intelligence based on the factor analysis of abilities is that it is made up of two components: one a general reasoning ability, largely innate, the other, the set of skills resulting from investing this ability in a particular way. These are the two most important abilities. Others are perceptual speed, visualization ability and speed of retrieval from memory, a factor which affects how fluent we are in our ideas and words.

We are now in a position to examine some crucial issues in the area of intelligence and intelligence testing, issues which have often aroused considerable emotion but have been dealt with from bases of ignorance and prejudice rather than knowledge.

The heritability of intelligence

Positions on this controversial question polarize unfortunately around political positions. Opponents of the hereditary hypothesis were heartened by the evidence (now generally accepted) that Sir Cyril Burt had manufactured his twin data which supported this hypothesis. However, there are other more persuasive data confirming this position – data coming from biometric analyses.

First, what is the hereditary hypothesis? It claims that the variance in measured intelligence in Britain and the USA is attributable about 70 per cent to genetic factors and 30 per cent to environmental. It is very important to note that this work refers to variance within a particular population. If the environment were identical for individuals, variation due to the environment would be nought. This means that figures cannot be transported from culture to culture or even from historical period to period. This variance refers to population variance; it does not state that 70 per cent of the intelligence in an individual (whatever that means) is attributable to genetic factors. Finally, a crucial point is that interaction takes place with the environment; there is no claim that all variation is genetically determined.

These figures have been obtained from biometric analysis (brilliantly explicated by Cattell 1982) which involve examining the relationship of intelligence test scores of individuals of differing degrees of consanguinity, thus allowing variance to be attributed to within-family (found to be important) and between-family effects, as well as enabling the investigator to decide whether, given the data, assortative mating, or other genetic mechanisms, can be implicated. Work deriving from this approach is difficult to impugn.

Racial differences in intelligence

This is an even more controversial issue with potentially devastating political implications. Some social scientists feel that this is a case where research should be stopped, as for example with certain branches of nuclear physics and genetic engineering. Whether suppression of the truth or the search for it is ever justifiable is, of course, itself a moral dilemma.

The root of the problem lies in the inescapable fact that in the USA Blacks score lower on intelligence tests than any other group. Fascists and members of ultra right-wing movements have immediately interpreted this result as evidence of Black inferiority. Opponents of this view have sought the cause in a variety of factors: that the tests are biased against Blacks, because of the nature of their items: that Blacks are not motivated to do tests set by Whites; that the whole notion of testing is foreign to Black American culture; that the depressed conditions and poverty of Black families contribute to their low scores; that the prejudice against Blacks creates a low level of self-esteem so that they do not perform as well as they might; that verbal stimulation in the Black home is less than in that of Whites.

Jensen (1980) investigated the whole problem in great detail and many of these arguments were refuted by experimental evidence, especially the final point, for Blacks do comparatively worse on non-verbal than verbal tests. But to argue that this is innate or biologically determined goes far beyond the evidence. Motivational factors and attitudes are difficult to measure and may well play a part in depressing Black scores. What is clear, however, is that on intelligence tests American Blacks perform markedly less well than other racial or cultural groups, while these tests still predict individual success in professional, high-status occupations.

Importance of intelligence

Intelligence as measured by tests is important because in complex technologically advanced societies it is a good predictor of academic and occupational success. That is why people attach great value to being intelligent. Cross-cultural studies of abilities in Africa, for example, have shown that the notion of intelligence is different from that in the west and is not there so highly regarded. Many skills in African societies may require quite different abilities. Thus as long as, in a society, it is evident that a variable contributes to success, that variable will be valued; and even though intelligence is but one of a plethora of personal attributes, there is, in the west, little hope that more reasoned attitudes to intelligence will prevail.

Two further points remain to be made. First, the fact that there is a considerable genetic component does not mean that the environment (family and education) do not affect intelligence test scores. It has clearly been shown that even with 80 per cent genetic determination, environmental causes can produce variations of up to 30 points.

Finally, the rather abstract statistically defined concept of intelligence is now being intensively studied in cognitive experimental psychology in an attempt to describe precisely the nature of this reasoning ability. Sternberg's (1982) analyses of analogous reasoning are good examples of this genre – the blending of psychometric and experimental psychology.

Paul Kline
University of Exeter

References

Cattell, R. B. (1971) *Abilities: Their Structure, Growth and Action*, New York.
—— (1982) *The Inheritance of Personality and Ability*, New York.
Jensen, A. R. (1980) *Bias in Mental Testing*, Glencoe, IL.
Sternberg, R. J. (ed.) (1982) *Handbook of Human Intelligence*, Cambridge, UK.

Further reading

Kline, P. (1992) *Intelligence: The Psychometric View*, London.

Resnick, R. B. (ed.) (1976) *The Nature of Intelligence*, Hillsdale, NJ.

Vernon, P. E. (1979) *Intelligence: Heredity and Environment*, San Francisco, CA.

interest

The charge made (or price paid) for the use of loanable funds is called interest. The rate of interest is the amount payable, usually expressed as a percentage of the principal sum borrowed, per period of time, usually per month, quarter or year. Financial intermediaries will commonly both borrow and lend funds, their profitability being dependent on the difference between the rate which they are willing to pay depositors and the rate they charge borrowers. Interest rates may be calculated on a simple or a compound basis. Simple interest involves a percentage return on the principal per period, whereas compound interest involves a return based on both the principal and accumulated interest, already paid in previous periods. Interest rates may be fixed, in which case they stay constant throughout the period of the loan, or they may be variable, in which case they may be changed during the period of the loan.

The supply of loanable funds will depend on: the level of savings in the private sector; the rate of growth of bank lending; and, less commonly, on the size of the public financial surplus, which depends on the excess of government revenue over its expenditure. Demand for loanable funds can come from consumers, businesses and the government, due to the need to finance the Public Sector Borrowing Requirement.

The charging of interest may be rationalized in a number of ways. First, the lender is entitled to a share of the profit resulting from the productive use of the loaned funds. Second, savers should be rewarded for abstaining from present consumption, which will probably be worth more to them than future consumption. Third, lenders should receive a fee for allowing someone else to borrow an asset which provides the service of liquidity. Fourth, lenders should be entitled to a risk premium, because they face the risk of non-repayment. These factors may also be used to explain the difference between lending and borrowing rates and the fact that different types of financial assets bear different interest rates. In general, the shorter the term of the loan and the lower the risk, the lower the rate of interest.

There have been criticisms of the morality of charging interest in the form discussed above. Marx, for example, regarded interest as an element of surplus value, together with rent and profit, which accrued to finance capitalists and as such it stemmed directly from the exploitation of labour by capitalists. Marxist-Leninist regimes have typically had low interest rates; nominally to cover some of the costs of running banks and the payments mechanism. The charging of interest has also been condemned, at times, by followers of various religions, for example, Christianity and Islam, the most reviled practices being those linked to private money lenders, usurers or Shylocks. Marxist objections, however, stem from social, rather than religious, ethics.

The growth of Islamic fundamentalism, in Iran, Pakistan and Sudan, for example, revived criticism of western-style interest charges. Islam clearly condemns usury, but there is some theological debate as to whether this means that interest rate charges in general should be prohibited. The reasons given for condemning such charges include their role in reinforcing the accumulation of wealth by the few, and thereby reducing people's concern for fellow humans; the fact that Islam does not permit gain from financial activity unless the beneficiary is also subject to risk of potential loss; and that Islam regards the accumulation of wealth through interest as selfish compared with that accumulated through hard work. These objections, especially the second, would rule out legally guaranteed regular interest payments. It would not, however, rule out equity investment, since this is subject to a return that varies with profit, and equity holders are subject to loss, although they are commonly protected through limited liability. In Pakistan attempts were made to develop an Islamic banking system in which returns are based on a profit and loss sharing principle, rather than regular guaranteed interest payments, and which are, therefore, akin to the returns on equities.

In western economies with numerous financial assets there is a whole array of interest rates. These do, however, tend to move up and down together, and so it is possible to consider, in the abstract, the determination of the level of the rate of interest. Keynesian economists regard the interest rate as being determined by the equation of the demand for and supply of money. Classical economists claimed that it was determined by the interaction of the demand for funds, by investors, and the supply of funds, by savers. Keynes criticized this view, arguing that changes in national income were primarily instrumental in bringing about an equilibrium between savings and investment through their influence on the supply of, and demand for, loanable funds.

A distinction is often made between the nominal and the real interest rate. The real rate is the nominal rate less the expected rate of inflation; although it is sometimes approximated by subtracting the actual rate of inflation from the nominal rate. The concept of the natural rate of interest is also often used. It is the rate of interest that would hold in an economy which was in a non-inflationary equilibrium. The rate of interest, being the contractual income expressed as a percentage of the nominal value of the security, is to be differentiated from the yield of a security, which is a percentage relationship of its income to its current market price. The 'yield curve' is used to depict the relationship between the yields of assets with different terms to maturity, that is, between short, medium and long-term financial assets.

Andy Mullineux
University of Birmingham

Further reading

Bain, A. D. (1981) 'Interest rates', in *The Economics of the Financial System*, Oxford.
Karsten, I. (1982) 'Islam and financial intermediation', *IMF Staff Papers* vol. 29.
Wilczynski, J. (1978) *Comparative Monetary Economics*, London.

See also: credit; financial system.

interest groups and lobbying

In broad terms interest groups (or pressure groups) are organizations which seek to influence public policy: that process of trying to achieve influence is 'lobbying'. American authors tend to use the term 'interest group' while traditional British literature tended to prefer 'pressure group'. There is no consensus as to whether these terms are describing discrete phenomena or whether they are synonymous. Though American data still dominate in this field, comparative approaches are available (Richardson 1993; Thomas 1993).

The most important reason for studying interest groups relates to notions of democracy. The main contributions come from Dahl (e.g. 1989) who argued that interest groups are generally – though not necessarily – beneficial because they sustain a policy debate. Of less theoretical significance but still important was Truman's *The Governmental Process* (1951) in which he defined interests in terms of shared attitudes. Interest group membership and the numbers of groups are generally thought to be on the increase (Baumgartner and Walker 1988, but cf. Smith 1990), but the assumption that increased group competition results in a more open policy-making system has been contested. Gray and Lowery (1993) argue that whatever the density of group coverage, lack of diversity means a flawed contest.

An important counter to Truman's work was Mancur Olson's *The Logic of Collective Action* (1965). Olson argued that to recruit members an organization had to supply *selective incentives* obtainable only by the membership and ·not rely on *collective goods* equally available to 'free riders' who did not join. Among explanations for group participation at levels higher than anticipated by the Olson argument are 'imperfect information' (the potential member is unaware of the irrelevance of their contribution) (Moe 1980); the avoidance of *collective bads* (Mitchell 1979); and the existence of an 'equity ethic' that drives individuals to make fair share contributions (Walker 1991). Walker (1991) also points out that some groups rely on the contribution from patrons rather than membership subscriptions. Most importantly, there has been the extension of the rational choice approach beyond the simple economic cost–benefit analysis envisaged by Olson to include 'soft incentives' (Opp 1986).

Much attention has been given to the distinction between a party and an interest group, but this may not be the most interesting boundary area. One stereotypical notion of the interest group defines it as a voluntary association of individuals existing for the purpose of securing political goals, though some authors include associations of organizations as well as individuals. However, Salisbury (1984) showed that associations (especially of individuals) might be numerically few and politically marginalized in policy making compared to state and local governments, corporations, think tanks, lobbyists, etc.

Authors who adopt a functional approach to the definition of an interest group include individual companies and bureaucratic units as such on the grounds that they attempt to influence policy. Such an approach is rejected by Rose (1989: 222) who complained that sometimes every political institution acting politically is then seen as an interest group. Jordan *et al.* (1992) have suggested reserving the term interest group for multi-member, politically oriented bodies and to use the term 'policy participant' for bodies such as a company acting politically.

If the collective (or otherwise) nature of the interest group has been controversial, another debate concerns the degree of organization. Those who accept the notion of the 'unorganized group' are operating in the same general area as those preferring the term 'social movement' (e.g. Melucci 1989).

Other important themes concern the relationship between the groups and government. In the 1980s this topic was dominated by the *corporatist* accounts of Schmitter and Lehmbruch (1979) and others who held that interest representation is organized in a formal way with the limited number of constituent units recognized by the state (Williamson 1989). In the 1990s more attention has been given in Britain to a *policy community* explanation that anticipates that there will be advantage to departments in co-operating over policy with specialist clienteles (Jordan and Richardson 1987: Marsh and Rhodes 1992).

The literature on lobbying echoes the same theme of mutual advantage between government and non-governmental bodies. The attention given to commercial or 'for hire' lobbyists (Jordan 1991) and lobbying of the legislature, should not obscure the direct and co-operative lobbying links between collective and corporate organizations and the relevant sections of the bureaucracy (Heinz *et al.* 1993 Schlozman and Tierney 1986). Lobbying is often not 'pressure' by external bodies on the executive, but the result of government looking for support and information among the affected groups.

Grant Jordan
University of Aberdeen

References

Baumgartner, F. and Walker, J. (1988) 'Survey research and membership in voluntary associations', *American Journal of Political Science* 32.

Dahl, R. (1989) *Democracy and its Critics*, New Haven, CT.

Gray, V. and Lowery, D. (1993) 'The diversity of state interest group systems', *Political Research Quarterly* 46(1).

Heinz, J., Laumann, E., Nelson, R. and Salisbury, R. (1993) *The Hollow Core: Private Interests in National Policy Making*, Cambridge, MA.

Jordan, G. (1991) *The Commercial Lobbyists*, Aberdeen.

Jordan, G., Maloney, W. and McLaughlin, A. (1992) *What is Studied When Pressure Groups are Studied*, Working Paper no. 1, British Interest Group Project, Aberdeen University.

Jordan, G. and Richardson, J. J. (1987) *Government and Pressure Groups in Britain*, Oxford.

Marsh, D. and Rhodes, R. (1992) *Policy Networks in British Government*, Oxford.

Melucci, A. (1989) *Nomads of the Present*, London.

Mitchell, R. C. (1979) 'National environmental lobbies and the apparent illogic of collective action', in C. Russell (ed.) *Collective Decision-Making*, Baltimore, MD.

Moe, T. M. (1980) *The Organization of Interests*, Chicago.

Olson, M. (1965) *The Logic of Collective Action*, Cambridge, MA.

Opp, K.-D. (1986) 'Soft incentives and collective action', *British Journal of Political Science* 16.

Richardson, J. (ed.) (1993) *Pressure Groups*, Oxford.

Rose, R. (1989) *Politics in England*, 5th edn, Basingstoke.

Salisbury, R. H. (1984) 'Interest representation: the dominance of interest groups', *American Political Science Review* 78(1).

Schlozman, K. and Tierney, J. (1986) *Organized Interests and American Democracy*, New York.

Schmitter, P. and Lehmbruch, G. (eds) (1979) *Trends toward Corporatist Intermediation*, Beverly Hills, CA.

Smith, T. (1990) 'Trends in voluntary group membership', *American Journal of Political Science*, 34(3).

Thomas, C. (ed.) (1993) *First World Interest Groups*, Westport, CT.

Truman, D. B. (1951) *The Governmental Process*, New York.

Walker, J. L. (1991) *Mobilizing Interest Groups in America*, Ann Arbor, MI.

Williamson, P. (1989) *Corporatism in Perspective*, London.

Further reading

Dunleavy, P. (1991) *Democracy, Bureaucracy and Public Choice*, London.

Grant, W. (1995) *Pressure Groups, Politics and Democracy in Britain*, Hemel Hempstead.

Key, V. O. (1958) *Politics, Parties and Pressure Groups*, 4th edn, New York.

Petracca, M. (ed.) (1992) *The Politics of Interests: Interest Groups Transformed*, Boulder, CO.

Rothenberg, L. S. (1992) *Linking Citizens to Government*, New York.

Wilson, G. K. (1990) *Interest Groups*, Oxford.

See also: public choice; representation, political.

International Monetary Fund

The International Monetary Fund (IMF), together with its sister organization the International Bank for Reconstruction and Development (World Bank), was established at the Bretton Woods international monetary conference in 1944 and became operational in 1946. It has around 180 country members. Its original purpose was to promote international monetary stability and co-operation between countries in general, and an orderly exchange rate regime and stable exchange rates in particular. The objective of the founding members – dominated by the USA (White) and the UK (Keynes) – was to avoid the instabilities in international monetary relations (especially with respect to exchange rates) that had characterized much of the interwar period. In particular, the Bretton Woods regime (in which the IMF was to play a central role) was based on the central feature of fixed but adjustable exchange rates with each member country agreeing a par value for its currency (formally against gold but in practice against the US dollar) with the Fund. The IMF would provide short-term balance of payments financing assistance for temporary deficits. The Fund would invariably set conditionality provisions when giving assistance and these conditions would relate to key aspects of economic policy (e.g. the conduct of fiscal and monetary policy, the size of budget deficits, etc.). A country in 'fundamental disequilibrium' was required, with the IMF's agreement, to change the par value of its currency. The IMF could, therefore, have a powerful surveillance role in the international monetary system and a decisive influence on the conduct of member government's economic policy. At times in its history this power has been substantial but has generally declined since the early 1980s.

At the outset there was to be a clear distinction between the role of the Fund and that of the World Bank. The IMF was created to provide short-term assistance for any country (developed and underdeveloped) in temporary balance of payment difficulty, while the World Bank was to provide long-term project finance to aid the longer-term development of economies. The distinction still exists, but over time, and most especially since the early 1980s, it has become less clear-cut in three respects: the Fund has extended the maturity of some of its facilities; the World Bank also makes non-project loans which amount to general balance of payment financing; and the financial facilities of the Fund have come to be used exclusively by less developed countries.

The IMF is essentially a fund. Each member country is assigned a quota the size of which is set mainly in relation to the importance of the country in world trade. The sum of quotas (all denominated in special drawing rights, a composite currency unit based on the world's major currencies) determines the size of the Fund. The five largest quotas (of the USA, Japan, Germany, France and the UK) account for 43 per cent of the total. The quotas are central to the Fund's operations in two major respects: they determine the extent to which each country has access to financing facilities, and also each member's voting rights on the executive board.

The financial resources of the IMF are derived from the contributions of members which pay in amounts equal to 25 per cent of quota in foreign currency (this becomes the country's reserve tranch and is included in the members' foreign currency reserves) and 75 per cent in its domestic currency. Technically, a country does not borrow from the IMF but draws or purchases foreign currency from the Fund with its own currency. While the detail is complex, the basic drawing capacity (access to foreign currency) of each member is limited by a requirement that the Fund's holding of a member's currency should not exceed 200 per cent of its quota. Given that each member contributes its own currency equal to 75 per cent of quota, and pays in 25 per cent in foreign currency, each country effectively has access to additional foreign currency to finance a balance of payments deficit equal to 100 per cent of its quota. This is divided into four credit tranches. In addition to this basic condition, countries have access to a series of additional financial facilities for specific purposes. These include the Extended Fund Facility (where repayments are required only after four and a half to ten years), the Compensatory and Contingency Financing Facility (designed to cover export shortfalls and other unforeseen shocks), and the Structural Adjustment Facility, which makes medium-term loans at concessional rates to low-income countries.

As members make use of the credit tranches the IMF imposes conditions with respect to the country's economic policy. The objective is to ensure that, as normally repayment has to be made between three and a half and five years, the country's balance of payments is improved over this period. In this way the IMF can exert considerable influence over a country's economic policy although this power exists only when a country seeks access to the Fund's financial facilities.

While access to the IMF's facilities is open to all members, and the UK and Italy made substantial use of them in the 1960s and 1970s, no developed country has made drawings since 1976. This is because exchange rates have become more flexible and industrialized countries have been able to borrow substantially from international banking and credit markets. Although IMF facilities usually carry a lower rate of interest than the market, governments usually prefer the latter as it avoids both the IMF's conditionality and the loss of esteem often associated with IMF borrowing. Overall, the Fund's influence on industrial countries has declined.

The role of the IMF has changed since its creation and reflects changes in the prevailing international monetary regime and world economic circumstances. It does not in practice perform a powerful disciplining, management or surveillance role in the international monetary system. It certainly does not in any way manage the system or have much influence on its evolution. Power resides with national governments. In general, its surveillance role in the international monetary system has declined with the move away from fixed exchange rates. Its role in balance-of-payments financing, while significant for some developing countries from time to time, has also become less decisive and, for many countries, the amounts that can be borrowed in the markets far exceeds the facilities of the Fund. Nevertheless, its normal and special lending facilities can be of value.

Other roles have become more significant. First, it is a forum for governments to exchange views about economic conditions, policy and their objectives. The IMF, through its annual consultations with each member, has more intelligence about world economic trends than any other organization. Its publications are authoritative. Second, it collects and publishes a substantial volume of data about global economic and financial trends. Third, it performs consultancy services for governments (most especially in developing countries) in all aspects of economic management. A fourth area of influence has been in acting as a forum for debt-restructuring exercises following the substantial market borrowing of some governments during the 1970s and 1980s, and the debt-servicing difficulties that many encountered in the 1980s. Finally, and an area of particular significance since 1990, there are the advice and financing facilities offered to the transitional-economies of eastern Europe as they cope with the structural problems of shifting from rigidly centrally planned economies toward market-orientated regimes.

The IMF has evolved in a way quite different from the conception of its founders. This is largely because the nature of the international monetary system has changed.

David T. Llewellyn
Loughborough University

Further reading

de Vries, M. G. (1976) *The International Monetary Fund 1966–71: The System under Stress*, 2 vols, Washington, DC.
—— (1985) *The International Monetary Fund 1972–78: Cooperation on Trial*, 3 vols, Washington, DC.
—— (1986) *The IMF in a Changing World, 1944–85*, Washington, DC.
—— (1987) *Balance of Payments Adjustment, 1945 to 1986: The IMF Experience*, Washington, DC.
Edwards, S. (1989) 'The International Monetary Fund and the developing countries: a critical evaluation', in *IMF Policy Advice, Market Volatility, Commodity Price Rules, and Other Essays*, Carnegie-Rochester Conference Series on Public Policy 31, Amsterdam.
Finch, C. D. (1989) *The IMF: The Record and the Prospects*, Essays in International Finance 175, Princeton, NJ.
Horsefield, J. K. (1969) *The International Monetary Fund 1945–65: Twenty Years of International Monetary Cooperation*, 3 vols, Washington, DC.
IMF (1985) 'The role and functions of the International Monetary Fund', Washington, DC.
Killick, T. (ed.) (1984) *The IMF and Stabilization: Developing Country Experiences*, New York.
—— (ed.) (1986) *The Quest for Economic Stabilisation: The IMF and the Third World*, London.
Llewellyn, D. T. (1986) 'The international monetary system since 1972: structural change and financial innovation', in M. Posner (ed.) *The Problems of International Money: 1972–85*, Washington, DC.
—— (1990) 'The international monetary system', in D. T. Llewellyn and C. R. Milner, *Current Issues in International Monetary Economics*, London.
Tew, J. H. B. (1988) *The Evolution of the International Monetary System 1945–1988*, London.

See also: international monetary system; OECD; World Bank.

international monetary system

The international monetary system encompasses the arrangements and mechanisms governing monetary and financial relationships between countries. Under alternative systems these may be either precise and reasonably well defined (as under the Gold Standard and, to a lesser extent, the Bretton Woods arrangements in the period 1944–73) or flexible, as has generally been the case since 1973. The monetary relationships between countries are different from those between regions of a country, and raise different issues of analysis and policy. This is because countries have degrees of policy autonomy (particularly with respect to monetary policy) not conferred upon regions of a nation-state; different currencies are involved and their exchange values may change in such a way as to alter the economic and financial relationship between countries; there is no automatic financing of countries' payments imbalances unlike between regions within a country, and, for this reason, there is pressure on nation-states to adjust balance of payments imbalances.

The arrangements within the international monetary system cover six main areas. In various ways, either explicitly or implicitly, it is these six issues that have dominated developments in the international monetary system and the various debates over reform of prevailing systems:

First, central to any system or set of arrangements are *exchange rates* and the extent to which, either because of agreed rules of behaviour or because *ad hoc* decisions are made, central banks intervene in the foreign exchange market to influence the level of exchange rates.

Second, coupled with the exchange rate is the question of *settlement obligations* when a deficit country's currency is purchased by other central banks. This became a major issue in the early 1970s with the breakdown of the Bretton Woods system following the substantial accumulation of US dollars by European and Japanese central banks.

A third element in the monetary relations between countries relates to the linked issues of the balance of pressures that exist as between balance of payments *financing and adjustment*, and the extent to which the pressure for adjustment is symmetrical between surplus and deficit countries. Balance of payments adjustment imposes costs on a deficit country both through the particular mechanism adopted, but also because it usually implies a smaller net absorption of real resources from the rest of the world.

Fourth, the way in which balance of payments *financing* is conducted is a significant issue for international monetary arrangements. In particular, whether financing is undertaken by transferring reserve assets or by borrowing has implications for the growth of international debt and confidence in the international monetary system. One of the factors behind the eventual breakdown of the Bretton Woods system was that a dominant country (the USA) had its persistent payments deficit financed by the central banks of surplus countries purchasing dollars in the foreign exchange market which were not converted by the US authorities into gold or other reserve asset. A *confidence problem* arose as by the early 1970s the volume of such

American liabilities came to exceed the value of the USA's gold stock. A notable feature of the international monetary system of the 1970s was the financing of balance of payments deficits through borrowing from banks.

Fifth, the arrangements for satisfying the requirements of central banks to hold *international liquidity* is a significant element. Central in this is the form in which international liquidity is held (and in particular whether certain national currencies are held for this purpose) and the extent to which there are arrangements for the conscious control of the volume of international liquidity, as against conditions where it is largely demand-determined.

Finally, pervading all of the issues identified, there is the question of *management* of the international monetary system and the extent to which it is based upon the acceptance by governments and central banks of agreed rules of behaviour. The management role of supranational organizations (such as the International Monetary Fund) is subject to considerable controversy given its potential implications for the perceptions of national sovereignty.

The six key issues arise because countries (monetary unions) have trade and financial links with one another. This in turn means that policy developments in one country can affect economic conditions in partner countries and, similarly, that the attainment of domestic policy targets can be thwarted by external developments. In practice, most of the problem issues in the international monetary system relate to the consistency of policy targets between countries.

International interdependence necessarily implies that in one way or another *ex post* compatibility is secured between countries with respect notably to the balance of payments, the exchange rate and the rate of growth of the money supply. However, these may be secured *ex post* at the expense of some *ex ante* plans not being achieved. This is obvious with respect to the balance of payments, as the sum of separate *ex ante* targets might imply an aggregate world surplus or deficit. In various ways *ex post* these inconsistencies are eliminated. But unless all central banks refrain from foreign exchange market intervention (or can successfully sterilize the monetary effects of such intervention), the same is also true of monetary policies. It is relevant, therefore, to consider how potential conflicts of policy and targets between countries might be minimized through various arrangements for ensuring either *ex ante* consistency, or minimizing the resistance to *ex post* equilibrating mechanisms. Logically, five broad mechanisms or options may be identified: first, automatic market mechanisms such as floating exchange rates or non-sterilization of balance of payments induced changes in the money supply; second, the

$(n - 1)$ approach, whereby one country in the system agrees not to have an external target; third, *ex ante* policy co-ordination designed to ensure consistent targets and compatible means of securing them; fourth, an agreement to a precise set of policy rules which indicate what is required of policy makers in specified circumstances; or fifth, a multilateral approach, whereby some supranational authority indicates (and possibly enforces) policy measures which have been calculated to ensure consistency and stability in the system. In practice, the mechanisms are likely to be a composite of several.

The Bretton Woods system as it developed in practice was based essentially upon the $(n - 1)$ arrangement, with the passive role being played by the USA. Such a system presupposes that the central country agrees not to have an external target, and partners are prepared to accept the hegemony of that country, particularly with respect to monetary policy. It was the latter that proved to be a major weakness in the final years of the Bretton Woods system. The major potential weakness of this mechanism is the moral hazard confronted by the key country, which can largely determine its own policy and targets and in the process impose costs (in terms of nonattainment of targets) on partner countries. For instance, in the monetary sector, with a fixed exchange rate, the rate of growth of the money supply in an integrated group can be determined by the dominant country if, like the USA in the 1960s, it chooses to sterilize the monetary effects of its balance-of-payments position.

Until the early 1970s, arrangements in the international monetary system were those outlined in the Bretton Woods agreement of 1944, though the system was operated in practice very differently from the intentions at the outset. The main elements were fixed, but adjustable, exchange rates, with most countries maintaining exchange rates fixed against the US dollar which became the pivotal currency. International liquidity was held predominantly in dollars which were supplied through a persistent US balance-of-payments deficit.

But the international monetary environment became considerably less certain and predictable over the 1970s, and early in the decade the Bretton Woods arrangements finally disintegrated after almost thirty years. At various times, the fixed-exchange-rate system came under strain as the volume of funds that could move between countries and currencies grew markedly after the general moves towards convertibility in the late 1950s. Towards the end of the 1960s it became increasingly apparent that fixed exchange rates, freedom of international capital flows, and independent national control over domestic money supplies were incompatible. The adoption of floating exchange rates in the early 1970s was partly associated with a desire on the part of governments in Europe and elsewhere to determine their monetary policy independently of the USA.

In itself, the Bretton Woods system was potentially stable and had much to commend it. It became, in effect, a dollar standard, and this could have proved durable had Europe been prepared to accept the permanent monetary dominance of the USA.

Since the breakdown of the Bretton Woods arrangements the international monetary system has operated in an *ad hoc* manner. Attempts at reform in the mid-1970s failed to produce a Grand Design new structure similar to that achieved in 1944 which was at the time a response to the turbulence of the 1930s. In the early 1980s, a new 'confidence problem' emerged, related to the external debt position of a few developing countries. This was a reflection of the shift in the balance of pressures between balance-of-payments financing and adjustment towards the former which had been a notable feature of the 1970s.

David T. Llewellyn
Loughborough University

Further reading

Tew, J. H. B. (1982) *Evolution of the International Monetary System 1945–81*, London.
Williamson, J. (1977) *The Failure of World Monetary Reform 1971–74*, London.

See also: International Monetary Fund; reserve currency; World Bank.

international relations

In the most general sense international relations have existed ever since people formed themselves into social groups, and then developed external relations with groups like themselves. Relationships were most frequently conflictual or warlike, although occasionally they were co-operative; but they took place in a system of anarchy and not within the framework of any political or legal or customary rules. These peculiar relationships were little considered by writers in the western world before Machiavelli, but from the seventeenth century onwards international law (Grotius, Pufendorf, Vattel) and the problems of war and peace (Rousseau, Kant) began to attract attention. These historical origins, combined with the horror of the First World War, led to the subject's emergence as a policy-making, prescriptive and normative study: war was an intolerable evil, its recurrence must forever be prevented, and the duty of international relations scholars was to show how to achieve this. It was assumed that nobody could want war, so if states were

democratic and governments were accountable to their peoples, and if the system's anarchy were ended (hence the League of Nations), war might be banished.

The diagnosis was too simple. The aspirations and actions of Hitler, Mussolini, the Japanese, and the Bolsheviks in Moscow showed the truth of the dictum of Morgenthau (1948) that peace and security is the ideology of satisfied powers. Scholars now turned their minds away from study of ways to achieve a supposedly universal goal to study of how things in the internal arena in fact were. The modern subject of international relations was born. From the outset, though at first not explicitly, the subject was approached by different scholars from two different points of view. The first sought to establish why the significant units (or actors) on the international stage behaved in the ways they did: most such scholars saw states as the significant actors, and this branch of the subject became foreign policy analysis. The second group focused on the arena within which relations occurred, and was concerned to identify the mechanisms by which patterned relationships with a fair degree of stability and order were able to be maintained in conditions which, formally at least, were anarchical.

The 1950s and 1960s saw a burgeoning of methodological experimentation and quasi-theoretical speculation, and a proliferation of journals. The behaviouralist revolution in the USA invaded international relations, as it did other social sciences, and a great debate with the so-called traditionalists raged through the 1960s and early 1970s, and is not yet concluded. But in the 1970s and 1980s disappointment at the relative lack of success in the creation of theories with explanatory power for real-world problems led to some redirection of attention towards substantive questions, to smaller-scale analyses and to theorizing over limited ranges of phenomena.

Foreign policy analysis is the branch of the subject in which most practical advances have occurred. Many conceptual frameworks have been developed, the most comprehensive probably being that of Brecher *et al.* (1969), but the central components of such frameworks are now widely agreed. States are conceived as having objectives of various kinds – political/security, economic, ideological. Objectives are not consistently compatible one with another, and a short-term objective may be inconsistent with a long-term goal. Objectives are ranked differently by different groups, organizations, and political leaderships within states, and rankings change over time. Explanation of policy decisions thus requires understanding of political interplay and bureaucratic process. But the determination of policy is conditioned also by states' capabilities – economic, demographic, political, military – and by decision makers' perceptions of the comparative efficacy of their own capabilities as against those of the other state(s) with which they are dealing, all in the context of support relationships (alliances, economic aid) and of respective commitments elsewhere in the system. Most, if not all, relationships have elements of conflict and common interest, and are essentially of a bargaining character; but the conflictual element usually predominates, and the concept of power is thus central to the analysis. A check-list of such considerations affecting foreign-policy decisions enables rudimentary comparisons of foreign policies to be made, but also makes possible greater awareness among policy makers of the likely consequences of their decisions.

The purposes of studies at the second or system level are to determine the factors that make the stability of the system more or less probable, and the effect on international outcomes of the system's structure. Essential structural components are the number of significant units (or actors) in the system, the nature, quality and quantity of interactions among the units, the distribution of capabilities among them, and the degree to which realignment of relationships is easy or is constrained (a system that is ideologically highly polarized, for example, is relatively inflexible). Analysis at the system level is commonly more highly abstract than analysis of state behaviour: this makes possible theory construction of a more rigorous kind, but by the same token makes application of theory to the real world more difficult.

At both levels statistical and mathematical techniques are used, as well as more traditional methods relying on historical and verbally described data. The distinction between the levels is, of course, analytical only. To take just one example of interdependence: at the unit behaviour level, the extent to which states are economically, militarily or ideologically interdependent will very greatly affect the policy choices that are open; at the system level, the extent to which the realignment of units is impeded by their interdependence will fundamentally affect both outcomes and the stability of the system. Mention of interdependence calls attention to the fact that while states are widely accepted as still the most significant actors in the international arena, there are now many other actors, including intergovernmental organizations (the International Monetary Fund) and non-governmental organizations (guerrilla groups or multinational corporations). The roles of these, in interplay with the behaviour of states, and as components of international systems, all form part – and some would say an increasingly important part – of the study of international relations.

P. A. Reynolds
Lancaster University

References

Brecher, M., Steinberg, B. and Stein, J. (1969) 'A framework for research in foreign policy behaviour', *Journal of Conflict Resolution* 13.
Morgenthau, H. J. (1948) *Politics Among Nations*, New York.

Further reading

Carr, E. H. (1939) *The Twenty Years' Crisis 1919–1939*, London.
Holsti, K. J. (1977) *International Politics*, Englewood Cliffs, NJ.
Reynolds, P. A. (1980) *An Introduction to International Relations*, London.
Rosenau, J. N. (1971) *The Scientific Study of Foreign Policy*, Glencoe, IL.
Smith, M., Little, R. and Shackleton, M. (1981) *Perspectives on World Politics*, London.
Waltz, K. N. (1979) *Theory of International Politics*, Reading, MA.

international trade

International trade is not intrinsically different from transactions in which commodities do not cross national boundaries. Nevertheless, the study of international trade has traditionally constituted a separate branch of microeconomics. It may be distinguished from other branches by its focus on situations where some but not all goods and factors are mobile between countries; and from international macroeconomics by its focus on real rather than nominal variables (trade flows and relative prices rather than exchange rates and money supplies), and by a tendency to examine medium-run issues using equilibrium analysis rather than short-run positions of disequilibrium.

One of the first and most durable contributions to the analysis of international trade is the principle of *comparative advantage* due to Ricardo (1817, ch. 7). This is the antecedent of both the normative and positive strands of international trade theory. At a normative level, it postulates that an absolutely inefficient country will nevertheless gain from trade; at a positive level, it predicts the direction of trade: each country will tend to export those goods which it produces relatively cheaply in the absence of trade. As an explanation of trade patterns, the principle has met with some success. However, in its classical form it is open to two objections: it assumes unrealistically that unit production costs are independent of scale or factor proportions; and it fails to explain why they differ between countries in the first place.

A theory which overcomes these deficiencies was developed by the Swedish economists Heckscher (1919) and Ohlin (1933), who stressed international differences in *factor endowments* as the basis for comparative advantage and trade. Thus a country which is relatively capital-abundant will tend to export goods which are produced by relatively capital-intensive techniques. Largely through the influence of Samuelson (1949), a highly simplified version of this theory, assuming only two goods and two factors in each country, has come to dominate the textbooks. In this form it is a useful teaching device for introducing some basic concepts of general equilibrium theory but, not surprisingly, it is overwhelmingly rejected by the data. The most notable example of this is the so-called *Leontief Paradox*, an early application by Leontief (1954) of his technique of input-output analysis, which found that the presumably capital-abundant USA exported labour-intensive commodities, thus contradicting the theory. Nevertheless, for most economists probably the preferred explanation of trade patterns between countries at different levels of economic development is an eclectic theory of comparative advantage along Heckscher-Ohlin lines, allowing for many factors of production, some of them (such as natural resources) specific to individual sectors.

Even this theory fails to account adequately for certain features of contemporary international trade, especially between advanced economies with similar technology and factor endowments. Such trade is frequently *intra-industry*, involving differentiated products within a single industry. Various theories explain such trade in terms of imperfectly competitive firms producing under conditions of increasing returns. Attention has also focused on the increased international mobility of factors (in part through the medium of *multinational corporations*) which in different circumstances may act as a substitute for or a complement to trade.

As well as attempting to explain the pattern of trade, positive trade theory also makes predictions about many aspects of open economies. Most notorious of these is the implication of the Heckscher-Ohlin model known as the *factor price equalization theorem*, which predicts that free trade will equalize the prices of internationally immobile factors. The theory also makes predictions concerning such issues as the effects of tariffs and international transfers on foreign and domestic prices, the effects of trade policy on domestic income distribution, and the consequences of structural change.

Turning to normative trade theory, its traditional focus has been the merits of free trade relative to autarky, stemming from increased specialization in production and increased efficiency and diversity of choice in consumption. Similar arguments favour partially restricted trade relative to autarky, although the benefits of selective trade liberalization (such as the formation of a customs union) are not as clear-cut. The persistence of protectionist sentiment, despite these theoretical arguments, may be explained by the fact that gains from trade accruing to the economy as a whole are not inconsistent with losses to individual groups, especially owners of factors specific to import-competing sectors.

Two exceptions to the case for free trade are normally admitted. The *optimal tariff argument* states that a country with sufficient market power can gain by behaving like a monopolist and restricting the supply of its exports. The *infant-industry argument* defends transitional protection to enable a new industry to benefit from learning and scale economies. (As with many arguments for trade restriction, the latter on closer examination is less an argument against free trade than against *laissez faire*.) Work on *strategic trade policy* has added to these arguments the possibility that a government's ability to pre-commit to tariffs or subsidies may allow it to give an advantage to home firms competing in oligopolistic markets.

Other special models have been developed to deal with important features of contemporary international trade. Thus, the growth of trade in intermediate goods (as opposed to goods for final consumption) has inspired the theory of *effective protection*, which builds on the insight that an industry benefits from tariffs on its outputs but is harmed by tariffs on its inputs. The postwar decline in importance of tariffs (at least between developed countries), due largely to international agreements such as the General Agreement on Tariffs and Trade (GATT) and the formation of free-trade areas and customs unions such as the European Union (formerly the EC), has focused attention on the widespread use of *non-tariff barriers* (such as quotas, health and safety regulations and government procurement policies) as methods of restricting trade.

J. Peter Neary
University College Dublin

References

Heckscher, E. (1919) 'The effect of foreign trade on the distribution of income,' *Ekonomisk Tidskrift* 11. Translated in H. Flam and M. J. Flanders (eds.) (1991) *Heckscher-Ohlin Trade Theory*, Cambridge, MA.

Leontief, W. (1954) 'Domestic production and foreign trade: The American capital position re-examined,' *Economia Internazionale* 7 reprinted (in part) in R. E. Caves and H. G. Johnson (eds) (1968): *Readings in International Economics*, Homewood, IL.

Ohlin, B. (1933) *Interregional and International Trade*, Cambridge, MA.

Ricardo, D. (1817) *On the Principles of Political Economy and Taxation*, Volume 1 of *The Works and Correspondence of David Ricardo*, P. Sraffa (ed.), Cambridge, UK.

Samuelson, P. A. (1949) 'International factor-price equalisation once again,' *Economic Journal* 59, reprinted in J. E.

Stiglitz (ed.): *The Collected Scientific Papers of Paul A. Samuelson, Volume II*, Cambridge, MA. MIT Press, 1966.

Further reading

Jones, R. W. and Kenen, P. B. (eds) (1984) *Handbook of International Economics: Volume 1*, Amsterdam (especially Chapter 1 by R. W. Jones and J. P. Neary and Chapter 2 by W. M. Corden).

Helpman, E. and Krugman, P. A. (1985) *Market Structure and Foreign Trade*, Cambridge, MA.

—— (1989) *Trade Policy and Market Structure*, Cambridge, MA.

interviews and interviewing

The use of surveys in social science research has expanded considerably in the last three decades, and with it the practice of interviewing. The interview is one of the most central parts of the survey-taking process: it is the source of information for the researcher who has carefully designed and integrated the components of a survey. A well-designed survey starts with an overall study design, a sample that fits the needs of the survey, a carefully drafted questionnaire, editing and coding rules to summarize the data collected, and an analysis plan. But even if these pieces are executed flawlessly, any survey can be a failure if the interviewing is poorly handled. The increased use of interviews has led to the development of multiple interviewing techniques, an improvement in methods used by interviewers, and the establishment of trained permanent staffs to conduct interviews.

Types of interviews

In survey research, there are essentially three techniques for gathering information from respondents: mail, telephone, and personal interviews. The choice between these techniques depends on the money and time available for collecting information, the types of questions being asked, and concerns about data quality. Mail interviews are usually conducted with a small to moderate length questionnaire; questions asked in a mail questionnaire should not be especially difficult and there should be relatively few places in the questionnaire where the respondent has to 'skip' to a different series of questions. Mail interviews are the cheapest of the methods used for interviewing, but in using them the researcher gives up control over the interview process. In a carefully designed study, research should be conducted under controlled conditions so that no factors extraneous to the topic being studied can intrude on the data collection. In the case of a mail interview, the researcher cannot determine who will fill out the questionnaire if sent to a home or business, nor can one use probing type statements to obtain more detailed answers to complex questions.

Telephone interviews resolve some of these problems. The interviewer can to some degree control who responds to the questions and can probe to obtain clarification of ambiguous responses. These interviews can be more detailed than mail interviews and more complicated questionnaire designs are possible, since the telephone interviewer can be trained in how the questionnaire should be completed. One disadvantage is that telephone interviews must be kept somewhat short, usually one-half hour or less, to avoid respondent fatigue; they also cost more than mail interviews – interviewers must be paid, and there are capital costs for telephone equipment and use.

As in the case of mail and telephone interviews, personal interviews have their trade-offs. Personal interviews can be substantially more expensive than telephone interviews because of the travel costs. But there are advantages: a much more detailed and lengthy interview can be conducted with a respondent; the personal interview allows the interviewer to use printed materials like flash cards to elicit responses; the interviewer is also able to see and interact with the respondent, which can be a help in determining whether the respondent is confused by, or bored with, the questions being asked. This mode allows the interviewer the most control over the interview process.

Ranking the three methods by cost, the postal interview is least expensive, followed by telephone and then personal interviews. There are exceptions to this ordering that depend on the circumstances of the survey. But in terms of the quality of the data, the interviewer has more control of and can ask more detailed questions in a personal interview. Telephone interviews offer some control of the interview, though less than the personal, and postal interviews offer the least control and the least opportunity for asking detailed questions. Again, this ranking will not always hold true, as there are circumstances and types of questions where the respondent will be more comfortable in responding by telephone or mail because of embarrassment or discomfort in talking to a stranger.

Another factor affecting the choice between the three interviewing modes is response rates. Responses to postal surveys have traditionally been lower than those obtained for telephone or personal interview surveys. This has led to the practice of mixed mode surveys, with an initial or multiple attempts to contact respondents by mail, followed by telephone and personal contacts to increase response.

Methods of interviewing

As in any area of scientific inquiry, the data collected in a survey need to be of the highest quality to enable the researcher to draw from them. Errors in the data, especially biases due to flaws in the collection process, can lead to erroneous conclusions in analysis. To improve further the quality of survey data, several modifications to the interview process have been introduced that increase response and enhance quality.

Two examples of these types of modifications will illustrate such improvements. The first is the use of diaries. In a broad range of surveys, from consumer behaviour to epidemiological studies, diaries have been introduced to improve the quality of the data gathered. Surveys that ask retrospective questions about behaviour frequently have problems with recall loss, that is, the respondent cannot remember all instances of a given action. To help the respondent, it is now a common practice to have an interviewer collect demographic and attitudinal information during a personal visit interview, and to leave a diary to be filled out by the respondent on a daily basis which would describe the type of behaviour being studied over a week or longer. This methodology has been especially useful in consumption studies and research on time usage.

A second method used for interviewing is an enhancement to the telephone interview. Traditional methods for interviewing have used paper questionnaires with the interviewer transcribing responses. The new method, computer-assisted telephone interviewing (CATI), uses the computer to give the interviewer questions on a display screen, and the interviewer types in the respondent's answers to be stored in computer memory. The computer controls the interview, using the responses to determine how to branch through skip patterns and providing some editing of data for inconsistent responses. Although the initial investment can be high, CATI allows for better control of the survey and leads to better quality in the data collected.

The interviewer

General survey practice for large and moderate-sized survey organizations has been to hire and train permanent interviewing staff. Interviewers are recognized as skilled professionals who contribute to the survey effort through their experience in contacting respondents, conducting interviews, and understanding what the researcher is attempting to study. In most survey organizations, the interviewer as a permanent staff member receives training in these skills, in methods for asking and coding questions, and in general principles of the conduct of a survey interview. For particular studies, the interviewer will receive training as to the intent of each question and the study as a whole, how to deal with difficult skip patterns, and other information relevant to the study. Many organizations have two interviewing staffs, one trained exclusively for telephone interviewing from a central location, the other a geographically dispersed group of interviewers who conduct personal interviews. These would be trained and supervised differently, as the interviewing techniques would be different.

Charles D. Cowan
Bureau of the Census, US Dept of Commerce

Further reading

Bradburn, N. M. and Sudman, S. (1979) *Improving Interview Method and Questionnaire Design*, San Francisco, CA.

Cannell, C. F., Oksenberg, L. and Converse, J. M. (1979) *Experiments in Interviewing Techniques*, Ann Arbor, MI.

Gorden, R. (1975) *Interviewing: Strategy, Techniques and Tactics*, Homewood, IL.

Hoinville, G., Jowell, R. and Associates (1978) *Survey Research Practices*, London.

Smith, J. M. (1972) *Interviewing in Market and Social Research*, London.

See also: methods of social research; questionnaires; sample surveys.

investment

Investment can be defined as the change in the capital stock over a period of time – normally a year for accounting purposes. It is not to be confused with financial investment, which involves the purchase of financial assets, such as stocks and shares, and is, therefore, more closely connected with the analysis of saving. It is also commonly distinguished from inventory investment, which involves changes in stocks of finished goods, work in progress and raw materials.

Capital investment goods differ from consumption goods in that they yield a flow of services, over a period of time, and these services do not directly satisfy consumer wants but facilitate the production of goods and services, or consumer goods. Although some consumer goods are perishable, a large number provide services over a period of time and are, therefore, akin to investment goods. Such goods are called consumer durables. The existence of various goods that provide flows of services over time presents problems for national income accounting. This is because it is not always clear whether such goods should be classified as investment or consumer goods. Expenditure on land and dwellings, by households, is an example. In the UK such expenditures are treated as investment. Expenditure on plant and machinery is, however, clearly part of (capital) investment, since it either replaces worn-out machinery or adds to productive capacity. Gross investment is total expenditure on capital goods per year, and net investment is gross investment net of depreciation – which is the decline in the capital stock due to wear and tear.

A distinction is often drawn between public investment, which is undertaken by the public sector, and private investment. Direct foreign, or overseas, investment involves the purchase of financial or productive assets in other countries and should be distinguished from overseas portfolio investment.

A number of theories have been developed to explain the determination of investment demand. These commonly relate to private-sector investment demand, since public-sector investment may involve other considerations. The importance of investment lies in the fact that a rise in the capital stock of an economy may increase its productive capacity and potential for economic growth. It should be noted that the capital stock is one of a number of factors of production, along with labour and raw materials, which contribute to production and, therefore, that investment is not the sole determinant of growth. Additionally, investment is a major route through which technical progress can be made.

Public investment may be guided by principles other than narrow profit maximization, since the government should take account of social costs and benefits as well as pecuniary ones. Public investment might, consequently, be undertaken to alleviate unemployment in depressed areas or to encourage technical change. Keynesian economists have argued that public investment can be an important catalyst to economic development and may have a significant role to play in leading an economy out of recession.

Economic literature postulates that there are two major determinants of private investment demand: the rate of interest, and the increase in national income. Other factors clearly influence investment as well: these include wage and tax rates, which affect the relative cost of capital and labour. Assuming that these other influences are constant, however, it is postulated that changes in the rate of interest or national income will cause a change in the desired capital stock and that this will lead to investment.

A change in the rate of interest will influence the desired capital stock by altering the expected profitability of various potential investment expenditures. This can be seen in various ways. Firms may be viewed as forecasting the revenues and costs over the life of the project in which the capital good is to be employed. To do this they must forecast the expected life of the project, the sales volumes and prices and various costs, in each year of the project. The expected project life will depend on both the physical life and the techno-

logical life of the capital good. A firm will not wish to operate with obsolete capital goods, since it will be at a cost disadvantage relative to its competitors. Having estimated the expected future flow of profits, and any scrap value that capital good might have at the end of the project's life, the firm will then *discount* this expected income stream. If it discounts it using the market rate of interest, then it will discover the gross present value of the project, and after subtracting the cost of the capital good it will have calculated the net present value. If this is positive, then the profit is acceptable given the risk involved and the attractiveness of alternative projects. A fall in the rate of interest will lead to a rise in the net present value of various projects and will, other things being equal, lead a number of firms to want to buy additional capital goods. In aggregate, the desired capital stock will rise. Keynes explained the influence of the interest rate on investment in a slightly different manner, based on the internal rate of return, or what he called the marginal efficiency of capital. This alternative suggests that firms will find the rate of discount which equates the (discounted) expected flow of returns to the cost of the capital good. If this rate is less than the market rate of interest, then the project is potentially profitable. A fall in the interest rate should, therefore, increase the number of potentially profitable projects and hence the aggregate desired capital stock. If a firm is borrowing funds to finance investment, the interest rate represents the cost of borrowing. If it is financing investment from internal funds, the interest rate represents the *opportunity cost*, since it represents the revenue the firm could, alternatively, receive from financial investment. Such explanations of the determination of investment demand are based on an assumption of fixed interest rates, throughout the life of the project. Financial institutions are, however, increasingly lending at variable rates, and this will further complicate the investment decision by requiring firms to form expectations of interest rates throughout the project's life. It is to be noted that expectations play a major role in determining investment demand, according to this analysis, and that, consequently, a government policy of trying to stimulate investment, by reducing the interest rate, might not have the desired effect in times of worsening expectations of future profits.

A second major influence on investment demand is believed to be the change in national income. A rise in national income might increase expected sales and lead to a desire to increase productive capacity. The accelerator theory is a more formal explanation of the influence of a rise in national income on investment. It postulates a fixed ratio of capital to output, based on technological considerations, so that output growth should lead to an increase in the desired capital stock.

It seems unlikely that an economy's capital to output ratio is fixed over time, since many factors will influence this ratio, such as the relative cost of capital and labour, technical progress, and changes in the relative importance of various sectors of the economy, which may have different capital/output ratios. In its crude form the accelerator theory does not perform well empirically, but in more flexible forms it is more successful at explaining investment.

It is, therefore, clear that a change in the rate of interest or in national income might influence the demand for capital goods and change the aggregate desired capital stock for the economy as a whole. The actual net investment that occurs each year in any economy depends on the rate of depreciation of capital stock, and on the extent to which the increased demand for capital stock is satisfied. This will in turn depend on the ability of the capital goods-producing industry to meet the increased demand; the extent to which the price of capital goods rises in response to the increased demand, thus raising the cost of capital goods and reducing the net present value of investment projects; and the extent to which suitable capital goods can be purchased from abroad.

Andy Mullineux
University of Birmingham

Further reading

Hawkins, C. J. and Pearce, D. W. (1971) *Capital Investment Appraisal*, London.
Junankar, P. N. (1972) *Investment: Theories and Evidence*, London.
Maurice, R. (ed.) (1968) *National Accounts Statistics: Sources and Methods*, London.

See also: capital theory; national income analysis.

J

James, William (1842–1910)

William James, eminent psychologist and philosopher, was born in New York City. He, his novelist brother, Henry, and his sister were the main recipients of an unusually unsystematic education supervised by their father which consisted largely of European travels and private tutors. After an interval in which he studied painting, James enrolled in the Lawrence Scientific School at Harvard in 1861. In 1864 he entered Harvard Medical School and received an MD in 1869. His life was marked by periods of acute depression and psychosomatic illnesses which occasioned solitary trips to Europe for rest and treatment. These periods, however, produced two benefits: they gave James first-hand experience of abnormal psychological states concerning which he was later to be a pioneer investigator; and they provided opportunities for extensive reading of science and literature in French, German and English. His marriage in 1878 appears to have been an important factor in improving his health and focusing his concentration on teaching and writing. His academic life was centred at Harvard where he became an instructor in psychology in 1875 and taught anatomy and physiology. Subsequently he offered courses in philosophy until his retirement in 1907.

James's work in psychology and philosophy was interfused and is not completely separable. His greatest effort and achievement was *The Principles of Psychology* (1890) which, some ten years in writing, made him world famous and is now regarded a classic in both fields of study. James stated his intention to establish psychology as a natural science. By this he meant that metaphysical questions would be avoided and, wherever possible, explanations in psychology should be based on experimental physiology and biology rather than on introspective procedures which had dominated philosophic psychology since Locke and Hume. In contrast to a widely prevailing conception of mind as composed of ideas, like atoms, ordered and compounded by association, James proposed that mentality is a 'stream of consciousness' including in it feelings and interests. For James, the mental is to be construed in evolutionary and teleological forms: mental activity is evidenced where there are selections of means to achieve future ends. Darwinian theory had an important influence on James's psychological and philosophical views. Ideas and theories are interpreted as instruments enabling us to adapt successfully to, and partly transform, reality according to our interests and purposes of action.

In an address of 1898, 'Philosophical Conceptions and Practical Results', James inaugurated the theory of pragmatism which soon became the major movement in American philosophy. He also drew attention to the neglected work of Charles S. Peirce whom he credited with having originated pragmatism. The main thesis is that the value and significance of concepts, their meaning and truth, is determined not by their origins but by their future practical consequences. An application of this view is found in 'The Will to Believe' (1896) and in James's Gifford Lectures (1901–2), 'The Varieties of Religious Experience'; it is argued explicitly in *Pragmatism* (1907) and *The Meaning of Truth* (1909). In his later writings and lectures, James refined and defended his metaphysical doctrines of the pluralistic character of reality, indeterminism, and 'radical empiricism' according to which the world is conceived as a growing continuous structure of experience.

H. S. Thayer
City University of New York

Further reading

Burkhardt, F. and Bowers, F. (eds) (1975–88), *The Works of William James*, 19 vols, Cambridge, MA.

Perry, R. B. (1935) *The Thought and Character of William James*, 2 vols, Boston, MA.

Skrupskelis, I. K. and Berkeley, E. M. (1992–), *The Correspondence of William James*, Charlottesville, VA.

Japanization

The term Japanization, derived from Turnbull's (1986) seminal article, embodies two related phenomena: first, emulation of Japanese manufacturing techniques and industrial relations, or human resource management systems, by western companies; second, direct investment and implantation by Japanese corporations outside Japan. Much of the focus in Britain and the USA has been fixed upon vehicle manufacture, such as Nissan, Toyota and Honda, as well as consumer electronics, with considerable investment by Japanese corporations into particular regions and joint projects.

In Japan the most successful corporations have usually been associated with two related systems. A system of 'lean management' in which waste of all kinds (including excess management) is progressively eliminated through Just-in-Time (JIT) systems, where, for instance, parts are delivered to the factory Just-in-Time to be used. This is associated with Total Quality Management (TQM) in which responsibility for permanent improvement and quality is pushed down upon the direct producers and not reserved for an autonomous quality control department. The other half of this system involves the 'four pillars' of Japanese management: first, permanent employment for the multi-skilled and highly mobile workforce (primarily restricted to men and available only for the minority in the largest corporations, though this also began to crumble in the early 1990s); second, seniority-based pay and promotion systems in organizations to complement the 'high-trust' culture – in contrast to the more meritocratic and low-trust 'value-added' systems which prevail in the west; third, enterprise-based trade unions; and fourth, a strongly mobilized and deeply entrenched unitary culture, conspicuously symbolized by the daily rendition of company songs and underpinned by the rich network of affiliate companies that encourage corporate employees to refer to themselves as belonging to the corporation. This familial attitude is reinforced daily through travel, health, education, housing and consumption patterns, which are often channelled through the corporate travel, health, education, housing and shopping complexes.

In the west those plants that have been Japanized have tended to accommodate both Japanese and western approaches in various hybrid forms. Thus, JIT and TQM systems have been eagerly adopted but the industrial relations and cultural aspects less so: secure – as opposed to permanent – employment exists in some plants; single unions or union-less plants are preferred to the more traditional multi-union western plants; seniority-based reward systems are rare; and attempts by management to impose unitary cultures on western workers have been generally unsuccessful in environments where corporate influence upon individuals is considerably reduced by the higher levels of public welfare.

There is considerable controversy as to the success rate of experiments in Japanization: many failures or poor results are laid at the door of intransigent and dichotomous cultural conflicts. It should be remembered, though, that however many of the ideas appear deeply embedded in Japan's Samurai past, some of the 'uniquely' Japanese methods and ideas have their origins in the west.

Keith Grint
University of Oxford

Reference

Turnbull, P. (1986) 'The "Japanization" of production and industrial relations at Lucas Electrical', *Industrial Relations Journal* 17.

Further reading

Oliver, N. and Wilkinson, B. (1988) *The Japanization of British Industry*, Oxford.

judicial process

As studied by contemporary social scientists, focusing primarily on liberal democracies, the judicial process is the complex of formal and informal operations by which tribunals adjudicate claims based on rules putatively authorized by the regime. The tribunals are differentiated and relatively autonomous from the rest of the polity, and typically do not initiate action, but respond when a claim fit for adjudication is presented to them through an adversarial presentation of evidence and argument. So defined, the judicial process is a relatively modern enquiry, dependent upon two intellectual developments: the emergence of the ideal concept of a distinct judicial function performed by a distinct institution; and the rise of a science of politics that emphasizes the informal processes over formal procedures of government and which, as applied to the study of the judiciary, questions the reality, attainability and intellectual sophistication of this conceptual ideal.

Although ancient and medieval political philosophers did distinguish a judicial function from other governmental functions, these distinctions were subordinated to a more fundamental one, that between legislation and politics. Legislation was regarded by the ancients as an extraordinary event, subject at most to rare and cautious amendment, while politics encompassed deliberations and actions within the framework of this legislation. Viewing God as the ultimate legislator, medieval thinkers regarded virtually all governmental functions as aspects of the judicial function.

Because the law was regarded as everlasting, yet the situations to which it was to be applied were ever-changing, the judicial function, both in ancient and medieval thought, included generous elements of practical wisdom and equity as essential supplements to the more literal terms of the law.

The more carefully defined and tightly circumscribed contemporary judicial function, performed by a specialized agency, arises concomitantly with the idea of law as the enactment of a sovereign legislator, or what students of political development call the shift of authority from a traditional to a constitutional basis. With authority to make law vested in a present institution having the capacity to change the law to meet new situations, the quasi-legislative character of the ancient and medieval judicial function would threaten to derange legislative authority and offend individual rights by effecting burdens and punishments retroactively. Ironically, this rigorous subordination of judgment to legislation also required the autonomy of the judiciary from the legislature, so that courts could be impartial to the parties before it and free from pressure to interpret the law other than as the legislature intended it at the time of enactment. From these conceptual and institutional developments there emerges, then, the idealized modern judicial function as one presupposing the existence of right answers at law, performed by a tribunal with sufficient autonomy to discern these answers in the resolution of disputes. We find numerous expressions of this ideal among theorists and jurists of liberal democracy; perhaps the most frequently quoted is that of Montesquieu, who held that judges were to be 'no more than the mouth that pronounces the words of the law, mere passive beings, incapable of moderating either its force or rigour'.

Influenced by evolutionary theory, jurists and social scientists during the late nineteenth and early twentieth centuries began shifting their focus from institutional forms and idealized purposes to the 'live forces' that were claimed to constitute the underlying reality. Those who called themselves realists provided the most radical onslaught on the ideal judicial function by dismissing the ontological claim of 'right answers'. In most instances, within wide boundaries, they maintained, there was no right answer to be discovered, no measure by which to assess the claims of one judge's opinion over another; what really constituted the law were the psychological traits of the judge. A distinct but related movement, sociological jurisprudence, emphasized not only the creative character of the judicial function, but also the need to consider both law and courts in the context of their larger political and social environments.

From this odd marriage of a judicial ideal, which is implicit in the theory and institutions of liberal democracy, and this realist assessment of that standard, is born the modern study of the judicial process. Bearing a greater likeness to its realist parent, it is predominantly an empirical enquiry. Central to its study are the following: the processes by which courts are staffed, the conditions of judicial tenure, and the effect of these on judicial decisions; how rules of procedure, both formal and informal, affect the definition and disposition of issues; the decision-making patterns of individual judges, the dynamics of collective decision making in juries and on appellate courts, patterns of interaction among the courts in appellate and federal systems; the impact and implementation of judicial decisions; and the comparative competence of judicial and non-judicial branches of government for effecting social change. Normative enquiries focus on modes of legal interpretation and, especially regarding constitutional law, the propriety of judicial activism and restraint. A long promising, but as yet underdeveloped, area is the comparative study of the judicial process, including the study of systems other than those in liberal democracies.

Stanley C. Brubaker
Colgate University

Further reading

Abraham, H. J. (1980) *The Judicial Process*, 4th edn, New York.
Horowitz, D. (1977) *The Courts and Social Policy*, Washington, DC.
Murphy, W. F. and Tanenhaus, J. (1972) *The Study of Public Law*, New York.

See also: law; sociolegal studies.

K

Keynes, John Maynard (1883–1946)

The son of John Neville Keynes, a Cambridge economist, philosopher and administrator, and Florence Ada (Brown), Cambridge's first woman town councillor and later its mayor, Maynard Keynes made contributions that extended well beyond academic economics. After an education at Eton and King's College, Cambridge (BA in Mathematics 1905), his first career was that of a civil servant in the India Office (1906–8). Although he soon returned to Cambridge to lecture in economics (1908–20) and be a Fellow of King's (1909–46), he never lost his connection with the world of affairs. He served as a member of the Royal Commission on Indian Finance and Currency (1913–14), was a wartime Treasury official eventually in charge of Britain's external financial relations (1915–19), a member of the Macmillan Committee on Finance and Industry (1929–31), a member of the Economic Advisory Council (1930–9), an adviser to the Chancellor of the Exchequer (1940–6) and a director of the Bank of England (1941–6). After 1919, he also had an active career in the world of finance as a company director, insurance company chairman and bursar of King's College, Cambridge. Moreover, under the influence of his Bloomsbury friends Vanessa Bell and Duncan Grant, as well as Lydia Lopokova of the Diaghilev Ballet whom he married in 1925, he played an active and important role in the cultural life of his time as a patron of the arts, founder of the Arts Theatre, Cambridge (which he gave to the city and university in 1938), trustee of the National Gallery, chairman of the Council for the Encouragement of Music and the Arts, and initiator and first chairman of the Arts Council of Great Britain.

Keynes's reputation as an academic economist arises from work that he started after his fortieth year and published after he was 47. Prior to that, he was much better known as a publicist and commentator on economic affairs, a career he began in 1919 after his resignation as the senior Treasury official at the Paris Peace Conference with his bestselling and influential indictment of the negotiation and terms of the Peace Treaty in *The Economic Consequences of the Peace* (1919). He continued in this popular vein with *A Revision of the Treaty* (1922), *A Tract on Monetary Reform* (1923), *The Economic Consequences of Mr Churchill* (1925), *The End of Laissez-Faire* (1926) and prolific journalism, notably for the liberal *Nation and Athenaeum* (1923–31) and the more socialist *New Statesman and Nation*, for both of which he was chairman of the board. This does not mean that he was unknown as an academic: he was editor of the Royal Economic Society's *The Economic Journal* (1911–45) and the author of *A Treatise on Probability* (1921), a philosophical examination of the principles of reasoning and rational action in conditions of incomplete and uncertain knowledge, the earliest ideas of which date after 1904 when Keynes was strongly influenced by G. E. Moore. Nevertheless, it would be fair to echo Sir Austin Robinson's comment (1947): 'If Maynard Keynes had died in 1925 it would have been difficult for those who knew intimately the power and originality of his mind to have convinced those who had not known him of the full measure of Keynes' ability.'

The bases for Keynes's academic reputation as an economist were his *Treatise on Money* (1930) and *The General Theory of Employment, Interest and Money* (1936). Both were stages in the development in theoretical terms of the principles which should underlie attempts by governments to achieve economic stability. In the *Treatise*, as in the more popular *Tract*, the main concern was with monetary and price stability and the role that monetary policy alone could play in achieving them. As was common in contemporary monetary economics, Keynes dichotomized the economy into its monetary and real sectors and, on the assumption that money was neutral in the long run, looked for the principles of monetary practice which would ensure price stability, in the *Treatise* case a monetary policy which made the long-term market rate of interest equivalent to the 'natural rate' at which savings equalled investment. This initial approach to the problem was found to be inadequate by Keynes's critics, who included R. G. Hawtrey, F. A. Hayek and D. H. Robertson, as well as a group of younger economists in Cambridge (R. F. Kahn, James Meade, Joan and Austin Robinson, and Piero Sraffa). When convinced of the inadequacies of the *Treatise*, Keynes began reformulating his ideas. The major breakthrough came in 1933 when, contrary to traditional theory, Keynes hit on the crucial role of changes in output and employment in equilibration savings and investment, thus providing the basis for a more general theory than his own or his predecessors' previous work. The new theory seemed to offer the possibility of equilibrium at less than full employment, something missing in previous work. From his 1933 breakthrough, which hinged on the consumption-income relationship implicit in the multiplier, after considerable further work, everything fell into place.

During the last ten years of his life, although his activities were inhibited by a severe heart condition after 1937, Keynes devoted less time to defending and somewhat refining his theoretical views than to seeing them implemented. Even before the outbreak of war in 1939, he had started to influence Treasury thinking in Britain, while his students and his writings were becoming influential in such places as Washington and Ottawa. However, the problems of war finance and post-war planning appear to have been crucial in the spread of his ideas into day-to-day policy making, for as he demonstrated in *How to Pay for the War* (1940) the new ideas when married to another contemporary development – national income and expenditure accounting – provided a powerful new way of thinking about the economy and its management. The resulting 'new economics' put less emphasis than Keynes would have done on the roles of monetary policy and the control of public investment in the achievement of full employment, yet, along with a political determination to avoid the wastes of the interwar years, it led to widespread official commitments to post-war policies of high or full employment. By then, however, Keynes was less involved in such matters: the last years of his life saw him devoting much more of his efforts to shaping other aspects of the post-war world, most notably the international monetary order of the International Monetary Fund and the World Bank, and to securing Britain's post-war international economic position. Gaining these, or at least a semblance of them, finally exhausted him.

Donald Moggridge
University of Toronto

Reference

Robinson, E. A. G. (1947) 'John Maynard Keynes, 1883–1946', *Economic Journal* 57.

Further reading

Harrod, R. F. (1951) *The Life of John Maynard Keynes*, London.
Keynes, J. M. (1971–89) *The Collected Writings of John Maynard Keynes*, ed. E. Johnson and D. Moggridge, 30 vols, London and New York. (Those approaching Keynes's ideas for the first time are advised to look at vol. 9, *Essays in Persuasion*.)
Moggridge, D. E. (1993), *Keynes*, 3rd edn, Toronto.
Skidelsky, R. (1983) *John Maynard Keynes*, vol. 1, London.
—— (1992) *John Maynard Keynes*, vol. 2, London.

See also: Keynesian economics.

Keynesian economics

Keynesian economics comprises a body of theory and ways of thinking about the functioning of the aggregate (macro) economy that derives its inspiration from J. M. Keynes's *General Theory of Employment, Interest and Money* (1936), and from the work of Keynes's younger contemporaries such as Sir Roy Harrod, Lord Kaldor, Lord Kahn, Joan Robinson and Michał Kalecki, who extended Keynes's analysis to the growing economy and to the question of the functional distribution of income between wages and profits which Keynes himself had neglected.

There was no formal macroeconomics before Keynes. The prevailing orthodoxy was that economic systems tend to a full employment equilibrium through the operation of the price mechanism, with the distribution of income determined by the payment to factors of production according to their marginal productivity. Growth was assumed to be a smooth continuous process. The twin pillars of classical employment theory were that savings and investment were brought into equilibrium at full employment by the rate of interest, and that labour supply and demand were brought into equilibrium by variations in the real wage. Anyone wanting to work at the prevailing real wage could do so. Keynes's *General Theory* was written as a reaction to the classical orthodoxy. The debate is still very much alive. Keynesians take issue with pre-Keynesian modes of thought relating to such issues as: the tendency of economies to long-run full employment equilibrium; the functioning of aggregate labour markets; the distribution of income, and to other matters such as the relation between money and prices.

There are at least four major differences between Keynesian and pre-Keynesian economics.

First, in pre-Keynesian economics, investment is governed by decisions to save. Variations in the rate of interest always ensure that whatever saving takes place can be profitably invested. There is no independent investment function. By contrast, Keynesian economics emphasizes the primacy of the investment decision for understanding the level of employment and growth performance. Investment determines output which determines saving, through a multiple expansion of income (called the 'multiplier process') at less than full employment, and through changes in the distribution of income between wages and profits at full employment. It is capitalists, not savers, that take the investment decision, and they live in historical time with their present actions determined by past decisions and an uncertain future. By the changing 'animal spirits' of decision makers, capitalist economies are inherently unstable. Keynes brought to the fore the role of expectations in economic analysis, and emphasized their key role in understanding capitalist development.

Second, in pre-Keynesian theory there is a divorce between money and value theory. Money is a 'veil' affecting only the absolute price level, not the relative prices of goods and services in the economic system. There is no asset demand for money. Money is demanded for transactions only, and increases in the money supply affect only the price level. In Keynesian economics, money is demanded as an asset, and in the *General Theory* itself, the rate of interest is determined solely by the supply of and demand for money for speculative purposes, with the effect of money on prices depending on how interest rates affect spending relative to output. Keynesian economics attempts to integrate money and value theory. Keynesian inflation theory stresses the strong institutional forces raising the price level to which the supply of money adapts in a credit economy.

Third, in pre-Keynesian economics, the aggregate labour market is assumed to function like any micro-market, with labour supply and demand brought into equality by variations in the price of labour, the 'real wage'. Unemployment is voluntary due to a refusal of workers to accept a lower real wage. Keynes turned classical voluntary unemployment into involuntary unemployment by questioning whether it was ever possible for workers to determine their own real wage since they have no control over the price level. Unemployment is not necessarily voluntary, due to a refusal to accept real wage cuts, if by an expansion of demand both labour supply and demand at the current *money* wage would be higher than the existing level of employment. There are still many economists of a pre-Keynesian persuasion who believe that the major cause of unemployment is that the aggregate real wage is too high and that workers could price themselves into jobs by accepting cuts in money wages to reduce real wages without any increase in the demand for output as a whole.

Fourth, Keynesian economics rejects the idea that the functional distribution of income is determined by factors of production being rewarded according to the value of their marginal product derived from an aggregate production function. This assumes a constant return to scale production function, otherwise factor income would not equal total output. More serious, since capital goods are heterogeneous they can be aggregated only once the price, the rate of interest or profit, is known. Therefore the marginal product cannot be derived independently. Keynesian distribution theory (as pioneered by Kalecki and Kaldor) shows the dependence of profits on the investment decision of firms and the savings propensities attached to wages and profits. This insight can be found in Keynes's earlier work, *The Treatise on Money* (1930), the story of the widow's cruse.

One unfortunate aspect of Keynes's economics was that, for the most part, it assumed a closed economy. A Keynesian approach to the functioning of capitalist economies cannot ignore the balance of payments, or more precisely the export decision relative to the propensity to import. This is the notion of the Harrod trade multiplier revived by Kaldor and Thirlwall. Keynesian economics now embraces analysis of the functioning of the world economy, recognizing the mutual interaction between countries. What unites Keynesian economists, however, is the rejection of the facile belief that we live in a world in which the functioning of markets guarantees the *long-run* full employment of resources, and, even if we did, that it would have any relevance. As Keynes said in his *Tract on Monetary Reform* (1923), 'Economists set themselves too easy a task if in tempestuous seasons they can only tell us that when the storm is long past the ocean is flat again.'

A. P. Thirlwall
University of Kent

Further reading

Clarke, P. (1988) *The Keynesian Revolution in the Making 1924–1936*, Oxford.

Coddington, A. (1983) *Keynesian Economics: The Search for First Principles*, London.

Fletcher, G. A. (1989) *The Keynesian Revolution and its Critics*, London.

Leijonhufvud, A. (1968) *On Keynesian Economics and the Economics of Keynes*, Oxford.

Patinkin, D. and Clarke Leith, J. (1977) *Keynes, Cambridge and the General Theory*, London.

See also: classical economics; Keynes, John Maynard; money.

kinship

'Kinship is the central discipline of anthropology,' one expert remarked in the mid-1960s. 'It is to anthropology what the nude is to art' (Fox 1967: 10). This comment was true then, but kinship studies have since become rather unfashionable. The promise of a unified and general theory of kinship has not been realized; indeed the very definition of the field is in dispute, some scholars arguing that the project of a comparative science of kinship rests on the illusion that in all societies 'kinship' systems are ordered on similar principles.

From about 1860 to 1920, the pioneer anthropologists attempted to chart the evolution of kinship and the family. Their characteristic concern was with the way in which marriage and the family had developed from what was assumed to be the promiscuous sexuality of early human bands. The gradual disillusionment of anthropologists with these speculative reconstructions led to a second phase (from about 1920 to 1970) when the central project was the classification of types of kinship systems.

The basis for most typologies was the kinship terminology, the native-speaker's classification of kin. A widely agreed typology of kinship terminologies emerged in the early twentieth century. The types were all named after native North American peoples, but the assumption was that virtually all kinship terminologies in the world would fit into this classification. Drawing on cross-cultural statistical comparisons, researchers have attempted to relate these types of kinship terminologies to particular forms of descent or marriage rules (see Murdock 1949). Two general theoretical frameworks emerged. One emphasized descent and descent groups in the classification of kinship systems, the other gave pride of place to marriage arrangements.

These typologies were subjected to challenges. Since the mid-1970s, a cultural discourse on kinship has dominated the field, and it has deconstructed the notion that kinship is the universal basis of a social subsystem.

The family, descent and alliance

One of the generally accepted theses of the evolutionist writers in the nineteenth century was that in early communities the domestic unit and the band had been based on unilineal descent groups, descent being traced in the male line only (patrilineal) or in the female line only (matrilineal). The family had developed at a late stage of human history. By the early twentieth century this conclusion had been rejected, and it was agreed that the family was a universal feature of

human societies. According to Malinowski, the family was a domestic institution, relying on affection, concerned above all with the nurture of children. The descent corporation was a public, political institution, with a role in the affairs of the community and in the regulation of property rights. However, Malinowski argued that the family was in a sense prior to the lineage, and that the descent group built upon the sentiments of solidarity generated within the domestic family (see esp. Malinowski 1929).

Radcliffe-Brown argued that the wider kinship system was built upon the foundation of the family; but while the family was universally bilateral – ties being recognized to both mother and father – most societies favoured one side of the family for public purposes. The essential function of descent was to regulate the transmission of property and rights in people from generation to generation (see Kuper 1977).

Fortes (1969) developed the idea that the social sphere should be analysed into two domains, defined as the domestic domain – the world of the family and household – and the politico-jural, or public, domain. General, biologically derived principles regulated domestic relationships and the developmental cycle of the family (Goody 1958).

The students of Malinowski and Radcliffe-Brown took the central importance of the family for granted, and were more concerned to develop the theory that large corporate groups of kin, recruited by unilineal descent, were the basic public institutions in most primitive societies. Even the bands of native Australians constituted descent corporations. In more complex societies, these corporations regulated political and economic life (Fortes 1969).

'Descent theory' claimed that it had identified a widespread type of social system, based on unilineal descent groups, that everywhere exhibited similar structural features. It seemed to many that a type of society – one of great historical importance – had been defined. Indeed a great deal of effort went into classifying this type of society into subtypes, on the basis of particular descent arrangements.

The main challenge to descent theory in this period was provided by 'alliance theory', launched by Claude Lévi-Strauss in 1949 in perhaps the most influential single work on kinship published in the twentieth century: *Les Structures élémentaires de la parenté*. Lévi-Strauss's project was to provide an explanation that accounted at once for the incest taboo and for systems of preferential marriage with a specific category of kin. The key was the principle of reciprocity, expressed in the most basic social rule, the incest taboo. The incest taboo prevents men from mating with their own sisters and daughters, and so obliges them to exchange these for wives. The obverse of this rule was a positive marriage rule, found in many societies, enjoining marriage with a particular category of kin. Lévi-Strauss constructed a classification of social systems based on the ways in which they ordered the exchange of women in marriage.

The cultural critique

The most fundamental critique of the orthodox tradition of kinship was launched by David Schneider (1984). He began with the most basic issue, challenging the notion that kinship is a universal subsystem of societies. Beliefs about reproduction varied greatly. The mother–child bond might be universally recognized and valued, but the role of the father was highly variable. Anthropologists were accustomed to distinguish the genitor (the biological father) from the pater (the socially recognized father) but the notion of the genitor was culturally variable, and some peoples denied that reproduction was a result (primarily or even necessarily) of sexual intercourse. The social responsibilities of a man for his wife's children also varied greatly. In consequence, there could be no cross-cultural definition of 'father'.

Similarly, ideas about consanguinity were not simply minor variations on a common theme, that a certain category of people were genealogically related blood-kin. The category translated as 'kin' might be built upon a variety of beliefs about common substance, and might incorporate ideas of spiritual relationship, relationships arising from initiation, shared domicile, commensality, etc.

Genealogies, which were based on the presumption that blood relationships structured kinship systems, simply imposed western categories on other peoples. Kinship terminologies, which were based on a genealogical grid, were accordingly artefacts of the observer. So-called 'kin' terms actually often had non-kinship connotations, and there was not necessarily a discrete domain of terms for consanguineal relatives. In sum, our notion of kinship encoded particular beliefs about the biology of reproduction. Other peoples had different biological theories and would not necessarily construct a comparable category of consanguineal relatives.

Contemporary research on kinship

The cultural critique had the effect of undermining the traditional cluster of interests that defined kinship studies. Moreover, feminist scholars appropriated some of the classical topics of kinship studies, though contextualizing them very differently (see e.g. Collier and Yanagisako 1987; Strathern 1993). In consequence there has been a loss of interest and of confidence in classical kinship studies, but some traditional research programmes nevertheless persist. First, ethnographic studies continue to describe the use of kinship values and kinship institutions in the business of social life. Second, particularly in France, some anthropologists pursue the agenda of Lévi-Strauss, constructing models that draw out the logic of systems of kinship classification and relate them to marriage rules. Third, there are studies concerned with what might be termed Schneider's agenda: the variety of ways in which peoples conceptualize relationship, encoding quite different biological notions. These studies tend to be critical of any genealogically based comparative approach to kinship. Fourth, some scholars have attempted to make comparative studies of kinship systems within a cultural area, so escaping some of the problems involved in the cross-cultural definition of kinship.

A somewhat neglected field is the application of the methods of anthropological analysis to kinship in contemporary industrial societies. Sociologists have tended to concentrate on the family, although some anthropologists had drawn attention to the salience of broader kinship relationships in modern western societies (see, e.g. Firth et al. 1969). However, most anthropologists who worked in European societies tended to concentrate on kinship relationships in rural communities. Kinship theory has been applied in a more imaginative way by historians, and a new field, 'family history', draws on anthropological models.

Despite these developments, theoretical debate has been muted, the main problem being the challenge of the cultural relativists that there is no universal field of kinship. The critical strategy of the relativists is, however, suspect. They emphasize the exceptions, the picturesque variations in conceptions of biological relationship and the variety of forms of mating. However, it is evident that rather similar ideas about marriage, descent, family organization and kinship morality can be found in the great majority of human societies, including China, India, Indonesia, Europe, much of Africa and the Near East – in other words, in the societies in which over 90 per cent of people live. Even in isolated Amazonian and New Guinea societies, ethnographers seem to have little difficulty in identifying 'family', 'marriage' or 'kin'. Indeed, the resemblances between domestic institutions in societies all over the world are so remarkable that it is hard to understand why anthropologists should have lost sight of commonalities. One reason is, perhaps, the persistent desire to emphasize that biology does not determine cultural forms; but it would be absurd to take the extreme position that institutions concerned with marriage and filiation are biologically determined or, on the contrary, that they are free from biological constraints.

In conclusion, there is surely room for comparison and generalization, and for a renewal of the theoretical study of kinship. It is likely that social anthropologists will once again recognize the central importance of subjects that have gripped historians, philosophers, dramatists and novelists in every literate civilization in every generation.

Adam Kuper
Brunel University

References

Collier, J. and Yanagisako, S. (eds) (1987) *Gender and Kinship: Essays Toward a Unified Analysis*, Stanford, CA.

Firth, R., Hubert, J. and Forge, A. (1969) *Families and their Relatives*, London.

Fortes, M. (1969) *Kinship and the Social Order*, London.

Fox, R. (1967) *Kinship and Marriage*, Harmondsworth.

Goody, J. (ed.) (1958) *The Developmental Cycle of the Domestic Group*, Cambridge, UK.

Kuper, A. (ed.) (1977) *The Social Anthropology of Radcliffe-Brown*, London.

Lévi-Strauss, C. (1969) *The Elementary Structures of Kinship*, Boston, MA. (Original French edn 1949.)

Malinowski, B. (1929) *The Sexual Life of Savages*, London.

Murdock, G. P. (1949) *Social Structure*, New York.

Schneider, D. (1984) *A Critique of the Study of Kinship*, Ann Arbor, MI.

Strathern, M. (1993) *After Nature*, Cambridge, UK.

Further reading

Barnard, A. and Good, A. (1984) *Research Practices in the Study of Kinship*, London.

Kuper, A. (1988) *The Invention of Primitive Society*, London.

Leach, E. R. (1961) *Rethinking Anthropology*, London.

Schneider, D. (1980) *American Kinship: A Cultural Account*, 2nd edn, Chicago.

See also: family; family history; genealogies; house; marriage.

L

labelling theory

Labelling theory has made a key contribution to the analysis of deviance by turning away from the study of the presumed 'deviant' (like the criminal or the drug user) and focusing instead upon reactions towards deviance. While major proponents include Cohen (1970), Erickson (1966), Goffman (1961a, 1961b), Lemert (1967), Matza (1969), Scheff (1966) and Schur (1963), the publication of Becker's influential *Outsiders* in 1963 helped the theory achieve prominence. In this study, ostensibly of drugs, Becker provides the canonical statement:

> deviance is *not* a quality of the act the person commits, but rather a consequence of the application by others of rules and sanctions to an 'offender'. The deviant is one to whom that label has successfuly been applied; deviant behaviour is behaviour that people so label.

In the critical and counter-cultural days of the mid-1960s, labelling theory was seen as the harbinger of radical new approaches. It focused upon the power of groups to define deviance. It championed the rights of groups designated deviant. It often celebrated the lifestyles of 'deviants' who had been inhumanely labelled. And it led to arguments for decriminalization, decarceration, destigmatization, deprofessionalization and demedicalization. Associated with the Society for the Study of Social Problems in the USA, it led to the growth of the National Deviancy Conference in Britain (Taylor and Taylor 1973).

In its most explicit form, labelling theory suggested that societal reactions, far from merely being responses to deviance, may often be causal in producing deviants. As Lemert (1967), another founder argued, the idea that 'social control leads to deviance' is a 'potentially richer premise for studying deviance'. An earlier formulation of this position by Tannenbaum (1938) suggested that the very 'process of making the criminal

is a process of tagging, defining, identifying, segregating, describing, emphasising, making conscious and self conscious; it becomes a way of stimulating, suggesting, emphasising, evoking the very traits that are complained of'.

In a more general form labelling theory argued for a reconceptualization of the entire field of deviance enquiry; instead of assuming definitions of deviance as objectively given and focusing thereafter on explaining the deviant, this approach recommended looking at deviance as subjectively problematic, relativistic and changing. In this general form, labelling theory suggests four key questions.

The first examines the nature of the societal reaction, problematizing the very categories associated with deviance. This means looking, for instance, at the labels used by various social control agents – such as the police or the courts – in recognizing and defining 'deviants'. It leads to research on the perceptions held of 'delinquents' by court officals (Emerson 1969), stereotypes of mentally ill people held by pyschiatrists (Scheff 1966) or the role of the media in depicting social problems (Cohen and Young 1975). The focus hence is shifted from deviant being to deviant construct and stereotyping is a major concern.

A second question is causal, asking why certain groups get stigmatized, criminalized or defined as sick. Usually, this involves historical questions – asking about the ways in which legislation came into being to define marijuana as criminal, the ways in which the category of 'the homosexual' was invented in the nineteenth century, or how notions of 'madness' entered civilization. Research also asks how groups and organizations come to create their own categories of deviance – in courtroooms, in the mass media, in classrooms or at home.

A third question examines the conditions by which deviants are selected for processing – the 'screening' process. Not only are the decisions of formal control agents examined (e.g. how police apprehend delinquents), but so too is the role of more informal definers, such as those of the family or friends who may protect or reject 'deviants' (Goffman 1961b).

A final and perhaps most common question concerns the impact of sanctions and labels on deviants. Sanctions could, for instance, deter crime; but labelling theorists usually argue that labelling may well exacerbate, amplify or even cause crime and deviance. Labelling may initiate deviant careers, generate deviant subcultures, and sometimes the overreach of the criminal law into areas of victimless crimes may create more problems than solved (Schur 1963). Finally, it is also concerned with the wider impact of labelling on the culture – the creation of a moral order, boundaries, and the good.

Despite its enormous popularity and influence, labelling theory has been heavily criticized (Taylor *et al.* 1973). It neglects a concern with the causes of deviance. It is too social psychological – neglecting wider concerns of power, structure and history – being too individualistic, subjective and relativistic. It is vague and lacks an objective foundation. From the left, it is accused of being insufficiently critical of the state; from the right it is seen as 'too soft' on criminals, too willing to side with the underdog, and too subversive. These critiques are generally unfounded and are answered in Plummer (1979). Despite many new developments in the study of deviance, labelling theory has remained prominent and influential, often under newer names such as 'social constructionism'. Indeed, and ironically – given its radical roots – it may have become something of a new orthodoxy in North America (Schur 1971).

Ken Plummer
University of Essex

References

Becker, H. S. (1963) *Outsiders: Studies in the Sociology of Deviance*, New York.
Cohen, S. (1970) *Folk Devils and Moral Panics*, London.
Cohen, S. and Young, J. (1975) *The Manufacture of News*, London.
Emerson, R. (1969) *Judging Delinquents*, Chicago.
Erickson, K. T. (1966) *Wayward Puritans*, London.
Goffman, E. (1961a) *Stigma*, Harmondsworth.
—— (1961b) *Asylums*, Harmondsworth.
Lemert, E. (1967) *Human Deviance, Social Problems and Social Control*, Englewood Cliffs, NJ.
Matza, D. (1969) *Becoming Deviant*, Englewood Cliffs, NJ.
Plummer, K. (1979) 'Misunderstanding labelling perspectives', in D. Downes and P. Rock (eds) *Deviant Interpretations*, Oxford.
Scheff, T. J. (1966) *Being Mentally Ill*, London.
Schur, E. (1963) *Crimes without Victims*, Englewood Cliffs, NJ.
—— (1971) *Labelling Deviant Behaviour*, Englewood Cliffs, NJ.
Tannenbaum, F. (1938) *Crime and the Community*, Cincinnati, OH.
Taylor, I. and Taylor, L. (1973) *Politics and Deviance*, Harmondsworth.
Taylor, I., Walton, P. and Young, J. (1973) *The New Criminology*, London.

See also: deviance; prejudice; stereotypes; stigma.

labour market analysis

Since before Adam Smith, labour markets have been known to differ greatly from other markets. Workers cannot be separated from the services they provide, and their motivation and beliefs critically affect how they work. Labour is not exchanged on a labour market: instead, people contract to supply labour in a form to be specified in detail (and within certain limits) only after they have been hired. The employment relation is often of considerable duration. In 1991, the percentage of workers with their current firms for ten years or more was UK, 29 per cent; US, 27 per cent; Germany, 41 per cent; and Japan, 43 per cent (OECD 1993). As many workers change firms only occasionally, it is clear that many employment problems are the result of a complex mix of market and organizational causes. Which of these we believe is the predominant cause will condition whether we start from price theory, stressing the analogy with other markets, as would most neo-classical economists, or from a more organizational or institutional approach. To explore the differences between these I shall look at labour allocation and work incentives.

The majority, 'neo-classical', tradition emphasizes competition and flexible prices, believing that these will, in the long run, provide the best overall outcomes for the greatest number. Because firms compete for workers, those with dangerous or unpleasant working conditions have to pay more to attract them. If they need workers with particular skills, then by offering higher wages, they provide an incentive for people to undertake the necessary training. The price mechanism works better than government educational planning based on surveys of skill needs because it forces firms to say not only what skills they would like, but also how much they would be worth to them. In the context of unemployment, with flexible wages and no restrictions on laying workers off, firms would hire extra labour until workers no longer thought the wages offered worthwhile.

Faced with bad working conditions, skill shortages or unemployment, neo-classical economists would generally look first for failures of, or obstacles to, the price mechanism. Is it better to seek to improve dangerous or unhealthy working conditions by means of government regulation which is costly to run and is often easily evaded, or to rely on the price mechanism? The latter means that employers have to pay more to attract workers, and so have a financial incentive to invest in technology to improve conditions. If accident rates remain high, is it because employers enjoy monopsonistic power in their local labour markets, or because of some perversity in the price mechanism? For example, employers may fear that if they are the first to invest in safer equipment they will attract the most accident-prone workers (Elliot 1991).

If an industry faces persistent problems of skill shortages, are the incentives for people to train right? Do the rewards for skilled jobs adequately compensate for the outlays involved? Are employers failing to get any return on training they provide because workers are leaving once their training is complete? If the skills are transferable, should the trainees bear most of the cost, perhaps as low trainee allowances? In the case of unemployment among low-skilled workers, are minimum wage laws or collective agreements setting pay levels which make it uneconomic to employ them – 'pricing them out of jobs'?

Treating wages as if they were market prices, and labour as a freely traded commodity, arguably comes closest to reality when looking at the markets for casual labour, where job durations are typically rather short, and for craft and professional occupations where skills are transferable between firms.

However, the clear analytical prescriptions of the theory become clouded when looking at relations within the enterprise, and when looking at the institutions which characterize modern labour markets such as trade unions and training organizations. A great number of job changes occur within firms, through promotions and job reassignments, as indeed do inter-regional job moves (about 40 per cent of such moves in the UK in the late 1980s). It has been common to contrast the allocation of labour between firms, on 'external' or 'local' labour markets, with that within the firm, on 'internal' labour markets (ILMs). Whereas the former involves movement between firms, or between unemployment and jobs, the latter involves movement between jobs or employment locations within firms.

Whether wages act in the same way on ILMs as they are reputed to do on local labour markets is hotly debated (e.g. Rosenberg 1989). Some argue that the force of competition among workers is weak compared with inter-group power relations, and once workers have been hired, management's primary task is to organize and motivate staff, not negotiate market prices.

The reasons that firms develop ILMs, and hence their overall significance for economic theory, are also under debate. Building on price theory, the neo-classical approach seeks to explain ILMs as a response to certain kinds of failure in the market system. For example, ILMs may develop in firms where the necessary skills are lacking on their local labour markets; or firms may develop ILMs to encourage workers to take a long-term interest in their firm's success. In the first case, many firms have their own unique production methods, or a particular style of service, and then develop their own training programmes linking these to job progression, thus creating an ILM (Doeringer and Piore 1971). In the second case, because workers have much better knowledge of their work and the production process than management, they have a strong incentive to manipulate information in order to negotiate a more favourable effort-bargain, but which reduces productivity. By creating an ILM, the employer gives workers a long-term stake in their firm's success so that they will wish to raise productivity (Williamson 1975). In both explanations, the ILM remains nested within the general framework of price theory.

An alternative, 'institutionalist' view of ILMs treats them as the normal pattern for firms to adopt unless there already exists a structure of occupational markets for qualified labour (OLMs). Inter-firm markets for labour with transferable skills are in fact like public goods and so depend upon a high degree of co-operation among employers to control 'free-rider' behaviour. Without this support, they are inherently unstable (Marsden 1986). Although in theory the trainee should bear the cost of wholly transferable training (Becker 1975), there are strong theoretical and practical reasons why employers commonly bear much of the cost.

The 'cost-sharing' mechanisms predicted by Becker tend to break down for a number of reasons. Relying on low trainee pay rates limits investments in transferable skills to what working-class families can afford to subsidize. Adult skilled workers may be leery of low trainee rates, fearing that trainees could be exploited as a form of cheap, substitute labour, and therefore either seek to restrict numbers, or to raise trainee pay rates. Employers may not be able to enforce apprenticeship contracts and recoup their training costs – the cause of its decline in the USA.

Hence, employers have an incentive to cut their own training expenditures and to 'poach' skilled labour from their competitors. This increases the costs for employers who continue to train, and thus further encourages poaching. Out of the resulting vicious circle the OLM atrophies and breaks up, and firms resort to ILM practices in order to be sure to capture the returns on their investment in skill formation.

Yet despite these problems, we observe a certain number of large OLMs for occupational skills in Germany, in parts of UK industry, and in many countries in the artisan sector. Their survival has depended largely upon a strong institutional infrastructure capable of controlling free-rider activities by employers, and of reassuring skilled workers that cost-sharing would not lead to their being substituted by cheap apprentice labour. In Germany, the local chambers of industry and commerce, of which all local employers have to be members, provide powerful channels for peer group pressures against free-riding, and strong supervisory powers exercised by the works councils, supported by the unions, have ensured that apprentices get their full training. In the absence of such structures, firms will generally adopt ILM strategies.

Thus to contrast the two approaches on labour allocation, neo-classical economists generally look for blockages in the price mechanism as potential causes of many of the serious labour market problems, and commonly identify institutional factors as one of the prime culprits. The institutionalist approach treats the institutional framework as a precondition for an effective price mechanism. Thus, in the case of skills training, the former stresses the need for low trainee rates of pay and high rewards for skilled workers, whereas the latter stresses the need to create the institutional structures under which adult workers will accept the cost-sharing solution, and employers will refrain from poaching (Marsden and Ryan 1990)

Turning to incentives within the firm, a revolution has taken place in economic thinking on wages. Neo-classical theorists have abandoned the idea that the market sets a single rate of pay for a given job as irrelevant to many jobs. Instead, they have argued that workers are attracted to jobs by the whole package of benefits on offer, be they short-term employment at a fixed wage or the prospect of career employment and salary progression. Employers adopt one or other model depending on the kind of worker they wish to recruit. Thus fast-food firms might have relatively simple incentive structures with a rate for the job, whereas retail banks might offer complex structures with career jobs, age or performance incremental pay scales, and so on, depending on the kind of recruit they want.

The kind of performance that employers require from their staff has also been examined (Akerlof and Yellen 1986). In many types of job, sub-standard performance by the employee does not become apparent for some time. By providing career employment, the employer has time to monitor performance, and to sanction good or bad results. Employees might be encouraged to stay by taking a starting salary below the value of their output in the expectation that, later in their career, they would be paid in excess of it. By offering such profiles, employers can attract employees who are looking for a long-term job. In addition, the penalty of dismissal for poor performance increases with seniority (since alternative jobs would pay them only the value of their output) so the incentive to work well increases. Some other theories look at how different kinds of salary and promotion systems encourage good rather than perfunctory performance. Competition for promotion can be organized as a 'tournament' to ensure high performance, thus top salaries may reflect less the value of the work done by top managers than that of those competing for the top jobs. Another theory looks at pay as involving a 'partial gift exchange' and reciprocity whereby employers offer better than average career conditions to their staff, and, in return, employees feel that they should reciprocate by giving better performance (Akerlof and Yellen 1986).

These theories rely mainly upon individual performance and individual incentives, and there is minimal reference to supporting institutional structures. An alternative approach is to look at collective incentives: at what is needed in order to promote co-operative exchange within the workplace. It can be argued that co-operative exchange leads to high productivity because it encourages flexible working and information sharing. Such practices are hard to obtain in many organizations because they affect small group power relations (Brown 1973). Since co-operation usually involves one party placing itself in a weak position *vis-à-vis* others (for example, by sharing information it controls) it exposes itself to exploitation. Therefore, parties will not normally adopt a co-operative stance unless they are confident the others will do likewise. The rise of 'lean production' and the increasing awareness of the greater job flexibility to be found in German and Japanese workplaces, as compared with the job demarcation rules common in Britain or the seniority rules common in the USA, have brought these issues to centre stage (Womack *et al.* 1990).

Game theory stresses the difficulty of obtaining stable co-operative exchange unless there is some kind of trust, and thus some kind of framework to support it (Dasgupta 1988). Two important conditions should be met: the parties need to know something about the motivations and intentions of the others, and they need some framework of guarantees to give them redress, and to enable them to exchange information so that genuine cases when *force majeure* prevents reciprocity can be distinguished from simple opportunism. Concrete examples of such frameworks can be found in the current practice of German co-determination, and in the relations between large Japanese firms, enterprise unions and their federations (Aoki 1988).

As for policy, the individualistic approach normally stresses the value of greater inequalities to reward higher levels of individual performance. Against this, if performance depends on co-operative team working, it could be argued that pay inequalities should be smaller. Since responsibility and decision making are shared in team working, there is less reason to focus incentives on key individuals. Strong individual incentives may be incompatible with co-operative exchange because they encourage people to conceal information which enables them to perform better than their colleagues.

Whatever the outcome of this debate, the idea of there being a single entity called the 'labour market', and that it sets prices for single units of work, is clearly too simplistic. There are many different kinds of employment relations. At the low paid–low skill end of the market, something approximating casual labour markets with short-term employment and competitive wage rates tied to individual jobs may exist. In the middle, where qualified blue and white collar skills are used, jobs tend to be fairly long term, and management are more concerned about motivation and efficient deployment of staff within their organizations than with the haggling of the market-place. Collective bargaining remains influential in many countries, and acts as a powerful force for shaping pay structures according to workers' views of fairness. Among management and higher professionals, collective bargaining is much weaker, and many workers have their own individual reputations which often have a market value. The policy problems raised by each of these are different, and, in the field of incentives, are potentially contradictory.

David Marsden
London School of Economics and Political Science

References

Akerlof, G. and Yellen, J. (eds) (1986) *Efficiency Wage Models of the Labour Market*, Cambridge, UK.

Aoki, M. (1988) *Information, Incentives, and Bargaining in the Japanese Economy*, Cambridge, UK.

Becker, G. S. (1975) *Human Capital: A Theoretical and Empirical Analysis, with Special Reference to Education*, Chicago.

Brown, W. E. (1973) *Piecework Bargaining*, London.

Dasgupta, P. (1988) 'Trust as a commodity', in D. Gambetta (ed.) *Trust: Making and Breaking Cooperative Relations*, Oxford.

Doeringer, P. B., and Piore, M. J. (1971) *International Labor Markets and Manpower Analysis*, Lexington, MA.

Elliott, R. F. (1991) *Labor Economics: A Comparative Text*, New York.

Marsden, D. W. (1986) *The End of Economic Man? Custom and Competition in Labour Markets*, Brighton.

Marsden, D. W. and Ryan, P. (1990) 'Institutional aspects of youth employment and training policy in Britain', *British Journal of Industrial Relations* 28(3).

OECD (1993) *Employment Outlook 1993*, Paris.

Rosenberg, S. (ed.) (1989) *The State and the Labor Market*, New York.

Williamson, O. E. (1975) *Markets and Hierarchies: Analysis and Antitrust Implications*, New York.

Womack, J., Jones, D. T. and Roos, D. (1990) *The Machine that Changed the World*, New York.

See also: employment and unemployment; factors of production; labour migration; matching; supply-side economics.

labour migration

All migration involves the reallocation of – actual or potential – labour, except in the case of retirees. The notion of labour migration focuses on the motivation of migrants. Labour migration may then be defined as migration prompted by the migrant's intent to relocate to a more or less distant labour market. Where labour is allocated through a labour market, most migration is prompted by the decisions of households and individuals to move in search of better work opportunities.

Labour migration reflects the spatial distribution and redistribution of economic opportunities among regions and nations. The decision to migrate is based on a comparison between the point of departure and possible destinations. Education and training, patronage, and gender are key variables affecting opportunities in different labour markets. Age, kinship support, and access to resources, especially control over land, are additional factors determining the costs and benefits of migration.

The Industrial Revolution attracted workers from agriculture in such numbers as to ensure the growth of cities at a time when urban mortality was high and urban natural population growth negative. Eventually, the countryside was depleted. In most industrialized countries, labour migration has been largely interurban for some time.

In less developed countries today, most labour migration still originates in rural areas – it is either intra-rural or rural–urban. Combined with rapid natural population growth, it feeds urban growth at a pace without precedent in human history. In most cities of the South, government administration, commerce, workshop production and repairs, and domestic work – rather than industry – dominate the labour market. Lipton's *Why Poor People Stay Poor* (1977) prompted considerable debate as to the extent to which public policy in less developed countries is guided by an urban bias which concentrates resources on the urban sector and hence exaggerates its attraction for migrants.

Distinct gender patterns characterize rural–urban migration in different countries. Men dominate among migrants in South Asia and in many Middle Eastern and African countries, but in Latin America, the Philippines, and Thailand women dominate. Many of these women come to town to work, at least initially, as domestics. Gender selectivity in rural–urban migration is reflected in urban sex ratios: women outnumber men in the urban population of every Latin American country, whereas men outnumber women by a substantial margin in the cities of every country in South Asia. An explanation for such distinct patterns may be found in cultural definitions of gender roles that affect both the mobility of women and their economic opportunities in different settings (Gilbert and Gugler 1992: 74–79).

In many less developed countries a good deal of labour migration is temporary. In South Africa (Hindson, 1987) and China (Blecher, 1988), government policies used to be expressly designed to bar labour migrants from moving permanently. In Indonesia, daily or weekly commuting from rural areas to urban jobs has become an increasingly common pattern (Hugo, 1995). Single men from the Deccan have come to work in Bombay on a temporary basis for over a century (Dandekar, 1996). In southeastern Nigeria, a pattern of temporary family migration has continued for a generation (Gugler, 1991). Some of these migration strategies are designed to reduce the living expenses of dependents and to maintain a source of rural income, all aim at ensuring a measure of security for labour migrants who as a rule can expect little social security in the city.

Some labour migration crossses international borders. The extreme disparities in standards of living between rich and poor countries beckon potential labour migrants. However, affluent countries have increasingly tightened restrictions on this potentially vast movement. They have succeeded to the extent that, compared to internal labour migration, the volume of international labour migration is quite insignificant.

International labour migration, as well as labour migration within regionally divided countries, brings together groups of different origins. They often affirm separate identities in the competition over jobs and housing and articulate political conflict in ethnic terms.

Josef Gugler
University of Connecticut

References

Blecher, M. (1988) 'Rural contract labour in urban Chinese industry: migration control, urban–rural balance, and class relations', J. Gugler (ed.) *The Urbanization of the Third World*, Oxford.

Dandekar, H. (1996) 'Changing migration strategies in Deccan Maharashtra, India, 1885–1990', J. Gugler (ed.) *Cities in Asia, Africa and Latin America: Multiple Perspectives*, Oxford.

Gilbert, A. and Gugler, J. (1992 [1982]) *Cities, Poverty and Development: Urbanization in the Third World*, 2nd rev. edn, Oxford.

Gugler, J. (1991) 'Life in a dual system revisited: urban–rural ties in Enugu, Nigeria, 1961–1987', *World Development* 19.

Hindson, D. (1987) *Pass Controls and the Urban African Proletariat in South Africa*, Johannesburg.

Hugo, G. (1995) 'Urbanization in Indonesia: city and countryside linked', J. Gugler (ed.) *The Urban Transformation of the Developing World: Regional Trajectories*, Oxford.

Lipton, M. (1977) *Why Poor People Stay Poor: Urban Bias in World Development*, London.

Further reading

Castles, S. and Miller, M. J. (1993) *The Age of Migration: International Population Movements in the Modern World*, Basingstoke.

Johnson, J. H. and Salt J. (eds.) (1990) *Labour Migration: The Internal Geographical Mobility of Labour in the Developed World*, London.

Kritz, M. M., Lim, L. L. and Zlotnik, H. (eds) (1992) *International Migration Systems: A Global Approach*, Oxford.

Sassen, S. (1988) *The Mobility of Labour and Capital*, Cambridge.

Stark, O. (1990) *The Migration of Labour*, Oxford.

United Nations (1993) *Internal Migration of Women in Developing Countries: Proceedings of the United Nations Expert Meeting on the Feminization of Internal Migration, Aguascalientes, Mexico, 22–25 October 1991*, New York.

See also: ethnicity; migration; urbanization.

labour relations *see* industrial relations; trade unions

landscape

Landscape in conventional usage is a spatial concept, denoting an area of land whose coherence sets it apart from surrounding territory. Its medieval origins as a legal term in Germanic language relate to the collective ownership and use of an area (for example, the cultivated lands of a parish or other community). Its parallels in the Romance languages (*pays, paesaggio, paisaje*) have a similar derivation. The suffix *scape* relates to the verb *shape*, implying intentional human organization and design of space. Since the sixteenth century, however, landscape and its parallels in other European languages have taken on a strongly visual dimension, largely from their use in painting, the coherence and design of a landscape now deriving from its framing and composition. From being a term of art, landscape evolved to denote actual scenery, spaces which either have the qualities of a painting, or which are viewed in a painterly way. Landscape gardening, which extended the aesthetic qualities of the garden beyond its traditional enclosure, played a role in this semiotic transformation. The meaning of landscape has been further extended, to refer to any area, aesthetically pleasing or otherwise. But it retains both strong visual reference and close connection to cultivated land, rather than urbanized or maritime spaces, to which the derivative terms townscape and seascape are applied. 'Wilderness' may be referred to as landscape when its visual qualities are being emphasized.

Among the social sciences, geography has paid greatest attention to landscape. Drawing on German geographical precedents, Carl Sauer and his students at Berkeley used it as an important concept in studies of human transformation of the natural world and its characteristic cultural expressions in particular regions (Leighly 1963). The cultural landscape was an empirical datum for assessing the changes wrought by material human culture on a pre-existing natural landscape, through such activities as cultivation, domestication, land drainage and forest clearance (Thomas 1956). Study of landscape as an expression of culture was extended to more contemporary and vernacular scenes by J. B. Jackson, founder of the journal *Landscape*, whose writings sought to explore changing American popular culture through such elements as the highway strip, the front yard and the shopping mall (Jackson 1984; Meinig 1979).

Since the mid-1980s increased academic emphasis has been placed on the cultural politics of landscape, with the recognition that the idea of landscape represents a way of seeing and representing area with close historical and conceptual connections to actual control and authority over space (Bender 1994; Cosgrove and Daniels 1988). The connections between landscape, mapping and property ownership have been explored (Cosgrove 1984), as have the roles of landscape representations in constructing, sustaining and contesting the identities of communities and places at different scales. Iconic landscapes such as Niagara Falls (McKinsey 1985), Constable's Suffolk (Daniels 1992), or the Danish heathlands (Olwig 1984) play a significant role in the construction of national identity. Construction and reproduction of such landscapes is as much an aspect of cultural imagination as of the material world, although studies of such landscapes have developed partly in response to a growing demand for environmental and heritage conservation and for marketing the past, all of which have brought landscape more centrally into the field of social policy and planning. As a concept which mediates nature and culture, landscape is of growing theoretical significance in an environmentally conscious age.

Denis Cosgrove
University of London

References

Bender, B. (ed.) (1994) *Landscape: Politics and perspectives*, London.

Cosgrove, D. (1984) *Social Formation and Symbolic Landscape*, London.

Cosgrove, D. and Daniels, S. J. (1988) *The Iconography of Landscape*, Cambridge, UK.

Daniels, S. J. (1992) *Fields of Vision: Landscape and National Identity in England and the United States*, London.

Jackson, J. B. (1984) *Discovering the Vernacular Landscape*, New Haven, CT.

Leighly, J. (1963) *Land and Life: Selections from the Writings of Carl Ortwin Sauer*, Berkeley, CA.

McKinsey, E. (1985) *Niagara Falls: Icon of the American Sublime*, Cambridge, UK.

Meinig, D. (1979) *The Interpretation of Ordinary Landscapes*, Oxford.

Olwig, K. (1984) *Nature's Ideological Landscape*, London.

Thomas, W. L. (1956) *Man's Role in Changing the Face of the Earth*, Chicago.

See also: cartography; cultural geography; environment; nature; space.

language

Language is the most human of all human abilities. It may be the defining characteristic of *Homo sapiens*. Wherever humans exist, language exists. Although no one knows the precise number of languages in the world, there are at least 3,000 and as many as 8,000 according to different estimates and depending on one's definition of language and dialect. Considering that the world is populated by billions of people, the number is actually rather small. One-half of the world's population (approximately 2,100 million) speak only fifteen of these thousands of languages. Of these, more than half of the world's population speak Mandarin Chinese than any other language (about 387 million). There are just a few speakers of languages like Apache, an Athabaskan language, or Menomini, an Algonquian language. These languages seem very different from each other and from Zulu, Lapp, Hebrew, Uzbek or English. Yet, despite these surface differences, all human languages are governed by universal properties and constraints, a fact that was understood as early as the thirteenth century by Roger Bacon, who pointed out that 'He that understands grammar in one language, understands it in another as far as the essential properties of grammar are concerned.' The similarities of human languages go beyond the spoken languages and include the sign languages used by deaf persons throughout the world. Research on these sign languages show that although gestures instead of sounds are utilized, and the visual perceptual system instead of the auditory system for comprehension, their systems of units, structures and rules are governed by the same underlying principles as are spoken languages.

All human languages are equally complex and equally capable of expression. There are no so-called primitive languages. If one can say something in one language, the same thought can be expressed in another although the form of expression may differ. The vocabulary, that is, the inventory of sound (or gesture)/meaning units of every language, can be expanded to include new words or concepts through borrowing words from another language, through combining words to form compounds such as *bittersweet* or *pickpocket*, through blending words together, such as *smog* from *smoke* and *fog*, through neologisms or the coining of new words, a common practice of manufacturers of new products, by the use of acronyms – words derived from the initials of several words such as *radar* from *Radio Detecting And Ranging*. Abbreviations of longer words or phrases may also become lexicalized, as exemplified by *ad* for *advertisement*, and proper names may be used as common terms, such as *sandwich*, named from the fourth Earl of Sandwich in England who, it is reported, ate his food between slices of bread so that he need not take time off from gambling to eat in normal fashion. Although these examples are all from English, all languages can expand vocabularies in similar fashion, as is shown by compounds such as *cure-dent* (toothpick) in French, *Panzerkraftwagen* (armoured car) in German or *četyrexetažnyi* (four-storeyed) in Russian. In Akan, a major language spoken in Ghana, the word meaning 'son' or 'child' – *ɔha* – is combined with *ɔhene*, which means 'chief', to form the compound *ɔheneba* meaning 'prince'.

One common or universal characteristic of all languages is that the form of vocabulary items is for the most part arbitrarily related to its referent or meaning. Thus, the word meaning 'house' in English is *house*, in French is *maison*, in Spanish is *casa*, in Russian is *dom* and in Akan is *ɔdaŋ*.

All human languages utilize a finite set of discrete sounds (or gestures) like 'c', 'm', 'a' and 't' which can be defined by a finite set of phonetic (or gestural) properties or features. The vowel and consonant sound segments combine to form meaningful units like *cat* or *mat* called *morphemes*. Some words consist of just one morpheme; others are complex morphological units, that is, simple morphemes can be combined to form words like *cats* or *catlike*. Each language has specific constraints on word formation. In English one can add *un-* as a prefix to negate the meaning of a word, as in *unlikely* or *unfortunate*, but cannot add it at the end as a suffix; *likelyun* and *fortunateun* are not words in English, nor are the units formed by prefixing the suffixes *-ly* or *-ate* as in *lylike* or *atefortune*.

Just as in word formation, there are constraints or rules which determine how words can be combined to form sentences. *The cat is on the mat* means something different from *The mat is on the cat* and *cat the on is mat the* means nothing because the words are not combined according to the syntactic rules of English.

The syntactic rules in every language are similar kinds of rules although they may differ in specific constraints. Thus, in English, adjectives usually precede the nouns they modify (as in *the red house*) whereas in French they usually follow (as in *la maison rouge*). But in all languages these rules of syntax include a principle of recursion which permits the generation of an infinite set of sentences. We know that this is so since any speaker of any language can produce and understand sentences never spoken or heard previously. This recursive aspect is also revealed by the fact that, in principle, there is no longest sentence in any language; one can keep adding additional words or phrases or conjoin sentences with words like *and* or *but* or relative clauses, such as *The cat is on the mat and the mat is on the floor*, or *The cat is on the mat that is on the floor*, or *The cat is on the mat and the mat is on the floor and the floor is made of wood which comes from the forest in the north of the country near the border*.

Speakers of a language know these rules; the system of knowledge which underlies the ability to speak and understand the infinite set of sentences constitutes the *mental grammar* of a language which is acquired by a child and is accessed and used in speaking and understanding. This linguistic knowledge is not identical to the processes used in speaking and understanding. In actual linguistic performance, however, we must access this mental grammar as well as other non-linguistic systems (motor, perceptual, cognitive) in order to speak and understand. This difference between the knowledge of language (the grammar) and linguistic performance accounts for why in principle there is no longest sentence and language is infinite, whereas in performance each sentence is finite and the total number of sentences produced and understood in any one lifetime is finite.

The universality of language and of the grammars which underlie all languages suggests that the human brain is uniquely suited for the acquisition and use of language. This view is receiving increasing support from research on child language acquisition.

Further support for the view that the human brain is a language-learning organ is provided by neurological studies of language disorders such as aphasia. No one now questions the position put forth by Paul Broca in 1861 that language is specifically related to the left hemisphere. Furthermore, there is converging evidence that focal damage to the left cerebral hemisphere does not lead to an across-the-board reduction in language ability, and that lesions in different locations in the left brain are quite selective and remarkably consistent in the manner in which they undermine language. This selectivity reflects the different parts of the grammar discussed above; access to and processing of the phonology (sound system), the lexicon (inventory of morphemes and words), the syntax (rules of sentence formation), and the semantics (rules for the interpretation of meanings) can all be selectively impaired. There is also strong evidence showing that the language faculty is independent of other mental and cognitive faculties. That is, language not only appears to be unique to the human species but also does not appear to be dependent on general intelligence. Severely retarded individuals can learn language; persons with brain lesions may lose language abilities and retain other cognitive abilities.

Victoria A. Fromkin
University of California

Further reading

Akmajian, A., Demers, R., Harnish, M. and Farmer, A. (1990) *Linguistics: An Introduction to Language and Communication*, 3rd edn, Cambridge, MA.

Chomsky, N. (1986) *Knowledge of Language: Its Nature, Origin, and Use*, New York.

—— (1988) *Language and Problems of Knowledge: The Managua Lectures*, Cambridge, MA.

Fromkin, V. and Rodman, R. (1993) *An Introduction to Language*, 5th edn, New York.

Jackendoff, R. (1994) *Patterns in the Mind: Language and Human Nature*, New York.

Klima, E. and Bellugi, U. (1979) *The Signs of Language*, Cambridge, MA.

Newmeyer, F. J. (1988) *Linguistics: The Cambridge Survey*, 4 vols, Cambridge, UK.

O'Grady, W., Dobrovolsky, M. and Atonoll, M. (1991) *Contemporary Linguistics: An Introduction*, New York.

Pinker, S. (1994) *The Language Instinct: How the Mind Creates Language*, New York.

See also: first language acquisition; language and culture; linguistics.

language acquisition *see* first language acquisition

language and culture

There are three major ways in which language is related to culture: language itself is a *part* of culture; every language provides an *index* of the culture with which it is most intimately associated; every language becomes *symbolic* of the culture with which it is most intimately associated.

Language as a part of culture

Most human behaviours are language-embedded, thus language is an inevitable part of culture. Ceremonies, rituals, songs, stories, spells, curses, prayers and laws (not to mention conversations, requests and instructions) are all speech acts or speech events. But such complex cultural arenas as socialization, education, barter and negotiation are also entirely awash in language. Language is, therefore, not only part of culture but also a major and crucial part. All those who

seek fully to enter into and understand a given culture must, accordingly, master its language, for only through that language can they possibly participate in and experience the culture. Language shift, or loss of a culture's intimately associated language, is indicative of extensive culture change, at the very least, and possibly of cultural dislocation and destruction, although a *sense* of cultural identity may, nevertheless, persist, as a conscious or unconscious attitudinal level.

Language as an index of culture

The role of language as an index of culture is a by-product (at a more abstract level) of its role as part of culture. Languages reveal the ways of thinking or of organizing experience that are common in the associated cultures. Of course, languages provide lexical terms for the bulk of the artefacts, concerns, values and behaviours recognized by their associated cultures. Above and beyond such obvious indexing, languages also reveal the native clusters or typologies into which the above referents are commonly categorized or grouped. Colours, illnesses, kinship relationships, foods, plants, body parts and animal species are all culture-bound typologies and their culturally recognized systematic qualities are revealed by their associated culture-bound languages. This is not to say that speakers of particular languages are inescapably forced to recognize only the categories encoded in their mother tongues. Such restrictions can be counteracted, at least in part, via cross-cultural and cross-linguistic experience, including exposure to mathematical and scientific languages which provide different categories from those encountered in ethnocultures and their associated mother tongues.

Language as symbolic of culture

Language is the most elaborate symbol system of humankind: it is no wonder that particular languages become symbolic of the particular ethnocultures in which they are embedded and which they index. This is not only a case of a *part* standing for the whole (as when Yiddish stereotypically stands for or evokes eastern European derived ultra-Orthodox Jewish culture when we hear it spoken or even mentioned), but also a case of the part becoming a rallying symbol for (or against) the whole and, in some cases, becoming a cause (or a target) in and of itself. Language movements and language conflicts utilize languages as symbols to mobilize populations to defend (or attack) and to foster (or reject) the cultures associated with them.

Joshua A. Fishman
Yeshiva University

Further reading

Cooper, R. L. and Spolsky, B. (eds) (1991) *The Influence of Language on Culture and Thought*, Berlin.
Dutton, T. (1992) *Culture Change, Language Change*, Canberra.
Hanks, W. F. (1990) *Referential Practice: Language and Lived Space Among the Maya*, Chicago.
Muhlhausler, P., Harre, R. *et al.* (1990) *Pronouns and People: The Linguistic Construction of Personal Identity*, Oxford.
Urban, G. (1991) *A Discourse-Centered Approach to Culture*, Austin, TX.

See also: culture; discourse analysis; language; sociolinguistics.

latency period

In Freud's theory of psychosexual development, the latency period comes between the time of childhood (or pre-genital) sexuality and the onset of adolescence when true genital sexuality becomes possible. At about the age of 5, sexual development enters a period of relative calm. The direct expression of sexuality is constricted, according to Freud (1905), by the gradual emergence, encouraged by education, of opposing mental forces such as feelings of shame, disgust, and moral and aesthetic ideals. Sexual energy is diverted into affection. Freud believed that this latency period is a necessary condition for the development of advanced civilization. As with the preceding stages of psychosexual development (oral, anal and phallic), Freud considered that the onset of the latency period is governed by a biological timetable. But it has been suggested that the latency period may be a feature of sexually repressive societies, rather than universal as Freud proposed. His assumption that it is a time of sexual quiescence has also been questioned (White 1960).

Although for Freud, the latency period is 'time out', characterized by lack of significant sexual development, Erikson (1950) regards it as of considerable significance for the development of ego. For the first time, children move firmly outside the orbit of their family to go to school. In social terms, as Erikson points out, this is a very decisive stage. Recognition now begins to rest on the exercise of skills; children may become aware of being judged on their performance in comparison with their peers. No longer can they live in the infant's world of fantasy, but have to develop their ability to deal with the challenges of the social world. They learn to *do* things and can identify with adults such as teachers who can show them *how* to do. Where children feel inadequate to their task, a sense of inferiority may be the result. But if a child is encouraged and given confidence, the ego quality which can emerge is a sense of lasting *competence*.

The social order interlinks with this stage through educational activities which are likely to reflect its particular technological ethos. Thus 'play is transformed into work, games into competition and co-operation'. There is a danger here of overemphasizing competence so that the later adult comes to place too great an importance on work and achievement and thus becomes 'the conformist and thoughtless slave of his technology and of those who are in a position to exploit it'. In Erikson's analysis, the latency period is relevant to neurosis, in that it is a time when ego strengths can develop which can help the growing child to learn to cope with emotional conflicts both within themselves and in their relation with others.

Richard Stevens
Open University

References

Erikson, E. H. (1950) *Childhood and Society*, New York.
Freud, S. (1905) *Three Essays on the Theory of Sexuality, Standard Edition of the Complete Psychological Works of Sigmund Freud*, ed. J. Strachey, vol. 7, London.
White, R. (1960) 'Competence and the psychosexual stages of development', in M. R. Jones (ed.) *Nebraska Symposium on Motivation*, Lincoln, NB.

See also: ego; Freud, Sigmund; libido; sexual behaviour.

law

Conceptions of what law is are culturally and historically specific, but legal 'theories' often claim for themselves a universalism that they do not really have. When scholars from the western European legal tradition study the laws and legal institutions of other cultures, what they look for are norms and institutions that are either in form or in function analogous to those in their own heritage. The category 'law' that they proceed from is a western cultural construct (Berman 1983).

Many of the arguments about what law is or should be are organized around a single dichotomy: whether the basis of law is a moral consensus or a matter of organized domination. Law is sometimes interpreted as an expression of cultural values, sometimes as a rationalized framework of power. In ethnographic fact it is usually both. Separating the two absolutely creates a false opposition. Friedman (1975) has argued that 'the function of the legal system is to distribute and maintain an allocation of values that society feels to be right ... allocation, invested with a sense of rightness, is what is commonly referred to as *justice*'. Society is thus anthropomorphized as a consensual entity having common values. But Friedman's more extended discussion indicates a clear awareness of social stratification, and sharp differences of interest and power. His social science approach tries to embrace both consensus and domination in the same analysis.

In the jurisprudence of the west there have been a number of competing scholarly paradigms of law. The four principal schools of thought with roots in the nineteenth century (and earlier) are conventionally designated natural law theory; analytical jurisprudence or legal positivism; historical jurisprudence (or legal evolutionism); and sociological jurisprudence. The various modern social science perspectives on law have been shaped by this intellectual history, as have modern works on jurisprudence and legal history. Current work is best understood in the light of earlier ideas.

Natural law thinking

In its various forms, this dominated western ideas about justice through the eighteenth century, and has not fully disappeared, being perhaps most evident in current arguments about universal human rights. It was once closely associated with the idea of divine law. Natural law theory postulates the existence of a universal, underlying system of 'justice' and 'right', which is distinguishable from mere human enactments, norms and judgements. The content of this natural law was thought to be discoverable by human beings through the exercise of reason. To be just, human laws should conform to natural law, but they do not always do so. Human law can be unjust.

Analytical jurisprudence or legal positivism

This was a nineteenth-century development that continues in new forms to the present, and attacked natural law thinking on the ground that it was unscientific, that it was grounded on a mythical entity, and that it confused law with morality. The notion was that only *law as it is* can be the subject of scientific inquiry, that the province of what law ought to be was not a matter for science, but for philosophers and theologians. It was Bentham's follower, John Austin, who first generated the 'science of positive law'. Austin's science was a 'conceptual jurisprudence' occupied with discovering the key doctrines and ideas actually used in the existing formal legal system.

Austin's most cited formulation is one in which law is treated as command, the source of law as 'the sovereign person or body' that sets it within a particular political society. Consistent with this position, Austin argued that international law was 'improperly so-called' because it was neither set nor enforced by a political superior. He invented a category, 'positive morality' to contrast with 'positive law' to accommodate the law-like quality of international law without having it disturb his model that associated law with sovereignty.

Later positivists were critical of Austin, and developed modifications. Hans Kelsen generated an analysis which he called 'the pure theory of law' in which he asserted that law consists of a hierarchy of norms to which sanctions are attached. The validity of lower-level norms is derived from higher norms, until ultimately at the top of the hierarchy is the basic norm on which the whole structure depends. The effect of that basic norm is to require people to behave in conformity to the legal order. It defines the limits of that order.

Another major positivist critic of the Austinian perspective is H. L. A. Hart, who also has reservations about the artificiality of Kelsen's idea of the basic norm, and proposes an alternative. Hart (1961) rejects a conception of law based on coercive order as one too much derived from the model of criminal law. He argues that in fact law does many more things than prohibit or command and punish. It also can empower persons to act, and can define the conditions under which such actions are legally effective. Hart points to three troublesome issues that frequently recur in the attempt to define the specifically legal and distinguish it from other domains: the relationship between law and coercive orders, between legal obligation and moral obligation, and the question whether law is to be understood as a set of rules. Plainly there are coercive orders, binding obligations and rules that are not matters of law, yet all three elements also are central to legal systems. How are these to be distinguished? Hart's resolution of this problem is to describe law as a set of social rules divided into two types: primary rules of obligation and secondary rules of recognition, change and adjudication. The secondary rules sort the legal from other rule orders. Since legal validity is established by formal criteria, according to Hart's definition, an immoral law can be legally valid. Original and elegantly formulated as Hart's discussion is widely acknowledged to be, it has been criticized for its exclusive focus on rules at the expense of other important dimensions of legal systems, particularly the fact that it is a formal internal definition that turns away from questions about the socioeconomic context, the institutional framework and cultural ideas that inform law in action. His is very much a formalist lawyer's definition, and emphatically not a sociological one. Much of the sociological perspective has emerged as a reaction against this kind of legal positivism.

Historical jurisprudence or legal evolutionism

This school developed as another nineteenth-century reaction to natural law thinking. It is much more society-conscious and culture-conscious than positivism. In Germany this took the form of an almost mystical conception of the cultural unity of a people. This was coupled with the idea that there was an organic mode in which a people's inherent destiny unfolded over time. For Savigny, law was the expression of the spirit (*Volksgeist*) of a particular people, the notion of *Volksgeist* being ambiguously associated with race as well as culture. In this interpretation, custom was the fundamental form of law since it originated in the life of the people. Legislated law was significant only when grounded in popular awareness, a kind of codification and refinement of legal ideas already in the popular consciousness.

In Britain, Maine (1861) constructed a very different historical approach. He rejected Savigny's idea of the *Volksgeist* special to each people, and tried to generalize about the evolution of law and legal ideas in universal terms. Using comparative examples of the legal institutions of a few peoples, he endeavoured to show the sequential steps in the legal development of progressive societies. His idea was that in the shift from kin-based to territorially based polities, collective family property faded out and private individual property came in, that there was a change in the conception of certain wrongs which ceased to be treated as torts and came to be treated as crimes, and that much of the law affecting persons shifted from status to contract. Many of these generalizations have been criticized in later work, but the questions they raise remain issues of importance.

Marx, though only peripherally concerned with law, has had such a profound effect on social thought that his ideas about law must be taken into account in any review of these matters. He resists compartmentalization, but could be suitably placed within the historical school as his is a theory of sequential developments. Since in his model of history, class struggle is the principal dynamic of change, law is a dependent variable, not an independent force. In Marx's thought, the mode and relations of production constitute the 'base' of any social formation, and politics, law and ideology are part of the superstructure of ideas and practices which maintain a given set of class relations. The state and law are seen essentially as instruments of class domination, and reflections of it. In the twentieth century, the expansion of the welfare state, largely the product of legislation, has often been referred to in order to call into question some of these ideas of Marx's about law, but some Marxists see no contradiction in the matter and argue that what has happened is simply that class domination has taken new forms.

Marxist and neo-Marxist ideas are extremely important in the development of current critical legal theory Marxist themes can be seen in the work of Abel (1982), Balbus (1977), and Kennedy (1980) among others. They interpret law as a mode of maintaining the inequalities inherent in capitalist economies, however seemingly ameliorative reformist laws sometimes appear on their face.

Sociological jurisprudence

By contrast, from the start, this school was wedded to the idea that progress could be made to occur through legal reform. Major species of legal sociology interpret law as the means of solving social problems. Jhering (1872) thought of society as an arena of competing interests, and that the function of law was to mediate among them. The purpose was to produce 'the security of the conditions of social life' as a whole. The good of the whole was to come above special interests. Pound (1911–12) came to be very much influenced by Jhering's ideas as he considered the function of law in a democracy. He added his own conception that the task of law was one of 'social engineering'. In order that law achieve a scientifically informed efficacy in this role, he urged that sociological studies be made of any social field to be regulated, and also of the actual impact of existing legal institutions, precepts and doctrines.

Ehrlich, another member of the sociological school, stressed the gap between law on the books and the 'living law', the actual conventional practices of a people. For Ehrlich (1926 [1913]) social practice was the true source of viable law. This 'living law' could come to be embodied in formal statutes and decisions, but law that did not have that anchoring lacked the social vitality to be just and effective. Consequently Ehrlich exhorted lawyers and jurists to make themselves aware of existing social conditions and practices in order to bring formal law into harmony with society. This explains Ehrlich's broad definition of law as 'the sum of the conditions of social life in the widest sense of the term'. 'Law' included rules made and enforced by private associations. His was not a definition focused on 'government', but on 'society'.

Ehrlich's contemporary, Weber (1954 [1922]), conceived of law equally broadly. Law, he said, involved a 'coercive apparatus', the purpose of which was norm-enforcement within a community, corporate organization or an institution. Thus law-like norms could be 'guaranteed' by a variety of social bodies, not only by the state, although the state differed from the others in having a monopoly on 'coercion by violence'. Weber made it clear that, despite the coercive apparatus, the motive for obedience to norms was not necessarily the existence of such a system of physical coercion. The motive could be 'psychological'.

In his models of government and society, his 'ideal types', Weber identified the bureaucratic state with a 'legal order' of 'rational' rules. As he saw it, the evolution of law was marked by a movement from formal and substantive irrationality to rationality. In this sense rationality meant a logically coherent system of principles and rules. Legal irrationality was the use of means other than logic or reason for the decision of cases. Ordeals and oracles were examples of formal irrationality. Arbitrary decisions in terms of the personal predilections of the judge constituted substantive irrationality. In his ideal types Weber postulated a consistency between the type of overall political organization of a society (its mode of 'imperative co-ordination'), its values and ideology, and its type of legal system.

Weber's ideas continue to influence the work of theorists of law. One revisionist writer is Unger (1976), who borrows 'ideal types' from Weber and postulates a multiplicity of them in historical sequence. But not only do his types differ from Weber's, but also he sees as the principal impetus to change an awareness of the dissonance between ideal and real in a particular social order. His is a very orderly, very personal vision. In his view, the problem of our time is the reconciliation of freedom and community.

Like Weber's, Durkheim's (1960 [1893]) legal theory had an evolutionary theme. He thought that primitive societies were held together by 'mechanical solidarity', a coherence produced by a homogeneity of culture and a sameness of all social units, while the cohesion of complex societies was one of 'organic solidarity' founded on the division of labour in society and a system of complementary differences. Associated with each of these was a type of law. He regarded punitive retribution as the mode of dealing with wrongs in primitive society, while restitutive justice was appropriate to repair many wrongs under conditions of 'organic solidarity'. While Durkheim's interpretation of law in primitive societies was quite wrong, as the anthropologist Malinowski (1926) later showed, the direction of his enquiry, the question to what extent law is an aspect of social cohesion, remains cogent.

Social scientists now approach law with a distilled and selective recombination of many of these classical ideas of nineteenth-century and early-twentieth-century scholars. They use these transformed paradigms in combination with new methods, new information and new preoccupations. These have been generated in a very much altered politico-economic setting. Statistical studies have become an essential concomitant in many analyses of law and its effect in mass society. Quantitative methods have also been applied to the study of legal institutions themselves, to the behaviour of courts, lawyers and administrative agencies. Legal arguments and rationales are not taken at face value, but are studied as texts, both as they reveal and as they obscure values and interests. Economic dimensions and consequences have loomed increasingly large in the study and evaluation of legal norms. The costs of 'justice' and the nature of access to 'justice' have become major issues. The high-flown values that legal principles express are examined by legal economists in the light of their 'efficiency' and their social effect, not just their self-defined moral content.

Anthropologists have substantially enlarged the existing body of knowledge regarding the social order of non-western societies, simple and complex. Ethnographic materials collected through direct observation have made plain the ways in which order is maintained without government in small-scale systems, and the way that disputes are negotiated in oral cultures. These works are pertinent to the operation of subsections of large-scale, complex societies. A knowledge of such subsystems illuminates the peculiar relation between national laws and local practices in many parts of the world.

The importance and widespread existence of plural legal systems has been acknowledged in the post-colonial world as never before. All the theories founded on a notion that consensus and common values necessarily underlie all effective legal systems have been brought into question in the many instances in which power, rather than consensus, underpins particular laws. The role of law in relation to dissensus and conflict, cultural pluralism and class stratification is an increasingly urgent question for social theorists. The difference between the way law is conceived in the west and elsewhere has also become important as the greater interdependence of all countries is manifest. The question whether there are overarching commonalities that are or could be embodied in international law bears on everything from international commerce to the rights of refugees.

Variously conceived by the professions that generate, apply and enforce it, law is obviously quite differently approached by those who observe, analyse and teach it. Thus there is the law of lawyers and judges, of governments, of legislators and administrators, the formal legal system, its concepts and doctrines, its institutions and workings. In a related, but not identical, territory is the law of legal theorists and legal scholars and social scientists, many of them teachers. Beyond that is the way that the legal order impinges on ongoing social life.

Social scientists study all of this wide range, with a great variety of purposes and perspectives. Some are occupied with assembling information which will be the basis for proposed reforms. Others are engaged in trying to understand the relation between the actual workings of legal institutions and the self-explanations that form its ideology, without any immediate application in mind, rather with the idea of enlarging knowledge, and refining theory. In the broadest sense, one might say that there are two general streams of modern research. One is a social problems/social engineering approach that proceeds from the assumption that law is a consciously constructed instrument of control which has the capacity to shape society and to solve problems, an instrument which can itself be reformed and perfected towards this end. Research is seen to serve these practical purposes. In contrast is the social context approach which assumes that law is itself a manifestation of the existing structure (or past history) of the society in which it is found, and tries to know, understand or explain its form, content and institutions by showing contextual connections. Instead of just one 'social science approach' to law, there are many.

Sally Falk Moore
Harvard University

References

Abel, R. (1982) 'The contradictions of informal justice', in R. Abel (ed.) *The Politics of Informal Justice, vol. I: The American Experience*, New York.

Balbus, I. D. (1977) 'Commodity form and legal form: an essay on the "relative autonomy" of the law', *Law and Society Review* 571.

Berman, H. J. (1983) *Law and Revolution; The Formation of the Western Legal Tradition*, Cambridge, MA.

Durkheim, E. (1960 [1893]) *The Division of Labour in Society*, Glencoe, IL. (Original edn, *De la division du travail social*, Paris.)

Ehrlich, E. (1936 [1913]) *Fundamental Principles of the Sociology of Law*, trans. Walter L. Moll, Cambridge, MA. (Original edn, *Grundlegung der Soziologie des Rechts*, Munich.)

Friedman, M. (1975) *The Legal System: A Social Science Perspective*, New York.

Jhering, R von (1872) *Der Kampf ums Recht*, Regensburg

Hart, H. L. A. (1961) *The Concept of Law*, New York.

Kennedy, D. (1980) 'Toward an historical understanding of legal consciousness: the case of classical legal thought in America 1850–1940', *Research in Law and Sociology* 3.

Maine, H. (1861) *Ancient Law*, London.

Malinowski, B. (1926) *Crime and Custom in Savage Society*, London.

Pound, R. (1911–12) 'The scope and purpose of sociological jurisprudence', *Harvard Law Review* 24 and 25.

Unger, R. (1976) *Law in Modern Society*, New York.

Weber, M. (1954 [1922]) *Max Weber on Law in Economy and Society*, ed. M. Feinstein, Cambridge, MA. (Original edn, *Wirtschaft und Gesellschaft*, Tübingen.)

Further reading

Black, D. (1976) *The Behavior of Law*, New York.

Cain, M. and Hunt, A. (1979) *Marx and Engels on Law*, London.

Friedman, L. M. and MacCaulay, S. (eds) (1977) *Law and The Behavioral Sciences*, 2nd edn, Indianapolis, IN.

Nader, L. and Todd, H. F. (eds) (1975) *The Disputing Process, Law in Ten Societies*, New York.

Nonet, P. and Selznick, P. (1978) *Law and Society in Transition*, New York.

See also: critical legal studies; law and economics; sociolegal studies.

law and economics

It is relatively easy to establish with some precision when economic analysis began to be applied to legal rules and legal procedures in a systematic way. In the immediate post-war period, the economist Aaron Director was appointed to the University of Chicago Law School to develop work in the area of political economy. This led to collaboration with the school's lawyers, and in 1958 the University of Chicago began publication of the *Journal of Law and Economics*. Economists such as George Stigler played a major role in this process, particularly in the development of a sceptical approach to the benefit of regulation. R. H. Coase joined the Law School in 1964 and became responsible for the Law and Economics Program. In 1971 the school began to publish a related scholarly periodical, the *Journal of Legal Studies*, edited by Richard Posner.

This frequently rehearsed 'Chicago' account of how law and economics began is substantially true. Significant contributions were made by other scholars, notably by Calabresi at Yale and by Oliver Williamson (later to found the *Journal of Law, Economics and Organisation*), who developed a distinctive 'transactions costs' approach to contractual relations. But Chicago formed the centre of gravity.

This had major consequences for the early development of the field. Chicago was the home of libertarians who deprecated all forms of government intervention. In his early text, *Economic Analysis of Law*, Posner (1970) had no hesitation in defining wealth maximization as the aim of the legal system, attainable by eliminating or minimizing restrictions on the operation of free markets. This led to heated controversy with legal philosophers. However, a less partisan approach has emerged, represented by the publication of an influential textbook by Cooter and Ulen (1988). The field also spread to Europe, as shown by the publication of at least two scholarly journals: the *International Journal of Law and Economics* and the *European Journal of Law and Economics*.

One of the earliest major contributions to law and economics was an article setting out what became known as the Coase theorem (Coase 1960) on social cost. Coase demonstrated that, in the absence of transactions costs, agents would bargain around any legal rules in order to secure an efficient outcome. If A's factory is polluting B's atmosphere, and B has the right to make A stop producing, A will buy that right from B if A's profits exceed the monetary value of B's injury. The result had two implications. At one level, it emphasized the law's role in defining property rights. Second, it implied that legal enactments had limited influence on the allocation of resources because parties could always bargain round particular entitlements. However, these rather simple lessons have now been modified in the more sophisticated analysis of liability rules described below.

Law and economics involves the application to the legal system (legal enactments and legal procedures) of the standard battery of economic techniques. Laws represent constraints governing the conduct of utility-maximizing or profit maximizing individuals or organizations. The interaction of the parties is modelled subject to the relevant legal constraint and the outcome is evaluated using the standard techniques of welfare economics.

A good example is provided by one of the most developed applications of law and economics – liability for accident. Consider an accident involving a driver and a pedestrian. The probability of its occurrence depends upon how much of the relevant activities (driving and walking) the parties undertake and how much care they exercise. On the economist's standard maximizing assumptions, the levels of activity and of care are determined by which liability rule (no liability, strict liability, negligence, etc.) the parties are subject to. It is thus possible to evaluate how alternative liability rules encourage the parties to take proper account of the consequences to others of their actions. If drivers are risk averse, they may wish to insure themselves against liability for damages. What effects will insurance have on incentives to avoid accidents? Could better results be achieved by regulation, criminal sanctions, or a combination of these two with civil liability? A particularly clear exposition of these issues can be found in Shavell (1993). A similar approach, though leading to less interesting conclusions, can be taken to the law of contract. Analysis here has focused upon efficient incentives for breach of contract.

The same techniques can also be applied to legal procedures. Rational litigants will pursue suits only when the expected benefits from doing so exceed the expected cost. In the case of the plaintiff, the latter will largely comprise the monetary costs of losing the case. Incentives to sue and settle therefore depend upon whether the loser of a case pays all costs, or whether each side pays its own, and on whether lawyers are allowed to charge clients on a contingent fee basis – claiming nothing if the case is lost but retaining a substantial proportion (normally one-third) of damages if the case is won. There will also be greater incentives to bring actions if plaintiffs can aggregate similar suits in a 'class' action. The cost of legal proceedings is also significantly affected by the extent of competition among lawyers. Analyses of these issues can be found in *OXREP* (1994).

It is apparent that most of the intellectual impetus within law and economics has come from the latter discipline. Its well-established analytical techniques have triumphed over the more empirical, classificatory approach which has characterized much legal scholarship. Many legal academics have sought to resist what they regard as the imperialist ambitions of the economists, but to little effect.

The influence of law and economics has been more mixed. It has had a significant impact in North America where courts are much more open to economic argument and judges more familiar with it. European courts have so far proved to be much more resistant and are likely to remain so.

Martin Cave
Brunel University

References

Coase, R. H. (1960) 'The problem of social cost', *Journal of Law and Economics* 3(1).
Cooter, R. and Ulen, T. (1988) *Law and Economics*, Chicago.
OXREP (1994) 'The Economics of Legal Reform', *Oxford Review of Economic Policy*, Spring.
Posner, R. (1970) *Economic Analysis of Law*, Boston, MA.
Shavell, S. (1993) 'The optimal structure of law enforcement', *Journal of Law and Economics* 36(1).

See also: law; regulation; sociolegal studies.

laws of returns *see* returns, laws of

leadership

Leadership is a one-way or mutual process of influence that obtains compliance. It may be focused in one individual, but does not have to be. Leadership is sometimes treated as though it were virtually coterminous with management, but increasingly studies of leadership tend to emphasize various aspects of change, while those of management stress the status quo (Yukl 1994). Scholarly interest in leadership has waxed and waned over time, but since the early 1980s there has been a virtual explosion in interest, especially in leadership as it operates in an organizational context.

Scholarly studies of leadership began around 1900 and focused on traits that distinguished great historical leaders from the masses. Related research, after the Second World War, began to emphasize the behaviour of leaders rather than the traits that distinguish leaders. A 'situational contingency perspective', ushered in by Fred Fiedler, stressed that in addition to these traits and forms of action such situational contingencies of leadership as the nature of the task must be taken into account (Bass 1990). Some have laid so much stress on situational contingencies, in particular the nature of the followers, or the characteristics of jobs and organizations, that they leave little or no room for the influence of leaders. While accepting that the substantive impact of leadership may be strongly restricted by other forces, some writers, however, emphasize the fact that people may attribute significant symbolic powers to their leaders, especially where it is difficult to determine the 'real' causes behind relative success and failure. What has been called the 'romance of leadership notion' (Hunt 1991) often helps to explain the replacement of corporate leaders or leaders of sports teams, where performance is poor for reasons that are not evident. Poor leadership is invoked to explain the failure, and almost magical powers may be attributed to replacement leaders under such circumstances.

The recognition of this process of attribution has revived interest in transformational or charismatic leadership since the 1970s. Under what Bryman (1992) terms 'new leadership', followers do not merely enter into day-to-day transactional dealings with leaders, in which rewards are offered for services; new leaders expand the goals of their followers, and give them confidence to exceed their own expectations of their potential. Vision, a sense of mission, and movement beyond the status quo are emphasized; extraordinary things are attributed to the leader.

A perceptual and information-processing framework is especially important in the study of strategic leadership (leadership *of* organizations) where the acceptance and impact of strategic leadership decisions is strongly influenced by perceptions of the leader (Lord and Maher 1991). The notion of strategic leadership is now increasingly important in research, despite the preponderance of studies that emphasize rather lower-level face-to-face leadership *in* organizations (Hunt 1991).

Numerous perspectives on strategic leadership are also being developed. One integrative framework (Hunt 1991) extends Jaques's (1989) work on the impact of strategic leadership as it cascades down the organization. This suggests that leadership requirements become increasingly complex as one moves up the hierarchy (Phillips and Hunt 1992).

A final, increasingly important perspective that encompasses many of these other approaches is concerned with leadership of high-performance teams (Yukl 1994). These teams are a response to more and more common thrusts to empower employees and to ensure their active participation in organizations. Like the strategic-leadership approach, studies of leadership of high-performance teams consider leadership to be embedded within an organization and recognize such factors as culture and organizational design. Moreover, using employee or formal management facilitators, the teams need both traditional and new leadership.

James G. Hunt
Texas Tech University

References

Bryman, A. (1992) *Charisma and Leadership in Organisations*, London.

Fiedler, F.E. (1967) *A Theory of Leadership Effectiveness*, New York.

Hunt, J. G. (1991) *Leadership: A New Synthesis*, Newbury Park, CA.

Jacques, E. (1989) *Requisite Organization*, Arlington, VA.

Lord, R. G. and Maher, K. J. (1991) *Leadership and Information Processing*, Boston, MA.

Phillips, R. L. and Hunt, J. G. (eds) (1992) *Strategic Leadership: A Multiorganizational-Level Perspective*, Westport, CT.

Yukl, G. (1994) *Leadership in Organizations*, 3rd edn, Englewood Cliffs, NJ.

See also: charisma; elites; entrepreneurship; group dynamics; management theory; organizations; political psychology; strategic management.

learning

For hundreds of years, learning meant the formation of associations, and was considered the means by which society transmitted its acquired cultural capital. Learning was the cliché which lay behind almost every explanation in the social sciences. Increasingly, however, the study of learning has been transformed into the study of the human mind. When one speaks of learning one must speak of representations, of knowledge, of modularity, of innate and specific structures of mind. While the new view of learning is mostly restricted to the cognitive sciences – the social sciences as a whole have not been affected – one would expect that it will ultimately have a powerful impact on the social sciences.

In philosophy and psychology, learning has traditionally been regarded as a potential solution to the problem of knowledge. How is it that a human being comes to have knowledge of the world? In this context, the study of learning has long been central to the study of the human mind. Empiricist philosophers, such as Locke and Hume, conceived of knowledge as a system of association of ideas. Hume invoked principles which explained how these associations were formed. For example, the principle of contiguity said that if two ideas occurred near each other in time, then it was likely that an association was formed between these ideas. In the latter part of the nineteenth century these principles became the focus of experimental study. With the behaviourist revolution in American psychology in the twentieth century, association theory was modified so that it no longer was ideas that were associated. Rather, a stimulus was associated with a response. But the basic underlying notions of association theory persisted: that human knowledge is to be represented as a system of associations and that these associations are learned.

The study of learning thus became the experimental study of the learning of associations. To make these associations experimentally testable, the learning of arbitrary associations was studied, for example, the associations between nonsense syllables, like *dax* and *gep*. From this emerged the famous learning curve, showing the probability of individuals forming an association as a function of the number of times the associated items were shown to them simultaneously. Not surprisingly, it was discovered that the more practice that people have on an association, the better they learn it.

Grand theoretical schemes developed to explain learning, for example, those of Hull. These envisioned learning as a unitary phenomenon. In essence, human and animal learning were conceived to be the same thing, though there might be a quantitative difference. Within a species, what appeared to be different kinds of learning really were not. In short, the principles of learning remained unchanged across species and content of what was learned. A number of theoretical disputes arose over the precise character of these principles, but the different theories shared many underlying assumptions of breathtaking simplicity and elegance. These were that all learning was the same and that there were a few general principles of learning. The theory must have had simplicity and elegance, for what else could explain the fact that learning theory in this form lasted for so long? For the matter, plain and simple, was that learning theory did not work. If one actually considered real domains of human knowledge, it quickly became apparent that learning theory could not explain how that knowledge was acquired. The nonsense syllables of the laboratory, like the 'ideas' of the philosophers (or the 'quality spaces' of Quine), were abstractions which lost the essence of the problem.

The ideas which have replaced association theory are rich and interconnected. There is no way here even to hint at the extensive justification that has been developed for them. We shall simply list some of the themes of the new study.

Language and innate principles

Perhaps the major critique of the adequacy of association theory, as well as the most extensive development of an alternative theory for human learning, has come from the field of linguistics, namely from Chomsky (1965; 1975). Chomsky argues that the structure of language is such that there is no way that a human could learn language given any of the traditional notions of learning (call these 'learning theory'). Since every normal person masters a natural language, learning theory could not possibly be correct. Chomsky argues that the only way that these structures could develop is if there is an innate basis for them in the human mind.

Conscious awareness

We are not aware of most of the knowledge that we possess. For example, most of the principles of language are beyond our conscious awareness. In broad terms, the modern innatist position is very much like that of the rationalist philosophers (Descartes, Leibniz). Probably the biggest single difference (besides the extensive detailed technical developments in the modern period) is that the philosophers generally seem to have believed that the principles of mind were available to conscious introspection. It also does not seem unreasonable to claim that even behaviourists would only invoke principles of explanation of which they were consciously aware, although they did not explicitly state this. According to the modern view, although principles of knowledge are not necessarily available to consciousness, they are still in the mind, and thus a matter of individual psychology. Giving up the assumption of the necessity of conscious awareness of principles of mind is a liberating force in learning theory, for it makes possible the development of theoretical constructs which traditionally would have been immediately ruled out on the basis of introspection.

Domain-specific and species-specific principles

The modern view violates the cardinal principle of the traditional view, that all knowledge except for some simple principles of association is learned. But it also violates the two subsidiary principles, that learning principles do not depend on the species or on the domain of knowledge. Principles of learning differ from species to species. Animals do not learn language, because the principles of language only occur in humans. Some scholars are quite willing to accept the innate character of principles of learning, but believe that these principles operate in all domains of knowledge. That is, the principles are some kind of complicated hypothesis-formation ability. But the modern view holds that there are different principles in different domains of knowledge. Thus those which underlie our ability to recognize objects are different from those which enable us to use language. This latter view has come to be called the *modular* view of cognition. In the entire history of learning theory, there are really only two general kinds of ideas about learning: the formation of associations, and some kind of hypothesis-formation. With the development of the modern view of domain-specific principles, it is possible to have a much more delineated learning theory with particular principles for particular domains of knowledge. Of course it is an open and empirical question whether more general principles of cognition and learning underlie the specific principles which have been discovered. On the evidence to date, it appears unlikely that the domains will be completely unified. For example, visual perception and language just *look* different.

Reinforcement

In many traditional views of learning, an organism could learn only if properly reinforced. For example, children were supposed to learn a response better if given a piece of candy when they made the correct response. The modern view, based on considerable evidence, is that reinforcement appears much less necessary for learning, although it may still be an effective motivator. Skinner (1957) argued that children learned to speak grammatically by being positively reinforced for correct sentences and negatively reinforced for incorrect sentences. But Brown and Hanlon (1970) and other investigators have shown that parents do not differentially reinforce grammatical and nongrammatical utterances of young children in the language learning period. Thus reinforcement does not appear to play a significant role in language learning, from the standpoint of giving information to the child. Its role as a motivator is more difficult to assess precisely.

Instruction

One of the surprising discoveries of the modern period is the degree to which children spontaneously develop cognitive abilities, with no special arrangements of the environment. The field of language acquisition, and cognitive development more generally, is replete with examples. It is clear that the rules of language, for example, are not taught to children. People in general do not know the rules, although they use them implicitly, so how could they teach them? Some scholars believe that although parents do not teach the rules of language, they nevertheless provide special instruction by presenting children with a particular simplified language that is fine-tuned to their levels of ability (Snow and Ferguson 1977). But the best evidence (Newport *et al.* 1977) seems to show that there is no such fine-tuning.

Certain abilities unfold naturally, with no special instruction. Language appears to be one of these. Principles of visual perception also follow this outline. The same may be true for certain basic principles of counting, although not for the learning of the names of numbers (Gelman and Gallistel 1978). Other abilities seem to stretch the ordinary limits of the human mind, and seem to demand instruction in the usual case. The learning of advanced mathematics, or many other subjects, seems to follow this pattern.

Learnability and feasibility

It has proved possible to define mathematically the question of the possibility of learning. Gold (1967) provided one of the first useful formalizations. Wexler and Culicover (1980) investigated the question of learnability for systems of natural language and showed that linguistic systems could be learned if language-specific constraints were invoked. They further investigated the problem of feasibility, that is, learnability under realistic conditions. Specific constraints can be invoked which allow for feasible learning systems, specifically, very complex systems which can nevertheless be learned from simple input. This would seem to mirror the situation for a child, who learns an essentially infinite system (say language) from exposure to only a fairly small part of the system.

Animal research

We have concentrated on learning in humans, especially the learning of language, the ability most centrally related to the human species. However, extensive modern research on animal learning also questions the traditional assumptions. It appears that traditional learning theory is not an adequate theory for animals.

Social implications

The assumption of innate principles of human cognition does *not* imply that there are innate differences between individuals or races. The central idea of the modern view is that the innate principles are part of the shared human endowment, just as the innate existence of a heart is. In fact, the existence of the innate principles of mind may be thought of as helping to define human nature, an old concept generally out of favour in the social sciences. Contemporary social scientists in general founded their theories of society and politics on a psychology closely associated with traditional learning theory. Thus, children are socialized into the values of their society. But it is conceivable that there are principles of mind (of human nature) which relate to the structure of society (or to interpersonal relations, or ethics). If so, the modern view of learning might one day be expanded to include these principles, and there may conceivably be a social science founded on the modern view of learning.

Kenneth Wexler
University of California

References

Brown, R. and Hanlon, C. (1970) 'Derivational complexity and the order of acquisition of child speech', in J. R. Hayes (ed.) *Cognition and the Development of Language*, New York.

Chomsky, N. (1965) *Aspects of the Theory of Syntax*, Cambridge, MA.

—— (1975) *Reflections on Language*, New York.

Gelman, R. and Gallistel, C. R. (1978) *The Child's Understanding of Number*, Cambridge, MA.

Gold, E. M. (1967) 'Language identification in the limit', *Information and Control* 10.

Newport, E., Gleitman, H. and Gleitman, L. R. (1977) 'Mother I'd rather do it myself: some effects and non-effects of maternal speech style', in C. E. Snow and C. A. Ferguson (eds) *Talking to Children*, Cambridge, UK.

Skinner, B. F. (1957) *The Behavior of Organisms*, New York.

Snow, C. E. and Ferguson, C. A. (eds) (1977) *Talking to Children: Language Input and Acquisition*, Cambridge, UK.

Wexler, K. and Culicover, P. W. (1980) *Formal Principles of Language Acquisition*, Cambridge, MA.

Further reading

Piatelli-Palmarini, M. (ed.) (1980) *Language and Learning*, Cambridge, MA.

See also: conditioning, classical and operant; educational psychology; first language acquisition; learning curve; motivation; Piaget, Jean.

learning curve

The concept of the learning curve was introduced in a study, concerning students on a typewriting course, of how (mathematically and statistically) to relate improvement in typing speeds to practice in typing since the start of the course (Thurstone 1919). The concept of relating performance to the extent of practice/experience was subsequently applied to the analysis of industrial production in the aircraft industry where it was shown that the labour cost required to construct each aircraft (in a series of the same type or model of aircraft) systematically decreased with the cumulative total number (of that type of aircraft) constructed (in the same plant) since the beginning of the production process (Wright 1936).

Because practice/experience (the basis of learning involving skill) is a cumulative phenomenon, the learning curve has the general form:

Performance = Function of
(*Cumulative total*: repetition of task; or output (number of items) produced)

The measure of performance may differ as circumstances require (so giving rise to a family of learning curves), but the key (and identifying) feature of a learning curve, as such, is that the argument of the function is the *cumulative total* since the initiation of the process.

For various reasons, it is preferable (although not essential) in learning curve analysis to use a measure of performance which varies *inversely* with performance. For example, unit labour (UL) requirement should be used rather than labour productivity. The labour-hours required for the production of the ith item may be denoted UL_i, where i (always an integer value) is measured in a (cumulative) series *since the start of production* (of that particular type of product in that particular plant).

The proper derivation of the learning curve must begin with the cumulative total labour input (Berghell 1944). The cumulative total labour-hours (CTL) used for the production of i items may be denoted $CTL_{(i)}$ where the brackets round the subscript i signify that this is the cumulative total for items 1 to i inclusive, where 1 refers to the first ever item of that particular type of product to be produced in that particular plant. We must begin at the plant level with the following function for the cumulative total labour-hours as related to i, the cumulative total output (number of items ever) produced:

$$CTL_{(i)} = UL_1 i^c$$

This power function may be called the cumulative total labour requirement function.

For $i = 1$, $CTL_{(i)}$ reduces to the unit labour requirement for the first ever item, UL_1. Thereafter, $CTL_{(i)}$ varies with i. If the parameter c takes the value 1, then $CTL_{(i)}$ is simply a multiple, i, of UL_1 and no 'learning' or improvement in performance occurs. But if $0<c<1$, then $CTL_{(i)}$ will vary less than proportionately with i, and learning, or performance improvement, will be occurring. The smaller the value of c, the more rapid the learning process with respect to the cumulative total. The magnitude of the parameter c is the crucial feature which captures or expresses the effect of the learning process.

The cumulative total labour requirement function is not a learning curve in the strict sense because cumulative total labour input is not a measure of performance. However, it is from this function that we may derive various family members of the learning curve, each with a recognizable measure of performance as the dependent variable.

The cumulative (or 'running') average unit labour requirement (CAL), defined and measured as $CTL_{(i)}/i$ and denoted $CAL_{(i)}$, is obviously a measure of performance, so one learning curve can be derived as:

$$CAL_{(i)} = CTL_{(i)}/i = UL_1 i^c/i = UL_1 i^{c-1}$$

This may be called the cumulative average unit labour requirement learning curve. The derived parameter as the exponent on i, namely $c - 1$, may be called the learning curve elasticity. When $0 < c < 1$, the learning curve elasticity is negative and so $CAL_{(i)}$ will decrease with i. The smaller is c, the more rapid is the decline in $CAL_{(i)}$ (the faster is the improvement in performance) with the increase in i.

A learning curve can also be derived for the unit labour requirement for the particular ith item, UL_i. This is commonly identified (in the literature on cost accounting, engineering economics, and management) as *the* learning curve, and it should explicitly be called the unit labour requirement learning curve. The proper derivation of this learning curve is as follows. By definition:

$$UL_i = CTL_{(i)} - CTL_{(i-1)}$$

By substitution of the cumulative total labour requirement function:

$$UL_i = UL_1 i^c - UL_1 (i-1)^c$$

By a first factorization:

$$UL_i = UL_1 [i^c - (i-1)^c]$$

By manipulation of the second expression in the square brackets leading to a second factorization:

$$UL_i = UL_1 [i^c - \{i(1 - 1/i)\}^c]$$
$$= UL_1 [i^c - i^c (1 - 1/i)^c]$$
$$= UL_1 i^c [(1 - (1 - 1/i)^c]$$

By the binomial theorem, where c is not a positive integer and $0 < |1/i| < 1$ (both of which conditions apply):

$$(1 - 1/i)^c \approx 1 - c/i$$

(using only the first two terms of the binomial expansion). Whence by substitution and simplification (and as an approximation, with the approximation being closer the larger the value of i or the smaller the value of $1/i$):

$$UL_i = UL_1 i^c [1 - (1 - c/i)]$$
$$= UL_1 i^c [c/i]$$
$$= UL_1 ci^{c-1}$$

The last line expresses the unit labour requirement learning curve and, by comparison with the cumulative average unit labour requirement learning curve, it has the same elasticity (namely, $c - 1$) but, it should be carefully noted, a different constant term, $UL_1 c$. Because of the negative elasticity (when $0 < c < 1$), UL_i will decrease (performance will improve) as cumulative total output, i, increases and the smaller is c the more rapid is the improvement.

The appropriate way of estimating the parameters required for the learning curve (namely, UL_1 and c, so giving the learning curve elasticity $c - 1$) is to apply the method of least squares to the cumulative total labour requirement function in log-linear form (the reported data for labour input are nearly always given in a manner such that both i and $CTL_{(i)}$ can readily be ascertained).

The learning curve elasticity is usually applied with respect to the improvement in performance consequent upon a doubling of cumulative total output (doubling being an arbitrary, but intuitively convenient, factor of relative increase). The ratios $CAL_{(2i)}/CAL_{(i)}$ or UL_{2i}/UL_i will each be equal to 2^{c-1}. To illustrate, if c takes the value 0.8, so that $c-1$ takes the value -0.2, then, consequent upon a doubling of cumulative total output, unit labour requirement will improve to $2^{0.8-1} = 2^{-0.2} = 0.87055$ or to 87.055 per cent of the initial value; that is, unit labour requirement will decline by 12.945 per cent whenever cumulative total output doubles. By a convention of the literature (originating with Wright), such a learning curve would be referred to as 'an 87.055 per cent learning curve'.

Dudley Jackson
University of Wollongong

References

Berghell, A. B. (1944) *Production Engineering in the Aircraft Industry*, New York.

Thurstone, L. L. (1919) *The Learning Curve Equation*, *Psychological Monographs* 26(3).

Wright, T. P. (1936), 'Factors affecting the cost of airplanes', *Journal of the Aeronautical Sciences* 3(4).

See also: learning.

legitimacy

The discussion of legitimacy in social and political theory seems to confirm Hegel's dictum that theoretical reflection begins only when a practice has completed its development and become problematic. Questions about the moral worth or rightness of different forms of rule were present at the very beginning of systematic thinking about human communities. In *The Politics*, for instance, Aristotle held that some constitutions were 'right' (those promoting the common interest of citizens), while others were 'perverted' (those serving only the particular interest of rulers), a distinction grounded in a teleological metaphysics. However, classical theory lacked an explicit language of legitimacy, relying instead on general conceptions of order and lawfulness. Notions of legitimacy and legitimation were to be an invention of modern thought, represented best in Rousseau's promise in the *Social Contract* to demonstrate how political authority could be rendered 'legitimate'. His speculative answer and argument resting on the *volonté générale* served as both an epitaph for the Aristotelian tradition and a warning about the contestability of legitimacy in the modern age. This shift from a metaphysical to a voluntaristic account prepared the way for the contribution of Max Weber, the greatest modern theorist of legitimacy.

All modern theory starts from the assumption that legitimacy has to do with the quality of authoritativeness, lawfulness, bindingness, or rightness attached to an order; a government or state is considered 'legitimate' if it possesses the 'right to rule'. Unfortunately, the definition begs the most crucial question: in what does 'right' consist, and how can its existence and meaning be determined? Generally speaking, this question has been answered in two ways. One school of thought has argued with Weber (1968 [1922]) that, 'It is only the probability of orientation to the subjective *belief* in the validity of an order which constitutes the valid order itself.' According to this view, 'right' reduces to belief in the appropriateness of an existing order and the 'right to rule'. The presence of objective, external or universal standards for judging rightness grounded in natural law, reason or some other transhistorical principle is typically rejected as philosophically impossible and sociologically naïve. In his sociology of legitimacy, Weber attempted to guard against the relativistic consequences of such a conception by identifying four *reasons* for ascribing legitimacy to any social order: tradition, affect, value-rationality and legality. This classification then served as the basis for his famous analysis of the ideal types of 'legitimate domination' (*legitime Herrschaft*): traditional, charismatic and legal-rational.

Since the appearance of Weber's work scholars have continued to debate the logic, meaning and application of his views. Some have sharply criticized the sociological approach for subverting a rational distinction between legitimate and illegitimate forms of rule; for failing to distinguish legitimacy from legality; and for confusing a distinction among belief elicited through coercion, habit or rational choice. (In what sense Weber may be guilty of these charges is also a matter of dispute.) Underlying these criticisms from the second school of thought is the conviction, expressed particularly in the work of Jürgen Habermas, that a satisfactory theory of legitimacy must be philosophically grounded in such a way as to render possible a 'rational judgement' about the 'right to rule'. For Habermas (1975 [1973]; 1984 [1981]), grounds have been sought in a complex 'consensus theory of truth', where 'truth' signifies 'warranted assertability' under conditions of *ideal* 'communicative competence'.

Whether Habermas or others sharing his assumptions have provided a coherent grounding for the theory of legitimacy remains a disputed issue. One difficulty with their attempt is that it comes at an awkward time, philosophically considered, for under the influence of particular interpretations of Nietzsche, Heidegger, Dewey and Wittgenstein, several contemporary thinkers have mounted a serious challenge to the project of identifying foundations of knowledge that can be used to achieve definitive criteria of rationality. Prominent examples include Rorty's 'pragmatism', Lyotard's 'post-modernism' and Foucault's 'genealogical critique of knowledge'. If such challenges succeed, then it becomes difficult to imagine any viable alternative to the Weberian typological approach.

In light of such an impasse in philosophy, since the mid-1970s work on legitimacy in the social sciences has proceeded generally in three directions. First, social scientists attracted to empirical investigation have either worked towards testing hypotheses about legitimation in experimental settings, or they have dropped the term legitimacy altogether, hoping to avoid troubling normative issues while searching for measurable levels of 'regime support'. Second, some have moved towards developing theories about *il*legitimacy or *de*-legitimation, arguing that the real problems of the modern state lie with its essential lack of legitimacy, as illustrated most dramatically by the collapse of the former Soviet Union and events in Europe after 1989. Third, in a related move, others have focused attention on state structure and policy or the relationship between state and civil society in an effort to understand the factors conditioning legitimacy. While a state-centred view is sometimes labelled Weberian and a state/civil society framework neo-Marxist, there seems little reason to suppose that they cannot be combined in a unified approach. One can investigate strategies used by the state (particularly in the domains of science, technology, communication and education) to shore up sagging belief in its right to rule, as well as sources of legitimation emergent in the group processes composing civil society that condition a public's degree and kind of support for existing political institutions.

Whatever the outcome of these contemporary debates and directions of inquiry, such diversification of viewpoints is a firm indication that the problem of legitimacy will remain centrally important in the social and political sciences, at least as long as the modern state-system remains intact.

Lawrence A. Scaff
Pennsylvania State University

References

Habermas, J. (1975 [1973]) *Legitimation Crisis*, Boston, MA. (Original edn, *Legitimationsprobleme im Spätkapitalismus*, Frankfurt.)

—— (1984 [1981]) *The Theory of Communicative Action*, 2 vols, Boston, MA. (Original edn, *Theorie des Kommunikativen Handelns*, Frankfurt.)

Weber, M. (1968 [1922]) *Economy and Society*, New York. (Original edn, *Wirtschaft und Gesellschaft*, Tübingen.)

Further reading

Barker, R. (1990) *Political Legitimacy and the State*, Oxford.

Denitch, B. (ed.) (1979) *Legitimation of Regimes*, Beverly Hills, CA.

Lehman, E. (1987) 'The crisis of political legitimacy', *Research in Political Sociology* 3.

Stryker, R. (1994) 'Rules, resources, and legitimacy processes', *American Journal of Sociology* 99.

Thomas, G., Walker, H. and Zelditch, M. (1986) 'Legitimacy and collective action', *Social Forces* 65.

See also: authority; state; Weber, Max.

leisure *see* work and leisure

Lévi-Strauss, Claude (1908–   )

Claude Lévi-Strauss was born in Brussels, of French parents. After attending the Lycée Janson de Sailly in Paris he studied at the Faculty of Law in Paris, where he obtained his license, and at the Sorbonne, where he received his teacher's qualification in philosophy (*agrégation*) in 1931. After teaching for two years at the lycées of Mont-de-Marsan and Laon, he was appointed to the French university mission in Brazil, serving as professor at the University of São Paulo from 1935 to 1938. Between 1935 and 1939 he organized and directed several ethnographic expeditions in the Mato Grosso and the Amazon. Returning to France on the eve of the war, he was mobilized. After the armistice, in June 1940, he succeeded in reaching the USA, where he taught at the New School for Social Research in New York. Volunteering for the Free French forces, he was attached to the French scientific mission in the USA and founded with H. Focillon, J. Maritain, J. Perrin and others the École Libre des Hautes Études in New York, of which he became secretary-general. In 1945 he was appointed cultural counsellor of the French Embassy to the USA but resigned in 1948 in order to devote himself to his scientific work.

Lévi-Strauss's doctoral thesis, submitted at the Sorbonne, was made up of his first two studies, *La Vie familiale et sociale des Indiens Nambikwara* (1948) and *Les*

Structures élémentaires de la parenté (1949) (*The Elementary Structures of Kinship*, 1969). In 1949 he became deputy director of the Musée de l'Homme, and later director of studies at the École Pratique des Hautes Études, chair of the comparative religion of non-literate peoples, in succession to Maurice Leenhardt. In 1959 he was appointed to the Collège de France, establishing a chair in social anthropology. He taught there until his retirement in 1982.

The name of Claude Lévi-Strauss has become linked indissolubly with what later came to be called 'structural anthropology'. Reading his first articles, such as 'Structural analysis in linguistics and anthropology' (1963 [1945]), one is struck by the clarity with which from the first he formulated the basic principles of structuralism. As the title of the essay suggests, he found his inspiration in the linguistics of Saussure and above all in the phonological method developed by Trubetzkoy and by Jakobson (with whom he was associated in New York during the Second World War). He drew from them rules of procedure: concentrate not on conscious phenomena but on their unconscious infrastructure; do not attribute an independent value to the elements of a system but rather a positional meaning, that is to say, the value of the elements is dependent upon the relations which combine and oppose them, and these relations must be the foundation of the analysis; recognize at the same time that these relations also have a merely positional significance within a system of correlations whose structure must be extracted.

Lévi-Strauss applied this method first to the study of kinship systems, demonstrating their formal analogy with phonetic systems. His article of 1945 paid especial attention to the problem of the avunculate, sketching some of the central themes of his *Elementary Structures*, which he was then elaborating. These included the central role of marriage exchange, which implies a prohibition on incest (of which exchange is, in a sense, the other, positive, side of the coin). Marriage exchange is the condition of kinship: 'Kinship is allowed to establish and perpetuate itself only through specific forms of marriage.' He also stressed the social character of kinship, which has to do not with 'what it retains from nature', but rather with 'the essential way in which it diverges from nature' (1963). Finally, Lévi-Strauss proposed the definition of kinship systems, and of social systems more generally, as systems of symbols.

Another influence which is also apparent, and which Lévi-Strauss has always acknowledged, is the work of Marcel Mauss. His sympathy for the thought of Mauss is apparent when he compares the method of analysis in Mauss's *Essai sur le don* with the approach of structural linguistics, or when, in the same essay, he charges anthropology with the task of studying 'the unconscious mental structures which one may discern by investigating the institutions, or better still the language', and which render intelligible the variety and apparent disorder of appearances (Lévi-Strauss 1983 [1950]).

This was the goal which had been set by the author of *The Elementary Structures of Kinship*:

> The diversity of the historical and geographical modalities of the rules of kinship and marriage have appeared to us to exhaust all possible methods for ensuring the integration of biological families within the social group. We have thus established that superficially complicated and arbitrary rules may be reduced to a small number. There are only three possible elementary kinship structures; these three structures are constructed by means of two forms of exchange; and these two forms of exchange themselves depend upon a single differential characteristic, namely the harmonic or disharmonic character of the regime considered. Ultimately, the whole imposing apparatus of prescriptions and prohibitions could be reconstructed *a priori* from one question, and one alone: in the society concerned, what is the relationship between the rule of residence and the rule of descent? (1969 [1949]: 493)

Furthermore, these kinship structures rest upon universal mental structures: the force of the rule as a rule, the notion of reciprocity, and the symbolic character of the gift.

Lévi-Strauss returned to deal with one unanswered question fifteen years later, in *The Raw and the Cooked* (1970 [1964]). Are these kinship structures really primary, or do they rather represent 'the reflections in men's minds of certain social demands that had been objectified in institutions'? Are they the effect of what one might term an external logic? His *Mythologiques*, of which this was the first volume, put this functionalist hypothesis out of court, demonstrating that in mythology, which, in contrast to kinship, 'has no obvious practical function ... is not directly linked with a different kind of reality', processes of the same order were to be found. Whether systems were actually 'lived', in the course of social life, or like the myths, simply conceived in an apparently spontaneous and arbitrary manner, they led back to the same sources, which one might legitimately describe as 'mental'. This answer had in fact been given earlier, in *Le Totémisme aujourd'hui* (*Totemism*, 1962) and *La Pensée sauvage* (*The Savage Mind*, 1966), the latter book asserting, in opposition to Lévy-Bruhl's notion of a 'prelogical mentality', that 'savage' forms of thinking are to be found in us all, providing a shared basis which is domesticated by our various cultures.

The issue was whether the structuralist method applied only to kinship structures, and moreover only to those Lévi-Strauss termed 'elementary', which are not universal, even among those societies which traditionally are called traditional. The re-examination of totemism demonstrated how successfully this method could be applied to the symbolic systems with the aid of which people structure their representations of the world. The analysis of myths demonstrated, further, that the method not only worked for closed systems, like kinship systems, but also applied to open systems, or at least to systems whose closure could not be immediately established and whose interpretation could be developed only in the manner of a 'nebula' in the absence of 'the general appearance of a stable and well-defined structure' (*The Raw and the Cooked*).

In his last lectures at the Collège de France, between 1976 and 1982, Lévi-Strauss took up problems of kinship once more, but moved on from the systems based on unilineal descent and preferential alliance, concerning which he had developed his theory of elementary structures in 1949. He now investigated societies whose fundamental grouping brought together 'either cognates and agnates, or else cognates and maternal kin', and which he termed the 'house', borrowing a term which was used in medieval Europe. These studies are described in his book, *Paroles données* (1984). Here he demonstrates that structuralism is by no means disqualified from the study of 'a type of institution which transcends the traditional categories of ethnological theory, combining descent and residence, exogamy and endogamy, filiation and alliance, patriliny and matriliny' and can analyse the complex matrimonial strategies which simultaneously or in succession employ principles 'which elsewhere are mutually exclusive'. What is the best alliance? Should one seek a spouse in the vicinity, or far away? These are the questions which dominate the myths. But they are not posed by savages alone. At a conference held in 1983 (whose proceedings were published in *Annales*, November–December 1983) Lévi-Strauss cited materials from Blanche de Castille, Saint-Simon and the peasant populations of Japan, Africa, Polynesia and Madagascar to show that 'between societies which are called "complex" and those which are wrongly termed "primitive" or "archaic", the distance is less great than one might think'.

It is therefore mistaken to criticize anthropologists, certainly if they are structuralists, for ignoring history and considering the societies that they study as though they were static, despite the fact that, like our own, they exist in time, even if they may not situate themselves in time in the same fashion. This criticism rests upon a misunderstanding which Lévi-Strauss, however, tried to forestall very early. It is significant that it was in 1949

– the year in which his *Elementary Structures* appeared – that he published an essay with a title – 'History and Ethnology' – which he was to use again for his conference paper in 1983. In his article of 1949 he emphasized that the difference between the two disciplines was a consequence of their very complementarity, 'history organizing its data with reference to conscious characterizations, ethnology with reference to the unconscious conditions of social life'. In 1983, taking into account what has come to be called the 'nouvelle histoire', this complementarity is restated, but at another level. In fact 'it was through their contact with ethnology that the historians recognized the importance of those obscure and partly submerged facets of life in society. In return, as a consequence of the renewal of its field of study and its methods, history, under the name of historical anthropology, has become a source of considerable assistance to ethnologists'. Thus anthropology and history can serve each other, at least if historians do not concern themselves only with the succession of kings and queens, with wars, with treaties and with the conscious motives of actors, but study customs, beliefs and all that which is covered by the vague term *mentalité*, in a given society at a given time; especially if the anthropologist recognizes that the past of so-called complex societies increases 'the number of social experiments which are available for the better knowledge of man'.

It is true that in his inaugural lecture at the Collège de France in 1960 Lévi-Strauss opposed 'cold' societies – those which chose to ignore their historical aspect, and which anthropologists had traditionally preferred to study – and 'hot' societies – those which, on the contrary, valued their historicity and which were of especial interest to historians. Nevertheless, this opposition did not put in question the historicity of one or other type of society, but rather their attitude to their respective pasts. Every society presents a double aspect: structural and historical. But while one aspect might be especially favoured, this does not lead to the disappearance of the other. And in truth, the cold societies do not deny the past: they wish to repeat it. For their part, hot societies cannot totally deny their 'coldness': the history that they value is theirs only by virtue of a certain continuity which guarantees their identity. This explains the paradox that the very peoples who are most concerned with their history see themselves through stereotypes. And recognizing, or desiring, a history, does not prevent them from thinking of others, and especially their neighbours, in a static mode. One might instance the set fashion in which, for example, the French and the English represent each other. Thus structuralism does not put history in question, but rather an idea of history which is so common: the idea that history can concern itself only with flux, and that

change is never-ending. Yet although nature does not, apparently, make jumps, history does not seem to be able to avoid them. Certainly one might interest oneself in the moments of transition. One might equally interest oneself in the intervening periods, and is history not in essence constituted by such periods? The times within which different states of society succeed each other are not less discontinuous than the space within which societies contemporary in time but equally different, often ignorant of each other, share a border. It matters little whether the distancing – which appears to ethnologists to be the condition of their research, since it is 'the other' as such which is the object of their research – is temporal or spatial.

Obviously it is not necessary to accept the notion of a possible fusion between anthropology, as conceived by Lévi-Strauss, and history. Historians strive to surmount discontinuity, their goal being to establish genealogical connections between one social state and another. Anthropologists, on the contrary, try to profit from discontinuity, by discovering, among distinct societies (without concerning themselves as to whether or not they figure in the same genealogical tree) homologies which attest to the reality of a shared foundation for humanity. Lévi-Strauss has always striven to recognize this 'original logic' beneath a diversity of expressions which have often been judged to be absurd, explicable only by positing the priority of affect over intellect, but which are 'a direct expression of the structure of the mind ... and not an inert product of the action of the environment on an amorphous consciousness' (*Totemism*, 1962).

If one might talk of a Kantian aspect to structuralism (and Lévi-Strauss has never denied it), one should note that its course inverts that of Kant in two ways. First, instead of positing a transcendental subject, it tries to detach, from the variety of concrete systems of representations, collective modes of thought. Second, from among these systems it selects those which diverge most from ours. Kantianism without a transcendental subject thus, although the ambition of discovering in this way 'a fundamental and communal matrix of constraints', or in other words invariants, would seem nevertheless at the least to evoke its shade.

Such an enterprise appears to dispose of subjectivity, or at least to put it within parentheses, and this has indeed been one of the reproaches directed at structuralism: that it does not deal with man as a subject. There is a misapprehension here. As Lévi-Strauss, indeed, remarked in his 'Introduction à l'oeuvre de Marcel Mauss' (1983 [1950]):

> Every society different from ours is an object; every group in our society, apart from our own, is an object; indeed, each usage, even of our own group,

which we do not share, is an object. Yet this unlimited series of objects, which together constitute the object of the ethnographer, whatever its historical or geographical features, is still, in the end, defined in relation to himself. However objective in analysis, he must in the end achieve a subjective reintegration of them.

Again, in the same text: 'In the last analysis, the ethnological problem is a problem of communication.' That is to say, communication between subjects, between 'the Melanesian of whatever island', as Mauss put it, 'and the person who observes him, listens to him . . . and interprets him'. A similar point was made in *La Pensée sauvage*, published twelve years later, which ended with a consideration of the convergence between the laws of 'savage thought' and modern theories of information, that is, of the transmission and reception of messages. Thus the subject is not neglected or denied, but (while avoiding a solipsism which would obviously be the negation of anthropology) one might say that there is always a plurality of subjects, without which indeed the problem of communication would not present itself, and it is their relations which are significant. This remains a constant principle of Lévi-Strauss's structuralism: it is the relations which matter, not the terms.

That is also the principle which has guided this brief review. It has been concerned less with the analysis of texts, each considered in itself, than with their relations – from a point of view as much synchronic as diachronic – the aim being to abstract the invariant features of a body of work which is at once complete yet always open.

Jean Pouillon
Collège de France, Paris

References

Lévi-Strauss, C. (1963 [1945]) 'Structural analysis in linguistics and anthropology', *Structural Anthropology*, New York. (Originally published as 'L'analyse structurale en linguistique et en anthropologie', *Word* 1.)
—— (1969 [1949]) *The Elementary Structures of Kinship*, London. (Original edn, *Les Structures élémentaires de la parenté*, Paris.)
—— (1983 [1950]) *Introduction to Marcel Mauss*, London. (Originally published as 'Introduction à l'oeuvre de Marcel Mauss', in Marcel Mauss, *Sociologie et anthropologie*, Paris.)
—— (1984) *Paroles données*, Paris.

Further reading

Hayes, E. N. and Hayes, T. (eds) (1970) *Claude Lévi-Strauss: The Anthropologist as Hero*, Cambridge, MA.
Lévi-Strauss, C. (1961 [1955]), *A World on the Wane*, New York. (Original edn, *Tristes Tropiques*, Paris.)

—— (1963 [1949]) 'History and ethnology', *Structural Anthropology*, New York. (Originally published as 'Histoire et ethnologie', *Révue de Métaphysique et de Morale*.)
—— (1963 [1958]) *Structural Anthropology*, New York. (Original edn, *Anthropologie structurale*, Paris.)
—— (1970 [1964]) *The Raw and the Cooked*, London. (Original edn, *Le Cru et le cuit* ([vol. 1 of *Mythologiques*]), Paris.)
—— (1972 [1966]) *From Honey to Ashes*, London. (Original edn, *Du Miel aux cendres* ([vol. 2 of *Mythologiques*]), Paris.)
—— (1978 [1968]) *The Origin of Table Manners*, London. (Original edn, *L'Origine des manières de table* ([vol. 3 of *Mythologiques*]), Paris.)
—— (1981 [1971]) *The Naked Man*, London. (Original edn, *L'Homme nu* ([vol. 4 of *Mythologiques*]), Paris.)
—— (1977) 'The scope of anthropology', *Structural Anthropology*, II. (Inaugural lecture, Collège de France, 1960; published in *Anthropologie structurale*, II, Paris, 1973.)
—— (1983) *Le Regard éloigné*, Paris.
Steiner, G. (1966) 'A conversation with Claude Lévi-Strauss', *Encounter* 26.

See also: structuralism.

liberalism

Although it is the predominant political ideology in the west, liberalism is a protean doctrine whose meaning can perhaps be conveyed only by the use of adjectives that describe its particular nuances. The two most familiar are social liberalism and economic liberalism.

The various liberalisms, nevertheless, derive from various interpretations of the morally appropriate relationship between the individual and the state, or organized community. Liberalism has traditionally presupposed that the individual is logically prior to society and that political forms should respect this by allocating a protected sphere within which the person should be free to pursue self-determined goals. It rests upon a belief in a pluralism of purposes such that none is entitled to special privilege, and claims that law and state should preserve an institutional framework of equal justice. It is therefore indissolubly connected to a form of constitutionalism which limits political authority.

Liberals vary in the extent to which they acknowledge the role of reason in human affairs. However, liberalism has always rejected conservative claims that traditional institutional arrangements are entitled to allegiance in advance of a consideration of the value they might have in the protection of individual self-fulfilment. There is also an implicit universalism in liberalism in that it proclaims a moral validity independently of particular historical and social circumstances. This purported validity is derived normally from either a utilitarian calculation of the advantages that accrue from individual self-determination or from a purely moral perspective that rests on the inviolability of the person.

John Locke (1690) was perhaps the originator of modern liberalism with his argument that government was bound by natural law and that its function was limited to the protection of individual rights, especially the entitlement to property which derived from individual appropriation, subject to moral law. Furthermore, his liberalism included a right to disobedience if government transgressed the boundaries of individualism specified by morality. Despite this, Lockean liberalism could be said to be embedded in the English common law tradition, which was maturing in the seventeenth century

However, the modern development of liberalism owes more to the influence of the Enlightenment on European thought. This produced a much more rationalistic version which explicity subjected all received social arrangements to the test of an abstract reason, uncontaminated by traditional practices. From Voltaire onwards French liberalism in particular was inherently distrustful of experience and supposed that liberty-enhancing institutions were to be designed from first principles. It was a form of liberalism that came to be significantly different from the cautious empiricism of David Hume and Adam Smith, who were distinctive in identifying liberty with the spontaneous growth of market institutions and their associated legal framework. This leaves a small role for government since the 'invisible hand' of the exchange system was thought to generate the public good out of the self-regarding actions of private agents (Smith 1776).

From the early nineteenth century, liberalism began to be associated explicitly with *laissez-faire* economics and utilitarianism, and its moral dimensions were limited to the promotion of happiness. However, Jeremy Bentham (1789), while still claiming that individuals were the units of social evaluation (for him collective entities such as the state and society were 'fictions' which were constructed out of the motivations of discrete, pleasure-seeking agents), maintained that there was a role for political direction in the creation of an artificial harmony of interests. This, theoretically, allowed an expanded role for the state. But throughout the century the natural processes of the market in the allocation of resources and in the determination of income became the key features of liberalism. The growth of free trade and the limiting of government to the provision of defence, law and order and other essential public goods, were practices associated exclusively with liberalism. The doctrine was also understood as the means for achieving universal peace, as well as prosperity. John Stuart Mill, although he thought of himself as a liberal utilitarian, was excep-

tional in stressing the moral value of individuality and in his *On Liberty* (1859) was as concerned to argue for freedom as a contribution to the development of the personality as well as for its role in wealth creation. The latter was, in fact, understated.

In the early twentieth century, liberalism began to take on a much more social orientation and the state was charged with the duty of providing conditions for the fulfilment of the good life. Under the influence of writers such as L. T. Hobhouse (1911), British liberal doctrine became associated with the rise of the welfare state. This could still claim to be individualistic in that the state was not understood to embody collective values irreducible to those of private agents, or as the source of a morality which could claim an unquestioned loyalty from citizens, but certainly the role of the state in creation of a more equal society became integral to liberalism. Economic liberty, the protection of property rights and the inviolability of contract, faded into the background. The great theorists of economic intervention, such as Keynes (1936), could all claim to be liberal, despite their rejection of the *traditional* liberal doctrine that a free market is automatically self-correcting. The creation of the general interest was now the direct responsibility of liberal governments.

In the contemporary world, liberalism has shed much of its earlier utilitarianism. This is largely because of its embrace of the theory of social justice. Thus Rawls (1971) argues that justice is the first virtue of society and its demands must be met (normally) before conditions of economic well-being become relevant to the evaluation of government policy. The doctrine remains rationalistic and critical of received institutions. Using the contractarian method, Rawls asks individuals which principles of social and economic organization they would adopt if they were ignorant of their present circumstances and the value of their particular talents. In addition to choosing the traditional liberal values of equality before the law and free expression, Rawls argues that rational agents would opt for a redistributive rule that would permit inequality only in so far as that is needed to ensure the greatest benefit to the least advantaged. This is seen to be consistent with rational self-interest since an individual may turn out to be the least advantaged in the conditions of the real world.

This approach has come to be definitive of late twentieth-century liberalism (especially in the USA). It is Kantian in foundation since it stresses the inviolability and separateness of persons. Individual interests cannot be conflated into a social utility function since this would put the ends of society in a privileged position. It is also 'neutral' about conceptions of the good. Ways of life are matters of individual determination, since for the state to favour any one would be to assume a moral knowledge which it cannot have. It would also involve the unequal treatment of people. It is permitted only to promote the primary goods, those encompassing the conditions of basic well-being, liberty, equality of opportunity and self-respect, and must eschew any ideas of perfectionism. In its original formulation it was heavily universalistic, since individuals are deliberately abstracted from any communal affiliations and asked to deliberate over moral rules which are applicable to all agents. The doctrine is heavily egalitarian because it denies the moral validity of, not merely inherited wealth, but also the advantages that accrue from the distribution of natural assets (skills and talents that are socially valuable). Nobody deserves their talents, they are the product of the random processes of nature. The original liberal notion of self-ownership is explicitly rejected. The earnings derived from natural assets constitute a common pool which is available for redistribution according to the principles of social justice. The only concession to the liberal utilitarian's notion of efficiency is that some inequality is required to ensure that the talented use their skills so that everybody (including the least advantaged) benefits. The final link between this liberalism and economic liberalism is broken with Rawls's claim that his system is consistent with either capitalist or socialist ownership of the means of production.

This is not specifically a natural rights doctrine because Rawls and his followers do not utilize a notion of individual claims prior to society, but its moral metaphysic provides liberalism with intellectual armoury to be used against positive law (legislation). The legalistic social liberals, especially Ronald Dworkin (1977), have been active in claiming rights against the state. These individual rights (though they do not include economic freedoms) take priority over communal interests or the will of the majority. This version of liberalism has prospered in the USA precisely because the written constitution there gives the judiciary considerable interpretative authority over the content of liberal rights.

Economic liberalism has undergone a minor revival since the mid-1970s. Here the emphasis has been either on individual rights to property, which social liberalism's egalitarianism severely attenuates, or on the alleged economic incoherence of liberal redistributivism. Thus Nozick (1974), in a revised version of Locke's doctrine, argues that individuals have rights to their natural talents and to the products of voluntary exchange and inheritance. For the state to intervene to create an egalitarian order would be to violate these rights and to use individuals (in a non-Kantian manner) as mere means to the ends of society. The state is limited to the enforcement of legitimately acquired property rights, to the protection of freedom of contract and to the correction of past wrongs.

Friedrich von Hayek (1976) takes a more economic view. For him there is no distinction between production and distribution: any redistribution of resources must have a feedback effect (through reduced incentives) on productive possibilities so that society as a whole is worse off. To entrust the state with redistributive powers is to pose serious threats to liberty and the rule of law. Justice is really a type of constitutionalism which forbids the state imposing various outcomes (particular patterns of income and wealth) on a natural market process. Furthermore, Hayek maintains that in a pluralistic, liberal society there is no agreement about the morality of distribution. For example, there is no theory of desert which can secure universal assent and any interference with the verdict of an anonymous market is a threat to the liberal order. Hayek's liberalism is firmly tied to market economics and the doctrine of the rule of law. What is surprising is his claim that these arrangements will emerge spontaneously if people are left some liberty. The role of reason in the evaluation of social order is seriously diminished.

Whatever their disagreements about economics, modern liberals are united at least in their opposition to that kind of conservatism which locates the identity of the individual within given social orders which are immune from rational criticism. The individual is accorded a peculiar kind of sovereignty which is resistant to the claims of community. Methodologically, almost all liberals doubt the explanatory value of collectivist or holistic theories. They also reject the moral implications that such models may have. Similarly, while not denying the legitimacy of democratic procedures, liberals are not willing to endanger the sanctity of the individual by unconstrained majority rule.

Norman Barry
University of Buckingham

References

Bentham, J. (1789) *An Introduction to the Principles of Morals and Legislation*, London.
Dworkin, R. M. (1977) *Taking Rights Seriously*, London.
Hayek, F. A. von (1976) *The Mirage of Social Justice*, London.
Hobhouse, L. T. (1911) *Liberalism*, London.
Keynes, J. M. (1936) *The General Theory of Employment, Interest and Money*, London.
Locke, J. (1690) *Two Treatises of Government*, London.
Mill, J. S. (1859) *On Liberty*, London.
Nozick, R. (1974) *Anarchy, State and Utopia*, New York.
Rawls, J. (1971) *A Theory of Justice*, Cambridge, MA.
Smith, A. (1776) *An Enquiry into the Nature and Causes of the Wealth of Nations*, London.

See also: Bentham, Jeremy; Hayek, Friedrich A.; Locke, John; Mill, John Stuart; pluralism, political.

libido

This term was used by Sigmund Freud to denote sexuality in its widest sense: that is, any kind of body stimulation which produces pleasure. Initially, Freud classified biological drives into two basic types: those concerned with the preservation of the individual such as the needs for food and sleep, and those concerned with the preservation of species (sexuality or libido). (With the impact of the First World War, Freud (1920) also postulated a death instinct or urge to self-destruction (thanatos) but this has never become a fully accepted part of psychoanalytic theory.)

Freud (1905) emphasized the psychological implications of the development of libido. During the first five years of life, he claimed, the source and nature of the body stimulation that is most pleasurable to the child changes as a result of biological development. For the very young infant, the mouth is the zone and pleasure is derived initially from sucking and, as teeth develop, from biting (the oral stage). Later, excretion becomes the focus of attention, pleasurable stimulation being derived from the retention and elimination of faeces (the anal stage). Still later, perhaps in about the fourth year, interest shifts to the genitals. This is reflected in curiosity about sex differences and pleasure in masturbation and physical stimulation from rough-and-tumble play (the phallic stage). From about the age of 5 until adolescence, there is a 'latency period'. At adolescence, sexuality becomes directed outwards and, instead of the child's own body being the primary source of gratification, becomes focused (if only in fantasy) on another partner. The 'pre-genital' modes of childhood sexuality will be incorporated into this. Thus, oral stimulation, for example in the form of kissing, is usually involved in sexual relations.

If a child is frustrated or over-indulged at a particular stage of development this may result in 'fixation' (or, later, 'regression'). Zone and physical mode fixation will result in a later tendency to sexual perversion (this being defined as where satisfaction is primarily obtained from a pre-genital form of stimulation). Fixation may also occur in relation to the psychological quality that characterizes each stage. Fixation at the oral stage, for example, may result not only in someone who enjoys oral stimulation but also in later dependency. At the anal phase, demands may be made on the child for control of body functions. It thus lays the basis for later attitudes of obedience and rebelliousness, as well as characteristics such as obsessiveness and creativity. The phallic phase is the time of Oedipal conflict when repression of desires which create anxiety may become a characteristic pattern of defence. Because neurotic symptoms (as well as personality characteristics) are also rooted in patterns of psychosexual development, Freud described neuroses as the 'negative of the perversions'.

The psychological significance of libido is that sexual energy can be repressed and transmuted into different forms. So, according to Freud, intellectual curiosity, appreciation of beauty, love, friendship and creativity may well represent *sublimations* of libido.

Several other psychoanalytic schools (e.g. Jung, Adler) have been critical of what they regard as Freud's over-concern with libido. In his later theorizing, Freud himself came to give more emphasis to the functioning of the ego.

Richard Stevens
Open University

References

Freud, S. (1905) *Three Essays on the Theory of Sexuality, Standard Edition of the Complete Psychological Works of Sigmund Freud*, ed. J. Strachey, vol. 7, London.
—— (1920) *Beyond the Pleasure Principle, Standard Edition of the Complete Psychological Works of Sigmund Freud*, ed. J. Strachey, vol. 13, London.

Further reading

Freud, S. (1916) *Introductory Lectures on Psychoanalysis, Standard Edition of the Complete Psychological Works of Sigmund Freud*, ed. J. Strachey, vol. 16, London.
Stevens, R. (1983) *Freud and Psychoanalysis*, Milton Keynes.

See also: Freud, Sigmund; latency period; sexual behaviour.

life cycle

The way in which the life cycle is divided up, and how its phases are represented, varies greatly between cultures. Culture imposes its own pattern on biological events and the process of maturation; it is society, not physiology, which through its rituals makes men of boys, or ancestors of elders. In many cultures an individual's progress through the sequence of life stages is represented as a series of jumps rather than as a steady undifferentiated flow. It may also be seen as a progress towards the acquisition of full personhood.

Very often the infant is not a person at all until named some weeks after birth; its death does not therefore occasion any public ritual or mourning. Weaning commonly marks the transition from infancy to childhood – the duration of which is culturally highly variable, as is the extent to which children are represented as inhabiting a separate sphere with needs and requirements quite different from those of adults (see Ariès 1962). In many traditional societies child labour has a significant role to play in the production process, and in some towards the reproduction of the symbolic order of the adult world. It may, for example, be crucial to the maintenance of purdah restrictions, for female seclusion could not be sustained without children to run errands and carry messages to other houses which adults cannot freely enter, and to market women's home production. While in contemporary western culture, adolescence is often represented as a phase of rebellious insubordination, experimentation and emotional turmoil, Wilder (1970) describes it as a time during which the rural Malay youth exhibits an extreme passivity amounting almost to suspended animation; and, in a now classic study, Mead (1928) argued that the 'crisis of adolescence' does not exist in Samoa (a conclusion for which the ethnographic basis has been forcefully – if inconclusively – contested by Freeman 1983).

The cultural definition of adult maturity is highly relative, but in many societies marriage marks the crucial transition for both sexes. Among certain groups of Australian Aborigines, a woman reverts to the status of 'girl' regardless of her chronological age as soon as her marriage is dissolved. In the age-set systems of East Africa, a man's marriage, which confers full adult status, may be delayed until he is 30 or 40 years old. After a Samburu boy's age-set have been circumcised they become *moran* or 'warriors' who will live for a decade or more in the bush away from the settlements of the elders and their polygynous households (Spencer 1965). Gerontocratic polygyny clearly depends on the prolonged bachelorhood of the warriors. Elsewhere a married man remains a jural minor so long as his father is alive (Fortes 1949).

Old age is an honoured condition in many traditional societies, and there appears to be a strong correlation between ancestor worship and reverence for elderly people. In many cases the authority of male elders is sustained by their monopoly over rights in women, and/or over the items required for marriage payments (Douglas 1958). In preliterate cultures, elderly people are also the repositories of tradition and of the sacred knowledge which ensure the abundance of the harvest, the fertility of the women and the health of the community. Sometimes the old are expected to withdraw progressively from practical life in order to devote themselves to spiritual matters. In the final phase of his life, the Hindu male should renounce the world and become a wandering ascetic (though it might be argued that the chief effect of this theory is to promote a thoroughly this-worldly ethic during the earlier 'householder' stage on the grounds that there will be time enough for other-

worldliness in one's dotage). Elsewhere the old are routinely neglected and treated with some callousness (see Ortner 1978 on the Sherpas). Among the pastoral Fulani of north-eastern Nigeria, each son owns a specified share of the herd managed by his father, from which he withdraws his cattle when he sets up an independent domestic unit after the birth of his first child. At the marriage of his youngest son a man's herd is finally completely dispersed, and he and his wife (or wives) each go to live with their eldest son (which, given high rates of divorce and polygyny, will probably mean that they go to different places). There the old man sleeps on the periphery of the homestead where he will eventually be buried. Socially he is already dead, and he makes his bed over his own grave (Stenning 1958).

J. P. Parry
London School of Economics and
Political Science

References

Ariès, P. (1962) *Centuries of Childhood*, New York.
Douglas, M. (1958) 'Raffia cloth distribution in the Lele economy', *Africa* 28.
Fortes, M. (1949) *The Web of Kinship among the Tallensi*, Oxford.
Freeman, D. (1983) *Margaret Mead and Samoa: The making and Unmaking of an Anthropological Myth*, Cambridge, MA.
Mead, M. (1928) *Coming of Age in Samoa*, London.
Ortner, S. (1978) *Sherpas through their Rituals*, Cambridge, UK.
Spencer, P. (1965) *The Samburu: A Study of Gerontocracy in a Nomadic Tribe*, London.
Stenning, D. (1958) 'Household viability among the Pastoral Fulani', in J. Goody (ed.) *The Developmental Cycle in Domestic Groups*, Cambridge, UK.
Wilder, W. (1970) 'Socialization and social structure in a Malay village', in P. Mayer (ed.) *Socialization: The Approach From Social Anthropology*, London.

See also: adolescence; age organization; childhood; gerontology, social; life history; life-span development; life tables and survival analysis; rites of passage.

life history

A life history may be defined as the sequence of events and experiences in a life from birth until death in social, cultural and historical contexts. Life histories can be studied not only with the 'life history method' of having a respondent recount the story of his or her life, but also with the full range of social scientific and historical methods, including archival research, participant observation, experimental methods and prospective longitudinal research.

Within the social sciences, it is possible to identify roughly three periods in the study of life histories. First, from approximately 1920 to the Second World War, there was a substantial and growing interest in life histories, much of it associated with oral histories and with the study of personal documents (Allport 1942; Langness and Frank 1981; Thomas and Znaniecki 1920). Second, from the Second World War to the late 1960s, interest declined and increased attention was given to more structured quantitative and experimental methods. Third, since 1970, however, there has been an enormous outpouring of work in the study of lives associated with developments in fields such as life history research in psychopathology (Roff and Ricks 1970), adult development (Levinson *et al.* 1978), sociological studies of the life course (Elder 1974), oral history and life stories (Bertaux 1981), personality psychology (Alexander 1990; McAdams and Ochberg 1988; Rabin *et al.* 1990) and psychobiography (Erikson 1975; Runyan 1982; 1988). Over the years, the study of individual life histories has survived challenges from Marxism, structuralism, quantitative scientism, and post-modernism, and continues to thrive as there is increased acceptance of narrative, contextualist and 'historical science' (Gould 1989) forms of research which study unique sequences of events in the physical, biological and social sciences.

Methodological critics sometimes argue that life history studies are ineffective in ruling out competing causal explanations and that it is unsafe to generalize from the study of a single case. Studies of individual life histories are, however, appropriately evaluated not on their effectiveness for testing causal generalizations (a criterion most appropriate for experimental studies), but rather on their ability to present and interpret information about the life of a single individual. Such studies can usefully be evaluated through a 'quasi-judicial' methodology (Bromley 1977), analogous to procedures in courts of law, where evidence, inferences and interpretations in a life history study are critically assessed by those with competing points of view who are free to present their own evidence, interpretations and conclusions and to contest alternative accounts.

The goals of psychology can be thought of as existing on three distinct levels: learning what is true of persons-in-general; what is true of groups of persons, distinguished by sex, race, social class, culture and historical period; and what is true of individual human beings. These three levels of analysis inform one another, but are also partially independent. The study of individual life histories is a necessary complement to the study of group differences and the search for universal generalizations.

William McKinley Runyan
University of California

References

Alexander, I. E. (1990) *Personology: Method and Content in Personality Assessment and Psychobiography*, Durham, NC.

Allport, G. W. (1942) *The Use of Personal Documents in Psychological Science*, New York.

Bertaux, D. (ed.) (1981) *Biography and Society: The Life History Approach in the Social Sciences*, Beverly Hills, CA.

Bromley, D. B. (1977) *Personality Description in Ordinary Language*, New York.

Elder, G. H. jr (1974) *Children of the Great Depression*, Chicago.

Erikson, E. H. (1975) *Life History and the Historical Moment*, New York.

Gould, S. J. (1989) *Wonderful Life: The Burgess Shale and the Nature of History*, New York.

Langness, L. L. and Frank, G. (1981) *Lives: An Anthropological Approach to Biography*. Novato, CA.

Levinson, D. *et al.* (1978) *The Seasons of a Man's Life*, New York.

McAdams, C. and Ochberg, R. (eds) (1988) *Psychobiography and Life Narratives*, Durham, NC.

Rabin, A. *et al.* (eds) (1990) *Studying Persons and Lives*, New York.

Roff, M. and Ricks, D. (eds) (1970) *Life History Research in Psychopathology*, vol. I, Minneapolis, MN.

Runyan, W. M. (1982) *Life Histories and Psychobiography: Explorations in Theory and Method*, New York.

—— (ed.) (1988) *Psychology and Historical Interpretation*, New York.

Thomas, W. I. and Znaniecki, F. (1920) *The Polish Peasant in Europe and America*, Boston, MA.

See also: case study; life cycle; life-span development; oral history.

life-span development

How does each person make the journey through the life-span? How can we characterize this journey? Is it meant to be a series of bumps and curves, or a smooth, unfolding line? Are there species-specific, universal patterns of travel or is it a purely personal, idiosyncratic affair? Even if it is an idiosyncratic one, is it set in advance, like a key lying within one's genes or even one's 'soul', or is it a process that is continually composed and recomposed as one goes along? Alternatively, is one's destiny determined by the stamp placed on one from the environment; that is, are our personalities and selves formed in childhood and destined to remain stable thereafter? Or, is it a highly malleable process moulded by societal roles and expectations in a given culture at a given moment in history?

These are the fundamental questions posed by researchers and theorists concerned with life-span development, although the questions may take different shape or form depending on the exact area of research or investigation. Although life-span considerations have enjoyed a long history, it is only since the mid-1960s that researchers have begun to take this approach seriously, following the lead of twentieth-century psychologists such as Buhler, Erikson, Hall, and Jung (Baltes *et al.* 1980; Featherman 1983). Life-span development cannot be characterized by one overarching theory. It incorporates a multitude of levels of analysis and encompasses a variety of academic and applied disciplines, each with its own sets of assumptions about and ways of defining the subject matter. Ideally, interdisciplinary co-operation is needed to understand the complexity of the process. Within the framework of life-span development lie a multitude of subdisciplines, ranging from such diverse ends of the spectrum as molecular biology to sociocultural, anthropological and historical perspectives on ageing. The field of psychology alone encompasses many areas, such as cognitive and intellectual ageing, attachment relationships across the life-span, change and stability in personality, and social influences on development. Researchers and theorists concerned with social-historical and cultural factors, physiological processes, anthropology and psychology have all made important contributions to our understanding of how change occurs across the life-span, as have philosophers of science, who analyse the metatheoretical presuppositions guiding our theories about child development and adult development.

Due to the complex findings which emerge from the life-span literature, three propositions can be made. First, there is considerable inter-individual variation in development. Whereas child developmentalists have typically sought unidirectional, universally applicable laws (though, increasingly, there are exceptions), adult developmentalists have noted greater diversity and plasticity (adaptability) of developmental patterns (Baltes 1993). Second, historical changes affect the path that development takes. The role of historical change has been studied, for example, with the use of age/cohort sequential methodology, where individuals from two or more cohorts (generations) are followed over a long period of time (Schaie 1979). Third, interdisciplinary collaboration is necessary in order to describe fully individual development within a changing world. Featherman (1983) illustrates the usefulness of such an interdisciplinary approach in the fields of psychology, sociology and economics. Jointly considered, these three propositions advanced in life-span research necessitate an emphasis on the interactive relationships between individual development and historical change, resulting in dialectical and contextualist (Kramer and Bopp 1989; Lerner and Kauffman 1985; Riegel 1976) conceptions of human development.

A fairly common view of development is that our personalities are fixed during childhood. Research does not generally bear this out, as indicated by considerable plasticity in development even at very young ages (Brim and Kagan 1980), between adolescence and adulthood (McFarlane 1964) and into old age (Fiske

and Chiriboga 1990). Research on personality development indicates that, while there may be some stability from one period to its adjacent age period, there is little overall stability across longer time periods; furthermore, there are a few periods of considerable and abrupt change even from one age period to the next such as between adolescence and early adulthood (Haan *et al.* 1986). Fiske and Chiriboga (1990) conducted a cohort-sequential study of ordinary people in four separate stages of life, all of whom were followed over a number of years. Using a multi-method approach to measurement, they found a complex pattern of both change and stability that could not be explained simply by considering the life stage, age, gender, previous patterns of development, life experiences, historical events, or personality traits of the individual. Rather, each person approached the complex task of development in a unique manner, and each life journey was a complex narrative in itself, one that was constantly revised and remolded. Hagestad (1990) describes an individual's life course as being as unique as fingerprint. She cites a study of 7,000 women and 6,700 men, who displayed no fewer than 1,180 and 1,100 patterns, respectively, of role sequences and transitions throughout the life-span. Thus, individual variability in development is the norm, rather than the exception. Furthermore, there is considerable variability across historical epochs in what constitutes a life 'stage', let alone the developmental tasks which accompany one (Gergen 1991; Neugarten 1977).

This is not to say that life roles, life stages, age, gender, personality traits, and life experiences are irrelevant to development. They all contribute. For example, difficulties in the early attachment relationship between the primary caretaker (who is usually the mother) and infant sets the stage for later development, whereby deficiencies in the early nurturing environment create initial vulnerabilities for the child which are compounded with each new life context. Dysfunctions in early parent–child interactions and/or in the attachment bond set the stage for later peer rejection, antisocial behaviour, coping difficulties and, possibly, difficulty in bonding with their own infants later (Grossmann and Grossmann 1990; Main and Cassidy 1988; van Lieshout *et al.* 1990). Main (1990) has argued that the 'primary' attachment system of the infant, which predisposes it to develop a secure attachment with its primary caretaker, may be overridden by a context-sensitive, 'secondary' system in which it is more adaptive for the infant to either show greater avoidance or dependence on the caretaker. The resulting attachment system serves as an organizing feature for social cognitive, perceptual, and attentional processes, leading the child to selectively focus on and/or ignore certain informational properties of its environment, that is, it creates intelligence for areas where it is most needed (Main 1990; Rieder and Cicchetti 1989). This is not without loss, however, as the secondary system can put the infant at later risk for maladjustment.

Clinical psychologists, particularly object relations theorists, have contributed a great deal to our understanding of how the early nurturing environment creates internal, mental representations of ourselves, others, and ourselves in relation to others, which form the backdrop of all later interactions (Kernberg 1975; Kohut 1978). However, through personal exploration, therapy, novel life experiences, unexpected events, new relationships, and creative undertakings, these inner representations can be repaired and/or restructured to allow for discontinuity with the past at any given time, thereby enabling the person to chart a new course. Hence, both continuity and discontinuity possibly may occur at any point in the lifespan (Brim and Kagan 1980; Haan *et al.* 1986; Main and Cassidy 1988; Macfarlane 1967). The self system continues to undergo transformation and change into old age (Baltes 1993; Labouvie-Vief 1994). Furthermore, it is profoundly influenced by gender at all points of development (Turner and Troll 1994).

Thus, in development through the life course, each of the person's experiences, roles, relationships, and existing characteristics form the strands of his or her life, which the person weaves together to comprise a unique fabric, a texture (Erikson 1988). They comprise the concrete experiences and particulars of a person's life, which are woven together into general patterns that may adhere broadly to laws of organization, such as those described by interactive dialectical and contextual models of development. While describing broad regularities in patterns of change, these models allow for a unique and creative synthesis of one's experiences to revise and 'rewrite' one's life narrative at any given moment. While offering continuity with the past, these models also allow for novelty in our developmental paths. Novel, unexpected events or shifts may occur. These may reflect personal, idiosyncratic events or cultural/ historical events; they may be pleasant or unpleasant events (Baltes *et al.* 1980). They may be seemingly normative events (like marriage or parenting) which happen to occur at non-normative times in the lifespan, such as the mid-forties for marriage or birth of the first child), 'off-time' events (Neugarten 1977). With the multitude of constantly shifting events, it is not surprising that there is continued opportunity for change and continuity in our developmental paths. While there are some guidelines put forth by life-span theorists for navigating the complex map of development, each person's path is unique, differing in some

degree or quality from each other. No two life-spans are exactly alike.

Deirdre A. Kramer
Rutgers University

References

Baltes, P. B. (1993) 'The aging mind: potential and limits', *The Gerontologist* 33.

Baltes, P. B., Reese, H. W. and Lipsitt, L. P. (1980) 'Life-span developmental psychology', *Annual Review of Psychology* 31.

Brim, O. G. jr and Kagan, J. (1980) *Constancy and Change in Human Development*, Cambridge, MA.

Erikson, J. M. (1988) *Wisdom and the Senses: The Way of Creativity*, New York.

Featherman, D. L. (1983) 'The life-span perspective in social science research', in P. B. Baltes and O. G. Brim jr (eds) *Life-span Development and Behavior*, vol. 5, New York.

Fiske, M. and Chiriboga, D. A. (1990) *Change and Continuity in Adult Life*, San Francisco, CA.

Gergen, K. J. (1991) *The Saturated Self: Dilemmas of Identity in Contemporary Life*, New York.

Grossmann, K. E. and Grossmann, K. (1990) 'The wider concept of attachment in cross-cultural research', *Human Development* 33.

Haan, N., Millsap, R. and Hartka, E. (1986) 'As time goes by: change and stability in personality over fifty years', *Psychology and Aging* 1.

Hagestad, G. O. (1990) 'Social perspectives on the life course', in R. H. Binstock and L. K. George (eds) *Handbook of Aging and the Social Science*, 3rd edn, New York.

Kernberg, O. F. (1975) *Borderline Conditions and Pathological Narcissism*, New York.

Kohut, H. (1978) 'Forms and transformations of narcissism', in P. H. Ornstein (ed.) *The Search for the Self-Selected Writings of Heinz Kohut: 1950–1978*, New York.

Kramer, D. A. and Bopp, M. J. (eds) (1989) *Transformation in Clinical and Developmental Psychology*, New York.

Labouvie-Vief, G. (1994) 'Women's creativity and images of gender', in B. F. Turner and L. E. Troll (eds) *Women Growing Older: Psychological Perspectives*, Thousand Oaks, CA.

Lerner, R. M. and Kauffman, M. B. (1985) 'The concept of development in contextualism', *Developmental Review* 5.

McFarlane, J. W. (1964) 'Perspectives on personality consistency and change from the Guidance Study', *Vita humana* 7.

Main, M. (1990) 'Cross-cultural studies of attachment organization: recent studies, changing methodologies, and the concept of conditional strategies', *Human Development* 33.

Main, M. and Cassidy, J. (1988) 'Categories of responses to reunion with the parent at age 6: predictable from infant attachment classifications and stable over a one-month period', *Developmental Psychology* 24.

Neugarten, B. (1977) 'Personality and aging', in J. E. Birren and K. W. Schaie (eds) *Handbook of the Psychology of Aging*, New York.

Rieder, C. and Cicchetti, D. (1989) 'Organizational perspective on cognitive control functioning and cognitive-affective balance in maltreated children', *Developmental Psychology* 25.

Riegel, K. F. (1976) 'The dialectics of human development', *American Psychologist* 31.

Schaie, K. W. (1979) 'The primary mental abilities in adulthood: an exploration in the development of psychometric intelligence', in P. B. Baltes and O. G. Brim jr (eds) *Life-Span Development and Behavior*, vol. 2, New York.

Turner, B. F. and Troll, L. E. (eds) (1994) *Women Growing Older: Psychological Perspectives*, Thousand Oaks, CA.

van Lieshout, C. F. M., van Aken, M. A. G. and van Seyen, E. T. J. (1990) 'Perspectives on peer relations from mothers, teachers, friends and self', *Human Development* 33.

See also: adolescence; age organization; childhood; gerontology, social; life cycle; life history; life tables and survival analysis.

life tables and survival analysis

Demographers' interests in mortality and cohort attrition come together in the life table, which provides a statistical description of the shrinking over time of a cohort of individuals, as they die. (The French, with a certain perverse pessimism, call this a 'death table'.) The life table itself is composed of a number of columns showing the values of the different life-table functions at each age, starting from birth. Basic columns show mortality rates at each age, and probabilities of dying between one birthday and the next. Another column, the stationary or life-table population, shows the numbers of people there would be at each age if deaths occurred according to the life table, fertility exactly balanced mortality, and if there was no migration. Another column, the expectation of life, shows the average number of years left to be lived by people who survive to a particular birthday. Perhaps the most important column shows the number of people out of the original cohort who survive to each birthday, its value at 'exact' age 0 (that is, the zeroth birthday, or birth) being the scaled size of the original birth cohort. When the size of the original birth cohort is unity, this function gives the probability of surviving to a particular birthday, and is known as the survivorship function or survival function.

The simplest life table to conceptualize is the cohort life table, a birth cohort being registered and then followed until all its members die. The life table is progressively constructed by relating to the number of individuals who survive to a particular birthday the number of deaths that occur during the following year, or period of years, until the next designated birthday. The method is generally impracticable for a human population, however, since the process of calculation, like the process of extinction of the cohort, takes about a century.

An alternative approach is to calculate a period life table based on the mortality rates of a particular year or calendar period. Such life tables are routinely produced by national statistical offices. The mortality rates are obtained by relating counts of deaths at particular ages, as obtained from vital statistics, to estimates of the population alive at those ages, as derived from a population enumeration. The cohort to which the life table refers is synthetic, in the sense that the rates are not derived from the experience of an actual cohort, nor would any real cohort necessarily have experienced the mortality rates measured over the calendar period in question. In industrialized countries, for example, the people who contribute to mortality rates at the oldest ages are survivors of much harsher conditions than are experienced by the infants and children. Thus the period life table is a model because it shows not the experience of a real cohort, but the implications of a particular schedule of mortality.

The standard period life table has many applications. Its mortality rates are input to population projections. It provides summary statistics, such as expectation of life at birth, that national governments use as indicators of population health: such statistics are tracked from year to year, and unexpected movements attract attention. Cross-national comparisons of life tables lead to a ranking of countries according to the favourability of their mortality experience.

There are many variants of the standard period life table. The most obvious is that life tables are almost invariably calculated separately by sex, since men generally suffer higher mortality than women. In addition, if similar discriminating information is provided on both death certificates and census schedules, then separate mortality rates, and hence life tables, can be calculated according, for example, to occupation, ethnicity or marital status. Also, cause-specific life tables can be calculated from mortality rates according to cause of death. Finally, multiple-decrement life tables can be calculated that show simultaneous cohort attrition from a number of causes.

Any cohort, however defined, suffers attrition. In the 1970s, demographers began to apply the mechanics of the cohort life table to other than birth cohorts, and to events other than death. People married during a particular calendar period, for example, form a marriage cohort, and, once married, might divorce; likewise, women who have borne a second child might bear a third. Further, depending on the particular cohort under examination, and the event which removes people from observation, the unit of time may be not just a year, but a month or even a day. Such applications, which are typically based on data from large specially designed population surveys, are known by the more general term of survival analysis, where 'survival' refers to the avoidance of the event of interest, whether it be divorce for a marriage cohort, or a third birth for women with two children.

Just as with applications of conventional period life tables, the observer may wish to compare the 'survival' experience of different sub-cohorts. When samples are sufficiently large and the desired comparisons fairly simple, statistical tests can be applied to determine whether differences between the patterns of attrition in each sub-cohort are attributable to chance alone. More generally, however, demographers employ a modelling procedure, made possible by a statistical breakthrough in the early 1970s that showed how to combine life tables with techniques of multivariate regression, known as 'event-history analysis'.

Gigi Santow
University of Stockholm

Further reading

Elandt-Johnson, R. C. and Johnson, N. L. (1980) *Survival Models and Data Analysis*, New York.
Keyfitz N. (1968) *Introduction to the Mathematics of Population*, Reading, MA.
Shryock, H. S., Siegel, J. S. and Associates (1973) *The Methods and Materials of Demography*, Washington, DC.

See also: cohort analysis; life cycle; life-span development; morbidity.

limited liability

The most common form of capitalist business enterprise, the limited liability company, has a legal status of a *persona* separate from owners or shareholders. Three features arise: debts incurred are the firm's, not the shareholders', whose maximum liability is restricted to their original financial outlay; the identity of the firm is unchanged should one shareholder transfer his or her ownership title to a third party; the firm's contractual relationships are entered into by its officers (for example, directors or managers).

These three characteristics were not originally co-existent. By the fifteenth century, English law had awarded limited liability to monastic communities and trade guilds for commonly held property. In the seventeenth century, joint stock charters were awarded by the crown as circumscribed monopoly privileges to groups such as the East India and Hudson's Bay Companies.

By the early nineteenth century, a joint stock company could be formed simply by registration, and no monopoly privileges were awarded. The merging of the features was completed by mid-century when incorporation with full limited liability became permissible and common in the UK and the USA, and in Europe a decade or so later.

It is widely agreed that the move to large-scale industrial enterprise was facilitated, and indeed made possible, by limited liability. The threat of potential confiscation of an individual's total wealth should part of it be invested in an unsuccessful company was removed. Moreover, the risk could be further reduced if the individual invested in several and not just one firm. Large sums of untapped personal financial capital became available. Transferability of shares permitted continuity of business operation not present in other forms of enterprise. The existence of the firm as a separate contracting *persona* permitted a productive division of labour between risk-bearing capitalists and business administrators.

Schumpeter (1950) criticized this latter development as having pushed 'into the background all . . . the institutions of property and free contracting . . . that expressed the needs . . . of economic activity'. Hessen (1979) took the contrary view: limited liability is a creature of private agreement, not the state. Freely negotiated contractual specialization is a device for greater efficiency in meeting private wants, not a shirking of responsibility, not a Schumpeterian 'absentee ownership' which because nobody is 'left . . . to stand for it' must evolve into a state-controlled bureaucracy.

W. Duncan Reekie
University of the Witwatersrand

References

Hessen, R. (1979) *In Defense of the Corporation*, Stanford, CA.
Schumpeter, J. (1950) *Capitalism, Socialism and Democracy*, New York.

See also: corporate enterprise; firm, theory of.

linguistics

Linguistics can be defined as the science of language. Language, however, may be approached from a number of different perspectives, and it plays such a central role in human life that many disciplines are concerned with language in one way or another. Indeed every science contains one linguistic component at the very least, the language of its theory and observations with which it may at times be concerned. What then distinguishes linguistics from other sciences?

There is one field which is particularly close to linguistics, and that is the study of literature, since its very material is verbal. However, even in this case the preoccupation with linguistic matters is different from that of linguistics itself. In all other fields, language is a means to an end; only in linguistics is it studied as an end in itself.

Like so many other sciences, linguistics took its modern form as a separate academic discipline in the nineteenth century, although it has a long prehistory.

In particular it was preceded by national philologies, which arose in literate societies such as those of India, China and Greece. Modern linguistics developed in Europe on the basis of the Graeco-Roman tradition with minor contributions from Semitic sources in the Renaissance. The most theoretically sophisticated of these national philologies was that of India, and yet it became known to Europe only in the nineteenth century, while an appreciation of its significance is even more recent.

Although the philological studies of the grammarians is the chief source for linguistics in the classical tradition, two other pursuits are worthy of mention. One is the philosophical concern with the nature of language. The main question was whether the relation between sound and meaning is natural or conventional and the most important discussion is Plato's *Cratylus*. The second source is rhetoric, the effective use of language in public speaking and writing. Some of the earliest analyses of linguistic phenomena, such as Protagoras' distinguishing of the various moods of the verb, grew out of this applied interest.

The most important, though, was the philological tradition of the grammarians which developed in the Alexandrian period. In common with other national philologies it displayed the following features: The study of languages has as its goal the understanding of certain highly valued texts, sacred or, in the case of the Greeks, profane, namely the Homeric poems. It involves concentration on a single language and a valuation of it as superior to all other forms of speech including the contemporary spoken language which inevitably, in the course of linguistic change, has come to differ from it. It views historic change not as a rational process but as a haphazard degeneration from a formerly ideal state. This in turn involves the notion of 'prescriptivism', an attempt to restore a particular norm which is contrary to existing usage. The concentration on written texts also makes the written form primary *vis-à-vis* the spoken, since sounds are merely the momentary realizations of the apparently stable and fixed written norms. That language is not here studied for its own sake is very strikingly expressed in the *Techne Grammatike* (attributed to Dionysius Thrax around 100 BC), itself the model of numerous subsequent grammars. After enumerating the various subdivisions of grammar, the last mentioned is 'the appreciation of literary composition which is the noblest part of grammar'.

Nevertheless this tradition made lasting contributions. It provided a comprehensive model for describing language which was well suited to Latin and Greek and is the source of a large part of current linguistic terminology. It may be called the 'word-paradigm model'. The sentence consists of words which are divisible on the basis of form and function into a small number of classes, the parts of speech. Further, each part of speech can be considered from two points of view, internal variability of form ('morphology') and functional relation to other words in the speech chain ('syntax'). In the area of morphology the lasting achievement was the discovery of the 'paradigm', literally 'example'. Inflectional parts of speech such as the noun vary according to a set of categories, for example, case and number, and the number of distinct models is very small. For instance, all Latin nouns of the first declension have similar variations of form and any one noun, such as *puella* ('girl'), can be viewed as an example to follow for the rest. This was no mean achievement and grew out of the dispute in the Alexandrian period between the analogists, who stressed regularity in language, and the anomalists, who denied it. It was the search for regularities by the analogists that revealed the existence of comprehensive patterns, namely paradigms.

In syntax, there was the classification of types of relationships among words such as 'government', as when a verb requires and hence 'governs' a particular case, and agreement, as when two words agree in having the same categories, for example, the adjectives agreeing with nouns in gender, number and case.

One further feature of this model should be mentioned. It involved a hierarchy of levels. Sounds made up words; words made up sentences. On this basis there were two main levels, the 'phonological' and 'grammatical', the latter divided, as has been seen, into morphology and syntax. Such a notion of levels has remained as part of linguistic theory. In particular the existence of phonological and grammatical levels, even though there are relationships between them, seems to be fundamental to any theory of language.

The model just described was not all discovered at once by the Greeks. It developed considerably in the Roman, medieval and the post-medieval periods. In particular the rise of *grammaire générale*, largely but not exclusively French, in the seventeenth and eighteenth centuries (though without medieval predecessors) deserves mention. It employed the word-paradigm model but sought to explain its structure by reference to universal reason and the very nature of the world and of thought as shown by metaphysics and logic. Thus the difference between nouns and adjectives mirrored the difference between substances and their qualities. Moreover, a number of languages were often compared on the assumption that such categories, inherent in human reason, must exist in all languages.

The nineteenth century was not marked merely by the rise of linguistics as a separate discipline but involved a revolution in the conception of language. As a result of exploration and colonization, Europe became acutely aware of the vast number and diversity of human languages. The traditional explanation was the biblical story of the Tower of Babel, and at first the main question was what language was spoken before the confusion of tongues, the *lingua Adamica*. However, it began to be noticed that the differences in language were not haphazard; they fall into groupings such as the Romance, Germanic and Semitic languages.

The basic explanation which developed about the turn of the nineteenth century was that just as Spanish was like Italian because they were both changed forms of an originally homogeneous language, Latin, so where the original language was not recorded, the explanation had to be similar. There must have been a 'Proto-Germanic' and a 'Proto-Semitic' and so on. Moreover this process of differentiation of an ancestral language was not confined to the most obvious groupings. In particular the discovery of Sankrit, the sacred language of India, with its obvious resemblance to Latin, Greek and other European languages, led to the hypothesis of an original Indo-European language which had branched into Latin, Greek, Indo-Iranian, Germanic, Slavic and so on, which then in most instances differentiated once more in a more recent period. The metaphor was that of a family tree.

The historical-comparative method that dominated nineteenth-century linguistics had as its goal the reconstruction of the original ancestral language and of the subsequent changes in it, which gave rise to later language. It was mainly applied to Indo-European but was also employed in the study of other language families. This way of looking at language was in many ways diametrically opposed to the traditional one inherited from classical philology. Change is not a haphazard degeneration but follows rational patterns, indeed, becomes the central object of linguistic science. Changes on the phonological level are understandable in terms of articulatory and auditory similarity. Hence the written form is equally valuable since change is not degeneration, and the logical basis for linguistic prescriptivism is destroyed.

During the nineteenth century and up to about 1920, the inherited pattern of grammatical description, though often modified, continued its sway because the focus of interest was historical change. However, in the late 1920s another basic revolution in linguistics occurred, which we may call the 'structural'. The first articulation of this was in 1915 in the posthumous *Cours de linguistique générale* (English translation, *Course in General Linguistics*, 1959) of Ferdinand de Saussure of Geneva. De Saussure, himself a historical linguist by training, introduced a terminology which has become general in the social sciences. Language can be studied 'diachronically' in its aspect of historical process, or 'synchronically' in terms of the internal relations within a state as abstracted from change. There were a number of structural schools, differing in many respects but united in finding in the 'synchronic structure' of language the central object of linguistic science. An important factor was the work of anthropologists on non-western languages where both the profound differences from western languages and the usual absence of historical records combined to concentrate attention on synchronic structure.

The nature of these new methods can be most easily illustrated from phonology, which was in fact the earliest area of interest for the structuralists. A mere enumeration of the sounds of the language without regard to their functional relations was unenlightening. Thus two languages might both have *p* and *b* sounds which were phonetically identical but, if a rule could be formulated that told us when *p* occurs and when *b* in terms of other sounds, there could never be a functional meaning contrast. This is the case for the Algonquian languages. In English, on the other hand, *pat* and *bat* are different words. For the Algonquian languages *p* and *b* belong to the same phoneme or functional unit, while in English they are two contrasting units.

Similarly, methods were extended to the grammatical level leading to the positing of functional units like the morpheme. Thus the English phonemic variants of the plural *-s*, *-z* and *-əz* are predictable on the basis of the final phoneme, the stem, and hence are members of the same functional unit.

In 1957, Chomsky's *Syntactic Structures* ushered in the period of 'generative grammar'. The basic concept uses not functional units but rules. Moreover, grammar was constructed not as in the American structural school of observation by induction from the bottom up, morphemes consisting of phonemes and so on, but from top down – from syntax, particularly relations among whole sentence patterns ('transformations') with appeals to native intuitions of grammaticality. The whole grammar was not unlike an axiomatic system. The basic formulas often called 'deep structure' such as subject + predicate occurred first and by rule-governed substitutions, and transformations ended up as strings which would then be realized as actual utterances by phonological rules. After some years it became apparent that describing languages with this basic approach also leads to differing theories as in structuralism, and at the time of writing no one version holds the field.

A basic question raised by both the structuralist and generative revolution was the role of interlinguistic comparisons. Historical linguistics was essentially comparative, but was it possible to compare structures ahistorically? Did one just end up with an indefinitely large number of non-comparable individual descriptions? The American structuralist school seemed on the whole content with these results. The only universals of the dominant view were those of methodology. Languages could differ to any degree so that no cross-linguistic generalization was possible. The Prague school stressed the possibility of comparing structures and made some beginnings, especially in phonology Chomsky had by 1965 (*Syntactic Structures*) moved to the notion of universal grammar and indeed hailed *grammaire générale* as a predecessor. All grammars had identical deep structures and these reflected a universal genetically based human endowment. This viewpoint ultimately had to be abandoned to be replaced by universal constraints on the forms of grammars. Finally there were those who approached language universals by noting the existence of recurring and limited sets of types based on observations close to the surface, for example, in word order. Such constraints were frequently in the form of implicational relationships. For instance, language of the VSO type (with basic order verb-subject-object) always had the dependent genitive after the noun, but not necessarily vice versa. There were also non-restricted universals, such as that all sound systems have at least two vowel levels and two series of stop sounds based on the point of articulation.

Linguistics is at present divided into a considerable number of subfields, some of which are interdisciplinary. Some linguists pursue historical comparison whose legitimacy has never been seriously questioned by structuralists, usually specializing in some particular historical family, or subfamily, of languages. Others, particularly anthropological linguists, concentrate on the synchronic description of unwritten languages often with an areal specialization and some historical-comparative interests. On the basis of linguistic structure, some specialize in phonology frequently involving laboratory phonetics. Others work on grammatical level, particularly the syntactic, and may have connections with computer science. Still others are chiefly interested in semantics, often in alliance with philosophy. More purely interdisciplinary fields include psycholinguistics involving an analysis of the psychological processes at work in language use, acquisition of language by the child or second-language learning. A further important interdisciplinary area is socio-linguistics, commonly divided into macro-socio-linguistics, for example, language in relation to ethnicity with its accompanying social, political and education problems, and micro-sociolinguistics, which is concerned with conversational interaction as related, for example, to situational factors and the relative social status of the participants.

Since the 1950s linguistics, usually a minor speciality in other departments, has had an almost explosive growth, particularly in the USA, with a corresponding expansion in the number and size of independent departments and reflecting both the intellectual development of the field itself and its numerous connections with other disciplines.

Joseph Greenberg
Stanford University

Further reading

Greenberg, J. H. (1977), *New Invitation to Linguistics*, Garden City, NY.

Greenberg, J. J. (ed.) (1978) *Universals of Human Language*, 4 vols, Stanford, CA.

Lyons, J. (1968) *Introduction to Theoretical Linguistics*, 2 vols, London.

Newmeyer, F. J. (1980) *Linguistic Theory in America*, New York.

Newmeyer, F. J. (ed.) (1988) *Linguistics, The Cambridge Survey*, 4 vols, Cambridge.

Robins, R. H. (1968) *A Short History of Linguistics*, Bloomington, IN.

Sampson, G. (1980) *Schools of Linguistics*, Stanford, CA.

Vachek, J. (1964) *A Prague School Reader in Linguistics*, Bloomington, IN.

See also: Chomsky, Noam; language.

linguistics, historical *see* historical linguistics

linguistics, structural *see* structural linguistics

liquidity

Liquidity is, to quote Kenneth Boulding, 'a quality of assets which . . . is not a very clear or easily measurable concept' (1995): all economists know what it is but few would want to define it. Nevertheless, a definition is necessary and, for most uses, the definition must allow it to be measured.

While liquidity usually refers to a 'quality of assets', it may also apply to markets or agents (i.e. individuals or firms). However, in these applications it remains the quality of the assets traded in the market, or owned by the agent, which determines their liquidity.

Two measurable definitions of liquidity stand out. Lippman and McCall (1986) discuss 'notions' of liquidity, which keeps their technical analysis in touch with more down-to-earth ideas. Their notions are that money is perfectly liquid; an illiquid asset cannot be sold; an asset is more liquid if it is traded in a market with a large number of participants; and liquidity depends on the desire of the holder to sell. They then include these notions in a model in which the seller maximizes the expected present value of the money received from the sale, and liquidity is measured by the *expected time taken to sell the asset*. The present value increases with the selling price, but decreases with the expected delay until the transaction.

Grossman and Miller (1988) measure liquidity in terms of '*immediacy*', that is, the ability of an asset to be sold immediately. In financial markets, immediacy is supplied by 'market makers' – intermediaries who declare a price at which they themselves are prepared to buy so that sellers can sell immediately at that price. The market makers then search for another buyer to take the assets at a higher price, the price difference being the intermediary's reward for providing liquidity, or immediacy. Liquidity increases with the number of market makers. Financial markets can be contrasted with the housing market in this respect. Intermediaries in the latter tend not to buy houses themselves; their concern is to ensure that potential buyers are aware that a house is for sale; for this they charge a commission. Consequently, this market, with few market makers, is not very liquid.

While economists continue to sort out the precise definition and measurement of liquidity, others have to use approximate measures. Economic forecasters often use a measure of the private sector's liquidity as an indicator of its future expenditure, while company treasurers and banking supervisers monitor various liquidity ratios as a means of assessing a company's ability to withstand sudden demands on its cash reserves. For example, banks have to ensure that they have sufficient liquidity to meet all reasonable expectations of cash withdrawals by their customers.

David Barr
Brunel University

References

Boulding, K. E. (1955) *Economic Analysis*, 3rd edition, New York.
Grossman, S. J. and Miller, M. H. (1988) 'Liquidity and market structure', *Journal of Finance*, July.
Lippman, S. A. and McCall, J. J. (1986) 'An operational measure of liquidity', *American Economic Review*, March.

See also: monetary policy; money.

literacy

In the mid-1960s the place and meaning of the concept and the fact of literacy in the social sciences was a simple and secure one. Tied closely to the liberal, post-Englightement synthesis of modernization theory, literacy was seen as a central variable among that complex of factors that distinguished modern, developed or developing, and advanced societies *and* individuals, from the lesser developed areas and persons of the world. Literacy, moreover, was typically conceptualized more as an independent variable than a dependent factor. Support for this set of propositions was drawn, on the one hand, from a set of once commonsensical assumptions and expectations, rooted in a special view of the nature of (historical) development that emphasized the linearity and certainty of progress and, on the other hand, from a number of aggregate macrolevel ecological correlations that saw literacy levels relatively highly associated with many of the other indicators of social development, ranging from fertility rates to measures of economic development. Although literacy itself was at best vaguely defined and variously measured, a diffuse positivism and functionalism undergirded the prominence accorded to it in many formulations. But despite strong assumptions, there were surprisingly few empirical or critical studies. Important questions were few: expectations of literacy's key contribution to social and economic development, political democratization and participant citizenship, widening awareness and identification, seizure of opportunities, and action orientations dominated. As such, promotion of literacy often featured as a central element in plans for the development of underdeveloped areas, especially by North American and western European social scientists, governments and foundations.

Such an understanding no longer maintains its hegemony. In fact, no central theory governs expectations about the roles and meanings of literacy, and its very nature has itself become problematic and arouses contention and increasingly critical attention. From its formerly secure status as critical independent variable, literacy is now conceptualized more as a dependent factor; the linearity of its contributions is also debated. Ironically, as the status – so to speak – of literacy as an independently determinative variable, necessary if not always sufficient, has declined, its place on the agenda of social science research and discussion has risen. There are lessons in that transformation.

Many sources account for this change. Among them are the discovery of the limits of modernization theory and the theoretical synthesis on which it was based; greater awareness of the differences (and different effects) among literacy, schooling and education – terms too often used interchangeably and confused conceptually; recognition of the problematic nature of literacy, and the conceptual and empirical difficulties that the subject represents. For example, by the 1960s, the severe problems of measuring literacy – comparing measures and resulting rates for different places and periods, and assessing associations and contributions – were frequently noted; a variety of measures and definitions, with a trend towards their inflation, proliferated. Whether literacy's impacts were attitudinal and ideational, cognitive, skill-linked, concrete or more abstract, all-pervasive or more selective, sparked further discussion and weakened common bases of understanding. In addition, the conservative functions and consequences of literacy and, indeed, certain 'non-effects' received renewed attention. Empirical studies became more sensitive to weak and contradictory findings; discussions of literacy 'gaps' and time 'lags' in association with other expected aspects and concomitants of development punctuated the literature. International attention increased: from the twin sources of UNESCO's calls for action and analysis and pathbreaking national literacy campaigns in the Third World. The discovery of persisting *il*literacy in the advanced societies led to the identification of *il*literacy, and sometimes literacy, too, as a social problem, and a late twentieth century threat to national security, economic productivity, national welfare and the promise of democratic life. Rapid changes in communications technology, especially of non-print and non-alphabetic forms (in contrast to the traditional bases of literacy) not only led to sometimes frenzied questions about the 'future' and 'decline' of literacy and print, but also stimulated more questions about definitions, measures and levels of individual and national skills requisite for survival and advancement in late modern societies. Whereas literacy was seldom deemed *un*important or non-consequential, or *il*literacy *not* an obstacle or liability, its precise contributions and impacts could no longer be assumed.

The challenge of a number of revisionist 'critical theories' was also important. So too was the development of a historical analysis of literacy and illiteracy, much of which aimed specifically at testing the literacy – modernization linkages. In a number of careful, often statistical, studies, historians throughout Europe and North America sharply qualified traditional expectations of a series of direct connections tying rising levels of literacy to developments in societies, economies, polities and cultures. This is one area in which historians and social scientists have had much of importance to contribute to one another. In part, historians discovered relatively high levels of literacy in advance of 'modernization'; they simultaneously located important 'take-offs' prior to mass or even moderately high literacy rates. Literacy's linkages to the spread of modern attitudes and its relationship to individual advancement have been questioned. Notions of stages or threshold levels have also been criticized. Many macrolevel correlations seem to break down in disaggregated testing.

There are, however, a number of critical points at which historical and social scientific analyses reflect one another conceptually and empirically. These include the nature of literacy as a *dependent* variable; its dependence on *context*; the *limits* of universal impacts and generalized consequences (which have major implications for literacy's place in social science theories); the epistemological complications of *defining and measuring* literacy levels at the societal plane or literacy abilities at the individual level; the weakness of the traditional literacy–illiteracy *dichotomy*; and the fact that changes in literacy levels may often *follow from*, rather than precede, basic social, economic, political or cultural transformations. Literacy, increasingly, is connected to the larger network of communicative competencies (the oral, for example), not contrasted dichotomously and developmentally from them; it is also conceptualized more as a *continuous, widely varying, and nonlinear* attribute. Its importance as shaper of attitudes and as a symbol and symbolic influence stands beside, in partial independence from, its role in cognitive and skill determination. To speak of literacy in the abstract is now considered hazardous, if not quite meaningless.

Among the most critical of contemporary research approaches to literacy is the emerging social psychology of literacy. Scribner and Cole (1981) document the limits of literacy by itself and the theoretical assumptions that link it universally to higher forms of thought and practice; they point towards a formulation of literacy as *practice and context* determined and determining. Anthropological studies have moved towards ethnographies of literacy in use and non-use (Heath 1983; Tannen 1982; Whiteman 1981). Historical studies continue their pathbreaking relevance (Graff 1979; 1981a; 1981b; 1987; Furet and Ozouf 1977). By contrast, the sociology and economics of literacy find their theoretical presuppositions and empirical methods challenged and seek new paradigms (Bataille 1976; *Harvard Educational Review* 1981; Stanley 1978). The future of literacy studies is an exciting and vastly important one.

Harvey J. Graff
University of Texas

References

Bataille, L. (ed.) (1976) *A Turning Point for Literacy*, Oxford.

Furet, F. and Ozouf, J. (1977) *Lire et écrire: l'alphabétisation des français de Calvin à Jules Ferry*, 2 vols, Paris. (English translation of vol. 1, Cambridge, 1983.)

Graff, H. J. (1979) *The Literacy Myth: Literacy and Social Structure in the Nineteenth Century City*, New York.

— (ed.) (1981a) *Literacy in History: An Interdisciplinary Research Bibliography*, New York.

— (ed.) (1981b) *Literacy and Social Development in the West: A Reader*, Cambridge, UK.

— (1987) *The Legacies of Literacy: Continuities and Contradictions in Western Society and Culture*, Bloomington, IN.

Harvard Educational Review (1981) 'Education as transformation: identity, change, and development' (entire issue), 51(1).

Heath, S. B. (1983) *Ways with Words*, Cambridge, UK.

Scribner, S. and Cole, M. (1981) *The Psychology of Literacy*, Cambridge, MA.

Stanley, M. (1978) *The Technological Conscience*, Glencoe, IL.

Tannen, D. (ed.) (1982) *Spoken and Written Language: Exploring Orality and Literacy*, vol. 9, *Advances in Discourse Processes*, Norwood, NJ.

Whiteman, M. F. (ed.) (1981) *Writing: The Nature, Development, and Teaching of Written Communication*, vol. I, *Variations in Writing*, Hillside, NJ.

Further reading

Baumann, G. (1986) *The Written Word*, Oxford.

Finnegan, R. (1988) *Literacy and Orality*, Oxford.

Goody, J. (ed.) (1968) *Literacy in Traditional Societies*, Cambridge, UK.

Graff, H. J. (1994) *The Labyrinths of Literacy: Reflections on Past and Present*, Pittsburgh, PA.

Street, B. (ed.) (1993) *Cross-Cultural Approaches to Literacy*, Cambridge, UK.

See also: mass media.

lobbying *see* interest groups and lobbying

Locke, John (1632–1704)

John Locke was born in 1632 at Wrington in Somerset. In 1652 he entered Christ Church College, Oxford, where he received his MA in 1658. In that same year he was elected student of Christ Church; in 1660 he became lecturer in Greek, lecturer in Rhetoric in 1662, and censor of Moral Philosophy in 1664. From 1667 to 1681 Locke was physician and secretary to Anthony Ashley Cooper, Lord Ashley (later First Earl of Shaftesbury). He was elected fellow of the Royal Society in 1668, and was secretary to the Lords Proprietors of Carolina from 1668 to 1675. In 1684 he was deprived of his appointment to Christ Church by royal decree. He lived in Holland from 1683 to 1689, was Commissioner on the Board of Trade from 1696 to 1700, and died at Otes (Oates) in the parish of High Laver, Essex, in 1704.

Locke's *Essay Concerning Human Understanding* (1690) made a major contribution to psychology and to philosophical psychology. That work offered the outlines of a genetic epistemology, and a theory of learning. Locke's interest in children is reflected not only in his pedagogical work, *Some Thoughts Concerning Education* (1693), but in many passages of the *Essay* where he traced the development of awareness in children. The oft-quoted metaphor used by Locke to characterize the mind as a blank tablet should not blind us to the fact that the Lockean mind comes equipped with faculties, that the child has specific 'tempers' or character traits which the educator must learn to work with, and that human nature for Locke has basic self-preserving tendencies to avoid pain and seek pleasure. These tendencies were even called by Locke 'innate practical principles'. The innate claim that his psychology rejected was for truths (moral and intellectual) and specific ideational contents.

Much of the *Essay* is occupied with discussing how we acquire certain ideas, with showing how a combination of physical and physiological processes stimulate and work with a large number of mental operations (for example, joining, separating, considering, abstracting, generalizing) to produce the ideas of particular sense qualities and many complex notions, such as power, existence, unity. One such complex notion is the idea of self or person.

The account of the idea of self – or rather, *my* idea of *my* self, for Locke's account of this notion is a first-person account – emerges out of a discussion of the question, 'Does the soul always think?' That question had been answered in the affirmative by Descartes. For Locke, not only was it empirically false that the soul always thinks, but also that question suggested wrongly that something in me (my soul), not me, thinks. *I* am the agent of my actions and the possessor of my thoughts. Moreover, all thinking is reflexive, when I think, I am aware that I am thinking, no matter what form that thinking takes (sensing, willing, believing, doubting or remembering). It is the awareness of my act of thinking which also functions in awareness of self. Consciousness appropriates both thoughts and actions. The self or person for Locke consists in that set of thoughts and actions which I appropriate and for which I take responsibility through my consciousness.

Appropriation is a fundamental activity for Locke. I appropriate my thoughts and actions to form my concept of self. The *Essay* details the appropriation by each of us of ideas and knowledge. Education is also an appropriation of information, but more importantly of habits of good conduct. Education is a socializing process. It takes place usually within the family, with a tutor (for Locke writes about the education of a gentleman's son). But the account of the socialization process extends to Locke's political writings, *Two Treatises on Government* (1690), where he discusses the family, duties that parents have to their children and to each other (a marriage contract is part of his account of the family), and the rights and duties of citizens in a political society. The appropriation of land, possessions and eventually money by the activities of the person constitutes an early stage in Locke's account of the movement from the state of nature to a civil (political) society.

The political society, as the pre-political state of nature, is grounded in law and order; order is respect and responsibility to each other and ultimately to God whose law of nature prescribes these duties. Locke's law of nature is a Christianized version of that tradition. The individual laws which he cites on occasion prescribe and proscribe the actions sanctioned or denied by the liberal religion of his day. These laws differed little in content from those innate moral truths Locke attacked; it was not the truths he rejects, only the claim that they were innate. Locke's society is fairly slanted in favour of the individual: preservation of the person, privacy of property, tacit assent, the right of dissent. At the same time, the pressures towards conformity and the force of majority opinion are also strong. The structure of his civil society, with its checks and balances, its separation of powers, its grounding on the law of nature, is designed to achieve a balance between the rights and needs of the individual and the need for security and order. His views on toleration (which were expressed in a series of tracts), while directed mainly against religious intolerance, match well with his insistence that government does not have the right to prescribe rites, rituals, dress and other practices in religion. Locke's toleration did not, however, extend to unbelief, to atheism.

The methodology for acquiring knowledge recommended by Locke and illustrated in his *Essay* stressed careful observation. Both in the physical sciences and in learning about ourselves and others, it was the 'plain, historical method' (that is, experience and observation) which holds the promise of accurate knowledge, or sound probability. Knowledge was not limited to demonstrative, deductive processes. Truth claims were always open to revision through further reports and observations. These concepts of knowledge and this experiential method were extended by Locke to what was later termed (for example, by Hume) 'the science of man' or 'of human nature'. His detailed attention to his own thought processes enabled him to map the wide variety of mental operations and to begin the development of a cognitive psychology. His interest in children, throughout his life, led to observations and descriptions of their behaviour. He had many friends who had children, and lived for several years on different occasions with families who had several young children. The *Essay* uses some of these observations as the basis for a brief genetic learning theory, and his *Some Thoughts* contains many remarks and recommendations for raising children based upon his firsthand experience with children in their natural environment.

Locke's social theory grew out of his reading and (more importantly) out of these habits of observing people in daily life. In his travels in France and Holland, he often recorded details of activities and practices, religious, academic and ordinary. Where direct observation was not possible, he used the new travel literature for reports on other societies, other customs and habits. He had his own biases and preferences, to be sure, but with his dedication to reason and rationality, he seldom allowed emotions to affect his observation or his conclusions. He was an articulate representative of the Royal Society's attitudes in the sciences, including what we know as the social sciences.

John W. Yolton
Rutgers University

References

Locke, J. (1689) *Epistola de Tolerantia*, Gouda.
—— (1689) *Letter Concerning Toleration*, London.
—— (1690) *Essay Concerning Human Understanding*, London.
—— (1690) *A Second Letter Concerning Toleration*, London.
—— (1690) *Two Treastises of Government*, London.
—— (1692) *Some Considerations of the Consequences of the Lowering of Interest and Raising the Value of Money*, London.
—— (1692) *A Third Letter for Toleration*, London.
—— (1693) *Some Thoughts Concerning Education*, London.
—— (1695) *The Reasonableness of Christianity, as Delivered in the Scriptures*, London.
—— (1695) *Short Observations on a Printed Paper, Intituled 'For Encouraging the Coining Silver Money in England, and After, for Keeping it Here'*, London.
—— (1695) *Further Considerations Concerning Raising the Value of Money*, London.
—— (1697) *A Letter to Edward Lord Bishop of Worcester*, London.
—— (1714) *Works*, 3 volumes, London.

Further reading

Aaron, R. I. (1971) *John Locke*, 3rd edn, Oxford.
Colman, J. (1983) *John Locke's Moral Philosophy*, Edinburgh.
Cranston, M. (1957) *John Locke: A Biography*, New York.
Dunn, J. (1969) *The Political Thought of John Locke*, Cambridge, UK.
Tully, J. (1980) *A Discourse on Property: John Locke and his Adversaries*, Cambridge, UK.
Yolton, J. W. (1956) *John Locke and the Way of Ideas*, Oxford.
—— (1970) *Locke and the Compass of Human Understanding*, Cambridge, UK.

See also: liberalism; social contract.

Lyotard, Jean François (1924–   )

The French philosopher Lyotard has become internationally famous for his work on post-modernity. In *The Postmodern Condition* (1979) he showed how the identification of knowledge with representation, characteristic of modern societies, reduces the variety of actions we perform in language to denotation. Language then becomes a set of statements that can be treated as things, as commodities in capitalist societies. For Lyotard, rational knowledge is no longer the basis for critique, nor does it hold out the possibility of emancipation, as the modern thinkers of the Enlightenment had promised. Auschwitz, he has said (Lyotard 1986), is the metaphor of modernity. Knowledge is a western narrative of terror, in so far as it aims at silencing the other possible stories by presenting itself as the only legitimate, true account of events (Lyotard 1979; 1986).

Born in Versailles on 10 August 1924, Lyotard studied philosophy with Ferdinand Alquié, Maurice de Gandillac and Maurice Merleau-Ponty. His first book was an introduction to phenomenology, and phenomenology remains a significant influence in all Lyotard's work. He accepts and develops the phenomenological idea that the Cartesian cogito, the reflective I, is an embodied, particular subject in a temporal 'situation'. Knowledge and truth are human, relative to a certain context, and derive from a lived world of experiences that are never fully comprehended. At the time of La Phénoménologie (1954), Lyotard was still trying to overcome what he saw as the major failure of phenomenology, namely its political ambiguities. The conclusion of the book was a militant appeal to recast phenomenology as a Marxist philosophy.

Nevertheless, Lyotard's relationship with Marxism was ambivalent. From 1956 to 1963 Lyotard contributed to the journal Socialisme and Barbarie, a publication well known for its trenchant, though still Marxist, critique of the USSR and the French Communist Party, and, in later writings (Dérive à partir de Marx et Freud, 1973) he began to argue that Marxist claims to possess a universal truth is not an alternative to ideology, to illusion, but a tool for domination.

For a while Lyotard celebrated instinctual desire as an alternative to reason, a position that makes Des dispositifs pulsionnels (1973) and Economie libidinale (1974) uncomfortable reading. It was only when he came to characterize judgement as a faculty of reason distinct from knowledge, that his critique of modernity, initially called 'paganism', and then 'post-modernity', gained its distinctive tone (Au Juste, Lyotard and Thébaud 1979).

Post-modernity does not speak 'in the name of' the people or for our emancipation. Politics is not a science; it is not the representation of the true nature of beings or the true will of the people. Politics is an arena where judgements must be made, without recourse to absolute criteria, universal theories, or ideal consensus. Lyotard's understanding of politics as the art of making judgements is an attempt to do justice to the heterogeneity and incommensurability of perspectives, and a challenge to the characteristic modern certainty that there are sure and reliable solutions to political problems (L'Inhumain, 1988).

Lyotard's writings on art and language are aspects of his concern with rhetorics, that is, with the expression of ideas and feelings that escape rational discourse. Art experiments with the possibility of representation, sometimes inventing new modes of representation (modernism), and sometimes presenting the unpresentable, showing what cannot be said (postmodernism) (Le Postmoderne expliqué aux enfants, 1986). Language does not simply denote a world of objects; rather, in language we perform a variety of actions, what Wittgenstein called 'language games'. Lyotard has stressed the agonistic dimension of these games and recognized the irreconcilable nature of what he calls 'phrases' in language (Le Différend, 1983).

It is still unclear whether in his critique of modernity Lyotard does indeed overcome relativism. His approach to language and human action as incommensurable, contextual games seems, inevitably, to lead to relativism. His refusal of the universal claims of grand theories as narratives that attempt to legitimize particular pespectives leaves him within the limits of his own small narrative. Given this framework, Lyotard's achievement is his demand to think anew what justice could mean when no longer associated with a theory of knowledge. This move brings the issues of ethics and politics back on to the postmodernist agenda.

Emilia Steuerman
Brunel University

References

Lyotard, J. F. (1954) *La Phénoménologie*, Paris.
—— (1973) *Dérive à partir de Marx et Freud*, Paris.
—— (1973) *Des dispositifs pulsionnels*, Paris.
—— (1974) *Economie libidinale*, Paris.
—— (1979) *La Condition postmoderne*, Paris. 1979. (*The Postmodern Condition*, Minneapolis, MN, 1983.)
—— (1983) *Le Différend*, Paris. (*The Different*, Minneapolis, MN, 1988.)
—— (1986) *Le Postmoderne expliqué aux enfants*, Paris. (*The Postmodern Explained*, Minneapolis, MN 1992.)
—— (1988) *L'Inhumain*, Paris. (*The Inhuman*, Cambridge, UK, 1991.)
Lyotard, J. F. and Thébaud, J. L. (1979) *Au Juste*, Paris. (*Just Gaming*, Minneapolis, MN, 1985.)

Further reading

Benjamin, A. (ed.) (1992) *Judging Lyotard*, London.
Lyotard, J. F. (ed.) (1985) *La Faculté de Juger*, Paris.
—— (1993) *Political Writings*, Minneapolis, MN.

See also: post-modernism; post-modernity.

M

Machiavelli, Niccolo (1469–1526)

Machiavelli was a Florentine patriot, civil servant and political theorist. Entering the service of the Council of Ten which ruled republican Florence in 1498, he was sent abroad on diplomatic missions which provided much of the experience later to be distilled as advice on political and military skill. In 1512 the republic crumbled and the Medici family, who had long dominated Florentine politics, returned to power. Accidentally and unjustly implicated in a plot against them, Machiavelli was arrested and tortured. On his release he was exiled from the city, and retired to a small farm in Sant' Andrea, seven miles south of the city. The remainder of a disappointed life was devoted to writings, some of them intended to persuade the new rulers to restore him to the centre of affairs which he so dearly loved.

The Prince (1513), written soon after his downfall, was a short work of advice to princes, focused in its last chapter on the local problem of liberating Italy from foreign domination. Some writers (Spinoza and Rousseau most notably) have taken the work as a satire on monarchy, but it seems evidently a piece of self-advertisement in the service of ingratiation. Settling in to a life of exile, Machiavelli farmed, and wrote the *Discourses on the First Ten Books of Titus Livius* ([1532] 1950), a sequence of reflections on political skill, largely as exemplified in the Roman republic. His republican sympathies are evident in this work, but the frank discussion of ruthless and immoral options, for which he is notorious, is no less to be found here than in *The Prince*. By 1520 he had written on *The Art of War* and commenced *The History of Florence*. His comedy *Mandragola* is one of the classics of Italian literature. In 1525, the Medici regime was overthrown and a republic restored, but the new regime failed to employ him. He died in 1526.

Machiavelli criticized previous writers on politics for dealing with ideal and imaginary states, and claimed himself to deal with the 'effective truth' (*verita effettuale*) of politics. Situated firmly within the tradition of civic humanism, he was deeply preoccupied with the constitution of cities and the glory of heroes. His contribution to the unblinking realism of the period was to recognize that the heroes of statesmanship had not invariably followed the moral advice current in a Christian community, and indeed that some of the maxims conventionally pressed upon princes might well lead directly to their ruin. A prince must therefore know, he argued, how not to be good, and to use this knowledge according to necessity. Beyond that, however, he thought that those rulers who are in the process of consolidating their power must know how to dominate the imaginations of men. One who did was Cesare Borgia, a prince with whom Machiavelli dealt while serving the Florentine republic. Borgia had used one of his lieutenants, Ramirro da Orca, to pacify, with all necessary brutality, the newly conquered Romagna; he then had da Orca killed, and his body cut in two, and left in the piazza at Cesena, to satisfy the grievances and no doubt dominate the imaginations of the people. The ferocity of this spectacle, he wrote in chapter VII of *The Prince*, 'caused the people both satisfaction and amazement'. It is often said that Machiavelli believed in one kind of morality for private life, another for statesmen. Yet for all his cynicism, there is nothing actually relativist to be detected in his straightforward recognition of good and evil. Rulers are not accorded a different morality; they are merely construed as the guardians of morality itself and accorded a licence to violate moral norms when necessary. Transposed out of the idiom of advice to princes and into a characterization of the emerging modern state (of which Machiavelli was an acute observer) this became the idea of reason of state.

Machiavelli was very far from encouraging any sort of enormity. Statesmen are the creators of civilization, and their ambitions are without glory unless they serve the public good. Machiavelli talked with some diffidence of the proper use of cruelty in politics. The test of necessary cruelty is that it is economical, and this combination of utility with an ethic of honour was highly distinctive of his attitude. 'When the act accuses him, the outcome should excuse him,' wrote Machiavelli, in a passage often translated as 'the end justifies the means'. But Machiavelli is concerned not with moral justification but with the proper judgement to be made by subjects, and historians. From this technical point of view, religion is important because it binds men to commitments and intensifies their virtue. Machiavelli is deeply anticlerical in a Latin style, and often directly hostile to Christianity because its ethic of humility weakens governments and discourages a serious military ferocity. His admiration goes to the heroic actor in this world rather than to the pious devotee of the next.

The Machiavelli of the *Discourses* is less well known but more enduring. Here we find a conflict theory of society, with men struggling to hold states together against the tendencies of dissolution. Machiavelli bequeathed to later thinkers the classical idea that any enduring constitution must balance monarchic, aristocratic and democratic elements. To create and sustain such a state, in which mere private and familial preoccupations are transcended in the public realm of citizenship, is the supreme human achievement, but contains its own ultimate doom. For states create peace, and peace allows prosperity, and when men grow accustomed to peace and prosperity, they lose their civic virtue and indulge private passions: liberty, to use Machiavelli's terms, gives way to corruption. This tradition of thought, with its emphasis on citizenly participation never ceased to be cultivated even in the absolute monarchies of early modern Europe, and became dominant from the time of the French Revolution onwards. It composes much of what the modern world calls 'democracy'.

The Machiavelli of popular imagination, however, has always been the exponent of the pleasures of manipulation, the supreme pornographer .of power. Many revolutionary adventurers have found in him conscious formulae to cover what they were inclined to do by instinct. In this role, Machiavelli has been remembered by social psychologists constructing a questionnaire to measure the manipulative tendencies of personality. Those who score high are called 'high machs', while less manipulative people are called 'low machs'.

Kenneth Minogue
London School of Economics and Political Science

Further reading

Chabrol, F. (1958) *Machiavelli and the Renaissance*, London.
Hale, J. R. (1961) *Machiavelli and Renaissance Italy*, London.
Parel, Anthony J. (1992) *The Machiavellian Cosmos*, Oxford.
Pocock, J. (1975) *The Machiavellian Moment*, Oxford.
Skinner, Q. (1981) *Machiavelli*, London.

McLuhan, Marshall (1910–80)

McLuhan was for a time one of the most cited authors in the field of study of mass communication, following the publication of his two main books, *The Gutenberg Galaxy* (1962) and *Understanding Media* (1964). Moreover, he was probably as well known outside the circle of academic media specialists as within it. After a fairly conventional career as a teacher of literature, he became a spinner of theory and publicist for his ideas about the consequences for culture and society of changes in communication technology – from writing to print and from print to electronic media. Although his assessment of television happened to be especially topical in the 1960s, he was also continuing a North American (perhaps especially Canadian) tradition of interest in technology, communication and the new. He owed much of his central thesis to a forerunner and colleague at the University of Toronto, the economic historian Harold J. Innis, who had traced the connection between changes in communication technology in the ancient and medieval world and changing forms of political and social power. Innis argued that each medium had a bias towards a certain kind of application, message and effect and thus, eventually, a bias towards a certain kind of society. A similar version of communication determinism was elaborated by McLuhan, with particular stress on the difference between the pictorial medium of television, which involves the spectator imaginatively and sensorily, and the medium of print, with its linear, sequential logic and its bias towards rationalism and individualism.

McLuhan's dicta are often best remembered summarily by his own catch-phrase 'the medium is the message'. He was a controversial figure and it is impossible in a few words to strike an adequate balance in assessing his work. On the positive side were a lively imagination; a striking and aphoristic turn of phrase; an ability to cross academic boundaries and synthesize his eclectic finds. Furthermore, he seems to have exerted charm as a person and influence as a teacher. The principal entry on the debit side is that he lacked any discernible system of thought or adherence to an established tradition of research method, so that his many ideas are often both questionable and untestable. It is still not clear whether or not he made a valid or original contribution to any precise understanding of media, yet he did call attention to the need to do this, at a good moment and in a way which could not be ignored. In respect of his own message, the manner of delivery may well have been more significant than the content. However, the increasing attention now being paid to the globalization of communication has raised McLuhan's stock, and he may also be seen as a precursor of post-modernist thinking about mass communication.

Denis McQuail
University of Amsterdam

References

McLuhan, M. (1962) *The Gutenberg Galaxy*, London.
—— (1964) *Understanding Media*, London.

Further reading

Miller, J. (1971) *McLuhan*, London.

See also: mass media; media effects.

macroeconomic policy

Government policy which is intended to influence the behaviour of the economy as a whole, in particular the level of economic activity, unemployment and the rate of inflation, is called *macroeconomic*. This is in contrast with *microeconomic* policy directed towards the development or efficiency of particular industries, regions, activities or markets. One of the main attractions of macroeconomic policy, it can be argued, is that it enables the government to point the economy as a whole in the right direction without interfering with the proper functioning of the market system.

Traditionally the goals of macroeconomic policy have been full employment and price stability. The stability of output from year to year, avoiding rapid booms or deep recessions, is an additional objective. The growth rate of output in the longer term, however, is commonly believed to depend on a quite different set of factors, such as technology, training and incentives, which fall rather within the domain of 'supply-side' or microeconomic policy. In an open economy, either the balance of payments position or the behaviour of the exchange rate in the foreign exchange market can be seen as a separate objective of macroeconomic policy, or else as a constraint on its operation.

The instruments of macroeconomic policy are both monetary and fiscal. Monetary policy is operated by the central bank, for example the US Federal Reserve Board or the Bank of England. The stringency of policy can be measured either by the level of real interest rates (that is nominal interest rates *minus* the rate of inflation) or by the growth of the money supply (variously defined). One advantage of monetary policy as a means of influencing the economy is that, unlike fiscal policy, it can be reviewed and changed almost continuously in the light of new information.

The instruments of fiscal policy are taxation and public spending, controlled by the government or federal administration subject to the important proviso of legislative support. Different taxes and expenditures affect the economy in different ways, but by 'fiscal policy' in the present context we mean the effect of the budget as a whole on the level of aggregate demand in the economy. Except in a dire emergency fiscal policies are usually changed only once a year. Their use for managing the economy is also limited by the need for prudence in the management of the public accounts themselves.

The use of public borrowing and interest rates to stabilize the economy was accepted as a principle of policy in the 1950s and the 1960s, as the ideas of Maynard Keynes converted most of the economics profession. Subsequently in the 1970s and 1980s there was a neo-classical or monetarist counter-revolution, originating in Chicago and led by Milton Friedman. The underlying issue in this debate concerns the relationship between the two goals of full employment and price stability. It may be possible, by cutting taxes or cutting interest rates, to increase employment in the short run without adding much to inflation straight away; however, in the longer term the neo-classical argument is that the situation will be reversed, with unemployment back at its 'natural' level and nothing to show for the expansionary policy except a burst of higher inflation.

An extensive literature on the theory of macroeconomic policy has appeared since the 1960s drawing on control engineering. The economy can be represented by a mathematical model in which the main behavioural relationships at the aggregate level are each described by a dynamic equation. By repeated simultaneous solutions of the model equations (using a reasonably fast computer) it can be shown how the economy might respond to shocks, for example an increase in the price of imports. Feedback rules for policy can then be devised, which will minimize the disruption, as measured by a combination of the deviations from desired levels of various economic indicators, such as output or inflation.

Especially since the mid-1970s, this mechanistic approach to policy design has been improved to take account of expectations, both in the specification of models and in the design of policy rules. If the use of policy instruments follows any logical rule then it will be understood and anticipated by those whose behaviour it is intended to control. This suggests that the creation of the right kind of expectations is itself an integral part of policy design. That conclusion, in turn, creates the problem of 'time inconsistency': a policy may be the best available at some initial period because it will create favourable expectations in, for example, financial markets. When the time comes to fulfil those expectations, however, the best policy may be to change course. The problem arises because the markets will realize in advance that the policy is time inconsistent and will not be misled in the first place. From this follows a case for making binding commitments, such as the enacting of a constitutional amendment, or membership of a monetary union.

In practice, the record of macroeconomic policy since the 1970s has been mainly one of failure rather than success. Inflation accelerated sharply in most countries, especially in the aftermath of the two dramatic increases in world oil prices, in 1974 and 1979. Since the 1980s inflation has been lower, but at the same time unemployment in many countries has been much higher. The response to these disappointments has been to introduce new policies designed to improve the 'trade-off' between the two objectives. In the 1970s, especially in Britain, the main emphasis was on prices and incomes policies. The other approach, which continues into the 1990s, involves special employment measures designed to help the unemployed directly either by providing training or by matching them more successfully to the vacancies which exist.

Andrew Britton
National Institute of Economic and Social Research, London

Further reading

Britton, A. J. C. (1991) *Macroeconomic Policy in Britain, 1974–1987*, Cambridge, UK.

Dornbusch, R. and Fischer S. (1987) *Macroeconomics*, New York.

Fisher, D. (1987) *Monetary and Fiscal Policy*, London.

Friedman, M. (1968) 'The role of monetary policy', *American Economic Review* March.

Goodhart, C. A. E. (1989) 'The conduct of monetary policy', *Economic Journal* 99(386).

Keynes, J. M. (1936) *The General Theory of Employment, Interest and Money*, London.

OECD (1988) *Why Economic Policies Change Course: Eleven Case Studies*, Paris.

Tobin, J. (1972) 'Inflation and unemployment', *American Economic Review* March.

See also: econometrics; employment and unemployment; inflation and deflation; macroeconomic theory; monetary policy; public goods; taxation.

macroeconomic theory

The term macroeconomics was coined by Ragnar Frisch in 1933 to apply to the study of the relationships between broad economic aggregates such as national income, inflation, aggregate unemployment, the balance of payments, and so on. It can be contrasted with the study of individual decision-making units in the economy such as households, workers and firms, which is generally known as microeconomics. It is no coincidence that the 1930s also saw the development of Keynesian economic theory, landmarked by the *General Theory of Employment, Interest and Money* (Keynes 1936) and the founding of the Econometric Society whose aim was to advance 'economic theory in its relation to statistics and mathematics'. Prior to this period, no explicit distinction was made between microeconomic and macroeconomic theory, although many classical analyses, such as Hume's specie-flow mechanism, or earlier studies of the relationship between the balance of trade and national wealth by mercantilists such as Mun, were couched in what are now recognizably macroeconomic terms. The real fillip to the development of macroeconomic theory, however, was the rise of Keynesian economics – the so-called Keynesian revolution. Classical economists such as Smith and Hume and neoclassical economists such as Marshall and Pigou saw the world in equilibrium terms where quantities flowed and prices moved as if in a large, well-oiled machine: '. . . it is impossible to heap up money, more than any fluid, beyond its proper level' (Hume 1752). In the long run, the classical or neoclassical view was that everything would, indeed, reach its 'proper level'. Thus, faced with the large-scale and chronic unemployment of the interwar years, an acceptable classical response to the question, 'What is the solution to the unemployment problem?' might have been 'a reduction in the population' – presumably brought about by conscripts to the army of unemployed falling below a subsistence level of income. While this would clearly be a very long-term solution, the retort would have been that unemployment is a very long-term problem: thus, Keynes's famous dictum that 'in the long run, we are all dead'. Keynesian macroeconomic theory argued that economies could go into 'underemployment equilibrium' and may require government intervention, particularly in the form of public spending, in order to move towards a full-employment equilibrium.

Another important school of macroeconomic theory, which is essentially classical in its outlook, is monetarism, of which the University of Chicago has traditionally been thought of as the intellectual home. The essential differences between Keynesian and monetarist macroeconomic theory can be sketched as follows. At its most fundamental level, macroeconomics can be thought of as dealing with the interactions of five aggregate markets: the goods market, the money market, the bond market, the foreign exchange market, and the labour market. Monetarists focus on only the second of these markets and are typically concerned with the supply of and demand for money. This is because a number of assumptions are implicitly made with respect to supply and demand in the various markets. The foreign exchange market is assumed to clear (supply is equal to demand) because the exchange rate is flexible. The wage rate is assumed to adjust so that there is no involuntary unemployment – everyone who wants to work at the going wage rate will find a job – so that the labour market clears. Similarly, goods prices are assumed to be flexible so that the goods market clears. This leaves only the bond market and the money market. But an important principle of economics, known as Walras's law, states that if n-1 markets of an n-market system clear, then the n-th must clear also (this is essentially the same as solving a simultaneous equation system). Thus, given the foregoing assumptions, the bond market can be ignored and equilibrium conditions in the entire macroeconomy can be characterized by equilibrium conditions in the money market alone. Typically, Keynesian macroeconomic theory will deny one or more of these underlying assumptions. For example, if, because of long-term labour contracts, wages are rigid, then there may be fewer vacancies than the number of people looking for work at the going wage rate – the labour market will not clear and there will be involuntary unemployment.

The high tide of Keynesian macroeconomic theory, in the 1950s and 1960s, was the counterpart to the apparent success of Keynesian macroeconomic policy, particularly in the US and the UK. Rising unemployment and inflation towards the end of the 1960s and into the early 1970s, however, generated a further crisis in macroeconomic theory, culminating in a monetarist counter-revolution. Indeed, by the time that Richard Nixon, in 1969, declared, 'we are all Keynesians now', the tide had probably already turned. Milton Friedman, the High Priest of monetarism had already given his inaugural lecture to the American Economic Association (Friedman 1968) in which he outlined his theory of the 'expectations-augmented Phillips curve', which appeared to explain the co-existence of inflation and unemployment in monetarist terms. Like the classical economists, monetarists assume that there is an equilibrium or natural rate of employment. According to this view, government can only increase employment beyond this level, say, by an expansionary monetary policy, by fooling workers into underestimating the level of inflation. Thus, if the government increases the

money supply and prices begin to rise, to the extent that workers underestimate next period's inflation rate, they will set their wage demands too low. Thus, in the next period, labour will appear cheap to producers and more workers will be taken on and the aggregate level of employment will rise. When inflation expectations catch up, however, workers will raise their wage claims accordingly, the real or price-adjusted wage rate will go back to its old level, and the economy returns to the natural rate of employment – albeit at a higher inflation rate.

In the 1970s, a third school of macroeconomic theory emerged, known as the New Classical School, and associated primarily with economists such as Robert Lucas and Thomas Sargent, then both at the University of Minnesota. New classical economists developed further the monetarist assertion that monetary policy is only effective in the short run into the key assertion that it is almost always ineffectual. They did this by taking the monetarist apparatus and grafting on the additional assumption of 'rational expectations'. According to the rational expectations hypothesis, agents' expectations of future macroeconomic variables are essentially the same as the true mathematical expectation based on all of the available information. Thus, in the example given above, agents would realize that the money supply has been increased and, using all of the available information, would form their best estimate of next period's price level. This is not to say that they would have perfect foresight, but that their best estimate is as likely to be an overestimate as an underestimate, since if they consistently underestimated price movements they would rationally revise their method of estimation. Thus, on average, agents' forecasts will be correct – wage increases will on average match price increases brought about by an expansionary monetary policy, the price-adjusted wage rate will stay the same, and the level of unemployment will not move. If traditional monetarism allowed a role for activist monetary policy only to the extent that agents could be fooled, new classical theory argued that it was extremely difficult to fool them. The rational expectations revolution of the 1970s fuelled a major industry in academic macroeconomics. Although there are many who would disagree, it is probably true to say that New Classical macroeconomics has now run its course, largely as a result of a general loss of faith in the assumption of rational expectations – itself occasioned by numerous empirical studies which reject the hypothesis in a number of contexts – and increasing evidence of the stickiness of wages and prices.

Where does this leave macroeconomic theory? To a large extent in a state of crisis. As the foregoing discussion should make clear, schools of macroeconomic theory may be broadly classified according to whether monetary 'non-neutralities' (i.e. the effects of monetary policy on real aggregate variables such as output and employment) arise for informational reasons – as in equilibrium schools of thought such as monetarist, new classical, or, more recently, real business cycle theory (see, e.g. Lucas 1987) or for other reasons such as price or wage rigidity, as in Keynesian macroeconomic theory. Because of a general loss of faith in the ability of econometrics to discriminate between alternative views of macroeconomics – not least because of their observational equivalence under certain conditions (Sargent 1976) – the ultimate preference for one macroeconomic theory over another probably has more to do with the economist's faith in a certain underlying view of the world rather than anything else. Thus, real business-cycle theorists continue to analyse dynamic models in which prices are flexible and economic agents are rational optimizers, while the primary task of the 'New Keynesian Economics' 'is to explain why changes in the aggregate price level are sticky' (Gordon 1990). Given that different macroeconomic policy prescriptions are forthcoming from each class of theory – typically interventionist for Keynesian or New Keynesian theory, non-interventionist for equilibrium theorists – the choice may lie as much in the domain of political ideology as in that of economic theory.

Mark Taylor
University of Liverpool

References

Friedman, Milton (1968) 'The Role of Monetary Policy', *American Economic Review* (58).
Gordon, Robert J. 'What is New Keynesian Economics?', *Journal of Economic Literature* (28).
Hume, David (1752) 'On the Balance of Trade', in David Rotwein (ed.) *Essays Moral, Political, and Literary*, London.
Keynes, John Maynard (1936) *The General Theory of Employment, Interest and Money*, London.
Lucas, Robert E. Jr (1987) *Models of Business Cycles*, Blackwell.
Sargent, Thomas J. (1976) 'On the Observational Equivalence of Natural and Unnatural Theories of Macroeconomics', *Journal of Political Economy* (84).

See also: classical economics; Keynesian economics; macroeconomic policy; microeconomics; monetarism; rational expectations.

magic

'Magick', says Aleister Crowley, its foremost modern exponent, 'is the Science and Art of causing Change to occur in conformity with Will.' This is possible because 'there is nothing in the universe which does not influence every other thing' (Crowley 1929). But for E. B. Tylor, generally considered the founding father of British anthropology, magic was 'one of the most pernicious delusions that ever vexed mankind' (Tylor 1871).

Tylor's study began the first phase in the modern scientific history of magic, which viewed magical ideas and practices as mistaken attempts by ignorant savages and backward and superstitious persons in European society to manipulate physical reality by non-physical means. Tylor's approach was taken up and elaborated by J. G. Frazer, who devoted two volumes of his master-work *The Golden Bough* (1890) to the analysis of a global range of magical material. Frazer concluded that magic was a mistaken application to the material world of the laws of thought so as to constitute 'a spurious system of natural law'. This 'pseudo-science' (a term first employed by Tylor) could everywhere be reduced to two basic principles: that like produced like, and that things which had once been in contact continued to act on each other at a distance. These two principles resulted respectively in *homeopathic* or *imitative* magic, and *contagious* magic. The two branches could finally be comprehended under the name *sympathetic magic*, 'since both assume that things act on each other at a distance through a secret sympathy, the impulse being transmitted from one to the other by means of what we may conceive as a kind of invisible ether' (Frazer 1932).

Frazer also saw the magical as the first of three great stages in the evolution of human thought. Magic, according to Frazer, was succeeded by religion, which in turn gave way to science, the characteristic mode of thought of modern times. When, in the early 1920s, anthropology abandoned the evolutionary approach to the study of society which had dominated nineteenth-century theorizing, it also turned aside from the Frazerian ambition of giving a universal account of magic. Instead of seeking for the general characteristics of magical thought, each local magical system was seen as being like a language, specific to a particular society and culture. The linguistic parallel was explicitly drawn by Marcel Mauss (Hubert and Mauss 1906). The functionalist Bronislaw Malinowski devoted two thick volumes of ethnography to the magical practices of the Trobriand islanders of Melanesia, and suggested that magic was always encountered where human technical resources were inadequate to attain human aims. Magic, he thought, would disappear with technological advance (Malinowski 1935). This plausible generalization has been shown to be invalid in the case of post-Renaissance England where, according to the historian Keith Thomas, echoing Max Weber, 'magic lost its appeal before the appropriate technical solutions had been devised to take its place'. In the home of the Industrial Revolution the rationalist tradition of classical antiquity had blended with the Christian doctrine of a single all-directing providence to produce the conception of an orderly and rational universe, in which effect followed cause in a predictable manner (Thomas 1971).

An important exception to the functionalist particularism that dominated the post-Malinowski era in social anthropology was the work of Lucien Lévy-Bruhl (1857–1939). This French philosopher and scholar sought to show that non-empirical behaviour in tribal societies reflected a general mode of thought which he called *pre-logical* (though he recanted this pejorative term in his posthumous *Carnets*). In a massively documented critique of Lévy-Bruhl, Malinowski's student, E. E. Evans-Pritchard (1937), demonstrated in the case of the Zande people of Central Africa that their 'magical' thought followed logical paths, even though embedded in non-rational premises, such as belief in witchcraft.

The functionalists shared with Tylor and Frazer the presumption that magic, and also religion (the two domains being often lumped together under the label 'magico-religious') were intrinsically delusions, however much they might be shown to contribute to the functioning of specific societies. This presumption of a basic nonsensicality in the magical has been challenged by some anthropologists, who see it as merely a symptom of scientistic, arrogant ethnocentricity in western scholarship. This novel willingness to credit the claims of magicians appears to herald an emergent third phase in the social-scientific approach to magic, one which also appears to mark a return to the universalism of Tylor and Frazer. The most influential contribution to this new genre is that of Carlos Castaneda, who in a series of unprecedentedly popular books has purported to describe his initiation into the paranormal world of experts in sorcery among the Yaqui Indians of Mexico, a world startlingly different from the 'reality' that the author's western education had conditioned him to accept without question. The veracity of Castaneda's account of his bizarre odyssey has been challenged by some scholars, particularly de Mille (1978). But as a reaffirmation from a repressed Third-World culture of a magical vision of the world which has disappeared from the cultural mainstream of western civilization since the Enlightenment, Castaneda's work has the symbolic truth of authentic myth. A comparable though more modest report from Africa is the archaeologist and ethnographer Adrian Boshier's (1974) description of his initiation into the world of Zulu magic. In a similar and more general vein, Drury (1982) has traced interesting parallels between anthropological accounts of tribal shamanism and ritual magic in Europe. This rehabilitation of the 'pseudo-science' of tribal peoples may also be associated with a convergence between the ideas of some western scientists and those of the European magical tradition. Experimental evidence has been taken to prove that sub-atomic particles that have once interacted can instantaneously respond to each other's motions thousands of years later when they are light-years apart. Considering this and other disconcerting results, the physicist David Bohm (1980) suggested that the apparent separation of objects in the universe may conceal an invisible 'implicate' order of a mental kind in which everything is intimately connected with everything else. Magic may be about to recover a scientific respectability lost since the Renaissance.

Roy Willis
University of Edinburgh

References

Bohm, D. (1980) *Wholeness and the Implicate Order*, London.
Boshier, A. (1974) 'African apprenticeship', in A. Angoff and D. Barth (eds) *Parapsychology and Anthropology*, New York.
Crowley, A. (1929) *Magick in Theory and Practice*, Paris.
Drury, N. (1982) *The Shaman and the Magician*, London.
Evans-Pritchard, E. E. (1937) *Witchcraft, Oracles and Magic among the Azande*, Oxford.
Frazer, J. G. (1890) *The Golden Bough*, London.
— (1932) *The Magic Art and the Evolution of Kings*, 2 vols, London.
Hubert, H. and Mauss, M. (1906) 'Esquisse d'une théorie générale de la magie' in M. Mauss *Sociologie et anthropologie*, Paris.
Malinowski, B. (1935) *Coral Gardens and their Magic*, 2 vols, London.
Mille, R. de (1978) *Castaneda's Journey: The Power and the Allegory*, London.
O'Keefe, D. (1982), *Stolen Lightning: The Social Theory of Magic*, Oxford.
Tambiah, S. J. (1990) *Magic, Science, Religion, and the Scope of Rationality*, Cambridge, UK.
Thomas, K. (1971) *Religion and the Decline of Magic*, London.
Tylor, E. B. (1871) *Primitive Culture*, 2 vols, London.

See also: reason, rationality and rationalism; religion and ritual.

Malinowski, Bronislaw Kasper (1884–1942)

Malinowski had a profound influence on British social anthropology through his innovative methods of field research, his wide-ranging theoretical writings, his inspired teaching, and his entrepreneurial promotion of a revitalized discipline. His Trobriand corpus remains the most comprehensive and widely read in world ethnography.

Born in Cracow, Malinowski studied mathematics, physics and philosophy at the Jagiellonian University. His doctoral thesis on the positivist epistemology of Mach and Avenarius foreshadowed his later formulations on 'functionalism', the methodological doctrine with which his name is associated.

After studying chemistry and psychology at Leipzig, Malinowski's interests turned decisively to anthropology, and in 1910 he became a student of ethnology under Seligman and Westermarck at the London School of Economics (LSE). He soon aspired to be 'Anthropology's Conrad'. Malinowski was in Australia when the First World War was declared in Europe but despite his status as an enemy alien he was permitted to do fieldwork in eastern Papua. It was during three expeditions between 1914 and 1918 that he reaped the ethnographic benefits of 'living right among the natives' and mastering their language. Intensive fieldwork involving participant observation was henceforth to become the hallmark of British anthropology, though Malinowski's posthumously published field dairies (1967) exploded his own myth of easy rapport and helped to precipitate the crisis of conscience which afflicted anthropology in the 1970s.

Returning to England in 1920 with his Australian bride, Malinowski began full-time teaching at the LSE in 1924, and was appointed to a professorship in 1927. He did much of his writing at his villa in the Italian Tyrol, but travelled widely in Europe, Africa and the USA. It was while on sabbatical in 1938 that the Second World War broke out in Europe, and he was advised to remain in the USA. In 1940 and 1941 he conducted fieldwork in Mexico, and just before his sudden death in 1942 he was appointed to a permanent professorship at Yale.

Aided by his sometime rival Radcliffe-Brown, Malinowski generated the most significant paradigm-shift in British anthropology since its creation in the mid-nineteenth century: from the speculatively pre-historical study of cultural traits as 'survivals' (whether in an evolutionist or diffusionist mode) to the empirical, synchronic study of social 'institutions' within living, functioning cultures. This shift was marked by the collection and synthesis of new kinds of data by increasingly professional academic investigators. Malinowski's lengthy, 'heroic' immersion in an exotic society was thus the culmination of a trend, and prolonged fieldwork thereafter became a rite of passage for entry into the profession.

Malinowski's theoretical contributions to anthropology lay in fields as disparate as the family, psychoanalysis, mythology, law, economic anthropology and pragmatic linguistic theory. Yet the key to understanding any culture, he taught, lay in the interrelation of its constituent 'institutions'; thus his demand for the empirical observation of social behaviour in concrete cultural contexts. His most compelling Trobriand works in this vein concerned the ceremonial exchange of the *Kula* (1922); kinship, sex and marriage (1929); and gardening, land tenure and the language of magic (1935). Although his literary romanticism exoticized their culture, Malinowski demystified the Trobrianders themselves: his exemplary 'Savages' were pragmatic, self-motivated, rational human beings.

The allure of Malinowski's sociological functionalism (and a timely turn to practical anthropology) won him generous Rockefeller funding for his students' fieldwork in Africa. As a prescription for gathering rich data, functionalism clearly worked. However, the schematized form in which Malinowski developed his biologically based cultural functionalism (1944a) did not outlive him.

Malinowski was a charismatic and challenging teacher – loved or loathed – who trained a generation of postgraduates in his famous Socratic seminar. Established in key academic posts in Britain and elsewhere, his students gave the discipline its distinctive intellectual profile until the 1960s.

As a publicist and polemicist, Malinowski wrote, lectured and broadcast on many social issues of his day. A romantic positivist, a scientific humanist, a linguistically gifted cosmopolitan and a political liberal, he passionately opposed totalitarianism (1944b) and was gratified when his books were burned by the Nazis. In the 1980s, re-evaluation by Polish scholars of his earliest work restored Malinowski's reputation in his homeland and placed him in the mainstream of European modernism.

Michael W. Young
Australian National University

References

Malinowski, B. (1922) *Argonauts of the Western Pacific*, London.
—— (1929) *The Sexual Life of Savages*, London.
—— (1935) *Coral Gardens and their Magic*, 2 vols, London.
—— (1944a) *A Scientific Theory of Culture*, Chapel Hill, NC.
—— (1944b) *Freedom and Civilization*, New York.
—— (1967) *A Diary in the Strict Sense of the Term*, London.

Further reading

Ellen, R., Gellner, E., Kubica, G., Mucha, J., (eds.) (1988) *Malinowski Between Two Worlds*, Cambridge, UK.
Firth, R. (ed.) (1957) *Man and Culture*, London.
Stocking, G. W. (1983) 'The ethnographer's magic', in G. W. Stocking (ed.) *Observers Observed*, Wisconsin, WI.
Young, M. W. (ed.) (1988) *Malinowski among the Magi*, London.

See also: social anthropology.

Malthus, Thomas Robert (1766–1834)

Thomas Robert Malthus, cleric, moral scientist and economist, was born near Guildford, Surrey. He entered Jesus College, Cambridge, in 1784, graduated in mathematics as ninth Wrangler in 1788 and was a non-resident fellow of his college from 1793 until his marriage in 1804. Originally destined for a career in the Church of England, he became curate of Okewood in Surrey in 1796, and Rector of Walesby in Lincolnshire in 1803; but from 1805 until his death he served as professor of history and political economy at Haileybury College, then recently founded by the East India Company for the education of its cadets.

The source of Malthus's reputation as a political economist lay in his *Essay on the Principle of Population* published in 1798; but this essay was originally written to refute the 'perfectibilist' social philosophies of such writers as Godwin and Condorcet, and as such was developed within the context of an essentially Christian moral philosophy, as was all of Malthus's writing. At the core of Malthus's argument was his theory that

> Population, when unchecked, increases in a geometrical ratio. Subsistence increases only in an arithmetical ratio. . . . By that law of our nature which makes food necessary to the life of man, the effects of these two unequal powers must be kept equal. This implies a strong and constantly operating check on population from the difficulty of subsistence.

In the first edition of his *Essay*, Malthus identified the checks to population as either preventive (keeping new population from growing up) or positive (cutting down existing population); hence followed the bleak conclusion 'that the superior power of population cannot be checked without producing misery or vice'. In the second, much enlarged, edition (1803) he extended the category of preventive checks to include 'moral restraint', thus admitting the possibility of population being contained without either misery or vice as necessary consequences. Even when thus modified, Malthus's population principle seemed to impose narrow limits to the possibilities of economic growth and social improvement, although he himself did not so intend it. Idealists and reformers consequently railed against the implications of the theory, but his fellow economists accepted both its premises and its logic and for most of the nineteenth century it remained one of the classical 'principles of political economy'.

His population principle was not Malthus's only contribution to economic thought: he was among the first to state (in 1815) the theory of rent as a surplus generally associated with the name of his friend and contemporary, David Ricardo. Both were followers of Adam Smith but Malthus's development of Smith's system differed significantly from Ricardo's, notably in his use of supply and demand analysis in the theory of value as against Ricardo's emphasis on labour-quantities, and his explanation of the 'historical fall' of profits in terms of competition of capitals rather than by the 'necessity of resort to inferior soils' which Ricardo stressed.

Malthus and Ricardo debated at length 'the possibility of a general glut' of commodities. Ricardo argued for the validity of Say's Law, that 'supply creates its own demand', while Malthus asserted the possibility of over-saving (and over-investment) creating an excess supply. Ricardo's apparently watertight logic won acceptance for Say's Law for over a century, until Keynes in 1933 drew attention to Malthus's use of the principle of 'effective demand' and contended that 'the whole problem of the balance between Saving and Investment had been posed' in the Preface to his *Principles of Political Economy* in 1820. Economists tend to see Malthus's *Principles* not so much as containing a notable foreshadowing of Keynes's theory of employment as presenting, albeit through a glass darkly, a subtle and complex analysis of the conditions required to initiate and maintain balanced growth in a market economy.

R. D. Collison Black
Queen's University Belfast

References

Keynes, J. M. (1933) *Essays in Biography*, London. Reprinted in *The Collected Writings of John Maynard Keynes*, Vol X, (1972) London.
Malthus, T. R. (1798) *An Essay on the Principle of Population*, 2nd edn 1803, 6th edn 1826, London.
—— (1820) *The Principles of Political Economy, considered with a View to their Practical Application*, 2nd edn 1836, London.
Sraffa, P. (ed.) (1951–2) Works and Correspondence of David Ricardo, Vol II, pp. 308, 312; Vol VIII, pp. 257, 285, 300–01; Vol IX, pp. 9–11; 15–17, 19–27.

Further reading

James, P. (1979) *Population Malthus, His Life and Times*, London.
Winch, D. (1987) *Malthus*, Oxford.

See also: demography.

management *see* human resource management; leadership; management theory; organizations; public management; strategic management

management theory

Management theory is a generalized term which is used loosely to refer to research findings, frameworks, propositions, beliefs, views, saws and suggestions, all of which seek to explain how managers should manage. It is an untidy hotchpotch of diverse offerings. Kramer (1975: 47) used the more specific term 'management idea'. He said that it

> derived from inductive and deductive reasoning. It is a systematically organized knowledge applicable to a relatively wide area of circumstances. As a system of assumptions, accepted principles and rules of procedures [it] assists managers to analyze and explain underlying causes of a given business situation and predict the outcome of alternate courses of action.

As an academic field of study, management dates back only to the beginning of the twentieth century. In that time, six relatively cohesive and distinct bodies or families of ideas have become established. It is these that are featured in management textbooks and which are discussed in management classes and journals. Although they represent only a fraction of the thinking and writing on management, they are held to constitute established management theory (Huczynski 1993). These five bodies of knowledge are, in broadly chronological order, bureaucracy (Max Weber); scientific management (Frederick Taylor); administrative theory (Henri Fayol); human relations (Elton Mayo); neo-human relations (Douglas McGregor). To these five, it is necessary to refer to a sixth, guru theory (Rosabeth Moss Kanter, Tom Peters and Lee Iaccoca). The writings of this school of management came into prominence during the 1980s, and have had a continuing impact on management thought and practice.

Bureaucracy theory

Max Weber's theory of bureaucracy was set in a historical-philosophical context. Weber was a German sociologist (1864–1920) and not a manager, engineer or management consultant. His interests were in the process of social change, and, in particular, in the effect of rationality on religious thought and capitalism. By rationality he meant the kind of action or mode of organizing in which goals are clearly conceived and all conduct, except that designated to achieve the particular goal, is eliminated. The application of his concept of rationality to the organizational context is what secured this social scientist's pre-eminent position in modern management thought. The term that Weber applied to the organizational form built upon pure legal-rational authority was

'bureaucracy'. The Weberian model of bureaucracy offers a stable and predictable world which provides the blueprint for 'rationally designed' structures in which rational individuals carry out their roles and actions. For Weber, the bureaucratic form of organization possessed the features of specialization, hierarchy, rules, impersonality, full-time officials, career focus and a split between public and private activity.

Scientific management theory

Developed at the beginning of the twentieth century, Frederick Winslow Taylor's theory of scientific management focused upon shopfloor organization, and upon the techniques that could be used to maximize the productivity of manual workers. His name is synonymous with work measurement and time-and-motion study. Taylor, an American, based his work on the accurate and scientific study of work. An engineer by training, he produced a template for much of the job design work done during the twentieth century. Scientific management principles such as a clear division of task and responsibilities between management and workers, scientific selection and training of workers, development of the one-best-way of working, and the application of economic incentives, all continue to be used to this day. Taylor's objective was to increase productivity and reduce cost.

Administrative theory

The primary focus of administrative theory was on the determination of which types of specialization and hierarchy would optimize the efficiency of organizations. The theory is built around the four central pillars – the division of labour, the scalar and functional processes, organizational structure, and the span-of-control. The individual most closely associated with administrative theory is Henri Fayol, who spent his career at a French mining company where he rose to the position of managing director. As a management practitioner, Fayol sought to discover and write down a set of successful management techniques that could be described and taught. In this sense, his interest in the structuring of the organization as a whole, complements Taylor's focus on worker organization. Fayol's ideas were diffused not by social scientists or business school faculty, but by management consultants and other managers.

Human relations theory

Human relations theory is associated closely with the name of Elton Mayo – an Australian by birth, but best known as a professor at the Harvard Business

School. Some commentators see human relations as a reaction against scientific management. Human relations ideas stressed the social nature of work, and focused on the worker, not as an individual, but as a member of a social group. It viewed employees as existing in an organizational context, recommended that managers should direct their motivational efforts towards the team, and saw individuals meeting their basic needs within the workplace. It recommended that managers control workgroups (both formal and informal) by the use of techniques such as friendly and relaxed supervision and employee counselling. The original research on which the theory is based was conducted during the 1930s, but the theory had its greatest organizational impact in the USA during the 1940s and 1950s.

Neo-human relations theory

During the late 1950s and early 1960s, Mayo's original ideas were developed and extended. A more psychological direction was taken, to complement his more sociological and social psychological perspective. Underlying this neo-human relations theory (NHR) was the view that, above all, company employees wanted the opportunity to grow and develop on the job. The NHR writers assumed that if workers were allowed to do responsible and meaningful work, their attitude to their company would be more positive, and they would come to share management goals. As a consequence, this state of circumstances would put an end to industrial conflict. Many observers cite the work of Abraham Maslow (1943) as the starting-point of the neo-human relations era. NHR theory underpinned most of the organizational development (OD) work which was to have such a great impact on the design of organizational structures and teams, technology implementation, and employee selection and development.

Guru theory

NHR and OD dominated management thought for almost two decades. It was not until the election of President Ronald Reagan in the USA and Prime Minister Margaret Thatcher in Britain at the start of the 1980s that it gave way to the enterprise culture on both sides of the Atlantic. Many observers have called the 1980s. 'The Business Decade'. One consequence of this was an explosion in the number of management ideas offered. Not only did the number of ideas increase, but also they flowed from diverse sources. It is difficult to pick out with confidence any single consistent theme from the torrent of writings, speeches, videos and audiotapes that, during the 1980s, sought

to tell managers how to manage more effectively. Perhaps it is the notion that the object of business was to compete with others for the favours of the customer, who was king, that comes closest to giving a flavour of the thinking at the time. Since so much of the impact of these ideas depended on the individuals who promoted them, this sixth body of management ideas is labelled guru theory. These management gurus came from three different backgrounds. First, there were the academic gurus who held posts in university business schools. Among, these one would include Rosabeth Moss Kanter and Michael Porter (Harvard Business School), Henry Mintzberg (McGill) and Philip Kotler (Northwestern). Working from an academic base, these writers have been influential in affecting how managers think about innovation, corporate strategy and marketing. Second in line are the consultant gurus, whose expertise and credibility come from having consulted for a wide number of different organizations. Here one would list Peter Drucker, Tom Peters, Philip Crosby and W. Edwards Deming. These writers have had a profound effect on the practice of management, the creation of excellence, and the improvement of product quality. The final grouping consists of 'hero-managers'. As the label suggests, these are the prescriptions of individuals who have held senior managerial positions in companies. Following in the tradition of Henri Fayol and Alfred P. Sloan, modern hero-managers make recommendations, based on their experiences, to their fellow managers. The most successful American hero-manager has been Lee Iacocca (Chrysler Corporation), while his British counterpart, Sir John Harvey-Jones (ex-ICI), has gained visibility through book publication and television appearances. Only time will tell if these three types of guru ideas will survive over the long term, and will be placed alongside the five established bodies of management ideas from the past.

Andrzej Huczynski
University of Glasgow

References

Huczynski, A. A. (1993) *Management Gurus: What Makes Them and How To Become One*, London.

Kramer, H. (1975) 'The philosophical foundations of management rediscovered', *Management International Review* 15(2–3).

Maslow, A. H. (1943) 'A theory of human motivation', *Psychological Review* 50(4).

Further reading

Clutterback, D. and Crainer, S. (1990) *Masters of Management*, Basingstoke.

Pugh, D. S., Hickson, D. J. and Hinings, C. R. (eds) (1983) *Writers on Organization*, Harmondsworth.

Wren, D. (1970) *The Evolution of Management Thought*, Chichester.

See also: bureaucracy; human resource management; leadership; public management; strategic management.

marginal analysis

Marginal analysis in economics attempts to explain the determination of prices and quantities on the basis of the comparisons of rewards and costs 'on the margin', that is, the rewards and costs of extending economic activity by small incremental amounts. It is an approach that follows naturally from the view that economic agents try to maximize some economic goal, such as utility or profits. They are assumed to possess the information that relates their activities to their goals, for example, the extent to which an increase in consumption increases their utility, or the effects of an increase in output on their profits. This is the cornerstone of neo-classical analysis, which dates from the marginal revolution of the 1870s set in motion by the writings of Jevons, Menger and Leon Walras. As opposed to classical analysis, which concentrated on questions of capital accumulation and growth, neo-classical analysis was concerned with the optimal allocation of given resources, and marginal techniques, with their accompanying mathematics of differential calculus, proved to be a fruitful way of dealing with these questions and appeared to provide economics with scientific precision.

Marginal analysis, although it assumed a central role in economic theory from the 1870s, appeared in economics writings in earlier periods. It was prominent in the work of Thünen, whose theory of distribution was based on the marginal productivity of the factors of production. Cournot discussed the behaviour of firms under the assumption of profit maximization, and he made use of marginal revenue and marginal cost to deduce the positions of equilibrium. Dupuit distinguished between the total and marginal utility of goods when he examined the social benefits derived from public goods such as bridges, and on this basis he arrived at measures of consumers' surplus from the existence of such goods. Gossen enunciated the principle of diminishing marginal utility, which he termed his First Law. He went on to state what has been called Gossen's Second Law, that the maximization of an individual's satisfaction from any good that can be used in different ways, requires that it be allocated among these uses in such a way that its marginal utility be the same in all its uses.

The marginal approach was also not unknown in classical economics. In Ricardo's theory, the rent of land is price-determined, not price-determining, since it is the price of corn, given the wage and interest rates, that determines the extent of cultivation and the rent that can be extracted from the cultivators. His treatment of this question is an example of marginal analysis, since this decision is based on considerations of the effects on the output of corn of incremental changes in inputs. The combined doses of labour and capital on land that is being cultivated are increased until the output from the final, or marginal, dose is just sufficient to cover the wage and interest costs of that dose. Rent can be extracted only from the products of the intramarginal inputs of labour-capital. Similarly, the extent to which less fertile, or more distant, land will be cultivated depends on the marginal product of labour-capital on this land. No-rent land is that land where output is just sufficient to compensate the labour and capital employed. Wicksteed, Wicksell, and J. B. Clark generalized Ricardo's approach to cover the case where all factors of production would be treated as being potentially variable, to arrive at a marginal productivity theory of distribution, and thus Blaug (1978) believes that Ricardo should be credited with 'having invented marginal analysis'.

The independent discovery by different theorists of the marginal productivity theory of distribution can be taken as a high point of marginal analysis, since it appeared to complete the marginal revolution by showing that not only are the prices of goods determined by marginal utility, but also the prices of the inputs used to produce these goods are determined in a similar manner by their marginal products. This theory of distribution can, however, also be used to show the limitations of marginal analysis. In order to apply marginal techniques exclusively, it is necessary that there exists a known function linking the variable whose value is to be determined (output of a good in this case) to *all* the variables (inputs of the elements of production in this case) on which its value depends. This function should be continuous and differentiable so that the marginal products of the inputs can be derived. These inputs must be measured in physical units, rather than in terms of money values, if their marginal products are to be taken as independent determinants of their prices. In general, however, these conditions are not all satisfied. If the inputs in any specific production process, whose number will be very large, are measured in physical units, then they are often connected by a relationship of complementarity, and separate marginal products cannot be calculated for them. If these inputs are combined to form the aggregate factors of production, labour and capital, as was done by Clark, then capital can be measured only in money-value terms. This means that the marginal analysis begins with the prices of capital goods, and cannot provide an explanation of their determination. In addition, some essential inputs into the productive activity of firms, such as business organization and ability whose importance was emphasized by Marshall (1920), cannot be measured in physical units and placed in a production function. Even though Marshall made extensive use of marginal analysis, and is often erroneously credited with having a marginal productivity theory of distribution, he was aware of the limitations of marginal productivity as the sole explanation of distribution.

Marginal analysis cannot deal fully with situations where future conditions are not known with certainty, or where they cannot be represented by some well-defined probability distribution, since the effects on the variables of interest of marginal changes cannot be determined. Questions having to do with capital accumulation cannot be handled adequately by these techniques, since investment depends on expectations of future conditions that in a fundamental sense cannot be known in a context of historical time. Those wedded to marginal analysis thus tend to assume conditions that permit marginal techniques to be employed, even though they represent serious departures from the reality the analysis is supposed to illuminate. This may be one reason for the predominance given in neoclassical theory to perfect competition, despite the fact that modern manufacturing industry is imperfectly competitive. Only in the case of perfect competition is profit maximization, which is concerned with maximizing the present value of the stream of profits over time, synonymous with short-period profit maximization, the maximization of the current period's profits.

A. Asimakopulos
formerly, McGill University

References

Blaug, M. (1978) *Economic Theory in Retrospect*, 3rd edn, Cambridge, UK.
Marshall, A. (1920) *Principles of Economics*, 8th edn, London.

Further reading

Black, R. D., Coats, A. W. and Goodwin, C. D. W. (eds) (1973) *The Marginal Revolution in Economics*, Durham, NC.
Howey, R. S. (1960) *The Rise of the Marginal Utility School 1870–1889*, Lawrence, KS.
Schumpeter, J. A. (1954) *History of Economic Analysis*, New York.

See also: maximization.

markets

Markets are institutions that enable exchange to take place through bargaining or auction. They play a crucial role in allocating resources and distributing income in almost all economies, and also help to determine the distribution of political, social and intellectual influence. Only complete markets, in which every agent is able to exchange every good directly or indirectly with every other agent, can secure optimal production and distribution.` Such markets must also be competitive, with many buyers and sellers, no significant barriers to entry or exit, perfect information, legally enforceable contracts, and an absence of coercion. While the obvious common-sense models of markets refer to those for widely used commodities, the same analysis can be applied to markets for capital, land, credit, labour and so on. A system of perfect markets provides a mechanism to co-ordinate the activities of individuals who pursue their own self-interest, and thus embodies the essential social and political institutional framework that allows economists' assumptions about human behaviour to result in optimal efficiency and welfare outcomes.

Inevitably, most economic analysis of markets, from Aristotle onwards, has focused on their imperfections, and something like the modern theory of oligopoly was propounded in the early nineteenth century by Cournot (1838). Modern discussion of incomplete markets has been dominated by the debates begun by the work of Arrow and Debreu (1954), which suggested that uncertainty would inhibit the securing of Pareto-optimal solutions, linking up with a complementary analysis of the consequences of imperfect competition, such as that set out in Stigler (1957). The absence of complete markets, especially the lack of information or enforceable contracts, or the presence of distortions caused by taxes or subsidies or imperfect property rights, is seen to lead to market failure: the circumstance in which allocations achieved by markets are not efficient.

Market imperfections and failures that result in inefficient and exploitative socioeconomic structures have been analysed in detail for developing economies in the Third World, especially for the agrarian institutions of their rural areas. While the older literature often stressed a lack of rationality or the survival of a non-material tradition to explain the absence of effective market institutions in Africa and Asia, it is now possible to see that the interlinking of markets where the same agents supply land, credit and employment under conditions of monopoly or oligopoly (see Bharadwaj 1974; Braverman and Stiglitz (1982) lies at the heart of the problems of food production and distribution in South Asia and elsewhere. As a result, those with labour to sell are not given adequate entitlements and those with land and capital use their social power to extract rents without effective competition. More generally, as Bardhan (1989) and others have argued forcefully, social institutions such as share-cropping and debt-bondage can distort land and labour markets to create a sub-optimal and static economic equilibrium, and should not simply be seen as second-best adaptions to imperfect market conditions brought about by exogenous uncertainty or imperfect information. The role of the state in substituting for missing markets was seen by development economists and policy makers in the 1950s and 1960s as justified by the inadequate or exploitative nature of market allocations. By the end of the 1970s, however, with the obvious distortions in prices that resulted from state intervention, and the heightened dangers of rent-seeking by which the owners of scarce factors of production such as capital and land were guaranteed returns that rewarded them for the ownership of their assets not the efficient use of them, a more neo-classical role of the relations between markets and governments was reasserted by Lal (1983) among others. This debate is complicated by the fact that many developing economies achieved independence and began their development policies at a time (the late 1940s and early 1950s) when national and international market institutions were badly damaged by the impact of the Great Depression and the Second World War (Tomlinson 1993).

Despite the resurgence of neo-classical rigour in development theory, awkward questions about the practical power of market arrangements to secure optimal solutions to economic problems have persisted. If all markets are in some sense imperfect, then questions remain about how best to complete them to ensure equity and efficiency by using other institutions. While some economists have suggested that complementary institutional change to reassign property rights or establish effective prices by removing all subsidies and distorting taxation is all that is necessary (Friedman and Friedman 1980), others have seen the problem as more complex than this.

In developed economies, doubts about the efficiency of markets to ensure dynamic structural change have been focused on the history of large corporations, especially in the USA. Here the work of Coase (1937; 1960) and others led to the identification of transactions costs that can inhibit the contractual arrangements on which competitive markets must be based, and provided a framework for analysing institutions as substitutes for missing markets in an environment of pervasive risks, incomplete markets, information asymmetry and moral hazard. Thus in the words of Williamson (1981), large firms have come to be seen as alternatives to markets, not monopolists but 'efficiency instruments' that can co-ordinate the economic activity needed for rapid structural and technological change through the visible hand of the corporation more effectively than the invisible hand of the market. The work of business historians that stresses the importance of firms' investments in managerial capabilities in constructing internationally competitive industries notably Chandler 1990) can be used to flesh out these points empirically. The emergence of efficient and rapidly growing industrial economies in East Asia has given another twist to this analysis. The market activity that has accompanied rapid technical change and dynamic growth in Japan, South Korea and Taiwan, in particular, has been seen as managed or governed by a developmental state (Wade 1990). This has produced the paradoxical situation that economies with apparently less competitive markets have outperformed those such as the USA in which free enterprise is still the ideal. Thus the question of whether the competitive market, as usually understood by Anglo-Saxon economists, was ever or is still the most effective way of securing economic growth and social justice is at the top of the agenda for social scientists once more.

B. R. Tomlinson
University of Strathclyde

References

Arrow, K. J. and Debreu, G. (1954) 'Existence of an equilibrium for a competitive economy', *Econometrica* 22.

Bardhan, P. (1989) 'Alternative approaches to the theory of institutions in economic development', in P. Bardhan (ed.) *The Economic Theory of Agrarian Institutions*, Princeton, NJ.

Bharadwaj, K. (1974) *Production Conditions in India Agriculture*, Cambridge, UK.

Braverman, A. and Stiglitz, J. E. (1982) 'Sharecropping and the interlinking of agrarian markets', *American Economic Review* 72.

Chandler, A. D. (1990) *Scale and Scope: The Dynamics of Industrial Capitalism*, Cambridge, MA.

Coase, R. (1937) 'The nature of the firm', *Economica*, ns 4.
—— (1960) 'The problem of social cost', *Journal of Law and Economics* 3.

Cournot, A. (1838) *Recherches sur les principles mathématiques de la théorie des richesses*, Paris.

Friedman, M. and Friedman, R. (1980) *Free to Choose: A Personal Statement*, New York.

Lal, D. (1983) *The Poverty of Development Economics*, London.

Ledyard, J. O. (1987) 'Market failure', in J. Eatwell, M. Milgate and P. Newman (eds) *The New Palgrave Dictionary of Economics*, London.

Stigler, G. J. (1957) 'Perfect competition, historically contemplated', *Journal of Political Economy* 43.

Tomlinson, B. R. (1993) *The Economy of Modern India, 1860–1970*, Cambridge, UK.

Wade, R. (1990) *Governing the Market: Economic Theory and the Role of Government in East Asian Industrialisation*, Princeton, NJ.

Williamson, O. E. (1981) 'The modern corporation: origin, evolution, attributes', *Journal of Economic Literature*.

Wilson, C. (1987) 'Incomplete markets', in J. Eatwell, M. Milgate and P. Newman (eds) *The New Palgrave Dictionary of Economics*, London.

See also: capital, credit and money markets; competition; derivative markets and futures markets; firm, theory of; general equilibrium theory; microeconomics; mixed economy; monopoly; prices, theory of; transaction costs.

marriage

Historically and cross-culturally marriage has taken many different forms. Anthropologists especially devoted much energy to specifying these forms and analysing the economic and social characteristics which generated distinct marriage systems. Frequently marriage was examined from a jural perspective with emphasis placed on the rights and responsibilities which marriage generated, not only between husbands and wives but also between their kin (Fortes 1962). Within this framework, matters such as control of sexuality, the legitimacy of children, the economic stability of households and the control and transmission of property were central.

The relationship between economic transformation and the form which marriage takes has also been the focus of much attention within the social sciences. In particular, sociologists have long been interested in the ways in which marriage was patterned by industrialization. The principal argument, put forcefully by writers like Goode (1963) and Stone (1979), is that the introduction of wage labour effectively breaks the control which the wider kin group, and especially parents, can exert over the younger generation's marital behaviour. Where individual welfare and lifestyles are dependent on resources generated through productive property controlled by other kin, marriage systems will tend to reflect collective rather than individual concerns. However, as wage labour increasingly dominates within the economic system, so individuals are freed from their dependence on inherited property and more able to exert their own will over marriage issues, including, of course, choice of spouse.

It is within this context that romantic love and compatibility come to dominate cultural images of the essential character of marriage. Within contemporary 'marital blueprints' (Cancian 1987), in the industrialized world at least, emotional satisfaction, intimacy and personal fulfilment are emphasized as both the rationale for marriage and the criteria of its success (Clark 1991). At an ideological level, it is love – the largely untheorized, supposedly special romantic and sexual attraction between two individuals – which is prioritized within marriage discourses. Indeed Giddens (1992), among others, has argued that the social and economic conditions of late modernity have further boosted the cultural significance of intimacy and romantic love through freeing sexual expression from reproduction. It is within this context that the current historically high levels of marital separation and divorce need to be understood: the more that emotional intimacy and personal fulfilment are seen as the *sine qua non* of marriage, the less acceptance there is of relationships where such feelings are absent.

Inherent in these views of marriage is the notion that it is a relationship increasingly characterized by equality. However, as feminist scholarship has consistently demonstrated, marriage continues to be marked by a high division of labour and an unequal distribution of resources. In this, marriage reflects the inequalities which exist outside the domestic arena. In particular, despite changes in employment practices, in most marriages wives continue to carry the primary responsibility for domestic organization and childcare. This is now commonly combined with some form of paid work, but the gendered hierarchies of employment (for a discussion of this in Britain, see Crompton and Sanderson 1990) usually result in women earning significantly less than their male partners, for whom employment is prioritized. The social organization of childcare also continues to be highly gendered, even if many fathers do play a more active part than in the past. In the early and arguably key phase of a marriage, the birth of children encourages a more tightly bound division of labour (Mansfield and Collard 1988), usually with negative consequences for women's social and economic participation.

If the interaction of labour market differentials and women's socialization as nurturers and carers results in a clear division of responsibility in marriage, it also has an impact on the allocation of resources between wives and husbands. Although obtaining appropriate data is not as straightforward as it might seem, the evidence from different countries indicates that men routinely have higher levels of personal expenditure than their female partners, more control over major decisions and higher priority given to their work and leisure projects. Given the differential character of their primary responsibilities, they also have somewhat more freedom over their use of time, especially, though not only, when there are children in the household. Although a range of other social, cultural and economic factors clearly impinge on this, women's leisure participation is often more constrained than that of their male partners by the disjointed and piecemeal nature of their domestic responsibilities, the need to combine this with involvement in paid work, and their lesser access to money for personal expenditure. Research, as well as media attention, has also continued to demonstrate the significant role that marital violence plays in sustaining male control and privilege in some marriages (Pahl 1985).

The claim that marriage is being undermined with modernity is a common one. The high levels of separation and divorce occurring in different industrial societies are one reason for this. So too, though, are the significant changes which have arisen in patterns of cohabitation, that is sexual and domestic unions which have not been legally sanctioned. However, while cohabitation has become far more common and much less stigmatized since the mid-1970s than previously, its consequences for marriage are more difficult to calculate. It would appear that for many people cohabitation serves as an alternative form of engagement rather than an alternative to marriage. In Britain, for example, by the late 1980s over 50 per cent of those marrying had previously cohabited compared with less than 5 per cent in 1966 (Haskey and Kiernan 1989). It remains an open question whether significant numbers of people will choose cohabitation rather than marriage as a form of union throughout their life course.

Graham Allan
University of Southampton

References

Cancian, F. (1987) *Love in America*, Cambridge, UK.

Clark, D. (1991) *Marriage, Domestic Life and Social Change*, London.

Crompton, R. and Sanderson, K. (1990) *Gendered Jobs and Social Change*, London.

Fortes, M. (ed.) (1962) *Marriage in Tribal Societies*, Cambridge, UK.

Giddens, A. (1992) *The Transformation of Intimacy*, Cambridge, UK.

Goode, W. J. (1963) *World Revolution and Family Patterns*, New York.

Haskey, J. and Kiernan, K. (1989) 'Cohabitation in Great Britain: characteristics and estimated number of cohabitation partners', *Population Trends* 58.

Mansfield, P. and Collard, J. (1988) *The Beginning of the Rest of your Life: A Portrait of Newly-Wed Marriage*, Basingstoke.

Pahl, J. (1985) *Private Violence and Public Policy*, London.

Stone, L. (1979) *The Family, Sex and Marriage in England 1500–1800*, Harmondsworth.

See also: divorce; family; family history; kinship; nuptiality.

Marshall, Alfred (1842–1924)

The British economist Alfred Marshall was one of the dominant figures in his subject during the late nineteenth and early twentieth centuries. His 1890 masterwork, the *Principles of Economics*, introduced many of the tools and concepts that economists use in price theory even today. The book also presented an influential synthesis of received theories of value and distribution.

Marshall was born on 26 July 1842 in Bermondsey, London, his father William being at the time a clerk at the Bank of England. Alfred was educated at Merchant Taylors' School, revealing there his aptitude for mathematics. Somewhat against his father's wishes, he entered St John's College, Cambridge, to embark on the mathematics tripos, graduating in 1865 as Second Wrangler. He was then elected to a fellowship at St John's. Soon abandoning mathematics for ethics and psychology, his growing interest in social questions led him to economics, which by 1870 he had chosen as his life's work. He took a prominent part in the teaching for the moral sciences tripos until leaving Cambridge in 1877 on marriage to his one-time student, Mary Paley.

Although Marshall published little, these early years were the formative ones for his economic views. He mastered the classical tradition of A. Smith, D. Ricardo and J. S. Mill and was encouraged towards a mathematical approach by early acquaintance with the works of A. A. Cournot and J. H. von Thünen. Priority for the marginal revolution of the early 1870s clearly goes to W. S. Jevons, L. Walras and C. Menger, but Marshall had been working on similar lines before 1870. However, his attitude towards these new developments remained somewhat grudging, and he was always reluctant to publish merely theoretical exercises. More general influences significant in this early period were those of H. Sidgwick (perhaps more personal than intellectual), H. Spencer and G. W. F. Hegel. The last two, in tune with the spirit of the age, led Marshall towards an organic or biological view of society. He found the early socialist writers emotionally appealing, but unrealistic in their views as to evolutionary possibilities for human nature. Somewhat later, he saw merit in the programme of the German Historical School of Economics, but deplored its anti-theoretical stance. It was from these and other varied sources, including energetic factual enquiry, that he distilled and long pondered his subtle, complex and eclectic approach to economic questions.

Marshall returned to Cambridge in 1885, from exile in Bristol and Oxford, as professor of political economy and the acknowledged leader of British economists. He had already commenced work on his *Principles*. His first two significant publications had appeared in 1879. One was a selection of theoretical chapters from a never-completed book on foreign trade, printed by Sidgwick for private circulation under the title *The Pure Theory of Foreign Trade: The Pure Theory of Domestic Values*. These superb chapters did much to establish Marshall's reputation among British economists. The other was an ostensible primer, the *Economics of Industry*, co-authored by his wife, which foreshadowed many of the ideas of the *Principles*. It was this work that first brought Marshall's views to the attention of foreign economists.

Marshall lived in Cambridge for the rest of his life, resigning his chair in 1908 to devote all his energies to writing. The years were externally uneventful and dominated by the internal struggle to give vent and adequate expression to his vast store of knowledge. The first volume of what was intended as a two-volume work on *Principles of Economics* appeared in 1890 and cemented his international reputation. Although this first volume went through eight editions, little progress was made with the second volume, which had been intended to cover money, business fluctuations, international trade, labour and industrial organization. Among the famous concepts introduced in the *Principles*, as it soon came to be known, were consumer surplus, long and short-period analysis, the representative firm, and external economies. The elucidation and criticism of these and related concepts were to occupy English-speaking economists for many years.

In 1903, under the influence of the tariff agitation, Marshall embarked on a tract for the times on national industries and international trade. This too grew vastly in his hands and, when it eventually appeared in 1919, *Industry and Trade* realized his earlier intentions only incompletely. The book's tone, historical and descriptive rather than theoretical, has made it better known among economic historians than among economists. The years that remained were devoted to a last-ditch effort to salvage some of his unpublished earlier work. Some important early contributions to the theories of money and international trade at last saw the light in *Money, Credit and Commerce* in 1923, but the book remains an unsatisfactory pastiche. Marshall died on 13 July 1924 at the age of 81 having failed to do much that he had wished, yet still having achieved greatness.

During his years as professor, Marshall was instrumental in establishing the specialized study of his subject at Cambridge, which eventually became a leading centre for economic study and research. As teacher and adviser he inspired his students with his own high and unselfish ambitions for his subject. Among the several students who were to attain professional prominence and influence, A. C. Pigou and J. M. Keynes should especially be mentioned. Nationally, Marshall was a public figure and played an important role in government inquiries and in the professionalization of economics in Britain. Internationally, he was cosmopolitan in outlook and kept close contact with economists and economic events abroad.

Marshall was anxious to influence events and deeply concerned for the future of Britain, and especially of its poorer and less privileged citizens. Yet he preferred to remain above the fray of current controversy, whether scientific or concerned with policy, trusting that constructive work and patient study would provide the surer if slower route towards the desired goals. His desire for historical continuity and the avoidance of controversy led him frequently to underplay the novelty of his ideas and to exaggerate their closeness to those of his classical forebears.

John K. Whitaker
University of Virginia

Further reading

Guillebaud, C. W. (ed.) (1965) *Marshall's Principles of Economics, Variorum Edition*, London.
Pigou, A. C. (ed.) (1925) *Memorials of Alfred Marshall*, London.
Whitaker, J. K. (ed.) (1975) *The Early Economic Writings of Alfred Marshall, 1867–1890*, London.

See also: Marshall-Lerner criterion; neo-classical economics.

Marshall-Lerner criterion

This criterion is named after the British economist Alfred Marshall and the US economist Abba Lerner. It is a simple condition which shows whether a devaluation of a country's currency will improve the country's balance of trade. Such an improvement need not necessarily follow, as a devaluation will normally cheapen the value of each unit of the country's exports in world currency and may not cheapen the value of each unit of its imports. If the balance of trade is to improve following the devaluation, export sales must increase enough, and/or import purchases diminish enough, to offset any such relative cheapening of exports. The relative cheapening of exports is called 'a worsening of the country's terms of trade'.

The Marshall-Lerner criterion states that 'a country's trade balance will improve following a depreciation of its currency if the (positive value of) the elasticity of foreign demand for its exports and the (positive value of) its elasticity of demand for imports together sum to more than unity'. (An elasticity of demand for a commodity shows the percentage increase in the quantity demanded following a 1 per cent fall in the commodity's price.) The Marshall-Lerner criterion is appropriate if the following simplifying assumptions are applicable: the country's exports are in infinitely elastic supply (export prices are constant in home currency); the world supply of imports to the country is infinitely elastic (import prices are constant in foreign currency); and the balance of trade is initially neither in surplus nor in deficit. In such circumstances an x per cent devaluation will cause an x per cent reduction in the foreign currency revenue from each unit of exports, and no change in the foreign currency revenue for each unit of imports; in other words, it will cause an x per cent worsening of the terms of trade. But, if the Marshall-Lerner criterion holds, it will also cause an increase in export volume and reduction in import volume which together sum to more than x per cent and so outweigh this worsening of the terms of trade.

Qualifications to the Marshall-Lerner criterion are required if the assumptions mentioned in the previous paragraph do not hold. If, for example, the prices of exports in foreign currency are in part tied to foreign competitors' prices in foreign currency, then the terms of trade loss following a devaluation will be smaller, and an improvement in the balance of trade will be easier to obtain. By contrast, a devaluation starting from an initial position of deficit will in general require larger volume responses if it is to improve the trade balance. The export and import elasticities then need to add up to more than unity for a devaluation to be successful.

Modern balance of payments theory, developed since the Second World War, has suggested some more fundamental modifications to the Marshall-Lerner criterion. First, a devaluation will normally lead to increases in domestic costs and prices. This domestic inflation may partly or fully upset the stimulus to export promotion and import reduction. The second modification is suggested by the techniques of Keynesian multiplier analysis: any improvement in the trade balance will increase domestic incomes and expenditures, sucking in more imports, so partly or fully undoing the initial improvement. The third amendment has been suggested by the monetary theory of the balance of payments. Any improvement in the trade balance may lead to monetary inflow, a stimulus to expenditures at home, and further increases in imports which may undo the initial improvement. These three developments have made it clear that the success of a devaluation depends not only on the size of export and import elasticities, as suggested by the Marshall-Lerner criterion, but also upon the domestic inflationary process, upon domestic income expansion, and upon what happens to domestic monetary conditions.

David Vines
University of Oxford

Further reading

Södersten, B. and Reed, G. (1994) *International Economics*, 3rd edn, London.

See also: balance of payments; international trade; Marshall, Alfred.

Marx, Karl Heinrich (1818–83)

Marx was a German social scientist and revolutionary, whose analysis of capitalist society laid the theoretical basis for the political movement bearing his name. Marx's main contribution lies in his emphasis on the role of the economic factor – the changing way in which people have reproduced their means of subsistence – in shaping the course of history. This perspective has had a considerable influence on the whole range of social sciences.

Karl Heinrich Marx was born in the town of Trier in the Moselle district of the Prussian Rhineland on 5 May 1818. He came from a long line of rabbis on both his father's and his mother's sides. His father, a respected lawyer in Trier, had accepted baptism as a Protestant in order to be able to pursue his career. The atmosphere of Marx's home was permeated by the Enlightenment, and he assimilated a certain amount of romantic and early socialist ideas from Baron von Westphalen – to whose daughter, Jenny, he became engaged in 1835 and later married. In the same year he left the local gymnasium, or high school, and enrolled at the University of Bonn. He transferred the following year to the University of Berlin, where he soon embraced the dominant philosophy of Hegelianism. Intending to become a university teacher, Marx obtained his doctorate in 1841 with a thesis on post-Aristotelian Greek philosophy.

From 1837 Marx had been deeply involved in the Young Hegelian movement. This group espoused a radical critique of Christianity and, by implication, a liberal opposition to the Prussian autocracy. Finding a university career closed to him by the Prussian government, Marx moved into journalism. In October 1842 he became editor, in Cologne, of the influential *Rheinische Zeitung*, a liberal newspaper backed by Rhenish industrialists. Marx's incisive articles, particularly on economic questions, induced the government to close the paper, and he decided to emigrate to France.

Paris was then the centre of socialist thought and on his arrival at the end of 1843, Marx rapidly made contact with organized groups of émigré German workers and with various sects of French socialists. He also edited the shortlived *Deutsch-französische Jahrbücher*, which was intended to form a bridge between nascent French socialism and the ideas of the German radical Hegelians. It was also in Paris that Marx first formed his lifelong partnership with Friedrich Engels. During the first few months of his stay in Paris, Marx rapidly became a convinced communist and set down his views in a series of manuscripts known as the *Ökonomisch-philosophische Manuskripte* (*Economic and Philosophic Manuscripts of 1844*). Here he outlined a humanist conception of communism, influenced by the philosophy of Ludwig Feuerbach and based on a contrast between the alienated nature of labour under capitalism and a communist society in which human beings freely developed their nature in co-operative production. For the first time there appeared together, if not yet united, what Engels described as the three constituent elements in Marx's thought – German idealist philosophy, French socialism, and English economics. It is above all these Manuscripts which (in the west at least) reoriented many people's interpretation of Marx – to the extent of their even being considered as his major work. They were not published until the early 1930s and did not attract public attention until after the Second World War; certain facets of the Manuscripts were soon assimilated to the existentialism and humanism then so much in vogue, and presented an altogether more attractive basis for non-Stalinist socialism than textbooks on dialectical materialism.

Seen in their proper perspective, these Manuscripts were in fact no more than a starting-point for Marx – an initial, exuberant outpouring of ideas to be taken up and developed in subsequent economic writings, particularly in the *Grundrisse* (1857–8) and in *Das Kapital* (1867). In these later works the themes of the '1844 Manuscripts' would certainly be pursued more systematically, in greater detail, and against a much more solid economic and historical background; but the central inspiration or vision was to remain unaltered: humankind's alienation in capitalist society, and the possibility of emancipation – of people controlling their own destiny through communism.

Because of his political journalism, Marx was expelled from Paris at the end of 1844. He moved (with Engels) to Brussels, where he stayed for the next three years. He visited England, then the most advanced industrial country in the world, where Engels's family had cotton-spinning interests in Manchester. While in Brussels, Marx devoted himself to an intensive study of history. This he set out in a manuscript known as *The German Ideology* (also published posthumously); its basic thesis was that 'the nature of individuals depends on the material conditions determining their production'. Marx traced the history of the various modes of production and predicted the collapse of the present one – capitalism – and its replacement by communism.

At the same time that he was engaged in this theoretical work, Marx became involved in political activity and in writing polemics (as in *Misère de la Philosophie* (1847) (*The Poverty of Philosophy*) against what he considered to be the unduly idealistic socialism of Pierre Joseph Proudhon. He joined the Communist League, an organization of German émigré workers with its centre in London, for which he and Engels became the major theoreticians. At a conference of the league in London at the end of 1847, Marx and Engels were commissioned to write a *Manifest der kommunistischen Partei* (1848) (*Manifesto of the Communist Party*), a declaration that was to become the most succinct expression of their views. Scarcely was the *Manifesto* published when the 1848 wave of revolutions broke in Europe.

Early in 1848, Marx moved back to Paris, where the revolution had first erupted. He then went on to Germany where he founded, again in Cologne, the *Neue Rheinische Zeitung*. This widely influential newspaper supported a radical democratic line against the Prussian autocracy. Marx devoted his main energies to its editorship, since the Communist League had been virtually disbanded. With the ebbing of the revolutionary tide, however, Marx's paper was suppressed. He sought refuge in London in May 1849, beginning the 'long, sleepless night of exile' that was to last for the rest of his life.

On settling in London, Marx grew optimistic about the imminence of a fresh revolutionary outbreak in Europe, and he rejoined the rejuvenated Communist League. He wrote two lengthy pamphlets on the 1848 revolution in France and its aftermath, entitled *Die Klassenkämpfe in Frankreich 1848 bis 1850* (1850) (*The Class Struggles in France*) and *Der achzehnte Brumaire des Louis Bonaparte* (1852) (*The Eighteenth Brumaire of Louis Bonaparte*). But he soon became convinced that 'a new revolution is possible only in consequence of a new crisis', and devoted himself to the study of political economy to determine the causes and conditions of this crisis.

During the first half of the 1850s the Marx family lived in three-room lodgings in the Soho district of London and experienced considerable poverty. The Marxes already had four children on their arrival in London, and two more were soon born. Of these, only three survived the Soho period. Marx's major source of income at this time (and later) was Engels, who was drawing a steadily increasing income from his father's cotton business in Manchester. This was supplemented by weekly articles he wrote as foreign correspondent for the *New York Daily Tribune*. Legacies in the late 1850s and early 1860s eased Marx's financial position somewhat, but it was not until 1869 that he had a sufficient and assured income settled on him by Engels.

Not surprisingly, Marx's major work on political economy made slow progress. By 1857–8 he had produced a mammoth 800-page manuscript – a rough draft of a work that he intended should deal with capital, landed property, wage-labour, the state, foreign trade, and the world market. This manuscript, known as *Grundrisse* (Outlines), was not published until 1941. In the early 1860s he broke off his work to compose three large volumes, entitled *Theorien über den Mehrwert* (1861–3) (*Theories of Surplus Value*), that discussed his predecessors in political economy, particularly Adam Smith and David Ricardo.

It was not until 1867 that Marx was able to publish the first results of his work in Volume 1 of *Das Kapital*, devoted to a study of the capitalist process of production. Here he elaborated his version of the labour theory of value, and his conception of surplus value and exploitation that would ultimately lead to a falling rate of profit and the collapse of capitalism. Volumes 2 and 3 were largely finished in the 1860s, but Marx worked on the manuscripts for the rest of his life. They were published posthumously by Engels. In his major work, Marx's declared aim was to analyse 'the birth, life and death of a given social organism and its replacement by another, superior order'. In order to achieve this aim, Marx took over the concepts of the 'classical' economists that were still the generally accepted tool of economic analysis, and used them to draw very different conclusions. Ricardo had made a distinction between use-value and exchange-value. The exchange-value of an object was something separate from its price and consisted of the amount of labour embodied in the objects of production, though Ricardo thought that the price in fact tended to approximate to the exchange-value. Thus – in contradistinction to later analyses – the value of an object was determined by the circumstances of production rather than those of demand. Marx took over these concepts, but, in his attempt to show that capitalism was not static but an historically relative system of class exploitation, supplemented Ricardo's views by introducing the idea of surplus-value. Surplus-value was defined as the difference between the value of the products of labour and the cost of producing that labour-power, that is, the labourer's subsistence; for the exchange-value of labour-power was equal to the amount of labour necessary to reproduce that labour-power and this was normally much lower than the exchange-value of the products of that labour-power.

The theoretical part of Volume 1 divides very easily into three sections. The first section is a rewriting of the *Zur Kritik der politischen Ökonomie* (1859) (*Critique of Political Economy*) and analyses commodities, in the sense of external objects that satisfy human needs, and their value. Marx established two sorts of value – use-value, or the utility of something, and exchange-value, which was determined by the amount of labour incorporated in the object. Labour was also of a twofold nature according to whether it created use-values or exchange-values. Because 'the exchange-values of commodities must be capable of being expressed in terms of something common to them all', and the only thing they shared was labour, then labour

must be the source of value. But since evidently some people worked faster or more skilfully than others, this labour must be a sort of average 'socially necessary' labour time. There followed a difficult section on the form of value, and the first chapter ended with an account of commodities as exchange values, which he described as the 'fetishism of commodities' in a passage that recalls the account of alienation in the *Pariser Manuskripte* (1844) (*Paris Manuscripts*) and (even more) the *Note on James Mill*. 'In order', said Marx here, 'to find an analogy, we must have recourse to the mist-enveloped regions of the religious world. In that world the productions of the human brain appear as independent beings endowed with life, and entering into relation both with one another and the human race. So it is in the world of commodities with the products of men's hands.' The section ended with a chapter on exchange and an account of money as the means for the circulation of commodities, the material expression for their values and the universal measure of value.

The second section was a small one on the transformation of money into capital. Before the capitalist era, people had sold commodities for money in order to buy more commodities. In the capitalist era, instead of selling to buy, people had bought to sell dearer: they had bought commodities with their money in order, by means of those commodities, to increase their money.

In the third section Marx introduced his key notion of surplus value, the idea that Engels characterized as Marx's principal 'discovery' in economics. Marx made a distinction between *constant* capital which was 'that part of capital which is represented by the means of production, by the raw material, auxiliary material and instruments of labour, and does not, in the process of production, undergo any quantitative alteration of value' and *variable* capital. Of this Marx said: 'That part of capital, represented by labour power, does, in the process of production, undergo an alteration of value. It both reproduces the equivalent of its own value, and also produces an excess, a surplus value, which may itself vary, may be more or less according to the circumstances.' This variation was the rate of surplus value around which the struggle between workers and capitalists centred. The essential point was that the capitalist got the worker to work longer than was merely sufficient to embody in the product the value of the labour power: if the labour power of workers (roughly what it cost to keep them alive and fit) was £4 a day and workers could embody £4 of value in the product on which they were working in eight hours, then, if they worked ten hours, the last two hours would yield surplus value – in this case £1.

Thus surplus value could arise only from variable capital, not from constant capital, as labour alone created value. Put very simply, Marx's reason for thinking that the rate of profit would decrease was that, with the introduction of machinery, labour time would become less and thus yield less surplus value. Of course, machinery would increase production and colonial markets would absorb some of the surplus, but these were only palliatives and an eventual crisis was inevitable. These first nine chapters were complemented by a masterly historical account of the genesis of capitalism which illustrates better than any other writing Marx's approach and method. Marx particularly made pioneering use of official statistical information that came to be available from the middle of the nineteenth century onwards.

Meanwhile, Marx devoted much time and energy to the First International – to whose General Council he was elected on its foundation in 1864. This was one of the reasons he was so delayed in his work on *Das Kapital*. He was particularly active in preparing for the annual congresses of the International and in leading the struggle against the anarchist wing of the International led by Mikhail Bakunin. Although Marx won this contest, the transfer of the seat of the General Council from London to New York in 1872 – a move that Marx supported – led to the swift decline of the International. The most important political event during the existence of the International was the Paris Commune of 1871, when the citizens of Paris, in the aftermath of the Franco-Prussian war, rebelled against their government and held the city for two months. On the bloody suppression of this rebellion, Marx wrote one of his most famous pamphlets – entitled *Address on The Civil War in France* (1871) – which was an enthusiastic defence of the activities and aims of the Commune.

During the last decade of his life Marx's health declined considerably, and he was incapable of the sustained efforts of creative synthesis that had so obviously characterized his previous work. Nevertheless, he managed to comment substantially on contemporary politics in Germany and Russia. In Germany he opposed, in his *Randglossen zum Programm der deutschen Arbeiterpartei* (1875) (*Critique of the Gotha Programme*), the tendency of his followers Wilhelm Leibknecht and August Bebel to compromise with the state socialism of Ferdinand Lassalle in the interest of a united socialist party. In Russia, in correspondence with Vera Sassoulitch, he contemplated the possibility of Russia's bypassing the capitalist stage of development and building communism on the basis of the common ownership of land characteristic of the village council or *mir*. Marx, however, was increasingly dogged by ill health, and he regularly travelled to European spas and even to Algeria in search of recuperation. The deaths of his eldest daughter and of his wife clouded the last years of his life, and he died in London on 13 March 1883.

The influence of Marx, so narrow during his lifetime, expanded enormously after his death. This influence was at first evident in the growth of the Social Democratic Party in Germany, but reached worldwide dimensions following the success of the Bolsheviks in Russia in 1917. Paradoxically, although the main thrust of Marx's thought was to anticipate that a proletarian revolution would inaugurate the transition to socialism in advanced industrial countries, Marxism was most successful in developing in Third-World countries, such as Russia or China. Since the problems of these countries are primarily agrarian and the initial development of an industrial base, they are necessarily far removed from what were Marx's immediate concerns: for him, the collapse of Soviet communism would have been a source neither of surprise nor of dismay. On a more general level, over the whole range of the social sciences, Marx's materialist conception of history and his analysis of capitalist society have made him probably the most influential figure of the twentieth century.

David McLellan
University of Kent

Further reading

Avineri, S. (1968) *The Social and Political Thought of Karl Marx*, Cambridge, UK.
Cohen, G. (1978) *Karl Marx's Theory of History: A Defence*, Oxford.
McLellan, D. (1974) *Karl Marx: His Life and Thought*, New York.
Marx, K. (1977) *Selected Writings*, ed. D. McLellan, Oxford.
Ollman, B. (1971), *Alienation, Marx's Conception of Man in Capitalist Society*, Cambridge, UK.
Peffer, R. (1990) *Marxism, Morality and Social Justice*, Princeton, NJ.
Plamenatz, J. (1975) *Karl Marx's Philosophy of Man*, Oxford.
Suchting, W. (1983) *Marx: An Introduction*, Brighton.

See also: alienation; Marx's theory of history and society; Marxian economics; Marxist history.

Marx's theory of history and society

Marx's general sociohistorical theory, often known as the materialist conception of history or historical materialism, seeks, in the words of Engels,

> the ultimate cause and the great moving power of all important historic events in the economic development of society, in the changes in the modes of production and exchange, and in the consequent division of society into distinct classes, and in the struggles of these classes against one another.

Marx first elaborated his theory, which became the guiding thread of his subsequent studies, in *Die Deutsche Ideologie (The German Ideology)* of 1845–6. A famous, but very compact, statement of it appears in Marx's Preface to *Zur Kritik der politischen Ökonomie* (1859) (*A Contribution to the Critique of Political Economy*).

There Marx contends that the economic structure of society, constituted by its relations of production, is the real foundation of society. It is the basis 'on which rises a legal and political superstructure and to which correspond definite forms of social consciousness'. On the other hand, society's relations of production themselves 'correspond to a definite stage of development of [society's] material productive forces'. In this manner 'the mode of production of material life conditions the social, political and intellectual life process in general'. As society's productive forces develop, they clash with existing production relations, which now fetter their growth. 'Then begins an epoch of social revolution' as this contradiction rifts society and as people become, in a more or less ideological form, 'conscious of this conflict and fight it out'. This conflict is resolved in favour of the productive forces, and new, higher relations of production, whose material preconditions have 'matured in the womb of the old society itself', emerge which better accommodate the continued growth of society's productive capacity. The bourgeois mode of production represents the most recent of several progressive epochs in the economic formation of society, but it is the last antagonistic form of production. With its demise the prehistory of humanity will come to a close.

According to Marx, the expansion of the productive forces (that is, of the means of production and of the skill and expertise of human labour power) determines society's relations of production because, as he wrote to Annenkov, 'Men never relinquish what they have won.' In order to retain 'the fruits of civilization' they will change their way of producing to accommodate the acquired productive forces and facilitate their continued advance. The relations of production, though, influence the momentum and qualitative direction of the development of the productive forces; capitalism in particular is distinguished by its tendency to raise society to a productive level undreamt of before. Still, Marx's materialist conception assigns explanatory primacy to the development of the productive forces, envisioning, for instance, the emergence of capitalism as a response to the level of the productive forces existing at the time of its origin.

The development of society's productive capacity thus determines the main contours of its socioeconomic evolution, while the various economic structures that result shape, in turn, society's legal and political institutions, or superstructure. Which other social institutions are properly part of the superstructure is a matter of debate, but Marx certainly thought that all the various spheres and realms of society reflect the dominant mode of production and that the general consciousness of an epoch is shaped by the nature of its production. The Marxist theory of ideology contends, in part, that certain ideas originate or are widespread because they sanction existing social relations or promote particular class interests. The economy's determination of legal and political forms, however, will tend to be relatively direct, while its influence over other social realms, culture, and consciousness generally is more attenuated and nuanced.

Because a superstructure is needed to organize and stabilize society, the economic structure brings about those institutions that are best suited to it. Law, in particular, is necessary to 'sanction the existing order' and grant it 'independence from mere chance and arbitrariness'. This function itself gives the legal realm some autonomy, since the existing relations of production are represented and legitimated in an abstract, codified form, which in turn fosters the ideological illusion that the law is entirely autonomous with respect to the economic structure. In addition, under capitalism the '*fictio juris* of a contract' between free agents obscures the real nature of production, in particular, the 'invisible threads' that bind the wage-labourer to capital. In pre-capitalist societies, for example in feudalism, tradition and custom perform a similar stabilizing function and may also win a degree of autonomy from the economic realm. There the true nature of the social relations of production is obscured by entanglement with the relations of personal domination which characterize the other spheres of feudal life.

In the social organization of production, people stand in different relations to the forces and products of production, and in any given mode of production these relations will be of certain characteristic sorts. One's economic position, as that is understood in terms of the existing social production relations, gives one certain material interests in common with others and determines one's class. Hence follow the familiar definitions of the bourgeoisie and proletariat by reference to the purchase and sale, respectively, of labour power (and the underlying ownership or non-ownership of the means of production).

A central thesis of Marx is that class position, so defined, determines the characteristic consciousness or world view of its members. For example, Marx's discussion of the Legitimists and Orleanists in *Der achzehnte Brumaire des Louis Bonaparte* (1852) (*The Eighteenth Brumaire of Louis Bonaparte*) emphasizes that on the basis of its socioeconomic position each class creates 'an entire superstructure of distinct and peculiarly formed sentiments, illusions, modes of thought and views of life'. The differing material interests of classes divide them and lead to their struggle. Classes differ in the extent to which their members perceive themselves as a class, so that antagonisms between classes may not be discerned by the participants, or may be understood only in a mystified or ideological manner.

The ultimate success or failure of a class is determined by its relation to the advance of the productive forces. In the words of *The German Ideology*, 'The conditions under which definite productive forces can be applied are the conditions of the rule of a definite class of society.' That class which has the capacity and the incentive to introduce or preserve the relations of production required to accommodate the advance of the productive forces has its hegemony ensured. Marx's theory views class rule, hitherto, as both inevitable and necessary to force the productivity of the direct producers beyond the subsistence level. The productive progress brought by capitalism, however, eliminates both the feasibility of, and the historical rationale for, class rule. Since the state is primarily the vehicle by which a class secures its rule, it will wither away in post-class society.

Marx's 'Preface' designates the Asiatic, ancient, feudal, and modern bourgeois modes of production as the major epochs in humanity's advance, but these mark the general stages of socioeconomic evolution as a whole – not the steps which history obliges every nation without exception to climb. In a famous letter of November 1877, Marx characteristically denied propounding 'any historic-philosophic theory of the *marche générale* imposed by fate upon every people', but this oft-quoted remark does not amount to a rejection of historical determinism. Although Marx's theory permits countries to lag behind or even skip steps, their course must still be accounted for within the overarching pattern of socioeconomic evolution, and that development is due to the productive forces. Marx could consistently believe in a necessary, productive-force-determined evolution of history without holding that every social group is preordained to follow the same course. It seems likely, in addition, that Marx would have been willing to revise his particular tabulation of historical periods (or at least the pre-feudal ones), since he did not analyse in detail humanity's early modes of production. Modification of Marx's schema, as well as of his analysis of capitalism (and the projected transition to socialism), is in principle compatible with his basic theory of society and history.

It should be borne in mind that Marx's theory does not pretend to explain every last detail of history and society. Certain social and cultural phenomena are beyond its explanatory range, and from its broad purview, many historical events, and certainly the specific forms they take, are accidental. Nor does the theory seek to explain fully and scientifically individual behaviour, though it attempts to situate that behaviour within its sociohistorical confines. In so far as there are ineluctable tendencies in history, these result from, not despite, the choices of individuals.

Marx's ideas have had an influence on the social sciences, the significance of which it is hard to exaggerate. Not only has his work inspired, to various extents, countless writers, but even those who reject Marx frequently find themselves obliged to define their own thought in relation to his. Despite the perennial attractions of Marx's approach and the fertility of his insights, controversy continues over the basic concepts and theorems of his theory, the relative importance of its various components, and the specific features that characterize his sociohistorical methodology. Given Marx's far-reaching claims and the lack of an interpretative consensus, a conclusive assessment of the viability of his general theory of society and history is exceedingly difficult.

William H. Shaw
San José State University

Further reading

Cohen, G. A. (1988) *History, Labour and Freedom*, Oxford.
Elster, J. (1985) *Making Sense of Marx*, Cambridge, UK.
Shaw, W. H. (1978) *Marx's Theory of History*, Stanford, CA.
Wood, A. (1981) *Karl Marx*, London.

See also: alienation; Asiatic Mode of Production; capitalism; economic history; feudalism; Marx, Karl Heinrich; Marxian economics; Marxist history; political economy; social history; social structure and structuration; stratification.

Marxian economics

Marxian economics traditionally begins from a general statement of the 'labour theory of value' (GLTV): that value in commodity exchange is grounded on exploitation in production. This leads to an account of the labour process, showing how exploitation takes place and how it can be measured by a rate of exploitation – the hours worked for the employers – divided by the hours worked to support the labourer. From this, a 'special labour theory of value' (SLTV) is developed: prices, or ratios of exchange between commodities, are proportioned to the hours of direct and indirect labour that went to produce them. These prices are easily calculable from input-output data, and have the important property that they are independent of the distribution of the surplus between the social classes. But, except in special cases, they are not consistent with a uniform rate of profit in capital, such as free competition would tend to establish (Steedman 1977). (The question of the relation between prices based on labour values and prices based on a uniform rate of profit is known as the 'transformation problem'.)

Important as they are, the theories of exploitation and labour value are foundations. The edifice itself centres upon the 'general law of capitalist accumulation' (GLCA), that the accumulation of capital is accompanied, *pari passu*, by an increase in the proletariat, maintaining, therefore, an industrial reserve army of unemployed people, proportioned in size to the total capital. The arguments for this proportion require a way of expressing prices which is independent of distribution (since, for example, when capital accumulates faster than the proletariat grows, wages rise and profits fall, slowing down accumulation), but do not otherwise depend on the SLTV. Having established the GLCA, Marx turned to the 'theory of circulation', the tendency of the rate of profit to fall, the behaviour of rents, the theory of crises, and the role of money, credit, and interest.

Since the mid-1960s there has been a great revival of Marxian economics, due chiefly to the work of Piero Sraffa (1960). Sraffa's construction of the standard commodity, which solves Ricardo's problem of the invariable measure of value, provides a way of expressing prices both consistent with a uniform rate of profit and invariant to changes in distribution. Hence, the SLTV can be discarded; the GLTV, on the other hand, remains unaffected, since the rate of exploitation, and the connection between exploitation and profits, can be shown more clearly than ever in equation systems based on Sraffa (Morishima 1973). Thus, the GLCA can be established on a firm foundation, permitting an analytical treatment of the effects of class conflict on wages and exploitation, although modern work normally gives much greater scope to demand factors than Marx did.

However, the very system of equations which establishes the validity of the basic Marxian scheme – the GLTV and the GLCA – undermines the Marxian argument for the tendency of the rate of profit to fall simply as a result of a rise in the organic composition of capital. For firms will not adapt a new technique unless it is cheaper than the old, at current prices. But it can be shown that if it is cheaper, then when adapted and the new prices are established, the new rate of profit will never be less than the old (Roemer 1981). Thus, the Marxian theory of crisis needs another foundation. This has led to interesting work on the theory of circulation, money and credit, bringing the Marxian tradition into contact with the work being done by the post-Keynesian school. In particular, Marxists and neo-Ricardians have been concerned with whether the rate of profit determines the rate of interest, or vice versa, or whether they are both determined together.

Questions of circulation and money lead to a re-examination of competition, and the tendency to greater centralization and concentration. Competition has been conceptualized as a form of strategic conflict, but there is as yet no generally accepted theory of the development and behaviour of the corporation. However, this is a rapidly developing field.

Marxian economics has greatly benefited from the classical revival instigated by Sraffa. But Marx founded his economic thinking on a critique of the classics, basically contending that they took relations of social power for the natural order of things, and attributed to mere tokens – money, capital, commodities – power which really resided in class relationships. Modern Marxian economics likewise both learns from the post-Keynesian and modern classical tradition, and establishes its separate identity through a critique of these schools. Its critique is essentially that of Marx: the economic system works according to laws, but these laws in turn depend on the nature of the political and social system, and cannot be fully understood apart from the whole. This critique has particular force when it comes to the theory of economic policy, for the post-Keynesians, in particular, tend to attribute to the state power and a degree of neutrality which Marxists do not believe possible under capitalism.

Edward J. Nell
New School for Social Research, New York

References

Morishima, M. (1973) *Marx's Economics: A Dual Theory of Value and Growth*, Cambridge, UK.

Roemer, J. (1981) *Analytical Foundations of Marxian Economic Theory*, Cambridge, UK.

Sraffa, P. (1960) *Production of Commodities by Means of Commodities*, Cambridge, UK.

Steedman, I. (1977) *Marx after Sraffa*, London.

See also: Marx, Karl Heinrich; Marx's theory of history and society; political economy; value and distribution.

Marxist history

When Karl Marx referred to his system as 'historical materialism' he was signalling his indebtedness to two important intellectual traditions. First, to the French Enlightenment with its emphasis on the determination of social attitudes and behaviour by material forces such as climate and the economy: intended initially to undermine established religious ways of thinking, this became the basis of a more positive method of systematic economic analysis. Second, to the German reaction against the Enlightenment, with its emphasis on the value of all modes of thought when understood within their original historical contexts: intended initially to defend inherited religious ways of thinking, this became the basis of a more general method of sympathetic cultural understanding. Though many later historians first encountered economic determinism and cultural historicism through the writings of Marx, these approaches did not originate with him and even their combination into historical materialism had been anticipated by Scottish Enlightenment thinkers such as Adam Smith who had developed their own accounts of the stages of social development. Marx himself was well aware of this and in his famous letter to Weydemeyer rejected any claim to have discovered the existence of classes and class struggle in history and emphasized that his own contribution was to show that 'the class struggle necessarily leads to the dictatorship of the proletariat' (1852). Thus while Marx has become the best known purveyor of historical materialism, the specifically Marxist element within this was his argument that, just as feudalism had unintentionally given rise to the bourgeoisie and its revolutionary transformation of society, so the economic development of capitalism would necessarily give rise to a united proletariat and its revolutionary expropriation of the means of production from the bourgeoisie.

For fifty years after his death in 1883, Marxist historical work was largely restricted to the writings of left-wing activists attempting to justify their political strategies by compiling material on the recent economic development of capitalism. However, the interwar depression and the rise of fascism, combined with the apparent success of socialism in the Soviet Union, made Marxism more plausible in the west and it began to pass into the mainstream of historical debate, particularly through the work of Maurice Dobb and Ernest Labrousse. Dobb was a Cambridge economist who became involved in history through his pioneering work on the Russian economy under the Soviet regime. More importantly, Dobb's (1946) essays on the economic development of capitalism set the agenda for research into the transition from feudalism to capitalism and into the economic formation of the modern working class which was to guide the next generation of British Marxist historians. Labrousse was a historian at the Sorbonne whose studies of economic cycles in eighteenth-century France were intended to uncover the precise material causes of the outbreak of the Revolution of 1789 (Labrousse 1943). More importantly, his pioneering application of sophisticated quantitative methods had a significant influence on the shift towards more rigorous demographic and econometric history among the next generation of French historians around the journal *Annales*.

The period after the Second World War therefore saw flourishing schools of Marxist historians in the western universities, focusing mainly on the analysis of the material structures underlying political developments. Important work on the origins of the English Revolution in the seventeenth century, on the development of the British labour movement in the nineteenth century, and on the economic and social history of the French départements in the early-modern and modern periods has since faced major challenges but has made a permanent contribution to the establishment of a more problem-oriented approach in place of the older narrative style of historical writing. This is best understood as part of a wider movement towards economic history which had equally important roots in radical-liberal work on the British Industrial Revolution beginning with Arnold Toynbee (1884), and in democratic work on material factors in US history beginning with the 'frontier thesis' of Frederick Jackson Turner (1893). Moreover, even at the moment of its apparent triumph, Marxist history was increasingly subject to internal tensions, particularly following the Soviet invasion of Hungary in 1956. This embarrassing failure of the major socialist regime raised questions about the political teleology which had underpinned the Marxist approach to history, and led to a re-examination of the confident economic determinism and a re-emphasis on the elements of cultural historicism in Marx's writings. This was particularly marked in Britain, with its strong native tradition of ethical and idealist socialism; one of the most influential contributions was Edward Thompson's (1963) study of the early-nineteenth-century English working class. This emphasized political and religious traditions as much as economic structures, and interpreted them in their own terms rather than with the advantage of hindsight, producing the famous manifesto about rescuing even those who had followed backward-looking or utopian ideas 'from the enormous condescension of posterity'. While undoubtedly leading to fresh insights into the experiences of ordinary people, this kind of work also launched Marxist history into an attempt to reconcile economic determinism and political agency, class structure and the autonomy of culture, within which it began to lose its coherence as a system.

The next great depression in the 1970s and 1980s then undermined rather than reinforced Marxism, as western labour movements suffered reverses at the hands of reactionary regimes and the Soviet Union was completely discredited as a viable political alternative to liberal democracy. Those historians in the Marxist tradition who were still concerned with concrete historical analysis moved away from the old teleological framework through the deconstruction of key materialist categories such as class, and the inclusion of the impact of state activity within their range of social forces. As a result, their work became increasingly reabsorbed into the liberal mainstream. Those historians in the Marxist tradition who attempted to maintain a distinctive unifying focus tended to emphasize the determining impact of language on consciousness, and, where this went beyond a suggestive new approach to popular movements and became the basis of a critical approach to historical method, it sheared away not only the old materialist teleology but also any falsifiable approach to the analysis of cultural contexts. Ironically, then, many of those historians who still professed loyalty to the critical heritage of Marx began to propose an increasingly ungrounded version of historicism.

Alastair J. Read
University of Cambridge

References

Dobb, M. (1946) *Studies in the Development of Capitalism*, London.
Labrousse, C. E. (1943) *La Crise de l'Économie française à la fin de l'Ancien Régime*, Paris.
Marx, K. (1852) 'Marx to Weydemeyer, 5 March 1852', in K. Marx and F. Engels, *Collected Works*, vol. 39, London.
Thompson, E. P. (1963) *The Making of the English Working Class*, London.
Toynbee, A. (1884) *Lectures on the Industrial Revolution of the Eighteenth Century in England*, London.
Turner, F. J. (1893) 'The significance of the frontier in American history', *Report of the American Historical Society*.

Further reading

Hobsbawn, E. (1978) 'The Historians' Group of the Communist Party', in M. Cornforth (ed.) *Rebels and their Causes*, London.
Prost, A. (1992) 'What has happened to French social history?', *Historical Journal* 35.

See also: economic history; Marx, Karl Heinrich; Marx's theory of history and society; social history.

mass media

Mass media together comprise a new social institution, concerned with the production and distribution of knowledge in the widest sense of the word, and have a number of salient characteristics, including the use of relatively advanced technology for the (mass) production and dissemination of messages; the systematic organization and social regulation of this work; and the direction of messages at potentially large audiences who are unknown to the sender and free to attend or not. The mass media institution is essentially open, operating in the public sphere to provide regular channels of communication for messages of a kind determined by what is culturally and technically possible, socially permitted and in demand by a large enough number of individuals.

It is usual to date the beginnings of mass media from the first recognizably modern newspaper, in the early seventeenth century, which in turn was a new application of the technology of printing, already in use for over 150 years for the multiple reproduction of book manuscripts. The audiovisual forms which have subsequently been developed, mainly since the end of the nineteenth century, have caused existing media to adapt and have enlarged the total reach of media, as well as extended the diversity of their social functions.

This history of media development is, nevertheless, more than a record of technical advance and of increasing scale of operation. It was a social innovation as much as a technological invention, and turning points in media history are marked, if not caused, by major social changes. The history of the newspaper, still the archetypal as well as the first, mass medium, illustrates the point very well. Its development is linked to the emergence to power of the bourgeois (urban-business-professional) class, which it served in cultural, political and commercial activities. It became an essential instrument in subsequent economic and political struggles, a necessary condition for economic liberalism, constitutional democracy and, perhaps, also, revolution and bureaucratic centralism. Its development thus reflects not only political and economic forces but also major social and cultural changes. The latter include urbanization; rising living standards and the growth of leisure; and the emergence of forms of society which are, variously, democratic, highly organized, bureaucratic, nationalistic and committed to gradual change. Consideration of newer media, especially film, radio and television, would not greatly modify this assessment, and these media have not greatly widened the range of functions already performed by the newspaper as advertiser, entertainer and forum for the expression of opinion and culture.

Early social science views of mass media reflect some of these historical circumstances. Commentators were struck by the immense popular appeal of the new media and by the power which they might exert in society. Beyond that, views divided sharply on whether to welcome or regret the new instruments of culture and information, and a division between pessimists and optimists has been an enduring feature of assessments of mass media, starting to fade only as the inevitability and complexity of the media are accepted. The pessimistic view stems partly from the pejorative connotations of the term 'mass', which includes the notions of vast scale, anonymity, impersonality, uniformity, lack of regulation and mindlessness. At the extreme, the media were regarded, sometimes by conservative and radical critics alike, as instruments for manipulation, a threat to existing cultural and spiritual values and to democracy. But optimists saw the mass media as a powerful means of disseminating information, education and culture to the previously excluded classes and of making feasible a genuine participatory democracy. By the 1930s some circumstantial evidence and enough theory supported both sides, but there was little systematic investigation.

The first period of scientific investigation of mass media undertaken between the mid-1930s and the late 1950s resulted in a much more modest estimate of media effects than was previously assumed, even a new myth of media powerlessness. The earlier stimulus-response model of influence was replaced by a model of indirect influence, according to which the media were seen to be subject to mechanisms of selective attention, perception and response, such that any effects would be more likely to reinforce existing tendencies than to cause any major change. Further, the working of media was seen to be subordinate to the existing patterns of social and personal influence and thus not well conceived of as an external influence. While the evidence reassured many critics and discomfited prophets of doom, it seemed to lead to no slackening of efforts to use media, in ever more subtle ways, for political and commercial ends. Since the 1960s there has been further development in the assessment of mass media effects in the direction of a renewed belief in their potency.

The earlier research, despite its reassuring message, left open the possibility that media effects could be considerable under certain conditions: first, where there exists a monopoly or uniformity of message content; second, where the messages seem to concern matters beyond immediate experience or direct relevance; and third, where there is a cumulation over a long period of time of similar messages. Research attention has thus shifted from the search for direct, short-time effects on individuals and towards the following: structures of ownership and control of media; patterns of ideology or culture in messages and texts; professional and organizational contexts in which media knowledge is manufactured. Experts assessing the influence of mass media emphasize what people learn from the media, thus cognitive effects in the widest sense. We may learn from the media what is normal or approved, what is right or wrong, what to expect as an individual, group or class, and how we should view other groups or nations. Aside from the nature and magnitude of media effects on people, it is impossible to doubt the enormous dependence of individuals, institutions and society as a whole on mass media for a wide range of information and cultural services.

If the mass media play an essential part in mediating a wide range of relationships within societies, they have also come to be seen as playing a comparable part in mediating relations between nation-states and world blocs. The flow of information and culture by way of mass media does much to establish and confirm patterns of perception, of hostility and attraction and also the relations of economic dependence and latent conflict between the different worlds of east and west, north and south. While mass media still largely consist of separate national systems, the increasing internationalization of networks and content is now interesting researchers.

The history of mass media has so far been fairly short and very eventful, but it already seems on the point of a new and significant departure which may change the essential character of mass communication. The most important developments are of smaller-scale, point-to-point and potentially interactive media, employing cable, satellite or computer technology. It is likely that there will be a move away from centralized and uniform media of distribution towards a more abundant and functionally diversified provision of messages based on receiver demand. The boundaries between mass communication and the emerging new forms of information transfer are likely to become even more blurred in what is being hailed as an emerging 'information society'. Nevertheless, the issues which shaped early debates about mass media are still somewhat relevant in the new conditions, especially those which concern the contribution of mass communication to equality or inequality, order or change, unity or fragmentation. Because of their public functions, nationally and internationally, mass media are unlikely to be replaced by the new media, although the balance of use and significance will change.

Denis McQuail
University of Amsterdam

Further reading

Curran, J. and Gurevitch, M. (eds) (1991) *Mass Media and Society*, London.
McQuail, D. (1994) *Mass Communication Theory: An Introduction*, London.

See also: communication networks; communications; literacy; McLuhan, Marshall; media and politics; media effects.

matching (two-sided matching)

One of the main functions of many markets and social processes is to match one kind of agent with another, for example, students and colleges, workers and firms, marriageable men and women. A class of two-sided matching models for studying such processes was introduced by Gale and Shapley (1962), who focused on college admissions and marriage.

A market is two-sided if there are two sets of agents, and if an agent from one side of the market can be matched only with an agent from the other side. Gale and Shapley proposed that a matching (of students and colleges, or men and women) could be regarded as *stable* only if it left no pair of agents on opposite sides of the market who were not matched to each other but would both prefer to be. They showed that a special property of two-sided (as opposed to one-sided or three-sided) markets is that stable matchings always exist (at least when agents' preferences are uncomplicated).

If we consider matching processes whose rules are that any two agents on opposite sides of the market can be matched to each other if they both agree, then, unless a matching is stable, there are players who wish to be matched to each other but who are not, even though the rules allow them to arrange such a match. So only stable matchings are likely to arise if the matching process is sufficiently 'free' as to allow all potential matchings to be considered.

A natural application of two-sided matching models is to labour markets. Shapley and Shubik (1972) showed that the properties of stable matchings are robust to generalizations of the model which allow both matching and wage determination to be considered together. Kelso and Crawford (1982) showed how far these results can be generalized when firms, for example, may have complex preferences over the composition of their workforce.

Two-sided matching models have proved useful in the empirical study of labour markets, starting with the demonstration in Roth (1984) that since the early 1950s the entry level labour market for US physicians has been organized in a way that produces (predominantly) stable matchings. Subsequent work has identified natural experiments which show that labour markets organized so as to produce *un*stable matchings suffer from certain kinds of difficulties which are largely avoided in comparable markets organized to produce stable matchings. This work combines the traditions of co-operative and non-cooperative game theory, by considering how the strategic environment faced by market participants influences the stability of the resulting market outcome.

Studies in the mid-1990s have focused on the timing of transactions. Bergstrom and Bagnoli (1993) model causes of delay in marriage, while Roth and Xing (1994) discuss several dozen matching markets in which there has been a tendency for transactions to become steadily earlier (e.g. clerks for Federal judges in the USA are now hired almost two years before they begin work, and similar phenomena are observed among British doctors, graduates of elite Japanese universities, etc.). An overview of matching can be found in Roth and Sotomayor (1990).

Alvin E. Roth
University of Pittsburgh

References

Bergstrom, T. and Bagnoli, M. (1993) 'Courtship as a waiting game', *Journal of Political Economy* 101.

Gale, D. and Shapley, L. (1962) 'College admissions and the stability of marriage', *American Mathematical Monthly* 69.

Kelso, A. S. Jr and Crawford, V. P. (1982) 'Job matching, coalition formation, and gross substitutes', *Econometrica* 50.

Roth, A. E. (1984) 'The evolution of the labor market for medical interns and residents: a case study in game theory', *Journal of Political Economy* 92.

Roth, A. E. and Sotomayor, M. (1990) *Two-Sided Matching: A Study in Game-Theoretic Modeling and Analysis*, Cambridge, UK.

Roth, A. E. and Xiaolin Xing (1994) 'Jumping the gun: imperfections and institutions related to the timing of market transactions', *American Economic Review* 84.

Shapley, L. S. and Shubik, M. (1972) 'The assignment game I: the core', *International Journal of Game Theory* 1.

See also: labour market analysis.

material culture

Material culture is an important source of evidence across the social sciences and humanities. It can be narrowly defined as the study of the material products of human manufacturing processes or, as George Kubler (1962) argues, more euphoniously, as 'the history of things'. As well as focusing on art and artefacts it usually encompasses the study of the technological processes involved in the manufacture of the objects and the conceptual systems within which they are embedded. It can also include the human construction of the environment as a cultural and economic landscape, since artefacts are instrumental in economic processes and landscapes are transformed through human action. In the social sciences, artefacts are viewed as part of culture and integral to the processes of social reproduction. They cannot be understood in isolation from the broader social and cultural contexts within which they exist.

In nineteenth-century anthropology, material objects were included with other cultural traits in the models of evolutionary theorists such as Pitt-Rivers, Tylor and Haddon. Material culture was taken to be an index of the level of social and cultural development of particular societies, and typological analyses established formal sequences which were assumed to demonstrate the evolution of societies from simple to complex forms. Diffusionist theorists, who were concerned to trace the origins of ideas, also used material culture as a major source of evidence. Probably because of its use as evidence in evolutionary and diffusionist theory and its association with 'speculative history', material culture was largely neglected by British anthropology for the first half of the twentieth century. As a consequence the study of material culture was missing from the fieldwork revolution that began to transform anthropology at the turn of the century, when interest shifted to studying contemporary societies in their own right as functioning wholes. In the USA the situation was more complex. Material culture was an integral part of culture-area theory and the ecological evolutionary anthropology of White and Steward. Moreover, US archaeology maintained theoretical interest in material culture at a time when it was largely neglected in the rest of the discipline. From the 1960s onwards it was in the branches of ethno-archaeology, 'new' archaeology and behavioural archaeology (Gould and Schiffer 1981) that much research into contemporary material culture was pursued.

The 1960s saw a general renewal of interest in the subject, stimulated by the growth of symbolic anthropology and the interest of archaeologists in the material culture of contemporary societies as a source of data for archaeological interpretation. Moreover, with the demise of functionalism and the move to a more historically informed theoretical framework, material culture came into its own again as a source of information that could add a time dimension to research (see Appadurai 1986). The separation of material culture from other social and cultural data is now recognized to be arbitrary, and objects have been reintegrated within social theory. This has had a dual effect: the opening up of a previously neglected body of data that provides insight into social processes, and a better understanding of the artefacts themselves. Material culture has been increasingly used as a source of evidence by social historians, psychologists and exponents of cultural studies. Research in material culture has contributed in particular to the literature on exchange, processes of value creation (Munn 1986) and to an understanding of processes of consumption.

The analytic core of research into material culture remains the explanation or interrogation of the form of material objects. Artefacts are uniquely material in nature: they can be recorded in detail and people can be questioned about their form (Ucko 1969). But the objective is, in part, to uncover through analysis the ideational systems that underlie the production and consumption of artefacts, to abstract from the surface concreteness of their form by connecting them to history and relating them to the diversity of social processes. Analysis has often been framed in terms of semiotics or meaning (see Hodder 1989). It is, however, important to take a broad perspective on meaning which can relate the instrumental functions of an object to other dimensions of its value which may include such factors as aesthetics, style, symbolism and economics.

The concept of objectification has proved useful in the study of material culture. Material objects can be viewed as objectifications of the systems of knowledge, methods of production and division of labour used in their manufacture, and as objectifications of the values that are represented in patterns of consumption and contexts of use. This positioning of objects at the fulcrum of a process linking production with consumption has made them a fruitful subject for analysis. The analysis of material culture provides information on value creation, on the expression of individual identity and on the motivations underlying consumer behaviour. Increasingly material culture is being used as a source of information in the study of complex societies and global patterns and processes (Miller 1987).

As in the nineteenth century, social scientists are once again viewing material culture as important evidence for historical and global processes, but they have adopted new and very different theoretical perspectives. While there is still interest in material culture objects as indices of cultural boundaries and markers of social categories, researchers have become equally concerned with transformations in the value and meaning of objects as they move from context to context, either as part of local exchange systems or global trading processes (Thomas 1991). Material objects frequently outlast their maker; thus they are both sources of evidence about previous lifeways and objects to be reflected on by the generations who succeed their makers. As time progresses, artefacts often get caught up in ideological process and find themselves incorporated in new contexts that were never envisioned by their original manufacturers. The study of material culture encompasses the analysis of ideological restructurings, whether in the form of present-day heritage industry or in the process of the reinterpretation of rock art over the generations and its consequences on the production of later paintings. Material culture not only creates potential for but also constrains human action, and it is subject to human agency; people make meaningful objects but they can also change the meaning of objects.

Howard Morphy
Pitt-Rivers Museum

References

Appadurai, A. (ed.) (1986) *The Social Life of Things*, Cambridge, UK.

Gould, R. and Schiffer, M. (1981) *Modern Material Culture Studies: The Archaeology of Us*, New York.

Hodder, I. (1989) *The Meaning of Things: Material Culture and Symbolic Expression*, London.

Kubler, G. (1962) *The Shape of Time*, New Haven, CT.

Miller, D. (1987) *Material Culture and Mass Consumption*, Oxford.

Munn, N. M. (1976) *Fame of Gawa*, Cambridge, UK.

Thomas, N. (1991) *Entangled Objects: Exchange, Material Culture and Colonialism in the Pacific*, Cambridge, MA.

Ucko, P. J. (1969) 'Penis sheaths: a comparative study', *Proceedings of the Royal Anthropological Institute for 1968*.

See also: archaeology.

mathematical economics

Mathematical economics has developed from being a relatively small branch of economic theory in 1950 to become almost coextensive with mainstream economic theory. Its success has been such that economists out of sympathy with the basic assumptions and models of so-called neo-classical economic theory have found themselves obliged to provide increasingly mathematical formulations of radical economic theory derived from the Marxian and Ricardian traditions. The reasons for the rapid expansion of mathematical economics after 1950 lie partly in the influx of ex-mathematicians to academic economics – Kenneth Arrow, Gérard Debreu, Frank Hahn, Werner Hildenbrandt – and partly in the increasing concern in all branches of economics with formal rigour and with the establishment of economics as a scientific discipline. Prior to the mathematical formalization of economic theory and the introduction of advanced techniques of mathematical analysis, economic theorists had relied primarily on graphical techniques of analysis and presentation. Up to a point these can be very effective, but they are inherently limited by the two-dimensional character of a piece of paper. More subtly, graphical techniques can introduce implicit assumptions whose significance may be neglected or very difficult to understand.

Historically, among the first applications of mathematical analysis in economics were Leon Walras's use of the theory of simultaneous equations to discuss the problem of equilibrium in several interrelated markets and Edgeworth's use of calculus to analyse consumer behaviour. These subjects remain at the heart of modern mathematical economics, though the mathematical techniques applied have changed totally. They also illustrate the increasingly close relationship between advances in certain areas of mathematical economics and pure mathematics. Walras's problem has stimulated the development of 'general equilibrium analysis' which focuses on the conditions for the existence of a set of prices, or other instruments, which ensure that supply and demand are equal in all markets simultaneously when the resources, technological possibilities and consumer preferences that determine supply and demand are specified in quite general terms. If a unique general equilibrium can be shown to exist, one may then use comparative statistics to examine how the character of the equilibrium is altered if some of the initial conditions are changed. From such comparisons it may – or may not – be possible to infer the response of prices and quantities to a variety of changes in the world. General equilibrium analysis has come to depend heavily on modern developments in topology and functional analysis, so that the dividing line between the more abstract type of mathematical economics and pure mathematics has almost vanished.

The theory of individual consumer – or producer – behaviour has both benefited from and stimulated advances in the theory of mathematical programming and of convex analysis. As a consequence, familiar results derived by the application of calculus have been subsumed within a much more general theory which is based upon the concept of a maximum/minimum value function – that is, a profit or cost function for a producer, an indirect utility or expenditure function for a consumer. This theory exploits a number of powerful duality results which characterize interrelated maximization and minimization problems and can be given straightforward economic interpretations, such as the association of 'shadow prices' with the constraints which limit the set of feasible choices. This approach to consumer and producer theory has important empirical implications which can in principle be tested. For example, the 'theory of optimal consumer choice' implies that compensated price responses must be symmetric – in other words, the change in the consumption of good i with respect to the price of good j must equal the change in the consumption of good j with respect the price of good i – and that the compensated substitution effect must be negative – an increase in the price of good i should reduce the consumption of i. In both cases, the compensated effect refers to the change after income has been adjusted so as to hold utillity constant. This compensation is obviously difficult to measure, so that it is not possible to test these predictions directly in experiments, but indirect tests of the hypothesis of maximizing behaviour have been devised. The results have been mixed, but the mathematical developments have stimulated much fruitful empirical work and have provided the basis for modern welfare economics.

The assumptions of equilibrium and maximization which underpin most of economic theory are controversial, especially as descriptions of short-run behaviour. As a result, mathematical economists have sought to construct theoretical models which weaken or dispense with these assumptions. Unfortunately, though these can provide useful insights into particular problems or phenomena, the models are always open to the criticism that they are *ad hoc*, in the sense that they rely upon specific types of behavioural responses, and that their results are not robust to even quite small changes in the characterization of these responses. At present there seem to be no powerful simplifying principles which enable economists to analyse models of disequilibrium or non-maximizing behaviour – or even to agree on what these models should look like. Hence most of the current effort of mathematical economists is devoted to modifying standard equilibrium and maximizing models by incorporating considerations of uncertainty and differential information, in the hope that this approach will provide the basis for reconciling the more obvious disparities between observed economic behaviour and theoretical predictions. None the less, the basic philosophical problem of how far useful economic models can be developed without the fundamental assumptions of maximization and equilibrium remains unanswered. What, for instance, does it mean to describe someone as 'choosing' a course of action which that person judges inferior to some other feasible alternative? Until a convincing solution to this problem is found, mathematical economists are likely to continue to rely upon equilibrium models of maximizing behaviour.

Gordon Hughes
University of Cambridge

Further reading

Arrow, K. J. and Intriligator, M. D. (eds) (1981; 1983; 1984) *Handbook of Mathematical Economics*, 3 vols., Amsterdam.
Cassels, J. W. S. (1981) *Economics for Mathematicians*, Cambridge, UK.
Varian, H. R. (1978), *Microeconomic Analysis*, New York.

See also: equilibrium; general equilibrium theory; mathematical models; maximization.

mathematical models

As mathematics is a powerful, flexible language and models are representations, mathematical models are representations framed in mathematical terms. A good metaphor for a mathematical model is a map. A map is a simple device for representing a complex geographical locality. Much of the richness of the locality is removed in the representation but enough remains for it to be recognized. Whether the map is a good one

depends not only on its properties but also on the use to which it is put. If you want to get through a city quickly, a simple map of the arterial routes suffices. For a walking tour of a city centre, a detailed map of the city centre is enough, and if you are hiking in open country a geological survey map works fine – if you know how to use it. Essentially, a model must make substantive sense, and be technically adequate. Additionally, the model may lead to identification of modes of implementation and intervention.

Discussions of mathematical models are frequently co-ordinated by at least two of the following distinctions. The first differentiates process models from structural models, the second deterministic models from probabilistic ('stochastic') models, and the third differentiates models using discrete variables from those using continuous variables. In principle, an eight-cell table can be constructed using these three criteria and each cell filled with mathematical models sharing the criteria defining the cell.

Models of processes explicitly attempt to model change and provide an understanding of the mechanisms of change. Among the frequently used tools are differential equations and difference equations. Models of structure attempt to represent and understand the structure of social relations. Frequently used mathematical tools include graph theory and matrix algebra; in addition, modern algebraic tools such as groups, semi-groups and Boolean algebras find applications in these structural analyses, as well as category theory and algebraic topology.

Stochastic models are used to model processes whose outcomes are governed by a probabilistic mechanism(s). Many types of stochastic models are available to social scientists (see Bartholomew 1982). Deterministic models eschew stochastic mechanisms in favour of deterministic mechanisms and relations. The process models of social change can be deterministic or stochastic. The structural models tend to be deterministic. If the models are discrete they use variables that can take only one of the small number of states, whereas continuous models use variables that are, or can be, treated usefully as if they are continuous. For the process models, a further distinction can be made concerning the representation of time: it, too, can be taken as discrete or continuous.

Mathematical models have wide-ranging applications in the social sciences. (For many examples see Fararo 1973; Rapoport 1983; Sørensen 1978.) A modeller selects the mathematical model best suited for a substantive problem where skill shows in knowledge of alternative model candidates and selection of the most fruitful one(s). Mathematical modellers tend to draw on mathematics already developed using models formulated in other disciplines. This is unproblematic if the model captures the crucial theoretical aspects, and critical empirical components, of the substantive problem. Indeed, mathematical models draw their power from being devoid of substantive content: a mathematical model can be used fruitfully in different areas of one field or even in different fields. Seldom have mathematics been invented because of social science needs, which contrasts with the physical science tradition exemplified by the invention of the differential-integral calculus by Newton and Leibniz. Exceptions include game theory, decision theory and some areas of artificial intelligence research. So much for models, but what is a good model?

Good models must be adequate in all components of its methodology. The Theory-Model-Data triangle of Leik and Meeker (1975) provides a way of discussing this. There are three pairs of mappings – between theory and model; between model and data; and between theory and data – and all are important (although different model builders may place differential emphasis on them).

The theory–model linkage is concerned with expressing a congruence between a theory and its representation in a mathematical model. The theory has to map into the model with little distortion or loss. Deductively, there is a mathematical formalization of the theory while, inductively, this can be a formal generalization of the theory. The mathematical model then has to be useful. Useful, here, means the machinery of the mathematical system has to be mobilized to derive or establish mathematical results. These results can be mapped to the theory and to the data. Deductively, the model maps to the (empirical) data by specifying, or predicting, empirical outcomes. The model is truly predictive if it makes predictions that can be checked empirically. Sometimes models are not predictive in this sense. Instead they lead to the construction of descriptions based on data. Also deductively, the mathematical results (theorems) map to the theory by specifying the theoretical implications of the derivations through the mappings linking theory and model.

When the empirical predictions and specifications stemming from the model are confronted with data, several outcomes are possible. First, the predictions made on the basis of the theory and the model may be borne out providing support for the model. The results are filtered back through the mappings and interpreted substantively. Second, if a model calls only for empirical descriptions, these by themselves are not, at face value, too important. However, they must make sense when interpreted theoretically. Third, the model may lead to predictions that are disconfirmed, calling the model into question. The model builder then has to establish if the model should be rebuilt or discarded.

This requires skill. Further, this decision has other important implications: measurements must be good and empirical evidence is decisive. Which brings us to statistical methodology.

The frequently made distinction between mathematical models and statistical analysis is a very blurred one. First, formal approaches can, and do, incorporate error specification (a theory of error) – which other approaches generally do not. This informs estimation. Second, the properties of the statistical tools are stated and established mathematically. Finally, new mathematical models and their uses generate estimation problems and statistical questions.

Space precludes discussion of the rest of the Theory-Model-Data triangle but each does constrain the others. The theory, the model, and the data have to make sense and be consistent with one another – which is the nub of evaluating models.

The charge is often made that mathematical models overlook much of the richness and texture of social life. They do, and this is a virtue (which is not to say that the richness and texture are irrelevant). The claim that social phenomena are incredibly complex and that this complexity cannot be captured via mathematical models need not detain us. While the basic laws of physics are simple, for example Newton's laws of motion, they generate behaviours that are, and appear to observers as, very complex. Note also that complex mathematical formulae are generated from simple start points. A direct attempt to model complexity, for example, to predict the exact trajectory of a snowflake in a storm or a leaf in a wind, would appear bizarre and fruitless. Yet in the social sciences there are many attempts to model, in one way or another, the surface phenomena of human life. Following the distinction between noise and true signals, the modeller and the critic need to evaluate the model on the basis of (good) measurement of signals rather than of noise. While empirical evidence is decisive, not all measurements count. That social behaviour is complex cannot be denied, but the principles governing this behaviour need not be complex. They may even permit a mathematical description (which does not mean we have slavishly to follow the mathematical antics of the natural sciences – or even use the same mathematics). In this context, computer simulation models are used fruitfully.

It does not follow that all social scientists should use mathematics, only that some do. While mathematical models are used quite frequently, only a minority of social scientists create and use them. Yet, even so, we can point to a powerful drive towards mathematical expression of and solutions to disciplinary, and, more strongly, interdisciplinary problems. Social science publications like the *Journal of Mathematical Sociology* and the *Journal of Mathematical Psychology* find counterparts among the natural sciences in the *Journal of Mathematical Physics* and *Mathematical Geology*. Of course, neither set validates the other. There are many publications without mathematics in their title but which, nevertheless, carry a heavy mathematical imprint. These include *Psychometrika, Sociological Methodology, Social Networks, Geographical Analysis, Econometrica* and *Environment and Planning*. Within all of these journals good mathematical social science can be found. What is less clear is whether all of this activity stems from an intrinsic need for the use of mathematics in a discipline at a certain stage, or crude imitation between fields, or even the carving out of a niche by the mathematically inclined. Probably a bit of each is involved, but while imitation and niche creation are not intellectually illegitimate, only the first provides the continuing basis and context for significant work.

The mathematically inclined members of the social science tribe talk largely to themselves, primarily because they have learned the language, but also because many other tribe members do not care to listen. To the extent that the mathematical folk are concerned only to build their models for the sake of building them, they will remain in their intellectual niche. This will change only with the construction of powerful and relevant (hence successful) mathematical models. Then, perhaps, the niche will expand to form the ecosystem.

Patrick Doreian
University of Pittsburgh

References

Bartholomew, D. J. (1982) *Stochastic Models for Social Processes*, 3rd edn, New York.
Doreian, P. and Hummon, N. P. (1976) *Modelling Social Processes*, New York.
Fararo, T. (1973) *Mathematical Sociology: An Introduction to Fundamentals*, New York.
Leik, R. K. and Meeker, B. F. (1975) *Mathematical Sociology*, Englewood Cliffs, NJ.
Rapoport, A. (1983) *Mathematical Models in the Sociol and Behavioural Sciences*, New York.
Sørensen, A. (1978) 'Mathematical models in sociology', *Annual Review of Sociology* 4.

Further reading

Coleman, J. S. (1964) *An Introduction to Mathematical Sociology*, New York.

See also: artificial intelligence; game theory; mathematical economics; methods of social research; statistical reasoning.

maximization

According to an oft-quoted view, economics is about 'doing the best one can in a situation of scarcity'. Many, if not most, problems in economics fall under this heading. For example, consumers are assumed to choose the best bundle of commodities out of the range possible given their income constraints. The government is assumed to choose its policies to do the best it can for society as a whole, again given the constraints it faces. Such optimization may be said to be at the heart of economic analysis. The mathematical counterpart of this essentially economic problem is the maximization of an objective function subject to constraints on the choice variables.

The general maximization problem may be written as

$$\text{Max}_{\underline{x}} \; W\,(\underline{x}) \text{ subject to } \underline{x} \in X$$

where $W(\cdot)$ is the objective function, $\underline{x}$ is the vector of control (or choice) variables. These are shown to be restricted to the set X, which therefore specifies the constraints of the problem. The *economics* of the problem lies in the specification of the objective function $W(\cdot)$ and the constraint set $\underline{X}$. However, once these are specified, we still have to solve the problem in order to derive further economic results of interest. This is where the mathematical theory of maximization comes in.

If $\underline{x}^*$ satisfies

$$W\,(\underline{x}^*) \geq W\,(\underline{x}) \text{ for all } \underline{x} \in X$$

then $\underline{x}^*$ is said to be a *global* solution to the problem. On the other hand, if the inequality holds only for $\underline{x}$ in a neighbourhood of $\underline{x}^*$, then $\underline{x}^*$ is said to be a *local* solution to the problem. The *Weierstrass theorem* in mathematics says that, if the set X is compact and non-empty, and if the objective function $W(\underline{x})$ is continuous on X, then a global solution exists for the above problem. Most economic problems satisfy these conditions. However, can we say more about the nature of the solution $\underline{x}^*$? The answer is that we can, if we define the set $\underline{X}$ in greater detail.

For many economic problems the constraint set $\underline{X}$ can be specified implicitly as a series of inequalities which the control variable has to satisfy. Consider, therefore, the problem

$$\text{Max } W\,(\underline{x}) \text{ subject to } \underline{g}(\underline{x}) \leq \underline{b}; \quad \underline{x} \geq \underline{0}$$

where $\underline{x}$ is a $n \times 1$ vector. The $\underline{b}$ and the $m \times 1$ vector of functions $\underline{g}$ define the constraints on $\underline{x}$. Consider now the following function

$$\mathscr{L}(\underline{x}, \underline{\lambda}) = W(\underline{x}) + \underline{\lambda} \cdot (\underline{b} - \underline{g}(\underline{x}))$$

where λ is a m $\times$ 1 vector of non-negative auxilliary variables. The m elements of λ are known as Lagrange multipliers and $\mathcal{L}(\underline{x}, \underline{\lambda})$ is known as the Lagrangian of the problem. The *Kuhn-Tucker theorem* in non-linear programming then provides the conditions which characterize the solution to the problem. These conditions are

$$\frac{\partial \mathcal{L}}{\partial \underline{x}} (\underline{x}^*, \underline{\lambda}^*) \leqslant \underline{0}; \quad \frac{\partial \mathcal{L}(\underline{x}^*, \underline{\lambda}^*)}{\partial \underline{x}} \cdot \underline{x}^* = \underline{0}; \quad \underline{x}^* \geqslant \underline{0}$$

$$\frac{\partial \mathcal{L}}{\partial \underline{\lambda}} (\underline{x}^*, \underline{\lambda}^*) \geqslant \underline{0}; \quad \underline{\lambda}^* \cdot \frac{\partial \mathcal{L}}{\partial \underline{\lambda}} (\underline{x}^*, \underline{\lambda}^*) = \underline{0}; \quad \underline{\lambda}^* \geqslant \underline{0}.$$

The first part of the Kuhn-Tucker theorem says that if there exist $\underline{x}^*$, $\underline{\lambda}^*$ satisfying the above conditions, then $\underline{x}^*$ is a solution to the problem. The second part say that if $W(\cdot)$ is concave, $g(\cdot)$ are convex and there is some point $\hat{\underline{x}}$ for which the constraint is satisfied with strict inequality, then, for $\underline{x}^*$ to be a solution to the problem, there must exist $\underline{\lambda}^*$ such that $\underline{x}^*$, $\underline{\lambda}^*$ satisfy the Kuhn-Tucker conditions.

The Kuhn-Tucker conditions provide the basis for characterizing the optimum in most economic models. For example, if $\underline{x}^* \geqslant \underline{0}$, then we must have that

$$\frac{\partial \mathcal{L}}{\partial \underline{x}} (\underline{x}^*, \underline{\lambda}^*) = \underline{0};$$

or

$$\frac{\partial W(\underline{x}^*)}{\partial x_i} = \lambda^* \cdot \frac{\partial g^*(\underline{x}^*)}{\partial \underline{x}_i} \quad \text{for } i = 1, 2, \ldots, n.$$

In the case where the problem is the consumer's problem of choosing quantities x_i to maximize the utility function $U(\underline{x})$ subject to a single budget constraint

$$\sum_{i=1}^{n} p_i x_i \leqslant y$$

these conditions become

$$\frac{\partial U(\underline{x}^*)}{\partial x_i} = \lambda p_i \quad i = 1, 2, \ldots, n$$

or

$$\frac{\partial U(\underline{x}^*)}{\partial x_i} = \frac{\partial U(\underline{x}^*)}{\partial x_j} = \frac{p_i}{p_j}$$

that is, the marginal rate of substitution between any pair of goods must equal the price ratio of those two goods. Similar conditions can be derived and interpreted for other problems. In fact the $\underline{\lambda}^*$ have interpretation in terms of shadow prices which tell us the values to the agent of releasing each constraint at the margin.

S. M. Ravi Kanbur
University of Essex

Further reading

Baumol, W. (1965) *Economic Theory and Operations Analysis*, 2nd edn, Englewood Cliffs, NJ.
Dixit, A. K. (1975) *Optimization in Economic Theory*, London.
Intriligator, M. D. (1971) *Mathematical Optimization and Economic Theory*, Englewood Cliffs, NJ.

See also: marginal analysis; mathematical economics.

media *see* mass media; media and politics; media effects

media and politics

In all technologically advanced countries, the media have become a central political arena. Their most obvious importance lies in the huge audiences they reach, and the way these audiences transcend and cut across other social divisions and political constituencies. Just as importantly, the massive presence of the media acts as a force for disclosure from official institutions, and so has transformed political processes and created tensions surrounding the control of information and impressions.

The development of the media has always been intertwined with aspirations for democracy and struggles for political control (Keane 1991). The press had a deeply ambiguous history, chequered with political patronage, official subservience and expedient compromises. The news was reported with both fear and favour, as independent journalistic functions emerged uncertainly and erratically within what were primarily political instruments. But whether under state despotism, party patronage or under more solidly commercial bases, with the growth of the press barons in the nineteenth and early twentieth centuries, newspapers never manifested any golden age of journalistic purity (Smith 1979). There have always been charges that the press appealed to 'baser' instincts, just as earlier forms of personal information exchange centred on salacious gossip (Stephens 1988) and that it indulged in sensationalism and wilful distortion.

The outcome from all these idiosyncrasies and expediencies was the invention of a qualitatively new institution, one devoted to disclosure and dependent on audience acceptance with its own priorities, incentives and constraints, whose growth was fanned by the competition for market share and/or political influence. One institutional dynamic was towards an ever increasing conception of what it could and should make public (Roshco 1975) and to do so in ways that had the greatest audience appeal. Such imperatives made the media's route to their current political centrality inevitable.

Access to the media is now a key political resource. Efforts to influence media content and to counteract the attempts at media manipulation by opponents are an important battleground in many political conflicts. While media analysts have hesitated in pronouncing upon the political impacts of media, political participants certainly act as if the media have great power. From the time, when in their very different ways, Franklin Roosevelt and the German Nazis recognized the importance of radio, political leaders and activists from all parts of the spectrum have devoted great energy to influencing or controlling the media. Some terrorist groups have demanded media access among their demands, while others have planned their actions to achieve maximum international media exposure. Coup leaders typically commandeer broadcasting stations as one of their early targets, based upon an appreciation of establishing the appearance of control and the elimination of opportunities for counter-mobilization. Leaders in liberal democracies have sizeable staffs and resources devoted to achieving the most favourable media coverage.

The grievances of disaffected groups with a political system typically now include dissatisfaction with the media and its treatment of them. Disadvantaged groups and embattled leaders commonly blame the media as one key reason for their problems. However, discontents with the media are not limited to the politically disadvantaged. The performance of the media has attracted a variety of powerful but contrasting critiques. Dissatisfactions cross the political spectrum, provoking ideological critiques from both left and right. More embracingly, broadcasting, in particular, has been blamed for a cheapening of political discourse (Postman 1986); for the dominance of entertainment over political priorities; for the sale of political influence through advertising; and for being cognitively disabling and increasing popular political alienation.

However, the views of the critics are as contentious and problematic as the performance of the media. The power of the media to control public thinking has proved more limited than some feared. Many of the claims about media influence confuse visibility with power. Reassuringly, efforts at media manipulation by political leaders have met with mixed success. The collapse of communist regimes in Eastern Europe demonstrated that not even a generation of media control could secure them legitimacy from the populace.

The problems with claims about unidirectional ideological effects of the media go beyond the frequent difficulties of demarcating criteria and the transparent biases of the observers. Solely textual approaches to news, casting it in terms of myth or ideology, fail to capture its impact as a central institution, whose functioning affects the actions and relationships of key political participants. The media have been the focus of new complexes of political activity, including the growth of 'spin doctors' and other 'minders'. An institution devoted to disclosure sets up tensions, and is ripe for unintended consequences, even when politically constrained.

Especially but not only in liberal democracies, the media's impact upon the processes of policy making and the operation of other political institutions has been many-sided (Tiffen 1989). It has increased the government's speed of response. Prominence in the news has often influenced the priorities of political decision making, media attention imparting 'heat as well as light' (Sigal 1973) upon issue agendas. When media attention changes the timing of decisions, their content and effectiveness may also change. Most fundamentally, news has enlarged the scope of information available to the public. It has broadened the geographic range of the world with which they are regularly acquainted and deepened their knowledge of their own societies and politics. An often overlooked consequence is that policy making, or at the least the presentation of policies, is more constrained towards options which are publicly acceptable.

In these ways, the political significance of the media is far more profound and pervasive than the occasional deliberate exercise of power by those who occupy strategic positions in it – proprietors, editors, journalists or advertisers. Moreover the attribution of manipulative manoeuvres to such media figures, when based solely upon external readings of content, often lack any grasp of the internal constraints and motivations.

Each new advent in media has been greeted by great hopes and fears. These are often to do with aspects of the quality of cultural and political life, not easily subjected to measurement. Nevertheless false forecasts have clearly abounded. Moreover, despite the importance of political influences on media developments, they typically unfold in ways not foreseen by media policy makers or would-be controllers. Media history bears ample testimony to the limited prescience of both policy makers and their critics. Despite the difficulties of predicting future developments, two current trends promise to be of increasing political importance – the multiplicity of media outlets and trends towards internationalization.

The enormously increased technological capacity to deliver numerous channels to households, via satellites, cable and terrestial services, has coincided with a trend, through most western countries and in newly democratized polities, towards deregulation as a general policy stance. This has been particularly manifested in media and telecommunications policies, even though market rhetoric, centring on the consumer sovereignty brought by open competition, has rarely fitted media developments very well. The huge start-up costs, the desirable economies of scale in supply, production and distribution, and the logic of advertising strategies, all seem to lend themselves to oligopoly.

Many countries have allowed new commercial broadcasters to enter, at the same time as the finance available for public-service broadcasters has been squeezed. Most obviously the increased outlets will increase consumer choice, but the end of the process and its political implications are hard to foresee. Some say broadcasting will give way, at least in niche markets, to narrowcasting. The traditional democratic concern with massification is already being replaced by a concern with fragmentation.

The second and partly related trend is an increase in media capacities to transmit information around the globe instantaneously. This is a central part of the growing political importance of transnational forces, and the increasing influence of international influences upon domestic politics. The media were one element, for example, in the international opinion which helped to buttress domestically reformist leaders like Gorbachev and Yeltsin, and one thread in the way international actions and support contributed to the success of the African National Congress and the relatively peaceful transition from apartheid in South Africa.

Increasingly, the audiences for news are becoming international, with consequences for the conduct of foreign policy and the control strategies of national regimes. The massive presence of the western media probably prevented a bloodier regime crackdown during the fall of the Marcos regime in the Philippines in 1986. Chinese protesters deliberately appealed to the western media in attempting to change domestic power balances during the protests which culminated in the 1989 Tiananmien Square massacres. The availability of satellite news services, copied on to videotapes and widely distributed among activists, was an ingredient in the victory of the 'mobile phone mob' in Bangkok's 1992 demonstrations. At the same time, such trends have made the international flow of news and information even more unbalanced, the control of technology and commercial capacity has become more concentrated, the forces for international integration have in some important ways eroded national sovereignty, and the presence of western advertising and programming will have unknown cultural effects upon new audiences.

The safest prediction is that the history of the media will continue to be ambiguous, with double-edged implications for many political ideals, and in an equally complicated and contentious but dynamic future, politics and the media will continue to develop inextricably bound to each other.

Rodney Tiffen
University of Sydney

References

Keane, J. (1991) *The Media and Democracy*, London.
Postman, N. (1986) *Amusing Ourselves to Death: Public Discourse in the Age of Entertainment*, London.
Roshco, B. (1975) *Newsmaking*, Chicago.
Sigal, L. (1973) *Reporters and Officials*, Lexington, MA.
Smith, A. (1979) *The Newspaper: An International History*, London.
Stephens, M. (1988) *A History of News: From the Drum to the Satellite*, New York.
Tiffen, R. (1989) *News and Power*, Sydney.

Further reading

Dyson, K. and Humphreys, P. with Negrine, R. and Simon, J. -P. (1988) *Broadcasting and New Media Policies in Western Europe*, London.
Gans, H. (1979) *Deciding What's News*, New York.
Head, S. (1985) *World Broadcasting Systems: A Comparative Analysis*, Belmont, CA.
McQuail, D. (1992) *Media Performance: Mass Communication and the Public Interest*, London.
Seymour-Ure, C. (1974) *The Political Impact of Mass Media*, London.
Tuchman, G. (1978) *Making News*, New York.

See also: mass media; media effects; public sphere.

media effects

The rise of mass media (press, film, radio, television, etc.) during the twentieth century has been accompanied by continuous claims and debate concerning their effects. The term 'effects' refers to two different things: the potential to inform and influence according to the wishes of mass media senders, and the many, often unintended, consequences for individuals and societies which may have followed the extensive availability and use of mass media. Belief in the power and effects of media in the two senses is founded on certain distinctive features of the new technologies for mass communication, especially their enormous capacity to carry information, sounds, images and ideas of all kinds; the possibility of reaching very large proportions of a national (and now a global) population almost simultaneously or in a very short time; the apparent capacity to overcome old barriers to communication, not only those of time and space, but also those of culture, age and economic differences; and the evidently great attraction of mass media to nearly everyone.

The potential of far-reaching effects of the two kinds mentioned is without question great and real. It is confirmed by everyday experience and simple observation of a world in which distant events are often common knowledge instantly, styles and fashions disseminated by the media are encountered in much the same form across the globe and the routine of daily life is nearly everywhere patterned by the ubiquitous and rather similar television screen, radio and newspaper. Furthermore, an additional witness to the power of media can readily be found in the vast sums which are spent by advertisers and by propagandists of all kinds on mass media.

We can, with some confidence, say that the mass media have, in general, the following main kinds of effects in significant measure. They provide us with much of our information about our near and extended environment; they influence our habits of consumption; they provide models and examples (positive or negative) which guide our development and behaviour; they help us to relax; they help us to participate in and relate more effectively to our social group and environment. At another level, it is also clear that the mass media now facilitate and influence the working of major social institutions, such as those of politics, government, the justice system and business. A longer term and more general effect of mass media is the influence they exert on culture, whether this is taken to mean social habits and practices, symbolic goods produced and consumed, values, language use or cultural identifications (to nation, locality, social group, etc.).

In respect of these different kinds of media effects (individual, institutional or cultural), there is some consensus on the general direction of effects to be expected. In relation to individual information, opinions and behaviour, it is thought that people are influenced according to the dominant emphasis and direction in the media to which they are most exposed. Whatever receives most attention and is portrayed in a positive light by trusted or liked sources is, other things being equal, likely to lead to effects in line with media message content. In respect of institutions, it begins to look as if the media, when taken up for institutional purposes, do serve these ends quite well, but they also have a significant effect on the institutions themselves as they adapt their activities to the potential and the demands of the media. In respect of culture, the main general effects of the media have been said to be in the direction of greater homogeneity of culture nationally and internationally (the phenomenon of cultural 'globalization'); the rise of a new form of media culture which is an outcome of technology, a new class of cultural producers, and a new industrial and commercial system.

This conventional wisdom concerning the effects of the mass media is often invoked as a general truth, largely because it is tried and tested and fits much everyday observation. It is only part of the story, however; it does not explain why there is so much dispute, debate and continued searching for harder evidence to back the general hypotheses formulated. The main reasons for uncertainty are as follows. Both intended and unintended effects of mass media can be perceived as either good or bad, and there are often vested interests in claiming or denying one or the other; mass media can rarely be separated out and measured as a single single causal factor, except in the most simple laboratory conditions; effects are far from one directional and are rarely predictable except in the most general terms; there are many and varied individual, social and cultural barriers to media effects; the mass media are also continually changing, as new technologies change the potental and as the societal context changes (societies do not stand still).

In respect of individuals, the main dispute has centred on the potential for mass media to encourage the imitation or learning (especially by young people) of aggressive, antisocial or undesirable values and behaviour. This charge by critics of the media has been answered by controls on content, inconclusive research and by claims that the mass media teach many more pro-social than antisocial messages. In general, they do seem to be on the side of the established order (a point of criticism by another group of critics). Advertising and political communication are the institutional forms which have received most scrutiny, and both have been criticized on the mutually inconsistent grounds that they are not really effective and are both inclined to mislead, trivialize and manipulate. The potential for mass communication to integrate society and homogenize culture has to be weighed against the view that mass media can have isolating and atomizing effects on social life, through encouraging privatization and individual consumerism. The media may offer a new global media culture to all, but they also undermine and weaken traditional and particular cultures. In most of these disputes, the standards of evidence required to settle questions of media effects cannot be attained by social research, even if the parties in dispute would be ready to listen.

In any case, it is clear (although only fragmentarily demonstrable) that mass media do normally have inconsistent and even contradicatory effects, which depend on the circumstances of context and place. At the root of this observation is the crucial fact (which has often been demonstrated) that effects are produced by people themselves, individually and in institutions, in interaction with media but not by the media directly. This applies, whether the effects are considered as information, behaviour, opinions or expressions of value. A one-sided media-centric view of social and cultural change has tended for too long to dominate discussion of media effects, although it has been clearly rejected by current theory and research. The expression media effects is itself misleading, although it will have to continue to serve as a signpost for a much more complex phenomenon which is rather older and will endure longer than the media.

Denis McQuail
University of Amsterdam

Further reading

Comstock, G., Chaffee, S., Katzman, N., McCombs, M. and Roberts, D. (1978) *Television and Human Behavior*, New York.

Curran, J. and Gurevitch, M. (eds) (1991) *Mass Media and Society*, London.

Gitlin, T. (1980) *The Whole World is Watching*, Berkeley, CA.

Hovland, C. I., Lumsdaine, A. A. and Sheffield, F. D. (1949) *Experiments in Mass Communication*, Princeton, NJ.

Lazarfeld, P. F., Berelson, B. and Gaudet, F. (1944) *The People's Choice*, New York.

McQuail, D. (1994) *Mass Communication Theory*, 3rd edn, London.

McQuail, D. and Windahl, S. (1993) *Communication Models*, 2nd edn, London.

See also: McLuhan, Marshall; mass media; media and politics; pornography; violence.

medical anthropology

Despite, or perhaps because, medical anthropology has already become the single most popular and populous subdiscipline of anthropology in the USA and is rapidly growing in importance elsewhere, it remains difficult to define its subject matter. There is no widely accepted definitive text on the field as a whole although the now dated Foster and Anderson (1978) has been influential in international public health; McElroy and Townsend (1985) describes ecological approaches, and Helman (1994) is useful for clinicians seeking pragmatic understanding of their own and their patients' culture; in addition, Johnson and Sargent (1990) provides a series of nineteen articles which cover theoretical perspectives, the description of diverse medical systems, the health of populations, methods, policy and advocacy.

Interest in the reactions of people in other societies and cultures to the occurrence of disorders centred on the body has marked anthropology from its inception until the present day. Physicians among the earliest anthropologists, W. H. R. Rivers for example, were interested in the native response to disease. They assumed the latter to be a natural occurrence, existing independently of specific cultural beliefs. Thus when Victor Turner (1964) was commissioned by the Rhodes-Livingstone Museum to study Lunda medicines, both he and his sponsors assumed that, while healing practice would be culturally variable, the diseases to which it was a response would be fixed. Turner himself was apologetic that his lack of medical knowledge would hinder his recognition of which diseases were being treated, and Janzen (1978) later enlisted the physician Arkinstall to save embarrassment in the same area. Frake's (1961) earlier work influenced another physician Fabrega in collaboration with Silver to recognize that the perception of disease entities and the measures taken against them might be seen as part of the same system of more or less consistent thought (Fabrega and Silver 1973). It could therefore be analysed and described as an ethnomedicine in its own right rather than seen as an inadequate, perhaps magico-religious, stage on the way to true definitive, scientific understanding. While Frake (1961) and his successors were able to perceive system in relatively unchallenged and unitary, pristine if complex form, scholars like Leslie (1978) in India and Kleinman (1978) in China were faced with complicated situations in which vast numbers of people seemed able to live with, and within, apparently incompatible systems of belief about bodily ills and how to heal them. This seemed to be achieved without apparent feelings of cognitive discomfort. 'Medical pluralism', as it came to be known, was similarly observed in Africa, where, despite political ambivalence (Comaroff 1981; McCullough 1983), western medicine was partially embraced while longer-existing, but seemingly inconsistent, views were developed instead of being abandoned.

The persistence of such pluralism, however, did cause discomfort to anthropologists about the adequacy of their own theories. In the English-speaking world a series of conferences in the early 1970s, also participated in by African, Antipodean, Asian and European scholars (see Leslie 1978; Loudon 1976) initiated a theoretical rethinking which is still vigorously in progress and which increasingly draws, in addition to anthropology, on contributions from, among others, philosophy, sociology, literary criticism, history and social studies of science and technology (see, e.g. Good 1994; Lindenbaum and Lock 1993). This has involved, sometimes in uneasy partnership even within the same person, both medically qualified and lay scholars recognizing the validity of different interpretations, of the same set of perceived deviations from a norm of physical health and well-being. Kleinman (1978) called these diverse perceptions *explanatory models*. He identified those who held them, within a culture, as variously using (relatively unsystematized) popular, folk and professional discourses to arrive at models which might be broadly centred either on views of the nature of physical bodily experience (*disease*) and/or on subjective experience of suffering (*illness*).

Others, influenced by ethnography and current ideas in medical sociology, emphasized, in addition to disease and illness, a separate category of *sickness* (Young 1982). This last was defined either as social causation (in the continuing tradition of eighteenth-century public health) or as cultural performance – building on Turner's (1982) later work – or as a combination of the two. First, it was intended to enable escape from the danger, fallen into by incautious, medically committed but anthropologically unsophisticated, readings, which represented illness and disease as merely a contrast in perceptions between an objective, true and realist medical analysis and a subjective, false and imaginary patient view; knowledge was contrasted with mere belief. Second, it allowed for the possibility even, and perhaps especially, in industrial society that the parameters of sickness might be seen as including not only technological, social and politico-economic factors before the event but also, after the event, ritual and instrumental elements of culturally legitimate healing processes. These might be as diverse as exorcism of spirits and hospitalization or the wearing of amulets and the incorporation of heart pacemakers or hip prostheses.

By the mid-1980s, two trends seemed to be dominating understanding of bodily disorder in its social and cultural context. The first, associated with the developing radical critique (mainly outside anthropology) of the political economy and social organization of biological medicine (termed 'biomedicine') which was in all societies centred round the concept of sickness. The second, originally suggested by Hahn (1983), focused not so much on illness as such, as on the cultural process by which it was given meaning by sufferers and their helpers. Here the crucial concept was suffering from whatever physical or other cause it had arisen.

While these intellectual debates were in train in the USA, much useful ethnography was being carried out and published (for two excellent monographs illustrating the trends here described see Farmer 1992; Scheper Hughes 1993) and professionalization was in process. A Society for Medical Anthropology had been formed within the American Anthropological Association and flourished to the extent of producing a newsletter and then transforming it into a fully fledged journal. The first article in this *Medical Anthropology Quarterly* was by Scheper Hughes and Lock (1987) and pointed out not that the emperor had no clothes but all too many. So much focus had been placed either phenomenologically, on how disorder was suffered, or critically, on how it was created, that the body which endured the ills had all but disappeared from view. They sought to remedy this by drawing from theories of Mauss, Mary Douglas and other symbolic anthropologists about the body social; from history and sociology about the body politic and social control; and above all, by drawing from non-western philosophy, western phenomenological writings, non-biomedical and minority biomedical views and feminist thought, in order to formulate a counter-theory to the dualistic thinking about the body and its ills which has dominated western culture at least since Descartes. Their article, and the discussions of which it formed the centre, served to reflect and to crystallize a much more widespread tendency to see sickness in terms of personal agency and lived cultural experience: the description of biological disease had been transcended, if not replaced, by the situated praxis of the embodied person in misfortune. In their theory and in their practice, medical anthropologists had come to argue that their concern with the multiple aspects of failure in the lived body had led them back from a biomedically dominated applied empiricism at the periphery of social and cultural anthropology to the centre of a more general anthropological discipline. Misfortune is seen as causing persons to question their cultural ability to produce and reproduce their social being and personal identity – a threat to ontological security. Its analysis helps to make possible for all, including those charged with the care and cure of the sick, self-understanding of the most profound aspects of shared human consciousness.

Ronald Frankenberg
Brunel University

References

Comaroff, J. (1981) 'Healing and cultural transformation: the Tswana of Southern Africa', *Social Science and Medicine* 15B(3).

Fabrega, H. and Silver, D. (1973) *Illness and Shamanistic Healing in Zinacantan: An Ethnomedical Analysis*, Stanford, CA.

Farmer, P. (1992) *AIDS and Accusation: Haiti and the Geography of Blame*, Berkeley, CA.

Foster, G. M. and Anderson, B. G. (1978) *Medical Anthropology*, New York.

Frake, C. O. (1961) 'The diagnosis of disease among the Subanum of Mindanao', *American Anthropologist* 63.

Good, B. J. (1994) *Medicine, Rationality and Experience: An Anthropological Perspective*, Cambridge, UK.

Hahn, R. (1983) 'Rethinking "illness and disease"', *Contributions to Asian Studies* 18.

Helman, C. G. (1994) *Culture, Health and Illness*, 3rd edn, London.

Janzen, J. M. (1978) *The Quest for Therapy in Lower Zaïre*, Berkeley, CA.

Johnson, T. M. and Sargent, C. F. (eds) (1990) *Medical Anthropology: Contemporary Theory and Method*, New York.

Kleinman, A. (1978) 'Concepts and a model for the comparison of medical systems as cultural systems' (see also commentary by Alan Thomas), in C. Leslie (ed.) (1978) *Theoretical Foundations for the Comparative Study of Medical Systems, Social Science and Medicine* (special issue) 12B.

Lindenbaum, S. and Lock, M. (eds) (1993) *Knowledge, Power and Practice: The Anthropology of Medicine and Everyday Life*, Berkeley, CA.

Loudon, J. (ed.) (1976) *Social Anthropology and Medicine*, London.

McCullough, J. (1983) *Black Soul, White Artifact: Fanon's Clinical Psychology and Social Theory*, Cambridge, UK.

McElroy, A. and Townsend, P. K. (1985) *Medical Anthropology in Ecological Perspective*, New York.

Scheper Hughes, N. (1993) *Death without Weeping: The Violence of Everyday Life in Brazil*, Berkeley, CA.

Scheper Hughes, N. and Lock, M. (1987) 'The mindful body: a prolegomenon to future work in medical anthropology', *Medical Anthropology Quarterly* vol 1.

Turner, V. (1964) *Lunda Medicine and the Treatment of Disease*, Rhodes-Livingstone Museum Occasional Paper no. 15, Livingstone, Northern Rhodesia.

—— (1982) *From Ritual to Theatre: The Human Seriousness of Play*, New York.

Young, A. (1982) 'Anthropologies of illness and sickness', *Annual Review of Anthropology* 11.

See also: body; cultural anthropology; disability; epidemiology; history of medicine; medical sociology; social anthropology.

medical sociology

Medical sociology is that branch of sociology concerned with the broad preserve of medicine in modern society. The subject has expanded so rapidly since the 1950s that it is now one of the largest (if not the largest) specialized areas of sociology. This growth is undoubtedly partly due to the realization that many of the problems contained within modern health care are essentially social in nature; however, it also reflects the growing interest of medicine itself in the social aspects of illness, particularly in relation to psychiatry, paediatrics, general practice (or family medicine), geriatrics and community medicine. Thus, while medical sociology has had general sociology as an intellectual parent, it has under the patronage of medicine enjoyed funding, appointments, an extended teaching role and ease of access for research which has arguably underpinned much of the expansion of the subject. But it has probably had to pay a price for this alliance (and reliance) on medicine in terms of a distortion of emphasis in the problems, methods and theories judged appropriate for the discipline.

Medical sociology as a distinct area of study is first recognizable in the 1950s and, if journals might be used as disciplinary markers, the founding of *Journal of Health and Human Behaviour* (later amended to *Journal of Health and Social Behaviour*) in 1960 represents the subject's first claim to autonomy. In these early years, despite the ascendancy of structural-functionalism, it seemed to be medical, psychological and, at best, psychosocial perspectives which predominated. The new post-war interest in social epidemiology, for example, which sought to identify the role of social factors in the causation of disease, was pursued by both interested physicians and sociologists. Early studies showed the influence of social structure, in particular of social class, in the aetiology of both psychiatric and organic disease, though identification of the relevant specific components of social structure proved more difficult.

The failure to establish the intervening variables between social structure and disease led many sociologists to explore aetiology at the more microlevel of stress. Although more the province of the psychologist, stress was seen to offer the possibility of bridging the gap between the social and the biological especially when refined to encompass life events and notions of loss. In early studies, research tended to concentrate on those illnesses, such as psychiatric disturbances, which seemingly lacked biological correlates and hence the possibility of a wholly biological aetiology. However, the net has widened considerably to embrace organic diseases with supposed biological causes, as it is recognized that this does not preclude an often important role for social factors in either establishing susceptibility or in actually triggering the onset.

The interest in social factors in illness, together with the contemporary findings (through morbidity surveys) by both sociologists and physicians of a symptom iceberg in the community, led to another important area in the early development of medical sociology, namely illness behaviour. Given that symptoms were so prevalent in the community, the traditional medical model which viewed symptoms as a simple stimulus to seek help seemed inappropriate. Why people consulted the doctor was therefore more complex; successive studies set out to explore the particular patterns of behaviour and reactions to stress and illness which affected the decision to seek medical help.

If social epidemiology and illness behaviour were subjects which emerged directly at the interface between medical sociology and medicine, other areas such as 'labelling', the sociology of the hospital and professions were obviously more closely drawn from general sociology. Thus 'labelling theory' and 'stigma', while developed within general sociology, were applied at an early stage to particular diagnostic groups such as physically handicapped and mentally ill people; likewise students of institutions, bureaucracies and organizations found, in the hospital, an ideal model through which to test and illustrate their arguments; in similar fashion the medical profession provided an archetypal occupational organization for those sociologists intent on exploring the role of professions in the occupational division of labour.

In time many of these various areas of general sociology became the specific province of medical sociology, though again, because of the early close alliance with medicine, these issues tended to be explored in a medico-centric way. Thus the medical profession with its supposed esoteric knowledge and altruistic service was seen as an ideal for the aspiring paramedical occupations; hospital structure was examined in terms of improving efficiency, and labelling in terms of treatment regimes and rehabilitation. If there is one contemporary slogan which sums up the early years, it is the classic difference between sociology *in* medicine and sociology *of* medicine, though arguably the latter was by far the weaker partner. Even so, by 1967 the field of medical sociology was sufficiently well expanded for the appearance of another journal, *Social Science and Medicine*, which in its title steered a neutral course between the conflicting claims of the two medical sociologies.

If it were possible to identify a year or a particular text as marking a watershed in medical sociology, there might well be agreement that the publication of Freidson's *Profession of Medicine* in 1970 was a significant event. It offered a synthesis of earlier studies on professions, labelling, medical organization, patient perceptions and so on, and it was to be marked out as a key text in establishing the formal identity of medical sociology; yet, as its subtitle – 'a study of the sociology of applied knowledge' – implied, it was the form of the analysis which underpinned that synthesis which pointed to a new direction. At root, both illness *and* disease were social constructs, reflections of social organization, professional interests, power relations and so on. Freidson's achievement was to liberate medical sociology from the confines of medically defined categories, whether it was in the profession's beneficent view of itself or in the supposed biological and objective nature of illness, and in so doing opened up patient experience and medical knowledge to more penetrating and systematic analysis.

During the 1970s and 1980s, health care delivery and health policy were subjected to a more critical theoretical approach, particularly from those sociologists of a Marxist persuasion who argued the case for fully resourced and equitable state provision. At a time when the idea of a right-wing intellectual seemed a contradiction in terms, this appeared to be a relatively uncontested position to take. However, the triumph of the market (on both sides of the Atlantic) as a means of distributing health care in the 1990s has placed the sociologist of health care in unfamiliar territory. The state still (and increasingly so in the USA) underwrites the resources, but 'controlled markets' are meant to provide the necessary consumer choice and competition. Yet, despite the rhetoric on what policy is or should be, sociologists are already discovering from more local and grounded studies that 'health policy-in-action' is a more negotiated and precarious process than official accounts might lead one to suppose.

Interest in the detail of social life has also found expression in patients' experience of illness. Patients' views of illness, which had been studied only as an adjunct of illness behaviour, have begun to be investigated in their own right. Medical theories of illness may claim coherence and validity, but it seems that patients' explanatory frameworks are equally sophisticated. Borrowing from medical anthropology, sociologists view patients as needing to know the answer to the questions 'Why me?', 'Why now?' and 'Why this (illness)?' The method of enquiry has further supported the development of qualitative methodologies.

The corollary of the acceptance that patients' theories of illness are as meaningful as medical ones is a recognition that medical knowledge itself can be the object of critical sociological enquiry. The fact that it is only since the end of the eighteenth century that medicine has reduced illness to an intra-corporal pathological lesion shows how medical knowledge is both culturally and historically located. This means, for example, that medical knowledge may be explored not as a form of superior scientific truth, but as a means available to controlled, alienated or depoliticized people in the conduct of their lives. Equally, it can be argued, through it core assumptions of corporal integrity, medical knowledge and practice play a crucial role in fabricating the analysable and calculable body in modern society.

Despite these many critical leanings, medical sociology has not become emancipated from medicine: there are too many ties and alliances for that. Many medical sociologists are employed by medical institutions or on medically defined tasks; indeed, many of them are directly concerned to ameliorate patient suffering, not least through the rapidly expanding field of health services research. Yet a more critical sociology has succeeded in widening the agenda such that the title of a new journal, *Sociology of Health and Illness*, first published in 1979, perhaps reflects more accurately the interests of this branch of sociology than the term 'medical sociology'.

David Armstrong
University of London

Reference

Freidson, E. (1970) *Profession of Medicine: A Study of the Sociology of Applied Knowledge*, New York.

Further reading

Aaron H. J. and Schwartz, W. B. (1984) *The Painful Prescription: Rationing Hospital Care*, Washington, DC.

Brown, G. W. and Harris, T. (1978) *Social Origins of Depression: A Study of Psychiatric Disorder in Women*, London.

Fitzpatrick, R. *et al.* (1984) *The Experience of Illness*, London.

Foucault, M. (1963) *The Birth of the Clinic: An Archaeology of Medical Perception*, London.

Freidson, E. (1970) *Profession of Medicine*, New York.

Goffman E. (1961) *Asylums: Essays on the Social Situation of Mental Patients and Other Inmates*, Harmondsworth.

Kleinman, A., Eisenberg, J. and Good B. (1978) 'Culture, illness and cure', *Annals of Internal Medicine* 88.

Starr, P. (1982) *The Social Transformation of American Medicine*, New York.

See also: disability; epidemiology; health economics; history of medicine; labelling; medical anthropology; morbidity; professions; public health.

medicine, history of *see* history of medicine

memory

The study of human memory investigates the reception and encoding of information and the later influence of retained information upon behaviour, either in the processes of remembering and recognizing, or in other more indirect ways. A useful distinction, generally accepted in the area and originally made more than 100 years ago by William James (1890), is that between *primary* and *secondary* memory. Primary memory refers to short-term retention whereas secondary memory refers to long-term retention. Both these broad domains of human memory have been extensively investigated since James's original proposal; they can be divided into a number of discrete types of memory, some of which are associated with distinct brain areas and others of which are distinguished by different types of knowledge and memory processes. Two major advances in the last 20 years have been the application of this understanding of human memory to neuropsychological disorders and to consciousness and memory.

The concept of primary memory encompasses the very brief retention of literal aspects of an event as well as the somewhat more durable retention of information in *working memory*. Temporary fast-decaying and easily overwritten sensory memory stores such as *iconic* and *echoic* memory retain perceptual and auditory information, respectively, in a literal manner for periods measured in fractions of a second. These sensory memory stores facilitate, for example, the smooth perception of films and unbroken perception of sequences of utterances and music. However, the human brain rapidly extracts information from sensory memory stores and recodes it into appropriate forms for retention in working memory, where it can be retained for a period of a few minutes, or longer if it is frequently rehearsed. For example, speech-based auditory information is recoded into phonological form for immediate output (as in repetition) or for further processing in terms of meaning. A structure called the *phonological loop* is thought to mediate this recoding; this structure has been identified as critical in the acquisition of language and vocabulary by children. Patients who have suffered damage to the phonological loop through brain injury, that is, in strokes, viral diseases, and through head injury, although still capable of producing speech, can no longer process novel speech input. For example, they cannot learn new languages.

In contrast the concept of secondary memory refers to long-term storage over periods of hours, months, years, decades and even a lifetime. Long-term memory is the terminus of information flow through the memory system and consists of a massively complex and extensive system of durable retention. Three classes of knowledge are often distinguished in long-term memory. First, *procedural memory* refers to knowledge that cannot be brought into consciousness but which underlies and supports the retention and execution of skilled and practised behaviour. For example, many people can whistle, ride a bicycle, or sign their name, but no one can introspect upon this; these skills are known only by being performed. In the later stages of degenerative brain diseases such as Alzheimer's disease, striking impairments of procedural memory are often evident. Second, *semantic memory* refers to facts and knowledge about the world. This knowledge can be consciously retrieved and stated. People know *a tiger is a cat, a robin is a bird*, or *London is the capital of England*, and can answer many additional questions about such facts. Interestingly, in some cases of brain injury the ability to make such judgements can be selectively lost. For instance, some brain-injured patients lose the ability to make correct semantic judgements about living things while retaining an ability to make comparatively normal judgements about artefacts. For other patients this pattern is reversed. Taken together, these sorts of findings suggest that the representation of semantic knowledge in the brain may be highly structured. Third, *episodic* or *autobiographical memory* refers to memory for experienced episodes and events. In amnesia this type of memory may become impaired so that although patients' ability to recall memories from the period before their injury or illness remains intact, their ability to create or encode new memories is totally lost. Such patients have intact short-term working memories and so can perform some everyday tasks and hold short conversations, but as they are unable to create new memories they remain unaware of tasks that have been completed and conversations that have been conducted, even when these occurred only a few minutes previously.

Perhaps the most intriguing and certainly the most hopeful finding is that amnesic patients who cannot create new autobiographical memories can none the less acquire new information. For instance, amnesic patients shown a list of words and some minutes or hours later asked to recall the list not only may fail to recall any words but may even fail to recall that they were shown any words. However, if instead of recall the patient is asked to make some response that does not entail explicit remembering then strong evidence of the retention of the original word list can be demonstrated. So powerful is this implicit learning or memory that amnesic patients have, for example, been taught to operate computers (when this was something they did not do prior to their injury), and, with appropriate social and memorial supports, some amnesic people have been able to return to work. The reality of implicitly remembering has now been extensively investigated in non-brain-damaged individuals where it is sometimes referred to as *fluency*. This captures the nature of implicitly remembering as, typically, some current task is speeded and made more fluent when it features items processed in an earlier episode, even though these are not consciously recalled at the time. Consider how quickly and fluently you can now read the word 'neuropsychological'.

Current understanding of human memory based on theories developed in the psychological laboratory is now providing important insights into memory dysfunctions following brain injury and age-related memory changes. The current research initiative into conscious and non-conscious aspects of memory promises to expand this understanding in important directions.

Martin A. Conway
University of Bristol

Further reading

Baddeley, A. D. (1990) *Human Memory: Theory and Practice*, Hove.

Collins, A. F., Gathercole, S. E., Conway, M. A. and Morris, P. E. (eds) (1993) *Theories of Memory*, Hove.

James, W. (1890) *Principles of Psychology*, Vol. 1, New York.

Parkin, A. J. (1993) *Memory: Phenomena, Experiment, and Theory*, Oxford.

See also: ageing; cognitive psychology; mental imagery; thinking.

Menger School *see* Austrian School

mental disorders

Descriptions of psychological behaviour and intellectual disturbances have existed in the literature of western civilizations since ancient times. Disturbances associated with the ageing process were among the first to be recorded. There are also descriptions of alcoholic deterioration, as well as phenomena which are now called delirium, affective disorder or psychoses. Depending upon the *Zeitgeist*, however, the phenomena were interpreted in many ways. Galen's Doctrine of the Four Humours was invoked as an explanation of psychological and behavioural disturbances well into the seventeeth century, while theories of the occult strongly influenced views of mental disturbances throughout the eighteenth century and into the early nineteenth century.

The origin of modern scientific psychiatry can be traced to the Enlightenment. During this era, the notion of mental disturbances as illnesses began to take hold with some intellectual force. By creating a climate which encouraged people to look upon the mental illnesses as natural phenomena, the rationalism of the age made the phenomena more accessible to systematic enquiry through observation, experimentation and classification. As with any scientific endeavours to study the human condition, efforts to delineate the mental disorders were influenced by, first, the dominant intellectual assumptions and attitudes which determine what data will receive attention and how the data will be ordered; second, the technologies and methodologies available for gathering the data, and, third, the setting or social context delimiting the universe of phenomena accessible to study.

Organic versus functional mental disorders

In the early nineteenth century, the care of mentally disturbed people gradually became the responsibility of the medical rather than the law enforcement or religious arms of society. Asylums and mental hospitals became the primary sites for the conduct of scientific enquiry. As a result, the phenomena under study represented the most severe examples of behavioural or psychological disturbances. A materialistic philosophical orientation dominated medical thinking. Research in the fields of physiology, bacteriology and pathology was quite productive in delineating the pathophysiology and aetiology of physical illnesses. The philosophical perspective and technological advances tended to promote a view of mental disorder as the expression of physical disease or biological disease processes.

The notion of biological causality was, and remains, a major orienting principle in efforts to understand the nature of mental illness. Then, as now, the existing technology was not adequate to the task of defining an invariable relationship between the behavioural and psychological phenomena under study and either anatomical lesions or pathophysiological processes. A useful convention was adopted, however, by segregating 'organic' from 'functional' mental disorders. This dichotomy is based upon an aetiological distinction: the presence or absence of a biological abnormality or dysfunction that fully accounts for the condition.

Psychotic versus non-psychotic functional disorders

Since an aetiological distinction based on biological causality could not be used as the basis for differentiating the functional mental disorders, a phenomenological approach was used. Essentially qualitative, the approach involved the careful observation of a clinical picture on a case-by-case basis. From the observations, relatively unique configurations of symptoms and symptom clusters were identified that suggested natural groupings of phenomena. In this manner, conditions where the dominant feature was a profound disturbance of mood were segregated from those where the dominant feature was a disturbance in the process and content of thought. This distinction between 'disorders of mood' and 'disorders of thought' received further corroboration when longitudinal data indicated that the course of the disorders also differed. Disorders of mood were more likely to remit, while those of thought were associated with progressive deterioration. For many years, these characteristics formed the primary basis for a distinction between what are now called schizophrenic and manic depressive disorders.

Regardless of the characteristics differentiating the disorders of thought and mood, individuals with both disorders shared three characteristics: behaviour that grossly violated social norms; the incorrect valuation of the accuracy of thoughts or perceptions; and the marked tendency to draw false inferences about external reality even in the face of incontrovertible evidence to the contrary. These latter two features constitute what is referred to as 'impaired reality testing'. This impaired reality testing, together with bizarre, disorganized behaviour well beyond the pale of social acceptability, became the cardinal features for designating functional disorders as psychotic rather than non-psychotic. The utility of this dichotomy as the basis for classification is a major source of debate within psychiatry; nevertheless, it is a useful convention for differentiating the most severe mental disorders – schizophrenic disorders, major affective disorders, and paranoid disorders – from the other non-organic psychological and behavioural phenomena that constitute the functional mental disorders.

Neurotic, personality and stress-related disorders

The further elaboration of conditions constituting the functional mental disorders was stimulated by two occurrences of particular importance in the field of psychiatry: the shift of the centre of academic enquiry from the asylum to the university psychiatric clinic, and the emergence of psychoanalysis. The former made an increasingly broad range of phenomena acceptable and accessible to study; the latter brought a conceptual framework and methodology for studying the psychogenic origins of disordered behaviour. In addition, the growing interaction among the clinical, behavioural, social and biological sciences that began at the end of the nineteenth century, and has carried through to the present, generated a number of useful paradigms. While facilitating an examination of the psychological and social origins of mental disorders, these paradigms contributed to the demarcation of three major clusters of non-psychotic functional mental disorders: neurotic, personality, and stress-related disorders.

Neurotic disorders

Just as the invention of the microscope expanded the scope of biology, so the techniques of medical hypnosis and free association opened new avenues for exploring mental functioning and rendered the unconscious accessible to scientific enquiry. An important corollary of these methodological advances was the identification of psychological process. This process is characterized by the existence of conflict within an individual, perceived as a potential threat or danger, which calls into play response patterns called defence mechanisms. These three events occur outside of the individual's conscious awareness. When the events lead to the formation of symptoms or symptom complexes that are distressing, recognized as unacceptable, and experienced as unhealthy or foreign, the outcome is a neurotic disorder.

Not everyone accepts the scientific validity of evidence derived through applying the psychoanalytic method. Some question the aetiologic paradigm described above and have offered other models, frequently based on learning theory, to explain the neuroses. Even so, few dispute the importance of psychological mechanisms in the genesis of these disorders. Further, evidence from clinical and epidemiologic literature indicates that neurotic disorders can be found in very different cultures, findings which support the view of the phenomena as a discrete class of mental disorders.

Neurotic disorders are identified primarily in terms of their mode of symptomatic or behavioural expression (for example, anxiety disorder, hypochondriasis, or dissociative state). While some of the behaviours at times appear bizarre, as in the case of obsessive, compulsive or phobic disorders, they do not grossly violate social norms. This circumstance, together with the absence of impaired reality testing, provides a basis for distinguishing neurotic from psychotic functional mental disorders.

Personality disorders

Originally, personality disorders were identified on the basis of overt behaviour that was associated with, or could lead to, frank violations of the formal rules and conventions established within a society to maintain social order. Criminal, sexually perverse and addictive behaviours fell most easily under this rubric, particularly in those instances where the individual manifesting the behaviours was not psychotic or neurotic, and did not suffer significant subjective distress.

The delineation of personality disorders solely on the basis of rule-breaking behaviour seemed well off the mark as more came to be understood about the social, cultural and psychological processes shaping personality development. Personality came to be viewed as a product of social interaction and individual experiences in a cultural environment. This notion led to a definition of personality as deeply ingrained patterns of behaviour that determine how individuals relate to, perceive, and think about themselves and the environment. Personality disorder was defined as the existence of persistent, inflexible and maladaptive patterns of behaviour that consistently and predictably were in violation of the rights of others; denigrating to oneself or others; destructive to interpersonal and social relationships or vocational performance; or undermining of the ability to meet day-to-day obligations or achieve life goals. Although conditions characterized primarily by socially deviant behaviour (such as perversions or antisocial personality disorder) are still considered personality disorders, so too are conditions where interpersonal relationships are significantly compromised (such as schizoid or explosive personality disorders), or where personality absorption is the dominant feature (such as aesthenic or inadequate personality disorders).

Stress-related disorders

The interest in the relationship between stress and mental illness, an outgrowth of the experience of military psychiatry in the First World War, has been sustained throughout the twentieth century. In the social sciences, research has focused on natural disasters; in the epidemiologic and clinical sciences, on life events and mental disorder; in the behavioural sciences, the emphasis is on coping and adaptation; and in the biological sciences, on homeostasis. A firmer understanding has developed about psychological vulnerability occurring during transitional states as well as normal developmental phases. In turn, the general systems theory has facilitated an examination of psychological factors as stressors that generate pathophysiological responses.

A related group of clinical phenomena was identified, not on the basis of their symptomatic manifestations (which are legion in their variations) but on the basis of the precipitants. These stress-related disorders include acute catastrophic stress reactions with clear environmental precipitants, such as war or natural disaster; post-traumatic stress disorders characterized by a re-experiencing of the trauma, reduced involvement with the external world, and a variety of autonomic, dysphoric or cognitive symptoms; adjustment disorders precipitated by an array of life events, family factors, developmental crises and the like, which act as psychosocial stressors; psychophysiological malfunctions of psychogenic origin which occur in the absence of tissue damage or a demonstrable disease process (for example, hyperventilation, neurocirculatory aesthenia or dysmenorrhoea); and psychic factors associated with physical disease – a category which conveys the notion that psychologically meaningful environmental stimuli can initiate or exacerbate certain physical disorders such as asthma, rheumatoid arthritis or ulcerative colitis.

Conclusion

By any criteria, since the 1830s there have been enormous strides in the delineation of mental disorders. With the exception of organic mental disorders, however, a knowledge of aetiology remains quite primitive. Behavioural, social and neuroscientists are searching for aetiologic factors. To the extent that the demonstration of aetiology allows us to make sharper distinctions among mental disorders than does a strictly descriptive approach, these efforts, if successful, would undoubtedly lead to further modification of our definitions of mental disorders.

Gary L. Tischler
Yale University

Further reading

Alexander, E. S. and Selasnick, S. T. (1966) *The History of Psychiatry*, New York.

American Psychiatric Association (1980) *DSM-III: Diagnostic and Statistical Manual of Mental Disorders*, 3rd edn, Washington, DC.

Brenner, C. (1973) *An Elementary Textbook of Psychoanalysis*, New York.

Gunderson, E. K. E. and Rahe, R. H. (1974) *Life Stress and Illness*, Springfield, IL.

Kraepelin, E. (1909) *Psychiatrie*, 8th edn, Leipzig.

Levy, R. (1982) *The New Language of Psychiatry*, Boston, MA.

Nichols, A. M. (1978) *The Harvard Guide to Modern Psychiatry*, Cambridge, MA.

Paykel, E. S. (1982) *Handbook of Affective Disorders*, New York.

Wang, J., Cooper, J. and Sartorius, N. (1974) *The Measurement and Classification of Psychiatric Symptoms*, Cambridge, MA.

Woodruff, R. A., Goodwin, D. W. and Guze, S. B. (1974) *Psychiatric Diagnosis*, New York.

See also: behaviour therapy; clinical psychology; cognitive-behavioural therapy; depressive disorders; DSM-IV; genetic aspects of mental illness; mental health; neuroses; psychiatry; psychopathic personality; psychoses.

mental health

The concepts of mental health and illness have come to play a central role in the way that western societies understand and regulate themselves. In the process, they have undergone a series of transformations. The view of mental disorders as 'illness' or 'disease' gained currency during the rise of the psychiatric profession in the mid-nineteenth century. It did not imply that all such disorders had a physical cause, for psychiatry recognized 'functional' as well as 'organic' types of mental illness. (In the early nineteenth century, indeed, asylum doctors often interpreted mental illness in terms of a breakdown of reason or morality, and the favoured way of dealing with it was called 'moral treatment'.) Nevertheless, the concepts of mental illness and health resembled their physical counterparts in one respect: they constituted a clear dichotomy.

From the beginning of the twentieth century the organization of mental health care – and with it the concept of mental health itself – changed drastically. New forms of treatment, such as psychoanalysis, were developed to replace incarceration, with the aim of intervening before disturbances became totally disabling. New professions (e.g. psychotherapy, social work and clinical psychology) came into being. Inspired by the dramatic results which hygienic measures had achieved in the fight against disease, the Mental Hygiene Movement in the USA set out to find the psychic equivalents of clean drinking water and good drainage. In the wake of these developments, mental health and illness lost their 'all-or-nothing' character and came to be regarded simply as two poles of a continuum, with an infinite number of gradations in between.

During the twentieth century three further developments have taken place. First, the range of conditions which can potentially be classified as mental illness has expanded dramatically to include almost every kind of failure to cope or deviation from normality: from drug abuse to broken marriages, from eating disorders to religious fundamentalism. Second, mental health professionals (like their counterparts in physical medicine) have devoted more attention to the healthy end of the continuum, i.e. to the 'normal' population and the way it lives. Third, all traces of moral content have gradually been expunged from the concepts of illness and health; in keeping with the positivist ideals of most psychiatrists and psychologists, the aim has been to provide a non-judgemental, scientifically objective account of human problems.

With these three changes, the concept of mental health has acquired crucial importance in the way that human problems are formulated and dealt with, and the associated professions have expanded greatly in power and numbers. Kittrie (1971) refers to 'the therapeutic state', Castel *et al.* (1982) to the 'psychiatric society'.

Modern perspectives on mental health

Social scientists have approached mental health in two main ways. Some ally themselves with psychiatry and carry out epidemiological research on the connection between mental illness and the social environment. Classic studies in this vein are those of Hollingshead and Redlich (1958), who found an increased incidence of mental illness in lower social classes, and Brown and Harris (1978), who identified predisposing and precipitating factors in women's depression.

Others, however, adopt a more critical stance. Some see the mental health professions as a vast apparatus of social control: these writers, following Szasz (1961), regard mental illness as a myth – a smokescreen for repressive interventions in people's personal lives. This critique came to the fore in the 1960s in the work of Goffman (1961), Scheff (1966) and the 'anti-psychiatrists'. However, the idea that psychiatry simply 'medicalizes' deviance never gained widespread acceptance. Such a notion seems warranted if one thinks of forcibly sedated prisoners, political activists or schoolchildren; but it runs into problems when treatment is actively sought by people anxious to get rid of their symptoms. Indeed, it is precisely when people appear to have no control over their behaviour and when it fails to make sense that the concept of mental illness is invoked (Ingleby 1982).

In the late 1970s a different critical approach to the mental health professions came to the fore. Foucault (1980) and his followers emphasized that power in the modern state is typically 'productive', not 'repressive': the discourses of psychiatry and psychology actively help people formulate their projects and their problems. They are not ideological *distortions* of reality: they help to *produce* reality itself. The sociologist De Swaan (Brinkgreve *et al.* 1979) coined the term 'proto-professionalization' to describe the way that lay people avidly internalize the viewpoint of professionals. However central the concept of mental health may be to the management of social problems, we cannot regard it as something imposed from above.

This, however, does not imply that there is no room for criticism. First, though modern professionals are more often seen as friendly partners than as police officers, they have considerable power in shaping the way that we make sense of our world. Writers such as Lasch (1977) have questioned whether we are wise to entrust such power to them. Second, the aura of moral neutrality which professionals cultivate is misleading; their views always contain an implicit normative commitment to certain ideals. Feminists, in particular, have shown up the patriarchal assumptions underlying supposedly objective analyses of women's psychological problems. Third, though the medical model may be much more complex and sophisticated than it was in the 1890s, it still takes the individual as its unit of analysis. If problems – such as those of young mothers, elderly people, migrants, homeless or unemployed people – are routinely reduced to personal ones, it is extremely hard to reconstruct them as collective ones. Although critical approaches to mental health have not figured prominently in social science since the 1970s, such a crucial and contentious concept is unlikely to escape attention indefinitely.

David Ingleby
University of Utrecht

References

Brinkgreve, C., Onland, J. and De Swaan, A. (1979) *De opkomst van het Psychotherapeutisch Bedrijf (The Rise of the Psychotherapy Industry)*, Utrecht.

Brown, G. and Harris, T. (1978) *Social Origins of Depression*, London.

Castel, F., Castel, R. and Lovell, A. (1982) *The Psychiatric Society*, New York.

Foucault, M. (1980) 'Truth and power', in M. Foucault, *Power/Knowledge: Selected Interviews and Other Writings 1972–1977*, Hassocks.

Goffman, E. (1961) *Asylums: Essays on the Social Situation of Mental Patients and Other Inmates*, New York.

Hollingshead, A. B. and Redlich, F. C. (1958) *Social Class and Mental Illness*, New York.

Ingleby, D. (1982) 'The social construction of mental illness', in A. Treacher and P. Wright (eds) *The Problem of Medical Knowledge: Examining the Social Construction of Medicine*, Edinburgh.

Kittrie, N. (1971) *The Right to be Different*, Baltimore, MD.

Lasch, C. (1977) *Haven in a Heartless World: The Family Besieged*, New York.

Scheff, T. (1966) *Being Mentally Ill: A Sociological Theory*, London.

Szasz, T. (1961) *The Myth of Mental Illness*, New York.

Further reading

Ingleby, D. (ed.) (1980) *Critical Psychiatry: The Politics of Mental Health*, New York.

See also: clinical psychology; mental disorders; neuroses; psychiatry; psychoses; social problems.

mental illness, genetic aspects of *see* genetic aspects of mental illness

mental imagery

The term mental imagery is used in two ways. It refers to a subjective experience, 'seeing with the mind's eye', 'hearing with the mind's ear', and so on. It is also used to refer to a specific way in which information is represented and processed, which happens to produce such experiences. In this latter sense, a mental image is a perceptual representation that is stored briefly in short-term memory. Most research is concerned with image representations. Imagery can be studied with a variety of techniques, which range from behavioural observations (e.g. the time required to use images in certain ways, or the effects of imagery on accuracy) to neuropsychological assessments (e.g. deficits following brain damage, or brain areas that are activated during imagery). Visual imagery has been the topic of most research.

Purposes of imagery

Imagery has at least seven functions. First, it plays a role in some forms of reasoning and problem solving by allowing one to predict the outcome of a specific action; for example, one can look in a crowded cupboard and see how to rearrange the contents to make space for another box. Second, one can use imagery to reason about abstract concepts by visualizing symbols, such as graphs or Venn diagrams. Third, imagery can help one to comprehend verbal descriptions of specific situations. Fourth, imagery is used when one recalls visual or spatial information that has not been verbally coded; for example, consider how you try to recall what was on your dinner table last night. Fifth, imagery can help one to memorize information; for example, memory for pairs of words increases substantially if one visualizes the named objects as if they were interacting in some way (see, e.g. Bower 1972; Paivio 1971). Sixth, imagery can be used to help one improve skills; by visualizing oneself practising an action, one can calibrate the stored information that directs that action. Finally, when subjects were asked to record their images on an hourly basis, they reported that most imagery occurred in daydreams (Kosslyn *et al.* 1990). However, the subjects reported that even such aimless imagery sometimes reminded them of an important oversight or gave them an idea.

Imagery relies on many of the same neural mechanisms that are used in like-modality perception. Visual images not only interfere with visual perception more than with auditory perception (and vice versa for auditory images), but also can be confused for actual stimuli (Craver-Lemley and Reeves 1987; Finke 1989; Johnson and Raye 1981). Some visual illusions also occur in imagery (e.g. Berbaum and Chung 1981); brain damage that disrupts perception also tends to disrupt imagery in the same way (Farah 1988). However, the two abilities are not identical, as witnessed by the fact that brain damage can sometimes affect them separately (Kosslyn 1994). Brain-scanning techniques have revealed that very similar parts of the brain are activated during visual imagery and visual perception. Indeed, it appears that visual memories are sorted in an abstract form, and at least some images are reconstructed in parts of the brain that are topographically organized; these images actually depict information. Other types of images, however, may not be picture-like in this way. This, though, is an area of controversy (Roland and Gulyas 1994).

Imagery processing

Once images are formed, they can 'stand in' for actual objects in many ways. One can scan over imaged objects, rotate them, 'zoom in' on them, fold them, and so on; in all cases, the more processing (scanning, rotating, zooming, etc.) that is required, the more time is required (Kosslyn 1994; Shepard and Cooper 1982).

Images occur when input is retained briefly or when one activates stored information to generate an image. An image of a single shape apparently is generated by the same mechanisms that prime one to see a specific object during perception, but in imagery this priming is so strong that the pattern is reconstructed. If one needs a detailed image, additional parts are added, one at a time, into the image (see Kosslyn *et al.* 1988). The processes used to add parts are complex, and draw on mechanisms in both cerebral hemispheres. Counter to

the common wisdom, imagery is not a right hemisphere process (for a review, see Kosslyn 1994).

Stephen M. Kosslyn
Harvard University

References

Berbaum, K. and Chung, C. S. (1981) 'Muller-Lyer illusion induced by imagination', *Journal of Mental Imagery* 5.
Bower, G. H. (1972) 'Mental imagery and associative learning', in L. Gregg (ed.) *Cognition in Learning and Memory*, New York.
Craver-Lemley, C. and Reeves, A. (1987) 'Visual imagery selectively reduces vernier acuity', *Perception* 16(5).
Farah, M. H. (1988) 'Is visual imagery really visual? Overlooked evidence from neuropsychology', *Psychological Review* 95.
Finke, R. A. (1989) *Principles of Mental Imagery*, Cambridge, MA.
Johnson, M. K. and Raye, C. L. (1981) 'Reality monitoring' *Psychological Review* 88.
Kosslyn, S. M. (1994) *Image and Brain: The Resolution of the Imagery Debate*, Cambridge, MA.
Kosslyn, S. M., Cave, C. B., Provost, D. and Von Gierke, S. (1988) 'Sequential processes in image generation', *Cognitive Psychology* 20.
Kosslyn, S. M., Segar, C., Pani, J. and Hillger, L. A. (1990) 'When is imagery used? A diary study', *Journal of Mental Imagery* 14.
Paivio, A. (1971) *Imagery and Verbal Processes*, New York.
Roland, P. E. and Gulyas, B. (1994) 'Visual imagery and visual representation', *Trends in Neurosciences* 17 (including commentaries).
Shepard, R. N. and Cooper, L. A. (1982) *Mental Images and their Transformations*, Cambridge, MA.

Further reading

Paivio, A. (1986) *Mental Representations* New York.
Tippett, L. (1992) 'The generation of visual images: a review of neuropsychological research and theory', *Psychological Bulletin* 112.
Tye, M. (1991) *The Imagery Debate*, Cambridge, MA.

See also: memory; sensation and perception.

methods of social research

The term method is widely used in social enquiry. A great range of research writing and teaching is provided in the social sciences under such titles as *Research Methods* (Burgess 1993), *Methods of Social Research* (Stacey 1969), *Sociological Research Methods* (Bulmer 1984), *Survey Methods in Social Investigation* (Moser and Kalton 1971), *A Methodology for Social Research* (Sjoberg and Nett 1968) and *Methods of Social Study* (Webb and Webb 1932). As a consequence, some clarification is required on the different terms that are used to discuss work on research methodology and research methods, given that both these terms are ambiguous and lack clarity. Some of the key terms that are used in discussions of methodology include *general methodology*, which is associated with the principles guiding an empirical enquiry; *research strategy* or *research procedure*, which refer to the way in which a particular study is designed and conducted; *research process*, which denotes the interrelationship between the activities that occur within a project and the principles and procedures that are used; and *research techniques or methods*, referring to specific fact-finding operations that yield social data. These issues are of equal importance in all forms of social research, and need to be considered in relation to each other. Techniques and methods of investigation should not therefore be seen in isolation. They must be linked to the substantive problems that the researcher wishes to investigate. The research problem in an investigation should determine the methods of investigation that are to be used. The methods that are used are also linked to the philosophical and epistemological issues that a project raises, and to the social processes that occur within a project. Issues relating to the research process may lead to the modification of the methods that are used.

Within the social sciences there are a range of methods that can be used, and it is the task of researchers to select which are most appropriate for their studies so that reliable and valid data are collected.

The choice of research methods that are available to social scientists has been well summarized by de Vaus (1986) in terms of experimental methods, survey methods and case study methods. To these approaches we must add documentary and historical methods. The range of methods that are available are outlined in Figure 1. As Figure 1 indicates, there is a range of different styles of investigation based on experiments, surveys, case studies (including ethnography) and documentary and historical methods that include the use of written texts as well as non-text materials. The researcher may use a combination of the different approaches available in order to deal with issues concerned with validity through methodological triangulation (the use of different methods, theories, investigators and data) (Denzin 1970).

Investigators who use different approaches to social research may use similar methods. Interviews, questionnaires, observation and documents are appropriate in many forms of social research. The distinguishing feature of research projects is the way in which the data are collected using these different approaches, and in turn the way in which analysis takes place. Interviews may be structured with specific questions, which include closed (fixed choice) as well as open-ended responses, or unstructured where similar topics are raised through an interview agenda. Structured interviews often involve the use of interview schedules that are completed by an interviewer, while unstructured interviews are frequently tape-recorded and subsequently transcribed (Burgess 1984; 1993; Hammersley and Atkinson 1983).

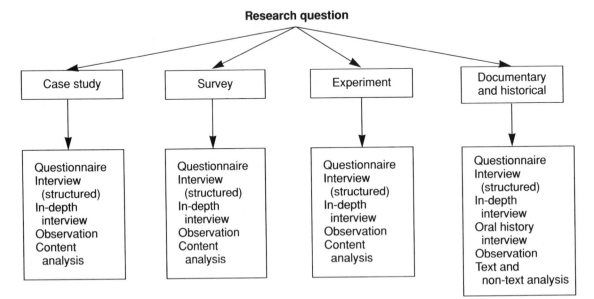

Source: Adapted from de Vaus 1986: 6

Figure 1 Research methods in the social sciences

Observation includes systematic observation which includes the use of particular schedules such as Flanders Interaction Analysis (Croll 1986), or may be closer to participant observation as used in many anthropological and some sociological studies (Burgess 1984). The collection of documentary evidence may take a variety of forms including written material, oral histories (collected by interview) and photographic and visual evidence (Scott 1990).

Some writers discuss social research in terms of opposing styles of investigations, and make comparisons to highlight the differences between them. However, researchers will get little benefit by engaging in arguments about the superiority of one technique as opposed to another. Instead, there is a need to focus on research problems using as wide a range of methods of research as are available. Indeed, Mitchell (1977) has highlighted the similarities involved in surveys and case study (ethnographic) research.

Figure 2 illustrates the importance of the researcher in social investigation. While researchers perform an important role in the conduct of social surveys, they play a greater part in ethnographic studies where they are central to data collection. In each case, the researcher has to consider the use of different methods in relation to the particular project. However, researchers also need a knowledge of the key methods associated with the principal styles of social investigation.

1 *Experiments* measure the effects of manipulating one variable on another. Usually, samples are taken from known populations and are allocated to different experimental conditions. Such an approach usually involves hypothesis testing. The problems that such an approach can deal with include internal validity, that is, the extent to which a study establishes that a factor or variable has caused the effect that is found, and external validity, that is, the degree to which findings can be generalized from a sample to a population. Researchers have also developed the quasi-experiment that has been designed to apply the principles associated with experimental work in laboratories to field situations so that comparisons are made between different groups within the field.

2 *The survey* is probably the most common method of social investigation that is used in social research. It is often associated with the use of a questionnaire or a formal interview. Such schedules are developed, piloted and finalized before a study is actually conducted. Accordingly, questionnaire design, attitude measurement and question wording are important aspects associated with social surveys that may take the form of face-to-face interviews, postal surveys or telephone interviews. Much of the work associated with the conduct of surveys includes the careful design of the questionnaire, the training of survey interviewers, the preparation of the interview schedule and the administration of the research instrument, which has to be coded and analysed. The use of technology increasingly plays a role in the development of such approaches as computer-based interviewing and data analysis using statistical packages.

3 *Ethnographic case* studies may involve the use of observation, and, more particularly, participant observation, together with unstructured interviews and conversations. The ethnographer is involved in using participatory techniques in order to understand the social situation in which those who are studied are involved. In particular, observation of people *in situ* forms a large part of this approach, in conjunction with conversational style interviews. Participant observers usually take a role in a particular setting which has resulted in a topology of researcher roles: complete participant, participant as observer, observer as participant, and complete observer. While these roles never exist in their pure form, they do provide an important framework for the ethnographer to use in a field setting. The methods used by the ethnographer to record data are particularly important, for fieldnotes and interview transcripts constitute the data that are subsequently coded and analysed. In the 1990s new technology has played a major role with software programs being developed to assist in the preparation and analysis of ethnographic data (Bryman and Burgess 1994).

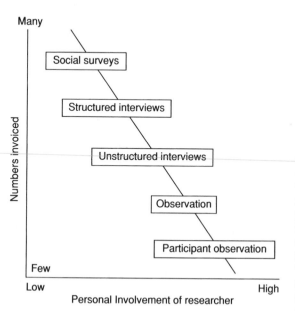

Source: Mitchell 1977: 89

Figure 2 Methods of data collection

4   *Documents* are produced in all organizations; they are therefore a major source of evidence for the social researcher. They can take a variety of forms and are often classified as primary source material or secondary source material. A distinction can be made between ready-made documents that are automatically available to a researcher, and specially commissioned documents where researchers invite the participants in their study to produce material (perhaps in the form of a diary) that is kept over a short period of time. Interest has been growing in oral-historical approaches, which are very similar to interview-based studies and have links with ethnographic and survey-based approaches of investigation. Increasing use is also being made of non-textual documentary materials, with visual evidence including photographs, film and videos playing an increasing role. In this respect, new technology again becomes an important resource that the social researcher can use (Scott 1990).

5   *Mixed Methods.* There is a tendency to subdivide the different approaches that have been used in social investigation. However, there are considerable links and overlaps between the different methods of investigation, so much so that some writers have talked about the importance of triangulation or multi-method strategies of investigation (Bryman 1988; Burgess 1984; Denzin 1970). In this respect, researchers need to evaluate the range of methodological tools that can be brought to bear upon the particular problem that they have to investigate. Ethnographic methods can be linked together with survey investigation and with documentary and historical methods, given that they may complement each other, with surveys prefacing fieldwork and informing fieldwork activity. Alternatively, fieldwork activity may generate concepts and questions that are then utilized within the framework of questionnaire design. Two key questions about the data that are collected demand consideration, namely, are they reliable? Are they valid? These are the fundamental issues that any method of social investigation must address.

Robert G. Burgess
University of Warwick

References

Bryman, A. (1988) *Quantity and Quality in Social Research*, London.

Bryman, A. and Burgess, R. G. (eds) (1994) *Analysing Qualitative Data*, London.

Bulmer, M. (ed.) (1984) *Sociological Research Methods*, 2nd edn, London.

Burgess, R. G. (1984) *In the Field*, London.

—— (1993) *Research Methods*, London.

Croll, P. (1986) *Systematic Classroom Observation*, Lewes.

Denzin, N. (1970) *The Research Act*, Chicago.

de Vaus, D. A. (1986) *Surveys in Social Research*, London.

Hammersley, M. and Atkinson, P. (1983) *Ethnography: Principles into Practice*, London.

Mitchell, C. (1977) 'The logic and methods of sociological enquiry', in P. Worsley (ed.) *Introducing Sociology*, Harmondsworth.

Moser, C. A. and Kalton, G. K. (1971) *Survey Methods in Social Investigation*, London.

Scott, J. (1990) *A Document of Record*, Oxford.

Sjoberg, G. and Nett, R. (1968) *A Methodology for Social Research*, New York.

Stacey, M. (1969) *Methods of Social Research*, Oxford.

Webb, S. and Webb, B. (1932) *Methods of Social Study*, London.

Further reading

Agnew, N. McK. (1994) *The Science Game: An Introduction to Research in the Social Sciences*, New York.

Reinharz, S. (1992) *Feminist Methods in Social Research*, New York.

Robson, C. (1993) *Real World Research*, Oxford.

Smith, H. W. (1975), *Strategies of Social Research: The Methodological Imagination*, Englewood Cliffs, NJ.

Yin, R. (1989) *Case Study Research*, Beverly Hills, CA.

metropolitan and urban government

Metropolitan and urban government refers to sub-national units of government and their associated political processes which frame public policy and deliver public services to relatively large and concentrated populations. Much of the writing on the subject may be grouped broadly around four questions. What is the appropriate structure of government for urban areas? What is the nature of urban politics? How is urban policy made? What services are delivered to whom and why?

Structure

As the population and geographic spread of urban areas grow, so does the need for larger units of local government. This raises a set of related questions about how many tiers of government there should be, the division of functions between them, and their relations to central government (Sharpe 1978). Some argue that large units of urban government will be undemocratic and inefficient – the justification for abolishing the top-tier units of the Greater London Council and the metropolitan counties of England. Others point out that small is not necessarily beautiful just as big is not necessarily ugly (Newton 1982). It is also said that modern urban society needs large urban units of government because cities and their hinterlands form indivisible social and economic entities which should be governed as a whole. The fragmentation of big city government in the USA causes huge problems for the organizing, financing and delivering of public services. The New York Metropolitan Region, with its 1,400 units of government, has been described as 'one of the great unnatural wonders of the world' (Wood 1961).

Urban politics

For some political scientists, local politics are national politics writ small, a convenient local research site in which to test general theories of politics. The enormous literature on community power is the best example. The elitists (Bachrach and Baratz 1970; Hunter 1953) found that small groups of professionals and business-people ran cities in their own interests. They were strongly challenged by the pluralists (Dahl 1961; Polsby 1980) who found that cities were run in a more open and democratic manner.

The crowding of the urban political arena with different social, economic and political interests makes it a major battleground of modern politics. For Marxists, coalitions of urban residents are the main opponents of the capitalist state (Castells 1976; Cockburn 1977). For others, urban government is the most immediate and accessible level of government and a good site for testing theories of modern politics and democracy (Newton 1976). However, another approach argues that urban politics has its own special nature, being concerned with 'low politics' (roads and parks, for example) while national government controls the 'high politics' of international affairs and economic management (Bulpitt 1983). According to the dual state thesis, local politics is likely to be open and pluralist, national government more closed and elitist (Saunders 1982).

Urban policy

Rational choice theorists argue that citizens (consumer-voters) move between urban municipalities in search of their optimum package of public goods at a given price (Tiebout 1956). Consequently, competing municipalities in the same urban area create a quasi-market for the allocation of costs and services. Although it has a large theoretical literature in the USA, the Tiebout hypothesis has not been subjected to proper empirical testing. In any case, it does not apply well to Britain, where urban and metropolitan government is far less fragmented. Even in the USA, Anthony Downs (1973: 11) argues that housing is allocated not by free market forces, but by municipal policies and local laws which are explicitly designed to prevent free markets from operating. Increasingly, urban government is seen as constrained by the external factors of national and international economic change, population movements and social forces, and

by the policies of national and international government (Peterson 1981).

Urban services

Many public services of the modern state are provided by city governments. Some have even defined urban government in terms of the collective consumption of public services (Dunleavy 1980). Research has therefore examined who gets what within the city. It has also compared the public service expenditures of different local authorities according to their social, economic and political features. The question of whether party political control makes any difference to urban services and spending has been extensively examined, and the conclusion seems to be that it does, but to a fairly limited extent (Sharpe and Newton 1984).

Kenneth Newton
University of Essex

References

Bachrach, P. and Baratz, M. S. (1970) *Power and Poverty*, London.
Bulpitt, J. (1983) *Territory and Power in the United Kingdom*, Manchester.
Castells, M. (1976) *The Urban Question*, Cambridge, MA.
Cockburn, C. (1977) *The Local State*, London.
Dahl, R. A. (1961) *Who Governs?*, New Haven, CT.
Downs, A. (1973) *Opening up the Suburbs: An Urban Strategy for America*, New Haven, CT.
Dunleavy, P. (1980) *Urban Political Analysis*, London.
Hunter, F. (1953) *Community Power Structure*, Chapel Hill, NC.
Newton, K. (1976) *Second City Politics*, Oxford.
—— (1982) 'Is small really so beautiful? Is big really so ugly? Size, effectiveness and democracy in local government', *Political Studies* 30.
Peterson, P. (1981) *City Limits*, Chicago.
Polsby, N. (1980) *Community Power and Political Theory*, New Haven, CT.
Saunders, P. (1982) *Social Theory and the Urban Question*, London.
Sharpe, L. J. (1978) 'Reforming the grass roots', in A. H. Halsey and D. Butler (eds) *Policy and Politics*, London.
Sharpe, L. J. and Newton, K. (1984) *Does Politics Matter?*, Oxford.
Tiebout, C. M. (1956) 'A pure theory of local expenditures', *Journal of Political Economy* 64.
Williams, D. P. *et al.* (1965) *Suburban Differences and Metropolitan Policies: A Philadelphia Story*, Philadelphia, PA.
Wood, R. C. (1961) *1400 Governments: The Political Economy of the New York Metropolitan Region*, Cambridge, MA.

Further reading

Wolman, H. and Goldsmith, M. (1992) *Urban Politics and Policy: A Comparative Approach*, Cambridge, MA.

See also: city; urban planning.

microeconomics

Microeconomics is that portion of economic theory concerned with the economic behaviour of individual units in the economy, and the factors determining the prices and quantities exchanged for particular goods and services. It can be contrasted with macro-economics, which is concerned with the determination of values for aggregates for the economy. For example, microeconomics examines the determination of the price of wheat, or the relative prices of wheat and steel, or employment in the steel industry, while macro-economics deals with the determination of the level of employment in a particular economy, or with the level of prices of all commodities. Although this distinction between two areas of economic analysis is useful for many purposes, and economic theory textbooks are usually devoted either to microeconomics (also known as 'price theory') or to macroeconomics, it should not be taken to imply that these two levels of analysis are independent. Micro-questions, such as those concerning the relative prices produced in competitive and monopolistic industries, cannot be answered without reference to the level of aggregate demand in the economy, while macroeconomics is built on micro-foundations that specify the nature of competition in different industries, for example, competitive or oligopolistic.

The development of microeconomics as a distinct area was part of the marginal or neo-classical approach that came to dominate economic theory after the 1970s. In contrast to classical economics, which was concerned with the economic growth of nations due to the growth of their productive resources, and which explained the relative prices of goods on the basis of the 'objective' conditions of their costs of production, neo-classical theory turned its attention to the efficient allocation of given resources (under the implicit assumption of full employment) and to the 'subjective' determination of individual prices based on marginal utility.

The topics dealt with by microeconomic analysis are often presented under the following six headings: theory of consumer behaviour; theory of exchange; theory of production and cost; theory of the firm; theory of distribution; and welfare economics. The common theme underlying these topics is the attempt of individual actors to achieve an optimal position, given the values of the parameters constraining their choices. Consumers try to maximize satisfaction (or utility), given their tastes, incomes and prices of all goods; firms try to maximize profits, and this means, among other things, that any rate of output is produced at least cost. The conditions for maximization are expressed in terms of marginal equalities. For example, for profit maximization a firm's rate of output should be such that marginal revenue is equal to marginal cost. In traditional approaches to microeconomics it is assumed that the self-seeking actions of individual units result in equilibrium positions where, given the values of the parameters, all participants are making the best of the situations facing them. They can be concerned either with partial equilibrium analysis (developed by Marshall) that concentrates on the determination of equilibrium values in a particular industry, assuming that the values in other industries are determined independently of these particular values, or with general equilibrium analysis (developed by Leon Walras), that provides full scope for the interdependence of all sectors of the economy, and deals with the simultaneous determination of all prices and quantities in the system. This generality is obtained at some cost, with the treatment being formal and mathematical, and important aspects of economic processes that occupy time are ignored.

A. Asimakopulos
formerly, McGill University

Further reading

Asimakopulos, A. (1978) *An Introduction to Economic Theory: Microeconomics*, Toronto.
Mansfield, E. (1982) *Microeconomics*, 4th edn, New York.

See also: consumer behaviour; cost-benefit analysis; econometrics; firm, theory of; markets; prices, theory of; supply-side economics; welfare economics.

migration

Migration is a generic term used to refer both to immigration (or in-migration) and to emigration (or out-migration). Formally, these terms may refer to various types of change of residence, but we customarily speak of immigration and emigration when the change of residence is between nations, and of in-migration and out-migration when the change of residence is between subunits of a nation. The term 'net migration' is used to denote the difference between the number of in-migratory events and the number of out-migratory events with respect to a particular geographic unit during a given time period.

Events of immigration (in-migration) and emigration (out-migration) constitute two of the four components of population change; the other two are births and deaths. For large areas, population change is generally determined predominantly by the balance of births and deaths ('natural increase'). However, for small areas the net migration is often larger than the natural increase.

A migration stream is defined as the total number of migratory events from Place A to Place B during a given time period. The counterstream is defined as the total number of migratory events from Place B to Place A. The sum of events in the stream and counterstream is termed the gross interchange between A and B. The effectiveness of migration is defined as the ratio of the net migration between A and B and the gross interchange between the two places. Logically, therefore, the effectiveness of migration can vary from a low of 0 to a high of 1. For most pairs of geographic units the effectiveness of migration tends to be much closer to 0 than to 1.

Certain types of migration are commonly distinguished. Petersen (1975) made useful distinctions between the concepts of free, impelled and forced migration. In free migration, the will of the migrant is the main factor. In impelled migration, the will of the migrant is subordinated to the will of other persons. In forced migration, the will of other persons is paramount, and the will of the migrant is of no weight at all. Return migration is defined as migration back to a place in which one had formerly resided. For most individuals who have migrated several times during their lifetime, return migrations are an important component of the total number of movements. Chain migration refers to the common pattern whereby individuals migrate to a particular destination in which they already have kin or friends who have previously migrated from the individual's own area of origin.

Migration differentials

It is universally observed that the propensity to migrate is strongest among young adults. Other differentials in migration tend to be limited to particular cultures or locales.

Determinants of migration

The determinants of migratory behaviour may conveniently be analysed in terms of a preference system; a price system; and the total amount of resources available for all goals (Heer 1975).

First, the *preference system* describes the relative attractiveness of various places as goals for potential migrants, compared to other goals which their resources would allow them to pursue. An area's attractiveness is the balance between the positive and negative values which it offers. Among the most important of the positive values is the prospect of a better-paying job. Other advantages achieved by migration include the chance to live in a more favourable climate, freedom from persecution, marriage and the continuation of marital ties, and the desire for more adequate housing, a factor particularly important with respect to central city to suburb movements.

However, migration also creates negative values. A major disincentive to migration is that it involves a disruption of interpersonal relationships with kin and old friends. Chain migration is so attractive precisely because it mitigates this disruption of relationships. Other negative aspects of migration are the necessity to learn new customs and sometimes a new language. Laws restraining legal entry or departure are also, of course, important deterrents to migration.

Second, *the price system* describes costs in money, energy and time (which cannot be used in the pursuit of other goals) imposed by a given migration decision. As the cost of migration generally varies in direct proportion to the distance travelled, the number of migrants to a given place tends to vary inversely with the distance.

Third, *the total resources available* for all goals also affect the decision to migrate. If the only drawback to migration is the expense of the move, then an increase in monetary income should increase the probability of migration. The secular increase in monetary income since the end of the nineteenth century in the developed nations should have increased rates of migration, provided that the value and price of migration had remained constant. However, to the extent that regional differences in job opportunities may also decline, the factor of increasing resources may be offset.

Consequences of migration

Migration has consequences for the areas of net out-migration and net in-migration, as well as for the larger social system, which includes both the area of out-migration and the area of in-migration.

First, net out-migration may have several important consequences for an area. It may relieve population pressure and cause the average level of wage and salary income to rise. However, it may cause the value of land and real estate to decline. Areas of net out-migration incur the loss of the investments made to raise and educate those children who spend their productive years elsewhere.

Second, net in-migration may also have important consequences. If the area is definitely underpopulated, the resultant population increase may help the area achieve economies of scale and thus raise the general standard of living. Under other circumstances, net in-migration may result in decline in average wage and salary income. In either case, a net flow of in-migrants will tend to raise the price of land and real estate. It is also possible that a high rate of in-migration fosters social disorganization, as social-control networks are not easily established among persons who are strangers to one another.

Third, for the system comprising the areas of both net inflow and net outflow, migration promotes a redistribution of population. If migrants have been responsive to differences in job opportunities, this redistribution will further the economic development of the total system. Usually, migration also has consequences for the degree of regional homogeneity within the total system. Since migrants tend to move from low to high income areas, regional income inequalities are generally reduced by migration. Moreover, migration often helps to reduce regional disparities in racial, ethnic and religious composition.

Migration policies and legislation affecting migration

It is useful to distinguish between migration policies, which are intentionally designed to influence migratory flows, and legislation affecting migration which in fact influences the flow of migrants even though it is designed to serve some other major goal or goals. Almost all nations have adopted policies with respect to international migration. Most such policies severely restrict immigration, so that the actual stream of legal immigrants is much smaller than it would have been if no barriers had been imposed (Davis 1981). As a result, many nations, particularly the USA, have a large number of illegal immigrants. However, certain nations have actively encouraged immigrants of a particular type. Australia, for example, in the twenty-year period following the Second World War, actively sought to increase its population through subsidizing immigration from Europe while at the same time discouraging immigration from Asia. Although most governments proclaim the right of their citizens to emigrate, many of them place restrictions on emigration of selected persons for reasons of national security. Moreover, restrictions on emigration can be very severe, as exemplified until recently in the former Soviet Union.

The stream of rural to urban migration has marked every nation, both developed and less developed, since the beginning of the Industrial Revolution. In the developed nations, the net stream of rural to urban migration has in most cases ceased; in many of the less developed nations, it is still of considerable magnitude.

Explicit policies concerning internal migration are less common than with respect to external migration, but in most nations there is a large body of legislation which affects internal migration either negatively or positively. Nations which do have explicit policies regarding internal migration have generally tried either to discourage the growth of their largest cities or to encourage settlement of scarcely populated regions with important natural resources.

David M. Heer
University of Southern California

References

Davis, K. (1981) 'Emerging issues in international migration', *International Population Conference, Manila, 1981*, vol. 2, Liège.

Heer, D. M. (1975) *Society and Population*, 2nd edn, Englewood Cliffs, NJ.

Petersen, W. (1975) *Population*, 3rd edn, New York.

See also: labour migration; population geography; population policy; population projections; refugees; vital statistics.

military regimes

There have been and still are several military governments; there have been few military regimes. Military governments are easily created in times of political crisis. They are the product of an intervention in the political arena aimed at displacing disliked politicians and calling new elections. Those interventions may immediately replace governing politicians with civilians more favourable to the interests of the military or to their conception of the political sphere. Or else military governments may just come into being in order to prevent the election of unacceptable politicians. In all these cases, military governments are shortlived. They will probably last only the time necessary to call new elections, no longer than six months to one year. The amount of bloodshed will be limited because the civilian opposition will be easily deterred and the military will receive some support even from some civilian quarters. In all likelihood, only a few military officers will occupy political positions (the most visible and the most prestigious ones) leaving to civilian politicians all the other ministries, particularly the economic ones. The military institution, the armed forces as such, will be only partially involved in the coup and in the government. Indeed, military officers in the government may be asked to resign from active duty. The relatively smooth return to the barracks of the interventionist officers is the natural outcome of a military government.

Military regimes are an entirely different story: they are the product of the intervention of the military institution as a whole, the armed forces. They receive practically no support from the civilians except in a severely polarized situation. Indeed, interventionist officers do not ask for the support of the civilians and decide to fill all ministerial positions, making perhaps an exception only for an economic ministry to be entrusted to a conservative civilian economist in order to keep the confidence of the international business community. Military regimes are created not to re-equilibrate the competition among different groups of politicians. On the contrary, they aim at restructuring their society, in order to prevent the re-emergence of conditions necessitating a further coup by the armed forces. Therefore, the tenure of military regimes may be long; in any event, it cannot be predetermined. The Latin American military have offered several examples, with varying degree of success, of institutional coups and military regimes: Brazil (1964–82), Peru (1968–80), Chile (1973–90) and perhaps even the shortlived case of Argentina (1976–82).

Military regimes are no more, and usually less, successful than their civilian counterparts. They do not reduce the level of domestic political conflict and are often obliged to resort to a very high degree of repression and torture. They fail to produce a high level of economic development. Even when they succeed in refuelling the economy, they do so at a very high price for the lower classes and, in some cases, denationalizing the structure of their economy. Nor are they able to reshape the political system: their civilian opponents are usually back in power a few years after the demise of the military regime.

Most military regimes come to an end when the officers themselves realize that the contradictions of their governing experience may endanger the integrity of the military institution. Always divided on the decision to intervene in the political arena and to remain there, the officers may thereafter opt for a unilateral withdrawal. In some cases, the extrication decision is forced on them if they lose a war. It was the case of the Argentine military after the Falkland War in 1982. In other cases, the military may feel confident in their ability to control a relatively demobilized society, as in the case of Brazil at the beginning of the 1980s. In most cases, their only and major problem before withdrawing is to acquire some sort of immunity for the violence and the crimes they have committed, as in Chile. In all cases, the withdrawal from the political arena becomes inevitable when many officers fear that the tensions within the military institution may lead to internal conflicts and even to a breakdown. In a few developing and most developed countries, powerful military institutions usually have other, less costly and dangerous means than open political intervention to satisfy their needs and to promote their political preferences and goals.

Gianfranco Pasquino
University of Bologna

Further reading

Kolkowicz, R. and Korbonski, A. (eds) (1982) *Soldiers, Peasants, and Bureaucrats: Civil–Military Relations in Communist and Modernizing Societies*, London.
Nordlinger, E. A. (1977) *Soldiers in Politics: Military Coups and Governments*, Englewood Cliffs, NJ.
Stepan, A. (1988) *Rethinking Military Politics: Brazil and the Southern Cone*, Princeton, NJ.

See also: authoritarian and totalitarian systems; democratization; military sociology.

military sociology

Military sociology is mainly concerned with the armed forces as a special type of organization with specific social functions. These functions flow from the purpose of the organization, namely security, and from the organizational means, force or violence. These matters have been the subject of discussion for centuries and were considered by the pioneer sociologists Comte and Spencer. An empirically grounded and theoretically informed military sociology became established, however, only during the Second World War. Pioneering studies were carried out by the Research Branch of the Information and Education Division of the US Armed Forces between 1942–5, and later published (Stouffer *et al.* 1949). The discipline is still most developed and differentiated in the USA, though there are institutions for research in military sociology in other countries.

There are five main fields of research.

Internal organisational problems in daily military life

Processes within small groups and military rituals are analysed in order to identify problems of discipline and motivation, and also to elucidate the way in which the military subculture is ordered.

Internal organizational problems in combat

Studies in this area concern the criteria for the selection of military leaders, including the lower ranks, and evaluate combat motivation.

The armed forces and the society

Military sociologists are interested in the image of the profession with respect to the impact of social and technological change, the recruitment profile of the armed forces, the broader structure of defence, problems of training and educating soldiers and, more recently, the role of women in the army.

The military and politics

The traditional question of the causes and functions of militarism has been broken down into more specific issues, and there is now a clear difference between the west and other parts of the world in the emphases chosen. In western democracies, research has come to focus on the political control of the military and the web of military, economic and administrative interests, which are difficult to disentangle. The sparse analyses of armed forces in the socialist countries address the political balance between the army and the party. In contrast, numerous studies devoted to the military in developing countries are concerned with the causes and consequences of military coups, with the ability of the armed forces to contribute to development, and with 'Praetorianism', the form typically taken by militarism in underdeveloped countries.

Armed forces in the international system

These studies deal with national and international aspects of security, with armaments and armament control, and with international peacekeeping operations. A proper sociology of war exists in only a rudimentary form.

This brief survey clearly indicates the interdisciplinary nature of the field. Military sociology is also in a special position because of widespread concern with its applied orientation, and with the conservative views of its main client, the armed forces. It is seldom taught in university departments of sociology, and most research is concentrated in extra-university institutions, often within the armed forces. Nevertheless, the best studies in the field have profitably explored this very tension between academic and liberal commitments and the applications of the research. Exemplary studies are Andreski (1954), Finer (1962), Huntington (1957), Janowitz (1960) and Moskos (1970).

The key issues for research in the immediate future relate to the most urgent problems of military organization. Such problems include the consequences of current technological developments and of changes in the civilian view of the functions of the military in industrial countries after the end of the east–west conflict, as well as the growing importance of military and paramilitary violence, especially in developing countries.

Wilfried von Bredow
Philipps University

References

Andreski, S. (1954) *Military Organization and Society*, London.
Finer, S. E. (1962) *The Man on Horseback*, London.
Huntington, S. P. (1957) *The Soldier and the State*, Cambridge, MA.
Janowitz, M. (1960) *The Professional Soldier*, Glencoe, IL.
Moscos, C. C. Jr (1970) *The American Enlisted Man*, New York.
Stouffer, S. A. (1949) *The American Soldier*, Princeton, NJ.

See also: military regimes; war studies.

Mill, John Stuart (1806–73)

John Stuart Mill, the classic exponent of liberalism, was brought up in utilitarian principles by his father, James Mill, a close friend and associate of Bentham. His rigorous childhood education, described in his *Autobiography* (1873), involved a brilliant and precocious mastery of classical languages by the age of 7. For most of his working life he was a clerk at India House in London, though briefly a Member of Parliament. After a long association, he married Harriet Taylor whom he always claimed as his inspiration and intellectual partner. On their marriage, in protest against the legal situation of women at the time, he wrote a formal renunciation of the property and similar rights bestowed on him as a husband.

Mill was a many-sided thinker and writer – a philosopher, social scientist and humanist. Among the subjects he treated were politics, ethics, logic and scientific method. He also wrote on the position of women (*The Subjection of Women*, 1859), constitutional reform (*Considerations on Representative Government*, 1861) and economics (*Principles of Political Economy*, 1848).

In *Utilitarianism* (1861) Mill expounded and defended the principle that the tendency of actions to promote happiness or its reverse is the standard of right and wrong. His version of utilitarianism was from a logical point of view possibly flawed, but from a moral point of view enhanced, by the notion that some forms of happiness are more worthwhile than others. *On Liberty* (1859) is the classic argument for the claims of the individual against the state, and in it Mill makes an impassioned defence of the principles of liberty and toleration. Isaiah Berlin writes of Mill that 'the highest values for him . . . were individual liberty, variety, and justice'. This is sometimes seen as inconsistent with his basic utilitarianism, but Mill believed that principles like liberty and justice were themselves important social instruments for utility. This follows from his view of human nature, and in particular from his belief that self-determination and the exercise of choice are themselves part of a higher concept of happiness, and that 'collective mediocrity' is a recipe for social stagnation and permanent cultural and economic arrest. Writing on toleration, Mill argued in favour of liberty of thought, speech and association, as well as for freedom to cultivate whatever lifestyle one chooses, subject only to the constraint of not harming others. It is often disputed whether there are any actions which do not affect other people in some way, but the distinction between other-regarding and self-regarding actions – the postulation of a public realm and a private realm – is an essential element of liberalism.

Mill applied these principles to education, defending a liberal and secular education. He considered compulsory education not an invasion of liberty but essential to it. However, he believed strongly that there should not be a 'state monopoly of education' but that state education should be one amongst a number of competing systems.

In *A System of Logic, Ratiocinative and Deductive* (1843), Mill defended a classical view of induction as empirical generalization, and held that this can supply a model for both logical deduction and scientific method. In some respects this may be seen as a classic version of British empiricism, and indeed Mill was an empiricist in the sense that he believed truth, including mathematical truth, was to be established by observation rather than intuition; however, because he was prepared to accept the uniformity of nature as a basic postulate, his account does not have the sceptical consequences that this position might otherwise seem to involve. Mill extended his discussion of methodology to cover the application of experimental method to social science and set out to provide 'a general science of man in society'. His argument is to be found in Book VI of *A System of Logic*, which has been called the most important contribution to the making of modern sociology until Durkheim's *Rules of Sociological Method*.

While some of his immediate successors saw Mill as the unfortunate propounder of views that are inherently irreconcilable, a number of modern commentators have offered a revisionist interpretation of Mill as a consistent thinker. This position was taken at one time by John Gray (1983), who argued that Mill's active rather than passive conception of happiness necessarily involves a social setting in which liberty and toleration are the norm. Later, however, Gray attacked his own revisionist interpretation – an interpretation shared also by, for example, Ryan (1987) and Berger – arguing that Mill's Victorian faith in progress obscured from him the truth that the empirical assumption that liberty will contribute to happiness is either unsupported or false. This breaking of the link between happiness and liberty, Gray suggests, together with the collapse of classical utilitarianism that results from recognising the ultimate incommensurability of pleasures of various kinds, is fatal to any form of liberalism. The revision of revisionism should not be taken, however, as anything more than a sign of the perennial interest of Mill's ideas; and Mill, more than any of his critics, would no doubt see this as another opportunity to insist

that no truth should ever be allowed to become a dead dogma, even the truth of liberalism itself.

Brenda Almond
University of Hull

References

Berger, F. (1984) *Happiness, Justice and Freedom: The Moral and Political Philosophy of John Stuart Mill*, Berkeley, CA.
Berlin, I. (1969) 'John Stuart Mill and the Ends of Life' in *Four Essays on Liberty*, Oxford.
Durkheim, E. (1950) The Rules of Sociological Method, trans. S. A. Solovay and J. H. Mueller, and ed. E. G. Catlin.
Gray, J. (1983) *Mill on Liberty: A Defence*, London.
Ryan, A. (1987) *The Philosophy of John Stuart Mill*, 2nd edn, London.

Further reading

Skorupski, J. (1989) *John Stuart Mill*, London.
Ten, C. L. (1980) *Mill on Liberty*, Oxford.

See also: liberalism; utilitarianism.

mind

'Mind' is derived from old Teutonic *gamundi*, meaning to think, remember, intend. These various senses are apparent in current phrases such as to bear in mind, remind, give one's mind to, make up or change one's mind. Most verbal forms are now obsolete or dialectal but remain in such phrases as 'never mind' or 'mind how you go' in the sense of attend. Traditionally 'mind' has been used to refer collectively to mental abilities such as perceiving, imagining, remembering, thinking, believing, feeling, desiring, deciding and intending. Sometimes an agent is implied: 'Mind is the mysterious something which feels and thinks' (Mill 1843); sometimes not: 'What we call mind is nothing but a heap or collection of different perceptions, united together by certain relations' (Hume 1740).

In classical Greece, questions about the mind were interwoven with those about the soul or spirit, as was the case in medieval Europe, where theological concerns predominated. Plato's tripartite division of the mind into cognitive, conative and affective functions lasted at least until the nineteenth century. Numerous classifications of mental faculties were offered in the eighteenth and nineteenth centuries. Although these were generally speculative, artificial and non-explanatory, they laid the ground for later work in psychometrics and cortical localization of function, and subsequently modularity (Fodor 1983) and neuropsychology.

Diverse criteria have been offered for distinguishing the mental from the physical (Feigl 1958) but there are problems associated with many of them. According to the first, mental phenomena are private whereas physical phenomena are public. Descartes (1953 [1641]) claimed that physical bodies were spatially extended and subject to deterministic laws, whereas minds were nonspatial and free. Brentano (1874) suggested intentionality as characteristic of the mental: perceiving, thinking, and desiring imply objects which may have no objective existence. Attempts have been made to distinguish mental and physical in terms of different logics, for example, intensional and extensional (Chisholm 1967) or linguistic conventions (Ryle 1949).

Traditionally the mind has been identified with conscious experience: 'Consciousness . . . is the condition or accompaniment of every mental operation' (Fleming 1858); 'No proposition can be said to be in the Mind which it was never conscious of' (Locke 1690). However, this proposition is patently false. Neurophysiologists and clinicians in the nineteenth century recognized different levels of functioning in the nervous system and acknowledged unconscious mental activity, although the idea has a much more venerable history dating back at least to classical Greek times. William James (1890) pointed out that it is only the perchings and not the flights of thought that are available to consciousness. The majority of mental processes take place outside awareness, for instance, large parts of perception, retrieval, skills and creative thinking. This fact is made even more obvious by consideration of such phenomena as hypnosis, subliminal perception, learning without awareness, split personality and blindsight (a clinical condition in which patients with damage to the occipital lobes may report no experience of seeing and yet be able to make correct discriminations in a forced choice situation).

If mind is characterized as the system that governs behaviour rather than being identified with the contents of consciousness, then the way is open for more mechanistic approaches to its study. With the rise of cognitive psychology, the most popular framework has been the computer metaphor, premised on a functionalist philosophy: what characterizes the mental is its functional organization rather than its material constitution. According to the computational model of mind, mental activity is computation – mental processes are operations performed on representations – and can be modelled by the manipulation of abstract symbols according to formal rules in a digital computer. The computational model has been criticized as being both behaviouristic and dualistic (Russell 1984). Functionalism cannot provide a satisfactory analysis of qualitative differences in experience; and mental processes are considered to be independent of any particular physical realization. It has been doubted whether the context-free, formal manipulation of abstract symbols can deal adequately with meaning and reference (Searle 1980). Orthodox artificial intelligence underemphasizes the dynamic interaction with the environment and ignores the developmental and biological dimensions of mental life.

A more biologically realistic alternative has regained popularity: neural networks, which employ connectionist principles and exhibit parallel distributed processing. They show such features as context addressability and resistance to local damage, and account well for many psychological phenomena such as pattern recognition, learning and memory. They have also enabled fruitful links to be established with neurophysiological research.

The mind can be modelled by a hierarchy of multiple parallel processors, enabling speed and flexibility, with interaction and dependencies within and between levels. At the lowest level they govern sensory and motor interactions with the external world. At the highest level overall goals are monitored. Some of the modules may be fairly general in function; the majority are probably relatively specialized. The evidence suggests a broad division of labour between those specialized for verbal processing and those specialized for spatial processing. A small subset of results, but not the inner workings, are available to consciousness in a limited capacity serial processor which interrelates products of parallel processors. The system can construct models of the external world (including one of itself), which influence its input and output. The contents of the mind appear to be images, propositions, models and procedures for carrying out actions. It is clear that 'mind' is a term which is too vague to be useful. The tools are now available for the detailed specification of its function, which will require the combined efforts of work in artificial intelligence, experimental psychology and neuroscience.

E. R. Valentine
University of London

References

Brentano, F. (1874) *Psychologie vom empirischen Standpunkt*, Leipzig.

Chisholm, R. M. (1967) 'Intentionality', in P. Edwards (ed.) *The Encyclopaedia of Philosophy* vol. 4, New York.

Descartes, R. (1953[1641]) *Discourse on Method*, London.

Feigl, H. (1958) 'The "mental" and the "physical" ', in H. Feigl et al. (eds) *Concepts, Theories and the Mind–Body Problem*, Minneapolis, MN.

Fleming, W. (1958) *The Vocabulary of Philosophy*, London.

Fodor, J. A. (1983) *The Modularity of Mind*, Cambridge, MA.

James, W. (1890), *Principles of Psychology*, New York.

Locke, J. (1690) *Essay Concerning Human Understanding*, London.

Mill, J. S. (1843) *A System of Logic*, London.

Russell, J. (1984) *Explaining Mental Life*, London.

Searle, J. R. (1980) 'Minds, brains and programs', *Behavioral and Brain Sciences* 3.

Further reading

Gregory, R. L. (ed.) (1987) *The Oxford Companion to the Mind*, Oxford.

Johnson-Laird, P. N. (1983) *Mental Models*, Cambridge, UK.

Valentine, E. R. (1992) *Conceptual Issues in Psychology*, 2nd edn, London.

See also: artificial intelligence; consciousness; nervous system.

mixed economy

A purely private right to a resource may be said to exist when an individual can select any use for that resource including the option of sale. This may be contrasted with other specifications of property rights like communal access to roads, state ownership of railways or, indeed, when any privately owned resource is subject to restrictions in the range of its use. The degree to which purely private rights prevail in an economy would reflect the degree to which an economy is mixed, but a precise measure has yet to be devised.

There are two broad ways of thinking about the mixed economy. One is to ask how and why the public sector has increased its share of property rights. The other way is to ask why the economy should be mixed, and this has been the main focus of debate in the post-war period up to about the late 1960s. It has been a debate partly about aims, but perhaps more about whether certain economic and social aims are better achieved by non-private rights to resources. In this sense, the mixed economy is the outcome of policies consciously espoused by parties, supported by a majority of voters and executed by governments. To understand the post-1945 growth of the public sector, one needs, in this light, first to emphasize the effect of the interwar years of large-scale unemployment. For many people, the low income levels and social tragedies seemed damning evidence of the inefficiencies and injustices of capitalism, to be remedied in part by public ownership of the means of production. Doubts that resources would be efficiently allocated in such a system disappeared for some by the demonstration that public ownership was consistent with the use of a price system (see, e.g. Lange 1936). The efficient allocation of resources which was theoretically obtainable in a perfectly competitive world was obtainable also by public firms adjusting output levels to the point where prices equalled marginal costs, but with the key difference that, with capital publicly owned, profits accrued to the nation rather than to a select few. Similarly, the Keynesian demonstration that unemployment could be an equilibrium feature of capitalism pointed to an enhanced role for the state. While an expansion of private investment would have beneficial effects on income and employment levels comparable to increased public spending, Keynes had stressed the role of pessimistic expectations in preventing a sufficiently low level of interest rates or in inhibiting a business investment expansion independently of interest-rate levels.

In the two decades from 1945, these arguments gradually lost some of their force. Rising living standards in economies where over 60 per cent of GDP still emanated from the private sector, financial losses in public enterprises, waiting-lists for certain public services together with some embryonic doubts, especially by American economists, about whether government deficit manipulation was actually the source of full employment, undermined some of the support for government economic activity. That support was, however, largely sustained, at least intellectually, by several strands of earlier thought receiving increased emphasis. It is clear, for example, that the analysis of public goods has a wider applicability than law, order and defence. In so far as the issue is one of spill-over effects in consumption and production, then, in a world of continuing urbanization, government corrective action for transport congestion, air pollution and safety regulation seemed vital. In a similar technical vein, while public ownership was no longer seen as the best vehicle for improving income distribution, a strand in the early support for such government intervention was to prevent private monopolistic exploitation of economies of scale common in fuel, transport and general infrastructure development. The arguments for public provision of education, health and even housing had never relied solely on the issue of income distribution; rather there were questions about the access to information, to capital markets and to the speed with which the price system could deal fairly with shortages. Finally, though perhaps least convincingly, the differential growth experience of the post-1945 economies entered the economist's agenda in the 1960s with government again seen as an important catalyst.

There has, however, always been the view that the above is a misconception both of how the private competitive system works and how public ownership works. Private monopoly in the field is quite consistent with competition for the field so that auction bidding for franchises for refuse collection, electricity supply and such services could eliminate monopoly profits. How, secondly, will private decision takers react to the existence of spill-over effects? If there are net gains to be exploited by public action on the height of chimneys or on river pollution by up-stream firms, how can we be sure that private decision takers have not already entered economic dealings to their joint satisfaction? And if the argument is that, especially with large groups, there are transaction costs in private exchange relations, so also are there costs to the government in acquiring information, casting doubt on whether its solution will be any better. More generally, why should the analysis of utility-maximizing behaviour stop at the door of the public sector? Civil servants, public industry managers and politicians are the relevant decision takers. In the Austrian tradition the cost of an activity is the value of the alternative foregone by the decision taker, not by some vague entity like the state. In summary, there is no guarantee on this line of thought that government action will yield a superior solution to the private sector solution with all its warts (see, e.g. Demsetz 1982). Such doubts mounted in the 1970s and 1980s fuelled in part by the increasing growth of government and the part this might have played as the source of monetary expansion in the late 1960s and early 1970s. By the mid-1970s, moreover, Keynesianism as a theoretical framework for analysing unemployment and inflation was under strong attack, precisely because of its deficient analysis of the micro behaviour of agents in the economy.

While such debates on policy have been continually supported by positive studies of how economic systems work, they have not fully confronted the basic question of why the public sector has grown. Indeed, much of the debate has treated the state as an autonomous force, as something separate from the features of the rest of the economy. Doubts about such a characterization should arise when it is recognized that the pre-nineteenth century, early modern European absolutist states had interventionist bureaucracies and armies where the attenuation of private rights, if we could only measure it, might bear comparison to modern state sectors. Many Marxists would certainly want to locate the characterization of the modern state in the capitalist mode of production, in the sense of the state being another form of monopoly capital or a collective form to secure for capitalism what private capital on its own cannot secure – legal system, control of trade unions, and so on. A longer-term view is also developing in other quarters (North and Wallis 1982; Olson 1982). The industrialization which started in the late eighteenth century meant a rapidly increasing division of labour, thereby enhancing the role of transaction costs and the supply of organized interest groups. The same forces which have advanced the middleman, the white-collar worker and those engaged in banking, accounting, law, insurance, property and trade are also important in prompting the provision of transaction cost reducing services by government, that is, basic transportation, justice, police, fire, defence, postal services, licensing, quality inspection and measurement standards. The attenuation of purely private rights usually requires group or collective action; there are in-built disincentives to such action which, in democracies, take a long time to overcome. It was in the latter part of the nineteenth century that the significant changes became observable. Over the years from 1869 to 1970 the percentage of the US labour force in government grew from 3.5 per cent to 18.1 per cent matching rises from 7.8 per cent to 19.1 per cent in retail trade, 0.4 per cent to 4.0 per cent in finance, insurance and real estate, and 11.1 per cent to 17.4 per cent in other services. It is probably only by a further analysis of such long-run trends that we shall fully understand the mixed economy.

Robert Millward
University of Manchester

References

Demsetz, H. (1982) *Economic, Legal and Political Dimensions of Competition*, Amsterdam.
Lange, O. (1936) 'On the economic theory of socialism', *Review of Economic Studies* 4.
North, D. C. and Wallis, J. J. (1982) 'American government expenditures: a historical perspective', *American Economic Association: Papers and Proceedings*.
Olson, M. (1982) *The Rise and Decline of Nations*, New Haven, CT.

Further reading

Lord Roll of Ipsden (ed.) (1982) *The Mixed Economy*, London.

See also: crowding out; markets; nationalization; planning, economic; prediction and forecasting; public goods.

mobility, social *see* social mobility

modernity

Modernity refers to a historical period which began in Western Europe with a series of cultural, social and economic changes during the seventeenth century, and it is usually characterized by three features: first, culturally, a reliance on reason and experience conditioned the growth of science and scientific consciousness, secularization and instrumental rationality; second, as a mode of life it was based on the growth of industrial society, social mobility, market economy, literacy, bureaucratization and consolidation of the nation-state; and third, it fostered a conception of the person as free, autonomous, self-controlled and reflexive. Opposed to traditional forms of thought and life, modernity can be conceptualized as a mode of social and individual experience that is shared by many men and women all over the world due to the expansion and prestige of scientific enquiry, technological innovation, political models of democracy and nation-state boundaries, and the subjective drive for self-development. Modernity is inherently globalizing. Giddens (1991) has argued that the globalizing tendencies of modern institutions is accompanied by continuous changes in the perception of the self and redefinitions of identities. From this perspective, modernity is more than a historical product; it is an uncompleted programme that can still play a very creative role in present-day societies. Modernity implies an openness towards a determinate future characterized by material progress, social stability and self-realization.

According to Berman (1982), to be modern is to live in an environment that, at the same time, promises adventure, growth, joy, power and transformation of the self and the world, and threatens to destroy everything we have and we are. Modernity is a paradoxical unity which has constantly been on trial. The paradoxes of modernity are closely related to the discontinuities between the growth of reason; the logic of industrialism; the power of the nation-state; and the personal quest for freedom and self-realization. Bauman (1991) has pointed out that modernity would be better defined by the consciousness of a universal order that allows no place within the boundaries of the nation-state for strangers, diversity and tolerance. In his perspective, the Holocaust is a product of modernity. Foucault (1977) has analysed the emergence of disciplinary powers (in psychology, penology and sexology) in circumstances of modernity. Wagner (1994) argues that the modern project is unable to reconcile its conflicting commitment to liberty and to discipline, and that its history is characterized by the coexistence of the discourses of liberation and control.

It has also been stated that in no contemporary society have religion or collective identities disappeared, and Mingione (1991) has shown that reciprocal obligations between individuals continue to be recognized in modern societies. Family or religious ties, ethnic solidarity, and gender and sexual identities play a very important role in the processes of allocating power and distributing resources. In contemporary societies, western and non-western, the realization of the self is often accompanied by loyalties, formerly seen as pre-modern, to different communal groups.

Eduardo P. Archetti
University of Oslo

References

Bauman, Z. (1991) *Modernity and Ambivalence*, Ithaca, NY.
Berman, M. (1982) *All that is Solid Melts into Air: The Experience of Modernity*, London.
Foucault, M. (1977) *Discipline and Punish: The Birth of the Prison*, London. (Original French edn, *Surveiller et punir*, Paris, 1975.)
Giddens, A. (1991) *Modernity and Self-Identity*, Cambridge, UK.
Mingione, E. (1991) *Fragmented Societies*. Oxford.
Wagner, P. (1994) *A Sociology of Modernity: Liberty and Discipline*, London.

Further reading

Lash, S. and Friedman, J. (eds) (1992) *Modernity and Identity*, Oxford.
Osborne, P. (1992) 'Modernity is a qualitative, not a chronological, category', *New Left Review* 192.
Turner, B. S. (ed.) (1990) *Theories of Modernity and Postmodernity*, London.

See also: modernization; post-modernism; post-modernity.

modernization

In academic development economics and related disciplines, and also in actual public policy on development, the word modernization slips and slides, alludes and obtrudes, both as a key or code term as well as a perfectly ordinary word meaning updating, upgrading, renovation, reconstruction or stabilization in the face of adverse social, physical or economic structures. In this ordinary usage, sometimes a particular history, political approach or ideology is intended, sometimes not. Often all that is meant is professionalism, rationality, planning or progress in general. Where no particular history or episode of development is taken to be at issue, probably any implied allusion to, say, the Russian debate about industrialization, or peasant participation in policy, will be sovietized, sanitized, populist perhaps, and certainly depoliticized. Where some particular historical reference *is* intended, such as to congeries of changes which included economic and demographic developments in western Europe from the sixteenth to the nineteenth centuries, unfortunately there is similarly likely to be much ellipsis and little historiography. As a result, the model matters alluded to tend in this literature to be more misunderstood than understood. For instance, 'industrialization' as in 'western industrial revolution' will be bandied about as if, for example, English, French and Dutch history in this regard had been the same, as if the Rochdale pioneers in the co-operative movement had not been non-agricultural, not engaged in political protest against a regime from which they felt excluded, not an urban class or class segment with a distinctive religious zeal.

Turning now to its other sense, before modernization as a technical and emotive key or code term or discourse emblem can do for one what it does already for others, some special initiation may be necessary. For example, modernization as a policy remedy for rural or some other backwardness problem may be proposed essentially as an alternative paradigm or option to another policy remedy: self-reliance (understood in a special sense) is the answer for another policy problem, dependency. Modernization theory and dependency theory are constantly pitted in the development studies literature as exclusive and hostile rivals. In development economics since Bretton Woods, this has served indeed as the principal polarization in this literature. Undoubtedly there are some striking contrasts between them with regard, for example, to the consequences for international relations, with each favouring recourse to its own pivotal terms about development problems and solutions. Exponents of modernization will preach dualism, diffusion of innovations, economies of scale, development administration, human resources development, financial and foreign aid. Believers in dependency theory will talk about core and periphery, world-system, unequal exchange, small is beautiful, delinking, or adjustment. Yet there are also some equally important, if seldom identified, similarities. Both schools of thought adopt comparable concepts of what one calls traditional, and the other pre-capitalist society and economy. Both are preoccupied with crises and turning-points and stages of development. Both put a heavy stress on First and Second World determinisms on the Third (and Fourth). Both tend to prefer structuralist analyses and to look for structural change.

Neo-classical economic studies of growth and development say they are or ought to be unadulterated by sociological, political and other non-economic variables. Is modernization neo-classical in the way in which *dependentia* often claim it is (and dependency is not)? Much will depend on the degree to which distinctions are drawn in each as regards dogma and actual practice, and one area or sector compared with another. Lack of stated institutional (as in institutional economics, comparative social institutions, and so on) analysis is not necessarily and equally a matter of implicit default as well, at least to the same extent or form. In modernization (and dependency) theory and practice, some institutional analysis goes – erroneously or otherwise – by omission as well as commission. For instance, nothing could be more institutionalist – and attitudinalist – than modernization's (and again dependency's) ideas of traditional society and economy (and underdevelopment). There is none the less much useful truth in the complaint that – in its coded sense – modernization 'crudely foreshortens the historical development of society ... is a technocratic model of society, conflict-free and politically neutral [which dissolves] genuine social conflict and issues in the abstractions of "the scientific revolution" [and] "productivity" [presuming] that no group in the society will be called upon to bear the costs of the scientific revolution'.

Modernization (like dependency yet again, so really there is very much similarity indeed) tends to self-correct its policies in the light of its disappointments with the actual development record as it unfolds: that is, it self-adjusts within its own shell of epistemological and other assumptions as further challenges present themselves. Thus, unfortunately, the historical perspectives and changes in the development studies are seldom those of the economies and policies to which they say they are addressed. So, and again as with dependency no less, modernization can often be best understood not as a particular development – or development theory or method for the study of development and development theory – but rather as a recurring pattern of perennial speech about such development, theory and method, and would-be practical action. In many development studies and policies this tends to be discourse about solutions which are more likely to be in search of, than for, problems. Whose discourse is this? On the whole this is the perennial speech *of* modernizing elites as well as *about* modernizing elites (neither of which, as most notably in Iran, might on empirical investigation turn out in effect to be modernizing). These are the writers and actors who align their own best efforts with state-building, but in the name of nation-building.

Raymond Apthorpe
Institute of Social Studies, The Hague

Further reading

Adams, A. (1979) 'Open letter to a young researcher', *African Affairs*.
Sunkel, O. (1979) 'The development of development thinking', in J. J. Villamil (ed.) *Transactional Capitalism and National Development*, Hassocks.
Wrigley, E. A. (1972) 'The process of modernization and the industrial revolution in England', *Journal of Interdisciplinary History* I.

See also: economic development; modernity; underdevelopment.

monetarism

Monetarism, a term coined by Karl Brunner in 1968, does not denote a tightly knit school. There are significant disagreements among monetarists. It is sometimes uncertain whether someone is a monetarist, a Keynesian or a neo-classical economist. In Britain monetarism became the doctrine of a political party (Conservatives), while in the USA and Canada it remained essentially an academic discipline. It also received some academic support in Germany. Its leading exponent is Milton Friedman, but another important branch of monetarism is due to Karl Brunner and Allan Meltzer. The leading elements of (academic) monetarism are the quantity theory of money, the use of the growth rate of money as the target of monetary policy, and advocating at least a relatively stable growth rate of money. These elements form a coherent whole, but one can accept the quantity theory without accepting the others, and conversely.

The quantity theory asserts that changes in prices and nominal income are explained primarily by changes in the money supply that are not themselves caused by changes in the demand for money. Suppose the central bank increases bank reserves, so that banks increase outstanding deposits. The public now holds more nominal money. Since its previous holdings corresponded to its desired holdings, it spends the extra money. With demand increasing, firms raise prices. Prices continue to rise as long as demand is excessive, that is, as long as the real money supply is greater than it was before. Eventually prices will have risen in proportion to the initial increase in the *nominal* money supply, so that the *real* money supply is back to where it was before. Prices then no longer rise.

Output and employment will also change in this process. Initially, as demand increases, firms respond by raising output and employment. However, once the real money stock, and hence aggregate demand, have returned to their previous levels output falls to its previous level.

The basic insight of the quantity theory is that the public wants to hold a certain quantity of *real* money. If the nominal money supply is greater, prices rise until the real quantity of money again equals what the public desires. Monetarists view the nominal demand for money as a stable function of nominal income and interest rates, so that if one knows the change in the supply of nominal money, one can predict how much nominal income will have to change for the public's money holdings to be in equilibrium. A similar analysis of the supply and demand for money can be used to explain the relative prices of different monies, that is, the exchange rate.

Keynesians do not deny that such a process occurs. But they reject the monetarist view that fluctuations in the money supply explain most of the fluctuations in nominal income. They attribute more importance to incentives to spend, such as the profitability of investment, or changes in government expenditures. They therefore ascribe a lesser role than monetarists to changes in the money supply. Furthermore, changes in the demand for money also matter. For example, if financial innovations reduce the demand for money, the public will spend more, even though the money supply is constant. Moreover, many believe that changes in the money supply are often due to changes in the demand for money. If the demand for money increases, interest rates rise, and the central bank increases the money supply to hold down interest rates temporarily. Hence, the observed correlation between

changes in money and income that monetarists point to does not indicate that money causes income. In addition, the definition of money is uncertain. Hence, some Keynesians argue, the growth rate of some particular measure of money tells us little.

It is therefore mainly empirical issues that distinguish the quantity theory from Keynesian theory: the stability and predictability of the demand for money, the independence of money supply changes from money demand changes, and the relative importance of the money supply and other expenditure motives as determinants of nominal income. Another difference is that monetarists believe that the private sector is essentially stable, something many Keynesians doubt. Monetarists also focus more on the long run than do Keynesians. A Keynesian may agree with a monetarist that in the long run deficits do not reduce unemployment, but focuses on the short run in which they may. This difference, too, largely reflects an empirical disagreement – the length of the short run. But empirical issues determine the research strategy, and hence the theoretical formulation one uses. Yet with empirical issues playing such a large role, it is not surprising that the distinction between Keynesians and quantity theorists is often not clear-cut.

Another rival to monetarism is new-classical theory that argues that when the public perceives a change in the money supply it adjusts prices and wages immediately instead of changing output. Many new-classical theorists attribute recessions to declines in productivity growth, not to declines in the growth rate of the money supply.

Monetarist and Keynesian views on policy also form a continuum. In the USA monetarists are *relatively* more concerned about inflation and *relatively* less about unemployment than Keynesians are. In Britain, while Keynesian stress demand management policies as the remedy for unemployment, monetarists stress labour-market policies. These disagreements, too, centre on empirical issues. Thus, monetarists believe that expansionary policies do not reduce unemployment for long, that fairly soon the Phillips curve becomes vertical. Keynesians typically argue that that takes a long time, or doubt that the Phillips curve is completely vertical even in the long run.

Monetarists naturally stress monetary policy, not fiscal policy. In Britain the two are closely connected, because the money supply responds strongly to government borrowing.

The central bank has to select one or several targets. Monetarists recommend a single target, the money supply, or the base (currency plus reserves). Others often argue that nominal income, interest rates or the exchange rate are better target, or that the central banks should use many targets.

The best known monetarist policy is to have money grow at a fixed rate, regardless of economic conditions. By no means all monetarists go that far; many just want the money supply to grow at a stabler rate than now. Those advocating a fixed rate maintain that in the past central banks' stabilization policies have *destabilized* the economy. They argue that changes in the money supply affect nominal income with long and variable lags, and that our ability to forecast is limited. Hence, any policy that the central bank selects based on prevailing conditions or on forecasts, may well be inappropriate and destabilizing when it takes effect. Moreover, central banks cannot be trusted. They are motivated by political pressures for inflation and for stable nominal interest rates and by their own bureaucratic interests. Thus they try to hold down interest rates in an expansion while moderating the decline of interest rates that typically occurs during recessions. This generates pro-cyclical fluctuations in the money supply.

To summarize the history of monetarism, after the Keynesian revolution (Keynes 1936) the quantity theory lost most of its support. It regained attention when Friedman (1956) redeveloped it in a form much influenced by Keynes. Subsequently it received strong support from the following sources: Friedman and Schwartz (1936) showed that monetary factors had played a very major role in the Great Depression, and more generally that they plausibly explain US macroeconomic history. Brunner and Meltzer (1989) demonstrated that the Federal Reserve was operating without a coherent framework for economic analysis. From the mid-1960s through the 1970s inflation was high and rising. Finally, from the 1950s through the 1970s the velocity of money was growing at a predictable rate. Monetarism therefore gathered converts.

This changed in the 1980s. In the USA and many other countries velocity became unstable, probably due mainly to financial innovations. The Federal Reserve lowered the inflation rate substantially. Among academic economists emphasis shifted away from the informal theory that monetarists use towards more formal theory. For these reasons monetarism declined. But another important reason is that Keynesian theory has absorbed much of monetarism. It now attributes much greater importance to the money supply than it once did. Keynesians also became much more concerned about political pressures on the central bank, and about its tendency to follow more inflationary policies than it has announced. There is widespread recognition of the difficulties of fine-tuning, and of the Phillips curve being vertical in the long run.

Will monetarism make a comeback as a major independent development? That depends in large part on whether the demand for money will become more predictable again.

Thomas Mayer
University of California

References

Brunner, K. and Meltzer, A. (1989) *Monetary Economics*, Oxford.
Friedman, M. (1956) *Studies in the Quantity Theory of Money*, Chicago.
—— (1968) 'The role of monetary policy', *American Economic Review* 58.
Friedman, M. and Schwartz, A. (1963) *A Monetary History of the United States*, Chicago.
Keynes, J. M. (1936) *The General Theory of Employment, Interest and Money*, London.
Laidler, D. (1982) *Monetarist Perspectives*, Cambridge, MA.
Mayer, T. *et al.* (1978) *The Structure of Monetarism*, New York.

See also: Chicago School; crowding out; demand for money; Friedman, Milton; inflation and deflation; monetary policy; money; money, quantity theory of.

monetary policy

Monetary policy refers to the setting of interest rates to achieve certain economic goals, usually the control of inflation or some measure of real activity. Control means short-term stabilization and/or the achievement of some target level over the longer term. The key issues concern the way in which the policy should be implemented, the choice of goals, and the authorities which should be empowered to take these decisions.

The main *instrument* of monetary policy is the rate of interest charged by the central bank on the money which it provides to the banking system. Whatever the policy goal, day-to-day policy decisions are often taken with reference to an *intermediate target* or *indicator*, such as the exchange rate or the rate of monetary growth.

The money supply itself is not an instrument of monetary policy as the central bank cannot exercise direct control over it. It can, however, exercise indirect control through its control of the rate which it charges to the banking system. At the heart of this system is a group of banks who keep deposit accounts at the central bank. The balances on these accounts, together with cash, constitute the monetary base. In the course of each business day, individuals and firms withdraw money from each of these banks and keep it as cash, or deposit it with the other banks. Towards the end of each day, the accumulation of these transactions leaves some banks owing money to others – money that must be delivered by the end of the day. The debtors usually obtain the necessary money by borrowing it from other banks through the interbank market. Occasionally, however, some of them will find by the close of business that they have not been able to borrow sufficient funds to cover their obligations. They must then turn to the central bank which, as *lender of last resort*, can supply money by buying some of the bank's assets (often Treasury Bills) or providing an overdraft. The interest rate on these funds will influence the rate that the banks charge on their loans to customers and the amount they are willing to lend.

Central banks may attempt to implement monetary policy through *open market operations*, that is, their purchase or sale of financial assets, usually government bonds. Each sale takes money out of the economy and deprives the banking system of some of the funds it will need later in the day to settle its internal debts, that is, the whole system will be short of funds. This ensures that some banks will have to get funds from the central bank which will allow the latter to force interest rates up if it so wishes. However, the central bank cannot refuse to make the funds available unless it is willing to let one or more banks become insolvent. Thus it is not possible for the bank to practise *monetary base control*, although it can of course use the monetary base as an intermediate target and adjust its lending rates accordingly.

It follows that the implementation of monetary policy does not depend upon the existence of *reserve requirements*, that is, the requirement that the banks hold a certain amount of their assets in the form of deposits at the central bank. Banks do, of course, have to borrow from the central bank if these deposits fall below the required level, but this is true even if the required level is zero. Changes in reserve requirements will have an effect on monetary growth but few central banks are willing to use them in such an active fashion. Required reserves provide the central bank with cheap deposits and act as a tax on the banking system.

Arguments about the goals of monetary policy became heated after the publication of Keynes's *General Theory* in 1936. Previously most economists had held the classical view that the level of economic activity could not be influenced by policy actions and that the target for monetary policy should be prices or inflation. Keynes took the opposite view and recommended management of aggregate demand as a means of stabilizing the economy. Keynesians, but not necessarily Keynes himself, also held the view that fiscal, rather than monetary, policy was the most effective demand management tool.

By the 1960s the battle appeared to have been won by the short-term activity stabilizers, and the opposition, by then labelled monetarists, were a dwindling band. However, the experiences of the 1970s began a move towards a long-term inflation goal. The issue turned on whether the economy is self-righting or not. The very essence of Keynesianism is that it is not, or at least not before we shall all be dead.

The monetarists, by now holed-up in Chicago and a few lonely outposts in England, attacked this view on two fronts. First, that it was in fact monetary policy which would have the greater effect on demand. Second, that the economy would always settle to a natural rate of activity and policy makers should attend to improving this natural rate rather than interfering with the market forces which lead the economy towards it. They also added the somewhat inflammatory opinion that the authorities were not competent to adjust demand at the right time. By taking this view, they condemned demand management by both monetary and fiscal policy, but were particularly agitated by the prospect of demand managers using the powerful monetary policy incompetently. Far better, they argued, to take such a potent weapon out of the hands of the managers and assign it to the long-term goal of low inflation by setting a fixed target for the rate of monetary growth.

Nestling between the two great pillars of the mechanics of monetary policy and the structure of the economy is an awkward little subject known as the 'transmission mechanism', by which changes in monetary policy come to affect output and jobs. Views on this changed enormously in the 1970s and 1980s. Previously, it had been thought that monetary policy changes simply caused people and firms to demand more, or less, domestically produced output, or to switch between domestic goods and imports if the policy action moved the exchange rate. Subsequently, it was argued that their behaviour would be influenced by both actual and *expected* policy, and that for a change in monetary policy to have an effect on activity it would have to come as a surprise. For example, if firms knew in advance that the authorities were going to relax monetary policy in an attempt to increase output beyond the natural rate, they would increase their prices in advance. To achieve a temporary increase in output the expansion would have to be greater than expected. To achieve a long-term expansion a sequence of accelerating monetary growth surprises would be necessary, with an accompanying acceleration of inflation.

Theoretical models were developed to analyse these expectational effects, culminating in the *rational expectations hypothesis*, which provided weapons for both sides. First, it was claimed that intelligent individuals could predict all the actions of a rational monetary authority, that is, that policy surprises were impossible. The activists countered that even expected policy can be effective if firms typically set prices before they become aware of future policy actions. Conversely, if the authorities are known to be committed to full employment, wage bargainers have little to fear in pressing for large pay increases because they know that if firms cannot afford them, and start laying off labour, the authorities will increase the level of demand so that they can increase prices to raise the money to meet the enlarged wage bill. Thus stabilization policy creates an *inflationary bias*. Furthermore, active policy makes it difficult for firms to distinguish between those increases in shop prices which indicate that their share of the natural rate of demand has increased, and those which reflect policy actions that will eventually lead to all prices increasing with no long-term demand change. Thus active monetary policy can reduce the efficiency of prices as a signalling mechanism.

The policy game also creates a difficulty for the implementation of a passive long-term inflation target, however. The optimal long-term strategy is to announce that low inflation will be maintained through thick and thin. However, should a recession emerge, the optimal short-term response of a government concerned about its election prospects might be to increase demand by a monetary relaxation. Thus the optimal long-term policy is not consistent with both the short-term objectives of the government and the events that may emerge over time, a problem known as *time inconsistency*.

This lack of *policy credibility* can be overcome by establishing a reputation for riding out recessions without a policy response. Alternatively, the time inconsistency can be removed by changing the objectives of the decision makers – possibly by changing the decision makers themselves, by handing the responsibility to an institution charged with keeping inflation down and with no interest in winning elections. The natural choice for this is, of course, the central bank. The successful anti-inflation performance of the relatively independent Bundesbank in the 1980s and 1990s offered strong support for this choice and was a key factor in the 1990 decision to make the European Central Bank independent of European governments.

David Barr
Brunel University

Reference

Keynes, J. M. (1936) *The General Theory of Employment, Interest and Money*, London.

Further reading

Blanchard, O. J. and Fischer, S. (1989) *Lectures on Macroeconomics*, Cambridge, MA.

Goodhart, C. A. E. (1984) *Monetary Theory and Practice*, Basingstoke.

See also: demand for money; liquidity; macroeconomic policy; monetarism; money, quantity theory of; supply-side economics.

money

Most of the disputes among various schools of thought on the role of money in an economy are due to differing conceptualizations of the functions and properties of money and its relations to the passage of time. Money can be defined only by its essential functions and properties.

In all neo-classical theories (for example, monetarism, general equilibrium theory, neo-Walrasian theory, rational expectations theory and neo-classical synthesis Keynesianism), historical time is treated as if it is irrelevant; all present and future activities are logically determined and paid for at the initial instant. Such theories assume that future events are either known with perfect certainty or known as statistically predictable according to the mathematical laws of probability. Consequently, the sole function of money is as a *numeraire*, that is, a yardstick upon which to measure the relative prices (and therefore scarcities) of the various goods that are produced. In the long run, real output, employment and economic growth are solely determined by the exogenous factors of technology and preferences, in other words, money can not affect long-run real outcomes. Thus while in the short run in neo-classical theory money may have a transient effect on employment, in the long run Say's Law prevails so that supply creates its own demand.

Keynes's revolution against neo-classical theory requires that a monetary economy operate quite differently from a non-monetary system so that in the short as well as the long run, real output, employment and growth are *not* determined solely (or even mainly) by technology and preferences. For Keynes and post-Keynesians, time is a device that prevents everything from happening at once. Production takes time; and money and forward contracts are human institutions created to organize (efficiently) production processes which will operate over an uncertain (not statistically predictable) future. (A forward contract is one that specifies the future date(s) for delivery and payment.) In such a monetary, contractual economy the concept of money requires two concomitant features, which in turn require two necessary properties.

These features were spelled out at the very beginning of Keynes's *Treatise on Money* (1930) 'Money [is] that by delivery of which debt-contracts and price-contracts are *discharged*, and in the shape of which a store of General Purchasing Power is held', that is, money is *the means of contractual settlement*, and a *store of value*, a vehicle for moving purchasing power over time – a time machine.

This second feature is known as *liquidity*. Liquidity can be possessed in various degrees by some, but not all, durables. Since any durable besides money can *not* (by definition) settle a contract, then for durables other than money to be a liquidity time machine they must be resaleable in well-organized, orderly spot markets. The degree of liquidity of any durable asset depends on its prompt resaleability in such markets. A fully liquid asset is always resaleable for a fixed quantity of money. A liquid asset is always resaleable, but its exact market price is uncertain. An illiquid asset is not readily resaleable at any money price.

For Keynes (1936), money (and all liquid assets) possess two essential properties which are inexorably tied to money's two features. These properties are that the elasticity of production is zero (or negligible), and that the elasticity of substitution is zero (or negligible). The meaning of these elasticity properties is, first, that 'Money [and other liquid assets] do not grow on trees' and hence cannot be harvested by the use of labour in the private sector whenever workers are made idle by a lack of effective demand for all other producible goods; and, second, that anything that is easily producible is not a good substitute for money for settling contracts or for use as a liquidity time machine. Consequently, when, in the aggregate, people want to spend some portion of the income they would earn at full employment levels of production on money or other liquid assets, that is, people do not want to commit themselves contractually to buy all the full employment output of industry but instead want to maintain purchasing power to have freedom of future choice while facing an uncertain future, then there will be an insufficient aggregate demand for the full employment output. Firms will not be able to market their full employment production flow profitably, and some workers will be involuntarily unemployed. These unemployed people can not be allocated to meeting the public demand for liquidity by being put to work by private entrepreneurs to harvest money from liquidity trees.

In sum, in a world of uncertainty, the existence of a nonproducible money and the fact that goods are priced via contacts 'in terms of money' is highly significant. Of all the various schools of economic thought, only Keynes (and his post-Keynesian followers) possess a conceptualization of money which reflects its role as a store of value in an uncertain world.

Paul Davidson
University of Tennessee

References

Keynes, J. M. (1930) *A Treatise on Money*, London.
— (1936) *The General Theory of Employment, Interest and Money*, London.

Further reading

Davidson, P. (1994), *Post Keynesian Macroeconomic Theory*, Cheltenham.
Friedman, M. (1974) 'A theoretical framework for monetary analysis', in R. J. Gordon (ed.) *Milton Friedman's Monetary Framework: A Debate with his Critics*, Chicago.
Hicks, J. R. (1977) *Causality in Economics*, New York.
Keynes, J. M. (1973) 'A monetary theory of production', in *The Collected Writings of John Maynard Keynes*, vol. 13, London.
Tobin, J. (1988) 'Theoretical issues in macroeconomics', in G. Feiwel (ed.) *Contemporary Macroeconomics and Distribution*, Albany, NY.

See also: gold standard; Keynesian economics; liquidity; monetarism; money, quantity theory of.

money, quantity theory of

The quantity theory of money is the proposition that there is a causal connection between the quantity of money and the general level of prices. The connection was well established by the middle of the seventeenth century: 'It is a common saying that plenty or scarcity of money makes all things dear or good cheap' (Thomas Mun 1928 [1664]). A modern version is 'Inflation is too much money chasing too few goods'. In its strongest version, not only is money the cause of price changes but also prices are supposed to change in proportion to the monetary change, in the long run. In the sixteenth and seventeenth centuries, discussion of the relation between money and prices could scarcely pass for a *theory*, because there was no articulation of the causal connection. Its status was more that of shrewd observation, the causal role of money made clear by the influx of precious metals from the New World.

The proportionality doctrine was started by John Locke (1923 [1691]). His purpose was to refute the mercantilist equation of money with national wealth by showing that money's value varied inversely with its quantity. His reasoning was based on an abstract comparison of the same economy with two different stocks of money (allowing for the velocity of money's circulation). Hume (1955 [1752]), however, asserted that proportionality applied in the long run to actual variations in the amount of money in real-world economies. This doctrine cannot be supported by Locke's method. No appropriate reasoning was offered by Hume or anyone since, though it is still widely asserted (as the 'neutrality of money').

Hume's treatment of the short-run effects of monetary changes was, in contrast, good theory – indeed the first *explanation* of the relation between money and prices. (In present-day language he explained the transmission mechanism.) An increase of money (from abroad, in exchange for exports) encourages greater output and employment, without, at first, any increase in wages. If workers become scarce, wages will increase (though Hume remarks that the manufacturer will also expect greater productivity). At first, prices of wage-goods are stable and production rises to meet demand. But gradually all prices rise and the situation prior to the monetary increase is restored. This line of reasoning is both congruent with Keynesian export-led growth and similar to the theory put forward by Milton Friedman (1969).

J. S. Mill (1857) provides the bridge to modern theory in two ways: he makes clear that the medium-of-exchange function of money is crucial to quantity theory and he deals with non-metallic, credit money (bank notes, cheques). The older theorists allowed for hoarding, which would dampen the effect on prices. Hoarding is plausible in the case of precious metals, but credit money has no alternative use, making hoarding more difficult to justify. Credit money also gives rise to the possibility that purchases could be made without possessing money at all.

These problems were relatively new. Irving Fisher (1911) formalized them, but did not solve them, by separating currency from bank-deposit money and postulating a different velocity of circulation for each. It is not obvious which should be the larger, or by how much.

An approach to the hoarding problem is provided by the development, in 'Cambridge quantity theory' (Marshall 1923), of the concept of a demand for money based chiefly on transactions needs. Expected expenditure levels were indicated by one's income and wealth. It was considered plausible that some money might be held idle (hoarded) if one had so little wealth that lending at interest was not open to one. This would affect the velocity of circulation but probably not substantially.

Friedman (1956), though beginning from the antithetical proposition that money is an asset to be held, contrives in the end to arrive at a formulation similar to earlier quantity theory. It is implied that an exogenous change in money will affect aggregate money-income, but the division between price and quantity in the long run is no more resolved than it was in Hume's time, and in the short run somewhat less resolved.

Keynes, although originally an adherent of the quantity theory (1923), broke with it in 1936 by providing a rationale for substantial hoarding of money when interest rates were expected to rise, in order to avoid capital losses.

The problem of credit raised by Mill is not amenable to analysis in the demand-for-money framework. It is being addressed by post-Keynesian work on endogenous money (Desai 1987).

Victoria Chick
University of London

References

Desai, M. J. (1987) 'Endogenous and exogenous money', in J. Entwell, M. Milgate and P. Pewman (eds) *The New Palgrave: A Dictionary of Economics*, London.

Fisher, I. (1911) *The Purchasing Power of Money*, New York.

Friedman, M. (1956) 'The quantity theory of money – a restatement', in M. Friedman (ed.) *Studies in the Quantity Theory of Money*, Chicago.

— (1969) 'The role of monetary policy', *American Economic Review* 58.

Hume, D. (1955 [1752]) *Of Money*, in E. Rotwein (ed.) [David Hume's] *Writings on Economics*, London.

Keynes, J. M. (1923) *A Tract on Monetary Reform*, London.

— (1936) *The General Theory of Employment, Interest and Money*, London.

Locke, J. (1923 [1691]) *Some Considerations of the Lowering of Interest and Raising the Value of Money, Works of John Locke*, vol. V, London.

Marshall, A. (1923) *Money, Credit and Commerce*, London.

Mill, J. S. (1857) *Principles of Political Economy*, 2 vols, London.

Mun, T. (1928 [1664]) *England's Treasure by Foreign Trade*, Oxford.

Further reading

Blaug, M. (1978) *Economic Theory in Retrospect*, 3rd edn, London.

Laidler, D. E. W. (1991) *The Golden Age of the Quantity Theory: The Development of Neoclassical Monetary Economics: 1870–1914*, Oxford.

See also: monetarism; monetary policy; money.

monopoly

A firm or individual (the monopolist) has a monopoly over the provision of a good or service when there is no alternative provider. The monopolist can select a combination of price and sales from all the market possibilities represented by the demand curve. There are two factors which limit the monopolist's power to extract profit by increasing price. First, if the product is not a necessity for them, consumers could reject the product and buy other goods; second, if there are close substitutes, for example different brands of the same kind of good, then the consumer can select one of these competing brands. Essentially the more the type of good is a necessity, and the less similar are alternative brands or products, the lower the fall in sales for a given price rise and the greater the monopolist's power to make profit (Chamberlin 1933; Robinson 1933). Advertising tends to increase perceptions of product differences, and increase brand loyalty. This may also prevent competitors from entering the market and thus preserve future monopoly power (Schmalensee 1978).

There are two main reasons why economic welfare may be reduced by the existence of monopoly. First, monopoly power allows price to be set above marginal cost. Thus further (unsupplied) units would cost less than the amount somebody would be willing to pay. The absence of these unsupplied units is an allocative inefficiency caused by the firm's desire to keep prices high. Second, without sufficient competition from other suppliers and with imperfect control by the firm's owners, costs may be inefficiently high. To offset these adverse factors, the firm's monopoly may allow greater economies of scale (in the limit there are cases of 'natural' monopoly where multiple suppliers of, say, piped water would be obviously inefficient). (Schmalensee and Willig 1989; Williamson 1968).

Whether any particular monopoly requires regulation to safeguard the consumers' interests is a matter for anti-trust policy (Scherer and Ross 1990). Regulation may take the form of prevention (by refusing permission for mergers), breaking up existing monopolies, price controls or restrictions on allowable profit. However, all monopoly regulation suffers from the fact that the monopolists know more about their markets than the regulator (asymmetric information).

Monopolists may not be private profit-maximizing firms, but rather state firms pursuing other objectives. Then the welfare arguments have to be reassessed. Also, monopolies (and monopoly power) may be the necessary outcome of the need for dynamic incentives. Thus a patent granted to an invention yields a monopoly to the inventor. Without such patent protection, the investment necessary to produce the invention may not occur. Thus some kinds of monopoly may be inevitable in order to yield appropriate incentives to obtain dynamic efficiency of economic growth through technical innovation.

Finally, monopoly has a natural inverse termed monopsony: only one buyer in a market. Analysis is very similar and examples include the state buying road construction and defence projects.

Norman Ireland
University of Warwick

References

Chamberlin, E. (1933) *The Theory of Monopolistic Competition*, Cambridge, MA.

Robinson, J. (1933) *The Economics of Imperfect Competition*, London.

Scherer, F. M. and Ross, D. (1990) *Industrial Market Structure and Economic Performance*, Boston, MA.

Schmalensee, R. (1978) 'Entry deterrence in the ready to eat breakfast cereal industry', *Bell Journal of Economics* (9).

Schmalensee, R. and Willig, R. D. (1989) *Handbook of Industrial Organization*, Amsterdam.

Williamson, O. (1968) 'Economics as an anti-trust defence: the welfare trade-offs', *American Economic Review* (58).

See also: cartels and trade associations; competition; corporate enterprise; markets; regulation.

morbidity

In literature the term morbidity describes a gloomy state of mind. In the social sciences it refers to health experience, more specifically to episodes of sickness. At any given time a population contains a certain number of sick people, who may be considered in terms of either the number of diseases and injuries or the amount of sickness time they experience. Those issues – sickness, its incidence and its duration – define the study of morbidity. As a subject of study morbidity addresses the quality of life, seeking to learn why sicknesses occur and what effects they have on individuals and society. In mortality studies the idea of prolonging life is familiar, and life expectancy at birth is often employed as a gauge of the success of mortality policies. In morbidity studies, the aim is rather to diminish the number of sickness episodes and to reduce the amount of sickness time that individuals experience. Whereas life expectancy estimates how long members of a population can be expected to live, a counterpart, health expectancy, estimates what portion of that lifetime will be spent in good health and what portion in bad health. In ideal circumstances individuals would live a long life in good health.

Mortality is declining in most world regions. For Western Europe, where the history is known in detail, that decline began in the late eighteenth century, a time when infectious diseases were commonplace. Since that time the risk of dying at any given age has diminished, and life expectancy has increased from about 30 or 35 years at birth to more than 75 years. Although in the past scholars often assumed that morbidity must have closely approximated mortality during the health transition, research into health experience suggests the contrary. At each age the likelihood of death has declined sharply, but the likelihood of falling sick – of initiating a new episode of disease or injury – has declined at a more gradual pace and along a different course. In other words, the likelihood of dying from any given sickness has changed over time, both for individual diseases and for all the ailments that people deem to be sickness. The lethality of diseases declined and humankind gained more control over the causes and risk factors associated with disease and injury. More surprising, the average duration of sickness episodes has increased. Thus health expectancy has not kept pace with the increase in life expectancy.

Several reasons have been advanced for the inverse trends of sickness time and of survival. First, the characteristics of the diseases that people suffer changed from mostly short to mostly prolonged maladies. In the past people were sick more often, but on average their sicknesses were much shorter than those of the late twentieth century. Second, a theory called 'heterogeneous frailty' explains rising sickness time by pointing to changes in population composition. 'New survivors', that is, those individuals who lived longer as mortality declined, appear to have suffered more sickness. Third, medicine has enjoyed notable success at deferring the resolution of long sicknesses, especially in adults. In addition, cultural factors have promoted a broader definition of sickness by the society and the individual.

Over the life course health experiences differ sharply between individuals and between men and women. Some people are often sick while others claim never to have been sick a day in their lives. These differences reflect varying attitudes towards whether a particular experience should be counted as sickness. They also reflect differences in exposure to disease and injury risks, and perhaps also differences in the degree to which prior health experience continues to influence subsequent health. Many diseases leave lasting effects after recovery, and the same is true of commonplace experiences (exposure to solar radiation) and behaviours (cigarette smoking). Those 'insults' appear to accumulate at differential rates. Health experience later in life, and the timing of death, may be due not only to differences in individuals that are present at birth, which is what the theory of heterogeneous frailty suggests, but also to differences acquired over the life course. In the past and the present alike, women report more sicknesses than men, but live longer.

In developed countries the leading problems for morbidity policy deal with the prevention of protracted sickness, including the increasingly elongated final episode of sickness that results in death. Costs of treating sickness have increased in the second half of the twentieth century at a pace faster than most other costs, resulting in a health sector that persistently eats up a growing share of resources. For developing countries the problems in this area are more complex. Especially in Africa and Asia acute infectious diseases, respiratory infections, and chronic degenerative diseases occur simultaneously, demanding a more varied and a costlier set of health policies. The task of research in the social sciences on morbidity is to treat sickness itself as an effect, and to search for the means to reduce its burden on the individual and society.

James C. Riley
Indiana University

Further reading

Alter, G. and Riley, J. C. (1989) 'Frailty, sickness and death: models of morbidity and mortality in historical populations', *Population Studies* 43.
Gruenberg, E. M. (1977) 'The failures of success', *Milbank Memorial Fund Quarterly / Health and Society* 55.
Riley, J. C. (1989) *Sickness, Recovery and Death: A History and Forecast of Ill Health*, London.
Verbrugge, L. M. (1985) 'Gender and health: an update on hypotheses and evidence', *Journal of Health and Social Behavior* 26.

See also: epidemiology; fertility; health transition; life tables and survival analysis; medical sociology; mortality; public health.

mortality

While individuals are born and die only once, populations experience a series of births and deaths of individuals. Social scientists study the rate of mortality, the social and economic determinants of mortality rates, and the ways in which societies deal with the death of an individual. The simplest summary measure of mortality is the crude death rate or CDR (the number of deaths per year per thousand population). It measures the effect of mortality on the population growth rate. However, the CDR is affected by the age distribution in the population. Therefore, it is not useful for comparing mortality levels in populations with different levels of fertility or populations affected by migration.

More refined comparisons use age-specific death rates (annual deaths per thousand in a specific age group). A related measure is the infant mortality rate (IMR). The IMR for a year is the number of infant deaths (deaths before the first birthday) during the year per 1,000 live births during the same year. For a cohort of live births, the IMR is the proportion who die before their first birthday. The IMR varies from a low of about 5 to over 300 per 1,000. The IMR is often used as an indicator of mortality in the whole population since estimates of infant mortality are available for many populations that lack reliable estimates of adult mortality.

A life table characterizes mortality in a period of years by showing what would happen to a group of newborns (a hypothetical cohort) if the current age-specific death rates at each age did not change during their lifetime. The expectation of life at birth or life expectancy (e_0) is the average age at death in a life table. In general, e_0 is not the most common age at death for the hypothetical cohort. For example, in the USA in 1989 the life expectancy was 75.3 years. However, the life table suggests that only about 24 per cent of hypothetical cohort would die when they were between ages 70 and 79 whereas 47 per cent would die over age 80. The value of e_0 is pulled down by the small number of individuals who die at very young ages.

Mortality has declined rapidly since the 1830s in European populations and more recently in non-European populations. Most of the decline resulted from reductions in deaths to infectious and parasitic diseases. Although modern medical advances such as antibiotics and vaccines have been important in declines in developing countries, they were less important in the mortality declines in populations of European origin. Mortality rates to such infectious diseases as tuberculosis, diphtheria, measles, diarrhoeas and pneumonia declined drastically before the development of effective medical measures to prevent or treat these diseases (Omran 1980). Most of these declines can be attributed to changes in nutrition, basic public health interventions such as improved water and sanitation and changes in personal behaviours such as basic cleanliness and child-feeding practices. The relative importance of behavioural change and medical advances in recent mortality declines in low mortality populations is a subject of debate (Blackburn 1989).

The mortality declines have encouraged changes in social structures (United Nations 1986). For example, in high mortality populations there are high proportions who are widowed and orphaned. These societies generally have strong social mechanisms for ensuring the welfare of widows and orphans. These often include rapid remarriage of widows or a sharing of the financial responsibility for children among the father's or the mother's brothers. In societies with low mortality, these mechanisms become less important and the support of elderly parents during a potentially long period of ill-health and low economic productivity becomes a more significant problem.

Although the age distribution of a population is an important factor in shaping social structure, mortality does not play the major role in this. In particular, the proportion of the population that is over 65 is largely determined by fertility rates which affect the ratio of the number of children to the number of persons of childbearing age. However, recent mortality declines have increased the proportion of the 'old' (over 65) who are among the 'oldest old' (over 85).

The age distribution of dying persons is also important. In a typical high mortality country about 15 per cent of the population and 40 per cent of the deaths are under age 5. In the USA in 1980 only 7 per cent of the population and 3 per cent of the deaths were under age 5. Most deaths in the USA are over age 75 (44 per cent) compared to only 11 per cent of the deaths in a typical high mortality population. This distribution has implications for cultural attitudes towards life and death. For example, in some high mortality societies children are not given a name until they have survived the first few weeks of life.

In most societies mortality rates vary with indicators of social status such as education, income and occupation. These differences are related to differences in nutrition, housing, access to and use of health services, and such behavioural differences as child-feeding practices, smoking and alcohol consumption (United Nations 1982).

Douglas C. Ewbank
University of Pennsylvania

References

Blackburn, A. (1989) 'Trends and determinants of CHD mortality: changes in risk factors and their effects', *International Journal of Epidemiology* 18 (supplement 1).

Omran, A. R. (1980) 'Epidemiologic transition in the U.S.', *Population Bulletin* 32.

United Nations (1982) *Levels and Trends of Mortality Since 1950*, Department of International Economic and Social Affairs (ST/ESA/SER.A/74), New York.

—— (1986) *Consequences of Mortality Trends and Differentials*, Department of International Economic and Social Affairs (ST/ESA/SER.A/95), New York.

Further reading

Gribble, J. and Preston, S. (eds) (1993) *The Epidemiological Transition: Policy and Planning Implications for Developing Countries*, Washington, DC.

Mosley, W. H. and Chen, L. C. (1984) 'An analytic framework for the study of child survival in developing countries', *Population and Development Review* 10 (supplement).

See also: demographic transition; gerontology, social; health transition; morbidity; population geography; population policy; population projections; public health; vital statistics.

motivation

Motivation, as the word implies, is what *moves* people. If most of psychology deals with 'How' questions, like 'How do people perceive?' or 'How do people learn habits?' the field of motivation is concerned with more fundamental 'Why?' questions. The most basic of these include 'Why does the organism behave at all?', 'Why does this behaviour lead in one direction rather than another at a particular time?' and 'Why does the intensity or persistence of the behaviour vary at different times?'

The main types of answers which have been given to these sorts of questions since the end of the nineteenth century can be listed roughly chronologically in terms of when they were first proposed. Although each approach was developed to some extent in reaction to what went before, and was seen by its adherents as superior in some respect to its predecessors, proponents of all these approaches will be found in one form or another in present-day psychology.

First, the earliest approach was that of *hedonism*, which said simply that people behave in such a way as to maximize pleasure and minimize pain. From this perspective individuals were seen as being essentially rational beings, making sensible decisions about what courses of action to take in the light of their likely consequences in relation to pleasure or pain.

Second, the development of *psychoanalysis* from the early twentieth century onwards marked a break with this commonsense view. Freud argued that people are irrational and that their behaviour is largely determined by the outcome of the continual struggle between the powerful unconscious urges of the id (especially the sexual drive or eros) and the individual's conscience, or superego, representing the dictates of society (see especially Freud 1933). Every subsequent form of depth psychology has had at least this in common with Freud's original version: that individuals are seen as being to some extent at the mercy of psychological forces which are outside their conscious control, and that they are usually unaware of the real reasons for their actions.

Third, *instinct* theorists, like William McDougall (1908), also emphasized the non-rational side of human nature, bringing out the continuity between animal and human motivation, and answering the 'Why' questions in the context of Darwinian biology. This general approach was readopted by ethologists like Tinbergen (1951), although the research techniques and interests of ethologists are remote from those of McDougall.

Fourth, as laboratory experimental work with animals came to dominate psychology, so another motivational concept began to hold sway: that of *drive*. This concept was introduced by Woodworth (1918) to describe the strength of internal forces which impel the organism into action. The main advantage of this concept was that drive could be defined operationally, for example, by the number of hours of food deprivation; in this way motivation could be quantified and made more amenable to rigorous scientific investigation. There was broad agreement that such biological

drives existed as a hunger drive, a thirst drive and a sexual drive; later some theorists added various social drives and even such drives as an exploratory drive. The use of the concept probably reached its high point in the elaborate learning theory of Clark Hull (1943), one of the basic ideas of which was that the aim of all behaviour is 'drive-reduction', this being 'reinforcing' to the organism.

Fifth, a major problem with the notion of drive-reduction was that the organism, especially the human organism, often seems to be engaged in attempts to increase its stimulation and to present itself with challenges, rather than always to maintain drive at as low a level as possible. This problem was overcome with *optimal arousal theory*, originally proposed by Hebb (1955), which suggested that the organism is seeking to attain, and maintain, some level of arousal which is intermediate on the arousal dimension. Thus, the organism is provoked into action not only when arousal is too high but also when it is too low (the latter being experienced, for example, by feelings of boredom). A further advantage of this theory was that the arousal concept provided a way of linking psychological and physiological research.

Sixth, a completely different approach to motivation was taken by Maslow (1954), with his notion of *self-actualization*, a concept which has subsequently become one of the mainstays of humanistic psychology. The general idea is that people have a fundamental need to grow psychologically in such a way that they become fully individual and fulfil their own potentials. According to Maslow there is a need hierarchy which ascends from physiological and safety needs, up through the need to belong and love and the need for self-esteem, to the highest level, that of self-actualization itself. Living involves a kind of snakes-and-ladders course up and down this hierarchy, but the aim is always to reach the top, success in which is marked by so-called peak experiences.

Finally, in the 1980s *reversal theory* (Apter 1989) made a radical challenge to the basic assumption on which all the other theories of motivation are based, namely, that of homeostasis (in its broadest systems-theory sense). This implies that there is some single preferred state which the organism attempts at all times to achieve, and to maintain once achieved. This may be, for example, low drive, intermediate arousal or the top of a need hierarchy. However it is defined, it remains a relatively unchanging end-point for the organism to strive towards. Reversal theory argues that this is an absurd oversimplification and that, at least in the human case, people want quite contrary things at different times and are in this respect inherently inconsistent. To give just one example, sometimes people want extremely low arousal (for example, when very tired) and at other times they want extremely high arousal (such as during sexual intercourse or while watching sport). The end-point, therefore, is dynamic rather than static, and the overall situation is better characterized as one of multistability than homeostasis.

Michael J. Apter
Yale University

References

Apter, M. J. (1989) *Reversal Theory: Motivation, Emotion and Personality*, London.
Freud, S. (1933) *New Introductory Lectures on Psychoanalysis*, New York.
Hebb, D. O. (1955) 'Drives and the C.N.S. (Conceptual Nervous System)', *Psychological Review* 62.
Hull, C. L. (1943) *Principles of Behavior*, New York.
McDougall, W. (1908) *An Introduction to Social Psychology*, London.
Maslow, A. H. (1954) *Motivation and Personality*, New York.
Tinbergen, N. (1951) *The Study of Instinct*, London.
Woodworth, R. S. (1918) *Dynamic Psychology*, New York.

Further reading

Evans, P. (1989) *Motivation and Emotion*, London.
Franken, R. E. (1988) *Human Motivation*, 2nd edn, Monterey, CA.
Houston, J. P. (1985) *Motivation*, New York.

See also: instinct; learning; psychoanalysis.

movements, social *see* social movements

multicultural education

'Multicultural education' began as an educational reform movement in the USA during the civil rights struggles of African Americans in the 1960s and 1970s. Substantial societal changes such as the integration of public schools and an ever-increasing immigrant population have had a profound impact on educational institutions. As educators struggle to explain the disproportionate failure and dropout rates of students from marginalized ethnic groups, some proposed that these students lack sufficient cultural knowledge for academic success. However, many multicultural theorists attribute school failure to institutional inequities that create obstacles to marginalized youths' academic success.

Banks (1993) has described the evolution of multicultural education in four phases. First, there are efforts to incorporate ethnic studies at all levels of the curriculum. Second, this is followed by multi-ethnic

education, an attempt to establish educational equity through the reform of the entire educational system. Third, other marginalized groups, such as women, people with disabilities, and gays and lesbians, begin to demand fundamental changes in educational institutions. The addition of various groups with differing needs and agendas has resulted in a myriad of theoretical focuses. However, during the fourth phase of theory development, research and practice, attention to the interrelationship of race, gender and class has resulted in a common goal for most theorists, if not practitioners, of multicultural education. This reform movement seeks nothing less than the transformation of the schooling process and educational institutions at all levels so that all students, whatever their race or ethnicity, disability, gender, social class or sexual orientation, will enjoy equal opportunities to learn.

Most proponents of multicultural education agree that their goal is an education that is anti-racist; attends to the basic skills and knowledge necessary to world citizenry; is important for all students; is pervasive throughout all aspects of the education system; develops attitudes, knowledge and skills that enable students to work for social justice; is a process in which staff and students together unlearn anti-democratic attitudes and behaviours and learn the importance of cultural variables for academic success; and employs a critical pedagogy that emphasizes the social construction of knowledge and enables students to develop skills in decision making and social action (Nieto 1992). They share also a view of the school as a social system of interrelated components such as staff attitudes and actions, school policy and politics, school culture and hidden curriculum, student learning styles, assessment and testing procedures, instructional materials, formalized curriculum of study, teaching styles and strategies, languages and dialects of the school, and community participation. Multicultural education, then, extends beyond reform of the curriculum to the transformation of all components in the system.

Ronald W. Wilhelm
University of North Texas

References

Banks, J. (1993) 'Multicultural education: historical development, dimensions, and practice', *Review of Research in Education* 19.
Nieto, S. (1992) *Affirming Diversity: The Sociopolitical Context of Multicultural Education*, New York.

Further reading

Banks, J. (1994) *An Introduction to Multicultural Education*, Needham Heights, MA.

Sleeter, C. and Grant, C. (1988) *Making Choices for Multicultural Education: Five Approaches to Race, Class, and Gender,* Columbus, OH.

See also: education; ethnic politics.

multinational enterprises

A multinational enterprise owns and controls productive activities located in more than one country. It owns the outputs of these activities even though it may not own the assets used: these may be hired locally in each country. The multinational does not necessarily transfer capital abroad; finance can often be obtained locally as well. The multinational is thus, first, an international producer, and only second, a foreign investor.

The activities of the multinational enterprise form an integrated system; they are not usually a mere portfolio of unrelated operations. The rationale for integration is that managerial control within the enterprise co-ordinates the activities more profitably than would arm's length contractual relations (Buckley and Casson 1991).

The antecedents of the modern multinational enterprise are found in the late nineteenth century, in British direct investments in the colonies, and in the merger movement in the USA from which the modern corporation evolved. In the interwar period, multinational operations focused upon backward integration into minerals (especially oil). Horizontal integration was effected through international cartels rather than multinational firms. After the Second World War, many US enterprises began to produce in Western Europe, particularly in high-technology industries producing differentiated products. They transferred to Europe new US technology, together with improved management and accounting practices, and the experience of selling to a multicultural market of the kind that was developing within the European Community. In the 1970s European firms began to produce in the USA on a larger scale than before, often in the same industries in which US firms were producing in Europe. At the same time, Japanese firms began to produce abroad on a large scale in low-wage South-East Asian countries, particularly in low-technology industries such as textiles.

The value added by some of the world's largest multinationals now exceeds the gross national products of some of the smaller countries in which they produce. However, there are increasing numbers of very small multinational firms: not all multinationals conform to the popular image of the giant corporation.

Multinational operations provide firms with a number of benefits in addition to the operating economies afforded by integration. Intermediate products transferred between the parent company and its overseas subsidiaries – or between one subsidiary and another – can be valued at transfer prices which differ from those prevailing in arm's length trade. The transfer prices can be set so as to minimize *ad valorem* tariff payments, to reallocate profits to subsidiaries in low-tax countries, and to allow the enterprise to bypass exchange controls by disguising capital transfers as income. Transfer prices are particularly difficult for fiscal authorities to detect when the resources transferred are inherently difficult to value: this is particularly true of payments for technology and management services which are very common in firms in high-technology industries. Reliable evidence on transfer pricing is difficult to obtain, though there are some proven instances of it.

Multinational operations also give the enterprise access to privileged information through membership of producers' associations in different countries, and enable it to co-ordinate internationally the lobbying of government for favourable changes in the regulatory environment. Multinationals are often accused of enlisting the support of powerful governments in the pursuit of their interests in foreign countries, though once again reliable evidence is difficult to obtain. The United Nations actively monitors the behaviour of multinationals through its Centre on Transnational Corporations.

Mark Casson
University of Reading

Reference

Buckley, P. J. and Casson, M. C. (1991) *The Future of the Multinational Enterprise,* 2nd edn, London.

Further reading

Buckley, P. J. and Casson, M. C. (1985) *Economic Theory of the Multinational Enterprise: Selected Papers,* London.
Dunning, J. H. (1992) *Multinational Enterprises and the Global Economy,* Wokingham.

See also: business concentration; cartels and trade associations; globalization; international trade.

myth *see* folklore and myth

N

national income analysis

In any economy every year there are millions of transactions which combine to give the overall level of economic activity. It is the classification, presentation and study of statistics relating to such transactions which is the concern of national income analysis. Such information is vital to policy makers in assessing what changes are needed in short-term economic policy and in assessing long-term performance of the economy, the latter being of particular interest to developing economies. International organizations may use national income as a basis for allocating aid or demanding contributions to their budget.

The first works in national income were by Sir William Petty and Gregory King in England in the seventeenth century. Modern pioneers include Kuznets in the USA and Bowley, Stamp and Clark in the UK. The development and use of Keynesian economics gave a great impetus to national income analysis during and after the Second World War with Richard Stone, Nobel Laureate 1984, as the leading figure (Stone and Stone 1965).

The central point of national income analysis is the measurement of the amount of economic activity or national product: that is, the value of all goods and services crossing the production boundary. There are three methods of arriving at this aggregate figure. First, the *income method* totals all incomes earned in economic activity in the form of wages, rent and profits (including undistributed amounts). Old-age pensions and similar transfer payments are excluded as not representing economic activity. Second, the *expenditure method* totals all items of final expenditure – private and government expenditure on current consumption and industrial and government purchases of capital equipment. Payments by one firm to another for raw materials or components or other inputs must be excluded. Such items of *intermediate expenditure* are used up in the production process and do not cross the production

boundary. Third, the *production method* looks at each firm and industry and measures its *value added* – the value of its output less the value of intermediate purchases from other firms. This represents an individual firm's contribution to the national product.

When due allowance is made for imports and exports, these three methods will, in principle, yield identical estimates of national income. In practice this is not always the case due to a less than perfect supply of information to government statisticians who are required often to reconcile three slightly differing estimates.

It is generally agreed that national income is a measure of economic activity. Unfortunately there is no general agreement about what constitutes economic activity, that is, where to draw the production boundary. Transfer payments and intermediate expenditures have been noted as transactions which are excluded because they do not cross the production boundary. Many countries follow the UN System of National Accounts (SNA) and include all goods and services (including the services of government employees) for which there is a payment, either in money or in kind. The principal difference occurs in the Soviet Material Product System (MPS) which emphasizes material output and excludes government services and many personal services such as entertainment and hairdressing.

Whatever definition is adopted, there are three different pairs of concepts of national income which can be used. First, a measure of *gross national product* makes no allowance for depreciation – wear and tear of capital equipment. *Net national product* subtracts an estimate of depreciation from the gross measure, and is a more accurate reflection of the achievement of the economy. Second, if expenditures are valued at the prices paid by purchasers they will include indirect taxes and will yield a measure of national income at *market prices*. For many purposes of comparison, both internally and externally, it is desirable to deduct indirect taxes (and add on any subsidies) and obtain a measure at *factor cost*, which is the essential costs of production. Such a measure is obtained automatically using the income or production methods. The third pair are measures of gross *domestic* product (GDP) and gross *national* product (GNP). The former relates to all economic activity taking place within the geographical limits of the economy. The latter measures economic activity carried out by the resources – labour and capital owned by national members of the economy. In many developing countries dependent on foreign capital, the outflow of profits means that GDP can exceed GNP by up to 20 per cent. These pairs of concepts can be combined in various ways, the most common being gross domestic product at factor cost.

The three methods of measuring national income serve as a focus for different analyses of the aggregate. The income accounts can be used to analyse the shares of wages and profits in total national income and the equality, or otherwise, of the distribution of this income to individuals. The details of the production accounts enable one to examine the relative importance of different industries (for example, manufacturing and services), of different regions in the country, or of privately and publicly owned production. On the expenditure side, much attention has focused in Western Europe on the split between private and public spending. In general, economists are interested in the division between consumption and investment (the purchase of new capital equipment). Here national income analysis is very closely related to macroeconomics and the study of what determines the size of these items and how changes in them affect the overall level of national income.

All transactions are measured in money terms and give national income in *current prices*, but it is necessary to allow for price changes when making comparisons between years. Values at current prices are adjusted by an appropriate index of prices in order to obtain estimates in *constant prices*. Any observed changes will then reflect only changes in quantity and not in price.

Table 1. Social accounting matrix UK 1982 (£ billion)

Payments by \ Payments to		Production		Consumption		Capital accumulation	Rest of the world	Totals
		Goods and services	Taxes on goods and services	Private sector	Public sector			
Production	Goods and services	–	–	136.5 CH	55.6 CG	37.8 V	67.8 X	299.7
	Taxes on goods and services	–	–	30.6	4.5	3.2	3.3	41.6
Consumption (income and outlay)	Private sector	192.3 YH	–	–	50.4 HG	–	1.6 E	244.3
	Public sector	7.2 YG	41.6	58.4 GH	–	–		107.2
Capital accumulation		33.0 D	–	18.5 SH	–5.1 SG	–	–	46.4
Rest of the world		67.2 M	–	0.3 TH	1.8 TG	5.4 B	–	74.7
Totals		299.7	41.6	244.3	107.2	46.4	74.7	

CH – household consumption; CG – government current expenditure; V – capital formation; X – exports of goods and services; YH – private sector incomes (wages; profit; rent); HG – transfers from government to private sector (including Social Security benefits); E – net income from abroad; YG – public sector trading surplus; GH – payments by private sector to government (taxes on income; Social Security contributions); D – depreciation or capital consumption; SH – private sector saving; SG – public sector saving; M – imports of goods and services; TH – private transfers abroad (net); TG – government transfers abroad; B – net investment abroad (= balance of payments on current account)

Gross domestic product at factor cost = YH + YG + D = 232.5

National income analysis originated in the measurement of production, income and expenditure aggregate flows, but gradually more and detailed transactions have been included. The analysis of transactions between firms and industries known as *input-output* analysis is a separate topic. Borrowing and lending, that is, transactions in financial assets, are analysed in a *flow-of-funds table*, and the accounting system can be extended to include stocks as well as flows. *National balance sheets* record the value of assets, financial and physical, held by members of the economy at the end of each accounting period. The presentation and analysis of this more complicated system of accounts is greatly facilitated by showing the data in a large square table (see Table 1) recording transactions between sectors of the economy in the columns and those in the rows. Known as a *social accounting matrix*, this is the most recent methodological development in this field.

A. G. Armstrong
University of Bristol

Reference

Stone, R. and Stone, G. (1965) *National Income and Expenditure*, 7th edn, London.

Further reading

Abraham, W. I. (1969) *National Income and Economic Accounting*, Englewood Cliffs, NJ.
Beckerman, W. (1976) *An Introduction to National Income Analysis*, London.

See also: investment; national wealth.

national wealth

The wealth of a nation comprises a wide range of assets including both physical capital and net claims on other countries. The physical capital itself is not easily quantified. The United Nations *System of National Accounts* (1968), however, provides conventional guidelines for building up an inventory of physical assets. Broadly, vehicles, plant and machinery, and buildings are entered at their market value, after allowing for depreciation. Land is valued at its improved value, but no allowance is made for unextracted minerals or growing crops and forests. Equally, and perhaps most importantly, no allowance is made for the human capital possessed by the nation, despite the fact that the productive skills of its people may be its most important resource. Wealth estimates for the UK are to be found in Revell (1967) while for the USA they are provided by Goldsmith (1982). In both cases annual statistical estimates are provided of some of the components of national wealth.

In an attempt to measure national wealth, net claims on other nations represent real resources available to the home country, and thus net fixed and portfolio investment must be counted together with foreign currency reserves and other lending to the rest of the world, net of borrowing from the rest of the world. But the network of financial claims within a country has no direct bearing on its national wealth. A country is not richer because the government has borrowed a large national debt from the private sector (although it may be if the government has invested the money it has borrowed more productively than the private sector would have). Individual holders of the national debt are, however, richer because they hold the debt, and in a full analysis of national wealth the economy is broken up into institutional sectors. The wealth of each sector includes not only its physical assets and its net claims on the rest of the world but also its net claims on the other sectors in the economy. Because only net claims are included, the sum of the net wealth of each institutional sector will equal the national wealth, in the same way as transfer payments have to be netted out when adding up institutional income to arrive at national income.

Just as some physical assets are conventionally omitted in the estimation of national wealth, so some financial claims are omitted in the compilation of estimates of sectoral wealth. Buiter (1983) presents a more general accounting framework which includes the capitalized value of social security and national insurance benefits as a liability of central government, and the capitalized value of future tax receipts as an asset, although such an approach can be criticized because future tax rates can change, and there is no obvious reason to capitalize these flows on the basis of any particular future path of tax and payment rates.

Martin Weale
University of Cambridge

References

Buiter, W. M. (1983) 'Measurement of the public sector deficit and its implications for policy evaluation and design', *International Monetary Fund Staff Papers*.
Goldsmith, R. W. (1982) 'The National Balance Sheet of the United States, 1953–1980', NBER.
Revell, J. L. (1967) *The Wealth of the Nation*, Cambridge, UK.
United Nations (1968) *System of National Accounts*, New York.

See also: national income analysis.

nationalism

Nationalism is the belief that each nation has both the right and the duty to constitute itself as a state. There are many difficulties in specifying what a nation is – in

Europe, for example, the candidates range from the Welsh and the Basques to Occitanians and Northumbrians – but some common culture is indispensable and a shared language highly desirable. The Swiss have so far got by without a common language, but its lack has sorely tried the rulers of Belgium. Nationalist theory usually attributes conflict to cross-national oppression, and thus offers a promise of world peace when self-determination has become a global reality.

Nationalism emerged in the hatred of cosmopolitanism which registered the resentment of Germans and other Europeans who were coming to feel marginal in terms of the universalistic rationalism of the French Enlightenment. The romantic idea that true humanity must be mediated by a deep involvement in one's own unique culture led to an admiration for songs, poems, stories, plays and other creations understood as emanations of the national soul. The language of a people was accorded a unique value, no less as the medium of cultural self-expression than as a practical rule of thumb about how far the boundaries of a putative nation might stretch. The conquests of Napoleon turned these particularistic passions in a practical direction, and Fichte's *Addresses to the German Nation* delivered at Berlin in 1807–8 struck a responsive chord throughout Germany. Italy and Germany were both plausible candidates for state creation and both duly became states, though Italy remains imperfectly national to this day, while German unity owed more to Bismarck than to popular passion for nationhood.

The spread of nationalist ideas to Eastern Europe and beyond, where very different peoples were inextricably intertwined, was bound to create difficulties. Doctrinal diffusion was facilitated by the growth of industry, and of cities. Teachers, journalists, clergy and other intellectuals found in nationalist ideas an identity for the present and a vision for the future. Some set to work writing down languages previously purely oral; others constructed a literature and elicited a suitable history. Opera and the novel were favourite vehicles of nationalist feeling. The politics of these endeavours triumphed with the Treaty of Versailles in 1918, which settled Europe in terms of the principle of national self-determination.

Throughout Africa and Asia, nationalist ideas fuelled the campaigns to replace the old European empires with home-grown rulers, but since there were few plausible nations in this area, successor states which had been constructed on a variety of principles claimed freedom in order to *begin* the process of cultural homogenization which might lead to nationhood. Pakistan, based upon the religious identity of Islam, attempted to hold together two separated areas inherited from the British Raj, and could not be sustained in that form; the eastern region broke off as Bangladesh in 1971. The artificial boundaries of imperial Africa have, however, been a surprisingly successful container of the often chaotic mixture of tribes they contained, though virtually all have had to compensate for lack of homogeneity by centralizing and frequently tyrannizing governments.

Political scientists often find in nationalism an attractive form of explanation because it promises to explain the hidden causes of conflict between different ethnic groups. In this usage, nationalism is not a belief, but rather a force supposed to move people to both action and belief. Such a concept provokes a search for the conditions under which the force is triggered. The promise of this research programme, like many another in political science, far exceeds the performance. Nationalism is better treated as a complex of ideas and sentiments which respond flexibly, decade by decade, to new situations, usually situations of grievance, in which peoples may find themselves.

Kenneth Minogue
London School of Economics and Political Science

Further reading

Anderson, B. (1991) *Imagined Communities*, London.
Gellner, E. (1983) *Nations and Nationalism*, Oxford.
Hertz, F. (1944) *Nationality in History and Politics*, London.
Kedourie, E. (1970) *Nationalism in Asia and Africa*, London.
Smith, A. D. (1971) *Theories of Nationalism*, London.

See also: ethnic politics; fascism; federation and federalism; tribe.

nationalization

At the heart of the term nationalization is the act of converting a privately owned resource into one owned by the central government (or local government in the case of 'municipalization'). One might then ask how the use and development of the resource and the economic organization of production may be predicted to change. Instead of exploring this issue, many economists in both Europe and North America have taken an essentially prescriptive stance. 'What advice can one give about the use of the resources?' they have asked, invariably on the presumption that the managers, civil servants and ministers are disinterested recipients of that advice. Since no one would want to deny that resources should be used efficiently, economists have translated their own concept of efficiency into guidelines of behaviour. Publicly owned industries should, as a first approximation, set user prices and extend the use of resources up to the point where the marginal cost of output equals price. The rationale for this is that no gains could then be made by switching resource usage in or out of the industry, since consumer valuation of the marginal dose of resources is just equal to its valuation in other activities. The implications of such a rule are quite striking, suggesting, for example, different electricity tariffs for different times of day, high fares and tariffs for transport, gas and electricity to high-cost rural areas, low fares and freight rates for bulky, long-distance rail journeys. Much work has been undertaken on the detailed implementation of these policy proposals, in terms of identifying short and long-run marginal costs, demand elasticities and time-stream aspects of investment projects. While many economists have not felt that the price at marginal cost rule should be modified to take into account questions of income distribution – on the grounds that the tax system is the way to handle that – they have not advocated the simple rule when spill-over effects exist or when information flows have been regarded as deficient. Health and education are therefore viewed as areas raising other considerations.

The forgotten question about how the use of resources would actually change under public ownership re-emerged in the 1970s, partly as a product of the growing influence of a persistent element in US economic thinking – the study of institutional behaviour – and partly because the economists' policy prescriptions were either ignored or found too difficult to implement. The restriction of a private interest to the end of promoting a public interest can be achieved in a variety of ways. Such 'regulation' has a long history in Britain, embracing areas like the factory inspectorate and the control of private railway and fuel companies in the interwar period. The shift in the immediate post-1945 period to public ownership of strategic industries may itself be a reflection of the siege mentality of the 1930s and 1940s. Study of such issues is still awaited. Instead the main thrust of 'positive' theories has come from US thinking on the property rights characteristics of public firms. For example, one approach stresses that citizen-owners can dispose of their rights in publicly owned activities only by engaging in high-cost activities like migration or concerted political action. This is contrasted with private ownership, where each owner has the unilateral ability to buy and sell shares, an act viewed as a capitalization of the expected results of current management action. A significant wedge between owner and management therefore arises in public firms, the nearest approximation to which for private firms is the cost to owners of monitoring management behaviour. In the former case the wedge permits scope for discretionary behaviour by civil servants, management and politicians. The precise outcome in each public firm would depend on the way in which property rights are specified and the constraints on the various parties in the pursuit of their own utility maximizing position. But the broad expectation is that productivity will be lower and unit costs higher in public than in private firms. Testing such theories is difficult, for when public

firms have product monopolies there is no contemporaneous private firm to act as benchmark, and in the absence of monopoly one has to separate the effects of competition from the effects of ownership. Because of the wide variety of institutional types within many of its industries, the USA is proving a fruitful data source with comparisons between publicly owned firms (municipal rather than national) and private firms, some of which are regulated. The evidence on productivity and unit costs shows a very varied pattern, with public firms coming out better in electricity supply, private firms in refuse collection and water supply, and with no clear-cut differences in transport. Pricing structures in public firms seem unambiguously to be less closely geared to the supply costs of particular activities, though whether this is due to electoral influences, empire building or a disinterested pursuit of fairness is not yet clear. Little work has yet been done on explaining why some activities are taken into public ownership whilst others are not.

Robert Millward
University of Manchester

Further reading

Chester, N. (1975) *The Nationalisation of British Industry 1945–51*, London.
Millward, R. and Parker, D. (1983) 'Public and private enterprise: relative behaviour and efficiency', in R. Millward and M. T. Sumner (eds) *Public Sector Economics*, London.

See also: mixed economy; privatization.

natural resource economics

The field of natural resource economics includes both descriptive and normative studies of the allocation of natural resources – resources created not through human actions but available from nature. Key issues relate the amounts of particular resources that will or should be transformed in economic processes rather than left in a natural state, and the balance in resource use between present and future years or generations.

Natural resources – particularly forests, fisheries, energy, and agricultural land – have interested economists since Adam Smith, but only recently have theories been developed that are specific to natural resources. Resource economics examines the development and use of natural resources: coal mines, forests, fisheries, petroleum and land. It is traditionally distinguished from environmental economics, which examines the impact of human activities on the natural environment, and, conversely, the influences of the natural environment on human activities, such as air and water pollution, waste disposal and biodiversity preservation.

The traditional distinction has blurred as the linkages between the two branches of economics have become more obvious. The materials balance concept reminds us that every ton of material initially from the natural environment may be cycled through the economy but ultimately returns as a ton of material to the natural environment, for example, coal from under the ground remains in the economic system until burned. It then returns to the natural environment as atmospheric carbon dioxide emissions, and as ash and sludge. The natural environment can be seen as providing limited waste disposal locations, and is thus a natural resource. Plant and animal populations of forests and fisheries are part of the natural environment.

A second distinction is between renewable and depletable resources. Renewable resources, such as forests, fisheries and clean air or water, are characterized by self-renewing resource stocks. The renewal rate may depend upon the stock size, environmental characteristics and human interventions. Depletable ('non-renewable') or ('exhaustible') resources, such as petroleum, iron ore, precious minerals or virgin wilderness, are characterized by resource stocks that are not self-renewing. For both renewable and depletable resources, the resource stock limits the maximum usage rate. A central issue is *when* natural resources should be used, because use reduces subsequent stock availability. Thus use incurs an opportunity cost, reflecting the economic value of the subsequent stock availability reduction. The issue is particularly salient for depletable resources that can be harvested or extracted only once.

A third distinction is whether a resource is managed as common property, available to everyone, or as private property, controlled by a few individuals. Typically, users of common property resources ignore their opportunity costs, leading to overuse. Conversely, firmly vested property rights lead potential users to incorporate opportunity costs and thus improve resource use.

Natural resource economics is inherently interdisciplinary. Study requires information from physics, engineering, chemistry, biology, ecology, political science, law and economics. Current theories reflect this interdisciplinary reality, for example, population dynamics models (drawn from biology and ecology) intertwine with economic models in renewable resource analysis.

James L. Sweeney
Stanford University

Further reading

Dasgupta, P. S. and Heal, G. M. (1979) *Economic Theory and Exhaustible Resources*, Cambridge, UK.

Kneese, A. V. and Sweeney, J. L. (eds) (1985; 1993) *Handbook of Natural Resource and Energy Economics*, 3 vols, Amsterdam.

See also: energy; environmental economics.

nature

The concept of nature is one of the most complex and tangled ideas in most societies, expressing as much about a society's self-image as about the world external to it. In western social and intellectual systems, nature is viewed as that part of the terrestrial world that is external to human society, containing its own laws, operating according to its own physical, chemical and biological processes. Such a radical separation of nature from society is historically novel and geographically specific, however. It became a dominant conception only with the advent of capitalist modernity between the sixteenth and eighteenth centuries in Europe and was consistent with the practical treatment and experience of nature in rapidly industrializing societies where indeed nature is increasingly rendered an object for human exploitation and transformation.

The intensity of human involvement with, and transformation of, nature has led to a compensatory treatment of nature in more universal rather than external terms: nature as all-encompassing, including human beings and the social domain. This universal concept of nature makes possible the idea of 'human nature' and inspires more recent ecological visions of the world. Together these external and universal conceptions frame contemporary western treatments of nature.

Ideologies of nature in social discourse traditionally appeal to the ambiguity of this dualistic conception of nature. That certain processes or relationships occur 'in nature' comes to vouch for their applicability in the social world. At the end of the nineteenth century, for example, Social Darwinism transferred the authority of 'natural' science to the realm of social behaviour in attempting to explain certain forms of competitive social behaviours as 'natural'. In this way, a specific concept of nature has very direct ideological and political implications. Fundamental social categories of race, gender and class, for example, or social actions such as economic competition, can thereby be attributed to 'natural' differences between people or natural impulses in all people. The pervasive equation of nature and woman expresses a simultaneous oppression of women and nature. Further, the universality of nature is a foundational assumption behind myriad romantic and utopian world-views.

Although scientific discourse is erected on the assumption of an external nature, it does not inherently deny the universality of nature. In the social sciences, especially in certain subfields of geography, psychology and anthropology – the disciplines most directly concerned to bridge the gap between social and natural events and processes – there is a stronger tradition of the connectedness of social and 'external' natures. Following Cicero, Hegel (1970) recognized a distinction between first and second nature. *First nature* was original, pristine, god-given, the stuff of natural science, while *second nature* comprised the system of social structures, economic institutions, legal and state edifices, and altered environments. More critical approaches in the social sciences have generally developed this distinction. For the Frankfurt School, social production necessarily involves the 'domination of nature', a particularly exploitative relation that was systematized with the advent of capitalist society. This has led some commentators to interpret the ecological destructiveness of western societies in a rather one-dimensional manner as heralding the 'end' of nature (McKibben 1989) . But the Frankfurt School presented a more complicated portrait. The domination of nature, they argue, is none other than a displaced means of dominating other human beings. Second nature now completely dominates first nature for purposes of controlling second nature itself. According to Horkheimer and Adorno (1972), therefore, human society is in the process of becoming little more than 'a massive racket in nature', to which the only response would be a 'revolt of nature'.

Others have questioned whether the externality of nature remains a viable concept at all given the global reach of social transformations of nature; Hegel's distinction in the 1840s should be overhauled (Smith 1984, Fitzsimmons 1989). It may now be more accurate to talk of the 'production of nature' whereby the whole global environment is, to differing degrees, the product of human activity. First nature is now produced and reproduced from within second nature. The crucial point here is that the global production of nature does not in any way presume the control of nature nor in any way deny the operation of 'natural' processes, from gravity to photosynthesis. Rather it implicates human societies directly in the future of natural change. Such a perspective has direct implications for the environmental movement, cutting off any access to a romanticized, primordial 'first' nature, and suggesting a practical source (human transformative labour) for the resolution of the dialectic of external and universal natures.

Neil Smith
Rutgers University

References

Fitzsimmons, M. (1989) 'The matter of nature', *Antipode* 21.
Hegel, G. W. F. (1970) *Philosophy of Nature*, London.
Horkheimer, M. and Adorno, T. (1972) *Dialectic of Enlightenment*, New York.
Marcuse, H. (1964) *One Dimensional Man*, London.
McKibben, B. (1989) *The End of Nature*, New York.
Smith, N. (1984) 'The production of nature', in N. Smith, *Uneven Development: Nature, Capital and the Production of Space*, Oxford.

Further reading

Evernden, N. (1992) *The Social Creation of Nature*, Baltimore, MD.
Glacken, C. (1967) *Traces on the Rhodian Shore: Nature and Culture in Western Thought from Ancient Times to the End of the Eighteenth Century*, Berkeley, CA.
Ortner, S. (1974) 'Is female to male as nature is to culture?', in M. Zimbalist Rosaldo and L. Lamphere (eds) *Woman, Culture and Society*, Stanford, CA.
Schmidt, A. (1971) *The Concept of Nature in Marx*, London.
Williams, R. (1980) 'Ideas of nature', in R. Williams, *Problems of Materialism and Culture*, London.

See also: environment; human nature; landscape.

needs *see* basic needs; human needs

neo-classical economics

The term neo-classical economics refers to the enhanced version of classical economics that was promoted and developed in the late nineteenth century, primarily by Alfred Marshall and Leon Walras. The most familiar versions were developed in the twentieth century by John Hicks (1946 [1939]) and Paul Samuelson (1965 [1947]). Despite what neo-classical might usually imply, neo-classical economics differs from the classical only in matters of emphasis and focus. Unlike classical methods of explaining the state of any economy in terms of seemingly mysterious forces like the 'invisible hand', neo-classical economics tries to provide a complete explanation by focusing on the actual mechanisms which lead to the explained state.

The pure world that neo-classical economists attempt to explain consists of independently minded individuals making decisions which can be completely rationalized in terms of aims and means, interacting with one another only by means of market competition, and all the while being limited only by the constraints provided by nature. It is important to note what is omitted from this world-view. There is no necessary role for social institutions such as churches or governments, except those that can be explicitly explained as the consequences of individual market choices. Likewise, there is no role for authorities. The individual or the decision-making unit such as a firm always knows what is best for him, her or it.

In the neo-classical world, whenever individuals are not satisfied with current affairs (say, not consuming enough bread), they allegedly enter the market and compete with other buyers by bidding up the price (of bread), thereby creating an incentive for at least one producer to sell to them rather than anyone else. This process of increasing the going market price raises the average selling price and thereby indicates to producers that more is wanted, and to other buyers that they should consider cheaper substitutes (for bread). If a sufficient amount of time is allowed for all such market activity to be worked out, eventually all individuals will be satisfied relative to what they can afford (to afford any more may mean that they would have had to work more than what they considered optimal). The market process is worked out to a point where one individual can gain only by causing others to lose and thereby leaving them unsatisfied. In other words, in the long run everyone is happy relative to their own personal aims and to their natural givens (for example, to their inherited resources or skills).

Since the 1930s, formal analyses of this very special neo-classical world have frequently demonstrated that any attempt to interfere with its preconceived free market mechanism – either by manipulating prices or by restricting market trading – can only lead to a world where some people are not being allowed to choose what they want and thus lead to a non-optimal state of affairs. Nevertheless, it has often been pointed out by critics, such as John Maynard Keynes, that the amount of time necessary for the market activity to be worked out is unrealistic. Other critics, such as Thorstein Veblen, merely claimed that the neo-classical world was fundamentally unrealistic as some individuals do not act independently, and thus there is no guarantee, even if there were enough time, that everyone will be satisfied. While there are a few exceptions, most neo-classical economists have been concerned with either the formal analytics of the special neo-classical world or the applicability of its many formal theorems to everyday world problems.

Few of the economists who focus on the analytical aspects of economic theory are actually attempting to answer their critics. Rather, most neo-classical economic theorists have been concerned with other equally important questions. Can we really confidently rely on a world view that allows only independent decision making and only free competition? How can one specify the details of the formal neo-classical world so as to justify such confidence? Critics still question the sufficiency of any purely competitive, individualist

world and ask whether other details are necessary. Does this world ask require that there be numerous individuals participating as buyers and as sellers? Does it require an infinity of time for the long run and thus by doing it so render an impossible world? While the necessity of such additional conditions remains somewhat in doubt, a few logically sufficient views of a world of individual decision makers have been worked out in great, yet tedious, detail.

Since, by methodological commitment, all events are ultimately to be explained in neo-classical economics as being the logical consequences of individual decision making guided by market events, the elements of individual decision making have had to yield to extensive formal analysis. Unfortunately, despite the many impressive displays of mathematical agility and prowess, not much has been accomplished beyond what can be learned from any elementary calculus textbook. Every individual is thought to be maximizing with respect to some particular quantitative aim (for example, utility, profit or net income) while facing specified natural constraints (such as technical knowledge or capabilities, or personal skills). It follows, then, whenever utility (the quantity representing the level of satisfaction achieved by consuming the purchased goods) is maximized, the formal relationship between the quantity of any good and the utility (the 'utility function') must be one where, over the relevant range of choice, each additional unit of the good must add slightly less to the total utility than did any previous unit. This is termed 'diminishing marginal utility' and it (or some multidimensional version such as 'diminishing marginal rates of substitution') is a necessary condition for each individual's utility function. Why any individual's marginal utility is diminishing has never been adequately explained using economics principles alone. It can be asserted only that it is a necessary condition for the viability of any neo-classical world. Similar analysis has been provided for the other aims that individuals might have (such as profit, wealth, welfare), although virtually all other aims can be reduced to the analytics of utility maximization (see Samuelson 1965 [1947]).

Other neo-classical economists have been trying indirectly to answer the critics by showing that, even without assurances that the neo-classical world is realistic or possible, it can be used to provide detailed explanations of current economic events. Countless academic articles have been written which demonstrate the robustness of neo-classical theories. All are of a form that implies that any desirable economic event must be the logical consequence of the aims and choices of individuals, and any undesirable event must be the result of unforeseen natural events or the consequence of interference in the market by well-meaning governments or corporations. So far, few critics have been convinced by the tedious formalities or even by the number of allegedly successful demonstrations.

Lawrence A. Boland
Simon Fraser University

References

Hicks, J. (1946 [1939]) *Value and Capital*, 2nd edn, Oxford.
Samuelson, P. (1965 [1947]) *Foundations of Economic Analysis*, New York.

Further reading

Boland, L. (1986) *Methodology for a New Microeconomics: The Critical Foundations*, London.
—— (1992) *The Principles of Economics: Some Lies my Teachers Told Me*, London.

See also: macroeconomic theory; Marshall, Alfred; microeconomics; prices, theory of.

nervous system

The nervous system has long been recognized as the locus of the control of human action, but the nature of its contribution and the mechanisms by which this is achieved are still a matter of active debate. The main thrust of investigation has been empirical, and has been initiated from two fields within psychology – physiological psychology and human neuropsychology.

Physiological psychology has investigated the influence of general physiological systems upon the fundamental aspects of behaviour, and has concentrated on affective and conative mechanisms rather than cognitive processes. Because the site of these mechanisms is in the central subcortical parts of the head, and in lower brain systems, they have generally been studied in animal preparations, for the survival of human cases with damage to these areas is relatively poor. Research has identified three major functional systems. First, the limbic system, which includes the cingulate gyrus, the septal region, the fornix, the hippocampus and the amygdala, is involved in the evaluation of experience as punishing or rewarding. It also maintains a memory of these evaluations, so that behaviour can be adaptive and appropriate to its context. Rage and fear, taming, flight and attack are all associated with this region, as is the regulation of psychological mood. Second, the medial forebrain bundle, grouped around the hypothalamus, is involved in the basic motivational systems for hunger, thirst and sexual behaviour. It can be convenient to think of subsystems within the hypothalamus which turn such drives on or off, although the system is in reality more complex. Related structures subserve the effects of reward and punishment, and also exert control on the endocrine system of hor-

mones, and on the autonomic nervous system involved in emotion and anxiety. If pleasure is generated anywhere within the brain, it is here. Third, the system in the brainstem governs the operation of reflex responses and maintains the general level of alertness and attention within the rest of the nervous system.

The other, and more recently prominent, field is that of *human neuropsychology*. This has mainly investigated cognitive functions, and in the cerebral cortex of human subjects. Its origins are in clinical neuropsychology, the study of patients with damage to the central nervous system. From the latter half of the nineteenth century, investigators recognized that fairly discrete behavioural defects could be associated with relatively localized injuries to the surface of the brain. This study of focal brain lesions, promoted by the observation of those injured in both World Wars, laid the basis of modern neuropsychology as both a research area and an applied clinical discipline. The most widely adopted functional model derived from this work is that of regional equipotentiality within an interactionist theory. Interactionist theory, originating with Hughlings Jackson and developed by Luria and Geschwind, proposes that higher abilities are built up from a number of more basic component skills which are themselves relatively localized. Regional equipotentiality argues for localization only within certain rather loosely defined regions. That higher functions appear incompletely localized in the brain may be due to the flexibility of cognitive systems in employing basic components in complex performance.

Three main approaches are adopted in modern clinical neuropsychology. First, behavioural neurology, derived from the work of Luria and most widely practised in the former Soviet Union, is individual-centred and aims at a qualitative analysis and description of the patient's problems rather than a quantitative assessment. The focus of interest is not only the level of performance, but also the way in which a given task is performed. Second, an approach, popular in the USA, concentrates on the use of test batteries. The two currently most important are the Halstead–Reitan and the Luria–Nebraska Neuropsychological Batteries. Such batteries, composed of a large number of standard tests, seek to give a complete description of the patient's level of performance across the whole spectrum of abilities, and use statistical methods. Diagnostic indicators are also usually a feature of the results. Third, the individual-centred, normative approach is most commonly practised in Britain. It relies to some extent upon formal psychometric assessment, but emphasizes the need to tailor the assessment to the nature of a particular patient's difficulties. The aim is an accurate description of the dysfunction being investigated, going beyond a simple diagnostic classification to an understanding in cognitive psychological terms. This approach is more efficient in terms of time and resources, but makes greater demands upon professional skill and clinical insight. The approaches are, of course, rather less distinct in clinical practice.

The clinical tradition in neuropsychology has developed since the mid-1960s through important contributions from cognitive experimental psychology. The stimulus for this development was undoubtedly the study of the commissurotomy or 'split-brain' patients by Sperry and Gazzaniga in the early 1960s. These patients, in whom the two lateral hemispheres of the cortex had been surgically separated for the treatment of epilepsy, provided a unique opportunity to study the functions of each hemisphere operating alone. It was demonstrated that each was capable of perceiving, learning and remembering, and that there were in addition relative specializations characteristic of each hemisphere: the left subserved speech and verbal, symbolic, logical and serial operations, while the right undertook spatial-perceptual, holistic and parallel processes. The split-brain patients also provided a milieu for the empirical investigation of the seat of consciousness, although the conclusions to be drawn are still very much a matter of debate. However, apart from the research findings directly derived from the split-brain patients which are sometimes difficult to interpret, this work demonstrated that methods already employed in a different context in experimental psychology could be used to investigate brain organization in normal intact human adults. An enormous literature has built up around these techniques, and the results, although far from unanimous, broadly support the conclusion derived from the split-brain patients. This is that the hemispheres possess relative specializations for cognitive function. While it was at one time thought that this might relate to the type of material processed, or the response mechanisms employed, it is now thought that the nature of the processing determines the relative proficiency of each hemisphere. No one specification of the relevant processing characteristics has yet been widely accepted.

Since about 1980, the specialism of *cognitive neuropsychology* has also become established out of a fruitful interchange between cognitive psychology and human neuropsychology. Data derived from the deficits exhibited by those with neuropsychological impairments are used to refine and test models of normal cognitive processes; cognitive models developed with normal subjects are applied to understand the cognitive deficits of those with injury or disease of the brain. This approach has been particularly successful in extending our understanding of the higher intellectual functions, notably including reading, writing, spelling and calculation. Clinical application of the approach

permits a precise analysis of a patient's disability in neuropsychological terms by reference to the processing elements which are dysfunctional. Allied to the cognitive neuropsychology approach are developments in *cognitive neuroscience* which have resulted in the creation of a new generation of models of brain function, variously referred to as 'neural networks', 'parallel distributed processing (PDP)' or 'connectionist' models. These models, which relate to advances in computer science and artificial intelligence, employ the concept of a connectionist matrix which has the ability to learn and to acquire intelligent functions, and to respond to malfunction, in a way which provides a persuasive analogy for human brain function. These models are likely to have an increasingly important role in advancing our understanding of higher functions.

Alongside these developments in experimental neuropsychology has been a renewed interest in electrophysiological processes. The technology of averaged evoked response recording, and different ways of looking at the ongoing electrical activity of the brain (EEG), have both produced significant advances in directly linking cognitive events in the psychological domain to observable concurrent events in the physiological domain. While this research is difficult in technological and methodological terms, it holds the promise of being able to identify accurately, with good temporal resolution, the concomitants of cognitive processes within the physiological activity of the brain. Despite inventive research, this promise is some way from being fulfilled. At the same time, psychophysiological studies, which have a longer history, have continued into the psychological correlates of autonomic nervous system functions. Much has been learned of the peripheral changes in heart rate, electrodermal response, respiration, blood pressure and vascular changes which accompany changes in emotion and mood, but the problems of individual and situational variability, and the poor temporal association between mental and physiological states because of the slow response of the autonomic processes, have led to a decline in interest.

Dramatic developments in medical imaging of brain structures – by nuclear magnetic resonance imaging (NMRI) and magnetic resonance imaging (MRI) – and of physiological brain processes – by positron-emission tomography (PET scan) and single photon emission computed tomography (SPECT) – are, however, providing new opportunities for the study of the association between neurological structures and psychological processes.

A number of fundamental problems face the apparently successful study of brain–behaviour relationships:

First, the philosophical issue of the mind–body problem. Most neuroscientists adopt a position of psychoneural monism, assuming that some identity can be established between mental and physiological events. This, of course, may be a conceptual error. It is possible that developments in electrophysiology may provide a means for the empirical investigation of this issue, till now primarily the domain of philosophers. Second, much of experimental neuropsychology proceeds by inference to, rather than direct observation of, physiological processes, so placing great importance upon methodological rigour. Third, it has to be admitted that we still have no real idea of how the brain operates to produce high-level cognition. A rather vague cybernetic-electronic model is often assumed, though this is being modified by the introduction of connectionist models, but there is no real certainty that this in any way reflects the actual principles of operation within the brain. Fourth, the nervous system is a very complex set of highly integrated subsystems. It is unlikely that significant progress will be made in our understanding of it until more adequate models can be developed, both of the physiological performance of large neural systems and of the psychological structure of cognitive abilities.

J. Graham Beaumont
Royal Hospital and Home, London

Further reading

Beaumont, J. G. (1988) *Understanding Neuropsychology*, Oxford.
Heilman, K. M. and Valenstein, E. (eds) (1993) *Clinical Neuropsychology*, 3rd edn, New York.
Kolb, B. and Whishaw, I. Q. (eds) (1990) *Fundamentals of Human Neuropsychology*, 3rd edn, San Francisco, CA.
McCarthy, R. A. and Warrington, E. K. (1990) *Cognitive Neuropsychology: A Clinical Introduction*, London.
Shallice, T. (1988) *From Neuropsychology to Mental Structure*, Cambridge, UK.
Zeki, S. (1994) *A Vision of the Brain*, Oxford.

See also: connectionism; mind; physiological psychology.

networks *see* communication networks; social networks

neuroses

Historically, the neuroses or psychoneuroses have constituted a major category of mental disorders in psychiatry and psychoanalysis. The term neuroses evolved from the belief that the symptoms of these disorders originate in neural disturbances. Later, the term psychoneuroses came into being to reflect the understanding that most neurotic symptoms have psychic or emotional origins. The two terms are nowadays used interchangeably. In fact, the *Diagnostic and Statistical Manual of Mental Disorders* (DSM – IV) of the

American Psychiatric Association – the organization's official manual for nomenclature published in 1994 – omits the classification of 'neuroses'; instead, the neuroses are included under the mood, anxiety, somatoform, factitious, dissociative, sexual and gender identity, and impulse-control disorders not elsewhere classified categories.

Traditionally, the neuroses have been categorized according to the symptoms or manifestations of anxiety, which is considered their common source. In these illnesses, the predominant disturbance is a symptom or a group of symptoms which cause distress to the individual and are recognized as unacceptable and alien. However, reality testing remains grossly intact and there is no demonstrable organic aetiology. Thus, a neurotic individual's behaviour remains largely normal. Without treatment, these conditions are relatively enduring or recurrent.

Because the definition of normality or health is difficult, one can assume that everyone is a potential neurotic. Individuals may be considered neurotic when their ego defences are quantitively excessive and disruptive to usual patterns of adaptive functioning. The neurotic process hinders one's freedom to change, limits the capacity to sustain effort, and reduces flexibility in the areas of thinking, behaviour and emotions. Neuroses can be circumscribed, affecting only one of these areas, or they may be more widespread, touching on several areas in the individual's life.

Psychoanalysts and dynamically oriented psychiatrists believe that the neuroses are caused by conflicts between the sexual and aggressive id drives and ego forces that are attempting to control and modify the drives. Neuroses may also arise from conflicts between the superego (or conscience) and the ego. Object relations theorists contend that neurotic conflicts may arise from incongruous self-representations within the ego and superego and their internal interactions, as well as from their interactions with the external environment.

According to the classic dynamic formulation, symptom formation is a consequence of the emergence into consciousness of the instinctual derivatives and memory traces producing anxiety. A danger is created, calling forth repression and other defensive mechanisms to ward off the anxiety. If these mechanisms are unsuccessful in containing anxiety, symptoms emerge which represent substitute expressions of the instinctual drives. The symptoms can be understood as compromise formations or attempts of the ego to integrate ego drives, superego and reality.

The appearance of a neurosis in a person usually indicates a fixation or regression to an earlier phase of infantile development. These illnesses may be precipitated by realistic situations that correspond to earlier traumatic life experiences. Unconscious fantasies and feelings are stirred up, activating the original conflict. While there is no definite evidence of biogenetic factors in the production of neurotic disorders, constitutional differences may be contributory.

Originally, Freud classified hysteria, phobias and the obsessive-compulsive neuroses under the heading 'transference neuroses', because patients with these conditions repeat childhood neurotic patterns within the transference during treatment. Since patients with melancholia and schizophrenia did not exhibit the same tendency in treatment, these entities were termed *narcissistic neuroses*. The term *symptom neuroses* corresponds to the present-day neurotic disorder, while *character neuroses* is roughly equivalent to the concept of personality disorder.

Freud's classification of neuroses was based both on his psychoanalytic understanding of the condition and his experience of those patients' responses to the treatment situation. The psychiatric establishment, unwilling to accept Freud's approach, found a compromise and classified the neuroses as different patterns for dealing with anxiety. Thus, hysterical neurosis, conversion type, implied that anxiety had been converted into a physical symptom, for example, a paralysis. Phobia assumed that anxiety was compartmentalized, and so on.

The more recent psychiatric classification, DSM-IV, has moved still further away from any theory of the underlying dynamics. Instead, the focus is descriptive and behavioural. The current diagnosis of what were once designated neuroses are panic disorder, generalized anxiety disorder, conversion disorder, psychogenic pain disorder, psychogenic amnesia, psychogenic fugue, multiple personality, sleepwalking disorder (in childhood), simple phobia, social phobia, agoraphobia with panic attacks, agoraphobia without panic attacks, separation anxiety disorder (in childhood), obsessive compulsive disorder, depersonalization disorder, and hypochondriasis. As this list demonstrates, the emphasis is not on the theory of aetiology; rather, classification depends on careful description of the symptoms of the disorder. Since DSM-III and DSM-III-R came into existence in 1980 and 1987, respectively, the new classification of acute stress disorders has been added in DSM-IV. In addition, two new classifications have been introduced: somatization disorder, and acute and chronic post-traumatic stress disorders.

Nevertheless, it is still true that in these conditions the individual experiences anxiety, directly or indirectly, in addition to one or several recognizable defence mechanisms that serve to identify the disorder. An example would be an obsessive-compulsive disorder in which the person is troubled by involuntary recurrent, persistent ideas, thoughts, images or impulses that are ego-dystonic (obsessions) and engages in repetitive and seemingly purposeful behaviours performed according to certain rules, or in a stereotyped fashion (compulsions). The individual recognizes that these obsessions and compulsions are senseless or unreasonable, but mounting tension ensues when the person attempts to resist the compulsion or to ignore the obsession. Common obsessions include thoughts of violence, contamination, and doubt, while common compulsions are hand-washing, checking, counting and touching.

The neuroses have responded well to psychoanalysis and other forms of dynamic psychotherapy such as individual reconstructive psychotherapy, supportive therapy and psychoanalytic group psychotherapy. Other modalities used in treatment of neuroses include behaviour modification, hypnosis, psychotropic medications and various non-dynamic approaches.

Normund Wong
Walter Reed Army Medical Center

References

Freud, S. (1959 [1926]) *Inhibitions, Symptoms and Anxiety, Standard Edition of the Complete Psychological Works of Sigmund Freud*, ed. J. Strachey, vol 20, London. (Original edn, *Hemmung, Symptom und Angst.*)
Shapiro, D. (1965) *Neurotic Styles*, New York.

See also: DSM-IV; mental disorders; mental health; psychoses.

non-verbal communication

The term non-verbal communication can refer to facial expression, eye contact, pupil dilation, posture, gesture and interpersonal distance. It can also refer to communication through touch or smell, through various kinds of artefacts such as masks and clothes, or through formalized communication systems such as semaphore. Sometimes it has been used to refer to the vocal features of speech, such as intonation, stress, speech rate, accent and loudness. Because the term non-verbal is a definition only by exclusion, the number of features which the term can embrace are virtually limitless.

However, not all non-verbal behaviour should be regarded as communication. For behaviour to be communicative, it needs to be shown that information has been both transmitted and received (referred to as 'systematic encoding' and 'appropriate decoding': Wiener *et al.* 1972). Even so, the concept of systematic encoding does not require that a behaviour should be *intentionally* communicative. Communication may take place without any conscious intention to communicate, or indeed, even against the express intentions of the encoder. For example, members of an audience may well show signs of boredom without any conscious intention to do so; indeed, a listener may even try to suppress such tell-tale cues by trying hard to appear attentive, but still be incapable of suppressing the occasional yawn. To the speaker, the listener may still communicate boredom, despite the best intentions not to do so (Bull 1987). Nor is awareness necessary to the concepts of systematic encoding and appropriate decoding, in the sense that neither encoder nor decoder needs to be able to identify the specific non-verbal cues through which a particular message is transmitted. For example, people may be left with the feeling that someone was upset or angry without being able to specify exactly what cues were responsible for creating that impression. In fact, it can be argued that a great deal of non-verbal communication takes this form, and that one task of the researcher is to try and identify more precisely the cues that are responsible for creating such impressions.

Non-verbal cues can be said to communicate information about emotion, speech, individual differences and interpersonal relationships. Particular importance is commonly ascribed to non-verbal cues in the communication of emotion, stemming from the observations of Charles Darwin (1872), who argued that the facial expressions of emotion constitute part of an innate, adaptive, physiological response. Current thinking has been heavily influenced by Ekman's 'neurocultural' model (Ekman 1972; Ekman and Friesen 1986), according to which there are at least seven fundamental emotions with innate expressions which can be modified through the learning of what he calls display rules (norms governing the expression of emotions in different social contexts). Indeed, research has shown that there are discernible differences between posed and spontaneous expressions, in that posed expressions are more asymmetrical (Skinner and Mullen 1991) – evidence supporting the assumption of the neurocultural model that facial expressions are both innate and learned.

Non-verbal behaviour has been shown to be related to speech in terms of syntax (Lindenfeld 1971), vocal stress (Bull and Connelly; Pittenger et al. 1960) and meaning (e.g. Bull 1987; Scheflen 1964). If non-verbal behaviour is so closely related to speech, what functions does it serve? According to one view, gesture is essentially secondary to speech, used as a means of elaborating the spoken message, or as a substitute when speech is difficult or impossible (e.g. Ekman and Friesen 1969). An alternative view stems from Kendon (1985), who points out that gesture as a silent, visual mode of expression has very different properties from those of speech; consequently, it is suitable for a different range of communication tasks. According to this view, gesture should be seen not as subordinate to speech, but as an additional resource, as part of a multichannel system of communication, which allows the skilled speaker further options through which to convey meaning.

Non-verbal cues also convey significant information about individual differences and interpersonal relationships. For example, it has repeatedly been shown (e.g. Hall 1984) that there are notable sex differences in non-verbal communication, such that women are clearer encoders than men (i.e. they transmit more information through non-verbal cues) and also better decoders. Furthermore, men and women differ in the non-verbal behaviour which they use. Women both smile more and gaze more at other people; they prefer closer interpersonal distances and are approached more closely than men; they also use smaller and less open body movements and positions (Hall 1984). In addition, it has been shown that non-verbal behaviour varies according to the nature of the relationship, and that decoders can utilize such information to discern the relationship between people in terms of sex, age and acquaintanceship (e.g. Abramovitch 1977; Benjamin and Creider 1975).

Thus, non-verbal communication is an important source of social information; as such, there is no doubt that its systematic study does have considerable practical significance. If communication can legitimately be regarded as a skill (e.g. Argyle and Kendon 1967), then with appropriate training or instruction it is possible for people to improve their performance as with any other skill. This learning might take the form of a systematic course in social skills training, or it might be beneficial simply to read a book on non-verbal communication. Social skills training has been widely used both as a therapy for psychiatric patients experiencing social difficulties, and as a form of professional training with, for example, teachers, doctors, nurses and police officers; its effectiveness in a number of different social contexts is attested by a substantive research literature (e.g. Kelly 1982). Social skills training typically includes a significant component on non-verbal communication; as such, it reflects our increased awareness and theoretical understanding of the role of non-verbal communication in social interaction.

Peter Bull
University of York, UK

References

Abramovitch, R. (1977) 'Children's recognition of situational aspects of facial expression', *Child Development* 48.

Argyle, M. and Kendon, A. (1967) 'The experimental analysis of social performance', in L. Berkowitz (ed.) *Advances in Experimental Social Psychology*, vol. 3, New York.

Benjamin, G. R. and Creider, C. A. (1975) 'Social distinctions in non-verbal behaviour', *Semiotica* 14.

Bull, P. E. (1987) *Posture and Gesture*, Oxford.

Bull, P. E. and Connelly, G. (1985) 'Body movement and emphasis in speech', *Journal of Nonverbal Behaviour* 9.

Darwin, C. (1872) *The Expression of the Emotions in Man and Animals*, London.

Ekman, P. (1972) 'Universal and cultural differences in facial expression of emotion', in J. R. Cole (ed.) *Nebraska Symposium on Motivation 1971*, Lincoln, NB.

Ekman, P. and Friesen, W. V. (1969) 'The repertoire of non-verbal behaviour: categories, origins, usage and coding', *Semiotica* 1.

—— (1986) 'A new pan-cultural facial expression of emotion', *Motivation and Emotion* 10.

Hall, J. A. (1984) *Nonverbal Sex Differences: Communication Accuracy and Expressive Style*, Baltimore, MD.

Kelly, J. A. (1982) *Social Skills Training: A Practical Guide for Interventions*, New York.

Kendon, A. (1985) 'Some uses of gesture', in O. Tannen and M. Saville-Troike (eds) *Perspectives on Silence*, Norwood, NJ.

Lindenfeld, J. (1971) 'Verbal and non-verbal elements in discourse', *Semiotica* 3.

Pittenger, R. E., Hockett, C. F. and Danehy, J. J. (1960) *The First Five Minutes: A Sample of Microscopic Interview Analysis*, Ithaca, NY.

Scheflen, A. E. (1964) 'The significance of posture in communication systems', *Psychiatry* 27.

Skinner, M. and Mullen, B. (1991) 'Facial asymmetry in emotional expression: a meta-analysis of research', *British Journal of Social Psychology* 30.

Wiener, M., Devoe, S., Robinson, S. and Geller, J. (1972) 'Non-verbal behaviour and non-verbal communication', *Psychological Review* 79.

See also: social psychology.

norms

Social norms exist in two basic forms. The first kind of norm refers to action that is common or typical. Such norms describe what most people do; they can be called *descriptive norms*. They motivate our behaviour by giving us evidence of what most other people think is effective conduct for them in a particular situation. By simply registering what most others are doing and imitating their actions, we can usually choose efficiently and correctly. Evidence of various sorts indicates that people are likely to follow the lead of the crowd. Researchers have repeatedly demonstrated that the perception of what most others are doing influences observers to behave similarly, even when the behaviours are as morally neutral as choosing a consumer product (Venkatesan 1966) or looking up at an empty spot in the sky (Milgram *et al.* 1969).

The second kind of norm refers to shared expectations within a society, organization or group as to what constitutes desirable conduct – the moral rules we agree to live by. Such norms reflect what most people approve or disapprove. They motivate our behaviour by promising informal social rewards and punishments for it. In contrast to descriptive norms, which are often termed the norms of 'is', these are often called the norms of 'ought'. Whereas descriptive norms inform our behaviour, these enjoin it; consequently, they can be labelled *injunctive norms*. Examples of often cited injunctive norms include the norm for reciprocity and the norm for social responsibility. According to Gouldner (1960), there is no human society that does not subscribe to the reciprocity norm, which obligates us to give back to others the kind of behaviour (e.g. gifts, favours or concessions) they have given to us. The norm of social responsibility, also called *the helping norm*, prescribes aid for those in need. It, too, has been reported across many cultures (Berkowitz 1972).

There is debate as to the usefulness of the concept of injunctive norms in explaining or predicting much of human behaviour. Some see widely shared moral rules as powerful and crucial to a full understanding of social conduct (eg Pepitone 1976). Others see them as ill defined and weak, at best, in their impact on human functioning (Krebs and Miller 1985). A way of resolving the debate comes from the recognition that the degree to which any norm is likely to guide a person's behaviour is dependent on the degree to which the person's attention is focused on the norm (Cialdini *et al.* 1991). That is, even though injunctive norms may be in place at all times within a society, organization or group, they are not in force at all times. It is only when a norm is activated (i.e. made prominent or focal) in an individual's consciousness that it will direct that individual's actions forcefully (Miller and Grush 1986; Rutkowski *et al.* 1983). We have reason to take heart, then, that social norms can be employed as a force for directing human conduct. However, this will apply primarily among those who focus naturally on normative considerations or who have had their attention temporarily directed to those considerations.

Robert B. Cialdini
Arizona State University

References

Berkowitz, L. (1972) 'Social norms, feelings, and other factors affecting helping and altruism', in L. Berkowitz (ed.) *Advances in Experimental Social Psychology*, vol. 6, New York.

Cialdini, R. B., Kallgren, C. A. and Reno, R. R. (1991) 'A focus theory of normative conduct', in M. Zanna (ed.) *Advances in Experimental Social Psychology*, vol. 24, New York.

Gouldner, A. W. (1960) 'The norm of reciprocity: a preliminary statement', *American Sociological Review* 25.

Krebs, D. L. and Miller, D. T. (1985) 'Altruism and aggression', in G. Lindzey and E. Aronson (eds) *The Handbook of Social Psychology*, New York.

Milgram, S., Bickman, L. and Berkowitz, O. (1969) 'Note on the drawing power of crowds', *Journal of Personality and Social Psychology* 13.

Miller, L. E. and Grush, J. E. (1986) 'Individual differences in attitudinal versus normative determination of behavior', *Journal of Experimental Social Psychology* 22.

Pepitone, A. (1976) 'Toward a normative and comparative biocultural social psychology', *Journal of Personality and Social Psychology* 34.

Rutkowski, G. K., Gruder, C. L. and Romer, D. (1983) 'Group cohesiveness, social norms and bystander intervention', *Journal of Personality and Social Psychology* 44.

Ventatesan, M. (1966) 'Study of consumer behavior, conformity and independence', *Journal of Marketing Research* 3.

See also: conformity; deviance; social psychology.

nuptiality

In the field of demography, the study of nuptiality refers to the study of the marital status composition of the population and the components of change of marital status, that is, first marriage, divorce (and separation), widowhood and remarriage. Defined in this way, a strict, legal interpretation of marital status is implied. However, in many societies, people's actual or *de facto* status is frequently different from their legal status. For example, in Latin America and the Caribbean and increasingly in the west, couples begin their partnership in a consensual union which may not later be formally legalized. In other places, several systems of marriage law, such as civil law, religious law and tribal or customary law, operate simultaneously. The decision to study legal status, *de facto* status, or both must therefore depend on the circumstances prevailing in the particular society.

At a broader level of conception, nuptiality may also cover the study of the balance of the sexes available for marriage (the marriage market), polygamy, and the relative characteristics of husbands and wives (assortive mating). At this point, it becomes apparent that patterns of nuptiality are merely a subset of the totality of a society's marriage customs. This recognition has directed research on nuptiality away from demography in isolation to the place or function of nuptiality patterns within the prevailing social structure. Particular attention has focused on nuptiality in relation to familial organization and religion.

Strongly patrilineal societies, as found in Africa, the Middle East, South Asia and East Asia, have traditionally been characterized by universal marriage for both sexes, early marriage for women but a relatively wide age difference between the sexes, and low rates of divorce and remarriage. A young girl was seen as a visitor in her parents' household, a person who would soon leave to join her husband's household. As such, her value to her parents was in the alliance with another family that her marriage effected, rather than in any direct services that she would provide to the household economy of her parents. Also, because at marriage she became the property of her husband's household, divorce and remarriage were difficult. In the Middle East, South Asia and in parts of Africa, these patterns are also reinforced by Islam and Hinduism, which place great significance on virginity at marriage for women and on the duty of parents to see their children married. In these religions, marriage is not regarded as a purely individual decision.

Where family structure is more loosely organized or is bilateral, as in European cultures, the Caribbean, Latin America and South-east Asia, marriage has tended to be less than universal and age at marriage somewhat later for women. There has been a smaller age difference between the sexes, and divorce, remarriage and informal unions have been more frequent. These patterns are reinforced by the individualism more prominent in the major religions of these areas, Christianity and Buddhism. However, Islamic societies in South-east Asia have universal and early marriage for women emphasizing the pre-eminence of religion in this regard.

These more traditional patterns are changing in many parts of the world. Most spectacularly, age at marriage for women in East Asia has risen substantially and has been accompanied by a major shift of single women into the paid, non-agricultural labour force. Alliance marriages have lost their force in the shift of power to the national level, and in the face of the growing earning potential of single women. In the west, age at marriage for both sexes has fluctuated violently in the twentieth century in relation to economic swings and societal changes in life course expectations. Age at marriage is also rising slowly in Africa, the Middle East and South Asia mainly because girls spend a longer period in school. However, the chances of any increase of women's age at marriage very much beyond age 20 in these countries are still fairly remote, because a change in the role of single women, similar to that which has occurred in East Asia, is likely to be more strongly resisted.

Peter McDonald
Australian Institute of Family Studies

Further reading

Dupâguier, J., Hélin, E., Laslett, P., Livi-Bacci, M. and Sogner, S. (1981) *Marriage and Remarriage in Populations of the Past*, London.

Goode, W. J. (1963) *World Revolution and Family Patterns*, Glencoe, IL.

McDonald, P. (1984) 'Social organisation and nuptiality in developing societies', in J. Cleland and J. Hobcraft (eds) *Reproductive Change in Developing Countries*, Oxford.

See also: divorce; fertility; marriage; vital statistics.

O

occupational psychology

Occupational psychology is a somewhat catch-all title
for an area which has variously been called industrial
psychology, organizational psychology, vocational
psychology and personnel psychology. Industrial psychology perhaps carries a hint of psychology in the
interests of management; organizational psychology
limits the field to a particular context; vocational
psychology tends to deal with individual careers outside
the organizational context in which they are usually
conducted, while personnel psychology possibly ignores
the non-organizational context. Thus occupational
psychology is a useful label, since it incorporates all of
these emphases.

Historically, we can view the development of occupational psychology as a product of the social, economic and cultural changes in western industrial
society. Sometimes, these effects were mediated through
parallel developments in mainstream psychology. A few
examples may make these relationships clearer.

The biological determinism of the nineteenth
century, exemplified in Galton's researches into the
supposed hereditary basis of outstanding intellectual
ability, coincided with the growth of 'scientific management'. As expounded by F. W. Taylor, this approach
assumed that work could be broken down into tasks for
which specific abilities were required. The First World
War led to the development of psychometric tests to
select for military functions, so the ideological justification and the practical tools were available for the
growth of the psychometric testing movement for
purposes of occupational selection. That this tradition
lives on is evident from the following quotation from
the doyen of American applied psychologists, Marvin
Dunnette: 'Human attributes do indeed exist to a sufficiently consistent degree across situations so that the
prediction of human work performance can realistically be undertaken on the basis of tested aptitudes
and skills apart from situational modifiers' (Dunnette

and Hough 1990). This statement clearly implies the
assumptions that individuals possess lasting characteristics; that these characteristics hold true across situations; that they are related to particular aspects of jobs,
and that jobs are definable in terms of the tasks they
involve.

A second influence upon occupational psychology
has been the emphasis during the first half of the twentieth century on the importance of the small group.
Again, the evidence of the Second World War indicated the value of group cohesiveness in achieving
certain sorts of objectives. The military idea of leadership and the post-war emphasis upon skills of people
management led to increased study of work groups.
The concept of the working group as dependent for its
success upon easy interpersonal relationships gained
credence, and managers were seen as oriented towards
the maintenance of these relationships as well as
towards the achievement of organizational goals.
Hence the leadership theories of Fred Fiedler, and the
theory x and theory y typology of management propounded by David McGregor fitted in well with the
current *zeitgeist*.

The third wave of development in occupational
psychology related to the strong cultural influence of
humanism in the 1960s, exemplified in the popular
text *The Greening of America* by Theodore Reich (1970).
Self-actualization, the reaching of one's full potential,
and other slogans gained support of such mainstream psychologists as Carl Rogers and Abraham
Maslow. Their influence spilled over into occupational
psychology in the form of various types of group
training in management development programmes. The
objective of many of these programmes was to
help individuals to get in touch with their 'real selves'
and as a consequence realize more of their true potential as individuals.

The history of occupational psychology can cynic-
ally be seen as a response to the opportunity to make
the most out of each current ephemeral cultural fad.

An alternative point of view might suggest that psychologists have been used for practical purposes when it was thought by the authorities that they could be of use.

Social psychology has much to say about the relationship between organizations and individuals in the theory of roles; about the meaning of work in the phenomenological approaches to cognition; about life careers in the life-span theories of human development; and about the relationships between organizations and between nation-states in the theories of conflict and negotiation. The focus is now less upon individuals in isolation from their context, and also less upon the primary working group. The organizational context of work, together with the values and image it implies, are much more to the fore. So too is the environment of organizations, to which they must continuously adapt if they are to survive. In particular, labour relations and economic and technological change are being brought into psychological focus. Cross-cultural studies are beginning to demonstrate how ethnocentric our theories have hitherto been, and how irrelevant they are to the needs of developing nations. Only if a broad perspective proves stronger than a parochial professionalism will occupational psychology come into its own.

Peter Herriot
Sundridge Park: Corporate Research

Reference

Dunnette, M. D. and Hough, L. M. (eds) (1990) *Handbook of Industrial and Organizational Psychology*, 2nd edn, 3 vols, Palo Alto, CA.

Further reading

Bass, B. M. and Barrett, G. V. (1981) *People, Work and Organizations*, 3rd edn, Boston, MA.
Katz, D. and Kahn, R. L. (1978), *The Social Psychology of Organizations*, 2nd edn, New York.

See also: aptitude tests; vocational and career development.

OECD

The Organization for Economic Co-operation and Development (OECD) was founded in 1961, replacing the Organization for European Economic Co-operation (OEEC) which had been set up to implement the Marshall Plan for European economic reconstruction, following the Second World War.

The OECD constitutes a forum where representatives of the governments of its member countries discuss and attempt to co-ordinate their economic and social policies. Membership of the OECD has been restricted to relatively industrialized pro-market economies, and hence has been labelled the rich man's club. Since 1973 the twenty-four members have been Australia, Austria, Belgium, Canada, Denmark, Finland, France, Germany, Greece, Iceland, Ireland, Italy, Japan, Luxembourg, The Netherlands, New Zealand, Norway, Portugal, Spain, Sweden, Switzerland, Turkey, the United Kingdom and the USA. In April 1994, Mexico joined the organization, and South Korea, Poland, Hungary and the Czech Republic are preparing their candidacies. The gradual inclusion of new members has offered a widening role for the OECD, but at the same time it raises questions as to its long-term mandate, for its functions and membership increasingly may be seen to overlap with those of the International Monetary Fund (IMF), World Bank and World Trade Organization.

Unlike the Bretton Woods institutions, the OECD has no money to lend or international agreements to negotiate. Its role is to provide a forum for the analysis and discussion of economic and social issues which are of mutual concern to its members. Its 1,900 employees (600 of whom are professionals, mostly economists) are based in Paris. They are the secretariat for over 200 intergovernmental committees and working parties which meet with varying regularity on subjects ranging from the co-ordination of international economic policy to the setting of common standards for development aid. Among its best known publications are its *Economic Outlook*, its regular surveys of individual member countries, its annual review of agricultural policies and subsidies, and its analysis of the implications of trade liberalization.

The Development Centre of the OECD (established in 1962) is a semi-autonomous institution which carries out and sponsors research on development issues that are of concern to the OECD members. The Club du Sahel (established in 1973) aims to co-ordinate OECD aid in the Sahara region. Other bodies associated with the OECD include the International Energy Agency, which was established in 1974 after the oil price shock, to improve co-ordination in the energy policies of its members and to co-ordinate petroleum sharing in event of emergencies, and the Nuclear Energy Agency (established in 1958), which aims to promote co-operation between OECD members for the development and application of nuclear power for peaceful purposes.

Ian Goldin
World Bank

Further reading

OECD, *OECD Economic Studies*, twice yearly, Paris.
—— *Agricultural Policies, Markets and Trade*, annually, Paris.
—— *Development Co-operation*, annually, Paris.

See also: International Monetary Fund; World Bank.

Oedipus complex

The Oedipus complex, reflecting the myth of Oedipus who unwittingly killed his father and married his mother, consists of a cluster of unconscious feelings of love for the parent of the opposite sex and hatred for the other. It is the focus of the phallic stage – the third phase in Freud's theory of psychosexual development. At around the age of 4 or 5, the developmental paths of boys and girls begin to diverge. The natural feelings of affection felt by the boy for his mother may now be intensified by erotic feelings aroused by masturbation. Feelings of rivalry with his father may arouse in the child both hostility and fear of loss of love, even of castration, given his focus of interest on his penis at this stage and his still largely autistic (i.e. fantasy-determined) view of reality.

Freud had suggested the importance of these feelings in a boy's sexual development as early as 1897 on the basis of his own self-analysis. He had been surprised at the hostility and guilt he had discovered in relation to his father and the almost erotic nature of his feelings for his mother. He later elaborated the notion and it became a core feature of early psychoanalytic theory. The way the boy handles the conflict, Freud believed, helps determine the sexual and emotional patterns of later life. (For example, ambivalence towards the mother created by conflict between the boy's desire for her and his fear of his father may lead to later difficulties in integrating affection and sexual need, so that women are either idealized or regarded as sex objects.) Satisfactory adjustment may be made by the boy intensifying his identification with his father. This results in introjection of parental attitudes and prohibitions and thus provides the basis for conscience or superego. Freud also regarded the Oedipal conflict as the nucleus of neurosis. It generates the need to repress desire and lays down a basis of guilt and anxiety over the consequences of illicit longings.

Freud considered it no coincidence that parricide is the theme not only of Sophocles' *Oedipus Rex* but also of two other masterpieces of literature, *Hamlet* and *The Brothers Karamazov*. As he also pointed out, 'The myths of every people, and not only of the Greeks are filled with examples of love-affairs between fathers and daughters and even between mothers and sons.' Freud was eventually to argue that the Oedipus complex is not just rooted in family relations but in the ancient history and conventions of society. In *Totem and Taboo* (1913), he speculated that the origins of the incest taboo lay in the killing, long ago, of the father-leader by the younger men of a primal horde.

Jung suggested the complementary notion for girls of an Electra complex. Although Oedipal themes do occur in Freud's analyses of women patients (see, for example, the case of Dora), Freud made clear that the key experience for girls at this stage is the sense of loss experienced when a girl realizes that she has no penis. Penis envy leads her to devalue her mother and shift the focus of her affection to her father. Such different paths of development suggest, because of the role of the Oedipus complex in the development of *superego*, that men are likely to possess a stronger moral conscience than women. Freud's ideas here have been strongly criticized by other psychoanalysts (e.g. Horney) as well as feminists.

Different views have been expressed by other psychoanalysts about the Oedipus complex. Klein (1948) asserts, for example, that its onset is much earlier; Kohut (1971) and White (1960) regard it as part of a broader set of identifications by means of which a male child comes to develop a sense of masculinity and self-confidence; and Horney (1939) not only denies that the Oedipus complex is universal but claims that it occurs only as a result of a more general disturbance in family relations. Anthropological evidence suggests that it is more likely a feature of a particular style of family structure, such as the patriarchal pattern of Freud's time.

Several psychological studies have produced results consistent with the idea. Young boys, for example, have been found to express more hostility to men than do young girls. Male dreams are more likely to include male strangers, aggressive encounters and content symbolic of castration and anxiety. However, none provides definitive support. Esterson (1993), after reviewing Freud's own accounts of the Oedipus complex, has even concluded that 'it is difficult to regard it as other than largely a figment of an extraordinarily colourful imagination. Not for the first time Freud erected a speculative . . . theory on the flimsiest of foundations and became utterly convinced of its validity'.

Richard Stevens
Open University

References

Esterson, A. (1993) *Seductive Mirage: An Exploration of the Work of Sigmund Freud*, Chicago.

Freud, S. (1897) *Extracts from the Fliess Papers, Standard Edition of the Complete Psychological Works of Sigmund Freud*, ed. J. Strachey, vol. 1, London.

—— (1913) *Totem and Taboo, Standard Edition of the Complete Psychological Works of Sigmund Freud*, ed. J. Strachey, vol. 13, London.

—— (1915) 'A Fragment of the Analysis of a Case of Hysteria', *The Case of Dora, Standard Edition*, vol. 7.

Horney, K. (1939) *New Ways in Psychoanalysis*, New York.

Jung, C. G. (1961) *Freud and Psychoanalysis, Complete Works*, vol. 4, transl. R. F. C. Hull, London.

Klein, M. (1948) *Contributions to Psychoanalysis 1921–45*, London.

Kohut, H. (1971) *The Analysis of the Self*, New York.

White, R. (1963) *Ego and Reality in Psychoanalytic Theory*, New York.

Further reading

Freud, S. (1916) *Introductory Lectures on Psychoanalysis, Standard Edition of the Complete Psychological Works of Sigmund Freud*, ed. J. Strachey, vol. 16, London.

Kline, P. (1981) *Fact and Fantasy in Freudian Theory*, 2nd edn, London.

Stevens, R. (1983) *Freud and Psychoanalysis*, Milton Keynes.

See also: Freud, Sigmund; incest; psychoanalysis.

opinion polls *see* public opinion polls; sample surveys

oral history

Oral history is the recording and interpretation of spoken testimonies about an individual's past. In contrast to oral tradition, it is more often concerned with experiences in the recent past than with the transmission of memories across generations (Henige 1982).

A variety of theories and methods fall within this rubric. Oral testimonies may be used to give a detailed account of an individual life (a 'life history' or 'personal narrative') or to facilitate historical reconstruction and the analysis of social change ('cross-analysis') (Bertaux 1981; Lummis 1987; P. Thompson 1988).

The life history method was pioneered by the Chicago School in studies of immigrant experience, youth culture, and crime and deviance (Plummer 1983). Life-history interviews are usually semi-structured or unstructured. They aim, as Malinowski (1922) put it, 'to grasp the native's point of view, his relation to life, to realise his vision of the world'.

Cross-analyses based on oral testimony typically use larger samples with more structured interviews. An influential UK example is Paul Thompson's (1993) study of social structure and social change in Edwardian Britain. Begun in 1968, this project gathered personal recollections from a representative sample (based on the 1911 census) of 500 people. In practice, despite these disparate foundations, techniques of cross-analysis and life history are often used together.

Oral testimony is one of the oldest and most widely used forms of historical evidence. It is the main form of historical record in non-literate societies, and was commonly used in European historical research before the mid-nineteenth century (for example in the work of the French historian Jules Michelet (1847)). As the influence of positivism grew, however, oral sources were increasingly viewed with suspicion on grounds of reliability (Henige 1982; P. Thompson 1988).

During the post-war period, oral history underwent a revival in Europe and the USA with the emergence of social history. The generation and preservation of oral sources was central to this history from below, with its concern to recover the experiences of those who had been marginalized from historical records. Oral history in this recovery mode remains a vitally important way of gathering evidence about non-elite social groups, who are often the subjects of legal, parliamentary or other official records, but for whom there is little evidence in their own words. Oral history of this kind has been undertaken on areas such as women and work (Davidoff and Westover 1986; Roberts 1984), local and occupational history (Samuel 1975; White 1980), rural history (Blythe 1977; Ewart-Evans 1975), childhood (Humphries 1981; T. Thompson 1981) and family history (Hareven 1982). A perceived strength of this kind of oral history is its capacity to elicit evidence both of past events and the individual's feelings about them.

Critics and advocates of oral history have debated the merits of this recovery mode. Its chronological scope will always be limited, given that evidence is usually confined to living memory. Sceptics also argue that the method is teleological, as narrators inevitably represent the past in terms of present concerns. Document-led historians have above all expressed concern about its reliability, given that there can be as much as seventy years between the experience and narration of an event. Oral historians have responded by pointing out that long-term memory remains accurate, and that written sources such as court records or eyewitness accounts are in any case often transcribed oral accounts (P. Thompson 1988).

With the emergence of cultural history during the 1980s and 1990s, advocates of oral history have criticized the recovery mode on the opposite grounds. Rather than seeking equivalence across documentary and oral sources, they emphasize the distinctiveness of speech as a mode of representing the past (Tonkin 1992). Rather than suppressing the effects of memory, they highlight the ways in which people may misremember, elide dates or suppress memories. Psychological or affective truths – which may well contradict historical ones – become objects of analysis (Samuel and Thompson 1990). For example, Alessandro Portelli (1991) has compared written accounts of the death of an activist in Terni, an Italian steelworks town, with the oral accounts of ex-communists. Underscoring their need to keep radical traditions alive, Terni's communists had revised the date and occasion of the death so that it coincided with a high-point in local labour militancy.

Portelli's work reflects a broader shift towards exploring the symbolic and subjective dimensions of oral testimony. Collective memories may be analysed, as in Portelli's study or Luisa Passerini's (1987) work on interwar Italian fascism. Alternatively, individual or family myths may be interpreted in terms of the psychic functions they serve (Fraser 1983; Samuel and Thompson 1990). A stress on language and narrative forms is common to these approaches. Cadences and patterns of speech, pauses and silences, and the interactions between interviewer and interviewee are seen as objects of analysis rather than obstacles to recall. Testimonies are interpreted as present cultural artefacts rather than as unmediated reflections of past experience.

More recent oral history work thus stresses the particular qualities of spoken testimonies such as retrospection, memory and a symbiotic relationship between source and interpreter. The interpretative focus has shifted from the past as lived to the past as represented. This has resulted in a more interdisciplinary approach to oral history, which now includes not only social history and sociology, but also feminist studies (especially Gluck and Patai, 1991), psychoanalysis, literary studies, anthropology and cultural studies.

Michael Roper
University of Essex

References

Bertaux, D. (ed.) (1981) *Biography and Society: The Life History Approach in the Social Sciences*, London.

Blythe, R. (1977) *Akenfield: Portrait of an English Village*, Harmondsworth.

Davidoff, L. and Westover, B. (eds) (1986) *Our Work, Our Lives: Women's History and Women's Work*, London.

Ewart-Evans, G. (1975) *Where Beards Wag All: The Days That We Have Seen*, London.

Fraser, R. (1984) *In Search of a Past*, London.

Gluck, S. B. and Patai, D. (1991) *Women's Words: The Feminist Practice of Oral History*, New York.

Hareven, T. (1982) *Family Time and Industrial Time*, New York.

Henige, D. (1982) *Oral Historiography*, London.

Humphries, S. (1981) *Hooligans or Rebels?*, Oxford.

Lummis, T. (1987) *Listening to History: The Authenticity of Oral Evidence*, London.

Malinowski, B. (1922) *Argonauts of the Western Pacific*, London.

Michelet, J. (1847) *Histoire de la Révolution Française*, Paris, Vol. 2. pp. 530.

Passerini, L. (1987) *Fascism in Popular Memory: The Cultural Experience of the Turin Working-Class*, Cambridge, UK.

Plummer, K. (1983) *Documents of Life: An Introduction to the Problems and Literature of a Humanistic Method*, London.

Portelli, A. (1991) *The Death of Luigi Trastulli and Other Stories: Form and Meaning in Oral History*, New York.

Roberts, E. (1984) *A Woman's Place: An Oral History of Working Class Women 1890–1940*, Oxford.

Samuel, R. (1975) 'Quarry roughs: life and labour in Headingham Quarry, 1860–1920', *Village Life and Labour*, London.

Samuel, R. and Thompson, P. (eds) (1990) *The Myths We Live By*, London.

Thompson, P. (1988) *The Voice of the Past: Oral History*, 2nd edn, Oxford.

—— (1993) *The Edwardians: The Remaking of British Society*, 2nd edn, London.

Thompson, T. (1981) *Edwardian Childhoods*, London.

Tonkin, E. (1992) *Narrating our Pasts: The Social Construction of Oral History*, Cambridge, UK.

White, J. (1980) *Rothschild Buildings: Life in an East London Tenement Block 1887–1920*, London.

See also: folklore and myth; life history; oral tradition; social history.

oral tradition

The use of oral tradition as a term of art in the social sciences became common after the publication in English (1973) of Jan Vansina's *De la tradition orale: essai de méthode historique* (1961). Here Vansina proposed systematic means of identifying, collecting and interpreting oral traditions so as to discover aspects of the past, especially where documentation is lacking. He defined them as 'verbal testimony transmitted from one generation to the next one or a later one' (1973: xiii).

Vansina exemplified his methodology through analysis of traditions he had himself collected in the 1950s in the then Belgian-controlled Ruanda-Urundi and Kuba kingdom of Congo. Influenced by British anthropologists, he nevertheless criticized them for assuming that traditions could only justify contemporary social structures (cf. Malinowski's influential notion that myths are charters for present action, 1926). Well versed in earlier German scholarship, he also argued that it was wrong to claim that oral traditions can not be validated internally, without reference to independent (usually written) accounts.

Vansina's propositions were immediately engaging and influential at a time when European colonization was ending and new nations sought an authenticating past; when historians in the USA and western Europe were beginning to investigate history from below through living memories; when new universities, and therefore research workers, proliferated. Above all, the tape recorder encouraged study of the oral. In Europe and the USA, oral history focused on experiences which were personally recalled. For Africa, oral tradition was sought, in the expectation that traditional societies would use it to transmit some record of their more distant past. Vansina argued that historical information from a generation before the speaker might be encoded in riddles, proverbs, praise names, dynastic poems, and the like.

Oral traditions had been recognized and studied much earlier. The term 'tradition' comes from the Latin *traditio*, transmission or 'handing down', and Francis Bacon used it to define 'the expressing or transferring of knowledge' (1605, Oxford English Dictionary). In Europe, collection and study of folksong and folklore, ballads, oral epics, customs and popular superstitions goes back to the eighteenth century and earlier. The search for an authentic stream of tradition, ideally rural, and uncontaminated by high culture, became one aspect of cultural nationalism in Europe, where the high culture could often be identified with imperial overrule, and 'the tradition' therefore has authorized a subordinate community's right to nationhood – in terms of its language, long history and native wisdom. Like the adjective 'traditional', the phrase offers a guarantee, but one that can be challenged.

The quest for oral tradition has been complementary or alternative to documentary history, and the relative lack of interest in Indian oral traditions may be due to the greater kudos of literary civilization. The first great survey of oral material was called *The Growth of Literature* (Chadwick and Chadwick 1932; 1936; 1940). The Chadwicks discussed their sources as preliterate evidence of morality and law as well as of verbal art. Studies of Balkan singers by Parry (1930; 1932) and Lord (1960) were undertaken so as to understand better the art of Homer, on the premise that the epic was a universal, originally oral genre. Lord shows how singers recoded new material through stock themes and fixed formulae, in an influential model of oral transmission. However, not all oral material is patterned in this way. Lord's case study also shows how orality can coexist with literacy for hundreds of years. Information from literate sources can appear in traditional material and vice versa, so that traditions are not insulated from change.

Lord's approach to traditions is unlike many purely textual accounts because it is derived from observing singers and discussing practices with them. Later researchers have focused on performances and the dynamics of the social situations in which tellers communicate their material to particular audiences. Vansina's initial contention that the teller of a tradition could be merely their conduit was essentially derived from structural-functional anthropology and assumes a fairly static intervening past, in which the same social conditions of transmission have recurred. Oral historians in Africa have not always found well-formed traditions and it has become clearer that these are not conservative by definition. We should look rather to social context so as to grasp the ideology informing an account. How is it authorized? 'Tradition bearers' may support official leaders, while in a non-centralized community, tellers may recall only that part of the past which explains or justifies their own small social unit. Past changes may be described in oblique, symbolic ways.

In many parts of the world, students of verbal arts may indeed find performers who work in a long-developed tradition. But some analysts stress that all utterances are actions, and can not simply be analysed as if they are written texts (and see Vansina 1985). Social and economic historians, like political scientists, have often recorded personal reminiscences rather than tradition. But these are not necessarily distinct forms, and an appearance of authorial spontaneity or impersonal timelessness may be misleading (see e.g. Tonkin 1992). The practical and analytical advice of Finnegan (1992) is useful to anyone with social or cultural interests who seeks to record and interpret oral performances. Finnegan also reviews the many academic approaches to tradition.

Elizabeth Tonkin
Queen's University Belfast

References

Chadwick, H. M. and Chadwick, N. K. (1932; 1936; 1940) *The Growth of Literature* 3 volumes, Cambridge, UK.
Finnegan, R. (1992) *Oral Traditions and the Verbal Arts*, London.
Lord, A. B. (1960) *The Singer of Tales*, Cambridge, MA.
Malinowski, B. (1926) *Myth in Primitive Psychology*, London.
Parry, M. (1930; 1932) 'Studies in the epic techniques of oral text making', *Harvard Studies in Classical Philosophy*, 41; 43, Cambridge, MA.
Tonkin, E. (1992) *Narrating our Pasts*, Cambridge, UK.
Vansina, J. (1961) 'De la tradition orale: essay de méthode historique' *Annales du Musée Royal de l'Afrique Centrale*.
—— (1973) *Oral Tradition*, Harmondsworth.
—— (1985) *Oral Tradition as History*, London.

Further reading

Dundes, A. (1980) *Interpreting Folklore*, Bloomington, IN.
Johnson, J. W. with Fa-Digi Sisòkò (1986) *The Epic of Son-Jara*, Bloomington, IN.
Tedlock, D. (1983) *The Spoken Word and the Work of Interpretation*, Philadelphia, PA.

See also: folklore and myth; oral history.

organization, industrial *see* industrial organization

organizational change

Change within organizations is at once one of the most pervasive yet elusive subjects within the social sciences. It is evidently a universal phenomenon, while at the same time it has been studied largely through indirect means. It was no surprise therefore that Bill Clinton used the image of change fourteen times during his presidential inauguration on 20 January 1993. However, academic understanding of change in organizations has developed through the study of related areas such as technological change. None the less, the problem has generated a core of specialist work which reveals a rich variety of approaches to understanding organizational change.

There is general agreement that organizational change may take on many forms. An organization could exhibit localized, incremental change or large-scale strategic change which involves the whole institution. Equally, staff may employ an anticipatory or a reactive approach to change. Combining such features leads to a fourfold classification of organizational change types (Nadler and Tushman 1990): *tuning*, where small, internally developed adjustments to existing policies or structures occurs; *adaptation*, as a firm is forced to react to external pressures such as legislation; *reorientation*, when a company plans a strategic shift in core activities; and *re-creation*, where the organization effects a fundamental reworking of its reason for existence. An additional and extreme form of change is the crisis which threatens such profound change that it endangers the existence of the organization. These distinctions and the resulting vocabulary are a vital means of comprehending the variety of types of change found within organizations and those who write about the subject.

Commentators on organizational change fall into four groups. The first set relates largely to the practitioners and consultants who seek to advise organizations on appropriate change techniques. In general, their preoccupation has been with change seen as an event and an essentially rational orientation to management. The most sophisticated version of this approach comes from Beckhard and Harris (1987) who emphasize the choices that organizations face when changing. In their view these choices should account for three distinct change conditions: the present state of the organization, the future state as defined by management, and the vital transition state, which enables the organization to proceed from the present to future desired condition.

A second group of academic writers place greater emphasis on change as a process rather than an event. Some dis-miss the idea that change in organizations can be direct or managed. Lindblom (1990), for example, saw the role of management as adapting to the irrational behaviour within organizations by developing a 'science of muddling through'. Others emphasize the part played by chance and serendipity in all aspects of organizational life. Quinn (1988) is distinctive, for he considers that strategies for changing organizations can be created, but they emerge in a fragmented, evolutionary and intuitive manner. In spite of their emergent nature, these strategies can be logically and incrementally generated in an informal yet purposeful manner.

During the 1980s a third, more assertive school of writing on organizational change arose which emphasized the creative opportunities and the capacity for commercial regeneration. The main impetus came from the reaction of US organizations to the increasing Japanese domination of international markets, notably in consumer goods and manufacturing industries. Writers such as Kanter (1990) see commercial competition as a spur to innovation within organizations. Her assumption is that integrative organizations link their structure, culture and reward systems to facilitate change. Key rules for changing organizations therefore emphasize problem definition, building coalitions and mobilizing completion.

A fourth group of writers working in the UK have pointed to the range of forces involved in organizational change. Studies of both manufacturing and service sectors suggest that organizational change has to be conceptualized as a multilevel problem and analysed as a multidimensional problem. Pettigrew and Whipp (1991) reveal how changes occur simultaneously at the organization, sector and economy levels. Moreover, change within an organization has to be understood by reference to the content of the change, the contexts in which it happens, and the process through which it occurs. These dimensions may be translated into three respective research questions: What is the nature of the change? Why has it arisen? How has it occurred? The emphasis for change managers becomes attention to the three corresponding analytical, educational and political problems of organizational change.

The future of the subject will, in many ways, be determined by the unravelling of the issues raised in the more recent Anglo-American studies. However, the isolated work of Carnall (1990) on the coping strategies of individuals in the face of organizational change will become central to the growing schedule of puzzles raised by the advent of the knowledge worker and network organizations.

Richard Whipp
University of Wales

References

Beckhard, R. and Harris, R. T. (1987) *Organizational Transitions: Managing Complex Change*. Reading, MA.

Carnall, C. A. (1990) *Managing Change in Organizations*, Hemel Hempstead.

Kanter, R. M. (1990) *The Change Masters: Corporate Entrepreneurs at Work*, London.

Lindblom, C. E. (1990) 'The science of "muddling through"', in D. S. Pugh (ed.) *Organization Theory: Selected Readings*, Harmondsworth.

Nadler, D. and Tushman, M. (1990) 'Beyong the charismatic leader: leadership and organizational change', *California Management Review*, Winter, 32, 2.

Pettigrew, A. M. and Whipp, R. (1991) *Managing Change for Competitive Success*, Oxford.

Quinn, J. B. (1988) 'Strategic change, "logical incrementalism"', in J. B. Quinn, H. Mintzberg and R. M. James (eds) *The Strategy Process: Concepts, Contexts, and Cases*, Englewood Cliffs, NJ.

See also: *organizations*.

organizations

Formal organizations emerged as the strategic social units within industrial capitalist societies in the latter half of the nineteenth century as the scale and complexity of socioeconomic and political activity moved beyond the administrative capacity of more personal and direct forms of control. The former provided a social technology through which human, capital and cultural resources could be assembled and co-ordinated in such a way that they fulfilled the material and social needs of dominant groups within industrial capitalist societies. In this respect, formal organizations provided a set of structures and practices through which the requirements for efficient large-scale production and administration, and the power interests which they served, could be realized.

At the core of this set of structures and practices lay the principles of standardization and centralization. Standardization was provided for by the development of an extremely detailed division of functional and administrative tasks such that the routinization of work performance could be pushed as far as was practically possible under prevailing conditions. Centralization became enshrined in the hierarchical mechanisms through which overall strategic command could be concentrated at the apex of the organization, while operational decision-making authority could be delegated downwards in a highly controlled and regulated manner. Thus, the combination of standardized work performance and centralized administrative control established a generic organizational framework through which the rational management of socioeconomic and political activity could be realized on a continuous basis within industrial capitalist societies.

This framework became modified in various ways from the 1960s onwards in order to respond to and cope with the destabilizing impact of technological and economic innovations that required more organic organizational forms which departed from the inherent logic of standardized work and centralized control (Burns and Stalker 1961). Over time, the modifications to highly specialized and centralized organizational designs suggested by the 'organic' model – involving a move towards much more flexible and adaptive ways of working and managing – began to raise some very serious questions about the theoretical cogency and practical utility of the orthodox bureaucratic or mechanistic form.

Nevertheless, functionally specialized and hierarchically structured organizational designs dominated the economic, social and political development of capitalist and subsequently socialist societies for much of the twentieth century. Both systems came to depend on the administrative machinery which formal or complex organizations provided as a necessary precondition for the management of large-scale economic and political activity, as well as for the disciplining of their populations in anomic urban conurbations, where the maintenance of social order became more problematic for ruling elites and classes (Cooper 1992). Indeed, the technical and political indispensability of formal organization for the rational administration and management of social life in modern societies led some commentators (Presthus 1962) to argue that the latter were all 'organized societies' – irrespective of their particular ideological features and historical trajectories. The twentieth century, it was argued, was the century of 'organization', in so far as modern industrial – or for that matter post-industrial (Bell 1973) – societies could not continue to exist in anything resembling their current institutional forms without the administrative mechanisms and techniques through which the rational direction and control of long-term socioeconomic and political development could be achieved (Kumar 1978). Formal organization provided the indispensable planning and steering mechanism which allowed modern industrial and post-industrial societies to exert a degree of self-control over their destinies which was simply inconceivable for traditional or, for that matter, 'market' societies.

However, later research and analysis suggests that the dominance of formal organization is at an end – or at the very least that its reign is in terminal decline. From the 1980s onwards, a number of highly influential studies have been published (Castells 1989; Lash and Urry 1987; 1994; Piore and Sabel 1984) which argue that a process of 'disorganization' has taken hold in all advanced industrial societies which fundamentally undermines the strategic role and significance of formal or complex organization. This is so to the extent that the underlying dynamic of late-twentieth-century technological, economic and cultural change is seen to push in the direction of ways of organizing that break with the standardizing and centralizing imperatives characteristic of earlier phases of capitalist-led development. Thus, the 'disorganizing dynamic' inherent in late twentieth-century capitalist accumulation seems to require much more flexible and fragmented forms of organizing, in which formalized administrative structures and practices give way to structureless flows of resources, people, ideas and technologies. As Castells puts it. 'There is, in fact, a shift away from the centrality of the organizational unit to the network of information and decision. In other words, *flows rather than organizations* become the units of work, decision and output accounting' (Castells 1989: 142).

If this intepretation is accepted, then the continued relevance of organizations to our understanding and management of social change becomes much more questionable and potentially redundant – in both an intellectual and practical sense. The social engineering ethos which informed so much of the long-term development of formal organization now seems pretentious, not to say powerless, in the face of radical change which fundamentally undermines the rationale for standardized work and centralized control. Yet, the disorganization thesis is open to challenge on a number of grounds. First, it tends to treat organization as being synonymous with bureaucratic organization. While there is some justification for this view, it seriously underestimates the extent to which alternative organizational forms, that break with established practice, have always been available and used. Second, it tends to neglect the issue of how flows become organized and how organizational forms – whatever their particular configuration – structure the processes through which change occurs. Finally, it risks the acceptance of a rather naïve and over-optimistic interpretation of long-term socioeconomic, political and cultural development, in which the power struggles that drive both the dynamics and outcomes of change are conspicous by their absence.

In short, a systematic consideration of the plurality of organizational forms through which social life is co-ordinated is likely to remain a major focus for social scientific research as it struggles to understand and explain the dynamics, structures and outcomes of socio-historical change in contemporary capitalist societies.

Michael I. Reed
Lancaster University

References

Bell, D. (1973) *The Coming of Post-Industrial Society*, New York.
Burns, T. K. and Stalker, G. M. (1961) *The Management of Innovation*, London.
Castells, M. (1989) *The Informational City*, Oxford.
Cooper, B. (1992) 'Formal organization as representation: remote control displacement and abbreviation', in M. Reed and M. J. Hughes (eds) *Rethinking Organization: New Directions in Organization Theory and Analysis*, London.
Kumar, K. (1978) *Prophecy and Progress: The Sociology of Industrial and Post-Industrial Society*, London.
Lash, S. and Urry, J. (1987) *The End of Organized Capitalism*, Cambridge, UK.
—— (1994) *Economies of Signs and Space*, London.
Piore, M. and Sabel, C. (1984) *The Second Industrial Divide*, New York.
Presthus, R. (1962) *The Organizational Society*, New York.

Further reading

Clegg, S. (1990) *Modern Organizations*, London.
Reed, M. (1992) *The Sociology of Organizations*, Hemel Hempstead.
Thompson, P. and McHugh, D. (1990) *Work Organizations*, London.

See also: firm, theory of; human resource management; industrial organization; leadership; organizational change.

orientalism

Orientalism is the extension and application to anthropology of the work of the literary and cultural critic Edward Said. His *Orientalism* (1978) describes how westerners have understood the Middle East, classically called the Orient, and particularly the understandings developed by the academic discipline called Oriental Studies. As a generic term in anthropology, orientalism refers to distortions in the perception and analysis of alien societies that resemble the distortions that Said discerns in Oriental Studies. These distortions, critics say, are found frequently in anthropology (see Clifford 1988; Fabian 1983).

One distortion is exaggerating 'the difference between the familiar (Europe, the West, "us") and the strange (the Orient, the East, "'them'")' (Said 1978: 43). This is found in ethnography that focuses on the exotic in the societies it describes. More subtly, it is found in theories or models that compare the west and the alien and that portray the alien as little more than a mirror-image of the western. Examples include the comparison of hierarchic (India) and egalitarian (western) societies (e.g. Dumont 1970; 1977) and the comparison of gift (Melanesian) and commodity (western) societies (e.g. Gregory 1982).

A second distortion is treating a society as though it is an unchanging expression of some basic essence or genius, a distortion sometimes called 'essentialism'. Here, social and cultural practices and institutions are portrayed or understood as being 'what they are *because* they are what they are for all time, for ontological reasons that no empirical matter can either dislodge or alter' (Said 1978: 70). This refers particularly to anthropologists who seek to discern a stable and coherent social order that somehow simply inheres in the society being described as part of its essence.

Closely related to this is a third distortion, portraying and analysing a society as though it is radically separated from the west. This occurs especially in ethnography that ignores points of contact between the society and the west, and so ignores the colonial relations that may have existed between the two societies, as it also ignores western intrusions in that society. These are ignored because they do not reflect what is taken to be the true essence of the society involved.

Although many condemn orientalism, it may be inescapable in anthropology. Groups commonly distinguish themselves from others by casting those others as exotic in some way, and there is no reason to expect that anthropologists are exempt from this tendency. Similarly, comparison is at the heart of anthropology, and to compare two societies is almost necessarily to stress their differences and slight their similarities, and to construe them in terms of fundamental attributes or essences.

James G. Carrier
University of Durham

References

Clifford, J. (1988) *The Predicament of Culture: Twentieth-Century Ethnography, Literature, and Art*, Cambridge, MA.

Dumont, L. (1970) *Homo Hierarchicus: The Caste System and its Implications*, London.

—— (1977) *From Mandeville to Marx: The Genesis and Triumph of Economic Ideology*, Chicago.

Fabian, J. (1983) *Time and the Other: How Anthropology Makes Its Object*, New York.

Gregory, C. A. (1982) *Gifts and Commodities*, London.

Said, E. (1978) *Orientalism*, Harmondsworth.

See also: cultural anthropology.

P

parapsychology

Strictly speaking, parapsychology refers only to the study of psychokinesis (PK) and extrasensory perception (ESP). *Psychokinesis* (literally *mind movement*) refers to the ability physically to affect objects or events by mental influence alone, known popularly as 'mind over matter'. *Extrasensory perception* refers to three different phenomena: *telepathy*, which is direct communication between two minds without the use of the known sensory channels; *clairvoyance*, which is awareness of objects and events at a distant location, without the use of the known sensory channels or logical inference; and *precognition*, which is knowledge of events before they happen, other than by logical inference. In practice, however, the term parapsychology is often used more widely to refer to the study of any paranormal events (i.e. events which cannot be explained in terms of the known laws of science). This wider definition would include such areas as astrology, the Bermuda triangle, biorhythm theory, firewalking, ghosts, Kirlian photography, UFOs (unidentified flying objects), unusual life-forms (for example, the yeti), and so on.

Although reports of paranormal events can be found in all cultures throughout history, widespread modern interest in the subject in the western world was sparked by the birth of spiritualism. In 1848, the Fox sisters, 11-year-old Kate and 13-year-old Margaret, in the small New York town of Hydesville, reported hearing a rapping sound in their home. It was claimed that these sounds were messages from the dead and thus the spiritualist movement was born. Within a relatively short period, seances were popular across both the USA and Europe and the range of phenomena produced at such events had gone beyond simple rapping. They included levitation, ectoplasmic manifestations, spirit voices, and so on. Many great scientists became interested in such phenomena leading to the formation in Britain of the Society for Psychical Research (SPR) in 1882. The American

Society for Psychical Research (ASPR) was founded in 1885. It was hoped at the time that the study of mediums and their abilities might provide proof that the soul survives after death, but convincing proof was never forthcoming. Many mediums were caught red-handed in the act of cheating, but this by no means persuaded their supporters, including some of the finest scientists of the time, that all of the effects produced by such mediums were fraudulent. Even the confession by Margaret Fox in 1888 that the apparent rapping which had given rise to spiritualism forty years earlier was nothing more than the noise produced by her 'cracking' her toes did little to shake the conviction of true believers.

Eventually, however, the need for more controlled testing of paranormal claims was recognized. A milestone in parapsychological investigation was the establishment in 1935 by Joseph Banks Rhine of the Parapsychology Laboratory at Duke University. Rhine, with the assistance of his wife Louisa and other colleagues, introduced quantitative studies rather than relying upon anecdotal evidence. He carried out studies of PK, in which subjects would attempt to influence the roll of a dice, and studies of ESP using a special pack of cards, known as a Zener pack. Each set of twenty-five cards contained five of each type of symbol (plus sign, square, circle, wavy line, and star). By chance alone, one would expect a subject to get about five correct if asked to guess the sequence of cards in a shuffled deck. Rhine's early research appeared to demonstrate that subjects could perform on both ESP and PK tasks at a level far higher than could be explained simply on the basis of chance expectation. However, his early work was criticized on both methodological and statistical grounds. When controls were tightened in response to such criticisms, significant results, although still produced, were harder to obtain. Since this pioneering research, however, the experimental sophistication of parapsychologists has increased tremendously. Two techniques which have been used widely are remote viewing (in which a 'sender' visiting a randomly selected remote site attempts to project mental impressions of the site back to a 'receiver') and the *ganzfeld* procedure (in which a sender attempts to transmit information telepathically to a receiver, the latter being under conditions of perceptual deprivation).

Critics of parapsychology remain unconvinced by the evidence produced. There is no doubt that many of the claimed phenomena subsumed under the wider definition of parapsychology are not genuine. For example, hundreds of empirical investigations of the claims of traditional astrology show conclusively that it lacks any validity, and neither Kirlian photography nor firewalking, contrary to popular belief, require any psychic explanation. Furthermore, the claims regarding PK and ESP at the core of parapsychology have not been proven to the satisfaction of the wider scientific community. Critics continue to highlight methodological and statistical problems in the area, pointing out that such extraordinary claims require a very high standard of evidence. After all, if parapsychological claims are true, the rest of science will require major revision. A further problem is the ever-present possibility of fraud. It is salutary to consider the case of S. G. Soal, a British investigator whose work in the 1940s was hailed by parapsychologists as providing incontrovertible evidence for the reality of telepathy. In the 1970s, however, it was shown conclusively that there were anomalies in the data set. Soal's results were apparently fraudulently obtained, although this was demonstrated only after several decades and might easily have never come to light. The single most damaging criticism of parapsychology, however, is that even after over a century of organized scientific research, and despite claims to the contrary, parapsychologists have been unable to specify the conditions that would be required for a reliably reproducible paranormal effect. Until this is achieved, critics will remain understandably reluctant to accept the reality of the paranormal.

Christopher French
University of London

Further reading

Edge, H. L., Morris, R. L., Palmer, J. and Rush, J. H. (1986) *Foundations of Parapsychology: Exploring the Boundaries of Human Capability*, London.
Kurtz, P. (ed.) (1985) *A Skeptic's Handbook of Parapsychology*, Buffalo, NY.

Pareto efficiency

Pareto efficiency is a concept used by economists to define the efficient organization of an economy. Roughly speaking, it requires not only that production should be organized in an efficient manner, but also that this production should be distributed efficiently among consumers. In formal terms, an allocation of resources, which specifies not only what is produced with the basic resources available to the economy, but also how that production is distributed among consumers, is Pareto efficient if the following holds: there is no other feasible allocation in which no individual is worse-off and at least one individual is strictly better-off than in the initial allocation (equivalently, it is impossible to make someone better-off without simultaneously making at least one individual worse-off). Here, 'feasible' refers to what can be produced given the available resources and technology.

The Italian sociologist and economist, Vilfredo Pareto (1848–1923), was the first to use this definition of efficiency, although Edgeworth had earlier employed the same idea without apparently realizing its general applicability. Pareto efficiency is too weak to be equated with optimality in any meaningful sense, and consequently the term has gradually replaced the misleading 'Pareto optimality' in usage. The weakness of the concept stems from the fact that it has nothing to say about distributional issues. To put the matter at its starkest, imagine an economy with a fixed amount of a single type of good, say apples. Suppose that all the apples are allocated to a particular individual, who likes to have as many apples as possible, and everyone else gets nothing. This allocation is Pareto efficient as any other allocation will make our individual worse-off, but it is certainly not optimum in any reasonable sense. This weakness, however, is also the reason why it is *the* accepted definition of efficiency within orthodox theory. It is held to be value-free because its application requires no opinion as to the relative merits of different welfare distributions. Moreover, its use requires relatively weak information about individual welfare: it is only necessary to know how individuals rank alternative allocations; neither cardinal information about intensities of preferences nor interpersonal comparabilty of individual welfare is required.

The concept plays a central role in modern welfare economics. A key result is the so-called first theorem of welfare economics, which asserts that a competitive market economy will under mild conditions lead to a Pareto efficient allocation of resources. This theorem is the formalization in a precise mathematical sense of Adam Smith's 'invisible hand', whereby a society of individuals, each behaving in a self-seeking manner, results in an outcome which is to the common good in some sense. Pareto attempted unsuccessfully to establish this result; it was left to a later generation of theorists to come up with a satisfactory derivation.

Jonathan Thomas
University of Warwick

References

Pareto, V. (1897) *Cours d'économie politique*, vol. 2 Lausanne.
Edgeworth. F. Y. (1881) *Mathematical Psychics*, London.
Smith, A. (1776[1981]) *An Inquiry into the Nature and Causes of the Wealth of Nations*, ed. R. H. Campbell, A. S. Skinner and W. B. Todd, New York.

Further reading

Little, I. M. D. (1950) *A Critique of Welfare Economics*, Oxford.
Sen, A. K. (1979) 'Personal utilities and public judgements: or what's wrong with welfare economics?', *Economic Journal* 89.

See also: economic efficiency; welfare economics.

Parsons, Talcott (1902–79)

Talcott Parsons, the son of a Congregational minister in Colorado, became the most important American sociologist. He studied biology and philosophy at Amherst College and then did graduate work in social science at the London School of Economics and at Heidelberg. In 1927, he joined the Harvard economics department and in 1931 switched to the sociology department, which had just been created. He became chairman of the sociology department in 1944 and then chairman of the newly-formed department of social relations in 1946, a position he retained until 1956. He officially retired in 1973 but continued writing until his death (in Munich) in 1979. His self-image was that of a theoretical synthesizer of social science in general and sociology in particular. Seeing sociocultural forces as the dominant ones shaping human activity, he assigned sociology the role of integrating the analyses of psychology, politics and economics into a science of human action. Sociology also had the role of providing other social sciences with their boundary assumptions (such as specifying what market imperfections exist).

Parsons's first book, *The Structure of Social Action* (1937), assesses the legacy to sociology of Marshall, Pareto, Durkheim and Weber. These thinkers, Parsons argues, converged from different directions on a solution to the problem of why society is not characterized by a Hobbesian war of all against all. According to Parsons, their solution is that people share common values and norms. Parsons's subsequent work, particularly *The Social System* (1951), *Towards a General Theory of Action* (1951), and *Family, Socialization and Interaction Process* (1955), develops the importance of the integration of a shared normative structure into people's need-dispositions for making social order possible. Structure, for Parsons, comprises the elements with greatest permanence in a society. These elements he identifies as the society's values, norms, collectivities and roles. The concern with people being socialized into a society's structure gives a conservative flavour to Parsons's thought.

Parsons argues that for a social structure to persist, four functions must be performed. These are adaptation, goal-attainment, integration and pattern-maintenance or tension-management. Societies tend to differentiate functionally to produce separate institutions specializing in each of these functions. The economy is adaptive, the polity specializes in goal-attainment, the stratification system is integrative, while education and religion are both concerned with pattern-maintenance. The most important social change in human history has been a gradual evolution of more functionally differentiated societies. For the evolution of a more differentiated structure to be successful, there must be adaptive upgrading, inclusion and value generalization. The increased specialization produced by functional differentiation makes adaptive upgrading possible. Inclusion refers to processes (such as extension of the franchise) that produce commitment by people to the new more specialized structures. Finally, values must be generalized or stated more abstractly in order to legitimize a wider range of activities.

Parsons sees money, power, influence and commitment as generalized symbolic media that mediate the interchanges among the differentiated sectors of society. Power is defined as the capacity to achieve results. He develops an analysis of power based on its being the political system's equivalent of money. Force is the equivalent of the gold backing of a currency – it provides a back-up to power, but if it has to be resorted to frequently then the political system is breaking down. Inflation can ruin power just as it may destroy a currency.

Parsons's substantive concerns have ranged from Nazi Germany to Ancient Greece to modern school classes. Many of his specific analyses have proved highly influential. Particularly noteworthy are his analysis of illness as legitimized deviance; of McCarthyism as a response to strains in American society resulting from the USA assuming the responsibilities of being a world power; of the pressures in American society pushing towards full citizenship for Black Americans; and of secularization as a result of increasing functional differentiation. Parsons's analysis of business and the professions involves the use of one of his best-known classifications, the pattern variables. The four pattern variables which can be used to describe any role relationship are affectivity v. neutrality, specificity v. diffuseness, universalism v. particularism, and quality v. performance. The relationship of business people to their clients is identical to professionals to their clients when this relationship is classified using the pattern variables. Each group relates neutrally, specifically, universalistically and in terms of the expected performance of the client. Understood this way, business people and professionals are similar, and their roles mesh easily together. Thus this analysis is better than one that sees professionals as altruistic and radically different from egotistical business people.

Parsons's influence on American sociology is immense. His *The Structure of Social Action* was the first major English-language presentation of the works of Weber and Durkheim and helped make their ideas central to American sociology's heritage. Many of Parsons's specific analyses and concepts are widely accepted, though few people accept his overall position. In the 1940s and 1950s, he was the dominant American theorist. In the 1960s his ideas came under increasing attack for being incapable of dealing with change. Since then, this criticism has come to be seen as simplistic. His work is increasingly being examined in terms of the solutions it offers to various dilemmas about how to theorize about society.

Kenneth Menzies
University of Guelph

Further reading

Bourricaud, F. (1981 [1977]) *The Sociology of Talcott Parsons*, Chicago. (Original edn, *L'individualisme institutionel: essai sur la sociologie de Talcott Parsons*, Paris.)
Menzies, K. (1977) *Talcott Parsons and the Social Image of Man*, London.
Wearne, Bruce C. (1989) *The Theory and Scholarship of Talcott Parsons to 1951*, Cambridge, UK.

parties, political

Scholars who have specialized in the study of political parties have found it difficult to agree on a definition of the term. The oldest definition, which emerged in the nineteenth century, may still be the best one: political parties are organizations that try to win public office in electoral competition with one or more similar organizations. The problem with this definition is that it is a narrow one. As Schlesinger (1968) points out, it excludes three kinds of organizations that are also usually referred to as parties: first, those that are too small to have a realistic chance to win public office, especially executive office, but that do nominate candidates and participate in election campaigns;

second, revolutionary parties that aim to abolish competitive elections; and third, the governing groups in totalitarian and other authoritarian one-party states. However, the inclusion of these three additional categories makes the definition overly broad. This difficulty may be solved partly by distinguishing two very different types of parties: the governing parties in one-party states and the competitive parties in two-party and multiparty democracies or near-democracies (that is, countries that are not fully democratic but that do allow free electoral competition).

The principal problem that remains is how to draw a distinction, in two-party and multiparty systems, between political parties and interest groups. Interest groups may sometimes also nominate candidates for public office without *ipso facto* changing their character from interest group to political party. Hence two further criteria have been proposed. One concerns the breadth of the interests represented by parties and interest groups. The typical function of interest groups is to articulate interests, whereas political parties serve the broader function of 'aggregating' the articulated interests (Almond 1960). This distinction is obviously one of degree rather than of a sharp dividing line. It also applies more clearly to two-party systems with broadly aggregative parties than to multiparty situations.

The second criterion, suggested by Blondel (1969), entails a combination of the kinds of goals that parties and interest groups pursue and the types of membership that they have. Interest groups tend to have either a promotional or protective character. Promotional associations tend to advance specific points of view (such as environmentalism or the abolition of capital punishment) and are in principle open to all citizens. Protective associations (such as trade unions or veterans' associations) defend certain groups of people; their membership is therefore more limited, but their goals are broader and may extend over the entire range of public policy issues. Political parties can now be distinguished from both promotional and protective groups: their goals are general (like those of protective associations), but their membership is open (like that of promotional groups). The borderline cases are single-issue parties, which resemble promotional groups, and cultural or ethnic minority parties, which are similar to protective groups.

Parties can be classified according to three principal dimensions. First, their form of organization, which distinguishes between mass and cadre parties. Mass parties have relatively many formal members and are centralized, disciplined and highly oligarchical; cadre parties have a much smaller formal membership and lower degrees of centralization, discipline and oligarchy. Second, the parties' programmes, which may be ideological or pragmatic, and which may reflect a leftist, centrist or rightist outlook. Third, the parties' supporters, who may be mainly working class or mainly middle class, or may be defined in terms other than the socio-economic spectrum, such as religion and ethnicity.

Duverger (1963) has shown that these dimensions are empirically related: socialists and other parties of the left tend to be based on working-class support, and are ideological mass parties; conservative and centre parties tend to be supported more by middle-class voters, and are pragmatic cadre parties. The link between party organizations and programmes in western democracies was stronger in the period before the Second World War than in the post-war era. The general post-war trend has been for parties to assume the character of mass parties but also to become more pragmatic. The relationship between programmes and supporters has also grown somewhat weaker, but it is still true that the parties of the left tend to be supported by working-class voters to a greater extent than the parties of the right. Social class is a good predictor of party choice in virtually all democracies, but in religiously or linguistically divided countries voting behaviour is more strongly determined by religion and language (Lijphart 1979).

The way in which a political party operates in a democracy depends not only on its own characteristics but also on its interaction with other parties. In this respect, the literature on political parties has emphasized the difference between two-party and multiparty systems. Here another definitional problem arises. How should we determine the number of parties in a party system? For instance, Britain is usually said to have a two-party system, although no fewer than eight different parties were elected to the House of Commons in the 1992 election. The usual practice is to count only the large and important parties and to ignore the small parties. But how large does a party have to be in order to be included in the count?

Sartori (1976) has proposed that only those parties should be counted that have either coalition potential or blackmail potential. A party possesses coalition potential if it has participated in cabinet coalitions (or in one-party cabinets) or if it is regarded as a possible coalition partner by the other major parties. A party without coalition potential may have blackmail potential: it may be ideologically unacceptable as a coalition partner, but it may be so large that it still exerts considerable influence (such as a large communist party). Sartori's counting rules therefore appear to be based on the two variables of size and ideological compatibility, but it should be pointed out that the size factor is the crucial one. A very small party with only a few parliamentary seats may be quite moderate and ideologically acceptable, but it will generally not have coalition potential simply because the support it can give to a cabinet is not sufficiently substantial. Hence the parties that Sartori counts are mainly the larger ones, regardless of their ideological compatibility. Moreover, although size is the dominant factor, he does not use it to make further distinctions among larger and smaller parties: they are all counted equally.

Blondel (1969) has tried to use both the number of parties and their relative sizes in classifying party systems. His four categories are two-party systems, two-and-a-half party systems, multiparty systems with a dominant party, and multiparty systems without a dominant party. Two-party systems, like those of Britain and New Zealand, are dominated by two large parties, although a few small parties may also have seats in parliament. A two-and-a-half party system consists of two large parties and one that, although considerably smaller, does have coalition potential and does play a significant role, such as the German Free Democrats and the Irish Labour Party. Multiparty systems have more than two-and-a-half significant parties. These may or may not include a dominant party. Examples of the former are the Christian Democrats in the Italian multiparty system and the Social Democrats in the Scandinavian countries. The French Fourth Republic offers a good example of a multiparty system without a dominant party.

The concepts of a dominant party and a half party serve the useful function of distinguishing between parties of different sizes, but they only offer a rough measurement. A more precise index is the effective number of parties (Taagepera and Shugart 1989). It is calculated according to a simple formula that takes the exact share of parliamentary seats of each party into consideration. For a pure two-party system with two equally strong parties, the effective number of parties is 2.0. If the two parties are highly unequal in size – for instance, if they have 65 and 35 per cent of the seats – the effective number of parties is 1.8. This is in agreement with the view that such a party system deviates from a pure two-party system in the direction of a one-party system. If there are three parties of equal strength, the index is 3.0. In a two-and-a-half party system in which the parliamentary seats are distributed in a 45:43:12 ratio, the effective number of parties is exactly 2.5.

Party systems have a strong empirical relationship with electoral systems and with cabinet coalitions and cabinet stability (Lijphart 1984). In four countries using plurality methods of election (Canada, New Zealand, the UK and the USA) the average effective number of parties in the 1945–80 period was 2.1; in fifteen, mainly west European, countries with proportional representation, the average effective number of parties was 3.8, almost twice as many. Moreover, as the effective number of parties increases, the probability that a coalition cabinet will be formed also increases, but the longevity of cabinets decreases.

Arend Lijphart
University of California

References

Almond, G. A. (1960) 'Introduction: a functional approach to comparative politics', in G. A. Almond and J. S. Coleman (eds) *The Politics of the Developing Areas*, Princeton, NJ.

Blondel, J. (1969) *An Introduction to Comparative Government*, London.

Duverger, M. (1963) *Political Parties: Their Organisation and Activity in the Modern State*, trans. B. North and R. North, New York.

Lijphart, A. (1979) 'Religious vs. linguistic vs. class voting: the "crucial experiment" of comparing Belgium, Canada, South Africa, and Switzerland', *American Political Science Review* 73.

——(1984) *Democracies: Patterns of Majoritarian and Consensus Government in Twenty-One Countries*, New Haven, CT.

Sartori, G. (1976) *Parties and Party Systems: A Framework for Analysis*, vol. 1, Cambridge, UK.

Schlesinger, J. A. (1968) 'Party units', in D. L. Sills (ed.) *International Encyclopedia of the Social Sciences*, vol. 11, New York.

Taagepera, R. and Shugart, M. S. (1989) *Seats and Votes: The Effects and Determinants of Electoral Systems*, New Haven, CT.

Further reading

Budge, I. and Keman, H. (1990) *Parties and Democracy: Coalition Formation and Government Functioning in Twenty States*, Oxford.

Butler, D., Penniman, H. R. and Ranney, A. (eds) (1981) *Democracy at the Polls: A Comparative Study of Competitive National Elections*, Washington, DC.

Janda, K. (1980) *Political Parties: A Cross-National Survey*, New York.

Laver, M. and Hunt, W. B. (1992) *Policy and Party Competition*, New York.

Lijphart, A. (1994) *Electoral Systems and Party Systems: A Study of Twenty-Seven Democracies, 1945–1990*, Oxford.

Lipset, S. M. and Rokkan, S. (eds) (1967) *Party Systems and Voter Alignments: Cross-National Perspectives*, New York.

Strom, K. (1990) 'A behavioral theory of competitive political parties', *American Journal of Political Science* 34(2).

Von Beyme, K. (1985) *Political Parties in Western Democracies*, New York.

See also: elections; voting.

pastoralism

Pastoralism is a form of livelihood based upon the management of herds of domestic animals, including, in the Old World, cattle, sheep, goats, horses, camels, yak and reindeer, and in the New World, llamas and alpacas. It is well adapted to semi-arid, mountainous or subarctic environments which are unsuited to agriculture. However, most pastoralists either cultivate a little themselves, or obtain part of their food from agricultural neighbours in exchange for animal produce. Not much is known about the historical origins of pastoralism, but in most parts of the world it has probably arisen as a by-product of agricultural intensification. Only in the Eurasian subarctic and possibly in the Peruvian Andes did pastoral economies follow directly on the hunting of wild herds of the same species.

Pastoralists are commonly supposed to be nomadic. Though the grazing requirements of their herds often necessitate frequent shifts of location, the nature and extent of this movement varies considerably from one region to another. Sometimes it takes the form of a regular seasonal migration, but in other cases the movement appears most irregular, though in fact it is conditioned by the erratic incidence of local rainfall. Some pastoralists spend much of their lives in settled communities, or move in order to combine the husbandry of flocks and herds with that of crops or orchards. Since domestic animals may provide not only food and raw materials, but also a means of transport, many pastoral peoples are heavily involved in long-distance trade. Their nomadic movement may also have political significance, as a strategy to escape domination by an encompassing state organization. People who move about are hard to tax and administer, and for this reason central governments have always had an interest in the settlement of nomads.

Most pastoral societies are markedly egalitarian. Local groups or camps are fluid in composition, and disputes are solved by the parties going their separate ways. However, the recognition of living animals as moveable, self-reproducing property opens up possibilities not only for their accumulation but also for their functioning as a medium of exchange. The transfer of animals from household to household as gifts, loans or marriage payments serves to cement enduring social relations. The possession of animal property further structures relations within, as well as between, domestic groups, allowing men to control their juniors who stand to inherit, and who may need animals in order to marry with bridewealth. Relations between men and women depend critically on whether women can own animals or can only mediate transactions of animal wealth between men.

Pastoral peoples are among the most vulnerable in the modern world. In the past they have often held the key to power in the regions they traversed, by virtue of their military superiority and control over trade. Their presence is now generally considered an embarrassment by the administrations of the territories they inhabit. Restrictions on movement, enforced settlement and commercialization have undermined traditional strategies of security, so that occasional ecological crises – previously endured – have turned into human disasters of catastrophic proportions.

Tim Ingold
University of Manchester

Further reading

Galaty, J. G. and Johnson, D. (eds) (1990) *The World of Pastoralism: Herding Systems in Comparative Perspective*, London.

Ingold, T. (1980) *Hunters, Pastoralists and Ranchers*, Cambridge, UK.

Khazanov, A. M. (1984) *Nomads and the Outside World*, Cambridge, UK.

See also: hunters and gatherers.

patriarchy

Patriarchy, literally meaning the rule of the father, is a term which has been widely used in a range of contrasting accounts which seek to describe or explain the conditions of male superiority over women. What is not always understood is that the different uses of the term reflect differing understandings of the relationship between nature and culture in the organization of social life.

The modern history of this term starts with the lawyer Henry Maine's *Ancient Law* (1861), which argued that 'The patriarchal family was the fundamental and universal unit of society' (Coward 1983: 18). Like many of his contemporaries, Maine defined human society as society with law, and saw legality as being historically founded on the authority which fathers exercised over their families.

Maine was quickly challenged by evolutionary theorists (influenced by Darwin), especially Bachofen (1968 [1861]), McLennan (1865) and Morgan (1877), who claimed that modern society developed through a succession of stages from nature to culture. This contradicted Maine's view that human organization had been fully social from its beginnings.

According to the evolutionists, the earliest stage of human organization was matriarchy based on biological links between mother and child rather than social links with the father (patriarchy), which was a later and more advanced stage.

The idea of patriarchy as a vital developmental stage can be seen in the social theory of Marx, Engels and Weber, and in the psychoanalytic theory constructed by Freud. Engels's (1884) writing focused on the connection between private property, the patriarchal family and the origins of female oppression. Patriarchal household heads controlled women as the reproducers of children.

Thus, in the tradition of Morgan, Engels saw women's social position, unlike men's, as structured by their physical nature. Engels's account provided the framework for Marxist feminist critiques of patriarchy. However, a continuing tension developed between Marxist historical materialism, which insisted that a change in class relations would free women of their oppression, and the implications of Engels's biologically based account, which inadvertently introduced the possibility that it would not.

Attempts to resolve this contradiction not only include the development of dual systems theory (e.g. Barrett 1988; Delphy 1970–7; Eisenstein 1979; Rubin 1975), but also have led some Marxist feminists to reject the use of the term patriarchy altogether.

Whereas the Marxist approach argues that material structures determine relations between men and women, radical feminists (e.g. Daly 1978; Dworkin 1981; Millett 1971; Rich 1979) reverse the equation. For them, patriarchal values structure relations between the sexes and these inequalities of gender become paradigmatic of all other social inequalities and are not reducible to any other causes. However, although this view of patriarchy is a social explanation of gender oppression, it also tends, despite itself, to take for granted a natural distinction between men and women due to its central focus on an antagonistic gender dichotomy.

In these debates, the question which was constantly being asked was both whether the oppression of women was universal and whether it was natural.

Because of its cross-cultural perspective, anthropology had always potentially offered a critique of assumptions that relations between men and women are everywhere the same. However, it was not until the 1970s that the discipline began to engage with feminist perspectives (e.g. Ortner 1974; Reiter 1974; Rosaldo and Lamphere 1974) and began to shift its focus away from kinship and towards gender. Drawing on ethnographic evidence from outside Europe, anthropologists increasingly suggested that the apparently obvious biological differences between men and women did not necessarily account for, or directly explain, the very many different ways in which relationships between the sexes can be envisaged and enacted. Non-western societies do not necessarily make a strong dichotomous distinction between male and female based in biology, nor opposed nature to culture (e.g. Atkinson and Errington 1990; MacCormack and Strathern 1980). The concept of patriarchal domination may therefore seriously misrepresent the complexity of sexual relations and gendered identity, both outside and within the west. Writing from the mid-1980s to the 1990s has therefore moved away from the question of the causes of patriarchy to a comparative ethnography of the different components of gendered identities, including, for example, race.

Fenella Cannell
London School of Economics and Political Science

Sarah Green
University of Cambridge

References

Atkinson, J. M. and Errington S. (eds) (1990) *Power, Difference and Gender in Island Southeast Asia*, Stanford, CA.

Bachofen, J. J. (1968) *Myth, Religion and Mother-Right*, selections of Bachofen's writings, including *Das Mutter-Recht* (1861), London.

Barrett, M. (1988) *Women's Oppression Today: The Marxist-Feminist Encounter*, London.

Coward, R. (1983) *Patriarchal Precedents: Sexuality and Social Relations*, London.

Daly, M. (1978) *Gyn-ecology: The Metaethics of Radical Feminism*, Boston, MA.

Delphy, C. (1970–7) *The Main Enemy*, London.

Dworkin, A. (1981) *Pornography: Men Possessing Women*, New York.

Eisenstein, Z. (ed.) (1979) *Capitalist Patriarchy and the Case for Socialist Feminism*, New York.

Engels, F. (1884) *The Origins of the Family, Private Property and the State, in the Light of the Researches of Lewis H. Morgan*, London.

MacCormack, C. and Strathern, M. (eds) (1980) *Nature, Culture and Gender*, Cambridge, UK.

McLennan, D. (1865) *Primitive Marriage*, London.

Maine, H. (1861) *Ancient Law*, London.

Millett, K. (1971) *Sexual Politics*, New York.

Morgan, L. H. (1877) *Ancient Society*, New York.

Ortner, S. B. (1974) 'Is female to male as nature is to culture?', in M. Z. Rosaldo and L. Lamphere (eds) *Woman, Culture and Society*, Stanford, CA.

Reiter, R. R. (ed.) (1974) *Toward an Anthropology of Women*, London.

Rich, A. (1979) *On Lies, Secrets and Silence*, New York.

Rosaldo, M. Z. and Lamphere, L. (eds) (1974) *Woman, Culture and Society*, Stanford, CA

Rubin, G. (1975) 'The traffic in women', in R. Reiter (ed.) *Toward an Anthropology of Women*, London.

See also: feminist theory; gender and sex; primitive society; women; women's studies.

patronage

An exchange relationship is called patronage when it shows several distinctive characteristics. Usually, patronage is precisely defined as the power to provide jobs in the bureaucratic machinery at all levels. However, in a broader sense patronage means the distribution of valued resources: pensions, licences or public contracts, according to political criteria. There is a patron who has power and wants to retain it and there are clients who are in a subordinate position, though not totally powerless or deprived of resources. The patron may need votes and political support in a variety of ways. The clients are in a position to provide votes and different forms of political support. As a consequence, the exchange relationship may be established. In some cases, patronage is perfectly legal. For example, elected office holders are allowed to make use of a spoils system in appointing loyal supporters to political and bureaucratic positions. In the USA the President, governors and mayors do have and exercise this ancient privilege, though in time seriously trimmed and carefully scrutinized. By so doing, they reward their supporters, are in a better position to steer their preferred political and bureaucratic course, and try to reach additional constituencies. As political patrons, they are rightly considered responsible for the performance of the people they have selected and appointed. This kind of patronage, then, is democratic and functional. Loyal people are needed as collaborators by elected officials to implement their programme. If they are competent, then the political system will work better.

In most cases, however, political patronage is neither democratic nor functional. Political leaders create more jobs for their supporters, distribute public resources to some of them in a selective way, with the only purpose to increase their votes while completely disregarding administrative procedures, legal rules and performance criteria. The political loyalty of the clients takes precedence over their competence, over citizens' rights and needs. Political patronage is utilized to produce and reproduce the votes and the consensus of incumbent office holders. In the Italian case, this very widespread type of patronage is called *lottizzazione*. That is, jobs in the large public sector of the economy and in all agencies controlled by the governing parties have been attributed with exclusive reference to party affiliation and in proportion to the electoral power of governing parties. As to the clients, they provide votes and mobilize support as long as jobs and other resources are given to them. The structure of political opportunities will determine whether patronage continues to be acceptable and effective. If and when political and socioeconomic alternatives materialize, some groups of clients may decide to emancipate themselves from the compelling ties of patronage.

Often patronage entails corruption. Public resources are used to bribe. Individuals who owe their careers to political patrons are coerced into performing illegal activities. Citizens' rights are subordinated to the clients' privileges. Some political patronage may be necessary for the functioning of all political systems. However, depending on its nature, quantity and visibility, political patronage is usually resented and, often, periodically rejected. Sooner or later all patronage systems reach a dimension incompatible with the functioning of democratic regimes.

Gianfranco Pasquino
University of Bologna

Further reading

Chubb, J. (1982) *Patronage, Power, and Poverty in Southern Italy*, Cambridge, UK.

Eisenstadt, S. N. and Lemarchand, R. (eds) (1981) *Political Clientelism, Patronage, and Development*, Beverly Hills, CA.

See also: corruption.

peace studies

Peace studies as an identifiable field of study has its origins in the period between the two world wars, especially in the work of Lewis Fry Richardson in Britain and Quincy Wright in the USA. Much of the early work was in reaction to the intense human destruction of the First World War and therefore focused on understanding the causes of war.

With the development of the Cold War in the 1950s, there was a new surge of interest in the study of peace, with the establishment of the Centre for Research on Conflict Resolution at the University of Michigan and the International Peace Research Institute in Oslo (PRIO). The Stockholm International Peace Research Institute (SIPRI) was established shortly afterwards and the two Scandinavian centres, together with the Polemological Institute at Groningen in The Netherlands, became the main European centres.

Michigan's *Journal of Conflict Resolution* and PRIO's *Journal of Peace Research* became the main academic outlets for an area of study developing primarily in Europe and North America and concerned centrally with east–west tensions and the nuclear threat.

For twenty years from the mid-1950s, the main concern of peace studies was with applying social science disciplines, such as political science, sociology and economics, to major problems of international conflict, principally those of the Cold War. This was considered to be in marked contrast to traditional strategic studies and international relations, which were regarded by peace researchers as relying too heavily on law, history and military strategy.

Peace studies developed further with an increasing concentration on attempts to visualize a truly peaceful society, extending far beyond the idea of peace as no more than the absence of war. Such 'negative peace' was considered fully capable of embodying societies with deep social and economic divisions, and peace research became implicitly concerned with analysing the socioeconomic conditions under which a harmonious order was possible, giving rise to the enhancement of human potential throughout a community. Principal writers included Kenneth and Elise Boulding in the USA, Johan Galtung in Norway and Bert Rolling in The Netherlands.

By the early 1970s, with the waning of Cold War tensions, the controversy in the USA over the Vietnam War and the failure of political liberation in the Third World to be accompanied by economic independence and progress, much of the focus of peace studies shifted to north–south issues, closely matching the more radical ideas in the field of development studies. At the same time, there remained a concern with the militarism of the Cold War and a continuing commitment to the study and practice of mediation and other forms of conflict resolution, much of this supported by individuals and charitable trusts associated with the Society of Friends (Quakers) in the USA and Britain.

During the 1970s there was a slow but steady increase in the number of centres devoted to peace studies, principally in Western Europe and North America, much of the focus being on issues concerned with liberation and development. Enduring conflicts in the Middle East and Northern Ireland attracted more attention as, increasingly, did issues of environmental security.

The heightened Cold War tensions of the early 1980s resulted in a huge increase in interest in peace studies, with the development of specialist degree courses in a number of western universities, and the widespread provision of courses in peace studies as minor components in general degree programmes. There was also extensive use of ideas of peace as a focus in many subjects in secondary and tertiary education including history, geography, theology, philosophy and even medicine and the natural sciences.

In parallel with this, there were extensive reactive attacks on peace studies from academics and politicians, especially in the USA and Britain where, at a time of intense east–west confrontation, peace studies was considered to be a subversive activity to be equated with appeasement. Interestingly, this focus on peace studies served mainly to increase its intellectual rigour, as scholars were faced constantly with critical scrutiny of their teaching and writing.

With the collapse of the Soviet Union and the ending of the Cold War at the end of the 1980s, the attacks on peace studies decreased and the subject found wider academic favour. As the post-Cold War world began to evolve not into a more peaceful international order, but rather a complex disorder of frequent ethnic, nationalist and resource-led conflicts, the need for a serious intellectual focus on issues of peace, conflict and violence became more readily apparent.

In this context, some of the main strands of peace studies since the late 1950s appeared to be acquiring a new salience. Concern with militarization, potential north–south conflict, the need for a more peaceful economy, and a much greater focus on the related issues of peacekeeping, mediation and conflict resolution, all contributed to an increasing acceptance of the view that peace studies was an intellectually legitimate focus for study.

If the main determinants of peace related to issues such as the avoidance of deep socioeconomic divisions, the management of environmental constraints and the control of militarization, then the interdisciplinary and applied outlook of peace studies appeared likely to make it peculiarly relevant in the search for a more peaceful world order.

Paul Rogers
University of Bradford

Further reading

Mack, A. (1991) 'Objectives and methods of peace research', in T. Woodhouse (ed.) *Peacemaking in a Troubled World*, Oxford.

O'Connell, J. (1991) 'Approaches to the study of peace in higher education: the tensions of scholarship', in T. Woodhouse (ed.) *Peacemaking in a Troubled World*, Oxford.

See also: conflict, social; war studies.

peasants

The basic problem arising from social scientists' use of the term peasants is this: should it be used, as in everyday parlance, to refer to a social type, or should it rather be used as an adjective to describe certain features of varying rural productive systems? In the absence of agreement on this (rarely discussed) point, discussion of substantive issues is clouded by arguments about 'what is a peasant' and about what distinguishes peasants from either proletarians or capitalist producers. The definitional arguments tend in particular to concentrate on an 'all or nothing' type of question, assuming that a producer is either a peasant or not, and as a result the substantive discussions resort to hybrid formulations such as semi-proletariat, petty bourgeoisie, petty commodity production, their attempts to fit an account of rapidly changing social and economic structure into a rigid framework of mutually exclusive social categories and productive systems.

The usage of the term in contemporary social science derives from the experience of Eastern Europe in the late nineteenth and early twentieth centuries: peasants are defined as people who organize production almost exclusively on the basis of the unpaid labour of a nuclear family or close kinship group; they are therefore assumed to be autarchic as far as labour is concerned. Furthermore, they either only produce for their own consumption or sell some of their products on the market solely in order to meet their culturally defined consumption requirements, which assumes them to be almost self-sufficient in production and consumption. This is the image of the peasantry developed by Russian populism during the nineteenth century and elaborated in an elegant economic theory of non-capitalist production systems by A. V. Chayanov (1966), whose work remains the classic in the field. Chayanov started out by assuming (implicitly) the existence of a peasant family production and consumption unit with common objectives and rationality, working and eating under the direction of an implicitly male head. He then combined this with a second assumption, that wage labour was almost entirely absent from peasant farms. This yielded the immediate conclusion that therefore they could not be profit-seekers, because the category of profit implies, by definition, the use of wage-labour, which was absent. This was reinforced by the implicit assumption that the labour of the family members had no alternative use, and therefore was cost-free as well as unpaid. From this basis, he reached the generalization that peasant farms produced only up to the point where the drudgery of an extra unit of labour was greater than the marginal utility of the corresponding extra unit of output – in other words, that once a family had produced enough to satisfy its subsistence needs its labour input would level off. The two categories drudgery and utility are essentially subjective in his model, which refers to a natural economy, and therefore unquantifiable – which makes the theory difficult to test. This in turn led him to interpret the inequalities observed in Russian peasant society in the period just before and after 1917 as an optical illusion, reflecting the movement of households through a life cycle rather than abiding class divisions: as the households were formed at marriage and passed through successive stages until old age and death, the ratio of consumers to workers (mouths-to-feed to arms-to-work) changed, and so did their requirements and therefore ownership of land. This process of demographic differentiation was reinforced by the practice of periodic redistributions of land according to need within the Russian peasant communities (*mir*).

Subsequently, the study of the peasantry has confronted two major areas of inquiry which have gradually forced a rethinking of these relationships and of those between peasantries and the wider society. These areas are, first, the effects of capitalist development on peasantries in poor and middle-income countries (commonly known as the Third World) and second, the identity of farming populations in advanced capitalist countries.

The central analytical question posed by the expansion of capitalism in the Third World, as far as this subject is concerned, is whether the peasantries in those countries merit the name at all. Vast numbers of studies have revealed the disintegration of the peasantry as defined above, and have shown that they frequently engage in the employment of wage labour, and/or that they depend significantly on income from wage labour in their – often unsuccessful – attempts to meet their subsistence requirements. Some people have seized on this as evidence which confirms the position adopted by the young Lenin 1964 [1896]) that the penetration of the money economy leads inexorably to social differentiation – the rise of opposing classes of capitalists and proletarians. Others, in particular writers who have taken a feminist view, have begun to question the standard model even more fundamentally: they question the image, assumed even by Lenin, of an arcadian, pre-capitalist 'peasant family' with common interests and a single central rationality and objectives which existed everywhere 'once upon a time'. In particular they have pointed out that the dominant position of the male head of the household, assumed in the standard definition, may be more a consequence arising from capitalist development than a reality of pre-capitalist society (Young *et al.* 1981). Yet the stark reality of mass poverty and proliferating tiny plots of land in poor countries has prevented the abandonment of the term, despite the evidence of rapid proletarianization. To cope with this inconsistency, some writers (de Janvry 1982; Vergopoulos 1978) have tried to show that this only undermines Lenin's thesis in a superficial sense. For them one main difference between dependent capitalism in contemporary peripheral countries and in advanced capitalism is that, while the latter destroys the peasantry, the former actually benefits from and assures their perpetuation. Theirs is an essentially functionalist model: impoverished rural populations are forced into high fertility by their poverty and by their uncertain expectation of life. This then ensures the reproduction of a mass of cheap potential migrant labour at little cost to capital in education or welfare; capital will further benefit from the cheapness of food produced by the surplus rural population, which applies vast amounts of labour to small plots of land and thus obtains high yields from it. This view is analytically controversial in many ways, but represents an interesting adaptation of the standard concept of peasants to a framework of analysis of class and exploitation. The problem which remains is whether the term peasantry as traditionally defined, with its strong implicit assumptions about family labour and self-consumption should be used to describe these populations.

Further difficulties arise for the standard view from the contemporary experience of advanced countries of Western Europe, North America and Australia, and even in some of the more developed agricultural regions of the Third World. Here, although farming is largely a family concern and uses very little wage labour, it does use vast amounts of fixed and liquid capital. These units resemble the standard image of peasant units in some ways, but seem to fly in the face of the usual assumption that peasants are impoverished and oppressed and possess hardly any capital base.

In conclusion, it seems best to discard the term 'peasant' as a comprehensive label of rural populations of any sort and to use it instead as an adjective describing features of rural production systems – without pretensions to exhaustive definition.

David Lehmann
University of Cambridge

References

Chayanov, A. V. (1966) *The Theory of Peasant Economy*, ed. D. Thorner *et al.*, Homewood, IL.

De Janvry, A. (1982) *The Agrarian Question in Latin America*, Baltimore MD.

Lenin, V. I. (1964 [1896]) *The Development of Capitalism in Russia*, Moscow.

Vergopoulos, K. (1978) 'Capitalism and peasant productivity', *Journal of Peasant Studies* 4.

Young, K., McCulloch, R. and Wolkowicz, C. (1981) *Of Marriage and the Market*, London.

Further reading

Harriss, J. (1982) *An Introduction to Rural Development*, London.

See also: agricultural economics; rural sociology.

penology

Penology is the study of penalties (from the Greek ποινή, penalty), although in its broadest sense it is also concerned with the consequences and merits of attempting to deal with various kinds of conduct by criminal prohibition ('criminalizing'). It includes not only the study of penal codes of law, but also the investigation of ways in which penal codes are applied by courts in practice, and the manner in which each type of penal measure is applied. For example, even when a penal code appears to oblige courts to pronounce a sentence (such as imprisonment for life in the case of murder), there are ways of avoiding this (such as convicting the offender of a less serious charge of homicide); most penal systems provide legal devices by which a sentence of imprisonment can be terminated before its nominal end. Penologists are interested in all such expedients, and in the criteria which are used by courts, administrators and other personnel to make distinctions between offenders, whether for such purposes or for other reasons. Other reasons may include the belief that certain types of offenders are more likely than others to respond to certain regimes, or that some prisoners are so dangerous that they must be given special sentences, detained longer than is normal for the offence, or given freedom only under specially strict conditions.

An important task of penologists is to provide answers to the question 'How effective is this (or that) measure?' Effectiveness is usually assessed by reconvictions or rearrests, although this is not without problems. For example it cannot take account of offences of which the offender is not suspected; the follow-up period must be substantial; in some jurisdictions rearrests or reconvictions for minor offences are not recorded centrally. The most serious problem, however, is the difficulty of being sure that offenders who remain free of rearrests during the follow-up period would not have remained free if otherwise dealt with: for example, if merely discharged without penalty. In consequence, follow-up studies must usually be content with *comparing* the reconviction rates after different measures. Even so, they have to take into account the fact that courts are selective, and do not allocate offenders randomly to different measures (a few random allocation studies have been achieved, but only for rather specific groups of offenders or offences: see Farrington 1983). The criteria used to allot offenders to different measures may themselves be associated with higher or lower reconviction rates. For instance, the more previous convictions that individuals have, the more likely they are to be reconvicted, quite apart from any effect which a sentence may have on them. Again, offenders whose offences usually involve theft, burglary, drunkenness or exhibitionism are more likely to be reconvicted than those who commit serious sexual offences or personal violence. Statistical devices have to be used to allow for this, for example, by subdividing samples into high-, medium- and low-risk groups. When such precautions are taken, the differences between reconviction rates following such different measures as imprisonment, fines and probation have tended to disappear, and the choice of sentence therefore seem to make no difference to a person's likelihood of reconviction, or not enough difference to justify expensive measures. But this is now regarded as an exaggeration: some types of offenders do respond to some techniques (McLaren 1992).

In any case, other possible aims of penal measures have to be taken into account. Psychiatrists, for example, usually regard themselves as primarily concerned with the mental health of those committed to their charge by criminal courts; and social workers – including many probation officers – regard their clients' financial and family problems as more important than their legal transgressions.

Whether these views are accepted or not, some penal measures are valued as general deterrents, in the belief that even if they do not often affect the conduct of those who have experienced them, they discourage potential offenders who have not yet committed offences (Beyleveld 1980). The efficacy of general deterrents has been exaggerated, for example, by the supporters of capital punishment: statistical comparisons of jurisdictions which have abolished or retained the death penalty, or of decades in the same jurisdiction preceding and following abolition, suggest that the substitution of long periods of imprisonment for the death penalty does not affect rates of intentional homicide. In plain terms, potential murderers who think before they kill are as likely to be deterred by 'life' as by death. Whatever the penalty, however, its deterrent efficacy depends to a great extent on people's own estimates of the probability of being detected and punished. For some people this seems immaterial; but they tend to be those who commit impulsive or compulsive crimes.

Another aim of some penal measures is simply to protect other people against a repetition of the offence by the offender concerned, usually by some degree of incapacitation. Incapacitation may take the form of long detention, disqualification from certain activities (such as driving or engaging in certain occupations) or surgery (for example, castration for rapists). The more severe types of incapacitating measures are controversial, the chief objection being that the probability of offenders' repeating their offence seldom approaches certainty, and is often less than 50:50 (Floud and Young 1981).

This illustrates a more general tendency to acknowledge the relevance of jurisprudence for penology. Scepticism about the efficacy of corrective or deterrent measures, together with the excessive use of very long detention in the name of therapeutic treatment, has revived the classical emphasis on the need for penalties to reflect the culpability of the offender. The underlying Kantian morality of this was never quite abandoned by jurists in the former West Germany; but the revival of it in the USA and Scandinavia is an important phenomenon, although lacking the sophistication of German jurists (Von Hirsch 1976).

English judges – and, quite independently, Durkheimian sociologists – have contributed yet another notion. Without necessarily accepting the retributive view (which has both difficulties and dangers) they hold that penalties have an important expressive or symbolic function, declaring publicly the moral disapproval with which most people regard harmful offences (Walker 1978). Some English judges have even stated that an important task of sentencers is to lead public opinion, although this seems to exaggerate the attention and respect which the public pay to sentences

(Walker and Marsh 1984). More tenable is the proposition that sentences *reflect* people's disapproval: the question is whether sentencers are selected or trained so as to be sure of reflecting the views of the law-abiding public, particularly in societies with heterogeneous moralities.

Other subjects in which penologists have interested themselves are the rights of offenders, especially those recognized by conventions (such as those of the United Nations or European Union); the protection of offenders against avoidable stigma; and the rights of victims to compensation, whether from the state or the offender, and to other forms of care.

Nigel Walker
University of Cambridge

References

Beyleveld, D. (1980) A *Bibliography on General Deterrence Research*, Westmead.

Farrington, D. P. F. (1983) 'Randomised experiments on crime and justice', in M. Tonry and N. Morris (eds) *Crime and Justice*, vol. 4, Chicago.

Floud, J. and Young, W. (1981) *Dangerousness and Criminal Justice*, London.

McLaren, K. (1992) *Reducing Reoffending: What Works Now*, Wellington, NZ.

Von Hirsch, A. (1976) *Doing Justice, the Choice of Punishments: Report of the Committee for the Study of Incarceration*, New York.

Walker, N. (1978) 'The ultimate justification', in C. F. H. Tapper (ed.) *Crime, Proof and Punishment: Essays in Memory of Sir Rupert Cross*, London.

Walker, N. and Marsh, C. (1984) 'Do sentences affect public disapproval?', *British Journal of Criminology*.

See also: capital punishment; crime and delinquency; criminology; punishment; rehabilitation.

perception *see* sensation and perception

periphery *see* centre and periphery

person

The sociological concept of the person embodies a complex and fruitful insight. First, all societies have some general ideas about the constitution of individual human beings and of the reasons they act as they do. All societies, in other words, have their own view of human psychology. Second, in all societies these psychological ideas are inextricably woven together with moral evaluations about what people should and should not do, especially to each other. All societies, that is, have a system of morality and law. This bundle of ideas and values, this combination of a psychology and a morality, comprises a society's concept of the person. Societies differ greatly in their concepts of the person, as shown by anthropologists, historians and sociologists studying a broad variety of cultures and periods of history.

Both the importance of the notion of person, and its historical and cultural mutability, were first recognized at the beginning of the twentieth century by Durkheim and his collaborator Mauss. They wrote of 'person' as a category of thought, by which they meant that it is a fundamental and inescapable constituent of human cognition, a framework without which thought itself would be impossible, like the categories of time and space. On this view it is inconceivable that any society could be without some concept of person, since such ideas render each of us mentally intelligible and morally accountable to others, thereby creating human societies as opposed to random collections of autistic individuals. Durkheim and Mauss laid down that the concept of the person differs sharply from the concept of individual human beings in their biological, or their purely idiosyncratic, constitution. Personhood is concerned with the moral nature of people, with their accountability and responsibility within society, with their capacities to achieve such accountability and responsibility, and therefore with the fundamental sense in which human beings are, in their thought and feeling, creatures of their society and its past.

The mutability of notions of the person from time to time and place to place makes the concept a splendid tool for comparative cultural and social analysis. Societies may differ, for example, in their concept of who is qualified for personhood: among the Lugbara of Uganda and some other African societies, men but not women are considered to have the necessary capacity for moral judgement and self-control to make them fully responsible members of society. Hence men but not women are – or can become, since judgement is considered to increase with age until death – full persons, and these conceptions have important implications for the way that society is organized and for the distribution of political and economic obligations and opportunities. In most North Atlantic societies, on the other hand, personhood is bestowed very early, with birth or even before, on people of both sexes. But whereas the Lugbara concept of personhood stresses responsibility to others, the North Atlantic tendency is to stress the rights of persons to individual goods – for example, to the pursuit of individual happiness. North Atlantic personhood therefore accompanies a very different form of economic and political life, one in which the very notions of social responsibility and of social groups beyond the individual may be little developed or problematical.

Michael Carrithers
University of Durham

Further reading

Carrithers, M., Collins, S. and Lukes, S. (1985) *The Category of the Person*, Cambridge.

personal construct theory

Personal construct theory was presented by Kelly (1955) as an alternative to existing psychological theories. Its basic philosophical assumption, constructive alternativism, asserts that all interpretations of the world are replaceable. People are regarded as operating like scientists, formulating hypotheses, testing these out, and revising those which are invalidated. This process involves the development of a hierarchical system of bipolar personal constructs (e.g. 'kind–unkind'), not all of which have verbal labels. Each construct offers a choice, in that an element of the individual's experience may be construed at one of its poles, the other, or neither, and Kelly considered that people make those choices which most facilitate the anticipation of events. Although there are commonalities between people's construing, particularly within the same culture, each individual's construct system is unique. The essence of all intimate relationships is the construal of another person's construction processes.

Personal construct theory views the person holistically, rejecting distinctions between cognition, conation and affect. Emotion is viewed as the awareness of a transition in construing. In threat, this transition is in core constructs, those central to one's identity. Guilt is the awareness of behaving in a way which is discrepant with one's core role, the constructions determining one's characteristic ways of interacting with others. Anxiety is the awareness that one's constructs do not equip one to anticipate events. Aggression is the active elaboration of construing, while hostility is the attempt to extort evidence for a prediction rather than revising it when invalidated. Other strategies used to cope with invalidation and inconsistencies in construing include constricting one's world to exclude unpredictable events, and, conversely, dilating in an attempt to develop a way of construing the new experiences which one confronts. One may also loosen construing, making one's predictions less precise, or tighten, and more clearly define these predictions. The optimally functioning person is characterized by interplay of such strategies while formulating and revising constructions. However, in psychological disorder the person continues to employ a certain construction despite consistent invalidation. Personal construct psychotherapy therefore aims to facilitate reconstruction.

As well as its extensive clinical applications (Winter 1992), the theory has been employed in numerous other areas, including educational (Pope and Keen 1981) and business (Jankowicz 1990) settings. A particularly popular technique derived from it is the repertory grid, a method of assessment of construing.

Although there have been attempts at integration of personal construct theory with alternative approaches, it contrasts with most other theories, particularly those with reductionist and mechanistic assumptions. However, it has been regarded as exemplifying an approach termed constructivism (Mahoney 1988), the influence of which has permeated numerous areas of psychology as well as other fields.

David Winter
Barnet Health Care

References

Jankowicz, D. (1990) 'Applications of personal construct psychology in business practice', in G. J. Neimeyer and R. A. Neimeyer (eds) *Advances in Personal Construct Psychology*, vol. 1, Greenwich, CT.

Kelly, G. A. (1955) *The Psychology of Personal Constructs*, New York.

Mahoney, M. J. (1988) 'Constructive metatheory: I. Basic features and historical foundations', *International Journal of Personal Construct Psychology* 1.

Pope, M. and Keen, T. (1981) *Personal Construct Psychology and Education*, London.

Winter, D. A. (1992) *Personal Construct Psychology and Clinical Practice: Theory, Research and Applications*, London.

See also: personality; personality assessment.

personality

Personality (from the Latin *persona*, an actor's mask) is an ill-defined concept embracing the entire constellation of psychological characteristics that differentiate people from one another. There is no consensus on its precise definition: in 1937 Gordon W. Allport quoted more than fifty distinct definitions, and the list has grown considerably since then. The underlying assumptions common to all definitions are that people have more or less stable patterns of behaviour across certain situations, and that these behaviour patterns differ from one person to the next. Whereas most areas of psychological research are concerned with universal aspects of behaviour and mental experience, the study of personality focuses specifically on individual differences.

The earliest personality theory of note, uncertainly attributed to Hippocrates (*c.*400 BC) and Galen (AD *c.*170) and widely accepted throughout the Middle Ages, is the doctrine of the four temperaments. People can be classified into four personality types according to the balance of humours or fluids in their bodies. Optimistic people are governed by blood (*sanguis*), depressive people by black bile (*melas chole*), short-tempered people by yellow bile (*chole*) and apathetic people by phlegm (*phlegma*). The physiological basis of this theory collapsed during the Renaissance with advances in biological knowledge, but the underlying typology survived in some modern personality theories.

The first systematic investigation of individual differences using modern empirical methods was Francis Galton's study of intelligence in England in 1884. A more reliable method of measuring intelligence, developed by the French psychologists Alfred Binet and Theodore Simon in 1905, stimulated research into other kinds of individual differences. Work on intelligence continued to flourish independently and is still (illogically) excluded from most academic discussions of personality.

The simplest personality theories focus on single traits or characteristics. Among the most extensively researched of the single-trait theories are those concerned with authoritarianism, field dependence, and locus of control.

Field dependence is a personality trait, first identified by Witkin in 1949, associated with the way in which people perceive themselves in relation to the environment. A field dependent person is strongly influenced by the environment and tends to assimilate information non-selectively; a field independent person, in contrast, is more reliant on internally generated cues and more discriminating in the use of external information. The trait was originally investigated with the rod and frame test, in which the subject, seated in a darkened room, tries to adjust a luminous rod to the vertical position within a tilted rectangular frame. Field dependent people are unduly influenced by the tilted frame, whereas field independent people are more able to discount the frame and concentrate on internal gravitational cues in judging the vertical. Researchers later developed more convenient measures of field dependence, notably the paper-and-pencil embedded figures test, which involves the identification of simple geometric figures embedded in larger, more complex diagrams. Scores on these tests are predictive of behaviour across a wide range of situations. Witkin and Goodenough (1977) concluded from the voluminous published research that field independent people are especially adept at certain forms of logical thinking, tend to gravitate towards occupations such as engineering, architecture, science teaching and experimental psychology, and are often regarded by others as ambitious, inconsiderate and opportunistic. Field dependent people excel at interpersonal relations and are generally considered to be popular, friendly, warm and sensitive; they are most usefully employed in such occupations as social work, elementary school teaching

and clinical psychology. Field dependence generally declines with age, and women are more field dependent, on average, than men.

Locus of control is a personality trait first described by Phares (1957) and incorporated by Rotter (1966) into his social learning theory. It indicates the degree to which people consider their lives to be under their own personal control. It is measured on a continuum from *internal* to *external* by means of questionnaires constructed by Rotter and others. People whose locus of control is internal tend to believe that they are largely responsible for their own destinies, whereas those whose locus is external tend to attribute their successes and failures to the influence of other people and uncontrollable chance events. According to Rotter and his followers, a person's locus of control affects the way that person will perceive most situations and influences behaviour in predictable ways. Research has consistently shown that people whose locus of control is internal, as compared to those whose locus is external, are more likely to adopt health-promoting activities such as weight-watching, giving up smoking, visiting dentists regularly, and taking exercise; they are relatively resistant to social influence and persuasion, and are generally better adjusted and less anxious than those whose locus of control is external. Mental disorders such as schizophrenia and depression are generally associated with external locus of control.

More ambitious multi-trait theories of personality are intended to account for human personality as a whole rather than just one aspect of it. Their aim is to identify the constellation of fundamental traits that constitute the structure of personality, and to explain differences between people according to their location on these dimensions. Allport and Odbert (1936) found 4,500 words denoting personality traits in a standard English dictionary. The first task of any multi-trait theory is to identify the most important of these, taking into account the considerable overlap between them. A statistical technique designed for this purpose, called factor analysis, reduces the measured correlations between a large number of traits to a relatively small number of dimensions or factors. These primary factors, which will generally be found to correlate with one another, can then be reduced to a still smaller number of higher-order factors. This is analogous to reducing the multitude of distinguishable shades of colour to the three dimensions of hue, saturation and brightness, which suffice to explain all the differences. The most influential multi-trait theories are those of Raymond B. Cattell, who has concentrated mainly on primary factors, and Hans J. Eysenck, who prefers higher-order factors.

Cattell's theory (Cattell and Kline 1977), which he outlined in the 1940s and elaborated over the succeeding decades, is based on 171 traits that are intended to encompass the entire sphere of personality. They represent the list of dictionary traits after the elimination of synonyms and the addition of a handful of technical terms. Factor analytic studies of ratings and questionnaires reduced the list to sixteen primary factors or source traits, measured by a standardized paper-and-pencil test called the Sixteen Personality Factor (16PF) questionnaire. They include easily recognizable characteristics such as intelligence, excitability, submissiveness/dominance and forthrightness/shrewdness, together with several others for which Cattell invented neologisms, such as sizia, threcta and zeppia.

An important aspect of personality in Cattell's theory, in addition to the temperament and ability factors that determine *how* people behave, is the analysis of motivational factors determining *why* they behave as they do. According to the theory, the ultimate sources of motivation, called ergs, are biologically based and culturally universal factors such as food-seeking, mating, gregariousness and acquisitiveness. The means by which they are satisfied are called sentiments; these are culturally variable and include such activities as sport, religion and work. Five ergs and five sentiments are measured by the Motivational Analysis Test (MAT). Factor analysis has revealed three basic dimensions of motivation, corresponding roughly to Freud's id, ego and superego. If a person is motivated to read a particular book, for example, this may be because of impulsive desire (id interest), rational choice (ego interest) or a sense of obligation (superego interest).

Eysenck's (1967) theory, which he has developed steadily since the 1940s, is simpler than Cattell's, partly because it is based on higher-order factors. The three major factors or dimensions of personality in this theory are extraversion (E), neuroticism (N) and psychoticism (P). They are measured by standardized scales such as the Eysenck Personality Questionnaire (EPQ). Traits associated with the extraversion factor are sociability, friendliness, enjoyment of excitement, talkativeness, impulsiveness, cheerfulness, activity and spontaneity. Traits associated with neuroticism include worrying, moodiness, tenseness, nervousness and anxiety. Psychoticism involves feelings of persecution, irrational thinking, a liking for very strong physical sensations, inhumane cruelty and lack of empathy.

According to Eysenck's theory, the location of a person on these three independent factors explains a great deal about that person's everyday behaviour. The theory also accounts for psychological disorders. Low E, high N and low P, for example, is suggestive of obsessional neurosis; high E, high N and low P points to hysteria; low E, low N and high P is characteristic of schizophrenia; and so on. Most people, of course, fall somewhere between the extremes on all three scales. Eysenck believes that the three factors are biologically based and largely hereditary, and he has devoted a great deal of attention to their possible locations in the brain and central nervous system.

One of Eysenck's most controversial applications of his theory is to the explanation of crime and antisocial behaviour (Eysenck 1977). He has argued that extreme extraversion, associated with a low level of arousal in the reticular formation of the brain stem, results in weak susceptibility to conditioning, which in turn leads to inadequate socialization and conscience development. Added to this, low arousal produces sensation-seeking behaviour. For both reasons, Eysenck believes, a great deal of criminal and antisocial behaviour is explicable in terms of the biologically based and largely hereditary extraversion factor in his personality theory.

The most important controversy in the field of personality, initiated by Mischel (1968), centres on the issue of consistency. Mischel summarized an impressive array of evidence that seemed to cast doubt on one of the underlying assumptions of all personality theories – that people display more or less stable patterns of behaviour across situations. He drew particular attention to the low correlations between personality test scores and behaviour, and concluded that behaviour can be more reliably predicted from past behaviour than from personality test scores. This suggestion implies that behaviour is merely predictive of itself, and that theories of personality are futile, at least for predicting behaviour. Mischel recommended that personality research should be abandoned in favour of the investigation of situational factors that influence behaviour.

The situationist (or contextualist) critique of personality generated a considerable amount of debate and research, much of it appearing to refute Mischel's arguments and evidence. The debate is unresolved, but the views of most authorities since the mid-1970s have tended towards interactionism. According to this view, human behaviour is dependent partly on internal personality factors, partly on external situational factors, and partly on interactions (in the statistical sense) between personality and situational factors.

Andrew M. Colman
University of Leicester

References

Allport, G. W. (1937) *Personality: A Psychological Interpretation*, New York.

Cattell, R. B. and Kline, P. (1977) *The Scientific Analysis of Personality and Motivation*, London.

Eysenck, H. J. (1967) *The Biological Basis of Personality*, Springfield, IL.

Eysenck, H. J. (1977) *Crime and Personality*, London.

Mischel, W. (1968) *Personality and Assessment*, New York.

Phares, E. J. (1957) 'Expectancy changes in skill and chance situations', *Journal of Abnormal and Social Psychology* 54.

Rotter, J. B. (1966) 'Generalized expectancies for internal versus external control of reinforcement', *Psychological Monographs* 80 (609).

Witkin, H. A. and Goodenough, D. R. (1977) 'Field dependence and interpersonal behavior', *Psychological Bulletin* 84.

Further reading

Hall, C. S. and Lindzey, G. (1978) *Theories of Personality*, 3rd edn, New York.

Hampson, S. (1982) *The Construction of Personality: An Introduction*, London.

See also: personal construct theory; personality assessment.

personality, psychopathic *see* psychopathic personality

personality assessment

There is little agreement among psychologists concerning the meaning of personality. However, one definition which underpins this article is that personality is the sum of an individual's attributes. The task of personality assessment is, therefore, to measure these attributes.

There are two basic approaches to the measurement of personality – the nomothetic and the idiographic. The former is concerned with the measurement of traits that are to be found in more or less degree among all individuals; the latter seeks to measure that which is specific to the individual concerned. Cutting across the nomethetic and idiographic distinction are the different methods of personality measurement. There are three basic methods which we shall discuss separately, together with some more general procedures which are, sometimes unwisely, used in personality assessment. The three types of personality tests are inventories or questionnaires, projective techniques and objective tests. Good measurement demands of tests high reliability (the capability of giving the same scores to individuals on repeated testing, and also internal consistency) and high validity (that is, the test clearly measures what it claims to measure). In addition to these methods, it is possible to use interviews, rating scales, semantic differentials and repertory grids, although these are not common in personality assessment.

Personality inventories or questionnaires consist of items, phrases or sentences about behaviour, to which subjects have to respond Yes/No, True/False, Like/Dislike, for example. The items are selected by two methods. In the first, criterion keying, items are selected if they can discriminate one group from another, for instance, schizophrenics from normals. A well-known test thus constructed is the Minnesota Multiphasic Personality Inventory (MMPI). The second method uses factor analysis to select the items. Factor analysis is a statistical technique which can evaluate dimensions underlying correlations (in this case between test items). Thus a factor analytic test, *ipso facto*, measures a dimension. The best-known examples of these are Cattell's Sixteen Personality Factor (16PF) questionnaire, the Eysenck Personality Questionnaire (EPQ) and the Personality Inventories constructed by Guilford. Personality inventories are reliable and reasonably valid, and have been found useful in industrial and educational psychology for guidance and selection. From these nomothetic tests two variables stand clear: extraversion and anxiety.

Projective techniques generally consist of ambiguous stimuli to which subjects have to respond more or less freely. There is much argument over their reliability and validity. These are essentially idiographic techniques; the Rorschach test, consisting of series of inkblots, is perhaps the most famous example.

Objective tests are a development in personality assessment stemming mainly from Cattell. They are defined as tests which can be objectively scored and whose purpose cannot be guessed, thus making them highly useful in selection. However, as yet there is little evidence concerning the validity of these nomothetic measures and thus they are definitely at the experimental stage only. Typical tests are: the fidgetometer (a chair which measures movement, for example, during an interview), the slow line drawing test, handwriting pressure test and a balloon-blowing measure.

Finally, rating scales and interviews and other methods (as mentioned above) are usually shown to be lacking in both reliability and validity. Personality tests are much to be preferred, allowing quantification for applied and research purposes.

Paul Kline
University of Exeter

Further reading

Cattell, R. B. and Kline, P. (1977) *The Scientific Analysis of Personality and Motivation*, London.

Kline, P. (1993) *Handbook of Psychological Testing*, London.

Vernon, P. E. (1964) *Personality Assessment*, London.

See also: personal construct theory; personality; projective methods.

personnel management *see* human resource management

phenomenology

As a philosophical movement, phenomenology was founded by Edmund Husserl, the German philosopher. Its main concern is to provide philosophy with a foundation that will enable it to be a pure and autonomous discipline free from all presuppositions. Its method is essentially descriptive, and its aims are to uncover the fundamental structures of intentionality, consciousness and the human life-world (*Lebenswelt*). The idea of the 'life-world' of 'lived experience' that is always 'taken for granted', even by the empirical sciences, is one of the main concepts of phenomenology which has interested many social scientists, including psychologists and psychiatrists. Nevertheless, critics have argued that when phenomenological concepts are transferred from their original domain to the context of social science, their meaning is radically transformed.

The key figure in the transition from pure phenomenology to modern sociology is undoubtedly Alfred Schutz. Schutz, with a background in law and social science, and personally acquainted with Husserl, arrived in the USA from Austria in 1939; from then on he considerably influenced successive generations of philosophers and social scientists at the New School for Social Research in New York. In his major work, *Der sinnhafte Aufbau der sozialen Welt*, 1932 (*The Phenomenology of the Social World*, 1967), Schutz examines Max Weber's ideas about the methodology of the social sciences. Central to Weber's account is the view that sociology is concerned with an 'interpretive understanding' of human 'social action'. Although this is essentially correct, in Schutz's opinion Weber's ideas require further clarification which is best achieved through a phenomenological analysis of the structure of social reality and of the interpretation of that reality.

Schutz's ideas are clearly set out – although his position remains unchanged – in his *Collected Papers* (3 vols. 1962–6). A central argument is that

> the thought objects constructed by the social scientist refer to and are founded upon the thought objects constructed by the common sense thought of man living his everyday life among his fellow-men. Thus the constructs used by the social scientist are, so to speak, constructs of the second degree, namely constructs of the constructs made by the actors on the social scene, whose behaviour the scientist observes and tries to explain in accordance with the procedural rules of his science.

The relationship between social scientists and their subject matter is totally unlike that between natural scientists and their subject matter. The social world is an interpreted world, and the facts of the social sciences are interpreted facts. According to Schutz, this essential characteristic of social reality provides social science with its central problem: attempting to construct objective accounts of a subjective reality.

In contemporary sociology, the use of Schutz's ideas has taken several directions. But common to all is an effort to clarify the philosophical and methodological foundations of sociological knowledge. These different trends are to be found in P. Berger and T. Luckmann's *The Social Construction of Reality* (1966), which is primarily concerned with how a phenomenological approach can redirect the traditional sociology of knowledge towards an investigation of the taken-for-granted world of common sense knowledge; in A. V. Cicourel's *Method and Measurement in Sociology* (1964), a critique of the research methods of conventional social science, which fails to recognize the implicit use of common sense knowledge; and in H. Garfinkel's *Studies in Ethnomethodology* (1967), the most radical use of phenomenological ideas resulting in fundamental scepticism of the achievements of conventional social science.

Inevitably, all who claim to be working within the broadly defined phenomenological tradition have radicalized or reinterpreted many of the original ideas of phenomenology. Most phenomenological sociologists have concentrated upon relatively small-scale problems and have been sceptical of the achievements of mainstream sociology and its concern with the macroanalysis of social structures. In part, this can be traced back to Schutz's analysis of Weber's work in which he discusses Weber's methodological essays without looking at Weber's own substantive sociology; but it also mirrors an underlying failure of the whole phenomenological project to understand the nature of science.

In a wider context, phenomenology has influenced philosophers interested in the nature of the human sciences, many of whom have tried to combine phenomenological ideas with those from other traditions such as, for example, Marxism. Representative figures here are M. Merleau-Ponty, J. P. Sartre and H. Arendt.

Peter Lassman
University of Birmingham

Further reading

Luckmann, T. (ed.) (1978) *Phenomenology and Sociology*, Harmondsworth.
Piucevic, E. (1970) *Husserl and Phenomenology*, London.
Wagner, H. R. (ed.) (1970) *Alfred Schutz: On Phenomenology and Social Relations*, Chicago.

See also: ethnomethodology.

philosophy of the social sciences

Philosophy of the social sciences is, in the bureaucratic jargon of academe, the study of the aims and methods of the social sciences (sociology, anthropology, political science, psychology, sometimes economics; borderline cases are history, geography, demography and linguistics); it constitutes a sub-specialty within philosophy of science – the study of the aims and methods of science in general. Standard anthologies organize their material around such questions as the following. Are natural things fundamentally different from social things? Must then the sciences of social things use different methods from the sciences of natural things? Are then sciences of the social at all possible? Alternatively, are social things mere aggregates? Do social things mix facts and values? Are values a social product? From this list it is apparent that the subject is engaged with traditional philosophical concerns – ontological, epistemological and normative.

Rarely is there a perfect fit between a subject as defined by academic bureaucracy and what its practitioners actually do. And when place is found for transcendental arguments to the effect that the subject is an impossibility, this cannot but affect an encyclopedia article. All alternative frameworks have their limitations. An Aristotelian matrix approach, dividing the subject up into orderly categories and concepts, conceals unruly and disorderly elements. The historical approach, treating it as a story with a beginning, a middle and, possibly, an end, risks identifying the subject with present preoccupations. The kinship approach, tracing all present elements to a common ancestor, risks merging and simplifying descent. The map-making approach, trying to give an overall picture, has to ignore continental drift. My choice is a metaphysical sketch map, supplemented by a little history. The result will be a trifle untidy, but the reader should be aware that this is because the terrain itself is mountainous, dotted with mists, and we are forced to map from sea-level, without radar.

Nature and convention

The phrase 'philosophy of the social sciences' itself suggests that there is scientific study of the social (denied by phenomenologists and some followers of Wittgenstein, see below), and that the aims and methods of such study may differ from those of science in general (denied by the logical positivists and others, see below). The very distinction between the natural and the social, between nature and convention, is deeply rooted in our thinking. It was not always so, but it is the notion of impersonal nature that is recent. Once, humankind took itself as the measure of all things and explained nature anthropomorphically; the result of the scientific revolution (in ancient Greece and post-Renaissance Western Europe – we concentrate on the latter) was to overthrow anthropomorphism, to depersonalize nature and explain it by postulating orderly and law-like processes unfolding mechanically (Dijksterhuis 1961). Such was the flush of seventeenth- and eighteenth-century enthusiasm for the new science that even humanity itself was to be treated as part of nature, or as 'a machine': its aims and its desires as motive forces – or motives for short – and its actions as movements, including social movements and social revolutions akin to the revolving of the heavens.

Such euphoria came to grief over such problems as how to maximize the creation of wealth; how to realize moral and political aims in social institutions; how to prevent suicide. These seemed to demand, if not anthropomorphism, then, at least, laws of human convention. If nature is taken to be those aspects of things that are more or less given, the laws and motive forces governing that which we cannot alter, then convention covers all forms of orderliness that is not constant from place to place and time to time, and which is humanly alterable. This division of our environment into unchanging and changing parts affects our efforts to explain it. It makes it our first task when facing a problem to decide to what extent it belongs to nature or to convention – usually a far from uncontroversial allocation.

Controversy over what is natural and what is conventional is heightened by the presence of established sciences of nature. A metaphysical issue is given a methodological twist. This comes about as follows: the rise and success of natural science is, it is widely held, to be explained as the application of a particular method, the empirical method. Thus, if a problem is identified as natural, the methods of the natural sciences are appropriate; but, having been so successful with nature, perhaps they are also appropriate for problems of convention. To the ancient Greeks this might have seemed absurd. But as European society under industrialization changed from *Gemeinschaft* to *Gesellschaft*, more systematic thought had to be given to altering current conventions and making them work better. As such, social thought grew in cognitive power and practical importance, debates about the boundary between nature and convention, and hence the appropriate methods with which to approach convention, took on a life of their own. Some philosophers of social science, greatly exercised over questions of method, are unaware that they debate a disguised metaphysical issue. One example of this is those who push the empirical method because they hold that nature is real and observable, whereas conventions are abstract unobservables (Kaufman 1944). A relic of this thinking is the individualism/holism dispute over what is more and what is less real among conventions. One party, the individualists, holds that only individual human beings are real and larger-scale social entities are aggregates which can be, for explanatory purposes, reduced to theories about individuals. The other party, the holists, questions the reality of individuals when they can be explained as creatures of society. Although there is some purely philosophical debate of such issues, under the influence of positivism they are usually joined in methodological form: which is more empirically observable – the individual or the whole? A convincing case can be made for either side.

Awkwardly cutting across all attempts to map this field are Marxist variants of each set of issues. Marx could be said to hold that there was only nature, not convention, and that his dialectical materialism should be seen as part of natural science. The cross-cutting occurs because Marxists will not permit him to be treated as just one of a succession of social scientists; hence some dispute the interpretation of Marx's writings, while others advance positions they claim are in the spirit of his work, if not within the letter. As a result almost every issue in the philosophy of the social sciences is duplicated within Marxism, but in a manner that exaggerates the importance of Marx. Mainstream philosophers of social science often mention Marx, but he is a pivotal figure only for Marxists.

Positivism and its legacy

Empiricist methodology always had its a priorist opponents, but the triumph of Newton's physics over Descartes was taken to be a triumph of empiricism over a priorism. From then on, despite Kant's valiant attempt at reconciliation, a priorist methodologies have grown increasingly estranged from science. That left humane studies and social studies as fields to continue the struggle between the rivals. Simmel (1950), Durkheim (1938 [1895]) and Weber (1949) all wrote their classics on the philosophy of the social sciences when the anti-science tendencies in German academic philosophy were at their peak. History done on Hegelian lines was the model for humanities and their a priorism was now known as hermeneutics. Both empiricism and a priorism are present in these classics.

The twentieth-century high tide of militant empiricism was the logical positivism movement that began in the 1920s. It appropriated all cognition into science, the success of which was attributed to the use of the empirical method. Theories not empirically verifiable were declared non-scientific and merely metaphysical. The battle line the positivists drew in social studies was, could the social sciences live up to their name by producing verifiable theories? If so, then the unity and identity of science and cognition could be upheld. In face of this challenge the a priorists took some time to regroup. Some, amazingly, retreated to the rather unpromising ground of Marxism (the Frankfurt School), which they tried to Hegelianize and a priorize (Frisby 1976).

The primary interests of the logical positivists were in the natural sciences, but their predilection for a hodgepodge of logic, economics, statistics, Marx (note again how he confuses all issues), psychoanalysis and linguistics ensured that attempts were made to give a positivist account of each that would secure their place in unified science.

So long as logical positivism flourished within philosophy (down to the early 1960s), intense debates took place over the degree to which the empirical method could be utilized in what were now unselfconsciously called 'the social sciences'. The limits of mathematical and quantitative methods and simplicity were explored, as was the problem of whether facts could be separated from values. If social phenomena resisted measurement and quantification, and if they were permeated by values, the verifiable empirical basis of the social sciences was undermined. Along with the classics, the literature generated in this period is the core of most readers and courses in philosophy of the social sciences.

Meanwhile, the regrouped opponents of logical positivism engaged with precisely the same problems. They considered the limits of empiricism to be much more severe, and the problem of values to be much more pervasive, however, than did the logical positivists. Indeed it was argued that the limits of empiricism were the limits of natural science. As for values, these were the tip of the iceberg. As soon as the conscious, self-conscious, meaning-generating, and reflexive activities of human beings were under study, a totally different order of things was involved, demanding a totally different approach. That approach involved historical imagination (*Verstehen*) which requires the scrutiny of texts (hermeneutics) and some phenomenological rather than any empirical method (Dallmayr and McCarthy 1977; Natanson 1963; Schutz 1962). Textualist studies have flourished since the mid-1980s (Clifford and Marcus 1986), often blended with historical rethinking (Geertz 1988).

Disguised under the dispute about method was another about aims. Social things being unlike natural things, it was possible that attempting to explain and predict them was not only erroneous but also inappropriate. Followers of the later Wittgenstein went even further than the continental a priorists and used the patron saint of logical positivism's later work to develop a transcendental argument against the very possibility of a science of the social. Winch (1958) and

Louch (1966), despite differences, converge on the idea that what makes social things social as opposed to inert are the meaning-generating activities of human beings which show themselves in rules of behaviour. Language, for example, is not random noises but patterns that make sense. Clearly such rules are not natural; rather they are activities that define and constitute human life together. We cannot then explain human conduct in the way that we offer mechanical causal explanation in science, but only by mastering from the inside the rules in use and their degrees of freedom. People do social things for reasons, not in obedience to laws. The large literature on Winch and on whether reasons are causes can be traced through *The Philosopher's Index*.

Methodological differences, rationality relativism

The logical positivists and their opponents agree in translating metaphysical and epistemological issues into methodology. They also agree on the pivotal role played for method by the possibility of human intervention, in particular that intervention which is an unintended consequence of having thoughts about society that alter people's behaviour. (Popper (1945) labels this the Oedipus effect, Merton (1957) labels it the self-fulfilling prophecy.) Both Marxists and conservatives like to play down the desirable or effective scope for intervention in society, but this argument traps them with their own theories. What is the purpose of theorizing about society if the best we can do to improve it is to let it alone? Moreover, how is that view to be sustained when adequate theorizing itself improves society? One reaction to this is to attribute a privileged status to theorizing, to see it as somehow underdetermined by the general processes of determinism in society. Efforts were made first by Marx and Durkheim, and then, under the label 'sociology of knowledge', by Mannheim, to connect forms of putative cognition with social forms, class interest and the like, meanwhile exempting from such determination the natural sciences and that theorizing itself (Mannheim 1936 [1929]). The 'strong programme' of the sociology of knowledge – first proposed by Merton, although he attributes it to Mannheim – embraces science and exempts nothing (Bloor 1991). This is supported by the idea that reality, especially what people take reality to be, is itself a social construction – an idea that may be ascribed to the school of phenomenology but which goes specifically to Berger and Luckmann (1966). This issue, however, gets debated directly rather than methodologically, with the marshalling of comparative evidence to show how reality can be constructed very differently in different times and places. (Radical psychological theorists – labelling theory, so-called – extended the argument to the boundary between normal and abnormal psychological states, suggesting that psychopathology too is a matter of convention.) Much of the evidence came from anthropology, which had described societies where world-views, counting, the very categories of language and hence of reality, were different from ours. Reality seemed socially relative. Winch (1964) extended his earlier work in this direction, arguing that Evans-Pritchard's (1937) classic study of Azande witchcraft was conceptually confused in comparing magic to science. Battle was joined by the anthropologist Horton, who had upheld the validity of such comparisons (W. R. Horton and Finnegan 1973). He thus followed Gellner, the leading critic of the various sociological idealisms (Gellner 1992; R. Horton 1993).

Anthropology also stimulated the overlapping and so-called rationality debate, another treatment of the issue of relativism. The search for a characterization of what constituted human rationality stemmed from Aristotle's suggestion that it was rationality that set the human animal apart from other animals. Rationality was for long taken to mean reasoning, ratiocination and logic. Mill (1843) took it for granted that logic was the laws of the human mind. Anthropologists had once held that uncivilized peoples lacked the ability to reason, were incapable, even, of coherent speech. In the twentieth century they reversed themselves and found 'primitive' peoples to be as rational, if not in some ways more rational, than us. Yet their societies were without science and full of superstition, making them by positivist standards (logic and empiricism) not rational. Relativists argued that standards of rationality were embodied in differing social arrangements and hence differed. Absolutists argued that a necessary minimum for rationality – logic – was a necessary minimum for social life to function at all, therefore no societies were not rational. Still others tried to model degrees of rationality (Elster 1983; Jarvie 1984; Wilson 1970). Since the mid-1980s, developments, as we shall see, reveal new vigour among the relativists.

Logical positivism in philosophy petered out in the 1960s. The social sciences lagged a little behind. Political science and psychology experienced in the 1950s the behavioural revolution (hence behavioural sciences was a briefly fashionable name), in which positivist notions of aims and methods came to dominate – just as the positivist hegemony over philosophy was crumbling. More subtly, in sociology and anthropology the early positivism and empiricism of Durkheim had been blended in the 1940s into structural-functionalism, a way of going about thinking about society that, despite serious logical flaws (Gellner 1973), survived in a modified form as the mainstream account of aims and methods. Although there was much debate about functionalism, it was endorsed as a method, perhaps because, stemming from a richer positivism, the extreme naturalism and inductivism of logical positivism rarely infected the work of sociologists and anthropologists – even if, sometimes, they echoed the rhetoric (Jarvie 1964).

Already in the 1940s there had been intervention in the debates about the aims and methods of the social sciences from another quarter. An economist, Hayek (1952), and an anti-positivist philosopher, Popper (1957), in articles that became new classics as books, argued that social scientists harboured mistaken views about the natural sciences. Hayek stressed that in science there were elements of a priori model building; Popper said that scientific method was trial and error. They thus criticized the identification of science with the positivist description of it. Both attacked the search for historical laws. Positivism was declared caricature and labelled 'scientism', then diagnosed not only as underlying the spurious claims of Marxists and positivists, but also as being what the continental a priorists were against.

Drawing primarily on the neglected example of economics, Hayek and Popper argued that the test of methods was results: by that test the freedom economists exercised to invent simplified models and work out their implications before complicating the models with real-world additions was one used generally in common sense and professional social thought. Their work was part of a vigorous methodological debate within economics stemming from Robbins (1932) and Hutchison (1938), later pressed further by Friedman (1953), Klappholz and Agassi (1959), and others (Blaug, 1992). Alas, to the other social sciences economics is like mathematics to the non-scientist: a basic subject everyone knows they should be conversant with, and about which they feel guilty because they are not. Moreover, there is ambivalence: economics has high status, yet whether economic theories are testable has been repeatedly questioned and still is. Hence the debates that go on in economics about model-building, rationality, realistic assumptions, whether theories should aim at truth or predictive success, and the value of mathematization (Boland 1982) are scarcely referred to in discussions of the aims and methods of the other social sciences. This is especially poignant, because the debates within economics presuppose that economic behaviour is conventional and hence that the methods of economics are free to be different from those of natural science.

The very important point about false images of science shared by positivists, Marxists and anti-science a priorists had little impact. With the correction made, Hayek and Popper argued that simple modifications of

method would allow the social sciences to belong to unified science. Instead, the most controverted point was an ontological one. First, do humans act rationally – do they act at all? In opposition to the Hegelian tendency in Marx to reify abstractions and endow them with causal force (relations of production, classes, and so on), Hayek and Popper sidestepped ontology (but see Gilbert 1989; Jarvie 1972) and proposed the principle of rational action or methodological individualism as more fruitful and in better conformity to the actual practice of the social sciences. This was the principle to attribute aims only to individuals and not to social wholes. Social institutions, they held, were real, but they were built, sustained and given aims only by individuals. A lively and extended debate continues (O'Neill 1973).

To a large extent Popper and Hayek did not carry the day, as positivist and behavourist and holistic social science has flourished since the 1960s. Early in that decade an essay on the history of science was published that was destined finally to purge logical positivism from the social sciences and yet which, like Popper, Hayek and the positivists, continued to urge the unity of science, while explicitly patronizing the social sciences as underdeveloped and hence not yet admissible. Its author, a physicist, was a self-taught historian utterly innocent of economics, sociology or any of the social sciences. The book was *The Structure of Scientific Revolutions*, the author, Thomas Kuhn (Barnes 1982).

Kuhn (1962) argued that what distinguished a science from a prescience or a nonscience was its domination by a paradigm, that is, a recognized piece of work in the field that people copy in method, style and substance. In science such paradigms are fully in place when they are incorporated in current standard textbooks and imposed on novices. Noticing the incessant warring about fundamentals in the social sciences, the existence of rival textbooks, Kuhn could not but characterize them as presciences. There is some irony in the way that social scientists have seized on Kuhn's ideas and reversed them, arguing that since the social sciences have textbooks they have paradigms, therefore they are sciences. But Kuhn specifically says there must be agreement among the leadership of a field on a single paradigm if that field is to count as scientific. Conclusion: there are as many social sciences, or branches of the social sciences, as there are paradigmatic works; once we declare that Freud and Piaget do not contest child psychology but that there are two fields, developmental psychology and cognitive psychology, a prescientific field is transformed into two paradigm-dominated scientific fields.

Once again the debate has been vigorous. Kuhn's critics have argued that there are textbooks of pseudoscience (astrology), non-science (theology) and doubtful cases (psychoanalysis). More telling, Kuhn provides a legitimation-procedure for the boundary-drawing of academic bureaucrats who wish to conceal debate, controversy and confusion and give the impression of the orderly march of progress in 'fields', 'subjects', 'areas' and so on. Yet the categories of natural and conventional, not to mention physical, chemical, biological or mathematical, may themselves stem from problems and hotly debated theories (Hattiangadi 1978/9).

A more relativist reading of Kuhn is that no special aims or methods characterize natural science, which is a subject much like any other, distinguishable if at all by its social status. Hence comparison with the social sciences was an empirical matter *for the social sciences* and the 'strong programme' of the sociology of knowledge vindicated itself (Bloor 1976). Whether the results point to identity or contrast, they belong to the sociology of knowledge, which thus is the truly comprehensive discipline. Social studies of science, then, under whatever rubric, have implications in all directions, in sociology as well as philosophy, in metatheory as well as theory.

I. C. Jarvie
York University, Canada

References

Barnes, B. (1982) *T. S. Kuhn and Social Science*, London.
Berger, P. and Luckmann, T. (1966) *The Social Construction of Reality*, New York.
Blaug, M. (1992) *The Methodology of Economics*, 2nd edn, London.
Bloor, D. (1976) *Knowledge and Social Imagery*, London.
Boland, L. A. (1982) *The Foundations of Economic Method*, London.
Clifford, J. and Marcus, G. E. (eds) (1986) *Writing Culture: The Poetics and Politics of Ethnography*, Berkeley, CA.
Dallmayr, F. and McCarthy, T. (1977) *Understanding Social Inquiry*, Washington, DC.
Dijksterhuis, E. J. (1961) *The Mechanization of the World Picture*, New York.
Durkheim, E. (1938 [1895]), *Rules of Sociological Method*, Glencoe, IL. (Original edn, *Les Règles de la méthode sociologique*, Paris.)
Elster, J. (1983) *Sour Grapes*, Cambridge, UK.
Evans-Pritchard, E. E. (1937) *Witchcraft, Oracles and Magic among the Azande*, Oxford.
Friedman, M. (1953) *Essays in Positive Economics*, Chicago.
Frisby, D. (ed.) (1976) *The Positivist Dispute in German Sociology*, London.
Geertz, C. (1988) *Works and Lives: The Anthropologist as Author*, Oxford.
Gellner, E. (1973) *Cause and Meaning in the Social Sciences*, London.
—— (1992) *Postmodernism, Reason and Religion*, London.
Gilbert, M. (1989) *On Social Facts*, London.
Hattiangadi, J. N. (1978/9) 'The structure of problems: I and II', *Philosophy of the Social Sciences* 8; 9.
Hayek, F. A. (1952) *The Counter-Revolution of Science*, Glencoe, IL.
Horton, Robin (1993) *Patterns of Thought in Africa and the West*, Cambridge, UK.
Horton, W. R. and Finnegan, R. (eds) (1973) *Modes of Thought*, London.
Hutchison, T. W. (1938) *The Significance and Basic Postulates of Economic Theory*, London.
Jarvie, I. C. (1964) *The Revolution in Anthropology*, London.
—— (1972) *Concepts and Society*, London.
—— (1984) *Rationality and Relativism*, London.
Kaufmann, F. (1944) *Methodology of the Social Sciences*, Oxford.
Klappholz, K. and Agassi, J. (1959) 'Methodological prescriptions in economics', *Economica* 26.
Kuhn, T. S. (1962) *The Structure of Scientific Revolutions*, Chicago.
Louch, A. R. (1966) *Explanation and Social Action*, Berkeley, CA.
Mannheim, K. (1936 [1929]) *Ideology and Utopia*, London. (Original edn, *Ideologie and Utopie*, Bonn.)
Merton, R. (1957) *Social Theory and Social Structure*, Glencoe, IL.
Mill, J. S. (1843) *A System of Logic*, London.
Natanson, M. (ed.) (1963) *Philosophy of the Social Sciences: A Reader*, New York.
O'Neill, J. (ed.) (1973) *Modes of Individualism and Collectivism*, London.
Popper, K. R. (1945) *The Open Society and its Enemies*, London.
—— (1957) *The Poverty of Historicism*, London.
Robbins, L. (1932) *Essay on the Nature and Significance of Economic Science*, London.
Schutz, A. (1962) *Collected Papers*, vol. 1: *The Problem of Social Reality*, The Hague.
Simmel, G. (1950) *The Sociology of George Simmel*, ed. K. H. Wolff, Glencoe, IL.
Weber, M. (1949) *Methodology of the Social Sciences*, ed. E. Shils, Glencoe, IL.
Wilson, B. (ed.) (1970) *Rationality*, Oxford.
Winch, P. (1958) *The Idea of a Social Science*, London.
—— (1964) 'Understanding a primitive society', *American Philosophical Quarterly* 1.

Further reading

Agassi, J. (1977) *Towards a Rational Philosophical Anthropology*, The Hague.
Bhaskar, R. (1979) *The Possibility of Naturalism: A Philosophical Critique of the Contemporary Social Sciences*, Brighton.
Borger, R. and Cioffi, F. (1970) *Explanation in the Behavioural Sciences*, Cambridge, UK.
Brodbeck, M. (ed.) (1968) *Readings in the Philosophy of the Social Sciences*, New York.
Brown, R. (1963) *Explanation in Social Science*, London.
Brown, S. C. (ed.) (1979) *Philosophical Disputes in the Social Sciences*, Brighton.
Collingwood, R. G. (1946) *The Idea of History*, Oxford.
Durkheim, E. (1915 [1912]) *Elementary Forms of the Religious Life*, London. (Original edn, *Les Formes elementaires de la vie religieuse*, Paris.)
Emmet, D. and MacIntyre, A. (1970) *Sociological Theory and Philosophical Analysis*, London.
Gellner, E. (1975) *Legitimation of Belief*, Cambridge, UK.
—— (1985) *Relativism and the Social Sciences*, Cambridge, UK.

Giddens, A. (1976) *New Rules of Sociological Method*, New York.

Hollis, M. and Lukes, S. (eds) (1982) *Rationality and Relativism*, Oxford.

Hollis, M. (1994) *The Philosophy of Social Sciences: An Introduction*, Cambridge, UK.

Hookway, C. and Pettit, P. (eds) (1978) *Action and Interpretation*, Cambridge, UK.

Krimerman, L. (ed.) (1969) *The Nature and Scope of Social Science: A Critical Anthology*, New York.

Simmel, G. (1980) *Essays on Interpretation in Social Science*, Totawa, NJ.

Skinner, Q. (ed.) (1985) *The Return of Grand Theory in the Human Sciences*, Cambridge, UK.

See also: Popper, Karl; positivism; sociology of science.

physiological psychology

Before 1879, when Wundt founded his psychological laboratory in Germany and initiated the contemporary era of scientific psychology as a distinct academic discipline, psychological issues had been investigated within the framework of physiology by pioneering sensory physiologists such as Helmholtz. Even Wundt – and many of his European and American followers – primarily regarded themselves as physiological psychologists, in that they were concerned with elucidating how the human brain and mind are related. Modern physiological psychology, however, relies heavily on the application of physiological measures and manipulations of animals (and particularly animal models of human psychology). For this reason, Thompson (1967) traces the subject's origins as a distinct psychological subdiscipline to Shepherd Franz's 1902 publication on the effects of frontal lobe lesions on simple animal learning tasks, devised by Thorndike at the turn of the century.

Then, as now, the subject was construed as the study of how the brain and endocrine system control those behaviours associated with perception, emotion, motivation, attention, thinking, language, learning and memory. For many years, because of the influence of Watsonian behaviourism, it suffered from a general unwillingness to postulate psychological processes mediating observable behaviour. This neglect, which arose from a justified mistrust of introspection as the royal road to the mind, was criticized by Hebb (1980), who argued that mental operations are essentially unconscious and can be inferred only from patterns of behavioural and related brain activity. As such inferences are hard to make, there exists an opposing tendency among physiological psychologists, in which, instead of making no theoretical postulates, they explain brain–mind relationships in terms of overly general intuitive psychological concepts, like attention. Success in the enterprise therefore requires both an adequate technology for influencing and measuring

brain processes, and also methods for measuring and interpreting behaviour. Exciting developments in techniques for exploring brain processes since the 1950s have not yet been matched by improvements in analysing behavioural processes, although these may come as artificial intelligence research has increasing impact.

The central issues of physiological psychology concern the extent to which the control of psychological functions is localized in the brain, how these functions are mediated, and how this control emerges in phylogeny and ontogeny. The first two of these issues have been polemical since the late eighteenth century with the emergence of phrenology, over a century before Franz began his research. The phrenologists believed that the control of complex psychological functions, such as philoprogenitiveness, was highly localized in the brain and that their degree of development was indicated by bumps on the overlying skull. Some nineteenth-century researchers, like Flourens (who lesioned pigeon brains to see what functions were lost), adopted a holistic position and argued that functional control was distributed, not localized. Others, such as the neurologists Broca and Wernicke, who found that specific left cortical lesions causes selective verbal impairments, argued that complex functions are indeed controlled by small brain regions. The controversy continued into the twentieth century when Karl Lashley formulated an influential holistic viewpoint, based on studies of the effects of lesions on learning in the rat, defined by his principles of mass action (efficiency of a given function depends on the amount of available brain tissue) and equipotentiability (widely distributed brain regions have equivalent function).

The longevity of the holistic v. localized dispute depended partly on an inadequate analysis of the nature of complex psychological functions, such as memory, and partly on the crudeness of physiological techniques before the Second World War. As Luria (1973) indicated, psychological goals, like remembering, may be achieved through a variety of routes, each using somewhat different subprocesses. Blocking a preferred route by a specific brain lesion may cause a less preferred one to be adopted and different (spared) subprocesses used. How the brain controls these subprocesses is the key issue. Componential analysis of complex behaviours into their functional atoms is based on criteria lacking universal agreement. This uncertainty permits the existence of a range of views about the reasons why partial recovery may occur after brain damage. Some propose that there is always functional loss so that recovered behaviours are performed differently, whereas others argue that functions genuinely recover and are mediated by surviving brain tissue (Stein *et al.* 1983). The uncertainty also explains the inchoate state of understanding of three other major issues. First, it relates to why early brain lesions sometimes have different effects than adult lesions. For example, does the fact that early left hemisphere lesions disturb verbal behaviour much less than adult lesions mean that certain processes have not yet been irreversibly assigned to that hemisphere, or that in early life verbal behaviour is achieved differently? Second, it relates to the issue of how different is the organization of people's brains. For example, Ojemann (1983) has reported that the ability to name things is disturbed by electrically stimulating different cortical regions in distinct individuals. Are their subprocesses differently located, or do they name in different ways? Third, the same question arises with the last issue, cross-species comparisons. Do species with radically differing brains, who can perform similar complex tasks, do so by using distinct systems of subprocesses?

The use of improved physiological techniques have, however, made clear that functions are more localized than Lashley believed. The brain is now seen as an enormous interlinked set of modules, each acting as a special-purpose computer. Roughly, the neocortex comprises a functional mosaic of modules, which process distinct aspects of sensory information in series and in parallel so that meaning can be extracted and spatial representations constructed by cross-modal integration. This information is stored mainly in the neocortex when further subcortical systems are activated. Further neocortical and subcortical modules programme appropriate behaviour, based on such sensory analysis and a determination (made largely subcortically) of the motivational significance of the information.

Detailed parts of this framework have sprung from the application of physiological techniques. These techniques are now sophisticated. Animal lesions can be precisely placed and identified, and accidental human lesions can now be better located in life using computed axial tomography, cerebral blood flow measurement and positron-emission computed tomography. The last technique, in particular, makes it possible to measure a lesion-induced disturbance of apparently healthy tissue. This bears on a major problem with lesion studies: a function may be lost either because it was controlled by destroyed tissue or because the destruction makes healthy tissue act abnormally. The difficulty can be resolved only by the supplementary use of other techniques like electrical or chemical stimulation of tissue, or recording electrophysiological, metabolic or biochemical activity of neurons whilst an animal (or human) subject is performing a selected task. If the use of these techniques yields consistent and convergent implications, an interpretation can be made of the function of a given brain region. Confidence in such interpretations can be further increased by improved knowledge of the brain's microanatomy and connections. Modern techniques have led to a massive surge in this knowledge, giving rise to the hope that by the turn of the century it will be possible to make detailed computer simulations of how activity in well-described brain regions mediates complex psychological abilities, such as the visual perception of objects.

Andrew Mayes
University of Manchester

References

Hebb, D. O. (1980) *Essay on Mind*, Hillsdale, NJ.
Luria, A. R. (1973) *The Working Brain*, Harmondsworth.
Ojemann, G. A. (1983) 'Brain organization for language from the perspective of electrical stimulation mapping', *Behavioral and Brain Sciences* 6.
Stein, D. G., Finger, S. and Hart, T. (1983) 'Brain damage and recovery: problems and perspectives', *Behavioral and Neural Biology* 37.
Thompson, R. (1967) *Foundations of Physiological Psychology*, London.

Further reading

Carlson, N. R. (1979) *The Brain: A Scientific American Book*, Oxford.
—— (1981) *Physiology of Behavior*, 2nd edn, Boston, MA.
Kolb, B. and Whishaw, I. Q. (1980) *Fundamentals of Human Neuropsychology*, San Francisco, CA.
Oatley, K. (1978) *Perceptions and Representations*, London.

See also: nervous system.

Piaget, Jean (1896–1980)

Jean Piaget, the Swiss psychologist, biologist and philosopher, was professor of experimental psychology at the University of Geneva (1940–71) and of developmental psychology at the Sorbonne in Paris (1952–63). As a psychologist, Piaget was influenced by Freud, Janet, J. M. Baldwin and Claparède. Piaget's theories and experiments, which he published in innumerable books and articles, place him among the foremost psychologists of the century.

Piaget's lifelong quest was for the origins of knowledge. Trained as a biologist, and initially influenced by Bergson's evolutionary philosophy, he sought to explain the conditions of knowledge by studying its genesis. Evolutionary theory, the developmental psychology of children's intelligence, and the history of science were to provide the scientific underpinnings of this epistemological project.

In his early work (1923–36), Piaget tried to gain insight into children's logic by studying their verbally expressed thought. Using a free method of interrogation, the 'clinical method', Piaget investigated children's reasoning about everyday phenomena, causality and moral problems. A leading idea expressed in Piaget's early books is that of egocentrism in early childhood and its gradual replacement by socialized, and therefore logical, thinking. Young children's egocentrism is revealed in their incapacity to differentiate between their own point of view and that of another. Neither experience nor the influence of adults are sufficient grounds for the attainment of logical thinking. Instead, Piaget explained the abandonment of egocentrism by the child's desire and need to communicate with children of the same age.

In the late 1920s and early 1930s Piaget made extensive observations of his own children as babies and elaborated his theory of sensorimotor intelligence in infancy. Contrary to contemporary conceptions, he considered babies as actively and spontaneously oriented towards their environment. As they 'assimilate' things to their action patterns, they at the same time have to 'accommodate' these patterns to the exigencies of the external world. In this process of interaction with the environment the child's innate reflexes and patterns of behaviour are altered, differentiated and mutually co-ordinated. The organization of action patterns gives rise to a 'logic of actions'. In his account of the development of the object concept, Piaget states that initially children do not appear to recognize a world existing independently of their actions upon it. A baby playing with a toy does not search for it when it is covered; according to Piaget, it ceases to exist for the baby. The concept of an independently existing world is gradually constructed during infancy and is attained only at about 18 months when the child becomes capable of representing things mentally.

The existence of a logic in action, demonstrated in the baby studies, made Piaget revise his earlier theories of the origins of logical thinking in early and middle childhood. Logical operations are prepared in sensorimotor intelligence and the former are the result of internalization of the latter. The attainment of logical thinking, therefore, is not the result of verbal interactions with other children, but of the child's reconstruction of the action logic on a new, mental plane. Piaget now viewed cognitive development as resulting in stages, characterized by a dynamic equilibrium between the child's cognitive structures and the environment. Development is the result of a process of equilibration, in which equilibria of a progressively more stable kind are sought and attained. Piaget distinguished three stages: the sensorimotor stage (0–18 months), the stage of concrete operations (about 7–11 years) and the stage of formal operations (from about 11 years). In each of these three stages children's thinking is characterized by its own kind of logic: an action logic in the sensorimotor stage, a logic applied to concrete situations in the concrete operational stage, and a logic applied to statements of a symbolic or verbal kind in the formal operational stage.

In the period between the sensorimotor and the concrete operational stage (which Piaget called the pre-operational period) the child's thinking lacks the possibility to carry out operations, that is, reversible mental actions. Piaget and his collaborators demonstrated in many simple yet elegant experiments the transition from pre-operational to concrete thinking about concepts such as number, velocity, space, and physical causality. In these experiments they no longer restricted themselves to verbal interaction, but introduced materials which the child could manipulate. In the famous conservation task, the child must judge whether the amount of fluid poured into a glass of different proportions changes or does not change. Pre-operational children are characteristically misled by the perceptual appearance of the situation. Only concrete operational children can reverse the transfer in thought and give the correct answer.

From 1950 onward Piaget produced his great epistemological studies, in which he rejected empiricism and rationalism. Consequently he opposed behaviourism, maturational theories of development and nativist ideas in Gestalt psychology. The newborn child is neither a *tabula rasa*, ready to receive the impression of the environment, nor endowed with a priori knowledge about the world. Piaget showed himself a pupil of Kant by assuming that our knowledge of the world is mediated by cognitive structures. But, unlike Kant, he did not consider these as fundamental ideas given at birth: he showed them to be the products of a lengthy process of construction in the interaction of subject and environment. He therefore coined his epistemology a *genetic* epistemology.

The aim of genetic epistemology is to reconstruct the development of knowledge from its most elementary biological forms up to its highest achievements, scientific thinking included. Psychology has a place in this project, in so far as it studies the development of biological structures in the human baby into sensorimotor and operational intelligence. But the enterprise is essentially a biological one, as the development of intelligence is conceived of as an extension of biological adaptation. Intelligence is the specific product in humans of the same biological principles applying to all living nature: adaptation resulting in structural re-organizations and in equilibria of increasing stability.

Piaget saw psychology as a necessary but limited part of his epistemology; and he always regretted the exclusive interest in the psychological component of his work. In the International Centre for Genetic

Epistemology, which he founded at the University of Geneva in 1955 and to which he attracted specialists in all fields of study, he stimulated the interdisciplinary study of epistemology. But the acclaim for his epistemological ideas was never more than a shadow of the universal enthusiasm for the *psychologist* Piaget.

Piaget's influence on developmental psychology can hardly be overestimated. His ideas were seen as a help in supplanting behaviouristic and psychoanalytic theories in psychology. He set the margins for discussions in cognitive developmental psychology from the 1960s up to the present time. But his ideas and methods have always been the object of sharp criticism. Many developmental psychologists think that Piaget underrated the cognitive capacities of young children, and he is reproached for neglecting in his later studies the social context of development in favour of an isolated epistemic subject. Therefore, many now go beyond the mature Piaget and find inspiration in his early works.

Ed Elbers
University of Utrecht

Further reading

Boden, M. (1979) *Piaget*, London.

Ducret, J.-J. (1984) *Jean Piaget*, Geneva.

Flavell, J. H. (1963) *The Developmental Psychology of Jean Piaget*, Princeton, NJ.

Gruber, H. E. and Vonèche, J. J. (eds) (1977) *The Essential Piaget: An Interpretive Reference and Guide*, London.

Piaget, J. (1923) *Le Langage et la pensée chez l'enfant*, Neuchâtel. (*The Language and Thought of the Child*, London, 1926.)

—— (1932) *Le Jugement moral chez l'enfant*, Paris. (*The Moral Judgment of the Child*, London, 1932.)

—— (1936) *La Naissance de l'intelligence chez l'enfant*, Neuchâtel. (*The Origin of Intelligence in the Child*, London, 1952.)

—— (1950) *Introduction à l'épistémologie génétique*, 3 vols, Paris.

—— (1967) *Biologie et connaissance*, Paris. (*Biology and Knowledge*, London, 1971.)

—— (1974) *La Prise de conscience*, Paris. (*The Grasp of Consciousness*, London, 1976.)

—— (1975) *L'Equilibration des structures cognitives*, Paris. (*The Development of Thought: Equilibration of Cognitive Structures*, Oxford, 1977.)

Piaget, J. and Inhelder, B. (1948) *La Représentation de l'espace chez l'enfant*, Paris. (*The Child's Conception of Space*, London, 1956.)

—— (1959) *La Génèse des structures logiques élémentaires*, Neuchâtel. (*The Early Growth of Logic in the Child*, London, 1964).

—— (1966) *La Psychologie de l'enfant*, Paris. (*The Psychology of the Child*, London, 1969.)

Rotman, B. (1977) *Jean Piaget: Psychologist of the Real*, Hassocks.

See also: developmental psychology; learning.

place

A place is an area in which people live together, and thus a key concept in geographic analysis. Much modern social science has emphasized compositional rather than contextual theories of social organization and life (Thrift 1983): people have been categorized according to who they are rather than where they come from, and sociological categories such as class and status have taken precedence over the geographical category of place. Since the mid-1980s, however, the importance of the contextual has been realized (Agnew and Duncan 1989): people are socialized as members of groups that are constituted in places, and the nature of those groups can vary from place to place.

A major impetus to this reincorporation of place within social science was given by Giddens's (1984) promotion of structuration theory, in which locale is a key concept. A locale is a situation within which social interaction occurs, and since virtually all interaction requires the individuals involved to be co-present in time and space, then most locales are necessarily places, which may vary in their spatial and temporal extent. Locales are thus crucial arenas within which interaction occurs and group identity develops.

Giddens drew considerably on the work of a Swedish geographer, Torsten Hagerstrand (1982), whose contextual theory of time geography asserts that projects involving interpersonal interaction can be realized only if the parties involved are co-present in a place. Whether this is possible depends on three constraints being overcome: capability constraints (Can an individual reach a certain place at a given time?); coupling constraints (Can all of the individuals concerned reach the place at the same time?); and authority constraints (Do all of the individuals involved have access to the place at the required time?). Operation of these constraints thus defines the possibilities for project realization. Each individual's biography is a constrained trajectory through time and space: where trajectories intersect, so interaction is enabled and biographies may be changed. The contents of a place – who is there, when – vary, therefore: when one is in a place, and who with, are major influences on individual and group socialization and behaviour.

Others have produced similar arguments. In her seminal *Spatial Divisions of Labour*, for example, Massey (1984) argues that the geography of industrial restructuring can be understood only if the context of the places within which it occurs is appreciated: the nature of social relations varies between places, with some consequently being much more attractive to investors than others. This has stimulated a substantial body of research in which place is usually treated as synonymous with locality: differences between localities in their economic, social, cultural and political structures have been sought as means of understanding how they differ and what this implies for future change.

The importance of the nature of a place to its economic future is a growing problem because of the increased mobility of two of the major factors of production, capital and labour: places have to attract and retain investments and people, and those involved in their management must operate accordingly. This has generated interest in the creation and selling of places among business and political groups, who may combine in a local alliance in order to sell 'their place' (Reynolds 1994). These local interest groups realize the importance of creating an image of 'their place', which may involve both restructuring of social relations and substantial investment in the built environment in order to effect the right conditions to attract capital investment. The changing geography of uneven development, at a variety of spatial scales, is thus closely linked to the success and failure of the politics of place.

For some authors the importance of place (locality, locale) in the processes of socialization and restructuring are illustrations of the validity of the arguments for post-modernism, which prioritizes difference, as do some feminist and other approaches which stress 'positionality': Jackson (1992: 211) notes that 'both movements challenge us to consider from where we speak and whose voices are sanctioned'.

R. J. Johnston
University of Bristol

References

Agnew, J. and Duncan, J. S. (eds) (1989) *The Power of Place: Bringing Together Geographical and Sociological Imaginations*, Boston, MA.

Giddens, A. (1984) *The Constitution of Society*, Cambridge, UK.

Hagerstrand, T. (1982) 'Diorama, path and project', *Tijdschrift voor Economische en Sociale Geografie* 73.

Jackson, P. (1992) 'Changing ourselves: a geography of position', in R. J. Johnston (ed.) *The Challenge for Geography – A Changing World: A Changing Discipline*, Oxford.

Massey, D. (1984) *Spatial Divisions of Labour: Social Structures and the Geography of Production*, London.

Reynolds, D. R. (1994) 'Political geography; the power of place and the spatiality of politics', *Progress in Human Geography* 19.

Thrift, N. J. (1983) 'On the determination of social action in space and time', *Society and Space: Environment and Planning D* 1.

Further reading

Duncan, S. and Savage, M. (1991) *New Perspectives on the Locality Debate*, London.

Johnston, R. J. (1991) *A Question of Place: Exploring the Practice of Human Geography*, Oxford.

See also: habitus; region.

planning, economic

Economic planning is the use of a systematic alternative method of allocating economic resources either to replace or supplement the market mechanism. Its main justification is when the market mechanism fails to supply the right signals to decision-makers. This may be because economies of scale render the atomistic market mechanism ineffective, or because the market is incapable of taking into account the long-run needs of the economy. The state may possess knowledge which the market does not, whether about general economic uncertainties, the preferences of the community as a whole, or the longer-run future. Alternatively, the state may simply reject the validity of the individual preferences which underlie the market system. Critics of planning have focused on the insuperable quantities of information that must be processed if the entire economy is to be organized by one body, and the undemocratic implications of the state's overruling individuals' choices. National economic planning fell into disrepute in the 1980s as a result of the perceived inability of the planned economies of the Soviet Union and Eastern Europe to adapt to changing technological and international competitive conditions.

In common usage, planning can mean either control or forecasting, and economic planning can be anything from consultation to coercion. It is possible in principle to distinguish three types of economic planning: *directive planning* involves administrative regulation from a central body entirely replacing autonomous profit-seeking behaviour in the market; *incentive planning* means the state attempts to achieve a desired outcome by using monetary rewards without coercion; with *indicative planning* the state confines itself to forecasting or consultation, hoping that persuasion and the provision of superior economic information will lead to better economic performance.

In reality, no single system falls into one only of the three categories. The former Soviet system was in principle directive with respect to enterprises, but the market mechanism was in fact allowed considerable sway in the USSR. Consumer goods were not administratively distributed and enterprise managers actually had considerable freedom of manoeuvre which the state tried to manipulate by incentives schemes.

In practice the state gave instructions to firms in annual operating plans rather than the Five Year Plans (which were very general). The Soviet state could not direct the whole of the production side of the economy because of the vast amount of information that it would have needed to handle, even if there had been no inherent uncertainty. Thus a key failure of planning has been the failure to realize that systematic planning is not the same thing as all-pervasive tight regulatory controls.

Many proposals were made for reforming planning in the USSR and Eastern Europe (most of which had copied the Soviet model after 1945) in order to replace the directive element by incentive-based systems, but with very little success. Only Hungary made any significant moves after 1969. A major problem with such reforms was that where the price incentives were set wrongly, a partially decentralized system may be even worse than a centrally planned one as managers follow the logic of bonuses rather than real market forces. It was also felt that even a trace of 'planning' made it hard to enforce the threat of bankruptcy, widely perceived as necessary to ensure the full play of market forces, and so most of the former socialist countries opted for a rapid transition to a wholly market economy after 1989. The Chinese economy was the major exception where an administratively directed state-owned sector coexists with a very rapidly growing private and locally controlled sector, which largely escapes state control and which by the early 1990s had overtaken the state sector in size. Cuba and North Korea remained traditional planned economies.

In the west, economic planning was essentially a wartime phenomenon. The Second World War saw the successful use of planning to achieve war priorities in the UK and USA. After 1945 some idea of planning was advocated by many in the west, incentive or indicative methods being seen as a way of combining the co-ordinating powers of both the market and the plan. But actual attempts at planning displayed a lack of coherence between policy instruments, and between the instruments and the desired objectives. State intervention in many countries and periods has often been very *ad hoc*. Indicative planning was attempted in France, where the Five Year Plan was intended to be a statement of the broad economic goals of the nation. In principle the planners forecast the best available growth path for the economy and influence people's expectations so as to realize this scenario with no coercion of economic actors. French planning appears to have had some real success before 1965, but it has atrophied since then. In practice it always involved far less coherence and more direct (but not always co-ordinated) intervention than the pure model of indicative planning. A misunderstanding of French experience led to total failure of the UK National Plan (1965–70); too much weight was placed on the idea that an optimistic plan could be self-fulfilling. Planning as pure forecasting continues in a number of countries, notably The Netherlands and Scandinavia, and was hotly debated in the USA during the mid-1970s, but planning in western industrial economies (outside wartime) typically does not try to forecast or control every microeconomic variable but rather to regulate the major aggregates such as inflation, overall investment, etc. Incomes policies are a form of macroeconomic planning where the free play of market forces in the labour market is held to be socially undesirable. The former socialist countries largely rejected the middle option of indicative planning on the grounds that, although the market system might bring them some problems of adjustment, their economies were so distorted that no one, and especially not the discredited state planners, was likely to do better than the trial and error process of market forces.

Economic planning may be carried out at a lower level than the national economy. There is regional and sectoral planning, which may or may not be made consistent with national planning. Large corporations also engage in planning, and there have been suggestions that the planning activities of large corporations can be building blocks for the creation of national plans. Critics of this view point out that usually corporate plans are speculative scenarios rather than fully worked out operational programmes.

Less developed countries have often engaged in development planning. This has rarely attempted to follow the directive model, because agriculture does not lend itself well to central planning and because the political and bureaucratic preconditions are such as to make it very hard to manage. India in the 1950s announced an intention to combine western parliamentary democracy with Soviet-type planning. In the end planning became little more than a system of forecasting designed to clarify national economic priorities alongside a widely criticized system of bureaucratic regulations, now rejected by policy makers. Some countries have been more successful (e.g. South Korea or Tunisia) though attempting less than India did initially. Considerable debate reigns over how far the newly industrializing countries of Asia, such as Korea or Taiwan, relied on pure market forces rather than on a form of planning through state influence over the banking system.

Probably the most fruitful use that can be made of economic planning lies in attempts to simulate and collectively consider the likely consequences of alternative future scenarios for the economy, and discussing and negotiating on the likely responses of major economic actors. The European Commission has occasionally attempted to organize such exercises of which perhaps the most striking concerned the attempt to alert economic actors to the potential significance of the '1992' Single Market plan and to induce changes in expectations and behaviour. But on the whole non-market reflection and analysis of this sort found little favour in Europe or the USA during the 1980s, when a consensus built up that private capital markets were uniquely qualified to process and generate economically valuable information about future investment and financial prospects, and that labour markets should be regulated solely by competitive pressures. Only experience rather than economic theorizing will determine whether the rejection of planning is a permanent or a cyclical phenomenon.

Peter Holmes
University of Sussex

Further reading

Bornstein, M. (ed.) 1994 *Comparative Economic Systems*, Homewood, IL.
Cave, M. E. and Hare, P. G. (1981) *Alternative Approaches to Economic Planning*, London.
Journal of Comparative Economics (1990) special issue on indicative planning, December.
Wade, R. (1990) *Governing the Economy*, Princeton, NJ.

See also: mixed economy; prediction and forecasting.

planning, urban *see* urban planning

Plato (428/7–348/7 BC)

Plato was born into a wealthy, well-connected family of the old Athenian aristocracy (Davies 1971). He and his elder brothers Adeimantos and Glaukon (both of whom figure in the *Republic*) belonged to the circle of young men attached to Socrates, as did his cousins Kritias and Charmides, who played a leading part in the oligarchic junta of the Thirty which seized power at the end of the Peloponnesian War in 404/3. In the seventh Letter (a sort of *apologia pro vita sua* by Plato himself or a disciple), Plato claims to have been quickly shocked by the tyrannous behaviour of the Thirty, and equally disgusted with the restored democracy when it condemned Socrates to death in 399; but his chances of playing any prominent part in Athenian politics had in any case been fatally compromised by his close connections with the junta. He settled down to the theoretical life of a philosopher and teacher, which he praises (for example, *Theaetetus* 172–6) as the highest form of human activity. In 367, however, after thirty years of highly productive theoretical activity, he

attempted to put some of the political ideas of the *Republic* into practice by training the young ruler of Syracuse, Dionysius II, for the role of philosopher-king. Not surprisingly, he failed; one of Plato's most obvious weaknesses as a political analyst was his neglect of external factors and relations with other powers, which in the fourth century BC constituted in fact the main problem for the Greek cities. While there are problems of detail in dating Plato's dialogues, one can perhaps say that in his work before the Sicilian episode he is still engaged in a vivacious debate with ideas current in the Athens of his youth, whereas in his later works (*Sophist, Statesman, Philebus, Timaeus, Critias, Laws*) he is addressing himself more specifically to fellow-philosophers, present and future. The philosophical centre he founded in the Academy – a sort of Institute for Advanced Study in rural surroundings – continued after his death.

The influences which shaped Plato's thought are thus the aristocratic milieu in which he grew up and the political events of his lifetime, the personality of Socrates, and the standards of systematic reasoning associated with the role of philosopher. His contributions to social thought as we would now define it lie mainly in the fields of political and moral philosophy, psychology and education; but these aspects of his thought cannot be detached from his epistemology and cosmology.

Part of the fascination of reading Plato comes from the dialogue form in which he presented his ideas. He was no doubt influenced in this choice by Socrates, who communicated his own ideas solely through argument and left no written works; more generally, the Athenians were used to hearing different points of view upheld by opposing speakers in political assemblies, in law courts and in drama. Socrates takes the leading part in Plato's earlier dialogues, and this enabled the author both to acknowledge his debt to his teacher and, perhaps, to avoid taking full responsibility for the ideas he was putting forward. Plato never figures in his own dialogues. The dialogue form also suited his gifts as a brilliantly natural and graceful writer, a skilful parodist and master of characterization and light-hearted conversation. The introductory scenes of his dialogues provide the historian with lively sketches of upper-class manners and mores in the late fifth century BC.

The key element in Plato's thought as it concerned social life was a widening of the gap between body and spirit. This enabled him to preserve an essential core of religious belief from the criticisms which had been directed against traditional religion, to ground Socrates' argument that virtue is a kind of knowledge in a general theory of epistemology which offered solutions to logical problems raised by earlier philosophers, and to provide a foundation for belief in the immortality of the soul; at the same time it formalized a psychological split between lower and higher elements in the personality, and linked this to a justification of social hierarchy, and to a theory of education in which censorship played an essential part.

Plato's early dialogues show Socrates attacking a traditional, unreflective upper-class practice of virtue as a routine response of the gentleman to predictable situations. When asked to define courage (*Laches*), piety (*Euthyphro*) or moderation (*Charmides*), his interlocutors give specific examples of brave, pious or self-controlled behaviour, and Socrates then proves to them that such acts would not in all circumstances be considered virtuous. Echoes of the same attitude can be found in Xenophon and Euripides.

Some of Plato's contemporaries went on from this criticism of traditional conceptions of virtue to deny its existence altogether: in the *Republic*, Thrasymachus argues that values and virtues are defined by the ruling class to suit their own interests, and Glaukon argues that they represent the interests of the majority. Plato therefore needed a concept of virtue which was flexible and abstract enough to satisfy Socratic criticism but nevertheless safe against relativist attack. His response was the theory of Forms or Ideas, existing at a level of ultimate, abstract reality which was only imperfectly reflected in the material world but of which the human mind could gradually acquire better knowledge through philosophical training.

Coming closer to the world of Ideas thus becomes both the highest aim of human life and the standard by which all kinds of knowledge are judged; it follows that human societies should be directed by philosophers or by laws formulated by philosophers. The human personality is divided into three elements: intelligence, *amour-propre* (*Thumos*) and the physical appetites. Education aims to train the first to dominate the other two.

Thumos refers to a set of qualities regarded somewhat ambiguously in Plato's culture (Dover 1974). It was the basis of the human pursuit of prestige and honour and thus – like the appetites – beneficial when exercised in moderation but dangerous when obsessive. Too eager a pursuit of honour led to tyranny or to a tendency to take offence for no reason. Thus there was a popular basis for the view that even ambition for what the ordinary person in the street considered the supreme good had to be controlled. This point was particularly important for Plato, because his belief that the good society was a society ruled by good and wise men meant that the essential problem of political organization was to prevent the ruling elite from becoming corrupted. This led him to formulate the idea of the 'mixed constitution', later to influence Polybius, Montesquieu, and the US Constitution.

Because a philosophical education involved training in subjects like astronomy and mathematics for which not all had equal interest or aptitude, and because philosophers had to detach themselves from activities and preoccupations likely to strengthen the influence of their *Thumos* and bodily appetites, the hierarchy of faculties in the psyche led to a hierarchy of groups in the ideal city. Philosophers would have supreme authority, semi-educated watch-dogs would act as a military and police force on their behalf, and those who supplied the economic needs of the city would have the lowest status of all. Education was to be carefully adjusted to the reproduction of the system; the lower class were to be trained to obedience and persuaded by a political myth that their status was due to natural causes; poets should represent only socially commendable behaviour; knowledge of alternative forms of society was to be carefully suppressed, except in the case of selected members of the ruling elite.

Such views have in the twentieth century led to attacks on Plato as a proto-fascist or Stalinist (Crossman 1937, Popper 1945). In the *Laws* the more extreme proposals of the *Republic* (in particular, the abolition of private property and the family) were dropped; it is interesting to see Plato grappling here with detailed problems of law-drafting, and the text is a key piece of evidence on Greek legal thought. Return to law as a source of authority was a capitulation to the rigid type of definition of virtue which Socrates had attacked (see the *Statesman*); but the argument which had seemed valid when applied to individuals would not work for collectivities. There was something wrong with the analogy between parts of the city and parts of the human psyche.

S. C. Humphreys
University of Michigan

References

Crossman, R. H. (1937) *Plato Today*, London.
Davies, J. K. (1971) *Athenian Propertied Families*, Oxford.
Dover, K. J. (1974) *Greek Popular Morality in the Time of Plato and Aristotle*, Oxford.
Popper, K. (1945) *The Open Society and its Enemies*, London.

Further reading

Gouldner, A. W. (1966) *Enter Plato: Classical Greece and the Origins of Social Theory*, New York.
Guthrie, W. K. C. (1975–8) *A History of Greek Philosophy*, vols 4 and 5, Cambridge, UK.
Ryle, G. (1966) *Plato's Progress*, Cambridge, UK.
Shorey, P. (1933) *What Plato Said*, Chicago.
Stalley, R. F. (1983) *An Introduction to Plato's Laws*, Oxford.
Taylor, A. E. (1926) *Plato: The Man and his Work*, London.
Wood, E. M. and Wood, N. (1978) *Class Ideology and Ancient Political Theory: Socrates, Plato and Aristotle in Social Context*, Oxford.

plural society

Since the early 1960s, the term plural society has been used to describe societies, usually at the level of independent states or colonial territories, characterized by sharp internal cleavages between ethnic, racial, religious or linguistic groups. By the criterion of 90 per cent or more of the population speaking the same language, at best 10 per cent of the 150-odd states represented at the United Nations are genuine nation-states. The remainder exhibit various degrees of cultural and social pluralism, ranging from the extreme fragmentation of countries like Nigeria, Zaïre, India and the former Soviet Union, with scores of ethnic groups, often unrelated to each other, to less hetero-geneous states like Belgium, Switzerland or Canada, made up of two or three related language groups.

That broad spectrum of societies has, of course, been studied from a wide variety of perspectives, each with its own vocabulary. Marxists have generally preferred the term 'multinational states', and the thrust of their analysis has been to explain the cleavages and conflicts of these societies by reference to a combina-tion of internal class cleavages and unequal exchanges between the 'core' and 'periphery' of the 'capitalist world-system' (Frank 1967; Lenin 1969 [1916]; Wallerstein 1974). They have treated ethnic, linguistic, racial or religious differences as either residues of past epochs with vanishing significance, or as labels of false consciousness masking class differences.

A number of liberal scholars, however, when dealing with 'bourgeois democracies' of Western Europe and North America have dealt with pluralism as a condi-tion of the political give-and-take of competition and conflict between contending interest groups (Kornhauser 1960; Lipset 1963). By pluralism, however, they have meant not so much ethnic or racial cleavages. Indeed, they often ignored these. Rather, they referred principally to the diversity of political views and of specialized interest groups competing for resources in the political arena of parliamentary democracies.

Yet another tradition has dealt with the accommo-dation of ethnic conflicts in what it called consocia-tional or proportional democracies (Lijphart 1977). Scholars in this tradition worked mostly in the advanced industrial countries of Europe (such as Belgium, The Netherlands, Switzerland and Austria), characterized by only a moderate degree of pluralism and a high degree of equality between the constituent linguistic or religious collectivities.

Most closely associated with the label plural society is a group of social scientists who have studied princi-pally the highly fragmented societies of Asia, Africa, the Caribbean and Latin America, societies generally characterized by a history of violent conquest, followed by colonialism, slavery, indenture and other forms of highly institutionalized segmentation and inequality between ethnic or racial groups (Furnivall 1948; Kuper and Smith 1969; Schermerhorn 1970; van den Berghe 1974). Not unexpectedly, these scholars stress conflict and the coercive role of the state in maintaining a system of social inequality and economic exploitation. Although their analysis shares a number of features with that of the Marxists, they tend to emphasize cultural and racial lines of cleavage more than class lines and to ascribe causal priority to political relations over economic relations. That is, they tend to regard unequal relations to the means of production as derivative of unequal power relations, rather than vice versa. They also generally insist on treating class and ethnicity as two distinct bases of social organization, which in practice overlap, but which can also vary independently.

Pierre van den Berghe
University of Washington

References

Frank, A. G. (1967) *Capitalism and Underdevelopment in Latin America*, New York.
Furnivall, J. S. (1948) *Colonial Policy and Practice*, London.
Kornhauser, W. (1960) *The Politics of Mass Society*, London.
Kuper, L. and Smith, M. G. (eds) (1969) *Pluralism in Africa*, Berkeley CA.
Lenin, V. I. (1969 [1916]) *Imperialism, The Highest Stage of Capitalism*, Peking.
Lijphart, A. (1977) *Democracy in Plural Societies*, New Haven, CT.
Lipset, S. M. (1963) *The First New Nation*, New York.
Schermerhorn, R. A. (1970) *Comparative Ethnic Relations*, New York.
van den Berghe, P. L. (1974) 'Pluralism', in J. J. Honigmann (ed.) *Handbook of Social and Cultural Anthropology*, Chicago.
Wallerstein, I. (1974) *The Modern World-System*, New York.

See also: colonialism; ethnic politics; pluralism, political; world-system theory.

pluralism, political

Political pluralism is a normative perspective in modern politics that emphasizes the importance for democracy and liberty of maintaining a plurality of relatively autonomous political and economic organ-izations. Political pluralists believe that in large-scale societies competing economic interests and differences of political opinion are unavoidable. In opposition to Marxists, political pluralists do not believe that these significant political cleavages are primarily or necessarily related to class. Nor do they believe that these sources of political conflict can be eliminated by bringing the means of production under public ownership. For the governmental system of large-scale societies to be democratic, political pluralists insist that there must be institutions through which divergent interests can articulate their views and compete for power. A system of competitive political parties is a hallmark of pluralist democracies. Such democratic polities are often referred to as liberal democracies.

Some political pluralists recognize that inequality in the distribution of political resources may mean that some social interests or groups in a liberal democracy have much more power and influence than others. Thus a political pluralist may advocate redistributive policies to reduce political inequalities (Dahl 1982). However much inequalities are reduced, democratic pluralists are still faced with the dilemma of how much autonomy should be extended to groups whose views differ from those of the majority. Federalism is one solution to this dilemma where significant societal differences coincide with territorial divisions. Another approach is consociational democracy in which national policy is arrived at through a consensus of elites drawn from the country's major cultural or ideological segments (Lijphart 1977).

Peter H. Russell
University of Toronto

References

Dahl, R. A. (1982) *Dilemmas of Pluralist Democracy*, New Haven, CT.
Lijphart, A. (1977) *Democracy in Plural Societies*, New Haven, CT.

Further reading

Connolly, W. E. (ed.) (1969) *The Bias of Pluralism*, New York.
Lipset, S. M. (1960) *Political Man: The Social Bases of Politics*, Garden City, NY.

See also: democracy; federation and federalism; liberalism; plural society.

Polanyi, Karl (1886–1964)

Polanyi, a charismatic teacher and original thinker whose ideas cut across both academic and political boundaries, grew up in the intellectual milieu of revisionist socialism in Hungary which also produced Georg Lukács and Karl Mannheim. To escape authoritarian regimes he moved in 1919 from Budapest to Vienna, where he worked as an economic journalist through the years of the depression, and again in 1933 from Vienna to England. His lectures in England for the Workers' Educational Association (he had earlier pioneered workers' education in Hungary with the Galilei Circle) grew into *The Great Transformation* (1944),

an analysis of the rise and fall of economic liberalism and the world economy from Ricardo's England to Hitler's Germany.

In 1947 Polanyi moved to Columbia University; the results of his seminars on the comparative study of economic institutions were outlined in *Trade and Market in the Early Empires* (1957). Through this volume and his influence on collaborators such as Paul Bohannan, George Dalton, Marshall Sahlins, A. L. Oppenheim and M. I. Finley, Polanyi's views have exerted a decisive influence both on economic anthropology and on the economic anthropology and the economic history of the ancient world.

Polanyi's belief that in pre-capitalist societies the economy (defined as institutionalized provision for human material needs) is embedded in social relationships governed by values other than concern for profit has clear affinities with the functionalism of Malinowski and Talcott Parsons. His views generated a heated but ephemeral debate between 'Substantivists' and 'Formalists' in economic anthropology in the 1960s; they also, however, aided Marxist anthropologists in their struggle to free themselves from crude economism (Godelier 1975). His work is rich in detailed insights into the working of money, trade and exchange centres in pre-capitalist economies; his Weberian typology of exchange systems (reciprocity, householding, redistribution, market exchange) has particularly stimulated research and criticism among historians of ancient Mesopotamia (Gledhill and Larsen 1982).

For Polanyi, the central problem of modern society was to combine socialist economic planning with individual freedom (Dumont 1983). In retirement, he worked to found the journal *Co-Existence* as a forum for truly international and intercultural discussion of such questions.

S. C. Humphreys
University of Michigan

References

Dumont, L. (1983) 'Preface' to K. Polanyi, *La Grande Transformation*, Paris.
Gledhill. J. and Larsen, M. T. (1982) 'The Polanyi paradigm and a dynamic analysis of archaic states', in C. Renfrew *et al.* (eds) *Theory and Explanation in Archaeology*, London.
Godelier, M. (1975) 'Introduction' to K. Polanyi, *Les Systèmes économiques dans l'histoire et dans la théorie*, Paris.

Further reading

Humphreys, S. C. (1969) 'History, economics and anthropology: the work of Karl Polanyi', *History and Theory* 8.
Polanyi, K. (1977) *The Livelihood of Man*, New York.

See also: exchange.

police

The idea of the police must be distinguished from the broader concept of policing, although in contemporary societies the two are commonly assimilated. Police refers to a specific kind of social institution, while policing implies a process with particular social functions. Police are not found in every society, and police organizations and personnel can take a variety of forms. It is arguable, however, that policing of some kind is a universal requirement of any social order, and may be carried out by a number of different institutional arrangements and social processes.

Policing connotes a set of activities *directed* at preserving the security of a particular social order. That order may variously be seen as resting upon a basic consensus of interests, or a manifest (and/or latent) conflict of interests between groups differentially placed in a hierarchy of power and privilege, or perhaps a complex intertwining of the two. As one analyst has put it, the police function may involve parking tickets *and* class repression (Marenin 1983). Whether particular policing activities actually succeed in securing social order is a moot point, as is the relationship between policing and other elements of social control.

Policing is a specific subset of social control processes. It must be distinguished from the broader elements of the creation of social order (for example, socialization and the creation and reproduction of cultural and ethical standards), as well as from institutions for adjudication and punishment of deviance.

Policing may be defined as surveillance coupled with the threat of the initiation of sanctions for any deviance that may be discovered thereby. The most familiar system of this kind is the one implied by the modern sense of police: this connotes a formal organization concerned primarily with regular uniform patrol of public space together with *post-hoc* investigation of reported or discovered crime or disorder. However, policing can be accomplished by a diverse array of people and techniques, of which the modern idea of policing is only one. Policing may be carried out by professional state employees with an omnibus policing mandate – the archetypal modern concept of *the* police (which itself can take a variety of forms) or by state agencies with other primary purposes, such as the Atomic Energy Authority, Customs and Excise, parks and transport constabularies, and other 'hybrid' bodies (Johnston 1992: ch. 6). Policing may also be done by professional employees of specialist private police agencies or by in-house security personnel hired by an organization whose main business is not policing (Shearing 1992; Shearing and Stenning 1987; South 1988).

Policing functions may also be performed by citizens in a voluntary capacity within state organizations, like the British Special Constabulary; in association with the state police, like Neighbourhood Watch schemes; or in volunteer bodies which are not under any state auspices. Sometimes such volunteer policing may be in tension with the state, like the Guardian Angels, and the various forms of vigilantism which have flourished in many times and places.

Policing may be carried out by state bodies with other primary functions (like the British army in Northern Ireland), or by employees (state or private) with other primary roles (like caretakers, shop assistants or porters). Policing may also be done by non-human processes: surveillance technology, architecture, or the security aspects of particular natural or built environments. All these strategies of policing are prevalent now as in the past, although it is only the state agency with the specific mandate of policing which is popularly understood by the label police.

Until modern times policing functions were carried out primarily as a by-product of other social relationships and by citizen volunteers or private employees. Anthropological studies have shown how many pre-literate societies have existed without any formalized system of policing. Specialized policing institutions emerge only in relatively complex societies (Schwartz and Miller 1964). This is not merely a reflex of a burgeoning division of labour. Policing may originate in collective and communal processes of social control, but specialized police forces develop together with social inequality and hierarchy. They are means for the emergence and protection of more centralized state systems. The development of specialized police 'is linked to economic specialisation and differential access to resources that occur in the transition from a kinship- to a class-dominated society' (Robinson and Scaglion 1987: 109; Robinson *et al.* 1994). In contemporary societies the police become the agency specialized in the handling of the state's distinctive capacity: the monopoly of legitimate force (Bittner 1974).

There are varying explanations for the creation of specialized police agencies in modern societies. Different countries have experienced divergent historical routes, and interpretations of the rise of the police will vary between different theoretical and political positions (Brogden *et al.* 1988: chs 4–5; Reiner 1992: chs 1–2). Anglo-American police ideology postulates a fundamental distinction between continental European police systems, which originate overtly as instruments of state control, and the British system, which is represented as a necessary adjustment of ancient forms of communal self-policing in the face of the exigencies of industrialization. More recent historical and comparative research has exposed the oversimplification of this orthodox perspective (Mawby 1990). The British, US and other common law systems of police may not have originated as direct and explicit tools of the state, but their emergence and development is closely related to shifting structures of state control and class conflict (Emsley 1991; Miller 1977). The supposedly community-based British model was in any case for home consumption only. A more militaristic and coercive state-controlled system of policing was always exported to colonial situations (Brogden 1987).

Since the mid-1960s a substantial body of research on police organization and practice has developed, primarily in Britain and North America, but increasingly elsewhere as well; this is now a major branch of criminology (Reiner 1994). The main source of police research was the growing awareness that the popular conception of the police as simply a law-enforcement agency was misleading in two ways. From the outset police research showed that the police performed a variety of order-maintenance and social service functions apart from dealing with crime and criminals (Banton 1964; Punch 1979; Waddington 1993). Moreover, in performing their various tasks the police exercised considerable discretion and regularly deviated from the rule of law (Holdaway 1983; Manning 1977; Skolnick 1966). The recognition of police discretion raised the questions – for research, policy and politics – of how it was exercised in practice, its relationship to legal and social justice, and how it could be made accountable (McConville et al. 1991; Reiner and Spencer 1993).

The development of police research has coincided with a period in which growing concern about rising crime and about police malpractice has kept law and order at the centre of political controversy. Police forces have grown in powers and resources as a consequence. However, the apparent failure of crime rates to respond to increased police capacity has called into question the actual and potential effectiveness of the police as a crime control mechanism. Researchers have shown that there is little scope for reducing crime by increasing police deployment (Clarke and Hough 1984), although innovative tactics may have a modest impact (Sherman 1992). Despite this evidence, in the early 1990s the British government launched a sweeping and highly controversial package of reforms on the premise that managerial reorganization on private sector businesslike lines can inject a higher level of efficiency which can make the police effective in dealing with crime (Reiner and Spencer 1993).

It is becoming increasingly apparent, however, that the police by themselves can play only a limited role in managing the problems of crime. Crime control involves a more complex mix of policing strategies involving the police in partnership with citizens, private security, and technological and environmental crime prevention methods. Above all, it requires social and economic policies which can tackle the roots of crime and reinvigorate informal social control processes. The police are becoming once more a part of a more complex web of policing processes.

R. Reiner
London School of Economics
and Political Science

References

Banton, M. (1964) *The Policeman in the Community*, London.

Bittner, E. (1974) 'Florence Nightingale in pursuit of Willie Sutton: a theory of the police' in H. Jacob (ed.) *The Potential for Reform of Criminal Justice*, Beverly Hills, CA.

Brogden, M. (1987) 'The emergence of the police: the colonial dimension', *British Journal of Criminology* 27(1).

Brogden, M., Jefferson, T. and Walklate, S. (1988) *Introducing Policework*, London.

Clarke, R. and Hough, M. (1984) *Crime and Police Effectiveness*, London.

Emsley, C. (1991) *The English Police: A Political and Social History*, Hemel Hempstead.

Holdaway, S. (1983) *Inside the British Police*, Oxford.

Johnston, L. (1992) *The Rebirth of Private Policing*, London.

McConville, M., Sanders, A. and Leng, R. (1991) *The Case for the Prosecution: Police Suspects and the Construction of Criminality*, London.

Manning, P. (1977) *Police Work: The Social Organisation of Policing*, Cambridge, MA.

Marenin, O. (1983) 'Parking tickets and class repression: the concept of policing in critical theories of criminal justice', *Contemporary Crises* 6(2).

Mawby, R. (1990) *Comparative Policing Issues*, London.

Miller, W. (1977) *Cops and Bobbies*, Chicago.

Punch, M. (1979) 'The secret social service', in S. Holdaway (ed.) *The British Police*, London.

Reiner, R. (1992) *The Politics of the Police*, 2nd edn, Hemel Hempstead.

——(1994) 'Policing and the police', in M. Maguire, R. Morgan and R. Reiner (eds) *The Oxford Handbook of Criminology*, Oxford.

Reiner, R. and Spencer, S. (eds) (1993) *Accountable Policing: Effectiveness, Empowerment and Equity*, London.

Robinson, C. and Scaglion, R. (1987) 'The origin and evolution of the police function in society', *Law and Society Review* 21(1).

Robinson, C., Scaglion, R. and Olivero, M. (1994) *Police in Contradiction: The Evolution of the Police Function in Society*, Westport, CT.

Schwartz, R. D. and Miller, J. C. (1964) 'Legal evolution and societal complexity', *American Journal of Sociology* 70(1).

Shearing, C. (1992) 'The relation between public and private policing', in M. Tonry and N. Morris (eds) *Modern Policing*, Chicago.

Shearing, C. and Stenning, P. (eds) (1987) *Private Policing*, Beverly Hills, CA.

Sherman, L. (1992) 'Attacking crime: police and crime

control', in Tonry, M. and Morris, N. (eds) *Modern Policing*, Chicago.

Skolnick, J. (1966) *Justice without Trial*, New York.

South, N. (1988) *Policing for Profit*, London.

Waddington, P. A. J. (1993) *Calling the Police*, Aldershot.

See also: crime and delinquency; criminology; social control.

policy making

Policy itself has three senses. In one sense it refers to the purposes for which people associate in the polis. A second sense has to do with the review of information and the determination of appropriate action. The third sense concerns the securing and commitment of resources.

Over the last century a distinction has been constructed between policy (in all these senses) and policy making, a dualism which has sundered the inclusive Baconian view of policy as reason of state. In consequence policy making itself has come to be conceived of as one peculiar process, while policy is something else: a symbolic entity 'out there' merely uttered, chosen or promised. 'We have galaxies of policies' (David Steel, UK General Election 1983).

Two factors determine this dichotomy. One has been the association of the modern state with nationalism, mobilization and elections and therefore with a mandate or platform. The second factor is that the modern state is 'not an enormous coercive power, but a vast and conscious organization' (Durkheim). Concomitant institutional developments provided bases for the classic dualistic formulations of Woodrow Wilson, opposing politics and administration, and of J. S. Mill, who contrasted politics and policy arguments from administrative practices, and of Bagehot, who envisaged a political minister who would be above the dirty business of policy making. The dichotomy was completely established between the philosophical radical decade and the mid-Victorian era.

This rationalistic estrangement of policy and policy making has been inescapable, but ultimately pernicious. It is necessarily premised on a non-political and technical model of policy making as an optimalizing search for the best means to realize a given platform. This has fostered in turn a peculiarly influential and dangerous dichotomy, between policy and implementation.

These dichotomies would have been impossible without the development of such social sciences as scientific management and classical public administration, and without the emergence of vocational rather than political social sciences. At the same time, the dichotomous model has provided the conditions for the development of the social sciences, and, in government machines themselves, for a distinction between policy and management, and so for a technologizing of policy making and of social science involvement, for example, in economic and welfare and other policy sectors.

However recent its involvement in policy making may be, these disciplines have managed to suppress any historical consciousness of what has happened, and argue for a favoured role, sector by sector, as though it were unproblematic, scientific and unique. In truth the role of specific social sciences in policy making is a consequence of political accidents. They share, none the less, a common subservience to the privileging of the politics of policy.

The dualistic concept of policy making as policy and implementation has, then, been the breeding ground for a dangerous dichotomizing with consequences for the data, problems and agendas of modern policy, and for the strategies and the highly sectoral constructions of modern policy, each with its dutifully innocent social science enshrined in techniques like social cost-benefit analysis, casework and extensions, and within hived-off devices for sectoral improvements, like planning cells, or separate foundations such as the many imitators of the RAND Corporation.

This splitting up of policy making into policy and implementation also led inevitably to the search for explanations of the unhappy differences between the experience of implementation and the policies which had been promised. Such explications are at once banal and erroneous, since policy is actually about securing and maintaining office, as it always has been. It is also dangerous, since the dichotomy between policy and implementation makes it difficult to determine responsibilty. Decision makers blame implementers, the outside advisers blame insiders, and the policy agencies even blame the poor intended target group members themselves.

The dominant record of the policy-making social sciences thus far has been to participate in the construction and enjoyment of these conveniently escapist dualisms. There have been some institutional descriptions and some survey work on public opinions of familiar policy themes. There has also been an effort to depoliticize the social science of public policy outright by treating policy making as a simulacrum of individual market choice.

Alternative approaches, which are concerned with the whole of policy-making practice, face two difficulties. One is that access to the inner institutional materials often requires acceptance of the fashions and legitimation of the politics of policy. The second difficulty is that an alternative social science of policy making must, at one and the same time, manage to see policy fashions, headlines or technologies for what they are and avoid the apparently harmless policy versus implementation dichotomy.

The alternative policy-making social science would also need to construct a grid for handling all the zones of policy practice. It could then expose the establishment and presentation of policy in terms of objective and unavoidable problems, like deficits and gaps, and in therapeutic and unobjectionable strategies, with heavily disguised favours or exclusions, costs and controls in the actual deliveries.

Such a social science would be a confrontational account of what is involved in policy making, not a co-opted, false or mythologizing discourse. However inconvenient for some social science relationships, it would challenge the unchallengeable, reveal what is hidden, and insist on considering precisely those effects, data, victims and possibilities which are ignored in orthodox social science discourse about policy making.

Bernard Schaffer
formerly, University of Sussex

Further reading

Appleby, P. (1949) *Policy and Administration*, Alabama.
Ballard, J. (ed.) (1981) *Policy Making in a New State*, St Lucia, Queensland.
Lindblom, C. E. (1968) *The Policy-Making Process*, Englewood Cliffs, NJ.
Self, P. (1975) *The Econocrats and the Policy Process*, London.

See also: policy sciences; public administration.

policy sciences

The policy sciences are concerned with understanding the decision processes of public and private institutions, and with assessing the significance of all knowledge for purposes of decision. The term policy sciences was introduced after the Second World War by Lerner and Lasswell (1951) to refer to the emergence of this focus on decision among specialists in many disciplines. Subsequent developments have been marked by the refinement of conceptual tools; the establishment of policy programmes in universities, government agencies, and the private sector; and by the explosive growth of policy analyses. Policy experts in the aggregate have not yet developed a distinctive professional identity or a shared understanding of their actual and preferred roles in the evolution of civilization.

Policy scientists are traditionally graduates from academic programmes in public or business administration, political science, economics, jurisprudence, and the like. Since the 1960s, policy scientists have also emerged from the physical and natural sciences in increasing numbers. These disciplines have had little contact with traditional policy theory but a great deal

to do with the major policy problems of our time. In a typical career pattern, scientists in a laboratory or research institute discover latent interests and talents in an initial attempt to relate their specialized knowledge to the broader environment. The environment tends to nurture and reinforce these initiatives to the extent that knowledge is expected to pay off in national security, domestic political advantage, wealth, well-being, prestige, or in other ways. The aspiring policy expert soon learns to sustain this expectation through delivery of partial results, and to justify further science and scholarship in terms that the environment rewards.

Policy scientists tend to converge on a common outlook, despite their different origins. A distinctive element of this common outlook is *contextuality*. An enquiry that reduces considerations of realism or worth to those of a single discipline, for example, may be acceptable to a manuscript editor who enforces that discipline's standards. However, it is not likely to be acceptable to a decision maker, unimpressed by the traditional academic division of labour, who cannot afford to ignore other considerations in the evaluation of alternative courses of action. Another element is a *problem-orientation* that includes the tasks logically entailed in a rational choice among alternatives. A rational choice entails projections of the probable consequences of alternatives, and preferences for the evaluation of those consequences. Thus specialists in preferences, including some philosophers, gradually learn that priorities among goals are contingent on projections, which in turn depend on the description of trends and the analysis of factors conditioning those trends. Conversely, specialists in projections, mostly scientists, gradually learn to clarify and make explicit their goals in order to guide empirical policy research. (The 'value free' connotation of 'science' is attenuated, while science as the pursuit of 'verifiable knowledge' is retained.) A third element is the synthesis of *multiple methods*. Each method of observation or analysis tends to divert attention from some potentially important aspects of the situation at hand. The use of multiple methods helps compensate for such blind spots. In general, over-reliance on any partial approach to policy analysis leads to mistakes in practice.

The integration of knowledge from many sources and the application of that knowledge to particular policy problems depends upon conceptual tools. Ideally, such tools crystallize and conveniently label the principal distinctions that have turned out to be useful across broad ranges of experience. They do not provide general answers to particular questions, as empirical and normative theories are sometimes purported to do. Rather, the conceptual tools are heuristics: as principles of procedure, they guide the search for data and insights pertinent to a specific decision. As principles of content, they outline the general considerations involved in a decision and help bring to bear the knowledge accumulated from different times, places and cultural contexts. As short lists of interrelated concepts, they anticipate or implement findings of cognitive psychology on the processing of information within the constraints of short-term memory (Simon 1981). Command of these conceptual tools enables a policy scientist to maximize the potential for rationality within the constraints of time, resources and other factors in the situation.

Lasswell (1971) and his collaborators (Lasswell and Kaplan 1950; Lasswell and McDougal 1992) have refined the most comprehensive set of conceptual tools since the 1940s, but approximate equivalents are persistently rediscovered by others. To understand behaviour, policy scientists postulate that people act selectively to maximize preferred outcomes according to their own perspectives; but the acts are less than fully rational because the relevant perspectives are incomplete, distorted, and unconscious in various respects and degrees. The perspectives are also subject to change. Lasswell's (1971) 'maximization postulate' and Simon's (1983) 'principle of bounded rationality' are essentially equivalent tools for understanding behaviour. To map the contexts that affect (and are affected by) the behaviour of individuals or groups, policy scientists use conceptual models of the decision process and of the broader social process. A model of the decision process, among other things, directs attention to the multiple points at which power has or might be used to shape decisions. A model of the broader social process, among other things, directs attention to the distinctive social bases, justifications, and strategies of the power elite and to the social outcomes and effects of decisions. To orient themselves in the context, policy scientists perform the intellectual tasks entailed in rational decision. These tasks have been conceptualized in nearly equivalent ways by Simon (1983) and many others.

While convergence towards a common outlook and equivalent conceptual tools will continue to be reinforced through practical policy experience, the process of convergence is far from complete (Brunner 1991). For example, disciplinary differences in outlook persist. They are still reflected to some extent in such terms as policy analysis (economics), policy studies (political science), socioeconomics (sociology) and philosophy and public affairs (philosophy). Moreover, restrictive assumptions about human behaviour endure. For narrowly scientific purposes, it is often assumed that behaviour is determined by invariant behavioural laws (despite the existence of choices) or by objective rationality (despite differences in perspectives and behaviour). In addition, reductionist approaches persist. For technical reasons, it is often convenient to exclude what is not easily quantified or formalized, to take preferences as fixed or given, or to assume that decisions are discrete (made once and for all) rather than revised as circumstances change. So long as such partial approaches persist, it is appropriate to restrict policy sciences to the integrative conception of Lasswell and his collaborators, and to refer to the collection of partial approaches as the 'policy movement'.

The rise of policy experts of all kinds has been expedited by the increasing complexity of modern society. Science-based technology continues to fragment the social division of labour into ever more specialized parts, and at the same time to interconnect the parts more densely and more quickly through modern means of communication and transportation. This complicates problems of decision in the public and private sectors, because more (and more specialized) considerations must be taken into account. In response, decision makers demand more assistance from experts, and educational and research institutions expand to meet the demand. Growth accelerated with the establishment of first-generation policy schools in major universities in the late 1960s. The graduates of these schools have been recruited into offices of planning or evaluation in government agencies, research divisions of organized political groups, private think tanks, and university policy programmes – all of which have expanded and multiplied since the 1970s. In reviewing the explosive rise of policy analyses, Rivlin (1984) found a paradox: no longer was any major issue in US government debated without reference to the many policy analyses of the participants involved. Yet there had been no obvious progress on major issues, like federal budget deficits, in which stalemate and a search for panaceas tended to prevail.

From a broader perspective, there is little doubt that the scientific revolution has failed to abolish zones of poverty amidst plenty, or to civilize the militant structure of world politics before or after the Cold War. In principle, the fruits of knowledge are available to all. In practice, knowledge is often selectively used for the benefit of the few. The rich and the powerful are in a position to compensate or command the services of policy experts. But policy scientists may also serve the weak, the poor, and others who are disadvantaged, as well as common interests. The question of whose interests are served is confounded with professional identities, which remain in flux. One of the continuing tasks of the policy sciences and the policy movement is to appraise their own impact on policy and society. For these appraisals, the search for authoritative criteria can be guided by the Universal Declaration of Human Rights.

Ronald D. Brunner
University of Colorado

References

Brunner, R. D. (1991) 'The policy movement as a policy problem', *Policy Sciences* 24.
Lasswell, H. D. (1971) *A Pre-View of Policy Sciences*, New York.
Lasswell, H. D. and Kaplan, A. (1950) *Power and Society*, New Haven, CT.
Lasswell, H. D. and McDougal, M. S. (1992) *Jurisprudence for a Free Society: Studies in Law, Science and Policy*, 2 vols, New Haven, CT.
Lerner, D. and Lasswell, H. D. (eds) (1951) *The Policy Sciences*, Stanford, CA.
Rivlin, A. (1984) 'A policy paradox', *Journal of Policy Analysis and Management* 4.
Simon, H. A. (1981) *The Sciences of the Artificial*, 2nd edn, Cambridge, UK.
—— (1983) *Reason in Human Affairs*, Stanford, CA.

See also: policy making; public administration.

political anthropology

Morgan's *The League of the Ho-de-ne-sau-nee, or Iroquois* (1851) is acknowledged as the first political ethnography, and his *Ancient Society* (1877) established a dominant evolutionary paradigm in political anthropology. Like Montesquieu, Morgan projected society progressing from savagery through barbarism to civilization, emerging from civil to political society based on territoriality and property. The first professional political studies were carried out through the Bureau of American Ethnology established when the US government was most concerned with law and order on Indian reservations. Morgan and Herbert Spencer provided the conceptual and classificatory underpinning; long periods of fieldwork provided the political ethnography.

It was, however, large centralized states, still functioning under conditions of indirect rule in British colonial Africa, that provided the impetus for the development of the subfield of political anthropology. The major work of this era, *African Political Systems* (1940) edited by Meyer Fortes and E. E. Evans-Pritchard, distinguished between states, and stateless and band societies. Structural analyses of the political constitutions of the Tallensi and Nuer led to the extensive adoption of typologies and the comparative method in political anthropology.

Criticized for its lack of distinction between 'society' and 'polity', and for its concentration on rules rather than the regularities of political action, systems analysis was challenged in the 1950s by a focus on process and action. Africa again provided the stimulus and in this period leading up to independence, anthropologists began to study interstitial, supplementary and parallel political structures and their relation to formal power. This served them well as practitioners of other disciplines, particularly political scientists, sociologists and historians entered the realm of non-western societies. The politics of ethnicity and of elites encouraged anthropologists to study political movements, leadership and competition. Immersed in field situations of rapid institutional change, they constructed their analyses around contradictions, competition and conflict (Vincent 1990).

'Action theory' (later called agency or practice theory) developed out of a concern with process most rigorously formulated in the work of Victor Turner. His field research among the Ndembu of Northern Rhodesia (now Zambia) was later formulated programmatically in *Political Anthropology* (Swartz, *et al.* 1966). Along with F. G. Bailey's trilogy on Indian caste, village and electoral politics, this encouraged a trend towards the study of individual actors, strategies and decision making in political arenas. Bailey's *Stratagems and Spoils* (1980) remains an excellent guide to the understanding of micropolitical action.

A turning point came in the late 1960s when a critique was mounted against individualistic analysis in the context of neo- or economic imperialism. Talal Asad (1973) drew attention to the problematic relationship of anthropology to British colonialism. Pierre Bourdieu scrutinized the vast legacy of French colonial scholarship to revolutionize orthodox Algerian ethnography. One of the most exciting trends took the form of 'subaltern studies'. Accounts of power relations in colonial India, particularly in the work of Bernard Cohn (1982), a Chicago anthropologist-cum-historian, further stimulated rethinking of imperialism, nationalism, peasant insurgency, class and gender.

Concern with the mechanics of power and the relation of power to knowledge (largely derived from Michel Foucault) halted the involution of disciplinary and subfield specialization in its tracks. Global transdisciplinary movements – such as subaltern, feminist and cultural studies – made problematic familiar political concepts. After a century in which the concept of society has predominated, power, history, and culture have become vital new concerns within political anthropology (Dirks *et al.* 1993) as the twentieth century draws to a close.

Joan Vincent
Columbia University

References

Asad, T. (ed.) (1973) *Anthropology and the Colonial Encounter*, London.
Bailey, F. G. (1980) *Stratagems and Spoils: A Social Anthropology of Politics*, Oxford.
Cohn, B. (1982) *An Anthropologist Among The Historians*, Oxford.
Dirks, N., Eley, G. and Ortner, S. (eds) *Culture/Power/History*, Princeton, NJ.

Fortes, M. and Evans-Pritchard, E. E. (eds) (1940) *African Political Systems*, London.

Vincent, J. (1990) *Anthropology and Politics: Visions, Traditions and Trends*, Tucson, AZ.

See also: divine kingship; social anthropology; state, origins of.

political culture

The term political culture has entered everyday language; as a concept, it has enjoyed a new lease of life in the social sciences in the 1980s and 1990s. The author of one of the most systematic explorations of the notion of political culture has suggested that 'the enduring nature of its appeal in the face of a large body of criticism' derives partly from 'a dissatisfaction both with an account of politics that ignores the issues of meanings and culture, and with an account of culture that ignores issues of politics and power' (Welch 1993).

Although some of the themes evoked by the concept of political culture were not unknown to classical political thought, the term political culture appears to have been first used by Herder (Barnard 1969), and its elaboration and development as a concept of modern political science dates from the 1950s (especially Almond 1956). Substantive empirical research organized around the concept began to appear in the 1960s (see e.g. Almond and Verba 1963; Pye and Verba 1965). These early applications of the concept were linked to questionable theories of political development, but the value of an understanding of political culture in no way depends upon its incorporation in a particular type of developmental, structure-functionalist or systems analysis.

While the concept of political culture had a generally lower salience in the 1970s than in the 1960s, it began to attract in that decade greater attention than hitherto from students of Communist systems. A number of them identified as a vital issue, of both theoretical and practical importance, the degree of consonance or dissonance between, on the one hand, the values and political doctrine being promulgated through the official agencies of political socialization by the Communist power-holders and, on the other, the values and fundamental political beliefs to be found among the mass of the people (Brown 1984; Brown and Gray 1977; White 1979). It had been argued that Communist states represented particularly successful cases of political socialization from above. Thus, for example, Huntington and Dominguez (1975) suggested that 'the most dramatically successful case of planned political cultural change is probably the Soviet Union' and that Communist systems had been an exception to a more general rule that conscious, mobilizational efforts to change political cultures had fared poorly (Greenstein and Polsby 1975). Studies of political culture in the European Communist countries called into question, however, the success there of official political socialization. A variety of sources of evidence were drawn upon by researchers, for in most Communist countries, relevant survey data were either unavailable or unreliable and overt political behaviour could also be misleading. Conformist political actions did not necessarily imply the internalization of Marxist–Leninist norms in highly authoritarian regimes where the penalties for political non-conformity were severe.

The collapse of most Communist systems by the beginning of the 1990s, while not providing conclusive evidence regarding popular values and beliefs in the late 1970s, tended to lend support to those who emphasized the relative failure of Communist political socialization efforts. Writing in 1983 – some years before the Communist regimes in Russia and Eastern Europe came to an end following a process of peaceful change – Gabriel Almond went so far as to see Communism as 'a test of political culture theory' and concluded:

> What the scholarship of comparative communism has been telling us is that political cultures are not easily transformed. A sophisticated political movement ready to manipulate, penetrate, organize, indoctrinate and coerce and given an opportunity to do so for a generation or longer ends up as much or more transformed than transforming.

Political culture has been defined in a variety of different ways and several distinctive approaches to the study of it may be identified. So far as definitions are concerned, they can be classified into two broad categories: those which confine the scope of political culture to the subjective orientation of nations, social groups or individuals to politics; and those which broaden the concept to include patterns of political behaviour. Most political scientists have favoured the more restrictive category. Representative definitions in this first group include those which see political culture as 'the system of empirical beliefs, expressive symbols and values which defines the situation in which political action takes place' (Verba 1965), or as 'the subjective perception of history and politics, the fundamental beliefs and values, the foci of identification and loyalty, and the political knowledge and expectations which are the product of the specific historical experience of nations and groups' (Brown 1977).

An example of a broader definition is that which views political culture as 'the attitudinal and behavioural matrix within which the political system is located' (White 1979). Scholars who prefer this second, broader type of definition of the concept have suggested that in characterizing political culture in subjective or psychological terms, 'political scientists have parted company with the great majority of anthropologists' (Tucker 1973). That view appears, however, not only to downplay the great diversity of definitions of culture among anthropologists but also to overlook a growing body of work within social and cultural anthropology. As Ladislav Holy (1979) has put it:

New insights into the working of social systems have been achieved in anthropology through following the implications of an analytical distinction between the conceptual and cognitive world of the actors and the realm of events and transactions in which they engage.

Definitions matter less than the use to which the concept of political culture is put and the extent to which its employment helps to illuminate important aspects of political life. As recently as 1990, an entire series of books entitled 'Political Cultures' was launched under the general editorship of the late Aaron Wildavsky. Its starting-point was that 'political cultures broadly describe people who share values, beliefs, and preferences legitimating different ways of life', but it stressed an 'openness to a variety of approaches to the study of political cultures'. The volume which launched the series (Thompson *et al.* 1990) draws extensively on the pioneering work of the anthropologist Mary Douglas. In contrast to the studies conducted in the 1960s, the authors emphasize the variety of political cultures to be found within each country and move the focus of attention from differences between nations to differences within nations. Having set out the case for 'the social construction of nature', Thompson *et al.* argue that if 'the boundaries between the political and the nonpolitical are socially constructed, then the study of political culture must assume a central place' in the discipline of political science.

This approach is consonant with the work of Welch (1993), who draws upon phenomenological social theory in claiming that 'the social environment through which people move is constituted and made meaningful by them'. Denying the 'givenness' of any part of that environment, he criticizes much of the existing body of work on political culture. 'Culture', Welch (1993) suggests, 'is not a set of givens of which political culture is a subset; it is a process, and "political culture" refers to that process in its political aspects.'

Among the many debates which surround the concept of political culture is an emerging one on the value of survey research as a way of eliciting and understanding political cultures. Some of the newer writing, which draws heavily on the insights of anthropology (see, e.g. Welch 1993) sees survey research as at best of marginal value as an aid to interpreting political cultures, while other scholars – in a more sociological tradition – emphasize the dangers of the subjective views of the social scientist being projected on to the social actors studied in the absence of well-grounded surveys. Increasingly, a valuable body of interpretative work on political culture is being built up, albeit from a variety of definitional and methodological starting-points.

Archie Brown
University of Oxford

References

Almond, G. A. (1956) 'Comparative political systems', *Journal of Politics* 18.
—— (1983) 'Communism and political culture theory', *Comparative Politics* 13.
Almond, G. A. and Verba, S. (eds) (1963) *The Civic Culture: Political Attitudes and Democracy in Five Nations*, Princeton, NJ.
Barnard, F. M. (1969) 'Culture and political development: Herder's suggestive insights', *American Political Science Review* 62.
Brown, A. (1984) *Political Culture and Communist Studies*, London.
Brown, A. 'Introduction' to: Brown, A. and Gray, J. (1977) *Political Culture and Political Change in Communist States*, London.
Douglas, M. (1975) *Implicit Meanings: Essays in Anthropology*, London.
—— (1982) *In the Active Voice*, London.
Holy, L. (1979) 'Changing norms in matrilineal societies: the case of Toka inheritance', in D. Riches (ed.) *The Conceptualization and Explanation of Processes of Social Change*, Belfast.
Huntington, S. and Dominguez, J. I. (1975) 'Political development', in F. I. Greenstein and N. W. Polsby (eds) *Macropolitical Theory*, vol. 3 of *Handbook of Political Science*, Reading, MA.
Thompson, M., Ellis, R. and Wildavsky, A. (1990) *Cultural Theory*, Boulder, CO.
Tucker, R. C. (1973) 'Culture, political culture and Communist society', *Political Science Quarterly* 88.
Verba, S. 'Conclusion: Comparative Political Culture' in Pye, L. W. and Verba, S. (eds) (1965) *Political Culture and Political Development*, Princeton, NJ.
Welch, S. (1993) *The Concept of Political Culture*, London.
White, S. (1979) *Political Culture and Soviet Politics*, London.

See also: communism; cultural anthropology; cultural history; cultural studies; culture; political science.

political economy

The term political economy came into general use in the eighteenth century and meant the measures taken by governments to regulate trade, exchange, money and taxes (roughly what would now be called economic policy). By a natural progression the term came to be applied to the study of these and other economic questions; political economy became a recognized academic profession and was increasingly considered a science. In some places (Scottish universities, for example) it is still the term normally used to denote what is elsewhere more usually called economics. But, especially under the influence of W. S. Jevons (1879; 1905) and Alfred Marshall (1890), 'economics' had for the most part replaced 'political economy' by the end of the nineteenth century, although some economists continued to distinguish between the two, reserving the term political economy for questions of policy (e.g. Robbins 1939).

The most significant distinctions to have been made between the two terms have, however, been associated with the history of Marxism. In 1843 Engels, shortly to become Marx's close collaborator, published an article with the title 'The outlines of a critique of political economy' (Engels 1975 [1844]). He argued that the new economic thinking, favouring competition and free trade, which began with Adam Smith, was 'half an advance' on the mercantilism which had gone before, but, by not questioning private property, was guilty of covering up the fact that capitalism necessarily led to social and economic evils. Such 'sophistry and hypocrisy' tended to increase with time so that Ricardo was more guilty than Smith, and Mill more guilty than Ricardo.

Over the next thirty-five years, Marx, in his own economic writings, greatly enlarged, deepened and refined this critique in works such as *Contribution to a Critique of Political Economy* (Marx 1980 [1859]), a precursor to *Capital* (Marx 1976 [1867]), which itself bears the subtitle, *A Critique of Political Economy*. By political economy Marx meant the body of economic thinking which began with Adam Smith and included Ricardo, Malthus and others, roughly corresponding to what are now known as the classical economists. In using the term, Marx was not departing from the general usage of the day but his critique paved the way for a change in meaning.

Marx was both a strong critic and an admirer of the tradition of political economy, especially of Smith and Ricardo. But he distinguished the honest, if sometimes mistaken, pursuit of truth by some political economists and those increasingly abundant economic writings whose purpose was merely to legitimize capitalism (which he sometimes called 'vulgar economics'). Marx and Engels believed that political economy as a science arose alongside capitalism: because the exploitative nature of pre-capitalist economic systems was transparent, they did not require a science to explain them, merely an ideology (generally a religion) to legitimize them; but, since the nature of capitalist exploitation

was opaque (being hidden behind the veil of money and market relations), it needed its own economic science (political economy) to reveal it.

For Marx, a truly scientific political economy, in order to reveal this hidden exploitation, must study not only exchange but also the nature of production and labour. Vulgar economics concealed capitalist exploitation by treating all relations as exchange; it was, therefore, an ideology rather than a science. Marx came apparently to recognize in classical political economy slightly more than Engels's 'half an advance' and dated its definitive vulgarization a little later than Engels had done in 1844.

This distinction between (scientific) political economy and (vulgar) economics has been a constant in critical, and especially Marxist, economic thinking. But there have been moments when the vocabulary has acquired a special importance. The revival of Marxist economic analysis in Western Europe and the USA from the late 1950s onwards took the term political economy as a kind of symbol. This reflected both the desire to re-emphasize methodological differences with an increasingly rampant (vulgar) economics and also the need for a code name in places, such as the USA, where Marxists were persecuted. There was an exceptional flowering of articles, books and university courses bearing the title of *The Political Economy of . . .* (a tendency strongly influenced by Baran 1957). Although this political economy expressed a renewed interest in the questions and methods of the classical economics and of Marx, the use of the term became increasingly loose, often simply denoting economic analysis which introduces non-economic (especially political) factors.

In this looser sense the term has come to have attractions for anyone whose view of economic life extends beyond the confines imposed by much orthodox economics. Since around 1980 the term political economy has spread on an unprecedented scale, partly losing its association with Marxism. The growing field of international political economy, for instance, tends to see political economy rather eclectically as a set of questions in which politics and economics are enmeshed and which can be answered via differing ideological approaches – liberal, nationalist, Marxist and others (see Gilpin 1987). On the other hand, some economists, without describing what they do as political economy, have concerned themselves increasingly with the kinds of issues which preoccupied the classical political economists, such as the relationship between the design of wage and labour systems and the profitability of capital (Bowles 1985). In these ways the distinction between political economy and economics is becoming more blurred.

The term has also undergone a number of mutations. In the USA political economics is sometimes preferred, as in the organization, the Union of Radical Political Economics and its *Review of Radical Political Economics*. Of more recent coinage is 'political ecology', an attempt to apply some of the methods of political economy, especially in its Marxist sense, to ecological questions. More confusingly, political economy is being used to connote the economic and political characteristics of a particular place (country, city, region). References to such concepts as 'the European political economy' (as a replacement for 'the European economy') are becoming increasingly common but have almost no relationship to the earlier, more analytical meanings and simply raise the level of incoherence in the use of the term.

Bob Sutcliffe
University of the Basque Country

References

Baran, P. A. (1957) *The Political Economy of Growth*, New York.

Bowles, S. (1985) 'The production process in a competitive economy: Walrasian, Neo-Hobbesian and Marxian models', *American Economic Review* 75(1).

Engels, F. (1975 [1844]) 'The outlines of a critique of political economy', in K. Marx and F. Engels, *Collected Works*, vol. 3, London.

Gilpin, R. (1987) *Political Economy of International Relations*, Princeton NJ.

Jevons, W. S. (1879) *Principles of Economics*, London.

—— (1905) *The Theory of Political Economy*, London.

Marshall, A. (1890) *Principles of Economics*, London.

Marx, K. (1976 [1867]) *Capital: A Critique of Political Economy*, Harmondsworth.

—— (1980 [1859]) *A Contribution to a Critique of Political Economy*, in K. Marx and F. Engels, *Collected Works*, vol. 16, London.

Robbins, L. C. (1939) *The Economic Basis of Class Conflict and Other Essays in Political Economy*, London.

Further reading

Groenewegen, P. (1987) 'Political economy' and 'Economics', in J. Eatwell, M. Milgate and P. Newman (eds) *The New Palgrave: A Dictionary of Economics*, London.

King, J. E. (1948) 'The origin of the term "political economy"', *Journal of Modern History* 20.

See also: Marx's theory of history and society; Marxian economics; Ricardo, David; Smith, Adam.

political geography

Defining political geography is a difficult task because its aims and purposes have altered in response to the changing nature of geography as a discipline. But the resulting political geographies have always been more than merely political aspects of contemporary geographical studies. There has been a common thread in all political geographies based upon concern for the nation-state as a territorial entity. Territory is interpreted as the fundamental link between state sovereignty and national homeland that lies at the heart of the legitimacy and practice of the modern state. The result has been spatially focused, state-centric analyses of power.

The interpretation and analysis of the basic trilogy, territory–state–nation, has varied widely in political geography. Since its inception as a coherent body of knowledge at the end of the nineteenth century, political geography has experienced four main phases of development: environmental, functional, spatial analysis, and pluralistic.

Environmental political geography

In 1897 the German geographer Friedrich Ratzel published his *Politsche Geographie* (1897) in which contemporary ideas of environmental determinism were applied to the study of the state. Focusing on strategic location at a global scale, in 1904 Halford Mackinder presented his 'pivot-area', later renamed 'heartland' theory, which became the foundation of geopolitical studies (1904). The apogee of this environmental geography came with Derwent Whittlesey's (1939) subtle study of politics and landscape in *The Earth and the State*; its nadir was German *geopolitik's* legitimation of the Third Reich's territorial expansion. This form of political geography declined as geographers in general tried to align their studies with developments in the social sciences. Environmental political geography was found wanting in terms of adequate social theory, and its ideas survived outside geography only when political scientists referred to environmental influences as geographical factors or when simplistic geopolitical ideas were used to justify aggressive Cold-War policies.

Functional political geography

Political geography was re-established in the early post-Second World War period by a series of papers focusing on the spatial integration of the state. The most influential was Richard Hartshorne's (1950) 'The functional approach in political geography' in which the state was viewed as existing in equilibrium between centrifugal and centripetal forces. Adding to this home-grown functionalism, political geographers borrowed ideas and concepts from contemporary political science. The apogee of this phase of political geography was 'A geographical model for political systems analysis' presented by Cohen and Rosenthal

(1971), which reordered earlier functionalism into systems thinking.

Spatial analysis in political geography

The rapid increase in quantitative studies in geography in general – usually referred to as 'the quantitative revolution' – had only a muted influence in political geography. In fact its main effect was to sideline political studies as largely unsuitable for quantitative analysis in geography. A secondary effect was to reorient political geography towards those areas where there were plentiful data for analysis. Two sets of researches benefited in particular. Spatial inequalities in social and economic well-being as detailed by state census returns were widely studied as welfare geography, thus covering an aspect of state activity neglected by the functionalists. There was a similar data-led expansion in electoral geography, where voting returns for (approximately) equal population areal units were found to be eminently suitable for spatial analysis.

Pluralistic political geography

The common criticism levelled at both functionalism and spatial analysis was that they produced apolitical studies in which analysis of power was neglected. Remedies of this deficiency have been many, producing the contemporary variety in political geography. The Marxist contribution has been to interpret state politics in terms of spatially-based class alliances. From a more cultural perspective nations and nationalism have been studied in terms of particular attachment to place. In addition a world-systems political geography has been constructed in which states and nations are seen as part of the social and spatial development of the modern world-system. All of these approaches share a common concern to tackle the problematic of the changing territorialization of contemporary world society.

Peter J. Taylor
University of Newcastle upon Tyne

References

Cohen, S. B. and Rosenthal, L. D. (1971) 'A geographical model for political systems analysis', *Economic Geography* 61.
Hartshorne, R. (1950) 'The functional approach in political geography', *Annals, Association of American Geographers* 40.
MacKinder, H. J. (1904) 'The Geographical pivot of history' *Geographical Journal* 23.
Ratzel, F. (1897) *Politische Geographie*, Munich.
Whittlesey, D. (1939) *The Earth and the State*, New York.

Further reading

Busteed, M. (1983) 'The developing nature of political geography', in M. Busteed (ed.) *Developments in Political Geography*, London.
Reynolds, D. R. and Knight, D. B. (1989) 'Political geography', in D. L. Gaile and C. J. Willmott (eds) *Geography in America*, Columbus, OH.
Taylor, P. J. (1993) *Political Geography: World-Economy, Nation-State and Locality*, London.

See also: social geography; space; territoriality.

political parties *see* parties, political

political pluralism *see* pluralism, political

political psychology

Political psychology is an interdisciplinary field whose basic substantive purpose is to uncover the interrelationships between psychological and political processes. The field draws on diverse disciplinary sources including cultural and psychological anthropology, economic psychology, sociology, psychology, and political science. The last two are especially important theoretical and methodological sources for the field.

The major theoretical contributions to the field from psychology have traditionally come from psychoanalytic theory, personality theory, social and developmental psychology, and increasingly from cognitive psychology. On the political science side, major theoretical frameworks have been drawn from the areas of mass political behaviour, political leadership and decision making, and political conflict both within and between nations.

At the methodological level also, the tools of data gathering and analysis in the field have been diverse. Intensive case studies, survey methods, and small group experimentation and analysis are a few of the major empirical tools that have been used with a variety of theoretical perspectives. Individual case studies of particular leaders, or particular types of leaders (e.g. revolutionary leaders, presidents and so on) using psychoanalytic theory have deepened our appreciation of specific individual leaders, similarities and variations within particular leadership roles, and the process of leadership itself. However, case studies employing the insights of group dynamics and personality theories have also deepened our appreciation of presidential and group decision making.

So too, systematic surveys of large populations have been instrumental in developing our understanding of the psychology of mass publics. They have as well cast light on the developmental and situational origins of public behaviour, including reactions to presidential candidates and in-office performance, evaluations of and responses to political events, and of course the choice of whether and how one chooses to participate in public affairs. Studies in these substantive areas have utilized numerically grounded data to provide insight into the cognitive understandings, personality dispositions, and developmental experiences which underlie the behaviour of mass publics.

In some cases particular theoretical or methodological frames seem more suited for particular substantive questions. A political psychology study of a specific president, foreign minister or other leader would seem to call for a more intensive individual focus resting on personality theory, broadly conceived. However, a study of why political decision-making groups do or do not follow procedures which will increase the possibility of arriving at satisfactory outcomes cannot depend on theories of individual psychology alone. Studying the pattern of mass political beliefs and behaviours must clearly aim for widely representative analysis which may need to be more extensively than intensively focused.

Studies in political psychology must also be sensitive to levels of analysis and contextual issues. Whether studies focus on an individual leader, small or larger groups, or larger collective processes, each is embedded in complex psychological and material contexts that must be considered. Leaders, for example, may choose a course of action consonant with their own psychologies, but they also do so with regard to consideration of such decisions on a range of other contexts. Or to take another example, governmental decision-making groups may make very productive use of good decision procedures, but outcomes in the real world will depend on variables that go well beyond whether the group utilized adequate procedures.

In short, the processes and substantive areas studied in political psychology are varied and complex. It is therefore not surprising that no one theoretical or methodological paradigm has emerged for the entire field. The diversity of theory and methods, with its resultant encouragement of substantive and methodological debate with a view towards ultimately refining theory, may therefore be as much a necessity as a stage in the development of the field.

Debate, however wide ranging, does not reflect lack of the theoretical or substantive progress. Like other interdisciplinary social science fields, the maturing of political psychology can be traced from its early broad general concerns. The philosophical roots of the field date back to the classical traditions in eastern and western cultures. Then as now, philosophers sought to understand basic human nature and the consequences of its relationship to different forms of political arrangements.

As a maturing field, political psychology is characterized by an increasing degree of theoretical *specification*; of the origins and developmental paths of the political psychology dynamics it uncovers, of the nature of the dynamics themselves, and finally of the contextual forces that sustain or inhibit these dynamics. Modern political psychology treats individual and group psychology as a variable, not a given.

While the field does not have one major paradigm, there is an emergent consensus on four basic frames of understanding: the developmental, the dynamic, the contextual, and the importance of composite theory. The first approaches political behaviour by examining the ways that the past has helped shape the present. The second examines political behaviour as stemming from multiple, not single, psychological and political factors, while the third examines the situational factors that either inhibit or facilitate the political behaviours in questions. Lastly, composite theory stresses the application of dual or multiple theoretical frames to address specific substantive areas. Thus, for example, studies of how children acquire politically relevant dispositions depend on concepts and models which must be integrated from developmental psychology, psychoanalytic theory and, depending on the particular focus of the study, cognitive psychology.

Theories of political psychology can not and do not aspire to explain everything of interest in the world of politics, but neither is it possible fully to understand political life without reference to the psychological processes that frame and often underlie them.

Stanley A. Renshon
The City University of New York

Further reading

Barber, J. D. (1993) *Presidential Character: Predicting Performance in the White House*, Englewood Cliffs, NJ.

George, A. L. (1980) *Presidential Decision Making in Forein Policy: The Effective Use of Information and Advice*, Boulder, CO.

Hermann, M. G. (ed.) (1986) *Political Psychology*, San Francisco, CA.

Jervis, R. (1976) *Perception and Misperception in International Politics*, Princeton, NJ.

Knutson, J. N. (ed.) (1973) *Handbook of Political Psychology*, San Francisco, CA.

Lasswell, H. D. (1948) *Power and Personality*, New York.

Renshon, S. A. (ed.) (1995) *The Clinton Presidency: Campaigning, Governing and the Psychology of Leadership*, Boulder, CO.

See also: charisma; leadership; political science.

political recruitment and careers

To study recruitment is to look at political events with an eye to how the participants got there, where they came from and by what pathways, and what ideas, skills and contacts they acquired or discarded along the way. Knowing their abilities, sensitivities, aims and credentials, one is better able to anticipate and interpret what they say and do. In turn, better evaluations can be made of the key consideration: performance, by elites and by the institutions and systems they run.

Everywhere political recruitment is a system maintenance process that is only partly institutionalized. The trade of politics is largely learned through an apprenticeship system. The career perspectives of each generation are moulded both by new priorities placed on skills and knowledge appropriate to meet changing needs and by the performance examples, good and bad, of men and women ahead of them on the political ladder. It is not uncommon to note that, even at early stages in their careers, tomorrow's leaders are being screened for capacities that their elders never had to possess. At the same time, elites persistently search for successors who are like themselves in style, judgement, temperament, beliefs and outlook. Elites are self-perpetuating.

The classic theorists, Mosca, Pareto and Michels, each explored the stultifying implications of incumbency. Governing elites are not necessarily adequate to the task. Too often, incumbency is a brake on efforts to update an institution's functional rationality, since performance norms and leadership objectives tend to be set by incumbents themselves.

Patterns of incumbency are called 'careers'. Subjectively, career perspectives are moving vantage points from which men and women in politics appraise their duties and opportunities, whether they treat public life as a calling or as a livelihood, or both. Objectively, individuals' life paths through the communal and corporate infrastructure of their society never cease to be apprenticeships that equip them with crucial skills and typical attitudes as well as with material resources and organizational sponsors – which are often necessary as credentials at subsequent major career thresholds.

Opportunities in politics are almost inevitably characterized by elements of co-optation. Aspirants for political careers cross an unmarked threshold when they are taken seriously for a given job by those who control the necessary political resources to get it and keep it. The intramural screening system for a neophyte legislator, official or party functionary is often a searching and unnerving process. Formal recruitment processes in politics – whether by election, examination, sponsorship or other credentialling procedures –

seldom bestow much interpersonal influence; rather, such influence comes when one can show special prowess, rally a following, claim inside knowledge, or otherwise impress one's colleagues.

Schlesinger (1966) has stressed the notion of a political opportunity structure. In different polities, the realistic routes to significant office can be identified, and both traffic flow and casualty rates can be calculated. For Seligman (1971) it is not offices but roles that define the opportunity structure. Both the supply of eligibles and the demand for people to fill political roles must be considered. Not only one's birth chances but also one's access to education, wealth or other avenues of mobility affect eligibility. Eligibles for any given role are those with appropriate resources and skills who are socialized, motivated and certified to fill it.

Careers also depend on the kind of sponsorship available and credentialling mechanisms involved. A minor position can often be seized successfully with no more than makeshift and temporary team efforts. To sustain a significant career of officeholding, however, implies sustained organizational support. Political career opportunities, as contrasted with *ad-hoc* chances to play roles or even briefly to hold formal posts, tend to be controlled by parties; cliques may help one start a career, or may cut it short, but rarely can they suffice to sustain one.

Typically, political parties control the high-risk thresholds that distinguish a local notable from a translocal functionary, a legislative career from a ministerial one. Once those who control the jobs and roles available at a given organizational node, in a given institutional setting, or at a given geographic locale, have taken eligible aspirants seriously enough to invest organizational resources by sponsoring them formally, the aspirants are probably certified for at least a modest career in the same orbit. To put the same person in transit to a different career orbit, however, takes venture capital – party resources more difficult to secure and more jealously husbanded.

If a number of rivals contend for a party's nomination, the pattern of risks – financial, programmatic, organizational and personal – for all contenders are a function of the field against them. Some candidates change the risks significantly for others but not for themselves; they may need the exposure and experience, and they and their backers may view the effort as a long-term investment rather than a demonstrable loss.

Using an opportunity structure/political risk schema prompts certain key questions. Who are the gatekeepers? What selection criteria do they use? What quasi-automatic credentialling practices narrow the field? Is self-promotion encouraged? Are aspirants sometimes conscripted? Is a job sought for its own sake, or as a stepping stone, or as a seasoning experience? Career opportunities are probably more agglutinated, more commingled and more presumptively closed to outsiders than the opportunity-structure schema suggest.

Motivations have been much studied also. Lasswell's 'displacement formula' (1930) (see Marvick 1977) is concerned with personality dynamics: private motives are displaced on to public objects and rationalized in terms of public purposes. Eldersveld (1964) has demonstrated the labile and complex patterns of activist motivations. Wilson (1962) argues that leaders can grant or withhold various incentives, and thus nurture distinctive kinds of organizations. The political pros in machine politics are accommodationist and success-minded. Quite different are the amateur volunteers, whose participation is principled and programmatic.

Dwaine Marvick
University of California

References

Eldersveld, S. J. (1964) *Political Parties: A Behavioral Analysis*, New York.
Marvick, D. (ed.) (1977) *Harold D. Lasswell on Political Sociology*, Chicago.
Schlesinger, J. (1966) *Ambition and Politics*, Chicago.
Seligman, L. (1971) *Recruiting Political Elites*, Morristown, NJ.
Wilson, J. Q. (1962) *The Amateur Democrat*, Chicago.

Further reading

Aberbach, J., Putnam, R. and Rockman, B. (1982) *Bureaucrats and Politicians*, Cambridge, MA.
Eulau, H. and Czudnowski, M. (eds) (1976) *Elite Recruitment in Democratic Polities*, New York.
Eulau, H. and Prewitt, K. (1973) *Labyrinths of Democracy*, New York.
Prewitt, K. (1970) *The Recruitment of Political Leaders*, New York.
Putnam, R. (1976) *The Comparative Study of Political Elites*, Englewood Cliffs, NJ.

See also: citizenship; elites; representation, political.

political representation *see* representation, political

political science

Political science is an academic discipline, devoted to the systematic description, explanation, analysis and evaluation of politics and power. Political science might be more accurately labelled 'politology', as indeed it is in some European countries, both because some of its practitioners reject the idea that their discipline is like

that of the natural sciences and because the subject does not have one unified body of theory or paradigm (unlike some of the natural sciences).

The historical antecedents of the discipline are most apparent in the works of western political philosophers in a canonical tradition stretching from Plato's *Republic* through to Machiavelli's *The Prince* and Hobbes's *Leviathan*. However, political science has also evolved from numerous other forms of ancient and medieval enquiry, especially history, political economy and jurisprudence. The ambition to create a science of politics is an old one, at least as old as Aristotle's *Politics*, but agreement on its scope, methods and results remains elusive.

The scope of the contemporary discipline of political science is extensive. The major subfields of inquiry include political thought, political theory, political history, political institutions, comparative political analysis, public administration, public policy, rational choice, political sociology, international relations, and theories of the state.

Political thought

The classics of western political thought, the accumulated body of texts and writings of great philosophers, still frame the intellectual education of many students of political science. The canon of great western thinkers includes texts from the ancient world such as the writings of Plato and Aristotle, from the medieval and early modern period the works of Aquinas, Augustine, Hobbes, Locke, Rousseau and Montesquieu, and finally the books of modern writers like Kant, Hegel, Marx, Tocqueville and John Stuart Mill.

This canon has, however, been regularly attacked as ethnocentric, because it ignores the philosophical traditions of non-occidental countries. It is additionally criticized as sexist because it is a canon of male writers who make contestable assumptions about men and women (Okin 1980; Pateman 1988); it is also condemned as biased towards liberal political assumptions. Finally, the canon is rejected by those who claim that a mature science should supersede its origins, and that therefore the study of political thought should be left to historians. In response, defenders of the study of political thought sometimes claim that the thoughts of the great thinkers have often transcended their times, and for that matter their geographical, ethnic and sexual origins. Moreover they claim that ancient, medieval and early modern political thought shared three common preoccupations, which are still live issues among political scientists: first, explaining the nature of the state and what makes a state legitimate and worthy of obedience; second, explaining the nature of justice and the role or otherwise of politics in securing justice; and third, explaining and speculating about the nature of a good political system.

Interpreters of political thought have always differed over the reasons they advance for continuing to pay detailed attention to classical texts. Some believe that the classics contain permanent truths, although they dispute which particular authors and texts contain them. They think it is the duty of educators to transmit these truths to subsequent generations, and regard much empirical political science as a betrayal of 'the great tradition'. A similar group of thinkers, influenced by Leo Strauss, maintain that the classics contain timeless truths but that they are accessible only to a civilized elite. By contrast other historians of political thought, while agreeing that the classics address timeless questions, maintain that the canon is more important for the questions it raises than the answers it provides; it is a starting-point rather than a set of lessons. For example, consider the abstract question, raised in diverse forms by Hobbes, Locke and Rousseau, 'Would rational persons in a state of nature agree to establish a state, and if so what type?' This question helps clarify the conceptions of human nature assumed in political thought as well as the nature of political obligation, political legitimacy and the state. Others, influenced by Quentin Skinner, argue that the classics, far from being timeless, are texts addressed to the authors' contemporaries, and that the authors were engaged in political arguments of specific relevance to their own times. For them the task of political thought is to recover the original meanings and contexts of classical discourses, often by focusing on forgotten and marginal writers. This contextualist and historicist approach is criticized for assuming radical discontinuities in the meaning and accessibility of texts, and for implying that we have to do the impossible – become contemporaries of the authors of great texts in order to understand them. Moreover, this approach is hoist by its own petard: critics ask 'Which contemporary political controversies are such historians addressing when they offer readings of canonical texts?'

Political theory

Contemporary political philosophers have appropriated the title of 'political theorists' for themselves, although other political scientists insist that they engage in positive political theory proper, that is, the search for regularities in and deductive propositions about politics and power. The best way to appreciate this controversy is to realize that self-styled political theorists are usually normative in orientation and that their political theory has evolved from the history of political thought.

Much contemporary Anglo-American theory (i.e. political theory written in the English language) has a deductive and analytical flavour – reflecting the rising ascendancy of rational choice within this field. It addresses, often with mathematical and logical rigour, many of the themes raised in the classics. Political theorists partly see their task as that of conceptual clarification, explicating the possibly contradictory meanings of key concepts, like democracy, liberty, equality, law, legitimacy and rights. However, their major concern is with normative questions, such as 'What is justice?', an issue most famously tackled in our times by John Rawls's (1971) book *A Theory of Justice*. In this text Rawls revived the idea of the social contract made famous by Hobbes, Locke and Rousseau, to ask what principles of justice would be adopted by rational individuals behind a 'veil of ignorance' in which they would not know what positions in society they themselves would subsequently occupy. Rawls's answer, much disputed, is that rational individuals would embrace (in the following order of importance) the principles of equal liberties for all, the meritocratic principle of equality of opportunity, and the 'difference principle' justifying inequalities in income and resources only if they better the condition of the worst off. These conclusions and the methods by which they are derived are the subject of an enormous critical literature. Seminal work in this area has now extended beyond justice within a given state and within a given generation to issues of distributive justice across generations and across the world.

Political history

Some political scientists describe themselves first and foremost as political historians – albeit with a bias towards contemporary history. They believe that the task of political science is to offer retrodictive explanations rather than predictions, and are critical of mere historians whom they accuse of being methodologically unselfconscious, overly descriptive, and naïve believers in the idea that truth lies in the governmental archives.

Political historians tend, crudely speaking, to be divided into two camps. Students of 'high politics' study elite decision makers; they believe that the personalities and machinations of key elites shape history and cannot be subsumed away as mere by-products of other causes. They also generally believe that self-aggrandizement and self-interest account for most elite behaviour. Exponents of high politics are sometimes denigrated by their colleagues in the profession as mere biographers. By contrast, exponents of 'low politics', or history from below, believe that mass political behaviour provides the key to explaining major political episodes, such as revolutions. For them the charisma, plots or blunders of political leaders are less important than major changes in the values, interests and actions of collectivities, and in charting the importance of such phenomena they make use of the methodological techniques common across the social sciences.

Political institutions

It was the study of political institutions, especially the roles of constitutions, executives, legislatures, judiciaries, bureaucracies, political parties and electoral systems, which first prompted the formal establishment of political science departments in many universities in liberal states at the end of the nineteenth century. The concerns of the first institutionalists were often indistinguishable from those of constitutional or public lawyers: mapping the formal and procedural consequences of political institutions. Contemporary political scientists still spend much of their time monitoring, evaluating and hypothesizing about the origins, development and consequences of political institutions, such as plurality-rule electoral systems or quasi-governmental organizations. The bulk of them are interested primarily in tracing the origins and developments of institutions, and providing 'thick' or 'phenomenological' (what it's really like) descriptions of these institutions, normally of the countries in which they reside. Some of their less tolerant colleagues claim they engage in thick description simply because they are thick rather than proper political scientists. Such critics are sceptical of the activities of their colleagues who are simply area specialists or knowledgeable about government or public administration in one country: they may provide essential data for political science, but they are not themselves scientific practitioners.

Comparative politics

These critics maintain that a comparative focus provides the only way to be genuinely social scientific. In their view political science is concerned with establishing universal laws or 'theories of the middle range', that is, generalizations which can provide rigorous and tested, albeit time-bound, explanations of political phenomena. In its narrowest form, comparative political institutions has developed as a discipline which compares constitutions, executives, legislatures and judiciaries – either within or across states – with a view to explaining differences in the way in which political issues are processed and resolved. Such work can deal with narrow questions – such as the repercussions of having bureaucracies staffed by those with a legal training as opposed to some other educational or professional background – or more broad-ranging

matters – such as the repercussions of having a separation of powers or a parliamentary system of government. Analysis also extends to the comparison of federations, consociations, militaries, political parties, electoral systems and systems of interest-representation. In its wider form, *comparative political analysis*, political scientists use general concepts which are not country-specific and are committed to positivist methods of enquiry.

Comparative political analysis developed as part of the behaviourist movement in the social sciences which criticized the formalistic and legalistic nature of institutional political science of the 1950s and 1960s. It sought to test and quantify propositions about mass and elite political behaviour, arguing that constitutional, legal and formal analyses frequently had little substantiated empirical support. The behavioural revolution was accompanied by rigorous quantitative research on electoral systems and electoral behaviour, the functioning of political parties and party systems, the role of interest groups, and the making of public policy, with the emphasis on studies of decision making. The antithesis between formal institutionalists and quantitative political scientists has mostly been overcome; modern empirical political scientists normally embrace methods and insights from both approaches.

The marriage between institutionalism and the use of modern empirical techniques (like survey research and statistical testing) is perhaps most fruitfully revealed in the testing of cross-national generalisations. Arend Lijphart's (1984) *Democracies: Patterns of Majoritarian and Consensual Government in Twenty One Democracies* is an exemplary work of comparative political analysis, indicating the fundamental consequences of choosing either majoritarian or consensual political institutions in democracies. Rein Taagepeera and Mathew Shugart's (1989) study of *Seats and Votes: The Effects and Determinants of Electoral Systems* is another example of rigorous positivist political science which has formalized and improved our knowledge of the workings of electoral systems, while Weaver and Rockman's (1993) edited text *Do Institutions Matter?* demonstrates the resurgence of interest in assessing exactly how institutions shape policy making in democratic states.

Two broad differences in methods employed by comparativists are well illustrated in the study of democratization: one school of thought seeks to provide global predictive explanations of democratization on the bases of simple indices of development or the distribution of power-resources (e.g. Vanhanen 1990), while another engages in comparative historical investigations of a more limited range of cases to provide more multidimensional and descriptively rich accounts of patterns of democratization (e.g. Moore 1966). A similar division in methods applies to students of revolutions. Comparative political analysis is also concerned to explain variations in the origins and repercussions of ethnic and national conflict, and the ways in which they are managed by states (see, e.g. Gurr 1993; Horowitz 1985; Lijphart 1977; McGarry and O'Leary 1993).

Public administration and public policy

These are empirical and normative branches of political science which overlap with law and economics. Whereas public administration focuses on the institutional arrangements for the provision of public services, and historically has been concerned with ensuring responsible and equitable administration, public policy specialists analyse the formation and implementation of policies, and address the normative and empirical merit of arguments used to justify policies.

The most vigorous intellectual debates in public administration presently centre on 'public management', the allegedly 'new public management', and the validity of rational choice interpretations of the workings of political institutions, especially public bureaucracies (Dunleavy 1991).

Neither public administration nor public policy have one dominant approach: exponents of pluralism, behaviourism, rational choice, Marxism and feminism are to be found engaged in debate with institutionalists who derive their inspiration from the work of the political sociologist Max Weber. These diverse frames of reference do, however, structure most policy advocacy in western liberal democracies (Bobrow and Dryzek 1987).

Conventional public policy analysis, especially in the USA, is of a quantitative bent, and is influenced by those with expertise in economics, decision analysis and social policy. The subject matter of this subdiscipline is the formulation, implementation and evaluation of public policies. Technical public policy analysts are well versed in cost-benefit, risk-benefit and sensitivity analysis as well as the more standard social scientific modelling and statistical techniques. The positivist and managerialist orientation of these analysts has been criticized by authors like Giandomenico Majone (1991) who maintain that arguments about policy can only rarely be satisfied by 'hard science'. Most of the time policy advocacy works through persuasion in the absence of determinate evidence, and so some conclude that democracies should be structured to ensure that persuasion is open and competitive, and that rhetoric in the best sense be openly encouraged in democratic fora – rather than having a policy process shrouded by 'decisionistic' technocrats with illegitimate claims to expertise (Majone 1991).

Public policy specialists examine who has the power to put policy proposals on the agenda, for example, voters, interest groups, ethnic groups, professional organizations, dominant classes, political parties, mass media (this is the field of policy formulation); how policies are made (the study of decision making) and executed by elected and unelected officials (the study of implementation); and whether public policies are effective and desirable (the field of evaluation). The distinction between area specialists, who focus on public policies in one country or one set of institutions (such as the European Union), and specialists in comparative public policy, who seek to be social scientists intent on establishing regularities, is characteristic of the field. In comparative public policy attempts are made to explain policy divergences and policy convergences both within and across states. Specialists in this field ask and attempt to answer questions such as 'Does it matter which political parties are in power in explaining policy outcomes?', which has led to intensive investigation of whether the presence of left-wing or right-wing parties in government makes any difference to policy outcomes (and if so by how much?), for example, in the domain of taxation or social welfare provision.

Political economy

An increasing number of political scientists work at the boundaries of politics and economics. Some believe that theories of political behaviour, just like theories of economic behaviour, should start from simple assumptions about human beings and should construct predictions about their behaviour from these assumptions. For exponents of rational choice, the test of a good theory is its predictive power rather than the incontestable truth of its assumptions. Their critics claim that exponents of rational choice share with economists the belief that human beings are simply overgrown pigs, insatiably pursuing their avaricious self-interest. Exponents of rational choice generally make the assumption that human beings are rational and self-interested agents. They build testable hypotheses on the assumption that voters wish to maximize their utility, that politicians are pure office-seekers who wish to maximize the votes they can win at elections, and that utility-maximizing bureaucrats seek to maximize their departmental budgets. Such thinking has generated an extensive literature, for example, on the political economy of the business cycle, in which theorists try to predict how politicians manipulate economic instruments to cement or create political support (e.g. Tufte 1978), and theories of regulation, in which analysts seek to predict which industries will be regulated by government (see the discussion in Hood 1994).

More generally political economists look for rent-seeking explanations of political and economic phenomena. They ask the questions 'Who benefits?' and 'Who pays?' in seeking to explain political outcomes. Rational choice investigations of domestic political economy are complemented by students of international political economy who seek to integrate the disciplines of politics and economics in research on international organizations like GATT, NAFTA and the European Union, as well as more general studies of the political economy of protectionism and free trade.

Confusingly, the label political economy is also used by political scientists working within the Marxist tradition. They generally accept the propositions of historical materialism and explain policy outcomes as responses to the imperatives of capital accumulation, class struggle and crisis-containment. They deploy Marxist theories of the state in their analyses of liberal democracies, and theories of imperialism and underdevelopment in their studies of the states of the ex-colonial world.

Political sociology is an important interdisciplinary interface of sociology and political science, which has evolved since the 1950s. Political sociologists reject the firm distinction between the political and the social, and stress the high degree of interaction between the two, which traditional approaches to both sociology and political science underemphasized. Political sociology draws upon arguments developed from the works of the most famous classical sociologists, notably Max Weber (particularly his writings on rationalization, bureaucratization and the sociology of domination), Emile Durkheim (especially his discussions of collective identifications and norms) and Karl Marx (especially his writings on state and class).

Political sociology's original focus upon the relationship between social structure (mainly economic class) and political behaviour (mainly voting) has expanded considerably since the mid-1960s to include all aspects of power relations between and within social groups. Debate in this field is often between those who treat political institutions as largely autonomous from social structural determination, those who believe that political institutions are largely reducible to social structural determination, and those who view the distinction between the political and social as fluid and indeterminate. The latter are presently dominant. For example, theorists of political and social movements like Charles Tilly distinguish between the polity, where formal political influence is concentrated, and the external society, but regard the processes of mobilizing resources in pursuit or defence of interests as essentially similar for both challengers and members of the polity – in line with pluralist conceptions of the state and society.

Another division within political sociology is between those who espouse functionalist theories, which treat conflict as an aberration from a normal state of equilibrium, and approaches of a Marxist or pluralist origin, which view conflict as a continuous and ubiquitous feature of politics.

Subjects studied in political sociology include the influence of childhood socialization on political beliefs; the importance of sex, ethnicity, religion and class in shaping and explaining political beliefs and preferences (especially voting preferences); the influence of the mass media in politics; and the definition and consequences of political culture.

International relations

The relations between states are the subject of international relations, which is a misleading title for the subdiscipline of political science which focuses on trans-state and inter-state relations in diplomacy, economic transactions, and war and peace. The origins of international relations lie in the works of theologians, who addressed arguments as to when and how war was just, of early modern jurists, like Grotius, Pufendorf and Vattel, who sought to establish that there was a law of nations co-equal to the domestic law of states, and of political philosophers, like Rousseau and Kant, who addressed the possibility of moral conduct in war and the need for a stable and just international order.

Practitioners of international relations focus on a diverse array of subjects – international organizations, international political economy, war studies, peace studies and foreign policy analysis – but normatively are divided into two principal schools of thought, that of idealists and realists. The former believe that states can and should conduct their affairs according to law and morality and that functional co-operation across state boundaries establishes the bases for moral conduct. Realists, by contrast, believe that states are fundamentally amoral in their foreign policy; relations between states are governed by interests rather than goodness; peace is the result of a balance of power between states rather than normative order and functional co-operation. Methodologically, international relations has followed the rest of political science, adopting behavioural and quantitative approaches in the 1950s and 1960s, and being subject to fragmentation since the 1970s as diverse pluralist, Marxist, structuralist, rational choice and feminist critics of disciplinary orthodoxies have vied with one another since the 1970s.

Theories of the state

Many would concur that the subject matter of theories of the state provide the most unified focus for contemporary political theory, political thought, public administration, public policy, political sociology and international relations. Given that the political world is constituted by states, and is likely to remain so for the foreseeable future, this is not surprising.

Defining the concept of the state is a matter of some controversy. On organizational definitions the state is a special type of government which must exercise sovereign authority over a specified territory and population and have that sovereignty recognized by other states. Internally a state must be the formal source of law, the monopolist of civil force and the ultimate extractor of taxation; externally it must, in principle, be capable of autonomous diplomacy if not war-making. On this organizational understanding states vary in the extent to which they are effectively internally and externally sovereign, centralized, bureaucratized, co-ordinated and subject to the control and direction of their citizens.

If states form the subject matter of political science, the question arises as to how long they have been in existence. It is widely argued that the modern state emerged in late medieval Europe through the supersession of feudal polities. It remains a moot point whether the ancient empires of the Mediterranean, the Middle East, India, China or pre-Columbian America should be described as states, given that features such as sovereignty, centralization, territoriality and bureaucratization were either non-existent or underdeveloped in such political systems. The most frequent argument is to maintain a sharp distinction between the city-states, feudal polities and empires of agrarian societies and the states and empires of commercial and industrial societies – with their more extensive capabilities to control and penetrate their societies.

Although states vary considerably in their origins and forms, almost all of them, leaving aside a few residual traditional monarchies, seek to legitimize themselves as emanations of their peoples, and they do so in two ways, which can be reinforcing or contradictory. On the one hand they claim to be expressions of popular or democratic sovereignty (even dictators now make this claim); on the other hand they usually claim to be the state of a nation, an emanation of the self-determination of the people of X. These two claims explain some of the dynamics of modern states: competition for definition and control of the state centres on claims to represent the popular will, while competition for definition and control of the territorial boundaries of the state centres on claims to represent the national will. These processes are reflected in the sometimes reinforcing and sometimes contradictory activities of state-building and nation-building, and their opposites, state-fragmentation and nationalist secession.

Much contemporary political science has focused on the organization of the state in liberal democracies, in part responding to the growth of state activities in the capitalist democracies of the west, which in the twentieth century have seen the state's functions expand beyond a minimal core (defence, order and law-making and protection of the dominant religion) to include extensive economic and social management and regulation. Five distinct schools of thought on the empirical workings of the democratic state are evident in modern political science: pluralism Marxism, rational choice, elite theory (sometimes called neo-statism or new institutionalism) and neo-pluralism. Some claim to have developed novel feminist and green theories of the state, though these claims are disputed, and such work for the present at least is much less extensively developed.

Each of these bodies of thought is divided about the extent to which the democratic state is controlled by its citizens and their voluntary organizations (Dunleavy and O'Leary 1987). Simplifying matters, three answers address this issue: there are those who think that states are controlled by their societies (or at least the most powerful in their societies); there are those who think that states are sufficiently autonomous to re-direct and reshape the pressures placed upon them by their societies (or the most powerful in their societies); and finally there are those who think that states are so autonomous that they can act directly against the pressures emanating from their societies (or the most powerful in their societies).

The present and future of the discipline

Political science is therefore both a multidisciplinary and multi-theoretical subject. It is a vibrant field of enquiry, and is not likely to disappear unless politics is abolished, a possibility which most of the profession happily regard as impossible. The classical preoccupations of political philosophers and historians remain, and political science departments generally resist the siren voices of irrationalist post-modernism. This disciplinary conservatism does not of course mean political conservatism. Political scientists vary considerably in their ideological orientations, while remaining committed to reason and dispassionate analysis; indeed they often see their role as 'speaking truth to power.' While some worry that the discipline is in danger of dividing into warring sects (Almond 1989), others see the lack of paradigmatic closure as beneficial for the subject, and they observe throughout the world comparative and empirical political analysts busying themselves in research on democracy, democratization, the prerequisites of legitimate and effective states, and the prospects for justice and conflict-resolution in the new international order – tasks which require little justification.

Brendan O'Leary
London School of Economics and Political Science

References

Almond, G. (1989) *A Discipline Divided: Schools and Sects in Political Science* London.

Bobrow, D. B. and Dryzek, J. S. (1987) *Policy Analysis by Design*, Pittsburgh, PA.

Dunleavy, P. (1991) *Democracy, Bureaucracy and Public Choice: Economic Explanations in Political Science*, Brighton.

Dunleavy, P. and O'Leary, B. (1987) *Theories of the State: The Politics of Liberal Democracy*, London.

Gurr, T. R. (1993) *Minorities at Risk: A Global View of Ethnopolitical Conflicts*, Washington, DC.

Hood, C. (1994) *Explaining Economic Policy Reversals*, Buckingham.

Horowitz, D. (1985) *Ethnic Groups in Conflict*, Berkeley, CA.

Lijphart, A. (1977) *Democracy in Plural Societies: A Comparative Exploration*, New Haven, CT.

—— (1984) *Democracies: Patterns of Majoritarian and Consensual Government in Twenty One Democracies*, New Haven, CT.

McGarry, J. and O'Leary, B. (eds) (1993) *The Politics of Ethnic Conflict Regulation*, London.

Majone, G. (1991) *Evidence, Argument and Persuasion in the Policy Process*, New Haven, CT.

Moore, B. (1966) *The Social Origins of Dictatorship and Democracy: Lord and Peasant in the Making of the Modern World*, Harmondsworth.

Okin, S. M. (1980) *Women in Western Political Thought*, London.

Pateman, C. (1988) *The Sexual Contract*, Cambridge, UK.

Rawls, J. (1971) *A Theory of Justice*, Cambridge, MA.

Taagepeera, R. and Shugart, M. (1989) *Seats and Votes: The Effects and Determinants of Electoral Systems*, New Haven, CT.

Tufte, E. (1978) *Political Control of the Economy*, Princeton, NJ.

Vanahanen, T. (1990) *The Process of Democratisation: A Comparative Study of 147 States*, New York.

Weaver, R. K. and Rockman, B. (eds) (1993) *Do Institutions Matter? Government Capabilities in the United States and Abroad*, Washington, DC.

Further reading

Bottomore, T. (1992) *Political Sociology*, London.

Dahl, R. (1984) *Modern Political Analysis*, Englewood Cliffs, NJ.

Weisberg, H. F. (ed.) (1986) *Political Science: The Science of Politics*, New York.

political theory

Political theory is an enterprise with a long and distinguished ancestry. Once our forebears had ceased to regard their social and political institutions simply as hallowed by tradition, and began to ask why they took the form that they did, and whether they might not be improved, political theory was born. What things should be allowed by law and what forbidden? Who should rule, and how far should the ruled accept an obligation to obey? What is justice, among individuals and in society? These questions and others like them inevitably arise whenever people begin to reflect critically on their practices and institutions, and political theory tries to answer them in a systematic way. Its methods have been drawn at different times from different disciplines: philosophy, theology, law, history and, more recently, the social sciences. So not only have political theories varied in their practical stance – ranging from, at one extreme, wholesale defences of the existing social and political order to, at the other, manifestos for revolutionary change – but also they have rested on different beliefs about how we should go about answering questions like those above. Some theories have started from a conception of human nature, and asked what political and social arrangements would best fulfil the needs and interests of human beings. Others have interpreted existing institutions as part of an overall pattern of historical development – either as the culmination of that pattern, or as a transient stage destined to be replaced by something higher. Others again have begun by asking what kind of knowledge is possible in political matters, and gone on to defend institutional arrangements which give power to people in proportion to their capacity to use it for the good of society as a whole.

In the twentieth century these methodological issues have come to the fore, propelled especially by the impact of positivism. Older political theories, from Plato and Aristotle down to Marx and Mill, sought to combine in a seamless whole an understanding of the existing social and political world with proposals for conserving or changing it. Central to positivism, however, was the claim that there could be no logical connection between empirical propositions describing the world as it is and normative propositions telling us how we ought to act. Acceptance of this claim implies that political theory as traditionally understood rested on a mistake. The mistake was to run together explanations of social and political relationships with recommendations about how those relationships should be conducted in future.

Positivism is no longer the dominant force that it once was in philosophy and the social sciences, but one of its legacies has been that the label 'political theory' is now often applied to three forms of theorizing – empirical, formal and normative – whose aims are somewhat different.

First, *empirical political theory* is a term commonly used to refer to the theoretical parts of political science. Political scientists are interested in describing and explaining particular political events, but they are also interested in developing broader explanatory theories which draw together a wide range of phenomena under a single umbrella. They have, for instance, tried to explain in general terms why revolutions occur, or what conditions are required to make stable democratic government possible. The issues that are considered are often similar to those addressed in the older tradition of political theory, but much greater use is typically made of quantitative evidence to test theoretical claims. Thus someone seeking to produce a theory about the causes of revolution would characteristically begin by looking for correlations between the outbreak of revolutions and other phenomena such as the extent of economic inequality in the societies under consideration.

Second, *formal political theory* is a burgeoning field which overlaps considerably with 'social choice theory', 'public choice theory', etc. It borrows from economics the idea of rational actors pursuing their goals under certain institutional constraints, and then attempts to model political systems as if they were made up of such actors in various roles – politicians, bureaucrats, voters, etc. Given rational actors and a set of procedural rules, what will the final configuration of the system be? Two major applications are to collective decision procedures and to party competition in a representative democracy. In the first case, the theorist postulates a population, each of whom has his or her own preferences as between a number of policies, and looks at how these preferences will be amalgamated into a 'collective choice' by various decision rules (such as majority voting). One well-known result of these investigations is Arrow's (1963) theorem, according to which *no* decision rule can simultaneously meet a number of reasonable-sounding conditions (such as that if each person taken separately prefers x to y, the decision procedure should also choose x in preference to y). In the second case, the theorist again assumes a population with given policy preferences, and looks at how parties will behave under a democratic electoral system on the assumption that each party's aim is to win the election and each voter's aim is to secure policies that correspond as closely as possible to his or her preferences. This application was originally developed by Antony Downs (1957) and has since been considerably elaborated.

Third, *normative political theory* remains closest in spirit to the traditional enterprise, in so far as it is directly concerned with the justification of political institutions and policies. It aims to lay down principles of authority, liberty, justice and so forth and then to specify what kind of social order would most adequately fulfil these principles. There is, however, deep disagreement among normative theorists about what kind of justification is possible here.

At one extreme stand those who adhere to some form of value-subjectivism. Ultimate political principles simply express the personal standpoint of those who espouse them and are incapable of further justification. The task of political theory is on this view twofold: it consists partly in clarifying the basic principles themselves – removing conceptual ambiguity, giving the principles a more formal statement – and partly in showing what they imply in practice. Thus some people may declare that the freedom of the individual is their fundamental political value, but this in itself does not settle whether such a person should be in favour (say) of a nightwatchman state or an interventionist welfare state. The theorist's job, on this view, is to explore what the idea of freedom means, and then to apply it to practical issues, such as whether redistributive taxation reduces the freedom of the wealthy, or increases the freedom of the poor, or does both. But if other people were to sidestep the argument by declaring that individual freedom had no value for them in the first place, the political theorist would have nothing further to say in reply.

At the other end of the spectrum stand those who adhere to some form of foundationalism, the view that it is possible to find objective grounds to support basic political principles. Prominent here have been various different versions of contractarian political theory. Contractarian theorists hold that there is a set of basic political principles which all rational people would agree to given appropriate conditions. The most influential example has been John Rawls's (1971) theory of justice, which understands justice as the principles that rational individuals would choose to be governed by in an 'original position' in which they were ignorant of their personal characteristics, their ideals of the good life and their social position. Somewhat similar in spirit is Jürgen Habermas's (1984) claim that legitimate norms are those that would be agreed to in an 'ideal speech situation' from which coercion and domination are absent and in which the participants have to persuade one another by the force of argument alone.

Not all foundationalists are contractarians. The other main option is naturalism, where a normative theory is supported by appeal to human needs and interests that are claimed to be universal. Some contemporary naturalists, such as Masters (1989), appeal to sociobiology and argue that our social and political institutions must be appropriate to our genetically given human nature. Others, such as MacIntyre (1981), are neo-Aristotelians who argue that the best social order is one that fosters to the greatest extent distinctively human capacities, such as powers of reason and virtue.

The main difficulty faced by foundationalists is that of responding to human variety, whether this is expressed in cultural differences between societies or in cultural cleavages within societies, along lines of class, gender, ethnicity and so forth. If human beings differ from one another in radical ways – in beliefs, in basic values, in identities – how can we claim that under suitable conditions of abstraction they would all agree to the same political principles, or that they share basic needs and interests that could be used to justify a determinate set of political arrangements? Foundationalists are accused, by post-modernists and others, of an unsustainable universalism which flattens out observable differences between human beings.

This line of thought leads political theory back to value-subjectivism. There is, however, a third possibility, which may be called an interpretative approach to political theory. Here it is claimed that societies are founded upon certain shared understandings which it is political theory's task to draw out and convert into explicit principles. These understandings are contained in a society's language, its conventions and practices; they vary from one society to the next, but in any given context they are relatively determinate and relatively stable. Thus the US Constitution, for example, interpreted over time, provides a rich source of common understandings on which the political theorist can draw, whereas in the UK the absence of a written constitution means that shared understandings take a different form, and have to be found in parliamentary debates, in public opinion, and so forth. Among the most influential of contemporary political theorists favouring an interpretative approach are Charles Taylor (1985) and Michael Walzer (1983).

The interpretative approach to political theory raises the question of how political theories are related to the world-views of ordinary men and women: the pictures of the social world that we all carry with us and use to make sense of everyday political events. In particular, how does political theory differ from ideology, understood as a more or less systematic and action-guiding framework for understanding the social world? The answer is that political theories invariably have an ideological content, but to a greater or lesser extent succeed in scrutinizing and testing those assumptions that ideologies take for granted. Thus liberal ideology might take it for granted that existing social inequalities reflected differences in individual merit, whereas a political theory of a liberal stripe would need both to scrutinize the idea of merit itself – in virtue of what should one person be considered more meritorious than another? – and to look for evidence that there was indeed a relationship between personal merit so defined and the possession of social advantages.

To distinguish itself from mere ideology, political theory must make use both of formal analysis and of the empirical evidence collected by the social sciences. This suggests that the distinction between empirical, formal and normative theory referred to earlier cannot be an absolute one. Rather we should distinguish between forms of political theory that are driven by an interest in explanation and those that are driven by an interest in justification. The distinction cannot be absolute because, on the one hand, normative theories make empirical assumptions about the kind of social order that will result if certain principles are acted upon; while, on the other hand, explanatory theories always rest upon judgements about which phenomena are significant enough to warrant our attempts to explain them (we try to develop theories of democracy or theories of revolution because we regard these as important phenomena, whether we approve of them or disapprove). Thus political theory continues to occupy an essential place in contemporary social science, and the idea, once touted, that it might disappear altogether now seems faintly ridiculous. As Isaiah Berlin (1962) remarked,

> So long as rational curiosity exists – a desire for justification and explanation in terms of motives and reasons, and not only of causes or functional correlations or statistical probabilities – political theory will not wholly perish from the earth, however many of its rivals, such as sociology, philosophical analysis, social psychology, political science, economics, jurisprudence, semantics, may claim to have dispelled its imaginary realm.

David Miller
University of Oxford

References

Arrow, K. (1963) *Social Choice and Individual Values*, New Haven, CT.

Berlin, I. (1962) 'Does political theory still exist?', in P. Laslett and W. G. Runciman (eds) *Philosophy, Politics and Society*, vol. 2, Oxford.

Downs, A. (1957) *An Economic Theory of Democracy*, New York.

Habermas, J. (1984) *The Theory of Communicative Action*, vol. 1, Boston, MA.

MacIntyre, A. (1981) *After Virtue*, London.

Masters, R. (1989) *The Nature of Politics*, New Haven, CT.

Rawls, J. (1971) *A Theory of Justice*, Cambridge, MA.

Taylor, C. (1985) *Philosophy and the Human Sciences: Philosophical Papers 2*, Cambridge, UK.

Walzer, M. (1983), *Spheres of Justice*, Oxford.

Further reading

Barry, B. (1990) *Political Argument*, 2nd edn, Hemel Hempstead.

Barry, N. (1981) *An Introduction to Modern Political Theory*, London.

Dunn, J. (1979) *Western Political Theory in the Face of the Future*, Cambridge, UK.

Held, D. (ed.) (1991) *Political Theory Today*, Cambridge, UK.

Kymlicka, W. (1990) *Contemporary Political Philosophy*, Oxford.

Miller, D. and Siedentop, L. (eds) (1983) *The Nature of Political Theory*, Oxford.

Plant, R. (1991) *Modern Political Thought*, Oxford.

Runciman, W. G. (1969) *Social Science and Political Theory*, Cambridge, UK.

politics, ethnic *see* ethnic politics

politics and media *see* media and politics

population and resources

The relationships of population size and growth to resources have been subject to intense debate and substantial confusion. Much of the debate centres on the *scarcity* of resources and whether they are running out, or being used up too fast, as a result of rapid population growth. Several insights are germane to analysing this issue.

First, for resources that are traded in well-functioning markets, the price of the resource is the best single assessment of its scarcity. Scarcity should *not* be measured simply by the amount of resources remaining or yet to be discovered, but rather by reference to demand or value to end-users. A resource with tiny supply and no demand is not scarce; a resource with substantial supply and huge demand may well be scarce.

Second, by the price measure, and based on historical evidence of relatively constant or declining real prices over time, most non-renewable resources are not particularly scarce, nor are they becoming increasingly scarce. Expansion of supply and/or curtailments of demand have been more than sufficient to maintain a long-run balance of resources *vis-à-vis* their use. Changes in demand and supply for resources have been heavily influenced by new discoveries, changes in technology resulting in reduced use of relatively scarce resources, and the capacity of consumers and producers to make appropriate substitutions of relatively abundant for relatively scarce resources.

Third, historically the major cause of an expanded demand for resources has not been rapid population growth, but rather rises in income. Prosperous countries, where population growth is slow, consume an inordinate amount of resources. In the future, as Third-World countries become more prosperous and given their predictably large populations resulting from rapid population growth in recent and future decades, upward pressures on resource prices will become considerably stronger. This resource scarcity will be increasingly costly to circumvent.

Fourth, over-use of resources due to population or income pressures is most likely to occur where market prices do not adequately reflect true present and future scarcity, and where governments are unable or unwilling to provide appropriate and offsetting regulations. Forests, fisheries, clean air, clean water, and even common land represent areas where markets and prices can fail to allocate resources well. This is because property rights are in some settings difficult to establish, monitor and enforce. After all, one cannot sell something that one does not own for a price; thus prices are not available to signal scarcity in such cases. Moreover, the true demand or value of some resources is quite uncertain. An important example is the value that individuals and/or societies place on the existence of plant and animal species, and on biological diversity. While population pressures are not the primary cause of over-use of resources where markets and government policies are deficient, population pressures are indeed an exacerbating cause, and sometimes an important one.

Very little is known operationally about the optimal size of population *vis-à-vis* resources, although there is much discussion about sustainable population levels. Estimates of the earth's carrying capacity for various important resources (mainly land and water for food production) vary from 5 billion to 30 billion people. Estimates of the capacity of biological and ecological systems to regenerate, or be sustainable on a long-term basis, are equally vague. Current predictions are for a world population of 9 billion to 12 billion by the end of the twenty-first century. Whether this population size will be sustainable – whether it will preserve over time a reasonable stock of resources for future generations – is not known with any degree of certainty.

Allen C. Kelley
Duke University

Further reading

Marquette, C. M. and Bilsborrow, R. (1994) 'Population and the environment in developing countries: literature survey and research bibliography', UN Document ESA/P/WP. 123, 16 February, New York.

Panayotou, T. (1993) *Green Markets: The Economics of Sustainable Development*, San Francisco, CA.

Simon, J. (1981) *The Ultimate Resource*, Princeton, NJ.

United Nations (1994) *World Resources 1994–95: People and the Environment*, New York.

See also: ecology; energy; population geography; population policy.

population census *see* census of population

population genetics

Population genetics is that branch of science concerned with the description of genetic variation in populations and probable causes of this variation. The former is usually called empirical or experimental and the latter theoretical population genetics.

Inherited variation had been studied in a formal way in the latter half of the nineteenth century, notably by Sir Francis Galton. The modern form of the subject originates with the rediscovery of Mendel's rules of genetic transmission and the enunciation by G. H. Hardy and W. Weinberg in 1908 of the famous Hardy-Weinberg law. This law relates allele frequencies to genotype frequencies at a single genetic locus in large populations that are not subject to natural selection on the gene in question.

The subsequent development of theoretical population genetics was led by R. A. Fisher and J. B. S. Haldane in the UK and Sewall Wright in the USA. Fisher's 1918 paper provided a far-reaching connection between simple Mendelian genetic variation and phenotypic variation whose description is essentially statistical. Fisher's approach, in terms of variance analysis, was adopted by agricultural researchers and later by behaviour geneticists. Although Fisher continued to work in all areas of theoretical population genetics, a split developed between the biometrically oriented agricultural geneticists and evolutionary theorists, a split which persists to this day. Fisher's 1930 book, *The Genetical Theory of Natural Selection*, outlines his way of applying mathematics to Darwin's concepts while incorporating genetic discoveries and field observations made up to that time. The book is still widely referred to and stands not only as one of the most significant biology books but also as one of the great scientific achievements of the twentieth century.

Haldane shared Fisher's interest in the construction and analysis of mathematical models of the evolutionary process. Haldane's (1924) series of papers in the *Proceedings of the Cambridge Philosophical Society* studied the changes in gene frequencies in populations subject to various forms of natural selection, inbreeding, mutation and migration. His 1932 book, *The Causes of Evolution*, is a brilliant survey of the issues in evolution raised by theoretical population genetics and foreshadows the theory of kin selection.

Sewall Wright began his career working on the genetics of coat colour in guinea pigs. His first contributions to theoretical population genetics were made in the 1920s. Much of his subsequent work is summarized in his four-volume treatise *Evolution and the Genetics of Populations* (published between 1969 and 1978). Initially Wright was interested in the effect of regular inbreeding on the amount of genetic variability in a population. His classic 1931 paper demonstrated that stochastic effects due to small population size must be considered in evolutionary theory. He termed these effects 'random genetic drift' and showed that the quantitative analysis of the consequences of genetic drift could best be accomplished using a class of parabolic differential equations. Mathematicians such

as William Feller became interested and subsequently developed an important part of probability theory in order to solve these equations. Although Wright's main contributions to theoretical population genetics were concerned with population structure, he also made fundamental contributions to statistics. He originated the idea of path analysis now widely used in sociology and econometrics as well as behaviour genetics.

Fisher, Haldane and Wright laid the foundations for theoretical population genetics. The tradition of building mathematical models whose aim is to clarify the populational and evolutionary significance of each newly discovered genetic phenomenon has continued. Since the mid-1960s, theory has addressed the roles of recombination, meiotic drive, sexual selection and assortative mating, as well as gene–gene interaction in fitness. Phylogenetic techniques have been developed that use genetic rather than phenotypic variation. Evolutionary changes occurring simultaneously at mutiple loci can now be studied mathematically, as can the joint effects of genetic and cultural transmission. Much of the theory has been developed in response to changes that have occurred since the mid-1960s in the picture of genetic variability that exists in nature.

That there is inherited variation in plants and animals has been known, at least implicitly, since agriculture originated. Empirical population genetics is concerned with the genetic basis for inherited variation and how the genes contributing to the observed variation vary among the members of a population. It is also concerned with how well explanations from theoretical population genetics fit these observations. For example, the ABO blood group is determined by antigens on the red blood cells and antibodies in the sera of humans. That the ABO genotype is inherited was known in 1911, but until 1924 it was thought to be controlled by two genes. Only when the mathematician Felix Bernstein compared population data on the frequencies of the ABO genotypes to expectations from theory was it proven that there was a single gene involved.

There are many human genes now known to control antigens on the red cells, and the frequencies of the genotypes vary across the world. Since the mid-1960s even more variation has been shown to exist for antigenic determinants on the white blood cells. The technique of gel electrophoresis made it possible for H. Harris (1966) working with humans, and J. L. Hubby and R. C. Lewontin (1966) working with Drosophila, to exhibit variation for genes which determine enzymes. There followed an explosion of information on the level of genetically based enzyme variation present in almost 2,000 species of plants and animals. In humans, for example, about 23 per cent of enzyme genes show population level variability while about 43 per cent are variable in Drosophila.

Since the mid-1960s the amount of genetic variability that exists in humans, either in blood groups or in enzyme determinants, has been shown to be great. While on the face of it some of this variation might be ascribed to racial differences, careful statistical examination has shown that this is misleading. In fact, about 85 per cent of human genetic variation (measured by any of a number of common statistics) is between individuals within a population (that is, a nation or tribe). Only about 5 per cent is between races.

Ultimately, all genetic variation is due to mutation. But what causes the variation to be maintained at a given level in a given population? It is here that the quantitative theory of population genetics is invoked, and it is here that major conceptual disagreements have occurred. On the one hand, Th. Dobzhansky and his students in the USA, and the British ecological geneticists following E. B. Ford, believe that most of the observed genetic variation is a direct response to natural selection acting on these variants. This position has been called the 'selectionist' school. The followers of the great geneticist H. J. Muller – most notably M. Kimura (1983) from Japan – hold that the genetic variants we see are transient and their frequencies are primarily the result of the interaction between mutation and random genetic drift. This is the 'neutralist' school.

We are not yet at the stage where a definitive numerical resolution between these philosophies can be made. In a few cases, most notably the case of the sickle cell haemoglobin in humans, the connection between an observed genetic polymorphism and natural selection has been established. For most observed polymorphisms, however, the physiological and fitness differences between genotypes have not been established.

Modern biochemical techniques have enabled examination of variation in the DNA itself. The resulting patterns of variation appear to be very difficult to reconcile with any mode of natural selection acting at this molecular level, although these types of data are still actively being collected.

Among the most active research areas, both empirical and theoretical, are the relationship between molecular variation and disease, statistical methodology related to behaviour genetics, the processes of speciation and the significance of molecular variation for classical evolutionary theory. In all of these the tendency since the mid-1970s has been to move away from earlier considerations of single genes acting in isolation, to genes in a milieu of other genes, of genotypes interacting with environments and towards the evolutionary basis of social structures.

Marcus W. Feldman
Stanford University

References

Fisher, R. A. (1918) 'The correlation between relatives on the supposition of Mendelian inheritance', *Transactions of the Royal Society* (Edinburgh) 52.

—— (1958 [1930]) *The Genetic Theory of Natural Selection*, 2nd edn, New York.

Haldane, J. B. S. (1924) 'A mathematical theory of natural and artificial selection', *Proceedings of the Cambridge Philosophical Society* 23.

—— (1932) *The Causes of Evolution*, New York.

Harris, H. (1966) 'Enzyme polymorphisms in man', *Proceedings of the Royal Society B*, 164.

Hubby, J. L. and Lewontin, R. C. (1966) 'A molecular approach to the study of genic heterozygosity in natural populations. I. The number of alleles at different-loci in *Drosophila pseudoobscura*', *Genetics* 54.

Kimura, M. (1983) *The Neutral Theory of Molecular Evolution*, Cambridge, UK.

Wright, S. (1969–78), *Evolution and the Genetics of Populations*, 4 vols, Chicago.

Further reading

Cavalli–Sforza, L. L. and Bodmer, W. F. (1971) *The Genetics of Human Populations*, San Francisco, CA.

Lewontin, R. C. (1974) *The Genetic Basis of Evolutionary Change*, New York.

See also: genetics and behaviour.

population geography

It is nearly as difficult to define, and give a table of contents for, population geography as it is for geography itself. The simplest approach is to distinguish between, first, the work of those who focus on the distribution of population and who seek to understand, by a variety of means, which factors affect variations in that distribution. Such enquiries tend to operate at a variety of scales, from the global to the local, to stress the significance of supportive or repellent environments for the development of human societies, and to deal particularly with the role of migration in the redistribution of population. Many would regard this as population geography proper. A second line of enquiry uses spatial arrangements, patterns and structures to identify those social, economic, political, environmental and other characteristics of human societies that influence the quantitative and qualitative attributes of populations. For example, geographical variations in the level of mortality may be influenced by economic development, access to health care, environmental hazards, and so forth. This strand of population geography tends to focus on variations in fertility and mortality, hence the term 'spatial demography' has been coined; to rely on ecological correlation; and to be associated with attempts to model or forecast changes in the spatial distribution of population using the three components of migration, mortality and fertility.

Both of these approaches would consider that the geography of population should occupy a distinct and separate place among the sub-fields of geography, but their practitioners would also emphasize the importance of links with demography and human biology, with the medical sciences, and with the other social sciences, but especially sociology and economics. Some have also claimed that population geography should represent the integrating core of the subject, since it is via the changing and varying distribution of population that the interplay between people and their environments may be interpreted.

In the mid-1990s the principal research problems facing population geographers could be classified in the following way.

First, the mapping of contemporary trends: this involves use of the most recently available sources of data, often the population census, to chart trends in the distribution of populations and their other characteristics, such as age, living arrangements, education, occupations, etc. Here the problems are ones of measurement, of representation and description, of topicality, of seeing the near future in the recent past. This may be seen as population geography's contribution to useful knowledge.

Second, population, development and resources: here the spatially articulated interplay between population growth, the prospects for economic growth and development, and access to and consumption of resources poses a series of technical and philosophical problems. In parts of Latin America, Africa, South and East Asia these issues have been seen in terms of the consequences of rapid population growth – in excess of 2.5 per cent per year – of famines, family planning programmes, urbanization, finite resource depletion, environmental degradation and, more recently, the impact of AIDS.

Third, the form and causes of long-term population change: population geography retains a clear temporal dimension in which the concepts of the demographic and mobility transitions figure prominently. The problems encountered by specialists in this area often relate to the difficulty of reconstructing past series and of expressing them in a sufficiently disaggregated way. Although this will only ever be possible for European societies over several centuries, there is an expanding field of interest in the historical population geography of those ex-European colonies that are now experiencing rapid population growth.

Fourth, the social geography of excluded or marginalized populations: here there is concern with refugees, homeless people, racial minorities, gay groups, etc.,

and their use of social and physical space, as well as the identification of appropriate spaces within which such groups are permitted to exist by authority organizations, such as governments. These four aspects of contemporary population geography do not cover the entire range, but they do illustrate the variety of work that is being undertaken, as well as the problems faced and the connections with other specialisms both within and outside geography.

Finally, what of population issues within geography? It is too easy to dismiss population geography as an old-style, highly empirical and positivist branch of a discipline that since the mid-1940s has experienced a sequence of methodological and philosophical realignments. Radical geographers are ever mindful of Marx's reaction to Malthus; blaming the victims for reproducing when it is the political and economic system that is at fault appears unjust. This has tended to exclude population matters from the politically correct geographical research agenda or to trivialize the issues through oversimplification. However, the study of population in a geographically sensitive way remains an important vehicle for both interpretation and change; there will be few that are more important for social scientists in the twenty-first century.

Robert Woods
University of Liverpool

Further reading

Brown, L. A. (1991) *Place, Migration and Development in the Third World*, London.
Clarke, J. I. (1972) *Population Geography*, 2nd edn, Oxford.
—— (ed.) (1984) *Geography and Population: Approaches and Applications*, Oxford.
Harvey, D. W. (1974) 'Population, resources and the ideology of science', *Economic Geography* 50.
Jones, H. (1990) *Population Geography*, London.
Woods, R. I. (1979) *Population Analysis in Geography*, London.
—— (1982) *Theoretical Population Geography*, London.
Woods, R. I. and Rees, P. H. (eds) (1986) *Population Structures and Models*, London.
Zelinsky, W. (1971) 'The hypothesis of the mobility transition', *Geographical Review* 61.

See also: fertility; migration; mortality; population and resources; population policy; population projections; social geography.

population policy

Population policy is government's articulated vision of goals that it wishes to achieve in respect of population. Systematic attention by governments to population as a matter for public policy is relatively new. Not much attention was paid by policy makers to population, as such, before 1945, although public policy concerns about mortality and migration have a long history in their own right. Although the science of demography addresses three elements of population change – fertility, mortality and migration – the thrust of modern population policy is usually on fertility and, in most cases, on reducing fertility. This is because the poorest countries of the world are experiencing unprecedented rates of population growth and it is widely believed that rapid population growth in poor countries has seriously undesirable consequences.

Population policies are necessarily adopted at national levels. Yet the modern phenomenon of adopting them has been heavily influenced by international opinions and considerations. It is no mere coincidence that attention to population policy, principally in the poorer countries, parallels the period of international assistance to development efforts of those countries. That period began roughly with the formation of the Organization for Economic and Social Development in 1961. Thus, the first of the serious consequences thought to be associated with rapid population growth in poor countries was arrested economic development.

Further consequences about which serious concern is expressed are environmental degradation, poor health of mothers and children, political unrest and insecurity, and inattention to human rights. Indeed, because doubt has been introduced about the validity of the concerns regarding economic development, these additional concerns have risen in importance.

Underlining the influence of international considerations on the adoption of national population policies is the series of international population conferences sponsored by the United Nations and attended by official delegations of the UN member states. The International Conference on Population and Development (ICPD), held in Cairo in September 1994, suggests the possibility that large-scale changes are about to occur in the international context in which national population policies are enacted. Whereas final documents from the earlier international conferences, in Bucharest in 1974 and Mexico City in 1984, focused most intensely on fertility targets, the draft final document for Cairo includes substantial attention to achieving, as matters of population policy, improvements in maternal and child health and in female education. Moreover, attention is devoted in the ICPD draft to issues of gender equality, equity and empowerment of women, and to reproductive rights and sexual and reproductive health. Questions are raised from time to time about whether these added attentions imply changes in policy goal, for example, from fertility reduction to, say, improved health of women, or whether they are to be understood as improved means toward attainment of the unchanged goal of fertility reduction. Such questions are likely to be the subjects

of considerable literature following from the adoption of a final document at Cairo in September 1994.

Often there is a gap between a country's stated population policy and its implementation. This sort of short-fall in performance is not, of course, exclusive to population policy. In every sphere and in every country, ambition may exceed capability. But in the field of population policy, it may be that the locally perceived weight of international interest in a poor country's fertility rates contributes more to the shortfall than in other fields.

George Zeidenstein
Harvard University

Further reading

Bongaarts, J. (1993) 'Population policy options in the developing world', *Science* 263.

Cohen, S. A. (1993) 'The road from Rio to Cairo: toward a common agenda', *International Family Planning Perspectives* 19.

Demeny, P. (1991) 'Tradeoffs between human numbers and material standards of living', in K. Davis and M. S. Berstam (eds) *Resources, Environment, and Population: Present Knowledge, Future Options, Population and Development Review, Supplement to vol. 16, 1990.*

Dixon-Mueller, R. (1993) *Population Policy and Women's Rights*, Westport, CT.

Finkle, J. L. and Crane, B. B. (1985) 'Ideology and politics at Mexico City: the United States at the 1984 International Conference on Population', *Population and Development Review* 11.

ICPD (May 1994) *Draft Programme of Action of the International Conference on Population and Development*, International Conference on Population and Development Secretariat, New York.

National Academy of Sciences (1986) *Population Growth and Economic Development: Policy Questions*, Washington, DC.

National Research Council (1986) 'National Research Council, population growth and economic development: policy questions', *Population and Development Review*, Review Symposium 12.

Preston, S. (1986) 'Are the economic consequences of population growth a sound basis for population policy?', in J. Menken (ed.) *World Population and U.S. Policy: The Choices Ahead*, New York.

Ross, J. A. and Mauldin, W. S. (eds) (1988) *Berelson on Population*, New York.

See also: demographic transition; fertility; migration; mortality; population and resources; population geography; population projections; vital statistics.

population projections

Population projections are calculations that illustrate the development of populations when certain assumptions are made about the course of future population growth. Projections can be made for the country as a whole, for major geographical or political subdivisions of a country, or for particular classes of a population. The assumptions of the projection may mirror patterns of growth observed in the past, may be based on an extrapolation of past trends, or may be conjectural, speculative or illustrative. The length of the projection period may vary from a few years to many decades, depending on the needs being served, the population in question and the availability of resources.

Several procedures for projecting populations can be distinguished. A total population can be projected forward in time by means of a balancing equation, whereby future population size is estimated by adding to a previously enumerated population changes over the intervening period due to natural increase (births less deaths) and net migration. The method demands a satisfactory initial population count and reliable estimates of the components of population growth, and is warranted only for fairly short projection periods.

A slightly different approach can be taken by projecting an initial population by reference to a rate of annual increase under the assumption of a mathematical model for the form of population growth. The most commonly used model is that of exponential growth. The technique also permits calculations of a population's doubling time, or the rate of growth that must have been operating to produce a particular population size after a certain number of years. Variants of the method incorporate other patterns of growth, such as the logistic, but have the common feature that future population size is estimated without regard to the components of growth.

If a population's age structure is not constant, because of past fluctuations in vital rates or age-selective migration, it is greatly preferable to extrapolate from a known age structure on the basis of age-specific fertility and mortality rates. This is known as the component method of population projection, and is performed in several steps. The first is to calculate the survivors of the initial population on the basis of an assumed or underlying life table, and the second is to calculate the children born and surviving over the projection period. Thus, for example, with a projection period of five years, one would calculate the survivors of people initially aged 0–4 years, 5–9 years, and so on, to give the numbers aged 5–9, 10–14 and so on, in the projected population, and then apply age-specific fertility rates to women in the childbearing years to derive the number of children whose survivors will go to make up the 0–4 age group in the projected population. A final refinement might be to adjust for known or assumed rates of immigration and emigration.

Demographers are perhaps best known for making population projections. Nevertheless, there is a considerable difference of opinion within the profession as to the role of the demographer in this regard, and even as to the function of a projection. According to Brass (1974), 'the forecasting of future populations would seem to many people the main practical justification for the science of demography'. Opposing this view Grebenik (1974) declared that 'it is perhaps salutary to remind ourselves that there is only one feature that all demographic predictions have had in common, and that is that they have all been falsified by events'. We can go some way towards reconciling these points of view by distinguishing, as does Keyfitz (1972), between a prediction of what will actually happen in the future, and a projection, which is merely the numerical consequence of a series of assumptions. A projection is bound to be correct (barring arithmetic error), while a single forecast is nearly certain to be invalidated by subsequent events. For example, a forecast might be based on current mortality which is subject to change, or on an assumed future level of mortality which proves to have been incorrect.

Whatever limitations or qualifications that demographers place on their projections, they cannot prevent their being used as forecasts. The most that demographers can do is to state their assumptions clearly, or perhaps even prepare a range of projections from a range of extreme assumptions, and leave the user to decide whether any sort of forecast is feasible.

Michael Bracher
University of Stockholm

References

Brass, W. (1974) 'Perspectives in population prediction: illustrated by the statistics of England and Wales' (with discussion), *Journal of the Royal Statistical Society A* 137(4).

Grebenik, E. (1974) 'Discussion', in W. Brass, *Journal of the Royal Statistical Society A* 137(4).

Keyfitz, N. (1972) 'On future population', *Journal of the American Statistical Association* 67.

Further reading

Dorn, H. F. (1950) 'Pitfalls in population forecasts and projections', *Journal of the American Statistical Association* 45.

Hajnal, J. (1955) 'The prospects for population forecasts', *Journal of the American Statistical Association* 50.

Shyrock, H. S., Siegal, J. S. and associates (1973) *The Methods and Material of Demography*, US Bureau of the Census, Washington, DC.

See also: fertility; migration; mortality; population geography; population policy; prediction and forecasting; vital statistics.

populism

Populism is one of the least precise terms in the vocabulary of social science. The political phenomena to which it refers are extraordinarily diverse, with few connecting links. Only one feature is shared by all so-called populists, namely a rhetoric of appeals to 'the people' understood in a variety of senses. However, a distinction can be drawn between two broad families of populisms, each of them internally differentiated: populism as a form of radical movement based on or oriented towards rural grievances, and populism as a style of politics.

Populism as rural radicalism has three variants, which overlap to some extent but also show sharp differences:

First, there are radical farmers' movements, of which the paradigm case is the US People's Party of the 1890s. This movement, whose adherents coined the label Populist, grew out of the economic grievances of farmers in the western and southern states, and for a time appeared to threaten the US two-party system. The Populists, whose manifesto declared 'We seek to restore the government of the Republic to the hands of "the plain people" ', demanded a variety of reforms, including monetary inflation by increased coinage of silver.

Second, there are movements of radical intellectuals, aiming at agrarian socialism and romanticizing the peasantry. The model here is *Narodnichestvo* (Populism), a phase of the nineteenth-century Russian revolutionary movement during which disaffected intellectuals went to the people to try to provoke them to revolution. At the height of the movement in 1874, thousands of young people flocked to the countryside to preach the gospel of agrarian socialism. They believed that since communal cultivation of land still survived in the Russian village, a new socialist society could be constructed upon this rural foundation once the state was destroyed. When the peasantry proved unresponsive, some of the *Narodniki* took to terrorism instead.

Third, there are spontaneous grassroots peasant movements, aimed at control of the land and freedom from elite domination. There is no acknowledged paradigm movement, but examples include the Zapatistas in the Mexican Revolution and the peasant parties of Eastern Europe after the First World War. Third World revolutionary movements with a peasant base, such as Maoism, may be regarded as a fusion of Marxism with populism. Agrarian populism is often thought to be characteristic of developing countries, and has been plausibly linked to the strains of economic and social modernization.

Populism as a political style includes a variety of diverse phenomena:

First, populist dictatorship includes cases in which a charismatic leader appeals beyond conventional politicians to the masses, and gains unconstitutional power by giving them 'bread and circuses'. Juan Peron,

who (with the help of his wife Eva) built up a loyal popular following in Argentina in the 1940s, is an obvious case.

Second, populist democracy is hostile to representation and seeks to keep as much power as possible in the hands of the people. Its characteristic institutional devices are the popular referendum on legislation passed by a representative assembly; popular initiative, whereby voters can bypass the assembly and initiate legislation to be voted on in a referendum; and the recall, whereby representatives can be forced by dissatisfied constituents to undergo an extra election before the end of their term of office. Some populists are attracted by the opportunities offered by modern technology for the electorate to offer instant judgements on political issues.

Third, 'reactionary populism' describes politicians who play to the prejudices of the masses in democratic countries against what are taken to be the more enlightened views of the political elite. Politicians who gain popularity by playing on ethnic hostilities or right-wing views about law and order are particularly liable to the charge of populism in this sense.

Finally, 'politicians' populism' is the style of politicians who avoid ideological commitments and claim to speak for the whole people rather than for any faction, and of catch-all people's parties that are short on principles, eclectic in their policies and prepared to accept all comers.

These populist political styles may be combined but do not necessarily occur together. Similarly, agrarian populists may use some populist political styles, as in the case of the American Populists of the 1890s.

When used to describe a political style, the term populist is usually derogatory. However, as democratization spreads, opportunities for political populism grow with it, because these political styles exploit the gap between democratic theory and practice. There is an unavoidable tension between democracy as a form of state and democracy's legitimizing principle, the sovereignty of the people. Populists mobilize support by appealing through past democratic institutions and politicians to the people they are supposed to represent. In doing so they make use of the ambiguities of the notion, 'people'. In English, this can refer to 'the united people', that is, the nation as a whole as opposed to squabbling factions; the 'common people', as opposed to the rich and powerful; 'ordinary people', as opposed to professional politicians; and 'our people', as opposed to foreigners or ethnic minorities. Populist politicians often use these ambiguities to appeal to a number of different constituencies simultaneously.

As political populists incline to a demagogic style and frequently mobilize support by playing on nationalist or ethnic hostilities, there are affinities with some versions of fascism. However, political populism can be distinguished from fascism in the strict sense by its characteristic lack of ideological commitments.

Margaret Canovan
University of Keele

Further reading

Canovan, M. (1981) *Populism*, New York.
Ionescu, G. and Gellner, E. (eds) (1969) *Populism: Its Meanings and National Characteristics*, London.

See also: democracy; fascism; radicalism.

pornography

The word pornography is derived from the ancient Greek *porne* and *graphos* meaning 'writing about whores'. From its origin in ancient Greece, where the *porne* were the lowest class of prostitute, to its present-day status in western capitalist society as a multi-billion pound international industry facilitated by developments in printing, video, computer and satellite broadcasting technologies, women's participation and exploitation in prostitution and pornography has been economically motivated and predicated on institutionalized systems of gendered power relations. The pornography industry is part of a wider sex industry based on the buying and selling of women and children internationally as sexual commodities, and the international traffic in women and children for prostitution.

Traditionally, pornography has been considered as a form of erotic and sexually explicit representation. A number of sharply diverging positions have evolved with respect both to pornography and representation: the liberal/libertarian left; the conservative/moral right; competing feminist theories; and theories that primarily interrogate power and domination. There have been critiques of representation as power or objectification (especially over, or of, women) in terms of sexuality, gender, race, class, politics and ideology in fields as diverse as psychoanalysis, discourse analysis, language, post-modernism, feminism and Marxism. Literary, cultural, lesbian/queer and women's studies have developed theories of creation/production, effect and reception of representation taking into account the role of the producer, the nature of the content, and the identity/position/consciousness of the consumer.

There have been three major theories about the effects of pornography. First, from the authoritarian, conservative, moral perspective, sexual representations have been defined as obscene and harmful to the moral fabric of society and this definition has been

institutionalized in the regulation of pornography by obscenity laws. Second, from within the liberal/libertarian perspective, pornography has been defined not only as sexual representation but also as a form of freedom of expression which operates in the realm of fantasy and is regarded as a reflection of individual freedom in society.

Third, some strands of feminism have defined pornography as act or product as well as representation and considered the function of representation in the construction of ideas, fantasy, imagination and desire, and the influence of representation (through these processes) on action and behaviour. Some feminist perspectives on pornography see pornography as a positive expression of women's sexuality. More generally, feminist and gay and lesbian campaigns have re-opened debates on pornography, transforming consciousness by making the connections between male power, male violence and pornography. One strand of feminism has defined pornography as 'a practice of subordination and sexual inequality' in terms of the harm experienced by women and children in the making and use of pornography. Harm is defined as including rape and sexual assault, child sexual abuse, sexual harassment and women's subordinate status in society to which pornography is both a causal and a contributing factor, the effects of which are evidenced from a number of sources, including the testimony of women and children who have experienced pornography-related abuse, clinical work and research with sex offenders, and social science and experimental psychological research.

Since the early 1980s, research has distinguished between three different kinds of sexually explicit representation – sexually explicit material which is violent; sexually explicit material which is non-violent but subordinating and dehumanizing; and sexually explicit material which is non-violent and non-subordinating called erotica – and consistently shown negative effects on attitudes and behaviour from the use of the first two categories, but not the third. Government inquiries in the USA (1986), Canada (1985), Australia (1988) and New Zealand (1989) have drawn conclusions about the harmful effects of these categories of pornography.

The current tensions between the competing perspectives on pornography are illustrated by two judicial decisions. A Federal court in the USA in 1985 found that pornography produced attitudes of bigotry and contempt, fostered acts of aggression and harmed women's opportunities for equality and rights of all kinds, but the court decided that this simply demonstrates the power of pornography as speech and ruled that the free speech rights of the pornography industry took precedence over women's rights to be free of sexual violence and inequality (Hudnut 1985). In 1992 the Canadian Supreme Court ruled unanimously that sexually violent pornography and non-violent but subordinating and dehumanizing pornography contributed to sexual violence and sex discrimination (HM v Butler 1992).

Catherine Itzin
University of Bradford

Further reading

Barry, K. (1979) *Female Sexual Slavery*, New York.
Donnerstein, E., Linz, D. and Penrod, S. (1987) *The Question of Pornography: Research Findings and Policy Implications*, New York.
Dworkin, A. (1981) *Pornography: Men Possessing Women*, London.
Gibson, P. C. and Gibson, R. (eds) (1993) *Dirty Looks, Women, Pornography, Power*, London.
Heathcote, O., Itzin, C., Jouve, N. W. and Saunders, S. (1994) 'Representation and Pornography', *Violence, Abuse and Gender Relations Strategy Seminar Report to the ESRC*.
Itzin, C. (ed.) (1992) *Pornography: Women, Violence and Civil Liberties*, Oxford.
Kappeler, S. (1986) *The Pornography of Representation*, Cambridge, UK.
Linz, D. and Malamuth, N. (1993) *Pornography*, New York.
Malamuth, N. M. and Donnerstein, E. (eds) (1984) *Pornography and Sexual Aggression*, New York.
Segal, L. and McIntosh, M. (eds) (1992) *Sex Exposed: Sexuality and the Pornography Debate*, London.
Zillmann, D. and Bryant, J. (eds) (1989) *Pornography: Research Advances and Policy Considerations*, Hillsdale, N J.

See also: gender and sex; media effects; sexual behaviour.

positivism

Although the explicit postulates of logical positivism are not accepted by most practising social scientists there remains an amorphous and implicit self-consciousness, a self-perception, that pervades contemporary social science practice which may be called the 'positivist persuasion'. The major postulates of this persuasion follow.

First, a radical break exists between empirical observations and non-empirical statements. This seems like a simple and rather commonsensical position, but it is actually a fundamental, specifically intellectual principle that has enormous ramifications.

Second, because of this assumed break between general statements and observations, it is widely believed that more general intellectual issues – philosophical or metaphysical – are not fundamentally significant for the practice of an empirically oriented discipline.

Third, as such an elimination of the non-empirical (purely intellectual) reference is taken to be the distinguishing feature of the natural sciences, it is believed that any objective study of society must assume a natural scientific self-consciousness.

Finally, questions which are of a theoretical or general nature can correctly be dealt with only in relation to empirical observations. There are three important corollaries of this fourth point. First, regarding the *formulation* of scientific theories, the positivist persuasion argues that the process of theory formation should be one of construction through generalization, a construction consisting of inductions from observation. Second, regarding the problem of theoretical *conflict*, the positivist persuasion argues that empirical tests must in every case be the final arbiter between theoretical disputes. It is crucial experiments rather than conceptual dispute that determine the outcome of competition between theories. Third, if the formulation of theories and the conflict between them can be entirely reduced to *empirical* material, there can be no long-term basis for structured kinds of scientific *disagreement*. Social-scientific development is viewed as a basically progressive one, that is, as linear and cumulative, and the segmentation or internal differentiation of a scientific field is viewed as the product of specialization rather than the result of generalized, non-empirical disagreement. It is viewed, in other words, as the result of focusing on different aspects of empirical reality rather than of seeking to explain the same element of empirical reality in different ways.

The ramifications of these beliefs about social science have been enormous: everywhere they have had an impoverishing effect on the social-scientific imagination, in both its empirical and theoretical modes.

By unduly emphasizing the observational and verificational dimensions of empirical practice, the positivist impetus has severely narrowed the range of empirical analysis. The fear of speculation has technicalized social science and driven it toward false precision and trivial correlational studies. This flight from generality has only contributed further to the inevitable atomization of social-scientific knowledge.

This positivist impetus has also led to a surplus of energy devoted to methodological rather than conceptual innovation, for the scientific challenge is increasingly understood to be the achievement of ever more pure forms of observational expression.

Finally, but perhaps most significantly, the positivist persuasion has crippled the practice of theoretical sociology as well. It has sharply reduced the quantity of discussion that directly concerns itself with the generalized elements of social-scientific thought. But it has also unmistakably reduced the quality. This has occurred because under the rubric of the positivist persuasion, it is much more difficult for theoretical analysis to achieve an adequate self-understanding. The positivist persuasion has caused a widespread failure of nerve in theoretical sociology.

What might an alternative position look like? Clearly, even in American social science since the 1950s, there has been some alternative put forward. What is usually proposed is some kind of humanistic as compared to scientific approach to empirical study: there is humanistic geography, sociology, political science, psychology and even the humanistic narrative approach in contrast to the analytic approach in history. These humanist alternatives have in common their anti-scientific stances, a position which is held to imply the following: a focus on people rather than external forces; an emphasis on emotions and morality rather than instrumental calculation; interpretative rather than quantitative methods; the ideological commitment to a moral society, one which fights the dangers of technology and positivist science. In the European tradition this purportedly vast dichotomy was formalized by Dilthey as the distinction between *Geisteswissenschaft* and *Naturwissenschaft*, between hermeneutics and science. In its most radical form, the hermeneutical position argues that the uniquely subjective topic of the 'human studies' makes generalizations impossible; in more moderate form it argues that even if some generalizations are possible, our effort must aim only at understanding rather than explanation, hence that causal analysis is the monopoly of natural science.

This distinction between social and natural sciences, which is at the heart of such a humanist position, is an invidious one. Such an alternative to the positivist persuasion is too timid, too self-effacing before the power of the 'big sciences'. It also implies a much too rigid connection between epistemology, method and ideology. Finally, and this is the important point, it is plainly wrong.

The humanistic or hermeneutical alternative to positivism suffers from a misunderstanding of natural science. The post-empiricist philosophy, history and sociology of science since the mid-1960s has conclusively demonstrated that the positivist persuasion has been vastly and irrevocably wrong, not just about the usefulness of the natural science guide to social science, but about natural science itself. From the wide range of this discussion there are certain basic points upon which most of the participants in this movement are agreed. These are the fundamental postulates of the 'post-positivist persuasion', and they all point to the rehabilitation of the theoretical.

First, all scientific data are theoretically informed. The fact/theory distinction is not concrete, does not exist in nature, but is analytic. Calling statements observational is a manner of speech. We use some theories to provide us with the 'hard facts', while we allow others the privilege of 'tentatively' explaining them.

Second, empirical commitments are not based solely on empirical evidence. The principled rejection of evidence is often the very bedrock upon which the continuity of a theoretical science depends.

Third, the elaboration of general scientific theory is normally dogmatic rather than sceptical. Theoretical formulation does not proceed, as Popper would have it, according to the law of the fiercest struggle for survival: it does not adopt a purely sceptical attitude to generalizations, limiting itself only to falsifiable positions. To the contrary, when a general theoretical position is confronted with contradictory empirical evidence which cannot be simply ignored (which is often the first response), it proceeds to develop *ad-hoc* hypotheses and residual categories which allow these anomalous phenomena to be 'explained' in a manner that does not surrender a theory's more general formulations.

Finally, fundamental shifts in scientific belief will occur only when empirical challenges are matched by the availability of alternative theoretical commitments. This background of theoretical change may be invisible, as empirical data give the *appearance* of being concrete (as representing external reality) rather than analytic (representing thought as well). But this appearance is not correct: the struggle between general theoretical positions is among the most powerful energizers of empirical research; it must be placed at the heart of major changes in the natural sciences.

These insights take us beyond the hermeneutics-versus-science dichotomy. We can see that science itself is a hermeneutical, subject-related activity. Social studies need not, therefore, withdraw itself from the greater ambitions of science. What they must do is to understand the nature of social science in a radically different way, as a science that must be, from the beginning, explicitly concerned with *theoretical* issues. No doubt this much more subjective understanding of the post-positivist position is depressing to those who hope for, and believe in, an objective science; positivists, indeed, might well view such a position as surrender or defeat. I would strongly disagree. As Raymond Aron once wrote in his elegy to the great positivist philosopher Michael Polanyi: 'To recognize the impossibility of demonstrating an axiom system is not a defeat of the mind, but the recall of the mind to itself.'

Jeffrey C. Alexander
University of California

Further reading

Alexander, J. C. (1983) *Theoretical Logic in Sociology*, 2 vols, London.
Frisby, D. (ed.) (1976) *The Positivist Dispute in German Sociology*, London.
Halfpenny, P. (1982) *Positivism and Sociology*, London.

See also: philosophy of the social sciences; sociology of science.

post-industrial society

The term post-industrial society seems to have originated with Arthur Penty, a Guild Socialist and follower of William Morris, at the end of the 19th century. Penty looked forward to a 'post-industrial state' based on the small craft workshop and decentralized units of government. The concept was not taken up again until the 1950s, when it was given an entirely new twist. It owes its present meaning largely to the writings of the Harvard sociologist, Daniel Bell.

In numerous works, especially *The Coming of Post-Industrial Society* (1973), Bell has argued that modern industrial societies are entering into a new phase of their evolution, a post-industrial phase. Post-industrial society is as different from classic industrial society as the latter was from pre-industrial agrarian society. It is concerned with the production of services rather than goods, the majority of its workforce is in white collar rather than manual occupations, and many of these workers are professional, managerial or technical employees. The old working class is disappearing, and with it many of the class conflicts of industrial society. New alignments, based on status and consumption, are supplanting those based on work and production.

Post-industrial society is a highly educated society; indeed, knowledge is its central resource, but knowledge in a special sense. Industrial society ran on practical knowledge, the knowledge that comes from doing rather than from pure research. Its representative figures are inventors like Watt and Edison. Post-industrial society depends on theoretical knowledge, the knowledge that is developed in universities and research institutes. It not only looks to theoretical knowledge for many of its characteristic industries, such as the chemical and aeronautical industries, but increasingly puts a good part of its national resources into developing such knowledge, in the form of support for higher education and research and development activities. This shift of emphasis is reflected in the growth in importance of the 'knowledge class' – scientists and professionals – and of 'knowledge institutions', such as universities. These will eventually displace businesspeople and business organizations as the ruling complex in society.

Bell's account of post-industrial society has been the most influential. It is based largely on generalization from American experience, but many European sociologists have found sufficient similarities in their own societies to concur: for instance, Alain Touraine in *The Post-Industrial Society* (1971), although he stressed more than Bell that conflicts in the new society will be as severe as in the old. Bell's ideas have been particularly acceptable to futurologists of both west and east, who have made the concept of post-industrial society central to their thinking. In Eastern Europe, post-industrialism has usually been given a Marxist gloss, as a 'higher stage' on the way to full socialism, but, with that necessary qualification, east European reception of the post-industrial idea has been remarkably warm.

How plausible is the post-industrial concept? Many of the changes that Bell notes in the economy and the occupational structure are undoubtedly occurring. Industrial societies are to a large extent now white collar, service societies. But that is largely because they have exported their manufacturing sectors to the countries of the Third World, without in any way giving up their control. Multinational corporations have their headquarters in the cities of the 'post-industrial' world, but set up their plants and recruit their workforce in the industrialized world, for obvious reasons of cheapness and political convenience. Hence post-industrial societies contain and continue the ethic and social purpose of industrialism, which in many cases overwhelms the striving towards the newer post-industrial ethic of social responsibility and professional commitment. The same feature is clear in the area to which great importance is attributed, white collar and professional work. We may be (almost) all professionals now, but much professional work has been 'industrialized' by bureaucratization and the application of computer technology, thus making professional workers increasingly like the proletarians of industrial society. The bulk of research in universities and the R&D (research and development) departments of industry and government is devoted to extensions and refinements of existing products and processes, such as newer car designs or higher-definition television sets. Additionally, research is directed towards newer and more efficient ways of waging war (defence and space research) or controlling the population (much applied social science). In neither case can we discern a new social principle at work, such as would signal the coming of a new social order.

In recent years, largely under the stimulus of the writings of Ivan Illich and E. F. Schumacher, a new concept of post-industrialism has grown. In many ways this harks back to the original usage of the term by Penty. It picks out the features of modern society which genuinely suggest a movement *beyond* industrialism, rather than, as with Bell, a continuation of it. Although nostalgia for pre-industrial life plays some part in this reformulation, the more serious thinkers look to the most advanced sectors of modern technology and organization to supply the building-blocks of the new society. They are especially impressed by the capacity of modern technology to abolish work: work, that is, as paid employment. Left to itself, this process can take the disastrous shape of mass unemployment and a reversion to the social conflicts of the 1930s. But they see also an opportunity which can be seized, given the political will. Work in the highly rationalized formal economy can be reduced to a minimum and shared out equally. From the wages for such work, together with some form of minimum income guarantee, we can purchase the 'appropriate' or 'intermediate' technology needed to deliver a good deal of the goods and services we require. Work can largely be organized in the informal economy around a revived local domestic or communal economy. If such a future society contains in it the elements of a pre-industrial way of life, reversing some of the tendencies towards centralization and large-scale bureaucratic organization inherent in industrialism, it is no less post-industrial for that.

In the 1980s Daniel Bell returned to the theme of the post-industrial society, which he now more firmly identified as the information society. Under this banner the concept has been given a new lease of life, as witness a flourishing literature on the subject.

Krishan Kumar
University of Kent

Further reading

Frankel, B. (1987) *The Post-Industrial Utopians*, Cambridge, UK.
Garshuny, J. (1978) *After Industrial Society?*, London.
Kumar, K. (1978) *Prophecy and Progress: The Sociology of Industrial and Post-Industrial Society*, Harmondsworth.
Toffler, A. (1981) *The Third Wave*, London.

See also: futurology; post-modernism; post-modernity.

post-modernism

The term post-modernism (and post-modern) has been used variably to refer to what are interpreted as major changes in the way the contemporary world can and ought to be represented. The term, introduced from architecture and art criticism which then passed into philosophy and literary studies, has now become something of a commonplace in the social sciences. In architecture, where it first gained currency, post-modernism referred to an active break with the principal tenets of modern architecture and the emergence of new combinations of older styles, the return of concrete as opposed to abstract forms, the active use of kitsch and pastiche. In a renowned programmatic statement, the French philosopher F. Lyotard (1984) announced the demise of the great paradigm of scientific rationality and the return of multiple wisdoms, cultures, a relativism of knowledges. Richard Rorty (1980), another early representative of philosophical post-modernism, stressed the impossibility of scientific models of progress and argued for 'edifying conversation' among paradigms rather than cumulative development. The early discussion in the social sciences was very much intertwined with the more general philosophical discussions and was especially focused on Habermas's (1981) critique of Lyotard, Bell (1973) and others, and the ensuing debate between proponents of post-modernism vs. modernism. For Habermas (1987), post-modernism was a dangerously conservative rejection of the incomplete modern project, a capitulation to the apparent failure of the emancipatory content of that project. For Lyotard (1984) it was a liberation from the straitjacket of rationalist purity of the master discourses of a totalitarian modernity.

The onslaught on hegemonic discourses has occurred across the whole of the social fabric. In anthropology, 'ethnographic authority' came under attack in the 1980s and was to be replaced by more dialogical approaches (Clifford 1988). More extreme, perhaps more consistent, versions of the attack on anthropological authority (Tyler 1990) questioned the very adequacy of written language to represent 'the other'. The attack on general scientific paradigms has been a central issue in sociology and other social sciences, but it has remained more varied and perhaps more general than in anthropology, where the question of authority and voice are central methodological issues. In sociology, especially cultural sociology, the issue of post-modernism has come increasingly to focus on a characterization of contemporary western societies, i.e. 'the post-modern condition'. This is evident in work by Lash and Urry (1987), Mingione (1991), Vattimo (1987), Baudrillard (1970; 1972; 1978), Featherstone (1991), and others whose approaches are often quite opposed to one another in spite of rather strong similarities with regard to the nature of the conditions they describe. Literary theorists and the growing field of cultural studies have had a significant place in many of these discussions (e.g. Jameson 1991). Numerous sets of oppositions have been used to characterize the difference between post-modernism and modernism. Among the most common are the following:

Modernism	Post-modernism
scientific knowledge	wisdom (cultural knowledge)
grand theory	relative cultural corpuses
universalism	particularism
mono-vocality	poly-vocality
symbolic meaning	simulacra
coherence	pastiche
holism	fragmentation
history	histories
rational ego	libidinal self
intellectual	tactile

We should distinguish between the terms post-modern and post-modernism. The former might be said to refer to a social and cultural condition, whereas the latter refers to a mode of thought, strategy or style. Very much of the discussion during the 1980s concerned the pros and cons of post-modernism as an intellectual position. More recently the discussion has begun to move towards an attempt at interpreting the social conditions themselves. There are numerous interpretations of the 'post-modern condition'. For some it is an aspect of what Bell (1973) referred to as post-industrialization, the movement from mass industrial towards information-based technology and the emergence of an information society in which control of communication was to become central. For Bell (1976) the post-modern is a product of modernism itself, the effect of the destruction of meaning, of morality of authoritative structures, leading ultimately to 'pornotopia'. Baudrillard's interpretation of the advent of information technology argues that symbolic meaning is disappearing, being replaced by a plethora of floating signifiers where the social is reduced to simulacra. The latter interpretation represents a world devoid of meaning in which there is little hope in the future, whereas for other approaches (e.g. Lyotard) the post-modern is the advent of a non-hegemonic political and intellectual strategy. It is not always easy to separate political identity from analysis in the discussions of the post-modern. Advocates of post-modernism have openly attacked modernism as a hegemonic discourse, a structure of control and domination in which discipline was instated by way of rationality itself. For Jameson (1991) and others, post-modernism is characterized, instead, as the 'cultural logic of late capitalism', a dissolution of modernism related to the breakdown of meaning structures, itself a product of disintegration of the modern 'Oedipal' self with a centre of authority and capable of symbolic practice. The result resembles Baudrillard's vision of superficiality and pastiche, but the explanation is explicitly Marxist, as opposed to the former's use of notions of consumer society and information society. Attempts to come to grips with the social

transformations underlying the apparent decline of modernity are represented by Lash and Urry (1987) and Harvey (1990). For Lash and Urry (1987) the decline of modernity is part of a general process of disorganization of capitalism, a fragmentation of formerly hierarchical processes leading to various forms of social disorder, and a demand for flexibility. For Harvey (1990) the major process involved is the time–space compression produced by an increasingly rapid process of capitalist reproduction on a global scale. Vattimo (1987), in another important analysis of the degeneration of modernity, has tried to link post-modernism to the decline of western hegemony and the emergence of multiple political voices in the centre itself. This interpretation is very close to Friedman's view of post-modernity as a label for the cultural aspect of the decline of hegemony itself, the fragmentation of a formerly homogeneous/ranked universe, both social and representational (Friedman 1988; 1992; 1994).

It could be argued that what is often designated as post-modernism is an aspect of the fragmentation of the global system. Here there is a link between the decentralization of capital accumulation, the decline of western hegemony, the decline of modernism as a strategic identity of self-development, and the emergence of multivocality, multiculturalism and of indigenous, Fourth-World movements. There is an interesting parallel among different sets of fragmentations: the fragmentation of knowledge into separate relative fields, the disintegration of the evolutionary scheme of social types into a plethora of different cultures which have been interpreted as incommensurable with respect to one another, the real 'ethnification' of the nation state, both as a result of regionalization and immigration, the apparent rise of so-called narcissistic disorders that might be indicative of the dissolution of individual ego structures. The individual is also subject to changes in conditions of existence which in their turn alter practices of identification and meaning construal. This is the key to understanding the relation between economic and social processes and cultural phenomena characteristic of post-modernity.

Post-modernism has had special significance for anthropology. This can be accounted for in terms of the special place of anthropology in western identity and its various discourses. Anthropology is that field which represents 'the others' of the world to the centre. These others have been part and parcel of our identification of the world and thus our self-identity. Whether evolutionist or relativist, anthropology has provided a scheme within which we could place ourselves. This was largely dependent upon the ability to represent the populations of the periphery in unproblematic terms. The attack on ethnographic authority began to undermine the capacity to represent. The anthropologist could no longer 'read' or simply represent in any other way. This hierarchical practice would have to be replaced by a more sensitive relation to our 'object', so that instead of translating 'them' into a homogeneous text we would have a multivocal representation of their reality. In numerous collections of articles (Clifford and Marcus 1986; Marcus and Fisher 1986), the question of authority, voice and text were discussed at length. While the initial work was very much self-centred on problems of the ethnographer it is also the case that Clifford, and later Marcus, were aware of the larger context of the shift from a homogeneous/neatly ranked and hegemonic world order to a situation of increasing fragmentation. Marcus explicitly speaks of the need to grasp the ethnographic realities of the world system, and it is clear that the purely methodological critiques of representativity in ethnography are critical for the field today. The re-evaluation of ethnographic method, especially as applied to contemporary heterogenous and multi-layered realities, may not have been the goal of post-modernist critiques, but it may prove to be their major contribution. The analysis of the contemporary world in anthropological terms has not, however, played a salient role in these discussions. Oblique reference to the decline of the colonial power structures is mere background material for the focus on voice and text that so preoccupies anthropologists of the post-modern. To the extent that anthropologists have begun to study the post-modern world rather than concentrating on post-modernist implications for method and questions of representation, they have taken to analysing various aspects of the changing global situation: the formation of diaspora cultures and multicultural contexts, the politics of identity, processes of social disintegration, 'balkanization', changing forms of consumption, etc. These studies might not have anything in particular to do with post-modernity as such. But in their concern with understanding contemporary situations in global terms and with doing ethnography that is concrete and multivocal, as is required by studies geared to revealing the complexity of these situations, they can be said to be contributing to an anthropology of the post-modern situation. There is thus a certain convergence here in the social sciences: an anthropology increasingly focused on the disjointed present, a sociology focusing on the social conditions involved in what appears to be a decline or at least radical transformation of modernity, a political science focused increasingly on aspects of multiculturalism, problems of democracy in the Second and Third Worlds, and the relation between culture and power (Apter 1993; Bayart 1989; Young 1993). It is likely that this orientation to an understanding of a world undergoing vastly changing power relations and their cultural consequences shall eventually replace or fill in the categories that are currently referred to as post-modernity and post-modernism.

Jonathan Friedman
University of Lund

References

Apter, A. (1993) *Democracy, Violence and Emancipatory Movements: Notes for a Theory of Inversionary Discourse*, Geneva.
Baudrillard, J. (1970) *La Société de consommation*, Paris.
—— (1972) *Pour une critique de l'économie politique du signe*, Paris.
—— (1978) *A l'ombre des majorités silencieuses ou La Fin du social*, Paris.
Bayart, F. (1989) *L'Etat en Afrique: la politique du ventre*, Paris.
Bell, D. (1973) *The Coming of Post-Industrial Society*, New York.
—— (1976) *The Cultural Contradictions of Capitalism*, London.
Clifford, J. (1988) *The Predicament of Culture: Twentieth Century Ethnography*, Cambridge, MA.
Clifford, J. and Marcus, G. (eds) (1986) *Writing Culture: The Poetics and Politics of Ethnography*, Berkeley, CA.
Featherstone, M. (1991) *Consumer Culture and Postmodernism*, London.
Friedman, J. (1988) 'Cultural logics of the global system', *Theory Culture and Society* 5(2–3).
—— (1992) 'Narcissism, roots and postmodernity', in S. Lash and J. Friedman (eds) *Modernity and Identity*, Oxford.
—— (1994) *Cultural Identity and Global Process*, London.
Habermas, J. (1981) 'Modernity versus postmodernity' *New German Critique* 22.
—— (1987) *The Philosophical Discourses of Modernity*, Cambridge, MA.
Harvey, D. (1990) *The Condition of Postmodernity*, Oxford.
Jameson, F. (1991) *Postmodernism, or the Cultural Logic of Late Capitalism*, London.
Lash, S. and Urry, J. (1987) *The End of Organized Capitalism*, Oxford.
Lyotard, J.-F. (1984) *The Postmodern Condition: A Report on Knowledge*, Minneapolis, MN.
Marcus, G. and Fisher, M. (1986) *Anthropology as Cultural Critique: An Experimental Movement in the Social Sciences*, Chicago.
Mingione, E. (1991) *Fragmented Societies*, Oxford.
Rorty, R. (1980) *Philosophy and the Mirror of Nature*, Oxford.
Tyler, S. (1990) *The Unspeakable: Discourse, Dialogue and Rhetoric in the Postmodern World*, Madison, WI.
Vattimo, G. (1987) *La Fin de la modernité: nihilisme et herméneutique dans la culture postmoderne*, Paris.
Young, C. (ed.) (1993) *The Rising Tide of Cultural Pluralism: The Nation State at Bay?*, Madison, WI.

See also: Habermas, Jürgen; Lyotard, Jean François; modernity; post-industrial society; post-modernity; reflexivity.

post-modernity

The term post-modernity usually refers to a fully developed modernity which emerged in the affluent societies of Western Europe and of European descent in the

1970s. As a social and cultural condition described by different theoreticians, post-modernity covers a wide range of phenomena: an architectural critique of modernism and a revalorization of pastiche; a fascination in literary circles for what is perceived as popular kitsch in TV soap operas, Hollywood B films or literary forms like the romance or the murder mystery; literary criticism that emphasizes the autonomy of texts in relation to the social reality or the human experience which lies behind the texts; a characterization of society as post-industrial or post-capitalist, where consumption, electronic technology and representation of reality by the media dominates; the idea that modern society does not guarantee the elimination of material scarcity, social conflicts or ecological disasters and the achievement of democracy; or, the critique of the modern ideology that assumes the universality of the individual ego, reason and scientific language.

According to Foster (1985) it is convenient to make a distinction between a post-modernity of resistance, which seeks to criticize modernity and existing social and cultural conditions, and a post-modernity that celebrates the new social order. The works of Lyotard and Bauman are examples of the former. Lyotard (1986 [1979]) has questioned the privileged position of scientific rationalism as the dominant form of knowledge in modernity. In his perspective, scientific language is primarily a strategy of power for a conventional division of 'reality' in various fields of specialization and the negation of other forms of knowledge that exist in society. Lyotard rejects the existence of universals and, more specifically, the universal validity of the discourse of western reason. Post-modernity is the acceptance of cultural differentiation based on the existence of different types of knowledge. Bauman (1992; 1993) sees post-modernity as a self-contained condition defined by distinctive features of its own: institutionalized pluralism, variety, contingency and ambivalence (against the postulated universality, homogeneity, monotony and clarity of the modern condition). He postulates the pluralism of authority and the autonomy of the agent which permits the exercise of ethical choices and reasserts emotional dignity. In the post-modern condition, the agent is not just an actor and decision maker, but a moral subject.

Jameson (1984; 1985) postulates a correlate between late capitalism and the idea of post-modernity. Post-modernity, especially in the arts and literature, is a cultural dominant form that celebrates consumer society. The post-modern condition is characterized by the 'death' of the autonomous subject and the emergence of new moral ideals and free-floating emotions; the fragmentation of codes and discursive heterogeneity without a clear norm; a nostalgic perception of history which legitimizes pastiche as an aesthetic form;

and a conception of reality as the reproduction of simulacra through the visual power of computers and media, which abolishes any sense of alternative collective projects for dominated groups.

Eduardo P. Archetti
University of Oslo

References

Bauman, Z. (1992) *Intimations of Postmodernity*, London.
—— (1993) *Postmodern Ethics*, Oxford.
Foster, H. (1985) 'Postmodernism: a preface', in H. Foster (ed.) *Postmodern Culture*, London.
Jameson, F. (1984) 'Postmodernism or the cultural logic of late capitalism', *New Left Review* 146.
—— (1985) 'Postmodernism and consumer society', in H. Foster (ed.) *Postmodern Culture*, London.
Lyotard, J.-F. (1984 [1979]) *The Postmodern Condition: A Report on Knowledge*, Minneapolis, MN. (Original edn, *La Condition postmoderne: rapport sur le savoir*, Paris.)

Further reading

Foster, H. (ed.) (1985) *Postmodern Culture*, London.
Giddens, A. (1990) *The Consequences of Modernity*, Cambridge, UK.
Tester, K. (1993) *The Life and Times of Post-modernity*, London.
Turner, B. S. (ed.) (1990) *Theories of Modernity and Postmodernity*, London.

See also: Lyotard, Jean François; modernity; post-industrial society; post-modernism.

poverty

The definition of poverty has attracted considerable political and social scientific controversy. However, the debate cannot be dismissed as being merely semantic. The social definition of poverty is crucial, first, because it determines to what extent, if any, governments accept that the problem itself exists, and, second, because it influences what policies, if any, are to be adopted to tackle poverty and, as a consequence, how the poor themselves will be treated.

Three different historical and scientific approaches may be distinguished in the contemporary debate about poverty: subsistence or absolute poverty, basic needs, and relative deprivation (Townsend 1993).

Subsistence or absolute poverty

Subsistence or absolute poverty implies that there is a fixed basic minimum income below which physiological efficiency cannot be maintained. Based on pioneering research by Charles Booth and Seebohm Rowntree at the turn of the nineteenth century, this approach entails the calculation of a poverty line based on the minimum necessities – such as food, housing, clothing, fuel and some household sundries – required to maintain physical efficiency (Rowntree 1901). The policy implications of this approach are that if society can provide an income sufficient to meet subsistence needs, then poverty can be eliminated. It is mainly for this reason that the subsistence approach has found favour with policy makers in industrial countries such as Britain and the USA, and in some Third-World countries such as India (Townsend 1993).

The subsistence approach has been criticized for being too simplistic and inflexible. It ignores the fact that individual needs, even for food, are determined more by social convention than by scientific or expert judgement. Thus, even if it was possible to construct a single measure of the necessities required for physical efficiency, the behaviour of those forced to rely on it would not necessarily conform to the rigid regime dictated by the measure. Inevitably, this measure proposes a style of life for poor people which is significantly different from the rest of society. None the less it has been influential in the determination of social security levels in many countries.

Basic needs

The concept of basic needs encompasses the idea of subsistence needs and has been used principally in discussions about poverty in Third-World countries. Proponents of this approach have argued that it 'should be placed within a context of a nation's economic and social development' (International Labour Office 1976). The basic needs approach comprises two key elements: first, insufficient income to maintain subsistence requirements for food, shelter, clothing and certain household goods, and, second, insufficient essential services such as safe drinking water, sanitation, public transport, health services and education (Townsend 1993). This concept has been operationalized by a number of international organizations such as the ILO, UNESCO and the World Bank.

The idea of basic needs has been criticized on the same grounds as subsistence poverty, both being absolute approaches. In addition, Townsend (1993) has argued that to restrict the human needs of poor people in Third-World countries to what is required for mere physical survival is a form of racism whereby 'unsophisticated' peoples are deemed to have lesser needs than those in complex 'civilizations'. However, the concept of universal basic needs has been revived by Doyal and Gough (1991) who assert, against relativism, that health and autonomy constitute the most basic of human needs and are the same for everyone. They argue that eleven second-order or intermediate needs, which are the same for all cultures, must also

be met as they 'universally and positively' contribute to physical health and autonomy. These are nutritional food and clean water; protective housing; a non-hazardous work environment; appropriate health care; security in childhood; significant primary relationships; physical security; economic security; appropriate education; and safe birth control and childbearing.

Relative deprivation

The third approach, relative deprivation, maintains that any measure of poverty and, therefore, the numbers of people regarded as being in poverty, can be determined only by reference to the standard of living of the members of a particular society. This measurement is based on the level of income necessary for individuals to participate in the wide range of roles, relationships and consumptions that constitute full membership of the society in which they live. Income is defined in its widest sense to include resources such as assets, housing, company fringe benefits, education, health and other social services. Thus, according to Townsend, who is most closely associated with the development of the relative concept of poverty, individuals and families are in poverty when 'their resources are so seriously below those commanded by the average individual or family that they are, in effect, excluded from ordinary living patterns, customs and activities' (Townsend 1979: 1). The adoption of the term 'social exclusion' by, for example, the European Union in preference to the term 'poverty' suggests common acceptance of this broader perspective, if not of Townsend's precise measure of poverty.

There are two main implications arising from the relative deprivation approach. First, that the eradication of poverty becomes much harder than under subsistence definitions and is dependent on a reduction of inequalities within societies: thus poverty is the other side of the coin to wealth and both are the products of structural inequality. Second, the relative approach points to different standards in different societies according to local customs and practices. However, this divergence should not be exaggerated because there is considerable overlap in the living standards between affluent and relatively poor countries. For example, the most prosperous fifth of the population in relatively poor countries such as Mexico, Malaysia and Turkey are much better off than the poorest fifth in Britain (Townsend 1993).

Early studies of relative poverty were based on incomes relative to national social assistance rates (Townsend and Abel-Smith 1965). More recently, half the average income has been used as a measure of poverty in most European countries. Researchers on poverty, who have tended to agree that a relative definition is the most appropriate (for a defence of the absolutist approach see Sen 1983), have used three different ways to measure it: *social consensus approach* (Mack and Lansley 1985), based on a common public agreement of what goods and services are deemed to be essential to everyday life; the *budget standard approach* (Bradshaw 1993), according to which experts make professional judgements as to how much different types of family units need to live on; and the *behavioural approach* (Townsend 1979), which examines how people actually behave in relation to different income levels.

Conclusion

While there are problems associated with each of these methods, there is no doubt about the renewed intensity of the search for an objective measure of poverty. However, it is important that the academic debate does not obscure the real problems: an increase in poverty within and between countries, and an increase in inequality which is creating a sharper divide between rich and poor people and rich and poor nations. At the same time, policy makers in some of the developed countries are more concerned to eliminate the problem of 'the poor', or the strata sometimes referred to as 'the underclass', rather than to prevent or eliminate poverty.

The whole issue of poverty – definition, extent, meaning and policy response – is a contested terrain in which policy makers can select the scientific definition of poverty and theory about causation to suit their policy intentions. When poverty is defined in absolutist terms, the policy response is likely to be a minimal and selective one: conditional welfare for the poorest. When poverty is defined in terms of relative deprivation, the policy response required is directed at significant change in the social structure, and particularly in the distribution of resources: distributional justice for all citizens.

Alan Walker
University of Sheffield

Carol Walker
Sheffield Hallam University

References

Abel-Smith, B. and Townsend, P. (1965) *The Poor and the Poorest*, London.
Bradshaw, J. (1993) *Household Budgets and Living Standards*, York.
Doyal, L. and Gough, I. (1991) *A Theory of Human Needs*, Basingstoke.
International Labour Office (1976) *Employment Growth and Basic Needs: A One-World Problem*, Geneva.
Mack, J. and Lansley, S. (1985) *Poor Britain*, London.
Rowntree, B. S. (1901) *Poverty: A Study of Town Life*, London.
Sen, A. (1983) 'Poor relatively speaking', *Oxford Economic Papers* 35.
Townsend, P. (1979) *Poverty in the United Kingdom*, Harmondsworth.
—— (1993) *The International Analysis of Poverty*, Hemel Hempstead.

Further reading

Debate between A. Sen and P. Townsend, reprinted in P. Townsend (1993) *The International Analysis of Poverty*, Hemel Hempstead.
Walker, A. and Walker, C. (eds) (1987) *The Growing Divide: A Social Audit 1979–87*, London.
Wilson, W. J. (1987) *The Truly Disadvantaged*, Chicago.

See also: human needs; social welfare policy; welfare economics; welfare state.

power

Definitions of power are legion. To the extent that there is any commonly accepted formulation, power is understood as concerned with the bringing about of consequences. But attempts to specify the concept more rigorously have been fraught with disagreements. There are three main sources of these disagreements: different disciplines within the social sciences emphasize different bases of power (for example, wealth, status, knowledge, charisma, force and authority); different forms of power (such as influence, coercion and control); and different uses of power (such as individual or community ends, political ends and economic ends). Consequently, they emphasize different aspects of the concept, according to their theoretical and practical interests. Definitions of power have also been deeply implicated in debates in social and political theory on the essentially conflicting or consensual nature of social and political order. Further complications are introduced by the essentially messy nature of the term. It is not clear if power is a zero-sum concept (Mills 1956; Parsons 1960); if it refers to a property of an agent (or system), or to a relationship between agents (or systems) (Arendt 1970; Lukes 1974; Parsons 1963); if it can be a potential or a resource (Barry 1976; Wrong 1979); if it is reflexive or irreflexive, transitive or intransitive (Cartwright 1959); nor is it clear if power can only describe a property of, or relationship between, individual agents, or if it can be used to describe systems, structures or institutions (Lukes 1978; Parsons 1963; Poulantzas 1979); furthermore, it is not clear whether power necessarily rests on coercion (Cartwright 1959) or if it can equally rest on shared values and beliefs (Beetham 1991; Giddens 1977; Parsons 1963). Nor is it at all clear that such disputes can be rationally resolved, since it has been argued that power is a theory-dependent term and that there are few, if any, convincing metatheoretical grounds for resolving disputes between competing theoretical paradigms (Gray 1983; Lukes 1974; Morriss 1987).

In the 1950s discussions of power were dominated by the conflicting perspectives offered by power-elite theories (Mills 1956), which stressed power as a form of domination (Weber 1978 [1922]) exercised by one group over another in the presence of fundamental conflicts of interests; and structural-functionalism (Parsons) which saw power as the 'generalized capacity of a social system to get things done in the interests of collective goals' (Parsons 1960). Parsons thus emphasized power as a systems property, as a capacity to achieve ends; whereas Mills viewed power as a relationship in which one side prevailed over the other. Mills's views were also attacked by pluralists, who argued that he assumed that some group necessarily dominates a community; rather, they argued, power is exercised by voluntary groups representing coalitions of interests which are often united for a single issue and which vary considerably in their permanence (Dahl 1957; 1961; Polsby 1963). Against class and elite theorists the pluralists posed a view of US society as 'fragmented into congeries of small special-interest groups with incompletely overlapping memberships, widely differing power bases, and a multitude of techniques for exercising influence on decisions salient to them' (Polsby 1963). Their perspective was rooted in a commitment to the study of observable decision making, in that it rejected talk of power in relation to nondecisions (Merelman 1968; Wolfinger 1971), the mobilization of bias, or to such disputable entities as 'real interests'. It was precisely this focus on observable decision making which was criticized by neo-elite and conflict theorists (Bachrach and Baratz 1970; Connolly 1974; Lukes 1974), who accused the pluralists of failing to recognize that conflict is frequently managed in such a way that public decision-making processes mask the real struggles and exercises of power; both the selection and formulation of issues for public debate and the mobilization of bias within the community should be recognized as involving power. Lukes (1974) further extended the analysis of covert exercises of power to include cases where A affects B contrary to B's real interests – where B's interests may not be obtainable in the form of held preferences, but where they can be stated in terms of the preferences B would hold in a situation where B exercises autonomous judgement. Radical theorists of power have also engaged with structural-Marxist accounts of class power over questions of whether it makes sense to talk of power without reference to agency (Lukes 1974; Poulantzas 1973; 1979). Although these debates have rather dominated discussions of power in social and political theory, we should not ignore the work on power in exchange and rational-choice theory (Barry 1976), nor the further criticisms of stratification theories of power which have been developed from positions as diverse as Luhmann's neo-functionalism (Luhmann 1979), and Foucault's rather elusive post-structuralism (Foucault 1980; but see Foucault 1982).

Definitional problems seem to be endemic to discussions of power. One major problem is that all accounts of power have to take a stand on whether power is exercised over B whether or not the respect in which B suffers is intended by A. Similar problems concern whether power is properly restricted to a particular sort of effect which A has on B, or whether it applies in any case in which A has some effect on B. These two elements, intentionality and the significance of effects, allow us to identify four basic views on power and to reveal some of the principal tensions in the concept (White 1972).

The first view makes no distinction between A's intended and unintended effects on B; nor does it restrict the term power to a particular set of effects which A has on B. Power thus covers phenomena as diverse as force, influence, education, socialization and ideology. Failing to distinguish a set of significant effects means that power does not identify a specific range of especially important ways in which A is causally responsible for changes in B's environment, experience or behaviour. This view is pessimistically neutral in that it characteristically assumes that power is an ineradicable feature of all social relations, while it makes no presumption that being affected by others in one way or in one area of life is any more significant than being affected in any other. One plausible version of this view is to see power as the medium through which the social world is produced and reproduced, and where power is not simply a repressive force, but is also productive (Foucault 1980). Note that with this conception there is no requirement that A could have behaved otherwise. Although this is an odd perspective, it is not incoherent, as it simply uses power to refer to causality in social and interpersonal relations.

The second view isolates a set of significant effects. Thus, A exercises power over B when A affects B in a manner contrary to B's preferences, interests, needs, and so on. However, there is no requirement that A affect B intentionally, nor that A could have foreseen the effect on B (and thus be said to have obliquely intended it). Poulantzas's Marxism provides one such view by seeing power in terms of 'the capacity of a social class to realize its specific objective interests' (Poulantzas 1973). Any intentional connotations are eradicated by his insistence that this capacity is determined by structural factors. The capacity of a class to realize its interests 'depends on the struggle of another class, depends thereby on the structures of a social formation, in so far as they delimit the field of class practices' (Poulantzas 1973). As agency slips out of the picture, so too does any idea of A intentionally affecting B. Although idiosyncratic, this view does tackle the problem of whether we can talk meaningfully of collectivities exercising power. If we want to recognize the impact which the unintended consequences of one social group's activities have over another, or if we want to recognize that some group systematically prospers while others do not, without attributing to the first group the intention of doing the others down, then we shall be pushed towards a view of power which is not restricted solely to those effects A intended or could have foreseen. The pressures against this restriction are evident in Lukes's and Connolly's work. Both accept unintended consequences so as to 'capture conceptually some of the most subtle and oppressive ways in which the actions of some can contribute to the limits and troubles faced by others' (Connolly 1974). Both writers, however, also recognize that attributions of power are also often attributions of responsibility, and that to allow unintended effects might involve abandoning the possibility of attributing to A responsibility for B's disbenefits. Consequently both equivocate over how far unintended effects can be admitted, and they place weight on notions of A's negligence with regard to B's interests, and on counterfactual conditionals to the effect that A could have done otherwise. Stressing 'significant effects' also raises problems, as the criteria for identifying such effects are hotly disputed. Thus radical theorists criticize pluralists for specifying effects in terms of overridden policy preferences, on the grounds that power is also used to shape or suppress the formation of preferences and the articulation of interests. Again, two pressures operate, in that it seems sociologically naïve to suppose that preferences are always autonomous, yet it is very difficult to identify appropriate criteria for distinguishing autonomous and heteronomous preferences. Taking expressed preferences allows us to work with clearly observable phenomena, since B can share the investigator's ascription of power to A – it thus has the advantage of methodological simplicity and congruence with the dependent actor's interpretation. However, taking 'repressed' preferences or real interests can be justified, since it provides a more theoretically persuasive account of the complexities of social life and of the multiple ways in which potential conflicts are prevented from erupting into crisis. Yet this more complex theoretical account is under pressure to identify a set of real interests, and the temptation is to identify them in terms of autonomous/rational preferences; the problem with this is that it often carries the underlying implication that power would not exist in a society in which all agents pursued their real interests. Power is thus used to describe our deviation from utopia (Gray 1983).

The second view is primarily concerned with identifying the victims of power – not the agents. The focus is on A's power *over* B. The third view, which attributes power only when A intends to affect B, but which does not place any restrictions on the manner in which A affects B, switches the focus from A's power *over* B to A's power *to* achieve certain ends (Russell 1938; Wrong 1979). Power is concerned with the agent's ability to bring about desired consequences – 'even' but not necessarily 'against the resistance of others' (Weber 1978 [1922]). This view has a long pedigree (Hobbes 1651) and it satisfies some important theoretical interests. In so far as we are interested in using A's power as a predictor of A's behaviour, it is clearly in our interests to see A's power in terms of A's ability to secure high net profit from an action – the greater the anticipated profit, the more likely A is to act (Barry 1976). Another reason for focusing on A's intention is the difficulty in identifying a range of significant effects which is not obviously stipulative. Concentrating on A's intended outcomes allows us to acknowledge that there are a number of ways in which A can secure B's compliance and thereby attain A's ends. Thus force, persuasion, manipulation, influence, threats, throffers, offers, and even strategic positioning in decision procedures may all play a role in A's ordering of A's social world in a way that maximally secures A's ends. But seeing power solely in terms of A's intentions often degenerates into an analysis where all action is understood in power terms, with behaviour being tactical or strategic to the agent's ends. On this view agents become, literally, game-players or actors, and we are left with a highly reductive account of social structures and institutions (Rogers 1980).

Finally, the fourth perspective analyses power in terms of both intentional action and significant effects. It concentrates on cases where A gets B to do something A wants which B would not otherwise do. Two sets of difficulties arise here. The first concerns the extensiveness of the concept of power and its relationship with its companion terms, authority, influence, manipulation, coercion and force. On some accounts power is a covering term for all these phenomena (Russell 1938); on others it refers to a distinct field of events (Bachrach and Baratz 1974). Getting B to do something that B would not otherwise do may involve mobilizing commitments or activating obligations, and it is common to refer to such compliance as secured through authority. We may also be able to get B to do something by changing B's interpretation of a situation and of the possibilities open to B – using means ranging from influence and persuasion to manipulation. Or we may achieve our will through physical restraint, or force. Finally, we may use threats and throffers in order to secure B's compliance – that is, we may coerce B

(Nozick 1969). In each case A gets B to do something A wants which B would not otherwise do, although each uses different resources (agreements, information, strength, or the control of resources which B either wants or wants to avoid), and each evidences a different mode of compliance (consent, belief, physical compliance or rational choice). Although exchange and rational choice theorists have attempted to focus the analysis of power on the final group of cases, to claim that the others are not cases of power is clearly stipulative. Yet it is these other cases which introduce some of the pressures to move away from a focus solely on intended effects and significant affecting. Where A's effect on B is intended, instrumental to A's ends and contrary to B's preferences, and where B complies to avoid threatened costs, we have a case which firmly ties together A's intention and the set of effects identified as significant (B's recognized costs are intended by A and functional to A's objectives). But the other cases all invite extensions, either in the direction of covering cases in which A secures A's will, disregarding the nature of the effects on B, or towards cases where B's options or activities are curtailed by others, either unintentionally, or unconditionally. Also, this view of power risks focusing on A's *exercise* of power over B, to the detriment of the alternative and less tautological view (Barry 1976) that power is a possession, that it may exist without being exercised, and that a crucial dimension of power is where A does not secure B's compliance, but is in a position to do so should he choose. Wealth, status, and so on, are not forms of power, but they are resources which can be used by A to secure B's compliance. An adequate understanding of power in a given society will include an account of any systematic inequalities and monopolies of such resources, whether they are being used to capacity or not. The pressure, once again, is against exclusive concentration on A's actual exercise and towards a recognition of A's potential. But once we make this step we are also likely to include cases of anticipatory surrender, and acknowledging these cases places further pressure on us to move beyond easily attributable, or even oblique, intention on A's part. These pressures are resisted mainly by those who seek to construct a clear and rigorous, if stipulative, theoretical model of power. But there is also some equivocation from those who seek to match ascriptions of power with ascriptions of moral responsibility. Part of the radical edge of Lukes's (1974) case stems precisely from the use of ascriptions of power as a basis for a moral critique. But much is problematic in this move. A may act intentionally without being sufficiently sane to be held morally responsible; A may intentionally affect B to B's disbenefit without violating moral norms (as in a chess game, competitions, some

exchange relations with asymmetrical results, and so on); it is also important to recognize that B's compliance must maintain proportionality with A's threat in order for B to be absolved of moral responsibility (Reeve 1982).

The theoretical and practical pressures which exist at the boundaries of these four possible interpretations of power account for much of the concept's messiness. Each has its attractions. The fourth view is most promising for model or theory building, the third for the prediction and explanation of action, the second for the study of powerlessness and dependency, and the first for the neutral analysis of the strategic but non-intentional logic of social dynamics. Although meta-theoretical grounds for arbitration between competing conceptions of power seem largely absent, we can make a few comments on this issue. Although restrictivist definitions of power may serve specific model and theory-building interests, they inevitably provide a much simplified analysis of social order and interaction. However, more encompassing definitions risk collapsing into confusion. Thus, while there are good theoretical grounds for moving beyond stated preferences to some notion of autonomous preferences – so as, for example, to give a fuller account of B's dependence – we should be cautious about claiming that A is as morally responsible for B's situation as when A intentionally disbenefits B. Indeed, depending on how we construe the relevant counterfactuals, we might deny that agents are liable for many of the effects of their actions. Thus, we might see social life as inevitably conflict ridden, and while we might recognize that some groups systematically lose out it might not be true that A (a member of the elite) intends to disadvantage any individual in particular, or that A could avoid harming B without allowing B to harm A (as in Hobbes's state of nature). Also, although we are free to use several different definitions of power (such as the three dimensions identified by Lukes 1974), we should recognize that each definition satisfies different interests, produces different results and allows different conclusions, and we need to take great care to avoid confusing the results. Finally, we should recognize that although definitions of power are theory-dependent, they can be criticized in terms of the coherence of the theory, its use of empirical data, and the plausibility of its commitments to positions in the philosophies of mind and action.

Mark Philp
University of Oxford

References

Arendt, H. (1970) *On Violence*, London.

Bachrach, P. and Baratz, M. S. (1970) *Power and Poverty, Theory and Practice*, Oxford.

Barry, B. (1976) 'Power: an economic analysis', in B. Barry (ed.) *Power and Political Theory* London.

Beetham, D. (1991) The *Legitimacy of Power*, New Brunswick, NJ.

Cartwright, D. (1959) 'A field theoretical conception of power', in D. Cartwright (ed.) *Studies in Social Power*, Ann Arbor, MI.

Connolly, W. (1974) *The Terms of Political Discourse*, Lexington, MA.

Dahl, R. (1957) 'The concept of power', *Behavioral Science* 2.

—— (1961) *Who Governs? Democracy and Power in an American City*, New Haven, CT.

Foucault, M. (1980) *Power/Knowledge*, Brighton.

—— (1982) 'The subject and power', in H. Dreyfus and P. Rabinow (eds) *Michel Foucault: Beyond Structuralism and Hermeneutics*, Brighton.

Giddens, A. (1977) ' "Power" in the writings of Talcott Parsons', in *Studies in Social and Political Theory*, London.

Gray, J. N. (1983) 'Political power, social theory, and essential contestability', in D. Miller and L. Siedentop (eds) *The Nature of Political Theory*, Oxford.

Luhmann, N. (1979) *Trust and Power*, London.

Lukes, S. (1974) *Power, A Radical View*, London.

—— (1978) 'Power and authority', in T. Bottomore and R. Nisbet (eds) *A History of Sociological Analysis*, London.

Merelman, R. M. (1968) 'On the neo-élitist critique of community power', *American Political Science Review* 62.

Mills, C. W. (1956) *The Power Elite*, London.

Morriss, P. (1987) *Power: A Philosophical Analysis*, Manchester.

Nozick, R. (1969) 'Coercion', in S. Morgenbesser *et al.* (eds) *Philosophy, Science and Method*, New York.

Parsons, T. (1960) 'The distribution of power in American society', in *Structure and Process in Modern Societies*, Glencoe, IL.

—— (1963) 'On the concept of political power', *Proceedings of the American Philosophical Society* 107.

Polsby, N. (1963) *Community Power and Political Theory*, New Haven, CT.

Poulantzas, N. (1973) *Political Power and Social Classes*, London.

—— (1979) *State, Power, Socialism*, London.

Reeve, A. (1982) 'Power without responsibility', *Political Studies* 3.

Rogers, M. F. (1980) 'Goffman on power hierarchy and status', in J. Ditton (ed.) *The View from Goffman*, London.

Russell, B. (1938) *Power*, London.

Weber, M. (1978 [1922]) *Economy and Society*, eds. G. Roth and G. Wittich, Berkeley, CA. (Original edn, *Wirtschaft und Gesellschaft*, Tübingen.)

White, D. M. (1972) 'The problem of power', *British Journal of Political Science* 2.

Wolfinger, R. E. (1971) 'Nondecisions and the study of local politics', *American Political Science Review* 65.

Wrong, D. (1979) *Power: Its Forms, Bases and Uses*, Oxford.

See also: authority; government.

pragmatics

Pragmatics is generally defined as the theory of utterance interpretation, and contrasted with semantics, the theory of sentence meaning. In interpreting an utterance, the hearer has to answer three main questions: What did the speaker intend to say? What did the speaker intend to imply? What was the speaker's intended attitude to what was said and implied? The goal of pragmatic theory is to explain how this is done.

A major influence has been the philosopher H. P. Grice, whose *William James Lectures* at Harvard in 1967 (Grice 1989) are fundamental. Grice argued that many aspects of utterance interpretation traditionally regarded as conventional, or semantic, could be more explanatorily treated as conversational, or pragmatic. For Grice, the crucial feature of pragmatic interpretation is its *inferential* nature: the hearer is seen as constructing and evaluating a hypothesis about the intended interpretation, based, on the one hand, on the meaning of the sentence uttered, and, on the other, on background or contextual assumptions and general communicative principles which speakers are normally expected to observe.

Most recent work in pragmatics takes the inferential nature of utterance interpretation for granted. Controversy exists, however, about the nature and number of communicative principles involved. Grice saw communication as both rational and co-operative, and proposed a co-operative principle and maxims of truthfulness, informativeness, relevance and clarity which he saw as universal. The universality of Grice's maxims has been questioned. It is sometimes claimed that different cultures have different principles or maxims (see e.g. Keenan 1979). An alternative view is that pragmatic variation results from differences in background or contextual assumptions rather than differences in the principles of communication themselves.

Grice's view that co-operation is essential to communication has also been questioned. Grice's fundamental communicative principle is the co-operative principle, which instructs speakers to make their conversational contribution such as is required by the accepted purpose or direction of the current talk exchange. An alternative approach is taken by relevance theory (Sperber and Wilson 1986), which argues that the key to communication lies in more basic facts about human cognition, and that communication which is not co-operative in Grice's sense is understood in exactly the same way as co-operative communication.

According to relevance theory, the human cognitive system automatically allocates attention to information that seems relevant. Any act of communication demands the audience's attention; as a result, it creates an expectation of relevance. In interpreting an utterance or other act of communication, the hearer should rationally choose the interpretation that best satisfies this expectation. Relevance theorists claim that no other principles of communication are needed. In this way, they reject Grice's co-operative principle and maxims while retaining his central insights about the inferential nature of communication and the importance of speaker intentions.

For a general survey and bibliography, see Levinson (1983) and Schiffrin (1994). Grice's collected papers on pragmatics are published in Grice (1989). For an introductory survey of relevance theory, see Blakemore (1992).

Deirdre Wilson
University of London

References

Blakemore, D. (1992) *Understanding Utterances*, Oxford.
Grice, H. P. (1989) *Studies in the Way of Words*, Cambridge, MA.
Keenan, E. (1979) 'The universality of conversational postulates' *Language in Society* 5.
Levinson, S. (1983) *Pragmatics*, Cambridge, UK.
Schiffrin, D. (1994) *Approaches to Discourse*, Oxford.
Sperber, D. and Wilson D. (1986) *Relevance: Communication and Cognition*, Oxford.

See also: discourse analysis; semantics; sociolinguistics; symbolic interactionism.

prediction and forecasting

The periods and time-horizons considered in relation to specific forecasting procedures may be short term (1 to 18 months), medium term (6 months to 5 years) or long term (over 5 years). Very long-term projections (15–25 years) tend to be more in the nature of perspective plans about the social and physical infrastructure of the country and, apart from the demographic projections, more politically conjectural. There are two basic analytical approaches to forecasting.

The first method tries to outline a pattern of responses by relating the variable to be predicted, such as prices or sales, to all the other significant variables, such as output, wage costs, exchange-rate variation and imports, that policy makers believe exert a strong influence on its behaviour. This approach rests on a view of what factors are important and the inter-relationships between them. A major problem, however, is that most endogenous and exogenous variables are not, in practice, independent. Directly and indirectly the various explanatory and dependent variables react on each other. For example, interest

rates in the USA affect interest rates and prices in Europe, which lead to exchange-rate adjustments. These influence capital flows, which in turn have repercussions on interest rates. The interaction between prices and wages is also well known and has led to bitter disputes as to cause and effect. To a certain extent, however, such difficulties can be handled (or their importance recognized) in the mechanical techniques chosen. Other features of a more psychological nature, involving expectations motivated by feelings of political uncertainty and individual caution, are less easy to accommodate in any mathematical schema.

The second approach produces forecasts on the basis of historical trends and patterns. The procedure tries to quantify and formalize experience in order to replicate, reproduce and extrapolate future trends in the socioeconomic variables of interest (income, production, crime, and so on). The length of past time series, the interval of the observations and their regularity should be closely related to the time horizon considered important. The relationships are rarely of a simple linear or quadratic form and will inevitably reflect a combination of trend, cyclical, seasonal and random shock disturbances.

A particular example of a large and complex economic model of the first kind concerned with short and medium-term projections is the OECD's (1979; 1982) INTERLINK model. This adopts relatively simple techniques to try and assess the overall international impact of various policy stimuli in different countries. The system links together a large number of individual country models through their international trade relations. Although the specifications of these large-scale national models differ widely, their approach is fundamentally Keynesian and mainly expenditure oriented. They are concerned essentially with the impact of government policies on consumption, investment and the balance of payments. This means that although the INTERLINK system focuses primarily on the broad macroeconomic aggregates necessary to produce the OECD's current individual country and overall economic projections, it still retains the same basic multiplier properties of the official national models. The significance of INTERLINK is that it draws the attention of policy makers to the fact that, increasingly, other countries' policies have an important impact on their own nation's demands and the levels of activity in the domestic economies. In the highly interrelated areas of budgetary finance, interest rates and currency exchange rates, such issues assume particular importance. The model also takes into account international feedback effects such as those that occur when the imports of certain countries (for example, Britain and the USA) are affected by the production and exports of another country (for example, Japan), to the extent that these adversely affect the output and exports of the importing countries (Britain and the USA). This leads to lower incomes in the importing countries as well as discriminatory trade policies, so that the demand for the goods produced by the exporting country is reduced and production (in Japan) has to be cut back (unless other new markets are found). National models, however sophisticated, rarely take into account these 'echo' effects, where economic disturbances elsewhere in the international system are subsequently transmitted back to their origin through related variables.

Fluctuations in economic activity associated with expansion, contraction and recovery in production and employment regularly occur in industrial countries; many internal and external factors have been advanced for the existence of such cycles. Whatever the reasons, it is apparent that the fluctuations touch on a wide range of statistical series: income, investment, prices, construction, share values, and so on. Some of these series appear to turn consistently a certain number of months before aggregate economic activity in general. This is not purely by chance; businesspeople themselves look for various signs to guide their current production, pricing and marketing strategies, and they react accordingly – often bringing about the particular outcomes they foresee.

In the area of short-term forecasting especially – the field which tends to dominate official policy concerns at the national level – systems of leading indicators are increasingly complementing the use of specified forecasting models. This is not so much because such indicators more accurately predict the values of economic variables, but because they better identify when and where cyclical changes are likely to take place. Leading indicators are also a convenient and economical way of obtaining an overall perspective of an economy from a large amount of detailed and potentially interconnected data. Good leading indicators should refer to variables which, historically, have had a strong and stable timing relationship with the turning-points of certain economic aggregates during the phases of a business cycle. Such indicators are therefore designed to provide very specific (interval) estimates of the dates for particular cyclical turning-points.

A leading indicator system is usually built around a basic economic aggregate or reference series, such as the gross domestic product (GDP) or total industrial production. Other economic series are then classified as to whether they are leading, coincident or lagging with respect to this predetermined benchmark variable. Among leading indicators are stock market prices (business confidence proxy), interest rates (investment and credit), inventories and orders (sales), over-time and short-time working (employment adjustment) and the money supply. Conceptually, all such variables must satisfy the requirement of some theoretical justification for the observed relationship. As more evidence is gathered over time and the links appear more sound, confidence in certain indicators increases and some series can be further refined to become better 'predictors'.

Michael Ward
University of Sussex

References

OECD (1979) *The OECD International Linkage Model*, Paris.
—— (1982) *OECD Interlink System*, vol. 1, *Structure and Operation*, Paris.

Further reading

Forrester, J. W. (1971) *World Dynamics*, Cambridge, MA.
Meadows, D. *et al.* (1972) *The Limits to Growth*, New York.
Theil, H. (1961) *Economic Forecasts and Policy*, Amsterdam.

See also: mixed economy; planning, economic; population projections.

prejudice

In the literal sense of the word, prejudice means prejudgement. Prejudiced individuals are people who have made up their minds about a certain topic before assessing the relevant information. This sense of prejudgement has formed an important part of the social psychological concept of prejudice. In addition, social psychologists have tended to use the term prejudice to refer to particular sorts of pre-judgements. Although logically it is possible to be prejudiced in *favour* of a group or person, psychologists tend to reserve the term for judgements which are unreasonably negative evaluations *against* a social group. Thus racist, anti-Semitic and sexist attitudes would all be considered prime examples of prejudice. The prejudiced person is seen as someone who has pre-judged a whole group unfavourably and who is likely to be biased against individual members of that group simply because of their group membership. Prejudiced beliefs are assumed to be erroneous or likely to lead the believer into making erroneous judgements. Moreover, prejudiced beliefs are seen as being resistant to change. Thus, Allport (1958), in his classic discussion of prejudice, wrote that 'pre-judgements become prejudices only if they are not reversible when exposed to new knowledge'.

Social psychologists have argued that the prejudiced person's error derives, in part, from a tendency to think about social groups in terms of stereotypes. In one of the first psychological investigations of stereotypes, Katz and Braly (1935) found that White US college students had a widespread tendency to ascribe clichéd descriptions, or stereotypes, to social groups. Blacks would be classed as 'superstitious' and 'lazy'; Jews as 'mercenary' and 'grasping'; Turks as 'cruel' and 'treacherous', and so on. By thinking in terms of such stereotypes, prejudiced people not only entertain unfavourable views about groups as a whole, but also exaggerate the percentage of individuals who might happen to possess the stereotyped trait.

Some of the most famous psychological theories of prejudice have offered motivational or psychoanalytic explanations to explain stereotyped thinking. For example, Adorno et al. (1950) argued that prejudiced people tended to have an authoritarian personality. The authoritarian, according to Adorno, was motivated by an intolerance of ambiguity, which stemmed from childhood experiences of rigid, loveless parents. The intolerance of ambiguity was reflected in a need to think about the world in rigid, hierarchical ways. Authoritarians sought hero figures to whom exaggerated respect could be shown; also they needed 'inferior' groups, on whom their own repressed insecurities and fears could be projected. The result was a brittle, suspicious personality, driven to despise and stereotype outgroups.

There is a fundamental problem with motivational explanations of prejudice, such as the theory of authoritarianism. They have difficulty explaining widespread prejudiced beliefs. For example, studies showed that racist beliefs among White South Africans could not be fully explained in terms of the authoritarian personality. Whereas most Whites in South Africa held prejudiced beliefs about blacks, only about 10 per cent could be said to have full authoritarian personalities. Racist, sexist or xenophobic prejudices are frequently not held for deep-seated motivational reasons, but because they form part of the 'common sense' which is generally accepted in racist, patriarchal or nationalist societies.

Many social psychologists have concentrated upon examining what Henri Tajfel (1981) called the 'cognitive aspects of prejudice'. This research has suggested that a considerable amount of prejudiced thinking is not the result of 'abnormal' psychological processes, but is a by-product of much more normal patterns of thinking. Thus, psychologists have sought to show how people's presuppositions affect the ways in which new information is interpreted. They have suggested that the act of categorizing stimuli leads to errors of simplification, resembling the errors of stereotyping. Moreover, experiments have demonstrated the extent to which people tend to search for evidence which confirms their presuppositions and to ignore contradictory

evidence; also there are findings about tendencies to overgeneralize, or draw confident conclusions from a small number of cases (Hamilton and Trolier 1986). For example, a person, who views a particular group as lazy, will often unconsciously interpret any ambiguous behaviour on the part of a group member as conforming to the stereotype of laziness. Similarly, the behaviour of the hard-working group member may pass unnoticed, or be discounted as 'exceptional'. Since majority groups in a society have the power to disseminate stereotypes about minority groups, stereotypes will often pass as common sense and believers will constantly be finding confirming evidence. They will be unaware of the extent to which their own cognitive biases, and the power of the majority group, have helped to create such apparent evidence.

There has been growing recognition that prejudiced thinking may not be as cognitively simple as earlier investigators had assumed. In particular, people can express prejudices without making unqualified statements about *all* Jews, *all* Blacks, or *all* women, etc. In fact, prejudiced persons often protect their stereotypes by admitting exceptions. For these reasons, a number of social psychologists have been paying close attention to the discourse which is used to formulate prejudiced views (van Dijk 1993; Wetherell and Potter 1993). Discourse studies have revealed the subtleties of prejudice. In contemporary western societies, there is a general acceptance that prejudice is wrong. Many speakers, wishing to avoid being seen as prejudiced, will not use blatant stereotyping to the same extent that, for example, the subjects in the Katz and Braly study did. In consequence, speakers will adopt complex discursive strategies to make negative evaluations of minority groups; they will disclaim prejudice, while simultaneously expressing prejudice (Billig 1991). Phrases such as 'I'm not prejudiced but . . .' are typically used to preface condemnatory remarks against outgroups. These phrases illustrate how the notion of prejudice itself has become very much part of the discourse of prejudice.

Michael Billig
Loughborough University of Technology

References

Adorno, T. W., Frenkel-Brunswik, E., Levinson, D. J. and Sanford, R. N. (1950) *The Authoritarian Personality*, New York.

Allport, G. W. (1958) *The Nature of Prejudice*, Garden City, NY.

Billig, M. (1991) *Ideology and Opinions*, London.

Hamilton, D. L. and Trolier, T. K. (1986) 'Stereotypes and stereotyping: an overview of the cognitive approach', in J. F. Dovidio and S. L. Gaertner (eds) *Prejudice, Racism and Discrimination*, Orlando, FL.

Katz, D. and Braly, K. W. (1935) 'Racial prejudice and racial stereotypes', *Journal of Abnormal and Social Psychology* 30.

Tajfel, H. (1981) *Human Groups and Social Categories*, Cambridge, UK.

van Dijk, T. A. (1993) *Elite Discourses and Racism*, Newbury Park, CA.

Wetherell, M. and Potter, J. (1993) *Mapping the Language of Racism*, London.

Further reading

Dovidio, J. F. and Gaertner, S. L. (eds) (1986) *Prejudice, Racism and Discrimination*, Orlando, FL.

See also: attitudes; labelling theory; racism; social psychology; stereotypes; stigma.

prestige

The word prestige comes from the medieval Latin *prestigiae*, meaning a conjurer's tricks or deception. There still clings to the term a rich hint of illusion. Present usage covers a variety of meanings, including the conception of prestige as a fixed attribute of positions in the stratification order (Rothman 1978), the conception that prestige is relational, based on the evaluation and recognition by the audience of the bearer's claims (Goode 1978; Simmel 1950), and a rarer view that prestige is the aura of success or glamour projected by the individual. On these definitions, the location of prestige could be in the social structure, or the relationship between bearer and audience, or the innate qualities of the person or group. Variations abound: for example, Eisenstadt (1968) mentions that prestige, a basic societal reward, is symbolic of the individual's status. Goldthorpe and Hope (1972) define prestige as a form of symbolic power that eventuates in structured relationships of deference and honour. T. H. Marshall (1964) addresses the problem of using prestige interchangeably with, or in place of, status. He sees prestige as less formal and institutionalized, more dynamic and person-centred than status. Hence, he calls prestige 'personal social status', distinguishing it from 'positional social status'.

Prestige can be achieved through personal effort or ascribed by inherited characteristics. It is usually demonstrated by material or symbolic rewards which the bearer sports or manipulates.

Prestige can be attributed to a person, a group or any social unit, varying along a continuum from high to low prestige; its acknowledgement might be limited to a small circle or expanded to a larger one. Prestige is always a scarce commodity, its allocation uneven. In every society, reflective of cultural values, some groups are defined as inherently worthy, and others are perceived as incapable of prestige.

People make evaluations of whether or not prestige is deserved. Even when claims are spurious, the audience can accept and anoint the undeserving prestigious; it can reject claims that at other times might have been seen as genuine. Important attributes of the audience are its values, size and its commitment to the prestige object. Attributes of the bearer centre on the basis of prestige, manner of expression, and response to the audience. Benefits acrue to both sets of participants: to the bearer go direct rewards, to the audience might come a sense of identification with the mighty or the beautiful or the talented (Turner 1964), and the possibility of community with each other.

The values which are considered worthy and which prestigious individuals come to symbolize vary from locale to locale, their number increasing with the complexity of the society. Each social hierarchy – class, status, power – can generate prestige. As C. Wright Mills (1963), tells us, 'A society may, in fact, contain many hierarchies of prestige, each with its own typical bases and areas of bestowal.'

A sizeable literature testifies that occupation is perceived by many sociologists as the primary source of prestige. The landmark study (National Opinion Research Center 1946), based on interviews in which people were asked to rank occupations, yielded a prestige scale. Many studies have replicated and extended the findings, establishing that nationally and internationally (Inkeles and Rossi 1956) people tend to agree on the relative prestige of occupations. However, a basic criticism has been posed (Goldthorpe and Hope, 1972; 1974): just what do the scales *actually measure*? The facile response that they reflect prestige values is open to question.

Charlotte Wolf
Memphis State University

References

Eisenstadt, S. N. (1968) 'Prestige, participation, and strata formation', in J. A. Jackson (ed.) *Social Stratification*, Cambridge, UK.

Gerth, H. and Mills, C. W. (1953) *Character and Social Structure*, New York.

Goldthorpe, J. H. and Hope, K. (1972) 'Occupational grading and occupational prestige', in K. Hope (ed.) *The Analysis of Social Mobility: Methods and Approaches*, Oxford.

—— (1974) *The Social Grading of Occupations: A New Approach and Scale*, Oxford.

Goode, W. J. (1978) *The Celebration of Heroes: Prestige as a Social Control System*, Berkeley, CA.

Inkeles, A. and Rossi, P. (1956) 'National comparisons of occupational prestige', *American Journal of Sociology* 61.

Marshall, T. H. (1964) *Class, Citizenship, and Social Development*, Garden City, NY.

Mills, C. W. (1963) 'The sociology of stratification', in I. L. Horowitz (ed.) *Power, Politics and People*, New York.

Reiss, A. J. Jr (1961) *Occupations and Social Status*, New York.

Rothman, R. (1978) *Inequality and Stratification in the United States*, Englewood Cliffs, NJ.

Simmel, G. (1950) *The Sociology of Georg Simmel*, trans. and ed. K. R. Wolff, Glencoe, IL.

Turner, R. (1964) *The Social Context of Ambition. A Study of High School Seniors in Los Angeles*, San Francisco, CA.

Further reading

Spier, H. (1937) 'Freedom and social planning', *American Journal of Sociology* 42.

Wolf, C. (1978) 'Social class, status, and prestige', *Social Control for the 1980's*, Westport, CT.

See also: hierarchy; status; stratification.

prices, theory of

The theory of prices lies at the heart of neo-classical economics. Its twin components of optimization and equilibrium form the basis of much of modern economic analysis. Not surprisingly, then, the theory of prices is also a showcase for economic analysis – reflecting its strength but also exposing its weaknesses.

The neo-classical theory of prices considers a stylized economy consisting of consumers and producers and the set of commodities which are consumed and produced. The object of the theory is to analyse the determination of the prices of these commodities. Given a set of prices, one for each commodity, consumers are assumed to decide on their consumption pattern in order to maximize a utility function representing their tastes between the different commodities. They are assumed to take prices as parametric and to choose commodity demands and factor supplies in order to maximize utility, subject to a budget constraint which says that expenditure (on commodities consumed) cannot exceed income (from selling factors, which are included in the list of commodities). Producers also take prices as parametric, but they maximize profits (revenue from selling commodities minus costs of purchasing factors of production), subject to technological constraints, these profits being distributed back to consumers. Consumers' commodity demands and factor supplies can be seen as functions of the parametric prices and producers' commodity supplies, and factor demands can also be seen as functions of these prices. Given these functions, derived from utility maximization and from profit maximization, we can ask the following question: does there exist a set of *equilibrium* commodity and factor prices, such that all markets clear, that is, the aggregate demand for each commodity and each factor equals aggregate supply?

If such a set of prices existed and if the economy tended towards these prices, then the above theory of prices (that they are determined in a manner so as to balance supply and demand) would have relevance. The existence question was settled in the early post-war period, culminating in the work of Debreu (1959) – for which he was awarded the Nobel Prize in Economics. Mathematically, the problem is one of finding a solution to a set of non-linear equations in the price vector. The major mathematical theorem that is invoked is the *fixed point theorem*, which says that any continuous map from a compact convex set into itself has a fixed point, that is, there is an element such that that element is mapped back into itself. The requirement that prices lie in a compact convex set is met if we notice that the entire system described above is homogeneous of degree zero in prices: scaling all prices by a given number leaves all decisions unaltered. For example, doubling all commodity and factor prices would not alter the optimal combinations of commodity supplies and factor demands: the profit at the old combinations would merely be doubled. Consumers' profit income would, therefore, double, as would their factor incomes and expenditures on commodities; the pattern of consumption and factor supply would be the same as it was before. Given such homogeneity of the system, we can in effect restrict prices to be such that they add up to unity. This, together with the fact that they are not allowed to be negative, restricts the price vector to lie in the unit simplex, which is a compact, convex set.

The next key requirement is that of continuity: we need individual demand and supply functions to be continuous in the prices which form their arguments. As shown in Figures 1a and 1b for a *single* market, a discontinuity in supply or demand functions could lead to there being no price at which supply equals demand. Continuity, along with the other assumptions of the fixed point theorem, guarantees existence of an equilibrium set of prices. But what guarantees continuity? Since the demand and supply curves are derived from the maximization decisions of producers and consumers, the answer must lie in the objective

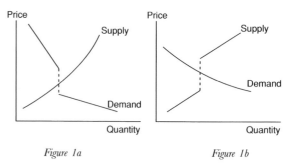

Figure 1a   *Figure 1b*

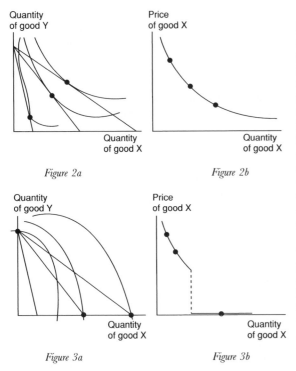

Figure 2a

Figure 2b

Figure 3a

Figure 3b

functions and in the constraints of these problems. In fact, it is convexity of individual indifference curves that guarantees continuity of commodity demands and factor supplies as functions of the price vector. Figures 2a, 2b, 3a and 3b show convex and concave indifference curves, together with the corresponding continuous and discontinuous demand functions. A similar analysis would apply to production technology, profit maximization and the continuity of the resulting supply functions.

If the equilibrium price vector exists, then we have a theory of prices, a theory which relies on the role of prices as co-ordinating the independent demand and supply decisions of individuals, which are based in turn on quite independent optimization. But will the equilibrium price vector be attained? For this we need to consider *dynamics*, how the economy moves when it is out of equilibrium. The simple way of thinking about this is to consider what happens in a given market when the price is such that supply exceeds demand. Then, it is argued, there will be a downward pressure on prices as the excess supply makes itself felt. Similarly, when price is such that demand exceeds supply, the price will rise and reduce this gap. The limit of this process, occurring in all markets simultaneously, will be to move the price vector to its equilibrium pattern. The 'invisible hand' of Adam Smith leads the market to a state of rest.

If the above account were acceptable, then we would have a theory of the determination of prices: the forces of supply and demand would move the economy towards a price such that all markets clear. There are, however, at least two flies in the ointment. First, recall the assumption of price taking behaviour, which formed the logical basis for deriving supply and demand curves. As Arrow once remarked, 'If everybody is a price taker, then who changes the price?' Second, if a market does not clear at the going price, some agents will be rationed: they will not be able either to purchase what they wish to purchase or to sell what they wish to sell. It then seems plausible that they will recalculate their demands on the basis of these new constraints, which, again, destroys the earlier basis for calculation of supply and demand curves.

Orthodox theory has invented the fiction of an 'auctioneer' who performs the twin tasks of adjusting prices in response to disequilibrium, along with the fiction that no trade can take place out of equilibrium, in order to overcome the above problems. But this is no more than a device to maintain the formal structure of the theory. Once the artificial construct of the auctioneer is removed, the theory breaks down. Since the theory cannot guarantee convergence to equilibrium prices within its own logical framework, it is a theory of prices only in so far as the economy is in equilibrium. This is fine for the theory, but supply and demand equilibrium has certain features which are directly at variance with observed reality – involuntary unemployment, for example. Since supply of labour equals demand for labour in equilibrium, and the theory of prices only permits considerations of supply and demand equilibrium, the theory which claims to account for the determination of prices cannot account for the phenomenon of unemployment. These features were stressed by Malinvaud (1977).

The orthodox theory of prices outlined here can and has been extended to cover time, by use of the device of 'dated goods'. A commodity is now defined in terms of its consumption characteristics as well as in terms of its location in time. The number of goods is thus increased by a factor equal to the number of time periods considered in the analysis. Markets are supposed to exist *now* for all future goods, and an equilibrium set of prices is determined in exactly the same way as before. A similar device is used to introduce uncertainty. Uncertainty is captured in terms of a probability distribution over which 'state of nature' will rule at a given point in time. Goods are then distinguished according to the time and the state of nature in which they are consumed: an umbrella today if the sun shines is a different good from an umbrella today if it rains, and each of these is, in turn, different from an umbrella tomorrow if it rains, and so on. Once again, markets are assumed to exist *now* for these future contingent commodities, and prices for these goods are determined by equilibrium of demand and supply. It is, of course, a major requirement of the theory that these markets for state contingent goods exist now. If they do not, then equilibrium may not exist, as shown, for example, by Hart (1975).

To summarize, the modern neo-classical theory of prices attempts to provide a rigorous basis for Adam Smith's claim that an 'invisible hand' leads markets to a situation in which the optimizing decisions of agents are rendered consistent with each other. The modern theory demonstrates precisely the conditions under which this must be true. In doing so in a formal and rigorous way, it shows how implausible it is that equilibrium, even if it exists, will be obtained. Of course, in conducting this analysis, the modern theory neglects institutional features of actual economics – the analysis is in an abstract setting. But it seems unlikely that if the validation of the co-ordinating role of markets is questionable in the abstract setting, it will be any more plausible once the institutional constraints have been introduced.

S. M. Ravi Kanbur
University of Essex

References

Debreu, G. (1959) *Theory of Value*, New Haven, CT.
Hart, O. (1975) 'On the optimality of equilibrium when the market structure is incomplete', *Journal of Economic Theory*.
Malinvaud, E. (1977) *The Theory of Unemployment Reconsidered*, Oxford.

See also: markets; microeconomics; neo-classical economics; value and distribution.

primitive society

Reflecting on the essential conditions of social existence, the philosophers of the European Enlightenment found it helpful to imagine what human life might have been like without government or society. They thought that before people came together to form civil societies, they must have lived in what they termed a state of nature. Individuals in the state of nature were free, independent and equal, but they were also insecure and uncultivated. Granted the capacity to reason, they would have been willing to exchange their rude independence for security and civilization. Yet this choice was not free of risk. Once native freedom was compromised, it might be totally extinguished by a powerful government.

The Darwinian revolution rendered these assumptions quite unacceptable. Early human society was not the product of reason, but must have been a modification of the social forms of other primates. Unfortunately, there were no fossils that preserved these ancient societies. Archaeology can reveal little about the structure of any human societies that existed more than some 7,000 years ago. However, anthropologists were challenged to reconstruct the forms taken by what they called (on evolutionary analogies) 'primitive society'.

A long-standing anthropological project has attempted to find contemporary surrogates for the vanished communities of the past. Perhaps contemporary societies (classically, the Australian aborigines, more recently the !Kung Bushmen or Yanomami Indians) may stand for those frustratingly unknown prehistoric societies. Such societies may be called 'primitive', if indeed they correspond to the primitive form that universally produced more advanced societies.

There are four main empirical reasons against adopting this approach. The first has already been noted: since we do not know what (for example) Upper Paleolithic societies were like, we cannot say which modern societies resemble them.

The second problem with this project is that technology, or even mode of subsistence, is an unreliable predictor of social, political and even economic institutions. It is difficult to make any generalization about all contemporary hunter-gatherers, or small-scale farmers, or herders. Most contemporary foragers do live in small-scale local communities and deploy simple technologies, though some Inuit communities, for example, have for centuries now used modern technologies and established large and complex local communities while continuing to depend on foraging. However, even the hunter-gatherers whose technologies are still apparently traditional and simple vary greatly in ideology, in organization, and in their relationships with neighbours.

The third objection is that the main long-term variations in cultural tradition appear to be regional. The Kalahari hunter-gatherers, or San, for example, have more in common on most measures with the Khoi herders of southern Africa than with the Hadza of Tanzania or the Pygmies of the Ituri, who also lived until recently largely by foraging. If regional cultural traditions are historically deep and shape the ways of life of peoples with very different technologies, then we should pay more attention to regional cultural history than to cross-cultural typologies.

The fourth objection is that there are no isolated modern communities of foragers, or herders, and that therefore the conditions under which such ways of life are now shaped are completely different from those that governed them in the distant past. Upper Paleolithic hunters and gatherers lived in a world of hunters. Modern communities of foragers do not. When they were first studied by ethnographers, all so-called 'primitive people' were subjects of colonial or settler states. All now live as citizens of modern states. They have also all, without exception, been engaged for many generations in social and economic relationships with neighbours who lived very differently.

The consequence is that Kalahari Bushmen, Congo Pygmies, Inuit, and so on, are all adapted socially and culturally to the economic, cultural and political pressures exerted upon them by their neighbours. According to one strand of contemporary thinking, the organization and ideology of foragers must be understood largely as the product of their relations with the larger societies in which they are embedded. Some hunter-gatherers have been driven to live by foraging after living for long periods by farming or herding. All this suggests that the way of life of modern hunters or herders may be a poor guide to that of hunters and herders who lived thousands of years ago.

The theoretical objection to the notion of primitive society has to do with the idea of evolution which it presumes. This is not Darwinian evolution, though the proponents of primitive society make rhetorical claims to the Darwinian legacy, but their assumptions of unilineal progress are foreign to Darwinian thinking. In general, proponents of 'primitive society' assume that all human societies – or, taking a very long view, the human population as a whole, with insignificant local exceptions – pass through a series of similar social and cultural stages. Primitive societies, living or dead, correspond in significant ways to the societies that existed at some unstated period in the distant past when everyone lived in the same way, worshipped the same gods, married by the same rules, voted in the same sorts of leaders, and obeyed the same laws. They then experienced similar revolutionary transformations, in a set sequence. There is no empirical foundation for this fantasy, and no theoretical justification for it in Darwinian theory. Similar objections hold against ideas of 'primitive mentality'. Such ideas have, however, served to legitimate many racialist and imperialist policies.

Adam Kuper
Brunel University

Further reading

Childe, G. (1951) *Social Evolution*, London.
Kuper, A. (1988) *The Invention of Primitive Society*, London.
—— (1994) *The Chosen Primate*, Cambridge, MA.
Stocking, G. (1987) *Victorian Anthropology*, New York.

See also: anthropology; evolutionism and progress; patriarchy; tribe.

principal and agent

Almost all economic activity involves interactions between principals, such as employers and agents who act on a principal's behalf. The employment relationship is just one example. A patient's relations with a doctor are another. More elaborate settings lead to chains of principal–agent relations. An individual may contribute to a pension fund whose manager invests in companies run by board members. The fund manager is an agent in one relation and a principal in another. A principal may have many agents, and be able to compare their performance. Similarly, multiple principals may compete for agents: for example, a household (here the agent) may seek the insurance company offering the most advantageous policy. The relationship is thus one of the most pervasive in economic life.

Although recognized for many centuries, the agency relationship began to be analysed formally in the 1970s as part of a revival of interest in the economics of incentives and of information. Ross (1973) first introduced the principal–agent terminology. This and other contemporary contributions identified imperfect information as a necessary prerequisite for problems to exist. In the case of the employment relationship, for example, the employer can often monitor the employee's output, but not the level of effort. In such cases the employer has to infer the unobservable variable, effort, from the observed one, output, and seek to construct an employment contract which reduces incentives to shirk.

These information problems fall into two distinct categories which Arrow (1991) calls 'hidden action' (or moral hazard) and 'hidden information' (or adverse selection). Examples of hidden action are provided by workers who shirk and by managers who place their own interests above those of the owners of their companies. A classic illustration of hidden information occurs in health insurance markets. Typically the agents (the insured) have better information about their own health states than the principal who recompenses them (the insurer). If everyone is charged the same premium, the sickly will buy more insurance than the healthy. At best this will lead to an inefficient allocation of risks; at worst, the health insurance market will unravel as rising premiums discourage all but the most sickly from purchasing it.

A number of mechanisms exist for dealing with both types of information problems in the agency relation. Shirking in employment can be combated either by direct monitoring of effort, or by a payment scheme in which the employer takes a given amount of revenue and hands the rest over to the employee. But employees are generally reluctant to assume so much risk. As a result, compromise arrangements are developed, such as sharecropping, in which the tenant passes over a proportion of crop to the landlord. When the relation is repeated, the principal can use information already derived from dealings with the agent. Thus an insurance company can raise the premiums of drivers making multiple claims, creating incentives to take care which would be absent in a one-off relation.

Hidden information creates greater problems. In the health insurance case, low-risk customers could be encouraged to disclose their private information by being offered policies under which to cover a larger amount of health costs themselves through a larger excess or deductible. The sickly would refuse such options. However, such desirable segmentation sometimes collapses under the pressure of competition.

Thus analysis of the agency relation has exposed the common nature of many economic problems, but failed to identify universal solutions.

Martin Cave
Brunel University

References

Arrow, K. (1991) 'The economics of agency', in J. W. Pratt and R. J. Zeckhauser (eds) *Principals and Agents: The Structure of Business*, Cambridge, MA.

Ross, S. (1973) 'The economic theory of agency: the principal's problem', *American Economic Review* 63(2).

Further reading

Stiglitz, J. (1987) 'Principal and agent', in J. Eatwell, M. Milgate and P. Newman (eds) *The New Palgrave: A Dictionary of Economics*, London.

prisoners' dilemma

The prisoners' dilemma (PD) is the most studied example of decision making in game theory. Game theory was invented by von Neumann and Morgenstern (1944) in order to examine human strategic interaction. The name 'prisoners' dilemma' derives from a story by Albert Tucker. The police are certain that two suspects together committed a major crime, but do not have sufficient evidence to convict. The suspects are separated and offered a deal. If one confesses allowing the police to convict the other, the police will argue for leniency for the confessor. If both confess, both will receive reduced sentences. If neither confesses, then the police will convict them both of a minor crime on trumped-up charges.

The PD is represented by the following matrix:

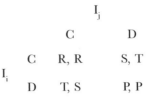

The two players, I_i and I_j, have two possible choices. They choose either C (co-operate with each other) or D (defect from co-operating). There are four possible outcomes represented by the letters T, R, P and S, interpreted as payoffs to each player. Each player orders these payoffs $\{T > R > P > S\}$ (where > means 'preferred to'). Choice D *dominates* choice C because *no matter what the other player does* each prefers D to C (T > R and P > S). Yet when both choose D they each receive their third-most-preferred payoff, P, whereas if both choose C, they receive their second-most-preferred payoff, R. Universal co-operation is universally preferred to universal defection, but universal co-operation is individually unstable (it is dominated) and individually inaccessible (it requires the co-operation of the other).

The game can represent numerous social and political situations such as the decision to join a trade union, whether or not to drop litter, or the decision of nations to co-operate in free trade. In many PD applications there are more than two players, which complicates the analysis. Moreover, in most social situations, the players do not face the decision once, but rather continually interact with each other. Such iterated games may allow co-operative solutions depending upon the degree of interaction, the value of the payoffs, and how much one discounts future benefits against current ones.

Axelrod (1984) ran a series of computer tournaments where game theorists pitted strategies against each other in an iterated PD. One strategy, TIT FOR TAT, which involves co-operating on the first round and then doing whatever one's opponent did on the previous round, won the tournaments. TIT FOR TAT does not allow non-co-operating strategies to exploit it, but is prepared to co-operate with other co-operators. Much has been made of this result to explain the development of both human and animal co-operation.

Keith Dowding
London School of Economics and Political Science

References

Axelrod, R. (1984) *The Evolution of Cooperation*, New York.
von Neumann, J. and Morgenstern, O. (1944) *Theory of Games and Economic Behavior*, Princeton, NJ.

Further reading

Heap, S. H. *et al.* (1992) *The Theory of Choice: A Critical Guide*, Oxford.
Rasmusen, E. (1989) *Games and Information: An Introduction to Game Theory*, Oxford.

See also: collective action; game theory; game theory, economic applications; rational choice theory.

privacy

Privacy as a value is often regarded as an essentially modern development, emerging out of the liberalism of nineteenth-century writers like J. S. Mill (1971 [1874]). In the Classical world, the private was associated with withdrawal from the public sphere and hence with deprivation (*privatus*), while the public arena was defined by positive values and was the social space which embraced freedom. The process of modernization has reversed this moral evaluation, as the public domain is often regarded as artificial and constraining in contrast to the freedom of the domestic domain. The home is a private castle, behind which men enjoy rewards of their labour outside the family. This cultural contrast which equates the public sphere with necessity and the private world with freedom is, from a feminist perspective, characteristic only of men. The private had largely negative connotations, whereas in contemporary society the notion of private is typically associated with privilege (Williams 1976), as in 'private property' or 'private club'. The existence of privacy as a moral criterion presupposes not only a clear institutional separation between the public and the private domain, but also a system of beliefs which emphasizes the importance of the private for the cultivation and protection of individuality. These two conditions developed in the nineteenth century with the separation of the family from the economy, allocating women and children to a space characterized by intimacy and seclusion, and with the articulation of the doctrine of individual liberties in opposition to the state. Like the doctrine of individualism, 'privacy' had a critical and oppositional role as a critique of standardization. While privacy and the private are firmly located in the nineteenth-century process of industrialization, they have many earlier precedents. For example, the Protestant Reformation of the sixteenth century, by emphasizing the importance of the private conscience in matters of doctrinal truth, isolated the individual from the authoritative institutions of the church. Alternatively,

it can be argued (Hepworth and Turner 1982) that the revolution in private consciousness can be traced back through the institution of confession to the penitential handbooks of the thirteenth century. Another indication of the growth of privacy as a moral standard is the emergence of the autobiography as the dominant form of literary expression by 1800. An important turning-point in this development was the retirement of Michel Eyquem de Montaigne in 1570 from public office and the publication of his *Essays de Montaigne*, which exhibit a modern sense of the subtlety of the interior, private person (Weintraub 1978). From a sociological perspective, the evolution of privacy is part of the complex development of individualism, subjectivity and the reflexive self.

While the nineteenth-century evaluation of privacy has precursors, the liberal view of private life is distinctive in that privacy became a peculiar point of anxiety. The private world was suddenly threatened by powerful social agencies: the extension of state power, the threat of mass democracy, the surveillance of the individual in schools, factories and hospitals, the increasing documentation of the individual by bureaucracy, and the professionalization of the police and other custodial occupations. In the heyday of liberalism, Alexis de Tocqueville (1947) noted the danger to personal freedoms which was the unintended consequence of mass politics. In sociology, Max Weber (1930) saw capitalism as an iron cage, which, through 'rationalization', would subordinate people to a new system of public domination and reduce the individual to a mere cog in the machine. Michel Foucault (1977 [1975]) and Jacques Donzelot (1977) have conceptualized modern society as a network of 'disciplines' which police the individual from the cradle to the grave: society, in this view, is a system of surveillance. Within this analysis, modern society is fundamentally paradoxical. A capitalist system requires individualism because the consumption of commodities depends on private hedonism, suitably stimulated by commercial advertising. At the same time, it produces individuation, that is, the standardization of persons for purposes of taxation, registration and surveillance. In this contradiction between private individualism and public individuation, the individuality of the private person is progressively undermined within an administered society. The growth of computer technology and systems of information storage and retrieval reinforces the process by which the public domain invades and undermines the privacy of individual citizens.

From a different perspective, privacy is itself treated as an ideology of capitalist society, specifically John Locke's theory of private property (Locke, 1960). The notion of the private individual is a fact of bourgeois ideology which legitimizes private property through the doctrine of individual rights. Privacy is seen as a primarily conservative belief – a necessary adjunct to private appropriation. The relationship between beliefs and social structure is, however, more complex than this view would suggest. 'Civil privatism' is partly undermined by the development of complex society, because urban life requires a social infrastructure (health, transportation, education, communication systems and leisure), much of which is provided by the state. In the language of Marxist urban sociology, there is a steady growth of collective consumption of urban facilities over private appropriation. The normative image of the private Robinson Crusoe becomes increasingly archaic with the development of capitalist society. However, in East European communism, privacy had been attacked by socialist governments as dangerous and subversive. Critics of state socialism and political centralisation often embraced the values of bourgeois privacy as an alternative to the collectivist values of the party system (Szelenyi 1988). Historical and sociological analysis of the relation between private and public spheres has been significantly influenced by J. Habermas's (1989 [1962]) *The Structural Transformation of the Public Sphere*, in which he argues that the expansion of the state has undermined the division of private and public. Genuine political debate in the polity has been corrupted by the public relations industry.

Bryan S. Turner
Deakin University

References

Donzelot, J. (1977) *The Policing of Families*, New York. (Original edn, *La Police des familles*, Paris.)

Foucault, M. (1977 [1975]) *Discipline and Punish: Birth of the Prison*, London. (Original edn, *Surveiller et punir: naissance de la prison*, Paris.)

Habermas, J. (1989 [1962]) *The Structural Transformation of the Public Sphere: An Inquiry into a Category of Bourgeois Society*, Cambridge, MA. (Original edn, *Strukturwandel der offentlichkeit: Untersuchung zu einer Kategorie der burgerlichen Gessellschaft*, Neuwied.)

Hepworth, M. and Turner, B. S. (1982) *Confession: Studies in Deviance and Religion*, London.

Locke, J. (1960[1690]) *Two Treatises on Government*, London.

Mill, J. S. (1971 [1874]) *Autobiography*, London.

Szelenyi, I. (1988) *Socialist Entrepreneur: Embourgeoisement in Rural Hungary*, Cambridge, UK.

Tocqueville, A. de (1947[1835–40]) *Democracy in America*, London.

Weber, M. (1930[1903–4]) *The Protestant Ethic and the Spirit of Capitalism*, London.

Weintraub, K. (1978) *The Value of the Individual, Self and Circumstance in Autobiography*, Chicago.

Williams, R. (1976) *Keywords: A Vocabulary of Culture and Society*, London.

See also: public sphere.

privatization

Strictly speaking privatization refers to the transfer of assets owned by the state to some form of private ownership, although it has been used more widely to denote any transfer of economic activity to the private sector, such as 'contracting out' of hospital cleaning and joint ventures using private capital. The focus here is on the narrower (ownership) definition, but many of the arguments apply equally to the wider usage.

The word privatization, as well as the concept, came to prominence in the 1980s. The previous term had been 'denationalization', which indicates both the nature of the process and the extent to which it was a reaction against earlier nationalization. However, this is only one of several reasons for the rise of privatization, both economic and political.

The basic economic argument is an efficiency one. Traditional theory has always favoured the competitive market solution to the problem of economic organization, but it also recognizes that the presence of monopoly may undermine this conclusion; this is especially true of 'natural monopolies', such as those in the energy, transport and communications sectors, where competition is not practicable. The choice between public and private ownership then comes down to a decision as to whether the benefits of private ownership in terms of greater incentives for economic efficiency and freedom from interference by civil servants and politicians outweigh the benefits of public ownership in terms of controlling a monopoly. For thirty years after the Second World War the consensus favoured public ownership; since the late 1970s many of the arguments for state ownership have faded from view as the *zeitgeist* of the 1980s led to a preference for private ownership and market solutions in general.

Thus one aim of privatization has been the promotion of wider share ownership. A more practical reason, hinted at earlier, was the perceived failure of nationalization. Also the natural monopoly argument for public ownership was weakened by technical change in some industries, and by the realization that it applied only to parts of others.

Finally there are financial objectives. The simplest is that privatization is a way of raising money for the government, permitting a reduction in other sources such as taxation. Also the industries are then able to use the normal capital markets for their investment needs. In some cases this is reinforced by national accounting conventions: in the UK, nationalized industry borrowing is included in the public sector borrowing requirement, and reducing this has been a major target of government policy.

Clearly not all the objectives on this list are mutually compatible: the more competition is introduced, for example, the lower the proceeds of a privatization are likely to be. The weights given to different objectives will be reflected in the method of privatization used. The most conspicuous has been the public flotation, where the industry is converted into a corporation and shares are then sold to the public. Alternatives include debt-financed management buy-outs, in which the firm is sold to its existing management, and trade sales to another private company.

Judging the success or otherwise of privatization is complicated by the need to disentangle the effects of the change of ownership from those of changes in the level of competition, and often in technology, which occurred at the same time. However, criticism has generally been strongest where monopolies were privatized without the introduction of any real competition, and where shares were heavily underpriced.

By definition privatization cannot continue indefinitely; eventually the supply of state-owned assets must run out. In the UK, for example, the majority had been sold by the mid-1990s. Worldwide, however, the policy seems set for a long run. The collapse of communism, and the opening up of much of Eastern Europe after 1989, led many countries there to see privatization as a fast route to a market economy, as well as attracting capital from the west. The policy has also had some support in developing countries, although the balance of the arguments there can be different. Often the share of investment accounted for by public enterprise is very high, and its role in national planning means that privatization is not seen as an attractive option.

Stephen Trotter
University of Hull

Further reading

Armstrong, M., Cowan, S. and Vickers, J. (1994) *Regulatory Reform: Economic Analysis and British Experience*, Cambridge, MA.

Curwen, P. (1986) *Public Enterprise: A Modern Approach*, Brighton.

Ott, A. F. and Hartley, K. (eds) (1991) *Privatization and Economic Efficiency*, Aldershot.

Parker, D. (1991) 'Privatisation ten years on', *Economics* 27.

Veljanovski, C. (ed.) (1989) *Privatisation and Competition*, London.

See also: nationalization; regulation.

problem solving

Problem solving is a major function of thought and has long been researched in cognitive psychology. Since the information-processing approach to cognitive psychology became theoretically dominant in the early 1960s, thinking has generally been regarded as a serial symbol manipulation process that makes use of a very limited working memory, supported by an extensive long-term memory. This approach has been fruitful and, by emphasizing both analysis and organization, largely avoids the dangers of elementarism and vagueness which had beset the earlier behaviourist and Gestalt approaches. Although connectionist approaches, which postulate considerable parallel processing among a large number of simple elements, have been put forward as latter-day versions of Gestalt theory, which may explain problem structuring and restructuring (Holyoak and Spellman, 1993), little detailed work has been carried out on this project. Most research on problem solving is still in the now classical tradition of serial symbol processing. Much research on problem solving has focused on move problems and reasoning problems.

Move problems

In this class of well-defined tasks, objects or quantities have to be manipulated (in reality or symbolically) in order to change some given starting configuration into a goal configuration. Normally, the available moves or actions are specified for the would-be solver at the start. Move problems may or may not involve an adversary. Non-adversary move puzzles have been extensively investigated. The importance of prior experience with the problem area has clearly emerged in the study of adversary move problems. De Groot (1965) found that both amateur and grandmaster chess players searched mentally to similar extents when asked to choose the best next move in a given board position; but the grandmasters always came up with a better move. A series of studies involving memory for realistic and randomly arranged chess boards showed that grandmasters have developed a very extensive network of familiar patterns in terms of which they can efficiently encode new positions (Chase and Simon 1973 de Groot 1965). More recent research, using larger numbers of subjects and a wider range of skill, has also shown that, in fact more skilled players search more deeply than less skilled players and are better at evaluating the potential of intermediate positions (Charness 1991; Holding 1985).

Reasoning problems

Deductive and inductive reasoning problems have been the focus of considerable attention. In the deductive area, the syllogism has been a favourite experimental task. The somewhat venerable 'atmosphere' hypothesis, according to which the presence of particulars or negatives in the premises colours the conclusions reached

(Woodworth and Sells 1935), still seems to be *descriptively* useful in summarizing error patterns (Begg and Denny 1969), although the explanation for these patterns remains controversial, for the following reasons.

The arguments of Henle (1962) for human rationality, which stressed the discrepancies between experimenters' and subjects' interpretations of syllogistic tasks, have been very influential. Phenomena that are not accounted for by the atmosphere hypothesis have been uncovered, for example Johnson-Laird's finding that the figure of the premises affects the nature of the conclusion drawn. Johnson-Laird (1983; 1993) was able to account for this 'figural bias' effect and for other fine grain results with a computer simulation that embodied his very influential 'theory of reasoning' as a process of working with *mental models* of the situations described by the premises. Poor performance is explained by failure of subject to consider all possible mental models that could be consistent with the premises. More difficult problems tend to have more alternative models to be considered. Wetherick (1989; Wetherick and Gilhooly 1990) has proposed a simpler explanation in terms of a matching bias where subjects match their conclusion to the logical form of the last possible premise in the argument.

Inductive reasoning has been intensively studied, especially in the contexts of concept learning and Wason's four-card task. In the case of concept learning, Bruner *et al.* (1956) noticed a reluctance among their subjects to attempt falsification of current hypotheses, and this apparent 'set' for verification was the starting-point for a long series of studies by Wason and others using the four-card task. In this task, subjects have to say which cards need to be turned over to test a conditional rule relating the showing and the not-showing faces of the cards. For example, the rule might be 'if there is an "A" on one side there is a "4" on the other side'. Given cards showing A, B, 4 and 7, which need be turned over? (Answer: A and 7). Most subjects do not choose the potentially falsifying '7' card. Johnson-Laird and Wason (1970) interpreted this result as showing 'verification bias'. A number of subsequent studies found improved performance if the materials were thematic rather than abstract (Wason and Shapiro 1971; but see Manktelow and Evans 1979 for a cautionary note). Facilitation was also found if the rules were of dubious truth-value (Pollard and Evans 1981) or if certain ambiguities in the standard task were clarified (Smalley 1974). While many have interpreted the above pattern of results in a manner akin to Henle's analysis of interpretation factors in syllogistic reasoning, Evans (1980) proposed that most responses to the standard abstract form of the task are due to an unconscious, non-rational, 'matching bias'. Supporting evidence comes from the high success rates found with negative 'if–then' rules, coupled with zero

transfer to positive rules. In the case of thematic versions of the rule, better performance seems to be due to the elicitation of a 'familiar reasoning schema' for 'permissions', which maps on to the conditional rule (Cheng and Holyoak 1985).

Conclusion

Overall, the results of research on problem solving are consistent with the standard information-processing assumptions of serial processing, limited working memory and vast long-term memory. Perhaps not surprisingly, data from studies of daydreaming and creative thinking suggest, however, that more complex models will be required to explain thought in general (Gilhooly 1988) than seem required for the special case of problem solving.

K. J. Gilhooly
University of Aberdeen

References

Begg, I and Denny, J. P. (1969) 'Empirical reconciliation of atmosphere and conversion interpretations of syllogistic reasoning errors', *Journal of Experimental Psychology* 81.

Bruner, J. S., Goodnow, J. J. and Austin, G. A. (1956) *A Study of Thinking*, New York.

Charness, N. (1991) 'Expertise in chess: the balance between knowledge and search' in K. A. Ericsson and J. Smith (eds) *Toward a General Theory of Expertise*, Cambridge.

Chase, W. G. and Simon, H. A. (1973) 'Perception in chess', *Cognitive Psychology* 4.

Cheng, P. W. and Holyoak, K. J. (1985) 'Pragmatic reasoning schema', *Cognitive Psychology* 17.

De Groot, A. D. (1965) *Thought and Choice in Chess*, The Hague.

Evans, J. St B. T. (1980) 'Current issues in the psychology of reasoning', *British Journal of Psychology* 71.

Gilhooly, K. J. (1988) *Thinking: Directed, Undirected and Creative*, 2nd edition, London.

Henle, M. (1962) 'On the relation between logic and thinking', *Psychological Review* 69.

Holding, D. H. (1985) *The Psychology of Chess Skill*, Hillsdale, NJ.

Holyoak, K. T. and Spellman, B. A. (1993) 'Thinking', *Annual Review of Psychology* 44.

Johnson-Laird, P. N. (1983) *Mental Models*, Cambridge, UK.
— (1993) *Human and Machine Thinking*, Hillsdale, NJ.

Manktelow, K. K. and Evans, J. St B. T. (1979) 'Facilitation of reasoning by realism: effect or non-effect?', *British Journal of Psychology* 70.

Pollard, P. and Evans, J. St B. T. (1979) 'The effects of prior beliefs in reasoning: an associational interpretation', *British Journal of Psychology* 72.

Smalley, N. S. (1974) 'Evaluating a rule against possible instances', *British Journal of Psychology* 65.

Wason, P. C. and Shapiro, D. (1971) 'Natural and contrived experience in a reasoning problem', *Quarterly Journal of Experimental Psychology* 23.

Wetherick, N. E. (1989) 'Psychology and syllogistic reasoning', *Philosophical Psychology* 2.

Wetherick, N. E. and Gilhooly, K. J. (1990) 'Syllogistic reasoning: effects of premise order', in K. J. Gilhooly, M. T. G. Keane, R. H. Logie and G. Erdos (eds) *Lines of Thinking*, vol. 1, Chichester.

Woodworth, R. S. and Sells, S. B. (1935) 'An atmosphere effect in formal syllogistic reasoning', *Journal of Experimental Psychology* 18.

Further reading

Garnham, A. and Oakhill, J. (1994) *Thinking and Reasoning*, Oxford.

Sternberg, R. J. and Smith, E. E. (1988) *The Psychology of Human Thought*, Cambridge, UK.

See also: thinking.

problems, social *see* social problems

production and cost functions

Production functions and cost functions are the cornerstones of the economic analysis of production. A *production function* is a mathematical relationship that captures the essential features of the technology by means of which an organization transforms resources such as land, labour and capital into goods or services such as steel or education. It is the economist's distillation of the salient information contained in the engineer's blueprints. Mathematically, let y denote the quantity of a single output produced by the quantities of inputs denoted $(x_1, ..., x_n)$. Then the production function $f(x_1, ..., x_n)$ describes the maximum quantity of output that can be produced by the input combination $(x_1, .., x_n)$, given the technology in use, and so $y \leq f(x_1, .., x_n)$. Several important features of the structure of the technology are captured by the shape of the production function. Relationships among inputs include the degree of substitutability or complementarity among pairs of inputs, as well as the ability to aggregate groups of inputs into a shorter list of input aggregates. Relationships between output and the inputs include economies of scale and the technical efficiency with which inputs are utilized to produce output.

Each of these features has implications for the shape of the cost function, which is intimately related to the production function. A cost function is also a mathematical relationship, one that relates the expenses an organization incurs to the quantity of output it produces, and to the unit prices it pays for the inputs it employs in the production process. Mathematically, let E denote the expense an organization incurs in the production of output quantity y when it pays unit prices $(p_1, ..., p_n)$ for the inputs it employs. Then the cost function $c(y, p_1, ..., p_n)$ describes the minimum expenditure required to produce output quantity y when input unit prices are $(p_1, ..., p_n)$, given the technology in use, and so $E \geq c(y, p_1, ..., p_n)$. A cost function is an increasing function of $(y, p_1, ..., p_n)$, but the degrees to which minimum cost increases with an increase in the quantity of output produced or in any input price depends on the features describing the structure of production technology. For example, scale economies enable maximum output to expand more rapidly than input usage increases, thereby causing minimum cost to increase less rapidly than output expands. Scale economies thus create an incentive for large-scale production, and by analogous reasoning scale diseconomies create a technological deterrent to large-scale production. For another example, if a pair of inputs are close substitutes in production, and the unit price of one of the inputs increases, the resulting increase in minimum cost is less than if the two inputs were poor substitutes, or complements. Finally, if waste in the organization causes actual output to fall short of maximum possible output, or if inputs are misallocated in light of their respective unit prices, then actual cost exceeds minimum cost; both technical and allocative inefficiency are costly.

As these examples suggest, under fairly general conditions the shape of the cost function is a mirror image of the shape of the production function. Thus the cost function and the production function generally provide equivalent information concerning the structure of production technology. This equivalence relationship between production functions and cost functions is known as 'duality', and it states that one of the two functions has certain features if, and only if, the other has certain features. Such a duality relationship has a number of important implications. Since the production function and the cost function are based on different data, duality enables us to employ either function as the basis of an economic analysis of production, without fear of obtaining conflicting inferences. The theoretical properties of associated output supply and input demand equations may be inferred from either the theoretical properties of the production function or, more easily, for those of the dual cost function. Empirical analysis aimed at investigating the nature of scale economies, the degree of input substitutability or complementarity, or the extent and nature of productive inefficiency, can be conducted using a production function or, again more easily, using a cost function.

If the time period under consideration is sufficiently short, then the assumption of a given, unchanging technology is valid. The longer-term effects of technological progress, or the adaptation of existing superior technology, can be introduced into the analysis. Technical progress increases the maximum output that can be obtained from a given collection of inputs, and so in the presence of unchanging unit prices of the inputs technical progress reduces the minimum cost that must be incurred to produce a given quantity of output. This phenomenon is merely an extension to the time dimension of the duality relationship that links production functions and cost functions. Of particular empirical interest are the magnitude of technical progress and its cost-reducing effects, and the possible labour-saving bias of technological progress and its employment effects that are transmitted from the production function, to the cost function and then to the labour demand function.

C. A. Knox Lovell
University of Georgia

Further reading

Danø, S. (1966) *Industrial Production Models*, New York.
Färe, R. (1988) *Fundamentals of Production Theory*, Berlin.
Färe, R., Grosskopf, S. and Lovell, C. A. K. (1994) *Production Frontiers*, Cambridge, UK.
Frisch, R. (1965) *Theory of Production*, Chicago.
Fuss, M. and McFadden, D. (eds) (1978) *Production Economics: A Dual Approach to Theory and Applications*, 2 vols, Amsterdam.
Johansen, L. (1972) *Production Functions*, Amsterdam.
Shephard, R. (1970) *Theory of Cost and Production Functions*, Princeton, NJ.

See also: factors of production; input-output analysis; productivity.

productivity

Productivity represents a relationship between the inputs used in a productive process and the output they generate. It is increases in productivity which make possible growth in income per head. A considerable amount of work has gone into an analysis of the historic growth process in the western world, in an attempt to unravel the extent to which the growth in output has been achieved through growth in productivity rather than through increases in inputs. Thus Kendrick (1961) looked at the USA, Denison (1967) tried to analyse the reasons for different growth rates in different countries, and Matthews *et al.* (1982) analysed the growth process in the UK. Since the oil crises of 1973–4, growth rates in many western countries have slowed down. Attempts to find explanations for what, to a casual observer, seems to be a reduction in productivity growth are found in Denison (1979) and Matthews (1982).

The essence of productivity analysis is a production function of the type $Y = f(K, L)$ where K, L are inputs of capital and labour respectively and Y is output. A simple notion of productivity growth would be one in which productivity grows in the same way as manna appears from heaven. Thus one may find the production function is in fact $Y = e^{at}f(K, L)$. Here output grows at the rate a, even though there need be no increase in the measured inputs. In his analyses Denison (1979) attempted to decompose this growth in productivity into changes arising from sources such as education, economies of scale, advances in knowledge, and so on. Courbis (1969) presented a clear framework showing how the index number problems of productivity measurement fit into a general scheme of index numbers.

The above production led to attempts to analyse neutral progress as that which is capital and labour saving in equal proportions. If there are constant returns to scale, the above production can be written as $Y = f(e^{at}K, e^{at}L)$, which represents Hicks's (1965) neutral technical progress. But the above approach does not take account of the fact that capital is a produced good. Rymes (1972; 1983) argued that Harrod (1961) produced a more suitable framework in order to allow for this. In such a framework one comes close to arguing that all increases in productivity are attributable to increases in labour productivity. Finally, Bruno and Sachs (1982) made the obvious point that capital and labour are not only inputs to production. Any analysis which fails to take account of changes in raw material inputs may give misleading results.

Martin Weale
University of Cambridge

References

Bruno, M. and Sachs, J. (1982) 'Input price shocks and the slowdown in economic growth: the case of UK manufacturing', *Review of Economic Studies*.
Courbis, R. (1969) 'Comptabilité nationale à prix constants et à productivité constante', *Review of Income and Wealth*.
Denison, E. F. (1967) *Why Growth Rates Differ*, Washington, DC.
—— (1979) 'Accounting for slower growth: the United States in the 1970s', Washington, DC.
Harrod, R. F. (1961) 'The neutrality of improvements', *Economic Journal*.
Hicks, J. R. (1965) *Capital and Growth*, Oxford.
Kendrick, J. W. (1961) 'Productivity trends in the United States', *National Bureau for Economic Research*, New York.
Matthews, R. C. O. (ed.) (1982) *Slower Growth in the Western World*, London.
Matthews, R. C. O., Feinstein, C. H. and Odling-Smee, J. C. (1982) *British Economic Growth, 1856–1973*, Oxford.
Rymes, T. K. (1972) 'The measurement of capital and total factor productivity in the context of the Cambridge theory of capital', *Review of Income and Wealth*.
—— (1983) 'More on the measurement of total factor productivity', *Review of Income and Wealth*.

See also: production and cost functions.

professions

The term profession originally denoted a limited number of vocations which were the only occupations in pre-industrial Europe that enabled people with no unearned income to make a living without engaging in commerce or manual work. Law, medicine and divinity constituted the three classical professions, but officers in the army and navy were also included in the ranks of the professions.

The process of industrialization was associated with major changes in the structure of these older professions, and with the rapid growth of new occupational groups, many of which subsequently claimed professional status. These changes within the occupational structure were reflected in the sociological literature in the attempt, for example in the classic study by Carr-Saunders and Wilson (1933), to define the distinguishing traits or characteristics of modern professions.

This approach – sometimes called the 'trait' or 'check-list' approach – has not, however, resulted in any widespread agreement as to what constitutes an adequate or useful definition of profession. For example, Millerson (1964), after a careful examination of the literature, listed no fewer than twenty-three elements, culled from the work of twenty-one authors, which have been included in various definitions of profession. No single item was accepted by every author as a necessary characteristic of a profession, and neither were any two authors agreed about which combination of elements could be taken as defining a profession. However, the six most frequently mentioned characteristics were: possession of a skill based on theoretical knowledge; provision of training and education; testing of competence of members; organization; adherence to a code of conduct; and altruistic service.

During the 1950s and 1960s many sociologists used this check-list approach to examine occupations such as social work, teaching, nursing and librarianship, in order to see whether such occupations could properly be regarded as professions. However, from the early 1970s, this largely descriptive approach was increasingly abandoned in the light of some telling criticisms, particularly from Freidson (1970) and Johnson (1972). It was argued that those traits held to define a profession were frequently analytically or empirically ambiguous, while the lists of defining elements appeared to be constructed in a largely arbitrary manner, with little attempt to articulate theoretically the relationships between the elements. Finally, critics felt that this approach reflected too closely the ideological image which professionals try to convey of their own work, with an uncritical acceptance of the professions' claims to such attributes as ethical behaviour, altruism and community service.

From the 1970s, the literature on professions became much more critical, and tended to focus on the analysis of professional power, and on the position of the professions in the labour market. In relation to the latter, Berlant (1975) saw professionalization as a process of monopolization, while Larson (1977) saw it as a process of occupational mobility based on securing control of a particular market. However, the dominant influence throughout the 1970s and 1980s was probably that of Freidson and Johnson, for both of whom the central problems concerned professional power.

Freidson argued that it is professional autonomy – the power of the professions to define and to control their own work – which is the distinguishing characteristic of the professions. In this perspective, specialized knowledge or altruistic behaviour are *not* seen as essential characteristics of professions. However, claims to such attributes – whether valid or not – may be important in the professionalization process in so far as they constitute the rhetoric in terms of which occupational groups seek to obtain from the state special privileges, such as a system of licensing and self-government, and a protected market situation. The professionalization process is thus seen as essentially political in character, a process 'in which power and persuasive rhetoric are of greater importance than the objective character of knowledge, training and work'.

Johnson's work centred on the analysis of practitioner–client relationships. He noted that those occupations which are conventionally labelled 'professions' have, at various times and in various places, been subject to a variety of forms of social control. Thus, in certain contexts, practitioners may be subject to control by powerful clients (patronage), or practitioner – client relationships may be mediated by a third party, such as the church or state (mediate control). The term 'professionalism' is reserved for a particular form of occupational control, involving a high degree of self-regulation and freedom from external control which, in its most developed form, was a product of the specific social conditions in nineteenth-century Britain and the USA.

Abbott (1988; 1991) has argued that professions are exclusive occupational groups which exercise jurisdiction over particular areas of work. This jurisdiction is held to rest on the control of a more-or-less abstract, esoteric and intellectual body of knowledge; groups lacking such knowledge (e.g. police as opposed to lawyers) have generally been unsuccessful in their attempts to professionalize. What is distinctive about Abbott's approach is not his definition of profession, but his insistence that professionalization cannot be understood as a simple linear development of individual occupations considered in isolation for, since the jurisdiction of one profession pre-empts that of others, the developments of the various professions must be seen as interdependent.

There remain numerous and sometimes conflicting definitions of profession. Abbott (1991) has noted this confusion and has suggested that 'to start with definition is thus not to start at all'. Perhaps more helpfully, Freidson (1986) has pointed to important differences between professions in Britain and the USA and high-status occupations in continental Europe, and has suggested that professionalism is 'an Anglo-American disease'. He argues that the problem is not created

> by including traits or attributes in a definition. The problem . . . lies much deeper than that. It is created by attempting to treat *profession* as if it were a generic concept rather than a changing historic concept with particularistic roots in those industrial nations that are strongly influenced by Anglo-American institutions.

Ivan Waddington
University of Leicester

References

Abbott, A. (1988) *The System of Professions: An Essay on the Expert Division of Labor*, Chicago.
—— (1991) 'The future of professions: occupation and expertise in the age of organization', *Research in the Sociology of Organizations* 8.
Berlant, J. L. (1975) *Profession and Monopoly: A Study of Medicine in the United States and Great Britain*, Berkeley, CA.
Carr-Saunders, A. M. and Wilson, P. A. (1933) *The Professions*, Oxford.
Freidson, E. (1970) *Profession of Medicine: A Study of the Sociology of Applied Knowledge*, New York.
—— (1986) *Professional Powers: A Study of the Institutionalization of Formal Knowledge*, Chicago.
Johnson, T. J. (1972) *Professions and Power*, London.
Larson, M. S. (1977) *The Rise of Professionalism*, Berkeley, CA.
Millerson, G. (1964) *The Qualifying Associations: A Study in Professionalization*, London.

profit

In terms of business accounting, gross profit is the difference between total sales revenue and expenditure on wages and salaries, rents and raw materials, and any other outlays incurred in the day-to-day operation of the firm. Net profit is gross profit net of money costs, such as interest payable on loans and depreciation allowance. After deduction of tax, profit may be distributed among the firm's owners or retained to contribute to reserve and investment funds.

In economics, profit is also regarded as revenue net of cost, but the costs concerned include imputed costs, as well as expenditures on inputs to the production process. A distinction is drawn between normal and supernormal (or excess) profit. Normal profit is regarded as the income accruing to the entrepreneur. It is the return that the entrepreneur must receive to cover the opportunity costs of the inputs employed. If actual profits are less than normal profits, then entrepreneurs will be able to switch their resources to a more profitable activity. The imputed costs, referred to above, are, therefore, the opportunity costs, namely the returns that could be earned by employing or hiring out the entrepreneur's assets to gain maximum pecuniary gain. Supernormal profits are profits earned in excess of normal profits. In competitive markets these should be zero, in the long run, but in markets with elements of monopoly (or oligopoly) they may be non-zero, hence they are often called monopolistic profits. In pure, perfectly, or imperfectly, competitive markets, excess profits can be made in the short run but, given the assumption of freedom of entry into the market, these will not persist in the long run. Similarly, less than normal profits may be earned in competitive markets, in the short run, provided that variable costs are being covered, but the assumption of freedom of exit will ensure that normal profits are made in the long run. A major factor leading to the persistence of excess profits in the long run, in monopolistic markets, is therefore the existence of barriers to entry to the market.

Profit has been variously regarded as the wages paid to the entrepreneur; as the rent paid for specialist knowledge possessed by the entrepreneur; as the interest on the entrepreneur's capital; as recompense for risk taking; as payment for management skills; and as surplus value expropriated by capitalists from workers.

In connection with modern firms, the view that profit is the return to entrepreneurial risk taking is complicated by the fact that the ownership of the firm is often divorced from its control. In the simple case of an entrepreneur who is both owner and manager of the firm, this return to risk view is attractive. In a limited company, however, the problem arises that it is not easy to see how the risk is divided between the shareholders, who receive the distributed profits, and the management, which may be regarded as essentially salaried employees. The matter is further confused when some of the management holds shares, in the form of directorships, and when the management is responsive to the wishes of shareholders, expressed at shareholders' meetings. It is also to be noted that not all risks need be borne by the firm, since many of them can be converted into a known cost through insurance.

F. H. Knight (1971) distinguished between risk and uncertainty. Risk entails events that occur with known probability and which can be insured against, in principle. Uncertainty occurs due to a change in the environment and entails unforeseeable events. The existence of uncertainty creates an environment in which, even in competitive markets, excess profits may be made in the short run. In the long run, when the change is understood, profits will return to normal. If the world is such that change is continually creating unforeseen events, or shocks, then there will always be newly created profitable opportunities. Change will be signalled by movements in the market price or in quantities, such as sales or inventories, and the firm must decide how to respond to such changes in order to take advantage of profitable opportunities. In order to do this the firm must form expectations of future changes and respond rapidly once prices or quantities deviate from expectations. In a competitive market, if a firm waits until the change is fully understood it will have missed the profitable opportunity, since others will have taken it up already. Lucas (1977) has developed a theory of the business cycle based on responses, in pursuit of profit, to price changes in the presence of rationally formed expectations.

Marx (1898) took a very different view of profit and its source. He argued that labour was only paid wages sufficient to maintain its labouring power. Normal profit then resulted from selling the product at its real value, which included surplus value resulting from unpaid labour. The whole of the expropriated surplus value or profit is not necessarily pocketed by the employing capitalist, however. The landlord may take one part, namely rent, and the money-lending or finance capitalist may claim a portion of surplus value, in the form of interest. The surplus value remaining in the hands of the employing capitalist may then be called industrial or commercial profit. Profit is not derived from land or capital as such, but is due to the fact that ownership of these factors enables capitalists to extract surplus value from workers. Clearly this view has had to be modified by Marxian theorists in the light of increasing ownership of capital, through direct or indirect shareholding, by workers.

Andy Mullineux
University of Birmingham

References

Knight, F. H. (1971) *Risk, Uncertainty and Profits*, Chicago.
Lucas, R. E. (1977) 'Understanding business cycles', in R. E. Lucas (1981) *Studies in Business Cycle Theory*, Oxford.
Marx, K. (1898) *Wages, Prices and Profit*, London.

Further reading

Dornbusch, R. and Fischer, S. (1994) *Macroeconomics*, (6th edn), New York.

See also: entrepreneurship; risk analysis.

progress *see* evolutionism and progress

projections, population *see* population projections

projective methods

Projective methods encompass a wide range of approaches to the assessment of individuals, all of which require the imposition of structure and/ or meaning upon ambiguous stimuli. In addition to this basic feature, projective methods are generally characterized by the lack of any one correct, true or obvious answer and usually provide the opportunity for open-ended, complex and expressive responses, as opposed to simple yes–no or true–false choices. Thus projective methods represent an indirect avenue to the assessment of a person. Personality characteristics are expressed while the person is engaged in doing something else, for example, describing a picture, completing a drawing, or classifying a set of objects. Projective methods involve going beyond the information given and filling in gaps in the evidence provided.

The concept of projection was introduced by Freud (1964 [1894]). It originally referred to a defensive attribution of personally unacceptable characteristics to other persons or objects. Thus an angry person would misperceive his or her anger in the expressions and actions of other people. Freud later recognized that projection could occur in the absence of defence or intrapsychic conflict. Rather, 'under conditions whose nature has not yet been sufficiently established, internal perception of emotional and thought processes can be projected outward [and] employed for building up the external world' (Freud, 1955 [1913]: 64).

Lawrence K. Frank (1939) identified projection as the common feature of an increasing number of personality assessment techniques, all of which provide 'relatively little structure and cultural patterning, so that the personality can project upon that plastic field his way of seeing life, his meanings, significances, patterns, and especially his feelings'. Frank (1939) also articulated three implications of this position. First, projection takes place with a minimum of awareness or conscious control. The person transcends the limits of self-knowledge and reveals more than he or she is capable of communicating directly. Second, the ambiguous stimuli of projective techniques serve mainly as stepping-stones for self-expression. Their specific characteristics are relatively unimportant.

Third, the responses to projective techniques are little influenced by the person's current psychological state or by the social context of their presentation; they principally reveal enduring personality characteristics.

This conceptualization is compatible with psychodynamic theories of personality, such as those of Freud and Jung. Responses to projective methods lend themselves easily to interpretation in terms of unconscious drives, intrapsychic conflicts, defences against them, and symbolic representation of these forces. For these reasons, projective methods have often been described as the 'road royal to the unconscious'.

Other formulations have shifted the focus to conscious operations and processes. Bruner (1948) forged links between responses to projective stimuli and the functionalist theory of perception. In Bruner's view, responses to ambiguous stimuli reflect hypotheses, based on past experience and present expectations. Fulkerson (1965) construed responding to projective methods as a series of decisions made under conditions of uncertainty. Two kinds of uncertainty were distinguished: those based, respectively, on stimulus ambiguity, amply emphasized by Frank and other traditional theorists, and on situational ambiguity, somewhat glossed over in these formulations. Fulkerson (1965) stressed cognitive choices open to the person: to emit or to withhold a response and how to present or communicate it to the examiner, all on the basis of the person's characteristic styles of coping with ambiguity in his or her life. Exner (1989) thoroughly analysed the process of responding to projective stimuli such as the Rorschach inkblots and concluded that only a small proportion of responses is traceable to projection. In the majority of cases, the process is based on the cognitive operations of encoding, classifying, selecting, and articulating responses.

Since 1900, a multitude of projective techniques have been developed. Of these, four varieties have become prominent: inkblots, story-telling tests, graphic techniques, and completion techniques. Projective methods have preponderantly relied upon the visual modality for the presentation or production of stimuli. Auditory techniques consisting of vague sounds difficult to recognize or structure have been repeatedly proposed, but have not gained wide acceptance. The same is true of several techniques that require tactile exploration of stimuli.

Inkblots were introduced by Hermann Rorschach of Switzerland, who developed a test consisting of ten cards. Rorschach also devised a multidimensional scoring system based on location (for example, whole, large, small or tiny detail), determinants (for example, form, movement, colour or shading) and content (for example, animal, human, plant or object). This test has been widely used in clinical and research settings; the

research literature comprises several thousand studies. The results of this work are divergent and complex; some of it supports and some of it refutes Rorschach's and other proponents' claims. In 1961, Wayne Holtzman at the University of Texas developed a statistically streamlined inkblot test. Consisting of two forms of forty-five inkblots each, it allows only one response per card, makes possible determination of test-retest reliability, and exhibits improved objectivity in scoring. Remarkably, it has supplemented (especially as a research tool) but has not replaced the Rorschach, which practising clinicians prefer because of its allegedly superior sensitivity and flexibility. Exner (1974; 1978) has devised a comprehensive Rorschach scoring system and has collected substantial contemporary developmental, clinical and normal normative data. These contributions have revitalized Rorschach usage, especially in the USA.

The Thematic Apperception Test (TAT) was introduced in 1935 by Henry A. Murray of Harvard University. It is still the most prominent story-telling technique in use. Twenty cards are administered; instructions invite the testee to extend the story into the past and the future and to relate the actions, thoughts and feelings of the people depicted. The resulting imaginative account reflects, in Murray's words, the person's 'regnant preoccupations', motives, feelings and fantasies. The voluminous TAT literature has provided support for these claims, but has not yet adequately specified how TAT productions relate to overt, observable behaviour.

Graphic projections are illustrated by the Draw-a-Person and House-Tree-Person techniques. Their interpretation proceeds from the assumption that the person's characteristics are projected into the drawings, produced in response to terse instructions, such as 'Draw a person, any kind of a person'.

In the sentence completion technique, more structure is provided. Despite its manifest transparency and the ease with which it can be faked, accumulated research with sentence completion has demonstrated its value as an auxiliary avenue of assessing personality.

Although projective techniques have been used since the end of the nineteenth century, these methods remain controversial. In general, they stand in a non-random, but highly imperfect, relationship to their non-test referents. They work better in identifying general dispositions or traits, such as aggression or anxiety, than in predicting specific acts, such as suicide or successful performance in a specific, stressful situation. Critics point to imperfect reliability, subjectivity of many interpretations, distortions produced by transient and situational influences, and, above all, by serious and intractable limitations of predictive and concurrent validity. Yet projective methods continue to be used and, after some loss of popularity in the 1970s, appeared to have experienced a degree of resurgence in the 1980s. Their survival as tools of personality assessment is linked to theoretical positions which emphasize the person's subjective experience not only as a determinant of behaviour, but also as a worthy subject of knowledge in its own right.

Juris G. Draguns
Pennsylvania State University

References

Bruner, J. S. (1948) 'Perceptual theory and the Rorschach test', *Journal of Personality* 17.

Exner, J. A. (1974) *The Rorschach: A Comprehensive System*, vol. 1, New York.

—— (1978) *The Rorschach: A Comprehensive System*, vol. 2, *Recent Research and Advanced Interpretation*, New York.

—— (1989) 'Searching for projection in the Rorschach', *Journal of Personality Assessment* 53.

Frank, L. K. (1939) 'Projective methods for the study of personality', *Journal of Psychology* 8.

Freud, S. (1955 [1913]) *Totem and Taboo, Standard Edition of the Complete Psychological Works of Sigmund Freud*, ed. J. Strachey, vol. 13, London.

—— (1964 [1894]) *The Neuro-psychoses of Defence, Standard Edition of the Complete Psychological Works of Sigmund Freud*, ed. J. Strachey, vol. 3, London.

Fulkerson, S. C. (1965) 'Some implications of the new cognitive theory for projective tests', *Journal of Consulting Psychology* 29.

Further reading

Groth-Marnat, G. (1991) *Handbook of Clinical Assessment*, 2nd edn, New York.

Rabin, A. J. (1981) *Assessment with Projective Techniques*, London.

See also: fantasy; free association; methods of social research; personality assessment.

psychiatry

Psychiatry is a speciality of medicine concerned with the diagnosis, treatment and study of mental diseases or disorders. Its practitioners are psychiatrists (in the USA, physicians with several years of approved training following their graduation from medical school). A number of professionals from other disciplines treat patients with psychiatric disorders. The most important of these are clinical psychologists, psychiatric social workers and psychiatric nurses. They commonly refer to those who seek help as clients rather than patients. These professionals may work in various collaborative relationships with psychiatrists or as independent practitioners. They employ the same verbal therapies as psychiatrists. Psychiatry differs from these specialities in being a medical discipline whose practitioners are physicians. As such, psychiatrists are specifically trained to make precise syndromal or aetiological diagnoses, whenever possible, and distinguish one syndrome from another; diagnose (or know when to refer to other physicians) those organic conditions which mimic psychiatric disorders such as brain tumour, cancer of the pancreas, and hyperthyroidism (these conditions can present as anxiety or depressive disorders); treat particular psychiatric disorders with psychotropic medications or other somatic treatments; manage untoward psychological reactions to medical illness; and integrate the biological with the psychological and social dimensions of mental disorders. In addition, the psychiatrist's training in medicine may encourage a research career in the biology of mental disorders. American psychiatrists as a whole have a high level of expertise in psychological treatments, particularly the psychodynamic approach. This is due to the impact of psychoanalytic theory on academic psychiatry especially since 1945, when many distinguished psychoanalysts assumed the chairs of academic departments.

Psychiatry relates closely to other medical specialities such as internal medicine, family medicine, neurology and paediatrics, as well as to many scientific disciplines that contribute to the understanding of mental disorders. These include psychology, epidemiology, anthropology, sociology, genetics and biochemistry.

The range of psychiatric disorders

Although abnormal states of thinking, feeling and behaving may be studied and treated in isolation, more often they are understood as part of specific syndromes, disorders or diseases. In the USA the most widely accepted classification of psychiatric disorders was presented in the American Psychiatric Association's (1980) third edition of the Diagnostic and Statistical Manual of Mental Disorders (DSM-III). Although developed by psychiatrists in the USA, this classification is widely used by psychiatrists in other countries, and by other mental health professionals. The classification attempts to provide a comprehensive description of the manifestations of mental disorders while remaining atheoretical with regard to aetiology. A related classification of mental disorders with broad international acceptance is the ninth edition of the International Classification of Disease (ICD-9).

The following are the major categories of psychiatric disorders according to DSM-III:

– Disorders Usually First Evident in Infancy,
   Childhood, or Adolescence
– Organic Mental Disorders

- Substance Abuse Disorders
- Schizophrenic Disorders
- Paranoid Disorders
- Psychotic Disorders Not Elsewhere Classified
- Affective Disorders
- Anxiety Disorders
- Somatoform Disorders
- Dissociative Disorders
- Psychosexual Disorders
- Factitious Disorders
- Disorders of Impulse Control Not Elsewhere Classified
- Adjustment Disorders
- Psychological Factors Affecting Physical Condition
- Personality Disorders

The manual describes subcategories of these major categories together with specific defining criteria for each disorder. There is a high degree of reliability for most of the disorders; that is, two observers of the same patient are likely to agree on the diagnosis. There is considerable variability in the established validity of these diagnostic categories.

Family and couple therapists criticize DSM-III on the grounds that they regard the couple or the family, not the patient, as the pathologic unit. Behaviour therapists criticize DSM-III on grounds that it is the thought, feeling or behaviour, not the syndrome or disease, that is the pathologic unit. Psychodynamic clinicians are apt to view psychopathology as part of a continuum based on the concept of developmental lines, rather than as discrete disease entities. In addition, they believe that each patient can be described only by a unique and complex formulation. Diagnostic categories are regarded therefore as both conceptually incorrect as well as oversimplifications of human problems. Despite these criticisms, there is a growing consensus among US psychiatrists that DSM-III will prevail and continue to grow in importance through future editions.

There are two extreme and opposing positions regarding psychiatric disease: that psychopathology, both social and individual, is everywhere and that therapeutic intervention may be useful for all human conditions; that mental illness is a myth, and therefore lies out of the purview of medicine.

Conceptual models in psychiatric thinking

There are many conceptual frameworks by which psychiatrists attempt to organize their thinking about patients with mental disorders. The presence of multiple approaches, particularly when they are not made explicit, commonly leads to misunderstanding among psychiatrists and between psychiatrists and other medical professionals, mental health professionals and patients. The four conceptual models most often used are biologic; psychodynamic; sociocultural; and behavioural.

First, according to the biologic model, psychiatric illness is a disease like any other. Its cause will be found to be related to disorders of genetics, biochemistry, and/or the functional anatomy of the brain. Abnormal behaviours are understood as partial manifestations of a syndrome or underlying disease process. In their relationship to patients, biologic psychiatrists behave like any other physicians: they elicit the history through careful questioning, establish a diagnosis and recommend a treatment plan which patients are expected to accept. The biologic approach, after giving psychiatry its classification of mental illness in the late nineteenth century, was generally unproductive until the 1950s. From that time until the present its contributions to psychiatry have included the development of antipsychotic, antidepressant and anti-mania medications; the increased understanding of the genetic transmission of some mental illness; and metabolic studies of depressive disorders. The biologic model has been least helpful in the study of the neuroses and personality disorders.

Second, according to the psychodynamic model, it is the development deficit, fixation, regressive response to current stress, and/or conflict within the mind that leads to psychiatric symptoms. The symptom represents both an expression of an underlying conflict as well as a partial attempt to resolve it. The concept of unconscious mental processes is all important. In their relationship to patients, therapists assume a nondirective posture in order to elicit meaningful associations, as well as to develop a transference reaction in which patients react to therapists as they would to other important people in their lives. The psychodynamic model had its origin with Sigmund Freud in the late nineteenth and early twentieth centuries. There have been significant theoretical developments since 1950 in ego psychology, object relations theory and self psychology. Although the psychodynamic model is a general psychology of normal and abnormal behaviour, it is most helpful in the understanding and treatment of neuroses and personality disorders.

Third, the sociocultural model focuses on the way that individuals function within their social systems. Symptoms are traced not to conflicts within the mind nor to manifestations of psychiatric disease, but to disruptions or changes in the social support system. According to the sociocultural approach, symptoms, disorders or the designation that someone is mentally ill may be seen as social phenomena: responses to breakdown or disorganization of social groupings, attempts at social communication, a cultural or ethnic expression of distress, or a message by the social group that certain behaviours are no longer acceptable. Treatment consists in helping patients to deal better with the existing social system. The sociocultural approach was reawakened in the 1950s. From that time until the present, the psychiatric ward was viewed as a social system, the relationship between social class and mental illness was established, and Federal legislation was enacted to provide psychiatric care for catchment areas in the community.

Fourth, the behavioural model regards symptoms in their own right as the problem. Symptoms are not manifestations of disease, intrapsychic conflict or social breakdown. In order to develop a treatment strategy, the behavioural formulation takes into account conditions antecedent to and reinforcing of the pathologic behaviours. The behavioural model, like the three models previously discussed, began its period of rapid growth in the late 1950s. Behavioural therapists are hopeful of offering several possible advantages to other forms of treatment including a shorter duration of treatment and applicability to a broad range of patients.

Which conceptual approach that psychiatrists use depends on several factors including their own training and ideology, the diagnosis of the patients, and the availability of clinical services. The use of a single approach to explain all psychopathology (including the belief that all psychopathology will ultimately be explained by biochemistry) is reductionistic. In optimal clinical practice, the psychiatrist attempts to understand the patient simultaneously by means of several conceptual approaches or frames of references, while conceding that even the four approaches described above may not exhaust the ways in which psychopathology of people can be understood. Various attempts to integrate several conceptual frameworks have been referred to as systems theory, biopsychosocial approach, multidimensional approach, or eclecticism.

Psychiatric treatments

Psychiatric treatments can be divided into two major categories: the biologic approaches (somatotherapy) and the psychologic or verbal therapeutic approaches. The most commonly used somatic treatments are drugs followed by electroconclusive treatments. Other somatic treatments much less used include insulin treatment and neurosurgery. Drugs may be divided into four major groups: anti-anxiety agents; antidepressant agents; antimanic agents; and antipsychotic agents. The anti-anxiety agents such as Librium and Valium are useful in the short-term treatment of some anxiety states. Their sedative-hypnotic effect makes them also useful for the short-term treatment of insomnia. This class of anti-anxiety agents (benzodiazepines), because of their relative safety, has rendered the barbiturates virtually obsolete. Antidepressant agents such as Tofranil and Elavil (tricyclics) and Nardil (MAO inhibiter) reverse depressive symptomatology, while the antimanic agents such as Lithium Carbonate reverse symptoms of mania or hypomania while sometimes functioning as an anti-depressant. The antipsychotic agents such as Haldol and Thorazine are useful in managing the excitement, delusions, hallucinations and disorientation of various psychotic states in schizophrenia, depressive psychoses and organic psychoses. With prolonged use, the antipsychotic agents can cause tardive dyskinesia, a permanent involuntary movement disorder involving primarily the tongue, neck and facial muscles. Electro-convulsive therapy, the passage of electrical current through the brain, is used primarily for depressed patients for whom drug therapy has failed, has or will produce serious side-effects, or will take too long before exerting a therapeutic effect.

There are hundreds of psychologic treatments. They may be classified according to theoretical approach, structure of the treatment, and duration. In terms of ideology the psychodynamic approach, based on the principles of psychoanalytic theory, is the most widely used. Behaviour therapies which include the specific techniques of relaxation, cognitive restructuring, and flooding have made major inroads in clinical practice since the late 1950s. In addition, there are various interpersonal, existential, Jungian, Adlerian and other therapies. To what degree specific dimensions of each ideological approach are uniquely therapeutic and to what degree there are common therapeutic dimensions of many approaches is a subject of considerable interest. As to structure, the therapist may treat the patient alone, with a spouse, as part of a family, together with a broader social network, or with a group of other patients. When therapy is provided to a couple or to a family, then the couple or family, not the individual, may be regarded as the patient. Most therapies take place once a week but may occasionally be as infrequent as once a month or as frequent as four or five times per week as in psychoanalysis. Depending on the goals of treatment, the sessions may range from one visit (evaluation), eight to twelve visits (brief or short-term therapy), one to four years (long-term therapy), or three to seven years (psychoanalysis). Treatment may take place in a private office, in a mental health centre, or in a psychiatric inpatient unit.

The therapeutic efficacy of the somatic treatments is well established. The efficacy of particular psychological treatments for designated symptoms or disorders has been receiving increasing confirmation since the early 1970s. For certain depressive and schizophrenic disorders, it has been established that a combination of drug and psychological or social treatments is more effective than either used alone. Psychiatric treatment has also been shown to diminish patients' use of medical facilities.

Psychiatry: past and future

Psychiatric illness is not new to modern society. In the Hippocratic writings (400 BC) there are clear descriptions of the major psychiatric disorders. Throughout the centuries psychopathology was described, explained and classified by the great physicians of the time. The degree of sophistication, or lack thereof, paralleled that for medicine in general. There was no autonomous discipline of psychiatry.

The historian George Mora divided modern scientific psychiatry into three overlapping periods. First, from 1800 to 1860, the mental hospital or asylum was the centre of psychiatric activity. It was staffed by a new type of physician, the alienist, totally devoted to the care of mentally ill people. The major accomplishments of this period were the practice of moral therapy, the description and classification of mental disorders, and the study of brain anatomy. Famous names associated with this period are Esquirol, Morel, Kahlbaum, Tuke, Rush and Ray. Second, from 1860 to 1920, the centre of psychiatry moved from the hospital to the university, which could simultaneously treat patients, teach, and do research. The important names of this era include Griesinger, Meynert, Forel, Bleuler, Charcot, Jackson, Kraepelin, A. Meyer and S. Freud. It was Kraepelin who provided a classification of mental disorders that is the intellectual precursor of DSM-III. Meyer developed the psychobiologic approach, trained a whole generation of leaders in American psychiatry and provided the fertile ground for the growth of psychoanalysis in the USA. Third, the period from 1920 to the present has been referred to as the psychiatric explosion. As described earlier, the greatest expansion of knowledge in psychodynamic, sociocultural, biologic and behavioural approaches began in the 1950s.

It is anticipated that by the end of the twentieth century there will be important new developments in psychiatry. These will include greater sophistication in nosology with improved validity for certain diagnostic categories; at the same time there will be philosophical and empirical sophistication in understanding the limitations of the diagnostic or categorical approach to other mental disturbances; significant advances in understanding the biology of mental processes in general and of the depressive and schizophrenic disorders in particular; significant advances in the evaluation of psychologic therapies so that more effective matches can be made between disorder and treatment; significant advances in the integration of biologic, psychodynamic, behavioural and social approaches to the diagnosis and treatment of mental disorders; advances in the integrative efforts between psychiatry and other medical disciplines such as neurology, medicine and paediatrics.

The advances described above will further define psychiatry both as a mental health profession and as a medical speciality.

Aaron Lazare
Massachusetts General Hospital

Reference

American Psychiatric Association (1980) *Diagnostic and Statistical Manual of Mental Disorders (DSM-III)*, 3rd edn, New York.

Further reading

Baldessarini, R. (1983) *Biomedical Aspects of Depression and its Treatment*, Washington, DC.

Brenner, C. (1982) *The Mind in Conflict*, New York.

Gedo, J. E. and Goldberg, A. (1973) *Models of the Mind: A Psychoanalytic Theory*, Chicago.

Greenhill, M. and Gralnick, A. (1983) *Psychopharmacology and Psychotherapy*, New York.

Lazare, A. (1973) 'Hidden conceptual models in clinical psychiatry', *New England Journal of Medicine* 288.

—— (1979) 'Hypothesis testing in the clinical interview', in *Outpatient Psychiatry: Diagnosis and Treatment*, Baltimore, MD.

Lishman, W. (1978) *Organic Psychiatry: The Psychological Consequences of Cerebral Disorder*, Oxford.

Papajohn, I. (1982) *Intensive Behavior Therapy: The Behavioral Treatment of Complex Emotional Disorders*, New York.

Rutter, M. and Hersov, L. (eds) (1984) *Child Psychiatry: Modern Approaches*, 2nd edn, Oxford.

See also: DSM-IV; *mental disorders; mental health; psychoanalysis; psychopharmacology.*

psychoanalysis

Psychoanalysis is a procedure for the treatment of mental and emotional disturbances. Sigmund Freud originated and developed psychoanalysis as a result of his individual researches into the causes of hysteria, one of the common forms of mental illness in Europe in the latter part of the nineteenth century (see Jones 1953).

The unique characteristic of psychoanalysis as a therapy derives from its theory of psychopathology. The central finding of psychoanalysis is that mental and emotional disturbances result from unconscious mental life. Treatment therefore depends upon the ability of the patient, with the help of the analyst, to reveal unconscious thoughts and feelings. The formula that propelled the psychoanalytic method from its inception ('what is unconscious shall be made conscious') remains vitally significant. The changes that have occurred in the formula have resulted from a broadened and deepened understanding of the nature of unconscious mental life and how it functions developmentally in relation to consciousness and to the environment.

According to Freud's first conception of symptom formation, morbid thought patterns occurred during a dissociated state and were prevented from normal discharge because of the altered states of consciousness. The undischarged tensions produced symptoms. The cure required some method of discharge – an abreaction or mental catharsis. By applying hypnosis, the noxious material could be brought to the surface and discharged through verbal association. This chain of inference, formulated first in collaboration with Joseph Breuer (1842–1925) who described his clinical experience in treating a female patient he named Anna O. (Freud 1955: vol. 2), was dependent upon a quantitative hypothesis concerning unconscious mental life and its relation to conscious states. In this pre-psychoanalytic period of research, excessive excitation and the blockage of discharge were thought to produce pathological effects.

A major shift occurred both in research and in the explanatory theory towards the turn of the century. Freud recognized, largely through his self-analysis but also through careful attention to what his patients told him, that a qualitative factor was as important as the quantitative in the pathological process. The unconscious thoughts and feelings contained sexual content and meaning which was linked to arousal, or in earlier language, the quantity of excitation.

The introduction of the qualitative factor altered the theory of neurosis and the therapeutic procedure and, indeed, the method of research. Instead of managing a procedure designed to discharge quantities of noxious excitation stored within the psyche, the problem shifted to uncovering the meaning of the symptoms, and through association, their roots in the unconscious. Hypnosis no longer served the purpose, since it was imperative that the entire treatment procedure elicit the full participation of the patient. Freud asked his patients to recline on the couch and to say whatever came to mind. This method, called free association, created a contradiction in terms. Freud discovered that it was difficult for the patient to carry out his request. Difficulty in associating did not seem to be a random effect, but along with the symptoms could be understood as an inherent aspect of the patient's manner of thinking and feeling and the particular form and content of the presenting symptoms. Freud visualized

the difficulties of free association as *resistance* and as part and parcel of the problem of unconscious content attempting to break through the barriers that guarded conscious mental life.

The research and treatment method, called psychoanalysis, replicated the individual's intrapsychic struggle with the unconscious. Freud's model of neurotic suffering combined both the quantitative and qualitative ideas in the concept of intrapsychic conflict. Symptoms, those alien and debilitating conditions, appear as a result of conflict within the psyche.

According to this model, the terms of neurotic conflict begin with desire; the aim is gratification. The impulse to act, to seek direct gratification of desire, is inhibited by restrictive forces within the psyche. The most familiar type of restriction arises from the individual's moral standards, which render unacceptable the direct gratification of desire. This opposition of the forces of desire and morality produces the debilitating symptoms but in forms that will allow a measure of gratification of desire, however small and costly. Symptoms, resulting from intrapsychic conflict, are the individual's best effort at compromise.

However, as Freud discovered, symptom formation, since it utilizes compromises, follows principles of mental function which apply across a broad spectrum of activity. Therefore, the dynamics of intrapsychic conflict go beyond the pathological and enter into the realm of a general psychology. Normal mental activity such as dreaming, to cite one illustration, follows the same principle as the activity that leads to symptom formation (Freud 1955: vols 4 and 5). A dream is a symptom of mental conflict since it represents a compromise among forces in the unconscious that simultaneously push toward gratification of desire while inhibiting this tendency. The symbolic content of the dream disguises the conflict but also expresses all the terms of the conflict – both desire and prohibition.

This model of intrapsychic conflict underwent a variety of modifications throughout Freud's lifetime. For example, the idea of desire shifted from a dual instinct theory of sex and self-preservation to a dual instinct theory of sex and aggression. Closer attention to the object of desire (in contrast to the aim of discharge) revealed that while its normal pathway was outward towards objects and the environment, it could turn inward, particularly during stressful episodes in the individual's life. But even where desire turned inward, the object remained important in the psychoanalytic theory of conflict because of the observation that the individual retained an internalized image of the object, while seemingly relinquishing it in its real form. Even in the case of the most severe psychological disturbances – psychoses – the individual may appear uninterested in the object world, but the internal conflict evolves around the representations of these objects both in their beneficent and malevolent forms.

The formalization of the model of conflict led to the structural hypothesis that postulates three parts of the psychic structure: id, superego and ego. The id is the part of the mind that generates desire, both sexual and aggressive impulses. The superego is the agency that involves the conscience (the imperatives of 'thou shalt not') and the ideals (the imperatives that one must achieve in order to feel loved and to experience self-esteem). The ego is the executive apparatus consisting of a variety of functions which together mediate the terms of the conflict between id, superego and, finally, reality.

Several problems arise in the application of the structural hypothesis, indeed, in working with all of these superordinate hypotheses in psychoanalytic theory. The hypothesis, which is part of the meta-psychology of psychoanalysis, poses a number of problems in application, both in strict scientific research as well as in clinical work. Some of these problems can be dismissed readily, such as the use of the structural hypothesis as though it referred to 'real' agencies of the mind. The id, superego and ego are abstract concepts, an attempt to organize a theory of conflict. They are not anatomical entities, nor are they especially valuable as a guide to the phenomenology of conflict. But the structural hypothesis and the concepts of id, superego and ego serve a number of intellectual purposes in the theory of psychoanalysis. One example is the concept of resistance, or what prevents unconscious content from direct appearance in conscious images and thoughts. The work of psychoanalysis indicates that the derivatives of unconscious mental life are omnipresent in consciousness, but in such indirect and disguised forms (except in the case of delusional thinking and hallucinations) as to stretch credulity about the idea of unconscious derivatives affecting conscious thinking and activity. The structural hypothesis organizes Freud's observations and conclusions about resistance as a part of unconscious mental life: he posited the need to broaden the term of resistance (from barriers to consciousness) to defence as an unconscious function of the ego to limit the danger that occurs when the pressure to act on impulses becomes great (Freud 1955: vol. 20).

Another problem with the structural hypothesis of psychoanalysis derives from the logical consequences of using this hypothesis to distinguish among and explain the forms and functions of various pathologies. Psychological conflict implies that a psychic structure exists within the individual, so that, for example, moral imperatives no longer depend upon the parents for their force. The individual has a conscience which inflicts some measure of painful anxiety and guilt when unconscious desire seeks gratification.

The classical theory of psychoanalysis presumes that psychic conflict and structure become established during the last stages of infantile development, which is called the Oedipal stage (Freud 1955: vol. 7). In relinquishing incestuous desire, the child of approximately age 5 identifies with the objects and consequently emerges from infancy with a reasonably self-contained psychic structure. The pathologies linked to conflict in psychic structure, the transference neuroses, include hysteria, obsessional neuroses and related character neuroses. These pathologies are called transference neuroses because they do not impair the patient's ability, despite pain and suffering, to establish attachments to objects. However, the attachments are neurotically based in that the patient shifts the incestuous struggle from parents to other people. In the transference neuroses, the relationship to objects is not totally determined by the persistence of neurotic disturbance. For example, a person may be able to function reasonably well with other people except that the person is incapable of sexual intimacy as a result of neurotic inhibition.

Psychoanalytic investigation, especially of the post-Second World War period, has given rise to doubt about some of the formulations of the structural hypothesis and some of its derivatives in the explanation of pathologies. For example, can one clearly differentiate structural conflict from earlier developmental problems which derive from the deficits of infancy? The investigation of borderline conditions (a consequence of developmental deficits) or narcissistic disturbances (the conditions of impaired self-esteem and painful self-awareness), suggest that early internalizations of objects so colour the later identifications as to minimize the effects of psychological structure (see Segal 1964). Critics argue that to treat such patients using classical techniques will prove futile. On the more theoretical plane, the critics also dispute the distinction between transference and narcissistic disturbances because of the importance of object attachments in the latter category of disturbance. Perhaps underlying the controversies within the psychoanalytic profession are more fundamental differences than the suggestion that one or more hypotheses are open to question. After all, any scientific endeavour attempts to disprove hypotheses and to modify the theory as a result of fresh observation and experimentation.

Almost from its inception, psychoanalysis has been the centre of debate in which the contenders, more than disputing particular hypotheses, are engaged in a test of contradictory world-views. As indicated earlier, a tension inherent in psychoanalytic observation and explanation pervades the field. The dialectics of quantity and quality, of mechanics and meaning, colour the evaluation and practice in the field. The tension extends into more abstract polarities: humanity between science and humanism, tragic and utopian views of humanity, and conservative versus imperialistic visions of the place of psychoanalysis in improving human relations.

Freud cautioned against abandoning points of view implicit in the quantitative and qualitative position in psychoanalysis. While he was an artist in his observation of pathology and mental function – (see, for example, Freud's exquisite narrative of an obsessional illness in his case 'The Rat Man' (Freud 1955: vol. 10)) – Freud never abandoned the theory of instincts and its grounding in biology. From early on, the disputes in psychoanalysis have resulted from attempts to frame the theories of pathology and therapy along a single dimension, what Freud called the error of *pars pro toto*, or substituting the part for the whole. Thus, in contemporary psychoanalysis, the stress on developmental deficits over structural conflict arises in part from a humanistic perspective and leads to the use of therapists not as objects in a transference drama that requires interpretation, but as surrogates who will use their beneficent office to overcome the malevolence of the past, particularly of early infancy. These debates within psychoanalysis have strong intellectual, as well as cultural and philosophical, foundations. Some investigators place psychoanalysis squarely in the midst of interpretive disciplines rather than the natural sciences (Ricoeur 1970). They link psychoanalysis to hermeneutics, linguistics and the humanities as against biology, medicine, psychiatry and the sciences. These debates also have economic and political ramifications concerning what constitutes the psychoanalytic profession and the qualifications of those who seek to enter its practice.

Psychoanalysis began as a medical discipline for the treatment of neurotic disturbances. It continues this therapeutic tradition of classical psychoanalysis in broadened application to the psychoses, borderline and narcissistic conditions through variants of psychoanalytic psychotherapy. As a result of its methods of investigation, its observations and theories, psychoanalysis has become a part of the general culture. The applications of psychoanalysis in literary criticism, history, political and social sciences, law and business are evidence of its infusion into the general culture. Writers, artists and critics, while debating the uses of psychoanalysis beyond the couch, understand the theory and experiment with its applications to the arts. Freud gave birth to a therapy and a theory and, perhaps beyond his intent, to a view of the world and the human condition.

Abraham Zaleznik
Harvard University

References

Freud, S. (1953–66) *Standard Edition of the Complete Psychological Works of Sigmund Freud*, ed. J. Strachey, 24 vols, London.
Jones, E. (1953) *Sigmund Freud: Life and Work*, 3 vols, London.
Ricoeur, P. (1970) *Freud and Philosophy: An Essay on Interpretation*, New Haven, CT.
Segal, H. (1964) *Introduction to the Work of Melanie Klein*. New York.

See also: ego; free association; Freud, Sigmund; id; motivation; Oedipus complex; psychiatry; transference; unconscious.

psycholinguistics *see* Chomsky, Noam; first language acquisition; language; pragmatics

psychological anthropology

Psychological anthropology is an area of anthropological theory concerned with relations between the individual and cultural systems of meaning, value and social practice. The field consists of a wide range of approaches to problems that arise in the intersections of mind, culture and society. It has been shaped particularly by interdisciplinary conversations between anthropology and other fields in the social sciences and humanities (Schwartz *et al.* 1992).

Because of anthropology's traditional focus on culture as shared, collective and public, psychological anthropology's concern with the individual in society has often fostered closer contacts with psychology and psychiatry than with the anthropological mainstream. Historically, psychological anthropology's fieldwork-based approach and emphasis upon naturalistic data aligned it more closely with psychoanalysis than with experimental psychology. However, the turn towards cognitive approaches in academic psychology produced new convergences with anthropology in both cognitive science (e.g. Holland and Quinn 1987) and the emerging area of 'cultural psychology' (Stigler *et al.* 1990).

The antecedents of psychological anthropology may be found in the earlier field of 'culture and personality' which emerged in mid-twentieth-century American anthropology. Associated most prominently with the work of Franz Boas's students Margaret Mead and Ruth Benedict, the field was influenced by an eclectic range of writers in anthropology, psychoanalysis and psychiatry, including Edward Sapir, A. I. Hallowell and Gregory Bateson. The long-term goal of culture and personality researchers was to develop a science of culture capable of identifying causal links between psychological processes and social and cultural forms.

Premised on the Parsonian division of the world into 'personality systems', 'cultural systems' and 'social systems', the niche for culture and personality studies was assured. The major questions posed by the culture and personality paradigm focused on the ways that individuals variously learn, adhere to, and/or resist normative values and beliefs. In focusing on tensions between the individual and society, the field studied both the effects of culture in shaping the personal world of the individual as well as the psychological underpinnings of collective norms, beliefs and practices. In its heyday culture and personality theory sought to represent cultural patterns of behaviour in terms of modal personality types, often assessed with projective tests and other psychodynamic methods. During the Second World War, culture and personality theorists were mobilized to work on analyses of the national character of distant enemies. Ruth Benedict's classic study of Japanese character, *Chrysanthemum and the Sword* (1946), was a product of these efforts.

From the 1940s onward, anthropologists using psychoanalytic concepts and methods analysed such varied cultural forms as religious beliefs, ritual practices and social norms as expressions of prevailing psychological processes. Socialization practices have been studied as a primary means for reproducing a society's dominant modes of personality and interaction. In work extending over several decades John and Beatrice Whiting applied methods of systematic comparison to study links between childrearing practices and social institutions and values (Whiting and Whiting 1975). In contrast with their observational methods, studies of individual life histories have been a methodological mainstay of psychological anthropology's attempts to explore cultural influences on individual identity and experience (e.g. Levy 1973).

As the field recognized problems of validity in applying personality concepts and methods across cultures, global studies of entire cultures were superseded by more circumscribed research on specific modes of thought, feeling and action. A number of new directions for psychological anthropology emerged, including greater interest in linguistic and cognitive approaches, studies of the self and ethnopsychology, and research on the culture and politics of the body (Schwartz *et al.* 1992).

The focus of interpretive anthropology in the 1960s and 1970s on problems of translation and representation, together with post-structural critiques of holistic concepts of culture, effectively problematized concepts of both 'culture' and 'psychology'. As images of culture as contested, variable and emergent displaced the view of culture as shared, normative and fixed, research in psychological anthropology became more interested in the interactive practices through which social realities acquire meaning and force for individuals and collectivities alike. This included attention to relations of power through which particular constructions become dominant and imbued with emotional meaning, as well as topics such as intracultural diversity, the politics of emotion, and the social ecology of cognition.

Instead of assuming the universal applicability of standard psychological concepts and methods, current studies examine the relevance of specific models of emotion and person across cultures. Similar to A. I. Hallowell's (1955) studies of the cultural construction of the self among the Ojibwa, research explores the terms and functions of local psychologies or 'ethnopsychologies'. In this regard, the entire field of cultural anthropology has become more psychological, spawning a large number of person-centred ethnographies concerned with cultural practices that create and manipulate social and emotional realities.

Comparative studies of concepts of personality and emotion in a variety of languages show a wide range of both intra- and intercultural variation. As anthropological studies of emotion multiplied, so did awareness of the semantic complexities of emotion across cultures, as well as of the social and political significance of emotion generally. Once regarded as the province of psychology concerned with the inner dynamics of the mind, emotions and motivations are now studied in ethnographic research examining their significance in ordinary talk and interaction. Questions about the universal versus culturally specific aspects of psychology are pursued in the context of research on the social and semiotic means through which people make sense of their lives.

Geoffrey M. White
East-West Center, Honolulu

References

Benedict, R. (1946) *The Chrysanthemum and the Sword*, New York.

Hallowell, A. I. (1955) *Culture and Experience*, Philadelphia, PA.

Holland, D. and Quinn, N. (eds) (1987) *Cultural Models in Language and Thought*, Cambridge, UK.

Levy, R. (1973) *The Tahitians: Mind and Experience in the Society Islands*, Chicago.

Schwartz, T., White, G. and Lutz, C. (eds) (1992) *New Directions in Psychological Anthropology*, Cambridge, UK.

Stigler, J., Shweder, R. and Herdt, G. (eds) (1990) *Cultural Psychology: Essays on Comparative Human Development*, Cambridge, UK.

Whiting, B. B. and Whiting, J. W. M. (1975) *Children of Six Cultures: A Psychocultural Analysis*, Cambridge, MA.

See also: cultural anthropology.

psychology

The word psychology has (at least in the UK), no legal definition. Although anyone can call themselves a psychologist, most of those who do so would relate the term to holding at least a university first degree or equivalent with that label, and many would consider a further qualification, and/or experience in a particular area, to be necessary also. They would regard psychology as the more-or-less scientific study of the behaviour and experience of human beings. They would distinguish themselves rather sharply from psychiatrists, that is, medically qualified persons specializing in mental and behavioural disorders, and very sharply from psychoanalysts, taken as practitioners of the particular treatment method derived from that of Freud (and, loosely, other related methods). Despite these conceptual distinctions, there is a degree of overlap in practice. Many psychologists deal with exactly the same kinds of problems as do psychiatrists, and both may employ psychoanalytic methodology. However, psychologists are found in a far wider range of activities. It is with psychology as academically qualified psychologists regard it that this entry is concerned.

The remark that 'psychology has a long past, but only a short history' was made by Hermann Ebbinghaus in 1908 and has been quoted ever since. It still has some force, inasmuch as what we conventionally label psychology, an attempt at a systematic scientific study analogous to other sciences, can be said to originate in the mid-nineteenth century. The accepted date for the first psychological laboratory, that of Wilhelm Wundt at Leipzig, is 1879, while the beginning of psychometric measurements is often taken as Francis Galton's book *Hereditary Genius* of 1869. However, the problems that psychologists face have been around presumably as long as the human race. All societies that we are aware of have tried to deal with them, with varying levels of sophistication. There is currently considerable interest in such 'indigenous psychologies', both in our own culture (lay theories) and in others.

The label, however, is ethnocentrically used for 'our' psychology. Like all such labels (history, chemistry, etc.) it is actually used to refer to several quite distinct areas. Three of them I distinguish as discipline, profession and subject. By *discipline* is meant a set of problems that seem to be related, and the methods and theories that have been developed in the attempt to solve them. By *profession* is meant a set of people who engage in such work, whether as researchers, teachers or practitioners; they may or may not be formally organized. By *subject* is meant the selection of material and resources for teaching and general dissemination. All of these can be

analysed further. Thus, within the discipline of psychology, the problems and their investigation have a reflexive relationship. What psychologists do and say is part of their own subject matter, indeed contributes to its changing nature. The bottom line in a sense is that every explanation is itself an explicandum; any theory about human behaviour is itself a piece of behaviour, which needs to be fitted into the theory. Thus no theory can ever by complete. More generally, there can be little doubt that (western) human behaviour now is not the same thing as it was in the mid-1890s and that this is at least partly due to the impact of psychological (and related) work; perhaps especially, psychoanalysis and psychometrics.

Psychology in turn changes because behaviour changes; human abilities exist now, for example for flying jet fighters or programming computers, that did not in the nineteenth century. It was not that there were a lot of frustrated would-be computer buffs, any more than there were machines in search of users. Without the hardware and software there was no corresponding mental activity, or, as it might be put, there can be no ability without achievement.

All the disciplines concerned with human behaviour necessarily overlap in scope, but each can be said to have a characteristic focus of interest and methodology. The focus of history is, rather simply, the past; that of medicine, disease, or health, or both. The focus of psychology may be regarded as the behaviour and experience of the individual. The general aim can be, variously, to understand, explain, predict and control these. Some psychological approaches emphasize an empathic, intuitive understanding, but the majority attempt something analogous to other sciences, based on the formulation of hypotheses that can be tested against objective empirical data, ideally by experiments in which relevant variables can be manipulated and extraneous ones controlled. Other human studies such as history or anthropology can rarely experiment. Even in psychology it is not always possible. There are many variables that cannot be manipulated for ethical or practical reasons. Some investigations have to employ naturally occurring variations, for example in examples of twins or of cultural differences in childrearing; some rely on observed correlations between variables; others may be largely descriptive. Some information can be got only by introspection – having people tell us what they are thinking, for example. However, all these methods can be used to gather data more or less systematically and objectively; most investigations seek to employ designs and statistical analyses that are sophisticated enough to allow it to be said with confidence whether the results are meaningful or accidental. It is this that most fundamentally differentiates a psychological approach from the traditional ways of dealing with human behaviour, which are based partly on reason but too often on convention, prejudice, hearsay, politics and so on. The reflexive nature of psychology may mean that complete objectivity is not possible, but few theorists would now claim this for any science; it does not mean that greater objectivity cannot always be sought.

There are numerous, if not infinite, ways of thinking about human behaviour, and psychology has tended at any one time to be dominated by one mode of thinking, although never exclusively, and in each case embracing quite wide variations. For most of the first part of the twentieth century (roughly 1910 to 1960) the dominant mode was the 'behaviourist' one. This ranged from the relatively simplistic view that behaviour was all that could be observed, and (thus) all that could be postulated or theorized about, to the far more sophisticated experimental analysis of behaviour developed by B. F. Skinner and followers. Since the 1950s a 'cognitive' mode has been dominant, which emphasizes the attempt to construct models of what goes on in the mind/brain, with an input from work on artificial intelligence. Rapidly coming to the fore in the 1990s, however, is what may be called a 'cultural' mode, which lays stress on the way in which human behaviour is not just influenced by, but symbiotically created by, its social context. The focus is on the individual, but as an aspect of a complex whole.

The *profession* of psychology, can be considered to comprise all those who are actively engaged with the problems of individual behaviour and experience, whether by way of teaching, research or practice. Most industrialized countries have developed a system of licensing professional psychologists, generally on the basis of a recognized degree plus specific further qualifications and experience. In some cases this is the responsibility of the central government, in others that of professional organizations. Some of the main recognized branches of professional work at present are clinical, educational, occupational, counselling, criminological, teaching of psychology, and research. The distinctions between these are often quite important to the practitioners, but to the observer may seem hard to follow. In any one of them, for example, a psychologist might be administering a test of intelligence or personality assessment and discussing it with a client, or designing and carrying out an experimental investigation, or teaching a graduate student. Conversely, two individuals even in the same branch might spend their working days in quite different activities. The distinctions lie rather in the context and in the main thrust of the work. Thus clinical psychologists generally work in association with hospitals or national health bodies, though some are in individual private practice, dealing with mental and behavioural disorders; occupational

psychologists mainly work in industry and deal mostly with 'normal' problems – personnel, work conditions, ergonomics, etc.; teachers of the subject are found in schools, colleges and universities. There are also quite numerous areas of professional work, such as market research, which are less distinctly defined and regulated.

A more abstract way of describing what psychologists do, suggested by the philosopher Richard Peters (1953), is that they have usually been concerned with one of four sorts of questions. One may be called questions of theory, that is, scientific questions about what is the case, what is generally true under what conditions, and why. Second, there are questions of technology: how to bring about specific practical ends, whatever the level of scientific knowledge. Third, there are questions of policy – of ethics and morality. Almost all psychological work raises such issues, both in dealing with individuals and in a wider context of effects on society. Fourth, there are philosophical or perhaps superordinate questions, including what kind of an activity psychology itself is, and what assumptions about human nature underlie its theories and methods. Many practical problems involve all four sorts of questions, for example, whether corporal punishment should be used on children (still an issue in the UK). It is a puzzle as to how scientific evidence is to be obtained, and how to show conclusively whether or not such punishment works; clearly ethical issues are involved, and indeed it may be a matter of our view of human nature – intrinsically good, bad or neutral.

At another level, one may say that psychologists have generally been engaged in one of four sorts of activities, or some combination of them. One might be called theorizing – trying to make sense of the state of knowledge at a particular time. A second is empirical – investigating under more-or-less controlled conditions, often, as already indicated, by experiment. A third is psychometric – measuring human differences and similarities using standardized instruments (popularly, tests). A fourth is clinical – seeking to help people with problems, without implying that these are necessarily pathological. Again in practice these may all overlap. A psychometric test may be used in many experiments, or in diagnosis of a problem. Experiments are used to test theories. But conceptually, and to a surprising degree historically, they are distinct approaches to the same subject matter, that is the behaviour of individual human beings.

Some of the main historical roots of psychology are to be found in Germany, France, Britain and Russia, but since the First World War it has been dominated by the USA in numbers and influence, although in recent decades the balance has begun to be somewhat restored. A different imbalance is still increasing:

psychology as a profession is becoming ever more female. Psychology degree courses in both the USA and Europe attract currently about 80 per cent female students. Psychology is seen, in fact, as largely a 'female' subject, and female students of it have increased as female entrants to higher education have caught up with and (1993 in the UK) passed male numbers. Views as to which subjects of study are appropriate to either sex tend to be formed quite early, probably before the teens, but the reasons for them are not well understood. The main distinction seems to be related to the idea that subjects and occupations are 'thing-oriented' or 'people-oriented'.

By a *'subject'* I refer to teaching but also to dissemination in a wider sense, e.g. through books and scientific journals. There is no agreed taxonomy of psychology, perhaps due to its reflexive nature, and new groupings of subject matter constantly emerge. However, recognized degree courses, and general textbooks, in psychology would all draw on at least the following areas: 1. Biological bases of behaviour – genetics, brain and nervous system, the senses, hormone systems; 2. Cognitive processes – perception, learning, memory, thinking, language; 3. Social processes – interactions between two or more individuals, e.g. parents and children, groups, mass media; 4. Emotion and motivation; 5. Individual differences, e.g. in intellectual abilities, personality; 6. Mental and behavioural disorders; 7. Development through the life-span from infancy to old age; 8. Theoretical, conceptual and historical issues in psychology; 9. Investigative methods both quantitative and qualitative; 10. Applications of psychology (though specific professional training is normally at postgraduate level). Psychology taught or presented for other purposes, such as pre-degree courses, usually involves a smaller selection from the same menu. Psychology is increasingly a part of many other trade or professional trainings, from hairdressing to police work. In the past, there is no doubt that some of what was offered was ill informed and irrelevant, but more recently there has been a very marked improvement. Rather than offering a potted version of 'psychology', teachers ask instead what are the problems of a particular occupation, and whether there is anything in the psychological cupboard, so to say, that may be of use. This is linked to the fact that psychology has steadily increased in popularity in nearly all the countries in which it is systematically taught, often being among the most frequently chosen of subjects at all levels.

In view of this, and a history of around a century and a half, it is somewhat surprising that the public image of psychology continues to be greatly at variance with that of psychologists themselves. Studies show that 'psychologists' are generally seen as kind of all-purpose counsellors, 'good with people' in a rather vague way but not particularly good at very much else. Psychology is seen to be an intuitive, non-scientific way of dealing with abnormal conditions, generally by recommending a woolly, 'soft' approach. In a rather contradictory way, psychology seems often to be viewed as simultaneously common sense and nonsense; and both ineffective yet dangerous. Psychology is frequently (though not always) ridiculed in the mass media, which use the word interchangeably with psychiatry. General bookshops often have a section labelled 'psychology' which is largely psychoanalysis, and there is little doubt that the immense cultural influence of Freud has coloured the popular view of what is really a very different enterprise. Perhaps uniquely among subjects, the same shops often have a further section labelled 'popular psychology' which is largely of the self-help variety. These books do sometimes draw on sound research, but more often rely on the centuries-old recipe of the author's own fantasies plus whatever gimmicks seem saleable at a particular time.

There is some evidence, indeed, of a rise in the popularity of what may be called 'pseudo-psychology', under the general banner of 'New Age' thinking. Academics report an increase in the numbers of students who overtly reject, not just particular findings, but the whole notion of seeking scientific objectivity. A similar attitude characterizes the growing numbers of religious fundamentalists. Even among the main body of psychology students, the scientific aspects are the least popular. At the same time, persons in authority, such as politicians and judges, freely pronounce with certainty on the causes and treatment of human behaviour, often plumping for one simple and, they no doubt hope, popular answer, with no better evidence than their own prejudices. This is not an argument for deference to a different authority, but for an awareness of what scientific knowledge is available. No responsible individuals would assert their own uninformed opinions as fact when it came to the treatment of cancer, say, or the construction of a road bridge.

Such attitudes may be partly due to the fact that psychology can seldom if ever provide simple panaceas, and often not even unequivocal answers in particular cases. The causes of behaviour are generally multiple; what the applied psychologist has to offer is a systematic, objective, patient but sophisticated methodology by which to disentangle the main threads. In all its forms psychology raises complex issues which are not easily solved. All along, consistent with the reflexive nature of the discipline, psychologists have puzzled as to whether they are engaged in a unitary activity, and if so what should be its scope and methods. A good deal of the puzzlement arises from failure to make the kinds of distinctions that have been suggested here. More comes from a tendency to reify labels: to write as though because there is a label 'psychology', there must be one thing corresponding to this label, defined by some simple characteristic, if only we could find out what it is. Psychology has accordingly usually been defined as the study, or the science, of behaviour, or of experience, or of both. Whichever version is adopted, there is then a further argument as to whether all species, or only the human, are to be included, and, if the latter, whether all peoples or only some. In practice, by far the greater number of psychological experiments have been done on American college students, almost as though they were test-tubes in which basic processes could be studied, though the balance is currently shifting rather markedly towards a far wider range.

It is suggested here that 'psychology' is a convenient label for a set of problems that do hang together, centring on the human individual. It is a reasonable scientific question to ask why William Shakespeare, and not any other member of his family, wrote outstanding plays, or why particular persons, and not others, abuse their children, suffer delusions or obtain a first class degree in mathematics at 13. To answer such questions we must address what Frederick Bartlett termed broadly 'the conditions of human behaviour'. One way to order these multifarious conditions is to consider three dimensions or 'levels', although such a topographical metaphor is misleading. These are the physiological, the individual *per se* (sometimes equated with cognitive or perhaps experiential), and the social. There can scarcely be any human behaviour that does not involve all of these, though not always to an equal degree. Shakespeare, for example, must have had a particular genetic potential (there is recent evidence on unique 'emergenic' genetic traits which may underlie genius), interacting with particular experiences to develop exceptional linguistic and dramatic skills, all in a social context in which poetry and plays were common currency as well as being richly rewarded in money and prestige. Some might add that a complete account of human beings should distinguish also what could be loosely called a spiritual dimension, without thereby necessarily implying anything supernatural. Western psychology, however, has so far had relatively little to say about this.

Some theorists have attempted to give accounts of behaviour that are consistent at the physiological, individual and social levels. Freud, for example, originally hoped to produce a neurological explanation which would be consistent with evidence at the other two levels, with which he did deal, but the neurology of his day was not adequate for the purpose. H. J. Eysenck's account of personality attempts a similar consistency: conditionability, considered to be an attribute of the nervous system, determines the degree of introversion/extraversion (individual personality) which in turn determines social behaviour, such as preferring solitude to company or committing crimes. Skinner similarly sought to take account of genetics, an individual's learning history, and the functional importance of social environments.

Psychologists are faced with a subject matter, namely individuals, that is apparently infinitely diverse; even 'identical' (monozygotic) twins are not literally identical. There are several possible strategies. One approach is that science cannot in principle deal with individual cases, but only with generalities. We can say accurately how many men will die of cancer by the age of 60, but it is unreasonable to seek more than a probabilistic prediction in any one case – a statement of the odds. An alternative, extreme, view is that since each individual is unique, she or he can be understood only in her or his own terms. However, understanding another person at all must involve at least the assumption that there is some commonality, which is generally taken for granted unless the behaviour of the other seems bizarre. It is the attempts to comprehend this more systematically, and thus to understand the particular individual in terms of the general, that are at the heart of psychology as a discipline. One strategy involves the assumption that, underlying behaviour, there must be some basic units or processes, just as chemists seek to reduce their subject matter to elements, and physicists to matter and forces. Thus Wundt and his followers, for example, tried to analyse the process of perception into simple sensations, and the more simplistic versions of Behaviourism sought to show how behaviour could be built up out of conditioned reflexes. Freud, a physiologist and physician, adopted a similar, although more sophisticated, strategy. His technique of drawing general conclusions from the analysis of just a few selected patients is often said to be 'unscientific', but it is in fact exactly analogous to the methods of physiology, specifically dissection. The same thing can be said of Piaget, another biologist. The current cognitive modelling approach similarly rests on the assumption that the minds of all individuals are sufficiently alike in important respects for a model to be generally applicable. Indeed this assumption underlies most of what has historically been labelled experimental psychology, as well as several approaches that have been considered to be quite different, such as psychoanalysis.

In contrast, the psychometric approach rests on the notion that human behaviour can only be assessed relatively, not absolutely. It was Galton who saw that a 'genius', for example, must essentially be defined as someone who is much better than others at some activity, though perhaps he did not see quite so clearly that it then depends on who those others are. Whatever the causes or the underlying mechanisms of genius (or any other level of behaviour), the performance itself must be defined relatively to what others can do. The direct descendant of Galton's pioneering work has been the widespread industry of psychological testing, using instruments (tests) standardized on particular populations, that is, groups of people for whom norms of performance on the test have been established. The use of tests to assess individuals and groups who may or may not have the same characteristics as the reference population has aroused violent controversy, most notoriously in the case of the intelligence test scores of non-White Americans. Conceptually, there has been argument as to whether measurements show that individuals fall into a number of relatively distinct groups (types); or whether each person manifests some of a number of possible characteristics (traits); or whether, rather, the differences can be subsumed in a small number of basic dimensions, a position on each of which would approximately describe every individual. H. J. Eysenck, among others, has sought to show that these approaches are in fact reconcilable. He has also argued that, on the one hand, much of the value of experimental work is lost if individual differences are not taken into account, while, on the other hand, it is possible to identify basic physiological mechanisms which underlie dimensions of difference such as intelligence and introversion/extraversion, thus integrating the experimental and psychometric approaches.

However, although physiological mechanisms may be common to all members of the human species, it is more difficult to maintain this of behaviour. Even such a basic operation as memory, for example, may serve different functions in oral and literate cultures, and employ different mechanisms. In our own, psychologically informed, culture, for many years it was believed that the immediate memory span for digits, that is the quantity of single-figure numbers that can be retained after one short presentation, was more or less fixed at around seven, plus or minus two – a range of five to nine. Numerous experiments demonstrated this. Since the mid-1980s it has been shown that with appropriate techniques and intensive practice the span can be raised even to seventy or eighty. Individuals have been publicly competing in such memory feats for cash prizes. Similarly, cultural studies show that other societies do not necessarily manifest the same groupings of behaviour as ours does, as for example in respect of what we label 'intelligence'. It is not that they count different things as 'intelligent', but rather that there is no equivalent classification or dimension. The debate as to whether there can be said to be cultural universals is a long one within anthropology and cannot be pursued here. From the psychological point

of view, it is important to realize that it cannot simply be taken for granted that the American college student – any more than the white rat – offers a convenient test tube in which to isolate pure samples of behaviour.

Indeed, as has already been suggested, it can be doubted whether there is a psychological subject matter that can be sampled in a way exactly analogous to that of the other natural sciences. Most of the successive prevailing modes of psychology, however, have been influenced by the immense practical success of those sciences, and psychologists have accordingly sought to employ comparable methods, especially that of the replicable experiment. In actual fact, no experiment is ever exactly replicable, but in many sciences the logical distinction can be ignored. This is not so with behaviour: it cannot be assumed that two random groups of people will be equivalent in the way that two chemical preparations are equivalent. It is not often possible to adopt the archetypal design of holding constant all variables but one, which is then varied in order to observe its effects. Recourse is often had to relatively complex methods of experimental design and multivariate statistical analysis. Drawing inferences from these, however, always rests upon the concept of statistical probability. Essentially this involves the calculation of the likelihood that results of a particular order would occur by chance. Thus, if on a single toss a coin turned up heads, it would be absurd to suggest that it must be biased. If the same result were to occur, say, one thousand times in succession, most observers would feel there must be some factor other than chance – although of course, logically, there need not be. In practice, experiments cannot be repeated many hundreds or thousands of times. Statistical methods allow for the calculation of the probability of the particular result being obtained, but what level of likelihood is acceptable is a matter of choice. Generally results are felt to be reliable when they have a probability that they would occur by chance only once in twenty, or more stringently once in a hundred, times.

While this is undoubtedly a fundamental advance on the traditional method of subjective judgement, there are further problems with it. One is that the acceptability of the statistical conclusion tends to be affected by the area of investigation. It may be important to have a higher level of probability if the consequences of error are serious, as in a drugs trial. Many psychologists are reluctant to accept the evidence of experiments in extrasensory perception (ESP) even though these yield statistical results that would be highly convincing in other areas, because they feel them to be inherently implausible. Another problem is that some investigations (ESP is again a case in point) yield results that are statistically significant, but only when there are extremely large numbers of observations. It seems odd to conclude that there is a causal factor that manifests itself so faintly, as it were. Again, a statistically significant result does not necessarily equate with a psychologically meaningful one. Another problem arises when successive studies show contradictory results. This is generally partly due to the difficulty of exact replication; but then it is difficult to see how to draw any general conclusions. A method that can be adopted to overcome this is that of the meta-analysis. The essence of this is that, rather than simply counting up studies that do or do not appear to support a particular conclusion, all available appropriate studies are viewed as a population to be systematically sampled and assessed. Together they yield a database that can be statistically analysed in much the same way as any other quantitative survey data. Such meta-analyses do, in fact, provide convincing evidence of the efficacy of psychological methods of intervention.

Some would argue that the ultimate test of a scientific enterprise is whether it works. On this criterion, psychology in the senses in which it has been considered here emerges as by far the most successful approach, indeed the only approach with any real chance of success, to a host of practical problems ranging from treatment of individual disorders and distress, to better teaching methods, to improving work conditions and job selection, to assessing the reliability of legal testimony and the efficacy of criminological methods, and innumerable others. If it also seems to fall short of finding solutions to the major problems that beset the human race, this is partly because of the immense complexity of such problems, and their inextricable entanglement with all sorts of uncontrollable factors such as the economic, political, religious, and so on. It is also because the answers to *some* problems can probably never be provided by science but will remain matters of philosophy or metaphysics. Yet the attempt, however difficult and limited it may be, at a more objective understanding of human behaviour and the human individual, is a better approach even to many of those problems than previous centuries have provided.

John Radford
University of East London

Reference

Peters, R. S. (1953) *Brett's History of Psychology*, London.

Further reading

Atkinson, R. L., Atkinson, R. C., Smith, E. E. and Bem, D. K. (1993) *Introduction to Psychology*, 11th edn, London.
Leahey, H. (1992) *A History of Psychology*, 3rd edn, New York.
Radford, J. and Govier, E. (eds) (1990) *A Textbook of Psychology*, 2nd edn, London.
Valentine, E. R. (1992) *Conceptual Problems in Psychology*, 2nd edn, London.

psychology, clinical *see* **clinical psychology**

psychology, cognitive *see* **cognitive psychology**

psychology, constitutional *see* **constitutional psychology**

psychology, counselling *see* **counselling psychology**

psychology, developmental *see* **developmental psychology**

psychology, educational *see* **educational psychology**

psychology, industrial and organizational *see* **industrial and organizational psychology**

psychology, occupational *see* **occupational psychology**

psychology, physiological *see* **physiological psychology**

psychology, political *see* **political psychology**

psychology, social *see* **social psychology**

psychopathic personality

The condition of the psychopathic personality has been variously labelled by psychiatrists over the past two hundred years as 'hereditary moral insanity', 'constitutional psychopathic inferiority', 'psychopathic personality', 'sociopath', and more recently, 'antisocial personality disorder'. Each of these labels suggests a different aetiology. The aetiology remains debatable, and even the condition itself defies precise description.

Some psychiatrists regard this disorder as an unreliable category, as a 'wastebasket' condition which lacks the features of a genuine mental disorder. Critics of the psychopath label also decry the use of this term as obscuring what, in their view is instead criminal, immoral or other situationally based behaviour. The supposed core of psychopathy includes egocentricity and lack of respect for the feelings and rights of others, coupled with persistent manipulative and/or antisocial behaviour – at times, of an aggressive, even violent, type. These core characteristics are manifested by certain criminals, but also by other, more outwardly successful, persons. As William McCord (1982) wrote, 'The psychopath simply does not care, one way or another, about the communality of human beings known as society.'

While appearing superficially normal (because cognition is intact and the individual does not manifest any obvious mental pathology) the psychopath's destructive pattern of activities is manifested over time, usually resulting in social and personal tragedies for both the psychopath and others.

The best-known modern criteria for psychopathic personality disorder were developed by Cleckley (1982). Cleckley's approach stresses the psychopath's persistent personality features such as untruthfulness and insincerity, poor judgement and failure to learn by experience, pathological egocentricity and incapacity for love, and inadequately motivated antisocial behaviour. Psychodynamically oriented psychiatrists explain these features as attributable to pathological superego development, inner emptiness and compensatory impulsivity. More 'objective', non-aetiological diagnostic approaches recommended by the American Psychiatric Association (DSM III) stressed a constellation of long-standing antisocial behaviour dating from childhood, and poor adult work behaviour, violation of social and interpersonal norms, and impulsivity.

The prevalence of psychopathy in normal and criminal populations is unknown. Over the centuries, the aetiology has been variously attributed to genetic predisposition or other constitutional problems and, more recently, to emotional deprivation in childhood with poor, inconsistent and sadistic parenting. Biological theories are related to the psychopath's putative brain immaturity, autonomic nervous system defects which inhibit learning of social norms, or hormonal defects. In some instances, aspects of the psychopathic syndrome may appear following brain injury. However, the aetiology of psychopathy remains obscure and controversial.

Little is known about treatment. The natural history of this disorder, however, includes attrition with age of certain diagnostic features and psychopathic behaviour. After age 40, the psychopath is said to 'burn out'. Current treatment approaches (usually not successful) include 'milieu therapy' to promote the psychopath's identification with better adjusted, more prosocial peers. From the psychological or behavioural perspective, consistent, limit-setting treatment approaches are advocated. Individual psychotherapeutic work directed towards uncovering and resolving inner conflicts is usually not successful. The psychopath is neither a neurotic nor a psychotic. The nature and extent of past social adjustment (not the mental status) best predict the psychopath's future adjustment.

The challenge of psychopathy, including the appropriateness of categorizing mental disorders along somewhat vague socially based criteria, will probably persist for a long time.

Loren H. Roth
University of Pittsburgh

References

Cleckley, H. (1982) *The Mask of Sanity*, New York.
McCord, W. (1982) *The Psychopath and Milieu Therapy*, New York.

See also: mental disorders; psychoses.

psychopharmacology

Since the mid-1950s there has been dramatic progress in our knowledge of drugs to treat the major psychiatric disorders. Prior to the 1950s, psychiatrists possessed only a few non-specific sedative and stimulant drugs to treat anxiety and depression. Electroconvulsive therapy (ECT) had also been found effective for patients with depressive illness, but it proved much less useful for patients with chronic schizophrenia. For many of the half-million patients in American mental hospitals in the 1950s, and hundreds of thousands more throughout the world, no effective treatment existed.

Then, in the space of only six years – from 1949 to 1955 – three pharmacological discoveries sparked a revolution in psychiatric treatment. These were antipsychotic drugs, antidepressant drugs and lithium.

Antipsychotic drugs

Antipsychotic drugs counteract delusions (beliefs in things which are not real) and hallucinations (seeing visions, hearing voices, and the like) – symptoms common in schizophrenia and manic-depressive illness. Within a few weeks, these drugs may bring patients from a floridly psychotic state, in which they must be confined to a locked ward of a mental hospital, to a state of near-remission, in which they can be discharged and return to normal social and occupational life. Indeed, the introduction of antipsychotic treatment is credited with decreasing the population of American mental hospitals from 550,000 to 430,000 in the twelve years after 1955, despite a steady rise in the population.

Remarkable as their effects may seem, however, all antipsychotic drugs may have annoying side-effects: sedation, muscle stiffness, restlessness, slowed physical and mental functioning, and other problems. Perhaps as a result of these side-effects, the antipsychotic drugs have often been misnamed 'major tranquillizers'. In fact, they are not tranquillizers at all; it is a serious misconception to think that they 'tranquillize' patients into being free of their symptoms. Rather, they seem to have specific and selective effects on the psychosis itself. Any sedative or tranquillizing properties of the antipsychotic drugs appear purely accidental. In fact, if normal individuals were to take even a small dose of one of the more potent antipsychotic drugs – such as fluphenazine or haloperidol – they would in all likelihood notice no tranquillization and, indeed, might possibly experience a jumpy, restless feeling called akathisia.

Newer antipsychotic drugs with potentially fewer side-effects, such as cloropine and risperidone, have been introduced for patients who cannot tolerate or respond poorly to conventional antipsychotic drugs.

Antidepressant drugs

Antidepressant drugs include the tricyclic antidepressants (such as impramine and amitriptyline) and the monoamine oxidase inhibitors (such as phenelzine and tranylcypromine), discovered in the 1950s, together with several newer families of agents. These include the 'serotonin reuptake inhibitors' (fluocetine, fluvoxamine, paroxetine, and sertraline) and several 'atypical' agents, such as bupropion and tazodone. These drugs provide relief for patients suffering from so-called major depression or from the depressed phase of manic depressive illness – conditions formerly responsive only to electroconvulsive therapy. The effect of antidepressants, like that of the antipsychotics, may be dramatic: patients too depressed to eat or sleep, unable to perform even the most rudimentary tasks, and thinking constantly of suicide, may respond so well that they are completely back to normal functioning in three or four weeks.

Like the antipsychotics, antidepressants are the subject of various misconceptions. In particular, they are not 'psychostimulants' or 'mood elevators'; a normal person taking them would typically notice some sedation, lightheadedness, dry mouth, and a few other side-effects, but no increased energy or euphoria. Antidepressants appear to act by correcting some underlying chemical imbalance in the brain, rather than propelling the patient into an artificial euphoria.

Lithium

Lithium is unique among psychiatric medications in that it is a simple ion, rather than a complex molecule. For reasons still poorly understood, it counteracts the manic phase of manic-depressive illness (it appears less effective in acute depression), and, taken over the long term, protects patients against relapses of mania or depression. Since it has relatively few side-effects, it may be taken for years at a time with few problems. Such long-term prophylactic use of lithium has transformed the lives of thousands of sufferers from manic-depressive illness and related disorders. Prior to lithium, many patients were accustomed to frequent psychiatric hospitalizations for the exacerbations of their illness, with severe disruption of their personal lives and their careers. Now they often enjoy partial or total protection against such occurrences.

Other psychiatric drugs

Other types of psychiatric drugs continue to be introduced. Benzodiazepines, such as chlordiazepoxide and diazepam, have been found safer and perhaps more effective than barbiturates for sedation in anxious patients; other benzodiazepines, such as flurazepam and temazepam, are excellent sleeping-pills. Stimulants, such as methylphenidate and magnesium pemoline, have ameliorated the symptoms of childhood hyperkinesis or minimal brain dysfunction, now called 'attention deficit disorder'. Anticonvulsant drugs, such as carbamazepine and sodium valproate, appear effective in some cases of manic-depressive illness. But none of these discoveries has matched the impact of the introduction of the antipsychotics, the antidepressants and lithium. Not only have the latter three classes of drugs greatly reduced the ravages of schizophrenia and manic-depressive illness, but they appear helpful for a number of other disorders, among them, panic disorder and agoraphobia, some forms of drug and alcohol abuse, anorexia nervosa and bulimia nervosa, certain organic mental disorders, and others.

The discovery of these medications has not only great clinical and public-health consequences, but also major theoretical implications. It is an important observation that the drugs have little psychiatric effect on normal individuals, but a profound effect on patients suffering from actual psychiatric disorders. In other words, unlike the non-specific sedative and stimulant medications, these compounds appear specifically to correct some underlying abnormality in the brain. This specificity not only suggests that there are biological abnormalities underlying many of the major psychiatric disorders, but also gives clues as to what the abnormalities may be. Studies of the action of psychopharmacologic agents have given impetus to the growing field of biological psychiatry. In time, this research may greatly enhance our knowledge of the aetiology of psychosis, depression, and other symptoms – and yield even more specific and effective treatments.

Harrison G. Pope
Mailman Research Center

Further reading

Baldessarini, R. J. (1977) *Chemotherapy in Psychiatry*, Cambridge, MA.

Davis, J. M. (1975) 'Overview: maintenance therapy in psychiatry. I: schizophrenia', *American Journal of Psychiatry* 132.

—— (1976) 'Overview: maintenance therapy in psychiatry. II: affective disorders', *American Journal of Psychiatry* 133.

Goodwin, F. K. (ed.) (1976) 'The lithium ion: impact on treatment and research', *Archives of General Psychiatry* 36.

Hollister, L. E. (1983) *Clinical Pharmacology of Psychotherapeutic Drugs*, 2nd edn, New York.

Jefferson, J. W. and Greist, J. H. (1977) *Primer of Lithium Therapy*, Baltimore, MD.

Klein, D. F., Gittleman, R., Quitkin, F. and Rifkin, A. (1980), *Diagnosis and Drug Treatment of Psychiatric Disorders: Adults and Children*, 2nd edn, Baltimore, MD.

See also: psychiatry.

psychoses

Psychosis (plural psychoses) is a nineteenth-century term for any kind of mental disturbance; its contemporary meaning is, however, restricted to a small number of mental disorders, in which there is thought to be a gross disruption in the faculties of thinking and perception. It can be argued, therefore, that psychosis is the technical term for madness (Frith and Cahill 1994). Psychotic symptoms (notably delusions and hallucinations), in contrast to the symptoms of the neuroses, are conventionally said to constitute a fundamental alteration in the person's knowledge of the world (Mullen 1979) and represent a 'gross impairment

in reality testing and the creation of a new reality' (American Psychiatric Association 1987). In the 'organic' psychoses (most of which are forms of dementia) there is a known physical cause, generally degenerative changes in the brain. For the 'functional' psychoses there is no general agreement as to cause.

The functional psychoses can be divided into a large number of diagnostic categories, but the most common major subdivisions are 'schizophrenia', 'delusional disorder' and the 'affective psychoses' (bipolar affective disorder, otherwise known as manic-depression, and mania and depression with psychotic symptoms). Full details of diagnostic classifications are given in standard manuals such as the *International Classification of Diseases* (version 10) used by British psychiatrists (World Health Organization 1992) or the American equivalent, the *Diagnostic and Statistical Manual of Mental Disorders* (American Psychiatric Association 1987; 1994).

On these conventional views, however, controversy rages. The extent and nature of the disturbances of thinking and perception in psychosis are disputed; the drawing of a clear line between psychosis and neurosis is questioned; and, within the broad category of psychosis, the diagnostic subdivisions of the contemporary psychiatric classification systems, and in particular the validity of the term schizophrenia, are vigorously contested. Curiously, in the context of these debates, while the meaning of the term is challenged, psychosis emerges as an acceptable general descriptor of an important group of disturbances in mental functioning which is relatively neutral in terms of assumptions about cause, and broad enough to avoid some of the problems of delineating the boundaries of the term. For while it is possible to formulate strict rules for diagnoses such as schizophrenia or bipolar affective disorder, these rules do not necessarily reflect the real life symptom clusters, and, it has been argued, notably by Bentall *et al.* (1988), these careful diagnostic rules do not 'cleave nature at its joints'. In some circles therefore, particularly among psychologists rather than psychiatrists, psychosis is the word used in preference to 'schizophrenia' and refers to the wider group of disorders listed above (Claridge 1993).

The key symptoms of psychosis are delusions and hallucinations. Briefly, a delusion is said to be a fixed false belief, held by a person despite evidence to the contrary and not shared by other members of the person's subculture. A hallucination is defined as an involuntary sense perception in the absence of an external stimulus, and can occur in any sensory modality (hearing, sight, touch, taste or smell). Although generally agreed to be less problematic than diagnostic categories like schizophrenia, psychotic symptoms do take many forms; delusion, in particular, poses definitional problems.

The causes of delusions are also disputed. In traditional psychiatry, delusions were thought to arise from profoundly disordered thinking or personality and to be not 'understandable' in a common-sense way or empathically (Jaspers 1913). Jaspers believed that delusions must therefore occur as a result of physical changes in the brain. Psychoanalytic thinking has proposed an alternative, suggesting that psychotic symptoms are reflections of personal unconscious states which are projected outwards in a primitive defence, because the early development of the individual has been seriously disturbed (Hingley 1992).

A third view of psychotic symptoms and their causes has been emerging from the work of psychologists and a smaller number of psychiatrists, drawing on the methods and models of cognitive psychology (Garety and Hemsley 1994; Oltmanns and Maher 1988; Slade and Bentall 1988). These authors challenge the view that delusions and hallucinations are not amenable to psychological understanding, even if their cause is in some cases or to some extent biological. They argue that psychotic symptoms may be viewed as on a continuum with normal experience and that the disturbances in thinking, emotion and perception found in people with psychosis are, in at least some cases, exaggerations of biases found in the general population. They also argue that these symptoms have multiple causes and that there are, in all probability, a number of different aetiological routes to the same or similar mental states. These writers therefore see psychosis as not always clearly distinguishable either from neurosis or from normality and as better understood in dimensional terms. Such views have implications for psychological therapy, and new psychological therapies are emerging which derive from cognitive behavioural approaches developed for neurotic disorders (e.g. Garety *et al.* 1994), in addition to the well-established therapeutic methods of medication, psychoanalysis (relatively rarely employed) and rehabilitative approaches.

Philippa A. Garety
University of London

References

American Psychiatric Association (1987) *Diagnostic and Statistical Manual of Mental Disorders*, 3rd edn revised (DSM-III-R), Washington, DC.
—— (1994) *Diagnostic and Statistical Manual of Mental Disorders*, 4th edn (DSM-IV), Washington, DC.
Bentall, R. P., Jackson, H. F. and Pilgrim, D. (1988) 'Abandoning the concept of "schizophrenia": some implications of validity arguments for psychological research into psychotic phenomena', *British Journal Clinical Psychology* 27.
Claridge, G. (1993) 'What is schizophrenia? Common theories and divergent views', *Journal of Mental Health* 2.
Frith, C. and Cahill, C. (1994) 'Psychotic disorders: schizophrenia, affective psychoses and paranoia', in A. M. Colman (ed.) *Companion Encyclopedia of Psychology*, London.
Garety, P. A. and Hemsley, D. R. (1994) *Delusions: Investigations into the Psychology of Delusional Reasoning*, Maudsley Monographs, Oxford.
Garety, P. A., Kuipers, L., Fowler, D., Dunn, G. and Chamberlain, F. (1994) 'Cognitive behaviour therapy for drug resistant psychosis', *British Journal Medical Psychology*.
Hingley, S. (1992) 'Psychological theories of delusional thinking: in search of integration', *British Journal Medical Psychology* 65.
Jaspers, K. (1959[1913]) *General Psychopathology*, trans. J. Hoenig and M. W. Hamilton, Manchester.
Mullen, P. (1979) 'Phenomenology of disordered mental function' in P. Hill, R. Murray and G. Thorley (eds) *Essentials of Postgraduate Psychiatry*, London.
Oltmanns, T. F. and Maher, B. A. (eds) (1988) *Delusional Beliefs*, New York.
Slade, P. D. and Bentall, R. P. (1988) *Sensory Deception: A Scientific Analysis of Hallucination*, London.
World Health Organization (1992) *International Classification of Diseases 10: Classification of Mental and Behavioural Disorders*, Geneva.

See also: depressive disorders; DSM-IV; genetic aspects of mental illness; mental disorders; mental health; neuroses; psychopathic personality; psychopharmacology; schizophrenia.

psychosomatic illness

In the broadest sense of the term, all human illness is psychosomatic, since the functions of mind and body are closely interwoven. Emotional disorders are commonly accompanied by bodily symptoms, and physical illness often leads to pathological emotional responses. Clinical practice reflects this duality. Psychiatrists working in general hospitals are often called upon to evaluate and treat not only patients whose illnesses are the response to an emotional stress, but also those for whom physical illness or injury is in itself a stressful precipitant of a pathological emotional reaction that, in turn, complicates the underlying physical disorder.

In the first category of psychosomatic illness, emotional factors may be a major precipitator of physical illness. In many patients with a variety of chronic bodily disorders (such as peptic ulcer, hyperthyroidism, and bronchial asthma), severe emotional stress (the loss of partner for example) appears to play a significant role in the onset and recurring episodes of the physical illness. Such patients often have major defects in their capacity to experience and express emotions aroused by stress. The arousal, barred from discharge over the psychological, emotional and behavioural channels that normally attenuate it, is shunted directly into nervous and endocrine pathways that control the body's organs. The resulting chronic stimulation of these organs leads to pathological changes manifested as physical illness. Modern scientific investigation of the psychosomatic process is beginning to uncover a wealth of facts that shed important light on the psychological, neuronal, endocrinal and immunological mechanisms at work in stress-induced psychosomatic illnesses. The knowledge thus gained will ultimately be translated into more effective treatment measures for a host of hitherto chronic, debilitating human diseases.

In the second category of psychosomatic illness, the individual patient's characteristic personality features help to determine the response to the stress of illness. As psychiatrists see it, these personality features often not only induce complications in the course of the illness, but also create problems in the medical management of the case. Dependency needs, in particular, pose a central psychological difficulty. The incapacitation resulting from a serious illness or injury compromises the patient's autonomy, independence, and self-sufficiency, and forces the patient into the role of an invalid who must look to others for help and care. Individuals who are fiercely independent may find it difficult to give up their autonomy. As a consequence, they deny the seriousness of their illness and refuse to comply with the treatment programme necessary for their recovery. In persons with strong, overt dependency needs, the symptoms of a physical disorder provide a means of gratifying those needs. As a result, both the symptoms and the incapacitation arising from the illness are intensified and often prolonged beyond the time when physical healing has taken place.

John C. Nemiah
Dartmouth Medical School

Further reading

Nemiah, J. C. (1961) 'Psychological complications of physical illness', in J. C. Nemiah, *Foundations of Psychopathology*, New York.
Taylor, G. J. (1987) *Psychosomatic Medicine and Contemporary Psychoanalysis*, Madison, CT.
Weiner, H. (1992) *Perturbing the Organism: The Biology of Stressful Experience*, Chicago.

See also: stress.

public administration

In what is probably still the most thoughtful and comprehensive work on the subject Dunsire (1973) identified no fewer than fifteen main meanings for the term administration. Given that the number of alternative definitions of public is not small either, it is unsurprising that the field of public administration

suffers identity problems. The development of public administration as a field of study (and, in parallel, as a field of practice) has been subject to constant incursions and borrowings. Public administration has long been disputed territory and its scholars (public administrationists) have frequently agonized over their intellectual parentage and prospects. Yet what the field may have lost through lack of a coherent identity it has – at least in the view of its enthusiasts – more than made up for by the richness of its polyglot theoretical baggage.

A typical contemporary text condenses the various meanings of public administration into just three: first, the *activity* of public servants; second, the *structure* of executive government; and third, the systematic study of the first two (Greenwood and Wilson 1989). We are naturally most concerned with the third of these meanings, but the nature of the field of study cannot be adequately comprehended without an appreciation of the continuous and close proximity of the *practice* of public administration, both as the day-to-day doings of countless public officials and the patterning and repatterning of a wide variety of state institutions. The development of the academic field has mirrored the growth of 'big government', a growth which, in many European and North American states, took off in the mid or late nineteenth century and continued (with occasional pauses) until the early 1980s.

As a proto social science, separate from the older study of the law, public administration can cite a number of distinguished ancestors. Frederick William I of Prussia (1713–40) created university chairs in 'cameralistics' or 'council studies', hoping to ensure a supply of adequately trained public officials. Napoleon Bonaparte developed a distinct and forceful system of state administration, including scientific training for elite civil servants and army officers. At least half of Jeremy Bentham's great *Constitutional Code* is concerned with the structures and procedures of government departments (Bowring 1843), and subsequently J. S. Mill theorized extensively on the ways in which administrative structures could influence administrative behaviours (Lerner 1961).

However, the best-known name in the early elaboration of administrative theory is probably that of Woodrow Wilson. In 1887 Wilson (later to become President of the United States) published a seminal paper entitled 'The study of administration'. Wilson argued that politics and administration could and should be separated from each other, and that administration could then be analysed and implemented in a wholly scientific manner. For example, 'If I see a murderous fellow sharpening a knife cleverly, I can borrow his way of sharpening the knife without borrowing his probable intention to commit murder'

(Wilson 1887: 220). In a strikingly analagous way contemporary politicians frequently argue that modern business methods may be imported to the public sector without also introducing the more inequitable and rapacious practices of the commercial world. Both the possibility and the desirability of such a separation remain the subjects of intense dispute.

Public administration scholars have always borrowed theories and approaches from larger and more prestigious academic neighbours. Law was probably the first of these, but since the 1920s, political studies, organization theory and management science have each in turn become more influential.

Law continues to contribute a particular concern with the correctness of procedures and with the accountability of public administrators to the appropriate public authorities. How are those who wield the resources and authority of the state to be held to account? How are those citizens who may have suffered at the hands of incompetent or corrupt officials to obtain redress? Where, and how, should administrative discretion be exercised?

The study of politics has had a particularly deep influence. Until recently, public administration scholars would most probably be located in university departments of government, politics or political science. Public administrationists from this background have tended to concentrate on 'higher' questions of the relationships between politicians and top civil servants, the role civil servants could or should play in the policy-making process, how public institutions could be structured so as to make them responsive to the objectives of politicians yet efficient, fair and free from partisan bias (a good example is Self 1972).

Organization theory is itself a relatively recent field of study, not without its own boundary disputes. Since the 1940s, however, it has generated many theories, concepts and taxonomies which have been gratefully taken up by public administrationists. Herbert Simon's (1947) analysis of the limits to rational decision making in organizational contexts was exceptionally fruitful. From the mid-1960s onwards a less elegant but nevertheless influential body of theory grew up around a series of research projects investigating the relationships between an organization's performance, its internal structures and the contingencies in its environment (Donaldson 1985).

Most recently, public administration has come under the influence, occasionally dominance, of management studies. The latter subject has expanded hugely in terms of publications and student numbers. In both American and British universities some public administration programmes have been absorbed within schools of management and business studies. This swallowing of public administration within the generic study of management was not unconnected with the contemporary political fashion for adopting private sector 'business methods' as the solution for many of the perceived problems of public governance. In the earlier stages of its growth, management studies tended to restrict itself to important but relatively mundane issues such as management information systems, operational logistics, recruitment policies, different approaches to planning and so on. By the mid-1980s, however, public administration was exposed to a much more ambitious managerial rhetoric of 'cultural change'. Western governments began to make extensive use of management consultants working to terms of reference so wide as to imply a substantial shifting of the public/private boundary and/or a fundamental re-structuring of many public institutions (Pollitt 1993).

In the mid-1990s it is exceptionally difficult to foresee the future of public administration as a distinct field of study. It is possible that it will disappear completely, consumed by not only the generic study of management but also the revived interest of political scientists in the actual implementation of political programmes and policies. More likely, perhaps, it will survive as a separate academic entity. In this modest scenario it will continue to eke out its existence on the margins of academically more prestigious and popular disciplines, defining itself in terms of the nature of its concerns and its substantive territory of interest rather than by laying claim to any unique conceptual or theoretical vocabulary.

To portray public administration in this way is not meant to belittle its importance. Public administrationists have struggled, with some considerable success, to make sense of the many and contrasting ways in which governments and their agents daily allocate and transfer huge sums of money, process millions of citizens through a myriad of transactions, embark upon vast infrastructural projects, issue numerous licenses, permits, refusals, fines and guidelines, and employ a sizeable proportion of the workforce in most modern economies. This is not a trivial endeavour.

Christopher Pollitt
Brunel University

References

Bowring, J. (ed.) (1843) *The Works of Jeremy Bentham*, 10 vols, Edinburgh.

Donaldson, L. (1985) *In Defence of Organization Theory: A Reply to the Critics*, Cambridge, UK.

Dunsire, A. (1973) *Administration: The Word and the Science*, London.

Greenwood, J. and Wilson, D. (1989) *Public Administration in Britain Today*, 2nd edn, London.

Lerner, M. (ed.) (1961) *Essential Works of John Stuart Mill*, New York.

Pollitt, C. (1993) *Managerialism and the Public Services*, 2nd edn, Oxford.

Self, P. (1972) *Administrative Theories and Politics*, London.

Simon, H. (1947) *Administrative Behavior: A Study of Decision-making Processes in Administrative Organization*, New York.

Wilson, W. (1887) 'The study of administration', *Political Science Quarterly* 2.

See also: bureaucracy; policy making; policy sciences; public management.

public choice

Public choice, or the economic theory of politics, is the application of the economist's way of thinking to politics. It studies those areas in which economic and political forces interact, and is one of the few successful interdisciplinary topics. The behaviour of the individual is taken to be rational, an assumption which political scientists and sociologists have also found to be fruitful.

While the term public choice was coined in the late 1960s, the type of politico-economic analysis has a long history. Condorcet was the first to recognize the existence of a voting paradox: in a system of majority voting, the individual preferences cannot generally be aggregated into a social decision without logical inconsistencies. Italian and Scandinavian public finance scholars have also explicitly dealt with political processes, in particular in the presence of public goods. Another forerunner is Schumpeter, who regarded the competition between parties as the essence of democracy.

There are four areas which are central to public choice.

First, *preference aggregation*. Condorcet's finding of a voting paradox has been generalized to all possible methods of aggregating individual preferences. The impossibility result remains in force, in particular when many issue-dimensions are allowed for.

Second, *party competition*. Under quite general conditions, the competition of two vote maximizing parties leads to an equilibrium: both parties offer the same policies in the median of the distribution of voters' preferences. The programmes proposed differ substantially when there are more than two parties competing, and when they can form coalitions.

Third, *interest groups*. The product of the activity of a pressure group is a public good, because even those not participating in its finance may benefit from it. Consequently, economic interests are in general not organized. An exception is when the group is small, when members only receive a private good from the organization, or when it is enforced by government decree.

Fourth, *public bureaucracy*. Due to its monopoly power in the supply of public services, the public administrations tend to extend government activity beyond the level desired by the population.

In recent years, the theories developed have been empirically tested on a wide scale. The demand for publicly provided goods and services has been econometrically estimated for a great variety of goods, periods and countries. An important empirical application is *politico-economic models* which explicitly study the interaction of the economic and political sectors. A vote maximizing government, which has to take into account the trade-off between inflation and unemployment, willingly produces a political business cycle. More inclusive politico-economic models have been constructed and empirically tested for various representative democracies: economic conditions such as unemployment, inflation and growth influence the government's re-election requirement, which induces in turn the government to manipulate the economy to secure re-election.

Viewing government as an endogenous part of a politico-economic system has far-reaching consequences for the theory of economic policy. The traditional idea of government maximizing the welfare of society has to be replaced by an emphasis on the consensual choice of the appropriate rules and institutions.

Bruno S. Frey
University of Zurich

Further reading

Frey, B. S. (1978) *Modern Political Economy*, Oxford.

Mueller, D. (1979) *Public Choice*, Cambridge, UK.

See also: interest groups and lobbying; public goods; supply-side economics; voting.

public goods

Public goods are characterized by non-excludability (individuals not paying for the good cannot be excluded) and by non-rivalry in consumption (that is, it does not cost anything when, in addition, other persons consume the good). The supply of a public good is Pareto-optimal (efficient) if the sum of the marginal utilities (or the sum of the marginal willingness to pay) of the persons benefiting equals the marginal cost of supply. This efficiency condition differs from the one of the polar opposite, private goods, where marginal utility has to equal marginal cost of supply.

The basic problem of public goods is that the prospective consumers have no incentive to reveal their preferences for such a good and are thus not ready to contribute towards financing the provision of the good. In the extreme case this incentive to act as 'free rider' leads to no supply of the public good at all, although everyone would potentially benefit from its provision.

Public goods is one of the few theoretical concepts in modern economics often used by other social sciences. One of the most important applications is to the problem of organizing economic interests. Pressure groups largely provide a public good because all persons and firms sharing these interests benefit from the activity. For that reason, there is little or no incentive to join. The (pure) public goods conditions apply, however, only when the interests are shared by a large number of persons or firms, for example by consumers and taxpayers, and when there are no exclusive benefits offered to members only.

The incentive to act as a free rider in a market setting may (partly) be overcome by resorting to the political process. The direct use of simple majority voting does not guarantee that the resulting public-good supply is Pareto-optimal. This is only the case if median voters (who throw the decisive vote) have a 'tax price' equal to their marginal willingness to pay. This will rarely be the case. In a representative democracy the competition between two parties leads under ideal conditions to the same outcome for public goods supply as simple majority voting. With more than two parties and/or imperfect political competition, the resulting public goods supply cannot in general be determined. Public goods should not be identified with public provision: some public goods are privately provided, and there are many non-public goods which are politically provided.

Decision-making procedures have been devised which solve the free rider problem. These preference-revealing mechanisms result in no one gaining by understating his or her preference for the public good. However, these proposals are difficult to understand by the participants and violate the principle of anonymity of voting.

In laboratory experiments, it appears that individuals are ready to contribute to the cost of providing a public good to some extent, even in the large number setting. Ethical considerations seem to play a significant role in the public goods context; many people appear to have moral qualms about behaving as free riders.

Bruno S. Frey
University of Zurich

See also: macroeconomic policy; mixed economy; public choice.

public health

The *Handbook on Training* of the Faculty of Public Health Medicine (1992) defines public health as 'the science and art of preventing disease, prolonging life and promoting health through organised efforts of society', and public health medicine as 'the branch of medical practice which specialises in public health'. It is concerned primarily with health and disease in populations, complementing clinical medicine with its concern of the health of individual patients. Its chief responsibilities are monitoring the health of a population, the identification of its health needs, the fostering of policies which promote health, and the evaluation of health services.

The fundamental science of public health is epidemiology. Epidemiology enables us to understand the determinants of health and disease, and the occurrence of various factors that produce disease in defined populations and groups. This enables us to decide what action can be taken to prevent disease and promote health, for example, through health education, social policies, modification of behaviour, immunization, screening for early identification of those at special risk or in need of special care and protection against specific environmental hazards.

In all societies, public health has always had the function of studying the nature and extent of disease and disability in a population, determining how it can vary with age and sex, with economic social circumstances, occupation and environment. Thus it defines the health needs of a particular area or population, setting priorities and reviewing the services that are needed. In addition, of course, it is essential to evaluate how effective the services in a community are, in terms of cure, care, the breadth of suffering, maintenance of working capacity, rehabilitation of the disabled and lowering of death and morbidity rates. One also needs to assess how efficiently such services are used in a community and, in particular, to determine the value for money.

The activities of public health will vary in different parts of the world. In the less developed parts, they will largely be concerned with the containment of environmental factors, improvement of sanitation, improvement of water supply, improvement of housing, as well as the containment of infectious diseases and their surveillance, for example, malaria, typhoid, diarrhoea. They will also be concerned with trying to determine the causes of malnutrition, and the causes of infant mortality, and determining the best ways of improving these, for example, through changing the patterns of feeding, changing the patterns of care for children and mothers, and the promotion of breast-feeding, as well as birth control.

In developed countries, the problems of public health will be somewhat different. The major causes of illness and death in developed countries are due to chronic disease such as cardiovascular disease, chronic respiratory disease, cancer, and motor vehicle accidents. Public health will be concerned with determining the appropriate methods and measures that need to be taken in order to contain these hazards, for example, through dissuading people from continuing to smoke, through developing effective policies for reducing the intake of fat in diet, through the containment of air pollution, and through the introduction of screening services for cancer of the cervix and breast, methods of identifying individuals at an early reversible stage of an illness.

Thus the most important aspects of current western public health policy are concerned with the development of methods of influencing behaviour and attitudes which are known to cause so much disease. In addition, it will be involved in determining the health care needs of a population, for example, in areas with large numbers of elderly people the services will be more concerned with those of the old than of the young, thus there will be need for more nursing homes and rehabilitive services than, say, obstetric facilities. Determining the effectiveness of services that are being provided is also important, such as case fatality ratios for cardiac operations, hip replacements, etc. Furthermore, there will be a need to advise on priorities, for example, between curative, rehabilitative and preventive services.

In the United Kingdom, public health is part of the National Health Service, and there are directors of public health, with staff in each district, who have specific responsibilities for reporting annually on the health of their population and for drawing attention to deficiencies of health provision and problems of health. They therefore have an extremely important role in combating disease. This powerful institutional model has not yet been adopted elsewhere. In other countries, the influence of public health is more diffuse.

Walter W. Holland
University of London

Reference

Faculty of Public Health Medicine (1992) *Handbook on Training and Examination for the Membership*, London.

See also: epidemiology; health economics; health transition; medical sociology; morbidity; mortality.

public management

The word management comes from the Italian *maneggiare*, meaning to ride a horse skilfully. In the eighteenth century, the term was often applied to political manipulation, and also to the superintendence of public services. The phrase 'administrative management' was coined by the US Brownlow Committee of 1937; 'public management' was revived in the 1980s to convey a politics-free 'production engineering' approach to public service provision (see Hood and Jackson 1991). Like public administration, to which it is closely related, public management has both ideological and analytic connotations. Ideologically, it denotes managerialism – the claim that public services ought to be run under the oversight of managers. This idea counters the rival doctrines of managing without managers (Martin 1983) and the view that public services should be run by professional experts, like hospital doctors. Another ideological element is the claim that efficiency means applying private sector management styles to public organization. This doctrine challenges an older monastic approach, which came to its height in the progressive era (late nineteenth/early twentieth century), which holds that to avoid corruption and politicization, the public service should be quite different from private business management, hiring and rewarding staff in different ways and operating in a legalistic style through general rules designed to promote equity and accountability.

Does public management have a distinctive analytic focus, distinguishing it from business management on the one hand, and from public administration on the other? Both issues are disputed. The first involves a debate over whether public management requires a different 'ABC' from that used for private sector management, or whether it simply represents a different area for applying the same basic techniques and ideas. Gunn (1987) identifies a spectrum of positions on public management distinctiveness, ranging from the view that 'public management is unique' to the view that public management is simply a less efficient form of public administration. Most commentators see public sector management's distinctiveness as lying in the way that multiple objectives and requirements for public accountability and political responsiveness shapes the operation of public services.

Whether public management is a subject and analytic approach distinct from public administration is also disputed. For some, public management is just a trendy 1980s term for what had previously been known as public administration, reflecting an era in which several OECD governments were antipathetic to public organization and aimed to make senior public servants see themselves as managers to combat the power of public-sector trade unions. Certainly, many college courses previously titled public administration were hastily re-titled as public management in that period (cf. Chandler 1991). But other interpretations are possible. One is that public management represented an attempt to pay more attention to the production function of public services, focusing on operational issues in contrast to the emphasis on public accountability and policy studies in conventional public administration at that time. An alternative view, coming midway between the other two, is that public management represented a return to earlier themes of public administration, particularly in the USA (cf. Overman 1984). Public administration as it developed in the progressive era was closely associated with the development of scientific management theory, reflecting the doctrine of a politics–administration dichotomy, that is, the view that organization and implementation embody professional skills which should be divorced from electoral politics.

The renewed emphasis on private-sector-style management approaches to public services – termed 'new public management' by some commentators (see Pollitt 1993) – in many OECD countries since the mid-1980s has provoked debates over the explanation of this development and about its normative appropriateness. New public management has been strongly defended, mainly by politicians and public servants, as a means of making modern government more efficient and customer-responsive. Critics question whether private-sector corporate management concepts can be effectively transferred to public services and whether the importation of private-sector mangement practices undermines the scope for using public organization as a key instrument for promotion of employment equity and other 'model employer' policies.

Christopher Hood
London School of Economics and Political Science

References

Chandler, J. A. (1991) 'Public administration: a discipline in decline', *Teaching Public Administration* 11(2).
Gunn, L. A. (1987) 'Perspectives on public management', in J. Kooiman and K. A. Eliassen (eds) *Managing Public Organizations*, London.
Hood, C. C. and Jackson, M. W. (1991) *Administrative Argument*, Aldershot.
Martin, S. (1983) *Managing without Managers*, Beverly Hills, CA.
Overman, S. (1984) 'Public management', *Public Administration Review* 44.
Pollitt, C. (1993) *Managerialism and the Public Services*, 2nd edn, Oxford.

Further reading

Osborne, D. and Gaebler, T. (1992) *Reinventing Government*, Reading, MA.

Wanna, J., O'Faircheallaigh, C. and Weller, P. (1992) *Public Sector Management in Australia*, Melbourne.

See also: bureaucracy; management theory; public administration; strategic management.

public opinion polls

Opinion polls are a form of sample survey. The term may be used to describe any survey designed to measure social and political attitudes, but it is most commonly applied to surveys of voting intention and political attitudes, conducted on behalf of the mass media.

The first attempts to gauge the balance of public opinion were made in nineteenth-century America but this was before the advent of sampling theory. Before the 1930s most polls were undertaken directly by newspapers themselves, the most famous for *The Literary Digest*. These relied on mail questionnaires sent to samples drawn from known population listings such as telephone directories or car registration lists.

The first professional polling organization independent of the media was not established until 1935 when George Gallup established the American Institute of Public Opinion. Its methods received early vindication when it correctly forecast Roosevelt's triumph over Landon in the 1936 presidential election. *The Literary Digest* poll, in contrast, put Landon ahead; telephone and car owners proved to be unrepresentative of the country as a whole. The following year Gallup's methods were imported into Great Britain by Henry Durant.

Gallup's methods rested on the foundation of 'random sampling theory'. Developed by statisticians at the turn of the century, its premise is that by selecting and interviewing a small sample of voters (provided that all voters have had an equal chance of being selected), the result of a poll will on average faithfully reflect the distribution of opinion within the electorate as a whole. Further, the poll's range of possible sampling error can be calculated, provided always that the sample to be interviewed has been selected at random from the known population.

But by no means are all modern polls based on the application of random sampling theory. For example, in Great Britain most opinion polls (like most market research but not most social surveys) are undertaken using 'quota sampling'. Instead of being allocated specific names or addresses to interview, interviewers are instead requested to contact a certain number of people with a given combination of characteristics such as age, gender and social class. These quotas are set to ensure that the total numbers of persons interviewed in each quota category reflects their known distribution in the population as a whole. While it lacks the statistical underpinning of random sampling, quota sampling has traditionally been defended on the grounds that in practice it seems to work as well. For instance, pre-election polls using the method have mostly proved to be reasonably close to the actual outcome.

In some countries such as France and Germany, the publication of opinion poll results in the period immediately before polling day is banned. But elsewhere, such as in Britain and America, opinion polls are themselves a major feature of the media coverage of campaigns until the final day. Indeed, reports of the results of opinion polls are the most common lead story in British newspapers at election times.

The prominence of opinion polls in modern elections has, however, been accompanied by several high-profile failures. The first such failure was in the US Presidential election of 1948, when all the polls suggested wrongly that Harry Truman would lose against Thomas Dewey. This encouraged US pollsters to improve their methods and in particular to ensure that they interviewed closer to election day itself. Similarly, in the British general election of 1970 all but one of the polls anticipated Labour's re-election to office, an error which was also blamed on concluding interviewing too early, thus missing an alleged late swing of popular support from Labour to the Conservatives.

The most recent embarrassment for the polls was in Britain's 1992 general election, when the polls suggested right until the last day that Labour were ahead of the Conservatives. This error could not be accounted for simply by a late swing of public opinion. Rather it has raised substantial doubts about the accuracy and effectiveness of the practice of quota sampling and left the market-research industry in a state of methodological flux.

The methodology of opinion polls is also influenced by changes in technology. Following the demise of *The Literary Digest* poll, polls were traditionally undertaken by interviewing people face-to-face in their own homes or, in the case of some quota samples, in the street. But the spread of telephone ownership to near saturation point in some countries such as the USA, Canada and parts of Northern Europe, has resulted in an increasing use of telephone interviews. One of the advantages of telephone interviewing is its greater speed and spread. But it has disadvantages too, notably its lower levels of response from potential respondents and, still in many countries, the unevenness of telephone ownership within the population. Both these factors can lead to biases in the resulting sample.

Opinion polls do not deal only with the subject of voting intention and they are certainly not confined to election periods. They deal, too, with a range of topical questions, attempting to inject the public's voice into current debates, whether about social, moral, political or economic issues. They also serve the purpose of monitoring the course of public opinion on such matters as the popularity of governments and party leaders, the images of parties, the salience of particular social or political problems, evaluations of the economy, and so on. The crafting of such questions requires considerable skill to ensure that they are comprehensible to all respondents and not biased towards one viewpoint or another.

Even the most carefully drafted questions may, however, produce misleading or spuriously precise answers, often suggesting a sense of certainty among the public about an issue that, in reality, most people know or care little about. None the less, the strength of polls lies in their ability to bring greater levels of accuracy than would otherwise be available about the ebbs and flows of public opinion. Even using as few as around one thousand interviews, the polls sometimes manage to read the mood of the whole adult population of a country (or even of several countries, as in the case of the European Union's regular Eurobarometer survey) on a range of social and political issues of the day.

John Curtice
University of Strathclyde

Roger Jowell
Social & Community Planning Research

Further reading

Jowell, R., Hedges, B., Lynn, P. and Heath, A. (1993) 'The 1992 British Election: the failure of the polls', *Public Opinion Quarterly* 57.

Roll, C. W. Jr and Cantril, A. H. (1972) *Polls: Their Use and Misuse in Politics*, New York.

Teer, F. and Spence, J. D. (1973) *Political Opinion Polls*, London.

The Opinion Polls and the 1992 General Election: A Report to the MRS (1994) London.

Worcester, R. M. (1991) *British Public Opinion: A Guide to the History and Methodology of Political Opinion Polling*, Oxford.

See also: questionnaires; sample surveys.

public sector economics

The term public sector economics has over a number of years gradually replaced the more traditional but narrower topic of public finance, which refers to the study of how best to design the means by which the activities of the public sector might be financed. Thus, while public finance examines the impact of alternative forms of taxation upon wider economic activity and also examines the economic effects of public sector borrowing, public sector economics adopts a wider perspective and incorporates the public expenditure side of the budget.

Because its perspective is wider, public economics encompasses many more fundamental issues such as why does the public sector exist; what is the economic role of the state and how large should the public sector be? Public finance's narrower scope confines it to an extension of price theory. That is to say, the economists' standard neo-classical framework is adapted to include taxes whose impact is examined in terms of their effects upon the allocation of resources, that is, upon price formation, the supply of labour and employment; risk taking, investment and savings. Public finance also tended to pay considerable attention to the legal and administrative details of alternative tax regimes. That remains a focus of interest for the public sector economics specialist but the emphasis has now shifted. Using the framework of neo-classical economics, the legislative and administrative infrastructure of alternative tax regimes are critically evaluated in an attempt to improve upon their design. In particular, their effects upon incentives and the behaviour that these incentives produce are examined. Public finance is, therefore, a subset of the more general topic of public sector economics.

Public sector economics, in addition to public finance, deals with cost benefit analysis; public and collective choice; fiscal federalism; public enterprises; the distribution of income and social economics as it applied to areas such as education, health, housing and defence. The boundaries of public sector economics become more amorphous as it strays into a number of different sub-branches of economics. That, however, is a reflection of the all-pervasiveness of the public sector in modern economies. Moreover, the boundaries between economics and other disciplines become fuzzy when discussing public sector issues. For example, public choice theory is partially economics and partially political science.

While the narrow topic of public economics has been enlarged to become public sector economics, the character of the subject has also changed in a number of important ways. These changes in some respects reflect the more general developments which have taken place in economic analysis. First, there has been a tendency towards greater emphasis upon the micro-economic perspective of the subject. Macroeconomic public sector economics is usually treated as a separate subject. Thus, monetary and fiscal policies, which were once regarded as separate from one another, are now treated together within macroeconomics rather than public sector economics. The implications for monetary policy of financing government deficits are now taken seriously when once they were ignored. Indeed, the subject of public sector deficits and their financing raises a number of issues brought together in the Barro-Ricardo equivalence theorem which shows, under restrictive assumptions, that government bonds do not represent an increase in net worth. Assuming no bequests between generations, that there is dynastic overlapping of generations, and that individuals have rational expectations regarding the future, then a tax financed increase in public spending is shown to be equivalent to bond financing.

Public sector economics with its emphasis upon microeconomics has, therefore, over the past years, tended to concentrate attention upon the government's allocative and distributional functions rather than the macroeconomic stabilization role (Musgrave 1959). The microeconomics of the public sector has also emphasized the use of normative theory, as in the optimal design of taxation and public expenditure policies. This is contrasted with positive analysis, which considers the reactions of households and firms to specific government policies (Atkinson and Stiglitz 1980; Tresch 1981).

The economic rationale for the public sector stems from the failure of markets to allocate resources efficiently or to distribute resources according to particular acceptable notions of social justice. Market failures originate in concentrations of economic power (as in the case of monopoly); poorly specified property rights (for example, pollution); high transactions costs (i.e. the costs of making markets and trading in them); the existence of externalities (e.g. third party effects of consumption and production decisions) and the presence of increasing returns to scale technologies (e.g. the network economies of public utilities).

Many market failures, departures from Pareto efficiency, are trivial and irrelevant and, therefore, do not warrant government intervention to correct them. Others are quite serious and require government policies to alleviate their effects. An extreme form of market failure is when markets fail to exist. This happens in the case of *public goods*, which have been defined as goods which once they are made available to one person, are made equally available to all others (Samuelson 1954). In that case, no profit maximizing private sector producer will have an incentive to produce the service because the production and/or consumption externalities of the public good do not enable the producer to exercise property rights to the good. If public goods are to be made available, then they need to be provided through the public sector which has the power of compulsory taxation to finance these activities. Certain other goods, such as education and health care, while they are private goods rather than public goods, nevertheless do have significant externalities associated with them. There will, therefore, be a tendency for individuals to consume amounts of these goods/services which, while they are privately optimal, are less than the amounts that correspond to a social optimum. In order to achieve a social optimum, government intervention either through direct provision or subsidy is required.

Government intervention is also justified in the case of monopolies where the prices charged by monopolists can greatly exceed marginal costs. The issue here is the form of the intervention and the definition of monopoly. A firm might have a significant share of a local market but face considerable foreign competition in global markets. Also, the threat of new entrants could force monopolists to keep their prices close to those of competitive firms. The government could choose to legislate against monopolies; it could choose to nationalize 'regulation of what'? Should prices or profits, for example, be regulated?

The distribution of incomes, and hence welfare, in a society depends on a variety of factors: the initial distribution of endowments, skills, abilities, age and health status and access to markets, to name but a few. The distribution of income generated by the complex interaction of such factors can end up being regarded as unjust: criteria for social justice vary from place to place and from time to time. There is no unanimity about what constitutes a socially just distribution of welfare. Governments can by means of their taxation and public spending decisions influence the distribution of welfare. Progressive taxation, social security spending on unemployment benefits and state pensions, health care and education spending all contribute to changing the final distribution of welfares.

While the public sector exists to combat market failures, the government machine is not perfect. The costs of market failure need to be balanced against government failure. Government interventions can destroy incentives; public sector bureaucrats can over-supply public goods; regulators can be captured by those, whom they are supposed to regulate. Government failure in its various forms has been the focus of attention of the libertarians and the public choice school (Buchanan and Tullock 1964).

The public sector is a significant part of most economies and, in most cases, grew since the 1940s. In the 1990s, however, as government failure and the public sector's inability to solve many social problems become more prevalent, focus is directed to rolling back the frontiers of the state; privatization, regulation and contracting out are high on the policy agenda of most countries. It is, therefore, likely that the public sector will diminish in size but not in importance.

P. M. Jackson
University of Leicester

References

Atkinson, A. B. and Stiglitz, J. (1980) *Lectures on Public Economics*, Maidenhead.
Buchanan, J. M. and Tullock, G. (1964) *The Calculus of Consent*, Ann Arbor, MI.
Musgrave, R. A. (1959) *The Theory of Public Finance*, Maidenhead.
Samuelson, P. A. (1954) 'The pure theory of public expenditure', *Review of Economics and Statistics* 36.
Tresch, R. W. (1981) *Public Finance: A Normative Theory*, Georgetown, Ont.

Further reading

Brown, C. V. and Jackson, P. M. (1990) *Public Sector Economics*, Oxford.
Jackson, P. M. (1982) *The Political Economy of Bureaucracy*, London.
—— (ed.) (1993) *Current Issues in Public Sector Economics*, London.
Jackson, P. M. and Price, C. M. (eds) (1994) *Privatisation and Regulation*, Harlow.

See also: macroeconomic policy; nationalization; privatization.

public sphere

The concept of the public sphere is used most commonly to refer to the realm of public discourse and debate, a realm in which individuals can discuss issues of common concern. The public sphere is generally contrasted with the private domains of personal relations and of privatized economic activity.

One of the most important accounts of the public sphere was provided by Jürgen Habermas in his classic work *The Structural Transformation of the Public Sphere* (1989 [1962]). Habermas traced the development of the public sphere (*Öffentlichkeit*) from Ancient Greece to the present. He argued that, in seventeenth- and eighteenth-century Europe, a distinctive type of public sphere began to emerge. This 'bourgeois public sphere' consisted of private individuals who gathered together in public places, like salons and coffee houses, to discuss the key issues of the day. These discussions were stimulated by the rise of the periodical press, which flourished in England and other parts of Europe in the late seventeenth and eighteenth centuries. The bourgeois public sphere was not part of the state but was, on the contrary, a sphere in which the activities of state authorities could be confronted and criticized through reasoned argument and debate.

The development of the bourgeois public sphere had important consequences for the institutional form of modern states. By being called before the forum of the public, Parliament became increasingly open to scrutiny; and the political role of the freedom of speech was formally recognized in the constitutional arrangements of many modern states. But Habermas argued that, as a distinctive type of public domain, the bourgeois public sphere gradually declined in significance. Many salons and coffee houses eventually disappeared, and the periodical press became part of a range of media institutions which were increasingly organized on a commercial basis. The commercialization of the press altered its character: the press gradually ceased to be a forum of reasoned debate and became more and more concerned with the pursuit of profit and the cultivation of images.

Habermas's argument concerning the transformation of the public sphere has been criticized on historical grounds (Calhoun 1992), and in terms of its relevance to the social and political conditions of the late twentieth century (Thompson 1991). But the concept of the public sphere remains an important reference point for thinkers who are interested in the development of forms of political organization which are independent of state power. It also remains a vital notion for theorists who are concerned with the impact of communication media in the modern world. The concept emphasizes the importance of open argument and debate – whether conducted in the media or in a shared locale – as a means of forming public opinion and resolving controversial political issues.

John B. Thompson
University of Cambridge

References

Calhoun, C. (ed.) (1992) *Habermas and the Public Sphere*, Cambridge, MA.
Habermas, J. (1989 [1962]) *The Structural Transformation of the Public Sphere: An Inquiry into a Category of Bourgeois Society*, Cambridge, UK.
Thompson, J. B. (1991) *Ideology and Modern Culture: Critical Social Theory in the Era of Mass Communication*, Cambridge, UK.

Further reading

Keane, J. (1991) *The Media and Democracy*, Cambridge, UK.
Landes, J. (1988) *Women and the Public Sphere in the Age of the French Revolution*, Ithaca, NY.
Sennett, R. (1974) *The Fall of Public Man*, Cambridge, UK.

See also: media and politics; privacy.

punishment

Punishment is an intended evil. At the macrolevel, discussion has centred on the reasons for punishment, its effects, the acceptable forms of punishment, and the relationships between social structure and level of punishment. At the microlevel – which will not be covered here – the discussion has concerned the effects of punishments as opposed to rewards on the ability to learn.

There are three main sorts of justification of punishment. The natural law position argues that we punish because we punish, or, in some formulations, we punish because it would be unjust not to do so. God or Nature demand it. Even if we live seconds before doomsday, the condemned murderer must be hanged, otherwise justice would not have been done. Often implicit in this model is a sort of equilibrium theory: evil balances out evil. The tariff, however, may change over time: an eye for an eye in biblical time becomes three years of imprisonment – or 500 dollars – in our time. The second major position is utilitarian: punishment has a purpose; we punish because it is necessary. Punishment is a means to get offenders (individual prevention) or potential offenders (general prevention) to obey the law. The magnitude of the pain inflicted is in this case not proportionate to the crime but to the intended social purposes. Legal philosophers often attempt to reconcile the two major positions, particularly by insisting that no more pain should be inflicted for reasons of utility than is acceptable according to just desert. The equally logical opposite position – that pain should not be inflicted if it serves no purpose – is more seldom expressed. The third position is related to the first, but emphasizes that the judicial process may serve to clarify values. Indeed, the process rather than the outcome may become the central issue. Courts may be compared to theatres, as arenas where social values are dramatized.

Criminologists have given much thought to the effects of punishment on offenders themselves. In general, they have not been able to identify any particular form of punishment that would seem to reduce the probability of relapse: no one measure (apart from death or castration, of course) appears to work better than any other. Some criminologists even claim that the only thing they have found is that punishments are likely to increase the danger of committing further crimes, because all punishments – even if they are called something else – imply stigma.

As far as the effects of punishment on other people's behaviour is concerned (that is, the general preventive effects), results of research are more complex both to describe and interpret. These effects are evident when we contrast extreme alternatives. Capital punishment for minor and easily detected offences will reduce them, while the absence of any sanction will encourage them – as we see in situations where the police are out of action. More commonly, the choice lies between degrees of punishment, for example, between one or two years' imprisonment. In such cases, there are few indications that one punishment is more effective than another. Even death penalties are not demonstrably more effective deterrents than long prison sentences.

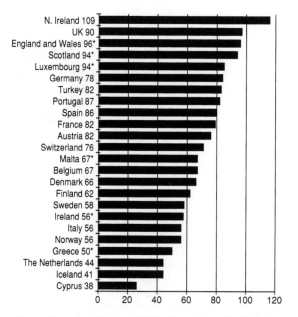

N. Ireland 109
UK 90
England and Wales 96*
Scotland 94*
Luxembourg 94*
Germany 78
Turkey 82
Portugal 87
Spain 86
France 82
Austria 82
Switzerland 76
Malta 67*
Belgium 67
Denmark 66
Finland 62
Sweden 58
Ireland 56*
Italy 56
Norway 56
Greece 50*
The Netherlands 44
Iceland 41
Cyprus 38

0   20   40   60   80   100   120

Source: Council of Europe (1992) *Prison Information Bulletin*
Note: *Figures for 1989. *Source*: Council of Europe (1990)
Prison Information Bulletin

Figure 1 Prisoners per 100,000 inhabitants in Western
European countries

Modern societies differ widely with respect to their penal traditions. Figure 1 gives the number of prisoners per 100,000 inhabitants in Western European countries in 1990 (Christie 1993).

Table 1 Prisoners per 100,000 inhabitants in
USSR/Russia and the USA

	.1979	1989	1993
USSR/Russia	660	353	470*
USA	230	426	550*

Note: *Estimates

Table 1 compares prison figures from some major industrial nations.

Taken together, Figure 1 and Table 1 indicate remarkably large variations in the use of imprisonment between countries and over time. It is difficult to explain these differences as a result of variation in the crime situation. Differences in social structure and penal traditions seems more promising as explanations. From Table 1, it is also clear that the number of prisoners now are on the increase, both in Russia and in the USA. In both countries, the prison industry is of particular importance as a driving force towards increase in the prison population: in Russia, due to what is produced within the prisons; in the USA, due to the consumption. The prison industry is constructing prisons, providing for equipment, food and service for the prisoners, as well as jobs for prison officers and other types of personnel. A joint feature of all these prison systems is that their inmates are heavily over-represented from the lower-lower classes, and from ethnic minorities.

Nils Christie
University of Oslo

Reference

Christie, N. (1993) *Crime Control as Industry: Towards Gulags Western Style?*, London.

Further reading

Hirsch, A. von (1976) *Doing Justice: Report of the Committee for the Study of Incarceration*, New York.
Mathiesen, T. (1974) *The Politics of Abolition*, Oxford.
Rawls, J. (1972) *A Theory of Justice*, Oxford.
Rutherford, A. (1993) *Criminal Justice and the Pursuit of Decency*, Foreword by Lord Scarman, Oxford.

See also: *capital punishment; crime and delinquency; criminology; penology; rehabilitation; social control.*

quantity theory of money *see* money, quantity theory of

questionnaires

Questionnaires pose a structured and standardized set of questions, either to one person, to a small population, or (most commonly) to respondents in a sample survey. Structure here refers to questions appearing in a consistent, predetermined sequence and form. The sequence may be deliberately scrambled, or else arranged according to a logical flow of topics or question formats. A questionnaire might, for example, commence with experiences from the subject's childhood, proceeding through time to the present. Questionnaire items follow characteristic forms: open-ended questions, where respondents fill in the blank, using an original choice of words; or the closed-response format, where responses must conform to options supplied by the interlocutor. Choices are frequently presented in the agree–disagree or yes–no form, or in extended multiple choice arrangements such as the Likert Scale, where several adverbs describe a hierarchy of sentiments such as agreement or favourability. Standardizing the phrasing for each question is a key phase in questionnaire design. Seemingly minor alterations in wording can substantially affect responses, a phenomenon which has generated much methodological research.

Questionnaires are distributed through the mail (perhaps the most usual method) or by hand, through arrangements such as the drop-off, where a fieldworker leaves the questionnaire for respondents to complete by themselves, with provision either for posting the complete form back to the research office, or for a return call by the fieldworker to collect the questionnaire. A questionnaire administered in a face-to-face interview, or over the telephone (growing in popularity among researchers), is generally termed a 'schedule'. In deciding upon one of these methods, researchers balance off costs, probable response rate, and the nature of the questions to be posed.

John Goyder
University of Waterloo

Further reading

Schuman, H. and Presser, S. (1981) *Questions and Answers in Attitude Surveys*, New York.

See also: interviews and interviewing; methods of social research; public opinion polls; sample surveys.

R

race

Few concepts in modern times have been less understood and few more liable to misuse than the concept of race when applied to humankind.

Such powerful feelings has it aroused that its use is sharply declining among the writers of physical anthropology textbooks in the USA. Of twenty such textbooks published between 1932 and 1969, thirteen (65 per cent) accepted that races of humans exist, three (15 per cent) claimed that they do not exist, while of the remaining four, two did not mention the subject while two stated that there was no consensus on the subject. Of thirty-eight such textbooks that appeared between 1970 and 1979, only twelve (32 per cent) stated that races of humans exist, whereas fourteen (37 per cent) claimed that races do not exist; of the remaining twelve texts, four were non-committal on the matter, three failed to mention race and five indicated that there was no consensus (Littlefield *et al.* 1982).

It is of course a moot point how much we may conclude from a study of the contents of textbooks, but it is, to say the least, striking that, during the 1970s, there was in the USA so marked a swing away from the earlier widespread acceptance of the existence of human races. Critics of the study cited have raised the question of the degree to which that change reflects new concepts flowing from new data and novel approaches, and the extent to which the change might have been predicated upon extraneous factors, such as a swing of fashion, political considerations, or the composition of classes of students to which the texts were directed. Nor is it clear whether the tendency in the USA typifies other parts of the world of physical anthropology.

Certainly the change tells us that, even among experts, no less than in the public mind, the concept of race is being critically re-examined and that no consensus, let alone unanimity, among specialists on the validity or the usefulness of the race concept appears to exist at the present time. It is worthwhile therefore to examine the meaning of race. Since race is basically a concept of biology in general, we shall start by examining race as a biological notion.

Race as a biological concept

Many, perhaps most, species of living things comprise numbers of populations which may be dispersed geographically and among varying ecological niches. To impart order to the subdivisions within a species, biologists have used several terms such as subspecies, race and population to classify the various groupings of communities that make up a species. Thus, in a species within which two or more subspecies are recognized, a race comprises populations or aggregates of populations within each formally designated subspecies. Often the term race is qualified: biologists recognize 'geographic races' (which may be synonymous with subspecies); 'ecological races' where, within a species, there occur ecologically differentiated populations; and 'microgeographic races' which refers to local populations (Mayr 1963).

Although students of any group of living things may differ from one another on the finer details of such intraspecific classifications, there has for some time been fairly general agreement that race is a valid biological concept. Classically, the differences among the races in a species have been identified by their morphology, that is, their observable physical structure.

Since the mid-1930s, and especially since 1950, biologists, not content with studying the morphological make-up of populations within species, have been studying the genetic composition of the subdivisions within species. These studies have directed attention to a number of non-morphological traits such as the genes for blood-groups and for specific proteins. When these hereditary characters are analysed, they reveal that there are no hard and fast boundaries between races and populations within a species. For any such genetic marker, it is not uncommon to find that the frequency of the trait in question is distributed along a gradient (or *cline*) which cuts across the boundaries of races, as delimited by morphology. Such gene clines often do not parallel any detectable environmental gradient; they appear to be neutral in relation to natural selective agencies in the environment.

Different genetic markers within a species may vary along different gradients. Thus, if one were to base one's thinking about the subdivisions of a species on the distribution of any one genetic marker, one would be liable to reach a different conclusion from that which might flow from the use of another genetic marker.

Hence, newer methods of analysis combine the frequencies of many different genetic markers, in the hope that the resulting sorting of populations will more nearly reflect the objective genetic relationship of the subgroups within a species.

Character-gradients apply as well to some morphological features. That is, some structural features such as body size, ear size, or colouring, change gradually and continuously over large areas. Such gradients, unlike the genetic clines, appear to parallel gradients in environmental features and have probably resulted from the action of natural selection (Huxley 1963). However, the frequencies of the genes governing morphological characters are less commonly used in the study of genetic interrelationships within a species, for several good reasons: first, such traits are often of complex, difficult and even uncertain genetic causation; second, many of them and, particularly, measurable characters are determined not by a single gene-pair, but by numbers of different gene-pairs; third, such characters are especially subject to environmental modification: for example, if animals live in a lush area and eat more food, they would be expected to grow bigger than those of the same species living in a more arid region. This 'eco-sensitivity' of the body's metrical traits renders them less useful in an analysis of genetic affinities.

In sum, race is a biological concept. Races are recognized by a combination of geographic, ecological and morphological factors and, since the 1970s, by analyses of the distribution of gene frequencies for numbers of essentially non-morphological, biochemical components. As long as one focused on morphological traits alone, it was sometimes not difficult to convince oneself that races were distinctly differentiated, one from another, with clear-cut boundaries between them; the progressive application of genetic insights and analyses to the problem revealed that recognizable gene variants (*or alleles*) are no respecters of such hypothetical boundaries. Often, indeed, one race merges

with the next through intermediate forms, while members of one race can and do interbreed with members of other races. Hence, the importation of genetic appraisal into the discussions on race has led to a definite blurring of the outlines of each race, and so to an attenuation of the concept of race itself.

Race in human biology

The biological concept of race, as just sketched, has been applied to the living populations of the human species. At least since the time of the Swedish naturalist and systematist Linnaeus (1707–78), all living human beings have been formally classified as members of a single species, *Homo sapiens*. The accumulation since the middle of the nineteenth century of fossil remains of the human family has revealed that earlier forms lived which could validly be regarded as different species of the same genus, for example *Homo habilis* and *Homo erectus*. Our species, *Homo sapiens*, probably made its appearance between one-half and one-third of a million years before the present.

As *Homo sapiens* spread across first the Old World and, more latterly, the New World, the species diversified, in varied geographical zones and ecological niches, into numerous populations. At the present time we have a situation in which living humanity is divided into several major and many minor subdivisions among which the same kinds of variation are encountered as apply to other living things. Thus, the populations show morphological variation, including some gradients associated with environmental gradients, and varying gene frequencies with clines of distribution that, for individual genetic markers, breach the limits of morphologically defined groups of populations.

Physical anthropologists, relying on morphological traits, have for long divided living humankind into great geographical races (also called major races, subspecies and constellations of races). Most classifications recognized three such major subdivisions, the Negroid, Mongoloid and Caucasoid; some investigators designated other major races, such as the Amerind and the Oceanian. Within the major races, several dozen minor races (or, simply, races) were recognized, the number identified varying with the investigator. As with other living groups, historically the classification of living *Homo sapiens* was based on morphological traits, such as skin colour, hair form and body size. As genetic analysis came to be applied, in respect first of blood-groups and later of a variety of proteins, clines were found which cut across the boundaries of minor and even of major races. Moreover, it was found that the genic variation between the major races was small in comparison with the intraracial variation. Doubts began to be expressed as to whether there was any biological basis for the classification of human races (for example, Lewontin 1972).

The problem is compounded by the fact that, even when genetical analysis became based not just on a few traits such as the ABO, MN and Rh blood-groups, but on a number of traits, different results were obtained according to which combinations and numbers of traits were used. For example, Piazza *et al.* (1975) analysed frequency data for eighteen gene loci in fifteen representative human populations: they found that the Negroid populations were genetically closer to the Caucasoid populations than either group of populations was to those populations classified as Mongoloid. This, in turn, was interpreted as signifying an earlier phylogenetic split between Mongoloid, on the one hand, and Negroid-Caucasoid on the other, and a later (more recent) split between Negroid and Caucasoid.

However, Nei's (1978) analysis, based on eleven protein and eleven blood-group loci in twelve human populations, revealed a first splitting between Negroid and Caucasoid-Mongoloid. Subsequently, Nei (1982) and Nei and Roychoudhury (1982) used a still larger number of genetic traits, namely sixty-two protein loci and twenty-three blood-group loci, that is eighty-five gene loci in all, for which data were available for some eighteen world populations. Interestingly, while the protein data revealed a first splitting between Negroid and Caucasoid-Mongoloid, the blood-group data suggest a slightly closer affinity and therefore a slightly more recent splitting between Negroid and Caucasoid.

Clearly, the last word has not been said on the exact pattern of affinities among the living races. Nor is there a consensus as to whether the large size of intraracial genetic variation, compared with interracial, vitiates any biological basis for the classification of human races. As two representative studies, we may cite Lewontin (1972) who believes there is no basis; and Nei and Roychoudhury (1982) who disagree with Lewontin and assert that, while the interracial genic variation is small, the genetic differentiation is real and generally statistically highly significant. Furthermore, it is clear that, by the use of genetic distance estimates, Piazza *et al.* (1975), Nei and Roychoudhury (1982) and others have been enabled to study the genetic relationships among the mainly morphologically defined human races, to construct dendrograms and to impart some understanding of the pattern of recent human evolution. Thus, the latter investigators have found evidence from protein loci to suggest that the Negroid and the Caucasoid-Mongoloid groups diverged from each other about $110,000 \pm 34,000$ years before present, whereas the Caucasoid and Mongoloid groups diverged at about $41,000 \pm 15,000$ years before present. These estimates do depend on a number of

assumptions and may be modified with the accretion of more data.

One further point may be mentioned here: the extent of genetic differentiation among the living human races, as determined by the study of protein loci, is not always closely correlated with the degree of morphological differentiation. Indeed, evolutionary change in morphological characters appears to be governed by quite different factors from those governing genetic differentiation in protein-forming genes of the human races, on presently available evidence. Genetic differentiation at protein loci seems to occur largely by such biological processes as mutation, genetic drift and isolation, with migration playing an important role in the establishment of current genetic relationships among human races. However, morphological characters have apparently been subject to stronger natural selection than 'average protein loci' (Nei and Roychoudhury 1972; 1982).

In short, the race concept can be applied to modern humans, even when one uses the most modern analytical procedures of population geneticists, and such application has been found of heuristic value. Nevertheless, irrespective of sociopolitical considerations, a number of modern investigators of human intraspecific variation find it more useful and more valid to base such studies on populations, as the unit of analysis, and to discard the race concept in these attempts.

Abuses and aberrations of the race concept

Among the various misconceptions that surround the concept of race are ideas about 'race purity', the effects of racial hybridization, superior and inferior races, race and mental differences, race and culture. A full review of this vast subject is not possible here: it has been dealt with in a number of studies such as those of Tobias (1970), Montagu (1972), Mead *et al.* (1968), Kagan (1968), Jensen (1969), Bodmer and Cavalli-Sforza (1970), Scarr-Salapatek (1971), Lochlin *et al.* (1975), Scarr (1980) and Gould (1981).

Although the foregoing selection of writers adopt widely differing standpoints, especially on the subject of race and intelligence (as supposedly reflected by IQ test results), it would not be unfair to claim that the following reflect the view of a great majority of physical anthropologists, human biologists and human geneticists at this time.

1 Race is an idea borrowed from biology.

2 At a stage when the study of human populations was primarily, if not exclusively, morphological and its objective classificatory, the race concept helped to classify the immense variety of living and earlier

human beings of the species *Homo sapiens*. With the advent of genetic analysis and the discovery that clines of genetic differentiation transcend the supposed boundaries of human races, the race concept has been appreciably weakened.

3 While some population geneticists have found that race still serves a useful purpose in the study of the genetic affinities of living populations, in the determination of the causal factors that have operated to produce genetic differentiation and in the reconstruction of the phylogenetic history of modern human diversity, others have found the concept of such negligible value in these studies as to have led them to discard race entirely. Time will tell whether we are witnessing 'the potential demise of a concept in physical anthropology' (as Littlefield *et al.* 1982 speculated), or whether the concept will survive the politico-social abuses to which it has been subject and which have been regarded by some as the primary cause of its decline from favour among many investigators and writers of textbooks.

4 If, for purposes of this analysis, we accept the existence of human races (as of other living things), we must note that races differ not in absolutes, but in the frequency with which different morphological and genetic traits occur in different populations.

5 The overwhelming majority of the genes of *Homo sapiens* are shared by all the mankind; a relatively small percentage is believed to control those features which differentiate the races from one another.

6 The formation of the modern human races is a relatively recent process, extending back in time for probably not much more than 100,000 years. As against this period of recent diversification, at least forty times as long a period of its hominid ancestry has been spent by each race in common with all other races, as it has spent on its own pathway of differentiation. This statement is based on the evidence that fossilized members of the human family (the *Hominidae*) are known from 4 million years before the present; molecular and some other evidence suggests that the appearance of the hominids may go back to 5 or more million years before the present.

7 Racially discriminatory practices make certain assumptions about race, some overt, some tacit. These include the assumptions that races are pure and distinct entities; that all members of a race look alike and think alike, which assumption, in turn, is based upon the idea that how one behaves depends entirely or mainly on one's genes; and that some races are better than others.

8 The scientific study of human populations has provided no evidence to validate any one of these assumptions.

9 Genetical and morphological analysis of human populations has failed to confirm that some races are superior and others inferior.

10 Accidents of geography and history, difficulties of terrain, physical environment and communication, are sufficient to account for the contributions which different populations have made to the varying advancement of human culture and to civilization.

11 Culture, language and outlook are not inseparably bound up with particular morphological or genetic racial features; for example, human culture is altering the direction of human evolution, as the species spreads into every corner of the world, and as cultural and racial divergence gives way over large areas to cultural and racial convergence.

12 The myth of the pure race has been thoroughly disproved. There are no pure (genetically or morphologically homogeneous) human races and, as far as the fossil record goes, there never have been.

13 Not only is purity of race a non-existent fantasy, but there is no evidence to support the notion that purity of race is a desirable thing.

14 Racial groups are highly variable entities; for many traits intraracial variability is greater than interracial variability. Intermediates exist between one race and the next.

15 Members of all races are capable of interbreeding with members of all others, that is, all that have been put to the test.

16 The supposed evils attendant upon race-crossing do not bear scientific scrutiny: neither sterility, diminished fertility, nor physical deterioration, has been proven to be a biological consequence of race-mixing. If there are unfortunate effects from such crossing, they are *social* (not biological) and they appear to result from the way in which other members of the populations in questions look at and treat the 'hybrids'.

17 The study of the races of humankind has been based on physical (that is morphological, physiological and biochemical) and genetic traits; mental characteristics have not been used in the classification of the human races, nor have they been found useful for such a purpose.

18 Scientific studies have not validly demonstrated any genetically determined variations in the kinds of nervous systems possessed by members of different human races, nor any genetically determined differences in the patterns of behaviour evinced by members of different races.

19 The claim that genetic factors contribute as much as 75 or 80 per cent of the variance of IQ test-score results and are therefore largely responsible for Black–White differences in mean test-score results has been seriously questioned in a number of investigations. It has been shown that a heritability estimate of 0.75 does not apply to American Blacks, among whom a much smaller percentage of the variance of test-score results has been shown to be genetically determined, and a

larger proportion environmentally determined. The immense literature that has accumulated since Jensen (1969) put forward his hypothesis that American Blacks are genetically inferior in intelligence to Whites has revealed many flaws that were implicit in the reasoning behind the hypothesis. The main conclusion that many of these studies have reached is that 'currently available data are inadequate to resolve this question in either direction' (Bodmer and Cavalli-Sforza 1970). A number of investigations have led to the development of environmental hypotheses. For example, Scarr (1980) found evidence in her studies to support a twofold hypothesis: such differences as exist between comparable populations she attributed partly to environmental factors and partly to cultural factors. On this additional cultural hypothesis, her work led her to stress a different relevance of extra-scholastic or home experience to scholastic aptitudes and achievement: 'The transfer of training from home to school performance is probably less direct for Black children than for White children' (Scarr-Salapatek 1971). Clearly, at this stage of our ignorance, it is unjustified to include intelligence, however tested, among the validly demonstrated, genetically determined differences among the races of humankind.

Phillip V. Tobias
University of the Witwatersrand

References

Bodmer, W. F. and Cavalli-Sforza, L. L. (1970) 'Intelligence and race', *Scientific American* 223.
Gould, S. J. (1981) *The Mismeasure of Man*, New York.
Huxley, J. S. (1963) *Evolution: The Modern Synthesis*, 2nd edn, London.
Jensen, A. R. (1969) 'How much can we boost IQ and scholastic achievement?', *Harvard Educational Review* 39.
Kagan, J. (1968) 'On cultural deprivation', in D. C. Glass (ed.) *Environmental Influences: Proceedings of the Conference*, New York.
Lewontin, R. C. (1972) 'The apportionment of human diversity', *Evolutionary Biology* 6.
Littlefield, A., Lieberman, L. and Reynolds, L. T. (1982) 'Redefining race: the potential demise of a concept in physical anthropology', *Current Anthropology* 23.
Lochlin, J. C., Lindzey, G. and Spuhler, J. N. (1975) *Race Differences in Intelligence*, San Francisco, CA.
Mayr, E. (1963) *Animal Species and Evolution*, London.
Mead, M., Dobzhansky, T., Tobach, E. and Light, R. E. (1968) *Science and the Concept of Race*, New York.
Montagu, A. (1972) *Statement on Race*, 3rd edn, London.
Nei, M. (1978) 'The theory of genetic distance and evolution of human races', *Japanese Journal of Human Genetics* 23.
—— (1982) 'Evolution of human races at the gene level', *Human Genetics, Part A: The Unfolding Genome*, New York.
Nei, M. and Roychoudhury, A. K. (1972) 'Gene differences between Caucasian, Negro and Japanese populations', *Science* 117.
—— (1982) 'Genetic relationship and evolution of human races', in M. K. Hecht, B. Wallace and C. T. Prance (eds) *Evolutionary Biology* 14.
Piazza, A., Sgaramella-Zonta, L. and Cavalli-Sforza, L. L. (1975) 'The fifth histocompatibility workshop: gene frequency data: a phylogenetic analysis', *Tissue Antigens* 5.
Scarr, S. (1980) *Race, Social Class and Individual Differences*, Hillsdale, NJ.
Scarr-Salapatek, S. (1971) 'Race, social class and IQ', *Science* 174.
Tobias, P. V. (1970) 'Brain size, grey matter and race – fact or fiction?', *American Journal of Physical Anthropology* ns 32.

racism

Racism, the idea that there is a direct correspondence between a group's values, behaviour and attitudes, and its physical features, is one of the major social problems confronting contemporary societies. Racism is also a relatively new idea: its birth can be traced to the European colonization of much of the world, the rise and development of European capitalism, and the development of the European and American slave trade. These events made it possible for colour and race to become pivotal links in the relations between Europeans, Americans and the people of Africa, Asia, Latin America and Australia. Though belief in the idea of the link between race and behaviour has never been proven, the tenaciousness of ideas supporting this connection has been elevated to a status of folk truth among the general population in many, if not most, countries (Williams 1990). Indeed, if the assertion of such a relationship were the only defining aspect of racism, its impact might be less damaging, though no less unacceptable. Instead, a more pernicious feature of racism entails the belief that some groups, those of a certain hue, with less power and low status, are inferior; others, of another hue, with greater power and high status, are deemed superior.

Racism is a highly complex and multifaceted concept and can be delineated into several areas, but it might be important to differentiate racism from ethnocentrism, a concept with which it is often confused and used, unfortunately, interchangeably. For example, Jones (1981) begins his critique of racism by distinguishing the two terms. Ethnocentrism entails the acceptance of the belief that individuals and groups seek to interpret events and situations, and to evaluate the actions, behaviour and values of other individuals and groups from their particular cultural perspectives. This view simply assumes that all insider values are 'acceptable', 'right' and 'good'; conversely, all outsider values are 'unacceptable', 'wrong' and 'bad'. What distinguishes ethnocentrism from racism is that in the former, there is no attempt to base insider/outsider differences along racial or colour lines. Oliver C. Cox

(1948) makes a similar point in his study of class, caste and colour: studies of early civilizations and empires demonstrated that ethnocentrism was clearly evident; the ethnocentrism focused solely on language and culture. That is, one was civilized if one understood the language and culture of the insider, but a barbarian if one did not. The early Greek idea of dividing the world into these two spheres, the civilized or the barbarian, was typical.

The Social Darwinism of the nineteenth century (Hofstadter 1955; Ryan 1981) laid the foundation for what is called 'ideological racism'. The logic is as follows: nature rewards groups which win the struggle for existence; strong groups, the winners, have won the right to control and, hence, decide the fate of the losers, the weaker groups. Those groups which lose in the struggle against other groups, by dint of this loss, confirm their weakness and inferiority. Since this ideology emerged simultaneously with the rise of European imperialism and the colonization of the continents, and gave credence to these events, and because the people and races being colonized and conquered were Africans, Asians and Native Americans, the close relationship between race, colour and ideas of superiority or inferiority was viewed by Europeans and Americans as having been confirmed.

As the European and American political, economic and cultural powers became more deeply entrenched in what DuBois called the 'coloured world', other attempts were made to justify the ever-increasing racial inequality. One new doctrine may be called 'scientific racism'. This racism entailed the use of 'scientific techniques', to sanction the belief in European and American racial superiority. The first technique was the use of 'objective' IQ tests, and their results, to confirm the high position of Europeans and the low positions of all other races in what its proponents called a racial hierarchy. Almost simultaneously with the use of 'scientific tests' was the use of brain size to prove inferiority or superiority. Those who believed in racial inequality were, thus, eager to use the lofty name of science to support their efforts to dominate and control other races and continents. In one of his studies, Pierre Van Den Berghe (1964) cut to the heart of the racist logic when he stated that despite all talk of inferiority or superiority, groups dominate other groups because only by doing so can they ensure and enforce inequality. But it can be said that this enforced inequality has yet a more ulterior motive which is even more central to the idea of racism: to isolate, penalize, ostracize and push the pariah group outside of the normal and ongoing social, political, economic and cultural discourse so that the pariah group will, in fact, be 'made' inferior.

During the 1960s when race and racism were crucial themes, Stokely Carmichael and Charles Hamilton (1967) coined the term 'institutional racism', using it in conjunction with 'individual racism' to differentiate the overwhelming importance of the former over the latter. An individual may be a racist and choose to discriminate against another individual or a group. This individual act is in contrast to institutional racism in which organizational networks linked to rules, procedures and guidelines make it difficult for members of one group to affiliate institutionally. In this case, it is not so much the individual who discriminates though individuals may do so as supervisors and managers for the company. In institutional racism, institutional rules and procedures which have been established on the basis of the qualifications and standards of the group in power serve to keep all other groups out, though this may not have been the intent of the original rules, procedures and guidelines. In fact, individuals employed in racist institutions may attest to their own lack of racism while proclaiming that they too are trapped and imprisoned by the laws, rules and procedures. There are other instances, however, when institutions willingly and knowingly discriminate. Since the mid-1980s, for example, the United States government has uncovered extensive patterns of institutional racism in housing, employment, education and banking, generally directed against racial minorities. Turner *et al.* (1984) presented a concise history of the interlocking networks which provide power and force to the racism which permeate institutions. One of the glaring consequences of the intensity of the traditional patterns of institutional racism has been the extent to which White Americans, and Whites in South Africa and Britain, have been the recipients of massive affirmative action programmes in which they, Whites, had a monopoly on jobs, incomes and bureaucratic positions, while those not White were removed from the competitive field. We have just recently begun to understand the extent to which centuries of affirmative action for Whites have consigned minorities to a secondary role in economics, politics, education and other areas of social life.

In the USA, some attention has focused on the idea of 'reverse racism'. Racism in any form, practised by any group, should be challenged and contested, but the idea that minorities in the USA now have sufficient power to injure the interests of the majority group is not consistent with the facts. In all areas of living (political, economic, educational, etc.) Whites continue to have a huge monopoly. When one looks closely at the data provided by those who claim that reverse racism is alive and real, one generally sees anecdotal evidence in which much of the information used is obtained third or fourth hand, that is, a friend of a friend said his friend did not get a job or lost a job to a Black. When these anecdotal sketches are used, the minority who gets the job or the promotion is invariably less qualified, very incompetent, etc. In the USA, a member of a minority group who is a racist may insult a member of the majority, but in no area of American life are minorities, who may be racists, in a position to control institutionally or determine the opportunity structure for the majority. When majorities are racists, and when they control the major institutions, as described by Turner *et al.* (1984), they can and do control the opportunity structure for minority people.

Since the 1960s when racial analysis became a major issue in social relations, ample data have been collected verifying the negative consequences of racism for minority groups. Generally, these negative consequences resonate around the theme of powerlessness in all areas. In the 1980s some sociologists began to focus on the impact of racism on Whites (Dennis 1981). This new twist on the consequences of racism shifts the focus somewhat, for it suggests that racism is not merely something which happens to the oppressed; rather there are social, emotional and ethical issues for the majority culture which controls the institutions which constitute the continuing source of racism. Attention has also been devoted to the idea that racism may be a more consciously directed act and idea than previously assumed. In the 1981 study (Dennis 1981), it was revealed that many parents did, in fact, socialize their children to be racists; racial training did not occur by chance. Children are guided in their racial training by adults, mainly parents (Dennis 1981; 1994). However, during their teen years, even the children from the most racist families tend to move away from the positions of parents and to assert their own views of other groups based on their relationship with these groups at school, work or in various social circles.

In the mid-1990s, the abolition of apartheid in South Africa will certainly alter the racial history in that country. But we now know, based on history in the USA and Britain, that the abolition of racially restrictive laws will not end all semblance of racism. Though much of the myth of race resides in institutional arrangements, another large part resides in patterns of racial thinking and the ideological orientation of individuals and groups in the society. Laws restricting discrimination may be effective to some degree, and groups may be frightened enough by the price they might pay for discriminating, yet ideological racism, enshrined in the deeply held racial myths in a society, may survive among the population in many forms. This then is the test for nations which contain diverse racial groups and which have had a history of racial domination and conflict: how to ensure individual and group equity; how to ensure that group cultural and racial differences be viewed as objective social and biological realities without the accompanying invidious distinctions.

Rutledge M. Dennis
George Mason University

References

Carmichael, S. and Hamilton, C. (1967) *Black Power*, New York.
Cox, O. C. (1959) *Caste, Class and Race*, New York.
Dennis, R. (1981) 'Socialization and racism: the white experience', in B. Bowser and R. Hunt (eds) *Impacts of Racism on White Americans*, Newbury Park, CA.
—— (1994) 'The racial socialization of white youth', in B. Bowser and R. Hunt (eds) *Impacts of Racism on White Americans*, 2nd edn, Newbury Park, CA.
Hofstadter, R. (1955) *Social Darwinism in American Thought, 1860–1915*, Boston, MA.
Jones, J. (1981) 'The concept of racism and its changing reality' in B. Bowser and R. Hunt (eds) *Impacts of Racism on White Americans*, Newbury Park, CA.
Ryan, W. (1981) *Equality*, New York.
Turner, J., Singleton, R. and Musick, D. (1984) *Oppression*, Chicago.
Van Den Berghe, P. (1964) *Caneville*, Middletown, CT.
Williams, R. (1990) *Hierarchial Structures and Social Values: The Creation of Black and Irish Identities in the United States*, Cambridge, UK.

See also: ethnicity; prejudice; Social Darwinism.

radicalism

Though social theories and philosophical analyses may be termed radical, the primary modern usage of the word radicalism is to designate basic or extreme political challenges to established order. The term (with an upper-case R) came into use in the late eighteenth and early nineteenth centuries to refer to an elite political faction which sought parliamentary and other rationalizing reforms, and became a key root of the Liberal Party in England. Almost immediately, a lower-case usage developed to describe all sorts of political orientations which shared either an analysis of current troubles claiming to go to their roots, or a programme deduced from first principles. Under pressure of the French Revolution and various English popular agitations, attention came increasingly to focus on actual mobilizations – radical actions – rather than merely radical ideas.

Social scientists are still divided in the extent of their emphasis on the importance of rationalistic analyses (for example, Marxist class consciousness) compared to other more directly social sources of radical actions. There are two conventional views among the latter group. One, now nearly discredited, holds that social atomization and marginalization dispose those cut off from the social mainstream to engage in protests which reveal more of their psychological troubles than any serious programme for social change. The other stresses the underlying interests which a common position in relation to some external factor, such as markets or means of production, gives to individuals. Both positions are challenged by empirical findings that a great deal of organization and internal cohesion are necessary to radical collective action. Common objective interests are not necessarily enough to produce concerted action. Activists can hope to achieve this coalescence through further organizational efforts, and they often see trade unions and similar organizations as way-stations on the road to class organization.

Traditional communities, however, have been the basis of more radical movements than class or any other abstract bonds and formal organizations. The popular radical movements (as opposed to elite radicals) of early industrial Britain acted on radical social roots in reaction to the disruptions of the Industrial Revolution. Though the members of these communities often lacked sophisticated radical analyses, they had visions profoundly at odds with conditions around them. Perhaps even more importantly, they had the social strength in their communal relations to carry out concerted action against great odds for long periods of time; few compromise positions were open to them, unlike the members of the modern working class. These sorts of social foundations continue to be central to radical movements around the world. Peasants and other traditional farmers along with artisans and craft workers form the mainstay of these radical movements.

Social revolutions, the most radical of actual political transformations, certainly have many causes besides anti-governmental radical movements. A state structure weakened by external conflicts or internal disunity may, for example, be essential to the success of a revolutionary movement. Where revolutions succeed, and transform societies rather than only change regimes, two sorts of radical groups have generally been involved. On the one hand, there has usually been a tightly organized, forward-looking, relatively sophisticated group of revolutionaries. On the other hand, there has also generally been a broad mass of protesters and rebels acting on the basis of strong local communities and traditional grievances. The latter are essential to making the revolution happen, to destabilizing the state. The former, however, are much better positioned to seize power during the transformation.

At least in the contemporary world of states and other large-scale abstract social organizations, there is a paradox to radicalism (which may of course be of the 'right' as well as the 'left'). Most radicalism is based on local bonds and tradition, yet when successful, it both disrupts tradition and displaces power towards the centre of society and its large-scale systems of control. This is true even of radical movements aimed at less extreme goals than revolutions. The US civil rights movement could succeed in ending local intolerance and oppression only by forcing an increase of central state power and its penetration into local life. But it could not at the same time make local communities democratic and preserve their autonomy as free realms of direct participation.

Craig Calhoun
University of North Carolina

Further reading

Calhoun, C. (1983) 'The radicalism of tradition', *American Journal of Sociology* 88.
Moore, B. Jr (1979) *Injustice: The Social Bases of Obedience and Revolt*, White Plains, NY.

See also: fascism; populism; revolutions; social movements.

rational choice theory

Rational choice theory (RCT) – or alternatively rational action theory (RAT) – adopts the view that behavioural units (usually individual people) optimize their choices (actions) under specific conditions. Colloquially, individuals (units) do the best they can given their conditions.

RCT is tied to no particular notion of what is 'best', but in the absence of any independent evidence to the contrary usually assumes that individuals look out for themselves (self-regard). There are, however, RCT models of altruism and malice. Evolutionary theory is often used to justify self-regard, by claiming to show that self-regard survives in competitive environments. This is, however, controversial.

It is the assumption of optimizing action, when conjoined with descriptions of the conditions of action, which gives RCT its predictive (explanatory) properties. It may also be used *normatively* to guide actions in an optimal direction. Differences in the conditions of action lead to variations in the type of theory which is analytically appropriate. The most basic distinction is between *parametric* and *strategic* conditions. The former implies that the focal decision/action taker, when optimizing, need make no calculation about how others will calculate about what the focal actor does, in taking the decision. When this is the case, the appropriate theory is *decision theory*. On the contrary, when the focal actor needs to calculate how others will choose (act) in taking their own decision (actions), then the conditions are strategic. Game theory is the theory of strategic choices/actions.

The conditions assumed in decision theory are as follows: first, the set of alternative actions available to the decision maker, second, the decision maker's *degree of certainty* about the relevant outcomes of each of the available actions, and third, the decision maker's *ranking* of the available actions on the basis of presumed rankings of relevant outcomes. It is conventional to divide the decision maker's degree of certainty into three types: decision under certainty where the actor (decision-maker) is certain about the relevant outcomes; decisions under risk where the decision maker can in some way assign probabilities to the outcomes; decisions under uncertainty where the decision maker cannot even assign probabilities. With decisions under certainty the optimal choice is the highest ranking action; with decisions under risk *expected utility theory* is usually deployed. The analysis of decisions under uncertainty is controversial but usually involves an attempt to assign some sort of probabilities.

Game theory extends RCT to strategic situations. Games may be classified in a number of ways, including zero-sum and non-zero sum; normal (or strategic) form and extensive form; complete and incomplete information; perfect and imperfect information; co-operative and non-co-operative; one shot and repeated (finite or infinite times). It is generally held that co-operative games can be reduced to non-co-operative ones, by including some initial bargaining moves. Nash equilibrium is the fundamental solution concept (predictive or normative). A Nash equilibrium is a set of (actions) strategies (one for each (actor) player) such that none has an incentive to change strategy given the other actors play the strategies specified in the set. Some games have more than one Nash equilibrium; then additional criteria must be applied for a solution (so-called equilibrium selection). Game theory is a theory of social interaction which is increasingly used in the social sciences, notably economics, but is now advancing in sociology and political science also.

Peter Abell
London School of Economics
and Political Science

Further reading

Abell, P. (ed.) (1991) *Rational Choice Theory*, Aldershot.

Coleman, J. S. and Fararo, T. J. (1992) *Rational Choice Theory, Advocacy and Critique*, Newbury Park, VT.

Moser, P. K. (ed.) (1990) *Rationality in Action*, Cambridge, UK.

See also: game theory; prisoners' dilemma; rational expectations.

rational expectations

Expectations of the future play an important part in economics. Investment, for example, is affected by expectations of demand and costs. The foreign exchange rate is affected by expectations of inflation and interest rates. The rational expectations hypothesis embodies the assumption that people do not make systematic errors in using the information which they have to predict the future. Some errors in prediction are generally inevitable due to lack of information and the inherent uncertainties of economic affairs. The rational expectations hypothesis postulates that, given the information used, the prediction errors are random and unavoidable.

Rational expectations are on average self-fulfilling. The term rational expectations equilibrium is used to describe situations in which expectations lead to actions which confirm the original expectations. For example, the expectation of a rise in stock market prices may itself generate the rise. The absence of systematic predictions errors in a rational expectations equilibrium suggests that people have no incentive to change the way they make predictions, and hence that the equilibrium is likely to persist unless disturbed by outside events.

The rational expectations hypothesis is seen by some economists, including Muth (1961), who coined the term rational expectations, as the extension to expectation formation of the assumption that people act 'rationally' in pursuit of their own self-interest, which forms the basis of neo-classical economics. However, a rational expectations equilibrium requires that agents are not only rational, in the sense of acting optimally given their own beliefs, but also that their beliefs are correct. Agents in a rational expectations equilibrium act as if they knew both the structural form, and the numerical values of the parameters, of the model which describes the economy in which they operate. Either agents are somehow endowed with the information and understanding which they need, or they have to learn about the model by some process of statistical inference, in which case a rational expectations equilibrium makes most sense in the context of a long-run stationary state. The inference problem faced by agents is greatly complicated by the assumption that expectations affect outcomes, so the way in which agents learn affects the data they observe, and standard results on the asymptotic properties of estimators do not apply. There are some examples in which agents derive a forecasting rule using ordinary least squares, which converges to the rational expectations equilibrium forecasting rule, despite the fact that the data are generated by an equation whose parameters change each time the agents revise their estimates (Marcet and

Sargent 1988). However, there are no general results. Nevertheless the rational expectations hypothesis is more appealing to many economists that any of the available alternatives, providing as it does a relatively simple and plausible description of expectation formation, which can be readily incorporated into mathematical economic models.

The concept of a rational expectations equilibrium has been applied extensively, particularly in finance and macroeconomics. The demand and therefore the price of financial assets depends upon investors' expectations of their future value. Thus the price itself is a source of information about the asset. This phenomenon has been modelled extensively as a rational expectations equilibrium, which has given useful insights into the circumstances in which various forms of the efficient markets hypothesis, that prices are perfect aggregators of information about assets, is valid.

The use of rational expectations equilibria in macroeconomics follows from the Lucas critique of econometric models (Lucas, 1976). This influential paper argued that the estimated relationships in Keynesian macroeconometric models are likely to break down when policy changes, because they fail to take account of the effect of the policy changes on the expectations and actions of optimizing agents. This led to the emergence of the 'new-classical' or 'rational expectations' school of macroeconomics, which developed rational expectations equilibrium models which incorporated the hypothesis that, in the absence of unanticipated inflation, there is a unique 'natural rate' of unemployment. The conjunction of the natural rate and rational expectations hypothesis is the basis for the claim of policy neutrality, that monetary policy can have no systematic and predictable effect on output and employment, and hence that there is no long-term trade-off between inflation and unemployment.

Margaret Bray
London School of Economics
and Political Science

References

Lucas, R. E. (1976) 'Econometric policy evaluation: a critique', in K. Brunner and A. H. Melzer (eds) *The Philips Curve and Labor Markets*, Amsterdam.

Marcet, A. and Sargent, T. J. (1988) 'The fate of systems with "adaptive" expectations', *American Economic Review*, Papers and Proceedings 78 (May).

Muth, J. F. (1961) 'Rational expectations and the theory of price movements', *Econometrica*, 29.

Further reading

Bray, M. (1989) 'Rational expectations, information and asset markets' in F. H. Hahn (ed.) *The Economics of Missing Markets Information and Games*, Oxford.

Miller, P. J. (1994) *The Rational Expectations Revolution*, Cambridge, MA.

Pesaran, M. H. (1987) *The Limits to Rational Expectations*, Oxford.

See also: game theory, economic applications; macroeconomic policy; rational choice theory.

rationalism *see* reason, rationality and rationalism

reason, rationality and rationalism

Rationality is a problem shared by the social sciences and philosophy. Before considering the various issues it raises, it is best to offer provisional definitions of the three related notions of reason, rationality and rationalism.

Reason is the name of an alleged human faculty capable of discerning, recognizing, formulating and criticizing truths. Philosophic disputes about reason concern its very existence (extreme irrationalism may deny that any such faculty exists at all); the nature of its operations (for example, can it actually secure data, or can it only make inferences; how powerful are the inferences it can make; can it make discoveries or can it only check discoveries made by other means?); the areas of its operations (is it restricted to deductive reasoning, or to science; can it be applied to moral, aesthetic, political issues; can it initiate conduct?).

Rationality is a trait which individuals or collectivities display in their thought, conduct or social institutions. Various features can be seen, singly or jointly, as marks or defining features of rationality:

1 A tendency to act only after deliberating and calculation, as opposed to acting impulsively or in obedience to unexamined intimations.
2 A tendency to act in accordance with a long-term plan.
3 A control of conduct by abstract and general rules.
4 Instrumental efficiency: the selection of means purely by their effectiveness in bringing about a clearly specified aim, as opposed to allowing means to be selected by custom or impulse.
5 A tendency to choose actions, institutions, and so on in terms of their contribution to a single and clearly specified criterion, rather than by evaluating them by multiple, diffuse and unclear criteria, or accepting them in virtue of their customariness.
6 A propensity to systematize convictions and/or values in a single coherent system.

7 An inclination to find human fulfilment in the exercise or satisfaction of intellectual faculties rather than in emotion or sensuality.

Rationalism is the name of a number of doctrines or attitudes:

1 The insistence of the authority of individual, independent, cognitive activity, as opposed to authority of some extraneous privileged sources (Revelation, Church).
2 The higher valuation of thought or inference as against sensation, observation or experiment, within cognitive activity.
3 The view that collectivities, or individuals, should best conduct their lives in accordance with explicit and intellectually chosen plans, rather than by custom, trial and error, or under guidance of either authority or sentiment.

It should be noted that doctrine (1) opposes the partisans of human reason, assumed to be fairly universally or evenly distributed among all people, to followers of privileged Authority. In other words, Rationalists in sense (1) include *both* sides of dispute (2), that is, both adherents of thinking and adherents of sensing as the main source of knowledge. In other words, issues (1) and (2) cut across each other. As 'rationalism' is widely used in both senses, and the issues are cross-related in complex ways, failure to see this ambiguity leads to confusion. A key figure in western rationalism was Descartes, who was a rationalist in both senses. On the one hand, he recommended that all traditional, inherited ideas be subjected to doubt, a kind of intellectual quarantine, and be awarded certificates of clearance only if they were found logically compelling to the enquiring mind. Though Descartes, when applying this method, did in fact eventually award just such a certificate to the theism of the faith of his birth, the sheer fact of making inner reason the first and last Court of Appeal in effect constituted and encouraged rationalism in sense (1). But he was also a rationalist in the second sense, and considered innate rational powers to be far more important than sensory information. His view of the human mind has been powerfully revived by the contemporary linguist, Noam Chomsky, notably in *Cartesian Linguistics* (1966) and supported by the argument that the amazing range of linguistic competence of most humans cannot be explained without the assumption of an innate grammatical structure present in all mind, which thus corresponds to one aspect of the old 'reason'.

In the seventeenth and eighteenth centuries, the programme of Descartes's rationalism (sense 1) was implemented, among others, by the school of 'British empiricists', of whom the greatest was probably David Hume. However, at the same time they repudiated rationalism (sense 2). Hume (1976 [1739–40]), for instance, basically considered thinking to be nothing but the aftertaste of sensations: thinking about a given object was like having an aftertaste of a dish when one is no longer eating.

The eighteenth century is often said to have been the Age of Reason; in philosophy, however, it was also the age of the Crisis of Reason. This was most manifest in the work of Hume. His main discovery was this: if rationalism (1), the subjection of all belief to evidence available to the individual, is combined with empiricism, the view that the senses alone supply the database at the individual's disposal, we end with an impasse: the database supplied by the senses simply is not strong enough to warrant our endorsement of certain convictions which seem essential for the conduct of life – notably, the presence of causal order in the world, or continuous objects, or of moral obligation. Hume's solution for this problem was that these crucial human tendencies, such as inferring from the past to the future, or feeling morally constrained, not being warranted by the only database available to us, were simply rooted in and justified by habit, a kind of Customary Law of the mind.

Immanuel Kant (1929 [1781]) tried to provide a stronger and less precarious refutation to Hume's scepticism. His solution was, in substance, that the human mind has a rigid and universal structure, which compels humans (among other things) to think in terms of cause and effect, to feel obliged to respect a certain kind of ethic (a morality of rule-observance and impartiality, in essence), and so on. So the inner logical compulsions on which Descartes relied as judges of culturally inherited ideas were valid after all, but they were only valid for the world as experienced by beings with our kind of mind; they were not rooted in the nature of things, as they were 'in themselves'. They were rooted in *us*.

It is among Kant's numerous intellectual progeny that the problem of reason becomes sociological. The two most important ones in sociology were Emile Durkheim and Max Weber. Each of them very obviously inherits the Kantian problem, but they apply it to society and to the diversity of human cultures in radically different, indeed almost diametrically opposed, ways. Durkheim followed Kant in being concerned with our conceptual compulsions, in holding conceptual compulsion to be central to our humanity. But where Kant was content to explain it by invoking an allegedly universal structure of the human mind, operating behind the scenes in each individual mind, Durkheim sought the roots of compulsion in the visible life of distinct communities and above all in ritual. The core of religion is ritual, and the function of ritual is to endow us with shared concepts, and to endow those concepts with a compelling authority for all members of a given community. This is the central argument of his *The Elementary Forms of Religious Life* (1915 [1912]). For Durkheim, all humans are rational, rationality manifests itself in conceptual compulsion, but the form that rationality takes varies from society to society. Sharing the same compulsions makes humans members of a social community.

If for Durkheim all humans are rational, for Weber some humans are more rational than others. He notes that the kind of rationality which Kant analysed – orderly rule-bound conduct and thought – is specially characteristic of one particular tradition, namely the one which engendered the modern capitalist and industrial society. (Weber is less explicitly concerned with Kant than is Durkheim, but the connection is nevertheless obvious.) Weber's problem is not why all humans are rational (all humans think in concepts and are constrained by them), but why some humans are *specially* rational, quite particularly respectful of rules and capable of selecting means for their effectiveness rather than for their congruence with custom, thereby becoming apt at establishing modern capitalist and bureaucratic institutions.

Weber (1961 [1924]; 1968 [1922]) noted that the kind of world codified by the great philosophers of the Age of Reason, a world amenable to rational orderly investigation and manipulation rather than propitiation, was not a world inhabited by all humankind, but only by the participants of the historical tradition which had engendered capitalism and large-scale bureaucracy. He believed that this kind of rational mentality was an essential precondition of a capitalist or bureaucratic civilization, and was *not* the necessary corollary of the other preconditions of that civilization: in other words, in opposition to historical materialism, he did not believe that the emergence of that civilization could be explained in terms of its material preconditions alone. One further and independent necessary factor was also required. (He modified rather than inverted the materialist position, in so far as he did not claim or believe that the nonmaterial necessary condition, or any set of such conditions, could ever be sufficient.) Hence in his hands the philosophical problem of rationality becomes a sociological one – how did rationality come to dominate one particular civilization and eventually, through it, the entire world?

The Durkheimian and Weberian traditions are not the only ones through which the philosophers' concern with Reason reaches the social sciences. There are at least two others.

In Kant, the attribution of rationality to a rigid and universal structure of the human mind, but *not*

to the material which that mind (or those minds) handled, led to a tense and uncomfortable dualism: the world was a blind, amoral machine, and the intrusion of either cognitive rationality or moral conduct into it was a mysterious imposition by our minds of order on to material indifferent and alien to that order. At the core of the philosophy of Hegel lay the supposition that Reason was not merely (as Kant thought) responsible for the individual striving for consistent behaviour and explanations, but that it was also a kind of grand and impersonal Puppet Master of History. In other words, the pattern of history had an underlying principle which was not alien to the rational strivings within us, but, on the contrary, provided a kind of guarantee for them. The idea is attractive, inherently and inescapably speculative, but it did seem to receive some support from the vision of history as Progress, which had become fashionable at about the same time. Marxism, while disavowing the mystical elements in Hegel, nevertheless took over the underlying intuition of a rational historic design. People who continue to uphold some version of this view are not normally called rationalists, but nevertheless their ideas are relevant to the debate about the relation of reason to life.

The other relevant tradition, in addition to the Marxist–Hegelian one, is associated with the great names of Schopenhauer, Nietzsche and Freud. Kant had identified Reason with all that was best in humankind. Schopenhauer (1958 [1819]) taught that humans were dominated by a blind irrational Will, whose power they could not combat in the world, though they could at best occasionally escape it through aesthetic contemplation and compassion. Nietzsche (1909–13) shared Schopenhauer's views, but inverted his values: why should the Will be condemned, in the name of a morality which was really the fruit of resentment, of a twisted and devious manifestation of that very Will which was being damned? Freud (1930) took over the insights of both thinkers (though not Nietzsche's values), provided them with an elaborate setting in the context of clinical practice and psychiatry, invented a technique purporting to alleviate at least some of the more pathological manifestations of irrational forces and set up an organization for the application and supervision of that technique. In so far as he did not applaud the dominance of irrational forces but on the contrary sought to mitigate them, he cannot (unlike Nietzsche) be accused of irrationalism; but his views of the devious and hidden control of seeming reason by hidden unreason closely resemble Nietzsche's, though as stated they are elaborated in what seems to be a far more specific form, and are linked to clinical practice.

The social scientist is likely to encounter the problem of Reason and Rationality (under a diversity of formulations) in connection with the various traditions and problems which have been specified. The main problem areas are

1 Innate reason vs experience as a source of cognition, the debate opposing thinkers such as Descartes and Chomsky to empiricists and behaviourists.
2 The anchoring of inner logical compulsions either to an allegedly universal human mental equipment, or to the specific culture – in other words the opposition of (say) Kant and Durkheim.
3 The question of a historically specific form of rationality, its roots, and its role in engendering modern civilization – what might be called the Weberian problem.
4 The feasibility, in principle or in particular cases, of locating a rational plan in history.
5 The debate as to whether the real driving force, and the location of genuine satisfaction, within the human psyche is to be sought in irrational drives or in rational aim, calculation, insight or restraint (or in what proportion).
6 Rationality in the sense of explicit criteria and conscious plan, as opposed to respect for tradition and continuity in the management of a polity.
7 Rationalism in the sense of favouring free enquiry as against the authority of either Revolution or Tradition.

These various issues are of course interrelated, although by no means identical, but they are often confused, and the lack of terminological consistency frequently furthers this confusion.

Ernest Gellner
University of Cambridge
Central European University

References

Chomsky, N. (1966) *Cartesian Linguistics: A Chapter in the History of Rationalist Thought*, New York.
Durkheim, E. (1915 [1912]) *The Elementary Forms of Religious Life*, London.
Freud, S. (1930[1930]) *Civilization and its Discontents*, London.
Hume, D. (1976 [1739–40]) *A Treatise on Human Nature*, 2 vols, London. (Original edn, *Das Unbehagen in der Kultur*, Leipzig.)
Kant, I. (1929 [1781]) *Immanuel Kant's Critique of Pure Reason*, Riga. (Original edn, *Kritik der reinem Vernunft*.)
Nietzsche, F. (1909–13) *Beyond Good and Evil and The Genealogy of Morals*, in O. Levy (ed.) *The Complete Works of Friedrich Nietzsche*, vols 12 and 13, Edinburgh.
Schopenhauer, A. (1958 [1819]) *The World as Will and Representation*, New York. (Original edn, *Die Welt als Wille und Vorstellung*, Leipzig.)
Weber, M. (1961 [1924]) *General Economic History*, London. (Original edn, *Wirtschaftsgeschichte*, Munich.)
—— (1968 [1922]) *Economy and Society*, New York. (Original edn, *Wirtschaft und Gesellschaft*, 2 vols, Tübingen.)

Further reading

Bartley, W. W. (1962) *The Retreat to Commitment*, New York.
Elster, J. (1978) *Logic and Society: Contradictions and Possible Worlds*, Chichester.
Hollis, M. and Lukes, S. (1982) *Rationality and Relativism*, Oxford.
MacIntyre, A. C. and Emmet, D. (1970) *Sociological Theory and Philosophical Analysis*, London.
Magee, B. (1963) *The Philosophy of Schopenhauer*, Oxford.
Wilson, B. (ed.) *Rationality*, Oxford.

See also: magic; sociology of science.

reference groups

Reference group refers to an individual or social grouping which either sets or maintains standards for the individual, or which acts as a frame of comparison relative to which individuals compare themselves.

Reference group theory and research developed out of the symbolic interactionist tradition within American social science. It was related to Charles Cooley's view that the self arises out of the ideas which others entertain of the given individual. The idea is also present in G. H. Mead's analysis of the differences between role-taking, the 'significant other' in the play stage, and the 'generalized other' in the game stage of human development. Being able to take on the role of the generalized other means that individuals are able to develop fully human characteristics, of effective selves able to look at, assess, control and direct their actions. The existence of the generalized other means that individuals can be the object of their own reflexive consciousnesses. Furthermore, Mead's discussion implies that it is because humans are able through symbols to take on the role of the other that they can refer their attitudes and behaviour to social groups with which they are not directly involved. Reference group analysis thus developed to take cognizance of the fact that people may refer for judgement to groups of which they are not and perhaps cannot be members.

H. H. Hyman first coined the term reference group in 1942 (Hyman and Singer 1968). He distinguished two different orientations that might be taken to such a group – the *identificatory* and the *judgemental*. In the former case, this produces a normative commitment to the group in question; in the latter, it entails actors evaluating themselves with respect to income, status, education, and so on by comparison with the achievements of the other group. This distinction was clarified by H. H. Kelly who distinguished between the normative and comparative function of any reference group; this in turn developed into the now commonplace distinction between the normative reference group and the comparative reference group.

Four other points should be noted. First, we should distinguish between different forms of the social object to which reference is made, that is, whether it is an individual, a group, a collectivity or a social category. Second, reference to any such social object should be viewed as either positive or negative, as in the case of the normative reference group involving respectively identification with or separation from the given social object. Third, we should also distinguish audience reference groups, namely those social objects which function as a source of evaluation and appraisal for the social actor but which are not bases of normative identification or social comparison. Fourth, there are highly complex and variable relations possible between an individual and a given group, ranging from formal membership, psychological membership, regular interaction, intermittent interaction, to no contact at all (Merton 1957).

There have been a number of attempts to identify universalistic explanations of the *selection* of normative reference groups. Some writers suggest that the acceptance of a reference group depends upon the ease with which satisfactory interpersonal contacts can be made. Others argue that the choice of normative references depends upon an individual's status-image and the function of the reference group in a process of status conferral. Others again argue that the selection of normative references will depend upon the degree of perceived interdependence between the individual and the group in question. And, finally, it is suggested that individuals are more likely to refer to a given group the more that the individuals are perceived to be socially valuable to the group in question. However, although these are all useful hypotheses, none has been seen to be universally valid.

The best known examination of the *consequences* of normative reference group selection is Theodore Newcomb's study of Bennington College (Hyman and Singer 1968). He observed that during four successive years, junior and senior students were markedly less conservative than freshmen in terms of a number of public issues; a cohort study over the same period showed the same trend. Moreover, non-conservatism was associated with high participation, involvement and status within the college. Hence, where the college acted as a normative reference group then the student's attitudes became less conservative; where this was not the case and the home and family remained as significant normative reference groups, then attitudes stayed more conservative. However, there are difficulties in this and related studies. First, it is often difficult to avoid circular argument, since the change of attitude both constitutes the explicandum *and* provides evidence for the patterning of normative group selection. Second, it is necessary to analyse an actor's *interpreta-tion* of competing normative reference groups rather than assume that particular consequences necessarily follow. Third, changing patterns of reference group selection have to be related to the temporal development of the self and especially to changes in the life cycle – hence reference group choices may be historically dependent one upon the other, as in Merton's (1957) analysis of anticipatory socialization.

Comparative reference group analysis is based on the argument that once clear physiological needs have been satisfied, then human beings require other bases by which to assess their achievements and satisfactions. In particular, it is argued, humans derive such assessments by comparing themselves with others. Many social philosophers from Aristotle onwards have noted these processes (Urry 1973). De Tocqueville analysed how the mass of the citizenry began to compare themselves with the newly emergent middle class who 'have no conspicuous privileges, and even their wealth . . . is impalpable and, as it were, *invisible*'. Marx in turn disputed this, arguing that 'although the pleasures of the labourer have increased, the social gratification which they afford has fallen in comparison with the increased pleasures of the capitalist'. He concludes that since our wants and pleasures 'are of a social nature, they are of a relative nature'. And, from a different tradition, Max Scheler maintained that

> The medieval peasant prior to the thirteenth century does not compare himself to the feudal lord, nor does the artisan compare himself to the knight . . . every comparison took place within a strictly circumscribed frame of reference. . . . In the 'system of free-competition', on the other hand . . . aspirations are intrinsically *boundless*, for they are no longer tied to any particular object or quality.

A version of this can be found in the famous intepretation of the 'promotion finding' in the *American Soldier* study, which established that those units where there was a high rate of promotion expressed *more* dissatisfaction about future promotion chances than units where promotion rates were lower. Hence, Robert Merton (1957) argued that higher mobility rates induced excessive hopes and expectations for further promotion, and more widespread comparisons were made. This view was amplified by W. G. Runciman (1972) who also, on the basis of a national sample survey, concluded that manual workers in the UK had fairly restricted comparative reference groups, especially with regard to class dimensions of inequality. Certain non-manual workers made wider and more class-conscious comparisons. An important reason for this was that there generally has to be some kind of basis or similarity along other dimensions of social inequality, apart from the one where the comparison is occurring, in order that wide-ranging comparisons can be made. For example, the Amba in East Africa were willing to work for Europeans at a much lower price than for employers from another tribe, because 'a European is on a much higher social plane, and therefore comparisons are out of the question'. There was no other similarity or basis for the comparison.

Most research indicates that actors normally operate in terms of fairly restricted patterns of social comparison. It is only in periods of rapid social change that these established patterns may be upset. John Urry (1973) distinguished between 'conventional comparisons', those used in everyday life and structured in terms of the actor's social network, and 'structural comparisons', those feasibly made when that everyday world is disrupted, and comparisons are structured by the environing patterns of social stratification. Urry also emphasized that relative deprivation involves a number of distinct stages of development, in particular, that there are varied conditions under which revealed deprivations are deemed unjust, and blame may be attributed to the dominant groups or the wider society. Ted Gurr (1970) has likewise elaborated an integrated theory of political violence, in which the first stage, the development of discontent, stems from the perception of relative deprivation between people's value expectations and value capabilities.

Overall, there is nothing which we might term 'reference group theory'. The term is, as Runciman argues, useful in describing certain processes of attitude formation within an individualistic social science, based on related notions of self, identity and role. The key idea is, as Thoreau puts it, 'If a man does not keep pace with his companions perhaps it is because he hears a different drummer.'

John Urry
University of Lancaster

References

Gurr, T. (1970) *Why Men Rebel*, Princeton, NJ.
Hyman, H. H. and Singer, E. (eds) (1968) *Readings in Reference Group Theory and Research*, New York.
Merton, R. K. (1957) *Social Theory and Social Structure*, New York.
Runciman, W. G. (1972) *Relative Deprivation and Social Justice*, Harmondsworth.
Urry, J. (1973) *Reference Groups and the Theory of Revolution*, London.

See also: groups; symbolic interactionism.

reflexivity

Reflexivity is a term used in a wide variety of senses. Two main tendencies can be discerned. First, reflex-ivity is used to characterize general features of (modern) social life. Second, reflexivity is used more specifically to refer to certain characteristics of social scientists' attempts to explain social life. It is not clear how these uses are interrelated: the definitively reflexive history of the term is yet to be written.

An example of the first usage is Beck's (1992) discussion of reflexive modernity. Here reflexivity refers to the fact that modern societies are now reaping the negative results of their mishandling of the environment, and to humankind's increasing awareness of these negative consequences. The supposed virtue of human dominance of nature is increasingly called into question. Beck also suggests that this leads to a form of personal reflexivity whereby members of mature modern societies question established patterns of life and social mores.

Arguably, what is missing from Beck's account is attention to the second main usage of reflexivity. What are the reflexive consequences of Beck's account? Does increasing personal reflexivity also mean that different forms of social science account are now appropriate (or necessary)? This second sense of reflexivity connotes the idea that the claims and arguments made by social science in some sense refer back to social science itself.

Classically, the second usage of reflexivity is associated with a species of philosophical paradox, the most well known of which is the Liar's Paradox. Thus, the statement that All Cretans Are Liars, when uttered by a Cretan, generates both false and true conditions for its evaluation: if the statement is true then it is false; if it is false, then it is true.

Notwithstanding the negative connotations associated with such aporia, reflexivity is sometimes encouraged as an aid to improved analysis. This form of reflexivity is benign introspection. Social scientists are encouraged to reflect upon the social circumstances of the production of their knowledge, either as a methodological corrective (often consigned to the appendix of research reports), or as part of a general injunction toward healthy awareness of the social and political context within which they operate.

In Garfinkel's (1967) discussion of ethnomethodology, reflexivity refers to the intimate interdependence between surface appearances (documents or accounts) and the associated underlying reality (a distinction which is characteristic of the documentary method of interpretation). The sense of the former is elaborated by drawing on knowledge of the latter, while at the same time, the sense of the latter is elaborated by what is known about the former. Accounts are thus 'constituent features of the settings they make observable'. Constitutive reflexivity has radical implications for social science's pretensions to causal argument, since it casts considerable doubt on the extent to which explanans and explanandum can be considered distinct elements in an explanation.

Reflexivity is often said to be engendered by all social science with relativizing tendencies. Any claim about the influence of social circumstances on a particular situation can be understood as also referring to the claim itself. This aspect of reflexivity comes into particular focus in work in the sociology of scientific knowledge. Whereas it has been convincingly demonstrated that natural scientific knowledge is a product of social, cultural, historical and political processes, rather little attention has been given to the fact that social science itself is an activity generated by these same forces. Sociology of science treats scientific knowledge in broadly relativist terms, but often continues to practise its own craft in realist terms. This has lead to criticisms of inconsistency, especially from objectivist philosophers of science. The recommended solution from this latter quarter is to abandon relativism. By contrast, a body of work has arisen which takes the opposite tack and upholds the principle of consistency by exploring ways of abandoning realist methods in the social study of science.

One source of antipathy to this reflexive project is the assumption that such work is incompatible with good (serious) research practice because of its self-regarding quality or because it leads to a regress of meta-studies. Such assumptions have led researchers interested in reflexivity to develop a practice in which the interrogation of the methods proceeds simultaneously with, and as an integral part of, the investigation of the object. This has lead to a variety of experimental textual forms ranging from the use of dialogue to the visible display of various material constraints on form, such as (following Ashmore 1989) the seven hundred and fifty word limit of this

Steve Woolgar
Brunel University

References

Ashmore, M. (1989) *The Reflexive Thesis: Wrighting Sociology of Scientific Knowledge*, Chicago.
Beck, U. (1992) *Risk Society: Towards a New Modernity*, London.
Garfinkel, H. (1967) *Studies in Ethnomethodology*, Englewood Cliffs, NJ.

Further reading

Bartlett, S. J. and Suber, P. (eds) (1987) *Self-Reference: Reflections on Reflexivity*, Dordrecht, The Netherlands.
Woolgar, S. (ed.) (1988) *Knowledge and Reflexivity: New Frontiers in the Sociology of Knowledge*, London.

See also: ethnomethodology; post-modernism; sociology of science.

refugees

The concept of refugee is at once a legal, political, cultural and sociological category. As a consequence, the attribution or label refugee carries with it not only common-sense cultural connotations and legal specificity, but also a great deal of analytical baggage (Marx 1990; Zetter 1988; 1991). Refugees are also heterogenous populations found across the world which have been singled out from ordinary migrants as a potential subject for study for all disciplines.

Legal and political dimensions

Although the phenomenon of refugees is not novel to the twentieth century (Marris 1985), the technical meaning, as it developed after the First World War, was mainly concerned with distinguishing those groups who had lost the protection of their own state (refugees) from ordinary migrants (immigrants). During this period, refugees were not simply defined as people seeking safety, but those who were forced to cross international boundaries under particular conditions of political duress (Skran 1989). The ascription refugee (as defined in the 1933 Refugee Convention) allocates this status according to specific nationalities, for example Russians, Armenians, Assyrians and Turks (Skran 1989: 21). This international convention also entailed an obligation of receiving states to provide assistance and protection. A separate category of people in need of international protection was identified by the 1938 Refugee Convention which concerns the status of de-nationalized Germans, mainly Jews (Goodwin-Gill 1990; Skran 1989). It is important to note that the pre-Second World War definitions identified refugees in terms of membership of particular national groups and the particular political situation which led to their flight.

The main international legal instrument – the 1951 UN Convention Relating to the Status of Refugees – emerged as a result of the European experience of the Second World War. The drafters of the convention – thirty-five primarily western-block countries (Weis 1994) – defined refugees as individuals, rather than groups, who had a 'well-founded fear of persecution for reasons of race, religion, nationality, membership of a particular social group or political opinion'. It was limited to people fleeing events occurring in Europe before 1 January 1951. Although governments were supposed to apply this definition to all asylum seekers in a neutral manner, and the Office of the UN High Commissioner for Refugees (UNHCR) was to be of an entirely non-political character, in fact this was not the case. Because of the politics of the Cold War, people fleeing communist countries were generally granted asylum and their acceptance was used for ideological purposes (Loescher 1993: 59; Loescher and Scanlan 1986).

In the aftermath of decolonization, refugees became a global problem and the 1967 Protocol extended the definition of a refugee beyond European boundaries. Both the Organization of African Unity's Convention and the Cartagena Declaration expanded the definition of a refugee to include those who fled their countries 'owing to external aggression, occupation, foreign domination or events seriously disturbing public order'. An important feature of all these international conventions is that they contain a negative stricture (the condition of *non-refoulement*) for the signatory states without, however, obliging them to grant asylum to a refugee. In contrast, asylum under Islamic law entails the duty of the state to grant asylum (Elmadmad 1993).

Although the 1951 Convention relating to the Status of Refugees was being prepared at the time of the 1948 expulsions of the Palestinians, the international community recognized the difficulty of incorporating them under the authority of the High Commissioner for Refugees, whose office was to be non-political, and the Arab states also resisted such an inclusion of Palestinians because they held the United Nations directly responsible for the creation of the refugee crisis and felt that the international community should bear the cost rather than placing it on them, the countries of refuge. As a consequence, an independent legal and assistance regime, the UN Relief and Works Agency (UNRWA) for Palestinian Refugees in the Near East, was created under the UN General Assembly Resolution 194(III) of 1948 to accommodate their case.

In its working definition, Palestinians were registered as refugees by UNRWA if they had lost *both* home and livelihood and had taken refuge in one of the countries or areas where this organization was providing relief. Furthermore, the status of a Palestinian refugee is transmitted to descendants through the male line. It is evident that both the determination of refugee status and the assistance and protection to which they are entitled are influenced by the prevailing geopolitical agenda.

The sociological dimension: the evolution of solutions to the refugee problem

The evolution of the term refugee as it has developed in the context of international humanitarian policy after the First World War falls into five main phases. In each one of these phases is found both a particular conceptualization of the refugee as a national and an international problem and the corresponding policy solution used to address it (Goodwin-Gill 1990).

Phase I

The interwar period was dominated by the spirit of the times which was nationalism, understood as one nation for each state and only one state for every nation, as Manzini put it. In this sense, refugees were defined in terms of their membership of a nation without a state, or without the protection of their state, and thus in need of international protection, for example, passports (travel documents for Russian refugees) (Skran 1992), and livelihood support (jobs for Armenian refugees). In some cases, settlement sponsorship schemes were supported for nation-states trying to absorb those refugees who had an ethnic claim (e.g. Greece and Greek refugees from Turkey) (Skran 1992: 28–30). Furthermore, since the protection and assistance was mainly provided by the receiving state, the dominant solution was primarily through the labour market.

Phase II

In the period following the Second World War, solutions were guided by the Cold War ideology and the west's preoccupation with the elimination of the enemy: fascism, whether right or left (Harrell-Bond 1985). Resettlement as a response to the vast refugee numbers was to be a *permanent* solution, involving the *assimilation* of the newcomers into the host society (Hathaway 1992; Kay and Miles 1988).

Phase III

By the 1970s, most of the situations giving rise to mass exodus were taking place in Asia and Africa. Refugees became identified as a Third World problem to be resolved in these regions (Zolberg *et al.* 1989). Asylum was perceived as temporary, as was (and still remains) the solution devised to address it: the refugee camp (Harrell-Bond 1986; Malkki 1989; 1990; Stein 1986; Voutira and Harrell-Bond 1994). Given that the weakest states had become the hosts of the vast majority of refugees, the refugee camp was perceived by the rich donor countries as a strategy of political containment, as an efficient mechanism for the delivery of humanitarian relief leading to economic self-sufficiency (Daley 1991; Harrell-Bond 1986; 1993). Neither of these objectives were, in fact, achieved. With respect to the political considerations, refugee camps became the seedbed for political foment (Malkki 1989; 1990). As far as economic self-sufficiency was concerned, for the most part, people living in refugee camps have been systematically impoverished (Clark and Stein 1985; Harrell-Bond 1986; Waldron 1987). Refugees became permanent cases for international welfare (Harrell-Bond and Voutira 1992; Harrell-Bond *et al.* 1992).

Phase IV

From the early 1980s, the recognition of the failures of temporary solutions led to series of attempts simply to eliminate the problem. These included efforts to undermine the legitimacy of the whole notion of refugee status by promoting the idea that refugees were not victims of circumstances but, in fact, individuals who had been attracted by the aid offered as a result of this status (Ruiz 1987). Such ideas have led to the very common popular misconception that all refugees are now job seekers rather than asylum seekers. With the increasing poverty and instability in the south, such beliefs are further reinforced by the general unwillingness to recognize the degree to which human rights issues underlie the diverse economic, environmental and civil unrest which cause refugee movements (Hathaway 1991).

The promotion of voluntary repatriation is the major solution marking Phase IV (Coles 1985; Harrell-Bond 1989), with many observers criticizing the coercion under which these programmes are implemented (Crisp 1984; Cuny and Stein 1990). Even repatriation back into conflict situations may be seen as legitimate (Cuny et al. 1992), and refoulement is legitimized by the concept of safe countries (Amnesty International 1992; EXCOM 1991).

Under the policies of perestroika, the waiving of restrictions on immigration and the international policy of rapprochement between east and west, the concept of voluntary repatriation was introduced to account for the large numbers of immigrants from the east. These included ethnic Germans, Armenians, Greeks, and Jews from the then Soviet Union, Hungarians from Romania, Germans from Poland, to mention only a few, who were defined as repatriating to their respective homelands (Bade 1993; Korcelli 1992; Voutira 1991).

Phase V

The 1990s marked the beginning of a new phase. On the one hand, UNHCR proclaimed it as the decade of repatriation. On the other, as a result of the war in the former Yugoslavia, refugees are once again a European problem demanding a common response. Methods were introduced to actively prevent threatened people from acquiring access to the territory of states bound to grant asylum by governments, united by their restrictionist policies (e.g. fortress Europe), and reinterpreted as protection of the right not to be uprooted. The international community now promotes the notion of preventive protection through safe havens (Jaeger 1993).

Sociocultural constructions of the refugee

Media images of refugees, often reinforced by charity fund-raising, characteristically focus on depictions of misery, destitution, helplessness and dependency (Benthall 1993). These familiar encodings of the global culture are far removed from anthropological analyses of the refugee experience in different cultural contexts. Accordingly, we need to identify the degrees to which the formal and technical meanings of the legal terms discussed vary with respect to different ideologies and local practices concerning strangers, foreigners and guests.

A number of cases point to the range of such cultural variations. In southern African societies, norms of hospitality to the stranger allowed western survivors of shipwrecks to be welcomed into local communities even as chiefs and benefactors of these regions. In South-east Asia, foreigners were regularly integrated into local communities through rituals of eating together, helping and entertaining neighbours according to Buddhist tradition. For the Sherpas in Nepal, the people are the hosts and the gods are their guests: making others comfortable pleases the gods, who, in turn, are expected to protect the hosts from demons. Among Afghan refugees, codes of honour ensured temporary shelter among kin, when they first arrived in Pakistan. On the ideological level, Koranic tradition includes the general obligation to grant asylum to the refugee (mohajer), guaranteeing the maintenance of this protection. Furthermore, because the refugee in this context is associated with Muhammad's flight from Mecca to Medina in AD 622, a refugee is not a term of shame but a term of honour. In each of these cases, the theme of exchange of social obligation and reciprocity supports the manifestation of 'this-worldly' or secular benevolent behaviour, which is legitimized by the belief in 'other-worldly' restitution or retribution to balance out the particular act.

In conclusion, refugees are people who have undergone a violent rite of separation and unless or until they are incorporated as members into their host state (or returned to their state of origin) find themselves in a perpetual state of liminality or between and betwixt (Malkki 1990). Their incorporation is an interactive process involving the adaptation of both refugees and their hosts.

Coming to terms with the different dimensions of human suffering that are encapsulated in the refugee experience has functioned as a corrective device for theory. The study of such disenfranchised and dispossessed populations has also provided an impetus for establishing social science more firmly within public affairs.

E. Voutira
B. E. Harrell-Bond
University of Oxford

References

Amnesty International (1992) 'Europe: harmonization of asylum policy. Accelerated procedures for "manifestly unfounded" asylum claims and the "safe country" concept'. London.

Bade, K. J. (1993) 'Re-migration to their Father's Land? Ethnic Germans from the East in the Federal Republic of Germany', *Refugee Participation Network* 14.

Benthall, J. (1993) *Disasters, Relief and the Media*, London.

Clark, L. and Stein, B. (1985) *Older Refugee Settlements in Africa: A Final Report*, Washington, DC.

Coles, G. (1985) 'Voluntary repatriation: a background study', *Round Table on Voluntary Repatriation*, UNHCR, San Remo.

Crisp, J. (1984) 'Voluntary repatriation programmes for African refugees: a critical examination', *Refugee Issues* 1(2).

Cuny, F., and Stein, B. (1990) 'Prospects for the promotion of spontaneous repatriation', in G. Loescher · and L. Monahan (eds) *Refugees and International Relations*, Oxford.

Cuny, F. Stein, B. and Reed, P. (1992) *Repatriation during Conflict in Asia and Africa*, Dallas.

Daley, P. (1991) 'Gender, displacement and social reproduction: settling Burundian refugees in Tanzania', *Journal of Refugee Studies* 4(3).

Elmadmad, K. (1993) *L'Asile dans les pays afro-arabes avec une reference speciale au Soudan*, PhD thesis, University Hassan II, Casablanca.

EXCOM (1991) (Executive Committee of the High Commissioner's Programme) 42nd Session, Sub-Committee of the Whole on International Protection: Background note on the 'safe country' concept and refugee status (EC/SCP/68 GE.91-02095).

Goodwin-Gill, G. (1990) 'Different types of forced migration movements as an international and national problem', in G. Rystad (ed.) *The Uprooted: Forced Migration as an International Problem in the Post War Era*, Lund.

Harrell-Bond, B. E. (1985) 'Humanitarianism in a straight-jacket', *African Affairs* 334.

—— (1986) *Imposing Aid*, Oxford.

—— (1989) 'Repatriation: under what conditions is it the most desirable solution for refugees? An agenda for research', *African Studies Review* 32(1).

—— (1993) 'Creating marginalised dependent minorities: relief programmes for refugees in Europe', *Regugee Participation Network* 15.

Harrell-Bond, B. E. and Voutira, E. (1992) 'Anthropology and the study of refugees', *Anthropology Today* 8(4).

Harrell-Bond, B. E., Voutira, E. and Leopold, M. (1992) 'Counting the refugees: gifts, givers, patrons and clients' *Journal of Refugee Studies* 5(3/4).

Hathaway, J. (1991) *The Law of Refugee Status*, Oxford.

—— (1992) 'The conundrum of refugee protection in Canada: from control to compliance to collective deterrence', in G. Loescher (ed.) *Refugees and the Asylum Dilemma in the West*, University Park, PA.

Jaeger, G. (1993) 'The recent concept of preventative protection', *Refugee Participation Network*.

Kay, D. and Miles, R. (1988) 'Refugees or migrant workers? The case of European volunteer workers in Britain (1946 1951)', *Journal of Refugee Studies* 1(3/4).

Korcelli, P. (1992) 'International migrations in Europe: Polish perceptives for the 1990s', *International Migration Review* 26(2).

Loescher, G. (1993) *Beyond Charity: International Cooperation and the Global Refugee Crisis*, Oxford.

Loescher, G. and Scanlan, J. (1986) *Calculated Kindness: Refugees and America's Half-Open Door*, New York.

Malkki, L. (1989) 'Purity and exile: transformations of historical-national consciousness among Hutu refugees in Tanzania', PhD thesis, Harvard University.

—— (1990) 'Context and consciousness: local conditions for the production of historical and national thought among Hutu refugees in Tanzania', in Richard Fox (ed.) *National Ideologies and the Production of National Cultures*, American Ethnological Society Monograph Series, no. 2.

Marris, M. (1985) *The Unwanted: European Refugees in the Twentieth Century*, Oxford.

Marx, E. (1990) 'The social world of refugees', *Journal of Refugee Studies* 13(3).

Ruiz, H. (1987) *When Refugees won't Go Home: The Dilemma of Chadians in the Sudan*, Washington, DC.

Skran, C. (1989) 'The international refugee regime and the refugee problem in interwar europe', D Phil dissertation, University of Oxford.

—— (1992) 'The international refugee regime: the historical and contemporary context of international responses to asylum problems', in G. Loescher (ed.) *Refugees and the Asylum Dilemma in the West*, University Park, PA.

Stein, B. N. (1986) 'Durable solution for developing country refugees', *International Migration Review* 20(2).

Voutira, E. (1991) 'Pontic Greeks today: migrants or refugees', *Journal of Refugee Studies* 4(4).

Voutira, E. and Harrell-Bond, B. H. B. (1994) 'In search of the locus of trust: the social world of the refugee camp', in E. Daniel and J. Knudsen (eds) *(Mis)Trusting Refugee Narratives*, Berkeley, CA.

Waldron, S. R. (1987) 'Blaming the refugees', *Refugee Issues* BRC/RSP.

Weis, P. (1994) *Commentary on the Convention Relating to the Status of Refugees*, Cambridge, UK.

Zetter, R. (1988) 'Refugees, repatriation and root causes', *Journal of Refugee Studies* 1(2).

—— (1991) 'Labelling refugees: forming and transforming an identity', *Journal of Refugee Studies* 4(1).

Zolberg, A., Suhrke, A. and Aguayo, S. (1989) *Escape from Violence: Globalized Social Conflict and the Refugee Crisis in the Developing World*, New York.

See also: migration.

regimes, military *see* **military regimes**

region

A region is an area of the earth's surface which is relatively homogeneous, and differs from its neighbours, on certain criteria. The definition and description of regions was a dominant concern of geographers during the central period of the twentieth century, who interpreted their role within the academic division of labour as accounting for the areal differentiation which characterizes the earth's surface. Thus for several decades regional geography was at the discipline's core: 'regional geography is at least a vital and indispensable part of the subject: . . . for the general reader it is and always has been geography *par excellence*' (Wooldridge and East 1958: 141).

The practice of regional geography involved selecting the criteria on which regional delimitation was to be based, applying those criteria in the field, and then describing the assemblage within each region. The latter involved synthesizing the results of systematic investigations of the different phenomena which make up the contents of a region, and Wooldridge (1956: 53) defined the geographer's task as gathering up 'the disparate strands of the systematic studies, the geographical aspects of other disciplines, into a coherent and focused unity, to see nature and nurture, physique and personality as closely related and interdependent elements in specific regions'. This defined geography as a synthesizing discipline, dependent on many others for much of its raw material.

The criteria for regional definition, and the form in which their synthesis should take in regional description, engendered substantial debate. For many authors, the physical environment was the key to regional understanding, and many regional definitions and descriptions were strongly underpinned by notions of environmental determinism – human activities are strongly conditioned, if not determined, by their physical context. Some authors distinguished between a 'natural region', for which physical characteristics alone were the defining criteria, and a 'geographical region', whose character reflected human response to the environment. Others went further, and likened the region to an organism.

Regional geography was structured on the concept of the region as a homogeneous spatial unit: as the core of the discipline, it was presented as the study of how parts of the world vary because of the uneven distribution of natural and human phenomena (including the interaction of the two). Different types of phenomena cluster in different areas, creating regions, so the study of regions both illuminates the reasons for the clustering and illustrates the unique features of the different parts of the world.

The region was thus perceived as an entity which was an important pedagogic device, and much published geographical work portrayed spatial variations through regional descriptions: this included substantial textbooks covering areas of continental or sub-continental scale. Others criticized such study,

however, as 'trying to put boundaries that do not exist around areas that do not matter' (Kimble 1951: 159).

This latter view gained increased acceptance by the late 1950s, and regional geography's dominance of geographical practice was challenged by those attracted to an alternative view of the discipline as spatial science. Regional geography was attacked as ill defined and poorly done, and rapidly fell into disrepute, although the concept of the region was retained in the new task of defining homogeneous areas for the practice of spatial analysis.

Although it is now extremely rare for regional geography as a research activity to be promoted, it retains supporters among those who identify a pedagogic role for the description of regions as a means of transmitting knowledge about areal differentiation, which task is 'popular and educational rather than practical or narrowly professional' (Paterson 1974: 21); indeed, one eminent US geographer has claimed that regional geography is 'the highest form of the geographer's art', involving the production of 'evocative descriptions that facilitate an understanding and appreciation of places' (Hart 1982: 2).

This siren call has attracted few disciples. Nevertheless, the increased focus on place (locale, locality, region) within geographical work has led to some calls for the study of regions, if not of regional geography as traditionally practised. Regions in that context are changing milieux within which social relations are forged and reforged, and individuals are socialized and resocialized: they are the local settings within which global processes are played out.

R. J. Johnston
University of Bristol

References

Hart, J. F. (1982) 'The highest form of the geographer's art', *Annals of the Association of American Geographers* 72.

Kimble, G. H. T. (1951) 'The inadequacy of the region', in L. D. Stamp and S. W. Wooldridge (eds) *London Essays in Geography*, London.

Paterson, J. L. (1974) 'Writing regional geography', in C. Board *et al.* (eds) *Progress in Geography*, vol. 6, London.

Wooldridge, S. W. (1956) *The Geographer as Scientist*, London.

Wooldridge, S. W. and East, W. G. (1958) *The Spirit and Purpose of Geography*, 2nd edn, London.

Further reading

Johnston, R. J. (1984) 'The region in twentieth century British geography', *History of Geography Newsletter* 4.

Johnston, R. J., Hauer, J. and Hoekveld, G. A. (eds) *The Challenge of Regional Geography*, London.

Lee, R. (1985) 'The future of the region: regional geography as education for transformation', in R. King (ed.) *Geographical Futures*, Sheffield.

Paassi, A. (1991) 'Deconstructing regions: notes on the scales of social life', *Environment and Planning A* 23.

See also: place.

regulation

Regulation, here defined as any rule laid down by the government which affects the activities of other agents in the economy, takes many forms, but in general the types of activities concerned and the methods of control vary together. Three broad areas can be identified.

The first is legislation: this approach is commonest for issues such as safety. Most countries have regulations concerning health and safety at work, such as protection for workers against dangerous machinery; other examples include the wearing of seatbelts in cars. Enforcement may be carried out by the normal police authorities or by special agencies such as factory inspectors.

The second category is the regulation of monopolies. A monopoly will charge higher prices than a competitive industry, so consumers' interests need some protection. It is useful to distinguish the general case, where action is infrequent, from the particular case of natural monopoly typified by public utilities, where regulation is more continuous.

General competition law operates when a company either has, or is about to acquire, a significant share of the market; then a body such as the Monopolies and Mergers Commission in the UK would determine whether a proposed merger or takeover should go ahead. However, the benefits of monopoly can also be gained by a group of firms acting collusively, and the threat of this has led to antitrust legislation such as the Sherman Act in the USA.

The second area of monopoly regulation is that applied to industries where competition is not feasible for structural reasons; this includes much of the transport, communications and energy sectors. Here a regulator is needed more or less permanently. The difficulty then is to control the monopoly sufficiently tightly without removing all its incentive to cut costs and develop new products. Two main methods have been used: rate-of-return regulation, where the firm may not exceed a given percentage return on its capital assets, and price-capping, which controls prices directly.

The final method of regulation is self-regulation, where an industry polices itself. This seems to occur where the problem is incomplete knowledge on the part of consumers. In areas such as medicine or the law, consumers depend on the doctor or lawyer making the right decision on their behalf. Some control of practitioners is therefore needed, and licensing is delegated to their professional bodies: someone 'struck off' their registers can no longer practise. Financial services markets are often self-regulatory too, requiring membership of the appropriate organization to work in the market, although the banking system is regulated by the government's central bank as part of its general responsibility for the stability of the financial system.

Stephen Trotter
University of Hull

Further reading

Crew, M. A. and Kleindorfer, P. R. (1986) *The Economics of Public Utility Regulation*, Basingstoke.

Francis, J. G. (1993) *The Politics of Regulation*, Oxford.

Gowland, D. (1990) *The Regulation of Financial Markets in the 1990s*, Aldershot.

Sherman, R. (1989) *The Regulation of Monopoly*, Cambridge, UK.

See also: cartels and trade associations; law and economics; monopoly; privatization; supply-side economics.

rehabilitation

Rehabilitation or reform (the terms can be used interchangeably) is most commonly associated with the rehabilitation of offenders. It can, however, be applied to all who need help or assistance with personal or social problems. When used in the content of offenders it operates as a philosophy of punishment. As such it stands in contrast to other philosophies of punishment such as deterrence or retribution, which are seen by rehabilitationists as wholly punitive. Supporters of rehabilitation often claim rehabilitation is not a philosophy of punishment but a theory of treatment. Yet such a claim cannot easily be sustained: rehabilitation can involve punishment, and often does, and can accompany punishment, and often does.

Rehabilitation has its philosophical roots in Plato, who saw wickedness – or crime – 'as a mental disease disintegrating and ultimately fatal'. Plato thought 'that no punishment inflicted by law should be for the sake of harm but to make the sufferer better, or to make him less bad than he would have been without it'. The modern version of rehabilitation is essentially the same; the aim is still to make the sufferer better, that is, improve the offender's social or personal position. Supporters of rehabilitation argue that the offence is merely a symptom of an underlying problem which itself occurs as a result of social or personality defects. If the underlying problem is removed (or cured) then so too will the symptom or the need to commit further crime. Following again from Plato, the emphasis remains on the offender: Plato did not say that crime was a disease but that the offender was diseased.

The methods used in modern rehabilitation follow Plato's mental disease model. The language of rehabilitation therefore follows the language of medicine and the methods also follow the medical approach. The offender's social situation and personality is first diagnosed and the reasons or causes of the crime are identified. A treatment plan is then devised where the aim is to provide new interpretations of past situations or relationships and/or provide effective management for future ones. Diagnosis and treatment are usually provided by experts trained in a certain type of therapeutic milieu; in the 1960s it was a Freudian-based therapy but it need not be. On successful completion of treatment, which may occur quite quickly or may last a number of years, the offender is said to be cured, that is, expected to be crime free.

The main appeal of rehabilitation is that it offers optimism and hope linked to a strong humanitarian emphasis on assisting the offender to achieve an improved way of life. Its second appeal is that rehabilitation uses the skills of professional workers whose training is based on contemporary social theories. This again is in contrast to deterrence or retribution, where the approach is to look only at the crime and where the aim is either to control action or to punish according to just deserts – both of which take no account of the offender's personal or social situation. Deterrence and retribution are seen as sterile and unimaginative compared to rehabilitation.

Yet in spite of these claims, very few rehabilitative programmes have produced results which suggest that they are more effective in treating offenders and reducing crime than any other type of appraisal. Moreover, the so-called expertise of those undertaking rehabilitation has begun to be questioned – it is now suggested that their expertise is less than is claimed. The humanitarian basis of the philosophy has also been challenged. Treatment can involve an open-ended commitment which can last as long as is required to treat the offender. This may be longer and more intense than other forms of punishment, so it is possible that minor offenders with serious personality problems can remain on treatment programmes longer than had they been sentenced otherwise. Or serious offenders with few problems can be treated speedily. This leads to accusations that rehabilitation is unfair and unjust. It also raises questions about the role of law in a democratic society. Does the law exist to enforce an agreed set of rules or to reshape people's temperaments? Critics of rehabilitation argue that the courts are supposed to assume we have free will and confine themselves to judgement of our actions. This

assumption too may be questioned but is considered less dangerous than presuming that the courts have a duty to rearrange our minds.

Philip Bean
Loughborough University of Technology

Further reading

Allen, F. A. (1959) 'Criminal justice legal values and the rehabilitative ideal', *Journal of Criminal Law, Criminology and Police Science* 50.
—— (1964) *The Borderland of Criminal Justice*, Chicago.
Bean, P. T. (1974) *Rehabilitation and Deviance*, London.
Lewis, C. S. (1971) 'The humanitarian theory of punishment', in C. Radzinowicz and M. Wolfgang (eds) *Crime and Justice*, vol. 2, New York.
Packer, H. L. (1969) *The Limits of the Criminal Sanction*, Oxford.

See also: penology; punishment.

relations, industrial *see* industrial relations

relations, international *see* international relations

religion and ritual

Anthropologists who specialize in the study of pre-literate societies have always been faced with the difficult problem of defining what kinds of phenomena can be called religious. At first sight, what religion is, in those places where the world religions occur, seems fairly straightforward. There are special places for it – temples, churches, mosques – and special people to deal with it – imams, rabbis, priests. Even in these cases, however, the matter is much less simple. If we take the example of Islam, we find that such activities as sleeping, waking, eating, defecating and washing all have a religious character; thus, even here, it is not clear where religion begins or where it ends.

The problem is even more complicated in the case of traditional societies, not only because phenomena which are easily referred to by the English word 'religion' are part and parcel of activities which we would not so label, but also because people in such societies, unlike the participants in a world religion, have no concept of religion as a distinct phenomenon. This has led social scientists to try a whole range of definitions, usually settling, with little conviction, on formulae such as: religion involves the belief in supernatural forces (see Goody 1961). The problem with this type of definition is in the difficulty of distinguishing between 'natural' and 'supernatural' knowledge. For example, are we to call the belief that one should respect one's father and mother a natural or a supernatural belief, since it refers to empirical beings, but cannot be justified on purely practical grounds? Another type of definition tries to deal with such difficulties. For example, Durkheim called religious all beliefs and practices which were believed to be right of themselves, not merely right because they were the best way of doing something according to practical criteria. The first type of beliefs and practices were, according to him, 'sacred'; the second 'profane' (Durkheim 1915 [1912]). But in practice it is impossible to distinguish on the basis of this criterion, as it separates what is not separated in ordinary life. This point is repeatedly made by Weber, who stresses how particular religions are coterminous with particular ways of acting, particular ways of life; as a result the 'sacred' and the 'profane' are ultimately inseparable (Weber 1930 [1905]). This, however, does not help in defining what religion is, and the only solution seems to be to abandon the notion of religion as an analytical category and to look at social reality in terms less closely tied to a particular cultural tradition. This is implicit in the work of Marx where religion is subsumed under the wider label of ideology, which also includes such ideas as the 'rightness' of competition in capitalist systems (Marx and Engels 1939 [1845–6]).

Even if we reject the notion of religion as an analytical tool, we can retain it as a general indication of an area of study. Taking this perspective, we may ask what kinds of topics seem to recur in the discussion of religion. What these areas are is well summarized in Plato's famous theory of ideas in *The Republic*. After considering the problems of the relation of humans to their environment and their biological and psychical nature, Plato argues that all we apprehend through our senses is in fact · a necessarily compromised and misleading shadow of a clearer, simpler and eternal reality which we may not see but which governs what we see. He concludes that there are some people who can see the truth better than others, and that therefore they can see more clearly what more ordinary people see only as distorted shadows. It follows, according to Plato, that these people should, because of their proximity to the true source of knowledge, be political leaders. We have here three of the typical ingredients of religion: philosophical or intellectual speculation; the denial of the validity of experience; and the legitimation of authority. We shall consider these three topics in turn.

Intellectual speculation about problems surrounding the human condition seem to be typical of all known societies, and they always focus around the same particularly fundamental problem: how far are humans separate or continuous with animals, plants and even geographical and cosmological events? The answer is, like any answer to this fundamental question, always unsatisfactory, and therefore such answers endlessly throw up further problems, thereby initiating an ongoing, never resolved, dialogue. Of course in most cases such speculation is not carried out in abstractions, but in terms of specific notions which seem to concretize the problem. What is the significance of cooking food as opposed to eating it raw? Is human copulation the same thing as animal copulation? What would copulation between different species mean? Does the fact that all human societies exchange – especially in marriage – finally differentiate humans from animals? What would happen to this difference if men copulated with their sisters? Are the cycles of life related to the cycles of plants, the seasons, the heavenly bodies? The continuing boldness of thought and fascination of human beings with such metaphysical questions is well illustrated by Lévi-Strauss's (1970–81 [1964–72]) work on the mythology of South and North American Indians, *An Introduction to the Science of Mythology*.

It is misleading to imagine that such intellectual pursuits are more typical of complex societies than simple ones. If anything, it is the other way round. Anthropologists' reports of the freest and boldest metaphysical speculation all relate to societies with the very simplest technology. This is because these societies are often the ones where institutionalized political inequality is least developed, and the accompanying regulation of speculation by means of authority leads to a diminution of the type of free speculative activities discussed by Lévi-Strauss for the Amerindians. When speculation does occur in more centralized society, it becomes quite separate from the main religious concerns which centre on ritual. How this happens will become clear when we consider the process by which the value of experience is denied in religion, and how this is linked with authority.

The organization of speculation by authority occurs through ritual. Ritual, like religion, is another word which has posed many problems for anthropologists. But for all anthropologists rituals are relatively fixed sequences of behaviour; as a result they are not individual and not *ad hoc*. Rituals are not legitimized in terms of an immediate instrumentality (Leach 1954); they convey meaning by means of symbols, defined by one anthropologist as minimal units of ritual (Turner 1967). If rituals are to be seen as a means of communication, they use very peculiar means, which has led Sperber (1975) to point out how misleading it is to see them as a kind of language. Rituals use symbols which seem to refer and connote only in the vaguest of ways. Rituals employ relatively fixed sequences of language, and, above all, singing, which hinders analytical communication (Bloch 1992). They use endless repetition (Leach 1966), reminding us again that they convey meaning in a different, less simple, way than other statements. For all these reasons, rituals seem to be the very opposite of the free speculation characteristic of the myth that Lévi-Strauss studied. They are invariant, they are unclear, there is little possibility for individual innovation and they are anti-intellectual.

In spite of this, a surprisingly similar pattern seems to emerge in all rituals, throughout the world, and they all seem to carry much the same message. This is Plato's message: do not trust the world of appearances for there is something truer, more permanent, that lies hidden beyond. If we do not accept the truth of this message, the question we must ask of rituals is not what they reveal of the beyond, but rather how they create the image of the beyond. In other words, anthropologists reverse the platonic assertion about rituals which state that this world is a shadow of another, but see rituals as creating an image of a shadow out of the reality of this world, although a shadow which is presented as the real thing.

There are a number of suggestions in the anthropological literature as to how rituals effect this inversion. Two French authors, Hertz (1960 [1928]) and Van Gennep (1960 [1909]), noted the tripartite division that seems to occur in many rituals. Van Gennep stressed how rituals often involve the idea of a journey which illustrates a social transformation; this would be the case for initiation rituals. The rituals enact children leaving their childhood state, then going through an intermediate stage, the liminal stage (after the Latin *limen*, meaning threshold, one of the commonest symbols of such a state) and finally entering the world of adulthood. Van Gennep called such rituals 'rites of passage' because they use the symbolism of a journey.

One of the usual ways of explaining such rituals has been to follow Van Gennep's lead and to see rites of passage as devices for the smooth transfer of social roles from individual to individual. It is clear, however, that such an explanation is insufficient, and that it ignores the religious aspects of such practices.

Other anthropologists have paid special attention to the middle liminal stage, noting that this stage is governed by rules which, in a number of ways, contrast, or are even totally opposed to, those of normal life (Gluckman 1963; Turner 1967). The liminal stage often seems to involve inversions of authority, for example, children ruling over adults; in some cases this stage also involves the chaotic suspension of normal behaviour in orgiastic sequences. This is a common feature of all ritual, for example, the Lent carnival in the Christian calendar. The explanation of such apparently bizarre behaviour goes to the very heart of ritual and religion. Ritual is a dramatic

commentary on life, which represents it as a mixture of two elements, pure and impure. The task of ritual is to separate the two so that the impure can be eliminated in order that the true – pure – can emerge. Or, looked at from an atheistic perspective, this antithetical process creates the illusion of the Other. In this light we can reinterpret the three stages of the rites of passage: the first acts out the mixed state; it is followed by the acting out of the impure chaotic state; this is then driven out and replaced by the contrasting image of the pure holy state.

We can see this three-stage schema in initiation rituals, whether they be Christian baptism or Australian aboriginal initiation ritual. The first stage is a fairly neutral representation of non-ritual, birth; the second stage involves the creation of an image of birth as a horrifyingly polluting event, so that the third stage can be staged as a cleansing of the child from the polluting effects of birth in order that the child be reborn again in a higher, purer, truer way. The same pattern can also be observed in funerary rituals, which involve stressing death as a dirty, polluting, horrifying event so that the latter part of the ritual can involve a victory over death in a superior world (Bloch and Parry 1982). This perspective enables us to understand one of the most puzzling features of religion. Although all religions proclaim the existence of a transcendental purity, which escapes the false reality of the shadows of this world (shadows which we would otherwise take for reality), they do this by emphasizing dirt, pollution, decay and corruption (Douglas 1966). Revelling in the idea of pollution is so typical of religion because the drama which creates the transcendental requires the representation of its antithesis. This also explains the repeated presence of the notion of cleaning in all types of religion – which often takes the somewhat extreme form of bodily mutilation, such as the ritual bleedings of New Guinea or of Jewish circumcision.

The basis of religious rituals is therefore an elaborate denial of the sufficiency of non-religious activity, especially a denial that the creative potential is in human hands. Birth is denied its creativity and death its finality, and, interestingly, these two ideas are usually closely linked in a total denial of the time-scale of human production and reproduction. Instead, and by means of the drama of ritual, a timeless order is created in which human life, birth and action are irrelevant. This image may be more or less elaborate. In the systems of ancestor worship found in many parts of Africa, an image is created of people surviving beyond their life-span, so that succeeding generations of a descent group are really the same moral entity reincarnated (Fortes 1959). In traditional Hindu belief, an image is created of great mystical cycles, of a length totally incomparable with the biological cycles of human life. These cycles, unlike human history, are represented as the 'real' basis of the cosmos.

The religious image involves identifying this life with death and decomposition, and the Other life with the victory over death, since the religious world is sufficiently timeless and unchanging for the human life-span to be meaningless. In order to convey this message, rituals juggle endlessly with the idea of death and birth by creating the image of a life-giving death (Frazer 1890). This appears to lie behind one of the commonest forms of ritual sacrifice, which seems to rest on the paradox that killing produces transcendental life (Hubert and Mauss 1964 [1899]; Robertson-Smith 1889).

The world created by ritual is, however, extremely vague. Rituals create by drama, not by exegesis. Consequently, when – as in world religions – there are also professional theologians trying to organize and systematize beliefs, their ideas seem curiously distant from the everyday religion of people (Geertz 1960; Tambiah 1969). Accordingly, some anthropologists distinguish between two types of religion, a folk religion and an official theological religion (Srinivas 1952). It is partly as a result of these problems that anthropologists and sociologists have found it almost impossible to agree about the notion of belief (Leach 1966). The messages of ritual are quite specific about what is *not* the real world, as was Plato, but much vaguer about what the real world is like. What seems to matter above all in religion is the declaration of the limitations, if not outright pointlessness, of conscious human action.

This last fact explains the close relation between religions and political systems. For political power to appear as more than mere coercion, but as a legitimize exercise, it must be represented as the instrument of something which transcends the here and now. This something need not always be religious, but it very often is. For example, African elders appear justified in their control of others because they are the representatives of the pure, death-defying ancestors. Medieval kings were Christ's representatives on earth. In some parts of the world, rulers are actually represented as gods. In cases such as these the religion will inevitably frown on metaphysical speculation involving a challenge to authority. However, the powers that be will enforce participation in rituals. The political significance of religion in such cases depends partly on the fact that religious rituals reinterpret existence as shadows, so that the true legitimacy of power lies beyond the actions of subordinates; but it also rests on the fact that religion is a reinterpretation and a deconstruction of real life. This means that the other world which religion creates is also partly the world we all know, but seen in another light, the distorting light of ritual; as a result the other world still appears to some extent true to our senses and our emotions. Religion, in order to be powerful and to perform its political role, must have this appearance of deep truth, and explanations of religion must explain not only how it maintains authority but also why it is so apparently necessary and comforting to the participants.

Yet it would be misleading to think that organized religion always supports authority. Indeed, the use of religion by those in authority means that it is likely also to be used in religious revolts. In such cases the rebels claim either that the present rulers are not the true representatives of the divine on earth, while they, the rebels, are (Ileto 1979), or more rarely, that they have discovered a superior source of divinity which therefore renders invalid the claims of the power holders (Lan 1985). But victory has little to do with the specifically religious claims of either side; it is a matter of who is strongest on the battlefield.

Maurice Bloch
London School of Economics
and Political Science

References

Bloch, M. (1992) *Prey into Hunter: The Politics of Religious Experience*, Cambridge, UK.

Bloch, M. and Parry, J. (eds) (1982) *Death and the Regeneration of Life*, Cambridge, UK.

Douglas, M. (1966) *Purity and Danger*, London.

Durkheim, E. (1915 [1912]) *The Elementary Forms of the Religious Life*, London.

Fortes, M. (1959) *Oedipus and Job in West African Religion*, Cambridge, UK.

Frazer, J. G. (1890) *The Golden Bough*, London.

Geertz, C. (1960) *The Religion of Java*, Glencoe, IL.

Gluckman, M. (1963) *Order and Rebellion in Tribal Africa*, London.

Goody, J. (1961) 'Religion and ritual: the definitional problem', *British Journal of Sociology* 12.

Hertz, R. (1960 [1928]) *Death and the Right Hand*, London. (Original edn, *Mélanges de la sociologie religieuse et folklore*, Paris.)

Hubert, J. and Mauss, M. (1964 [1899]) *Sacrifice: Its Nature and Function*, London. (Original edn, *Essai sur la nature et la fonction du sacrifice*, Paris.)

Ileto, R. C. (1979) *Pasyon and Revolution: Popular Movements in the Philippines 1840–1910*, Manila.

Lan, D. (1985) *Guns and Rain: Guerillas and Spirit Mediumship in Zimbabwe*, London.

Leach, E. R. (1954) *Political Systems of Highland Burma*, London.

—— (1966) 'Ritualisation in man in relation to conceptual and social development', in J. Huxley (ed.) *A Discussion on Ritualization of Behaviour in Animal and Man*, London.

Lévi-Strauss, C. (1970–81 [1964–72]) *An Introduction to the Science of Mythology*, 4 vols, London. (Original edn, *Mythologiques*, Paris.)

Marx, K. and Engels, F. (1939 [1845–6]) *The German Ideology*, parts 1 and 3, New York. (Full text first published in 1932 as *Die Deutsche Ideologie*.)

Robertson-Smith, W. (1889) *Lectures on the Religion of the Semites*.

Sperber, D. (1975) *Rethinking Symbolism*, Cambridge, UK.

Srinivas, M. N. (1952) *Religion and Society among the Coorgs of South India*, Oxford.

Tambiah, S. J. (1969) *Buddhism and the Spirit Cult*, Cambridge, UK.

Turner, V. (1967) *The Forest of Symbols*, Ithaca, NY.

Van Gennep, A. (1960 [1909]) *The Rites of Passage*, London. (Original edn, *Les Rites de passage*, Paris.)

Weber, M. (1930 [1905]) *The Protestant Ethic and the Spirit of Capitalism*, London. (Original edn, *Die protestantische Ethik und der 'Geist' des Kapitalismus*, Tübingen.)

Further reading

Leach, E. R. (1966) 'Virgin Birth', *Proceedings of the Royal Anthropological Institute*.

Tambiah, S. J. (1990), *Magic, Science, Religion, and the Scope of Rationality*, Cambridge, UK.

Turner, V. (1969) *The Ritual Process*, Chicago.

See also: magic; rites of passage; sects and cults; totemism.

representation, political

The history of political representation is that of the rise of European parliaments, through the transformation of the sovereign's councillors into a sovereign assembly.

The medieval monarch used to seek advice from persons chosen at his discretion for their competence and trust. But since he wanted them to report from all the land and then to convey his orders and tax demands back to 'their' people, he tended to pattern his selection after the actual social hierarchy, choosing those in the nobility and high clergy, whose fiefs and dioceses constituted his kingdom, and (as early as the thirteenth century in England) important commoners.

During crises, when the king most needed their co-operation, the councillors demanded and obtained the right to be convened periodically and to be masters of their agenda. Also, instead of answering individually to the king for their particular community (which was soon to be reapportioned into electoral districts), they made collective deliberations and rendered them obligatory and compelling. They were now acting as one single assembly (whose number, election, immunity and so on had to be formalized) and speaking for the people as a whole; thus the king, who had been seen as the head, and natural representative, of his people, implicitly began to speak only for himself.

Not only political legitimacy, but also power, had shifted: in the name of political representation they had in fact established their rule. For example, the slogan of the American Revolution did not mean 'no taxation without our spokesman to the king' but 'without our share of power', indeed 'without governing ourselves'. Parliament, instead of the king, was sovereign.

Whatever its constitutional formula, representative government is an awkward proposition, first, because the more faithful the representation, the less the ability to rule, that is, to make choices or even compromises or coercions; and second, because the demands of modern politics have both glorified government (the rise everywhere of the executive branch which executes always less and rules always more) and diminished the role of parliaments based on territorial representation. When the representational logic of the former royal councillors came to its democratic triumph with their election according to the principle 'one man, one vote', it appeared that one vote is too little to be correctly represented: all people want to press for their multifaceted interests through specific spokesmen or organizations which will fight the suppressions, amalgamations and distortions that territorial representation implies in each electoral district and then at the legislative level, whatever the endeavours of special and minority groups to force their 'quotas' into elected or appointed bodies.

Political representation takes an ironical turn, first, when advocates of functional representation criticize parliaments for disregarding obvious demands of the people and arbitrarily imposing their idea of the common interest (much like the kings had been criticized as unrepresentative); second, when parliamentary elections often become geared to the nomination of a government rather than of representatives; and third, when the executive branch surrounds itself more and more formally with 'councillors' drawn from the most important interest groups in the country and whose 'advice' tends to become obligatory and compelling.

Jean Tournon
University of Grenoble

Further reading

Birch, A. H. (1971) *Representation*, London.

International Commission for the History of Representative and Parliamentary Institutions (1984) *Assemblee di Stati e istituzioni rappresentative nella storia del pensiero politico moderno (secoli XV – XX)*, Rimini.

Morgan, E. S. (1989) *Inventing the People: The Rise of Popular Sovereignty in England and America*, New York.

Pennock, J. and Chapman, J. (1968) *Representation*, New York.

Pitkin, H. (1967) *The Concept of Representation*, Berkeley, CA.

Reid, J. (1989) *The Concept of Representation in the Age of the American Revolution*, Chicago.

Schmitt, C. (1988) *The Crisis of Parliamentary Democracy*, London.

See also: citizenship; democracy; interest groups and lobbying; political recruitment and careers.

repression

Repression, in psychoanalytic theory, is when a desire, thought or feeling that causes conflict and therefore anxiety is banished from or denied access to conscious awareness. Repressed desires continue to press for expression, however, and may manifest themselves if only indirectly at times when the censor or defensive processes of the ego are relaxed; for example, in sleep in the form of dreams, or in mistaken actions and words (parapraxes or 'Freudian slips'). The concept of repression necessarily implies a psychodynamic model of the psyche in which two or more mental systems interact. Conflict arises when urges which are pleasurable for the id run counter to the reality orientation of the ego or the 'moral' concerns of the superego. Repression requires the expenditure of psychic energy and hence can be neurotically debilitating. It is important to distinguish repression from suppression. In repression, the individual has no consciousness of desire. In suppression, while the urge may not be acted on, the person is aware of it.

Freud's early work with Breuer focused on the role of repression in neurosis, especially in the production of the symptoms of hysteria (Breuer and Freud 1896). The difficulty in drinking experienced, for example, by one of Breuer's patients, Anna O (Bertha Pappenheim), they attributed to the feelings of disgust which she had experienced on seeing her governess's dog being encouraged to drink from a glass. Unable to express these, she had repressed them from her consciousness. The repressed feelings produced her hysterical symptoms of hydrophobia. The difficulty that another patient, Elizabeth von R, experienced in walking Freud traced to the fact that she had become aware of her forbidden feelings for her brother-in-law during a walk with him in the woods. These had caused her intense feelings of guilt when her sister had subsequently died, and Freud believed that it was the repression of these guilty thoughts that led to the symptoms.

The focus of Freud's early therapeutic technique was lifting the repressions. His aim was to encourage emotional expression ('catharsis') of the repressed feelings. In Freud's later theorizing, repression still retained its primacy as a defensive process though it was seen as often accompanied by other mechanisms of defence such as projection. But, for Freud, repression is an intrinsic feature of civilized life, for socialization inevitably involves some frustration of the fulfilment of desires.

Although it forms the cornerstone of psychoanalytic theory, repression is a hypothetical concept which can be defined only in terms of other concepts from psychoanalytic theory such as id, ego, superego and the theory of the unconscious. It is one of the relatively few areas, however, for which there is undoubted support from experimental work. In studies of perceptual defence, for example, subjects are found to have higher thresholds for potentially traumatic stimuli. Blum (1955) has also shown that defence comes into operation much as psychoanalytic theory might predict, that is when subjects who tend to use repression as a defence are confronted with stimuli which arouse conflict.

Richard Stevens
Open University

References

Blum, G. S. (1955) 'Perceptual defense revisited', *Journal of Abnormal and Social Psychology*, 51.
Breuer, J. and Freud, S. (1896) *Studies in Hysteria, Standard Edition of the Complete Psychological Works of Sigmund Freud*, ed. J. Strachey, vol. 2, London.

Further reading

Freud, S. (1916) *Introductory Lectures on Psychoanalysis, Standard Edition of the Complete Psychological Works of Sigmund Freud*, ed. J. Strachey, vol. 16, London.
Stevens, R. (1983) *Freud and Psychoanalysis*, Milton Keynes.

See also: defences; unconscious.

research and development (R&D)

Research and development activity lies at the heart of economic growth, even if spending on R&D on its own accounts for only a small percentage of national income. Putting research together with development is, however, to group two rather different activities. Basic research produces new scientific knowledge, hypotheses and theories which are expressed in research papers and memoranda, while inventive work drawing on this basic research produces patentable inventions. Development work takes this stock of knowledge and patentable inventions as its raw materials and develops blueprints, specifications and samples for new and improved products and processes (Freeman 1982; Nelson 1959). Grouping R and D together also hides the fact that most corporate spending on R&D should properly be described as D rather than R.

Allied with this is the distinction between 'invention' and 'innovation'. Inventions are the culmination of research activity and are ideas, sketches or models for a new product or process that may often be patented. An innovation in the economic sense takes place when a new product is marketed or a new process is put to commercial use, and as such represents the culmination of development, production and marketing. Many inventions never turn into innovations, and for those that do there can be a long and complex chain of events between invention and innovation.

R&D is often used as a measure of comparative innovative activity (OECD 1981), but it is an input measure rather than an output measure. For that reason, some prefer to measure innovative activity by counting innovations, though this is a very labour-intensive activity (Townsend *et al.* 1981).

As an intermediate measure of innovative activity, many researchers have made use of patent data (Griliches 1990; Patel and Pavitt 1989). The patent gives a firm a monopoly right to commercial use of a particular invention (embodied in a product or process) for a given period. The rationale for this is that in the absence of a patent, some inventions might be copied comparatively freely by many firms other than the originator, and the inventor would not recoup the costs of invention. Hence, the aim of the patent is to sustain the incentive to innovate. It is recognized, however, that the value of different patents is highly variable, with a large majority having little or no economic value – whatever their technological merit – while a few are of huge value.

The economic importance of R&D is not to be judged simply in terms of the inventions and innovations to which it gives rise. First, as Cohen and Levinthal (1989) argue, there are two sides to R&D: the first is generation of inventive output, while the second is learning. Much R&D may be carried out to learn from the R&D efforts of others.

Second, patents can have important implications for the competitive environment, even if they do not always translate into innovative outputs. Patents can act as a barrier to entry, although they can sometimes be invented around. If, however, firms hold patents that they do not use, this may constitute 'pre-emptive patenting', and anti-trust authorities may call for compulsory licensing of these patents.

Third, research activity can have significant implications for the competitive environment, even if its outputs are not registered as patents. Firms may announce how much R&D resources they are committing to a particular area as a signal to potential entrants. In these circumstances, accumulated R&D activity can be a deterrent to entry, and hence influence the competitive environment, even if the firm is not actually selling any products currently that use this accumulated technological knowledge.

Finally, it is often argued that the fruits of R&D efforts spill over outside the originating firm (Jaffe 1986). As is well known from the basic economic analysis of externalities, this may mean that the private incentive for firms to invest in R&D is less than the social value of that R&D, because some of the benefit

is not captured by the investor. This is a part of the rationale for favourable tax treatment of R&D (Stoneman 1987). However, Geroski (1994) has cast doubt on how serious this problem is in practice.

P. Swann
London Business School

References

Cohen, W. M. and Levinthal, D. A. (1989) 'Innovation and learning: the two faces of R&D', *Economic Journal* 99.

Freeman, C. (1982) *The Economics of Industrial Innovation*, London.

Geroski, P. A. (1994) 'Markets for technology: knowledge, innovation and appropriability', in P. Stoneman (ed.) *Handbook of the Economics of Innovation and Technical Change*, Oxford.

Griliches, Z. (1990) 'Patent statistics as economic indicators: a survey', *Journal of Economic Literature* 28.

Jaffe, A. (1986) 'Technological opportunity and spillovers of R&D: evidence from firm's patents, profits and market value', *American Economic Review* 76.

Nelson, R. R. (1959) 'The simple economics of basic research', *Journal of Political Economy* 67.

OECD (1981) *The Measurement of Scientific and Technical Activities: Proposed Standard Practice for Surveys of Research and Experimental Development (The 'Frascati' Manual)*, Paris.

Patel, P. and Pavitt, K. (1989) 'The technological activities of the UK: a fresh look', in A. Silberston (ed.) *Technology and Economic Progress*, Basingstoke.

Stoneman, P. (1987) *The Economic Analysis of Technology Policy*, Oxford.

Townsend, J., Henwood, F., Thomas, G., Pavitt, K. and Wyatt, S. (1981) *Innovations in Britain since 1945*, Occasional Paper 16, University of Sussex.

reserve currency

Governments hold reserves of foreign currencies to enable them to intervene in the foreign exchange markets, in order to try to influence the exchange rate of the domestic currency against foreign currencies by buying and selling various currencies. The need for such reserves would not arise if currencies were allowed to float freely. The fixed exchange-rate system existed from 1944, following the Bretton Woods agreement, until 1973; it was succeeded by the 'dirty' floating system in which governments frequently intervene to influence exchange rates rather than let them float freely. Both systems require governments to hold foreign exchange reserves that enable them to influence exchange rates through foreign exchange intervention. Reserve currencies are currencies widely held by governments as part of their foreign exchange reserves.

Given that the Bretton Woods agreement resulted in the major countries fixing the exchange rates of their currencies against the US dollar, and given the significance of the USA in the world economy, the US dollar became the major reserve currency throughout the world. Sterling had been a major reserve currency prior to the Second World War but its role declined significantly in the post-war period. Following the collapse of the fixed exchange-rate system in 1973, there has been a move to diversify foreign currency holdings by governments. The Deutschmark (especially with the post-1979 European monetary system where it has played the role of an 'anchor currency' much like the US dollar in the Bretton Woods system), the Swiss franc and the Japanese yen have all emerged as widely held reserve currencies.

There is some debate as to whether this diversification of foreign currency holdings is optimal or whether internationally created reserve assets, such as the Special Drawing Right or the European Currency Unit, might provide a better basis for the international monetary system.

Andy Mullineux
University of Birmingham

Further reading

Grubel, H. (1984) *The International Monetary System*, 4th edn, Harmondsworth.
Kenen, P. B. (1983) *The Role of the Dollar as an International Currency*, New York.
Roosa, R. V. *et al.* (1982) *Reserve Currencies in Transition*, New York.

See also: gold standard; international monetary system.

resource management, human *see* human resource management

resources and population *see* population and resources

returns, laws of

Among the abstract generalizations for which economists have at some time or another claimed explanatory or predictive powers analogous to those inherent in the natural or scientific laws of the physical sciences, the laws of returns have the longest history. They describe the relationship between the rate of growth of output for an expanding industry and the rate of increase in the inputs of the required factors of production (land, labour and capital), and they provide an instructive illustration of the way so-called economic 'laws' are in practice circumscribed by the organiza-

tional and technological conditions in which they operate.

In principle there are three ways in which the output of an industry might expand as a result of the injection of additional inputs into the production process. In the case of constant returns, output increases in proportion to the increase in total inputs. In the case of increasing returns, the rate of growth of output is greater than the rate of increase in inputs. In the case of diminishing returns, the rate of growth of output will fall short of the rate of growth in inputs. In practice an expanding industry may be subject to successive phases of increasing, constant and diminishing returns. In the early stages of its growth, when all factor inputs are in elastic supply and there are economies to be gained by increasing the scale of operations, increasing returns would be the norm. Where there is an important factor of production in limited supply (for example, land in the case of agriculture), there will come a point beyond which adding equal doses of the other factors to a fixed quantity of, say, land, will yield a declining rate of return to the variable factors – unless of course there are advances in knowledge (technological progress) compensating for the scarcity of land and possibly generating further economies of scale.

Cases of increasing returns in manufacturing were noticed by seventeenth- and eighteenth-century observers. Adam Smith, for example, explained a tendency for output to grow faster than inputs in manufacturing industry partly in terms of the scope offered for division of labour (improved organization) in factory industry, and partly in terms of what would now be classified as technological progress (advances in knowledge, improved machinery, and so on). Other eighteenth-century writers were more concerned with the evidence for diminishing returns in agriculture and its implications for an economy experiencing a rising population. Turgot, for example, pointed out that if increasing amounts of capital are applied to a given piece of land, the quantity of output resulting from each additional dose of capital input will first increase and then, after a certain point, decrease towards zero.

Most English nineteenth-century classical economists readily accepted the assumption that diminishing returns prevailed in agriculture, and increasing returns in manufacturing. Few of them expected much technological progress in agriculture and were consequently pessimistic about the long-term consequences of a sustained increase in population. According to J. S. Mill, for example, 'This general law of agricultural industry is the most important proposition in political economy.' The neo-classical economists, such as Alfred Marshall, writing later in the century when it was evident that economic progress involved a high degree of industrialization, were more optimistic about the outcome of what they saw as the conflict between the two forces of diminishing returns in the primary product industries and increasing returns, reinforced by technical progress, in the manufacturing sector. Their problem, however, was that the only assumption about laws of returns which was consistent with the long-term competitive equilibrium analysis on which the neo-classical theory of value depended was the unrealistic assumption of constant returns. For as Piero Sraffa showed, in an article published in the 1926 *Economic Journal*, if increasing returns to scale prevailed, the profit-maximizing firm would be driven to expand indefinitely, thus destroying the basis for perfect competition; while the existence of diminishing returns would mean that costs and prices would be interdependent for all those industries competing for a factor in scarce supply, thus invalidating the Marshallian technique of partial equilibrium analysis.

Meanwhile, however, leading economic historians had already questioned the empirical validity of the laws of returns. In a famous article on 'empty economic boxes' published in the 1922 *Economic Journal*, Clapham had complained that, 'A great deal of harm has been done through omission to make clear that the Laws of Returns have never been attached to specific industries, that we do not, for instance, at this moment *know* under what conditions of returns coal or boots are being produced.'

The concept of diminishing returns is still sometimes invoked in support of Malthusian polemics by those who insist on the limits to growth, or as ready-made explanations for such events as the spectacular rise in commodity prices in the early 1970s; similarly those wishing to promote policies favouring some branch of manufacturing may justify their case by categorizing it as subject to increasing returns. However, modern economic theorists have effectively abandoned the idea that it is either useful or possible to formulate a theoretical justification for broad, generalizable laws of returns. More significant has been research focused on whether and when particular industries experience constant or increasing or decreasing returns to scale; these are essentially empirical issues which raise complex technical and analytical problems and yield results valid only for highly differentiated sectors of industries. In this context the laws of returns are demoted to tentative hypotheses which provide the starting-point for a programme of theoretical and/or empirical research into the characteristics of a particular production function.

Phyllis Deane
University of Cambridge

revolutions

A revolutionary crisis, or revolution, is any political crisis propelled by illegal (usually violent) actions by subordinate groups which threatens to change the political institutions or social structure of a society.

Some revolutionary crises result in great changes in politics and society, as the Russian and Chinese Revolutions; some result in great political changes but few changes in social life outside of politics, as the English Revolution; some result in hardly any change at all and are hence considered unsuccessful revolutions, as the revolutions of 1848 in Germany.

The word revolution first appeared in political writing in fourteenth-century Italy and denoted any overturning of a government; such events were seen as part of a cycle in the transfer of power between competing parties, with no great changes in institutions implied. However, since the French Revolution, revolution has become associated with sudden and far-reaching change. It is this particular sense of the word that has been carried to fields other than politics, as in the Industrial Revolution or scientific revolutions.

Revolutions have causes, participants, processes of development and outcomes. No two revolutions are exactly alike in all these respects, thus no general theory of revolutions has proven satisfactory. Understanding revolutions requires theories of causes, of participants, of processes and of outcomes of revolutions that stress the variations in each element and how they combine in specific historical cases.

Many of the key issues in studies of revolution were set out in the nineteenth century by Marx and Engels (1968 [1848]). Marx viewed Europe's history since the Middle Ages as a progression through various modes of production, each one more fruitful than the last. Bourgeois revolutions, exemplified by the French Revolution of 1789, were necessary to destroy the privileged feudal aristocracy and the agrarian society over which it presided. However, the resulting political freedom and material benefits would extend only to the class of professionals and businessmen who controlled the succeeding capitalist society; thus a further revolution in the name of labourers remained necessary to extend self-determination and the material benefits of modern industrial technology to all. The major elements of this view – that revolution is a necessary agent of change; that such change is progressive and beneficial; and that revolutions, in both cause and effect, are intimately related to great historical transitions – pose the articles of faith for practising revolutionaries and the chief research problems for academic analysis.

The work of Tocqueville (1856) has assumed increasing importance. Tocqueville's analysis of the French Revolution stressed the continuity of the old regime and the post-revolutionary state, and the greater centralization of state power that followed from the revolution. Similar continuities have occurred elsewhere: the Russian imperial bureaucracy and secret police, the Chinese imperial bureaucracy, and the Iranian personal authoritarian state have been replaced by similar, albeit more powerful, post-revolutionary versions. Thus the extent of the historical transformation associated with revolutions appears less striking in practice than in Marxist theory.

Since the mid-1960s, social scientists seeking the causes of revolutions first focused on changes in people's expectations and attitudes, but later moved to an emphasis on institutions and the resources of states. Gurr (1970) argued that when people's social opportunities no longer accorded with their expectations, either because expectations were rising too quickly, or welfare was falling, feelings of 'relative deprivation' would make fertile ground for popular opposition to governments. Johnson (1966) suggested that any large and sustained 'disequilibrium' between the economic, political and cultural sectors of a society – such as education increasing more rapidly than economic output, or economic organization changing more rapidly than political organization – could lead many individuals to withdraw their allegiance to the current regime. Huntington (1968) emphasized expectations in the political sphere, arguing that if popular expectations for participation in politics came to exceed a country's institutional procedures for political participation, unmet demands for political participation could lead to an explosion of popular activity directed against the current regime. However, Tilly et al. (1975), in empirical studies of collective violence, found that strikes and riots did not occur most frequently during times of deprivation, such as periods of falling real wages or falls in economic output. Nor were strikes and riots especially common during times of disequilibrium, such as periods of rapid urbanization or industrialization. Instead workers acted to protect and defend their interests whenever the opportunity was available; those opportunities depended on shifts in the balance of power between workers and the employers and states that they faced. Tilly's 'resource mobilization' view argued that whenever conflict arose over economic or political issues, the incidence of popular protest depended chiefly on how the abilities and the range of actions open to those at odds with the current regime compared with the resources of the regime and its supporters. Skocpol (1979), emphasizing the differences between states and the importance of international competition, led the way in developing a social-structural perspective on revolutions, which views revolutions as a consequence of state weaknesses combined with institutions that provide aggrieved elites

and popular groups with opportunities for effective collective action.

The origins of revolutions do not appear to reside in an exceptional level of deprivation or disequilibrium. Instead, revolutions occur when difficulties that are successfully coped with in other times and places – wars and state fiscal crises – occur in states with institutions particularly vulnerable to revolution. Skocpol identified three institutional features that make for such vulnerability:

1 A state military machine considerably inferior to those of nations with which the state is normally in competition.
2 An autonomous elite able to challenge or block implementation of policies sought by the central administration.
3 A peasantry with autonomous village organization.

One could also add:

4 large concentrations of artisans and labourers in and near inadequately policed political centres.

These elements, in various combinations, have played a role in the origins of the major revolutions of modern times: England 1640 (1, 2, 4); France 1789 (1, 2, 3, 4); Mexico 1910 (1, 2, 3); China 1911 (1, 2); Russia 1917 (1, 3, 4); Iran 1979 (2, 4). Peasant organization has often been supplied by a revolutionary party, rather than automonous village organization. This functional substitution has led to different, characteristically peasant-party-based, revolutions: China 1949; Vietnam 1972; Nicaragua 1979.

A military or fiscal crisis in an institutionally vulnerable state may begin a revolution; however, the process of revolution and the roles of various participants vary greatly. Certain processes appear to be, if not universal, extremely common: an initial alliance between moderates seeking reform and radicals seeking far-reaching change; involvement in international war (in part because nearby states fear the revolution spreading, in part because revolutionary leaders find the nationalist fervour generated by external wars useful); a gradual fission between moderates and radicals, with the latter triumphing; a civil war as leaders of the revolutionary parties seek to extend their control throughout the nation and eliminate opposition; the emergence of authoritarian rule by a single dominant leader. Other variables – the extent and autonomy of popular participation, the extent of civil war, the degree and permanence of radical triumph, and the duration of autocratic rule – range from high to low across revolutions, depending on the resources available to various groups, the skills of individuals, and the luck of political and military battles.

The outcomes of revolutions are equally diverse. These depend not only on the factors that caused the revolution, but also on the vagaries of the revolutionary process, the influence wielded by external countries and the problems and resources faced by the eventual victors in the revolutionary struggle. The French and English revolutions, though differing greatly in the level of popular uprisings, resulted eventually in similar regimes: monarchies in which possession of private property was the key to political participation and social status. By contrast, the Russian and Chinese (1949) revolutions, the former with a level of autonomous popular participation, both rural and urban, akin to that of France, the latter with a chiefly rural peasant-party revolution, both resulted eventually in socialist party-states, in which membership and rank in the state party are the keys to political participation and social status. Mexico's revolution led to a hybrid capitalist party-state, in which political participation is directed by and through the state party, but private wealth is the chief criterion of social status.

Evaluations of the material progress made under post-revolutionary regimes are also mixed. There are cases of great progress in health and literacy, such as Cuba; but the ability of post-revolutionary regimes to provide a generally higher material standard of living than similarly situated non-revolutionary regimes is yet to be demonstrated (Eckstein 1982).

The role of ideological changes in causing revolutions and shaping their outcomes is hotly debated. Most revolutionaries have proven quite pragmatic in modifying revolutionary programmes as seemed necessary; Russia under the New Economic Plan of the 1920s, and China in the 1980s, have embarked on such pragmatic paths. At other times ideological fervour has taken precedence, as in the Jacobin years of the French Revolution, and the Great Leap Forward and Cultural Revolution in China. Ideological programmes are thus a rather unpredictable, if far from dominant, element in shaping revolutions.

Ideology in a broader sense, as an overall cultural perspective, has been a more uniformly important factor. Eisenstadt (1978) has noted that the key to revolution lies in the coalescence, in a time of political crisis, of diverse movements – peasant uprisings, elite political revolts, religious heterodoxies – into a widespread attack on the institutions of the old regime. Thus the main role of ideologies in revolutions has been to bring together diverse grievances and interests under a simple and appealing set of symbols of opposition. For this purpose, any ideology that features a strong tension between good and evil, emphasizes the importance of combating evil in this world through active remaking of the world, and sees politics as simply one more battlefield between good and evil, may serve as the foundation for a revolutionary ideology. Thus puritanism, liberalism, communism, anti-colonialism and Islam have all proved adaptable to providing symbols for revolutions. Studies of peasants' and workers' revolts have stressed that traditional ideologies – the communal ideology of 'members' against 'outsiders' of the peasant village and the craft guild – can also motivate actors in revolutionary crises. None of these ideologies of themselves brought down governments; but they were crucial in providing a basis for uniting diverse existing grievances under one banner and encouraging their active resolution.

Revolutions have occurred in a remarkably varied range of societies. Pre-industrial monarchies, Third-World colonies of industrialized states, modernizing dictatorships, and totalitarian party-states have had their governments suddenly overturned by popularly backed movements for change. What all regimes that have fallen to revolutions had in common was a closed state with limited elite access and few channels for the populace to influence changes in leadership. If this pattern holds, the arena for future revolutions will be the remaining authoritarian states of Africa, the Middle East, Latin America, and South-east Asia, and the party-dictatorships of Communist China and Cuba. The advanced industrial democracies may see strikes and demonstrations, but are unlikely to witness revolutions.

The degree of violence in revolutions is also highly variable, and this seems rooted in the diverse nature of the societies in which revolutions have occurred. Societies with higher levels of industrialization and education, and with less influential conservative and counter-revolutionary forces, seem to be able to sustain popular revolutions without descending into mass violence and terror. This is the hopeful basis for expecting positive results from the revolutions in the Czech Republic, Poland and Hungary. However, societies with large agricultural populations, low-to-moderate levels of literacy, or a large proportion of powerful conservative or counter-revolutionary elites, tend to fall into revolutionary spirals of struggles for power and internal violence, sometimes escalating to civil war. This suggests that new crises may be anticipated in parts of Africa, Latin America, the Middle East and Asia. Even in parts of Eastern Europe, including many of the successor states to the Soviet Union, the clash between reformers and still powerful conservatives may ignite new explosions. Revolutions are thus likely to continue to shape, and reshape, world politics for years to come.

Jack A. Goldstone
University of California, Davis

References

Eckstein, S. (1982) 'The impact of revolution on social welfare in Latin America', *Theory and Society* 11.

Eisenstadt, S. N. (1978) *Revolution and the Transformation of Societies*, New York.

Gurr, T. R. (1970) *Why Men Rebel*, Princeton, NJ.

Huntington, S. (1968) *Political Order in Changing Societies*, New Haven, CT.

Johnson, C. (1966) *Revolutionary Change*, Boston, MA.

Marx, K. and Engels, F. (1968 [1848]) *The Communist Manifesto*, London. (Original edn, *Manifest der Kommunistischen Partei*, London.)

Skocpol, T. (1979) *States and Social Revolutions*, Cambridge, UK.

Tilly, C., Tilly, L. and Tilly, R. (1975) *The Rebellious Century 1830–1930*, Cambridge, MA.

Tocqueville, A. de (1856) *The Old Regime and the French Revolution*, New York.

Further reading

Goldstone, J. A., Gurr, T. R. and Moshiri, F. (eds) (1994) *Revolutions of the Late Twentieth Century*, Boulder, CO.

Moore, B. Jr (1966) *Social Origins of Dictatorship and Democracy*, Boston, MA.

Wolf, E. R. (1969) *Peasant Wars of the Twentieth Century*, New York.

See also: radicalism; terrorism.

revolutions, industrial *see* industrial revolutions

Ricardo, David (1772–1823)

David Ricardo was born in London on 18 April 1772, the third son of Abraham Israel Ricardo, a Sephardic Jew who had moved from Amsterdam to London around 1760. The young Ricardo was groomed to follow his father on the London Stock Exchange. Although his education was by no means negligible, it appears to have been somewhat narrow, perhaps explaining in part his later outbursts of despair over his literary ability.

Ricardo worked with his father for seven years until, at the age of 21, he married a Quaker and disavowed the Jewish faith. Estranged from his parents, Ricardo pursued a brilliant career as a jobber and loan contractor. Through a combination of fine judgement and good luck he soon amassed a considerable fortune and began a gradual retirement from business in 1814.

It was in 1799 that his interest in Political Economy was aroused by a chance perusal of Adam Smith's (1981 [1776]) *The Wealth of Nations*. His first rash of publications came ten years later with letters and pamphlets addressed to the 'Bullion Controversy'. Ricardo, always a strict quantity theorist, sought to expose the inflationary consequences of the Bank Restriction Act 1797, which had suspended the free convertibility of paper currency into gold. He argued that the government had been mistaken in suspending convertibility and even more wayward in trusting ignorant Bank of England officials with monetary control. The remedy for inflation was a return to convertibility, ideally accompanied by the establishment of an independent authority to oversee monetary management.

Following the Bullion Controversy, Ricardo's next important publication, *An Essay on the Influence of a Low Price of Corn on the Profits of Stock* (1815), was one of many pamphlets spawned by the Tory government's controversial proposal to impose a new scale of duties on the importation of foreign corn. Borrowing and adapting the theory of differential rent, rediscovered by his contemporary and friend, Thomas Robert Malthus, Ricardo inveighed against protection. His principal argument was that a protection-induced expansion of domestic cultivation would tend to run up against diminishing returns, thus resulting in a rising corn price, higher money wages, a falling general rate of profit and a slackening pace of capital accumulation. The only true gainers would be the landlords, whose rents would increase as general profitability declined.

Ricardo's major work, *The Principles of Political Economy and Taxation* (three editions: 1817, 1819, 1821), was initially conceived as an expanded *Essay* and, although its scope was broader, the contents of the core theoretical chapters reflect that early conception. In particular, Ricardo now sought to demonstrate beyond logical doubt that diminishing agricultural returns *must* (permanently) depress general profitability in the absence of technological advances and the free importation of foreign grain. Since, as far as he was concerned, rising corn prices posed the sole empirical threat of permanently declining profitability, the clear message of his work was that the newly revised corn law should be scrapped.

Prominent among the theoretical innovations in the *Principles* was the development of a pure labour theory of value according to which permanent changes in exchange relationships between most commodities result from alterations in direct or indirect *quantities* of labour expended on their production. At the same time, Ricardo had discovered various limitations to the theory, later reduced by him to differences in the 'time profiles' of labour inputs. Pressed by Malthus to justify a theory which he had himself undermined, Ricardo embarked on his futile quest for a perfect measure of value which would magically restrict (permanent) variations in exchange relationships to those resulting from altered expenditures of labour-time, and this *without* assuming identical time profiles of labour inputs. That bizarre line of enquiry found expression in an extensively rewritten chapter 'On Value' for the third edition of the *Principles*, in which Ricardo also asserted the empirical relevance of the 'pure' labour theory. The complexities of value continued to trouble him until his death, not least because of his muddled attempt to reconcile 'value' in the sense of expended labour with 'value' in the more conventional sense of cost-of-production.

Adumbration of a theory of comparative advantage in international trade, the treatment of profit of as a residual or 'surplus', consideration of the possibility of labour displacement following the introduction of new machinery (in the third edition of the *Principles*) and a strict adherence to the 'law of markets' (in short, the doctrine that 'supply creates its own demand'), all count among the distinctive features of the *Principles*. Mention should also be made of Ricardo's austere, logico-deductive style of reasoning, for which he has been often condemned as an ultra-abstractionist. Despite superficial appearances, however, Ricardo's political economy was mostly addressed to the concrete issues of his time; with the partial exception of his later deliberations on 'value', his was not an interest in theory for its own sake.

The success of the *Principles* was decisive in persuading Ricardo that he should follow the advice of his mentor, James Mill, to enter Parliament. So it was that in 1819 he took his seat as the member for the small pocket borough of Portarlington in Ireland. From the floor of the Commons, Ricardo was untiring in his efforts to disseminate the scientific truths of political economy, as he saw them. With an almost fanatical belief in the efficiency and wealth-generating potential of competitive capitalism, he campaigned vigorously against monopolies, international trade restrictions, the poor laws, relief works and government borrowing generally (he boldly proposed that the national debt should be paid off over a two or three-year period by the imposition of a property tax). As a convert to the Bentham-Mill cause of parliamentary reform, though always remaining a moderate reformer, he also argued for a (very) limited extension of the electoral franchise, triennial parliaments and, most important of all in his view, the introduction of a secret ballot. He apparently believed, and certainly hoped, that those reforms would bring about a Parliament free from party and factional interest: a legislative environment which would promote the greatest happiness of the greatest number. When, at some future point in time, the working class came to appreciate the unique benefits of *laissez-faire* capitalism, they too could be trusted with democratic participation.

Ricardo's 'Political Economy' has attracted and repelled, both in his lifetime and subsequently. Nor is there any consensus over his location in the history of economic thought: some have claimed him for the neo-classical school, others for the Marxian, others still for a Neo-Ricardian (or Sraffian) school. Part of the reason for the seemingly endless debate over his doctrinal home can be traced to the presence of a confusion and ambiguity in his writings which facilitates contradictory readings. But it is also the fate, perhaps even the hallmark, of great historical figures that they should be enlisted in support of causes held dear by subsequent generations. By that criterion, David Ricardo is one of the greatest Political Economists ever.

Terry Peach
University of Manchester

References

Ricardo, D. (1951–73) *The Works and Correspondence of David Ricardo*, ed. P. Sraffa with M. H. Dobb, 10 vols, Cambridge, UK.

Smith, A. (1981 [1776]) *An Inquiry into the Nature and Causes of the Wealth of Nations*, ed. R. Campbell and A. Skinner, Indianapolis, IN.

Further reading

Blaug, M. (1958) *Ricardian Economics: A Historical Study*, New Haven, CT.

Hollander, J. H. (1910) *David Ricardo: A Centenary Estimate*, Baltimore, MD.

Hollander, S. (1979) *The Economics of David Ricardo*, Toronto.

Peach, T. (1993) *Interpreting Ricardo*, Cambridge, UK.

Sraffa, P. (1951) Introduction, *The Works and Correspondence of David Ricardo*, vol. 1, Cambridge, UK.

See also: political economy; value and distribution.

risk analysis

Risk and uncertainty are an integral part of most human behaviour, as only rarely are the outcomes of human actions predictable with complete certainty. They are particularly evident in economic and financial affairs, with risk and uncertainty forming the basis of financial contracts and the role of financial institutions, instruments and markets. Thus financial markets exist in part to enable people to deal with risk and uncertainty in their financial affairs, and many instruments (insurance, futures, options contracts, etc.) exist in order for risk and uncertainty to be managed. If risk and uncertainty were removed entirely there would be little for the financial system to do, or what it would do would be fundamentally different from the role it actually plays.

It is not surprising, therefore, that much of the formal analysis of risk and uncertainty has been undertaken in the area of finance. However, while finance has its own special characteristics, the relevant analysis and axioms derived in this area apply, in varying degrees and forms, to other areas of behaviour.

Although in common usage the two are frequently interchanged and regarded as alternative terms for the same phenomenon, this is erroneous as they are distinct concepts. *Uncertainty* arises when the future is unknown but no actual probabilities (either objective or subjective) are attached to alternative outcomes. *Risk* arises when specific numerical probabilities are attached to alternative outcomes. Thus the foundation of a large part of risk analysis lies in probability theory. The starting-point is that, in most areas, economic agents are risk-averse in that they gain no intrinsic welfare from knowingly taking risk. It follows from this that, other things being equal, agents prefer less risky to more risky projects and behaviour, and that attempts are frequently made to avoid or limit risk. However, other things are not equal, and agents can be, and need to be, compensated for taking risk. The risk premium that is received is such a compensation. Thus, other things being equal, agents prefer high to low rates of return and low rather than high risk. This means that agents are prepared to pay a higher price for less risky assets with a given expected rate of return, and that higher returns are available only if more risk is taken.

A distinction is also drawn between *risk* and *seriousness*. The former relates to the measurable (actual or assumed) probability of event X happening, while *seriousness* relates to the impact on the agent if X does occur. Thus assuming X is an undesired outcome, agents will avoid exposing themselves to the possibility of X occurring: the higher is its probability, and the more serious the outcome would be for the agent, the less is the compensation offered. Thus, we are not indifferent between two risks with the same probability (say an earthquake occurring and the chance of it raining) when their seriousness differs, and conversely we are not indifferent between two risks that have the same degree of seriousness but different probabilities. Behaviour is, therefore, influenced both by the risk of an event or outcome and the potential seriousness of it if it occurs.

This, in turn, gives rise to the concept of *disaster myopia* where, confronted with low-probability/high-seriousness risks, agents behave as if the probability were zero rather than low and, in the event that the risk materializes, the impact on the agent is very serious. Because the probability is viewed as being zero (rather than very low) no protection is taken. There must be a greater than zero probability that reading this article will induce acute schizophrenia and yet one reader is doing so. Many banks and other financial institutions that get into serious difficulty do so because they accept low-probability/high-seriousness risks but behave as if the risk were zero. An example would be

banks making loans to a small number of developing countries to an extent that greatly exceeded their capital: while the probability of default might be low it would be very serious (and in fact was serious when it occurred in the 1980s) if a default were to occur.

Risk analysis is applied to situations which have multiple, uncertain outcomes. Leaving aside the special area of finance, it involves four major processes: specifying the relevant attributes of various outcomes; establishing the probability distribution of outcomes associated with each attribute (often by analysing past periods); an evaluation of the uncertain outcomes so that choices can be made, and analysis of methods to reduce or shift risk to other agents.

The essential elements of risk analysis and management are captured in a review of the issues that are considered in banking. Banks are necessarily in the risk business because they issue debt contracts on both sides of the balance sheet, because the characteristics of these contracts are different on the assets and liabilities side (their traditional *asset transformation* role), and because they are highly geared institutions: a high ratio of debt liabilities to equity capital. The ultimate risk is that, because of non-repayment of loans, the bank becomes insolvent as the value of its assets falls below that of its debt liabilities. In practice, banks are subject to many different kinds of risk: credit, price, foreign currency, liquidity, operational, forced-sale, etc. For expositional purposes, we restrict the discussion to credit-risk, that is, the risk that a loan is not repaid.

Risk analysis and management for a bank involves five key processes: first, identification and measurement of risks, that is, a calculation of the probability of default; second, what can be done to lower the probability of default; third, measures to limit the damage in the event that the risk materializes, that is, default occurs; fourth, action to shift risk on to others, that is, risk-sharing, and fifth, how the residual risk is absorbed.

The first procedure is to identify and quantify the risk. The bank will use its expertise and past experience to calculate the probability of a default. This involves a screening of potential borrowers and projects and the acquisition of information to ascertain the nature and magnitude of the risk. Banks may have a comparative advantage over others in this process because of their skills and experience.

Second, the bank will seek to reduce the probability of the risk by, for instance, monitoring the behaviour of borrowers, setting conditions on the loan, devising incentive-compatible contracts to ensure that the behaviour of the borrower is such as to lower the probability of default (e.g. by requiring the borrower to invest personal resources in the project), taking collateral from the borrower so that the borrower also loses if the loan is not repaid, credit rationing, taking an equity stake in the project so that the bank has some say in its management, and so on. In these ways a lender can attempt to reduce the probability of a default. An incentive-compatible contract can also be used to reduce the potential moral hazard of the borrower: an incentive a borrower may have to deliberately default. The contract must be structured so that there is a greater incentive for the borrower to repay than to default deliberately.

Third, a bank, lender or purchaser of a financial asset will seek to limit the damage in the event of a default or fall in the price of an asset. The standard procedure is to include the loan or asset within an efficiently diversified portfolio where the individual risks are less than perfectly correlated. In this way the overall portfolio is less risky than any particular asset within it: what remains is *systematic* risks, that is, the part of an investment's total risk that cannot be avoided by combining it with other investments in a diversified portfolio. In this procedure the value of a particular investment or loan is measured in terms of its contribution to the overall risk of the portfolio rather than its inherent riskiness. Thus a risk-averse investor may rationally choose an investment which has a higher inherent risk than the existing risk of the portfolio (on the face of it, counter-intuitive) if it has the effect of lowering overall portfolio risk. A bank may construct a diversified portfolio of loans by either making different types of loans (e.g. to different types of borrowers) or by having several similar loans but to different borrowers. This is an application of the law of large numbers. Thus, if there is a 10 per cent probability that a $1,000 loan will not be repaid, the expected future value of the loan is indeterminate: either 0 or $1,000. On the other hand, with the same probabilities, if ten loans of $100 are made, the expected future value of the portfolio becomes $900. A bank may also seek to limit the damage of a default by, for instance, requiring collateral to be lodged (the collateral is retained in the event of a default), or by restricting the size of individual loans relative to the bank's equity capital so that it does not become insolvent if the borrower does not repay. A bank may also limit damage through a hedge contract.

The fourth component of risk analysis and management is to shift risks on to others. The standard procedure is insurance. Here a risk-averse agent pays a premium to pass the risk to an insurance company. This is possible only if it is profitable for both parties. The gain to the insured is the passing of the risk for which benefit the insured is prepared to pay a premium. It is advantageous to insurers if they can charge premiums which generate profits after claims have been met. This will be possible if the insurer is able to acquire a diversified structure of risks. Not all risks are, however, insurable. The necessary conditions are: first, the insured risk is observable and verifiable (thus we cannot insure against having a headache) whereas we can for a broken leg); second, the risk must be diversifiable by the insurer; and third, there must be no moral hazard, that is, there must be no incentive for the insured to cause the risk to materialize. With respect to the last mentioned, for instance, a house will not be insured for more than its value as this could create an incentive for the owner to burn it down, even allowing for the transactions costs of replacing it. In principle a bank could seek to insure its loans, though in practice this is rare as the bank is itself usually a more efficient insurance vehicle, implying that, given the size and diversity of its loan portfolio, the risk premiums it can profitably build into its own loan interest rates are lower than the premiums that would be charged by an external insurer. In addition, if loans are externally insured a moral hazard is created, in that there may be an incentive for the bank to make high-risk loans in a situation where it has superior information to that of the insurance company. A bank may also effectively insure against a price risk by becoming a counter-party in a forward, futures or options contract.

Summarizing the analysis, a bank or investor will identify and measure risks, consider how to reduce the probability of a default, seek to limit the damage in the event of a default, and consider alternative mechanisms for shifting risk. Any remaining risk has to be absorbed and a bank will handle this through the pricing of its loans (i.e. set a risk premium in the loan interest rate to cover expected risk which amounts to internal insurance), and by holding an equity capital cushion to absorb potential unexpected risks.

The analysis has been conducted primarily by reference to risks in finance. However, the same principles apply in all risk analysis. As has been argued, risk analysis is inseparable from risk management.

David T. Llewellyn
Loughborough University

Further reading

Arrow, K. J. (1971) *Essays in the Theory of Risk-Bearing*, Chicago.

Balch, M. *et al.* (eds) (1974) *Essays on Economic Behaviour under Uncertainty*, Amsterdam.

Borch, K. H. (1990) *Economics of Insurance*, Amsterdam.

Brealey, R. and Myers, S. (1988) *Principles of Corporate Finance*, New York.

Diamond, P. and Rothschild, M. (eds) *Uncertainty in Economics: Readings and Exercises*, New York.

Dreze, J. (1987) *Essays on Economic Decisions under Uncertainty*, Cambridge, UK.

Ehrlich, I. and Becker, G. (1972) 'Market insurance, self-insurance and self-protection', *Journal of Political Economy* 80(4).

Hirshleifer, J. and Riley, J. (1970) 'The analysis of uncertainty and information: an expository survey', *Journal of Economic Literature*, 17.

Knight, F. (1921) Risk, *Uncertainty and Profit*, Boston, MA.

Markowitz, H. (1959) *Portfolio Selection: Efficient Diversification of Investment*, New Haven, CT.

Sinkey, J. F. (1992) *Commercial Bank Financial Management in the Financial Services Industry*, New York.

Smith, C. W. *et al.* (1990) *Managing Financial Risk*, New York.

Tobin, J. (1958) 'Liquidity preference as behaviour toward risk', *Review of Economic Studies* 25.

von Neumann, J. and Morgensten, O. (1953) *Theory of Games and Economic Behaviour*, Princeton, NJ.

Williams, A. and Heins, R. (1989) *Risk Management and Insurance*, New York.

See also: credit; entrepreneurship; profit; risk society.

risk society

The term risk society is associated with the German sociologist Ulrich Beck. In a risk society the future has become uncertain. Possible events which technology unintentionally generates cannot be insured against because they have unimaginable implications (e.g. the 1986 explosion at the Chernobyl nuclear reactor). For example, with nuclear power Beck identifies suspension of 'the principle of insurance not only in the economic, but also in the medical, psychological, cultural and religious sense. *The residual risk society has become an uninsured society*' (Beck 1992b: 101). Instead of belief in progress and the future, risk society is experienced in terms of short-term calculations of danger: 'In this sense, one could say that the calculus of risk exemplifies a type of ethics without morality, the mathematical ethics of the technological age' (Beck 1992b: 99).

Beck's exploration of the role, status and implications of technology inspired lively debate. First, his work relates to themes of post-modernity and the post-modern. Beck's argument that risk society has torn up the insurance contract between present and future bears comparison with post-modern doubt about the meta-narrative of progress. Yet Beck is no post-modernist. He has faith in the potential of a self-critical technological enterprise to solve risk problems. Secondly, Beck emphasizes the sociological significance of the environment and ecology. In Germany, Beck had a major impact on environmentalist politics and thinking, but in the English-speaking world that impact has been considerably lessened by the gap between original publication and translation (Beck's book was published in Germany in 1986; the English translation appeared in 1992).

Risk is also a theme in the work of Anthony Giddens. He distinguishes pre-modern (traditional) and modern environments of risk: 'The risk environment of traditional cultures was dominated by hazards of the physical world' while the modern risk environment is 'structured mainly by humanly created risks' (Giddens 1990: 106; 111). Giddens stresses the importance of the environment, war and personal relationships in modern experiences and constructions of risk. In so doing, Giddens makes it plain that 'Risk is not just a matter of individual action. There are "environments of risk" that collectively affect large masses of individuals' (Giddens 1990: 35).

The risk society debate is a major attempt to understand new social movements and emergent social problems. However, its residual faith in the ability of technology to insure society against the very risks that technology has created makes it improbable that the debate will be able to break out of a circle in which blindly accepted technology leads to a risk, which only a self-critical technology might be able to resolve.

Keith Tester
University of Portsmouth

Further reading

Beck, U. (1992a) *Risk Society: Towards a New Modernity*, London.
—— (1992b) 'From industrial society to the risk society: questions of survival, social structure and ecological enlightenment', *Theory, Culture and Society* 9(1).
Giddens, A. (1990) *The Consequences of Modernity*, Cambridge, UK.

See also: risk analysis.

rites of passage

'The life of an individual in any society is a series of passages from one age to another and from one occupation to another' (Van Gennep 1960 [1909]). Since the publication in 1909 of Arnold Van Gennep's *Les Rites de passage*, this term has been used primarily to refer to life-crisis rituals, such as those accompanying birth and death, puberty, marriage, initiation into adulthood or entry to priestly or political and other secular offices. Also included are those individual or collective rites which mark changes in the season or calendar. The common element in such rites, Van Gennep argued, is that they effect a transition from one social condition to another and, as a consequence, display a definite three-phase structure, with *rites of separation, transition* and *aggregation*. This pattern, though discernible to some extent in all, tends to be most fully realized in initiation rites where it may be given added force in the symbolism of death and rebirth. The *rites of separation* thus enact a symbolic death which removes individuals from society and their old social status before they are transformed in the subsequent *rites of transition* and, finally, reborn into a new social position and back into the community in the culminating *rites of aggregation.*

For Van Gennep the theme of passage provided the clue to the diverse symbolic devices employed in such rites. For example, the ritual movements may be represented in spatial terms, by exits and entrances, crossings and journeys, and in the general significance attached to crossroads, boundaries and thresholds. Of much current interest is Van Gennep's identification of the mid or transitional period as one of marginality or liminality (from the Latin, *limen* meaning threshold). It represents, he writes, the point of inertia for the novices between contrary ritual movements; they are regarded as outside society, untouchable and dangerous, sacred as opposed to profane. Sharing with Van Gennep a similar concern with social classification and the cultural imposition of order on natural and social affairs, structuralist anthropologists such as Mary Douglas (1966) and Edmund Leach (1976) have argued that ideas of danger attach to any situation or object which transgresses or cannot be placed within the dominant system of social classification. Novices, betwixt-and-between defined social positions, are inherently anomalous and thus likely to be regarded as both polluted and polluting. Outside and opposed to normal social life, liminality is also given ritual expression in licence, disorder and role reversal.

From a functionalist perspective, Max Gluckman (1963) sees such inversional elements as motivated by underlying conflicts in the structure of social relations. Proposing the idea of 'rituals of rebellion', he argues that they give a voice to those usually held inferior and oppressed. For example, Zulu women, never full citizens in the villages of their husbands, dressed up as men in a first sowing rite and were given licence to behave obscenely and ape the ways of their menfolk. This interpretation has been influential but meets with difficulties in dealing with ritual situations where superiors assume the style and behaviour of inferiors. Victor Turner (1969), taking a new approach and exploring the experiential implications of liminality, sees the key process in initiations as one of ritual levelling, with the person stripped of social insignia and signs of secular status, reduced to nakedness and subject to humiliation by ordeal, test and trauma. Socially invisible, dead to the normal world, the initiate is at the same time united with fellow initiates. This humbling process, he suggests, contains a revitalizing element, 'giving recognition to an essential and generic human bond, without which there could be *no* society' (Turner 1969). In this context he asks us to consider

two modalities of social experience, of 'structure' where people are differentiated by social role and position and linked in an often hierarchical political system, as opposed to what he calls 'communitas', as it presents itself in an undifferentiated community of equals who may recognize each other in an immediate and total way. 'Communitas emerges where social structure is not,' says Turner, reaffirming the bonds of essential unity upon which the social order ultimately rests. While he feels that communitas finds its most characteristic expression in the liminal period of *rites de passage* where the individual is divested of normal social attributes, he argues that it may be engendered also in role reversals in seasonal rites and be an attribute more generally of structural marginality and inferiority, exemplified by such figures as sacred clowns and holy beggars.

In contrast to psychoanalytic accounts, anthropological theory has made relatively little of the dramatic ordeals and mutilations which are commonly found in association with initiations. For example, circumcision for Van Gennep is best explained as a separation rite, while for Turner it is an aspect of ritual levelling. Such symbolism is seen as essentially arbitrary – Van Gennep (1960 [1909]) writes, 'The human body has been treated like a simple piece of wood which each has cut and trimmed to suit him.' Psychoanalytic accounts of initiation, of course, take the opposed view that genital mutilation is central to the development and purpose of such rites. Neo-Freudian explanations diverge, with some regarding circumcision as a symbolic castration, while Bettelheim (1954) has suggested that it is best regarded as a mimetic menstruation, representing male envy of female reproductive powers. Seen as a response to universal problems, such explanations fail to account for the cross-cultural variability in incidence and type of such ordeals. However, a more psychologically informed anthropology seems to be developing, aiming to explore the subjective experience of initiation as this is encoded in different cultural idioms. It is perhaps no accident that interesting work here is coming from New Guinea societies with their plethora of explicit sexual symbolism (see Herdt 1982).

To conclude, two broad approaches to the study of *rites de passage* can be distinguished. The first looks to social classification and, with Van Gennep, gives primacy to the idea of transition. This gives a unity to the category but, in so far as it portrays rituals as static dramas of form, tends to underplay the creative intent of such rites in pre-industrial society and the culturally specific ways in which this is conceived and realized. As Turner reminds us, many *rites de passage* intend an active transformation of the person. The second approach looks to the subjective effects of ritual and the concepts of personhood mediated by the ritual process. To some extent this harks back to earlier functionalist concerns with the efficacy of ritual (prefigured, for example, in Richards 1982 [1956]), but it promises to be a far more eclectic venture, drawing freely upon other disciplines.

Suzette Heald
Lancaster University

References

Bettelheim, B. (1954) *Symbolic Wounds*, Glencoe, IL.

Douglas, M. (1966) *Purity and Danger: An Analysis of Concepts of Pollution and Taboo*, London.

Gluckman, M. (1963) *Order and Rebellion in Tribal Africa*, London.

Herdt, G. H. (1982) *Rituals of Manhood: Male Initiation in Papua New Guinea*, Berkeley, CA.

Leach, E. (1976) *Culture and Communication; The Logic by which Symbols are Connected*, Cambridge, UK.

Richards, A. I. (1982 [1956]) *Chisungu: A Girl's Initiation among the Bemba of Northern Rhodesia*, London.

Turner, V. W. (1969) *The Ritual Process*, London.

Van Gennep, A. (1960 [1909]) *The Rites of Passage*, London. (Original edn, *Les Rites de passage*, Paris.)

Further reading

Crapanzano, V. (1992) 'Rite of return', in *Hermes' Dilemma and Hamlet's Delight*, Cambridge, MA.

Gluckman, M. (ed.) (1962) *Essays on the Ritual of Social Relations*, Manchester.

Heald, S. and Deluz, A. (eds) (1994) *Anthropology and Psychoanalysis: An Encounter through Culture*, London.

Turner, V. W. (1967) *The Forest of Symbols*, Ithaca, NY.

See also: age organization; life cycle; religion and ritual.

ritual and religion *see* religion and ritual

role

A role is the expected behaviour associated with a social position. People from Outer Mongolia visiting the courts of justice in Britain and observing a series of criminal trials would not understand what they saw until they appreciated that people in court proceedings have to play particular roles: judge, prosecutor, defence advocate, accused, witness, juror, usher, spectator and so on. The interpretation of behaviour in a courtroom provides a good example of the utility, indeed the necessity, of a concept of role. Its positive features will be discussed first before considering whether the selection of some other example might not cast doubt upon the value of the concept.

Were they able to overhear conversations in various parts of the court building, the visitors would be able to discover the number and names of the positions that have to be occupied if the proceedings are to be lawful; the names of the individuals occupying these positions on particular occasions; and how well particular individuals were thought to perform their roles. Over a long period of time, the visitors could watch particular barristers pleading before various judges and taking different kinds of cases; some would advance their careers more rapidly than others.

Watching individual lawyers after they had become judges, the observers might conclude that they had taken certain of the other judges as models of what to emulate and what to avoid. In such ways the observers could ascertain the processes by which individuals learn to play roles according to the satisfaction or dissatisfaction of others. The observers would also learn about the processes by which individuals come to occupy the various positions.

To start with, the observers might be surprised to notice that the barrister who had spoken for the prosecution in a case that had just been completed was appearing for the defence in the next case. They would learn that it is the role of barristers to speak for whichever client they are engaged (by a solicitor) to represent; their personal opinions of their clients' moral merits are irrelevant, while the uniform they wear (wig, gown and standardized costume) reinforce the message that their personality is subordinated to their role. Observation would also show that barristers are punished for infringing the rules (one who asks leading or irrelevant questions will be rebuked by the judge) and rewarded for doing well (by being asked to take more cases, and cases bringing higher fees). Every now and again an unusual event would reveal some other kind of rule showing that two roles may not be held by the same person if there is any suspicion that their obligations may conflict. Judges may not preside over a case in which they have a personal interest. A barrister may be unable to represent both of two people jointly charged with an offence, since the two may dispute with each other as to their relative culpability. Judges and barristers would be criticized were they, in their leisure time, to associate with known criminals.

The roles of judge and barrister are assumed willingly, that of the accused is usually not. Sometimes accused persons deny the authority of the court to try them, but they are still tried. However reluctant people may be to feature as accused persons, once they have been arraigned it is usually in their interest to play the expected role in the hope that they may be able to utilize it in a manner that will enable them either to escape conviction or to secure a lighter sentence. Thus it may be possible to obtain a better understanding of the way such people behave if it is assumed that they comprehend what is expected of them and are seeking to turn those expectations to their advantage.

Court proceedings illustrate the utility of the role concept for the additional reason that they can be given a historical dimension that reveals the steady differentiation and sharper definition of the roles involved. In many societies at one stage of their history, cases were settled by *kadi*-justice (to use an expression of Arabic origin employed by Max Weber). In *kadi*-justice a politically powerful person makes an informal decision according to ethical or practical values, rather than by reference to previous decisions or to statute law. In such circumstances political and judicial roles are not distinguished. Even in the mid-seventeenth century, English criminal trials were, by modern standards, very brief: the Surrey assizes tried on average per day fourteen defendants charged with serious offences. Nowadays the proceedings are more complex. The evidence of each witness can be examined at length; there is time to evaluate the evidence in terms of the roles the witnesses were playing; while everyone in court will be conscious that the judge, the lawyers and the witnesses are taking part in a drama and interpreting their roles in a way that can be compared with actors on a stage. A higher material standard of living permits people to be more self-conscious about their behaviour.

In *Games People Play*, Eric Berne (1964) describes and assigns names to the various characteristic disputes arising in families. One of them is 'Uproar', occurring most frequently between a domineering father and an adolescent daughter bidding for greater freedom. It has sexual undertones. It derives its name from the fact that the dispute is often terminated by one or both parties shouting angrily, retiring to a bedroom and slamming the door. It is possible to see Uproar as a game in which two people play distinctive roles (even though these roles are not defined by rights and obligations, which has been the traditional way of conceptualizing role in anthropology and much of sociology). If, however, the players have read an analysis of the game, they are much more likely to recognize what is happening if they themselves are drawn into a dispute of this kind. They will have an insight into the dynamics of the relationship and the way in which they are contributing to it. Not only may they find themselves playing a role but also they will be conscious of themselves as doing so, and in some circumstances they may even distance themselves from their role by signalling that their behaviour is not completely serious. This awareness is facilitated by the use of the word 'role' in ordinary language and by the availability of books analysing behaviour in role terms, a feature

of European and North American culture in the second half of the twentieth century.

'Father' and 'adolescent daughter' can both be considered social positions, but the behaviour expected of people occupying these positions is much less well defined than in the case of the judge and the barrister. Until relatively recently in Britain (and in many parts of Europe), adolescent daughters were constrained much more narrowly than their brothers. When they reached marriageable age, middle-class young women put their hair up to indicate their change of status. The dressing of their hair was a role sign; the alteration in it was a minor ceremonial of role-changing (as a wedding is a major ceremonial of it). An unmarried woman was not supposed to meet a man unless a chaperone was present. These role expectations have since changed, along with other changes in the social structure, but the speed and extent of their change in particular households will have been an outcome of a conflict between fathers and daughters, each seeking to impose their own definitions of expected behaviour. Indeed, changing expectations with respect to gender roles have been an occasion for intense discussion. What the sociologist or social psychologist can do is to ascertain the expectations of a role such as 'adolescent daughter' held by people in other, related positions. An examination of these expectations and their determinants could contribute to an analysis of the more general problem and indicate ways in which it could most easily be resolved. This could be particularly relevant to the domestic problems of immigrant Muslim groups in European cities. In the father–daughter relationship within these groups, the conflicts between two value systems are brought to a head.

The various senses of the word 'expect' in English conceal a particular difficulty. Someone may expect a doctor to be male and a nurse to be female simply because most people in these two positions are of those genders. This is a purely *statistical* expectation. Someone else may expect a doctor to be male and a nurse female because of a belief that this is right and proper (just as the office of priest in the Catholic Church is limited to males). This is a *normative* expectation. The two kinds of expectations go together in the sense that someone growing up in a society in which all doctors are male may come to believe that all doctors should be male. Anyone who makes use of the concept of role may need to explain whether the expectations associated with a position are of the one kind or the other; both can be comprehended in role analysis.

Role as a concept in social science cannot be compared to an elementary particle in physics. It is not possible to list all the roles in a particular society, because there are no clear principles for deciding what is a social position: in the end it is a question of discovering whether it is useful in given circumstances to regard, say, pedestrian, as a role. In so far as people are conscious of themselves and others as occupying positions with generally known rights and duties, then their behaviour cannot be understood without reference to their expectations about how they should behave and others should behave towards them. The research worker may ask them what their expectations are; the researcher may observe their behaviour and deduce their expectations from it; or the researcher may do both and find out that when their stated expectations are not met they do not necessarily do anything about it (a serious breach will be another matter). In order to analyse actual behaviour, the concept of role is only a beginning which must be supplemented by a battery of related concepts which give it greater utility. Biddle (1979) defines 334 such concepts.

Biddle also comments upon research work showing that boys and girls are treated somewhat differently in the classroom. In the USA, boys (who are taught mostly by women teachers) do less well in reading than girls, whereas in Germany (where the teachers are more likely to be male) boys do better than girls. One possible explanation of this finding is that schoolchildren take teachers as role models. Female pupils can identify with female teachers, but male pupils experience a conflict between their masculinity and their relationship to a female role model. This conflict can stimulate them to behave in ways that the school system defines as deviant. A similar argument is heard in societies like the USA and Britain, in which Black people constitute a minority of the population. The poor performance in examinations by Black children may be ascribed to the dearth of suitable role models, such as Black teachers, Black newsreaders on television and Black popular heroes. This kind of hypothesis can be tested by the methods of social science. Evidence also suggests that the absence of good male and female role models in the home can have a negative effect upon the personality development of children.

Writers who are concerned about social harmony are readily drawn to a conception of society as a unit in which everyone has a series of roles to play and where all the main roles are clearly defined. For them the concept of role helps describe the relation between the individual and society. But for those who see society as an arena in which groups with opposed interests clash with one another, such a view is regarded as suspect; they are most inclined to picture individuals as coerced by injustifiable role expectations which exact compliance, or to maintain that the very concept of role is redundant. These are criticisms of an unimaginitive use of the concept of role (seen as a representation of social relations) rather than of a problem-solving approach to role which seeks to elucidate a particular pattern of behaviour. When social scientists start from a set of observations and seek to account for what people do, they regularly have to explain behaviour in terms of people's conforming with rules. The barrister does not ask a leading question in circumstances where it is forbidden. Any explanation of why people follow rules implies a concept of role, because the rules apply to those who occupy particular social positions. Depending on the nature of the problem, it then becomes necessary to make use of other concepts from the vocabulary of role analysis particularly as it has been developed by social psychologists. By discovering which formulations are most effective in providing explanations, the present confusion about alternative definitions will eventually be dispelled.

Michael Banton
University of Bristol

References

Berne, E. (1964) *Games People Play*,
Biddle, B. J. (1979) *Role Theory: Expectations, Identities and Behaviour*, London.

Further reading

Banton, M. (1965) *Roles: An Introduction to the Study of Social Behaviour*, London.
Goffman, E. (1959) *The Presentation of Self in Everyday Life*, New York.
Jacksons, J. A. (ed.) (1972) *Role*, Cambridge, UK.

See also: social structure and structuration; status.

Rousseau, Jean-Jacques (1712–78)

Rousseau's contribution to the social sciences has been a paradoxical one. In his first *Discours*, 'Discours sur les sciences et les arts' (1964 [1750] 'On science and art'), Rousseau argued that scientific enquiry in general tends rather to corrupt than to enlighten, and that public virtue would be better served by ignorance than by systematic knowledge. In his second *Discours*, 'Sur l'origine et les fondements de l'inégalité parmi les hommes' (1964 [1775], 'On the origins of inequality'), Rousseau himself offered a pioneering work in social theory that generations of social scientists have considered crucial to the founding of such disciplines as sociology and social anthropology – the very sorts of theoretical enquiry that Rousseau had virtually ruled out in his first *Discours* as inimical to the public good (see Derathé 1970; Durkheim 1965 [1953]; Lévi-Strauss 1962).

Furthermore, whereas Rousseau argued in the second *Discours* that humans are not originally social beings and that sociability is fundamentally alien to human nature, his argument in *Du contrat social* (1978 [1762], *The Social Contract*), his main work of political philosophy, is that one can conceive of a legitimate state only where the members are wholeheartedly devoted to the good of the community and are able to identify their own interests with those of the whole society. It would seem that an author whose work is rooted in such basic contradictions would be incapable of producing a cogent and consistent social philosophy, and indeed many critics would dismiss Rousseau's achievement on just these grounds. However, one of the central claims of Rousseau's thought is that society itself is founded on irresolvable contradiction, and that therefore paradox may be the most appropriate medium in which to understand the essence of social life.

It is in his magnificent treatise on education, *Émile, ou traité de l'éducation* (1979 [1762], *Emile, or On Education*), that Rousseau states the basic insight of his social theory – the impossibility of reconciling the contradiction between nature and society:

> He who would preserve the supremacy of natural feelings in social life knows not what he asks. Ever at war with himself, hesitating between his wishes and his duties, he will be neither a man nor a citizen. He will be of no use to himself nor to others. He will be a man of our day, a Frenchman, an Englishman, one of the great middle class.

This insight is further developed in *The Social Contract* (published in the same year as *Émile*).

The core idea of *The Social Contract* is a very simple one: it is that no polity can be considered legitimate except in so far as its laws issue from the will of its members; that citizens are entitled to renounce natural liberty only for the sake of a superior freedom; and that the touchstones of politics based on right are law, democratic will and popular sovereignty. Rousseau managed to articulate a vision of politics as a moral community, even though he remained suspicious of all social relationships and held to the view that society as such is inevitably corrupting. His solution to the problem lay in substituting the power of law for the power of people, thus making people independent of one another by making them all equally dependent on the laws of the republic.

Although Rousseau categorically repudiated the conditions of political life in modernity, many of the fundamental ideas of liberal democracy are owed to him: the idea that the overarching function of government is legislation; the idea that political legitimacy flows from the will of the people; and the idea that formal equality and the rule of law are essential to democratic liberty.

From the first *Discours* onwards, Rousseau's work represented a lifelong battle against the assumptions and aspirations of the Enlightenment. Although Rousseau knew, and had been personally close to, many of the leading members of the French Enlightenment, his ideas led him into increasingly heated and passionate controversies with the champions of Enlightenment. Of these, the most significant product was Rousseau's *Lettre à d'Alembert sur les spectacles* (1960 [1758], *Letter to D'Alembert*), debating the issue of whether the theatre should be introduced into Rousseau's native city of Geneva. In general, the spokesmen of the Enlightenment sought to refashion the nature of humankind and society by constructing scientific principles of social existence. Rousseau, by contrast, thought that humans are best as they are by nature, that human nature is invariably deformed by life in society, and that such a science of society could only deepen the corruption and debasement of humankind. This was, in fact, the central insight of his social and moral philosophy, the foundation upon which all his political principles and psychological analyses are built.

Despite recurrent attempts to expose totalitarian traits within Rousseau's political thought, the ever-present concern throughout his political writings was with republican liberty. Rousseau feared that without the sustaining nourishment of genuine citizenship and civic virtue, humans in society would become slaves to social conformity, that they would (in the words of the second *Discours*) always live outside of themselves rather than within themselves, and that they would forfeit their natural liberty without attaining the higher condition of civil freedom, thus being worse off rather than better for having left nature to enter social existence. Notwithstanding the supposed romanticism attributed to Rousseau's thought, he possessed a sober and clear-headed insight into the possibility that post-Enlightenment science and technological civilization would pose an ever-greater threat to freedom and civic solidarity.

Even though Rousseau's literary and autobiographical writings have established the image of him as an unworldly and misanthropic dreamer, his political discernment is testified to by his acute diagnosis of the crumbling social order in Europe: in *Considérations sur le gouvernement de la Pologne* (1972 [1782] *The Government of Poland*), Rousseau writes, 'I see all the states of Europe hastening to their doom'; in *Émile*, he predicts, 'The crisis is approaching, and we are on the edge of a revolution'; 'In my opinion it is impossible that the great kingdoms of Europe should last much longer.'

There remains, of course, the predictable complaint that Rousseau's social theory is irretrievably utopian, and cannot in any sense be applied to modern conditions. For Rousseau himself, given the conception of political philosophy that he adheres to, and steeped as he is in the classical utopianism of Plato, this does not necessarily count as a very telling objection. As he remarks in *Émile*, 'We dream and the dreams of a bad night are given to us as philosophy. You will say I too am a dreamer; I admit this, but I do what the others fail to do. I give my dreams as dreams, and leave the reader to discover whether there is anything in them which may prove useful to those who are awake.'

Ronald Beiner
University of Southampton

References

Derathé, R. (1970) *Jean-Jacques Rousseau et la science politique de son temps*, Paris.

Durkheim, E. (1965 [1953]) *Montesquieu and Rousseau: Forerunners of Sociology*, trans. R. Manheim, Ann Arbor, MI. (Original edn, *Montesquieu et Rousseau, précursors de la sociologie*, Paris.)

Lévi-Strauss, C. (1962) 'Jean-Jacques Rousseau, fondateur des sciences de l'homme', in S. Baud-Bovy *et al.*, *Jean-Jacques Rousseau*, Neuchâtel.

Rousseau, J.-J. (1964 [1750; 1775]) *The First and Second Discourses*, ed. R. D. Masters, trans. R. D. and J. R. Masters, New York.

—— (1960 [1758]) *Letter to D'Alembert*, Glencoe, IL.

—— (1972 [1782]) *The Government of Poland*, trans. W. Kendall, Indianapolis.

—— (1978 [1762]) *On the Social Contract*, ed. R. D. Masters, trans. J. R. Masters, New York.

—— (1979 [1762]) *Emile, or On Education*, trans. A. Bloom, New York.

Further reading

Masters, R. D. (1968) *The Political Philosophy of Rousseau*, Princeton, NJ.

Rousseau, J.-J (1960 [1758]) *Politics and the Arts*, trans. A. Bloom, Glencoe, IL.

Wokler, R. (1995) *Rousseau*, Oxford.

See also: social contract.

rural sociology

From a mainstream social science perspective, rural sociology has often been considered somewhat marginal to the central theoretical interests of sociology and anthropology. It seemed of little interest to general sociology, which was mostly concerned with the larger questions of industrial and urban change or with the search for grand-theoretical schema aimed at providing a broad understanding of social behaviour. Anthropology was too committed to the investigation of the peculiarities of non-western societies and cultures to find much of interest in a field which focused primarily on rural situations in the industrialized west. In addition, rural sociology has frequently been criticized for its heavy empiricist and naïve positivist approach and for being too ready to undertake applied research for government or agri-business. Although these criticisms have been voiced most vehemently against the American rural sociological tradition, some traces of the same tendency and argument can be found with respect to certain types of European rural sociology. In Britain the situation was rather different, in that apart from the early development of rural community studies (most in fact carried out by social anthropologists and social geographers in the 1950s and early 1960s), rural sociology has hardly developed at all as a specialism, and it was left to agricultural economists and rural planners to investigate the social problems of the countryside.

Specialized departments of rural sociology first appeared in the USA from the 1930s onwards when a number of Land Grant Colleges were set up under the auspices of the US Department of Agriculture to research rural problems and to train rural extensionists and sociologists to work closely with government agencies and farmers' organizations (see Hightower 1973 for a trenchant critique of this policy). This initiative was consolidated after the Second World War with the emergence of a specific style of research focusing upon such questions as the spread of technological innovations, the disparities between rural and urban lifestyles, educational and occupational mobility patterns, and the impact of community development programmes. These various dimensions were, in the main, explored employing a methodology based on questionnaires, formal interview techniques, and quantitative analysis. The dominant framework for analysing the empirical findings was the idea of a rural–urban continuum, which sought to explain differences in social and cultural patterns by reference to the place of communities along a continuum that ran from the most urban to the most rural type of settlement. During the 1950s and 1960s, a great deal of rural-sociological research became organized around this specific conceptual schema, so successfully in fact that it was exported to other countries. As Hofstee (1963) observed, this package came to Europe in the form of a kind of 'mental Marshall aid'. It was also diffused to parts of Latin America and Asia. Indeed, the founding of various international associations specializing in rural sociology, such as the International Rural Sociological Association (IRSA), which holds a world congress every four years, is in great measure due to the enthusiasm and institutional resources of senior members of the American rural-sociology tradition.

By the end of the 1960s, the notion of a rural–urban continuum was theoretically bankrupt. Several studies had demonstrated that differences in social and cultural patterns did not simply coincide with spatial or ecological milieux (Pahl 1966). Diffusion studies were becoming increasingly complex in terms of trying to isolate the critical socio-psychological factors explaining the spread and adoption rate of innovations among farmers, but these studies had failed to deal with the wider structural conditions affecting the propensity of farmers to respond to new opportunities; nor was there any analysis of the structure and content of social networks among farmers and extensionists that might also affect the adoption pattern (Rogers and Shoemaker 1971). These limitations, together with others such as the neglect of comparative work on different forms of agricultural production (for example, family farms, capitalist enterprise and collective farms), on the effects of different government policies towards agriculture, and on questions of regional inequality, led to the beginnings of new ways of conceptualizing rural sociology.

Whereas the early tradition had assumed that there was something especially distinctive about rural locations which made them socially and culturally different from urban forms of social life, researchers increasingly took the view that rural locations were merely empirical or geographical entities in which one worked. Being 'rural' carried no special theoretical or methodological implications for the research. The significance of one's work and its relevance to other rural sociologists or to sociologists and others working in different types of empirical contexts depended essentially on the kinds of theoretical and methodological questions posed, and not merely on the fact of having had common rural experience.

In an attempt to resolve these various issues, and at the same time preserve some professional and institutional distinctiveness, several rural sociologists proposed, in the late 1970s and 1980s, a realignment of the field in order to articulate its findings more directly with general theoretical and policy debates, and to stimulate new lines of sociological enquiry (Newby 1980; 1981; Newby and Buttel 1980). Several promising new directions for empirical and theoretical analysis were suggested, each one necessitating an appreciation of developments in other fields.

Although rural sociology – especially in the USA – was born out of an interest in agricultural policy questions, it was surprising in fact that so little systematic comparison was undertaken of the characteristics, means of implementation, and social outcomes of different policies. It was argued therefore that a more adequate sociology of agricultural and rural development required theoretically informed analysis of policy problems: for example, one needed to be able to characterize differences in the nature and activities of different political regimes and policy communities in order to explain the ways in which various rural populations and different social classes were affected by, and responded to, planned intervention. This stimulated a number of interesting studies on this theme dealing with various European and American situations (e.g. Mann and Dickinson 1980; Sinclair 1980). But often the work fell short by failing to take full cognizance of existing sociological, economic and anthropological analyses of similar problems in Third-World countries (Harriss 1982, Long 1977) where a wide range of policies had been tried and analysed (for example, small-farmer, 'green revolution', large-scale settlement and land-reform programmes, and a large variety of marketing and fiscal measures). Since the late 1980s there has been a better cross-fertilization of these different research traditions, resulting in a number of theoretically interesting empirical studies (e.g. de Vries 1992; Porter *et al.* 1991; van der Ploeg 1990).

Another important new area for research concerned the impact of world food trade and agricultural aid flows between the richer and poorer nations. Initiated by sociologists and political economists (Friedmann 1981), this opened up research that focused on both ends of the process, that is, on European and American interests and policies as well as those of the Third-World countries. This has led to a burgeoning of interest in the analysis of the restructuring of international food systems and of the relationship between crises at the farm level and shifts in the patterns of food consumption, labour, investment and food processing (Goodman and Redclift 1992; Marsden and Little 1990).

The exploration of these and related issues (such as questions of technology development, in particular, biotechnology, and deficiencies in international food regulation and distribution) has prompted a rethinking of the scope of rural sociology, since farm behaviour and the livelihoods and welfare of rural populations are increasingly affected by these more global structures. Since the mid-1980s, conventional boundaries of analysis have been questioned by work on ecological change and environmental pollution. Although rural populations are not always the worst affected by these problems, there are a number of critical situations in which they are, with the devastation brought by oil exploration and the pollution of water and soils through dumping of industrial waste or excessive use of chemical farming inputs. The analysis of these processes and situations requires both an understanding of broad, cumulative ecological processes, as well as the politics of natural resource use and sustainable development. Rural sociologists have an important role to play in such research, but any conclusions they may reach must draw upon the work of environmental scientists, technologists and political scientists (Redclift 1984; see also Murdoch and Clark 1994 for a thoughtful discussion of issues of 'sustainable knowledge').

In the early 1980s, Howard Newby (1980; 1981) suggested that one of the most disquieting aspects in the history of rural sociology was its failure to develop a systematic analysis of agricultural production, at the level of either the enterprise or the overall agrarian structure. Despite the important early attempts to look at different forms of agricultural production, at contrasting patterns of land tenure and their influence on local social organization and power systems, and at the question of capitalist penetration in agriculture, it was only from the late 1970s onwards that a genuine sociology of agriculture begun to emerge. Comparing the work carried out on agricultural populations within industrialized countries with similar research in the Third World, the latter it seems (at least initially) made more progress in understanding these dimensions. This was no doubt partly due to the fact that the sociology of development and social anthropology were quicker to respond to the new developments in Marxist theory emanating from the French structuralists (Oxaal *et al.* 1975), and to the discourse on 'dependency' and 'underdevelopment'. This generated a whole range of Third-World rural studies dealing with structures on inequality and patterns of uneven development, which built upon the early European debates on the development of capitalism in agriculture to lay the foundations for a comparative political economy of agriculture. This type of analysis brought forth, in the 1980s, many rural sociological studies focusing upon industrialized agriculture that explored the different ways in which capital controlled and the state managed agricultural production (for example, through stimulating vertical integration of production and through the application of pricing and subsidy measures). Some of this work also took a closer look at the internal workings and power differentials within the farm/household enterprise, thus analysing how gender ideology and relations shaped the organization of labour, decision making and distribution of rewards (Whatmore 1991). This work, in turn, provided useful theoretical inputs into Third-World agricultural research: throughout the 1980s, the main journals *Sociologia Ruralis* and *Rural Sociology* published many articles addressing these new comparative issues.

At about the same time as this drive towards establishing a comparative political economy of agriculture was underway, so an increasing scepticism towards modes of analysis based upon conventional political-economic categories arose. This was reflected in the ongoing debate about 'agency' and 'structure' (i.e. the significance of farmer strategies versus external constraints). One school of thought has strongly argued the case for a fundamental reconstruction of theoretical and methodological concepts from an actor-oriented social constructivist perspective (Long 1984; Long and Long 1992). This, it is maintained, would make room for a fuller analysis of the differentiated nature of styles of farming, agrarian enterprise and organizing practices. It would also reveal how external intervention and agrarian change are composed of socially constructed and continuously renegotiated processes. Such an approach would imply a major rethinking of certain critical concepts such as agrarian development, state intervention, commoditization, and agricultural knowledge; as well as provide new insights into the intricate relations between processes of 'globalization' and 'localization'.

Rural sociology, then, is presently caught up in a number of controversies and expectations. Throughout its history it has never effectively been able to claim the status of a distinctive discipline with its own special object of investigation and mode of explanation. Instead, it has constantly been forced to engage in a number of interchanges with other disciplines working on similar analytical problems. In this way, its identity has been outward looking and bound up with the theoretical and empirical findings of studies that fall under such fields as peasant studies, economic anthropology, sociology of development, economic history, political economy, policy studies, science and technology, and environmental and natural resource management studies. Some rural sociologists look upon this broadening out of theoretical and empirical concerns as evidence of the general disarray of the field. Others look to the future believing that rural sociology is that much more alive and exciting because of its catholic attitude. They also contend that we are presently witnessing the emergence of a theoretically better informed and more socially relevant comparative rural sociology which is beginning to make important inroads into mainstream social science.

Norman Long
University of Bath

References

de Vries, P. (1992) 'Unruly clients', PhD thesis, Wageningen Agricultural University.

Friedmann, H. (1981) 'State policy and world commerce: the case of wheat, 1815 to the present', Working Paper 14a, University of Toronto.

Goodman, D. and Redclift, M. (1992) *Refashioning Nature: The Modern Food System*, Oxford.

Harriss, J. (1982) *Rural Development: Theories of Agrarian Change and Peasant Economy*, London.

Hightower, J. (1973) *Hard Tomatoes, Hard Times*. Cambridge, MA.

Hofstee, W. W. (1963) 'Rural sociology in Europe', *Rural Sociology* 28.

Long, N. (1977) *An Introduction to the Sociology of Rural Development*, London.

—— (1984) 'Creating space for change: a perspective on the sociology of development', *Sociologia Ruralis* 24 (3/4).

Long, N. and Long, A. (eds) (1992) *Battlefields of Knowledge: The Interlocking of Theory and Practice in Social Research and Development*, London.

Mann, S. A. and Dickinson, J. A. (1980) 'State and agriculture in two eras of American capitalism', in H. Newby and F. Buttel (eds) *The Rural Sociology of Advanced Societies: Critical Perspectives*, Montclair, NJ.

Marsden, T. and Little, J. (1990) *Political, Social and Economic Perspectives on the International Food System*, Aldershot.

Murdoch, J. and Clark, J. (1994) 'Sustainable knowledge', Centre for Rural Economy, Working Paper 9, University of Newcastle upon Tyne.

Newby, H. (1980) 'Rural sociology; a trend report', *Current Sociology* 28.

—— (1981) 'Rural sociology and its relevance to the agricultural economist: a review', *Journal of Agricultural Economics* 12.

Newby, H. and Buttel, F. (eds) (1980) *The Rural Sociology of Advanced Societies: Critical Perspectives*, Montclair, NJ.

Oxaal, I. *et al.* (1975) *Beyond the Sociology of Development*, London.

Pahl, R. (1966) 'The rural–urban continuum', *Sociologia Ruralis* 6.

Porter, D., Allen, B. and Thompson, G. (1991) *Development in Practice: Paved with Good Intentions*. London.

Redclift, M. (1984) *Development and the Environmental Crisis*, London.

Rogers, E. and Shoemaker, F. (1971) *Communication of Innovations: A Cross-Cultural Approach*, Glencoe, IL.

Sinclair, P. R. (1980) 'Agricultural policy and the decline of commercial family farming; a comparative analysis of the US, Sweden and the Netherlands', in H. Newby and F. Buttel (eds) *The Rural Sociology of Advanced Societies: Critical Perspectives*, Montclair, NJ.

van der Ploeg, J. D. (1990) *Labor, Markets and Agricultural Production*, Boulder, CO.

Whatmore, S. (1991) *Farming Women: Gender, Work and Family Enterprise*, London.

See also: agricultural economics; peasants.

S

sample surveys

The modern sample survey evolved from the Victorian social survey movement, which assembled facts about urban poverty. Other sources were the development of the statistical theory of probability, and the early attempts to carry out straw polls before elections. In the twentieth century, Bowley and others used samples in preference to attempts (on the model of Booth) to survey entire populations. Gradually (and particularly in the USA) the survey was broadened to include questions about attitudes as well as about facts. The surveys increasingly came to focus on the individual rather than on a sometimes eclectic combination of units of analysis; the survey now normally studies people ('respondents'). Respondents may be questioned about their own lives or asked about the society around them. Information is elicited in answers to questions, often ordered in the formal structure of a questionnaire; but the information may be combined with the fieldworker's own observations. The resulting body of variables (the items of information classified by respondents) is then arranged in a matrix amenable to statistical analysis. Some writers – a minority however – also use the term surveys for other kinds of data sets, such as aggregated statistics for organizations, social groups or areal units. In this sense a survey is a non-experimental (*ex post facto*) analysis, to be distinguished from an experimental design.

Sample surveys are intended to provide information about a larger population. The probable accuracy of generalizations from a sample survey to its population can be calculated using the mathematics of significance testing, if certain conditions are met. The most important condition is random sampling, that is, every member of the population sampled must stand an equal chance of being selected for the sample. For some populations, students enrolled in a school, for instance, random selection poses no obstacle, but for more diverse constituencies true random sampling

is virtually impossible. In a national population, which changes constantly as individuals are born, age and die, a sampling frame (a list of all members of the population from which to sample) becomes outdated before it can be used, and it requires a massive effort to compile in the first place. In practice, short-cut approximations to random sampling are generally employed for surveying. Special procedures are then used to estimate the correction factor ('design effect'), to permit the application of significance tests.

Human subjects not only complicate sampling by ageing, changing social characteristics, and shifting residence, but also are sometimes not available or not willing to respond to surveys. The study of this non-response preoccupies many survey methodologists, and is motivated by both technical and ethical considerations. Technically, only a minor inconvenience – the erosion of the sample case base – results as long as non-response occurs at random. Much evidence, however, shows that non-response to surveys follows predictable lines. Even if non-response derives from a simple availability factor, such as the difficulty of contacting night-shift workers at home during the conventional leisure hours, the resulting uncompleted questionnaires or interview schedules constitute a form of sampling error not accommodated in standard significance testing. An enormous literature on maximizing survey response has accumulated, particularly with reference to mailed questionnaires. Postal surveying counteracts the availability problem, to the extent that people read their mail at a time of their own choosing. Consequently, the elasticity of response due to conditioning becomes evident. Response to mailed questionnaires increases, sometimes dramatically, when follow-up mailings are carried out, or prizes or cash incentives are included with the questionnaire, or even after tests have been conducted to allow for improvements in the covering letter sent out with the questionnaire.

The pursuit of maximum response is sometimes carried to such lengths that ethical issues are raised. If people ignore calls by interviewers or solicitations through the mail by considered choice, should their wishes not be respected? This depends in part on their motives for non-response. Many researchers regard principled refusal as very rare, so that in their view the survey fieldworker may be justified in employing persuasive tactics – or as justified as the car salesperson or the life-insurance representative. There is increasing sensitivity to the rights of the citizen to privacy and confidentiality, however, and these rights are now emphasized by the granting agencies which fund much survey research.

Despite problems of these kinds, the sample survey has developed into the dominant method of research in sociology (particularly in the USA), and in several of the other social sciences. Not all methodologists applaud this development, and a substantial group prefer such alternatives as participant observation. The survey is especially useful in the collection of comprehensive information about naturally occurring social phenomena. The resultant data may be used either for detailed description or for multivariate analysis, where statistical techniques are used to weigh the influence of various factors on the dependent (to be explained) variable. In either case, the attraction of the survey method lies in its promise to generalize from a sample to a population. A practical difficulty is that survey designs must be determined in advance, and can be altered in mid-study only with great difficulty and expense. Consequently, surveys tend to be employed largely for purposes of confirmation rather than exploration. The logic of the sample survey seems ideally suited to research topics where it is defensible to assume that every sample member's responses are of equal social importance and analytical utility.

One reason that the survey continues to attract social scientists is that it satisfies some key conditions for scientific procedures. The procedures used in a sample survey can be codified, scrutinized, and replicated with a precision denied to less formal methods. The rules for reaching conclusions about the association between variables measured in a survey can be specified in advance (as, for example, when a significance level upon which a hypothesis test will hinge is selected). Social scientists who take the second word of their title literally (too literally, some would argue) tend to be drawn to sample surveys.

John Goyder
University of Waterloo

Further reading

Babbie, E. (1973) *Survey Research Methods*, Belmont, CA.
Gordon, M. (1973) 'The social survey movement and sociology in the United States', *Social Problems* 21.
Kish, L. (1965) *Survey Sampling*, New York.
Marsh, C. (1982) *The Survey Method: The Contribution of Surveys to Sociological Explanation*, London.

See also: interviews and interviewing; methods of social research; public opinion polls; questionnaires.

Saussure, Ferdinand de (1857–1913)

Although linguistics existed as a science as early as the beginning of the nineteenth century, Ferdinand de Saussure, born in 1857 in Geneva, son of an eminent Swiss naturalist, is generally regarded as the founder of modern linguistics. Saussure's *Cours de linguistique générale* (1959 [1916], *Course in General Linguistics*) is the most important of all linguistic works written in western Europe in the twentieth century. Yet it was first published only after his death and was an edited version of notes taken by his students of lectures he gave in Geneva between 1907 and 1911. After having spent ten productive years (1881–91) teaching in Paris (before returning to a chair at Geneva, where he remained until his death), Saussure became increasingly perfectionist, and this prevented him from presenting any treatment of linguistics in the form of a book, since he found it impossible to write anything at all, on such a difficult subject, which he regarded as worthy of publication. This combination of modesty and painful consciousness may explain why he produced only two books in his lifetime, both of them when he was still young, and both in comparative and Indo-European grammar, and not in theoretical linguistics. His first book, published in 1879 when he was only 21, was written in Leipzig while he was attending the lectures of two important Neo-grammarians, Leskien and Curtius. His brilliant insights into the vexed question of the Indo-European resonants brought him immediate fame. The second book was his doctoral dissertation (1880), and was concerned with the absolute genitive in Sanskrit.

Saussure's major contribution is to theoretical linguistics. Yet his writings on the subject are confined to the *Cours*, and then only in the introduction, in Part 1, 'Principes généraux', and in Part 2, 'Linguistique synchronique', the remainder of the book, albeit suggestive, not having enjoyed equivalent fame. His theory is characterized by the famous distinctions he introduced, which were adopted later by all linguists, and by his conception of the linguistic sign.

After distinguishing the study of all social institutions from semiology, as the study of sign systems, then semiology itself from linguistics, and finally the study of language in general from the study of specific human languages, Saussure arrives at the three distinctions which have deeply influenced all linguistic thinking and practice in the twentieth century.

First, *langue* versus *parole*, that is, a distinction between, on the one hand, language as a social resource and inherited system made up of units and rules combining them at all levels, and, on the other hand, speech as the concrete activity by which language is manifested and put to use by individuals in specific circumstances. Saussure states that linguistics proper is linguistics of *langue*, even though we may speak of a linguistics of *parole* and despite the fact that the use of speech alters language systems themselves in the course of history. In fact, he considers only linguistics of *langue* in the *Cours*.

Second, *synchrony* versus *diachrony*: Saussure repeatedly emphasizes that linguistics, like any other science dealing with values (see below), must embrace two perspectives. A synchronic study is conducted without consideration of the past and it deals with the system of relationships which is reflected in a language as a collective construct. A diachronic study deals mostly with unconscious historical change from one state to another.

Third, *syntagmatic* versus *associative* relationships: a syntagm is defined as a combination of words in the speech chain, and it ties together elements that are effectively present, whereas the relationships called *associative* by Saussure (and, later, paradigmatic by Hjelmslev) unite absent terms belonging to a virtual mnemonic series. Thus, the word *teaching* has an associative relationship with the words *education, training, instruction*, and so on, but a syntagmatic relationship with the word *his* in the syntagm *his teaching*. Saussure adds that the very best type of syntagm is the sentence, but he says that sentences belong to *parole* and not to *langue*, so that they are excluded from consideration. This attitude, although consistent, was to have serious consequences for structural linguistics, as it is the reason for its almost total neglect of syntax.

Saussure defines the linguistic sign as a double-faced psychic entity which comprises the concept and the acoustical image. These he calls the *signifié* and the *signifiant*. The sign has two fundamental material characteristics. First, it is arbitrary. There is no internal and necessary relationship between the signifié and the signifiant; if there were any, then, to take an example [ks] would be the only possible signifiant for the meaning 'ox'. Thus different languages would not exist in the world. Second, the signifiant is linear: it is uttered along the time dimension, which is a line, and it is not possible to utter more than one sign at the same time. Saussure adds that the whole mechanism of language relies on this essential principle.

Saussure then goes on to treat the notion of *value* (*valeur*), which is the status of a linguistic unit in rela-

tion to other units, from the very existence of which it draws its definition, so that value and identity are two notions that can be equated. Therefore, in language, as Saussure says in a formula that was to become very famous, 'there are only differences'. For example, since English *sheep* coexists, in the language, with *mutton*, whereas there is nothing comparable as far as the French *mouton* is concerned, *sheep*, although meaning *mouton*, has a different value.

Saussure's theory, despite its uncompleted form, has been very influential. The phonology of the Prague School and Hjelmslevian glossematics, to mention only two examples, owe much to it. Even some of the gaps have been indirectly useful. Thus, the absence of the sentence has been compensated for by transformational syntax, and the nontreatment of the linguistics of *parole* by the development of pragmatics.

Claude Hagège
Ecole Pratique des Hautes Etudes

References

Saussure, F. de (1879) *Mémoire sur le système primitif des voyelles dans les langues indo-européennes*, Leipzig.
—— (1880) *De l'emploi du génitif absolu en sanscrit*, Geneva.
—— (1959 [1916]) *Course in General Linguistics*, New York. (Original edn, *Cours de linguistique générale*, Paris.)

Further reading

Amacker, R. (1975) *Linguistique saussurienne*, Paris.
Culler, J. (1976) *Saussure*, Glasgow.
Engler, R. (ed.) (1968–74) *Ferdinand de Saussure, Cours de linguistique générale*, Wiesbaden.

See also: semiotics; structural linguistics; structuralism.

schizophrenia

The technical term for madness, psychosis, refers to a mental state in which a person perceives, thinks and/ or behaves in strange ways. Thus, the psychotic person may hear voices that other people do not perceive (auditory hallucinations), have beliefs that others would consider irrational (delusions), behave in strange ways, such as carrying around a bag with small bits of paper, or have difficulties in thinking clearly, such as having thoughts follow each other in a disorganized fashion.

Schizophrenia is one form of madness or psychosis. It is the disorder marked by a psychotic state or states and identified especially by certain characteristic symptoms. These symptoms include particular kinds of auditory hallucinations and certain delusions, such as feeling controlled by an outside force. Bizarre behaviour and formal thought disorder are also common.

However, since these symptoms can also be found in other types of psychoses, the diagnosis of schizophrenia is frequently one of exclusion – having a psychosis in which affective symptoms (depression or elation) are not predominant, and where no organic origin has been identified. Another criterion often included for diagnosing schizophrenia is that the condition continue for at least several months.

Perhaps because it is such a terrifying disorder, there are many existing beliefs about schizophrenia that far outdistance the available information. Thus, for example, people who are not mental health professionals often believe that schizophrenia means a split personality, or that it involves only people who are 'totally out of touch with reality'. Such views are either incorrect and/or oversimplifications, and thus neither do justice to the complexities of the disorder nor to the basic humanity of the people afflicted with it.

Other common but distorted beliefs about schizophrenia are that it is entirely hereditary, that patients never recover, and that people who have it are totally incapacitated. Although research suggests that there may be a genetic component in the causation of schizophrenia, it is likely that those genetic characteristics make a person vulnerable to developing schizophrenia rather than causing the disorder as such. In fact, schizophrenia appears to be caused by a wide range of biological factors and life experiences, probably acting together in ways that are not currently understood.

It was often believed that people with schizophrenia do not recover, but a group of longitudinal studies demonstrated the inaccuracy of this notion. While many patients have the disorder over a long period of time, about 60 per cent of people diagnosed as schizophrenic recover completely or have only limited residual impairment.

Finally, although many people with schizophrenic disorders are impaired severely, at least for periods of time, with treatment and rehabilitation it is often possible for such persons to return to the community and function effectively.

Certain hallucinations, delusions, bizarre behaviour, and 'formal' thought disorder are indicative of schizophrenia, but it is important to note that this condition is not totally different from more normal human experience. There are, for example, degrees of intermediate states between florid schizophrenia and normal behaviour, and many of these states are considered normal. The existence of these intermediate states suggests that many manifestations of schizophrenia and other psychoses may be extremes on continua of functioning, functioning that may be found in people who are normal and not psychotic. Thus, people who have been paged by name all day on a loudspeaker system may hear their name being called at night after leaving the building where the system operates. Sometimes people believe that someone in their organization is out to ruin them when there is little evidence for this. There are particular types of religious beliefs that may or may not be based in reality. Some behaviours which appear strange may nevertheless have a purpose. People who have just heard some shocking news or encounter some other kind of highly unusual situation may be disorganized in their thinking for a brief period.

Treatments of schizophrenia focus both on direct control of symptoms and on countering the underlying causes, although it is not certain that treatments supposedly directed at the causes do in fact operate in that way. Antipsychotic medications are pre-eminent among the treatments focused more directly on symptom reduction or elimination. These do not merely tranquillize or sedate the person generally, but appear to have a more specific action tending to reduce the psychotic symptoms themselves, at least in some patients. Although the development of these medications has been an important advance in the treatment of schizophrenia, there is a growing opinion that they do not resolve the basic processes of the disorder. There has also been increasing concern about the side-effects of these medications. Some of these effects, such as abnormal involuntary movements of the face and other parts of the body, may not appear until after a prolonged use and then may be irreversible.

There is evidence to suggest that certain kinds of personal or social treatments are also helpful for schizophrenia. Thus, hospitalization that temporarily provides an environment with reduced stimulation, and the more reality-oriented forms of group and individual psychotherapy appear to be helpful. The acquisition of insight and interpersonal and occupational skills may help reduce the person's vulnerability to recurrence of psychosis. If a particular stressful event or situation appears to have contributed to a recurrence of the psychotic state, it may also be helpful to assist the person to understand and/or change that circumstance.

Schizophrenia is a shocking and striking condition, causing much agony for the individual, as well as for family, friends and co-workers. Because schizophrenia relates to the human condition more generally in so many ways, it also has much to teach us about biology, psychology and social attachments. Considerable progress has been made in understanding and treating this condition, but much remains to be learned.

John S. Strauss
Yale University

Further reading

Kaplan, H. and Sadock, B. (1989) *Comprehensive Textbook of Psychiatry*, 5th edn, Baltimore, MD.

Strauss, J. S. and Carpenter, W. T. Jr (1982) *Schizophrenia*, New York.

See also: DSM-IV; psychoses.

science, cognitive *see* cognitive science

science, sociology of *see* sociology of science

Scottish Enlightenment, social theory

The Scottish Enlightenment (*c*.1740–90) encompassed many facets of thought of which social theory was only one. That theory itself incorporated a wide range of intellectual enquiry going beyond the well-known work of Hume (1987 [1741–42]) and Smith (1981 [1776]) to the sociology of Ferguson (1966 [1767]) and Millar (1960 [1779]), the anthropology of Kames (1774) and Monboddo (1773) and many works of socially informed history (e.g. Robertson 1972 [1769]).

The Scots take human sociality to be an evidentially warranted fact. A common explanation of this fact was that humans possessed a social instinct or appetite, but reference was also made to non-instrumental social ties such as friendship and loyalty. Part of the significance of this commitment to evidence was the deliberate rejection of the conceptions of a state of nature and a social contract. Not only were these notions fanciful but also they over-emphasized the role of purposive rationality. For the Scots the scope of reason was circumscribed by habit and social convention; social norms, for example, were the product of socialization. This also meant that the Scots were sceptical of the supposed achievements of great legislators like Lycurgus in moulding social institutions. Instead the Scots drew attention to the accidental and gradual formation of the institutions; in a phrase of Ferguson's, co-opted by later theorists like Hayek (e.g. 1960), 'nations stumble upon establishments which are indeed the result of human action, but not the execution of any human design.' This is an exemplification of the 'law of unintended consequences' of which the other classic formulation in the Scottish Enlightenment is Smith's 'invisible hand', whereby pursuit of self-interest by individuals furthers the public interest.

This diminution of the role of rationalistic individualism is part of the Scots' endeavour to explain social institutions as the effects of correspondingly social causes. They sought to go beyond the mere cataloguing of facts to tracing the chain of causes and effects. This was typically executed by writing 'natural histories', which traced the development of key institutions like property, government, ranks, the status of women and religion from simplicity to complexity or from rudeness to civilization. As an organizing device this development was seen to fall into stages that corresponded to different modes of subsistence – hunting, herding, farming and exchanging. In outlining this development, evidence from contemporary ethnography and classical history were combined in a deliberate utilization of the comparative method. The overall aim of the enquiry was to render explicable the 'amazing diversity' (as Millar termed it) of social life.

The Scots regarded their own society as belonging to the fourth commercial stage. This meant that in contrast to earlier savage societies it was 'polished', its values were more humane and the rule of law operated. The decisive ingredient of this stage was the extent of the division of labour, which although it had greatly increased the material well-being of the inhabitants also had deleterious effects. Ferguson and Kames evaluated these using the longstanding vocabulary of corruption, and Smith too noted the adverse consequences upon the labourer's virtues but he advocated a remedy in the form of primary education provided at the public's expense. This mixture of analysis and judgement is characteristic of the social theory of the Scottish Enlightenment.

Christopher J. Berry
University of Glasgow

References

Ferguson, A. (1966 [1767]) *An Essay on the History of Civil Society*, ed. D. Forbes, Edinburgh.

Hayek, F. (1960) *The Constitution of Liberty*, London.

Hume, D. (1987 [1741–42]) *Essays Moral Political and Literary*, ed. E. Miller, Indianapolis, IN.

Kames, H. Home, Lord (1774) *Sketches on the History of Man*, Edinburgh.

Millar, J. (1960 [1779]) *The Origin of the Distinction of Ranks*, 3rd edn, repr. in W. Lehmann, *John Millar of Glasgow*, Cambridge, UK.

Monboddo, J. Burnett, Lord (1773) *Origin and Progress of Language*, vol. 1, Edinburgh.

Robertson, W. (1972 [1769]) *The Progress of Society in Europe*, ed. F. Gilbert, Chicago.

Smith, A. (1981 [1776]) *An Inquiry into the Nature and Causes of the Wealth of Nations*, ed. R. Campbell and A. Skinner, Indianapolis, IN.

Further reading

Campbell, R. and Skinner, A. (eds) (1982) *The Origins and Nature of the Scottish Enlightenment*, Edinburgh.

Hont, I. and Ignatieff, M. (eds) (1983) *Wealth and Virtue: The*

Shaping of Political Economy in the Scottish Enlightenment, Cambridge, UK.

Sher, R. (1985) *Church and University in the Scottish Enlightenment*, Edinburgh.

See also: Hume, David; Smith, Adam.

sects and cults

The sociological concepts of sect and cult usually refer to religious groups or quasi-groups – which may be large or small, with complex or simple forms of organization – that are regarded, by members and non-members alike, as deviant in relation to a wider cultural or doctrinal context. The deviance in question has negative connotations for non-adherents and positive connotations for adherents. It is necessary in this stipulation to mention quasi-groups as well as groups: groups regarded as sectarian tend to promote intra-group solidarity and personal identification with the group, while cultic quasi-groups do not systematically encourage group cohesion and explicit sharing of ideas.

Sects have been more frequently studied than cults, for two reasons. First, for some purposes, it has often been found unnecessary to make a distinction between the two forms, and the more generic 'sect' has in that case been used by social scientists. Second, even though sect has a clear history as a pejorative term (for long used within Christendom to denote heretical departures from official doctrine), sociologists in the twentieth century have used the term more or less non-judgementally. That orientation has arisen from the scholarly view that the history of Christianity (and perhaps other major religious traditions) has been characterized by an interplay between *sectarian heterodoxy* and *churchly orthodoxy*, and from the argument that certain kinds of sectarian movements have been crucial in the development of western conceptions of individualism, voluntary organization and democracy – notably Protestant sects of the seventeenth century.

In contrast, cults have not as such had an innovative impact on the wider society. They tend not to be solitary groups. Cults have typically offered particular, concrete benefits to their adherents rather than the comprehensive world-views and conceptions of salvation typical of religious sects. A complication in distinguishing between sects and cults became particularly evident in the 1970s, with the proliferation in a number of societies of controversial 'new religious movements' (many of them inspired by non-western ideas or leaders). These became labelled as cults by journalists and leaders of movements which developed for the purpose of stimulating legal control of their activities, most notably their conversion techniques and methods of retaining recruits. But many of these new movements are, more accurately, sects from a sociological standpoint.

Yet the term *cultus* is probably much older than words linked to sect. That status derives from the fact that the traditional connotation of words linked to cult has focused upon religious rituals and practices (often of a magical, instrumental rather than a religious, celebratory kind); while sect has a shorter, clear-cut history because of its primary reference to deviant religious doctrines. The history of religious doctrines (intellectually systematized bodies of knowledge elaborated by religious specialists as orthodoxies) is confined to the period since the rise of the great world-religious traditions, such as Judaism, Christianity, Islam and Buddhism; while in periods and areas relatively untouched by the major religions of world significance, the more typical form of orientation to the super-empirical world has taken the form of an emphasis on ritual practice and concrete religious action – within the context of, or in relation to, mythologies which have tended not to emphasize the notion of the salvation of the individual. In the mythological, as opposed to the doctrinal, context a variety of different rituals and practices – including magical ones directed at the obtaining of immediate, concrete (rather than long-term salvational) benefits – have typically arisen.

This does not mean that cultic phenomena have not appeared outside the relatively primitive contexts of predoctrinal mythology and orthopraxis. In fact we may illuminate an important aspect of the difference between sects and cults by pointing to the fact that while in medieval Christianity sect was used as a condemnatory way of talking about movements which were regarded officially as heretic (displaying undesirable heterodoxical tendencies) the Church could at the same time tolerate and even encourage cults devoted to the veneration of individuals who had been sanctified, often posthumously, as saints. Indeed the problem of heterodoxy (sectarian departure from official doctrine) was alleviated in the traditional Catholic Church by the carefully monitored sanctioning of cultic practices – often of a more-or-less magical character – in such a way as to institutionalize heteropraxis (departure from official conceptions of religious ritual and concrete action). However, within the Christian Church of that time and within Catholicism since the Protestant Reformation of the sixteenth century, the tolerance of orders of priests and monks has constituted a form of institutionalized sectarianism – specifically, the incorporation within the official conception of variations on and departures from doctrinal orthodoxy.

In the wake of the Reformation – and most particularly in those societies which became strongly influenced by Protestantism – social and cultural circumstances arose which encouraged the flowering of a great variety of religious beliefs and practices, notably because those societies witnessed a considerable growth of religious individualism. Thus, whereas the notion of sect had developed almost entirely for the purpose of depicting violation of the dominant, official religious beliefs and values of the Church, in societies extensively affected by Protestantism the relevance of a distinction between sect and Church was greatly reduced, most notably in the USA after that country achieved independence from Britain in the late eighteenth century and established a wall separating religion from the state. As a consequence the idea of Church lost most of its sociological significance in the USA.

The modern study of deviant religious groups was initiated in Germany early in the twentieth century by Max Weber (1930 [1922]) and Ernst Troeltsch (1931 [1908–11]). Weber, as a historical sociologist, was interested in the contribution of sectarian Christian movements to the development of modern conceptions of rationality and economic individualism; Troeltsch was, as a sociologically informed theologian, particularly interested in the interplay in Christian history between churchly orthodoxy and sectarian heterodoxy, with particular reference to the ways in which religion had in the past and could continue to have an impact on secular institutions. In spite of frequent references to Weber and/or Troeltsch, the typical student of religious movements since the mid-twentieth century has been interested in different kinds of questions.

Much of the modern perspective can be traced to the influence of Richard Niebuhr, whose book, *The Social Sources of Denominationalism* (1929), crystallized interest in the kinds of social and economic circumstances which pushed individuals into joining deviant religious movements, and in the degree to and manner in which religious sects moved away from a deviant to a more mainstream position within the wider society. Under Niebuhr's influence, and with particular reference to North American and British societies, this position has been characterized in terms of religious organizations of the *denominational* type. In this perspective denominations are seen as standing midway between the sect, which demands a great deal of involvement from its participants and stands in a negative relationship to the wider society, and the Church, which is more central to the society and therefore does not typically demand that its members discipline themselves strongly against the culture of the wider society. Sociologists, investigating these issues, concluded that sects which seek to convert as many members as possible are most likely to relinquish their original commitments, while those which emphasize esoteric doctrines are much less likely to do so (for

which they 'pay' by remaining relatively small). More recently, however, the study of sects has taken a new turn, while the study of cults – including the circumstances under which cults may become transformed into sects – has been revived.

Sociological focus upon sects and cults now tends to be less directly concerned with the conceptual identification of sects and/or cults as distinctive types of religious organizations than with the ways in which new religious movements arise, their methods of organizing their memberships, and the critiques which they frequently offer with respect to modern societies. More specifically, whereas until recently the major sociological interest in sects and cults centred upon their esoteric nature and the conditions of their persistence or demise, the proliferation of many new religious movements in the early 1970s, and the rise to prominence of what are often called 'fundamentalist' religious movements since the late 1970s, has given rise to a broader set of sociological concerns about the nature and direction of change of modern societies. Among those concerns have been the relationship between religious movements and the modern state (not least because in some societies the state has sought to regulate the activities of new movements), and the extent to which the proliferation of new religious movements (and the revival of older ones) signals a global resurgence of religiosity.

The pejorative meaning often attached to the term sect and, more particularly, cult has largely resulted from the controversial nature of many of these movements' practices. Some of them have been charged with 'brainwashing' their converts or engaging in deviant sexual behaviour. Such movements have on occasion become involved in dramatic incidents of physical violence, the most notable recent cases in the Western world being the suicide, or murder, of more than 900 adherents to the People's Temple in Jonestown, Guyana in 1978; the deaths of 78 members of the Branch Davidians in Waco, Texas in 1993; and the demise of about 50 members of the Solar Temple in Chiery, Switzerland in 1993. These and a number of other violent occurrences in different parts of the world have become a significant aspect of the social-scientific study of religion.

Roland Robertson
University of Pittsburgh

References

Niebuhr, H. R. (1929) *The Social Sources of Denominationalism*, New York.

Troeltsch, E. (1931 [1908–11]) *The Social Teachings of the Christian Churches*, London. (Original edn, *Die Soziallehren der christlichen Kirchen und Gruppen*, Tübingen.)

Weber, M. (1930 [1922]) *The Protestant Ethic and the Spirit of Capitalism*, London. (Original edn, *Die protestantische Ethik und der 'Geist' des Kapitalismus*, Tübingen.)

Further reading

Beckford, J. A. (1985) *Cult Controversies*, London.
Bromley, D. G. and Hadden, J. K. (eds) (1993) *The Handbook of Cults and Sects*, 2 vols, Greenwich, CT.
Robbins, T. (1988) *Cults, Converts and Charisma*, London.
Robbins, T. and Anthony, D. (eds) (1990) *In Gods We Trust*, New Brunswick, NJ.
Robertson, R. (1970) *The Sociological Interpretation of Religion*, Oxford.
Stark, R. and Bainbridge, W. S. (1986) *The Future of Religion*, Berkeley, CA.

See also: cargo cults; religion and ritual; syncretism.

self-concept

The self-concept has had a diversity of meanings, due in part to its multidisciplinary heritage. Philosophy and theology have emphasized the self as the locus of moral choices and responsibility. Clinical and humanistic psychologies have stressed the self as the basis of individual uniqueness and neurosis. Within sociology the self-concept has acquired an indelibly social character, with the emphasis on language and social interaction as the matrix for the emergence and maintenance of the self. The current popularity of self-concept within experimental social psychology places greater emphasis on its cognitive and motivational aspects, such as the self-concept as a source of motivation, as a performance aimed at managing impressions, and as a source of perceptual and cognitive organization.

At its core, the idea of self-concept or self-conception is based on the human capacity for reflexivity, frequently considered the quintessential feature of the human condition. Reflexivity, or self-awareness, the ability of human beings to be both subjects and objects to themselves, can be conceptualized as the dialogue between the 'I' (for example, the self-as-knower) and the 'me' (the self-as-known), an internal conversation, which emerges (at both the ontogenetic and the phylogenetic levels) with the emergence of language – an argument extensively developed by G. H. Mead (1934). Language requires us to take the role of the other with whom we are communicating, and in the process enables us to see ourselves from the other's perspective.

Properly speaking, this process of reflexivity refers to the concept of self. The self-concept, on the other hand, is the *product* of this reflexive activity. It is the conception that individuals have of themselves as physical, social, moral and existential beings. The self-concept is the sum total of individuals' thoughts and feelings about themselves as objects (Rosenberg 1979).

It involves a sense of spatial and temporal continuity of personal identity, a distinction of 'essential' self from mere appearance and behaviour, and is composed of the various attitudes, beliefs, values and experiences, along with their evaluative and affective components (such as self-evaluation or self-esteem), in terms of which individuals define themselves. In many respects the self-concept is synonymous with the concept of ego (Sherif 1968), although psychologists have preferred the latter term and sociologists the former. The various aspects of the self-concept can be grouped into two broad categories: identities and self-evaluations.

First, the concept of identity focuses on the meanings constituting the self as an object, gives structure and content to the self-concept, and anchors the self to social systems. 'Identity' has had its own interesting and complex history in the social sciences. In general, it refers to who or what one is, to the various meanings attached to oneself by self and others. Within sociology, identity refers both to the structural features of group membership which individuals internalize and to which they become committed (for example, various social roles, memberships and categories) and to the various character traits that individuals display and that others attribute to actors on the basis of their conduct in particular social settings. The structure of the self-concept can be viewed as the hierarchical organization of a person's identities, reflecting in large part the social and cultural systems within which it exists (Stryker 1980).

Second, self-evaluation (or self-esteem) can occur with regard to specific identities which an individual holds, or with regard to an overall evaluation of self. People tend to make self-evaluations on the basis of two broad criteria: their sense of competence or efficacy, and their sense of virtue or moral worth (Gecas and Schwalbe 1983; Wells and Marwell 1976).

Several processes have been identified as important to the development of self-concepts: reflected appraisals, social comparisons, self-attributions and role-playing. The most popular of these in sociology is 'reflected appraisals'. Based on Cooley's (1902) influential concept of the 'looking-glass self' and Mead's (1934) theory of role-taking as a product of symbolic interaction, reflected appraisals emphasize the essentially social character of the self-concept, such as the idea that our self-conceptions reflect the appraisals and perceptions of others, especially significant others, in our environments. The process of reflected appraisals is the basis of the 'labelling theory' of deviance in sociology, and of self-fulfilling processes in social psychology.

Social comparison is the process by which individuals assess their own abilities and virtues by comparing them to those of others. Local reference groups or persons are most likely to be used as a frame of reference for these comparisons, especially under conditions of competition, such as athletic contests or classroom performance. Self-attributions refer to the tendency to make inferences about ourselves from direct observation of our behaviour. Bem's (1972) 'self-perception theory' proposes that individuals determine what they are feeling and thinking by making inferences based on observing their own overt behaviour. Role-playing as a process of self-concept formation is most evident in studies of socialization. It emphasizes the development of self-concepts through the learning and internalizing of various social roles (for example, age and sex roles, family roles, occupation roles).

The self-concept is both a product of social forces and, to a large extent, an agent of its own creation. Along with the capacity for self-reflexivity discussed earlier, the agentive aspect of the self-concept is most evident in discussions of self-motives (that is, the self-concept as a source of motivation). Three self-motives have been prominent in the social psychological literature: self-enhancement or self-esteem motive; self-efficacy motive; and self-consistency motive.

First, the self-enhacement or self-esteem motive refers to the motivation of individuals to maintain or to enhance their self-esteem. It is manifest in the general tendency of persons to distort reality in the service of maintaining a positive self-conception, through such strategies as selective perception, reconstruction of memory, and some of the classic ego-defensive mechanisms.

Second, the self-efficacy motive refers to the importance of *experiencing* the self as a causal agent, that is, to the motivation to perceive and experience oneself as being efficacious, competent and consequential. The suppression or inhibition of this motive has been associated with such negative consequences as alienation, learned helplessness, and the tendency to view oneself as a pawn or victim of circumstances (Gecas and Schwalbe 1983).

Third the self-consistency motive is perhaps the weakest of the three, yet it continues to have its advocates. Lecky (1945), an early advocate, viewed the maintenance of a unified conceptual system as the overriding need of the individual. Those theorists who view the self-concept primarily as an organization of knowledge, or as a configuration of cognitive generalizations, are most likely to emphasize the self-consistency motive. The self-concept as an organization of *identities* also provides a motivational basis for consistency, in that individuals are motivated to act in accordance with the values and norms implied by the identities to which they become committed.

In the past, the bulk of research on the self-concept has focused on self-esteem (see Wells and Marwell 1976; Wylie 1979), that is, on the antecedents of self-esteem, the consequences of self-esteem, and the relationships between self-esteem and almost every other aspect of personality and behaviour. Much of this research focus continues to be evident. But there are noticeable trends in other directions as well. The most evident are the dynamics of self-presentation and impression management in naturalistic and experimental settings; the development and the consequences of commitment to specific identities (especially gender, ethnic group, deviant, and age-specific); historical and social structural influences on self-conceptions (such as wars, depressions, cultural changes, and organizational complexity); and, increasingly, we find a focus on the effect of self-concept on social structure and social circumstances. The self-concept is rapidly becoming the dominant concern within social psychology (both the sociological and the psychological varieties), as part of the general intellectual shift from behavioural to cognitive and phenomenological orientations in these disciplines.

Viktor Gecas
Washington State University

References

Bem, D. J. (1972) 'Self-perception theory', in L. Berkowitz (ed.) *Advances in Experimental Social Psychology*, vol. 6, New York.

Cooley, C. H. (1902) *Human Nature and the Social Order*, New York.

Gecas, V. and Schwalbe, M. L. (1983) 'Beyond the looking-glass self: social structure and efficacy-based self-esteem', *Social Psychological Quarterly* 46.

Lecky, P. (1945) *Self-Consistency: A Theory of Personality*, New York.

Mead, G. H. (1934) *Mind, Self and Society*, Chicago.

Rosenberg, M. (1979) *Conceiving the Self*, New York.

Sherif, M. (1968) 'Self-concept', in D. K. Sills (ed.) *International Encyclopedia of the Social Sciences*, vol. 14, New York.

Stryker, S. (1980) *Symbolic Interactionism: A Social Structural Version*, Menlo Park, CA.

Wells, L. E. and Marwell, G. (1976) *The Self-Esteem: Its Conceptualization and Measurement*, Beverly Hills, CA.

Wylie, R. C. (1979) *The Self-Concept*, Lincoln, NB.

Further reading

Gecas, V. (1982) 'The self-concept', *Annual Review of Sociology* 8.

Rosenberg, M. (1979) *Conceiving the Self*, New York.

See also: labelling; person; social identity; social psychology.

semantics

Any system used to carry information must be characterized syntactically, defining its grammatical expressions, and semantically, defining how they are used to express meaning. Its semantics is distinguished in addition from its phonology, the sound structure a system may have, and from its pragmatics, including the rules of social interaction between its users. The interface between the syntax, semantics, phonology and pragmatics of an information system is a core concern of theoretical research.

A very strict view of the relation between syntax and semantics is based on the principle of 'compositionality', stemming from Gottlob Frege's (1960 [1892]) work, according to which the meaning of an expression is a function derived from the meaning of its parts and the way they are put together. Several logicians adopted it as a methodological principle in the late 1960s to characterize the syntax and semantics of a fragment of English in a logically precise way. Several other assumptions were inherited from Frege, including the idea that clauses refer to truth-values, that the substitution of logically equivalent expressions preserves truth-value in extensional contexts, but that intensional contexts require substitution of expressions with the same sense, not merely co-reference, to preserve truth-value. A flourishing research programme ensued on the logical semantics of natural language with a categorial syntax and a truth-conditional semantics. Interpretation was considered a structure preserving mapping from a syntactic tree of a clause to its truth-conditions in a set-theoretic possible worlds model. The central notion of logical entailment was characterized by truth-preserving operations on the 'logical form' of the premises. Logical entailments disregard context, for no matter what additional information is obtained, they are always preserved. Core issues in this research programme were scope ambiguities, binding of pronouns, and generalized quantifiers.

First, scope ambiguities: quantificational expressions can be found in various linguistic categories. Noun phrases (NPs) contain 'universal quantifiers', *every student* or *all books*, and 'existential quantifiers', *a student* or *three books*. 'Modal quantification' is expressed in adverbials, *possibly, necessarily, allegedly, hypothetically*, and modal auxiliary verbs, *may, must, can, might*, or attitude verbs with clausal complements, *doubt that, believe that, consider that* and *know that*. Any clause that contains at least one universal and one existential quantificational expression exhibits a scope ambiguity, requiring disambiguation by systematically permuting their order in the logical form. To obtain different orders in a compositional semantics the technique of 'quantifying in' combines the quantifier Q_1 to occur first with an expression containing the other quantifiers $Q_2, \ldots, Q_n$ and a free variable, to be bound by Q_1. This proved to be widely applicable not only to linguistic quantification, but also to relative clauses and bound pronouns.

Second, binding of pronouns: a pronoun may refer to different referents, depending on the linguistic context in which it occurs. The inviting analogy between free variables in logic and pronouns in natural language constituted a very fruitful heuristic, despite its obvious shortcomings, e.g. a proper name binds a pronoun in *John loves his mother*, but an individual constant cannot bind a free variable in logical systems. If an NP is quantified in, it binds all free occurrences of the same variable, expressing co-reference. However, scope conflicts may arise, for instance, in the interpretation of *Every student who read a book liked it*. When *a book* is quantified into *Every student who read it liked it* to bind both occurrences of *it*, *a book* cannot refer to different books depending on which student is meant, but implies that all students who read a book, read the same one and liked it. Similar problems arise in expressing co-reference of individuals across intensional contexts, as in *A student believed he read a novel, but John thought it was a short story*. Furthermore, pronouns can be bound only by existential NPs or proper names across clauses, but in logic no quantifier can bind a variable in another formula. These three kinds of problems facing truth-conditional semantics lead eventually to the dynamic semantic systems, defining interpretation as a process of incremental updates of information.

Third, generalized quantifiers: initiated by R. Montague, all NPs are interpreted by sets of sets of individuals. The universal quantifier *every student* requires a set containing all sets that include all students, the existential *a student* requires a set containing all sets that include at least one (possibly different) student, and a proper name *John* requires a set of all sets that have John as an element. All kinds of natural, non-logical determiners lend themselves to such set-theoretic interpretation, enriching our understanding of the variety of quantification in natural languages.

After two decades the truth-conditional approach proved to face insuperable technical difficulties in accounting for the linguistic principles binding pronouns within a clause as well as between clauses and for the meaning of any context-sensitive expressions. To remedy this, the concept of interpretation had to be changed fundamentally, argued some semanticists in the early 1980s, including J. Barwise, I. Heim, H. Kamp and B. Partee. Rather than consider it a static relation between a syntactic analysis of an isolated expression and its truth-conditions in a model, interpretation should be viewed as a dynamic process updating the information available at a certain stage, using connected discourse or texts. The reference of a pronoun and, in general, the content of an expression often depend on the current context, the information available, and the external situation in which it is used. Various logical systems, designed for dynamic interpretation, broadened the concerns of semantics beyond coreference of pronouns, scope ambiguities and logical entailments, to include new topics on how context is affected by interpretation. Core issues in this research programme of dynamic semantics are dynamic binding of pronouns, context shifts, and hybrid forms of reasoning.

First, dynamic binding of pronouns: co-reference of pronouns within a clause as well as between clauses in discourse motivated the development of dynamic semantics. Some systems require a pronoun to co-refer with a definite description in which the information about the intended referent is accumulated. Other systems design structured representations of the information available so that only some of the descriptive conditions determine the referent. This constitutes a very lively area of research, combining logical and computational techniques with linguistic data.

Second, context shifts: a dynamic semantics must determine how information is preserved while the interpretation proceeds, requiring a precise understanding of how the presuppositions of expressions (conditions which must be satisfied for the expression to be evaluated) are projected in a clause, and preserved or lost during the interpretation of discourse. This issue was raised originally in linguistic theory by L. Karttunen and S. Peters in the 1970s, as a pragmatic issue, but resurfaced in dynamic semantics. The interpretation of indefinites, and tense and aspect also gives rise to specific rules for shifting contexts when descriptive information is given about different individuals or events.

Third, hybrid forms of reasoning: reasoning may mix descriptive information with assumptions on what the words mean, how causal correlations are structured, what we see or hear and our private information. To design logical systems that model such hybrid forms of inference constitutes a major challenge for dynamic semantics. This concept of inference must be sensitive to various forms of context-change, for different conclusions are drawn at different times depending on what information is available. Though logical entailments are immune to changes in context, our reasoning is not, even if linguistic means exist to immunize information against context-sensitivity.

In dynamic semantics the old boundary disputes between syntax, phonology, semantics and pragmatics have turned into more fruitful collaborations on representational interfaces of the modular system. The information one expresses in using language may also depend on intonation, social status and power, on traditions and cultural values. Ultimately, a comprehensive semantic theory of meaning and interpretation should encompass all such issues and yet represent a precise system of inference.

Alice G. B. ter Meulen
Indiana University

Reference

Frege, G. (1960 [1892]) 'On sense and reference', in P. Geach and M. Black (eds) *Translations from the Philosophical Writings of Gottlob Frege*, Oxford.

Further reading

Barwise, J. and Perry, J. (1983) *Situations and Attitudes*, Cambridge, MA.
Benthem, J. van (1986) *Essays in Logical Semantics*, Dordrecht, The Netherlands.
Davidson, D. and Harman, G. (1972) *Semantics of Natural Language*, Dordrecht, The Netherlands.
Gårdenfors, P. (ed.) (1987) *Generalized Quantifiers: Linguistic and Logical Approaches*, Dordrecht, The Netherlands.
Kamp, H. and Reyle, U. (1993) *From Discourse to Logic*, Dordrecht, The Netherlands.
Keenan, E. and Faltz, L. (1985) *Boolean Semantics of Natural Language*, Dordrecht, The Netherlands.
Meulen, A. ter (1994) *The Representation of Time in Natural Language: The Dynamic Interpretation of Tense and Aspect*, Cambridge, MA.
Montague, R. (1972) *Formal Philosophy*, ed. R. Thomason, New Haven, CT.
Oehrle, D., Bach, E. and Wheeler, D. (eds) (1988) *Categorial Grammars and Natural Language Structures*, Dordrecht, The Netherlands.
Partee, B., Meulen, A. ter and Wall R. (1990) *Mathematical Methods in Linguistics*, Dordrecht, The Netherlands.

See also: linguistics; pragmatics; semiotics.

semiotics

Semiotics is an ancient mode of enquiry which incorporates all forms and systems of communication as its domain. The development of semiotic theory and methods took place within specific fields, first in medicine, then in philosophy and, in the twentieth century, in linguistics. The rapid development of semiotics since 1950 spans several fields, including sociology, anthropology, literary and cultural criticism, linguistics and psychoanalysis.

The central idea in semiotics is a particular conception of the structure of the *sign* which is defined as a bond between a signifier and a signified: for example, the bond that exists between a series of sounds (signifier) and their meaning (signified) in a given language, or the social convention that the colour red stands for danger. Semiotic research involves the study of conventions, codes, syntactical and semantic elements, and logic: in short, all the mechanisms which serve both to produce and obscure meanings, and to change meanings in sign systems. As such, semiotics is uniquely adapted to research on several questions which fall in the domain of the social sciences: communication conduct, myth, ritual, ideology, and sociocultural evolution and change. Major contributions to socio-semiotic research include Erving Goffman's studies of face-to-face interaction, Roland Barthes's critique of modern material culture, Lévi-Strauss's research on American Indian myths, and Jacques Lacan's psycho-analytic investigations.

Historical origins

The first known synthesis of semiotic principles was accomplished in Classical Greek medicine, a branch of which dealt with the symptoms and signs of illness. It was in this applied context that the Greeks made explicit the *principle of the arbitrariness of the relationship of the signifier to the signified* that became the basis for the first accurate diagnosis of disease. The Greeks noted, for example, that a pain in the wrist may indicate a problem with the vital organs, not the wrist, and began to base their diagnosis on the pattern of *relationship between signs*. The combination of arm pains, pale skin, and difficult breathing was given a more nearly correct medical meaning in the place of the incorrect array of meanings they might have for someone operating within the primitive framework of a concrete, analogical connection between signifiers and signified. This effected a transfer of phenomena that formerly could be understood only within a religious framework into the scientific domain.

Semiotics flourishes during times, such as the present, when there is general anxiety about the capacity of western science to solve important problems, or when there is widespread questioning of the ultimate validity of western cultural and philosophical values. When there is an intellectual crisis, the problematical relationship of the signifier to the signified is not a secret buried deep in the heart of the sign and social consensus. Rather the signifier/signified relationship appears to almost everyone as a series of discontinuities between events and their meanings.

Peirce's typology of signs

The intellectual base of current semiotic activity is mainly the writings of the Swiss linguist, Ferdinand de Saussure, and the American pragmatist philosopher, Charles S. Peirce. Following Peirce's synthesis of semiotic principles, there are three major types of signs based on the structure of the relationship of the signifier to the signified: icons, indices, and symbols. An *iconic* sign depends on a bond of resemblance between the signifier and the signified and requires social and legal arrangements and agreements concerning authenticity and originality. *Indices* are produced by the direct action of that which they represent, such as the line left at high tide, and they engage scientific, historical and other forms of curiosity and detective work. *Symbols* are arbitrary and conventional (such as the words in a language) and they require community consensus on proper meanings. Since any object or idea can be represented by each of the three types of signs, the mode of representation implies the form of interpretation and specific social arrangements as well. In short, every mode of scientific and other discourse is the result of (unconscious) decisions that reflect basic, often unstated, social values. Semiotics can function as a metalanguage by analysing the ways the various fields and disciplines represent their subject matter, for example, the frame of mind and form of social relationship that is implicit in experimental science or in Marxist theory.

The semiotic critique of 'rational' science

Semioticians often make a claim to be both more rigorous and more politically engaged than their colleagues in disciplines which base their methods on Cartesian rationalism. The source of this seemingly paradoxical claim is found in the contrast of the *signifier/signified* relationship which is the basis of semiotics, and the *subject/object* relationship which is the basis of rational science. According to the semiotic critique of rationalism (and its offspring, positivism), the *subject/object* opposition takes the form of an imperative to establish a hierarchy in which scientific subjectivity dominates its empirical object. This originally innocent formulation, which unleashed enormous intellectual energy, contains no safeguards against excesses and abuse. Specifically, the subject/object split is the ultimate philosophical justification for one group or class (for example, the 'west' or the 'east') to claim the right to dominate others, to assert that the *meanings* they provide are the only correct meanings from the range of possible meanings. Of course it is possible to advance scientific understanding and social thought within this paradigm by policing deviant intellectual tendencies and precisely calibrating social ideology to scientific theory, but the successes of this approach should not render it less suspect. From the perspective provided by the signifier/signified relationship, it appears more a moral or political *position* than a rigorous analytical mode.

Dean MacCannell
University of California

Further reading

Barthes, R. (1972 [1957]) *Mythologies*, trans. A. Lavers, New York.

Baudrillard, J. (1981) *For a Critique of the Political Economy of the Sign*, trans. C. Levin, St Louis, MO.

Burke, K. (1973 [1941]) *The Philosophy of Literary Form: Studies in Symbolic Action*, Berkeley, CA.

Eco, U. (1976) *A Theory of Semiotics*, Bloomington, IN.

Goffman, E. (1974) *Frame Analysis: An Essay on the Organization of Experience*, New York.

Greimas, A. J. and Courtès, J. (1979) *Sémiotique: dictionnaire raisonné de la théorie du langage*, Paris.

Lacan, J. (1966) *Ecrits*, Paris. (Trans. A. Sheridan, 1977, London.)

Lévi–Strauss, C. (1976 [1958–73] 'The scope of anthropology', in *Structural Anthropology, vol. II*, New York. (Original edn, *Anthropologique structurale*, 2 vols, Paris.)

MacCannell, D. and MacCannell, J. F. (1982) *The Time of the Sign: A Semiotic Interpretation of Modern Culture*, Bloomington, IN

Peirce, C. S. (1940; 1955), *Selected Writings*, selected and edited by J. Buchler, New York.

Saussure, F. de (1959 [1916]) *Course in General Linguistics*, New York. (Original edn, *Cours de linguistique générale*, Paris.)

Sebeok, T. A. (ed.) (1978) *Sight, Sound and Sense*, Bloomington, IN.

See also: Saussure, Ferdinand de; semantics; symbolism.

sensation and perception

Sensation and perception refer to the mechanisms by means of which we are aware of and process information about the external world. Aristotle classified the senses into the five categories of seeing (vision), hearing (audition), smelling (olfaction), tasting (gustation), and the skin senses. It is now commonplace to subdivide further the skin senses into separate categories of pain, touch, warmth, cold, and organic sensations. In addition, two senses of which we are not normally aware are also included – kinesthesis, or the sense of position of our limbs, and the vestibular sense, which provides information regarding movement and position of the head.

Early theorists often regarded sensation as more elementary and less complex than perception, but the distinction has not proven to be useful. Physical energies such as light, sound waves, acceleration, are *transduced* by the sensory end organs so as to activate nerves which carry the signals to the central nervous system. The properties of the sense organs determine the acceptable range of physical stimuli. For example, the human ear responds to vibrations of the air only between 20 and 20,000 cycles per second. The minimum physical energy required to activate the sensory end organs is referred to as the *absolute threshold*. Thresholds for hearing depend systematically on the frequency of the vibrations, being minimal in the intermediate frequency range which involves speech sounds, and progressively higher for both lower and higher frequencies. Similarly, within the range of wave lengths which activate the eye, the visual system is most sensitive to yellow and yellow-green, and less sensitive to red and blue. Wave lengths outside of this range do not activate the visual system although infra-red radiation may be perceived as heat.

The quality of sensation – whether it is perceived as light, sound, pain, smell and so on – is not determined directly by the nature of the physical stimulus but rather by the nervous pathways being activated. Under normal conditions, light energy will typically stimulate visual pathways because the light threshold for the eyes is much lower than for any other form of physical energy. Pressure on the eyeball, however, will elicit a light sensation. Similarly, all the sense organs have the lowest thresholds for the appropriate forms of stimulus energy. The relationship between the quality of sensory experience and the specific nervous pathways activated is referred to as Mueller's doctrine of *specific nerve energies*. This concept was important in the early history of psychology because it focused attention on the role of the nervous system in mediating experience. We do not perceive the external world directly, but rather are aware of the activity of the nerves. Since awareness and knowledge depend on nervous activity, the study of the nervous system is fundamental to the science of psychology.

The intensity of sensation is not predictable from the absolute energy in the stimulus but is rather related to some multiple of stimulus energy. For example, the energy required for a light to appear just noticeably brighter than another light is closely predicted by the *ratio* of energies. An increment of a light unit which is just noticeable when viewed on a 10 light unit back-ground will not be visible when viewed on a 100 light unit background. The just noticeable difference is closely predicted by the ratio of energies. The *differential threshold* for the 100 unit background would, in this case, be 10. To a first approximation, the ratio of the just noticeable difference to the background, historically known as *Weber's law*, is a constant. In the nineteenth century, the physicist Fechner argued, on the basis of Weber's law, that the subjective magnitude of sensation is determined by the logarithm of the stimulus energy. This relationship was viewed by Fechner as representing a quantification of the mind and the solution of the mind–body problem. The procedures devised to study sensory functions, known as *psychophysics*, provided an important methodology in support of the founding of experimental psychology as an independent laboratory science in the late nineteenth century.

Information from the senses is combined with past experience, either consciously or unconsciously, to construct our awareness of the external world and to guide our motor responses. For the most part, these perceptions are accurate, but there are instances in which they are in error. Incorrect perceptions are referred to as *illusions*, which may result when normal mechanisms are inappropriately activated. When viewing two-dimensional photographs or drawings, distortions of size, shape and direction may occur because of the misapplication of sensory and perceptual mechanisms which normally subserve three-dimensional vision. Illusions should be differentiated from hallucinations, which refer to perceptions which have no basis in the external world. Hallucinations are typically associated with psychopathology, drugs, or pathology of the nervous system.

The theoretical importance of sensation and perception derives from the empirical point of view in philosophy which maintains that knowledge is mediated by the senses. In this context, limitations of sensory systems, illusions, and distortions by past experience or bias relating to motivational factors play a central role, because they determine the content of the mind. The predominance of the empirical view was responsible for the emphasis on the study of sensation and perception during the early history of experimental psychology.

Sensory systems can act independently or in conjunction with other senses. The 'taste' of food results from the combination of inputs from olfaction, gustation, the skin senses, and kinesthesis. This can be demonstrated by comparing the taste of foods when the nasal passages are blocked. In this case, taste is reduced to a less complex combination of the four basic gustatory qualities of salt, bitter, sour and sweet. The wide variety of food qualities is made possible in large part by olfactory cues. The appearance of food, its temperature, and resistance to chewing also contribute to these complex sensations.

Spatial orientation depends on the integration of visual, vestibular and proprioceptive information, all of which contribute to the maintenance of erect posture and location. The interactive nature of the sensory systems subserving spatial orientation is responsible for the fact that overactivation of the vestibular sense can lead to the illusory sensation that the visual world is moving. Similarly, if a large area of the visual environment is moved, an objectively stationary observer will experience a compelling illusory sensation of body motion (vection).

The correspondence between the physical pattern of stimulation and our corresponding perception of the world has remained a problem of major interest in perception. If two adjacent stationary lights are alternately flashed, the observer will report apparent movement between them. This phenomenon was cited by the *Gestalt* psychologists in support of their position that perception consists of more than the elements of stimulation. It is also the basis for the perceived movement in motion pictures and television. The contribution of the observer to perceptual experience is emphasized in numerous theoretical analyses of perception. In the case of *Gestalt* psychology, the organization is provided by inherent properties of the nervous system. Within the context of theories which stress the role of attention

or motivation, the observer 'selects' only certain aspects of the environment for processing, in other words, we tend to see and hear what we want to see and hear and actively exclude information which is potentially embarrassing or unpleasant. The phenomenon of selective perception is illustrated by the reaction to painful stimuli which may be minimized or ignored if associated with an otherwise pleasant event such as victory in an athletic contest, but may be reported as very painful under unpleasant circumstances. Since the study of human perception frequently depends on the verbal report of an observer, it can not be evaluated directly and is therefore subject to modification by motivational states.

The active contribution of the observer to perception is also illustrated by the phenomenon of perceptual constancy. The first stage of sensing or perceiving visual stimuli is the formation of an optical image in the eye. This image is determined by geometric principles so that its size will be inversely proportional to the distance from the observer. In spite of wide variation in retinal image size, the perceived sizes of objects tend to remain constant and to correspond to their true dimensions. The tendency to perceive the veridical sizes of objects in spite of the continually changing pattern of the retinal image is referred to as perceptual 'constancy'. Other perceptual attributes also demonstrate constancy effect. The foreshortening of the retinal image resulting from oblique viewing is not perceived. Circular objects appear round even though the retinal image is elliptical, for example, shape constancy. When we move our eyes, the retinal image also moves but the perception of the environment remains stationary, for example, space constancy. A white object appears 'white' and a dark object appears 'dark' even under wide ranges of ambient illumination, for example, brightness constancy. Similarly, the colours of objects tend to remain the same even though the spectral quality of the light reflected from them varies as they are illuminated by the different wave-lengths provided by natural and artificial illumination, for example, colour constancy. Perceptual constancies are essential in biological adjustment because they permit the organism to be aware of and to respond to the biologically relevant, permanent physical characteristics of objects in the environment. The eye has been likened to a camera, and they are similar, as both have an optical system for focusing an image on a light sensitive surface. However, whereas the camera is passive, the eye, as well as other sensory systems, is connected to the brain so that the final perception is a result of the active combination of physical stimuli with information from the observer's past experience, motivation and emotions.

Sensation and perception have been of interest, not only because of their central role in the acquisition of knowledge and in mediating awareness, but also because they play an essential role in many aspects of human and animal behaviour. Pain is an essential protective mechanism which is normally activated whenever the integrity of the organism is in danger. Olfaction provides warning against ingestion of poisons. Serious threats to health are a consequence of the fact that no information is provided by our sensory systems for some dangers, for example, ionizing radiation, carbon monoxide, early stages of some diseases.

Knowledge of sensation and perception is important in performance evaluation and prediction and in medical diagnosis. Many tasks in modern society place unusual demands on the individual's sensory capacities as, for example, in aviation. Consequently sophisticated batteries of tests have been developed to identify those individuals with the superior visual and perceptual capacities necessary to operate high-performance aircraft. In a technologically oriented society, the ability to acquire information from reading is indispensable and has led to the development of an extensive visual health-care system. The systematic changes in vision, balance and hearing which occur as a consequence of ageing are relevant to the design of safe environments and the successful adjustment of the elderly. Visual tests are sensitive to pathology and are used in evaluating the consequences of disease, in diagnosis, and in the evaluation of therapy.

Perceptual tests provide a methodology for evaluating group dynamics and personality. If a single stationary point of light is viewed in an otherwise dark room, it will appear to move. The extent of this reported *autokinetic* movement has been shown by Sherif to depend on the magnitude of apparent movement reported by other observers and their social status. The extent to which one's reports are influenced by others is taken as a measure of social pressure and conformity. Ambiguous stimuli are also used to evaluate personality. In the Rorschach test, subjects are asked to describe what they see in patterns formed by inkblots. It is assumed that the reports will be a reflection of the individual's personality dynamics which are attributed or 'projected' unconsciously into the ambiguous stimulus.

Herschel W. Leibowitz
Pennsylvania State University

Further reading

Boring, E. G. (1942) *Sensation and Perception in the History of Experimental Psychology*, New York.
—— (1950) *A History of Experimental Psychology*, 2nd edn, New York.
Carterette, E. C. and Friedman, M. P. (eds) *Handbook of Perception* (1974) vol. 1, *Historical and Philosophical Roots of Perception*; (1973) vol. 3, *Biology of Perceptual Systems*; (1978)

vol. 4, *Hearing*; (1975) vol. 5, *Seeing*; (1978) vol. 6A, *Tasting and Smelling*; (1978) vol. 6B, *Feeling and Hurting*; (1978) vol. 8, *Perceptive Coding*; (1978) vol. 9, *Perceptual Processing*.
Held, R. H., Leibowitz, H. W. and Teuber, H. L. (1978), *Handbook of Sensory Physiology*, vol. 8, *Perception*, Heidelberg.
Kling, J. W. and Riggs, L. (eds) (1971) *Woodworth and Schlosberg's Experimental Psychology*, 3rd edn, New York.
Pastore, N. (1971) *Selective Theories of Visual Perception: 1650–1950*, London.

See also: mental imagery; social psychology; vision.

sex *see* gender and sex; homosexualities; pornography; sexual behaviour.

sexual behaviour

Among humans sexual behaviour extends far beyond the mere act of copulation between a male and a female resulting in offspring. An elaborate superstructure has evolved out of the basic facts of female capacity to bear children, and the necessity, until the merest moment ago in historical time, for male impregnation. Sexual intercourse in humans may occur throughout the female ovulatory cycle. Though usually described as continuous female receptivity, this may equally well be considered a highly atypical manifestation of continuous sexual interest (irrespective of female readiness for impregnation) on the part of the human male.

While a great deal of sexual behaviour must have gone on throughout history, since without it there would have been no perpetuation of the human species, it is by no means easy either to define or to quantify it. The occurrence of pregnancy is an almost certain indication that some kind of sexual activity has occurred, but its absence hardly indicates the converse. Thus quantification of the extent of same-sex erotic practices, and of non-coital heterosexual behaviour, is extremely difficult, while abortion and infanticide, and various forms, more and less effective, of deliberate birth control, have additionally acted to render recorded birth rates a dubious guide to the extent of sexual activity.

Activities involving the genital, and secondary sexual, areas between members of opposite sexes and of the same-sex, may serve various social and personal purposes which have no necessary connection with the primary reproductive purpose of such acts: economic survival, the assertion of power, and pleasure. Within all known human societies, sexual activity has been subjected to various restrictions and taboos, such as who constitutes an appropriate partner, defined by factors such as gender, race, relative social status, age, and degree of kinship. Other areas subject to societal rulings are specific sexual acts, and where and when they take place.

It is relatively easy to establish attitudes towards sexual behaviour as recorded in legal codes, and texts of moral and religious prescription, but whether such codes and taboos have been representative of the views of more than an articulate and literate elite (usually ruling-class males) is much more questionable, and their relation to actual practice even more so. Certain acts or forms of relationship being outlawed, however, does not mean that they were not occurring: the very existence of overt proscription or deprecation of certain types of conduct indicates that a possibility, if no more, was felt to exist. Contemporary descriptions of a society's mores tend to exaggerate either the degree to which it adhered to accepted standards of sexual propriety, or, conversely, flouted them, to make a moral point.

As a topic for study, sex in the human has been a site of constant speculation, taboo, stigma and controversy, and the work of scholars in a wide variety of disciplines has failed to produce a clearly descriptive whole. It has been much easier to describe phenomena conceivable as 'other', either among non-human animals, remote tribes, or traditional enemy nations (in Britain, sexual vice or unorthodoxy has been persistently ascribed to the French), or to define manifestations as pathological or exceptional, than to attempt to study, rather than make assumptions about, normal conduct.

It is practically impossible to establish a baseline of 'normal', 'natural' human sexual behaviour, given how widely this has varied between cultures and throughout history. Has there been roughly the same amount of all kinds of sexual behaviour going on at all times and all places, or has behaviour been determined by current ideologies and assumptions? We may perhaps assume that neither of these positions is entirely the case, although historical evidence, except for that relating to occurrence of pregnancy or sexually transmitted disease, will seldom reveal much about ordinary, rather than exceptional, sexual activity. Anecdotal evidence and prescriptive agendas have beset attempts at clarification. Extremely specific local conditions have been assumed to represent a universal norm. To become visible certain forms of sexual conduct have generally had to be perceived as both transgressive and the domain of legal action, as in sodomy trials or the divorce court, or else practised by high-status figures within society.

Human sexuality was a latecomer to the nineteenth-century physiological mapping of the human body, and social sciences were equally reluctant to grapple with it. Early investigators, if they did not fall foul of the legal system, found that interest in such a subject excluded them from professional rewards. The study was thus sporadic and uncoordinated, with individual researchers considering different problems and asking different questions and therefore producing results not comparable. Accounts of human sexual activity have suffered from male bias, only recently subjected to a more gender-sensitive revision, although Herschberger (1948) made an early (and witty) assault on the sexism of their language and assumptions. Attempts to interpret sexual mores among humans by the use of the less sensitive, and more readily observable, behaviour of animals of a variety of species must raise serious questions of validity. There is little reliable evidence available (even in contemporary society) about what people are actually doing sexually, and the very attempt to find out is branded as unacceptable, however necessary such findings may be for wider questions of health (Wellings et al. 1994).

The uncoupling of sexual responsiveness in both sexes from the reproductive cycle of the female has had profound consequences for human social arrangements. However, throughout history, and even in the late twentieth century, in spite of occasional reports of scientific advances in bringing about 'male pregnancy', it has been women who have physically undergone pregnancy and childbirth and who, in the social arrangements of most cultures, are primarily responsible for their rearing. The male contribution, physically, is fleeting and need have no further repercussions for the individual male beyond the moment's pleasure.

It has been argued that men are continuously manufacturing sperm (and ejaculate a vastly redundant number during the sexual act), while women are born with a finite number of ova, and therefore men are biologically programmed to maximize the scattering of their genetic potential, through promiscuity. The aim of women, conversely, is to obtain the support of a (genetically superior) partner during childrearing, thus they are innately monogamous. There have, however, been suggestions that given the impossibility of reliable ascription of paternity for most of history, women have made their contribution to maintaining sexual diversity and obtaining superior paternal genes for their children through clandestine adultery. But whatever the innate dispositions of the two sexes, however, throughout history and in diverse cultures, environmental and social factors, which are themselves often hard to disentangle, have operated to such an extent that the concept of some innately 'natural' sexual behaviour is exceedingly problematic.

Attempts to establish an explanatory model for sexual behaviour either heterosexual or homosexual on the basis of biological factors, be these hormonal, differences in brain structure, or genetic, operate in the face of a lack of a reliable generally valid picture of what constitutes 'normal' human sexual behaviour. That such attempts continue, and generate massive media attention, suggests enormous bewilderment, and continuing curiosity, about the entire subject.

Lesley A. Hall
Wellcome Institute for the History of Medicine

References

Herschberger, R. (1948) *Adam's Rib*, New York.
Wellings, K., Field, J., Johnson, A. M. and Wadsworth, J. (1994) *Sexual Behaviour in Britain: The National Survey of Sexual Attitudes and Lifestyles*, Harmondsworth.

Further reading

Johnson, A. M., Wadsworth, J., Wellings, K. and Field, J. (1994) *Sexual Attitudes and Lifestyles*, Oxford.
Porter, R. and Hall, L. (1995) *The Facts of Life: The Creation of Sexual Knowledge in Britain 1680–1950*, New Haven, CT.

See also: feminist theory; homosexualities; incest; latency period; libido; pornography.

simulation, computer *see* computer simulation

skills, social *see* social skills and social skills training

slavery

The definitions of slavery are as numerous as the societies in which slavery was to be found, and for good reason. The rights which owners had over their slaves and the duties by which they were bound constituted a bundle whose composition varied from society to society, although the slave's rights were always heavily circumscribed. Nevertheless, certain elements can probably be considered part of all these bundles. First, the slaves were initially outsiders, brought by force to serve their new master, or they were in some way expelled from full membership of their society, for instance, because of debt or as the result of a criminal trial. They might of course be the descendants of such individuals, depending on the degree to which a given society was prepared to assimilate slaves and their offspring to full membership. Second, at least in the first generation, slaves were marketable commodities, at any rate where commercialization was present in any recognizable form. In other words, they were a species of property and it was this which distinguished slaves

from other forms of forced labour. Third, slaves had specific, generally inferior, occupations within the total division of labour. Finally, slaves were held in their status only by force or the threat of it, and in many ways the ending of the necessity for this marked a slave's full assimilation into the society.

Within this broad framework, the variations were enormous. This is to be expected from an institution which, in its various forms, existed all over the world – Australia is the only large and inhabited land mass where slavery never occurred – and from the beginnings of recorded human history until the twentieth century. Indeed, vestiges still survive, particularly in parts of the Islamic world and in various prostitution rackets. Nevertheless, the various slave systems may perhaps be distinguished according to two criteria, namely the degree of openness and the extent to which the system of production was organized around it.

As regards the former question, particularly in societies whose social systems were organized around kinship groups, slavery could be a valued means of expanding the size of that group and the number of dependants an important individual had beyond the limits set by the natural processes of reproduction. Since slaves were by definition outsiders, and thus people without kin of their own, they and their descendants could be incorporated into their owners' group, albeit often in an inferior position. Where there was no premium on the number of kin an individual might have, or where the rules for the division of property made it advantageous to cut down the number of co-sharers, then slaves and their descendants could rarely gain admission to the higher ranks of society. In such circumstances, slaves would be freed only as a result of a formal act of manumission. These might occur with greater or lesser frequency, but in all such cases the ex-slave began his or her life of freedom in a lowly status, often still formally dependent on his or her former owner.

With regard to the second criterion, while slavery as such has existed in an enormous number of societies, the number in which it has been crucial to the organization of production has been relatively few. Ancient Greece, Ancient Rome and, in modern times, the southern USA, the Caribbean and parts of Brazil are the best known of these, although there were a number of other parts of the world, such as seventh-century Iraq, eighteenth-century colonial South Africa, Zanzibar in the nineteenth century, and parts of the western and central Sudan in the same period, for which a convincing case could be made. The emergence of economies based on slave labour depended on at least three conditions: first, private property rights, above all land, had to be established, and concentrated to the extent that extra-familial labour was required; second, internal labour had to be insufficiently available, often as the result of the emancipation of earlier labourers, whether they were bonded peasants as in Ancient Greece or indentured servants as in colonial America – in other words, large-scale slavery was a consequence of large-scale freedom. Third, since slaves generally had to be bought, commercial market production had to be sufficiently developed. Although the demand for slaves on a grand scale may well have been logically prior to their supply, the continued existence of a slave society required the regular importation of new slaves, almost invariably through an organized slave trade, as – with the exception of the USA – slave populations were unable to reproduce themselves naturally.

In those cases where slavery was an integral part of the organization of labour, it tended to be rather towards the closed pole of the assimilation continuum, even though the distinction between slave and free was nowhere as harsh as in the USA. For this reason, it was only in these societies (and not always even there) that a genuine slave culture was able to develop, as something distinct from that of the owners. Therefore, it was only in such societies that slaves were able to organize sufficiently for a large-scale rebellion to be possible, although individual acts of resistance were to be found wherever slavery existed. Very often, the major revolts were none the less the work of newly imported slaves, as the efficacy of repression tended to persuade second generation slaves of the futility of a rising, and led them to adopt an ambivalent attitude, which combined outward acquiescence with the effort to create a way of life for themselves that was as free and as comfortable as the circumstances permitted. In this way they tended to confirm the paternalist ideology of their masters, although this would then be rudely shattered by the general refusal of ex-slaves to remain in their former owners' service when, after the abolition of the institution, there was no longer legal compulsion for them to do so.

Robert Ross
University of Leiden

Further reading

Miller, J. C. (1985) *Slavery: A World-wide Bibliography*, White Plains, KS. (Continued in annual instalments in *Slavery and Abolition*.)
Patterson, O. (1982) *Slavery and Social Death: A Comparative Study*, Cambridge, MA.

sleep

Sleep is an area of human behaviour which occupies one-third of the total life span and occurs throughout all societies and all of history. Despite its pervasiveness it was largely ignored by social scientists until the mid-twentieth century. As laboratory-based studies began in earnest in the early 1950s to describe the nature and dimensions of sleep as a regularly recurring behaviour (Aserinsky and Kleitman 1953; Dement and Kleitman 1957), it became clear that this period was far from a passive state of quiescence or non-behaviour. By recording the electroencephalogram (EEG), electrooculogram (EOG) and electromyogram (EMG) continuously throughout the time period from waking into sleep until the final reawakening, it was found that there were regular cyclic changes within sleep itself. The discovery that sleep consists of two distinct types, rapid eye movement (REM) sleep and non-rapid eye movement (NREM) sleep, which differed as much from each other as each did from wakefulness, led to a series of studies detailing the properties of these two states and their interactions within the context of the whole circadian (sleep–wake) rhythm. Each hour and a half the shift from a synchronized, physiologically quiescent, NREM sleep in which motor activity is intact, to the desynchronized, physiologically active, REM state accompanied by motor paralysis, became known as the 'ultradian rhythm'. Within NREM sleep, variations in EEG pattern were further differentiated by convention into numerical sleep stages 1, 2, 3, 4. This laid the basis for the descriptive mapping of a night's sleep by the number of minutes spent in each sleep stage across the hours of the night and by the length of the ultradian cycle. This plot is referred to as 'sleep architecture'. Once these conventions were established (Rechtschaffen and Kales 1968) age norms for these sleep characteristics were also established (Williams *et al.* 1974). Study of these developmental changes provided insight into sleep–wake relations. Individual differences in sleep parameters were also explored and related to variations in intelligence, personality and lifestyle. For example, although it is still a matter of some debate, long sleepers (those sleeping in excess of nine hours per night) were found to differ reliably from short sleepers (who sleep less than six hours per night) in psychological makeup, with long sleepers being more introverted, with lower energy and aggressive drive than short sleepers. It is clear that there is a selective difference in the type of sleep that is increased for these people. Long and short sleepers have the same amount of stages 3 and 4, but long sleepers have twice the amount of REM sleep and their REM sleep has increased eye movement density. Thus it is in the area of REM function that the need of long sleepers for more sleep must be explored. Other variations also occur, for example, in depth of sleep. These have been studied using the degree of auditory stimulation needed to produce an arousal as the measurement. This procedure has established that all sleep stages become progressively lighter with age, making sleep more fragile in the elderly.

Beyond the descriptive and correlational studies there has been the continuing challenge concerning the question of sleep function. This question has been approached most often by looking into the effects on waking behaviour of sleep deprivation, either total or selective. Until recently these studies have been hampered by the limits to which human subjects could be subjected. Short studies of sleep loss have produced only small and equivocal results. These have been summed up ironically as: the effects of sleep deprivation are to make one more sleepy. However, the effects on subsequent sleep are clear. After total sleep loss, sleep architecture is changed. REM sleep is postponed in favour of a prolonged period of stages 3 and 4 sleep. It appears that this synchronized sleep is pre-emptive and is recouped first. In fact, if the degree of sleep loss has been more than a night or two, the first night of recovery sleep may contain no REM sleep at all. This may not reappear until a second recovery night. The opposite is true of the recovery following a period of selective REM sleep deprivation. On the first night of ad-lib sleep, REM sleep appears earlier in the architectural plot and the total amount may be increased above the usual proportion when total sleep time is controlled. In other words, both NREM stages 3 and 4 and REM sleep act as if they have the properties of needs requiring they be kept in homeostatic balance. A long-term sleep deprivation study using rats and employing yoked non-sleep-deprived animals as controls established that extreme sleep loss results in debilitative organic changes and death (Rechtschaffen *et al.* 1983). This is the first study to establish that sleep is necessary to sustain life. How much sleep of what kind is necessary at the human level to ensure well-being will probably be determined not from experimental studies, but may come from the many clinical studies being carried out of patients suffering from various disorders of sleep and of sleep–wake relations.

Against the background knowledge of normative sleep architecture, for each sex across the whole life-span, significant deviations in amount and type of sleep can now be identified, as well as differences in the distribution of sleep across the circadian cycle. Studies that have sought to relate waking psychopathology to sleep pathology have been most productive in the area of depression. Although it has been well known that most persons suffering from affective disorders also suffer from insufficient and poor quality sleep, the detailed laboratory monitoring has revealed the nature of this dysfunction to be specific to REM sleep. This is found to be significantly displaced in the overall architecture. The first REM sleep occurs too soon, at half the normal cycle length, is often abnormally prolonged on first occurrence, from a norm of ten to as much as forty minutes, and with an increase in the density of eye movements within this time period and a change in total time distribution. Instead of REM being predominant in the second half night, as in normal individuals, in the depressed the distribution in the first and second halves of the night is equal (Kupfer *et al.* 1983). Since REM deprivation is known to increase waking appetite and sexual activity in cats and depression is associated with reduction of these behaviours, the finding of a specific REM dysfunction in these patients hints that this sleep stage is implicated in the regulation of appetitive behaviours.

Studies of sleep under time-free conditions have established that the normal human circadian rhythm is not twenty-four hours but slightly greater than twenty-five. This finding suggest that social learning has played a part in entraining sleep to a twenty-four-hour cycle. Loss of these social cues (*zeitgebers*) during vacation time or when unemployed, for example, often leads to later sleep onset time and longer sleep periods leading to later arousal hours. Most normal individuals have little trouble becoming re-entrained. However, some individuals with withdrawn schizoid personalities, or perhaps some neurological deficit, have no established sleep–wake rhythm. These people suffer from an inability to function in regular occupations due to the unpredictability of their time periods for active prosocial behaviours.

Nocturnal sleep studies of persons whose waking life is interrupted by uncontrollable episodes of sleep have revealed several different types of sleep disturbance that are responsible for these intrusions, including narcolepsy and sleep apnœa syndromes. The study of sleep and its interaction with waking behaviour has enlarged the capacity of the social and behavioural scientist to account for some aspects of human behaviour previously poorly understood and has changed the time frame of observation to one including the full circadian cycle.

Rosalind D. Cartwright
Rush-Presbyterian-St Luke's Medical Center

References

Aserinsky, E. and Kleitman, N. (1953) 'Regularly occurring periods of eye motility and concomitant phenomena during sleep', *Science* 118.

Dement, W. and Kleitman, N. (1957) 'Cyclic variations in EEG during sleep and their relation to eye movements, body motility and dreaming', *Electroencephalography and Clinical Neurophysiology* 9.

Kupfer, D., Spiker, D., Rossi, A., Coble, P., Ulrich, R. and Shaw, D. (1983) 'Recent diagnostic treatment advances in REM sleep and depression', in P. J. Clayton and J. E.

Barretts (eds) *Treatment of Depression: Old Controversies and New Approaches*, New York.

Rechtschaffen, A. and Kales, A. (eds) (1968) *A Manual of Standardized Terminology, Techniques and Scoring System for Sleep Stages of Human Subjects*, Los Angeles, CA.

Rechtschaffen, A., Gilliland, M., Bergmann, B. and Winter, J. (1983) 'Physiological correlates of prolonged sleep deprivation in rats', *Science* 221.

Williams, R., Karacan, I. and Hursch, C. (1974) *Electroencephalography (EEG) of Human Sleep: Clinical Applications*, New York.

Further reading

Cartwright, R. (1978) *A Primer on Sleep and Dreaming*, Reading, MA.

Dement, W. (1972) *Some Must Watch While Some Must Sleep*, San Francisco, CA.

Hartmann, E. (1973) *The Functions of Sleep*, New Haven, CT.

Kryger, M., Roth, T. and Dement, W. (1994) *Principles and Practice of Sleep Medicine*, 2nd edn, Philadelphia, PA.

Webb, W. (1975) *Sleep, the Gentle Tyrant*, Englewood Cliffs, NJ.

See also: dreams.

Smith, Adam (1723–90)

Adam Smith was born in Kirkcaldy, on the east coast of Scotland, in 1723. After attending the Burgh School, Smith proceeded to Glasgow University (1737–40) where he studied under Francis Hutcheson. Thereafter he took up a Snell Exhibition in Balliol College, Oxford (1740–6). In 1748 Henry Home (Lord Kames) sponsored a course of public lectures on rhetoric and Smith was appointed to deliver them. The course was successful and led, in 1751, to Smith's election to the chair of logic in Glasgow University where he lectured on language and on the communication of ideas. In 1752 Smith was transferred to the chair of moral philosophy where he continued his teaching in logic, but extended the range to include natural theology, ethics, jurisprudence and economics.

Smith's most important publications in this period, apart from two contributions to the *Edinburgh Review* (1755–6), were the *Theory of Moral Sentiments* (1759, later editions, 1761, 1767, 1774, 1781, 1790) and the *Considerations Concerning the First Formation of Languages* (1761).

The *Theory of Moral Sentiments* served to draw Smith to the attention of Charles Townsend and was to lead to his appointment as tutor to the Duke of Buccleuch in 1764, whereupon he resigned his chair. The years 1764–6 were spent in France, first in Bordeaux and later in Paris, where Smith arrived after a tour of Geneva and a meeting with Voltaire. The party settled in Paris late in 1765 where Smith met the leading *philosophes*. Of especial significance were his contacts with the French economists, or Physiocrats, notably Quesnay and Turgot, who had already developed a sophisticated macroeconomic model for a capital using system.

Smith returned to London in 1766, and to Kirkcaldy in the following year. The next six years were spent at home working on his major book, which was completed after a further three years in London (1773–6). The basis of Smith's continuing fame, *An Inquiry into the Nature and Causes of the Wealth of Nations*, was published on 9 March 1776. It was an immediate success and later editions (of which the third is the most important) appeared in 1778, 1784, 1786 and 1789.

In 1778 Smith was appointed Commissioner of Customs and of the Salt Duties, posts which brought an additional income of £600 per annum (to be added to the continuing pension of £300 from Buccleuch) and which caused Smith to remove his household to Edinburgh (where his mother died in 1784). Adam Smith himself died, unmarried, on 17 July 1790 after ensuring that his literary executors, Joseph Black and James Hutton, had burned all his manuscripts with the exception of those which were published under the title of *Essays on Philosophical Subjects* (1795). He did not complete his intended account of 'the general principles of law and government', although generous traces of the argument survive in the lecture notes.

The broad structure of the argument on which Smith based his system of social sciences may be established by following the order of Smith's lectures from the chair of moral philosophy. The ethical argument is contained in *Theory of Moral Sentiments* and stands in the broad tradition of Hutcheson and Hume. Smith was concerned, in large measure, to explain the way in which the mind forms judgements as to what is fit and proper to be done or to be avoided. He argued that people form such judgements by visualizing how they would behave in the circumstances confronting another person or how an imagined or 'ideal' spectator might react to their actions or expressions of feeling in a given situation. A capacity to form judgements on *particular* occasions leads in turn to the emergence of *general rules* of conduct which correct the natural partiality for self. In particular Smith argued that those rules of behaviour which related to justice constitute the 'main pillar which upholds the whole edifice' of society.

Smith recognized that rules of behaviour would vary in different communities at the same point in time as well as over time, and addressed himself to this problem in the lectures on jurisprudence. In dealing with 'private law' such as that which relates to life, liberty or property, Smith deployed the analysis of *The Theory of Moral Sentiments* in explaining the origin of particular rules in the context of four socioeconomic stages – those of hunting, pasture, agriculture and commerce. In the lectures on 'public' jurisprudence he paid particular attention to the transition from the feudal-agrarian state to that of commerce; that is, to the emergence of the exchange economy and the substitution of a cash for a service nexus.

The economic analysis which completed the sequence and which culminated in the *Wealth of Nations* is predicated upon a system of justice and takes as given the point that self-regarding actions have a social reference. In fact the most complete statement of the psychology on which the *Wealth of Nations* relies is to be found in Part VI of *The Theory of Moral Sentiments* which was added in 1790.

The formal analysis of the *Wealth of Nations* begins with an account of the division of labour and of the phenomenon of economic interdependence and then proceeds to the analysis of price, the allocation of resources and the treatment of distribution. Building on the equilibrium analysis of Book I, the second book develops a version of the Physiocratic *model* of the circular flow of income and output before proceeding to the analysis of the main theme of economic growth. Here, as throughout Smith's work, the emphasis is upon the unintended consequences of individual activity and leads directly to the policy prescriptions with which Smith is most commonly associated: namely, the call for economic liberty and the dismantling of all impediments, especially mercantilist impediments, to individual effort.

Yet Smith's liberalism can be exaggerated. In addition to such necessary functions as the provision of defence, justice and public works, Jacob Viner (1928) has shown that Smith saw a wide and elastic range of governmental activity.

The generally optimistic tone which Smith uses in discussing the performance of the modern economy has also to be qualified by reference to further links with the ethical and historical analyses. Smith gave a great deal of attention to the social consequences of the division of labour, emphasizing the problem of isolation, the breakdown of the family unit, and the mental mutilation (affecting the capacity for moral judgement) which follows from concentrating the mind on a restricted range of activities. If government has to act in this, as in other spheres, Smith noted that it would be constrained by the habits and prejudices of the governed. He observed further that the type of government often found in conjunction with the exchange or commercial economy would be subject to pressure from particular economic interests, thus limiting its efficiency, and, also, that the political sphere, like the economic, was a focus for the competitive pursuit of power and status.

A. S. Skinner
University of Glasgow

References

Smith, A. (1976 [1759]) *Theory of Moral Sentiments*, ed. D. D. Raphael and A. L. Macfie.
—— (1976 [1776]) *Wealth of Nations*, ed. R. H. Campbell, A. S. Skinner and W. B. Todd.
—— (1977) *Correspondence of Adam Smith*, ed. E. C. Mossner and I. S. Ross. This includes: *A Letter from Governor Pownall to Adam Smith* (1776); Smith's *Thoughts on the State of the Contest with America* (1778); Jeremy Bentham's *Letters to Adam Smith on Usury* (1787; 1790).
—— (1978) *Lectures on Jurisprudence*, ed. R. L. Meek, D. D. Raphael and P. G. Stein. This includes two sets of students notes.
—— (1980) *Essays on Philosophical Subjects*, ed. W. P. D. Wightman: 'The History of Astronomy'; 'The History of the Ancient Physics'; 'History of the Ancient Logics and Metaphysics'; 'Of the External Senses'; 'Of the Imitative Arts'; 'Of the Affinity between Music, Dancing and Poetry'.
   This also includes 'Contributions to the *Edinburgh Review*' (1755–6) and 'Of the Affinity between certain English and Italian Verses', ed. J. C. Bryce; Dugald Stewart, *Account of the Life and Writings of Adam Smith*, ed. I. S. Ross.
—— (1983) *Lectures on Rhetoric and Belles Lettres*, ed. J. C. Bryce. This includes the *Considerations Concerning the First Formation of Languages*.
Viner, J. (1928) 'Adam Smith and laissez faire', in J. Hollander *et al.*, *Adam Smith, 1776–1926*, Chicago.

Further reading

Campbell, T. D. (1971) *Adam Smith's Science of Morals*, London.
Haakonssen, K. (1981) *The Science of the Legislator: The Natural Jurisprudence of David Hume and Adam Smith*, Cambridge, UK.
Hollander, S. (1973) *The Economics of Adam Smith*, Toronto.
Lindgren, R. (1975) *The Social Philosophy of Adam Smith*, The Hague.
Macfie, A. L. (1967) *The Individual in Society: Papers on Adam Smith*, London.
O'Driscoll, G. P. (ed.) (1979) *Adam Smith and Modern Political Economy*, Iowa.
Rae, J. (1965 [1895]) *Life of Adam Smith*, London. (Reprinted with an introduction by J. Viner, New York.
Reisman, D. A. (1976) *Adam Smith's Sociological Economics*, London.
Scott, W. R. (1937) *Adam Smith as Student and Professor*, Glasgow.
Skinner, A. S. and Wilson, T. (1975) *Essays on Adam Smith*, Oxford.
Winch, D. (1965) *Classical Political Economy and the Colonies*, London.
—— (1978), *Adam Smith's Politics*, Cambridge, UK.

See also: political economy; Scottish Enlightenment, social theory.

social anthropology

The term social anthropology began to be used for a branch of anthropology in the early twentieth century. Initially – when used, for instance, by James George

Frazer – it described an evolutionist project. The aim was to reconstruct the original 'primitive society' and to chart its development through various stages to civilization. In the 1920s, under the influence of Bronislaw Malinowski and A. R. Radcliffe-Brown, the emphasis in British social anthropology (the dominant school) shifted to the comparative study of contemporary societies: Radcliffe-Brown suggested that it was essentially a comparative sociology. 'Social anthropology' was now contrasted with 'cultural anthropology', as practised in the USA especially, which was concerned with ethnohistory, cultural diffusion, language and, increasingly, with issues of culture and personality.

The British School drew particularly on the sociology of Durkheim and Mauss, who had pioneered the systematic application of sociological theories to ethnographic reports on non-western societies. The borderline between sociology and social anthropology was a permeable one, and when sociology was belatedly established as a university discipline in Britain some of the early chairs went to social anthropologists. Such modern figures as Pierre Bourdieu, Fredrik Barth and Ernest Gellner moved across the boundary between the disciplines in both directions.

As it crystallized, social anthropology became essentially a combination of Durkheimian sociology and ethnographic field research by participant observation. This synthesis came to be known as 'functionalism', a vague and contentious label. Malinowski himself stressed personal agency and the conflicts between social norms and individual interest, while the followers of Radcliffe-Brown were more inclined to abstract systems of values and norms. Although there was a great deal of internal debate, from the mid-1920s until the 1960s the small but productive band of British social anthropologists appeared to informed observers to be engaged in a single, specialized project. The main aim was to analyse the synchronic relationships between institutions within a society, and to classify institutions or whole societies into types.

Fieldwork by participant observation, on the model pioneered by Malinowski in the Trobriand Islands (1915–18), became the characteristic mode of ethnographic research. Ideally a trained social anthropologist spent one to two years in the community being studied, integrating with the local people and working in the vernacular language. This research strategy became a defining feature of functionalist anthropology, but it outlived functionalist theory and was diffused to other disciplines, so-called 'ethnographies' becoming a feature of various schools of social research.

The major achievement of functionalist anthropology was a series of authoritative, sociologically informed ethnographic studies of societies in Africa, the Pacific and India. Ethnographic studies were increasingly made in Europe, but generally in rural settings. Comparative studies were also fostered, and typologies flourished, based either upon cross-cultural categories or upon the comparison of societies within a particular region (see e.g. Fortes and Evans-Pritchard 1940; Radcliffe-Brown and Forde 1950).

In post-war France, Claude Lévi-Strauss (1963) developed a 'structuralist' approach, which aimed to make general statements about the mentality of human beings as expressed in social institutions and mythologies, drawing not only on Mauss but also on linguistics. Lévi-Strauss influenced some leading British social anthropologists, notably Edmund Leach, Mary Douglas and Rodney Needham. However, both 'functionalism' and 'structuralism' came under attack in the 1970s. Marxist critics accused both schools of being ahistorical, and of neglecting macrosociological processes. Varieties of Marxist theory and dependency theory became influential. Feminist critics introduced fresh perspectives.

In the 1980s, however, a more fundamental shift became apparent, from the dominantly sociological orientation that had characterized social anthropology for most of the century to a fresh concern with problems of meaning and with 'culture', which had been treated as a residual category by the comparative sociologists. American theorists in the tradition of cultural anthropology – notably Clifford Geertz and David Schneider – were increasingly influential in Europe. Later, the post-modernist turn taken by some younger American scholars made converts. This theoretical upheaval was accompanied by a loss of confidence in the objectivity and reliability of established ethnographic field methods. The typological projects of the functionalists and structuralists were often rejected for their positivism and for the perhaps arrogant transposition of western cultural categories to other ways of life.

At the same time, however, the Anglo-French tradition of social anthropology had diffused through much of Western Europe. In 1989 the European Association of Social Anthropologists was established. Judging from the conferences and publications of this flourishing association (see the journal *Social Anthropology*, which began publishing in 1992), a new synthesis is being established. Modern social anthropologists draw upon a variety of contemporary social theories (see Kuper 1992), and they experiment with a wide range of comparative, historical and ethnographic research strategies. The tradition of ethnographic field research remains strong (with Europe now a major focus of research). Field studies are now often long term and historically informed. The density of ethnographic research in many regions and the presence of local communities of scholars have also made field studies more specialized and, often, more sophisticated.

Despite the theoretical turmoil, social anthropology is more popular than ever before, and perhaps more influential, particularly in the fields of history, sociology, geography and cultural studies. Social anthropologists are also more open than ever to ideas from these and other disciplines (including, most notably, psychology and linguistics), and to interdisciplinary collaboration. They contribute to applied research studies on such questions as ethnic relations, immigration, the effects of medical and educational provision, and even marketing; they are involved in community development projects all over the world.

The fundamental object of modern social anthropology is to confront the models current in the social sciences with the experiences and models of peoples all over the world. While no theoretical perspective dominates the field, contemporary social anthropologists produce sociologically informed, culturally sophisticated, studies of a great variety of social processes; their training provides them with an invaluable comparative perspective on the range of human social behaviour.

Adam Kuper
Brunel University

References

Fortes, M. and Evans-Pritchard, E. E. (eds) (1940) *African Political Systems*, London.
Kuper, A. (ed.) (1992) *Conceptualizing Society*, London.
Lévi-Strauss, C. (1963) *Structural Anthropology*, London.
Radcliffe-Brown, A. R. and Forde, D. (eds) (1950) *African Systems of Kinship and Marriage*, London.

Further reading

Carrithers, M. (1993) *Why Humans have Cultures*, Oxford.
Evans-Pritchard, E. E. (1951) *Social Anthropology*, London.
Hastrup, K. (ed.) (1992) *Other Histories*, London.
Kuper, A. (1983) *Anthropology and Anthropologists: The Modern British School*, London.
Stocking, G. (ed.) (1984) *Functionalism Historicized: Essays on British Social Anthropology*, Madison, WI.

See also: anthropology; cultural anthropology; cultural history; economic anthropology; Malinowski, Bronislaw Kasper; political anthropology.

social class *see* class, social

social conflict *see* conflict, social

social contract

The doctrine that government should be for and by the people informs the constitution of all countries claiming to be democratic, even when the precept is not observed in practice. Democratic governments rest their claims to legitimacy and obedience on electoral consent, but the concept of consent itself derived originally from contract theory which discovered the origins of government in a primal act of consent, 'the social contract'. The foremost exponents of contract theory, Hobbes, Locke and Rousseau, did not believe that savages had literally congregated and agreed to set up governments; contract was, rather, a hypothetical device. Its purpose was to show that governments should be viewed *as if* they had been established by the people and evaluated according to whether they served the purpose of protection for which they were instituted. In Hobbes's case the theory had illiberal implications: almost any government, however bad, would serve to keep anarchy at bay. But for Locke, the people had the right to resist a government which failed to protect their lives and property. Whether the conclusions of contract theory were reactionary or revolutionary depended on its basic assumptions.

In *Leviathan* (1968 [1651]), Hobbes, fresh from the horrors of civil war, imagined people in an anarchic state of nature, living in fear of sudden death. These people would eventually make a contract to guarantee peace, for their own protection. But since none would trust their fellows, they would then appoint a sovereign, independent of the contract, to enforce it and maintain order by all necessary means, including coercion. Because Hobbes sees authorization as a blank cheque, imposing no accountability on those in authority, his sovereign would have unqualified power over those who authorized him.

Locke's contract theory (1924 [1690]) was developed partly in protest against Hobbes's absolutist conclusions, partly to vindicate the revolution of 1688, which replaced the Stuarts with a constitutional monarchy. His state of nature is peaceful and orderly; people follow natural, moral laws and cultivate land and acquire property. But the absence of laws to resolve disputes leads people to establish a government by agreement. In making the contract, individuals surrender their natural rights, receiving instead civil rights and protection. The government thus created has a limited, fiduciary role. Its duty is the preservation of 'life, liberty and estate', and if it reneges, the people have the right to overthrow it. Although Locke argued that the contract enforced consent to majority rule, his was not a theory of democracy but an argument for a balanced constitution with a people's legislature, an executive monarch and an independent judiciary. This innovatory constitutionalism was a far cry from Hobbes's axiom that sovereignty was necessarily indivisible. Locke's doctrine that post-contract generations must consent to government, either actively or tacitly, later gave rise to 'consent theory'.

Contractualism is developed in a different direction by Rousseau (1913 [1762]), who argued that governments originally resulted from conspiracies of the rich to protect their property. But through an ideal social contract, individuals would freely consent to exchange their natural autonomy for a share in government. This could be achieved only by a direct, participatory democracy, which would be directed by the 'General Will'. The General Will is 'that which wills the common good', the decision which all citizens would accept if they laid aside personal interests. Dissenters from the General Will could be 'forced to be free', that is, compelled to obey laws for the public good which, if less self-interested, they would themselves freely have chosen. The General Will thus represents our 'better selves', but liberal theorists have often regarded it as a potential justification for authoritarianism or for totalitarian regimes claiming to act in the 'real interests' of the people (although undoubtedly this was not Rousseau's intention) and have therefore rejected Rousseau's contract theory.

Despite their differences, all three theories reflect the same desire to make the legitimacy of governments rest on the people's choice. The cultural environment which produced this desire was one of increasing individualism, secularization and legalism: the doctrine of individual free will dictated that no persons should be governed without their own consent, while the decline of the 'divine right of kings' dogma meant that a secular justification for political power was needed. The recourse to a contractual justification mirrored the growing reliance on contracts in the expanding commercial world, and a new, anti-feudal, legalistic attitude to public affairs.

The central fallacy of contract theories, as T. H. Green stated (1901), is that they presuppose 'savage' people with notions of rights and legality which could be generated only *within* a society. More damning for critics such as Hume, Bentham and Paine was the fact that existing governments were blatantly based on coercion, not consent, and operated largely for the benefit of the governors. History too suggested that most governments had been established through conquest and force. Such criticisms explain why contract theory was later replaced by the more plausible idea of democratic consent. However, contractarianism was revived in Rawls's *Theory of Justice* (1971), which identified the principles of justice as those to which people would consent, if deliberating in a state-of-nature-like vacuum. Rawls's work, which vindicates a broadly liberal view of justice, illustrates again how the original assumptions, especially those concerning human nature, determine the form and the contents of a hypothetical social contract. Contract theory is not abstract speculation, but a political myth tailored to prove a point.

Post-Rawlsian debate has been informed by 'rational choice theory'. In particular, the Prisoners' Dilemma model, which shows that it is rarely in the interests of individuals to co-operate, has been used to confront social contract theory. But Gauthier (1986), Taylor (1987) and others have invoked rational choice techniques to illustrate the possibility of co-operation and a rolling social contract, based on self-interest, for the provision of public goods, including government.

Despite the logical and empirical shortcomings of contract theory, it deserves serious attention because of its relation to central political ideas such as the will of the people, legitimacy and political obligation. All these have been employed manipulatively, often by regimes which have no basis in the people's choice. To avoid such ideological manoeuvres and sleights of hand, we need to reject the rhetorical invocation of implicit, tacit or imaginary social contracts and to develop a doctrine of meaningful and participatory choice and consent.

Barbara Goodwin
Brunel University

References

Gauthier, D. (1986) *Morals by Agreement*, Oxford.

Green, T. H. (1901) *Lectures on the Principles of Political Obligation*, London.

Hobbes, T. (1968 [1651]) *Leviathan*, ed. C. B. Macpherson, London.

Locke, J. (1924 [1690]) *An Essay Concerning the True Original, Extent and End of Civil Government*, London.

Rawls, J. (1971) *A Theory of Justice*, Cambridge, MA.

Rousseau, J. J. (1913 [1762]) *The Social Contract*, trans. G. D. H. Cole, London. (Original edn, *Du contrat social*, Paris.)

Taylor, M. (1987) *The Possibility of Cooperation*, Cambridge, UK.

Further reading

Riley, P. (1982) *Will and Political Legitimacy: A Critical Exposition of Social Contract Theory in Hobbes, Locke, Rousseau, Kant and Hegel*, Cambridge, MA.

See also: Hobbes, Thomas; Locke, John; political theory; Rousseau, Jean-Jacques.

social control

The concept of social control is widely and variously used in the social sciences. In sociology and anthropology it is used as a generic term to describe the processes which help produce and maintain orderly social life. In the specialist field of criminology, it usually carries a narrower meaning, referring to the administration of deviance by criminal justice, social welfare and mental health agencies. Sometimes the term takes on a critical sense, for example in social history and women's studies, where the notion of social control has been used to point to the subtle constraints and forms of domination present in institutions such as the family or the welfare state.

The breadth and imprecision of the social control concept has meant that it has tended to work as an orienting device for thinkers and researchers, rather than as an explanatory tool of any refinement. Sociologists in the early twentieth century developed the concept to explore the problem of social order in the industrialized, urbanized societies then emerging. Criminologists in the 1960s used the term to redirect attention away from an exclusive focus upon the individual criminal and to stress the role which social rules and reactions play in the process of criminalizing particular behaviours and persons. Social historians in the 1970s employed the notion of social control as a means of subverting and revising orthodox accounts of social reform which had tended to overlook the hidden class-control aspects of many reform programmes.

However, once such reorientations have been achieved, the general concept of social control often ceases to be useful and gives way to more specific questions about the different forms, objectives, supports and effects of the control practices under scrutiny. Like many sociological concepts, social control is a subject of continuing contestation, either by those who deny the appropriateness of this approach to particular phenomena, or else by those who find the term insufficiently precise to do the analytical and critical work required. That the concept is also and inevitably tied into political debates – either as part of a conservative quest for social order, or else in support of a radical critique of social institutions – serves to deepen the controversy surrounding its use. So too does the semantic proximity of the term to other concepts such as socialization, regulation, domination, power and culture. Social scientists who use this concept are obliged to define it for their own purposes or else invite misunderstanding.

Given this conceptual state of affairs, the most illuminating way of understanding the term is to summarize its intellectual history rather than adopt a purely analytical exposition (Coser 1982; Janowitz 1975a). However, one should bear in mind that contemporary usage still draws upon all of these past conceptions, and often reinvents under a different name many of the ideas and distinctions which earlier writers first established.

The classical social theorists of the nineteenth century – Comte, Marx, Durkheim, Weber, Simmel, etc. – did not employ the term social control, although their work certainly dealt with the issues of social self-regulation, enforcement of norms, and class domination which social control theorists were later to address. Instead, the concept was first developed by the sociologists of early-twentieth-century USA, particularly by E. A. Ross and W. G. Sumner, who sought to identify the myriad ways in which the group exerts its influence upon the conduct of the individual. Ross's (1901) *Social Control* took as its starting-point the shift from small-scale, agrarian, face-to-face communities to dense, industrialized urban societies, and argued that this shift entailed a qualitative transformation in the bonds which made social order possible. Whereas the earlier *gemeinschaft* communities had been held together by what Ross regarded as a 'living tissue' of natural controls such as sympathy, sociability and a shared sense of justice, social control in the newer *Gesellschaft* societies was a matter of 'rivets and screws' which had to be consciously created and maintained if order was to be achieved within these complex and conflictual social settings. Ross's work catalogued and anatomatized these foundations of order, dealing in turn with public opinion, law, belief, education, religion, art and social ceremony. In much the same way, Sumner's (1906) *Folkways* described how usages, manners, customs and morals provided the basic underpinning of social regulation, upon which the more formal system of law was built.

Underlying this early work is a Hobbesian conception of individual human nature as disruptive and anti-social, to be reined in by the imposition of group controls and sanctions – as well as an anxiety that deliberate social control was more than ever necessary in burgeoning metropolises such as Chicago and New York, with their masses of newly arrived immigrants and diverse ethnic groups. Later work, by writers such as G. H. Mead (1925) and C. H. Cooley (1920), developed a different conception of the individual's relation to society in which social control was accomplished not by suppressing individuality but rather in its very creation. For these writers, the self emerges through a process of interaction with others, out of which develops the individual's capacity to take the point of view of other people. To the extent that this socialization process is successful, individuals are constituted as social selves, internalizing the norms of the wider society ('the generalized other'), and adapting their conduct to the various roles demanded by social interaction. Thus the social control which permits co-ordination and integration operates in and through the individual, rather than over against individuality, and the internal self-control of the individual is as much a social matter as the rules and regulations which constrain individuals from the outside. (In somewhat different language, and from somewhat different premises, Durkheim, Freud and Piaget had come to a similar conclusion: see Coser (1982). See also Elias's (1979; 1981 [1939]) *The Civilizing Process*, which sets out a sociohistorical account of how social controls and self-controls change over time.)

For Chicago sociologists such as Park and Burgess (1925), 'all social problems turn out finally to be problems of social control'. By this they meant that the practical problems of administering social institutions and governing populations, as well as the theoretical problems of understanding the dynamics of social organizations, turn on the ability of the analyst or policy maker to comprehend the mechanisms which permit groups to regulate their own activities without recourse to violence and in accordance with specified moral ideals. In this conception, social control is contrasted with coercive control, (and indeed, with minority or class domination) and is viewed as an integral part of purposive social planning and the rationalization of social institutions. Moreover, it can take both positive and negative forms, operating to elicit and evoke action in individuals through rewards, persuasion or education, or else to restrain and repress by means of gossip, satire, laughter and criticism (see Lumley 1925). For the early American Pragmatists and Progressives – and, indeed, for a few later sociologists such as Janowitz (1975b) and Melossi (1990) – social control was thus an ideal to strive after. (One version of this ideal was the Welfare State, which utilized controls such as Keynesian demand management, insurance-based protections, personal social services, and processes of democratic opinion formation, in an attempt to govern in the interests of a positive ethic of solidarity and security.) By the 1970s, many writers had come to regard the history of twentieth-century rationalization and social engineering in a much more negative light, with the consequence that social control came to be regarded by some as a regrettable feature of social organization and a subject for critical attack.

In anthropology, the issue of social control was first explicitly addressed as part of a controversy about the social organization of 'primitive' societies. In his account of *Crime and Custom in Savage Society* (1926) Malinowski attacked the then orthodox view that small-scale, pre-industrial societies were held together by virtue of the 'spontaneous obedience' of group members, whose individuality was stifled by the operation of a harshly conformist *conscience collective* (cf. Durkheim 1984 [1893]). Against this view, Malinowski

argued that social control was embedded in the reciprocity of routine social relations, and was supported by the self-interest of each individual in maintaining his or her place in the system of exchange and reputation, as well as by the ceremonial enactment of social obligations, which ensured that individual deviance was made visible to others. Social control involved not only the individual internalization of social norms, but also the active pursuit of self-interest, and occasionally the operation of coercive sanctions. As Etzioni (1961) later pointed out, social organizations can be distinguished in terms of the three modes of control which Malinowski identifies. Thus prisons, mental hospitals and concentration camps are founded primarily (though not exclusively: see Sykes 1958) on coercive controls; organizations such as the workplace depend upon the utilitarian controls of remuneration; while others – such as religious, voluntary and political associations – maintain their cohesion primarily through the normative commitment of their members.

In the 1950s Parsons (1951) defined the theory of social control as 'the analysis of those processes in the social system which tend to counteract ... deviant tendencies'. Social control thus came to refer to a subsystem or, at most, a special remedial aspect of social relations, rather than the patterning effect of social relations as such. This narrower usage has tended to prevail in the specialist field of criminology, where it has spawned a large literature analysing the effects – especially the unintended effects – of the actions of 'agencies of social control' such as the police, prisons, psychiatrists, etc. (However Hirschi's (1969) influential control theory of crime utilizes the term in its older sociological sense to argue that the key variable in explaining offending is the strength of the social bonds which tie individuals into patterns of conformity.) In the 1960s Lemert (1967) and Becker (1963) transformed that field by arguing that 'social control leads to deviance' rather than the reverse, and by stimulating research on the ways in which the 'labelling' and 'stigmatizing' of deviant conduct by officials tends to reinforce and amplify deviant identities and behaviour.

In the 1970s, this critical attitude towards the practices of social control came to take a more radical form, partly under the influence of Marxist theories of the state, and partly as a result of the new social history which argued that the emergence of modern institutions such as the reformatory prison, the asylum, and the social welfare system ought to be seen not as humane and progressive reforms but instead as strategic measures to consolidate the subordination and control of the lower classes (Donajgrodzki 1977). In the 1980s there emerged a new specialism, the sociology of social control, focused upon the developmental forms and functioning of the 'control apparatus' (Cohen 1985; Cohen and Scull 1983). An influential thesis which has emerged from this work – and which resonates with the dystopian themes of Orwell's (1949) *Nineteen Eighty-Four* and Huxley's (1932) *Brave New World* – asserts that, since the 1960s, there has been an 'increasing expansion, widening, dispersal, and invisibility' of the 'net of social control' (Cohen 1985: 14). The assumption underlying this thesis is that modern society is increasingly governed by reference to expert knowledge, classification systems, and professional specialists in the administration of deviance. Styles of social control may change, (e.g. the shift from reliance upon closed institutions to greater use of community-based provision for mentally ill people), as may the ideologies which gloss these practices (e.g. the decline of 'rehabilitative' philosophies in the penal system), but the build up of the control apparatus is viewed as a secular trend.

Critics of the concept (see Miller and Rose 1986) object to its tendency to imply that diverse strategies and practices of governance – operating in different social sites, involving different personnel, different techniques and different programmatic objectives – can somehow be said to share a common source (usually the state or the ruling class) and a common purpose (integration or domination). To lump all of these together as social control is to impart a spurious unity to a variety of problems and practices which may have little in common. Others (e.g. Thompson 1981; van Krieken 1991) object to the implication that social controls are imposed upon the subordinate classes, rather than negotiated or invited by the groups concerned, and to the frequently made assumption that the social control objectives implicit in a reform programme are automatically realized just because laws are passed or agencies set up. In this respect, the alleged 'social control' effects of reform measures often function as a *post-hoc* explanation for a theoretically predicted event (usually a revolution) which failed to occur. Like its more Marxist cognates 'ideology' and 'hegemony', social control can operate as a device to protect a theory from falsifying evidence rather than as a tool for exploring the social world.

David Garland
University of Edinburgh

References

Becker, H. (1963) *Outsiders*, New York.
Cohen, S. (1985) *Visions of Social Control*, Cambridge, UK.
Cohen, S. and Scull, A. (eds) (1983) *Social Control and the State*, Oxford.
Cooley, C. H. (1920) *Social Process*, New York.
Coser, L. A. (1982) 'The notion of control in sociological theory', in J. P. Gibbs (ed.) *Social Control: Views From the Social Sciences*, Beverly Hills, CA.
Donajgrodzki, A. P. (ed.) (1977) *Social Control in Nineteenth Century Britain*, London.
Durkheim, E. (1984 [1893]) *The Division of Labour in Society*, trans. W. D. Halls, London.
Elias, N. (1979; 1981 [1939]) *The Civilizing Process*, 2 vols, London.
Etzioni, A. (1961) *A Comparative Analysis of Complex Organisations*, New York.
Hirschi, T. (1969) *Causes of Delinquency*, Berkeley, CA.
Huxley, A. (1932) *Brave New World*, London.
Janowitz, M. (1975a) 'Sociological theory and social control', *American Journal of Sociology* 81.
—— (1975b) *Social Control of the Welfare State*, Chicago.
Lemert, E. (1967) *Human Deviance, Social Problems and Social Control*, Englewood Cliffs, NJ.
Lumley, F. E. (1925) *Means of Social Control*, New York.
Malinowski, B. (1926) *Crime and Custom in Savage Society*, London.
Mead, G. H. (1925) 'The genesis of the self and social control', *International Journal of Ethics* 35.
Melossi, D. (1990) *The State of Social Control*, Cambridge, UK.
Miller, P. and Rose, N. (eds) (1986) *The Power of Psychiatry*, Cambridge, UK.
Orwell, G. (1949) *Nineteen Eighty-Four*, London.
Park, R. E. and Burgess, E. W. (1925) *Introduction to the Science of Sociology*, Chicago.
Parsons, T. (1951) *The Social System*, London.
Ross, E. A. (1901) *Social Control*, New York.
Sumner, W. G. (1906) *Folkways*, Boston, MA.
Sykes, G. (1958) *The Society of Captives*, Princeton, NJ.
Thompson, F. M. L. (1981) 'Social control in Victorian Britain', *Economic History Review* 34.
Van Krieken, R. (1991) 'The poverty of social control: explaining power in the historical sociology of the welfare state', *Sociological Review* 39.

See also: police; punishment.

Social Darwinism

Social Darwinism refers loosely to various late nineteenth-century applications (mostly misapplications) to human societies of ideas of biological evolution associated (often erroneously) with Darwin. Though often associated with conservatism, *laissez-faire* capitalism, fascism and racism, Social Darwinism was, in fact, a pervasive doctrine of the late nineteenth and early twentieth centuries, especially in Britain and North America, and its influence covered the entire political spectrum, including, for example, British Fabian socialism.

Its two leading intellectual proponents were the British philosopher Herbert Spencer (who coined the phrase 'survival of the fittest') and William Graham Sumner, a professor of anthropology at Yale University. To Spencer (1864; 1873–85), we owe the misleading analogy that a society is like an organism (hence, the term 'organicism' sometimes used to describe his theories). Just as an organism is composed of inter-dependent organs and cells, a human society is made up of specialized and complementary institutions and individuals, all belonging to an organic whole.

Spencer himself was never very clear about his analogy: he claimed that society was both 'like an organism' and that it was a 'super-organism'. His central notion, however, was that the whole (organism-society) was made up of functionally specialized, complementary and interdependent parts. Thus, he is also considered to be one of the main fathers of sociological functionalism.

Sumner's concept of 'mores' (his term, by the way) and his turgid disquisitions on morality are his most lasting contributions. What his writings have to do with Darwinism is questionable. 'Bad mores are those which are not well fitted to the conditions and needs of the society at the time. . . . The taboos constitute morality or a moral system which, in higher civilization restrains passion and appetite, and curbs the will' (Sumner 1906). Sumner uses terms such as 'evolution' and 'fitness' to be sure, but his moralistic pronouncements and his repeated emphasis on the 'needs of the society' are the very antithesis of Darwin's thinking. Spencer was also prone to inject ethics into evolution, seeing an 'inherent tendency of things towards good'. Darwin saw evolution as a random process devoid of ethical goals or trends, and natural selection as a blind mechanism discriminating between individual organisms on the basis of their differential reproductive success.

Another central theme in Sumner is that 'stateways cannot change folkways', meaning that state action is powerless to change the underlying mores. This certainly made him an apostle of *laissez-faire*. Indeed, he went so far as to contradict himself and suggest that state intervention is worse than useless: it is noxious. These propositions probably form the core of the doctrine associated with Social Darwinism, namely, that the existing social order with its inequalities reflects a natural process of evolution in which the 'fitter' rise to the top and the 'unfit' sink to the bottom. Any attempt, through social welfare, for example, to reduce inequalities is seen as noxious because it allows the unfit to 'breed like rabbits'. Indeed Spencer, as a good Victorian puritan, believed that intelligence and reproduction were inversely related. Overproduction of sperm, he thought, leads first to headaches, then to stupidity, then to imbecility, 'ending occasionally in insanity' (Spencer 1852).

Again, these ideas are quite antithetical to those of Darwinian evolutionary theory. If the lower classes reproduce faster than the upper classes, it means they are *fitter*, since, in evolutionary theory, the ultimate measure of fitness is reproductive success. To say that the unfit breed like rabbits is a contradiction in terms.

Social Darwinism, in short, is a discredited moral philosophy that bears only a superficial terminological resemblance to the Darwinian theory of evolution, and is only of historical interest.

Pierre van den Berghe
University of Washington

References

Spencer, H. (1852) 'A theory of population deduced from the general law of animal fertility', *Westminster Review* 1.
—— (1864) *Principles of Biology*, London.
—— (1873–85) *Descriptive Sociology*, London.
Sumner, W. G. (1906) *Folkways*, Boston, MA.

Further reading

Hofstadter, R. (1959) *Social Darwinism in American Thought*, New York.
Ruse, M. (1982) *Darwinism Defended*, Reading, MA.

See also: evolutionism and progress; race.

social democracy

Social democracy is a party-based political movement, inspired by socialism, which has held different meanings in different times and places. It has remained a substantially European movement, with Australia, New Zealand and Israel as the main exceptions. Not all social democratic parties have adopted the name, the most common alternatives being Socialist Party (France) and Labour Party (The Netherlands, Britain and Norway).

Three phases can be distinguished: from 1875 when the German Social Democratic Party (SPD) was founded to 1914; between the World Wars; and the period since 1945.

The first period, one of expansion and consolidation of the movement, coincided with the industrialization of Europe and the formation of a large proletariat. Social democrats (or socialists – the terms were then interchangeable) were then members of centralized and nationally based parties, loosely organized under the banner of the Second International (1889) supporting a form of Marxism popularized by Friedrich Engels, August Bebel and Karl Kautsky. This held that capitalist relations of production would dominate the whole of society, eliminating small producers until only two antagonistic classes, capitalists and workers, would face each other. A major economic crisis would eventually open the way to socialism and common ownership of the means of production. Meanwhile, social democrats, in alliance with trade unions, would fight for democratic goals such as universal suffrage and a welfare state and traditional workers' demands such as a shorter working day. It was assumed that in democratic countries power could be achieved peacefully, though participation in bourgeois governments was ruled out. Some (e.g. Rosa Luxemburg) proposed the mass general strike as the best revolutionary weapon.

The SPD provided the main organizational and ideological model though its influence was less pronounced in southern Europe. In Britain the powerful trade unions tried to influence the Liberals rather than forming a separate working-class party. Not until 1900 was a Labour Party created. It was never Marxist and adopted a socialist programme only in 1918.

The First World War and the October Revolution divided the movement, setting the supporters of Lenin's Bolsheviks against the reformist social democrats, most of whom had backed their national governments during the war. Thereafter the rivalry of social democrats and communists was interrupted only occasionally, as in the mid-1930s, in order to unite against fascism. Between the wars socialists and social democrats formed governments in various countries including Britain, Belgium and Germany. In Sweden, where social democrats have been more successful than elsewhere, they governed uninterruptedly from 1932 to 1976.

After 1945, while in northern Europe socialists called themselves social democrats, in other countries, notably in Britain, France and Italy, social democrat was the label given to right-wing socialists who sided with the USA in the Cold War, objected to extensive nationalization, and were hostile to Marxism. In practice the differences between various tendencies were never as significant as internal doctrinal debates suggest. Eventually all social democratic parties discarded Marxism, accepted the mixed economy, loosened their links with the trade unions and abandoned the idea of an ever-expanding nationalized sector. In the 1970s and 1980s they adopted some of the concerns of middle-class radicals, such as feminism and ecologism. Socialism was no longer a goal at the end of a process of social transformation but the process itself, in which power and wealth would gradually be redistributed according to principles of social justice and equality – a position advocated by Eduard Bernstein (1993 [1899]) in the 1890s. The success of capitalism in the 1950s favoured such revisionism, enshrined in the SPD at its Bad Godesberg Conference in 1959 and popularized in Britain by Anthony Crosland (1956). All social democrats assumed that continuous economic growth would sustain a thriving public sector, assure full employment and fund a burgeoning welfare state. These assumptions corresponded so closely to the actual development of European societies that the period 1945–73 has sometimes been referred as the era of 'social democratic consensus'. Significantly, it coincided with the 'golden age' of capitalism.

Since 1973, left-wing parties obtained power where they had never held it before, in Portugal, Spain, Greece and France (except briefly in 1936–7). But social democracy faced a major crisis of ideas. Contributing factors were the end of continuous economic growth, massive unemployment (which made the welfare state more difficult to fund), global economic interdependence (which made national macroeconomic management inadequate), popular resistance against high levels of taxation, a sharp fall in the size of the factory-based proletariat, and the challenge of neo-liberal and anti-statist ideas of deregulation and privatization. The collapse of communism and the transformation of communist parties into social democratic ones provided little comfort for social democrats when the ideology of the free market appeared stronger than ever before.

Donald Sassoon
University of London

References

Bernstein, E. (1993 [1899]) *The Preconditions of Socialism*, ed. H. Tudor, Cambridge, UK.
Crosland, A. (1956) *The Future of Socialism*, London.

Further reading

Gay, P. (1952) *The Dilemma of Democratic Socialism: Eduard Bernstein's Challenge to Marx*, New York.
Padget S. and Paterson, W. E. (1991) *A History of Social Democracy in Postwar Europe*, London.
Sassoon, D. (1995) *One Hundred Years of Socialism*, London.
Schorske, C. (1972) *German Social Democracy 1905–1917: The Development of the Great Schism*, New York.

See also: communism; socialism.

social geography

Social geography is a subdiscipline of geography as a whole, a subject which spans the natural and social sciences, and covers topics ranging from plate tectonics to psychoanalysis. Some authors equate social geography with the entirety of human geography, that is, with the social science arm of the discipline. In first coining the term 'social geography' in 1884, for instance, Elisee Reclus referred to it as the intricate relationship between 'man' (meaning people) and nature (Dunbar 1977). Others have defined the field more narrowly, following Fitzgerald's (1946) view that an interest in the social can be pursued in its own right, as an area distinct from studies of the political and economic aspects of life. Most analysts, however, see the domain of social geography as lying somewhere between these extremes.

The main definitions of social geography which now exist may be grouped in a variety of ways. There are, however, two key (interrelated) focuses for the work of the subdiscipline. They reflect, first, a preoccupation dating from the 1960s and 1970s to align the project of geography more fully with the social science mainstream, and, second, a commitment on the part of a number of key individuals to develop a radical, socially relevant area of study.

Geography has always had close links with sociology, and the development of social geography since the mid-1950s has, in part, been an exploration of the complementarity of the two disciplines. Thus Jones (1985: 3) sees social geography as concerned with 'describing and explaining spatial elements of the society in terms of the structure of that society', while Jackson and Smith (1984: vii) regard it as the study of 'how social life is constituted geographically through the spatial structure of social relations'. This orientation has given social geography an interest and a role in a range of philosophical and methodological debates, notably those concerning the autonomy of human agency relative to structural forces and spatial constraints. Social geography has, by exploring these themes, played a key role in what Eyles (1986) terms the reconstitution of human geography as a social science.

A second part of this reconstitution concerns the quest for relevance at the end of a period of progressivism. Towards the end of the 1960s, it became evident that the world's social problems were getting worse, not better, and that social inequalities were escalating rather than ameliorating, even in the so-called welfare states. During the 1970s, two key texts helped social geographers develop a critical and constructive role in an apparently unjust society.

The first, David Harvey's (1973) *Social Justice and the City*, not only exploded the myth of value-free social science, but also carried a powerful political message about the way in which a radical and committed social geography could inform the process of social change. This book drew social geography into the realms of critical social science and harnessed it to the transformative aspirations of what was then thought of as the New Left.

The second key text, David Smith's (1977) *Human Geography: A Welfare Approach*, raised the question of who gets what, where, and so stimulated the development of a welfare-oriented, policy relevant social geography. This early work underpins the problem-based approach to social geography taken up in the collection edited by Pacione (1987) and developed by Cater and Jones (1989). This approach conceptualizes social geography as an enquiry into resource allocation, enticing geographers to study spatial inequalities in housing and employment opportunities, crime, health and a range of other social issues. More recently research in this vein has focused on aspects of racism and gender inequality, ageing and disability, and has produced a critique of the constitution and manipulation of power relations in a socially unjust world.

In the past, the term social geography has more often been associated with European, and especially British, geography than with North American scholarship. This reflects the more ready incorporation of New Left thinking into European social science, and the closer contact of European scholars with the strengths and weaknesses of the welfare state ideal. It reflects, too, the extent to which North American human geography has been dominated by the tradition of cultural geography favoured by Carl Sauer. Thus apart from a few early attempts to carve out a niche for the subdiscipline (e.g. Buttimer 1968; Watson 1953), it was not until the publication in 1983 of David Ley's *A Social Geography of the City* that the idea caught on in the USA (see Johnston 1986). Since the late 1980s, however, geographers with an interest in both social and cultural studies on both sides of the Atlantic have attempted to bring these themes together and to develop a more integrated social science component to the discipline. This is reflected, for instance, in the merger of the Social and Cultural Geography Study groups of the Institute of British Geographers, and in the orientation of their first publication *New Words, New Worlds* (Philo 1991).

Susan Smith
University of Edinburgh

References

Buttimer, A. (1968) 'Social geography', in D. L. Sills (ed.) *International Enyclopedia of the Social Sciences*, vol. 6, New York.

Cater, J. and Jones, T. (1989) *Social Geography: An Introduction to Contemporary Issues*, London.

Dunbar, G. (1977) 'Some early occurrence of the term "social geography" ', *Scottish Geographical Magazine* 93.

Eyles, J. (ed.) (1986) *Social Geography in International Perspective*, London.

Fitzgerald, W. (1946) 'Geography and its components', *Geographical Journal* 197.

Harvey, D. (1973) *Social Justice and the City*, London

Jackson, P. and Smith, S. J. (1984) *Exploring Social Geography*, London.

Johnston, R. J. (1986) 'North America', in J. Eyles (ed.) *Social Geography in International Perspective*, London.

Jones, E. (ed.) (1985) *Readings in Social Geography*, Oxford.

Ley, D. (1983) *A Social Geography of the City*, New York.

Pacione, M. (1987) *Social Geography: Progress and Prospect*, London.

Philo, C. (ed.) (1991) *New Words, New Worlds*, Lampeter.

Smith, D. M. (1977) *Human Geography: A Welfare Approach*, London.

Watson, J. W. (1953) 'The sociological aspects of geography', in G. Taylor (ed.) *Geography in the Twentieth Century*, London.

See also: *cultural geography; economic geography; geography; political geography; population geography; sociology; space; territoriality.*

social gerontology *see* gerontology, social

social history

The most famous definition of social history is attributed to G. M. Trevelyan: 'history with the politics left out'. Like many often repeated quotes it is a misquotation. What Trevelyan (1942) actually wrote in the introduction to his *English Social History* was not so silly: 'Social history might be defined negatively as the history of a people with the politics left out'. He went on to suggest that this was an inadequate definition, but since so many works of history had consisted of politics with society left out there was a case for redressing the balance, for 'without social history, economic history is barren and political history is unintelligible'. He went on:

> social history does not merely provide the required link between economic and political history. Its scope may be defined as the daily life of the inhabitants of the land in past ages: this includes the human as well as the economic relation of different classes to one another, the character of family and household life, the conditions of labour and leisure, the attitude of man to nature, the culture of each age as it arose out of these general conditions of life and took ever-changing forms in religion, literature and music, architecture, learning and thought.

Trevelyan sought in his survey of six centuries to retrieve what he could of the lives of rich and poor, women and men, children and parents, to analyse as well as to tell a story, seeking to define and to celebrate the characteristics of Englishness as a contribution to wartime morale-building. He was preoccupied with the problems of coherence and periodization in social history which 'cannot like the web of political history be held together by the framework of well-known names of kings, Parliaments and wars'; aware that important changes in attitudes and practices (towards childrearing for example) occurred gradually, the old surviving alongside, and interacting with, the new. These preoccupations have endured.

Although, as Trevelyan indicated, the writing of history had previously been dominated by political narrative, alternative strands had emerged. First, in Britain social history developed along with economic history. The first generation of classics in economic history written in the interwar years, a striking number of them by women, including Eileen Power, professor of economic history at the London School of Economics (to whom Trevelyan dedicated his *Social History*), were as much concerned with social as with strictly economic history, for example Power's (1922) *Medieval English Nunneries* (Berg 1992).

Second, intellectuals associated with the early Labour Party sought to analyse social inequality and institutions historically to suggest how they might be changed, in particular Barbara and J. L. Hammond's books on the impact of industrialization on the labouring poor (Hammond and Hammond 1911; 1917; 1919) and Beatrice and Sidney Webb's histories of trade unionism and of local government (Webb and Webb 1894; 1929).

Around the same time in France a similar reaction against history as the history of political events gave birth to the journal *Annales d'histoire economique et sociale* in 1929. The *Annalistes* had a definite programme not merely to explore societies and the economies of the past but also to integrate the study of society, economy, politics, intellectual life, geography and demography all in their broadest sense, ideally over long time periods (if sometimes of very small places) in order to understand, as they put it, 'civilization', the complex network of interactions which constitutes a society. In 1946 the title of the journal was changed to *Annales: Economies, Sociétés, Civilisations* (as it remains). This aspiration to total .history was an influential stimulus internationally for many decades – especially under the direction of Braudel (1949) in the 1950s and 1960s – reminding historians that they could be bold, though relatively few took up the challenge and fewer still could match practice with ambition. But it provided a new rigour both in the definition of social history and its methods. Above all it was systematic. French historians were the first to apply quantitative techniques to the study of politics, social structure and demography. They were strongly positivist in rarely questioning how the structures which they studied or their data were constructed. Driven by *Annales*, social history acquired greater and earlier legitimacy and prominence in French academic life than elsewhere (Prost 1992).

British social history did not advance so tidily. After 1945 the tradition of Labour intellectuals writing the history of the labour movement and of the working class, notably G. D. H. Cole (1948), and later Asa Briggs (1991), continued as did the close association of economic and social history, though they moved apart from the 1960s.

A new and important stimulus was the Communist Party History Group, several of whom achieved a remarkable international eminence: Hilton (1987), Kiernan (1988), Hill (1986), Hobsbawm (1978; 1987), E. P. Thompson (1992) and Dorothy Thompson. All had interests in the history of radical ideas, social protest and subordinate groups, and a preference for literary over quantitative sources.

The liberal strand, to which Trevelyan and G. M. Young (1936) belonged, carried on. One of its important products, G. Kitson Clark's (1962) *The Making of Victorian England*, was dedicated to Trevelyan. Clark was 'primarily a political historian', but 'anxious to write what might be called "history in depth" ', combining demographic, economic and political history with the study of socioeconomic groups at all levels and central aspects of culture such as religion. This he felt 'quite sure . . . is the right line of development for historiography'. H. J. Perkin (1969) was already working on his study of *The Origins of Modern British Society 1780–1880* and defining social history as a 'vertebrate discipline' built around the theme of the history of social structure (Perkin 1962), rather than as the 'shapeless container for everything from changes in human physique to symbol and ritual' that some perceived (Hobsbawm 1980). Perkin (1992) sought to analyse how a 'viable class society' emerged amid the change of industrialization, while others emphasized conflict. Social history was stronger and more varied in Britain by the early 1960s than subsequent commentators have suggested.

The expansion of the social sciences in the postwar period, especially sociology, influenced historical work. A successful example was the work of the Cambridge Group for the History of Population and Social Structure, formed in 1964 by Peter Laslett and E. A. Wrigley. This set out to apply quantitative techniques developed in France and questions and concepts previously largely confined to sociologists and anthropologists to the study of demography and social structure over long time periods (Laslett 1965; 1988). The outcome has transformed our understanding of the process of population change (Wrigley and Schofield 1981) and household structure (Laslett and Wall 1972) in Britain over several centuries and has been widely influential elsewhere. This work has raised important general questions about the relationship between economic and social change especially during the process of industrialization (Wrigley 1988), and more specific ones, such as about the relative roles of family and welfare agencies in support for the poor in European societies. In the USA quantitative historical sociology particularly influenced studies of social mobility (Thernstrom 1964) and of social protest (Tilly and Shorter 1974).

Also important from the mid-1960s was the growing oppositional culture in sections of the academy. This attracted historians in Britain and elsewhere to social history, especially 'history from below', also much influenced by the publication of E. P. Thompson's (1963) *The Making of The English Working Class*.

Social history in the 1960s, from whatever perspective it was written, was centrally organized around a conception of society as hierarchically structured, with class as the primary organizing category. In the 1970s and 1980s more historians became aware that behaviour and beliefs (about politics for example) could not be explained as satisfactorily in terms of socioeconomic position as had been thought. Growing attention to women's history made it clear that gender was as important a social category as class. Changing ideological preoccupations, combined with a wider academic challenge to structuralism in all its forms, made social historians more sensitive to the variety of divisions within societies and the variety of identities each individual possessed related to race, nation, age-group and religion as well as gender and class.

This greatly complicated the writing of social history, leading some to fear that it was about to collapse into random empiricism. Others turned to anthropology for help in understanding social complexity, in particular to the cultural ethnography of Geertz and the insights of Mary Douglas. The task was further complicated by the growing influence in the academy of Foucault and of sociolinguistics, semiotics and literary theory: Saussure, Derrida, Bakhtin, Baudrillard and Bourdieu pre-eminently. The impacts of these very different theorists were controversial (*American Historical Review* 1989; *Past and Present* 1991). At their best they challenged historians to recognize that the objects of their investigation – social groups, madness, sexuality, the state or any other – are not givens as they had implicitly supposed but constructs whose construction in time must be interpreted; so also are the languages of written sources, which contributed to the construction of, and are not merely the expression of, feeling and action. And they could provide a richer range of resources for interpreting the wide range of sources used by social historians, oral, visual and material as well as documentary.

Under these influences, historians (more in some countries than in others, more slowly in the UK than the USA or Australia, slower still in Germany) began to talk of studying 'culture' rather than 'society' (Hunt 1989) or in France '*mentalités*' (Chartier 1982). The value of this approach is that it enables historians to conceptualize values, beliefs, language, political organization, economic activity and much else as interacting elements of the same system rather than as isolated features of human activity. The danger is that, like 'total history', it becomes so inclusive that specificity is lost, it can remain a desirable aspiration within which social historians can continue to pursue a variety of themes. But it can develop independent theories and concepts which learn from but are not parasitic upon other disciplines; and it can provide their indispensable contribution to the social sciences: analysis over time, long-run as well as short-run time.

Pat Thane
University of Sussex

References

Berg, M. (1992) 'The first women economic historians', *Economic History Review* 2.

Braudel, F. (1949) *La Méditerranée et le monde méditerranéen à l'époque de Philippe II*, Paris.

Briggs, A. (1991) Videotaped interview with J. Harris, *Interviews with Historians*, Institute of Historical Research, London.

Chartier, R. (1982) 'Intellectual history or sociocultural history? The French trajectories', in D. LaCapra and S. Kaplan (eds) *Modern European Intellectual History: Reappraisals and New Perspectives*, Ithaca, NY.

Clark, G. Kitson (1962) *The Making of Victorian England*, London.

Cole, G. D. H. (1948) *A Short History of the British Working Class Movement, 1789–1947*, London.

Hammond, B. and Hammond, J. L. (1911) *The Village Labourer*, London.

—— (1917) *The Town Labourer*, London.

—— (1919) *The Skilled Labourer*, London.

Hill, C. (1986) Videotaped interview with P. J. Corfield, *Interviews with Historians*, Institute of Historical Research, London.

Hilton, R. (1987) Videotaped interview with J. Hatcher, *Interviews with Historians*, Institute of Historical Research, London.

Hobsbawm, E. (1978) 'The Historians Group of the Communist Party', in M. Cornforth (ed.) *Rebels and their Causes*, London.

—— (1980) 'The revival of narrative: some comments', *Past and Present* 86.

—— (1987) Videotaped interview with P. Thane, *Interviews with Historians*, Institute of Historical Research, London.

Hunt, L. (ed.) (1989) *The New Cultural History*, Berkeley, CA.

Kiernan, V. G. (1988) *The Duel in European History; Honour and the Reign of Aristocracy*, Oxford.

Laslett, P. (1965) *The World We Have Lost*, London.

—— (1988) Videotaped interview with K. Wrightson, *Interviews with Historians*, Institute of Historical Research, London.

Laslett, P. and Wall, R. (1972) *Household and Family in Past Time*, Cambridge, UK.

Perkin, H. (1962) 'What is social history?', in H. Finberg (ed.) *Approaches to History*, London.

—— (1969) *The Origins of Modern English Society*, London.

—— (1992) Videotaped interview with P. Thane, *Interviews with Historians*, Institute of Historical Research, London.

Power, E. (1922) *Medieval English Nunneries, c.1275–1535*, Cambridge, UK.

Prost, A. (1992) 'What has happened to French social history?', *Historical Journal* 35(2).

Thernstrom, S. (1964) *Poverty and Progress: Social Mobility in a Nineteenth Century City*, Cambridge, MA.

Thompson, E. P. (1963) *The Making of the English Working Class*, London.

—— (1992) Videotaped interview with P. J. Corfield, *Interviews with Historians*, Institute of Historical Research, London.

Tilly, C. and Shorter, E. (1974) *Strikes in France, 1830–1848*, Cambridge, UK.

Trevelyan, G. M. (1942) *English Social History: A Survey of Six Centuries*, London.

Webb, B. and Webb, S. (1894) *The History of Trade Unionism, 1666–1920*, London.

—— (1929) *English Local Government*, London.

Wrigley, E. (1988) *Continuity, Chance and Change: The Character of the Industrial Revolution in England*, Cambridge, UK.

Wrigley, E. and Schofield, R. (1981) *The Population History of England*, London.

Young, G. M. (1936) *Victorian England: Portrait of an Age*, London.

Further reading

Corfield, P. J. (1991) *Language, History and Class*, Oxford.

See also: cultural history; historical geography; history; history of medicine; Marx's theory of history and society; Marxist history; oral history.

social identity

In its most general sense, social identity refers to a person's self-definition in relation to others. Within social psychology, however, it usually has a more specific connotation, namely, a self-definition in terms of one's membership of various social groups. This sense of the term owes much to G. H. Mead, who emphasized a social conception of the self, arguing that individuals experience themselves 'from the standpoint of the social group as a whole' to which they belong (Mead 1977). It is important to distinguish this public (or social) aspect of identity from the more private (or personal) aspects. Indeed, Mead himself, in stressing the importance of the group, can be seen as contrasting his approach from the more individualistic psychodynamic formulations. Thus, it has become common to refer to social identity in the manner above, and to personal identity as reflecting those parts of one's self-definition which have to do with personality traits, physical attributes, inter-personal styles and the like. Brown and Turner (1981) argued that this is not merely an abstract theoretical distinction but one which, following Tajfel (1978), may have important behavioural implications: according to whether 'personal' or 'social' identities are psychologically uppermost in any situation may determine whether people exhibit sporadic and idiosyncratic 'interpersonal' behaviours, *or* organized and socially uniform 'intergroup' behaviours.

Historically, the concept of social identity has occupied a central place in both social-psychological and sociological theorizing. For instance, Lewin (1948), whose 'field theory' inspired a whole generation of post-war social psychologists, wrote and researched extensively on the psychological significance of group affiliations, especially for minority and marginal groups. Within a more psychoanalytic tradition, the work of Erikson (1960) on identity conflicts and identity diffusion in the individual's life cycle has had important clinical applications. Within sociology, too, social identity has not gone unnoticed. For example, in Parson's 'general theory of action' it is defined as a subsystem of personality and assigned a major role in determining a person's participation in the social system (see, e.g. Parsons 1968).

Reflecting these theoretical concerns, much empirical research attempted to measure different components of identity. The bulk of this work concentrated on aspects of personal identity focusing on such topics as self-esteem, locus of control, and level of aspiration. These methodologies were reviewed by Wylie (1974). In contrast, very few attempts have been made to measure social identity. One of the earliest, and still widely used, techniques is the Twenty Statements Test devised by Kuhn and McPartland (1954). This simply involves a respondent giving up to twenty responses to the question 'Who am I?' These responses may be analysed to reveal the nature of that person's social and personal identity referents, the evaluative quality of the terms used, and the importance attributed to different elements. A typical finding is that social identity referents emerge earliest in response protocols, the most commonly mentioned categories being sex and occupational role. Zavalloni (1971) proposed a technique for investigating a person's social identity idiographically. This method allows the respondent to differentiate between different subgroups within a larger category, sometimes attaching very different valence and meaning to those subgroup identifications. However, both of these techniques yield essentially qualitative data and, in the latter case, are time-consuming to administer and analyse. A simpler and more practicable instrument was suggested by Driedger (1976). This consists of a short scale in which the respondent is permitted to affirm or deny, in varying degrees of strength, different aspects of ingroup membership. Although designed to measure ethnic identity, the technique has been extended to measure the strength of other group identifications also (Brown *et al.* 1986).

Despite these methodological difficulties, the concept of social identity continues to excite considerable research interest. Much of this has been stimulated by Tajfel's 'social identity' theory, e.g. Tajfel, 1978), which proposed a causal link between social identity needs and various forms of intergroup behaviour. Central to this theory is the hypothesis that people's social identities are sustained primarily through social comparisons, which differentiate the ingroup from relevant outgroups. From this simple idea it has proved possible to explain the prevalence of intergroup discrimination, even in the absence of real conflicts of interest, and to provide persuasive analyses of the plight of minority groups, industrial conflicts over pay differentials, and linguistic differentiation between ethnic groups.

Rupert Brown
University of Kent

References

Brown, R. J. and Turner, J. C. (1981) 'Interpersonal and intergroup behaviour', in J. C. Turner and H. Giles (eds) *Intergroup Behaviour*, Oxford.

Brown, R. J., Condor, S., Mathews, A., Wade G. and Williams, J. A. (1986) 'Explaining intergroup differentiation in an industrial organisation', *Journal of Occupational Psychology* 59.

Driedger, L. (1976) 'Ethnic self-identity: a comparison of ingroup evaluations', *Sociometry* 39.

Erikson, E. H. (1960) 'The problem of ego identity', in M. R. Stein, A. J. Vidich and D. M. White (eds) *Identity and Anxiety*, New York.

Kuhn, M. H. and McPartland, T. S. (1954) 'An empirical investigation of self attitudes', *American Sociological Review* 19.

Lewin, K. (1948) *Resolving Social Conflicts*, New York.

Mead, G. H. (1977) *On Social Psychology*, ed. A. Strauss, Chicago.

Parsons, T. (1968) 'The position of identity in the General Theory of Action', in C. Gordon and K. J. Gergen (eds) *The Self in Social Interaction*, New York.

Tajfel, H. (1978) *Differentiation between Social Groups: Studies in the Social Psychology of Intergroup Relations*, London.

Wylie, R. C. (1974) *The Self Concept*, London.

Zavalloni, M. (1971) 'Cognitive processes and social identity through focussed introspection', *European Journal of Social Psychology* 1.

Further reading

Hogg, M. and Abrams, D. (1988) *Social Identifications*, London.

See also: person; self-concept.

social mobility

Social mobility has long been a central topic of sociological speculation, and since the 1940s, the object of many empirical enquiries. Interest in the topic arises in part from its supposed relation to justice and efficiency in societies, and in part from the relative ease with which mobility may be quantified. Numerous hypotheses have been advanced which turn on the extent or pattern of mobility, trends in mobility over time, and comparisons of mobility across countries (Lipset and Bendix 1966). For example, it is argued that the relative ease of upward movement in nineteenth-century USA helps to explain the absence of a significant socialist movement (Sombart 1976 [1906]). However, empirical enquiry does not unequivocally support the proposition that there was more mobility in the USA than in Europe. Indeed, the results from most empirical investigations are inconclusive.

Nevertheless, certain propositions have emerged with some degree of support. Since the mid-1960s it has been established that among males, there is a strong, but by no means perfect, correlation between level of education obtained and social standing of occupation (Blau and Duncan 1967). It also appears that measured intelligence (IQ) in childhood is the best single predictor of both educational achievement and the occupation level of men (Duncan 1966).

Painstaking collection of mobility data for the past enables us to say that in sixteenth-century Norwich a freeman had a fifty-fifty chance of being in the same trade as his father, but if he left that trade it was pure chance which other trade he entered. In the twentieth century, North American mobility has been highly asymmetric, as the USA changed from a rural to an urban society, and boys leaving the land slotted into the non-farm occupational structure at all levels. This accounts for the notion that the USA is a peculiarly open society.

These findings, together with a few more based on less quantified material (Kaelble 1977; 1985), constitute the sum of our knowledge of what mobility has actually occurred in recent centuries – and few of them are immune to refutation.

When, however, we turn from matters of empirical fact to matters of theoretical interpretation, we come up against problems of measurement, models and meaning. One such problem is that of the theoretical distinction between mobility in the sense of *generalized* upward movement in a society such as nineteenth-century North America, and movement which consists of equal upward and downward flows between any two social categories. A society manifesting this latter type of bilateral equal exchange in any high degree is said to be open or fluid (Thernstrom 1973). Within both generalized upward shift and fluidity (whether these are high or low in degree) we must distinguish between movement occasioned by universalistic qualities (merit)

and movement, or lack of it, based on ascriptive qualities (such as father's class).

The argument that high mobility inhibited the development of socialism in the USA is usually based on the observation that few middle-class Americans moved down into the working class, whereas many sons and daughters of farmers (and also many immigrants who started in menial jobs) moved up into the middle class. Latter-day claims that the USA is a more open and 'meritocratic' society than Britain are based on the belief that there is more bilateral exchange in the USA, and that those who rise in the North American social scale do so because they have acquired good educational credentials and therefore deserve their mobility. In fact it would appear that British men (data for women are harder to interpret) are no less mobile than American men, when allowance is made for the relative concentration of Britons in the working class, and for the flight from the land in the USA. It also seems that, under the selective system of education, the able British son of a working-class father had a better chance than his American analogue of getting a good job, because he was more likely to receive a good education and to be groomed by his secondary school for the higher occupations (Hope 1984).

Broadly speaking, European and North American writers appear to diverge on the topic of mobility. On the whole, Americans are interested in the question of how individuals take up positions in a vertical hierarchy which is mainly a matter of material advantage. When they find that position in that hierarchy is determined, to quite a high degree, by level of education attained, they claim that their society is a meritocracy, where universalistic rather than ascribed qualities are the basis of achievement. They tend to think that this model adequately describes the social structure for white males, though not for blacks and females (Blau and Duncan 1967; Featherman and Hauser 1978). European researchers, by contrast, more often consider the life-chances and the degree of class-consciousness of collectivities with a view to predicting whether these aggregates are likely to undertake class-action. They ask whether mobility disrupts class solidarity and induces alienation of one sort or another (Dahrendorf 1959). In both Europe and the USA political scientists speculate anxiously on the relation between mobility, particularly the downward movement of whole categories of persons, and support for fascism (Lipset 1981). This fear is likely to be much exacerbated by Ross Perot's populist candidacy in the 1992 US presidential election, and by the even greater success of Silvio Berlusconi's *Forza Italia* in 1994. Turner (1992) reports work on political attitudes in many countries.

The main criticism that can be levelled against mobility research in so far as it deals with transmission between generations is that it entirely ignores genetic transmission. Logically, you cannot say that transmission is social unless your research design allows you also to estimate genetic transmission. While biologists hunt the human genome, sociologists cling doggedly to environmentalism. Within the social realm, the main criticism is that wealth is rarely measured. This is important in the study of poverty because a serious aspect of poverty is the hand-to-mouth existence that occurs when your stored wealth is depleted (no spare pair of shoes, no money for fares to seek work). A further criticism is that equations that include income are based more or less on assumptions of normal distribution, but inequality in US society takes the form of wildly discrepant remuneration running as high as $200 million in a single year. A model of positive feedback may be invoked to explain both the political success of populist media-based political candidates, and the distribution of rewards to celebrities.

The main conclusion of mobility research in the USA is that North American society is 'universalistic' and rewards are rationally allocated. In fact, by analysing data from the General Social Surveys it is possible to show that there are very great discrepancies by religious and ethnic affiliation, even within the group of White males. This is not surprising. In a pluralist society, 'You help your friends and kill your enemies' (to quote a former president of the American Trial Lawyers Association). Furthermore a society in which there are 497,697 elected officials in 83,236 governments, many of which appoint scores or thousands to boards and commissions, cannot possibly be universalistic (Sterba 1992). Sociologists claim to have established universalism, even while political scientists celebrate American pluralism. In fact sociologists are well aware of the barriers to universalism. Of the sixteen areas into which Chicago may be divided, four are 87–98 per cent Black and three are 0 per cent Black. Mean per capita income varies from $3,952 to $35,275 (Reardon 1994).

Keith Hope
Southern Illinois University

References

Blau, P. M. and Duncan, O. D. (1967) *The American Occupational Structure*, New York.
Dahrendorf, R. (1959) *Class and Class Conflict in Industrial Society*, London.
Duncan, O. D. (1966) 'Ability and achievement', *Eugenics Quarterly* 15.
Featherman, D. L. and Hauser, R. M. (1978) *Opportunity and Change*, New York.
Hope, K. (1984) *As Others See Us*, New York.
Kaelble, H. (1977) *Historical Research on Social Mobility*, New York.
—— (1985) *Social Mobility in the 19th and 20th Centuries: Europe and America in Comparative Perspective*, Leamington Spa.
Lipset, S. M. (1981) *Political Man: The Social Bases of Politics*, Baltimore, MD.
Lipset, S. M. and Bendix, R. (1966) *Social Mobility in Industrial Society*, Berkeley, CA.
Reardon, P. T. (1994) 'Chicago more like 16 cities', *Chicago Tribune* 13 March.
Sombart, W. (1976 [1906]) *Why is there No Socialism in the United States?*, trans. P. M. Hocking and C. T. Husbands, New York.
Sterba, J. P. (1992) 'Election spending during four years may top $6 billion' *Wall Street Journal* 1 September.
Thernstrom, S. (1973) 'Urbanization, migration, and social mobility in late nineteenth century America', in H. G. Gutman and G. S. Kelley (eds) *Many Pasts: Readings in American History*, Englewood Cliffs, NJ.
Turner, F. C. (ed.) (1992) *Social Mobility and Political Attitudes*, New Brunswick, NJ.

Further reading

Payne, G. and Abbott, P. (1990) *The Social Mobility of Women: Beyond Male Mobility Models*, London.

See also: elites; stratification.

social movements

For Lorenz von Stein (1855: vi), *the* social movement of the nineteenth century was the working class. Scholarship and social change in the twentieth century have pluralized the term, loosening it from its historical connotations and applying it to a variety of phenomena from unstructured collective behaviour to cults and religious sects to issue-oriented protest movements all the way .to organized revolutions. The only common denominators in the variety of definitions that have resulted is that social movements are uninstitutionalized groups of unrepresented constituents engaged in sequences of contentious interaction with elites or opponents (Tarrow 1994; Tilly 1978; 1986).

With so broad a focus and so unconstrained a definition, empirical richness has been gained at the cost of agreed-upon methodological canons. Although organizational analyses and survey studies are more and more employed, the typical approach remains the configurational case study, often of a movement with which the author has had a personal relationship. The resulting mass of case studies has fed the urge to typologize, based in part on the empirical properties of groups and in part on their relation to existing society. Following the Tillys' lead, a number of scholars have experimented with collective action event analysis over more or less long time periods (Tilly et al. 1975).

Theoretically, the field has focused on three major questions.

First, what kind of people are recruited into social movements? In the past, these were often seen as fanatics or social isolates in search of new collective identities, but since the mid-1970s research has shown that movement activists come from almost any sector of the population. They are most often recruited out of social networks and tend to stay active in one form or another of movement activity after their initial recruitment experience (McAdam 1988).

Second, how does the appearance of a movement relate to cycles in economic growth and changes in class relations? It used to be thought that economic deprivation was the main source of movement formation, but the movements of the 1960s led to the opposite hypothesis – that movements are the result of 'post-material' attitudes that grow out of affluence (Inglehart 1977). With the decline of Marxism, analysts have become wary of ascribing causal priority to such macrostructural factors as economic cycles, and have been increasingly turning to the changes in political opportunities that lower the costs of collective action (Eisinger 1973; Tarrow 1994).

Third, how do relations between leaders and followers affect the outcomes of movement activity and the careers of social movements? Here the classical Michelsian insight about the displacement of group goals by leaders has been a guiding star, but research since the 1960s suggests that such institutionalization is far from preordained (Zald and Ash 1966). The problem of leader–follower relations has been recast in the form of the now-familiar problem of the free rider (Olson 1968). But since people *do*, increasingly, engage in contentious collective action, doubt has been cast on the applicability of Olson's theory to movements.

Social movement theory and research have had two main historical sources: first, the conservative reaction to the French and the industrial revolutions (see Oberschall 1973 for sources); and second, the rise of the socialist movements of the late nineteenth century. After the decline of anarchism and the rise of collective bargaining, a slow-growing belief in the rationality of collective action combated the earlier presumption that it was irrational. The great cataclysms of the twentieth century – fascism and the Russian revolution – revived the earlier view of movements as catchment areas for people seeking new identities, but in newer, post-Freudian forms (Fromm 1969). This was particularly the case in the USA. Influenced by a generation of exiles who brought with them nightmarish memories of the 'mob', and lacking the strong Marxist matrix of European theorists, North American social movement researchers were particularly vulnerable to the

persuasion that social movements are an expression of dysfunctions in society (Smelser 1963).

The decade of the 1960s contested this vision and revivified a field that had been sinking into marginality. As the student, anti-war, women's and environmental movements developed concrete and purposive critiques of elites and authorities, the result for social movement research was the 'normalization' of collective action. There was a growing tendency to see movements as the outcome of the instrumental mobilization of resources and collective action as an element – albeit a turbulent and uncivil one – in the political process (McAdam 1982; McCarthy and Zald 1977).

The analytical gains brought by these new models have been enlightening for US research, but have been purchased at the cost of obscuring the special character of social movement activity. Europeans, in particular, have criticized the North American approaches for neglecting the ideological projects of movements and for becoming insensitive to their impact on culture. The response of some scholars has been to revive social psychological approaches to movements and, of others, to pay greater attention to how movements construct meaning (Klandermans 1992).

The impact of the movements of the 1960s was somewhat different in Europe, where the structuralist persuasion, stripped of its Marxist integument, led to the theory of 'new' social movements. This has French (Touraine 1988), German (Offe 1985) and Italian (Melucci 1989) variants, with somewhat less impact on British researchers. The theory holds that the growth of the Keynesian welfare state and the centralization of advanced capitalist economies have brought about a constriction of individual life-spaces, but have *not* led to the formation of ideologically coherent movements. The result is movements that address life-space concerns but nothing resembling the class/mass party-movements of the nineteenth and early twentieth centuries.

The theory of new social movements is attractive, but it has been criticized for operating at too high a level of generalization to capture the variations in movement formation that have been observed in various countries – all of which have similar states of centralization and welfare but different levels and strengths of movement activity. It also seems to reify the new in new social movements, overlooking the considerable overlay between their properties and those of the old social movements of both past and present. And, of course, it has little to say about the new 'new' social movements of less industrialized societies or of the former state socialist world.

An important heritage of the 1960s movements was to underscore the remarkable diffusion of contentious collective action among a variety of social groups and nation-states in broad cycles of protest that appeared to follow a dynamic that was not predictable from either macrosocietal trends or from state policies (Tarrow 1994). Analysts have also observed a growing appearance of hybrid forms of interest group/social movement-type organizations which combine a capacity for contentious collective action with more traditional lobbying and educational activities.

McCarthy and Zald (1977) called these new forms of movement 'professional movement organizations', but they often encompass part-time and amateur activists using the widely diffused organizational skills and communication resources available to quite ordinary people acting collectively. The capacity of these groups to overcome their paucity of resources, to use innovative forms of collective action, and to gain access to the media differentiates them from earlier forms of social movement (Klandermans 1992).

Two contradictory trends mark social movements: first, there has been so great a diffusion of movement activity that the world may be entering a stage in which collective action has become an accepted part of routine politics; but, second, there has been a spread of violent, intolerant and mutually exclusive movements like Islamic fundamentalism, the ethnic violence in Eastern Europe and anti-immigrant and racist movements. While the last phase of social movement research took its cues from the largely civil, national and purposive movements of the 1960s, the next phase will have to come to grips with these contradictory aspects of a movement society.

Sidney Tarrow
Cornell University

References

Eisinger, P. K. (1973) 'The conditions of protest behavior in American cities', *American Political Science Review* 67.

Fromm, E. (1969) *Escape from Freedom*, New York.

Inglehart, R. (1977) *The Silent Revolution: Changing Values and Political Styles among Western Publics*, Princeton, NJ.

Klandermans, B. (1992) 'The social construction of protest and multiorganizational fields', in A. Morris and C. McClurg Mueller (eds) *Frontiers in Social Movement Theory*, New Haven, CT.

McAdam, D. (1982) *The Political Process and the Development of Black Insurgency*, Chicago.

—— (1988) *Freedom Summer*, New York.

McCarthy, J. and Zald, M. (1977) 'Resource mobilization and social movements: a partial theory', *American Journal of Sociology* 82.

Melucci, A. (1989) *Nomads of the Present: Social Movements and Individual Needs in Contemporary Society*, Philadelphia, PA.

Oberschall, A. (1973) *Social Conflict and Social Movements*, Englewood Cliffs, NJ.

Offe, C. (1985) 'New social movements: challenging the boundaries of institutional politics', *Social Research* 52.

Olson, M. (1968) *The Logic of Collective Action*, Cambridge, MA.

Smelser, N. (1963) *The Theory of Collective Behavior*, New York.

Stein, L. von (1855) *Geschichte der Socialen Bewegung Frankreichs von 1789 bis auf unsere Tage*, Berlin.

Tarrow, S. (1994) *Power in Movement: Collective Action, Social Movements and Politics*, Cambridge, UK.

Tilly, C. (1978) *From Mobilization to Revolution*, Reading, MA.

—— (1986) *The Contentious French*, Cambridge, MA.

Tilly, C., Tilly, L. and Tilly, R. (1975) *The Rebellious Century, 1830–1930*, Cambridge, MA.

Touraine, A. (1988) *Return of the Actor: Social Theory in Postindustural Society*, Minneapolis, MN.

Zald, M. and Ash R. (1966) 'Social movement organizations: growth, decay and change', *Social Forces* 44.

Further reading

Evans, S. M. and Boyte, H. C. (1992) *Free Spaces: The Sources of Democratic Change in America*, Chicago.

Gamson, W. (1990) *The Strategy of Social Protest*, 2nd edn, Belmont, CA.

Gurr, T. R. (ed.) (1980) *Handbook of Political Conflict: Theory and Research*, New York.

Marx, G. T. and Wood J. L. (1975) 'Strands of theory and research in collective behavior', *Annual Review of Sociology*.

Zald, M. and McCarthy, J. (1987) *Social Movements in an Organizational Society*, New Brunswick, NJ.

See also: collective action; radicalism.

social networks

A social network is any articulated pattern of connections in the social relations of individuals, groups and other collectivities. The relations concerned may be interpersonal relations or they may be economic, political or other social relations. Social network analysis is a mathematical method for describing the structures exhibited by social networks. While it plays a role in the development of theories concerning social networks, social network analysis itself is method and not a theory.

Social network analysis originated in a non-technical form in social psychology and in anthropology, but it has now developed into an advanced area of mathematical applications. From the 1930s many social scientists began to take seriously the metaphors of the 'web' or 'fabric' of social life as ways of understanding social structure. From these textiles metaphors, aimed at understanding the interweaving and interlocking relations through which social actions were organized, the metaphor of the social network emerged. Radcliffe-Brown in anthropology and Jacob Moreno in social psychology began to employ this metaphor, and in Moreno's hands it evolved into the new discipline of sociometry and, from there, into group dynamics. It was Moreno who introduced the idea of representing a social network as a diagram (a 'sociogram') in which points (representing people) were connected by lines (representing their social relationships).

Radcliffe-Brown's ideas were taken up by W. Lloyd Warner in his research into American communities and, in particular, in the experimental studies undertaken with Elton Mayo at the Hawthorne electrical plant in Chicago. In these Hawthorne experiments, the informal social relations of work groups were, once again, mapped in diagrammatic form. In Warner's community studies, such ideas as the 'clique' made their first appearance as ways of understanding the formation of cohesive groupings within a social network.

Until the 1950s, however, no distinct methodology of social network analysis existed, and the ideas remained metaphorical and programmatic. A beginning was made in the formalization of the network metaphor in the work of George Homans (1951), who tried to synthesize the results of anthropological and small group research, later recasting these ideas in the framework of exchange theory. It was in the hands of British social anthropologists, however, that the greatest strides were made. John Barnes, Elizabeth Bott and Clyde Mitchell were all associated, to varying degrees, with Max Gluckman's department at Manchester University and were heavily influenced by Siegfried Nadel. Nadel's (1957) pioneering work gave voice to earlier works by Barnes, Bott and Mitchell. Barnes (1954) explicitly used the network idea in reporting his fieldwork on a Norwegian fishing village, Bott (1957) analysed kinship and friendship networks of married couples in London, and Mitchell (1969) undertook and supervised research on urban social networks in Central Africa. In the work of Mitchell, such ideas as 'density', 'durability' and 'reachability' were used to analyse the structure of social networks in formal terms.

The major breakthrough in social network analysis occurred in the USA during the 1960s, when a number of sociologists associated with Harrison White at Harvard began to use sophisticated mathematics and computing techniques to examine social networks. Many of these studies concerned interlocking directorships in business, but their studies ranged over such areas as the search for work and the search for illegal abortions (Wellman and Berkowitz 1988). The development of computer technology and the easier availability of computers allowed formal network techniques to be more widely employed in numerous areas, and a number of standard packages are now available. Despite this proliferation of formal and quantitative techniques, much qualitative research on social networks is still undertaken.

The basis of many ideas in network analysis is the mathematical theory of graphs, though ideas from algebraic topology and multidimensional scaling are also employed. Fundamental to the method is the idea of a social network as comprising points connected by lines, and the pattern of lines connecting the points can be represented in a matrix ready for mathematical processing. The principal measures that can be used are those of density, centrality, components, cliques, blocks, and various ideas of social distance. The basic techniques and measures are fully discussed in Scott (1991).

John Scott
University of Essex

References

Barnes, J. A. (1954) 'Class and committee in a Norwegian island parish', *Human Relations* 7.
Bott, E. (1957) *Family and Social Network*, London.
Homans, G. (1951) *The Human Group*, London.
Mitchell, J. C. (ed.) (1969) *Social Networks in Urban Situations*, Manchester.
Nadel, S. F. (1957) *The Theory of Social Structure*, Glencoe, IL.
Scott, J. P. (1991) *Social Network Analysis: A Handbook*, London.
Wellman, B. and Berkowitz, S. D. (eds) (1988) *Social Structures*, Cambridge, UK.

See also: communication networks; methods of social research.

social problems

The study of social problems has undergone a major and exciting shift in direction since the 1970s. The field was once dominated by approaches that treated social problems as objective and observable aspects of reality. Social problems were defined as conditions that are undesirable, unjust, dangerous, offensive or in some way threatening to the smooth functioning of society. The primary concern for those adopting an objectivist or realist approach was to identify such conditions and to get at the underlying forces contributing to the problem, often with a view to recommending ameliorative action.

Since the 1970s an alternative perspective has emerged. 'Social constructionism' (as it is generally called) starts from the premise that what gets viewed as a social problem is a matter of definition. Many of the conditions and behaviours that are now regarded as social problems were not always considered problematic. Parents once had the right to discipline their children as they saw fit. We now regard certain forms of discipline as child abuse. Date rape, the environmental crisis, drunk driving, homelessness and AIDS have all become an integral part of public consciousness and debate, yet until recently were unnamed or unnoticed. Other conditions and behaviours such as homosexuality and pre-marital or extramarital sex might have been considered social problems in the past but are now less likely to be viewed in these terms. These examples show that our experiences and interpretations of conditions change and that what constitutes a social problem is essentially a subjective judgement. If this is the case, how can social problems be studied?

Rather than focusing on objective conditions, constructionists direct attention to the social process by which conditions come to be seen as problems. In *Constructing Social Problems*, a book that has been described as a 'watershed in the development of the contemporary sociology of social problems' (Miller and Holstein 1989: 2), Spector and Kitsuse (1977) encouraged sociologists to abandon the notion of social problems as a kind of *condition* and suggested in its place a conception of social problems as an *activity*. They defined social problems as the activities of groups expressing grievances and making claims about putative conditions. The task for sociologists of social problems, they suggested, was not to evaluate or assess such claims but to account for claims-making activity and its results. Indeed, to guard against the tendency to slip back into an analysis of conditions, Spector and Kitsuse insisted that all assumptions about the objective conditions, including assumptions about their very existence, be suspended. To the extent that sociologists address the conditions themselves, they become participants in, rather than analysts of, the process they should be studying. This orientation to the study of social problems and especially the concept of 'claims making' have become the heart of the constructionist approach. In contrast to objectivists, then, who look at social conditions, their causes and solutions, constructionists are interested in the claims making about conditions, the ways in which meanings concerning undesirable conditions are produced and the responses that these activities generate.

The significance of this new thrust in the study of social problems is not only that it has given sociologists and other social scientists a way to deal with the subjective nature of social problems, but also that in so doing it has provided a distinctive subject matter for the field. The traditional objectivist approaches produced analyses of social conditions bound together by nothing more than the analyst's assessment of these conditions as undesirable. The conditions themselves had little in common, so that an understanding of any one condition contributed little to an understanding of others. In conceptualizing the field in terms of claims-making activity, constructionism provides a separate focus, a specific set of questions to guide research, and the framework for building a theory of *social problems* as distinct from theories about undesirable *conditions* (Best 1989: xvii; Schneider 1985: 210).

Since its emergence, the constructionist perspective has revitalized the study of social problems. It has generated a large body of empirical work examining claims-making efforts around issues ranging from prostitution, missing children, smoking, coffee drinking, sexual harassment, and toxic work environments to homosexuality, AIDS, teenage drinking, rock music, the marketing of infant food formulas in the Third World, and child, spousal and elderly abuse. The literature covers not only contemporary issues but also historical efforts such as the construction of margarine as a social problem in the nineteenth century and the early eugenics campaigns against impoverished women. Increasingly there are studies that look at the social problems process in cross-cultural contexts. A prominent theme since the early 1980s is the increasing 'medicalization' of social problems. Medicalization refers to the tendency to view undesirable conditions and behaviours as medical problems and/or to seek medical solutions or controls (Conrad and Schneider 1980). Constructionists have examined the medicalization of such conditions as alcoholism, drug addiction, cult membership, academic underachievement, crime control, compulsive gambling, sudden infant death, transsexualism and physician impairment. (Most of these studies have been published in the journal *Social Problems*; see also the JAI research annual *Perspectives on Social Problems*; Best 1989; Schneider and Kitsuse 1984 for collections; for a selective review, see Schneider 1985.)

The ever-growing number of case studies is providing the field with a strong foundation for theorizing about the unique role played by public agencies, government, social movements, the media, 'experts' including social scientists, and other participants in the social problems process, the rhetorical strategies and vernacular resources (Ibarra and Kitsuse 1993) that claims makers use, and the consequences of claims making in terms of who gains ownership over social problems and what policies and institutionalized procedures they establish to deal with them.

The constructionist approach to social problems has also generated lively theoretical debates about the assumptions that the approach makes, the way it is applied, and the future directions that it might take. Much of the debate has centred around the extent to which sociologists have remained true to the original formulation of the approach with its requirement that any reference whatever to objective conditions be avoided. Some sociologists have made the effort to maintain complete impartiality with respect to the validity of claims and the nature of the conditions about which claims are made, restricting their analyses solely to the definitional activities and interpretations of claims makers. Others do not see the need for such a strict interpretation and allow themselves to challenge the truth value of claims they 'know' to be false (Gusfield 1985; Rafter 1992). There are disagreements about whether the radically subjectivist position that Spector and Kitsuse (1977) called for is desirable or even possible (Best 1989; Troyer 1992; Woolgar and Pawluch 1985). From those working outside a constructionist perspective there are still questions about the real social problems that have an existence independent from how they might be seen and the moral obligation social scientists have to speak out and even to act against conditions they consider to be unjust (Eitzen 1984). Despite these debates, what remains clear is that the constructionist approach has been and will probably continue to be a productive source of social problems theorizing and research.

Dorothy Pawluch
McMaster University

References

Best, J. (ed.) (1989) *Images of Issues: Typifying Contemporary Social Problems*, New York.

Conrad, P. and Schneider, J. W. (1980) *Deviance and Medicalization: From Badness to Sickness*, St Louis, MO.

Eitzen, S. (1984) 'Teaching social problems', *Society for the Study of Social Problems Newsletter* 16.

Gusfield, J. R. (1985) 'Theories and hobgoblins', *Society for the Study of Social Problems Newsletter* 17.

Ibarra, P. R. and Kitsuse, J. I. (1993) 'Vernacular constituents of moral discourse: an interactionist proposal for the study of social problems', in G. Miller and J. A. Holstein (eds) *Constructionist Controversies: Issues in Social Problems Theory*, New York.

Miller, G. and Holstein, J. A. (1989) 'On the sociology of social problems', in J. A. Holstein and G. Miller (eds) *Perspectives on Social Problems*, vol. 1, Greenwich, CT.

Rafter, N. H. (1992) 'Some consequences of strict constructionism', *Social Problems* 39.

Schneider, J. W. (1985) 'Social problems theory: the constructionist view', *Annual Review of Sociology* 11.

Schneider, J. W. and Kitsuse, J. I. (eds) (1984) *Studies in the Sociology of Social Problems*, Norwood, NJ.

Spector, M. and Kitsuse, J. I. (1977), *Constructing Social Problems*, New York.

Troyer, R. (1992) 'Some consequences of contextual constructionism', *Social Problems*, 39.

Woolgar, S. and Pawluch, D. (1985) 'Ontological gerrymandering: the anatomy of social problems explanations', *Social Problems*, 32.

Further reading

Holstein, J. A. and Miller, G. (eds) (1993) *Reconsidering Constructionism: Debates in Social Problems Theory*, New York.

See also: crime and delinquency; deviance; domestic violence; mental health; suicide; violence.

social psychology

Social psychology is the study of the nature, functions and phenomena of social behaviour and of the mental experience of individuals in social contexts. It includes the study of social effects on aspects of behaviour and mental experience that are studied more generally in other branches of psychology. It also includes a number of psychological phenomena that do not arise, or in some cases cannot even be delineated, in individuals outside of their social contexts. Among these distinctively social psychological phenomena are aggression and anger, altruism and helping behaviour, social attitudes and persuasion, attraction and social relationships, attribution and social cognition, bargaining and negotiation, conformity and social influence processes, co-operation and competition, group decision making, group dynamics, language and speech, leadership and group performance, non-verbal communication and body language, obedience to authority, prejudice and intergroup conflict, self-presentation and impression management, sex roles, sexual behaviour, social learning and socialization.

Most authorities agree that social psychology is the biochemistry of the social sciences, a field lying between sociology and individual psychology. The field is in this sense interstitial, and it plays a pivotal role as a major social science discipline. In its theories and research, social psychology provides vital information about how social factors influence individual thoughts, feelings and actions.

Although there remain a number of highly resonant pockets of overlapping interest in sociology, most of the research literature and most of the recent texts in social psychology have been written by psychologists. It is also the case that the early development of social psychology was dominated by theories and research generated in the USA. Many of the seminal figures behind this array of contributions did, however, emigrate from Europe in the 1930s: they included Brunswik, Heider, Katona, Lazarsfeld and Lewin. Under the stimulus of the European Association of Experimental Social Psychology (founded in 1967), there has been considerable momentum towards redressing the imbalance represented by the pre-eminence of the USA. The European tradition of social psychology has tended to place more emphasis on such non-experimental approaches as discourse analysis, social representations research, and various qualitative research methodologies, in addition to experimental social psychology.

Social psychology evolved out of a recognition of human diversity within cultural uniformity. It focuses on choices and behavioural decisions among the competing options that confront us all in complex contemporary societies, and on the rich complexity of human social life. It has become a field that, more than any other, deals with the psychology of everyday life.

Historical outline

In the mid-1950s, Gordon Allport (1954) argued that most of the major problems of concern to contemporary social psychologists were recognized as problems by social philosophers long before psychological questions were joined to scientific methodology. Perhaps the most fundamental question was posed by Comte: how can people simultaneously be the cause and the consequence of society? Although many textbook authors conveniently identify the birth date of social psychology as 1908, when two influential early texts by McDougall and Ross were published, in a very real sense the field began to cohere and develop its own identity only in the mid-1930s and did not really take on momentum until after the Second World War. This coherence and subsequent momentum depended largely on the development of genuinely social theories and methods, the most influential early examples of which were the contributions of Kurt Lewin in the late 1930s and early 1940s.

Partly through sustained advocacy and partly through example, Lewin championed the possibilities of experimentation in social psychology. His experimental studies of autocratic, democratic and *laissez-faire* leadership atmospheres (with Lippitt and White in 1939) showed how complex situational variables could be manipulated, validated, and shown to produce distinctive but orderly consequences. Lewin hoped to solve the problems of generalizing from the laboratory to the 'real world' by advocating not only the linkage of experimentation · to theory but also the parallel conduct of laboratory and field experimentation on conceptually cognate problems.

Although there would be wide agreement that Kurt Lewin deserves the title of the father of *experimental* social psychology, there were many other influences gathering under the social psychology umbrella during the 1920s and 1930s in the USA. These included a sustained series of empirical studies on group problem solving, the invention by Thurstone and Chave (1929) and Likert (1932) of ingenious attitude measurement techniques, and the development of respondent sampling and survey research methodologies.

The central identity of social psychology was to remain anchored in the experimental approach. One of Lewin's students, Leon Festinger, exemplified Lewin's emphasis on going back and forth between the laboratory and the field, and showed in particular how experimentation made sense only when it was wedded to theory. Between the mid-1940s and the mid-1960s, when he was active as a social psychologist, Festinger (1954; 1957) developed two theories that had a profound impact on the field. The first was a theory of 'social comparison processes', a detailed set of postulates and propositions concerning the consequences for social interaction of people's need for the kinds of information about themselves and the outer world that only other people could provide. The second was a theory of 'cognitive dissonance', which portrayed the various mental and behavioural manoeuvres by which people attempt to maintain and restore cognitive consistency. The power of this theory was greatly enhanced by Festinger's recognition that some cognitions are more resistant to change than others, and that behavioural commitment is a potent source of such resistance. This recognition permitted rather precise predictions to be made concerning the form that dissonance reduction would take in different situations, in particular that changes would usually be observed in the least resistant cognition. The ideas informing both of these theories remain important in much current social psychological thinking and have become a part of our cultural wisdom. Equally important, perhaps, the voluminous research generated by the theory of cognitive dissonance provided a clear example of coherent progress through experimental research in social science, research yielding cumulative insights that helped to refine and amplify the theory that inspired it.

Just as enthusiasm for investigating dissonance phenomena began to wane in the late 1960s, a very different kind of theoretical orientation became prominent in social psychology. This was the 'attributional approach' to social cognition, an approach pioneered by Fritz Heider and identified with his seminal treatment of the *Psychology of Interpersonal Relations* (1958). The basic premise of the attributional approach is that people are motivated to understand behaviour, and readily do so by viewing it within a meaningful causal context. Our responses to others, in other words, are a function of the causes we attribute to explain their behaviour. Although initially the focus of attribution theory was almost exclusively on the perception of other people, Kelley (1967) and Bem (1967) extended the attributional orientation to include self-perception. The perception of our own inner dispositions and emotions may sometimes be mediated by our causal evaluations of our own behaviour, taking into account relevant features of the situational context.

As the attributional orientation flourished in the early 1970s, it fed and was fed by a broad revival of interest in *social cognition*. Social psychology (at least since the subjectivism championed by W. I. Thomas) has always been interested in the ways in which people interpret their social environments, but an emphasis on detailed analyses of information processing and social cognition has become more dominant since the late 1980s (see e.g. Fiske and Taylor 1991). The influence of the attributional approach has been reflected in a concern with attributional biases and errors in the application of inference strategies (Nisbett and Ross 1980; Schneider 1994).

While these developments in social cognition were occurring within the mainstream of experimental social psychology, some social psychologists continued to concentrate on the traditional problems of social influence and group processes. Asch's (1956) classic studies of conformity and Milgram's (1974) research into obedience to authority have become standard textbook topics. In different ways, their findings showed the remarkable sensitivity of normal adults to social influence pressures. The nature of group processes was especially informed by Thibaut and Kelley's (1959) analysis of outcome exchanges in dyads and larger groups. This analysis capitalized on the contingency matrices of game theory, as well as building on both reinforcement and social comparison theories within psychology. It provided a rich and provocative framework for dealing with power relations, roles, and the development of norms, and it also influenced the development of the distinctively European social identity theory of intergroup relations. Many publications since the 1960s have dealt with complex interpersonal conflict situations that might be resolved through bargaining and negotiation. Throughout this period, also, a steady stream of articles has appeared shedding light on such social phenomena as aggression, helping behaviour, attitude change, jury decision making, crowding, social discrimination, sex-role stereotypes, the impact of television, and a variety of other applied topics. More comprehensive historical overviews – both general and within specific content areas – may be found in the *Handbook of Social Psychology* (Lindzey and Aronson 1985) and *Advances in Experimental Social Psychology* (Zanna 1990; 1991; 1992; 1994).

Current status of the field

Any brief characterization of such a complex discipline must be arbitrary and selective in many respects. It is nevertheless possible to venture a few generalizations on the current status of the field that would probably recruit a reasonable consensus among social psychologists. The emphasis on experimentation has been buffeted by critical winds from several directions. Some critics have concluded that the problem of generalizing from artificial laboratory situations is insurmountable, and that there is no way to extrapolate meaningfully from the historical and contextual particularities of any

given experiment. Other critics have been concerned with the ethics of those deceptive cover stories that used to be common in social psychological experiments but have become much less so with the tightening up in the USA, Britain, and elsewhere of ethical guidelines for the conduct of research with human subjects. Still others are bothered by the treatment of research subjects as manipulable objects rather than autonomous agents with whom one negotiates appropriate explanations for behaviour. Finally, there are those who feel that experimentation implies a highly restrictive form of one-way causation, misrepresenting the normal processes of situation selection and movement through complex feedback loops in which the behaviour of actors is both causal and caused.

Although many of these criticisms raise vital concerns, neither singly nor in combination are they likely to relegate the experimental approach to a secondary position in the armamentarium of social psychology. The viability of the experimental approach may be even more assured as its practitioners more clearly realize its particular strengths and its limitations. Even if the generalization problem seems insurmountable, on occasion, the design of experiments are often useful in facilitating and disciplining conceptual thought. There is no doubt, however, that non-experimental approaches will continue to make important contributions to social psychology.

The current flowering of cognitive social psychology seems to be producing new intellectual alliances and breaking down old boundaries between general experimental and social psychology. Certainly social psychologists are borrowing paradigms from the traditions of general research on attention, memory and thinking; cognitive psychologists in, turn are showing greater sensitivity to the influences of social factors. In a similar fashion, social psychological theory has shed light on such clinical phenomena as depression, alcohol and drug abuse, obesity, and a range of problems associated with symptom labelling. Although social psychology may in some respects play the role of a gadfly within the social sciences, borrowing here and lending there, it is not likely to lose its special identity as the one field especially concerned with the details of interpersonal influence. During the 1980s, the pendulum seemed to swing away from a concern with social interdependence and group phenomena towards a concern with individual information processing, but many cognitive psychologists later began to move away from the entirely non-social implications of the information-processing metaphor. Here there seems to be some divergence between the more 'individualistic' Americans and the more 'groupie' Europeans. It would be interesting if the more blatantly *social* psychology of the Europeans influenced an American revival of interest in groups. This seems to be an old story in social psychology: the study of individuals must be informed by a clear understanding of the matrices of social interdependence within which they function; the study of groups must comprehend the cognitive and motivational processes of group members. The tension between these two focuses, in the long run, may be what keeps the field on its relatively straight track, in spite of temporary deviations in course.

Edward E. Jones
formerly, Princeton University

Andrew M. Colman
University of Leicester

References

Allport, G. W. (1954) 'The historical background of modern social psychology', in G. E. Lindzey (ed.) *Handbook of Social Psychology*, 1st edn, vol. I, Cambridge, MA.

Asch, S. E. (1956) 'Studies of independence and conformity: a minority of one against a unanimous majority', *Psychological Monographs* 70.

Bem, D. J. (1967) 'Self-perception: an alternative interpretation of cognitive dissonance phenomena', *Psychological Review* 74.

Festinger, L. (1954) 'A theory of social comparison processes', *Human Relations* 7.

—— (1957) *A Theory of Cognitive Dissonance*, Evanston, IL.

Fiske, S. T. and Taylor, S. E. (1991) *Social Cognition*, 2nd edn, New York.

Heider, F. (1958) *The Psychology of Interpersonal Relations*, New York.

Kelley, H. H. (1967) 'Attribution theory in social psychology', *Nebraska Symposium on Motivation* 14.

Lewin, K., Lippitt, R. and White, R. K. (1939) 'Patterns of aggressive behavior in experimentally created "social climates"', *Journal of Social Psychology* 10.

Likert, R. (1932) 'A technique for the measurement of attitudes', *Archives of Psychology* 140.

Lindzey, G. E. and Aronson, E. (eds) (1985) *Handbook of Social Psychology*, 3rd edn, 2 vols, New York.

McDougall, W. (1908) *An Introduction to Social Psychology*, London.

Milgram, S. (1974) *Obedience to Authority: An Experimental View*, New York.

Nisbett, R. E. and Ross, L. (1980) *Human Inference: Strategies and Shortcomings of Social Judgment*, Englewood Cliffs, NJ.

Ross, E. A. (1908) *Social Psychology: An Outline and a Source Book*, New York.

Schneider, D. J. (1994) 'Attribution and social cognition', in A. M. Colman (ed.) *Companion Encyclopedia of Psychology*, vol. 2, London.

Thibaut, J. W. and Kelley, H. H. (1959) *The Social Psychology of Groups*, New York.

Thurstone, L. L. and Chave, E. J. (1929) *The Measurement of Attitude*, Chicago, IL.

Zanna, M. P. (ed.) (1990, 1991, 1992, 1994) *Advances in Experimental Social Psychology*, vols 23–6, San Diego, CA.

See also: aggression and anger; altruism; attitudes; conformity; group dynamics; non-verbal communication; norms; prejudice; self-concept; sensation and perception; stereotypes.

social research methods *see* methods of social research

social science

Social science is the ambitious concept to define the set of disciplines of scholarship which deal with aspects of human society. The singular implies a community of method and approach which is now claimed by few; thus the plural, social sciences, seems more appropriate. The social sciences include economics, sociology (and anthropology) and political science. At their boundaries, the social sciences reach into the study of the individual (social psychology) and of nature (social biology, social geography). Methodologically, they straddle normative (law, social philosophy, political theory) and historical approaches (social history, economic history). In terms of university departments, the social sciences have split up into numerous areas of teaching and research, including not only the central disciplines, but also such subjects as industrial relations, international relations, business studies and social (public) administration.

The term social science(s) does not sit easily in the universe of scholarship, especially not in English. *Sciences sociales* and *Sozialwissenschaften* are somewhat happier expressions, though they too have suffered from being interpreted either too widely or too narrowly. Frequently, social science is meant to define either sociology, or synthetic social theory only. Everywhere, the implied analogy to the natural sciences has been contested. In 1982, the British government challenged the name of the publicly financed Social Science Research Council, arguing *inter alia* that 'social studies' would be a more appropriate description for disciplines of scholarship which cannot justly claim to be scientific. (The council is now called Economic and Social Research Council.)

The history of the concept does not help much in trying to make sense of it. Social sciences have grown out of moral philosophy (as the natural sciences emerged from natural philosophy). It has often been observed that their separate identity owes much to the great revolutions of the eighteenth century, the Industrial (English) and the bourgeois (French) Revolutions. Among the Scottish moral philosophers of that time, the study of political economy was always coupled with that of wider social issues (though not called social science). With the ascendancy of positivism in the early nineteenth century, especially in France, positive philosophy, or social science, took the place of moral philosophy. Positivism, according to Auguste Comte (1830–42; 1844), emphasizes the factual as against the speculative, the useful as against the idle, the certain as against the indecisive, the precise as against the vague, the positive as against the negative or critical. It is thus both science in the sense of nineteenth-century materialism and prescription. Comte borrowed the term, *science social*, from Charles Fourier (1808) to describe the supreme synthetic discipline of the edifice of science. At the same time, he had no doubt that the method of social science (which he also called social physics) was in no way different from that of the natural sciences.

Five developments either stemming from Comte, or encouraged by different traditions, have helped confuse the methodological picture of the social sciences.

First, many of those who took the analogy to the natural sciences seriously engaged in social research. The great factual surveys of Charles Booth in Britain, and of the Chicago School in the USA, bear witness to this trend. Frederic Le Play had started a similar tradition in France. In Germany, the *Verein für Socialpolitik* adopted the same research techniques. Such often large-scale descriptive enterprises are the precursors of modern ('empirical') social research and analysis.

Second, science, of course, is more than fact-finding. Thus a natural science notion of theoretical social science has informed at least two of the heroes of sociology, Emile Durkheim (1895) and Vilfredo Pareto (1916). Durkheim in particular was impressed by the need to study 'social facts', whereas Pareto stimulated both metatheoretical insights and specific theories. They have had few followers.

Third, by the turn of the century, a methodological dichotomy was born which gave rise to another aspect, or notion, of social science. Against the ambitions of those who tried to emulate the natural sciences in the study of social phenomena, the German School of thought gained ground, according to which social phenomena do not lend themselves to such rigid analysis, but require a different approach, one of *Verstehen*, of empathy and understanding. Max Weber (1921) straddles different approaches, but introduced into social science what were later called 'hermeneutic' or 'phenomenological' perspectives.

Fourth, it will readily be seen that all three approaches mentioned so far are most closely associated with the subject of sociology and its history. Indeed, economics soon began to go its own way. Ever since the decline of the German historical ('romantic') school of economists, it developed as the discipline which of all the social sciences most nearly deserves the name, science. Economic knowledge is to a considerable extent cumulative; theories are developed and tested, if not always against reality, then at least against models and their assumptions. *Verstehende* economics, even descriptive economics, have become the exception.

Finally, Max Weber also insisted on another distinction which defines the fifth aspect of social science, that between knowledge, however gained, and values. Prescription and description (or theory) belong to different universes of discourse. The distinction was explosive at the time (*Werturteilsstreit*), and continues to be that, although political theory, moral philosophy, and jurisprudence have gone their own ways, and the study of social policy has shifted from the prescriptive to the analytical.

These then are the disparate methodological elements of social science: empirical social science, descriptive in character if not in intention, increasingly sophisticated in its techniques which are themselves manifold; rare attempts at developing theories in the strict sense, attempts which are neither universally recognized nor cumulative; *verstehende Sozialwissenschaft*, perhaps best described as the historical analysis of the present, often full of empirical data as well as attempts at explanation, the bulk of social science; economics; and explicitly prescriptive social theory, often political in substance and intent.

Looking at the social sciences as a whole, this is quite a pell-mell, and is perceived as such. However, all attempts to produce a new synthesis have failed. The most ambitious examples are those by Karl Popper (1945; 1959 [1934]) and Talcott Parsons (1937; 1951; 1956). Popper insists that there is one logic of scientific inquiry. It is the logic of progress by falsification: we advance hypotheses (theories), and progress by refuting accepted hypotheses through research, that is, by trial and error. Popper did not primarily have the social sciences in mind, but it is here that his language has created havoc. Everybody now 'hypothesizes', though few such projects are even capable of falsification. More importantly, Popper's logic, if misinterpreted as practical advice to scholars, leads to an arid notion of scholarly activity, especially in the social sciences. If hypothetico-deductive progress is all there is, then 99 per cent of all social science is useless. Popper's logic of scientific enquiry provides but one measure of advancement; it is not a litmus test for distinguishing between what is and what is not social science. Indeed, Popper himself has written important works of social, or at any rate social-philosophical, analysis.

Talcott Parsons's attempted synthesis is even more ambitious in that it is addressed to the theoretical substance of social science. Throughout his numerous abstract analyses, Parsons has argued that the substance of social science is one, social action, and that even the incarnations of social action stem from the same general model, the social system. The social system has four subsystems: the economy, the polity, the cultural system, and the 'integrative' systems. Economics, political science, the study of culture and that of social integration (sociology) are thus related, and interdependent, disciplines. Descending from the social system, all subsystems require similar analysis. Parsons's claims have had little effect on social sciences other than sociology. Economists in particular have largely ignored them. Their central weakness may be that while society can be looked at in this way, it need not be. In any case, different social sciences have continued to go their own way. Have they progressed? It would be vain to deny this, though concepts of progress differ with different methods. At the same time, the social sciences have probably given us *multa non multum*. Perhaps, a more modest approach is indicated today. In the absence of a synthesis, it is desirable to let a hundred flowers bloom. Each of the social sciences will continue to contribute to knowledge. It is not unlikely that important developments will occur at the boundaries of different disciplines. It is also probable that most social sciences will incorporate several of the approaches which have split the subjects. Though the search for synthesis will never cease, in fact the social sciences will for some time remain a variegated and somewhat disparate group of intellectual endeavours.

Ralf Dahrendorf
St Antony's College, Oxford

References

Comte, A. (1830–42) *Cours de philosophie positive*, Paris. (English translation, *The Positive Philosophy of Auguste Comte*, London, 1896.)
—— (1844) *Discours sur l'ésprit positif*, Paris. (English translation, *Discourse on the Positive Spirit*, 1903. London.)
Durkheim, E. (1895) *Les Règles de la méthode scientifique*, Paris. (English translation, *The Rules of Sociological Method*, Chicago, 1938.)
Fourier, C. (1808) *Théorie des quatre mouvements et des destinées générales*, Lyon.
Pareto, V. (1916) *Trattato die sociologia generale*, Rome. (English translation, *The Mind and Society: Treatise on General Sociology*, 4 vols, London, 1935.)
Parsons, T. (1937) *The Structure of Social Action*, New York.
—— (1951) *The Social System*, Glencoe, IL.
Parsons, T. and Smelser, N. (1956) *Economy and Society*, New York.
Popper, K. (1945) *The Open Society and its Enemies*, London.
—— (1959 [1934]) *The Logic of Scientific Discovery*, New York. (Original edn, *Logik der Forschung*, Vienna.)
Weber, M. (1921), *Wirtschaft und Gesellschaft*, Tübingen. (English translation, *Economy and Society*, New York, 1968.)

social skills and social skills training

The meaning and assessment of social competence

A socially competent person is someone who possesses the necessary social skills to produce the desired effects on other people in social situations. These may be the professional skills of teaching, selling, interviewing and so on, or the everyday skills of communicating effectively, being persuasive, and maintaining social relationships. Social competence can be assessed by objective measures of success, for example, in selling, or self-rating scales, such as for assertiveness, or the amount of difficulty experienced in different situations. Social skills can also be assessed by ratings made by supervisors or others. Interviews can find out more details about areas of social difficulty. Role-playing in laboratory or clinic can provide information about specific areas of deficit. In the case of clients for social skills training (SST), the particular goals of treatment can then be decided upon.

Social skills are important because of the effects which they have. In everyday life lack of skills can lead to social isolation, breakdown of marriage, and unhappiness. At work the lack of skills results in ineffectiveness on the part of supervisors, teachers, and anyone whose work involves dealing with people.

Social inadequacy of different degrees is widespread. Among children, some are isolated, others aggressive. Over 50 per cent of students say they often feel lonely, 15–20 per cent seriously so, and 40 per cent of students say that they are shy. Between 7 and 10 per cent of adults are handicapped by an inability to establish or sustain normal relationships or cope with common social situations. Among outpatient neurotics the corresponding figure is 20 per cent, while for hospitalized psychotics it is probably 100 per cent. Failures of social competence can lead to rejection and social isolation, and ultimately to the development of anxiety, depression and other symptoms of mental disorder.

For any particular professional social skill, such as selling, teaching or supervising working groups, some people are far less effective than others. Some salespersons may sell 25 per cent of what the better ones sell, poor supervisors may generate four times as much absenteeism and labour turnover, and much less output than better supervisors. Among people who go to work abroad, for example, for those going to parts of the Middle or Far East for commercial firms or the Peace Corps, as many as 60 per cent may fail, and return home early.

There are a number of basic components of social skills, which may need to be trained differently, such as rewardingness, assertiveness, non-verbal communication, verbal communication skills, empathy and co-operation, social problem solving, self-presentation, and the skills of different situations and relationships.

Role-playing is now the most widely used training method. An area of skill is briefly described, such as how to combine a principle with an example (teaching) or how to make someone talk more (interviewing). This is followed by a demonstration, live or on film ('modelling'). The contents of this teaching depend on the results of research into the most effective way of performing the skill, for example, which teaching methods get the best results. A trainee then role-plays in front of video cameras for 5–10 minutes, with another trainee, or with a prepared stooge. Finally, there is a feedback – consisting of playback of video-tape, and comments from the trainer. Between sessions trainees are encouraged to try out the new skills (homework) and report back on how they got on.

Supplementary exercises for special aspects of social skills can also be used. These include training to send and receive non-verbal communications from face and voice, in the conduct of conversations, in appearance and other aspects of self-presentation, and the handling of particular situations and relationships. These specialized methods make use of research into, for example, non-verbal communication and conversational analysis.

Educational methods are a valuable addition to, but not a substitute for, more active methods of training. The 'Culture Assimilator' for intercultural skills consists of instruction on the situations which have been found to cause most difficulty in the other culture. Training for situation and relations can include instructions on the rules and other basic features, and can correct common misunderstandings.

The current extent of social skills training

SST is being increasingly used for neurotics, disturbed adolescents, depressives, alcoholics, drug addicts and prisoners, usually as part of a larger treatment package. Training usually consists of role-played sessions, once or twice a week, for one to one-and-a-half hours, in groups of four to ten with two trainers, sometimes combined with individual treatment.

SST is now widely used for people at work, especially teachers, interviewers, supervisors and managers, doctors and nurses, sales staff, police, and those going to work overseas. Training for everyday social skills is less readily available. However, in North America there is widespread assertiveness training, mainly for women, occasional training in heterosexual skills for students with 'minimal dating' problems, and training for making friends for young people who are lonely. While

Americans are very interested in assertiveness, British clients for SST are more interested in making friends.

The effectiveness of SST

Does it work? For socially inadequate neurotics, SST does a little better than behaviour therapy aimed to reduce anxiety: SST improves the skills, and may later reduce the anxiety. The worse the patients are, the more sessions are needed. Mental patients of all kinds can be helped by SST, preferably as part of a larger package.

Professional social skills, and intercultural skills, can be trained in quite a short course of role-playing – typically six sessions. Success is also found with training in marital skills.

However, it should be emphasized that most follow-up studies have been carried out on earlier and fairly simple versions of SST. Research has now made possible much more sophisticated training, such as that embodied in the various supplementary exercises listed earlier.

Michael Argyle
University of Oxford

Further reading

Hollin, C. R. and Trower, P. (eds) (1986) *Handbook of Social Skills Training*, 2 vols, Oxford.

L'Abate, L. and Milan, M. A. (eds) (1985) *Handbook of Social Skills Training and Research*, New York.

Spence, S. and Shepherd, G. (1983) *Developments in Social Skills Training*, London.

Trower, P., Bryant, B. and Argyle, M. (1978) *Social Skills and Mental Health*, London.

Wine, J. D. and Smye, M. D. (eds) (1981) *Social Competence*, New York.

See also: vocational and career development.

social structure and structuration

The idea that social structure can be studied as though it has formal attributes without reference to the agency of actors has had a strong influence on social thought and sociological theory. Until comparatively recently, it was taken to be an essential concept for sociology, although its deployment was very much conditioned by the strategic concerns of the theorist. By this is meant that for some practitioners, social structure is simply a background assumption made in the course of undertaking a theoretical or empirical investigation, while for others, it constitutes the central focus of their theoretical commitment.

In the first instance, social science investigators expect to discover evidence of pattern and relationship in the social world. They may believe, for example, that crime rates have some kind of link to unemployment, although not necessarily claiming that this linkage or correlation reveals structure. Certainly, correlations are not unambiguous measures of structure, but without them it is not easy to see how a structurally informed analysis can proceed.

In the second instance, structure is often given a strong determinative causal status, albeit this formulation is sometimes softened by substituting structure for 'constraint'. A fully fledged structural theory does not allow much leeway for agency and intention. Individuals are structurally located, and this profoundly limits the range of their experience and behaviour. Not only is such a position inherently improbable, but also it fails to take into account the possibility that there may be more than one structure impinging on individuals. Moreover, different structures may make contradictory demands that severely subvert and disrupt a person's sense of her or his location. Indeed, any theorization of industrial society is inevitably concerned with the fragmentation and differentiation of structures, and the way in which they change in response to technological, economic and ecological factors.

Minimally, social structure may be conceived of as being a constraint on behaviour. What is at issue here is not constraint *per se*, but rather the alternative strategies used by practitioners to give it theoretical plausibility. For various interpretive and phenomenological sociologies, the problem of constraint is focused on the procedures used by social actors in order to produce a structured world. Social structures have no real existence, except in the minds of the actors who give them meaning. From this perspective, structural explanations are conceived of as having validity only in so far as they are experienced subjectively. Structures, therefore, are what actors say they are. If they influence practice, then this is because they are perceived as having some kind of reality, but a reality that is dependent, in the last analysis, on the 'constructions' of individuals. However, there are sociological positions that grant reality to structures. Durkheim, Marx, Althusser, Lévi-Strauss, among others, have all been associated with a strong view of structure, although Durkheimian and Marxist versions start from different premises.

The net result of this theoretical confrontation is conceptual confusion, often leading to the implicit acceptance of a reductive dualism in which one side or the other claims logical and empirical priority. While there have always been attempts to reconcile these positions, they have not been systematically explored in sociology. Giddens (1976; 1984; 1987) has attempted to remedy this by providing an analytical framework in which both structure and action are aspects of the same conceptual universe. In what he calls the 'duality of structure', both action and structure entail each other. Social actors, in the conduct of their everyday lives, actively produce meaning within settings that they themselves have given meaning to; simultaneously, they are influenced by the way in which these meanings have become routinized and reproduced in time and space. Put differently, social structure is produced and reproduced in the 'practices of' people in everyday activities.

Practices play a key role in Giddens's discussion. What people do and say has consequences for social structures. This is not to be taken to mean that their intentions must be included in the analysis, but rather to emphasize the fact that when people interact they bring into play resources, skills and knowledge that they have acquired in previous interactions. Social structuring practices, therefore, are always partly rooted in face-to-face encounters, but these encounters never take place in some kind of structureless void; they are mediated and affected by resources that already have social and cultural significance. In this respect structure is a dialectical process in which what people practice is also what they construct. This in essence is what structuration is about.

Structuration also involves the interfusion of intended and unintended consequences. What people want and do may result in the consolidation of what they do not want. This is a familiar enough theme in mainstream sociology, but in Giddens's frame of reference, it provides a fruitful way of suggesting that structures are resources that both enable and constrain people. Traditionally, most views of social structure have concentrated on its restrictive and constraining attributes. For Giddens this is completely to misunderstand how power and structure operate in social life. To insist on a social structure's negative aspect is to deny human beings any social potency. It is to claim that they cannot reflexively dissent from and actively oppose these constraints.

It may be objected that what Giddens is doing here is to underplay the significance of historical and global factors on social life, and that he overemphasizes the valency of practice. Whether this is the case is beyond the scope of such a short discussion, but a relevant question is whether his account does not itself sometimes slip back into stressing the logical priority of structure. Connell (1987), for example, argues that Giddens, and also Bourdieu, do not give themselves much leeway to 'let history in'. While Giddens's duality of structure notion helps us to retreat from our obsession with categorical models of social relationships, he nevertheless does not pay enough attention to the effect that practice has on practice. In the case of gender, for example, how does the divorce rate influence the practice of marriage counsellors? And how is this practice related to government policy and feminist theory and practice? In Giddens's defence it can be argued that structuration does involve the introduction of reflexivity into the very fabric of social constraints.

Arthur Brittan
University of York, UK

References

Connell, R. W. (1987) *Gender and Power*, Cambridge, UK.
Giddens, A. (1976) *New Rules of Sociological Method*, London.
—— (1984) *The Constitution of Society*, Cambridge, UK.
—— (1987) *Social Theory and Modern Sociology*, Cambridge, UK.

Further reading

Cohen, I. J. (1989) *Structuration Theory: Anthony Giddens and the Constitution of Social Life*, Basingstoke.
Craib, I. (1992) *Anthony Giddens*, London.

See also: Durkheim, Emile; Marx's theory of history and society; role; stratification.

social survey *see* public opinion polls; sample surveys

social welfare

The adjective 'economic' is perhaps more appropriate, since when it is discussed by economists, 'social' welfare encompasses goods and services but not wider social issues. The modern approach is a fusion of two earlier approaches, a rough-and-ready statistical approach and a finely-honed welfare analytic approach.

The statistical approach measures social welfare in terms of just two parameters: real income and its distribution. One's overall judgement is then to some degree subjective, depending upon how real income gains (or losses) are valued as against egalitarian losses (or gains). To capture the whole income distribution in one parameter is, of course, extremely arbitrary, but for many purposes (for example, cross-country comparisons) it is reasonably safe to take some measure of real income per head and an index of inequality like the Gini coefficient. The measurement of real income itself is not unambiguous because its composition changes over time as does its distribution. The composition aspect is intimately connected with both the theory of index numbers and the theory of consumer behaviour. To use current prices as weights for the different commodities is, however, a reasonable practical approximation to changes in real income. Distributional changes are more serious, and only in the rare case where real income had increased to the same degree for everyone could they be ignored. All this is essentially an elaboration of Pigou's double criterion that real income increase without the poor being worse off *or* that the poor be better off and real income not decrease.

It was thought for some time – by Kaldor and Hicks – that it would be desirable to use real income alone, without distributional judgements, to evaluate economic policies. This is because interpersonal comparisons were said to be 'unscientific'. The 'new welfare economics' advocated the use of a compensation principle: if adoption of a policy enabled the gainers to compensate the losers and still be better off, then the policy would bring an improvement. Later, due to Scitovsky, it had to be added that the losers could not then bribe the gainers to return to the original position. Controversy arose as to whether the principle was merely a test for real income increases or a criterion for improvement. Part of the difficulty lay in whether compensation was to be actual or merely hypothetical. In the 1950s, Little insisted, successfully, that distributional considerations would have to be reintroduced. Though the attempt to jettison distribution failed, there is still a feeling that real income is somehow more important and more fundamental, especially in the longer term (it is, after all, a *sine qua non*). The compensation principle was intended to be a test of economic efficiency from which it is not desirable to depart too far.

The other, welfare analytic, approach starts from the preferences of individuals rather than from aggregate income. Individual utilities are a function of individuals' goods and services, and social welfare is a function of individual utilities (Bergson 1938). Together with competitive theory, this construction enables one to draw out certain optimality properties of markets – this is especially so if lump-sum redistributions (almost impossible in practice) are permitted. Most of these propositions, except those to do with redistribution, are independent of distributional weights and therefore robust against distributional preferences. Whatever these preferences, efficiency requires equality of marginal rates of substitution in production and consumption. So if lump-sum redistributions are possible, social welfare is maximized under competition with distribution being a separate 'political' matter. Unfortunately the dichotomy cannot be sustained, and there are no truly simple rules for maximizing social welfare.

A second use of the welfare analytic approach which has so far proved to be strongly negative (though usefully so) is relating social choice to individual preferences. There should, it was felt, be some method for moving from the latter to the former. Arrow (1951) showed that no such transition rule was possible.

Starting from individual preference orderings, it is impossible to derive a social ordering without violating at least one of a number of perfectly reasonable axioms, for example, that the ordering be not imposed, not dictatorial, not restricted in domain, and so on. To give examples, a competitive mechanism has to be rejected because the domain is restricted to Pareto-improvements on the original allocation, and a Bergsonian welfare function because it would have to be imposed (by an economist?). Social choice cannot therefore be grounded in individual preferences except for relatively trivial cases.

The modern reaction to these two weaknesses of the welfare analytic approach (the impossibility of lump-sum redistributions or of acceptable transition rules) is to be very much more explicit about distributional judgements and interpersonal comparisons. Failing that, work on social choice remains barren and formal. Following Atkinson (1970) a great deal of technical work has been done on the relationships between social-welfare functions and indices of inequality. There is scope within the approach for a whole spectrum of value judgements running from a zero preference for equality to Rawlsian emphasis on the income of the poorest. The modern approach moves away from Arrow's assumption that we have only ordinal information about individuals, without reverting to crude utilitarianism. In the same spirit it ventures to make statements about equivalence between individuals and to compare 'needs'. Social welfare can then be indexed (always provisionally) by statistical measures which certainly carry recognized value judgements with them but have good foundations in consumer theory. The measures are a compromise between statistical convenience and (possibly sterile) theoretical purity.

David Collard
University of Bath

References

Arrow, K. J. (1951) *Social Choice and Individual Values*, New York.
Atkinson, A. B. (1970) 'On the measurement of inequality', *Journal of Economic Theory* 2.
Bergson, A. (1938) 'A reformulation of certain aspects of welfare economics', *Quarterly Journal of Economics* 52.

Further reading

Mishan, E. J. (1981) *Introduction to Normative Economics*, Oxford.
Sen, A. K. (1982) *Choice, Measurement and Welfare*, Oxford.

See also: poverty; social welfare policy; social work; welfare economics; welfare state.

social welfare policy

In the long boom succeeding the Second World War, social welfare policy was widely seen as the state's intervention in society to secure the well-being of its citizens. This progressivist interpretation of increasing social expenditure by the state was sustained by the writings of key post-war welfare theorists such as Titmuss (1950) and Marshall (1967). The former welcomed increasing collectivism as a necessary and desirable means of enhancing social integration; the latter saw in the developing British welfare state the extension of citizenship through the acquisition of social rights. The Beveridge-Keynes welfare state, which had been called into existence by the exigencies of war and the balance of social forces in the post-war situation, came to assume an ideological significance, both as the exemplar against which other welfare states were to be assessed, and also as an explanation of the development of the welfare state itself. This ideological construction had few means of accounting for developments in other countries such as the pioneering achievements in social policy in New Zealand, nor of specifically conservative political strategies such as those of Bismarck's Germany, in which social insurance was conceived of as a mechanism to weaken the working-class movement and inhibit the spread of socialist ideas. For that matter, its emphasis on the peculiarly British nature of the achievement led to difficulties in explaining the rather better performance by most indicators of Britain's new partners when it joined the European Community, a phenomenon which was received with some shock by British political culture.

Relatively early on in the post-war period, social democratic theorists such as Crosland (1956) acknowledged the significance of social welfare policy and the achievement of the full employment economy in modifying a basically capitalist social formation. None the less, redistribution was to be secured through growth, thus avoiding the political opposition of the rich – a strategy which was thrown into question as economic growth faltered and even declined. The significance of these policies for structuring sex-gender relations within the home and within the labour market was grasped very much more slowly (Wilson 1977). None the less, the achievement of the welfare state or welfare capitalism, as it has been variously termed, was aided by the discourse and practices of social policy in which 'need' was set as morally and administratively superior to the market as the distributive principle for welfare. Thus integral to the achievement of welfare capitalism and institutional welfare was a concept of need which stood as an antagonistic value to that of capitalism with its, at best, residual welfare.

Need was at the same moment emancipatory and constrained within the dominant social relations. In its emancipatory aspect, need fostered the language of rights, not only in theoretical writing but also within the popular demands of the new social movements which rose during the late 1960s and early 1970s within North America and Europe (Piven and Cloward 1971; Rose 1973). Aided by the 'rediscovery of poverty' in the 1960s (Abel-Smith and Townsend 1965; Harrington 1962), large-scale mobilization around income maintenance and housing exerted substantial pressure on governments to offer more, and more responsive, welfare provision. Thus, the new social movements shared with institutional welfare an opposition to mere residual welfare, but continuously sought to go beyond not only the level of existing provisions but also the organizational forms through which they were realized. Instead – and this tendency was to become magnified as the welfare movements were joined by the 1970s wave of feminism – existing forms of welfare were seen as coercive, inadequate and statist. In contrast, the oppositional forms developed by the movements themselves emphasized democratic accountability, and nonhierarchical ways of working. Freire's (1972) thesis of conscientization as the politically creative strategy for the poor in the Third World was shared by the new social movements as they sought to develop an alternative practice of welfare to what was usual in the old industrialized societies. At their most radical the new movements sought that society itself should be organized around the meeting of human need.

While the boom lasted, this critique of institutional welfare as statist and bureaucratic made relatively little impact on either mainstream social welfare policy thinking or on political culture: ideological support for a more or less institutional welfare overlaid the deeper antagonism between need and the market. The separation of need from market values was further facilitated by the separation between economic and social policy discourses. Social policy felt able to ignore economic policy since it was confident that Keynesian demand management techniques had delivered and would continue to deliver the precondition of the welfare state, namely, the full employment economy. Economists largely ignored the discussion of social welfare policy as of no interest to other than social ameliorists, until the crisis of the mid-1970s during which the loss of confidence in Keynesian techniques fostered a return to an endorsement of the market and an increasingly open opposition to state welfare expenditure (Friedman 1962). Where institutional welfare had seen expanded welfare policies as socially integrative, a radical political economy had emphasized their contribution to capital accumulation and social control

(Gough 1979; O'Connor 1973); now monetarism and the advent of a new right saw such expenditures as harming individualism and competitiveness and thus weakening the central dynamic of capitalism. With considerable populist skill the new right acknowledged the critique of the coercive character of public welfare, and offered an increase in personal liberty through rolling back the (welfare) state, restoring the market and the family as the paramount providers of welfare.

The very depth of the current crisis which has provided the conditions for the rise of the new right, none the less serves as a major constraint for its remedies. Global restructuring of manufacturing is associated with widespread and foreseeably long-term unemployment in the de-industrializing countries. Unemployment, averaging around 12 per cent in the OECD countries in 1982 and with few clear indications of a significant improvement, requires, even in the most residual conception of welfare, substantial expenditure for both maintenance and control of an expanding surplus population. This situation is aggravated by the large numbers of young people among the unemployed, among whom ethnic and racial minorities are over-represented.

Despite these political constraints, since 1975 most western governments have reduced the rate of growth of their social welfare budgets. Thus, up to 1975 the real rate of social expenditure growth in the seven largest OECD countries was no less than 8 per cent per annum (15 per cent growth at 1985 prices); between 1975 and 1981 the real rate was halved. While all countries have experienced difficulties in maintaining their social welfare budget in the face of the reduction of the growth of the overall economy, governments with a specifically anti-welfare ideology such as the USA and Britain have made substantial inroads. Thus, in the case of Britain an institutional system of welfare moves increasingly towards a residual model, particularly in the area of social security. The Nordic countries stand apart as the last bastion of the most highly developed expression of the old welfare state, although the mix of labour market and social policies through which they achieve this varies substantially between them. Given the double significance for women of the existence of the welfare state, as potential provider of both employment and services, it is perhaps not by chance that those Nordic countries with a continuing commitment to welfare have also an unusually high proportion of women representatives in their parliaments and upper houses. It is noteworthy that writers from these countries, such as Himmelstrand and his co-workers (1981), are taking an active part in the current international debate concerning the possible future direction open to a post-welfare state society. These writers seek to develop a theory which looks beyond welfare capitalism, to a new but very much more democratically based corporatism. Such post-welfare state theorists are typically not unsympathetic to the claims of the new social movements (Gorz 1982). However, they seem not to have fully appreciated the significance of feminist theorizing concerning the relationship between paid and unpaid labour within the development of the welfare state, and thus the advantage to the dominant gender of retaining the present arrangements. Thus, even though the precondition of the old welfare state, the full employment of one gender with welfare flowing through the man to the dependent family, no longer fits the actuality of either domestic or labour market structures, the ideological defence of those arrangements persists. Faced with the growing 'feminization of poverty' (Pearce 1978), and the profoundly segregated (by both occupation and between full and part-time employment) labour market, there is a serious question concerning the extent to which the needs of women are met by the new post-welfare state theorizing.

These are cautious, even sceptical, reflections on the debate around the welfare state and the place of social welfare policy (Glennister 1983). How far any of the new theories can offer to serve as the new fusion of the social and the economic the contemporary historical equivalent of the old welfare state of Keynes and Beveridge is not yet clear. What is clear, however, is that social welfare policy having spent its years of greatest growth relatively detached from economic policy has now been forcibly rejoined by circumstance. Together they occupy the centre of an intensely debated political arena.

Hilary Rose
University of Bradford

References

Abel-Smith, B. and Townsend, P. (1965) *The Poor and the Poorest*, London.
Crosland, A. (1956) *The Future of Socialism*, London.
Freire, P. (1972) *Cultural Action for Freedom*, Harmondsworth.
Friedman, M. (1962) *Capitalism and Freedom*, Chicago.
Glennister, H. (ed.) (1983) *The Future of the Welfare State*, London.
Gorz, A. (1982) *Farewell to the Working Class*, London.
Gough, I. (1979) *The Political Economy of Welfare*, London.
Harrington, M. (1962) *The Other America*, Harmondsworth.
Himmelstrand, U., Ahrne, G., Lundberg, L. and Lundberg, L. (1981) *Beyond Welfare Capitalism; Issues Actors and Social Forces in Societal Change*, London.
Marshall, T. H. (1967) *Social Policy*, 2nd edn, London.
O'Connor, J. (1973) *The Fiscal Crisis of the State*, New York.
Pearce, D. (1978) 'The feminization of poverty: women, work and welfare', *Urban and Social Change Review*.
Piven, F. F. and Cloward, R. (1971) *Regulating the Poor: The Functions of Public Welfare*, New York.
Rose, H. (1973) 'Up against the Welfare State: the claimant unions', in R. Miliband and J. Saville (eds) *The Socialist Register*, London.
Titmuss, R. M. (1950) *Problems of Social Policy*, London.
Wilson, E. (1977) *Women and the Welfare State*, London.

See also: human needs; human rights; poverty; social welfare; social work; welfare economics; welfare state.

social work

It is perhaps not surprising that the term social work, combining the rich ambiguity of 'social' with the misleading and somewhat deterrent simplicity of 'work', has undergone considerable change in usage since it first appeared in England towards the end of the nineteenth century. It was then used to describe a perspective applicable from a number of different occupations rather than to announce the arrival of a particular new occupation. This perspective derived from the serious reconsideration of the role of citizen, and it can be illustrated from the dedication of a book entitled *The Spirit of Social Work* (Devine 1911) to

social workers, that is to say, to every man and woman, who, in any relation of life, professional, industrial, political, educational or domestic; whether on salary or as a volunteer; whether on his own individual account or as a part of an organized movement, is working consciously, according to his light intelligently and according to his strength persistently, for the promotion of the common welfare.

(The fact that Devine was an American indicates the speed with which social work was exported to the USA and, thence, eventually to many other societies, developed and developing.)

This broadly brushed backcloth has been more or less evident in the twentieth century as social workers have attempted to claim a role that is specialized and professional. It is perhaps one reason why an agreed and satisfactory definition of social work is not yet forthcoming. Other features of social work activity have also contributed to this lack of agreement about the nature of social work. The broad purposes of social work have become more ambiguous as social workers increasingly became state employees rather than volunteers or paid workers in non-statutory agencies. Sometimes public appreciation of social work has been blunted by the large claims made on behalf of social workers (for instance, that social work can cure a considerable range of private sorrows and public ills or simply that social workers represent the conscience of society). Changes in the dominant theories said to underpin social work – economics or sociology or psychoanalytic theories – and confusion between espoused theories and those actually informing practice have created at least the impression of significant ruptures as a tradition of practice struggles to assert itself. Finally, social work, like teaching, is both an 'attempting' and a 'succeeding' term: on occasions practitioners will deny the term to activity that was not particularly successful or that infringed one of the contested maxims that figure largely in professional talk.

A rough description of the contemporary social worker is of a person who as a representative of some statutory or non-statutory agency delivers a wide range of services, from income maintenance and welfare commodities, to directive and non-directive counselling. These services are directed or offered to individuals or to groups of different kinds, based on kinship, locality, interest or common condition. For the efficient and effective delivery of such services, social workers claim to use skills of various kinds, a range of theoretical and practical knowledge, and a set of values specific to social work.

Definition or general description take us some way towards grasping social work, but a more productive approach is to examine certain key questions concerning the form and the purposes of social work that have arisen at different times in the present century. In relation to form, two questions predominate: is social work to be treated as a profession (and if so, what kind of profession); is social work to be practised as an applied science, as an art, or as some kind of ministration? Flexner's (1915) consideration of the professional nature of social work raised questions that may still fruitfully be pursued. He concluded that social work met some of the criteria for professional status, but that social workers were mediators rather than full professional agents, that they pursued no distinctive ends, and that they were required to possess certain personal qualities rather than expertise in scientifically-derived technical skills. More recently, it has been suggested that social work can most easily be viewed as a semi-profession or as a bureau-profession. The characterization of social work as part of a humanistic as contrasted with a scientific movement is best studied through the work of Halmos (1965).

Controversy within social work is somewhat rare, but important questioning concerning the purpose of social work can be appreciated through three major debates (Timms 1983). The first, between leaders of the influential Charity Organization Society and the Socialists at the turn of the century, concerned the emphasis to be given to the individual and to his social circumstances and to preventive as opposed to curative work. The second, between two American schools of social work, the Functionalists and the Diagnosticians in the middle of the century, raised questions concerning the independence of social work as a helping process contrasted with a process of psychological treatment. The third, most immediate, controversy revolves around the possibility of a social work that is politically radical or, specifically, Marxist.

Noel Timms
University of Leicester

References

Devine, E. (1911) *The Spirit of Social Work*, New York.
Flexner, A. (1915) 'Is social work a profession?', *Proceedings of the 42nd National Conference of Charities and Correction.*
Halmos, P. (1965) *The Faith of the Counsellors*, London.
Timms, N. (1983) *Social Work Values: An Enquiry*, London.

Further reading

Timms, N. and Timms, R. (1982) *Dictionary of Social Welfare*, London.
Younghusband, E. (1978) *Social Work in Britain: 1950–1975*, 2 vols, London.

See also: social welfare; social welfare policy.

socialism

Socialism is a political theory the central tenets of which are that the means of production should be taken into collective or common ownership and that, as far as possible, market exchange should be replaced by other forms of distribution based on social needs. Socialism was brought into existence by the industrial revolution and it was designed to appeal to the mass working class of the new factory towns created by machine production. Before the development of modern industry, radical conceptions of the reorganization of society were predominantly egalitarian and democratic republican, committed to empowering artisans and peasants. Socialism aimed to solve the problems of modern industry and a competitive market society and was thus a new departure in political ideas.

Socialist ideas and political movements began to develop in the early nineteenth century in England and France. The period between the 1820s and the 1850s was marked by a plethora of diverse socialist systems proposed by Saint-Simon, Fourier, Owen, Blanc, Proudhon, Marx and Engels, and many lesser thinkers. Most of these systems were utopian and many of their advocates were middle-class philanthropists committed to improving the lot of the workers. Most socialists sought a more organized society that would replace the anarchy of the market place and the mass poverty of the urban masses.

Socialist solutions varied enormously: some were strongly in favour of state ownership while others favoured co-operative and mutual ownership, some favoured a decentralized and mutualist economy while others supported centralized economic planning. Socialism in this period did not develop strong political movements; rather it relied on the formation of model communities by wealthy patrons like Robert Owen, on winning established elites to reform, as with the Saint-Simonians in France, or with proposing projects for state action, as with Louis Blanc's National Warshops after the 1848 revolution in France.

The radical and revolutionary mass movements in this period were not socialist. Rather they were nationalist in countries like Hungary or Poland or Italy under foreign domination; in England and France they were popular-radical, committed to democratic republican reform. Between 1848 and 1871 the popular democratic and revolutionary traditions exhausted themselves in the European countries in a series of political defeats, at the barricades in countries like France, or through less violent political containment by the established parties and classes, as was the case with the Chartists in England.

In the period between 1848 and 1871 Marx and Engels in particular attempted radically to recast socialist theory. They attacked the utopianism of their predecessors, refusing to promulgate schemes of social reform. In essence they argued that the class struggle arising from the system of capitalist production is the objective basis of socialist victory, socialism is to be identified with the cause of the proletariat, and its aim is to overthrow the ruling class and create a new society without economic exploitation or state domination. Marx and Engels consistently advocated revolution and the seizure of power by the working class, but they did recognize that universal suffrage might facilitate the downfall of capitalism.

Actually, it did nothing of the sort. Between 1870 and 1914 the institutional foundations of modern socialism were developed in Britain and Germany. Universal suffrage created the modern political party – a permanent machine with paid officials whose task was to mobilize the mass electorate. The Social Democratic Party (SPD) became the dominant force in German socialism, not primarily because it adopted Marxism party orthodoxy, but because it started early and was effectively competing for votes in national elections. In Britain and Germany large-scale industrialism was accompanied by the growth of trade unionism, The British Labour Party was created to facilitate the parliamentary representation of the trade unions, and the links between the SPD and the unions were similarly close.

As a mass electoral party and the political representative of unionized labour, any socialist movement in an advanced industrial country had to relegate to virtual impotence the popular insurrectionary politics of the old European 'left'. Even Engels conceded as much, and one of Marx's disciples, Eduard Bernstein, did no more than carry the conclusion to its logical extreme. Bernstein's (1993 [1899]) *Preconditions of Socialism* represented the first articulate advocacy of 'social democracy' as against revolutionary socialism. It displaced the goal of 'revolution' in favour of a never-ending struggle for attainable reforms. Others, like Karl Kautsky, orthodox but politically cautious, argued that by parliamentary and acceptable political means the workers could engineer a revolutionary change in the social system.

To the mass party and the labour union must be added as a key institutional support of modern socialist movements the rise of big government. In the period 1870–1914 in Britain and Germany, governments came to provide, administer and organize an increasing range of activities, mass schooling, social insurance, public health, public utilities, etc. This provided another base for socialist advocacy and practice. British Fabian socialism sought to intervene in shaping central and local government's provision, aiming to provide an organizing core of the practical intellectuals. The success of Fabianism stands in stark contrast to the failure of its competitors, such as the anti-statist and decentralist doctrines of the Guild Socialists. For all the forceful advocacy by able thinkers like G. D. H. Cole (1953–61), the Guild Socialist movement was dead by the early 1920s. Likewise, British labour syndicalism (strong in the run-up to 1914 and during the First World War) perished in at same time, while conventional institutional trade unionism survived and continued to flourish.

Western European socialism was exported to the periphery, and to rapidly industrializing Russia in particular. Russian socialists adopted Marxism. Some like the Mensheviks remained faithful to German social democratic models, emphasizing an evolutionary strategy and co-operation with capitalistic modernization. Lenin and the Bolshevik faction came to favour an immediate revolutionary overthrow of tsarism and capitalism, and aimed to build a socialist society rapidly without long intermediary stages. Lenin's seizure of power in the Russian Revolution was a victory over social democrats and agrarian socialists as much as anything else. It was condemned by many western socialists, notably both the parliamentarist Kautsky and the revolutionary Rosa Luxemburg, as leading to authoritarian rule that would betray the interests of the workers.

These criticisms proved prescient. Before 1914 the socialist movement was essentially, despite differences, one enterprise. The First World War produced a split in socialism and a communist regime implacably opposed to European democratic socialism. European communist parties created after 1918 were under Soviet tutelage. Communist parties in the 1920s and early 1930s emphasized insurrectionary politics, going so far as to stigmatize democratic socialist parties like the SPD as 'social fascist'. The aftermath of the Second World War, with the consolidation of Soviet rule in Eastern Europe and the restoration of parliamentary democracy in Western Europe, led to a radical change in communist parties. In France and Germany they became mass electoral parties and sought to participate in government. The split between communism and socialism in Europe, bitter into the 1950s, ceased to have much meaning with the rise of Eurocommunism in the 1970s.

After 1945 social democratic parties in Europe participated in government to a hitherto unprecedented degree. The post-1945 boom was a period of intensification of big government and welfarism. In Scandinavia, the UK and Germany, socialist parties became accepted parties of government. Radical socialist ideas declined in favour of social democratic objectives of redistribution and welfare in a state-managed full-employment capitalist system. For example, Anthony Crosland's *Future of Socialism* (1956) advocated a basic change in Labour Party doctrine.

In the 1970s Western European social democracy entered a period of profound crisis from which it has failed to emerge. Socialists had become dependent on Keynesian national economic management to deliver the growth and full-employment necessary to make their welfare and redistribution strategies possible. With the oil crisis of 1973 and the collapse of the long postwar boom, western economies entered into a period of economic turbulence, uncertain growth, and the internationalization of major markets that made social democrats little more than crisis managers. For a period the fashionable monetarist and free-market doctrines seemed to threaten to wipe out socialism or social democracy completely. These new doctrines have failed in large measure too and their destructive social consequences have provoked a renewed concern for social justice. Nevertheless the socialist parties in western societies still have no coherent strategies. This is not only due to the absence of an alternative economic programme, but also because social changes have fatally undermined the constituency to which reformist and revolutionary socialists alike appeal, a large and relatively homogenous manual working class. The occupational structure had diversified, and with it the socialist claim to represent the majority has lost its force.

The spectacular collapse of communism after 1989 has further undermined western socialism. Even if most socialists in Europe rejected the Soviet model, it always remained the one 'actually existing' socialism which had replaced the market by planning and it was repellent to most free people. Its collapse makes the idea of a fundamental social change to a non-market system seem unsustainable. The future of socialism is thus uncertain.

Paul Hirst
University of London

References

Bernstein, E. (1993 [1899]) *The Preconditions of Socialism*, ed. H. Tudor, Cambridge, UK.
Cole, G. D. H. (1953–61) *A History of Socialist Thought*, 5 vols, London.
Crosland, A. (1956) *The Future of Socialism*, London.

Further reading

Lichtheim, G. (1970) *A Short History of Socialism*, London.
Wright, A. W. (1986) *Socialisms: Theories and Practices*, Oxford.

See also: capitalism; communism; fascism; social democracy.

society, civil *see* civil society

society, information *see* information society

society, post-industrial *see* post-industrial society

society, primitive *see* primitive society

society, risk *see* risk society

sociobiology

Sociobiology is used in both a wide and a narrow sense. As Ernst Mayr (1982: 598) put it, 'Sociobiology, broadly speaking, deals with the social behavior of organisms in the light of evolution.' This definition would include ethology, biopolitics, primatology, behavioural zoology, eugenics, population genetics, biosocial anthropology, evolutionary ecology, and all the disciplines that accept the neo-Darwinian mandate.

In the narrow sense, following the coinage of E. O. Wilson in his *Sociobiology: The New Synthesis* (1975), it refers to the application of theories of evolutionary genetics, stemming from the work of the modern synthesists of the 1930s and 1940s (Huxley, Haldane, Fisher, Wright) as modified by Hamilton, Williams, Maynard Smith and Trivers in the 1960s and 1970s. Here we shall explore both senses of the word.

All the sociobiological disciplines derive ultimately from Darwin's (1859) theory of natural selection (as modified by later discoveries in genetics), differing only in their interpretations. Thus they should not be confused with so-called Social Darwinism, which was in fact derived more from Herbert Spencer's developmental and progressive theories than from Darwin's essentially non-progressive theory of 'descent by modification'. In keeping with Darwin's own approach, especially in *The Descent of Man* (1871) and *The Expression of the Emotions in Man and Animals* (1872), sociobiology maintains that humankind is part of the natural world, and that therefore human behaviour is subject to analysis by the principles of natural science. Thus it stands firmly on the side of human sciences as natural sciences, as opposed to the view of them as purely cultural sciences: in terms of the traditional debate as set by Dilthey in the 1880s, it is for *Naturwissenschaft* as against *Geisteswissenschaft* (or *Kulturwissenschaft* in Dilthey's later formulation). It thus stands also in firm opposition to many current anti-positivist trends in philosophy and the social sciences and humanities. Whatever the differences among themselves, and these can be quite profound despite outside perceptions of homogeneity, the sociobiological sciences have a common aim of developing theories that apply to social behaviour in general, whether human or non-human. Human behaviour has unique qualities, but is not therefore exempt from the laws of natural selection, and even those unique qualities must be explained on its principles.

There are several strands or traditions that follow in the Darwinian tradition. One is the *natural history* tradition: the careful observation of the behaviour of both domestic and wild animals, birds and fish, from the lowest organisms to the higher mammals. Much of this was carried on outside the academy by dedicated amateurs, as it had been since long before Darwin. Indeed Darwin could be counted as a member of its ranks. But like the other strands, it was to receive much new impetus, and above all a working theory, from Darwinism. Whitman in the USA and Spaulding in the UK, whose work influenced William James, were followed by such notables as Lack on the robin and Fraser Darling on the red deer. During the 1930s, this observational tradition developed an academic base under Heinroth and Lorenz in Germany, Tinbergen in

The Netherlands, Huxley in Britain and Allee in the USA. The academic development came to be known as *ethology* (a word originally coined by John Stuart Mill). (For a general summary see Eibl-Eibesfeldt's *Ethology*, 1975.) Its general principle was that behaviour throughout the life cycle of an organism emerged according to an evolved programme, but a programme that needed releasers or stimuli from the environment for its completion, as in the classic case of 'imprinting' – by young animals on their parents – for example. The environment included other organisms, and the main stress was on the *communication mechanisms* that evolved to make social interaction possible. After the Second World War it was joined by remarkable developments in *primatology* stemming from both zoology and anthropology, principally under Hall, Kummer, Washburn and the Japanese students of their indigenous macaque populations. Later Jane Goodall (under the direct influence of Louis Leakey and the investigation of human origins) was to pioneer the field study of chimpanzees, and George Schaller that of gorillas.

The involvement of anthropologists as well as the growing interest in human behaviour among the ethologists proper, led to various attempts to apply principles derived from animal behaviour studies (which continued across many species) to human behaviour ('comparative ethology'). These involved such areas as territorialism (Ardrey), dominance hierarchies (Chance, Barkow, Chase), mother–infant bonding (Count, Harlow), male bonding, female hierarchies, optimism (Tiger), aggression (Lorenz), ritualization (Huxley), attention structure (Chance and Larsen), kinship, incest avoidance, social categories (Fox), attachment (Bowlby), facial expression (Ekman), courtship (Eibl-Eibesfeldt, Lockard), childhood behaviour (Blurton Jones, Chisholm, Konner), art (Morris, Disanayake), fathering (Mackey) and politics (Somit, Masters), to name but a few. The first general attempt at synthesis for social scientists came with Tiger and Fox's *The Imperial Animal* (1971). The general attempt to use theories and methods of ethology to study human behaviour and society – either through interpretation or by direct study – came to be known as *human ethology* (see Fox and Fleising 1976 – note that this review article considers 'sociobiology' a recent subfield of human ethology – and Eibl-Eibesfeldt's definitive *Human Ethology*, 1989) and continues as a lively tradition, especially in Europe.

Primatology has developed almost as a separate discipline from ethology and includes field studies of primate kinship and mating, ecology, communication, politics, and the linguistic abilities of apes. Studies of captive colonies and laboratory animals, as in the work of Hinde and Harlow, for example, have been important. Because of the heavy input from anthropology and the nearness of relationship between humans and the other primates, the relevance of primate studies for the study of the evolution of human behaviour has always been central. In the spirit of comparative ethology, anthropologists have continued to examine the social life of primates for clues to the evolution of human social organization (DeVore, Wrangham, Hardy, Fox, Kinzey, etc.) Human ethology also maintains a continuing close relationship with studies of hominid evolution generally, and such developments in the neurosciences as the study of the complex relationships between hormones, neurotransmitters, and social behaviour ('neuroethology'). The work of Chomsky and the transformational grammarians and such biolinguists as Lenneberg, for example, was important in bringing human verbal communication under the aegis of ethological interpretation, and away from the purely cultural.

Another major tradition stems from the rediscovery of Mendel and the growth of genetics. This was an independent development in its origins, but once married to Darwin's theory of natural selection (after an initial confusing period when it was thought of as a rival to that theory: see Mayr 1982) it developed an impressive field of *evolutionary population genetics* which was concerned with the causes of the shifting of gene frequencies in populations over time. There was a remarkable convergence of these ideas in the 1930s which, following the title of a book by Julian Huxley (1942), has come to be known as the 'modern synthesis' and involved the work of among others, R. A. Fisher, J. B. S. Haldane and Sewall Wright. What the synthesis did was to marry the population concerns of the naturalists with the mathematical concerns of the geneticists and show how natural selection was the bridge. It did not, however, concern itself overly with the evolution of behaviour in the manner of the ethologists. The latter continued to operate largely under the aegis of 'group selection' theory, although this was often unstated. In the clear case of Wynne-Edwards in his *Animal Dispersion in Relation to Social Behaviour* (1962) it was central, stating that conventional behaviours evolved, for example, *in order to* achieve the control of populations.

During the 1960s a reaction set in to this form of thinking that was to have profound effects for the future of human behavioural evolutionary studies. Williams (1966) produced an elegant series of arguments insisting that natural selection could work only on individual organisms, not groups, and Hamilton (1963; 1964), in an attempt to produce an answer to Darwin's unsolved puzzle of the existence of sterile castes in insects, demonstrated that such 'altruism' (i.e. sacrifice of one's own reproductive fitness to further

that of others) could spread in populations if certain conditions were met. Haldane had made the half-serious suggestion that while he would not lay down his life for his brother, he would for two brothers or eight first cousins. Hamilton (along with Maynard Smith 1964) worked out the mathematical genetics of this self-sacrificial behaviour in which it paid altruists, in terms of their own reproductive fitness, to sacrifice their immediate fitness (offspring) in so far as in doing so they preserved the fitness of enough relatives, who carried genes identical by descent with their own, to compensate. The logic of this implied that the real units of evolution were in fact the genes themselves, and that organisms were the mechanisms, or vehicles, by which the genes ensured that replicas of themselves were reproduced. This logic was beautifully worked out by Dawkins (1976) who coined the now popular term 'selfish gene'.

The originality of Hamilton's position, however, was to show how 'altruism' and 'selfishness' were two sides of the same coin, and not necessarily incompatible. In helping relatives we were, in genetic terms at least, helping ourselves. To this interesting mix Trivers (1971) added the necessary formula to deal with altruism towards strangers, again demonstrating how this could evolve if there were a pay-off for the altruist. Maynard Smith had shown how game theory could handle much of the conceptual and mathematical elements of this theory, and the philosopher's favourite paradox of the 'Prisoners' Dilemma' became the foundation of theories of what Trivers dubbed 'reciprocal altruism'. A major element of this theory involved the possibility of cheating, since freeloaders could always take the benefits without paying the costs. They could not, however, do this to excess since there would then be no altruists to cheat. Hence arose the concept of the *evolutionary stable strategy* (ESS), in which two such behaviours could evolve in tandem.

Thus two powerful new concepts were developed: the concept of *inclusive fitness*, the fitness of the individual plus that of those with whom the individual shared genes in common by descent; and the concept of *reciprocal altruism*. A corollary of inclusive fitness was *kin selection*, which sounds like group selection in that it sees selection working essentially on units of related organisms. The difference essentially is that kin selection does not need to assume that behaviours evolve *for* these groups, but only for the benefit of individuals and their gene replicas in other organisms. Trivers (1972) further added the concept of *parental investment* (PI), which clarified the differing roles of the sexes in the rearing to viability of their offspring and hence the problems of parent–offspring and sibling–sibling conflict, as well as the profound asymmetry in male and female mating strategies. As a consequence attention was called to Darwin's neglected concept of *sexual selection* especially as it affected differential male–female reproductive strategies

One might say that sociobiology in the narrower sense was born when E. O. Wilson (1975) took these theoretical concepts, married them to the data of entomology, ethology and primatology, and produced a 'new synthesis' to replace and advance the 'modern synthesis' of Huxley. Wilson's ambition (which was anything but narrow) was to order all behaviour across species, from insects through primates to humans, according to the set of principles deriving from the precepts of Williams, Maynard Smith, Hamilton and Trivers. The influence of his massive synthesis has been profound, not only on the science of human behaviour, but also throughout the biological sciences. We, however, are concerned here with the subsequent developments in the study of human social behaviour.

Largely under the influence of Alexander (1974), a school of sociobiological thought emerged which took as its central precept the *maximization of reproductive success*. Its main assumption is that such maximization – deriving directly from Darwinian fitness – is a basic motive and can explain a whole range of human mating and kin-related behaviours. It married this idea to the basic ideas of kin altruism ('nepotism'), inclusive fitness, parental investment and *paternity certainty*. Thus organisms – humans included – would strive to maximize reproductive success through inclusive fitness, and attempt to ensure (largely in the case of males) that the genes they 'invested' in were their own, that is, ensure the certainty of paternity. Ethnographic, sociological and historical examples were ransacked to discover examples of these principles at work. Thus the problem of the avunculate (the special relationship between mother's brother and sister's son) and hence the origins of matrilineal descent were attributed to 'low paternity certainty' in promiscuous societies where males would prefer to invest in sisters' sons with a low but definite degree of genetic relationship, rather than their own sons whose degree of relationship could be zero (Alexander, Kurland, Hartung; for a critique see Fox 1993). The logic of this general position has been applied to hypergamy (Dickeman), despotic polygyny (Betzig), child abuse (Daly and Wilson), legal decisions (Beckstrom), kin support in illness (McGuire), family structure (van den Berghe), cross-cousin marriage (Alexander), mate competition, kin-term manipulation (Chagnon), polyandry (Crook), bridewealth (Irons, Mulder), morality (Alexander), parental care (Hames, Turke, Hill, Kaplan), among many others. (See, e.g. Betzig *et al.* 1988; Chagnon and Irons 1979; for a review of the state of the art, see King's College Sociobiology Group 1982; issues of the journal *Ethology and Sociobiology*.)

Another tradition, however, rejects the primacy of reproductive fitness maximizing. It argues that while differential reproductive success *in the past*, and particularly in the species' *environment of evolutionary adaptation* (EEA), certainly led to specific adaptations, no such generalized motive can explain ongoing behaviour. The motive, it is argued, does not give specific enough instructions to the organism, which is more likely to act on proximate motives like desire for sex, avoidance of cheaters, accrual of resources, achievement of status, etc. These may well lead to reproductive success, but they are not based on any general desire for its maximization. Studies, then, of contemporary behaviour which demonstrate – as do many of the studies cited above – that certain practices in certain circumstances lead to reproductive success, or that they involve nepotistic actions towards kin, tell us only that ongoing behaviour shows ingenious *adaptability*, but tell us nothing about whether or not these practices stem from genuine evolutionary *adaptations* (see Symons 1992).

The influence, among other things, of cognitive science, has led many sociobiologists then to reject the 'adaptation agnostic' stance of their other brethren and to look for specific adaptational mechanisms in human perception and cognition ('information processing mechanisms'), whether or not these lead to *current* reproductive success. This school of *evolutionary psychology* has attempted to devise means of testing for 'domain specific algorithms' in the human mind, and is firmly opposed to 'domain general mechanisms' such as are proposed, for example, by many artificial intelligence theorists. It is sympathetic to those philosophers of mind like Fodor who prefer a modular to a unitary model of mind, and echoes, for example, Lumsden and Wilson's idea of 'epigenetic rules' or the 'biogrammar' of Tiger and Fox, and various other developments in the field of 'cognitive ethology' and transformational grammar ('the language acquisition device'). For example, Tooby and Cosmides have looked for cognitive mechanisms for social exchange and the detection of cheating, Buss for mate-preference mechanisms, Wilson and Daly for male proprietary behaviour, Silverman and Eals for sex differences in spatial ability, Profet for pregnancy sickness as an adaptive response to teratogens, and Orians and Heerwagen for evolved responses to landscape (see Barkow *et al.* 1992). Linguists, like Pinker, adhering to this approach, take issue with Chomsky and others who, while seeing linguistic competence as innate, do not see it as a product of natural selection. Evolutionary linguists see language, on the contrary, as having all the design hallmarks of an evolved adaptation. The 'adaptationist' school, however, like the one it rejects, is itself largely brain agnostic in that it does not try to link its domain specific modules to brain functions. But developments in neuroscience and artificial intelligence, particularly theories of parallel distributed processing (PDP), may well show the way to a future melding of these approaches (see Churchland 1993).

Sociobiology, both broadly and narrowly speaking, shows then a continuing vigorous development with influences in all the social sciences as well as philosophy and literature. Even criticisms of it have developed beyond simple-minded objections to genetic determinism or Social Darwinism to become serious attempts to grapple with the real issues (see Kitcher 1985). The general issue of conceptualizing the relation of genes and culture continues to be contentious (Boyd and Richerson 1985; Durham 1991), and the issue of group selection is by no means settled, but the future holds promise for the development of a normal science paradigm within which constructive disputes will be possible and cumulative progress made. The big question mark for the social sciences is the degree of their willingness to enter into a constructive debate with the sociobiologists now firmly established in their midst.

Robin Fox
Rutgers University

References

Alexander, R. D. (1974) 'The evolution of social behavior', *Annual Review of Ecology and Systematics* 5.

Barkow, J., Cosmides, L. and Tooby, J. (eds) (1992) *The Adapted Mind: Evolutionary Psychology and the Generation of Culture*, New York.

Betzig, L., Mulder, M. B. and Turke, P. (1988) *Human Reproductive Behaviour: A Darwinian Perspective*, Cambridge, UK.

Boyd, R. and Richerson, P. J. (1985) *Culture and the Evolutionary Process*, Chicago.

Chagnon, N. and Irons, W. (1979) *Evolutionary Biology and Human Social Behavior*, North Scituate, MA.

Churchland, P. S. (1993) *Neurophilosophy: Toward a Unified Science of the Mind/Brain*, Cambridge, MA.

Darwin, C. (1859) *On the Origin of Species by Means of Natural Selection*, London.

Dawkins, R. (1976) *The Selfish Gene*, Oxford.

Durham, W. H. (1991) *Coevolution: Genes, Culture and Human Diversity*, Stanford, CA.

Eibl-Eibesfeldt, I. (1975) *Ethology: The Biology of Behavior*, New York.

—— (1989) *Human Ethology*, New York.

Fox, R. (1993) *Reproduction and Succession*, New Brunswick, NJ.

Fox, R. and Fleising, U. (1976) 'Human ethology', *Annual Review of Anthropology*, 5, Palo Alto, CA.

Hamilton, W. D. (1963) 'The evolution of altruistic behavior', *American Naturalist* 97.

—— (1964) 'The genetical evolution of social behavior', *Journal of Theoretical Biology* 7.

Huxley, J. (1942) *Evolution: The Modern Synthesis*, London.

King's College Sociobiology Group (eds) (1982) *Current Problems in Sociobiology*, Cambridge, UK.

Kitcher, P. (1985) *Vaulting Ambition*, Cambridge, MA.

Maynard Smith, J. (1964) 'Group selection and kin selection', *Nature* 289.

Mayr, E. (1982) *The Growth of Biological Thought*, Cambridge, MA.

Symons, D. (1992) 'On the use and abuse of Darwinism in the study of human behavior', in Barkow *et al.* (eds) *The Adapted Mind*, New York.

Tiger, L. and Fox, R. (1971) *The Imperial Animal*, New York.

Trivers, R. L. (1971) 'The evolution of reciprocal altruism', *Quarterly Review of Biology* 46.

——(1972) 'Parental investment and sexual selection', in B. Campbell (ed.) *Sexual Selection and the Descent of Man 1871–1971*, Chicago.

Williams, G. C. (1966) *Adaptation and Natural Selection*, Princeton, NJ.

Wilson, E. O. (1975) *Sociobiology: The New Synthesis*, Cambridge, MA.

Wynne-Edwards, V. C. (1962) *Animal Dispersion in Relation to Social Behaviour*, Edinburgh.

See also: altruism; ethology; genetics and behaviour; human nature; instinct; social Darwinism.

sociolegal studies

Sociolegal studies is both a body of knowledge and a set of institutions and it has different significance in the USA and UK. Many commentators have explicitly declined to define the discipline that they acknowledge sociolegal studies to be (see (ESRC) Economic and Social Research Council 1994; Genn and Partington 1993). Definitions that are offered tend to be highly abstracted formulations such as 'the study of the law and legal institutions from the perspectives of the social sciences' (Harris 1983) or work bearing on 'the relationship between society and the legal process' (Law and Society Review 1994). Institutionally sociolegal studies reflects the work that is carried on by members of the Law and Society Association (LSA) in the USA and the Socio-Legal Studies Association (SLSA) in the UK. Although the discipline has roots both in law faculties and social science departments, it tends not to encompass scholars who are not affiliated with the LSA or SLSA even though they work on the social underpinnings and consequences of law. Thus researchers who do law and economics in the USA and criminology and conventional sociology of law in the UK are not likely to label themselves as sociolegal scholars.

For many years US scholars interested in the interactions between law and its social environment considered themselves to be affiliated with the law and society movement. The leading journal in both the USA and UK has 'law' and 'society' in its title. However, law and society is problematic as a description of the field on two accounts. It carries the unfortunate implication that law is distinct from, rather than a constitutive part of, society; historically it has implied a research strategy involving positivist assumptions and normal science models. In the USA sociolegal studies has then become a term of refuge for scholars who wish to emphasize the interpenetration of law and society and to make clear their tolerance of, even commitment to, interpretative and other forms of post-positivist enquiry. In addition, for these scholars sociolegal studies has become self-referential: their professional references and affiliations are to other sociolegal scholars and sociolegal studies rather than to the disciplines in which they were trained and generally teach. In the UK, sociolegal studies described the discipline from the start and was accorded the definitive imprimatur in the 1970s when Oxford's ESRC-supported programme was labelled the Centre for Socio-Legal Studies.

The traditional concerns of sociolegal scholars can be characterized as either peeling back law's façade or filling in its blanks. The first focus has directed attention to the differences between prescription and behaviour, commonly denominated the gap between 'law on the books' and 'law in action'. The second concern has produced empirical descriptions and analyses of areas of legal life that have not been systematically studied. These traditional interests have led to important research on fields such as the social structure of the legal profession, access to justice and the tolerance of inequality, the level and direction of discretion exercised by legal authorities, historical and cultural variation in legal practices, doctrines and ideologies, the consumers' perspective of law, the indirect and unanticipated consequences of regulation, the transformation of disputes over time, and the symbolic dimensions of social problems.

While there is no reason to believe that interest and productivity in traditional concerns will diminish, a new set of questions about theory, methods and politics are increasingly debated. The new theoretical issues arise from the engagement of sociolegal scholars with the ideas of continental social theorists such as Foucault, Habermas, Bourdieu and Luhmann and with the work of feminist and race theorists. While the impact of each of these currents is different, all prompt a serious reconsideration of accepted sociolegal assumptions about law. More specifically, two important emergent issues concern the 'constitutive' approach and the 'globalization' perspective (the proliferation of world-level rule systems to regulate transnational social, economic and political relations). The constitutive perspective has been developed in studies of lower courts, and welfare and education law. Its lesson is that law is not simply applied to people, but is to a large degree 'constituted' or made meaningful

within citizens' encounters with law and their use of it. This insight has led to an analysis of the plurality of meanings people attribute to law and of the ways people resist the taken-for-granted reality promoted by formal legal institutions. The globalization perspective encourages an examination of the expansion of regulatory structures developed to co-ordinate global and regional economic relations and to deal with the transnational dimensions of crime, the environment and social and ethnic conflict.

Second, although methodological pluralism has always been a hallmark of sociolegal work, questions of method have increasingly come to occupy a central point of discussion within the field. This development is best understood as an outgrowth of the movement towards interpretative forms of inquiry occurring throughout the social sciences, including a philosophical critique of empiricism. The traditional view had led sociolegal analysts to examine the objective features of law, such as its formal structures, and to explain such structures by identifying objective non-legal 'social factors' that are correlated with them. Interpretivist approaches, on the other hand, rest upon the idea that law cannot be understood solely in terms of its material manifestations. Thus, interpretivist sociolegal scholars are fundamentally concerned with questions of meaning. In their view even the 'objective' manifestations of law are symbolically constructed. The task of the sociolegal investigator then is to examine the range of meanings found in law and the consequences of those meanings for the constitution of law's subjects.

The final issue is that of politics. Because sociolegal studies represent a 'second kind of learning about law and legal institutions' (Galanter 1985) – distinct from the professional image of law – and because critical legal studies and Marxist sociology of law have been a strong presence, questions of politics have always been an important part of the field. But an increasingly large component of the sociolegal community is reluctant to engage unreflectively in the politics inherent in policy work and legal reform campaigns. Scholars involved in such work often must accept official criteria and definitions of legal problems. These efforts also have historically been confounded with 'liberal legalism' – the unequivocal acceptance of the desirability of enhancing the effectiveness of law. To many contemporary sociolegal scholars these connections create impediments to developing truly critical appraisals of the operation of law in society.

W. L. F. Felstiner
University of California, Santa Barbara

Ryken Grattet
Louisiana State University

References

Economic and Social Research Council (1994) *A Review of Socio Legal Studies*, London.

Galanter, M. (1985) 'The legal malaise or justice observed', *Law and Society Review*, 537.

Genn, H. and Partington, M. (1993) *Socio-Legal Studies: A Review by the ESRC*, London.

Harris, D. (1943), 'The development of socio-legal studies in the United Kingdom', *Legal Studies* 547.

Law and Society Review (1994) 'Policy', *Law and Society Review*.

Further reading

Cotterrell, R. (1984) *The Sociology of Law*, London.

Hunt, A. (1993) *Explorations in Law and Society*, New York.

Lempert, R. O. and Sanders, J. (1986) *An Invitation to Law and Social Science*, New York.

See also: criminology; critical legal studies; judicial process; law; law and economics.

sociolinguistics

When the founder of modern linguistics, Saussure (1966 [1916]), divided the concept of language into *langue*, language as an idealized system, and *parole*, speech or the realization of the system in what people actually say in defined circumstances, he used another term as well – *langage* – for systematized speech: the system which lies behind the variations in language use by individuals in different circumstances. Language use, without the stylistic preferences, quirks and performance errors of the individual speaker, but taking note of systematic differences correlating with systematic variation of social setting, is at the heart of sociolinguistics.

Sociolinguistics can be tackled from the sociology end or the linguistics end of the spectrum. Sociology is concerned with social structure and social groups, institutions and processes, so sociolinguistics will examine questions about how language mediates these: how language expresses power relationships between social groups, reflects the characteristics of institutions like the law or government, and how language socializes children into accepting the behavioural norms of society or organizes them into workplace roles. Contributions from sociolinguistics to sociology may particularly illuminate the study of social processes and theories of social cohesiveness or conflict.

Linguistics is concerned with language and languages, and sociolinguistics viewed from this end of the disciplinary spectrum will compare and contrast the linguistic choices people and groups make, consciously or unconsciously, by virtue of belonging or wishing to belong to different social categories, and by virtue of their intention within the communicative situation in which they find themselves. Choices between different languages (French or English in Quebec), styles or varieties of language (Yorkshire dialect or standard English), or variants of language variables (presence or absence of 'ne' in negation in French) are conditioned by the communication situation and have consequences for meaning: different choices convey different messages to interlocutors. Contributions from sociolinguistics to linguistics will be oriented towards the study of meaning, investigating rules, grammars, change always in their social setting. Sociolinguistics and functional linguistics go well together (Halliday 1985).

But since sociolinguistics is sociolinguistics, and not sociology nor linguistics, it combines the insights of linguistics with those of sociology in examining the speech (or, better, communicative) behaviour of human beings. Individual scholars and studies range across a wide field, from macrosociolinguistics, large-scale surveys of group attitudes and uses, employing the field methods of relevant social sciences (particularly quantitative methods), to microsociolinguistics, concerned with small-scale interaction, close to conversation analysis and ethnomethodology, and usually using mainly qualitative methods. Similarly, sociolinguistics ranges from attempts, close to language planning and the sociology (and politics) of language, to understand society, social institutions and social processes as mediated by language (how the discourse of the powerful dominates the powerless), to investigations of language use by social forces (how the powerful manipulate discourse).

In a seminal study in the mid-1960s, William Labov (1966) examined how a particular language variable was differently realized by different social strata. In the New York urban environment, different pronunciations of 'r' systematically correlated with setting (formality and informality) and social class (working and middle) and Labov was able to show therefore that there existed an identifiable social dialect. Differences in pronunciation – the variants of the language variables – were systematically correlated to variants of social variables through quantitative measurement of both.

Underlying Labovian sociolinguistics was 'consensual' sociology: social strata could coexist, both structural and individual mobility are possible, and society is organized around an assumed social contract enabling its components to function as a coherent whole. 'Variationist' studies have remained a significant part of sociolinguistics (Gardner-Chloros 1991; Trudgill 1974).

In Britain meanwhile, Basil Bernstein (1971–5) correlated language use with social class, finding that working-class children used a 'restricted', while middle-class children controlled an 'expanded' language code. Interpretations of his work concluded that social dialects were determined by social cirumstances, and that working-class dialects were deficient (or even defective).

The implications of correlational sociolinguistics were worked out in educational programmes in both the USA and Britain: to conquer the language deficit of working-class children, education would have to compensate – by teaching them the language of the middle class. In the USA, and later in Britain and Europe generally, 'social class' and 'ethnic group' – Blacks in the USA, immigrants in Europe – quickly became equivalent, and synonyms for 'socially disadvantaged'. Reaction set in to the 'deficit' hypothesis: difference, not deficit, was the byword, and educational priorities shifted during the 1980s to accepting language variety in the classroom – teaching the standard ('white middle class') language was regarded as an assimilationist approach, often racist in purpose. Educational sociolinguistics has remained a main focus for study, and has brought sociolinguistics into policy studies and politics (e.g. Fairclough 1989).

In sociolinguistics, research started to question the point and purpose of correlational study. Data were necessary, but what did the data show? 'Pure', 'core' or 'mainstream' linguistics, concentrating on the idealized speaker-hearer and the abstract language system, although generally ignoring sociolinguistics, wanted to know how sociolinguistics could identify systematicity: what was a minimal unit for sociolinguistics? Sociology wanted to know how language use related to a theory of society: how did social institutions and processes relate to language?

To the latter question, Habermas (1979), Foucault (1970) and Bourdieu (1982) provided some answers from 'conflict' sociology: language use was a major site for the struggle of historical social forces. The dominating social class ensured its own reproduction through hegemony: the incorporation of its ideology in accepted discourse. The standard language was nothing more than the discourse style of the elite, language standardization was the linguistic parallel of economic rationalization, and social struggle for domination and reproduction was represented through mastery of the 'social capital' of elite language. Education was a process of elimination: those who succeeded joined the elite and preserved their exclusiveness, if necessary even by changing the discourse style of the elite. Underlying sociolinguistics was a constant tension and struggle between the dominated and the dominating.

Sociolinguistics hence, for some scholars, became the study of the domination of social groups through discourse, whether the groups are differentiated by social status (classes), language (regional or non-territorial minorities), or gender (examining inherent gender bias in language, particularly from a feminist standpoint).

Is there a minimal unit for sociolinguistics, that is, a basic element uniting language and setting in such a way that one could characterize contrasts between individual occurrences? Early work identified the communicative competence of individuals in communication settings as a basis for a more comprehensive approach than the fragmented identification of language variables. Perhaps, now, we need to retain four aspects of the setting for language (and perhaps all social) behaviour: the expression of self, of (social) identity, of habit and of intention, and their expression in communication (not necessarily uniquely through language) as forming the basis for such a minimal unit.

D. E. Ager
Aston University

References

Bernstein, B. (1971–5) *Class, Codes and Control*, London.

Bourdieu, P. (1982) *Ce que parler veut dire*, Paris.

Fairclough, N. (1989) *Language and Power*, London.

Foucault, M. (1970) *The Order of Things*, London.

Gardner-Chloros, P. (1991) *Language Selection and Switching in Strasbourg*, Oxford.

Habermas, J. (1979) *Communication and the Evolution of Society*, Oxford.

Halliday, M. A. K. (1985) *Introduction to Functional Grammar*, London.

Labov, W. (1966) *The Social Stratification of English in New York City*, Washington, DC.

Saussure, F. de (1966 [1916]) *Course in General Linguistics*, New York.

Trudgill, P. (1974) *The Social Differentiation of English in Norwich*, Cambridge.

Further reading

Ammon, U., Dittmar, N. and Mattheier, K. J. (eds) (1988) *Sociolinguistics: An International Handbook of the Science of Language and Society*, Berlin.

Newmeyer, F. (ed.) (1988) *Language: The Socio-Cultural Context*, vol. 4 of *Linguistics: The Cambridge Survey*, Cambridge, UK.

See also: discourse analysis; language and culture; pragmatics.

sociology

More intimately than any other discipline that investigates the patterns of human interaction, sociology is associated with the advent of modernity, and this for several reasons.

First, perhaps the only common denominator of the great number of schools of thought and research strategies that claim sociological provenance is their focus on *society*. This focus may take one of two forms. Some sociologists have taken as their subject those structures and processes that can properly be conceived only as the attributes of a 'totality' (that is, shown not to be reducible to the traits of the individuals or associations whose interlocking and mutually dependent actions form that totality). Others have been concerned rather with the difference that is made to the condition and the conduct of individuals and groups of individuals by virtue of the fact that they form part of such a totality, called 'society'. But society, understood as the supra-individual, *anonymous*, and not immediately visible site of powerful forces that shape individual fates and prompt or constrain individual actions, is a *modern* creation (distinct both from the *polis*, the site of articulated intentions, open debate, decision making and explicit legislation, and the *household*, the sphere of free exercise of individual will, both of which are rooted in pre-modern history). Within society, actions tend to take the form of conditioned and determined (and thus more or less predictable) modes of conduct, shaped as they are by a constant pressure towards uniformity. But because society is 'the rule of nobody' with no fixed address, the mechanisms underlying this conditioning, the source of pressures towards uniformity, are far from evident. They are not represented in the awareness of the actors whose behaviour they shape. They must first be discovered in order to be grasped. Only once statistics had been developed did it become possible to set apart society as an autonomous object of study, as an entity distinct from individual, motivated actions, since statistics allowed for the uniform representation of a mass of actions, stripped of individuality.

Second, another typically modern phenomenon is the constant tension between humans uprooted from their traditional and communal settings, transformed into 'individuals' and cast into the position of autonomous subjects of action, and 'society', experienced as a daily constraint upon, and ultimately the outer limit to, the action of individual will. The paradox is that the modern individual neither can be fully at home and at peace with society, nor can he or she exist (indeed, come into being as an *individual*) outside society. In consequence, the study of society and of the tension between its capacity both to constrain and to enable, has been prompted throughout modern history by two diverse though connected interests, in principle contradictory to each other in their practical applications and consequences. On the one hand there is an interest in manipulating social conditions in such a way as to elicit more uniform behaviour of the kind desired by those in positions of power. The central question here is one of *discipline*, that is of coercing people to behave in certain ways even if they do not share, or even reject, the goals set by the designing and controlling agencies. On the other hand, there is an interest in understanding the mechanisms of social regulation so that, ideally, their enabling capacity can be revealed, allowing people better to resist constraints and pressures towards uniformity.

It goes without saying that these two interests are at cross-purposes. One aims to limit the very human freedom that the other is designed to promote. More precisely, there is a clash between the two kinds of freedom that the respective interests require, and in the end they undermine each other. The pursuit of enhanced uniformity is conducted in the name of improving human control over nature, that is, in the name of a *collective* freedom to shape the world in conformity with a vision of human needs or human nature. Yet the objective of controlling nature also inevitably entails the control of *human* nature (in practice, of human *individuals*), that is, of imposing patterns of conduct which would not necessarily be followed if matters were left to take what we call their natural course.

The inherent ambivalence of the modern human condition, situated in a society that simultaneously constrains and enables, was reflected in the self-definition of sociology as *the scientific study of society and of the aspects of human life that derive from 'living in society'*. Much sociological work has been inspired by a variety of controlling agencies, which sought precise and efficient instruments for eliciting disciplined and manageable behaviour. Above all, the modern state had to install and sustain 'law and order' through the rational design of an institutional network that would constrain individual life. Theoretical models of society constructed by sociology more often than not presented a view from the top, from, as it were, the control room. Society was perceived as an object of social engineering, while 'social problems' were depicted as in the first place problems of administration, to be met by legal rules and the redeployment of resources. On the other hand, sociology responded willy-nilly to the resentment felt against the oppression entailed in social engineering, for it inevitably exposed the artificial, arbitrary, 'man-made' and contrived character of social institutions, which the powers that be claimed were objectively necessary or rational. That is why throughout its history sociology has attracted criticism from both sides of the political divide. Power-holders will go on accusing sociologists of relativizing the kind of order they are sworn to promote and defend, and so of undermining their hold over their subjects, and inciting what they see as unrest and subversion. People defending their way of life or their ideals against what they experience as oppressive, stifling constraints imposed by resourceful powers are likely to object that sociology serves as a counsellor to their adversaries. The intensity of these charges will in each case reflect not so much the state of sociology as the state of social conflict in which, by virtue of the very nature of its work, it is inescapably enmeshed.

Understandably, both sets of adversaries would like to delegitimize the validity of sociological knowledge and to deny its scientific authority. Such assaults make sociologists acutely sensitive about their scientific status. They prompt ever renewed, yet forever inconclusive attempts to convince both academic opinion and the lay public that the knowledge produced by sociologists, as a result of the application of sociological methods, is superior to unaided and freely formed popular opinions, and that it can even claim truth values equivalent to those imputed to the findings of science.

The boundaries of sociological discourse

The term sociology has been in use since the second quarter of the nineteenth century, mostly through the influential work of August Comte, who not only coined the name for a not-yet-practised area of study but also claimed for the future science the status of a generalized and generalizing knowledge of the laws governing the progressive yet orderly development of human society (in his terms, the laws of social dynamics and social statics) – knowledge that would be obtained by deploying universally applicable scientific methods of observation and experiment. When attempts to establish sociology as a superior source of comment on human experience (as scientific knowledge in general is superior to folk beliefs), and particularly to introduce it as a separate academic discipline into a field of study already occupied by subjects that had become established and recognized at an earlier stage, were undertaken in Europe and the USA at the turn of the century, the pioneer sociologists chose to spell out the genuine or putative differences between the subject-matters or approaches of sociology and its older and established competitors. These pioneer sociologists wished to define and fence off an area of reality that none of the established disciplines had explored, and/or a type of knowledge that no discipline had hitherto provided.

Emile Durkheim, retrospectively acclaimed as one of the founding fathers of sociology as an academic discipline, followed the French positivist tradition and postulated the existence of specifically social facts, which had been left out (and by their very nature could not but be neglected) by other types of human studies, and particularly by psychology, the most obvious

competitor for the job of explaining the observed regularities in human conduct. Durkheim postulated the objective status of such social facts, that is their irreducibility in principle to the data of individual, subjective experience. (By objectivity he meant the assumed independence of social facts from the self-consciousness of human actors, and also their power to coerce the conduct of individuals and to bring them into line should they veer from socially accepted standards.) This necessarily implied that such facts should be treated in the way all respected sciences study their areas of reality: *objectively*, from the point of view of an external observer, without reference to subjectively experienced 'states of mind' and the motives of the actors.

At the same time, another founding father of academic sociology, Max Weber, inspired by the German *Geisteswissenschaften* and *Kulturlehre* traditions, attempted to set the new discipline apart by following what was virtually the opposite strategy. Sociology was to be distinguished by its approach and interpretative stance, rather than by claiming that a separate set of 'facts' constituted an exclusive domain for its study. For Max Weber, sociology was distinguished by its attempt to *understand* human conduct (always a *meaningful* – purposive – phenomenon, unlike the behaviour of inanimate bodies that can be explained, but not understood) in terms of the meanings that actors invest in their actions. Unlike the natural-scientific explanation of events with reference to external causes, sociological understanding was to be an inside job. What set apart properly sociological explanations was that they operated 'at the level of meaning'. To understand social action one had to postulate the meanings that 'made sense' of the observed conduct.

The differences between the disciplines collectively designated as social sciences (of which sociology is one, alongside psychology, anthropology, political science and various others) were, however, originally determined by the kinds of questions they posed about humans, regarded as social beings, that is, as entities whose conduct is regular, by and large predictable, and also potentially (given the availability of adequate resources) controllable, and who are for these reasons potential objects of study in the sense defined by the strategies of modern science. These questions were in turn dictated by the often practical and policy-oriented interests of the modern state and other agencies. Only later were the originally contingent differences reinforced through the progressive departmentalization of academic research and teaching, and it was then argued that each dealt with an allegedly distinct and autonomous aspect of human reality.

The core of the discourse of sociology has been relatively well defined by a distinctive written tradition, but it has been, and remains, notoriously frayed at the edges, despite the fact that for most of its history it struggled to set itself apart from related academic enterprises, and thus to demarcate the area over which it exercised exclusive sovereignty. The frontiers of sociology are porous, letting in materials formed within other interpretive traditions and other discourses. It is also far from clear (let alone universally agreed) what sort of propositions belong to sociology proper, and from which 'sites' such propositions can be formulated if they are to be accepted as being sociologically relevant. Little wonder that there are few, if any, themes, topics, questions or practical interests that may be classified as unambiguously and exclusively sociological without their assignment being contested by other discourses within the humanities or social sciences. Moreover, as commentators on human experience, sociologists share their subject-matter with countless others, not only members of other social scientific communities but also with novelists, poets, journalists, politicians, religious thinkers and the educated public in general.

There is another reason that sociology has been unable to make the transition from the status of a discourse to what Michel Foucault terms a discursive formation. It is characterized by what Anthony Giddens (1976) describes as a 'double hermeneutics'. The object of sociological commentary is always an already experienced experience, filled with meaning, interpreted and narrated even while it is still (for a sociologist) raw material. Unlike the objects dealt with by the natural sciences, which are not as a rule part of the daily practice and experience of non-specialists, the objects of the sociologists' hermeneutical efforts are the products of a competent, wide-ranging and incessant – though largely unreflective – hermeneutical activity on the part of the lay members of society.

Apart from the fact that the data of sociology are in this way secondary or second level, the interpretative operations of the sociologist do not differ in kind from the lay hermeneutic practices that are already embedded in the objects of its study – that are, indeed, responsible for the constitution of these objects. It is not immediately apparent – and must therefore be proven – that professional sociological interpretations are necessarily superior, more credible, trustworthy and otherwise privileged than the primary, lay meanings that they are intended to improve upon or to replace. Hence – again in striking contrast to the practices of most natural sciences, but in common with the experience of many human sciences – the clarification of its relationship to common sense (that is, lay sense, beliefs that have been denied the status of professional knowledge) and intensive methodological self-reflection

constitute an integral, and inordinately prominent, aspect of sociological work.

The most common strategy of sociologists is to denigrate popularly held opinion, and to cast doubt upon the introspective capacity of actors. However profound the other differences between them may be, most schools of thought in sociology agree that the actors hold at best a hazy, at worst a mistaken, image of the true motives and reasons for their conduct, and that they cannot reliably represent the social forces that affect their lives, for they reason from within the confines of their own, always partial and fragmentary, life experiences. On that view, common sense is incoherent and internally contradictory, vulnerable to distorting influences, and always in need of correction. Being mere opinions, popular interpretations should be treated as *objects* of research and not as a *source* of true knowledge. This strategy of denigrating common sense is supplemented by the effort to elaborate methods of data collection and an interpretive methodology that might claim the authority of established scientific procedures, so assuring a degree of reliability of sociological knowledge to which mere opinions, which are not formed in a similarly methodical fashion, cannot aspire.

The formative interests of sociology

The projects of research and teaching that were collected under the name of 'sociology' in the USA were stimulated by concerns about the turbulence that was caused by rapid industrialization and the massive immigration in the urban areas of the American Mid-West in the early twentieth century. These concerns were shared initially by politicians, social reformers and religious preachers (the first academic sociologists being drawn from their ranks). The constantly changing social world seemed to be poorly integrated, the direction of change unconstrained by shared traditions or by self-regulating communal mechanisms. Consequently the options were apparently wide open, offering a perhaps dangerous freedom for social experiment. The social setting, and therefore also human conduct, seemed to be flexible and pliable – available for rational design and for social engineering. In this context, the emerging 'science of society' regarded itself as first and foremost an instrument of policy for local governments and social workers. The policies to be designed with social-scientific inspiration and assistance were intended to deal with 'deviation', 'abnormality' and 'pathology'. In short, they aimed to resolve social problems. Society was seen, indeed, as first and foremost a collection of *problems*, and the science of society was accordingly asked to deliver a theoretical guide to practical problem solving.

A similar practical bias also characterized continental European sociology when, like its North American counterpart, it began to be assimilated into the universities at the end of the nineteenth century. However, the Europeans did not concentrate on problem solving. Rather, the emerging social science was intended to enable rational human beings to play a conscious part in the large movements of history, movements that were believed to exhibit a direction and logic, if one that had yet to be revealed. Sociology would therefore enable people to feel more at home in an unfamiliar world, more in control of their own actions and – collectively and obliquely – of the conditions under which they were obliged to act. In other words sociology, it was hoped, would discover the historical tendency of modern society, and modify it. In the place of a spontaneous, elemental, poorly understood process, it would set an orderly, monitored development. It was also widely assumed from the start that not all modern transformations were unambiguously beneficial and desirable. Sociology therefore had to alert the public, at all levels but in particular at the level of the law-makers, to the dangers hidden in uncontrolled social processes, and it had to propose ways of preventing such undesirable processes from materializing, or to propose ways of repairing the damage.

The founders of the new discipline and their successors, whose ideas were later to be absorbed into its canon, agreed on this understanding of the calling of sociology, even if they differed in their interpretation of the crucial features and guiding factors of the historical trends that they all wished to grasp. Comte (1798–1857) identified the moving force of history in the progress of scientific knowledge and, more generally, in the 'positive spirit'. Herbert Spencer (1820–1903) envisaged the passage of modern society from the conflict-ridden military stage to a peaceful 'industrial' stage, where a multitude of products became available for distribution. He foresaw a continuous progress towards the increasing complexity of society, paired with the growing autonomy and differentiation of individuals. Karl Marx (1818–83) expected the progressive control over nature to result eventually in the complete emancipation of society from the constraints of necessity arising from want – a redemption from misery and strife, which would put an end to the alienation of products from their producers and to the transformation of those products into capital deployed to enslave and further expropriate the producers, eventually putting to an end all exploitation. Ferdinand Tönnies (1855–1936) conceived of a historical succession whereby the original *Gemeinschaft* – the natural togetherness of communities held together by mutual sympathy, solidarity and co-operation –

would be replaced in modern times by *Gesellschaft* – a web of partial, purposeful, impersonal and contractual bonds. Emile Durkheim (1855–1917) focused his analysis of historical trends upon the progressive division of labour and thus the growing complexity of the social whole. He proposed a model of society integrated first by the 'mechanical' solidarity of similar segments and later by the 'organic' solidarity of functionally differentiated yet complementary classes and professional groups. Max Weber (1864–1920) represented modernity mainly in terms of an ubiquitous rationalization of all spheres of social life, thought and culture, and the increasing role played by action grounded in the calculation of means and ends at the expense of the non-rational or irrational, custombound or affective forms of conduct. George Simmel (1859–1918) emphasized the passage from qualitative and differentiated to quantitative and uniform relations, and underlined the new and growing role played by universalizing and disembedded forces, best exemplified by the institution of money and by abstract, categorical thought.

The appearance of sociology coincided in continental Europe with a wave of optimism in the creative, life-improving potential and the universal destiny of European civilization, which was identified in the public mind with civilization as such. That faith drew inspiration and apparent confirmation from the rapid and unresisted global expansion of European rule and influence. The profusely demonstrated practical superiority of the European way of life seemed to offer the budding social science an uncontroversial model of social development in general, and a standard by which to measure other societies and to anticipate their future development. Then, as later, sociology was in tune with the general intellectual mood of the time, sharing the widespread belief in progress, the expectation of constant improvement, the conviction that all present or future problems could be solved through the advance of science and technical know-how, if the political will existed, and the expectation that rationally organized, humane societies would come to dominate the world. Sociology aimed to be a part of this progressive change, through reflecting upon the course history had taken and was likely to take in the future, and thereby supplying the standards by which practical measures might be evaluated. The identification of unsolved and potentially dangerous problems, and criticisms of misguided or ineffective ways of handling social problems, was seen as an integral constituent of the task of sociology.

At the time of the establishment of continental sociology, Britain was the centre of a worldwide empire. The principle of indirect rule in the colonies presupposed that the conquered populations were enclosed and by and large self-reproducing totalities – societies in their own right. Evidently different from metropolitan societies, yet viable and retaining their own distinctive traits, they put on the agenda the task of the comparative study of societies – a task undertaken by what came to be known as 'social anthropology'. Until the middle of the twentieth century, social anthropology dominated social science in Britain, thereby delaying the establishment of academic sociology. The emergence of sociology in Britain coincided with the dismantling of the empire and the concomitant concern with the study of Britain itself. The circumstance that sociology entered public debate in Britain at a time of retreat and retrenchment, rather than at a time of expansion and optimism, as had been the case in continental Europe and the USA, was to have consequences for the status and public reception of sociology in Britain for a long time to come.

The changing profile of sociology

Attempts are often made, misleadingly, to reduce the variegated and open sociological discourse to a succession of clearly demarcated periods, each distinguished by the dominance, or at least prevalence, of a single paradigm – a coherent and circumscribed body of interrelated concepts. Yet one can hardly think of sociology as a discursive formation with boundaries, let alone as characterized by the practice of 'normal science' in Thomas Kuhn's sense, focused upon a shared paradigm. Always part and parcel of the intellectual life of its time and place, the shifts in the interests of sociological discourse and in the tasks that sociology sets itself reflect more than anything else general cultural changes.

By common consent, the second part of the twentieth century has brought the most radical of all shifts to which modern culture has been exposed since its inception. The most seminal, and the most important of its intellectual consequences, was the collapse of the hierarchy of values that had hitherto underpinned modern culture. A new scepticism became established, that put in question all modern certainties, above all the conviction that the western type of society represents the form of civilization that will eventually achieve universal dominion, and that (notwithstanding temporary slow-downs and occasional set-backs) a continuous progress towards a more rational and accident-proof society has already been assured. Closely connected with this crisis of confidence has been the retreat of the powers from the project of global domination, as well as the gradual yet relentless fall from grace of the ideal of an all-regulating, ubiquitous, obsessively legislating state engaged upon great enterprises of social engineering.

The most momentous consequence for the shape and status of sociology was the disappearance of the vantage point from which most of the orthodox sociological work had been done: that of the cockpit, or control room, of an administrative centre willing and resourceful enough to treat society as an object that could be closely monitored and managed, once social processes had been analysed into a series of definable and in principle resolvable problems. To be sure, much of the work done in sociology departments retains the impress of the past of the discipline, when it was sustained by demands emanating from expanding warfare and welfare bureaucracies. None the less the overall trend is away from the old ways and towards new 'cognitive' perspectives. There can be no doubt that the nature and tasks of sociological work are now understood in a very different way from that taken for granted in the first half of the twentieth century.

To sum up, the focus of sociological interests is shifting from *structure* to *agency*, from society understood primarily as a set of external constraints that restrict the field of choices available to the members of society, and to a large extent determine their behaviour, to social settings that are understood primarily as pools of enabling resources from which the actors draw in order to pursue their own goals. Society is conceived of less as a self-perpetuating pattern of social positions and functions, more as an ongoing process, which in its course puts together and dismantles (always temporary) networks of dependency and stages for action. Though the category of society is not likely to vanish from sociological discourse, its meaning is undergoing fateful changes. Increasingly, the category is used in the sense of 'sociation' (actors entering into or abandoning relationships) or – yet more symptomatically – in the sense of 'sociality' (meaning the very capacity of actors to sociate). This is arguably the crucial shift: other new traits or new emphases that will be listed below, and which set contemporary sociological discourse apart from the received tradition of modern sociology, may be represented as its manifestations or consequences.

Where once sociology was concerned above all with stability, self-reproduction and repetitiveness, and with the ways and means of securing these (the central preoccupation of the once dominant 'systems theory' of Talcott Parsons and equally of the opponents of his structural functionalism), attention is moving towards the study of innovation. It is understood that every action is to an extent a creative act, though it always takes account of extant, already meaningful patterns.

The emphasis is also shifting away from the search for laws and regularities. These were conceived of as preceding the action, affecting its course while themselves remaining unaffected. Actions are no longer portrayed as *determined* but rather as *contingent*, each a unique creation and therefore not truly predictable. Doubt is also cast upon the predictive value of statistics. It is accepted that the most frequent or numerous phenomena will not necessarily represent the trends of the future. In consequence, there seem to be no clear-cut criteria by which to anticipate the consequences of events, their impact and durability, and thus to judge their significance. This in turn leads to the erosion of once central, privileged objects or areas of sociological study. Since sociologists no longer evoke 'basic conflicts', 'main links' or 'steering processes', it is not obvious why certain topics, actors or events ought to be given priority by the sociologist.

The attention of sociologists is accordingly shifting from the control room (from issues like the impact of the state, class domination, etc.) to mundane, elementary interactions, to the grassroots level of social reality, to what actors do to one another and to themselves in the context of face-to-face interaction. Largely under the influence of Alfred Schütz's argument that the 'world within reach' supplies the archetype for the actors' model of all other 'universes of meaning' (Schütz 1982), it is assumed that the essential skills and knowledge reflectively or unreflectively deployed by the actors in their daily life are ultimately responsible for what is perceived in retrospect to be a global, impersonal trend, or the persistence of objective structures.

Once actors were conceived of as knowledgeable and in principle prone to self-monitoring, the prime task of sociological investigation became the reconstruction of their knowledge. This dramatically alters the role assigned to common sense in sociological discourse. Initially conceived of as alternative, poorly informed and essentially false interpretation of social reality (to be criticized, corrected or supplanted) it now becomes the major resource for sociological interpretation. To an unprecedented degree, sociology now assumes a hermeneutical stance. It emphasizes that social realities are intrinsically meaningful (endowed with meaning by the actors who produce them), and that in consequence to understand those realities one must reconstruct the actors' meanings. This does not necessarily mean that the sociologist strives to achieve empathy: to discover what is going on in the minds of the actors, to bring to light their conscious motives and explicit goals. Sociologists still tend to deny that the actors are necessarily the best judges of sociological interpretations. But the hermeneutical approach does mean that explanations or interpretations of social realities must treat the actors as meaning-driven and meaning-creating, rather than as being pushed and pulled by impersonal, objectively describable forces and constraints.

Another intimately related trend is the switch in interest from external coercion and constraint to the actor's self-construction and self-definition. Actions are meaningful, actors are knowledgeable, reflecting constantly upon their own identity and motives. One might say that if human beings were seen by orthodox sociology as driven primarily by necessity and as the target of social forces, they tend to be construed now, more often than not, as identity-driven and motivated, choosing subjects.

The most general trend is to move down the levels of social organization in search of the genuine levers of social actions. Contemporary sociologists accordingly pay particular attention to *community* at the expense of 'society' (which in modern sociology was assumed to be, for all practical purposes, identical with the nation-state). For a long time, sociologists believed that community was a relic of pre-modern times, bound to disappear in the course of modernization. It is now being restored to a central position in sociological analysis, and is regarded as the ultimate source of actors' meanings, and thus of social reality itself. Communities are considered to be the bearers of tradition, which is sustained and recreated by the actions of their members; to be the ultimate source of whatever commonality and sharing is to be found in the actors' meanings; and to be the point of reference in the process whereby the actors define themselves and construct their identities (and so, reciprocally, sustain the community). Unlike 'society', which is identified with the nation-state, communities have no objective boundaries (that is, boundaries guarded by coercive powers). They are fluid, and the strength of the grip in which they hold their members may vary too (that grip being none other than the intensity of the actors' emotional identification with what they conceive as, or imagine to be, community).

Sociologists say that communities are *imagined*. As conceived in contemporary sociology, community is postulated – the postulate becoming reality where actions are undertaken as if it *was* a reality. There is therefore a constant interplay between actors and 'their' communities, neither being assigned priority in sociological analysis.

Alternative sociologies

The perspectival shift in contemporary sociology – the new self-awareness that admits the community-, culture-, time-bound nature of any sociological discourse and body of knowledge – is simultaneously responsible for, and a response to, the emergence of alternative sociologies that promote different interpretations of shared social realities. These insist that a plurality of interpretations is inevitable, given the difference between the experiential vantage points from which interpretive efforts are launched. To be sure, earlier social theorists sometimes argued that there was an intimate affinity between position-related experience and the style and content of sociological knowledge. Most notably, this is true of the Marxist thesis that there is an unbridgeable opposition between the 'bourgeois' and 'proletarian' view of society. The novelty consists, first, in an extension of the perspectival principle from two opposing classes to a multitude of categories distinguished by ethnic, gender, or cultural characteristics, and the overt acceptance of the *interested* nature of each perspective (for each serves the needs of a group whose collective experience it claims to articulate, and each is necessary for the integration of the group and the sustenance of group tradition). Moreover, the alternative sociologies abandon the claim to objectivity and to exclusive truth, openly admitting the relativity of any interpretation. However strong the mutual interest (both approving and critical) that various alternative sociologies show in the assertions of others, little progress has been made so far towards a genuine synthesis of interpretive standpoints. Given their strategies and their understanding of the nature of sociological work, it is legitimate to doubt whether such a synthesis is a realistic objective. More likely the coexistence of alternative perspectival sociologies will be a lasting (nay constitutive) condition of sociology.

Arguably the most prolific and influential among alternative sociologies has been born of the new awareness of the specificity of gender-related experience, inspired by the feminist movement of the second half of the twentieth century. Feminist sociology, like other alternative sociologies, assumes that all knowledge is socially situated. In other words, it is related in both its subject-matter and its interpretive angle to an experience unique to a specific group or category, distinguished by the content of its life concerns. Mainstream sociology, on this view, has been situated in the essentially male context of the 'relations of ruling' (Smith 1987) – in the world of paid labour, politics and formal organizations. Emerging in this context, and serving it, the mainstream, male sociology produces 'rulership texts' that masquerade as objective knowledge. They construct and impose general identities and classifications, and deploy abstract, impersonal and anonymous categories that denigrate or exclude from the realm of the significant all real, personal life experience. The assumed objectivity of such knowledge, feminist sociologists aver, is a mere pretence; its allegedly non-partisan viewpoint can be seriously asserted only in so far as male domination itself has been exempted from the discourse, while providing its tacit premise. Once that premise is questioned, it becomes clear that mainstream sociology is but one of the many potential situated sociologies – one that focuses on a selected part of 'the social', excluding other parts. In particular it leaves out – and fails to account for – the social world as it is experienced and lived by women. For this reason, a sociology by women and for women needs to be developed to supplement the extant male sociology, and simultaneously to expose its limited scope, its situatedness, and its unwarranted bid for monopoly, reflecting as it does at the level of theory the practice of male domination.

On this view, the part of the 'social' on which the new female sociology must be constructed is the sphere of daily domestic life, childcare, service-oriented activities, in which women's roles are cast and moulded. But female sociology is not set apart only by concentrating on a specific, often underplayed area of experience. The different experience of women must also be processed in a new way, steering clear of the male inclination to abstract, depersonalize and categorize. Such a sociology should aim to return to the real and the concrete. Women are immersed in the practical context of the everyday/everynight world, the world of the actual and specific, which they never leave (at least in their gender-specific capacity). This kind of experience, marginalized and declared out of court by the dominant sociological discourse, must be granted social significance so that women's lives can be brought back from the margins to which they have been exiled to the centre of social life and of the knowledge of the social.

The feminist-inspired alternative sociology takes 'gender' as the key differentiator of social situatedness and situated experience. It considers gender to be the constitutive factor of the most consequential social division and social conflict, as well as the basis of the critical dimension of social domination and oppression – that is, of patriarchal rule. Other alternative sociologies select their key differentiator differently – most often from class, ethnic or racial attributes – but on the whole they share the assumption that all knowledge of the social is position bound, situated and interested, and treat with reserve any claims of unencumbered objectivity, suspecting that behind such claims must lurk a bid for domination, and an apology for oppression.

Areas of sociological study

Sociology is a widely ramifying discipline, subdivided into numerous fields of specialized study, often united quite loosely by little more than shared hermeneutic strategies and an ambition to correct common beliefs. The demarcation of these fields follows quite closely the institutionalized, functional divisions in organized society, answering the effective or assumed demand of the established areas of management. Thus specialized bodies of knowledge have accumulated that focus on deviance and corrective or punitive policies, politics and political institutions, army and war, race and ethnicity, marriage and the family, education, the cultural media, information technologies, religion and religious institutions, industry and work, urban living and its problems, health and medicine.

Not all specific research interests, however, can be referred unambiguously to administrative demands. The endemic ambivalence of sociology, which can be traced back to the ambivalent response of the early sociologists to the rationalization project of modernity, manifests itself in the persistence of areas of study that have no direct administrative application, and are even potentially disruptive from the managerial point of view. To be sure, the distinction between the potentially stabilizing and destabilizing, overt or latent intentions and effects of sociological knowledge cuts across the thematic divisions, none of the specialized fields being entirely free from ambivalence. Still, certain areas of sociological thought address themselves more explicitly than others to individuals resisting managerial manipulation and attempting to assert control over their own lives. Relevant areas of study include social inequality (whether based on class, gender or race), identity-formation, interaction in daily life, intimacy and depersonalization, etc. In contrast to management-oriented areas of study, there is a pronounced tendency to cross-fertilize, to borrow insights, to dismantle boundaries between different areas of expertise. This is in keeping with the overall strategic aim of restoring the wholeness of life and personality, which are fragmented and separated by institutionalized divisions.

Major theoretical influences in contemporary sociology

The formative, classic ideas of Marx, Weber, Durkheim or Simmel continue to constitute the backbone of sociological discourse, providing the reference point for self-identification over the wide range of schools and styles between which sociological practice is divided. The classic works are frequently revisited, reread and reinterpreted in the light of changing experiences, interests and priorities. Given the spread of interpretations imposed upon the variety of original classical insights, revivals of classic sources may serve the integration of sociological work or sustain the division between different schools of thought. Talcott Parsons's social action and system theory, which under the name of 'structural functionalism' dominated the sociological scene in the 1950s and 1960s, was constructed as a (highly idiosyncratic) interpretation of the classic

sociological tradition. So was the opposition to Parsons – by C. Wright Mills, Ralf Dahrendorf, David Lockwood, John Rex and others – which prepared the ground for the eventual replacement of the Parsonian version of sociology by providing new insights into the classical foundations of the discipline.

The most seminal of departures that led in the course of the 1970s to widespread criticism and rejection of what Anthony Giddens termed the 'orthodox consensus' was the phenomenological revolution. Initiated by Berger and Luckmann (1966), the revolution was sustained by a spate of radical reformulations of the subject-matter and proper strategy of sociological work. The posthumously published work of Alfred Schütz served as the main theoretical inspiration and authority. It prepared the way for the influence of the continental philosophies of Husserl and Heidegger, and their hermeneutical applications in the writings of Paul Ricoeur and Hans Gadamer. The effect of the exposure to phenomenology was to shift interest from external, extra-subjective structural constraints to the interpretation of the subjective experience of actors; and from the determination to arbitrate between objective truth and prejudiced opinion to the effort to reveal the conditions of knowledge rooted in communally transmitted traditions. Harold Garfinkel's 'ethnomethodology' (that treated the social as the accomplishment of knowledgeable actors, in the course of their everyday work) added further impetus to the reorientation of sociology away from 'objective' systems and structures and towards 'social agency', self-reflexive, intentional action and its unanticipated consequences, a move most emphatically expressed in the work of Anthony Giddens.

There has been a greater openness of sociology to developments and fashions in other disciplines, and more generally in other areas of culture. Apart from phenomenology and hermeneutics, powerful influences have been Adorno and Horkheimer's critical theory, Wittgenstein's philosophy, Lévi-Strauss's and Barthes's semiotics, Foucault's philosophy of knowledge, Braudel's historiography, Lacan's psychoanalysis and Derrida's deconstruction – to name but the most obvious instances.

Two other developments should also be noted. First, North American sociology lost the dominant position that it had gained in the years following the Second World War. It has been in retreat at home, due to the diminishing resources of its sponsoring bureaucracies, while its empirical methodology, once the source of its greatest strength and appeal, has found less application in European sociology due to its changed concerns and strategies. Second, there has been a growing interchange between national sociologies, sociological discourse acquiring increasingly a transnational character. Examples are the worldwide impact of Jürgen Habermas's (1979) 'communication theory', Niklas Luhmann's 'revised system theory', Ulrich Beck's (1992) *Risikogesellschaft*, Frederik Barth's analysis of ethnic boundaries, or Pierre Bourdieu's (1985) notions of 'cultural capital' and 'habitus'.

The post-modern controversy

Through the works of Charles Jencks, Jean-François Lyotard, Jean Baudrillard, Gianni Vattimo, Alberto Melucci, Michel Maffesoli and other writers, the twin issues of the reassessment of the current trends of modern society and of the aim and function of sociological work have moved to the centre of sociologists' concerns, expressed in what came to be called the 'post-modern debate'.

The nub of the debate concerns the thesis that the modern project has ground to a halt or exhausted itself, being displaced by 'post-modernity' – a non-systemic condition of multiple realities, of change without direction, with no prospect of being controlled. Doubts are voiced as to whether the present condition is so distinctive and novel as to warrant the description post-modern. Habermas (1979) and Giddens (1993), for instance, insist that the features described as post-modern are traits of a late or mature modernity, and that the modernist project is still far from exhausted. Others, however, argue that the demise of utopias, of the trust in progress and in historical direction, as well as the collapse of projects to impose universal and uniform cultural standards and structural patterns, testify to a decisive break.

Both sides in the debate invoke the concept of the 'society of risk', originally introduced by Ulrich Beck (1992) and now very generally accepted. One view is that the modern forces of science and technology have further reinforced their central position, since only techno-science can locate, articulate and deal with the new, global risks. The contrary view is that present-day society is shaped by its responses to the new risks created mostly by past responses to risks previously revealed – a process that feeds post-modern fragmentation.

With respect to the microsocial level, some maintain that the notorious fluidity of individual identity, the instability of personal relationships, signal the fulfilment of the long modern development towards individual freedom. The alternative view is that the current human condition is marked above all, in characteristic post-modern fashion, by the difficulty of holding on to already acquired identities.

Finally, another hotly contested issue is the connection between the condition called 'post-modern' and the affluence of certain highly developed consumer societies. Doubts are accordingly raised as to the global significance of the post-modern condition.

The views adopted as to what are the appropriate strategies for sociology in the new circumstances are closely related to the stands taken in the debate between modernists and post-modernists. Those who argue that contemporary society is increasingly post-modern maintain that sociology ought to take stock of the multiplicity of cultures, traditions and forms of life, and thus concentrate its efforts on facilitating communication and understanding between distinct realities rather than continue the search for a unique and universally binding truth, in defiance of communally grounded and tradition-bound local, lay knowledge. Those who hold this view are ready to accept that sociology is essentially an attempt to replicate, somewhat more systematically, the interpretive activity in which all members of society are engaged, in the daily activities of sociation. Not everyone, however, is prepared to abandon the modernist ambition of social science to provide privileged knowledge, which is bound to expose the frailty of lay beliefs and eventually to replace them with scientifically grounded, objective truth, and which aspires to co-operate in political and legislative efforts to establish rational structures that will make possible and promote the replacement of lay enterprises with rational, scientific projects.

Zygmunt Bauman
University of Leeds

References

Berger, P. and Luckmann, T. (1966) *The Social Construction of Reality*, New York.

Giddens, A. (1976) *New Rules of Sociological Method: A Positive Critique of Interpretive Sociology*, London.

Schütz, A. (1982) *Life Forms and Meaning Structure*, London.

Smith, D. E. (1987) *The Everyday World as Problematic: A Feminist Sociology*, Boston, MA.

Further reading

Bauman, Z. (1991) *Intimations of Postmodernity*, London.

Beck, U. (1992) *Risk Society: Towards a New Modernity*, New York.

Bourdieu, P. (1985) *Languages as Symbolic Power*, Oxford.

Coser, L. A. and Rosenberg, B. (1985) *Sociological Theory: Selected Readings*.

Fay, B. (1975) *Social Theory and Political Practice*, London.

Giddens, A. (1993) *Sociology*, Cambridge, UK.

Habermas, J. (1979) *Communication and the Evolution of Society*, Oxford.

Heritage, J. (1984) *Garfinkel and Ethnomethodology*, Oxford.

Mestrovic, S. G. (1991) *The Coming Fin de Siècle*, London.

Turner, B. S. (1990) *Theories of Postmodernity*, New York.

Whistler, S. and Lasch, S. (1987) *Max Weber: Rationality and Modernity*, London.

sociology, industrial see industrial sociology

sociology, medical see medical sociology

sociology, military see military sociology

sociology, rural see rural sociology

sociology of art see art, sociology of

sociology of science

The sociology of science comprises a broad church of approaches concerned to discern the nature and consequences of the social relations associated with the practice and culture of science. Since the early 1970s the sociology of science has acquired a special significance arising from its particular attention to the content of scientific knowledge. By contrast with earlier modes of sociological analysis of science (such as those championed by Merton 1973), the more recent variants have not only examined the sets of institutional and other social relations between those who happen to be scientists, but also attempted to articulate the consequences of these relations for the nature, direction, content and truth status of scientific knowledge itself. The shift in focus from the social relations between those who just happened to be scientists to the character of the knowledge itself marked a significant metamorphosis in the field. The sociology of science (which was more exactly a sociology of scientists) became the 'sociology of scientific knowledge' (SSK).

The claim that the truth value of the content of scientific knowledge is dependent on (or, less strongly, associated with) the social circumstances of its production is of course highly controversial. This form of relativist claim is most famously associated with the 'strong programme in the sociology of knowledge' (Bloor 1976). Under this rubric sociologists were enjoined to adopt a symmetrical approach to explaining the emergence of scientific knowledge: the occurrence of both true and false scientific knowledge, it was suggested, could be explained by invoking the same kinds of sociological factors. Moreover, the strong programme argued that this sociological approach

could be extended to the heartland of rationality, namely to logic and mathematics. Whereas true scientific and mathematical knowledge is traditionally defined in terms of the absence of social factors, this approach argues that science is constitutively social. Unsurprisingly, this and the related work of other British sociologists of science engendered considerable debate between sociologists and philosophers of science throughout the 1970s and early 1980s. Sociology was intruding upon philosophers' turf: philosophers were no longer the (sole) arbiters of which standards and practices could ensure reliable scientific knowledge.

The work of this period both contributed to and derived from earlier debates in the history of science about the relative merits of internalist and externalist explanations of the genesis of scientific knowledge. In particular, the arguments of SSK resonated with the more radical interpretations of Thomas Kuhn's (1970) general description of the dynamics of scientific change, although these were subsequently largely disavowed by their author.

Until this point, SSK was largely based on detailed historical case studies of specific episodes in science: famous experiments; controversies over the interpretation of observations, and so on. Social studies of science depended largely on interviews with scientists who were themselves public spokesmen on behalf of science. In line with Kuhn's adage about the problems of rational reconstruction in the history of science, the accounts resulting from this work often embodied confusions between historical and logical accuracy. In the context of injunctions that sociology should take the 'content' of scientific argument into account, a further formidable barrier to understanding the social basis of science was the fact that its practitioners enjoyed lengthy and intensive specialized technical training. The move by sociologists to study science 'naturalistically' turned this barrier to advantage. Science was studied 'ethnographically': sociologists adopted the stance of an anthropologist joining a strange tribe, engaging in prolonged participant observation of the day-to-day activities of the scientific laboratory (Knorr-Cetina 1981; Latour and Woolgar 1986; Lynch 1985). This afforded the possibility of being deliberately sceptical about just those knowledge claims which seemed most evident and obvious to members of the tribe.

It was evident from the first moment that sociology of science embraced a form of relativism, that significant questions of reflexivity were implicated: in its simplest form, if the claim of sociology of science was that knowledge depended on social factors, then this also applied to the claims of the sociology of science. Many philosophers (incorrectly) seized upon this argument from reflexivity as the basis for the charge that relativistic sociology of science is inconsistent and self-refuting. But, of course, refutation follows only if the presence of social factors entails falsehood and distortion, and it was just this asymmetric approach to the sociology of science which its proponents were at pains to disavow. The point they insisted upon was that social circumstances were implicated in the genesis of scientific knowledge whether it subsequently be designated true or false.

Since the 1980s the sociology of science has both derived from and contributed to several parallel intellectual movements, including post-structuralism, constructivism, feminism, discourse analysis, ethnomethodology and post-modernism. Against this background the further significance of the sociology of science has become evident. The strategic value of SSK is that in demonstrating the relativist basis of scientific knowledge – a particularly hard case of knowledge production – it makes more plausible arguments for the social basis of other forms of knowledge (Collins 1985). However, over and above its epistemologically contentious claims about the social basis for scientific knowledge, the sociology of science (and technology) has relevance for broader questions in social theory. This arises directly from the growing emphasis on 'epistemic' questions, from its attention to the reflexive implications of arguments about the social basis of explanatory adequacy, and from the basic point that 'science' is conventionally defined in opposition to the 'social'. As a result, sociology of science is no longer concerned merely to convey substantive findings about the nature of science, but instead finds itself involved in attempts to respecify key notions such as 'social', 'society' and 'agency'. One example of the last derives from the movement known as 'actor network theory' or the 'sociology of translation' (Callon 1986; Latour 1987; 1991; Law 1991).

Actor network theory posits a description of scientific (and technological) process whereby an array of heterogeneous elements are defined, identified and aligned into a network. In this view successful scientists are those able to enrol the best and most elements into a network. In particular, successful scientists are no longer necessarily those who follow (or, as recommended by Feyerabend, deliberately flout) the rules of scientific method prescribed by philosophers. Instead, in this view, scientists strive to provide effective representation – in a way which conflates the epistemological and political meanings of the term – of an endless variety of esoteric elements: electrons, microbes, scallops and so on. The fidelity of these allies is what holds the network together; the strength of the network is the direct correlate of the robustness of the scientific fact. Scientific and technical facts are not, in this view, derived from adherence to special or

superior methodology. The 'hardness' of a fact is a reflection of subsequent usage rather than of its correspondence to a pre-existing nature; hardness is simply a measure of the work required to unpack and dissolve the network. People are not convinced because something is a fact; rather, a claim becomes a fact in virtue of the conviction of sufficient numbers of allies.

Developments like actor network theory suggest that sociology of science is an important source of new ideas for social theory. Given the basic premise of liberal intellectual enquiry that 'it could be otherwise', sociology of science explores the possibility and problems of a form of relativist enquiry which urges a reconsideration of the nature and scope of social theory. In particular, it provokes an examination of a form of social theory which includes non-human elements as part of an extended conceptualization of the social. What would a social theory look like which attempts to revise basic preconceptions about the nature of 'social' and of 'agency' (Woolgar 1995)?

Whereas the sociology of science in the 1970s and 1980s exhibited considerable solidarity in its antipathy to 'realist' and 'objectivist' philosophies of science, controversy over the later developments has exposed significant fissions in the post-Kuhnian relativist bloc. For example, there is debate over the ways in which Wittgensteinian philosophy can be used as a progenitor of a sceptical sociological programme of enquiry (Lynch 1993); about the extent to which reflexivity and actor network theory take relativism too far (see contributions to Pickering 1992); about whether and to what extent SSK's engagement with relativism and constructivism prevents it from having relevance for moral, political and policy questions.

These questions both underscore the pertinence of sociology of science for theoretical issues beyond the substantive focus upon science, and promise increasing engagement with related intellectual movements – constructivism, feminism, post-modernism, and so on. Over a relatively short space of time sociology of science has undergone several major transformations. This trajectory has involved the successive questioning of a series of asymmetric assumptions about the nature of scientific knowledge and the scope of social study: Merton (1973) problematized the asymmetric notion that science could not be understood as a social institution on a par with others; the strong programme criticized the assumption that truth and false knowledge could not be treated symmetrically; the reflexive project purveys symmetrical treatments of author and object; and actor network theory attempts to redress asymmetries between human and non-human objects.

It is entirely consistent with its relativist commitment that no one of these trends in the brief history of the sociology of science can claim to be the ultimate social perspective on science. Rather, the value of the endeavour is constantly to provoke, re-energize and question accepted views.

Steve Woolgar
Brunel University

References

Bloor, D. (1976) *Knowledge and Social Imagery*, London.
Kuhn, T. S. (1970) *The Structure of Scientific Revolutions*, Chicago.
Latour, B. (1987) *Science in Action*, Milton Keynes.
—— (1991) 'Technology is society made durable' in J. Law (ed.) *A Sociology of Monsters*, London.
Latour, B. and Woolgar, S. (1986) *Laboratory Life: The Construction of Scientific Facts*, Princeton, NJ.
Law, J. (ed.) (1991) *A Sociology of Monsters: Essays on Power, Technology and Domination*, London.
Lynch, M. (1985) *Art and Artefact in Laboratory Science: a study of shop work and shop talk in a research laboratory*, London.
—— (1993) *Scientific Practice and Ordinary Action: Ethnomethodology and Social Studies of Science*, Cambridge, UK.
Lynch, M. and Woolgar, S. (eds) (1990) *Representation in Scientific Practice*, Cambridge, MA.
Merton, R. K. (1973) *The Sociology of Science: Theoretical and Empirical Investigations*, Chicago.
Pickering, A. (ed.) (1992) *Science as Practice and Culture*, Chicago.
Woolgar, S. (1995) 'Science and technology studies and the renewal of social theory', in S. Turner (ed.) *Social Theory at the End of the Century*, Oxford.

Further reading

Woolgar, S. (1988) *Science: The Very Idea*, London.

See also: communication networks; philosophy of the social sciences; positivism; reason, rationality and rationalism; reflexivity; technology.

sociology of sport *see* sport, sociology of

sorcery and witchcraft *see* witchcraft and sorcery

space

Space is everywhere, and the events and behaviours that interest social scientists occur in and through space. The natural sciences claim that for most terrestrial events and processes this space can be characterized geometrically as Euclidean. Space provides an essential means for identifying and individuating among things (Strawson 1959), and cartography is the principal device in our society for portraying these relationships. Space also exerts a ubiquitous and fundamental effect on all behaviour. Examining these effects is one of the principal tasks of human geography (Haggett 1965).

The effects of space stem from its role in causality, which assumes that spatial contact must be made between and among interacting objects. These contacts are becoming ever more indirect with developments in technology, transportation and communication; still, flows of energy, material, and information must be uninterrupted through space for effects to take place. The effect of space depends on how the spatial arrangement of these objects influences their interactions.

Isolating this effect for social systems is extremely difficult. Although the spatial configurations of elements of a social system can be described in geometric terms, geometric properties such as distance do not have a simple effect (as it does in the inverse square law of gravity). This is because the significance of distance for terrestrial events is always modified by the medium through which the interaction flows (*the relational concept of space principle*: Sack 1980), and modern technology provides numerous and shifting channels for interaction.

Even more complex are the effects resulting from humanly created boundaries in space that filter, impede or sever contact. These boundaries are associated with each and every territorial unit in the world, from the nation-state to rights of property and zoning, and laws and rules about appropriate behaviour in streets, building and rooms. The territorial segments of space with their rules clear portions of space so that things can take place (Sack 1986). The territorial rules about in/out of place not only enable the elements of a system and the flows within it to take place, but also constrain or prevent other interactions through space. The door to a room and the boundaries to a nation are opened or closed to constrain and enable specific spatial interactions. The fact that each of these places often serves numerous functions further complicates the analysis of how spatial relations affect the interactions of a system.

Such complications depend on how society organizes territories and develops mechanisms for interaction, and so they are examples of the *social construction of space* (Harvey 1985). 'Spatiality' is the term used to describe the dynamic and interdependent relationship between society's construction of space, and the effects of space on society (Soja 1985). The concept spatiality applies not only to the social level, but also to the individual, for it draws attention to the fact that this relationship takes place through individual human actions, and also constrains and enables these actions (Giddens, 1984).

Robert Sack
University of Wisconsin

References

Giddens, A. (1984) *The Constitution of Society* Berkeley, CA.

Haggett, P. (1965) *Locational Analysis in Human Geography*, London.

Harvey, D. (1985) *Consciousness and the Urban Experience*, Baltimore, MD.

Sack, R. (1980) *Conceptions of Space in Social Thought: A Geographical Perspective*, London.

—— (1986) *Human Territoriality: Its Theory and History*, Cambridge, UK.

Soja, E. (1985) 'The spatiality of social life: towards a transformative retheorisation', in D. Gregory and J. Urry (eds) *Social Relations and Spatial Structures*, Basingstoke.

Strawson, P. (1959) *Individuals: An Essay in Descriptive Metaphysics*, New York.

Further reading

Entrikin, J. (1991) *The Betweenness of Place*, Baltimore, MD.

Tuan, Yi-Fu (1977) *Space and Place*, Minneapolis, MN.

—— (1982) *Segmented Worlds and Self*, Minneapolis, MN.

See also: landscape; political geography; social geography; spatial analysis; territoriality.

spatial analysis

Spatial analysis is an approach within geography and associated disciplines, such as archaeology, which uses statistical methods to generalize about spatial patterns. Geographers have a continuing interest in establishing correlations between phenomena which vary over space, such as rainfall amounts and crop yields. Those who see this as the prime purpose of geography argue that it should be developed as a spatial science, 'concerned with the formulation of the laws governing the spatial distribution of certain features on the surface of the earth.' (Schaefer 1953: 227). There has been much technical and substantive experimentation, assisted by the rapid development of computing technology, into both the mathematical modelling strategies and the statistical procedures that can be employed in reaching such generalizations (see Johnston 1991).

The difficulties of spatial analysis, and hence the challenges that it poses to scholars with certain intellectual predilections, are of two major types.

First, there are the difficulties constituted by the nature of spatial phenomena, their measurement and correlation. Haggett (1965) produced a pioneering classification of the phenomena into point patterns (which may or may not be hierarchically organized); line patterns; areal patterns; flow patterns; and patterns of change in all four. Some of these are relatively easy to measure (a point pattern such as the distribution of shops in a town, or stations along a railway line,

for example), but others are less so, such as the amount of rainfall over an area, which has to be estimated from measurements at a sample of points. (For an introduction to these measurement methods, see Unwin 1981.)

Correlation of measurements of two or more spatial patterns is often difficult because the data have necessarily been collected within different spatial templates. Rainfall amount may be measured at a sample of points, for example, and crop yields by farms: how does one superimpose the one on the other and obtain a measure of their correspondence? As importantly, what are the errors involved in establishing correlations through procedures which combine different frameworks? In many such studies, spatial analysts have to use aggregate data for territorial units – such as counties or countries – when what they are really interested in are the individuals. A good example is provided by students of migration behaviour, who may be interested in the relationship between a person's occupation and propensity to migrate, but can analyse the relationship only between the percentage of people in an area in certain occupations and the percentage of those same people who migrate during a defined period. They have to infer an individual relationship (between class and migration) from an aggregate one, which can involve errors often termed 'ecological' (Alker 1969). Furthermore, the relationship between those two variables can vary according to both the scale of the areas used (in general, the larger the area and the coarser the aggregation the higher the correlation) and the actual configuration of areas (there are thousands of ways in which twenty-nine wards in a city can be combined to form six parliamentary constituencies, for example): together these produce what is known as the 'modifiable areal unit problem' (Openshaw and Taylor 1991).

Advances in attacking these problems have been substantially assisted since the mid-1980s by the development of 'geographical information systems' (GIS) technology. These combined hardware and software packages allow the integration and analysis of data sets on different spatial structures.

The second set of difficulties involves the use of classical (parametric) statistical procedures in the analysis of spatial data. These have a particular property ('spatial autocorrelation') which can introduce bias and error to the statistical estimates of relationships. Spatial autocorrelation is a two-dimensional extension of a widely appreciated, and fairly readily resolved, issue in the analysis of temporal data: the value of a variable at one point in time can be strongly influenced by its value at the previous point, hence introducing an element of double-counting. With temporal data, autocorrelation extends in one direction only; with spatial data it extends in all directions. For this reason, some argue that conventional statistical procedures cannot be applied to many geographical data sets, hence the exploration of specific methods for spatial analysis (Cliff and Ord 1981).

The near-hegemony which spatial science held over the practice of geography in some countries in the 1960s and 1970s has since been challenged by proponents of alternative views. But it continues to attract practitioners seduced by the possibility of identifying and accounting for 'spatial order' (Haggett 1990).

R. J. Johnston
University of Bristol

References

Alker, H. R. (1969) 'A typology of ecological fallacies', in M. Dogan and S. Rokkan (eds) *Quantitative Ecological Analysis in the Social Sciences*, Cambridge, MA.

Cliff, A. D. and Ord, J. K. (1981) *Spatial Process*, London.

Haggett, P. (1965) *Locational Analysis in Human Geography*, London.

—— (1990) *The Geographer's Art*, Oxford.

Johnston, R. J. (1991) *Geography and Geographers: Anglo-American Human Geography since 1945*, 4th edn, London.

Openshaw, S. and Taylor, P. J. (1981) 'The modifiable areal unit problem', in N. Wrigley and R. J. Bennett (eds) *Quantitative Geography: A British View*, London.

Schaefer, F. K. (1953) 'Exceptionalism in geography: a methodological examination', *Annals of the Association of American Geographers* 43.

Unwin, D. J. (1981) *Introductory Spatial Analysis*, London.

Further reading

Haining, R. P. (1990) *Spatial Data Analysis in the Social and Environmental Sciences*, Cambridge, UK.

See also: space.

sport, sociology of

As sport is a central component of popular culture, it is inevitably a suitable target for sociological analysis. Among the many varying detailed definitions of sport, there are two main common elements. First, sport entails physical activity in the form of skill, prowess or exertion, and on this count board games such as chess are usually excluded. Second, sport involves competition based on a formal set of rules. In other words it is institutionalized physical activity.

Social scientific study of sport was slow to develop. To a large extent this reflected a cultural bias in favour of intellectual rather than physical activity. Following the rapid expansion of academic sociology in the 1960s, and the increased television coverage of sport at the same time, the sociology of sport began to develop as a recognized specialism.

Up until the 1970s work in the sociology of sport fell within the two dominant paradigms or schools of sociological thought. Most of the early textbooks were functionalist in their theoretical framework (e.g. Loy and Kenyon 1969) and adopted a positive view of sport as beneficial to society. Sport was seen as functional to the social system in that it encouraged social integration, socialized individuals into obeying rules, and facilitated the release of tension and the channelling of aggression.

By contrast, conflict theory (derived from traditional Marxist thought) emphasized the negative consequences of sport. Sport was regarded as an opiate, which enabled people to escape from the problems of everyday reality. Individuals hooked on sport are less likely to question the existing economic and political structures and thus the inherent inequalities in capitalist societies are maintained. Furthermore, it is argued that the organization of sport inculcates work discipline, encourages aggressive individualism and ruthless competition, traits deemed beneficial to a successful capitalist economy (Brohm 1978).

From the 1970s onwards many sociologists became less concerned with the search for universal grand theories and devised more flexible theoretical approaches, which led to new bodies of research in the sociology of sport. Symbolic interactionists argue that sport is not just a reflection of society but is socially constructed through individual choices and interactions. They take actors' meanings or definitions of the situation as the starting-point for analysis. An example of this kind of work is to study the meanings and identities involved in the process of becoming an athlete (Stevenson 1990).

Diverse strands from neo-Marxism, feminism and cultural studies contribute to the application of critical theory to the sociology of sport. A major theme asserts that the dominant forms of sport in a given society are socially constructed, and sport plays a role in reproducing the dominant social and cultural relations in the wider society (Hargreaves 1986). Critical theory stresses the importance of grounding analysis within specific historical and cultural contexts. Much of the research asks why sport has taken certain forms and organized in different ways in different locations and at different times. Mention should be made also of attempts to analyse sport in relation to 'figurational theory' derived from the work of Elias on the civilizing process (Dunning and Rojek 1992).

In terms of more specific topics of research in the sociology of sport, stratification issues have figured prominently. Social differentiation and social inequality in sports participation have been analysed with reference to social class, race and ethnicity (Jarvie 1991) and gender. Others have examined the relationship between sport and politics, the economy, education, the media and religion (Hoffman 1992). Valuable contributions to the study of sport have been made by historians (e.g. Mason 1980) and geographers (e.g. Bale 1989). An important subdiscipline has developed particularly in Europe on the sociology of football, concentrating initially on football hooliganism (e.g. Dunning *et al.* 1988) and in the 1990s branching into wider aspects (Duke 1991).

Vic Duke
University of Salford

References

Bale, J. (1989) *Sports Geography*, London.
Brohm, J. M. (1978) *Sport: A Prison of Measured Time*, London.
Duke, V. (1991) 'The sociology of football: a research agenda for the 1990s', *Sociological Review* 39.
Dunning, E. and Rojek, C. (eds) (1992) *Sport and Leisure in the Civilising Process*, London.
Dunning, E. *et al.* (1988) *The Roots of Football Hooliganism*, London.
Hargreaves, J. (1986) *Sport, Power and Culture*, Cambridge, UK.
Hoffman, S. (ed.) (1992) *Sport and Religion*, Champaign, IL.
Jarvie, G. (ed.) (1991) *Sport, Racism and Ethnicity*, London.
Loy, J. and Kenyon, G. (eds) (1969) *Sport, Culture and Society*, London.
Mason, T. (1980) *Association Football and English Society 1863–1915*, Brighton.
Stevenson, C. (1990) 'The early careers of international athletes', *Sociology of Sport Journal* 7.

See also: work and leisure.

stagflation

Stagflation is a form of inflation which occurs or persists despite the presence of a substantial or even increasing percentage of measured unemployment of the labour force. The measured inflation rate may, however, be decreasing. Stagflation is therefore not inconsistent with a substantial degree of disinflation, provided only that the residual inflation rate remains significantly positive.

The term stagflation (stagnation plus inflation) came into common usage in the USA in the late 1960s and early 1970s to describe the state of the US economy as American involvement in Indo-China was reduced substantially, and the US government sought to reduce or reverse the so-called 'Vietnam' inflation by fiscal and particularly by monetary measures. But aspects of the stagflation phenomenon itself were known earlier under other names, such as 'cost-push inflation', 'sellers' inflation', 'administered-price inflation', and even 'new inflation'. The novelty was that the inflation rate seemed resistant to reductions in aggregate demand from whatever source.

Stagflation is in any case inconsistent with thoroughgoing price flexibility in input and output markets – in other words, with pure competition. But such flexibility had been assumed, as regards outputs though not the wages of labour, by the expository or 'textbook' Keynesianism of the immediate post-war period (1945–55). Its policy recommendation had been for fiscal and monetary expansion (particularly the former, in the form of higher public expenditures and deficits) as a remedy for unemployment, and for fiscal and monetary contraction as a remedy for inflation, which was itself assumed to arise from the excess demand of 'too much money chasing too few goods'. The uselessness and irrelevance of such recommendations in the face of unemployment with inflation (that is, of stagflation) led to widespread public, political and journalistic dissatisfaction with both Keynesian theory and macroeconomics generally, and to demands for its complete scrapping or restructuring.

Macroeconomics offers no unified counsel as to how stagflation should be dealt with. In particular, counsel which assumes low employment as the major problem, which concentrates on short-run solutions, which is not averse to living with inflation, differs from counsel which assumes inflation to be the major problem, which concentrates on long-run solutions to squeeze inflation out of the economy, and which is not averse to living with unemployment. The problem, in short, is one of social and economic priorities.

In this discussion we shall deal separately with two related scenarios of stagflation. The first type begins with a failure or refusal of the monetary and fiscal systems – particularly the former – to respond to or 'accommodate' an exogenous and often external inflationary shock. The second type begins with monetary and fiscal measures – again, primarily the former – to decelerate or reverse an inflation already in progress. These two stagflation scenarios are often found together, and much of the technical analysis of the two cases is quite similar.

A standard example of the first type of stagflation, the exogenous shock, begins with a rapid and unanticipated rise in the price of an imported raw material like petroleum (the OPEC oil shocks of 1973 and 1979), although a domestic catastrophe like drought or earthquake could serve as well on the supply side. (On the demand side, the US involvement in Vietnam provided a similar shock to the Canadian economy in the middle and later 1960s.) To make the analysis clearer but at considerable cost in realism, we suppose a starting position marked by both high employment and price-level stability. The price of crude oil and petroleum-intensive products (fuels, petrochemicals) rises. The reduced supply of petroleum also lowers the country's real income. Nothing, however, is done to ease either fiscal policy (by tax cutting or increased expenditures) or monetary policy (higher monetary growth rates or lower interest rates). The price increase in the economy's petroleum-intensive sector leads to inflation unless other sectors cut their prices and allow their profit margins to be squeezed, and unless labour accepts some part of the real income cost in lower money and real wages. In these circumstances, any inflation is of the stagflation variety because there is no monetary or fiscal 'validation' of the higher price level at the going high level of employment. Without such validation, the employment and capacity-utilization levels will fall.

In a pressure-group economy, a price rise in one sector does not in the short run trigger price declines in other sectors, in profit margins, or in the wages of organized labour. As we have said, without increased purchasing power to carry the higher price level at the previous level of employment, the employment level will fall. The stagflation scenario is then largely complete. Not entirely complete, however, for we can inquire further into the reasons and rationalizations for the failure of non-oil sectors and of labour to accept price, profit and wage reductions and maintain employment despite the higher oil price and its repercussions through the economy. There are three explanations: forecasting; distributional considerations; and a 'strike' against the monetary and fiscal policy of the government in power. These three reactions are often simultaneous, and it is difficult to distinguish between them.

First, the 'forecasting' reaction is nothing more than a rational belief (in the light of recent history in many countries) that government monetary and fiscal policy will soon 'accommodate' higher oil prices. In which case, prices and wages lowered now would shortly rise again anyway, and patience is preferable to controversial concessions. (We should also remember that much of the initial unemployment consequent upon stagflation is concentrated upon youth not yet hired, youth employed only recently, temporary employees, and employees of concerns in financial difficulty. The bulk of the labour force is protected by 'seniority' institutions.)

Second, as for the 'distribution' reaction, it is very well to argue in the abstract for wage-price-profit concessions in non-oil sectors to maintain employment and avoid inflation, or for the equitable sharing of the real income loss which results from reduced oil supplies. But what does all this mean in the concrete? What constitutes 'equity'? How much of the cost is to be borne by whom? What wages and profit margins

are to be cut, and by how much? The purely competitive market has its own rough-and-ready, quick-and-dirty solutions for such problems, but these are solutions which, for reasons of 'fairness', 'equity', and/or 'compassion', pressure-group economics and collective bargaining are designed to avoid. The distribution argument against deflationary adjustment is, in simple terms, that the group bargaining and negotiation procedures necessary to allocate the oil-shock losses are too costly in time, acrimony, nervous strain, and possible output losses through strikes and bankruptcies, to be undertaken before they have become practically necessary as well as theoretically desirable.

Third, the 'strike' reaction can be understood if we suppose a monetarist government in power, which cannot be expected to yield to group pressure or 'adjust' its fiscal and especially its monetary policies to the higher price of oil. But if we also suppose a regime of parliamentary democracy, subject to periodic elections, then there is likely to exist, or to arise if stagflation persists, an opposition party or faction which advocates accommodative policies of monetary and fiscal ease. Does it not then make good *Realpolitik* deliberately to refuse concessions to the current hard-nosed, anti-inflationist regime, and even facilitate its overthrow by making the stagflation worse and its alternative more attractive? This is what is meant by a political 'strike' against government fiscal and monetary policies, to facilitate the government's replacement by the 'accomodationist' opposition. Until the accommodationist pressure groups have faced and lost at least one general election, it is unlikely that they will themselves accept the adjustments required to end stagflation.

We turn now to the second type of stagflation (which is not fundamentally different), namely, a situation in which a government tightens its monetary and fiscal policy, particularly the former, with the aim of decelerating or reversing an inflationary process in being. We again assume initial high employment and also a situation when some prices (including wages and interest rates) have already been adjusted to next year's anticipated inflation, while others have not yet been adjusted for last year's inflation. Relative prices, wages, and interest rates, in other words, are 'wrong' from the viewpoint of the omniscient economist. In this situation stagnation results from the 'leading' prices and (especially) wage rates being too high and rigid downward. The inflation results from the 'lagging' prices and wages receiving an additional upward fillip in the interests of 'fairness', 'equity', or simply high inflationary expectations. The stagflation results, of course, from the conjunction of the stagnation and inflation factors.

Once again, competitive market forces would provide a rough-and-ready solution if unchecked. This solution would presumably feature the decline of those prices and wages that had risen too high under the influence of over-sanguinary expectations, and the rise of those which had been restrained by caution, money illusion, or long-term contracts. But, once again, power or pressure economics have partially replaced market forces in the short run. The rationalizations of the first type of stagflation, which we have classified as forecasting, distributional disagreement and strikes against controls, take over just as in the second type. There is, however, a minor difference, in that any distributional 'losses' to be allocated are not actual losses as in the first type but the non-achievement of the gains anticipated from outpacing inflation.

Incomes policies are advocated widely as remedies for stagflation, as well as for inflation in the large by writers fearing stagflation. Some of these involve direct controls over prices, wages, interest rates, and/or profit margins. Others are associated with tax penalties for firms raising the wages they pay or the prices they charge beyond levels approved by government agencies. (In the USA, such systems are known generically as TIPs or Tax-Induced Incomes Policies.) The only reason why stagflation requires different remedies than inflation generally is that the greater need to avoid increasing unemployment demands greater delicacy in tightening constraints. Similarly, remedies for the unemployment aspects of stagflation are no different from those for unemployment generally, except for a greater delicacy required to avoid igniting or accelerating inflation.

Martin Bronfenbrenner
Duke University

Further reading

Cornwall, J. (1983) *Post-Keynesian Analysis of Stagflation*, London.

See also: employment and unemployment; inflation and deflation.

state

State refers, in its widest sense, to any self-governing set of people organized so that they deal with others as a unity. It is a territorial unit ordered by a sovereign power, and involves officeholders, a home territory, soldiers distinctively equipped to distinguish them from others, ambassadors, flags, and so on. Since the 1880s, the inhabitable land of the world has been parcelled up into such units; before that, quite large areas had been either unclaimed and uninhabited, or inhabited by nomadic and wandering peoples who were not organized as states. Most states are now represented at the United Nations, and they vary in size and significance from China and the USA at one extreme, to Nauru and the Seychelles at the other.

More specifically, however, the term state refers to the form of centralized civil rule developed in Europe since the sixteenth century. This model has been imitated, with varying success, by all other peoples in the modern world. What most distinguishes the state as an organizational entity is the freedom and fluency with which it makes and unmakes law. The empires of the east, by contrast, were predominantly bound by custom, while in Europe in the medieval period, authority to rule was dispersed among different institutions, and in any case took long to acquire the habits of fluent legislation.

The modern European state came into being gradually, and has never ceased to evolve. Its emergence can in part be traced in each of the major European realms by way of the growing currency of the word 'state', along with its analogues in other European languages: *stato, état, estado, Reich* and so on. The idea, however, has played a varying role in different countries – much less, for example, in Britain than in some continental countries. Machiavelli in *The Prince* (1513) exhibits a clear grasp of the emerging realities of central power, but while he sometimes talks of *lo stato*, he can also use expressions like *loro stato* (your state) which suggest that he is not altogether clear about the difference between a state and a regime. In Jean Bodin's *Six Livres de la République* (1578) later in the sixteenth century, the French state was explicitly theorized in terms of the idea of sovereignty, as the absolute and perpetual power of both making and unmaking laws. The *un*making of laws is important, because it constitutes one reason why the growth of absolute power could be welcomed as a liberation from the dead hand of inherited rules. A weariness with the civil strife of the sixteenth and seventeenth centuries further disposed many people to welcome absolute rulers as guarantors of peace. Monarchs were, of course, far from loathe to acquire this power, and set to work diminishing the co-ordinate powers, and jurisdictions inherited from earlier times. The Church was perhaps the most important of these jurisdictions, and lost power no less in realms that remained Catholic than in those which became Protestant. Parliamentary institutions fell into desuetude everywhere except in England. The nobility, which had been turbulent in the exercise of its feudal powers, were domesticated as courtiers, most famously at the Versailles of Louis XIV. Monarchy became strictly hereditary and evolved mystiques both of blood and divine right. The absolute power thus generated was often used with a ruthless cynicism typified in the motto 'canons are the arguments of princes' and exemplified in the careers of spectacularly aggrandizing monarchs like Charles XII of Sweden and Frederick the Great of Prussia. But all states alike tried to expand their power both by mobilizing the resources available and by conquering new territory. It would be a mistake, however, to think that this early modern absolutism became indistinguishable from despotism. The sovereigns remained subject to myriad customary restrictions and had to operate for the most part in terms of law, whose abstractness limits its usefulness as an instrument of pure policy. Further, as the new system settled down in the later seventeenth century, the more powerful classes, such as the nobility, clergy and the bourgeoisie in the towns, solidified into corporations which sensibly limited the freedom of action exercised by monarchs who found in Enlightenment rationalism a doctrine highly conducive to their dreams of mobilizing national power. What emerged was the *ancien régime*, a social form so immobile it needed a French Revolution and a Napoleon to destroy it.

The issues raised by the emergence of this quite new form of civil association can best be grasped by their reflection in European political philosophy. A pure theory of the state was presented by Thomas Hobbes in *Leviathan* (1651). Hobbes argued that subjection to a sovereign ruling by law was the only alternative to the incessant discord created when proud and insecure individuals jostled together. Hobbes was clear, as Machiavelli was not, that the state (or *Leviathan*) is an abstract and impersonal structure of offices conditionally exercised by particular individuals. People must, as subjects, rationally consent to the absolute power of the sovereign, but this consent lapses if the sovereign cannot protect them, or if the sovereign begins directly to threaten their lives. The boldness of the Hobbesian conception, which reflects the thoroughness with which Hobbes thought the issue through, lies in the extrusion of any external limitations on the sovereign power: what the sovereign declares to be just is *ipso facto* just, and the sovereign has the right to determine religious belief, and what may be taught in the schools. Liberty is the private enjoyment of the peace brought by civil association, a peace in which alone culture and material prosperity may be garnered.

Being a philosophical work, the *Leviathan* explained but did not justify, and fragments of its argument were appropriated by both sides in the English civil war. Both sides were offended by it. The *Leviathan* was publicly burned at Oxford in 1685. Immediately after the revolution of 1688, John Locke published *Two Treatises on Government*, which softened the intolerably austere picture of the state Hobbes gave. This was an occasional work which popularized the notion that governments rested upon the consent of their subjects, and were limited by natural rights (to life, liberty and property) with which people entered civil society. Their business was to protect such rights. Locke avoided the idea of sovereignty altogether and emphasized that

the rulers *represented* the ruled. The spread of liberalism in the next two centuries extended this idea, both in theory and in practice.

In the course of the eighteenth century, it became clear that the modern European state raised quite new problems, both practical and theoretical. It was a free association of individuals claiming the power to legislate for themselves, without any necessary moral, religious or metaphysical commitments. Two ideas, potentially disharmonious, consequently dominated further development: community and freedom. The best formulation of the problem is in Chapter 6 of Rousseau's *Social Contract* (1762):

> How to find a form of association which will defend the person and goods of each member with the collective force of all, and under which each individual, while uniting himself with others, obeys no one but himself, and remains as free as before.

Rousseau's solution focused on a general will constituting a community of citizens devoted to the public interest. Such a conception clearly emerged from the ancient conception of the virtuous republic which had haunted European thought since Machiavelli's *Discourses on the First Ten Books of Livy* (1518), and which was unmistakably subversive of the European system of extended monarchies. Just how subversive it was soon became evident, both in the thought of Immanuel Kant, who argued that republics were the condition of perpetual peace, and in the French Revolution, whose protagonists adopted Rousseau posthumously as one of their own.

The problem was that the classical republic was possible only in a small city with a homogeneous population. Montesquieu had argued in *De l'esprit des lois* (1748) (*The Spirit of the Laws*) that no such thing was possible in the conditions of modern Europe. In the 1820s Hegel presented in the *Philosophy of Right* (1821) an account of the modern state as the objective embodiment of the fully developed subjective freedom towards which the human spirit had always been tending. At the time, however, a whole group of writers emerged to emphasize the misery and repression, as they saw it, of modern life and the iniquity of the state. Marx and Engels argued that the state was an illusion masking the domination of the bourgeois class, and predicted that after a proletarian revolution, the state would wither away. A newly homogeneous humankind would be able to surpass the unity and virtue of the classical republics on a worldwide scale.

The actual history of states has been one of a continuous growth, both in their claim to regulate the lives and property of their subjects, and in their physical capacity to enforce such claims. It is, for example, possible to regulate a literate society much more completely than an illiterate one. The propensity of European states to engage in war with one another has provided frequent emergencies in which necessity trained governments in how to regulate; and all states now have bureaucracies and other instruments of control. Yet, paradoxically, the increase in the state's range and power has produced countervailing decreases in effectiveness. When its functions were limited to guaranteeing order and security, the state was accorded immunity from some of the moral restraints binding on individuals. The doctrine called 'reason of state' authorized the breaking of treaties, deceit, and the employment of violence, when necessary. From the nineteenth century onwards, some extensions of state power (especially the redistributions of wealth which began to constitute the state as a system of welfare for all members of society) were justified on the ground that the state stood for a higher morality. Citizens thus came to believe that they had rights *against* the state. The state's claim to suspend law, to guard its own secrets, to the use of non-legal measures in dealing with enemies who themselves resorted to terror – all the traditional apparatus of *raison d'état* – was challenged, and it was felt to be the duty of the state to represent the highest moral standards even against those who violated them. In developments such as this, and in the persistently transforming dynamism of the idea of democracy, will be found reasons for seeing the modern state, at least in its European heartland, not as an abstract idea, but as an institution ceaselessly responsive to the beliefs that move its subjects.

Kenneth Minogue
London School of Economics and Political Science

Further reading

Dunleavy, P. and O'Leary, B. (1987) *Theories of the State*, London.
d'Entreves, A. P. (1967) *The Notion of the State*, London.
Mabbott, J. D. (1967) *The State and the Citizen*, 2nd edn, London.
Maritain, J. (1951) *Man and the State*, London.
Oakeshott, M. (1975) *On Human Conduct*, London.

See also: citizenship; civil society; federation and federalism; government; legitimacy; political theory; state, origins of; welfare state.

state, origins of

Since the seventeenth century, much western scholarship has focused on the origin of the state, a form of political organization in which power rests in the hands of a small governing group that monopolizes the use of coercive force to maintain internal order and cope with neighbouring peoples. This type of government is found in all large-scale societies, which are also invariably characterized (even in socialist examples) by marked political and economic disparities.

Theorizing has centred on whether states evolve primarily through consent or conflict and as a result of internal or external factors. It has also been debated keenly whether states have improved or degraded the human condition by comparison with smaller, seemingly more natural societies. 'Social contract' theorists, including Thomas Hobbes and John Locke, believed that individuals submitted willingly to the state in return for the protection it offered their persons and property. Karl Wittfogel and Julian Steward argued that the state first evolved to manage large irrigation systems in arid regions. Others see the state developing in order to regulate the production, importation and redistribution of valuable materials.

The oldest 'conflict' theories postulated that states originated as a result of conquest, especially of agricultural peoples by pastoralists. Marxists view agricultural and craft specialization as producing socioeconomic differentiation that results in class conflict and ultimately the formation of the state as a means to maintain ruling-class dominance. Robert Carneiro argues that population increase within geographically or socially circumscribed areas results in warfare over arable land and the emergence of the state. More generally, Mark Cohen maintains that population increase leads to the intensification of food production and eventually to competition for arable land, population agglomeration, and the development of the state. In each of these theories, the state evolves at least in part to protect social and political inequalities.

None of these theories explains satisfactorily the origin of the state. Marxists assume that emergent classes developed prior to the state, a position that is not widely accepted. Other explanations do not appear to cover all, or even most, cases. 'Prime-mover' theories of the origins of the state have been rejected. Synthetic theories, which combine a number of causal variables, have not proved more successful. It is widely accepted that many different factors promote the development of larger and more differentiated societies which require state controls. This has led interest to shift away from explaining why the state develops to how.

Increasing use has been made of 'information theory' to account for the development of the state. It is argued that the delegation of decision making to central authorities becomes increasingly necessary for political systems to function adequately as their size and complexity increase. Centralized control requires the collection of information from all parts of the system and the effective transmission of orders from the centre to these parts. Archaeologists have argued that the state can be equated with settlement hierarchies of at least three levels, corresponding to an equal number of levels of decision making. This does not explain, however, why early civilizations were characterized by marked economic and status disparities rather than simply by functionally differentiated leadership roles.

A further application of information theory suggests that gossip, ridicule, accusations of witchcraft and other economic and political levelling mechanisms that are found in small, egalitarian societies work only when people are known to one another. As larger societies develop, leaders can use their newly acquired control of public information to weaken opposition and silence critics. This facilitates the concentration of political and economic power among an elite and the development of conspicuous consumption as a feature of elite lifestyles.

At the same time, it is recognized that rulers must curb the predatoriness of officials and excessive increases in the bureaucracy and distribution of state largess if exactions are to remain within limits that are acceptable to the taxpayer. This assumes that the state provides services, such as defence and internal order, which the bulk of the population accepts as essential. If exactions are kept within accepted limits, most people will continue, at least passively, to support the state.

Additional theories stress the emulation of inegalitarian behavioural patterns within extended and nuclear families and other spheres of personal interaction. This strengthens the power of the state by making domination appear universal and natural from each person's earliest infancy. Attention is also paid to hegemonic ideologies which elites employ to naturalize inequality and enhance their own power. There is, however, disagreement about the extent to which dominated classes accept elite claims or construct counter ones. The latter position rejects theocratic explanations of state power. While the state is not coterminous with human societies, discussions of its origins remain intimately tied to an understanding of human nature.

Bruce G. Trigger
McGill University

Further reading

Clastres, P. (1977) *Society against the State*, New York.
Flannery, K. V. (1972) 'The cultural evolution of civilizations', *Annual Review of Ecology and Systematics* 3.
Haas J. (1982) *The Evolution of the Prehistoric State*, New York.
Johnson, G. A. (1973) *Local Exchange and Early State Development in Southwestern Iran*, Ann Arbor, MI.
Patterson, T. C. and Gailey, C. W. (eds) (1987) *Power Relations and State Formation*, Washington, DC.
Tainter, J. A. (1988) *The Collapse of Complex Societies*, Cambridge, UK.

See also: political anthropology; state.

state of nature *see* primitive society; social contract

statistical reasoning

Statistical reasoning (SR) is a form of reasoning with probabilistic features, applicable to inference and decision making in the presence of an uncertainty that cannot be expressed in terms of known and agreed chance probabilities. Thus SR is not relevant to games of pure chance, such as backgammon with well-engineered dice, but is likely to be involved in guessing the voting intentions of an electorate and fixing an advantageous polling date.

Its application is usually mediated by some standard statistical method (SM) whose prestige and convenience, especially if computerized, can induce a neglect of the associated SR. Even when explicitly formulated, SR may be plausible (or not) in appearance and efficacious (or not) in its ultimate influence. The evolutionary theory of SR (Campbell 1974) postulates that it is a genetically controlled mental activity justified by survival advantage. A related black-box view of the efficacy of SR may be useful in deciding between the claims of different SR schools that their respective nostrums are found to work in practice. We shall concentrate here, however, on the plausibility of the types of SR usually associated with particular statistical methods, and go on to consider principles that may assist in the continually required discrimination in favour of good SR. Our i^{th} example of method is denoted by SMi and the jth example of possible reasoning for it is denoted by SRi_j. Undefined terms will be supposed to have their ordinary interpretations.

SM_1: The incorporation of an element of objective random sampling in any observations on a population of identifiable items, that ensures for each item a specified, non-negligible probability of being included in the sample.

$SR1_1$: Without the element of random sampling, it is impossible for the sampler to justify the selection of items without reference to some systematic, comprehensive theory, which may be erroneous or, worse, subject to undeclared or subconscious bias.

$SR1_2$: With the element, it is maintainable by probabilistic argument that the unobserved items should not be systematically different from those observed. This permits tests of hypotheses about the population as a whole.

$SR1_3$: The power of such tests may be enhanced by the device of restricted randomization which excludes in advance the selection of samples that would only weakly discriminate among alternative hypotheses.

SM2: Random manipulation of controllable independent variables in the treatment of experimental units, and the analysis of the effect of this manipulation on dependent variables.

$SR2_1$: If the effect referred to were reliably established, this could be described as causal, operating either directly or through the agency of other variables. The use of an isolated random manipulator – uninfluenceable and influential only through controllable independent variables – is necessary in order to rule out the hypothesis of spurious correlation between the dependent variables and naturally occurring variation of the independent variables. As a bonus, it also rules out the possibility of the experimenter using 'inside knowledge' to produce such a correlation by unconscious or deliberate choice of the values of the control variables.

$SR2_2$: The extent to which such causal inference is possible in non-experimental investigation depends on the extent to which changes in the independent variables are induced by factors judged to be equivalent to an isolated random manipulator, as in *quasi-experimental studies* (Blalock 1972).

SM3: Evaluation of the achieved significance level P for the observed value t of a test statistic T whose (null) distribution is specified by a (null) hypothesis H_0, i.e.

$$P = Pr (T \geqslant t \mid H_0).$$

$SR3_1$: When it is small, P provides a standardized interpretable encoding of the deviation of t from the values of T that would be expected if H_0 were true. Increasing values of t are encoded as decreasing values of P which induce increasing dissatisfaction with H_0. A small value of P forces the simple dichotomy: either H_0 is true and a rare event has occurred, or H_0 does not describe the actual distribution of T.

$SR3_2$: P is not the 'probability that H_0 is true', which probability is not definable in the set-up of SM3.

$SR3_3$: The 'dissatisfaction' in $SR3_1$ increases smoothly: there is no critical value, 0.05 for example, at which P suddenly becomes scientifically important.

$SR3_4$: The provenance of T should be taken into account in the calculation of P when, for example, T has been selected as a result of a search for any interesting feature of the data.

SM4: Calculation, from the data x, of a 95 per cent confidence interval $(\ell(x), u(x)$ for a real-valued parameter θ in a statistical model defined as a set $\{Pr_\theta\}$, indexed by θ, of probability distributions of X, the random generic of x.

$SR4_1$: The particular interval $(\ell(x), u(x))$ is regarded as relevant to inference about the true value θ because of the coverage property.

$$Pr (\ell(X) \leqslant \theta \leqslant u(X)) = 0.95$$

$SR4_2$: The value 0.95 is not the 'probability that θ lies in the particular interval $(\ell(x), u(x))$', which probability is not definable in the set-up of SM4.

$SR4_3$: Can the 'relevance' mentioned in $SR4_1$ be reasonably maintained when, as may happen, the calculated interval turns out to be the whole real line, or the empty set, or when it may be logically established that the interval contains θ? Such counter-examples to $SR4_1$ do not arise in the commoner applications of the confidence interval method.

SM5: Given data x for a statistical model indexed by a parameter θ, a posterior probability distribution for θ is calculated by the Bayesian formula

$$posterior\ density \propto prior\ density \times Pr_\theta(x)$$

and used freely for purposes of inference and decision.

$SR5_1$: There are now several nearly equivalent formulations of the Bayesian logic (Fishburn 1970) whose upshot, roughly, is that any individual, willing to accept a few qualitative axioms about 'probability' and to give expression to them in a rich enough context, will discover that she or he has a subjective probability distribution over everything – or at least over everything related to x. The formula in SM5 is particularly convenient if the first fruits of the introspective process for determining this distribution are not only the assignment of probability 1 to the assertion that data x was indeed randomly generated by the statistical model but also the probability distribution of θ which is the 'prior density'.

$SR5_2$: If the 'process' in $SR5_1$ were faithfully undertaken by a very large number of Bayesians in a range of contexts, then, if the statistical models to which unit probability is assigned were indeed correct, it would be a consequence of the supposed randomness in the models that the data x would, with high probability, show significant departure from its associated model in a specifiable proportion of cases. This would be so, even if the Bayesians were fully aware of the features of their data at the time of their probability assignments.

It may therefore be necessary to defend the rights of Bayesians to use statistical models that would be rejected by other statistical methods.

SR5$_3$: The difficulty for the Bayesian approach just described may be overcome by the assignment of a probability of $1 - \epsilon$ rather than unity to the statistical model: awkward data can then be accommodated by reserving the prior probability ϵ for any ad hoc models.

SR5$_4$: A similar loophole may be employed in dealing with the paradox created by data that simultaneously deviates highly significantly from what is expected under a sharp sub-hypothesis, $\theta = \theta_0$, say, of the model, while increasing the odds in favour of θ_0 (Lindley 1957). For example, suppose a 'psychic' correctly predicts 50,500 out of 100,000 tosses of a fair coin and the statistical model is that the number of correct guesses is binomially distributed with probability. For the prior that puts prior possibility $\frac{1}{2}$ at $\theta = \frac{1}{2}$ and $\frac{1}{2}$ uniformly over the interval $(0,1)$, the posterior odds in favour of $\theta = \frac{1}{2}$ are $1.7/1$, although the outcome has an achieved significance level of 0.0008.

SR5$_5$: Bayesians claim that all probabilities are subjective with the possible exception of the quantum theoretic sort. At best, subjective probability distributions may agree to assign unit probability to the same statistical model but, even then, the posterior distributions would differ, reflecting individual priors. Such differences have not succumbed to extensive but largely abortive efforts to promulgate objective priors (Zellner 1980), just as attempts to formalize the apparently reasonable slogan 'Let the data speak for themselves!' have proved nugatory.

SM6: Given are

1 a statistical model$\{Pr_\theta\}$
2 a set $\{d\}$ of possible decisions
3 a loss function $L(d, \theta)$, the loss if decision d is taken when θ is true
4 a set $\{\delta\}$ of decision rules, each of which individually specifies the decision to be taken for each possible x.

Deducible are the risk functions of θ, one for each δ, defined by the expectation under Pr_θ of the randomly determined loss $L(\delta(X),\theta)$ The method, not completely specified, consists in selecting a decision rule from $\{\delta\}$ that has a risk function with some optimal character.

SR6$_1$: The ambiguity of choice of T for the 'achieved significance level' method (SM3), coupled with that method's lack of concern about its performance when H_0 does not hold, led Neyman and Pearson to treat testing a hypothesis as what may now be viewed as a special case of SM6. This has, simply, $\{d\} = \{$Accept H_0, Reject $H_0\}$, $L = 0$ or 1 according as d is right or wrong and, as a consequence, a risk function equivalent to a statement of the probabilities of error 'size' and '1 – power'.

SR6$_2$: A difficulty with the risk function approach to inference that is implicit in the Neyman-Pearson treatment of hypothesis testing was pointed out by Cox (1958). It can be illustrated with a simple story. Two pollsters A and B wanted to test the hypothesis that no more than half the electors of a large city, willing to respond to a particular Yes – No question, would do so affirmatively (Cohen 1969). Pollster A suggested that the poll would require only 100 randomly chosen respondents, whereas B wanted to get 10,000 responses. They agreed, first, to toss a fair coin to decide the sample size, second, to employ the 5 per cent hypothesis test, most powerful in detecting a Yes:No ratio of 2:1, with probabilities of error defined before the outcome of the toss is known. They check with a statistician that this test would have an overall power of 99 per cent for the alternative hypothesis that the proportion of yeses was 2/3. In the event, the sample size was 10,000 and the number of yeses was 5,678. Both A and B were astonished when advised that this number was too small to reject the hypothesis by the agreed test, even though, had it been obtained in a survey with a non-random choice of the sample size 10,000, it would have had an achieved significance level (SM3) of less than 1 in a million!

The reason for this behaviour is that the Neyman-Pearson lemma, justifying the test, ignores all possibilities other than the null and alternative hypotheses, under both of which any outcome in the region of 5,678 yeses has only the remotest possibility of occurring.

SR6$_3$: Another apparent difficulty for risk functions arose in connection with the widespread use of least squares estimates for normal models. Taking risk as mean square error, James and Stein (1961) found that improvements could be made, whatever the true values of the parameters, by means of a special estimator even when this combined the data of quite unrelated problems. This striking phenomenon may be regarded as providing a criticism of least squares estimation viewed as a form of restriction on $\{\delta\}$: a

Bayesian approach whose prior insists that the problems are indeed unrelated will not allow any pooling of information – but will also not produce least squares estimates.

The above examples of SR were elicited in response to statements of representative statistical methods and are of a somewhat *ad-hoc*, fragmentary character. Are there no general principles that can be brought to bear on any problem of statistical methodology of whatever size and shape? The answer depends very much on the extent to which the 'uncertainty' in the problem has been crystallized in the form of an agreed statistical model $\{Pr_\theta\}$. Given the latter, the ideas of Birnbaum (1969) and Dawid (1977) deserve wider appreciation.

In Dawid's terminology, an 'inference pattern' is any specified function $I(\xi,x)$ of the two arguments: a 'potential experiment' ξ and associated potential data x (the value of variable X). For each ξ in a specified class, a statistical model $\{Pr_\theta\}$ is provided for X, where the parameter θ indexes the supposed common uncertainty in all the potential experiments considered. These are the defining conditions under which a number of principles require that I be the same for data x in ξ and data x′ in $\xi′$:

Principle	Conditions for $I(\xi,x) = I(\xi',x')$
'Distribution'	ξ and ξ' have the same $\{Pr_\theta\}$ and $x = x'$
'Transformation'	ξ' is given by a 1 – 1 transformation t of the data in ξ and $x' = t(x)$
'Reduction'	$I(\xi,x)$ is a function of $r(x)$, ξ' is given by reporting the value of r, and $x' = r(x)$
'Ancillarity'	$a(X)$ has a constant distribution (independent of θ), ξ' is the experiment whose statistical model is the set of probability distributions of X given $a(X) = a$, $a(x) = a$ and $x' = x$
'Sufficiency'	ξ' reports the value of a sufficient statistic $t(x)$ and $x' = t(x)$
'Likelihood'	the likelihood functions of θ, given x in ξ and given x′ in ξ', are proportional

There are implications among such principles so that if one accepts the weaker looking ones, one is then obliged to accept the stronger ones – such as the likelihood principle. Very many statistical methods violate the latter.

When there is no agreed statistical model, however, SR cannot receive the (occasionally doubtful) benefit of mathematical support. Perhaps as a consequence, it has not received much attention in the literature, except in the popular texts excellently represented by Huff (1973) or the occasional philosophical article (most philosophical discussions of SR are implicitly model-dependent). At this pre-modelling level, there is a broad consensus among the statistically minded as to what constitutes poor SR: it is much more difficult to characterize good SR. The latter is required to avoid the elementary logical pitfalls but has to go well beyond that in constructive directions. A paradoxical snag in statistical thinking about some problems is how to recognize that the data are inadequate to support such thinking: imaginative SR is often needed to specify the kind of data needed to support the embryonic inferences being formulated.

Pre-modelling SR stands to gain much from the recent advances in 'descriptive statistics' largely associated with the work of Tukey (1977). The techniques of 'exploratory data analysis' and 'computer-intensive methods' (Diaconis and Efron 1983) extend the range of statistical activity ultimately subject to SR scrutiny but, at the same time, they enhance the risks that SR will be neglected by methodologists fascinated by the complexity of such techniques.

M. Stone
University of London

References

Birnbaum, A. (1969) 'Concepts of statistical evidence', in S. Morgenbesser *et al.* (eds) *Philosophy, Science and Method: Essays in Honor of E. Nagel*, New York.

Blalock, H. M. (1972) *Causal Models in the Social Sciences*, London.

Campbell, D. T. (1974) 'Evolutionary epistemology', in P. A. Schilpp (ed.) *The Philosophy of Karl Popper*, La Salle, IL.

Cohen, J. (1969) *Statistical Power Analysis for the Behavioral Sciences*, New York.

Cox, D. R. (1958) 'Some problems connected with statistical inference', *Annals of Mathematical Statistics* 29.

Dawid, A. P. (1977) 'Conformity of inference patterns', in J. R. Barra *et al.* (eds) *Recent Developments in Statistics*, Amsterdam.

Diaconis, P. and Efron, B. (1983) 'Computer-intensive methods in statistics', *Scientific American* 248.

Fishburn, P. C. (1970) *Utility Theory for Decision Making*, Publications in Operations Research 18, New York.

Huff, D. (1973) *How to Lie with Statistics*, Harmondsworth.

James, W. and Stein, C. (1961) 'Estimation with quadratic loss', *Proceedings of the 4th Berkeley Symposium of Mathematical Statistics and Probability* 1.

Lindley, D. V. (1957) 'A statistical paradox', *Biometrika* 44.

Tukey, J. W. (1977) *Exploratory Data Analysis*, Reading, MA.

Zellner, A. (1980) *Bayesian Analysis in Econometrics and Statistics: Essays in Honor of Harold Jeffreys*, Amsterdam.

See also: mathematical models; methods of social research.

status

Difficult to conceptualize and often elusive to the empirical grasp, yet the idea of status is essential to an understanding of social stratification. It has been apparent to social scientists that members of all known societies are stratified to some extent, that sometimes the basis of this order has been relatively simple, such as sex and age, and sometimes the divisions are many and complex.

In the past, status was a juristic term connoting individuals' rights and duties as relevant to their condition and station in life. However, in the nineteenth century, after social upheavals had shaken the old order to its foundations, Alexis de Tocqueville commented that among the repercussions could be noted a quickening in the scramble for status. To people of higher status, the inherited right to privileges and honour seemed to be slipping away; and to those of lower status, there was suddenly hope of changing their lot. The sharp changes in status fortunes that emerged from the erosion of privilege could not be encompassed by the old legalistic definition of the term, yet it was some time before it was broadened sufficiently to be useful as a tool for analysis.

This came with Max Weber, who pointed out that status, class or income, and political power are the three major dimensions of social stratification. It is unclear which had priority but Weber implied that if an individual has high status, wealth would follow, although they usually overlap, both being products of the distribution of power. In saying that status is 'an effective claim to social esteem in terms of positive or negative privileges' (Weber 1978 [1922]), Weber emphasized its relational base and that a status claimant must have an audience from which to receive or to demand deferential response. Gerth and Mills (1953) emphasized that a status situation is not fixed, but tends to be played out on the uncertain grounds of claimant and audience negotiation and compromise. Harold Garfinkel (1956), in his work on status degradation, underlines the crucial role a fickle audience can play in determining the destiny of a claimant.

A different interpretation has distinguished the work of anthropologist Ralph Linton (1936). For him, status is primarily a position in a social structure, involving rights, duties, and reciprocal expectations of behaviour, none of which depends on the personal characteristics of the status occupant. Davis (1948) further developed this idea for sociology. Merton (1957) went on to postulate that individuals have an array of social positions, forming a composite or status set. Lenski (1954) studied disjunction between the status and class positions of individuals and groups, called 'status crystallization', in which rewards in one do not correspond to rewards in the other. He found that when this is perceived as an inequity, it elicits dissatisfaction and responses of anger and desire to change the system, or withdrawal and apathy.

In summary, two major conceptualizations of status have emerged: status, as seen by Weber and his followers, is relational and intersubjective; status, as outlined by Linton and others, is positional and highly structured. Much research takes an uneasy path between the two.

Types

Although the literature is replete with typologies of status, among the most important are those of 'ascribed' and 'achieved' status. Ascribed status is that which is inherited, such as sex, race, or ethnicity, or over time, or age, and is crucial to defining the basic patterns of people's lives. Achieved status is acquired through personal effort or chance, possibly from occupational or educational attainment. Both of these types are bases for the formation of 'status communities'.

Status communities

From collections of individuals who have commonalities of occupation or education or experience, communities tend to develop. Members, becoming cognizant of their similarities, of shared styles of living and interests, come to identify with one another (Bensman 1972). The status community organizes to defend the 'good life', to capture and monopolize whatever privileges and rewards it can, to block entry to lower-status invaders, and to press and push ever upward to higher-status heights. It is a power base eventually devolving upon its members the moral sense of *deserved* honour and superiority.

Lower-status groups, which Weber (1946) calls 'negatively privileged', might also cohere into an 'ethnic community'. Just as with status communities, ethnic members believe in their own dignity and honour, though perhaps necessarily rooted elsewhere than in the misery of the present; the past, perhaps, or even in a millenarian vision of the future. For many of these groups – Blacks, Jews, lower-caste Indians, women, and so on – it is the lack of social power and the marks of ascriptive status that have bound them to the wheel of ill fortune.

Status symbols

'Status symbols' are those visible marks that celebrate the individual's or group's difference and superiority. Erving Goffman (1972) calls status symbols 'specialized means of displaying one's position'. Symbolic value can be lent to almost any object or situation. Language, etiquette, gestures, material objects, particularly if they are difficult to acquire, can distinguish a group and set it apart. Whatever connotes the individual's or group's place in the social order can be used to elevate it symbolically and, by reference, to demean outsiders. During periods of rapid social change or in urban settings where the individual's status is unknown, status symbols can be manipulated and fraudulently used by individuals laying claim to higher status, and indeed the bearer can gain greater deference and privilege than deserved.

A major criticism of status theory is that it is politically conservative, that the gradations of increasing or decreasing status obscure the reality of sharp class lines (Vanneman and Pampel 1977). Yet inequality is hardly explicable by reference *only* to a class system of discrete categories, nor, for that matter, to a concept emphasizing achieved status positions. Neither adequately accounts for the continuing troubles of subordinate groups. Status analysis, which emphasizes the relations between groups and the long-term effects of ascriptive status, might more effectively explain a world piloted by organized honour, privilege, and power when used together with other stratification theory.

Charlotte Wolf
Memphis State University

References

Bensman, J. (1972) 'Status communities in an urban society: the musical community', in H. R. Stub (ed.) *Status Communities in Modern Society*, Hinsdale, IL.

Davis, K. (1948) *Human Society*, New York.

Garfinkel, H. (1956) 'Conditions of successful degradation ceremonies', *American Journal of Sociology* 61.

Gerth, H. and Mills, C. Wright (1953) *Character and Social Structure*, New York.

Goffman, E. (1972) 'Symbols of class status', in H. R. Stub (ed.) *Status Communities in Modern Society*, Hinsdale, IL.

Lenski, G. E. (1954) 'Status crystallization, a non-vertical dimension of social status', *American Sociological Review* 19.

Linton, R. (1936) *The Study of Man*, New York.

Merton, R. K. (1957) *Social Theory and Social Structure*, 2nd edn, Glencoe, IL.

Vanneman, R. and Pampel, F. C. (1977) 'The American perceptions of class and status', *American Sociological Review* 42.

Weber, M. (1946) *Max Weber; Essays in Sociology*, trans. and ed. H. Gerth and C. Wright Mills, New York.

—— (1978 [1922]) *Economy and Society, I and II*, Berkeley, CA. (Original edn, *Wirtschaft und Gesellschaft*, Tübingen.)

Further reading

Berger, J. M., Fiski, M. H., Norman, R. Z. and Zeldich, M. (1977) *Status Characteristics and Social Interaction*, New York.

Blumberg, P. (1974) 'The decline and fall of the status symbol: some thoughts on status in a post industrial society', *Social Problems* 21.

Jackman, M. R. and Jackman, R. W. (1973) 'An interpretation of the relation between objective and subjective social status', *American Sociological Review* 38.

Jackson, E. F. (1962) 'Status consistency and symptoms of stress', *American Sociological Review* 27.

Wolf, C. (1978) 'Social class, status and prestige', in J. S. Roucek (ed.) *Social Control for the 1980's*, Westport, CT.

See also: prestige; role; stratification.

stereotypes

Stereotypes are usually defined as relatively fixed and oversimplified generalizations about groups or classes of people. In practice, they generally focus on negative, unfavourable characteristics, although some authorities include in their conceptions of stereotypes positive social overgeneralizations as well.

The term derives from the Greek *stereos*, meaning solid, and *tupos*, meaning image or impression, from *tuptein*, to strike. A stereotype was originally a solid printing mould or plate which, once cast, was difficult to change, but the word was adapted for its present usage by Walter Lippmann in his classic book, *Public Opinion* (1922). Lippmann was the first to articulate the 'cognitive miser' theory, according to which stereotypes serve an important function as cognitive simplifications that are useful for the economical management of a reality that would otherwise overwhelm us with its complexity. The phenomenon of stereotyping has become a standard topic in sociology and social psychology. Early empirical studies (e.g. Katz and Braly 1933) stressed the surprising degree of consensus in the stereotypes depicting different ethnic groups. Labelling theorists in sociology have emphasized the power of stereotypes in generating invidious emotional responses to deviant individuals or minority group members. Frustration-aggression theory in psychology also stimulated interest in the dynamics of prejudice and emphasized the motivated nature of many of our stereotypes (Dollard *et al.* 1939).

Two important developments in social psychology shortly after the Second World War accelerated interest in the processes of stereotyping. One was a growth of interest in the role of motivation and past experience as determinants of our perceptions. A capstone of this development was an article by Jerome S. Bruner (1957) linking perception to the concept of pre-established cognitive categories. Bruner explicitly stressed the assimilation of incoming information to the 'typical instance' of a category, thus providing a fruitful context for the discussion of stereotyping.

The second development was the hugely influential research project, *The Authoritarian Personality* (Adorno *et al.* 1950). This represented an attempt to illuminate some of the hidden dynamics of anti-semitism, ethnocentrism, and of more general predispositions towards oversimplified thinking associated with fascist belief systems. Stereotypic thinking was found to characterize high scorers on the F scale, which was designed to measure authoritarianism.

Gordon Allport's (1954) analysis of prejudice and stereotyping began a general movement towards treating stereotypes as a consequence of normal cognitive functioning rather than looking at them as a by-product of frustration or pathological defensiveness. In this and subsequent treatments, stereotypes have been viewed as the often unfortunate end-products of useful and even necessary strategies of information processing.

As the field of social psychology has become explicitly more cognitive, there has been renewed interest in stereotypes and the experiences and settings that contribute to them. The edited volumes by Mackie and Hamilton (1993) and Zanna and Olson (1994) summarize much of the research into the phenomenon of stereotyping; for a critical perspective based on social identity and self-categorization theories see also the monograph by Oakes *et al.* (1994). Although it is still generally acknowledged that stereotypes may at times be motivated and serve as a justification for hostile or prejudiced attitudes, more stress is currently being placed on the contention that processes of prejudgement and categorization are built into every act of perception or information processing. Thus stereotypes are nothing more than cognitive categories that often satisfy emotional needs, prove quite resistant to disconfirming information, and operate as powerful cognitive magnets to which such information is assimilated.

Although stereotypes are generally viewed as the maladaptive extreme of the cognitive processing continuum, and serve to perpetuate social conflict and discrimination, there is also much evidence that they may be readily discarded when judging individual group members. Thus it appears that some individuals are quite capable of maintaining strong and rather rigid views of typical group members even when these views do not necessarily influence how a particular member is perceived or evaluated.

Edward E. Jones
Princeton University

Andrew M. Colman
University of Leicester

References

Adorno, T. W., Frenkel-Brunswik, E., Levinson, D. J. and Sanford, R. N. (1950) *The Authoritarian Personality*, New York.
Allport, G. W. (1954) *The Nature of Prejudice*, Cambridge, MA.
Bruner, J. S. (1957) 'On perceptual readiness', *Psychological Review* 64.
Dollard, J., Doob, L. W., Miller, N. E., Mowrer, O. H. and Sears, R. L. (1939) *Frustration and Aggression*, New Haven, CT.
Katz, D. and Braly, K. (1933) 'Racial stereotypes in 100 college students', *Journal of Abnormal and Social Psychology* 28.
Lippmann, W. (1922) *Public Opinion*, New York.
Mackie, D. M. and Hamilton, D. L. (eds) (1993) *Affect, Cognition, and Stereotyping: Interactive Processes in Group Perception*, San Diego, CA.
Oakes, P. J., Haslam, S. A. and Turner, J. C. (1994) *Stereotyping and Social Reality*, Oxford.
Zanna, M. P. and Olson, J. M. (eds) (1994) *The Psychology of Prejudice*, Hillsdale, NJ.

See also: labelling theory; prejudice; social psychology; stigma.

stigma

The sociologist Erving Goffman is usually credited with introducing the term stigma into the social sciences. He began his influential text, *Stigma: Notes on the Management of Spoiled Identity* (1963), with a brief etymological summary:

> The Greeks . . . originated the term *stigma* to refer to bodily signs designed to expose something unusual and bad about the moral status of the signifier. The signs were cut or burnt into the body and advertised that the bearer was a slave, a criminal, or a traitor – a blemished person, ritually polluted, to be avoided, especially in public places. Today the term . . . is applied more to the disgrace itself than to the bodily influence of it.
>
> (Goffman 1963)

The concern with stigma fits well into a broader and older concern with deviance and its labelling. The labelling perspective favoured by many sociologists of deviance (especially those who share the orientation of symbolic interactionism) emphasizes the social construction of boundaries separating the normal from the deviant. These boundaries serve an important symbolic function of affirming in-group values and are relevant in several different domains. Goffman distinguished between blemishes of character (for example, mental illness, homosexuality, criminal behaviour), abominations of the body (physical deformities of various kinds) and the tribal stigma of race, nation or religion. Although it is important to note that stigma can emerge in each of these domains, it should also be recognized that the tendency to avoid disabled or deviant persons may stem from the awkwardness of not knowing how to act in their presence, rather than being a reflection of the drastic discredit usually associated with the term stigma.

Cutting across the content domains of potential stigma, a number of dimensions may be identified that affect the degree of discredit likely to result from the process. One such dimension is *concealability*. A condition that can be concealed in normal circumstances raises the possibility of 'passing' as someone without the condition, about whether or when to disclose the condition. Another dimension is *origin*: how did the condition come about and to what extent was the person responsible? People tend to attribute greater responsibility for obesity, alcoholism, or AIDS than for mental retardation or the paraplegia of a combat veteran. Other dimensions of variation include *aesthetic* concerns, the extent to which the condition actually or symbolically *imperils* others, and to which it may *disrupt* normal social interaction. Deafness, for example, is typically more socially disruptive than blindness, although particular interaction contexts may make blindness more salient as a disability.

In spite of these sources of variation and their important differential consequences, the stigmatizing process has a number of features that transcend the particularities of any single deviant condition. Associated with a crucial act of categorizing or labelling the deviant person, there is an arousal of emotions typically featuring a mixture of revulsion and sympathy. Discussions of stigma (Ainlay *et al.* 1986; Jones *et al.* 1984; Lee and Loveridge 1987) have made much of the ambivalence involved in stigma. The act of labelling often sets in motion a process of devastating cognitive reconstruction that gives innocent behavioural data an ominous, tell-tale meaning. Thus there are strong tendencies for stigmatizing reactions to move in the direction of stereotypes that rationalize or explain the negative affect involved. Many stigmatizing reactions, however, are initially characterized by vague discomfort and unjustified 'primitive' affect.

Edward E. Jones
formerly, Princeton University

References

Ainlay, C., Becker, G. and Coleman, L. M. (eds) (1986) *The Dilemma of Difference: A Multidisciplinary View of Stigma*, New York.

Goffman, E. (1963) *Stigma: Notes on the Management of Spoiled Identity*, Englewood Cliffs, NJ.

Jones, E. E., Farina A., Hastorf, A., Marcus, H., Miller, D. and Scott, R. A. (1984) *Social Stigma: The Psychology of Marked Relationships*, New York.

Lee, G. and Loveridge, R. (eds) (1987) *The Manufacture of Disadvantage: Stigma and Social Closure*, Milton Keynes.

See also: deviance; labelling theory; prejudice; social psychology; stereotypes.

stock-flow analysis

Economic variables can be classified into two basic forms: 'flow variables' (such as income) and 'stock variables' (such as wealth). Other variables may be formed as a ratio between flows (such as the proportion of income saved), a ratio between stocks (such as proportion of wealth held as liquid assets) or a ratio between a flow and a stock (such as the ratio between capital and output). Clarity in economic analysis requires that a clear distinction between flows and stocks be maintained at all times. A flow should always have attached to it the relevant time period *during* which the flow occurs (to say that a person's income is $500 is meaningless until one adds 'per week' or 'per month' or whatever the relevant period). For precision, a stock variable should always have attached to it the date at which the stock existed or was valued. A change between a stock at one date and the stock at a later date will be a flow during the period covered by the dates (see Fisher 1906)..

Stock-flow analysis is concerned with the relationship between stock variables and flow variables: there are two basic branches. The first branch comprises causal stock-adjustment models in which a flow is causally related to changes in a 'desired' or 'equilibrium' stock. The second branch is concerned with valuation models in which a stream of future flows is discounted and summed to a present-value stock equivalent.

An important feature of stock-adjustment models is that adjustment to change may be spread over several time periods, so giving rise to lags, distributed variously over those time periods, in the impact on flows. Hence the analysis of distributed lags tends to be a feature of stock-adjustment models.

Examples of stock-adjustment models are, in macroeconomics, the accelerator principle in which the aggregate flow of fixed-capital formation is related to changes in the 'desired' stock of fixed capital, and, in microeconomics, the relationship of the flow of demand for new cars to the pre-existing stock of cars (partly because of replacement demand). Bringing stocks into the analysis of flows has proved a powerful explanatory device and has served greatly to elucidate the variance in flows. For example, it is likely that a full understanding of personal sector savings flows (particularly in conditions of inflation) will require more information on personal sector stocks of financial assets, and for this we will have to await the regular compilation of national and sectoral balance sheets to complement the national income flow accounts.

Valuation models, based on the operation of discounting, are a form of stock-flow analysis in which a stream of future flows is rendered into a stock-equivalent at the present date. In this way, a series of flows (or entitlement thereto) may be given a single valuation or 'price'. Accordingly, discounting is a common technique of financial analysis.

Dudley Jackson
University of Wollongong

Reference

Fisher, I. (1906) *The Nature of Capital and Income*, New York.

See also: capital consumption.

strategic management

The subject of strategic management is the positioning of the firm in its broadest sense – its relationship with its customers, suppliers and competitors. Strategic management is therefore a discipline very different from those concerned with the functional activities of the firm – accounting, marketing, scheduling and control of operations, personnel and human relations – although all of these will be influenced by the firm's strategy.

Writers on strategic management commonly distinguish three phases of the process. The first is an appreciation of the internal and external environment within which the firm operates. The second is the choice of a strategy to match that environment, and the third is the implementation of the preferred strategy within the firm. This distinction is somewhat artificial; the selection of strategy must be determined by the business environment within which the company operates, and it is impossible to make sensible choices of strategy in the absence of an analysis of the means by which alternative strategies are to be implemented.

Strategic management was first recognized as a subject in the early ·1960s. It originated in integrative management courses taught at the Harvard Business School, and in works such as Ansoff (1965) and Andrews (1980). Strategic management was then equated with corporate planning – the preparation of quantitative forecasts or targets for five or more years ahead. Scepticism about the practical value of such exercises in the face of changing economic conditions and competitive behaviour has steadily diminished the influence of such strategic plans, and the resources which firms devote to them.

In the early 1970s, new thinking in strategic management came from consulting companies such as McKinsey and the Boston Consulting Group which developed tools of market and competitor analysis. Conventional scholarship emphasizes the evolutionary nature of scientific knowledge, while the commercial orientation of strategic management has established a subject in which the dependence of new thinking on old is often concealed, and slight differences in approach are much exaggerated. This manner of evolution has seriously inhibited the establishment of an agreed structure or body of knowledge in strategic management, and calls into question the claims of the subject to be regarded as an academic discipline.

Porter (1980) is the most comprehensive exposition of strategy as competitor analysis. But since the early 1980s there have been reactions against analytic styles of strategic management. Softer approaches are in vogue, which attach greater importance to human factors in understanding the position of the firm. There is wide agreement that implementation is the most neglected of the three components of strategy. Yet the difficulties of implementing strategy are perhaps more appropriately seen as criticisms of the process of strategy formulation itself.

The most important developments on strategic management concern resource-based theories of strategy. The strategy of the firm is, in this view, dependent on the match between the unique capabilities of the firm and the external environment within which it operates. While reasserting the prescriptive focus of strategic management, this approach emphasizes the firm-specific nature of valid prescription and, by focusing on the relationships between individuals and markets, links the economic and the sociological dimensions of strategy.

John Kay
London School of Economics and Political Science

References

Andrews, K. R. (1980) *The Concept of Corporate Strategy*, rev. edn, Homewood, IL.
Ansoff, H. I. (1965) 'The firm of the future', *Harvard Business Review* 43(5).
Porter, M. E. (1980) *Competitive Strategy: Techniques for Analyzing Industries and Competitors*, New York.

Further reading

Kay, J. A. (1983) *Foundations of Corporate Success*, Oxford.
Quinn, J. B., Mintzberg, H. and James, R. M. (1980) *The Strategy Process*, Englewood Cliffs, NJ.

See also: human resource management; leadership; management theory; public management.

stratification

Social stratification refers to the division of people into layers or strata which may be thought of as being vertically arranged, in the same way that layers of the earth are arranged above or below other layers. Although the geological metaphor which sociologists use draws attention to a striking feature of many, if not most, societies, there are limits beyond which its use becomes misleading. The arrangement of persons in a society is enormously more complex than the arrangement of the layers of the earth, and social strata are not visible to the naked eye in the way that geological strata are.

When we talk of social stratification we draw attention to the unequal positions occupied by individuals in society. Sometimes the term is used very broadly to refer to every kind of inequality, although it may be useful to restrict it to inequalities between groups or categories of persons with a definite or at least a recognizable identity. Thus we speak of stratification between manual and non-manual workers or between Blacks and Whites, but not usually of stratification between the members of a family. The implication of this is that one may reasonably describe such simple societies as of the Andaman Islanders or the !Kung Bushmen as being unstratified although there certainly are inequalities in these societies.

There is disagreement as to whether stratification is a universal feature of all human societies (Bendix and Lipset 1967). While some of this disagreement may be traced to divergent uses of the same terms, there are also genuine differences in point of view. The so-called functional theory of stratification maintains that stratification in the broad sense not only is universally present but also performs a definite social function. Others maintain that just as there have been societies in the past where stratification in the strict sense was absent or rudimentary, so also there can be societies in the future where it will be absent or inconsequential. It is not easy to see how societies which are at present stratified will cease to be stratified in the future or to prove that stratification has a determinate social function because it is present everywhere, or nearly everywhere.

The geological metaphor of stratification tends to obscure the fact that in a given society the same individuals may be differently ranked depending upon the criteria selected. Every society uses more than one criterion of ranking, and different societies do not give prominence to the same criteria. It requires much skill and judgement to identify the significant criteria in each case and to determine their degree of consistency. While some scholars stress the consistency between the different dimensions of stratification or even the determining role of one or another among them, others argue that, though related, these dimensions are mutually irreducible (Béteille 1977).

The economic aspect or dimension of stratification is important in all societies and manifestly so in modern societies. But we see how complex the problem is as soon as we try to specify the nature of the economic dimension, for it may refer to either wealth or income or occupation which, although closely related, are not one and the same. Wealth and income are relatively easy to measure, but, since their distribution is continuous, there is no easy way to draw lines between people on the basis of how much of the one or the other they have. Moreover, what matters is not simply how much wealth or income people have but also how it is acquired and how it is used.

In past societies, wealth in some forms, such as land, was valued more than wealth in other forms, such as money, and inherited wealth more than wealth acquired by trade or commerce. Capitalism reduces the significance of such distinctions but does not eliminate them altogether. And while the accumulation and transmission of wealth might be severely restricted in socialist societies, disparities of income are important there as well.

All industrial societies, whether of the capitalist or the socialist type, show a certain family resemblance in their occupational structure. The occupational role acquires far greater salience in these societies than in all other societies known to history. As the separation of the occupational from the domestic domain becomes more complete, more and more people come to have definite occupations, and their social identity comes increasingly to be defined in terms of these. Much of an adult's life is spent in the pursuit of an occupation in a factory or an office, and the person's early life is largely a preparation for it. The occupational structure itself becomes more differentiated and more complex.

While all occupations may in some sense be equally useful, they are not all equally esteemed by members of society. The commonsensical view of this, at least in capitalist societies, is that occupations are differentially esteemed because they are unequally paid; but this leaves unexplained why some occupations are better paid than others. The ranking of occupations is in fact a very complex phenomenon, being governed partly by considerations of scarcity and partly by the values distinctive to the society concerned (Bendix and Lipset 1967; Goldthorpe and Hope 1974). In all modern societies, occupational ranking is complicated by the variability of values among sections of the same society and by the rapid replacement of old occupations by new ones.

While there obviously is some correspondence between the esteem enjoyed by an occupation and the income it provides, this correspondence is not perfect (Cole 1955). This is partly due to the changes continuously taking place in the modern world among the various occupations in regard to both income and esteem. But there may be other, more fundamental, reasons behind the lack of perfect correspondence.

Disparities of income between manual and non-manual occupations have been greatly reduced in most industrial societies, but manual occupations continue to be less esteemed than non-manual ones, sometimes even when they are better paid. This is true not only of capitalist but also of socialist societies, despite the bias for the manual worker in socialist ideology.

Occupation is closely linked with education in all industrial societies but probably more so in socialist than in capitalist ones (Cole 1955; Wesolowski 1979). Obviously, education is valued because it provides access to well-paid occupations but it is valued for other reasons as well. Education gives people access to knowledge and to the inner meaning of life both within and outside their own occupational sphere; all of this is valued for its own sake and not merely for the financial returns it provides.

Education, occupation and income enter as important ingredients in the styles of life adopted by men and women. Social stratification manifests itself typically through differences in styles of life among members of the same society (Bottomore 1965; Heller 1969). Such differences relate to both the material and the non-material sides of life and may manifest themselves in gross or subtle ways Habitation, dress and food all indicate differences in styles of life and, as is well known, language divides people no less than it unites them. Groups differentiated by their styles of life, particularly when they are ranked among themselves, are generally referred to as status groups.

Popular usage does not distinguish systematically between classes and status groups, but it is useful to do so. According to a famous distinction, a class is defined by its position in the system of production, whereas what characterizes a status group is its pattern of consumption (Weber 1978 [1922]). A class is conceived of as being a somewhat larger aggregate than a status group, and classes acquire their identity in opposition to each other in the political arena. Whereas the relations between classes are typically relations of conflict, the relations between status groups are relations of emulation. Emulation by inferiors of the styles of life of their superiors provides stability to the prevailing system of stratification.

Income, occupation and education are not the only things that count in regard to status or style of life, even in modern societies. Race and ethnicity have independent significance in regard to both. Although differences of race are biological in origin, how much they count in stratification depends on the value assigned to these differences in the society in question. The very existence of sharp differences of race as in South Africa and, to some extent, the USA indicates the restriction by law or custom of intermarriage between members of different races. Such restriction is usually, if not

invariably, associated with feelings of superiority and inferiority between the races concerned.

Endogamy, as either a rule or a tendency, is perhaps the most effective mechanism for maintaining the boundaries between social strata (Ghurye 1969; Weber 1958 [1920]). On the whole it is more strictly practised between groups based on race, caste and ethnicity than between those that are defined solely in terms of income, occupation and education. Where boundaries are strictly maintained between racial or ethnic groups through endogamy, through residential segregation and in other ways, access to higher education and employment tends to be more difficult for members of some than of other groups. In such cases equality of opportunity can do very little to prevent the reproduction of the existing system of stratification.

Stratification by race is seen in its clearest and most extreme form in South Africa. There the segregation of races is not only a widespread social practice, but until recently, was also accepted as a basic social principle. Segregation or apartheid – literally meaning 'apartness' – was the official norm of South African society, and it sought to regulate every sphere of social life from marriage to politics. The roots of apartheid, as of a great deal of stratification by race, go back to the experience of colonial rule. In South Africa the unequal relationship between a settler and an indigenous population was imposed by the former on the latter and perpetuated until 1994 through the principle and practice of segregation.

Power plays a part in the maintenance and reproduction of social stratification everywhere (Béteille 1977; Dahrendorf 1968). First, there is the use of the apparatus of state for enforcing the privileges and disabilities of superior and inferior strata, as in pre-1994 South Africa. But violence may also be used for the same end outside the framework of the state as in the case of lynching, whether of Blacks by Whites in the USA or of untouchables by caste Hindus in India. Whereas power is important everywhere in upholding the existing order, the extent to which force is openly used to the advantage of superior against inferior strata varies. The naked use of force becomes common where agreement breaks down in a society about the ranks to be occupied by its different members.

Race is often compared with caste, since both forms of stratification are marked by great rigidity. Indeed, the term caste has become a synonym for rigid social stratification. The caste system was found in its most characteristic form in traditional India among the Hindus, although divisions of a broadly similar kind were found also among other religious groups in India as well as in other South-Asian countries. Until recently the divisions of caste were very elaborate among the Hindus, and they were kept in place by a variety of rules and restrictions. Each caste or subcaste had in the course of time developed its own style of life through which it maintained its social identity, and Max Weber thought that castes were best characterized as status groups.

Many changes are taking place in the caste system. The division into castes in contemporary India – like the division into races in the USA – coexists with many other divisions and inequalities whose roots lie elsewhere. An important aspect of the traditional order of Indian society was that inequalities between people not only existed in fact but also were accepted as a part of the natural scheme of things. To a large extent this was true also of medieval Europe where the hierarchical conception of society was supported by both law and religion. Things have changed considerably, and in most societies inequality or stratification exists within a legal and moral environment in which equality is the dominant value. This means that stratification in most contemporary societies is far more amorphous and fluid than the division of past societies into orders or estates or castes whose hierarchy was recognized and acknowledged by most, if not all, members of society.

André Béteille
University of Delhi

References

Bendix, R. and Lipset, S. M. (eds) (1967) *Class, Status and Power: Social Stratification in Comparative Perspective*, London.
Béteille, A. (1977) *Inequality Among Men*, Oxford.
Bottomore, T. B. (1965) *Classes in Modern Society*, London.
Cole, G. D. H. (1955) *Studies in Class Structure*, London.
Dahrendorf, R. (1968) 'On the origin of inequality among men', in R. Dahrendorf, *Essays in the Theory of Society*, London.
Ghurye, G. S. (1969) *Class, Caste and Occupation*, Bombay.
Goldthorpe, J. H. and Hope, K. (1974) *The Social Grading of Occupations: A New Approach and Scale*, Oxford.
Heller, C. S. (ed.) (1969) *Structured Social Inequality: A Reader in Comparative Social Stratification*, London.
Weber, M. (1958 [1920]) *The Religion of India*, New York. (Original edn, section of *Gesammelte Aufsätze zur Religionsoziologie*.)
—— (1978 [1922]) *Economy and Society*, 2 vols, Berkeley, CA. (Original edn, *Wirtschaft und Gesellschaft*, Tübingen.)
Wesolowski, W. (1979) *Classes, Strata and Power*, London.

Further reading

Jencks, C. *et al.* (1972) *Inequality*, New York.
Marshall, T. H. (1977) *Class, Citizenship and Development*, Chicago.

See also: caste; class, social; elites; equality; hierarchy; Marx's theory of history and society; prestige; social mobility; social structure and structuration; status.

stress

The breadth of the topic of stress is reflected both in the diversity of fields of research with which it is associated and in the difficulty of finding an adequate definition. Some stresses such as noise, heat or pain might best be considered as properties of the environment which represent departure from optimum and which differ only in intensity from levels which are normally tolerable. Thus, stress could be seen as a stimulus characteristic, perhaps best defined as an 'intense level of everyday life'. In contrast, it is possible to envisage stress as a pattern of responses associated with autonomic arousal. Initial impetus for this approach was provided by Selye (1956), who proposed that stress is the nonspecific response of the body to any demand made upon it. Physiologically committed, it assumed that the stress response was not influenced by the nature of the stressful event, but was part of a universal pattern of defence termed the 'General Adaptation Syndrome'. Selye demonstrated a temporal pattern in cases of prolonged stress. There were three identifiable phases: alarm, resistance and exhaustion. The capacity of the organism to survive was assumed to be a function of exposure time; resistance to further stress was lowered in the alarm phase, raised in the subsequent resistance phase and further lowered in the exhaustion phase.

Neither stimulus-based nor response-based definitions cope well with varied and complex stresses such as taking an examination, parachute jumping, surgical operations and public speaking. The problem that 'one man's stress is another man's challenge' is partly solved by a definition which presupposes that stress is the result of imbalance between demand and capacity, and, more importantly, by the *perception* that there is imbalance. The factors which create ambition and translate into intentions are as important in determining stress levels as those which affect capacity.

A number of models have been proposed which assume that the conditions for stress are met when demands tax or exceed adjustive resources (Cox and Mackay 1978; Lazarus 1966; 1976). In particular, Lazarus has proposed that several appraisal processes are involved in the assessment of threat. The intensity of threat depends not only on stimulus features, but also on the perceived ability to cope. In turn, coping may take the form of direct action or avoidance and may involve anticipatory preparation against harm, or the use of cognitive defence strategies.

Fisher (1984) proposed that mental activity in the perception and response to stress forms the essential basis of worry and preoccupation, and is likely to be concerned with the assessment and establishment of control. The perception of personal control not only is a likely determinant of psychological response, but also has been shown to determine hormone pattern. For example, applied and laboratory studies have suggested that control over the work pace dictates the pattern of noradrenaline and adrenaline balance, and may determine the degree of experienced anxiety.

Working conditions and events in life history together form an important source of potential stress and may have a pervasive influence on mental state and physical health in the long term. Stress at work is no longer thought to be the prerogative of white-collar and professional workers. Repetitive manual work is associated with high adrenaline levels, paced assembly-line workers have been found to be very anxious, and computer operators who spend more than 90 per cent of their time working at the interface may be tense for 'unwind periods' after work. Depression is likely when personal discretion is reduced, when there is lack of social support, or when social communication is impaired, as in conditions of high machine noise.

A significant additional feature of life history is the adjustment required by change. Two important consequences of change are interruption of previously established activity and the introduction of uncertainty about future control. Studies of homesickness in university students have suggested the importance of worry and preoccupation as features of adjustment to change. Grieving for the previous lifestyle is as much a feature as concern about the new, and in some individuals this may be an important prerequisite for the establishment of control (Fisher 1984; Fisher et al. 1985).

Competence is a necessary condition of the exercise of personal control, but it may be difficult to maintain in stressful circumstance. Studies of the effects of environmental stress on attention and memory have indicated changes in function in relatively mild conditions of stress. Although the changes may not always be detrimental in mildly stressful conditions, at high levels of stress, behavioural disorganization and consequent loss of control are characteristic. It has been found that performance is related to arousal level in the form of an inverted 'U' curve. Mild stresses, by increasing arousal, are likely to improve performance, whereas severe stresses are more likely to cause deterioration. However, the assumption of a single dimension of arousal has been undermined by physiological evidence suggesting that there are arousal patterns which may be stimulus or response specific. The concept of compatibility between concurrent and stress-produced arousal levels was proposed by Fisher (1984) as part of a composite model of the relationship between stress and performance. The model also takes into account the influence of worry and mental preoccupation associated with stress and the establishment of control as joint determinants of performance change.

In both occupational and life-stress conditions, the pattern of behaviour – and hence the accompanying hormone balance which features in a particular stress problem – may result from decision making about control. A critical decision concerns whether a person is helpless or able to exercise control. The mental processes involved in control assessment may involve detecting and summarizing the relationship between actions and consequences over a period of time. In dogs, prior treatment by inescapable shock was shown to produce inappropriate helplessness in later avoidance learning (Seligman 1975), which led to the hypothesis that depression and helplessness are closely associated, and may be transmitted as expectancies about loss of control. The question 'Why are we not all helpless?' is appropriate, given the high probability that most people experience helplessness on occasions in their lives; it has been partly answered by research which suggests that normal subjects resist helplessness and depression by overestimating control when rewards are forthcoming (Alloy and Abramson 1979). Equally, they may put more effort into a task, or find other evidence suggesting that control is possible, thus raising self-esteem (Fisher 1984). By contrast, those already depressed assess control levels accurately, but are more likely to blame themselves for circumstances which indicate that there is no control. Therefore, lack of optimistic bias and lack of objectivity in attributing the cause of failure distinguishes the depressed from the non-depressed person.

These considerations suggest that analysis of decisions about control in different stressful circumstances may provide the key to understanding the risks attached to long-term health changes in an individual. A person who is too readily helpless may be depressed and may incur the punishment produced by control failure, and thus experiences distress. A person who struggles against the odds of success incurs the penalty of high effort. A person who practises control by avoidance may need to be constantly vigilant, and to evolve elaborate techniques for avoidance, and, if successful, will never receive the information which indicates control is effective.

The outcome of decision making about control could have implications for physical health because of the mediating role of stress hormones. Repeated high levels of catecholamines may, because of functional abuse of physical systems, increase the risk of chronic illness such as heart disease. High levels of corticoid hormones may change the levels of antibody response, thus changing the risk associated with virus and bacterial borne illness, as well as diseases such as cancer (Cox and Mackay 1982; Totman 1979).

The process of deciding about control may underline worry activity and may be prolonged or attenuated as a function of environmental contingencies. Worrying may be a very effective way of solving problems because it is an intense period of ruminative thinking. However, during the process of worrying, due to hormone levels that create and sustain suppression of the immune response, vasoconstriction and increased blood clotting tendency are likely. The worried person provides a perfect method for raising the hormone focused risk of illness (Fisher and Reason 1989). Worry levels are self reported as very high following major changes associated with moves and losses (Fisher 1990; Fisher and Cooper 1991).

Shirley Fisher
University of Strathclyde

References

Alloy, L. B. and Abramson, L. Y. (1979) 'Judgements of contingency in depressed or non-depressed students: sadder but wiser?', *Journal of Experimental Psychology (General)* 108.

Cox, T. and Mackay, C. (1982) 'Psychosocial factors and psychophysiological mechanisms in the aetiology and development of cancers', *Society of Science and Medicine* 16.

Fisher, S. A. (1984) *Stress and the Perception of Control*, Hillsdale, NJ.

—— (1990) *Homesickness, Cognition and Health*, Hillsdale, NJ.

Fisher, S. and Cooper, C. (1991) *On the Move: The Psychology of Change and Transition*, Chichester.

Fisher, S. and Reason, J. (1989) *Life Stress, Cognition and Health*, Chichester.

Fisher, S., Murray, K. and Frazer, N. (1985) 'Homesickness, health and efficiency in first year students', *Journal of Environmental Psychology* 5.

Lazarus, R. (1966) *Psychological Stress and the Coping Process*, New York.

—— (1976) *Patterns of Adjustment*, Tokyo.

Seligman, M. E. P. (1975) *Helplessness: On Depression Development and Death*, San Francisco, CA.

Selye, H. (1956) *The Stress of Life*, New York.

Totman, R. (1979) *The Social Causes of Illness*, London.

See also: activation and arousal; anxiety; psychosomatic illness.

structural linguistics

Structural linguistics, the study of languages through observation and description of their basic units and the relationships of same, may be said to have begun with the great Sanskrit grammar of Panini (*c.*300 BC). This work was not known in the west until the end of the eighteenth century. The foundations of modern structural linguistics were laid in the later nineteenth century by Jan Baudouin de Courtenay, a Pole teaching in the Russian University of Kazan, and Ferdinand de Saussure, a Swiss. Baudouin, working closely with his Polish graduate student (and successor in the Kazan chair), Mikolaj Kruszewski, approached the notion of a system of basic units of sound ('phonology') and form ('morphology') which derive their informative power from the fact of their opposition (or contrast) to each other. It was at Kazan that the terms *phoneme* and *morpheme* were first used in approximately their present sense. Saussure, whose work was known in Kazan, was working along the same lines, and he, who knew no Russian or Polish, was acquainted with the Kazan ideas through German translations of two works by Kruszewski. Kruszewski died early and Saussure's lectures were published only after his death by devoted students. Since Baudouin de Courtenay, because of his concern for social and psychological factors in language use, came to define phonological and morphemic units as, at least in part, mental constructs, he lost touch with the main body of structuralists, who were led by Edward Sapir and Leonard Bloomfield in the USA and by N. S. Trubetzkoy, Roman Jakobson and L. V. Shcherba in Europe. Shcherba remained in the Soviet Union, while Trubetzkoy (from Vienna) and Jakobson helped to found the Prague Circle, where structural linguistics was stretched to include 'structural' studies of literature. An offshoot of the Prague Group was the Copenhagen Circle, of which the leading figures were Louis Hjelmslev and Hans Uldall.

A major difference between the formulations of the Prague School (as exemplified in the work of Jakobson) and the New World structuralists is the definition of the basic units of phonology (phonemes) as *bundles of distinctive features* by the former, and as *classes of sounds and phones* by the latter (exemplified particularly in the work of Bernard Bloch, Bloomfield's successor at Yale). An interesting development of the Prague doctrines was offered by the Frenchman André Martinet who sought, in the phonological structure of a language, the 'pressures' or impulses for future phonological development. In the Bloomfield-Sapir tradition, universals of phonological structure have been sought notably by C. F. Hockett, and of morphosyntax by J. H. Greenberg, while efforts at writing a distribution-based grammar (with minimal recourse to meaning) were made by Zellig Harris.

Much of the linguistic work ever done has been accomplished in the twentieth century as a result of the efforts of Kenneth Pike, a student of Sapir's, who has trained hundreds of missionary linguists at the Summer Institute of Linguistics. Thus, structural linguistic analysis, as a prerequisite to Bible translation, has given us excellent accounts of many languages from the preliterate world.

D. L. Olmsted
University of California

Further reading

Hymes, D. and Fought, J. (1981) *American Structuralism*, The Hague

Rieger, J., Szymcak, M. and Urbanczyk, S. (eds) (1989) *Jan Niecislaw Badouin de Courtenay, a Lingwistika Swiatowa* (Conference Proceedings), Warsaw.

Stankiewicz, E. (ed. and trans.) (1972) *A Baudouin de Courtenay Anthology: The Beginnings of Structural Linguistics*, Bloomington, IN.

See also: Saussure, Ferdinand de; structuralism.

structuralism

Since the 1940s the term structuralism has become generally used for a certain approach (not a school or dogma), particularly in linguistics, social anthropology and psychology. Although there is some difference between the way it is applied in these disciplines, and between American and European usage, it generally refers to types of research in which the object of investigation is studied as a system. Because a system is a 'set of connected things or parts' (Oxford English Dictionary), this entails concentration on the relations between the elements which constitute the system; in the words of Dumont (1970 [1966]):

> We shall speak of structure exclusively . . . when the interdependence of the elements of a system is so great that they disappear without residue if an inventory is made of the relations between them: a system of relations, in short, not a system of elements.

Ferdinand de Saussure (1931 [1916]), who is generally regarded as the founder of structural linguistics, makes a basic distinction between the study of language as *parole* (speech, that is, language as produced by a speaking individual) and of language as *langue*: as a system. The *system* is essential, while *parole* is 'contingent and more or less fortuitous'.

The structuralist emphasis on the relations between the elements in a system appears, for example, in Saussure's discussion of the value (*valeur*) of words:

> the value of words in a language which express similar ideas limit each other's scope. The value of synonyms, like 'to fear', 'to dread', 'to be afraid of' is entirely determined by their mutual opposition. If 'to dread' did not exist, its meaning would be adopted by its neighbours.

The field most developed by later linguists is structural phonetics, usually termed 'phonology' in Europe and 'phonemics' in the USA. The aim of phonetics, as a *parole* discipline, is to give the most accurate description of speech sounds; phonology, on the *langue* level, is concerned with the question of which speech sounds function as phonemes, in other words, the smallest units which differentiate between the meanings of words. That is to say, it is not the phonologist's concern whether there is a phonetic difference between the English -p- sounds in *pin, prone, up*, etc. It is his concern that the opposition between -p- and -b-, -d-, -f-, for example, makes for the distinction between words with different meanings such as *pin* and *bin, pin* and *din, pin* and *fin*, and so on, that is, that the -p- in English is a phoneme.

Roman Jakobson developed a means to specify what distinguishes each phoneme, that is, what are any phoneme's 'distinctive features': 'The inherent distinctive features which have so far been discovered in the languages of the world . . . amount to twelve basic oppositions, out of which each language makes its own selection' (Jakobson and Halle 1971). These basic oppositions are, for example, vocalic versus non-vocalic, abrupt versus continuant, voiced versus voiceless, and so on. This approach is typically structural, as it defines phonemes as the elements in a system, by considering what distinguishes each element from the others, that is to say, by concentrating on the relations between the elements. The relations, in this case, are of the most elementary type: binary oppositions. It is not surprising that this linguistic method made an impression on the structural anthropologist Lévi-Strauss. Another aspect of the distinctive feature analysis affected Lévi-Strauss more than any other anthropologist, namely its universal applicability: it refers, as we saw, to '*the* languages of the world'.

Two other concepts which anthropology owes to structural linguistics are 'syntagmatic' and 'paradigmatic' relations. Elements in a language, for example, words in a sentence which are arranged in a certain sequence, form a *syntagmatic chain*. A paradigmatic (or, in Saussure's now obsolete terminology, 'associative') set comprises elements, for example, words, which are equivalent in one or more respects. For example, 'impardonable, intolerable, indefatigable . . .' and 'teach, teacher, taught . . .' are two paradigmatic sets (de Saussure 1931). These concepts have been applied, again particularly by Lévi-Strauss, in the analysis of myths. The events narrated in any single myth form a syntagmatic chain, while the personages and events occurring in a myth, or a corpus of myths, can be studied as members of paradigmatic sets.

It is not unlikely that Saussure was familiar with the works of Emile Durkheim, which were very influential in his time. Durkheim can be considered as one of the founding fathers of modern sociology, but structural anthropology can also trace back its origins to him, his collaborators, united around the journal *Année Sociologique*, and his pupil and successor Marcel Mauss. The work of this school can be exemplified by

Durkheim and Mauss's joint publication 'De quelques formes primitives de la classification'. The opening sentences of this long article are typical.

Contemporary psychology has shown how very complex apparently simple mental operations really are, but 'this operation . . . has been only very rarely applied as yet to operations which are properly speaking logical'. The authors then demonstrate such logical operations in several non-western societies by describing systems of territorial classification:

> In totemic societies it is a general rule that the tribe's constituent groups, namely moieties, clans, sub-clans, arrange the territorial sectors which each of them occupies in accordance with their mutual social relationships and the resemblances and differences between their social functions.
>
> Durkheim and Mauss (1963 [1903])

For example, when the entire Wotjoballuk tribe of New South Wales is (temporarily) united in one territory, one of the tribe's moieties must always occupy the northern, the other moiety the southern area. The two clans with the sun as their totem occupy the eastern portion of the settlement, and so on.

It was particularly this work from the French school which served as an inspiration and an example to (amateur, and later professional) anthropologists in what was to become the other consistently active centre of structural anthropology, The Netherlands. Their earlier (roughly pre-1950) works, usually based on data from Indonesia, give clear evidence of their origin. They are concerned with orderliness or system as it appears in the deeds, words and works of the members of the investigated societies – this is common to all structural anthropology. But the earlier Dutch writers, like their *Année Sociologique* exemplars, concentrated on 'ordering' rather than on 'order'; on structures of which the social participants are aware, and which they deliberately construct. In addition, the nineteenth-and early twentieth-century structuralists in both countries shared the idea that social structure serves as the model for all other classification systems. From the study of territorial classification, Dutch structural research fanned out, as it were, to the structural principles, particularly binary oppositions, in Javanese material culture, traditional theatre, and mythology. In the 1930s, however, kinship and marriage systems became the focus of interest. A major discovery was the frequent occurrence of 'asymmetric connubium', a system whereby marriages between individuals are so arranged that they conform to a regular connubial relationship between groups (clans or clan segments): one group always acts as 'bride-giver' to a second, while this 'bride-receiving' group gives women in marriage to the males of a third group (de Josselin de Jong 1977). This brings us to more recent times, and back to France.

Claude Lévi-Strauss is the foremost exponent of structural anthropology. His first major work (1969 [1949]) might be called a rediscovery of asymmetric connubium (which he terms *échange généralisé*), but he places it in a much wider and richer context: ethnographically, by using material from Siberia, China, India, South East Asia and Australia, and, above all, theoretically, by making the *échange* system shed light on the concepts of incest and exogamy, and on the opposition, which is to be fundamental in all his subsequent work, between 'nature' and 'culture'.

'In language there are only differences' (de Saussure 1931 [1916]); Lévi-Strauss applied this typically structural viewpoint in his book on totemism (1962 [1962]). Totemism does not associate each clan with one animal species as its totemic ancestor, but consists of a classification of the animal world, based on the 'distinctive features' of each species, and a classification of clans on the same basis. When the two classification systems are associated with each other, the result is totemism, in which 'it is the differences which are similar' (1962). Lévi-Strauss's study of a set of cultural phenomena as a system of variations has its climax in the four volumes of *Mythologiques* (1970–9 [1964–71]).

Myths are the purest manifestation of *La Pensée sauvage* (1966 [1962]): thought which, in contrast to 'domesticated thought' does not aim at practical results, but tries to solve problems as an end in itself. The problems dealt with in the 813 myths of South and North American Indians analysed in *Mythologiques* are, principally: Why do we humans prepare our food, and animals not? Why can we take off our clothing and ornaments, and barter them with foreign groups, while the animals can not? How did this come about? In other words, the problem of culture versus nature.

In analysing myths, a basic precept for the investigator is to avoid 'mythomology', that is, the interpretation of each single mythical personage or event in isolation (the heroine 'stands for' fertility, travelling by boat 'stands for' long life, and so on). Here again, it is not the elements, but the relations between the elements that is essential (for example: the lizard, as a land animal, stands in opposition to the aquatic crocodile; hence they are also in opposite relationships to the human hero: the hero of Myth 1 chases lizards, the hero of Myth 124 is chased by a crocodile).

By the same token, a myth can never be understood in isolation, but should be studied in its relation to other myths. All the American Indian myths studied in the book are to be considered as variant versions of one another, linked together by 'transformations'. That is to say, one does not compare myths when, and because, they are similar, but because of their differences: the myth corpus, like a language, is a system of differences – sometimes even of perfect oppositions.

Lévi-Strauss uses the same method in *La Voie des masques* (1975). A certain type of mask used by the Salish Indians of British Columbia is his starting-point for a study of comparable masks in the same region: comparable, not on the grounds of similarity, but of systematic 'transformations'. Part II of the book discusses the *Dzonokwa*, a type of mask which is the opposite of the Salish mask in every respect: in form and colour, in its ritual function and performance, in the myths about its origin, and in the way it is obtained and inherited. By introducing the concept of transformation, Lévi-Strauss has added a new dimension to comparative studies in general, and revivified comparative anthropology. Also in contrast to the earlier French and Dutch structuralists, he does not confine his research to structures of which the cultural participants are aware. On the contrary, his frequent references to the *'structure inconsciente de l'esprit humain'* indicate his particular interest in not only unconscious structures, but also in basic structuring principles which are not culture-specific, but (probably) of universal occurrence.

Outside anthropological circles there is a tendency to equate structural anthropology with Lévi-Strauss; this is a popular misconception. It is striking that, while Lévi-Strauss has a tendency (stronger in some works than in others) to study the products of the 'unconscious structure of the human mind' as closed systems, the aim of many of his French congeners is to link the conceptual structures more closely to social problems. Georges Balandier demonstrated that three binary oppositions (male–female, elder–younger, superior–inferior) are frequently the basis of conflicts. Roger Bastide applied the insights of structural anthropology to the problems in developing countries. Louis Dumont (1970 [1966]) demonstrated the fundamental difference between inequality and hierarchy: the latter is exemplified by India, for 'the caste system is above all a system of ideas and values, a formal, comprehensible, rational system'. Maurice Godelier remedied structuralism's neglect of economic factors, and thereby achieved a synthesis between structuralist and Marxist anthropology. Although Roland Barthes can also be mentioned in this context, as he studied the effect of 'mythologies' on modern western societies, his principal achievement was his comparison between myth-as-language and natural language, thus making good use of the old association between structural linguistics and anthropology. Georges Condominas also closed a circuit, by directing the research of his active Centre for South-East Asian Studies to the topic of *l'espace social*, that is, territorial classification.

Among British anthropologists there are several whose works are typically structural, although they might not call themselves structuralists. In view of the British tradition of *social* anthropology, it is not surprising that the tendency, just discussed in connection with the French group, also appears in British structuralist publications, be it in a different form.

Rodney Needham's works on matrilateral cross-cousin alliance started from a position very close to Lévi-Strauss's *Les Structures élémentaires de la parenté*, but diverged sharply with the introduction of the concepts of 'prescriptive' and 'preferential' alliance. E. R. Leach's position moved in the opposite direction: sharply critical of the *Structures* (which he called a 'splendid failure'), he came to be more and more in sympathy with Lévi-Strauss's views in his later publications on myths and belief systems. While one of Mary Douglas's (1966) best-known books could be called 'Lévi-Straussian', the social context (in the form of the pressure exerted on an individual by his 'group' and the society's 'grid') plays a dominant role in a later work (Douglas 1970). Victor Turner's principal works are concerned with ritual. Lévi-Strauss has only very seldom dealt with this subject, perhaps because rituals, by their very nature, have also to be studied as socially operative. Turner devoted much attention to this aspect, for example, in the case of 'rituals of affliction'.

Of structuralists outside linguistics and anthropology, the most prominent are the psychologist Jean Piaget, the historian Fernand Braudel and other members of the *Annales* group. As a structuralist, Piaget is noted for his emphasis on self-regulation as a characteristic of structures. Braudel is very close to Lévi-Strauss when he recognizes *structures* as one of the three types of history, history *de langue durée*, of which the participants in the events are not conscious.

P. E. de Josselin de Jong
University of Leiden

References

Douglas, M. (1966) *Purity and Danger*, London.
—— (1970) *Natural Symbols*, London.
Dumont, L. (1970 [1966]) *Homo Hierarchicus*, London. (Original edn, *Homo Hierarchicus*, Paris.)
Durkheim, E. and Mauss, M. (1963 [1903]) *Primitive Classification*, London. (Original edn, 'De quelques formes primitives de la classification', Paris.)
Jakobson, R. and Halle, M. (1971) *Fundamentals of Language*, The Hague.
Josselin de Jong, P. E. de (ed.) (1977) *Structural Anthropology in the Netherlands*, The Hague.
Lévi-Strauss, C. (1969 [1949]) *The Elementary Structures of Kinship*, London. (Original edn, *Les Structures élémentaires de la parenté*, Paris.)

—— (1962 [1962]) *Totemism*, London. (Original edn, *Le Totémisme aujourd'hui*, Paris.)

—— (1966 [1962]) *The Savage Mind*, London. (Original edn, *La Pensée sauvage*, Paris.)

—— (1970–9 [1964–71]) *Introduction to a Science of Mythology*, London. (Original edn, *Mythologiques*, 4 vols, Paris.)

—— (1982 [1975]) *The Way of the Masks*, Seattle. (Original edn, *La Voie des masques*, Geneva.)

Saussure, F. de (1931 [1916]) *Course in General Linguistics*, New York. (Original edn, *Cours de linguistique générale*, Paris.)

See also: Lévi-Strauss, Claude; Saussure, Ferdinand de; structural linguistics.

structure, social *see* social structure and structuration

subculture

In common parlance the term subculture is used most often to describe those special worlds of interests and identifications that set apart some groups and/or larger aggregations from others. Social science use of the term is somewhat more specific. Here subcultures denote shared systems of norms, values, interests or behaviours that distinguish individuals, groups and/or larger aggregations from the larger societies in which they also participate. Physical contiguity is not required of those who identify with a subculture, for individuals may share interests, and so on, with others who are not members of their community of residence.

While we speak of 'youth subcultures', 'ethnic subcultures', 'delinquent subcultures' and various 'professional subcultures', it is important to note that neither membership in a particular category (such as age or ethnicity) nor behaviour (delinquency, bird watching, or professional practice) is sufficient to account for or to characterize a subculture. The critical element, rather, is the degree to which values, artefacts and identification are shared among and with other members of a category, or among and with those who engage in a particular type of behaviour.

No general theory of subcultures has emerged (but see Yinger 1960; 1977). Instead, following research documenting enormous variation in the form and content of subcultures, theory has proceeded by illustration and analogy, with little progress in measurement or formal theoretical development. Principles of subcultural formation have been identified, however.

A large body of research suggests that a major contributor to subcultural formation is *social separation*. Social separation tends to produce cultural differentiation (Glaser 1971). More is required, however. The crucial condition for the emergence of new cultural forms appears to be interaction regarding special interests or problems among persons in socially separated categories (Cohen 1955). Social structural characteristics such as age, race, ethnicity, social class and specialized training or interests, as well as particular types of behaviour, have become major bases for social separation and subcultural formation.

Subcultures exist in relation to larger cultures and social systems. The nature of these relationships is critical to the origin, development, and the status of subcultures. They may be merely different, and be viewed indifferently; they may be viewed positively; or, because defined as deviant, viewed negatively. Some are not merely different, but oppositional to major cultural values, in which case they are properly termed contra- or counter-cultures. Definitions and experiences involving subcultural 'outsiders' and 'insiders' – between and among them – exert powerful, often determining, influences on subcultures. Suspicion, distrust and fear of the different, deviant and/or unknown may lead to rejection by the dominant society, particularly when those who are so defined also lack power. A cycle of interaction may thus be set in motion in which those who are defined as different, and so on, are increasingly thrown on their own resources, develop their own values, beliefs, roles and status systems. Examples are various delinquent and lower-class subcultures, religious sects and other groups that withdraw from the larger society. Conversely, powerful groups are able to command the resources necessary to avoid many of the negative effects, if not always the negative definitions, of their differences. 'High society', the professions and the learned disciplines come to mind. As these examples suggest, organizational forms and subcultures should not be confused, though they are often mutually reinforcing.

Macroeconomic, political and cultural conditions provide the background against which subcultural formation takes place. Structural differentiation associated with changing technology and the advent of capitalism in western Europe, for example, changed traditional economic and social relationships, which in turn led to new bases for social separation and subcultural formation. Subcultures thus are linked to social change, serving at times as the engines of social change and at times as resisters to change. The esoteric knowledge, language and techniques of the sciences, for example, promote the discovery of further knowledge and applications; but vested interests associated with occupations and professions – and identification with the past, which is often associated with subcultures – often resist change.

Subcultures vary along many dimensions: rigidity of separation, degree of exclusivity, how much of the lives of participating individuals is encompassed, the extent to which they are group centred or more diffuse among those who identify or are identified with them, and the extent to which they overlap with other subcultures. Numerous theories have attempted to account for these and other characteristics and variations of subcultures, but scientific work in this area remains at a primitive level.

James F. Short, Jr
Washington State University

References

Cohen, A. K. (1955) *Delinquent Boys: The Culture of the Gang*, New York.
Glaser, D. (1971) *Social Deviance*, Chicago.
Yinger, J. M. (1960) 'Contraculture and subculture', *American Sociological Review* 25.
—— (1977) 'Presidential address: countercultures and social change', *American Sociological Review* 42.

Further reading

Schwartz, G. (1987) *Beyond Conformity or Rebellion: Youth and Authority in America*, Chicago.
Schwendinger, H. and Schwendinger, J. S. (1985) *Adolescent Subcultures and Delinquency*, New York.

See also: gangs.

subsidies

Subsidies are negative taxes which may be put on consumption goods or investment goods or factor services. Specific examples include subsidies on welfare goods and housing, accelerated depreciation provisions for investment, general wage subsidies, wage subsidies for specific purposes such as training, deficiency payments to farmers, and payments to public utilities for providing services in sparsely populated areas.

Whereas taxes generally reduce taxed activities, subsidies normally increase the subsidized activity and are sometimes justified because the activity concerned generates external benefits. For example, a training subsidy might be introduced to encourage a better-trained labour force. When subsidies are introduced to aid the poor, an important issue is whether the subsidy should be paid in cash or in kind – for example, through food vouchers. Payments in kind make it more likely that the subsidy is used as desired, such as on food purchases, but is open to objections on paternalistic grounds and because such payments prevent people from spending their income as they themselves prefer.

Subsidies frequently present problems of public accountability because it may be difficult to discover or control the extent of the subsidy. For example, support for a subsidy to a branch railway line does not necessarily mean unlimited support for losses on railway lines. Subsidies are of course open to all sorts

of political pressures, but the force of this argument is for subsidies to be open and known. It may, for example, be difficult to discover if housing subsidies go mainly to those who live in publicly owned housing or who have subsidized rents, or to owner-occupiers with subsidized mortgages and who escape income taxation on the implicit income from home ownership. In the absence of knowledge, both renters and owner-occupiers may feel that the other group is the more heavily subsidized.

C. V. Brown
University of Stirling

Further reading

Musgrave, R. A. (1959) *The Theory of Public Finance*, New York.

See also: taxation.

suicide

The term suicide refers to the death of a person that is the result of behaviour undertaken by that person in the knowledge or expectation of that result. Some forms of suicide are direct, such as hanging or shooting oneself. Other forms are indirect, such as going on hunger strike or refusing to take life-preserving medication. Many of the behaviours to which the words suicide or suicidal are attached, however, appear not to be motivated by the wish to die. Often they are not even intended to harm oneself, but only to express or communicate feelings such as despair, hopelessness and anger. Contemporary scientific literature, therefore, acknowledges, apart from suicide, two other categories of suicidal behaviour. First, *suicidal communication or ideation* refer to cognitions that can vary from fleeting thoughts that life is not worth living via well thought-out plans to kill oneself, to an intense delusional preoccupation with self-destruction. Second, the terms *suicide attempt or parasuicide* cover behaviours that can vary from what is sometimes labelled as suicidal gestures or manipulative attempts to serious but unsuccessful attempts to kill oneself. Research has shown that considerable overlap exists between the populations of persons involved in the three classes of suicidal behaviour. There is also some evidence of developmental pathways that sequentially link suicidal ideation to parasuicide to suicide. Yet little is known of the causes and patterns of recruitment from suicidal ideation to parasuicide, and from parasuicide to suicide, and on the factors that precipitate or protect against these transformations.

The use of mortality statistics for the scientific study of suicide, initiated by Emile Durkheim in his famous book *Le Suicide* (1951 [1897]) has been subject to intense debate and criticism as to their validity ever since. There seems to be a general consensus that although suicide is generally underreported, national statistics can be used for analysis of trends between countries, within them, and over time.

Generally speaking, suicide appears to be a relatively rare event. In most countries suicide ranks as the ninth or tenth cause of death for all age groups taken together, accounting for slightly more than (an averaged) 1 per cent of all deaths in females and 2 per cent in males. There are, however, substantial international differences. Some countries, such as Hungary, Japan and Denmark, traditionally have a suicide mortality three to five times as high as, for example, England, Wales and Ireland, suggesting that cultural characteristics play a significant role.

Since the time mortality statistics have been kept, which for some countries goes back to the first half of the nineteenth century, one of the most basic facts about suicide is that its risk increases as a function of age. Suicide is extremely rare in children under the age of 12 and becomes more common after puberty, with its incidence increasing in the following years. In almost all countries the highest suicide rates are among elderly people, for men usually in the age category 75 years and over, but for women often at a considerably younger age, between 55 and 74 years. In the latter half of the twentieth century, however, the median age of persons who died by suicide lowered significantly, due to the fact that in many countries in Europe, North America and Asia suicide mortality reached an all time high among people aged 15–34 years, and consequently ranked among the top three causes of death in that age group. Research indicates that this development can partially be explained by a simultaneous dramatic increase in the incidence of attempted suicide or parasuicide, a behaviour that is particularly common among adolescents and young adults, with lifetime prevalence rates ranging from 5 to 20 per cent. The risk of suicide among those who have made a previous non-fatal suicide attempt is many times higher than among the general population. Both fatal and non-fatal suicidal behaviour – with a ratio of between twenty and forty non-fatal suicidal acts to every suicide – appear to be related to a number of largely overlapping but partially different social, psychological and physical risk factors. Among the social risk factors are weak or absent social ties or low social participation. The risks may arise from social isolation as a consequence of detention, divorce, being unemployed, being a member of an ethnic minority or migrant group, or belonging to an underprivileged group. Among the psychological factors are the presence of a psychiatric illness, particularly depression, psychoactive substance abuse and personality disorders. Research indicates that these three disorders have become more common over the course of the twentieth century and that they appear

earlier in the life cycle, possibly as a consequence of the lowering age of puberty. Among the physical risk factors are chronic illness and physical handicaps. In addition, it has been shown that short-term factors also play a role in the probability of suicide, such as the portrayal of suicides in the media and the occurrence of suicidal behaviour in one's peer group, perhaps a school community, where one suicidal act might spark off an epidemic of such acts. Given the fact that there are many pathways to suicide or parasuicide and that these are multifactorial behaviours, their prevention must also be multifactorial. Most prevention and intervention efforts, however, have been unifactorial or focus on just one category of factors, particularly psychological factors. Consequently, there is still lack of empirical evidence concerning the impact of preventive programmes and projects on suicide mortality and on the incidence of parasuicide at the population level and even at the clinical level.

René F. W. Diekstra
University of Leiden

Reference

Durkheim, E. (1951 [1897]) *Suicide: A Study in Sociology*, New York. (Original edn, *Le Suicide*, Paris.)

Further reading

Blumenthal, S. J. and Kupfer, D. J. (eds) (1990) *Suicide over the Lifecycle: Risk factors, Assessment and Treatment of Suicidal Patients*, Washington, DC.

Diekstra, R. F. W. (1994) *The Anatomy of Suicide: A Treatise on Historical, Social, Psychological and Biological Aspects of Suicidal Behaviours and their Preventability*, Dordrecht, The Netherlands.

Douglas, J. D. (1967) *The Social Meanings of Suicide*, Princeton, NJ.

See also: social problems.

supply-side economics

The term supply-side economics has both a general and a specific meaning. At its most general, the term relates to analyses that stress the importance of supply factors in determining output and economic growth in the long run. In its specific sense, the term is associated with US economic policy of the 1980s, sometimes referred to as Reaganomics, which held as one of its more extreme beliefs that tax cuts need not be matched by expenditure cuts because the tax cuts will cause enough growth to restore tax revenues. We consider these aspects in turn.

Modern supply-side economics is built on analysis of individual choice. It is fundamentally microeconomic in nature – a factor which might explain its neglect in macroeconomics until comparatively recently. Major factors in the supply-side determination of output include the effect of incentives on production, the efficiency of the labour market, the avoidance of over-regulation and the level of saving. These ideas lie at the heart of economics. Writers include Kuznets (1971) on economic development, Kendrick (1961) and Denison (1962) on growth and productivity, Mincer and Polachek (1974) on the sensitivity of women's labour supply to post-tax wages, Becker (1964) on human capital, and Schultz (1974) and Becker (1981) on the economics of the family. Friedman's (1968) demonstration of the illusory nature of the long-run Phillips curve trade-off between unemployment and inflation also relies on supply-side (individual-choice) analysis: he showed how the curve depended on workers and firms being surprised by the current rate of inflation. Thus monetary policy could not effect a permanent reduction in unemployment, which required instead long-run policies such as improved education opportunities that would reduce the constraints faced by unemployed people. Buchanan and Tullock (1962) and the economists of the public choice school can also be said to have made a contribution to supply-side economics. Their conclusion that government intervention, rather than increasing national output and economic growth, can often have the reverse effect (governments as well as markets can fail), places an important limit on the role of government in promoting economic growth.

In macroeconomic analysis, the demand side has tended to overshadow the supply side, particularly since the great depression and the rise of Keynesianism. For much macroeconomic policy, aggregate demand has been viewed as the determining factor of output, with aggregate supply established in the main simply by labour supply and labour productivity trends. In this context, the long-run effect of aggregate demand management in reducing output via increased taxes and a bigger share of government in national income tends to be ignored. Higher marginal tax rates on personal and corporate incomes can impact adversely on national output and growth by lowering labour force participation, worker effort and capital accumulation. The clear failure of demand-side policies in the face of the 'stagflation' of the 1970s led academic economists such as Feldstein (1981) to reassert the need to address neglected supply-side issues.

Supply-side economics, in its more specific meaning, was developed by economists such as Arthur Laffer, Jude Wanniski, Michael Evans and Paul Craig Roberts, who worked more in the government policy arena rather than the academic arena. These economists are often referred to as 'supply-siders'. Accounts of their ideas can be found in Roberts (1984) and Bartlett and Roth (1984). The Economic Recovery Tax Act (1981) was strongly influenced by supply-sider arguments and included saving and investment incentives, reduced capital gains taxes and reductions in personal taxation. Advocacy of reduced personal taxation was associated with the supply-siders' most widely-known contribution, the Laffer curve. The Laffer curve posits an inverted-U relation between the total tax revenue and marginal tax rates. With a zero tax rate, the tax yield will be zero. With a 100 per cent tax rate, the financial incentive to work will be absent and tax yield will again be zero. Between these two points tax yield will at first rise with increasing tax rates, but then fall as the incentive to work decreases. If the economy is operating beyond the maximum point of this curve, tax cuts will increase rather than decrease revenue. The supply-siders asserted that this was the case.

However, the shape of such a Laffer curve, and the position of countries upon it, is not clear empirically. Stuart (1981) examined the case of Sweden. He estimated that the maximum point of the Laffer curve occurred at a marginal tax rate of 70 per cent, whereas at the time of his study actual rates were slightly in excess of 80 per cent. He therefore concluded that Sweden was on the downward-sloping part of the curve. Lindsey (1987) analysed data for the USA and concluded that the maximum point of the curve lay at a 40 per cent marginal tax rate. Looking at the US tax rate reductions from 1982 to 1984, which involved a 23 per cent reduction of tax rates over three years, and a reduction of the top rate in the first year from 70 to 50 per cent, he concluded that up to a quarter of the revenue loss from these reductions that simple arithmetic would suggest would be recouped by 'changes in taxpayer behaviour'. Evidence for the UK was examined by Brown (1988). He rejected completely any view that the reduction of the UK basic rate from 27 to 25 per cent in 1988 could lead to increased revenue, but argued that it is possible that reducing the higher rate from 60 to 40 per cent could lead to more revenue. Broadly, the empirical evidence refutes the more extravagant supply-sider claims that major reductions in basic tax rates could be self-financing, but lends support to the view that this is likely to work for reductions in higher rate taxation.

Overall, there is now more emphasis on the importance of supply side issues in economics, and the extreme neglect of the supply side, seen in the heyday of Keynesian demand management has decreased. However, the wilder claims of supply-siders associated with the US tax reform of 1981 have not been found to have been realized.

S. Siebert
P. A. Watt
University of Birmingham

References

Bartlett, B. and Roth, T. P. (1984) *The Supply-Side Solution*, London.

Becker, C. (1964) *Human Capital*, New York.

—— (1981) *A Treatise on the Family*, Cambridge, MA.

Brown, C. (1988) 'Will the 1988 income tax cuts either increase work incentives or raise more revenue?', *Fiscal Studies* 9.

Buchanan, J. and Tullock, G. (1962) *The Calculus of Consent*, Ann Arbor, MI.

Denison, E. (1962) 'Education, economic growth, and gaps in information', *Journal of Political Economy* 70.

Feldstein, M. (1981) 'The retreat from Keynesian economics' *Public Interest* 64.

Friedman, M. (1968) 'The role of monetary policy', *American Economic Review* 58.

Kendrick, J. W. (1961) *Productivity Trends in the United States*, Princeton, NJ.

Kuznets, S. (1971) *Economic Growth of Nations*, Cambridge, MA.

Lindsey, L. B. (1987) 'Individual taxpayer response to tax cuts: 1982–1984', *Journal of Public Economics* 33.

Mincer, J. and Polachek, S. (1974) 'Family investments in human capital: earnings of women', *Journal of Political Economy* 82.

Roberts, P. C. (1984) *The Supply Side Revolution: An Insider's Account of Policymaking in Washington*, Cambridge, MA.

Schultz, T. (1974) *The Economics of the Family*, Chicago.

Stuart, C. E. (1981) 'Swedish tax rates, labour supply and tax revenues', *Journal of Political Economy* 89.

See also: economic growth; inflation and deflation; labour market analysis; microeconomics; monetary policy; public choice; regulation; taxation.

survey *see* public opinion polls; sample surveys

symbolic interactionism

Symbolic interactionism is the title that was awarded belatedly and retrospectively to the ideas of a group of sociologists and social psychologists once centred on the University of Chicago. As that group evolved during the 1920s, 1930s and 1940s, its members began to scatter throughout the universities of North America, bearing interactionism with them. The critical early generation of George Mead, William James, Charles Cooley, William Thomas and Robert Park was succeeded first by that of Herbert Blumer and Everett Hughes and then by third and fourth generations populated by such people as Erving Goffman, Howard Becker, Anselm Strauss and Eliot Freidson.

Interactionism itself alludes to a deliberately unsystematic and often vague method of interpreting the ways in which people do things together, a method that has flowed from the theoretical and practical work of the Chicago School (of Sociology). Because it is unsystematic, there are a number of versions of interactionism. There is no one orthodoxy, and any published account must therefore be a little partial.

Theoretically, interactionism was shaped by pragmatism. It has been framed by a series of special perspectives on the possibilities of knowledge and the limits of enquiry. It not only describes the character of social life but also suggests how it should be studied: problems of definition and method have been collapsed into one, it being argued that sociologists and the persons whom they observe follow the same procedures. Society and sociology are produced by special processes of knowledge, and it is those processes which must be understood before sociology can proceed. Knowledge itself is described as belonging neither to the surveying mind alone nor to the world alone. On one level, interactionists contend that it is misleading to imagine that people's interpretations of events and things are free: interpretations are restrained by the capacity of those events to 'answer back'. On another level, it is claimed that knowledge is not a simple mirror of its objects: people actively create, shape and select their response to what is around them. Knowledge is then presented as an active process in which people, their understanding and phenomena are bound together in what has been called the 'knowing–known transaction'. That transaction is exploratory, emergent and situated, lending a dialectical structure to all activity. Interactionists argue that practical knowledge does not arise in seclusion. Rather, it addresses specific problems and purposes, those problems establishing distinctive questions and perspectives that illuminate some facets of the world and not others. Illumination, in its turn, will disclose new ideas which can return to transform problems and purposes, leading to another shift of question and another train of ideas. And so it goes on in an indefinite regress that will end only when exhaustion, boredom or practical satisfaction has been attained. It is evident that there cannot be a logical terminus for investigation or activity. All knowledge is destined to be provisional, liable to reformulation with the answering of just one more question. All knowledge is a novel and often unanticipated synthesis of what has gone before. Moreover, all knowledge is embedded in its own context and history of development. There are limits to generalization and abstraction.

Chief among the problems that confront individuals is the character that they possess. People do not always understand themselves, their past and their possible futures. Facts about the self are revealed with each new action and they cannot always be predicted or assimilated. Yet it is vital to learn what one is and what one might become. Without that knowledge, there would be no appreciation of how one's actions will affect others and how others will affect oneself. It is necessary to place oneself. Just as people observe the world about them, so they observe themselves, composing a series of running conjectures about identity. The process of self-exploration translates the subject into an examining 'I' and an examined 'me', the 'me' being an objectification of inferences made by oneself and others. Indeed, the responses of others are critical because they may be used to construct a sense of how one appears, a 'looking-glass self'. Over time, the symbolic effects worked by such responses can become relatively anonymous, depersonalized and standardized, the basis of an abstract representation called the 'generalized other'. This whole process is itself orchestrated and mediated by language, and most of its constituent forms have been likened to those of a conversation. Interactionists have given great emphasis to words as a means of animating, stabilizing and objectifying what would otherwise be fleeting and private experience. It is in the work done by words that people can share a community of perspectives about themselves, one another and the objects which are in their environment.

The prime vehicle of social action is the 'significant gesture', an expression or display which incorporates replies to the responses which others might make to it. In its anticipation of others' answering behaviour, the significant gesture ties people together, allowing lines of conduct to converge and unite. Society itself tends to be seen as a mosaic of little scenes and dramas in which people make indications to themselves and others, respond to those indications, align their actions, and so build identities and social structures.

The task of the interactionist is to describe that activity, and it is also thought to be emergent and anchored in its contexts. Enquiry is frequently tentative, open and exploratory, deploying a variety of strategies but leaning towards ethnography and participant-observation. It is held to be the job of sociologists to enter the social situations of their subjects, observe their conduct, understand their practices and the symbolic work that accompanies them, and then retire to report what has been seen. Those descriptions of conduct are frequently built up into larger portraits of social worlds, reference being made to the patterns which seem to organize them. There is interest in such ordering processes as the career, conflict and the division of labour. Any resulting analysis may be tested by its plausibility, its ability to provide scripts for behaviour, and by the criticism supplied by the subjects themselves.

Interactionists would maintain that sociology resides in research, not in schematic treatises about society, epistemology and methodology. All argument, including interactionism, must be rooted in the elucidation of particular problems in specific contexts. Attempts to render it universal or apart from concrete experience will deny it authenticity. The conventional interactionist territory has then been the small world of an occupation, institution or social group. Interactionism itself has been most conspicuous in those sectors of sociology which dwell on substantive areas, medicine, deviance, education and careers being instances. In the main, the approach has been closely identified with US scholars who are linked at first or second hand with the University of Chicago. Its greatest impact was probably achieved in the 1960s and 1970s when it changed the form of the sociology of deviance, Becker and Goffman acting as especially important figures.

Paul Rock
London School of Economics
and Political Science

Further reading

Becker, H. (1970) *Sociological Work*, Chicago.
Blumer, H. (1969) *Symbolic Interactionism: Perspective and Method*, Englewood Cliffs, NJ.
Goffman, E. (1959) *The Presentation of Self in Everyday Life*, New York.
Hughes, E. (1958) *Men and their Work*, Glencoe, IL.
Rock, P. (1979) *The Making of Symbolic Interactionism*, London.
Rose, A. (ed.) (1962) *Human Behavior and Social Processes*, Boston, MA.

See also: pragmatics; symbolism.

symbolism

The various notions of symbolism developed in the social sciences constitute different responses to a central, apparently inevitable, tension in a scientific description of culture. Most cultural productions convey some meaning, yet a social science cannot readily accept these overt meanings as a sufficient explanation for those manifestations. To close this gap is the main point of developing a notion of symbolism. The point is argued forcefully by Durkheim; consider for instance his famous statement, that a human institution like religion 'cannot be founded on an error and a lie. . . . One must know how to go underneath the symbol to the reality which it represents' (Durkheim 1947 [1915]: 14). This statement also introduces the ambiguity, to be found in most discussions of symbolism, between three different understandings of the term. Cultural manifestations are called symbolic, first, because they can be interpreted as indices of underlying social realities by social scientists, or second, because they are expressive of particular concerns of the actors, or, finally, in the sense that they are *prima-facie* irrational. These different understandings are at the foundation of three major approaches to cultural symbolism – sociological, hermeneutic and psychological respectively.

The first, *sociological* stance is principally associated with the name of Durkheim, although the notion of cultural productions as signs or symptoms of social relations was forcefully articulated in Hegelian and Marxist approaches to culture. In Marx in particular, the uneasy definition of ideology reflects a central ambiguity in the study of symbolism. Ideology is often described as an exercise in camouflage, as the representations whereby a social class explicitly portrays the social order in which it dominates as the only possible one. But ideology is also part of a broader, historically determined form of consciousness, which includes all the representations that make social interaction possible. While Marx concentrated his activity as a decoder of cultural forms on the first, narrower domain of ideology, Durkheim extended the notions of symbol and referent to the whole of human culture. The main thrust of this approach was a rejection of Tylorian intellectualism (Skorupksi 1976). The contrast is particularly evident in the domain of religion, seen by Tylor as a misguided attempt at explaining the natural world, while for Durkheim it is a 'figurative expression' of social structure. In the Durkheimian system, however, symbols cannot be seen as just projections of pre-existing social forms. Religion in particular creates social cohesion by enforcing its ideal counterpart, conceptual cohesiveness.

One may argue that the Durkheimian symbolist tradition tends to confuse two quite different aspects of cultural symbols, namely, their use as a source of information for the sociologist and their meaning for the social actors. Consider for instance Leach's statement, that 'the various *nats* [i.e. spirits] of Kachin religious mythology are, in the last analysis, nothing more than ways of describing the formal relationships that exist between real persons and real groups in ordinary human Kachin society' (Leach 1954: 182). The explanation proposed may well exhaust the sociological significance of the various spirit-notions of the Kachin. But this leaves untouched the particular meanings they articulate for Kachin actors. Such considerations found the second, *hermeneutic* stance in the approach to symbolism, in which the main problem is to translate the meanings of cultural symbols, not to explain their occurrence. For Geertz, for instance, the study of culture is 'not an experimental science in search of law but an interpretive one in search of meaning' (Geertz 1973: 5). In such authors as Turner (1967; 1974) or Fernandez (1986), the emphasis lies on the figurative power of cultural symbols, on their effects as both expressive figures and organizing principles for inchoate or unstructured feelings and thoughts.

It is possible, however, to approach meanings without taking this hermeneutic stance, and consider the production of meaning as a psychological process, amenable to scientific investigation like any other such process. This leads us to the third, *cognitive* understanding of symbolism, intrinsically related to considerations of rationality. From Lévy-Bruhl or Rivers down to modern cognitive approaches, anthropology has tried to provide some description of the cognitive processes whereby people can be led to hold beliefs for which rational justifications seem either impossible or unavailable. So symbolism could be construed as the product of a special 'mode of thought', with particular functional properties. An echo of this conception can be found in Lévi-Strauss's notion of a *pensée sauvage*. Here symbols are produced by the application of universal, formal operations, such as binary opposition and analogy, to a set of 'concrete' categories: nature and culture, male and female, the raw and the cooked, etc. (Lévi-Strauss 1966; see also Leach 1976). In the absence of precise psychological models, however, the idea of particular modes of thought leads to a conception of symbolism as a residual category, justifying Gellner's comment that 'in social anthropology if a native says something sensible it is primitive technology, but if it sounds very odd then it is symbolic' (Gellner 1987: 163). An important attempt to go beyond this characterization can be found in Sperber's (1975) cognitive account of symbolism. For Sperber, certain cultural phenomena are 'symbolic' to particular actors if their rational interpretation does not lead to a limited and predictable set of inferences. This triggers a search for possible, generally conjectural representations which, if true, would make a rational interpretation possible. This conception has two interesting corollaries for the social scientist. First, it implies that it is futile to provide keys or translations for cultural expressions. The fact that a phenomenon is treated symbolically precisely excludes the possibility of a single, exhaustive interpretation. Second, while symbolism exists as a psychological process, there are no such things as 'symbols', as a particular class of cultural products. Any conceptual or perceptual item can become symbolic, if there is some index that a rational interpretation is unavailable or insufficient. In this framework, a proper account of cultural symbolism will be found, not in the social sciences as such, but in the empirical and theoretical developments of cognitive science.

Pascal Boyer
University of Cambridge

References

Durkheim, E. (1947 [1915]) *The Elementary Forms of the Religious Life*, London.

Fernandez, J. W. (1986) *Persuasions and Performances: The Play of Tropes in Culture*, Bloomington, IN.

Geertz, C. (1973) *The Interpretation of Culture*, New York.

Gellner, E. (1987) *Culture, Identity and Politics*, Cambridge, UK.

Leach, E. R. (1954) *The Political Systems of Highland Burma: A Study of Kachin Political Systems*, London.

—— (1976) *Culture and Communication: The Logic by which Symbols are Connected*, Cambridge, UK.

Lévi-Strauss, C. (1966) *The Savage Mind*, London.

Skorupski, J. (1976) *Symbol and Theory: A Philosophical Study of Theories of Religion in Social Anthropology*, Cambridge, UK.

Sperber, D. (1975) *Rethinking Symbolism*, Cambridge, UK.

Turner, V. (1967) *The Forest of Symbols: Aspects of Ndembu Ritual*, Ithaca, NY.

—— (1974) *Dramas, Fields and Metaphors*, Ithaca, NY.

See also: semiotics; symbolic interactionism.

syncretism

Syncretism denotes the mixture of different religious traditions, but the term is frequently extended to describe hybridity in a number of other domains such as medicine, art or culture generally. It is important to be aware of the word's original religious associations, however, because these have not always been positive, and they have generated some uncertainty among social scientists as to whether the term can be used in a neutral, non-evaluative way.

In the seventeenth century the Catholic Church branded 'syncretists' those Protestants who wished to sink their differences with each other and with the Catholics and establish a new ecumenical Christianity (Martin 1983). Catholic theologians rejected any compromise form of Christianity as an inconsistent jumble of theological ideas – a syncretism. A negative assessment of religious mixture was perhaps to be expected from a Church interested in safeguarding the integrity of its doctrine and practice throughout the world.

Syncretism retained its negative connotations during missionary expansion. It served to excoriate unauthorized local appropriations of Catholicism or Protestantism where missionaries deemed the missionized to have distorted the truth of Scripture through the introduction of elements from indigenous religions. An example is Sundkler's (1961) characterization of Zulu Zionism as a nativistic-syncretistic bridge which carried its practitioners back from their foothold in true Christianity to 'the African animism from where they once started'. Sundkler wrote as a missionary in the service of the Church of Sweden Mission (Lutheran). For the most part, subsequent Africanist anthropologists did not contest or revise this European, Church-controlled, negative definition of syncretism. Instead they have let it stand and sought to demonstrate that Independent African Churches are not syncretic, but rather faithful translations of Christianity into African contexts.

On the other side of the Atlantic, the general attitude of social scientists towards syncretism has been more positive, perhaps because until the last quarter of the twentieth century many North and South American countries publicly espoused melting-pot ideologies as a strategy of nation-building. The melting-pot is the analogue of syncretism in the ethnopolitical domain, and it would have been difficult to criticize the one without simultaneously undermining the other. Thus, for example, the influential mid-century anthropologist Melville Herskovits (1958) considered syncretism a valuable concept for specifying the degree to which diverse cultures had integrated; it was not a bridge leading to religious relapse, but rather a stage (for Negroes and other minorities) on the road towards the ideal of cultural assimilation and integration. It becomes apparent, then, that syncretism can receive positive or negative connotations depending on the regional scholarly tradition within which one encounters it.

Historians of religion for the most part agree that *all* religions are syncretic: all have mixed with other religious traditions and incorporated exogenous features during their history. Such an observation would seem to diminish the importance of syncretism since the term says nothing new or special. This does not, however, change the manifest fact that religions constantly come into contact with each other, or break apart and reform under internal pressures, all the more so in an age of increased multiculturalism and global intercommunication. Syncretism thus furnishes a potentially useful term in the analytical vocabulary of contemporary social science alongside 'creolization', 'hybridization' and 'interculturation'. Religions should perhaps be viewed less as fixed systems, and more as traditions in a continual process of change, dynamically coping with the tensions generated by internal social developments or the challenges of alternative religious traditions. Syncretic appropriations of new forms are thus part of the very nature of religion at any point in time and may be a means of resisting domination and preserving cultural autonomy.

Although nearly every religion may be objectively characterized as syncretic, such an observation conflicts with the subjective opinion that individuals frequently have of their own religious traditions (Droogers 1989). Followers of doctrinal religions of the Book, such as Christianity and Islam, are very unlikely to regard their religions as other than authentic and even pure. Having accepted the proposition that all religious traditions are syncretic, anthropologists and sociologists are now increasingly turning to ethnographic analyses of power, rhetoric and subjectivity, which motivate people to accept or reject the description of their practice as syncretic (Stewart and Shaw 1994).

Charles Stewart
University of London

References

Droogers, A. (1989) 'Syncretism: the problem of definition, the definition of the problem', in J. Gort, H. Vroom, R. Fernhout and A. Wessels (eds) *Dialogue and Syncretism: An Interdisciplinary Approach*, Grand Rapids, MI.

Herskovits, M. (1958) *The Myth of the Negro Past*, 2nd edn, Boston, MA.

Martin, L. (1983) 'Why Cecropian Minerva? Hellenistic religious syncretism as system', *Numen* 30: 131–45.

Stewart, C. and Shaw, R. (ed.) (1994) *Syncretism/Anti-Syncretism: The Politics of Religious Synthesis*, London.

Sundkler, B. (1961) *Bantu Prophets in South Africa*, 2nd edn, London.

See also: sects and cults.

T

taboo

The term taboo derives from various Polynesian languages where it has the sense of 'forbidden'. More specifically, what is forbidden and dangerous is unregulated contact between the everyday world and the sacred, which includes both the holy (for example, the person of a chief) and the unclean (for example, a corpse). Most modern anthropological thinking about taboo derives from Durkheim (1976 [1912]), for whom this disjunction between profane and sacred was the cornerstone of religion – the sacred being secondarily divided between the 'auspiciously' and 'inauspiciously' sacred. Taboos have the function of keeping separate what must not be joined – of policing the boundaries between sacred and profane, and between 'good' and 'bad' sacred – while rites in general re-create the solidarity of the group. Developing this second proposition, Radcliffe-Brown (1952) argued that taboo behaviour expresses and reinforces the values and sentiments essential to the maintenance of society. Other work, however, has taken as its starting-point the notion that taboos mark the boundaries between a culture's fundamental categories.

This line of thought was brilliantly exploited by Douglas (1966; 1975). Dirt, said Lord Chesterfield, is 'matter out of place'. It implies disorder and a confusion of cherished categories. Pollution behaviour and taboo focus on that which is ambiguous in terms of such categories. There is even a sense in which taboos entrench the categories by highlighting and defining the boundaries between them. Margins and boundaries tend therefore to be populated by anomalous creatures of various kinds, and if they don't exist they have to be invented. In myth, for example, the elephant-headed Hindu deity Ganesa often appears – in keeping with his physical character – as an ambivalent trickster. It is he who marks the boundaries between sacred and profane space and time, for he conventionally stands at the entrances to temples, and is worshipped at the beginning and end of major rituals.

Anomalies can be dealt with in various ways: first, they can be suppressed or eradicated. In some societies twins are destroyed for they are seen as blurring the boundary between humans (characterized by single births) and animals (characterized by multiple births). As products of the same parturition, they are mystically one but physically two; in a society which attaches much importance to the birth order of siblings they are doubly ambiguous, for there are two physical beings to occupy one structural role in the kinship system (Turner 1969). A second possibility is to regard the anomaly as filthy and unclean – as in the 'abominations' of Leviticus. Here, for example, land animals are divided into the clawed and hoofed; the latter having the linked characteristics of being ruminant and cloven-hoofed, and being rated as the only legitimate meat. Creatures like the pig (which divide the hoof but do not chew the cud), or the camel, hare and hyrax (which chew the cud but are not cloven-hoofed) are abominated and tabooed. Third, the anomaly may be welcomed as a positive mediator between, say, the sacred and the profane, or between nature and culture. Thus, in the taxonomic system of the Congolese Lele the pangolin is a highly ambiguous creature. It is an arboreal animal with the scaly body and tail of a fish, and is credited with a number of anthropomorphic qualities, the most important of which are a sense of sexual 'modesty' and the reproduction of only one offspring at a time. It therefore stands in the same kind of relationship to humans as begetters of twins stand to animals. Both mediate between nature and culture and are the focus of cult groups which control hunting and fertility.

What the theory fails to explain, however, is why some anomalous creatures are filthy abominations while others are positive mediators. Douglas (1973) tried to solve this puzzle, though not entirely satisfactorily, by suggesting that attitudes to boundary crossing in the social sphere are reflected in attitudes towards potential mediators in other spheres (evaluation of creatures – like pigs – which straddle the Jewish insistence on endogamy, for example, going with the negative evaluation of creatures which straddle conceptual boundaries). More plausibly, she notes that that which is anomalous and marginal is not only the focus of pollution and danger, but also a source of extraordinary power. The Aghoris are a small sect of Hindu ascetics who perform austerities at, and may live on, the cremation grounds. They rub their bodies with cremation ash, use shrouds for loin-cloths, cook their food on wood pilfered from the pyres, consume it out of a human skull; and they are *supposed* to meditate while seated on top of a corpse, and to eat and drink all manner of foul substances including urine, excrement and the putrescent flesh of corpses. By such austerities ascetics are held to acquire extraordinary supernatural powers by which they can surmount the ordinary physical limitations of the mortal condition (Parry 1981). The categories are safe and orderly, but imply restriction. What lies outside is dangerous, but also highly potent.

J. P. Parry
London School of Economics
and Political Science

References

Douglas, M. (1966) *Purity and Danger: An Analysis of Concepts of Pollution and Taboo*, London.
—— (1973) *Natural Symbols*, Harmondsworth.
—— (1975) *Implicit Meanings: Essays in Anthropology*, London.
Durkheim, E. (1976 [1912]) *The Elementary Forms of the Religious Life*, London.
Parry, J. P. (1981) 'Sacrificial death and the necrophagous ascetic', in M. Bloch and J. Parry (eds) *Death and the Regeneration of Life*, Cambridge, UK.
Radcliffe-Brown, A. (1952) *Structure and Function in Primitive Society*, London.
Turner, V. (1969) *The Ritual Process: Structure and Anti-Structure*, Chicago.

taxation

Taxes are the main source of government revenue. Among the OECD countries in 1981 taxes accounted for between one-fifth (in the case of Turkey) and one-half of gross domestic product (in the case of Sweden).

There is considerable variation in the relative importance of different kinds of taxes. In 1981 France raised only 13 per cent of tax revenue from personal income tax, while New Zealand raised 61 per cent. Neither the USA nor the UK appears unusual either in the total amount of tax that it collects or in the composition of the tax burden, except that both raise a high share of revenue from property taxes, and the USA raises a low share from taxes on goods and services.

It is assumed here that it has been decided how much total revenue the government requires. This makes it possible to concentrate on how best this revenue requirement can be met. This question is considered under three headings: allocative effects, distributional effects and administrative effects.

Allocative effects

Taxes will in general cause people to change their behaviour. If there are two activities (or goods), A and B, and A is taxed while B is not, then, unless their incomes change, people will normally do (or buy) less of A and more of B. An important exception is where it is not possible to do less of A. For example, a tax on each person (a head or poll tax) cannot legally be avoided except by dying.

If A is an activity which has harmful side-effects – for example, a chimney that smokes – then reducing activity A may be desirable. In general, however, it is preferable to tax activities where the reduction in production or consumption will be small. One aspect of this concerns the effects of taxes on prices of goods. Taxes will normally raise prices (though not usually by the amount of the tax). The increase in price will cause people to reduce consumption, especially where the quantity demanded is very sensitive to price. Because high consumption is generally to be preferred to low consumption, this leads to the proposition that taxes should tend to be concentrated on goods where demand is relatively insensitive to price changes.

It is also interesting to look at an example where people's incomes are *not* held constant, for instance, a tax on income from work. A tax on the income from work will have two effects on the amount of work people will want to do. It will reduce take-home pay and thus encourage them to want to work more to maintain their real income ('the income effect'). But it will also reduce the amount that people receive for giving up an hour of their leisure and so encourage them to work less ('the substitution effect'). This means that an income tax distorts the work–leisure choice. If the tax base included leisure as well as income, this distortion could be avoided, as in the case of the head tax mentioned above. The difficulty with head taxes is that it is impractical to vary them in accordance with a person's capacity to earn income.

Distributional effects

Taxes generally change the distribution of income. This is fairly obvious if we think about the distribution of income after tax, but taxes can also influence the distribution of income before tax. If, for example, income taxes change the amount of work people do, this will change the distribution of pre-tax income.

A common fallacy is that in order to redistribute income towards the poor, it is necessary to have a schedule of rates which increase as income rises. However, provided that tax receipts are used to finance a benefit which is equally available to all, there is no need for a rising schedule of tax rates.

Many people would like to see taxes make the distribution of net income more equal. 'More equal' is of course a very vague phrase, and there are clearly differences as to how far towards equality people would like society to go.

Achieving the balance between allocative and distributional effects of taxes is the subject-matter of the field of 'optimal taxation'. In the case of income tax, the problem is to find the structure of rates that provides the best balance between high rates to provide revenue for redistribution and low rates to ensure that the income available for redistribution does not fall too much. More crudely, the problem is to balance the size of the cake against its distribution. It has been argued that the schedule of tax rates against income should start at zero, rise, and then at some high level of income fall again to zero. This optimal schedule thus looks rather like an upside-down U, whereas the actual tax schedule in some countries is U-shaped if one includes means-tested state benefits on low incomes as well as income taxes.

Administrative effects

Collecting taxes imposes costs on both the public and private sector which can vary widely. For example, the USA and UK have very nearly the same number of people collecting income tax, but the US population is roughly four times the UK population. (It may be that private sector costs of income tax compliance are lower in the UK than in the USA.)

One of the main determinants of administrative costs is the complexity of the tax law. Very often these complexities are introduced to attempt to make the law fairer, but ironically the complexities may reduce public awareness to the point where, for example, the poor do not make full use of provisions that could benefit them.

One of the most important sources of complexities is multiplicity of rates as between different kinds of income such as earnings and real capital gains. Where the rate of tax on capital gains is relatively low, there is a strong incentive for those with high earnings to convert income into capital gains. A single uniform rate on all income would be a considerable simplification. It would also be a move in the direction of the optimal schedule of income tax rates discussed above.

C. V. Brown
University of Stirling

Further reading

Brown, C. V. (1983) *Taxation and the Incentive to Work*, 2nd edn, London.

Kay, J. A. and King, M. A. (1983) *The British Tax System*, 3rd edn, London.

Musgrave, R. A. (1959) *The Theory of Public Finance*, New York.

See also: distribution of incomes and wealth; macroeconomic policy; subsidies; supply-side economics.

Taylorism

Taylorism refers to a form of systematic management whose principal aim is to remove control over the organization of work from those who actually do the work. The separation of thinking about how to perform a particular task from its actual execution lies at the heart of Taylorism, and in Frederick Taylor's day at the turn of the twentieth century, it was a radical innovation. In a world of craft knowledge and internal contracts, the manufacturing workshop at the end of the nineteenth century was one organized and largely run by craftsmen in their respective trades. Taylor's (1911) notion of 'scientific management' represented a direct challenge to this form of organization and laid the basis of the modern factory system.

Scientific management, as professed by Taylor, involves wresting control from the workforce of what they do and how they do it, and passing this knowledge to a group of workers whose sole task it is to manage. Management thus becomes a distinct activity (separate from ownership) whose function is to establish a set of work standards, lay down how they should be achieved, and select the most appropriate workers to perform them. To achieve this process of task management it was necessary to analyse the existing labour process: breaking jobs down into their component parts and then calculating how to get the best out of each component. Time and motion studies were used by management to obtain detailed knowledge about each step of the work process. Taylor himself was fond of telling the story of Schmidt, a pig iron handler at the Bethlehem Steel Company, to convey the principles of his system.

After watching a gang of workmen loading pig iron on to railway cars at the rate of $12\frac{1}{2}$ tons per person each day, Taylor's first act was to select 'scientifically' the appropriate workmen. Schmidt was selected for his physical and social attributes. After a series of time and motion studies, where the details of picking up pig iron and walking with it were recorded, Schmidt was instructed to load pig iron in a systematic way, his every movement timed, and a piece rate wage system offered as an incentive to improve his output. The end result, according to Taylor, was that Schmidt was able to carry $47\frac{1}{2}$ tons of pig iron each day. The broader message, however, was that it was now possible to break down jobs into their minimum skill requirements, reduce training times, and still improve productivity levels. It also implied that cheaper, unskilled labour could be hired to perform the tasks.

It is debatable how much influence Taylorism has had upon patterns of work organization in the industrialized world, especially outside of the USA. It is apparent, however, that Taylor's ideas on the rationalization of work did influence Henry Ford's engineers at Detroit in 1913–14 and contributed towards the rise of mass production techniques at the Highland Park Factory. What distinguishes Ford's innovations from those of Taylor, however, is that whereas Taylor took for granted the existing level of technology and sought greater productivity from labour, Ford used technology to mechanize the labour process and to eliminate labour. *Fordism*, as exemplified by the moving assembly line, represents the dominance of machinery over labour and is thus a step beyond Taylor in the organization of work and the development of modern industry.

John Allen
Open University

Reference

Taylor, F. W. (1911) *Principles of Scientific Management*.

Further reading

Littler, C. R. (1978) 'Understanding Taylorism', *British Journal of Sociology* 29.
—— (1985) 'Taylorism, Fordism and job design', in D. Knights, H. Willmott and D. Collinson (eds) *Job Redesign: Critical Perspectives on the Labour Process*, Aldershot.

See also: Fordism; industrial relations; industrial sociology.

technical assistance

Technical assistance – or technical co-operation as it is now more often called, partly in deference to the susceptibilities of its recipients – is part of foreign aid.

Its purpose is to create the skills and institutions needed for faster development, also referred to as 'capacity building'. Technical co-operation (TC) consists partly of people sent to countries in need of particular kinds of technical or other professional expertise, and partly of training or education in the donor countries. Sometimes the technical assistance takes the form of a brief visit by consultants. More typically, foreign experts stay for a year or longer – to work as economists in the Ministry of Finance, as science teachers, as agronomists or to set up a rural development project. Much technical assistance comes as part of a project that also contains financial aid. A new computer system in the statistical office, financed by foreign aid, may require experts to install it and to train local staff in its operation. Increasingly, technical assistance is provided under the aegis of non-governmental organizations like Oxfam or Médicins Sans Frontières.

Taking the OECD countries as a whole, technical co-operation now accounts for some 25 per cent of their total foreign aid. But that percentage is an average, with large variations between member states. For instance, 43 per cent of UK bilateral aid takes the form of TC, while in Norway, Sweden and Japan it accounts for only about 14 per cent of total aid. In 1991 there were some 150,000 trainees or students from Third-World countries in the OECD countries, while 80,000 TC personnel were working overseas (OECD 1994).

Technical assistance, like the rest of foreign aid, began after the end of the Second World War. Before that, colonial governments had often provided such assistance, but on a much smaller scale. Technical assistance received a great boost in 1949 when President Truman delivered his Inaugural Address and under Point Four urged 'a wider and more vigorous application of modern and technical knowledge' in the interests of Third-World countries. Much of it came through the specialized agencies of the newly established United Nations; some of the agencies devoted themselves very largely to providing technical assistance. The Food and Agricultural Organization and the World Health Organization are just two cases in point. Much of the funding for UN technical assistance comes from the UN Development Programme (UNDP). World Bank projects also often contain large elements of technical assistance.

One major problem with technical assistance is that it is often inappropriate to conditions in the recipient countries. The technology used in advanced industrial countries tends to reflect the fact that labour has become expensive in relation to capital. It is therefore capital intensive. It also reflects these countries' affluence. This technology may be quite inappropriate in countries in which it is capital that is scarce and expensive, not labour, and which cannot afford, for example, the standards of medical care found in countries with a much higher income per head. Much technical assistance has unfortunately been insensitive to these considerations. Nor is it the donor countries alone that have been responsible for the transfer of inappropriate technologies. Often governments and others in Third-World countries have put pressure on donors to provide the very latest technology, regarding anything less as part of an attempt by advanced industrial countries to perpetuate the backwardness of the recipients. Inappropriate technology is also sometimes transferred by returning students, who want to put into practice what they have learned, however inappropriate.

The most common model of technical assistance is the expatriate expert working with a local counterpart who will eventually take over. The efficacy of this model has been questioned. To induce foreign experts to live and work overseas they have to be highly paid and comfortably housed, but this is often resented by their locally paid counterparts, and that impedes the effective transfer of knowledge. Moreover, not all experts are good at imparting their expertise to others. The increasing use made of volunteers is in part a response to the difficulties experienced with technical assistance.

Walter Elkan
Brunel University

Reference

OECD Development Assistance Committee (1994) *Development Cooperation 1993 Report* Paris.

Further reading

Berg, E. J. (ed.) (1993) *Rethinking Technical Cooperation*, UNDP Regional Bureau for Africa, New York.
Cassen, R. (1986) *Does Aid Work?*, Oxford.
Mosley, P. (1987) *Overseas Aid: Its Defence and Reform*, Hemel Hempstead.
Seers, D. (1962) 'Why visiting economists fail', *Yale University Growth Center Paper* 10, New Haven, CT.

See also: aid; economic development; technical progress; technology; underdevelopment.

technological progress

The importance of technological progress for economic and social development is undeniable, but it is a field where understanding and analytical effort have lagged far behind other areas, such as short-term supply–demand analyses. This is due at least partly to the complexity of the process of technical change and the difficulty of obtaining precise definitions and measurements of it. Important advances have been made since the 1970s, but it remains a relatively neglected field.

Schumpeter, one of the few distinguished economists to put technological progress at the centre of his analysis, stressed the importance of new products, processes, and forms of organization or production – factors which have clearly been associated with enormous changes in the economic structures of developed economies since the Industrial Revolution. The rise of major new industries, such as railways and steel in the nineteenth century, and automobiles, synthetic materials and electronics in the twentieth, depended upon a complex interaction of inventions, innovations and entrepreneurial activity, which Freeman (1982) aptly described as 'technological systems'. Since the onset of the post-1973 recession, the idea that developed capitalist economies are subject to long waves of alternating periods of prosperity and stagnation, each wave being of around fifty to sixty years' duration, has been revived: some commentators argue that new technological systems are primarily responsible for the onset of an upswing, which begins to slow down as the associated technologies and industries reach maturity. Other economists, while accepting the notion of such cycles, argue that technological progress is a consequence, rather than a cause, of them. Outside the long-wave literature, there is an ongoing debate concerning the direction of causality regarding observed statistical associations between the growth of an industry and the pace of technical innovation.

At the macroeconomic level, the traditional, neo-classical growth models treat technological progress as part of a residual factor in 'explaining' increases in output, after accounting for the effects of changes in the volume of the factors of production (capital, labour and so on). This residual is normally large, and implicitly incorporates factors such as the education of the workforce and management expertise which contribute to improvements in efficiency, in addition to technological progress. In such approaches technological change is purely 'disembodied', that is, unrelated to any other economic variables. The class of so-called vintage capital models, which have become quite widely used since the early 1970s, treat technological progress as at least partly embodied in new fixed investment: plant and machinery are carriers of productivity improvements and the gains from technological progress depend on the level of investment in them. Even the latter approach, however, does not go far in capturing the processes and forces by which new techniques are absorbed into the production system; the 'evolutionary' models pioneered by Nelson and Winter (1982) attempt to explore the conditions under which entrepreneurs will strive to adopt improved techniques. Such approaches are, however, in their infancy.

Discussion of how new techniques are generated and adopted is typically conducted at a more micro-economic case-study level. An *invention* is a new or improved product, or a novel procedure for manufacturing an existing product, which may or may not become translated into an *innovation*, that is, the (first) commercial adoption of the new idea. In many cases, scientific discoveries pave the way for inventions which, if perceived as having potential market demand, are adopted commercially; in the nineteenth century, the inventor/innovator was frequently an independent individual, but in the nineteenth century the emphasis has moved to scientific and technological work being carried out in-house by large firms. If an innovation is successful, a period of *diffusion* often follows, where other firms adopt or modify the innovation and market the product or process. It is at this stage that the major economic impact frequently occurs. Freeman illustrated this process in the case of plastics, where fundamental scientific research work in Germany in the early 1920s on long-chain molecules led directly to the innovation of polystyrene and styrene rubber, and indirectly to numerous other new products in the 1930s. Further innovations and massive worldwide diffusion took place after the Second World War, facilitated by the shift from coal to oil as the feedstock for the industry. In the 1970s the industry appeared to have matured with a slow-down in demand and in the rate of technological progress.

The measurement of inventive and innovative activity is beset with difficulties. Input measures include the personnel employed and financial expenditure, although there is necessarily a degree of arbitrariness in defining the boundary of research and development activity. Output measures of invention include patent statistics, but these need to be interpreted with caution, owing to the differences in propensity to patent between firms, industries and countries with different perceptions of whether security is enhanced by patent protection or not, and differences in national patent legislation. The use of numbers of innovations as an output measure normally requires some – necessarily subjective – assessment of the relative 'importance' of the individual innovations. Despite their limitations, however, the use of several indicators in combination can provide a basis for comparisons between industries or between countries.

Over the post-war period, governments increasingly recognized the importance of attaining or maintaining international competitiveness in technology. The emergence of Japan as a major economic power owed much to a conscious policy of importing modern foreign technology and improving it domestically. Most coun-tries have a wide variety of schemes to encourage firms to develop and adopt the new technologies, and policies for training or retraining the workforce in the skills needed to use new techniques. In the current context, attention is, of course, focused particularly on micro-electronics-related technologies; and – whatever their validity – fears that these technologies could exacerbate unemployment problems generally take second place to fears of the consequences of falling behind technologically, in the eyes of governments and trade unions alike.

Forecasts of the impact of new technologies are notoriously unreliable. The cost-saving potential of nuclear power was dramatically overstated in the early stages, while the potential impact of computers was first thought to be extremely limited. For good or ill, we can, however, say that technological progress shows no sign of coming to a halt.

J. A. Clark
University of Sussex

References

Freeman, C. (1982) *The Economics of Industrial Innovation*, 2nd edn, London.
Nelson, R. R. and Winter, S. G. (1982) *An Evolutionary Theory of Economic Change*, Cambridge, MA.

Further reading

Heertje, A. (1977) *Economics and Technical Change*, London.

See also: technical assistance; technology.

technology

Technology admits a wide variety of definitions. First, it refers to physical objects or artefacts, for example, a car. Second, it refers to activities or processes – the system of car production, the pattern of organization around vehicle technologies, the behaviour and expectations of car users, and so on. Third, it can refer to the knowledge and skills associated with the production or use of technologies – the expertise associated with car design and use, as well to broader cultural images generated and sustained by the car industry.

Conventionally, technology has been the focus of social science interest from the point of view of its actual and potential impacts on society, or more specifically on work and the organization of labour. This follows the well-known position of technological determinism associated with some forms of Marxism: that technologies have the capacity to determine the course of historical evolution. In this view, then, the proper focus of social science attention is the effects of technology upon society. This position also draws upon views of the evolution of technology as a process whereby new developments are extrapolated from the existing (technical) state of affairs.

Against this it can be pointed out that technology is not independent of society; that 'society' can also have a significant impact upon the course of technological development; and that the determinist thesis is undermined by the many myriad examples where the effects of a technology diverge from the intended effects, or where a whole series of different effects result from the same technology (MacKenzie 1987; MacKenzie and Wajcman 1985).

These criticisms underpin the 'social shaping' approach to technology, wherein the central question is what shapes technology in the first place, before it has 'effects'? What role does society play in shaping technology? Axiomatic to this approach is the presumption that technologies can not be considered neutral, but are the upshot of various social and political forces. A celebrated example is Winner's (1985 [1980]) analysis of Robert Moses's bridges on Long Island, New York: the apparently unremarkable structural form of these bridges is said in fact to embody the social class bias and racial prejudice of their designer. The bridges were designed with a low headway; buses could not pass under them, so that poor people and Blacks, who were habitually dependent on bus transportation, were kept off the roads. Hence the technology embodies sociopolitical factors.

A similar theme occurs in attempts to apply social constructivism as developed for the analysis of scientific knowledge (Bijker and Law 1992; Bijker et al. 1987). We thus find the same post-Kuhnian critique of preconceptions of technology as was applied to scientific knowledge: the role of the great individual inventor must be seen in social context; technological growth can no longer be seen as a linear accumulation of artefacts each extrapolated from an existing corpus of technological achievement; technology involves social process as well as product. In short, technology is to be regarded as the upshot of a process of social construction: a stabilized design or artefact is the contingent product of social circumstances rather than the logical outcome of technical trajectory.

Similarily, technology has been construed as a cultural artefact. In this way of thinking, technology is congealed social relations, that is, a frozen assemblage of the practices, assumptions, beliefs, language, and so on, involved in its design and manufacture. Technology is thus a cultural artefact or system of artefacts which provides for certain new ways of acting and relating. The apposite slogan is that technology is society made durable: technology re-presents a form of social order (a defined concatenation of social relations) in material form (Latour 1991). It freezes and offers this fixed version of social relations such that its adequately configured users re-enact the set social arrangements. They can only 'adequately' (that is, socially accountably) use/make sense of the technology if they conform to the community of social relations which the technology makes available (cf. Cooper and Woolgar 1993; Woolgar 1993).

It is unclear to what extent these social science perspectives pose a radical challenge to widely entrenched preconceptions about the nature of technology. The key point of the social science critique is that technologies do not contain intrinsic (or given) technical capacities and potential; these qualities are the upshot of contingent social shaping and/or their interpretation and use. Yet, arguably, critics themselves deploy uninterrogated versions of 'what the technology can do'. At one level, there is the danger that the social study of technology becomes a mere application of the constructivist formula, thereby overlooking the strategic significance of this form of relativism for fundamental questions about the adequacy of social science explanation.

In order further to stress the interpretive flexibility of technology, the wide and contingent variety of possible designs and uses, it has been useful to deploy the metaphor of technology as a 'text'. The analogy highlights the social contingency of the processes of both designing (writing) and using (consuming, interpreting, reading) technology. In particular, it draws attention to the complex social relations between producers and consumers, and points to the importance of conceptions of user which are embodied by the technology text. The technology text makes available a particular reading which can be drawn upon by adequately configured users.

One benefit of this perspective is that it sets technology within a more theoretical frame of understanding how cultural artefacts in general are created and used. The production and consumption of cultural artefacts in general can be understood as occurring in virtue of the reorganization of sets of social relations. However, by comparison with other cultural artefacts, technology and science are particularly hard: that is, the congealed social relations are especially costly to unpack; by contrast, for example, cultural artefacts such as social science texts comprise social relations which seem relatively easy and cheap to dismantle.

It is a truism that technology is increasingly central to modern social life. But from an analytic point of view, there is a useful sense in which it is useful to recognize that this has always been the case; it is just that features of life once popularly regarded as technology have now been absorbed into routine. For example, writing is not now commonly thought of as a technology, yet it is a practice and system whose initial introduction provoked profound questions about the nature of reason and practice (Ong 1982). This way of broadening our conception of technology – from physical objects and their associated patterns of social organization to a more general notion of 'a system of social arrangements' – allows us to extend the perspective developed for the sceptical analysis of inherent technical qualities.

This perspective on technology has important implications for current thinking about the relation between technology and work. On the whole, this latter tradition has followed a determinist line by concentrating on the effects upon work organization of the introduction of new technologies. The sociology of technology proposes considerably more flexibility in the interpretation, use and implementation of technology in work situations.

Technology is also an important focus for examining and confronting deeply-held preconceptions about human nature. This follows from the fact that the emergence and evolution of a new technology can become the focus of discussion and concern about potential changes to the established order of social relationships. Thus, for example, just as seventeenth-century mechanical puppets aroused substantial moral concern about the implications for qualities defined as uniquely human, so too recent debates about artificial intelligence can be understood as discussions about what, after all, are the quintessential features of human (that is, non-mechanical) nature.

Steve Woolgar
Brunel University

References

Bijker, W. E. and Law, J. (eds) (1992) *Shaping Technology, Building Society: Studies in Socio-technical Change*, Cambridge, MA.

Bijker, W. E., Hughes, T. P. and Pinch, T. (eds) (1987) *The Social Construction of Technological Systems*, Cambridge, MA.

Cooper, G. and Woolgar, S. (1993) 'Software is society made malleable: the importance of conceptions of audience in software and research practice', PICT Policy Research Paper 25, Uxbridge.

Latour, B. (1991) 'Technology is society made durable', in J. Law (ed.) *A Sociology of Monsters: Essays on Power, Technology and Domination*, London.

MacKenzie, D. (1987) *Inventing Accuracy: A Historical Sociology of Nuclear Missile Guidance*, Cambridge, MA.

MacKenzie, D. and Wajcman, J. (eds) (1985) *The Social Shaping of Technology*, Milton Keynes.

Ong, W. (1982) *Orality and Literacy: The Technologizing of the Word*, London.

Winner, L. (1985 [1980]) 'Do artefacts have politics?' in D. MacKenzie and J. Wajcman (eds) *The Social Shaping of Technology*, Milton Keynes.

Woolgar, S. (1993) 'The user talks back', CRICT Discussion Paper 40, Uxbridge.

See also: sociology of science; technical assistance; technological progress.

territoriality

Territoriality is a strategy which uses bounded spaces in the exercise of power and influence; this can take place at a great variety of spatial scales, ranging from the student in a library who spreads books on a desk so as to prevent others sitting nearby, to a state apparatus which delineates and defends its national borders.

The use of territoriality has been identified in a range of animal species, leading some scientists to argue that it is a genetically inherited trait. Most social scientists avoid this claim, however, and instead focus on the efficiency of territoriality as a strategy, in a large variety of circumstances, involving the exercise of power, influence and domination.

Sack (1986) defines territoriality as the establishment of differential access to people and things. It comprises three necessary facets: a classification of space (i.e. the definition of the relevant territory); communication of that classification by the means of boundaries (so that you know whether you are within or outside the relevant territory); and enforcement or control of membership (i.e. subjection to certain rules if within the territory and limits on crossing its boundary).

The value of this strategy in enforcing control rests on a number of characteristics of bounded spaces. First, as a classification a territory is an extremely efficient way of defining membership – those inside a territory are subject to the controls therein – which can readily be communicated by boundary markers (which might be as effective as walls, as in prisons). Territoriality is also a means of reifying and depersonalizing power, associating it with the space rather than with the individuals who implement it, and therefore can be used to deflect attention from the reality of unequal relationships.

The efficiency of territoriality is exemplified by the large number of 'containers' into which the earth's surface is divided. By far the best example of its benefits to those wishing to exercise power is the state, which is necessarily a territorial body. Within its territory, the state apparatus assumes sovereign power: all residents are required to 'obey the laws of the land' in order for the state to undertake its central roles within society; boundaries are policed to control people and things entering and leaving. Some argue that territoriality is a necessary strategy for the modern state, which could not operate successfully without it (Johnston 1991; Mann 1984).

Many social groups use territoriality, either formally (with delineated boundaries, as with estate walls) or informally (as with the 'turfs' of street gangs), to advance their interests. These may involve defensive strategies, as when minority groups retreat into ghettos the better to withstand threats.

Territoriality is important in the creation and maintenance of group consciousness – as in nationalism, which often involves people being socialized into allegiance to a territory rather than to a human institution (i.e. the state apparatus in control of that territory). As people identify with one territory, they define others as not of that territory, and therefore different from themselves. This can be a major cause of tension: the definition of 'in-groups' (associated with positive characteristics) and 'out-groups' (with negative features) leads to a polarization of social attitudes at a variety of scales (and so some argue for social engineering which will reduce the polarization by mixing rather than separating groups, that is, by removing the use of territoriality: Sennett 1970). Those in control of state apparatus may well build on this polarization of attitudes in, for example, the development of support for foreign policies (as with US President Reagan's presentation of the Soviet Union as the 'evil empire').

R. J. Johnston
University of Bristol

References

Johnston, R. J. (1991) 'The territoriality of law: an exploration', *Urban Geography* 12.
Mann, M. (1984) 'The autonomous power of the state: its origins, mechanisms and results', *European Journal of Sociology* 25.
Sack, R. D. (1986) *Human Territoriality: Its Theory and History*, Cambridge.
Sennett, R. (1970) *The Uses of Disorder*, London.

Further reading

Johnston, R. J. (1991) *A Question of Place: Exploring the Practice of Human Geography*, Oxford.
Taylor, P. J. (1994) 'The state as container: territoriality in the modern world-system', *Progress in Human Geography* 19.
—— (1995) 'Beyond containers: inter-nationality, inter-state-ness, inter-territoriality', *Progress in Human Geography* 20.
Wolch, J. and Dear, M. J. (eds) (1989) *The Power of Geography: How Territory Shapes Social Life*, Boston, MA.

See also: political geography; space.

terrorism

Terrorism consists of a series of acts intended to spread intimidation, panic, and destruction in a population. These acts can be carried out by individuals and groups opposing a state, or acting on its behalf. The amount of violence is often disproportionate, apparently random, deliberately symbolic: to hit a target which would convey a message to the rest of the population. Violence perpetrated by the state or by right-wing terrorist groups is anonymous. Its goals are to shift sectors of public opinion to support the restoration of law and order and repressive measures, at the same time physically destroying political opponents and intimidating their actual and potential supporters. Violence from left-wing groups is usually 'signed'. Its goals are the awakening of public opinion to the injustices of the system, the punishment of hated representatives of the 'system' and their lackeys, and the expansion of political support for, and/or the defence of, their organizations. The ultimate goal is to muster enough support to overthrow the regime or, at least, to produce a revolutionary situation. An intermediate stage might be the unmasking of the 'fascist face' of the regime and the revelation to the population of its repressive reality.

Terrorism by the state or against it must be considered rational behaviour within the context of alternative options. It is suggestive of the lack of vast support both for the state and for terrorist organizations. Otherwise, both would utilize different political means. It is indeed a short cut to the problem of the creation of the necessary support. Sociopolitical terrorism may arise both in democratic and non-democratic states. It is more frequent in the former because of the relative ease with which terrorist organizations can be created in an atmosphere of freedom, when their appearance is unexpected. In non-democratic states, of course, it may be the state apparatus itself which resorts to terrorist activities. In any event, the lack of peaceful alternatives to change is likely to radicalize the situation and to push some opponents towards violent, clandestine activities.

There is not a single cause of terrorism: several conditions and determinants must be present. For state terrorism, the most important conditions are the willingness and determination of the dominant groups to retain power against mounting opposition, even by violent means. For sociopolitical terrorism, it is the inability to acquire sufficient support for radical changes in the light of mass passivity and elite unresponsiveness. However, terrorism is never simply the response to socioeconomic conditions of marginality: it is always the product of a political project. Be they at the service of the state or against the state, the terrorists pursue political goals.

According to their goals, one can define and identify several types of terrorism: repressive, revolutionary and secessionist. It is also possible to speak of international terrorism – though somewhat inappropriately

– for those groups staging their activities on the international scene. They want to dramatize their plight and obtain international visibility, recognition, and support (such as some sectors of the Palestine Liberation Organization (PLO), the Armenians, the Ustasha). However, most terrorist organizations are indigenous, such as the Irish Republican Army (IRA), the German Rote Armee Fraktion, the Italian Brigate Rosse and the neo-fascist Ordine Nuovo, the French Action Directe and the Basque ETA. They have roots and pursue goals that are inherently national, even though they might enjoy some (reciprocal) international support.

On the basis of the superior technical strength of modern states and of the legitimacy of democratic ones, it is often said that political terrorism cannot win. However, terrorism by the state can achieve significant results, and political terrorism against non-democratic regimes can severely weaken them (though, in order to win, the terrorist group will have to transform itself into guerrilla bands).

Terrorism, even if it is defeated, is not without consequences. The dynamics of political competition, the structures of the state, the relationships between citizens and political-administrative bodies will be changed to an extent that has thus far not been assessed. Therefore, political terrorism will endure as the weapon of groups that have neither the capability, the possibility, nor the patience to utilize other instruments to pursue their goals and implement their strategies.

Gianfranco Pasquino
University of Bologna

Further reading

Crenshaw, M. (ed.) (1983) *Terrorism, Legitimacy and Power*, Middletown, CT.
Eckstein, H. (1963) *Internal War*, New York.
Laqueuer, W. (1977) *Terrorism: A Study of National and International Political Violence*, Boston, MA.
Lodge, J. (ed.) (1981) *Terrorism: A Challenge to the State*, London.
Moss, D. (1989) *The Politics of Left-Wing Violence in Italy*, London.
Schmidt, A. P. (1983) *Political Terrorism: A Research Guide to Concepts, Theories, Data Bases and Literature*, New Brunswick, NJ.
Stohl, M. (ed.) (1979) *The Politics of Terrorism*, New York.
Wardlaw, G. (1982) *Political Terrorism: Theory, Tactics and Countermeasures*, Cambridge, UK.

See also: revolutions; violence.

therapeutic community

The use of community social processes for the treatment of mentally ill and personality disordered patients has been labelled 'therapeutic community'. Factors which have led to this approach include a growing dissatisfaction with the results of individual psychotherapy, the recognition of some harmful effects of institutionalization itself, and the realization of the importance of social experiences in learning and, therefore, in therapy.

The impetus for the therapeutic community came during and after the Second World War with the development of therapeutic units for soldiers suffering combat fatigue. In these army centres every aspect of the soldiers' hospital life was designed to counteract the socialization experience involved in being defined as mentally ill. The success of these units in returning soldiers to full activity was in sharp contrast with previous experience, and led to efforts at their replication in the civilian community.

Procedures in therapeutic communities derive from three sources: first, group therapy, in which patients receive continuous feedback on their behaviour as seen by others and their maladaptive use of defence mechanisms; second, democratic traditions of self-government, including a sharing of facilities, the use of first names, and frank expressions of thoughts and feelings between patients and staff; and, third, the importance of being part of a social unit to counteract alienation and promote rehabilitation. The power of peer group pressure has long been used in self-help groups, such as Alcoholics Anonymous.

The tone of the therapeutic community is often set by a daily meeting where all patients, ward staff, and doctors openly discuss problems and psychopathology.

Problems of the therapeutic community include the blurring of roles which makes it possible for staff to evade responsibility and authority. Also, the community approach may become a vehicle for the patient's rationalizing hostility towards authority or leadership in any form.

Despite difficulties, the concept has added to the effectiveness and humanity of the psychiatric unit. Those therapeutic communities which have achieved stability have incorporated professional control while permitting patients an active voice in their own care.

Bernard S. Levy
Harvard University

Further reading

Almond, R. (1974) *The Healing Community*, New York.
Caudill, W. (1958) *The Psychiatric Hospital as a Small Society*, Cambridge, MA.
Cumming, J. and Cumming, E. (1962) *Ego and Milieu*, New York.
Jones, M. (1953) *The Therapeutic Community*, New York.

therapy *see* behaviour therapy; cognitive-behavioural therapy; family therapy

thinking

Human thinking has been the subject of study by both philosophers and psychologists since the time of Aristotle. As a topic for investigation, however, thinking is rather different from most other subjects since we lack, even now, a clearly agreed definition of what it is. The way in which the topic has been discussed and studied implies several different notions of human thought. Of these, the oldest – and the most common-sensical – is that thinking corresponds to the 'contents of consciousness'. There is a long philosophical tradition dating from the Aristotle through the British Empiricist school of Locke, Berkeley, Hume and Mill that takes this perspective and that encouraged a methodology of *introspectionism* in which the mind studies itself directly. Common-sense views of thinking, embedded in the folk psychology of our culture, also has it that we are beings whose decisions and actions are controlled by conscious thoughts. In folk psychology, we attribute the causes of behaviour to a variety of conscious mental states which we label with such terms as beliefs, motives, intentions, decisions, and so on.

The modern conception of thought within the dominant methodology of cognitive science is a functional one, based on the idea of the brain as a computer-like information processing system. Hence, thinking is seen as no more or less than the high-level information processing required for problem solving, reasoning, decision making, creativity and so on. In this approach, thinking is more or less defined by exclusion, as a residual category of processes that we would not wish to include among those responsible for perception, memory or language. The role of consciousness is of little or no interest to most cognitive scientists. While this view of human thought is accepted by some contemporary philosophers of mind, it is strongly disputed by others (e.g. Searle 1992). The radical shift away from both the common sense of folk psychology and the philosophical tradition of almost two millennia occurred within the past century and it is of interest to dwell briefly on how this came about.

Faith in introspection as a method of studying thought declined progressively for a variety of reasons. When psychology emerged as a separate discipline from philosophy in the late nineteenth century, the first schools were based upon the use of the introspective method. One of these schools, based in the German university of Würzburg around the turn of the century, produced surprising and – at the time – mystifying results (Humphrey 1951). Subjects asked to describe the thought processes experienced while performing simple tasks were often unable to identify any images or other concrete forms of thought; sometimes thoughts were present but 'indescribable', sometimes the subjects could not identify any experience which mediated their behaviour. The findings of these early psychologists are confirmed by many modern psychological studies in which, for example, it is relatively easy to demonstrate that people's behaviour, such as decision making, is controlled by features of the environment of which they show no awareness in their introspective reports. Moreover, it appears that when asked to explain their thinking, people often rationalize or theorize, constructing after the event and often giving self-flattering accounts of their own behaviour (see Evans 1989: ch. 5).

Apart from the doubts engendered by experimental studies of introspection, the equation of consciousness with thinking was undermined by two major psychological schools. The first was the psychoanalytic (Freudian) movement in which the notion of unconscious thinking was strongly promoted. The second was that of behaviourism founded by J. B. Watson in the 1920s and highly influential in experimental psychology until the late 1950s. In this approach mentalistic accounts of human behaviour were discarded on the grounds that all scientific observations had to be objective and replicable – qualities which could not be claimed for the introspective method. Behaviourism attempted to describe all behaviour, including thinking, in terms of observable stimuli and responses.

In the 1960s cognitive psychology appeared as a new approach and later joined up with relevant approaches to linguistics, philosophy, artificial intelligence and neuroscience to form the multidisciplinary endeavour known as 'cognitive science'. In this approach intelligence is defined as computational processes at an abstract level which may be manifest in both biological systems (i.e. brains) and machines (i.e. computers). By use of the computer metaphor and the idea of thinking as information processing, modern cognitive psychologists rediscovered the notion of internal thought processes, the absence of which had so impoverished behaviouristic accounts of complex behaviour. At the same time, few were willing to reintroduce the notion against which the behaviourists had reacted – that of conscious intentional mental states as the causes of behaviour.

It is recognized that much everyday thinking is of an apparently aimless and unguided nature and there is a field of study concerned with daydreaming.

However, the great majority of contemporary studies of human thought are concerned with *directed* thought, which is focused on achievement of goals. One large area of study is that of problem solving which is concerned with the processes by which people are able to achieve goals by indirect means. Most studies have used *well-defined* problems, such as anagram solving or chess playing, where everything is clear from the outset – the goals, the constraints, the means available to change the current situation. Solutions of problems like this are normally described as a search through a problem space consisting of an initial state, one or more goal states, and any number of intermediate states through which one can pass. This led to a parallel programme of artificial intelligence work concerned with the development of *heuristic* procedures thought to reduce intelligently the search required in large problem spaces in a human-like manner (Newell and Simon 1972). Since the mid-1970s psychologists have shown more interest in ill-defined problem solving, where the solver has to supply parts of the problem specification typically on the basis of prior knowledge and experience. This is more representative of the requirements of real-world thinking in areas such as medical problem solving or engineering design.

Decision making differs from problem solving in that individuals have to commit themselves to an action at one point in time, the consequences of which will become apparent only at a later time. Hence, rational decision making requires the ability to judge the probability of future events and weigh these against the desirability of possible outcomes in making choices. A large field of research developed since the early 1970s suggests that people judge probabilities by use of rather crude heuristics which lead to many systematic errors and biases, such as overconfidence in judgement, extrapolation from small or biased samples of evidence, and neglect of base rate information in judgements about specific cases. This has led many psychologists to the conclusion that people are fundamentally irrational decision makers.

Another important contemporary field of work that has also produced a large catalogue of errors and biases in its experimental finding is that of deductive reasoning. In this area, subjects are asked to draw inferences on the basis only of the presented information (premises) with their performance assessed by the norms of formal logic. Almost all studies of this kind – conducted mostly on adults of above average intelligence – show extensive logical errors. For example, people frequently draw inferences which are 'fallacious' in logic, that is, which do not necessarily follow from the information given. Their responses may be biased by many factors, including the linguistic form of the premises and the prior 'believability' of the conclusions. For discussion of biases in both deductive reasoning and probability judgement, see Evans (1989).

It is probably true to say that concerns about rationality have displaced the discussion of consciousness as the dominant philosophical issue concerning psychological studies of human thinking. The problem is that the success of the human species suggests that we have evolved to have a highly adaptive intelligence, yet we have these numerous laboratory demonstrations of erroneous thought. A rationality debate has developed since the mid-1980s with philosophers mostly arguing for human rationality in spite of the psychological evidence and with psychologists being divided on the issue (see Manktelow and Over 1993). One line of argument from the rationalists is that the normative systems used – such as probability theory and formal logic – are inappropriate or inadequate measures of rationality; another is that psychological experiments study 'cognitive illusions' which have limited implications for everyday reasoning. In response, however, it is not too difficult to demonstrate that many of the observed effects apply equally to expert subjects making decisions within their own domains of knowledge.

Jonathan St B. T. Evans
University of Plymouth

References

Evans, J. St B. T. (1989) *Bias in Human Reasoning: Causes and Consequences*, Brighton.

Humphrey, C. (1951) *Thinking: An Introduction to its Experimental Psychology*, London.

Manktelow, K. I. and Over, D. (eds) (1993) *Rationality*, London.

Newell, A. and Simon, H. A. (1972) *Human Problem Solving*, Englewood Cliffs, NJ.

Searle, J. (1992) *The Rediscovery of Mind*, Cambridge, MA.

Further reading

Ericsson, K. A. and Simon, H. A. (1984) *Protocol Analysis: Verbal Reports as Data*, Cambridge, MA.

Garnham, A. and Oakhill, J. (1994) *Thinking and Reasoning*, Oxford.

See also: cognitive psychology; cognitive science; memory; problem solving.

Third World

The term Third World was first used by the French demographer, Alfred Sauvy, in August 1952, to describe the new nation-states, mostly in Asia and Africa, which had begun to emerge at the end of the Second World War (e.g. Sri Lanka and India) but which became much more numerous when the 'winds of change' blew over Africa: seventeen countries became independent in 1961 alone. Latin American countries, though mostly equally underdeveloped in economic terms, were not involved until the 1970s, as they had long been independent.

At that time, the world was polarized into two camps, headed by the rival superpowers. But most of the new states went out of their way to avoid identification with either camp: as states, they claimed to be non-aligned in international politics (though some, in fact, did align themselves with one camp or the other), and, internally, to be trying to find a third way, avoiding not only the authoritarian, planned and centralized Soviet model, but also the western market economy and political pluralism one. The more radical of them claimed to be developing socialist humanism, which attracted interest in western countries, too (the concept, indeed, derives from the *tiers état* of pre-revolutionary France: the estate of ordinary people who lacked the privileges of the other two estates, the clergy and the nobility). Now it was used in relation to states, not estates.

By 1955, the Afro-Asian Conference, held in Bandung, Indonesia, which Nehru persuaded Zhou Enlai to attend, brought together representatives of the majority of the world's population. To many, especially on the left, the non-aligned movement (it refused the title of bloc) seemed to be growing into a new force capable of changing the world balance of power, and much more likely, now, to be the grave-diggers of capitalism than either the communist countries or the working class in developed capitalist countries.

The first concern of the new states was to secure the liberation of the remaining colonies and, above all, to break the South African apartheid regime. Radical leaders like Nkrumah further hoped to develop new, positive alternatives: to overcome the colonial legacy of the balkanization of the continent via the new Organization of African Unity (OAU).

But that organization quickly became primarily concerned with the opposite: maintaining the boundaries of its member states which had been constructed by the colonial powers. Given the multi-ethnic composition of these states, secession movements emerged, often, as in Katanga, manipulated by the former colonial power. Conflicts between countries broke out, too: Tanzania, where Julius Nyerere had initially wondered whether the country would need an army, found itself invaded by Idi Amin's Uganda. Increasingly, country after country was sucked into what were often proxy wars, fought with high-tech armaments supplied by one or other of the superpowers (in the case of Somalia, first by the USSR, then by the USA).

Increasingly, though, the major problems that these countries faced, and which they discussed at successive conferences in Cairo, Lusaka, Algiers, Sri Lanka, Havana and elsewhere, were economic rather than political. As producers of raw materials and importers of high-priced manufactured goods and, most of them, of oil, they found themselves at an increasing disadvantage, in an increasingly global market: not 'developing', but 'underdeveloping'.

The first victory achieved by the non-aligned on the economic front was the success of seventy-seven underdeveloped countries in winning UN backing for a World Conference on Trade and Development, in 1962. The second major breakthrough came in 1974, when the oil-producing states formed OPEC, with severe effects even on western economies.

A few countries – notably the 'four Little Tigers' of East Asia (Taiwan, South Korea, Hong Kong and Singapore) – have, moreover, succeeded in developing their economies along capitalist lines, first as newly industrializing countries (NICs), and later so massively (and others somewhat less dramatically) that they are no longer part of the Third World (even if, as in the cases of Brazil and Mexico, they have incurred phenomenal levels of debt in the process, and still harbour huge sectors of rural and urban poverty). But most of the Third World has not developed so spectacularly, particularly most of Black Africa, which, in many respects, has 'underdeveloped'.

The term therefore seems likely to persist, even though it has always attracted criticism from those who see it as a badge of inferiority (because 'First' and 'Second' seem to them to imply superiority). They see underdevelopment, too, as a consequence of western colonization, rather than attributing it – as many in the west do – to factors internal to the Third World itself, some in terms of unfavourable natural environments in which periodic famine is believed to be endemic; others in terms of social factors, such as traditional institutions (e.g. caste or patriarchalism) which are thought to hinder progress, as well as more modern hindrances to development such as dictatorial regimes.

Finally, some argue that there is only one 'world system' (especially since the collapse of communism), so that countries can be ranked, statistically, only as richer or poorer, not classified as belonging to one world or another. Most world-system theorists, however, argue that the status of a country depends on its place in the world system as a whole: whether it is central, peripheral or semi-peripheral.

Peter Worsley
University of Manchester

Further reading

Fanon, F. (1961) *The Wretched of the Earth*, London.
Singham, A. W. and Hune, S. (1986) *Non-Alignment in an Age of Alignments*, New York.

Worsley, P. (1964) *The Third World*, London.
—— (1984) *The Three Worlds*, London.

See also: centre and periphery; underdevelopment; world-system theory.

time

Social time comes in many different guises, is used for a multitude of purposes, and underpins the various social science perspectives in specific ways. The complexity of time is retained irrespective of whether the dominant time expression of a society revolves around the clock, the calendar, religious festivals, or other sources for the scheduling of social life.

For all societies, time constitutes a parameter within which life is structured, organized and synchronized. This time frame may be constituted on the basis of calendars, clocks, seasons, the life-span from birth to death, personal biographical events, or publicly available social markers such as elections, world championships, religious festivals, university terms/semesters, and bank opening times. As parameter, time allows for the estimation of duration – the reckoning of time – be this through the movement of the planets, regularly recurring events, processes of set duration, or devices such as clocks.

Time is further constituted through irreversible change. We know the passage of time through the difference between the past, present and future: through the decay of organic matter, the development and ageing of our fellow beings, through life and death. Social scientists have two principal means of dealing with such temporality. They can chart it objectively on a before-and-after basis and locate it historically with reference to calendar and clock time. This is the dominant social science approach to temporality, utilized in empirical research, historical accounts, and in both functionalist and Marxist perspectives. Alternatively, social scientists can use the subjective positioning of the now, the present, yesterday or tomorrow which is always person/event specific and has flexible boundaries. This interpretative/constitutive approach tends to emphasize the creative moment, the fact that the present is always more than that which preceded it, that time is constitutive of events.

While all known societies seem to recognize change and reckon time in some way, not all societies have created an independent, abstract time which is quantifiable and can be used as both resource and medium of exchange. In industrial and industrializing countries this clock time underpins social interactions in general and employment relations in particular. As abstract exchange value it can be sold, allocated and controlled.

As such, 'clock time' is intimately tied to relations of power and has significance not only for employers and employees but also for members of society whose time is not exchanged for money: those caring at home for their kin and, for example, young, elderly and unemployed people. People whose time cannot be so quantified and translated into money live in the shadows of economic relations of clock time, simultaneously excluded from its benefits and affected by its all-pervasive meaning and power.

Barbara Adam
University of Wales

Further reading

Adam, B. (1990) *Time and Social Theory*, Cambridge, UK.
—— (1990) *Timewatch: The Social Analysis of Time*, Cambridge, UK.
Davies, K. (1990) *Women and Time: The Weaving of the Strands of Everyday Life*, Aldershot.
Elias, N. (1992) *Time*, Oxford.
Kern, S. (1983) *The Culture of Time and Space 1880–1918*, London.
Rivkin, J. (1987) *Time Wars*, New York.
Time and Society (1992–) London.
Young, M. (1988) *The Metronomic Society*, London.

totalitarian regimes *see* authoritarian and totalitarian systems; military regimes

totemism

The anthropological notion of totemism was invented by McLennan (1869–70) and condemned to oblivion by Lévi-Strauss (1963). During its life-span, however, it became a major focus for debates between celebrated European and North American anthropologists, who tried repeatedly, and unsuccessfully, to give it an appropriate definition and explanation. Its very birth was the product of a misunderstanding. The word 'totem' was coined at the end of the eighteenth century by J. Long from an expression in the Ojibwa language, *ototeman*, denoting the existence of a kinship relationship between two members of the same clan. The clans of the Ojibwa (of the region of the Great Lakes) were named mainly after animals, and these eponyms could thus be used to specifiy common membership of a clan. Long mistakenly merged this practice of collective naming with a belief, common among North American Indians, according to which each individual is associated with an animal that acts as its guardian spirit: from this confusion stemmed his interpretation of the Ojibwa 'totem' as a mystic link between an animal spirit and an exogamous clan. This initial ethnographic blunder was amplified by McLennan (1869–70), who argued that totemism was the first religion of humankind and the source of primitive institutions: the fetishist worship of plant and animals had been the cement of clan exogamy and matrilineal descent.

Following McLennan, Rivers (1914) formulated a definition widely accepted by the anthropological community at the turn of the century. Totemism combines three elements: the connection between a natural species and an exogamous group; the belief that the members of the group are descended from this species; a ritualized behaviour towards the totemic species. Blinded by their quest for a single origin of religion, and by their obsession with the pristine naturalness of primitive societies, the main theorists of totemism (Durkheim 1915; Frazer 1910) did not pay attention to Tylor, who had suggested as early as 1899 that the phenomenon might best be explained by a tendency of the mind to 'classify out the universe'. The expansion of ethnographic knowledge soon revealed that the classical definition of totemism could not accommodate the diversity of empirical facts (Goldenweiser 1910). Increasingly, totemism was stripped of all concrete content and came to be considered as a mnemonic method, among others, for naming exogamous units (Boas 1916). With the decline of evolutionism, interest in totemism waned, until Lévi-Strauss (1963) took up the argument where Boas had left it, and showed why natural species are commonly used as labels for social groups. The natural kingdom offers to the mind a spontaneous model of ordered discontinuity, which also suggests a way of conceptualizing clan segmentation, by homology. Reduced to a denotative relation between a natural species and an exogamous unit, totemism is thus simply one of various possible types of association between person and groups (in the human domain) and individual and species (in the natural domain). While dissolving the totemic illusion into a general theory of classification, Lévi-Strauss nevertheless left in the shadow all those phenomena that have been described in the context of individual totemism (relations between a human person and a natural species or a member of a species). In these ritualized interactions, plants and animals are not treated by humans as mere cognitive devices for social classification, but as persons, endowed with a spiritual principle and social attributes, with whom relations (of protection, seduction, hostility, alliance or exchange of services) may be established. Such 'animic relations' (Descola 1992) can be considered as symmetrical inversions of totemic classifications: they do not exploit the differential relations between natural species to confer a conceptual order on society, but rather use the elementary categories structuring social life to organize, in conceptual terms, the relations between humans and natural species.

Philippe Descola
Ecole des Hautes Etudes en Sciences Sociales

References

Boas, F. (1916) 'The origin of totemism', *American Anthropologist* 18.
Descola, P. (1992) 'Societies of nature and the nature of society', in A. Kuper (ed.) *Conceptualizing Society*, London.
Durkheim, E. (1915) *The Elementary Forms of the Religious Life*, London.
Frazer, J. G. (1910) *Totemism and Exogamy*, London.
Goldenweiser, A. A. (1910) 'Totemism, an analytical study', *Journal of American Folklore* 23.
Lévi-Strauss, C. (1963) *Totemism*, London.
McLennan, J. F. (1869–1870) 'The worship of animal and plants: totems and totemism', *Fortnightly Review* 6–7.
Rivers, W. H. R. (1914) *The History of Melanesian Society*, Cambridge, UK.
Tylor, E. B. (1899) 'Remarks on totemism', *Journal of the Royal Anthropological Institute* 1.

See also: religion and ritual.

trade *see* cartels and trade associations; international trade; trade unions

trade unions

A trade union is a combination of employees for the purpose of regulating the relationship between employees and employer so that the pay and conditions of the employees may improve. Such regulation can be brought about in three main ways: unilateral regulation by the trade union; bargaining with the employer by the employees collectively; and statutory regulation (Clegg 1976).

Historically, unilateral regulation was used by unions of skilled craftsmen who would agree among themselves not to accept employment unless certain terms were met by the employer. Subsequently, with the extension of trade unions to cover nearly all sections of the workforce, collective bargaining over pay and conditions became the major activity of trade unions in most countries, with trade union officers also acting to resolve any grievances of individual members, or of small groups, within the workplace. The process of collective bargaining now has very wide scope, and trade union officers frequently exert considerable control and management of the internal labour markets of the members' employing organization (in regard to such things as recruitment, promotion, discipline, and task allocation). The state has tended to intervene not only in the employee–employer relationship but also in the process of collective bargaining by legislation and through judicial or quasi-judicial procedures. Thus trade unions have developed their legal expertise and their political connections to operate (and occasionally to resist) and to influence legislation in their members' interests.

Most countries have some statutory legislation concerning the formation of a trade union and the conduct of its affairs (paralleling company or partnership legislation). Generally, a trade union is required to be registered, to have rules conforming to certain standards (for example, for the election of a governing body and the appointment of officers), and to keep and submit (audited) accounts. In return, a registered trade union may be granted certain legal immunities or privileges, the most important being the right not to be sued for breach of contract as a result of action taken in the course of collective bargaining. In some countries, deregistration (or the threat thereof) has been used by governments to influence the behaviour of trade unions.

The logic of collective bargaining (and of its corollary, that agreements must be honoured by both sides) requires that, when necessary, the employee members of a trade union will act together in a united front and that no members will break ranks either by refusing to take, say, strike action when instructed by trade union officers, or by taking strike action when this has not been instructed. A trade union must, therefore, have some method of ensuring that all members do what is required of them. A trade union can usually rely on voluntary compliance based on fraternal solidarity or ideological commitment, but the use of sanctions against recalcitrant members always raises difficult questions of the rights of individuals against the needs of the collectivity.

In general, trade unions have become an integral and accepted part of the economies in which they work. This has caused controversy among those who have other views of the functions of trade unions. Marx and Engels saw trade unions as developing inevitably and together with capitalism and (optimistically from their viewpoint) as being in the vanguard of the revolutionary process to overthrow the capitalist system. Marx and Engels subsequently observed the tendency of trade unions, especially in Britain, to become 'corrupted': by concentrating on improving the condition of workers through collective bargaining, they were, by implication, accepting the capitalist system.

Although Marx and Engels observed these tendencies towards the 'embourgeoisement' of the working class, it was Lenin who argued that trade unions tended to become integrated into the capitalist system and that

there was therefore a need 'to divert the working-class movement from this spontaneous, trade-unionist striving to come under the wing of the bourgeoisie, and to bring it under the wing of revolutionary Social-Democracy' (Lenin 1902). Subsequently, Trotsky extended Lenin's thesis of trade union integration into the capitalist system to an attack on trade union leaders who used their authority actively to assist capitalism in controlling the workers, so ensuring trade unions' full incorporation into the system. Seen from another point of view, Trotsky's attack is simply a criticism of the role of trade unions in enforcing collective agreements. The view that trade unions render capitalism 'safe' by institutionalizing conflict may meet with approval or disapproval, but it is central in understanding the role of trade unions in many countries.

Given that trade unions, as an integral part of the market economy, bargain effectively, the question arises as to their economic impact. There are two broad issues of interest: their impact on the general level of wages and their impact on the structure of earnings within the labour market. In situations of full employment, the process of collective bargaining (or the 'power' of trade unions) has been blamed for causing inflation by increasing remuneration per employee by more than the increase in real output per employee, so leading to rising unit labour costs, rising prices, and loss of 'competitiveness' (at an unchanged exchange rate) in world markets, with consequent loss of jobs. In response, governments have sometimes attempted to agree with (or to impose on) trade unions an incomes policy, usually comprising some limitation on collectively bargained pay increases together with other measures more acceptable to the unions.

On the issue of pay structures, there is evidence to show that (at least during certain periods – especially of high unemployment) average earnings for unionized groups of employees tend to be higher than average earnings for employees who are not unionized. Some argue that trade unions (or rather, the consequences of collective bargaining) have been at least partly responsible, in co-operation with many other influences, for creating and maintaining labour market 'segmentation'. This is the situation where employment is divided between a relatively unionized 'primary' labour market comprising well-paid jobs with good conditions of employment (short hours, holidays with pay, promotion prospects, pensions) in large firms and in the public sector, and a peripheral relatively non-unionized 'secondary' labour market, with low pay and inferior conditions. This strand of criticism of trade unions has been developed both in industrial countries and also in Third-World countries where, it has been argued, trade unions serve to enhance the real incomes of an employed urban elite at the expense of the rural peasantry: incomes policies in Third-World countries have as often been aimed at this problem as at controlling inflation.

Dudley Jackson
University of Wollongong

References

Clegg, H. (1976) *Trade Unionism under Collective Bargaining: A Theory Based on Comparisons of Six Countries*, Oxford.
Lenin, V. I. (1902 [1963]) *What Is To Be Done?* Moscow

See also: corporatism; industrial relations; industrial sociology.

transaction costs

Transaction costs represent the cost of the resources (physical as well as human) deployed to complete an exchange of goods and services between parties (individuals and/or organizations), in a way that leaves them satisfied. Such resources are not wasted: if successfully invested in smoothing transactions they keep markets, firms and the economy in general efficient. Costless transactions obtain only in an ideal world. Factors that may contribute to the cost of a transaction in the real world are the search for the 'true' price at which the sale/purchase ought to take place, since prices are never known by the agents in a complete and real way; discovering the 'true' quality of the good or service (their quality is often not fully known to some of the parties); checking the reputation of the partners in order to avoid subsequent surprises; carefully crafting the contract that regulates the exchange, so as to avoid later claims; and monitoring its execution so as to pinpoint responsibilities and dues if modifications have to be added to the original contract. Resources have to be devoted both to overcome natural deficiencies in information and to maintain a reasonable perception of equity among partners who do not necessarily share the same goals or trust each other. Trust is an important source of transaction costs. There are natural difficulties that arise from the lack of information, or its asymmetric distribution, and, furthermore, strategic or opportunistic behaviour may also drive up the costs of the transaction. For example, one party may be willing to exploit privileged information about the quality of a good or its value in order to profit from the transaction, and this may lead to litigation if discovered.

The imperfections that may endanger real as opposed to ideal transactions cause friction in the functioning of the economy. As a consequence, the functioning of economic institutions, and in particular the market, may be endangered. However, as in mechanics, friction may also create movement.

Institutional economists have pointed out that the failure of the market, due to excessive transaction costs, need not completely impede transactions. The exchange process may simply be transferred to other institutions, such as the hierarchy or the clan. These 'non-price' institutions internalize market transactions by governing them through long-term, open contracts that create mutual dependence between the parties, improve reciprocal control, curb opportunism, and allow for better co-operation. One way to avoid costly litigation or disappointments that may endanger the repetition of the exchange over time is for some of the parties to internalize the supplier, that is, to transform the supplier into an internal department, so that the production of the good may be monitored more closely. In any case, costs have to be borne, either because of haggling in a malfunctioning market or through the setting up of administrative controls and monitoring apparatus (the hierarchy).

The strength of the transaction costs perspective is that it offers a compact set of concepts and a unifying language to analyse and interpret a variety of micro and macro phenomena, such as vertical integration between firms; the employment contracts and the internal labour relations; anti-trust laws and interventions; and even the emergence and failure of economic institutions. Nevertheless, it has two major limitations. First, transaction costs economics is based on a more sophisticated, but still narrow view of the agent as 'economic man', who maximizes utility despite the limits of his or her rationality. Therefore altruistic behaviour, for example, is beyond its scope. Second, the approach presents a static, comparative view of why different economic institutions exist, develop or decay. Transaction costs economics indicates that for a given level of uncertainty and amount of trust between the parties there is usually a limited number of governance structures that are more efficient and will survive in the long run. When circumstances change, efficient governance structure must adapt swiftly, or it will be swept away by competition. The approach is silent, however, on the forces that make certain organizations stickier than others. In sum, transaction costs economics seems to assume an implicit notion of frictionless change. It may, however, be ignoring the widespread role of transition costs in socioeconomic organizations undergoing continuous change.

Claudio Ciborra
University of Bologna

Further reading

Barney, J. B. and Ouchi, W. G. (eds) (1986) *Organisational Economics*, San Francisco, CA.
Ciborra, C. U. (1993) *Teams, Markets and Systems*, Cambridge, UK.

Williamson, O. E. (1985) *The Economic Institutions of Capitalism*, New York.

See also: economic man; institutional economics; markets; trust and co-operation.

transference

The concept of transference was formally brought into psychiatry by Sigmund Freud, who discovered empirically that his patients' perceptions of him during analysis were coloured, distorted, and even completely fabricated in relation to the patients' early feelings towards important figures in their own past: parents, siblings, caretakers and the like.

These early, often infantile, feelings were transferred to the analyst *unconsciously*; the patient initially believed that these essentially internal perceptions were valid reflections of the therapist himself. At times, they were recognized as internal and inappropriate to the real situation; for example, a patient might say: 'This is strange, but I seem to feel toward you as I did toward my mother.'

At first it seemed to Freud that transference feelings were an obstacle and impediment to the rational progress of the analysis. However, he came to recognize that the transference was a repetition of earlier conflicts and feelings, and thus the analysis of the transference became the central task of the analyst. Modern psychoanalysts consider the transference even more important for therapeutic exploration and treatment.

Such transference feelings were later discovered to play a part in almost all human relationships, at least to some degree. A common example is a person's tendency to see various authority figures in parental terms and to experience feelings for them which are derived from childhood. To take an extreme case, love at first sight is a phenomenon almost entirely composed of transference feelings; since this sort of attachment owes nothing to the *real* aspects of the loved one, the feelings must originate from elsewhere, in the past.

A number of dynamic psychiatrists hold the view that, for operational purposes, everything that occurs within the analytic or therapeutic session may be viewed as a manifestation of transference feelings by one or the other parties. More recently, two areas relevant to this issue have become the focus of attention. The first is the so-called 'real relationship', that is, those elements of the therapeutic relationship that are transference-free (or relatively so). The second is the idea that certain psychological entities may best be diagnosed by noting the specific types of transference formed during therapy itself (for example, narcissistic personality disorders).

The usual form of transference in therapy (and life in general) might be described as 'neurotic transference', in the sense that the feelings transferred derive from the original neurotic conflicts of the individual. One characteristic of this sort of transference is that it is testable: patients can correct their own misperception once attention is called to the nature and form of the error. Thus, a patient might say in such a situation, 'I see that I was automatically expecting you to reject me as my father once did.' On occasion, however, the transference perception is *not* testable, and resists reality testing. Such a fixed transference is called a 'psychotic transference', in which the patient is unalterably convinced of the reality of the transference perception: thus the patient might say, 'You *are* rejecting, there is no doubt about it; my father's nature is irrelevant to the matter.' These psychotic transferences are quite common among patients with the borderline syndrome, and contribute to the difficulty of therapeutic work with them.

It may be a safe generalization that the major source of difficulty with all parts of therapy, especially the therapeutic alliance, is the feelings that derive from the transference. This problem is balanced by the fact that the ability to work successfully with transference material is often the hallmark of the successful therapist.

Thomas G. Gutheil
Harvard University

Further reading

Freud, S. (1958) *The Dynamics of Transference*, London.

Greenacre, P. (1954) 'The role of transference', *Journal of the American Psychoaralytic Association* 2.

Greenman, R. R. (1965) 'The working alliance and the transference neurosis', *Psychoanalytic Quarterly* 34.

Orr, D. (1954) 'Transference and countertransference: an historical survey', *Journal of the American Psychoanalytic Association* 2.

See also: psychoanalysis.

transition, demographic *see* demographic transition

transition, health *see* health transition

transport, economics and planning

Transport forms a major part of any economic system. Economists have traditionally looked at ways in which markets for transport industries (the railways, shipping, airlines, and so on) could be improved to maximize the benefits derived from public and private transport operations. They have sought to develop techniques to help improve pricing and investment decisions. Transport planners have been more concerned with provision of public infrastructure (such as roads) and with the co-ordination in its supply and use. There has been something of a change in emphasis in both fields as environmental considerations, including issues of greenhouse gas emissions, have played an increasing role in decision-making processes.

The demand for transport is derived from the demand for some final activity and, hence, the quality and form of transport supply can be influential on where people decide to live and where firms locate. Transport, consequently, is often seen as a key tool in development strategies even though its exact link with location decisions is still comparatively poorly understood by economists. Transport economics and planning, therefore, try to treat transport in the broader context of industrial and social activities. In consequence, there are strong ties between these subjects and work in fields such as regional science, land-use planning and spatial economics.

The continued expansion of urbanization, especially in Third-World countries, poses particular problems for the transport system. The central location of many employment opportunities, the inflexible nature of much existing transport infrastructure, and the pollution and noise associated with concentrated traffic flows generate problems of pure economic efficiency and of extensive external costs. Policies such as pollution pricing to limit the environmental intrusion associated with urban roads have been developed by economists, while costs-benefit and similar procedures are now widely used to appraise investments in new urban transport infrastructure. At the same time, transport planning has been developed alongside land use and environmental planning to take a more integrated approach, so as to meet the wider social objectives associated with the provision of urban transport without incurring a significant loss in economic efficiency. The transport planning process has evolved since the mid-1940s from an exercise in drawing up physical plans for the utopian transport system into modern structure planning, where the emphasis is on the interaction of transport with the urban economy in general and with the operation of all transport modes.

Economics has contributed to the modern transport planning process in a number of ways. First, it provides practical tools for placing monetary values on non-traded attributes such as noise, pollution and safety. In particular, the development of stated-preference approaches to valuation (involving confronting individuals with hypothetical trade-offs to elicit the values placed on external effects), to supplement the more established revealed preference techniques (involving observing actual trade-offs), has enabled a wider range of costs and benefits to be evaluated. Second, economic models provide the foundation for many of the traffic forecasting models employed in urban planning. In particular, discrete choice models, based upon individual behaviour and the assumption that forms of transport are desired not as entities in themselves but because of their attributes (such as speed, reliability, economy and safety), are now widely used. Third, pricing instruments are now generally seen as one of the most effective ways of ensuring that the urban transport system is used to its greatest effect, and these are now being added to the portfolio of physical traffic management controls. Examples here include road (or congestion) pricing and optimal subsidy policy.

A major interest of transport economists has been the question of deregulation (the removal of long-standing price and market entry controls) and privatization. Following advocacy of such reforms in the USA, and the passing of the Airline Deregulation Act 1978, market-liberalizing policies have become widespread in the transport field. The Single European Act 1986 has, for example, brought wide measures of liberalization to European transport markets. The motivation for change has partly been stimulated by the appreciation by political economists that regulatory systems can be captured by those whom they are intended to regulate and that regulators themselves may not be motivated to serve the public interest. While conventional economic theories of competitive markets have played a part in moving towards greater liberalization in these situations, the development of contestability theory (Baumol et al. 1982), and the appreciation of the power of potential as well as actual competition, has provided a rationale for some of the more recent policy initiatives.

The justification for public ownership of parts of the transport system has long been debated. It does permit easier planning and co-ordination, but equally can lead to slack management (so-called X-inefficiency) and the excessive intrusion of political considerations in policy making. Privatization of transport infrastructure has gradually occurred in many countries as concerns over efficiency has outweighed other factors. Transport economists have mixed views on the effectiveness of this, since the privatization movement has occurred at a time of significant regulatory change, and to date little analytical evidence is available separating the impacts of the two parallel trends.

K. J. Button
University of Loughborough

Reference

Baumol, W. J., Panzar, J. C. and Willig, R. D. (1982) *Contestable Markets: An Uprising in the Theory of Industry Structure*, New York.

Further reading

Banister, D. (1994) *Transport Planning*, London.

Banister, D. and Button, K. J. (eds) (1991) *Transport in a Free Market Economy*, London

Button, K. J. (1993) *Transport Economics*, London

Mohring, H. (ed.) (1994) *The Economics of Transport*, 2 vols, Aldershot.

Small, K. A. (1992) *Urban Transport Economics*, Chur.

See also: economic geography.

tribe

The term tribe was initially used by Victorian scholars as part of their attempt to construct a science of so-called 'primitive' societies. Pioneer anthropologists laboured to identify core features of the wide array of indigenous societies in areas such as Africa, the Americas and Melanesia. The term tribe (or sometimes 'clan') was applied to major social groups, but it was soon apparent that there was considerable diversity, and some effort was devoted to deciding which groups should properly be called tribes, and what their defining characteristics were. The term passed into common usage and persisted in anthropology for many years (as late as the 1960s in some cases, e.g. Lewis 1968), but it fell increasingly into disuse when it became apparent that the societies described as tribes had little in common. Moreover, intellectuals in de-colonizing states argued that western scholars, especially anthropologists, had colluded in the colonial invention of tribe, in order to divide people and hinder nation-building.

In the 1960s and 1970s many anthropologists embarked on a reflexive exercise to discover why the notion of tribe had exerted such a hold on the discipline and, indeed, western public imagination. Part of the answer, they decided, lay in nineteenth-century fascination with ideas of social evolution. The armchair ethnographers had not been careful empiricists; on the contrary, they had constructed an image of primitive society through *a priori* inversion of certain traits of their own society, and had then selected evidence to prove their vision.

Early ethnographers had noted that recruitment to significant groups in industrial society turned on criteria of achievement, contract and choice, and they speculated that 'primitive' groups were recruited by ascription, on the basis of status. Evidence that kinship played some part in constituting these social groups led them to conclude that tribes were ascriptive groups based solely on kinship. This was patently untrue, but it allowed people in the west to believe that primitive and civilized worlds were fundamentally different, and that the latter had evolved superior forms of social existence.

From the reflexive vantage of the 1970s, 'tribe' was part of an intellectual process that had imposed 'other-ness' (difference *and* inferiority) on people in certain parts of the world.

Imposing otherness had also been a practical process. Imbued with nineteenth-century notions of tribe, administrators had forced tribes on people throughout the colonial world. It was convenient to believe that the groups they constructed were actually natural groups that had existed since time immemorial. Early-twentieth-century anthropology had not challenged this fiction seriously, because its supposedly neutral research was integral to the colonial enterprise, and to the way that the west used its image of 'the Rest' to justify inequality and exploitation.

In the 1960s and 1970s scholars proclaimed that tribes had never existed, except in the minds of observers. This went too far, and was insulting to the people whose plight it sought to explain. It implied that they had passively allowed tribe, and related para-phernalia of otherness, to be imposed.

In the 1980s, scholars from various disciplines sought a more nuanced analysis of the practical ways in which the idea of tribe was imposed by diverse agents of colonialism. This allowed exploration of how colonized people responded – by adapting new ideas and practices to old ways, transforming them while adopting them, and subverting them to their own ends. In the Comaroffs' (1991) phrase, attention has been given to both the 'colonization of consciousness' and the 'consciousness of colonization'.

Since the mid-1980s, research has revealed who led responses of adaption, adoption and subversion, and why others followed. In doing so, it has also uncovered the ambiguity of tribe. Tribe involved ideas that were new to much of the world – primordiality, ascription, and absolute boundaries. But, once adopted, these ideas could not be contained at one level of society. The associated mode of thinking informed new perceptions of smaller and larger groups. This mode was often used to construct images of ethnic groups and nations, and to separate difference from inferiority. People were enabled to claim, and redeem, their otherness in various contexts. Tribe was one key to a Pandora's box of claims about identities.

The repercussions are still evident, and gain significance in a post-industrial world where popular dreams of progress and social mobility turn sour. There is now wide tendency to emphasize identities and groups for which people qualify by ascription rather than achievement. Belonging to such groups is a way to assert dignity and compete for resources in national and global contexts. Tribe is only one label that can be applied, and in Africa it is likely, for historical reasons, to be subordinate to cognates such as ethnic group, nation and race. But, in the 1990s, it would be foolhardy to proclaim the idiom of tribe dead.

John Sharp
University of Cape Town

References

Comaroff, J. and Comaroff, J. (1991) *Of Revelation and Revolution: Christianity, Colonialism and Consciousness in South Africa*, Chicago.
Lewis, I. M. (1968) 'Tribal society', in D. Sills (ed.) *International Encyclopedia of the Social Sciences*, New York.

Further reading

Fried, M. H. (1975) *The Notion of Tribe*, Menlo Park, CA.
Helm, J. (ed.) (1968) *Essays on the Problem of Tribe*, Seattle, WA.
Skalnik, P. (1988) 'Tribe as colonial category', in E. Boonzaier and J. Sharp (eds), *South African Keywords*, Cape Town.
Vail, L. (ed.) (1989) *The Creation of Tribalism in Southern Africa*, Berkeley.

See also: ethnic politics; ethnicity; nationalism; primitive society.

trust and co-operation

Most students of trust would agree that trust makes co-operation possible and thus improves the general welfare of society. Without trust, people will avoid potentially rewarding but risky interactions (Hardin 1992; Orbell and Dawes 1993). However, beyond this general sense of the importance of trust as a facilitator or lubricator of interpersonal and inter-organizational relations, there is little consensus concerning the nature and functions of trust.

Economists often consider that trust is ultimately grounded in a trustee's self-interests, and this view is also shared by some political scientists and sociologists (e.g. Coleman 1990; Hardin 1992). In this view, a truster trusts a trustee to perform an action X when and only when the truster knows that the trustee's self-interest is met by the consequence of X. One can prove her trustworthiness in this sense by having a lie detector surgically implanted in her brain that automatically detonates a small implanted bomb as soon as she lies: no one would ever doubt her words. Various 'hostages' such as warranty for used cars play the role of such a 'bomb', and provide a sign of trustworthiness. One who can benefit from proving oneself trustworthy has an incentive to post such a hostage. Trustworthiness is thus grounded in a trustee's self-interests.

It should be noted that this 'grounded-in-self-interest theory' of trust is a theory of trustworthiness, not of trust *per se*. Trust plays no independent role in this theory, or 'trust by itself constitutes nothing' (Hardin 1992: 512). A truster's trust is simply a more-or-less accurate assessment of trustee's trustworthiness.

In contrast, most psychologists believe trust begins where the cold calculation of self-interests ends. As Lewis and Weigert (1985) state, 'knowledge alone can never cause us to trust' and 'trust begins where simple prediction ends' (1985: 970, 976). Psychologists are generally interested in individual differences in trust as a personal trait. For example, Rotter (1967: 653) defines trust as 'a *generalized expectancy* that oral or written statements of other people can be relied upon'. Whereas trust is simply a reflection of a person's trustworthiness in the grounded-in-self-interest approach, according to the psychological approach trust involves more than objective assessments of a person's trustworthiness.

According to the 'groundedness' approach, the trust of a *truster* and co-operativeness of a *trustee* are two sides of the same coin. A person co-operates if and only if co-operation is consistent with that person's self-interests. Both a truster's trust and a trustee's trustworthy action are ultimately grounded in the trustee's self-interests. In contrast, psychologists focus more on the relationship between trust and co-operation in the behaviour of a single person. Many empirical studies have repeatedly demonstrated a positive correlation between trust (i.e. the expectation of a partner's co-operative action) and co-operative behaviour (see Dawes 1980 for a review of this literature). The causal direction between the two has not yet been settled. Pruitt and Kimmel (1977) believe that trust is a critical condition for co-operation: actual co-operation takes place when one who has developed co-operative motivation can trust others and expect them not to act exploitatively. Orbell and Dawes (1993), however, argue that these expectations are a 'projection' of one's own trustworthiness.

Since the early 1990s, there has been a third approach which grounds trust in *truster's*, rather than trustee's, self-interest (e.g. Orbell and Dawes 1993; Yamagishi and Yamagishi 1994). Trust in this approach can be defined as a cognitive bias in the assessment of trustee's intent based on imperfect information. This approach claims that such cognitive bias or heuristic has a 'survival value' in particular social environments.

Toshio Yamagishi
Hokkaido University

References

Coleman, J. S. (1990) *Foundations of Social Theory*, Cambridge, MA.

Dawes, R. M. (1980), 'Social dilemmas', *Annual Review of Psychology* 31.

Hardin, R. (1992) 'The street-level epistemology of trust', *Politics and Society* 21.

Lewis, J. D. and Weigert, A. (1985) 'Trust as a social reality', *Social Forces* 63.

Orbell, J. M. and Dawes, R. M. (1993) 'Social welfare, co-operators' advantage, and the option of not playing the game', *American Sociological Review* 58.

Rotter, J. B. (1967) 'A new scale for the measurement of inter-personal trust', *Journal of Personality* 35.

Yamagishi, T. and Yamagishi, M. (1994) 'Trust and commitment in the United States and Japan', *Motivation and Emotion*.

Further reading

Barber, B. (1983) *The Logic and Limit of Trust*, New Brunswick, NJ.

Gambetta, D. (ed.) (1988) *Trust*, Oxford.

See also: altruism; transaction costs.

U

unconscious

Perhaps the single most important idea in Freud's theory is that human beings are influenced by ideas, feelings, tendencies and ways of thinking of which they are not conscious. Freud's original topography of the mind had three divisions: the conscious, the preconscious, and the unconscious. His theory can be pictured as follows: the mind is like a darkened theatre, with a single spotlight to illuminate the actors on the stage. Consciousness is equivalent to the actor in the spotlight at any moment. All of the other actors who can be illuminated as the spotlight moves across the stage are equivalent to the preconscious. To complete Freud's picture we must imagine that there are many actors who are off-stage, in the unconscious. Unless they make the transition to the stage, the light of consciousness cannot illuminate them. Seen or unseen, on-stage or off, all the actors take part in the play of psychic life. The barrier between off-stage and on-stage is removed or weakened in dreams, and by free association, which is the basic technique of psychoanalysis.

Freud understood the unconscious as dynamic. Unconscious impulses were thought to be constantly active, influencing the preconscious and conscious – sometimes in discernible ways. Freud's explanation for slips of the tongue (now commonly called Freudian errors) is the substitution of an unconscious thought for what was consciously intended. By considering these unconscious influences, Freud found meaning in what others saw as trivial mistakes – for example, when a man calls his wife by his mother's name. Freud's theory of humour is similarly based on the dynamic interaction between conscious and unconscious. The joke allows the pleasurable release of some repressed idea or feeling; aggressive sexual jokes are thus a classic example.

Freud's theory of the unconscious became more complex in the course of his writings. At first he assumed that everything which was unconscious had

once been conscious and had been repressed. The paradigmatic example was the subject who under hypnosis could be given some post-hypnotic suggestion, such as to open an umbrella indoors, but told to *forget* that he had been given that instruction. When the trance was ended, the subject would comply with the suggestions and open the umbrella indoors, but be unable to explain why he had done such a silly thing. Thus his behaviour was influenced by an idea about which he had no conscious awareness. Freud believed that his patients, like hypnotic subjects, were capable of splitting off from consciousness certain ideas and feelings by a defensive process he called repression. These repressed unconscious ideas could influence the patient's behaviour, producing neurotic symptoms without his awareness.

Freud's clinical work demonstrated that the most significant repressed ideas led back to childhood experiences. The content of the unconscious seemed to be ideas and tendencies, mainly sexual and aggressive – which he thought of as instinctual and biological – which were repressed under the moral influence of the environment. But the repressed remained active in the unconscious and continued in dynamic interaction with the conscious. Thus Freud's conception of the unconscious emphasized the continuing and irrational influence of the past on the present.

The idea of the splitting of consciousness was not original to Freud, nor was that of an instinctive unconscious. These ideas in some form go back at least as far as Plato. The German philosophers of the nineteenth century, Schopenhauer and Nietzsche, had a view of human nature which, in many ways, anticipated Freud. Freud's theory of the unconscious none the less met with intense philosophical criticism, even ridicule. The idea that what was mental was not identical with consciousness and that the mental might be a mystery to consciousness was problematic for certain philosophical notions. Descartes had said, 'I think therefore I exist.' He used this introspective claim as the basis of a theory of knowledge. Freud's concept of the unconscious challenged the certitude of all such introspective claims about the certainty of self-knowledge. The idea of unconscious influences also called into question the notion of free will. Perhaps because Freud emphasized the sexual aspects of the unconscious, his views were easy for philosophers to ridicule. The philosopher Sartre, who was in many ways more sympathetic than most contemporary philosophers to Freud's emphasis on the importance of sex, still found it necessary to reject Freud's fundamental concept of the unconscious. He interpreted repression as self-deception; asserting that it is impossible to lie to oneself, he described repression as bad faith.

Freud's concept of the unconscious derived from his study of dreaming. He viewed the unconscious (associated with the infantile, the primitive, and the instinctual) as striving towards immediate discharge of tension. Dreaming and unconscious thinking are described as primary process thought, that is, they are unreflective, concrete, symbolic, egocentric, associative, timeless, visual, physiognomic and animistic, with memory organized about the imperative drive, in which wishes are equivalent to deeds and there is a radical departure from norms of logic – for example, contradictory ideas exist side by side. Primary process thought is contrasted with the modulated and adaptive discharge of tension in secondary process. By contrast, conscious thinking is reflective or directed, abstract, specific and particular, situation oriented, logical, chronological, auditory, verbal and explanatory. Memory is organized around the conscious focus of attention; thought and actions are clearly distinguished; thinking is rational and logically oriented. Freud's view was that although the child advances from primary process to secondary process thinking, primary process does not disappear, but remains active in the unconscious. It can be revealed in dreams, in psychotic thinking, and in other regressed mental states. Preconscious thinking was characterized as intermediate between these two types. The distinction between primary and secondary process is a key development in Lacan's linguistic reinterpretation of Freud.

Carl Jung, probably the greatest figure in psychoanalysis next to Freud, was an early advocate of what he called the collective unconscious. He assumed that in addition to repressed content, there was an inherited component to the unconscious shared by the human race. He based this conception on the evidence that certain symbols and complexes endlessly recur in the history of civilization. The Oedipus myth of the Greeks is the Oedipal dream of modern times. Freud and Jung took these ideas quite literally, believing that the individual was born not only with instinctual tendencies, but also with inherited complexes and symbols – for example, the serpent as a phallic symbol. Despite his eventual break with Jung, Freud maintained his own version of a collective unconscious, which also included the idea that certain moral concepts such as taboos had been inherited.

Freud subsequently reconceptualized his ideas about the unconscious in terms of the ego, the superego and the id. The id and the unconscious are now often used interchangeably in the psychiatric and psychoanalytic literature. While the theory of the unconscious remains controversial even now, the intuition that consciousness does not fully grasp the deeper mystery of our mental life continues to play an important role in twentieth-century thought.

Alan A. Stone
Harvard University

Further reading

Ellenberger, H. F. (1970) *The Discovery of the Unconscious: The History and Evolution of Dynamic Psychiatry*, New York.
Freud, S. (1953 [1900]) *The Interpretation of Dreams, Standard Edition of the Complete Psychological Works of Sigmund Freud*, ed. J. Strachey, vol. 4, London.

See also: consciousness; defences; free association; hypnosis; psychoanalysis; repression.

underdevelopment

The original meaning of underdevelopment was a neutral one, simply defining the condition of poorer countries which then were called underdeveloped countries. However, this term was felt to be derogatory and has since disappeared from the international vocabulary, being replaced by the more euphemistic 'developing countries'. As a result the term underdeveloped has assumed a specific and rather different meaning. It is now closely associated with the so-called dependency school, and it indicates a belief that in the world economy there are centrifugal forces at work, strengthening the position of the already rich core while keeping the periphery poor and in a state of permanent underdevelopment. The chief author using and building on this term was André Gunder Frank (1967). Frank was also the first to speak of 'development of underdevelopment', meaning the development of a rich country/poor country or core/periphery relationship which results in the impoverishment of the poor or periphery partner.

There are a number of variants within the underdevelopment school. These range from the radical wing which identifies underdevelopment with neo-colonial relationships and is an outgrowth of Marxist thinking, to non-political or non-ideological explanations such as the principle of cumulative causation developed by Gunnar Myrdal (1956). The principle of cumulative causation states that in the case of poor countries or poor groups a vicious circle is at work keeping them poor (for example, low income causing low savings and low investment, in turn causing low income in the next round; or low income leading to poor health leading to low productivity and low income). By contrast, in rich countries, or among rich groups, a reverse beneficial circle enables them to go from strength to strength and to improve their condition progressively. The strict Marxian view is perhaps best represented by Rodney (1972) in *How Europe Underdeveloped Africa*: 'An indispensable component of modern underdevelopment is that it expresses a particular relationship of exploitation: namely the exploitation of one country by another.' This view logically also leads to the use of the concept in describing domestic relations within developing countries (as in relations between an urban elite and the rural poor), but in practice the term is now associated with an international context of relations between countries. In between these two extremes are various other schools of thought explaining that the system of international trade relations has a tendency to benefit rich countries more than poor countries. The best known of these schools is the Prebisch-Singer theory according to which the terms of trade of primary products tend to deteriorate in relation to the prices of manufactured goods (Prebisch 1964; Singer 1950).

The radical view that any international contact between rich and poor countries will be to the disadvantage of the latter, obviously leads to the policy conclusion that poorer countries should either try to be self-sufficient or inward-looking in their development; while in the case of smaller countries, where this is not feasible, regional groupings of developing countries are advocated. One does not have to be an advocate of the underdevelopment school, however, to support such policies; it is clear that trade, investment and other economic relations among the developing countries are conspicuously and abnormally sparse compared with relations between rich and poor countries. It can be argued that it is also in the interest of the richer industrialized countries to support such closer south–south co-operation.

The milder variation is that international contacts are advantageous for both partners, in accordance with liberal doctrine and the law of comparative advantage, but that the benefits are unequally distributed.

The belief of the more radical underdevelopment school that international relations are positively harmful to the poorer partners can in turn lead to two different policy conclusions. One is to reduce north–south contacts and instead develop south–south relations; the other is to reform the international

system so that its benefits are more equally distributed. The latter approach is implied in the pressure of the developing countries for a New International Economic Order which has dominated the international discussions since the mid-1970s and also in such reform proposals as the two Brandt Reports (Brandt 1980; 1983).

H. W. Singer
University of Sussex

References

Brandt (1980) *North–South: A Programme for Survival* (Report of the Independent Commission on International Development Issues under the Chairmanship of Willy Brandt), London.

—— (1983) *Common Crisis, North–South: Co-operation for World Recovery*, Brandt Commission, London.

Frank, A. G. (1967) *Capitalism and Underdevelopment in Latin America*, New York.

Myrdal, G. (1956) *Development and Underdevelopment*, Cairo.

Prebisch, R. (1964) *Towards a New Trade Policy for Development*, New York.

Rodney, W. (1972) *How Europe Underdeveloped Africa*, Dar-es-Salaam.

Singer, H. W. (1950) 'The distribution of gains between investing and borrowing countries', *American Economic Review*.

Further reading

Frank, A. G. (1991) *The Underdevelopment of Development*, Stockholm.

Harrison, D. (1988) *The Sociology of Modernization and Development*, London.

Stewart, F. (1984) 'New theories of international trade: some implication for the South', in H. Kierzowski (ed.) *Monopolistic Competition and International Trade*, London.

See also: aid; centre and periphery; economic development; modernization; technical assistance; Third World; world-system theory.

unemployment *see* employment and unemployment

urban geography

Urban geography is concerned with the spatial attributes of towns and cities and with the ways in which they affect – and are affected by – physical, demographic, economic, social, cultural and political processes. Like other aspects of human geography, urban geography is concerned with local variability within a general context (Johnston 1984). This means that it is concerned with an understanding of both the distinctiveness of individual towns and cities and the regularities that exist within and between them in terms of the spatial relationships between people and their environment.

For urban geographers, some of the most important questions therefore include: what attributes make cities and neighbourhoods distinctive? How did these distinctive identities evolve? Are there significant regularities in the spatial arrangement of towns and cities across particular regions or nations? Are there significant regularities in the spatial organization of land use within cities, or in the patterning of neighbourhood populations by social status, household type or race? How do people choose where to live within cities, and what are the constraints on their choices? How does a person's area of residence affect his or her behaviour? What groups, if any, can manipulate the spatial organization of towns and cities? Who profits from such manipulation?

In pursuing these questions, urban geographers have adopted a variety of different approaches to knowledge and understanding. Several have been particularly influential. The first is a straightforward descriptive approach that stems from geographers' traditional concern with areal differentiation and the distinctiveness of place. Individual towns and cities are thus treated as mosaics of distinctive neighbourhoods and morphological units, or as parts of city-systems, to be classified and regionalized according to their economic functions or their quality of life relative to other cities. The second is an analytical quantitative approach, based on a positivist philosophy in which the geographer's role is understood to pivot on modelling the spatial organization of society. Third is the so-called behavioural approach, where the emphasis is on the study of people's activities and decision-making processes (where to·live, for example) and on the significance of the meanings that they attach to their urban surroundings. Fourth is the structuralist approach, which stresses the constraints imposed on individual behaviour by the organization of society as a whole and by the activities of powerful groups and institutions within it. Finally, there are post-structuralist approaches, which attempt to reconcile the interaction of meta-structures (economic, political, etc.) with human agency, and to explain the development of localized systems of shared meanings within larger sociocultural frameworks.

Whatever the approach, cities are never regarded by urban geographers simply as stages on which social, economic and political processes are acted out. Rather, urban settings are studied in terms of their contribution to patterns of development and to the nature of the relationships between different social groups and economic activities within the city. While not necessarily the dominant factor in shaping patterns of development and interaction, spatial organization is undeniably important as a determinant of business and social networks, friendships, marriages, and so on. Similarly, territoriality is frequently the basis for the development of distinctive social milieux which, as well as being of interest in themselves, are important because of their capacity to mould the attitudes and shape the behaviour of their inhabitants. In short, urban spaces are created by people, and they draw their character from the uses to which they are put and from the people that inhabit them. As people live and work in urban spaces, they gradually impose themselves on their environment, modifying and adjusting it, as best they can, to suit their needs and express their values. Yet at the same time people themselves gradually accommodate both to their physical environment and to the people around them. There is thus a continuous two-way process, a 'sociospatial dialectic' (Soja 1980) in which people create and modify urban spaces while at the same time being conditioned in various ways by the spaces in which they live and work.

Distance also emerges as a significant determinant of the quality of life in different parts of the city because of variations in physical accessibility to opportunities and amenities such as jobs, shops, schools, clinics, parks and sports centres. Because the benefits conferred by proximity to these amenities contribute so much to people's welfare, locational issues also often form the focus of inter-class conflict within the city, thus giving the spatial perspective a key role in the analysis of urban affairs. The partitioning of space through the establishment of *de jure* territorial boundaries also represents an important spatial attribute which has direct repercussions on several spheres of urban life. The location of local authority boundaries helps to determine their fiscal standing, for example; while the boundaries of school catchment areas have important implications for community status and welfare; and the configuration of electoral districts is crucial to the outcome of formal political contests in the city.

Paul L. Knox
Virginia Polytechnic Institute and
State University

References

Johnston, R. J. (1984) 'The world is our oyster', *Transactions; Institute of British Geographers* 9.
Soja, E. (1980) 'The socio-spatial dialectic', *Annals; Association of American Geographers* 70.

Further reading

Berry, B. J. L. (1988) *The Geography of Market Centers and Retail Distribution*, Englewood Cliffs, NJ.

Cadwallader, M. T. (1985) *Analytical Urban Geography*, Englewood Cliffs, NJ.

Hart, J. F. (ed.) (1991) *Our Changing Cities*, Baltimore, MD.

Harvey, D. W. (1989) *The Urban Experience*, Oxford.

Johnston, R. J. (1980) *City and Society*, Harmondsworth.

Knox, P. L. (1993) *Urbanization: An Introduction to Urban Geography*, Englewood Cliffs, NJ.

Vance, J. E., Jr (1988) *The Continuing City*, Baltimore, MD.

See also: city; urban planning; urbanization.

urban planning

Urban planning is as old as civilization. The cities of antiquity reflected the glorification of rulers and their military and religious needs. The first working-class town was designed to provide labour for the building of an Egyptian royal pyramid. More democratic influences entered with the Greek *agora* and Roman *forum*. Hydraulic engineering was always a major influence upon urban planning from the ancient empires of Egypt and Mesopotamia, to the development of cities in The Netherlands. The planning of medieval cities was governed by their walls and fortifications. The founding of colonies and military centres produced many examples of planned towns.

From the later Middle Ages onwards, the patronage of rulers, corporations of merchants and individual landowners enabled architect-planners to create or reshape many famous cities. Examples are the work of Bernini and others in Rome, of the two Woods in Bath, of Craig in Edinburgh, and the baroque-style cities of southern Germany and Austria.

The industrial revolution and the consequent growth of vast, sprawling cities changed the character of urban planning quite radically. Planning developed along three different but related lines.

First, the detailed regulation of land uses was a feature of many old cities, but it became minimal during the earlier *laissez-faire* period of industrialization. Health and sanitary problems compelled the adoption of building codes and regulations about street widths and housing layouts. Subsequently, statutory planning schemes were introduced which separated incompatible land uses, specified housing densities, and reserved land for open space and other public purposes.

This hygienic type of planning has been much criticized for spoiling the 'muddled variety' of urban life. The protective effect of zoning laws has been strongest in upper-class residential suburbs. Elsewhere, planning controls have been kept more flexible by the pressures of the private land market. This was particularly true of the USA, where the regular gridiron layout of cities assisted land speculation, and where the first zoning code for New York City permitted a maximum population of 365 million. By contrast, development

has been controlled quite closely in The Netherlands, and some other European states, but the fragmentation of land ownership and the existence of speculative values are widespread obstacles to planning and also to participation.

Political attempts have been made to tax and control development values so as to facilitate planning; for example, there were three such attempts in the UK between 1945 and 1980. These had some success in limiting planning compensation, thus helping the protection of rural areas and green belts, but little success in collecting betterment or assisting urban renewal. Some European countries, particularly after the Second World War, have pooled and reallocated land holdings so as to aid redevelopment. However, the implementation of regulatory plans depends upon either private or public initiatives. To be effective, government planning requires integrated policies and complex co-ordination, and in western societies urban change depends increasingly upon business and financial interests.

Second, the historical architectural tradition continued in new ways. Modern cities are usually no longer dominated by great public works, save in autocratic states or special cases like Brasilia. Highway planning has become more influential or even dominant over the design of cities. Haussmann's boulevards restructured Paris, largely for purposes of crowd control. The 'city beautiful' movement, exemplified in Burnham's Chicago plan, included boulevards, parks and museums, but ignored the decaying ghettoes behind the city frontage. Regional parkways combined roads and parks, sometimes attractively. Robert Moses in New York built a career around linking planning with the co-ordination of public works. Monumental designs for cities of the future, such as those of Le Corbusier, belong with the historic architectural tradition, but are likely to be realized only in specialized projects.

Third, there have emerged the planned public developments such as the British new towns, Canberra in Australia, and many examples of municipal enterprise. These towns represent massive exercises in public estate development, which carry on older traditions of private or corporate land management. Public land ownership is the key, when combined with the vesting of wide responsibilities for city development in the same agency. Stockholm's post-war development, when the city owned most vacant land, sponsored or provided most of the housing, and owned and developed the transportation system, is a good example of comprehensive planning for urban growth. Many other European and British cities possessed many similar powers, although rarely so completely. Changes in the political climate, and the replacement of strong city governments by two-tier metropolitan systems, had by 1980 largely brought to an end the era of the city planning and development machines (Self 1982). Comprehensive planning by *ad hoc* bodies like new town corporations has also proved politically vulnerable.

Planned public developments have often provided improved social and environmental standards and better access to facilities for aged people, teenagers, and working wives; but they have also imposed technocratic concepts upon a passive clientele. The failings have been most marked in redevelopment schemes, which have produced much unpopular high-rise housing, a neglect of social facilities, and in the USA extensive displacement of the poor in the interests of subsidized commercial development.

The profession of town planning was dominated historically by architects but has increasingly utilized the skills of engineers, valuers, economists, sociologists and others. Regional planning, a particular interest of geographers, has grown in importance. Planning has been closely linked with other major functions, such as housing at one time and, more recently, transportation. There is much disagreement about the best education for a town planner, and about the separability of his role from the general task of urban management.

The modern development of planning has been much influenced by imaginative writers such as Geddes, Mumford (1961), and practical idealists such as Ebenezer Howard and Sir Frederic Osborn, who initiated two garden cities. Concepts of balanced growth, limitation of urban size, new communities, and rural protection were important for the major advance in town planning powers after 1940. Social ideals, although subdued by market pressures, remain important for planning and also for professional planners.

Planning systems have grown in complexity, often involving national guidelines, regional outline plans, subregional or county plans, and detailed local plans. These various plans sometimes conflict and are often outflanked by both public and private developers. Planning has built up complex techniques of forecasting and modelling, and become increasingly concerned with steering and monitoring exogenous economic and social trends.

None the less, urban planning remains highly political and reflective of the dominant values of a society. In communist systems, strong public powers for planning existed, but these were often applied in a monolithic way which ignored private preferences. In capitalist democracies, the planner has become either a specialist in land-use regulation, or a rather weak generalist articulating a community interest. Much has been written about spatial inequalities in cities, and the dominance of capitalist interests (Harvey 1973).

Effective urban planning depends upon a mixture of public regulation and public initiative. It is increasingly important for coping with such problems as traffic congestion and pollution, wasteful urban sprawl, overbuilt central areas, degraded neighbourhoods; for improving access to employment and social facilities by the development of new centres; and for establishing satisfactory standards of housing and environmental amenity. Increasingly traditional town planning needs to be integrated with environmental goals. While planning has some achievements to its credit – such as the protection of historic centres, protection of the countryside and some well-planned new towns – it falls a long way short of the above goals. Progress depends not only upon the recruitment of broadly educated planners with a dedication to basic goals, but (still more) upon stronger political support and a political willingness to overcome the often destructive and divisive impacts of modern market economics.

Peter Self
Australian National University

References

Harvey, D. (1973) *Social Justice and the City*, London.
Mumford, L. (1961) *The City in History*, London.
Self, P. (1982) *Planning the Urban Region*, London.

See also: city; metropolitan and urban government; urban geography; urbanization.

urbanization

The term urbanization appears in the literature of nearly every social science; within each it is used loosely when the theories of the particular field are applied to the study of urban units, their populations or individuals living in urban places. The term does, however, have two interrelated, more specific, meanings. First, demographers, who use it to refer to the redistribution of population between rural and urban areas, have given it its most specific meaning at a conceptual level, but the demographic study of urbanization has failed to produce an internationally accepted set of criteria defining urban. Second, in a number of other social sciences, most notably economics, geography and sociology, urbanization refers to the changing morphological structure of urban agglomerations and its development. Indeed, within the social sciences one of the major research issues centres around the separation of the causes and consequences of urbanization as a demographic phenomenon and the emergent morphology of large urban complexes in the western world.

Population redistribution

The demographic study of urbanization has concentrated on the movement of people between rural and urban areas on a world scale, and on the differential level, pace and pattern of this redistribution between the more and less developed countries. As late as 1950 only 28 per cent of the world's population is thought to have been living in urban sectors. At mid-decade over one half of the population in the more developed countries lived in urban areas, but only a little more than 15 per cent of the population of the less developed regions. By 1980 estimates suggest that the level of urbanization in the more developed regions reached 70 per cent, and in the lesser developed regions over 30 per cent. These redistributions are a consequence of the differential rates of increase in the rural and urban populations of the more and less developed countries. Between 1950 and 1980, for example, the urban population increased by some 85 per cent in the more developed regions while the rural population actually decreased by over 10 per cent. Among the less developed regions the urban population increased by more than 250 per cent and the rural population increased by more than 60 per cent. While the differential pace of urbanization can be directly linked to the differential rates of urban and rural growth, it is considerably more difficult to identify the differentials in the components of urban and rural population change. This is largely due to the fact that urban and rural population growth, in addition to being affected by natural increase and net migration, is also affected by changing boundaries (or area reclassification) of what are defined as urban and rural areas.

The dominant historical trend of population redistribution has been towards an increasing concentration of population in urban areas. However, within urban areas themselves, there has been movement away from urban centres towards the suburban periphery. Definitions of urban, suburban and rural vary markedly from country to country; still, strong indications are that in many western countries this decentralization of population is occurring, and that increasingly it involves movement beyond large agglomeration (metropolitan) boundaries into the non-metropolitan sector.

Urbanization and urban morphology

The link between urbanization as a strictly demographic phenomenon and urbanization as a morphological phenomenon has its roots in the early works of European economists such as Weber, Gras (1922) and Christaller (1966 [1933]), and in the US intellectual tradition known as human ecology. Traditional approaches linking population redistribution to urban structure tried to account for the concentration of population in large urban agglomerations and the development of urban systems. Large agglomerations developed around a single urban centre which attracted the excess rural population and absorbed it into an economy based on production and manufacturing and the associated services and product distribution industries.

While these urban centres were developing, a second area or outer ring grew up around them. This ring was increasingly dominated by the centre, as the ecological distance between previously independent communities and the centre was reduced through technological innovations in transport and communication. As the total area expands, formerly independent and quasi-independent communities lose many of their specialized functions and services to the centre where the full advantages of external economies offered by location can be had. Once economic activity and jobs are centralized in the agglomeration centre, the outer area becomes primarily a residential suburb, increasingly dependent on and oriented to the centre.

With three sources of change (other than natural change) contributing to their population growth (migration from the centre, migration from rural areas and other agglomerations, the incorporation of new territory and its population), suburban areas begin to grow at a faster rate than either agglomeration centres or rural areas. The structural limits to growth and expansion are thus set by the economy's capacity to support population and the centre's ability to co-ordinate, control and integrate wider territory, while the territorial limits to growth are determined by transportation technology and the need to be able to move people routinely to the centre.

This traditional approach depicts suburban areas and their populations as almost totally dependent on urban centres. It also focuses attention on the concentration of services and economic activity in the centre and on the decentralization of population or places of residence. Research has shown that population is now decentralizing beyond traditional agglomeration boundaries, while services and economic activity are reconcentrating in traditional suburban territory. These observations, which contradict the traditional approach, have led some researchers to suggest that there are limits to the size of agglomerations under the control of a single centre: once the point is reached where the cost of moving people, goods and information is too high to support continued growth of the decentralizing structure, nucleation begins and there is a return to scale, and a number of smaller centres emerge. Within each of these centres, a surrounding population can satisfy all its routine and daily needs.

Alternatively, others have argued that the reconcentration of services and economic activity within the suburban ring and the further decentralization of population is merely an extension of the traditional expansion model. It represents a new stage in the agglomeration process culminating in an urban structure dominated by an inner ring which will perform the functions and assume the characteristics of city centres in the past. This, it is argued, will facilitate greater residential expansion and make old city centres dependent on this inner suburban ring, similar to the earlier dependence of suburbs on cities. Beyond this inner ring, traditional population decentralization will continue leading to greater expansion of metropolitan territory.

David F. Sly
Florida State University

References

Christaller, W. (1966 [1933]) *The Central Places of Southern Germany*, trans. C. W. Baskin, Englewood Cliffs, NJ. (Original edn, *Die Zentralen Orte in Suddentschland*, Jena.)
Gras, N. S. B. (1922) *An Introduction to Economic History*, New York.

Further reading

Berry, B. J. L. (1981) *Comparative Urbanization: Divergent Paths in the Twentieth Century*, New York.
Burnley, I. H. (ed.) (1974) *Urbanization in Australia: The Post-War Experience*, Cambridge, UK.
Goldstein, S. and Sly, D. F. (eds) (1977) *Patterns of Urbanization: Comparative Country Studies*, Liège.
Hawley, A. (1981) *Urban Society: An Ecological Approach*, New York.
Sly, D. F. (1982) 'The consequences of metropolitan decentralization for personal gasoline consumption', *Population Research and Policy Review 1*.
Sly, D. F. and Tayman, J. (1980) 'Metropolitan morphology and population mobility: the theory of ecological expansion reexamined', *American Journal of Sociology 86*.

See also: city; labour migration; urban geography; urban planning.

utilitarianism

Utilitarianism is the doctrine that decisions should promote good consequences. It is a normative theory, meant to guide conduct and to serve as the basis of sound evaluations. It does not assume that actual decisions or judgements always satisfy that standard.

Like other important philosophical ideas, utilitarianism has many variations. The founders of modern utilitarianism, Bentham (1789) and J. S. Mill (1861), assumed that good consequences are, at bottom, desirable conditions of individuals (perhaps including animals other than humans). Bentham's hedonistic utilitarianism called for the promotion of pleasure and the prevention of pain. Mill, who distinguished higher and lower pleasures, seems to have held that human good consists in the free development of individuals' distinctive, and distinctively human, capacities. Ideal utilitarians believe that what is most fundamentally of value can include such things as beauty, which need not be defined in terms of human good or conscious states.

Utilitarianism in its various forms can be understood to combine a theory of intrinsic value with some notion of how stringently and directly it should be served, for example, whether good consequences must be maximized or need only be promoted to a lesser degree, and whether each and every decision should be so regulated ('act' utilitarianism) or rather that acts should conform to useful patterns ('rule' utilitarianism).

Utilitarians often claim as a virtue of their theory that it bases evaluations on ascertainable facts, such as how much pleasure and pain would result from alternative courses of action. But the calculations require interpersonal comparisons of utility, of which many are sceptical. This has led some theorists to develop normative standards in terms of less demanding notions of efficiency, as in welfare economics.

Utilitarians have generally favoured social reforms (because, for example, income transfers from rich to poor are supposed to promote welfare overall), and they have championed political rights and personal liberty (because, for example, paternalistic interference is supposed to be counter-productive). Critics charge, however, that utilitarianism lacks principled commitment to all such values: it cares only how much good is produced, but not about equitable distribution, respect for personal desert, or the security of freedom and individual integrity.

Most generally, critics charge that utilitarianism distorts sound moral judgement: to promise to do something, for example, is deliberately to place oneself under an obligation, the demands of which (it is argued) are greater and more specifically directed than utilitarianism allows. They claim that utilitarianism fails to take obligations (or for that matter rights) seriously.

Utilitarianism nevertheless remains a widely accepted theory of central importance, though its status – like that of any normative principle – is uncertain. The idea that principles merely express more or less arbitrary attitudes seems largely based upon an exaggerated contrast between ethics and science, which suffers from overly simple conceptions of empirical knowledge and discovery. Developments in the theory of reference and justification, along with the decline of logical positivism, have revived interest in moral realism (or cognitivism) and in the possibility of rationally defending either utilitarianism or some competing doctrine.

David Lyons
Cornell University

References

Bentham, J. (1789) *An Introduction to the Principles of Morals and Legislation*, London.
Mill, J. S. (1861) *Utilitarianism*, London.

Further reading

Brandt, R. B. (1979) *A Theory of the Good and the Right*, Oxford.
Sen, A. and Williams, B. (eds) (1982) *Utilitarianism and Beyond*, Cambridge, UK.
Smart, J. J. C. and Williams, B. (eds) (1973) *Utilitarianism, For and Against*, Cambridge, UK.

See also: Bentham, Jeremy; Mill, John Stuart.

Utopianism

Utopianism is a form of social theory which attempts to promote certain desired values and practices by presenting them in an ideal state or society. Utopian writers do not normally think of such states as realizable, at least in anything like their perfectly portrayed form. But nor are they engaging in a merely fanciful or fantastic exercise, as the popular use of the term suggests. Often, as in Plato's *Republic*, the first true Utopia, the aim is to show something of the essential nature of a concept – justice or freedom – by painting it large, in the form of an ideal community based on such a concept. At other times, as with Sir Thomas More's *Utopia* (1516), the object is primarily critical or satirical, to scourge the vices of the writer's society by an artful contrast with the virtuous people of Utopia. Only rarely – Edward Bellamy's *Looking Backward* (1888) is a good example – do Utopian writers seek to transform society according to the blueprint painstakingly drawn in their Utopia. Essentially the function of Utopias is heuristic.

Until the seventeenth century, Utopias were generally located in geographically remote areas of the globe. The European voyages of discovery of the sixteenth and seventeenth centuries killed off this useful device by making the world too familiar. From then on Utopias were spatially displaced: to outer space – journeys to the moon begin in the seventeenth century – or beneath the sea, as in the frequent discovery of the sunken civilization of Atlantis, or deep below the earth's crust. But increasingly too the displacement was temporal rather than spatial, a move encouraged first by the seventeenth-century idea of progress and later by the vastly expanded notion of time offered by the new geology and biology of Lyell and Darwin. Instead of Utopia being the better place, it became the better time. H. G. Wells took his Time-Traveller billions of years into the future, and Olaf Stapledon in *Last and First Men* (1930) employed a timescale of 2,000 million years to show the ascent of humans to full Utopian stature.

The displacement of space by time also produced a new sociological realism in Utopias. Utopias were now placed in history and, however distant the Utopian consummation, it could at least be presented as something that humankind was tending towards, perhaps inevitably. The link with science and technology in the seventeenth century – as in Bacon's *New Atlantis* (1627) and Campanella's *City of the Sun* (1637) – strengthened this development. With the rise of nineteenth-century socialism, itself heavily Utopian, Utopianism became increasingly a debate about the possible realization of socialism. The Utopias of Bellamy and Wells (*A Modern Utopia*, 1905) were the most powerful pleas on behalf of orthodox socialism, but William Morris offered an attractive alternative version in *News from Nowhere* (1890). An alternative of a different kind came with the invention of the dystopia or anti-Utopia, an inversion and a savage critique of all Utopian hopes. Foreshadowed in Samuel Butler's anti-Darwinian *Erewhon* (1872), it reached its apogee in the 1930s and 1940s, especially with Aldous Huxley's *Brave New World* (1932) and George Orwell's *Nineteen Eighty-Four* (1949). Only B. F. Skinner's *Walden Two* (1948) kept the Utopian torch alight in these dark years, and there were many who saw in this Utopia of behavioural engineering a nightmare worse than the blackest dystopia. Utopianism, however, revived strongly in the 1960s, in such works as Herbert Marcuse's *An Essay on Liberation* (1969), and is to be found alive and flourishing in the futurological and ecological movements.

Perhaps Utopianism is inherent in the human condition, perhaps only in those cultures affected by the classical and Christian traditions; but one might well agree with Oscar Wilde that 'a map of the world that does not include Utopia is not worth even glancing at'.

Krishan Kumar
University of Kent

Further reading

Kumar, K. (1987) *Utopia and Anti-Utopia in Modern Times*, Oxford.
Manuel, F. E. and Manuel, F. P. (1979) *Utopian Thought in the Western World*, Cambridge, MA.

V

value and distribution

Early nineteenth-century theorists who shared Adam Smith's focus on macroeconomic problems also followed his example by using a cost of production framework of analysis to address questions of what determined the relative exchange values of goods on the one hand and the distribution of those values among factors of production on the other. Accordingly they defined the value of each commodity (and of national output as a whole) as the sum of the rewards accruing to the labourers, landlords and capitalists involved in producing it.

Since labour generally accounted for the bulk of these costs, classical economic analysis tended to use a simplified version of the cost of production approach that approximated to a labour theory of value. Ricardo, for example, justified leaving rent out of his account of value by adopting a theory of differential rents in agriculture, which enabled him to conclude that rent was price determined rather than price determining. He then dealt with capital by arguing that, in the long run, the relative exchange values of goods could be expected to vary in proportion not only to their direct labour costs but also to the cost of labour embodied in the fixed capital used up in producing them. That gave him a rough but reasonable measure of the relative exchange values of commodities in terms of the person-hours of labour used up in their production.

This convenient simplification provided the springboard for the Marxian theory of capitalist economic development based on exploitation of labour by owners of the means of production. Marx postulated that the labour embodied in commodities represented not merely a rough measure but the whole essence of value in a capitalist economic system. He then developed a theory of surplus value in which the share of profits in the value of output was explained by the historically specific characteristics of mature capitalism, wherein powerful entrepreneurs could divert the community's social surplus into their own pockets. In so doing he elevated a spectre which classical political economists had typically refused to acknowledge – that of an inevitable conflict between the interests of capital and labour.

A cost of production theory of value and distribution effectively underpinned both orthodox and unorthodox economic doctrine until the 1870s when some theorists began to analyse the theory of value in a market-oriented rather than a production-oriented framework. It was Marshall who first systematically explored the new perspectives opened up by marginal analysis and laid the foundations of neo-classical economics which rapidly assumed the mantle of orthodoxy in mainstream economic thought. The crucial distinguishing characteristic of the new economics was a shift away from the broad macroeconomic concerns of classical political economy in order to focus, with increasing mathematical rigour and social detachment, on a systematic analysis of market prices in long-term competitive equilibrium. It involved interpreting the behaviour of both consumers and producers in terms of their marginal utility and cost functions. Thus the individual parties to an exchange transaction were assumed to adjust the quantities offered or demanded to the point where their marginal preferences and costs coincided with given market prices and these in turn were assumed to reflect combined preferences and costs over the whole economy. The prices of factors of production (and hence their distributive shares) were explained in terms of a similar mechanism. Profit-maximizing entrepreneurs were seen as engaged in a continuous process of substitution between factors of production – weighing up costs and returns of alternative combinations of, say, machinery and labour or skilled and unskilled labour – so as to achieve the most profitable technique (defined as that which equated costs and return at the margin). In short, the neo-classical theorists derived their answer to the question of what determined the relative shares of factors of production as a purely logical byproduct of their assumptions about market prices in competitive equilibrium.

Twentieth-century economists have therefore inherited two different traditions of analysis of value and distribution. The neo-classical system of ideas matured elegantly in the middle decades of the century into the Arrow-Debreu model of general equilibrium yielding mathematically consistent, highly abstract results without normative or descriptive implications for applied economics. Debreu (1959), for example, subtitled his monograph on value *An Analysis of Economic Equilibrium*. Meanwhile economists whose research programmes are driven by contemporary macroeconomic policy problems have sought to be realistically selective in their choice of assumptions and in consequence have tended to be more eclectic and less rigorous in their analyses than the high theorists. Keynes, for example, who had been brought up on currently orthodox Marshallian economics had been persuaded by the 1930s that, in a world characterized by chronic unemployment and fluctuating money values, its postulates concerning the operations of the labour market were profoundly unrealistic and its theory of value and distribution was uncoordinated with its theory of money and prices. It was to rectify these flaws in the neo-classical economic theory that Keynes (1936) formulated his own *General Theory of Employment Interest and Money* and generated the so-called Keynesian revolution in economic doctrine.

Pure theories of value and distribution – new and old – continue to inspire serious (if often inconclusive) debates at academic conferences in the second half of the twentieth century and to suggest potentially fruitful doctoral research topics. For applied economists the present rapidly changing political, institutional and technological problem situations in which contemporary economic agents take their decisions makes it inappropriate to seek overarching, general purpose theories in the area of value and distribution. However, inspired perhaps by the example of Keynes, there is increasing evidence of imaginative cross-fertilization of ideas between schools of thought which were once inhibited from effective communication by the presumed ideological undertones of radically different perspectives.

Phyllis Deane
University of Cambridge

References

Debreu, G. (1959) *Theory of Value*, New York.
Keynes, J. M. (1936) *General Theory of Employment Interest and Money*, London.

Further reading

Baranzini, M. and Scazzieri, R. (eds) (1986) *Foundations of Economics*, London.
Black, R. C., Coats, A. W. and Goodwin, C. D. W. (eds) (1973) *The Marginal Revolution in Economics*, Durham, NC.
Dobb, M. (1973) *Theories of Value and Distribution since Adam Smith*, Cambridge, UK.

See also: general equilibrium theory; Marxian economics; prices, theory of; Ricardo, David.

Vienna School *see* Austrian School

violence

Violence entails inflicting emotional, psychological, sexual, physical and/or material damage. It involves the exercise of force or constraint perpetrated by individuals, on their own behalf or for a collective or state-sanctioned purpose. Research on violence includes its definition, its psychological impact, its origins, its collective expressions, its cultural meanings and its relevance to law.

Definitions of violence range widely. We usually associate violence and its use with individually motivated action, although a great deal of violence is committed by individuals on behalf of others. The violence of institutions, such as within prison, or that of state-sanctioned agencies, such as the use of deadly force by police, are examples of the use of violence by the state for the constraint of its citizens. Too few definitions characterize negligent or reckless driving, or negligent deaths at work as violence, yet these actions may involve intentional disregard for the safety of others. The violence arising from war or actions of civil insurgency have dramatic impacts on the psychological and physical well-being of countless people.

Developing and developed countries often cite the lower incidence of violence as a barometer of democracy and freedom. Yet countries, such as Bosnia, previously characterized as peaceful, sometimes erupt into brutality and violence. Nationalism, cultural intolerance and fundamentalism continue to fuel political conflicts and violence. Questions linger about collective violence: under what conditions does violence serve as an agent of control or an agent of resistance to particular sets of beliefs?

Criminal violence, and the fear of it, has a particular niche within discourses of and about civility, especially within countries largely considered peaceable. Violence in such places is considered to be the actions of errant or unsocialized individuals. At the same time, such jurisdictions are characterized as safe, although research suggests that there is a great deal of violence – defined by individual acts of threat and assault – which occur in so-called peaceable societies. Physical and sexual assault of girls and women, for example, are commonplace in many societies.

In 'developed' countries, people themselves largely manage violence on their own. In effect, most violence is decriminalized, either because recipients fail to report it to authorities, such as the police, in the first place, or because they refuse to co-operate with the justice system when they or others do report. The context within which violence occurs influences how individuals define and respond to violence. Crime surveys consistently show that incidents of violence are reported far less frequently than other forms of crime. Truer data about the incidence of violence can be found in crime surveys rather than police statistics, which suggests that violent crime constitutes approximately 6 per cent of all reported serious crime.

Gender-specific differences in the nature and rate of violence and victimization are especially important in understanding violence. Generally speaking, men are the overwhelming perpetrators and recipients of violence and are as likely to be assaulted and killed by acquaintances as they are by strangers. Women encounter physical and sexual violence most often in and around their own homes, and their assailants are typically intimates, former intimates and other acquaintances. However, both women and men cite stranger violence as that which they fear the most. Research consistently shows that the fear of violence restricts women's lives much more than men's, and that women report higher levels of fear of violence than do men, despite the much higher official statistics indicating men's experiences of violence.

Whether physical or psychological, the harm felt by the recipient of violence varies, as does the long-term impact on his or her everyday life. A recent experience of violence, or its threat, may have significant effects, altering an individual's routines and personal lifestyle or it may have little noticeable influence on daily life. Studies of post-traumatic stress disorder, for instance, often explore the impact of violence upon individuals' lives.

Typically, in law and in popular culture, the focus for explaining violence is on the behaviour of specific, criminally defined offenders. Debates continue about how to account for the violence of individuals. Biological explanations suggest that violence is rooted in hormonal imbalances, low intelligence, or brain injury. Psychology provides another route to interpretations of acts of violence. Low self-esteem, feelings of inadequacy, and depression are found among the explanations given for those who commit violence. Evolutionary psychology, too, provides a framework for explaining violence, such as the analysis of homicide by Daly and Wilson (1988). These researchers suggest that competition, status and control over reproductivity provide men with strong legacies within which contemporary, individually committed violence should be placed.

Sociological explanations, such as those which examine the links with economic deprivation, gang involvement, dominant social groups and use of violence in the informal economy, provide descriptions of the context within which violence occurs, but fail to predict which individuals within those environments will commit violence. Analysis of structural vulnerability, such as, for example, the violence towards women by men, racial attacks, and homophobic violence, displays the use of violence to maintain dominance. Violence which is specifically targeted against particular groups or individuals because of their beliefs, their skin colour, their gender, their sexuality, or their social class works to remind those more vulnerable that they will be constrained by those structurally advantaged. Violence does succeed in achieving dominance through force. But violence may also be a sign of resistance as well. The violence of civil insurgents demonstrates the use of violence for this purpose.

Naming actions as violence or resistance to oppression demonstrates how explanations of violence are subjective. Resistance to violence can be on an individual basis, as in situations where battered women kill their assailants, or they can be on a collective basis, as in armed insurgencies against state regimes. Public debates, as well as criminal trial defences, revolve around the use, meaning and consequences of violent actions. Often the subjective meanings of violence, and the social and political contexts within which violence arises, are contested and contestable. The meanings of violence are socially constructed.

Violence continues to fascinate people, as the proliferation of violence on television, the cinema, in books and in the news attests. The effects of viewing violence is hotly contested among researchers. Debates continue about how much of this type of violence we should be viewing on our televisions each evening. We are now able to witness the brutality and violence that others commit, in living colour. How this affects viewers, whether and how actual experiences of violence affect individuals future behaviour, and how violence prevention can increase the quality of life of many people are crucial debates for social scientists.

Elizabeth A. Stanko
Brunel University

Reference

Daly, M. and Wilson, M. (1988) *Homicide*, New York.

Further reading

Dobash, R. E. and Dobash, R. P. (1992) *Women, Violence and Social Change*, London.
Newburn, T. and Stanko, E. A. (1994) *Just Boys Doing Business*, London.
Stanko, E. A. (1990) *Everyday Violence*, London.

See also: domestic violence; social problems; terrorism.

vision

Perception is a process for obtaining knowledge of the world, and more than 80 per cent of it is accounted for by vision. It is a skill, not simply the passive recording of external stimulation (E. J. Gibson 1988). A perceiving organism is more like a map-reader than a camera. The early investigation of perception started with philosophical speculation about what role the senses might play in the acquisition of knowledge. It was only about a century and a half ago that the scientific and experimental study of these matters came into being (Boring 1950).

Nativism and empiricism

Two themes derived from established philosophical traditions dominated the early psychological research on vision. Empiricism started with the work of the British philosophers of the seventeenth and eighteenth centuries, principally Locke (1632–1704), Berkeley (1685–1753) and Hume (1711–76). It states that all understanding is based on elementary sensations, the building blocks of knowledge. In contrast, the nativist position, deriving from the rationalism of the French philosopher René Descartes (1596–1650), claimed that all true knowledge needs to be grounded in clear thinking, and the innate capacity to order and refine the messages of the senses. Such opposed views are still echoed in the theoretical and practical activities of modern psychologists.

It would be difficult now to find a supporter of either of these positions in their simple form. Nowadays we investigate the manner in which innate processes interact with experience of different kinds; in this regard much progress has been made.

The physiology of the visual system

The central nervous system is made up of many sorts of specialized cells, or neurons. Neurons in the retina of the eye receive light, and cause neural signals to be generated that are transmitted through various pathways to the posterior portion of the brain. The anatomical and physiological basis for vision is one of extraordinary complexity and delicacy, and it is mainly since the early 1960s that a detailed knowledge of how it works has been attained.

The major breakthrough came in the work of David Hubel and Torsten Wiesel, who first reported on recordings from single neurons in the brain cortex of the cat (Hubel and Wiesel 1962). They discovered that the function of individual visual neurons is usually not too difficult to describe and analyse. Before them it had been widely accepted that the connections between neurons at birth must be essentially random; experience would 'tune up' the system so that it could deal adequately with the information supplied through the senses, a form of empiricism (Hebb 1949). These developments are discussed in Dodwell (1970).

Hubel and Wiesel showed that most neurons in the primary visual area of the brain are specialized to respond to quite specific features of the environment, and do so even from birth. For example, there are cells that respond to short horizontal lines at the centre of the field, others prefer vertical or diagonal lines in other positions and so on. The important point is that they all have a definite preference. What the role of these *feature detectors* may be in the larger scheme of visual perception, and how they are to be understood as the building blocks for the development of a mature perceiving organism, are still open questions. The empiricism of the psychologist Hebb was thus to a great extent overtaken by the discoveries of Hubel and Wiesel (and subsequently very many other investigators) concerning innate physiological coding mechanisms.

The different sensory qualities of contour, movement, colour and depth have all been found to be processed in anatomically distinct channels which even have separate maps in different parts of the brain cortex (Maunsell and Newsome 1987). Certain higher order neurons that are sensitive to more complicated aspects of the visual field than simple oriented line segments have been identified, even some that respond to hands, moving human bodies, and faces (Perrett *et al.* 1985). This physiological knowledge is only a beginning, however; there is much more to say about the nature of seeing.

The visual world: space and object perception

The spatial character of vision is first registered in the formation of a sharp image of the visual scene on the retina of the eye, the retinal image. The size of the retinal image depends on the distance between eye and object, but *perceived* size does not vary so directly. Your friends do not suddenly shrink in size as they move away from you! This discrepancy between what the retinal image might lead one to expect, how things really appear to the observer is called *perceptual constancy*. It occurs not only for size, but also for shape, colour and brightness. In each case what is meant by constancy is the fact that what one sees (the phenomenon) is far *less* variable than what an analysis of the optical and other physical features of the stimulating environment would lead one to expect.

Our perceptual world is usually very stable – constant – yields few surprises, and is not subject to misinterpretation. It is stable because most of our percepts are *overdetermined*; visual cues are mutually consistent and are reinforced by tactile, auditory and other information. Only a philosopher would question whether the object in front of us is really a solid table, or the person we are talking to a robot (Rock 1984).

Perceptual illusions

Far from being mere party amusements, illusions can help us to understand quite a bit about perception. They are called illusions because there is a discrepancy between what common sense, habit, or geometrical intuition tells us should be seen, and what we actually see. It has been proposed that some illusions are induced by false intimations of perspective, yet this cannot be the whole story, as many illusions do not have a perspective interpretation. Illusions may be caused by the way information is coded by physiological mechanisms, by the way the spatial layout is interpreted, or by simple misinterpretation of distance cues. No one theory of the illusions has gained universal acceptance. Perhaps their main challenge is in reminding us of the many different factors that can enter into perceptual processing.

Gestalt psychology

The study of illusions certainly favours an eclectic and empiricist approach to perception. Yet some influential movements in psychology deny that position. Gestalt psychology which asserted the primacy of organizational phenomena, denied the role of experience in building up perception. The German word *Gestalt* means configuration. The main tenet of that school of psychology was that perception is *holistic*; it is not to be understood by breaking it into elementary parts. For the Gestalt psychologists the visual field was determined by a set or organizational principles that are simply a part of the way the brain works (Köhler 1929).

Gestalt psychologists held theories about brain activity that are now known to be false, so the school fell into disrepute, but it provided many demonstrations of organizational phenomena in perception that still pose a challenge.

Gibson's perceptual theory

J. J. Gibson (1950; 1966), like the Gestalt theorists, was also disenchanted by the traditional empiricist approach in which elements of sensory experience are somehow glued together to yield the coherent, one-piece perceptual world of normal experience. What is this glue? Nobody knows. Gibson argued that it is unnecessary to know, because the glue does not exist. Gibson concentrated his attention on movement, and concluded that information contained in moving displays (in traditional terms, the motion of the retinal image) was of decisive general importance in most visual tasks. He argued that information in 'whole field' displays gives valid and salient information about the true state of the world.

Gibson insisted on the organized quality of our perceptions, but in contrast to the Gestalt psychologists, he was not interested in the physiological substrate; undue concern with that, he argued, would tend to make us ask the wrong questions about perception. He insisted that perception is to be understood as the basis for action, and for understanding both organism and environment as a single interacting biological system; too much concern with the physiology would simply displace concern from the places where it was most useful.

The nature of perceptual learning

Unlike the Gestalt psychologists, Gibson accepted that perceptual learning has a role to play in the production of a mature organism. However, he maintained that the nature of this learning is quite different from what the traditional empiricist tells us. Perceptual learning, according to him, consists not in the gluing together of sensory atoms, but in coming to differentiate and discriminate among the features of the environment. Very likely there are two different sorts of perceptual learning, one constructive, or synthetic, and another that, while not destructive, is analytic in the Gibsonian sense. For example: synthetic perceptual learning might well be needed to account for the infant's ability to co-ordinate sights and sounds in forming concepts of *object permanency*, whereas analytic processes might be involved in learning to discriminate between the faces of two distinct adults in the infant's environment. Debate on this matter is still active.

Conclusion

The wide scope of research in perception, the ways it can aid us in understanding the intricacies of the perceptual apparatus, how it is used to inform us about the world, and how it is tuned up in the course of development have been touched on. If my emphasis has seemed to be heavily on the physiological side, this is because advances in understanding of the physiological substrate of vision have been so impressive since the 1950s. Yet it is clear that not all we need to know about perception is exhausted by this knowledge.

Perception is a many-faceted beast, and answers to its many questions need to be sought in different places, and at different levels of function; sensory, organizational, cognitive. To perceive seems effortless. To understand perception is nevertheless a great challenge.

Peter C. Dodwell
Queen's University, Kingston

References

Boring, E. (1950) *A History of Experimental Psychology*, New York.
Dodwell, P. C. (1970) *Visual Pattern Recognition*, New York.
Gibson, E. J. (1988) 'Exploratory behaviour in the development of perceiving, acting and acquiring of knowledge', *Annual Review of Psychology* 39.
Gibson, J. J. (1950) *The Perception of the Visual World*, Boston, MA.
—— (1966) *The Senses Considered as Perceptual Systems*, Boston, MA.
Hebb, D. O. (1949) *The Organization of Behavior*, New York.
Hubel, D. H. and Wiesel, T. N. (1962) 'Receptive fields, binocular interaction and functional architecture in the cat's visual cortex', *Journal of Physiology* 160.
Köhler, W. (1929) *Gestalt Psychology*, New York.
Maunsell, J. H. R. and Newsome, W. T. (1987) 'Visual processing in monkey extrastriate cortex', *Annual Review of Neuroscience* 10.
Perrett, D. I., Smith, P. A. J., Potter, D. D., Mistlin, A. J., Head, A. S., Milner, A. D. and Jeeves, M. A. (1985) 'Visual cells in the temporal cortex sensitive to face view and gaze direction', *Proceedings of the Royal Society of London* B 223.
Rock, I. (1984) *Perception*, New York.

Further reading

Blakemore, C. (1978) 'Maturation and modification in the developing visual system', in R. Held, H. Liebowitz and H. Teuber (eds) *Handbook of Sensory Physiology*, vol. 8, *Perception*, New York.
Dodwell, P. C. (1990) 'Perception', in R. Lockhart, J. Grusec and J. Waller (eds) *Foundations of Perception*, Toronto.
Gregory, R. L. (1966) *Eye and Brain*, New York.
Held, R. (1965) 'Plasticity in sensorimotor systems', *Scientific American* 213(5).
Hubel, D. H. (1987) *Eye Brain and Vision*, New York.

Kohler, I. (1964) 'The formation and transformation of the perceptual world', *Psychological Issues* 3.
Michael, C. F. and Carello, C. (1981) *Direct Perception*, Englewood Cliffs, NJ.
Rock, I. (1984) *Perception*, New York.
Schiffman, H. R. (1982) *Sensation and Perception: An Integrated Approach*, 2nd edn, New York.

See also: sensation and perception.

vital statistics

An individual's entry into or departure from life, or change in civil status, is known as a vital event. In demographic applications the term most commonly encompasses births, marriages and deaths, including stillbirths as well as live births, and divorces as well as marriages. An exhaustive list of such events would also contain annulments, adoptions, legitimations, recognitions and legal separations, but these latter vital events are less commonly the subject of demographic analysis. Vital statistics are the basic or derived data regarding vital events.

Christenings, marriages and burials were recorded in European parish registers as long ago as the sixteenth century. The first serious study of vital statistics, that of John Graunt in 1662, was based upon burial and christening records and presented the first crude life tables. Civil registration of vital events became compulsory in Scandinavia and some of the American colonies fairly early in the seventeenth century but in England not until 1837, although England was the first country to produce regular publications of vital statistics. In contrast, most developing countries have either a defective system of vital registration, or none at all.

The information contained in a registration document includes the date and place of the vital event being registered, and the date and place of registration. The sex of the child and names and ages of parents are included on a birth certificate, and the cause of death, and age, marital status and occupation of the deceased on a death certificate. Other information on background characteristics is also obtained, the exact inventory varying with the type of event being registered, and from country to country.

Demographic data are of two types, stock and flow, the stocks being population totals at a particular moment and the flows represented by movements into and out of a population over a period of time. Information on stocks is obtained from periodic population censuses or population registers, and on flows from a system of registration of vital events. The most obvious examples of flows are births and deaths, although marriage is also a flow as it represents movement from the unmarried to the married state. The most basic demographic measures incorporate both types of information, with a flow in the numerator and a stock in the denominator. Thus, for example, the crude birth rate, the simplest fertility measure, is calculated as the ratio of births which occurred during a particular year, as obtained from registration data, to the estimated mid-year population. Similarly, the total number of deaths in a particular year is related to the mid-year population in order to estimate the crude death rate.

Such measures can be made more informative by taking into account additional attributes such as age or, depending on the background information collected on the registration forms and its comparability with census information, other characteristics as well. Some examples are life tables for different occupational groups or regional age-specific fertility rates.

Most developing countries lack a comprehensive system of vital registration. In an attempt to compensate for this deficiency, since the mid-1960s a number of techniques have been developed by which vital rates can be estimated from fairly simple questions appended to a census schedule. Vital rates are also estimated, with varying degrees of success, from specially designed sample surveys.

Gigi Santow
University of Stockholm

Further reading

Brass, W. and Coale, A. J. (1968) 'Methods of analysis and estimation', in W. Brass *et al.* (eds) *The Demography of Tropical Africa*, Princeton, NJ.

Graunt, J. (1939) *Natural and Political Observations Made upon the Bills of Mortality*, ed. W. F. Willcox, Baltimore, MD.

Shryock, H. S., Siegel, J. S. and associates (1973) *The Methods and Materials of Demography*, Washington, DC.

Spiegelman, M. (1968) *Introduction to Demography*, Cambridge, MA.

Wrigley, E. A. and Schofield, R. S. (1983) 'English population history from family reconstitution: summary results 1600-1799', *Population Studies* 37.

See also: census of population; fertility; migration; mortality; nuptiality; population policy; population projections.

vocational and career development

The field of vocational and career development concerns itself with how and why individuals develop preferences for one or another type of work and how they eventually choose an occupation and seek satisfaction from their work. It has produced instruments and procedures to assist individuals via education, consultation, and counselling to optimize their vocational and career potential.

The field cuts across many different domains: developmental psychologists are interested in the developmental antecedents of important vocational and career decisions; test and measurement specialists create instruments to measure such domains as vocational interests, personality, and vocational maturity; sociologists study the impact of family and the sociocultural environment on careers; organizational psychologists focus their attention on career development in organizations, and counselling psychologists and guidance counsellors develop and apply methods to intervene in the vocational and career-development process.

Important theories in the field of vocational and career development have been summarized by Osipow (1983). Since the late 1960s, the developmental theory of Super (1990) and the person-environment-fit theory of Holland (1985), both originally formulated during the 1950s, have been the most prominent theories in the field. Super's (1990) original self-concept theory, which viewed vocational development as being inextricably linked to the development of a person's self-concept, was subsequently expanded to include consideration of the changing life roles of individuals throughout their life-span. Holland's (1985) theory rests on the assumption that there are a finite number of different work environments which attract different personalities. If the work environment matches the personality of the person choosing it, this can lead to a successful career. Both Super's and Holland's theories have stimulated a great deal of research, the majority of which has supported the basic theoretical formulations.

Other important approaches to vocational and career development include Krumboltz's (1979) social-learning theory and Dawis and Lofquist's (1984) theory of work adjustment. Interest in the field is growing rapidly, in part because of its attention to the vocational and career development of women and minorities (Betz and Fitzgerald 1987). There is also growing recognition of the fact that career development is a life-span process, not a single decision regarding an occupational choice. It is a process, occurring over the course of a lifetime, during which the person's unique attributes of individuality dynamically interact with multiple levels of the environment in producing, among other things, the person's vocational development or the person's career (Vondracek *et al.* 1986). Finally, another noteworthy perspective focuses not on the traditional quantitative aspects of career development, but on the meaning of vocation, the meaning of career, within the individuals' overall life-span development (e.g. Cochran 1990).

Fred W. Vondracek
Pennsylvania State University

References

Betz, N. E. and Fitzgerald, L. F. (1987) *The Career Psychology of Women*, New York.

Cochran, L. (1990) *The Sense of Vocation: A Study of Career and Life Development*, Albany, NY.

Dawis, R. V. and Lofquist, L. H. (1984) *A Psychological Theory of Work Adjustment: An Individual Differences Model and its Applications*, Minneapolis, MN.

Holland, J. L. (1985) *Making Vocational Choices: A Theory of Vocational Personalities and Work Environments*, 2nd edn, Englewood Cliffs, NJ.

Krumboltz, J. D. (1979) 'A social learning theory of career decision-making', in H. Mitchell *et al.* (eds) *Social Learning and Career Decision Making*, Cranston, RI.

Osipow, S. H. (1983) *Theories of Career Development*, 3rd edn, Englewood Cliffs, NJ.

Super, D. E. (1990) 'A life-span, life-space approach to career development', in D. Brown *et al.* (eds) *Career Choice and Development*, San Francisco, CA.

Vondracek, F. W., Lerner, R. M., and Schulenberg, J. E. (1986) *Career Development: A Life-Span Developmental Approach*, Hillsdale, NJ.

See also: aptitude tests; occupational psychology; social skills and social skills training.

voting

Voting is a means of expressing and aggregating a choice of party or candidate in elections. Ancient Greeks voted by placing a pebble (*psephos*) in an urn, giving rise to the term psephology, or study of elections. By the end of the nineteenth century most western states had granted the vote to most adult males and in the first few decades of the twentieth century it was extended to women on the same terms. Free competitive elections are regarded as the key to representative democracy.

Electoral systems and constitutions prescribe the conduct of elections. They cover such features as

1 Frequency: e.g. fixed calendar elections as in the USA or elections which have to be held within a fixed time period (e.g. Britain).
2 Occasions: for local, regional and national legislatures and head of state; they can also be held on policy questions, via referendums, or nominations, via primaries.
3 Eligibility: virtually all states confine the right to vote to adult citizens, although they may differ in their criteria for adulthood and citizenship.
4 Registration: voters have to be registered on an electoral roll or register; in the USA registration is more complex than in other states.
5 The weight of the vote: the extent to which the system approximates to one person, one vote, one value depends on the type of electoral system and size of constituencies.

The study of voting behaviour has gone through several stages and employed different approaches. These are various models, drawn from different intellectual backgrounds, including historical, aggregate data, sociological, party identification, and issue voting approaches.

First, the historical approach considers that it is easily overlooked that voters are usually presented at elections with a fixed choice of parties: these are the product of historical forces which long preceded the birth of the present-day electors. Important work by Lipset and Rokkan (1967) has traced the origins of many party systems to such key historical events as the Reformation and Counter-Reformation, the industrial revolution, the early stages of nation-building and the French revolution. These formative events have given rise to party systems which are variously based on religious allegiance, class interest and centre versus periphery loyalties. Once created some parties endure beyond the circumstances which gave rise to them. They adapt to new interests and issues and socialize voters into voting for them.

Second, the aggregate data approach analyses census data for the particular unit (which may be a region, constituency or ward) to establish correlations between the dominant social factors of the population and the strength of a political party. It was well established in the USA and France in the first decades of the twentieth century and André Siegfried used it to describe the geographical division of France into political left and right regions. The approach is more useful where the unit under study has a pronounced social character (e.g. a mining or a farming community). The problem is to move from aggregate to individual data correlations.

Third, the sociological approach, using sample surveys to interview voters, was pioneered in the USA in the 1940s (Lazarsfeld *et al.* 1948) and enabled studies to be made of individual voters. This work showed that such social background factors as class, religion and residence predisposed people to vote Republican or Democrat. It was also useful in showing the extent to which the parties drew on attitudinally integrated groups of support. In Britain the pioneering study by Butler and Stokes (1969) showed the importance of social class and of religion in shaping party votes.

Fourth, the party identification approach, borrowed from psychology, was developed by Angus Campbell (1960) and his colleagues at the University of Michigan. They found that most US voters were attached to a political party; they had a party identity, often inherited from parents, and reinforced by occupation, class and neighbourhood. It was a force for continuity in voting behaviour. The party identification approach has had a major impact on electoral studies, on cross-national research and on developing typologies of elections. In the USA in the 1970s and 1980s identification declined as a predictor of party vote. Although the Democrats enjoyed a clear lead on identification over Republicans they regularly lost presidential elections. The concept is also useful in helping to construct a *normal* vote for a party.

Fifth, the issue voting approach has been inspired by Downs (1957) and applied by Himmelweit and Jaeger (1985). It emphasizes the importance of issue preferences to the voter. For Himmelweit, who terms it the *consumer model of voting*, it is issue preferences, moderated by the strength of party identification and habit of voting for one party rather than another, which shapes the vote decision. Students specify three conditions for issue voting: the voter must be aware of the issue, care about the issue, and perceive the parties as taking different stands on the issue, with one party representing their issue preference. If party identification leads to *expressive* voting, then rational choice leads to instrumental voting. Early voting studies pointed to the apathy and ignorance of many voters and suggested that only a small minority of voters were able to satisfy the conditions for issue voting. But more recent research, which allows voters to suggest their own important issues, finds that issue voting is more widespread.

Other approaches have stressed the importance of how the economy is performing. Economic-based explanations of voting have to come to terms with the fact that key indicators vary over time; unemployment, inflation, take-home pay or economic optimism differ in their salience from one election to another. Carried to extremes, models which link voting behaviour to rates of unemployment and inflation would predict that continued economic decline would lead to the demise of established political parties. But in times of economic depression voters' expectations may be scaled down, other concerns may become more significant, or alternative parties viewed as less attractive to the government of the day. In the British general election in 1992 voters' perceptions of Labour as untrustworthy on economic management was important in delivering a surprise election victory to the Conservatives.

Scholars also differ as to whether voting is primarily *retrospective*, that is, based on the perceived record of the government, or *prospective*, in which the citizen votes on the basis of the policy proposals of the parties. A neo-Marxist or radical approach emphasizes the voter's relationship to the state as an employer or consumer of services. This approach cuts across conventional social class analysis and emphasizes the importance of employment in the private or the public sector, or dependence on public or private housing, transport, education and so on.

The concept of the *normal vote* is crucial for developing a typology of elections and interpreting the outcome of an election. If the change proves to be durable then the election has been *critical*, or realigning, inaugurating a long term change in the strength of the parties. Thus, the Democrats became the clear majority party in the USA after Roosevelt's *critical* 1932 election, and the Conservative victory in 1979 seems to have been a critical one in Britain. A *maintaining* election is one in which the great majority of voters follow their traditional party loyalties and the majority party wins. A *deviating* election is one in which the usual minority party wins, in response to short-term factors associated with the campaign (e.g. Eisenhower's victories in the 1952 and 1956 US presidential contests).

More rapid social and economic change is weakening the bases of traditional voting. In turn, this loosening of allegiance gives more scope to short-term factors such as the mass media, economic trends and the campaign and candidates. The availability of different models of voting behaviour and the development of more sophisticated techniques of data analysis have greatly enriched our knowledge of voting. On the whole, what emerges is a more complex pattern. For example, is party identification, outside of the USA anything more than a reflection of the party vote? How does one establish the direction of influence between issue preferences and party loyalty? Debate is sure to continue.

Dennis Kavanagh
University of Nottingham

References

Butler, D. and Stokes D. (1969) *Political Change in Britain*, London.

Campbell A. (1960) *The American Voter*, New York.

Downs, A. (1957) *An Economic Theory of Democracy*, New York.

Himmelweit, H. and Jaeger, M. (1985) *How Voters Decide*, Milton Keynes.

Lazarsfeld, P. *et al.* (1948) *The People's Choice*, New York.

Lipset, S. and Rokkan, S. (1967) *Party Systems and Voter Alignments*, New York.

See also: elections; parties, political; public choice.

W

war studies

The study of war is still dominated by Carl von Clausewitz's reflections based on his experience of the Napoleonic campaigns *On War* (Clausewitz 1976). The book was still being revised when he died in 1831 so that only the first chapters reflect his developed thought, and this has led to a debate (familiar to students of Marx) over whether the early or later Clausewitz represents a truer or better picture. As the Napoleonic Wars were held to represent a shift in the character of war towards total confrontations involving the mobilization of whole societies, and as Clausewitz was the most influential expositor of this shift, he was often blamed for the wars that followed, especially as his early writings can be taken to legitimize a drive for a decisive battle. Yet he can also be used as a source of caution, in that the later Clausewitz became more concerned with the tension between an inherent nature of war, which can take over and push it to absolute levels of violence, and the limiting factors, of which the most important was the definition of war aims which led to his famous injunction that war is the continuation of politics by other means (Gat 1989).

While politics might provide the purposes of war, its actual conduct was a military responsibility. Some, such as the Swiss Henri de Jomini (1971 [1862]), another veteran of the Napoleonic Wars, believed that success in war was governed by the application of general principles. On a more modest scale, investigations into past campaigns were undertaken by the military so as to be able to apply any lessons when developing new doctrine and tactics. The German Hans Delbruck was almost unique as an academic military historian. He distinguished between wars of annihilation, directed largely at the decisive destruction of the enemy armies, and those of exhaustion, where resources are limited and battle has to be complemented by attempts to destroy the economic base of the opponent, for example, by destroying crops or blockade (Craig 1985).

Otherwise, the origins of particular wars were studied by historians but theories of war's causation were few and far between.

By the turn of the century, there was some understanding of how the combination of the revolutions in industrialization and transport were leading to a revolution in warfare. Even some military planners understood that at issue was whether the new capacity for manoeuvre could produce results before the new capacity for attrition took over. The absolute nature of the First World War transformed the study of war.

One consequence of this was that the problem of war was put at the centre of the new study of international relations and at the centre of the practice of international law. It was treated as an inter-state crime. The objective was to design an international order in which disputes would be settled without resort to arms and so war could be prohibited. The study of its conduct was tantamount to endorsing its continued place in human affairs. Causation came to be understood in terms of irrational factors, such as an arms race, more than deliberate state policy.

Even those who were not convinced that war could be abolished, and pursued studies of its conduct, were profoundly influenced by the desire to avoid the carnage of the First World War. Most were veterans of the war, though they were also often disaffected or retired. There were those such as the Italian Douhet, and the American Billy Mitchell (Warner 1943), who believed that air power now offered a way to bring wars to a swift conclusion, possibly without any encounters on land, while others, such as the British writers 'Boney' Fuller and Basil Liddell Hart, believed that the key innovation was the tank (Bond 1977).

The Second World War did not conform exactly to the expectations of any pre-war theorist. Moreover its finale, with the atomic destruction of Nagasaki and Hiroshima, suggested that previous types of warfare might have all been rendered obsolete. For students of war, the events of the 1930s and their consequences produced a new seriousness. International relations moved from idealist to realist mode. An interest in the theory of war was reflected in the major collection on *Makers of Modern Strategy* put together by Edward Meade Earle, almost as part of the war effort, but which served as a standard text for four decades until superseded by a new collection under the same name (Earle 1943; Paret 1985). In Chicago Quincy Wright (1942) produced his monumental *Study of War*, thereby demonstrating the importance of serious empirical analysis.

Another important feature of the Second World War was the growing relevance of science, and the scientific method, in the development of both weapons and tactics, marked by developments in radar, missiles and jet engines as well as nuclear fission. This in itself ensured that the study of the conduct of, and preparations for, war would have a distinctive civilian quality. The awesome dilemmas of the nuclear age accelerated this civilian tendency. Following the adoption of the doctrine of massive retaliation by the Eisenhower Administration in 1954, a boom in strategic studies took place. It appeared as if US security policy was going to depend on a threat to inflict terrible damage on the Soviet Union and its allies as punishment for even the smallest transgression. This was despite the declining credibility of such a threat as the Soviet capacity for counter-punishment grew.

It was initially students of history and politics who worried most as to the sense of all this. Those from this background tended to doubt whether nuclear strength could be turned into a decisive military asset when faced with an adversary of some – even if inferior – nuclear strength. But the two sides were acting and talking as if nuclear weapons had superseded all other types of weapons, and commitments to allies had been made on exactly this supposition. So the classical strategists found themselves in a conundrum for which their intellectual traditions left them unprepared (Freedman 1989).

Into the breach stepped a new breed of strategists, often from schools of economics and engineering rather than politics and history, who sought to demonstrate how a wholly novel situation might be mastered by exploiting novel methodologies. As this logic led to co-operative attempts to manage superpower antagonism through arms control negotiations, studies of strategic matters came to be seen as an almost exclusively civilian – and academic – domain.

Because of the catastrophic consequences of a superpower confrontation, there appeared to be grounds for believing that war was close to abolishing itself. Certainly, the importance of avoiding war meant that its study became overtaken by the study of deterrence. In terms of the theory of war, this could be accommodated within a realist model which assumed that great powers would pursue their interests in a rational manner (Waltz 1960).

In this context the study of war came to revolve around three distinct questions. First, was there a possibility that developments in nuclear weapons technology could produce conditions for a meaningful victory in a superpower confrontation? Second, failing that, and assuming that nuclear arsenals continued to neutralize each other, how significant were developments with conventional military forces? Third, how much was it possible to rely on rational behaviour at times of crisis, when such factors as poor information and misperception, flaws in decision-making processes and the psychology of individual leaders, as well as overdependence on automatic early warning and launch procedures, could all have catastrophic consequences?

This last question in particular encouraged detailed empirical studies on past successes and failures in deterrence (Jervis, *et al.* 1985). This work raised important methodological issues concerning the possibility of generalizing from a series of distinct events in quite different historical periods and geopolitical settings. There has been since the 1960s one distinct approach to war studies marked by a rigorous empiricism (Midlarsky 1989). This has included a major investigation into the 'correlates of war' (Small and Singer 1980).

With the end of the Cold War all approaches to the study of war had to undergo some reappraisal. The Gulf War suggested that classical studies on the conduct of war still might have their place, yet the overall thrust of much analysis was to suggest that the great power encounters which had dominated the study of war since the time of Clausewitz were becoming consigned to history. If any military tradition remained relevant it was that of the irregular/guerrilla war. These had been fought in the name of anti-colonialism but, now that the processes of decolonization was all but complete, were largely bound up with conflicts within and between the newly independent, and often quite weak, states.

This tradition of writing on war tends to take large-scale land operations as the starting-point. Indeed, thinking on war has been dominated by a focus on large-scale acts of aggression and decisive battles (including the avoidance thereof). To some this also meant the end of Clausewitz's influence and the irrelevance of his intellectual schema (Creveld 1991; Keegan 1993). However, even so-called ethnic conflicts and civil wars are waged for political purposes and require some understanding of the effective manipulation of the means of violence. This aspect still ensures some continuity in the study of war, even in the light of the enormous changes in the international environment, social and economic conditions, and the advance of military technology.

Lawrence Freedman
University of London

References

Bond, B. (1977) *Liddell Hart: A Study of his Military Thought*, London.

Clausewitz, C. von (1979) *On War*, ed. and trans. M. Howard and P. Paret, Princeton, NJ.

Craig, G. (1985) 'Delbruck: the military historian', in P. Paret (ed.) *Makers of Modern Strategy*, Princeton, NJ.

Creveld, M. van (1991) *The Transformation of War*, New York.

Earle, E. M. (ed.) (1943) *Makers of Modern Strategy*, Princeton, NJ.

Freedman, L. (1989) *The Evolution of Nuclear Strategy*, 2nd edn.

Gat, A. (1989) *The Origins of Military Thought*, Oxford.

Jervis, R., Lebow, R. N., and Stein, J. G. (eds) (1985) *Psychology and Deterrence*, New York.

Jomini, Baron H. de (1971 [1862]) *The Art of War*, Westport, CT. (Original edn, trans. G. H. Wendell and W. P. Craighill, Philadelphia, PA.)

Keegan, J. (1993) *History of Warfare*, London.

Midlarsky, M. (ed.) (1989) *Handbook of War Studies*, Boston, MA.

Paret, P. (ed.) (1985) *Makers of Modern Strategy*, Princeton, NJ.

Small, M. and Singer, J. D. (1980) *Resort to Arms: International and Civil Wars, 1816–1980*, Beverly Hills, CA.

Waltz, K. (1960) *Man, the State and War: A Theoretical Analysis*, New York.

Warner, E. (1943) 'Douhet: Mitchell, Seversky: theories of air warfare', in E. M. Earle (ed.) *Makers of Modern Strategy*, Princeton, NJ.

Wright, Q. (1942) *The Study of War*, Chicago.

Further reading

Aron, R. (1968) *On War*, New York.

Blainey, G. (1988) *The Causes of War*, London.

Cowley, R. (ed.) (1992) *Experience of War*, New York.

Gilpin, R. (1983) *War and Change in World Politics*, Cambridge, UK.

Jones, A. (1987) *The Art of War in the Western World*, Oxford.

Liddell Hart, B. H. (1968) *Strategy: The Indirect Approach*, London.

Luttwak, E. (1987) *Strategy: The Logic of War and Peace*, Cambridge, MA.

McInnes, C. and Sheffield, G. D. (eds) (1988) *Warfare in the Twentieth Century: Theory and Practice*, London.

Schelling, T. (1963) *The Strategy of Conflict*, New York.

Walzer, M. (1980) *Just and Unjust Wars*, Harmondsworth.

See also: conflict, social; feud; military sociology; peace studies.

Weber, Max (1864–1920)

Max Weber, the son of a member of the Reichstag and an activist Protestant mother, grew up in Berlin in an intellectually lively home frequently visited by the Bismarckian era's leading politicians and intellectuals. After receiving an outstanding secondary education in languages, history and the classics, he studied law, economics, history and philosophy at the universities of Heidelberg, Strasbourg, Göttingen and Berlin. Although his first appointments, at the universities of Freiburg (1894) and Heidelberg (1897), were in the faculty of economics, he is best known as one of the major founders of modern sociology and as one of the intellectual giants of interdisciplinary scholarship. As strange as it may sound, he ranged freely across the entire palette of written history, from the ancient Greeks to the early Hindus, from the Old Testament prophets to the Confucian literati, from the economic organization of early Near Eastern civilizations to the trading companies of the medieval west, and from the origins of continental law to comparative analyses of the rise of the modern state.

The diversity of these themes – only a small sampling – should not lead us to view Weber as a scholar of unlimited energies frantically leaping about for its own sake. Rather, when looked at closely, a grand design becomes visible in his writings, yet one that remained incomplete and whose inner coherence can be plotted only against the inner torments of their author. Weber and others of his generation in Germany viewed the dawning of rapid industrialization and the modern age itself with profound ambivalence rather than as a first step towards a new era of progress. While welcoming the possibilities it offered for a burgeoning of individualism and an escape from the feudal chains of the past, he saw few firm guidelines in reference to which modern people might be able to establish a comprehensive meaning for their lives or even their everyday actions (Weber 1946). Moreover, the overpowering bureaucracies indispensable to the organization of industrial societies were endowed with the capacity to render people politically powerless as well as to replace creative potential with stifling routine and merely functional relationships. These developments threatened to curtail the flowering of individualism.

Just such quandaries stood behind all of Weber's sociological writings, particularly those undertaken after 1903. In these studies he wished to define precisely the uniqueness of western civilization and to understand on a universal scale the manner in which people, influenced by social constellations, formulate *meaning* for their lives that guides action. A curiosity founded in such questions instilled in him an amazing capacity to place himself, once he had constructed a 'mental image' of another era and civilization, into the minds of those quite unlike himself. This aim to understand how values, traditions and actions made sense to their beholders, however foreign they were to the social scientist investigating them, formed the foundation for Weber's *verstehende* sociology.

Perhaps it was this sensitivity, as well as a sheer respect for meanings formulated over centuries, that prompted Weber to construct one of his most famous axioms, one debated heatedly to this day. To him, all scientific judgements must be value-free: once researchers have selected their themes of enquiry, then personal values, preferences and prejudices must not be allowed to interfere with the collection and evaluation of empirical data (Weber 1949). All people involved in scientific work should avoid an inadvertent intermixture of their values with those of the actors being studied. To Weber, even scientists who happened to be Calvinists were duty-bound – as long as they wished to pursue science – to describe, for example, tribal sexual practices accurately and to interpret them in reference to their indigenous cultural significance, however repugnant they seemed personally. This axiom also implied a strict division between that which *exists* (the question for scientific analysis) and that which *should be* (the realm of personal values).

In explicitly circumscribing the legitimate domain of science and denying it the right to produce ideals and values, Weber had a larger purpose in mind. He hoped to establish an inviolable realm within which individuals would be forced to confront themselves and autonomously formulate a set of personal values capable of guiding their actions and endowing them with meaning. Nothing less was required as a counterforce in an age in which bureaucratization and the scientific world-view threatened to encroach upon decision making, thus threatening viable individualism. Weber's own adherence to a value-free science, particularly in his studies of pre-modern and non-western societies, the penetration of his insight into the diverse ways in which meaning could be formed and patterned action ensued, and the universal-historical scope of his investigations, enabled him to write – however fragmented, incomplete and poorly organized – a comparative-historical sociology of civilizations unique in the history of sociology.

Even though his interest focused upon comparisons between civilizations and causal analyses of differences, Weber's emphasis upon individual meaning and patterned action prevented him from taking the Hegelian absolute spirit, the Marxian organization of production and class struggle, or the 'social facts' of Durkheim as his point of departure. Nor was he inclined, due to his continuous accentuation of the conflicts between diverse spheres of life (religious, political, economic, legal, aesthetic) and the centrality of power and domination, to view societies, like Parsons, as basically integrated wholes. In fact, Weber's

orientation to individuals and the meaning they attach to their action would seem to carry him dangerously close to a radical subjectivism. Two procedures guarded against this possibility.

First, in his substantive studies, it was the patterned actions of individuals in groups, and not individuals acting alone, that captured his attention. It was only this regular action that, according to Weber, proved to be culturally significant and historically powerful. Individuals tended to become knit together into collectivities primarily in six ways: acknowledgement of common material interests (as occurred when classes were formed), recognition of common 'ideal interests' (as took place when status groups arose), adherence to a single world-view (as occurred in religious groups), acknowledgement of affectual feelings (as found in person-oriented groups, such as the household, the clan and the neighbourhood), awareness of relationships of legitimate domination (as took place in the charismatic, patriarchal, feudal, patrimonial and bureaucratic forms of domination), and recognition of traditions. However massive and enduring an institution might appear, it must not, according to Weber, be understood as more than the orientations of individuals acting in common.

The second means employed by Weber to avoid lapsing into a radical subjectivism involves his major methodological tool: the 'ideal type' (Weber 1949). Indeed, this heuristic construct so effectively guarded against this possibility that a number of commentators have accused Weber – particularly in his later work – of moving away from a *verstehende* sociology and of reifying the social phenomena he studies. In part, Weber himself is to blame. Instead of discussing, for example, bureaucratically-oriented action, he uses the term bureaucracy, and rather than using class-oriented action, he speaks of classes.

Perhaps the ideal type can be best understood against the backdrop of Weber's view of social reality. For him, when examined at its basic level, social reality presents a ceaseless flow of occurrences and events, very few of which, although repeatedly interwoven, seem to fall together coherently. Due to its infinite complexity, no investigator can expect to capture reality exhaustively, nor even to render accurately all its contours.

Weber propounded the use of the ideal type to confront this conundrum. This purely analytic tool enables a purchase upon reality through its simplification. Far from arbitrary, however, the procedures for doing so involve a deliberate *exaggeration of the essence* of the phenomenon under study and its reconstruction in a form with greater internal unity than ever appeared in empirical reality. Thus, Weber's conceptualization, for example, of the bureaucracy or the Calvinist does not aim to portray accurately all bureaucracies or

Calvinists, but to call attention only to essential aspects. As an artificial construct, the ideal type abstracts from reality and fails to define *any* particular phenomenon. None the less, it serves crucial purposes: it allows us, once an entire series of ideal types appropriate for a theme under investigation have been formed, to undertake comparisons; and, when used as a heuristic yardstick in comparison to which a specific bureaucracy or Calvinist church can be defined and its deviation assessed, it enables an isolation and clear conceptualization of distinctive attributes. Only after a number of ideal-typical 'experiments' have been conducted can we move on to questions regarding the purely empirical *causes* for the uniqueness of the particular case. For Weber, causal questions remained central rather than ones of definition alone.

Although he outlined a methodology – only hinted at above – that would allow him to investigate the manner in which individuals formulated meaning in different civilizations and epochs as well as to define precisely the uniqueness of the modern west, it must be concluded that, when viewed in reference to these broad aims, his various writings constitute mere fragments. Most, including his comparative studies on the *Economic Ethics of the World Religions* (*EEWR*) – these include *The Religion of China* (1951), *The Religion of India* (1958) and *Ancient Judaism* (1952) – and *Economy and Society* (*E&S*) (1968 [1922]), were published in incomplete form. None the less, the discrete elements of the whole have stood on their own and become classics in their own right. Broadly speaking, Weber's works divide into more empirical investigations on the one hand and analytical models on the other (*E&S*).

By far his most famous, debated and readable book, *The Protestant Ethic and the Spirit of Capitalism* (1930 [1922]), falls into the former category. In this classic, Weber sought to understand certain origins of modern capitalism. For him, this form of capitalism was distinguished by a systematic organization of work, the replacement of a 'traditional economic ethic' among workers as well as entrepreneurs by methodical labour, and a systematic search for profit. Thus, Weber saw a particular *attitude* towards work and profit – 'a spirit of capitalism' – as important, and denied that the influx of precious metals, increased trade, technological advances, population increases, the expansion of banking techniques, the universal desire for riches, or the Herculean efforts of 'economic supermen' (Carnegie, Rockefeller, Fugger) were alone adequate to explain the origin of modern capitalism.

Religious roots, according to Weber, anchored this spirit, namely the doctrines of the ascetic Protestant sects and churches, particularly the pastoral exhortations of Calvinism. The deep anxiety introduced by this religion's predestination doctrine in respect to the overriding question of one's personal salvation proved more than believers could reasonably bear. As a result of revisions introduced by Richard Baxter, a seventeenth-century minister, worldly success came to be viewed as a *sign* that God had bestowed his favour and, thus as evidence of membership among the predestined elect. In this way, since it allowed the devout to believe they belonged among the chosen few and thereby alleviated intense anxiety, worldly success itself became endowed with a religious – indeed, a salvation – 'premium'. Methodical labour in a calling (*Beruf*) proved the surest pathway towards worldly success, as did the continuous reinvestment of one's wealth – an unintended consequence of this attitude – rather than its squandering on worldly pleasures. To Weber, the medieval monk's other-worldly asceticism became, with Calvinism, transformed into an 'inner-worldly asceticism'.

In calling attention to this *cultural* cause of modern capitalism, Weber (1930 [1922]) in no way sought to substitute an idealist for a materialist explanation. Rather, he aimed only to point out the heretofore neglected idealist side in order to emphasize that a comprehensive explanation of modern capitalism's origins must include consideration of the economic ethic as well as the economic form. Moreover, far from claiming that Calvinism led to modern capitalism in a monocausal fashion, Weber (1961 [1927]) asserted that the rise of this type of capitalism can be explained adequately only through multidimensional models (Cohen 1981; Collins 1980; Kalberg 1983). Indeed, as Weber (1930 [1922]) noted in his discussion of 'backwoods Pennsylvania' and as Gordon Marshall (1980; 1982) has demonstrated in the case of Scotland, a constellation of material factors must exist in a manner such that a conducive context is formulated, for without this context the spirit of capitalism is powerless to introduce modern capitalism. Once firmly entrenched, however, modern capitalism perpetuates itself on the basis of secularized socialization processes as well as coercive mechanisms and no longer requires its original spirit.

While adressing the rise of modern capitalism in a novel manner, *The Protestant Ethic* failed to grapple with the larger, comparative issue: the distinctiveness of the Occident, Weber knew well, could be defined only through a series of comparisons with non-western civilizations. In turning to China and India, he again took the issue of modern capitalism as his focus, though here he posed the negative question of why, in these civilizations, this type of capitalism had failed to develop. Moreover, far from attempting to assess only whether Confucian, Taoist, Hindu and Buddhist teachings introduced or inhibited methodical economic action, these studies turned as well to the materialist side and sought to discuss the economic ethics of non-western world religions in the context of a whole series of social structural and organizational dimensions. This comparative procedure enabled Weber also to isolate the array of material factors in the west that proved conducive to the development of modern capitalism. These empirical studies, in addition to his investigations of ancient Judaism, carried him a giant step further as well in his attempt to understand the manner in which social configurations influence the formation of meaning.

Yet these studies remained, as Weber himself repeatedly emphasized (1930 [1922]; 1972 [1920]) drastically incomplete, especially if examined in reference to his overall goals. They are, furthermore, too poorly organized to provide us with a distinctly Weberian approach for an unlocking of the elusive relationship between ideas and interests. These empirical investigations must be read through the lens of the analytical categories and models Weber develops for the analysis of social action on a universal-historical scale in one of the genuine classics of modern social science, *Economics and Society E&S* (1968 [1922]).

At first glance, this three-volume tome seems to conceal thoroughly Weber's larger aims. Part One is concerned primarily with the articulation of a broad series of sociological concepts. Although empirically based, each of these ideal types, since formulated on a universal-historical scale, remains at a high level of abstraction. None the less, each can be utilized as a heuristic yardstick that serves as a point of reference for the definition of particular cases. The ideal types of Part Two are less all-encompassing and relate generally to specific epochs and civilizations (Mommsen 1974). This section reveals on every page how its author, in considering historical examples, extracted their essence and constructed ideal types. Just this perpetual movement between the historical and ideal-typical levels, as well as Weber's unwillingness to formulate an ideal type before scrutinizing innumerable cases, accounts for its exceedingly disjointed character. His failure to discuss his overriding themes in a synoptic fashion has also decreased the readability of *E&S*.

These problems have blinded most Weber specialists to the 'analytic' of social action buried between the lines of this treatise and utilizable for the comparative and historical study even of entire civilizations (Kalberg 1980; 1983; 1990; 1994). Consequently, each chapter has been read and debated apart from its broader purposes in the Weberian corpus and in an ahistorical fashion. None the less, standing on their own, the separate chapters have attained classical status in a wide variety of sociology's subfields, such as the sociology of religion, urban sociology, stratification, economic sociology, modernization and development,

the sociology of law, and political sociology. In each chapter, Weber lays out, in light of the specific problematic involved, a universal-historical analytic that includes a differentiated discussion of the ways in which, at each stage, social action becomes patterned in response to diverse internal and external forces and acquires specific status groups and organizations as 'social carriers'.

Only the typology of rulership (*Herrschaft*) can be given special attention here. (This translation has been suggested by Benjamin Nelson and appears to me preferable to either 'domination', which captures the element of force yet weakens the notion of legitimacy, or 'authority', which conveys legitimacy but downplays the component of force.) In this voluminous section Weber wishes to define the major empirical bases for the legitimation of rulership and to articulate, for each, the typical relationships between rulers, administrative bodies, and the ruled. Charismatic rulership is based upon the attribution of extraordinary personal qualities; traditional rulership (patriarchal, feudal, and patrimonial) rested upon custom and the belief that 'time immemorial' itself provided a justification for continued rule; and rational-legal (bureaucratic) rulership was legitimized through enacted laws, statutes and regulations. Crucial for the endurance of all types is at least a minimum belief on the part of the ruled that the rulership is justified; only then will obedience be rendered. While many interpreters have reified these ideal types, Weber designed them exclusively as heuristic yardsticks.

Throughout *E&S*, as well as *EEWR*, a subtle and dialectical view of the relationships between value-oriented, interest-oriented, and tradition-oriented action prevails. As opposed to the EEWR studies, these relationships in *E&S* are dealt with as models which not only combine ideal types in relationships of 'elective affinities', but also chart the patterned 'relations of antagonisms' between discrete ideal types and even differentiated spheres of life. At this point E&S moves far beyond mere concept-formation and classification to the level of the *dynamic* interaction of constellations. At this 'contextual' level Weber shifts repeatedly back and forth between ideal types of varying range, all of which aim to articulate 'developmental sequences': entire series of ideal types that, on the basis of a developmental dimension as well as a focus upon the religion, economy, law and rulership spheres of life, seek to conceptualize epochal change. Whether the change hypothesized by these research instruments in fact took place in the history of a particular epoch and civilization remained for Weber an empirical question, one that involved, above all, the strength of 'carrier' strata, the success of new groups and organizations in establishing their rulership, and sheer power (Kalberg

1994). Despite his awareness of the inflexibility of tradition and the manner in which millennia-long histories remained within civilizational 'tracks' or world-views, Weber's conviction that power and unexpected historical 'accidents' could always introduce a significant realignment of configurations prevented him from constructing global formulas that promised to forecast the unfolding of societies. To Weber, the materialist interpretation of history, for example, provided a useful hypothesis rather than a scientific explanation.

This sketch of Weber's sociology has touched upon only a few of its major contours. The intensity of Weber's persistent struggle with the immense complexity, unresolved paradoxes, and even contradictory drifts of social reality, and his refusal to simplify on behalf of doctrinal or ideological positions, can be appreciated only by those who directly confront his writings. Fortunately, in turning towards systematic analyses of the major underlying themes in his corpus as a whole, the ongoing Weber renaissance (Weiss 1989) promises to knit together its fragments and to reveal the concerns that literally possessed one of the twentieth century's most remarkable scholars.

Stephen Kalberg
Boston University

References

Cohen, I. J. (1981) 'Introduction to the Transaction Edition', in M. Weber, *General Economic History*, New Brunswick, NJ.

Collins, R. (1980) 'Weber's last theory of capitalism', *American Sociological Review* 56.

Kalberg, S. (1980) 'Max Weber's types of rationality: cornerstones for the analysis of rationalization processes in history', *American Journal of Sociology* 85.

—— (1983) 'Max Weber's universal-historical architectonic of economically-oriented action: a preliminary reconstruction', in S. G. McNall (ed.) *Current Perspectives in Social Theory*, Greenwood, CT.

—— (1990) 'The rationalization of action in Max Weber's sociology of religion', *Sociological Theory* 8.

—— (1994) *Max Weber's Comparative-Historical Sociology*, Oxford.

Marshall, G. (1980) *Presbyteries and Profits: Calvinism and the Development of Capitalism in Scotland, 1560–1707*, Oxford.

—— (1982) *In Search of the Spirit of Capitalism*, London.

Mommsen, W. (1974) *Max Weber: Gesellschaft, Politik und Geschichte*, Frankfurt.

Weber, M. (1930 [1922]) *The Protestant Ethic and the Spirit of Capitalism*, London. (Original edn, *Die protestantiscche Ethik und der 'Geist' des Kapitalismus*, Tübingen.)

—— (1946) *From Max Weber*, ed. H. H. Gerth and C. W. Mills, New York.

—— (1949) *The Methodology of the Social Sciences*, selection and trans. E. Shils, New York.

—— (1951) *The Religion of China*, New York.

—— (1952) *Ancient Judaism*, New York.

—— (1958) *The Religion of India*, New York.

—— (1961 [1927]) *General Economic History*, London. (Original edn, *Wirtschaftsgeschichte*, Munich.)

—— (1968 [1922]) *Economy and Society*, New York. (Original edn, *Wirtschaft und Gesellschaft*, Tübingen.)

—— (1972 [1920]) *Collected Papers on the Sociology of Religion*, London. (Original edn, *Gesammelte Aufsatze zur Religionssoziologie*, vol. 1, Tübingen.)

Weiss, J. (1989) *Max Weber heute*, Frankfurt.

See also: authority; bureaucracy; charisma; legitimacy.

welfare, social see social welfare

welfare economics

If economics is the study of how to make the best, or optimal, use of limited resources, welfare economics is concerned with the meaning of the term 'optimal' and with the formulation of statements that permit us to say that a given policy or event has improved or reduced social welfare.

Optimality is defined in terms of maximizing social welfare, so that the focus of concern is on what comprises the latter concept. Typically, it is taken to be the sum of the welfares of all members of a defined society. By adopting the value judgement that it is individuals' own judgements of their welfare that is to count in the formulation of a measure of social welfare, we have the basis for Paretian welfare economics (after Vilfredo Pareto). In this case, to say that individual A's welfare has improved is to say no more than A prefers one situation to another. To say that *social* welfare has improved requires a further definitional statement, namely, that the improvement in A's welfare has occurred without any other individual being worse off. Thus social welfare has improved if, and only if, at least one individual's welfare has improved and no one's has decreased. It may be noted that while the first requirement is a value judgement, the second is a matter of definition. It is not an additional value judgement.

Paretian welfare economics is almost self-evidently sterile, since we can envision few situations in which no one is harmed by a policy. Some individuals gain and some lose. The sterility of the pure Paretian principle arises because of the alleged difficulty of comparing one person's gain in welfare and another's loss: the so-called fallacy of interpersonal comparisons of utility. If this is accepted, there are obvious difficulties for the formulation of criteria for a gain in social welfare. The principle emerging from the work of Kaldor (1939) and Hicks (1939) declares that there is a net gain in social welfare if those who gain can use part of their gains to compensate the losers and still have something left over. In other words, *if* compensation occurred, those who stand to lose would be fully compensated and their welfare would accordingly be the same before and after the policy in question. Gainers would still be better off provided the required compensation is less than their gross gains. This is the Kaldor-Hicks compensation principle.

Scitovsky (1941) pointed out that a further condition is required, since a policy may alter the distribution of income in such a way that those who lose may be able to pay those who gain sufficient to induce them back to the initial situation. The requirement that this should *not* be the case defines the Scitovsky reversal test for a state of affairs to be defined as a (modified) Pareto-improvement. Since *actual* compensation mechanisms are complex, all compensation criteria are typically formulated in terms of the potential for compensation. There is no requirement for the compensation to occur. This provides the complete separation from the Pareto principle: the compensation principle may sanction a policy that leads to a (strict) Pareto deterioration in social welfare. Scitovsky's work opened the way for an explicit treatment of the distribution of income. Little (1957) defined various alternatives whereby social welfare can be said to increase according to the fulfilment of the compensation criterion (the efficiency test) and an improvement in the distribution of income (an equity test). The seminal work of Rawls (1971), however, best defines the turning-point in welfare economics, whereby there is explicit and simultaneous attention paid to both efficiency and equity through the adoption of Rawls's 'maximin' principle of benefiting the least well off in society.

The historical oddity of welfare economics remains that it has survived as an elaborate framework in itself, and as the foundation of practical techniques such as cost-benefit analysis, despite severe and arguably fatal criticism in the 1950s – notably in the work of de Graaf (1957). Arrow's (1963) famous 'impossibility theorem' also indicates the problems of defining any social welfare function based on the fundamental Paretian value judgement about consumer sovereignty.

The basic analysis of welfare economics has remained largely unchanged since the mid-1970s. It has formed the foundation for *environmental economics* as well as cost-benefit analysis. Recent work has integrated psychological concepts, notably in work on the divergence found in practice between the Hicksian concepts of *compensating and equivalent variations (CV and EV)*, two measures of consumer surplus. Theoretically, the two measures should be nearly the same. In practice, EV appears to be substantially above CV, or, in plain language, 'willingness to accept compensation' to tolerate a welfare loss greatly exceeds 'willingness to pay' for an equivalent environmental improvement. Some work speculates that these differences amount to

non-reversible indifference curves, that is, consumers' valuations are heavily dependent on where they are to begin with. If this is correct, not just welfare economics, but demand theory generally, rests on a fallacy.

David W. Pearce
University of London

References

Arrow, K. (1963) *Social Choice and Individual Values*, 2nd edn, New York.
Hicks, J. (1939) 'Foundations of welfare economics', *Economic Journal* 49.
Kaldor, N. (1939) 'Welfare propositions of economics and interpersonal comparisons of utility', *Economic Journal* 49.
Little, I. M. D. (1957) *A Critique of Welfare Economics*, 2nd edn, Oxford.
Rawls, J. (1971) *A Theory of Justice*, Oxford.
Scitovsky, T. (1941) 'A note on welfare propositions in economics', *Review of Economic Studies*.

Further reading

Just, R. E., Hueth, D. H. and Schmitz, A. (1982) *Applied Welfare Economics and Public Policy*, Englewood Cliffs, NJ.
Sudgen, R. (1981) *The Political Economy of Public Choice: An Introduction to Welfare Economics*, Oxford.

See also: cost-benefit analysis; economic efficiency; environmental economics; microeconomics; Pareto efficiency; poverty; social welfare; social welfare policy; welfare state.

welfare state

The term welfare state refers to the role that states have played in providing welfare services and benefits for their citizens primarily in income maintenance and health care but also in housing, education and social work. From the end of the nineteenth century, the states of most industrialized countries involved themselves, with varying degree, form and effect, in such provision. In 1884 Germany introduced the first system of compulsory national insurance against sickness. Shortly afterwards Denmark, New Zealand and Australia introduced non-contributory old-age pensions. In Britain a series of similar welfare reforms was enacted by the Liberal government between 1906 and 1914. However, the most significant developments took place in the 1930s and 1940s with, for example, the New Deal in the USA, the People's Home in Sweden, and post-war welfare reforms in Britain, France and Germany. Most of these reforms centred upon the goal of full male employment supported by family allowances and insurance benefits for sickness, unemployment and old age. This particular historical development of what is sometimes called the Keynesian welfare state underpins the meaning of the term welfare state.

However, this general understanding of the welfare state conceals a number of important issues. First, not all welfare provision emanates from the state, nor do all citizens benefit equally. The market, the voluntary sector and the family, especially the unpaid work of women, also provide welfare. Second, there are different political standpoints and explanations for the role of welfare in society. Third, since the 1980s the post-war welfare settlement has faced major challenges.

Up until the 1970s the study of welfare states was dominated by a Fabian or social-democratic approach in which the extension of state-provided welfare was seen as the key to a more egalitarian and integrated socialist society (Titmuss 1958). Not all those who favoured state welfare intervention were necessarily socialist. The architect of the British post-war settlement, Beveridge, was a Liberal who believed in state intervention to remove the warts from the face of capitalism.

The rise to power in Britain (and the USA) in the 1980s of a New Right government marked the articulation and practice of a particular form of anti-collectivist approach to welfare. According to this approach the welfare state is seen not as a solution to society's ills but as a cause: it creates high taxation, interferes with the market, acts as a disincentive to economic growth; it creates a culture of dependency (an underclass) sapping individual initiative, and is wasteful, inefficient and bureaucratic (Friedman 1962).

Critical analyses of the welfare state have also emerged from the left. A political economy of welfare explains the development of the welfare state as an uneasy truce between conflicting interests: the interests of capitalism in accumulating profit and in having a healthy, cared-for and appropriately skilled workforce; the interests of the working class in improving their conditions, and the interests of the state in maintaining political stability and its own legitimacy (Gough 1979). The development of social movements around gender, race and disability has put further issues on the welfare agenda. Feminist analyses, in particular, argue that while welfare provisions have the capacity to give women greater autonomy (e.g. contraception or childcare), at the same time many policies have reinforced women's dependency (Pascall 1986). The social insurance policies of the post-war settlements assumed a woman's financial dependence upon a male breadwinner and her primary role as wife and mother. Similar critiques have emerged in relation to the racist underpinnings of welfare citizenship (Williams 1989) and the role of the welfare state in constructing a dependent form of disability (Oliver 1990).

Since the 1980s a number of developments have cast doubt on the appropriateness of the term 'welfare state'. First, a number of social changes in the industrialized west have challenged the future viability of the post-war welfare states: economic recession, increasing unemployment, an ageing population, changing family structure, increased poverty and class, gender and racial inequalities, and the fragmentation of class support for universal welfare policies. Second, many European countries have begun to place greater emphasis upon developing a welfare mix between state, private, voluntary and informal sectors, and most have introduced charging and greater selectivity. Third, the creation of the European Union in 1993 has created debate about how far a supranational state will produce convergent social policies. Finally, although some argue that reports of the death of the post-war welfare state have been greatly exaggerated (e.g. Hills 1993), these developments have created an increasing awareness of the diversity of state interventions in welfare, so that rather than talk of an implicitly uniform welfare state it is more accurate to refer to a variety of welfare regimes.

One major comparative study of eighteen advanced capitalist democracies argues that their welfare systems cluster around three distinct welfare regimes: liberal (USA, Canada, Australia, Japan, Switzerland), conservative (France, Germany, Italy, Austria, Belgium) and social-democratic (Sweden, Norway, Denmark, Finland, The Netherlands) (Esping-Andersen 1990). What distinguishes the three regimes most are their political histories, especially working-class mobilization and the capacity for class coalitions, the relative influence of the state and the market, and the extent to which access to social security benefits effectively cushion citizens from dependence upon the market. Other comparative studies (Ginsburg 1992) have focused upon mobilization and inequalities around class, race/ethnicity and gender, and the relationship between the state, the market and the family, showing, for example, the different degrees to which welfare states have modified the male-breadwinner model of female dependency over the post-war period. Such studies yield an increasingly complex picture of the roles that welfare systems play in the dynamics of a patriarchal and racially structured capitalism of the late twentieth century.

Fiona Williams
Open University

References

Esping-Andersen, G. (1990) *The Three Worlds of Welfare Capitalism*, Cambridge, UK.

Friedman, M. (1962) *Capitalism and Freedom*, Chicago.

Ginsburg, N. (1992) *Divisions of Welfare: A Critical Introduction to Comparative Social Policy*, London.

Gough, I. (1979) *The Political Economy of Welfare*, London.

Hills, J. (1993) *The Future of Welfare*, York.

Oliver, M. (1990) *The Politics of Disablement*, London.

Pascall, G. (1986) *Social Policy: A Feminist Analysis*, London.

Titmuss, R. M. (1958) *Essays on the Welfare State*, London.

Williams, F. (1989) *Social Policy: A Critical Introduction. Issues of Race, Gender and Class*, Cambridge, UK.

See also: poverty; social welfare; social welfare policy; state; welfare economics.

witchcraft and sorcery

Beliefs in witchcraft and sorcery are one way of explaining the inexplicable, controlling the uncontrollable, and accounting for the problem of evil. By attributing unmerited misfortune or unwonted success to the illicit use of occult powers and substances by human beings motivated by malice, greed or envy, the beliefs help to explain, not simply how something happened, but *why* it happened as it did and, thus, to provide moral and psychological theories of causation. Such beliefs may be only one explanatory mode in a cosmology which offers other (and sometimes competing) causal explanations; and recourse to diviners, oracles or witchdoctors may be necessary before a particular event is attributed to witchcraft and action taken to redress the situation.

Anthropologists and others following them, such as historians (Mair 1969; Marwick 1982), often distinguish between the witch, who possesses an innate, mystical power, and the sorcerer, who employs technical, external means such as destructive magic to gain his or her nefarious ends, though the distinction is not always so clear-cut. It is the witch in this narrow sense who is often spoken of as the ·epitome of evil, the negation of the human being, the cancer within the society or the external enemy intent on destruction, whose image has been said to represent the 'standardized nightmares of the group' (Monica Wilson in Marwick 1982) and to embody the obverse of accepted moral and physical norms. These role types derive from Evans-Pritchard's (1937) *Witchcraft, Oracles and Magic among the Azande*, a seminal study in the sociology of knowledge, though he expected neither the Zande distinction to be universally valid, which it is not, nor anthropologists to use it thus; indeed, even his own interpretation of the Zande has been questioned. The definitional problems are formidable, and some would in any case regard the search for universals as a fruitless and invalid exercise (MacGaffey 1980) and would construe the general and wide-ranging use of the terms here as misleading.

The distinction between mystical and technical means has been found useful, though again problematical. Some writers have stressed that while empirical, if doubtful, evidence of sorcery might be found, witchcraft powers and acts are 'all-in-the-mind', unverifiable and unbelievable to the outside observer. Therefore, confession of such powers and activities (and the search for them) has been taken sometimes as evidence of delusion or psychopathology, as in some interpretations of the European witch-hunts of the fifteenth to seventeenth centuries. But although doubt may be cast on confessions produced under torture or other forms of pressure, in some circumstances confession or self-accusation may be used as a protest, as an appeal and as a weapon, for example, by subordinate and frustrated women (Mair 1969; Wyllie in Marwick 1982). In Western Europe and North America, where beliefs in witchcraft are confined to the religious and occult fringe, and in rural cultures, proponents of such beliefs may be regarded generally as eccentric if not deluded, as would be anyone who attributed personal misfortunes to the occult powers of colleagues. But in witch-believing cultures the believer is rational; it is non-believers who may be seen as deviant, misguided or irrational by their peers, and it is unbelief or disbelief which requires explanation (Evans-Pritchard 1937; Hirst and Woolley 1982).

Witch beliefs may postulate that anyone, anywhere, may practise witchcraft and sorcery, or that only persons in specified social categories or possessing specified attributes will pose a threat. However, the sociology of the beliefs (the patterns of allegations, accusations and confessions) shows the selection of targets (whether witch or victim) to be the outcome of quarrels, grudges and strained relations between suspect, accuser and victim. These charges are mainly made about and between people who are not separated by any great social, structural or spatial distance. And yet, there are some differences, depending upon whether the witch-hunt is an individual or communal affair. Many such ethnographic studies of witchcraft have been in effect structural-functional studies of micropolitics, relating the beliefs and accusations to social-structural factors, showing how they contribute to the maintenance of the system and demonstrating their reactionary and conservative functions, although sometimes they have been shown to be radical forces acting as vehicles of social change (Mair 1969; Marwick 1982).

Cognitive, symbolic, semantic and rationalist perspectives have begun to remedy some of the omissions and defects of their functionalist predecessor (Marwick 1982). One such approach involves looking at witches and witchcraft as part of a wider frame of reference such as person categories and concepts of human action. MacGaffey (1980) has shown how comparative analysis of religious structures is facilitated by examining the role of the witch/sorcerer as just one in a set of religious commissions associated with occult powers (such as witch-finder, diviner, magician, priest, prophet, chief). These roles may be differentiated by criteria such as means used (mystical or technical), ends sought (public or private), effects intended (death or life, destruction or protection) and legitimacy (good or bad). This approach, too, allows us more easily to take into account the 'moral ambiguity' of power, that the 'same' power may be good or bad, licit or illicit, and its deployment social or antisocial according by whom it is used and for what ends. In a different vein, witchcraft and sorcery are being analysed within the wider context of social control systems and categories of deviance, in relation to law, criminology and madness in early modern Europe and in colonial contexts (Hirst and Woolley 1982). Yet another approach is to set witch-finding movements within the context of other religious movements and of cults explaining misfortune. Such developments require witchcraft and sorcery to be seen not as isolated elements, as empirical realities, but as aspects of wider classifications and of action systems.

Anne Akeroyd
University of York, UK

References

Evans-Pritchard, E. E. (1937) *Witchcraft, Oracles and Magic among the Azande*, Oxford.

Hirst, P. and Woolley, P. (1982) *Social Relations and Human Attributes*, London.

MacGaffey, W. (1980) 'African religions: types and generalizations', in I. Karp and C. S. Bird (eds) *Explorations in African Systems of Thought*, Bloomington, IN.

Mair, L. (1969) *Witchcraft*, London.

Marwick, M. G. (ed.) (1982) *Witchcraft and Sorcery: Selected Readings*, 2nd edn, Harmondsworth.

Further reading

Douglas, M. (ed.) (1970) *Witchcraft Confessions and Accusations*, London.

Favret-Saada, J. (1980) *Deadly Words: Witchcraft in the Bocage*, Cambridge, UK.

See also: magic; witch-hunts.

witch-hunts

Witch-hunting, the search for the agent(s) responsible for individual and communal afflictions, is a corollary of beliefs in witchcraft and sorcery. In *individual witch-seeking* the cause of a particular affliction is sought from specialists such as diviners who, if witchcraft is diagnosed, may indicate the witch responsible.

Whether the complainant confronts the suspect will depend on whether such an action is necessary for effecting a cure and for averting future danger, and on the complainant's (and others') assessment of the practicality and costs (social, political, economic and legal) of an overt accusation. A widespread series of misfortunes may so perturb a community that *communal witch-testing* will occur, initially directed against those thought to be responsible for the crisis-precipitating events. But should panic grow, and further evidence of witching activity appear and/or past events be reinterpreted in that light, then a small witch-hunt may develop. *Mass witch-hunting* takes three main forms: the summoning of an individual witch-finder by a community or its representatives; the acceptance of a peripatetic witch-finder or witch-cleansing cult, such as those of Central Africa which may recur every ten to fifteen years as their predecessor's millenarian claims are seen to have been false; and a hunt organized and orchestrated by an elite primarily for its own ends. Such hunts aim to protect a community (or polity) by uncovering all witches and either neutralizing their occult powers and destroying their materials, or eliminating the witches by expulsion, imprisonment or execution.

The great European witch panics of the fifteenth to seventeenth centuries exemplify the elite mass witch-hunt. Arising out of actions against heretics, those purges were perpetrated by the religious and secular educated literate elite against a witch of their own making: the satanic witch, the agent of the Devil, was the creation of the Inquisition, of torture and of theological demonology (Cohn 1975). Explanations for those horrific events range from collective psychopathology, to misogyny, minority persecutions and class conflict; but while such multiple explanations are necessary to a fuller understanding, particularly crucial is the fact that the persecutions were coterminous with attempts to establish and maintain Christianity as a political ideology (see Larner 1981).

Elite witch-hunts have analogies with 'moral panics', and actions against 'deviants', 'public menaces' and 'enemies of the state/people' (such as communists, intellectuals, capitalists, Jews, heretics, 'unpatriotic subversives', and 'thought-criminals' and other social categories made scapegoats). The term 'witch-hunt' is actually a twentieth-century American word describing the pursuit of a group for its beliefs or characteristics, or of an individual on trumped-up charges, the victimization of those selected as ideological or political enemies, as occurred during McCarthyism in the USA, the Cultural Revolution in Maoist China, and similar political witch-hunts. Such purges may be shortlived and they, or their excesses, repudiated, but often rehabilitation comes too late for the many victims of such elite obsessions (Shils 1956) with secrecy, subversion, conspiracy and xenophobia.

Anne Akeroyd
University of York, UK

References

Cohn, N. (1975) *Europe's Inner Demons: An Enquiry Inspired by the Great Witch-Hunt*, London.
Larner, C. (1981) *Enemies of God: The Witchhunt in Scotland*, London.
Shils, E. A. (1956) *The Torments of Secrecy: The Background and Consequences of American Security Policies*, London.

Further reading

Marwick, M. G. (ed.) (1982) *Witchcraft and Sorcery: Selected Readings*, 2nd edn, Harmondsworth.
Trevor-Roper, H. R. (1967) *The European Witch-craze of the Sixteenth and Seventeenth Centuries*, Harmondsworth.

See also: witchcraft and sorcery.

Wittgenstein, Ludwig Josef Johann (1889–1951)

Wittgenstein was born in Vienna and though originally trained as an engineer became a pupil of Bertrand Russell at Cambridge. He returned to Austria to serve in the First World War, and in 1921 published the German edition of the *Tractatus Logico–Philosophicus*. He then became a schoolteacher in Lower Austria. In this, as in everything else, he was an intense and demanding man, and soon resigned his post. After that, he became involved in the design of a house which still stands in Vienna, a monument to the aesthetic austerity that he championed. Around this time he rejected the *Tractatus* and began to articulate his later philosophy. He returned to Cambridge in 1929 and held the chair of philosophy from 1939 to 1947.

In the *Tractatus* the essence of language is assumed to reside in its fact-stating function. This is said to rest on the capacity of sentences to 'picture' facts. Pictures consist of parts which correspond to the parts of the thing pictured. The parts of a picture stand to one another in a certain relation, and this says how the corresponding objects are arranged if the picture is true. In language the parts are names, and elementary sentences are arrangements of names. More complicated sentences can then be built up by using the rules of Russell's logic. Wittgenstein may have based his picture theory on the way in which systems of material points have a symbolic representation in sophisticated versions of theoretical mechanics. Certainly the conclusion he drew was that the only meaningful language was the language of science. All attempts to transcend this and express what is 'higher' – namely, ethics, aesthetics and the meaning of life – are doomed. Even the attempt to state the relation of language to the world tries to go beyond these limits, so the doctrines of the *Tractatus* itself are meaningless. Those who understand my propositions correctly, said Wittgenstein, will surmount them like a ladder, and then throw them away.

Is this an attack on everything non-scientific? Wittgenstein's friend, Paul Engelmann, tells us that it is the exact opposite. The aim is not to dismiss what cannot be said, the 'higher', but to *protect* it. The *Tractatus* is an ethical document which must be understood in terms of Wittgenstein's involvement with the great Viennese critic Karl Kraus and the influential architect Adolf Loos. Kraus exposed moral corruption which shows itself in the corruption of language. Loos conducted a campaign against aesthetic corruption which shows itself in the confusion of art with utility and the pollution of functional simplicity by needless decoration. The *Tractatus* likewise expressed the ethics of purity, separation, simplicity and the integrity of silence.

Why Wittgenstein became dissatisfied with this position is unclear, but some light may be shed by relating his shift of opinion to a broad cultural change in which he participated. If the *Tractatus* addressed the issues that exercised pre-war Viennese intellectuals, the late philosophy addressed the problems that confronted them in the post-war years. We know that the military defeats and economic and constitutional problems in Europe were accompanied by an acute sense of cultural crisis. One symptom of this was the enormous popularity of Spengler's irrational life-philosophy with its conservative pessimism. Wittgenstein is known to have been impressed by Spengler, and the later work can be seen as a brilliant expression of this form of conservative irrationalism. All the features of this style – the priority of the concrete over the abstract, of practice over norms, life over reason and being over thought – are prominently displayed.

In his later work Wittgenstein rejected the idea that language has a single essential function. It is not structured by correspondence with objects but by its role in the stream of life. There are as many ways for words to carry meaning as there are ways of organizing action. The picture theory gave way to the idea of 'language-games'. We must not theorize about language but observe its diversity as we name, count, instruct, question, promise, pray and so on. The real heart of the late philosophy, however, is the analysis of rule following. It is tempting to explain human behaviour in terms of our capacity to follow rules. In § 201 of the *Investigations* Wittgenstein argued that no course of action can be determined by rules, because any course of action could be said to accord with the rule. Any non-standard interpretation of a rule could be justified by a non-standard interpretation of the rules for following the rule. Ultimately it must be said of all rules that they are obeyed blindly. At every point, rules, and the application of the concepts in them, depend on taken for granted practices or customs. Wittgenstein used this insight to bring out the conventional character of all knowledge and discourse, whether it was an introspective report or a mathematical truth.

For the later Wittgenstein, then, the notion of meaning is explained in terms of *use*. Meaningless or metaphysical discourse is language 'on holiday', that is, not employed in a language game that has a genuine role in a form of life. The job of the philosopher is to inhibit our tendency to detach words from their real use. In this the philosopher is like a doctor who must bring language back to its healthy everyday life. What had to be accepted as given, said Wittgenstein, was the 'form of life'. Other than this all belief is groundless: this is the end-point of all justification. Nothing could be a clearer expression of the conservative thinker's belief in the priority of life over reason.

It is only now that this European dimension of Wittgenstein's thinking, both in its early and late phase, is beginning to emerge. This offsets the somewhat narrow readings that have been given them as forms of logical and linguistic 'analysis'. Nevertheless the full potential of the late philosophy, as the basis of a social theory of knowledge, still awaits exploitation.

David Bloor
University of Edinburgh

Further reading

Bloor, D. (1983) *Wittgenstein: A Social Theory of Knowledge*, London.
Engelman, P. (1967) *Letters from Ludwig Wittgenstein with a Memoir*, Oxford.
Janik, A. and Toulmin, S. (1973) *Wittgenstein's Vienna*, London.
Monk, R. (1990) *Ludwig Wittgenstein: The Duty of Genius*, London.
Specht, E. K. (1963) *The Foundations of Wittgenstein's Late Philosophy*, Manchester.
Winch, P. (1958) *The Idea of a Social Science and its Relation to Philosophy*, London.

As Wittengstein's unpublished writings gradually appear in print, the corpus of his work now stands at over a dozen volumes. Nevertheless, the main texts of the early and late philosophy, respectively, are still:

Wittgenstein, L. (1961) *Tractatus Logico-Philosophicus*, trans. D. F. Pears and B. F. McGuinness, London.
—— (1953) *Philosophical Investigations*, trans. G. E. M. Anscombe, Oxford.

women

Feminists have pointed out that women are always defined in relation to men, who are taken as the norm. Women are 'the other': they are defined by the absence of male characteristics, and the absence of these characteristics is seen as making them inferior to men. Men as the producers of knowledge have defined 'women': women are the object of knowledge rather than its subject, even to themselves.

'Woman' is defined as the female of 'man'. The human race is divided into two mutually exclusive categories – men and women. These two categories are seen as biologically determined. Women are said to be naturally caring and subservient, suited to their role as homemakers. They have been seen as more governed by emotions than men, a less developed form of the species and closer to nature because they are the childbearing and childrearing gender. Until the 1970s social scientists tended implicitly to accept without consideration the view that women's social roles are biologically determined. There were notable exceptions, such as Margaret Mead (e.g. 1928), but in general the theorization of women's roles was not on the agenda.

Women's biological role as childbearers and subsequent social role as childrearers has been seen as providing the basis for their subordination (see, e.g. Parsons and Bales 1955). Women, it is argued, are forced into a reliance on men to protect and provide for them while they are bearing and rearing children (see, e.g. Firestone 1974). Men need to control women in order to ensure that they know who their offspring are in order to pass on property.

The majority of feminists have rejected the essentialist view that 'woman' is a natural category and have argued that it is socially constructed. Materialist feminists such as Christine Delphy (1984) have argued that the basis of women's oppression is the domestic mode of production: women are exploited by men, who appropriate the domestic labour of women. 'Woman' is an economic and political category: women form a social class which is subordinated to and exploited by another social class, men. Women are in a specific social relationship to men, however, having personal and physical obligations to them as well as an economic relationships – a quasi-feudal relationship.

Men, as the producers of knowledge, construct society and women's subordinate role within it. Beyond the political and economic subordination of women, women are subordinated by men's preferred mode of sexuality; men have created a social world in which heterosexuality is compulsory. This structures relationships not only in domestic life and between particular men and women, but also in all aspects of everyday life. It is evident in workplace relationships, judicial decisions, the behaviour of the police and the use that is made of women in advertising and the service industries.

Beyond this, post-modern feminists have argued that defining women as a unitary category glosses over the multitude of different experiences that women have of sexism and oppression. The fractured and divergent experiences of actual women are submerged in the category woman. Women's experiences are structured by race/ethnicity, age, sexuality and so on; it is therefore necessary to deconstruct the category. It is necessary to acknowledge that there are relations of power *between* women – between Black and White women, middle- and working-class women, women in the First and the Third World, and so on (see, e.g. Barrett and Phillips 1992).

Avtar Brah (1992), however, while accepting that 'women' is not a *uniting* category, suggests that it is none the less a *unifying* one. She argues that heterogeneity of the conditions of being a woman results in differences but not necessarily in divisions; there are commonalities of experience. To treat 'woman' as an entirely fictional category is to ignore the material relations that construct women into membership of the category.

Pamela Abbott
University of Derby

References

Barrett, M. and Phillips, A. (eds) (1992) *Destabilising Theory*, Oxford.
Brah A. (1992) 'Questions of difference and international feminism', in J. Aaron and S. Walby (eds) *Out of the Margins*, Basingstoke.
Delphy, C. (1984) *Close to Home*, London.
Firestone, S. (1974) *The Dialectic of Sex: The Case for Feminist Revolution*, New York.
Mead, M. (1928) *Coming of Age in Samoa: A Psychological Study of Primitive Youth for Western Civilization*, New York.
Parsons, T. and Bales, R. (1955) *Family, Socialisation and Interaction Process*, New York.

See also: feminist practice; feminist research; feminist theory; gender and sex; patriarchy; women's studies.

women's studies

The area of academic study which has become known as Women's Studies grew out of the feminist movement in the USA and western Europe in the late 1960s and early 1970s. The movement had close intellectual and political links with the various campaigns of the time to democratize the universities, and as such one of the first targets of contemporary feminism was the sexism and misogyny of much of traditional scholarship. While feminism as a political movement campaigned around

issues of sexuality (access to abortion and contraception and the deconstruction of heterosexuality as the single permissible form of sexual practice) and unequal power relations between the sexes (in both the household and the public worlds of politics and paid work) feminism within the academy questioned the ways in which knowledge was constructed. Initially, campaigns were organized around the issue of the absence of women from the curriculum. If one subject dominated feminist critiques of the academy it was that the human subject (in any discipline) was always, and uncontentiously, male.

The radicalism and the creativity of feminism of the early 1970s brought to academic debates and discussion profoundly innovative questions. For example, Kate Millett (1971) and Germaine Greer (1970) – both trained within the discipline of English literature – examined the ways in which official versions of culture marginalized and/or excluded women. Sheila Rowbotham's (1973) *Hidden from History* claimed the existence of another history – that of women. Across the range of disciplines taught in universities women academics turned to examine what they had been taught and found it both exclusive (in that it was largely blind to the existence of women) and informed by assumptions about the relative importance of women and men. Although feminists did uncover, and recover, a feminist tradition in which women had written about women (in the academy women such as Viola Klein, Alice Clark and Mirra Komarovsky and outside it figures such as Virginia Woolf and Simone de Beauvoir) a great deal of energy was also devoted to documenting the lives of women. The political slogan 'the personal is political' informed the studies by women of women within the household and personal relationships. As the boundaries between the public and the private started to shift, what was to emerge was public discussion of both pathological forms of male–female relationships (such as violence against women) and the more ordinary day-to-day responsibilities carried by women. Childcare, the care of sick and elderly people, and housework itself became part of the remit of the social sciences. Within the same context, feminist academics also turned to examine the ways in which information about the social world was collected. Personal experience and subjectivity were validated as legitimate forms of research data and research practice: as in previous debates about the objectivity of the social sciences, the case was made against the apparently disinterested social investigator. Thus just as the object of study shifted, so too did the subject.

This considerable and diverse project of the documentation of women's lives has continued since the late 1960s. However, as it has grown older, so two developments have become marked. The first, identifiable in the earliest days of women's studies, is debate around the issue of the theoretical systems underlying and informing the collection of information. In the early 1970s the term 'patriarchy' was widely used as an explanation for what was assumed to be the universal subordination of women. Feminist writers, within and outside the academy, used the term widely to indicate a male epistemology which inevitably led to the oppression of women. Within this theoretical stance were coined such vivid phrases as 'all men are rapists' and 'male power is the *raison d'être* of pornography'. A fundamental social and psychological distinction was assumed between women and men, from which followed an ongoing campaign by men to secure their domination.

The polarity explicit in this view has never lost its radicalizing impact, and despite the sophistication and diversity which now informs theoretical debates within women's studies the idea of a basic division between women and men still retains its intellectual as well as its political impact. But what has happened since the late 1960s in academic feminism is that the category of 'woman' has lost its initial homogeneity. Two developments in particular have been significant here: the first is the influence of psychoanalysis, the second the challenge to western feminism by women of the south and women of minority groups within the north. The first major shift towards the integration of psychoanalysis into women's studies and feminism occurred in 1976 when Juliet Mitchell published *Psychoanalysis and Feminism*. In this she initiated a debate which still continues about the relationship between biological sex and sexuality. Written as a defence of Freud against those traditions in feminism which defined his work as misogynist, Juliet Mitchell (and subsequently numerous other women) turned to Freud in order to re-examine both the ways in which individual sexual identity is created and the construction of the symbolic order of sexuality. Both themes have remained central to women's studies. In 1980 Adrienne Rich attacked what she termed 'compulsory heterosexuality' and throughout the 1970s and 1980s French feminists, informed by Freud and Lacan, re-examined the assumed stability (and indeed existence) of femininity and the feminine.

The impact of psychoanalysis and psychoanalytically informed feminism on women's studies has been immense, and particularly so in the case of the study of literature. Whereas feminists in the early 1970s had worked to establish the existence of women writers, by the 1980s the canon of literature was to be further re-examined by feminist readings of the 'great tradition'. Women literary critics re-read and reinterpreted literature and in doing so demonstrated the diversity of interpretation made possible by feminism.

That theme of diversity has been equally significant in terms of the challenge to, and by, women's studies of ethnocentric perceptions of the social world. When Ester Boserup's *Women's Role in Economic Development* was published in 1970, the impact of the north on the south as a modernizing, and universally progressive, force was seldom questioned. 'Development' was widely read as positive. But after Boserup's intervention, anthropologists and economists were held accountable for the extent to which their understanding of other cultures was not merely ethnocentric in its conclusions but also sexist. In the 1970s feminists from cultures other than those of the White northern middle class were to attack vehemently what they saw as the internal colonization of their cultures: imperialism was seen not only in terms of politics in subject territories but also in terms of the domination within societies of one culture over all others. In Britain and the USA in particular women of colour initiated campaigns to reclaim their past and construct their future. Another movement slogan 'finding our voice' became the organizing focus for the documentation of the lives of non-white women.

By the mid-1980s women's studies was established as an area of study in higher education throughout the north. An initial attack on the empirical absence of women as both objects of academic study and active subjects in the construction of knowledge had established the validity of each critique. While the northern academy did not change its practices or curriculum, women academics established a space within universities for the legitimate discussion of issues affecting women and relevant to sexual difference. Nevertheless, although women now constitute about half of all students in higher education, they are still a small proportion (in all western societies) of academics.

Despite the massive under-representation of women in the western academy, women's studies (with which only some women academics identify) has made a significant impact on diverse disciplines and established new methodological and epistemological models. What has been put on the academic agenda is sexual difference, and the implications of sexual difference for the social experiences of the two sexes. In recent women's studies literature new departures can be detected in terms of both the subject matter and the discussion of sexual difference. In terms of the first, what can be seen is a gradual development of interest in the issue of how sexual difference affects not only what we think about, but also the very processes through which knowledge in our society is collected and systematized. Women academics have turned to philosophy and the natural sciences (traditionally subjects in which the actual presence of women has been even more limited than in the social sciences and the humanities) to examine the dominating epistemologies of the west and post-Enlightenment thought. In part through the impact of post-modernism as a disempowering agency on all synthesizing 'grand theories' but equally through feminist scepticism about claims to universalism of all theoretical traditions, feminist scholars have taken to task the underlying claims to universal explanation and validity of a range of moral and methodological assumptions. For example, Sandra Harding (1986) has argued that natural science is 'gendered'; that is, that its method and its object is structured by organizing distinctions between male and female. In other contexts, a range of authors have made similar claims: that the great, supposedly abstract and objective systems of law, political science and medicine formed within a post-Enlightenment discourse are deeply gendered and founded upon an assumed, and certainly unnegotiated, distinction between female and male.

This radical attack on the very foundations of the western academy has proceeded alongside the equally energetic, and equally radical, critique by feminists of the construction of sexual identity. This theme has been consistent within women's studies, but the most recent work in the area has stressed less the difference between women and men than what is regarded as the generally oppressive assumption that sexual desire must always be directed towards individuals of the opposite sex. The assumed logic of this position, and its social institutionalization, has been undermined by writers such as Judith Butler (1990) who have argued for the recognition of the instability of desire. Her work, like that of many women working in this area (on studies of lesbian sexuality, the sexuality of adolescent girls and the visual representation of women) has been informed by the writing of Michel Foucault. His studies of sexuality and incarceration have widely informed feminist academic work, not least because his repeated attack on the ideas of progress and enlightenment allowed a space in the historical record for women to record their interventions as dissenters from masculinist discourses.

It is thus that the practice of women's studies which initially set out to correct an academic absence has come to constitute a major and increasingly global academic presence. Clearly, resistance still remains to accepting and integrating the substantial critique of the traditional academy accumulated within women's studies. This resistance remains particularly marked in those societies without an indigenous feminist movement or tradition. Nevertheless, what has been put on the academic record is the issue of sexual difference; the homogeneity of the historical subject has been replaced by the diversity of the present and future subject.

Mary Evans
University of Kent

References

Boserup, E. (1970) *Women's Role in Economic Development*, New York.
Butler, J. (1990) *Gender Trouble*, London.
Greer, G. (1970) *The Female Eunuch*, London.
Harding, S. (1986) *The Science Question in Feminism*, Ithaca, NY.
Millett, K. (1971) *Sexual Politics*, London.
Mitchell, J. (1976) *Psychoanalysis and Feminism*, London.
Rich, A. (1980) 'Compulsory heterosexuality', *Signs* 5.
Rowbotham, S. (1973) *Hidden from History*, London.

Further reading

Barrett, M. and Phillips, A. (1992) *Destabilising Theory*, Cambridge, UK.
Brown, L., Collins, H., Green, P., Humm, M. and Landells, M. (eds) (1992) *The International Handbook of Women's Studies*, Hemel Hempstead.
Humm, M. (ed.) (1992) *Feminisms: A Reader*, Hemel Hempstead.
Marks, E. and de Courtivron, I. (eds) (1981) *New French Feminisms*, Brighton.
Mitter, S. (1986) *Common Fate, Common Bond: Women in the Global Economy*, London.
Pateman, C. (1988) *The Sexual Contract*, Oxford.
Rose, J. (1986) *Sexuality in the Field of Vision*, London.
Sayers, J. (1992) *Mothering Psychoanalysis*, London.
Showalter, E. (1976) *A Literature of their Own*, Princeton, NJ.
Stanley, L. and Wiseman, S. (1993) *Breaking Out Again*, London.

See also: division of labour by sex; domestic violence; feminist practice; feminist research; feminist theory; gender and sex; patriarchy; women.

work and leisure

Work can refer to any physical and/or mental activities which transform natural materials into a more useful form, improve human knowledge and understanding of the world, and/or provide or distribute goods to others. The definition of work cannot be limited to references to activities alone, however, but most also consider the purposes for which, and the social context within which, those activities are being carried out. For some people their 'work' is to play games to entertain spectators, games such as football, tennis or snooker which many others play for their own pleasure and relaxation; to read a book for interest or amusement has a different significance from reading the same book in order to prepare a lecture. Work activities are instrumental activities: they are undertaken in order to meet certain individual needs either directly, or indirectly by providing for the needs of others so that goods and services, or the means to purchase them, are received in exchange. Work activities may also be valued for their own sake, but they always have an extrinsic purpose.

In industrial societies the most socially prominent and economically important forms of work are those activities which occur within relationships of employment, or self-employment, and provide goods and services for sale in the market in return for a wage, salary or fee. This predominance of one social context and form of organization of work is a relatively recent development; within human history as a whole the direct provision of a family's or a community's needs (as in peasant societies), or production carried out under coercion (for example serfdom, or slavery), have been much more common. Indeed the development of industrial societies necessitated not only considerable social innovation in forms of work organization (such as factories and offices) but also the emergence and internalization of new values regarding work, ones which provided the necessary sense of obligation to work hard and in a rational and regular way under the control of others (Thompson 1967). Such a 'work ethic', whose origins were seen by Weber (1930 [1922]) as lying particularly in certain forms of Protestantism, has, however, coexisted with the more traditional view of work as a necessity. Whereas when work is viewed as a moral duty, of value in itself, not to work is to be idle; when work is a tiresome necessity, not to work is to have leisure.

The current importance of work within an employment relationship and a market context should not obscure those forms of work which are differently structured and located. Of particular importance is domestic work, which is often very time consuming and clearly makes a considerable and absolutely essential contribution to the economy, though one which is only rarely acknowledged. Also part of the so-called informal economy are other household activities such as do-it-yourself home improvements and exchanges of help and services between relatives and neighbours; activities in the wider community such as voluntary work; and work in the hidden economy: jobs on the side for pay which is not taxed, and the clearly illegal work of criminals (Gershuny and Pahl 1980).

A definition of leisure is equally difficult. It can be used to refer to a quality of life (leisure as the mark of a 'gentleman'), or to refer to some combination of time, activity and experience: time free from work and other necessary activities such as eating and sleeping; 'play' activities which are outside normal routines; and experiences which are intrinsically rewarding (Parker 1971; Roberts 1981). While leisure can fairly clearly be distinguished from paid employment, it may be much more difficult to separate it from other forms of work such as housework or voluntary work. Leisure is also differently experienced and unevenly available: people with

jobs have more clearly demarcated leisure time and activities than those with domestic responsibilities, whose 'work is never done'.

A major preoccupation has been with unemployment, the lack of paid work for all those able and willing to do it. In so far as levels of unemployment are seen as due to structural changes in the economies of industrial societies, and especially the use of minicomputers, robots and so on to replace human labour, they have raised the question of whether we may be seeing the start of a 'leisure society', one in which it will no longer be normal for all adults to work, and where there will be far more leisure and maybe even the need to 'work' at one's leisure activities (Jenkins and Sherman 1979; 1981). There are, of course, a lot of unresolved questions about such a future for work and leisure. It is far from clear that the potential of the new technology is as great as has been claimed, and, if it is, whether that potential can be realized in ways which will release people from employment. There are considerable problems in ensuring that the economic benefits of the new technology are distributed in ways which reward people generally rather than just the few: existing fiscal and tax arrangements are certainly far from adequate.

Even if many people can be provided with a high standard of living without the need to undertake (much) paid employment, there is a motivational problem: who is going to be prepared to do the remaining heavy, repetitive, unpleasant or unrewarding jobs once pay is no longer an incentive?

Most important of all, we need to consider the social and psychological functions currently filled by work, and especially paid employment, and to ask whether leisure, even if it is 'worked at', or any other activities, can provide alternatives. Can leisure structure the day as work and employment do; provide social contacts outside the immediate family and locality; link individuals to goals and purposes outside themselves; give a sense of identity and status; and enforce activity and through that some sense of control over events (Jahoda 1982)? Work provides a sense of necessity and constrains what we can do; for this reason it is often resented and contrasted unfavourably with leisure and 'free time'; paradoxically without the constraint the sense of freedom may also be lost.

Richard K. Brown
University of Durham

References

Gershuny, J. I. and Pahl, R. E. (1980) 'Britain in the decade of the three economies', *New Society* 3.

Jahoda, M. (1982) *Employment and Unemployment*, Cambridge, UK.

Jenkins, C. and Sherman, B. (1979) *The Collapse of Work* London.

—— (1981) *The Leisure Shock*, London.

Parker, S. R. (1971) *The Future of Work and Leisure*, London.

Roberts, K. (1981) *Leisure*, London.

Thompson, E. P. (1967) 'Time, work discipline and industrial capitalism', *Past and Present* 38.

Weber, M. (1930 [1922]) *The Protestant Ethic and the Spirit of Capitalism*, London. (Original edn, *Die protestantische Ethik und der 'Geist' des Kapitalismus*, Tübingen.)

Further reading

Abrams, P. and Brown, R. K. (eds) (1984) *UK Society: Work, Urbanism and Inequality*, London.

Anthony, P. D. (1977) *The Ideology of Work*, London.

Esland, G. and Salaman, G. (1980) *The Politics of Work and Occupations*, Milton Keynes.

Gershuny, J. (1978) *After Industrial Society*, London.

Hedges, N. and Beynon, H. (1982) *Born to Work*, London.

See also: sport, sociology of.

World Bank

Along with the International Monetary Fund, the International Bank for Reconstruction and Development (IBRD or World Bank) was established in 1944 and began operations in 1946. It is essentially an international development agency whose primary role is to make long-term development project loans in foreign currency to member governments. It is the largest of all official development agencies. Since its creation its role has changed substantially.

Its original role (as suggested by its original name) was to facilitate the reconstruction of European economies after the Second World War. It originally had 45 members compared with around 150 in the mid-1990s. The bulk of its early lending was to Europe and even by the mid-1950s lending to Europe accounted for two-thirds of its total. As the post-war reconstruction of the European economies was rapid (due partly to bilateral Marshall Plan assistance rather than the activities of the IBRD) the World Bank's focus changed. It was in this process that it emerged as the world's leading economic development agency making loans to developing countries. Its focus remains the making of loans to foster economic development. It has become the world's largest official lender for the development of low-income countries. As well as finance, the Bank also provides substantial technical assistance on the projects it finances.

In 1956 the Bank was expanded by the establishment of the International Finance Corporation whose purpose is to provide and facilitate finance exclusively for the development of private enterprise in member countries. A further extension was made in 1960 with the creation of the International Development Agency focused on low-income borrowers with loans made on more concessionary terms. In 1988 the Multilateral Investment Guarantee Agency was established as part of the World Bank group to facilitate and encourage foreign direct investment in developing countries. It does this partly by an insurance programme to alleviate perceived political risks by potential investors. The World Bank group is, therefore, a bank, a broker, a consultant, and an insurance agency.

Its loans are usually for large-scale projects in the area of energy, transportation, infrastructure, communications and public utilities. Such loans alleviate domestic savings and foreign currency constraints to borrowing countries' economic development. A characteristic of developing countries is that the optimum level of capital formation exceeds the capacity of the country to generate domestic savings, and foreign currency reserves are insufficient to fill the gap on a continuing basis. The World Bank acts as an intermediary by channelling savings generated in the developed world towards investment in developing countries. All loans of the World Bank are made to either governments or to entities guaranteed by governments (e.g. public utilities).

Typically, loans are repayable over a period of ten to fifteen years and carry interest rates which reflect the cost of funds to the Bank. The Bank has never suffered a default on a loan and it has never had to call on any part of its capital. The World Bank has the highest possible credit-rating in the world's capital markets.

While historically development projects have dominated its lending, priorities and focus have changed over time. Increasing emphasis has been given to alleviating poverty *per se* and this is reflected in the expansion of lending to the rural sector. In its 1991 *Annual Report* it stated that 'the eradication of poverty remains the World Bank's top priority'. This shift in emphasis, a reflection also of the ability of higher-income developing countries to tap international banking and capital markets directly, is seen in the increasing proportion of lending to low-income countries. Thus, in 1981, 35 per cent of loans were made to this group of countries while by 1991 the proportion had risen to over 40 per cent. Lending has been directed to health and nutrition projects as well as to education. Environmental issues have also been given an increased priority.

Since 1988, the Bank has also participated in debt-reduction and debt-restructuring programmes of those developing countries which encountered severe debt-servicing problems following many years of massive private market borrowing.

The Bank is owned by its member governments who provide the Bank's capital. Its main lending operations, however, are financed by its own borrowing on the international capital markets. It has become one of the world's largest single issuers of bonds. It can borrow on very fine terms not only because of its untarnished record of repayments and debt-servicing, but also because it has never borrowed amounts in excess of its own capital. This gearing ratio of 1:1 makes it the most cautious and prudent bank in the world. In effect, the World Bank borrows in its own name and makes loans to countries which are unable to gain direct access to private markets or can do so only on less advantageous terms than the World Bank.

The World Bank inevitably has its critics from across the political spectrum. It is criticized from one end of the spectrum for being an agent of capitalism and imperialism and for creating conditions on its lending that unduly interfere with governments' social and political priorities. This alleged bias arises because it is controlled by wealthy developed countries with poorer borrowing nations having little voice in its decision-making progress. At the other end of the spectrum the criticism is that it is too passive, and not sufficiently responsive to market forces in economic development. This school also argues that it has a bias towards public sector rather than private enterprise projects and has not been sufficiently vigorous in fostering de-regulation.

Whatever the merits of the conflicting criticisms, the fact remains that the World Bank has become both the world's largest development agency and one of the largest borrowers in international capital markets.

David T. Llewellyn
Loughborough University

Further reading

Baum, W. C. and Tolbert, S. M. (1985) *Investing in Development: Lessons of World Bank Experience*. New York.

de Vries, B. A. (1987) *Remaking the World Bank*, Washington, DC.

Fried, E. R. and Owen, H. D. (eds) (1982) *The Future of the World Bank*, Washington, DC.

Mason, E. S. and Asher, R. E. (1973) *The World Bank since Bretton Woods*, Washington, DC.

World Bank, *Annual Reports*, Washington, DC.

World Bank, *World Development Reports*, Washington, DC.

See also: International Monetary Fund; international monetary system; OECD.

world-system theory

The sociologist Immanuel Wallerstein developed world-system theory in the early 1970s in an attempt to explain the origins and processes of capitalism, the industrial revolution, and the complex interconnections of the First, Second and Third Worlds. The multidisciplinary research of world-system theory focuses on historical studies of the growth of the world-system and on contemporary processes within it.

The modern world-system arose in western Europe about 500 years ago. It was based on capitalist trade networks which transcended state boundaries, hence it is called the capitalist world-economy. The drive for capital accumulation via production for exchange caused increasing competition among capitalist producers for labour, materials and markets. As competition waxed and waned through repeated crises of overproduction, various regions of the world were incorporated into the unevenly expanding world-economy. These cyclic processes are a fundamental property of the world-system.

Uneven expansion differentiates the world into three central, or 'core', interrelated types of societies. The central or 'core' societies specialize in industrial production and distribution, have relatively strong states, a strong bourgeoisie, a large wage-labour class, and are heavily involved in the affairs of non-core societies. At the other extreme, in the 'periphery', societies concentrate on the production of raw materials, have weak states, a small bourgeoisie, a large peasant class, and are heavily influenced by core societies. The remaining societies form the semiperiphery, which shares characteristics of both the core and periphery. Semiperipheral societies are typically rising peripheral societies, or declining core societies. The semiperiphery blocks polarization between core and periphery, thus stabilizing the system. The economic and political interrelations of the core and periphery are the presumed sources of development in the core, and the lack of development in the periphery.

A key assumption of world-system theory is that the world-economy must be studied as a whole. The study of social change in any component of the system – nations, states, regions, ethnic groups, classes – must begin by locating that component within the system. The typical component analysed is a state. Thus world-system theory has a dual research agenda. It examines the consequences of dynamic changes in its components (such as states) for evolution of the system and for the movement of various components within the system. It also examines the consequences of dynamic changes in the world-system for the internal dynamics and social structure of its various components.

Case studies investigating the emergence and evolution of the world-system offer finer-grained analyses of various components of the system and complement global analyses. Controversy surrounds the measurement and explanation of the system and its parts, and centres on two major issues: first, to what degree and how is underdevelopment in the periphery necessary to the development of the core; and second, whether market (exogenous) factors or social-structural (endogenous) factors, especially class, are the primary agents of change.

World-system literature is complicated by a number of intertwined polemics, which focus on the role of socialist states in the contemporary world-system; the probability of a world socialist revolution; the degree to which underdevelopment is a necessary consequence of core development; the effects of various policies on the evolution of the world-system; and whether world-system theory is a useful extension or crude distortion of Marxist theory.

Since the mid-1980s world-system theory has begun to address a number of issues which critics have noted it had neglected. So much new work has been done that these criticisms are losing salience. Indeed, a scholar who consulted only the works of Wallerstein, or summary works written in the early 1980s, would be poorly informed. Some new topics are various cyclical processes in the world-system; the consequences of the collapse of the Soviet Union; the roles of women, households, and gender in the world-economy; the role of culture in the world-economy; case studies of slavery, agrarian capitalism, and the incorporation of aboriginal populations into the world-economy; and pre-capitalist world-systems.

The last topic has generated a great deal of work and debate among anthropologists and archaeologists. Debates centre around whether there has been one sporadically growing world-system since the origin of states or several types of world-systems, of which the modern world-system is only one. These new evolutionary studies open a number of assumptions about the modern world-system to empirical, historically grounded investigation, often done with an eye to foreseeing possible future transformations of the contemporary system.

Polemical debates notwithstanding, world-system theory has generated many studies of long-term social change. These studies use techniques from all the social sciences and are published in a wide range of journals. Several journals have devoted special issues to world-system issues. *Review*, published by the Fernand Braudel Center at the State University of New York, Binghamton, is devoted to world-system studies.

Thomas D. Hall
DePauw University

Further reading

Abu-Lughod, J. (1989) *Before European Hegemony*, Oxford.
Arrighi, G. (1994) *The Long Twentieth Century*, London.
Chase-Dunn, C. (1989) *Global Formation*, Oxford.
Chase-Dunn, C. and Grimes, P. (1995) 'World-systems analysis', *Annual Review of Sociology* 21.
Hall, T. (1989) *Social Change in the Southwest, 1350–1880*, Kansas.
Hall, T. and Chase-Dunn, C. (1993) 'The world-systems perspective and archaeology: forward into the past', *Journal of Archaeological Research* 1.
Hopkins, T. K., Wallerstein, I. and associates (1977) 'Patterns of development of the modern world-system', *Review* 1.
Kiser, E. and Drass, K. (1987) 'Changes in the core of the world-system and the production of utopian literature in Great Britain and the United States, 1883–1975', *American Sociological Review* 52.
McMichael, P. (1984) *Settlers and the Agrarian Question*, Cambridge, UK.
Martin, W. G. (1994) 'The world-systems perspective in perspective: assessing the attempt to move beyond nineteenth-century eurocentric conceptions', *Review* 17.
Shannon, T. (1996) *An Introduction to the World-System Perspective*, 2nd edition, Boulder, CO.
Suter, C. (1992) *Debt Cycles in the World-Economy*, Westview, BC.
Tomich, D. (1990) *Slavery in the Circuit of Sugar*, Baltimore, MD.
Wallerstein, I. (1974) *The Modern World-System I*, New York.
—— (1979) *The Capitalist World-Economy*, Cambridge, UK.
—— (1980) *The Modern World-System II*, New York.
—— (1984) *The Politics of the World-Economy*, Cambridge, UK.
—— (1989) *The Modern World-System III*, New York.
—— (1991) *Geopolitics and Geoculture*, Cambridge, UK.
Ward, K. (1993) 'Reconceptualizing world-system theory to include women', in P. England (ed.) *Theory on Gender/Feminism on Theory*, Aldine.

See also: capitalism; centre and periphery; globalization; imperialism; Third World; underdevelopment.